HARRAP'S CONCISE
FRENCH AND ENGLISH
DICTIONARY

HARRAP'S CONCISE
FRENCH AND ENGLISH
DICTIONARY

FRENCH–ENGLISH, ENGLISH–FRENCH
IN ONE VOLUME

ABRIDGED BY

R. P. JAGO

FROM

HARRAP'S STANDARD FRENCH
AND ENGLISH DICTIONARY

HARRAP   LONDON

First published in Great Britain 1949
by GEORGE G. HARRAP & CO. LTD
182–184 High Holborn, London WC1V 7AX

Reprinted: 1952; 1954; 1956; 1957;
1960; 1961; 1963; 1964; 1966;
1967; 1970; 1971; 1972; 1973

ISBN 0 245 55654 0

Printed in Great Britain by
Redwood Press Limited
Trowbridge, Wiltshire

PREFACE

HARRAP'S CONCISE FRENCH AND ENGLISH DICTIONARY has been built on the solid foundation provided by the two dictionaries edited by the late J. E. Mansion, M.A. The first of these, Harrap's STANDARD FRENCH AND ENGLISH DICTIONARY, in two volumes, is the most complete and scholarly work of its kind. The second, Harrap's SHORTER FRENCH AND ENGLISH DICTIONARY, also in two volumes, provides a work of smaller compass, yet sufficiently comprehensive to cover most of the needs of the advanced student. This third Dictionary, Harrap's CONCISE FRENCH AND ENGLISH DICTIONARY, abridged from the SHORTER DICTIONARY, and containing the French-English and English-French parts in one volume, is designed especially for use in schools and by those whose requirements do not call for the more advanced volumes. It contains many noteworthy features of the STANDARD and SHORTER Dictionaries, and yet is not much larger than the average novel. It should make a useful addition to the home library, where its scope will be found to be quite sufficient for normal requirements.

In abridging the SHORTER DICTIONARY, it was necessary to exclude more than one-half of the material contained therein. It was therefore decided to reduce the number of headwords, leaving out the more uncommon entries, rather than to reduce the many illustrative examples which form so valuable a feature of the STANDARD and the SHORTER DICTIONARIES.

The plan and general arrangement of the CONCISE DICTIONARY remain substantially the same as in the STANDARD and the SHORTER DICTIONARIES. The following explanations are worth noting:

1. Bracketed words which complete examples are not exclusive. In most cases any suitable word may be substituted for them.
2. In Part I difficult points of pronunciation and departures from the normal conjugation of verbs are indicated.

The publishers would like to pay a tribute to Mr R. P. Jago, who has carried out the task of compiling the CONCISE DICTIONARY with remarkable consistency and perseverance. Mr Jago worked for many years on the STANDARD and SHORTER DICTIONARIES and has brought his great experience to bear in solving the problem of what to include and exclude. He has carried out the difficult task of abridging the SHORTER DICTIONARY in a masterly fashion.

REPRESENTATION OF THE PRONUNCIATION
VOWELS

[i] vite, cygne
[iː] rire, lyre, Moïse
[e] été, donner, j'ai
[ɛ] elle, très, peine, mais, Noël
[ɛː] terre, père, paire
[a] chat, là, femme, toit
[aː] rare, tard, noir
[ɑ] pas, âgé, le bois
[ɑː] sable, âge, tâche
[ɔ] donne, Paul, album
[ɔː] fort, Laure
[o] dos, impôt, chaud
[oː] fosse, fausse, rôle
[u] tout, goût, août
[uː] cour, Douvres
[y] cru, eu, ciguë

[yː] mur, ils eurent
[ø] feu, ceux, nœud
[øː] meule, jeûne
[œ] jeune, œuf, cueillir
[œː] fleur, sœur, œuvre
[ə] le, ce, entremets
[ɛ̃] vin, plein, main, chien, examen, faim, thym
[ɛ̃ː] prince, ceindre, plaindre
[ã] enfant, temps, paon
[ãː] danse, centre, ample
[ɔ̃] mon, plomb
[ɔ̃ː] honte, nombre, comte
[œ̃] lundi, à jeun, parfum
[œ̃ː] humble

CONSONANTS

[p] pain, absolu
[b] beau, bleu, abbé
[m] mou, flamme, prisme
[f] feu, bref, phrase
[v] voir, vivre, wagon
[t] table, net, théâtre
[d] donner, sud
[n] né, canne, automne
[s] sou, rébus, cire, scène, action, six
[z] cousin, zéro, deuxième

[l] lait, aile, table
[ʃ] chose, chercher, schisme
[ʒ] Jean, gilet, manger
[k] camp, képi, quatre, écho
[g] garde, guerre, second
[ɲ] campagne, gniaf
[r] rare, marbre, rhume
[ks] accident, extrême
[gz] exister

SEMI-CONSONANTS

[j] yacht, piano, ration, voyage, travailler, cahier
[w] ouate, ouest, noir, pingouin, tramway
[ɥ] muet, huit, lui

DIPHTHONGS

[iːj] fille, famille
[ɛːj] soleil, veille, paye
[aːj] travail, muraille
[ɑːj] il bâille, ferraille
[œːj] fauteuil, œil, je cueille

ABBREVIATIONS

A:	Archaism; ancient; in former use	conj.	Conjunction
Abs.	Absolutely, absolute use	Conj. like	Conjugated like
		Const:	Construction
Ac:	Acoustics	Coop:	Cooperage
acc.	Accusative	Corr:	Correspondence
a., adj.	Adjective	Cost:	Costume
Adm:	Administration	Cr:	Cricket
adv.	Adverb	Crust:	Crustacea
Aer:	Aeronautics	Cryst:	Crystallography
Agr:	Agriculture	Cu:	Culinary; cuisine
Alg:	Algebra	Cust:	Customs
Amph:	Amphibia	Cy:	Cycles; cycling
Anat:	Anatomy		
Ann:	Annelida	Danc:	Dancing
Ant:	Antiquity, -ies	dat.	Dative
Anthr:	Anthropology	def.	(i) Definite; (ii) defective
Ap:	Apiculture		
Ar:	Arithmetic	dem.	Demonstrative
Arach:	Arachnida	Dent:	Dentistry
Arb:	Arboriculture	Dial:	Dialectical
Arch:	Architecture	Dipl:	Diplomacy
Archeol:	Archeology	Dist:	Distilling
Artil:	Artillery	Dom.Ec:	Domestic Economy
Astr:	Astronomy	Draw:	Drawing
Astrol:	Astrology	Dressm:	Dressmaking
attrib.	Attributive	Dy:	Dyeing
Aut:	Automobilism		
aux.	Auxiliary	E:	Engineering
Av:	Aviation	Ecc:	Ecclesiastical
		Echin:	Echinodermata
B:	Biblical; Bible	El:	Electricity; electrical
Bac:	Bacteriology	El.-Ch:	Electro-Chemistry
Ball:	Ballistics	Eng.	English; England
Bank:	Banking	Engr.	Engraving
Bib:	Bibliography	Ent:	Entomology
Bill:	Billiards	Equit:	Equitation
Bio-Ch:	Bio-Chemistry	esp.	Especially
Biol:	Biology	etc.	Et cetera
Bookb:	Bookbinding	Eth:	Ethics
Book-k:	Book-keeping	Ethn:	Ethnology
Bootm:	Bootmaking	excl.:	Exclamation; exclamatory
Bot:	Botany		
Box:	Boxing	Exp:	Explosives
Breed:	Breeding		
Brew:	Brewing	f.	Feminine
		F:	Familiar
		Farr:	Farriery
card.a.	Cardinal adjective	Fb:	Football
Carp:	Carpentry	Fenc:	Fencing
Cav:	Cavalry	Fin:	Finance
Cer:	Ceramics	Fish:	Fishing
Ch:	Chemistry	For:	Forestry
Chr:	Chronology	Fort:	Fortification
Cin:	Cinematography	Fr.	French; France
Civ.E:	Civil Engineering	fu.	Future
Cl:	Classical	Fung:	Fungi
Clockm:	Clock and watch making	Furn:	Furniture
		Gasm:	Gasmaking
Coel:	Coelenterata	Geog:	Geography
cogn.acc.	Cognate accusative	Geol:	Geology
Coll:	Collective	Geom:	Geometry
Com:	Commerce	ger.	Gerund
Comest:	Comestibles	Glassm:	Glassmaking
comp.	Comparative	Gr.	Greek
Conch:	Conchology	Gr.Alph:	Greek Alphabet
condit.	Conditional		

Gr.Civ:	Greek Civilization
Gram:	Grammar
Gym:	Gymnastics
Hairdr:	Hairdressing
Harn:	Harness
Hatm:	Hatmaking
Her:	Heraldry
Hist:	History; historical
Hor:	Horology
Hort:	Horticulture
Hum:	Humorous
Husb:	Husbandry
Hyd:	Hydraulics; hydrostatics
Hyg:	Hygiene
i.	Intransitive
I.C.E:	Internal Combustion Engines
Ich:	Ichthyology
imp.	Imperative
impers.	Impersonal
ind.	Indicative
Ind:	Industry
indef.	Indefinite
ind.tr.	Indirectly transitive
inf.	Infinitive
Ins:	Insurance
int.	Interjection
interr.	Interrogative
inv.	Invariable
Iron:	Ironical(ly)
Join:	Joinery
Journ:	Journalism
Jur:	Jurisprudence; law
Lap:	Lapidary Arts
Laund:	Laundering
Leath:	Leatherwork
Ling:	Linguistics
Lit:	Literary use; literature; literary
Lith:	Lithography
Log:	Logic
Lt.	Latin
m.	Masculine
Magn:	Magnetism
Mapm:	Mapmaking
Mch:	Machines
Meas:	Weights and measures
Mec:	Mechanics
Mec.E:	Mechanical Engineering
Med:	Medicine
Metall:	Metallurgy
Metalw:	Metalworking
Metaph:	Metaphysics
Meteor:	Meteorology
Mil:	Military
Mill:	Milling
Min:	Mining and quarrying

vii

Miner :	Mineralogy	phr.	Phrase	Sp :	Sport
M.Ins :	Maritime Insurance	Physiol :	Physiology	Spong :	Sponges
Moll :	Molluscs	Pisc :	Pisciculture	St.Exch :	Stock Exchange
Moss :	Mosses	pl.	Plural	sth.	Something
Mth :	Mathematics	Plumb :	Plumbing	sub.	Subjunctive
Mus :	Music	P.N :	Public notices	Sug.-R :	Sugar-Refining
Myr :	Myriapoda	Poet :	Poetical	sup.	Superlative
Myth :	Myth and legend; mythology	Pol :	Politics	Surg :	Surgery
		Pol.Ec :	Political Economy	Surv :	Surveying
		poss.	Possessive	Swim :	Swimming
n.	Nous (= we)	Post :	Postal Service		
N.	North	p.p.	Past participle	Tail :	Tailoring
N.Arch :	Naval Architecture	pr.	(i) present ; (ii) pro- nominal	Tan :	Tanning
Nat.Hist :	Natural History			Tchn :	Technical
Nau :	Nautical	pred.	Predicate ; predica- tive	Televis :	Television
Needlw :	Needlework			Ten :	(i) Tennis ; (ii) law tennis
neg.	Negative	prep.	Preposition		
neut.	Neuter	Pr.n.	Proper name	Tex :	Textiles
nom.	Nominative	pron.	Pronoun	Tg :	Telegraphy
Num :	Numismatics	Pros :	Prosody	Th :	Theatre
num.a.	Numeral adjective	Prot :	Protozoa	Theol :	Theology
		Prov :	Proverb	thg	Thing
Oc :	Oceanography	Psy :	Psychology	Tls :	Tools
occ.	Occasionally	Publ :	Publishing	Toil :	Toilet
Onomat :	Onomatopoeia	Pyr :	Pyrotechnics	Tp :	Telephony
Opt :	Optics			tr.	Transitive
Orn :	Ornithology	qch.	Quelque chose	Tram :	Tramways
Ost :	Ostreiculture	qn	Quelqu'un	Trig :	Trigonometry
				Typ :	Typography
p.	(i) Participle ; (ii) past	Rac :	Racing		
		Rail :	Railways	U.S :	United States
P :	Popular ; slang	R.C.Ch :	Roman Catholic Church	usu.	Usually
Paint :	Painting trade				
Pal :	Paleography	rel.	Relative	v.	Verb
Paleont :	Paleontology	Rel :	Religion(s)	v.	Vous (= you)
Paperm :	Papermaking	Rel.H :	Religious History	V :	Vulgar
Parl :	Parliament	Rept :	Reptilia	Veh :	Vehicles
p.d.	Past descriptive ; imperfect tense	Rh :	Rhetoric	Ven :	Venery
		Row :	Rowing	Vet :	Veterinary science
Pej :	Pejorative			Vit :	Viticulture
perf.	Perfect	S.	South	Voc :	Vocative
pers.	Person ; personal	s., sb.	Substantive		
p.h.	Past historic ; past definite	S.a.	See also	W.Tel :	Wireless Telephony and Telegraphy
		Sch :	Schools and universi- ties		
Ph :	Physics			W.Tg :	Wireless Telegraph
Pharm :	Pharmacy	Scot :	Scottish	W.Tp :	Wireless Telephony
Phil :	Philosophy	Sculp :	Sculpture	Wr :	Wrestling
Phot :	Photography	sg.	Singular		
Phot.Engr :	Photo-Engraving ; process work	Sm.a :	Small arms	Y :	Yachting
		s.o.	Someone	Z :	Zoology

The symbol = is used to indicate a correspondence between French and English institutions, where the terms thus brought together cannot be considered strictly as translations one of the other. Thus *Procureur général* = Attorney General. *Procureur de la République* = Public Prosecutor.

CONCISE
FRENCH AND ENGLISH DICTIONARY

PART ONE
FRENCH—ENGLISH

A, a[1], *s.m.* (The letter) A, a.

a[2]. See AVOIR.

à, *prep.* (Contracts with the article *le* into **au,** with the article *les* into **aux.**) I. **I.** (*a*) *Aller à l'école,* to go to school. *Voyage à Paris,* journey to Paris. (*b*) *Au voleur!* stop thief! (*c*) *Nous sommes point à point, F:* nous sommes point à, the score is even. *Ten:* **Quinze A,** fifteen all. **2.** *Attendre à plus tard,* to wait until later. *A jeudi!* see you on Thursday! **3.** *Être au jardin,* to be in the garden. *Avoir qch. à la main,* to have sth. in one's hand. **4.** *A deux heures,* at two o'clock. *Au mois de juillet,* in the month of July. **5.** *Vendre des marchandises à la douzaine,* to sell goods by the dozen. *Nous l'avons fait à trois,* there were three of us at it. *A la française,* (in the) French fashion. *Nager à la chien,* to swim dogwise. *Manger à sa faim,* to eat one's fill. **6.** *Penser à qch.,* to think of sth. **7.** (*a*) *Tasse à thé,* tea-cup. (*b*) *Machine à vapeur,* steam-engine. (*c*) *Homme à barbe noire,* man with a black beard. (*d*) *Le livre est à Jean,* the book is John's. **8.** (*a*) *C'est très gentil à vous,* that's very kind of you. (*b*) *C'est à vous de décider,* it is for you to decide. *C'est à vous,* it is your turn. II. **I.** *Il me reste à vous remercier,* I still have to thank you. **2.** *J'ai à faire,* I have work to do. **3.** *J'ai une lettre à écrire,* I have a letter to write. *Un spectacle à ravir,* a delightful sight. *Machine à coudre,* sewing-machine. **4.** *Je suis prêt à vous écouter,* I am ready to listen to you. **5.** (*a*) *Il est à travailler,* he is at (his) work. (*b*) *A partager les mêmes périls on apprend à se connaître,* by sharing the same dangers we learn to know each other. **6.** *Elle est laide à faire peur,* she is frightfully ugly.

abaissant, *a.* Lowering.

abaissement, *s.m.* **I.** *A. du bras, des prix,* lowering of the arm, of prices. **2.** Falling, abatement, sinking. *A. des prix,* dropping of prices. **3.** Dip (of the ground). **4.** Abasement.

abaisser, *v.tr.* **I.** To lower. *A. les yeux sur la foule,* to look down on the crowd. **2.** To lower (one's voice); to reduce, lessen (prices). **3.** To humble, bring low, abase.

s'abaisser. I. To slope downward, go down. *Ses paupières s'abaissèrent,* her eyelids drooped. **2.** To humble oneself. **3.** *S'a. à faire qch.,* to stoop to doing sth.

abandon, *s.m.* **I.** (*a*) Surrender, renunciation. (*b*) *Sp:* Giving up, withdrawal. **2.** Forsaking, desertion, neglect. **3.** Forlornness, neglect. *A l'abandon,* neglected, in utter neglect. **4.** Lack of restraint; abandon.

abandonnement, *s.m.* **I.** = ABANDON I, 2, 4. **2.** Profligacy, shamelessness.

abandonner, *v.tr.* **I.** To forsake, desert, abandon; to leave. *Abandonné de tous,* forsaken by all. *Abandonné par les médecins,* given up by the doctors. **2.** To surrender, renounce, give up. **3.** To let go (a rope).

s'abandonner. I. (*a*) To neglect oneself, to be careless of oneself. (*b*) To give way (to grief). **2.** To be unconstrained. **3.** *S'a. à qch.,* to give oneself up to sth.

abandonné, *a. & s.* **I.** Forsaken (person). *Navire a. en mer,* derelict (ship). **2.** Profligate, shameless, abandoned (person).

abaque, *s.m.* (*a*) Abacus, counting frame. (*b*) Chart, graph, scale; plotter.

abasourdir, *v.tr* To dumbfound, astound, bewilder.

abasourdissant, *a.* Astounding.

abasourdissement, *s.m.* Bewilderment, stupefaction.

abat. See ABATTRE.

abatis, *s.m.* = ABATTIS.

abat-jour, *s.m.inv.* (*a*) Lamp-shade. (*b*) Eye-shade. (*c*) Sun-blind, awning.

abattage, *s.m.* **I.** (*a*) Knocking down. (*b*) Felling. **2.** Slaughtering.

abattant. I. *a.* (*a*) Depressing. (*b*) **Siège abattant,** tilting seat (of car). **2.** *s.m.* Flap (of table, envelope).

abattement, *s.m.* (*a*) Prostration. (*b*) Despondency, depression, low spirits.

abattis, *s.m.* **I.** (*a*) Felling (of trees). (*b*) Slaughter (of game). **2.** *A. de maisons,* heap of fallen houses. **3.** *pl. Cu:* Giblets.

abattoir, *s.m.* Slaughter-house; abattoir.

abattre, *v.tr.* (Conj. like BATTRE) **I.** (*a*) To knock down, pull down; to overthrow. *F:* Abattre de la besogne, to get through a lot of work. (*b*) To fell, cut down. (*c*) To cut off. **2.** To slaughter, kill. **3.** To bring down. (*a*) *A. un avion,* to bring down an aeroplane. (*b*) *A. violemment le couvercle,* to bang down the lid. **4.** To lower. *A. les tentes,* to strike tents. **5.** To lay (dust). **6.** To blow down. **7.** To dishearten, depress. Ne vous laissez pas abattre! bear up!

s'abattre. I. To fall. **2.** *S'a. sur qch.,* to pounce upon sth. **3.** To abate, to subside. *Le vent s'abat,* the wind is falling. **4.** To become depressed.

abattu, *a.* Dejected, low-spirited. *Visage a.,* drawn face.

abbaye, *s.f.* Abbey, monastery.

abbé, *s.m.* **I.** Abbot. **2.** *R.C.Ch:* Priest.

abbesse, *s.f.* Abbess.

abcès [apsɛ], *s.m.* Abscess, gathering.

abdication, *s.f.* (*a*) Abdication. (*b*) Renunciation, surrender (of authority).

abdiquer, *v.tr.* To abdicate (throne); to renounce, surrender (rights).

abdomen [-mɛn], *s.m.* Abdomen.

abdominal, -aux, *a.* Abdominal.

abeille [abɛːj], *s.f.* Bee. *A. mâle,* drone. *A. mère,* queen-bee.

aberration, *s.f.* Aberration.

abhorrer, *v.tr.* To abhor, loathe.

abîme, *s.m.* Abyss, chasm.

abîmer, *v.tr.* To spoil, damage, injure.

s'abîmer. I. (*a*) *S'a. dans les flots,* to be swallowed up by the sea. (*b*) *S'a. dans la douleur,* to be sunk in grief. **2.** To spoil.

abject [-ʒɛkt], *a.* Abject (poverty); mean, contemptible, despicable (person, conduct).

abjectement, *adv.* Abjectly.

abjuration, *s.f.* Abjuration; recantation.

abjurer, *v.tr.* To abjure; to recant.

ablution, *s.f.* Ablution, washing.

abnégation, *s.f.* Abnegation, self-sacrifice.

aboi, *s.m.* Aux abois, at bay; hard pressed.

aboiement, aboîment, *s.m.* Bark, barking.

abolir, *v.tr.* To abolish, suppress.

abolition, *s.f.* Abolition, suppression.

abominable, *a.* Abominable; heinous.

abominablement, *adv.* Abominably.

abomination, *s.f.* Abomination, abhorrence, detestation.

abominer, *v.tr.* To abominate, abhor.

abondamment, *adv.* Abundantly.

abondance, *s.f.* **I.** Abundance, plenty. **2.** Wealth (of details). Parler avec abondance, to have a great flow of words. Parler d'abondance, to speak extempore. **3.** *F:* Wine diluted with water.

abondant, *a.* Abundant, copious, plentiful; rich (style). *A. en qch.,* abounding in sth.

abonder, *v.i.* **I.** To abound (*en,* in); to be plentiful. **2.** Abonder dans le sens de qn, to be entirely of s.o.'s opinion.

abonnement, *s.m.* **I.** Subscription (to paper). **2.** (Carte d')abonnement, season-ticket. *Prendre un a.,* to take a season.

abonner (s'), *v.pr.* **I.** *S'a. à un journal,* to subscribe to a paper. **2.** To take a season-ticket.

abonné, *s.* **I.** Subscriber (to paper). **2.** Season-ticket holder.

abord, *s.m.* **I.** Access, approach (to land). Ile d'un a. difficile, island difficult of access. **2.** *pl.* Approaches (*d'un endroit,* to a place); surroundings. **3.** (*a*) Manner in which a person approaches another. *Son a. fut respectueux,* he greeted me respectfully. (*b*) Manner in which a person receives others. Avoir l'abord facile, to be easy to approach. **4.** *Adv. phr.* D'abord, tout d'abord, first, in the first place. Dès l'abord, from the outset. A l'abord, at first sight, to begin with.

abordable, *a.* **I.** Easy to land on; easy of access; accessible. **2.** Easily approached; accessible, affable.

abordage, *s.m.* *Nau:* **I.** Boarding (as an act of war). **2.** Collision.

aborder. I. *v.i.* To land; to make land. *A. à quai,* to berth. **2.** *v.tr.* (*a*) To accost, approach (s.o.). (*b*) *A. une question,* to approach, tackle, a question. (*c*) To board (ship in a fight). (*d*) To collide with (ship).

aborigène. I. *a.* Aboriginal; native. **2.** *s.* Aboriginal. *pl.* Aborigènes, aborigines.

Aboukir. *Pr.n.m. Geog:* Abukir. *Hist:* La bataille d'Aboukir, the battle of the Nile.

aboutir, *v.i.* **I.** *A. à, dans, en, qch.,* to end at, in, sth.; to lead to sth.; to result in sth. *Une pyramide aboutit en pointe,* a pyramid ends in a point. *N'a. à rien,* to lead, come, to nothing. **2.** *Abs.* To succeed. Faire aboutir qch., to bring sth. to a successful issue.

aboutissant, *a.* Bordering, abutting (*à,* on).

aboutissement, *s.m.* Issue, outcome.

aboyer, *v.i.* (j'aboie) (Of dog) To bark; (of hound) to bay.

aboyeur, -euse. I. *a.* Barking (dog). **2.** *s. F:* (*a*) Fault-finder. (*b*) Tout (in front of booth).

abrégement, *s.m.* Abridging; shortening.

abréger, *v.tr.* (j'abrège; n. abrégeons; j'abrégerai) **I.** To shorten, to cut short. Pour abréger . . ., to be brief . . . **2.** To abridge, cut down (article); to abbreviate.

s'abréger. (Of days) To grow shorter.

abrégé, *s.m.* Abridgment, précis, summary, epitome. *A. d'histoire de France,* short history of France.

abreuvage, abreuvement, *s.m.* Watering (of horses).

abreuver, *v.tr.* **I.** To water (horses). **2.** To flood, irrigate. *L'Égypte est abreuvée par le Nil,* Egypt is watered by the Nile.

s'abreuver, (of horse) to drink; (of pers.) to quench one's thirst.

abreuvoir, *s.m.* (*a*) Watering-place; horse-pond. (*b*) Drinking-trough.

abréviation, *s.f.* Abbreviation.

abri, *s.m.* Shelter, cover. **Prendre abri,** to take cover. **A l'abri,** sheltered, under cover. *Se mettre à l'a.,* to take shelter. **A l'abri de** qch., sheltered, screened, from sth. *Nau: A l'a. de la côte,* under the lee of the shore.

abricot, *s.m.* Apricot.

abricotier, *s.m.* Apricot-tree.

abriter, *v.tr.* To shelter, screen, shield. **s'abriter,** to take shelter (*contre,* from).

abrogation, *s.f.* Abrogation, repeal (of law).

abroger, *v.tr.* (n. abrogeons) To abrogate, rescind, repeal (law).

abrupt [-rypt], *a.* **1.** Abrupt, steep (descent). **2.** Abrupt, blunt; short of speech.

abruptement, *adv.* Abruptly.

abrutir, *v.tr.* To brutalize, stupefy. *Abruti par la boisson,* sodden with drink. **s'abrutir,** to become sottish, to get stupid.

abruti, *s.m.* **1.** *F:* Sot. **2.** *P:* Idiot.

abrutissant, *a.* Stupefying; deadly dull.

abrutissement, *s.m.* **1.** Degradation. **2.** Sottishness.

absence [aps-], *s.f.* **1.** Absence. *Remarquer l'a. de qn,* to miss s.o. **2.** *A. d'imagination,* want of imagination.

absent [apsã]. **I.** *a.* (*a*) Absent, away (*de,* from). (*b*) Missing, wanting, absent. (*c*) *Son esprit est a.,* his thoughts are far away. **2.** *s.* (*a*) (The) absent one. (*b*) Absentee.

absenter (s') [saps-], *v.pr.* **I.** To absent oneself; to go from home. **2.** *S'a. de l'école,* to stay away from school.

abside [apsid], *s.f. Ecc.Arch:* Apse.

absinthe [apsɛ̃:t], *s.f.* **1.** *Bot:* Wormwood. **2.** Absinth(e).

absolu [aps-], *a.* Absolute. (*a*) *Refus a.,* flat refusal. (*b*) *Pouvoir a.,* absolute power. *Caractère a.,* autocratic nature. (*c*) Positive, peremptory (tone).

absolument [aps-], *adv.* (*a*) (To reign) absolutely. (*b*) Entirely; utterly. (*c*) Peremptorily. *Je le veux a.,* I insist upon it.

absolution [aps-], *s.f. Theol:* Absolution.

absolv-ant, -ons, etc. See ABSOUDRE.

absorbant [aps-], *a.* **1.** Absorbent (substance). **2.** Absorbing, engrossing (book).

absorber [aps-], *v.tr.* **1.** To absorb, soak up. **2.** To imbibe. **3.** To absorb, engross. **s'absorber,** to become absorbed.

absoudre [aps-], *v.tr.* (*pr.p.* absolvant; *p.p.* absous, *f.* absoute; *pr. ind.* j'absous) (*a*) To exonerate. (*b*) To absolve.

abstenir (s') [saps-], *v.pr.* (Conj. like TENIR) *S'a. de qch.,* to abstain from sth.; to forgo sth.

abstention [aps-], *s.f.* Abstaining, abstention.

abstiendr-ai, -as, etc. See ABSTENIR (S').

abstien-ne, -s, -t. See ABSTENIR (S').

abstinence [aps-], *s.f.* Abstinence. **1.** Abstemiousness. **2.** Abstention (*de,* from).

abstin-s, -t. See ABSTENIR (S').

abstraction [aps-], *s.f.* Abstraction. (*a*) *Faire abstraction de qch.,* to leave sth. out of account. (*b*) *Dans un moment d'a.,* in a moment of abstraction.

abstraire [aps-], *v.tr.* (Conj. like TRAIRE) To abstract.

abstrait, *a.* **1.** Abstracted. **2.** Abstract (idea); abstruse (question).

abstraitement [aps-], *adv.* **1.** In the abstract. **2.** Abstractedly.

abstray-ons, -ez. See ABSTRAIRE.

absurde [aps-]. **1.** *a.* Absurd, nonsensical. **2.** *s.m.* L'absurde, absurdity.

absurdement [aps-], *adv.* absurdly.

absurdité [aps-], *s.f.* **1.** Absurdity. **2.** *Dire des absurdités,* to talk nonsense.

abus, *s.m.* **1.** (*a*) Abuse, misuse (*de,* of). *Employer un terme par abus,* to misuse a term. (*b*) Over-indulgence (*de,* in). (*c*) Violation (of rights). **Abus de confiance,** breach of trust. **2.** Abuse; corrupt practice. **3.** Error, mistake.

abuser. I. *v.i. A. de qch.* (*a*) To misuse sth. *Vous abusez de vos forces,* you are over-exerting yourself. (*b*) To take advantage of sth. *A. de l'amabilité de qn,* to impose upon s.o.'s kindness. **2.** *v.tr.* To deceive, delude. **s'abuser,** to delude oneself; to be mistaken.

abusif, *a.* **1.** Contrary to usage. *Emploi a.,* wrong use, misuse. **2.** Excessive.

abusivement, *adv.* Improperly, wrongly.

acabit, *s.m. F:* Nature. **Ils sont du même acabit,** they are all of a piece.

acacia, *s.m. Bot:* Acacia.

académicien, *s.m.* Academician.

académie, *s.f.* Academy. **1.** University college or centre. **2.** Society. **3.** (*a*) Riding school. (*b*) *A. de musique,* school of music.

académique, *a.* Academic(al).

acajou, *s.m.* Mahogany.

acanthe, *s.f.* Acanthus.

acariâtre, *a.* Bad-tempered, shrewish.

accablant, *a.* **1.** Overwhelming. **2.** Overpowering (heat).

accablement, *s.m.* Dejection, despondency.

accabler, *v.tr.* To overpower, overwhelm, crush. **accablé,** *a.* **1.** Overwhelmed (with work); overcome (with grief); tired out. **2.** *A. par la chaleur,* prostrated by the heat.

accalmie, *s.f.* Lull (in the storm).

accaparer, *v.tr.* To corner, hoard (wheat). *F: A. la conversation,* to monopolize the conversation.

accapareur, -euse, *s.* Monopolist.

accéder, *v.i.* (j'accède) *j'accéderai)* **1.** To have access (*à,* to). **2.** *A. à une requête,* to accede to, comply with, a request.

accélérateur, -trice. I. *a.* Accelerative, accelerating. **2.** *s.m. Aut:* Accelerator.

accélération, *s.f.* (*a*) Acceleration. (*b*) Hastening, speeding up (of work).

accélérer, *v.tr.* (j'accélère; j'accélérerai) To accelerate, quicken; to speed up. **s'accélérer,** to become faster; to accelerate.

accéléré, *a.* **1.** Accelerated (motion). **2.** Quick, fast.

accent, *s.m.* Accent. **1.** Stress. **2.** *A. aigu,* acute accent. **3.** Pronunciation. **4.** Tone of voice. **5.** *pl.* (*a*) *Les accents du désespoir,* the accents of despair. (*b*) *Les accents de la Marseillaise,* the strains of the Marseillaise.

accentuation, *s.f.* **1.** Stressing (of syllables). **2.** Accentuation; placing of accents.

accentuer, *v.tr.* **1.** To stress (syllable). **2.** To mark (vowel) with an accent; to accentuate. **3.** To emphasize. *Traits fortement accentués,* strongly marked features.

s'accentuer, to become accentuated, more pronounced, more marked.

acceptabilité, *s.f.* Acceptability.

acceptable, *a.* **1.** Acceptable (*à,* to). **2.** In fair condition.

acceptablement, *adv.* Acceptably.

acceptation, *s.f.* Acceptance.

accepter, *v.tr.* To accept. *A. que qch. se fasse,* to agree to sth. being done.

acception, *s.f.* Acceptation, meaning.

accès, *s.m.* **1.** Access, approach. **Trouver accès auprès de qn,** to gain admission to s.o. **2.** Fit, attack, outburst. **Travailler par accès,** to work by fits and starts.

accessibilité, *s.f.* Accessibility.

accessible, *a.* **1.** Accessible. **2.** (*a*) Approachable. (*b*) *A. à la pitié,* open to pity.

accession, *s.f.* **1.** Accession. **2.** Union. **3.** Adherence, adhesion (to a party).

accessit [-sit], *s.m.* Honourable mention.

accessoire. **1.** (*a*) Accessory. **2.** *s.m.* Accessory, appurtenance. *pl. Th:* Properties.

accident, *s.m.* **1.** Accident. (*a*) **Je l'ai retrouvé par accident,** I found it accidentally. (*b*) Mishap. *A. mortel,* fatality. **Nous sommes arrivés sans accident,** we arrived safely. **2.** *Mus:* Accidental. **3.** **Accident de terrain,** undulation of the ground.

accidenté. **1.** *a.* (*a*) Eventful (life). (*b*) Uneven, broken (ground). **2.** *s.* Victim of an accident. *Les accidentés,* the injured.

accidentel, -elle, *a.* **1.** Accidental, undesigned. **2.** *Mus:* **Signes accidentels,** (i) accidentals, (ii) key-signature.

accidentellement, *adv.* Accidentally.

acclamation, *s.f.* Acclamation, cheering.

acclamer. **1.** *v.tr.* (*a*) To acclaim, applaud, cheer. (*b*) *Pred. A. qn empereur,* to hail s.o. as emperor. **2.** *v.ind.tr. A. à une proposition,* to greet a proposal with cheers.

acclimatation, *s.f.* Acclimatization.

acclimatement, *s.m.* Acclimatization.

acclimater, *v.tr.* To acclimatize (*à,* to).

s'acclimater, to become acclimatized.

accointances, *s.f.pl.* Intimacy; dealings.

accointé, *s.* Partner (in fraud).

accolade, *s.f.* **1.** (*a*) Embrace. (*b*) *F:* Hug or kiss. **2. Recevoir l'accolade,** to be knighted. **3.** *Mus:* Bracket.

accoler, *v.tr.* To couple.

accommodable, *a.* Adjustable (quarrel).

accommodant, *a.* Good-natured, easygoing, accommodating.

accommodement, *s.m.* Compromise, arrangement.

accommoder, *v.tr.* **1.** (*a*) To make (s.o.) comfortable. (*b*) To suit (s.o.). *Difficile à a.,* difficult to please. **2.** To cook, dress (food). **3.** *A. qch. à qch.,* to fit, adapt, sth. to sth.

s'accommoder. **1.** To make oneself comfortable. *Il s'accommode partout,* he is very adaptable. **2.** *S'a. de qch.,* to make the best of sth. **3.** *S'a. à qch.,* to adapt, accommodate, oneself to sth. **4.** *S'a. avec qn,* to come to an agreement with s.o.

accompagnateur, -trice, *s.* Accompanist.

accompagnement, *s.m.* **1.** Accompanying. **2.** *Mus:* Accompaniment.

accompagner, *v.tr.* To accompany. (*a*) To go, come, with (s.o.). (*b*) To escort, attend (s.o.). (*c*) *A. qn au piano,* to accompany s.o. on the piano.

accomplir, *v.tr.* **1.** To accomplish, achieve; to carry out, perform, fulfil. **2.** To complete, finish.

accompli, *a.* Accomplished (musician).

accomplissement, *s.m.* **1.** Accomplishment, performance (of duty); fulfilment (of wish). **2.** Completion.

accord, *s.m.* **1.** Agreement. (*a*) Settlement. (*b*) Harmony. **D'accord,** in agreement, in accordance (*avec,* with). **Se mettre d'accord avec qn,** to come to an agreement with s.o. **D'accord!** agreed! quite so! (*c*) *Gram:* Concordance. **Les règles d'accord,** the concords. **2.** *Mus:* Chord. **3.** *Mus:* Pitch, tune. **Être d'accord,** to be in tune.

accordéon, *s.m.* Accordion.

accorder, *v.tr.* **1.** To reconcile. **2.** *Mus:* To tune. **3.** To grant, concede; to award.

s'accorder. **1.** (*a*) To agree, come to an agreement. (*b*) To get on (*avec qn,* with s.o.). **2.** To accord, harmonize; to be in keeping. **3.** *Gram:* To agree. **4.** (Of dress) To go (*avec,* with). **5.** (Of instruments) To tune (up).

accordeur, *s.m.* Tuner.

accort, *a.* Pleasing, trim.

accostage, *s.m. Nau:* Boarding (of ship); drawing alongside (of quay).

accoster, *v.tr.* **1.** To accost; to go, come, up to. **2.** To berth (a boat). **3.** *Nau:* To come on board.

accoter (s'), *v.pr. S'a. à un mur,* to lean against a wall.

accoucher, *v.i.* To be confined.

accouder (s'), *v.pr.* To lean on one's elbows.

accouplement, *s.m.* **1.** (*a*) Coupling, join(ing), link(ing). (*b*) *El:* Connecting. **2.** Pairing, mating.

accoupler, *v.tr.* (*a*) To couple; to yoke (oxen). (*b*) To couple (up) (parts). (*c*) *El:* To connect (batteries).

accourir, *v.i.* (Conj. like COURIR). To hasten (up). *Ils ont accouru, sont accourus, à mon secours,* they came running to my help.

accoutrement, *s.m.* Dress, garb; *F:* get-up.

accoutrer, *v.tr.* To rig (s.o.) out, get (s.o.) up (*de,* in).

accoutumer, *v.tr.* A. *qn à qch.,* to accustom s.o. to sth. ; to inure s.o. (to hunger).

s'accoutumer. *S'a. à qch.,* to get accustomed to sth. ; to become inured to sth.

accoutumé. *a.* (*a*) Accustomed, used (*à,* to) ; inured (to). (*b*) Accustomed, customary, usual. *Adv. phr.* **Comme à l'accoutumée,** as usual.

accréditer, *v.tr.* **1.** (*a*) To accredit (an ambassador). (*b*) To cause (sth.) to be credited. **2.** To credit, believe (sth.).

s'accréditer, (of news) to gain credence.

accroc [akro], *s.m.* **1.** Tear, rent (in clothes). **2.** Hitch, difficulty.

accrocher, *v.tr.* (*a*) To hook. *A. sa robe à un clou,* to catch one's dress on a nail. (*b*) *A. une voiture au train,* to hitch, couple, a carriage on to the train. (*c*) *A. sa robe à un clou,* to hang (up) one's dress on a nail. (*d*) *W.Tel: A. un poste,* to pick up, tune in, a station.

s'accrocher. **1.** *S'a. à qch.,* to fasten on to, cling to, sth. **2.** To get caught (*à,* on).

accroire, *v.tr.* *Faire a. à qn,* to cause s.o. to believe. *En faire a. à qn,* to delude s.o. *S'en faire a.,* to think too much of oneself.

accroiss-e, etc. See ACCROÎTRE.

accroissement, *s.m.* **1.** (*a*) Growth (of plant). (*b*) Increase. **2.** (Amount of) increase, growth.

accroître, *v.tr.* (*pr.p.* accroissant; *p.p.* accru; *pr.ind.* j'accroîs, il accroît) To increase, augment; to enhance (reputation).

s'accroître, to increase, grow.

accroupir (s'), *v.pr.* To squat, to crouch (down). *Accroupi,* squatting, crouching.

accru, -s, -t, etc. See ACCROÎTRE.

accu, *s.m.* El: F: = ACCUMULATEUR.

accueil [akœj], *s.m.* Reception, welcome. *Faire bon accueil à qn,* to welcome s.o.

accueillant [akœjᾶ], *a.* Gracious, affable.

accueillir [akœji:r], *v.tr.* (Conj. like CUEILLIR) To receive, greet.

acculer, *v.tr.* To drive (s.o.) back (*contre,* against) ; to bring (animal) to bay.

s'acculer, *à, contre, qch.,* to set one's back against sth. ; to stand at bay.

accumulateur, -trice, *s.* **1.** Accumulator, hoarder. **2.** *s.m.* El: Accumulator.

accumulation, *s.f.* **1.** Accumulating (of energy). **2.** Accumulation, hoard.

accumuler, *v.tr.* To accumulate, amass; to hoard ; to heap up.

s'accumuler, to accumulate.

accusateur, -trice. **1.** *a.* Accusatory, incriminating. **2.** *s.* Accuser, impeacher.

accusatif, *a. & s.m. Gram:* Accusative.

accusation, *s.f.* **1.** Accusation, charge. **2.** *Pol:* Impeachment, arraignment.

accuser, *v.tr.* **1.** *A. qn de qch.,* to accuse s.o. of sth. ; to charge, tax, s.o. with sth. **2.** *A. qch.,* to own to, to profess, sth. *Fenc: A. un*
coup, to acknowledge a hit. **3.** To define, show up, accentuate. *L'indicateur accuse une vitesse de . . .,* the speedometer shows a speed of. . . . **4. Accuser réception de qch.,** to acknowledge (receipt of) sth.

accusé. **1.** *a.* Prominent, pronounced, bold (feature). **2.** *s.* Accused.

acerbe, *a.* **1.** Tart, sour. **2.** Sharp, harsh.

acerbité, *s.f.* Acerbity. **1.** Tartness, sourness. **2.** Sharpness, harshness.

acérer, *v.tr.* (j'acère; j'acérerai) To sharpen.

acéré, *a.* (*a*) Sharp(-pointed). (*b*) Sharpedged, keen (blade).

acétate, *s.m. Ch:* Acetate.

acétique, *a. Ch:* Acetic.

acétylène, *s.m.* Acetylene.

achalandage, *s.m. Com:* **1.** Working up of a connection. **2.** Customers, connection.

achalander, *v.tr.* To provide (shop) with custom.

acharnement, *s.m.* (*a*) Desperate eagerness. (*b*) Relentlessness. *A. au travail, pour le travail,* passion for work. *Travailler avec a.,* to work (desperately) hard.

acharner (s'), *v.pr.* **1.** *S'a. après, contre, sur, qn,* to be dead set against s.o. *Le malheur s'acharne après lui,* misfortune dogs his footsteps. **2.** *S'a. à, sur, qch.,* to work unceasingly at sth.

acharné, *a.* **1.** Eager in pursuit. *Hommes acharnés les uns contre les autres,* men fighting desperately against each other. **2.** *Joueur a.,* inveterate, keen, gambler. **3.** *Lutte acharnée,* stubborn, desperate, contest.

achat, *s.m.* Purchase. **1.** Buying. **2.** Thing bought.

acheminer (s'), *v.pr. S'a. vers sa maison,* to proceed, to wend one's way, homeward.

acheter, *v.tr.* (j'achète) (*a*) *A. qch.,* to buy, purchase, sth. (*b*) *A. qch. à qn,* to buy sth. from, of, s.o. (*c*) *Je vais lui a. un livre,* I am going to buy him a book.

acheteur, -euse, *s.* Purchaser, buyer.

achèvement, *s.m.* Completion, finishing.

achever, *v.tr.* (j'achève). **1.** To end, finish (off), complete. *A. de faire qch.,* to finish doing sth. *Achève de boire ton café,* drink up your coffee. **2.** To dispatch (animal).

s'achever. **1.** To draw to a close ; to end. **2.** (Of work) To reach completion.

achevé, *a.* **1.** (*a*) Accomplished (horseman); perfect (piece of work). (*b*) *F:* **Sot achevé,** downright fool. **2.** *s.m.* Finish, perfection (of work of art).

achoppement, *s.m.* Knock, stumble. **Pierre d'achoppement,** stumbling-block.

acide. **1.** *a.* Acid, sharp, sour. **2.** *s.m.* Acid.

acidité, *s.f.* Acidity, sourness, tartness.

acier, *s.m.* Steel. *Lame d'a., en a.,* steel blade. *Regard d'acier,* steely glance.

acolyte, *s.m.* **1.** *Ecc:* Acolyte. **2.** *F:* (*a*) Assistant, acolyte. (*b*) Confederate.

acompte, [akɔ̃:t], *s.m.* Instalment, payment on account.

aconit [-nit], *s.m. Bot:* Aconite.

Açores (les). *Pr.n.f.pl.* The Azores.

à-coup, *s.m.* Jerk; sudden stoppage. Il travaille par à-coups, he works by fits and starts.

acoustique. I. a. Acoustic. Cornet acoustique, ear-trumpet. Tuyau acoustique, speaking-tube. **2.** *s.f.* Acoustics.

acquéreur, -euse, *s.* Acquirer, purchaser.

acquérir, *v.tr. (pr.p.* acquérant; *p.p.* acquis; *pr.ind.* j'acquiers, n. acquérons, ils acquièrent; *pr.sub.* j'acquière, n. acquérions, ils acquièrent; *fu.* j'acquerrai) To acquire, obtain, get, win, gain, secure. *Sa protection m'est acquise,* I can count on his protection.

acquis. I. a. (a) Acquired (knowledge). **(b)** Droits acquis, vested interests. **2.** *s.m.* Acquirements, experience.

acquiescement, *s.m.* Acquiescence, assent.

acquiescer, *v.ind.tr.* (n. acquiesçons) *A. à qch.,* to acquiesce in sth.; to agree to sth.

acqui-s, -t, etc. See ACQUÉRIR.

acquisition, *s.f.* Acquisition. **I.** Acquiring. **2.** Thing bought or obtained; purchase.

acquit, *s.m.* **I.** *Com:* Receipt, acquittance. "Pour acquit," 'paid.' **2.** Release (from promise). Faire qch. par manière d'acquit, to do sth. as a matter of form.

acquittement, *s.m.* **I.** Discharge, payment (of debt). **2.** *Jur:* Acquittal.

acquitter, *v.tr.* **I.** (a) *A. qn (d'une obligation),* to release s.o. (from an obligation). (b) *A. un accusé,* to acquit an accused person. **2.** (a) *A. une dette,* to discharge a debt. (b) *A. une facture,* to receipt a bill.

s'acquitter. I. *S'a. d'un devoir,* to discharge a duty. *Se bien a.,* to acquit oneself well.

âcre, *a.* Acrid, bitter, tart, pungent.

âcreté, *s.f.* Acidity, bitterness, pungency.

acrimonie, *s.f.* Acrimony, acrimoniousness.

acrimonieusement, *adv.* Acrimoniously.

acrimonieux, *a.* Acrimonious.

acrobate, *s.m. & f.* Acrobat, tumbler.

acrobatie, *s.f.* (a) Acrobatics. (b) Acrobatic feat.

acrobatique, *a.* Acrobatic.

acrostiche, *a. & s.m.* acrostic.

acte, *s.m.* **I.** Action, act, deed. Faire acte de bonne volonté, to give proof of good will. **2.** *Jur:* (a) Deed, title. *A. de vente,* bill of sale. (b) Acte judiciaire, writ. Acte d'accusation, bill of indictment. (c) Record. Acte de décès, death-certificate. Acte de dernière volonté, last will and testament. **3.** *Th:* Act.

acteur, -trice, *s.* Actor, actress; player.

actif. I. a. (a) Active. *Armée active,* regular army. (b) Active, brisk, alert. **2.** *s.m. Com:* Assets; credit (account).

action, *s.f.* **I.** (a) Action, deed, exploit. **2.** (a) (i) *A. sur qch.,* effect on sth. (ii) *A. sur qn,* influence over s.o. Sans action, ineffective. (b) *A. de l'eau,* agency of water. (c) Action, motion. **3.**

(a) Action, gesture. (b) *Th:* Action. **4.** *Fin:* Share. Compagnie par actions, joint-stock company. **5.** *Jur:* Action, lawsuit, trial. **6.** *Mil:* Action, engagement.

actionnaire, *s.m. & f.* Shareholder.

actionner, *v.tr.* **I.** *Jur:* To sue. **2.** *Mec.E:* To set in action.

s'actionner, to bestir oneself.

actionné, *a.* Busy, brisk.

activement, *adv.* Actively, briskly.

activer, *v.tr.* To quicken, stir (up), urge on. *A. un travail,* to expedite a piece of work.

s'activer, to bestir oneself.

activité, *s.f.* Activity. **I.** *A. chimique d'un corps,* chemical activity of a body. **2.** Quickness, dispatch. **3.** En activité, in progress, at work. *L'usine est en a.,* the mill is working.

actrice. See ACTEUR.

actuaire, *s.m. Ins:* Actuary.

actualité, *s.f.* **I.** Actuality, reality. **2.** Question, event, of the moment. Les actualités, current events.

actuel, -elle, *a.* Of the present day; existing, current. *A l'heure actuelle,* at the present time.

actuellement, *adv.* (Just) now, at present, at the present time, at the moment.

acuité, *s.f.* Acuteness, sharpness (of point). *A. d'un son,* high pitch of a sound.

adage, *s.m.* Adage, common saying; saw.

adaptable, *a.* Adaptable (à, to).

adaptation, *s.f.* Adaptation, adjustment.

adapter, *v.tr. A. qch. à qch.,* (i) to fit, adjust sth. to sth.; (ii) to adapt sth. to sth.

s'adapter. I. *S'a. à qch.,* to fit, suit, sth. **2.** *S'a. aux circonstances,* to adapt oneself to circumstances.

addenda, *s.m.inv.* Addendum (à, to).

addition, *s.f.* **I.** Addition, (i) adding (à, to); (ii) adding up, totting up. **2.** (a) Accession, accretion. (b) *Ar:* Addition, cast, tot. (c) (In restaurant) Bill, reckoning.

additionnel, -elle, *a.* Additional.

additionner, *v.tr.* **I.** To add up, cast. **2.** *Lait additionné d'eau,* watered milk.

adepte, *s.m. & f.* Adept.

adhérence, *s.f.* Adherence, adhesion.

adhérent. I. a. Adherent (à, to); adhesive. **2.** *s. A. d'un parti,* adherent of a party.

adhérer, *v.i.* (j'adhère; j'adhérerai) **I.** To adhere, stick. (Of wheels) *A. à la route,* to grip the road. **2.** To adhere (to opinion). **3.** *A. à un parti,* to join (a party).

adhésif, *a. & s.m.* Adhesive.

adhésion, *s.f.* **I.** Adhesion, sticking. **2.** Adhesion, adherence (à, to). *A. à un parti,* joining of a party.

adieu, *pl.* -eux. **I.** *adv.* Good-bye, farewell. **2.** *s.m.* Farewell, parting, leave-taking. Faire ses adieux à qn, to take leave of s.o.

adipeux, *a.* Adipose, fatty (tissue).

adjacent, *a.* Adjacent, contiguous (à, to); adjoining; bordering (à, on).

adjectif. 1. *a.* Adjectival. **2.** *s.m.* Adjective.

adjectivement, *adv.* Adjectivally.

adjoign-e, etc. See ADJOINDRE.

adjoindre, *v.tr.* (Conj. like JOINDRE) **1.** *A. qch. à qch.,* to unite sth. with sth. **2.** *A. qn à un comité,* to add s.o. to a committee.

　s'adjoindre *à d'autres,* to join (in) with others.

adjoint. 1. *a.* Assistant (professor). **2.** *s.* Assistant; deputy. **3.** *s.m. Adjoints du verbe,* adjuncts of the verb.

adjoin-s, -t. See ADJOINDRE.

adjudant, *s.m.* **1.** *Mil:* (*a*) Company sergeant-major. (*b*) **Adjudant-major,** adjutant. **2.** *Navy:* Warrant-officer.

adjudicataire. 1. *a. Partie a.,* contracting party. **2.** *s.* Highest bidder (at auction).

adjudicateur, -trice, *s.* Adjudicator, awarder (of contract).

adjudication, *s.f.* (*a*) Adjudication, award. (*b*) Knocking-down (of sth. to s.o.).

adjuger, *v.tr.* (n. adjugeons) *A. qch. à qn,* (i) to adjudge, award, allocate, sth. to s.o.; (ii) to knock down sth. to s.o.

adjurer, *v.tr. A. qn de faire qch.,* to adjure, beseech, s.o. to do sth.

admettre, *v.tr.* (Conj. like METTRE) **1.** To admit; to let (s.o.) in. *Être admis à un examen,* to pass an examination. **2.** *A. qn à faire qch.,* to permit s.o. to do sth. **3.** (*a*) *A. qch.,* to admit, permit sth. L'usage admis, the accepted custom. (*b*) *J'admets que j'ai tort,* I admit that I am in the wrong.

administrateur, -trice, *s.* **1.** Administrator (of colony). **2.** Director (of bank).

administratif, *a.* Administrative.

administration, *s.f.* **1.** Administering (of justice). **2.** (*a*) Administration (of business). Conseil d'administration, board of directors. (*b*) Governing. **3.** (*a*) Governing body. (*b*) Government service. (*c*) The officials.

administrativement, *adv.* Administratively.

administrer, *v.tr.* **1.** To administer, conduct (business); to govern (country). **2.** *A. qch. à qn,* to administer sth. to s.o.

　administré, *s.* Person under s.o.'s administration or jurisdiction.

admirable, *a.* Admirable, wonderful.

admirablement, *adv.* Admirably, wonderfully.

admirateur, -trice. 1. Admiring. **2.** *s.* Admirer.

admiratif, *a.* Admiring (gesture).

admiration, *s.f.* Admiration. **Être l'admiration de qn,** to be admired by s.o.

admirer, *v.tr.* To admire.

admis, admisse, etc. See ADMETTRE.

admissibilité, *s.f.* Admissibility.

admissible, *a.* (*a*) Admissible. (*b*) *A. à un emploi,* eligible for an occupation.

admission, *s.f.* Admission (*à, dans,* to).

admit. See ADMETTRE.

admonestation, *s.f.* Admonition.

admonester, *v.tr.* To admonish, censure.

adolescence, *s.f.* Adolescence, youth

adolescent, *s.* Adolescent.

adonner (s'), *v.pr. S'a. à qch.,* to give oneself up to sth. *S'a. aux sports,* to go in for sport.

adopter, *v.tr.* **1.** *A. un enfant,* to adopt a child. **2.** *A. un projet de loi,* to pass a bill.

adoptif, *a.* Adopted, adoptive (child).

adoption, *s.f.* Adoption (of child). *Parl:* Passage, carrying (of bill).

adorable, *a.* Adorable; charming.

adorablement, *adv.* Adorably.

adorateur, -trice, *s.* Adorer, worshipper.

adoration, *s.f.* Adoration.

adorer, *v.tr.* To adore, worship.

adosser, *v.tr.* To place back to back.

　s'adosser *à, contre, qch.,* to set, lean, one's back against sth.

　adossé, *a. A. à qch.,* with one's back against sth.

adoucir, *v.tr.* **1.** To soften; to tone down; to subdue; to sweeten. **2.** To alleviate, relieve. **3.** To pacify, mollify

　s'adoucir. 1. (Of voice) To grow softer. **2.** (Of weather) To grow milder. **3.** (Of pain) To grow less.

adoucissement, *s.* **1.** Softening (of voice). **2.** Alleviation (of pain).

adresse, *s.f.* **1.** Address, destination. **Lettre à l'adresse de qn,** letter addressed to s.o. *F:* Une observation à votre adresse, a hit at you. **2.** (*a*) Skill, dexterity. (*b*) Shrewdness, adroitness. (*c*) Craftiness, cunning.

adresser, *v.tr.* **1.** To address, direct (letter). **2.** *On m'a adressé à vous,* I have been recommended to come to you. **3.** To aim, address (remarks).

　s'adresser. 1. To apply (*à,* to). "S'adresser ici," 'apply, enquire, here.' **2.** *S'a. à qn,* to address s.o., to speak to s.o.

Adrien. *Pr.n.m.* **1.** Adrian. **2.** Hadrian.

adroit, *a.* **1.** (*a*) Dexterous, deft, skilful, handy. (*b*) *Phrase adroite,* neat way of putting it. **2.** Shrewd, adroit (answer).

adroitement, *adv.* **1.** Skilfully. **2.** Adroitly.

adulateur, -trice. 1. *a.* Adulatory, flattering, sycophantic. **2.** *s.* Sycophant; flatterer.

adulation, *s.f.* Adulation; sycophancy.

adulte, *a. & s.m. & f.* Adult, grown-up.

adultération, *s.f.* Adulteration (of food); falsification (of document).

adultère¹. 1. *a.* Adulterous. **2.** *s.* Adulterer, *f.* adulteress.

adultère², *s.m.* Adultery.

adultérer, *v.tr.* (j'adultère; j'adultérerai) To adulterate; to falsify (document).

advenir, *v.* (Conj. like VENIR) To occur, happen; to come (about). **1.** *v.i. Je ne sais ce qui en adviendra,* I don't know what will come of it. **Le cas advenant que** + *sub.,* in the event of (something happening). **2.** *v. impers.* Or, *il advint,* now it came to pass. **Advienne que pourra,** come what may.

adventice, *a.* Adventitious; casual.
adverbe, *s.m.* Adverb.
adverbial, -aux, *a.* Adverbial.
adverbialement, *adv.* Adverbially.
adversaire, *s.m.* Adversary, opponent.
adverse, *a.* (*a*) *Jur:* La partie a., the other side. (*b*) Adverse, unfavourable.
adversité, *s.f.* 1. Adversity. Être dans l'adversité, to be in straitened circumstances. 2. Misfortune, trial.
adviendra, advienne, advient, advint. See ADVENIR.
aérage, *s.m.* **aération,** *s.f.* 1. Ventilation (of room). 2. Aeration (of bread).
aérer, *v.tr.* (j'aère, j'aérerai) 1. (*a*) To ventilate. (*b*) To air. 2. To aerate.
aérien, -ienne, *a.* 1. Aerial (phenomenon). Raid aérien, air-raid. 2. (Light and) airy.
aérodrome, *s.m.* Aerodrome, flying-ground.
aérolithe, *s.m.* Aerolite, meteorite.
aéronaute, *s.m. & f.* Aeronaut.
aéronautique. 1. *a.* Aeronautical; air (service). 2. *s.f.* Aeronautics
aéroplane, *s.m.* Aeroplane.
aéroport, *s.m.* Air-port, air-station.
aéroporté, *a.* Airborne.
aérostatique. 1. *a.* Aerostatic(al). 2. *s.f.* Aerostatics.
affabilité, *s.f.* Graciousness, affability.
affable, *a.* Gracious, affable.
affaiblir, *v.tr.* To weaken. (*a*) To enfeeble. (*b*) To lessen. A. le courage de qn, to damp s.o.'s courage.
s'affaiblir, to become weak(er); to lose one's strength.
affaiblissement, *s.m.* 1. (*a*) Weakening. (*b*) Lessening, reducing. 2. Enfeeblement.
affaire, *s.f.* 1. (*a*) Business, affair. Ce n'est pas votre a., it's no business of yours. J'en fais mon a., leave it to me; I will deal with it. Savoir son affaire, to know what one is about. (*b*) Question, matter, affair. Affaire de cœur, love-affair. A. de goût, matter of taste. Ce n'est que l'affaire d'un instant, it won't take a minute. (*c*) Thing (required). J'ai votre a., I have the very thing you want. Faire l'affaire de qn, to answer the purpose of s.o. Son affaire est faite, he is done for. (*d*) (i) Business, matter. Ce n'est pas une affaire, it's no great matter. La belle affaire! pooh, is that all! En voici une affaire! here's a pretty kettle of fish! (ii) S'attirer une (mauvaise) affaire, to get into trouble. 2. (*a*) Affair, business, transaction. Faire une bonne a., to do a good stroke of business. C'est une affaire d'or, it will be a gold mine. Venir pour affaire(s), to come on business. C'est une affaire faite! done! that's settled! (*b*) Avoir affaire à, avec, qn, to have to deal with s.o. C'est a. à un médecin, it is a case for a doctor. 3. *pl.* (*a*) Things, belongings. (*b*) Business, trade. Faire de bonnes affaires, to be successful in business. Homme d'affaires, (i) business man, (ii) agent,

(iii) steward, (iv) lawyer. (*c*) Les affaires de l'État, State affairs. Le Ministère des Affaires étrangères, the Foreign Office. 4. *Jur:* Case, lawsuit. 5. (*a*) Affaire d'honneur, duel. (*b*) *Mil:* Engagement.
affairé, *a.* Busy. Faire l'affairé, to pretend to be busy, to fuss around.
affaissement, *s.m.* 1. Subsidence; collapse (of floor). 2. Depression, despondency.
affaisser (s'), *v.pr.* (*a*) (Of thg) To subside, give way, collapse; (of material) to give, yield. (*b*) (Of pers.) To collapse.
affamer, *v.tr.* To starve (s.o.).
affamé, *a* Hungry, starving, famished. Être a. de qch., to hunger after sth.; to long for sth.
affectation, *s.f.* 1. Affectation. (*a*) Affectedness. Sans affectation, unaffectedly. (*b*) Simulation, pretence. 2. A. de qch. à qch., assignment of sth. to a purpose; appropriation for a purpose.
affecter, *v.tr.* 1. A. qch. à un certain usage, to assign sth. to a certain use. 2. To affect, simulate. A. la mort, to feign death. 3. To affect; to have a partiality for. A. les grands mots, to affect big words. 4. To assume, take on (shape). 5. (*a*) To affect, move, touch (s.o.). (*b*) To affect (career).
affecté, *a.* Affected (person); mincing.
affection, *s.f.* Affection. 1. Fondness, attachment, liking (pour, for). Avoir qn en affection, to be fond of s.o. 2. *Med:* Complaint.
affectionner, *v.tr.* A. qn, to have an affection for s.o.
affectionné, *a.* Affectionate, loving.
affectueusement, *adv.* Affectionately, lovingly.
affectueux, *a.* Affectionate, loving.
afférent, *a.* 1. Assignable (à, to). Traitement a. à un emploi, salary attaching to a post. 2. Relating (à, to).
affermer, *v.tr.* 1. To lease (farm). 2. To rent; to take (land) on lease.
affermir, *v.tr.* 1. To strengthen, steady, make firm. 2. To strengthen, consolidate.
s'affermir, to become stronger, firmer.
affermissement, *s.m.* 1. Strengthening. 2. Support.
afféterie, *s.f.* Affectation, primness.
affichage, *s.m.* Bill-sticking; placarding. *Sp:* Tableau d'affichage, telegraph board.
affiche, *s.f.* (*a*) A. murale, placard, poster, bill. A. de théâtre, play-bill. (*b*) Stamp, mark, sign (of quality).
afficher, *v.tr.* 1. To stick (up), placard, display (notice). A. une vente, to advertise a sale. "Défense d'afficher," 'stick no bills.' 2. To parade; to make a show of (sth.).
s'afficher, to show off; to seek notoriety.
afficheur, *s.m.* Bill-sticker, bill-poster.
affilage, *s.m.* Whetting, sharpening.
affiler, *v.tr.* To sharpen, set, whet (blade).
affilé, *a.* Sharp.

affiliation, *s.f.* Affiliation (*à,* with).

affilier, *v.tr.* To affiliate (*à,* to, with).

affinage, *s.m.,* **affinement,** *s.m.* **1.** Improvement, refining. **2.** Sharpening (of the intelligence). **3.** Thinning.

affiner, *v.tr.* **1.** To improve, refine. **2.** To sharpen (the intelligence). **3.** To thin.
　s'affiner. To gain in refinement.

affinité, *s.f.* Affinity. (*a*) Relationship by marriage. (*b*) Similarity of character. (*c*) *Ch:* *A. pour un corps,* affinity for a body.

affirmatif. **1.** *a.* Affirmative, positive. **Signe affirmatif,** nod. **2.** *s.f.* L'**affirmative,** the affirmative.

affirmation, *s.f.* Affirmation; assertion.

affirmativement, *adv.* Affirmatively; positively.

affirmer, *v.tr.* (*a*) To affirm, assert. (*b*) *Théorie affirmée par l'expérience,* theory supported by experience.

affixe. **1.** *a.* Affixed. **2.** *s.m.* Affix.

affleurement, *s.m.* **1.** *Carp:* Levelling, making flush. **2.** *Geol:* Outcrop.

affleurer. **1.** *v.tr.* To bring to the same level. **2.** *v.i.* To be level, flush.

affliction, *s.f.* Affliction, tribulation, sorrow.

affligeant, *a.* Distressing, sad (news).

affliger, *v.tr.* (n. affligeons) **1.** To afflict (*de,* with). **2.** To pain, distress, grieve.
　s'affliger, to grieve, to sorrow (*de,* at, about, over).

affligé, *a.* **1.** Afflicted. *Être a. d'une infirmité,* to suffer from an infirmity. **2.** *Être a. d'une nouvelle,* to be grieved at a piece of news.

affluence, *s.f.* **1.** Flow, flood. **2.** Affluence, abundance. **3.** Crowd, concourse. **Heures d'affluence,** rush hours.

affluent, *s.m.* Tributary, affluent (of river).

affluer, *v.i.* **1.** (Of water) To flow. **2.** To abound; to be plentiful. **3.** *A. à, dans, un endroit,* to crowd to a place.

affolement, *s.m.* **1.** Distraction, panic. **2.** Racing (of engine).

affoler, *v.tr.* **1.** To madden, distract. **2.** *Mch:* To let (machine) race.
　s'affoler. **1.** To fall into a panic; to stampede. **2.** To become infatuated (*de,* with).

affolé, *a.* Crazy, distracted.

affranchir, *v.tr.* **1.** To free; to set free; to emancipate. **2.** To pay the postage on; to stamp (letter).
　s'affranchir, to become free, independent. *S'a. de qch.,* to shake off sth.

affranchi, *a.* (*a*) Freed, emancipated (slave). (*b*) Free (*de,* of, from).

affranchissement, *s.m.* **1.** Emancipation (of slave). **2.** Stamping (of letter).

affranchisseur, *s.m.* Liberator.

affre, *s.f.* Usu. *pl.* Anguish, spasm.

affrètement, *s.m.* Chartering (of ship).

affréter, *v.tr.* (j'affrète; j'affréterai) To charter (ship).

affreusement, *adv.* Terribly, frightfully.

affreux, *a.* **1.** Frightful, hideous. **2.** Frightful, shocking (crime).

affront, *s.m.* Affront, indignity, snub.

affronter, *v.tr.* To face, confront (s.o.); to affront (danger). *A. les périls d'un voyage,* to dare the perils of a journey.

affublement, *s.m.* Get-up, rig-out.

affubler, *v.tr.* *A. qn de qch.,* to dress s.o. up in sth. ; to rig s.o. out in sth.
　s'affubler, to rig oneself out (in sth.).

affût, *s.m.* **1.** Hiding-place. **Être, se mettre, à l'affût de qn,** to lie in wait for s.o. *A l'a. de nouvelles,* on the look-out for news. **2.** Gun-carriage.

affûter, *v.tr.* To sharpen (tool); to set (saw).

afin, *adv.* **1.** Afin de (*faire qch.*), to, in order to, so as to (do sth.). **2.** Afin que + *sub.,* so that, in order that.

africain, *a. & s.* African.

Afrique. *Pr.n.f.* Africa.

agaçant, *a.* **1.** Annoying, irritating. **2.** Provocative.

agacement, *s.m.* Irritation; setting (of teeth) on edge.

agacer, *v.tr.* (n. agaçons). **1.** To set (teeth) on edge; to jar, grate, upon (nerves). **2.** *A. qn,* to provoke s.o.
　s'agacer, to become irritated.

agacerie, *s.f.* Provocation, rousing.

agate, *s.f. Miner:* Agate.

âge, *s.m.* **1.** Age. (*a*) **Quel âge avez-vous?** how old are you? *Être d'âge à faire qch.,* to be of an age to do sth. *Mourir avant l'âge,* to die before one's time. (*b*) **Le bas âge,** infancy. **Être à l'âge de raison,** to have arrived at years of discretion. (*c*) Old age. **Prendre de l'âge,** to be getting on in years. **2.** Generation. **3.** Period, epoch. *Hist:* **Le moyen âge,** the Middle Ages.

âgé, *a.* Old, aged. **1.** **Âgé de dix ans,** aged ten, ten years old. **2.** Advanced in years.

agence, *s.f.* Agency.

agencement, *s.m.* Arrangement (of a house); fitting up (of parts of machine).

agencer, *v.tr.* (n. agençons). To arrange (house); to adjust (parts of machine).

agenda, *s.m.* Memorandum-book; engagement-book; diary.

agenouillement, [-ujmã], *s.m.* Kneeling.

agenouiller (s') [-uje], *v.pr.* To kneel (down).
　agenouillé, *a.* Kneeling.

agent, *s.m.* **1.** Agent, agency. **2.** (*a*) Agent. **Agent d'affaires,** man of business. (*b*) **Agent (de police),** policeman. (*c*) **Agent de change,** stock-broker.

agglomération, *s.f.* Agglomeration.

agglomérer, *v.tr.* (j'agglomère, j'agglomérerai) To agglomerate; to mass together.
　s'agglomérer, to agglomerate; to cohere.

agglutiner, *v.tr.* To agglutinate; to bind.

aggravation, *s.f.* **1.** Aggravation (of disease). **2.** Increase (of taxation).

aggraver, *v.tr.* **1.** To aggravate (disease); to worsen. **2.** To increase, augment (penalty).
　s'aggraver, to worsen; to grow worse.

agile, *a.* Agile, nimble; active.
agilement, *adv.* Nimbly.
agilité, *s.f.* Agility, nimbleness, litheness.
agir, *v.i.* To act. **I.** *A. de soi-même,* to act on one's own initiative. **Faire agir qch.,** to set sth. going, working. **Est-ce ainsi que vous en agissez avec moi?** is that how you treat me? **2.** To act, operate, take effect. *A. sur qn,* to bring an influence to bear upon s.o. **3.** *Jur:* To take proceedings.
  s'agir (*de*), *v.impers.* (*a*) To concern; to be in question; to be the matter. *De quoi s'agit-il?* what is the question? what is it all about? *Voici de quoi il s'agit,* the thing is this. *Il s'agit de votre avenir,* your future is at stake. *Il ne s'agit pas de cela,* that is not the question. (*b*) **S'agir de faire qch.,** to be a matter of doing sth.
agissant, *a.* Active, busy, bustling.
agitateur, -trice. I. *s.* (Political) agitator. **2.** *s.m.* Stirrer, stirring-rod.
agitation, *s.f.* Agitation. **I.** (*a*) Shaking, stirring; waving (of flag); wagging (of tail). (*b*) Discussing (of question). (*c*) *L'a. ouvrière,* labour unrest. **2.** (*a*) (State of) perturbation. (*b*) Restlessness. (*c*) Roughness (of sea).
agiter, *v.tr.* **I.** (*a*) To agitate; to wave (handkerchief). *Le chien agite sa queue,* the dog wags its tail. (*b*) To shake (bottle). (*c*) To stir (mixture). **2.** To agitate, excite. **3.** To debate (question).
  s'agiter. (*a*) To be agitated, in movement. *S'a. dans son sommeil,* to toss in one's sleep. (*b*) To become agitated, excited.
agité, *a.* **I.** Choppy, rough (sea). **2.** Agitated, restless (night); troubled (sleep). **3.** Excited.
agneau, *s.m.* Lamb.
agonie, *s.f.* Death agony; pangs of death. *Être à l'agonie,* to be at one's last gasp.
agonisant. I. *a.* Dying; in the throes of death. **2.** *s.* Dying person.
agoniser, *v.i.* To be dying.
agrafe, *s.f.* Hook, fastener; clasp (of album); buckle (of strap); clip (for papers). **Agrafes et portes** (*de couturière*), hooks and eyes.
agrafer, *v.tr.* To fasten by means of a hook, clasp, or clip.
agraire, *a.* Agrarian.
agrandir, *v.tr.* (*a*) To make larger; to enlarge. (*b*) To magnify.
  s'agrandir. I. To grow larger; to increase; to expand. **2.** To become richer, more powerful.
agrandissement, *s.m.* **I.** (*a*) Enlarging, extending. (*b*) Enlargement, extension (of factory). *Phot:* Enlargement. **2.** Increase in power; aggrandizement.
agréable, *a.* Agreeable, pleasant, nice. *Si cela peut vous être a.,* if you like. **Faire l'agréable,** to make oneself pleasant (*auprès de,* to). *Pour vous être a.,* to oblige you.
agréablement, *adv.* Agreeably, pleasantly.
agréer. I. *v.tr.* To accept, approve (of), agree to. **Agréez mes salutations empressées,**

believe me yours sincerely **2.** *v. ind. tr.* To suit, please.
  s'agréer *à qch.,* to take pleasure in sth.
agrégation, *s.f.* (*a*) Aggregation, binding. (*b*) Aggregate, agglomeration.
agréger (*s'*)**,** *v.pr.* (Of matter) To unite, join together; to aggregate.
  agrégé. I. *a.* Aggregate (matter). **2.** *a. & s. Sch:* (Professeur) agrégé, teacher who has qualified for a post in a Lycée.
agrément, *s.m.* **I.** (*a*) Pleasure, amusement. *Voyage d'agrément,* pleasure-trip. **Ouvrages d'agrément,** fancy work. (*b*) Attractiveness, charm. **2.** Usu. *pl.* Amenities (of place); charms (of person). **3.** *A. donné à qch.,* assent, consent, to sth.
agrémenter, *v.tr.* To embellish, ornament, adorn (*de,* with).
agrès, *s.m.pl.* Tackle, gear (of ship).
agresseur, *s.m.* Aggressor.
agressif, *a.* Aggressive, provocative.
agression, *s.f.* Aggression.
agressivement, *adv.* Aggressively.
agreste, *a.* **I.** Rustic; rural (site). **2.** Uncouth, countrified (person).
agricole, *a.* Agricultural (produce).
agriculteur, *s.m.* Agriculturist, farmer.
agriculture, *s.f.* Agriculture, farming.
agripper, *v.tr.* *F:* To clutch, grip.
  s'agripper. *S'a. à qch.,* to cling to sth.
agronomie, *s.f.* Agronomy, husbandry.
aguerrir, *v.tr.* To train (troops).
  aguerri, *a.* Seasoned, trained (army).
aguets, *s.m.pl.* **Aux aguets,** watchful (*de,* for). *Avoir l'oreille aux a.,* to keep one's ears open.
ah, *int.* Ah! oh!
ahurir, *v.tr.* *F:* To bewilder. **I.** To dumbfound. **2.** To confuse, daze.
  ahuri, *a.* *F:* Bewildered. (*a*) Dumbfounded. (*b*) Confused, dazed.
ahurissant, *a.* Bewildering.
ahurissement, *s.m.* Bewilderment.
ai. See AVOIR
aide¹, *s.f.* (*a*) Help, assistance, aid. **Venir en aide à qn,** to help s.o. **A l'aide!** help! *Prep.phr.* **A l'aide de qch.,** with the help, assistance, of sth. (*b*) Relief, succour.
aide², *s.m. & f.* Assistant, helper. **Aide de camp,** aide-de-camp.
aider. I. *v.tr. Aider qn,* to help, assist, aid, s.o. **Je me suis fait aider,** I got some help. *S'a. de qch.,* to make use of sth. **Le temps aidant,** with the help of time. **2.** *v.ind.tr. A. à qch.,* to help towards sth.
aie, -s, -nt. See AVOIR.
aïe [aj] *int.* (Indicating twinge of pain) Oh!
aïeul [ajœl] *s.m.* **I.** (*pl.* aïeuls) Grandfather. **2.** (*pl.* aïeux) Ancestor.
aïeule [ajœl] *s.f.* **I.** Grandmother. **2.** Ancestress.
aigle. I. (*a*) *s.m. & f. Orn:* Eagle. *Un regard d'a.,* keen glance. (*b*) *s.m. Lit:* Genius. *F:* **Ce n'est pas un aigle,** he is not brilliant. **2.** *s.m.* Lectern, reading-desk. **3.** *s.m. or f. Mil:* Eagle, standard.

aiglefin, *s.m. Ich:* Haddock.
aiglon, *s.* Eaglet; young eagle.
aigre, *a.* (*a*) Sour, acid, tart. *s.m.* **Tourner à l'aigre,** to turn sour. (*b*) Sour(-tempered), crabbed. (*c*) Shrill, sharp (sound).
aigre-doux, -douce, *a.* Bitter-sweet (fruit). *F: Ton a.-d.,* subacid tone.
aigrefin¹, *s.m. Ich: =* AIGLEFIN.
aigrefin², *s.* Sharper, swindler.
aigrelet, -ette, *a.* Sourish, tart.
aigrement, *adv.* Acrimoniously, bitterly.
aigrette, *s.f.* **I.** (*a*) Aigrette (of heron); tuft. (*b*) *Cost:* Aigrette, plume. **2.** *Orn:* Egret.
aigreur, *s.f.* Sourness, tartness, acidity.
aigrir. I. *v.tr.* (*a*) To make sour. (*b*) To sour, embitter. **2.** *v.i.* To turn sour.
  s'aigrir. I. To turn sour. **2.** To become soured, embittered.
aigrissement, *s.m.* Embitterment.
aigu, -uë, *a.* **I.** Sharp, pointed (instrument). *Geom:* **Angle aigu,** acute angle. **2.** Acute, sharp; keen. **3.** Shrill, piercing, high-pitched. **4.** **Accent aigu,** acute accent.
aiguille [egɥi:j], *s.f.* **I.** Needle. *A. à coudre,* sewing needle. **Travailler à l'aiguille,** to do needlework. **2.** (*a*) **Aiguille de pin,** pine-needle. (*b*) *Rail:* Point. **3.** Needle, point. *A. d'un clocher d'église,* church spire. **4.** (*a*) (Swinging) needle (of compass). (*b*) Index, pointer (of balance). (*c*) Hand (of clock). **Petite aiguille,** hour-hand. **Grande aiguille,** minute-hand. *A. trotteuse,* second-hand.
aiguillette [egɥijɛt], *s.f. Nau:* Lanyard.
aiguilleur [egɥijœ:r], *s.m. Rail:* Pointsman.
aiguillon [egɥijɔ̃], *s.m.* **I.** (*a*) Goad. *F:* **L'aiguillon du remords,** the pricks of remorse. (*b*) Spur, incentive. **2.** (*a*) *Bot:* Prickle, thorn. (*b*) Sting (of wasp).
aiguillonnement [egɥij-], *s.m.* **I.** Goading (of horse). **2.** Pricking (of conscience).
aiguillonner [egɥijɔne], *v.tr.* **I.** To goad. **2.** To urge on, incite; to rouse; to whet.
aiguiser [eg(ɥ)ize], *v.tr.* **I.** (*a*) To whet; to sharpen. (*b*) To point. *A. un crayon,* to sharpen a pencil. **2.** To make keen; to whet.
  s'aiguiser, (of wits) to become keen.
ail [a:j], *s.m.* Garlic.
aile, *s.f.* **I.** Wing, pinion. **Battre de l'aile,** (i) to flutter; (ii) *F:* to be exhausted. **Ne (plus) battre que d'une aile,** *F:* (of pers.) to be on his last legs. **2.** Wing (of aeroplane); sail (of windmill); arm (of semaphore); blade (of propeller); mudguard.
ailé, *a.* Winged, feathered.
aileron, *s.m.* **I.** (*a*) Pinion (of bird). (*b*) Fin (of shark). **2.** *Av:* Aileron, wing-tip.
aill-e, -es, etc. [a:j]. See ALLER.
ailleurs [ajœ:r], *adv.* **I.** Elsewhere, somewhere else. **2.** *Adv. phrs.* (*a*) **D'ailleurs,** (i) besides, moreover; (ii) from another place. (*b*) **Par ailleurs,** (i) by another route, (ii) in other respects.
aimable, *a.* **I.** Amiable, agreeable; kind; nice. **Vous êtes bien aimable, c'est très aimable à vous,** that is very kind of you.

Peu aimable, ungracious. **2.** Lovable, attractive.
aimablement, *adv.* Amiably, kindly, nicely.
aimant¹, *a.* Loving, affectionate.
aimant², *s.m.* Magnet.
aimanter, *v.tr.* To magnetize. **Aiguille aimantée,** magnetic needle.
Aimée. *Pr.n.f.* Amy.
aimer, *v.tr.* **I.** (*a*) To like, care for, to be fond of. **Se faire aimer de qn,** to win s.o.'s affection. *A. faire qch.,* to like to do sth. (*b*) **Aimer autant.** *S'aime(rais) autant rester ici (que de . . .),* I would just as soon stay here (as . . .). (*c*) **Aimer mieux.** *J'aime mieux qu'il vienne,* I would rather he came. **2. Aimer qn (d'amour),** to love s.o.
aine, *s.f. Anat:* Groin.
aîné, *a.* (*a*) Elder (of two); eldest. *s.* **Il est mon aîné,** he is older than I. (*b*) Senior. *M. Dumont a.,* Mr Dumont senior.
aînesse, *s.f.* **I.** Primogeniture. **Droit d'aînesse,** (i) Law of Primogeniture, (ii) birthright. **2.** Seniority.
ainsi. I. *adv.* Thus; so; in a like manner. **S'il en est ainsi,** if such is the case, if (it is) so. **Et ainsi de suite,** and so on. **Pour ainsi dire,** so to speak, as it were. **Ainsi soit-il,** (i) so be it, (ii) *Ecc:* amen. **2.** *conj.* So, thus. *A. vous ne venez pas?* so you are not coming? **3.** *Conj.phr.* **Ainsi que,** (just) as. *Cette règle a. que la suivante me paraît, me paraissent, inutile(s),* this rule, as also the next one, seems to me to be unnecessary. (The concord is usu. in the *pl.*)
air, *s.m.* **I. I.** (*a*) Air, atmosphere. *Sortir prendre l'air,* to go for a breath of fresh air. *F:* **Vivre de l'air du temps,** to live upon (next to) nothing, on air. **Au grand air, en plein air,** in the open air. *Jeux en plein air,* outdoor games. (*b*) **En l'air,** in the air. **Être en l'air,** to be in a state of confusion. **Paroles en l'air,** idle talk. **2.** Wind, draught. **Il fait de l'air,** it is breezy.
  II. air. I. (*a*) Appearance, look. **Avoir bon air,** (i) to look distinguished; (ii) (of dress) to look well. **Air de famille,** family likeness. (*b*) **Avoir l'air,** to look, seem. (The predicative adj. may agree either with *air* or with the subject.) *Elle a l'air fatigué(e),* she looks tired. *Cela en a tout l'air,* it looks like it. **2.** Manner, way. **Se donner des airs,** to give oneself airs.
  III. air. Tune, air, melody. *F:* **Je connais des paroles sur cet air-là,** I've heard that tale before.
airain, *s.m.* Bronze, brass. **Avoir un cœur d'airain,** to have a heart of stone. *Avoir un front d'a.,* to be brazen-faced.
aire, *s.f.* **I.** Surface; flat space; floor. *A. d'une grange,* threshing-floor. *Av: A. d'embarquement,* tarmac. **2.** Area. **3.** Eyrie. **4.** *Nau:* **Les aires de vent,** the points of the compass. *F:* **Prendre l'aire du vent,** to see which way the wind is blowing.
airelle, *s.f. Bot:* Whortleberry, bilberry.

aisance, *s.f.* **1.** Ease. *(a)* Freedom (of movement). *Donner de l'a. à qch.,* to ease sth. *(b)* Jouir de l'aisance, to be in easy circumstances. **2.** Easing. Lieu, cabinet, d'aisances, public convenience.

aise. 1. *s.f.* Ease, comfort. Être à l'aise, à son aise, (i) to be comfortable ; (ii) to be well-off. *Ne pas être à son a.,* (i) to feel uncomfortable ; (ii) to feel ill. Il en prend à son aise, (i) he takes it easy ; (ii) he is a cool customer. A votre aise ! just as you like ! **2.** *a.* Bien aise, very glad.

aisé, *a.* **1.** *(a)* Easy, free (manner) ; comfortable (clothes). *(b)* Well-to-do (person). **2.** Easy (task). *C'est plus aisé à dire qu'à faire,* it is more easily said than done.

aisément, *adv.* **1.** Comfortably. **2.** Easily.

aisselle, *s.f.* Armpit.

ait [ɛ]. See AVOIR.

ajonc [aʒɔ̃], *s.m.* *Bot:* Furze, gorse, whin.

ajour, *s.m.* **1.** Opening (which lets the light through). **2.** Openwork (in wood-carving).

ajouré, *a.* Perforated, pierced. *Woodw:* Travail ajouré, fretwork.

ajournement, *s.m.* Postponement, adjournment.

ajourner, *v.tr.* To postpone, put off, adjourn, defer.

    s'ajourner, to adjourn.

ajouter, *v.tr.* To add. **1.** *A. des chiffres,* to add up figures. Ajouter l'action aux paroles, to suit the action to the word. **2.** *"Venez aussi,"* ajouta-t-il, "you come too," he added.

ajustable, *a.* Adjustable.

ajustage, *s.m.* **1.** Fitting (of dress). **2.** Assembly (of machine).

ajustement, *s.m.* Adjusting, adjustment.

ajuster, *v.tr.* **1.** *(a)* To adjust, set (tool). *(b)* To fit together (machine). *(c)* *A. son fusil,* to take aim with one's gun. *A. qn (avec un fusil),* to aim (a gun) at s.o. *(d)* *A. qch. à qch.,* to fit, adapt, sth. to sth. **2.** To put right, straight ; to settle.

alacrité, *s.f.* Alacrity, eagerness.

alambic, *s.m.* *Ch:* Still.

alanguir, *v.tr.* To make languid.

    s'alanguir, to languish, droop.

alanguissement, *s.m.* Languor, weakness ; drooping, decline.

alarmant, *a.* Alarming ; startling.

alarme, *s.f.* Alarm. *Rail:* Tirer la sonnette d'alarme, to pull the communication-cord.

alarmer, *v.tr.* **1.** To give the alarm to. **2.** To frighten, startle, alarm.

    s'alarmer, to take fright (*de,* at).

alarmiste, *a. & s.* Alarmist ; scaremonger.

albanais, *a. & s. Ethn:* Albanian.

Albanie. *Pr.n.f.* Albania.

albâtre, *s.m.* Alabaster.

albatros [-tros], *s.m. Orn:* Albatross.

albinos [-noːs], *s. & a. inv.* Albino.

album [-bɔm], *s.m.* **1.** Album, sketch-book. **2.** Trade catalogue. *pl. Des albums.*

albumine, *s.f. Biol:* Albumin.

albumineux, *a. Biol:* Albuminous.

alcade, *s.m.* Alcalde, magistrate (in Spain).

alcali, *s.m. Ch:* Alkali.

alcalin, *a.* Alkaline.

alchimie, *s.f.* Alchemy.

alchimiste, *s.m.* Alchemist.

alcool [-kɔl], *s.m.* Alcohol, *F:* spirit(s). *A. à brûler,* methylated spirit.

alcoolique [-kɔl-]. **1.** *a.* Alcoholic, spirituous. **2.** *s.* Drunkard.

alcôve, *s.f.* Alcove, (bed-)recess.

alcyon, *s.m. Myth:* Halcyon.

aléa, *s.m.* Risk, hazard, chance.

aléatoire, *a.* Hazardous, risky.

alène, *s.f. Tls:* Awl. *A. plate,* bradawl.

alentour. 1. *adv.* Around, round about. *Prep. phr.* Alentour de la maison, round about the house. **2.** *s.m.pl.* Alentours (*d'une ville*), environs, surroundings (of a town).

alerte. 1. *int.* Up ! to arms ! **2.** *s.f.* Alarm, warning. *Tenir l'ennemi en a.,* to harass the enemy. **3.** *a.* *(a)* Alert, brisk. *(b)* Vigilant.

alerter, *v.tr.* To warn.

alezan, *a. & s.* Chestnut (horse).

alfa, *s.m. Bot:* Alfa(-grass), esparto.

algarade, *s.f.* **1.** Storm of abuse. **2.** Escapade ; prank.

algèbre, *s.f.* Algebra.

algébrique, *a.* Algebraic.

Alger. *Pr.n.* Algiers.

Algérie. *Pr.n.f. Geog:* Algeria.

algérien, -ienne, *a. & s.* Algerian.

algue [alg], *s.f. Bot:* Alga, seaweed.

aliénation, *s.f.* Alienation. **1.** *Jur:* Transfer (of property). **2.** Estrangement. **3.** Aliénation mentale, insanity.

aliéner, *v.tr.* (j'aliène ; j'aliénerai) **1.** *Jur:* To alienate, part with (property). **2.** To alienate, estrange (a friend).

    aliéné, *a. & s.* Lunatic ; insane (person).

aliéniste, *s.m. & f.* Mental specialist.

alignement, *s.m.* *(a)* Alignment. *Mil:* A droite alignement ! right dress ! *(b)* Making up (of accounts). **2.** Row (of trees).

aligner, *v.tr.* To align, draw up, line up ; to put (thgs) in a line, in a row.

    s'aligner, to fall into line.

aliment, *s.m.* Aliment, food.

alimentaire, *a.* **1.** *Jur:* Pension alimentaire, alimony ; allowances for necessaries. **2.** Alimentary, nourishing (product).

alimentation, *s.f.* *(a)* Alimentation, feeding ; supply (of town). *(b)* Nourishment.

alimenter, *v.tr.* To feed, nourish (s.o.) ; to supply (market) with food.

alinéa, *s.m. Typ:* **1.** First line of paragraph. En alinéa, indented. **2.** Paragraph.

alitement, *s.m.* Confinement to bed.

aliter, *v.tr.* To keep (s.o.) in bed.

    s'aliter, to take to one's bed.

    alité, *a.* Confined to (one's) bed.

alizé, *a. & s.m.* Les (vents) alizés, the trade-winds.

allaitement, *s.m.* Nursing, suckling.

allaiter, *v.tr.* To suckle (child).

allant. I. *a.* Active ; spirited. *s.m.* **Avoir de l'allant,** to have plenty of go. **2.** *s.m.pl.* **Allants et venants,** comers and goers.

allèchement, *s.m.* Allurement, attraction.

allécher, *v.tr.* (j'allèche ; j'allécherai) To allure, attract, entice, tempt.

allée, *s.f.* **I.** Allées et venues, coming and going. **2.** (*a*) Walk (esp. lined with trees). (*b*) Path (in garden). (*c*) Entrance, alley ; carriage-drive.

allège, *s.f. Nau:* Lighter.

allégement, *s.m.* (*a*) Lightening (of vessel). (*b*) Relief (of pain).

alléger *v.tr.* (j'allège, n. allégeons ; j'allégerai) (*a*) To lighten. (*b*) To relieve (pain).

s'alléger, to become lighter or easier.

allégorie, *s.f.* Allegory.

allégorique, *a.* Allegorical.

allègre, *a.* Lively, gay, cheerful.

allégresse, *s.f.* Gladness, liveliness.

alléguer [-ge], *v.tr.* (j'allègue ; j'alléguerai) **I.** To allege, urge, plead. **2.** To quote.

Allemagne. *Pr.n.f. Geog:* Germany.

allemand. I. *a. & s.* German. **2.** *s.m.* L'allemand, the German language.

aller. I. *v.i.* (*pr. ind.* je vais, tu vas, il va, n. allons, ils vont ; *pr. sub.* j'aille ; *imp.* va (vas-y), allons ; *fu.* j'irai. Aux. *être*) **I.** To go. (*a*) *A. et venir,* to come and go. **Je ne ferai qu'aller et revenir,** I shall come straight back. **Il va sur ses dix ans,** he is nearly ten (years old). *F:* **Faire aller qn,** to order s.o. about. (*b*) *Allez, je vous écoute,* go on, I am listening. **2.** (*a*) To go, be going (well). *Les affaires vont,* business is brisk. *Ça ira!* we'll manage it ! *Je vous en offre cinq francs.—Va pour cinq francs!* I'll give you five francs for it.—Five francs be it ! *Cela va sans dire,* cela va de soi, that's understood, that is a matter of course. (*b*) (Of machine) To go, work, run. *La pendule va bien,* the clock is right. *F:* comment allez-vous? *F:* comment cela va-t-il? how are you? how do you do? **Je vais bien,** *F:* ça va, I am well, I am all right. **3. Aller à qn.** (*a*) (Of clothes) To suit, become, s.o. (*b*) (Of food) To agree with s.o. (*c*) (Of clothes) To fit s.o. (*d*) To be to s.o.'s liking. *F:* **Ça va!** all right ! O.K. ! **4.** (Of colours) **Aller avec qch.,** to go well with sth. ; to match sth. **5.** (*a*) *A. voir qn,* to go and see s.o. ; to call on s.o. *A. trouver qn,* to go to s.o. (*b*) To be going (to do sth.). *Il va s'en occuper,* he is going to see about it. *Elle allait tout avouer,* she was about to confess everything. *A. en augmentant,* to increase. **6. Y aller.** (*a*) *A. voir qn,* on y va ! coming ! (*b*) **Y aller de tout son cœur,** to put one's back into it. **Allons-y!** well, here goes ! **Vas-y! allez-y!** go it ! go ahead ! (*c*) *F:* **Y aller de sa personne,** to take a hand in it oneself. **7.** *v.impers.* **Il va de soi,** it stands to reason, it goes without saying. **Il en va de même pour lui,** it's the same with him. **Il y**

allait de la vie, it was a matter of life and death. **8.** *int.* **Allons,** *dépêchez-vous!* come, make haste ! **Allons donc!** (i) come along ! (ii) nonsense ! **Allons bon!** there now ! **Mais va donc!** get on with it ! *J'ai bien souffert,* **allez!** I have suffered much, believe me ! **s'en aller.** (*pr. ind.* je m'en vais ; *imp.* va-t'en, allons-nous-en, *perf.* je m'en suis allé(e)). **I.** To go away, to depart. *Il faut que je m'en aille,* I must be going. **Le malade s'en va,** the patient is sinking. **2.** *F: Je m'en vais vous raconter ça,* I'll tell you about it.

II. **aller,** *s.m.* **I.** Going ; outward journey. **Billet d'aller et retour,** return ticket. *Sp:* Match aller, away match. **2. Pis aller,** last resort ; makeshift. **Au pis aller,** if the worst comes to the worst.

alliage, *s.m.* **I.** Alloying, blending. **2.** Alloy.

alliance, *s.f.* **I.** Alliance. (*a*) Match, marriage, union. (*b*) Union, blending. **2.** Wedding-ring.

allier, *v.tr.* **I.** To ally, unite. **2.** To alloy, mix ; to match (colours) (*d*, with).

s'allier. (*a*) To form an alliance. (*b*) *S'a. à une famille,* to marry into a family.

allié. I. *a.* Allied. **2.** *s.* (*a*) Ally. (*b*) Relation by marriage.

alligator, *s.m. Rept:* Alligator.

allitératif, *a.* Alliterative.

allitération, *s.f.* Alliteration.

allô, allo, *int. Tp:* Hullo ! hallo !

allocation, *s.f.* **I.** Allocation, assignment (of supplies). **2.** Allowance, grant.

allocution, *s.f.* Short speech ; allocution.

allongement, *s.m.* **I.** Lengthening (of dress). **2.** Extension (of time).

allonger, *v.tr.* (n. allongeons) **I.** To lengthen (garment). **2.** To stretch out (one's arm). **3.** To protract, prolong.

s'allonger. I. (Of days) To grow longer. *F: Son visage s'allongea,* he pulled a long face. **2.** *F:* **S'allonger par terre,** to fall flat on the ground.

allumage, *s.m.* Lighting (of lamp). *I.C.E.:* Ignition. **Raté d'allumage,** misfire.

allumer, *v.tr.* **I.** To light ; to kindle. *Abs.* To switch on the light ; to light up. **2.** To inflame, excite (passion).

s'allumer. I. To kindle, to take fire. **2.** To warm up to one's subject.

allumette, *s.f.* Match. *A.* suédoise, safety match.

allumette-bougie, *s.f.* Wax-vesta. *pl. Des allumettes-bougies.*

allumeur, -euse, *s.* Lighter ; igniter.

allure, *s.f.* **I.** (*a*) Walk, carriage, bearing. (*b*) Pace. *Marcher à une vive a.,* to walk at a brisk pace. (*c*) Speed. **A toute allure,** at full speed. (*d*) Working (of engine). **2.** (*a*) Demeanour, behaviour. (*b*) Aspect, look.

allusion, *s.f.* Allusion ; hint, innuendo.

alluvial, -iaux, *a.* Alluvial.

alluvion, *s.f. Geol:* Alluvium.

almanach [-na], *s.m.* Almanac ; calendar.

aloès [alɔɛs], *s.m. Bot:* Aloe.
aloi, *s.m.* Standard, quality. **De bon aloi,** genuine.
alors, *adv.* **1.** Then; at the time. **2.** (a) Then. *A. vous viendrez?* well then, you are coming? (b) Therefore, so. *Il n'était pas là, a. je suis revenu,* he wasn't there, so I came back again. **3.** *Conj. phr.* Alors que, when. Alors même que, even though. **4.** (= EN-SUITE) Then, next.
alouette, *s.f. Orn:* Lark.
alourdir, *v.tr.* **1.** To make heavy. **2.** To make dull. **3.** To weigh down (s.o.).
  s'alourdir, to grow (i) heavy, (ii) stupid.
alourdissant, *a.* Oppressive (heat).
alourdissement, *s.m.* (Growing) heaviness.
aloyau, -aux, *s.m.* Sirloin (of beef).
alpaga, *s.m.* Alpaca.
alpe, *s.f.* Alp, mountain.
alpestre, *a.* Alpine (scenery).
alphabet, *s.m.* **1.** Alphabet. **2.** *Sch:* Spelling-book, primer.
alphabétique, *a.* Alphabetical.
alpin, *a.* Alpine (troops).
alpinisme, *s.m.* Mountaineering.
alpiniste, *s.m. & f.* Mountaineer.
alsacien, -ienne, *a. & s.* Alsatian.
altérable, *a.* Liable to deterioration.
altérant, *a.* Thirst-producing.
altération, *s.f.* **1.** Change (for the worse); deterioration (of food). **2.** Adulteration (of food); falsification (of document).
altercation, *s.f.* Altercation, dispute.
altérer, *v.tr.* (j'altère; j'altérerai) **1.** To change (for the worse); to impair (health). **2.** To tamper with. **3.** To make thirsty.
  s'altérer. 1. To change (for the worse); to deteriorate. *Sa voix s'altéra,* his voice faltered. **2.** To grow thirsty.
  altéré, *a.* **1.** Faded (colour); broken (voice); drawn (face). **2.** Thirsty.
alternance, *s.f.* Alternation.
alternatif, *a.* **1.** (a) Alternate. (b) *El.E:* Alternating (current). **2.** Alternative. **3.** *s.f.* Alternative, alternative.
alternativement, *adv.* Alternately, in turn.
alterne, *a.* Alternate (angles).
alterner, *v.i.* (a) To alternate. (b) To take turns (*pour,* in + *ger.*); to take it in turns (*pour,* to + *inf.*). *Ils alternent pour veiller,* they take it in turns to sit up.
altesse, *s.f.* Highness.
altier, *a.* Haughty, proud.
altièrement, *adv.* Haughtily, proudly.
altitude, *s.f.* Altitude, height.
alto, *s.m. Mus:* **1.** Alto (voice). **2.** Viola.
altruisme, *s.m.* Altruism.
altruiste. 1. *a.* Altruistic. **2.** *s.* Altruist.
aluminium [-njom], *s.m.* Aluminium.
alun, *s.m.* Alum.
alvéole, *s.m. or f.* **1.** (a) Alveole; cell (of honeycomb). (b) Pigeon-hole (of desk). **2.** Socket (of tooth). **3.** Cavity (in stone).
alvéolé, *a.* **1.** Honeycombed. **2.** Pitted.

amabilité, *s.f.* **1.** Amiableness, amiability; kindness. **2.** *pl.* Civilities.
amadou, *s.m.* Amadou; touchwood.
amadouer, *v.tr.* **1.** To coax, wheedle, persuade. **2.** To draw (customers).
amaigrir, *v.tr.* To make thin; to emaciate.
  s'amaigrir, to grow thin, to lose flesh.
amaigrissement, *s.m.* Loss of flesh, wasting away.
amalgamation, *s.f.* Amalgamation.
amalgame, *s.m.* Amalgam.
amalgamer, *v.tr.* To amalgamate.
  s'amalgamer, to amalgamate; to blend.
amande, *s.f.* Almond.
amandier, *s.m.* Almond-tree.
amant, *s.* Lover.
amarante. 1. *s.f. Bot:* Amarant(h). **2.** *a.inv.* Amaranth; purplish.
amarrage, *s.m.* (a) Mooring. *Aer:* Mât d'amarrage, mooring mast. (b) Berth, moorings.
amarre, *s.f.* (a) (Mooring) rope; painter; *pl.* moorings. (b) Cable, hawser.
amarrer, *v.tr.* To make fast, to moor.
  s'amarrer, to make fast; to moor.
amas, *s.m.* Heap, pile, accumulation.
amasser, *v.tr.* **1.** To heap up, pile up. **2.** To store up; to amass (a fortune). **3.** To gather (troops) together.
  s'amasser, to pile up, accumulate.
amateur, -trice, *s.* **1.** Lover (of sth.). *A. de chiens,* dog-fancier. **2.** Amateur.
amazone, *s.f.* **1.** (a) *Myth:* Amazon. *Geog:* Le fleuve des Amazones, the (River) Amazon. (b) Horsewoman. **2.** (Lady's) riding-habit.
ambages, *s.f.pl.* Circumlocution. Parler sans ambages, to speak to the point.
ambassade, *s.f.* Embassy.
ambassadeur, *s.m.* Ambassador.
ambassadrice, *s.f.* Ambassadress.
ambiance, *s.f.* Surroundings, environment.
ambiant, *a.* Surrounding, encompassing
ambigu, -uë, *a.* Ambiguous.
ambiguïté, *s.f.* Ambiguity, ambiguousness.
ambigument, *adv.* Ambiguously.
ambitieusement, *adv.* Ambitiously.
ambitieux, 1. *a.* Ambitious. **2.** *s.* Ambitious person.
ambition, *s.f.* Ambition (de, of, for).
ambitionner, *v.tr.* To be ambitious of; to covet.
amble, *s.m. Equit:* Amble; (ambling) pace.
ambler, *v.i.* To amble.
ambre, *s.m.* **1.** Ambre gris, ambergris. **2.** Ambre jaune, yellow amber.
ambré, *a.* **1.** Perfumed with amber(gris). **2.** Warm (complexion).
ambroisie, *s.f. Gr.Myth.:* Ambrosia.
ambrosiaque, *a.* Ambrosial.
ambulance, *s.f.* Ambulance.
ambulancier, *s. Mil:* Hospital orderly; *f.* nurse.
ambulant, *a.* Itinerant, peripatetic. Marchand ambulant, pedlar.

âme, *s.f.* **1.** Soul. (*a*) **Rendre l'âme,** to give up the ghost. (*b*) (Departed) soul, spirit. (*c*) Heart, feeling. **2.** (*a*) Bore (of gun). (*b*) Sound-post (of violin).

amélioration, *s.f.* Amelioration, improvement; change for the better.

améliorer, *v.tr.* To ameliorate, to improve.
s'améliorer, to get better; to improve.

amen [amɛn], *int. & s.m.inv.* Amen.

aménagement, *s.m.* Fittings (of office).

aménager, *v.tr.* (n. aménageons) To fit up.

amende, *s.f.* **1.** Fine. **Être condamné à une amende,** to be fined. *Games:* **Être mis à l'amende,** to have to pay a forfeit. **2. Faire amende honorable,** to apologize.

amendement, *s.m.* Improvement.

amender, *v.tr.* (*a*) To improve (soil). (*b*) *Parl:* To amend (bill).
s'amender, to improve.

amener, *v.tr.* (j'amène) **1.** To bring; to lead (hither). **Amener qn à faire qch.,** to get, induce, s.o. to do sth. **2.** *A. une mode,* to bring in a fashion. **3.** *Nau:* To strike (colours); to lower (sail).

aménité, *s.f.* **1.** Amenity, charm (of manners); grace (of style). **2.** *pl.* Compliments.

amer[1] [amɛːr]. **1.** *a.* (*a*) Bitter. (*b*) *Ironie amère,* biting irony. **2.** *s.m.* Bitter(s).

amer[2], *s.m. Nau:* Sea-mark, landmark.

amèrement, *adv.* Bitterly.

américain, *a. & s.* American.

Amérique. *Pr.n.f.* America.

amerrir, *v.i. Av:* To alight (on the sea).

amerrissage, *s.m. Av:* Alighting (on sea).

amertume, *s.f.* Bitterness.

améthyste, *s.f.* Amethyst.

ameublement, *s.m.* **1.** Furnishing (of house). **2.** Furniture.

ameublir, *v.tr.* To loosen, break up (soil).

ameuter, *v.tr.* To collect (riotous crowd).
s'ameuter, to gather into a mob.

ami. 1. *s.* Friend. **Nos amis et parents,** our kith and kin. **Mon ami,** (i) my dear fellow, (ii) my good man, (iii) my dear. **Mon amie,** my dear, my love. *Adv.phr.* **En ami(e),** in a friendly manner. **2.** *a.* Friendly (*de,* to).

amiable, *a. Jur: Arrangement à l'a.,* amicable arrangement. *Vente à l'a.,* private sale.

amiante, *s.m. Miner:* Asbestos.

amical, -aux, *a.* Friendly.

amicalement, *adv.* In a friendly way.

amidon, *s.m.* Starch.

amidonner, *v.tr.* To starch.

amincir, *v.tr.* To make thinner. *Taille amincie,* slender figure.
s'amincir, to grow thinner, more slender.

amincissement, *s.m.* Thinning down.

amiral, -aux, *s.m.* **1.** Admiral. **2.** Flagship.

amirauté, *s.f.* Admiralty.

amitié, *s.f.* **1.** Friendship, friendliness, affection. **Prendre qn en amitié,** to take to s.o. **Se lier d'amitié avec qn,** to strike up a friendship with s.o. **Par amitié,** out of friendliness. **2.** (*a*) Kindness, favour. (*b*) *pl.* **Avec mes sincères amitiés,** with kind regards.

ammoniac, -aque [-jak], *a.* Gaz ammoniac, ammonia.

ammoniaque, *s.f. Ch:* Ammonia.

amnésie, *s.f. Med:* Amnesia.

amnistie, *s.f.* Amnesty; general pardon.

amnistier, *v.tr.* To amnesty, pardon.

amoindrir. 1. *v.tr.* To reduce, diminish, belittle. *A. un mal,* to mitigate an evil. **2.** *v.i. & pr.* To diminish, to grow less.

amoindrissement, *s.m.* Reduction, diminution.

amollir, *v.tr.* **1.** To soften **2.** To weaken, enervate.
s'amollir. 1. To become soft. **2.** To grow weak, effeminate.

amollissement, *s.m.* **1.** Softening. **2.** Weakening.

amonceler, *v.tr.* (j'amoncelle) To pile up, heap up, bank up.
s'amonceler, to pile up.

amoncellement, *s.m.* **1.** Heaping (up), piling (up). **2.** Heap, pile.

amont, *s.m.* Upper waters (of river). **En amont,** up-stream. **En amont du pont,** above (the) bridge.

amorçage, *s.m.* **1.** Beginning (of sth.). **2.** Baiting (of hook).

amorce, *s.f.* **1.** Beginning (of sth.). **2.** (*a*) *Exp:* Detonator. (*b*) *Sm.a:* Percussion cap. **3.** Bait. **Se laisser prendre à l'amorce,** to swallow the bait.

amorcer, *v.tr.* (n. amorçons) **1.** To begin (building). **2.** (*a*) To bait. (*b*) To allure.

amorphe, *a.* Amorphous.

amortir, *v.tr.* **1.** To deaden (pain); to damp (ardour); to break (fall). **2.** To slake (lime). **3.** To redeem, pay off (debt).
s'amortir, to become deadened.

amortissable, *a.* Redeemable.

amortissement, *s.m.* **1.** Deadening (of pain), damping (of ardour), breaking (of fall). **2.** Redemption (of debt). **Fonds, caisse, d'amortissement,** sinking-fund.

amour, *s.m.* (Usu. *f.* in *pl.* in 1, 2.) **1.** Love, affection, passion. **Mariage d'amour,** love match. **Pour l'amour de qn,** for the sake of, for love of, s.o. **2.** *Mon a.,* my love, my sweetheart. **3.** Cupid. *Quel a. de bijou!* what a lovely jewel!

amoureusement, *adv.* Lovingly.

amoureux. 1. (*a*) Loving. *Être a. de qn,* to be in love with s.o. **2.** *s.* Lover, sweetheart.

amour-propre, *s.m.* (*a*) Self-respect; pride. (*b*) Self-esteem, vanity.

amovible, *a.* **1.** Removable (official). **2.** (Of parts of machine) Detachable.

ampère, *s.m. El.Meas:* Ampere.

amphibie. 1. *a.* Amphibious. **2.** *s.m.* Amphibian.

amphithéâtre, *s.m.* Amphitheatre.

amphore, *s.f.* **1.** *Archeol:* Amphora. **2.** Jar.

ample, *a.* **1.** Ample; full (dress). **2.** Roomy, spacious. **3.** Full (account).

amplement, *adv.* Amply, fully.
ampleur, *s.f.* Fullness (of garment); volume (of voice).
amplificateur, -trice. 1. *(a) a.* Magnifying. *(b) s.* Magnifier (of trifles). **2.** *s.m. (a) Phot :* Enlarger. *(b) W.Tel:* Amplifier.
amplification, *s.f* **1.** Amplification. **2.** *Phot :* Enlarging.
amplifier, *v.tr.* **1.** To amplify; to expand (thought). **2.** *Opt :* To magnify.
ampoule, *s.f.* **1.** *(a)* Bulb (of electric light). *(b)* Container (of vacuum-flask). **2.** Blister.
amputation, *s.f.* Amputation.
amputer, *v.tr.* To amputate (limb).
amulette, *s.f.* Amulet, charm.
amusant, *a.* Amusing, funny.
amusement, *s.m.* *(a)* (Action of) entertaining. *(b)* Amusement, recreation.
amuser, *v.tr.* To amuse, entertain.
　　s'amuser, to amuse, enjoy, oneself. *Bien s'a.,* to have a good time.
amygdale [amidal], *s.f.* Tonsil.
an, *s.m.* Year. **Bon an, mal an,** taking one year with another. **En l'an 1200,** in the year 1200. **Le jour de l'an,** New Year's day.
anachorète, *s.m.* Anchorite, recluse.
anachronisme, *s.m.* Anachronism.
anagramme, *s.f.* Anagram.
analogie, *s.f.* Analogy.
analogue. 1. *a.* Analogous; similar (à, to). **2.** *s.m.* Analogue, parallel.
analyse, *s.f.* Analysis. **1.** *(a) A. grammaticale,* parsing. *(b) Ch: A. quantitative,* quantitative analysis. **2.** Abstract, précis.
analyser, *v.tr.* To analyse. *A. une phrase,* (i) to parse, (ii) to analyse, a sentence.
analytique, *a.* Analytical.
analytiquement, *adv.* Analytically.
ananas [anana(:s)], *s.m.* Pine-apple.
anarchie, *s.f.* Anarchy.
anarchique, *a.* Anarchic(al).
anarchiste, *a. & s. Pol:* Anarchist.
anathématiser, *v.tr.* To anathematize.
anathème, *s.m.* Anathema; ban, curse.
anatife, *s.m. Crust:* Barnacle.
anatomie, *s.f.* Anatomy.
anatomique, *a.* Anatomical.
anatomiste, *s.m.* Anatomist.
ancestral, -aux, *a.* Ancestral.
ancêtre, *s.m. & f.* Ancestor, ancestress.
anchois, *s.m.* Anchovy. **Beurre d'anchois,** anchovy paste.
ancien, -ienne, *a.* **1.** Ancient, old. *Amitié ancienne,* friendship of long standing. **2.** Ancient, old(en), early. **L'Ancien Testament,** the Old Testament. *s.m.pl.* **Les anciens,** the ancients. **3.** Former, old; ex-. *A. élève,* old boy (of a school). *Anciens combattants,* ex-service men. **4.** Senior (officer). *Les (élèves) anciens,* the senior boys. **Il est votre ancien,** he is senior to you.
anciennement, *adv.* Anciently, formerly.
ancienneté, *s.f.* **1.** Antiquity (of monument). **2.** Seniority; length of service.

ancillaire, *a.* Ancillary.
ancrage, *s.m.* **1.** Anchoring. **2.** Anchorage.
ancre, *s.f.* Anchor. **Jeter, mouiller, l'ancre,** to anchor.
ancrer, *v.tr.* To anchor.
andalou, -ouse, *a. & s.* Andalusian.
Andorre. *Pr.n.* (Republic of) Andorra.
andouille [-du:j], *s.f. Cu:* Chitterlings.
andouiller [-duje], *s.m. Ven:* Tine (of antler).
André. *Pr.n.m.* Andrew.
Andrinople. 1. *Pr. n. f. Geog:* Adrianople. **2.** *s.f.Tex:* Turkey-red cotton.
âne, *s.m.* **1.** Ass; *F:* donkey. *(a)* **Faire une promenade à âne,** to go for a donkey ride. *(b)* **En dos d'âne,** ridged. *Pont en dos d'âne,* hog-backed bridge. **2.** *F:* Fool, ass, dunce. **Bonnet d'âne,** dunce's cap.
anéantir, *v.tr.* To reduce to nothing; to annihilate. *F: Je suis anéanti,* I am dead-beat.
　　s'anéantir, to come to nothing.
anéantissement, *s.m.* **1.** Annihilation. **2.** Prostration.
anecdote, *s.f.* Anecdote.
anémie, *s.f. Med:* Anaemia.
anémique, *a.* Anaemic, bloodless.
anémone, *s.f.* **1.** Anemone, wind-flower. **2.** *Coel:* **Anémone de mer,** sea-anemone.
ânerie, *s.f.* Foolish act or remark.
anéroïde, *a.* Aneroid (barometer).
ânesse, *s.f.* She-ass.
anesthésie, *s.f. Med:* Anaesthesia.
anesthésique, *a. & s.m.* Anaesthetic.
anfractuosité, *s.f.* **1.** Anfractuosity, sinuosity. **2.** Cragginess, unevenness.
ange, *s.m.* **1.** Angel. *F:* **Être aux anges,** to walk on air. **2.** **Ange (de mer),** angel-fish.
Angèle. *Pr.n.f.* Angela.
angélique. 1. *a.* Angelic(al). **2.** *s.f. Bot:* Angelica.
angélus [-ly:s], *s.m.* Angelus(-bell); ave-bell.
angine, *s.f. Med:* **1.** Quinsy; tonsillitis. **2.** *A. de poitrine,* angina pectoris.
anglais. 1. *a.* English (language); British (army). *F:* **Filer à l'anglaise,** to take French leave. **2.** *s.* Englishman; Briton. **3.** *s.m.* English (language).
angle, *s.m.* **1.** Angle. **A angles droits,** rectangular. **2.** Corner, angle (of wall).
Angleterre. *Pr.n.f.* England.
anglican, *a. & s. Rel:* Anglican. *L'Église anglicane,* the Church of England.
anglicisme, *s.m.* Anglicism; English idiom.
anglo-normand, *a. & s.* **Les îles Anglo-normandes,** the Channel Islands.
anglophile, *a. & s.* Anglophil(e), pro-English.
angoissant, *a.* Distressing (news); tense.
angoisse, *s.f.* Anguish; distress; agony.
angoisser, *v.tr.* To anguish; to distress.
anguille [ãgi:j], *s.f. Ich:* *(a)* Eel. *Soupçonner a. sous roche, F:* to smell a rat. *(b)* **Anguille de mer,** conger-eel.
angulaire, *a.* Angular. **Pierre angulaire,** corner-stone.

angularité, s.f. Angularity.
anguleux, a. Angular, bony (face); rugged (outline).
anhydre, a. *Ch:* Anhydrous.
anhydride, s.m. *Ch:* Anhydride. *A. carbonique,* carbon dioxide.
anicroche, s.f. Difficulty, hitch, snag.
ânier, s. Donkey-driver.
aniline, s.f. *Dy:* Aniline.
animal¹, -aux, s.m. Animal. *F:* **Quel animal!** what a brute! what a beast!
animal², -aux, a. **1.** Animal (kingdom). **2.** Sensual, brutal (instinct).
animation, s.f. **1.** Quickening; bringing to life. **2.** Animation, liveliness.
animer, v.tr. **1.** To animate, quicken. **2.** To actuate; to move, propel. **3.** To enliven. **s'animer. 1.** To come to life. **2.** To become animated, lively.
animé, a. Animated, lively.
animosité, s.f. Animosity, spite.
anis, s.m. (a) *Bot:* Anise. (b) **Graine d'anis,** aniseed.
anisette, s.f. Anisette (cordial).
ankyloser, v.tr. *Med:* To anchylose; to stiffen.
annales, s.f.pl. Annals; (public) records.
annaliste, s.m. Annalist.
anneau, -eaux, s.m. **1.** Ring. **2.** (a) Link (of chain). (b) Ringlet. (c) Coil (of serpent).
année, s.f. Year, twelvemonth. *Pendant toute une a.,* for a whole twelvemonth.
annelé, a. Ringed (column).
annexe, s.f. **1.** Annex(e), outbuilding. **2.** Enclosure (with letter).
annexer, v.tr. **1.** To annex (territory). **2.** To append, attach (document).
annexion, s.f. Annexation.
Annibal. Pr.n.m. *A.Hist:* Hannibal.
annihilation, s.f. Annihilation.
annihiler, v.tr. To annihilate, destroy.
anniversaire. 1. a. Anniversary (festival). **2.** s.m. *F: L'a. de qn,* s.o.'s birthday.
annonce, s.f. **1.** (a) Announcement, notice. (b) *Cards:* Declaration; call. (c) Sign, indication. **2.** Advertisement.
annoncer, v.tr. (n. annonçons) **1.** To announce, give notice of, give out. *Cards: A. son jeu,* to declare. **2.** To advertise (sale). **3.** (a) To promise, foretell. *Cela n'annonce rien de bon,* it bodes no good. (b) To show, evince. *Visage qui annonce l'énergie,* face that indicates energy. **4.** To announce (s.o.). **s'annoncer. 1.** To announce oneself. **2.** To augur (well). *Le temps s'annonce beau,* the weather promises to be fine.
annonciateur, -trice, s. **1.** Announcer; harbinger. **2.**s.m. *Tp:* Indicator-board.
annonciation, s.f. **Fête de l'Annonciation,** Feast of the Annunciation; Lady day.
annotateur, -trice, s. Annotator (of text).
annotation, s.f. Annotation.
annoter, v.tr. To annotate (text).
annuaire, s.m. **1.** Annual, year-book. **2.** Calendar. **3.** (Yearly) list; (telephone) directory.

annuel, -elle, a. Annual, yearly.
annuellement, adv. Annually, yearly.
annuité, s.f. **1.** Annual instalment (in repayment of debt). **2.** (Terminable) annuity.
annulaire. 1. a. Annular, ring-shaped. **2.** s.m. The ring-finger.
annulation, s.f. Annulment, repeal.
annuler, v.tr. To annul; to render void; to repeal (law), quash (judgment), set aside.
anoblir, v.tr. To ennoble.
anoblissement, s.m. Ennoblement.
anode, s.f. *El:* Anode; positive pole.
anodin. 1. a. Anodyne, soothing. **2.** s.m. Palliative; pain-killer
anomalie, s.f. Anomaly.
ânon, s.m. Ass's foal, ass's colt.
ânonner, v.tr. To stumble through (speech); to hum and haw; to mumble.
anonymat, s.m. Anonymity.
anonyme. 1. a. (a) Anonymous (letter). (b) *Com:* **Société anonyme,** limited(-liability) company. **2.** s.m. Anonymity.
anonymement, adv. Anonymously.
anormal, -aux, a. Abnormal, irregular.
anormalement, adv. Abnormally.
anse, s.f. **1.** Handle (of basket). **2.** Loop, bight (of rope). **3.** *Ph.Geog:* Bight, bay.
antagonisme, s.m. Antagonism.
antagoniste. 1. a. Antagonistic, opposed. **2.** s. Antagonist, opponent.
antan (d'). A. & *Lit:* Of yester year.
antarctique, a. Antarctic.
antécédent. 1. a. Antecedent, previous. **2.** s.m. (a) *Gram:* Antecedent. (b) pl. Antecedents.
antédiluvien, -ienne, a. Antediluvian.
antenne, s.f. **1.** *W.Tel:* Aerial (wire). **2.** Antenna, feeler (of insect).
antépénultième, a. Ante-penultimate.
antérieur, a. **1.** (a) Anterior; former (period); earlier (date). (b) *Gram:* **Futur antérieur,** future perfect. **2.** Fore-(limb); front-(wall).
antérieurement, adv. Previously.
anthologie, s.f. *Lit:* Anthology.
anthracite, s.m. Anthracite.
anthrax [-aks], s.m. *Med:* Carbuncle.
anthropoïde. a. & s.m. Anthropoid.
anthropologue, s.m. Anthropologist.
anthropophage. 1. a. Cannibalistic; man-eating. **2.** s. Cannibal.
anthropophagie, s.f. Cannibalism.
anti-aérien, -ienne, a. Anti-aircraft (gun).
antichambre, s.f. Ante-room; waiting-room.
anticipatif, a. Anticipatory.
anticipation, s.f. Anticipation.
anticiper. 1. v.tr. To anticipate; to forestall **2.** v.i. *A. sur les événements,* to anticipate events.
anticlérical, -aux, a. Anti-clerical.
antidater, v.tr. To antedate.
antidérapant, a. *Aut:* Non-skid(ding).
antidote, s.m. *A. d'un poison, contre un poison,* antidote for, against, a poison.

Antilles [ãti:j]. *Pr.n.f.pl.* **Les Antilles,** the West Indies. **La Mer des Antilles,** the Caribbean Sea.

antilope, *s.f. Z :* Antelope.

antimoine, *s.m. Ch :* Antimony.

antinomie, *s.f.* Antinomy ; paradox.

Antioche. *Pr.n.f. A.Geog :* Antioch.

antipathie, *s.f. A. pour qn,* antipathy to s.o. ; aversion for s.o.

antipathique, *a.* Antipathetic.

antipodes. *s.m.pl.* **Les antipodes,** the Antipodes.

antiquaire, *s.m.* Antiquary, antiquarian.

antique. *a.* (*a*) Ancient ; pertaining to the ancients. (*b*) Antique (furniture).

antiquité, *s.f.* **1.** Antiquity. **2.** Ancient times ; antiquity. **3.** *pl.* Antiquities.

antisémitisme, *s.m.* Anti-Semitism.

antiseptique, *a. & s.m. Med :* Antiseptic

antithèse, *s.f.* **1.** *Rh :* Antithesis. **2.** Direct contrary (*de,* to, of).

antithétique, *a.* Antithetic(al).

antitoxine, *s.f. Med :* Antitoxin.

Antoine. *Pr.n.m.* Ant(h)ony.

antonyme, *s.m.* Antonym ; counter-term.

antre, *s.m.* Cavern ; den, lair.

Anvers. *Pr.n.m. Geog :* Antwerp.

anxiété [ãks-], *s.f.* Anxiety, concern.

anxieusement [ãks-], *adv.* Anxiously.

anxieux [ãks-], *a.* Anxious, uneasy.

aorte, *s.f. Anat :* Aorta.

août [u], *s.m.* August.

Apache, *s.m.* **1.** *Ethn :* Apache. **2.** *F :* **Un apache,** a hooligan, a rough (of Paris).

apaisement, *s.m.* **1.** Pacifying. **2.** Abatement.

apaiser, *v.tr.* **1.** *A. qn,* to appease, pacify, calm, s.o. **2.** To allay ; to quell.

s'apaiser, to calm down.

apanage, *s.m.* Attribute, prerogative.

aparté, *s.m. Th :* Aside ; stage-whisper.

apathie, *s.f.* Apathy ; listlessness.

apathique, *a.* Apathetic ; listless.

apathiquement, *adv.* Apathetically, listlessly.

apercevable, *a.* Perceivable, perceptible.

apercevoir, *v.tr.* (Conj. like RECEVOIR). To perceive, see ; to catch sight of.

s'apercevoir *de qch.,* to perceive, notice, sth ; to become aware of sth. *Sans s'en a.,* without noticing it.

aperçu, *s.m.* **1.** Glimpse. **2.** Outline, sketch, summary.

apéritif, *s.m.* Appetizer.

aphorisme, *s.m.* Aphorism.

api, *s.m. Hort :* (**Pomme d')api,** lady-apple.

apiculteur, *s.m. Husb :* Bee-keeper.

apiculture, *s.f.* Bee-keeping.

apitoyer, *v.tr.* (j'**apitoie**) To move (to pity) ; to incite to pity.

s'apitoyer *sur le sort de qn,* to commiserate with s.o.

aplanir, *v.tr.* **1.** To flatten (surface) ; to plane (wood) ; to smooth away (difficulties). **2.** To level (road).

s'aplanir. **1.** To grow smoother ; (of difficulties) to disappear. **2.** To become level.

aplanissement, *s.m.* **1.** Smoothing (of surface), planing (of timber). **2.** Levelling.

aplatir, *v.tr.* To flatten.

s'aplatir. **1.** To become flat ; to go flat. **2.** *S'a. devant qn,* to grovel before s.o.

aplati, *a.* (*a*) Flattened. (*b*) Deflated.

aplomb, *s.m.* **1.** Perpendicularity ; uprightness ; balance (of pers.). **D'aplomb,** upright ; vertical(ly) ; plumb. *Voilà qui vous remettra d'a.,* that will set you up. **2.** Assurance. **Perdre son aplomb,** to lose one's self-possession.

apocalypse, *s.f. B :* **L'Apocalypse,** the Book of Revelation ; the Apocalypse.

apocryphe, *a.* Apocryphal.

apogée, *s.m. Astr :* Apogee ; *F :* height, zenith (of one's glory).

Apollon. *Pr.n.m. Myth :* Apollo.

apologie, *s.f.* Defence, vindication. NOTE. Never = EXCUSE, *q.v.*

apologiste, *s.m.* Apologist.

apologue, *s.m. Lit :* Apologue, fable.

apoplectique, *a. & s. Med :* Apoplectic.

apoplexie, *s.f. Med :* Apoplexy.

apostat, *a. & s.* Apostate ; *F :* Turncoat.

apostolique, *a.* Apostolic.

apostrophe, *s.f.* Apostrophe.

apothéose, *s.f.* **1.** Apotheosis ; deification. **2.** *Th :* Grand finale.

apothicaire, *s.m.* Apothecary.

apôtre, *s.m.* Apostle.

apparaiss-ant, etc. See APPARAÎTRE.

apparaître, *v.i.* (Conj. like CONNAÎTRE. Aux. usu. *être,* occ. *avoir*) **1.** To appear ; to come into sight. **2.** To become evident.

apparat, *s.m.* State, pomp, show, display.

appareil [-rɛːj], *s.m.* **1.** Display, pomp. **2.** (*a*) Apparatus, outfit. *A. de pêche,* fishing-tackle. (*b*) Device, appliance ; mechanism. *Appareils à gaz,* gas-fittings. (*c*) Machine, instrument. *W.Tel :* A. à lampes, valve set. *Phot :* **Appareil (photographique),** camera.

appareillage[1] [-rɛj-],*s.m.* **1.** (*a*) Installation, fitting up (of wireless station). (*b*) *Nau :* Getting under way. **2.** (*a*) Outfit ; fittings ; equipment. (*b*) *Ind :* Plant.

appareillage[2]**,** *s.m.* Matching (of colours).

appareiller[1] [-rɛjɛ], *v.tr.* **1.** To install, fit up (workshop). **2.** *Nau :* (*a*) *A. une voile,* to trim a sail. (*b*) *Abs :* To get under way.

appareiller[2]**,** *v.tr.* = APPARIER.

apparemment, *adv.* Apparently, to all appearances.

apparence, *s.f.* **1.** (*a*) Appearance ; look. **Selon toute apparence,** to all appearances. (*b*) (**Fausse**) **apparence,** false, fallacious, appearance. **En apparence,** in semblance ; on the surface. **2. Sauver les apparences,** to keep up appearances.

apparent, *a.* **1.** (*a*) Visible, conspicuous, apparent. *Peu a.,* inconspicuous. (*b*) Obvious, evident. **2.** Apparent, not real.

apparenté, *a.* Related, akin. **Bien apparenté,** well connected.

apparier, *v.tr.* To match (socks); to pair off (opponents).

apparition, *s.f.* 1. Appearance; coming out; publication. 2. Apparition, ghost.

appartement, *s.m.* Flat; suite of rooms.

appartenir, *v.i.* (Conj. like TENIR) 1. To belong (*à*, to). 2. *v. impers. Il lui appartient de* . . ., it behoves him to . . . .

     s'appartenir, to be one's own master.

appas, *s.m.pl.* 1. (Physical) charms. 2. Lure, attraction (of wealth).

appât, *s.m.* (a) Bait. (b) Lure (of success); attraction (of pleasure).

appauvrir, *v.tr.* To impoverish.

     s'appauvrir, to grow poor(er).

appauvrissement, *s.m.* Impoverishment.

appel, *s.m.* 1. Appeal. (a) Faire appel à qn, to appeal to s.o. (b) *Jur:* Appeal at law. 2. Call; (vocal) summons. Appel d'incendie, fire-alarm. 3. Roll-call, call-over. Faire l'appel, to call (over) the roll. *Répondre à l'a.,* to answer (to) one's name.

appelant. (a) *a.* Appealing (party). (b) *s. A. d'un jugement,* appellant against a judgment.

appeler, *v.tr.* (j'appelle) 1. (a) To call, call to (s.o.). (b) *A.* qn de la main, to beckon (to) s.o. 2. (a) To call in, send for, summon. Faire appeler un médecin, to call in a doctor. *Jur: A.* qn en justice, to summons s.o. (b) Être appelé à qch., to be destined for sth. 3. To call (by name); to name. 4. (a) To appeal to, call on. (b) To call for. *Ce problème appelle une solution immédiate,* the problem calls for an immediate solution. 5. (a) To provoke, arouse. (b) *Corps appelé par une force,* body pulled, attracted, by a force. 6. *v.i.* (a) *Jur: A. d'un jugement,* to appeal against a sentence. (b) En appeler à qn, to appeal to s.o.

     s'appeler, to be called, named. Comment vous appelez-vous? what is your name?

appendice, *s.m.* 1. Appendix (of book). 2. Annex(e). 3. *Anat:* Appendix.

appendicite, *s.f.* Appendicitis.

appentis, *s.m. Const:* (a) Penthouse. Toit en appentis, lean-to roof. (b) Outhouse.

appesantir, *v.tr.* 1. To make heavy; to weigh down. 2. To dull.

     s'appesantir. 1. To become heavy. 2. *S'a. sur un sujet,* to dwell on a subject.

appétissant, *a.* Tempting, appetizing.

appétit, *s.m.* 1. Appetite. Avoir bon appétit, to have a hearty appetite. 2. Desire, lust. *A. du gain,* greed of gold.

applaudir. 1. *v.tr.* (a) To applaud, clap. Se faire applaudir à tout casser, to bring the house down. (b) To applaud, commend. 2. *v.ind.tr. A. à qch.,* to approve sth.

     s'applaudir de qch., to congratulate oneself on sth.

applaudissement, *s.m.* Usu. *pl.* 1. Applause; clapping. 2. Approval, approbation.

applicable, *a.* Applicable. Mot a., appropriate word.

application, *s.f.* Application. 1. *A. d'un bandage à une blessure,* applying of a bandage to a wound. 2. Diligence.

applique, *s.f.* (a) (Wall-)bracket (for lamps). (b) Sconce, bracket-lamp.

appliquer, *v.tr.* To apply.

     s'appliquer. 1. *S'a. à qch.,* to apply oneself to sth.; to work hard at sth. 2. *A qui s'applique cette remarque?* to whom does this remark apply?

     appliqué, *a.* 1. Studious, diligent. 2. Sciences appliquées, applied sciences.

appoint, *s.m.* 1. *Com:* Balance. 2. Contribution.

appointements, *s.m.pl.* Salary, emoluments. *Ecc:* Stipend.

appontement, *s.m.* 1. Gang-plank. 2. (Wooden) wharf; landing-stage.

apport, *s.m. Com:* Initial share (in undertaking).

apporter, *v.tr.* To bring. 1. *A. des nouvelles,* to bring news (*à*, to). 2. *A. du soin à faire qch.,* to exercise care in doing sth.

apposer, *v.tr.* To affix, place, put.

apposition, *s.f. Gram:* Apposition.

appréciable, *a.* Appreciable.

appréciateur, -trice. 1. *a.* Appreciative. 2. *s.* Appreciator (*de*, of).

appréciation, *s.f.* 1. Valuation, estimate, appraising. 2. Appreciation (of work of art). Une affaire d'a., a matter of opinion. 3. Rise in value.

apprécier, *v.tr.* 1. (a) To appraise; to value. (b) To determine, estimate (distance). 2. To appreciate (good thing).

appréhender, *v.tr.* 1. Appréhender qn (au corps), to arrest s.o. 2. To dread, apprehend.

appréhensif, *a.* Apprehensive (*de*, of); fearful, timid.

appréhension, *s.f.* 1. Understanding. 2. Dread.

apprendre, *v.tr.* (Conj. like PRENDRE) 1. (a) To learn (lesson). *A. à faire qch.,* to learn (how) to do sth. (b) To learn, hear of. 2. *A. qch. à qn.* (a) To teach s.o. sth. (b) To tell s.o. sth.

appris, *a.* Bien appris, well-bred.

apprenti, *s.* (a) Apprentice. (b) Articled clerk. (c) *F:* Novice, tyro.

apprentissage, *s.m.* (a) Apprenticeship. (b) (In professions) Articles. *F:* Faire l'apprentissage de la vie, to learn by experience.

apprêt, *s.m.* 1. *pl.* Preparations (for journey). 2. Affectedness. 3. *Cu:* Dressing (of food).

apprêter, *v.tr.* To prepare; to make ready.

     s'apprêter. 1. To prepare oneself, get ready. 2. (Of trouble) To be brewing.

     apprêté, *a.* Affected, stiff (manner).

apprêteur, -euse, *s. Ind:* Finisher.

apprîmes, appris. See APPRENDRE.

apprivoisement, *s.m.* Taming, domestication.

apprivoiser, *v.tr.* To tame (animal); to win over (s.o.).

     s'apprivoiser, to become tame.

apprivoisé, *a.* Tame.
approbateur, -trice. 1. *a.* Approving (gesture). **2.** *s.* Approver.
approbatif, *a.* Approving.
approbation, *s.f.* Approval, approbation.
approbativement, *adv.* Approvingly.
approchable, *a.* Approachable, accessible.
approchant. *a.* Approximating, similar (*de,* to). *Couleur approchante du bleu,* colour approximating to blue.
approche, *s.f.* **1.** Approach, drawing near. *D'une* **approche difficile,** difficult of access. **2.** *pl.* Approches, approaches (of a camp).
approcher. 1. *v.tr.* (*a*) *A. qch. de qch.,* to bring, draw, sth. near (to) sth. *Approchez votre chaise,* draw up your chair. (*b*) To approach, come near; to come close to. **2.** *v.i.* (*a*) To approach, draw near. (*b*) *A. de qn,* to approach s.o. *Nous approchons de Paris,* we are getting near Paris. (*c*) *A. de qch.,* to resemble sth.; to approximate to sth.
   s'approcher, to come near; to approach. *S'a. de qch.,* to draw, come, near (to) sth.
approfondir, *v.tr.* **1.** To deepen, excavate (river-bed). **2.** To go thoroughly into (sth.).
   s'approfondir, to grow deeper; to deepen.
approfondi, *a.* Careful (study). *Connaissance approfondie du français,* thorough command of French.
approfondissement, *s.m.* **1.** Deepening (of canal). **2.** Investigation (of question).
appropriation, *s.f.* **1.** Appropriation. **2.** *A. de qch. à qch.,* adaptation of sth. to sth.
approprier, *v.tr.* **1.** *S'a. qch.,* to appropriate sth. (to oneself). **2.** To make appropriate.
   s'approprier, to adapt oneself (*à,* to).
approprié, *a.* Appropriate, adapted (*à,* to); proper, suitable.
approuver, *v.tr.* **1.** (*a*) *A. qch.,* to approve of, be pleased with, sth. *A. de la tête,* to nod approval. **2.** To agree to, sanction (expenditure). *A. un contrat,* to ratify a contract.
approvisionnement, *s.m.* **1.** Provisioning, victualling (of town); stocking (of shop). **2.** Supply, stock, store.
approvisionner, *v.tr.* To supply (*de,* with); to furnish with supplies; to provision.
   s'approvisionner, to take in, lay in, a supply (*en, de,* of); to lay in stores.
   approvisionné, *a.* Stocked (*de,* with).
approximatif, *a.* Approximate; rough.
approximation, *s.f.* Approximation.
approximativement, *adv.* Approximately, roughly.
appui, *s.m.* **1.** (*a*) Prop, stay. (*b*) Rest. *Arch:* Balustrade. *A. de fenêtre,* window-ledge. *A. d'escalier,* banisters. **2.** Support. (*a*) *Mur d'appui,* supporting wall. **Barre d'appui,** hand-rail. **A hauteur d'appui,** breast-high. (*b*) *A. moral,* moral support. *Être sans appui,* to be friendless. **3.** *A. de la voix sur une syllabe,* stress on a syllable.
appuyer, *v.tr.* (j'appuie) **1.** To support. (*a*) To prop (up). (*b*) *A. une pétition,* to support

a petition. **2.** (*a*) *A. qch. contre qch.,* to lean sth. against sth. *A. son opinion sur qch.,* to base one's opinion on sth. (*b*) *Mus: A. (sur) une note,* to dwell on, sustain, a note. **3.** *Abs. A. sur le bouton,* to press the button. *A. sur une syllabe,* to lay stress on a syllable. *A. à droite,* to bear to the right.
   s'appuyer. *S'a. sur, contre, à, qch.,* to lean, rest, on, against, sth.
âpre, *a.* **1.** Rough, harsh. **2.** Biting, sharp (rebuke). *Temps â.,* raw weather. **3.** Keen (competition).
âprement, *adv.* **1.** Harshly. **2.** Keenly.
après. I. *prep.* **1.** (*a*) After. (*b*) *Je viens a. lui,* I come next to him. **2.** *Épingler une carte après le mur,* to pin a card to the wall. **3.** *Courir après qn,* to run after s.o. *Il est toujours après moi,* he is always nagging at me. **4.** *Prep.phr.* **D'après,** according to; after; from. *Paysage d'a.* Turner, landscape after Turner. **5.** *Après avoir dîné, il sortit,* after dining he went out.
   II. après, *adv.* **1.** (*a*) Afterwards, later. *Le jour* (d')**après,** the next day; the day after. **Et après?** what then? (*b*) *Conj.phr.* **Après que,** after, when. **2.** *F:* **Tout le monde leur court après,** everybody runs after them.
après-demain, *adv.* The day after to-morrow.
après-guerre, *s.m.inv.* Post-war period.
après-midi, *s.m.* or *f. inv.* Afternoon.
âpreté, *s.f.* **1.** Roughness, harshness (of voice). **2.** Bitterness (of weather). **3.** *A. à faire qch.,* keenness in doing sth.
à-propos, *s.m.* **1.** Aptness, suitability (of an expression). **2.** Opportuneness.
apte, *a.* **1.** Apte à qch., fitted, qualified, for sth. *Élève apte,* apt, gifted, pupil. **2.** Apt, suitable (example).
aptitude, *s.f.* Aptitude, fitness (*à pour,* for). *Il a des aptitudes,* he is naturally gifted.
aquarelle [akwa-], *s.f.* Water-colour.
aquarium [akwarjɔm], *s.m.* Aquarium.
aquatique [akwa-], *a.* Aquatic (bird).
aqueduc [-dyk], *s.m.* Aqueduct.
aqueux, *a.* Aqueous, watery.
aquilin, *a.* Aquiline. *Nez a.,* Roman nose.
arabe. 1. *a. & s.* (*a*) Arab. (*b*) *a.* Arabian (customs). **2.** *a. & s.m.* Arabic.
arabique, *a.* **Gomme arabique,** gum-arabic.
arable, *a.* Arable, tillable (land).
arachide, *s.f. Bot:* Pea-nut, earth-nut.
araignée, *s.f.* Spider. **Toile d'araignée,** cobweb. *F:* **Avoir une araignée au plafond,** to have a bee in one's bonnet.
aratoire, *a.* Agricultural.
arbalète, *s.f.* Cross-bow.
arbalétrier, *s.m. A:* Cross-bowman.
arbitrage, *s.m.* Arbitration.
arbitraire, *a.* **1.** Arbitrary; discretionary. **2.** Arbitrary, despotic.
arbitrairement, *adv.* Arbitrarily.
arbitre[1], *s.m.* (*a*) *Jur:* Arbitrator, referee. (*b*) *Games:* Referee, umpire. (*c*) Arbiter.

arbitre², *s.m. Phil:* Libre arbitre, free will.
arbitrer, *v.tr.* **1.** *Jur:* To arbitrate.
2. *Games:* To referee, umpire (match).
arborer, *v.tr.* To raise; to hoist (flag).
arbre, *s.m.* **1.** (*a*) Tree. *A. fruitier*, fruit-tree. *A. vert*, evergreen (tree). (*b*) **Arbre généalogique**, genealogical tree. (*c*) **Arbre de Noël**, Christmas-tree. **2.** *Mec.E:* Shaft, axle.
arbrisseau, *s.m.* Shrub.
arbuste, *s.m.* Bush; shrub.
arc [ark], *s.m.* **1.** Bow. **Tir à l'arc**, archery. **2.** Arch. **3.** Arc.
arcade, *s.f.* (*a*) Archway. (*b*) *pl.* **Arcades**, arcade.
arc-boutant, *s.m.* **1.** Flying-buttress. **2.** Strut, stay, spur. *pl. Des arcs-boutants.*
arc-bouter, *v.tr.* To buttress, shore up.
s'arc-bouter, to brace oneself (to resist a shock).
arceau, *s.m.* **1.** Arch (of vault). **2.** Ring bow (of padlock); (croquet) hoop.
arc-en-ciel, *s.m.* Rainbow. *pl. Des arcs-en-ciel* [arkɑ̃sjɛl].
archaïque [ark-], *a.* Archaic.
archaïsme [ark-], *s.m.* Archaism.
archange [ark-], *s.m.* Archangel.
arche¹, *s.f.* L'arche de Noé, Noah's Ark.
arche², *s.f.* Arch (of bridge); (croquet) hoop.
archéologie [ark-], *s.f.* Archaeology.
archéologue [ark-], *s.m.* Archaeologist.
archer, *s.m.* Archer, bowman.
archet, *s.m.* Bow. *A. de violon*, violin bow.
archevêché, *s.m.* **1.** Archbishopric. **2.** Archbishop's palace.
archevêque, *s.m.* Archbishop.
archidiacre, *s.m. Ecc:* Archdeacon.
archiduc [-dyk], *s.m.* Archduke.
Archimède. *Pr.n.m. Gr.Hist.:* Archimedes.
archipel, *s.m. Geog:* Archipelago.
architecte, *s.m.* Architect.
architecture, *s.f.* Architecture.
archives, *s.f.pl.* Archives; records.
archiviste, *s.m. & f.* **1.** Archivist; keeper of public records. **2.** Filing clerk.
arçon, *s.m. Harn:* Saddle-bow. **Vider les arçons**, to be unhorsed.
arctique, *a.* Arctic.
ardemment, *adv.* Ardently, warmly.
ardent, *a.* **1.** Burning, scorching; blazing (fire). *Charbons ardents*, live coals. **2.** Ardent, passionate, eager.
ardeur, *s.f.* **1.** Heat. **2.** Eagerness, ardour.
ardoise, *s.f.* Slate. **Crayon d'ardoise**, slate-pencil.
ardoisière, *s.f.* Slate-quarry.
ardu, *a.* **1.** Steep, abrupt, difficult (path). **2.** Arduous, difficult (task).
arduité, *s.f.* Arduousness, difficulty.
are, *s.m. Meas:* 100 square metres.
arec [arek], *s.m.* Areca palm.
arène, *s.f.* **1.** *Lit:* Sand. **2.** Arena. *F:* **Descendre dans l'arène**, to enter the lists.
aréole, *s.f.* Halo, nimbus, ring.
aréomètre, *s.m. Ph:* Hydrometer.
aréquier, *s.m. Bot:* Areca palm.

arête, *s.f.* **1.** (Fish-)bone. **Grande arête**, backbone (of fish). **2.** Line; edge. *A. d'une chaîne de montagnes*, ridge of a mountain range. *A. du nez*, bridge of the nose. **3.** Beard, awn (of ear of wheat).
argent, *s.m.* **1.** Silver. **2.** Money, cash. *A. liquide*, ready money, cash (in hand). **En avoir pour son argent**, to have one's money's worth. **Avoir toujours de l'argent à la main**, to be always paying out.
argenter, *v.tr.* To silver.
    argenté, *a.* Silver-plated.
argenterie, *s.f.* (Silver-)plate.
argentin¹, *a.* Silvery (waves); tinkling (bell).
argentin², *a. & s.* Argentine, of Argentina.
argile, *s.f.* (*a*) Clay. (*b*) **Argile cuite**, terra-cotta, earthenware.
argileux, *a.* Clayey (soil).
argonaute, *s.m. Myth:* Argonaut.
argot, *s.m.* Slang.
arguer [argɥe], *v.* (j'argüe) **1.** *v.tr.* To infer, assert. **2.** *v.i.* To argue.
argument, *s.m.* **1.** Argument. **2.** Outline, summary (of book).
argumenter, **1.** *v.i.* (*a*) To argue (*contre*, against). (*b*) *F:* To argufy. **2.** *v.tr.* *A. qn*, to remonstrate with s.o.
Argus [argys]. *Pr.n.m. Myth:* Argus. *F:* A. de la police, police spy.
Ariane. *Pr.n.f. Gr.Myth:* Ariadne.
aride, *a.* Arid, dry, barren.
aridité, *s.f.* Aridity, barrenness.
Arioste (l'). *Pr.n.m.* Ariosto.
aristo, *s.m.* *P:* Toff, swell.
aristocrate, *s.m. & f.* Aristocrat.
aristocratie, *s.f.* Aristocracy.
aristocratique, *a.* Aristocratic.
Aristophane. *Pr.n.m.* Aristophanes.
Aristote. *Pr.n.m.* Aristotle.
arithmétique. **1.** *a.* Arithmetical. **2.** *s.f.* Arithmetic.
arlequin, *s.m.* (*a*) *Th:* Harlequin. (*b*) *F:* Inconsequent person, weathercock.
arlequinade, *s.f.* Harlequinade.
armateur, *s.m. Nau:* (*a*) Fitter-out (of ship). (*b*) (Ship-)owner.
armature, *s.f.* **1.** Framework (of window). *A. d'une raquette*, frame of a racquet. **2.** *El:* Armature. **3.** *Mus:* Key-signature.
arme, *s.f.* **1.** Arm, weapon. **Armes à feu**, fire-arms. **Armes portatives**, small-arms. **Armes blanches**, side-arms. **Faire des armes**, to fence. **Salle d'armes**, (i) armoury, (ii) fencing-school. **Maître d'armes**, fencing-master. **Faire ses premières armes**, to go through one's first campaign. **Place d'armes**, parade-ground. **Passer par les armes**, to be (court-martialled and) shot. **2.** Arm (as a branch of the army). **3.** *pl. Her:* Arms.
armée, *s.f.* Army.
armement, *s.m.* **1.** (*a*) Arming. (*b*) *pl.* Armaments. **2.** Fortifying, strengthening. **3.** *Nau:* Commissioning, fitting out. **Port d'armement**, port of registry.
Arménie. *Pr.n.f. Geog:* Armenia.

arménien, -ienne, *a. & s.* Armenian.
armer. I. *v.tr.* **1.** To arm (*de*, with). **2.** To fortify, strengthen. **Béton armé,** reinforced concrete. **3.** *Nau:* To equip, commission (ship). **4.** (*a*) *A. un canon,* to load a gun. (*b*) To cock (fire-arm).
II. **armer,** *v.i.* To arm, prepare for war.
armistice, *s.m.* Armistice.
armoire, *s.f.* **1.** Wardrobe. **2.** Cupboard.
armoiries, *s.f.pl. Her:* (Coat of) arms; armorial bearings.
armoricain, *a. & s.* Armorican.
armorier, *v.tr.* To (em)blazon.
armure, *s.f.* Armour.
armurerie, *s.f.* **1.** Manufacture of arms. **2.** Arms factory.
armurier, *s.m.* **1.** Gunsmith. **2.** Armourer.
arnica, *s.f. Pharm:* Arnica.
aromate, *s.m.* Aromatic; spice.
aromatique, *a.* Aromatic.
arome, *s.m.* **1.** Aroma. **2.** *Cu:* Flavouring.
aronde, *s.f.* **1.** *Orn: A:* Swallow. **2.** *Carp:* Queue d'aronde, dovetail.
arpège, *s.m.* Arpeggio; spread chord.
arpent, *s.m.* (Old measure, roughly =) Acre.
arpentage, *s.m.* (Land-)surveying.
arpenter, *v.tr.* **1.** To survey, measure (land). **2.** *F:* Arpenter le terrain, to stride along.
arpenteur, *s.m.* (Land-)surveyor.
arquebuse, *s.f. A:* (H)arquebus.
arquer. I. *v.tr.* To bend, curve (wood). *A. le dos,* to hump the back. **2.** *v.i.* To bend. **s'arquer,** (of the legs) to become bent.
arqué, *a.* Arched, curved.
arrache-pied (d'), *adv.phr.* Without interruption. *Travailler d'a.-p.,* to work steadily.
arracher, *v.tr.* To tear (out); to pull (up). *A. qch. à qn,* to snatch sth. from s.o. *Se faire a. une dent,* to have a tooth out. *S'a. les cheveux,* to tear one's hair.
arrangeant, *a.* Accommodating, obliging.
arrangement, *s.m.* Arrangement; agreement.
arranger, *v.tr.* (n. arrangeons) To arrange. **1.** To set in order. *A. une chambre,* to tidy up a room. **2.** To contrive. *A. une fête,* to get up an entertainment. **3.** To settle.
s'arranger. 1. To manage, contrive. *Il s'arrange de tout,* he is very adaptable. *Qu'il s'arrange!* that's his look-out! **2.** *S'a. avec qn,* to come to an agreement with s.o.
arrérages, *s.m.pl.* Arrears.
arrestation, *s.f.* Arrest. En état d'arrestation, under arrest.
arrêt, *s.m.* **1.** Stop, stoppage; stopping, arrest (of motion). **Point d'arrêt,** stopping place. *Trajet sans a.,* non-stop journey. *Dix minutes d'a.,* ten minutes' stop. *Rail:* Signal à l'arrêt, signal at danger. "Arrêt fixe," 'all cars stop here.' **2.** (*a*) Decree. (*b*) *Jur:* Judgment. **Arrêt de mort,** sentence of death. **3.** Seizure. **Mettre arrêt sur un navire, to** put an embargo on a ship. **4.** Arrest. Garder les arrêts, to be under arrest. **5.** Chien d'arrêt, setter, pointer.

arrêter. I. *v.tr.* **1.** To stop; to check; to hinder; to detain. *A. qn tout court,* to stop s.o. short. **2.** To fix, fasten (shutter). *A. l'attention,* to arrest attention. **3.** To arrest, seize. **Faire arrêter qn,** to give s.o. into custody. **4.** (*a*) To engage, hire. (*b*) To decide. *A. un jour,* to fix a day.
II. **arrêter,** *v.i.* To stop, halt. *Arrêtez un moment,* stop a moment.
s'arrêter. 1. To stop; to come to a stop, to a standstill. *S'a. en route,* to break one's journey. **2.** (*a*) *S'a. à un sujet,* to dwell on a subject. (*b*) *Son regard s'arrêta sur moi,* he eyed me intently.
arrêté. 1. *a.* (*a*) (Of ideas) Fixed, decided. (*b*) *Sp:* Départ arrêté, standing start. **2.** *s.m.* Decision, decree.
arrhes [a:r], *s.f.pl.* (*a*) Earnest (money). (*b*) Deposit.
arrière. 1. *adv.* (En) arrière. (*a*) Behind. *Prep.phr.* En arrière de qch., behind sth. *En a. de son siècle,* behind the times. (*b*) In arrears. (*c*) Backwards; backward (motion). **Arrière!** back! *Nau:* En arrière à toute vitesse! full speed astern! **Faire marche arrière,** to back; *Aut:* to reverse. **2.** *a.inv.* Back. *Aut:* Lanterne arrière, rear light. **3.** *s.m.* (*a*) Back, back part (of house). (*b*) Stern (of ship). **4.** *Fb:* Back.
arriéré, *a.* **1.** In arrears; (payment) overdue. **2.** Backward; behind the times. **3.** *s.m.* Arrears. **Avoir de l'arriéré,** to be behindhand.
NOTE. In all the following compounds ARRIÈRE is inv., the noun takes the plural.
arrière-boutique, *s.f.* Back-shop.
arrière-bras, *s.m.* Upper arm.
arrière-cour, *s.f.* Back-yard.
arrière-garde, *s.f.* **1.** *Mil:* Rear-guard. **2.** *Navy:* Rear-division (of squadron).
arrière-goût, *s.m.* After-taste, faint taste.
arrière-grand'mère, *s.f.* Great-grandmother. *pl.* Des arrière-grand'mères.
arrière-grand-père, *s.m.* Great-grandfather. *pl. Des arrière-grands-pères.*
arrière-main, *s.m. or f.* **1.** Back of the hand. **2.** (Hind)quarters (of horse).
arrière-pensée, *s.f.* (*a*) Mental reservation. (*b*) Ulterior motive.
arrière-petite-fille, *s.f.* Great-granddaughter. *pl. Des arrière-petites-filles.*
arrière-petit-fils, *s.m.* Great-grandson.
arrière-plan, *s.m.* Background. *Th: A l'a.-p.,* up-stage, at the back.
arrière-port, *s.m.* Inner harbour.
arrière-rang, *s.m.* Rear rank.
arrière-saison, *s.f.* Late season.
arrière-scène, *s.f. Th:* Back of the stage.
arrière-train, *s.m.* **1.** (Hind)quarters (of animal). **2.** *Veh:* Waggon-body.
arrimage, *s.m.* (*a*) Stowing (of cargo). (*b*) Trimming (of ship).
arrimer, *v.tr.* (*a*) To stow (cargo). (*b*) To trim (ship).

arrimeur, *s.m.* (*a*) Stower. (*b*) Stevedore.

arrivant, *s.* Person arriving; arrival.

arrivée, *s.f.* Arrival, coming, advent. *A mon a.,* on my arrival.

arriver, *v.i.* (Aux. *être*) **1.** (*a*) To arrive, come. *Il arriva en courant,* he came running up. *F: Arrivez!* come on ! *La nuit arriva,* night came on. *Impers. Il arriva un soldat,* there came a soldier, (*b*) *A. à un endroit,* to reach a place. **Arriver à bon port,** to arrive safely. (*c*) *Il faudra bien en a. là,* it must come to that. **2.** To succeed. (*a*) *Il n'arrivera jamais à rien,* he will never achieve anything. (*b*) **Arriver à faire qch.,** to manage to do sth. **3.** To happen. *Cela arrive tous les jours,* it happens every day. *Impers. Il lui est arrivé un accident,* he has met with an accident. *Faire a. un accident,* to cause an accident.

arriviste, *s.m. & f.* Thruster.

arrogamment, *adv.* Arrogantly.

arrogance, *s.f.* Arrogance.

arrogant, *a.* Arrogant, overbearing.

arroger (s'), *v.tr.pr.* (n.n. arrogeons) *S'a. un droit,* to arrogate a right to oneself.

arrondir, *v.tr.* (*a*) To round (off) ; to make round. (*b*) *Phrase bien arrondie,* well-rounded sentence.
    s'arrondir, to become round ; to fill out.

arrondi, *a.* Rounded, round (chin).

arrondissement, *s.m.* **1.** Rounding (off). **2.** Administrative area ; ward (in Paris).

arrosage, *s.m.,* **arrosement,** *s.m.* (*a*) Watering. (*b*) Irrigation.

arroser, *v.tr.* (*a*) To water (plants). *A. un rôti,* to baste a joint. *F: Yeux arrosés de larmes,* eyes bathed in tears. (*b*) *A. une prairie,* to irrigate a meadow.

arroseur, *s.m.* Street-orderly.

arrosoir, *s.m.* Watering-can.

arsenal, -aux, *s.m.* Arsenal.

arsenic [-ik], *s.m.* Arsenic.

art, *s.m.* **1.** Art. (*a*) **Arts d'agrément,** accomplishments. (*b*) **Beaux-arts,** fine arts. **Œuvre d'art,** work of art. **2.** Skill ; artistry. *Civ.E:* Travaux, ouvrages, d'art, constructive works.

artère, *s.f.* Artery.

artériel, -elle, *a.* Arterial.

artésien, -ienne, *a. & s.* Artesian.

arthrite, *s.f. Med:* Arthritis.

artichaut, *s.m.* Globe artichoke.

article, *s.m.* **1.** (*a*) *Ent:* Joint. (*b*) **Être à l'article de la mort,** to be at the point of death. **2.** (*a*) Article, clause (of treaty). (*b*) *Articles de dépense,* items of expenditure. (*c*) Article (in newspaper). **3.** *Com:* Article, commodity; *pl.* goods, wares. **Article(s) de Paris,** fancy goods. **4.** *Gram:* Article.

articulation, *s.f.* **1.** (*a*) *Anat:* Articulation, joint. *Bot:* Node. (*b*) Connection, joint. **2.** Articulation, utterance.

articuler, *v.tr.* **1.** To articulate, joint. **2.** To articulate ; to utter or pronounce distinctly.
    articulé, *a.* (*a*) Articulate(d) ; jointed. (*b*) Articulate ; distinct (utterance).

artifice, *s.m.* **1.** Artifice ; guile ; contrivance. **2. Feu d'artifice,** fireworks.

artificiel, -elle, *a.* Artificial. **1.** (*a*) *Lumière artificielle,* artificial light. (*b*) *Rire a.,* forced laugh. **2.** Imitation (pearl).

artificiellement, *adv.* Artificially.

artificieux, *a.* Crafty, cunning, guileful.

artillerie [-tijri], *s.f.* **1.** Artillery. **2.** Gunnery.

artilleur [-tij-], *s.m.* Artilleryman ; gunner.

artimon, *s.m.* (**Mât d'**)**artimon,** mizzen-mast.

artisan, *s.m.* **1.** Artisan, craftsman. **2.** Maker, contriver. *Il a été l'a. de sa fortune,* he is a self-made man.

artiste. 1. *s.m. & f.* (*a*) Artist (including musician, etc.). (*b*) *Th: Mus:* Performer. (*c*) *Th:* Artiste. **2.** *a.* Artistic.

artistement, *adv.* Skilfully, cleverly.

artistique, *a.* Artistic (furniture).

artistiquement, *adv.* Artistically.

aryen, -yenne, *a. & s.* Aryan ; Indo-European.

as¹ [ɑːs], *s.m.* **1.** Ace. **As de pique,** ace of spades. **2.** Ace, *F:* First-rater.

as² [a]. See AVOIR.

asbeste, *s.m. Miner:* Asbestos.

ascendance, *s.f.* **1.** *Astr:* Ascent. **2.** Ancestry.

ascendant. 1. *a.* Ascending, upward. *Av:* Vol ascendant, climbing flight. **2.** *s.m.* (*a*) **Astre qui est à l'ascendant,** star in the ascendant. (*b*) Ascendancy, influence. (*c*) *pl.* **Ascendants,** ancestry.

ascenseur, *s.m.* Lift.

ascension, *s.f.* Ascent, ascension ; rising (of sap). **Faire l'ascension d'une montagne,** to climb a mountain.

ascensionnel, -elle, *a.* Ascensional ; upward. *Aer:* Force ascensionnelle, lift.

ascète, *s.m. & f.* Ascetic.

ascétique, *a. & s.* Ascetic(al).

ascétisme, *s.m.* Asceticism.

aseptique, *a. Med:* Aseptic.

asiatique, *a. & s.* Asiatic.

Asie. *Pr.n.f. Geog:* Asia.

asile, *s.m.* Shelter, home, refuge. **Sans asile,** homeless. *A. d'aliénés,* mental hospital.

aspect [aspɛ], *s.m.* **1.** Sight, aspect. **Au premier aspect,** at first sight. **2.** Aspect, appearance, look. **Considérer une affaire sous tous ses aspects,** to look at a thing from all points of view.

asperge, *s.f.* Asparagus.

asperger, *v.tr.* (n. aspergeons) To sprinkle with water.

aspérité, *s.f.* Asperity. **1.** Ruggedness, roughness (of surface). **2.** Harshness.

asphalte, *s.m.* Asphalt.

asphodèle, *s.m. Bot:* Asphodel.

asphyxiant, *a.* Asphyxiating, suffocating.

asphyxie, *s.f.* Asphyxiation, suffocation.

asphyxier, *v.tr.* To asphyxiate, suffocate.

aspic¹ [aspik], *s.m. Rept:* Asp. *F:* Langue d'aspic, venomous tongue.

aspic², *s.m.* *Cu:* Aspic(-jelly).

aspirant. I. *a.* Sucking. **Pompe aspirante**, suction pump. **2.** *s.* (*a*) Aspirant; candidate. (*b*) *Navy:* Midshipman.

aspirateur, -trice. I. *a.* Aspiratory. **2.** *s.m.* *A. de poussières*, vacuum-cleaner.

aspiration, *s.f.* **I.** Aspiration (*à*, for, after). **2.** *Ling:* Aspiration; rough breathing. **3.** (*a*) Inspiration, inhaling. (*b*) Suction.

aspirer. I. *v.ind.tr.* To aspire. **2.** *v.tr.* (*a*) To inspire, inhale. (*b*) To suck up (water). (*c*) *Ling:* To aspirate, breathe.

    aspiré, *a.* *Ling:* Aspirate(d).

    aspirée, *s.f.* *Ling:* Aspirate.

aspirine, *s.f.* *Pharm:* Aspirin.

assagir, *v.tr.* To make wiser; to sober.

    s'assagir, to become wiser.

assagissement, *s.m.* **I.** Making wiser. **2.** Growing wiser.

assaillant [-ajɑ̃], *s.m.* Assailant.

assaillir [-aji:r], *v.tr.* (*pr.p* **assaillant**; *pr. ind.* **j'assaille**) To assail, assault, attack.

assainir, *v.tr.* To make healthier; to purify (atmosphere).

assainissement, *s.m.* Cleansing, purification.

assaisonnement, *s.m.* **I.** (Action of) seasoning (dish). **2.** Condiment, seasoning.

assaisonner, *v.tr.* To season (*de*, with).

assassin. I. *s.* Assassin; murderer. **2.** *a.* (*a*) Murderous (horde). (*b*) Killing (smile).

assassinat, *s.m.* Assassination, murder.

assassiner, *v.tr.* **I.** To assassinate, murder. **2.** *F:* To worry to death (*de*, with).

assaut, *s.m.* **I.** Assault, attack, onslaught. **Troupes d'assaut**, storm-troops, shock troops. **2.** Match, bout.

assèchement, *s.m.* Drying, drainage.

assécher, *v.* (j'assèche; j'assécherai) **I.** *v.tr.* To dry, drain. **2.** *v.i.* & *pr.* To dry up.

assemblage, *s.m.* **I.** Assemblage, gathering. **2.** Assembling (of parts of machine). **3.** *El.E:* Connection, joining up.

assemblée, *s.f.* Assembly. **I.** Meeting. *A. de famille*, family gathering. **2.** *Mil:* *Battre l'a.*, to beat the assembly.

assembler, *v.tr.* **I.** To assemble; to call (people) together; to collect, gather. **2.** To assemble, fit together (machine). *El.E:* To connect, join up (cells).

    s'assembler, to assemble, meet, gather. *Prov:* **Qui se ressemble s'assemble**, birds of a feather flock together.

assener, *v.tr.* (j'assène) To deal, strike (blow).

assentiment, *s.m.* Assent, consent.

asseoir, *v.tr.* (*pr.p.* asseyant, assoyant; *p.p.* assis; *pr.ind.* j'assieds; ils asseyent, or j'assois, ils assoient; *pr.sub.* j'asseye, or j'assoie; *p.h.* j'assis; *fu.* j'assiérai, j'asseyerai, j'assoirai) **I.** To set, seat. **2.** To lay (foundations). *A. un camp*, to pitch a camp. *Av:* *A. l'appareil*, to pancake.

    s'asseoir, to sit down.

    assis, *a.* Seated. **Demeurer assis**, to

remain seated; to keep one's seat. *Il n'y a plus de places assises*, 'standing room only.'

assermentation, *s.f.* Swearing in.

assermenter, *v.tr.* To swear in; to administer the oath to.

    assermenté, *a.* Sworn (in).

asservir, *v.tr.* To enslave.

    asservi, *a.* *Être a. à l'étiquette*, to be a slave to etiquette.

asservissement, *s.m.* (*a*) Reduction to slavery. (*b*) State of bondage.

assesseur, *s.m.* Assessor.

assey-ant, -e, -ons, etc. See ASSEOIR.

assez, *adv.* **I.** Enough, sufficient, sufficiently. (*a*) *J'aurai a. de cent francs*, I shall have enough with a hundred francs. (*b*) *Avez-vous a. d'argent?* have you enough money? *Oui, j'en ai a.*, yes, I have sufficient. *F:* **J'en ai assez!** I have had enough of it, I am sick of it! (*c*) *C'est a. parler*, I, you, have said enough. (*d*) *Être a. près pour voir*, to be near enough to see. **2.** Rather, fairly. *Elle est a. jolie*, she is rather pretty. **3.** **Est-il assez enfant!** how childish of him!

assidu, *a.* Assiduous. (*a*) Sedulous, industrious. *Être a. à qch.*, to be persevering in sth. (*b*) Unremitting, unceasing. (*c*) Regular (visitor).

assiduité, *s.f.* Assiduity. **I.** (*a*) Sedulousness. (*b*) *Sch:* **Prix d'assiduité**, attendance prize. **2.** Constant care.

assidûment, *adv.* Assiduously, sedulously.

assied, -s. See ASSEOIR.

assiégeant. I. *a.* Besieging (army). **2.** *s.m.* Besieger.

assiéger, *v.tr.* (j'assiège, n. assiégeons; j'assiégerai) **I.** (*a*) To besiege. (*b*) *F:* *A. qn de questions*, to besiege s.o. with questions. **2.** To beset, crowd round.

assiér-ai, -as, etc. See ASSEOIR.

assiette, *s.f.* **I.** Stable position. (*a*) *F:* **N'être pas dans son assiette**, to be out of sorts. (*b*) *Golf:* *A. d'une balle*, lie of a ball. **Prendre son assiette**, to set, to settle. **2.** Support, basis. **3.** Plate. **Assiette creuse**, soup-plate.

assiettée, *s.f.* Plate(ful).

assignation, *s.f.* **I.** *Fin:* Assignment. **2.** *Jur:* Writ; summons; subpoena.

assigner, *v.tr.* **I.** To assign. **2.** *Jur:* (*a*) To summon, subpoena. (*b*) To issue a writ against.

assimilation, *s.f.* Assimilation.

assimiler, *v.tr.* **I.** To assimilate. **2.** To liken, compare (*à*, to, with).

assis. See ASSEOIR.

assise, *s.f.* **I.** Laying (of foundation). **2.** (*a*) *Les assises de la société*, the foundations of society. (*b*) Seat (on horseback). **3.** *pl.* *Jur:* **Les assises**, the assizes.

assistance, *s.f.* **I.** Presence, attendance (of magistrate). **2.** (*a*) Audience, company. (*b*) Spectators, onlookers. **3.** Assistance, help.

assistant, *s.* **1.** Usu. *pl.* (*a*) Bystander, onlooker, spectator. (*b*) Member of the audience. **2.** Assistant (professor).

assister. 1. *v.i.* *A. à qch.*, to attend sth.; to be present at sth. **2.** *v.tr.* To help, assist.

association, *s.f.* **1.** (*a*) Association (of words). (*b*) *El:* Connecting (of cells). **2.** (*a*) Society, company; association. (*b*) *Com:* Partnership.

associer, *v.tr.* To associate, unite, join. *A. des idées,* to connect ideas.

s'associer. 1. *S'a. à qch.*, to share in, join in, sth. **2.** *S'a. à, avec, qn.* (*a*) To enter into partnership with s.o. (*b*) To associate with s.o.

associé, *s.* (*a*) *Com:* Partner. (*b*) Associate member (of learned body).

assoiffé, *a.* *Être a. de qch.*, to be thirsty, thirsting, eager, for sth.

assoir-ai, -as; assoi-s, -t. See ASSEOIR.

assombrir, *v.tr.* (*a*) To darken, obscure. (*b*) To cast a gloom over (company).

s'assombrir. (*a*) To darken; to cloud over. (*b*) To become gloomy, sad.

assombrissement, *s.m.* **1.** Darkening. **2.** Gloom.

assommant, *a.* **1.** Overwhelming. **2.** *F:* Boring, tedious.

assommer, *v.tr.* **1.** (*a*) *A. un bœuf,* to fell an ox. **2.** *F:* To bore; to tire to death.

assommeur, -euse. 1. *s.m.* Slaughterman. **2.** *s.* *F:* Quel assommeur que votre ami! your friend is a terrible bore!

assommoir, *s.m.* **1.** (*a*) Pole-axe. (*b*) Club, bludgeon. **2.** Low tavern.

assomption, *s.f.* Assumption.

assortiment, *s.m.* **1.** Matching. *A. parfait de couleurs,* perfect match(ing) of colours. **2.** Assortment. *Ample a. d'échantillons,* wide range of patterns.

assortir, *v.tr.* (*a*) To assort, sort, match (colours). (*b*) To stock (shop).

s'assortir, to match; to harmonize.

assorti, *a.* **1.** Matched, paired. **2.** Assorted, mixed. **3.** Bien assorti, well stocked.

assoupir, *v.tr.* (*a*) To make drowsy. (*b*) To allay, lull (pain).

s'assoupir. 1. To drop off to sleep; to doze off. **2.** (Of pain) To wear away.

assoupi, *a.* **1.** Dozing. **2.** Dormant.

assoupissant, *a.* Soporific.

assoupissement, *s.m.* **1.** Allaying (of pain). **2.** Drowsiness; dozing.

assouplir, *v.tr.* To make supple.

s'assouplir, to become supple.

assouplissement, *s.m.* **1.** Assuaging (of pain). **2.** Drowsiness.

assourdir, *v.tr.* **1.** To make deaf; to deafen. **2.** (*a*) To deaden (sound). (*b*) To soften, subdue (colour).

s'assourdir, (of sound) to grow fainter.

assourdissant, *a.* Deafening.

assourdissement, *s.m.* (*a*) Deafening. (*b*) Deadening (of sound).

assouvir, *v.tr.* To appease.

s'assouvir, to satiate oneself.

assouvissement, *s.m.* Satisfying, satisfaction (of hunger).

assoy-ant, -ons, etc. See ASSEOIR.

assujettir, *v.tr.* **1.** To subdue, subjugate (province). *A. ses passions,* to curb one's passions. **2.** To fix, fasten (*à,* to).

assujetti, *a.* Subject (*à,* to).

assujettissement, *s.m.* **1.** Subjection. **2.** Fixing, fastening.

assumer, *v.tr.* To assume; to take upon oneself.

assurance, *s.f.* **1.** Assurance. **2.** (*a*) Making sure or safe. (*b*) *Com:* Insurance, assurance. *A. sur la vie,* life-assurance.

assurément, *adv.* **1.** *Marcher a.,* to tread firmly. **2.** Assuredly, surely, undoubtedly.

assurer, *v.tr.* **1.** (*a*) To make firm; to fix, secure. (*b*) *A. un résultat,* to ensure a result. *A. un pays,* to make a country secure. (*c*) *A. son visage,* to put on a firm countenance. **2.** *A. qn de son affection,* to assure s.o. of one's affection. **3.** *Com:* To insure. **Se faire assurer sur la vie,** to have one's life insured.

s'assurer. 1. *S'a. sur ses pieds,* to take a firm stand. **2.** *S'a. de qch.,* to make sure, certain, of sth. *S'a. que + ind.,* to make sure, ascertain, that. . . . **3.** *S'a. de qch.,* to make sure of, to secure, sth. **4.** *Com:* To get insured.

assuré, *a.* Firm, sure (step); assured, confident (air); certain (cure). *Voix mal assurée,* unsteady voice.

Assyrie. *Pr.n.f.* *A.Geog:* Assyria.

astérisque, *s.m.* *Typ:* Asterisk.

astéroïde, *s.m.* *Astr:* Asteroid.

asthmatique [asmatik], *a.* Asthmatic(al).

asthme [asm], *s.m.* Asthma.

asticot, *s.m.* Maggot.

astiquage, *s.m.* Polishing, furbishing.

astiquer, *v.tr.* To polish, furbish (belt).

astrak(h)an, *s.m.* Astrakhan (fur).

astral, -aux, *a.* Astral (body).

astre, *s.m.* Heavenly body; star.

astreign-ant, -ez, etc. See ASTREINDRE.

astreindre, *v.tr.* (Conj. like PEINDRE) To compel, oblige; to tie down.

astringent, *a. & s.m.* Astringent.

astrologie, *s.f.* Astrology.

astrologue, *s.m.* Astrologer.

astronome, *s.m.* Astronomer.

astronomie, *s.f.* Astronomy.

astronomique, *a.* Astronomical.

astuce, *s.f.* **1.** Astuteness; artfulness. **2.** Wile.

astucieusement, *adv.* Astutely, artfully.

astucieux, *a.* Astute, artful, crafty.

asymétrique, *a.* Unsymmetrical.

atavique, *a.* Atavistic.

atavisme, *s.m.* Atavism.

atelier, *s.m.* **1.** (*a*) (Work)shop, work-room. (*b*) Studio (of artist). **2.** Shop-staff, work-room staff.

athée, I. *a.* Atheistic(al). **2.** *s.* Atheist.
athéisme, -s.m. Atheism.
athénée, s.m. Athenaeum.
Athènes. *Pr.n.f. Geog:* Athens.
athénien, -ienne, *a. & s.* Athenian.
athlète, s.m. Athlete.
athlétique, *a.* Athletic.
athlétisme, -s.m. Athleticism; athletics.
atlantique, *a.* *L'océan A.,* *s.m.* l'Atlantique, the Atlantic (Ocean).
Atlas [atlɑːs]. **I.** *Pr.n.m. Myth:* Atlas. **2.** *s.m.* Atlas, book of maps.
atmosphère, s.f. Atmosphere.
atmosphérique, *a.* Atmospheric. *Pression a.,* air-pressure.
atoll, s.m. *Geol:* Atoll; coral island.
atome, s.m. *Ph:* Atom.
atomique, *a.* Atomic.
atomiser, v.tr. To atomize, to spray (liquid).
atone, *a.* **I.** Dull, vacant (look). **2.** Un-stressed, atonic (syllable).
atour, s.m. Usu. *pl. A:* Finery.
atout, s.m. *Cards:* Trump.
âtre, s.m. Fireplace, hearth(-stone).
atroce, *a.* Atrocious, heinous. *Douleur a.,* agonizing pain.
atrocement, adv. I. Atrociously, shockingly. **2.** Dreadfully.
atrocité, s.f. I. Atrociousness. **2.** Atrocity.
atrophie, s.f. *Med:* Atrophy.
atrophier, v.tr. To atrophy (limb).
   s'atrophier, to atrophy; to waste (away).
attabler (s'), v.pr. To sit down to table.
attachant, *a.* **I.** Interesting (book); arresting (spectacle). **2.** Engaging (personality).
attache, s.f. I. Fastening; tying up. *Nau:* Port d'attache, home port. **2.** Tie, fastener, fastening. (*a*) Head-rope (of horse); leash (of dog). (*b*) Paper-fastener, clip.
attachement, s.m. *A. pour qn,* attachment, affection, for s.o.
attacher, v.tr. To attach. (*a*) To fasten, bind; to tie (up). (*b*) *Spectacle qui attache l'attention,* spectacle that rivets the attention.
   s'attacher. I. To attach oneself, to cling, stick. *F: S'a. aux pas de qn,* to dog s.o.'s footsteps. **2.** *S'a. à une tâche,* to apply oneself to a task.
   attaché, *a.* (*a*) Fastened, tied-up. (*b*) *Être a. à qn,* to be attached, devoted, to s.o. (*c*) *Il est a. à mes pas,* he dogs my footsteps. **2.** *s.m. A. militaire,* military attaché.
attaque, s.f. I. (*a*) Attack, onslaught. (*b*) *Med: A. de goutte,* attack of gout. **2.** *Mec.E: A. directe,* direct drive (of motor).
attaquer, v.tr. I. To attack, assail. **2.** To begin, *F:* to tackle (piece of work). **3.** (Of piece of mechanism) To drive, operate.
   s'attaquer *à qn,* to attack s.o. *S'a. à plus fort que soi,* to meet more than one's match.
attarder, v.tr. To keep (s.o.) late.
   s'attarder, to linger, dally, loiter; to stay late.
   attardé, *a.* **I.** Belated (traveller); late.

2. Behind the times. **3.** Backward (child).
atteign-ant, -ez, etc. See ATTEINDRE.
atteindre, v. (Conj. like PEINDRE) **I.** *v.tr.* To reach; to overtake. (*a*) *A. la ville,* to reach the town. *A. son but,* to attain one's end. (*b*) *A. le but,* to hit the target. *Le poumon est atteint,* the lung is affected. **2.** *v.ind.tr. A. à qch.,* to reach, attain (to) sth.
atteinte, s.f. I. Reach. **2.** Blow, hit. *Porter a. aux intérêts de qn,* to injure s.o.'s interests.
attelage, s.m. I. (*a*) Harnessing. (*b*) Way of harnessing. **Attelage à quatre,** four-in-hand. **2.** Team; yoke (of oxen). **3.** *Rail:* Coupling.
atteler, v.tr. (J'attelle) **I.** To harness (horses); to yoke (oxen). **2.** *A. une voiture,* to put horses to a carriage. **3.** *Rail: A. des wagons,* to couple (up) waggons.
attelle, s.f. *Surg:* Splint.
attenant, *a.* Contiguous; abutting (*à,* on).
attendre, v.tr. I. To wait for, to await. *Faire attendre qn,* to keep s.o. waiting. *Se faire a.,* to be late. **Attendez donc!** wait a bit! **En attendant,** meanwhile, in the meantime. *Conj.phr.* **En attendant que** + *sub.,* till, until. **2.** To expect.
   s'attendre. *S'a. à qch.,* to expect sth. *Je m'y attendais,* I thought as much.
attendrir, v.tr. I. To make (meat) tender. **2.** To soften (s.o.'s heart).
   s'attendrir, to be moved (to pity).
   attendri, *a.* Fond, compassionate (look).
attendrissant, *a.* Moving, touching.
attendrissement, s.m. (Feeling of) pity.
attendu. I. *prep.* Considering (the circumstances); owing to (the events). **2.** *Conj. phr.* Attendu que + *ind.,* considering that . . ., seeing that. . . .
attentat, s.m. (Criminal) attempt; outrage.
attente, s.f. I. Wait(ing). **Salle d'attente,** waiting-room. **2.** Expectation(s), anticipation. **Contre toute attente,** contrary to all expectations. **"Dans l'attente de votre réponse,"** 'awaiting your reply.'
attenter, v.ind.tr. To make an attempt (*à,* on).
attentif, *a.* Attentive (*à,* to); heedful (*à,* of); careful.
attention, s.f. Attention, care. (*a*) **Attention suivie,** close attention. **Attirer l'attention,** to catch the eye. **Faites attention!** take care! **Attention!** look out! (*b*) *Être plein d'attentions pour qn,* to show s.o. much attention.
attentionné, *a.* Attentive. *Être a. pour qn,* to be considerate towards s.o.
attentivement, adv. Attentively, carefully.
atténuant, *a.* *Jur:* Extenuating.
atténuation, s.f. I. Attenuation, lessening. **2.** Extenuation (of crime).
atténuer, v.tr. I. (*a*) To attenuate, lessen; to mitigate (punishment). *A. une chute,* to break a fall. (*b*) *Phot:* To reduce (negative). **2.** To extenuate (offence).
   s'atténuer, to lessen; to diminish.

atterrant, *a.* Overwhelming, crushing, staggering (piece of news).

atterrement, *s.m.* Stupefaction, consternation.

atterrer, *v.tr.* To overwhelm, astound; to strike with consternation.

atterré, *a.* Utterly crushed (by news).

atterrir, *v.i.* (*a*) *Nau:* To make a landfall. (*b*) (Of boat) To ground. (*c*) *Av:* To land.

atterrissage, *s.m.* **1.** *Nau:* (*a*) Landfall. (*b*) Grounding (of boat). **2.** *Av:* Landing. **Terrain d'atterrissage,** landing-ground.

attestation, *s.f.* Attestation.

attester, *v.tr.* **1.** *A. qch.*, to attest sth.; to testify to sth. **2.** *J'en atteste les cieux,* I call heaven to witness.

attiédir, *v.tr.* To make tepid, lukewarm.

s'attiédir, to grow lukewarm.

attiédissement, *s.m.* Cooling.

attifage, *s.m.,* **attifement,** *s.m.* **1.** Dressing up. **2.** Get-up, rig-out.

attifer, *v.tr.* To dress (s.o.) up (*de,* in).

s'attifer, to dress oneself up.

attique, *a.* Attic, Athenian.

attirail [-ra:j], *s.m.* Apparatus, gear; outfit.

attirant, *a.* Attractive, drawing (force); alluring, engaging (manners).

attirer, *v.tr.* **1.** (*a*) (Of magnet) To attract, draw. (*b*) *A. qch. à, sur, qn,* to bring sth. on s.o. *S'a. un blâme,* to incur a reprimand. **2.** *A. qn dans un piège,* to lure s.o. into a trap.

attiser, *v.tr.* To stir (up), poke (fire).

attitré, *a.* Regular, appointed (agent).

attitude, *s.f.* Attitude, posture. **Être toujours en attitude,** to be always posing.

attouchement, *s.m.* Touching, contact.

attraction, *s.f.* (*a*) Attraction (of magnet). (*b*) Attractiveness (of person).

attrait, *s.m.* Attraction, lure; allurement.

attrape, *s.f.* (*a*) Trap, snare (for birds). (*b*) *F:* Trick, catch.

attrape-mouches, *s.m.inv.* **1.** Fly-trap; fly paper. **2.** *Bot:* Catchfly.

attrape-niais, *s.m.inv.,* **attrape-nigaud,** *s.m. F:* Booby-trap. *pl. Des attrape-nigauds.*

attraper, *v.tr.* To catch. **1.** (*a*) To (en)trap, (en)snare. (*b*) *A. qn,* to trick, cheat, s.o. **Attrapé!** sold again! (*b*) Des attrape-nigauds. **Attrape!** take that! (*b*) *Une pierre l'a attrapé au front,* a stone hit him on the forehead. (*c*) *A. un rhume,* to catch cold.

attrayant, *a.* Attractive, engaging, alluring.

attribuable, *a.* Attributable.

attribuer, *v.tr.* **1.** To assign, allot (*à,* to). **2.** To attribute, ascribe (fact); to impute (crime). **3.** *S'a. qch.*, to lay claim to sth.

attribut, *s.m.* **1.** Attribute. **2.** Predicate.

attributif, *a.* Predicative.

attribution, *s.f.* **1.** Assigning, attribution; allocation. **2.** Usu. *pl.* (*a*) Prerogative; powers. (*b*) Sphere of duties; functions.

attrister, *v.tr.* (*a*) To sadden, grieve. (*b*) To give a gloomy appearance to.

s'attrister, to grow sad.

attrition, *s.f.* Attrition; wearing away.

attroupement, *s.m.* (Unlawful) assembly.

attrouper, *v.tr.* To gather (mob) together.

s'attrouper, to gather into a mob.

au = *à le.* See **À** and **LE.**

aubaine, *s.f.* Windfall, godsend.

aube¹, *s.f.* **1.** Dawn. **2.** *Ecc:* Alb.

aube², *s.f.* Paddle, blade (of wheel). **Roue à aubes,** paddle-wheel.

aubépine, *s.f.* Hawthorn, whitethorn.

auberge, *s.f.* Inn.

aubergine, *s.f. Bot:* Aubergine, egg-plant.

aubergiste, *s.m. & f.* Innkeeper.

aubier, *s.m. Bot:* Sap-wood.

aucun. 1. *pron.* (*a*) Anyone, any. (*b*) (i) No one, nobody. (ii) None, not any (*c*) *pl. Lit:* Some people, some folk. **2.** *a.* (*a*) Any. (*b*) *Le fait n'a aucune importance,* the fact is of no importance.

aucunement, *adv.* **1.** In any way, at all. *Le connaissez-vous a.?* do you know him at all? **2.** In no way, in no wise; not at all. *Je ne le connais a.*, I don't know him at all.

audace, *s.f.* Audacity, audaciousness. **1.** Boldness, daring. *N'ayez pas l'a. de le toucher!* don't you dare touch him! **2.** Impudence. *Vous avez l'a. de me dire cela!* you have the face to tell me that!

audacieusement, *adv.* Audaciously. **1.** Boldly. **2.** Impudently.

audacieux, *a.* Audacious. **1.** Bold, daring. **2.** Impudent; brazen (lie).

au-dessous, *adv.* **1.** (*a*) Below (it); underneath. *Les locataires a.-d.*, the occupiers below. (*b*) *Les enfants âgés de sept ans et a.-d.*, children of seven years old and under. **2.** *Prep. phr.* **Au-dessous de.** (*a*) Below, under. *Il est a.-d. de lui de se plaindre,* it is beneath him to complain. (*b*) *Épouser qn a.-d. de soi,* to marry beneath one. (*c*) *A.-d. de cinq ans,* under five (years of age).

au-dessus, *adv.* **1.** (*a*) Above (it). (*b*) *Mille francs et a.-d.*, a thousand francs and upwards. **2.** *Prep.phr.* **Au-dessus de.** (*a*) Above. *Il est a.-d. de cela,* he is above doing such a thing. (*b*) *A.-d. de cinq ans,* over five (years of age). (*c*) **Au-dessus de tout éloge,** beyond all praise.

au-devant, *adv.* **1.** Aller au-devant, to go to meet (sth.). **2.** *Prep.phr.* **Au-devant de.** *Aller a.-d. de qn,* to go to meet s.o. *Aller a.-d. des désirs de qn,* to anticipate s.o.'s wishes.

audibilité, *s.f.* Audibility.

audible, *a.* Audible.

audience, *s.f.* (*a*) Hearing. **Vous avez audience,** I am ready to hear you. (*b*) *Jur:* Hearing (by the court); sitting, court. **Lever l'audience,** to close the session.

audit. See **LEDIT.**

auditeur, -trice, *s.* Hearer, listener.

audition, *s.f.* **1.** Hearing (of sounds); audition. **2.** (*a*) Trial hearing (of singer). (*b*) *Jur:* Audition des témoins, hearing of the witnesses.

auditoire, *s.m.* **1.** Auditorium. **2.** Audience.

auge, *s.f.* Feeding-trough.

augmentation, *s.f.* Increase, augmentation. *A. de prix,* advance in prices.

augmenter. I. *v.tr.* To increase, augment. *Édition augmentée,* enlarged edition. *F:* Augmenter qn, to raise s.o.'s salary or rent. **2.** *v.i.* To increase. *La rivière a augmenté,* the river has risen.

augure[1], *s.m. Rom.Ant:* Augur.

augure[2], *s.m.* Augury, omen. **Oiseau de mauvais augure,** bird of ill omen.

augurer, *v.tr.* To augur, forecast.

Auguste[1]. *Pr.n.m.* Augustus.

auguste[2], *a.* August, majestic.

aujourd'hui, *adv.* To-day. *Cela ne se pratique plus a.,* this is not done nowadays.

aumône, *s.f.* Alms. *Réduit à l'a.,* reduced to beggary.

aumônier, *s.m.* **I.** Almoner. **2.** Chaplain.

aumônière, *s.f.* Chain purse; mesh-bag.

aunaie, *s.f.* Plantation of alders.

aune[1], *s.m. Bot:* Alder.

aune[2], *s.f. A:* Ell. *F:* **Mesurer les autres à son aune,** to judge others by oneself.

auparavant, *adv.* Before(hand), previously. *Un moment a.,* a moment before.

auprès, *adv.* **I.** Close to. **2.** *Prep. phr.* **Auprès de.** (a) Close to, by, beside, near. *Il vit a. de ses parents,* he lives with his parents. (b) *Être bien a. de qn,* to be in favour with s.o. (c) Compared with. *Nous ne sommes rien a. de lui,* we are nothing beside him.

auquel. See LEQUEL.

aur-a, -ai, -ons. See AVOIR.

auréole, *s.f.* (a) Aureole, halo **(of saint).** (b) Halo (of moon).

auréolé, *a.* Haloed.

auriculaire. I. *a.* Auricular. *Témoin a.,* ear-witness. **2.** *s.m.* The little finger.

Aurigny. *Pr.n.m. Geog:* Alderney.

auriste, *s.m. Med:* Ear specialist.

aurore. I. *s.f.* (a) Dawn, day-break; break of day. (b) **Aurore boréale,** aurora borealis; northern lights. **2.** *Pr.n.f. Myth:* Aurora.

auscultation, *s.f. Med:* Auscultation.

ausculter, *v.tr. Med:* To sound (patient).

auspice, *s.m.* Usu. *pl.* (a) *Rom. Ant:* Auspice. (b) Omen, presage. **Faire qch. sous les auspices de qn,** to do sth. under s.o.'s patronage.

aussi. I. *adv.* (a) As. *Il est a. grand que son frère,* he is as tall as his brother. (b) So. *Après avoir attendu a. longtemps,* after waiting so long. (c) (i) Also, too. (ii) So. *J'ai froid.— Moi a.,* I am cold.—So am I. (d) *Conj.-phr.* **Aussi bien que,** as well as. **2.** *conj.* (a) Therefore, consequently, so. (b) **Aussi bien,** moreover, for that matter, besides.

aussière, *s.f. Nau:* Hawser.

aussitôt. I. *adv.* (a) Immediately, directly, at once, forthwith. **Aussitôt dit, aussitôt fait,** no sooner said than done. (b) *Conj.phr.* **Aussitôt que** + *ind.,* as soon as. **2.** *prep.*

Aussitôt son départ, *je reviens,* as soon as he is gone I shall come back.

austère, *a.* Austere (life); severe (style).

austèrement, *adv.* Austerely.

austérité, *s.f.* Austerity.

austral, -als, -aux, *a.* Austral, southern.

Australasie. *Pr.n.f.* Australasia.

Australie. *Pr.n.f.* Australia.

australien, -ienne, *a. & s.* Australian.

autant, *adv.* **I.** (a) As much, so much; as many, so many. **Autant en emporte le vent,** it is all idle talk. **Encore autant, une fois autant,** twice as much; as much again. *Il se leva, j'en fis autant,* he got up and I did the same. (b) (i) **Autant vaut.** *Le travail est fini ou a. vaut,* the work is as good as finished. *A. vaut rester ici,* we may as well stay here. **Autant vaudrait dire,** one might as well say. (ii) *A. dire mille francs,* we might as well say a thousand francs. **2. Autant que.** (a) As much as, as many as. (b) As far as, as near as. **Autant qu'il m'en souvienne,** as far as I can remember. **3. Autant de,** as much, as many, so much, so many. **C'est autant de fait,** it is so much done. **4.** (a) *Conj.phr.* **D'autant que,** more especially as. (b) **D'autant plus,** (all, so much) the more. **Je l'en aime d'autant plus,** I like him (all) the better for it. (c) **D'autant plus . . . que,** (all) the more . . . as.

autel, *s.m.* Altar. **Maître autel,** high altar.

auteur, *s.m.* **I.** Author, perpetrator; promotor. *A. d'un accident,* party at fault in an accident. **2.** Author, writer. **Droit d'auteur,** copyright. **Droits d'auteur,** royalties.

authenticité, *s.f.* Authenticity, genuineness.

authentique, *a.* Authentic, genuine.

auto, *s.f. F:* Motor car. **Faire de l'auto,** to go in for motoring.

autobiographie, *s.f.* Autobiography.

autobiographique, *a.* Autobiographic(al).

autobus [-by:s], *s.m.* Motor (omni)bus.

autocar, *s.m.* Motor coach.

autocrate. I. *s.m.* Autocrat. **2.** *a.* Autocratic.

autocratie, *s.f.* Autocracy.

autocratique, *a.* Autocratic.

autocratiquement, *adv.* Autocratically.

autodafé, *s.m. Hist:* Auto-da-fé.

autodrome, *s.m.* Motor-racing track.

autographe. I. *a.* Autograph(ic) (letter). **2.** *s.m.* Autograph.

autographier, *v.tr.* To autograph.

autogyre, *s.m. Av:* Autogyro.

automate, *s.m.* Automaton.

automatique, *a.* Automatic; self-acting.

automnal, -aux, *a.* Autumnal.

automne [otɔn], *s.m. or f.* Autumn.

automobile. I. *a.* Self-propelling. **Voiture automobile,** motor vehicle. [*Canot a.* motor boat. **2.** *s.f.,* occ. *m.* (Motor) car.

automobilisme, *s.m.* Motoring.

automobiliste, *s.m. & f.* Motorist.

automoteur, -trice, *a.* Self-propelling.

autonome, *a.* Autonomous, self-governing.
autonomie, *s.f.* Autonomy, self-government.
autopsie, *s.f.* Autopsy; post-mortem (examination).
autorisation, *s.f.* **1.** Authorization, authority; permit. **2.** Licence.
autoriser, *v.tr.* To authorize. **1.** To invest with authority. *A. qn à faire qch.,* to authorize s.o. to do sth. **2.** To sanction.
 autorisé, *a.* Authorized, authoritative.
autoritaire, *a.* Authoritative, dictatorial.
autorité, *s.f.* **1.** (*a*) Authority. Il veut tout emporter d'autorité, he wants his own way in everything. (*b*) Faire autorité *en matière de* faïence, to be an authority on china. *Sa parole a de l'a.,* his word carries weight. **2.** Les autorités, the authorities (of a town).
autour¹, *adv* **1.** Round; about. **2.** *Prep.phr.* Autour de, round, about. *Assis a. de la table,* seated round the table. **Tourner autour du** pot, to beat about the bush.
autour², *s.m. Orn:* Goshawk.
autre, *a. & pron.* **1.** (*a*) Other, further. D'autres vous diront, others will tell you. *Sans a. perte de temps,* without further loss of time. **Parler de choses et d'autres,** to talk about one thing and another. **C'est une raison comme une autre,** it's a good enough reason. (*b*) Nous autres Anglais, we English. (*c*) Cela *peut arriver* d'un jour à l'autre, it may happen any day. *Je le vois* de temps à autre, I see him now and then. (*d*) L'un et l'autre, both. Les uns et les autres, (i) all and sundry, (ii) both parties. (*e*) L'un ou l'autre, either. Ni l'un ni l'autre, neither. (*f*) *L'un dit ceci, l'a. dit cela,* one says this and the other says that. Les uns . . ., les autres . . ., some . . ., some. . . . (*g*) L'un l'autre, each other, one another. Elles se moquent les unes des autres, they make game of each other. (*h*) L'un dans l'autre, *on se fait trente francs,* one thing with another, on an average, we earn thirty francs. **2.** (*a*) Other, different. Une tout(e) autre femme, quite a different woman. *J'ai des idées autres,* my ideas are different. **J'en ai vu bien d'autres,** that's nothing; I've been through worse than that. Il n'en fait jamais d'autres! that's just like him! (*b*) (Someone, something) else. *Adressez-vous à* quelqu'un d'autre, ask someone else. Nul autre, personne (d')autre, *ne l'a vu,* no one else, nobody else, saw him. (*Dites cela*) à d'autres! nonsense! tell that to the marines! (*c*) *indef.pron.m.* Autre chose, something else. C'est tout autre chose! that's quite a different matter!
autrefois, *adv.* Formerly; in the past. *Livre a. si populaire,* book once so popular. *Les hommes d'a,* the men of old.
autrement, *adv.* Otherwise. **1.** (*a*) Differently. (*b*) C'est bien autrement sérieux, that is far more serious. **2.** *Venez demain,* autrement il sera trop tard, come to-morrow, or else it will be too late.

Autriche. *Pr.n.f. Geog:* Austria.
autrichien, -ienne, *a. & s.* Austrian.
autruche, *s.f. Orn:* Ostrich.
autrui, *pron.indef.* Others; other people.
auvent, *s.m.* (*a*) Penthouse, open shed. (*b*) Porch roof.
auvergnat, *a. & s.* (Native) of Auvergne, Auvergnat.
aux = *à les.* See **à** and LE.
auxiliaire. 1. *a.* Auxiliary (verb). **Bureau auxiliaire,** sub-office. **2.** *s.* Auxiliary. (*a*) Aid, assistant. (*b*) *s.m.pl.* Auxiliaries.
auxquels, -elles. See LEQUEL.
aval, *s.m.* Lower part (of stream). **En aval,** down-stream. *En a. du pont,* below the bridge.
avalanche, *s.f.* Avalanche.
avaler, *v.tr.* **1.** To swallow (down); to drink up; to devour. **C'est dur à avaler,** that's a bitter pill; I can hardly stomach that. **2.** To lower, let down.
avance, *s.f.* **1.** Advance, lead. Avoir de l'avance sur qn, to be ahead of s.o. *Arriver avec cinq minutes d'a.,* to arrive five minutes before time. *F:* **La belle avance!** much good that will do you! **2.** Projection. **Balcon qui forme avance,** balcony that juts out. **3.** (*a*) Avance de fonds, advance, loan. (*b*) *pl.* **Faire des avances à qn,** to make advances to s.o.; to make up to s.o. **4.** *Adv. phr.* (*a*) **Payer qn d'avance,** to pay s.o. in advance. (*b*) **Se réjouir par avance,** to rejoice beforehand. (*c*) **Payable à l'avance,** payable in advance. (*d*) L'horloge est en avance, the clock is fast. *Nous sommes en a.,* we are before our time.
avancement, *s.m.* **1.** (*a*) Advancing, putting forward. (*b*) Putting forward (of dinner-hour); hastening (of event). (*c*) Furtherance (of plan). (*d*) Promotion, preferment. **2.** Advance(ment), progress. **3.** Projection, jutting out. **4.** Pitch (of screw).
avancer, *v.* (n. avançons) I. *v.tr.* **1.** (*a*) To advance, put forward (one's hand). (*b*) *A. une proposition,* to put forward a proposal. **2.** To make (sth.) earlier; to hasten (sth.) on. **3.** *A. de l'argent à qn,* to advance money to s.o. **4.** To promote. À quoi cela vous avancera-t-il? what good will that do you?
 II. **avancer,** *v.i.* **1.** To advance. (*a*) To move forward. *Montre qui avance d'une minute par jour,* watch that gains a minute a day. (*b*) To progress; to make headway. **2.** (*a*) To be ahead of time. *L'horloge avance,* the clock is fast. (*b*) To jut out, project.
 s'avancer. 1. To move forward, to advance. **2.** To progress. **3.** To jut out.
 avancé, *a.* (*a*) *Position avancée,* advanced position. (*b*) *Opinions avancées,* advanced ideas. (*c*) *Élève a.,* forward pupil. (*d*) *A une heure avancée de la nuit,* at a late hour of the night. (*e*) Avancé en âge, well on in years. (*f*) *F:* Vous voilà bien avancé! a lot of good that has done you!

avanie, *s.f. F :* Insult, affront.

avant. I. **1.** *prep.* Before. (Surtout et) **avant tout,** first of all ; above all. **2.** (*a*) *Prep.phr.* **Avant de** + *inf. Je vous reverrai a. de partir,* I shall see you before leaving. (*b*) *Conj.phr.* **Avant que** + *sub. Je vous reverrai a. que vous (ne) partiez,* I shall see you again before you leave. (*c*) **Pas avant de, que,** not before, not until. **3.** *adv.* **Il était arrivé quelques mois avant,** he had arrived some months before. **4.** *adv.* (*a*) Far, deep. **Pénétrer très avant dans les terres,** to penetrate far inland. (*b*) Far, late. **Bien avant dans la nuit,** far into the night. **5.** *Adv. phr.* **En avant,** in front ; before ; forward. *Nau :* **En avant à toute vitesse,** full steam ahead. *Prep.phr.* **En avant de,** in front of, ahead of. **6.** (In adj. relation to sb.) (*a*) Fore, forward, front. **Essieu avant,** fore-axle. (*b*) **La nuit d'avant,** the night before.

II. **avant,** *s.m.* **1.** (*a*) *Nau :* Bow. *Le logement de l'équipage est à l'avant,* the crew's quarters are forward. **Aller de l'avant,** to go ahead. (*b*) Front. **2.** *Fb :* Forward.

avantage, *s.m.* **1.** Advantage. **Tirer avantage de qch.,** to turn sth. to account. **Il y a avantage à** + *inf.,* it is best to + *inf.* **Avoir l'avantage,** to have the best of it. **2.** *Ten :* (Ad)vantage.

avantager, *v.tr.* (n. avantageons) (*a*) To favour ; to give an advantage. (*b*) *L'uniforme l'avantage,* he looks well in uniform.

avantageusement, *adv.* Advantageously, favourably.

avantageux, *a.* Advantageous, favourable.

NOTE. In all the following compounds AVANT is inv., the noun or adj. takes the plural.

avant-bassin, *s.m.* Outer basin or dock.
avant-bras, *s.m.* Forearm.
avant-corps, *s.m.* Fore-part, projecting part.
avant-cour, *s.f.* Fore-court.
avant-coureur. **1.** *s.m.* Forerunner, harbinger. **2.** *a.m.* Premonitory (symptom).
avant-dernier, *a. & s.* Last but one.
avant-garde, *s.f.* Advanced guard.
avant-goût, *s.m.* Foretaste.
avant-guerre, *s.m.* Pre-war period.
avant-hier, *adv.* The day before yesterday.
avant-plan, *s.m.* Foreground.
avant-port, *s.m.* Outer harbour.
avant-poste, *s.m. Mil :* Outpost.
avant-propos, *s.m.* Preface, foreword.
avant-scène, *s.f. Th :* Apron, fore-stage. Loge d'avant-scène, stage-box.
avant-train, *s.m.* (*a*) Front of carriage. (*b*) *Artil :* Limber.
avant-veille, *s.f.* Two days before.
avare. **1.** *a.* (*a*) Miserly. (*b*) *Être a. de paroles,* to be sparing of words. **2.** *s.* Miser.
avarice, *s.f.* Avarice.
avaricieusement, *adv.* Avariciously.
avaricieux, *a.* Avaricious, stingy.

avarie, *s.f.* Damage, injury.
avarier, *v.tr.* To damage, injure, spoil.
s'avarier, to deteriorate, go bad.
avatar, *s.m.* Transformation. Esp. in *pl.* Avatars, (varied) experiences.
avec. **1.** *prep.* (*a*) With. *Et avec cela, madame?* anything else, madam? (*b*) *Cabane construite avec quelques planches,* hut built out of a few boards. (*c*) *Cela viendra avec le temps,* that will come in time. (*d*) *Combattre avec courage,* to fight with courage. (*e*) *Avec cela, avec ça. Je suis grande et avec ça mince,* I am tall, and slender to boot. (*f*) **D'avec,** from. *Séparer le bon d'avec le mauvais,* to separate the good from the bad. **2.** *adv.* With it, with them.
avenant, *a.* **1.** Comely, pleasing, prepossessing. **2.** **A l'avenant,** in keeping, correspondingly. *Et un chapeau à l'a,* and a hat to match.
avènement, *s.m.* (*a*) Advent (of Christ). (*b*) Accession (to the throne).
avenir, *s.m.* Future. *Jeune homme d'un grand a.,* youth of great promise. **Dans l'avenir,** at some future date. **A l'avenir,** in (the) future, henceforth.
Avent, *s.m. Ecc :* Advent.
aventure, *s.f.* **1.** Adventure. **2.** Chance, luck, venture. **Tenter l'aventure,** to try one's luck. **A l'aventure,** at random ; at a venture. **Par aventure, d'aventure,** by chance, perchance. **3.** **Dire la bonne aventure (à qn),** to tell fortunes ; to tell (s.o.'s) fortune.
aventurer, *v.tr.* To venture, risk (one's life).
s'aventurer, to venture ; to take risks.
aventureusement, *adv.* Adventurously, venturesomely.
aventureux, *a.* Adventurous, venturesome ; rash ; reckless.
aventurier, *s.* Adventurer. **C'est une aventurière,** she is an adventuress.
avenu, *a.* **Non avenu,** not having occurred ; cancelled.
avenue, *s.f.* Avenue ; carriage drive.
avéré, *a.* Authenticated, established (fact). *Ennemi a.,* avowed enemy.
averse, *s.f.* Sudden shower ; downpour.
aversion, *s.f.* Aversion (*envers, pour,* to, for, from) ; dislike (*pour,* to, for, of). **Prendre qn en aversion,** to take a dislike to s.o.
avertir, *v.tr.* A. qn de qch., to warn, notify, s.o. of sth. *Se tenir pour averti,* to be on one's guard. *Prov :* **Un homme averti en vaut deux,** forewarned is forearmed.
averti, *a.* Experienced, wide-awake (observer) ; well-informed.
avertissement, *s.m.* Warning ; notice. **Avertissement au lecteur** foreword (to book).
avertisseur, *s.m.* **1.** Warner. *Th :* Call-boy. **2.** Warning signal ; alarm.
aveu, -eux, *s.m.* **1.** Consent, authorization. **2.** Avowal, confession.
aveuglant, *a.* Blinding ; dazzling.

aveugle, *a.* Blind, sightless. **1.** (*a*) *Devenir a.,* to go blind. (*b*) *s.* **Un aveugle,** a blind man. **2.** *Arch:* **Fenêtre aveugle,** blind window. **3.** Blind, unreasoning (hatred); implicit (confidence).

aveuglement, *s.m.* **1.** Blinding. **2.** (Mental) blindness; infatuation.

aveuglément, *adv.* Blindly.

aveugler, *v.tr.* **1.** (*a*) To put (s.o.'s) eyes out. (*b*) To dazzle, blind. **2.** *Nau:* A. *une voie d'eau,* to stop a leak.

aveuglette (à l'), *adv.phr.* Blindly.

aveulir, *v.tr.* To enervate.

s'aveulir, to sink into sloth (of mind).

aveulissement, *s.m.* Enervation.

aviateur, -trice, *s.* Aviator; airman, -woman.

aviation, *s.f.* Aviation.

avide, *a.* Greedy. *A. de qch.,* (i) greedy of sth.; (ii) eager for sth.

avidement, *adv.* Greedily; eagerly.

avidité, *s.f.* Avidity, greed(iness).

avilir, *v.tr.* **1.** To render vile; to degrade. **2.** *Com:* To depreciate (prices).

avilissant, *a.* Debasing, degrading.

avilissement, *s.m.* **1.** Debasement. **2.** Depreciation.

avion, *s.m.* Aeroplane; *F:* plane. *A. de combat,* fighter. "Par avion," 'by air-mail.'

aviron, *s.m.* **1.** Oar. *A. de couple,* scull. Armer les avirons, to ship the oars. **Engager son aviron,** to catch a crab. **2.** L'aviron, rowing.

avis, *s.m.* **1.** (*a*) Opinion, judgment. **A, selon, mon avis,** in my opinion. De l'avis de tous, in the opinion of all. **J'ai changé d'avis,** I have changed my mind. **Je suis d'avis qu'il vienne,** in my opinion he ought to come. (*b*) Advice, counsel. *Demander l'a. de qn,* to ask s.o.'s advice. **2.** Notice, warning, announcement. **Avis au lecteur,** foreword (to book). **Jusqu'à nouvel avis,** until further notice.

aviser. **1.** *v.tr.* (*a*) To perceive. (*b*) *A. qn de qch.,* to inform s.o. of sth. **2.** *v.i. A. à qch.,* to deal with (situation).

s'aviser *de qch.,* to bethink oneself of sth. *Ne vous en avisez pas!* you'd better not!

avisé, *a.* Prudent, circumspect; far-seeing. **Bien avisé,** well-advised.

aviso, *s.m. Navy:* Despatch-vessel; sloop.

aviver, *v.tr.* **1.** To quicken; to revive, brighten (colours); to irritate (wound). **2.** To put a keen edge on (tool).

avocat, *s.* **1.** Barrister; counsel. **Être reçu avocat,** to be called to the bar. **2.** Advocate.

avoine, *s.f.* Oat(s). **Farine d'avoine** oatmeal.

avoir. **I.** *v.tr.* (*pr.p.* ayant; *p.p.* eu; *pr.ind.* j'ai, tu as, il a, n. avons, ils ont; *pr.sub.* j'aie, il ait; *p.d.* j'avais; *fu.* j'aurai). **1,** (*a*) To have, possess. (*b*) *Elle avait une robe bleue,* she had on a blue dress. (*c*) *Pred. A. les yeux bleus,* to have blue eyes. (*d*) **Avoir dix ans,** to be ten years old. **2.** To get, obtain. *Il a eu le prix,* he got the prize. **3.** *F:* To get the better of. **On vous a eu!** you've been had! **4.** *Il eut un mouvement brusque,* he made a sudden gesture. **5.** To ail. **Qu'avez-vous? qu'est-ce que vous avez?** what is the matter with you? **6.** (*a*) *Nous en avons pour deux heures,* it will take us two hours. (*b*) **En avoir à, contre, qn.,** to have a grudge against s.o. *Quoi qu'il en ait,* whatever he may say. **7.** **Avoir qch. à faire,** to have sth. to do. *Vous n'avez pas à vous inquiéter,* you have no need to feel anxious. **8.** *impers.* **Y avoir.** (*a*) *Combien y a-t-il de blessés?* how many wounded are there? *Il y en a qui disent,* there are some who say. **Il n'y a pas de quoi,** pray don't mention it. (*b*) **Qu'est-ce qu'il y a?** what is the matter? (*c*) Il y a deux ans, two years ago. *Il y avait six mois que j'attendais,* I had been waiting for the last six months. (*d*) *Combien y a-t-il d'ici à Londres?* how far is it (from here) to London? **9.** *J'ai fini,* I have done. *Quand il eut fini de parler, il vint à moi,* when he had finished speaking he came to me.

II. avoir, *s.m.* Property. *Tout mon a.,* all I possess. *Com:* **Doit et avoir,** debit and credit.

avoisinant, *a.* Neighbouring; near by.

avoisiner, *v.tr. A. qch.,* to be near sth., close, adjacent, to sth.

s'avoisiner. **1.** To be adjacent. **2.** (Of event) To approach, draw near.

avortement, *s.m.* Failure, falling through.

avorter, *v.i.* To miscarry. *Faire a. un dessein,* to frustrate a plan.

avorton, *s.m.* Puny, stunted, man.

avoué, *s.m. Jur:* = Solicitor.

avouer, *v.tr.* **1.** To acknowledge. *S'a. coupable,* to admit one's guilt. **2.** To confess, to own (a misdeed).

avril [-ril], *s.m.* April. **Le premier avril,** (i) the first of April; (ii) April-fool-day; All Fools' day. **Donner un poisson d'avril à qn,** to make an April-fool of s.o.

axe, *s.m.* **1.** Axis (of ellipse). **2.** Axle, spindle. **3.** *Pr. n. m. Pol:* Axis.

axiomatique, *a.* Axiomatic(al).

axiome, *s.m.* Axiom.

ayant. **1.** See AVOIR. **2.** *s.m. Jur:* **Ayant droit,** rightful claimant or owner; interested party; beneficiary. *pl. Des ayants droit.*

ay-ez, -ons. See AVOIR.

azalée, *s.f. Bot:* Azalea.

Azincourt. *Pr.n.m.* Agincourt.

azotate, *s.m. Ch:* Nitrate.

azote, *s.m. Ch:* Nitrogen.

azoté, *a.* Nitrogenous.

azoteux, *a. Ch:* Nitrous.

azotique, *a. Ch:* Nitric.

aztèque, *a. & s. Ethn:* Aztec.

azur, *s.m.* Azure, blue. *Geog:* **La Côte d'Azur,** the Riviera.

azyme, *a.* Unleavened (bread).

B, b [be], *s.m.* (The letter) B, b.

baba, *s.m.* *Cu:* Sponge-cake (usu. with currants) steeped in rum syrup; baba.

babil [-bi(l)], *s.m.*, **babillage** [-bij-], *s.m.* **1.** Prattling; twittering (of birds); babbling (of a brook). **2.** Prattle (of children).

babillard [-bij-]. **1.** *a.* Talkative. **2.** *s.* Tattler, chatterbox.

babillement [-bij-], *s.m.* = BABILLAGE.

babiller [-bije], *v.i.* To prattle; to babble.

babines, *s.f.pl.* *Z:* Pendulous lips (of monkey, dog, cat); chops (of ruminants).

babiole, *s.f.* Curio, knick-knack, bauble.

bâbord, *s.m.* *Nau:* Port (side).

babouche, *s.f.* Turkish slipper; babouche.

babouin, *s.m.* Baboon.

babylonien, -ienne, *a. & s.* Babylonian.

bac [bak], *s.m.* **1.** (*a*) Ferry-boat. (*b*) Ferry. *Passer le bac,* to cross the ferry. **2.** Tank, vat.

baccalauréat, *s.m.* *B. ès lettres, ès sciences,* school leaving-certificate.

bacchanale [-kan-], *s.f.* **1.** *Rom.Ant:* Les **Bacchanales,** the Bacchanalia. **2.** (*a*) Drinking song. (*b*) Orgy, drunken revel.

bacchante [-kan-], *s.f.* *Ant:* Bacchante.

bâche, *s.f.* **1.** Tank, cistern. **2.** Tarpaulin; tilt (of cart).

bachelier, *s.m.* (*a*) **Bachelier en droit,** bachelor of law. (*b*) **Bachelier ès lettres, ès sciences,** bachelor of letters, of science.

bachique, *a.* Bacchic.

bachot¹, *s.m.* Wherry, punt.

bachot², *s.m.* *P:* = BACCALAURÉAT.

bacille, *s.m.* *Biol:* Bacillus.

bâcler, *v.tr.* **1.** To bar, bolt (door). **2.** *Nau:* To close (harbour). **3.** *F:* To scamp (work).

bactérie, *s.f.* Bacterium.

bactérien, -ienne, *a.* Bacterial.

bactériologie, *s.f.* Bacteriology.

badaud, *s.* Saunterer, stroller.

Bade. *Pr.n.f.* *Geog:* Baden.

badigeonner, *v.tr.* To distemper (a wall).

badinage, *s.m.* (*a*) Trifling, jesting. (*b*) Banter.

badine, *s.f.* Cane, switch.

badiner. **1.** *v.i.* To jest, trifle. **2.** *v.tr.* To tease, banter.

badois, *a. & s.* *Geog:* (Native) of Baden.

bafouer, *v.tr.* To scoff, jeer, at.

bafouiller [-fuje], *v.tr. & i.* *F:* To splutter, stammer.

bâfrer. *F:* **1.** *v.i.* To gormandize, guzzle. **2.** *v.tr.* To stuff, guzzle.

bagage, *s.m.* **1.** Baggage. **Plier bagage,** to decamp. **Avec armes et bagage,** with all one's belongings. **2.** *pl.* Luggage.

bagarre, *s.f.* Affray, brawl; free fight.

bagatelle, *s.f.* Trifle.

bagne, *s.m.* *A:* Convict prison; hulks.

bague, *s.f.* (*a*) (Jewelled) ring. (*b*) B *d'un cigare,* band round a cigar.

baguenauder, *v.i. & pr.* *F:* To fool around.

baguette [-gɛt], *s.f.* Rod, wand, stick. **Passer par les baguettes,** to run the gauntlet.

bah, *int.* **1.** Nonsense! **2.** You don't say so!

bahut, *s.m.* Cupboard, cabinet.

bai, *a.* Bay (horse).

baie¹, *s.f.* *Geog:* Bay, bight.

baie², *s.f.* *Arch:* Bay, opening.

baie³, *s.f.* *Bot:* Berry.

baignade, *s.f.* **1.** Bathe. **2.** Bathing-place.

baigner. **1.** *v.tr.* (*a*) To bathe, steep; to dip. (*b*) (Of sea) To wash (coast); (of river) to water (a district). (*c*) To bath (baby). **2.** *v.i.* To soak, steep (in sth.). **se baigner. 1.** To take a bath. **2.** To bathe; to have a bathe.

baigneur, -euse, *s.* **1.** Bather. **2.** Bath attendant. **3.** *s.f.* **Baigneuse,** bathing-costume.

baignoire, *s.f.* **1.** Bath; (bath-)tub. **2.** *Th:* Ground-floor box (behind the pit).

bail [ba:j], *pl.* **baux,** *s.m.* Lease (to tenant). **Prendre une maison à bail,** to lease a house.

bâillant [bajɑ̃], *a.* Gaping; yawning.

bâillement [-ɑj-], *s.m.* **1.** Yawn. **2.** Gaping.

bailler [baje], *v.tr.* *F:* **Vous me la baillez belle!** tell that to the marines!

bâiller [baje], *v.i.* **1.** To yawn. **2.** To gape.

bailli [baji], *s.m.* *A:* Bailiff, magistrate.

bâillon [bajɔ̃], *s.m.* Gag.

bâillonner [-jɔ-], *v.tr.* To gag.

bain, *s.m.* Bath. (*a*) **Salle de bains,** bathroom. (*b*) **Bains publics,** public baths. (*c*) *pl.* Watering-place; spa. (*d*) Bathing. **Bains de mer,** (i) sea-bathing; (ii) seaside resort.

bain-marie, *s.m.* **1.** *Ch:* Water-bath. **2.** Jacketed saucepan. *pl.* **Des bains-marie.**

baïonnette [bajɔ-], *s.f.* Bayonet. *B. au canon!* fix bayonets!

baiser. **I.** *v.tr.* *Lit:* = EMBRASSER. *B. qn sur, à, la joue,* to kiss s.o. on the cheek. **II. baiser,** *s.m.* Kiss.

baissant, *a.* Declining; setting (sun).

baisse, *s.f.* **1.** Subsidence (of water); ebb (of tide). **2.** Fall, drop (in prices).

baisser. **I.** *v.* **1.** *v.tr.* To lower (price); to let down (carriage window). *B. les lumières,* to lower the lights. *Donner tête baissée dans un piège,* to fall headlong into a trap. **Baisser les yeux,** to cast down one's eyes; to look down. **2.** *v.i.* (*a*) To be on the decline; to ebb; (of flood) to abate. *Le soleil baisse,* the sun is sinking. *Sa vue baisse,* his sight is failing. (*b*) (Of prices) To fall. **se baisser,** to stoop; to bend down. **II. baisser,** *s.m.* *Th:* **Baisser du rideau,** fall of the curtain.

bajoues, *s.f.pl.* Cheeks, chaps (of pig).

bal, *pl.* **bals,** *s.m.* **1.** Ball. **2.** Bal public, dance hall.

balader. *F:* **1.** *v.i. & pr.* To stroll, saunter. **2.** *v.tr.* To take for a walk.

baladeur, -euse, s. I. F: Wanderer, saunterer. 2. s.f. Baladeuse. (a) Trailer (of motor car). (b) Costermonger's barrow.

balafre, s.f. I. Slash, gash (esp. in face); sabre-cut. 2. Scar.

balafrer, v.tr. I. To gash, slash (esp the face). 2. Visage balafré, scarred face.

balai, s.m. Broom Manche à balai, (i) broomstick, (ii) Av: P: joy-stick.

balance, s.f. I. (a Balance; (pair of) scales. Faire penchei la ba.ance, to turn the scale. (b) Scale(-pan). 2. B. d'un compte, balancing of an account. Faire la balance, to strike the balance.

balancement, s.m. I. Balancing. 2. Swinging, rocking (of boat).

balancer, v. (n. balançons) I. v.tr. I. To balance. (a) B. un compte, to balance an account. (b) To poise. 2. To swing, rock. II. **balancer,** v.i. To swing. se **balancer,** to swing; to sway, rock.

balancé, a. I. Well-balanced; well-poised. 2. Swinging (blow).

balançoire, s.f. (a) See-saw. (b) (Child's) swing.

balayage, s.m. Sweeping (of room).

balayer, v.tr. (je balaie, je balaye) To sweep; to sweep out (room); to sweep up (dirt). Balayer la mer, to scour the sea.

balayeur, -euse, s. I. Sweeper. 2. s.f. Balayeuse. Carpet sweeper.

balayures, s.f.pl. Sweepings.

balbutiement, s.m. Stammering, stuttering.

balbutier, I. v.i. To stammer, mumble. 2. v.tr To stammer out (sth.).

balcon, s.m. I. Balcony. 2. Th: Dress-circle.

baldaquin, s.m. Canopy; tester (of bed).

Bâle. Pr.n.f. Geog: Basel, Basle.

baléare, a. Geog: Les îles Baléares, the Balearic Isles.

baleine, s.f. I. Whale. Blanc de baleine, spermaceti. 2. Whalebone. Baleines d'un parapluie, ribs of an umbrella.

baleinier, I. a. Whaling (industry). 2. s.m. Whaler. 3. s.f. Baleinière, whale-boat.

balise, s.f. Nau: Beacon; sea-mark.

baliser, v.tr. Nau: To buoy, mark out.

balistique, s.f. Ballistics; gunnery.

baliveau, s.m. I. Sapling. 2. Scaffold-pole.

baliverne, s.f. F: (a) Idle story. (b) pl. Twaddle, nonsense.

balkanique, a. Balkan (state).

ballade, s.f. Lit: I. Ballade. 2. Ballad (poem, not song).

ballant, a. Swinging, dangling (arms).

ballast [-ast], s.m. I. Ballast, bottom (of road). 2. Ballast-tank (of submarine).

balle, s.f. I. Ball. B. de tennis, tennis-ball. Renvoyer la balle à qn, F: to give s.o. tit for tat. Games: Balle au camp, rounders. Balle au mur, fives. 2. Bullet; shot. B. perdue, stray bullet. Tirer à balle, to fire ball-cartridge. 3. Com: Bale (of cotton).

ballet, s.m. Th: Ballet.

ballon, s.m. I. Balloon. Envoyer un ballon d'essai, F: to put out a feeler. 2. Football.

ballonner, v.i. & pr. To swell (out); (of skirt) to balloon out.

ballot, s.m. Bundle, bale; (pedlar's) pack.

ballottement, s.m. Tossing (of ship).

ballotter, I. v.tr. To toss (about), shake (about). 2. v.i. (a) (Of door). To rattle (b) To toss (on the water).

balnéaire, a Station balnéa re. watering-place.

balourd. I. a. Awkward, lumpish. 2. s. Awkward person; yokel.

balourdise, s.f. I. Awkwardness. 2. Stupid blunder; bloomer.

balsamique [balz-], a. Balmy; aromatic.

Balthazar. Pr.n.m. Belshazzar.

Baltique. Geog: I. a. Baltic. 2. Pr.n.f. La Baltique, the Baltic (Sea).

balustrade, s.f. I. Balustrade 2. (Hand-)rail; railing.

balustre, s.m. (a) Baluster. (b) pl. Banisters.

bambin, s. F: Little child; tiny tot.

bamboche, s.f. I. Puppet. 2. F: Spree.

bambou, s.m. Bot: Bamboo(-cane).

ban, s.m. I. (a) (Public) proclamation. (b) Roll of drum. (c) F: Round of (rhythmical) applause. Accorder un ban à qn = to give three cheers for s.o. (d) pl. Banns (of marriage). 2. Hist: (Proclamation of) banishment; ban. F: Être en rupture de ban to be on the loose.

banal, -aux, a. Commonplace, trite.

banalité, s.f. I. Banality, triteness. 2. Commonplace remark.

banane, s.f. Banana.

bananier, s.m. Banana-tree.

banc [bã], s.m. I. Bench, seat, form. B. d'église, pew. B. de nage, thwart (of boat). B. des prévenus, dock. B. du jury, jury-box. 2. B. de sable, sand-bank. B d'huîtres, oyster-bed. 3. Shoal (of fish).

bancal, pl. -als, a. (a) Bandy-legged. (b) Rickety (furniture).

bandage, s.m. I. Bandage. 2. Tyre.

bande[1], s.f. I. (a) Band, strip (of cloth); belt (of land); (trouser) stripe. (b) Bill: Cushion. 2. Nau: (a) Side (of ship). (b) Heel, list(ing).

bande[2], s.f. I. Band, party, troop. 2. Flight, flock; pack; school (of porpoises).

bandeau, s.m. I. Bandeau, head-band. 2. Bandage (over the eyes).

bandelette, s.f. (a) Narrow band; strip; bandage. (b) pl. Wrappings (of mummy).

bander[1], v.tr. I. To bandage, bind (up) (wound). B. les yeux à qn, to blindfold s.o. 2. B. une roue, to put a tyre on a wheel. 3. B. un arc, (i) to bend, (ii) to string, a bow.

bander[2] (se), v.pr. To combine, to band together, form a league (contre, against).

banderole, s.f. Banderole, streamer.

bandit, s.m. (a) Bandit, brigand. (b) F: Ruffian.

bandoulière, *s.f.* **1.** Shoulder-strap. **Porter qch. en bandoulière,** to carry sth. across one's back. **2.** Bandoleer.

banlieue, *s.f.* Suburbs; outskirts.

bannière, *s.f.* Banner.

bannir, *v.tr.* To banish; to exile; to outlaw.

banni. 1. *a.* Banished, outlawed. **2.** *s.* Exile, outlaw.

bannissement, *s.m.* Banishment.

banque, *s.f.* **1.** (a) Bank. (b) Banking. **2.** *Cards:* Bank. **Faire sauter la banque,** to break the bank.

banqueroute, *s.f.* Bankruptcy.

banquet, *s.m.* Banquet, feast.

banquette, *s.f.* **1.** Bench, seat, form; wall-sofa (in restaurant). *Th:* **Jouer devant les banquettes,** to play to empty benches. **2.** *Golf:* Bunker.

banquier. 1. *a.* Banking (house). **2.** *s.* Banker.

banquise, *s.f.* Ice-floe, ice-pack.

baptême [bat-], *s.m.* Baptism, christening. **Nom de baptême,** Christian name.

baptiser [bat-], *v.tr.* To baptize; to christen. *F:* **Baptiser son vin,** to water down one's wine.

baptismal, -aux [bat-], *a.* Baptismal.

baquet, *s.m.* **1.** Tub, bucket. **2.** *Aut:* Bucket-seat.

bar[1], *s.m.* *Ich:* Sea-perch.

bar[2], *s.m.* (Public) bar.

baragouin [-gwɛ̃], *s.m.* *F:* Gibberish.

baragouiner [-gwi-], *v.tr. & i.* *F:* To talk gibberish, to jabber.

baraque, *s.f.* (a) Hut, shanty. *pl. Mil:* Huts, hutments. (b) Booth (at fair).

baratte, *s.f.* Churn.

baratter, *v.tr.* To churn.

barbacane, *s.f.* *A.Fort:* Barbican.

Barbade (la). *Pr.n.* Barbados.

barbare. 1. *a.* (a) Barbaric; uncouth. (b) Barbarous, inhuman. **2.** *s.m.* Barbarian.

barbarement, *adv.* **1.** Barbarically. **2.** Barbarously.

barbarie[1], *s.f.* **1.** Barbarism. **2.** Barbarousness, barbarity, cruelty.

Barbarie[2]. *Pr.n.f.* *A.Geog:* Barbary.

barbarisme, *s.m.* *Gram:* Barbarism.

barbe[1], *s.f.* Beard. (a) *F:* **Rire dans sa barbe,** to laugh in one's sleeve. **Faire qch. à la barbe de qn,** to do sth. to s.o.'s face. **Faire la barbe à qn,** to shave s.o. (b) Wattle (of bird); awn, beard (of wheat).

barbe[2], *s.m.* Barb; Barbary horse.

barbeau[1], *s.m.* *Ich:* Barbel.

barbeau[2], *s.m.* Bluebottle, cornflower.

Barbe-bleue. *Pr.n.m.* Bluebeard.

barbelé, *a.* Barbed. **Fil de fer b.,** *s.m.* **barbelé,** barbed wire.

Barberousse. *Pr.n.m.* Barbarossa.

barbiche, *s.f.* (a) Short beard. (b) Goatee.

barbier, *s.m.* Barber.

barbillon [-bijɔ̃], *s.m.* (a) Wattle (of cock). (b) Barb (of fish-hook).

barbon, *s.m.* Greybeard.

barboter, *v.i.* To paddle, splash (about).

barbouiller [-buje], *v.tr.* (a) To daub; to smear (*de,* with). (b) To smear (one's face); to blur (printing). **se barbouiller,** to dirty one's face.

barbouilleur, -euse [-buj-], *s.* *F:* **1.** Dauber, inferior artist. **2.** Scribbler.

barbu. 1. *a.* Bearded. **2.** *s.f.* *Ich:* Barbue, Brill.

bardane, *s.f.* *Bot:* Burdock.

barde, *s.m.* Bard, poet.

barème, *s.m.* **1.** Ready-reckoner. **2.** Scale (of salaries). **3.** Printed table (of fares).

baril, *s.m.* Barrel, cask, keg.

bariolage, *s.m.* **1.** Variegation. **2.** Medley (of colours).

barioler, *v.tr.* To variegate; to paint (sth.) in many colours, in gaudy colours. **bariolé,** *a.* Gaudy, motley; splashed with colour.

barnache, *s.f.,* **barnacle,** *s.f.* Barnacle-goose.

baromètre, *s.m.* Barometer.

barométrique, *a.* Barometric(al).

baron, *s.m.* Baron.

baronne, *s.f.* Baroness.

baronnet, *s.m.* Baronet.

baroque, *a.* Quaint, odd, baroque.

barque, *s.f.* Boat.

barquette, *s.f.* Small craft; skiff.

barrage, *s.m.* **1.** (a) Barring, stopping (of road); damming (of valley). (b) Crossing (of cheque). **2.** (a) Barrier, obstruction; dam, weir. (b) *Mil:* Barrage.

barre, *s.f.* **1.** (a) Bar, rod (of metal). (b) Bar, barrier. B. *d'appui,* hand-rail. **Paraître à la barre,** to appear before the Court, at the bar. (c) (Harbour) boom. (d) Bar (of river or harbour). B. *d'eau,* (tidal) bore. **2.** *Nau:* Bar, tiller (of boat); helm (of ship). (Of ship) **Sentir la barre,** to answer to the helm. **Homme de barre,** man at the wheel; helmsman. **3.** Line, dash, stroke, bar. **4.** Stripe. *Étoffe à barres,* striped cloth. **5.** *Games:* **Jeu de barres,** prisoners' base.

barreau, *s.m.* **1.** (a) Small bar; rail. *Barreaux d'une échelle,* rungs of a ladder. (b) Grate-bar, fire-bar. **2.** *Jur:* Bar. **Être reçu au barreau,** to be called to the bar.

barrer, *v.tr.* **1.** To strengthen by means of a bar or bars. **2.** (a) To fasten with a bar; to bar. (b) To bar, obstruct; to dam. "**Rue barrée,**" "no thoroughfare." **3.** To cross (a t). B. *un chèque,* to cross a cheque. **4.** To cross out, strike out (word). **5.** *Nau:* To steer.

barrette, *s.f.* Biretta; (cardinal's) cap.

barreur, *s.m.* *Row:* Coxswain; *F:* cox.

barricade, *s.f.* Barricade.

barricader, *v.tr.* To barricade.

barrière, *s.f.* **1.** Barrier. **2.** Gate (of town); toll-gate, turnpike.

barrique, *s.f.* Large barrel; cask.

barrir, *v.i.* (Of elephant) To trumpet.

barrissement, *s.m.,* **barrit,** *s.m.* Trumpeting (of elephant).

Barthélemy. *Pr.n.m.* Bartholomew.

baryton, *a. & s.m.* Barytone (voice).

baryum [-jɔm], *s.m. Ch:* Barium.

bas, basse. I. *a.* **1.** Low. *Voix basse,* low, deep, voice. *Conversation à voix basse,* whispered conversation. **Enfant en bas âge,** child of tender years. **Avoir la vue basse,** to be short-sighted. **2.** Mean, base, low. **3.** Low(er). **Au bas mot** at the lowest estimate.
II. **bas,** *adv.* **1.** Low (down). *Nau:* Haler bas une voile, to haul down a sail. **2. Mettre bas.** (*a*) To take off (one's) hat. (*b*) To overthrow. (*c*) **Mettre bas les armes,** to lay down one's arms. **3. Parler tout bas,** to speak in a whisper.
III. **bas,** *s.m* **1.** Lower part (of sth.). *F:* Les hauts et les bas de la vie, life's ups and downs. *Adv.phr.* **En bas,** (down) below. *Aller en b.,* to go downstairs. *Tomber la tête en bas,* to fall head foremost. *Prep.phr.* **En bas de,** at the foot of. *En bas de l'escalier,* downstairs. *Adv.phr.* **A bas,** down. **A bas les mains!** hands off! **Tomber à bas de son cheval,** to fall off one's horse. **2. Bas de l'eau,** low water. **3.** Stocking.
IV. **basse,** *s.f. Mus:* Bass.

basalte, *s.m.* Basalt.

basaner, *v.tr. F:* To bronze, tan.

basané, *a.* Sunburnt, tanned, swarthy.

bas-bleu, *s.m.* Blue-stocking. *pl. Des bas-bleus.*

basculant, *a.* Rocking, tilting.

bascule, *s.f.* Rocker; see-saw. **Chaise à bascule** rocking-chair. **Wagon à bascule,** tip-waggon.

basculer, *v.tr. & i.* **1.** (*a*) To rock, swing; to see-saw. (*b*) To tip (up). (*Faire*) *b. une charrette,* to tip a cart. **2.** To topple over.

base, *s.f.* **1.** Base (of triangle). *B. d'aviation,* aviation base. **2.** Lower part, foot, base (of mountain). **3.** Basis, foundation. **Sans base,** ungrounded (suspicions). **4.** Radix, root, basis (of logarithm). **5.** *Ch:* Base (of salt).

baser, *v.tr.* To base, found (opinion). **se baser** *sur qch.,* to found upon (a principle).

bas-fond, *s.m.* **1.** Low ground, hollow; swamp. **2.** Shallow, shoal.

basilic[1] [-ik], *s.m. Bot:* Basil.

basilic[2], *s.m. Myth: Z:* Basilisk.

basilique, *s.f. Arch:* Basilica.

basique, *a.* Basic (salt).

basque[1], *a. & s. Ethn:* Basque.

basque[2], *s.f.* Skirt, tail (of coat).

bas-relief, *s.m.* Bas-relief, low-relief.

bass, *s.m. Ich:* Bass

basse. See BAS.

basse-cour, *s.f.* Farm-yard, poultry-yard. *pl. Des basses-cours.*

basse-fosse, *s.f.* Dungeon. **Cul de basse-fosse,** deepest dungeon. *pl. Des basses-fosses.*

bassement, *adv.* Basely, contemptibly.

bassesse, *s.f.* **1.** Baseness, lowness. **2.** Low, mean, contemptible, action.

basse-taille, *s.f. Mus:* Basso-profondo. *pl. Des basses-tailles.*

bassin, *s.m.* **1.** Basin, bowl, pan. **2.** (*a*) Ornamental lake. (*b*) *Hyd.E:* Reservoir, tank. **3.** Dock, basin. **4.** (*a*) *B. d'un fleuve,* drainage basin of a river. (*b*) *B. houiller,* coal-field. **5.** *Anat:* Pelvis.

bassiner, *v.tr.* **1.** To bathe (wound). **2.** *B. un lit,* to warm a bed (with a warming-pan).

bassinoire, *s.f.* Warming-pan.

basson, *s.m. Mus:* Bassoon.

baste, *int.* Pooh! nonsense!

bastingage, *s.m. Nau:* **1.** *A:* Hammock netting. **2.** *pl.* Bulwarks, topsides.

bastion, *s.m. Fort:* Bastion.

bastonnade, *s.f.* Bastinado.

bat, -s. See BATTRE.

bât, *s.m.* **1.** Pack-saddle. **Cheval de bât,** pack-horse. *F: C'est là que le bât le blesse,* that's where the shoe pinches. **2.** Pack.

bataille [-taːj], *s.f.* Battle. *Le fort de la b.,* the thick of the fight.

batailler [-taje], *v.i.* To fight, battle.

batailleur, -euse [-taj-], *a.* Fighting, pugnacious.

bataillon [-tajɔ̃], *s.m. Mil:* Battalion. **Chef de bataillon,** major.

bâtard, *a. & s.* Bastard. (*a*) Illegitimate. (*b*) Mongrel (*c*) *Race bâtarde,* degenerate race.

bâtardise, *s.f.* Bastardy.

bateau, -eaux, *s.m.* Boat; merchant vessel. **Pont de bateaux,** pontoon-bridge. *Rail:* Le train du bateau, the boat-train. **Aller en bateau,** to go boating; to boat.

bateau-citerne, *s.m.* Tank boat; tanker. *pl. Des bateaux-citernes.*

bateau-feu, *s.m.* Lightship. *pl. Des bateaux-feux.*

bateleur, -euse, *s.* Juggler, tumbler.

batelier, *s.* Boatman; waterman; ferryman.

bâter, *v.tr. F: C'est un âne bâté,* he's a perfect ass.

bâti, *s.m.* Frame(-work), structure, support.

batifoler, *v.i. F:* To frolic, skylark.

bâtiment, *s.m.* **1.** Building trade. **2.** Building, edifice, structure. **3.** Ship, vessel. *Bâtiment de guerre,* warship.

bâtir, *v.tr.* To build, erect, construct. *Homme bien bâti,* well-set-up man. **Terrain à bâtir,** building-site.

bâtisse, *s.f.* **1.** Masonry; bricks and mortar. **2.** *F:* Gimcrack building.

batiste, *s.f. Tex:* Batiste, cambric.

bâton, *s.m.* **1.** Stick, staff, rod. (*a*) *B. ferré,* alpenstock. *Bâton de vieillesse,* support, prop, of old age. *Coup de bâton,* blow with a stick. *F: Mettre des bâtons dans les roues,* to put a spoke in (s.o.'s) wheel; to interfere. (*b*) *F: Conversation à bâtons rompus,* desultory conversation. (*c*) Staff, pole. *B. de* *pavillon,* flagstaff. *(d)* (Wand of office) *B. pastoral,* pastoral staff, crozier. *B. de chef d'orchestre,* conductor's baton. **2.** Stick, roll. *B. de cire à cacheter,* stick of sealing-wax. **3.** Stroke (of the pen).

bâtonner, *v.tr.* To beat, cudgel, cane.

bâtonnet, *s.m.* *(a)* Square ruler. *(b) Games :* Tip-cat.

batraciens, *s.m.pl.* *Z :* Batrachia(ns).

battage, *s.m.* Beating; threshing (of corn).

battant. **I.** *a.* Beating. **Pluie battante,** driving rain; downpour. *Mener les choses tambour b.,* to hustle things on. *F :* **Tout battant neuf,** brand-new.
II. battant, *s.m.* **1.** Clapper, tongue. **2.** *(a)* Leaf, flap (of table). **Porte à deux battants,** folding doors. *(b)* Door (of cupboard).

battement, *s.m.* *(a)* Beat(ing) (of drum); stamp(ing) (of feet); clapping (of hands); flutter(ing) (of wings); flapping (of sails). *(b) Mus :* Beat. *(c)* Beat(ing), throb(bing). *Chaque b. de cœur,* every heart-beat.

batterie, *s.f.* **1.** Fight, scuffle, rough-and-tumble. **2.** Beat (of drum). **3.** *Artil :* Battery. *Pièces en b.,* guns in action. **Montrer, démasquer, ses batteries,** to show one's hand. **4.** *(a)* Set, collection. *B. de cuisine,* (set of) kitchen utensils. *(b)* **Batterie électrique,** electric battery.

batteur, -euse, *s.* **1.** *(a) B. en grange,* thresher. *(b) Ven :* Beater. *(c) F :* **Batteurs de pavé,** loafers, idlers. **2.** *s.f.* **Batteuse,** threshing-machine; thresher.

battoir, *s.m.* **1.** Washerwoman's beetle. **2.** (Wooden) bat (for ping-pong).

battre, *v.* *(pr.ind.* **je bats, il bat)** To beat. **1.** *v.tr.* *(a)* To beat, thrash, flog. *B. du blé,* to thresh corn. *B. de la monnaie,* to coin, mint, money. *F :* **Battre monnaie,** to raise the wind. *(b)* To beat, defeat. *(c)* **Battre la campagne,** *F :* to wander (in one's mind). *Ven :* *B. un bois,* to beat a wood. *(d) Nau :* **Battre un pavillon,** to fly a flag. *(e)* **Battre les cartes,** to shuffle the cards. **2.** *v.tr. & i.* *(a) B. la mesure,* to beat time. *La montre bat,* the watch ticks. *(b) B. l'alarme,* to beat the alarm. *Le tambour bat,* the drum is beating. *Le cœur lui battait,* his heart was going pit-a-pat. *(c) Porte qui bat,* banging door. *(d) B. des mains,* to clap one's hands. *B. du pied,* to stamp one's foot. **se battre,** to fight.

battu, *a.* **1.** *Avoir les yeux battus,* to have rings, circles, round one's eyes. **2.** *Metalw :* **Fer battu,** wrought iron. **3.** *F :* *Suivre le chemin b.,* to follow the beaten track.

battue, *s.f. Ven :* Battue, beat.

baudet, *s.m.* **1.** (He-)ass; donkey. **2.** *F :* (Jack)ass, dolt.

Baudouin. *Pr.n.m.* Baldwin.

baudrier, *s.m.* Cross-belt; shoulder-belt.

baudruche, *s.f.* Gold-beater's skin.

bauge, *s.f.* Lair (of wild boar).

baume, *s.m.* Balm, balsam. *Pharm :* *B. de benjoin,* friar's balsam.

baux. See BAIL.

bauxite [boks-], *s.f. Miner :* Bauxite

bavard. **1.** *a.* *(a)* Talkative, garrulous. *(b)* Tale-bearing, gossiping. **2.** *s.* Chatterbox.

bavardage, *s.m.* Chatter(ing), chit-chat.

bavarder, *v.i.* **1.** To chatter. **2.** To gossip. **3.** To blab, to tell tales.

bavarois, *a. & s.* Bavarian.

bave, *s.f.* Slaver, dribble.

baver, *v.i.* To slaver; to slobber.

bavette, *s.f.* **1.** Bib. **2.** *Cy :* *B. garde-boue,* mud-flap.

baveur, -euse. **1.** *a.* Drivelling, slobbering. **2.** *s.* Dribbler, slobberer.

Bavière. *Pr.n.f. Geog :* Bavaria.

bavure, *s.f.* Wire-edge, burr.

bayadère, *s.f.* Nautch-girl.

bayer, *v.i.* **(je baye, baie)** *A :* To stand gaping. **Bayer aux corneilles,** to gape at the moon.

bazar, *s.m.* **1.** (Oriental) bazaar. **2.** Bazaar, emporium; cheap stores.

bê, *onomat.* Baa.

béant, *a.* Gaping (wound); yawning (chasm).

béat, *a.* **1.** *Optimisme b.,* complacent optimism. **2.** Sanctimonious, smug.

béatement, *adv.* **1.** Blissfully, complacently. **2.** Smugly.

béatification, *s.f.* Beatification.

béatifier, *v.tr. Ecc :* To beatify.

béatifique, *a.* Beatific.

béatitude, *s.f.* **1.** *(a)* Beatitude. *(b)* Bliss. **2.** Smugness, complacency.

beau, bel, *f.* **belle,** *pl.* **beaux, belles.** (The form *bel* is used before *m.sg.* sbs beginning with a vowel or a 'mute' *h*). **I.** *a.* **1.** Beautiful, handsome, fair. *Un bel homme,* a handsome, good-looking, man. **Le beau sexe,** the fair sex. *De beaux arbres,* handsome, fine, trees. **2.** Fine. *(a) De beaux sentiments,* fine, noble, lofty, feelings. *(b) Beau danseur,* fine dancer. *Un bel esprit,* a wit. *Prov :* **Les beaux esprits se rencontrent,** great minds think alike. *Belle occasion,* fine opportunity. **Avoir beau jeu à faire qch.,** to have every opportunity to do sth. **Un beau joueur,** a good loser. **Voir tout du beau côté,** to see the bright side of everything. *(c)* Smart, spruce. **Le beau monde,** society; the fashionable set. **Se faire beau,** to smarten oneself up. *(d)* **Beau temps,** fine weather. *(e)* **Tout cela est bel et bon,** that is all well and good. **Il en a fait de belles,** pretty things he's been up to ! **En voici d'une belle !** here's a how-d'ye-do ! *(f)* **J'ai eu une belle peur !** I got an awful fright ! **Au beau milieu de la rue,** right in the middle of the street. **Il y a beau jour qu'il est parti,** it's many a long day since he went away. **3.** *Adv.phrs.* **Bel et bien,** entirely, fairly, quite. **Tout beau !** steady ! gently ! **De plus belle,** more than ever. **4.** *V.phrs.* *(a)* **L'échapper belle,** to have a narrow escape. **La manquer belle**, to miss a brilliant opportunity. (*b*) **Il ferait beau voir cela**, that would be a fine thing to behold. (*c*) **Il fait beau (temps)**, it is fine (weather). (*d*) **Avoir beau faire qch.**, to do sth. in vain. *J'avais beau chercher, je ne trouvais rien*, search as I might, I found nothing. II. **beau, belle**, *s.* **I.** (*a*) Fair one, beauty. *La Belle au bois dormant*, the Sleeping Beauty. (*b*) **Un vieux beau**, an old beau. **2.** *s.m.* (*a*) **Le beau**, the beautiful. (*b*) **Le plus beau de l'affaire c'est que**, the best of the thing is that. (*c*) Fine (weather). **Le temps est au beau (fixe)**, the weather is set fair. **3.** *s.f.* **Belle**. *Jouer la belle*, to play the deciding game or set.

beaucoup, **I.** *s.m.inv.* (*a*) Much, a great deal, *F:* a lot. (*b*) (A great) many, *F:* a lot. **Beaucoup de**, much; (a great) many; a great deal of, *F:* lots of. *Avec b. de soin*, with much care. **Beaucoup d'entre nous**, many of us. (*c*) *Adv.phr.* **De beaucoup**, much, by far, by a great deal. *C'est de b. le meilleur*, it is far and away the best. **2.** *adv.* Much. *Elle parle b.*, she talks a great deal.

beau-fils, *s.m.* Stepson. *pl. Des beaux-fils.*

beau-frère, *s.m.* Brother-in-law. *pl. Des beaux-frères.*

beau-père, *s.m.* **I.** Father-in-law. **2.** Stepfather. *pl. Des beaux-pères.*

beaupré, *s.m. Nau:* Bowsprit.

beauté, *s.f.* **I.** Beauty, loveliness. **Grain, tache, de beauté**, beauty spot. **De toute beauté**, extremely beautiful. **Institut de beauté**, beauty parlour. **2.** Beauty; beautiful woman. **La beauté du bal**, the belle of the ball.

beaux-arts, *s.m.pl.* Fine arts. **École des beaux-arts**, art-school.

beaux-parents, *s.m.pl.* Parents-in-law.

bébé, *s.m.* Baby.

bec [bɛk], *s.m.* **I.** Beak; bill (of bird). **Coup de bec**, peck. **Il a bec et ongles**, he can look after himself. **Attaquer qn du bec et des ongles**, to go for s.o. tooth and nail. **2.** *F:* Mouth or nose. **Fin bec**, gourmet. *F:* **Tenir qn le bec dans l'eau**, to keep s.o. in suspense. *Laisser qn le bec dans l'eau*, to leave s.o. in the lurch. **Prise de bec**, altercation, squabble. **3.** (*a*) Nose (of tool); spout (of coffee-pot); cut-water (of bridge pier). (*b*) **Bec de plume**, pen-nib. (*c*) **Bec de gaz**, gas burner. **Bec Bunsen**, Bunsen burner.

bécane, *s.f. P:* Bicycle, *F:* bike.

bécarre, *s.m. Mus:* Natural (sign).

bécasse, *s.f. Orn:* Woodcock.

bécassine, *s.f. Orn:* Snipe.

bec-croisé, *s.m. Orn:* Crossbill. *pl. Des becs-croisés.*

bec-de-lièvre, *s.m.* Hare-lip. *pl. Des becs-de-lièvre.*

becfigue, *s.m. Orn:* (Familiar name for) the warbler, the fly-catcher, etc.

bêche, *s.f.* Spade.

bêche-de-mer, *s.f.* Sea-slug, sea-cucumber, bêche-de-mer. *pl. Des bêches-de-mer.*

bêcher, *v.tr.* To dig.

bêcheur, -euse, *s.* Digger (of the soil).

bécoter, *v.tr. F:* To give a little kiss, a peck.

becquée, *s.f.* **I.** Beakful. **2.** *L'oiseau donne la b. à ses petits*, the bird feeds its young.

becqueter, *v.tr.* (je becquète) **I.** (Of birds) (*a*) To pick up (crumbs). (*b*) To peck at (sth.). **2.** *F:* To kiss.

bedeau, *s.m.* **I.** *A:* Beadle. **2.** *Ecc:* Verger.

bédouin, *a. & s.* Bedouin.

bée, *a.f.* Gaping. **Bouche bée**, agape.

beffroi, *s.m.* **I.** Belfry. **2.** Alarm-bell.

bégaiement, bégayement, *s.m.* Stammering.

bégayer, *v.* (je bégaye, bégaie) **I.** *v.i.* To stutter, stammer. **2.** *v.tr.* To stammer out (one's lesson).

bégayeur, -euse. **I.** *a.* Stuttering, stammering. **2.** *s.* Stutterer, stammerer.

bègue [bɛg]. **I.** *a.* Stammering. *Il est b.*, he stammers. **2.** *s.* Stammerer.

bégueule [-gœl]. **I.** *s.f.* Prude. **2.** *a.* Prudish, prim; strait-laced.

béguine [-gin], *s.f.* **I.** *Ecc:* Beguin(e) (nun). **2.** *F:* Very devout woman.

beige, *a.* Beige; natural, raw (wool).

beignet, *s.m. Cu:* Fritter.

béjaune, *s.m.* **I.** Young bird. **2.** Ninny, greenhorn.

bel. See BEAU.

bêlement, *s.m.* Bleating, bleat.

bêler, *v.i.* To bleat.

belette, *s.f.* Weasel.

belge, *a. & s.* Belgian.

Belgique, *Pr.n.f.* Belgium.

bélier, *s.m.* **I.** *Z:* Ram. **2.** *A:* Battering ram. **3.** *Astr:* **Le Bélier**, the Ram; Aries.

belladone, *s.f. Bot:* Belladonna.

belle. See BEAU.

belle-fille, *s.f.* **I.** Step-daughter. **2.** Daughter-in-law. *pl. Des belles-filles.*

bellement, *adv.* Gently, softly.

belle-mère, *s.f.* **I.** Step-mother. **2.** Mother-in-law. *pl. Des belles-mères.*

belles-lettres, *s.f.pl.* Humanities, belles-lettres.

belle-sœur, *s.f.* Sister-in-law. *pl. Des belles-sœurs.*

belligérance, *s.f.* Belligerency.

belligérant, *a. & s.m.* Belligerent.

belliqueux, *a.* Warlike, bellicose.

belvédère, *s.m.* **I.** Belvedere; view-point; observation tower. **2.** Summer-house.

Belzébuth. *Pr.n.m.* Beelzebub.

bémol, *s.m. Mus:* Flat.

bénédicité, *s.m.* Grace (before meat).

bénédictin, *a. & s.* **I.** Benedictine (monk). **2.** *F:* **Bénédictine**, benedictine (liqueur).

bénédiction, *s.f.* Blessing, benediction. **Quelle bénédiction!** what a blessing!

bénéfice, *s.m.* **I.** Profit, gain. **Je suis en bénéfice**, I am in pocket. **2.** Benefit. **Faire**

qch. au bénéfice de qn, to do sth. for s.o.'s
benefit. **3.** *Ecc:* Living, benefice.

bénéficier, *v.i.* (*a*) To profit (*de*, by).
(*b*) To make a profit (*sur*, on).

benêt. I. *a.* Stupid, simple-minded. **2.** *s.m.*
Booby, simpleton, ninny.

bénévole, *a.* **1.** Benevolent; kindly; indulgent. **2.** Gratuitous, unpaid (service).

bénévolement, *adv.* **1.** Kindly, benevol-
ently. **2.** Gratuitously.

Bengale. *Pr.n.m.* Bengal. **Feu de Bengale**,
Bengal light.

bénignement, *adv.* Benignly, kindly.

bénignité, *s.f.* (*a*) Benignity, kindness.
(*b*) Mildness.

bénin, -igne, *a.* (*a*) Benign, kindly. (*b*) Mild,
gentle (remedy). *Hiver b.,* mild winter.

bénir, *v.tr.* (*p.p.* **béni, bénit.** The latter used
chiefly as an adj.) **I.** (*a*) To bless. (*Que*)
Dieu vous bénisse! God bless you! (*b*) To
pronounce a blessing on. (*c*) **Le ciel en soit
béni!** heaven be thanked for it! **2.** To consecrate.

　　bénit, *a.* Consecrated, blessed **Eau
bénite,** holy water.

bénitier, *s.m.* Holy-water basin; stoup.

benjoin [bɛ̃-], *s.m.* Gum benzoin.

benne, *s.f.* Flat hamper, basket.

Benoist, Benoît. *Pr.n.m.* Benedict.

benzène [bɛ̃-], *s.m. Ch:* Benzene.

benzine [bɛ̃-], *s.f.* Benzine.

béquille [-ki:j], *s.f.* Crutch.

berbère, *a. & s. Eth:* Berber, Kabyle.

bercail [-ka:j], *s.m.* (*a*) *Husb:* (Sheep)fold.
(*b*) The fold (of the Church).

berceau, *s.m.* **I.** Cradle; (swing-)cot.
2. *Hort:* Arbour, bower.

bercer, *v.tr.* (n. **berçons**) **I** To rock.
2. To lull; to send to sleep.
　se bercer. **I.** To rock, swing, sway.
2. *Se b. d'une illusion,* to cherish an illusion.

berceuse, *s.f.* **I.** (*a*) Swing-cot. (*b*) Rocking-
chair. **2.** Lullaby, cradle-song.

béret, *s.m.* Beret. *B. écossais,* tam-o'-shanter.

bergamot(t)e, *s.f.* Bergamot (orange).

berge, *s.f.* (Steep) bank (of river); banked
edge (of road). *Mil:* Rampart, parapet.

berger, *s.* **I.** Shepherd. **L'Étoile du Berger,**
the Evening Star. **2.** *s.f.* **Bergère.** (*a*) Easy-
chair. (*b*) *Orn:* Wagtail.

bergerie, *s.f.* Sheep-fold; pen.

bergeronnette, *s.f. Orn:* Wagtail.

berline, *s.f. Aut:* Limousine.

berlinois, *a.* **I.** Of Berlin. **2.** Berliner.

berlue, *s.f. Med:* False vision. *F: Avoir
la berlue,* to be blind to the facts.

Bermudes. *Pr.n.f.pl.* **Les (îles) Bermudes,**
the Bermudas.

bernache, *s.f.,* **bernacle,** *s.f.* **I.** *Crust:*
Barnacle. **2.** Bernacle goose.

bernard-l'ermite, *s.m.* Hermit-crab.

berne[1], *s.f.* **I.** Tossing-blanket. **2.** (*a*)
Tossing in a blanket. (*b*) *F:* Chaff, banter.

berne[2], *s.f. Nau:* **En berne,** at half-mast.

Berne[3]. *Pr.n. Geog:* Berne.

berner, *v.tr.* **I.** To toss in a blanket.
2. To chaff, banter.

bernique, *int. F:* Not a bit of use!

Berthe. *Pr.n.f.* Bertha.

béryl [-ril], *s.m. Miner:* Beryl.

besace, *s.f. A:* Beggar's wallet.

besicles, *s.f.pl.* **I.** *A:* Spectacles. **2.** Goggles.

bésigue, *s.m. Cards:* Bezique.

besogne, *s.f.* Work; task, job. **Se mettre à
la besogne,** to set to work. *Une rude b.,* a
stiff piece of work.

besogneux, *a.* Needy, impecunious.

besoin, *s.m.* Want, need. **I.** Necessity,
requirement. (*a*) *Pourvoir aux besoins de qn,*
to provide for s.o.'s wants. **Au besoin, en
cas de besoin,** in case of need; if necessary;
when required. (*b*) **Avoir besoin de qch.,**
to need, want, sth. *Je n'avais pas b. qu'on me
le rappelât,* I did not need to be reminded of
it. (*c*) *impers.* **Il n'est pas besoin,** there is no
need. **Si besoin est,** if need be. **2.** Poverty,
indigence. **Être dans le besoin,** to be in want.

bestial, -aux[1], *a.* Bestial, beastly, brutish.

bestialité, *s.f.* Bestiality.

bestiaux[2], *s.m.pl.* Cattle, beasts.

bestiole, *s.f.* Tiny beast.

bétail [-ta:j], *s.m. Coll.* (No *pl.*) Cattle;
live-stock. **Gros bétail,** cattle. **Menu bétail,**
smaller live-stock.

bête, *s.f.* **I.** Beast, animal; dumb creature.
(*a*) *B. à cornes,* horned beast. (*b*) *F:* Chercher la petite bête, to be over-critical. **Bête
à bon Dieu,** lady-bird. **2.** *F:* (*a*) Fool,
simpleton. (*b*) *a.* Stupid, foolish. **Pas si bête!**
I am not such a fool!

bétel, *s.m.* Betel.

bêtement, *adv.* Stupidly.

bêtise, *s.f.* **I.** Stupidity, silliness. **2.** Nonsense, absurdity. *Dire des bêtises,* to talk
nonsense. **Faire des bêtises,** to play the fool.
3. Blunder; piece of stupidity.

bétoine, *s.f. Bot:* Betony.

béton, *s.m.* Concrete.

bette, *s.f. Bot:* Beet.

betterave, *s.f.* Beet(root).

beuglement, *s.m.* **I.** Lowing (of cattle);
bellowing (of bull). **2.** Bellow.

beugler, *v.i.* To low; to bellow.

beurre, *s.m.* Butter. *Cu:* **Au beurre,** cooked
in butter.

beurrée, *s.f.* Slice of bread and butter.

beurrer, *v.tr.* To butter.

bévue, *s.f.* Blunder, mistake. *Sch:* Howler.

biais. I. *a.* Oblique, slanting, bevelled.
2. *s.m.* (*a*) Slant (of wall); bias (of bowl). **En
biais,** on the slant, slantwise; askew. **Regarder
qn de biais,** to look sideways at s.o. (*b*) Indirect
means, expedient. **Prendre une affaire du
bon biais,** to go the right way to work.

biaiser, *v.i.* **I.** To slant; to lean over.
2. To use evasions; to shuffle.

bibelot, *s.m.* **I.** Curio, knick-knack, trinket. **2.** *pl.* Odds and ends.

bibeloter, *v.i.* F: (a) To collect curios. (b) To do odd jobs.

biberon¹, -onne, s. **I.** *a.* Tippling, wine-bibbing. **2.** *s.* Tippler, wine-bibber.

biberon², *s.m.* Feeding-bottle.

Bible, *s.f.* La Bible, the Bible.

bibliographe, *s.m.* Bibliographer.

bibliographie, *s.f.* Bibliography.

bibliographique, *a.* Bibliographical.

bibliomane, *s.m.* Bibliomaniac.

bibliomanie, *s.f.* Bibliomania.

bibliophile, *s.m.* Bibliophile, book-lover.

bibliothécaire, *s.m.* Librarian.

bibliothèque, *s.f.* **I.** (a) Library (building). (b) Library (room). **2.** Bookcase, book-stand. **3.** Library; collection of books.

biblique, *a.* Biblical.

bicarbonate, *s.m.* Ch: Bicarbonate.

biceps [-seps], *s.m.* Anat: Biceps.

biche, *s.f.* Z: Hind, doe.

bichon, -onne, s. Maltese dog; lap-dog.

bichromate, *s.m.* Ch: Bichromate.

bicoque, *s.f.* F: Poky little house; shanty.

bicorne, *s.m.* (Two-pointed) cocked hat.

bicyclette, *s.f.* Bicycle, cycle.

bicycliste, *s.m. & f.* (Bi)cyclist.

bidet, *s.m.* Nag; pony.

bidon, *s.m.* (a) Can, drum (for oil). (b) Mil: Water-bottle.

bief [bjɛf], *s.m.* **I.** (Canal) reach, level. **2.** Mill-course, (mill-)race.

bielle, *s.f.* B. motrice, driving-rod.

bien. I. *adv.* **I.** Well. *Il faut b. les soigner,* we must look after them well. *Vous avez b. fait,* you did right. *Tout va b.,* all's well. *Aller, se porter, b.,* to be well, in good health. **Bien!** (i) good! (ii) that's enough! (iii) all right! **Très bien!** very good! well done! **2.** (With adj. function) (a) Right, proper. *Comme c'est b. à vous d'être venu!* how nice of you to come! (b) Comfortable. *Vous ne savez pas quand vous êtes b.,* you don't know when you are well off. F: **Vous voilà bien!** now you're in a fine fix! (c) **Je ne me sens pas bien,** I don't feel well. (d) **Être bien avec qn,** to be on good terms with s.o. (e) Of good appearance, position, etc. Il est très bien, he is very gentlemanly. **Ce sont des gens bien,** they are people of good position. **Donnez-moi quelque chose de bien,** give me something good. **3.** (a) Indeed, really, quite. *Je l'ai regardé b. en face,* I looked him full in the face. *Est-ce b. vous?* is it really you? **Je l'avais bien dit!** didn't I say so! *J'espère b. qu'il viendra,* I do hope he will come. **Bien entendu,** of course. *Il est b. venu, mais j'étais occupé,* he did come, but I was busy. (b) Very. *B. malheureux,* very unhappy. (c) Much, many, a great deal, a great many. (i) *J'ai b. envie de lui écrire,* I have a good mind to write to him. (ii) **Je l'ai vu bien des fois,** I have seen him many times.

Bien d'autres, many others. **4.** *Adv.phr.* (a) **Tant bien que mal,** somehow (or other). (b) **Bien plus,** nay more. **5.** *Conj.phr.* (a) **Bien que** + *sub.,* though, although. (b) **Si bien que** + *ind.,* so that, and so. *Il ne reparut plus, si b. qu'on le crut mort,* he failed to reappear and so he was thought dead. (c) **Ou bien** or else. **6.** *int.* **Eh bien!** well!

II. **bien,** *s.m.* **I.** **Le bien public,** the public weal, the commonweal. **Homme de bien,** good, upright, man. *C'est pour votre b.,* it is for your good. **Grand bien vous fasse!** much good may it do you! **2.** (a) Possession, property, wealth. F: **Avoir du bien au soleil,** to be a man of property. (b) *Jur:* **Biens mobiliers,** personal estate. **Biens immobiliers,** real estate. **3.** *Adv.phr.* (a) **En bien.** *Prendre la chose en b.,* to take the matter in good part. *Changement en b.,* change for the better. (b) **A bien.** *Mener une affaire à b.,* to bring a matter to a successful issue.

bien-aimé, *a. & s.* Well-beloved. *pl. Des bien-aimés.*

bien-être, *s.m.* No *pl.* (a) Well-being; comfort. (b) Welfare.

bienfaisance, *s.f.* Beneficence, charity.

bienfaisant, *a.* **I.** Beneficent, charitable. **2.** Beneficial, salutary.

bienfait, *s.m.* **I.** Benefit, kindness, service, good turn. **2.** Gift, blessing, boon.

bienfaiteur, -trice, s. Benefactor, benefactress.

bien-fondé, *s.m.* No *pl.* *Jur:* Justice, merits (of case).

bien-fonds, *s.m.* Real estate; landed property. *pl. Des biens-fonds.*

bienheureux, *a.* **I.** Blissful, happy. **2.** *Ecc:* Blessed.

biennal, -aux, *a.* Biennial, two-yearly.

bienséance, *s.f.* Propriety, decency.

bienséant, *a.* Seemly, decorous, proper.

bientôt, *adv.* (Very) soon; before long. F: **A bientôt!** good-bye, see you again soon! *C'est bientôt dit!* it is easier said than done!

bienveillance [-vɛjɑ̃-], *s.f.* Benevolence, kindness (envers, pour, to); good-will.

bienveillant [-vɛjɑ̃], *a.* Kind, kindly, benevolent (envers, pour, to).

bienvenir, *v.i.* **Se faire bienvenir de qn,** to ingratiate oneself with s.o.

bienvenu, *a. & s.* Welcome. **Soyez le bienvenu, la bienvenue!** welcome!

bienvenue, *s.f.* Welcome. **Souhaiter la bienvenue à qn,** to welcome s.o.

bière¹, *s.f.* Beer.

bière², *s.f.* Coffin.

biffer, *v.tr.* To cross out, cancel (word).

biffure, *s.f.* Erasure; cancelling stroke.

bifteck [-tɛk], *s.m.* Beefsteak.

bifurcation, *s.f.* Bifurcation, fork (of road). *Rail:* (Gare de) bifurcation, junction.

bifurquer, *v.tr. & i.* To fork, bifurcate, divide; to branch off.

bigame. **I.** *a.* Bigamous. **2.** *s.* Bigamist.

bigamie, *s.f.* Bigamy.
bigarreau, *s.m.* White-heart cherry.
bigarrer, *v.tr.* To variegate, mottle.
bigarrure, *s.f.* (*a*) Medley; mixture (of colours). (*b*) Slash (of colour).
bigle, *s.m. Ven:* Beagle.
bigorneau, *s.m. Moll:* Winkle.
bigot. I. *a.* (Over-)devout. **2.** *s.* Zealous church-goer; religious bigot.
bigoterie, *s.f.* Religious bigotry.
bigre, *int. P:* **Bigre!** *qu'il fait froid!* by Jove, it is cold!
bigrement, *adv. Vous avez b. raison!* you are jolly well right!
bijou, -oux, *s.m.* Piece of jewellery; jewel, gem. *F:* **Mon bijou!** my pet!
bijouterie, *s.f.* **I.** Jeweller's trade or shop. **2.** Jewellery; jewels.
bijoutier, *s.* Jeweller.
bilan, *s.m. Com:* **I.** Balance-sheet. **2.** Déposer son bilan, to file one's petition.
bilatéral, -aux, *a.* Bilateral, two-sided (contract).
bilboquet, *s.m. Toys:* (*a*) Cup-and-ball. (*b*) Tumbler (weighted figure).
bile, *s.f.* (*a*) Bile, gall. (*b*) Bile; bad temper. *S'échauffer la bile,* to worry, fret, get angry. *Ne te fais pas de bile!* don't worry!
bilieux, *a.* **I.** Bilious. **2.** (*a*) Choleric, irascible, testy. (*b*) Morose.
bilingue, *a.* Bilingual.
billard [-jaːr], *s.m.* **I.** (Game of) billiards. **2.** Billiard-table. **3.** Billiard-room.
bille¹ [biːj], *s.f.* (Small) ball. **I.** Billiard-ball. **2.** Marble, taw, alley. **3.** *Mec.E:* Roulement à billes, ball-bearing(s).
bille², *s.f.* Billet (of timber).
billet [bijɛ], *s.m.* **I.** Note, short letter. **Billet doux,** love-letter. **2.** Notice, invitation-card, circular. **Billet de faire part,** notice announcing a family event (birth, marriage, death). **3.** Ticket. *B. simple,* single ticket. *B. d'aller et retour,* return ticket. *B. de quai,* platform ticket. (In lottery) **Tirer un billet blanc,** to draw a blank. **4.** *Com:* (*a*) Promissory note, bill. (*b*) **Billet de banque,** bank-note. **5.** Billet de santé, bill of health. **6.** Permit, permission. *Sch: B. de sortie,* exeat.
billevesée [bil-, bij-], *s.f.* Crack-brained notion; nonsense.
billion [biljɔ̃], *s.m.* One thousand million.
billon [bijɔ̃], *s.m.* **I.** Balk (of timber). **2.** (Monnaie de) billon, copper or nickel coinage.
billot [bijo], *s.m.* Block (of wood).
bimbelot, *s.m.* **I.** Toy. **2.** Bauble.
bimbeloterie, *s.f.* **I.** Toy business. **2.** Toys, knick-knacks, odds and ends.
bimensuel, -elle, *a.* Fortnightly.
bimoteur, *a.m. Av:* **Appareil bimoteur,** twin-engine machine.
bine, *s.f. Agr:* Hoe.
biner, *v.tr. Agr:* To hoe.
binette, *s.f.* Hoe.

biniou, *s.m.* Breton (bag-)pipes.
binocle, *s.m.* Eye-glasses, pince-nez.
binôme, *a. & s.m.* Binomial. **Le binôme de Newton,** the binomial theorem.
biographe, *s.m.* Biographer.
biographie, *s.f.* Biography.
biographique, *a.* Biographical.
biologie, *s.f.* Biology.
biologique, *a.* Biological.
biologiste, *s.m.,* **biologue,** *s.m.* Biologist.
bioxyde, *s.m. Ch:* Dioxide.
biparti, *f.* **-ite,** *a.* Bipartite.
bipède. I. *a.* Two-legged. **2.** *s.m.* Biped.
biplace, *a. & s.m. Aut:* Two-seater.
biplan, *s.m. Av:* Biplane.
bique, *s.f. F:* She-goat, nanny-goat.
biquet, -ette, *s. F:* Kid.
birman, *a. & s.* Burmese.
Birmanie. *Pr.n.f.* Burma.
bis¹, *a.* Greyish-brown. **Toile bise,** unbleached linen. **Pain bis,** whole-meal bread.
bis² [biːs]. *Lt.adv.* Twice. **I.** *No.* 10 *bis* = No. 10A (of street). **2.** (After a line of a song) Repeat. **3.** *Th:* Encore!
bisaïeul, *s.* Great-grandfather, -grandmother.
bisannuel, -elle, *a.* Biennial.
biscornu, *a. F:* **I.** Mis-shapen; irregular (building). **2.** Distorted; crotchety (mind).
biscotte, *s.f.* Rusk.
biscuit, *s.m.* Biscuit or plain cake. **Biscuit de Savoie,** sponge-cake.
bise, *s.f.* (*a*) North wind. (*b*) *Lit:* Winter.
biseau, *s.m.* Chamfer, bevel. **Taillé en biseau,** bevel-edged.
biseauter, *v.tr.* To bevel, chamfer.
bismuth, *s.m. Ch:* Bismuth.
bison, *s.m. Z:* Bison.
bisséqué, *a.* Bisected.
bisser, *v.tr.* To encore (song).
bissextile, *a.f.* **Année bissextile,** eap-year.
bistouri, *s.m. Surg:* Bistoury, lancet.
bistre. I. *s.m.* Bistre. **2.** *a.* Blackish-brown; sepia; swarthy.
bitte, *s.f. Nau:* Bitt; bollard (on ship).
bitume, *s.m. Miner:* Bitumen, asphalt.
bitumer, *v.tr.* **I.** To asphalt (road). **2.** Carton bitumé, tarred felt.
bitumineux, *a.* **I.** Bituminous. **2.** Tarry.
bivalve, *s.m. Moll:* Bivalve.
bivouac [-wak], *s.m. Mil:* Bivouac.
bivouaquer [-wake], *v.i.* To bivouac.
bizarre, *a.* Peculiar, odd, queer, bizarre.
bizarrement, *adv.* Queerly, oddly.
bizarrerie, *s.f.* **I.** Peculiarity, oddness. **2.** Whimsicalness; extravagance; oddity.
black-out [-ut], *s.m.* Black-out.
blafard, *a.* Pallid, wan; lambent (flame).
blague, *s.f.* **I.** **Blague à tabac,** tobacco-pouch. **2.** *F:* (*a*) Tall story, humbug. **Sans blague?** really? (*b*) Joke. *Quelle b.!* what a joke!
blaguer [-ge]. *F:* **I.** *v.i.* (*a*) To draw the long bow. (*b*) To joke. **2.** *v.tr.* To chaff, banter; to make fun of.
blagueur, -euse [-gœ-,-gø-]. *F:* **I.** *s.* (*a*)

Humbug. (*b*) Wag, joker. (*c*) Scoffer. **2. *a.*** Bantering, scoffing.

blaireau, *s.m.* **1.** Badger. **2.** Shaving-brush.

blâmable, *a.* Blameworthy.

blâme, *s.m.* **1.** Blame, disapprobation. **Vote de blâme,** vote of censure. **2.** *Adm:* S'attirer un b., to incur a reprimand.

blâmer, *v.tr.* **1.** To blame; to find fault with. **2.** *Adm:* To reprimand.

blanc, blanche. I. *a.* **1.** White. *Vieillard à cheveux blancs,* white-haired old man. **2.** Light-coloured; pale. *s.* Un blanc, a white man. Blanc comme un linge as white as a sheet. **3.** Clean, white, pure, stainless. *Linge b.,* clean, unsoiled, linen. *F:* C'est bonnet blanc et blanc bonnet, it is six of one and half a dozen of the other. **Montrer patte blanche,** to show one's credentials. **4.** Blank (paper). **Nuit blanche,** sleepless night. **Voix blanche,** toneless voice. **Vers blancs,** blank verse. **5.** Fer blanc, tin-plate. *Boîte en fer b., F:* tin box; tin.
II. **blanc,** *s.m.* White. **1.** *Robe d'un b. sale,* dingy white dress. **2.** (*a*) Le blanc des yeux, the white of the eyes. (*b*) B. d'une cible, bull's-eye of a target. (*c*) Blank. **Chèque en blanc,** blank cheque. **3.** (*a*) Saigner qn à blanc, to bleed s.o. white. (*b*) Cartouche à blanc, blank cartridge. **4.** (*a*) B. de volaille, breast of chicken. **Un blanc d'œuf,** the white of an egg. (*b*) Blanc d'Espagne, whiting. (*c*) (Articles de) blanc, linen drapery.
III. **blanche,** *s.f.* **1.** *Bill:* White ball. **2.** *Mus:* Minim.

blanc-bec [-bɛk], *s.m.* *F:* Callow youth; greenhorn. *pl.* Des blancs-becs.

blanchaille [-ʃɑːj], *s.f.* **1.** *Fish:* Small fry. **2.** *Cu:* Whitebait.

blanchâtre, *a.* Whitish, whity.

blancheur, *s.f.* **1.** Whiteness, paleness. **2.** Purity, spotlessness.

blanchir. **1.** *v.tr.* (*a*) To whiten; to make white. (*b*) *Tex:* To bleach. (*c*) To wash, launder. *Donner du linge à b.,* to send clothes to the wash. (*d*) To whitewash. (*e*) *Cu:* To blanch. **2.** *v.i.* To whiten; to turn white. *Il commence à b.,* he is going white.

blanchissage, *s.m.* Washing, laundering. *Elle fait le b.,* she takes in washing.

blanchisserie, *s.f.* (*a*) Laundering. (*b*) Laundry.

blanchisseur, -euse, *s.* (*a*) Laundryman, *f.* laundress. (*b*) *s.f.* Washerwoman.

blanc-manger, *s.m.* Blancmange. *pl.* blancs-mangers.

blaser, *v.tr.* To surfeit.
se blaser, to become blasé, indifferent.
blasé, *a.* Blasé, indifferent.

blason, *s.m.* (*a*) Coat of arms, armorial bearings, blazon. (*b*) Blazon(ry), heraldry.

blasphémateur, -trice. I. *s.* Blasphemer. **2.** *a.* Blaspheming, blasphemous.

blasphème, *s.m.* Blasphemy.

blasphémer, *v.tr. & i.* (Je blasphème; je blasphémerai) To blaspheme.

blatte, *s.f.* *Ent:* Cockroach, black-beetle.

blé, *s.m.* **1.** (*a*) Corn. Halle aux blés, corn-exchange. *F:* Manger son blé en herbe, to spend one's money before one gets it. (*b*) Corn-field. *Faire les blés,* to cut the corn. **2.** Blé (froment), wheat.

blême, *a.* **1.** (*a*) Livid, ghastly. (*b*) Cadaverous (face). **2.** Pale; wan (light).

blêmir, *v.i.* **1.** To turn pale, livid. **2.** (Of light) To grow faint.

blêmissement, *s.m.* Turning pale, paleness.

blessant, *a.* Offensive, cutting (remark).

blesser, *v.tr.* **1.** (*a*) To wound, hurt. Blessé à mort, mortally wounded. (*b*) (Of saddle) To gall (horse). **2.** To offend; to wound the feelings of (s.o.). **3.** To hurt (s.o.'s interests).
se blesser. **1.** To injure, wound, oneself. **2.** To take offence (*de*, at).
blessé, *s.* Wounded person. *Mil:* Casualty.

blessure, *s.f.* Wound, hurt, injury.

blet, *f.* **blette,** *a.* Over-ripe, sleepy.

bleu, *pl.* **bleus.** **1.** *a.* Blue. Conte bleu, fairy tale. J'en suis resté bleu, I was flabbergasted. Il en a vu de bleues, he has had some queer experiences. **2.** *s.m.* (*a*) Blue. *F:* Mon bras est couvert de bleus, my arm is all black and blue. (*b*) *F:* Tout cet argent a passé au bleu, all this money has vanished. N'y voir que du bleu, (i) to be all at sea; (ii) to remain blissfully unconscious of sth. **3.** *s. F:* Tyro, greenhorn. *Mil:* Recruit. **4.** *s.m.* (*a*) Tchn: Blue print. (*b*) *F:* Petit bleu, express letter.

bleuâtre, *a.* Bluish.

bleuir. **1.** *v.tr.* To blue; to make blue. **2.** *v.i.* To become blue.

blindage, *s.m.* **1.** Timbering (of trench). **2.** Armour-plating (of ship).

blinder, *v.tr.* **1.** To timber (trench). **2.** To armour-plate (ship).

blindé, *a.* **1.** Timbered (shaft). **2.** Train blindé, armoured train.

bloc [blɔk], *s.m.* **1.** Block, lump (of wood). Acheter qch. en bloc, to buy sth. in the lump. **2.** *Pol:* Coalition. Faire bloc, to unite. **3.** Pad (of writing-paper). B. à dessin, drawing-block.

blocage, *s.m.* **1.** Clamping; locking (of part). **2.** *Mch:* Sticking, jamming.

blockhaus [-koːs], *s.m.* **1.** *Fort:* Block-house. **2.** *Navy:* Conning-tower.

blocus [-kyːs], *s.m.* Blockade, investment. Forcer le blocus, to run the blockade.

blond. **1.** *a.* Fair, flaxen (hair); blond (person). Bière blonde, pale ale. **2.** *s.* Fair(-haired) man, woman; blond(e). **3.** *s.m.* Blond, flaxen (colour). *Cheveux (d'un) b. doré,* golden hair.

blondin, *a. & s.* Fair-haired (person).

bloquer, *v.tr.* **1.** To jam on (brake). B. les roues, to lock the wheels. **2.** (*a*) To block, obstruct; to stop (cheque). (*b*) To blockade.

blottir (se), *v.pr.* To cower, crouch. *Blotti dans un coin*, huddled in a corner.

blouse, *s.f.* Loose overgarment; overall, smock(-frock), blouse.

bluet, *s.m.* *Bot:* Cornflower, bluebottle.

bluffer. 1. *v.tr.* *F:* To bluff. **2.** *v.i.* *F:* To try it on.

bluter, *v.tr.* *Mill:* To bolt, sift.

boa, *s.m.* *Rept:* Boa.

bobèche, *s.f.* Socket, sconce (of candlestick).

bobine, *s.f.* (a) Bobbin, spool, reel. (b) Reel, drum (for wire). *Phot:* Spool, roll of film. (c) *El:* B. d'induction, spark-coil.

bobiner, *v.tr.* To wind (silk on bobbin).

bocage, *s.m.* Grove, coppice, copse.

bocal [-kal], **-aux,** *s.m.* (a) Bottle or jar (for sweets). (b) (Glass) globe.

Boccace. *Pr.n.m.* Boccaccio.

bock, *s.m.* Glass of beer.

bœuf, *pl.* **bœufs** [bœf, bø], *s.m.* **1.** Ox, bullock. *Jeune b.*, steer. *Bœuf musqué*, musk-ox. **2.** Beef. *B. à la mode*, stewed beef.

Bohême, Bohème[1]. *Pr.n.f.* Bohemia.

bohème[2], *a. & s.* Bohemian. *Mener une vie de bohème*, to lead a Bohemian life.

bohémien, -ienne, *a. & s.* **1.** *Geog:* Bohemian. **2.** Gipsy.

boire. I. *v.tr.* (*pr.p.* buvant; *p.p.* bu; *pr.ind.* ils boivent; *pr.sub.* e boive) **1.** To drink. *B. qch. à petits coups*, to sip sth. **Boire un coup**, to have a drink. **Boire un affront**, to swallow, pocket, an insult. **2.** (Of plants) To absorb, drink up (moisture); (of boots) to take in water. **3.** To drink (alcoholic beverages). *Il a trop bu*, he is the worse for drink *Abs. Il boit*, he drinks. **4.** To drink in (with one's eyes). **Boire qn des yeux**, to devour s.o. with one's eyes.
II. boire, *s.m.* Drink, drinking. **Le boire et le manger**, food and drink.

bois[1], *s.m.* **1.** Wood, forest. *Petit b.*, spinney. **2.** Timber(-tree). *B. en état*, standing timber. *F:* Abattre du bois, to work hard. **3.** Wood, timber. *B. de chauffage*, firewood. **Chantier de bois**, timber-yard. **Gravure sur bois**, woodcut. **Je leur ferai voir de quel bois je me chauffe**, I'll show them what stuff I'm made of. **4.** *Engr:* Woodcut. **5.** *pl.* Bois de cerf, horns, antlers, of a stag. **6.** Bois de lit, bedstead.

bois[2]. See BOIRE.

boiser, *v.tr.* **1.** (a) To panel (room). (b) To prop (mine). **2.** To afforest.

boisé, *a.* **1.** Wooded, well-timbered (country). **2.** Wainscoted, panelled.

boiserie, *s.f.* **1.** Joiner's work. **2.** *Const:* Woodwork, panelling.

boisseau, *s.m.* *A:* Bushel. *F:* 13 litres.

boisson, *s.f.* Beverage, drink. **Pris de boisson**, the worse for drink.

boîte, *s.f.* **1.** Box. *B. de, en, fer blanc*, tin box; canister, *F:* tin. **Conserves en boîte**, tinned foods. **En boîte,** boxed. *B. aux lettres*, letter-box. *Anat:* **Boîte du crâne**, brain-pan.
2. *Aut:* *B. de vitesses*, gear-box. *El.E:* *B. à fusible*, fuse-box. **3.** *P:* (a) One's office, shop, school. (b) **Boîte de nuit**, night-club. (c) *Mil:* Guard-room, cells.

boiter, *v.i.* To limp; to hobble. *B. d'un pied*, to be lame in one foot *Lit:* Vers qui boitent, halting verse.

boiteux, *a.* (a) Lame, limping. (b) Rickety.

boîtier, *s.m.* Case. *B. de montre*, watch-case.

boiv-e, -es. See BOIRE

bol [bɔl], *s.m.* (a) Bowl, basin. (b) Fingerbowl.

bolchevisme, *s.m.* Bolshevism.

bolcheviste, *a. & s.* Bolshevist.

bolide, *s.m.* Meteor. *Lancé comme un b. sur la route*, hurtling along the road.

bolivien, -ienne, *a. & s.* *Geog:* Bolivian.

bombance, *s.f* *F:* Feast(ing); carousing. **Faire bombance**, to feast, to junket.

bombardement, *s.m.* Bombardment.

bombarder, *v.tr.* To bombard, shell. *F:* B. qn de demandes d'argent, to pester s.o. for money.

bombardier, *s.m.* **1.** Bomber, trench-mortarman. **2.** *Av:* Bomber.

bombe, *s.f.* **1.** Bomb. *F:* **Entrer en bombe**, to come bursting in. **2.** Bombe glacée, ice-pudding.

bomber. 1. *v.tr.* (a) To cause (sth.) to bulge. *B. la poitrine*, to throw out one's chest. (b) To bend, arch (one's back). (c) To camber (road). **2.** *v.i.* To bulge (out).

bombé, *a.* Convex, bulging. *Avoir le dos b.*, to be round-shouldered.

bon, bonne. I *a.* **1.** Good, upright, honest. **2.** Good, nice, pleasing. *La bonne société*, well-bred people. *F:* **Cela est bon à dire**, it's easier said than done. **3.** Clever, capable. **4.** Right, correct, proper. *Suis-je dans le bon train?* am I in the right train? *Typ:* Bon, stet. **5.** Good, kind (*pour, envers*, to). *Vous êtes bien bon de m'inviter*, it is very kind of you to invite me. **Faire bon visage à qn**, to be gracious to s.o. *Une bonne âme*, a simple soul. **6.** Good, advantageous. *bon à savoir*, it is worth knowing. **Acheter qch. à bon marché**, to buy sth. cheap. **A quoi bon?** what's the good of it? **Puis-je vous être bon à quelque chose?** can I do anything for you? **7.** Good, fit, suitable. *Être bon à qch.*, to be good for sth. *Mil:* **Bon pour le service**, fit for duty. **Je ferai comme bon me semblera**, I shall do as I think fit. **8.** Good, favourable. **Souhaiter la bonne année à qn**, to wish s.o. a happy New Year. *Nau:* Bon vent, fair wind. **9.** Good, sound, safe. *En bon état*, sound; in working order. **Billet bon pour trois mois**, ticket available for three months. *F:* **Son affaire est bonne!** he's in for it! **10.** *F:* *J'ai attendu deux bonnes heures*, I waited a full two hours. **11.** *adv.* **Tenir bon**, to stand fast, to hold one's own. **Sentir bon**, to smell nice. **Il fait bon ici**, it is pleasant, comfortable, here. **12.** **Pour de bon,** for good (and all); *Il pleut pour de bon,* it is raining in real earnest. **Est-ce pour de bon?** are you in earnest? **En voilà une bonne!** that's a good one! **C'est bon!** that will do! **13.** *int.* **Bon!** good! agreed! **14.** *s.* *F:* **Mon bon,** my dear fellow. **Ma bonne,** my dear.

II. **bon,** *s.m.* **1.** Order, voucher, ticket. **Bon de poste,** postal order. **2.** *Fin:* Bond, bill, draft.

III. **bonne,** *s.f.* (a) Maid(servant), servant. **Bonne à tout faire,** maid-of-all-work. (b) **Bonne d'enfants,** nursery-maid, nurse. (c) Waitress.

bonbon, *s.m.* Sweetmeat, *F:* sweet.

bonbonnière, *s.f.* **1.** Sweetmeat box. **2.** Neat little house or flat.

bond, *s.m.* **1.** Bound, leap, jump, spring. **Franchir qch. d'un bond,** to clear sth. at one bound. **2.** (Of ball) Bounce. **Faire faux bond,** (of ball) to break.

bonde, *s.f.* **1.** (a) Bung (of cask). (b) Plug (of sink). **2.** Bung-hole, plug-hole.

bonder, *v.tr.* To fill chock-full.

bondé, *a.* Chock-full, crammed, packed.

bondir, *v.i.* **1.** (a) To leap, bound; to spring up. **B. sur qch.,** to spring at, pounce on, sth. (b) To gambol, skip, caper. **2.** (Of ball) To bounce.

bondissant, *a.* (a) Bounding, leaping. (b) Skipping, frisking.

bondissement, *s.m.* (a) Bounding, leaping. (b) Skipping, frisking.

bonheur, *s.m.* **1.** Good fortune, good luck, success. **Être en bonheur,** to be in luck. **Porter bonheur,** to bring (good) luck. **Quel bonheur!** what a blessing! **Jouer de bonheur,** to be lucky, in luck. **2.** Happiness. **Faire le bonheur de qn,** to be the source of s.o.'s happiness.

bonhomie, *s.f.* Simple good-heartedness; good nature.

bonhomme, *s.m.,* **bonne femme,** *s.f.* (a) Simple, good-natured, man, woman. **Faux bonhomme,** sly, shifty, customer. *Pourquoi pleures-tu, mon b.?* why are you crying, my little man? **Il va son petit bonhomme de chemin,** he is jogging quietly along. *a.* **Prendre un air bonhomme,** to put on an air of simplicity, of good nature. (b) **Bonhomme en pain d'épice,** gingerbread man. *pl.* **Des bonshommes.**

bonifier, *v.tr.* **1.** To improve (land). **2.** *Com:* To make up (shortage).

boniment, *s.m.* (Showman's) patter.

bonjour, *s.m.* Good day, good morning, good afternoon.

Bonne-Espérance. *Pr.n.* **Le Cap de Bonne-Espérance,** the Cape of Good Hope.

bonne femme, *s.f.* See BONHOMME.

bonne-maman, *s.f.* *F:* Grand(mam)ma. *pl.* **Des bonnes-mamans.**

bonnement, *adv.* **Tout bonnement,** simply, plainly.

bonnet, *s.m.* **1.** (Close-fitting and brimless) cap. **Donner un coup de bonnet à qn,** to touch one's cap to s.o. *F:* **Avoir la tête près du bonnet,** to be hot-tempered. **Avoir mis son bonnet de travers,** to be in an ill humour. *Mil:* B. *de police,* forage-cap. B. *à poil,* busby. *F:* **Gros bonnet,** bigwig, big pot. **2.** B. *de nourrice,* nurse's cap. *F:* **Elle a jeté son bonnet par-dessus les moulins,** she has thrown propriety to the winds.

bonneterie, *s.f.* Hosiery; knitted goods.

bonnetier, *s.* Hosier.

bon-papa, *s.m.* *F:* Grand(pa)pa, grandad. *pl.* **Des bons-papas.**

bonsoir, *s.m.* Good evening, good night.

bonté, *s.f.* **1.** (a) Goodness, kindness; kindly feeling. (b) *pl.* Kindnesses, kind actions. **2.** Goodness, excellence.

bonze, *s.m.* **1.** Bonze, Buddhist priest. **2.** *P:* **Vieux bonze,** old dodderer.

boqueteau, *s.m.* Small wood; copse.

borax [-aks], *s.m.* *Ch:* Borax.

bord, *s.m.* **1.** *Nau:* (a) Board, side (of ship). **Moteur hors bord,** outboard motor. **Le b. du vent,** the weather-side. **Le b. sous le vent,** the lee-side. **Faux bord,** list. **Le long du bord,** alongside. (b) Tack, leg. **Courir un bord,** to make a tack. (c) **Les hommes du bord,** the ship's company. **2.** Edge; border, hem; brink, verge; brim. **Remplir les verres à pleins bords,** to fill the glasses brim-full. **3.** Shore, strand; bank (of river). **Aller au bord de la mer,** to go to the seaside.

bordeaux, *s.m.* Bordeaux (wine). B. *rouge,* claret.

bordelais, *a. & s.* (Native) of Bordeaux.

border, *v.tr.* (a) To border. (b) B. *qch. de qch., avec qch.,* to edge, fringe, sth. with sth. (c) B. *un lit,* to tuck in the bed-clothes.

bordée, *s.f.* *Nau:* **1.** Broadside. *F:* **Lâcher une bordée de jurons,** to let fly a volley of oaths. **2.** Board, tack. **Tirer des bordées,** to tack; to beat up to windward. **3.** Watch. B. *de tribord, de bâbord,* starboard watch, port watch.

bordereau, *s.m.* Memorandum; consignment note; schedule; bordereau.

bordure, *s.f.* **1.** (a) Border, rim; fringe; kerb; skirt (of a wood). **2.** Frame.

bore, *s.m.* *Ch:* Boron.

boréal, -aux, *a.* Boreal, north(ern).

borgne, *a.* **1.** (a) One-eyed; blind in one eye. (b) **Rue borgne,** blind alley. **2.** Disreputable, shady (public house).

borique, *a.* Boric, *F:* boracic (acid).

borne, *s.f.* **1.** (a) Boundary-mark, -stone. (b) *pl.* Boundaries, limits. **Cela passe les bornes,** that is going too far, beyond a joke. **2.** (Stone) corner-post. **3.** *El:* Terminal.

borne-fontaine, *s.f.* Street fountain, drinking-fountain. *pl.* **Des bornes-fontaines.**

borner, *v.tr.* **1.** (a) To mark out the boundary of (field). (b) To form the boundary of (country). **2.** To limit, restrict (power); to set limits, bounds, to (ambition).

se borner, to restrict oneself, to exercise self-restraint. *Je me suis borné à (vous) faire remarquer,* I merely observed.

borné, *a.* Limited, restricted. *Homme (d'un esprit) b.,* narrow-minded man.

Boschimans, *s.m.pl.* Bushmen.

Bosphore (le). *Pr.n.m.* The Bosphorus.

bosquet, *s.m.* Grove, th'cket.

bosse, *s.f.* **I.** Hump (of camel). **2.** (a) Bump, swelling, lump. (b) Unevenness, bump. **3.** Dent. **4.** Boss. **En bosse,** in relief.

bosselage, *s.m.* Embossing.

bosseler, *v.tr.* (**je bosselle**) **I.** To emboss (plate). **2.** To dent.

bossellement, *s.m.* **I.** Denting, bruising. **2.** = BOSSELURE.

bosselure, *s.f.* Dent, bruise.

bossoir, *s.m.* *Nau:* **I.** (a) Cathead. (b) Bow (of ship). **2.** Davit.

bossu. I. *a.* Hunch-backed (person); humped (animal). **2.** *s.* Hunchback.

bot [bo], *a.* **Pied bot,** club-foot.

botanique. I. *a.* Botanical. **2.** *s.f.* Botany.

botaniser, *v.i.* To botanize.

botaniste, *s.m. & f.* Botanist.

botte¹, *s.f.* Bunch (of carrots); truss, bundle.

botte², *s.f.* High boot, Wellington (boot). *F:* **Elle nous a dit cela à propos de bottes,** she said this without rhyme or reason.

botte³, *s.f.* *Fenc:* Thrust, lunge, hit.

botter, *v.tr.* (a) To put boots, shoes, on (s.o.). **Le Chat botté,** Puss in Boots. (b) *Être bien botté,* to be well shod.

bottier, *s.m.* Bootmaker, shoemaker.

Bottin, *s.m.* (Trade mark) Directory.

bottine, *s.f.* (Half-)boot; ankle-boot.

bouc [buk], *s.m.* He-goat; *F:* billy-goat. **(Barbe de) bouc,** goatee (beard).

boucan, *s.m.* *P:* Row, din, uproar.

boucaner, *v.tr.* To smoke-dry, cure (meat).

boucané, *a.* Swarthy (complexion).

boucanier, *s.m.* Buccaneer, pirate.

bouche, *s.f.* Mouth. **I. Garder qch. pour la bonne bouche,** to keep something as a tit-bit. **Faire la petite bouche,** to be dainty, fastidious. **Manger à pleine bouche,** to eat greedily. **C'est une fine bouche,** he is a gourmet. **2.** Mouth (of horse, cattle, fish. NOTE. Of a dog and carnivorous animals *gueule* is used.) **3.** Mouth, opening, aperture (of well); muzzle (of gun). **Bouche à feu,** gun, piece of artillery. **Bouche d'eau,** hydrant. *B. d'incendie,* hydrant. **Les Bouches du Gange,** the mouths of the Ganges.

bouchée, *s.f.* **I.** Mouthful. **2.** *Cu:* B. aux *huîtres,* oyster patty. **Bouchée à la reine,** vol-au-vent of chicken.

boucher¹, *v.tr.* B. **un trou,** to stop (up) to plug, a hole. *Cela servira à b. un trou,* it will serve as a stop-gap. *Se b. le nez,* to hold one's nose. *Se b. les oreilles,* to stop one's ears, to refuse to hear.

bouché, *a.* **I.** Plugged up. **2. Cidre bouché,** bottled cider.

boucher², *s.* Butcher.

boucherie, *s.f.* **I.** (a) Butcher's shop. (b) Butcher's trade. **2.** Butchery, slaughter.

bouche-trou, *s.m.* Stop-gap, substitute; makeshift. *pl. Des bouche-trous.*

bouchon, *s.m.* **I.** (a) Bush, sign (of tavern). (b) Tavern, public house. **2.** Wisp, handful (of straw). **3.** Stopper, plug, bung. *B. de liège,* cork. *B. de verre,* glass stopper.

boucle, *s.f.* **I.** Buckle, shackle. *B. de ceinture,* belt-buckle. **2.** (a) Loop, bow (of ribbon). (b) Loop, sweep (of river). **3.** Ring. **Boucles d'oreilles,** ear-rings. **4.** Curl, ringlet, lock (of hair).

boucler. I. *v.tr.* (a) To buckle (belt); to fasten (strap). *F:* **Boucler une affaire,** to clinch a matter. (b) To loop, tie up, knot (ribbon). **Boucler la boucle,** to loop the loop. (c) To lock up, imprison. (d) B. *(les cheveux de)* qn, to curl s.o.'s hair. **2.** *v.i.* (a) (Of metal) To buckle. (b) (Of hair) To curl, to be curly.

bouclé, *a. Cheveux bouclés,* curly hair.

bouclier, *s.m.* Buckler, shield.

Bouddha. *Pr.n.m.* Buddha.

bouddhiste, *a. & s.* Buddhist.

bouder. I. *v.i.* To sulk. *Dominoes:* "Je boude," 'pass!' 'go!' **2.** *v.tr.* B. qn, to be sulky, in the sulks, with s.o.

bouderie, *s.f.* Sulkiness; sulks.

boudeur, -euse. I. *a.* Sulky. **2.** *s.f.* **Boudeuse,** double back-to-back settee.

boudin, *s.m.* **I.** (a) *Cu:* Black-pudding. (b) *F:* **Boudins,** fat, podgy, fingers. **2.** (a) Corkscrew curl; roll, twist (of tobacco). (b) *Mec.E:* Fillet, beading; flange.

boudoir, *s.m.* Boudoir.

boue, *s.f.* **I.** Mud, mire; filth, dirt. **Tirer qn de la boue,** to raise s.o. from the gutter. **2.** (Building) mud, clay. **3.** Sediment, mud, deposit. **Bain de boues,** mud-bath.

bouée, *s.f.* *Nau:* Buoy. **I.** B. à cloche, bell-buoy. **2. Bouée de sauvetage,** life-buoy.

boueur, *s.m.* Scavenger, dustman.

boueux, *a.* (a) Muddy, miry. (b) Smudgy, thick (writing).

bouffant, *a.* Puffed (sleeve); baggy.

bouffée, *s.f.* Puff (of smoke); whiff.

bouffer. I. *v.i.* (Of dress) To puff (out), swell out. **2.** *v.tr.* B. les joues, to puff out one's cheeks.

bouffir. I. *v.tr.* To swell, blow out. **2.** *v.i.* To become swollen, puffed up, bloated.

bouffi, *a.* Puffy, puffed, swollen (eyes); bloated (face).

bouffissure, *s.f.* Swelling; puffiness.

bouffon. I. *s.m.* Buffoon, clown, fool jester. **2.** *a.* (f. bouffonne) Farcical.

bouffonnerie, *s.f.* Buffoonery; antics.

bouge, *s.m.* Den, slum, hovel.

bougeoir, *s.m.* Flat candlestick.

bouger, *v.* (n. bougeons) **I.** *v.i.* To budge

stir, move. **2.** *v.tr.* *F: Il ne faut rien b.*, you must not move anything.

bougie, *s.f.* **I.** Candle. *B. de cire*, wax-candle. *A la bougie*, by candlelight. **2.** *Ph.Meas:* Candle-power. **3.** *I.C.E:* Bougie (d'allumage), sparking-plug.

bougon, -onne. *F:* **I.** *s.* Grumbler, grouser. **2.** *a.* Grumpy.

bougonner, *v.i.* *F:* To grumble; to scold.

bougran, *s.m.* *Tex:* Buckram.

bouillabaisse [buja-], *s.f.* *Cu:* Provençal fish-soup; *bouillabaisse.*

bouillant [bujã], *a.* **I.** Boiling. **2.** Fiery, hot-headed, impetuous.

bouillir [bujiːr], *v.i.* (*pr.p.* bouillant; *pr.ind.* je bous) To boil. *Faire bouillir qch.*, to boil sth.

bouilli, *s.m.* *Cu:* Boiled beef.

bouillie, *s.f.* Pap; gruel, porridge.

bouilloire [bujwaːr], *s.f.* Kettle.

bouillon [bujɔ̃], *s.m.* **I.** (*a*) Bubble. *Bouillir à gros bouillons*, to boil fast. (*b*) *Cost:* *Manches à bouillons*, puffed sleeves. **2.** *Cu:* Bouillon gras, clear (meat-)soup; beef-tea.

bouillonnement [bujɔ-], *s.m.* Bubbling; boiling; seething.

bouillonner [bujɔ-], *v.i.* To bubble, boil up, seethe.

boulanger, *s.* Baker.

boulangerie, *s.f.* **I.** Bread-making, baking. **2.** Bakery; baker's shop.

boule, *s.f.* **I.** (*a*) Ball, sphere, globe. *B. de hockey*, hockey ball. (*b*) *Boule de scrutin*, ballot-ball. **2.** *Games: Jouer aux boules*, to play bowls. *Jeu de boules*, bowling-green. *Partie de boules*, game of bowls.

bouleau, *s.m.* Birch(-tree).

boule-de-neige, *s.f.* *Bot:* Guelder-rose. *pl. Des boules-de-neige.*

bouledogue, *s.m.* Bulldog.

boulet, *s.m.* (*a*) *A:* Boulet de canon, cannon-ball. (*b*) *F:* Traîner le boulet, to be tied down to an uncongenial occupation.

boulette, *s.f.* **I.** Pellet (of paper). **2.** *Cu:* Force-meat ball; rissole.

boulevard, *s.m.* Boulevard.

boulevardier, *s.m.* Man about town.

bouleversant, *a.* Upsetting, bewildering.

bouleversement, *s.m.* (*a*) Overthrow, up-setting. (*b*) Confusion, upheaval.

bouleverser, *v.tr.* (*a*) To upset, overthrow; to throw into confusion. (*b*) To upset, discompose.

bouline, *s.f.* *Nau:* Bowline.

boulon, *s.m.* Bolt, pin.

boulot, -otte, *a.* & *s.* Dumpy, chubby.

boum [bum], *int.* Bang! boom!

bouquet, *s.m.* **I.** (*a*) Bunch of flowers, nosegay, posy, bouquet. (*b*) Cluster, clump (of trees); plume, tuft (of feathers). **2.** Aroma (of cigar); bouquet (of wine). **3.** *F:* Réserver qch. pour le bouquet, to keep sth. for the last.

bouquetier. **I.** *s.* Flower-seller. **2.** *s.m.* Flower vase.

bouquetin, *s.m.* *Z:* Ibex.

bouquin, *s.m.* Old book; book of no value.

bouquiner, *v.i.* **I.** To hunt after old books. **2.** To pore over old books.

bouquineur, *s.m.* Lover of old books.

bouquiniste, *s.m.* Second-hand bookseller.

bourbe, *s.f.* Mud (of pond); mire.

bourbeux, *a.* Muddy, miry.

bourbier, *s.m.* Slough, mire. *F: Se tirer d'un bourbier*, to get out of a scrape.

bourde, *s.f.* *F:* **I.** Fib, falsehood. *Débiter des bourdes*, to tell fibs. **2.** Blunder, bloomer. *Faire une bourde*, to put one's foot in it, to drop a brick.

bourdon, *s.m.* **I.** *Mus:* Drone (of bagpipes). **2.** Great bell. **3.** *Ent:* Humble-bee.

bourdonnement, *s.m.* Humming, buzzing (of insects); booming (of bell).

bourdonner. **I.** *v.i.* (Of insects) To buzz, hum. **2.** *v.tr.* To hum (tune).

bourg, *s.m.* Small market-town.

bourgade, *s.f.* Important village.

bourgeois. **I.** *s.* **I.** (*a*) *A:* Burgher, citizen. (*b*) Commoner. *Agent de police en b.*, plain-clothes detective. **2.** Middle-class man, woman. *Les petits bourgeois*, the lower middle class; small shopkeepers. **3.** *P:* (As used by workmen) Governor, boss.
II. **bourgeois,** *a.* **I.** Middle-class (family). **2.** Homely, simple, plain (cooking). *Pension bourgeoise*, private boarding-house. **3.** Common, unrefined, vulgar.

bourgeoisie, *s.f.* The middle class.

bourgeon, *s.m.* **I.** Bud. **2.** *F:* Pimple; grog-blossom.

bourgeonnement, *s.m.* **I.** Budding, sprout-ing. **2.** *F:* Breaking out into pimples.

bourgeonner, *v.i.* **I.** *Bot:* To bud, shoot. **2.** *F:* To become pimply.

bourgmestre, *s.m.* Burgomaster.

Bourgogne. **I.** *Pr.n.f.* *Geog:* Burgundy. **2.** *s.m.* (Vin de) Bourgogne, Burgundy (wine).

bourguignon, -onne [-gi-], *a.* & *s.* Bur-gundian.

bourrache, *s.f.* *Bot:* Borage.

bourrade, *s.f.* Blow; thrust; thump.

bourrasque, *s.f.* Squall; gust of wind.

bourre, *s.f.* **I.** Flock (for stuffing); waste (of cotton). **2.** Plug, wad (of fire-arm).

bourreau, *s.m.* Executioner; hangman. *F: B. que vous êtes!* inhuman wretch that you are!

bourreler, *v.tr.* (je bourrèle) To torment (s.o. mentally).

bourrelet, *s.m.* **I.** Pad, wad, cushion. *B. de porte*, draught-excluder. **2.** Rim, flange.

bourrelier, *s.m.* Harness-maker; saddler.

bourrer, *v.tr.* **I.** To stuff, pad (cushion); to fill (pipe with tobacco). *F: Bourrer le crâne à qn*, to stuff s.o. with false stories. **2.** *Mil:* To ram (charge) home. **3.** *F:* Bourrer qn (de coups), to trounce s.o.

bourriche, *s.f.* Basket, hamper (for game).
bourricot, *s.m.* P: Donkey.
bourrique, *s.f.* (*a*) She-ass; donkey.
(*b*) F: Dunce, duffer, ignoramus.
bourriquet, *s.m.* Ass's colt.
bourru, *a.* Rough, rude, surly, churlish.
bourse, *s.f.* **1.** (*a*) Purse, bag, pouch. **Sans
bourse délier,** without spending a penny.
Faire bourse commune, to share expenses.
(*b*) Z: Pouch (of marsupial). **2.** *Sch:* B.
d'études, scholarship. **3.** Stock exchange.
Bourse du Travail, Labour Exchange.
boursier, *s.* Holder of a bursary.
boursoufler, *v.tr.* To puff up, swell (flesh);
to blister (paint).
    se boursoufler, to rise, swell; to
increase in volume; (of paint) to blister.
    boursouflé, *a.* Swollen; bloated. *Style
b.,* inflated, turgid, style.
boursouflure, *s.f.* **1.** Swelling, puffiness (of
the face); turgidity, inflation (of style).
2. Blister (on paint).
bous. See BOUILLIR.
bousculade, *s.f.* Scrimmage; scuffle, hustle.
L'heure de la bousculade, the rush hour.
bousculer, *v.tr.* **1.** *B. des objets,* to upset
things. **2.** *B. qn,* to jostle, hustle, s.o.
bouse, *s.f.* **Bouse de vache,** cow-dung.
bousiller [-zije], *v.tr.* F: *B. un ouvrage,* to
bungle, botch, scamp, a piece of work.
boussole, *s.f.* Compass.
bout[1], *s.m.* **1.** Extremity, end. *Au b. de la
rue,* at the bottom of the street. **Le haut bout
de la table,** the head of the table. *Écouter qn
jusqu'au b.,* to hear s.o. through. **Au bout
du compte,** after all. *Adv.phr.* **De bout en
bout,** from beginning to end, from end to
end. **Être à bout,** to be exhausted. *Pousser
à b. la patience de qn,* to exhaust s.o.'s patience.
Nous sommes à b. d'essence, we have run out
of petrol. *Venir à b. de faire qch.,* to succeed
in doing sth. **2.** End, tip, end-piece. *B. de
pipe,* mouthpiece of a pipe. **A bout portant,**
point-blank. *F:* **Prendre qch. par le bon
bout,** to tackle sth. the right way. **3.** Bit, fragment. *Nous avons un b. de jardin,* we have a
bit of garden. *B. de papier,* scrap of paper.
C'est un bon bout de chemin, it is a good
step to go.
bout[2]. See BOUILLIR.
boutade, *s.f.* **1.** Whim, caprice. **2.** Sudden
outburst. **3.** Sally; flash of wit.
boute-en-train, *s.m.inv.* **Le b.-en-t. d'une
société,** the life and soul of a party.
bouteille [butɛːj], *s.f.* Bottle. *B. isolante,*
vacuum flask. *El:* **Bouteille de Leyde,**
Leyden jar.
boutique, *s.f.* (*a*) Shop. **Tenir boutique,** to
keep a shop. *F:* **Parler boutique,** to talk
shop. (*b*) Market stall.
boutiquier, *s.* Shopkeeper; tradesman.
bouton, *s.m.* **1.** Bud. **En bouton,** budding,
in bud. **2.** Button. *B. de plastron,* stud.
B. de col, collar-stud. *Boutons de manchettes,*

cuff-links. **3.** (*a*) Knob, handle (of door);
button (of foil). **Tourner le bouton,** to
switch (the wireless) on or off. (*b*) **"Appuyez
sur le bouton,"** 'press the button.' **4.** Pimple
(on face). **5.** *Bot:* **Bouton d'or,** buttercup.
boutonner. 1. *v.i. Bot:* To bud. **2.** *v.tr.*
To button (up).
boutonnière, *s.f.* **1.** Button-hole. **2.**
Rosette (of Legion of Honour, etc.).
bouture, *s.f. Hort:* Slip, cutting.
bouturer, *v.tr.* To propagate (plants) by
cuttings.
bouvier, *s.m.* (*a*) Cowherd. (*b*) Drover.
bouvreuil [-rœːj], *s.m. Orn:* Bullfinch.
bovin, *a.* Bovine.
boxe, *s.f.* Boxing.
boyau, -aux, *s.m.* **1.** *F:* Bowel, gut. **Corde
de boyau,** (cat)gut. **2.** Hose-pipe. **3.** Narrow
thoroughfare. *Mil:* Communication trench.
brabançon, -onne, *a. & s* Brabantine,
Belgian. **La Brabançonne,** the Belgian
national anthem.
bracelet, *s.m.* **1.** Bracelet, bangle. **2.** Metal
band, ring.
brachycéphale [braki-], *a.* Brachycephalic,
short-headed.
braconnage, *s.m.* Poaching.
braconner, *v.tr. & i.* To poach.
braconnier, *s.m.* Poacher.
bractée, *s.f. Bot:* Bract.
brahmane, *s.m.* Brahmin, brahman.
brai, *s.m.* Pitch, tar.
braillard [-ɑjɑːr]. **1.** *a. F:* Vociferous,
bawling. **2.** *s.* Bawler; brawler.
brailler [brɑje], *v.i. F:* To bawl, shout.
braillerie [-ɑjri], *s.f. F:* Shouting, bawling.
braiment, *s.m.* Braying.
braire, *v.i.def.* To bray.
braise, *s.f.* **1.** (Glowing) embers. **2.** Small
cinders; breeze.
braiser, *v.tr. Cu:* To braise.
bramement, *s.m.* Belling (of stag).
bramer, *v.i.* (Of stag) To bell.
brancard, *s.m.* **1.** *Veh:* Shaft (of carriage).
2. Stretcher.
brancardier, *s.m.* Stretcher-bearer.
branchage, *s.m. Coll.* Branches, boughs.
branche, *s.f.* **1.** (*a*) Branch, bough. **Avoir
de la branche,** to look distinguished. (*b*)
Notre b. de la famille, our branch of the
family. (*c*) *B. d'un fleuve,* branch of a river.
(*d*) *Les différentes branches des sciences,* the
various branches of learning. **2.** Leg (of
compasses); blade (of propeller).
brancher. 1. *v.i. & pr.* (Of bird) To perch
on a branch. **2.** *v.tr. El:* To plug in.
branchies, *s.f.pl.* Branchiae, gills (of fish).
brande, *s.f.* **1.** Heather. **2.** Heath.
brandir, *v.tr.* To brandish, flourish.
brandissement, *s.m.* Brandishing, flourishing.
brandon, *s.m.* (Fire-)brand. **C'est un brandon de discorde,** he is a fire-brand.

branlant, *a.* Shaky; loose (tooth); tottery; rickety, crazy (chair).

branle, *s.m.* **1.** (*a*) Oscillation, swing (motion). (*b*) Impulse, impetus. **Mettre qch. en branle,** to set sth. going. **2. Mener .e branle,** to set the ball a-rolling.

branle-bas, *s.m.inv.* **1.** *Navy:* (Beat, pipe, to) quarters. **Faire le branle-bas de combat,** to clear for action. **2.** *F:* Bustle, commotion.

branlement, *s.m.* Oscillation, shaking.

branler. 1. *v.tr.* To swing, shake (one's legs); to wag (one's head). **2.** *v.i.* To shake; to be loose.

braquage, *s.m.* Aiming, evelling, pointing.

braquer, *v.tr.* (*a*) B. un fusil sur qch., to point a gun at sth. (*b*) B. les yeux sur qn, to fix one's eye(s) on s.o.

bras, *s.m.* Arm. **1.** (*a*) *Il a le(s) bras long(s),* he is long in the arm. *F:* **Avoir le bras long,** to have a wide influence. **Les bras m'en tombent,** I am dumbfounded. **Cette nouvelle m'a cassé bras et jambes,** this piece of news stunned me. **Avoir qn sur les bras,** to have s.o. on one's hands. **Voiture à bras,** handcart. *Prendre qn à pleins b.,* to hug s.o. **Saisir qn à bras-le-corps,** to grapple with s.o. **Bras dessus bras dessous,** arm in arm. (*b*) *pl.* Hands, workmen. **Manquer de bras,** to be short-handed. **2.** *B. d'une chaise,* arm of a chair.

braser, *v.tr.* To braze.

brasero, *s.m.* Brazier, charcoal-pan.

brasier, *s.m.* **1.** = BRASERO. **2.** (*a*) Fire of live coals. (*b*) Source of intense heat.

brasiller [-zije]. **1.** (*a*) *v.tr.* To grill, broil. (*b*) *v.i.* To sizzle. **2.** *v.i.* (Of sea) To gleam.

brassage, *s.m.* **1.** Brewing. **2.** Mixing, stirring.

brassard, *s.m.* Armlet, arm-badge. *B. de deuil,* mourning-band; arm-band.

brasse, *s.f.* **1.** Span (of the arms). *Nau:* Fathom. **2.** *Swim:* Stroke. **Nager à la brasse,** to swim hand over hand.

brassée, *s.f.* Armful.

brasser, *v.tr.* **1.** To brew (beer). **2.** To mix, stir (up). *F:* **Brasser des affaires,** to handle a lot of business.

brasserie, *s.f.* **1.** Brewery. **2.** Brewing. **3.** Beer-saloon (often also a restaurant).

brasseur, -euse, *s.* **1.** Brewer. **2.** Mixer. *F:* **Brasseur d'affaires,** man who handles a lot of business.

brassière, *s.f.* **1.** Child's vest. **2.** *pl.* (*a*) *F:* **Être en brassières,** to be in leading-strings. (*b*) Shoulder-straps.

bravache. 1. *s.m.* Braggadocio, bully. **2.** *a.* Swaggering, blustering, bullying.

bravade, *s.f.* Bravado, bluster.

brave, *a.* **1.** Brave, bold, gallant. **Un (homme) brave,** a brave, courageous, man. **2.** Good, honest, worthy. **C'est un brave homme,** he's a worthy man. *s.m. Je vous félicite,* **mon brave,** I congratulate you, my good man.

bravement, *adv.* Bravely, boldly, stoutly.

braver, *v.tr.* To brave. **1.** To face (sth.) bravely. **2.** To defy, dare.

bravo¹. 1. *int.* Bravo! well done! hear, hear! **2.** *s.m.* Cheer. *pl* Des bravos.

bravo², *s.m.* Bravo, hired assassin. *pl. Des bravi.*

bravoure, *s.f.* Bravery, gallantry.

brebis, *s.f.* **1.** Ewe. **2.** Sheep.

brèche, *s.f.* Breach, opening, gap (in hedge); notch (in blade). *F:* **Battre qn en brèche,** to disparage s.o.

bredouille [-du:j], *a.inv. F:* **Être bredouille,** to have failed completely (in sth.).

bredouiller [-duje], *v.i.* To mumble. *v.tr. B. une excuse,* to stammer out an excuse.

bref, (f. brève. 1. *a.* Brief, short. **Raconter qch. en bref,** to relate sth. in a few words. **2.** *adv.* Briefly, in short. **Parler bref,** to speak curtly. **3.** *s.m.* (Papal) brief. **4.** *s.f.* Brève, short syllable.

breloque, *s.f.* **1.** Charm, trinket; watch-charm. **2.** *Mil:* Dismiss.

brème, *s.f. Ich:* Bream.

Brême. *Pr.n.m. Geog:* Bremen.

Brésil [-zil]. *Pr.n.m. Geog:* Brazil.

brésilien, -ienne, *a. & s.* Brazilian.

Bretagne. *Pr.n.f. Geog:* Brittany.

brétailleur [-tɑj-], *s.m. F:* Swashbuckler.

bretelle, *s.f.* **1.** Strap, sling, suspender. **2.** (Paire de) bretelles, (pair of) braces.

breton, -onne, *a. & s.* Breton.

breuvage, *s.m.* **1.** Beverage, drink. **2.** *Med:* Draught, potion.

brève. See BREF.

brevet, *s.m.* **1.** Brevet d'invention, (letters) patent. **2.** Diploma, certificate.

breveter, *v.tr.* (je brevète, je brevette) To patent (invention).
    breveté. 1. (*a*) *s.* Patentee. (*b*) *a.* (i) Fournisseur breveté de sa Majesté, (tradesman) by special appointment to His Majesty. (ii) Patent. **2.** *a.* Certificated.

bréviaire, *s.m. Ecc:* Breviary.

brévité, *s.f.* Shortness.

bribes, *s.f.pl.* Scraps, fragments. *Bribes de conversation,* snatches of conversation.

brick [brik], *s.m. Nau:* Brig.

bricole, *s.f.* **1.** Breast-strap. **2.** *Bill:* **Jouer la bricole,** to play off the cushion. **3.** *Usu. pl. F:* Odd jobs.

bricoler. (*a*) *v.tr. C'est une affaire bricolée,* it's a put-up job. (*b*) *v.i.* To do odd jobs.

bricoleur, *s.m. F:* Potterer.

bride, *s.f.* (*a*) Bridle. (*b*) Rein(s). **Aller à bride abattue,** to ride at full speed. *Lâcher la b. à sa colère,* to give full vent to one's anger. *F:* **Tenir qn en bride,** to keep a tight hand over s.o.

brider, *v.tr.* **1.** (*a*) To bridle (horse). (*b*) B. ses passions, to curb one's passions. **2.** To tie up, fasten (up).

brièvement, *adv.* Briefly, succinctly.

brièveté, *s.f.* **1.** Shortness, brevity (of time). **2.** Brevity, briefness, conciseness.

brigade, *s.f.* **1.** *Mil:* Brigade. **2.** Squad, detachment (of gendarmes).

brigadier, *s.m.* (*a*) Corporal (of mounted arms). (*b*) B. *de police,* police sergeant.

brigand, *s.m.* Brigand, robber; ruffian.

brigandage, *s.m.* Brigandage, highway robbery.

brigue [brig], *s.f.* Intrigue; underhand work.

briguer [-ge], *v.tr.* To solicit, to court (s.o.'s favour). B. *des voix,* to canvass (for votes).

brillamment [brij-], *adv.* Brilliantly.

brillant [brijɑ̃]. **1.** *a.* Brilliant. (*a*) Sparkling, glittering (gem); glossy. (*b*) *Spectacle b.,* splendid sight. (*c*) B. *de santé,* radiant with health. **2.** *s.m.* (*a*) Brilliancy, brilliance, brightness. (*b*) Polish, shine (on boots). **3.** *s.m.* Brilliant (diamond).

briller [brije], *v.i.* To shine, sparkle, glitter, glisten. *F:* **Briller par son absence,** to be conspicuous by one's absence.

brimade, *s.f.* Rough joke.

brimbale, *s.f.* Handle (of pump).

brin, *s.m.* **1.** (*a*) Shoot (of tree). (*b*) Blade (of grass). **2.** *F:* Bit, fragment. B. *de consolation,* crumb of comfort. B. *de malice,* touch of malice. **3.** Strand (of rope).

brindille [-di:j], *s.f.* Sprig, twig, branchlet.

brio, *s.m.* *Mus:* Vigour, go, dash; *brio.*

brioche, *s.f.* *Cu:* Brioche; bun. *P:* **Faire une brioche,** to drop a brick.

brique, *s.f.* **1.** Brick. **2.** *Nau:* Brique à pont, holystone.

briquet, *s.m* (*a*) Flint and steel. (*b*) Cigarette-lighter.

briqueterie, *s.f.* Brick-field.

brisant. 1. *a.* Shattering, disruptive. **2.** *s.m.* (*a*) Reef, shoal. (*b*) Breaker.

brise, *s.f.* Breeze.

brise-lames, *s.m.inv.* Breakwater.

briser, *v.tr.* To break, smash, shatter. (*a*) B. *une porte,* to break open a door. (*b*) To crush (ore). **Brisé par la douleur,** crushed by grief. (*c*) To break (treaty). B. *toute résistance,* to break down all resistance. (*d*) To break off (conversation). *Abs.* **Brisons là,** let us say no more about it. **se briser,** to break. **brisé,** *a.* Broken. **Brisé de fatigue,** tired out.

brisées, *s.f.pl.* *F:* **Suivre les brisées de qn,** to follow in s.o.'s footsteps. **Aller sur les brisées de qn,** to compete with s.o.

brise-vent, *s.m.inv.* Wind-screen.

brisure, *s.f.* Break, crack.

britannique, *a.* British.

broc [bro], *s.m.* Pitcher; (large) jug.

brocanter, *v.i.* To deal in second-hand goods; to buy and sell.

brocanteur, -euse, *s.* Second-hand dealer.

brocart, *s.m.* *Tex:* Brocade.

broche, *s.f.* **1.** *Cu:* (*a*) Spit. (*b*) Meat skewer. **2.** Peg, pin. B. *de charnière,* hinge-pin. **3.** *Tex:* Spindle. **4.** *Cost:* Brooch.

brocher, *v.tr.* *Bookb:* To stitch, sew (book). **Livre broché,** paper-bound book.

brochet, *s.m.* *Ich:* Pike.

brochette, *s.f.* *Cu:* Skewer.

brocheur, -euse, *s.* *Bookb:* Sewer.

brochure, *s.f.* Pamphlet, brochure.

brodequin, *s.m.* Laced boot; ankle-boot.

broder, *v.tr.* To embroider

broderie, *s.f* (*a*) Piece of embroidery. (*b*) Embroidery work.

brodeur, -euse, *s* Embroiderer

broiement, *s.m.* Grinding, crushing.

brome, *s.m.* *Ch:* Bromine.

bromure, *s.m.* *Ch:* Bromide.

broncher, *v.i.* **1.** (Of horse) (*a*) To stumble. (*b*) To shy. **2.** *F:* (*a*) **Sans broncher,** without flinching. (*b*) To budge, stir.

bronchial, -aux, *a.* Bronchial.

bronchite, *s.f.* *Med:* Bronchitis.

bronze, *s.m.* **1.** Bronze. **2.** **Bronze à canon,** gun-metal.

bronzer, *v.tr.* To tan, sunburn. **se bronzer,** to tan; to bronze.

brosse, *s.f.* **1.** Brush. (*a*) **Donner un coup de brosse à qn,** to give s.o. a brush-down. **Cheveux taillés en brosse,** hair cut short. (*b*) Paint-brush. **Passer la brosse sur qch.,** to paint sth. out. **2.** *pl.* Brushwood.

brosser, *v.tr.* To brush; to scrub (floor). *F:* **Brosser qn,** to give s.o. a good thrashing.

brosseur, *s.m.* **1.** (*a*) Brusher. (*b*) *Mil:* Servant, batman. **2.** Scene-painter.

brou, *s.m.* **1.** Husk (of walnut). **2.** **Brou de noix,** walnut stain.

brouette, *s.f.* Wheelbarrow.

brouhaha, *s.m.* *F:* Hubbub; hullabaloo; hum (of conversation).

brouillage [bruja:ʒ], *s.m.* *W.Tel:* Jamming; interference.

brouillard [bruja:r], *s.m.* **1.** Fog, mist, haze. **2.** *Com:* Day-book.

brouiller [bruje], *v.tr* **1.** To mix up, jumble. B. *des œufs,* to scramble eggs. **Brouiller les cartes,** (i) to shuffle the cards; (ii) *F:* to spread confusion. *W.Tel:* **Brouiller un message,** to jam a message. **2.** To set (people) at loggerheads. **se brouiller. 1.** To become mixed, confused. **Le temps se brouille,** the weather is breaking up. **2.** To quarrel, to fall out.

brouillé, *a.* **1.** Jumbled, mixed, confused. **Œufs brouillés,** scrambled eggs. **2.** *Être b. avec qn,* to have fallen out with s.o.

brouillon [brujɔ̃], **-onne. 1.** *a.* Muddle-headed. **2.** *s.m.* (Rough) draft.

broussaille [-sɑ:j], *s.f.* Usu. *pl.* Brushwood. **Cheveux en broussaille,** unkempt hair.

brousse, *s.f.* (In Australia) (The) bush.

brouter, *v.tr.* B. *l'herbe,* to browse on the grass; to graze.

broutilles [-ti:j], *s.f.pl.* Sprigs, twigs.

broyer, *v.tr.* (je broie) To pound, pulverize.

bru, *s.f.* Daughter-in-law.

bruant, *s.m.* *Orn:* Yellow-hammer. *B. des neiges,* snow-bunting.

brugnon, *s.m.* *Hort:* Nectarine.

bruine, *s.f.* Fine rain; drizzle.

bruiner, *v.impers.* To drizzle.

bruire, *v.i.def.* (*pr.p.* **bruissant;** *fr.ind.* Il bruit, ils bruissent; *p.d.* il bruyait, il bruissait) To rustle; to rumble; to hum; (of brook) to murmur.

bruissement, *s.m.* Rumbling; brawling (of brook); surging (of sea); rustling.

bruit, *s.m* **I.** (*a*) Noise; din; report (of a gun). **Faire du bruit,** to make a noise. (*b*) Noise, fuss. **Beaucoup de bruit pour rien,** much ado about nothing. **2.** Rumour, report. **Faire courir un bruit,** to set a rumour afloat.

brûlant, *a.* Burning; on fire. *Larmes brûlantes,* scalding tears.

brûle-gueule, *s.m.inv.* Short clay pipe.

brûle-pourpoint (à), *adv.phr.* Point-blank.

brûler. **I.** *v.tr.* To burn. **I.** To burn (down) (house); to burn (up) (rubbish). **2.** To scorch. (*a*) *Le lait est brûlé,* the milk has caught. *F:* **Brûler le pavé,** to tear along the road. (*b*) *Aut:* *B. un village,* to pass through a village without stopping. (*c*) (Of frost) To bite, nip (buds). *La fumée me brûlait les yeux,* the smoke made my eyes smart.
II. brûler, *v.i.* **I.** To burn; to be on fire. *Games:* *Tu brûles,* you are getting hot. **2.** *B. de curiosité,* to be aflame with curiosity. **Les mains lui brûlent,** *F:* he is all impatience to be up and doing. **3.** (Of meat) to burn; (of milk) to catch.

brûlé. **I.** *a.* Burnt. *F:* **Cerveau brûlé,** dare-devil. **Homme brûlé,** man who has lost his reputation. **2.** *s.m.* *Odeur de b.,* smell of burning. *F:* **Sentir le brûlé,** (of opinions) to smack of heresy.

brûlot, *s.m.* *Hist:* Fire-ship.

brûlure, *s.f.* **I.** Burn, scald. **2.** (*a*) Frost-nip. (*b*) Blight; smut (on corn).

brume, *s.f.* Thick fog, haze, or mist.

brumeux, *a.* Foggy.

brun. **I.** *a.* Brown; dark (complexion). **2.** *s.m.* Brown (colour). **3.** *s.f.* **A la brune,** at dusk.

brunâtre, *a* Brownish.

brunet, -ette. **I.** *a.* Brownish. **2.** *s.f.* *Jolie brunette,* pretty brunette.

brunir. **I.** *v.i.* & *pr.* To become dark. **2.** *v.tr.* (*a*) To brown, darken. (*b*) To burnish (gold). (*c*) To polish (metal).

brunisseur, -euse, *s.* Burnisher.

brusque, *a.* **I.** Abrupt, blunt, brusque (manner). **2.** Sudden. *Aut:* **Tournant brusque,** 'sharp turn.'

brusquement, *adv.* **I.** Abruptly. **2.** Suddenly.

brusquer, *v.tr.* **I.** *B. qn,* to be abrupt with s.o. **2.** *B. les choses,* to precipitate matters.

brusquerie, *s.f.* Abruptness, bluntness.

brut [bryt], *a.* **I.** *Force brute,* brute force. **2.** Raw, unmanufactured; unpolished;

unrefined; crude; rough, uncut (diamond). **3.** *Com:* Gross (weight). **4.** *s.f.* **Brute.** (*a*) Brute beast. (*b*) Ruffian.

brutal, -aux, *a.* (*a*) Brutal, brutish. (*b*) Coarse, rough. *Force brutale,* brute force. *Coup b.,* savage blow.

brutalement, *adv.* (*a*) Brutally. (*b*) Bluntly.

brutaliser, *v.tr.* To ill-treat; to bully.

brutalité, *s.f.* **I.** (*a*) Brutality, brutishness. (*b*) Brutality, savagery. **2.** Brutal act.

Bruxelles [brysɛl]. *Pr.n.f.* Brussels.

bruyamment, *adv* **I.** Noisily. **2.** Clamorously.

bruyant, *a.* **I.** Noisy; resounding (success). **2.** Loud; boisterous (laughter).

bruyère, *s.f.* **I.** (*a*) Heather, heath. (*b*) Heath(-land). **2.** Briar. **Pipe en bruyère,** briar pipe.

bryone, *s.f.* *Bot:* Bryony.

bu. See BOIRE.

buanderie, *s.f.* Wash-house.

bubonique, *a.* *Med:* Bubonic (plague).

bucarde, *s.f.* *Moll:* Cockle.

bûche, *s.f.* (*a*) (Fire-)log. *B. de Noël,* yule-log. (*b*) *F:* Dolt, blockhead.

bûcher[1], *s.m.* **I.** Wood-shed. **2.** (*a*) **Mourir sur le bûcher,** to be burnt at the stake. (*b*) Funeral-pyre.

bûcher[2], *v.tr.* & *i.* To work hard; to swot.

bûcheron, *s.m.* (*a*) Woodcutter. (*b*) Lumberman.

bûcheur, -euse, *s.* *F:* Plodder, hard worker, swotter.

bucolique, *a.* Bucolic, pastoral.

budget, *s.m.* Budget; estimates.

budgétaire, *a.* Budgetary.

buée, *s.f.* Steam, vapour (on window-panes).

buffet, *s.m.* **I.** Sideboard. *B. de cuisine,* dresser. **2.** Buffet (at ball). *Rail:* Refreshment room.

buffle, *s.m.* *Z:* Buffalo.

buffleterie, *s.f.* *Mil:* Leather equipment.

bugle[1], *s.m.* *Mus:* Flugel horn

bugle[2], *s.f.* *Bot:* Bugle.

buglosse, *s.f.* *Bot:* Bugloss, alkanet.

bugrane, *s.f.* *Bot:* Rest-harrow.

buis, *s.m.* **I.** *Bot:* Box(-tree). **2.** Box(-wood).

buisson, *s.m.* **I.** Bush. **2.** Brake, spinney.

buissonnier, *a.* That lives in the bush. **Faire l'école buissonnière,** to play truant.

bulbe. **I.** *s.m.* or *f.* *Bot:* Bulb. **2.** *s.m.* *Anat:* Bulb *B.pileux,* root of a hair.

bulbeux, *a.* Bulbous (plant).

bulgare, *a.* & *s.* Bulgarian.

Bulgarie. *Pr.n.f.* Bulgaria.

bulle, *s.f.* **I.** (Papal) bull. **2.** Bubble.

bulletin, *s.m.* **I.** Bulletin; report. *B. d'actualité,* news bulletin. **2.** Ticket, receipt, certificate; (telegraph) form. *B. de vote,* voting paper. *B. de commande,* order form.

bûmes. See BOIRE.

buraliste, *s.m.* & *f.* (*a*) Clerk (in post office). (*b*) Collector of taxes.

bure, *s.f.* *Tex:* Frieze; homespun.

bureau, *s.m.* **1.** Writing-table, -desk ; bureau. *B. américain,* roll-top desk. **2.** (*a*) Office. *B. personnel,* private office. **"Bureau restant,"** 'to be called for.' *Th:* **Bureau de location,** box-office. **Bureau de tabac,** tobacconist's shop. (*b*) Board, committee.

bureaucrate, *s.m.* Bureaucrat.

bureaucratie, *s.f.* Bureaucracy ; *F:* red tape.

burette, *s.f.* **1.** Cruet. **2.** Oil-can ; oiler.

burin, *s.m.* Graver ; etcher's needle.

buriner, *v.tr.* To engrave.

burlesque, *a.* **1.** Burlesque. **2.** Comical, ludicrous.

bus. See BOIRE.

busard, *s.m.* *Orn:* Buzzard, harrier.

buse¹, *s.f.* **1.** *Orn:* Buzzard. **2.** *F:* Blockhead, dolt, fool.

buse², *s.f.* Nose-piece, nozzle (of bellows).

busqué, *a.* Aquiline, hooked (nose).

buss-e, -ent, -ions. See BOIRE.

buste, *s.m.* Bust.

but¹, *s.m.* **1.** Mark (to aim at) ; target, objective. **2.** Goal. *F:* **Aller droit au but,** to go straight to the point. **3.** Object, aim, purpose. **Dans le but de faire qch.,** with the object of doing sth. **Errer sans but,** to wander about aimlessly. **4.** *Adv.phr.* (*a*) **But à but,** even ; without any advantage to either party. (*b*) *F:* **Faire une offre de but en blanc,** to make an offer on the spur of the moment.

but². See BOIRE.

buter, *v.i.* To strike, knock (*contre,* against) ; to stumble (*contre,* over). (Of beams) To abut, rest (*contre,* against).

se buter. (*a*) *Se b. à un obstacle,* to come up against an obstacle. (*b*) *Se b. à faire qch.,* to be set on doing sth.

buté, *a.* Fixed, set. *Caractère b.,* obstinate nature.

butin, *s.m.* Booty, spoils, plunder.

butiner, *v.tr. & i.* (Of bees) *B. les fleurs,* to gather honey from the flowers.

butoir, *s.m.* Stop, check ; buffer.

butor, *s.m.* **1.** *Orn:* Bittern. **2.** *F:* Lout.

butte, *s.f.* **1.** Knoll, hillock, mound. **2.** *Mil:* Butts (of range). *F:* **Être en butte à qch.,** to be exposed to sth.

buv-ant, -ons, etc. See BOIRE.

buvard. 1. *a.* **Papier buvard,** blotting-paper. **2.** *s.m.* Blotter ; blotting-pad.

buvette, *s.f.* Refreshment bar (at station).

buveur, -euse, *s.* **1.** Drinker. **2.** Toper, drunkard, wine-bibber.

Byzance. *Pr.n. A.Geog:* Byzantium.

byzantin, *a. & s.* Byzantine.

C

C, c [se], *s.m.* (The letter) C, c.

c'. See CE¹.

ça. See CELA.

çà. 1. *adv.* Hither. **Çà et là,** here and there. **2.** *int. Ah çà!* now then !

cabale, *s.f.* Cabal. (*a*) Intrigue. (*b*) Clique.

cabaler, *v.i.* To cabal, intrigue.

cabane, *s.f.* (*a*) Hut, shanty. (*b*) Cabin (of barge).

cabanon, *s.m.* **1.** Small hut. **2.** (Lunatic's) padded cell.

cabaret, *s.m.* (*a*) Public-house, tavern. (*b*) Inn, eating-house.

cabaretier, *s.* Inn-keeper.

cabestan, *s.m.* Capstan, windlass, winch.

cabillaud [-ijo], *s.m.* Codfish ; fresh cod.

cabine, *s.f.* Cabin. (*a*) *Nau:* **C. de luxe,** state-room. (*b*) (Telephone) call-box. *Rail:* **C. à signaux,** signal-box.

cabinet, *s.m.* **1.** Closet ; small room. **C. de toilette,** dressing room. **C. de travail,** study. *Phot:* **C. noir,** dark-room. **2.** Office, room. **3.** Collection (of works of art). **4.** (*a*) *Foreign Pol:* Government. (*b*) *Pol:* Cabinet. (*c*) **C. d'un ministre,** minister's departmental staff.

câble, *s.m.* (*a*) Cable, rope. (*b*) Cable. **C. sous-marin,** submarine cable. **Aviser qn par le câble,** to cable to s.o.

câbler, *v.tr.* To cable (message).

câblogramme, *s.m.* Cablegram ; *F:* cable.

cabosser, *v.tr. F:* **1.** To bump, bruise. **2.** To dent (silverware).

cabotage, *s.m.* Coastwise trade.

cabrer. 1. *v.tr. Av:* To elevate (plane). **2.** *v.pr.* (Of horse) To rear.

cabriole, *s.f.* Leap, caper.

cabriolet, *s.m. Veh:* Gig.

cacahuète, *s.f.* Peanut.

cacao, *s.m. Bot:* Cacao. *Com:* Cocoa.

cacatoès [-tɔɛːs], *s.m. Orn:* Cockatoo.

cachalot, *s.m.* Cachalot ; sperm whale.

cache, *s.f. Phot:* Hiding-place ; cache (of explorer).

cache-cache, *s.m.* Hide-and-seek.

Cachemire. 1. *Pr.n.m. Geog:* Cashmere. **2.** *s.m. Tex:* Cashmere.

cache-nez, *s.m.inv.* Muffler, comforter.

cacher, *v.tr.* (*a*) To hide, secrete. (*b*) To hide (one's face) from view. **C. qch. à qn,** to hide sth. from s.o.

se cacher. 1. To hide, lie in hiding. **2.** (*a*) *Se c. à qn,* to hide from s.o. (*b*) *Je ne m'en cache pas,* I make no secret of it.

cachet, *s.m.* **1.** (*a*) Seal. (*b*) Mark, stamp, impress. **C. de la poste,** postmark. *Œuvre qui manque de c.,* work that lacks character.

2. (a) Stamp, seal (implement). (b) Signet (-ring). **3.** Voucher (for lessons).

cacheter, *v.tr.* (je **cachette**) To seal (up).

cachette, *s.f.* Hiding-place. **En cachette,** secretly; on the sly; on the quiet.

cachot, *s.m.* Dungeon.

cadavre, *s.m.* (a) Corpse; dead body. (b) Carcase (of animal).

cadeau, *s.m.* Present; gift.

cadenas, *s.m.* **1.** Padlock. **2.** Clasp, snap (of bracelet).

cadence, *s.f.* **1.** Cadence, rhythm. **2.** (a) *Mus:* Cadence. (b) Intonation (of voice).

cadet, -ette, *s.* (a) (The) younger, junior. (b) Junior (in rank). (c) *F:* The youngest (of a family).

cadmium [-mjɔm], *s.m.* *Ch:* Cadmium.

cadran, *s.m.* **1.** Dial. **Cadran solaire,** sundial. **2.** Face (of clock).

cadre, *s.m.* **1.** (a) Frame (of picture). (b) Border (of map); setting (of scene). (c) Compass, limits. **2.** Frame(work) (of bicycle). **3.** *Mil:* Cadre. *C. de réserve,* reserve list.

caduc, -uque [kadyk], *a.* **1.** (a) Decaying (house). (b) (Of pers.) Decrepit. **2.** *Bot:* Deciduous. **3.** Null and void (legacy).

cafard. **1.** *s. Sch:* Sneak. **2.** *s.m.* (a) Cockroach. (b) *F:* **Avoir le cafard,** to have the hump.

café, *s.m.* **1.** Coffee. (a) **Grain de café,** coffee-bean. (b) *Café noir, café nature,* black coffee. **Café complet,** coffee, hot milk, rolls and butter. (c) *a.inv.* Coffee-coloured. **2.** Café.

cafetier. **1.** *s.* Owner of a café. **2.** *s.f.* Cafetière, coffee-pot.

cafre, *a. & s. Ethn:* Kaffir.

cage, *s.f.* **1.** Cage. **2.** Cover, case. **3.** Well(-hole) (of stairs); shaft (of lift).

cagneux, *a. & s.* Knock-kneed.

cagnotte, *s.f. Games:* Pool, kitty, pot.

cagot. **1.** *s.* (Canting) hypocrite. **2.** *a.* Sanctimonious.

cagoule, *s.f.* (a) Cowl. (b) Penitent's hood.

cahier, *s.m.* Exercise book.

cahin-caha, *adv. Marcher c.-c.,* to limp along.

cahot, *s.m.* Jolt; bump (of vehicle).

cahotement, *s.m.* Jolting, bumping.

cahoter, *v.tr. & i.* To bump along (in cart).

cahute, *s.f.* **1.** Hut. **2.** Cabin (on barge).

caille [kɑːj], *s.f.* *Orn:* Quail.

cailler [kɑje], *v.tr., i., & pr.* To clot, curdle; (of blood) to congeal.

caillou, *pl.* **-oux** [kaju], *s.m.* (a) Pebble. (b) Boulder. (c) *pl.* Cobble-stones.

caillouteux [-ju-], *a.* Flinty, stony (road); pebbly, shingly (beach).

caïman, *s.m.* *Rept:* Cayman, caiman.

Caire (le). *Pr.n.* Cairo.

caisse, *s.f.* **1.** (a) (Packing-)case. (b) Box, chest (of tea). **2.** Body (of vehicle). **3.** *Com:*

(a) Cash-box; till. *C. enregistreuse,* cash-register. (b) (i) Pay-desk. (ii) Counting-house. (c) **Petite caisse,** petty cash. **Livre de caisse,** cash-book. (d) Fund. *C. d'amortissement,* sinking-fund. (e) Bank. **Caisse d'épargne,** savings-bank. **4.** **Grosse caisse,** big drum.

caissier, *s.* Cashier.

caisson, *s.m.* Box. **1.** *C. à munitions,* ammunition waggon. **2.** *Nau:* Locker, bin.

cajoler, *v.tr.* To cajole, coax.

cajolerie, *s.f.* Cajolery, coaxing.

cal, *s.m.* Callosity. *pl. Des cals.*

calamité, *s.f.* Calamity, disaster.

calamiteux, *a.* Calamitous.

calandre, *s.f.* (a) Roller. (b) Mangle.

calandrer, *v.tr.* (a) To calender, roll. (b) *Laund:* To mangle.

calcaire. **1.** *a.* Calcareous. **2.** *s.m.* Limestone.

calcédoine, *s.f.* *Miner:* Chalcedony.

calciner, *v.tr.* (a) To calcine. (b) *Être calciné,* to be burnt to death.

calcium [-sjɔm], *s.m.* *Ch:* Calcium.

calcul, [-kyl], *s.m.* (a) Calculation, reckoning. *Tout calcul fait,* taking everything into account. (b) Arithmetic.

calculer, *v.tr.* To calculate, compute. **calculé,** *a.* Premeditated; deliberate.

cale¹, *s.f.* **1.** Hold (of ship). **2.** *C. de construction,* slip(way). **Cale sèche,** dry dock.

cale², *s.f.* Wedge, chock, block.

calebasse, *s.f.* Calabash, gourd.

calèche, *s.f.* Light four-wheeled carriage.

caleçon, *s.m.* (Pair of men's) drawers.

calembour, *s.m.* Pun; play on words.

calendrier, *s.m.* Calendar, almanac.

calepin, *s.m.* Note-book.

caler, *v.tr.* **1.** To chock (up), wedge (up) (piece of furniture). **2.** *Aut:* To stall (the engine). *v.i.* (Of engine) To stall.

calfater, *v.tr.* To caulk.

calfeutrer, *v.tr.* To stop (up) (chinks).

calibre, *s.m.* **1.** Calibre, bore (of fire-arm). **2.** *Tls:* Gauge.

calibrer, *v.tr.* To gauge.

calice¹, *s.m.* Chalice.

calice², *s.m.* *Bot:* Calyx, flower-cup.

calicot, *s.m.* Calico.

calife, *s.m.* Caliph.

califourchon (à), *adv.phr.* Astride.

câlin, *a.* Caressing, winning (way).

câlinerie, *s.f.* **1.** Caressing. **2.** Caress.

calleux, *a.* Horny, callous.

callosité, *s.f.* Callosity, callus.

calmant, *a.* Calming; soothing.

calme¹, *s.m.* Calm, calmness.

calme², *a.* Calm; still, quiet (air); cool (manner).

calmement, *adv.* Calmly, coolly.

calmer, *v.tr.* To calm, quiet, still, allay (fears); to soothe (pain). **se calmer,** to become calm; (of storm) to abate.

calomniateur, -trice. I. *s.* Calumniator, slanderer. **2.** *a.* Slanderous, libellous.

calomnie, *s.f.* Calumny, slander, libel.

calomnier, *v.tr.* To slander, libel.

calomnieux, *a.* Slanderous, libellous.

calorie, *s.f. Ph.Meas:* Calorie.

calot, *s.m. Mil:* Forage-cap.

calotte, *s.f.* Skull-cap.

calque, *s.m.* Tracing; traced design.

calquer, *v.tr.* To trace (*sur*, from); to make a tracing of (drawing).

calvaire, *s.m. R.C.Ch:* Calvary.

calviniste, *s.* Calvinist.

calvitie, *s.f.* Baldness.

camail [-ma:j], *s.m.* Cape, cloak.

camarade, *s.m. & f.* Comrade; mate.

camaraderie, *s.f.* Comradeship; good fellowship.

cambrer, *v.tr.* To bend. *C. la taille,* to throw out one's chest.

  se cambrer, to brace oneself back; to draw oneself up.

  cambré, *a.* **I.** Cambered, arched. **2.** Bent, warped, crooked.

cambriolage, *s.m.* Housebreaking, *F:* burgling.

cambrioler, *v.tr.* To break into (house), to burgle.

cambrioleur, -euse, *s.* Housebreaker; burglar.

camée, *s.m.* Cameo.

caméléon, *s.m.* Chameleon.

camélia, *s.m. Bot:* Camellia.

camelot, *s.m. F:* (*a*) Hawker. (*b*) Newsvendor.

camion, *s.m.* Dray, waggon, lorry.

camionnage, *s.m.* Cartage, haulage.

camionneur, *s.m.* Carrier, carman.

camisole, *s.f.* **I.** (Woman's) dressing-jacket. **2.** *C. de force,* strait-waistcoat.

camomille [-mi:j], *s.f.* Camomile.

camouflage, *s.m.* Disguising; camouflage.

camoufler, *v.tr.* To disguise; to fake. *Mil:* To camouflage.

camp, *s.m.* Camp. **I.** *Mil:* **Asseoir le camp,** to pitch camp. *F:* **Fiche(r) le camp,** to clear out. **2.** (*a*) Party, faction. (*b*) *Games:* Side.

campagnard. I. *a.* Country (gentleman); rustic. **2.** *s.* Countryman; rustic.

campagne, *s.f.* **I.** (*a*) Plain; open country. **En pleine campagne,** in the open (country). (*b*) Country(-side). **Partie de campagne,** picnic. **2.** *Mil:* (The) field. **Entrer en campagne,** to take the field. **3.** Campaign.

campagnol, *s.m. Z:* (Field)-vole.

campanile, *s.m.* Campanile; bell-tower.

campanule, *s.f. Bot:* Campanula.

Campêche, *Pr.n. Geog:* Campeachy. **Bois de Campêche,** logwood.

campement, *s.m.* **I.** Encamping. **2.** Encampment.

camper. I. *v.i.* To (en)camp. **2.** *v.tr.* To encamp (troops).

  se camper. I. To encamp. **2.** *F: Se c. devant qn,* to plant oneself in front of s.o.

camphre, *s.m.* Camphor.

camus, *a.* Flat-, snub-nosed (person).

Canada. *Pr.n.m.* Canada.

canadien, -ienne, *a. & s.* Canadian.

canaille [-na:j]. *s.f.* Rabble.

canal, -aux, *s.m.* **I.** Channel. **2.** Canal.

canalisation, *s.f.* **I.** Canalization (of river). **2.** Pipes. *C. électrique,* wiring.

canaliser, *v.tr.* **I.** To canalize (river). **2.** To lay down pipes.

canapé, *s.m.* **I.** Sofa, couch, settee. **2.** *Cu: C. d'anchois,* anchovy on toast.

canard, *s.m.* **I.** Duck; drake. *C. sauvage,* wild duck. **2.** *F:* False report, *canard.*

canarder, *v.tr. Mil:* To snipe.

canari, *s.m. Orn:* Canary.

cancan, *s.m.* **I.** *F: pl.* Tittle-tattle, gossip. **2.** Cancan (dance).

cancer [-sɛːr], *s.m.* **I.** *Astr:* **Le Cancer,** the Crab; Cancer. **2.** *Med:* Cancer.

cancéreux, *a.* Cancerous.

candélabre, *s.m.* Candelabrum.

candeur, *s.f.* Ingenuousness, artlessness.

candidat, *s.m.* Candidate, applicant.

candidature, *s.f.* Candidature.

candide, *a.* Ingenuous, guileless, artless.

cane, *s.f.* Duck (as opposed to drake).

caneton, *s.m.,* **canette,** *s.f.* Duckling.

canevas, *s.m.* Canvas.

caniche, *s.m. & f.* Poodle.

caniculaire, *a.* Sultry (heat).

canicule, *s.f.* The dog-days.

canif [-nif], *s.m.* Penknife.

canin. I. *a.* Canine. **Exposition canine,** dog-show. **2.** *s.f.* Canine, canine (tooth).

caniveau, *s.m.* Gutter.

canne, *s.f.* **I.** Cane, reed. **2.** Walking-stick; cane. **3.** *Canne à pêche,* fishing-rod.

cannelle, *s.f.* Cinnamon (bark).

cannelure, *s.f.* (*a*) Groove, channel, slot. *Arch:* Fluting. (*b*) Corrugation.

cannibale, *s.m.* Cannibal.

cannibalisme, *s.m.* Cannibalism.

canon[1], *s.m.* **I.** Gun, cannon. **2.** Barrel (of rifle).

canon[2], *s.m.* **I.** *Ecc:* Canon, rule (of an order). **2.** *Mus:* Canon, round, catch.

canonique, *a.* Canonical (book). **Age canonique,** *F:* respectable age.

canonnade, *s.f.* Cannonade; gun-fire.

canonnier, *s.m.* Gunner.

canonnière, *s.f. Navy:* Gunboat.

canot, *s.m.* (Open) boat; dinghy.

canotage, *s.m. Sp:* Boating, rowing.

canotier, *s.m.* **I.** Oarsman. **2.** Straw-hat.

cantate, *s.f. Mus:* Cantata.

cantatrice, *s.f.* (Professional) singer.

cantine, *s.f.* Canteen.

cantinier, *s.* Canteen-keeper.

cantique, *s.m.* (*a*) Canticle. **Le Cantique des cantiques,** the Song of Songs. (*b*) Hymn.

canton, *s.m.* Canton, district.

cantonade, *s.f. Th:* (The) wings. **Parler à la cantonade,** to speak 'off.'

cantonnement, *s.m.* **1.** Billeting. **2.** Cantonment, billets, quarters.
cantonner, *v.tr.* To quarter, billet (troops).
cantonnier, *s.m.* Roadman, road-mender.
caoutchouc, *s.m.* (India-)rubber.
cap [kap], *s.m.* **1.** Cape, headland. **La colonie du Cap,** Cape Colony. **2.** Head (of ship). *Changement de cap,* change of course.
capable, *a.* Capable.
capablement, *adv.* Capably, ably.
capacité, *s.f.* **1.** Capacity (of vase). **2.** Capacity, ability.
caparaçon, *s.m.* Caparison, trappings.
cape, *s.f.* (Hooded) cape, cloak. *F:* **Rire sous cape,** to laugh up one's sleeve.
capeline, *s.f.* Hooded cape.
capillaire. 1. *a.* Capillary (tube). **2.** *s.m.* Maidenhair fern.
capitaine, *s.m.* (*a*) Captain. *C. de port,* harbour-master. *Certificat de c.,* master's certificate. (*b*) Chief, head, leader.
capital, -aux. 1. *a.* (*a*) Capital (punishment). (*b*) Essential, principal. *La ville capitale, s.f.* **la capitale,** the capital. (*c*) *Lettre capitale, s.f.* **une capitale,** capital (letter). **2.** *s.m.* Capital, assets.
capitalisme, *s.m.* Capitalism.
capitaliste, *s.m. & f.* Capitalist.
capiteux, *a.* (Of wine) Heady.
capitonner, *v.tr.* To upholster (furniture).
capitulation, *s.f.* Capitulation, surrender.
capituler, *v.i.* To capitulate; to surrender.
caporal, -aux, *s.m.* **1.** Corporal. **2.** Cut tobacco.
capot, *s.m.* **1.** Hooded great-coat. **2.** Bonnet (of car).
capote, *s.f.* **1.** *Mil:* Great-coat. **2.** (Baby's) bonnet. **3.** *Veh:* Hood. **4.** Cowl (of chimney).
capoter, *v.i.* **1.** *Nau:* To capsize; to turn turtle. **2.** *Aut:* To overturn.
câpre, *s.f. Bot:* Caper.
caprice, *s.m.* Caprice, whim.
capricieusement, *adv.* Capriciously, whimsically.
capricieux, *a.* Capricious, whimsical.
capsule, *s.f.* Capsule.
capter, *v.tr.* **1.** To obtain by insidious means. *Tp:* To tap (messages). **2.** To recover (by-product).
captieux, *a.* Fallacious, captious (argument).
captif, *a. & s.* Captive; prisoner.
captivant, *a.* Captivating; winsome.
captiver, *v.tr.* To captivate, charm.
captivité, *s.f.* Captivity.
capture, *s.f.* **1.** Capture, seizure (of ship). **2.** Capture, prize.
capturer, *v.tr.* To capture (ship).
capuchon, *s.m.* **1.** (*a*) Hood. (*b*) *Ecc:* Cowl. **2.** Cap (of fountain-pen); chimney-cowl.
capucin, *s.m.* Capuchin friar.
capucine, *s.f.* **1.** Capuchin nun. **2.** *Bot:* Nasturtium.
caque, *s.f.* Keg; herring-barrel.

caquet, *s.m.* Cackle, cackling (of hens).
caquetage, *s.m.* **1.** Cackling (of hens). **2.** Chatter(ing).
caqueter, *v.i.* (je **caquète,** je **caquette**) **1.** (Of hen) To cackle. **2.** *F:* To chatter.
car, *conj.* For, because.
carabine, *s.f.* (Cavalry) carbine; rifle.
caracole, *s.f. Equit:* Caracol(e); half-turn.
caractère, *s.m.* **1.** Character; graphic symbol. *Typ:* (Metal) type. **2.** (*a*) Characteristic, feature. (*b*) Official capacity. **Avoir caractère pour faire qch.,** to be entitled to do sth. **3.** (*a*) Nature, disposition. (*b*) Personality, character. *Montrer du c.,* to show spirit.
caractériser, *v.tr.* To characterize. **se caractériser. 1.** To assume character. **2.** To be distinguished.
caractéristique. 1. *a.* Characteristic, distinctive. **2.** *s.f.* Characteristic.
carafe, *s.f.* Decanter; carafe.
carafon, *s.m.* Small carafe.
caraïbe. 1. *a.* Caribbean. **2.** *s.* Carib.
carambolage, *s.m. Bill:* Cannon.
caramboler, *v.i. Bill:* To cannon.
caramel, *s.m.* Caramel; burnt sugar.
carapace, *s.f.* Carapace, shell.
carat, *s.m.* Carat.
caravane, *s.f.* **1.** Caravan, desert convoy. **2.** Caravan (vehicle).
caravansérail [-ra:j], *s.m.* Caravanserai.
carbonate, *s.m. Ch:* Carbonate.
carbone, *s.m.* Carbon.
carbonique, *a. Ch:* Carbonic.
carboniser, *v.tr.* (*a*) To char (wood). (*b*) *Être carbonisé,* to be burnt to death.
carburant, *s.m.* Motor-fuel.
carburateur, *s.m. I.C.E:* Carburettor.
carbure, *s.m. Ch:* Carbide.
carcasse, *s.f.* **1.** Carcase. **2.** Framework.
cardiaque, *a.* Cardiac (murmur). **Crise cardiaque,** heart attack.
cardinal, -aux. 1. *a.* Cardinal (point). **2.** *s.m. Ecc:* Cardinal.
carême, *s.m.* Lent. *F:* **Figure de carême,** dismal face.
carénage, *s.m.* **1.** Careening (of ship). **2.** Stream-lining.
carène, *s.f.* Hull (of ship).
caréner, *v.tr.* (je **carène,** je **carénerai**) **1.** To careen (ship). **2.** To stream-line.
caresse, *s.f.* Caress.
caresser, *v.tr.* **1.** To caress, fondle. **Caresser qn du regard,** to look fondly at s.o. **2.** To cherish (hope).
cargaison, *s.f.* Cargo, freight.
cargo, *s.m.* Cargo-boat; tramp (steamer).
caricature, *s.f.* Caricature.
caricaturer, *v.tr.* To caricature.
caricaturiste, *s.m.* Caricaturist.
carie, *s.f.* Caries, decay (of bone).
carillon [-ij3], *s.m.* Chime(s), carillon.
carillonner [-ij3-], *v.i.* (*a*) To chime the bells; to ring a peal. (*b*) (Of bells) To chime.

carlingue [-ɛ̃g], *s.f. Av:* (*a*) Fuselage. (*b*) *F:* Cockpit; cabin.
carme, *a. & s.m.* Carmelite (friar).
carmélite, *s.f.* Carmelite (nun).
carmin, *s.m.* Carmine (colour).
carnage, *s.m.* Carnage, slaughter.
carnassier. **1.** *a.* Carnivorous. **2.** *s.m.* Carnivore. **3.** *s.f.* **Carnassière**, game-bag.
carnation, *s.f. Art:* Flesh-tint.
carnaval, *pl.* **-als**, *s.m.* Carnival.
carnet, *s.m.* Note-book. *C. de banque*, pass-book. *C. de chèques*, cheque-book.
carnivore, *a.* Carnivorous.
Caron. *Pr.n.m. Myth:* Charon.
carotte, *s.f.* **1.** Carrot. *a.inv. F:* Ginger (hair). **2.** Plug (of tobacco).
Carpathes. *Pr.n.m.pl.* **Les (monts) Carpathes**, the Carpathian Mountains.
carpe, *s.f. Ich:* Carp. *F:* **Faire des sauts de carpe**, to flop about, to somersault.
carpette, *s.f.* Rug.
carquois, *s.m.* Quiver.
carré. **1.** *a* (*a*) Square. *Mth:* **Nombre carré**, square number. **Tête carrée**, (i) level-headed man; (ii) stubborn man. (*b*) *F:* Plain, blunt (answer). **2.** *s.m.* (*a*) *Mth:* Square. (*b*) Landing (of a staircase). *C. de choux*, cabbage-patch. **Carré des officiers**, *Navy:* ward-room.
carreau, *s.m.* **1.** Small square. **2.** (*a*) (Flooring) tile. (*b*) **Carreau de vitre**, window-pane. **3.** Floor (of room). **4.** *Cards:* Diamonds.
carrefour, *s.m.* Cross-roads; (in town) square, circus. *F:* **Musicien de c.**, street musician.
carrelage, *s.m.* **1.** Tiling. **2.** Pavement or floor(ing).
carreler, *v.tr.* (je carrelle) **1.** To lay (floor) with tiles; to pave. **2.** Étoffe carrelée, check material.
carrelet, *s.m. Ich:* Plaice; dab.
carrément, *adv.* Square(ly). *Parler c.*, to speak (i) straightforwardly, (ii) bluntly.
carrer, *v.tr.* To square.
carrier, *s.m.* **1.** Quarryman. **2.** Quarry-owner.
carrière[1], *s.f.* **1.** Career. **Soldat de carrière**, regular (soldier). **2.** *F:* **Donner libre carrière à son imagination**, to give free play to one's fancy.
carrière[2], *s.f.* Stone-pit, quarry.
carriole, *s.f. Veh:* Light cart.
carrosse, *s.m. A:* Coach.
carrosserie, *s.f.* Coach-work.
carrossier, *s.m.* Coach-builder.
carrousel, *s.m.* **1.** *A:* (*a*) Tournament. (*b*) Tilt-yard. **2.** Merry-go-round.
carrure, *s.f.* Breadth across the shoulders. *Homme d'une belle c.*, well-built man.
cartable, *s.m.* **1.** Writing-pad. **2.** (Card-board) portfolio. **3.** School satchel.
carte, *s.f.* **1.** **Carte blanche**, full warrant to act for the best. **2.** Map. *C. d'état-major*, ordnance survey map. *C. routière*, road-map.

Perdre la carte, to lose one's bearings. **3.** (Piece of) cardboard. **Carte à jouer**, playing-card. *Jouer aux cartes*, to play cards. **Jouer cartes sur table**, (i) to show one's hand; (ii) to act fairly and above-board. *F:* **Connaître le dessous des cartes**, to be in the know. **Carte de visite**, visiting-card. *C. d'entrée*, admission card. **Carte postale**, post-card. **Carte de restaurant**, bill of fare; menu. *C. du jour*, menu for the day.
cartel, *s.m.* (*a*) Dial-case (of clock). (*b*) Wall-clock.
carter [-tɛːr], *s.m.* **1.** *Cy:* Gear-case. **2.** Casing (of crank). *Cin:* Spool-box.
carthaginois, *a. & s.* Carthaginian.
cartilage, *s.m.* Cartilage; *F:* gristle.
cartilagineux, *a.* Cartilaginous; *F:* gristly.
cartographe, *s.m.* Map-maker.
cartographie, *s.f.* Map-making, mapping.
cartomancie, *s.f.* Fortune-telling (by cards).
carton, *s.m.* **1.** Cardboard; paste-board. **2.** Cardboard box. *C. d'écolier*, satchel. *C. de bureau*, filing-case. **3.** *Art:* Cartoon; small sketch.
cartonnage, *s.m. Coll.* (Cardboard) boxes.
cartonner, *v.tr.* To bind (book) in boards.
cartonnier, *s.m.* (Cardboard) file.
carton-pâte, *s.m. inv.* Papier mâché.
cartouche. **1.** *s.m.* Scroll (round title, etc.); cartouche. **2.** *s.f.* Cartridge.
cartouchière, *s.f.* Cartridge-pouch.
carvi, *s.m. Bot:* Caraway.
cas, *s.m.* **1.** Case, instance. *Cas limite*, border-line case. *Cas imprévu*, emergency. *F:* **C'est bien le cas de le dire**, . . . and no mistake. **2.** Case, matter, affair. **3.** **Faire cas de qch.**, to value sth. **4.** *Gram:* Case. **5.** **En ce cas**, in that case. **Dans, en, aucun cas**, in no circumstances, on no account. **En tout cas**, **dans tous les cas**, in any case, at all events. **Le cas échéant**, should the occasion arise.
casanier, *a.* Home-loving; stay-at-home.
casaque, *s.f.* **1.** *Mil:* Cloak. *F:* **Tourner casaque**, to turn one's coat. **2.** (*a*) Coat, jacket (of jockey). (*b*) (Woman's) jumper.
casaquin, *s.m.* Dressing-jacket.
cascade, *s.f.* Cascade, waterfall.
case, *s.f.* **1.** Small dwelling; hut, cabin. **2.** (*a*) Compartment; pigeon-hole. (*b*) Division (on printed form). (*c*) Square (of chess-board).
caser, *v.tr.* To put away; to file (papers). *F: C. qn*, to find a place for s.o. **se caser**, to settle down.
caserne, *s.f.* (*a*) Barracks. (*b*) *C. de pompiers*, fire(-brigade) station.
caserner, *v.tr.* To quarter in barracks.
casier, *s.m.* **1.** Set of pigeon-holes. **2.** (*a*) Bin, rack. (*b*) *C. à musique*, music-cabinet.
casino, *s.m.* Casino.
casoar, *s.m. Orn:* Cassowary.
caspien, **-ienne**, *a.* **La mer Caspienne**, the Caspian (Sea).

casque, *s.m.* (*a*) Helmet. *C. blindé,* crash-helmet. (*b*) *W. Tel:* Casque téléphonique, head-phones.
casquette, *s.f.* Peaked cap.
cassage, *s.m.* Breaking.
cassant, *a.* **1.** (*a*) Brittle. (*b*) Crisp (biscuit). **2.** Curt, abrupt (tone of voice).
cassation, *s.f.* **1.** *Jur:* Cour de cassation, Supreme Court of Appeal. **2.** Reduction to the ranks.
casse[1], *s.f.* **1.** Cassia. **2.** *Pharm:* Senna.
casse[2], *s.f.* Breakage, damage. *F:* Il y aura de la casse, there will be trouble.
casse-cou, *s.m.inv.* **1.** Death-trap. **2.** Dare-devil.
casse-croûte, *s.m.inv.* Snack.
casse-noisette(s), *s.m.inv.* **1.** (Pair of) nut-crackers. **2.** *Orn:* Nuthatch.
casse-noix, *s.m.inv.* (Pair of) nut-crackers.
casse-pierre(s), *s.m.inv.* *Bot:* Saxifrage.
casser, *v.tr.* **1.** To break, snap; to crack (nuts). Se casser la tête, (i) to break one's head; (ii) *F:* to cudgel one's brains. Applaudir à tout casser, to bring down the house (with applause). **2.** To cashier, break. **3.** *Jur:* To quash, set aside (verdict).
se casser, to break, snap, give way.
cassé, *a.* Broken, worn out (voice).
casserole, *s.f.* (Sauce)pan, stewpan.
casse-tête, *s.m.inv.* **1.** Club; loaded stick; truncheon. **2.** Puzzling task.
cassette, *s.f.* (*a*) Casket. (*b*) Money-box.
casseur, -euse, *s.* Breaker.
cassis [-sis], *s.m.* **1.** Black-currant. **2.** Black-currant liqueur.
cassonade, *s.f.* Brown sugar, moist sugar.
cassure, *s.f.* **1.** (*a*) Break, fracture. (*b*) Fractured edge. **2.** Broken fragment.
castagnettes, *s.f.pl.* Castanets.
caste, *s.f.* Caste. Esprit de caste, class consciousness. Hors caste, outcaste.
castillan [-tijõ], *a. & s.* Castilian.
castor, *s.m.* Beaver.
casuel, -elle [-ɥɛl]. **1.** (*a*) Fortuitous, accidental. (*b*) *Gram:* Flexions casuelles, case-endings. **2.** *s.m.* Perquisites.
casuellement [-ɥɛl-], *adv.* Fortuitously, accidentally.
casuiste, *s.m.* Casuist.
casuistique, *s.f.* Casuistry.
cataclysme, *s.m.* Cataclysm, disaster.
catacombes, *s.f.pl.* Catacombs.
catafalque, *s.m.* Catafalque.
cataire, *s.f. Bot:* Catmint.
catalan, *a. & s.* Catalan, Catalonian.
catalepsie, *s.f.* Catalepsy.
cataleptique, *a. & s.* Cataleptic (patient).
Catalogne, *Pr.n.f.* Catalonia.
catalogue [-lɔg], *s.m.* Catalogue, list.
cataloguer [-ge], *v.tr.* To catalogue; to list.
catalogueur [-gœ:r], *s.m.* Cataloguer.
catalyse, *s.f. Ch:* Catalysis.
catalytique, *a. Ch:* Catalytic.
cataplasme, *s.m.* Poultice.

cataracte, *s.f.* **1.** Cataract, falls. **2.** *Med:* Cataract.
catarrhe, *s.m. Med:* Catarrh.
catastrophe, *s.f.* Catastrophe.
catéchiser, *v.tr.* **1.** (*a*) *Ecc:* To catechize. (*b*) *F:* To coach (s.o.) up (in what to say). **2.** (*a*) To reason with. (*b*) To lecture.
catéchisme, *s.m.* Catechism.
catéchiste, *s.m. & f.* Catechizer.
catégorie, *s.f.* Category.
catégorique, *a.* Categorical. *Refus c.,* flat refusal.
catégoriquement, *adv.* (*a*) Categorically. (*b*) Clearly, explicitly.
cathédrale, *s.f.* Cathedral.
cathode, *s.f. El:* Cathode.
catholicisme, *s.m.* (Roman) Catholicism.
catholique. **1.** Orthodox. **2.** *a. & s.* (Roman) Catholic.
catimini (en), *adv.phr.* Stealthily.
Caton. *Pr.n.m. Rom. Hist:* Cato.
Caucase (le). *Pr.n.* The Caucasus.
cauchemar, *s.m.* Nightmare.
caudal, -aux, *a. Z:* Caudal.
cauri, *s.m.* Cowrie.
causal, *a.* No *m.pl.* Causal, causative.
cause, *s.f.* **1.** Cause. Être cause de qch., to be the cause of sth. *Il ne viendra pas et pour cause,* he will not come and for a very good reason. *Prep.phr.* A cause de, on account of; owing to. **2.** (*a*) *Jur:* Cause, suit, action. *Avocat sans cause,* briefless barrister. Être en cause, (i) to be a party to a suit; (ii) *F:* to be concerned in sth. *Mettre en c. la probité de qn,* to question s.o.'s honesty. Questions hors de cause, irrelevant questions. Mettre qn hors de cause, to exonerate s.o. Agir en connaissance de cause, to act with full knowledge of the case. (*b*) Faire cause commune avec qn, to make common cause with s.o.; to side with s.o.
causer[1], *v.tr.* To cause; to bring about.
causer[2], *v.i.* To converse, chat. Causer de la pluie et du beau temps, to indulge in small talk.
causerie, *s.f.* (*a*) Talk, chat. (*b*) Chatty lecture.
causette, *s.f. F:* Little chat.
causeur, -euse. **1.** *a.* Talkative, chatty. **2.** *s.* Talker, conversationalist.
caustique. **1.** *a.* (*a*) *Ch:* Caustic. (*b*) Caustic, cutting (remark). **2.** *s.m. Pharm:* Caustic.
caustiquement, *adv.* Caustically, bitingly.
cauteleusement, *adv.* **1.** Cunningly, slyly. **2.** Warily, cautiously.
cauteleux, *a.* **1.** Cunning, wily, sly. **2.** Wary, cautious.
cautériser, *v.tr.* To cauterize (wound).
caution, *s.f.* **1.** Security, guarantee. Donner caution pour qn, to go bail for s.o. Mettre qn en liberté sous caution, to let s.o. out on bail. *Com: Verser une c.,* to pay a deposit. *F:* Sujet à caution, unconfirmed (news). **2.** Surety, guaranty. Se rendre caution de

qn, (i) to go bail for s.o. ; (ii) *Com:* to stand surety for s.o.

cautionnement, *s.m. Com:* Guarantee.

cavalcade, *s.f.* **1.** Cavalcade. **2.** Pageant.

cavale, *s.f. Lit:* Mare.

cavalerie, *s.f.* Cavalry.

cavalier. 1. *s.* Rider; horseman. *a.* **Piste cavalière,** riding track. **2.** *s.m. (a) Mil:* Trooper. *(b) Chess:* Knight. *(c)* Gentleman, gallant. *(d)* Partner (to lady at ball). **3.** *s.m. (a)* Staple. *(b)* Rider (of balance). **4.** *a.* Cavalier, off-hand. **A la cavalière,** in a cavalier, off-hand, manner.

cavalièrement, *adv.* Cavalierly, off-handedly.

cave¹, *a.* Hollow, sunken (cheeks).

cave², *s.f.* Cellar, vault. **Avoir une bonne cave,** to keep a good cellar (of wine).

caveau, *s.m.* **1.** Small (wine-)cellar; vault. **2.** Burial vault.

caver, *v.tr.* To hollow (out), undermine. **se caver,** to become hollow.

caverne, *s.f. (a)* Cave, cavern. *(b)* Den.

caverneux, *a.* Hollow, sepulchral (voice).

caviar, *s.m.* Caviar(e).

cavité, *s.f.* Cavity, hollow.

ce¹, *dem.pron.neut.* (C' before parts of *être* beginning with a vowel. Also *ç'a été, ç'aura été.*) It, that. (a) *C'est faux!* it is untrue ! *Est-ce assez?* is that enough ? *(b)* (With a 3rd pers. pl. complement the verb should be in the plural, but familiar usage allows the singular.) *C'est moi, c'est nous, ce sont eux, F: c'est eux,* it is I, we, they. **Si ce n'est,** except, unless (This phr. is invariable.) *(c)* **Ce . . . ici** = CECI. *Ce n'est pas ici une auberge!* this is not an inn ! *(d)* **Ce . . . là** = CELA. *Ce n'est pas là mon parapluie,* that is not my umbrella. *(e) Paris, c'est bien loin!* it's a far cry to Paris ! *(f) C'est demain dimanche,* to-morrow is Sunday. *(g)* (i) *F: C'était inutile de sonner,* you need not have rung. (ii) *C'est assez qu'il veuille bien pardonner,* that he is willing to forgive is enough. *(h)* **C'est . . . que.** *C'est un bon petit garçon que Jean,* a fine little chap is John ! (i) (i) *C'est qu'il fait froid!* it is cold and no mistake ! (ii) *Est-ce que je peux entrer?* may I come in ? **2.** *(a) Vous devriez rougir, ce me semble,* it seems to me that you ought to blush. *(b)* **Ce disant,** so saying. **3.** *(a)* **Ce qui, ce que,** etc. = what *Je sais ce qui est arrivé,* I know what has happened. **Ce que c'est que de nous!** what poor mortals we are ! *(b)* **Ce qui, ce que,** etc. = which. *Il est parti, ce que je ne savais pas,* he has gone, which I did not know. *(c)* **Tout ce qui, que,** everything, all (that). *Tout ce que vous voudrez,* whatever you like. *(d) F: Ce qu'elle a changé!* how she has changed ! **4. Sur ce,** thereupon. **5.** *Conj.phr. Tenez-vous beaucoup à ce qu'il vienne?* are you very anxious for him to come ? **6.** *Prep. phr.* **Pour ce qui est de cela,** for that matter.

ce² (**cet**), **cette, ces,** *dem. a.* (The form **cet** is used before a sb. or adj. beginning with a vowel or *h* 'mute'.) This, that, *pl.* these, those. **1.** *Un de ces jours,* one of these days. **Ce dernier,** the latter. **2.** *pl.* (Deferential use) *Ces dames sont au salon,* the ladies are in the drawing-room. **3. Ce . . . -ci,** this. **Ce . . . -là,** that. *Prenez cette tasse-ci,* take this cup.

ceci, *dem. pron. neut.* This (thing). NOTE : An adjective qualifying *ceci* is partitive. **Le cas offre ceci de particulier,** the case is peculiar in this.

cécité, *s.f.* Blindness.

céder, *v.* (je **cède** ; je **céderai**) **I.** *v.tr. (a)* (i) To give up, yield. **Céder le pas à qn,** to give way to s.o. (ii) To transfer, assign. **Maison à céder,** business for sale. *(b)* **Le céder à qn en qch.,** to be inferior to s.o. in sth. **2.** *v.i.* To yield, give way. *Le câble céda sous l'effort,* the rope parted under the strain. *C. aux circonstances,* to yield to circumstances.

cédille [-di:j], *s.f. Gram:* Cedilla.

cédrat, *s.m. Bot:* Citron.

cédratier, *s.m. Bot:* Citron(-tree).

cèdre, *s.m. Bot:* Cedar(-tree, -wood).

ceign-ais, -ant, -e, -is, etc. See CEINDRE.

ceindre, *v.tr.* (Conj. like PEINDRE) **1.** To gird. *(a) C. une épée,* to buckle on a sword. *(b) C. qn de qch.,* to gird, encircle, s.o. with sth. **2.** To encompass (a town with walls).

ceinture, *s.f.* **1.** *(a)* Girdle ; (leather) belt ; (silk) sash ; waistband. *C. de sauvetage,* life-belt. *(b)* Waist, middle (of the body). **2.** Girdle, circle (of walls) ; belt (of hills). **3.** *Rail:* Chemin de fer de petite, grande, ceinture, inner-, outer-circle railway.

ceinturon, *s.m.* Waist-belt, sword-belt.

cela, *F:* **ça,** *dem. pron. neut. (a)* That (thing). **Qu'est-ce que c'est que cela,** *F:* **que ça?** what is that? NOTE. An adj. qualifying *cela* is partitive. *S'il n'y a que cela de nouveau,* if that is all that is new. *(b)* That, it. *Cela ne vous regarde pas,* it is no business of yours. *(c) F: Comment allez-vous?—*Comme **ci comme** ça, how are you?—So so. *(d)* **C'est ça,** that's it, that's right. **C'est cela même!** the very thing ! **Il n'y a que ça,** there's nothing like it. **Et avec cela, madame?** and what else, madam? *F:* **Allons, pas de ça!** come, none of that ! **Où ça?** where? **Comment ça?** how?

célébration, *s.f.* Celebration.

célèbre, *a.* Celebrated, famous (*par,* for).

célébrer, *v.tr.* (je **célèbre** ; je **célébrerai**) **1.** To celebrate ; (i) to solemnize (rite) ; (ii) to observe, keep (feast). **2.** To extol. *C. les louanges de qn,* to sing s.o.'s praises.

célébrité, *s.f.* Celebrity.

celer, *v.tr.* (je **cèle**) *A:* To conceal, keep secret (*à,* from).

céleri, *s.m.* Celery. **Pied de c.,** head of celery.

célérité, *s.f.* Celerity, dispatch.

céleste, a. Celestial, heavenly.

célibat, s.m. Celibacy.

célibataire, a. & s. Unmarried, single (man, woman). s.m. Bachelor. s.f. Spinster.

celle, celle-ci, celle-là. See CELUI.

cellulaire, a. 1. Cellular (tissue). 2. Voiture cellulaire, police-van; F: Black Maria.

cellule, s.f. Cell.

celluloïd(e), s.m. Ind: Celluloid.

cellulose, s.f. Com: Cellulose.

celte. 1. a. & s.m. Ling: = CELTIQUE. 2. s.m. & f. Celt.

celtique, a. & s.m. Celtic (language).

celui, celle, pl. **ceux, celles,** dem. pron. 1. (a) The one; those. Celui qui était parti le dernier, the one who started last. (b) He, she, those. C. qui mange peu dort bien, he who eats little sleeps well. 2. Mes livres et ceux de Jean, my books and John's. 3. Les rails en acier et ceux en fer, steel rails and iron ones. 4. Celui-ci, ceux-ci, this (one), these; the latter. Celui-là, ceux-là, that (one), those; the former. 5. Celui-là is used for celui 1, when the rel. pron. does not follow at once. Celui-là est heureux qui, he is happy who.

cénacle, s.m. 1. Ant: Supping-room; 'upper chamber.' 2. C. littéraire, literary group; coterie.

cendre, s.f. Ash(es), cinders. Mercredi des Cendres, Ash-Wednesday. Visage couleur de c., ashen face.

cendré, a. (Ash-)grey; ashy.

cendrée, s.f. Sp: Piste en cendrée, (i) cinder-track; (ii) dirt-track.

cendreux, a. 1. Ashy; ash-grey. 2. Full of ashes; gritty.

cendrier, s.m. (a) Ash-bin; ash-box (of locomotive). (b) Ash-tray.

Cendrillon [-ijɔ̃]. Pr.n.f. Cinderella.

cène, s.f. (a) La (Sainte) Cène, the Last Supper. (b) Holy Communion.

cénotaphe, s.m. Cenotaph.

censé, a. Supposed. Je ne suis pas c. le savoir, I am not supposed to know.

censément, adv. F: Il est c. le maître, (i) he is supposed to be the master; (ii) he is virtually the master.

censeur, s.m. 1. Critic, F: fault-finder. a. Esprit c., carping spirit. 2. (a) Censor. (b) Fin: Auditor. 3. Sch: Vice-principal (of lycée).

censurable, a. Censurable; open to censure.

censure, s.f. 1. (a) Censorship. (b) Audit (of accounts). 2. Censure, blame.

censurer, v.tr. 1. To censure. 2. To censor.

cent. 1. (a) num. a. (Takes a plural s when multiplied by a preceding numeral but not followed by another numeral. Does not vary when used as an ordinal) (A, one) hundred. Deux cents hommes, two hundred men. Deux cent cinquante hommes, two hundred and fifty men. La page deux cent, page two hundred. Faire les cent pas, to pace up and down. (b) s.m.inv. A hundred. Sept pour cent,

seven per cent. 2. s.m.var. Un cent d'œufs, a hundred eggs.

centaine, s.f. Une c. de francs, a hundred francs or so. Atteindre la centaine, to live to be a hundred.

centaure, s.m. Myth: Centaur.

centaurée, s.f. Bot: Centaury.

centenaire. 1. a. Ancient. 2. s.m. & f. Centenarian. 3. s.m. Centenary.

centennal, -aux, a. Centennial.

centième. 1. num. a. & s. Hundredth. 2. s.m. Hundredth (part).

centigrade, a. Centigrade.

centigramme, s.m. Centigramme.

centilitre, s.m. Centilitre.

centime, s.m. Centime.

centimètre, s.m. 1. Centimetre. 2. F: Tape-measure.

centipède, s.m. Centipede.

central, -aux. 1. a. Central. (a) Middle (point). (b) Principal, head (office). 2. (a) s.m. Central téléphonique, telephone exchange. (b) s.f. Centrale (électrique), power station.

centralement, adv. Centrally.

centralisation, s.f. Centralization.

centraliser, v.tr. To centralize.

centre, s.m. Centre; middle.

centrer, v.tr. To centre, adjust (wheel).

centrifuge, a. Centrifugal (force).

centripète, a. Centripetal (force).

centuple, a. & s.m. Centuple; hundred-fold.

cep [sɛ(p)], s.m. Vine-stock.

cépage, s.m. Vine-plant.

cèpe, s.m. Bot: Flap mushroom.

cependant. 1. adv. Meanwhile; in the meantime. 2. conj. Yet, still, nevertheless.

céramique. 1. a. Ceramic (arts). 2. s.f. Ceramics; pottery.

Cerbère. Pr.n.m. Myth: Cerberus.

cerceau, s.m. Hoop.

cercle, s.m. 1. Circle. (a) C. d'activités, circle, sphere, of activities. (b) Circle, set (of friends). (c) Club. 2. Hoop, ring, tyre. 3. (a) Dial. (b) Quart de cercle, quadrant.

cercler, v.tr. 1. To encircle, to ring. 2. To hoop (barrel); to tyre (wheel).

cercueil [-kœ:j], s.m. Coffin; casket.

céréale, a.f. Plantes céréales, s.f.pl. céréales, cereal plants; cereals.

cérébral, -aux, a. Cerebral. Fatigue cérébrale, brain-fag.

cérémonial, -aux. 1. a. Ceremonial. 2. s.m. No pl. Ceremonial.

cérémonie, s.f. Ceremony. Visite de cérémonie, formal call. F: Faire des cérémonies, to stand on ceremony.

cérémonieusement, adv. Ceremoniously.

cérémonieux, a. Ceremonious, formal.

cerf [sɛːr, occ. sɛrf, pl. sɛːr], s.m. Stag, hart.

cerfeuil [-fœ:j], s.m. Bot: Chervil.

cerf-volant [sɛrvɔlɑ̃], s.m. 1. Ent: Stag-beetle. 2. (Paper) kite. pl. Des cerfs-volants.

cerisaie, s.f. Cherry-orchard.

cerise. 1. *s.f.* Cherry. *F:* **Faire deux morceaux d'une cerise,** to take two bites at a cherry. **2.** *s.m. & a.inv.* Cherry-red, cerise.

cerisier, *s.m.* Cherry-tree, -wood.

cerne, *s.m.* Ring, circle (round eyes).

cerneau, *s.m.* Green walnut.

cernement, *s.m.* Surrounding (of army); investing (of town).

cerner, *v.tr.* **1.** To encircle, surround (army); to invest (town). **Avoir les yeux cernés,** to have rings under the eyes. **2.** To husk (walnuts). **3.** To girdle, ring (tree).

céroplastique, *s.f.* Wax-modelling.

certain. 1. *a.* (a) Certain, sure. **Tenir qch. pour certain,** to look on sth. as a certainty. (b) *Il est c. de réussir,* he is sure he will succeed. (c) Fixed, stated (date). **2.** *indef. a. & pron.* Some, certain. *Certains affirment,* some (people) maintain. *Après un c.: emps,* after a certain time.

certainement, *adv.* Certainly, assuredly.

certes [sɛrt], *adv.* (Oui) **certes!** yes indeed!

certificat, *s.m.* Certificate, testimonial.

certification, *s.f.* Certification.

certifier, *v.tr.* To certify, attest. *C. qch. à qn,* to assure s.o. of sth.

certitude, *s.f.* Certainty. **J'en ai la certitude,** I am sure of it.

céruse, *s.f.* White lead.

cerveau, *s.m.* (a) Brain. **Rhume de cerveau,** cold in the head. *F:* **Vous me rompez le cerveau,** you give me a headache. (b) *F:* Mind, intellect, brains. **Cerveau creux,** dreamer. **Cerveau brûlé,** hot-head.

cervelas, *s.m. Cu:* Saveloy.

cervelle, *s.f.* **1.** *Anat:* Brain(s) (as matter). **Brûler la cervelle à qn,** to blow s.o.'s brains out. **2.** *F:* Mind, brains. **Se creuser la cervelle pour,** to rack one's brains to.

Cervin. *Pr.n.m.* **Le Mont Cervin,** the Matterhorn.

ces. See CE[2].

cessation, *s.f.* Cessation, ceasing.

cesse, *s.f.* Cease, ceasing. **Sans cesse,** unceasingly.

cesser, *v.* To cease, leave off, stop. **1.** *v.i.* **Faire cesser qch.,** to put a stop to sth. *C. de faire qch.,* to cease doing sth. **2.** *v.tr. C. le travail,* to cease, leave off, work.

cession, *s.f.* **1.** *Jur:* Transfer, assignment. **2.** Delivery (of heat); supply (of power).

cessionnaire, *s.m. Jur:* Transferee.

c'est-à-dire, *conj.phr.* **1.** That is (to say); *i.e.;* in other words. **2.** *F:* **C'est-à-dire que** + *ind.,* the fact is that . . . .

césure, *s.f. Pros:* Caesura.

cet. See CE[2].

cétacé, *a. & s.m.* Cetacean.

cette. See CE[2].

ceux. See CELUI.

Ceylan. *Pr.n.m.* Ceylon.

chablis, *s.m.* Chablis (wine).

chabot, *s.m. Ich:* Chub.

chacal, *pl.* **-als** [-kal], *s.m.* Jackal.

chacun, *pron.* **1.** Each; every one; each one. *Trois francs c.,* three francs each. **2.** Everybody, everyone. **Chacun son goût,** every man to his taste.

chafouin, *a. & s.m. F:* Sly-looking (person).

chagrin[1], *s.m.* (a) Grief, sorrow, affliction, trouble. (b) Vexation, annoyance.

chagrin[2], *s.m.* Shagreen; grain-leather.

chagrin[3], *a.* **1.** Sad; troubled (de, at); distressed (de, at). **2.** Peevish, fretful.

chagrinant, *a.* (a) Distressing, sad. (b) Provoking, vexing.

chagriner, *v.tr.* **1.** To grieve, distress. **2.** To vex, annoy.

se chagriner, to grieve; to fret.

chah, *s.m.* Shah.

chahut, *s.m. F:* Rag; rowdyism. **Faire du chahut,** to kick up a shindy.

chahuter, *v.i. F:* To kick up a shindy.

chaîne, *s.f.* **1.** (a) Chain. *Nau:* Cable. (b) Shackles, fetters, bonds. **2.** **Chaîne de montagnes,** mountain range. **C. d'idées,** train of thought. **3.** *Tex:* Warp.

chaînette, *s.f.* Small chain.

chaînon, *s.m.* Link (of chain).

chair, *s.f.* Flesh. **1.** *Blessure dans les chairs,* flesh-wound. *F:* **Voir qn en chair et en os,** to see s.o. in the flesh. **Être (bien) en chair,** to be nice and plump. *F:* **Chair de poule,** goose-flesh. **2.** (a) Meat. *F:* **Battre qn en chair à pâté,** to make mincemeat of s.o. **Chair à canon,** cannon-fodder. (b) Pulp (of peach).

chaire, *s.f.* **1.** Chair, throne. **2.** Pulpit. **3.** (a) Chair, desk, rostrum (of lecturer). (b) Professorship.

chaise, *s.f.* **1.** (a) Chair, seat. *Ecc:* **Chaise de chœur,** stall. (b) *C. roulante,* Bath-chair. **2.** *A:* **Chaise à porteurs,** sedan-chair. **Chaise de poste,** post-chaise.

chaise-longue, *s.f.* Lounge-chair; couch. *pl. Des chaises-longues.*

chaland[1], *s.m.* Lighter, barge.

chaland[2], *s.* Customer, purchaser.

chaldéen, -enne [kal-], *a. & s.* Chaldean.

châle, *s.m.* Shawl.

chalet, *s.m.* (a) Chalet. (b) Country cottage.

chaleur, *s.f.* (a) Heat, warmth. "Craint la chaleur," 'to be kept in a cool place.' *pl.* **Les chaleurs,** the hot weather. (b) Ardour, zeal. **Parler avec chaleur,** to speak warmly.

chaleureusement, *adv.* Warmly, cordially.

chaleureux, *a.* Warm (thanks); cordial (welcome); gushing (compliments).

chaloupe, *s.f.* Launch; long-boat.

chalumeau, *s.m.* **1.** Straw (for drinking). **2.** *Mus:* Pipe. **3.** Blow-pipe; blow-lamp.

chalut, *s.m. Fish:* Drag-net; trawl.

chalutage, *s.m.* Trawling.

chaluter, *v.i.* To trawl.

chalutier, *s.m.* Trawler or drifter.

Cham [kam]. *Pr.n.m. B.Hist:* Ham.

chamailler [-ɔje], *v.tr. F:* To nag at, squabble with (s.o.).

se chamailler, to bicker, squabble.

chamaillerie [-ojri], *s.f.* **1.** Bickering, quarrelling. **2.** Squabble, wrangle.

chamarrer, *v.tr.* To bedizen, bedeck.

chamarrure, *s.f.* Bedizenment.

chambard, *s.m.* P: Upset, upheaval; row.

chambarder. P: **1.** *v.tr.* (*a*) To sack, rifle. (*b*) To smash up. **2.** *v.i.* To racket.

chambardeur, *s.m.* Rowdy.

chambellan, *s.m.* Chamberlain.

chambranle, *s.m.* **1.** Frame (of door). **2.** Mantelpiece.

chambre, *s.f.* **1.** Room, chamber. (*a*) *C. à deux lits,* double(-bedded) room. *C. d'ami,* spare (bed)room. *C. d'enfants,* nursery. Faire une chambre, to clean out, tidy, a room. (*b*) *C. de chauffe,* boiler-house. **2.** *Adm:* Chamber, house. Chambres du Parlement, Houses of Parliament. **3.** *Tchn:* Chamber, cavity, space. Chambre à air, inner tube (of tyre). *Phot:* Chambre noire, (i) camera (body); (ii) dark-room.

chambrée, *s.f.* **1.** Roomful (of people sharing a room). **2.** Barrack-room.

chambrette, *s.f.* F: Little room; attic.

chameau, *s.m.* **1.** (*a*) Camel. (*b*) P: (Of man) Dirty dog. **2.** Shunting engine.

chamelier, *s.m.* Camel-driver; cameleer.

chamelle, *s.f.* She-camel.

chamois, *s.m.* Chamois. Peau de chamois, wash-leather, chamois leather, shammy.

champ[1], *s.m.* Field. **1.** (*a*) Prendre, couper, à travers champs, to go, cut, across country. *F:* Prendre la clef des champs, to decamp, abscond. A tout bout de champ, repeatedly; at every turn. (*b*) *C. d'aviation,* flying ground. *C. de tir,* rifle-range. *Mil:* Battre aux champs, to beat the general salute. **2.** (*a*) Field of action; range, scope. *F:* Le champ est libre, the coast is clear. Être à bout de champ, to be at the end of one's tether. (*b*) *C. d'une lunette,* field of a telescope.

champ[2], *s.m.* Edge, side.

Champagne. **1.** *Pr.n.f.* Champagne. **2.** *s.m.* (Also vin de Champagne) Champagne. **3.** *s.f.* Fine champagne, liqueur brandy.

champenois, *a. & s.* (Native) of Champagne.

champêtre, *a.* Rustic, rural. Garde champêtre, rural policeman.

champignon, *s.m.* **1.** (*a*) *C. comestible,* mushroom. (*b*) *C. vénéneux,* fungus, toadstool. **2.** *F:* Thief, stranger (in candle).

champion, -ionne, *s.* Champion.

championnat, *s.m.* Championship.

chance, *s.f.* **1.** Chance. *Il a peu de chances de réussir,* he has little chance of succeeding. **2.** Luck, fortune. Souhaiter bonne chance à qn, to wish s.o. good luck. Avoir de la chance, to be in luck's way.

chancelant, *a.* Staggering, tottering.

chanceler, *v.i.* (je chancelle) To stagger, totter.

chancelier, *s.m.* Chancellor

chancelière, *s.f.* Foot-muff.

chancellerie, *s.f.* **1.** Chancellery. **2.** Secretaryship (of a legation).

chanceux, *a.* F: **1.** Hazardous. **2.** Lucky.

chancre, *s.m.* **1.** Canker. **2.** Ulcer.

chancreux, *a.* (*a*) Cankerous. (*b*) Cankered.

chandail [-da:j], *s.m. Cost:* Sweater.

Chandeleur (la), *s.* Candlemas.

chandelier, *s.m.* **1.** Candle-maker. **2.** Candlestick.

chandelle, *s.f.* **1.** (*a*) (Tallow) candle. *F:* Économies de bouts de chandelle, cheese-paring economy. Voir trente-six chandelles, to see stars. (*b*) (Church) candle, taper. *F:* Je vous dois une fière chandelle, I owe you more than I can repay. **2.** Chandelle de glace, icicle. **3.** (Of aeroplane) Monter en chandelle, to zoom.

chanfrein[1], *s.m.* Forehead (of horse).

chanfrein[2], *s.m.* Chamfer, bevelled edge.

chanfreiner, *v.tr.* To chamfer, bevel.

change, *s.m.* **1.** *Fin:* Exchange. Lettre de change, bill of exchange. **2.** Donner le change à qn, to deceive s.o.

changeable, *a.* **1.** Changeable. **2.** Exchangeable.

changeant, *a.* Changing. *D'humeur changeante,* fitful. Taffetas changeant, shot silk.

changement, *s.m.* Change; alteration. *C. de marée,* turn of the tide. *C. en mal,* change for the worse. *Mch:* Changement de marche, reversing; reversing gear.

changer, *v.* (n. changeons) **1.** *v.tr.* To change or exchange. **2.** *v.tr.* To change, alter. *F: La campagne me changera,* the country will be a change for me. **3.** *v.i.* To undergo a change. *Le temps va c.,* the weather is going to change

se changer. 1. To change; to alter. **2.** To change one's clothes; *F:* to change.

changeur, *s.m.* Money-changer.

chanoine, *s.m. Ecc:* Canon.

chanson, *s.f.* **1.** Song. *C. de bord,* sea-shanty. *F:* C'est toujours la même chanson! it's the same old story. **2.** Song, lay.

chansonnette, *s.f.* Comic song with patter.

chansonnier, *s.* **1.** Song-writer. **2.** *s.m.* Song-book.

chant, *s.m.* **1.** Singing; song. Leçon de c., singing lesson. Chant du coq, crowing of the cock. **2.** Melody, air. **3.** Canto (of poem).

chantage, *s.m.* Blackmail, extortion.

chantant, *a.* (*a*) Sing-song. (*b*) *Soirée chantante,* musical evening. (*c*) Melodious, tuneful.

chanteclair, *s.m. Lit:* Chanticleer.

chantepleure, *s.f.* Spout (of gutter).

chanter, *v.tr.* To sing. **1.** Chanter victoire sur qn, to crow over s.o. Faire chanter qn, to blackmail s.o. Qu'est-ce que vous me chantez? what fairy-tale is this you are telling me? Si ça me chante, if it suits me. **2.** (Of birds) To sing; (of cock) to crow; (of cricket) to chirp.

chanteur, -euse, *s.* Singer, vocalist. Maître chanteur, *F:* blackmailer.

chantier, *s.m.* Yard. *C. de construction,* (i) ship(-building) yard; (ii) slip-way.

F: Avoir une œuvre sur le chantier, to have a piece of work in hand, *F:* on the stocks.

chantonnement, *s.m.* Humming (of tune).

chantonner, *v.tr. & i.* To hum; to sing softly.

chantourner, *v.tr.* To cut, saw (sth.) round a curved outline.

chantre, *s.m.* (a) Cantor. **Grand chantre,** precentor. (b) *Lit:* Singer (of the past).

chanvre, *s.m.* Hemp. **Cheveux couleur de chanvre,** flaxen hair.

chaos [kao], *s.m.* Chaos, confusion.

chaotique [kao-], *a.* Chaotic, confused.

chape, *s.f.* **1.** *Ecc:* Cope. **2.** Covering. (a) Tread of a tyre. (b) Coping (of bridge).

chapeau, *s.m.* **1.** Hat. **C. mou,** soft felt hat. **C. gibus, c. mécanique,** opera-hat. **Saluer qn d'un coup de chapeau,** to raise one's hat to s.o. **Chapeau bas,** hat in hand. **2.** Cover. (a) *Cu:* Piecrust. (b) Cap (of fountain-pen). (c) Hood, cowl (of chimney).

chapelet, *s.m.* (String of) beads. **Égrener son chapelet,** to tell one's beads. **C. d'oignons,** string, rope, of onions.

chapelier, *s.* Hatter.

chapelle, *s.f.* (a) Chapel. **C. de la Vierge,** Lady chapel. (b) *Ecc:* **Maître de chapelle,** choir-master.

chapellerie, *s.f.* Hat-trade, -shop.

chaperon, *s.m.* **1.** Hood. **Le Petit Chaperon rouge,** Little Red Riding Hood. **2.** Chaperon. **3.** Coping (of wall).

chaperonner, *v.tr.* **1.** To hood (falcon). **2.** To chaperon. **3.** *Const:* To cope (wall).

chapiteau, *s.m.* Capital (of column).

chapitre, *s.m.* **1.** *Ecc:* Chapter. *F:* **Tenir chapitre,** to deliberate. **2.** (a) Chapter (of book). (b) Head(ing); item (of expenditure).

chapon, *s.m.* *Cu:* Capon.

chaque, *a.* Each, every.

char, *s.m.* **1.** Chariot. **2.** Waggon. **C. funèbre,** hearse. *Mil:* **Char d'assaut,** tank.

charade, *s.f.* Charade.

charançon, *s.m.* *Ent:* Weevil.

charbon, *s.m.* **1.** (a) **Charbon de bois,** charcoal. *F:* **Être sur des charbons ardents,** to be on tenter-hooks. (b) *Ch:* Carbon. (c) **Charbon de terre,** coal. **2.** Carbuncle.

charbonnage, *s.m.* **1.** Coal-mining. **2.** Usu. *pl.* Collieries, coal-field. **3.** Coal-depot.

charbonner, *v.tr.* **1.** To carbonize, char. *v.i.* **La lampe charbonne,** the lamp is smoking. **2.** *Se c. le visage,* to black one's face.

charbonnier. 1. *s.m.* *Nau:* Collier. **2.** *s.* (a) Charcoal-burner. *Prov:* **Charbonnier est maître chez soi,** a man's house is his castle. (b) Coal-merchant.

charcuterie, *s.f.* **1.** Pork-butcher's shop. **2.** Pork-butcher's meat; pig-meat.

charcutier, *s.* Pork-butcher.

chardon, *s.m.* Thistle.

chardonneret, *s.m.* Goldfinch.

charge, *s.f.* **1.** Load, burden. **Cheval de charge,** sumpter-horse. **Être à charge à qn,** to be a burden to s.o. **2.** *El.E:* Charge. **3.** Charge (of furnace). **4.** (a) Charge, responsibility, trust. **Cela est à votre charge,** that is part of your duty. **Femme de charge,** housekeeper. (b) Office. **Charges publiques,** public offices. **5.** Charge, expense. **Charges de famille,** dependents. *Prep. phr.* **A (la) charge de,** on condition of. **A charge de revanche,** on condition that I may do as much for you. **6.** Loading, charging. **7.** Exaggeration (of story). **8.** *Mil:* Charge. **9.** *Jur:* Charge, indictment. **Témoin à charge,** witness for the prosecution.

chargement, *s.m.* **1.** (a) Loading (of waggon); charging (of accumulator). (b) Registration (of letter). **2.** Cargo, freight, load.

charger, *v.tr.* (n. **chargeons**) **1.** To load (*de,* with). (a) **C. qn. de reproches,** to heap reproaches on s.o. (b) **C. qch. sur son dos,** to take sth. on one's back. (c) To fill (pipe); to load (gun); to charge (accumulator). **2.** **Charger qn de (faire) qch.,** to instruct s.o. to do sth. **3.** *Mil:* To charge (the enemy). **4.** *Jur:* To indict. **5.** To register (letter).

se charger. 1. *Le temps se charge,* the weather is becoming overcast. **2.** (a) *Se c. d'un fardeau,* to shoulder a burden. (b) *Se c. de qch.,* to undertake sth.

chargé, *a.* **1.** Loaded, laden. *Jour c.,* busy day. **Temps chargé,** heavy, overcast, weather. **2. Lettre chargée,** registered letter. **3.** *s.* **Chargé d'affaires,** ambassador's deputy.

chariot, *s.m.* **1.** (a) Waggon. (b) (Child's) go-cart. (c) Truck, trolley. **2.** (a) Carriage (of typewriter). (b) *Av:* **C. d'atterrissage,** under-carriage; landing gear.

charitable, *a.* Charitable (*envers,* to, towards).

charitablement, *adv.* Charitably.

charité, *s.f.* **1.** Charity, love. **Dame de charité,** district-visitor. **2.** Act of charity; alms(-giving). **Maison de charité,** alms-house.

charivari, *s.m.* Discordant music; din.

charlatan, *s.* Charlatan, quack.

charlatanisme, *s.m.* Charlatanism, quackery.

charmant, *a.* Charming, delightful.

charme¹, *s.m.* **1.** Charm, spell. **2.** Charm, attraction, seductiveness.

charme², *s.m.* *Bot:* Hornbeam, yoke-elm.

charmer, *v.tr.* **1.** To charm, bewitch, fascinate. **2.** To charm, please, delight.

charmeur, -euse, *s.* **1.** Charmer. **2.** Charming person.

charmille [-mi:j], *s.f.* (a) Hedge(-row). (b) Bower, arbour.

charnel, -elle, *a.* Carnal; sensual.

charnellement, *adv.* Carnally, sensually.

charnier, *s.m.* Charnel-house.

charnière, *s.f.* Hinge.

charnu, *a.* Fleshy. **Bras c.,** plump arm.

charogne, *s.f.* **1.** Carrion; decaying carcase. **2.** *P:* Scoundrel.

charpente, *s.f.* Frame(work), framing. **Bois**

de charpente, timber. (Of pers.) Avoir la charpente solide, to be solidly built.

charpenter, *v.tr.* **1.** To cut (timber) into shape. **2.** To frame (up) (roof).
   charpenté, *a.* Built, framed.

charpenterie, *s.f.* **1.** Carpentry. **2.** Carpenter's shop.

charpentier, *s.m.* Carpenter.

charpie, *s.f.* Lint. *F:* **Mettre qn en charpie,** to make mincemeat of s.o.

charretée, *s.f.* Cart-load, cartful.

charretier. 1. *s.m.* Carter, carrier, carman. **2.** *a.* **Porte charretière,** carriage gate(way).

charrette, *s.f.* Cart. *C. à bras,* hand-cart; barrow.

charriage, *s.m.* Cartage, haulage.

charrier, *v.tr.* To cart, carry, transport.

charron, *s.m.* Cartwright; wheelwright.

charroyer, *v.tr.* (je charroie) To transport (sth.) in a cart; to cart (sth.).

charrue, *s.f.* Plough. *F:* **Mettre la charrue devant les bœufs,** to put the cart before the horse.

charte, *s.f.* Charter.

chartreux. 1. *s.* Carthusian. **2.** *s.f.* Chartreuse, chartreuse (liqueur).

Charybde [kar-]. *Pr.n.m.* Charybdis.

chas, *s.m.* Eye (of needle).

chasse, *s.f.* **1.** (a) Hunting. *C. au tir,* shooting. **Aller à la chasse,** to go hunting or shooting. (b) *Louer une c.,* to rent a shoot. (c) *Nau:* **Donner chasse à un navire,** to give chase to a ship. **2.** **Chasse d'eau,** flush, scour. **3.** *Mec.E:* Play (of wheels).

châsse, *s.f.* **1.** Reliquary, shrine. **2.** Mounting; frame (of spectacles).

chasse-marée, *s.m.inv.* **1.** Fish-cart. **2.** Coasting lugger.

chasse-mouches, *s.m.inv.* Fly-killer.

chasser. 1. *v.tr.* (a) To chase, hunt. *C. à courre,* to ride to hounds; to hunt. *C. au fusil,* to shoot. (b) To drive out, away; to expel; to dismiss. *Nuages chassés par le vent,* wind-driven clouds. *C. un clou,* to drive a nail. **2.** *v.i.* (a) To hunt; to shoot. *C. au lion,* to hunt lions. (b) To drive. (c) *Nau:* (Of anchor) To drag.

chasseur, -euse, *s.* **1.** (a) Huntsman; hunter. (b) Shooter. *a. Chien c.,* sporting dog. **2.** *s.m.* (a) Footman, lackey. (b) *C. d'hôtel,* commissionaire; porter; page-boy. **3.** *s.m. Mil:* Rifleman. **Chasseurs à pied,** light infantry. **4.** *s.m. Av:* Fighter.

chassie, *s.f.* Rheum, matter (in the eyes).

chassieux, *a.* Rheumy (eyes).

châssis, *s.m.* (a) Frame. *C. de porte,* door-frame. *C. de fenêtre,* window-sash. (b) *Aut:* Chassis. *Av:* Under-carriage. *C. d'atterrissage,* landing-gear.

chaste, *a.* Chaste, pure.

chastement, *adv.* Chastely, purely.

chasteté, *s.f.* Chastity, purity.

chat, *f.* **chatte,** *s.* **1.** Cat; *m.* tom-cat; *f.* tabby(-cat). **Le Chat botté,** Puss in Boots. *F: Mon petit c., ma petite chatte,* darling.

Acheter chat en poche, to buy a pig in a poke. *Prov:* **Ne réveillez pas le chat qui dort,** let sleeping dogs lie. **A bon chat bon rat,** tit for tat. **Chat échaudé craint l'eau froide,** once bitten twice shy. **2.** **Chat à neuf queues,** cat(-o'-nine-tails).

châtaigne, *s.f. Bot:* Chestnut.

châtaignier, *s.m.* Chestnut-tree, -wood.

châtain, *a.* (Chestnut-)brown (horse). **Cheveux châtain clair,** light brown hair.

château, *s.m.* **1.** Castle. *F:* **Bâtir des châteaux en Espagne,** to build castles in the air. **2.** (a) Country seat; manor, hall. (b) Palace. **3.** **Château d'eau,** water-tower; *Rail:* tank.

châteaubriant, *s.m.* Grilled steak.

châtelain, *s.m.* (a) Castellan. (b) Lord (of manor).

châtelaine, *s.f.* **1.** Lady (of manor). **2.** Chatelaine (for keys).

chat-huant, *s.m.* Tawny owl; brown owl. *pl. Des chats-huants.*

châtier, *v.tr.* To punish, chastise; to chasten. *Prov:* **Qui aime bien châtie bien,** spare the rod and spoil the child.

chatière, *s.f.* (a) Hole (for cat in door). (b) *F:* Secret entrance.

châtiment, *s.m.* Punishment, chastisement.

chatoiement, chatoîment, *s.m.* (a) Shimmer; sheen. (b) Glistening.

chaton¹, -onne, *s.* **1.** Kitten. **2.** *s.m. Bot:* Catkin.

chaton², *s.m.* **1.** Bezel (of ring). **2.** Gem (in ring).

chatouillement [-ujmã], *s.m.* Tickling.

chatouiller [-uje], *v.tr.* To tickle. **Chatouiller les côtes à qn,** *F:* to give s.o. a thrashing.

chatouilleux [-ujø], *a.* **1.** (a) Ticklish. (b) Sensitive, touchy. **2.** Sore (point).

chatoyant, *a.* Iridescent, chatoyant.

chatoyer, *v.i.* (il chatoie) (a) To shimmer. (b) To glisten, sparkle.

chatte. See CHAT.

chat-tigre, *s.m.* Tiger-cat. *pl. Des chats-tigres.*

chaud. 1. *a.* Warm or hot. *F:* **Avoir la tête chaude,** to be hot-headed. *Affaire chaude,* brisk engagement. **Pleurer à chaudes larmes,** to weep bitterly. *V.phr.* **Il fait chaud,** it is warm (weather). **2.** *s.m.* (On label) **Tenir au chaud,** to be kept in a warm place. **Cela ne me fait ni chaud ni froid,** it is all the same to me. **Marqué à chaud,** branded. **Avoir chaud,** (of pers.) to be warm.

chaudement, *adv.* Warmly.

chaudière, *s.f.* **1.** Copper (for washing). **2.** Boiler.

chaudron, *s.m.* Cauldron.

chaudronnier, *s.* **1. Chaudronnier ambulant,** tinker. **2.** Boiler-maker.

chauffage, *s.m.* (a) Warming, heating (of room). (b) Firing, stoking (of boiler). (c) *P:* Cramming (of student).

chauffe, *s.f.* **1.** Heating. **2.** *Mch:* Stoking.

chauffe-pieds, *s.m.inv.* Foot-warmer.

chauffer. 1. *v.tr.* (*a*) To warm, heat. *C. du linge,* to air linen. (*b*) *Chauffé au rouge,* red-hot. *C. une chaudière,* to stoke up a boiler. *C. un examen,* to swot for an examination. **2.** *v.i.* To get, become, warm, hot. *P.:* Ça va chauffer, things are getting warm.

chauffeur, -euse, *s.* **1.** (*a*) Stoker, fireman. (*b*) *Sch:* *P:* Crammer. **2.** *Aut:* Driver; chauffeur, chauffeuse

chaulier, *s.m.* Lime-burner.

chaume, *s.m.* (*a*) Straw; haulm. (*b*) Thatch. *Toit de c.,* thatched roof. (*c*) Stubble.

chaumière, *s.f.* Thatched cottage.

chausse, *s.f.* *A:* *Des chausses,* hose, breeches.

chaussée, *s.f.* **1.** (*a*) Sea-wall. (*b*) Causeway (across marsh). **2.** (*a*) Roadway, carriageway. (*b*) Road; high road.

chausse-pied, *s.m.* Shoe-horn. *pl. Des chausse-pieds.*

chausser, *v.tr.* **1.** To put on (foot-wear). *C. les étriers,* to put one's feet into the stirrups. **2.** (*a*) To put shoes on (s.o.). (*b*) To supply, fit, with footwear. *Être bien chaussé,* to be well shod. *F:* Cela me chausse, that suits me.

chausse-trape, *s.f.* **1.** Trap (for wolves). *F:* Ruse. **2.** *Mil:* *A:* Caltrop. **3.** *Bot:* Star-thistle. *pl. Des chausse-trapes.*

chaussette, *s.f.* Sock.

chausson, *s.m.* **1.** (*a*) *C. de lisière,* list slipper. (*b*) Gymnasium shoe. **2.** *Cu:* Turnover.

chaussure, *s.f.* Foot-wear. *Fabricant de chaussures,* boot and shoe manufacturer.

chauve. 1. *a.* (*a*) Bald. (*b*) Bare, denuded (mountain). **2.** *s.m.* Bald person.

chauve-souris, *s.f.* *Z:* Bat. *pl. Des chauves-souris.*

chauvin. 1. *s.* Chauvinist, jingo. **2.** *a.* Chauvinist(ic), jingoist(ic).

chauvinisme, *s.m.* Chauvinism; jingoism.

chaux, *s.f.* Lime. **Chaux vive,** quicklime. *C. éteinte,* slaked lime. **Blanchir un mur à la chaux,** to whitewash a wall.

chavirement, *s.m.* Capsizing, upsetting.

chavirer. 1. *v.i.* (Of boat) To capsize, upset. **2.** *v.tr.* To turn (sth.) upside down; to upset, capsize (boat).

chef [ʃef], *s.m.* **1.** Head (of family); chief (of tribe); principal, head, chief (of business house); *C. de bureau,* head clerk. *C. de bande,* ring-leader. **Chef de cuisine,** chef. **Chef de musique,** bandmaster. *Row:* **Chef de nage,** stroke(-oar). *Sp:* **Chef d'équipe,** captain. *Rail:* **Chef de gare,** stationmaster. **Chef de train,** guard. **2.** Authority, right. **Faire qch. de son (propre) chef,** to do sth. on one's own (authority). **3.** Head(ing).

chef-d'œuvre [ʃedœːvr], *s.m.* Masterpiece. *pl. Des chefs-d'œuvre.*

chef-lieu [ʃefljø], *s.m.* Chief town (of department). *pl. Des chefs-lieux.*

cheik [ʃɛk], *s.m.* Sheik(h).

chélidoine, *s.f.* *Bot:* Great celandine.

chemin, *s.m.* **1.** (*a*) Way, road. *Il y a dix minutes de c.,* it is ten minutes away. **Faire son chemin,** to make one's way. **Chemin faisant,** on the way. **Faire un bout de chemin avec qn,** to accompany s.o. a little way. **Se mettre en chemin,** to set out. **Demeurer en chemin,** to stop in mid-career. **Ne pas y aller par quatre chemins,** to go straight to the point. (*b*) Road, path, track. *C. piéton,* footpath. **Grand chemin,** highway, high road. **2. Chemin de fer,** railway.

chemineau, *s.m.* Tramp, vagrant.

cheminée, *s.f.* **1.** (*a*) Fireplace. **Pierre de la cheminée,** hearthstone. (*b*) (**Manteau de**) **cheminée,** chimney-piece, mantelpiece. **2.** (*a*) Chimney (flue or stack). (*b*) Funnel (of locomotive).

cheminement, *s.m.* Tramping, walking; progress.

cheminer, *v.i.* To tramp, walk, proceed.

cheminot, *s.m.* Railwayman; plate-layer.

chemise, *s.f.* **1.** (*a*) Shirt. *C. molle,* soft shirt. *C. empesée,* stiff shirt. (*b*) **Chemise de nuit,** night-shirt; night-dress. (*c*) Chemise. *C. de tricot,* under-vest. **2.** (*a*) Jacket (for MS. matter); folder. (*b*) Dust-jacket (of book). (*c*) **Pommes de terre en chemise,** jacket potatoes.

chemiserie, *s.f.* Shirt factory or shop.

chênaie, *s.f.* Oak-grove, -plantation.

chenal, -aux, *s.m.* **1.** Channel, fairway (of river). **2.** Mill-race.

chenapan, *s.m.* Rogue, scoundrel.

chêne, *s.m.* Oak. **Chêne vert,** holm-oak.

chêne-liège, *s.m.* Cork-oak. *pl. Des chênes-lièges.*

chenet, *s.m.* Fire-dog; andiron.

chènevière, *s.f.* Hemp-field.

chènevis, *s.m.* Hempseed.

chenil, *s.m.* Kennels (of hunt).

chenille [-niːj], *s.f.* **1.** (*a*) Caterpillar. (*b*) Band of caterpillar tractor. **2.** *Tex:* Chenille.

chénopode [ke-], *s.m.* *Bot:* Goosefoot.

chenu, *a.* (Of hair) Hoary.

cheptel, *s.m.* (Live-)stock.

chèque, *s.m.* Cheque. *C. barré,* crossed cheque.

cher [ʃɛːr], *a.* **1.** Dear, beloved. *s.* Mon cher, my dear fellow. Ma chère, my dear. **2.** Dear, expensive, costly. *adv.* Il me le payera cher, I will make him pay dearly for it.

chercher, *v.tr.* **1.** To search for, look for; to seek. *Je l'ai cherché partout,* I have hunted for it everywhere. **Chercher aventure,** to seek adventures. **2. Aller chercher qn,** to (go and) fetch s.o. **Allez c. le médecin,** go for a doctor. **Envoyer chercher qn,** to send for s.o. **3. Chercher à faire qch.,** to endeavour, attempt, to do sth.

chercheur, -euse, *s.* Seeker, searcher; investigator. *a.* **Esprit c.,** enquiring spirit.

chère, *s.f.* Cheer, fare, living. **Faire bonne chère,** to fare sumptuously.

chèrement, *adv.* **1.** Dearly, lovingly. **2.** Dearly; at a high price.

chérir, *v.tr.* To cherish; to love dearly. **chéri. 1.** *a.* Cherished, dear. **2.** *s.* Dear one. **Ma chérie,** dearest.

cherté, *s.f.* Dearness, expensiveness.

chérubin, *s.m.* Cherub.

chétif, *a.* **1.** Weak, puny, sickly (person). **2.** Poor, miserable, wretched.

chétivement, *adv.* **1.** Weakly. **2.** Miserably.

cheval, -aux, *s.m.* **1.** Horse. (*a*) *C. de chasse,* hunter. *C. de course,* race-horse. **A cheval,** on horseback. *Aller à c.,* to ride. **Être à cheval sur qch.,** to sit astride sth. **Être à cheval sur l'algèbre,** to be well up in algebra. **Monter sur ses grands chevaux,** to ride the high horse. **Fièvre de cheval,** raging fever. (*b*) *Ich:* **Cheval marin,** sea-horse. **2. Cheval de bois,** wooden horse; *Gym:* vaulting horse. *C. à bascule,* rocking-horse. **Chevaux de bois,** roundabout, merry-go-round. **3.** *Mec:* Horse-power. *F:* **Une vingt chevaux,** twenty horse-power motor car.

chevalement, *s.m.* **1.** Shoring, props (of wall). **2.** Winding-plant; derrick.

chevaleresque, *a.* Chivalrous, knightly.

chevaleresquement, *adv.* Chivalrously.

chevalerie, *s.f.* **1.** Knighthood. **2.** Chivalry. **Chevalerie errante,** knight-errantry.

chevalet, *s.m.* Support, stand. (*a*) Trestle, frame, stand. (*b*) *C. de peintre,* easel. (*c*) Clothes-horse. (*d*) Bridge (of violin).

chevalier, *s.m.* **1.** (*a*) Knight. **Créer qn chevalier,** to knight s.o. **Chevalier d'industrie,** adventurer, sharper. (*b*) Rider, horseman. **2.** *Orn:* Sandpiper.

chevalière, *s.f.* (**Bague à la**) **chevalière,** signet-ring.

chevalin, *a.* Equine. **Boucherie chevaline,** horse-butcher's shop.

cheval-vapeur, *s.m.* *Mec:* Horse-power. *pl. Des chevaux-vapeur.*

chevauchage, *s.m.* Riding.

chevauchant, *a.* Overlapping.

chevauchée, *s.f.* **1.** Ride. **2.** Cavalcade.

chevauchement, *s.m.* **1.** Riding. **2.** Overlapping.

chevaucher. 1. *v.i.* (*a*) To ride (on horse). (*b*) *C. sur un mur,* to sit astride a wall. (*c*) To overlap. **2.** *v.tr.* To ride (on), straddle, to be astride.

chevelu, *a.* **1.** Long-haired. **2.** Hairy.

chevelure, *s.f.* **1.** (Head of) hair. **Chasseurs de chevelures,** scalp-hunters. **2.** Tail (of comet).

chevesne [-vɛːn], *s.m. Ich:* Chub.

chevet, *s.m.* (*a*) Bed-head. *Livre de c.,* bedside book. (*b*) Bolster.

cheveu, -eux, *s.m.* **1.** (A single) hair. **Couper un cheveu en quatre,** to split hairs. **Comme un cheveu dans la soupe,** very inappropriate. **Voilà le cheveu!** there's the rub! **2. Les cheveux,** the hair.

chevillage [-vij-], *s.m.* **1.** Pegging, bolting. **2.** Plugging.

cheville [-viːj], *s.f.* **1.** Peg, pin. *C. en fer,* bolt. **Cheville ouvrière,** *F:* mainspring (of enterprise). **2.** Peg, plug. **3.** *Anat:* Ankle. *F:* **Il ne vous vient pas à la cheville,** he can't hold a candle to you.

cheviller [-vije], *v.tr.* **1.** To pin, bolt, peg, together. *F:* **Avoir l'âme chevillée au corps,** to be hard to kill. **2.** To peg, plug (up).

chèvre, *s.f.* **1.** Goat, esp. she-goat, *F:* nanny-goat. **Barbe de chèvre,** goatee. *F:* **Ménager la chèvre et le chou,** to run with the hare and hunt with the hounds. **2.** (*a*) *Mec.E:* Derrick. (*b*) *Veh:* Jack.

chevreau, *s.m.* Kid.

chèvrefeuille [-fœːj], *s.m.* Honeysuckle.

chevrette, *s.f.* **1.** Kid; young goat. **2.** (*a*) Tripod, trivet. (*b*) Carriage-jack. **3.** *F:* Shrimp or prawn.

chevreuil [-rœːj], *s.m.* Roe-deer. **Peau de chevreuil,** buckskin.

chevrier, *s.* Goatherd; *f.* goat-girl.

chevron, *s.m.* **1.** Rafter (of roof). **2.** *Her:* Chevron. **3.** *Mil:* Long-service stripe.

chevrotain, *s.m.* Musk-deer.

chevrotant, *a.* Quavering, tremulous (voice).

chevrotement, *s.m.* Quavering, tremulousness (of voice).

chevroter, *v.i.* To sing, speak, in a quavering voice; to quaver.

chevrotine, *s.f.* Buck-shot.

chez, *prep.* **1.** (*a*) **Chez qn,** at s.o.'s house, home. *Je vais c. moi,* I am going home. *Acheter qch. c. l'épicier,* to buy sth. at the grocer's. (On letters) **Chez . . .,** care of . . . . **Faire comme chez soi,** to make oneself at home. (*b*) **Son chez-soi,** one's home, one's house. **2.** With, among. *Il en est ainsi c. les Français,* it is so among Frenchmen. *C. les animaux,* in the animal kingdom.

chic [ʃik]. **1.** *s.m.* (*a*) Skill, knack. **Il a le chic pour (faire) cela,** he has the knack of doing that. (*b*) Smartness, stylishness. **Il a du chic,** he has style. **2.** *a. inv. in f., var. in pl.* (*a*) Smart, stylish. *Les gens chics,* the smart set. (*b*) *P:* Fine, first rate. *Sois c.!* come, be a sport!

chicane, *s.f.* **1.** (*a*) Chicanery, pettifoggery. (*b*) Quibbling, wrangling. (*c*) (At bridge) Chicane. **2.** (*a*) Joints en chicane, staggered joints. (*b*) *Mil:* Zigzag trench.

chicaner. 1. *v.i.* To chicane, quibble. **2.** *v.tr.* *C. qn,* to wrangle with s.o. (*sur,* about).

chicanerie, *s.f.* Chicanery, quibbling.

chicaneur, -euse, *1.* *s.* Quibbler, caviller. **2.** *a.* Quibbling, haggling, captious.

chicanier = CHICANEUR.

chiche, *a.* (*a*) (Of thg) Scanty, poor. (*b*) (Of pers.) Stingy, niggardly.

chichement, *adv.* Stingily, meanly.

chicorée, *s.f.* Chicory.

chicot, *s.m.* Stump (of tooth).

chien, *f.* **chienne,** *s.* **1.** Dog; *f.* bitch.

Chien de berger, sheep-dog. *C. de garde*, watch-dog. Chien courant, hound. *F:* Se regarder en chiens de faïence, to glare at one another. Avoir d'autres chiens à fouetter, to have other fish to fry. Entre chien et loup, in the twilight. *Prov:* Qui veut noyer son chien l'accuse de rage, give a dog a bad name and hang him. Quel temps de chien! what beastly weather! 2. (a) Hammer (of gun). (b) Chien d'arrêt, pawl, catch.

chiendent, *s.m.* *Bot:* Couch-grass *P:* Voilà le chiendent! there's the rub!

chiffe, *s.f.* Rag.

chiffon, *s.m.* 1. (a) Rag. (b) Piece of lace, of ribbon. 2. *Tex:* Chiffon.

chiffonner, *v.tr.* (a) To rumple (dress); to crumple (piece of paper). (b) To annoy, vex.

chiffonnier. 1. *s.* Rag-and-bone man. 2. *s.m.* Small chest of drawers; chiffonier.

chiffrage, *s.m.* 1. Reckoning. 2. Numbering. 3. Coding.

chiffre, *s.m.* 1. (a) Figure, number, numeral. *Com:* Marqué en chiffres connus, marked in plain figures. (b) Amount, total. *Com:* C. d'affaires, turnover. 2. Cipher, code. 3. (a) Monogram. (b) *Typ:* Colophon.

chiffrer. 1. *v.i.* To calculate, reckon. 2. *v.tr.* (a) To number (pages of book). (b) To work out (amount). *Détails chiffrés*, figures (of scheme). (c) To cipher; to write (despatch) in code. Mot chiffré, code word. (d) To mark (linen). (e) *Mus:* To figure (the bass).

chiffre-taxe, *s.m.* Postage-due stamp. *pl. Des chiffres-taxes.*

chignon, *s.m.* Coil of hair; chignon, *F:* bun.

chimère, *s.f.* Chimera.

chimérique, *a.* 1. Visionary, fanciful (mind). 2. Chimerical.

chimie, *s.f.* Chemistry.

chimique, *a.* Chemical. Un produit chimique, a chemical.

chimiste, *s.m.* Chemist. (*Not* pharmaceutical.)

chimpanzé, *s.m.* Chimpanzee.

Chine. Pr.n.f. *Geog:* China. Encre de Chine, Indian ink. Papier de Chine, rice-paper.

chinois. 1. *a.* Chinese. 2. *s.* Chinaman, Chinese woman; Chinese.

chinoiserie, *s.f.* 1. Chinese curio. 2. *F:* Monkey trick. *Chinoiseries de bureau*, red tape.

chiourme, *s.f.* Gang of convicts.

chipage, *s.m.* Scrounging.

chiper, *v.tr.* *P:* To pinch, sneak, scrounge.

chipeur, -euse, *s.* Filcher; scrounger.

chipotage, *s.m.* 1. Wasting time. 2. Haggling.

chipoter. 1. *v.i.* (a) To waste time. (b) To haggle. 2. *v.tr.* To peck at (food).

chipotier, *s.* (a) Fiddle-faddler. (b) Quibbler.

chique[1], *s.f.* Quid (of tobacco).

chique[2], *s.f.* *Ent:* Chigoe, jigger.

chiquement, *adv.* *P:* 1. Smartly, stylishly. 2. Like a sport.

chiquenaude, *s.f.* Fillip, flick (of the finger).

chiquer, *v.tr.* To chew (tobacco).

chiqueter, *v.tr.* (je chiquette) To tear into shreds; to shred.

chiromancie [kir-], *s.f.* Chiromancy, palmistry.

chiromancien, -ienne [kir-], *s.* Palmist.

chirurgical, -aux, *a.* Surgical.

chirurgie, *s.f.* Surgery

chirurgien, -ienne, *s.* Surgeon.

chirurgique, *a.* Surgical.

chiure, *s.f.* Fly-speck, -mark.

chloral, *s.m.* *Ch:* Chloral.

chlorate, *s.m.* *Ch:* Chlorate.

chlore, *s.m.* *Ch:* Chlorine.

chlorhydrate, *s.m.* *Ch:* Hydrochlorate.

chlorhydrique, *a.* *Ch:* Hydrochloric (acid).

chloroforme, *s.m.* Chloroform.

chloroformer, *v.tr.* To chloroform.

chlorophylle, *s.f.* Chlorophyl(l).

chlorure, *s.m.* *Ch:* Chloride.

choc, *s.m.* 1. Shock, impact. *C. des verres*, clink of glasses. 2. Shock (to nervous system).

chocolat, *s.m.* Chocolate.

chœur, *s.m.* 1. Chanter en chœur, to sing in chorus. 2. Choir.

choisir, *v.tr.* To choose, select. *C. ses mots*, to pick one's words.

choisi, *a.* 1. Selected, 2. Select, choice.

choix, *s.m.* Choice, selection. *Je vous laisse le c.*, choose for yourself. Nous n'avons pas le c., we have no option. Avancer au choix, to be promoted by selection. *Com:* "Au choix," 'all at the same price.'

choléra [kɔl-], *s.m.* *Med:* Cholera.

chômage, *s.m.* 1. Abstention from work. *C. du dimanche*, Sunday closing. 2. Secours de chômage, unemployment benefit.

chômer, *v.i.* 1. To take a holiday (on feast-days). 2. To be idle. *Les usines chôment*, the works are at a standstill.

chômeur, *s.m.* Unemployed workman.

chopine, *s.f.* Half-litre mug.

choquant, *a.* Shocking, offensive.

choquer, *v.tr.* 1. To strike, knock (sth. against sth.). *Nous choquâmes nos verres*, we clinked glasses. 2. To shock. *Idée qui choque le bon sens*, idea that offends common sense. se choquer. 1. To come into collision (*contre*, with). 2. To be shocked.

choral, *pl.* -als [kɔr-], *a.* Choral.

choriste [kɔr-], *s.m.* Chorus-singer (in opera).

chose. 1. *s.f.* Thing. Dites des choses aimables de ma part à . . ., remember me kindly to. . . . La chose en question, the case in point. Je vois la chose, I see how matters stand. 2. *a.inv.* *F:* Être tout chose, to feel queer.

chou, *pl.* -oux, *s.m.* 1. Cabbage. *F:* Planter ses choux, to live retired in the country. Faire ses choux gras, to feather one's nest. Faire chou blanc, (at games) to make a duck. Mon petit chou, my dear. 2. *Cu:* Chou à la crème, cream bun.

choucas, s.m. Orn: (Jack)daw.

choucroute, s.f. Cu: Sauerkraut.

chouette[1], s.f. Owl.

chouette[2], a. & int. P: Fine, topping.

chou-fleur, s.m. Cauliflower pl. Des choux-fleurs

choyer, v.tr. (je choie) To pet, coddle (s.o.).

chrétien, -ienne, a. & s. Christian

chrétienté, s.f. Christendom.

Christ, s.m. I. Le Christ. Christ. 2. F: Crucifix.

christianisme, s.m. Christianity.

chromate, s.m. Ch: Chromate.

chromatique, a. Chromatic.

chrome, s.m. I. Ch: Chromium. 2. Com: Chrome.

chromique, a. Chromic (acid).

chromo, s.m. F: Chromo(lithograph).

chronique[1], a. Chronic (disease).

chronique[2], s.f. I. Chronicle. 2. Journ: News, reports.

chroniqueur, s.m. Chronicler.

chronologie, s.f. Chronology.

chronologique, a. Chronological.

chronomètre, s.m. (a) Chronometer (b) Stop-watch.

chrysalide, s.f. Ent: Chrysalis, pupa.

chrysanthème, s.m. Bot: Chrysanthemum.

chuchotement, s.m. Whispering, whisper.

chuchoter, v.i. & tr. To whisper

chuinter, v.i. (Of owl) To hoot

chut [ʃyt, ʃt], int. Hush! ssh!

chute, s.f. I. (a) Fall. Chute du jour, night-fall. Chute d'eau, waterfall. Com: C. de prix, fall, drop, in prices. (b) (Down)fall. 2. C. des reins, small of the back. 3. Ind: Shoot.

Chypre. Pr.n.f. L'île de Chypre, Cyprus.

ci[1], adv. Par-ci par-là, here and there.

ci[2], dem. pron inv. Comme ci, comme ça, so so.

ci-après, adv. Hereafter; later, further on.

cible, s.f. Target.

ciboire, s.m. Ecc: Pyx, ciborium.

ciboule, s.f. Spring onion.

ciboulette, s.f. Bot: Cu: Chive(s).

cicatrice, s.f. Scar.

cicatriser. I. v.tr. (a) To heal (wound). (b) To scar (face). 2. v.i. & pr. (Of wound) To heal (up).

Cicéron. Pr.n.m. Lt.Lit: Cicero.

ci-contre, adv. (a) Opposite. (b) Annexed (circular). (c) On the other side (of the sheet).

ci-dessous, adv. Hereunder; under-mentioned.

ci-dessus, adv. Above(-mentioned).

ci-devant, adv. Previously, formerly.

cidre, s.m. Cider.

ciel, pl. cieux, s.m. I. (a) Sky, firmament, heaven. A ciel ouvert, out of doors. (b) (pl. often ciels) Climate, clime, sky. 2. Heaven. F: Tomber du ciel, to come as a godsend. (Juste) ciel! (good) heavens! 3. (pl. ciels) Ciel de lit, bed-tester.

cierge, s.m. Ecc: Wax candle; taper.

cieux. See CIEL.

cigale, s.f. Ent: Cicada.

cigare, s.m. Cigar

cigarette, s.f Cigarette.

ci-gisent, ci-gît. See GÉSIR.

cigogne, s.f. Stork.

ciguë, s.f. Bot: Hemlock.

ci-inclus, a. (Inv. when it precedes the noun) La copie ci-incluse, the enclosed copy.

ci-joint, a. (Inv. when it precedes the noun) Subjoined, herewith.

cil [sil], s.m. (Eye-)lash.

cilice, s.m. Hair-shirt.

cime, s.f. Summit (of hill); top (of tree).

ciment, s.m. Cement. C. armé, reinforced concrete. Béton de ciment, concrete.

cimenter, v.tr. To cement.

cimeterre, s.m. Scimitar.

cimetière, s.m. Cemetery, graveyard.

cinabre, s.m. (a) Cinnabar. (b) Art: Vermilion.

ciné, s.m. F: = CINÉMATOGRAPHE.

ciné-actualités, s.m. News theatre. pl. Des cinés-actualités.

cinéma, s.m. F. Cinema.

cinématographe, s.m. Cinematograph.

cinéraire. I. a. Cinerary (urn) 2. s.f. Bot: Cineraria.

cinétique. Mec: I. a. Kinetic, motive (energy). 2. s.f. Kinetics.

cinglant, a. Lashing (rain); cutting, biting (wind); bitter (cold); scathing

cingler, v.tr. To lash, cut (horse) with a whip. F: La grêle lui cinglait le visage, the hail stung his face.

cinnamome, s.m. Cinnamon.

cinq [sɛ̃(:)k], num. a. inv. & s.m. inv. (As card. adj. before a noun or adj. beginning with a consonant sound [sɛ̃]) Five. C. hommes [sɛ̃kɔm], five men. J'en ai c. [sɛ̃:k], I have five. Le c. mars [sɛ̃kmars], March the fifth.

cinquantaine, s.f. (About) fifty.

cinquante, num. a. inv. Fifty.

cinquième. I. num. a. & s. Fifth. 2. s.m. Fifth (part).

cintre, s.m. I. Curve, bend. 2. Arch (of tunnel). 3. Coat-hanger.

cintrer, v.tr. To bend (bar) to the desired shape.

cintré, a. (a) Arched (window). (b) Curved.

cipaye [-pa:j], a. & s.m. Sepoy.

cirage, s.m. I. Waxing (of floors); blacking (of boots). 2. Polishing wax.

circoncire, v.tr. (p.p. circoncisant; p.p. circoncis; p.h. je circoncis) To circumcise.

circoncision, s.f. Circumcision.

circonférence, s.f. Circumference.

circonflexe, a. Circumflex (accent).

circonlocution, s.f. Circumlocution.

circonscription, s.f. I. Circumscription, circumscribing. 2. Division, district.

circonscrire, v.tr. (Conj. like ÉCRIRE) To circumscribe.

circonspect, *a.* Circumspect, prudent.

circonspectement, *adv.* Circumspectly.

circonspection, *s.f.* Circumspection.

circonstance, *s.f.* Circumstance, event. En pareille circonstance, in such a case. A la hauteur des circonstances, equal to the occasion.

circonstancié, *a.* Circumstantial, detailed (account).

circonstanciel, -ielle, *a.* (*a*) Circumstantial. (*b*) *Gram:* Adverbial (complement).

circonvenir, *v.tr.* (Conj. like VENIR) To circumvent, thwart; outwit (s.o.).

circuit, *s.m.* Circuit. **1.** Circumference. **2.** Deviation. *Circuits d'une rivière,* windings of a river. **3.** *El:* **Mettre (une lampe) en circuit,** to switch (a lamp) on.

circulaire. 1. *a.* Circular. **2.** *s.f.* Circular (letter).

circulation, *s.f.* **1.** Circulation. **2.** Traffic. *Arrêt de c.,* traffic block. **"Circulation interdite,"** 'no thoroughfare.'

circuler, *v.i.* **1.** (Of blood) To circulate, flow. **2.** To circulate, move about. **"Circulez!"** 'pass along!'

cire, *s.f.* Wax.

cirer, *v.tr.* To wax (thread); to polish (floors). *C. des chaussures,* to black shoes.

ciré, *a.* Waxed. **Toile cirée,** oilcloth.

cireur, -euse, *s.* **1.** Polisher. **2.** Shoeblack.

cirque, *s.m.* **1.** Circus. **2.** Cirque; amphitheatre (of mountains).

cisaille [-zɑːj], *s.f. sg. or pl.* Shears; nippers.

cisailler [-zɑje], *v.tr.* To shear (metal).

ciseau, *s.m.* **1.** Chisel. **2.** *pl.* Scissors. (*b*) Shears.

ciseler, *v.tr.* (je cisèle, je ciselle) To chase (gold); to chisel (wood).

ciselure, *s.f.* **1.** Chisel(l)ing. **2.** Chasing.

cistercien, -ienne, *a. & s. Ecc:* Cistercian.

citadelle, *s.f.* Citadel, stronghold.

citadin, *s.* Citizen, townsman.

citation, *s.f.* **1.** (*a*) Quoting. (*b*) Quotation. **2.** *Jur:* (*a*) Summons. (*b*) Subpoena.

cité, *s.f.* City. (*a*) (Large) town. (*b*) Housing estate.

citer, *v.tr.* **1.** To quote, cite. **2.** *Jur:* To summon; to subpoena. **3.** Citer qn (à l'ordre du jour) = to mention s.o. in dispatches.

citerne, *s.f.* Cistern, tank.

cithare, *s.f. Mus:* Zither(n).

citoyen, -enne, *s.* Citizen.

citrate, *s.m. Ch:* Citrate.

citrique, *a. Ch:* Citric (acid).

citron, *s.m.* Lemon; citron.

citronnade, *s.f.* Lemonade.

citronnier, *s.m.* Lemon-tree; citron-tree.

citrouille [-truːj], *s.f.* Pumpkin, gourd.

civet, *s.m. Cu:* Stew. *C. de lièvre,* jugged hare.

civette, *s.f.* Civet-cat.

civière, *s.f.* **1.** Hand-barrow. **2.** Stretcher, litter. **3.** Bier (for coffin).

civil [-vil], *a.* Civil. **1.** (*a*) Civic (rights). (*b*) *Jur:* Droit civil, common law. (*c*) Lay secular; civilian. **En civil, in plain clothes. 2.** Polite.

civilement, *adv.* Civilly.

civilisation, *s.f.* Civilization.

civiliser, *v.tr.* To civilize.

civilité, *s.f.* Civility, courtesy.

civique, *a.* Civic (duties); civil (rights).

clac [klak], *s.m. & int.* Crack.

claie, *s.f.* **1.** (*a*) Hurdle. (*b*) *C. à fruits,* (wicker) fruit-tray. **2.** Screen, riddle.

clair. 1. *a.* Clear. (*a*) Unclouded, limpid. (*b*) Obvious, plain (meaning). *Explication claire,* lucid explanation. (*c*) Bright, light (room). *Il ne fait pas c. ici,* you can't see here. (*d*) Light (colour). **2.** *adv.* Plainly, clearly. **3.** *s.m.* (*a*) Light. **Au clair de (la) lune,** in the moonlight. (*b*) Clearing (in wood). (*c*) **Message en clair,** message in plain language. **Sabre au clair,** with drawn sword.

Claire. *Pr.n.f.* Clara, Clare.

clairement, *adv.* Clearly, plainly.

claire-voie, *s.f.* Open-work, lattice(-work). **Caisse à claire-voie,** crate. *pl. Des claires-voies.*

clairière, *s.f.* Clearing, glade.

clairon, *s.m.* (*a*) Bugle. (*b*) Bugler.

claironnant, *a.* Loud, brassy (sound).

clairsemé, *a.* Scattered, sparse; thin (hair).

clairvoyance, *s.f.* **1.** Perspicacity, clearsightedness. **2.** Second-sight, clairvoyance.

clairvoyant. 1. *a.* Perspicacious, clearsighted. **2.** *a. & s.* Clairvoyant.

clameur, *s.f.* Clamour, outcry.

clandestin, *a.* Clandestine, secret.

clandestinement, *adv.* Clandestinely, secretly.

clapet, *s.m.* Valve.

clapier, *s.m.* **1.** Rabbit-warren. **2.** Rabbit-hutch.

clapotement, *s.m.* Plash(ing), lap(ping) (of waves).

clapoter, *v.i.* (Of sea) To chop, plash.

clapotis, *s.m.* Plash(ing), lap(ping) (of waves).

claque. I. *s.f.* **1.** Smack, slap. **2.** *Th:* Hired clappers (in Fr. theatres). **II. claque,** *s.m.* (*a*) Opera-hat. (*b*) Cocked hat.

claquement, *s.m.* Clapping (of hands); slamming (of door); cracking (of whip).

claquemurer, *v.tr.* To immure, mew up.

claquer. 1. *v.i.* To clap; (of door) to bang. *Il claque des dents,* his teeth are chattering. **2.** *v.tr. & i.* (Faire) claquer, to slam (the door); to crack (a whip). **3.** *v.tr.* (*a*) To slap (child). (*b*) *Th:* To clap (an actor).

clarifier, *v.tr.* To clarify.

clarinette, *s.f.* Clarinet.

clarté, *s.f.* **1.** Clearness, clarity. **Avoir des clartés sur un sujet,** to have some knowledge of a subject. **2.** Light, brightness.

classe, *s.f.* **1.** Class, division. *Les hautes*

classes, the upper classes. **2.** *Sch:* (*a*) Class, form. *Les hautes classes*, the upper school. (*b*) Aller **en classe**, to go to school. **3.** *Mil:* Annual contingent (of recruits).

classement, *s.m.* **I.** Classification, classing. **2.** (*a*) Sorting out. (*b*) Filing (of documents).

classer, *v.tr.* **I.** To class(ify). **2.** (*a*) To sort out (articles). (*b*) To file (documents). *F:* Classer **une affaire**, to pigeon-hole an affair.

classeur, *s.m.* **I.** Filing-cabinet, file **2.** (Pers.) Sorter (of letters).

classification, *s.f.* **I.** Classification, classifying (of plant) **2.** Sorting out.

classifier, *v.tr.* **I.** To classify (plant). **2.** To sort (out) (articles).

classique, *a.* **I.** For school use. **2.** (*a*) Classic(al). (*b*) Standard (work). *F:* C'est un coup classique, that's an old dodge. **3.** *s.m. Les classiques grecs*, the Greek classics.

clause, *s.f. Jur:* Clause. *C. additionnelle*, rider.

claustral, -aux, *a.* Claustral, monastic.

claveau, *s.m. Const:* Arch-stone.

clavecin, *s.m. A:* Harpsichord.

clavette, *s.f.* Key(-bolt), cotter(-pin), pin.

clavicule, *s.f.* Clavicle; *F:* collar-bone.

clavier, *s.m.* **I.** Keyboard (of typewriter). **2.** Range, compass (of clarinet).

clé, *s.f.*, **clef**, *s.f.* **I.** Key. (*a*) Fermer une porte à clef, to lock a door. Tenir qch. sous clef, to keep sth. under lock and key. (*b*) C. *d'une position*, key to a position. (*c*) Key (to a cipher). **2.** *Mus:* (*a*) Clef. (*b*) Keysignature. **3.** Clef de voûte, keystone. **4.** *Tls:* Key, wrench, spanner Clef anglaise, monkey-wrench.

clématite, *s.f. Bot:* Clematis.

clémence, *s.f.* **I.** Clemency (*pour, envers*, to, towards). **2.** Clemency, mildness.

clément, *a.* **I.** Clement (*pour, envers*, to, towards). **2.** Mild.

cleptomane, *s.m. & f.* Kleptomaniac.

cleptomanie, *s.f.* Kleptomania.

clerc, *s.m.* Clerk (in lawyer's office). *F:* Faire un pas de clerc, to make a blunder.

clergé, *s.m.* (The) clergy, priesthood.

clérical, -aux, *a.* Clerical.

clic [klik], *s.m. & int.* Click.

cliché, *s.m.* **I.** *Typ:* Plate (of type); block (of illustration). **2.** *Phot:* Negative. **3.** *Lit:* *F:* Stock phrase.

client, *s.* Client, customer, (cabman's) fare; (hotel) visitor.

clientèle, *s.f.* (*a*) Practice (of doctor). (*b*) *Com:* Customers; goodwill.

clignement, *s.m.* Blink(ing), wink(ing).

cligner, *v.tr. & i.* **I.** (*a*) Cligner les yeux, to screw up one's eyes. (*b*) C. les yeux, les paupières, to blink. **2.** Cligner de l'œil à qn, to wink at s.o.

clignotant, *a.* Blinking; twinkling (star).

clignotement, *s.m.* Blinking; twinkling.

clignoter, *v.i.* (*a*) Clignoter des yeux, to blink. (*b*) To twinkle. (*c*) (Of eyelid) To twitch.

climat, *s.m.* **I.** Climate. **2.** Region, climate.

clin d'œil [klɛ̃dœːj], *s.m.* Wink. Esp. En un clin d'œil, in the twinkling of an eye.

clinique. (*a*) Nursing-home. (*b*) (Doctor's) surgery.

clinquant, *s.m.* Tinsel.

clique, *s.f.* (Disreputable) gang, set.

cliquet, *s.m. Mec.E:* Catch, pawl.

cliqueter, *v.i.* (il cliquette) (Of chains) To clank; (of keys) to jingle.

cliquetis, *s.m.* Rattling (of chain); chinking (of glasses); jingling (of keys).

clivage, *s.m.* Cleavage (of rocks).

cloaque, *s.m.* Cesspool. *F:* Cloaque de vices, sink of iniquity.

cloche, *s.f.* **I.** Bell. *F:* Déménager à la cloche de bois, to do a moonlight flit. **2.** *Ch:* Bell-jar. *Hort:* Bell-glass, cloche. *Dom. Ec:* Dish-cover. **3.** Blister.

cloche-pied (à), *adv.phr.* Sauter à cloche-pied, to hop (on one foot).

clocher¹, *s.m.* Belfry, bell-tower; steeple. Esprit de clocher, parochialism. Course au clocher, point-to-point race.

clocher², *v.i.* To limp, hobble.

clocheton, *s.m.* Pinnacle; bell-turret.

clochette, *s.f.* Small bell; hand-bell.

cloison, *s.f.* **I.** Partition, division. Mur de cloison, dividing wall. **2.** *Nau:* Bulkhead.

cloisonner, *v.tr.* To partition (off) (room).

cloisonné, *a.* Cloisonné (enamel).

cloître, *s.m.* Cloister(s).

cloîtrer, *v.tr.* To cloister (s.o.).

clopin-clopant, *adv. F:* Aller clopin-clopant, to limp along, hobble about.

clopiner, *v.i.* To hobble, limp.

cloporte, *s.m. Crust:* Wood-louse.

clore, *v.tr.def.* (= FERMER, which has taken its place in most uses) (*p.p* clos; *pr.ind.* je clos, il clôt, ils closent) (*a*) To close (up) (*b*) To end (discussion).

clos. **I.** *a.* (*a*) Closed; shut up. A la nuit close, after dark. (*b*) Concluded. **2.** *s.m.* Enclosure. Clos de vigne, vineyard.

clôture, *s.f.* **I.** Enclosure, fence, fencing. **2.** (*a*) Closing (of offices). (*b*) Conclusion (of sitting).

clôturer, *v.tr.* **I.** To enclose (field). **2.** (*a*) To close down (factory). (*b*) To end (session).

clou, *s.m.* **I.** (*a*) Nail. *F:* Mettre qch. au clou, to pawn sth. (*b*) Clou à crochet, hook. (*c*) Star turn, chief attraction (of entertainment). **2.** Clou de girofle, clove.

clouer, *v.tr.* **I.** To nail (sth.). **2.** Rester cloué sur place, to stand rooted to the spot. *Être cloué à son lit*, to be bed-ridden.

clovisse, *s.f. Moll:* Cockle.

coagulation, *s.f.* Coagulation.

coaguler, *v.tr.* To coagulate (albumen); to curdle (milk).

se coaguler, (of blood) to coagulate, clot; (of milk) to curdle.

coaliser (se), *v.pr.* To form a coalition; to unite.

coalition, *s.f.* **1.** Coalition, union. **2.** (Hostile) combination; conspiracy.

coassement, *s.m.* Croak(ing) (of frog).

coasser, *v.i.* (Of frog) To croak.

cobalt [-balt, , *s.m.* Cobalt.

cobaye, *s.m.* Z: Guinea-pig; cavy.

cobra, *s.m.* Rept: Cobra.

cocagne, *s.f.* Mât de cocagne, greasy pole. Pays de cocagne, land of plenty.

cocaïne, *s.f.* Pharm: Cocaine.

cocarde, *s.f.* Cockade, rosette.

cocasse, *a.* P: Droll, laughable.

coccinelle, *s.f.* Ent: Lady-bird.

coche, *s.f.* Notch, nick.

cochenille [-ni:j], *s.f.* Cochineal.

cocher, *s.m.* Coachman, driver.

cochère, *a.f.* Porte cochère, carriage gateway, main entrance.

cochon, *s.m.* **1.** Pig, hog. Cochon de lait, sucking-pig. **2.** Cochon d'Inde, guinea-pig.

coco, *s.m.* **1.** Noix de coco, coco(a)-nut. **2.** F: Liquorice water.

cocon, *s.m.* Cocoon.

cocorico, *onomat. & s.m.* Cock-a-doodle-doo !

cocotier, *s.m.* Coco-nut palm.

code, *s.m.* Code. **1.** Statute-book. C. de commerce, commercial law. **2.** C. télégraphique, telegraphic code.

codicille, *s.m.* Codicil.

codifier, *v.tr.* **1.** To codify (laws). **2.** To code (message).

coefficient, *s.m* Coefficient. C. de sûreté, safety factor.

cœur, *s.m.* Heart. **1.** (a) En cœur, heart-shaped. F: Faire la bouche en cœur, to make a pretty mouth. (b) Avoir mal au cœur, to feel sick. Cela soulève le cœur, it makes one's gorge rise. **2.** Soul, feelings, mind. (a) Avoir qch. sur le cœur, to have sth. on one's mind. En avoir le cœur net, to clear the matter up. Parler à cœur ouvert, to speak freely, with open heart. Avoir le cœur gros, to be sad at heart. Avoir trop de cœur, to be too tender-hearted. Si le cœur vous en dit, if you feel like it. Je n'ai pas le cœur à faire cela, I am not in the mood to do that. Avoir à cœur de faire qch., to be bent on doing sth. (b) Apprendre qch. par cœur, to learn sth. by heart. **3.** Courage, spirit, pluck. Donner du cœur à qn, to hearten s.o. F: Avoir du cœur au ventre, to have plenty of spunk. Faire contre mauvaise fortune bon cœur, to put a brave face on things. **4.** (a) Avoir le cœur à l'ouvrage, to have one's heart in one's work. Travailler, y aller, de bon cœur, to work heartily, with a will. (b) A vous de tout cœur, yours affectionately. (c) Il a le cœur bien placé, his heart is in the right place. **5.** Middle, midst. Au cœur de l'hiver, in the depth of winter. **6.** Cards: Hearts.

coffre, *s.m.* (a) Chest, bin. (b) Boot (of carriage).

coffre-fort, *s.m.* Safe. pl. Des coffres-forts.

coffret, *s.m.* Small box; tool-chest.

cognac [-nak], *s.m.* Cognac; brandy.

cognassier, *s.m.* Quince(-tree).

cognée, *s.f.* Axe or hatchet.

cogner. **1.** v.tr. (a) To drive in, hammer in (sth.). (b) To knock, thump. **2.** v.i. To knock, thump; to bump.

cohérence, *s.f.* Coherence.

cohérent, *a.* Coherent.

cohésion, *s.f.* Cohesion, cohesiveness.

cohue, *s.f.* Crowd, mob, throng.

coi, *f.* **coite**, *a.* Se tenir coi, to lie low.

coiffe, *s.f.* **1.** Head-dress. cap. **2.** Caul (of new-born child).

coiffer, *v.tr.* **1.** (a) To cover (the head). Montagne coiffée de neige, snow-capped mountain. (b) C. un chapeau, to put on a hat. **2.** C. qn, to dress s.o.'s hair. se coiffer. **1.** To put one's hat on. **2.** To do one's hair.

coiffé, *a.* **1.** Être c. d'un chapeau, to be wearing a hat. Il est né coiffé, F: he was born with a silver spoon in his mouth. **2.** Être bien c., to have one's hair well dressed.

coiffeur, -euse, *s.* Hairdresser.

coiffure, *s.f.* **1.** Head-dress, head-gear. **2.** Hairdressing.

coin, *s.m.* **1.** (a) Corner. Place de c., corner seat. (b) Coins et recoins, nooks and corners. (c) Furn: Corner cupboard. (d) Coin du feu, ingle-nook. Au coin du feu, by the fireside. (e) C. de ciel bleu, patch of blue sky. **2.** Wedge. **3.** Stamp, die.

coincer, *v.* (n. coinçons) **1.** v.tr. To wedge (up), chock (up) (rails) **2.** v.i. & pr. (Of machine parts) To jam.

coïncidence, *s.f.* Coincidence.

coïncident, *a.* Coincident, coinciding.

coïncider, *v.i.* To coincide.

coing, *s.m.* Bot: Quince.

coite. See coi.

col, *s.m.* **1.** Neck (of bottle). **2.** Cost: Collar. (a) Faux col, detachable collar. (b) Col de dentelle, lace collar. **3.** Geog: Pass, col.

colback [-bak], *s.m.* Mil: Busby.

coléoptère, *s.m.* Coleopter, beetle.

colère. **1.** s.f. Anger. F: Colère bleue, towering passion. Se mettre en colère, to lose one's temper. **2.** a. Angry (voice); irascible (person).

coléreux, *a.* Quick-tempered, irascible, choleric (person).

colérique, *a.* Choleric, fiery (disposition).

colibri, *s.m.* Humming-bird.

colifichet, *s.m.* Trinket, bauble.

colimaçon, *s.m.* Snail. (Escalier en) colimaçon, spiral staircase, winding stairs.

colin-maillard, *s.m.* Blind-man's-buff.

colique, *s.f.* Colic ; F: stomach-ache.

colis, *s.m.* **1.** Parcel, package. **2.** (Article of) luggage. Les gros c., heavy luggage.

collaborateur, -trice, *s.* Collaborator.

collaboration, *s.f.* Collaboration.

collaborer, *v.i.* To collaborate (*avec*, with), *C. à un journal,* to contribute to a newspaper.

collant, *a.* (*a*) Sticky. (*b*) Close-fitting (garment).

collatéral, -aux, *a.* Collateral.

collation, *s.f.* **1.** Granting (of degree). **2.** Collation (of documents). **3.** Light meal.

colle, *s.f.* **1.** (i) Paste; (ii) glue; (iii) size. *C. forte,* glue. **2.** *Sch :* Poser.

collecte, *s.f.* **1.** *Ecc :* Collection (for the poor). **2.** *Ecc :* Collect.

collectif, *a.* Collective, joint (action).

collection, *s.f.* **1.** Collecting. **2.** Collection.

collectionnement, *s.m.* Collecting (of curios).

collectionner, *v.tr.* To collect (stamps).

collectionneur, -euse, *s.* Collector (of curios).

collectivement, *adv.* Collectively, jointly.

collectivité, *s.f.* Collectivity. **1.** Community. **2.** Common ownership.

collège, *s.m.* **1.** College. **2.** School.

collégien, -ienne, *s.* Schoolboy, -girl.

collègue, *s.m. & f.* Colleague.

coller. 1. *v.tr.* To paste, stick, glue. *F : C. son visage à la vitre,* to press one's face to the window. **2.** *v.i.* To stick, adhere, cling. **se coller,** to stick, adhere closely. *Se c. contre un mur,* to stand close to a wall.

collet, *s.m.* **1.** Collar (of coat). *a.inv.* **Elle est très collet monté,** she is very prim (and proper), very formal. **2.** Flange, collar (of pipe). **3.** Snare, noose. **Prendre des lapins au collet,** to snare rabbits.

colleur, *s.m.* *C. d'affiches,* bill-sticker.

collier, *s.m.* **1.** Necklace. **2.** *C. de chien,* dog-collar. *F :* **Donner un coup de collier,** to put one's back into it. **3.** Collar, ring (on birds).

colline, *s.f.* Hill.

collision, *s.f.* Collision. **Entrer en collision avec qch.,** to collide with sth.

colloque, *s.m.* Colloquy, conversation.

collusion, *s.f.* Collusion.

colmater, *v.tr.* To clog (filter); to choke (pipe).

Colomb [kɔlɔ̃]. *Pr.n.m.* **Christophe Colomb,** Christopher Columbus.

colombe, *s.f.* *Orn :* Pigeon, dove.

colombier, *s.m.* Dovecot; pigeon-house.

Colombine. *Pr.n.f.* *Th :* Columbine. *s.f. Bot :* Columbine.

colon, *s.m.* **1.** Husbandman; farmer. **2.** Colonist, settler.

colonel, *s.m.* Colonel.

colonial, -aux. 1. *a.* Colonial. **2.** *s.m.pl.* *F :* Coloniaux, colonials.

colonie, *s.f.* Colony, settlement. **Colonie pénitentiaire,** reformatory school.

colonisation, *s.f.* Colonization, settling.

coloniser, *v.tr.* To colonize (region).

colonnade, *s.f.* *Arch :* Colonnade.

colonne, *s.f.* **1.** Column, pillar. *F : Lit à colonnes,* four-poster bed. **2.** *Mil :* Column.

colophane, *s.f.* Rosin, colophony.

coloration, *s.f.* **1.** Colouring. **2.** Colour.

colorer, *v.tr.* To colour, tint.

coloré, *a.* Coloured. *Teint c.,* florid complexion.

colorier, *v.tr.* To colour (drawing). *Colorié à la main,* hand-coloured.

coloris, *s.m.* Colour(ing) (of painting).

colossal, -aux, *a.* Colossal, gigantic, huge.

colosse, *s.m.* Colossus.

colporter, *v.tr.* (*a*) To hawk (goods). (*b*) *F :* To spread abroad (news).

colporteur, -euse, *s.* Packman, pedlar.

coma, *s.m.* Coma.

comateux, *a.* Comatose.

combat, *s.m.* **1.** Combat, fight, contest. **Engager le combat,** to go into action. **Hors de combat,** disabled. **2.** *F :* Conflict; contest (of wits).

combattant, *s.m.* Fighting man; combatant. **Anciens combattants,** ex-service men.

combattif, *a.* Combative, pugnacious.

combattre, *v.* (Conj. like BATTRE) **1.** *v.tr.* To combat, to fight (against) (enemy). **2.** *v.i.* To fight, strive.

combe, *s.f.* Dale, dell, coomb, combe.

combien, *adv.* **1.** (Exclamative) (*a*) How (much)! (*b*) How many! **Combien de gens!** what a lot of people! **2.** (Interrogative) (*a*) How much? **C'est combien?** how much is it? (*b*) How many? *F :* **Le combien sommes-nous?** what day of the month is it?

combinaison, *s.f.* **1.** (*a*) Combination, arrangement. (*b*) *F :* Plan, scheme. (*c*) *Ch :* Combination. **2.** (Pair of) combinations.

combiner, *v.tr.* **1.** (*a*) To combine, unite (forces); to arrange (ideas). (*b*) *Ch :* To combine. **2.** To contrive (plan).

comble¹, *s.m.* **1.** Heaped measure. *F :* Ça, **c'est le comble!** that beats all! **2.** (*a*) Roofing. **De fond en comble,** from top to bottom. (*b*) *F :* Highest point; height (of happiness).

comble², *a.* (*a*) (Of measure) Heaped up. (*b*) (Of hall) Packed.

combler, *v.tr.* **1.** To fill in (ditch); to make good (a loss); to fill (a vacancy). **2.** To fill (measure) to overflowing. *C. qn de bienfaits,* to heap kindness on s.o.

comburant, *a.* Combustive.

combustible. 1. *a.* Combustible. **2.** *s.m.* Fuel.

combustion, *s.f.* Combustion, burning.

comédie, *s.f.* (*a*) Comedy. *F :* **C'était une vraie comédie!** it was as good as a play. (*b*) **Faire la comédie,** to pretend.

comédien, -ienne, *s.* Comedian; player.

comestible. 1. *a.* Edible, eatable. **2.** *s.m.* (*a*) Article of food. (*b*) *pl.* Provisions.

comète, *s.f.* Comet.

comice, *s.m.* **Comice agricole,** agricultural show.

comique. 1. *Th :* *Lit :* (*a*) *a.* Comic (actor). **Le genre comique,** comedy. (*b*) *s.m.* (i) Comedy. (ii) Comedian. **2.** (*a*) *a.* Comical,

funny. (*b*) *s.m. Le c. de l'histoire c'est que
. . .,* the joke is that. . . .

comiquement, *adv.* Comically, ludicrously.

comité, *s.m.* Committee, board. *F:* Être en
petit comité, to be at an informal gathering.

commandant. 1. *a.* Commanding (officer).
2. *s.m.* Commander; commanding officer;
Mil: Major. *Av:* Squadron-leader.

commande, *s.f.* **1.** *Com:* Order. Fait sur
commande, made to order. Payable à la
commande, cash with order. **2.** *Mec.E:*
(*a*) Control, operation. Organes de commande, controls.

commandement, *s.m.* **1.** Command, order.
2. (Position of) command, authority.

commander. 1. *v.tr.* (*a*) To command,
order. *C. à qn de faire qch.,* to command,
order, s.o. to do sth. *Apprendre à se commander,* to learn to control oneself. (*b*) To
govern; to be in command of (army).
(*c*) *C. le respect,* to command respect. (*d*) (Of
fort) To command, dominate (town). **2.**
v.ind.tr. C. à son impatience, to control one's
impatience.

commanditaire, *a. & s.m. Com:* (Associé)
commanditaire, sleeping partner.

comme¹, *adv.* **1.** (*a*) As, like. *Faites c. moi,*
do like me; do as I do. Tout comme un
autre, (just) like anyone else. Comme ça vous
venez de Paris? and so you come from Paris?
(*b*) *Blanc c. neige,* snow-white. (*c*) Comme (si),
as if, as though. *Il resta c. pétrifié,* he stood
as if petrified. *F:* C'est tout comme, it
amounts to the same thing. **2.** (Before verbs)
As. Faites comme il vous plaira, do as you
please. **3.** As; in the way of. Qu'est-ce que
vous avez comme légumes? what have you
got in the way of vegetables? **4.** *Excl.* How!
C. il est maigre! how thin he is!

comme², *conj.* **1.** As; seeing that. *C. vous
êtes là,* since you are here. **2.** (Just) as.

commémoratif, *a.* Commemorative.

commémoration, *s.f.* Commemoration.

commémorer, *v.tr.* To commemorate.

commençant, *s.* Beginner.

commencement, *s.m.* Beginning, commencement. Au commencement, at the
outset.

commencer, *v.tr. & i.* (*n.* commençons)
To begin, commence. *Abs.* Pour commencer,
to begin with.

commensurable, *a. Mth:* Commensurable.

comment, *adv.* **1.** *Interr.* How. *C. allez-
vous?* how are you? Comment cela? how
so? Comment (dites-vous)? I beg your
pardon? Comment faire? what is to be
done? **2.** *Excl.* What! why! Comment!
vous n'êtes pas encore parti! what, haven't
you gone yet! Mais comment donc! why,
of course!

commentaire, *s.m.* **1.** Commentary. **2.**
Comment. Voilà qui se passe de commentaire, comment is needless.

commentateur, -trice, *s.* Commentator,
annotator.

commenter, *v.tr. & i.* **1.** To comment
(up)on, annotate (text). **2.** *F: C. (sur) qn,
qch.,* to pass remarks upon s.o., sth.

commérage, *s.m.* (Ill-natured) gossip.

commerçant. 1. *a.* Commercial, business.
2. *s.* Merchant, tradesman.

commerce, *s.m.* **1.** Commerce; trade.
Faire le commerce du thé, to deal in tea.
2. Intercourse, dealings. *C. du monde,*
human intercourse. Être en commerce avec
qn, to be in touch with s.o.

commercial, -aux, *a.* Commercial; trading, business (relations).

commère, *s.f.* (*a*) Gossip, busybody (*b*)
Crony.

commettre, *v.tr.* (Conj. like METTRE) **1.** (*a*)
Il eut soin de ne pas se c., he was careful not to
commit himself. (*b*) *C. qch. à qn,* to entrust
sth. to s.o. **2.** To commit, perpetrate (crime).

commis¹, -isse, etc. See COMMETTRE.

commis², *s.m.* **1.** Clerk; book-keeper.
2. (*a*) (Shop-)assistant. (*b*) Commis voyageur,
commercial traveller.

commisération, *s.f.* Commiseration, pity.

commissaire, *s.m.* Commissioner. Com-
missaire de police = police superintendent.
Commissaires d'un bal, stewards of a ball.
C. d'un navire, purser.

commissariat, *s.m.* Commissariat de police,
central police station.

commission, *s.f.* Commission. **1.** *C. de
deux pour cent,* commission of two per cent.
2. Message, errand. **5.** Committee, board.

commissionnaire, *s.m.* **1.** *Com:* Commission-agent. **2.** Messenger, commissionaire.

commode. 1. *a.* (*a*) Convenient; handy.
(*b*) Convenient, comfortable (house). (*c*) Accommodating (disposition). *C. à vivre,* easy
to live with. **2.** *s.f.* Chest of drawers.

commodément, *adv.* Conveniently, comfortably.

commodité, *s.f.* **1.** Convenience; comfort.
2. Commodiousness.

commotion, *s.f.* **1.** Commotion, disturbance, upheaval. **2.** *Med:* Concussion.

commuer, *v.tr.* To commute (penalty)
(*en*, to).

commun. 1. *a.* (*a*) Common. Faire bourse
commune, to share expenses. D'un commun
accord, with one accord. (*b*) Universal,
general (custom). Le sens commun, common
sense. (*c*) Usual, everyday (occurrence).
(*d*) Vulgar. **2.** *s.m.* Common run (of persons).
Œuvre au-dessus du commun, work above the
average.

communal, -aux, *a.* **1.** Common (land).
2. Communal.

communauté, *s.f.* **1.** Community (of interests). **2.** Society.

commune, *s.f.* **1.** La Chambre des Communes, the House of Commons. **2.** *Fr.Adm:*
Commune.

ommunément, *adv.* Commonly, generally.

ommuniant, *s.* *Ecc:* Communicant.

communicant, *a.* Communicating (rooms).

ommunicatif, *a.* Communicative.

ommunication, *s.f.* Communication. **1.** (a) Donner communication de qch. à qn, to communicate sth. to s.o. (b) **Entrer en communication avec qn,** to get into communication with s.o. *Tp:* **Fausse communication,** wrong number. **2.** Message.

ommunier, *v.i.* *Ecc:* To communicate.

communion, *s.f.* Communion.

ommuniquer, *v.* To communicate. **1.** *v.tr.* To impart, convey (heat). **2.** *v.i.* *Porte qui communique au jardin,* door that communicates with the garden.

    communiqué, *s.m.* Official statement.

communisme, *s.m.* Communism.

communiste, *s.m. & f.* Communist.

commutateur, *s.m.* (Electric-light) switch.

commutation, *s.f.* Commutation.

compact [-pakt], *a.* Compact, close, dense.

compagne, *s.f.* (Female) companion.

compagnie, *s.f.* **1.** Company. **Fausser compagnie à qn,** to give s.o. the slip. **Dame de compagnie,** (lady) companion. **2.** Company; party. **3.** *Com:* **La maison Durand et Compagnie** (usu. et Cie), the firm of Durand and Company. **4.** *Mil:* Company.

compagnon, *s.m.* (a) Companion, comrade. **C. de bord,** shipmate. (b) (Workman's) mate.

comparable, *a.* Comparable (à, with).

comparaison, *s.f.* **1.** Comparison. *Prep.phr.* **En comparaison de qch.,** in comparison with sth. **2.** *Rh:* Simile.

comparaître, *v.i.* (Conj. like CONNAÎTRE) *Jur:* **Comparaître (en justice),** to appear before a court of justice.

comparatif, *a. & s.m.* Comparative.

comparativement, *adv.* Comparatively.

comparer, *v.tr.* To compare.

compartiment, *s.m.* Compartment; partition.

compas, *s.m.* **1.** (Pair of) compasses. **C. à pointes sèches,** dividers. **2. Compas de mer,** mariner's compass. **3.** Standard, scale (of measurement).

compasser, *v.tr.* To regulate (one's actions); to weigh (one's words).

    compassé, *a.* **1.** Stiff, formal (manner). **2.** Regular, set (life).

compassion, *s.f.* Compassion, pity.

compatibilité, *s.f.* Compatibility.

compatible, *a.* Compatible.

compatissant, *a.* Compassionate (*pour,* to, towards); tender-hearted.

compatriote, *s.m. & f.* Compatriot.

compendieusement, *adv.* Compendiously.

compendieux, *a.* Compendious, concise.

compensateur, -trice. 1. *a.* Compensating (spring). **2.** *s.m.* Compensator.

compensation, *s.f.* (a) Compensation; set-off. **Cela fait compensation,** that makes

up for it. *Bank:* **Chambre de compensation,** clearing-house. (b) Equalization (of forces).

compenser, *v.tr.* (a) To compensate; to make up for (sth.). (b) To compensate, set off (debts).

compère, *s.m.* **1.** Confederate. **2. Un bon compère,** a jolly good fellow.

compétemment, *adv.* Competently.

compétence, *s.f.* **1.** Competence, jurisdiction (of court). **Sortir de sa compétence,** to exceed one's powers. **2.** Competence, ability; proficiency.

compétent, *a.* Competent.

compilateur, -trice, *s.* Compiler.

compilation, *s.f.* Compilation.

compiler, *v.tr.* To compile.

complaire, *v.ind.tr.* (Conj. like PLAIRE) **C. à qn,** to please, humour, s.o.

    se complaire à *faire qch.,* to take pleasure in doing sth.

complaisamment, *adv.* **1.** Obligingly. **2.** Complacently.

complaisance, *s.f.* **1.** Complaisance, obligingness. **2.** Complacency.

complaisant, *a.* (a) Obliging, complaisant. (b) Complacent.

complément, *s.m.* Complement.

complémentaire, *a.* Complementary.

complet, -ète. 1. *a.* (a) Complete, entire. (b) Full (bus, *Th:* house, etc.). **2.** *s.m.* (a) Suit (of clothes). (b) *Adj.phr.* **Au complet,** complete, full.

complètement, *adv.* Completely; utterly.

complètement, *s.m.* Completion.

compléter, *v.tr.* (je complète; je compléterai) To complete; to finish off.

complexe. 1. *a.* Complex; complicated. **Nombre complexe,** compound number. **2.** *s.m.* *Psy:* Complex.

complexion, *s.f.* Constitution, temperament.

complexité, *s.f.* Complexity.

complication, *s.f.* **1.** Complication. **2.** Intricacy.

complice, *a. & s.* Accessory (*de,* to); accomplice, abettor (*de,* of).

complicité, *s.f.* Complicity.

compliment, *s.m.* **1.** Compliment. **2.** *pl.* Compliments, greetings. "Mes compliments à . . .," 'my kind regards to. . . .'

complimenter, *v.tr.* To compliment.

compliquer, *v.tr.* To complicate.

    compliqué, *a.* Complicated, intricate.

complot, *s.m.* Plot, conspiracy.

comploter, *v.tr.* To plot, to scheme.

complu, -s, -t, etc. See COMPLAIRE.

componction, *s.f.* Compunction.

comporter, *v.tr.* **1.** To allow (of), to admit of (sth.). **2.** To call for, require (sth.). **3.** To comprise (sth.). *Les fatigues que comporte un voyage,* the fatigue incidental to a journey.

    se comporter, to behave.

composant, *a. & s.m.* Component, constituent.

composer. I. *v.tr.* (a) To compose; to form. (b) To set (type). *Tp:* Composer le numéro, to dial the number. (c) *C. son visage*, to compose one's countenance. 2. *v.i.* To compound, come to terms.

se composer (*de*), to consist (of).

composé. I. *a.* (a) Compound. *Ch:* Corps composé, compound. (b) *Bot:* Composite (flower). (c) Composed, demure. 2. *s.m.* Compound.

compositeur, -trice, *s.* I. *Mus:* Composer. 2. *Typ:* Compositor.

composition, *s.f.* I. (a) Composing, composition. (b) Composing (of type). 2. (a) Composition, mixture. (b) *Mus:* Composition. *Sch:* Essay: test-paper. 3. Arrangement, compromise.

compote, *s.f.* Stewed fruit.

compréhensible, *a.* Comprehensible.

compréhensif, *a.* I. Comprehensive (statement). 2. Understanding (mind).

compréhension, *s.f.* Understanding.

comprendre, *v.tr.* (Conj. like PRENDRE) I. To comprise, include. Y compris . . ., including. . . . 2. To understand, comprehend. Je n'y comprends rien, I can't make it out. Cela se comprend, of course; naturally.

compressible, *a.* Compressible.

compression, *s.f.* Compression; squeezing.

comprimer, *v.tr.* To compress. *Outil à air comprimé*, pneumatic tool.

comprimé, *s.m.* *Pharm:* Tablet.

compr-îmes, -is, -it, etc. See COMPRENDRE.

compromettre, *v.* (Conj. like METTRE) I. *v.tr.* (a) To compromise (s.o.). (b) To endanger (life). 2. *v.i.* To compromise.

se compromettre, to compromise oneself.

comprom-is, -it, etc. See COMPROMETTRE.

comptabilité [kɔ̃t-], *s.f.* I. Book-keeping, accountancy. 2. Accountancy department. *Com:* Counting-house.

comptable [kɔ̃t-], *s.m.* Accountant, book-keeper.

comptant [kɔ̃t-]. I. *a.* Argent comptant, ready money. 2. *adv.* Payer comptant, to pay (in) cash. 3. *s.m.* Vendre au comptant, to sell for cash.

compte [kɔ̃t], *s.m.* Account. (a) Reckoning. Faire son compte de qch., to count on sth. Cela fait mon compte, that is the very thing I wanted. Y trouver son compte, to get sth. out of it. Le compte y est, the account is correct *F:* Il a son compte, he is done for. Son compte est bon, I'll settle his hash for him. En fin de compte . . ., tout compte fait . . ., all things considered. . . . (b) *Box:* Count. (c) Régler de vieux comptes, to pay off old scores. Compte en banque, banking account. Donner son compte à qn, to pay s.o. off (on dismissal). Pour mon compte, . . ., for my part. . . . (d) Compte rendu, report, review. Se rendre compte de qch., to realize sth.

compter [kɔ̃te]. I. *v.tr.* (a) To count (up reckon (up). Dix-neuf tous comptés, ninetee all told. Marcher à pas comptés, to wal with measured tread. Sans compter que . . not to mention that. . . . *Prep.phr.* compter de . . ., (reckoning) from. . . (b) *C. cent francs à qn*, to pay s.o. a hundre francs. (c) *Com:* To charge. (d) To valu (e) Compter faire qch., to reckon on doin sth. 2. *v.i.* (a) Vous pouvez y compter, yo may depend upon it. (b) *C. avec qn*, to recko with s.o. (c) Ne compter pour rien, to stan for nothing.

compteur [kɔ̃t-], *s.m.* (a) Meter. (b) Calcu lating machine.

comptoir [kɔ̃t-], *s.m.* I. *Com:* Counter Garçon de comptoir, bar-tender. 2. Comptoi d'escompte, discount bank.

compulser, *v.tr.* To examine, check.

computation, *s.f.* Computation.

computer, *v.tr.* To compute.

comte, *s.m.* Count.

comté, *s.m.* County.

comtesse, *s.f.* Countess.

concasser, *v.tr.* To crush, break (ore).

concave, *a.* Concave.

concavité, *s.f.* Concavity.

concéder, *v.tr.* (je concède; je concéderai) I. To concede (privilege). 2. *C. qu'on a tort*, to admit that one is wrong.

concentration, *s.f.* Concentration.

concentrer, *v.tr.* I. To concentrate. 2. To contain (one's feelings).

concentré, *a.* I. Concentrated. 2. *F:* Homme concentré, reserved man.

concentrique, *a.* *Geom: etc:* Concentric.

conceptible, *a.* Conceivable.

conception, *s.f.* I. Conception, conceiving. 2. Conception, idea.

concernant, *prep.* Concerning, about.

concerner, *v.tr.* (Used in third pers. only) To concern, affect.

concert, *s.m.* Concert. I. Harmony, agreement. 2. Musical entertainment.

concerter, *v.tr.* (a) To concert (plan). (b) To compose (one's countenance).

se concerter (*avec qn*), to act in concert (with s.o.).

concessif, *a.* Concessive.

concession, *s.f.* Concession.

concevable, *a.* Conceivable, imaginable.

concevoir, *v.tr.* (Conj. like RECEVOIR) (a) To conceive (idea). (b) To conceive, understand. (c) Ainsi conçu, (letter) worded as follows.

concierge, *s.m. & f.* (House-)porter; caretaker (of flats); keeper (of prison).

concile, *s.m.* *Ecc:* Council, synod.

conciliant, *a.* Conciliating, conciliatory.

conciliation, *s.f.* Conciliation.

concilier, *v.tr.* I. To conciliate, reconcile. *C. un différend*, to adjust a difference. 2. To win over, gain (esteem).

concis, *a.* Concise, terse.

concision, *s.f.* Conciseness, brevity.

concitoyen, -enne, s. Fellow-citizen.
concluant, a. Conclusive, decisive.
conclure, v.tr. (p.p. **conclu**) To conclude.
1. (a) To end, finish. (b) C. un marché, to drive a bargain. 2. (a) To decide, infer. (b) C. à qch., to conclude in favour of sth.
conclusif, a. Conclusive.
conclusion, s.f. Conclusion. 1. Close, end. 2. Concluding (of treaty). 3. Inference.
conçoi-s, -t, -ve, etc. See CONCEVOIR.
concombre, s.m. Cucumber.
concordance, s.f. 1. Concordance, agreement. 2. Gram: Concord, agreement; sequence (of tenses).
concorde, s.f. Concord, harmony.
concorder, v.i. To agree, to tally.
concourir, v.i. (Conj. like COURIR) 1. To converge; to coincide. 2. To combine, unite. 3. C. pour un prix, to compete for a prize.
concours, s.m. 1. (a) Concourse (of people). (b) Coincidence (of events). 2. Co-operation, help. 3. (a) Competition. Hors concours, not competing. (b) C. hippique, horse-show.
concret, -ète, a. Concrete, solid.
concrétion, s.f. Concrete mass, concretion.
conçu, -s, -t, etc. See CONCEVOIR.
concurremment, adv. 1. Concurrently, jointly. 2. Competitively.
concurrence, s.f. 1. Concurrence, coincidence (of events). 2. Competition, rivalry.
concurrent. 1. a. (a) Co-operative. (b) Competitive. 2. s. Competitor; candidate.
concussion, s.f. Extortion (by official).
condamnable [-dɑn-], a. Blamable, blameworthy.
condamnation [-dɑn-], s.f. Condemnation. 1. (a) Conviction, judgment, sentence. C. à mort, sentence of death. (b) Putting (of door) out of use. 2. Reproof, censure.
condamner [-dɑn-], v.tr. To condemn. 1. (a) To convict, sentence. Le médecin l'a condamné, the doctor has given him up. (b) Condamner une porte, to block up a door. 2. To censure, reprove.
  condamné, s. Condemned person.
condensation, s.f. Condensation.
condenser, v.tr. To condense (en, into).
condescendance, s.f. Condescension.
condescendre, v.i. To condescend.
condiment, s.m. Condiment, seasoning.
condisciple, s.m. Fellow-student.
condition, s.f. Condition. 1. (a) State. En condition, in (good) condition. (b) pl. Conditions, circumstances. (c) Rank, station. Gens de condition, people of quality. 2. Condition, stipulation. Conditions de faveur, preferential terms. Marchandises à condition, goods on approval. A condition de + inf., provided that. . . . 3. Être en condition (chez qn), to be in service (with s.o.).
conditionnel, -elle. 1. a. Conditional. 2. s.m. Conditional mood.
conditionner, v.tr. To condition (wool); to season (wood).

condoléance, s.f. Condolence.
condor, s.m. Orn: Condor.
conducteur, -trice. 1. s. (a) Leader, guide. (b) Driver. 2. a. Conducting, transmitting. 3. s.m. Conductor (of heat).
conduire, v.tr. (pr.p. **conduisant**; p.p. **conduit**; p.h. je **conduisis**) 1. (a) To conduct; to lead. C. à bien une affaire, to bring off an affair. (b) C. qn à faire qch., to induce s.o. to do sth. 2. To drive (car). 3. To convey, conduct. 4. To conduct, manage.
  se conduire, to conduct oneself, to behave.
conduit, s.m. Passage, conduit, pipe.
conduite, s.f. 1. (a) Conducting, leading (of s.o.). (b) Driving (of cart); navigation (of boat). 2. Direction (of affairs). 3. Conduct, behaviour. Changer de c., to mend one's ways. 4. Piping, tubing.
cône, s.m. Cone. C. de pin, pine cone.
confection, s.f. 1. Making (of machine); manufacture (of goods); drawing up (of document). 2. Ready-made suit or gown.
confectionner, v.tr. To make (up) (dress); to construct (machine). Article confectionné, ready-to-wear article.
confédération, s.f. (Con)federation.
confédérer, v.tr. (je **confédère**; je **confédérerai**) To confederate, unite.
  confédéré, a. Confederate.
conférence, s.f. 1. Conference, discussion. 2. Lecture.
conférencier, s.m. Lecturer.
conférer, v. (je **confère**; je **conférerai**) 1. v.tr. To confer (privileges). 2. v.i. To confer.
confesse, s.f. Aller à confesse, to go to confession.
confesser, v.tr. 1. To confess, own; to own (up) to (sth.). 2. To confess (one's sins). 3. (Of priest) To confess (penitent).
  se confesser, to confess one's sins.
confesseur, s.m. (Father-)confessor.
confession, s.f. Confession.
confessionnal, -aux, s.m. Confessional.
confiance, s.f. 1. Confidence, trust, reliance. Acheter qch. de confiance, to buy sth. on trust. Abus de confiance, breach of trust. Commis de confiance, confidential clerk. 2. Confidence, sense of security.
confiant, a. 1. Confiding, trustful. 2. Confident. 3. Self-confident.
confidence, s.f. Confidence. Dire qch. en confidence, to say sth. in confidence.
confident, .. Confidant, f. confidante.
confidentiel, -elle, a. Confidential.
confidentiellement, adv. Confidentially.
confier, v.tr. 1. To trust, entrust. 2. To confide, disclose.
  se confier à qn, (i) to put one's trust in s.o.; (ii) to take s.o. into one's confidence.
configuration, s.f. Configuration; lie (of the land).
confiner. 1. v.i. C. à un pays, to border upon a country. 2. v.tr. To confine, imprison.

confins, *s.m.pl.* Confines (of country).
confire, *v.tr.* (*pr.p.* confisant; *p.p.* confit;
pr.ind. ils confisent) To preserve (fruit).
  confit, *a.* Fruits confits, preserved fruit(s).
confirmatif, *a.* Confirmative.
confirmation, *s.f.* Confirmation.
confirmer, *v.tr.* To confirm.
confis-ant, -ons, etc. See CONFIRE.
confiscation, *s.f.* Confiscation.
confiserie, *s.f.* (*a*) Confectioner's shop.
  (*b*) Confectionery, preserves.
confiseur, -euse, *s.* Confectioner.
confisquer, *v.tr.* To confiscate, seize.
confit. See CONFIRE.
confiture, *s.f.* Preserve, jam.
conflagration, *s.f.* Conflagration, blaze.
conflit, *s.m.* Conflict; clash (of interests).
confluent, *s.m.* Confluence (of rivers).
confluer, *v.i.* (Of rivers) To meet, join.
confondre, *v.tr.* To confound. **I.** (*a*) To
  mingle. (*b*) To mistake, confuse. **2.** To
  discomfit; to abash. *C. la calomnie,* to silence
  calumny.
  se confondre. I. (*a*) To blend (*en,* into).
  (*b*) (Of streams) To intermingle. **2. Se**
  confondre en excuses, to apologize profusely.
  confondu, *a.* **I.** Disconcerted, abashed.
  2. Dumbfounded (*de,* at).
conformation, *s.f.* Conformation.
conforme, *a.* Conformable; consistent (*à,*
  with).
conformément, *adv.* Conformably (*à,* to);
  in conformity (*à,* with). *Mil: C. au plan,*
  according to plan.
conformer, *v.tr.* (*a*) To form, shape.
  (*b*) *C. qch. à qch.,* to conform sth. to sth.
  se conformer *à qch.,* to conform to sth.
conformité, *s.f.* Conformity.
confort, *s.m.* Comfort(s).
confortable, *a.* Comfortable, snug, cosy.
confortablement, *adv.* Comfortably,
  snugly.
confraternité, *s.f.* **I.** Confraternity,
  brotherhood. **2.** Brotherliness.
confrère, *s.m.* Colleague, fellow-member.
confrérie, *s.f.* Confraternity.
confronter, *v.tr.* To confront.
confus, *a.* **I.** Confused (heap); indistinct
  (noise); obscure (style). **2.** Confused,
  abashed.
confusément, *adv.* Confusedly; vaguely.
confusion, *s.f.* Confusion. **I.** (*a*) Disorder,
  jumble. *Mettre tout en c.,* to upset everything. (*b*) Mistake, error. *C. de dates,* confusion of dates. **2.** Confusion, embarrassment.
congé, *s.m.* **I.** (*a*) Leave (to depart). **Prendre**
  congé de qn, to take leave of s.o. (*b*) Leave
  (of absence). **2.** (*a*) (Notice of) dismissal.
  (*b*) *Donner c. à un locataire,* to give a tenant
  notice.
congédier, *v.tr.* **I.** To dismiss (servant).
  2. To take leave of, dismiss; discharge.

congélation, *s.f.* Congelation; freezing (of
  water).
congeler, *v.tr.* (il congèle) To congeal; to
  freeze (water). Viande congelée, frozen meat.
congénital, -aux, *a.* Congenital.
congestion, *s.f.* *Med:* Congestion. Congestion cérébrale, *F:* stroke.
congestionner, *v.tr.* *Med:* To congest.
  congestionné, *a.* Flushed, red (face).
conglomérer, *v.tr.* (je conglomère; je con-
  glomérerai) To conglomerate.
congre, *s.m.* Conger-eel.
congrégation, *s.f.* *Ecc:* Congregation.
congrès, *s.m.* Congress.
congru, *a.* Sufficient, adequate.
congruent, *a.* *Mth:* Congruent (*à,* with).
conifère. *Bot:* **I.** *a.* Coniferous, cone-bearing.
  2. *s.m.pl.* Conifères, conifers.
conique, *a.* Cone-shaped, conical.
conjectural, -aux, *a.* Conjectural.
conjecture, *s.f.* Conjecture, surmise, guess.
conjecturer, *v.tr.* To conjecture, surmise.
conjoint, *a.* United, joint.
conjointement, *adv.* (Con)jointly.
conjonctif, *a.* **I.** Connective (tissue).
  2. Conjunctive (phrase).
conjonction, *s.f.* **I.** Union, connection.
  2. *Gram:* Conjunction.
conjoncture, *s.f.* Conjuncture.
conjugaison, *s.f.* Conjugation.
conjugal, -aux, *a.* Conjugal. Vie conjugale, married life.
conjuguer, *v.tr.* *Gram:* To conjugate.
conjuration, *s.f.* **I.** Conspiracy, plot.
  2. Incantation. **3.** *pl. F:* Entreaties.
conjurer, *v.tr.* & *i.* **I.** To plot. **2.** (*a*) To
  conjure up (spirits); to exorcise. (*b*) To
  ward off. **3.** *C. qn de faire qch.,* to entreat s.o.
  to do sth.
  conjuré, *s.m.* Conspirator.
connais. See CONNAÎTRE.
connaissance, *s.f.* **I.** (*a*) Acquaintance,
  knowledge. *Avoir c. de qch.,* to be aware of
  sth. **En connaissance de cause,** with full
  knowledge of the facts. **Une personne de**
  ma connaissance, someone I know. **Une**
  figure de connaissance, a familiar face.
  (*b*) *C'est une de mes connaissances,* he is an
  acquaintance of mine. **2.** Knowledge, understanding. **3.** Consciousness.
connaiss-e, -es, etc. See CONNAÎTRE.
connaissement, *s.m.* Bill of lading.
connaisseur, -euse, *s.* Expert, connoisseur,
  judge (of wine).
connaître, *v.tr.* (*pr.p.* connaissant; *p.p.*
  connu; *pr.ind.* je connais, il connaît) To
  know. **I.** To be acquainted with (sth.). **Il**
  en connaît bien d'autres, he has plenty more
  tricks up his sleeve. **2.** To be acquainted
  with (s.o.). **Gagner à être connu,** to improve
  on acquaintance. **Ça me connaît,** you can't
  teach me anything about that. **Connu !** that's

an old story ! **3.** To be versed in, to have a thorough knowledge of (sth).
se connaître. 1. *Se c. à, en, qch.*, to know all about sth. *Je ne m'y connais plus,* I am all adrift, all at sea. **2.** Il ne se connaît plus, he has lost control of himself. Il ne se connaît plus de joie, he is beside himself with joy.
connexion, *s.f.* **1.** Connection (of ideas). **2.** Connecting organ or part.
connivence, *s.f.* Connivance, complicity.
connu, -s, -t, etc. See CONNAÎTRE.
conque, *s.f.* Conch ; marine shell.
conquérant, *a.* Conquering (nation).
conquérir, *v.tr.* (Conj. like ACQUÉRIR) *(a)* To conquer, subdue (country). *(b)* To win (over) (s.o.).
conquête, *s.f.* **1.** (Act of) conquest. **2.** Conquered territory.
conquiers, conquis, etc. See CONQUÉRIR.
consacrer, *v.tr.* **1.** *(a)* To consecrate. *C. toute son énergie à une tâche,* to devote (all) one's energies to a task. **2.** To sanctify.
consacré, *a.* **1.** Consecrated ; hallowed. **2.** Established. Expression consacrée, stock phrase.
consciemment, *adv.* Consciously.
conscience, *s.f.* **1.** Consciousness. Avoir conscience de qch., to be aware of sth. **2.** *(a)* Conscience. Faire qch. par acquit de conscience, to do sth. for conscience' sake. *(b)* Conscientiousness. Faire qch. en conscience, to do sth. conscientiously.
consciencieusement, *adv.* Conscientiously.
consciencieux, *a.* Conscientious.
conscient, *a.* Conscious ; fully aware (of).
conscription, *s.f.* Conscription.
conscrit, *s.m.* *Mil :* Conscript.
consécration, *s.f.* Consecration.
consécutif, *a.* Consecutive.
consécutivement, *adv.* Consecutively.
conseil [-sɛːj], *s.m.* **1.** Counsel ; (piece of) advice. Homme de bon conseil, man worth consulting. **2.** *(a) Jur :* Counsellor, counsel. *(b) Ingénieur c.,* consulting engineer. **3.** Council, committee. Tenir conseil, to hold a council. Le conseil des ministres, the Cabinet. *Com :* *C. d'administration,* board of directors. Conseil de guerre, (i) war-council, (ii) court-martial. *C. d'enquête,* court of enquiry.
conseiller[1] [-sɛj-], *v.tr.* To advise, counsel.
conseiller[2], *s.* **1.** Counsellor, adviser. **2.** *C. municipal,* town-councillor.
consentement, *s.m.* Consent, assent.
consentir, *v.* (Conj. like MENTIR) **1.** *v.i.* To consent, agree. *Prov :* Qui ne dit mot consent, silence gives consent. **2.** *v.tr.* C. un prêt, to grant a loan.
conséquemment, *adv.* **1.** Consistently. **2.** Consequently.
conséquence, *s.f.* *(a)* Consequence, result. En conséquence, accordingly. *(b)* Inference. Tirer une conséquence de qch., to draw an inference from sth. *(c)* Importance,

consequence. *F :* Tirer à conséquence, to be of importance.
conséquent. 1. *a. (a)* Consistent (mind). *(b)* Following. **2.** *s.m.* Consequent. *Adv.phr.* Par conséquent, consequently, accordingly.
conservateur, -trice. 1. *s. (a)* Conservator, keeper. *C. d'un musée,* curator of a museum. *(b) Pol :* Conservative. **2.** *a.* Preserving (process).
conservation, *s.f.* **1.** *(a)* Preserving (of fruit). *(b)* Preservation (of buildings) ; keeping (of archives). Instinct de la conservation, instinct of self-preservation. *(c)* Retaining (of rights). **2.** (State of) preservation.
conservatoire, *s.m.* School, academy (of music).
conserve, *s.f.* **1.** Preserve ; preserved food. *Conserves au vinaigre,* pickles. **2.** *pl.* Dark or tinted spectacles. **3.** *Nau :* Convoy, consort.
conserver, *v.tr.* **1.** *(a)* To preserve (fruit). *(b)* To preserve (building). *C. le gibier,* to preserve game. **2.** To keep, retain (rights).
se conserver, (of goods) to keep.
considérable, *a.* Considerable. **1.** Eminent ; well-to-do (person). **2.** Extensive (property).
considération, *s.f.* Consideration. **1.** Attention, thought. **2.** Reason, motive. **3.** Regard, esteem. Agréez l'assurance de ma haute considération, I am yours very truly.
considérer, *v.tr.* (je considère ; je considérerai) To consider. **1.** Ce n'est pas à considérer, it is not to be thought of. **2.** To contemplate, gaze on. **3.** To regard, deem.
considéré, *a.* **1.** Circumspect (behaviour). **2.** Esteemed (person).
consignataire, *s.m. & f. Com :* Consignee.
consignateur, *s.m.* Consignor.
consignation, *s.f.* **1.** Deposit (of money). **2.** *Com :* Consignment (of goods).
consigne, *s.f.* **1.** *(a)* Order(s), instructions (to sentry). Manquer à la consigne, to disobey orders. Être de consigne, to be on duty. *(b)* Password, countersign. **2.** *(a) Mil :* Confinement (to barracks). *(b) Sch :* Detention. **3.** Cloak-room ; left-luggage office.
consigner, *v.tr.* **1.** *(a)* To deposit (money). *(b) Com :* To consign (goods). **2.** *(a)* To keep in (pupil). *(b)* To refuse admittance to (s.o.). *C. un cabaret,* to put a public-house out of bounds.
consistance, *s.f.* **1.** *(a)* Consistency (of syrup). *(b)* Stability (of mind). **2.** Credit. *Bruit sans c.,* unfounded rumour.
consistant, *a.* Firm (substance). Homme c., man who knows his own mind.
consister, *v.i.* C. en qch., to consist of sth.
consolateur, -trice. 1. *s.* Comforter. **2.** *a.* Consoling, comforting.
consolation, *s.f.* Consolation, solace.
consoler, *v.tr.* To console, solace, comfort.
consolidation, *s.f.* **1.** Consolidation, strengthening. **2.** Healing (of wound). **3.** Funding (of floating debt).

consolider, *v.tr.* **1.** To consolidate, strengthen. **2.** To fund (debt). **se consolider,** to grow firm.

consommateur, -trice, *s.* (*a*) Consumer. (*b*) Customer (in café).

consommation, *s.f.* **1.** Consummation, accomplishment (of work). **2.** Consumption (of petrol). **3.** Drink (in café).

consommer, *v.tr.* **1.** To consummate, accomplish. **2.** To consume (food). **consommé. 1.** *a.* Consummate. **2.** *s.m. Cu:* Stock, beef-tea; clear soup.

consomption, *s.f.* **1.** (*a*) Consumption (of food). (*b*) Consuming (by fire). **2.** *Med:* Consumption.

consonant, *a.* Consonant.

consonne, *s.f. Ling:* Consonant.

conspirateur, -trice, *s.* Conspirator.

conspiration, *s.f.* Conspiracy, plot.

conspirer, *v.i.* **1.** To conspire, plot. **2.** To conspire, tend (à, to).

conspuer, *v.tr.* **1.** To decry, run down (s.o.). **2.** To boo, hoot (play).

constamment, *adv.* **1.** Steadfastly. **2.** Continually.

constance, *s.f.* **1.** Constancy, steadfastness. **2.** Constancy (of temperature).

constant, *a.* **1.** (*a*) Constant, steadfast. (*b*) Firm, unshaken. **2.** Established (fact). **3.** Constant, uniform.

constatation, *s.f.* Verification, establishment (of fact).

constater, *v.tr.* **1.** To establish (fact). *C. une erreur,* to find out a mistake. **2.** To state, record (sth.).

constellation, *s.f.* Constellation.

consternation, *s.f.* Consternation, dismay.

consterner, *v.tr.* To dismay.

constituant, *a.* Constituent. **1.** Component (part). **2.** *s. Pol:* Elector.

constituer, *v.tr.* To constitute. **1.** (*a*) To form, make (up). (*b*) To set up, institute. **2.** (*a*) *C. qn son héritier,* to make s.o. one's heir. (*b*) *C. une rente à qn,* to settle an annuity on s.o.

constitution, *s.f.* **1.** Constituting, establishing. *C. de pension,* settling of an annuity. **2.** Constitution. **3.** Composition (of air).

constitutionnel, -elle, *a.* Constitutional.

constructeur, *s.m.* Constructor.

constructif, *a.* Constructive.

construction, *s.f.* Construction. **1.** Constructing. **2.** Structure, building.

construire, *v.tr.* (Conj. like CONDUIRE) To construct. **1.** To build; to make. **2.** To assemble (machine).

consul, *s.m.* Consul.

consulaire, *a.* Consular.

consulat, *s.m.* Consulate.

consultant. 1. *a.* Consulting. **2.** *s.* (*a*) Person consulted. (*b*) Consulter.

consultatif, *a.* Advisory (committee).

consultation, *s.f.* Consultation.

consulter, *v.tr.* To consult. *Ouvrage à c.,* work of reference.

consumer, *v.tr.* To consume. **1.** To wear away. *Consumé par l'ambition,* eaten up with ambition. **2.** To use up (fortune). **se consumer,** to waste away.

contact [-takt], *s.m.* **1.** Contact, touch. *Garder le contact,* to keep touch. **2.** *El:* (*a*) Connection, contact. Établir le contact, to switch on. (*b*) Switch.

contagieux, *a.* **1.** Contagious (disease). **2.** Noxious (air).

contagion, *s.f.* Contagion.

contamination, *s.f.* (*a*) Contamination. (*b*) *Med:* Infection.

contaminer, *v.tr.* (*a*) To contaminate. (*b*) *Med:* To infect.

conte, *s.m.* **1.** Story, tale. **Contes de bonne femme,** old wives' tales. **2.** *F:* Story, yarn. Conte à dormir debout, cock-and-bull story.

contemplation, *s.f.* Contemplation.

contempler, *v.tr.* To contemplate.

contemporain. 1. *a.* (*a*) Contemporary. (*b*) Contemporaneous (de, w . **2.** *s.* Contemporary.

contenance, *s.f.* **1.** Ca~ ~ty (of bottle). **2.** Countenance, bearing. **Faire bonne contenance,** to put a good face on it.

contenir, *v.tr.* (Conj. like TENIR) **1.** To contain. **2.** To restrain; to control. **se contenir,** to keep one's temper. **contenu. 1.** *a.* Restrained; pent-up. **2.** *s.m.* Contents (of parcel).

content, *a.* (*a*) Content. (*b*) Pleased (de, with). (*c*) Pleased. *Je suis très c. de vous voir,* I am very pleased to see you. (*d*) Glad. *Comme elle était contente!* how glad she was!

contentement, *s.m.* (*a*) Contentment. (*b*) Satisfaction (de, at, with).

contenter, *v.tr.* To content, satisfy (s.o.); to gratify (curiosity). **se contenter** de qch., to be satisfied with sth.

contentieux, *a.* Contentious.

conter, *v.tr.* To tell, relate. **En conter (de belles) à qn,** to take s.o. in.

contestable, *a.* Debatable.

contestation, *s.f.* Contestation, dispute.

conteste, *s.f.* **Sans conteste,** indisputably.

contester. 1. *v.tr.* To contest, dispute. **2.** *v.i.* To dispute.

conteur, -euse, *s.* **1.** Narrator, teller. **2.** Story-teller, romancer.

contexte, *s.m.* Context.

contien-s, -t, -ne. See CONTENIR.

contigu, -uë, *a.* Contiguous, adjoining.

contiguïté, *s.f.* Contiguity, adjacency.

continence, *s.f.* Continence.

continent¹, *a.* Continent, chaste.

continent², *s.m.* **1.** Continent. **2.** Mainland.

continental, -aux, *a.* **1.** Continental. **2.** Belonging to the mainland.

contingent. 1. *a.* Contingent. **2.** *s.m.* (*a*) *Mil:* Contingent. (*b*) Quota.

contin-s, -t. See CONTENIR.

continu, *a.* Continuous, unceasing.

continuation, *s.f.* Continuation; long spell (of bad weather).
continuel, -elle, *a.* Continual, unceasing.
continuellement, *adv.* Continually.
continuer, *v.tr. & i.* To continue. *C. sa route,* to proceed on one's way. **Continuez!** go on!
continuité, *s.f.* Continuity.
continûment, *adv.* Continuously.
contorsion, *s.f.* Contortion.
contour, *s.m.* **1.** Outline. **2.** *Surv:* Contour (-line). **3.** Circuit (of town).
contourner, *v.tr.* **1.** To shape (design). **2.** To pass round, skirt. **3.** To twist, distort.
contourné, *a.* **1.** Shaped. **2.** Twisted.
contracter¹, *v.tr.* **1.** (*a*) To contract (alliance). (*b*) To incur (debt). **2.** To contract (habit).
contracter², *v.tr.* To contract. *Traits contractés par la douleur,* features drawn with pain.
 se contracter, to contract; to shrink.
contraction, *s.f.* Contraction; shrinking.
contradiction, *s.f.* **1.** Contradiction. *Esprit de contradiction,* contrariness. **2.** Inconsistency; discrepancy.
contradictoire, *a* (*a*) Contradictory; conflicting.
contraign-ant, -e, etc. See CONTRAINDRE.
contraindre, *v.tr.* (Conj. like CRAINDRE) To constrain. **1.** To restrain. **2.** To compel. *Je fus contraint d'obéir,* I was obliged to obey.
 contraint, *a.* Constrained; forced (smile).
contrainte, *s.f.* Constraint. **1.** Restraint. **2.** Compulsion, coercion.
contraire, *a.* **1.** (*a*) Contrary; opposite. *Jusqu'à avis contraire,* until further notice. (*b*) *s.m.* **Au contraire,** on the contrary. **2.** Adverse. *s.m.* **Aller au contraire de qn,** to run counter to s.o.
contrairement, *adv.* Contrarily.
contrariant, *a.* Provoking; annoying.
contrarier, *v.tr* **1.** To thwart, oppose. **2.** To vex, annoy.
 contrarié, *a.* **1.** Thwarted. **2.** Annoyed, vexed.
contrariété, *s.f.* **1.** (*a*) Contrariety. (*b*) *Esprit de contrariété,* contrariness. **2.** Vexation, annoyance.
contraste, *s.m.* Contrast; set-off.
contraster, *v.i. & tr.* To contrast.
contrat, *s.m.* Contract, agreement. *C. de mariage,* marriage settlement. *C. d'assurance,* insurance policy.
contravention, *s.f.* Contravention, breach. *F:* **Dresser une contravention à qn,** to take s.o.'s name and address.
contre. 1. *prep.* Against. (*a*) *C. toute attente,* contrary to all expectation. (*b*) *S'assurer c. l'incendie,* to insure against fire. (*c*) (In exchange) for. *Livraison c. remboursement,* cash on delivery. (*d*) To. *Parier à cinq c. un,*

to bet five to one. (*e*) Close to, by. **2.** *adv.* Against. **Parler pour et contre,** to speak for and against. **3.** *s.m.* (*a*) **Par contre,** on the other hand. (*b*) *Bill:* Kiss. (*c*) *Cards:* Double.

NOTE. In all the following compounds CONTRE is inv.; the noun takes the plural.

contre-amiral, -aux, *s.m.* Rear-admiral.
contre-attaque, *s.f.* Counter-attack.
contre-attaquer, *v.tr.* To counter-attack.
contre-balancer, *v.tr.* (n. **contre-balançons**) To counterbalance, offset.
contrebande, *s.f.* **1.** Contraband, smuggling. **2.** Contraband goods.
contrebandier, *s.m.* Smuggler.
contre-bas (en), *adv.phr.* **1.** (Lower) down; below. **2.** Downwards, down.
contre-bouter, *v.tr.* To buttress.
contrecarrer, *v.tr.* To cross, thwart (s.o.).
contre-cœur (à), *adv.phr.* Unwillingly, reluctantly, grudgingly.
contre-coup, *s.m.* (*a*) Rebound (of bullet); recoil. (*b*) Jar (of blow). (*c*) Repercussion. (*d*) *F:* After-effects.
contredanse, *s.f.* **1.** Quadrille (dance, air). **2.** (In Eng.) Country dance.
contredire, *v.tr.* (*pr.ind.* v. **contredisez;** otherwise like DIRE) To contradict.
contredit. *Adv.phr.* **Sans contredit,** assuredly, unquestionably.
contrée, *s.f.* (Geographical) region; country.
contre-espion, *s.m.* Counter-spy.
contrefaçon, *s.f.* **1.** Counterfeiting; infringement of patent). **2.** Counterfeit, forgery.
contrefaire, *v.tr.* (Conj. like FAIRE) **1.** (*a*) To imitate. (*b*) To feign. *C. le mort, F:* to sham dead. **2.** To counterfeit (coin); to pirate (book).
 contrefait, *a.* **1.** Feigned (zeal); disguised (writing). **2.** Counterfeit (coin). **3.** Deformed (person).
contre-ficher, *v.tr.* To strut, truss.
contre-fil, *s.m.* Opposite direction, wrong way (of watercourse, stuff, etc.).
contrefort, *s.m.* **1.** Abutment. **2.** *Geog:* Spur (of mountain); *pl.* foot-hills.
contre-jour, *s.m.* **Assis à c.-j.,** sitting with one's back to the light.
contremaître, -tresse. 1. *s.* Foreman, forewoman; overseer. **2.** *s.m.* Boatswain's mate. *Navy:* Petty officer.
contremander, *v.tr.* To countermand, cancel, revoke (order).
contremarche, *s.f.* **1.** *Mil:* Countermarch. **2.** *Const:* Rise (of stair).
contre-ordre, *s.m.* Counter-order.
contre-partie, *s.f.* **1.** Other party (in transaction). **2.** (*a*) *Book-k:* Contra. (*b*) Counterpart (of document). **3.** *Sp:* Return match.
contre-pied, *s.m.* No *pl.* **A contre-pied de,** contrary to.

contrepoids, *s.m.* Counterbalance; counterpoise.

contre-poil (à), *adv.phr.* F: **Prendre qn à contre-poil,** to rub s.o. the wrong way.

contrepoint, *s.m.* *Mus:* Counterpoint.

contre-poison, *s.m.* Antidote.

contrer. I. *v.tr.* *Box:* To counter (blow). 2. *v.i.* *Cards:* To double.

contre-saison (à), *adv.phr.* Out of season.

contrescarpe, *s.f.* Counterscarp.

contre-sens, *s.m.* I. Misinterpretation. 2. Wrong way (of stuff). **A contre-sens,** in the wrong sense, direction. 3. **A contre-sens de,** in the contrary direction to.

contresigner, *v.tr.* To countersign.

contretemps, *s.m.* I. (*a*) Mishap, hitch. (*b*) Delay, inconvenience. 2. *Adv.phr.* **A contretemps,** unseasonably, inopportunely.

contre-torpilleur, *s.m.* Destroyer.

contrevenir, *v.ind.tr.* (Conj. like VENIR. Aux. *avoir*) To contravene, infringe (*à un arrêté,* an order).

contrevent, *s.m.* Outside shutter.

contribuable, *s. m. & f.* Taxpayer or ratepayer.

contribuer, *v.i.* I. To contribute funds. 2. To contribute, conduce.

contribution, *s.f.* I. Tax or rate. 2. Contribution, share.

contrister, *v.tr.* To sadden, grieve.

contrit, *a.* Contrite, penitent.

contrition, *s.f.* Contrition, penitence.

contrôle, *s.m.* I. (Muster) roll; list. 2. (*a*) Testing, assaying (of gold). (*b*) Hall-marking. 3. (*a*) Checking. (*b*) *Adm:* Inspection, supervision.

contrôler, *v.tr.* I. To hall-mark (gold). 2. To inspect (work); to check (tickets); to verify (a fact). 3. To hold (s.o.) in check.

contrôleur, -euse, *s.* Inspector, examiner. *Rail:* Ticket-collector.

controverse, *s.f.* Controversy.

contumace, *s.f.* **Condamné par contumace,** sentenced in his absence.

contus, *a.* Contused, bruised.

contusion, *s.f.* Contusion, bruise.

contusionner, *v.tr.* To contuse, bruise.

convaincant, *a.* Convincing.

convaincre, *v.tr.* (Conj. like VAINCRE) I. To convince. 2. To convict.

convalescence, *s.f.* Convalescence.

convalescent, *a. & s.* Convalescent.

convenable, *a.* I. Suitable (*à,* for, to); becoming, proper. 2. Decent; seemly.

convenablement, *adv.* I. Suitably. 2. Decorously.

convenance, *s.f.* I. Conformity (of tastes). 2. Suitability, fitness. **Être à la convenance de qn,** to meet s.o.'s fancy. 3. Propriety. **Manque de convenance,** breach of (good) manners.

convenir, *v.i.* (Conj. like VENIR) I. (Conj. with *avoir*) (*a*) To suit, fit. *Sa figure me convient,* I like his face. **Si cela vous convient,** if that is agreeable to you. (*b*) *Impers.* **Il convient de : . .,** it is advisable to. . . . 2. (Conj. with *avoir,* and with *être* to denote a state of agreement) (*a*) To agree. *C. de qch.,* to agree on, about, sth. *Impers. Il fut convenu que . . .,* it was agreed that. . . . (*b*) *C. de qch.,* to admit sth. *J'ai eu tort,* **j'en conviens,** I confess I was wrong.

convenu, *a.* Agreed (price); appointed (time). **C'est convenu!** that's settled !

convention, *s.f.* Convention. I. Covenant, agreement. 2. *Les conventions sociales,* the social conventions. *Adj.phr.* **De convention,** conventional.

conventionnel, -elle, *a.* Conventional (symbol).

convergence, *s.f.* Convergence.

convergent, *a.* Convergent, converging.

converger, *v.i.* (**convergeant; ils convergeaient**) To converge.

conversation, *s.f.* Conversation, talk. **Avoir de la conversation,** to be a good conversationalist.

converser, *v.i.* To converse, talk.

conversion, *s.f.* I. Conversion (to a faith). 2. Conversion, change (*en,* into).

convertible, *a.* Convertible (*en,* into).

convertir, *v.tr.* To convert. I. *C. qn à ses opinions,* to bring over s.o. to one's opinions. 2. *C. qch. en qch.,* to convert, turn, sth. into sth.

se convertir, to become converted.

converti, *s.* Convert.

convexe, *a.* Convex.

conviction, *s.f.* I. Conviction; firm belief. 2. *Jur:* **Pièce de conviction,** exhibit.

convien-s, -t, etc. See CONVENIR.

convier, *v.tr.* I. To invite (s.o. to a marriage). 2. To invite (s.o. to do sth.).

convié, *s.* Guest.

convin-s, -t, etc. See CONVENIR.

convive, *s.m. & f.* (*a*) Guest (at table). (*b*) Table-companion.

convocation, *s.f.* Convocation, summons; convening (of assembly).

convoi, *s.m.* I. Convoy. 2. **Convoi funèbre,** funeral procession. 3. Train, convoy.

convoiter, *v.tr.* To covet, desire.

convoiteux, *a.* Covetous.

convoitise, *s.f.* Covetousness.

convolution, *s.f.* Convolution.

convoquer, *v.tr.* To summon, convoke (assembly); to convene (meeting).

convoyer, *v.tr.* (**je convoie**) To convoy (merchant fleet).

convulser, *v.tr.* To convulse.

convulsif, *a.* Convulsive.

convulsion, *s.f.* Convulsion. **Donner des convulsions à qn,** to throw s.o. into convulsions. **Convulsion politique,** political upheaval.

convulsionner, *v.tr.* (*a*) To convulse. (*b*) To make (muscles) twitch.

convulsivement, *adv.* Convulsively.

coopératif, *a.* Co-operative (society).
coopération, *s.f.* Co-operation.
coopérer, *v.i.* (je coopère ; je coopérerai)
To co-operate ; to work together.
coordination, *s.f.* Co-ordination.
coordonner, *v.tr.* To co-ordinate.
copain, *s.m. F:* Chum, pal.
copeau, *s.m.* Shaving (of wood) ; chip.
Copenhague. *Pr.n.f.* Copenhagen.
copie, *s.f.* 1. Copy, transcript. 2. Copy,
reproduction (of picture).
copier, *v.tr.* 1. To copy, transcribe. *C. qch.
au propre,* to make a fair copy of sth. 2. To
copy (picture). *C. qch. sur qch.,* to copy sth.
from sth. 3. To copy (s.o.).
copieusement, *adv.* Copiously.
copieux, *a.* Copious.
copiste, *s.m. & f.* Copier. 1. Transcriber.
Faute de copiste, clerical error. 2. Imitator.
copra(h), *s.m. Com:* Copra.
coq[1] [kɔk], *s.m.* (a) Cock. *Jeune coq,* cockerel.
Au chant du coq, at cock-crow. *Vivre comme
un coq en pâte,* to live like a fighting-cock.
Coq du village, cock of the walk. *Box: Poids
coq,* bantam-weight. (b) Cock, male (of
birds). *Coq-faisan,* cock-pheasant. *Coq de
bruyère,* (great) grouse.
coq[2], *s.m. Nau:* (Maître-)coq, (ship's) cook.
coq-à-l'âne, *s.m. inv.* Cock-and-bull story.
coque, *s.f.* 1. (a) Shell (of egg). *Un œuf à la
coque,* a boiled egg. (b) Shell, husk (of nut).
F: Se renfermer dans sa coque, to retire
into one's shell. 2. Hull (of ship).
coquelicot, *s.m. Bot:* Red poppy.
coqueluche, *s.f.* (W)hooping cough.
coquerico, *s.m.* Cock-a-doodle-doo.
coquet, -ette. 1. *a.* (a) Coquettish. (b)
Smart, dainty (garment). 2. *s.f.* Coquette.
(a) Flirt, coquette. (b) (Botanist's) vasculum.
coqueter, *v.i.* (je coquette) To coquet(te) ;
to flirt.
coquetier, *s.m.* Egg-cup.
coquettement, *adv.* Smartly (dressed).
coquetterie, *s.f.* 1. (a) Coquetry. (b) Love
of finery. 2. Smartness (of dress).
coquillage [-kij-], *s.m.* 1. Shell-fish. 2.
(Empty) shell (of shell-fish).
coquille [-ki:j], *s.f.* 1. Shell (of snail). 2.
Coquille de Saint-Jacques, scallop. 3. (a)
Shell (of nut). (b). *C. de buerre,* flake of
butter.
coquin. 1. *s.* Rogue, rascal ; *f.* hussy.
2. *a. F:* Roguish.
cor, *s.m.* 1. Tine (of antler). 2. (a) Cor de
chasse, hunting-horn. (b) *Mus: Cor d'harmonie,* French horn. 3. Corn (on the toe).
corail [-ra:j], **-aux,** *s.m.* Coral.
corbeau, *s.m.* 1. *Orn:* Crow ; raven.
2. *Arch:* Corbel, bracket.
corbeille [-bɛ:j], *s.f.* (Open) basket. *La
corbeille de noces,* presents (given to bride
by bridegroom).
corbillard [-bij-], *s.m.* Hearse.
cordage, *s.m.* 1. Roping (of bales). 2. (a)

Rope. *Vieux cordage,* junk. (b) *pl.* Cordage,
ropes.
corde, *s.f.* 1. (a) Rope, cord, line. *C. à linge,*
clothes-line. *Sauter à la corde,* to skip.
(b) String. *Corde de boyau,* catgut. *Corde
à piano,* piano wire. (c) Hangman's rope ;
gallows. *F: Se mettre la corde au cou,* to
put a halter round one's own neck. *Supplice
de la corde,* death by hanging. (d) *Tenir la
corde, F:* to have the advantage of s.o.
(e) *Tex:* Thread. *Drap qui montre la corde,*
threadbare cloth. 2. *Geom:* Chord. 3. *Anat:
Cordes vocales,* vocal cords.
cordé, *a.* Cordate ; heart-shaped.
cordeau, *s.m.* 1. Tracing-line, chalk-line.
F: Tiré au cordeau, perfectly straight.
2. *Min:* Match, fuse.
corder, *v.tr.* To cord (bale).
cordée, *s.f.* Line of roped climbers.
cordial, -aux. 1. Stimulating. *s.m.* Cordial ;
stimulant. 2. Cordial, hearty (welcome).
cordialement, *adv.* Cordially, heartily.
cordialité, *s.f.* Cordiality, heartiness.
cordon, *s.m.* 1. (a) Cord. *C. de la porte,*
door-pull (controlled by the *concierge*). (b) *C.
de soulier,* shoe-lace. (c) Ribbon (of an order).
(d) *El: C. souple,* flex wire. 2. Row, line ;
cordon (of police).
cordonnier, *s.m.* Shoemaker, bootmaker.
coriace, *a.* Tough, leathery (meat).
Corinthe. *Pr.n.f. Geog:* Corinth. *Raisins
de Corinthe,* currants.
cormoran, *s.m. Orn:* Cormorant.
cornac [-nak], *s.m.* Elephant-keeper ; mahout.
corne, *s.f.* 1. (a) Horn. *Montrer les cornes,
F:* to show fight. (b) Horn (of snail).
F: Rentrer les cornes, to draw in one's horns.
2. *Chapeau à cornes,* cocked hat. *C. d'un livre,*
dog's-ear of a book. 3. *Corne d'abondance,*
cornucopia.
corné, *a.* Corneous, horny.
corneille [-nɛ:j], *s.f. Orn:* Crow, rook.
C. d'église, jackdaw.
cornemuse, *s.f. Mus:* Bagpipes.
corner, *v.tr.* 1. (a) To trumpet ; proclaim
(sth.). (b) *Abs. Aut:* To sound the horn ;
to hoot. 2. *Page cornée,* dog's-eared page.
cornet, *s.m.* 1. *Mus:* Cornet à pistons,
cornet. 2. (a) *C. acoustique,* ear-trumpet. (b)
C. à dés, dice-box. *C. de papier,* screw of paper.
corniche, *s.f.* 1. *Arch:* Cornice. 2. Ledge
(of rock).
cornichon, *s.m. Hort:* Gherkin.
Cornouaille(s) [-nwɑ:j]. *Pr.n.f.* Cornwall.
cornouiller [-nuje], *s.m. Com:* Dogwood.
cornu, *a.* Horned.
cornue, *s.f. Ch:* Retort.
Corogne (la). *Pr.n. Geog:* Corunna.
corollaire, *s.m.* Corollary.
corolle, *s.f. Bot:* Corolla.
corporatif, *a.* Corporate.
corporation, *s.f.* Corporation.
corporel, -elle, *a.* Corporeal (substance) ;
corporal (punishment).

corps [kɔːr], *s.m.* **1.** Body. Saisir qn au corps, to arrest s.o. Prendre du corps, to put on flesh. Prendre corps, to take, assume, shape. *Mil:* Les gardes du corps, the body-guards, the life-guards. Saisir qn à bras le corps, to grapple with s.o. Lutter corps à corps, to struggle hand to hand. **2.** Corpse. **3.** (*a*) C. *célestes*, heavenly bodies. (*b*) *Vin qui a du c.*, full-bodied wine. **4.** Main part (of sth.). Faire corps avec qch., to be an integral part of sth. *Nau:* Perdu corps et biens, lost with all hands. **5.** Le c. *diplomatique*, the diplomatic corps. Corps d'armée, army corps.

corps-de-garde, *s.m.inv. Mil:* Guard-room.

corps-mort, *s.m. Nau:* Moorings.

corpulence, *s.f.* Stoutness, corpulence.

corpulent, *a.* Stout, fat, corpulent.

corpuscle, *s.m.* Corpuscle.

correct [-ɛkt], *a.* Correct, proper; accurate.

correctement, *adv.* Correctly, accurately.

correction, *s.f* **1.** Correction, correcting. **2.** Reproof. Maison de correction, reformatory. **3.** Correctness (of speech).

corrélatif, *a. & s.m.* Correlative.

corrélation, *s.f.* Correlation.

correspondance, *s.f.* **1.** Correspondence, agreement. **2.** (*a*) Communication (between places). (*b*) *Rail:* Connection (between trains). **3.** (*a*) Intercourse. (*b*) Correspondence (by letter).

correspondant. **1.** *a.* (*a*) Corresponding (*à*, to, with). (*b*) *Rail:* Train c., connection. **2.** *s.* Correspondent.

correspondre, *v.i.* **1.** To tally, agree (*à*, with); to correspond (*à*, to, with). **2.** To correspond (by letter).

corridor, *s.m.* Corridor, passage.

corriger, *v.tr.* (n. corrigeons) **1.** To correct; to rectify (mistake). **2.** To chastise.

 se **corriger** *d'une habitude,* to break oneself of a habit.

corroboration, *s.f.* Corroboration.

corroborer, *v.tr.* To corroborate.

corroder, *v.tr.* To corrode, eat away.

corrompre, *v.tr.* To corrupt; to deprave.

 corrompu, *a.* (*a*) Corrupt, depraved. (*b*) Tainted, putrid.

corrosif, *a. & s.m.* Corrosive.

corrosion, *s.f.* Corrosion.

corrupteur, -trice. **1.** *s.* Corrupter; briber (of witness). **2.** *a.* Corrupt (influence).

corruptible, *a.* Corruptible.

corruption, *s.f.* **1.** Corruption; bribing (of witnesses). **2.** Corruption, corruptness.

corsage, *s.m.* **1.** Bust (of woman). **2.** Bodice, body (of dress).

corsaire, *a. & s.m.* **1.** Privateer (ship). **2.** Privateer(sman).

corse¹, *a. & s.* Corsican.

Corse² (la). *Pr.n.* Corsica.

corset, *s.m.* Corset.

cortège, *s.m.* **1.** Train, retinue. **2.** Procession. Cortège funèbre, funeral.

corvée, *s.f.* **1.** *Mil:* (*a*) Fatigue. Être de corvée, to be on fatigue (duty). (*b*) Fatigue party. **2.** *F:* Irksome task.

cosaque, *s.m.* Cossack.

cosinus [-nyːs], *s.m. Mth:* Cosine.

cosmétique, *a. & s.m.* Cosmetic.

cosmique, *a.* Cosmic(al).

cosmopolite, *a. & s. m. & f.* Cosmopolitan.

cosse, *s.f.* Pod, husk, hull

cossu, *a. F:* Well-to-do (person)

costume, *s.m.* Costume, dress.

costumer, *v.tr.* To dress (s.o.) (up).

 costumé, *a.* Bal costumé, fancy-dress ball

cote, *s.f.* **1.** (*a*) Quota, share. (*b*) *Adm:* Assessment. **2.** Quotation. C. *des prix*, list of prices.

côte, *s.f.* **1.** Rib. Côte à côte, side by side. **2.** (*a*) Slope (of hill). (*b*) Hill. *A mi-côte*, half-way up the hill. **3.** Coast, shore.

côté, *s.m.* **1.** Side. Assis à mes côtés, sitting by my side. *Nau: Présenter le c. à qch.*, to be broadside on to sth. Le vent vient du bon côté, the wind is in the right quarter. C'est son côté faible, that is his weak spot. D'un côté . . . . on the one hand. . . De tous (les) côtés, on all sides; far and wide. Courir de côté et d'autre, to run about in all directions. De quel côté est l'hôtel? whereabouts is the hotel? Se ranger d'un côté, to take sides. **2.** *Adv.phr.* (*a*) De côté, on one side; sideways. Mettre qch. de côté, to put sth. aside. (*b*) A côté, to one side; near. Tirer à côté, to miss the mark. A côté de, by the side of; next to; beside.

coteau, *s.m.* **1.** Hillside. **2.** (Small) hill.

côtelette, *s.f.* (Mutton) cutlet; chop.

coter, *v.tr.* **1.** To assess. **2.** *Com:* To quote.

coterie, *s.f.* (Literary) set, coterie.

côtier. **1.** *a.* Coast(ing). **2.** *s.m.* Coaster; coasting vessel.

cotillon [-tijɔ̃], *s.m. Danc:* Cotill(i)on.

coton, *s.m.* Cotton Fil de coton, sewing cotton.

cotonnier, *s.m.* Cotton plant.

coton-poudre, *s.m.* Gun-cotton.

côtoyer, *v.tr.* (je côtoie). **1.** To keep close to, hug (shore); to skirt (forest). **2.** To border on (river).

cotre, *s.m. Nau:* Cutter.

cotte, *s.f.* (*a*) Cotte de mailles, coat of mail. (*b*) Short skirt; petticoat.

cou, *s.m.* Neck. La peau du cou, the scruff of the neck. Couper le cou à qn, to behead s.o. Prendre ses jambes à son cou, to take one's heels.

couard. **1.** *a.* Cowardly. **2.** *s.m.* Coward

couardise, *s.f.* Cowardice.

couchant. **1.** *a.* Soleil couchant, setting sun. **2.** *s.m.* (*a*) Sunset. (*b*) Le couchant, the west.

couche, *s.f.* **1.** Faire ses couches, to be confined. **2.** (*a*) Bed, layer. *F: Couches sociales*, classes of society. (*b*) Coat (of paint).

coucher. I. *v.* **1.** *v.tr.* (*a*) To put (child) to

bed. (b) *La pluie a couché les blés*, the rain has laid the corn. **Coucher un fusil en joue**, to aim a gun. **2.** *v.i. C. à l'hôtel*, to sleep at the hotel.

se coucher. (a) To go to bed. (b) To lie down. (c) (Of sun) To set, go down.
  II. **coucher**, *s.m.* **1.** *L'heure du coucher*, bedtime. **2.** Setting (of sun).

couchette, *s.f.* **1.** (Child's) cot, crib. **2.** Berth (on train).

coucou, *s.m.* **1.** (a) *Orn:* Cuckoo. (b) Cuckoo-clock. **2.** *Bot:* Cowslip.

coude, *s.m.* **1.** Elbow. **Coude à coude**, side by side. **Coup de coude.** nudge. **2.** Bend, elbow (of road).

coudées, *s.f. pl.* **Avoir ses coudées franches**, (i) to have elbow-room, (ii) to have a free hand.

cou-de-pied, *s.m.* Instep. *pl. Des cous-de-pied.*

coudoiement, *s.m.* Elbowing.

coudoyer, *v.tr.* (je coudoie) To elbow (s.o.).

coudre, *v.tr.* (*pr.p.* cousant; *p.p.* cousu; *pr.ind.* ils cousent) To sew, stitch.
  cousu, *a.* Sewn. *F:* **Avoir la bouche cousue**, to keep one's mouth shut tight.

coudrier, *s.m.* Hazel(-tree).

couguar [-gaːr,-gwaːr], *s.m.* Cougar, puma.

coulant. 1. *a.* Running, flowing (liquid). *Nœud c.*, slip-knot; noose. **2.** *s.m.* Sliding ring; scarf-ring.

couler. 1. *v.tr.* (a) To run, pour (liquid). (b) **Couler (à fond) un navire**, to sink a ship. (c) *C. une pièce dans la main de qn*, to slip a coin into s.o.'s hand. **2.** *v.i.* (a) (Of liquids) To flow, run. (b) (Of ship) **Couler bas**, to founder.
  se couler, to glide, slip. *Se c. entre les draps*, to slip into bed.

couleur, *s.f.* Colour. **1.** (a) Tint, hue. *F:* **En avoir vu de toutes les couleurs**, to have had all sorts of experiences. (b) Complexion. **Être haut en couleur**, to have a high colour. (c) *pl. Nau:* Colours, flag. **2.** Colour, paint. "Attention à la couleur!" 'wet paint.' **Boîte de couleurs**, box of paints. **3.** *Cards:* Suit.

couleuvre, *s.f.* Snake. *F:* **Avaler une couleuvre**, to pocket an affront.

coulisse, *s.f.* **1.** (a) Groove, slot. **Porte à coulisse**, sliding door. (b) Slide. **2.** *Th:* Les coulisses, the wings.

couloir, *s.m.* **1.** Strainer. **2.** Corridor. *Rail:* **Wagon à couloir**, corridor carriage. **3.** Channel (for water); mountain gorge.

coup, *s.m.* **1.** (a) Knock, blow. *C. de bec*, peck. **Coup de couteau**, stab. **Coup de baïonnette**, bayonet-thrust. **Tenir le coup**, to withstand the blow. **En venir aux coups**, to come to blows. **Faire d'une pierre deux coups**, to kill two birds with one stone. *Prep. phr.* **A coups de**, with blows from (sth.). (b) **Coup de feu**, shot. (c) **Coup de vent**, gust of wind. **2.** Stroke (normal action of sth.). (a) **Coup d'aile**, stroke of the wing. **Coup de**

dents, bite. **Boire qch. à petits coups**, to sip sth. **Coup de plume**, stroke of the pen. *Sur le c. de midi*, on the stroke of twelve. (b) *Games:* (i) Stroke. (ii) *Fb:* Kick. *C. d'envoi*, kick-off. (c) *C. de bonheur*, stroke of luck. (d) Clap, peal (of thunder). **3.** Influence. *Agir sous le c. de la peur*, to act out of fear. **4.** (a) Attempt; deed. **Coup de tête**, impulsive act. *Il médite un mauvais c.*, he's up to mischief. (b) **Tout d'un coup**, **d'un seul coup**, at one go. **Il fut tué sur le coup**, he was killed outright. **Pour le coup**, for the moment. **Après coup**, after the event. **Tout à coup**, suddenly. **Coup sur coup**, in rapid succession.

coupable. 1. *a.* (a) Guilty. (b) Culpable (act). **2.** *s. m. & f.* Culprit.

coupant. 1. *a.* Cutting, sharp. *Outils coupants*, edge-tools. **2.** *s.m.* Edge.

coupe¹, *s.f.* Cup. (a) *C. à champagne*, champagne glass. (b) *Sp:* (Gold) cup.

coupe², *s.f.* **1.** (a) Cutting (of hay); cutting out (of garment). *C. de cheveux*, hair-cut. (b) Cut (of a coat). (c) Section. **2.** *Cards:* Cut, cutting.

coupée, *s.f.* *Nau:* Gangway.

coupe-gorge, *s.m.inv.* Death-trap.

coupe-papier, *s.m.inv.* Paper-knife.

couper, *v.tr.* To cut. **1.** *Se c. au doigt*, to cut one's finger. *C. la tête à qn*, to cut off s.o.'s head. *C. un vêtement*, to cut out a garment. *Cards: Couper les cartes*, to cut. **2.** To cut, cross. *v.i.* **Couper au plus court**, to take a short cut. **3.** To cut off, interrupt. (a) **Couper la parole à qn**, to interrupt s.o. **Couper la respiration à qn**, to take s.o.'s breath away. (b) To turn off. *El: C. le courant*, to switch off the current. (c) *Cards:* To trump.
  coupé. 1. *a.* Cut up; broken (sleep). **2.** *s.m. Veh:* Brougham. *Aut:* Coupé.

couperosé, *a.* Blotchy (complexion).

couple. 1. *s.m.* Pair, couple. **2.** *s.f.* (a) Two, couple. (b) Leash (for dogs).

coupler, *v.tr.* To couple.

couplet, *s.m.* Verse (of song).

coupole, *s.f.* Cupola.

coupon, *s.m.* **1.** Cutting. *Coupons d'étoffe*, remnants. **2.** *Fin:* Coupon.

coupure, *s.f.* **1.** Cut (on finger). **2.** Piece cut out. *C. de journal*, newspaper cutting.

cour, *s.f.* **1.** Court. (a) *A la cour*, at court. (b) **Faire la cour à une jeune fille**, to court a young lady. **2.** *C. de justice*, court of justice. **3.** Court, yard. *C. de récréation*, school playground.

courage, *s.m.* Courage, valour. **Du courage!** cheer up!

courageusement, *adv.* Courageously, bravely.

courageux, *a.* Courageous, brave.

couramment, *adv.* **1.** Easily, readily; fluently. **2.** *C. employé*, in current use.

courant. 1. *a.* (a) Running. **Chien courant,**

hound. (b) Flowing. **Chambre avec eau courante,** bedroom with running water. (c) Current. **Le cinq courant,** the fifth inst. **Fin courant,** at the end of this month. **2.** *s.m.* (a) Current, stream. **Courant d'air,** draught. (b) Course. **Être au courant de l'affaire,** to know all about the matter.

courbature, *s.f.* Stiffness, tiredness. *Avoir une c.,* to be stiff all over.

courbe. 1. *a.* Curved. **2.** *s.f.* (a) Curve; sweep (of road). (b) Curve, graph.

courber. 1. *v.tr.* To bend, curve. *C. le front,* to bow one's head. **2.** *v.i.* To bend; to sag.

se courber, to bend, stoop.

courbure, *s.f.* Curvature.

coureur, -euse, *s.* **1.** Runner. **2.** (a) Wanderer, rover. *C. de routes,* tramp. (b) Gadabout. *C. de spectacles,* playgoer. (c) *C. de dots,* fortune-hunter.

courge, *s.f. Bot:* Gourd; vegetable marrow.

courir, *v.* (*pr.p.* **courant;** *p.p.* **couru;** *pr.ind.* je **cours;** *fu.* je **courrai.** The aux. is *avoir*) **1.** *v.i.* To run. (a) **J'y cours,** I'm going directly. *Arriver en courant,* to come running up. (b) *Sp:* To race; to run (in a race). (c) (Of ship) To sail. *C. au large,* to stand out to sea. (d) To be current. *Le bruit court que . . .,* there is a report abroad that. . . . **Par le temps qui court,** nowadays. **2.** *v.tr.* (a) To hunt (animal). (b) *C. un risque,* to run a risk. **3.** (With cogn. acc.) (a) *C. une course,* to run a race. (b) **Courir le monde,** to roam the world over.

couru, *a.* Popular (preacher).

courlis, *s.m. Orn:* Curlew.

couronne, *s.f.* **1.** Wreath (of flowers). **2.** (King's) crown; (ducal) coronet. **3.** *Num:* Crown.

couronnement, *s.m.* Coronation (of king).

couronner, *v.tr.* (a) To crown (with a wreath). (b) **Couronner qn roi,** to crown s.o. king.

courr-ai, -ons, etc. See COURIR.

courrier, *s.m.* **1.** Courier; messenger. **2.** Mail, post. **Par retour du courrier,** by return of post. **Faire son courrier,** to do one's correspondence.

courroie, *s.f.* Strap.

courroux, *s.m. Lit:* Anger, wrath.

cours, *s.m.* **1.** (a) Course; flow (of river). **Cours d'eau,** stream. **Donner libre cours à son imagination,** to give free play to one's imagination. **En cours de route,** on the way. **Au cours de l'hiver,** during the winter. (b) *Voyage au long c.,* ocean voyage. **2.** Circulation, currency (of money). **Avoir cours,** to be legal tender. **3.** *C. du change,* rate of exchange. **4.** Course (of lectures). **Finir ses cours,** to finish one's studies.

cour-s, -t. See COURIR.

course, *s.f.* **1.** Run, running. **2.** Race, racing. *C. de vitesse,* sprint. **3.** (a) Excursion, outing. (b) Journey. *Payer (le prix de) sa c.,*

to pay one's fare. (c) (Business) errand. **Faire des courses,** to run errands. **4.** Path, course (of planet).

court. 1. *a.* Short. (a) **Avoir l'esprit court,** to be of limited understanding. *s.m.* **Se trouver à court,** to find oneself short (of money). (b) (In time) *C. intervalle,* short interval. *De courte durée,* short-lived. **2.** *adv.* Short. *Tourner c. à droite,* to turn sharp to the right. **Tout court,** simply.

courtaud, *a. & s.* Dumpy, squat (person).

courtepointe, *s.f.* Counterpane.

courtier, *s.m. Com:* Broker. **Courtier maritime,** ship-broker.

courtisan, *s.m.* Courtier.

courtisane, *s.f.* Courtesan.

courtiser, *v.tr.* To court (s.o.).

courtois, *a.* Courteous; polite, urbane.

courtoisement, *adv.* Courteously.

courtoisie, *s.f.* **1.** Courtesy; politeness. **2.** (Act of) courtesy.

couseuse, *s.f.* Sewer, seamstress.

cous-ez, -ons, etc. See COUDRE.

cousin¹, *s.* Cousin.

cousin², *s.m. Ent: F:* Gnat, midge.

coussin, *s.m.* Cushion.

coussinet, *s.m.* **1.** Small cushion; pad. **2.** *Mec.E:* Bearing. **Coussinets à billes,** ball-bearings.

coût, *s.m.* Cost.

couteau, *s.m.* Knife. *F:* **Figure en lame de couteau,** hatchet face. **Ils sont à couteaux tirés,** they are at daggers drawn.

coutelas, *s.m. Nau:* Cutlass.

coutelier, *s.m.* Cutler.

coutellerie, *s.f.* **1.** Cutlery (trade or wares). **2.** Cutler's shop.

coûter, *v.i.* **1.** To cost. **Coûter cher,** to be expensive. **Coûte que coûte,** at all costs. **2.** *Cela me coûte à dire,* it pains me to have to say this.

coûteux, *a.* Costly, expensive.

coutil, *s.m. Tex:* Drill, twill; duck.

coutume, *s.f.* Custom, habit. **Avoir coutume de faire qch.,** to be in the habit of doing sth. **Comme de coutume,** as usual.

coutumier, *a.* Customary. **Droit coutumier,** common law.

couture, *s.f.* **1.** Sewing, needlework. **2.** Seam (in dress). *F:* **Battre qn à plate(s) couture(s),** to beat s.o. hollow.

couturier, *s.* (a) *s.m. & f.* Dressmaker. (b) *s.f.* Seamstress; needlewoman.

couvée, *s.f.* **1.** Sitting, clutch (of eggs). **2.** Brood, hatch(ing) (of chicks).

couvent, *s.m.* (a) Convent, nunnery. (b) Monastery.

couver. 1. *v.tr.* (a) (Of hen) To sit on (eggs). (b) To incubate, to hatch (out) (eggs). (c) *F:* **Couver le feu,** to brood over the fire. **Couver qn des yeux,** to look fondly at s.o. **2.** *v.i.* (Of fire) To smoulder.

couvercle, *s.m.* Lid, cover.

couvert, See COUVRIR.

couverture, *s.f.* **1.** Covering, cover; blanket. **Sous couverture d'amitié,** under the cloak of friendship. **2.** Roofing.

couveuse, *s.f. Husb:* **1.** Sitting hen. **2.** *C. artificielle,* incubator.

couvre-feu, *s.m.inv.* Curfew.

couvre-lit, *s.m.* Bedspread, counterpane. *pl. Des couvre-lits.*

couvre-pied(s), *s.m.* (a) Coverlet. *C. piqué,* (eider-down) quilt. (b) Bedspread. *pl. Des couvre-pieds.*

couvre-théière, *s.m.* Tea-cosy. *pl. Des couvre-théières.*

couvrir, *v.tr.* (Conj. like OUVRIR) To cover (*de,* with). **1.** *C. les pauvres,* to clothe the poor. *Mur couvert de lierre,* wall overgrown with ivy. *C. la table,* to lay the table. *C. une enchère,* to make a higher bid. **2.** *C. une maison,* to roof a house. *Maison couverte en chaume,* thatched house.

se couvrir. 1. (a) To clothe oneself. (b) To put on one's hat. **2.** (Of weather) To become overcast.

couvert[1], *a.* **1.** *Allée couverte,* shady walk. *Ciel c.,* overcast sky. **2.** *Rester c.,* to keep one's hat on. **3.** Clad.

couvert[2], *s.m.* **1.** Cover(ing), shelter. *Se mettre à couvert,* to take cover. **Sous le couvert de la nuit,** under cover of night. **2.** (a) Fork and spoon. (b) Cover, place (at table). **Mettre le couvert,** to lay the table. *La table est de vingt couverts,* the table is laid for twenty. (c) (In restaurant) Table-money.

coyote, *s.m. Z:* Coyote; prairie wolf.

crabe, *s.m.* Crab.

crac [krak], *int. & s.m.* Crack, snap.

crachat, *s.m.* Spittle, spit.

cracher. 1. *v.i.* (a) To spit. *F: Il ne faut pas cracher dessus,* it is not to be sneezed at. (b) (Of pen) To splutter. **2.** *v.tr.* To spit (out). *C. des injures,* to hurl abuse.

craché, *a. F: C'est son père tout craché,* he's the dead spit of his father.

crachin, *s.m.* Mizzle, fine drizzle.

Cracovie. *Pr.n.f. Geog:* Cracow.

craie, *s.f.* Chalk.

craign-ant, -e, -ons, etc. See CRAINDRE.

craindre, *v.tr.* (*pr.p.* craignant; *p.p.* craint; *pr.ind.* je crains; *p.h.* je craignis) (a) To fear, dread; be afraid of (sth.). *Je crains qu'il (ne) soit mort,* I fear he is dead. *Il est à c. que . . .,* it is to be feared that. . . . *Faire craindre qch. à qn,* to put s.o. in fear of sth. (b) *Com:* "Craint l'humidité," 'to be kept dry.'

crainte, *s.f.* Fear, dread; awe. **De crainte de tomber,** for fear of falling. **De crainte que . . .** (ne) + *sub.,* lest. . . .

craintif, *a.* Timid, timorous.

craintivement, *adv.* Timidly.

cramoisi, *a. & s.m.* Crimson.

crampe, *s.f. Med:* Cramp.

crampon, *s.m.* **1.** Cramp(-iron); clamp. **2.** Climbing-iron.

cramponner (se) *à qch.,* to hold on to sth.

cran, *s.m.* **1.** Notch. (a) Cog (of wheel). *Au c. sûreté,* at half-cock. (b) Distance between holes (in strap). **Descendre d'un cran,** to come down a peg. **2.** *F: Avoir du cran,* to have plenty of pluck.

crâne. 1. *s.m.* Skull; brain-pan. **2.** *a. F:* (a) Plucky (conduct). (b) Jaunty (air).

crânement, *adv. F:* (a) Pluckily. (b) Jauntily.

cranien, -ienne, *a. Anat:* Cranial.

crapaud, *s.m.* **1.** Toad. *F: Avaler un crapaud,* to pocket an insult. **2.** *Pyr:* Jumping cracker. **3.** Tub easy-chair.

crapaudine, *s.f.* Toadstone.

crapuleux, *a.* Debauched, dissolute.

craquer, *v.i.* To crack; to crackle; (of hard snow) to crunch (under the feet); (of shoes) to creak.

crasse. 1. *a.f.* Gross, crass. **2.** *s.f.* (Body) dirt. *F: Né dans la crasse,* born in squalor.

crasseux, *a.* Dirty, filthy (hands); squalid (dwelling).

cratère, *s.m.* Crater.

cravache, *s.f.* Riding-whip; hunting-crop.

cravate, *s.f.* (Neck-)tie; scarf.

crayeux, *a.* Chalky.

crayon, *s.m.* (a) Pencil. *C. à mine de plomb,* lead pencil. *C. pastel,* crayon. (b) Pencil-drawing; -sketch.

crayonner, *v.tr.* To pencil; to write, jot (sth.) down (on paper).

créance, *s.f.* **1.** Belief, credit. **Trouver créance,** to be believed. **2.** Trust. **Lettre(s) de créance,** credentials. **3.** Debt.

créancier, *s.* Creditor.

créateur, -trice. 1. *a.* Creative (power). **2.** *s.* Creator.

création, *s.f.* **1.** (a) Creation, creating. (b) Founding (of institution). **2.** *Les merveilles de la c.,* the wonders of creation.

créature, *s.f.* Creature.

crécelle, *s.f.* (Hand-)rattle.

crécerelle, *s.f. Orn:* Kestrel.

crèche, *s.f.* **1.** Manger, crib. **2.** (a) (Child's) crib. (b) (Public) day-nursery, crèche.

crédibilité, *s.f.* Credibility.

crédit[1], *s.m.* Credit, repute; prestige.

crédit[2], *s.m.* Credit. **Vendre qch. à crédit,** to sell sth. on credit. **Faire crédit à qn,** to give s.o. credit.

créditer, *v.tr. C. qn du montant d'une somme,* to credit s.o. with a sum.

créditeur, -trice, *s.* Creditor.

credo [kre-], *s.m.inv.* Creed.

crédule, *a.* Credulous.

crédulité, *s.f.* Credulity.

créer, *v.tr.* To create. *Se c. une clientèle,* to build up a connection.

crémaillère, *s.f.* **1.** Pot-hanger, -hook. *F: Pendre la crémaillère,* to have a house-warming. **2.** *Chemin de fer à crémaillère,* rack-railway.

crémation, *s.f.* Cremation.
crématorium [-jɔm], *s.m.* Crematorium.
crème, *s.f.* Cream. (*a*) *C. fouettée,* whipped cream. **Fromage à la crème,** cream-cheese. *a.inv.* **Rubans crème,** cream(-coloured) ribbons. (*b*) *Cu:* Custard, cream.
crémer, *v.tr.* (je **crème**; je **crémerai**) To cremate.
crémerie, *s.f.* **I.** Creamery, dairy; milkshop. **2.** Small restaurant.
crémeux, *a.* Creamy.
crémier, *s.* Dairyman, dairy-woman.
créneau, *s.m.* Crenel; *pl.* battlements.
crénelé, *a.* **I.** Crenellated, battlemented (wall). **2.** Toothed, notched.
créole, *a. & s. Ethn:* Creole.
crêpe. I. *s.f.* Pancake. **2.** *s.m.* (*a*) Crape. (*b*) **Crêpe de caoutchouc,** crêpe-rubber.
crépir, *v.tr.* To rough-cast (wall).
crépitement, *s.m.* Crackling; sputtering.
crépiter, *v.i.* To crackle; (of rain) to patter; (of candle) to sputter.
crépu, *a.* Crisp, frizzy, fuzzy (hair).
crépusculaire, *a.* Twilight, crepuscular.
crépuscule, *s.m.* Twilight; dusk.
cresson, *s.m. Bot:* Cress. *C. de fontaine,* water-cress.
crête, *s.f.* **I.** Comb, crest (of bird). **2.** (*a*) Crest (of wave). (*b*) Crest, ridge (of mountain).
crétin, *s.m.* (*a*) Cretin, idiot. (*b*) *F:* Hopeless ass.
crétois, *a. & s.* Cretan.
cretonne, *s.f. Tex:* Cretonne.
creuser, *v.tr.* **I.** To hollow (out); to plough (a furrow). **Front creusé de rides,** brow furrowed with wrinkles. *Se c. le cerveau,* to rack one's brains. **2.** To excavate.
creuset, *s.m.* Crucible, melting-pot.
creux. I. *a.* Hollow. *Chemin c.,* sunk(en), road. *Yeux c.,* deep-set eyes. *Voix creuse,* deep voice. **Avoir la tête creuse,** to be empty-headed. *adv.* **Sonner creux,** to sound hollow. **2.** *s.m.* Hollow (of the hand); hole (in the ground); trough (of wave).
crevaison, *s.f.* (*a*) Puncture (in tyre). (*b*) Bursting (of tyre).
crevasse, *s.f.* Crack (in skin); crevice (in wall); crevasse (in glacier). *Avoir des crevasses aux mains,* to have chapped hands.
crève-cœur, *s.m.inv.* Keen disappointment.
crever, *v.* (je **crève**) **I.** *v.i.* (*a*) To burst, split. **Crever de rire,** to split (one's sides) with laughter. (*b*) (Of animals) To die. *F:* **Crever de faim,** to be starving. **2.** *v.tr.* To burst (bag); to puncture (tyre). **Crever un œil à qn,** to put out s.o.'s eye. *F:* **Ça vous crève les yeux,** it's staring you in the face.
crevette, *s.f. C. grise,* shrimp. *C. rouge,* prawn.
cri, *s.m.* (*a*) Cry; chirp (of bird). *Cri perçant,* shriek (of person); squeal (of animal). (*b*) Shout, call. **Pousser les hauts cris,** to make shrill protest. *F:* **Le dernier cri,** the latest fashion.

criailler [kriɑje], *v.i.* **I.** To cry out, bawl. **2.** To whine, complain.
criard, *a.* (*a*) Squalling, peevish. (*b*) *Voix criarde,* shrill voice. *Dettes criardes,* pressing debts. *Couleur criarde,* loud colour.
crible, *s.m.* Sieve, riddle.
cribler, *v.tr.* **I.** To sift, riddle. **2.** *C. qn de balles,* to riddle s.o. with bullets.
criblé, *a.* **Criblé de dettes,** head over ears in debt.
cric [krik], *s.m.* (Lifting) jack.
cricri, cri-cri, *s.m.* **I.** Chirping (of cricket). **2.** *Ent:* *F:* Cricket.
criée, *s.f.* Auction. **Vente à la criée,** sale by auction.
crier. I. *v.i.* (*a*) To cry; to call out, to shout. *C. après qn,* to carp at s.o. *C. au secours,* to shout for help. (*b*) (Of mouse) To squeak; (of cricket) to chirp. (*c*) (Of door) To creak. **2.** *v.tr.* To cry, hawk (vegetables). *F:* *C. qch. sur les toits,* to cry sth. from the house-tops.
crime, *s.m.* Crime; *Jur:* felony.
criminel, -elle, *a.* **I.** (*a*) Guilty. (*b*) *s.* Criminal, felon. **2.** Criminal (attempt).
crin, *s.m.* Horsehair. *Les crins,* the mane and tail. *F:* **Révolutionnaire à tous crins,** out and out revolutionary.
crinière, *s.f.* Mane.
crique, *s.f.* Creek, cove.
criquet, *s.m. Ent:* Locust.
crise, *s.f.* **I.** Crisis. **2.** Attack (of gout). *Avoir une crise de larmes,* to have a fit of crying.
crispation, *s.f.* (*a*) Shrivelling up (of leather). (*b*) Nervous twitching, clenching (of the hands).
crisper, *v.tr.* To contract, clench.
criss, *s.m.* Creese, kris, Malay dagger.
crissement, *s.m.* Grating, grinding (of teeth); squeak (of brakes).
crisser, *v.tr. & i.* To grate.
cristal, -aux, *s.m.* **I.** Crystal. **2.** Crystal (-glass). *C. taillé,* cut glass.
cristallin, *a.* Clear as crystal.
cristallisation, *s.f.* Crystallization.
cristalliser, *v.tr. & i.* To crystallize.
critérium [-rjɔm], *s.m.,* **critère,** *s.m.* Criterion; test.
critique[1]. I. *a.* Critical. (*a*) Decisive, crucial. (*b*) *Examen c. d'un ouvrage,* critical examination of a work. **2.** *s.m.* Critic.
critique[2], *s.f.* Criticism. **I.** **Faire la critique d'une pièce,** to write a criticism of a play. **2.** Censure.
critiquer, *v.tr.* (*a*) To criticize. (*b*) To censure.
croassement, *s.m.* Caw(ing); croak(ing).
croasser, *v.i.* To caw; to croak.
croate. I. *a.* Croatian. **2.** *s.* Croat.
croc [kro], *s.m.* **I.** (*a*) Hook. (*b*) Pawl, catch. **2.** Canine tooth; fang (of wolf).
croc-en-jambe [krɔkɑ̃ʒɑ̃b], *s.m.* Trip. *Faire un c.-en-j. à qn,* to trip s.o. up.

croche, *s.f. Mus:* Quaver. **Double croche,** semiquaver.

crochet, *s.m.* Hook. **I.** Crochet-hook. Dentelle au crochet, crochet-work. **2.** *C. de serrurier,* picklock. *C. d'arrêt,* pawl, catch. **3.** Poison fang (of serpent). **4.** **Faire un crochet,** (of road) to take a sudden turn.

crochu, *a.* **I.** Hooked (nose). **2.** Crooked (stick).

crocodile, *s.m.* Crocodile.

croire, *v.* (*pr.p.* croyant; *p.p.* cru) **I.** *v.tr.* (*a*) *C. qch.,* to believe sth. **Il est à croire que** + *ind.,* it is probable that. . . . *Je ne crois pas que cela suffise,* I don't think that will be enough. **Je (le) crois bien!** I should think so! *Je crois que oui,* I believe so. **N'en croyez rien!** do not believe it! **A ce que je crois** . . ., to the best of my belief. . . . *Il se croit tout permis,* he thinks he may do anything. *F:* **Quel temps, croit-tu!** what beastly weather! (*b*) *C. qn,* to believe s.o. **Me croira qui voudra, mais . . .,** believe me or not, but. . . . *F:* **Je te crois!** rather! *Croyez-m'en,* be advised by me. *Je ne pouvais en c. mes yeux,* I couldn't believe my eyes. **2.** *v.i.* (*a*) *C. à qch.,* to believe in (the existence of) sth. *C'est à ne pas y croire,* it is beyond all belief. *C. au témoignage des sens,* to trust the evidence of one's senses. (*b*) *C. en qn,* to believe in, have faith in s.o.

crois. See CROÎTRE.

croisade, *s.f. Hist:* Crusade.

croisement, *s.m.* **I.** Crossing, meeting (of traffic). **2.** Crossing, intersection (of roads).

croiser. **I.** *v.tr.* To cross. **Rester les bras croisés,** to stand with arms folded. *C. qn sur l'escalier,* to pass s.o. on the stairs. *Leurs regards se croisèrent,* their eyes met. **2.** *v.i. Nau:* To cruise.

croisé. **I.** *a.* Crossed. *Pros: Rimes croisées,* alternate rhymes. *Husb: Race croisée,* cross-breed. **2.** *s.m.* Crusader.

croisée, *s.f.* **I.** **Croisée des chemins,** cross-roads. **2.** Casement-window.

croiseur, *s.m. Navy:* Cruiser.

croisière, *s.f.* Cruise.

croisillon [-zijɔ̃], *s.m.* Cross-piece; window bar.

croissance, *s.f.* Growth. **Arrêté dans sa croissance,** stunted.

croissant¹, *a.* Growing (plant); increasing (anxiety, etc.); rising (prices).

croissant², *s.m.* **I.** Crescent (of moon). **2.** *Cu:* Crescent(-roll).

croiss-e, -es, etc. See CROÎTRE.

croît. See CROÎTRE.

croître, *v.i.* (*pr.p.* croissant; *p.p.* crû, *f.* crue; *pr.ind.* je crois, il croît) To grow, increase. *La rivière a crû,* the river has risen. *Aller croissant,* to go on increasing.

croix, *s.f.* Cross. **I. La mise en croix,** the crucifixion. *Faire le signe de la c.,* to cross oneself. **La Croix rouge,** the Red Cross. *Mil:* **La Croix de guerre,** the Military Cross.

Croix ou pile, heads or tails. **2.** *Typ:* Dagger.

croquant, *a.* Crisp (biscuit).

croque-mitaine, *s.m. F:* Bogy(-man), bugaboo. *pl. Des croque-mitaines.*

croque-mort, *s.m.* (Undertaker's) mute. *pl. Des croque-morts.*

croquer, *v.tr.* (*a*) To crunch, munch. Chocolat à croquer, eating chocolate. (*b*) To sketch. *F:* **Elle est gentille à croquer,** she is perfectly sweet.

croquet, *s.m. Games:* Croquet.

croquis, *s.f.* Sketch.

crosse, *s.f.* **I.** Crosier. **2.** *Sp:* (Hockey-) stick; (golf-)club. **3.** (*a*) Crook. (*b*) Butt (of rifle).

crotale, *s.m.* Rattlesnake.

crotte, *s.f.* **I.** Dung. **2.** Mud, dirt.

crotter, *v.tr.* To dirty, soil.

crouler, *v.i.* (Of building) (*a*) To totter. (*b*) To collapse. *Th: F:* **Faire crouler la salle,** to bring down the house.

croupe, *s.f.* **I.** Croup, rump (of horse). *Prendre qn en c.,* to take s.o. up behind. **2.** Ridge, brow (of hill).

croupier, *s.m.* Croupier (of gaming-house).

croupir, *v.i.* **I.** To lie, wallow (in filth). *C. dans l'oisiveté,* to lie sunk in sloth. **2.** (Of water) To stagnate.

croupi, *a.* Stagnant, foul.

croustillant [-tijã], *a.* Crisp, crusty (pie).

croûte, *s.f.* **I.** Crust (of bread); rind (of cheese). *F:* **Casser une croûte,** to have a snack. **2.** Scab (on wound). **3.** *F:* Daub.

croyance, *s.f.* Belief (à, in).

croy-ant¹, -ons, -ez, etc. See CROIRE.

croyant², **I.** *a.* Believing. **2.** *s.* Believer.

cru¹, *a.* **I.** Raw (meat); crude (colour). **2.** *Adv.phr.* A cru, next to the skin.

cru², *s.m.* Vin du cru, local wine. **Sentir le cru,** to smack of the soil. *F: Une histoire de son cru,* a story of his own invention.

cru³, cru-s, -t, etc. See CROIRE.

crû, crû-s, -t. See CROÎTRE.

cruauté, *s.f.* Cruelty (*envers,* to).

cruche, *s.f.* Pitcher, jug.

cruchon, *s.m.* **I.** Small jug; pot (of beer). **2.** (Stoneware) hot-water bottle.

crucifères, *s.f.pl. Bot:* Cruciferae.

crucifier, *v.tr.* To crucify.

crucifix, *s.m.* Crucifix.

crucifixion, *s.f.* Crucifixion.

cruciforme, *a.* Cruciform; cross-shaped.

crudité, *s.f.* Crudity.

crue, *s.f.* Rising (of river); flood. **Rivière en crue,** river in spate.

cruel, -elle, *a.* Cruel (*envers,* to).

cruellement, *adv.* Cruelly.

crûment, *adv.* Crudely, roughly.

cruss-e, -es, etc. See CROIRE.

crûss-e, -es, etc. See CROÎTRE.

crustacés, *s.m.pl.* Crustacea; shellfish.

crypte, *s.f.* Crypt.

cryptogramme, *s.m.* Cryptogram; cipher.

cubain, *a. & s. Geog:* Cuban.

cube. 1. *s.m.* Cube. **2.** *a.* **Mètre cube,** cubic metre.

cuber, *v.tr.* To cube (number).

cubique, *a.* (*a*) Cubic(al). (*b*) *Mth:* **Racine cubique,** cube root.

cueillage [kœja:ʒ], *s.m.* Picking, gathering (of fruit).

cueiller-ai, -as, etc. See CUEILLIR.

cueillette [kœjɛt], *s.f.* Gathering, picking (of fruit).

cueillir [kœji:r], *v.tr.* (*pr.p.* **cueillant;** *pr.ind.* **je cueille;** *fu.* **je cueillerai**) To pick, pluck (fruit). *C. des lauriers,* to win laurels.

cuiller, cuillère [kyjɛ:r, kɥijɛ:r], *s.f.* Spoon. *C. à bouche,* table-spoon.

cuillerée [kyj-, kɥij-], *s.f.* Spoonful.

cuir, *s.m.* **1.** Hide (of elephant). **2.** (*a*) Leather. *C. vert,* raw hide. *C. verni,* patent leather. (*b*) **Cuir à rasoir,** razor-strop.

cuirasse, *s.f.* **1.** Cuirass. *F: Trouver le défaut dans la c. de qn,* to find s.o's weak spot. **2.** Armour (of warship).

cuirassé. 1. *a.* Armoured. **2.** *s.m.* Armoured ship; battleship.

cuirassier, *s.m. Mil:* Cuirassier.

cuire, *v.* (Conj. like CONDUIRE) **1.** *v.tr.* (*a*) To cook. *Cuit à point,* done to a turn. (*b*) To bake (bricks). **2.** *v.i.* (*a*) (Of food) To cook. *C. à petit feu,* to cook slowly; to simmer. **Faire cuire un bifteck,** to cook a steak. (*b*) To burn, smart. *Il vous en cuira,* you shall smart for it; you'll be sorry.

cuisant, *a.* Smarting, burning (pain); biting (cold).

cuisine, *s.f.* **1.** Kitchen. *Nau:* (Cook's) galley. **2.** (*a*) Cookery. **Faire la cuisine,** to do the cooking.

cuisinier, *s.* **1.** Cook. **2.** *s.f. Cuisinière à gaz,* gas-cooker.

cuisse, *s.f.* Thigh. *Cu: C. de poulet,* chicken leg.

cuistre, *s.m. F:* Cad; ill-mannered cur.

cuit, cuite. See CUIRE.

cuivre, *s.m.* **Cuivre rouge,** copper. **Cuivre jaune,** brass.

cuivré, *a.* **1.** Copper-coloured. *Teint c.,* bronzed complexion. **2.** *Mus: Sons cuivrés,* brassy tones.

cul [ky], *s.m.* **1.** (*a*) *V:* Backside, bottom. **2.** Bottom (of bottle).

culasse, *s.f.* Breech (of gun).

cul-blanc, *s.m. Orn:* Wheatear, stonechat. *pl. Des culs-blancs.*

culbute, *s.f.* (*a*) Somersault. **Faire la culbute,** to turn a somersault. (*b*) Tumble; heavy fall.

culbuter. 1. *v.i.* To turn a somersault. **2.** *v.tr.* To knock over, upset (sth.).

cul-de-jatte, *s.m.* Legless cripple. *pl. Des culs-de-jatte.*

culinaire, *a.* Culinary.

culminant, *a.* **Point culminant,** highest point; height, climax.

culot, *s.m.* **1.** (Metal) base (of cartridge). *P:*

Avoir du culot, to have plenty of cheek. **2.** Dottle.

culotte, *s.f.* **1.** *Cu:* Rump (of beef). **2.** **Une culotte,** a pair of breeches.

culpabilité, *s.f.* Culpability, guilt.

culte, *s.m.* **1.** Worship. **Avoir un culte pour qn,** to worship s.o. **2.** Form of worship; cult.

cultivateur, *s.m.* Cultivator; farmer.

cultiver, *v.tr.* **1.** To cultivate, farm, till (the soil). **2.** To cultivate (plants).

cultivé, *a.* **1.** Cultivated. **2.** Cultured.

culture, *s.f.* **1.** (*a*) Cultivation, tilling (of the soil). (*b*) *pl.* Land under cultivation. **2.** Cultivation, culture (of plants).

cumulus [-ly:s], *s.m.inv.* Cumulus; cloud-rack.

cunéiforme, *a.* Wedge-shaped, arrow-headed; cuneiform (writing).

cupide, *a.* Covetous, greedy, grasping.

cupidité, *s.f.* Cupidity, greed.

cupidon. *Pr.n.m.* Cupid.

cupule, *s.f.* Cupule; cup (of acorn).

curable, *a.* Curable (disease).

curateur, -trice, *s. Jur:* Trustee, administrator; guardian.

curatif, *a. & s.m.* Curative.

cure, *s.f.* **1.** Care. *Personne n'en a c.,* nobody cares. **2.** *Med:* (Course of) treatment; cure.

curé, *s.m.* Parish priest.

cure-dents, *s.m.inv.* Tooth-pick.

curée, *s.f.* (i) *Ven:* Quarry; (ii) **Être âpre à la curée,** to be eager for gain.

curieusement, *adv.* **1.** (*a*) Inquiringly. (*b*) Inquisitively. **2.** Curiously, quaintly.

curieux, *a.* Curious. (*a*) Interested. *Je serai c. de voir cela,* I shall be interested to see it. (*b*) Inquisitive (*de,* about). (*c*) Odd, peculiar.

curiosité, *s.f.* Curiosity. **1.** (*a*) Interested-ness. (*b*) Inquisitiveness. (*c*) Oddness, peculiarity. **2.** Curio.

cursif, *a.* (*a*) Cursive, running (handwriting). (*b*) Cursory.

curviligne, *a.* Curvilinear, rounded.

cutané, *a.* Cutaneous.

cuticule, *s.f.* Cuticle, epidermis.

cuve, *s.f.* Vat, tun.

cuver, *v.tr.* To ferment (wine). *F:* **Cuver son vin,** to sleep off one's drink.

cuvette, *s.f.* **1.** Wash-basin. **2.** Dish.

cyanhydrique, *a. Ch:* Hydrocyanic (acid).

cyanure, *s.m. Ch:* Cyanide.

cycle, *s.m.* **1.** Cycle (of events). **2.** (Bi-, tri) cycle.

cyclisme, *s.m. Sp:* Cycling.

cycliste, *s.m. & f.* Cyclist.

cyclone, *s.m. Meteor:* Cyclone.

cyclope, *s.m. Myth:* Cyclops.

cyclopéen, -enne, *a.* Cyclopean, gigantic.

cygne, *s.m.* Swan. *Jeune c.,* cygnet.

cylindre, *s.m.* Cylinder.

cylindrique, *a.* Cylindrical.

cymbale, *s.f. Mus:* Cymbal.

cynique. 1. *a.* (*a*) *A.Phil:* Cynic(al). (*b*) Shameless (morals); brazen (insolence).

2. *s.m.* (*a*) *A.Phil:* Cynic. (*b*) Shameless person.
cynisme, *adv.* Shamelessly.
cynisme, *s.m.* **I.** *A.Phil:* Cynicism. **2.** Shamelessness, effrontery.

cyprès, *s.m.* *Bot:* Cypress-(tree).
cypriote, *a. & s.* *Geog:* Cyprian, Cypriot; of Cyprus.
cytise, *s.m.* *Bot:* **I.** Cytisus. **2.** Laburnum.

D

D, d [de], *s.m.* (The letter) D, d.
dactylo, *s.m. & f.* *F:* Typist.
dactylographe, *s.m. & f.* Typist.
dada, *s.m.* *F:* **I.** Gee-gee. **2.** Hobby.
dague, *s.f.* Dagger; *Navy:* dirk.
dahlia, *s.m.* *Bot:* Dahlia.
daigner, *v.tr.* To deign, condescend.
daim, *s.m.* (Fallow-)deer; buck.
dais [dɛ], *s.m.* Canopy.
Dalila. *Pr.n.f.* *B.Hist:* Delilah.
dallage, *s.m.* **I.** Paving. **2.** Tiled floor.
dalle, *s.f.* (*a*) Flag(stone). (*b*) Slab.
daltonisme, *s.m.* Colour-blindness.
Damas. **I.** *Pr.n.m.* *Geog:* Damascus. **2.** *s.m.* (*a*) *Tex:* Damask. (*b*) Damson.
damasquiner, *v.tr.* To inlay (blade).
dame[1], *s.f.* **I.** (*a*) (Noble) lady. *F:* Elle fait la (grande) dame, she puts on airs. (*b*) Lady. *Que prendront ces dames?* what will you take, ladies? (*c*) (Married) lady. *F:* Votre dame, your good lady. (*d*) Dame d'honneur, lady-in-waiting. Dame de compagnie, (paid) companion. Dames de charité, district-visitors. (*e*) (Gentleman's) partner (at dance). **2.** *Games:* (*a*) Jeu de dames, (game of) draughts. (*b*) King (at draughts); queen (at cards and chess). **3.** Rowlocks.
dame[2], *int.* Dame oui! well, yes! rather!
damier, *s.m.* Draught-board (in Fr. with 100 squares). Étoffe en damier, chequered material.
damner [dɑne], *v.tr.* To damn.
damné, *a. & s.* Damned. Être l'âme damnée de qn, to be a tool in the hands of s.o.
dandiner, *v.tr.* To dandle (baby).
se dandiner, to have a rolling gait.
Danemark [-mark]. *Pr.n.m.* Denmark.
danger, *s.m.* Danger, peril. *A l'abri du d.,* out of harm's way. Courir danger de . . ., to run the risk of. . . . *F:* Pas de danger! never fear! *Il n'y a pas de d. qu'il vienne,* there is no fear of his coming.
dangereusement, *adv.* Dangerously.
dangereux, *a.* Dangerous (*pour,* to).
danois. **I.** *a.* Danish. Chien danois, Great Dane. **2.** *s.* Dane. **3.** *s.m. Ling:* Danish.
dans, *prep.* **I.** (*a*) In. (*b*) Within. *D. un rayon de dix kilomètres,* within a radius of ten kilometres. (*c*) Into. *Tomber d. l'oubli,* to sink into oblivion. (*d*) Out of. *Boire d. un verre,* to drink out of a glass. (*e*) *Il a voyagé*

d. le monde, he has travelled about the world. **2.** (*a*) In, within, during. Dans le temps, formerly. *Je serai prêt à partir d. cinq minutes,* I shall be ready to start in five minutes. (Cp. *On peut aller à Londres en cinq heures,* it takes five hours to get to London.) **3.** (*a*) Être d. le commerce, to be in trade. (*b*) Être d. la nécessité de, to be under the necessity of. *D. cette occasion,* on that occasion.
dansant, *a.* **I.** Dancing. **2.** Thé dansant, dance tea.
danse, *s.f.* Dance, dancing. Aimer la d., to be fond of dancing. Danse de Saint-Guy, St. Vitus's dance.
danser, *v.tr.* **I.** To dance. Ne savoir sur quel pied danser, to be all at sea. **2.** (Of horse) To prance.
danseur, -euse, *s.* **I.** Dancer. **2.** Partner (at dance).
dard, *s.m.* (*a*) Sting (of insect); forked tongue (of serpent). (*b*) Tongue (of flame). (*c*) Piercing ray (of sun).
darder, *v.tr.* To shoot forth. *F: Il darda sur moi un regard chargé de haine,* he shot a glance of hatred at me.
dare-dare, *adv.* In hot haste.
date, *s.f.* Date. Prendre date pour qch., to fix a date for sth. (Of event) Faire date, to mark an epoch. Être le premier en date, to come first. Je le connais de longue date. I have known him for a long time.
dater. **I.** *v.tr.* To date (letter). **2.** *v.i.* A dater de ce jour, from to-day. *A d. du 15,* on and after the 15th.
datif, *a. & s.m.* *Gram:* Dative (case).
datte, *s.f.* *Bot:* Date.
dattier, *s.m.* *Bot:* Date-palm.
dauphin, *s.m.* **I.** Dolphin. **2.** Dauphin.
davantage, *adv.* More. *Il m'en faut d.,* I need still more. *Je n'en dis pas d.,* I shall say no more.
de. (Before vowels and h 'mute' d'. *De + def. art. le, les,* are contracted into du, des.) **I.** *prep.* **I.** (*a*) From. *Du matin au soir,* from morning till night. *De vous à moi,* between ourselves. *De jour en jour,* from day to day. (*b*) *Il partit de nuit,* he left by night. (*c*) *Accompagné de ses amis,* accompanied by his friends. *La statue est de Rodin,* the statue is by Rodin. *J'ai fait cela de ma*

propre main, I did it with my own hand.
Vivre de sa plume, to live by one's pen.
(d) *Répondre d'une voix douce,* to answer in a
gentle voice. (e) *Sauter de joie,* to leap for
joy. (f) *Je suis âgé de seize ans,* I am sixteen
years old. *Ma montre retarde de dix minutes,*
my watch is ten minutes slow. (g) *Altéré
de sang,* thirsting for blood. **2.** (a) *Le livre
de Pierre,* Peter's book. *Le toit de la maison,*
the roof of the house. (b) *Un pont de fer,*
an iron bridge. (c) *Le chien de berger,*
the sheep-dog. (Cp. *Le chien du berger,* the
shepherd's dog.) *Le journal d'hier,* yesterday's paper. (d) *Un verre de vin,* a glass of
wine. *Quelque chose de bon,* something good.
3. *Près de la maison,* near the house. *Autour
du jardin,* round the garden. **4.** *Manquer
de courage,* to lack courage. *Convenir d'une
erreur,* to admit an error.
　II. **de,** serving as a link word. **1.** (a) *Le
mieux était de rire,* it was best to laugh. *Ils
sont indignes de vivre,* they are unfit to live.
(b) *Ainsi dit le renard, et flatteurs d'applaudir,*
thus spoke the fox, and his flatterers applauded.
2. *La ville de Paris,* the town of Paris. *Un
drôle de garçon,* a funny chap. *Il y eut trois
hommes de tués,* three men were killed. F: *Si
j'étais de vous,* if I were you.
　III. **de,** partitive particle, not prepositional.
(Used also as *pl.* of *un, une) N'avez-vous pas
des amis?* have you not got friends? *Sans
faire de fautes,* without making any mistakes.
Donnez-nous de vos nouvelles, let us hear from
you. *Vous êtes des lâches,* you are cowards.
dé[1], *s.m.* Gaming: Die. *Dés pipés,* loaded
dice. **Coup de dé,** cast of the die. F: **Le dé
en est jeté,** the die is cast.
dé[2], *s.m. Dé (à coudre),* thimble.
débâcle, *s.f.* **1.** Break(ing) up. **2.** (a) Downfall, collapse.
déballer, *v.tr.* To unpack (goods).
débandade, *s.f.* Rout (of army); stampede
(of horses). **A la débandade,** in confusion.
débander, *v.tr.* To disband (troops).
　se débander, to disband; (of crowd)
to disperse.
débarbouiller [-buje], *v.tr.* To wash (s.o.'s)
face.
　se débarbouiller, to wash one's face.
débarcadère, *s.m.* Landing-stage, wharf.
débarder, *v.tr. Nau:* To unload (timber).
débardeur, *s.m.* Docker, stevedore.
débarquement, *s.m.* Unloading (of cargo);
landing, disembarkment (of persons).
débarquer. **1.** *v.tr.* To unload (cargo);
to disembark, land (passengers), to drop
(pilot). **2.** *v.i.* To land, disembark (from
boat); to alight (from train).
débarras, *s.m.* Riddance. **Chambre de
débarras,** lumber-room.
débarrasser, *v.tr.* To disencumber; to clear
(table). *D. qn de qch.,* to relieve s.o. of sth.
　se débarrasser *de qch.,* to get rid of sth;
to extricate oneself from sth.

débat, *s.m.* **1.** Debate. **2.** Dispute.
débattre, *v.tr.* (Conj. like BATTRE) To
debate, discuss.
　se débattre, to struggle.
débauche, *s.f.* Debauch(ery).
débaucher, *v.tr.* To lead (s.o.) astray.
　débauché. **1.** *a.* Debauched, profligate.
2. *s.* Debauchee; *s.m.* rake.
débile, *a.* Weakly (child); sickly (plant).
débilité, *s.f.* Debility, weakness.
débiliter, *v.tr.* To debilitate, weaken.
débit[1], *s.m.* (a) (Retail) sale. (b) (Retail) shop.
Esp. **Débit de tabac,** tobacconist's. **Débit de
boissons,** public house.
débit[2], *s.m. Com:* Debit.
débitant, *s.* Retail dealer; retailer.
débiter[1], *v.tr.* **1.** To retail; to sell (goods)
retail. **2.** To cut up (meat). **3.** *D. des
histoires,* to spin yarns.
débiter[2], *v.tr. Com:* To debit.
débiteur[1], -euse, *s.* Usu. *Pej: D. de
calomnies,* scandal-monger.
débiteur[2], -trice. **1.** *s.* Debtor. **2.** *a.*
Compte débiteur, debit account.
déblai, *s.m. Rail:* Cut(ting).
déblayer, *v.tr.* (je déblaye, je déblaie) **1.** To
clear away (snow). **2.** *D. un terrain,* to clear
a piece of ground.
déboire, *s.m.* F: Disappointment.
déboiser, *v.tr.* To deforest (land).
déboîter, *v.tr.* To dislocate (joint).
débonnaire, *a.* Good-natured, easy-going.
débordant, *a.* **1.** Overflowing (de, with).
2. Projecting, protruding; overlapping.
déborder. **1.** *v.tr. & i.* To overflow, run
over. *Elle déborde de vie,* she is bubbling
over with vitality. **2.** *v.tr.* (a) To project,
stick out; to overlap (sth.). (b) To outflank
(the enemy).
débouché, *s.m.* **1.** Outlet (of passage).
2. Opening; chance of success.
déboucher[1], *v.tr.* **1.** To clear (choked pipe).
2. To uncork (bottle).
déboucher[2], *v.i.* To emerge, issue (forth).
déboucler, *v.tr.* To unbuckle (belt).
débourber, *v.tr.* **1.** To cleanse; to clean
out. **2.** To haul (carriage) out of the mire.
débours, *s.m.* Usu. *pl.* Disbursement; out-
of-pocket expenses.
débourser, *v.tr.* To disburse (money).
debout, *adv.* **1.** (a) (Of thg) Upright, on
end; (of pers.) standing. **Se tenir debout,** to
stand. *Argument qui ne tient pas d.,* argument
that won't hold water. **"Places debout seulement,"** 'standing room only.' F: **Conte à
dormir debout,** silly story. (b) (Of pers.)
Être debout, to be up. **Allons, debout!** come,
get up! **2.** *Nau:* **Vent debout,** head wind.
déboutonner, *v.tr.* To unbutton.
débraillé [-raje], *a.* Untidy (person). *Mœurs
débraillées,* bohemian habits.
débrider, *v.tr.* To unbridle (horse), (hence)
to halt.
débris, *s.m.pl.* Remains, debris.

débrouillard [-brujaːr], *a. F:* (a) Resourceful. (b) Clear-headed.

débrouiller [-bruje], *v.tr.* To unravel (thread). *D. une affaire*, to straighten out an affair.

se débrouiller. 1. (Of the sky) To clear (up). **2.** To extricate oneself (from difficulties); to manage.

début, *s.m.* **I.** First appearance (of actor). **2.** Beginning, start, outset. **Appointements de début,** commencing salary.

débutant, *s.* Beginner, tyro.

débuter, *v.i.* **I.** To make one's first appearance (on the stage). **2.** To begin, start.

deçà, *adv.* On this side. **Deçà et delà,** here and there, on all sides.

décacheter, *v.tr.* (Conj. like CACHETER) To unseal, break open (letter).

décade, *s.f.* Decade.

décadence, *s.f.* Decadence, decline, decay.

décadent, *a.* Decadent; in decay.

décagone, *s.m. Geom:* Decagon.

décamper, *v.i.* To decamp, make off.

décanter, *v.tr.* To decant, pour off.

décapitation, *s.f.* Decapitation, beheading.

décapiter, *v.tr.* To decapitate, behead.

décapode, *s.m. Crust:* Decapod.

decauville, *s.m.* Also **Chemin de fer Decauville,** narrow-gauge railway.

décéder, *v.i.* (Conj. like CÉDER. Aux. *être*) To die, to decease.

décédé, *a. & s.* Deceased, defunct.

déceler, *v.tr.* (je décèle) To disclose (fraud); to divulge, betray (secret).

déceleur, -euse, *s.* Divulger.

décembre, *s.m.* December.

décemment, *adv.* Decently.

décence, *s.f.* (a) Decency. (b) Propriety. *Choquer la d.,* to shock the proprieties.

décennal, -aux, *a.* Decennial.

décent, *a.* (a) Decent; modest (attire). (b) Proper, seemly (behaviour).

décentralisation, *s.f.* Decentralization.

décentraliser, *v.tr.* To decentralize.

déception, *s.f.* Disappointment.

décerner, *v.tr.* To award, bestow (a prize).

décès, *s.m.* Decease, death. **Acte de décès,** death certificate.

décevant, *a.* **I.** Deceptive; delusive (appearance). **2.** Disappointing (result).

décevoir, *v.tr.* (Conj. like RECEVOIR) **I.** To deceive, delude. **2.** To disappoint.

déchaînement, *s.m.* **I.** Letting loose, unchaining. **2.** (a) Breaking loose (b) Outburst.

déchaîner, *v.tr.* To unchain, to let loose.

se déchaîner, to break out. *La tempête se déchaîna,* the storm broke.

décharge, *s.f.* **I.** (a) Unloading (of cart); discharging (of cargo). (b) Discharge (of firearm). (c) *El:* Discharge. **2.** (a) Relief, easing. (b) *Obtenir une d. sur un impôt,* to obtain a rebate on a tax. (c) *Témoin à décharge,* witness for the defence. (d) Release (of accused person). **3.** Discharge, outlet.

déchargement, *s.m.* Unloading (of cart).

décharger, *v.tr.* (n. **déchargeons**) **I.** (a) To unload (cart); to discharge (cargo). (b) To unload (fire-arm). (c) *D. son cœur,* to unburden one's heart. (d) *Décharger son fusil sur qn,* to fire one's gun at s.o. *D. sa colère sur qn,* to vent one's anger on s.o. **2.** (a) To lighten (ship). (b) *D. qn d'une accusation,* to acquit s.o. of a charge. *D. qn d'une dette,* to remit a debt.

se décharger. I. (a) (Of gun) To go off. (b) (Of anger) To vent itself. **2.** *Se d. d'un fardeau,* to lay down a burden. **3.** *Le fleuve se décharge dans la mer,* the river empties itself into the sea.

décharné, *a.* Emaciated (limbs); gaunt (face); bony (fingers).

déchausser, *v.tr.* To take off (s.o.'s) shoes.

se déchausser, to take off one's shoes.

déchéance, *s.f.* **I.** Nation en déchéance, nation on the down-grade. **2.** Lapse (of rights).

déchet, *s.m.* Usu. *pl.* Waste, refuse.

déchiffrable, *a.* Decipherable; legible.

déchiffrer, *v.tr.* To decipher, make out (inscription); to decode (message).

déchiqueter, *v.tr.* (je déchiquette) To cut (flesh) into strips, into shreds.

déchiqueté, *a.* Jagged (edge).

déchirant, *a.* Heart-rending, harrowing.

déchirement, *s.m.* Tearing, rending. *D. de cœur,* heart-break.

déchirer, *v.tr.* To tear (garment); to tear up (paper); to tear open (envelope). *Sons qui déchirent l'oreille,* ear-splitting sounds. *Cris qui déchiraient le cœur,* heart-rending cries.

déchoir, *v.i.* (*pr.p.* **déchéant**; *p.p.* **déchu**; *pr.ind.* n. **déchoyons,** ils **déchoient**; *fu.* je **décherrai**) To fall (from high estate). *Ce quartier a déchu,* the neighbourhood has gone down.

déchu, *a.* Fallen; lapsed (policy).

de-ci de-là, *adv.phr.* Here and there.

décidément, *adv.* **I.** Resolutely, firmly. **2.** Decidedly, positively.

décider, *v.tr.* **I.** (a) To decide, settle. *Voilà qui décide tout!* that settles it! (b) *L'Assemblée décida la guerre,* the Assembly decided on war. **2.** *Décider qn à faire qch.,* to persuade, induce, s.o. to do sth. **3.** *Abs.* (a) *Il faut que je décide,* I must make up my mind. (b) *Décider de qch.,* to decide sth. **4.** *Décider de + inf.,* to decide (after deliberation) to (do sth.). **Décider que + ind.,** to decide, settle, that. . . .

se décider. I. To make up one's mind. **2.** *Je ne puis pas me d. à le faire,* I cannot bring myself to do it. **3.** *Se d. pour qn,* to decide in favour of s.o.

décidé, *a.* **I.** *Chose décidée,* settled matter. **2.** Resolute (person); determined (character). **3.** *Être décidé à faire qch.,* to be determined to do sth. **4.** *Avoir une supériorité décidée sur qn*, to have a decided superiority over s.o.

décimal, -aux, *a.* Decimal.

décimale, *s.f.* Decimal (fraction).

décimation, *s.f.* Decimation.

décime, *s.m.* Ten-centime piece.

décimer, *v.tr.* To decimate.

décisif, *a.* **1.** Decisive (battle); conclusive (evidence). **2.** Peremptory (tone).

décision, *s.f.* Decision. **1.** Forcer une décision, to bring matters to a head. **2.** Resolution, determination.

décisivement, *adv.* Decisively, peremptorily.

déclamation, *s.f.* **1.** Oratory. **2.** (*a*) Declamation, harangue. (*b*) Ranting.

déclamatoire, *a.* Declamatory (style).

déclamer, *v.tr.* **1.** To declaim (speech). **2.** To rant, spout. *D. contre qn*, to inveigh against s.o.

déclancher, *v.tr.* **1.** To unlatch (door). **2.** *F:* To set (apparatus) in motion. *Mil: D. une attaque*, to launch an attack.

déclaration, *s.f.* Declaration. (*a*) Proclamation, announcement. *D. de guerre*, declaration of war. (*b*) Notification (of birth). (*c*) Déclaration sous serment, affidavit. (*d*) *D. d'amour*, declaration of love.

déclarer, *v.tr.* **1.** (*a*) To declare, make known (one's intentions). (*b*) *Cards: D. trèfle*, to call clubs. **2.** To declare, announce. (*a*) *Pred. Déclaré coupable*, found guilty. (*b*) To notify (birth). (*c*) *D. la guerre à qn*, to declare war on s.o. (*d*) *Cust: Avez-vous quelque chose à d.?* have you anything to declare?

se déclarer. 1. (*a*) *Se d. pour qch.*, to declare for sth. (*b*) To declare one's love. **2.** (Of fire) To break out.

déclasser, *v.tr.* To bring (s.o.) down in the world.

déclassé, *a. & s.* **1.** (One) who has come down in the world. **2.** Obsolete (ship).

déclic [-klik], *s.m.* Pawl, catch; trigger.

déclin, *s.m.* Decline, close (of day). *Au déclin de sa vie*, in his declining years.

déclinaison, *s.f.* *Gram:* Declension.

décliner. I. *v.i.* To wane.
II. **décliner,** *v.tr.* **1.** To decline, refuse (offer). **2.** (*a*) *Gram:* To decline (noun). (*b*) *Décliner son nom*, to give one's name.

déclivité, *s.f.* Declivity, slope, incline.

décocher, *v.tr.* *F:* Décocher un coup à qn, to hit out at s.o. *D. un juron*, to rap out an oath.

décoiffer, *v.tr.* To remove (s.o.'s) hat.

se décoiffer, to remove one's headdress.

déçoi-s, -t, -ve. See DÉCEVOIR.

décolérer, *v.i.* (je décolère; je décolérerai) *F:* To calm down. *Il ne décolérait pas, F:* he was in a fine way about it.

décoller, *v.tr.* (Of aeroplane) To take off.

décollé, *a.* (Of ears) Standing out.

décolleté, *a. Femme décolletée*, woman in low-necked dress. *Robe décolletée*, low-necked dress.

décoloration, *s.f.* Discolouration.

décombres, *s.m.pl.* Rubbish, debris.

décommander, *v.tr.* To countermand.

décomposer, *v.tr.* To decompose.

se décomposer. 1. To decompose, to rot, decay. **2.** (Of face) To become convulsed.

décomposé, *a. Visage d.*, drawn face; face distorted by grief or terror.

décomposition, *s.f.* **1.** Decomposition. **2.** Distortion (of features).

déconcertant, *a.* Disconcerting.

déconcerter, *v.tr.* **1.** To upset (s.o.'s plans). **2.** To disconcert (s.o.).

se déconcerter, to lose one's assurance. *Sans se déconcerter*, unabashed.

déconfit, *a.* Crest-fallen, discomfited.

déconfiture, *s.f.* Collapse, failure.

déconseiller [-sɛje], *v.tr. D. qch. à qn*, to advise s.o. against sth.

décontenancer, *v.tr.* (n. décontenançons) To put (s.o.) out of countenance.

décontenancé, *a.* Abashed; put out.

déconvenir, *v.i.* (Conj. like VENIR. Aux. *avoir) Je n'en déconviens pas,* I do not deny it.

déconvenue, *s.f.* Disappointment; mortification; mortifying set-back.

décor, *s.m.* **1.** Decoration (of house). Peintre en décor, house-painter. **2.** *Th: pl.* Scenery. Pièce à décors, spectacular play.

décorateur, *s.m.* (House-)decorator.

décoratif, *a.* Decorative, ornamental.

décoration, *s.f.* Decoration. **1.** Ornamentation. **2.** Medal; ribbon, star (of an order).

décorer, *v.tr.* **1.** To decorate, ornament. **2.** To decorate (s.o.).

décorner, *v.tr. F: Il fait un vent à décorner les bœufs*, it is blowing great guns.

décorum [-rɔm], *s.m.* Decorum; the proprieties.

découcher, *v.i.* To sleep away from home.

découper, *v.tr.* **1.** To cut up (paper), to carve (fowl). Couteau à découper, carving-knife. **2.** To cut out (design). *D. un article dans un journal*, to cut an article out of a newspaper. Scie à découper, fret-saw.

se découper, to stand out, show up, project (sur, against).

découpler, *v.tr.* **1.** To slip (hounds). **2.** To uncouple (trucks).

découplé, *a. Bien découplé*, well set up.

découpure, *s.f.* **1.** Fretwork. **2.** Cutting. **3.** Indentation (in coastline).

découragement, *s.m.* Discouragement.

décourager, *v.tr.* (n. décourageons) **1.** To discourage, dishearten. **2.** *D. un projet*, to discountenance a scheme.

se décourager, to become disheartened.

découragé, *a.* Discouraged, despondent, downhearted.

décousu, *a.* Disconnected, disjointed (words); scrappy (conversation).

découverte, *s.f.* **1.** Discovery (of land). **Aller à la découverte,** to explore, prospect. **2.** Discovery.

découvrir, *v.tr..* (Conj. like OUVRIR) **1.** (*a*) To uncover. (*b*) To lay bare; to unveil (statue); to disclose (secret). *D. ses dents,* to show one's teeth. **2.** To perceive, discern. **3.** (*a*) To discover (plot); to detect (criminal). (*b*) To discover (oxygen). **se découvrir.** **1.** To take off one's hat. **2.** (Of sky) To clear up. **découvert.** **1.** *a.* (*a*) Uncovered. **A visage découvert,** openly, frankly. (*b*) Open (country). **2.** **A découvert,** uncovered, unprotected. **Parler à découvert,** to speak openly. **Mettre qch. à découvert,** to expose sth. to view.

décrasser, *v.tr.* To clean, cleanse, scour.

décrépit, *a.* Decrepit, senile.

décrépitude, *s.f.* Decrepitude.

décret, *s.m.* Decree; fiat, order.

décréter, *v.tr.* (**je décrète; je décréterai**) To decree; to enact (law).

décrier, *v.tr.* To disparage, decry (s.o.); to run (s.o.) down.

décrire, *v.tr.* (Conj. like ÉCRIRE) **1.** To describe (a sight). **2.** To describe (circle).

décrocher, *v.tr.* To take down (coat from peg); to disconnect (railway carriages). **Décrocher le grand succès,** to make a big hit.

décroissance, *s.f.* Decrease; diminution; wane (of the moon).

décroiss-ons, -ez, etc. See DÉCROÎTRE.

décroître, *v.i.* (Conj. like CROÎTRE, except *p.p.* **décru**) To decrease, diminish. *Aller (en) décroissant,* to decrease.

décrotter, *v.tr.* To clean (boots).

décrotteur, *s.m.* Shoeblack, boot-black.

décrottoir, *s.m.* Door-scraper.

décru, -s, -t, etc. See DÉCROÎTRE.

déçu, -s, -t, etc. See DÉCEVOIR.

décuple, *a. & s.m.* Decuple; *a.* tenfold.

décupler, *v.tr. & i.* To increase tenfold.

dédaigner, *v.tr.* To scorn, disdain. **Cette offre n'est pas à dédaigner,** this offer is not to be disdained.

dédaigneusement, *adv.* Disdainfully.

dédaigneux, *a.* Disdainful; scornful.

dédain, *s.m.* Disdain, scorn. **Avoir le dédain de qch.,** to have a contempt for sth.

dédale, *s.m.* Labyrinth, maze (of streets).

dedans. **1.** *adv.* Inside; within; in (it). *F:* **Mettre qn dedans,** to humbug s.o. **Donner dedans,** to fall into the trap. **En dedans,** inside; within. **En dedans de,** within. **2.** *s.m.* Inside, interior (of house). **Au dedans,** (on the) inside; within. **Au dedans de,** inside, within.

dédicace, *s.f.* Dedication.

dédier, *v.tr.* To dedicate.

dédire (se), *v.pr.* (Conj. like DIRE, except *pr.ind.* v.v. **dédisez**) *Se d. d'une promesse,* to go back on one's word.

dédit, *s.m.* **1.** Retraction, withdrawal. **2.** Breaking (of promise).

dédommagement, *s.m.* **1.** Indemnification. **2.** Indemnity, compensation, damages.

dédommager, *v.tr.* (n. **dédommageons**) To indemnify, compensate (s.o.). *D. qn de qch.,* to compensate s.o. for sth.

déductif, *a.* *Phil:* Deductive (reasoning).

déduction, *s.f.* **1.** Deduction, inference. **2.** *Com:* Deduction, allowance. "Sans déduction," 'terms net cash.'

déduire, *v.tr.* (Conj. like CONDUIRE) **1.** To deduce, infer. **2.** To deduct.

déesse, *s.f.* Goddess.

défaillance [-faj-], *s.f.* (*a*) *La d. de ses forces,* the failing of his strength. *Moment de d.,* weak moment. *D. de mémoire,* lapse of memory. (*b*) Fainting fit; swoon. **Tomber en défaillance,** to faint.

défaillir [-faj-], *v.i.* def. (*pr.p.* **défaillant**; *pr. ind.* **je défaux;** *fu.* occ. **je défaudrai**) (*a*) To become feeble. (*b*) **Sans défaillir,** without flinching. (*c*) To faint, swoon.

défaire, *v.tr.* (Conj. like FAIRE) **1.** To demolish; to cancel. **2.** (*a*) To undo; to untie. (*b*) *D. qn de qn,* to rid s.o. of s.o. **3.** To defeat (army). **se défaire.** **1.** To come undone. **2.** (*a*) *Se d. de qn,* to get rid of s.o. (*b*) *Je ne veux pas m'en d.,* I don't want to part with it. **défait,** *a.* (*a*) Discomposed (features). (*b*) Dishevelled (hair).

défais-ant, -ons. See DÉFAIRE.

défaite, *s.f.* Defeat.

défalquer, *v.tr.* To deduct (sum).

défass-e, -es, etc. See DÉFAIRE.

défaut, *s.m.* **1.** Default, absence, lack (of sth.). **Faire défaut,** (i) to be absent, (ii) to fail, to give out. *Le temps me fait d.,* I cannot spare the time. *Les provisions font d.,* there is a scarcity of provisions. **A défaut de qch.,** for lack of, failing, sth. **2.** (*a*) Fault, shortcoming. **C'est là son moindre défaut,** that is the last thing one can reproach him with. (*b*) Defect, flaw. *F:* **Mettre qn en défaut,** to put s.o. on the wrong track; to baffle s.o. **Prendre qn en défaut,** to catch s.o. napping.

défaveur, *s.f.* Disfavour, discredit.

défavorable, *a.* Unfavourable.

défectif, *a.* Defective (verb).

défection, *s.f.* Defection from, desertion of, a cause.

défectueux, *a.* Defective, faulty.

défectuosité, *s.f.* **1.** Defectiveness. **2.** Defect, flaw.

défendable, *a.* Defensible.

défendeur, -eresse, *s.* *Jur:* Defendant.

défendre, *v.tr.* **1.** (*a*) To defend (cause); to uphold (right). (*b*) To protect (*contre,* against, *from*). **2.** To forbid, prohibit. *D. qch. à qn,* to forbid s.o. sth. **se défendre.** **1.** To defend oneself. **2.** *Se d. de qch.,* to protect oneself from sth.

Il ne put se d. de sourire, he could not refrain from smiling.

défense, *s.f.* **1.** Defence. **Sans défense,** unprotected, defenceless. **Défense passive,** civil defence. *Poste de d. passive,* warden's post. **2.** *pl.* (*a*) Defences, defensive works. (*b*) Tusks (of elephant). **3.** Prohibition, interdiction. **"Défense d'entrer, de fumer,"** 'no admittance,' 'no smoking.'

défenseur, *s.m.* (*a*) Protector, defender. (*b*) Supporter, upholder (of a cause).

défensif, *a. & s.f.* Defensive.

défer-ai, -as, etc. See DÉFAIRE.

déférence, *s.f.* Deference, respect, regard.

déférer, *v.* (je **défère;** je **déférerai**) I. *v.tr.* *D. qn à la justice,* to give s.o. up to justice.
II. **déférer,** *v.i. D. à qn,* to defer to s.o.

déferler. **1.** *v.tr. Nau:* To unfurl (sail). **2.** *v.i.* (Of waves) To break.

défi, *s.m.* (*a*) Challenge. **Relever un défi,** to take up a challenge. (*b*) Defiance. **En défi de,** in defiance of.

défiance, *s.f.* **1.** Mistrust, distrust, suspicion. **2.** *D. de soi-même,* diffidence.

défiant, *a.* Mistrustful, distrustful.

déficit [-sit], *s.m.* Deficit; shortage.

défier, *v.tr.* (*a*) To challenge. (*b*) To defy, set at defiance. (*c*) To brave, to face (danger).
se **défier** *de qn,* to mistrust, distrust, s.o.

défigurement, *s.m.* Disfigurement. *D. d'une statue,* defacement of a statue.

défigurer, *v.tr.* To disfigure (sth.); to distort (the truth).

défiler, *v.i.* (*a*) To march past. (*b*) To walk in procession.
défilé, *s.m.* **1.** Defile, gorge. **2.** March past; procession. *D. de mannequins,* mannequin parade.

définir, *v.tr.* To define.
se **définir,** to become clear, distinct.

défini, *a.* Definite.

définitif, *a.* Definitive; final; permanent. *Adv.phr.* **En définitive,** finally.

définition, *s.f.* Definition.

définitivement, *adv.* Definitively.

défi-s, -t, etc. See DÉFAIRE.

déflation, *s.f.* Deflation (of the currency).

déflorer, *v.tr.* **1.** To strip (plant) of its blooms. **2.** To take the freshness off (news).

défoncer, *v.tr.* (n. **défonçons**) **1.** To stave in (boat); to smash in (box). **2.** To break up.
défoncé, *a.* **1.** Stove in; battered. **2.** *Chemin d.,* broken, bumpy, road.

déforestation, *s.f.* Deforestation.

déformation, *s.f.* (*a*) Deformation. (*b*) *Phot:* Distortion (of image).

déformer, *v.tr.* To deform; to put (hat) out of shape. *Phot: Image déformée,* distorted image.

défraîchir, *v.tr.* To take away the freshness of (sth.).
défraîchi, *a. Articles défraîchis,* (shop-) soiled goods.

défrayer, *v.tr.* (je **défraie,** je **défraye**) *D. qn,* to defray, pay, s.o.'s expenses. *Être défrayé de tout,* to have all expenses paid.

défricher, *v.tr.* To bring (land) into cultivation; to break (new ground).

défroque, *s.f.* Usu. *pl.* Cast-off clothing.

défunt, *a. & s.* Defunct, deceased.

dégagement, *s.m.* **1.** Redemption (of pledge). **2.** (*a*) Disengagement, release. *Mil:* Extrication (of troops); relief (of town). (*b*) Clearing (of road). **3.** Escape, release (of steam).

dégager, *v.tr.* (n. **dégageons**) **1.** To redeem (mortgage). **2.** (*a*) To disengage. *D. une ville,* to relieve a town. (*b*) To clear (road). **3.** To emit, give off (vapour).
se **dégager.** **1.** To free oneself, to get free. **2.** (Of gas) To be given off (*de,* by). **3.** To emerge, come out.
dégagé, *a.* (*a*) Free, untrammelled (movements). *Allure dégagée,* swinging stride. (*b*) Free and easy (manner).

dégainer, *v.tr.* To unsheathe, draw (sword).

dégarnir, *v.tr.* To dismantle (room); to strip (bed).
dégarni, *a.* Empty; stripped.

dégâts, *s.m.pl.* Damage.

dégel, *s.m.* Thaw.

dégeler, *v.tr. & i., v.impers.* (il **dégèle**) To thaw.

dégénération, *s.f.* Degeneration, degeneracy.

dégénérer, *v.i.* (je **dégénère;** je **dégénérerai**) To degenerate (*de,* from; *en,* into).
dégénéré, *a. & s.* Degenerate.

dégingandé, *a. & s. F:* Awkward, ungainly person).

dégivrage, *s.m.* De-icing.

dégivrer, *v.tr.* To de-ice.

dégivreur, *s.m* De-icer.

dégonflement, *s.m.* Deflation (of tyre).

dégonfler, *v.tr.* To deflate.
se **dégonfler,** (of tyre) to collapse, to go flat.

dégorger, *v.* (n. **dégorgeons**) **1.** *v.tr.* To disgorge. **2.** *v.i. & pr.* (Of pond) To discharge.

dégourdir, *v.tr.* To remove stiffness from (the limbs); to revive (by warmth).
se **dégourdir,** to restore the circulation; to lose one's numb, stiff feeling.

dégoût, *s.m.* Disgust, distaste.

dégoûtant, *a.* Disgusting, nasty.

dégoûter, *v.tr.* To disgust. *D. qn de qch.,* to disgust s.o. with sth.
se **dégoûter** *de qch.,* to take a dislike to sth.
dégoûté, *a.* **1.** Disgusted (*de,* with); sick (of). **2.** Overnice, squeamish.

dégoutter, *v.i.* **1.** To drip, trickle. **2.** To be dripping (*de,* with).

dégradant, *a.* Degrading, lowering.

dégradation, *s.f.* **1.** Degradation (from rank). *D. civique,* loss of civil rights. **2.**

(Moral) degradation. **3.** (a) Defacement. (b) Usu. pl. Damage, dilapidation.

dégrader, v.tr. **1.** To degrade (s.o.). **2.** To degrade, besot. **3.** To deface, dilapidate.

   se dégrader, to lower oneself.

dégrafer, v.tr. To unfasten, undo (dress).

degré, s.m. **1.** (a) Step (of stair); degree (of musical scale). (b) Degree (of heat) **2.** Degree (of relationship). **Par degrés,** by degrees, gradually. *Équation du second d.,* quadratic equation.

dégringolade, s.f. F: **1.** Tumble (downstairs). **2.** Collapse (of prices).

dégringoler, v.tr. & i. F: To tumble down, to come clattering down.

dégriser, v.tr. To sober (s.o.).

   se dégriser. (a) To sober down. (b) F: To come to one's senses.

déguenillé [-gnije], a. Ragged, tattered.

déguerpir [-ger-], v.i. (a) (Of tenant) To move out. (b) To clear out, decamp.

déguisement [-gi-], s.m. **1.** Disguise. **2.** Sans déguisement, plainly.

déguiser [-gi-], v.tr. **1.** To disguise. **2.** To disguise, conceal (truth).

déguster, v.tr. To taste, sample (tea). F: D. sa liqueur, to sip one's liqueur.

dehors. 1. adv. (a) Out, outside. *Coucher d.,* to sleep, (i) out of doors, (ii) away from home. "Ne pas se pencher dehors!" 'do not lean out of the window!' (b) En dehors, (on the) outside; outwards. *En d. du sujet,* beside the question. **2.** s.m. (a) Outside, exterior. (b) Usu. in pl. (Outward) appearance. **3.** prep. Dedans et dehors le royaume, within and without the realm.

déifier, v.tr. To deify ; to make a god of (s.o.).

déité, s.f. Deity.

déjà, adv. **1.** Already. **2.** Before, previously. *Je vous ai d. vu,* I have seen you before. **3.** Ça n'est déjà pas si mal, indeed it is not at all bad (for a start).

déjeuner. I. v.i. (a) To breakfast (de, off). (b) To lunch ; to have, take, lunch.

   II. déjeuner, s.m. (a) (Premier) déjeuner, breakfast. Petit déjeuner, coffee with rolls, etc. (b) (Second) déjeuner, lunch.

déjouer, v.tr. To thwart, (plan) ; to baffle, foil (the police) ; to frustrate (plot).

delà. Beyond. **1.** prep. Par delà les mers, beyond the seas. **2.** adv. Au delà, beyond. En delà, further away. s.m. L'au-delà, the beyond. Au delà de, beyond. *N'allez pas au d. de dix francs,* don't go above ten francs.

délabrement, s.m. Disrepair, decay.

délabrer, v.tr. To dilapidate ; to wreck, ruin (health).

   se délabrer, (of house) to fall into decay ; (of health) to become impaired.

   délabré, a. Out of repair ; tumble-down (house) ; impaired (health).

délacer, v.tr. (n. délaçons) To unlace.

délai, s.m. **1.** Delay. **2.** Respite, time al-lowed. A court délai, at short notice. Dans le plus bref délai, as soon as possible.

délaissement, s.m. **1.** (a) Desertion, neglect (of children). (b) Loneliness. **2.** Relinquishment (of right).

délaisser, v.tr. To forsake, desert, abandon.

délassement, s.m. Rest, relaxation.

délasser, v.tr. To rest, refresh (s.o.).

   se délasser, to take some relaxation.

délateur, s.m. Informer, spy.

délayer, v.tr. (je délaie, délaye) To add water to (powdered material) ; to water (liquid).

délectable, a. Delightful, pleasant.

délégation, s.f. Delegation.

déléguer, v.tr. (je délègue ; je déléguerai) **1.** D. qn pour faire qch., to delegate s.o. to do sth. **2.** To delegate (powers).

   délégué, a. & s. (a) Delegate (at meeting). (b) Deputy (professor).

délétère, a. Deleterious ; pernicious (doctrine).

délibération, s.f. **1.** Deliberation, discussion. **2.** Reflection, cogitation. **3.** Resolution, decision (of an assembly).

délibérément, adv. Deliberately.

délibérer, v. (je délibère ; je délibérerai) **1.** v.i. (a) To deliberate ; to take counsel. (b) To reflect, ponder. **2.** v.tr. (a) To deliberate over (a question). (b) To discuss (a matter).

   délibéré, a. Deliberate.

délicat, a. Delicate. **1.** Dainty (dish). **2.** Fine, refined (taste). **3.** Sensitive (skin) ; delicate, frail (health). **4.** Difficult, critical. **5.** Scrupulous (conscience). D. sur la nourriture, dainty about one's food.

délicatement, adv. Delicately.

délicatesse, s.f. Delicacy. **1.** Fineness, softness (of colouring). *Délicatesses de table,* table delicacies. **2.** Refinement (of taste). Avec délicatesse, tactfully. Fausse délicatesse, false modesty. **3.** Fragility ; delicate state (of health). **4.** Difficulty, awkwardness (of situation).

délices, s.f.pl. Delight(s), pleasure(s).

délicieusement, adv. Deliciously ; delightfully.

délicieux, a. Delicious ; delightful.

délié, a. Slender, fine. *Avoir la langue déliée,* to have a glib tongue.

délier, v.tr. To untie, undo. *Le vin délie la langue,* wine loosens the tongue.

délimiter, v.tr. To delimit, demarcate (territory) ; to define (powers).

délinquant, s. Offender, delinquent.

délire, s.m. Delirium. Avoir le délire, être en délire, to be delirious.

délirer, v.i. To be delirious ; to rave.

délit, s.m. Misdemeanour, offence.

délivrance, s.f. **1.** Deliverance, rescue. **2.** Delivery (of property) ; issue (of tickets).

délivrer, v.tr. **1.** To deliver ; to rescue (captive). **2.** To deliver, hand over (goods).

déloger, v. (Conj. like LOGER) **1.** v.i. To go

off. **2.** *v.tr.* To eject (tenant); to dislodge.

déloyal, -aux, *a.* Disloyal, false (friend); unfair (practice). *Sp : Jeu d.,* foul play.

déloyauté, *s.f.* Disloyalty, perfidy.

delphien, *a.* Delphic (oracle).

delta, *s.m. Gr.Alph : Geog :* Delta.

déluge, *s.m.* (a) Deluge, flood ; torrent (of abuse). (b) *F :* Downpour (of rain).

déluré, *a.* Sharp, knowing, smart.

démagogie, *s.f.* Demagogy.

démagogue, *s.m.* Demagogue.

demain, *adv. & s.m.* To-morrow. **A demain!** good-bye till to-morrow.

démancher, *v.tr. Se d. le bras,* to put one's arm out (of joint).

demande, *s.f.* **I.** (a) Request, application. **Faire la demande de qch.,** to ask for sth. (b) *Com :* Demand. **2.** Question, enquiry.

demander, *v.tr.* **I.** To ask (for). *D. la paix,* to sue for peace. **On vous demande,** somebody wants to see you. **Demander qch, à qn.** to ask s.o. for sth. *On nous demanda nos passeports,* we were asked for our passports. *Je demande à être entendu,* I ask to be heard. **2.** To desire, require. **3.** To ask, enquire. *D. à qn son avis,* to ask s.o.'s opinion. *Je me demande pourquoi,* I wonder why.

démangeaison, *s.f.* Itching. *F : Une d. de faire qch.,* a longing to do sth.

démanger, *v.i.* (il demangea(it)). With dative of person) To itch. *L'épaule me démange,* my shoulder is itching.

démarcation, *s.f.* Demarcation. **Ligne de démarcation,** dividing line.

démarche, *s.f.* **I.** Gait, walk. **2.** Step. **Faire les démarches nécessaires,** to take the necessary steps.

démarrer. **I.** *v.tr.* To unmoor, cast off (ship). **2.** *v.i.* (a) (Of boat) To cast off. (b) (Of train) To start ; (of driver) to drive off.

démasquer, *v.tr.* To unmask ; to expose.

démêler, *v.tr.* (a) To disentangle (string); to comb out (hair). *F : D. un malentendu,* to clear up a misunderstanding. (b) *F : D. qn dans l'ombre,* to make out s.o. in the gloom.

se démêler, to extricate oneself.

démembrement, *s.m.* Dismemberment.

démembrer, *v.tr.* To dismember.

déménagement, *s.m.* Removal. **Voiture de déménagement,** furniture van.

déménager, *v.tr. & i.* (n. déménageons) D. (ses meubles), to move house, to remove. *P :* **Déménager à la cloche (de bois),** to do a moonlight flit.

démence, *s.f.* Insanity, madness.

démener (se), *v.pr.* (Conj. like MENER) **I.** To throw oneself about ; to struggle. **2.** *F :* To bestir oneself.

dément, *a. & s.* Crazy, mad (person).

démentir, *v.tr.* (Conj. like MENTIR) **I.** To contradict (s.o.) ; to deny (fact). **2.** To belie.

se démentir, to contradict oneself.

Politesse qui ne se dément jamais, unfailing courtesy.

démenti, *s.m.* Denial, contradiction.

démesuré, *a.* Inordinate ; unbounded.

démesurément, *adv.* Inordinately ; enormously.

démettre¹, *v.tr.* (Conj. like METTRE) To dislocate (joint).

démettre² (se), *v.pr.* (Conj. like METTRE) *Se d. de ses fonctions,* to resign one's post.

demeure, *s.f.* (Place of) residence, dwelling place; abode. **Livraison à demeure,** goods delivered at any address.

demeurer, *v.i.* **I.** (Aux. *être*) To remain ; to stay (in a place). *Demeurons-en là,* let us leave it at that. *Ne pouvoir d. en place,* to be unable to keep still. **2.** (Aux. *avoir*) To live, reside.

demi. **I.** *a.* Half. *Deux heures et demie,* (i) two and a half hours ; (ii) half-past two. **2.** *s.m.* (a) *Deux plus un demi,* two plus one half. (b) **A demi.** half. *A d. mort,* half-dead. **Faire les choses à demi,** to do things by halves. **3.** *s.f.* **Demie,** half-hour. **Il est la demie,** it is half-past.

NOTE. In all the following compounds DEMI is inv.; the second component takes the plural.

demi-cercle, *s.m.* Semicircle, half-circle.

demi-circulaire, *a.* Semicircular.

demi-dieu, *s.m.* Demigod.

demi-frère, *s.m.* Half-brother ; step-brother.

demi-heure, *s.f. Une d.-h.,* half an hour.

demi-monde, *s.m.* Outskirts of society.

demi-mot (à), *adv.phr. Entendre (qn) à d.-m.,* to (know how to) take a hint.

demi-place, *s.f.* Half-fare (when travelling); half-price (at theatre).

démis. See DÉMETTRE.

demi-sœur, *s.f.* Half-sister ; step-sister.

demi-solde, *s.f. Mil :* Half-pay.

démission, *s.f.* Resignation.

demi-tour, *s.m. Mil :* Half-turn. *Faire faire d.-t. à son cheval,* to turn one's horse.

demi-voix (à), *adv.phr.* In an undertone ; under one's breath.

démobilisation, *s.f.* Demobilization.

démobiliser, *v.tr.* To demobilize.

démocrate, *s.m. & f.* Democrat.

démocratie, *s.f.* Democracy.

démocratique, *a.* Democratic.

démoder (se), *v.pr.* To go out of fashion.

démodé, *a.* Old-fashioned ; obsolete.

demoiselle, *s.f.* **I.** (a) Spinster. (b) **Demoiselle d'honneur,** bridesmaid. *D. de magasin,* shop-girl. **2.** Young lady. **3.** Dragon-fly.

démolir, *v.tr.* To demolish, pull down.

démolition, *s.f.* Demolition.

démon, *s.m.* Demon, devil, fiend.

démoniaque, *a.* Demoniac(al).

démonstratif, *a.* Demonstrative.

démonstration, *s.f.* Demonstration.

démonter, *v.tr.* **1.** To unhorse, unseat (rider). **Se laisser démonter,** to get upset. **2.** To take down, dismantle; to remove (pneumatic tyre); to release spring of (clock).
  démonté, *a.* **1.** Dismounted (cavalry). **2.** Stormy (sea). **3.** (Of pers.) Abashed. **4.** (Of clock) Run down.

démontrable, *a.* Demonstrable.

démontrer, *v.tr.* **1.** To demonstrate. **2.** *Action qui démontre la bonté,* act that betokens, evinces, kindliness.

démoralisation, *s.f.* Demoralization.

démoraliser, *v.tr.* To demoralize. **1.** To corrupt, deprave. **2.** To dishearten.
  se démoraliser, to become demoralized.

démordre, *v.i.* *F:* **Ne pas démordre de ses opinions,** to stick to one's opinions.

démunir (se), *v.pr.* *Se d. de qch.,* to part with sth.
  démuni, *a.* **1.** Unprovided (*de,* with). **2.** *Com:* *Être d. de qch.,* to be out of sth.

dénaturer, *v.tr.* To misrepresent, distort (words). *D. les faits,* to garble the facts.
  dénaturé, *a.* Unnatural; hard-hearted (father); perverted (taste).

dénégation, *s.f.* Denial.

dénicher, *v.tr.* (a) To find, discover. *F: Nous avons déniché un bon chauffeur,* we have unearthed a good chauffeur. (b) To dislodge (bird); to rout out (animal).

denier, *s.m.* **1.** *F: Le d. de la veuve,* the widow's mite. **2.** Money, funds.

dénier, *v.tr.* To deny (crime).

dénigrement, *s.m.* Disparagement; running down.

dénigrer, *v.tr.* To disparage; to run down.

dénombrement, *s.m.* Enumeration, counting.

dénombrer, *v.tr.* To count, enumerate.

dénominateur, *s.m.* Denominator.

dénomination, *s.f.* Denomination, name.

dénommer, *v.tr.* To denominate, name.

dénoncer, *v.tr.* (n. dénonçons) **1.** To declare, proclaim. **2.** (a) To denounce (s.o.). *Se d.,* to give oneself up. (b) To expose (vice).

dénonciateur, -trice. **1.** *s.* Informer, denouncer. **2.** *a.* Tell-tale (look).

dénonciation, *s.f.* **1.** Notice of termination (of treaty). **2.** Denunciation.

dénoter, *v.tr.* To denote, betoken.

dénouer, *v.tr.* **1.** To unknot; to untie, undo. *D. une intrigue,* to unravel a plot. **2.** To loosen (the tongue).

denrée, *s.f.* Commodity; food-stuff.

dense, *a.* Dense, crowded; close.

densité, *s.f.* Denseness, density.

dent, *s.f.* **1.** Tooth. **Avoir mal aux dents,** to have toothache. *Se faire arracher une d.,* to have a tooth out. **Coup de dent(s),** bite. **N'avoir rien à se mettre sous la dent,** to have nothing to eat. **Jouer des dents,** to ply one's teeth. **Rire à belles dents,** to laugh heartily. **Manger du bout des dents,** to pick at one's food. **Rire du bout des dents,** to force a laugh. **Avoir les dents longues,** to be very hungry. **Avoir une dent contre qn,** to have a grudge against s.o. **Être sur les dents,** to be worn out. **2.** Tooth (of saw); cog (of wheel); prong (of fork).

dental, -aux. **1.** *a.* Dental. **2.** *s.f.* **Dentale,** dental consonant.

denté, *a.* Cogged, toothed (wheel); dentate (leaf). **Roue dentée,** cog-wheel.

denteler, *v.tr.* (je dentelle) To notch, jag.
  dentelé, *a.* Notched, indented; serrated.

dentelle, *s.f.* Lace.

dentellière, *s.f.* Lace-maker.

dentelure, *s.f.* Indentation; ins and outs (of coast-line).

dentifrice, *s.m.* Tooth-paste, -powder; mouth-wash.

dentiste, *s.m.* Dentist.

denture, *s.f.* **1.** Set of (natural) teeth. **2.** Serrated edge. **3.** *Mec.E:* Cogs.

dénuder, *v.tr.* To denude, to lay bare.
  dénudé, *a.* Bare, denuded.

dénuement, *s.m.* Destitution, penury, need. *D. d'idées,* dearth of ideas.

dénuer, *v.tr.* To divest, strip.
  dénué, *a.* (a) *D. d'argent,* without money. (b) *D. de raison,* senseless.

dépareiller [-rɛje], *v.tr.* To break (set).
  dépareillé, *a.* Odd, unmatched.

départ, *s.m.* **1.** Division, sorting (out). **2.** Departure, starting. **Point de départ,** starting point.

département, *s.m.* (a) *Adm:* Department. (b) Subdivision (of France); department.

départemental, -aux, *a.* Departmental.

départir, *v.tr.* (Conj. like MENTIR) (a) To divide (property). (b) To dispense (favours).
  se départir, (Conj. like FINIR) **1.** *Se d. de qch.,* to give up sth. **2.** *Se d. de son devoir,* to deviate from one's duty.

dépasser, *v.tr.* **1.** (a) To pass beyond; to run past (signal). **Dépasser le but,** to overshoot the mark. **Dépasser les bornes,** to overstep the bounds. (b) *D. qn (à la course),* to overtake s.o. **2.** *D. qn de la tête,* to stand a head taller than s.o. *F: Cela me dépasse,* it is above my comprehension. **3.** To exceed. *D. la limite de vitesse,* to exceed the speed-limit.

dépayser, *v.tr.* **1.** To remove (s.o.) from his usual surroundings. **2.** To bewilder (s.o.).
  dépaysé, *a.* Out of one's element.

dépècement, *s.m.* Cutting up; dismemberment.

dépecer, *v.tr.* (je dépèce) To cut up (carcass); to dismember (fowl).

dépêche, *s.f.* (a) (Official) despatch. (b) *D. télégraphique,* telegram.

dépêcher, *v.tr.* To dispatch.
  se dépêcher, to hasten, to make haste. *Dépêchez-vous!* hurry up!

dépeigner, *v.tr.* To ruffle, rumple (s.o.). *Personne dépeignée,* unkempt person.

dépeindre, *v.tr.* (Conj. like PEINDRE) To depict, picture, describe.

dépenaillé [-nɑj-], *a.* Ragged, tattered.
dépendance, *s.f.* **1.** Dependence, depending. **2.** (*a*) Dependency (of a country). (*b*) *pl.* Outbuildings, offices. **3.** Dependence, subjection.
dépendant, *a.* Dependent (*de*, on).
dépendre, *v.i.* To depend (*de*, on). *Il dépend de vous de + inf.*, it lies, rests, with you to . . . . *Cela dépend*, that depends.
dépens, *s.m.pl. Com:* Cost, expenses. *Aux dépens de*, at the expense of (s.o.).
dépense, *s.f.* Expenditure, outlay (of money).
dépenser, *v.tr.* **1.** To spend (money). **2.** To spend, consume (energy).
　se dépenser. *Se d. en vains efforts*, to waste one's energy.
dépérir, *v.i.* To waste away; to wither.
dépérissement, *s.m.* Wasting away; withering.
dépeupler, *v.tr.* To depopulate.
dépiécer, *v.tr.* (je dépièce, n. dépiéçons; je dépiécerai) To cut to pieces; to dismember.
dépit, *s.m.* Spite, chagrin. *Par dépit*, out of spite. *Pleurer de dépit*, to cry with vexation. *En dépit de . . .*, in spite of. . . .
dépiter, *v.tr.* To vex.
　se dépiter, to take offence; to be vexed.
déplacement, *s.m.* **1.** Displacement; transfer (of official). **2.** Travelling; moving. *Frais de déplacement*, travelling or removal expenses. **3.** *N.Arch:* Displacement.
déplacer, *v.tr.* (n. déplaçons) **1.** To displace, shift. *D. un fonctionnaire*, to transfer a civil servant. **2.** To oust, take the place of (s.o.).
　se déplacer. (*a*) To change one's place. (*b*) To move about, to travel.
　déplacé, *a.* Out of place.
déplaire, *v.ind.tr.* (Conj. like PLAIRE) (*a*) To displease. *Ils se déplaisent*, they dislike each other. (*b*) *Impers.* *N'en déplaise à la compagnie*, with all due deference to those present. *Ne vous en déplaise*, if you have no objection.
　se déplaire, to be dissatisfied.
déplaisant, *a.* Unpleasing, unpleasant.
déplaisir, *s.m.* Displeasure, chagrin.
déplier, *v.tr.* To unfold, spread out.
　se déplier, to unfold; to open out.
déploiement, *s.m.* **1.** Spreading out, unfolding; unfurling. **2.** Display, show.
déplorable, *a.* Deplorable, lamentable.
déplorer, *v.tr.* To deplore, lament.
déployer, *v.tr.* (je déploie) **1.** To unfold, spread out; to unfurl. **2.** To display (goods).
déplu, -s, -t, etc. See DÉPLAIRE.
déplumer, *v.tr.* To pluck (chicken).
dépopulation, *s.f.* Depopulation.
déportation, *s.f.* Deportation.
déporter, *v.tr.* To deport.
déposer, *v.tr.* **1.** (*a*) To deposit; to set (sth.) down. *D. les armes*, to lay down one's arms. (*b*) (Of liquid) To deposit (sediment). **2.** (*a*) *D. son argent à la banque*, deposit one's money at the bank. (*b*) *Com:* To register

(trade-mark). (*c*) *Jur:* *D. une plainte*, to lodge a complaint. (*d*) *Abs.* **Déposer** (en justice), to give evidence. **3.** To depose (king).
dépositaire, *s.m. & f.* Depositary, trustee.
déposition, *s.f.* **1.** *Jur:* Deposition; statement. **2.** Deposing, deposition (of king).
dépôt, *s.m.* **1.** (*a*) Depositing. (*b*) Deposit. **2.** Depository, depot; police station. *D. de marchandises*, warehouse. **3.** Deposit, sediment.
dépouille [-puːj], *s.f.* **1.** Skin, hide (taken from animal). *Dépouille mortelle*, mortal remains. **2.** Usu. *pl.* Spoils, booty.
dépouiller [-puje], *v.tr.* To deprive, strip. *D. un pays*, to despoil a country.
　se dépouiller. *Se d. de qch.*, to divest oneself of (sth.).
dépourvu, *a.* Destitute, bereft, devoid. *Être pris au dépourvu*, to be caught unawares.
dépravation, *s.f.* Depravation.
dépraver, *v.tr.* To deprave.
dépréciateur, -trice. **1.** *s.* Disparager. **2.** *a.* Disparaging.
dépréciation, *s.f.* **1.** Depreciation; fall in value. **2.** (*a*) Underrating. (*b*) Disparagement.
déprécier, *v.tr.* **1.** To depreciate. **2.** (*a*) To underrate. (*b*) To disparage.
　se déprécier. **1.** To depreciate. **2.** To make oneself cheap.
déprédation, *s.f.* **1.** Depredation. **2.** Peculation; misappropriation.
dépression, *s.f.* **1.** Hollow, dip. **2.** Depression; dejection.
déprimer, *v.tr.* To depress.
　déprimé, *a.* Depressed.
depuis, *prep.* **1.** (*a*) (Of time) Since, for. *D. quand êtes-vous ici?* how long have you been here? *D. son enfance*, from a child. (*b*) *adv.* Since (then); afterwards, later. (*c*) **Depuis que** + *ind.*, since. . . . **2.** From. *D. le matin jusqu'au soir*, from morning till night.
députation, *s.f.* (*a*) Deputing, delegating. (*b*) Deputation, delegation.
députer, *v.tr.* To depute (s.o.).
　député, *s.m.* Deputy, delegate.
déraciner, *v.tr.* **1.** To uproot. *Se sentir déraciné*, to feel like a fish out of water. **2.** To eradicate (fault).
dérailler [-raje], *v.i.* (Of train) To become derailed.
déraisonnable, *a.* Unreasonable; unwise.
déraisonner, *v.i.* To talk nonsense.
dérangement, *s.m.* Derangement.
déranger, *v.tr.* (n. dérangeons) To derange. (*a*) To disarrange (papers). (*b*) To disturb, trouble. (*c*) To upset (plans).
　se déranger, to move, stir. *Ne vous dérangez pas*, please don't move. *Se d. pour obliger qn*, to go out of one's way to oblige s.o.
déraper, *v.tr. & i.* *Aut:* To skid, to sideslip.

derechef [-ʃef], *adv.* Yet again ; once more.

dérèglement, *s.m.* **1.** Disordered state ; irregularity. **2.** Dissoluteness, profligacy.

dérégler, *v.tr.* (je dérègle ; je déréglerai) To upset, disarrange.

   déréglé, *a.* **1.** Out of order. **2.** Lawless, wild (life) ; immoderate (desires).

dérider, *v.tr.* To smoothe.

   se dérider, to brighten up.

dérision, *s.f.* Derision, mockery. *Tourner qn en dérision,* to hold s.o. up to ridicule.

dérisoire, *a.* Ridiculous, laughable (offer).

dérivation[1]**,** *s.f.* **1.** Diversion (of watercourse). **2.** Derivation (of word).

dérivation[2]**,** *s.f.* *Nau :* Drift.

dérive, *s.f.* Leeway, drift. *Aller en dérive,* to drift. *A la dérive,* adrift.

dériver[1]**. 1.** *v.tr.* (*a*) To divert (stream). (*b*) *Ling :* To derive. **2.** *v.i.* To be derived (from a source).

   dérivé, (*a*) *a.* Derived. (*b*) *s.* Un dérivé, a derivative.

dériver[2]**,** *v.i.* *Nau :* To drift.

dernier, *a. & s.* **1.** Last, latest. (*a*) *Faire un d. effort,* to make a final effort. *Il arriva le d.,* he arrived last. *Dans ces derniers temps,* latterly. *La dernière mode,* the latest fashion. (*b*) (Last of series) *Le mois d.,* last month. *Le d. élève de la classe,* the bottom boy in the form. (*c*) *Ce dernier répondit . . .,* the latter answered. . . . **2.** (*a*) Utmost, highest. *Au d. degré,* to the highest degree. *Entrer dans les derniers détails,* to enter into the minutest details. (*b*) Lowest, worst. *Le d. prix,* the lowest price. *Le dernier de mes soucis,* the least of my worries. *Le dernier des derniers,* the lowest of the low.

dernièrement, *adv.* Lately, latterly.

dérober, *v.tr.* **1.** (*a*) To steal, to make away with (sth.). (*b*) *D. qn au danger,* to save s.o. from danger. **2.** To hide, conceal.

   se dérober. 1. To escape, steal away, slip away (à, from). **2.** To give way.

   dérobé, *a.* Hidden, concealed (door). *A la dérobée,* stealthily, secretly.

déroger, *v.i.* (n. dérogeons) (*a*) *D. à une condition,* not to conform to a condition. (*b*) To derogate (à, from). *D. à son rang,* to lose caste.

dérouler, *v.tr.* To unroll ; to unwind.

   se dérouler, to unfold. *Le paysage se déroule devant nous,* the landscape stretches out before us.

déroute, *s.f.* Rout. *Être en (pleine) déroute,* to be in (full) flight.

dérouter, *v.tr.* **1.** Dérouter les soupçons, to throw people off the scent. **2.** To confuse, baffle, nonplus.

derrière. 1. *prep.* (*a*) Behind, at the back of (sth.).) *Laisser qn d. soi,* to leave s.o. behind. (*b*) *Nau :* Abaft. **2.** *adv.* (*a*) Behind, at the back, in the rear. *Attaquer qn par derrière,* to attack s.o. from behind. *Pattes de derrière,* hind legs. (*b*) *Nau :* Aft. **3.** *s.m.* (*a*) Back,

rear (of building, etc.). (*b*) *F :* Behind, backside.

derviche, *s.m.* Dervish.

des = *de les.* See DE, LE[1], and UN.

dès, *prep.* Since, from ; as early as. *Dès sa jeunesse . . .,* from childhood. . . *Dès l'abord,* from the outset. *Dès le matin,* first thing in the morning. *Je commencerai dès aujourd'hui,* I will begin this very day. *Conj.phr.* Dès que + *ind.* Dès qu'il sera arrivé, as soon as he arrives. *Adv.phr.* Dès lors, ever since (then).

désabuser, *v.tr.* To disabuse, disillusion, undeceive (de, with regard to).

   se désabuser (de qch.), to have one's eyes opened.

désaccord, *s.m.* **1.** (*a*) Disagreement, dissension. (*b*) Clash (of interests). **2.** *Mus :* Discord. *En désaccord,* out of tune.

désaccoutumer, *v.tr.* To disaccustom.

   se désaccoutumer de faire qch. To get out of the habit of doing sth.

désaffection, *s.f.* Disaffection (envers, to).

désagréable, *a.* Disagreeable, unpleasant, surly.

désagréablement, *adv.* Disagreeably, unpleasantly.

désagrégation, *s.f.* Disintegration.

désagréger, *v.tr.* (je désagrège, n. désagrégeons ; je désagrégerai) To disintegrate.

   se désagréger, to break up.

désagrément, *s.m.* Source of annoyance ; unpleasant occurrence.

désaligné, *a.* Out of alignment ; out of line.

désaltérant. 1. *a.* Thirst-quenching. **2.** *s.m.* Thirst-quencher.

désaltérer, *v.tr.* (je désaltère ; je désaltérerai) To quench (s.o.'s) thirst.

   se désaltérer, to quench one's thirst.

désappointement, *s.m.* Disappointment.

désappointer, *v.tr.* To disappoint.

désapprobateur, -trice. 1. *s.* Disapprover. **2.** *a.* Disapproving, censorious.

désapprobation, *s.f.* Disapproval, disapprobation.

désapprouver, *v.tr.* To disapprove of, object to (sth.).

désarmement, *s.m.* **1.** Disarming. **2.** Disarmament. **3.** Paying off (of ship).

désarmer. 1. *v.tr.* (*a*) To disarm. (*b*) To unload (gun). **2.** *v.i.* To disarm.

   désarmé, *a.* **1.** Disarmed. **2.** Unarmed, defenceless.

désarroi, *s.m.* Disarray, disorder.

désassocier, *v.tr.* To dissociate.

désastre, *s.m.* Disaster, calamity.

désastreusement, *adv.* Disastrously.

désastreux, *a.* Disastrous, calamitous.

désavantage, *s.m.* Disadvantage, drawback.

désavantageusement, *adv.* Disadvantageously.

désavantageux, *a.* Disadvantageous.

désaveu, *s.m.* Disavowal, denial ; disclaimer.

désavouer, *v.tr.* To disavow, repudiate.

descendance [des-,de-], *s.f.* **1.** Descent, lineage. **2.** *Coll:* Descendants.

descendant [des-,de-]. **1.** *a.* Descending; downward. **Train descendant,** down-train. **2.** *s.* Descendant.

descendre [des-,de-]. I. *v.i.* (Aux. *être,* occ. *avoir*) **1.** (*a*) To descend; to come, go, down. *Le baromètre descend,* the glass is falling. (*b*) To come, go, downstairs. *Il n'est pas encore descendu,* he is not down yet. **2.** (*a*) To alight. *D. de cheval,* to dismount. *"Tout le monde descend!"* 'all change!' (*b*) *D. à un hôtel,* to put up at a hotel. **3.** To extend downwards. **4.** To be descended (from). II. **descendre,** *v.tr.* (Aux. *avoir*) **1.** *D. les marches,* to go down the steps. **2.** (*a*) To take, bring, (sth.) down. *D. les bagages,* to bring down the luggage. (*b*) To lower, let down. (*c*) To shoot down, bring down (partridge).

descente [des-,de-], *s.f.* Descent. **1.** (*a*) Coming, going, down. (*b*) Raid. **2.** Letting down, lowering. **3.** (*a*) *D. dangereuse,* dangerous hill. (*b*) **Descente de bain,** bath-mat. **Descente de lit,** (bed-side) rug.

descriptif [des-], *a.* Descriptive.

description [des-], *s.f.* Description.

désenchantement, *s.m.* (*a*) Disenchantment. (*b*) Disillusion.

désenchanter, *v.tr.* (*a*) To disenchant. (*b*) To disillusion.

désencombrer, *v.tr.* To disencumber.

déséquilibrer, *v.tr.* To unbalance.

    déséquilibré, *a.* Unbalanced (mind).

désert¹, *a.* **1.** Deserted (place). **2.** Desert (island); lonely (spot).

désert², *s.m.* Desert, wilderness.

déserter, *v.tr.* To desert.

déserteur, *s.m.* Deserter.

désertion, *s.f.* Desertion.

désespérant, *a.* Heart-breaking; that drives one to despair.

désespérément, *adv.* **1.** Despairingly, hopelessly. **2.** Desperately (in love).

désespérer, *v.* (je désespère; je désespérerai) **1.** *v.i.* To despair. **2.** *v.tr.* To drive (s.o.) to despair.

    se désespérer, to be in despair.

    désespéré. 1. *a.* Desperate. (*a*) Hopeless. (*b*) *Lutte désespérée,* desperate struggle. **2.** *s.* Desperate person.

désespoir, *s.m.* **1.** Despair. **2.** Desperation. *En désespoir de cause,* in desperation.

déshabiller [-bije], *v.tr.* To undress (s.o.).

    se déshabiller, to undress.

    déshabillé, *s.m.* Boudoir wrap, tea-gown.

déshabituer, *v.tr. D. qn de qch.,* to break s.o. of (the habit of) doing sth.

déshériter, *v.tr.* To disinherit (s.o.).

déshonneur, *s.m.* Dishonour, disgrace.

déshonorant, *a.* Dishonouring, discreditable.

déshonorer, *v.tr.* To dishonour, disgrace.

désignation, *s.f.* Designation.

désigner, *v.tr.* **1.** To designate, show, indicate. **2.** (*a*) To appoint, fix (day). (*b*) *D. qn à, pour, un poste,* to appoint s.o. to a post.

désillusion, *s.f.* Disillusion.

désillusionnement, *s.m.* Disillusionment.

désillusionner, *v.tr.* To disillusion.

désinfectant, *a. & s.m.* Disinfectant.

désinfecter, *v.tr.* To disinfect.

désinfection, *s.f.* Disinfection.

désintéressement, *s.m.* Disinterestedness.

désintéresser, *v.tr.* To buy out (partner).

    se désintéresser *de qch.,* to take no further interest in sth.

    désintéressé, *a.* **1.** Not involved. **2.** (*a*) Disinterested, unprejudiced. (*b*) Unselfish.

désinvolte, *a.* (*a*) Easy, free (gait). (*b*) Airy, detached (manner).

désinvolture, *s.f.* (*a*) Unconstraint; ease (of movement). (*b*) Free and easy manner. (*c*) *Avec désinvolture,* airily.

désir, *s.m.* Desire (*de,* for); wish.

désirable, *a.* Desirable.

désirer, *v.tr.* To desire, want; to wish for (sth.). *Cela laisse à désirer,* it is not quite satisfactory. *Com: Madame désire?* what can I show you, madam?

désireux, *a.* Desirous.

désister (se), *v.pr. Se d. d'une demande,* to waive a claim.

désobéir, *v.ind.tr. D. à qn,* to disobey s.o. (May be used in the passive) *Je ne veux pas être désobéi,* I won't be disobeyed.

désobéissance, *s.f.* Disobedience.

désobéissant, *a.* Disobedient.

désobligeance, *s.f.* (*a*) Disoblingness. (*b*) Disagreeableness (*envers qn,* to s.o.).

désobligeant, *a.* (*a*) Disobliging. (*b*) Disagreeable, ungracious.

désobliger, *v.tr.* (n. désobligeons) **1.** To disoblige (s.o.). **2.** To offend.

désœuvré, *a.* (Of pers.) Unoccupied, idle.

désœuvrement, *s.m.* Idleness. **Par désœuvrement,** for want of something to do.

désolant, *a.* Distressing, sad.

désolation, *s.f.* Desolation.

désoler, *v.tr.* To desolate. **1.** To devastate (country). **2.** To distress.

    se désoler, to grieve.

    désolé, *a.* **1.** (*a*) Desolate (region). (*b*) Devastated (country). **2.** Grieved.

désordonner, *v.tr.* To throw into disorder.

    désordonné, *a.* **1.** Disordered. **2.** Disorderly, dissolute.

désordre, *s.m.* **1.** (*a*) Disorder, confusion. *Cheveux en d.,* untidy hair. (*b*) *Med: D. nerveux,* nervous disorder. **2.** Disorderliness. **3.** *pl.* Disturbances, riots.

désorganisation, *s.f.* Disorganization.

désorganiser, *v.tr.* To disorganize.

désorienter, *v.tr.* To make (s.o.) lose his bearings.

désorienté, a. F: At a loss. *Je suis tout d.*, I am all at sea.

ésormais, adv. Henceforth; in future.

espote, s.m. Despot.

espotique, a. Despotic (power).

espotiquement, adv. Despotically.

espotisme, s.m. Despotism.

essaisir [des-], v.tr. To dispossess (s.o. of sth.).

   se dessaisir *de qch.*, to relinquish sth.

essèchement [des-], s.m. **1.** Drying up (of pond). **2.** Withering (of plants).

esséscher [des-], v.tr. (je dessèche; je dessécherai) **1.** To dry up (ground). **2.** To season (wood); to desiccate (food-stuffs).

   se dessécher. 1. To dry up. **2.** To wither.

   desséché, a. **1.** Dry (pond). **2.** Withered.

essein, s.m. **1.** Design, plan. **2.** Intention, purpose. *Dans ce dessein . . .*, with this intention. . . : *A dessein*, on purpose.

esserrer, v.tr. To loosen (screw); to slacken (belt). *D. son étreinte*, to relax one's hold.

essert¹, s.m. Dessert.

essert². See DESSERVIR.

esservir¹, v.tr. (Conj. like SERVIR) (Of railway) To serve (district).

esservir², v.tr. (Conj. like SERVIR) To clear (the table).

essiccation, s.f. *Ind:* Desiccation, drying.

essin, s.m. **1.** (a) (Art of) drawing, sketching. (b) Drawing, sketch. **2.** Design, pattern.

essinateur, -trice, s. **1.** Sketcher, drawer. **2.** Designer. **3.** Draughtsman, -woman.

essiner, v.tr. **1.** To draw, sketch. *D. qch. d'après nature*, to draw sth. from nature. **2.** To design, lay out (garden). **3.** To show, delineate (sth.).

   se dessiner, to stand out, take form.

essous. 1. adv. Under(neath), below, beneath. *Marcher bras dessus bras dessous*, to walk arm-in-arm. **Vêtements de dessous**, underclothing. **En dessous**, underneath; down(wards). *Regarder qn en d.*, to look at s.o. furtively. **2.** s.m. (a) Lower part. **Dessous de plat**, table-mat. F: **Avoir le dessous**, to get the worst of it. *Cost:* **Dessous de robe**, (under-)slip.

essus. 1. adv. Above, over; (up)on (it, them). *Mettre la main d.*, to lay hands on it. **En dessus**, on top; above. **2.** s.m. (a) Top, upper part. **Dessus de lit**, bedspread. **Dessus de cheminée**, mantelpiece. F: **Le dessus du panier**, the pick of the basket. (b) **Avoir le dessus**, to have the upper hand. **3.** **De dessus**, from, off. *Tomber de d. sa chaise*, to fall off one's chair.

estin, s.m. Fate, destiny.

estinataire, s.m. & f. Addressee (of letter); consignee (of goods).

estination, s.f. **1.** Destination. **Trains à** **destination de Paris**, trains for Paris. **2.** Intended purpose.

destinée, s.f. (a) Destiny. (b) pl. Destinies, fortunes.

destiner, v.tr. **1.** To destine. **2.** *D. qch. à qn*, to intend sth. for s.o.

destituer, v.tr. To dismiss, discharge (s.o.); to remove (official) from office.

   destitué, a. Deprived (*de*, of); lacking (*de*, in); without.

destitution, s.f. Dismissal (of official).

destructeur, -trice. 1. a. Destroying; destructive. **2.** s. Destroyer.

destructif, a. Destructive.

destruction, s.f. Destruction, destroying.

désuet, -ète, a. Obsolete (word).

désuétude, s.f. Disuse, desuetude.

désunir, v.tr. To disunite, divide (people).

   désuni, a. Disunited, at variance.

détachement, s.m. **1.** Detaching (of sth.). **2.** Indifference (*de*, to); detachment (*de*, from). **3.** Detachment (of troops).

détacher, v.tr. To detach. (a) To (un)loose; to unfasten. (b) To separate; to cut off. *D. un chèque du carnet*, to tear out a cheque from the book. (c) F: *Détacher un coup à qn*, to hit out at s.o.

   se détacher. 1. To come undone. **2.** To break off. *Un bouton s'est détaché*, a button has come off. **3.** *Se d. sur le fond*, to stand out against the background.

   détaché, a. **1.** (a) Loose. (b) Isolated. **2.** Detached, unconcerned (manner).

détail [-ta:j], s.m. **1.** (a) Dividing up. (b) *Com:* Retail. **Marchand au détail**, retailer. **2.** Detail. *Donner tous les détails*, to go into all the details.

détaillant [-tajã], s. Retailer.

détailler [-taje], v.tr. **1.** (a) To divide up. (b) To retail. **2.** To detail, enumerate.

détaler, v.i. To decamp; to scamper away.

dételer, v.tr. (je dételle) **1.** To unharness. **2.** *Rail:* To uncouple (trucks).

détendre, v.tr. To slacken, relax. *D. l'esprit*, to calm the mind.

   se détendre, to slacken, relax.

   détendu, a. Slack.

détenir, v.tr. (Conj. like TENIR) **1.** *D. le record*, to hold the record. **2.** (a) To detain (s.o.). (b) To withhold, keep back.

   détenu, s. Prisoner.

détente, s.f. **1.** Relaxation, loosening. **2.** Trigger (of gun).

détenteur, -trice, s. Holder (of securities).

détention, s.f. **1.** Holding (of securities). **2.** Detention (of s.o.).

détenu. See DÉTENIR.

détérioration, s.f. Deterioration.

détériorer, v.tr. To make worse.

   se détériorer, to deteriorate; to spoil.

détermination, s.f. Determination.

déterminer, v.tr. **1.** To determine (species); to settle (meeting-place). **2.** To cause; to bring (sth.) about. **3.** *D. de faire qch.*, to resolve to do sth.

déterminé, *a.* **I.** Determined, definite. *Dans un sens d.,* in a given direction. **2.** Determined, resolute.

déterrer, *v.tr.* To dig up, unearth; to exhume, disinter.

détestable, *a.* Detestable, hateful.

détestation, *s.f.* Detestation.

détester, *v.tr.* To detest, hate. **Se faire détester de tous, par tout le monde,** to get oneself disliked by everyone.

détonant. I. *a.* Detonating, explosive. **2.** *s.m.* Explosive.

détonateur, *s.m.* Detonator.

détonation, *s.f.* (*a*) Detonation. (*b*) Report (of fire-arm).

détoner, *v.i.* To detonate, explode.

détour, *s.m.* **I.** Turning, deviation; round-about way. **Sans détour(s),** plainly, frankly. **2.** Turn, curve (in river).

détournement, *s.m.* **I.** Diversion (of water-course). **2.** Misappropriation (of funds).

détourner, *v.tr.* **I.** (*a*) To divert (water-course); to turn (weapon) aside. *D. la conversation,* to change the conversation. (*b*) To turn away, avert (one's eyes). **2.** To misappropriate, embezzle (funds).

se détourner, to turn away.

détourné, *a.* Indirect, circuitous.

détracteur, -trice, *s.* Detractor.

détraquer, *v.tr. Son intervention a tout détraqué,* his intervention has upset everything. *Se d. les nerfs,* to wreck one's nerves.

détrempe, *s.f.* Paint: Distemper.

détremper, *v.tr.* To moisten, soak.

détresse, *s.f.* Distress. **I.** Grief, anguish. **2.** (*a*) (Financial) straits. (*b*) *Nau:* Signal de détresse, distress signal; *F:* S O S.

détriment, *s.m.* Detriment, loss.

détroit, *s.m. Ph.Geog:* Strait, straits.

détromper, *v.tr.* To undeceive.

détrôner, *v.tr.* To dethrone.

détruire, *v.tr.* (Conj. like CONDUIRE) **I.** To demolish. **2.** To destroy, ruin.

dette, *s.f.* Debt. **Avoir des dettes,** to be in debt.

deuil [dœ:j], *s.m.* **I.** (*a*) Mourning, sorrow. *F:* **Faire son deuil de qch.,** to give sth. up as lost. (*b*) Bereavement. **2.** (*a*) Mourning (clothes). **Grand deuil,** deep mourning. **Être en deuil de qn,** to be in mourning for s.o.

deux [dø; before a vowel sound in the same word group, døz], *num.a.inv. & s.m.* Two. *Charles Deux,* Charles the Second. **Deux fois,** twice. **Tous (les) deux,** both. **Tous les deux jours,** every other day. **Entre deux âges,** of uncertain age. **A nous deux maintenant!** now we two will have it out! *Ten:* **A deux,** deuce. **A deux de jeu,** five (games) all.

deuxième, *num. a. & s.* Second. *Appartement au d.* (*étage*), flat on the second floor.

deuxièmement, *adv.* Secondly.

deux-points, *s.m.* Colon.

dévaler. I. *v.i.* To descend. **2.** *v.tr. D. la colline,* to hurry down the hill.

dévaliser, *v.tr.* To rob (s.o. of his money).

devancer, *v.tr.* (n. devançons) **I.** To precede. **2.** To leave behind; to outstrip. **3.** To forestall. *D. les désirs de qn,* to anticipate s.o.'s desires.

devancier, *s.* (*a*) Precursor. (*b*) Predecessor.

devant[1]. **I.** *prep.* Before, in front of. *Marchez tout droit d. vous,* go straight ahead. **2.** *adv.* Before, in front. **Aller devant,** to go in front. **3.** *s.m.* Front (part), fore-part. **Devant de chemise,** shirt front. **Devant de cheminée,** fire-screen. **Prendre les devants,** to go on ahead. **Gagner les devants,** to take the lead.

devant[2]. See DEVOIR.

devanture, *s.f.* (*a*) Front(age) (of building). (*b*) *D. de magasin,* shop-front.

dévastateur, -trice. I. *s.* Devastator, ravager. **2.** *a.* Devastating.

dévastation, *s.f.* Devastation.

déveine, *s.f. F:* (Run of) ill-luck. **Avoir la déveine,** to be out of luck.

développement, *s.m.* **I.** Spreading out. **2.** Development, growth (of the body); development (of flower).

développer, *v.tr.* **I.** To spread out. **2.** To develop (a negative).

devenir, *v.pred.* (Conj. like VENIR. Aux. *être*) (*a*) To become. *Qu'est-il devenu?* what has become of him? (*b*) To grow into. (*c*) *C'est à devenir fou!* it is enough to drive one mad!

dévergonder (se), *v.pr.* To fall into dissolute ways.

dévergondé. I. *a.* Licentious, profligate, shameless. **2.** *s.* Profligate.

déverser, *v.tr.* **I.** To divert (channel). **2.** To discharge (water).

se déverser, to flow, pour.

dévêtir, *v.tr.* (Conj. like VÊTIR) (*a*) To undress (s.o.). (*b*) To take off (garment).

se dévêtir. I. To undress. **2.** *Se d. de son bien,* to divest oneself of one's property.

déviation, *s.f.* Deviation; curvature (of the spine).

dévider, *v.tr.* (*a*) To unwind. (*b*) To reel off (thread).

dévier, *v.i.* To deviate, swerve, diverge. **Faire dévier une balle,** to deflect a bullet.

devin, devineresse, *s.* Soothsayer. *F:* **Je ne suis pas devin,** I'm not a wizard.

deviner, *v.tr.* To guess. *F:* **Cela se devine,** that's obvious.

devinette, *s.f.* Riddle, conundrum.

dévisager, *v.tr.* (n. dévisageons) To stare at.

devise, *s.f.* (*a*) *Her:* Device. (*b*) Motto. (*c*) *F:* Slogan.

deviser, *v.i.* To chat, gossip.

dévoiler, *v.tr.* **I.** To unveil. **2.** To reveal, disclose (secret).

devoir. I. *v.tr.* (*pr.p.* devant; *p.p.* dû,

*. due; *pr.ind.* je dois, ils doivent; *p.h.* je
dus; *fu.* je devrai) **I.** (Duty) Should, ought.
(a) (General precept) *Tu dois honorer tes
parents,* you should honour your parents.
(b) (Command) *Vous devez vous trouver à
votre poste à trois heures,* you must be at your
post at three o'clock. (c) *Il aurait dû
m'avertir,* he should have warned me.
2. (Compulsion) Must, have to. *Enfin j'ai
dû céder,* at last I had to yield. **3.** (Futurity)
Am to. (a) *Je dois partir demain,* I am to
start to-morrow. *Dût-il m'en coûter la vie,*
were I to die for it. (b) *Cela devait être,* it
was meant to be. **4.** (Opinion expressed)
Must. *Vous devez avoir faim,* you must be
hungry. **5.** Devoir qch. à qn, to owe s.o. sth.
La peine due à ces forfaits, the penalties which
these crimes deserve.

    II. devoir, *s.m.* **I.** (a) Duty. Se mettre
en devoir de *faire qch.,* to prepare to do sth.
Il est de mon devoir de . . ., it is my duty
to. . . . (b) *Sch:* Exercise, task. **2.** *pl.* Mes
devoirs à madame votre mère, my duty to your
mother. Rendre à qn les derniers devoirs,
to pay the last honours to s.o.

dû, due. I. *a.* Due. (a) Owing. (b)
Proper. En temps dû, in due course. **2.** *s.m.*
Due. *F:* A chacun son dû, give the devil
his due.

évorant, *a.* Ravenous (wolf); consuming
(thirst); devouring (passion).

évorer, *v.tr.* To devour. *La soif me dévore,*
I am consumed with thirst. *D.* la route, to
eat up the miles.

évot. I. *a.* Devout, religious. **2.** *s.* Devout
person. Faux dévot, hypocrite.

évotement, *adv.* Devoutly.

évotion, *s.f.* Devotion; esp. piety.

évouement, *s.m.* **I.** Self-sacrifice; devotion to duty. **2.** *Croyez, monsieur, à mon
entier d.,* I am yours obediently.

évouer, *v.tr.* **I.** To dedicate. **2.** To devote.
se dévouer. **I.** To devote oneself.
2. Se d. pour qn, to sacrifice oneself for s.o.
    dévoué, *a.* Devoted, staunch, loyal.
Votre tout dévoué, yours faithfully.

evr-a, -ai, -as, etc. See DEVOIR.

extérité, *s.f.* Dexterity, skill (à, in).

iabète, *s.m. Med:* Diabetes.

iable, *s.m.* **I.** Devil. Faire le diable à
quatre, to kick up a shindy. Tirer le diable
par la queue, to be hard up. Du diable si je
le sais! hanged, blowed, if I know! Aller
au diable vauvert, to disappear *C'est au d.
auvert,* it's miles from anywhere. Ce n'est
pas le diable, it is nothing to worry about.
Bruit de tous les diables, devil of a din. A la
diable, anyhow. Pauvre diable! poor beggar!
Un grand d., a big, strapping, fellow. Ce
diable de parapluie, that wretched umbrella.
Il n'est pas aussi diable qu'il est noir, he is
not so black as he is painted. **2.** *Toys:*
Diable (à ressort), Jack-in-the-box.

iablement, *adv.* Awfully (funny).

diablotin, *s.m.* Little devil; imp.

diabolique, *a.* Diabolical, fiendish.

diacre, *s.m. Ecc:* Deacon.

diadème, *s.m.* Diadem.

diagnostic, *s.m. Med:* Diagnosis.

diagnostiquer, *v.tr. Med:* To diagnose.

diagonal, -aux, **I.** *a.* Diagonal. **2.** *s.f.*
Diagonale, diagonal (line).

diagonalement, *adv.* Diagonally.

diagramme, *s.m.* Diagram.

dialecte, *s.m.* Dialect.

dialogue, *s.m.* Dialogue.

diamant, *s.m.* Diamond.

diamétral, -aux, *a.* Diametrical.

diamètre, *s.m.* Diameter.

diane¹, *s.f. Mil:* Reveille.

Diane², *Pr.n.f.* Diana.

diapason, *s.m. Mus:* **I.** Diapason, pitch.
2. Tuning-fork.

diaphane, *a.* Diaphanous.

diaphragme, *s.m.* **I.** *Physiol:* Diaphragm,
midriff. **2.** *Tchn:* Diaphragm, dividing
plate.

diaprer, *v.tr.* To variegate.

diarrhée, *s.f. Med:* Diarrhoea.

dicotylédone. *Bot:* **I.** *a.* Dicotyledonous.
2. *s.f.* Dicotyledon.

dictagraphe, *s.m.* Dictagraph.

dictateur, *s.m.* Dictator.

dictatorial, -aux, *a.* Dictatorial.

dictature, *s.f.* Dictatorship.

dicter, *v.tr.* To dictate.
    dictée, *s.f.* Dictation.

diction, *s.f.* Diction; delivery. Professeur
de diction, teacher of elocution.

dictionnaire, *s.m.* Dictionary, lexicon.
D. de géographie, gazetteer.

dicton, *s.m.* Common saying; (wise) saw.

dieppois, *a. & s.* (Native) of Dieppe.

dièse, *s.m. Mus:* Sharp

diète, *s.f.* Diet, regimen.

dieu, -ieux, *s.m.* God. **I.** Grands dieux!
heavens! **2.** (a) S'il plaît à Dieu, God willing;
D.V. (b) *F:* Le bon Dieu, God. (c) *F:* Dieu
merci! thank heaven! Pour l'amour de Dieu,
for goodness' sake. Dieu sait *si j'ai travaillé,*
heaven knows I have worked hard enough!
3. *int. F:* Mon Dieu! dear me! *Mon D.,
oui!* why, yes!

diffamant, *a.* Slanderous, libellous.

diffamateur, -trice, *s.* Slanderer, libeller.

diffamation, *s.f.* Defamation, slander, libel.

diffamatoire, *a.* Defamatory, slanderous,
libellous.

diffamer, *v.tr.* To slander, libel.

différemment, *adv.* Differently.

différence, *s.f.* Difference. *Quelle d. avec
. . .!* what a difference from . . .! A la
différence de . . ., unlike . . . . A la
différence que . . ., with this difference
that. . . .

différenciation, *s.f.* Differentiation.

différencier, *v.tr.* To differentiate.

différend, *s.m.* Difference, dispute.

différent, *a.* Different. **A différentes reprises,** at various times.

différentiel, -elle, *a.* Differential; discriminating (tariff).

différer, *v.* (je diffère; je différerai) **I.** *v.tr.* To defer; to put off (payment). **2.** *v.i.* To differ. *D. d'opinion,* to differ in opinion.

difficile, *a.* **I.** Difficult. *Les temps sont difficiles,* times are hard. **2.** *F: Il est d. à vivre,* he is difficult to get on with. *s.* **Faire le difficile,** to be hard to please.

difficilement, *adv.* With difficulty.

difficulté, *s.f.* Difficulty. *Susciter des difficultés à qn,* to put difficulties in s.o.'s way.

difforme, *a.* Deformed, misshapen.

difformité, *s.f.* Deformity.

diffus, *a.* Diffused (light). *F: Style d.,* diffuse, prolix, style.

diffusément, *adv.* Diffusely, verbosely.

diffuser, *v.tr.* **I.** To diffuse (light). **Lumière diffusée,** flood-lighting. **2.** *W.Tel:* To broadcast (news).

diffuseur, *s.m. W.Tel:* (Of pers.) Broadcaster.

diffusion, *s.f.* **I.** Diffusion (of light); spread (of disease). **2.** Broadcasting (of news). **3.** Verbosity, diffuseness.

digérer, *v.tr.* (je digère; je digérerai) **I.** To digest. **2.** *F:* To stomach (insult).

digestible, *a.* Digestible.

digestif, *a.* Digestive.

digestion, *s.f.* Digestion.

digital, -aux. I. *a.* **Empreinte digitale,** finger-print. **2.** *s.f.* **Digitale.** *Bot:* Foxglove.

digne, *a.* **I.** (*a*) Deserving, worthy. *F:* **C'est bien digne de lui,** that's just like him. (*b*) *F:* **Un digne homme,** a worthy man. **2.** Dignified.

dignement, *adv.* **I.** Suitably. **2.** With dignity; worthily.

dignitaire, *s.m.* Dignitary.

dignité, *s.f.* **I.** Dignity. *Air de d.,* dignified air. **2.** High position; dignity.

digression, *s.f.* Digression. **Faire une digression,** to digress.

digue, *s.f.* (*a*) Dike, dam; embankment (of waterway). (*b*) Breakwater; sea-wall.

dilapidation, *s.f.* **I.** Wasting, squandering (of fortune). **2.** Peculation.

dilapider, *v.tr.* **I.** To waste, squander (fortune). **2.** To misappropriate (funds).

dilatation, *s.f.* (*a*) Dila(ta)tion, expansion. (*b*) Distension (of stomach).

dilater, *v.tr.* To dilate, expand.

dilemme, *s.m.* Dilemma. **Enfermé dans un dilemme,** on the horns of a dilemma.

dilettante, *s.m.* Dilettante, amateur.

diligemment, *adv.* Diligently.

diligence, *s.f.* **I.** (*a*) Diligence, application. (*b*) Haste, dispatch. **2.** (Stage-)coach.

diligent, *a.* Diligent, industrious.

diluer, *v.tr.* To dilute (*de,* with).

dilution, *s.f.* Dilution; watering down.

dimanche, *s.m.* Sunday. *Observer le d.,* to keep the sabbath.

dimension, *s.f.* Dimension, size.

diminuer. I. *v.tr.* To lessen; to diminish. **2.** *v.i.* To diminish, lessen; to abate. *Les jours diminuent,* the days are drawing in.

diminutif, *a. & s.m.* Diminutive.

diminution, *s.f.* Diminution, lessening; abatement; slackening (of speed).

dinde, *s.f.* Turkey-hen. *Cu:* Turkey.

dindon, *s.m.* Turkey-cock.

dindonneau, *s.m.* Young turkey.

dîner. I. *v.i.* To dine. *D. en ville,* to dine out.

II. dîner, *s.m.* Dinner.

dîneur, -euse, *s.* Diner.

diocésain, *a. & s.m. Ecc:* Diocesan.

diocèse, *s.m. Ecc:* Diocese.

Diogène. *Pr.n.m. Gr.Hist:* Diogenes.

diphtérie, *s.f. Med:* Diphtheria.

diphtongue, *s.f. Ling:* Diphthong.

diplomate, *s.m.* Diplomatist.

diplomatie, *s.f.* **I.** Diplomacy. **2. Entrer dans la d.,** to enter the diplomatic service.

diplomatique, *a.* Diplomatic.

diplôme, *s.m.* Diploma.

dire. I. *v.tr.* (*pr.p.* **disant;** *p.p.* **dit;** *pr. ind.* **vous dites, ils disent**) **I.** To say, tell. (*a*) *D. qch. à qn,* to tell s.o. sth. *Envoyer d. à qn que . . .,* to send word to s.o. that. . . . *Ce disant . . .,* with these words. . . . **Qu'en dira-t-on?** what will people say? *Il n'y a rien à d. à sa conduite,* no fault can be found with his behaviour. *D. ce qu'on pense,* to speak one's mind. *Je vous l'avais bien dit!* didn't I tell you so? **Comme on dit,** as the saying goes. *Cela ne se dit pas,* that is not said. *F:* **A qui le dites-vous?** don't I know it? **Dites toujours!** go on! say it! *D.* **que oui,** to say yes. **Je ne sais comment dire,** I don't know how to put it. **A vrai dire . . .,** to tell the truth. . . . **Tout est dit,** that is an end to the matter. **Pour ainsi dire,** so to speak. **Comme qui dirait . . .,** as you might say. . . . *A ce qu'il dit,* according to him. **Vous l'avez dit,** quite so. **Ainsi dit, ainsi fait,** no sooner said than done. **Cela va sans dire,** that goes without saying. **Il n'y a pas à dire,** there is no denying it. **Dites donc,** *en voilà assez!* look here, I say, that's enough! (*b*) **On le dit mort,** he is reported (to be) dead. (*c*) **Il ne se le fit pas dire deux fois,** he didn't wait to be told twice. (*d*) **Faire dire qch. à qn,** to make s.o. tell sth. **2.** (*a*) **Dire à qn de faire qch.,** to tell s.o. to do sth. (*b*) **Dire que** + *sub.* **Dites qu'on le fasse entrer,** bid them show him in. **3. Dire des vers,** to recite poetry. *D. son chapelet,* to tell one's beads. **4.** (*a*) To express, betoken. **Cela en dit beaucoup sur son courage,** it speaks volumes for his courage. (*b*) **Cette musique ne me dit rien,** I don't care for this music. **5.** (*a*) **Vouloir dire,** to mean. (*b*) **Qu'est-ce à dire?** what does this mean?

II. **dire**, *s.m.* Statement, assertion. **Selon son dire** . . ., according to him. . . .

dit, *a.* (*a*) Settled, fixed. (*b*) (So-)called. *La zone dite tempérée*, the so-called temperate zone.

direct [-ekt], *a.* Direct, straight. *Rail:* Train direct, through train.

directement, *adv.* Directly, straight.

directeur, -trice. I. *s.* Director, directress; head (of industrial concern); principal (of school). **Directeur général des postes, télégraphes, et téléphones**, Postmaster General. **2.** *a.* Directing, controlling (force).

directif, *a.* Directing, guiding (rule).

direction, *s.f.* **I.** (*a*) Guidance, direction. (*b*) Board of directors. **2.** Direction, driving (of engine). **3.** Direction, course. *Train d. de Bordeaux*, train for Bordeaux. **4.** *pl.* Directions, instructions.

directorat, *s.m.* (*a*) Directorate; directorship. (*b*) Managership.

dirigeable. I. *a.* Dirigible. **2.** *s.m. Aer:* Dirigible.

dirigeant, *a.* Directing, guiding (power). *Classes dirigeantes*, ruling classes.

diriger, *v.tr.* (n. dirigeons) **I.** To direct, control. **2.** (*a*) To direct, guide. (*b*) **Diriger ses pas vers** . . ., to direct one's steps towards. (*c*) To level, point (telescope) (*sur*, at).

se diriger. I. *Se d. vers un endroit*, to make one's way towards a place. **2.** (Of river) *Se d. du nord au sud*, to run north and south.

dis, -ais, -ant, -e, -ons, etc. See DIRE.

discernable, *a.* Discernible, visible.

discernement, *s.m.* **I.** Perception; discrimination. **2.** Discernment, judgment.

discerner, *v.tr.* To discern, distinguish (sth.). *D. le bien du mal*, to tell right from wrong.

disciple, *s.m.* Disciple, follower.

disciplinaire. I. *a.* Disciplinary (punishment). **2.** *s.m.* Disciplinarian.

discipline, *s.f.* Discipline.

discipliner, *v.tr.* To discipline.

discontinuation, *s.f.* Discontinuance.

discontinuer, *v.tr. & i.* To discontinue.

discordance, *s.f.* Discordance, dissonance.

discordant, *a.* Discordant.

discorde, *s.f.* Discord, dissension, strife.

discourir, *v.i.* (Conj. like COURIR) To discourse.

discours, *s.m.* **I.** Talk. **2.** Discourse. **3.** Speech, address. **4. Parties du discours**, parts of speech.

discourtois, *a.* Discourteous.

discrédit, *s.m.* Discredit; disrepute.

discréditer, *v.tr.* To disparage; to throw discredit on.

discret, -ète, *a.* (*a*) Discreet. (*b*) Quiet, unobtrusive.

discrètement, *adv.* **I.** Discretely. **2.** Unobtrusively.

discrétion, *s.f.* Discretion. **I.** Prudence.

2. *Se rendre à d.*, to surrender unconditionally.

disculpation, *s.f.* Exculpation.

disculper, *v.tr.* To exculpate, exonerate.

discursif, *a.* Discursive.

discussion, *s.f.* Discussion, debate. *La question en discussion*, the question at issue. *Sans d. possible*, indisputably.

discutable, *a.* Debatable, arguable.

discuter, *v.tr.* (*a*) To discuss, debate. *Discutons la chose*, let us talk it over. (*b*) To question, dispute.

disette, *s.f.* Scarcity, dearth.

diseur, -euse, *s.* (*a*) **Diseuse de bonne aventure**, fortune-teller. (*b*) **Beau diseur**, fine talker.

disgrâce, *s.f.* Disfavour, disgrace.

disgracier, *v.tr.* To dismiss from favour. **disgracié**, *a.* Out of favour.

disgracieux, *a* **I.** Uncouth. **2.** Ungracious.

disjoindre, *v.tr.* (Conj. like JOINDRE) To disjoin, sever, disjoint.

disjonctif, *a.* Disjunctive.

dislocation, *s.f.* Dislocation.

disloquer, *v.tr.* To dislocate.

disparaître, *v.i.* (Conj. like CONNAÎTRE. Aux. *avoir* or *être*) To disappear. *D. aux yeux de qn*, to vanish before s.o.'s eyes. **disparu**, *a.* **I.** Missing. **2.** Extinct.

disparate. I. *a.* (*a*) Dissimilar. (*b*) Ill-matched. **2.** *s.f.* (*a*) Disparity. (*b*) Incongruity.

disparition, *s.f.* Disappearance.

dispendieux, *a.* Expensive, costly.

dispensaire, *s.m.* (Public) dispensary.

dispensation, *s.f.* **I.** Dispensation; distribution. **2.** *Pharm:* Dispensing.

dispenser, *v.tr.* **I.** *D. qn d'une tâche*, to let s.o. off a task. **2.** (*a*) To dispense (charity). (*b*) *Pharm:* To dispense (medicine).

disperser, *v.tr.* To disperse, scatter. **se disperser**, to disperse, scatter.

dispersion, *s.f.* Dispersion; scattering.

disponibilité, *s.f.* **I.** Availability (of seats). **2.** *pl.* Available time or means.

disponible, *a.* Available; at (s.o.'s) disposal.

dispos, *a.m.* Fit, well, in good form.

disposer. I. *v.tr.* (*a*) To dispose, arrange. (*b*) *D. qn à qch.*, to dispose, incline, s.o. to sth. **2.** *v.ind.tr. D. de qch.*, to dispose of sth. *Disposez de moi*, I am at your service. *Les moyens dont je dispose*, the means at my disposal.

se disposer *à faire qch.*, to make ready to do sth.

dispositif, *s.m.* Apparatus, device.

disposition, *s.f.* Disposition. **I.** Arrangement (of house). *D. du terrain*, lie of the land. **2.** (*a*) State (of mind). (*b*) Predisposition; tendency. (*c*) *pl.* Natural aptitude. **3.** *pl.* (*a*) Arrangements. *Prendre toutes dispositions utiles*, to take all useful steps. (*b*) Provisions (of will). **4.** Disposal. **Libre disposition de soi-même**, self-determination.

disproportionné, *a.* Disproportionate.
disputable, *a.* Disputable, debatable.
dispute, *s.f.* Altercation, quarrel.
disputer, *v.tr. & i.* **1.** *Disputer qch.,* to dispute sth. *D. qch. à qn,* to contend with s.o. for sth. **2.** *v.i.* To quarrel, wrangle.
  se disputer, to quarrel (*pour,* over, about).
disque, *s.m.* (*a*) Disk, disc. (*b*) *D. de phonographe,* gramophone record.
disquisition, *s.f.* Disquisition.
dissection, *s.f.* Dissection.
dissemblable, *a.* Dissimilar; unlike.
dissemblance, *s.f.* Dissimilarity.
dissémination, *s.f.* Scattering (of seeds); spreading (of ideas); dissemination.
disséminer, *v.tr.* To scatter (seeds); to spread, disseminate (ideas).
dissension, *s.f.* Dissension, discord.
dissentiment, *s.m.* Disagreement, dissent.
disséquer, *v.tr.* (**je dissèque; je disséquerai**) To dissect.
dissertation, *s.f.* Dissertation.
dissidence, *s.f.* Dissidence; dissent.
dissident. 1. *a.* Dissident, dissentient. **2.** *s.* (*a*) Dissentient. (*b*) *Ecc:* Dissenter.
dissimilaire, *a.* Dissimilar, unlike.
dissimulation, *s.f.* **1.** Dissimulation; deceit. **2.** Concealment (of the truth).
dissimuler, *v.tr.* To dissemble, dissimulate, conceal (feelings). *Abs.* To dissemble.
  se dissimuler *derrière les rideaux,* to hide behind the ins.
  dissimulé, *a.* ₍ssimulating, secretive.
dissipation, *s.f.* **1.** (*a*) Dissipation, dispersion (of clouds). (*b*) Dissipation, wasting (of time). **2.** Dissipation, dissolute living.
dissiper, *v.tr.* (*a*) To dissipate, disperse (clouds); to dispel (fears). (*b*) To dissipate, waste (time).
  se dissiper. 1. (Of suspicions) To vanish; (of fog) to clear. **2.** To amuse oneself.
  dissipé, *a.* (*a*) Dissipated; gay (life). (*b*) *Sch:* Inattentive.
dissolu, *a.* Dissolute, loose, profligate.
dissolution, *s.f.* **1.** Disintegration, dissolution. **2.** (*a*) Dissolving. (*b*) Solution. **3.** Dissolution (of marriage).
dissolv-ant¹, -ez, -ons. See DISSOUDRE.
dissolvant², *a. & s.m.* (Dis)solvent.
dissonance, *s.f.* **1.** Dissonance. **2.** *Mus:* Discord.
dissonant, *a.* Dissonant, discordant.
dissoudre, *v.tr.* (*pr.p.* dissolvant; *p.p.* dissous, *f.* dissoute; *pr.ind.* je dissous, il dissout) To dissolve. **1.** To melt (substance) in a liquid. **2.** (*a*) To disintegrate, decompose. (*b*) To dissolve (partnership).
  se dissoudre. 1. *Se d. dans l'eau,* to dissolve in water. **2.** (Of assembly) To break up.
dissuader, *v.tr. D. qn de qch.,* to dissuade s.o. from sth.

dissyllabe, *s.m.* Dissyllable.
distance, *s.f.* Distance. **Suivre qn à distance,** to follow s.o. at a distance. **De distance en distance,** at intervals.
distancer, *v.tr.* (n. distançons) To outdistance, outrun, outstrip.
distant, *a.* Distant.
distendre, *v.tr.* To distend.
distension, *s.f.* Distension.
distillateur, *s.m.* Distiller.
distillation, *s.f.* Distillation, distilling.
distiller, *v.tr.* (*a*) To distil, exude. (*b*) *Ind:* To distil (spirits).
distillerie, *s.f.* Distillery.
distinct [-tɛ̃kt], *a.* **1.** Distinct, separate. **2.** Distinct, clear.
distinctement, *adv.* Distinctly, clearly.
distinctif, *a.* Distinctive, characteristic.
distinction, *s.f.* Distinction. **1. Sans distinction,** indiscriminately. **2.** (*a*) Distinction, honour. (*b*) Decoration. **3.** Distinction, eminence.
distinguable, *a.* Distinguishable.
distinguer, *v.tr.* To distinguish. **1.** To mark, characterize. **2.** To honour. **3.** *D. qch. de qch.,* to distinguish sth. from sth. **4.** To discern.
  se distinguer. 1. To distinguish oneself. **2.** To be distinguishable (from others). **3.** To stand out.
  distingué, *a.* Distinguished.
distique, *s.m. Pros:* Couplet.
distraction, *s.f.* **1.** Absence of mind, inadvertence. **2.** Diversion, amusement.
distraire, *v.tr.* (Conj. like TRAIRE) **1.** To distract, divert (s.o.'s attention). **2.** To divert, amuse.
  se distraire, to take relaxation; to amuse oneself.
  distrait, *a.* Absent-minded.
distraitement, *adv.* Absent-mindedly.
distray-ais, -ez, -ons, etc. See DISTRAIRE.
distribuer, *v.tr.* To distribute. *D. les cartes,* to deal out the cards.
distributeur, -trice, *s.* Distributor.
distribution, *s.f.* Distribution; allotment (of duties); issue (of rations); *Sch:* *D. de prix,* speech-day. *D. d'eau,* water supply. *El.E:* Tableau de distribution, switchboard.
dit, dites, dîtes. See DIRE.
divaguer, *v.i. F:* (*a*) To digress. (*b*) To ramble (in delirium).
divan, *s.m.* Divan; couch.
divergence, *s.f.* Divergence.
divergent, *a.* Divergent.
diverger, *v.i.* (n. divergeons) To diverge.
divers, *a. pl.* (*a*) Diverse, varied. (**Frais**) divers, sundry expenses. *Journ:* **Faits divers,** news items. (*b*) *Indef. adj.* (Always preceding the sb.) Various, sundry. **En diverses occasions,** on divers occasions.
diversement, *adv.* Diversely.
diversifier, *v.tr.* To diversify, vary.
diversion, *s.f.* Diversion, change.

diversité, *s.f.* Diversity.
divertir, *v.tr.* To divert, entertain, amuse.
se divertir, to amuse oneself.
divertissant, *a.* Diverting, amusing.
divertissement, *s.m.* **1.** Misappropriation (of funds). **2.** Diversion; entertainment.
dividende, *s.m.* Dividend.
divin, *a.* Divine.
divinateur, -trice, *s.* Divines.
divinité, *s.f.* Divinity.
diviser, *v.tr.* To divide.
se diviser, to divide, to break up.
diviseur, *s.m.* *Mth:* Divisor.
divisible, *a.* Divisible.
division, *s.f.* Division. **1.** Partition; dividing. **2.** Part; department, branch. **3.** Dissension.
divorce, *s.m.* Divorce.
divulguer, *v.tr.* To divulge, disclose.
dix, *num.a.inv. & s.m.* **1.** card *a.* Ten. (At the end of the word-group [dis]; before sb. or adj. beginning with a vowel sound [diz]; before sb. or adj. beginning with a consonant [di]) **2.** (Always [dis]) (*a*) *Dix et demi,* ten and a half. (*b*) *Le dix mai,* the tenth of May.
dix-huit. 1. Eighteen. **2.** *Le dix-huit mai,* the eighteenth of May.
dix-huitième. Eighteenth.
dixième. 1. *num. a. & s.* Tenth. **2.** *s.m.* Tenth (part).
dix-neuf. 1. Nineteen. **2.** *Le dix-neuf mai,* the nineteenth of May.
dix-neuvième. Nineteenth.
dix-sept [-sɛ(t)]. **1.** Seventeen. **2.** *Le dix-sept mai,* the seventeenth of May.
dix-septième. Seventeenth.
dizaine, *s.f.* (About) ten; half a score.
do, *s.m. Mus:* (The note) C.
docile, *a.* Docile.
docilement, *adv.* Submissively.
docilité, *s.f.* Docility.
docte, *a. Iron:* Learned.
docteur, *s.m.* Doctor. **1.** *D. en droit,* Doctor of Laws. *D. ès lettres,* Doctor of Literature. **2.** *Docteur* **(en médecine),** doctor (of medicine); physician.
doctoral, -aux, *a.* Doctoral; pompous.
doctrine, *s.f.* Doctrine, tenet.
document, *s.m.* Document.
documentaire, *a.* Documentary.
dodo, *s.m.* (Of child) **Faire dodo,** to go to sleep.
dodu, *a.* Plump.
dogmatique, *a.* Dogmatic.
dogme, *s.m.* Dogma, tenet.
dogue, *s.m.* Mastiff.
doigt, *s.m.* Finger; *Z:* digit. (*a*) *F:* **Mon petit doigt me l'a dit,** a little bird told me so. **Promener ses doigts sur qch.,** to finger sth. **Donner sur les doigts à qn,** to rap s.o. over the knuckles. **Savoir qch. sur le bout du doigt,** to have sth. at one's finger tips. **Se**

mordre les doigts, to bite one's nails with impatience. (*b*) **Être à deux doigts de la mort,** to be within an ace of death. (*c*) **Doigt de pied,** toe.
doigtier, *s.m.* Finger-stall.
doi-s, -t, -ve. See DEVOIR.
doléances, *s.f.pl.* Complaints; whining.
dolent, *a.* **1.** Whining, doleful. **2.** Painful.
domaine, *s.m.* **1.** Domain; estate, property. **Domaine public,** public property. **2.** *F:* Field, scope (of a science).
dôme, *s.m.* (*a*) *Arch:* Dome, cupola. (*b*) *F:* Vault, canopy (of heaven).
domestique. 1. *a.* Domestic. **2.** *s.m. & f.* (Domestic) servant.
domicile, *s.m.* Residence. *Jur:* Domicile. **A domicile,** at one's private house. **Franco à domicile,** carriage paid. **Institutrice à domicile,** visiting governess.
domicilié, *a.* Resident, domiciled (*d,* at).
dominance, *s.f.* Dominance, sway.
dominant, *a.* Dominating, dominant.
dominateur, -trice, *a.* Domineering.
domination, *s.f.* Domination, rule, sway.
dominer. 1. *v.i.* To rule, hold sway. **2.** *v.tr.* To dominate. (*a*) To rule, sway. *Sa voix dominait toutes les autres,* his voice rose above all others. (*b*) To tower above (sth.); to overlook.
dominicain, *a. & s.* Dominican.
dominical, -aux, *a.* *L'oraison dominicale,* the Lord's prayer.
domino, *s.m.* Domino.
dommage, *s.m.* **1.** (*a*) Damage, injury. (*b*) *F:* **Quel dommage!** what a pity! **2.** *pl.* (*a*) Damage (to property). (*b*) *Jur:* **Dommages-intérêts,** damages.
domptable [dɔ̃t-], *a.* Tamable.
dompter [dɔ̃te], *v.tr.* To tame; master.
dompteur, -euse [dɔ̃t-], *s.* Tamer.
don, *s.m.* **1.** Giving. **2.** (*a*) Gift, present. (*b*) Gift; talent.
donation, *s.f.* Donation, gift.
donc [dɔ̃:k]. **1.** *conj.* Therefore, consequently. **2.** *adv.* [dɔ̃] (Emphatic) *Mais taisez-vous d.!* do hold your tongue! *Allons d.!* (i) nonsense! (ii) come on! *Pensez d.!* just think!
donjon, *s.m.* Keep (of castle).
donner, *v.tr.* To give. **1.** *D. un bal,* to give a ball. *D. le bonjour à qn,* to wish s.o. good day. *D. à boire à qn,* to give s.o. something to drink. *Je vous le donne en vingt,* I give you twenty guesses. *F:* **C'est donné,** it's dirt cheap. **S'en donner (à cœur joie),** to have a good time. *D. les cartes,* to deal (the cards). **2.** (*a*) To provide, furnish; (of crops) to yield. *Cela donne à penser,* this gives food for reflection. *D. un bon exemple,* to set a good example. *A un point donné,* at a given point. *Étant donné qu'il est mineur,* inasmuch as he is not of age. (*b*) **Donner faim à qn,** to make s.o. hungry. **3.** To attribute (sth. to s.o.). *Je lui donne vingt ans,* I put him down as twenty. **Donner raison à qn,** to

agree with s.o. **4.** (a) **Fenêtre qui donne sur la cour,** window that looks out on the yard. (b) **D. de la tête contre qch.,** to knock one's head against sth. **D. dans le piège,** to fall into the trap. **F: Donner dedans,** to walk right into the trap. **Il me donne sur les nerfs,** he gets on my nerves. **F: Donner dans l'œil de, à, qn,** to strike s.o.'s fancy.

données, s.f. pl. Data.

dont, rel.pron. (= de qui, duquel, desquels, etc.) (a) From, by, with, whom or which. **La chaîne d. il était attaché,** the chain by which he was fastened. (b) (Of) whom, which. **Le livre d. j'ai besoin,** the book (that) I want. **Voici ce d. il s'agit,** this is what it is all about. (c) Whose. **La dame d. je connais le fils,** the lady whose son I know.

dorénavant, adv. Henceforth.

dorer, v.tr. To gild. **doré,** a. Gilded, gilt.

dorloter, v.tr. To fondle; to pamper.

dormant, a. (a) Sleeping. (b) Dormant.

dormeur, -euse, s. Sleeper.

dormir, v.i. (pr.p. **dormant;** pr.ind. **je dors**) **1.** To sleep; to be asleep. **Dormir la grasse matinée,** to lie late abed. **Ne dormir que d'un œil,** to sleep with one eye open. **Vous pouvez dormir sur les deux oreilles,** you need have no cause for uneasiness. **Il dormait debout,** he couldn't keep his eyes open. **2.** To be dormant. Prov: **Il n'y a pire eau que l'eau qui dort,** still waters run deep.

dortoir, s.m. Dormitory.

dorure, s.f. **1.** Gilding. **2.** Gilt.

dos [do], s.m. Back. **1.** Avoir le dos rond, to be round-shouldered. **Faire le gros dos,** (of cat) to arch its back; (of pers.) to put on important airs. **F: Avoir qn sur le dos,** to be saddled with s.o. **2.** Back (of chair). **"Voir au dos,"** 'turn over.'

dose, s.f. Dose (of medicine).

dossier, s.m. **1.** Back (of seat). **2.** (a) Documents, file (relating to an affair). (b) Record (of official).

dot [dɔt], s.f. Dowry. **F: Coureur de dots,** fortune-hunter.

doter, v.tr. (a) To dower (bride). (b) To endow (hospital).

douaire, s.m. **1.** (Widow's) dower. **2.** Jointure; marriage settlement.

douairière, a. & s.f. Dowager.

douane, s.f. Adm: Customs. **Visite de la d.,** customs examination. **(Bureau de) douane,** custom-house.

douanier. 1. a. **Tarif d.,** customs tariff. **2.** s.m. Custom-house officer.

double. 1. a. Double, twofold. **Faire coup double,** to kill two birds with one shot. **2.** adv. **Voir double,** to see double. **3.** s.m. (a) Double. **Bontés rendues au double,** kindnesses returned twofold. (b) Duplicate, counterpart. **Facture en double,** invoice in duplicate.

doublement, adv. Doubly.

doubler. 1. v.tr. (a) To double (the size). (b) To fold in two; to double. **Nau: D. un cap,** to double a cape. **Th: D. un rôle,** to understudy a part. **Aut: Défense de doubler,** overtaking forbidden. (c) To line (coat). **2.** v.i. To double, to increase twofold.

doublure, s.f. **1.** Lining (of garment). **2.** Th: Understudy.

douce. See DOUX.

douce-amère, s.f Bot: Woody nightshade.

doucement, adv. Gently, softly. **Allez-y doucement!** gently does it! Prov: **Qui va doucement va loin,** slow and steady wins the race.

doucereux, a. **1.** Sweetish, sickly. **2.** Mealy-mouthed, smooth-tongued.

douceur, s.f. **1.** (a) Sweetness. (b) pl. Sweet things. **2.** Softness. **3.** (a) Pleasantness. (b) Pleasant thing. **4.** Gentleness; sweetness; mildness.

douche, s.f. Shower-bath.

douer, v.tr. To endow (s.o.) (de, with). **doué,** a. Gifted.

douillet, -ette [duj-], a. (a) Soft, downy. (b) (Of pers.) Soft.

douleur, s.f. Suffering. **1.** Pain, ache. **2.** Sorrow, grief, woe.

douloureusement, adv. **1.** Painfully. **2.** Sorrowfully.

douloureux, a. Painful. **1.** Aching; sore. **2.** Sad, distressing.

doute, s.m. Doubt, misgiving. **Avoir des doutes sur qch.,** to have misgivings about sth. **Sans doute,** (i) doubtless(ly); (ii) no doubt, I dare say, to be sure.

douter, v.i. To doubt. **D. de qn,** to mistrust s.o. **F: Il ne doute de rien,** he is full of self-confidence.

se douter de qch., to suspect sth. **Je ne me doutais pas qu'il fût là,** I had no idea that he was there.

douteusement, adv. Doubtfully.

douteux, a. Doubtful, uncertain.

douve, s.f. **1.** Moat. **2.** Coop: Stave.

Douvres, Pr.n.f. Geog: Dover.

doux, f. douce, a. (a) Sweet; smooth, soft. **Eau douce,** fresh water. (b) Pleasant, agreeable. (c) Gentle; mild. (d) Gentle; meek. (e) adv. **Tout doux!** gently!

douzaine, s.f. Dozen. **Une d. de personnes,** about a dozen people. **A la douzaine,** by the dozen.

douze, num.a.inv. & s.m.inv. Twelve. **Le d. mai,** the twelfth of May.

douzième. 1. num. a. & s. Twelfth. **2.** s.m. Twelfth (part).

doyen, -enne, s. **1.** Dean. **2.** Être le d., la doyenne, de qn,** to be s.o.'s senior.

dragage, s.m. **1.** Dredging. **2.** Mine-sweeping; dragging (of river).

dragée, s.f. (a) Sugar(ed) almond. (b) Pharm: Sugar-coated pill.

dragon, s.m. **1.** Dragon. **2.** Mil: Dragoon.

drague, s.f. Dredger.

draguer, *v.tr.* **1.** To dredge. **2.** To drag (pond); to sweep (channel).

dragueur, *a. & s.m.* (*a*) (Bateau) dragueur, dredger. (*b*) *D. de mines,* mine-sweeper.

dramatique, *a.* Dramatic. *Auteur d.,* playwright.

dramatiquement, *adv.* Dramatically.

dramatiser, *v.tr.* To dramatize.

dramaturge, *s.m. & f.* Dramatist, playwright.

drame, *s.m.* **1.** (*a*) Drama. (*b*) Play. **2.** *F:* Sensational affair; drama.

drap, *s.m.* **1.** Cloth. *D. fin,* broadcloth. *D. mortuaire,* pall. **2.** Drap de lit, bed-sheet. *F:* **Être dans de beaux draps,** to be in a sorry plight.

drapeau, *s.m.* Flag; (regimental) colour. **Être sous les drapeaux,** to serve with the colours.

draper, *v.tr.* To drape (furniture).

draperie, *s.f.* Drapery.

drapier, *s.* Draper, clothier.

drelin, *onomat. & s.m.* Ting-a-ling.

Dresde. *Pr.n.f. Geog:* Dresden.

dresser, *v.tr.* **1.** To erect, set up. *D. les oreilles,* to prick up one's ears. **2.** To draw up (plan). **3.** To adjust. **4.** To train (animal). **se dresser.** (*a*) To stand up, rise. (*b*) To sit up, straighten up; to become all attention.

dressoir, *s.m.* Sideboard, dresser.

drille [dri:j], *s.f. Tls:* Hand-drill.

drogue, *s.f.* (*a*) Drug. (*b*) Chemical (as a commercial article).

droit[1], *a.* **1.** Straight, upright. *Col d.,* stand-up collar. *Angle d.,* right angle. **2.** (*a*) Direct, straight. (*b*) *Ligne droite, s.f.* **droite,** straight line. (*c*) *adv. Allez tout d.,* keep straight on. **3.** Straightforward, upright. **4.** (*a*) Right (hand). (*b*) *s.f.* **Droite,** right hand.

droit[2], *s.m.* **1.** Right. *D. de cité,* freedom of a city. **Avoir droit à qch.,** to have a right to sth. **Donner droit à qn,** to give a decision in favour of s.o. **S'adresser à qui de droit,** to apply to the proper quarter. **A bon droit,** with good reason. **Faire droit à une demande,** to accede to a request. **2.** Charge, fee, due. **3.** Law. **Faire son droit,** to study law.

droiture, *s.f.* Uprightness, rectitude.

drolatique, *a.* (*a*) Comic. (*b*) Ribald (tale).

drôle[1], *s.m.* Rascal, knave, scamp.

drôle[2], *a.* Funny, droll, odd. **Un drôle de garçon,** *F:* a queer fish. *Quelle d. d'idée!* what a funny idea!

drôlement, *adv.* Funnily, drolly.

dromadaire, *s.m. Z:* Dromedary.

drosère, *s.f. Bot:* Sundew.

dru. **1.** *a.* Thick, close-set; dense. **2.** *adv. Tomber dru,* to fall thick and fast.

druide, *f.* **druidesse,** *s.* Druid, druidess.

du = *de le.* **dû.** See DEVOIR.

duc, *s.m.* **1.** Duke. **2.** Horned owl.

ducal, -aux, *a.* Ducal.

duché, *s.m.* Duchy, dukedom.

duchesse, *s.f.* Duchess.

ductile, *a.* Ductile; *F:* tractable (nature).

ductilité, *s.f.* Ductility; *F:* pliableness.

due. See DEVOIR.

duègne, *s.f.* (*a*) Duenna. (*b*) *F:* Chaperon.

duel, *s.m.* Duel, encounter.

duelliste, *s.m.* Duellist.

dûment, *adv.* Duly; in due form.

dûmes. See DEVOIR.

dune, *s.f.* Dune, sand-hill; down.

Dunkerque. *Pr.n.f. Geog:* Dunkirk.

duo, *s.m. Mus:* Duet.

dupe, *s.f.* Dupe, *F:* gull.

duper, *v.tr.* To dupe, to gull, to fool (s.o.).

duperie, *s.f.* **1.** Dupery, deception. **2.** Take-in.

duplicité, *s.f.* Duplicity, deceit.

duquel. See LEQUEL.

dur, *a.* **1.** Hard; tough (meat, wood). **Être dur à cuire,** *F:* (of pers.) to be a tough nut. **2.** Hard, difficult. *adv.* **Travailler dur,** to work hard. **3.** **Avoir l'oreille dure,** to be hard of hearing. **4.** Hard, harsh.

durabilité, *s.f.* Durability.

durable, *a.* Durable, lasting.

durant, *prep.* During. *Parler des heures d.,* to talk for hours on end.

durcir. **1.** *v.tr.* To harden. **2.** *v.i. & pr.* To grow hard.

durcissement, *s.m.* Hardening.

durée, *s.f.* **1.** Lasting quality; wear. **Essai de durée,** endurance test. **2.** Duration.

durement, *adv.* **1.** Hard; hardly. **2.** Harshly, severely.

durent. See DEVOIR.

durer, *v.i.* To last, endure.

dureté, *s.f.* **1.** Hardness; toughness. **2.** Difficulty (of task). **3.** Harshness, callousness.

durillon [-rijɔ̃], *s.m.* Corn (on sole of foot).

du-s, -t, etc.; **dusse, -s,** etc. See DEVOIR.

duvet, *s.m.* Down (on chin).

dynamique. **1.** *a.* Dynamic(al). **2.** *s.f.* Dynamics.

dynamite, *s.f.* Dynamite.

dynamo, *s.f. El.E:* Dynamo.

dynastie, *s.f.* Dynasty.

dysenterie, *s.f. Med:* Dysentery.

dyspepsie, *s.f.* Dyspepsia.

E, e [e], *s.m.* (The letter) E, e.

eau, *s.f.* Water. **1.** Laver le plancher à grande eau, to swill the floor. Ville d'eau, watering-place; spa. Aller aux eaux, to go to a watering-place. **2.** (*a*) Cours d'eau, water-course, stream. (*b*) Le temps est à l'eau, it is wet weather. (*c*) *Service des eaux,* water supply. Conduite d'eau, water-main. *Eau courante dans les chambres,* hot and cold water in the rooms. **3.** Diamant de la première eau, diamond of the first water. *F:* Cela lui fait venir l'eau à la bouche, it makes his mouth water. Être tout en eau, to be dripping with perspiration.

eau-de-vie, *s.f.* Spirits; brandy.

eau-forte, *s.f.* **1.** *Ch:* Nitric acid. **2.** *Engr:* Etching. *pl. Des eaux-fortes.*

ébahir, *v.tr.* To astound, flabbergast.

ébahissement, *s.m.* Amazement.

ébats, *s.m.pl.* Gambols, revels.

ébauche, *s.f.* Rough sketch (of picture). *É. d'un sourire,* suspicion of a smile.

ébaucher, *v.tr.* To sketch out (plan). *É. un sourire,* to give a faint smile.

ébène, *s.f.* Ebony.

ébéniste, *s.m.* Cabinet-maker.

éblouir, *v.tr.* To dazzle.

éblouissement, *s.m.* **1.** Dazzling. **2.** Dizziness, vertigo.

ébonite, *s.f.* Ebonite, vulcanite.

éborgner, *v.tr. É. qn,* to put s.o.'s eye out.

éboulement, *s.m.* **1.** Caving in (of wall). **2.** Land-slide, landslip.

ébouler (s'), *v.pr.* To crumble, cave in.

éboulis, *s.m.* **1.** Mass of debris. **2.** Scree.

ébouriffer, *v.tr.* To dishevel, ruffle.

ébranlement, *s.m.* **1.** Shaking; shock. **2.** Perturbation, commotion.

ébranler, *v.tr.* **1.** To shake. **2.** To set in motion.
 s'ébranler. 1. To shake, totter. **2.** (Of train) To start.

ébrécher, *v.tr.* (j'ébrèche; j'ébrécherai) (*a*) To notch; to make a notch in (sth.); to chip (a plate); to break (a tooth). *Couteau ébréché,* jagged knife. (*b*) *F:* To damage, impair (reputation); to make a hole in (fortune).

ébriété, *s.f.* Inebriety; drunken state.

ébrouer (s'), *v.pr.* **1.** (Of horse) To snort. **2.** (Of bird) To take a bath.

ébruiter, *v.tr.* To noise abroad.

ébullition, *s.f.* Ebullition, boiling.

écaille, [ekɑːj], *s.f.* **1.** Scale (of fish). **2.** Shell (of oyster).

écale, *s.f.* Shell (of nut).

écaler, *v.tr.* To shell (nuts).

écarlate, *s.f. & a.* Scarlet.

écarquiller [-kije], *v.tr.* To open (the eyes) wide.

écart¹, *s.m.* **1.** Divergence. **2.** Deviation. Faire un écart. to step aside; (of horse) to shy. **3.** A l'écart, aside. Se tenir à l'écart, to keep out of the way; to stand aside.

écart², *s.m. Cards:* **1.** Discarding. **2.** Discard.

écartement, *s.m.* **1.** (*a*) Separation. (*b*) Setting aside. **2.** Space, gap.

écarter¹, *v.tr.* **1.** To separate, part. **2.** To move (s.o., sth.) aside. *É. un coup,* to ward off a blow. **3.** To divert (suspicion).
 s'écarter. 1. To move aside. **2.** To move apart, diverge. **3.** To deviate, stray.
  écarté, *a.* **1.** Isolated, lonely, secluded, remote. **2.** (Far) apart.

écarter², *v.tr. Cards:* To discard.

ecclésiastique. 1. *a.* Ecclesiastical; clerical. **2.** *s.m.* Ecclesiastic, clergyman.

écervelé, *a.* Thoughtless, hare-brained.

échafaud, *s.m.* **1.** Scaffolding, staging; stand. **2.** Scaffold.

échalas, *s.m.* (*a*) Vine-prop. (*b*) Hop-pole.

échalote, *s.f. Bot:* Shallot.

échancrer, *v.tr.* To notch. *Littoral échancré,* indented coastline.

échancrure, *s.f.* Notch, nick (in wood); indentation (in coast-line).

échange, *s.m.* Exchange.

échanger, *v.tr.* (n. échangeons) To exchange.

échantillon [-tijɔ̃], *s.m.* Sample.

échappement, *s.m.* Escape, leakage

échapper, *v.i.* (Aux. *être* or *avoir*) To escape. **1.** (*a*) *É. à qn,* to escape s.o. *Ce propos m'a échappé,* I failed to hear this remark. *Il est vrai que ce propos m'est échappé,* it is true that I let slip this remark. *É. à toute définition,* to baffle definition. (*b*) (Aux. *avoir*) *F:* Vous l'avez échappé belle, you have had a narrow escape. (*c*) *Laisser é. une larme,* to let fall a tear. **2.** *É. de qch.,* to escape from sth.
 s'échapper, to escape; to break free.

échappée, *s.f.* Space, interval. *É. de vue,* vista; *É. de beau temps,* spell of fine weather.

écharpe, *s.f.* (*a*) Sash. (*b*) (Lady's) scarf. (*c*) *Surg:* Arm-sling. (*d*) En écharpe, slantwise.

échasse, *s.f.* Stilt.

échauder, *v.tr.* To scald.

échauffant, *a.* **1.** Heating. **2.** *F:* Exciting.

échauffement, *s.m.* **1.** Heating. **2.** Overexcitement.

échauffer, *v.tr.* (*a*) To overheat. *F:* Échauffer la bile de qn, to anger s.o. (*b*) To warm.
 s'échauffer. (*a*) To get overheated. Ne vous échauffez pas, *F:* don't get excited. (*b*) To warm (up).

échéance, *s.f.* **1.** Date (of payment). **Venir**

à l'échéance, to fall due. **2.** Expiration (of tenancy).

échéant. 1. *a.* Falling due. **2.** See ÉCHOIR.

échec [-ɛk], *s.m.* **1.** (*a*) Check (at chess). Échec et mat, checkmate. (*b*) *F:* Check, failure. **2.** *pl.* (*a*) Chess. (*b*) Chessmen.

échelle, *s.f.* **1.** (*a*) Ladder. *É. à incendie, é. de sauvetage,* fire-escape. **Faire la courte échelle à qn,** to give s.o. a helping hand. *F:* Après lui il faut tirer l'échelle, we can never better that. (*b*) Scale (of prices). (*c*) Ladder (in stocking). **2.** Scale (of map).

échelon, *s.m.* Rung, round (of ladder).

échelonner, *v.tr.* To space out (objects); to stagger (holidays).

écherra, échet. See ÉCHOIR.

écheveau, *s.m.* Hank, skein (of yarn).

échevelé, *a.* (*a*) Dishevelled (hair). (*b*) Wild, disorderly (dance).

échine, *s.f.* Spine, backbone. **Avoir l'échine souple,** to be obsequious.

échiquier, *s.m.* Chess-board. **En échiquier,** chequered.

écho [eko], *s.m.* Echo.

échoir, *v.i.* (*pr.p.* échéant; *p.p.* échu; *pr.ind.* il échoit, il échet, ils échoient, ils échéent; *p.d.* il échoyait, il échéait; *fu.* il écherra. Aux. usu. *être*) **1.** Échoir en partage à qn, to fall to s.o.'s share. **Le cas échéant,** in case of need. **2.** (*a*) (Of bill) To fall due. (*b*) (Of tenancy) To expire.

échoppe, *s.f.* Booth; street stall.

échouer. 1. *v.i.* (*a*) *Nau:* To run aground, to ground. (*b*) To fail. *L'affaire échoua,* the business fell through. **2.** *v.tr.* To run (ship) aground.

échu. See ÉCHOIR.

éclaboussement, *s.m.* (Be)spattering.

éclabousser, *v.tr.* To splash, (be)spatter.

éclaboussure, *s.f.* Splash, spatter.

éclair, *s.m.* **1.** Flash of lightning; *pl.* lightning. **2.** Flash (of a gun). **3.** *Cu:* Éclair.

éclairage, *s.m.* Lighting; illumination.

éclaircie, *s.f.* **1.** Break, opening, rift (in clouds). **2.** Clearing (in forest).

éclaircir, *v.tr.* **1.** To clear (up). **2.** To solve, explain. *É. qn sur qch.,* to enlighten s.o. on sth.

　s'éclaircir. (*a*) (Of the weather) To clear (up). (*b*) *Je veux m'é. sur ce point,* I wish to enlighten myself on this point.

éclaircissement, *s.m.* (*a*) Enlightenment. (*b*) Clearing up (of mystery).

éclairer. 1. *v.tr.* (*a*) To light, illuminate. *Maison éclairée à l'électricité,* house lighted by electricity. (*b*) To enlighten. **2.** *v.impers.* Il éclaire, it is lightning.

　éclairé, *a.* Enlightened; well-informed.

éclaireur, *s.m.* Scout.

éclat, *s.m.* **1.** Splinter. **Voler en éclats,** to fly into pieces; to be shattered. **2.** Burst (of thunder). **Rire aux éclats,** to laugh heartily. **Faire (de l')éclat,** to create a stir. **3.** (*a*) Flash (of light). (*b*) Glitter; brilliancy.

éclatant, *a.* **1.** Bursting. **2.** Loud (sound). **3.** Dazzling (light); vivid (colour); sparkling (jewels); brilliant (deed).

éclatement, *s.m.* Bursting; shivering.

éclater. 1. *v.tr.* To split; to burst. **2.** *v.i.* To burst, explode; (of glass) to fly (into pieces). **Éclater de rire,** to burst out laughing. **3.** *v.i.* (Of jewels) To sparkle.

éclipse, *s.f.* Eclipse.

éclipser, *v.tr.* To eclipse.

　s'éclipser, to disappear, vanish.

éclisse, *s.f.* *Surg:* Splint.

éclore, *v.i. def.* (*p.p.* éclos; *pr.ind.* il éclôt, ils éclosent; *p.d.* il éclosait; no *p.h.*; Aux. usu. *être,* occ. *avoir*) **1.** (Of eggs) To hatch (out). **2.** (Of flowers) To open.

écluse, *s.f.* **1.** (*a*) (Canal) lock. (*b*) Sluice (-gate). **2.** *Geog:* L'Écluse, Sluys.

éclusier, *s.* Lock-keeper.

écœurant, *a.* Disgusting; sickening.

écœurement, *s.m.* Disgust.

écœurer, *v.tr.* **1.** To disgust. **2.** To dishearten.

école, *s.f.* **1.** (*a*) School, elementary school. **Aller à l'école,** to go to school. (*b*) **L'École polytechnique** = the Military Academy. **École supérieure de Guerre** = Staff College. **2.** School (of thought).

écolier, *s.* (*a*) Schoolboy, -girl; scholar. *F:* **Le chemin des écoliers,** the longest way round. (*b*) Novice.

éconduire, *v.tr.* (Conj. like CONDUIRE) To show (s.o.) the door.

économe. 1. *s.m. & f.* Bursar (of college); steward. **2.** *a.* Economical, thrifty.

économie, *s.f.* **1.** Economy, management. **2.** Economy, thrift. **Faire une économie de temps,** to save time. **3.** *pl.* Savings.

économique, *a.* **1.** Economic (doctrine). **2.** Economical, inexpensive.

économiser, *v.tr.* To economize, save.

écoper, *v.tr.* To bail out.

écorce, *s.f.* Bark (of tree); rind, peel.

écorcher, *v.tr.* **1.** To flay; to skin. **2.** To graze, rub off (the skin).

écorchure, *s.f.* Scratch, graze.

écorner, *v.tr.* **1.** *F:* Vent à écorner les bœufs, tearing wind. **2.** *É. un livre,* to dog('s)-ear a book.

écossais. 1. *a.* Scotch, Scottish. **2.** *s.* Scot; Scotsman, -woman.

Écosse. *Pr.n.f. Geog:* Scotland. **La Nouvelle-Écosse,** Nova Scotia.

écosser, *v.tr.* To shell (peas).

écot, *s.m.* **1.** Share, quota. **2.** Score, reckoning (of meal).

écoulement, *s.m.* (Out)flow, discharge. **Waste-pipe** (of bath).

écouler. 1. *v.pr.* (*a*) To flow out, run out. (*b*) (Of time) To pass, elapse. **2.** *v.tr.* To sell (off).

écourter, *v.tr.* To shorten.

écoute, *s.f.* **1.** *F:* **Se tenir aux écoutes,** to keep one's ears open. **2.** *W.Tel:* Receiving, listening in.

écouter, *v.tr.* **I.** (*a*) To listen to. Écouter de toutes ses oreilles, to be all ears. Écoutez! look here! (*b*) *W.Tel:* To listen in. **2.** To pay attention to.

écran, *s.m.* Screen.

écrasant, *a.* Crushing (weight).

écrasement, *s.m.* Crushing, squashing.

écraser, *v.tr.* To crush; to squash. Se faire écraser, to get run over.
  s'écraser, to collapse, crumple up. (Of aeroplane) To crash.

écrevisse, *s.f.* (Fresh-water) crayfish.

écrier (s'), *v.pr.* (*a*) To cry (out). (*b*) To exclaim.

écrin, *s.m.* (Jewel-)case.

écrire, *v.tr.* (*pr.p.* écrivant; *p.p.* écrit; *p.h.* j'écrivis) To write. (*a*) Machine à écrire, typewriter. Écrire une lettre à la machine, to type a letter. (*b*) To write (sth.) down. (*c*) To write (book).
  écrit. I. *a.* Written. **2.** *s.m.* Writing. Coucher qch. par écrit, to set down sth. in writing.

écriteau, *s.m.* Placard, bill, notice.

écriture, *s.f.* **I.** (Hand-)writing. **2.** (*a*) *pl.* Papers, documents. (*b*) L'Écriture sainte, Holy Scripture.

écrivain, *s.m.* Author, writer.

écrou, *s.m. Mch:* (Screw-)nut.

écroulement, *s.m.* Collapse; downfall.

écrouler (s'), *v.pr.* To collapse, give way.

écu, *s.m.* **I.** (*a*) *Archeol:* Shield. (*b*) *Her:* Escutcheon; coat of arms. **2.** *A:* Crown (= three francs).

écueil [ekœ:j], *s.m.* Reef, shelf. (Of ship) Donner sur les écueils, to strike the rocks.

écuelle, *s.f.* Bowl, basin.

écume, *s.f.* **I.** (*a*) Froth; foam; lather. (*b*) Scum. **2.** Écume de mer, meerschaum.

écumer. I. *v.tr.* To skim (soup). *F:* Écumer les mers, to scour the seas. **2.** *v.i.* To foam, froth.

écureuil [-rœ:j], *m.* Squirrel.

écurie, *s.f.* (*a*) Stable. (*b*) Boxing school.

écusson, *s.m. Her:* Escutcheon.

écuyer, *s.* **I.** *s.m.* Equerry. **2.** *s.* Rider, horseman.

édifiant, *a.* Edifying (example, etc.).

édification, *s.f.* **I.** Erection, building. **2.** (*a*) (Moral) edification. (*b*) Enlightenment.

édifice, *s.m.* Building, edifice.

édifier, *v.tr.* **I.** To erect, set up. **2.** (*a*) To edify. (*b*) To enlighten.

Édimbourg. *Pr.n. Geog:* Edinburgh.

édit, *s.m.* Edict.

éditer, *v.tr.* To edit (text).

éditeur, -trice, *s.* **I.** Editor (of text). **2.** Publisher.

édition, *s.f.* **I.** Edition. **2.** Publishing.

Édouard. *Pr.n.m.* Edward.

édredon, *s.m.* Eider-down.

éducation, *s.f.* (*a*) Education, bringing up. *É. physique,* physical training. (*b*) Training

(of animals). (*c*) Upbringing, breeding. Personne sans éducation, ill-bred person.

effacement, *s.m.* **I.** Obliteration. **2.** Retirement; self-effacement.

effacer, *v.tr.* (n. effaçons) **I.** To efface, obliterate. **2.** To throw in the shade.
  s'effacer. I. To become obliterated. **2.** To stand aside.

effarement, *s.m.* Fright, alarm.

effarer, *v.tr.* To frighten, scare, startle.
  s'effarer, to be frightened, scared, startled (*de,* at, by); to take fright (*de,* at).

effaroucher, *v.tr.* To startle, scare away.
  s'effaroucher, to be startled (*de,* at, by); to take fright (*de,* at).

effectif. I. *a.* (*a*) Effective, efficacious. (*b*) Effective, actual. **2.** *s.m. Mil:* Effective (force). Crise d'effectifs, shortage of manpower.

effectivement, *adv.* **I.** Effectively. **2.** Actually. **3.** (As an answer) That is so.

effectuer, *v.tr.* To effect, carry out.

efféminé, *a.* Effeminate, unmanly.

effervescence, *s.f.* **I.** Effervescence. **2.** *F:* Excitement; restlessness.

effervescent, *a.* Effervescent.

effet, *s.m.* **I.** Effect, result. A cet effet, to this end. **2.** (*a*) Action, operation. Prendre effet, to become operative. (*b*) En effet, as a matter of fact; indeed. *Vous oubliez vos paquets!—En e.!* you are forgetting your parcels!—So I am! **3.** (*a*) Impression. *Cela fait bon e.,* it looks well. Manquer son effet, to fall flat. (*b*) *Art: E. de lune,* moonlight effect or study. **4.** *Effets à payer,* bills payable. **5.** *pl.* Possessions, belongings.

efficace, *a.* Efficacious, effectual.

efficacité, *s.f.* Efficacy; efficiency.

effigie, *s.f.* Effigy.

effiler, *v.tr.* **I.** *Tex:* To unravel. **2.** To taper. **3.** To string (beans).
  effilé, *a.* **I.** *Tex:* Fringed (material). **2.** Slender (figure); tapering (fingers).

efflanqué, *a.* Lean(-flanked), *F:* skinny.

effleurement, *s.m.* **I.** (*a*) (Light) touch. (*b*) Skimming. **2.** Graze.

effleurer, *v.tr.* To touch lightly; to skim; to graze.

effloraison, *s.f. Bot:* Flowering.

effluve, *s.m.* Effluvium, emanation.

effondrement, *s.m.* Breaking down; subsidence; collapse.

effondrer, *v.tr.* To break (sth.) down.
  s'effondrer, to fall in; to break down.

efforcer (s'), *v.pr.* (n.n. efforçons) *S'e. de faire qch.,* to strive to do sth.

effort, *s.m.* **I.** Effort, exertion. *Faire un e. sur soi-même,* to try to control oneself. **2.** *Mec.E:* Strain, stress.

effraie, *s.f.* Barn owl, screech owl.

effrayamment, *adv.* Frightfully, dreadfully.

effrayant, *a.* **I.** Frightful, terrifying, dreadful, appalling. **2.** *F:* Tremendous, awful.

effrayer, v.tr. (j'effraie, j'effraye) To frighten, scare, startle (s.o.).
s'effrayer, to take fright.
effréné, a. Unbridled; frantic.
effriter, v.tr. To cause (sth.) to crumble.
s'effriter, to crumble (to dust).
effroi, s.m. Fright, terror, fear.
effronté, a. Shameless, bold; impudent.
effrontément, adv. Shamelessly.
effronterie, s.f. Effrontery, insolence. Payer d'effronterie, to brazen it out.
effroyable, a. Frightful, dreadful; hideous.
effroyablement, adv. Frightfully.
effusion, s.f. **1.** Effusion, outpouring. Effusion de sang, bloodshed. **2.** Effusiveness.
égal, -aux, a. **1.** (a) Equal. Toutes choses égales (d'ailleurs), other things being equal. Prep. phr. A l'égal de, equally with. (b) Level, even. **2.** (All) the same. Cela m'est (bien) égal, it is all the same to me.
également, adv. **1.** Equally, alike. **2.** Also, likewise.
égaler, v.tr. To equal, be equal to (sth.).
égaliser, v.tr. **1.** To equalize. **2.** To level.
égalité, s.f. **1.** Equality. Ten: deuce. A égalité de . . , where there is equality of. . . . **2.** Evenness, regularity.
égard, s.m. Consideration, respect. (a) Avoir égard à qch., to pay regard to sth. Eu égard à . . ., having regard to. . . . A l'égard de, with respect to. (b) Être plein d'égards pour qn, to be full of attentions to s.o.
égarement, s.m. **1.** (a) Miscarriage (of letter). (b) Mislaying. (c) Bewilderment. Égarement d'esprit, mental aberration. **2.** Deviation; wildness (of conduct). **3.** Frenzy.
égarer, v.tr. To mislead (s.o.).
s'égarer. 1. To lose one's way. **2.** Son esprit s'égare, his mind is becoming unhinged.
égaré, a. **1.** Stray, lost. Village é., out-of-the-way village. **2.** Distraught.
égayant, a. Cheerful, lively.
égayement, s.m. Enlivenment.
égayer, v.tr. (j'égaie, j'égaye) To enliven; to brighten (up).
s'égayer, to amuse oneself.
églantier, s.m. Wild rose; sweet briar.
église, s.f. Church.
égoïsme, s.m. Selfishness.
égoïste. 1. s.m. & f. Selfish person. **2.** a. Selfish.
égoïstement, adv. Selfishly.
égorger, v.tr. (n. égorgeons) To butcher, slaughter (persons).
égout, s.m. Sewer; drain.
égouttement, s.m. Drip(ping) (of water).
égratigner, v.tr. To scratch.
égratignure, s.f. Scratch.
Égypte, Pr.n.f. Geog: Egypt.
égyptien, -ienne, a. & s. Egyptian.
eh, int. Hey! Eh bien! well! now then!
éjection, s.f. Ejection.
élaborer, v.tr. To elaborate.

élan¹, s.m. **1.** (a) Spring, bound, dash. Prendre son élan, to take off (for a spring). (b) Impetus. **2.** Burst, outburst.
élan², s.m. Z: Elk, moose.
élancer, v.i. (n. élançons) To throb.
s'élancer. 1. S'é. en avant, to spring forward. S'é. sur qn, to rush at s.o. **2.** To shoot up.
élancé, a. Tall and slim; slender.
élargir, v.tr. **1.** (a) To widen; to stretch. (b) To enlarge, extend. **2.** To release (prisoner).
s'élargir. (a) To widen out. (b) To grow, extend.
élargissement, s.m. Enlarging.
élasticité, s.f. Elasticity.
élastique, a. & s.m. Elastic.
électeur, -trice, s. Elector, voter.
élection, s.f. **1.** Pol: Election. **2.** Election, choice, preference.
électoral, -aux, a. Electoral.
électorat, s.m. Electorate.
électricien, s.m. Electrician.
électricité, s.f. Electricity.
électrifier, v.tr. To electrify.
électrique, a. Electric.
électrisation, s.f. Electrification.
électriser, v.tr. To electrify.
électrocution, s.f. Electrocution.
électrolyse, s.f. Electrolysis.
élégamment, adv. Elegantly.
élégance, s.f. Elegance; stylishness.
élégant, a. Elegant, stylish, fashionable.
élégie, s.f. Elegy.
élément, s.m. **1.** Element. **2.** (a) Ingredient (of medicine). (b) El: Cell (of battery). **3.** pl. Rudiments.
élémentaire, a. Elementary.
éléphant, s.m. Elephant.
éléphantesque, a. F: Elephantine, gigantic, enormous.
élevage, s.m. Breeding, raising.
élévation, s.f. **1.** (a) Elevation, lifting. (b) Erection, setting up. **2.** Rise. **3.** Loftiness, height. **4.** High ground, eminence.
élève, s.m. & f. Pupil; student.
élever, v.tr. (j'élève) **1.** To elevate, raise. **2.** (a) To erect, set up. (b) É. une objection, to raise an objection. **3.** To bring up, rear (child); to breed (horses).
s'élever. 1. To rise (up). Le compte s'élève à mille francs, the bill comes to a thousand francs. **2.** To raise oneself.
élevé, a. **1.** High; noble, lofty. **2.** Bien élevé, well-bred.
éleveur, -euse, s. Stock-breeder. É. de chiens, dog-fancier.
elfe, s.m. Elf, brownie.
éligibilité, s.f. Eligibility.
éligible, a. Eligible.
élimination, s.f. Elimination.

éliminer, v.tr. To eliminate, get rid of; to weed out.

élire, v.tr. (Conj. like LIRE) To elect, choose.

élu. 1. a. Chosen; successful (candidate). **2.** s. Nouvel élu, newly elected member.

élision, s.f. Ling: Elision.

élite, s.f. Élite; flower, pick.

elle, elles, pers.pron.f. **1.** (Unstressed) (Of pers.) She, they; (of thg) it, they. **2.** (Stressed) (a) (Subject) She, it, they. C'est elle, it is she. (b) (Object) Her, it, them. Chez elle, with her, at her house.

ellébore, s.m. Bot: Hellebore.

ellipse, s.f. **1.** Gram: Ellipsis. **2.** Ellipse.

élocution, s.f. Elocution.

éloge, s.m. **1.** Eulogy. **2.** Praise.

éloignement, s.m. **1.** Removal, putting away (of sth.); postponement. **2.** (a) Absence. (b) Distance, remoteness. (c) Aversion.

éloigner, v.tr. (a) To remove (sth.); to get (sth.) out of the way. É. une pensée, to dismiss a thought. (b) To postpone, put off.

s'éloigner, to move off, withdraw.

éloigné, a. Far (away); distant; remote.

éloquemment, adv. Eloquently.

éloquence, s.f. Eloquence.

éloquent, a. Eloquent.

élu, -s, -t, etc. See ÉLIRE.

élucidation, s.f. Elucidation.

élucider, v.tr. To elucidate, clear up.

éluder, v.tr. To elude, evade, dodge.

émaciation, s.f. Emaciation.

émacié, a. Emaciated; wasted (face).

émail [emaːj], pl. **émaux,** s.m. Enamel.

émailler [emaje], v.tr. **1.** To enamel. **2.** (Of flowers) To dot (the fields).

émanation, s.f. Emanation.

émancipation, s.f. Emancipation.

émanciper, v.tr. To emancipate.

s'émanciper, to free oneself from control.

émancipé, a. F: Holding advanced opinions.

émaner, v.i. To emanate, to issue.

émaux. See ÉMAIL.

emballage, s.m. **1.** (a) Packing, wrapping. (b) Packing-cases; wrappings. **2.** Rac: Spurt.

emballer, v.tr. **1.** To pack (goods); to wrap up. **2.** Abs. Rac: To spurt. **3.** To fire (s.o.) with enthusiasm.

s'emballer. (a) (Of horse) To bolt. (b) (Of engine) To race. (c) F: To be carried away (by excitement). Ne vous emballez pas! keep cool!

embarcadère, s.m. Landing-stage; wharf, quay.

embarcation, s.f. Boat; esp. ship's boat.

embardée, s.f. Nau: Yaw, lurch.

embarder, v.i. (Of ship) To yaw, lurch.

embargo, s.m. Embargo.

embarquement, s.m. Embarkation.

embarquer. 1. v.tr. To embark (passengers); to ship (goods); to hoist in (boat). F: Embarquer de l'eau, to ship a sea. **2.** v.i. & pr To embark. Embarquez! all aboard!

embarras, s.m. **1.** Obstruction, obstacle, encumbrance. **2.** (a) Difficulty, trouble. Se trouver dans l'embarras, to be in difficulties. (b) F: Faire des embarras, to be fussy. **3.** Embarrassment. (a) Perplexity, hesitation. (b) Confusion, abashment.

embarrassant, a. **1.** Cumbersome. **2.** (a) Perplexing. (b) Embarrassing, awkward.

embarrasser, v.tr. To embarrass. **1.** To (en)cumber; to obstruct. **2.** (a) To trouble, inconvenience. (b) To perplex. (c) To confuse (s.o.).

embarrassé, a. **1.** Encumbered, obstructed. **2.** Embarrassed. (a) Perplexed. (b) Bashful, diffident.

embaucher, v.tr. To engage; take on; to hire.

embaumer, v.tr. **1.** To embalm (corpse). **2.** To perfume, scent. Sa chambre embaumait la violette, her room was fragrant of violets.

embellir. 1. v.tr. To embellish; to beautify. **2.** v.i. To improve in looks.

embellissement, s.m. **1.** Embellishment. **2.** Improvement (in looks).

embêtant, a. **1.** Annoying. **2.** Tiresome.

embêtement, s.m. **1.** Bother. **2.** Boredom.

embêter, v.tr. **1.** To annoy, vex. **2.** To bore.

emblée (d'), adv.phr. Directly; straight off.

emblématique, a. Emblematic(al).

emblème, s.m. **1.** (a) Emblem, device. (b) Badge, crest. **2.** Symbol, sign.

emboîter, v.tr. (a) To pack in tins, boxes. (b) To fit (things) together; to joint. (c) Emboîter le pas, to fall into step (d, sur, with).

embonpoint, s.m. Stoutness. Prendre de l'embonpoint, to put on flesh.

embouchure, s.f. **1.** Mouthpiece. **2.** (a) Opening, mouth (of sack). (b) Mouth (of river).

embourber, v.tr. To bog (vehicle).

s'embourber, to stick in the mud.

embouteiller [-tɛje], v.tr. To bottle.

embranchement, s.m. **1.** Branching (off). **2.** Branch. (a) Road junction. (b) Rail: Branch-line.

embrasement, s.m. Conflagration.

embraser, v.tr. To set fire to; to set ablaze.

s'embraser, to catch fire, to blaze up.

embrasé, a. Blazing; glowing; fiery.

embrassement, s.m. Embrace.

embrasser, v.tr. To embrace. **1.** (a) To put one's arms round (sth.). (b) To kiss. (Letter formula) "Je vous embrasse de tout mon cœur," 'with much love.' (c) To adopt (career). **2.** To contain, include.

embrasure, s.f. (a) Embrasure; window-recess. (b) Nau: Gun-port.

embrocher, v.tr. F: To run (s.o.) through.

embrouillement [ãbrujmã], *s.m.* **1.** Entanglement. **2.** Confusion (of ideas).
embrouiller [ãbruje], *v.tr.* **1.** To tangle (thread). **2.** To confuse, muddle.
  s'embrouiller. (*a*) To get muddled. (*b*) *L'affaire s'embrouille,* the affair is getting intricate.
embrumer, *v.tr.* To cover with mist.
  embrumé, *a.* Misty; clouded.
embrun, *s.m.* Spray, spindrift.
embryon, *s.m. Biol:* Embryo.
embûche, *s.f. F: Dresser une embûche à qn,* to lay a trap for s.o.
embuscade, *s.f.* Ambush, ambuscade.
embusquer, *v.tr.* To place in ambush.
  s'embusquer, to lie in ambush.
  embusqué, *s.m.* **1.** Man in ambush. **2.** *F:* Shirker (from active service).
émeraude. 1. *s.f.* Emerald. **2.** *a.inv.* Emerald green.
émergence, *s.f.* Emergence; emersion.
émerger, *v.i.* (n. émergeons) **1.** To emerge. **2.** To come into view.
émeri, *s.m.* Emery; emery-powder.
émerveillement [-vɛj-], *s.m.* Amazement.
émerveiller [-vɛje], *v.tr.* To amaze; to fill (s.o.) with wonder, with admiration.
  s'émerveiller, to marvel (*de,* at).
  émerveillé, *a.* Amazed, wonder-struck.
émétique, *s.m.* Emetic.
émetteur, -trice. 1. *s.m. W.Tel:* Transmitter. **2.** *a.* Issuing (bank). *W.Tel:* **Poste émetteur,** broadcasting station.
émettre, *v.tr.* (Conj. like METTRE) **1.** (*a*) To emit; to give off. (*b*) *W.Tel:* To broadcast. **2.** To issue.
émeu, *s.m. Orn:* Emu. *pl. Des émeus.*
émeu-s, -t, etc. See ÉMOUVOIR.
émeute, *s.f.* Riot. **Chef d'émeute,** ringleader.
émiettement, *s.m.* Crumbling.
émietter, *v.tr.* To crumble.
émigrant. 1. *a.* Emigrating; migratory (bird). **2.** *s.* Emigrant.
émigration, *s.f.* **1.** Migration (of birds). **2.** Emigration.
émigrer, *v.i.* **1.** (Of birds) To migrate. **2.** (Of pers.) To emigrate.
  émigré, *s.* (*a*) Emigrant. (*b*) Émigré.
éminemment, *adv.* Eminently.
éminence, *s.f.* Eminence. (*a*) Rising ground. (*b*) Superiority, prominence.
éminent, *a.* Eminent; distinguished.
émi-s, -t, etc. See ÉMETTRE.
émissaire, *s.m.* Emissary. *a.* **Bouc émissaire,** scapegoat.
émission, *s.f.* **1.** (*a*) Emission; utterance (of sound). (*b*) *W. Tel:* (i) Transmission; (ii) broadcasting. **2.** Issue (of tickets).
emmagasiner, *v.tr.* **1.** To store, warehouse. **2.** To accumulate (energy).
emmailloter [ãmaj-], *v.tr.* To swaddle (infant); tobind (up) (limb).
emmêler, *v.tr.* (*a*) To tangle. (*b*) To mix up (facts); to muddle (story).

emmener, *v.tr.* (j'emmène) To take (s.o.) away. *Je vous emmène avec moi,* I am taking you with me.
emmitoufler, *v.tr.* To muffle (s.o.) up.
émoi, *s.m.* Emotion, agitation. *Toute la ville était en é.,* the whole town was in a commotion.
émollient, *a. & s.m.* Emollient.
émoluments, *s.m.pl.* Emoluments.
émotion, *s.f.* Emotion; excitement.
émotionnant, *a.* Exciting, thrilling.
émotionner, *v.tr. F:* To thrill, move.
émoudre, *v.tr.* (Conj. like MOUDRE) To grind, sharpen, whet (tool).
émoulu. See ÉMOUDRE.
émousser, *v.tr.* (*a*) To blunt; to take the edge off. (*b*) To dull, deaden.
  émoussé, *a.* Blunt.
émouvant, *a.* Moving. (*a*) Touching. (*b*) Stirring, thrilling.
émouvoir, *v.tr.* (*p.p.* ému; otherwise conj. like MOUVOIR) To move. (*a*) To stir up, rouse. (*b*) To affect, touch. **Facile à émouvoir,** emotional.
  s'émouvoir. 1. To get excited. **2.** To be touched. *Sans s'é.,* calmly.
  ému, *a.* Affected (by emotion); moved.
empailler [ãpaje], *v.tr.* To stuff (animal).
empaqueter, *v.tr.* (j'empaquette) To pack (sth.) up.
emparer (s'), *v.pr. S'e. de qch.,* to take possession of sth.
empêchement, *s.m.* Obstacle, hindrance, impediment.
empêcher, *v.tr.* To prevent, hinder, impede. *Impers.* (Il) n'empêche que cela nous a coûté cher, all the same, it has cost us dear.
  s'empêcher, (always in the negative) to refrain. *Je ne pus (pas) m'e. de rire,* I couldn't help laughing.
empereur, *s.m.* Emperor.
empeser, *v.tr.* (j'empèse) To starch (linen).
  empesé, *a. F:* Stiff, starchy, formal.
empester, *v.tr. Air empesté par le tabac,* air reeking of tobacco.
empêtrement, *s.m.* Entanglement.
empêtrer, *v.tr.* **1.** To hobble (animal). **2.** To entangle; to trammel.
emphase, *s.f.* Bombast, grandiloquence.
emphatique, *a.* Bombastic, grandiloquent.
empiétement, *s.m.* Encroachment.
empiéter, *v.* (j'empiète; j'empiéterai) *v.i. E. sur le terrain de qn,* to encroach (up)on s.o.'s land. *E. sur les droits de qn,* to infringe s.o.'s rights.
empiler, *v.tr.* To stack, to pile (up).
empire, *s.m.* **1.** (*a*) Dominion; sway. (*b*) Influence, control. **Empire sur soi-même,** self-control. **2.** Empire.
empirer, *v.* **1.** *v.tr.* To make (sth.) worse. **2.** *v.i.* To grow worse.
emplacement, *s.m.* (*a*) Site. (*b*) Location. (*c*) Place, spot.
emplâtre, *s.m. Pharm:* Plaster.

emplette, *s.f.* Purchase. **Aller faire ses emplettes,** to go shopping.

emplir, *v.tr.* To fill (up). **s'emplir,** to fill up.

emploi, *s.m.* **I.** Use, employment (of sth.). *Emploi du temps,* time-table (of work). **2.** Employment, occupation, post.

employer, *v.tr.* (j'emploie) **I.** To employ, use (sth.). **2.** To employ (workmen). **employé,** *s.* Employee, assistant. *E. de banque,* bank clerk.

empocher, *v.tr.* To pocket (money).

empoigner, *v.tr.* **I.** (*a*) To grasp, seize. (*b*) *F :* *Ils se sont empoignés,* they had a set-to. **2.** To arrest (criminal). **3.** To thrill, grip (reader).

empois, *s.m.* (*a*) Starch(-paste).

empoisonner, *v.tr.* To poison (s.o.). **s'empoisonner,** to take poison. **empoisonneur, -euse,** *s.* Poisoner.

emportement, *s.m.* Transport. *Dans l'e. de la discussion,* in the heat of debate.

emporter, *v.tr.* **I.** To take away. *F :* (Que) le diable l'emporte! the devil take him! **2.** (*a*) *Le vent emporta son chapeau,* the wind blew off his hat. (*b*) *E. un fort,* to take a fort (by assault). **3.** *Se laisser emporter à la colère,* to give way to anger. **4.** *L'emporter sur qn,* to get the better of s.o. **s'emporter,** to lose one's temper. **emporté,** *a.* Quick-tempered.

empourprer, *v.tr* To tinge with crimson. **s'empourprer.** **I.** (Of pers.) To flush (up). **2.** (Of sky) To turn crimson. **empourpré,** *a.* Crimson.

empreindre, *v.tr.* (Conj. like PEINDRE) To impress, stamp. *Visage empreint de terreur,* face full of terror. **empreinte,** *s.f.* Impress(ion), (im)print. *E. des roues,* track of the wheels. *E. de pas,* footprint.

empressement, *s.m.* Eagerness, readiness, alacrity.

empresser (s'), *v.pr.* **I.** To hurry, hasten (*de faire qch.,* to do sth.). **2.** *S'e. à faire qch.,* to show zeal in doing sth. *S'e. auprès de qn,* to dance attendance on s.o. **empressé.** **I.** *a.* Eager, zealous. *Corr :* "Agréez mes salutations empressées," 'I am yours faithfully.' **2.** *s.* Busybody.

emprisonnement, *s.m.* Imprisonment.

emprisonner, *v.tr.* To imprison.

emprunt, *s.m.* Borrowing or loan. *Faire un emprunt à qn,* to borrow (money) from s.o. *Nom d'emprunt,* assumed name.

emprunter, *v.tr.* To borrow (*à,* from). *E. un nom,* to assume a name. **emprunté,** *a.* (*a*) Assumed (name); (*b*) Borrowed.

emprunteur, *s.* Borrower.

ému. See ÉMOUVOIR.

émulateur, -trice, *s.* Rival, competitor.

émulation, *s.f.* Emulation, rivalry.

émule, *s.m. & f.* Emulator, rival.

émulsion, *s.f.* Emulsion.

en[1], *prep.* **I.** (*a*) In, (in)to. *Venir en tramway,* to come by tram. *En tête,* at the head. (With *f.* names of countries) *Aller en France,* to go to France. (*b*) *Un homme en qui j'ai confiance,* a man whom I trust. (*c*) *En l'honneur de qn,* in honour of s.o. *Regarder en l'air,* to look up at the sky. **2.** In. *En été,* in summer. *D'aujourd'hui en huit,* to-day week. *On peut aller à Londres en cinq jours,* one can go to London in five days. **3.** (*a*) *Être en deuil,* to be in mourning. *En réparation,* under repair. *En faction,* on guard. (*b*) *Montre en or,* gold watch. (*c*) *Escalier en spirale,* spiral staircase. *Docteur en médecine,* doctor of medicine. (*d*) Into. *Briser qch. en morceaux,* to break sth. into bits. (*e*) *De mal en pis,* from bad to worse. **4.** *Prendre la chose en philosophe,* to take the thing philosophically. **5.** *Travailler en chantant,* to sing at one's work. *En attendant,* in the meantime. *Elle sortit en dansant,* she danced out.

en[2], *unstressed adv. and pron.* **I.** *adv.* **I.** From there; thence. *Vous avez été à Londres?* —*Oui, j'en arrive,* you have been to London? —Yes, I've just come from there. **2.** On that account. *Si vous étiez riche, en seriez-vous plus heureux?* if you were rich, would you be any the happier? II. **en,** *pron.inv.* **I.** (*a*) *J'aime mieux n'en pas parler,* I would rather not speak about it. *Les rues en sont pleines,* the streets are full of it, of them. *Il l'aime et il en est aimé,* he loves her and is loved by her. (*b*) *Combien avez-vous de chevaux?—J'en ai trois,* how many horses have you got? I have three. (*c*) *Nous avons visité l'église et en avons admiré les vitraux,* we visited the church and admired its stained glass. (*d*) *Vous remplacer, il n'en est pas capable,* he is not fit to take your place. **2.** Some, any. *J'en ai,* I have some. **3.** *Si le cœur vous en dit,* if you feel so inclined. **4.** *Prenez-en dix,* take ten.

enamourer (s'), *v.pr* To fall in love (*de,* with)

encadrement, *s.m.* **I.** Framing. **2.** Framework ; frame ; setting.

encadrer, *v.tr.* To frame (picture). *Jardin encadré de haies* garden enclosed by hedges.

encaisser, *v.tr.* (*a*) To pack (goods). (*b*) To encash, collect (bill).

encan, *s.m.* (Public) auction.

enceindre, *v.tr.* (Conj. like PEINDRE) To gird. **enceinte,** *s.f* **I.** Surrounding wall. **2.** Enclosure.

encens, *s.m.* Incense.

encercler, *v.tr.* To encircle ; to shut in.

enchaînement, *s.m.* **I.** Chaining (up). **2.** Chain, series ; sequence.

enchaîner, *v.tr.* **I.** To chain up **2.** To link (up), connect (ideas).

enchantement, *s.m* **I.** Enchantment; spell **2.** Charm ; glamour. **3.** Delight

nchanter, *v.tr.* I. To enchant. 2. To charm, delight.

enchanté, *a.* I. Enchanted. 2. Être enchanté de qch., to be delighted with sth.

nchanteur, -eresse. I. *s.* Enchanter, enchantress; *F:* charmer. 2. *a.* Bewitching.

enchère, *s.f.* Bid(ding). Mettre qch. aux enchères, to put sth. up for auction.

enchérir, *v.i.* (*a*) To go up in price. (*b*) Enchérir sur qn, to outbid s.o.

enchérissement, *s.m.* Rise (in price).

enchérisseur, -euse, *s.* Bidder.

enchevêtrement, *s.m.* Tangle (of traffic).

enchevêtrer, *v.tr.* To mix up, confuse.

enchevêtré, *a.* Tangled (skein); confused (style).

enclin, *a.* Inclined, disposed.

enclos, *s.m.* Enclosure; paddock.

enclume, *s.f.* Anvil. *F:* Être entre l'enclume et le marteau, to be between the devil and the deep sea.

encoignure, *s.f.* Corner, angle (of room).

encolure, *s.f.* I. *Turf:* Gagner par une e., to win by a neck. 2. Size in collars.

encombrant, *a.* Cumbersome; (man) always in the way.

encombre, *s.m.* Sans encombre, without let or hindrance.

encombrement, *s.m.* (*a*) Litter; congestion (of traffic). (*b*) Overcrowding.

encombrer, *v.tr.* To encumber. E. le marché, to glut the market. "N'encombrez pas le passavant," 'stand clear of the gangway.'

encontre (à l'), *adv.phr.* A l'encontre de, against; in opposition to. Aller à l'e. du danger, to go out to meet danger.

encore, *adv.* I. (*a*) Still. Hier encore je lisais un de ses livres, only yesterday I was reading a book of his. (*b*) Yet. Pas encore, not yet. (*c*) More, again. E. une tasse de café, another cup of coffee. Quoi encore? what else? Encore une fois, once more. 2. Non seulement . . ., mais encore . . ., not only . . ., but also. . . . 3. (Restrictive) (*a*) Encore si on pouvait lui parler, if even one could speak to him. (*b*) (With inversion) Je n'ai qu'un ciseau, e. est-il émoussé, I have only one chisel and even that is a blunt one. (*c*) *Conj.phr.* Encore (bien) que + *sub.*, (al)though; even though. Temps agréable e. qu'un peu froid, pleasant weather if rather cold.

encourageant, *a.* Encouraging, cheering.

encouragement, *s.m.* Encouragement.

encourager, *v.tr.* (n. encourageons) To encourage.

encourir, *v.tr.* (Conj. like COURIR) To incur. E. un risque, to take a chance.

encrasser, *v.tr.* To dirty, soil.

encre, *s.f.* Ink. E. de Chine, Indian ink. E. sympathique, invisible ink.

encrier, *s.m.* Inkpot; inkstand; ink-well.

encyclopédie, *s.f.* Encyclopedia.

endémique, *a.* Endemic.

endetter (s'), to get, run, into debt.

endiablé, *a.* (*a*) Reckless, devil-may-care. (*b*) Wild, frenzied (music).

endiguer, *v.tr.* I. To dam up (river). 2. To (em)bank (river).

endimancher, *v.tr* To dress (s.o.) in (his, her) Sunday best.

endolorir, *v.tr.* To make (limb) ache.

endolori, *a.* Painful, sore; tender.

endommager, *v.tr.* (n. endommageons) To damage, injure.

endormir, *v.tr.* (Conj. like DORMIR) I. (*a*) To put (s.o.) to sleep. (*b*) *F:* To bore (s.o.). 2. To deaden (pain). 3. *F:* E. les soupçons, to allay suspicion.

s'endormir, to fall asleep.

endormi, *a.* I. (*a*) Asleep, sleeping. (*b*) Sleepy, drowsy. (*c*) Dormant (passion). 2. (Of limb) Numb.

endosser, *v.tr.* I. To put on (clothes). *F:* E. une responsabilité, to shoulder a responsibility. 2. *Com:* To endorse (cheque).

endroit, *s.m.* I. Place, spot. Par endroits, here and there. 2. Side, aspect. Prendre qn par son endroit faible, *F:* to get on the soft side of s.o.

enduire, *v.tr.* (Conj. like CONDUIRE) To smear, coat.

enduit, *s.m.* Coat, coating (of paint).

endurable, *a.* Endurable.

endurance, *s.f.* Endurance. I. Longsuffering. 2. Resistance to wear and tear.

endurant, *a.* Patient; long-suffering.

endurcir, *v.tr.* I. To harden. 2. To inure.

endurci, *a.* I. Hardened. 2. Callous.

endurcissement, *s.m.* I. (*a*) Hardening. (*b*) Inuring. 2. (*a*) Hardness (of heart). (*b*) Obduracy.

endurer, *v.tr.* To endure, bear.

énergie, *s.f.* Energy; force, vigour.

énergique, *a.* (*a*) Energetic. (*b*) Strong, drastic (measure).

énergiquement, *adv.* Energetically.

énervement, *s.m.* State of nerves; nervous irritation.

énerver, *v.tr.* I. To enervate, weaken. 2. É. qn, to get on s.o.'s nerves.

enfance, *s.f.* I. (*a*) Childhood. Première enfance, infancy. (*b*) Boyhood; girlhood. 2. Seconde enfance, dotage.

enfant, *s.m. & f.* Child; boy or girl. Enfant trouvé, foundling. *F:* Allons-y, mes enfants! come on, lads! *a.* Bon enfant, good-natured.

enfantement, *s.m.* Childbirth.

enfanter, *v.tr.* To give birth to (child).

enfantillage [-tij-], *s.m.* Childishness.

enfantin, *a.* I. Infantile. 2. Childish (voice).

enfer, *s.m.* Hell. Les enfers, the underworld; Hades. Aller un train d'enfer, to ride hell for leather.

enfermer, *v.tr.* I. To shut (sth.) up. (Of room) Sentir l'enfermé, to smell stuffy. 2. To shut (sth.) in; to enclose.

enfiévrer, *v.tr.* (j'enflèvre; j'enfiévrerai)

1. To give (s.o.) fever. **2.** *F:* To fire, animate (s.o.).

enfiler, *v.tr.* **1.** To thread (needle); to file (papers); to string (beads). **2.** To take, go along (a street). **3.** *E. ses vêtements,* to slip on one's clothes.

enfin. 1. *adv.* (*a*) Finally, lastly. (*b*) In fact, in a word, in short. (*c*) At last. **2.** *int.* (*a*) At last! (*b*) *Mais e., s'il acceptait!* but still, if he did accept!

enflammer, *v.tr.* To inflame. **1.** To ignite. **2.** To inflame (wound). **3.** To excite.
   s'enflammer. 1. To catch fire. **2.** *F:* (Of pers.) To flare up.
   enflammé, *a.* **1.** Burning, blazing; fiery (sun). **2.** Glowing (cheeks).

enflement, *s.m.* Swelling.

enfler. 1. *v.tr.* To swell. *E. les joues,* to puff out one's cheeks. **2.** *v.i. & pr.* To swell.
   enflé, *a.* Swollen.

enflure, *s.f.* Swelling (of cheek).

enfoncement, *s.m.* **1.** Driving (in); breaking open. **2.** Depression (in the ground). *Arch:* Alcove, recess.

enfoncer, *v.tr.* (n. **enfonçons**) (*a*) To drive (in). *E. la main dans sa poche,* to thrust one's hand into one's pocket. (*b*) To break open. *E. un carreau,* to break a window-pane.
   s'enfoncer, to penetrate, go deep.
   enfoncé, *a.* **1.** Smashed (in). **2.** Sunken, deep (cavity). *Yeux enfoncés,* deep-set eyes.

enfouir, *v.tr.* To hide (sth.) in the ground.

enfourcher, *v.tr.* (*a*) To bestride, mount (horse). (*b*) *F:* To ride (hobby) to death.

enfourchure, *s.f.* Fork, crotch.

enfreindre, *v.tr.* (Conj. like PEINDRE) To infringe, transgress (the law).

enfuir (s'), *v.pr.* (Conj. like FUIR) **1.** To flee, fly; to run away. **2.** (Of liquid) To run out.

enfumer, *v.tr.* To fill with smoke.
   enfumé, *a.* **1.** Smoky. **2.** Smoke-blackened.

engageant, *a.* Engaging, prepossessing, winning (manners); inviting (meal).

engagement, *s.m.* **1.** Pawning. **2.** (*a*) Engagement, promise. (*b*) Engagement, appointment. **3.** Engagement, action.

engager, *v.tr.* (n. **engageons**) **1.** To pawn. *E. sa parole,* to pledge one's word. **2.** To engage (servant). **3.** (*a*) To catch, entangle (rope). *E. un aviron,* to catch a crab. (*b*) *E. la clef dans la serrure,* to fit, insert, the key in the lock. **4.** To begin, start; to open (conversation). **5.** *E. qn à faire qch.,* to urge s.o. to do sth.
   s'engager. 1. *S'e. à faire qch.,* to undertake to do sth. *Je suis trop engagé pour reculer,* I have gone too far to draw back. **2.** (*a*) To take service (*chez qn,* with s.o.). (*b*) To enlist. **3.** (*a*) (Of rope) To foul. (*b*) *L'armée s'engagea dans le défilé,* the army entered the pass. (*c*) (Of battle) To begin.

engelure, *s.f.* Chilblain.

engendrer, *v.tr.* **1.** To beget (child). **2.** To engender; to generate.

engin, *s.m.* Engine, machine; device. *Engin de pêche,* fishing tackle.

engloutir, *v.tr.* **1.** To swallow. **2.** To engulf; to swallow up (ship, fortune).

engloutissement, *s.m.* Swallowing up; engulfment.

engluer, *v.tr.* (*a*) To lime (twigs). (*b*) *F: Se laisser e.,* to allow oneself to be caught.

engorger, *v.tr.* (n. **engorgeons**) To choke (up), stop (up); to block, clog.

engouement, *s.m.* Infatuation.

engouffrer, *v.tr.* To engulf.

engoulevent, *s.m. Orn:* Nightjar.

engourdir, *v.tr.* To (be)numb.
   s'engourdir. 1. (Of limb) To grow numb. **2.** (Of the mind) To become dull.
   engourdi, *a.* **1.** Numb(ed). **2.** Dull, sluggish (mind).

engourdissement, *s.m.* **1.** Numbness. **2.** Dullness, sluggishness (of mind).

engrais, *s.m.* Manure. *E. chimique,* fertilizer.

engraisser. 1. *v.tr.* (*a*) To fatten. (*b*) To manure (land). **2.** *v.i.* To grow stout.

engrener, *v.tr.* (**j'engrène**) *F: E. une affaire,* to set a thing going.

enhardir, *v.tr.* To embolden.
   s'enhardir, to pluck up courage.

énigmatique, *a.* Enigmatic(al).

énigme, *s.f.* Enigma, riddle.

enivrant, *a.* Intoxicating, heady.

enivrement, *s.m.* **1.** Intoxication. **2.** *F:* Ecstasy (of joy).

enivrer, *v.tr.* To intoxicate.

enjamber, *v.tr.* (*a*) To bestride (horse). (*b*) To step over (obstacle). *Trois ponts enjambent le fleuve,* three bridges span the river.
   enjambée, *s.f.* Stride.

enjeu, -eux, *s.m. Gaming:* Stake.

enjoindre, *v.tr.* (Conj. like JOINDRE) To enjoin.

enjôler, *v.tr.* To coax, wheedle.

enjôleur, -euse. 1. *s.* Coaxer. **2.** *a.* Coaxing.

enjoliver, *v.tr.* To beautify, embellish.

enjoué, *a.* Playful, sprightly.

enjouement, *s.m.* Sprightliness.

enlacer, *v.tr.* (n. **enlaçons**) **1.** To interlace. **2.** (*a*) To entwine. (*b*) To clasp in one's arms.

enlaidir. 1. *v.tr.* To make ugly; to disfigure. **2.** *v.i.* To grow ugly.

enlèvement, *s.m.* **1.** Removal. **2.** Kidnapping; carrying off. **3.** *Mil:* Storming (of position).

enlever, *v.tr.* (**j'enlève**) **1.** (*a*) To remove. *E. le couvert,* to clear the table. *Enlevé par la mer,* carried away by the sea. (*b*) *E. qch. à qn,* to take sth. from s.o. **2.** To carry off; to kidnap s.o. *Se faire enlever par qn,* to elope with s.o. **3.** *Mil:* To storm (position). **4.** To raise. *E. le couvercle,* to lift the lid.

nliser (s'), *v.pr.* To sink (into quicksand); (of car) to get bogged.

nnemi. I. *s.* Enemy. **2.** *a.* Hostile (*de,* to).

nnui, *s.m.* **I.** Worry, anxiety. **Créer des ennuis à qn,** to make trouble for s.o. **Quel ennui!** what a nuisance! **2.** Boredom.

nnuyant, *a.* Annoying, vexing.

nnuyer, *v.tr.* (j'ennuie) **I.** (*a*) To annoy, worry. (*b*) To importune. **2.** To bore, weary.
    s'ennuyer, to be bored; to weary.

nnuyeux, *a.* **I.** (*a*) Boring, tedious. (*b*) Importunate. **2.** Annoying.

noncer, *v.tr.* (n. énonçons) **I.** To state (opinion). **2.** To articulate (word).

nonciation, *s.f.* **I.** Stating, expressing (of fact). **2.** Enunciation; articulation.

norgueillir [-gœj-], *v.tr.* To make proud.
    s'enorgueillir. *S'e. de qch.,* to pride oneself on sth.

norme, *a.* Enormous, huge.

normément, *adv.* **I.** Enormously. **2.** A great deal, a great many.

normité, *s.f.* **I.** (*a*) Enormity. (*b*) Vastness. **2.** *F:* Commettre une énormité, to make a gross blunder.

nquérir (s'), *v.pr.* (Conj. like ACQUÉRIR) To inquire, make inquiries (*de,* after).

nquête, *s.f.* Inquiry, investigation.

nqui-s, -t, etc. See ENQUÉRIR (s').

nraciner, *v.tr.* *F:* To establish (principles).
    s'enraciner, to take root.
    enraciné, *a.* Deep-rooted; deep-seated.

nrager, *v.* (n. enrageons) **I.** *v.tr.* To enrage. **2.** *v.i.* To (fret) and fume.
    enragé, *a.* (*a*) Mad (dog). (*b*) *F:* Rabid; enthusiastic.

nregistrement, *s.m.* Registration; booking (of an order).

nregistrer, *v.tr.* **I.** To register, record. **2.** *Musique enregistrée,* music on (gramophone) records.

nrhumer, *v.tr.* To give (s.o.) a cold.
    s'enrhumer, to catch (a) cold.

nrichir, *v.tr.* To enrich.
    s'enrichir, to grow rich.

nrichissement, *s.m.* Enrichment.

nrôlement, *s.m.* Enrolment.

nrôler, *v.tr.* To enrol.

nroué, *a.* Hoarse, husky.

nrouement, *s.m.* Hoarseness, huskiness.

nrouler, *v.tr.* (*a*) To roll up (map). (*b*) To wrap up.

nsanglanter, *v.tr.* To cover with blood.

nseigne, *s.f.* (*a*) Sign, index. (*b*) Sign (-board). *F:* Nous sommes tous logés à la même enseigne, we are all in the same boat. *Prov:* A bon vin point d'enseigne, good wine needs no bush.

nseignement, *s.m.* **I.** Teaching. **2.** Education, instruction.

nseigner, *v.tr.* **I.** To show; to point out. **2.** (*a*) E. les enfants, to teach children. (*b*) E. à qn à faire qch., to teach s.o. to do sth

ensemble. I. *adv.* Together. Être bien ensemble, to be good friends. Le tout ensemble, the general effect. Agir d'ensemble, to act in concert. **2.** *s.m.* (*a*) Whole, entirety. Vue d'ensemble, general view. (*b*) Cohesion, unity. Avec ensemble, all together.

enserrer, *v.tr.* (*a*) To enclose. (*b*) To squeeze.

ensevelir, *v.tr.* To bury.

ensevelissement, *s.m.* Burial.

ensoleillé [-lεje], *a.* Sunny.

ensorceler, *v.tr.* (j'ensorcelle) To bewitch.
    ensorcelé, *a.* Bewitched; under a spell.

ensuite, *adv.* After(wards), then. Et ensuite? what then?

ensuivre (s'), *v.pr.* (Conj. like SUIVRE. Used only in the third pers.) To follow, ensue, result.

entacher, *v.tr.* To sully, besmirch.

entaille [ătɑ:j], *s.f.* (*a*) Notch, nick, cut; groove. (*b*) Gash, cut, slash.

entailler [ătaje], *v.tr.* (*a*) To notch, nick. (*b*) To gash, cut, slash.

entamer, *v.tr.* **I.** To cut into (loaf); to open (bottle). E. son capital, to break into one's capital. **2.** To begin (conversation). E. un sujet, to broach a subject.

entassement, *s.m.* Accumulation.

entasser, *v.tr.* (*a*) To accumulate; to heap (up). (*b*) To pack together.
    s'entasser. I. (Of thgs) To accumulate. **2.** To crowd together.

entendement, *s.m.* Understanding.

entendre, *v.tr.* **I.** To intend, mean. J'entends que vous veniez, I expect you to come. **2.** (*a*) To hear. Entendre parler de qch., to hear of sth. Entendre dire qch. à qn, to hear s.o. say sth. (*b*) To listen to. Veuillez m'e., give me a hearing. A vous entendre . . ., according to you. **3.** (*a*) E. une langue, to understand a language. Il n'entend pas la plaisanterie, he can't take a joke. C'est entendu, agreed. Bien entendu! of course! (*b*) To know all about (sth.).
    s'entendre. I. To agree. **2.** To be skilled (*à,* in).
    entendu, *a.* (*a*) Business-like, sensible (person). (*b*) Knowing, shrewd.

entente, *s.f.* **I.** (*a*) Understanding. (*b*) Mot à double entente, word with a double meaning. **2.** Agreement, understanding. Entente cordiale, friendly understanding.

entérique, *a.* *Med:* Enteric.

enterrement, *s.m.* Burial, interment.

enterrer, *v.tr.* To bury, inter.

en-tête, *s.m.* Heading (of letter). *pl.* Des en-têtes.

entêtement, *s.m.* Obstinacy, stubbornness.

entêter (s'), *v.pr.* To be obstinate, stubborn.
    entêté, *a.* Obstinate, headstrong.

enthousiasme, *s.m.* Enthusiasm.

enthousiasmer, *v.tr.* To fire (s.o.) with enthusiasm.

enthousiaste. I. *s.m. & f.* Enthusiast. **2.** *a.* Enthusiastic.

entier, *a.* **I.** Entire, whole. *Payer place entière,* to pay full fare. **2.** Complete, full. **3.** *Adv.phr.* **En entier,** entirely, in full.

entièrement, *adv.* Entirely, wholly.

entomologie, *s.f.* Entomology.

entomologique, *a.* Entomological.

entonner, *v.tr. Mus:* **I.** To intone. Entonner les louanges de qn, to sing s.o.'s praises. **2.** To strike up (a song).

entonnoir, *s.m.* **I.** Funnel. **2.** Shell-hole, crater.

entorse, *s.f.* Sprain, wrench, twist.

entour, *s.m.* A l'entour, around, round about. A l'entour de, round (the town).

entourage, *s.m.* **I.** Surroundings. **2.** Set, circle (of friends); environment.

entourer, *v.tr.* To surround (*de*, with).

entr'acte, *s.m. Th:* **I.** Interval. **2.** Entr'-acte, interlude. *pl. Des entr'actes.*

entr'aider (s'), *v.pr.* To help one another.

entrailles [ɑ̃traːj], *s.f.pl.* **I.** Entrails, bowels. **2.** *F:* Bowels of mercy; compassion. Être sans entrailles, to be ruthless.

entr'aimer (s'), *v.pr.* To love one another.

entrain, *s.m.* Liveliness, briskness; spirit. Faire qch. sans entrain, to do sth. in a half-hearted manner.

entraînement, *s.m.* **I.** (*a*) Dragging along; carrying away. (*b*) Enthusiasm. **2.** Leading astray; allurement. *E. d'une mélodie,* lure of a tune. **3.** *Sp:* Training.

entraîner, *v.tr.* **I.** To carry along; to carry away. **2.** Se laisser entraîner, to allow oneself to be led astray, carried away. **3.** To entail, involve. **4.** *Sp:* To train.

entrave, *s.f.* **I.** Shackle. **2.** *E. à qch.,* impediment to sth.

entraver, *v.tr.* **I.** To shackle; to hobble (a horse). **2.** To hinder, impede.

entre, *prep.* **I.** Between. *Femme e. deux âges,* middle-aged woman. **Entre les deux,** betwixt and between. **2.** (*a*) Among(st). *Ce jour e. tous,* this day of all days. (*b*) *Tomber e. les mains de l'ennemi,* to fall into the enemy's hands. (*c*) D'entre, (from) among. *L'un d'e. eux,* one of their number. **3.** *Ils s'accordent e. eux,* they agree among themselves.

entrebâiller[-bɑje], *v.tr.* To half-open.

entre-choquer (s'), *v.pr.* (*a*) To collide. (*b*) To knock against one another.

entrecôte, *s.f. F:* Rib of beef.

entrecouper, *v.tr.* **I.** To intersect. **2.** To interrupt.

entrecoupé, *a.* Interrupted, broken (sleep).

entrée, *s.f.* **I.** Entry, entering. *Faire son e.,* to make one's entrance. **2.** Admission, admittance (to club). **"Entrée interdite,"** 'no admittance.' **3.** Way in; entrance. **4.** *Cu:* Entrée.

entrefaite, *s.f.* Sur ces entrefaites, meanwhile.

entrelacement, *s.m.* Interlacing; network.

entrelacer, *v.tr.* (Conj. like LACER) To interlace.

entremêlement, *s.m.* **I.** (Inter-)mingling. **2.** (Inter)mixture, medley.

entremêler, *v.tr. E. qch. de qch.,* to (inter) mix sth. with sth.

s'entremêler. **I.** To (inter)-mingle. **2.** *S'e. dans une affaire,* to interfere.

entremise, *s.f.* (*a*) Intervention. (*b*) Media-tion.

entrepôt, *s.m.* Warehouse, store.

entreprenant, *a.* Enterprising.

entreprendre, *v.tr.* (Conj. like PRENDRE) **I.** To undertake; to take (sth.) in hand. **2.** To contract for (piece of work).

entrepreneur, -euse, *s.* Contractor.

entreprise, *s.f.* Undertaking; venture.

entrer, *v.i.* (Aux. *être*) **I.** (*a*) To enter; to go in, to come in. "Défense d'entrer," 'no admittance.' *E. en courant,* to run in. (*b*) *E. en fonction,* to enter upon one's duties. (*c*) To enter into, take part in (sth.). *Vous n'entrez pour rien dans l'affaire,* you are in no way concerned with the business.

entre-regarder (s'), *v.pr.* To look at one another.

entresol, *s.m.* Entresol; mezzanine (floor).

entretenir, *v.tr.* (Conj. like TENIR) **I.** To maintain; to keep (sth.) up. *S'e. la main* to keep one's hand in. **2.** (*a*) To maintain (family). (*b*) *E. des soupçons,* to entertain suspicions. **3.** *E. qn (de qch.),* to talk to s.o. (about sth.).

s'entretenir, to talk, converse.

entretien, *s.m.* **I.** Upkeep, maintenance. **2.** Support (of family). **3.** Conversation; interview.

entreverr-ai, -as, etc. See ENTREVOIR.

entrevi-s, -t, etc. See ENTREVOIR.

entrevoir, *v.tr.* (Conj. like VOIR) To catch sight, catch a glimpse, of. *Laisser e. qch. à qn,* to drop a hint of sth. to s.o

entrevue, *s.f.* Interview.

entr'ouvrir, *v.tr.* (Conj. like OUVRIR) To half-open; to set (door) ajar.

entr'ouvert, *a.* **I.** Half-open (window). **2.** Gaping, yawning (chasm).

énumérateur, -trice, *s.* Enumerator.

énumération, *s.f.* Enumeration.

énumérer, *v.tr.* (j'énumère; j'énumérerai) To enumerate; to count up.

envahir, *v.tr.* **I.** To invade. **2.** To encroach upon.

envahissement, *s.m.* Invasion.

envahisseur, *s.m.* Invader.

enveloppe, *s.f.* **I.** Envelope, cover(-ing); wrapper. **2.** Exterior.

enveloppement, *s.m.* Envelopment.

envelopper, *v.tr.* To envelop. (*a*) To wrap up. *Enveloppé de brume,* shrouded in mist. (*b*) To cover. (*c*) To surround.

envenimer, *v.tr.* **I.** To envenom. **2.** To aggravate (quarrel).

enverr-ai, -as, etc. See ENVOYER.

envers¹, *s.m.* Wrong side, reverse. *F: L'e.*

de la vie, the seamy side of life. **A l'envers**, (i) inside out; (ii) wrong way up.

envers², *prep.* Towards.

envie, *s.f.* **1.** Desire, longing. **Avoir envie de qch.**, to want sth. **Avec envie**, longingly. **2.** Envy. **Faire envie à qn**, to make s.o. envious. **Porter envie à qn**, to envy s.o.

envier, *v.tr.* To envy. **1.** To covet **2.** To be envious of (s.o.).

envieusement, *adv.* Enviously

envieux, *a.* Envious.

environ. 1. *adv.* About. **2.** *s.m.pl.* **Environs**, surroundings, neighbourhood, environs.

environnement, *s.m.* Environment.

environner, *v.tr.* To surround.

envisager, *v.tr.* (n. envisageons) To face, envisage. (*a*) To look (s.o.) in the face. (*b*) To consider (possibility). *E. l'avenir*, to look to the future. *Cas non envisagé*, unforeseen case.

envoi, *s.m.* **1.** Sending, consignment. **Envoi de fonds**, remittance (of funds) **2.** Consignment, parcel.

envol, *s.m.* **1.** (*a*) (Of birds) Taking flight. (*b*) (Of aeroplane) Taking off **2.** (*a*) Flight. (*b*) Take-off.

envoler (s'), *v.pr.* (*a*) (Of bird) To fly away; to take flight. (*b*) (Of aeroplane) To take off. (*c*) (Of hat) To blow off.

envoyer, *v.tr.* (j'envoie; *fu.* j'enverrai) To send. **Envoyer chercher qn**, to send for s.o. *F:* **Je ne le lui ai pas envoyé dire**, I told him straight. *F:* **Envoyer promener qn**, to send s.o. to the right-about.

envoyé, *s.m.* Envoy; messenger, representative.

éon, *s.m.* Aeon, eon.

épagneul, *s.* Spaniel.

épais, -aisse, *a.* Thick. **Avoir la langue épaisse**, to be thick of speech.

épaisseur, *s.f.* **1.** Thickness; depth. **2.** Density, thickness (of fog).

épaissir. 1. *v.tr.* To thicken. **2.** *v.i. & pr.* To thicken, become thick; (of darkness) to deepen.

épanchement, *s.m.* Outpou.ing, effusion (of feeling).

épancher, *v.tr.* To pour out (liquid); to shed (blood).

s'épancher, to unbosom oneself.

épandre, *v.tr.* To spread.

s'épandre, (of water, fire) to spread.

épanouir, *v.tr.* To cause to open out.

s'épanouir. 1. To open out, bloom. **2.** (Of face) To light up

épanoui, *a.* In full bloom; full-blown. *Visage épanoui*, beaming face.

épanouissement, *s.m.* **1.** (*a*) Opening out (of flowers). (*b*) Beaming (of the face). **2.** (Full) bloom.

épargne, *s.f* **1.** Saving, thrift. **2. Vivre de ses épargnes**, to live on one's savings. **Bon d'épargne**, savings certificate.

épargner, *v.tr* **1.** To save (up) (money).

É. ses forces, to husband one's strength. **2.** To save, spare (time). **3.** To spare, have mercy on (prisoner, etc.).

éparpiller [-pije], *v.tr* To disperse, scatter

épars, *a.* Scattered.

épatant, *a.* *F:* Wonderful; fine, capital

épater, *v.tr.* *F:* To astound, flabbergast.

épaulard, *s.m.* *Z:* Grampus, orc.

épaule, *s.f.* Shoulder. **Coup d'épaule**, shove.

épauler, *v.tr.* To bring to the shoulder.

épaulette, *s.f.* *Cost:* (*a*) Shoulder-strap (*b*) *Mil:* Epaulet(te).

épave, *s.f.* (*a*) Wait. (*b*) *Nau:* Wreck; derelict. (*c*) *pl.* Wreckage.

épée, *s.f.* Sword; rapier. **Poursuivre qn l'épée dans les reins**, to press hard upon s.o. *F:* **Coup d'épée dans l'eau**, wasted effort.

épeler, *v.tr.* (j'épelle) **1.** To spell (word) **2.** To spell out (message).

éperdu, *a.* Distracted, bewildered *Résistance éperdue*, desperate resistance.

éperdument, *adv.* Distractedly, madly

éperlan, *s.m.* *Ich:* Smelt.

éperon, *s.m.* **1.** *Equit:* Spur. **2.** Spur (of mountain range); ram (of warship); cut-water (of bridge).

éperonner, *v.tr.* (*a*) To spur. (*b*) To ram

épervier, *s.m.* *Orn:* Sparrow-hawk

épeuré, *a.* Frightened, scared.

éphémère. 1. *a* Ephemeral. **2.** *s.m Ent:* May-fly.

épi, *s.m.* Ear (of grain); spike (of flower).

épice, *s.f.* Spice. **Pain d'épice**, gingerbread

épicer, *v.tr.* (n. épiçons) To spice

épicé, *a.* Highly spiced

épicerie, *s.f.* **1.** Spices. **2.** (*a*) Groceries (*b*) Grocer's shop.

épicier, *s.* Grocer.

épicurien, -ienne. 1. *a. & s.* Epicurean **2.** *s. F:* Epicure.

épidémie, *s.f.* Epidemic; outbreak

épiderme, *s.m.* Epiderm(is).

épier, *v.tr.* **1.** To watch; to spy upon **2.** To be on the look-out for (opportunity)

épigramme, *s.f.* Epigram

épilepsie, *s.f.* Epilepsy

épileptique, *a & s.* Epileptic.

épilogue, *s.m.* Epilogue.

épinard, *s.m.* *Bot:* Spinach.

épine, *s.f.* **1.** Thorn-bush. **2.** Thorn, prickle. **Une épine au pied**, a thorn in one's side. **3. Épine dorsale**, spine, backbone.

épineux, *a.* Thorny, prickly *F:* **Affaire épineuse**, ticklish matter.

épingle, *s.f.* Pin. *F:* **Tiré à quatre épingles**, spick and span. **Tirer son épingle du jeu**, to get out of a venture without loss. **Coups d'épingle**, pin-pricks petty annoyances.

épingler, *v.tr.* To pin.

Épiphanie, *s.f.* Epiphany; Twelfth Night.

épique, *a.* Epic.

épiscopal, -aux, *a.* Episcopal

épisode, *s.m.* Episode.
épitaphe, *s.f.* Epitaph.
épithète, *s.f.* Epithet.
épitomé, *s.m.* Epitome, abridgment.
épître, *s.f.* Epistle.
éploré, *a.* Tearful, weeping.
éplucher, *v.tr.* To peel (potatoes).
épluchures, *s.f.pl.* Peelings, parings.
éponge, *s.f.* Sponge. *F:* Passons l'éponge là-dessus, let us say no more about it.
éponger, *v.tr.* (n. épongeons) *S'é. le front,* to mop one's brow.
épopée, *s.f.* Epic (poem).
époque, *s.f.* **1.** Epoch, era, age. Faire époque, to mark an epoch. **2.** A l'époque de sa naissance, at the time of his birth.
épouse. See ÉPOUX.
épouser, *v.tr.* **1.** To marry, wed. **2.** To espouse (cause).
épousseter, *v.tr.* (j'époussette) To dust (furniture).
épouvantable, *a.* Dreadful, frightful.
épouvantail [-ta:j], *s.m.* **1.** Scarecrow. **2.** *F:* Bugbear.
épouvante, *s.f.* Terror, fright.
épouvanter, *v.tr.* To terrify. s'épouvanter, to take fright.
époux, -ouse, *s.* Husband, *f.* wife; spouse.
éprendre (s'), *v.pr.* (Conj. like PRENDRE) To become enamoured. épris, *a.* *É. de qn,* in love with s.o.
épreuve, *s.f.* **1.** *(a)* Proof, test, trial. Amitié à l'épreuve, staunch friendship. A l'épreuve de qch., proof against sth. *(b) Sch:* (Examination) paper. *(c) Sp:* Event. **2.** Trial, affliction, ordeal. **3.** *(a) Typ:* Proof. *(b) Phot:* Print.
épris. See ÉPRENDRE (s').
éprouver, *v.tr.* **1.** To test, try. **2.** To feel, experience (sensation). éprouvé, *a. Remède é.,* well-tried remedy.
éprouvette, *s.f.* Test-tube.
épuisant, *a.* Exhausting.
épuisement, *s.m.* **1.** Exhausting, using up; emptying. **2.** Exhaustion.
épuiser, *v.tr.* To exhaust. **1.** To use up, consume; to drain, empty (well). **2.** To wear, tire, (s.o.) out. s'épuiser, to become exhausted. épuisé, *a.* Exhausted.
équanimité, *s.f.* Equanimity.
équarrir, *v.tr.* To square (timber).
équateur [ekwa-]. **1.** *s.m.* Equator. *Sous l'é.,* at the equator. **2.** *Pr.n.m. Geog:* Ecuador.
équation [ekwa-], *s.f. Mth:* Equation.
équatorial, -aux [ekwa-], *a.* Equatorial.
équerre, *s.f. Tls:* Square.
équestre, *a.* Equestrian (statue).
équilatéral, -aux [ekɥi-], *a.* Equilateral.
équilibre, *s.m.* Equilibrium, balance.
équilibrer, *v.tr.* To balance, (counter-)poise. équilibré, *a.* In equilibrium; balanced.
équinoxe, *s.m.* Equinox.

équinoxial, -aux, *a.* Equinoctial.
équipage, *s.m.* **1.** *Nau:* Crew; ship's company. **2.** Train des équipages = Army Service Corps. **3.** Equipage. **4.** Apparel, attire.
équipe, *s.f.* **1.** Gang (of workmen). *Mil:* Working party. Travailler par équipes, to work in shifts. Chef d'équipe, foreman. **2.** *Sp:* Team; side.
équipement, *s.m.* Equipment. **1.** Fitting out. **2.** Outfit. *Petit é.,* kit.
équiper, *v.tr.* To equip; to fit out. équipée, *s.f.* *F:* Escapade, lark.
équitable, *a.* *(a)* Equitable, fair. *(b)* Fairminded.
équitablement, *adv.* Equitably, fairly.
équité, *s.f.* Equity, fairness.
équivalent, *a. & s.m.* Equivalent.
équivaloir, *v.i.* (Conj. like VALOIR) To be equivalent, equal in value.
équivaut. See ÉQUIVALOIR.
équivoque. **1.** *a.* *(a)* Equivocal, ambiguous. *(b)* Questionable, dubious (conduct). **2.** *s.f.* Ambiguity.
équivoquer, *v.i.* To equivocate.
érable, *s.m. Bot:* Maple(-tree, -wood).
éradication, *s.f.* Eradication.
érafler, *v.tr.* To scratch, graze.
éraflure, *s.f.* Slight scratch; graze.
érailler [-aje], *v.tr.* To graze, chafe. éraillé, *a.* **1.** Frayed (collar); scratched (surface). **2.** Raucous (voice).
ère, *s.f.* Era; epoch.
érection, *s.f.* Erection; setting up.
éreintement, *s.m. F:* Exhaustion.
éreinter, *v.tr. F:* To exhaust; to tire out.
ergot, *s.m.* Spur (of cock). *F:* Se dresser sur ses ergots, to bristle up.
ériger, *v.tr.* (n. érigeons) **1.** To erect, set up, raise. **2.** To establish, set up.
ermitage, *s.m.* Hermitage.
ermite, *s.m.* Hermit, eremite.
éroder, *v.tr.* To erode, abrade.
érosion, *s.f.* Erosion; wearing away.
érotique, *a.* Erotic; amatory (poem).
errant, *a.* **1.** Rambling, roving, wandering. **2.** Erring, misguided (person).
erre, *s.f. Nau:* (Head)way (of ship).
errer, *v.i.* **1.** To roam, wander (about). **2.** To err; to be mistaken.
erreur, *s.f.* Error. **1.** Mistake, blunder, slip. Sauf erreur, if I am not mistaken. **2.** False belief, delusion.
erroné, *a.* Erroneous, wrong, mistaken.
érudit. **1.** *a.* Erudite. **2.** *s.* Scholar.
érudition, *s.f.* Erudition, learning.
éruption, *s.f.* Eruption.
es [ɛ]. See ÊTRE.
ès [ɛs], contracted article = en les. *Docteur ès lettres,* doctor of literature.
escabeau, *s.m.* (Wooden) stool.
escadre, *s.f. Navy:* Squadron.
escadrille [-ri:j], *s.f. Navy:* Flotilla.
escadron, *s.m. Mil:* Squadron (of cavalry).

escalade, *s.f.* (*a*) Scaling, climbing. (*b*) Climb.

escalader, *v.tr.* To scale, climb.

escale, *s.f.* **1.** Port or place of call. **2.** Call.

escalier, *s.m.* Staircase ; (flight of) stairs. *E. roulant,* escalator.

escalope, *s.f.* Cutlet (of veal).

escamotage, *s.m.* **1.** Conjuring, sleight of hand. **2.** *F:* Sneaking, filching.

escamoter, *v.tr.* **1.** To conjure away ; to make vanish. **2.** *F:* To sneak, filch.

escamoteur, *s.m.* Conjuror.

escapade, *s.f.* Escapade ; prank.

escarbille [-bi:j], *s.f.* (*a*) (Half-burnt) cinder. (*b*) *pl.* Clinkers, ashes ; sparks (from engine).

escarboucle, *s.f. Lap:* Carbuncle.

escargot, *s.m.* Snail.

escarmouche, *s.f.* Skirmish.

escarpé, *a.* Steep, precipitous, abrupt.

escarpement, *s.m.* **1.** Steepness. **2.** Abrupt descent.

escarpin, *s.m.* (Dancing-)shoe ; pump.

Escaut (l'), *Pr.n.m.* The (river) Scheldt.

escient, *s.m.* Knowledge, cognizance. **A bon escient,** wittingly.

esclaffer (s'), *v.pr. F:* To burst out laughing.

esclavage, *s.m.* Slavery.

esclave, *s.m. & f.* Slave.

escompte [ɛskɔ̃:t], *s.m. Com:* Discount, rebate.

escompter [-kɔ̃te], *v.tr.* **1.** *Com:* To discount (bill). **2.** *F: E. un succès,* to reckon upon a success.

escorte, *s.f.* Escort. *Navy:* Convoy.

escorter, *v.tr.* To escort. *Navy:* To convoy.

escouade, *s.f.* Squad, gang.

escrime, *s.f.* Fencing, swordsmanship.

escrimeur, *s.m.* Fencer, swordsman.

escroc, *s.m.* Swindler, sharper ; crook.

escroquer, *v.tr.* **1.** *E. qch. à qn,* to cheat s.o. of sth. **2.** *E. qn,* to swindle s.o.

escroquerie, *s.f.* **1.** Swindling. **2.** Swindle.

esculent, *a.* Esculent, eatable.

Ésope, *Pr.n.m. Gr.Lit:* Aesop.

espace, *s.m.* Space. **1.** Distance, interval. **2.** Void, infinity.

espacer, *v.tr.* (n. **espaçons**) To space (out). **espacé,** *a.* Far between, far apart ; at wide intervals.

espadon, *s.m.* Sword-fish.

espadrille [-ri:j], *s.f.* (*a*) Canvas shoe. (*b*) Bathing sandal.

Espagne, *Pr.n.f.* Spain.

espagnol. **1.** *a.* Spanish. **2.** *s.* Spaniard. **3.** *s.m. Ling:* Spanish.

espèce, *s.f.* **1.** (*a*) Kind, sort. *F:* **Espèce de . . .,** takes the gender and number of the following noun. *Cet e. d'idiot, cette e. d'idiote,* that silly fool. (*b*) *pl. Fin:* Espèces (monnayées), specie, cash, coin. **2.** *Nat.Hist:* Species. **L'espèce humaine,** mankind.

espérance, *s.f.* Hope. **Garçon de grande espérance,** promising lad.

espérer, *v.tr.* (j'espère ; j'espérerai) To hope. *E. qch.,* to hope for sth. *E. en qn,* to hope, trust, in s.o.

espiègle, *a. & s.* Mischievous, roguish.

espion, -onne, *s.* Spy.

espionnage, *s.m.* Espionage, spying.

espionner, *v.tr.* To spy (up)on. *Abs.* To spy.

esplanade, *s.f.* Esplanade ; promenade.

espoir, *s.m.* Hope. **Avoir bon espoir,** to be full of hope.

esprit, *s.m.* **1.** Spirit. (*a*) **Le Saint-Esprit,** the Holy Ghost. **Rendre l'esprit,** to give up the ghost. **L'Esprit malin,** the Evil One. (*b*) Ghost, phantom. (*c*) Sprite. **2.** (*a*) **Recueillir ses esprits,** to pull oneself together. **Reprendre ses esprits,** to regain consciousness ; to come to. (*b*) *Ch:* (Volatile) spirit. **3.** (*a*) Mind. *Elle avait l'e. ailleurs,* her thoughts were elsewhere. **Avoir l'esprit des affaires,** to have a turn for business. (*b*) Wit. **Il fait de l'esprit,** he is trying to be funny. **4.** Spirit, feeling.

Esquimau, -aux, *s. & a.* Eskimo.

esquisse, *s.f.* Sketch ; draft ; outline.

esquisser, *v.tr.* To sketch, outline. *E. un sourire,* to give the ghost of a smile.

esquiver, *v.tr.* To avoid, dodge, evade. **s'esquiver,** to slip away ; to steal off.

essai, *s.m.* **1.** (*a*) Trial, test(ing). **Prendre qch. à l'essai,** to take sth. on approval. (*b*) *Metall:* Assay(ing). **2.** (*a*) Attempt(ing), try. **Coup d'essai,** first attempt. (*b*) *Lit:* Essay.

essaim, *s.m.* Swarm (of bees).

essaimer, *v.i.* (Of bees) To swarm.

essayer, *v.tr.* (j'essaie, j'essaye) **1.** (*a*) To test, try. (*b*) To try on (garment). (*c*) *Metall:* To assay. (*d*) *E. de qch.,* to try, make trial of sth. **2.** *E. de faire qch.,* to try to do sth.

essence, *s.f.* **1.** (*a*) (Essential) oil ; attar (of roses). (*b*) Motor spirit, petrol. (*c*) Essence, extract. **2.** (*a*) Nature, spirit, natural quality. *L'e. de l'affaire,* the gist of the matter. (*b*) *For:* Species (of tree).

essentiel, -elle. **1.** *a.* Essential. **2.** *s.m.* **L'essentiel,** the great thing.

essentiellement, *adv.* Essentially.

essieu, -eux, *s.m.* Axle(-tree).

essor, *s.m.* Flight, soaring.

essoufflement, *s.m.* Breathlessness.

essouffler, *v.tr.* To blow, wind (horse). **s'essouffler,** to get out of breath. **essoufflé,** *a.* Out of breath.

essuie-main(s), *s.m.inv.* Towel.

essuyer [esɥije], *v.tr.* (j'essuie) **1.** To wipe ; to wipe up. **2.** To suffer, endure (defeat). *E. un refus,* to meet with a refusal.

est[1] [ɛst]. **1.** *s.m.* No *pl.* East. **2.** *a.inv. Les régions est de la France,* the easterly parts of France.

est[2] [ɛ]. See ÊTRE.

estaminet, *s.m.* **1.** Public house. **2.** Bar (in hotel) ; tap-room.

estampe, *s.f.* Print, engraving.

estamper, *v.tr.* To stamp, emboss.

esthète, *s.m. & f.* Aesthete.

esthétique. 1. *a.* Aesthetic. **2.** *s.f.* Aesthetics.

stimable, *a.* Estimable.

stimateur, -trice, *s.* Appraiser, valuer.

estimation, *s.f.* (*a*) Valuing, appraising. (*b*) Estimate, valuation.

estime, *s.f.* **1.** Guesswork. *Nau:* Reckoning. **2.** (*a*) Estimation, opinion. (*b*) Esteem, regard.

estimer, *v.tr.* **1.** (*a*) To estimate; to value. (*b*) To calculate (distance). **2.** (*a*) To consider, deem. (*b*) To esteem (s.o.).

estomac, *s.m.* Stomach. *Creux de l'e.,* pit of the stomach.

Estonie. *Pr.n.f. Geog:* Esthonia.

estonien, -ienne, *a. & s. Geog:* Esthonian.

estrade¹, *s.f.* Battre l'estrade, to be on the tramp.

estrade², *s.f.* Dais; platform, stage.

estropier, *v.tr.* To cripple, lame, maim. **estropié,** *a.* Crippled, maimed.

estuaire, *s.m.* Estuary.

esturgeon, *s.m. Ich:* Sturgeon.

et [e], *conj.* And. *Et son frère et sa sœur,* both his brother and his sister. *J'aime le café; et vous?* I like coffee; do you? Note. There is no 'liaison' with *et.*

étable, *s.f.* Cow-shed; cattle-shed. *É. à porcs,* pigsty.

établi, *s.m.* (Work-)bench.

établir, *v.tr.* **1.** (*a*) To establish; to fix (one's place of abode). *É. un camp,* to pitch a camp. (*b*) To establish, prove (fact). **2.** To draw up (plan). *Com: É. un compte,* to draw up an account. **3.** To institute, create (tribunal); to lay down (rule); to found (colony). **4.** To set up in business. **s'établir,** to establish oneself, to take up one's abode.

établissement, *s.m.* Establishment. **1.** (*a*) Setting up; establishing. (*b*) Proving. **2.** Forming (of government); laying down (of rules); founding (of colony). **3.** (*a*) Institution. (*b*) Premises.

étage, *s.m.* **1.** Stor(e)y, floor (of building). **2.** (*a*) Tier, step. (*b*) *F:* Degree, rank.

étai, *s.m. Const:* Stay, prop.

étain, *s.m.* **1.** Tin. **2.** Pewter.

étalage, *s.m.* Display, show (of goods).

étaler, *v.tr.* (*a*) *Com:* To display (goods). (*b*) To spread out. (*c*) To flaunt, show off.

étalon¹, *s.m.* Stallion; stud-horse.

étalon², *s.m.* Standard (of weights).

étameur, *s.m.* (*a*) Tinsmith. (*b*) *É. ambulant,* tinker.

étamine, *s.f. Bot:* Stamen.

étampe, *s.f.* **1.** Stamp, die. **2.** *Tls:* Punch.

étanche, *a.* Tight, impervious. *É. à l'eau,* watertight.

étancher, *v.tr.* (*a*) To sta(u)nch (blood). (*b*) To quench (one's thirst).

étang, *s.m.* Pond, pool, mere.

étape, *s.f.* Stage (of journey). (i) Halting-place. (ii) Distance between two halting-places.

état, *s.m.* **1.** State, condition. **Mettre ses affaires en état,** to put one's affairs in order. *F:* Être dans tous ses états, to be in a great state. **2.** (*a*) Statement, return. État des dépenses, statement of expenses. (*b*) Faire état de qch., to take sth. into account. Faire grand état de qn, to think highly of s.o. (*c*) *Adm:* État civil, civil status. **3.** Profession, trade. *Il est épicier de son é.,* he is a grocer by trade. **4.** State; government.

état-major, *s.m.* (*a*) (General) staff. Carte d'état-major, ordnance map. (*b*) Head-quarters. *pl. Des états-majors.*

États-Unis (les). *Pr.n.m.pl.* The United States (of America).

étau, -aux, *s.m. Tls:* Vice.

étayer, *v.tr.* (j'étaie, j'étaye) To stay, prop (up).

été¹, *s.m.* Summer

été². See ÊTRE.

éteign-ant, -is, -ons, etc. See ÉTEINDRE.

éteignoir, *s.m.* (Candle) extinguisher.

éteindre, *v.tr.* (Conj. like PEINDRE) **1.** To extinguish, put out. **2.** To pay off (a debt); to abolish (a right). **s'éteindre.** (*a*) (Of fire) To die out. (*b*) (Of colour) To fade ; (of sound) to die away. **éteint,** *a.* (*a*) Extinguished. *Le feu est é.,* the fire is out. (*b*) Extinct (race). (*c*) Dull (colour). *Voix éteinte,* faint voice.

étendard, *s.m. F:* (War-)flag, standard.

étendre, *v.tr.* **1.** To spread, stretch. *É. le bras,* to stretch out one's arm. **2.** *É. ses connaissances,* to extend one's knowledge. **s'étendre. 1.** (*a*) To lie down at full length. (*b*) *S'é. sur un sujet,* to expatiate (up)on a subject. **2.** (*a*) To extend, stretch. (*b*) To spread. **étendu. 1.** *a.* (*a*) Extensive (knowledge); far-reaching (influence); wide (plain). (*b*) Outstretched (hands). **2.** *s.f.* Etendue, extent; stretch (of water). *É. d'une voix,* compass of a voice.

éternel, -elle, *a.* (*a*) Eternal. (*b*) Ever-lasting, endless.

éternellement, *adv.* (*a*) Eternally. (*b*) Endlessly.

éternité, *s.f.* Eternity.

éternuer, *v.i.* To sneeze.

éternûment, *s.m.* **1.** Sneezing. **2.** Sneeze.

éther [ete:r], *s.m. Med:* Ether.

éthéré, *a.* Ethereal, airy.

Éthiopie. *Pr.n.f.* Ethiopia; Abyssinia.

éthiopien, -ienne, *a. & s.* Ethiopian; Abyssinian.

éthique. 1. *a.* Ethical. **2.** *s.f.* Ethics.

ethnologie, *s.f.* Ethnology.

Étienne. *Pr.n.m.* Stephen.

étinceler, *v.i.* (il étincelle) **1.** To throw out sparks. **2.** (Of diamond) To sparkle, flash.

étincelle, *s.f.* Spark.

étincellement, *s.m.* Sparkling (of gem).

étioler, *v.tr.* To make (s.o.) weakly, pale.

étiqueter, *v.tr.* (j'étiquète) To label (luggage); to ticket (goods).

étiquette, *s.f.* **1.** Label, ticket. **2.** Etiquette.

étirer, *v.tr.* To stretch; to draw out.
     s'étirer, to stretch oneself, one's limbs.

étoffe, *s.f.* Stuff, material; fabric.

étoile, *s.f.* Star. **1.** *F:* Coucher à la belle étoile, to sleep in the open. **2.** (a) Decoration. *É. de la Légion d'honneur,* cross of the Legion of Honour. (b) *Typ:* Asterisk, star. **3.** *Th:* Star.

étoiler, *v.tr.* To stud, bespangle, with stars.
     étoilé, *a.* Starry, starlit (sky).

étole, *s.f.* *Ecc:* Stole.

étonnamment, *adv.* Astonishingly.

étonnant, *a.* Astonishing, surprising.

étonnement, *s.m.* Astonishment, surprise, wonder, amazement.

étonner, *v.tr.* To astonish, amaze, surprise. *Cela m'étonne que + sub.,* I am astonished that. . . .
     s'étonner, to be astonished, surprised, to wonder (de, at).

étouffant, *a.* Stifling, suffocating, stuffy (atmosphere); sultry (weather).

étouffer. 1. *v.tr.* (a) To suffocate, smother (s.o.). (b) To stifle (cry); to suppress (revolt). *É. une affaire,* to hush up a matter. **2.** *v.i. & pr.* (a) To suffocate, choke. (b) *On étouffe ici,* it is stifling here.

étourderie, *s.f.* **1.** Thoughtlessness. **2.** Thoughtless action; careless mistake.

étourdiment, *adv.* Thoughtlessly.

étourdir, *v.tr.* **1.** To stun, daze. **2.** To deaden (pain).
     étourdi. 1. *a.* Thoughtless; foolish (answer). **2.** *s.* Scatter-brain.

étourdissant, *a.* **1.** Deafening, ear-splitting. **2.** *F:* Staggering (news).

étourdissement, *s.m.* **1.** Giddiness, dizziness. **2.** Deadening (of pain); dazing.

étourneau, *s.m.* *Orn:* Starling.

étrange, *a.* Strange, peculiar, queer.

étrangement, *adv.* Strangely.

étranger. 1. (a) *a.* Foreign. (b) *s.* Foreigner, alien. (c) *s.m.* Foreign parts. *Vivre* à l'étranger, to live abroad. **2.** (a) *a.* Strange, unknown. (b) *s.* Stranger. **3.** *a.* Extraneous, foreign; not belonging (to sth.); irrelevant.

étrangeté, *s.f.* Strangeness, oddness.

étranglement, *s.m.* **1.** (a) Strangling. (b) Constriction. **2.** Narrows (of river); bottle-neck (of thoroughfare).

étrangler, *v.tr.* **1.** (a) To strangle, throttle. (b) *v.i. É. de colère,* to choke with rage. **2.** To constrict.
     étranglé, *a.* Constricted; choking (voice).

étrave, *s.f.* Stem, stern-post (of ship).

être. 1. *v.i. & pred.* (*pr.p.* étant; *p.p.* été; *pr.ind.* je suis, tu es, il est, n. sommes, v. êtes, ils sont; *pr. sub.* je sois, n. soyons, ils soient;

imp. sois, soyons; *p.h.* je fus; *fu.* je serai) **1.** To be, to exist. *Cela étant,* that being the case. **Eh bien, soit!** well, so be it! *Ainsi soit-il,* so be it; *Ecc:* amen. **2.** (a) *Il est chef de gare,* he is a stationmaster. *Nous étions trois,* there were three of us. *Nous sommes le dix,* to-day is the tenth. *Quand il fut pour sortir,* just as he was about to leave. *Il est d'un bon caractère,* he is good-tempered. *Il est de mes amis,* he is a friend of mine. (b) *Il fut trois ans à l'écrire,* he took three years to write it. (c) (i) (With *ce* as neuter subject) See CE¹. (ii) (With ellipsis of *ce*) *N'était mon rhumatisme,* were it not for my rheumatism. (d) (i) *Il est midi,* it is twelve o'clock. *Il est de mon devoir de + inf.,* it is my duty to + inf. **Comme si de rien n'était,** as if nothing had happened. *Abs. Trois à quinze francs, soit 45 fr.,* three at fifteen francs, that is 45 fr. **Soit dit sans offense,** be it said without offence. (ii) *Il était une fois une fée,* there was once upon a time a fairy. *Un héros,* **s'il en fut jamais,** a hero, if ever there was one. (e) (i) **Où en sommes-nous?** how far have we got? (ii) **J'en suis pour mille francs,** I am the poorer by a thousand francs. (iii) **J'en suis!** I'm game! I'm on! (iv) **C'en est trop!** this is past bearing. (v) **Il n'en est rien!** nothing of the kind! (vi) *Il en est qui disent que . . .,* there are some who say that. . . . **3.** (a) **Être à qn,** to belong to s.o. **Je suis à vous dans un moment,** I shall be at your service in a moment. (b) **C'est à vous de jouer,** it is your turn to play. **4.** (Aux. use) (a) *Il est arrivé,* he has arrived. (b) *Elle s'est fait mal,* she (has) hurt herself. **5.** *J'entends être obéi,* I mean to be obeyed. **6.** *F:* (a) = ALLER (in compound tenses and in *p.h.*) *J'ai été voir Jones,* I've been to see Jones. (b) = S'EN ALLER (in *p.h.* only) *Il s'en fut ouvrir la porte,* he went off to open the door.
     II. être, *s.m.* **1.** Being, existence. **2.** Being, nature. **3.** Being, individual. *Pauvres petits êtres!* poor little creatures!

étrécir, *v.tr.* To narrow.
     s'étrécir. 1. To narrow; to contract. **2.** (Of material) To shrink.

étrécissement, *s.m.* Narrowing.

étreign-ant, -is, -ons, etc. See ÉTREINDRE.

étreindre, *v.tr.* (Conj. like PEINDRE) **1.** To embrace; to clasp. *É. qch. dans la main,* to grasp sth. **2.** To fetter, impede.

étreinte, *s.f.* (a) Embrace. (b) Grasp, grip.

étrenne, *s.f.* Usu. *pl.* New-Year's gift.

étrier, *s.m.* Stirrup. **A franc étrier,** at full gallop.

étrille [-tri:j], *s.f.* Curry-comb.

étriller [-rije], *v.tr.* **1.** To curry(-comb) (horse). **2.** *P:* To thrash (s.o.).

étroit, *a.* **1.** Narrow; confined (space). **2.** Tight; tight(-fitting).

étroitement, *adv.* **1.** Narrowly. **2.** Tightly, closely.

étude, *s.f.* **1.** (*a*) Study. **Faire son étude de qch.,** to make sth. one's study. (*b*) Research. **2.** Office (of notary).

étudiant, *s.* Student.

étudier, *v.tr.* (*a*) To study. (*b*) To investigate, go into.

étui, *s.m.* Case, box. *É. à cigares,* cigar-case.

étymologie, *s.f.* Etymology.

étymologiste, *s.m. & f.* Etymologist.

eu [y]. See AVOIR.

eucalyptus [-ty:s], *s.m.* Eucalyptus; gum-tree.

eucharistie (l') [-ka-], *s.f. Ecc:* The eucharist.

euh [ø], *int.* (Expressing surprise, incredulity) Hm!

eûmes [ym]. See AVOIR.

eunuque, *s.m.* Eunuch.

euphémique, *a.* Euphemistic.

euphémisme, *s.m.* Euphemism.

euphonie, *s.f.* Euphony.

euphonique, *a.* Euphonic, euphonious.

eurent [y:r]. See AVOIR.

Europe. *Pr.n.f.* Europe.

européen, -enne, *a. & s.* European.

euss-e, -es, etc. [ys]. See AVOIR.

Eustache. *Pr.n.m.* Eustace.

eut [y], **eûtes** [yt]. See AVOIR.

eux. See LUI².

évacuation, *s.f.* (*a*) Removal, clearing out; evacuation. (*b*) Vacating (of apartment).

évacuer, *v.tr.* To evacuate, withdraw.

évader (s'), *v.pr.* To escape (by stealth).

évadé, *a. & s.* Escaped (prisoner).

évaluation, *s.f.* Valuation, appraisement; estimate.

évaluer, *v.tr.* To value, appraise; to estimate.

évangélique, *a.* Evangelical.

évangile, *s.m.* Gospel.

évanouir (s'), *v.pr.* **1.** To vanish, disappear. **2.** To faint, swoon.

évanouissement, *s.m.* **1.** Vanishing, disappearance. **2.** Faint(ing fit); swoon.

évaporation, *s.f.* Evaporation.

évaporer (s'), *v.pr.* To evaporate.

évasif, *a.* Evasive.

évasion, *s.f.* **1.** Escape (from prison). **2.** Quibble, evasion.

évasivement, *adv.* Evasively.

Ève. *Pr.n.f.* Eva. *B.Lit:* Eve.

évêché, *s.m.* **1.** Bishopric, diocese, see. **2.** Bishop's palace.

éveil [ve:j], *s.m.* **1.** (*a*) Awakening. (*b*) **Être en éveil,** to be wide-awake. *Tenir qn en é.,* to keep s.o. on the alert. **2.** Warning. **Donner l'éveil,** to raise the alarm.

éveiller [veje], *v.tr.* To wake (s.o.) up.

s'éveiller, to wake (up).

éveillé, *a.* **1.** Awake. **2.** Wide-awake.

événement, *s.m.* Event. **1. Dans l'événement,** as things turned out. **2.** Occurrence, incident.

éventail [-ta:j], *s.m.* Fan.

éventer, *v.tr.* **1.** To air. **2.** To fan.

éventrer, *v.tr.* To disembowel; to rip open; to break open.

éventualité, *s.f.* Possibility, eventuality.

éventuel, -elle. **1.** *a.* Possible, contingent. **2.** *s.m.* Eventuality, contingency.

éventuellement, *adv.* Possibly, contingently; on occasion.

évêque, *s.m.* Bishop.

évertuer (s'), *v.pr.* To do one's utmost; to exert oneself.

éviction, *s.f.* Eviction.

évidemment, *adv.* **1.** Evidently, obviously. **2.** Certainly; of course.

évidence, *s.f.* (*a*) Obviousness, clearness (of fact). **Se rendre à l'évidence,** to bow to the facts. **Il est de toute évidence que . . .,** it is obvious that. . . . (*b*) Conspicuousness. **Être en évidence,** to be in a conspicuous position.

évident, *a.* Evident, obvious, plain. **C'est évident,** that stands to reason.

évier, *s.m.* (Scullery) sink.

évincer, *v.tr.* (n. évinçons) **1.** To evict. **2.** To oust, supplant.

évitable, *a.* Avoidable.

éviter, *v.tr.* (*a*) To avoid, shun. *É. un coup,* to dodge a blow. *Évitez qu'on ne vous voie,* avoid being seen. (*b*) *F: É. une peine à qn,* to spare s.o. trouble.

évocation, *s.f.* (*a*) Evocation; conjuring up (of spirits) (*b*) Calling up (of the past).

évoluer, *v.i.* **1.** To perform evolutions. **2.** To evolve, develop.

évolution, *s.f.* Evolution.

évoquer, *v.tr.* (*a*) To evoke, call forth. (*b*) To call to mind.

exact [-zakt], *a.* Exact. (*a*) Accurate, correct. **C'est exact,** it is quite true. (*b*) Strict, rigorous. (*c*) Punctual.

exactement, *adv.* Exactly.

exaction, *s.f.* Exaction.

exactitude, *s.f.* (*a*) Exactness, accuracy, exactitude. (*b*) Punctuality.

exagération, *s.f.* Exaggeration.

exagérer, *v.tr.* (j'exagère; j'exagérerai) To exaggerate, magnify (danger).

exaltation, *s.f.* **1.** Exalting, glorifying. **2.** Exaltation; excitement.

exalter, *v.tr.* **1.** To exalt, magnify. **2.** To excite, inflame. **3.** To exalt, dignify.

s'exalter, to grow enthusiastic.

exalté. **1.** *a.* (*a*) Impassioned (speech). (*b*) Hot-headed. (*c*) Uplifted (state of mind). **2.** *s.* Fanatic.

examen, *s.m.* Examination. (*a*) Investigation. (*b*) *E. pour permis de conduire,* driving-test.

examinateur, -trice, *s.* Examiner.

examiner, *v.tr.* To examine.

exaspération, *s.f.* Exasperation, irritation.

exaspérer, *v.t.* (j'exaspère; j'exaspérerai) **1.** To exacerbate (pain). **2.** To exasperate, irritate.

exaucer, *v.tr.* (n. exauçons) To fulfil (wish).

excavation, *s.f.* **1.** Excavation, digging (out). **2.** Excavation, hollow.

excaver, *v.tr.* To excavate, to dig out.

excédent, *s.m.* Excess, surplus. *E. de poids,* overweight.

excéder, *v.tr.* (j'excède; j'excéderai) **1.** To exceed, go beyond. **2.** (*a*) To tire (s.o.) out. *Excédé de fatigue,* worn out. (*b*) To overtax (s.o.'s) patience.

excellemment, *adv.* **1.** Excellently. **2.** Eminently.

excellence, *s.f.* **1.** Excellence, pre-eminence. **Par excellence,** pre-eminently. **2. Votre Excellence,** your Excellency.

excellent, *a.* Excellent.

exceller, *v.i.* To excel.

excentricité, *s.f.* Eccentricity, oddity.

excentrique. 1. *a.* Eccentric, odd (person). **2.** *s.* Odd, eccentric, person.

excepter, *v.tr.* To except, exclude. **excepté,** *prep.* Except(ing), but, save. *Conj.phr.* **Excepté que** + *ind.,* except that.

exception, *s.f.* **1.** Exception. **Faire exception à une règle,** to be an exception to a rule. **Sauf exception,** with certain exceptions. **2.** Exception; protest.

exceptionnel, -elle, *a.* Exceptional; out of the ordinary.

exceptionnellement, *adv.* Exceptionally.

excès, *s.m.* (*a*) Excess. *Scrupuleux à l'e.,* scrupulous to a fault; over-scrupulous. (*b*) *pl.* **Commettre des excès,** to commit excesses.

excessif, *a.* Excessive, extreme; undue.

excessivement, *adv.* Excessively, exceedingly.

excision, *s.f.* Excision, cutting out.

excitabilité, *s.f.* Excitability.

excitable, *a.* Excitable.

excitant, *a.* Exciting, stimulating.

excitation, *s.f.* **1.** Excitation (of the senses). *E. à la révolte,* incitement to rebellion. **2.** (State of) excitement.

exciter, *v.tr.* To excite. (*a*) To arouse, stir up. (*b*) To inflame; to incite. (*c*) To stimulate (thirst).

exclamatif, *a.* Exclamatory.

exclamation, *s.f.* Exclamation.

exclamer (s'), *v.pr.* (*a*) To exclaim. (*b*) To protest loudly.

exclure, *v.tr.* (*p.h.* j'exclus) To exclude, shut out, leave out.

exclusif, *a.* Exclusive, sole.

exclusion, *s.f.* Exclusion, excluding. **A l'exclusion de . . .,** exclusive of. . . .

exclusivement, *adv.* Exclusively, solely.

excommunication, *v.tr.* Excommunication.

excommunier, *v.tr.* To excommunicate.

excrément, *s.m.* *Physiol:* Excrement.

excréter, *v.tr.* (j'excrète; j'excréterai) *Physiol:* To excrete.

excrétion, *s.f.* *Physiol:* Excretion.

excroissance, *s.f.* Excrescence.

excursion, *s.f.* Excursion; (i) tour, trip; (ii) outing. *E. à pied,* walking tour.

excursionniste, *s.m. & f.* Excursionist, tourist.

excusable, *a.* Excusable, pardonable.

excusablement, *adv.* Excusably.

excuse, *s.f.* **1.** Excuse. *F:* **Faites excuse!** pardon me! **2.** *pl.* Apology.

excuser, *v.tr.* **1.** To make excuses for (s.o.). **2.** To excuse, pardon. **s'excuser,** to excuse oneself; to apologize. **Se faire excuser,** to decline.

exécrable, *a.* Execrable; abominable.

exécrablement, *adv.* Execrably, abominably.

exécration, *s.f.* Execration, detestation.

exécrer, *v.tr.* (j'exècre; j'exécrerai) To execrate, loathe, detest.

exécutant, *s.* *Mus:* Performer (in band).

exécuter, *v.tr.* **1.** To execute; to carry out (plan); to perform. **2.** (*a*) To execute; to put to death. (*b*) To distrain upon. **s'exécuter. 1.** To comply. **2.** To pay up.

exécuteur, -trice, *s.* Executor, executrix.

exécutif, *a.* Executive.

exécution, *s.f.* **1.** Execution, performance. **Mettre une idée à exécution,** to carry an idea into effect. **2.** (*a*) *E. capitale,* execution. **Ordre d'exécution,** death-warrant. (*b*) *Jur:* Distraint, distress.

exemplaire¹, *a.* Exemplary.

exemplaire², *s.m.* (*a*) Specimen (of work). (*b*) Copy (of book).

exemple, *s.m.* Example. **1. Prêcher d'exemple,** to practise what one preaches. **Joindre l'exemple au précepte,** to suit the action to the word. **2.** Lesson, warning. **3.** Instance, precedent. **Par exemple,** for instance. *int.* **Par exemple!** the idea! *Ah non, par e.!* no indeed!

exempt [egzã], *a.* Exempt, free. *E. de soucis,* carefree.

exempter [-zãte], *v.tr. E. qn (de qch.),* to exempt, excuse, s.o. (from sth.).

exemption, *s.f.* Exemption; immunity (from service); freedom (from anxiety).

exercer, *v.tr.* (n. exerçons) To exercise. **1.** *E. son oreille,* to train one's ear. **2.** To exert, make use of. **3.** To practise (profession). **s'exercer.** *S'e. à qch.,* to practise sth. **exercé,** *a.* Practised (à, in).

exercice, *s.m.* Exercise. **1.** (*a*) **Prendre de l'exercice,** to take exercise. (*b*) *Mil:* Drill (-ing). **Faire l'exercice,** to drill. **2.** (*a*) (Putting into) practice; use (of power). **Entrer en exercice,** to enter upon one's duties. (*b*) *L'e. du culte,* public worship. **3.** Financial year.

exhalaison, *s.f.* Exhalation, effluvium.

exhalation, *s.f.* Exhalation, exhaling.

exhaler, *v.tr.* To exhale, emit.

exhaussement, *s.m.* **1.** Raising. **2.** *E. du terrain,* rise in the ground.

exhiber, *v.tr.* **I.** To present, show, produce. **2.** To exhibit, show.

exhibition, *s.f.* **I.** Producing, showing. **2.** Show; exhibition.

exhortation, *s.f.* Exhortation.

exhorter, *v.tr.* To exhort, urge.

exhumation, *s.f.* Exhumation, disinterment.

exhumer, *v.tr.* (*a*) To exhume, disinter. (*b*) *F:* To unearth, bring to light.

exigeant, *a.* Exacting; hard to please.

exigence, *s.f.* **I.** Exactingness. **2.** (*a*) Unreasonable demand. (*b*) Exigency, requirement(s). **Selon l'exigence du cas,** as may be required.

exiger, *v.tr.* (n. **exigeons**) **I.** To exact, require; to insist upon. **2.** To require, call for.

exigible, *a.* Exigible.

exigu, -uë, *a.* Exiguous, tiny (abode); scanty (resources); slender (income).

exiguïté, *s.f.* Exiguity (of abode); scantiness.

exil, *s.m.* Exile, banishment.

exiler, *v.tr.* To exile, banish.
  exilé, *s.* Exile.

existant, *a.* (*a*) Existing, existent. (*b*) (Supplies) on hand.

existence, *s.f.* (*a*) Existence. (*b*) Life. **Moyens d'existence,** means of subsistence.

exister, *v.i.* To exist, be; to live.

exode, *s.m.* Exodus.

exonération, *s.f.* Exoneration.

exonérer, *v.tr.* (**j'exonère; j'exonérerai**) To exonerate.

exorbitant, *a.* Exorbitant.

exorciser, *v.tr.* To exorcize (demon).

exorcisme, *s.m.* **I.** Exorcizing. **2.** Exorcism.

exotique, *a.* Exotic.

expansif, *a.* Expansive.

expansion, *s.f.* **I.** Expansion. **2.** *F:* Expansiveness.

expatriation, *s.f.* Expatriation.

expatrier, *v.tr.* To expatriate.
  s'expatrier, to leave one's own country.

expectant, *a.* Expectant (attitude).

expectoration, *s.f.* Expectoration.

expectorer, *v.tr.* To expectorate.

expédient. I. *a.* Expedient. **2.** *s.m.* Expedient, device, shift. *Vivre d'expédients,* to live by one's wits.

expédier, *v.tr.* To dispatch. **I.** To get rid of, dispose of. **2.** To expedite, hasten on. **3.** To forward, send off (letter).

expéditeur, -trice, *s.* Sender.

expéditif, *a.* Expeditious.

expédition, *s.f.* **I.** Expedition, dispatch (of business). **2.** (i) Copying, (ii) copy (of deed). **3.** (*a*) Dispatch(ing), forwarding. (*b*) Consignment. **4.** *E. au pôle sud,* expedition to the South Pole.

expéditionnaire. I. *s.m.* Sender. **2.** *a.* Expeditionary (force).

expérience, *s.f.* **I.** Experience. *Il a l'e. du monde,* he is a man of the world. **2.** Experiment, test.

expérimental, -aux, *a.* Experimental.

expérimenter, *v.tr.* To test, try (remedy). *Abs.* To make an experiment.
  expérimenté, *a.* Experienced; skilled.

expert. I. *a.* Expert, skilled; able. **2.** *s.m.* Expert; connoisseur. *Com:* Valuer, appraiser.

expertement, *adv.* Expertly.

expiation, *s.f.* Expiation. *Theol:* Atonement.

expiatoire, *a.* Expiatory.

expier, *v.tr.* To expiate, atone for.

expiration, *s.f.* Expiration. **I.** Breathing out. **2.** Expiry.

expirer, *v.* To expire. **I.** *v.tr.* To breathe out (air). **2.** *v.i.* (*a*) To die. (*b*) To come to an end.

explétif, *a. & s.m.* Expletive.

explicable, *a.* Explicable, explainable.

explicatif, *a.* Explanatory.

explication, *s.f.* Explanation. **Demander une explication à qn,** to call s.o. to account.

explicite, *a.* Explicit, clear, plain.

explicitement, *adv.* Explicitly, plainly.

expliquer, *v.tr.* (*a*) To explain, elucidate. (*b*) To explain, account for. *Je ne m'explique pas pourquoi . . .,* I can't understand why. . .
  s'expliquer, to explain oneself. *S'e. avec qn,* to have it out with s.o.

exploit, *s.m.* Exploit; feat; achievement.

exploitation, *s.f.* Exploitation, exploiting.

exploiter, *v.tr.* To exploit.

explorateur, -trice. I. *s.* Explorer. **2.** *a.* Exploring, exploratory.

exploration, *s.f.* Exploration.

explorer, *v.tr.* To explore.

explosible, *a.* Explosive.

explosif, *a. & s.m.* Explosive.

explosion, *s.f.* Explosion. **Faire explosion,** to explode, blow up.

exportateur, -trice. I. *s.* Exporter. **2.** *a.* Exporting.

exportation, *s.f.* Exportation.

exporter, *v.tr.* To export.

exposer, *v.tr.* **I.** (*a*) To exhibit, show. (*b*) To set out (plans). *Je leur ai exposé ma situation,* I explained to them how I was placed. **2.** To expose; to lay open. *E. sa vie,* to imperil one's life. **3.** To expose (hypocrite).
  exposé. I. *a.* (*a*) In an exposed position. (*b*) Liable, apt. **2.** *s.m.* Statement, account.

exposition, *s.f.* **I.** (*a*) Exhibition, show. (*b*) Exposure (to danger). (*c*) Exposition, statement. **2.** Aspect, exposure.

exprès¹, -esse. I. *a.* Express, explicit (order). "*Défense expresse de fumer,*" 'smoking strictly prohibited.' **2.** [ɛksprɛːs], *a. & s.m.* Express (messenger).

exprès² [ɛksprɛ], *adv.* Designedly, intentionally. *Je ne l'ai pas fait e.,* I didn't do it on purpose.

express, *a. & s.m.* Express (train).

expressément, *adv.* Expressly, explicitly.

expressif, *a.* Expressive.

expression, *s.f.* Expression. **I.** Squeezing out (of juice). **2.** Utterance, voicing; show, manifestation. **3.** Term, phrase.

exprimable, *a.* Expressible

exprimer, *v.tr.* To express. **I.** To squeeze out (juice). **2.** (*a*) To voice. (*b*) To show, betoken.

exproprier, *v.tr.* To expropriate.

expulser, *v.tr.* To expel; to eject.

expulsion, *s.f.* Expulsion; deportation (of alien); eviction (of tenant).

expurgation, *s.f.* Expurgation.

expurger, *v.tr.* (n. expurgeons) To expurgate.

exquis, *a.* Exquisite.

exquisement, *adv.* Exquisitely.

exsangue [-sɑ̃:g] *a.* Bloodless.

exsuder, *v.tr. & i.* To exude.

extase, *s.f.* Ecstasy; *Psy:* trance.

extasier (s'), *v.pr.* To go into ectasies.

extatique, *a.* Ecstatic.

extensible, *a.* Extending; expanding.

extension, *s.f.* **I.** Extension. (*a*) Stretching. (*b*) Spreading, enlargement. **2.** Extent.

exténuation, *s.f.* **I.** Extenuation, softening. **2.** Exhaustion (of mind).

exténuer, *v.tr.* **I.** To extenuate. soften. **2.** To exhaust.

extérieur. I. *a.* (*a*) Exterior, outer, external. (*b*) Foreign (trade). **2.** *s.m.* Exterior, outside.

extérieurement, *adv.* **I.** Externally, outwardly. **2.** On the surface; in appearance.

extermination, *s.f.* Extermination.

exterminer, *v.tr.* To exterminate, destroy.

externat, *s.m.* Day-school.

externe. I. *a.* (*a*) External, outer. *Angle e.,* exterior angle. *Pharm:* Pour l'usage externe, for outward application (*b*) Malade e., out-patient (at hospital). **2.** *s.* Day-pupil.

extincteur, *s.m.* Fire-extinguisher.

extinction, *s.f.* Extinction. **I.** (*a*) Extinguishing, putting out. (*b*) Abolition; paying off (of debt). **2.** (*a*) Dying out (of species). (*b*) Loss (of voice).

extirpation, *s.f.* Extirpation; eradication

extirper, *v.tr.* To extirpate, eradicate.

extorquer, *v.tr.* To extort; to wring (promise) (*à qn,* from s.o.)

extorsion, *s.f.* Extortion.

extra. I. *s.m.* Usu. *inv.* Extra. *Du vin d'e.,* extra-special wine. *Payer les extra(s),* to pay for the extras. **2.** *a.inv.* Extra-special.

extraction, *s.f.* Extraction. **I.** Extracting. **2.** Descent, lineage, origin.

extrader, *v.tr. Jur:* To extradite.

extradition, *s.f. Jur:* Extradition.

extra-fin, *a.* Superfine.

extraire, *v.tr.* (Conj. like TRAIRE) To extract, draw out, take out.

    extrait, *s.m.* **I.** Extract, essence. **2.** Extract, excerpt (from book).

extraordinaire, *a.* Extraordinary. Par extraordinaire, (i) for a wonder; (ii) for once in a while.

extraordinairement, *adv.* Extraordinarily.

extravagamment, *adv.* Extravagantly.

extravagance, *s.f.* Extravagance; absurdity.

extravagant, *a.* Extravagant; absurd.

extray-ant, -ons, etc. See EXTRAIRE.

extrême. I. *a.* Extreme. (*a*) Farthest, utmost. (*b*) Intense, excessive. (*c*) Drastic, severe. **2.** *s.m.* Extreme limit. *Pousser les choses à l'e.,* to carry matters to extremes.

extrêmement, *adv.* Extremely.

extrême-Orient (l'), *s.m.* The Far East

extrémiste, *s.m. & f* Extremist

extrémité, *s.f.* (*a*) Extremity, end; tip; point. (*b*) Extremity, extreme (of misery). Pousser qch. à l'extrémité, to carry sth. to extremes.

exubérance, *s.f.* Exuberance

exubérant, *a.* Exuberant.

exultation, *s.f.* Exultation.

exulter, *v.i.* To exult, rejoice.

Ézéchias [-kjɑ:s]. *Pr.n.m. B.Hist:* Hezekiah.

F

F, f [ɛf], *s.f.* (The letter) F, f.

fa, *s.m.inv. Mus:* (The note) F.

fable, *s.f.* (*a*) Fable. (*b*) Story, tale.

fabricant, *s.* Maker, manufacturer.

fabrication, *s.f.* **I.** Manufacture, making. **2.** C'est de la pure f., it's pure fabrication.

fabrique, *s.f.* **I.** Making, manufacture. Marque de fabrique. trade-mark. **2.** Factory, works.

fabriquer, *v.tr* **I.** To manufacture. **2.** *Pej:* To fabricate; to invent

fabuleux, *a.* **I.** Fabulous. **2.** *F:* Incredible.

façade, *s.f.* Facade, front(age).

face, *s.f.* Face. **I.** La f. des eaux, the face of the waters. **2.** (*a*) Face (of sth.). *F. avant,* front. (*b*) Head side (of coin). (*c*) Disque à double f., double-sided record. **3.** (*a*) Faire f. à des difficultés, to cope with difficulties. (*b*) Portrait de face, full-face portrait. *Vue de f.,* front-view. La maison (d')en face, the house opposite. Regarder qn (bien) en face, to look s.o. full in the face. **4.** *Prep.phr.* Face à, facing. En face de, opposite; over against.

face-à-main, s.m. Lorgnette. pl. Des faces-à-main.

facétie, s.f. Joke, jest.

facétieusement, adv. Facetiously.

facétieux, a. Facetious, waggish.

facette, s.f. Facet.

fâcher, v.tr. 1. To grieve. 2. To anger. Soit dit sans vous fâcher, if I may say so without offence. **se fâcher.** 1. To get angry. 2. Se f. avec qn, to fall out with s.o. **fâché,** a. 1. Sorry. Être f. de qch., to be sorry about sth. 2. Angry. Être f. contre qn, to be annoyed with s.o. 3. Être f. avec qn, to have fallen out with s.o.

fâcheusement, adv. Tiresomely; awkwardly.

fâcheux, a. Troublesome, tiresome. Position fâcheuse, awkward position. Il est f. que + sub., it is a pity that. . . .

facile, a. 1. Easy. (a) C'est f. à dire, it is more easily said than done. (b) (i) Homme f. à vivre, man easy to get on with. (ii) Pliable, weak. 2. Facile, ready, quick.

facilement, adv. Easily, readily.

facilité, s.f. 1. (a) Easiness (of task). Avec facilité, with ease. (b) Avoir la facilité de faire qch., to enjoy facilities for doing sth. 2. Aptitude, talent, facility. 3. Pliancy.

faciliter, v.tr. To facilitate.

façon, s.f. 1. (a) (i) Making, fashioning; (ii) make; workmanship. F. d'un habit, cut of a coat. "On prend à façon," 'customers' own materials made up.' (b) Cuir f. porc, imitation pigskin. 2. (a) Manner, mode, way. Je le ferai à ma façon, I shall do it (in) my own way. Je lui dis, façon de rire, que . . ., I said to him, by way of a joke, that. . . . De la bonne façon, properly. Arranger qn de (la) belle façon, to give s.o. a good dressing down. (b) Il entra sans façon(s), he entered unceremoniously. Sans plus de façons, without more ado. (c) De cette façon, thus. De toute façon j'irai, anyhow, I shall go. En aucune façon! by no means! 3. Conj.phr. De façon à, so as to.

faconde, s.f. Fluency of speech; F: the gift of the gab.

façonner, v.tr. To work, shape; to fashion.

fac(-)similé, s.m. Facsimile; exact copy. pl. Des fac(-)similés.

facteur, -trice, s. 1. (a) Carrier. (b) Carman (delivering parcels). (c) Postman. 2. Com: Agent, middleman. 3. s.m. Mth: Factor. F: Le facteur humain, the personal factor.

factice, a. Factitious; artificial, imitation.

factieux, a. Factious.

faction, s.f. 1. Sentry-duty, guard. 2. Faction; factious party.

factionnaire, s.m. Sentry, sentinel.

factotum [-tɔm], s.m. Factotum; handy man.

facture, s.f. Com: Invoice; bill (of sale).

facturer, v.tr. To invoice.

facultatif, a. Optional, facultative.

faculté, s.f. 1. (a) Option, right. (b) Faculty, ability. L'aimant a la f. d'attirer le fer, the magnet has the property of attracting iron. (c) pl. Resources, means. 2. Faculty (of medicine).

fade, a. Insipid, flavourless.

fadeur, s.f. Insipidity; sickliness.

fagot, s.m. Faggot; bundle of firewood. Sentir le fagot, to savour of heresy.

faible. 1. a. (a) Feeble, weak. (b) Brise f., light breeze. F. son, faint sound. Faibles ressources, scanty means. 2. s.m. Weakness, failing, foible. Avoir un faible pour qch., to have a weakness for sth.

faiblement, adv. Feebly, weakly; faintly.

faiblesse, s.f. 1. (a) Feebleness, weakness. (b) La f. humaine, human weakness. (c) Smallness (of sum). 2. F. chez qn, failing in s.o.

faiblir, v.i. To weaken; to grow weak(er). Ma vue faiblit, my sight is failing.

faïence, s.f. Crockery; earthenware.

faille [faːj]. See FALLOIR.

faillibilité [faji-], s.f. Fallibility.

faillible [faji-], a. Fallible.

faillir [fajiːr], v.i. (pr.p. faillant; pr.ind. je faux, il faut; fu. je faillirai, je faudrai) 1. To fail. F. à une promesse, to fail to keep a promise. Sans faillir, without fail. 2. Faillir + inf. (only in past hist. and compound tenses) J'ai failli manquer le train, I nearly missed the train.

failli, s. Bankrupt.

faillite [fajit], s.f. Com: Failure, bankruptcy, insolvency. Faire faillite, to go bankrupt, to fail.

faim, s.f. Hunger. Avoir faim, to be hungry. Manger à sa faim, to eat one's fill.

faîne, s.f. 1. Beech-nut. 2. pl. Beech-mast.

fainéant. 1. a. Idle, lazy, slothful. 2. s. Idler, sluggard.

faire, v.tr. (pr.p. faisant [fəzɑ̃]; p.p. fait; pr.ind. v. faites, ils font; pr.sub. je fasse; p.h. je fis; fu. je ferai) I. To make. 1. Ces vieilles gens sont ainsi faits, old people are like that. 2. (a) Statue faite en, de, marbre, statue made of marble. Vêtements tout faits, ready-made clothes. (b) Le mariage ne se fera pas, the marriage will not take place. 3. (a) Se f. des amis, to make friends. (b) Faire des provisions, to lay in provisions.

II. **faire,** to do. 1. (a) Que faire? what is to be done? Faites vite! look sharp! Vous allez avoir de quoi faire, you have your work cut out. Bonne à tout faire, general servant. Grand bien vous fasse! much good may it do you! C'est bien fait! it serves you right! (b) (To say) "Vous partez demain!" fit-il, "you leave to-morrow!" he said. 2. (a) F. la ronde, to go one's rounds. Voilà qui est fait, that's done, settled. Toute réflexion faite . . ., all things considered. . . . (b) F. de l'auto, to go in for

motoring. *Il fait son droit*, he is reading law.
3. *F. une promenade*, to go for a walk.
4. *Combien cela fait-il?* how much does that
come to? **5.** To be, constitute. **Cela fera
mon affaire**, that will suit me. **6.** To matter.
Qu'est-ce que ça fait? what does it matter?
Si cela ne vous fait rien, if you don't mind.
Cela ne fait rien, never mind. **7.** (Faire
replacing a head verb in the second term of
a comparison) *Pourquoi agir comme vous le
faites?* why do you act as you do?
III. faire. 1. To form. *Démarche faite
pour m'étonner*, step calculated to astonish
me. **2.** To arrange. *F. sa malle*, to pack one's
trunk. **A qui de faire?** whose deal is it?
3. *Qu'allez-vous f. de votre fils?* what are
you going to make of your son? **N'avoir que
faire de qch.**, to have no occasion for sth.
4. *F. le malade*, to sham illness. *F. l'imbécile*,
to play the fool.
IV. faire. 1. En faire. (a) *N'en faites
rien*, do no such thing. (b) **C'(en) est fait de
lui**, it's all up with him. **2. Y faire. Rien n'y
fit**, nothing availed. **Qu'y faire?** how can it
be helped? **3.** *F:* **La faire.** *On ne me la fait
pas!* nothing doing!
V. faire, *impers.* **1. Quel temps fait-il?**
what is the weather like? *Par le froid qu'il
fait*, in this cold weather. **2.** *Il fait mauvais
voyager par ces routes*, it is hard travelling
on these roads.
VI. faire. (Syntactical constructions)
1. *Je n'ai fait que le toucher*, I only touched it.
2. Je ne fais que d'arriver, I have only just
arrived. **3. Vous n'aviez que faire de parler**,
you had no business to speak.
VII. faire + *inf.* = causative verb. **1.**
(The noun or pron. object is the subject of
the inf.) (a) *Je le fis chanter*, I made him sing.
Faites-le entrer, show him in. (b) **Faire**
+ *v.pr.* (i) (Reflexive pron. omitted) *F.
asseoir qn*, to make s.o. sit down. (ii) Reflexive pron. retained) *Je le fis s'arrêter*, I
made him stop. **2.** (The noun or pron. is
the object of the inf.) (a) **Faire faire deux
exemplaires**, to have two copies made.
(b) **Se faire** + *inf.* *Un bruit se fit entendre*,
a noise was heard. **3. Faire faire qch. à qn**,
to cause, get, s.o. to do sth. *Faites-lui lire
cette lettre*, get him to read this letter.
se faire. 1. (a) To develop, mature.
Son style se fait, his style is forming. (b) To
become. *La nuit se fait*, night is falling.
(c) To adapt oneself. **Se faire à qch.**, to get
used to sth. (d) *La mer se fait*, the sea is
getting up. **2.** *Impers.* (a) **Il se fait tard**, it
is growing late. (b) *Il se fit un long silence*,
a long silence followed. **Comment se fait-il
que vous soyez en retard?** how is it that you
are late?
fait¹, *a.* Fully developed. *Homme f.*,
(full-)grown man.
fait², *s.m.* **1.** Act, deed. **Prendre qn sur
le fait**, to catch s.o. in the act. **Dire son fait

à qn, *F:* to talk straight to s.o. **2.** (a) Fact.
Prendre fait et cause pour qn, to take up the
cudgels for s.o. **Il est de fait que** + *ind.*, it
is a fact that. . . . **Aller droit au fait**, to go
straight to the point. **Être au fait de la
question**, to know how things stand. *Adv.phr.*
(i) **Au fait**, *que venez-vous faire ici?* after all,
what have you come here for? (ii) **En fait,
de fait**, as a matter of fact. *De f. cela est un
refus*, that is in effect a refusal. (iii) **De ce
fait**, thereby. *Prep.phr.* **En fait de**, as regards.
(b) Occurrence, happening.
fais, fais-ais, -ant, etc. See FAIRE.
faisan, *s.m.* (Coq) faisan, (cock-)pheasant.
faisceau, *s.m.* Bundle (of sticks). *F. d'ampoules électriques*, cluster of electric bulbs.
Mil: *Former les faisceaux*, to pile arms.
fait. See FAIRE.
fait-divers, *s.m.* *Journ:* News item. *Faits-
divers*, news in brief.
faîte, *s.m.* **1.** *Const:* Ridge (of roof). **2.** Top,
summit (of tree).
faites. See FAIRE.
faix, *s.m.* Burden, load.
falaise, *s.f.* Cliff.
fallacieux, *a.* Fallacious, misleading.
falloir, *v. impers. def.* (No *pr.p*; *p.p.* fallu;
pr.ind. il faut; *pr.sub.* il faille; *p.d.* il fallait;
fu. il faudra) **1.** To be wanting, lacking,
necessary. *Il lui faut un nouveau pardessus*, he
wants a new overcoat. *Il m'a fallu trois jours
pour le faire*, it took me three days to do it.
S'en falloir, to be lacking, wanting. *Je ne suis
pas satisfait, tant s'en faut*, I am not satisfied,
far from it. **Comme il faut**, proper(ly).
2. (a) **Falloir** + *inf.*, **falloir que** + *sub.*, to be
necessary. *Il nous faut le voir, il faut que nous
le voyions*, we must see him. **Il fallait voir ça!**
you ought to have seen it! **Il fallait le dire!**
why didn't you say so! *F:* *Faut-il qu'il soit
bête!* well, he *is* a fool! *F:* *C'est ce qu'il
faudra voir!* we must see about that!
(b) (With *le* = noun-clause) *Il viendra s'il
le faut*, he will come if necessary.
falsification, *s.f.* Falsification; forgery;
adulteration.
falsifier, *v.tr.* To falsify; *F:* to fake
(document); to adulterate.
fameusement, *adv.* *F:* Famously. *On s'est
f. amusé*, we had rare fun.
fameux, *a.* **1.** Famous. **2.** *F:* *Fameuse idée*,
capital idea. **Vous êtes un fameux menteur!**
you are a precious liar!
familial, -aux, *a.* Family (life).
familiariser (se), *v.pr.* To familiarize
oneself.
familiarité, *s.f.* Familiarity.
familier, *a.* **1.** Domestic; of the family.
Dieux familiers, household gods. **2.** Familiar.
(a) *Être f. avec qn*, to be on familiar terms, to
be intimate, with s.o. *Expression familière*,
colloquialism. *s.* *Un des familiers de la maison*,
a regular frequenter of the house. (b) *Visage
qui lui est f.*, face which is familiar, well-known,
to him.

5

familièrement, *adv.* Familiarly.
famille [-mi:j], *s.f.* Family; household. **Fils de famille,** youth of good social position. **En famille,** as a family party. **Cela tient de famille,** it runs in the family. **Esprit de famille,** clannishness.
famine, *s.f.* Famine, starvation.
fanal, -aux, *s.m.* (a) Lantern, light. *F. de tête,* head-light. (b) Beacon-light.
fanatique. 1. *a.* Fanatic(al). **2.** *s.* Fanatic.
fanatisme, *s.m.* Fanaticism.
faner (se), *v.pr.* To droop, wither, fade.
fanfare, *s.f.* **1.** (a) Flourish (of trumpets). (b) Fanfare. **2.** Brass band.
fanfaronnade, *s.f.* Piece of brag.
fange, *s.f.* Mud, mire, filth.
fangeux, *a.* Miry, muddy.
fantaisie, *s.f.* **1.** (a) Imagination, fancy. **De fantaisie,** imaginary. (b) *Mus:* Fantasia. **2.** Fancy, whim.
fantasque, *a.* Odd, whimsical.
fantassin, *s.m.* Foot-soldier, infantryman.
fantastique, *a.* Fantastic; fanciful.
fantoche, *s.m.* Marionette, puppet.
fantôme, *s.m.* Phantom, ghost, spectre. **Le Vaisseau Fantôme,** the Flying Dutchman.
faon [fã], *s.m.* Fawn.
farce, *s.f.* (a) *Th:* Farce. (b) *F:* Practical joke; prank.
farceur, -euse, *s.* **1.** Practical joker. **2.** Wag, joker, humorist; humbug.
farcir, *v.tr. Cu:* To stuff (poultry).
fard, *s.m.* Paint, rouge, make-up.
fardeau, *s.m.* Burden, load.
farder (se), *v.pr.* To make up; to rouge.
farinacé, *a.* Farinaceous, flour-like.
farine, *s.f.* Flour or meal. *F. de riz,* ground rice. *F:* **Ce sont gens de (la) même farine,** they are birds of a feather.
farouche, *a.* **1.** Fierce, wild, savage. **2.** (a) Shy, timid, coy. (b) Unsociable.
fascicule, *s.m.* Instalment (of publication).
fascination, *s.f.* Fascination, charm.
fasciner, *v.tr.* (a) To fascinate. (b) *F:* To bewitch.
fascisme, *s.m. Pol:* Fascism.
fasciste, *s.m. & f. Pol:* Fascist.
fass-e, -ions, etc. See FAIRE.
faste, *s.m.* Ostentation, display.
fastidieusement, *adv.* Fastidiously.
fastidieux, *a.* **1.** Dull, tedious, wearisome, irksome. *Besognes fastidieuses,* drudgery. *Orateur f.,* prosy speaker. **2.** (Food) that palls; fulsome (compliments).
fastueusement, *adv.* Ostentatiously; sumptuously.
fastueux, *a.* Ostentatious; sumptuous.
fat [fat]. **1.** *a.m.* Conceited, foppish. **2.** *s.m.* Conceited ass; fop.
fatal, -als, *a.* **1.** Fatal. *Coup f.,* mortal blow. **2.** Fated, inevitable. **C'est fatal,** it is bound to happen.
fatalement, *adv.* **1.** Fatally, mortally. **2.** Inevitably.

fatalisme, *s.m.* Fatalism.
fataliste. 1. *s.* Fatalist. **2.** *a.* Fatalistic.
fatalité, *s.f.* **1.** Fate, fatality. **2.** Mischance, calamity.
fatigant, *a.* **1.** Tiring, fatiguing. **2.** Tiresome, tedious.
fatigue, *s.f.* Fatigue, weariness.
fatiguer, *v.tr.* To fatigue, tire. **se fatiguer,** to tire; to get tired.
fatuité, *s.f.* Self-conceit, self-complacency.
faubourg, *s.m.* Suburb.
faubourien, -ienne, *a.* Suburban.
faucher, *v.tr.* **1.** To mow, cut, reap (field). **2.** To mow down (troops).
faucheur, -euse, *s.* **1.** Mower, reaper. **2.** *s.f.* Faucheuse, mowing-machine.
faucille [-si:j], *s.f.* Sickle; reaping-hook.
faucon, *s.m. Orn:* Falcon, hawk.
faudr-a, etc. See FAILLIR and FALLOIR.
faufiler, *v.tr.* (a) To tack, baste (seam). (b) To introduce stealthily; to slip in. **se faufiler,** to thread one's way. *Se f. le long du mur,* to creep along the wall.
faune[1], *s.m. Myth:* Faun.
faune[2], *s.f.* Fauna, animal life.
faussaire, *s.m. & f.* Forger.
fausse. See FAUX[1].
faussement, *adv.* Falsely, erroneously.
fausser, *v.tr.* To make false. **Fausser parole à qn,** to break one's word to s.o.
fausset[1], *s.m. Mus:* Falsetto.
fausset[2], *s.m.* Spigot.
fausseté, *s.f.* **1.** Falseness, falsity. **2.** Falsehood, untruth. **3.** Duplicity
faut. See FAILLIR and FALLOIR.
faute, *s.f.* **1.** Lack, need, want. **Faire faute,** to be lacking. **Sans faute,** without fail. **Faute de,** for want of. **Faute de quoi . . .,** failing which. . . . **2.** (a) Fault, mistake. (b) Transgression, offence.
fauteuil [-tœ:j], *s.m.* **1.** Arm-chair, easy-chair. *Th:* F. *d'orchestre,* orchestra stall. *F. de balcon,* dress-circle seat. **2.** Chair (at meeting).
fautif, *a.* **1.** Faulty, incorrect **2.** In fault.
fauve. 1. *a.* Fawn-coloured. **2.** *s.m.* (a) Fawn (colour). (b) *Les (grands) fauves,* wild beasts (lions, tigers, etc.).
fauvette, *s.f. Orn:* Warbler.
faux[1]**, fausse. I.** *a.* False. **1.** Untrue. **2.** Not genuine. (a) **Fausse monnaie,** counterfeit coin(age). *adv.* **Rire qui sonne faux,** laugh that has a false ring. (b) Treacherous. *F:* **Faux bonhomme,** shifty customer. **3.** Wrong, mistaken. **Présenter la conduite de qn sous un faux jour,** to place s.o.'s conduct in a false light. **Faire un faux pas,** to blunder. **Faire fausse route,** *F:* to be on the wrong track. *adv.* **Chanter faux,** to sing out of tune. *Adv.phr.* **A faux,** wrongly.
II. faux, *s.m.* **1.** Le *f.,* the false. **2.** *Jur:* Forgery.
faux[2]**,** *s.f.* Scythe.
faux[3]**.** See FAILLIR.

faux-monnayeur, *s.m.* Coiner.
faveur, *s.f.* Favour. *(a) Com :* **Prix de faveur,** preferential price. **Billet de faveur,** complimentary ticket. **A la faveur de,** by the help of. *(b)* **Faire une faveur à qn,** to do s.o. a kindness.
favorable, *a.* Favourable.
favorablement, *adv.* Favourably.
favori, -ite. **1.** *a. & s.* Favourite. **2.** *s.m.pl.* (Side-)whiskers.
favoriser, *v.tr.* To favour, to be partial to.
favoritisme, *s.m.* Favouritism.
fébrile, *a. F:* Feverish (preparations).
fécond, *a.* Prolific, fruitful, fertile.
fécondité, *s.f.* Fecundity **1.** Fruitfulness. **2.** Fertility.
fédéral, -aux, *a. & s.m.* Federal.
fédération, *s.f.* Federation.
fée, *s.f.* Fairy.
féerie, *s.f.* **1.** Enchantment. **2.** Fairyland.
féerique, *a.* Fairy-like, enchanting.
feign-ant, -ais, -is, etc. See FEINDRE.
feindre, *v.* (Conj. like PEINDRE) *v.tr.* To feign, simulate, sham. **Feindre de faire qch.,** to pretend to do sth.
feinte, *s.f.* Feint, pretence.
fêler, *v.tr.* To crack (glass).
fêlé, *a.* Cracked ; crack-brained (inventor). *Il a le cerveau f.,* he is a bit cracked.
félicitations, *s.f. pl.* Congratulations.
félicité, *s.f.* Felicity, bliss(fulness).
féliciter, *v.tr. F. qn de qch.,* to congratulate s.o. on sth.
se féliciter *de qch.,* to be pleased with sth.
félin, *a.* Feline. *(a) Z :* Cat (family). *s. Les grands félins,* the great cats. *(b) F :* Catlike.
fêlure, *s.f.* Crack (in china) ; split (in wood). *F :* Il a une fêlure, he's a bit cracked.
femelle, *s.f. & a.* Female (animal) ; she-(animal) ; cow-(elephant) ; hen-(bird).
féminin. **1.** *a.* Feminine. **2.** *s.m. Gram :* Feminine gender.
femme [fam], *s.f.* **1.** Woman. **2.** Wife. **3.** **Femme de chambre,** housemaid ; *Nau :* stewardess. **Femme de charge,** housekeeper.
fenaison, *s.f.* Haymaking ; hay-harvest.
fendre, *v.tr.* To split. *F. l'air,* to rend the air. **Fendre la foule,** to force one's way through the crowd. **Il gèle à pierre fendre,** it is freezing hard.
fenêtre, *s.f.* Window. **Mettre la tête à la fenêtre,** to thrust one's head out of the window.
fenouil [-nu:j], *s.m. Bot :* Fennel.
fente, *s.f. (a)* Crack, crevice, chink. *(b)* Slot.
féodal, -aux, *a.* Feudal.
fer, *s.m.* **1.** Iron. **2.** *(a)* **Fer de lance,** spearhead. *(b)* Sword. **Croiser le fer avec qn,** to cross swords with s.o. **3.** *Tls :* **Fer à souder,** soldering-iron. **Marquer au fer chaud,** to brand. **4.** *pl.* Irons, chains, fetters. **Être aux fers,** to be in irons. **5.** **Fer à, de, cheval,** horseshoe. *F :* **Tomber les quatre fers en l'air,** to go sprawling.
fer-ai, -as, etc. See FAIRE.
ferblantier, *s.m.* Tinman, tinsmith.

férié, *a.* Jour férié, (general) holiday.
férir, *v.tr.* (Used only in inf. and in *p.p.* **féru**) To strike. **Sans coup férir,** without striking a blow ; without firing a shot. **Être féru d'une idée,** to be set on an idea.
ferler, *v.tr.* To furl (sail).
ferme[1]. **1.** *a.* Firm, steady. *F:* **Attendre qn de pied ferme,** to wait resolutely for s.o. **2.** *adv.* Firmly. **Tenir ferme,** to stand fast. **J'y travaille ferme,** I am hard at it.
ferme[2], *s.f.* Farm.
fermement, *adv.* Firmly, steadily.
ferment, *s.m.* Ferment.
fermentation, *s.f.* Fermentation.
fermenter, *v.i.* To ferment.
fermer. **1.** *v.tr. (a)* To close, shut. **Fermer sa porte à qn,** to close one's door against s.o. **F. les rideaux,** to draw the curtains. **Fermer boutique,** to shut up shop. *On ferme !* closing time ! **Fermer l'électricité,** to switch off the light. *(b)* **Fermer la marche,** tc bring up the rear. **2.** *v.i.* (Of door) To close, shut.
se fermer, to close, shut.
fermé, *a.* **1.** Closed. **A la nuit fermée,** when night had fallen. **2.** Visage fermé, inscrutable countenance.
fermeté, *s.f.* Firmness ; steadfastness.
fermeture, *s.f.* **1.** Closing, shutting. **F. de la pêche,** close of the fishing season. **2.** Closing apparatus. **Fermeture éclair,** zip fastener.
fermier, *s. (a)* Tenant (of farm). *(b)* Farmer ; *f.* farmer's wife.
fermoir, *s.m.* Clasp, catch, fastener.
féroce, *a.* Ferocious, savage, wild, fierce.
férocement, *adv.* Ferociously.
férocité, *s.f.* Ferocity, ferociousness.
ferraille [fɛrɑ:j], *s.f.* Old iron, scrap-iron.
ferrer, *v.tr.* To fit, mount, (sth.) with iron. **Ferrer un cheval,** to shoe a horse.
ferré, *a.* Iron-shod. **Être ferré en mathématiques,** to be well up in mathematics.
ferret, *s.m.* Tag, tab.
ferrugineux, *a.* Ferruginous.
fertile, *a.* Fertile, fruitful.
fertilisation, *s.f.* Fertilization, fertilizing.
fertiliser, *v.tr.* To fertilize ; to make fruitful.
fertilité, *s.f.* Fertility ; fruitfulness.
féru. See FÉRIR.
fervemment, *adv.* Fervently.
fervent. **1.** *a.* Fervent, ardent. **2.** *s.* Devotee.
ferveur, *s.f.* Fervour ; ardour.
fesse, *s.f.* Buttock.
fesser, *v.tr.* To spank (s.o.).
festin, *s.m.* Feast, banquet.
feston, *s.m.* Festoon.
festoyer, *v.i.* (je festoie) To feast, carouse.
fête, *s.f.* **1.** Feast, festival. Jour de fête, holiday. **Fête de qn,** s.o.'s name-day. **Souhaiter la fête à qn.** to wish s.o. many happy returns. **Ce n'est pas tous les jours fête,** we'll make this an occasion. **2.** Fête, entertainment. **3.** Festivity. **Le village était en fête,** the village was holiday-making.

fêter, *v.tr.* **1.** Fêter la naissance de qn, to celebrate s.o.'s birthday. **2.** Fêter qn, to fête s.o.

fétiche, *s.m.* Fetish.

fétide, *a.* Fetid, stinking.

feu¹, feux, *s.m.* Fire. **1.** (*a*) *F:* Il fait feu de tout bois, nothing comes amiss to him. Visage en feu, flushed face. Prendre feu, (i) to catch fire ; (ii) *F:* to fly into a passion. Faire la part du feu, *F:* to cut one's losses. Voulez-vous bien me donner du feu? will you kindly give me a light? (*b*) Heat, ardour. **2.** (*a*) *Faire du feu,* to light a fire. (*b*) J'en mettrais la main au feu, I would swear to it. Faire mourir qn à petit feu, to kill s.o. by inches. (*c*) N'avoir ni feu ni lieu, to have neither hearth nor home. **3.** Armes à feu, fire-arms. Faire feu, to fire. Faire long feu, to hang fire. Tué au feu, killed in action. **4.** (*a*) Light (of lighthouse). *Adm:* Feux de circulation, traffic lights. (*b*) N'y voir que du feu, to be dazzled.

feu², *a.* Late (= deceased). **1.** (Between article and sb., and variable) *La feue reine,* the late queen. **2.** (Preceding the article and inv.) *Feu la reine,* the late queen.

feuillage [fœja:ʒ], *s.m.* Foliage.

feuille [fœ:j], *s.f.* **1.** Leaf (of plant). **2.** *F. de métal,* sheet of metal. **3.** *F. de papier,* sheet of paper. Feuille de route, *Mil:* Marching orders.

feuilleter [fœjte], *v.tr.* (je feuillette) To turn over the pages of (book).

feutre, *s.m.* **1.** Felt. **2.** Felt hat.

feutrer, *v.tr. F:* A pas feutrés, with noiseless tread.

fève, *s.f.* Bean.

février, *s.m.* February.

fez [fɛ:z], *s.m.* Fez.

fi, *int.* Fie ! for shame ! Faire fi de qch., to turn up one's nose at sth.

fiacre, *s.m.* Cab.

fiançailles [-sɑ:j], *s.f.pl.* Betrothal (*avec,* to).

fiancer (se), *v.pr.* To become engaged.

fiancé, *s.* Fiancé, fiancée.

fiasco, *s.m.inv.* Fiasco.

fibre, *s.f.* Fibre.

fibreux, *a.* Fibrous, stringy.

ficeler, *v.tr.* (je ficelle) To tie up.

ficelle, *s.f.* String, twine.

fiche, *s.f.* (*a*) Slip (of paper). (*b*) Card, ticket (of membership). (*c*) Index card.

ficher, *v.tr.* (*a*) *F:* Fichez-moi la paix ! shut up ! (*b*) Fichez(-moi) le camp ! out you go ! **se fiche(r).** *F:* Je m'en fiche (pas mal) ! I don't care a rap !

fichier, *s.m.* Card-index.

fictif, *a.* Fictitious, imaginary.

fiction, *s.f.* Fiction, invention, fabrication.

fidèle, *a.* Faithful, loyal, staunch.

fidèlement, *adv.* Faithfully.

fidélité, *s.f.* Fidelity, faithfulness. Serment de fidélité, oath of allegiance.

fiel, *s.m.* Gall.

fielleux, *a. F:* Rancorous, bitter (remark).

fier¹ [fjɛ:r], *a.* **1.** Proud. **2.** Haughty, stuck-up. **3.** *F: Tu m'as fait une fière peur,* a rare fright you gave me.

fier² (se), to trust. Se fier à qn, to trust s.o. Fiez-vous à moi, leave it to me.

fièrement, *adv.* **1.** Proudly. **2.** Haughtily.

fierté, *s.f.* **1.** Pride, self-respect. **2.** Pride, haughtiness.

fièvre, *s.f.* Fever.

fiévreusement, *adv.* Feverishly.

fiévreux, *a.* Feverish.

fifre, *s.m.* Fife.

figer, *v.tr.* (figeant) To coagulate, congeal. **se figer,** to coagulate. Sourire figé, set smile.

figue, *s.f.* **1.** Fig. **2.** Figue de Barbarie, prickly pear.

figuier, *s.m.* **1.** Fig-tree. **2.** *F. de Barbarie,* prickly pear.

figuratif, *a.* Figurative, emblematic.

figurativement, *adv.* Figuratively.

figure, *s.f.* **1.** Figure, form, shape. *Figures de cire,* waxworks. Figure de mots, figure of speech. **2.** (*a*) Face, countenance. *Cards:* Les figures, the court-cards. (*b*) Appearance.

figurer. 1. *v.tr.* To represent. **2.** *v.i.* To appear, figure. *Th:* Figurer sur la scène, to walk on. **se figurer** qch., to imagine sth. *Figurez-vous la situation,* picture the situation to yourself. **figuré,** *a.* Figurative. *Adv.phr.* Au figuré, in the figurative sense ; figuratively.

fil [fil], *s.m.* **1.** (*a*) Thread. *Fil d'Écosse,* sewing-cotton. Finesses cousues de fil blanc, obvious tricks. Brouiller les fils, to muddle things up. Fils de la Vierge, gossamer. (*b*) *Fil métallique,* wire. Fil de fer, iron wire ; *F:* wire. *Tp:* Être au bout du fil, to be on the phone. **2.** Grain (of wood). **3.** Fil de l'eau, current. Au fil de l'eau, with the stream. **4.** (Cutting) edge.

filament, *s.m.* Filament.

filant, *a.* Étoile filante, shooting star.

filasse, *s.f.* **1.** Tow. **2.** Oakum.

file, *s.f.* File (of soldiers). En file indienne, in single file. Deux heures à la file, two hours on end.

filer. I. *v.tr.* **1.** To spin (flax). *F:* Filer doux, to sing small. **2.** (*a*) Nau : To pay out (cable). (*b*) To prolong, draw out. **3.** (Of detective) To shadow. **II. filer,** *v.i.* To slip by. *Les autos filaient sur la route,* cars were bowling along the road. *F:* Filer (en vitesse), to cut and run. Filer à l'anglaise, to take French leave.

filet¹, *s.m.* **1.** Small thread. (*a*) *F. de lumière,* thin streak of light. *F. d'eau,* thin trickle of water. (*b*) *F:* Avoir le filet, to be tongue-tied. **2.** *Cu:* F. de bœuf, fillet, undercut, of beef.

filet², *s.m.* Net(ting). *Rail:* F. à bagages, luggage rack.

filial, -als, -aux. **I.** *a.* Filial. **2.** *s.f.* Filiale. Branch (of association).
filigrane, *s.m.* **I.** Filigree (work). **2.** Watermark (of bank-notes).
fille [fi:j], *s.f.* **I.** Daughter. **2.** Girl. Jeune fille, girl, young woman. Nom de jeune fille, maiden name. Vieille fille, old maid. Rester fille, to remain single.
filleul [fijœl], *s.* God-child.
film [film], *s.m.* Film. *F. d'actualité,* news film, news reel.
filmer, *v.tr. Cin:* To film (scene).
filon, *s.m. Min:* Vein, seam, lode (of metal).
filou, *s.m.* Pickpocket, thief.
filouter, *v.tr.* F. qn, to swindle, cheat, s.o.
fils [fis], *s.m.* Son. C'est bien le fils de son père, he's a chip of the old block. Être le fils de ses œuvres, to be a self-made man. M. Duval fils, Mr Duval junior.
filtre, *s.m.* Filter, percolator.
filtrer. **I.** *v.tr.* To filter, strain. **2.** *v.i. & pr.* To filter, percolate.
fin[1], *s.f.* **I.** End, close, termination. Mener une affaire à bonne fin, to bring a matter to a successful issue. *F:* Tu es stupide à la fin! you really are very stupid! **2.** End, aim, purpose. A quelle fin? for what purpose? A deux fins, serving a double purpose. *Prov:* Qui veut la fin veut les moyens, where there's a will there's a way.
fin[2], *a.* (a) Fine, first class. Vins fins, choice wines. *s.f. F:* Une fine, a liqueur brandy. (b) Subtle, shrewd. Avoir l'oreille fine, to be quick of hearing. Fin comme l'ambre, sharp as a needle. *s.m.* Jouer au plus fin, to have a battle of wits. (c) Fine, small (rain). Traits fins, delicate features.
final, -als, *a.* Final.
finalement, *adv.* Finally.
finalité, *s.f.* Finality.
finance, *s.f.* Finance. *pl.* Finances, resources.
financer, *v.tr.* (n. finançons) To finance.
financier. **I.** *a.* Financial. **2.** *s.m.* Financier.
finement, *adv.* **I.** Delicately. **2.** Shrewdly.
finesse, *s.f.* Fineness. **I.** Good quality (of material); delicacy (of execution). **2.** (a) Subtlety, shrewdness. *F. d'ouïe,* quickness of hearing. (b) Cunning, guile. (c) Piece of cunning. **3.** Fineness (of dust).
finir. **I.** *v.tr.* To finish, end. **2.** *v.i.* To end, finish. Il finira mal, he will come to a bad end. En finir avec qch., to have done with sth. Cela n'en finit pas, there is no end to it. Pour en finir, to cut the matter short.
fini, *a.* **I.** Finished, ended. **2.** (a) Accomplished. Acteur f., consummate actor. (b) *s.m.* Finish. Articles d'un beau f., highly finished goods. **3.** Finite.
finlandais. **I.** *a.* Finnish. **2.** *s.* Finn.
Finlande. *Pr.n.f. Geog:* Finland.
finnois. **I.** *a.* Finnish. **2.** (a) *s.* Finn. (b) *s.m.Ling:* Finnish.

firmament, *s.m.* Firmament, sky.
fi-s, -t. See FAIRE.
fiscal, -aux, *a.* Fiscal.
fiss-e, -es, etc. See FAIRE.
fission, *s.f.* Splitting.
fissure, *s.f.* Fissure, cleft.
fixe, *a.* **I.** Fixed, firm. Regard f., intent gaze. **2.** Fixed, regular, settled. Beau (temps) fixe, set fair. *P.N:* Arrêt fixe, all cars stop here.
fixement, *adv.* Fixedly.
fixer, *v.tr.* **I.** To fix; to make (sth.) firm, fast. Fixer l'attention de qn, to hold s.o.'s attention. Fixer qn, to stare at s.o. **2.** To fix, determine.
fixité, *s.f.* Fixity.
flaccidité, *s.f.* Flaccidity, flabbiness.
flacon, *s.m.* Bottle; flask.
flagellation, *s.f.* Flagellation, scourging.
flageller, *v.tr.* To scourge, flog.
flagorner, *v.tr.* To flatter; to toady to.
flagorneur, -euse, *s.* Flatterer, toady.
flagrant, *a.* Flagrant, glaring. Pris en flagrant délit, caught in the act.
flair, *s.m.* (a) (Of dogs) Scent, (sense of) smell. (b) *F:* (Of pers.) Flair.
flairer, *v.tr.* (a) (Of dog) To scent. *F: F. le danger,* to smell danger. (b) To smell (flower).
flamand. **I.** *a.* Flemish. **2.** *s.* Fleming. **3.** *s.m. Ling:* Flemish.
flamant, *s.m. Orn:* Flamingo.
flambant, *a.* Blazing, flaming. *adv.* Habit (tout) flambant neuf, brand-new coat.
flambeau, *s.m.* **I.** Torch. **2.** Candlestick.
flamber. **I.** *v.i.* To flame, blaze. **2.** *v.tr.* To singe (fowl). Il est flambé, his goose is cooked.
flamboyant, *a.* **I.** Flaming, blazing (fire); fiery (eyes). **2.** Flamboyant.
flamboyer, *v.i.* (il flamboie) To blaze.
flamme, *s.f.* **I.** Flame. Tout en flammes, ablaze. Par le fer et la flamme, with fire and sword. **2.** Pennant, streamer.
flanc, *s.m.* Flank, side. Prêter le flanc à la critique, to lay oneself open to criticism.
Flandre. *Pr.n.f. Geog:* Flanders.
flanelle, *s.f.* Flannel. F. de coton, flannelette.
flâner, *v.i.* To lounge about; to stroll.
flânerie, *s.f.* Dawdling, idling.
flâneur, -euse, *s.* (a) Idler, dawdler; stroller. (b) Loafer.
flanquer, *v.tr. F:* To throw. Flanquer un coup de pied à qn, to land s.o. a kick. Flanquer qn à la porte, to throw s.o. out.
flaque, *s.f.* **I.** Puddle, pool. **2.** Flaque de neige, patch of snow.
flasque, *a.* Flaccid (flesh); flabby (hand). Se sentir f., to feel limp.
flatter, *v.tr.* **I.** To stroke, caress. **2.** To delight. Flatter les caprices de qn, to humour s.o.'s fancies. **3.** To flatter.
se flatter, to flatter oneself, delude oneself.
flatterie, *s.f.* Flattery, blandishment.
flatteur, -euse. **I.** *a.* (a) Pleasing (taste); fond (hope). (b) Flattering. **2.** *s.* Flatterer.

fléau, -aux, *s.m.* **1.** *Husb:* Flail. **2.** Scourge ; plague. **3.** Beam, arm (of balance).

flèche, *s.f.* **1.** (*a*) Arrow. **Faire flèche de tout bois,** to use every means to attain an end. (*b*) Direction-sign, arrow. (*c*) Pointer (of balance). **2.** (*a*) Spire (of church). (*b*) *Conduire en flèche,* to drive tandem.

fléchir. 1. *v.tr.* (*a*) To bend. (*b*) To move to pity. **2.** *v.i.* To give way, bend ; to sag.

fléchissement, *s.m.* **1.** Bending. **2.** Sagging.

flegmatique, *a.* Phlegmatic. **1.** Lymphatic. **2.** *F:* Imperturbable, stolid.

flegme, *s.m.* Phlegm.

Flessingue. *Pr.n. Geog:* Flushing.

flétan, *s.m. Ich:* Halibut.

flétrir[1], *v.tr.* To blight (hopes).
se flétrir, to fade ; to wither.

flétrir[2], *v.tr. F. la réputation de qn,* to cast a slur on s.o.'s character.

fleur, *s.f.* **1.** Flower. (*a*) Blossom, bloom. (*b*) *F:* **Être dans la fleur de l'âge,** to be in the prime of life. (*c*) Bloom (on peach). **2.** (= SURFACE) **A fleur d'eau,** at water-level. **Voler à fleur d'eau,** to skim the water. **Yeux à fleur de tête,** prominent eyes

fleuret, *s.m.* (Fencing) foil.

fleurir, *v.i.* (*a*) (Of plants) To flower, bloom. (*b*) (*pr.p.* **florissant**) To flourish, prosper.
fleuri, *a.* **1.** In bloom. **2.** *Teint f.,* florid complexion.

fleuriste, *s.m. & f.* Florist

fleuve, *s.m.* (Large) river.

flexibilité, *s.f.* Flexibility ; pliability.

flexible, *a.* Flexible, pliable.

flibustier, *s.m.* Freebooter, buccaneer.

flirt [flœrt], *s.m. F:* **1.** Flirtation, flirting. **2.** Philanderer.

flirter, *v.i.* To flirt.

flocon, *s.m.* (*a*) Flake. (*b*) *F. de laine,* tuft, flock, of wool.

floconneux, *a.* Fleecy, fluffy.

floral, -aux, *a.* Floral.

flore, *s.f. Bot:* Flora.

floriss-ait, -ant, etc. See FLEURIR.

florissant, *a.* Flourishing, prosperous.

flot, *s.m.* **1.** (*a*) Wave. (*b*) *F:* Flots de larmes, floods of tears. *Couler à flots,* to gush forth. **2.** Floating. **A flot,** afloat. *F:* **Remettre qn à flot,** to restore s.o.'s fortunes.

flottaison, *s.f.* Floating.

flottant, *a.* Floating. *Robe flottante,* flowing robe.

flotte, *s.f.* Fleet.

flotter. 1. *v.i.* (*a*) To float. (*b*) To wave (in the wind). (*c*) To waver. **2.** *v.tr. F. du bois,* to float timber.

flotteur, *s.m.* **1.** Raftsman. **2.** Float.

flottille [-tiːj], *s.f. Navy:* Flotilla.

flou, *a.* Woolly (outline) ; hazy (horizon). *Cheveux flous,* fluffy hair.

fluctuation, *s.f.* Fluctuation.

fluctuer, *v.i.* To fluctuate.

fluet, -ette, *a.* Thin, slender.

fluide, *a. & s.m.* Fluid.

fluidité, *s.f.* Fluidity.

fluor, *s.m. Ch:* Fluorine.

flûte, *s.f.* **1.** Flute. *Petite f.,* piccolo. **2.** Long thin roll (of bread). **3.** *int. P:* = ZUT.

flûté, *a. Voix flûtée,* (i) soft, flute-like, voice ; (ii) piping voice.

fluvial, -aux, *a.* Fluvial ; river (police)

flux [fly], *s.m.* Flow ; flood.

fluxion, *s.f. Med:* Fluxion, inflammation

focal, -aux, *a.* Focal

foi, *s.f.* Faith. **1.** *Manque de foi,* breach of faith. **Ma foi, oui!** indeed, yes! **Foi d'honnête homme,** on the word of a gentleman. **2.** Belief, trust. **Avoir foi en qn,** to have faith in s.o. **3.** (Religious) faith, belief.

foie, *s.m.* Liver.

foin, *s.m.* Hay. *F:* **Mettre du foin dans ses bottes,** to feather one's nest.

foire, *s.f.* Fair.

fois, *s.f.* Time, occasion. **Une fois,** once. **Deux fois,** twice. **Encore une fois,** once more. **Une (bonne) fois pour toutes,** once (and) for all. **De fois à autre,** from time to time. **A la fois,** at one and the same time.

foison, *s.f.* **A foison,** plentifully ; in abundance.

foisonner, *v.i.* To abound (*de,* in, with).

fol, *a.* See FOU.

folâtre, *a.* Playful, frisky, frolicsome.

folâtrer, *v.i.* To sport, romp, frolic.

folie, *s.f.* **1.** Madness. **Être pris de folie,** to go mad. **2.** Folly ; piece of folly. **Dire des folies,** to talk wildly.

folio, *s.m.* Folio.

folle. See FOU.

follement, *adv.* Madly. **1.** Foolishly, unwisely. **2.** Extravagantly.

follet, -ette, *a.* **1.** **Feu follet,** will-o'-the-wisp. **2.** *Cheveux follets,* stray lock(s) of hair.

fomenter, *v.tr.* To foment.

foncer, *v.i.* (n. fonçons) *F. sur qn,* to rush, swoop (down), upon s.o.
foncé, *a.* Dark (colour). **Des rubans bleu foncé,** dark-blue ribbons.

foncier, *a.* **1.** Of the land. **Propriété foncière,** landed property. **2.** *Bon sens f.,* innate common sense.

foncièrement, *adv.* Fundamentally ; at bottom.

fonction, *s.f.* Function, office. (*a*) **Entrer en fonctions,** to take up one's duties. **Faire fonction de . . .,** to act as. . . . (*b*) *Fonctions du cœur,* functions of the heart.

fonctionnaire, *s.m.* Civil servant ; official.

fonctionnement, *s.m.* Functioning, working.

fonctionner, *v.i.* **1.** To function. **2.** To act, work. *Les trains ne fonctionnent plus,* the trains are no longer running.

fond, *s.m.* **1.** (*a*) Bottom (of well). *F. d'une culotte,* seat of a pair of breeches. **Au fin fond de . . .,** at the very bottom of. . . . (*b*) Bottom, bed (of the sea). *Grands fonds,* ocean deeps. *Hauts, petits, fonds,* shallows.

Adv.phr. **A fond**, thoroughly. *Visser une pièce à f.*, to screw a piece home. **2.** Foundation. **Rebâtir une maison de fond en comble**, to rebuild a house from top to bottom. **Faire fond sur qch.**, to rely on sth. **Cheval qui a du fond**, horse with staying power. *Journ:* **Article de fond**, leading article. **Au fond, at bottom. 3.** Back, far end. *F. d'un tableau*, background of a picture.

fondamental, -aux, *a.* Fundamental; basic. **Couleurs fondamentales**, primary colours.

fondant. 1. *a.* Melting. **2.** *s.m.* Fondant.

fondateur, -trice, *s.* Founder.

fondation, *s.f.* (*a*) Founding. (*b*) (Fund for) endowment; foundation. (*c*) (Endowed) establishment, institution.

fondement, *s.m.* Foundation; base.

fonder, *v.tr.* To found. *F. un commerce*, to start a business.
    se fonder *sur qch.*, to place one's reliance on sth.
    fondé, *a.* Founded, justified.

fondre. 1. *v.tr.* (*a*) To smelt. (*b*) To melt. (*c*) To cast (bell). (*d*) To dissolve, melt. (*e*) To blend (colours). **2.** *v.i.* (*a*) To melt. (*b*) To melt, dissolve. *F:* **Fondre en larmes**, to dissolve in(to) tears. **3.** *v.i.* To swoop down (upon the prey).

fondrière, *s.f.* (*a*) Hollow (in ground). (*b*) Bog, quagmire. (*c*) Muddy hole (in road).

fonds, *s.m.* **1.** (*a*) **Fonds de commerce**, business. (*b*) Stock(-in-trade). **2.** (*a*) Funds. **Rentrer dans ses fonds**, to get one's money back. (*b*) Means, resources. **Placer son argent à fonds perdu**, to purchase a life annuity.

font. See FAIRE.

fontaine, *s.f.* **1.** Spring, source, well. **2.** Fountain.

fonte¹, *s.f.* **1.** (*a*) Melting (of snow). (*b*) Smelting. (*c*) Casting, founding. **2.** Cast iron. **3.** *Typ:* Fount.

fonte², *s.f.* **1.** Holster. **2.** Leather pocket.

fonts, *s.m.pl. Ecc:* Font.

for, *s.m.* **Dans son for intérieur**, in his heart of hearts.

forain, *a.* **Spectacle forain**, travelling show.

forban, *s.m.* Corsair, pirate, buccaneer.

forçat, *s.m.* Convict.

force, *s.f.* **1.** Strength, force, vigour. (*a*) **Mourir dans la force de l'âge**, to die in the prime of life. **Être à bout de forces**, to be exhausted. **Tour de force**, feat (of strength or skill). (*b*) Force, violence **Force majeure**, circumstances outside one's control. **Force lui fut d'obéir**, he had no alternative but to obey. *Prov:* **La force prime le droit**, might is right. **De gré ou de force**, willy-nilly. **De toute force il nous faut . . .**, we absolutely must. . . . **2.** Force, power. **3.** *a.inv.* **Force gens**, many people. **4.** **A force de**, by dint of, by means of.

forcément, *adv.* Perforce.

forcené. 1. *a.* Frantic, mad, frenzied. **2.** *s.* Madman, madwoman.

forcer, *v.tr.* (n. **forçons**) To force. **1.** To compel. **2.** (*a*) **Forcer qch.**, to do violence to sth. **Forcer la consigne**, to force one's way in. (*b*) *F:* **Forcer la note**, to overdo it. **3.** *v.i. F. de vitesse*, to increase speed.
    forcé, *a.* Forced. **1.** Compulsory. **2.** Strained. *Exemple f.*, far-fetched example.

forer, *v.tr.* To drill, bore; to sink (a well).

forestier, *a.* Pertaining to a forest.

foret, *s.m. Tls:* Drill.

forêt, *s.f.* Forest.

forfait¹, *s.m.* Heinous crime.

forfait², *s.m.* Contract. **Acheter qch. à forfait**, to buy sth. outright.

forfaitaire, *a.* Contractual. **Marché forfaitaire**, (transaction by) contract; outright purchase.

forge, *s.f.* **1.** Smithy. **2.** Usu. *pl.* Ironworks.

forger, *v.tr.* (n. **forgeons**) To forge. **1.** *Fer forgé*, wrought iron. *Prov:* **En forgeant on devient forgeron**, practice makes perfect. **2.** To forge (document); to make up (excuse).

forgeron, *s.m.* (Black)smith.

formaliste, *a.* Formal, stiff.

formalité, *s.f.* **1.** Formality. *F:* **Sans autre formalité**, without further ado. **2.** *F:* **Sans formalité(s)**, without ceremony.

formation, *s.f.* Formation. **1.** Forming; moulding (of character). **2.** Make-up (of train).

forme, *s.f.* **1.** Form, shape. **2.** Form; method of procedure. **Renvoyer qn sans autre forme de procès**, to dismiss s.o. without ceremony **Faire qch. dans les formes**, to do sth. with due decorum. **Pour la forme**, for form's sake. **3.** *Ind:* Last; *pl.* boot-trees. **Chapeau haut de forme**, top hat. **4.** *F. d'un lièvre*, hare's form.

formel, -elle, *a.* Formal, strict (order); explicit (declaration); categorical.

formellement, *adv.* Formally. **Il est formellement interdit de . . .**, it is strictly forbidden to. . . .

former, *v.tr.* To form. **1.** To make, create. **2.** To shape, fashion.

formidable, *a.* (*a*) Formidable. (*b*) *F:* Tremendous. **C'est formidable!** well, I never!

formule, *s.f.* **1.** (*a*) Formula. (*b*) (Set) form of words. **2.** *Adm: etc:* (Printed) form.

formuler, *v.tr.* To formulate; to draw up; to give expression to.

fort. 1. *a.* **1.** (*a*) Strong. **Trouver plus fort que soi**, to meet one's match. **C'est une tête forte**, he has a good head on his shoulders. *Forte mer*, heavy sea. *D'une voix forte*, in a loud voice. **C'est plus fort que moi!** I can't help it! *Ce qu'il y a de plus f., c'est que . . .* the best part of it is that. . . . (*b*) **Ville forte**, fortified town. (*c*) **Se faire fort de faire qch.**, to undertake to do sth. **2.** Large. *Femme forte,* stout woman.

II. **fort,** *adv.* **1.** Strongly. **Frapper fort,** to strike hard. **2.** Very, extremely. **J'ai fort à faire,** I have a great deal to do.

III. **fort,** *s.m.* **1.** Strong part. *Le f. de l'hiver,* the depth of winter. **Au (plus) fort du combat,** in the thick of the fight. **2.** Fort, stronghold.

fortement, *adv.* Strongly; stoutly.

forteresse, *s.f.* Fortress, stronghold.

fortifiant. 1. *a.* Fortifying, strengthening, invigorating. **2.** *s.m.* Tonic.

fortification, *s.f.* Fortification. **1.** Fortifying (of town, etc.). **2.** Defence work(s).

fortifier, *v.tr.* To strengthen; to fortify.

fortuit, *a.* Fortuitous; (by) chance. **Cas fortuit,** accident.

fortuité, *s.f.* Fortuitousness.

fortuitement, *adv.* Fortuitously, accidentally.

fortune, *s.f.* **1.** Fortune, chance, luck. **Compagnons de fortune,** chance companions. **Dispositif de fortune,** makeshift. **2.** Piece of luck. **3.** Fortune, riches.

fortuné, *a.* **1.** Fortunate, happy, successful. **2.** Rich, well-off, well-to-do.

fosse, *s.f.* **1.** Pit, hole. **2.** Grave.

fossé, *s.m.* Ditch, trench.

fossette, *s.f.* Dimple.

fossile, *a. & s.m.* Fossil.

fossoyeur, *s.m.* Grave-digger.

fou, fol, folle. (The form 'fol,' used in the *m.* before a vowel within the word-group, is confined to sense I (*b*).) **1.** *a.* (*a*) Mad, insane. **Fou à lier,** raving mad. **Fou de joie,** beside oneself with joy. **Être fou de qn,** to be madly in love with s.o. (*b*) Foolish, silly. *Un fol espoir,* a mad hope. (*c*) Prodigious. **Succès fou,** tremendous success. *Il gagne un argent fou,* he makes no end of money. *A une allure folle,* at a break-neck speed. (*d*) Wafted here and there; not under control. *Herbes folles,* rank weeds. **2.** *s.* (Never *fol*) (*a*) Madman, madwoman; lunatic. (*b*) Fool. **Plus on est de fous plus on rit,** the more the merrier. **3.** *s.m.* *Chess:* Bishop.

foudre, *s.f.* Thunderbolt, lightning. **Coup de foudre,** thunderbolt.

foudroiement, *s.m.* Blasting.

foudroyant, *a.* Crushing; overwhelming.

foudroyer, *v.tr.* (je foudroie) To strike down; to blast. *J'étais foudroyé de ses paroles,* I was thunderstruck at his words

fouet, *s.m.* Whip, lash. **Coup de fouet,** (i) cut of whip; (ii) stimulus.

fouetter, *v.tr.* To whip, flog, lash; to beat. **Fouette, cocher!** off we go! **Avoir d'autres chiens à fouetter,** to have other fish to fry.

  fouettée, *s.f.* Whipping, spanking.

fougère, *s.f.* *Bot:* Fern; bracken.

fougue, *s.f.* Fire, ardour, spirit.

fougueux, *a.* Fiery, ardent, spirited.

fouille [fu:j], *s.f.* Excavation.

fouiller [fuje]. **1.** *v.tr.* (*a*) To dig, excavate. (*b*) To search. *F. un tiroir,* to ransack a drawer. **2.** *v.i. F. dans une armoire,* to rummage in a cupboard.

fouine, *s.f.* *Z:* Stone-marten. *F:* A figure de fouine, weasel-faced.

foulard, *s.m.* **1.** *Tex:* Foulard. **2.** Silk neckerchief.

foule, *s.f.* Crowd; throng.

fouler, *v.tr.* **1.** To press; to crush; to trample (down). **2.** To sprain, strain, wrench.

foulure, *s.f.* Sprain, wrench.

four, *s.m.* **1.** (*a*) Oven. (*b*) **Petits fours,** fancy biscuits. **2.** Kiln, furnace.

fourbe, *a.* Rascally, knavish.

fourberie, *s.f.* **1.** Deceit, cheating. **2.** Swindle.

fourche, *s.f.* (Pitch)fork.

fourcher, *v.i.* To fork, branch.

fourchette, *s.f.* (Table) fork. **Repas à la fourchette,** knife-and-fork meal.

fourchu, *a.* Forked, bifurcated. **Pied fourchu,** cloven hoof.

fourgon, *s.m.* Van, wag(g)on.

fourmi, *s.f.* *Ent:* Ant. *F:* **Avoir des fourmis dans les jambes** to have pins and needles in one's legs.

fourmilière, *s.f.* Ant-hill, ants' nest.

fourmillement [-mij-], *s.m.* **1.** Swarming. **2.** Tingling; pins and needles.

fourmiller [-mije], *v.i.* To swarm; to teem.

fournaise, *s.f.* *Lit:* (Fiery) furnace.

fourneau, *s.m.* (*a*) Furnace (of boiler); bowl (of pipe). (*b*) *F. à gaz,* gas-stove.

fournée, *s.f.* Batch (of loaves).

fournir, *v.tr.* To supply, furnish, provide. *Magasin bien fourni,* well-stocked shop. *v.ind.tr. F. aux besoins de qn,* to supply s.o.'s wants.

fournisseur, -euse, *s.* (*a*) Purveyor, caterer. (*b*) **Les fournisseurs,** the tradesmen.

fourniture, *s.f.* **1.** Supplying, providing. **2.** *pl.* Supplies, requisites.

fourrager, *v.i.* (n. fourrageons) To forage.

fourreau, *s.m.* Sheath, cover, case.

fourrer, *v.tr.* To stuff, cram. **Fourrer son nez partout,** to poke one's nose into everything.

fourré, *s.m.* (*a*) Thicket (*b*) Jungle.

fourreur, *s.m.* Furrier.

fourrure, *s.f.* (*a*) Fur, skin. (*b*) Hair, coat.

fourvoyer, *v.tr.* (je fourvoie) To mislead.

fox, *s.m.. F:* Fox-terrier.

foyer, *s.m.* **1.** Fire(-place), hearth, grate. **2.** (*a*) *F:* **Un foyer d'érudition,** a centre of learning. **3.** (*a*) Hearth, home. (*b*) *Th:* **Foyer du public,** foyer. **Foyer des acteurs,** green-room. **4.** Focus (of lens).

frac [frak], *s.m.* Dress-coat.

fracas, *s.m.* Din; (sound of a) crash.

fraction, *s.f.* Fraction; fractional part.

fracture, *s.f.* **1.** Breaking open, forcing. **2.** Fracture (of bone).

fracturer, *v.tr.* **1.** To force (lock); to break open (door). **2.** To fracture (bone).

fragile, *a.* **1.** Fragile; brittle. **2.** Frail.

fragilité, *s.f.* **1.** Fragility; brittleness. **2.** Frailty.

fragment, *s.m.* Fragment.

frai, *s.m.* Spawn.

fraîche. See FRAIS[1].

fraîchement, *adv.* **1.** Coolly. **2.** Freshly, recently.

fraîcheur, *s.f.* **1.** Coolness, chilliness. **2.** Freshness.

frais[1], fraîche. 1. *a.* Fresh. (*a*) Cool. (*b*) New, recent. Œufs frais, new-laid eggs. "Peinture fraîche," 'wet paint.' (*c*) Teint *f.*, fresh complexion. **2.** *s.m.* Prendre le frais, to take the air. A mettre au frais, to be kept in a cool place. De frais, freshly.

frais[2], *s.m.pl.* Expenses, cost. Faire les frais de la conversation, (i) to contribute a large share of the talk; (ii) to be the subject of the conversation. J'en suis pour mes frais, I've had all my trouble for nothing.

fraise, *s.f.* Strawberry.

fraisier, *s.m.* Strawberry-plant.

framboise, *s.f.* Raspberry.

framboisier, *s.m.* Raspberry-cane.

franc[1], *s.m.* Franc.

franc[2], franche, *a.* **1.** Free. **2.** (*a*) Frank; open, candid. Avoir son franc parler, to speak one's mind. Y aller de franc jeu, to be quite straightforward about it. (*b*) Real, true, downright.

français. 1. *a.* French. **2.** *s.* Frenchman, Frenchwoman. **3.** *s.m.* French (language).

France. *Pr.n.f. Geog:* France.

franche. See FRANC[2].

franchement, *adv.* **1.** Frankly, candidly, openly. **2.** *F:* Really, quite.

franchir, *v.tr.* (*a*) To clear (obstacle); to jump (over); to get over. (*b*) To pass through; to cross.

franchise, *s.f.* **1.** Freedom. **2.** Exemption. Importer qch. en franchise, to import sth. free of duty. En *f.*, post-free. **3.** Frankness, candour.

franc-maçon, *s.m.* Freemason. *pl.* Des francs-maçons.

franc-maçonnerie, *s.f.* Freemasonry.

franco, *adv.* Free, carriage-free.

François. *Pr.n.m.* Francis, Frank.

Françoise. *Pr.n.f.* Frances.

franc-parler, *s.m.* Frankness, candour; bluntness of speech; plain speaking.

frange, *s.f.* Fringe.

frappant, *a.* Striking (likeness).

frapper, *v.tr.* **1.** (*a*) To strike, hit. Frapper des marchandises d'un droit, to impose a duty on goods. On frappe, there's a knock. Frapper du pied, to stamp (one's foot). (*b*) To strike (coin). **2.** To ice (champagne).

fraternel, -elle, *a.* Fraternal, brotherly.

fraternellement, *adv.* Fraternally.

fraternisation, *s.f.* Fraternizing.

fraterniser, *v.i.* To fraternize.

fraternité, *s.f.* Fraternity, brotherhood.

fraude, *s.f.* **1.** Fraud, deception; smuggling. **2.** Fraudulence, deceit.

frauder. 1. *v.tr.* To defraud, cheat. **2.** *v.i.* To cheat.

fraudeur, -euse, *s.* **1.** Defrauder, cheat. **2.** Smuggler.

frauduleusement, *adv.* Fraudulently.

frauduleux, *a.* Fraudulent.

frayer, *v.tr.* (je fraye, je fraie) Se frayer un passage, to clear a way (for oneself).

frayeur, *s.f.* Fright; fear, dread.

fredonner, *v.tr.* To hum (tune).

frégate, *s.f.* Frigate. Capitaine de frégate, commander.

frein, *s.m.* **1.** Bit; (in wider sense) bridle. *F:* Mettre un frein aux désirs de qn, to curb s.o.'s desires. **2.** Brake.

freiner, *v.tr.* **1.** *Abs.* To put on the brakes. **2.** *F.* la production, to check production.

frêle, *a.* Frail, weak.

frelon, *s.m. Ent:* Hornet.

frémir, *v.i.* **1.** To quiver; (of leaves) to rustle. **2.** To tremble, shake, shudder.

frémissement, *s.m.* **1.** Quivering, rustling. **2.** (*a*) Shuddering. (*b*) Shudder, tremor.

frêne, *s.m.* Ash(-tree or timber).

frénésie, *s.f.* Frenzy, madness. Applaudir avec frénésie, to applaud frantically.

frénétique, *a.* Frantic, frenzied.

frénétiquement, *adv.* Frantically.

fréquemment, *adv.* Frequently.

fréquence, *s.f.* Frequency.

fréquent, *a.* Frequent.

fréquentation, *s.f* Frequentation.

fréquenter. 1. *v.tr.* (*a*) To frequent. (*b*) *F.* qn, to associate with s.o. **2.** *v.i. F. chez* qn, to be on visiting terms with s.o.

frère, *s.m.* Brother. Frère de lait, foster-brother.

fresque, *s.f. Art:* Fresco.

fret, *s.m.* Freight. **1.** Freightage. **2.** Chartering. **3.** Load, cargo.

frétillant [-tijã], *a.* **1.** (Of fish) Wriggling. **2.** Full of life; lively.

frétiller [-tije], *v.i.* (Of fish) To wriggle. *F. d'impatience,* to quiver with impatience.

fretin, *s.m. Fish:* Fry.

friabilité, *s.f.* Friability, friableness.

friable, *a.* Friable, crumbly.

friand, *a.* (*a*) Fond of delicacies. (*b*) Morceau *f.*, dainty morsel.

friandise, *s.f.* **1.** Love of good food. **2.** Dainty, delicacy, tit-bit.

friche, *s.f.* Waste land; fallow land.

fricot, *s.m. F:* Made-up dish; stew.

fricoter, *v.tr. & i. F:* To stew; to cook.

friction, *s.f.* Friction.

frileusement, *adv.* Cosily, snugly.

frileux, *a.* Sensitive to the cold; chilly.

frimas, *s.m.* (Hoar-)frost; rime.

friperie, *s.f.* (a) Second-hand goods. (b) *F:* Rubbish, frippery.
fripier, *s.* Wardrobe dealer.
fripon, -onne. 1. *s.* Rogue, rascal, knave. 2. *a.* Roguish, knavish.
frire, *v.tr. & i.def.* (*p.p.* frit) To fry. Je fais frire *des pommes de terre,* I am frying potatoes. **frit,** *a.* Fried.
frise¹, *s.f. Arch:* Frieze.
frise², *s.f. Tex:* Frieze.
Frise³. *Pr.n.f. Geog:* Friesland. *Mil:* Chevaux de frise, portable wire entanglement.
friser. 1. (a) *v.tr.* To curl, wave. (b) *v.i.* (Of hair) To curl. 2. *v.tr.* To touch, skim. Il frisait la soixantaine, he was bordering on sixty.
frisé, *a.* Curly; crisp (hair).
frisson, *s.m.* (a) Shiver (from cold). (b) Shudder, thrill. J'en ai le frisson, it gives me the shudders. (c) Thrill (of pleasure).
frissonnement, *s.m.* 1. Shivering; shuddering. 2. Slight shiver, shudder.
frissonner, *v.i.* (a) To shiver, shudder. (b) To be thrilled (with delight). (c) To quiver (with impatience).
frit. See FRIRE.
frivole, *a.* Frivolous, shallow.
frivolité, *s.f.* (a) Frivolity (b) Trifle.
froc [frɔk], *s.m.* (Monk's) frock. Jeter le froc aux orties, (i) of monk) to throw one's frock away; (ii) *F:* to change one's profession.
froid. I. *a.* 1. Cold. Il fait froid, it is cold. J'ai froid aux mains, my hands are cold. *F:* Il n'a pas froid aux yeux, he has plenty of cheek. 2. Cold (person); chilly (manner). *Sourire f.,* frigid smile. Battre froid à qn, to cold-shoulder s.o.
II. **froid,** *s.m.* 1. Cold. 2. Coldness. Il y a du froid entre eux, there is a coolness between them.
froidement, *adv.* Coldly, frigidly.
froideur, *s.f.* 1. Coldness (of temperature). 2. Coldness, frigidity (of manner).
froissement, *s.m.* 1. Crumpling (of paper); rustle (of silk). 2. Giving offence.
froisser, *v.tr.* 1. To crumple (up). *F. qn en passant,* to brush past s.o. 2. *F. qn,* to give offence to s.o.
se froisser, to take offence.
frôlement, *s.m.* Slight rubbing; light touch(ing).
frôler, *v.tr.* To touch lightly; to brush.
fromage, *s.m.* Cheese.
froment, *s.m.* Wheat.
froncement, *s.m. F. de(s) sourcils,* frown; scowl.
froncer, *v.tr.* (n. fronçons) *F. les sourcils,* to knit one's brows; to frown.
fronde, *s.f.* (a) Sling. (b) (Toy) catapult.
front, *s.m.* 1. Forehead, brow. Et vous avez le front de me dire cela! you have the face to tell me that! 2. Face, front. *F. de bataille,* battle front. Faire front à qch., to face sth. 3. De front, abreast.

frontal, -aux, *a.* Frontal, front.
frontière, *s.f.* Frontier(-line); border(-line).
frontispice, *s.m.* Frontispiece.
frottement, *s.m.* 1. Chafing. 2. Friction.
frotter, *v.tr.* To rub. *F:* Frotter les oreilles à qn, to warm s.o.'s ears.
froufrou, *s.m.* Rustle, rustling, swish.
fructifier, *v.i.* To fructify; to bear fruit.
fructueusement, *adv.* Fruitfully.
fructueux, *a.* Fruitful, advantageous.
frugal, -aux, *a.* Frugal.
frugalement, *adv.* Frugally.
frugalité, *s.f.* Frugality.
fruit, *s.m.* Fruit.
fruitier. 1. *a.* Arbre fruitier, fruit-tree. 2. *s.* Fruiterer, greengrocer.
fruste, *a.* Worn; rough.
frustration, *s.f.* 1. Frustration. 2. Cheating, defrauding (of creditors).
frustrer, *v.tr.* To frustrate, disappoint.
fugitif, *a. & s.* 1. Fugitive; runaway. 2. *Désir f.,* passing desire.
fuir, *v.* (*pr.p.* fuyant) 1. *v.i.* (a) To flee, fly, run away. (b) (Of horizon) To recede. (c) (Of tap) To leak. 2. *v.tr.* To shun, avoid.
fuite, *s.f.* 1. Flight, running away, absconding. 2. Leak; escape (of steam); leakage. 3. Shunning, avoidance.
fuligineux, *a.* Fuliginous, sooty, smoky; murky (sky).
fulmicoton, *s.m. Exp:* Gun-cotton.
fulminer, *v.i.* 1. *F. contre un abus,* to fulminate, inveigh, against an abuse. 2. To fulminate, detonate.
fume-cigarette, *s.m.* Cigarette-holder. *pl. Des fume-cigarette(s).*
fumée, *s.f.* (a) Smoke. Noir de fumée, lamp-black. (b) Steam (of soup). *Les fumées du vin,* the fumes of wine.
fumer. 1. *v.i.* (a) To smoke. (b) (Of soup) To steam. *F:* Fumer de colère, to fume, to rage. 2. *v.tr. F. une pipe,* to smoke a pipe. Défense de fumer, no smoking.
fûmes. See ÊTRE.
fumet, *s.m.* (Pleasant) smell (of cooking); bouquet (of wine).
fumeur, -euse, *s.* Smoker.
fumeux, *a.* Smoky, smoking.
fumier, *s.m.* 1. Manure, dung. 2. Dunghill; manure heap.
fumoir, *s.m.* Smoking-room.
funèbre, *a.* 1. Funeral (ceremony). *Marche f.,* dead-march. 2. Funereal, gloomy.
funérailles [-rɑːj], *s.f.pl.* Funeral.
funéraire, *a.* Funeral.
funeste, *a.* Deadly, fatal. *Influence f.,* baneful influence.
funiculaire. 1. *a.* Funicular. 2. *s.m.* Funicular railway.
fur, *s.m. Adv.phr.* Au fur et à mesure, (in proportion) as. *Fournir des articles au fur et à mesure des besoins,* to supply articles as they are wanted.
furent. See ÊTRE.

furet, *s.m.* (*a*) *Z:* Ferret. **Jeu du furet,** hunt-the-slipper. (*b*) *F:* Inquisitive person.

fureter, *v.i.* (**je furette**) (*a*) To ferret, go ferreting. (*b*) *F: F. dans les armoires,* to ferret, pry about in the cupboards.

fureur, *s.f.* **1.** Fury, rage, wrath. **2.** Fury, passion. **Avoir la fureur de bâtir,** to have a craze for building. **Chanson qui fait fureur, song** that is all the rage.

furibond, *a.* Furious; full of fury.

furie, *s.f.* **1.** *F:* C'est **une furie,** she's a fury. **2.** (*a*) Fury, rage.

furieusement, *adv.* Furiously, passionately.

furieux, *a.* Furious; in a passion.

furoncle, *s.m. Med:* Boil.

furtif, *a.* Furtive, stealthy.

furtivement, *adv.* Furtively, stealthily.

fus. See ÊTRE.

fuseau, *s.m. Tex:* Spindle.

fusée, *s.f.* (*a*) Rocket. *F. éclairante,* flare. *F. porte-amarre,* rocket apparatus. (*b*) Fuse.

fuselé, *a.* Spindle-shaped. *Aut:* Streamlined. *Doigts fuselés,* tapering fingers.

fusible. 1. *a.* Fusible; easily melted. **2.** *s.m. El.E:* Fuse.

fusil, *s.m.* Gun. *F. à répétition,* magazine-rifle. **A une portée de fusil d'ici,** within a gunshot from here.

fusilier, *s.m.* Fusilier.

fusillade [-zij-] *s.f.* Fusillade, rifle-fire.

fusiller [-zije], *v.tr.* (*a*) To shoot (down) (men). (*b*) To execute (by shooting); to shoot (spy).

fusion, *s.f.* **1.** Fusion, melting. **2.** Coalescing.

fuss-e, -ions, fut, fût¹. See ÊTRE.

fût², *s.m.* **1.** Stock (of rifle). **2.** (*a*) Shaft (of column). (*b*) Bole (of tree). **3.** Cask, barrel.

futaie, *s.f.* Wood, forest.

fûtes. See ÊTRE.

futile, *a.* Futile, trifling; idle (pretext).

futilement, *adv.* Futilely.

futilité, *s.f.* Futility.

futur, *a.* Future.

fuy-ais, -ons, etc. See FUIR.

fuyant, *a.* **1.** Fleeing (animal); fleeting (moment). **2.** Receding (forehead). **3.** *Yeux fuyants,* shifty eyes.

fuyard, *s.* Runaway.

G

G, g [ʒe], *s.m.* The letter G, g.

gâcher, *v.tr.* To spoil (sheet of paper); to bungle (job). *G. sa vie,* to make a mess of one's life.

gâchis, *s.m. F: Quel g.!* what a mess!

gaélique, *a. & s.m.* Gaelic.

gaffe, *s.f.* **1.** (*a*) Boat-hook. (*b*) *Fish:* Gaff. **2.** *F:* **Faire une gaffe,** to put one's foot in it; to make a blunder.

gage, *s.m.* **1.** Pledge, security. **Mettre qch. en gage,** to pawn sth. **Prêteur sur gages,** pawnbroker. **2.** Token, sign. **3.** Forfeit. **4.** *pl.* Wages, pay.

gager, *v.tr.* (n. **gageons**) To wager, bet. (To bet at races, etc., is PARIER.)

gageure, *s.f.* Wager, bet.

gagnant. 1. *a.* Winning (ticket). **2.** *s.* Winner.

gagne-pain, *s.m.inv.* **1.** (Means of) living. **2.** Bread-winner.

gagner, *v.tr.* **1.** (*a*) To earn. (*b*) To gain. **C'est autant de gagné,** it is so much to the good. *J'y gagnerai,* I shall gain by it. **2.** (*a*) To win, gain (a victory). (*b*) *G. la partie,* to win the game. (*c*) *G. tous les cœurs,* to win all hearts. **3.** To reach, arrive at. **4.** To gain (up)on, overtake. *Gagné par le sommeil,* overcome by sleep.

gai, *a.* Gay. (*a*) Merry, lively. (*b*) Bright, cheerful.

gaiement, *adv.* Gaily, brightly.

gaieté, gaîté, *s.f.* Gaiety, mirth, cheerfulness. **Faire qch. de gaîté de cœur,** to do sth. out of sheer wantonness.

gaillard [gaj-], **1.** *a.* (*a*) Strong, vigorous. (*b*) Merry, cheery. **2.** *s.m.* (*a*) (Merry) fellow. (*b*) Sharp fellow. **3.** *s.m. Nau:* Gaillard d'avant, forecastle. **Gaillard d'arrière,** quarter-deck.

gaîment, *adv.* = GAIEMENT.

gain, *s.m.* **1.** (*a*) Gain, profit. (*b*) Earnings. **2.** (*a*) Winning (of contest). **Avoir gain de cause,** to win one's case. (*b*) Winnings.

gaine, *s.f.* Sheath, casing.

gala, *s.m.* Festivity, fête, gala.

galamment, *adv.* **(*a*)** Politely, courteously. (*b*) Bravely, honourably.

galant. 1. *a.* (*a*) Gay, elegant. (*b*) Attentive to women; gallant. (*c*) Galant homme, man of honour. **2.** *s.m.* Lover, gallant.

galanterie, *s.f.* **1.** Politeness (esp. to ladies). **2.** Usu. *pl.* Love-affair.

galère, *s.f. Nau:* Galley. *F:* **Vogue la galère!** let's chance it! **Mais que diable allait-il faire dans cette galère?** but what the deuce was he doing there?

galerie, *s.f.* **1.** (*a*) Gallery. (*b*) **Jouer pour la galerie,** to play to the gallery. (*c*) Arcade. **2.** *Th:* Balcony, gallery. **Second g.,** upper circle. *Troisième g.,* gallery. **3.** *Min:* Gallery.

galet, *s.m.* (*a*) Pebble. *Gros g.,* boulder. (*b*) *pl.* Shingle.

galetas, *s.m.* (*a*) Garret, attic. (*b*) Hovel.
galette, *s.f.* Girdle-cake.
galeux, *a.* Mangy. *F:* Brebis galeuse, black sheep.
Galilée[1]. *Pr.n.f. B.Geog:* Galilee.
Galilée[2]. *Pr.n.m. Hist:* Galileo.
galimatias, *s.m.* Farrago; jumble of words.
galle, *s.f. Bot:* Gall(-nut).
Galles. *Pr.n.f.* Le pays de Galles, Wales.
gallique, *a. Hist:* Gallic; of Gaul.
gallois. 1. *a.* Welsh. **2.** *s.* Welshman, -woman. Les Gallois, the Welsh.
galoche, *s.f.* (*a*) Clog (with wooden sole and leather upper). (*b*) Overshoe.
galon, *s.m.* **1.** Braid. **2.** *pl.* (N.C.O.'s) stripes; (officer's) bands, gold braid.
galop, *s.m.* **1.** Gallop. Au petit galop, at a canter. **2.** *Danc:* Galop.
galoper, *v.i. & tr.* To gallop.
galopin, *s.* Urchin; young scamp.
galvanique, *a.* Galvanic.
galvaniser, *v.tr.* **1.** To galvanize. *F:* To give new life to (undertaking). **2.** *Metall:* To galvanize.
gambade, *s.f.* Leap, gambol.
gambader, *v.i.* To leap, caper; to gambol.
gamelle, *s.f.* Pannikin; mess-tin, -kettle.
gamin, *s.* (*a*) Street-arab, urchin. (*b*) *F:* Youngster.
gamme, *s.f.* **1.** *Mus:* Scale, gamut. **2.** Range, series (of colours).
gammée, *a.f.* Croix gammée, swastika.
Gand. *Pr.n.m. Geog:* Ghent.
gant, *s.m.* Glove. Jeter le gant à qn, to throw down the gauntlet to s.o.
gantelé, *a.* Gauntleted.
ganter, *v.tr.* To glove. G. du sept, to take sevens in gloves.
gantier, *s.* Glover.
garage, *s.m.* **1.** *Rail:* Shunting. Voie de garage, siding. **2.** Storage (of bicycles). **3.** Garage.
garagiste, *s.m. Aut:* Garage keeper.
garant, *s.* (*a*) Guarantor, surety, bail. Être garant pour ses faits, to be answerable for one's actions. (*b*) Authority, guarantee.
garantie, *s.f.* Guarantee. Donner une garantie pour qn, to stand security for s.o.
garantir, *v.tr.* **1.** To warrant, guarantee. G. un fait, to vouch for a fact. **2.** To shelter, protect.
garçon, *s.m.* **1.** (*a*) Boy, lad. *F:* C'est un garçon manqué, she's a tomboy. (*b*) *F:* Son. **2.** Young man. Garçon d'honneur, best man. *F:* Brave garçon, bon garçon, decent chap. **3.** Bachelor. **4.** Servant, employee; waiter; steward.
garde[1], *s.m. & f.* **1.** (*a*) Keeper. (*b*) Watchman. Garde champêtre, rural policeman. G. forestier, ranger. **2.** *Mil:* Guardsman.
garde[2], *s.f.* **1.** (*a*) Guardianship, care, custody. Chien de garde, watch-dog. Être sous bonne garde, to be in safe custody. Avoir qch. en garde, to have charge of sth. (*b*) Nursing. (*c*) Guarding, protection. (*d*) Keeping.

2. (*a*) Watch(ing). (*b*) Care, guard. Être sur ses gardes, to be on one's guard. Garde à toi! look out! *Mil:* "Garde à vous!" 'attention!' **3.** Prendre garde. (*a*) Prendre g. à qch., to beware of sth. (*b*) Prendre g. à qch., to attend to sth. Faire qch. sans y prendre garde, to do sth. without meaning it. (*c*) Prendre g. à, de, faire qch., to be careful to do sth. (*d*) Prendre g. de faire qch., to be careful not to do sth. Prenez garde de tomber, mind you don't fall. (*e*) Prendre g. que . . . (ne) + *sub.*, to be careful lest (sth. should happen). **4.** Guard. (*a*) Être de garde, to be on guard. (*b*) La garde, the Guards. **5.** Jusqu'à la garde, up to the hilt.
garde-à-vous, *s.m.* No *pl. Mil:* Attention.
garde-barrière, *s.m. & f.* Gate-keeper (at level-crossing). *pl. Des gardes-barrière(s).*
garde-boue, *s.m.inv.* Mudguard.
garde-chasse, *s.m.* Gamekeeper. *pl. Des gardes-chasse(s).*
garde-corps, *s.m.inv.* Railing (of bridge).
garde-côte, *s.m.* **1.** Coast-guard(sman). *pl. Des gardes-côte(s).* **2.** *Inv.* (*a*) Coast-guard vessel. (*b*) Coast-defence ship.
garde-feu, *s.m.inv.* (*a*) Fender. (*b*) Fire-guard.
garde-fou, *s.m.* **1.** Parapet. **2.** Railing (of bridge). *pl. Des garde-fous.*
garde-malade. 1. *s.m.* Male nurse. **2.** *s.f.* (Sick-)nurse. *pl. Des gardes-malades.*
garde-manger, *s.m.inv.* Larder, pantry.
garder, *v.tr.* **1.** To guard, protect. Garder qn à vue, to keep a close watch on s.o. **2.** (*a*) To retain. G. un vêtement, (i) to keep a garment; (ii) to keep on a garment. (*b*) To preserve. *F:* Garder une poire pour la soif, to put by something for a rainy day. **3.** To remain in (a place). G. le lit, to be laid up. **4.** To observe, respect. G. un secret, to keep a secret.
se garder. 1. To protect oneself. Garde-toi! look out for yourself! **2.** (*a*) Se garder de qch., to beware of sth. (*b*) Se garder de faire qch., to take care not to do sth.
garde-robe, *s.f.* (*a*) Wardrobe. (*b*) Clothes. *pl. Des garde-robes.*
gardien, -ienne, *s.* Guardian, keeper; care-taker.
gare[1], *int.* Look out! mind yourself! G. à lui si . . ., woe betide him if. . . .
gare[2], *s.f.* (Railway) station.
garenne, *s.f.* (Rabbit-)warren.
garer, *v.tr.* **1.** To shunt (train). **2.** (*a*) To garage (car). (*b*) To park (car).
gargouille [-guːj], *s.f.* (*a*) (Water-)spout (of roof-gutter). (*b*) *Arch:* Gargoyle.
garnement, *s.m. F:* Mauvais garnement, scapegrace, scamp, rogue.
garnir, *v.tr.* **1.** To furnish, provide (de, with). **2.** To trim (dress).
garni, *a.* **1.** Bourse bien garnie, well-lined purse. **2.** Chambres garnies, furnished apartments.
garnison, *s.f.* Garrison.

garniture, *s.f.* **1.** Fittings. **2.** (*a*) Trimming (of dress). (*b*) Trimming(s).

garrotter, *v.tr.* **1.** To pinion (prisoner). **2.** To gar(r)otte, strangle.

garrulité, *s.f.* Garrulousness, garrulity.

gars, gas [gɑ], *s.m.* *F:* Young fellow; lad. **Allons-y, les gars!** come on, boys.

Gascogne. *Pr.n.f.* *Geog:* Gascony. **Le Golfe de Gascogne,** the Bay of Biscay.

gascon, -onne, *a. & s.* *Ethn:* Gascon.

gaspiller [-pije], *v.tr.* To squander; to waste, spoil.

gastrique, *a.* Gastric.

gastronomie, *s.f.* Gastronomy.

gâteau, *s.m.* **1.** Cake; (open) tart. **2. Gâteau de miel,** honeycomb.

gâter, *v.tr.* To spoil. **1. Cela ne gâte rien,** that won't do any harm. **2.** To pamper. **se gâter,** to spoil, deteriorate. *Les affaires se gâtent,* things are going wrong. **gâté,** *a.* Spoilt. **Enfant gâté,** (i) spoilt child. (ii) Pet.

gauche, *a.* **1.** Warped; out of true. **2.** Awkward, clumsy. **3.** Left. (*a*) *Main g.,* left hand. (*b*) *s.f.* **Assis à ma gauche,** seated on my left. **4.** *Adv.phr.* **A gauche,** on the left, to the left.

gauchement, *adv.* Awkwardly, clumsily.

gaucherie, *s.f.* **1.** Left-handedness. **2.** Awkwardness, clumsiness, *gaucherie.*

gaufre, *s.f.* *Cu:* Waffle.

gaufrer, *v.tr.* (*a*) To emboss (leather). (*b*) To corrugate.

gaufrette, *s.f.* *Cu:* Wafer biscuit.

gaule, *s.f.* (Long thin) pole, stick.

gaulliste, (*a*) *s.m. & f.* Gaullist, follower of General de Gaulle. (*b*) *a.* Gaullist.

gaulois. 1. *a.* Gallic; of Gaul. **2.** *s. Les Gaulois,* the Gauls.

Gautier. *Pr.n.m.* Walter.

gaver, *v.tr.* To cram (poultry). *F:* **Se gaver de nourriture,** to gorge.

gaz [gɑːz], *s.m.* Gas.

gaze, *s.f.* Gauze. *G. métallique,* wire gauze.

gazelle, *s.f.* *Z:* Gazelle.

gazette, *s.f.* Gazette; news-sheet.

gazeux, *a.* **1.** Gaseous. **2.** Aerated (water); fizzy (drink).

gazon, *s.m.* **1.** (*a*) (Fine, short) grass; turf, sward. (*b*) Lawn, green. **2.** Turf, sod.

gazonner, *v.tr.* To cover with sods or turf.

gazonneux, *a.* Turfy.

gazouillement [-ʒuj-], *s.m.* Twittering; babbling.

gazouiller [-zuje], *v.i.* (Of bird) To twitter; to babble; to prattle.

gazouillis [-zuji], *s.m.* = GAZOUILLEMENT.

geai, *s.m.* *Orn:* Jay.

géant. 1. *s.* Giant, giantess. *Gym:* **Pas de géant,** giant's stride. **2.** *a.* Gigantic.

géhenne, *s.f.* Gehenna, Hell.

geign-ais, -ant, -is, etc. See GEINDRE.

geindre, *v.i.* (Conj. like PEINDRE) To whine, whimper.

gel [ʒɛl], *s.m.* Frost, freezing.

gélatine, *s.f.* Gelatin(e).

gélatineux, *a.* Gelatinous.

geler, *v.* (je gèle) **1.** *v.tr.* To freeze. **2.** *v.i.* (*a*) To become frozen; to freeze. (*b*) *Impers.* **Il gèle à pierre fendre,** it is freezing hard. **se geler,** to freeze, solidify. **gelé,** *a.* **1.** Frozen. **2.** Frost-bitten. **gelée,** *s.f.* **1.** Frost. **Temps à la gelée,** frosty weather. **2.** Jelly.

gelinotte, *s.f.* Hazel-grouse, hazel-hen.

gelure, *s.f.* *Med:* Frost-bite.

gémir, *v.i.* To groan, moan, wail.

gémissement, *s.m.* Groan(ing), moan(ing).

gemme, (*a*) *s.f.* Gem; precious stone. (*b*) *a.* **Sel gemme,** rock-salt.

gênant, *a.* **1.** Cumbersome; in the way. **2.** Embarrassing, awkward.

gencive, *s.f.* *Anat:* Gum.

gendarme, *s.m.* Gendarme.

gendarmerie, *s.f.* **1.** The force of gendarmes. **2.** Headquarters (of the gendarmes).

gendre, *s.m.* Son-in-law.

gêne, *s.f.* **1.** Discomfort, er''narrassment. **Sans gêne,** free and easy. **2.** Want; financial embarrassment.

généalogie, *s.f.* Genealogy; pedigree.

généalogique, *a.* Genealogical. **Arbre généalogique,** family-tree; pedigree.

gêner, *v.tr.* **1.** To constrict, cramp. *Mes souliers me gênent,* my shoes pinch. **2.** To hinder, impede; to be in (s.o.'s) way. **3.** To inconvenience, embarrass. **se gêner.** *Je ne me suis pas gêné pour le lui dire,* I did not scruple to tell him so. **gêné,** *a.* Embarrassed; ill at ease.

général, -aux. 1. *a.* General. **En règle générale,** as a general rule. *Th:* **Répétition générale,** *s.f.* générale, dress-rehearsal. **2.** *s.m. Mil:* General. **3.** *s.f.* **Générale.** (*a*) The general's wife. (*b*) Alarm call.

généralement, *adv.* Generally.

généralisation, *s.f.* **1.** Generalizing. **2.** Generalization.

généraliser, *v.tr.* To generalize.

généralité, *s.f.* Generality. *Dans la g. des cas,* in most cases.

générateur, -trice. 1. *a.* Generating; generative. **2.** *El.E:* Generator.

génération, *s.f.* Generation.

générer, *v.tr.* (je génère; je générerai) To generate.

généreusement, *adv.* Generously; liberally.

généreux, *a.* **1.** Noble, generous (soul). **2.** Liberal, generous.

générique, *a.* Generic (term).

générosité, *s.f.* Generosity; munificence.

Gênes. *Pr.n.f. Geog:* Genoa.

genèse, *s.f.* Genesis, origin, birth. *B:* **La Genèse,** (the Book of) Genesis.

genêt, *s.m.* *Bot:* Broom.

gêneur, -euse, *s.* Spoil-sport; intruder.

Genève. *Pr.n.f. Geog:* Geneva.
genévrier, *s.m. Bot:* Juniper(-tree).
génial, -aux, *a.* Full of genius.
génie, *s.m.* **1.** *(a)* (Guardian) spirit; (presiding) genius. *(b)* Genie, jinnee. **2.** *Homme de g.,* man of genius. **3.** (Pers.) Genius. **4.** *(a)* Engineering. *(b) Mil:* **Le génie,** the engineers.
genièvre, *s.m.* **1.** *Bot:* Juniper-berry; juniper-tree. **2.** Gin, Hollands.
génisse, *s.f.* Heifer.
génital, -aux, *a.* Genital.
génois, *a. & s.* Genoese.
genou, -oux, *s.m.* Knee. **A genou(x)!** down on your knee(s)! kneel down!
genre, *s.m.* **1.** Genus, kind. **Le genre humain,** the human race; mankind. **2.** Kind, manner. **C'est plus dans son genre,** that's more in his line. **3.** (Artistic) style, manner. **4.** Gender.
gens, *s.m.pl.* (The plural of GENT, *q.v.* Most attributive adjectives preceding *gens* take the feminine form, but the word-group is felt as masculine. *Ces bonnes gens sont venus me trouver. Quels sont ces gens? Quels* or *quelles sont ces bonnes gens? Tout* varies according as the attributive adjective has a distinctive feminine ending or not: *Toutes ces bonnes gens,* but *tous ces pauvres gens. Jeunes gens,* and the compounds of group 2 *(b)* below, never have a feminine adjective. *De bons petits jeunes gens. Les malheureux gens de lettres.*) **1.** People, folk(s), men and women. **2.** *(a)* **Jeunes gens,** (i) young people, young folk; (ii) young men. *(b) G. du monde,* society people. *G. de bien,* honest folk. *G. de robe,* lawyers. *(c)* Servants, domestics. **3. Le droit des gens,** the law of nations.
gent, *s.f. Hum: La g. ailée,* the feathered tribe.
gentiane, *s.f. Bot:* Gentian.
gentil¹, -ille [ʒɑ̃ti, -iːj], *a. (a)* Pleasing, nice. **C'est gentil à vous de m'écrire,** it is very kind of you to write to me. *(b) Sois gentil(le),* be a good boy, a good girl.
gentil², *s.m. Hist:* Gentile.
gentilhomme [-tij-], *s.m.* Man of gentle birth; gentleman (in this sense). *pl. Des gentilshommes* [ʒɑ̃tizɔm].
gentillesse [-tij-], *s.f.* **1.** *(a)* Prettiness, engaging manner. *(b)* **Auriez-vous la gentillesse de . . .,** would you be so very kind as to. . . . **2.** *pl.* **Dire des gentillesses,** to say nice things.
gentiment, *adv.* Nicely; prettily.
Geoffroi [ʒɔf-]. *Pr.n.m.* Godfrey, Geoffrey.
géographie, *s.f.* Geography.
géographique, *a.* Geographic(al). *Carte g.,* map.
geôlier [ʒolje], *s.m.* Gaoler, jailer, turnkey.
géologie, *s.f.* Geology.
géologique, *a.* Geological.
géologue, *s.m.* Geologist.
géométrie, *s.f.* Geometry. *G. dans l'espace,* solid geometry.

géométrique, *a.* Geometric(al).
Georges [ʒɔrʒ]. *Pr.n.m.* George.
géranium [-jɔm], *s.m. Bot:* Geranium.
gérant, *s.* Manager, director; *f.* manageress.
gerbe, *s.f.* Sheaf (of corn). *G. d'étincelles,* shower of sparks. *G. d'eau,* column of water
gerçure, *s.f.* Crack, cleft; chap (in skin).
gérer, *v.tr.* **(je gère; je gérerai)** To manage (hotel).
gerfaut, *s.m. Orn:* Gerfalcon.
germain, *a. Frère g.,* own brother, full brother. *Cousin g.,* first cousin.
germanique, *a.* Germanic.
germe, *s.m. Biol:* Germ.
germer, *v.i.* To germinate; to shoot.
germination, *s.f.* Germination.
gésier, *s.m.* Gizzard.
gésir, *v.i. def. (pr.p.* **gisant**; *pr.ind.* **il gît,** *n.* **gisons)** To lie. (On gravestone) **Ci-gît** here lies.
geste¹, *s.m.* **1.** Gesture, motion, movement. **D'un geste de la main,** with a wave of the hand. **Faire un geste,** to make a gesture. **2. Beau geste,** gesture of sympathy.
geste², *s.f.* **Faits et gestes,** doings, exploits.
gesticulation, *s.f.* Gesticulation.
gesticuler, *v.i.* To gesticulate.
gestion, *s.f.* Management; administration.
geyser [-zeːr], *s.m. Geol:* Geyser.
gibecière [ʒips-], *s.f.* **1.** Game-bag. **2.** Satchel.
gibet, *s.m.* Gibbet, gallows.
gibier, *s.m. Ven:* Game. *F:* **Gibier de potence,** gallows-bird.
giboulée, *s.f.* Sudden shower (usu. with snow or hail).
giboyeux, *a.* Well stocked with game.
gibus [-byːs], *s.m.* Crush-hat, opera-hat.
gicler, *v.i.* To squirt out.
gicleur, *s.m. I.C.E:* (Spray) nozzle; jet.
gifle, *s.f.* Slap in the face; box on the ear.
gifler, *v.tr.* To slap, smack, (s.o.'s) face; to box (s.o.'s) ears.
gigantesque, *a.* Gigantic; huge.
gigot, *s.m.* Leg of mutton.
gigue¹, *s.f. Danc:* Jig.
gigue², *s.f.* Haunch (of venison).
gilet, *s.m.* Waistcoat, vest. *G. tricoté,* cardigan.
Gilles. *Pr.n.m.* Giles.
gingembre, *s.m.* Ginger.
girafe, *s.f. Z:* Giraffe.
giration, *s.f.* Gyration.
giratoire, *a.* Gyratory.
girofle, *s.m. Bot:* Clove. **Un clou de girofle,** a clove.
giroflée, *s.f. Bot: G. des jardins,* stock. *G. des murailles,* wallflower.
giron, *s.m.* Lap. **Le giron de l'Église,** the bosom of the Church.
girouette, *s.f.* Weathercock; vane.
gisais, gisent, etc. See GÉSIR.

gisement, *s.m.* (*a*) *Geol:* Layer, bed. (*b*) *Min:* Lode, vein.

gît. See GÉSIR.

gîte, *s.m.* **I.** (*a*) Resting-place. *N'avoir pas de g.,* to have nowhere to lay one's head. (*b*) Form (of hare). **2.** Stratum, deposit.

givre, *s.m.* Hoar-frost, rime.

glabre, *a.* *Nat.Hist:* Glabrous, smooth. *F:* Visage glabre, clean-shaven face.

glace, *s.f.* **I.** Ice. **Retenu par les glaces,** ice-bound. **2.** (*a*) (Plate-)glass. (*b*) (Looking-) glass, mirror. (*c*) *Rail:* Window. **3.** *Cu:* Ice(-cream).

glacer, *v.tr.* (n. glaçons) (*a*) To freeze. (*b*) To ice (water). (*c*) To ice (cake).

glacé, *a.* **I.** (*a*) Frozen. (*b*) J'ai les pieds glacés, my feet are as cold as ice. (*c*) Iced (coffee). **2.** Glazed, glossy.

glacial, -als, *a.* Icy; frosty. **La Zone glaciale,** the Frigid Zone.

glacier, *s.m.* *Geol:* Glacier.

glaçon, *s.m.* (*a*) Block of ice; floe. (*b*) Icicle.

gladiateur, *s.m.* Gladiator.

glaïeul, *s.m.* *Bot:* Gladiolus. *G. des marais,* sword-flag.

glaire, *s.f.* White of egg; glair.

glaise, *s.f.* Clay, loam.

gland, *s.m.* **I.** Acorn. **2.** Tassel.

glande, *s.f.* Gland.

glaner, *v.tr.* To glean.

glaneur, -euse, *s.* Gleaner.

glapir, *v.i.* To yelp, yap; (of fox) to bark.

glapissement, *s.m.* Yapping, yelping; barking (of fox).

glas, *s.m.* Knell.

glauque, *a.* Glaucous; sea-green.

glissade, *s.f.* **I.** Slip. **2.** Sliding. **Faire une glissade,** to have a slide. **3.** Slide.

glissant, *a.* **I.** Slippery. **2.** Sliding.

glissement, *s.m.* **I.** (*a*) Sliding; slip. (*b*) Gliding. **2.** Landslip, land-slide.

glisser. **I.** *v.i.* **I.** To slip. **2.** To slide. **3.** To glide.
　　II. glisser, *v.tr.* *G. qch. dans la poche de qn,* to slip sth. into s.o.'s pocket.
　　se glisser, to creep, steal.

glissoire, *s.f.* Slide (on ice).

global, -aux, *a.* Total, aggregate, inclusive (sum); lump (payment).

globe, *s.m.* **I.** (*a*) Globe, sphere. (*b*) Orb (of regalia). **2.** Globe de l'œil, eyeball.

globulaire, *a.* Globular.

globule, *s.m.* Globule.

globuleux, *a.* Globular.

gloire, *s.f.* **I.** Glory. **2.** Boast, pride. **Se faire gloire de qch.,** to glory in sth. **3.** Glory, halo, nimbus.

glorieusement, *adv.* **I.** Gloriously. **2.** Proudly.

glorieux, *a.* **I.** Glorious. **2.** Proud. *G. de qch.,* vain of sth. **3.** *s.m.* Boaster. **Faire le glorieux,** to brag, to swagger.

glorifier, *v.tr.* To praise, glorify. **se glorifier,** to boast.

glossaire, *s.m.* Glossary, dictionary.

glouglou, *s.m.* Gurgle, bubbling.

gloussement, *s.m.* Clucking (of hen); gobbling (of turkey); chuckling.

glousser, *v.i.* (Of hen) To cluck; (of turkey) to gobble; (of pers.) to chuckle.

glouton, -onne. **I.** *a.* Greedy, gluttonous. **2.** *s.* (*a*) Glutton, gormandizer. (*b*) *s.m.* *Z:* Glutton, wolverine.

gloutonnement, *adv.* Gluttonously.

gloutonnerie, *s.f.* Gluttony.

glu, *s.f.* Bird-lime. *F:* Il a de la glu aux mains, money sticks to his fingers.

gluant, *a.* Sticky, gummy.

glutineux, *a.* Glutinous.

glycérine, *s.f.* Glycerin(e).

glycine, *s.f.* *Bot:* Wistaria.

gnome [gno:m], *s.m.* Gnome.

gnou [gnu], *s.m.* *Z:* Gnu, wildebeest.

go. *F:* **Tout de go.** **I.** Easily. **2.** All of a sudden.

gobelet, *s.m.* Goblet, cup.

gobe-mouches, *s.m.inv.* **I.** *Orn:* Fly-catcher. **2.** *Bot:* Fly-trap.

gober, *v.tr.* To swallow, gulp down. *F:* Gober des mouches, to stand gaping.

Godefroi. *Pr.n.m.* Godfrey.

godille [-di:j], *s.f.* Stern-oar; scull.

goéland, *s.m.* *Orn:* (Sea-)gull.

goélette, *s.f.* Schooner.

goémon, *s.m.* Seaweed.

goguenard, *a.* Mocking, bantering.

goitre, *s.m.* Goitre; *F:* wen.

golf, *s.m.* Golf. **Terrain de golf,** golf-links.

golfe, *s.m.* Gulf, bay. **Le Courant du Golfe,** the Gulf-Stream.

gomme, *s.f.* **I.** Gum. **2.** *G. élastique, à effacer,* (india-)rubber.

gomme-gutte, *s.f.* Gamboge.

gommeux, *a.* Gummy, sticky.

gommier, *s.m.* *Bot:* Gum-tree.

gond, *s.m.* Hinge-pin (of door). *F:* Sortir (hors) de ses gonds, to lose one's temper.

gondole, *s.f.* Gondola.

gonflage, *s.m.* Inflation.

gonflement, *s.m.* Inflating, inflation; distension.

gonfler. **I.** *v.tr.* (*a*) To inflate, distend; to pump up (tyre); to puff out (one's cheeks). (*b*) To swell. **2.** *v.i.* & *pr.* To become inflated.

goret, *s.m.* Little pig.

gorge, *s.f.* **I.** (*a*) Throat, neck. (*b*) Bosom, bust (of woman). **2.** Throat, gullet. **Avoir la gorge serrée,** to have a lump in one's throat. **Crier à pleine gorge,** to shout at the top of one's voice. **Rire à gorge déployée,** to laugh heartily. **Rire sous gorge,** to chuckle. **3.** *F:* **Faire des gorges chaudes de qch.,** to gloat over sth. **4.** Gorge, pass, defile.

gorgée, *s.f.* Mouthful, draught.

gorger, v.tr. (n. gorgeons) To stuff, gorge.
Gorgone, s.f. Myth: Gorgon.
gorille [-ri:j], s.m. Z: Gorilla.
gosier, s.m. Throat; gullet.
gosse, s.m. & f. P: Youngster, kid.
gothique, a. Gothic.
gouailler [gwaje], v.tr. To banter, chaff.
gouaillerie [gwajri], s.f. Banter, chaff.
gouailleur, -euse [gwaj-]. I. a. Waggish; bantering. 2. s. Banterer.
gouape, s.f. F: Blackguard, bad lot.
goudron, s.m. Tar.
goudronner, v.tr. To tar.
gouffre, s.m. Gulf, pit, abyss.
goujat, s.m. Boor, churl, cad.
goujon, s.m. Ich: Gudgeon.
goule, s.f. Ghoul.
goulet, s.m. Narrow part, neck (of object); gully (in mountains).
goulot, s.m. Neck (of bottle).
goulûment, adv. Greedily, gluttonously.
goupille [-pi:j], s.f. (Linch)pin.
goupillon [-pijɔ], s.m. I. Sprinkler (for holy water). 2. Brush (for gum).
gourde, s.f. I. Bot: Gourd. 2. Calabash, water-bottle.
gourdin, s.m. Club, cudgel, bludgeon.
gourmand. I. a. (a) Greedy. (b) Fond of sweet things. 2. s. Gourmand, glutton.
gourmander. I. v.i. To guzzle. 2. v.tr. (a) To rebuke. (b) To treat roughly.
gourmandise, s.f. I. Greediness, gluttony. 2. pl. Sweetmeats, dainties.
gourme, s.f. Jeter sa gourme, to sow one's wild oats.
gourmet, s.m. Gourmet, epicure.
gousse, s.f. Pod, shell, husk (of peas). G. d'ail, clove of garlic.
gousset, s.m. (a) Gusset. (b) Waistcoat pocket.
goût, s.m. I. (Sense of) taste. 2. Flavour, taste. 3. Prendre goût à qch., to develop a taste for sth. Prov: il ne faut pas disputer des goûts, everyone to his taste; there is no accounting for tastes. 4. Les gens de goût, people of taste.
goûter. I. v.tr. I. To taste (food). 2. To enjoy, appreciate. 3. Goûter à qch., to take a little of sth.
II. **goûter,** s.m. (Afternoon) snack.
goutte, s.f. I. Drop (of liquid). 2. Spot, splash (of colour). 3. F: Small quantity. 4. Adv.phr. F: Ne . . . goutte, not at all (thus used to-day only with comprendre, entendre, voir). Je n'y vois goutte, I can make nothing of it. On n'y voyait g., it was pitch-dark. 5. Med: Gout.
gouttelette, s.f. Droplet, globule.
goutteux, a. Gouty.
gouttière, s.f. I. Const: Gutter, guttering. 2. Spout, rain-pipe.
gouvernail [-na:j], s.m. Nau: Rudder, helm. Roue du gouvernail, (steering-)wheel.
gouvernante, s.f. Housekeeper.

gouverne, s.f. Guidance, direction.
gouvernement, s.m. I. (a) Government, management. (b) Governorship. (c) Steering. 2. (The) Government.
gouvernemental, -aux, a. Governmental.
gouverner, v.tr. I. Nau: To steer (ship). 2. To govern, rule. 3. (a) To manage, administer. (b) To govern (country).
gouverneur, s.m. Governor.
goyave, s.f. Bot: Guava (fruit).
grabat, s.m. Mean bed; pallet.
grâce, s.f. I. Grace, charm. (a) F: Faire des grâces, to attitudinize. (b) De bonne grâce, willingly. (c) Myth: Les trois Grâces, the three Graces. 2. Favour. Rentrer en grâce, to reingratiate oneself (auprès de, with). De grâce! for pity's sake! 3. (a) (Act of) grace. Demander une g. à qn, to ask a favour of s.o. (b) F: A la grâce de Dieu, we must trust in God. 4. (a) Jur: Free pardon. F: Je vous fais g. cette fois-ci, I will let you off this time. (b) Demander grâce, to cry for mercy. Je vous fais g. du reste, you needn't do any more. 5. Thanks. (a) pl. Action de grâces, thanksgiving. (b) Prep.phr. Grâce à, thanks to, owing to.
gracier, v.tr. To pardon.
gracieusement, adv. I. Gracefully. 2. Graciously. 3. Gratuitously.
gracieux, a. I. Graceful. 2. (a) Gracious. (b) A titre gracieux, as a favour; gratis.
gradation, s.f. Gradation; gradual process.
grade, s.m. I. Rank, dignity, grade. 2. (University) degree. 3. Mil: Rank.
gradé, s.m. Mil: Non-commissioned officer. Tous les gradés, all ranks (commissioned and non-commissioned).
gradin, s.m. Step, tier.
graduation, s.f. I. Graduation. 2. Scale.
gradué, a. (a) Graduated. Verre g., measuring glass; graduated measure. (b) Graded, progressive (exercises, etc.).
graduel, -elle, a. Gradual, progressive.
graduellement, adv. Gradually.
grain[1]**,** s.m. I. (a) Grain. G. d'orge, barleycorn. (b) Corn. 2. Berry, bean (of coffee). G. de raisin, grape. F: Grain de beauté, beauty spot; mole. 3. Particle, atom; grain (of salt). 4. Bead. 5. Grain, texture.
grain[2]**,** s.m. Squall; gust of wind.
graine, s.f. Seed (of plants). G. de lin, linseed. Monter en graine, to run to seed.
graissage, s.m. Greasing, lubrication.
graisse, s.f. Grease, fat. G. de rôti, dripping.
graisser, v.tr. To grease, lubricate. Graisser la patte à qn, to grease s.o.'s palm.
graisseux, a. (a) Greasy, oily, unctuous. (b) Fatty, adipose.
graminé. Bot: I. a. Graminaceous. 2. s.f.pl. Graminées, graminaceae, grasses.
grammaire, s.f. Grammar. Classes de grammaire, lower forms.
grammairien, -ienne, s. Grammarian.
grammatical, -aux, a. Grammatical.

grammaticalement, *adv.* Grammatically.

gramme, *s.m. Meas:* Gram(me).

gramophone, *s.m.* Gramophone.

grand, *a.* **1.** (*a*) Tall (in stature); large, big (in size). *Homme g.,* tall man. *Grands bras,* long arms. *Grands pieds,* big feet. (*b*) Chief, main. *G. chemin,* main road. *Nau: Le g. mât,* the mainmast. *G. ressort,* mainspring. (*c*) *Quand tu seras g.,* when you are grown up. *Les grandes personnes,* the grown-ups. *Sch:* **Les grandes classes,** the upper forms. (*d*) *adv. Porte(s) grande(s) ouverte(s),* wide-open door(s). *Adv.phr.* **En grand,** (i) on a large scale; (ii) full size. **2.** Large, many. *Le g. public,* the general public. **En grande partie,** to a great extent. **3.** *Les grands hommes,* great men. **Le grand monde,** (high) society. *Grands vins,* high-class wines. **4.** *Grandes pensées,* great, noble, thoughts. **5.** *Il fait g. jour,* it is broad daylight. *Il est g. temps de partir,* it is high time we were off. **6.** *s.m. Les grands de la terre,* the great ones of the earth.

grand'chose, *indef. pron. m.* (Nearly always coupled with *pas* or *sans*) Much.

grand-duc, *s.m.* **1.** Grand duke. **2.** Eagle-owl, great horned owl. *pl. Des grands-ducs.*

Grande-Bretagne. *Pr.n.f.* Great Britain.

grandeur, *s.f.* **1.** (*a*) Size; height (of tree). **De grandeur naturelle,** full-size(d). (*b*) Extent; scale. **2.** Greatness. (*a*) Importance; grandeur. (*b*) Majesty, splendour, grandeur. (*c*) Nobility.

grandiose, *a.* Grand, imposing.

grandir. **1.** *v.i.* (i) To grow tall; (ii) to grow up. **2.** *v.tr.* (*a*) To make (sth.) greater; to increase. (*b*) To magnify.

grandissement, *s.m.* Growth, increase.

grand(-)livre, *s.m.* Ledger. *pl. Des grands-livres.*

grand'maman, *s.f. F:* Grandmamma. *pl. Des grand'mamans.*

grand'mère, *s.f.* Grandmother. *pl. Des grand'mères.*

grand'messe, *s.f. Ecc:* High mass. *pl. Des grand'messes.*

grand-oncle, *s.m.* Great-uncle. *pl. Des grands-oncles.*

grand-papa, *s.m. F:* Grandpapa. *pl. Des grands-papas.*

grand'peine (à), *adv.phr.* With great difficulty.

grand-père, *s.m.* Grandfather. *pl. Des grands-pères.*

grand'route, *s.f.* Highway, high road. *pl. Des grand'routes.*

grand'rue, *s.f.* High street, main street. *pl. Des grand'rues.*

grands-parents, *s.m.pl.* Grandparents.

grand'tante, *s.f* Great-aunt. *pl. Des grand'-tantes.*

grange, *s.f.* Barn.

granit, *s.m.* Granite.

granulaire, *a* Granular.

granuler, *v.tr.* To granulate.

granuleux, *a.* Granular.

graphique. **1.** *a.* Graphic. **2.** *s.m.* Diagram, graph.

graphiquement, *adv.* Graphically.

graphite, *s.m.* Graphite, plumbago.

grappe, *s.f.* Cluster, bunch (of grapes).

grappin, *s.m. Nau:* Grapnel, hook.

gras, grasse, *a.* **1.** (*a*) Fat; fatty. (*b*) Rich (food). *Régime g.,* meat diet. **Faire gras,** to eat meat. (*c*) *s.m.* Fat (of meat). **2.** Fat, stout. **3.** Greasy, oily. **4.** Thick. *Boue grasse,* thick, slimy, mud.

grasseyer, *v.i.* To roll one's r's.

gratification, *s.f.* (*a*) Gratuity. (*b*) Bonus.

gratifier, *v.tr. G. qn de qch.,* (i) to bestow sth. upon s.o.; (ii) *F:* to attribute sth. to s.o.

gratis [-tis], *adv.* Gratis; free of charge.

gratitude, *s.f.* Gratitude, gratefulness.

gratte-ciel, *s.m.inv.* Sky-scraper.

grattement, *s.m.* Scratching; scraping.

gratter, *v.tr.* **1.** To scrape, scratch. *F:* **Gratter le papier,** to drive a quill. **2.** To erase (a word).

grattoir, *s.m.* Scraper.

gratuit, *a.* Gratuitous. (*a*) Free. (*b*) *Insulte gratuite,* gratuitous, wanton insult.

gratuitement, *adv.* Gratuitously.

grave, *a.* **1.** (*a*) Grave; solemn; sober. (*b*) Important, severe. **2.** *Voix g.,* deep voice. **3.** *Gram:* Accent grave, grave accent.

gravement, *adv.* **1.** Gravely. **2.** Seriously.

graver, *v.tr.* To cut, engrave, carve. *G. à l'eau forte,* to etch.

graveur, *s.m.* Engraver; carver. *G. à l'eau-forte,* etcher.

gravier, *s.m.* Gravel, grit.

gravir, *v.tr.* To climb; to ascend.

gravité, *s.f.* **1.** *Ph:* Gravity. **2.** Gravity, seriousness.

graviter, *v.i.* **1.** To gravitate. **2.** To revolve.

gravure, *s.f.* **1.** Engraving. *G. à l'eau-forte,* etching. **2.** Print, picture, engraving, etching. *Livre plein de gravures,* book full of illustrations.

gré, *s.m.* **1.** Liking, taste. **Au gré de mes désirs,** just as I could wish. **2.** Will, pleasure. **De mon plein gré,** of my own accord. **Bon gré mal gré,** whether we like it or not; willy-nilly. **Au gré des flots,** at the mercy of the waves. **3.** **Savoir (bon) gré à qn de qch.,** to be grateful to s.o. for sth.

grèbe, *s.m. Orn:* Grebe.

grec, grecque. **1.** *a.* Greek. **2.** *s.* Greek. **3.** *s.m.* **Le grec,** (the) Greek (language).

Grèce. *Pr.n.f. Geog:* Greece.

grecque. See GREC.

gredin, *s.* Rogue, scoundrel.

gréement, *s.m. Nau:* Rigging.

gréer, *v.tr. Nau:* To rig.

greffe, *s.f.* **1.** *Arb:* Graft, slip. **2.** Grafting.

greffier, *s.m.* **1.** Clerk (of the court). **2.** Registrar.

grégaire, *a.* Gregarious.

Grégoire. *Pr.n.m.* Gregory.

grêle[1], *a.* Slender, thin (leg); high-pitched (voice).

grêle[2], *s.f.* (*a*) Hail. (*b*) F: G. *de coups*, shower of blows.

grêler, *v.impers.* Il grêle, it hails.

grêlon, *s.m.* Hail-stone.

grelot, *s.m.* (Small globular) bell. F: Attacher le grelot, to bell the cat.

grelotter, *v.i.* 1. To tremble, shake, shiver. 2. To jingle.

grenade[1], *s.f.* 1. *Bot:* Pomegranate. 2. (*a*) Grenade, bomb. (*b*) G. *sous-marine*, depth-charge.

Grenade[2]. *Pr.n.f.* Granada (in Spain).

grenat. 1. *s.m.* Garnet. 2. *a.inv.* Garnet-red.

grenier, *s.m.* 1. Granary, storehouse. 2. Attic, garret.

grenouille [-nu:j], *s.f.* 1. Frog. 2. P: Funds (of a society). Manger la grenouille, to make off with the cash.

grès, *s.m.* 1. Sandstone. 2. Poterie de grès, stoneware.

grésil, *s.m.* Frozen pellets of snow.

grésillement [-zij-], *s.m.* Crackling, chirping (of crickets).

grésiller [-zije], *v.i.* (*a*) To crackle; (of frying-pan) to sizzle. (*b*) (Of crickets) To chirp.

grève, *s.f.* 1. Strand; (sea-)shore; (sandy) beach. 2. Strike (of workmen).

grever, *v.tr.* (je grève) Grevé *d'un impôt*, saddled with a tax.

gréviste, *s.m. & f.* Striker.

grief [grief], *s.m.* Grievance.

grièvement, *adv.* Severely, grievously.

griffe, *s.f.* Claw; talon. Coup de griffe, scratch.

griffon, *s.m.* 1. Griffin, gryphon. 2. *Orn:* Griffon-vulture.

griffonnage, *s.m.* 1. Scribbling. 2. Scrawl.

griffonner, *v.tr.* To scrawl, scribble.

grignotement, *s.m.* Nibbling.

grignoter, *v.tr.* To nibble.

gril [gri], *s.m. Cu:* Grid(iron), grill.

grillade [grijad], *s.f.* Grill, grilled steak.

grillage [grija:ʒ], *s.f.* (Metal) grating; wire-netting.

grille [gri:j], *s.f.* (*a*) (Iron) bars. (*b*) Iron gate. (*c*) Railings. (*d*) Fire-grate.

griller [grije], *v.tr.* 1. To grill (meat); to toast (bread). 2. To burn, scorch. 3. *v.i.* (*a*) *Cu:* To grill; to toast. (*b*) F: La lampe a grillé, the bulb has burnt out.

grillon [grijɔ̃], *s.m. Ent:* Cricket.

grimace, *s.f.* Grimace, grin, wry face.

grimacer, *v.i.* (n. grimaçons) To grimace; to grin; to make faces.

grimper, *v.i.* To climb (up). G. *à un mât*, to swarm up a pole. *v.tr* G. *une montagne*, to climb a mountain.

grimpeur, -euse. 1. *a.* Climbing. 2. *s.m.* Climber.

grincement, *s.m.* Grinding; creaking; gnashing.

grincer, *v.i.* (n. grinçons) To grate; to grind; to creak. G. *des dents*, to grind, gnash, one's teeth.

grincheux. 1. *a.* Grumpy, crabbed. 2. *s.* Grumbler, grouser.

grippe, *s.f.* 1. Dislike, aversion. 2. *Med:* Influenza.

gris, *a.* 1. (*a*) Grey. (*b*) Grey-haired. *Barbe grise*, grey beard. (*c*) *Temps g.*, dull weather. Faire grise mine, to look anything but pleased. 2. F: Intoxicated.

grisâtre, *a.* Greyish.

griser, *v.tr.* F: To intoxicate. se griser, to get tipsy, fuddled.

griserie, *s.f.* 1. Tipsiness. 2. Intoxication, exhilaration.

grisou, *s.m. Min:* Fire-damp.

grive, *s.f. Orn:* Thrush.

grivois, *a.* Licentious, loose.

Groenland [-ɛn-], *Pr.n.m.* Greenland.

grog [grog], *s.m.* Toddy; grog.

grognard. F: 1. *a.* Grumbling. 2. *s.* Grumbler, grouser.

grognement, *s.m.* 1. (*a*) (i) Grunting; (ii) grunt. (*b*) (i) Growling; (ii) growl. 2. F: (*a*) Grumbling. (*b*) Snarling; snarl.

grogner, *v.i.* 1. (*a*) To grunt. (*b*) To growl. 2. To grumble; to grouse.

groin, *s.m.* Snout (of pig).

grommeler, *v.i.* (je grommelle) To grumble, mutter.

grondement, *s.m.* 1. Growl(ing), snarl(ing). 2. Rumbling; booming.

gronder. 1. *v.i.* (*a*) To growl, snarl. (*b*) To rumble; to boom. (*c*) G. *contre* qn, to grumble at s.o. 2. *v.tr.* To scold.

gronderie, *s.f.* Scolding; rating.

grondeur, -euse. 1. *a.* Grumbling, scolding. 2. *s.* Grumbler; F: scold.

gros, grosse. 1. *a.* (*a*) Big, bulky, stout. G. *bout*, thick end (of stick). G. *sel*, coarse salt. *Grosse voix*, gruff voice; big voice. Gros mot, coarse expression. Grosse cavalerie, heavy cavalry. Jouer gros (jeu), to play for high stakes. Gros temps, heavy, bad, weather. F: Les gros bonnets, the bigwigs. (*b*) *Action grosse de conséquences*, action big with consequences. (*c*) *adv.* Gagner gros, to earn a great deal. 2. *s.m.* (*a*) Bulk, chief part. Le plus gros est fait, the hardest part of the job is done. G. *de l'été*, height of summer. (*b*) En gros. (i) Roughly, broadly. (ii) *Acheter en g.*, to buy in bulk. (*c*) *Com:* Wholesale (trade). 3. *s.f.* Grosse. *Com:* Gross; twelve dozen.

gros-bec, *s.m. Orn:* Grosbeak; hawfinch. *pl. Des gros-becs.*

groseille [-zɛ:j], *s.f.* 1. Currant. 2. Groseille à maquereau, gooseberry.

groseillier [-zeje], *s.m.* 1. Currant-bush. 2. Groseillier à maquereau, gooseberry-bush.

grosse. See GROS.

grosseur, *s.f.* Size, bulk, volume.

grossier, *a.* (*a*) Coarse, rough. (*b*) *Ignorance*

grossière, crass ignorance. *Faute grossière*, glaring blunder. (c) Rude, unmannerly (*envers*, to).

grossièrement, *adv.* **1.** Coarsely. **2.** Rudely.

grossièreté, *s.f.* (a) Coarseness, roughness. (b) Rudeness, coarseness. (c) Grossness, glaring nature.

grossir. **1.** *v.tr.* To enlarge, magnify. *Torrent grossi par les pluies*, torrent swollen by the rain. **2.** *v.i.* To increase, swell.

grossissant, *a.* **1.** Growing, swelling. **2.** Magnifying, enlarging.

grossissement, *s.m.* **1.** Increase in size. **2.** Magnifying, enlargement.

grotesque, *a.* (a) *Art:* Grotesque. (b) *F:* Ludicrous, absurd.

grotte, *s.f.* Grotto.

grouiller [gruje], *v.i.* To crawl, swarm (*de*, with).

groupe, *s.m.* Group; clump; cluster.

groupement, *s.m.* **1.** Grouping. **2.** Group.

grouper, *v.tr.* To group, to arrange (in groups).
  se grouper, to gather; to bunch (together).

gruau, *s.m.* **1.** (a) (Finest) flour of wheat. (b) **Gruau d'avoine**, groats. **2.** *Cu:* Gruel.

grue, *s.f.* **1.** *Orn:* Crane. *F:* **Faire le pied de grue**, to be kept waiting. **2.** (Hoisting) crane.

gruyère, *s.m.* Gruyere (cheese).

gué, *s.m.* Ford.

guenille [-ni:j], *s.f.* Tattered garment, old rag. **En guenilles**, in rags (and tatters).

guenon, *s.f.* She-monkey.

guépard, *s.m.* *Z:* Cheetah.

guêpe, *s.f.* *Ent:* Wasp.

guêpier, *s.m.* **1.** Wasps' nest. *F:* **Donner dans un guêpier**, to bring a hornets' nest about one's ears. **2.** *Orn:* Bee-eater.

guère, *adv.* (Always with neg. expressed or understood) Hardly; not much, not many. *Il en tardera g. à venir*, he will not be long in coming. **Il ne s'en faut de guère**, there is not much wanting.

guéridon, *s.m.* Pedestal table.

guérilla [-rija, -illa], *s.f.* Band of guerrillas.

guérir. **1.** *v.tr.* To cure, heal. **2.** *v.i.* (a) To be cured; to recover. (b) (Of wound) To heal.

guérison, *s.f.* **1.** Recovery. **2.** (a) Cure (of disease). (b) Healing (of wound).

guérite, *s.f.* **1.** Sentry-box. **2.** Cabin (for watchman). *G. téléphonique*, call-box.

Guernesey. *Pr.n.m. Geog:* Guernsey.

guerre, *s.f.* War, warfare. **1.** **Se mettre en guerre**, to go to war. **Faire la guerre à, contre, un pays**, to make war on, against, a country. **2.** Strife, feud. *Adv.phr.* **De guerre lasse** j'y consentis, for the sake of peace I gave in.

guerrier. **1.** *a.* Warlike. **2.** *s.m.* Warrior.

guet, *s.m.* Watch(ing); look-out. **Avoir l'œil au guet**, to keep a sharp look-out.

guet-apens, *s.m.* Ambush, ambuscade, snare. *pl.* Des guets-apens.

guêtre, *s.f.* Gaiter. *Demi-guêtres*, spats.

guetter, *v.tr.* To lie in wait for, to be on the look-out for.

gueule, *s.f.* **1.** (a) Mouth (of dog). (b) **Casser la gueule à qn**, to bash s.o.'s face. **2.** Mouth (of sack); muzzle (of gun).

gueule-de-lion, *s.f.*, **gueule-de-loup**, *s.f. Bot:* Antirrhinum, snapdragon. *pl. Des gueules-de-lion(-loup).*

gueux, *s.* Beggar; tramp.

gui, *s.m. Bot:* Mistletoe.

guichet, *s.m.* **1.** (a) Wicket(-gate). (b) Grating (in door). **2.** Turnstile. **3.** (a) Pay-desk (of bank). (b) (Booking-office) window. **4.** *Cr:* Wicket.

guide[1], *s.m.* **1.** Guide; conductor. **2.** Guide (-book).

guide[2], *s.f.* Rein.

guider, *v.tr.* To guide, direct, lead.

guidon, *s.m.* **1.** *Cy:* Handle-bar. **2.** Fore-sight (of gun). **3.** *Nau:* Burgee.

guigne[1], *s.f.* (Black-)heart cherry.

guigne[2], *s.f. F:* Bad luck, ill-luck.

guignol, *s.m.* (a) Punch. (b) Punch and Judy show.

Guillaume [gij-]. *Pr.n.m.* William.

guillemets [gijmɛ], *s.m.pl. Typ:* Inverted commas, quotation marks.

guillemot [gij-], *s.m. Orn:* Guillemot.

guillotine [gij-], *s.f.* **1.** Guillotine. **2.** **Fenêtre à guillotine**, sash-window.

guillotiner [gij-], *v.tr.* To guillotine.

guimauve, *s.f. Bot:* Marsh-mallow.

guimpe, *s.f.* (Nun's) wimple.

guindé, *a.* Stiff, *F:* starchy; stilted.

Guinée. **1.** *Pr.n.f. Geog:* Guinea. **2.** *s.f. Num:* Guinea.

guinguette, *s.f.* Place of refreshment (with music and dancing); pleasure gardens.

guirlande, *s.f.* Garland, festoon, wreath.

guise, *s.f.* Manner, way, fashion. **A votre guise!** please yourself! **En guise de**, (i) by way of; (ii) instead of.

guitare, *s.f. Mus:* Guitar.

guttural, -aux. **1.** *a.* Guttural; throaty. **2.** *s.f. Ling:* Gutturale, guttural.

Guyane (la). *Pr.n.f. Geog:* Guiana.

gymnase, *s.m.* Gymnasium.

gymnaste, *s.m.* Gymnast.

gymnastique. **1.** *a.* Gymnastic. **2.** *s.f.* Gymnastics.

gypse, *s.m.* **1.** *Miner:* Gypsum. **2.** *Com:* Plaster of Paris.

gyro, *a. Adm:* Sens gyro, roundabout.

gyroscope, *s.m.* Gyroscope.

Words beginning with an 'aspirate' h are shown by an asterisk.

H, h [aʃ], *s.m. & f.* (The letter) H, h.
*****ha,** *int.* **1.** Ah ! oh ! **2.** *Ha, ha !* ha, ha !
habile, *a.* Clever, skilful, able ; cunning, artful.
habilement, *adv.* Cleverly, ably, capably.
habileté, *s.f.* (*a*) Ability, skill, skilfulness. (*b*) Cleverness, smartness.
habillement [abij-], *s.m.* **1.** Clothing, dressing. **2.** Clothes, dress ; apparel.
habiller [abije], *v.tr.* (*a*) To dress. (*b*) To clothe.
   s'habiller, to dress.
   habillé, *a.* Dressed.
habit, *s.m.* **1.** Dress, costume ; *pl.* clothes. **2.** (*a*) Coat. (*b*) **Être en habit,** to be in evening-dress. **3.** (Monk's, nun's) habit.
habitable, *a.* Habitable.
habitant, *s.* (*a*) Inhabitant ; resident, dweller. (*b*) Occupier. (*c*) Inmate.
habitation, *s.f.* **1.** Habitation ; dwelling. **2.** Dwelling(-place), residence.
habiter. 1. *v.tr.* (*a*) To inhabit, to live in (a place). (*b*) To occupy (house). **2.** *v.i.* To live, reside, dwell.
habitude, *s.f.* (*a*) Habit, custom. **Se faire une habitude de,** to make it one's practice to. **D'habitude,** usually, ordinarily. **Comme d'habitude,** as usual. (*b*) Knack. *Je n'en ai plus l'h.,* I'm out of practice.
habituel, -elle, *a.* Usual, customary ; habitual.
habituellement, *adv.* Habitually, usually.
habituer, *v.tr.* To accustom, habituate.
   s'habituer, to get used, to get accustomed.
   habitué, *s.* Frequenter ; regular customer.
*****hache,** *s.f.* Ax(e). *H. de guerre,* tomahawk.
*****hacher,** *v.tr.* (*a*) To chop (up). **Hacher menu,** to mince. (*b*) To hack (up), mangle.
   haché, *a.* **1.** Staccato, jerky (style). **2.** *Mer hachée,* cross sea ; choppy sea.
*****hachette,** *s.f.* Hatchet.
*****hachis,** *s.m. Cu :* Mince.
*****hagard,** *a.* Haggard, wild(-looking).
*****haie,** *s.f.* (*a*) Hedge(-row). *H. vive,* quickset hedge. (*b*) Line, row (of troops).
*****haillon** [ajɔ̃], *s.m.* Rag (of clothing).
*****haine,** *s.f.* Hatred ; detestation.
*****haineux,** *a.* Full of hatred.
*****haïr,** *v.tr.* (je hais, n. haïssons ; *imp.* hais) To hate, detest.
*****haïssable,** *a.* Hateful, detestable.
*****halage,** *s.m.* Towing. **Chemin de halage,** tow(ing)-path.
*****hâle,** *s.m.* (*a*) Tanning ; sunburn. (*b*) Tan.
haleine, *s.f.* Breath. **Tout d'une haleine,** all in one breath. **Travail de longue haleine,** long and exacting labour.

*****haler,** *v.tr.* To tow ; to haul.
*****hâler,** *v.tr.* (Of sun) To tan.
   se hâler, to get sunburnt.
   hâlé, *a.* Sunburnt, tanned, weather-beaten.
*****haletant,** *a.* Panting, breathless, out of breath ; gasping (for breath).
*****halètement,** *s.m.* Panting ; gasping.
*****haleter,** *v.i.* (je halète) To pant ; to gasp (for breath).
*****halle,** *s.f.* (Covered) market.
*****hallebarde,** *s.f. Archeol :* Halberd, halbert ; bill. *F :* **Il tombe des hallebardes,** it is raining cats and dogs.
*****hallier,** *s.m.* Thicket, copse, brake.
hallucination, *s.f.* Hallucination, delusion.
*****halo,** *s.m. Meteor :* Halo.
*****halte,** *s.f.* **1.** Stop, halt. **Faire halte,** (of train) to stop, to call (at station). **Halte là !** halt ! **2.** Stopping-place, resting-place.
haltère, *s.m.* Dumb-bell.
*****hamac** [amak], *s.m.* Hammock.
hamadryade, *s.f.* **1.** *Gr.Myth :* Hamadryad, wood-nymph ; **2.** King-cobra.
*****hameau,** *s.m.* Hamlet.
hameçon, *s.m.* (Fish-)hook. **Mordre à l'hameçon,** to nibble at the bait.
*****hampe,** *s.f.* Staff, pole (of flag) ; shaft (of spear).
*****han,** *int. Pousser un han à chaque coup,* to give a grunt at every stroke.
*****hanche,** *s.f.* **1.** Hip. **Les (deux) poings sur les hanches,** with arms akimbo. **2.** Haunch (of horse) ; *pl.* hind-quarters.
*****hangar,** *s.m.* **1.** (Open) shed ; lean-to. *H. à bateaux,* boat-house. **2.** *Av :* Hangar.
*****hanneton,** *s.m. Ent :* Cockchafer.
*****hanter,** *v.tr.* To frequent, haunt. *Être hanté par une idée,* to be obsessed by an idea.
*****hantise,** *s.f.* Haunting memory ; obsession.
*****happer,** *v.tr.* (Of birds) To snap up, seize (insects).
*****harangue,** *s.f.* Harangue ; speech.
*****haranguer,** *v.tr.* To harangue.
*****harassement,** *s.m.* **1.** Harassing. **2.** Fatigue.
*****harasser,** *v.tr.* (*a*) To tire (out), exhaust. (*b*) To harass, worry.
*****harcelant,** *a.* Harassing, tormenting.
*****harceler,** *v.tr.* (Je harcèle) To harass, torment ; to harry. *H. qn de questions,* to pester s.o. with questions.
*****hardes,** *s.f.pl.* (Worn) clothes ; wearing apparel.
*****hardi,** *a.* Bold, audacious. (*a*) Daring, fearless. (*b*) Rash (*c*) Impudent. (*d*) *int.* Courage ! go it !
*****hardiesse,** *s.f.* **1.** Boldness, hardihood. (*a*) Daring, pluck. **Prendre la hardiesse**

de faire qch., to make so bold as to do sth. (b) Impudence, forwardness, effrontery. *Il a eu la h. de m'écrire*, he had the audacity, F: the cheek, to write to me. 2. Bold, daring, act.

*hardiment, adv. Boldly.

*harem [arɛm], s.m. Harem.

*hareng, s.m. Herring. *H. saur*, red herring.

*hargneux, a. Snarling; peevish, cross; nagging.

*haricot, s.m. H. (*blanc*), haricot bean. *Haricots verts*, French beans. *Haricots d'Espagne*, scarlet runners.

harmonie, s.f. 1. (a) Harmony; agreement. *En harmonie avec . . .*, in keeping with. . . . (b) Harmoniousness. 2. *Mus:* Harmony.

harmonieusement, adv. Harmoniously.

harmonieux, a. (a) Harmonious, tuneful (sound). (b) Harmonious (family).

harmoniser, v.tr. To harmonize; to match (colours).

*harnachement, s.m. 1. Harnessing. 2. (a) Harness, trappings. (b) Saddlery.

*harnacher, v.tr. To harness.

*harnais, s.m. (a) Harness. (b) Saddlery.

*haro, int. & s.m. *Crier haro*, to raise a hue and cry (*sur*, against).

*harpe, s.f. *Mus:* Harp.

*harpie, s.f. 1. (a) *Myth:* Harpy. (b) F: Harpy, shrew. 2. Harpy-eagle.

*harpon, s.m. Harpoon.

*harponner, v.tr. To harpoon.

*hasard, s.m. (a) Chance, luck, accident. *Le hasard fit que + ind. or sub.*, chance so ordained that. . . . *Au hasard*, at a guess, at random. Par hasard, by accident, by chance. (b) Risk, danger. *A tout hasard*, (i) at all hazards; (ii) on the off chance.

*hasarder, v.tr. To risk, venture. se hasarder, to take risks. *Se h. à faire qch.*, to venture to do sth.

*hasardeux, a. 1. Hazardous, perilous. 2. Daring, foolhardy.

*hâte, s.f. Haste, hurry. *Avoir hâte de faire qch.*, to be in a hurry to do sth. *A la hâte*, in haste. *En toute hâte*, with all possible speed.

*hâter, v.tr. To hasten; to expedite. *Hâter le pas*, to quicken one's pace. se hâter, to hasten, hurry.

*hâtif, a. (a) Forward, early (spring, fruit); premature (old age); precocious (fruit, mind). (b) Hasty, hurried, ill-considered.

*hâtivement, adv. (a) Prematurely. (b) Hastily.

*hauban, s.m. *Nau:* (a) Shroud. (b) Guy, stay.

*hausse, s.f. Rise, rising. *H. des prix*, advance of prices.

*haussement, s.m. Raising; lifting. *Haussement d'épaules*, shrug.

*hausser. 1. v.tr. To raise, lift. *Hausser les épaules*, to shrug (one's shoulders). 2. v.i. To rise.

*haut. I. a. 1. High. (a) Tall; lofty. *Haute mer*, open sea. *A mer haute*, at high water. (b) Exalted, important. (c) Raised. *Marcher la tête haute*, to carry one's head high. *Lire à haute voix*, to read aloud. (d) Être haut en couleur, to have a high colour. 2. Upper, higher.
II. haut, adv. 1. High (up), above, up. *Haut les mains!* hands up! *Parler haut*, to speak loudly. *Parlez plus h.!* speak up! 2. Back. *Comme il est dit plus h.*, as aforesaid.
III. haut, s.m. 1. Height. 2. Top; upper part. *Les hauts et les bas*, the ups and downs (of life). 3. *Regarder qn de h. en bas*, to look at s.o. contemptuously; *to look down on s.o. Du haut en bas*, from top to bottom. *En haut*, (i) above; (ii) upstairs.

*hautain, a. Haughty.

*hautbois, s.m. *Mus:* Oboe.

*hautement, adv. 1. Highly (esteemed). 2. (a) Loudly. (b) Openly, boldly. 3. Loftily.

*hauteur, s.f. 1. (a) Height, elevation. *A la hauteur de qch.*, abreast of, level with, sth. *Se montrer à la hauteur de la situation*, to prove equal to the occasion. (b) *Mus:* Pitch (of note). (c) Loftiness (of ideas). 2. Haughtiness. 3. High place; eminence.

*haut-fond, s.m. Shoal, shallow. *pl. Des hauts-fonds.*

*haut-le-corps, s.m.inv. Sudden start, jump.

*haut-parleur, s.m. *W.Tel:* Loud-speaker. *pl. Des haut-parleurs.*

*Havane. 1. *Pr.n.f.* *La Havane*, Havana. 2. s.m. Havana (cigar).

*hâve, a. Haggard, gaunt; sunken (cheeks).

*havre. 1. s.m. Harbour, haven, port. 2. *Pr.n.m.* *Le Havre*, Havre.

*havresac [-sak], s.m. Knapsack.

hawaïen, -ïenne, a. & s. *Geog:* Hawaiian.

*Haye (la). *Pr.n.f.* The Hague.

*hé, int. 1. (To call attention) Hullo! I say! 2. (Surprise) Hey! 3. *Hé! hé!* well, well! 4. *Hé bien . . .*, well. . . .

hebdomadaire. 1. a. Weekly. 2. s.m. F: Weekly (paper).

héberger, v.tr. (n. hébergeons) To harbour; to lodge, shelter.

hébétement, s.m. Stupefaction.

hébéter, v.tr. (j'hébète; j'hébéterai) To dull, stupefy; to daze.

hébété, a. Dazed, vacant, bewildered.

hébétude, s.f. F: Dazed, stunned, condition.

hébraïque, a. Hebraic, Hebrew.

hébreu, -eux. 1. a.m. (HÉBRAÏQUE is used for the f.) Hebrew. 2. s.m. *Ling:* Hebrew.

hécatombe, s.f. (a) Hecatomb. (b) F: Great slaughter.

*hein, int. (a) (Expressing surprise) Eh? what? (b) = *n'est-ce pas.*

hélas [elɑːs], int. Alas!

Hélène. *Pr.n.f.* Helen, Helena; F: Ellen.

*héler, v.tr. (je hèle; je hélerai) To hail, call (a taxi); to hail (a ship).

hélianthe, *s.m.* Helianthus, sunflower.
hélice, *s.f. Nau:* (Screw-)propeller, screw;
Av: air-screw.
héliographe, *s.m.* Heliograph.
héliostat, *s.m. Mil:* Heliograph.
héliotrope, *s.m.* (*a*) *Bot:* Heliotrope.
(*b*) *a.inv.* Heliotrope(-coloured).
hellène. 1. *a.* Hellenic. **2.** *s.* Hellene.
helvète, *a. & s. Ethn:* Helvetian.
helvétique, *a.* Helvetic, Swiss.
*****hem** [em], *int.* (A)hem ! hm !
hématite, *s.f. Miner:* Haematite.
hémisphère, *s.m.* Hemisphere.
hémisphérique, *a.* Hemispheric(al).
hémorragie, *s.f. Med:* Haemorrhage;
bleeding.
*****henné,** *s.m. Toil:* Henna.
*****hennir,** *v.i.* To whinny; to neigh.
*****hennissement,** *s.m.* (*a*) Whinnying, neigh-
ing. (*b*) Whinny, neigh.
Henri. *Pr.n.m.* Henry.
Henriette. *Pr.n.f.* Henrietta.
héraldique. 1. *a.* Heraldic. **2.** *s.f.* Heraldry.
*****héraut,** *s.m.* (*a*) Herald. (*b*) Harbinger.
herbacé, *a. Bot:* Herbaceous.
herbage, *s.m.* **1.** Grass-land; pasture.
2. Grass, herbage.
herbe, *s.f.* **1.** Herb, plant, weed. **Herbes
potagères,** pot-herbs. **Fines herbes,** herbs for
seasoning. *Omelette aux fines herbes,* savoury
omelet. **Mauvaise herbe,** weed. **2.** Grass.
F: **Couper l'herbe sous le pied à qn,** to cut
the ground from under s.o.'s feet. **3. En
herbe,** *F:* budding (poet).
herbeux, *a.* Grassy.
herbier, *s.m.* (*a*) Herbal. (*b*) Herbarium.
herbivore. *Z:* **1.** *a.* Herbivorous, grass-
eating. **2.** *s.m.* Herbivore.
herboriste, *s.m. & f.* Herbalist.
Hercule. *Pr.n.m.* Hercules.
herculéen, -enne, *a.* Herculean.
*****hère,** *s.m. F: Un pauvre h.,* a luckless wight.
héréditaire, *a.* Hereditary.
hérédité, *s.f.* **1.** Heredity. **2.** Heirship.
hérésie, *s.f.* Heresy.
hérétique. 1. *a.* Heretical. **2.** *s.* Heretic.
*****hérissement,** *s.m.* Bristling.
*****hérisser,** *v.tr.* (*a*) To bristle (up). (*b*) To
make (sth.) bristle; to cover with spikes.
se hérisser, to bristle (up); (of hair) to
stand on end.
hérissé, *a.* **1.** Bristling (*de,* with).
2. Bristly (moustache).
*****hérisson,** *s.m. Z:* Hedgehog.
héritage, *s.m.* Inheritance, heritage.
hériter. 1. *v.i. H. d'une fortune,* to inherit
a fortune. **2.** *v.tr. H. qch. de qn,* to inherit
sth. from s.o.
héritier, *s.* Heir, *f.* heiress.
hermétique, *a.* Tight(-closed), hermetically
sealed.
hermétiquement, *adv.* Hermetically.
hermine, *s.f.* **1.** *Z:* Stoat, ermine. **2.** *Com:*
Ermine (fur).

héroïne[1]**,** *s.f.* Heroine.
héroïne[2]**,** *s.f. Ch:* Heroin.
héroïque, *a.* Heroic(al).
héroïquement, *adv.* Heroically.
héroïsme, *s.m.* Heroism.
*****héron,** *s.m. Orn:* Heron.
*****héros,** *s.m.* Hero.
*****herse,** *s.f.* **1.** *Agr:* Harrow. **2.** *A.Fort:*
Portcullis.
*****herser,** *v.tr. Agr:* To harrow.
hésitant, *a.* Hesitating.
hésitation, *s.f.* Hesitation, hesitancy.
hésiter, *v.i.* **1.** To hesitate, waver. **2.** To
falter.
hétérodoxe, *a.* Heterodox.
hétérodoxie, *s.f.* Heterodoxy.
hétérogène, *a.* (*a*) Heterogeneous, dissimilar. (*b*) *F:* Incongruous; mixed.
*****hêtraie,** *s.f.* Beech-grove, -plantation.
*****hêtre,** *s.m.* Beech (tree or timber).
*****heu,** *int.* (*a*) Ah ! (*b*) (Doubt) H'm ! (*c*) (Con-
tempt) Pooh ! (*d*) (In speech) . . . er. . . .
heure, *s.f.* Hour. **1.** (*a*) **Deux lieues à l'heure,**
five miles an hour. *Journ:* **La dernière
heure,** (i) the latest news; (ii) stop-press
news. *Ind:* **Heures supplémentaires,** overtime. (*b*) (Time of day) **Quelle heure est-il?**
what is the time? **Cinq heures moins dix,**
ten minutes to five. *Ecc:* **Livre d'heures,**
prayer-book. (*c*) (Appointed hour) *Aut:*
H. d'éclairage, lighting-up time. *A l'h. dite,*
at the appointed time. **Être à l'heure,** to be
punctual. (*d*) (Present time) **Pour l'heure,**
for the present. **A l'heure qu'il est,** (i) by
this time; (ii) nowadays, just now. (*e*) Time.
2. *Adv.phrs.* **De bonne heure,** early. *De
meilleure h.,* earlier. **Faire qch.,** sur l'heure,**
to do sth. right away. **Tout à l'heure,** (i) just
now, a few minutes ago; (ii) presently, *F:*
directly. **A tout à l'heure!** so long ! see you
later ! **3.** *int.* **A la bonne heure!** well done !
heureusement, *adv.* Happily. (*a*) Suc-
cessfully. (*b*) Luckily, fortunately. (*c*) *Commencer h.,* to begin auspiciously.
heureux, *a.* **1.** Happy. *Nous serions h. si
vous acceptiez,* we should be glad if you would
accept. **2.** (*a*) Successful. *L'issue heureuse
des négociations,* the happy issue of the negotiations. (*b*) Lucky, favoured. *H. au jeu,*
lucky at cards. **3.** (*a*) Favourable, lucky,
fortunate. (*b*) *Début h.,* auspicious beginning.
4. Felicitous, happy, apt.
*****heurt,** *s.m.* Shock, knock. **Tout s'est fait
sans heurt,** everything went smoothly.
*****heurter,** *v.tr. & i.* **1.** (*a*) To knock (against),
run into. **H. du pied contre une pierre,** to stub
one's toe against a stone. (*b*) **H. à la porte,**
to knock at the door. **2.** To shock, offend.
se heurter. 1. *Se h. à une difficulté,* to
come up against a difficulty. **2.** To collide.
hexagonal, -aux, *a.* Hexagonal.
hexagone. 1. *a.* Hexagonal. **2.** *s.m.* Hexagon.
hexamètre. *Pros:* **1.** *a.* Hexametric(al).
2. *s.m.* Hexameter.

hiatus [-tyːs], *s.m.* **1.** Gap, break (in narrative). **2.** *Pros:* Hiatus.

hibernal, -aux, *a.* Hibernal; wintry.

hibernant, *a.* Hibernating (animal).

hibernation, *s.f.* Hibernation.

hiberner, *v.i.* To hibernate.

*hibou, -oux, *s.m.* *Orn:* Owl. *Jeune h.,* owlet.

*hic [ik], *s.m.* *F:* Voilà le hic! there's the rub!

*hideur, *s.f.* (a) Hideousness. (b) Hideous sight.

*hideusement, *adv.* Hideously.

*hideux, *a.* Hideous.

hier [iɛːr], *adv.* Yesterday. *H. soir,* last night.

*hiérarchie, *s.f.* Hierarchy.

*hiérarchique, *a.* Hierarchical. **Par voie hiérarchique,** through the official channels.

*hiérarchiquement, *adv.* Hierarchically; through the usual channels.

hiéroglyphe, *s.m.* (a) Hieroglyph. (b) *pl.* Hieroglyphics.

hiéroglyphique, *a.* Hieroglyphic(al).

*hi-han, *onomat.* (Donkey's) Hee-haw.

hi hi, *onomat.* (Sound of tittering) He, he!

hilarant, *a.* Mirth-provoking. *Ch:* **Gaz hilarant,** laughing gas.

hilare, *a.* Hilarious, mirthful.

hilarité, *s.f.* Hilarity, mirth, laughter.

hindou, *a. & s.* *Ethn:* Hindu.

hippique, *a.* Relating to horses; equine. **Concours hippique,** horse-show.

hippodrome, *s.m.* Hippodrome, circus.

hippopotame, *s.m.* *Z:* Hippopotamus.

hirondelle, *s.f.* **1.** *Orn:* Swallow. *H. de fenêtre,* house-martin. *H. de rivage,* sand-martin. **2.** Small river steamboat.

hirsute, *a.* **1.** Hirsute, hairy, shaggy. **2.** *F:* Rough, boorish.

*hisser, *v.tr.* To hoist (up), pull up. **se hisser.** *Se h. le long du mur,* to climb up the wall. *Se h. sur la pointe des pieds,* to stand on tiptoe.

histoire, *s.f.* **1.** (a) History. (b) **Histoire naturelle,** natural history. **2.** Story, tale. *Livre d'histoires,* story-book. *F:* **C'est toujours la même histoire,** it's the old, old story. *F:* **Il est sorti, histoire de prendre l'air,** he went out just to get some air. *F:* **En voilà une histoire!** here's a pretty go! *Iron:* **La belle histoire!** what about it? **3.** *F:* Fib, story. *Tout ça c'est des histoires,* that's all bunkum. **4.** *F:* **Faire des histoires,** to make a fuss. *Il faut éviter d'avoir des histoires,* we must keep out of trouble.

historien, -ienne, *s.* Historian.

historique. **1.** *a.* Historic(al). *F:* **C'est historique,** it actually happened. **2.** *s.m.* Recital of the facts.

historiquement, *adv.* Historically.

histrionique, *a.* Histrionic; stagy.

hiver [ivɛːr], *s.m.* Winter. **A l'hiver,** when winter is at hand. *Temps d'h.,* wintry weather.

hivernage, *s.m.* **1.** Wintering. **2.** Winter season.

hivernal, -aux, *a.* Winter; wintry.

hiverner, *v.i.* To winter.

*ho, *int.* **1.** (Call) Hi! **2.** (Surprise) Oh!

*hobereau, *s.m.* *F:* Small landed proprietor.

*hochement, *s.m.* Shaking, tossing.

*hochequeue, *s.m.* *Orn:* Wagtail.

*hocher, *v.tr. & i.* *H.* (de) *la tête,* (i) to shake one's head; (ii) to nod; (iii) to toss the head.

*holà, *int.* **1.** Hallo! **2.** Stop! enough!

*hollandais. **1.** *a.* Dutch. **2.** *s.* Dutchman, -woman. **3.** *s.m.* *Ling:* Le Hollandais, Dutch.

*Hollande. *Pr.n.f.* Holland.

holocauste, *s.m.* Holocaust.

*homard, *s.m.* Lobster.

homélie, *s.f.* Homily.

homéopathe. *Med:* **1.** *a.* Homoeopathic. **2.** *s.m.* Homoeopath.

homéopathie, *s.f.* Homoeopathy.

homéopathique, *a.* Homoeopathic.

Homère. *Pr.n.m.* *Gr.Lit:* Homer.

homérique, *a.* Homeric.

homicide[1]. **1.** *s.m. & f.* Homicide. **2.** *a.* Homicidal.

homicide[2], *s.m.* Homicide (as a crime). *H. involontaire,* manslaughter.

hommage, *s.m.* **1.** Homage. **2.** *pl.* Respects, compliments. **3.** Tribute, token. *H. de l'éditeur,* presentation copy.

homme, *s.m.* Man. (a) Mankind. **De mémoire d'homme,** within living memory. (b) **Homme fait,** grown man. *F:* **Mon homme,** my husband. (c) (Individual) *Il n'est pas mon h.,* he is not the man for me. **Trouver son homme,** to meet one's match.

homogène, *a.* Homogeneous.

homonyme. **1.** *a.* Homonymous. **2.** *s.m.* (a) Homonym. (b) *F:* Namesake.

homuncule, *s.m.* *F:* Manikin, dwarf.

*Hongrie. *Pr.n.f.* Hungary.

*hongrois, *a. & s.* *Geog:* Hungarian.

honnête, *a.* **1.** Honest, honourable, upright. **2.** Courteous, well-bred; civil (*envers,* to). **3.** Decent, seemly. **4.** Reasonable, fair.

honnêtement, *s.m.* **1.** Honestly. **2.** Civilly. **3.** Reasonably. **4.** Fairly.

honnêteté, *s.f.* **1.** Honesty, uprightness. **2.** Courtesy, civility. **3.** Decency, propriety. **4.** Fairness.

honneur, *s.m.* Honour. **1.** **(Ma) parole d'honneur!** on my word of honour! **Se faire honneur de qch.,** to be proud of sth. **Piquer qn d'honneur,** to put s.o. (up)on his mettle. **Tenir à honneur de faire qch.,** to consider oneself in honour bound to do sth. *Cour d'h.* (*d'un lycée*), main quadrangle. **2.** (a) *F:* **Faire h. au dîner,** to do justice to the dinner. *J'ai l'h. de vous faire savoir que . . .,* I beg to inform you that. . . . *Jouer pour l'honneur,* to play for love. (b) Il en est sorti à son honneur, he came out of it with credit. **3.** *pl.* (Marks of esteem)

Faire à qn les honneurs de la maison, to do the honours of the house to s.o. **4.** Faire honneur à sa signature, to honour one's signature. **5.** *Cards:* Les honneurs, honours.

*****honnir,** *v.tr.* Honni de tous, spurned by all.

honorabilité, *s.f.* (*a*) Honourable character. (*b*) Respectability.

honorable, *a.* (*a*) Honourable. *Vieillesse h.,* respected old age. (*b*) Respectable; creditable.

honorablement, *adv.* (*a*) Honourably. (*b*) Creditably.

honoraire, **I.** *a.* Honorary. **2.** *s.m.pl.* Fee(s) (of professional man); honorarium.

honorer, *v.tr.* **I.** (*a*) To honour; to respect. *Com:* Votre honorée du . . ., your favour of the. . . . (*b*) To do honour to (s.o.). (*c*) *Com:* To honour, meet (bill). **2.** To do credit to s.o.

s'honorer. (*a*) To gain distinction. (*b*) To consider oneself honoured (*de,* by).

honorifique, *a.* Honorary.

*****honte,** *s.f.* **I.** (*a*) (Sense of) shame. Honte à vous! shame (on you)! Avoir honte, to be ashamed. Faire honte à qn, to put s.o. to shame. (*b*) Fausse honte, bashfulness. **2.** (Cause of) shame, disgrace. *Couvrir qn de h.,* to bring shame on s.o.

*****honteusement,** *adv.* **I.** Shamefully. (*a*) Disgracefully. (*b*) Ignominiously **2.** Bashfully.

*****honteux,** *a.* **I.** Ashamed. **2.** Bashful, shamefaced. **3.** Shameful, disgraceful.

hôpital, -aux, *s.m.* **I.** Hospital, infirmary. Faire les hôpitaux, to walk the hospitals. **2.** *H. des orphelins,* orphans' home. *F:* Prendre le chemin de l'hôpital, to be on the road to ruin.

*****hoquet,** *s.m.* **I.** Hiccough, hiccup. **2.** Gasp.

horaire, **I.** *a.* Horary. *Signal h.,* time-signal. **2.** *s.m.* Time-table.

*****horde,** *s.f.* Horde.

*****horion,** *s.m.* Blow, punch, knock.

horizon, *s.m.* Horizon, sky-line.

horizontal, -aux. **I.** *a.* Horizontal. **2.** *s.f.* Horizontale, horizontal line.

horizontalement, *adv.* Horizontally.

horloge, *s.f.* Clock. *Il est deux heures à l'h.,* it is two by the clock.

horloger, *s.m.* Clock and watch-maker.

horlogerie, *s.f.* **I.** Clock-making. Mouvement d'horlogerie, clockwork. **2.** Clockmaker's shop.

hormis, *prep.* (No liaison) Except, but, save. Hormis que ne + *sub.* unless, except.

horoscope, *.m.* Horoscope.

horreur, *s.f.* Horror. **I.** Frappé d'h., horror-stricken. **2.** Repugnance, disgust. Avoir qch. en horreur, to have a horror of sth. **3.** Awfulness. **4.** Quelle h. d'enfant! what a horrid child! Oh, la vilaine h.! the horrid thing!

horrible, *a.* Horrible, awful.

horriblement, *adv.* Horribly, dreadfully.

horrifier, *v.tr.* *F:* To horrify.

horrifique, *a.* *F:* Horrific, hair-raising.

horripilant, *a.* Hair-raising.

*****hors,** *prep.* (Liaison with *r*: hors elle [ɔrɛl]) **I.** (*a*) Out of, outside. *Longueur h.* tout, over-all length. (*b*) Except. *Tous h. un seul,* all but one. *Conj.phr.* Hors que . . . ne + *sub.,* unless, except. **2.** *Prep.phr.* Hors de, out of, outside (of). Hors d'ici! begone! Être hors d'affaire, to have got through one's difficulties. Être hors de soi, to be beside oneself.

*****hors-bord,** *s.m.inv.* Speed-boat.

*****hors-d'œuvre,** *s.m.inv.* *Cu:* Hors-d'œuvre, side-dish.

*****hors-la-loi,** *s.m.inv.* Outlaw.

horticole, *a.* Horticultural.

horticulture, *s.f.* Horticulture, gardening.

hospice, *s.m.* **I.** Hospice. **2.** Alms-house, home, asylum.

hospitalier, *a.* Hospitable.

hospitalité, *s.f.* Hospitality.

hostie, *s.f.* (Eucharistic) host.

hostile, *a.* Hostile; unfriendly.

hostilité, *s.f.* **I.** Hostility (*contre,* to); enmity, ill-will. **2.** *pl.* Hostilities.

hôte, hôtesse, *s.* **I.** Host, *f.* hostess; entertainer; landlord, landlady. **2.** (*a*) Guest, visitor. (*b*) Dweller; denizen.

hôtel, *s.m.* **I.** Mansion, town-house. **2.** Public building. Hôtel de ville, town-hall. L'Hôtel des Monnaies, the Mint. **3.** (*a*) Hotel. (*b*) *H. meublé, garni,* hotel (providing lodging but not board).

hôtelier, *s.* Innkeeper; landlord, landlady; host, hostess (of an inn).

hôtellerie, *s.f.* Hostelry, inn.

*****hotte,** *s.f.* Basket (carried on the back); (mason's) hod.

*****hottentot,** *a. & s.* Hottentot.

*****houblon,** *s.m.* *Bot:* Hop(s).

*****houe,** *s.f.* *Tls:* Hoe.

*****houer,** *v.tr.* To hoe.

*****houille** [uːj], *s.f.* **I.** (Pit-)coal. **2.** Houille blanche, water-power.

*****houiller** [uj-]. **I.** *a.* Coal-bearing. **2.** *s.f.* Houillère coal-mine; colliery.

*****houilleur** [ujœːr], *s.m.* Collier, (coal-)miner.

*****houilleux** [ujø], *a.* Coal-bearing.

*****houle,** *s.f.* Swell, surge (of sea).

*****houlette,** *s.f.* (Shepherd's) crook.

*****houleux,** *a.* Swelling, surging (sea).

*****houp** [up]. *int* Allons h.! now then, heave!

*****houppe,** *s.f* (*a*) Bunch, tuft; pompon. H à poudrer, powder-puff. (*b*) Tassel.

*****houppé,** *a* Tufted, crested.

*****houri,** *s.f.* Moham.Rel: Houri.

*****hourra,** *int. & s.m.* Hurrah! huzza!

*****houspiller** [-pije], *v.tr.* To hustle; to jostle; to handle roughly.

*****housse,** *s.f.* Covering; (furniture) cover.

*****houssine,** *s.f.* Switch.

*****houx,** *s.m.* *Bot:* Holly.

*****hublot,** *s.m.* *Nau:* Scuttle, port-hole.

indication, *s.f.* Indication. **1.** Indicating, pointing out. **2.** (*a*) (Piece of) information. (*b*) Sign, token; clue. **3.** *pl.* Instruction(s).
indice, *s.m.* **1.** Indication, sign; mark, token. **2.** Index.
indicible, *a.* (*a*) Inexpressible, unutterable; unspeakable. (*b*) Indescribable.
indiciblement, *adv.* Inexpressibly.
indien, -ienne. 1. *a.* & *s.* Indian. **2.** *s.f.* *Tex:* Indienne, chintz.
indifféremment, *adv.* Indifferently.
indifférence, *s.f.* Indifference (*pour* to).
indifférent, *a.* **1.** (*a*) Indifferent; unconcerned. (*b*) Cold, insensible. **2.** Immaterial, unimportant.
indigence, *s.f.* Poverty, indigence, want.
indigène. 1. *a.* Indigenous; native. **2.** *s.* Native.
indigent, *a.* Poor, needy, indigent.
indigeste, *a.* Indigestible.
indigestion, *s.f.* Indigestion.
indignation, *s.f.* Indignation.
indigne, *a.* Unworthy. **1.** Undeserving. **2.** Shameful.
indignement, *adv.* **1.** Unworthily. **2.** Shamefully.
indigner, *v.tr.* To make (s.o.) indignant.
s'indigner, to become indignant.
indigné, *a.* Indignant (*de*, at).
indignité, *s.f.* **1.**(*a*) Unworthiness. (*b*) Baseness. **2.** *Souffrir des indignités*, to suffer indignities.
indigo, *s.m.* Indigo. *a.inv. Des rubans indigo*, indigo-blue ribbons.
indiquer, *v.tr.* To indicate. (*a*) To point out. *I. qch. du doigt*, to point to sth. (*b*) To mark, show. (*c*) To betoken. (*d*) To appoint, name. (*e*) *C'était indiqué*, it was the obvious thing to do.
indirect [-rekt], *a.* (*a*) Indirect. (*b*) Circumstantial (evidence).
indirectement, *adv.* Indirectly.
indiscipliné, *a.* Undisciplined, unruly.
indiscret, -ète. *a.* Indiscreet. (*a*) Imprudent, unguarded. (*b*) Pushing; tactless. (*c*) (Person) given to blabbing.
indiscrètement, *adv.* Indiscreetly.
indiscrétion, *s.f.* Indiscretion.
indiscutable, *a.* Indisputable, unquestionable.
indiscutablement, *adv.* Indisputably, unquestionably.
indispensable, *a.* Indispensable **1.** Obligatory. **2.** Essential.
indisposer, *v.tr.* To upset (s.o.).
indisposé, *a.* **1.** Indisposed, unwell. **2.** *I. contre qn*, unfriendly to s.o.
indisposition, *s.f.* Indisposition, illness.
indisputable, *a.* Indisputable, unquestionable.
indisputablement, *adv.* Indisputably, unquestionably.
indissoluble, *a.* Insoluble.
indistinct [-ɛ̃(ː)kt], *a.* Indistinct; hazy.

indistinctement, *adv.* Indistinctly.
indistinguible [-gi-], *a.* Indistinguishable.
individu, *s.m.* **1.** Individual. **2.** *F:* Usu *Pej:* Individual, person.
individualité, *s.f.* Individuality.
individuel, -elle, *a.* Individual; personal.
individuellement, *adv.* Individually.
indivisible, *a.* Indivisible.
Indo-Chine. *Pr.n.f.* Indo-China.
indo-européen, -enne, *a.* & *s.* Indo-European.
indolemment, *adv.* Indolently.
indolence, *s.f.* Indolence, apathy, sloth.
indolent, *a.* Indolent, apathetic, slothful.
indomptable [-dɔ̃t-], *a.* Unconquerable; untam(e)able; unmanageable.
indompté [-dɔ̃te], *a.* Unconquered; untamed.
indu, *a.* **1.** Not due. **2.** Undue; unwarranted.
indubitable, *a.* Beyond doubt, indubitable, unquestionable.
indubitablement, *adv.* Indubitably.
induction, *s.f.* Induction.
indulgence, *s.f.* Indulgence, leniency.
indulgent, *a.* Indulgent, lenient.
indûment, *adv.* Unduly; improperly.
industrialisation, *s.f.* Industrialization.
industrie, *s.f.* **1.** (*a*) Activity; industry. (*b*) Ingenuity. *Vivre d'industrie*, to live by one's wits. **2.** Industry, trade, manufacture.
industriel, -elle. 1. *a.* Industrial. **2.** *s.m.* Manufacturer.
industrieusement, *adv.* Busily, industriously.
industrieux, *a.* Busy, industrious.
inébranlable, *a.* Unshak(e)able. (*a*) Immovable, firm. (*b*) Resolute, steadfast.
inédit, *a.* **1.** Unpublished (book). **2.** *F:* New, original (plan).
ineffable, *a.* Ineffable, unutterable.
ineffaçable, *a.* Ineffaceable; indelible.
inefficace, *a.* Ineffectual; inefficacious.
inégal, -aux, *a.* **1.** Unequal. **2.** (*a*) Uneven, rough. (*b*) Irregular.
inégalé, *a.* Unequalled.
inégalement, *adv.* Unequally, unevenly.
inégalité, *s.f.* **1.** Inequality, disparity. **2.** Unevenness.
inélégant, *a.* Inelegant.
inéligible, *a.* Ineligible.
inemployé, *a.* Unemployed, unused.
inepte, *a.* Inept, foolish, idiotic.
ineptement, *adv.* Ineptly, foolishly.
ineptie, *s.f.* Ineptitude.
inépuisable, *a.* Inexhaustible; unfailing.
inéquitable, *a.* Inequitable, unfair.
inéquitablement, *adv.* Inequitably, unfairly.
inerte, *a.* Inert; sluggish; dull.
inertie, *s.f.* **1.** Inertia. **2.** Sluggishness.
inespéré, *a.* Unhoped-for, unexpected.
inestimable, *a.* Inestimable, invaluable.
inévitable, *a.* **1.** Unavoidable. **2.** Inevitable

invention, *s.f.* **1.** (*a*) Invention, inventing. (*b*) Imagination, inventiveness. **2.** (*a*) Invention, device. (*b*) Fabrication, lie.

inverse. 1. *a.* Inverse, opposite. **2.** *s.m.* Opposite, reverse.

inversement, *adv.* Inversely.

inversion, *s.f.* (*a*) *Gram:* Inversion. (*b*) Transposition.

invertébré, *a.* Invertebrate.

investigateur, -trice. 1. *a.* Investigating. **2.** *s.* Investigator, inquirer.

investigation, *s.f.* Investigation.

investir, *v.tr.* To invest.

investiture, *s.f.* Investiture.

invétéré, *a.* Inveterate.

invincibilité, *s.f.* Invincibility.

invincible, *a.* Invincible, unconquerable.

invinciblement, *adv.* Invincibly.

inviolable, *a.* Inviolable; sacred.

invisibilité, *s.f.* Invisibility.

invisible, *a.* Invisible.

invitation, *s.f.* Invitation.

invite, *s.f.* Invitation, inducement.

inviter, *v.tr.* To invite. **1.** *I.* qn à entrer, to invite s.o. in. **2.** (*a*) *I.* le désastre, to court disaster. (*b*) *I.* qn à faire qch., to request s.o. to do sth.

invocation, *s.f.* Invocation.

involontaire, *a.* Involuntary, unintentional.

invoquer, *v.tr.* **1.** To call upon, to invoke. **2.** *I. une raison*, to put forward a reason.

invraisemblable, *a.* Unlikely, improbable.

invraisemblance, *s.f.* Unlikeliness, improbability.

invulnérabilité, *s.f.* Invulnerability.

invulnérable, *a.* Invulnerable.

iode, *s.m.* Iodine.

iodure, *s.m. Ch:* Iodide.

ion, *s.m. El:* Ion.

ionique, *a. Arch:* Ionic (order).

iota, *s.m. F:* Pas un iota, not a jot, not an iota.

ir-ai, -as, etc. See ALLER.

Irak. *Pr.n.m. Geog:* Irak, Iraq.

irakien, -ienne, *a. & s.* Iraqi.

irascibilité, *s.f.* Irascibility.

irascible, *a.* Irascible.

iridescent, *a.* Iridescent.

Iris [iris]. **1.** *Pr.n.f. Myth:* Iris. **2.** *s.m.* (*a*) Iris (of eye). **3.** *s.m. or f. Bot:* Iris, flag. Racine d'iris, orris-root.

irisé, *a.* Iridescent, rainbow-hued.

irlandais. 1. *a.* Irish. **2.** *s.* Irishman; Irishwoman. **3.** *s.m. Ling:* Irish, Erse.

Irlande. *Pr.n.f. Geog:* Ireland.

ironie, *s.f.* Irony.

ironique, *a.* Ironic(al).

ironiquement, *adv.* Ironically.

irradier, *v.i.* To (ir)radiate.

irrationnel, -elle, *a.* Irrational.

irréalisable, *a.* Unrealizable.

irréconciliable, *a.* Irreconcilable.

irrécouvrable, *a.* Irrecoverable.

irréel, -elle, *a.* Unreal.

irréfléchi, *a.* **1.** Unconsidered, thoughtless. **2.** Hasty, rash.

irréflexion, *s.f.* Thoughtlessness.

irréfutable, *a.* Irrefutable.

irrégularité, *s.f.* **1.** Irregularity. **2.** Unpunctuality.

irrégulier, *a.* (*a*) Irregular. (*b*) Unpunctual.

irrégulièrement, *adv.* **1.** Irregularly. **2.** Unpunctually.

irrémédiable, *a.* Irremediable.

irrémédiablement, *adv.* Irremediably.

irremplaçable, *a.* Irreplaceable.

irréparable, *a.* Irreparable.

irréprochable, *a.* Irreproachable.

irrésistible, *a.* Irresistible.

irrésistiblement, *adv.* Irresistibly.

irrésolu, *a.* Irresolute, wavering (nature); faltering (steps).

irrésolument, *adv.* Irresolutely.

irrespectueusement, *adv.* Disrespectfully.

irrespectueux, *a.* Disrespectful.

irresponsabilité, *s.f.* Irresponsibility

irresponsable, *a.* Irresponsible.

irrévérence, *s.f.* Irreverence.

irrévérencieux, *a.* Irreverent.

irrévocable, *a.* Irrevocable.

irrévocablement, *adv.* Irrevocably.

irrigation, *s.f. Agr:* Irrigation.

irriguer, *v.tr. Agr:* To irrigate.

irritabilité, *s.f.* Irritability.

irritable, *a.* Irritable.

irritant, *a.* Irritating.

irritation, *s.f.* Irritation.

irriter, *v.tr.* To irritate. **s'irriter,** to grow angry.

irruption, *s.f.* Irruption. **Faire irruption dans une salle,** to burst into a room.

Isaïe. *Pr.n.m. B.Hist:* Isaiah.

isard, *s.m. Z:* Izard; wild goat.

islandais. *Geog:* **1.** *a.* Icelandic. **2.** *s.* Icelander.

Islande. *Pr.n.f. Geog:* Iceland.

isocèle, *a. Geom:* Isosceles (triangle).

isolant. 1. *a.* (*a*) Isolating. (*b*) Insulating.

isolateur, -trice. *El:* **1.** *a.* Insulating. **2.** *s.m.* Insulator.

isolement, *s.m.* **1.** Isolation, loneliness **2.** *El.E:* Insulation.

isolément, *adv.* Separately; singly.

isoler, *v.tr.* **1.** To isolate. **2.** *El.E:* To insulate.

isolé, *a.* **1.** Isolated; lonely. **2.** *El.E:* Insulated.

Israélite. *B.Hist:* **1.** *s.m. & f.* Israelite, Jew. **2.** *a.* Israelitish.

issu, *a.* Descended; born.

issue, *s.f.* **1.** Issue, end, conclusion. **2.** Exit; outlet.

Istamboul. *Pr.n.m. Geog:* Istanbul.

isthme, *s.m. Geog:* Isthmus.

Italie. *Pr.n.f.* Italy.

italien, -ienne, *a. & s.* Italian.

Voir qch. *sous* son vrai jour, to see sth. in its true light. *Vous êtes dans mon j.*, you are standing in my light. **2.** (a) Aperture, opening. **Jour de l'escalier**, well-hole (of stair). **Bas à jour(s)**, open-work stockings. (b) **Se faire jour**, to make a way for oneself. **3.** (Period of time) **Prendre jour pour qch.**, to appoint a day for sth. **Plat du jour** (*dans un restaurant*), F: 'to-day's special.' **Être de jour**, to be on duty for the day. **De nos jours**, nowadays. **Vivre au jour le jour**, to live from hand to mouth. **Du jour au lendemain**, at a moment's notice. **A un de ces jours!** F: so long! **Mettre à jour**, to bring up to date.

journal, -aux, *s.m.* **1.** Journal, diary, record. *Nau:* *J. de navigation*, log(-book). *J. de bord*, log-book. **2.** Newspaper, journal. **Les journaux**, the Press. *W.Tel:* **Journal parlé**, 'news.'

journalier. 1. a. Daily; everyday. **2.** *s.m.* Day-labourer.

journalisme, *s.m.* Journalism. *L'influence du j.*, the influence of the Press.

journaliste, *s.m. & f.* Journalist; reporter.

journée, *s.f.* **1.** Day(time). *Dans la j.*, in the course of the day. **2.** (a) Day's work. **Travailler à la journée**, to work by the day. **Femme de journée**, charwoman, daily help. **Aller en journée**, to go out charring. (b) Day's wages. (c) Day's march. **Voyager à petites journées**, to journey by easy stages. (d) Day (of battle). **Gagner la journée**, to win the day.

journellement, *adv.* Daily; every day.

joute, *s.f.* Contest, match.

jovial, -aux, *a.* Jovial, jolly, merry.

jovialement, *adv.* Jovially, merrily.

jovialité, *s.f.* Joviality, jollity.

joyau, -aux, *s.m.* Jewel. **Les joyaux de la Couronne**, the regalia.

joyeusement, *adv.* Joyously, joyfully.

joyeux, *a.* Merry, mirthful, joyous.

jubilant, *a.* F: Jubilant; in high glee.

jubilation, *s.f.* Jubilation; high glee.

jubilé, *s.m.* Jubilee.

jubiler, *v.i.* To exult, jubilate.

jucher, *v.i.* To go to roost; to perch.

se jucher. 1. To go to roost. **2.** To perch oneself.

juchoir, *s.m.* Perch (for fowls); hen-roost.

judaïque, *a.* Judaic.

Judas. 1. *Pr.n.m.* F: **Poil de Judas**, carroty hair. **2.** *s.m.* (a) F: Traitor, betrayer. (b) Spy-hole (in door).

judiciaire. 1. a. Judicial, judiciary, legal. **2.** *s.f.* (Sound) judgment.

judiciairement, *adv.* Judicially.

judicieusement, *adv* Judiciously, discreetly.

judicieux, *a.* Judicious, discerning.

juge, *s.m.* Judge. **Juge de paix**, police-court magistrate. F: **Je vous en fais juge**, I appeal to you.

jugement, *s.m.* Judgment. **1.** *Jur:* (a) Trial (of case). **Mettre en jugement**, to bring to trial. **Le jugement dernier**, doomsday. (b) Decision, award; sentence. **2.** Opinion, estimation. **3.** Discernment, discrimination.

juger. I. *v.tr.* (n. jugeons) **1.** (a) To judge; to try (case); to pass sentence on; to adjudicate. (b) To pass judgment on; to criticize. **2.** (a) To think, believe. *On le jugeait fou*, people took him to be mad. (b) **Juger de qch.**, to judge of sth. **A en juger par . . .**, judging by. . . . **II. juger, jugé**, *s.m.* **Faire qch. au jugé**, to do sth. by guess-work.

jugoslave, *a. & s.* Jugo-Slav.

jugulaire. 1. a. & *s.f.* Jugular (vein). **2.** *s.f.* Chin-strap.

juif [ʒɥif]. **1.** a. Jewish; Jew. **2.** s. Jew, f. Jewess. F: **Le petit juif**, the funny-bone.

juillet [ʒɥijɛ], *s.m.* July.

juin [ʒɥɛ̃], *s.m.* June.

jumeau, -elle. I. a. & s. Twin. *Trois jumeaux*, triplets. **II. jumelles**, *s.f.pl.* Binoculars. *Jumelles de théâtre*, opera-glasses.

jument, *s.f.* Mare.

Junon. *Pr.n.f. Myth:* Juno.

jupe, *s.f.* (Woman's) skirt. F: **Pendu aux jupes de sa mère**, tied to his mother's apron-strings.

Jupiter [ʒypitɛːr]. *Pr.n.m.* Jupiter, Jove.

jupon, *s.m.* Petticoat, underskirt.

jurement, *s.m.* (Profane) swearing; oath.

jurer, *v.tr.* To swear. **1.** *J. le ciel*, to call heaven to witness. **2.** (To promise) **Faire jurer le secret à qn**, to swear s.o. to secrecy. **3.** (To assert) **J'en jurerais**, I would swear to it. **4.** *Abs.* (a) To swear (profanely); to curse. F: **Jurer comme un charretier**, to swear like a trooper. (b) (Of colours) To clash.

juré. 1. a. *Ennemi j.*, sworn enemy. **2.** *s.m.* Juryman. **Les jurés**, the jury.

juridiction, *s.f.* Jurisdiction.

juridique, *a.* Judicial; legal.

juron, *s.m.* (Profane) oath.

jury, *s.m.* *Jur:* Jury.

jus, *s.m.* **1.** Juice. **2.** Gravy.

jusant, *s.m.* Ebb(-tide).

jusque, *prep.* **1.** As far as; up to. *Jusqu'ici*, thus far, so far. *Ils furent tués jusqu'au dernier*, they were killed to a man. **2.** Till, until. *Jusqu'ici*, till now, as yet. **3.** (Intensive) *Il sait jusqu'à nos pensées*, he knows our very thoughts. **4.** *Conj.phr.* **Jusqu'à ce que**, usu. + *sub.*, till, until.

jusquiame, *s.f. Bot:* Henbane.

juste, *a.* **1.** Just, right, fair. (a) *J. colère*, righteous anger. **Rien de plus juste**, nothing could be fairer. (b) *Magistrat j.*, upright judge. **2.** Right, exact, accurate. (a) *Le mot j.*, the exact word, the right word. **C'est juste**, that is so! that's right! **Rien de plus juste**,

I am off duty. *Je suis l. de mon temps*, my time is my own. (*b*) *L. de soucis*, carefree. (*c*) *Conversation l.*, free, broad, conversation. **2.** Clear, open (space); vacant. *Tp :* **"Pas libre,"** 'line engaged.' (Taxi sign) **"Libre,"** 'for hire.'

libre-échange, *s.m.* Free trade.

librement, *adv.* Freely.

libretto, *s.m.* Libretto. *F :* book (of an opera). *pl. Des libretti, des librettos.*

licence, *s.f.* Licence. **1.** (*a*) Leave, permission. (*b*) *Sch :* **Passer sa licence**, to take one's degree. **2.** (*a*) Abuse of liberty. (*b*) Licentiousness.

licencié, *s.* Licentiate, *L. ès lettres*, (approx. =) master of arts.

licencieusement, *adv.* Licentiously.

licencieux, *a.* Licentious.

lichen [likɛn], *s.m. Bot :* Lichen. *L. d'Islande*, Iceland moss.

licite, *a.* Licit, lawful, permissible.

licol, *s.m. Harn :* Halter; head-stall.

licorne, *s.f. Myth :* Unicorn.

licou, *pl.* **-ous,** *s.m.* = LICOL.

lie, *s.f.* Lees, dregs. **Lie de vin**, *a.inv.* purplish red.

liège, *s.m.* **1.** *Bot :* Cork-oak. **2.** Cork.

lien, *s.m.* Tie, bond.

lier, *v.tr.* **1.** To bind, tie, tie up. *L'intérêt nous lie*, we have common interests. *L. des idées*, to link ideas. **2. Lier conversation avec qn**, to enter into conversation with s.o. **se lier.** *Se l. (d'amitié) avec qn*, to form a friendship with s.o.

lié, *a.* **1.** Bound. **Avoir la langue liée**, to be tongue-tied. **2.** *Être (très) lié avec qn*, to be intimately acquainted with s.o.

lierre, *s.m.* Ivy.

lieu, -eux, *s.m.* **1.** Place. (*a*) Locality, spot. **En tout lieu**, everywhere. **En haut lieu**, in high places. *Je tiens ce renseignement de bon l.*, I have this information from a good source. **En (tout) premier lieu**, in the first place, first of all. (*b*) *pl.* House, premises. (*c*) *pl. F : Lieux (d'aisances)*, privy, w.c. **2.** (*a*) **Avoir lieu**, to take place. (*b*) Ground(s), cause. **Il y a (tout) lieu de supposer que** + *ind.*, there is (every) reason for supposing that. . . . **Donner lieu à des désagréments**, to give rise to trouble. (*c*) **Tenir lieu de qch.**, to take the place of. **Au lieu de**, instead of. **Au lieu que** + *ind.*, whereas. **3. Lieux communs**, commonplaces, platitudes.

lieue, *s.f.* League (= 4 kilometres).

lieutenant, *s.m.* (*a*) *Mil :* Lieutenant. *Navy: L. de vaisseau*, lieutenant. (*b*) *Mercantile Marine:* Mate. **Premier l.**, second mate. (*c*) *L. de port*, harbour-master.

lièvre, *s.m. Z :* Hare. **Courir deux lièvres à la fois**, to try to do two things at once. **Mémoire de lièvre**, memory like a sieve.

ligament, *s.m.* Ligament.

ligature, *s.f.* **1.** Tying, binding. **2.** *Typ :* Ligature.

lignage, *s.m.* Lineage, descent.

lignard, *s.m. F :* Soldier of the line.

ligne, *s.f.* Line. **1.** (*a*) Cord. **Ligne de pêche**, fishing-line. (*b*) *L. droite*, straight line. (*c*) **Auto qui a de la ligne**, car with clean lines. **Grandes lignes d'une œuvre**, broad outline of a work. (*d*) *L. de flottaison*, water-line (of ship). *Descendre en l. directe de . . .*, to be lineally descended from. . . . (*e*) *L. de maisons*, row of houses. **Question qui vient en première ligne**, question of primary importance. **Hors ligne**, out of the common. (*f*) **Écris-moi deux lignes**, drop me a line. **2.** *Mil : Lignes de retranchement*, the lines. **Rentrer dans ses lignes**, to retire within one's lines. **Infanterie de ligne**, infantry of the line. **3.** (*a*) **Ligne de chemin de fer**, railway line. (*b*) *L. télégraphique*, telegraph line.

lignée, *s.f.* Issue; (line of) descendants.

ligoter, *v.tr.* To bind (s.o.) hand and foot; to lash (thgs) together.

ligue, *s.f.* League, confederacy.

liguer, *v.tr. Être ligué avec qn*, to be in league with s.o.

lilas. **1.** *s.m. Bot :* Lilac. **2.** *a.inv.* Lilac.

lilliputien, -ienne, *a. & s.* Lilliputian.

limace, *s.f. Moll :* Slug.

limaçon, *s.m.* **1.** Snail. **Escalier en limaçon**, spiral staircase.

limande, *s.f. Ich :* Dab.

limbe, *s.m.* **1.** *Astr :* Rim, edge (of the sun). **2.** *Theol :* **Les Limbes**, limbo.

lime[1], *s.f. Tls :* File.

lime[2], *s.f. Bot :* Sweet lime.

limer, *v.tr.* To file; to file down.

limier, *s.m.* Bloodhound; sleuth-hound.

limitation, *s.f.* **1.** Limitation, restriction. **2.** Marking off (of ground).

limite, *s.f.* **1.** Boundary; limit. *F : Dépasser les limites*, to pass all bounds. **2. Cas limite**, border-line case. **Vitesse limite**, maximum speed.

limiter, *v.tr.* **1.** To bound, to mark the bounds of. **2.** To limit; to restrict.

limité, *a.* Limited, restricted.

limitrophe, *a.* Adjacent; abutting; bordering (on).

limon[1], *s.m.* Mud, silt.

limon[2], *s.m. Veh :* Shaft.

limon[3], *s.m. Bot :* Sour lime.

limonade, *s.f.* **1.** Lemonade. **2.** *pl.* Mineral waters; *F :* minerals.

limoneux, *a.* Muddy; charged with mud.

limonier[1], *s.m.* Shaft horse; wheeler.

limonier[2], *s.m. Bot :* Sour-lime (tree).

limousin. **1.** *a. & s.* (Native) of Limoges. **2.** *s.f. Aut :* Limousine, limousine (car).

limpide, *a.* Limpid, clear.

limpidité, *s.f.* impidity, clarity.

lin, *s.m.* **1.** Flax. **Graine de lin**, linseed. **Huile de lin**, linseed oil. **2.** (**Tissu de**) **lin**, linen.

linceul, *s.m.* Winding-sheet, shroud.

linéaire, *a.* Linear. *Mesures linéaires*, measures of length.

exercise; tactical exercise; manœuvre. (d) Shunting (of trains). (e) F: Scheme, manœuvre. (f) pl. Scheming. **2.** s.f. Nau: Rope; rigging. **3.** s.m. Labourer.

manœuvrer. I. v.tr. (a) To work, operate. (b) To handle (ship). (c) Rail: To shunt. **2.** v.i. (a) Mil: To manœuvre. (b) F: To scheme, manœuvre.

manoir, s.m. (a) Manor-house. (b) F: Country-house, country-seat.

manquant. I. a. (a) Missing. (b) Wanting, lacking. **2.** s. Absentee; defaulter.

manque, s.m. Lack, want; deficiency. M. de parole, breach of faith.

manquement, s.m. Failure, shortcoming, lapse. M. au devoir, breach of duty.

manquer. I. v.i. **1.** (a) M. de qch., to lack, be short of, sth. (b) Il a manqué (de) tomber, he nearly fell. (c) Impers. **Il s'en manque de beaucoup,** far from it. **2.** To fail. (a) To be wanting, deficient. Les vivres commencent à m., provisions are running short. F: **Il ne manquait plus que cela!** that's the last straw! (b) To give way. Son cœur lui manqua, his heart failed him. (c) To be absent, missing. Manquer à qn, to be missed by s.o. (d) To fall short. M. à sa parole, to break one's word. M. à une règle, to violate a rule. M. à qn, to be disrespectful to s.o. Abs. Le coup a manqué, the attempt miscarried. (e) Ne manquez pas de nous écrire, be sure to write to us.
II. manquer, v.tr. **1.** To miss (train). **Il l'a manqué belle,** he missed a splendid chance. **2.** M. sa vie, to make a failure of one's life.

manqué, a. **1.** Missed; unsuccessful. **Coup manqué,** (i) miss; (ii) failure. Vie manquée, wasted life. **2.** F: C'est un garçon m., she's a regular tomboy.

mansarde, s.f. Arch: **1.** (Fenêtre en) mansarde, dormer-window. **2.** Attic, garret.

manteau, s.m. **1.** Cloak, mantle, wrap. **2.** Manteau de cheminée, mantelpiece.

mantelet, s.m. **1.** Cost: Tippet. **2.** (Carriage-)apron. **3.** Shutter; Nau: dead-light.

mantille [-ti:j], s.f. Cost: Mantilla.

manucure, s.m. & f. Manicurist.

manuel, -elle. 1. a. Manual (labour). **2.** s.m. Manual, handbook.

manufacture, s.f. (Manu)factory; mill; works.

manufacturer, v.tr. To manufacture.

manufacturier. 1. a. Manufacturing. **2.** s.m. Manufacturer; mill-owner.

manuscrit, a. & s.m. Manuscript.

manutention, s.f. **1.** Management, administration. **2.** Handling (of stores).

maori, a. & s. Ethn: Maori.

mappemonde, s.f. Map of the world in two hemispheres. M. céleste, planisphere.

maquereau, s.m. Mackerel.

maquignon, -onne, s. **1.** Horse-dealer; coper. **2.** (Shady) go-between.

maquillage [-kij-], s.m. Th: (a) Making up. (b) Make-up.

maquiller [-kije], v.tr. Th: To make up (face).

maquis, s.m. Scrub, bush (in Corsica); underground forces; prendre le m., to go underground, to take to the maquis.

maquisard, s.m. Man of the maquis.

maraîchage, s.m. Market-gardening.

maraîcher, s. Market-gardener.

marais, s.m. Marsh(land); bog, fen.

marâtre, s.f. (Cruel) stepmother or mother.

maraude, s.f. (a) Marauding, plundering. (b) F: Taxi en m., cruising taxi.

marauder, v.i. (a) To maraud, plunder. (b) F: (Of taxicabs) To cruise (in search of fares).

maraudeur, -euse, s. Marauder, plunderer.

marbre, s.m. (a) Marble. (b) Marble (statue).

marbrer, v.tr. To marble; to mottle; to vein.

marbré, a. Marbled; mottled; veined.

marbrure, s.f. Marbling, veining. Mottling (of the skin).

marc [ma:r], s.m. **1.** Marc (of grapes). **2.** (Used) tea-leaves; coffee-grounds.

marcassin, s.m. Young wild boar.

marchand. 1. s. Dealer, shopkeeper, merchant; tradesman. M. de poisson, fishmonger. M. de tabac, tobacconist. M. des quatre saisons, costermonger; hawker (of fruit and vegetables). **2.** a. (a) Saleable, marketable. (b) Trading. Place marchande, shopping centre. **Navire marchand,** merchant ship.

marchander, v.tr. (a) To haggle. (b) Il ne marchande pas sa peine, he spares no pains.

marchandise, s.f. Merchandise, goods, wares.

marche, s.f. **1.** (a) Step, stair. La m. du bas, the bottom stair. (b) Treadle (of lathe). **2.** (a) Walking. Aimer la m., to be fond of walking. Ralentir sa marche, to slacken one's pace. **Se mettre en marche,** to set out, start off. (b) March. (i) **Ouvrir la marche,** to lead the way. (ii) Mus: M. funèbre, dead march. **3.** (a) Running (of trains); sailing (of ships). (b) Entrer dans le garage en m. arrière, to back into the garage. **4.** (a) Running, going, working (of machine). (b) Course (of events); march (of time).

marché, s.m. **1.** (a) Dealing, buying. (b) Deal, bargain. **C'est marché fait,** it is a bargain; F: done! **Par-dessus le marché,** into the bargain. (c) **Bon marché,** cheapness. A meilleur m., cheaper. Articles bon m., low-priced goods, F: bargains. (d) **Marché noir,** black market. **2.** Market.

marchepied, s.m. (a) Step (of carriage). (b) Veh: Footboard. Aut: Running-board.

marcher, v.i. **1.** To tread. **2.** (a) To walk, go. Deux choses qui marchent toujours ensemble, two things that always go together. (b) F: To obey orders. **Faire marcher qn,** (i) to

*huche, *s.f.* **1.** Kneading-trough. **2.** Bin. *La h. au pain*, the bread-bin.

*huer. **1.** *v.i.* (*a*) To shout, halloo. (*b*) To hoot. **2.** *v.tr.* To boo (actor).

huées, *s.f. pl.* Booing, hooting.

*huguenot, *a. & s.* Huguenot.

*Hugues. *Pr.n.m.* Hugh.

huile, *s.f.* Oil. **Peinture à l'huile**, oil-painting. *F:* **Huile de bras**, elbow-grease.

huiler, *v.tr.* To oil ; to lubricate, grease.

huileux, *a.* Oily, greasy.

huis, *s.m.* **Entretien à huis clos**, conversation behind closed doors.

huissier, *s.m.* **1.** (Gentleman) usher. **2.** *Jur:* (*a*) Process-server ; bailiff. (*b*) Usher.

*huit [ɥit], *num.a.inv. & s.m.inv.* (As card. adj. before a noun or adj. beginning with a consonant sound [ɥi]) Eight. **Huit jours**, a week. **D'aujourd'hui en huit**, to-day week.

*huitaine, *s.f.* **1.** (About) eight. **2.** Week. **Dans la huitaine**, in the course of the week.

*huitième. **1.** *num. a. & s.* Eighth. **2.** *s.m.* Eighth (part).

huître, *s.f.* Oyster.

*huit-reflets [ɥirəflɛ], *s.m.inv.* *F:* Top hat.

*hulotte, *s.f.* *Orn:* Common wood-owl.

*hum ['m, ɔm], *int.* Hem ! hm !

humain, *a.* **1.** Human. *Le genre h.*, mankind. **2.** Humane.

humainement, *adv.* **1.** Humanly. **2.** Humanely.

humaniser, *v.tr.* To humanize.

humanitaire, *a. & s.* Humanitarian.

humanité, *s.f.* **1.** Humanity. (*a*) Human nature (*b*) Mankind. (*c*) Humaneness. **2.** *pl.* *Sch:* *Les classes d'humanités*, the classical side.

humble, *a.* Humble, lowly.

humblement, *adv.* Humbly.

humecter, *v tr.* To damp, moisten.

*humer, *v.tr.* To suck in, up. *H. une prise*, to take a pinch of snuff.

humeur, *s.f.* (*a*) Humour, mood. *De méchante h.*, out of temper. **Être en humeur de faire qch.**, to be in the mood to do sth. (*b*) Temper. *Avoir l'h. vive*, to be quick-tempered. **Avec humeur**, testily.

humide, *a.* Damp, moist, humid. *Temps h. et chaud*, muggy weather. *Temps h. et froid*, raw weather.

humidité, *s.f.* Humidity, damp(ness), moisture. "Craint l'humidité," 'to be kept dry.'

humiliant, *a* Humiliating, mortifying.

humiliation, *s.f.* Humiliation, mortification ; affront.

humilier, *v.tr.* To humiliate, humble. **s'humilier** *usqu'à faire qch.*, to stoop to doing sth.

humilité, *s.f.* Humility, humbleness.

humoriste. **1.** *a.* Humorous. **2.** *s* Humorist.

humoristique, *a.* Humorous.

humour, *s.m.* Humour.

humus [ymy:s], *s.m.* *Hort:* Humus, leaf-mould.

*hune, *s.f.* *Nau:* Top.

*huppe[1], *s.f.* *Orn:* Hoopoe.

*huppe[2], *s.f.* Tuft, crest (of bird).

*huppé, *a.* **1.** *Orn:* Tufted, crested. **2.** *F:* Smart, well-dressed.

*hure, *s.f.* Head (of boar).

*hurlement, *s.m.* Howl(ing) ; roar(ing).

*hurler. **1.** *v.i.* To howl ; to roar. **2.** *v.tr.* To bawl out (song).

*hurleur, -euse. **1.** *a.* Howling, yelling. **2.** *s.* Howler, yeller.

*hussard, *s.m.* *Mil:* Hussar.

*hutte, *s.f.* Hut, shed, shanty.

hybride, *a. & s.m.* Hybrid.

hydrate, *s.m.* *Ch:* Hydrate, hydroxide.

hydraulique. **1.** *a.* Hydraulic. **2.** *s.f.* Hydraulics.

hydravion, *s.m.* Sea-plane, hydroplane.

hydre, *s.f.* Hydra.

hydrogène, *s.m.* *Ch:* Hydrogen.

hydrophile, *a.* Absorbent (cotton-wool).

hydrophobie, *s.f.* Hydrophobia, rabies.

hydropisie, *s.f.* *Med:* Dropsy.

hydroplane, *s.m.* Hydroplane, sea-plane.

hydroplaner, *v.i.* *Av:* To taxi along (on water).

hydrostatique. **1.** *a.* Hydrostatic(al). **2.** *s.f.* Hydrostatics.

hyène, *s.f.* *Z:* Hyena.

hygiène, *s.f.* Hygiene. *H. publique*, public health.

hygiénique, *a.* Hygienic ; healthy ; sanitary.

hymen [imɛn], *s.m.*, hyménée, *s.m.* *Poet:* Marriage.

hymne. **1.** *s.m.* Patriotic song. *H. national*, national anthem. **2.** *s.f.* *Ecc:* Hymn.

hyperbole, *s.f.* **1.** *Rh:* Hyperbole, exaggeration. **2.** *Geom:* Hyperbola.

hypercritique, *a.* Hypercritical, over-critical.

hypnotique, *a.* Hypnotic.

hypnotiser, *v.tr.* To hypnotize.

hypnotisme, *s.m.* Hypnotism.

hypnotiste, *s.m. & f.* Hypnotist.

hypocondriaque. **1.** *a.* Hypochondriac(al). **2.** *s.* Hypochondriac.

hypocrisie, *s.f.* Hypocrisy ; cant.

hypocrite. **1.** *a.* Hypocritical. **2.** *s.* Hypocrite.

hypocritement, *adv.* Hypocritically.

hypodermique, *a.* Hypodermic.

hyposulfite, *s.m.* *Ch:* Hyposulphite. *H. de soude*, hyposulphite of soda ; *Phot: F:* hypo.

hypoténuse, *s.f.* Hypotenuse.

hypothécaire, *s.* Mortgagee.

hypothèque, *s.f.* Mortgage.

hypothéquer, *v.tr.* (j'hypothèque i'hypothéquerai) To mortgage.

hypothèse, *s.f.* Hypothesis, assumption.

hypothétique, *a.* Hypothetical.

hysope, *s.f.* *Bot:* Hyssop.

hystérie, *s.f.* *Med:* Hysteria.

hystérique, *a.* *Med:* Hysteric(al).

I]   **I**

I, i [i], *s.m.* **1.** (The letter) I, i. **2.** i grec, (the letter) Y, y.

ïambique, *a. Pros:* Iambic.

ibère, *a. & s. Ethn:* Iberian.

ibérique, *a. Geog:* Iberian. **La péninsule** Ibérique, the Spanish, Iberian, Peninsula.

ibex [-ɛks], *s.m. Z:* Ibex.

ibis [-is], *s.m. Orn:* Ibis.

iceberg [-bɛrk], *s.m.* Iceberg.

ici, *adv.* **1.** Here. **Ici-bas,** here below, on earth. *Passez par ici,* step this way. *Tp: Ici Dupont,* Dupont speaking. *W.Tel: Ici Toulouse,* Toulouse calling. **2.** Now. **Jusqu'ici,** up to now; hitherto. *D'ici (à) lundi,* by Monday. **D'ici peu,** before long.

icone, *s.f. Ecc:* Icon, ikon.

iconoclaste. 1. *a.* Iconoclastic. **2.** *s.m.* Iconoclast.

idéal. 1. *a.* (*pl. idéaux*) Ideal. **Le beau idéal,** the ideal of beauty. **2.** *s.m.* (*pl. idéals, idéaux*) Ideal.

idéalement, *adv.* Ideally.

idéaliser, *v.tr.* To idealize.

idéalisme, *s.m.* Idealism.

idéaliste. 1. *a.* Idealistic. **2.** *s.* Idealist.

idée, *s.f.* **1.** Idea. (*a*) Notion. **On n'a pas idée de cela,** you can't imagine it. **Quelle idée!** the idea! **Voir qch. en idée,** to see sth. in the mind's eye. **Idée fixe,** obsession. (*b*) View, opinion. *En faire à son i.,* to do just what one likes. (*c*) Whim, fancy. **Comme l'idée m'en prend,** just as the fancy takes me. **2.** Mind. **J'ai dans l'idée que . . .,** I have a notion that. . . .

identification, *s.f.* Identification.

identifier, *v.tr.* To identify. **s'identifier** *à une cause,* to identify oneself with a cause.

identique, *a.* Identical (*à*, with).

identiquement, *adv.* Identically.

identité, *s.f.* Identity.

idiomatique, *a.* Idiomatic(al).

idiome, *s.m.* (*a*) Idiom, dialect. (*b*) Language.

idiosyncrasie, *s.f.* Idiosyncrasy.

idiot. 1. *a.* (*a*) Idiot. (*b*) *F:* Idiotic; senseless. **2.** *s.* (*a*) Idiot, imbecile. (*b*) *F:* Idiot, fool.

idiotement, *adv. F:* Idiotically.

idiotie, *s.f.* **1.** (*a*) Idiocy, imbecility. (*b*) Mental deficiency. **2.** *F:* Rank stupidity.

idiotisme, *s.m.* Idiom.

idolâtre. 1. *a.* Idolatrous. **2.** *s.* Idolater, *f.* idolatress.

idolâtrie, *s.f.* Idolatry.

idole, *s.f.* Idol, image. **Faire une idole de qn,** to idolize s.o.

idylle, *s.f.* Idyll; romance.

idyllique, *a.* Idyllic.

if, *s.m.* Yew(-tree).

igname, *s.f.* Yam; Indian potato.

ignare. 1. *a.* Ignorant. **2.** *s.* Ignoramus.

igné [igne], *a. Geol:* Igneous.

ignition [ig-], *s.f.* (State of) ignition. (Cp ALLUMAGE = act of ignition.)

ignoble, *a.* (*a*) Ignoble; base; disgraceful (*b*) Wretched (dwelling).

ignominie, *s.f.* Ignominy, shame.

ignominieusement, *adv.* Ignominiously.

ignominieux, *a.* Ignominious, shameful disgraceful.

ignoramment, *adv.* Ignorantly.

ignorance, *s.f.* **1.** Ignorance. **2.** *pl.* Errors mistakes.

ignorant. 1. *a.* Ignorant, uninstructed **2.** *s.* Ignoramus, dunce.

ignorer, *v.tr.* Not to know; to be ignoran of (sth.).

ignoré, *a.* Unknown.

iguane, *s.m. Rept:* Iguana.

il, ils. 1. *pers. pron. nom. m.* (Of pers.) He they; (of thg) it, they. **2.** *inv.* It, there (*a*) *Il est honteux de mentir,* it is shameful tc lie. *Il était une fois une fée,* there was once upon a time a fairy. (*b*) (With impers. vbs) *Il faut partir,* we must start. *Il y a quelqu'un à la porte,* there is someone at the door.

île, *s.f.* **1.** Island, isle. *Habiter dans une île,* to live on an island. **2.** Island site.

ilex [-ɛks], *s.m.* Ilex. **1.** Holly. **2.** Holm-oak.

Iliade (l'), *s.f. Gr.Lit:* The Iliad.

illégal, -aux, *a.* Illegal, unlawful.

illégalement, *adv.* Illegally.

illégalité, *s.f.* Illegality.

illégitime, *a.* Illegitimate; unlawful.

illégitimité, *s.f.* Illegitimacy; unlawfulness.

illettré, *a.* Illiterate, uneducated.

illicite, *a.* Illicit, unlawful.

illicitement, *adv.* Illicitly.

illimitable, *a.* Illimitable, boundless.

illimité, *a.* Unlimited, boundless.

illisibilité, *s.f.* Illegibility.

illisible, *a.* Illegible, unreadable.

illisiblement, *adv.* Illegibly.

illogique, *a.* Illogical; inconsequent; inconsistent.

illogiquement, *adv.* Illogically.

illuminant. 1. *a.* Illuminating. **2.** *s.m.* Illuminant.

illumination, *s.f.* Illumination.

illuminer, *v.tr.* **1.** (*a*) To illuminate. (*b*) Tc light up. **2.** To enlighten.

illusion, *s.f.* **1.** Illusion. **Se faire illusion à soi-même,** to deceive oneself. **2.** Delusion **Se faire illusion,** to labour under a delusion

illusoire, *a.* Illusory; illusive.

illustrateur, *s.m.* Illustrator.

illustration]   155   [impair

illustration, *s.f. Art:* Illustration. *(a)* Illustrating. *(b)* Picture.
illustre, *a.* Illustrious, famous, renowned.
illustrer, *v.tr.* **1.** To render illustrious. **2.** To illustrate.
  s'illustrer, to become famous (*par,* for, through); to win fame, renown.
illustré, *s.m.* Pictorial paper.
îlot, *s.m.* Islet, small island.
ilote, *s.m. Gr.Hist:* Helot.
image, *s.f.* Image. **1.** Reflection. **2.** *(a)* A l'image de qn, in the likeness of s.o. *(b)* Picture, figure. *Livre d'images,* picture-book. **3.** Mental picture, impression. **4.** Simile, metaphor.
imagé, *a.* Vivid; full of imagery.
imaginable, *a.* Imaginable.
imaginaire, *a.* Imaginary; fancied.
imaginatif, *a.* Imaginative.
imagination, *s.f.* Imagination.
imaginer, *v.tr.* To imagine. **1.** To invent, devise. **2.** To fancy, picture. Tout ce qu'on peut imaginer de plus beau, the finest thing imaginable.
imbécile. 1. *a. (a)* Imbecile, half-witted. *(b) F:* Silly, idiotic. **2.** *s. (a)* Imbecile. *(b) F:* Idiot, fool.
imbécilement, *adv. F:* Idiotically.
imbécillité, *s.f.* **1.** *(a)* Imbecility. *(b) F:* Silliness, stupidity. **2.** *F:* Stupid act or speech.
imberbe, *a.* Beardless; callow (youth).
imbiber, *v.tr.* **1.** *I. qch. de qch.,* to soak sth. in sth. **2.** (Of liquid) To permeate, soak. **3.** To soak up, imbibe.
  s'imbiber. 1. To become saturated (*de,* with); to absorb. **2.** To sink in.
imbu, *a.* Imbued, soaked. *I. de préjugés,* steeped in prejudice.
imbuvable, *a.* Undrinkable.
imitateur, -trice. 1. *s.* Imitator. **2.** *a.* Imitative, apish.
imitatif, *a.* Imitative.
imitation, *s.f.* Imitation. **1.** *(a)* Imitating, copying. *(b)* Mimicking. *(c)* Forging. **2.** *(a)* Copy. *(b)* Forgery, counterfeit.
imiter, *v.tr.* To imitate. *(a)* To copy. *(b)* To mimic. *(c)* To forge.
immaculé, *a.* Immaculate; stainless.
immanent, *a.* Immanent.
immangeable, *a.* Uneatable.
immanquable, *a.* Certain, inevitable.
immanquablement, *adv.* Inevitably.
immatérialité, *s.f.* Immateriality.
immatériel, -elle, *a.* **1.** Immaterial, unsubstantial. **2.** Intangible.
immaturité, *s.f.* Immaturity.
immédiat, *a.* Immediate. **1.** *(a)* Direct (cause). *(b)* Close at hand; near. *(c)* Urgent. **2.** Without delay.
immédiatement, *adv.* Immediately.
immémorial, -aux, *a.* Immemorial.
immense, *a.* **1.** Immeasurable. boundless. **2.** Immense, vast, huge.
immensément, *adv.* Immensely, hugely.

immensité, *s.f.* **1.** Immensity, infinity. **2.** Vastness, boundlessness.
immerger, *v.tr.* (n. immergeons) *(a)* To immerse, plunge, dip. *(b)* To drop overboard (in funeral at sea).
immérité, *a.* Unmerited, undeserved.
immersion, *s.f.* **1.** Immersion, dipping. **2.** Submergence. **3.** *Nau:* Committal to the deep.
immesurable, *a.* Immeasurable.
immeuble. *Jur:* 1. *a.* Real, fixed. **2.** *s.m.* *(a)* Real estate, landed property. *(b) F:* House, mansion (in flats). *(c)* Premises (of business).
immigrant, *a. & s.* Immigrant.
immigration, *s.f.* Immigration.
immigrer, *v.i.* To immigrate.
  immigré, *s.* Immigrant, settler.
imminence, *s.f.* Imminence.
imminent, *a.* Imminent, impending.
immiscer, *v.tr.* (n. immisçons) To mix up, involve (s.o.).
  s'immiscer *dans une affaire,* to interfere in an affair.
immobile, *a.* **1.** Motionless, still. *Visage i.,* set face. **2.** Immovable; firm.
immobilier, *a. Jur:* Real. Société immobilière, building society.
immobilisation, *s.f.* Immobilization.
immobiliser, *v.tr.* To immobilize.
immobilité, *s.f.* Immobility; fixity.
immodéré, *a.* Immoderate, excessive, inordinate.
immodérément, *adv.* Immoderately, excessively.
immodeste, *a.* Immodest, shameless.
immodestement, *adv.* Immodestly.
immodestie, *s.f.* Immodesty.
immolation, *s.f.* Immolation.
immoler, *v.tr.* To immolate, sacrifice.
immonde, *a.* Filthy; vile.
immondices, *s.f.pl.* Dirt, refuse.
immoral, -aux, *a.* Immoral.
immoralement, *adv.* Immorally.
immoralité, *s.f.* **1.** Immorality. **2.** Immoral act.
immortaliser, *v.tr.* To immortalize.
immortalité, *s.f.* Immortality.
immortel, -elle. 1. *a.* Immortal; undying. **2.** *s.m.pl.* Les immortels, the immortals, *F:* the members of the Académie française. **3.** *s.f.* Immortelle, everlasting (flower).
immortellement, *adv.* Immortally.
immuabilité, *s.f.* = IMMUTABILITÉ.
immuable, *a.* Immutable, unalterable; fixed, unchanging.
immuablement, *adv.* Immutably.
immuniser, *v.tr. Med:* To render immune (*contre,* from).
immunité, *s.f.* Immunity.
immutabilité, *s.f.* Immutability.
impact [ε̃pakt], *s.m.* Impact, shock.
impair. 1. *a.* Odd, uneven (number). **2.** *s.m. F:* Blunder, bloomer.

impalpable, *a.* Impalpable, intangible.
impardonnable, *a.* Unpardonable.
imparfait, *a.* **1.** Unfinished, uncompleted. **2.** Imperfect, defective.
imparfaitement, *adv.* Imperfectly.
impartial, -aux, *a.* Impartial, unbiassed, fair-minded, unprejudiced.
impartialement, *adv.* Impartially.
impartialité, *s.f.* Impartiality.
impassable, *a.* Impassable; unfordable.
impasse, *s.f.* **1.** Blind alley, dead-end. *P.N:* Impasse, no thoroughfare. **2.** Deadlock. *Se trouver dans une i.,* to find oneself in a dilemma.
impassibilité, *s.f.* Impassibility.
impassible, *a.* Impassive. **1.** Unmoved. **2.** Unimpressionable.
impassiblement, *adv.* Impassively.
impatiemment, *adv.* Impatiently.
impatience, *s.f.* (*a*) Impatience. (*b*) Eagerness.
impatient, *a.* (*a*) *I. du joug,* chafing under the yoke. (*b*) Impatient. (*c*) *Être i. de faire qch.,* to be eager to do sth.
impatienter, *v.tr.* To put out of patience; to provoke.
  s'impatienter, to lose patience.
impayable, *a.* **1.** Inestimable, invaluable, priceless. **2.** *F:* Highly amusing.
impeccabilité, *s.f.* Impeccability.
impeccable, *a.* Impeccable.
impécunieux, *a.* Impecunious.
impénétrabilité, *s.f.* **1.** Impenetrability. **2.** Inscrutability.
impénétrable, *a.* **1.** Impenetrable. *I. à l'eau,* impervious to water. **2.** Inscrutable.
impénitence, *s.f.* Impenitence; obduracy.
impénitent, *a.* Impenitent, unrepentant.
impératif, *a.* Imperious, imperative, peremptory.
impérativement, *adv.* Imperatively.
impératrice, *s.f.* Empress.
imperceptible, *a.* Imperceptible.
imperceptiblement, *adv.* Imperceptibly.
imperfection, *s.f.* Imperfection. **1.** Incompleteness. **2.** (*a*) Defectiveness. (*b*) Defect.
impérial, -aux. 1. *a.* Imperial. **2.** *s.f.* Impériale. Outside, top(-deck) (of tram).
impérialisme, *s.m.* Imperialism.
impérieux, *a.* **1.** Imperious, haughty. **2.** Imperative, pressing.
impérissable, *a.* Imperishable.
imperméable. 1. *a.* Impervious; impermeable. *I. à l'eau,* waterproof **2.** *s.m. Cost:* Waterproof; rain-coat.
impersonnel, -elle, *a.* Impersonal.
impertinemment, *adv.* Impertinently, rudely.
impertinence, *s.f.* Impertinence. **1.** *Jur:* Irrelevance. **2.** Pertness, rudeness.
impertinent, *a.* Impertinent. **1.** *Jur:* Irrelevant. **2.** Pert, rude.

imperturbabilité, *s.f.* Imperturbability.
imperturbable, *a.* Imperturbable, unruffled.
imperturbablement, *adv.* Imperturbably.
impétueusement, *adv.* Impetuously.
impétueux, *a.* Impetuous; impulsive.
impétuosité, *s.f.* Impetuosity; impulsiveness.
impie, *a.* Impious, ungodly; blasphemous.
impiété, *s.f.* Impiety, godlessness.
impitoyable, *a.* (*a*) Pitiless (*à, envers,* towards); ruthless. (*b*) Relentless.
impitoyablement, *adv.* (*a*) Pitilessly. (*b*) Relentlessly.
implacabilité, *s.f.* Implacability.
implacable, *a.* Implacable, relentless.
implacablement, *adv.* Implacably.
implanter, *v.tr.* To plant; to implant.
  s'implanter, to take root. *F: S'i. chez qn,* to foist oneself on s.o.
implicite, *a.* Implicit. (*a*) Implied (intention). (*b*) Absolute (faith).
implicitement, *adv.* Implicitly. (*a*) By implication. (*b*) Unquestioningly.
impliquer, *v.tr.* To implicate, involve.
implorer, *v.tr.* To implore, beseech.
impoli, *a.* Impolite, rude (*envers, avec,* to).
impoliment, *adv.* Uncivilly, impolitely.
impolitesse, *s.f.* **1.** Impoliteness. (*a*) Discourtesy. (*b*) Rudeness, ill-breeding. **2.** Act of discourtesy.
impolitique, *a.* Impolitic, ill-advised.
impopulaire, *a.* Unpopular.
impopularité, *s.f.* Unpopularity.
importance, *s.f.* Importance. (*a*) Consequence, moment. *Rail: I. du retard,* number of minutes (train is) late. *I. du dommage,* extent of the damage. *Adv.phr. Rosser qn d'i.,* to thrash s.o. soundly. (*b*) Social importance, position.
important, *a.* (*a*) Important; considerable (sum). (*b*) Consequential, self-important.
importateur, -trice, *s.* Importer.
importation, *s.f.* Importation. **1.** Importing. **2.** (Thing imported) Import.
importer[1], *v.tr.* To import (goods).
importer[2], *v.i.* (Only used in the third pers., participles, and inf.) To be of importance; to matter. **1.** *Les choses qui importent,* the things that matter. **2.** *Impers.* Il importe que + *sub.,* it is essential that. . . . N'importe, no matter, never mind. *Venez n'importe quel jour,* come any day.
importun. 1. *a.* Importunate; tiresome; unwelcome. *Je crains de vous être i.,* I am afraid I am disturbing you. **2.** *s.* Nuisance.
importunément, *adv.* Importunately.
importuner, *v.tr.* To importune. (*a*) To bother, pester. (*b*) To annoy, trouble.
importunité, *s.f.* Importunity; dunning.
imposant, *a.* Imposing; stately.
imposer. I. *v.tr.* **1.** To impose, prescribe; to set (task). *I. une règle,* to lay down a rule. *I. (le) silence à qn,* to enjoin silence on s.o.

I. le respect, to command respect. **2.** *Adm:*
(*a*) *I. des droits sur qch.*, to tax sth. (*b*) *I. qn*,
to tax s.o.
II. imposer, *v.i.* **1.** (En) imposer, to
inspire respect. **2.** (En) imposer à qn, to
impose on s.o.
s'imposer. 1. To assert oneself. **2.** *S'i.
à qn*, to thrust oneself upon s.o. **3.** To be
indispensable.
imposition, *s.f.* Imposing, laying down;
setting. (*a*) Imposition; taxation. (*b*) Assessment (of property).
impossibilité, *s.f.* Impossibility.
impossible, *a.* Impossible. *Il m'est i. de le
faire*, I cannot do it. *C'est i. à faire*, it cannot
be done. *Si par impossible il est encore vivant*,
if, by any remote chance, he is still alive.
imposteur, *s.m.* Impostor, humbug.
imposture, *s.f.* Imposture. **1.** Deception,
trickery. **2.** Swindle.
impôt, *s.m.* Tax, duty.
impotence, *s.f.* Helplessness, infirmity.
impotent, *a.* Helpless, crippled.
impraticable, *a.* **1.** Impracticable, un-
workable. **2.** Impassable.
imprécation, *s.f.* Imprecation, curse.
imprécis, *a.* Vague, indefinite.
imprégnation, *s.f.* Impregnation; permeation.
imprégner, *v.tr.* (j'imprègne; j'imprégnerai)
To impregnate (*de*, with).
imprémédité, *a.* Unpremeditated.
imprenable, *a.* Impregnable.
impression, *s.f.* **1.** Impressing. *Typ:*
Printing. *Faute d'impression*, misprint.
2. Impression. *I. de pas*, footprints. **3.** (Mental) impression.
impressionnable, *a.* Impressionable.
impressionnant, *a.* Impressive; moving.
impressionner, *v.tr.* To impress, affect;
to make an impression upon (s.o.).
imprévoyable, *a.* Unforeseeable.
imprévoyance, *s.f.* (*a*) Want of foresight.
(*b*) Improvidence.
imprévoyant, *a.* (*a*) Wanting in foresight.
(*b*) Improvident.
imprévu. 1. *a.* Unforeseen, unexpected.
2. *s.m.* (*a*) Unexpected character (of event).
(*b*) Unforeseen events. *Sauf imprévu*, barring
accidents.
imprimer, *v.tr.* **1.** To communicate (direction). *I. le respect*, to inspire respect. **2.** To
(im)print, impress, stamp. **3.** *Typ:* To print.
  imprimé, *s.m.* Printed paper or book.
"**Imprimés**," 'printed matter.'
imprimerie, *s.f.* **1.** (Art of) printing.
2. Printing-office, -works, -house; press.
imprimeur, *s.m.* (*a*) (Master-)printer. Im-
primeur-libraire, printer and publisher.
(*b*) (Working) printer.
improbabilité, *s.f.* Improbability.
improbable, *a.* Improbable, unlikely.
improbité, *s.f.* Dishonesty.
improductif, *a.* Unproductive.

impromptu. 1. *adv.* Without preparation;
impromptu. **2.** *a.inv.* Unpremeditated;
impromptu; extempore.
impropre, *a.* (*a*) Incorrect, wrong. (*b*) *I. à
qch.*, unfit for sth.
improprement, *adv.* Incorrectly, improperly.
impropriété, *s.f.* Impropriety.
improviser, *v.tr.* **1.** To improvise. **2.** *Abs.*
To speak extempore.
improviste (à l'), *adv.phr.* Unexpectedly.
Prendre qn à l'i., to take s.o. unawares.
improvoqué, *a.* Unprovoked.
imprudemment, *adv.* Imprudently; rashly.
imprudence, *s.f.* Imprudence; rashness.
imprudent, *a.* Imprudent, rash; unwise.
impudemment, *adv.* Shamelessly, impudently.
impudence, *s.f.* Impudence. (*a*) Effrontery. (*b*) Shamelessness.
impudent, *a.* **1.** Shamelessly immodest.
2. Impudent, insolent.
impuissance, *s.f.* Impotence, powerlessness,
helplessness.
impuissant, *a.* (*a*) Impotent, powerless,
helpless. (*b*) Unavailing, ineffective.
impulsif, *a.* Impulsive.
impulsion, *s.f.* **1.** (*a*) *Mec:* Impulse.
(*b*) *F:* Impulse, impetus. **2.** *Sous l'impulsion
du moment*, on the spur of the moment.
impunément, *adv.* With impunity.
impuni, *a.* Unpunished.
impunité, *s.f.* Impunity.
impur, *a.* Impure.
impureté, *s.f.* Impurity.
imputable, *a.* Imputable, attributable.
imputation, *s.f.* Imputation, charge.
imputer, *v.tr.* To impute, attribute. *I. à qn
d'avoir fait qch.*, to charge s.o. with doing sth.
inabordable, *a.* Unapproachable, inaccessible.
inaccentué, *a.* **1.** Unaccented (vowel).
2. Unstressed (syllable).
inacceptable, *a.* Unacceptable.
inaccessibilité, *s.f.* Inaccessibility.
inaccessible, *a.* Inaccessible, unapproachable.
inaccompagné, *a.* Unaccompanied.
inaccoutumé, *a.* Unaccustomed. **1.** Unused. **2.** Unusual, unwonted.
inachevé, *a.* Unfinished, uncompleted.
inactif, *a.* Inactive; idle.
inaction, *s.f.* Inaction, idleness.
inactivité, *s.f.* Inactivity.
inadmissibilité, *s.f.* Inadmissibility.
inadmissible, *a.* Inadmissible. *C'est i.!*
who ever heard of such a thing!
inadvertamment, *adv.* Inadvertently.
inadvertance, *s.f.* **1.** Inadvertency. **2.** (*a*)
Oversight, mistake. (*b*) Lapse of attention.
inadvertant, *a.* Inadvertent, heedless.
inaltérable, *a.* **1.** That does not deteriorate.
I. à l'air, unaffected by air. **2.** (*a*) Unalterable. (*b*) Unfailing, unvarying.

inamovible, *a.* Irremovable.
inanimé, *a.* **1.** Inanimate, lifeless. **2.** Senseless, unconscious.
inanité, *s.f.* **1.** Inanity, futility. **2.** Inane remark.
inapaisable, *a.* Inappeasable.
inapaisé, *a.* Unappeased.
inaperçu, *a.* (*a*) Unseen, unperceived, unobserved. (*b*) Unnoticed, unremarked.
inapplicable, *a.* Inapplicable.
inappréciable, *a.* **1.** Inappreciable. **2.** Inestimable, invaluable.
inapprécié, *a.* Unappreciated.
inapte, *a.* Inapt; unfit (*à*, for); unsuited (*à*, to).
inaptitude, *s.f.* Inaptitude; unfitness (*à*, for).
inarticulé, *a.* Inarticulate.
inassouvi, *a.* Unappeased; unquenched.
inattaquable, *a.* Unassailable.
inattendu, *a.* Unexpected, unforeseen.
inattentif, *a.* Inattentive; heedless (*à*, of).
inaudible, *a.* Inaudible.
inaugural, -aux, *a.* Inaugural.
inauguration, *s.f.* Inauguration.
inaugurer, *v.tr.* To inaugurate.
inauthentique, *a.* Unauthentic.
inautorisé, *a.* Unauthorized, unwarranted.
incalculable, *a.* Incalculable.
incandescence, *s.f.* Incandescence.
incandescent, *a.* Incandescent.
incantation, *s.f.* Incantation.
incapable, *a.* **1.** Incapable, unfit; inefficient. **2.** *I. de faire qch.,* unable to do sth.
incapacité, *s.f.* **1.** Incapacity, unfitness, inefficiency. **2.** *Adm:* *I. permanente,* permanent disablement.
incarcération, *s.f.* Incarceration.
incarcérer, *v.tr.* (j'incarcère; j'incarcérerai) To incarcerate, imprison.
incarnat. 1. *a.* Rosy, pink. **2.** *s.m.* Rosy tint (of dawn).
incarnation, *s.f.* (*a*) Incarnation. (*b*) *F:* Embodiment (of vice).
incarner, *v.tr.* To incarnate, embody.
   incarné, *a.* Incarnate.
incartade, *s.f.* (Verbal) attack, outburst; violent tirade.
incendiaire. 1. *a.* Incendiary; inflammatory. **2.** *s.* (*a*) Incendiary. (*b*) Fire-brand.
incendie, *s.m.* (Outbreak of) fire; conflagration. **Pompe à incendie,** fire-engine. *I. volontaire,* arson.
incendier, *v.tr.* To set on fire; to set fire to.
   incendié, *a.* Burning; burnt down.
incertain, *a.* (*a*) Uncertain, doubtful. (*b*) Unreliable.
incertitude, *s.f.* (*a*) Uncertainty, incertitude, doubt. (*b*) Indecision.
incessamment, *adv.* **1.** Unceasingly, incessantly. **2.** Immediately, forthwith.
incessant, *a.* Unceasing, ceaseless.
inceste, *s.m.* Incest.
incidemment, *adv.* Incidentally.

incidence, *s.f.* Incidence.
incident, *s.m.* Incident. (*a*) Occurrence, happening. (*b*) Difficulty, hitch.
incinération, *s.f.* (*a*) Incineration. (*b*) Cremation.
incinérer, *v.tr.* (j'incinère; j'incinérerai) (*a*) To burn to ashes. (*b*) To cremate.
inciser, *v.tr.* To incise, cut.
incisif, *a.* Incisive, sharp, cutting.
incision, *s.f.* Incision. **1.** Cutting. **2.** Cut.
incisivement, *adv.* Incisively.
incitant, *a.* Inciting, stimulating.
incitation, *s.f.* Incitement (*à*, to).
inciter, *v.tr.* To incite; to urge (on).
incivil, [-vil], *a.* Uncivil, rude, discourteous.
incivilement, *adv.* Uncivilly.
incivilisé, *a.* Uncivilized.
incivilité, *s.f.* Incivility, rudeness.
inclémence, *s.f.* Inclemency.
inclément, *a.* Inclement; severe.
inclinaison, *s.f.* (*a*) Tilting, canting. (*b*) Incline, slope; slant.
inclination, *s.f.* Inclination. **1.** Bending, bow(ing) (of body); nod (of head). **2.** (*a*) Bent, propensity. (*b*) Attachment, love.
incliner. 1. *v.tr.* To incline. (*a*) To slant, slope. (*b*) To tip up; to tilt. (*c*) To bend, bow (the head). (*d*) *I. qn à faire qch.,* to predispose s.o. in favour of doing sth. **2.** *v.i.* (*a*) To lean, slope. (*b*) *I. à la pitié,* to incline to pity.
   s'incliner. 1. To slant, slope. **2.** *S'i. devant qn,* to bow before s.o.
   incliné, *a.* **1.** Inclined. (*a*) *La tête inclinée,* with bowed head. (*b*) Sloping. **2.** *I. à, vers, qch.,* inclined to sth.
inclus, *a.* (*a*) Enclosed (in letter) (*b*) Included.
inclusif, *a.* Inclusive.
inclusion, *s.f.* (*a*) Enclosing. (*b*) Inclusion.
inclusivement, *adv.* Inclusively.
incohérence, *s.f.* Incoherence; disjointedness.
incohérent, *a.* Incoherent.
incolore, *a.* Colourless.
incomber, *v.i.* (Used only in third pers.) *I. à qn,* to devolve upon, be incumbent on.
incombustible, *a.* Incombustible; uninflammable, fireproof.
incommensurable, *a.* **1.** Incommensurate. **2.** *F:* Immeasurable, huge.
incommode, *a.* Inconvenient; uncomfortable; awkward.
incommodément, *adv.* Inconveniently, uncomfortably, awkwardly.
incommoder, *v.tr.* To inconvenience, incommode. *La fumée ne vous incommode pas?* you don't mind my smoking?
incomparable, *a.* Incomparable, unrivalled, matchless.
incomparablement, *adv.* Incomparably.
incompatibilité, *s.f.* Incompatibility.
incompatible, *a.* Incompatible.
incompatiblement, *adv.* Incompatibly.

incompétence, *s.f.* Incompetence, incompetency.

incompétent, *a.* Incompetent. (*a*) Inefficient. (*b*) *Jur:* Not qualified.

incomplet, -ète, *a.* Incomplete.

incomplètement, *adv* Incompletely.

incompréhensibilité, *s.f.* Incomprehensibility.

incompréhensible, *a.* Incomprehensible.

incompréhensiblement, *adv.* Incomprehensibly.

incompris, *a.* Misunderstood; unappreciated.

inconcevable, *a.* Inconceivable, unthinkable, unimaginable.

inconcevablement, *adv.* Inconceivably

inconciliable, *a.* Irreconcilable.

inconditionnel, -elle, *a.* Unconditional.

inconditionnellement, *adv.* Unconditionally.

inconduite, *s.f.* Loose living; laxity of conduct. *Jur:* Misconduct.

incongru, *a.* **1.** Incongruous, foolish. **2.** Improper.

incongruité, *s.f.* (*a*) Incongruity, absurdity. (*b*) Impropriety.

inconnu. **1.** *a.* Unknown. **2.** *s.* (*a*) Unknown person; (i) stranger, (ii) (mere) nobody. (*b*) *s.m.* L'inconnu, the unknown.

inconsciemment, *adv.* Unconsciously.

inconscience, *s.f.* Unconsciousness (*de.* of).

inconscient, *a.* Unconscious (act).

inconséquemment, *adv* Inconsistently, inconsequently.

inconséquence, *s.f.* Inconsistency, inconsequence.

inconséquent, *a.* Inconsistent, inconsequent.

inconsistance, *s.f.* Inconsistency.

inconsistant, *a.* Inconsistent.

inconsolable, *a.* Unconsolable.

inconstance, *s.f.* **1.** Inconstancy, fickleness. **2.** Changeableness.

inconstant, *a.* **1.** Inconstant. **2.** Changeable.

incontestable, *a* Incontestable, undeniable.

incontinent¹, *a.* Incontinent.

incontinent², *adv.* At once, forthwith.

inconvenance, *s.f* (*a*) Unsuitableness (*b*) Impropriety.

inconvenant, *a.* Improper, unseemly.

inconvénient, *s.m.* Disadvantage, drawback.

incorporation, *s.f.* Incorporation.

incorporer, *v.tr.* To incorporate.

incorrect [-rɛkt], *a.* Incorrect. (*a*) Inaccurate, wrong. (*b*) Untrue.

incorrectement, *adv.* Incorrectly.

incorrigible, *a.* Incorrigible; irreclaimable.

incorruptibilité, *s.f.* Incorruptibility

incorruptible, *a.* Incorruptible.

incrédibilité, *s.f.* Incredibility.

incrédule, *a* Incredulous (*à l'égard de*, of).

incrédulité, *s.f.* Incredulity.

incrément, *s.m. Mth:* Increment.

incrimination, *s.f.* Incriminating.

incriminer, *v.tr. Jur:* To incriminate.

incroyable, *a.* Incredible, unbelievable.

incroyablement, *adv.* Incredibly.

incrustation, *s.f.* Incrustation. **1.** Encrusting. *Join:* Inlaying. **2.** Inlaid work.

incruster, *v.tr.* To encrust.

incubation, *s.f.* (*a*) Incubation, hatching. (*b*) Sitting (of hens).

incube, *s.m.* Incubus, nightmare.

inculpation, *s.f.* Indictment, inculpation.

inculper, *v.tr.* To indict, charge.

inculquer, *v.tr.* To inculcate (*à,* upon).

inculte, *a.* Uncultivated, wild ; waste (land).

incultivé, *a.* Uncultivated.

incurable, *a. & s.* Incurable.

incursion, *s.f.* Inroad, foray, incursion

Inde. *Pr.n.f.* (*a*) India. (*b*) Les Indes, the Indies.

indécemment, *adv.* Indecently.

indécence, *s.f.* Indecency, immodesty.

indécent, *a.* Indecent, improper.

indécis, *a.* **1.** Unsettled, open (question); doubtful; vague. **2.** (Of pers.) (*a*) Undecided, in two minds. (*b*) Irresolute.

indécisif, *a.* Indecisive.

indéfendable, *a.* Indefensible.

indéfini, *a.* **1.** Indefinite. **2.** Undefined.

indéfiniment, *adv.* Indefinitely.

indéfinissable, *a.* Indefinable ; nondescript.

indélébile, *a.* Indelible (ink, stain)

indélicat, *a.* Indelicate ; coarse

indélicatesse, *s.f.* Indelicacy ; tactlessness.

indemne, *a.* (*a*) Without loss. (*b*) Undamaged. (*c*) Uninjured.

indemnisation, *s.f.* Indemnification.

indemniser, *v.tr* To indemnify. compensate.

indemnité, *s.f* (*a*) Indemnity, compensation. (*b*) Penalty (for delay). (*c*) Allowance, grant.

indéniable, *a* Undeniable.

indentation, *s.f.* Indentation.

indépendamment, *adv* Independently.

indépendance, *s.f.* Independence.

indépendant, *a.* **1.** (*a*) Independent ; free. (*b*) Self-reliant. **2.** Self-contained (flat).

indescriptible, *a.* Indescribable.

indésirable, *a. & s.* Undesirable

indestructible, *a.* Indestructible.

indéterminé, *a.* Undetermined, indefinite.

index [-ɛks], *s.m.inv.* **1.** (*a*) Forefinger. (*b*) Pointer (of balance); indicator **2.** Index (of book).

indicateur, -trice. **1.** *a.* Indicatory. Poteau indicateur, sign-post. Lampe indicatrice, tell-tale lamp. **2.** *s.* Informer **3.** *s.m.* (*a*) (Railway) time-table, guide ; (street) directory. (*b*) Indicator, pointer.

indicatif, *a.* Indicative.

indication, *s.f.* Indication. **I.** Indicating, pointing out. **2.** (a) (Piece of) information. (b) Sign, token; clue. **3.** *pl.* Instruction(s).

indice, *s.m.* **I.** Indication, sign; mark, token. **2.** Index.

indicible, *a.* (a) Inexpressible, unutterable; unspeakable. (b) Indescribable.

indiciblement, *adv.* Inexpressibly.

indien, -ienne. I. *a. & s.* Indian. **2.** *s.f.* *Tex:* Indienne, chintz.

indifféremment, *adv.* Indifferently.

indifférence, *s.f.* Indifference (*pour* to).

indifférent, *a.* **I.** (a) Indifferent; unconcerned. (b) Cold, insensible. **2.** Immaterial, unimportant.

indigence, *s.f.* Poverty, indigence, want.

indigène. I. *a.* Indigenous; native. **2.** *s.* Native.

indigent, *a.* Poor, needy, indigent.

indigeste, *a.* Indigestible.

indigestion, *s.f.* Indigestion.

indignation, *s.f.* Indignation.

indigne, *a.* Unworthy. **I.** Undeserving. **2.** Shameful.

indignement, *adv.* **I.** Unworthily. **2.** Shamefully.

indigner, *v.tr.* To make (s.o.) indignant. **s'indigner,** to become indignant.

indigné, *a.* Indignant (*de*, at).

indignité, *s.f.* **I.** (a) Unworthiness. (b) Baseness. **2.** *Souffrir des indignités,* to suffer indignities.

indigo, *s.m.* Indigo. *a.inv Des rubans indigo,* indigo-blue ribbons.

indiquer, *v.tr.* To indicate. (a) To point out. *I. qch. du doigt,* to point to sth. (b) To mark, show. (c) To betoken. (d) To appoint, name. (e) *C'était indiqué,* it was the obvious thing to do.

indirect [-rɛkt], *a.* (a) Indirect. (b) Circumstantial (evidence).

indirectement, *adv.* Indirectly

indiscipliné, *a.* Undisciplined, unruly.

indiscret, -ète. *a.* Indiscreet. (a) Imprudent, unguarded. (b) Pushing; tactless. (c) (Person) given to blabbing.

indiscrètement, *adv.* Indiscreetly.

indiscrétion, *s.f.* Indiscretion.

indiscutable, *a.* Indisputable, unquestionable.

indiscutablement, *adv* Indisputably, unquestionably.

indispensable, *a.* Indispensable **I.** Obligatory. **2.** Essential.

indisposer, *v.tr.* To upset (s.o.).

indisposé, *a.* **I.** Indisposed, unwell. **2.** *I.* contre s.o., unfriendly to s.o.

indisposition, *s.f.* Indisposition, illness.

indisputable, *a.* Indisputable, unquestionable.

indisputablement, *adv* Indisputably, unquestionably.

indissoluble, *a.* Insoluble.

indistinct [-ɛ̃(:kt)], *a* Indistinct; hazy.

indistinctement, *adv.* Indistinctly.

indistinguible [-gi-], *a.* Indistinguishable.

individu, *s.m.* **I.** Individual. **2.** *F:* Usu *Pej:* Individual, person.

individualité, *s.f.* Individuality.

individuel, -elle, *a.* Individual; personal.

individuellement, *adv.* Individually.

indivisible, *a.* Indivisible.

Indo-Chine. *Pr.n.f.* Indo-China.

indo-européen, -enne, *a. & s.* Indo-European.

indolemment, *adv.* Indolently.

indolence, *s.f.* Indolence, apathy, sloth.

indolent, *a.* Indolent, apathetic, slothful.

indomptable [-dɔt-], *a.* Unconquerable; untam(e)able; unmanageable.

indompté [-dɔte], *a.* Unconquered; untamed.

indu, *a.* **I.** Not due. **2.** Undue; unwarranted.

indubitable, *a.* Beyond doubt, indubitable, unquestionable.

indubitablement, *adv.* Indubitably.

induction, *s.f.* Induction.

indulgence, *s.f.* Indulgence, leniency.

indulgent, *a.* Indulgent, lenient.

indûment, *adv.* Unduly; improperly.

industrialisation, *s.f.* Industrialization.

industrie, *s.f.* **I.** (a) Activity; industry. (b) Ingenuity. *Vivre d'industrie,* to live by one's wits. **2.** Industry, trade, manufacture.

industriel, -elle. I. *a.* Industrial. **2.** *s.m.* Manufacturer.

industrieusement, *adv.* Busily, industriously.

industrieux, *a.* Busy, industrious.

inébranlable, *a.* Unshak(e)able. (a) Immovable, firm. (b) Resolute, steadfast.

inédit, *a.* **I.** Unpublished (book). **2.** *F:* New, original (plan).

ineffable, *a.* Ineffable, unutterable.

ineffaçable, *a.* Ineffaceable; indelible.

inefficace, *a.* Ineffectual; inefficacious.

inégal, -aux, *a.* **I.** Unequal. **2.** (a) Uneven, rough. (b) Irregular.

inégalé, *a.* Unequalled

inégalement, *adv.* Unequally, unevenly.

inégalité, *s.f.* **I.** Inequality, disparity. **2.** Unevenness.

inélégant, *a.* Inelegant.

inéligible, *a.* Ineligible.

inemployé, *a.* Unemployed, unused.

inepte, *a.* Inept, foolish, idiotic.

ineptement, *adv.* Ineptly, foolishly.

ineptie, *s.f.* Ineptitude.

inépuisable, *a.* Inexhaustible; unfailing.

inéquitable, *a.* Inequitable, unfair.

inéquitablement, *adv* Inequitably, unfairly.

inerte, *a.* Inert; sluggish; dull.

inertie, *s.f.* **I.** Inertia. **2.** Sluggishness.

inespéré, *a.* Unhoped-for, unexpected.

inestimable, *a.* Inestimable, invaluable.

inévitable, *a.* **I.** Unavoidable. **2.** Inevitable

inévitablement, *adv.* Inevitably.
inexact [-zakt], *a.* **1.** Inexact inaccurate.
2. Unpunctual.
inexactitude, *s.f.* **1.** Inaccuracy inexactitude **2.** Unpunctuality
inexcusable, *a.* Inexcusable
inexcusablement, *adv.* Inexcusably.
inexistant, *a.* Non-existent.
inexorable, *a.* Inexorable, unrelenting.
inexorablement, *adv.* Inexorably
inexpérience, *s.f* Inexperience.
inexpérimenté, *a.* Inexperienced.
inexplicable, *a.* Inexplicable, unaccountable.
inexploré, *a.* Unexplored.
inexprimable, *a.* Inexpressible.
inexpugnable, *a.* Impregnable.
inextinguible, *a.* Inextinguishable.
inextricable, *a.* Inextricable.
inextricablement, *adv.* Inextricably.
infaillibilité [ɛ̃faji-], *s.f.* Infallibility.
infaillible [ɛ̃fajibl], *a.* Infallible **1.** Unerring. **2.** Certain, sure, unfailing.
infailliblement [-faji-], *adv.* Infallibly.
infâme, *a.* Infamous; unspeakable.
infamie, *s.f.* **1.** Infamy, dishonour. **2.** Vile, foul, deed.
infanterie, *s.f.* Infantry.
infantile, *a.* Infantile.
infatigable, *a.* Indefatigable, untiring, tireless.
infatigablement, *adv.* Indefatigably.
infatuation, *s.f.* (*a*) Infatuation (*de*, for, over). (*b*) Self-conceit.
infatuer, *v.tr.* To infatuate.
    s'infatuer *de, pour, qn,* to become infatuated with s.o.
infect [ɛ̃fɛkt], *a.* Stinking; foul; noisome.
infecter, *v.tr.* **1.** To infect (*de*, with). **2.** To pollute, taint.
infectieux, *a* Infectious.
infection, *s.f.* **1.** Infection. **2.** Stink, stench.
inférence, *s.f. Log:* Inference.
inférer, *v.tr.* (j'**infère**; j'**inférerai**) To infer.
inférieur, *a.* Inferior. **1.** (*a*) (In place or amount) Lower. (*b*) (In quality) Poor (goods). (*c*) (In position) *D'un rang i.,* of a lower rank. **2. Inférieur à,** inferior to; below. **3.** *s.* Inferior.
infériorité, *s.f.* Inferiority. *I. du nombre,* inferiority in numbers.
infernal, -aux, *a.* Infernal.
infertile, *a.* Unfruitful, barren.
infertilité, *s.f* Unfruitfulness, barrenness.
infester, *v.tr.* To infest, overrun.
infidèle. **1.** *a.* Unfaithful. (*a*) False; unfaithful. (*b*) Dishonest. (*c*) Misleading. **2.** *s.* Infidel.
infidélité, *s.f.* Infidelity (*envers*, to). (*a*) Unfaithfulness. (*b*) Dishonesty (*c*) Inaccuracy. (*d*) (Religious) unbelief.
infime, *a.* **1.** Lowly, mean. **2.** *F:* Tiny, minute.
infini. **1.** *a.* Infinite; boundless, innumerable. **2.** *s.m.* **L'infini,** the infinite. *Adv.phr.* **A l'infini,** to infinity, boundlessly

infiniment, *adv.* Infinitely *Je regrette i.,* *F:* I am awfully sorry
infinité, *s.f* (*a*) *Mth:* etc: Infinity (*b*) *F:* *Une i. de raisons,* no end of reasons.
infinitésimal, -aux, *a.* Infinitesimal
infinitif, *a. & s.m* *Gram:* Infinitive (mood).
infirme. **1.** *a.* (*a*) Infirm (*b*) Disabled, crippled. (*c*) Weak, feeble frail **2.** *s.* (*a*) Invalid. (*b*) Cripple.
infirmerie, *s.f.* Infirmary.
infirmier. **1.** *s.m.* Hospital attendant; male nurse. **2.** *s.f.* **Infirmière,** (hospital) nurse; sick-nurse.
infirmité, *s.f.* (*a*) Infirmity. (*b* Physical disability. (*c*) Weakness, frailty.
inflammabilité, *s.f.* Inflammability.
inflammable, *a.* Inflammable.
inflammation, *s.f.* **1.** Ignition, firing (of explosives). **2.** *Med:* Inflammation
inflation, *s.f* *Pol.Ec:* Inflation.
inflexibilité, *s.f.* Inflexibility.
inflexible, *a.* Inflexible, unbending; unyielding (will); rigid (virtue); (heart) not to be swayed. *I. à toutes les prières,* inexorable to all entreaties.
inflexiblement, *adv.* Inflexibly.
inflexion, *s.f.* Inflexion, inflection.
infliction, *s.f.* *Jur:* Infliction (of penalty) (*à*, upon).
infliger, *v.tr.* (n. **infligeons**) To inflict.
influence, *s.f.* Influence. *Avoir peu d'i.,* to have little weight.
influencer, *v.tr.* (n. **influençons**) To influence; to sway
influent, *a.* Influential.
informateur, -trice, *s.* Informant.
informatif, *a.* Informative, informatory.
information, *s.f.* (*a*) Inquiry. **Prendre des informations (sur qn),** to make inquiries (about s.o.). (*b*) **Je vous envoie, pour votre information . . .,** I am sending you for your information . . .
informe, *a.* (*a*) Formless, shapeless. (*b*) Ill-formed; mis-shapen.
informer. **1.** *v.tr.* *I. qn de qch.,* to inform s.o. of sth. **2.** *v.i.* *Jur:* *I. contre qn,* to inform against s.o.
    s'informer, to make inquiries.
infortune, *s.f.* Misfortune, calamity
infortuné, *a.* Unfortunate, unlucky
infraction, *s.f.* Infraction. **1.** Infringement. **2.** *I. à la paix,* breach of the peace.
infranchissable, *a.* Impassable.
infréquent, *a.* Infrequent, rare.
infréquenté, *a.* Unfrequented.
infructueusement, *adv.* Fruitlessly; unprofitably.
infructueux, *a.* (*a*) Unfruitful, barren. (*b*) Fruitless, unavailing. (*c*) Unprofitable.
infuser, *v.tr* To infuse **1.** To instil (*à*, into). **2.** To steep, macerate.
    s'infuser, to infuse; (of tea) to draw.
infusion, *s.f* Infusion.
ingambe, *a.* Nimble, alert; still active.

6

ingénier (s'), *v.pr.* *S'i. à faire qch.,* to exercise one's wits to do sth.

ingénieur, *s.m.* Engineer.

ingénieusement, *adv.* Ingeniously, cleverly.

ingénieux, *a.* Ingenious, clever.

ingéniosité, *s.f.* Ingenuity; cleverness.

ingénu, *a.* Ingenuous, artless, simple. **Faire l'ingénu,** to affect simplicity.

ingénuité, *s.f.* Ingenuousness, artlessness.

ingénument, *adv.* Ingenuously, artlessly.

ingérer (s') *d'une affaire, dans une affaire,* to (inter)meddle with a business.

inglorieusement, *adv.* Ingloriously.

inglorieux, *a.* Inglorious.

ingouvernable, *a.* Ungovernable, unruly.

ingrat, *a.* **1.** Ungrateful (*envers*, to, towards). **2.** Intractable; thankless. **3.** (*a*) Unpleasing, repellent. (*b*) **L'âge ingrat,** the awkward age.

ingratitude, *s.f.* **1.** Ingratitude, ungratefulness. **2.** Thanklessness (of task).

ingrédient, *s.m.* Ingredient, constituent.

inguérissable, *a.* Incurable.

inhabile, *a.* Inapt; unskilled (in); unfitted (to); clumsy.

inhabilement, *adv.* Unskilfully; awkwardly.

inhabitable, *a.* Uninhabitable.

inhabité, *a.* Uninhabited.

inhaler, *v.tr.* To inhale.

inhérent, *a.* Inherent (*à*, in).

inhospitalier, *a.* Inhospitable.

inhumain, *a.* Inhuman; unfeeling.

inhumanité, *s.f.* Inhumanity.

inimaginable, *a.* Unimaginable; unthinkable.

inimitable, *a.* Inimitable; matchless.

inimitié, *s.f.* Enmity, hostility, ill-feeling.

inintelligent, *a.* Unintelligent; obtuse.

inintelligible, *a.* Unintelligible.

ininterrompu, *a.* Uninterrupted; unbroken.

inique, *a.* Iniquitous.

iniquement, *adv.* Iniquitously.

iniquité, *s.f.* Iniquity.

initial, -aux. 1. *a.* Initial; starting. **2.** *s.f.* **Initiale,** initial (letter).

initiateur, -trice. 1. *s.* Initiator. **2.** *a.* Initiatory.

initiation, *s.f.* Initiation (*à*, into).

initiative, *s.f.* Initiative.

initier, *v.tr.* To initiate (s.o.) (*à*, in). **initié,** *s.* (*a*) Initiate. (*b*) *F:* Person in the know.

injecter, *v.tr.* To inject. **injecté,** *a.* Inflamed, injected. *Yeux injectés de sang,* bloodshot, jaundiced, eyes.

injection, *s.f.* Injection.

injonction, *s.f.* Injunction, behest.

injudicieusement, *adv.* Injudiciously.

injudicieux, *a.* Injudicious.

injure, *s.f.* **1.** Wrong, injury. **2.** Insult; *pl.* abuse.

injurier, *v.tr.* To abuse; to call names.

injurieusement, *adv.* Injuriously, insultingly.

injurieux, *a.* Insulting, abusive.

injuste, *a.* Unjust, unfair.

injustement, *adv.* Unjustly, unfairly.

injustice, *s.f.* Injustice, unfairness.

injustifiable, *a.* Unjustifiable, unwarrantable.

injustifié, *a.* Unjustified, unwarranted.

inlassable, *a.* Untiring, unwearying; tireless.

inlassablement, *adv.* Untiringly, tirelessly.

inné, *a.* Innate, inborn.

innocemment, *adv.* Innocently.

innocence, *s.f.* Innocence. (*a*) Guiltlessness. (*b*) Simplicity. (*c*) Harmlessness.

innocent, *a.* **1.** Innocent; guileless. **2.** (*a*) Simple, artless. *s.* Simpleton. (*b*) Harmless. (*c*) *s.* Innocent, idiot.

innocuité, *s.f.* Innocuousness, harmlessness.

innombrable, *a.* Innumerable, numberless.

innovateur, -trice. 1. *a.* Innovating. **2.** *s.* Innovator.

innovation, *s.f.* Innovation.

inoccupé, *a.* Unoccupied. **1.** Idle. **2.** Vacant; uninhabited (house).

inoculation, *s.f.* *Med:* Inoculation.

inoculer, *v.tr.* To inoculate.

inodore, *a.* Odourless; scentless.

inoffensif, *a.* Inoffensive; innocuous.

inoffensivement, *adv.* Inoffensively, harmlessly.

inondation, *s.f.* Inundation; flood.

inonder, *v.tr.* To inundate, flood; to glut. **inondé,** *a.* Flooded.

inopiné, *a.* Sudden, unexpected.

inopportun, *a.* **1.** Inopportune. **2.** Unseasonable, ill-timed.

inopportunément, *adv.* **1.** Inopportunely. **2.** Unseasonably.

inorganique, *a.* Inorganic.

inoubliable, *a.* Unforgettable.

inouï, *a.* Unheard of. (*a*) Unparalleled, extraordinary. (*b*) *F:* Outrageous.

inqualifiable, *a.* Beyond words.

inquiet, -ète, *a.* (*a*) Restless, fidgety. (*b*) Anxious, uneasy.

inquiétant, *a.* Disquieting, disturbing.

inquiéter, *v.tr.* (**j'inquiète; j'inquiéterai**) To disquiet, trouble, disturb. **s'inquiéter,** to become anxious; to worry, to get uneasy.

inquiétude, *s.f.* Disquiet. (*a*) Restlessness. (*b*) Anxiety, uneasiness.

inquisiteur, *a.m.* (*a*) Inquisitorial. (*b*) *F:* Inquisitive, prying.

inquisition, *s.f.* Inquisition.

insaisissable, *a.* (*a*) Elusive. (*b*) Imperceptible.

insanité, *s.f.* Insanity.

insatiable, *a.* Insatiable.

nsatiablement, *adv.* Insatiably.
nscription, *s.f.* **1.** (*a*) Writing down, inscribing. (*b*) Registration, enrolment. (*c*) *Gramophones:* I. *sur cire,* wax recording. **2.** (*a*) Inscription. (*b*) Directions (on signpost); notice.
nscrire, *v.tr.* (*pr.p.* inscrivant; *p.p.* inscrit; *p.h.* j'inscrivis) **1.** (*a*) To inscribe, write down. (*b*) To register; to enter (s.o.'s) name. **2.** To inscribe, engrave.
  s'inscrire, to put down one's name.
nscrutable, *a.* Inscrutable.
nscrutablement, *adv.* Inscrutably.
nsecte, *s.m.* Insect.
nsécurité, *s.f.* Insecurity.
nsensé, *a.* (*a*) Mad, insane. *s.* Madman, -woman. (*b*) Senseless, foolish (*c*) Extravagant.
nsensibilité, *s.f.* Insensitiveness. (*a*) Insensibility. (*b*) Indifference, callousness.
nsensible, *a.* Insensible **1.** (*a*) Insensitive. (*b*) Indifferent; callous. **2.** Imperceptible; hardly perceptible.
nsensiblement, *adv.* Imperceptibly, insensibly.
nséparable. 1. *a.* Inseparable. **2.** *s.m.pl.* *Orn:* Love-birds.
nsérer, *v.tr.* (j'insère; j'insérerai) To insert.
nsertion, *s.f.* Insertion.
nserviable, *a.* Disobliging.
nsidieusement, *adv.* Insidiously.
nsidieux, *a.* Insidious.
nsigne¹, *a.* **1.** Distinguished (*par,* for); remarkable. *Faveur i.,* signal favour. **2.** *Pej:* Notorious, arrant.
nsigne², *s.m.* Usu. *pl.* Distinguishing mark; badge.
nsignifiance, *s.f.* Insignificance, unimportance.
nsignifiant, *a.* **1.** Insignificant, unimportant. **2.** Vacuous; lacking in personality.
nsinuant, *a.* Insinuating.
nsinuation, *s.f.* Insinuation.
nsinuer, *v.tr.* To insinuate. **1.** To insert (gently). **2.** To hint at (sth.).
  s'insinuer, to penetrate; to creep (in).
nsipide, *a.* Insipid. (*a*) Tasteless. (*b*) Dull, vapid, flat; tame (story).
nsipidité, *s.f.* Insipidity. (*a*) Tastelessness. (*b*) Dullness, flatness.
nsistance, *s.f.* Insistence. **Avec insistance,** earnestly, insistingly.
nsister, *v.i.* To insist. *I. sur un fait,* to dwell (up)on a fact.
nsociable, *a.* Unsociable.
nsolation, *s.f.* **1.** Sun-bathing. **2.** Sunstroke.
nsolemment, *adv.* Insolently.
nsolence, *s.f.* Insolence, impertinence.
nsolent, *a.* (*a*) Insolent, impertinent (*envers, avec,* to). (*b*) Haughty, overbearing.
nsolite, *a.* Unusual, unwonted.
nsoluble, *a.* Insoluble.
nsolvable, *a.* *Com:* Insolvent.

insomnie, *s.f.* Insomnia, sleeplessness.
insondable, *a.* Unfathomable.
insouciamment, *adv* Unconcernedly, heedlessly.
insouciance, *s.f* (*a*) Freedom from care. (*b*) Thoughtlessness, casualness.
insouciant, *a.* (*a*) Careless, free from care. (*b*) Heedless, thoughtless, casual.
insoucieux, *a.* Heedless.
insoumis, *a.* **1.** Unsubdued **2.** Unsubmissive, unruly.
insoupçonné, *a.* Unsuspected (*de,* by).
insoutenable, *a.* **1.** Untenable; indefensible. **2.** Unbearable.
inspecter, *v.tr.* To inspect; to examine.
inspecteur, -trice, *s.* Inspector; overseer; shop-walker; surveyor.
inspection, *s.f.* **1.** (*a*) Inspection, inspecting; survey (*b*) Tour of inspection. **2.** Inspectorship; surveyorship.
inspirateur, -trice, *a.* Inspiring, inspiriting.
inspiration, *s.f.* Inspiration. **1.** Inhaling. **2.** Suggestion, prompting.
inspirer, *v.tr.* To inspire. **1.** *I. le respect,* to inspire respect. **2.** To inhale.
instabilité, *s.f.* Instability.
instable, *a.* Unstable.
installation, *s.f.* **1.** Installation. **2.** (*a*) Arrangements, appointments; fittings (*b*) *Ind:* Plant.
installer, *v tr.* (*a*) To install. (*b*) To set up; to fit up, equip.
  s'installer, to install oneself.
instamment, *adv.* Insistently, earnestly.
instance, *s.f.* (*a*) Instancy, solicitation. (*b*) *pl.* Requests, entreaties.
instant¹, *a.* Pressing, urgent, instant.
instant², *s.m.* Moment, instant. **Par instants,** off and on. **Un instant!** wait a moment!
instantané. 1. *a.* Instantaneous. **2.** *s.m.* *Phot:* Snapshot.
instantanément, *adv.* Instantaneously.
instar de (à l'), *prep.phr.* After the fashion, manner, of; like.
instaurer, *v.tr.* To found, to set up.
instigateur, -trice, *s.* Instigator.
instigation, *s.f.* Instigation, incitement.
instiller, *v.tr.* To instil.
instinct [ɛ̃stɛ̃], *s.m.* Instinct. **D'instinct,** instinctively.
instinctif, *a.* Instinctive.
instinctivement, *adv.* Instinctively.
instituer, *v.tr.* To institute. (*a*) To establish. (*b*) To appoint (official).
institut, *s.m.* Institute, institution.
instituteur, -trice, *s.* **1.** Founder, foundress. **2.** (*a*) (School-)teacher. (*b*) *s.f.* Institutrice, governess.
institution, *s.f.* **1.** Institution. **2.** Establishment; academy.
instructeur, *s.m.* **1.** Instructor, teacher. *Sergent i.,* drill-sergeant. **2.** *Jur:* Juge instructeur, examining magistrate.

instructif, *a.* Instructive.

instruction, *s.f.* Instruction. **1.** (*a*) Travailler à l'instruction de qn, to work under s.o.'s direction. (*b*) *pl.* Instructions, directions. **2.** Education. Avoir de l'instruction, to be well educated. **3.** Juge d'instruction, examining magistrate.

instruire, *v.tr.* (*pr.p.* instruisant; *p.p.* instruit; *p.h.* j'instruisis) **1.** *I.* qn de qch., to inform s.o. of sth. **2.** To teach, instruct.
  instruit, *a.* Educated; well-read.

instrument, *s.m.* (*a*) Instrument, implement. (*b*) (Musical) instrument. (*c*) (Legal) instrument.

instrumental, -aux, *a.* Instrumental (music).

insu, *s.m.* A l'insu de, without the knowledge of.

insubordination, *s.f.* Insubordination.

insubordonné, *a.* Insubordinate.

insuccès, *s.m.* Unsuccess; failure.

insuffisamment, *adv.* Insufficiently, inadequately.

insuffisance, *s.f.* **1.** Insufficiency; inadequacy. **2.** Incapacity, incompetence.

insuffisant, *a.* **1.** Insufficient; inadequate; short (weight). **2.** Incapable, incompetent.

insulaire, **1.** *a.* Insular. **2.** *s.* Islander.

insultant, *a.* Insulting, offensive.

insulte, *s.f.* Insult.

insulter, *v.tr.* To insult, affront (s.o.).

insupportable, *a.* Unbearable, unendurable; intolerable.

insupportablement, *adv.* Unbearably; insufferably.

insurger (s'), *v.pr.* (n. n. insurgeons) To rise (in rebellion); to revolt.
  insurgé, *s.* Insurgent, rebel.

insurmontable, *a.* Insurmountable.

insurrection, *s.f.* Insurrection, rising.

intact [ětakt], *a.* Intact. (*a*) Untouched; unbroken. (*b*) Unsullied, unblemished.

intangible, *a.* Intangible.

intégral, -aux, *a.* Integral, entire, whole. Paiement i., payment in full.

intégralement, *adv.* Wholly, fully, in full.

intégrant, *a.* Integral. Faire partie intégrante de . . ., to be part and parcel of. . . .

intégrité, *s.f.* **1.** Integrity, entirety, wholeness. **2.** Uprightness, honesty.

intellect [-lekt], *s.m.* Intellect, understanding.

intellectuel, -elle, *a.* Intellectual; mental. Travail i., F: brainwork.

intellectuellement, *adv.* Intellectually.

intelligemment, *adv.* Intelligently.

intelligence, *s.f.* **1.** Understanding, comprehension. **2.** Intelligence, intellect. **3.** Vivre en bonne intelligence avec qn, to live on good terms with s.o. Être d'intelligence avec qn, to have an understanding with s.o.

intelligent, *a.* Intelligent; sharp, clever.

intelligible, *a.* (*a*) Intelligible, understandable. (*b*) Clear, distinct.

intelligiblement, *adv.* **1.** Intelligibly, plainly. **2.** Clearly.

intempérance, *s.f.* Intemperance.

intempérant, *a.* Intemperate.

intempérie, *s.f.* Inclemency (of weather).

intempestif, *a.* Untimely; inopportune.

intenable, *a.* Untenable.

intendant, *s.m.* Intendant. (*a*) Steward, bailiff. (*b*) Manager.

intense, *a.* Intense; severe; deep (blue).

intensif, *a.* Intensive.

intensifier, *v.tr.* To intensify.

intensité, *s.f.* Intensity; force (of wind).

intention, *s.f.* Intention. (*a*) Purpose, design. (*b*) Will, wish. Accepter l'intention pour le fait, to take the will for the deed. A l'intention de, for (the sake of).

intentionné, *a.* Bien intentionné, well-disposed.

intentionnel, -elle, *a.* Intentional, deliberate.

intentionnellement, *adv.* Intentionally, deliberately.

intercéder, *v.i.* (Conj. like CÉDER) To intercede (auprès de, with).

intercepter, *v.tr.* To intercept; to cut off.

interception, *s.f.* Interception.

interdiction, *s.f.* Interdiction; prohibition.

interdire, *v.tr.* (Conj. like DIRE, except pr.ind. and imp. interdisez) **1.** To forbid, prohibit. "Entrée interdite (au public)," 'no admittance.' "Passage interdit," 'no thoroughfare.' *I.* à qn de faire qch., to forbid s.o. to do sth. **2.** To disconcert, bewilder.
  interdit, 1. *a.* Disconcerted; taken aback. **2.** *Ecc:* Interdict.

intéressant, *a.* Interesting. Prix intéressants, attractive prices.

intéresser, *v.tr.* To interest. (*a*) To give a financial interest. (*b*) To affect, concern. (*c*) To be interesting to. (*d*) *I.* qn à une cause, to interest s.o. in a cause.
  s'intéresser, to become interested; to take an interest.

intéressé, *a.* **1.** Interested. **2.** Selfish, self-seeking. Amour intéressé, cupboard love.

intérêt, *s.m.* Interest. **1.** Share, stake (in business). **2.** Advantage, benefit. Il y a intérêt à . . ., it is desirable to. . . . *Rail:* Ligne d'intérêt local, branch-line. **3.** (Feeling of) interest. Porter intérêt à qn, to take an interest in s.o. **4.** *Fin:* *I.* composé, compound interest.

intérieur. 1. *a.* (*a*) Interior; inner; internal. (*b*) Inward (feelings). **2.** *s.m.* (*a*) Interior, inside. A l'intérieur, inside. (*b*) Home, house. Vie d'i., home life, domestic life.

intérieurement, *adv.* Inwardly, internally.

interjection, *s.f.* *Gram:* Interjection.

interloquer, *v.tr.* To disconcert, abash.

intermède, *s.m.* **1.** Medium, intermediary. **2.** *Th:* Interlude.

intermédiaire. 1. *a.* Intermediate, intervening. **2.** *s.m.* Agent, intermediary. *Com:* Middleman. **3.** *s.m.* Intermediary, agency.
interminable, *a.* Interminable; endless.
interminablement, *adv.* Interminably, endlessly.
intermittemment, *adv.* Intermittently.
intermittent, *a.* Intermittent.
internat, *s.m.* **1.** Living in. **2.** Boarding-school.
international, -aux, *a.* International.
interne. 1. *a.* Internal. **2.** *s.* (*a*) *Sch:* Boarder. (*b*) Resident medical student.
internement, *s.m.* Internment.
interner, *v.tr.* To intern.
interpeller, *v.tr.* To call upon. *Mil:* To challenge.
interpoler, *v.tr.* To interpolate.
interposer, *v.tr.* To interpose.
s'interposer, to interpose, intervene.
interprétation, *s.f.* **1.** Interpreting (of speech). **2.** Interpretation.
interprète, *s.m. & f.* Interpreter.
interpréter, *v.tr.* (j'interprète; j'interpréterai) To interpret.
interrogateur, -trice. 1. *a.* Interrogatory, inquiring. **2.** *s.* Questioner, interrogator.
interrogatif, *a.* *Gram:* Interrogative.
interrogation, *s.f.* Interrogation. **1.** Questioning. *Gram:* Point d'interrogation, question-mark. **2.** Question, query.
interroger, *v.tr.* (n. interrogeons) To examine, interrogate.
interrompre, *v.tr.* (Conj. like ROMPRE) (*a*) To interrupt. (*b*) To intercept. (*c*) To stop, suspend (traffic); to break (journey).
s'interrompre, to break off.
interruption, *s.f.* (*a*) Interruption. (*b*) Stoppage, break; breaking off.
intersection, *s.f.* (*a*) Intersection. (*b*) Crossing (of roads).
interstice, *s.m.* Interstice; chink.
intervalle, *s.m.* Interval. **1.** Distance, gap, space. **2.** Period (of time).
intervenir, *v.i.* (Conj. like VENIR. Aux. *être*) **1.** To intervene. (*a*) To interpose. (*b*) To interfere. **2.** To happen, occur, arise.
intervention, *s.f.* **1.** Intervening, intervention. **2.** Interference.
intestin, *s.m.* *Anat:* Intestine, bowel, gut. **Les intestins,** the bowels.
intimation, *s.f.* Notification.
intime, *a.* Intimate. **1.** Interior, inward. **2.** Close. *s.* Un, une, intime, an intimate friend.
intimement, *adv.* Intimately, closely.
intimidant, *a.* Intimidating.
intimidation, *s.f.* Intimidation.
intimider, *v.tr.* To intimidate. *Nullement intimidé,* nothing daunted.
intimité, *s.f.* **1.** Depths (of one's being). **2.** Intimacy. (*a*) Close connection. (*b*) Closeness (of friendship). (*c*) Privacy.

intolérable, *a.* Intolerable, unbearable.
intolérablement, *adv.* Intolerably, unbearably.
intoléramment, *adv.* Intolerantly.
intolérance, *s.f.* Intolerance.
intolérant, *a.* Intolerant.
intoxicant, *a.* Poisonous, toxic.
intoxication, *s.f.* Poisoning.
intoxiquer, *v.tr.* To poison.
intraitable, *a.* (*a*) Intractable, unmanageable. (*b*) Obstinate.
intransigeance, *s.f.* Uncompromisingness.
intransigeant, *a.* Uncompromising, strict.
intransitif, *a.* *Gram:* Intransitive.
intrépide, *a.* Intrepid, dauntless, fearless.
intrépidement, *adv.* Intrepidly, fearlessly.
intrépidité, *s.f.* Intrepidity, fearlessness.
intrigant. 1. *a.* Intriguing, scheming. **2.** *s.* Intriguer, schemer.
intrigue, *s.f.* Intrigue. **1.** (*a*) Plot, scheme. (*b*) (Love-)affair. **2.** Plot (of play).
intriguer. 1. *v.tr.* To puzzle. **2.** *v.i.* To scheme, plot, intrigue.
intrinsèque, *a.* Intrinsic.
intrinsèquement, *adv.* Intrinsically.
introduction, *s.f.* Introduction.
introduire, *v.tr.* (*pr.p.* introduisant; *p.p.* introduit; *p.h.* j'introduisis) To introduce. (*a*) To insert. (*b*) To bring in; to admit.
s'introduire, to get in, enter.
introspectif, *a.* Introspective.
introuvable, *a.* (*a*) Undiscoverable; not to be found. (*b*) *F:* Peerless, matchless.
intrus. 1. *a.* Intruding. **2.** *s.* Intruder.
intrusion, *s.f.* Intrusion.
intuitif, *a.* Intuitive.
intuition, *s.f.* Intuition.
inusable, *a.* Hard-wearing; everlasting.
inusité, *a.* (*a*) Unusual. (*b*) Not in common use.
inutile, *a.* (*a*) Useless, unavailing; vain. (*b*) Needless, unnecessary.
inutilement, *adv.* (*a*) Uselessly. (*b*) Needlessly.
invaincu, *a.* Unconquered, unvanquished.
invalide. 1. *a.* (*a*) Invalid, infirm. (*b*) *Jur:* Invalid (will). **2.** *s.* (*a*) Invalid. (*b*) *s.m.* Disabled soldier; pensioner.
invalider, *v.tr.* To invalidate.
invariable, *a.* Invariable, unvarying.
invariablement, *adv.* Invariably.
invasion, *s.f.* Invasion; inroad.
invective, *s.f.* (*a*) Invective. (*b*) *pl.* Abuse.
invectiver. 1. *v.i.* I. contre qn, to inveigh against s.o. **2.** *v.tr.* *F:* To abuse.
invendable, *a.* Unsaleable.
inventaire, *s.m.* Inventory.
inventer, *v.tr.* To invent. (*a*) To find out, discover. *F:* Il n'a pas inventé la poudre, he will never set the Thames on fire. (*b*) To devise; to make up (story).
inventeur, *s.m.* Inventor, discoverer.
inventif, *a.* Inventive.

invention, s.f. **I.** (a) Invention, inventing. (b) Imagination, inventiveness. **2.** (a) Invention, device. (b) Fabrication, lie.
inverse. I. a. Inverse, opposite. **2.** s.m. Opposite, reverse.
inversement, adv. Inversely.
inversion, s.f. (a) Gram: Inversion. (b) Transposition.
invertébré, a. Invertebrate.
investigateur, -trice. I. a. Investigating. **2.** s. Investigator, inquirer.
investigation, s.f. Investigation.
investir, v.tr. To invest.
investiture, s.f. Investiture.
invétéré, a. Inveterate.
invincibilité, s.f. Invincibility.
invincible, a. Invincible, unconquerable.
invinciblement, adv. Invincibly.
inviolable, a. Inviolable ; sacred.
invisibilité, s.f. Invisibility.
invisible, a. Invisible.
invitation, s.f. Invitation.
invite, s.f. Invitation, inducement.
inviter, v.tr. To invite. **I.** I. qn à entrer, to invite s.o. in. **2.** (a) I. le désastre, to court disaster. (b) I. qn à faire qch., to request s.o. to do sth.
invocation, s.f. Invocation.
involontaire, a. Involuntary, unintentional.
invoquer, v.tr. **I.** To call upon, to invoke. **2.** I. une raison, to put forward a reason.
invraisemblable, a. Unlikely, improbable.
invraisemblance, s.f. Unlikeliness, improbability.
invulnérabilité, s.f. Invulnerability.
invulnérable, a. Invulnerable.
iode, s.m. Iodine.
iodure, s.m. Ch: Iodide.
ion, s.m. El: Ion.
ionique, a. Arch: Ionic (order).
iota, s.m. F: Pas un iota, not a jot, not an iota.
ir-ai, -as, etc. See ALLER.
Irak. Pr.n.m. Geog: Irak, Iraq.
irakien, -ienne, a. & s. Iraqi.
irascibilité, s.f. Irascibility.
irascible, a. Irascible.
iridescent, a. Iridescent.
Iris [iris]. **I.** Pr.n.f. Myth: Iris. **2.** s.m. (a) Iris (of eye). **3.** s.m. or f. Bot: Iris, flag. Racine d'iris, orris-root.
irisé, a. Iridescent, rainbow-hued.
irlandais. I. a. Irish. **2.** s. Irishman ; Irishwoman. **3.** s.m. Ling: Irish, Erse.
Irlande. Pr.n.f. Geog: Ireland.
ironie, s.f. Irony.
ironique, a. Ironic(al).
ironiquement, adv. Ironically.
irradier, v.i. To (ir)radiate.
irrationnel, -elle, a. Irrational.
irréalisable, a. Unrealizable.
irréconciliable, a. Irreconcilable.
irrécouvrable, a. Irrecoverable.

irréel, -elle, a. Unreal.
irréfléchi, a. **I.** Unconsidered, thoughtless. **2.** Hasty, rash.
irréflexion, s.f. Thoughtlessness.
irréfutable, a. Irrefutable.
irrégularité, s.f. **I.** Irregularity. **2.** Unpunctuality.
irrégulier, a. (a) Irregular. (b) Unpunctual.
irrégulièrement, adv. **I.** Irregularly. **2.** Unpunctually.
irrémédiable, a. Irremediable.
irrémédiablement, adv. Irremediably.
irremplaçable, a. Irreplaceable.
irréparable, a. Irreparable.
irréprochable, a. Irreproachable.
irrésistible, a. Irresistible.
irrésistiblement, adv. Irresistibly.
irrésolu, a. Irresolute, wavering (nature) ; faltering (steps).
irrésolument, adv. Irresolutely.
irrespectueusement, adv. Disrespectfully.
irrespectueux, a. Disrespectful.
irresponsabilité, s.f. Irresponsibility
irresponsable, a. Irresponsible.
irrévérence, s.f. Irreverence.
irrévérencieux, a. Irreverent.
irrévocable, a. Irrevocable.
irrévocablement, adv. Irrevocably.
irrigation, s.f. Agr: Irrigation.
irriguer, v.tr. Agr: To irrigate.
irritabilité, s.f. Irritability.
irritable, a. Irritable.
irritant, a. Irritating.
irritation, s.f. Irritation.
irriter, v.tr. To irritate.
s'irriter, to grow angry.
irruption, s.f. Irruption. **Faire irruption** dans une salle, to burst into a room.
Isaïe. Pr.n.m. B.Hist: Isaiah.
isard, s.m. Z: Izard ; wild goat.
islandais. Geog: **I.** a. Icelandic. **2.** s. Icelander.
Islande. Pr.n.f. Geog: Iceland.
isocèle, a. Geom: Isosceles (triangle).
isolant. I. a. (a) Isolating. (b) Insulating. **2.** s.m. Insulator.
isolateur, -trice. El: **I.** a. Insulating. **2.** s.m. Insulator.
isolement, s.m. **I.** Isolation, loneliness **2.** El.E: Insulation.
isolément, adv. Separately ; singly.
isoler, v.tr. **I.** To isolate. **2.** El.E: To insulate.
isolé, a. **I.** Isolated ; lonely. **2.** El.E: Insulated.
Israélite. B.Hist: **I.** s.m. & f. Israelite, Jew. **2.** a. Israelitish.
issu, a. Descended ; born.
issue, s.f. **I.** Issue, end, conclusion. **2.** Exit; outlet.
Istamboul. Pr.n.m. Geog: Istanbul.
isthme, s.m. Geog: Isthmus.
Italie. Pr.n.f. Italy.
italien, -ienne, a. & s. Italian.

italique, *a. & s.m.* *Typ:* Italic (type); italics.
item [itɛm], *adv.* Item, likewise, also.
itinéraire, *s.m.* Itinerary. (a) Route, way. (b) Road-book.
itinérant, *a.* Itinerant.
ivoire, *s.m.* Ivory. *Geog:* La Côte d'Ivoire, the Ivory Coast.

ivraie, *s.f.* *Bot:* (a) Corn-cockle. (b) *B.Lit:* Tares.
ivre, *a.* Drunk, intoxicated. *I. de joie,* mad with joy.
ivresse, *s.f.* (a) Intoxication, inebriety. (b) *Lit:* Rapture.
ivrogne. **1.** *s.m.* Drunkard. **2.** *a.* Addicted to drink.

J

J, j [ʒi], *s.m.* The letter J, j.
jabot, *s.m.* **1.** Crop (of bird). **2.** *Cost:* Shirt-frill, ruffle.
jacasser, *v.i.* *F:* To chatter, jabber.
jacinthe, *s.f.* **1.** *Bot:* Hyacinth. *J. des bois,* blue-bell. **2.** *Miner:* Jacinth.
Jacques. *Pr.n.m.* James. *F:* Maître Jacques, Jack-of-all-trades.
Jacquot. **1.** *Pr.n.m.* *F:* Jim, Jimmy. **2.** *s.m.* Poll(-parrot), Polly.
jactance, *s.f.* Boastfulness, boasting, brag.
jade, *s.m.* Jade(-stone).
jadis [ʒadis], *adv.* Formerly, once, of old.
jaguar [-gwaːr], *s.m.* Jaguar; American tiger.
jaillir [ʒajiːr], *v.i.* To spring (up); to shoot forth; to gush (forth); (of sparks) to fly.
jaillissement [ʒaji-], *s.m.* Gush(ing), spout(ing).
jais, *s.m.* *Miner:* Jet.
jalonner, *v.tr.* *Surv:* To lay out, stake out.
jalousement, *adv.* Jealously.
jalousie, *s.f.* **1.** Jealousy. **2.** Venetian blind.
jaloux, *a.* (a) Jealous. (b) Zealous, careful.
Jamaïque (la). *Pr.n.f.* Jamaica.
jamais, *adv.* **1.** Ever. A tout jamais, for ever and ever. **2.** (With neg. expressed or understood) Never. *C'est le cas ou j.,* now or never. Jamais de la vie! never! out of the question! **3.** *s.m.* Au grand jamais! never, never!
jambe, *s.f.* **1.** Leg. *F:* Prendre ses jambes à son cou, to take to one's heels. Avoir les jambes rompues, to be worn out. N'avoir plus de jambes, to be tired out. **2.** Jambe de force, strut, prop, brace.
jambon, *s.m.* Ham.
jante, *s.f.* Rim (of wheel).
janvier, *s.m.* January.
Japon (le). *Pr.n.m.* *Geog:* Japan. *Au.J.,* in, to, Japan.
japonais, *a. & s.* Japanese.
jappement, *s.m.* Yelp(ing), yap(ping).
japper, *v.i.* To yelp, yap.
jaquette, *s.f.* (a) (Man's) tail-coat, morning coat. (b) (Woman's) jacket.

jardin, *s.m.* Garden. *Sch:* Jardin d'enfants, kindergarten.
jardinage, *s.m.* (a) Gardening. (b) Garden-stuff.
jardiner, *v.i.* To garden.
jardinier. **1.** *a.* Plantes jardinières, garden plants. **2.** *s.* Gardener. **3.** *s.f.* Jardinière, flower-stand.
jargon, *s.m.* (a) Jargon. (b) Cant, slang.
Jarnac [-ak]. *Pr.n.m.* (Used in) Coup de Jarnac, treacherous stroke; stab in the back.
jarret, *s.m.* Bend of the knee; hock (of horse). Plier le jarret, to bend the knee. Avoir le jarret solide, to be strong on one's legs.
jarretelle, *s.f.* (Stocking) suspender.
jarretière, *s.f.* Garter.
jars, *s.m.* Gander.
jaser, *v.i.* (a) To chatter; to gossip. Jaser comme une pie (borgne), to talk nineteen to the dozen. (b) To blab; to tell tales.
jaseur, -euse. **1.** *a.* Talkative. **2.** *s.* Chatter-box; gossip.
jasmin, *s.m.* *Bot:* Jasmine, jessamine.
jaspe, *s.m.* *Miner:* Jasper.
jatte, *s.f.* Bowl; (milk-)pan, basin.
jauge, *s.f.* **1.** (a) Gauge (of cask). (b) *Nau:* Tonnage (of ship). **2.** (a) Gauging-rod. (b) *Mec.E:* Gauge.
jauger, *v.tr.* (n. jaugeons) To gauge.
jaunâtre, *a.* Yellowish; sallow.
jaune. **1.** *a.* Yellow. *Chaussures jaunes,* brown shoes. *a.inv.* Des gants jaune paille, straw-yellow gloves. *adv.* Rire jaune, to give a sickly smile. Voir jaune, to see everything with a jaundiced eye. **2.** *s.m.* (a) Yellow (colour). (b) Jaune d'œuf, yolk (of egg).
jaunir, *v.tr. & i.* **1.** To colour (sth.) yellow. **2.** To grow, turn, yellow.
jaunisse, *s.f.* *Med:* Jaundice.
javeline, *s.f.,* **javelot,** *s.m.* Javelin.
je, before vowel sound j', *pers.pron.nom.* I.
Jean [ʒɑ̃]. *Pr.n.m.* John. La Saint-Jean, Mid-summer Day.
Jeanne [ʒan]. *Pr.n.f.* Jane, Joan.
Jeannette [ʒan-]. *Pr.n.f.* Jenny, Janet.

Jeannot]

168

[jour

Jeannot [ʒano]. *Pr.n.m. F:* Johnny, Jack.
Jérémie. *Pr.n.m.* Jeremiah.
jersiais, *a. & s.* (Native) of Jersey.
jésuite, *s.m. Ecc:* Jesuit.
jésuitique, *a.* Usu. *Pej:* Jesuitic(al).
Jésus. *Pr.n.m.* Jesus. **Jésus-Christ,** Jesus Christ.
jet, *s.m.* **1.** (*a*) Throwing, casting; throw, cast. (*b*) *Metall:* Cast, casting. *F:* Faire qch. d'un seul jet, to do sth. at one go. (*c*) Jet (*de marchandises*) à la mer, jettison(ing), throwing overboard (of cargo). **2.** (*a*) Jet, gush (of liquid); flash (of light). Jet d'eau, fountain. (*b*) Young shoot (of tree). **3.** Spout.
jeter, *v.tr.* (je jette) To throw, fling, cast. Jeter un cri, to utter a cry. *J. les fondements d'un édifice,* to lay the foundations of a building. *Nau: J. la sonde,* to heave the lead.
  se jeter *Se j. à bas de son lit,* to jump out of bed. *Se j. sur qn,* to attack s.o.
jetée, *s.f.* **1.** Jetty, pier. **2.** Breakwater.
jeton, *s.m. Cards:* Counter.
jeu, jeux, *s.m.* **1.** (*a*) Play, sport. Jeu de mots, play on words; pun. Jeu d'esprit, witticism. Se faire (un) jeu de qch., to make light of sth. (*b*) (Manner of) playing. *Jeu muet.* dumb show. **2.** (*a*) *Terrain de jeux,* sports-ground. Ce n'est pas de jeu, that's not fair. Jouer beau jeu, to play fair. *Prov:* A beau jeu beau retour, one good turn deserves another. *F: Vous avez beau jeu,* now's your chance. (*b*) (Place) *Jeu de tennis,* (lawn-)tennis courts. *Jeu de boules,* bowling-green. **3.** Set. *Jeu d'échecs,* set of chessmen. *Jeu de cartes,* pack of cards. **4.** Gaming, gambling, play. Jouer gros jeu, to play high. Faites vos jeux! put down your stakes! **5.** Les forces en jeu, the forces at work.
jeudi, *s.m.* Thursday.
jeun (à), *adj.phr.* Fasting.
jeune, *a.* (*a*) Young; juvenile or youthful. Jeunes gens, young folk. (*b*) Younger. *M. Dupont Jeune,* Mr Dupont junior.
jeûne, *s.m.* (*a*) Fast. (*b*) Fasting.
jeûner, *v.i.* To fast.
jeunesse, *s.f.* (*a*) Youth; boyhood, girlhood. Il faut que jeunesse se passe, youth will have its fling. (*b*) Youthfulness.
joaillerie [ʒwajri], *s.f.* **1.** Jeweller's trade. **2.** Jewellery.
joaillier [ʒwaje], *s.* Jeweller.
jobarder, *v.tr. F:* To dupe, gull.
joie, *s.f.* **1.** Joy; delight; gladness. Feu de joie, bonfire. *Adv.phr.* A cœur joie, to one's heart's content. **2.** Mirth, merriment.
joign-ant, -ons, -is, etc. See JOINDRE.
joindre, *v.tr.* (*pr.p.* joignant; *p.p.* joint; *pr.ind.* je joins, il joint; *p.h.* je joignis) **1.** To join. (*a*) To bring together. (*b*) To add. *J. le geste à la parole,* to suit the action to the word. (*c*) *J. son régiment,* to join one's regiment. **2.** To adjoin.
  se joindre, to join, unite.

joint. **1.** *a.* Joined, united. Pieds joints, feet close together. *Conj.phr* Joint (à ce) que besides which. **2.** *s.m.* Joint, join.
jointure, *s.f.* Joint, join. *J. du genou,* knee-joint. Les jointures des doigts, the knuckles.
joli, *a.* Pretty; nice. Jolie à croquer, pretty as a picture. *Iron: Voilà du j.!* here's a pretty state of things!
joliment, *adv.* **1.** Prettily, nicely. **2.** *F: J. amusant,* very amusing, awfully funny.
Jonas [-as]. *Pr.n.m. B.Hist:* Jonah.
jonc [ʒɔ̃], *s.m.* (*a*) *Bot:* Rush. (*b*) Canne de jonc, Malacca cane.
joncher, *v.tr. J. la terre de fleurs,* to strew the ground with flowers.
jonction, *s.f.* Junction, joining.
jongler, *v.i.* To juggle.
jonglerie, *s.f.* **1.** Juggling. **2.** Trickery.
jongleur, *s.m.* Juggler, mountebank.
jonque, *s.f. Nau:* (Chinese) junk.
jonquille [-kij], *s.f. Bot:* Jonquil.
Josué. *Pr.n.m. B.Hist:* Joshua.
joubarbe, *s.f. Bot:* Houseleek.
joue, *s.f.* Cheek. Coucher qn en joue, to aim (with a gun) at s.o.
jouer, *v.* To play. I. *v.i.* **1.** (*a*) *J. avec qn,* to play with s.o. (*b*) *J. aux cartes,* to play cards. (*c*) *J. du piano,* to play the piano. *J. des coudes,* to elbow one's way. *J. des dents,* to ply one's teeth. **2.** To gamble. **3.** To come into play; to work, to act. Faire j. un ressort, to release a spring. II. **jouer,** *v.tr.* **1.** To stake. *J. gros jeu,* to play for high stakes. *J. de malheur,* to be unlucky. **2.** (*a*) To play (card). (*b*) To act, play, perform (a play). *F:* Jouer la surprise, to feign surprise. **3.** To trick, fool.
  se jouer. **1.** Faire qch. en se jouant, to do sth. with great ease. **2.** Se j. de qn, to make game of s.o. **3.** Se j. au feu, to play with fire.
jouet, *s.m.* Toy, plaything.
joueur, -euse, *s.* **1.** (*a*) Player (of game). Être bon j., to be a good loser. (*b*) Performer, player (on an instrument). **2.** Gambler, gamester.
joufflu, *a.* Chubby.
joug, *s.m.* Yoke.
jouir, *v.i.* To enjoy. (*a*) *J. de la vie,* to enjoy life. (*b*) *J. d'une bonne réputation,* to bear a good character.
jouissance, *s.f.* Enjoyment. (*a*) Pleasure. (*b*) Possession, tenure. Avoir la jouissance de certains droits, to enjoy certain rights.
joujou, -oux, *s.m. F:* Toy, plaything.
jour [ʒuːr], *s.m.* Day. **1.** (Day)light. (*a*) Le petit jour, the morning twilight. Chambre qui prend jour sur la cour, room that looks out on the yard. Il fait jour, it is growing light. Il fait grand jour, it is broad daylight. (*b*) Mettre qch. au jour, to bring sth. to light; to publish (fact). Attenter aux jours de qn, to make an attempt on s.o.'s life. (*c*) Lighting.

Voir qch. sous son vrai jour, to see sth. in its true light. *Vous êtes dans mon j.*, you are standing in my light. **2.** (*a*) Aperture, opening. **Jour de l'escalier,** well-hole (of stair). **Bas à jour(s),** open-work stockings. (*b*) **Se faire jour,** to make a way for oneself. **3.** (Period of time) **Prendre jour pour qch.,** to appoint a day for sth. **Plat du jour** (*dans un restaurant*), F: 'to-day's special.' **Être de jour,** to be on duty for the day. **De nos jours,** nowadays. **Vivre au jour le jour,** to live from hand to mouth. **Du jour au lendemain,** at a moment's notice. **A un de ces jours!** F: so long! **Mettre à jour,** to bring up to date.

journal, -aux, *s.m.* **I.** Journal, diary, record. *Nau:* **J. de navigation,** log(-book). **J. de bord,** log-book. **2.** Newspaper, journal. **Les journaux,** the Press. *W.Tel:* **Journal parlé,** 'news.'

journalier. I. *a.* Daily; everyday. **2.** *s.m.* Day-labourer.

journalisme, *s.m.* Journalism. *L'influence du j.,* the influence of the Press.

journaliste, *s.m. & f.* Journalist; reporter.

journée, *s.f.* **I.** Day(time). *Dans la j.,* in the course of the day. **2.** (*a*) Day's work. **Travailler à la journée,** to work by the day. **Femme de journée,** charwoman, daily help. **Aller en journée,** to go out charring. (*b*) Day's wages. (*c*) Day's march. **Voyager à petites journées,** to journey by easy stages. (*d*) Day (of battle). **Gagner la journée,** to win the day.

journellement, *adv.* Daily; every day.

joute, *s.f.* Contest, match.

jovial, -aux, *a.* Jovial, jolly, merry.

jovialement, *adv.* Jovially, merrily.

jovialité, *s.f.* Joviality, jollity.

joyau, -aux, *s.m.* Jewel. **Les joyaux de la Couronne,** the regalia.

joyeusement, *adv.* Joyously, joyfully.

joyeux, *a.* Merry, mirthful, joyous.

jubilant, *a.* F: Jubilant; in high glee.

jubilation, *s.f.* Jubilation; high glee.

jubilé, *s.m.* Jubilee.

jubiler, *v.i.* To exult, jubilate.

jucher, *v.i.* To go to roost; to perch. **se jucher. I.** To go to roost. **2.** To perch oneself.

juchoir, *s.m.* Perch (for fowls); hen-roost

judaïque, *a.* Judaic.

Judas. I. *Pr.n.m.* F: **Poil de Judas,** carroty hair. **2.** *s.m.* (*a*) F: Traitor, betrayer. (*b*) Spy-hole (in door).

judiciaire. I. *a.* Judicial, judiciary, legal. **2.** *s.f.* (Sound) judgment.

judiciairement, *adv.* Judicially.

judicieusement, *adv.* Judiciously, discreetly.

judicieux, *a.* Judicious, discerning.

juge, *s.m.* Judge. **Juge de paix,** police-court magistrate. *F:* **Je vous en fais juge,** I appeal to you.

jugement, *s.m.* Judgment. **I.** *Jur:* (*a*) Trial (of case). **Mettre en jugement,** to bring to trial. **Le jugement dernier,** doomsday. (*b*) Decision, award; sentence. **2.** Opinion, estimation. **3.** Discernment, discrimination.

juger. I. *v.tr.* (*n.* **jugeons**) **I.** (*a*) To judge; to try (case); to pass sentence on; to adjudicate. (*b*) To pass judgment on; to criticize. **2.** (*a*) To think, believe. *On le jugeait fou,* people took him to be mad. (*b*) **Juger de qch.,** to judge of sth. **A en juger par . . .,** judging by. . . . **II. juger, jugé,** *s.m.* **Faire qch. au jugé,** to do sth. by guess-work.

jugoslave, *a. & s.* Jugo-Slav.

jugulaire. I. *a. & s.f.* Jugular (vein). **2.** *s.f.* Chin-strap.

juif [ʒɥif]. **I.** *a.* Jewish; Jew. **2.** *s.* Jew, *f.* Jewess. *F:* **Le petit juif,** the funny-bone.

juillet [ʒɥijɛ], *s.m.* July.

juin [ʒɥɛ̃], *s.m.* June.

jumeau, -elle. I *a. & s.* Twin. *Trois jumeaux,* triplets. **II. jumelles,** *s.f.pl.* Binoculars. *Jumelles de théâtre,* opera-glasses.

jument, *s.f.* Mare.

Junon. *Pr.n.f. Myth:* Juno.

jupe, *s.f.* (Woman's) skirt. *F:* **Pendu aux jupes de sa mère,** tied to his mother's apron-strings.

Jupiter [ʒypitɛːr]. *Pr.n.m.* Jupiter, Jove.

jupon, *s.m.* Petticoat, underskirt.

jurement, *s.m.* (Profane) swearing; oath.

jurer, *v.tr.* To swear. **I.** *J. le ciel,* to call heaven to witness. **2.** (To promise) **Faire jurer le secret à qn,** to swear s.o. to secrecy. **3.** (To assert) **J'en jurerais,** I would swear to it. **4.** *Abs.* (*a*) To swear (profanely); to curse. **Jurer comme un charretier,** to swear like a trooper. (*b*) (Of colours) To clash.

juré. I. *a. Ennemi j.,* sworn enemy. **2.** *s.m.* Juryman. **Les jurés,** the jury.

juridiction, *s.f.* Jurisdiction.

juridique, *a.* Judicial; legal.

juron, *s.m.* (Profane) oath.

jury, *s.m. Jur:* Jury.

jus, *s.m.* **I.** Juice. **2.** Gravy.

jusant, *s.m.* Ebb(-tide).

jusque, *prep.* **I.** As far as; up to. *Jusqu'ici,* thus far, so far. *Ils furent tués jusqu'au dernier,* they were killed to a man. **2.** Till, until. *Jusqu'ici,* till now, as yet. **3.** (Intensive) *Il sait jusqu'à nos pensées,* he knows our very thoughts. **4.** *Conj.phr.* **Jusqu'à ce que,** usu. + *sub.,* till, until.

jusquiame, *s.f. Bot:* Henbane.

juste, *a.* **I.** Just, right, fair. (*a*) *J. colère,* righteous anger. **Rien de plus juste,** nothing could be fairer. (*b*) *Magistrat j.,* upright judge. **2.** Right, exact, accurate. (*a*) *Le mot j.,* the exact word, the right word. **C'est juste,** that is so! that's right! **Rien de plus juste,**

you are perfectly right. **Comme de juste,** of course. (b) *Bottines trop justes,* tight boots. **C'est tout juste s'il ne me frappa pas,** he all but struck me. **3.** *adv.* (a) Rightly. *Frapper j.,* to strike home. *Chanter j.,* to sing in tune. (b) Exactly, precisely. (c) Barely. **Échapper tout juste,** to escape by the skin of one's teeth. **4.** *Adv.phr.* **Je ne sais pas au juste si . . .,** I do not exactly know whether. . . . **Comme de juste,** as is only fair.

justement, *adv.* **1.** Justly, rightly, deservedly. **2.** Precisely, exactly, just.

justesse, *s.f.* **1.** Exactness, accuracy. *Raisonner avec j.,* to argue soundly. **2. Arriver de justesse,** to arrive just in time.

justice, *s.f.* **1.** Justice. *C'est justice que + sub.,* it is only right that. . . . **En toute justice,** by rights. *Se faire j. à soi-même,* to take the law into one's own hands. **Faire justice de qch.,** to make short work of sth. **2.** Law. **Citer qn en justice,** to go to law with s.o.

justifiable, *a.* Justifiable, warrantable.

justification, *s.f.* **1.** Justification, vindication. **2.** Proof (of fact).

justifier, *v.tr.* **1.** To justify, vindicate ; to warrant. **2.** To prove, make good (assertion). **se justifier,** to clear oneself ; to justify oneself.

jute, *s.m.* *Tex :* Jute. *Sac en j.,* gunny bag.

juteux, *a.* Juicy.

juvénile, *a.* Juvenile ; youthful.

juxtaposer, *v.tr.* To place side by side ; to juxtapose.

juxtaposition, *s.f.* Juxtaposition.

K

K, k [ka], *s.m.* (The letter) K, k.

kaki, *s.m. & a.inv.* *Tex :* Khaki.

kaléidoscope, *s.m.* Kaleidoscope.

kangourou, *s.m.* *Z :* Kangaroo.

Kenya. *Pr.n.m.* *Geog :* Kenya (Colony).

képi, *s.m.* Kepi ; peaked cap.

kermesse, *s.f.* Village fair.

kilogramme, *s.m.* Kilogram(me).

kilomètre, *s.m.* Kilometre.

kilométrique, *a.* Borne kilométrique, kilometre stone.

kimono, *s.m.* *Cost :* Kimono.

king-charles [kiɲ-], *s.m.inv.* King Charles spaniel.

kiosque, *s.m.* **1.** (a) Kiosk. *K. de musique,* bandstand. *K. de jardin,* summer-house, (b) Newspaper- or flower-stall. **2.** *Nau :* Conning-tower (of submarine).

kiwi, *s.m.* *Orn :* Kiwi, apteryx.

klaxon, *s.m.* *Aut :* Klaxon, hooter.

klaxonner, *v.i.* *Aut :* To hoot, sound the hooter.

kleptomane, *a. & s.* Kleptomaniac.

kopeck [-ɛk], *s.m.* *Num :* Copeck, kopec(k).

korrigan, *s.* (In Brittany) Goblin ; evil sprite.

kourde, *a. & s.* *Ethn :* Kurd.

Kourdistan. *Pr.n.m.* Kurdistan.

krach [krak], *s.m.* (Financial) crash ; failure.

kyrielle, *s.f.* *F :* Rigmarole. *Toute une k. de noms,* a whole string of names.

kyste, *s.m.* *Med :* Cyst.

L

L, l [ɛl], *s.f.* (The letter) L, l.

l'. See LE[1, 2].

la[1], *def.art. & pron.f.* See LE[1, 2].

la[2], *s.m.inv.* *Mus :* (The note) A.

là, *adv.* **1.** There. (a) *Les choses en sont là que . . .,* matters are at such a point that. . . . *F : Otez-vous de là !* get out of that ! **Passer par là,** go that way. (b) *C'est là la question,* that is the question. *Que dites-vous là?* what is that you are saying? *Ce, cette, etc.,* . . . *-là,* see CE[1] 1, CE[2] 3. *Celui-là, celle-là,* see CELUI 4. **2.** Then. **D'ici là,** between now and then. **3.** (= CELA) *Qu'entendez-vous par là?* what do you mean by that? **4.** *int.* (a) *Là !* there now ! (b) *Oh là là !* oh dear me !

là-bas, *adv.* (Over) yonder.

labeur, *s.m.* Labour, toil, hard work.

laboratoire, *s.m.* Laboratory.

laborieusement, *adv.* Laboriously.

laborieux, *a.* **1.** Toilsome, arduous. **2.** Laborious, hard-working. *Les classes laborieuses,* the working classes.

labour, *s.m.* Tilling ; ploughing. **Terres de labour, les labours,** ploughed land.

labourable, *a.* Arable.

labourer, *v.tr.* To till ; to plough. *Les*

chagrins ont labouré son front, sorrow has furrowed his brow.

laboureur, *s.m.* Farm-labourer; ploughman.

labyrinthe, *s.m.* Labyrinth, maze.

lac [lak], *s.m.* Lake.

lacer, *v.tr.* (n. laçons) To lace (up).

lacération, *s.f.* Laceration.

lacérer, *v.tr.* (je lacère; je lacérerai) To tear, lacerate.

lacet, *s.m.* 1. Lace (of shoe). 2. Hairpin bend. *Sentier en lacet(s),* zigzag path. 3. Noose, springe, snare.

lâche, *a.* 1. Loose, slack; lax. 2. Cowardly; dastardly. *s.m.* Un lâche, a coward; a dastard.

lâchement, *adv.* 1. Indolently, slackly. 2. In a cowardly manner.

lâcher, *v.tr.* To release. (*a*) To slacken. *L. un coup de fusil à qn,* to fire a shot at s.o. (*b*) To let go; to drop. *Lâcher pied,* to give ground. (*c*) To set free. *L. un chien,* to let loose a dog. *F: L. un juron,* to let out an oath.

lâcheté, *s.f.* 1. (*a*) Cowardice. (*b*) Act of cowardice. 2. (*a*) Dastardliness. (*b*) Dastardly action.

laconique, *a.* Laconic.

laconiquement, *adv.* Laconically.

là-contre, *adv.* To the contrary. *Je n'ai rien à dire là-contre,* I have nothing to say against it.

lacs [lɑ], *s.m.* Noose, snare.

lacté, *a.* Lacteous, milky. *Astr:* La Voie lactée, the Milky Way, the Galaxy.

lacune, *s.f.* Lacuna, gap.

là-dedans, *adv.* In there; within.

là-dehors, *adv.* Without, outside.

là-dessous, *adv.* Under that, under there.

là-dessus, *adv.* On that.

ladite. See LEDIT.

ladre. 1. *a.* Niggardly, mean, stingy. 2. *s.* (*f.* ladresse) Niggard, skinflint.

ladrerie, *s.f.* Meanness, stinginess.

lagune, *s.f.* Lagoon.

là-haut, *adv.* Up there.

lai¹, *s.m.* *Pros:* Lay (in eight-foot verse).

lai², 1. *a.* Frère lai, lay-brother. 2. *s.m.* Layman.

laîche, *s.f.* *Bot:* Sedge.

laid, *a.* (*a*) Ugly; unsightly; plain. (*b*) Unseemly, mean, shabby.

laideur, *s.f.* 1. Ugliness; plainness. 2. Unseemliness, meanness.

laie, *s.f.* (Wild) sow.

laine, *s.f.* 1. Wool. 2. Woolly hair.

laineux, *a.* Fleecy; woolly.

laïque. 1. *a.* Laic; secular. 2. *s.* Les laïques, the laity.

laisse, *s.f.* Leash, lead.

laisser, *v.tr.* 1. To let, allow. **Je les ai laissés dire,** I let them talk away. **Laisser voir qch.,** to reveal sth. **Se laisser aller,** to get into slovenly ways. *S. l. aller dans un fauteuil,* to sink into an arm-chair. *Ne vous laissez pas aller comme ça!* don't carry on like that! **Laissez-le faire!** leave it to him! *Il se laissa faire,* he offered no resistance. 2. (*a*) To leave. *L. sa valise à la consigne,* to leave one's bag in the cloak-room. **Laisser là qn,** to leave s.o. in the lurch. *L. là qch.,* to give up doing sth. (*b*) (i) *Je vous laisse libre d'agir,* I leave you free to act. (ii) To leave (sth.) alone. *L. les détails,* to pass over the details. **Laissez donc!** please do not trouble. (iii) **Vous pouvez nous laisser,** you may leave us. (*c*) *Laissez-moi vos clefs,* leave me your keys. *Je vous le laisserai à bon compte,* I will let you have it cheap. **Cela laisse (beaucoup) à désirer,** it leaves much to be desired. (*d*) **Ne pas laisser de faire qch.,** not to fail to do sth. *Cela ne laisse pas (que) de m'inquiéter,* I feel anxious all the same.

laisser-aller, *s.m.inv.* 1. Unconstraint. 2. Carelessness, slovenliness.

laisser-faire, *s.m.* Non-interference.

laissez-passer, *s.m.inv.* Pass, permit.

lait, *s.m.* Milk. 1. Frère de lait, foster-brother. Cochon de lait, sucking-pig. 2. *L. de coco,* coco-nut milk.

laitage, *s.m.* Dairy produce.

laitance, *s.f.,* **laite,** *s.f.* *Ich:* Milt. *Cu:* Soft roe.

laiterie, *s.f.* 1. Dairy. 2. (*a*) Dairy-work. (*b*) Dairy-farming.

laiteux, *a.* Milk-like, milky.

laitier, *s.* (*a*) Milkman; milkwoman, milkmaid. (*b*) Dairymaid; dairyman.

laiton, *s.m.* Brass.

laitue, *s.f.* Lettuce. *L. pommée,* cabbage lettuce.

lama¹, *s.m.* (Buddhist) lama.

lama², *s.m.* *Z:* Llama.

lambeau, *s.m.* Scrap, bit, shred. *Vêtements en lambeaux,* clothes in tatters.

lambrequin, *s.m.* *Furn:* Valance, pelmet.

lambris, *s.m.* Panelling, wainscoting. *L. d'appui,* dado.

lame, *s.f.* 1. (*a*) Lamina, thin plate, strip. *L. de jalousie,* slat of a Venetian blind. (*b*) Blade. *Visage en lame de couteau,* hatchet-face. 2. Wave. **Lame de fond,** ground-swell.

lamentable, *a.* Lamentable, deplorable; woeful (voice).

lamentablement, *adv.* Lamentably; woefully.

lamentation, *s.f.* Lamentation. 1. (Be)-wailing. 2. Lament.

lamenter (se), *v.pr.* To lament; to wail. *Se l. sur son sort,* to bewail one's lot.

lampadaire, *s.m.* *Furn:* 1. Standard lamp. 2. Candelabrum.

lampe, *s.f.* 1. Lamp. 2. (*a*) *L. de poche,* electric torch; flash-lamp. (*b*) (Wireless) valve. 3. *L. d alcool,* spirit-lamp or -stove.

lampée, *s.f.* Draught, gulp (of wine).

lamper, *v.tr.* To swig, toss off (drink).

lampion, *s.m.* (*a*) Fairy light (for illuminations). (*b*) Chinese lantern.

lamproie, *s.f. Ich:* Lamprey.
lance, *s.f.* (a) Spear. (b) Lance.
lance-bombes, *s.m.inv.* **1.** *Artil:* Trench mortar. **2.** *Av:* Bomb rack.
lance-pierres, *s.m.inv.* Catapult.
lancer, *v.tr.* (n. lançons) **1.** To throw, fling, hurl. *L. un avion,* to catapult a plane. *L. un coup d'œil à qn,* to dart a glance at s.o. **2.** To start, set going. (a) *L. un cheval,* to start a horse off at full gallop. *L. un chien contre qn,* to set a dog on s.o. (b) To launch (ship); to release (bomb); to float (company). *Av: L. l'hélice,* to swing the propeller.
   se lancer *en avant,* to rush forward. *Se l. dans les affaires,* to launch out into business.
   lancé, *a.* Train *à toute vapeur,* train going at full speed. *Sp:* Départ lancé, flying start. *Il est éloquent une fois l.,* he is eloquent when once he gets going.
lancette, *s.f. Surg:* Lancet.
lancier, *s.m.* **1.** *Mil:* Lancer. **2.** (Quadrille des) lanciers, lancers.
lancinant, *a.* Shooting (pain).
lande, *s.f.* Sandy moor; heath; waste.
langage, *s.m.* Language; speech (of the individual). **Tenir un langage aimable,** to speak amiably. *F:* **Changer de langage,** to sing another tune. *En voilà un l.!* that's no way to talk!
lange, *s.m.* (a) Baby's napkin. (b) *pl.* Swaddling-clothes.
langoureusement, *adv.* Languidly, languishingly.
langoureux, *a.* Languid, languorous. *Amant l.,* languishing lover.
langouste, *s.f.* Spiny lobster; *F:* crayfish.
langue, *s.f.* **1.** Tongue. **Tirer la langue,** (i) to put out one's tongue; (ii) (of dog) to hang out its tongue. **Donner sa langue au chat,** (with reference to riddle) to give it up. **Mauvaise langue,** backbiter. **2.** Tongue (of flame); spit (of land). **3.** Language, speech, tongue (of a people). *Professeur de langues vivantes,* modern-language master. *F:* **Langue verte,** slang.
languette, *s.f.* Small tongue (of wood); strip (of tin-foil); tongue (of shoe).
langueur, *s.f.* Languor; listlessness. *Regard plein de l.,* languishing look.
languir, *v.i.* To languish, pine. **Ne nous faites pas languir,** don't keep us on tenterhooks. *Th: L'action languit,* the action drags.
languissant, *a.* **1.** Languid. **2.** Languishing.
lanière, *s.f.* Thin strap; thong; (leather) lace; lash (of whip).
lanterne, *s.f.* (a) Lantern. *L. vénitienne,* Chinese lantern. *L.* (de) tempête, hurricane-lamp. (b) *Aut: L. à feu rouge,* tail-light.
laper, *v.tr.* (Of dog) To lap (up).
lapereau, *s.m.* Young rabbit.
lapidaire, *s.m.* Lapidary.
lapider, *v.tr.* To stone to death; *F:* to throw stones at (dog).

lapin, *s.* Rabbit. *L. mâle,* buck rabbit. *L. de garenne,* wild rabbit. *F: L. de choux,* tame rabbit. **C'est un rude lapin,** he is a fine fellow.
lapon, 1. *a.* Lapp. **2.** *s.* Lapp, Laplander.
Laponie. *Pr.n.f.* Lapland.
laps [laps], *s.m.* **Un laps de temps,** a space of time.
laquais, *s.m.* Lackey, footman.
laque. 1. *s.f.* Lac. (b) *Paint:* Lake. **2.** *s.m.* Lacquer. **Laque de Chine,** japan.
laquelle, *pron.f.* See LEQUEL.
laquer, *v.tr.* To lacquer, to japan.
larcin, *s.m. Jur:* Larceny; petty theft.
lard, *s.m.* Bacon.
larder, *v.tr. F: L. qn de coups,* to shower blows on s.o.
large. 1. *a.* (a) Broad, wide. *L. d'épaules,* broad-shouldered. *D'un geste l.,* with a sweeping gesture. *adv. Portes larges ouvertes,* wide-open doors. (b) Large, big, ample. **2.** *s.m.* (a) Room, space. (b) *Nau:* Open sea. **Brise du l.,** sea-breeze. **Prendre le large,** to put to sea. *Au l. de Cherbourg,* off Cherbourg. (c) Breadth. **Se promener de long en large,** to walk up and down.
largement, *adv.* (a) Broadly, widely. *Services l. rétribués,* highly-paid services. (b) Amply.
largesse, *s.f.* Liberality.
largeur, *s.f.* Breadth, width.
larguer, *v.tr.* **1.** *Nau:* (a) To let go (rope). (b) To unfurl (sail). **2.** To let off (steam).
larme, *s.f.* Tear.
larmoyant, *a.* **1.** Weeping, tearful. **2.** *Pej:* Doleful; maudlin.
larmoyer, *v.i.* (je larmoie) **1.** (Of the eyes) To water. **2.** *Pej:* To snivel.
larron, *s.m.* (a) *F:* **S'entendre comme larrons en foire,** to be as thick as thieves. (b) Thief (in candle).
larve, *s.f.* Larva; grub (of insect).
larynx [-rĕ̃ks], *s.m. Anat:* Larynx.
las, lasse, *a.* Tired, weary.
lascar, *s.m.* **1.** Lascar. **2.** *P:* Clever fellow.
lascif, *a.* Lascivious, lewd.
lascivement, *adv.* Lasciviously, lewdly.
lasser, *v.tr.* To tire, weary.
   se lasser, to grow weary; to tire.
lassitude, *s.f.* Lassitude, weariness.
lasso, *s.m.* Lasso.
latent, *a.* Latent; hidden, concealed.
latéral, -aux, *a.* Lateral. *Rue latérale,* side-street.
latin. 1. (a) *a. & s.* Latin. **Le Quartier latin,** the students' quarter of Paris. (b) *a. Voile latine,* lateen sail. **2.** *s.m. Ling:* Latin. *F:* **Latin de cuisine,** dog-Latin. **Être au bout de son latin,** to be at one's wits' end. **J'y perds mon latin,** I can't make head or tail of it.
latitude, *s.f.* Latitude. **1.** Scope, freedom. **2.** *Geog:* Latitude.
Latran. *Pr.n.m.* **Le palais de Latran,** the Lateran Palace.
latrines, *s.f.pl.* Latrines.

latte, *s.f.* Lath, batten, slat.
laudanum [-nom], *s.m.* Laudanum.
laudatif, *a.* Laudatory.
lauréat, *s.* Laureate, prizeman.
Laurent. *Pr.n.m.* Lawrence.
laurier, *s.m.* *Bot:* Laurel.
lavabo, *s.m.* **1.** Wash-hand basin. **2.** Lavatory.
lavande, *s.f.* *Bot:* Lavender.
lavandière, *s.f.* **1.** Washerwoman; laundress. **2.** *Orn:* (Grey) wagtail.
lave, *s.f.* *Geol:* Lava.
laver, *v.tr.* To wash. *(a) Se l. les mains,* to wash one's hands. *L. la vaisselle,* to wash up. *F: Laver la tête à qn,* to haul s.o. over the coals. *(b)* (Of stream) *L. un pré,* to flow along a meadow.
  se laver, to wash (oneself).
lavoir, *s.m.* Wash-house.
laxatif, *a. & s.m.* *Med:* Laxative, aperient.
le[1]**, la, les,** *def.art.* (*Le* and *la* are elided to l' before a vowel or h 'mute.' *Le* and *les* contract with *à, de,* into **au, aux; du, des.**) The. **1.** (Particularizing) *(a) J'apprends le français,* I am learning French. **L'un . . . l'autre,** (the) one . . . the other. *Il est arrivé le lundi,* he arrived on Monday. *(b) La France,* France. *(c) Le roi Édouard,* King Edward. *Le colonel Chabot,* Colonel Chabot. *Le petit Robert,* little Robert. *(d) Le Dante,* Dante. *Le Havre,* Havre. *(e)* (With most feast-days) *F: A la Noël,* at Christmas. *(f)* (Often with parts of the body) *Hausser les épaules,* to shrug one's shoulders. *Elle ferma les yeux,* she closed her eyes. **2.** (Forming superlatives) *Mon amie la plus intime,* my most intimate friend. *C'est elle qui travaille le mieux,* she works best. **3.** (Generalizing) *Je préfère le café au thé,* I prefer coffee to tea. **4.** (Distributive) *Cinq francs la livre,* five francs a pound. **5.** Partitive **du, de la, des.** See DE III.
le[2]**, la, les,** *pers.pron.* **1.** (Replacing sb.) Him, her, it, them. *(a) Je ne le lui ai pas donné,* I did not give it to him. *Les voilà!* there they are! *(b)* (Following the vb.) *Donnez-le-lui,* give it to him. **2.** *Neut. pron.* **Le.** *(a)* (Replacing an adj. or a sb. used as an adj.) *Êtes-vous mère?—Je le suis,* are you a mother?—I am. *(b)* (Replacing a clause) (i) So. *Il me l'a dit,* he told me so. (ii) *Vous le devriez,* you ought to.
lécher, *v.tr.* (je lèche; je lécherai) To lick. *F: Il s'en léchait les doigts,* he smacked his lips over it.
leçon, *s.f.* **1.** *Ecc:* Lesson. **2.** *Sch:* Lesson. *L. de choses,* object-lesson. *Faire la leçon à qn,* to sermonize s.o.
lecteur, -trice, *s.* Reader.
lecture, *s.f.* Reading.
ledit, ladite, *pl.* **lesdits, lesdites,** (Contracted with *à* and *de* to audit, auxdit(e)s, dudit, desdit(e)s) *a.* The aforesaid.
légal, -aux, *a.* Legal; statutory. *Fête légale,* statutory holiday.

légalement, *adv.* Legally, lawfully.
légaliser, *v.tr.* **1.** To legalize. **2.** To attest, certify.
légalité, *s.f.* Legality, lawfulness. **Rester dans la légalité,** to keep within the law.
légataire, *s.m. & f.* *Jur:* Legatee.
légation, *s.f.* Legation.
légendaire, *a.* Legendary.
légende, *s.f.* **1.** Legend; fable. **2.** *(a)* Inscription (on coin). *(b)* List of references.
léger, *a.* **1.** *(a)* Light. **Avoir le sommeil léger,** to be a light sleeper. **Avoir la main légère,** to be quick with one's hands. *Conduite légère,* flighty conduct. *(b)* Slight (pain); gentle (breeze); faint (sound). **2.** *Adv.phr.* *A la légère,* lightly. *Conclure à la légère,* to jump to conclusions.
légèrement, *adv.* **1.** *(a)* Lightly. *(b)* Slightly. **2.** Without consideration.
légèreté, *s.f.* **1.** *(a)* Lightness. *(b)* Slightness. **2.** Levity; flightiness.
légion, *s.f.* Legion. *F: L. de moucherons,* swarm of gnats. **Ils s'appellent légion,** their name is legion.
légionnaire, *s.m.* Soldier of the Foreign Legion.
législateur, -trice. 1. *s.* Legislator, lawgiver. **2.** *a.* Legislative.
législatif, *a.* *(a)* Legislative. *(b) Élection législative,* parliamentary election.
législation, *s.f.* Legislation.
législature, *s.f.* Legislature; legislative body.
légitimation, *s.f.* **1.** Legitimation. **2.** Official recognition.
légitime, *a.* **1.** Legitimate, lawful. **2.** Justifiable; well-founded. *Jur: Légitime défense,* self-defence.
légitimement, *adv.* Legitimately, lawfully, rightfully.
légitimité, *s.f.* **1.** Legitimacy. **2.** Lawfulness.
legs [lɛ], *s.m.* Legacy, bequest.
léguer, *v.tr.* (je lègue; je léguerai) To bequeath.
légume, *s.m.* **1.** Vegetable. *Légumes verts,* greens. **2.** *F: Gros légume,* P: *grosse légume,* bigwig.
Léman. *Pr.n.m.* *Le lac Léman,* the Lake of Geneva.
lémur(e), *s.m.* *Z:* Lemur.
lendemain, *s.m.* Next day; morrow. *Le l. matin,* the next morning, the morning after. *Des succès sans lendemains,* short-lived successes.
lent, *a.* Slow.
lentement, *adv.* Slowly.
lenteur, *s.f.* **1.** Slowness. **2.** *pl.* Delays, dilatoriness.
lentille [-ti:j], *s.f.* **1.** *Bot:* *(a) Cu:* Lentil. *(b)* Lentille d'eau, duckweed. **2.** Bob, ball (of pendulum). **3.** *Opt:* Lens.
léonin, *a.* Leonine, lion-like.
léopard, *s.m.* Leopard.

lépidoptère. *Ent:* **1.** *a.* Lepidopterous. **2.** *s.m. pl.* **Lépidoptères,** lepidoptera.

lèpre, *s.f.* Leprosy.

lépreux. 1. *a.* Leprous. **2.** *s.* Leper.

lequel, laquelle, lesquels, lesquelles. (Contracted with *à* and *de* to auquel, auxquel(le)s, duquel, desquel(le)s **1.** *rel.pron.* Who, whom; which. (*a*) (Of thgs after prep.) *Décision par laquelle . . .,* decision whereby. . . . (*b*) (Of pers.) *La dame avec laquelle elle était sortie,* the lady with whom she had gone out. (*c*) (To avoid ambiguity) *Le père de cette jeune fille, lequel est très riche,* the girl's father, who is very rich. (*d*) (Adjectival) *Il écrira peut-être, auquel cas . . .,* perhaps he will write, in which case. . . . **2.** *interr.pron.* *Lequel d'entre nous?* which one of us?

les¹. See LE¹ ².

lesdit(e)s. See LEDIT.

lèse-majesté, *s.f.* High treason, lese-majesty.

lésiner, *v.i.* To be stingy, close-fisted.

lésion, *s.f.* Injury, hurt.

lesquels, -elles. See LEQUEL.

lessive, *s.f.* **1.** Lye. **2.** (Household) washing. (*a*) **Faire la lessive,** to do the washing. (*b*) Articles washed.

lest [lɛst], *s.m.* No *pl.* Ballast.

leste, *a.* Light; nimble, agile. *F:* **Avoir la main leste,** to be free with one's hands.

lestement, *adv.* Lightly, nimbly, smartly.

léthargie, *s.f.* Lethargy, apathy.

léthargique, *a.* Lethargic(al).

letton. 1. *a. & s.* (*a*) *Ethn:* Lett. (*b*) *Geog:* Latvian. **2.** *s.m. Ling:* Lettish.

Lettonie. *Pr.n.f. Geog:* Latvia.

lettre, *s.f.* Letter. **1.** Écrire **qch. en toutes lettres,** to write sth. out in full. **2. Au pied de la lettre,** literally. **3.** (*a*) Epistle, missive. (*b*) *pl.* **Lettres patentes,** letters patent. **4.** *pl.* Literature, letters.

lettré. 1. *a.* Lettered, well-read. **2.** *s.* Scholar.

leu, *s.m.* A la queue leu leu, in Indian file.

leur¹. 1. *poss.a.* Their. *Leurs père et mère,* their father and mother. **2.** Le leur, la leur, les leurs. (*a*) *poss.pron.* Theirs. (*b*) *s.m.* (i) Their own. *Ils n'y mettent pas du leur,* they don't pull their weight. (ii) *pl.* Their own (friends). *Je m'intéresse à eux et aux leurs,* I am interested in them and in theirs. (iii) *F:* *Ils continuent à faire des leurs,* they go on playing their old tricks.

leur², *pers.pron.* See LUI¹.

leurre, *s.m.* (*a*) Bait, lure. (*b*) Allurement.

leurrer, *v.tr.* (*a*) To lure. (*b*) *F:* To allure.

levain, *s.m.* Leaven.

levant. 1. *a.m.* Soleil levant, rising sun. **2.** *s.m.* (*a*) Le levant, the east. (*b*) *Geog:* Le Levant, the Levant.

levantin, *a. & s.* Levantine.

lever. I. *v.tr.* (je lève) **1.** (*a*) To raise, to lift (up). *L. les yeux,* to look up. **Lever l'ancre,** to weigh anchor. (*b*) To raise (siege); to close (meeting). (*c*) *L. une difficulté,* to

remove a difficulty. **2.** To collect, gather (crops). **3. Lever un plan,** to draw a plan.

se lever. (*a*) To stand up. *Se l. de table,* to leave the table. (*b*) To get up (from bed); to rise. *F:* **Se lever du pied gauche,** to get out of bed on the wrong side. (*c*) *Le vent se lève,* the wind is rising.

II. lever, *s.m.* **1.** (*a*) Rising; getting up (from bed). (*b*) Levee. (*c*) **Lever du soleil,** sunrise. **2.** *Th:* **Un lever de rideau en un acte,** a one-act curtain-raiser.

levé, *a.* (*a*) Raised. **Voter à main levée,** to vote by a show of hands. **Dessin à main levée,** free-hand drawing. (*b*) Up; out of bed.

levée, *s.f.* **1.** (*a*) Raising, lifting. (*b*) Gathering (of crops). *Post:* Collection (of letters). *La l. est faite,* the box has been cleared. **2.** (*a*) Embankment, sea-wall. (*b*) *Cards:* **Faire une levée,** to take a trick.

levier, *s.m.* **1.** Lever. **Force de levier,** leverage. **2.** Crow-bar.

lévite, *s.m. B:* Levite.

levraut, *s.m.* Leveret; young hare.

lèvre, *s.f.* **1.** Lip. **Du bout des lèvres,** in a forced manner. **Pincer les lèvres,** to purse one's lips. **2.** Rim (of crater).

lévrier, *s.m.* Greyhound.

levure, *s.f.* Yeast.

lexique, *s.m.* (*a*) Lexicon. (*b*) Glossary; vocabulary.

Leyde. *Pr.n.f. Geog:* Leyden.

lézard, *s.m.* Lizard.

lézarde, *a.* (Of wall) Cracked, full of cracks.

liaison, *s.f.* **1.** (*a*) Joining, binding. (*b*) *Ling:* Liaison. (*c*) *Mil:* Liaison, touch (between units). **2.** Intimacy.

liane, *s.f. Bot:* Liana; (tropical) creeper.

liard, *s.m. F:* **Il n'a pas un (rouge) liard,** he hasn't a red cent.

liasse, *s.f.* Bundle (of letters); file (of papers).

Liban. *Pr.n.m. Geog:* Lebanon.

libation, *s.f.* Libation; drink-offering.

libellule, *s.f. Ent:* Dragon-fly.

libéral, -aux. 1. *a.* Liberal. **2.** *a. & s. Pol:* Liberal.

libéralement, *adv.* Liberally.

libéralité, *s.f.* Liberality.

libérateur, -trice. 1. *a.* Liberating. **2.** *s.* Liberator, deliverer.

libération, *s.f.* (*a*) Liberation, freeing, releasing. (*b*) Payment in full.

libérer, *v.tr.* (je libère; je libérerai) (*a*) To liberate, release. (*b*) To free from debt.

liberté, *s.f.* **1.** Liberty, freedom. *Jur:* (Mise en) **liberté provisoire sous caution,** bail. **Parler en toute liberté,** to speak freely. *Mon jour de l.,* my day off. **2. Prendre des libertés avec qn,** to take liberties with s.o.

libertin. 1. *a.* Licentious, dissolute. **2.** *s.* Libertine, rake.

libidineux, *a.* Libidinous, lustful.

libraire, *s.m.,f.* Bookseller.

librairie, *s.f.* (*a*) Book-trade, bookselling. (*b*) Bookshop.

libre, *a.* Free. **1.** (*a*) *Quand je suis l.,* when

I am off duty. *Je suis l. de mon temps,* my time is my own. (*b*) *L. de soucis,* carefree. (*c*) *Conversation l.,* free, broad, conversation. **2.** Clear, open (space); vacant. *Tp:* "Pas libre," 'line engaged.' (Taxi sign) **"Libre,"** 'for hire.'

libre-échange, *s.m.* Free trade.

librement, *adv.* Freely.

libretto, *s.m.* Libretto. *F:* book (of an opera). *pl. Des libretti, des librettos.*

licence, *s.f.* Licence. **1.** (*a*) Leave, permission. (*b*) *Sch:* **Passer sa licence,** to take one's degree. **2.** (*a*) Abuse of liberty. (*b*) Licentiousness.

licencié, *s.* Licentiate, *L. ès lettres,* (approx. =) master of arts.

licencieusement, *adv.* Licentiously.

licencieux, *a.* Licentious.

lichen [liken], *s.m. Bot:* Lichen. *L. d'Islande,* Iceland moss.

licite, *a.* Licit, lawful, permissible.

licol, *s.m. Harn:* Halter; head-stall.

licorne, *s.f. Myth:* Unicorn.

licou, *pl.* **-ous,** *s.m.* = LICOL.

lie, *s.f.* Lees, dregs. **Lie de vin,** *a.inv.* purplish red.

liège, *s.m.* **1.** *Bot:* Cork-oak. **2.** Cork.

lien, *s.m.* Tie, bond.

lier, *v.tr.* **1.** To bind, tie, tie up. *L'intérêt nous lie,* we have common interests. *L. des idées,* to link ideas. **2. Lier conversation avec** qn, to enter into conversation with s.o.

se lier. *Se l. (d'amitié) avec qn,* to form a friendship with s.o.

lié, *a.* **1.** Bound. **Avoir la langue liée,** to be tongue-tied. **2.** *Être (très) lié avec qn,* to be intimately acquainted with s.o.

lierre, *s.m.* Ivy.

lieu, -eux, *s.m.* **1.** Place. (*a*) Locality, spot. **En tout lieu,** everywhere. **En haut lieu,** in high places. *Je tiens ce renseignement de bon l.,* I have this information from a good source. **En (tout) premier lieu,** in the first place, first of all. (*b*) *pl.* House, premises. (*c*) *pl. F:* Lieux (d'aisances), privy, w.c. **2.** (*a*) **Avoir lieu,** to take place. (*b*) Ground(s), cause. **Il y a (tout) lieu de supposer que** + *ind.,* there is (every) reason for supposing that. . . . **Donner lieu à des désagréments,** to give rise to trouble. (*c*) **Tenir lieu de qch.,** to take the place of. **Au lieu de,** instead of. **Au lieu que** + *ind.,* whereas. **3.** **Lieux communs,** commonplaces, platitudes.

lieue, *s.f.* League (= 4 kilometres).

lieutenant, *s.m.* (*a*) *Mil:* Lieutenant. *Navy: L. de vaisseau,* lieutenant. (*b*) *Mercantile Marine:* Mate. **Premier l.,** second mate. (*c*) *L. de port,* harbour-master.

lièvre, *s.m. Z:* Hare. **Courir deux lièvres à la fois,** to try to do two things at once. **Mémoire de lièvre,** memory like a sieve.

ligament, *s.m.* Ligament.

ligature, *s.f.* **1.** Tying, binding. **2.** *Typ:* Ligature.

lignage, *s.m.* Lineage, descent.

lignard, *s.m. F:* Soldier of the line.

ligne, *s.f.* Line. **1.** (*a*) Cord. **Ligne de pêche,** fishing-line. (*b*) *L. droite,* straight line. (*c*) *Auto qui a de la ligne,* car with clean lines. **Grandes lignes d'une œuvre,** broad outline of a work. (*d*) *L. de flottaison,* water-line (of ship). *Descendre en l. directe de* . . ., to be lineally descended from. . . . (*e*) *L. de maisons,* row of houses. **Question qui vient en première ligne,** question of primary importance. **Hors ligne,** out of the common. (*f*) **Écris-moi deux lignes,** drop me a line. **2.** *Mil: Lignes de retranchement,* the lines. **Rentrer dans ses lignes,** to retire within one's lines. **Infanterie de ligne,** infantry of the line. **3.** (*a*) **Ligne de chemin de fer,** railway line. (*b*) *L. télégraphique,* telegraph line.

lignée, *s.f.* Issue; (line of) descendants.

ligoter, *v.tr.* To bind (s.o.) hand and foot; to lash (thgs) together.

ligue, *s.f.* League, confederacy.

liguer, *v.tr. Être ligué avec qn,* to be in league with s.o.

lilas, **1.** *s.m. Bot:* Lilac. **2.** *a.inv.* Lilac.

lilliputien, -ienne, *a. & s.* Lilliputian.

limace, *s.f. Moll:* Slug.

limaçon, *s.m.* **1.** Snail. **Escalier en limaçon,** spiral staircase.

limande, *s.f. Ich:* Dab.

limbe, *s.m.* **1.** *Astr:* Rim, edge (of the sun). **2.** *Theol:* **Les Limbes,** limbo.

lime¹, *s.f. Tls:* File.

lime², *s.f. Bot:* Sweet lime.

limer, *v.tr.* To file; to file down.

limier, *s.m.* Bloodhound; sleuth-hound.

limitation, *s.f.* **1.** Limitation, restriction. **2.** Marking off (of ground).

limite, *s.f.* **1.** Boundary; limit. *F: Dépasser les limites,* to pass all bounds. **2. Cas limite,** border-line case. **Vitesse limite,** maximum speed.

limiter, *v.tr.* **1.** To bound, to mark the bounds of. **2.** To limit; to restrict.

limité, *a.* Limited, restricted.

limitrophe, *a.* Adjacent; abutting; bordering (on).

limon¹, *s.m.* Mud, silt.

limon², *s.m. Veh:* Shaft.

limon³, *s.m. Bot:* Sour lime.

limonade, *s.f.* **1.** Lemonade. **2.** *pl.* Mineral waters; *F:* minerals.

limoneux, *a.* Muddy; charged with mud.

limonier¹, *s.m.* Shaft horse; wheeler.

limonier², *s.m. Bot:* Sour-lime (tree).

limousin. **1.** *a. & s.* (Native) of Limoges. **2.** *s.f. Aut:* Limousine, limousine (car).

limpide, *a.* Limpid, clear.

limpidité, *s.f.* Limpidity, clarity.

lin, *s.m.* **1.** Flax. **Graine de lin,** linseed. **Huile de lin,** linseed oil. **2. (Tissu de)** lin, linen.

linceul, *s.m.* Winding-sheet; shroud.

linéaire, *a.* Linear. *Mesures linéaires,* measures of length.

linéal, -aux, a. Lineal (heir).

linéament, s.m. Lineament, feature.

linge, s.m. **1.** (Made-up) linen or calico. *L. de table,* napery; table-linen. **2.** Piece of linen or calico. *Essuyer qch. avec un l.,* to wipe sth. with a cloth.

lingère, s.f. (a) Wardrobe keeper. (b) Sewing-maid.

lingerie, s.f. (a) Linen-drapery. (b) Under-clothing, linen.

lingot, s.m. *Metall:* Ingot. **Or, argent, en lingots,** bullion.

lingual, -aux [-gwal,-o]. **1.** a. Lingual. **2.** s.f. Linguale. *Ling:* Lingual.

linguiste [-gɥist], s.m. & f. Linguist.

linguistique [-gɥis-]. **1.** a. Linguistic. **2.** s.f. Linguistics.

liniment, s.m. *Med:* Liniment.

linoléum [-ɔm], s.m. Linoléum incrusté, linoleum.

linotte, s.f. *Orn:* Linnet. *F:* **Tête de linotte,** feather-brained person.

linteau, s.m. Lintel.

lion, -onne, s. **1.** (a) Lion, f. lioness. (b) **Lion marin, lion de mer,** sea-lion. **2.** *Geog:* **Le golfe du Lion,** the Gulf of Lions.

lionceau, s.m. Lion's cub.

lippe, s.f. Thick (lower) lip.

lippu, a. Thick-lipped.

liquéfaction, s.f. Liquefaction.

liquéfier, v.tr. To liquefy.

liqueur, s.f. (a) Liquor, drink. *Liqueurs fortes,* strong drink. (b) Liqueur.

liquidateur, s.m. *Jur:* Liquidator.

liquidation, s.f. **1.** Liquidation. **2.** *Com:* Selling off; clearance sale.

liquide. 1. a. Liquid. *Argent l.,* ready money **2.** s.m. (a) Liquid. (b) Drink. **3.** s.f. Liquid consonant.

liquider, v.tr. **1.** To liquidate. (a) To wind up (a business). (b) To settle (account). **2.** To realize (one's fortune); to sell off.

lire, v.tr. (pr.p. lisant; p.p. lu) To read. **1. Avoir beaucoup lu,** to be well read. *L. dans la pensée de qn,* to read s.o.'s thoughts. **"Dans l'attente de vous lire,"** 'hoping to hear from you.' **2.** *L. une communication,* to read out a notice.

lis, s.m. Lily.

lis-ant, -e, -ons, etc. See LIRE.

Lisbonne. Pr.n.f. *Geog:* Lisbon.

lise[1], s.f. Quicksand.

Lise[2]. Pr.n.f. *F:* Eliza, Lizzie.

liseron, s.m. Bindweed, convolvulus.

Lisette. Pr.n.f. *F:* Lizzie, Eliza.

lisibilité, s.f. Legibility.

lisible, a. Legible.

lisiblement, adv. Legibly.

lisière, s.f. **1.** (a) Selvedge (of cloth). **Chaussons de lisière,** list slippers. (b) *F:* **Mener qn en lisière,** to keep s.o. in leading-strings. **2.** Edge, border (of field).

lisse, a. Smooth, glossy, polished; sleek.

lisser, v.tr. To smooth, gloss, polish. (Of bird) *Se l. les plumes,* to preen its feathers.

liste, s.f. List, roll, register. *Mil:* Roster. **Grossir la liste,** to swell the numbers.

lit, s.m. **1.** Bed. (a) *Lit clos,* box-bed. *Lit à colonnes,* four-poster. *Lit d'ami,* spare bed. **Prendre le lit,** to take to one's bed. **Garder le lit,** to be laid up. **Cloué au lit,** bed-ridden. **Enfant du second lit,** child of the second marriage. (b) **Bois de lit,** bedstead. **2.** (a) Bed, layer. (b) Bed, bottom (of river). **3.** Set (of the tide). **Dans le lit du vent,** in the wind's eye.

litanie, s.f. (a) pl. Litany. (b) sg. *F:* Rig-marole, rambling story. *Réciter toujours la même l.,* to keep harping upon one string.

literie, s.f. Bedding.

lithium [litjɔm], s.m. *Ch:* Lithium.

lithographe, s.m. Lithographer.

Lithuanie [litɥani]. Pr.n.f. *Geog:* Lith-uania.

lithuanien, -ienne [-tɥan-], a. & s. Lithuanian.

litière, s.f. **1.** (Stable-)litter. **2.** Litter, palanquin.

litige, s.m. Litigation; suit. **Cas en litige,** case at issue.

litigieux, a. Litigious.

litre, s.m. *Meas:* Litre (about 1¾ pint).

littéraire, a. Literary.

littéral, -aux, a. Literal.

littéralement, adv. Literally.

littérateur, s.m Literary man; man of letters.

littérature, s.f. Literature.

littoral, -aux. 1. a. Littoral, coastal. **2.** s.m. Coastline; littoral; seaboard.

liturgie, s.f. Liturgy.

liturgique, a. Liturgical.

livide, a. Livid; ghastly (pale).

lividité, s.f. Lividity; ghastliness.

Livourne. Pr.n. *Geog:* Leghorn.

livraison, s.f. **1.** Delivery (of goods). **2.** Part, instalment (of book published in parts).

livre[1], s.f. Pound. **1.** (Weight) **Vendre qch. à la livre,** to sell sth. by the pound. **2.** (Money) (a) *L. sterling,* pound ster-ling. (b) *A:* Franc.

livre[2], s.m. Book. (a) *Jouer un morceau à livre ouvert,* to play a piece at sight. (b) **Tenue des livres,** book-keeping.

livrée, s.f. Livery. **Porter la livrée de qn,** to be in s.o.'s service.

livrer, v.tr. **1.** (a) To deliver, surrender; to give up. *Livré à soi-même,* left to oneself. *L. ses secrets à qn,* to confide one's secrets to s.o. (b) **Livrer bataille,** to join battle (à, with). **2.** To deliver (goods). **se livrer. 1.** *Se l. à la justice, F:* to give oneself up. **2.** *Se l. au désespoir,* to give way to despair.

livret, s.m. **1.** Small book, booklet. *L. de banque,* pass-book. **2.** *Mus:* Libretto.

lobe, *s.m.* Lobe (of ear).

lobélie, *s.f.* *Bot:* Lobelia.

local, -aux. **1.** *a.* Local. **2.** *s.m.* Premises, building.

localement, *adv.* Locally.

localiser, *v.tr.* **1.** To localize. **2.** To locate.

localité, *s.f.* Locality, place, spot.

locataire, *s.m. & f.* **1.** Tenant, occupier. **2.** Lodger.

location, *s.f.* (*a*) (i) Hiring; (ii) letting out on hire. (*b*) (i) Renting; (ii) letting. **Agent de location,** house-agent. (*c*) *Th:* **Bureau de location,** box-office.

loch [lɔk], *s.m.* *Nau:* (Ship's) log. **Filer le loch,** to heave the log.

loche, *s.f.* *Ich:* Loach.

locomotif. **1.** *a.* (*a*) Transportable. **Grue locomotive,** travelling crane. (*b*) *Physiol:* Locomotive (organs). **2.** *s.f* *Rail:* Locomotive, locomotive, engine.

locomotion, *s.f.* Locomotion.

locution, *s.f.* Expression, phrase.

logarithme, *s.m.* Logarithm.

loge, *s.f.* **1.** Hut, cabin; lodge. **2.** *Th:* Box.

logement, *s.m.* **1.** Lodging, housing; billeting (of troops). **2.** (*a*) Accommodation; lodgings. **Logement garni,** furnished apartment(s). **Le logement et la nourriture,** board and lodging. (*b*) *Mil:* Quarters; billet.

loger, *v.* (n. logeons) **1.** *v.i.* To lodge, live; to be billeted. **L. en garni,** to be in lodgings. **2.** *v.tr.* (*a*) To lodge, house; to billet. **(Ici) on loge à pied et à cheval,** good accommodation for man and beast. (*b*) To place, put. **L. une balle dans la cible,** to plant a shot on the target.

  se loger, to lodge.

logicien, -ienne, *s.* Logician.

logique. **1.** *a.* Logical; reasoned. **2.** *s.f.* Logic.

logiquement, *adv.* Logically.

logis, *s.m.* Home, house, dwelling. **Garder le logis,** to stay in. **Corps de logis,** main building.

loi, *s.f.* **1.** (*a*) Law. **Faire la loi à qn,** to lay down the law to s.o. **Se faire une loi de faire qch.,** to make a rule of doing sth. **Hors la loi,** outlawed. (*b*) Act (of Parliament); law, statute. **Projet de loi,** bill. **2.** **Les lois du jeu,** the rules of the game.

loin, *adv.* Far. **1.** (*a*) **Jeune homme qui ira l.,** young man who will go a long way. **Il y a loin de la coupe aux lèvres,** there's many a slip 'twixt the cup and the lip. *Conj.phr.* **Loin que les crimes aient diminué ils ont augmenté,** far from diminishing, crime has increased. (*b*) *s.m.* **Admirer qn de loin,** to admire s.o. from afar. *Conj.phr.* **Du plus loin qu'il les voit,** as soon as he sees them. **2.** **Ce jour est encore l.,** that day is still distant. *Conj.phr.* **(D')aussi loin qu'il me souvienne,** as far back as I remember. **De loin en loin,** at long intervals.

lointain. **1.** *a.* Distant, remote. **2.** *s.m.* **Dans le lointain,** in the distance.

loir, *s.m.* *Z:* Dormouse.

loisible, *a.* Permissible, optional **Il lui est l. de refuser,** it is open to him to refuse.

loisir, *s.m.* Leisure. **Avoir des loisirs.** to have some spare time.

lombes, *s.m.pl.* Lumbar region; loins.

londonien, -ienne. **1.** *a.* Of London. **2.** *s.* Londoner.

Londres. *Pr.n.* Usu. *f.* *Geog:* London.

long, longue. **1.** *a.* (*a*) (Of space) **Ruban l. de cinq mètres,** ribbon five metres long. (*b*) (Of time; PROLONGÉ is preferable after a noun) **L. soupir,** long-drawn sigh. **Elle fut longue à s'en remettre,** she was a long time getting over it. **A la longue,** in the long run. **2.** *s.m.* Length. (*a*) (Of space) **Table qui a six pieds de l.,** table six foot long. **En long, lengthwise.** **De long en large,** up and down, to and fro. **Étendu de tout son long,** stretched at full length. **S'amarrer le long d'un navire,** to moor alongside a ship. **Se faufiler le l. du mur,** to creep along the wall. **Raconter qch. (tout) au long,** to relate sth. at full length. (*b*) (Of time) **Tout le l. du jour,** all day long. (*c*) (Of amount) **Inutile d'en dire plus l.,** I need say no more. **Regard qui en dit long,** look which speaks volumes.

longanimité, *s.f.* Forbearance, longanimity.

longe¹, *s.f.* Leading-rein, head-rope.

longe², *s.f.* *Cu:* Loin (of veal).

longer, *v.tr.* (n. longeons) To keep to the side of (road); to skirt.

longévité, *s.f.* Longevity, long life.

longitude, *s.f.* Longitude.

longitudinal, -aux, *a.* Longitudinal.

longtemps, *adv.* **1.** Long; a long time. **2.** **Il y a longtemps,** long ago. **Avant qu'il soit longtemps,** ere long.

longuement, *adv.* **1.** For a long time. **2.** Slowly, deliberately. **3.** **Plaider l. une cause,** to argue a case at length.

longueur, *s.f.* Length. **1.** **Couper qch. en longueur,** to cut sth. lengthwise. **Tirer un discours en longueur,** to spin out a discourse. **2.** (*a*) **Cette scène fait longueur,** this scene drags. (*b*) **Gagner par une l.,** to win by a length.

longue-vue, *s.f.* Telescope, field-glass, *F:* spy-glass. *pl.* **Des longues-vues.**

lopin, *s.m.* **L. de terre,** plot of ground; allotment.

loquace [-kwas], *a.* Loquacious, talkative.

loquacité [-kwas-], *s.f.* Loquacity, talkativeness.

loque, *s.f.* Rag. *F:* (Of pers.) **Être comme une loque,** to be absolutely limp.

loquet, *s.m.* Latch (of door).

loqueteux. **1.** *a.* In rags. **2.** *s.* Tatterdemalion.

lorgner, *v.tr.* To stare at (s.o.) through a lorgnette.

lorgnette, *s.f.* (Pair of) opera-glasses.

lorgnon, *s.m.* (*a*) Pince-nez, eye-glasses. (*b*) (Handled) lorgnette.

loriot, *s.m.* *Orn:* Oriole.

lorrain. **1.** *a.* Lorrainese. **2.** *s.* Lorrainer.
lors, *adv.* (*a*) **Depuis lors,** ever since then.
F: **Pour lors . . .,** then. . . . (*b*) **Lors . . .**
que, when. **Lors même que** *nous sommes*
heureux, even when we are happy. **Lors de**
sa naissance, when he was born.
lorsque, *conj.* When. *L. j'entrai,* when I
entered.
losange, *s.m.* **1.** *Her*: Lozenge. **2.** *Geom*:
Rhomb(us).
lot [lo], *s.m.* **1.** (*a*) Share; portion, lot.
(*b*) Prize (at a lottery). **Gros lot,** first prize.
2. Lot, parcel (of goods).
loterie, *s.f.* (*a*) Lottery. (*b*) Raffle, draw.
lotion, *s.f. Pharm*: Lotion.
lotionner, *v.tr.* To wash, bathe (wound).
lotir, *v.tr.* **1.** To divide (sth.) into lots.
2. *F*: **Être bien loti,** to be well provided for;
to be favoured by fortune.
lotissement, *s.m.* (*a*) Parcelling out. (*b*) Allotment. (*c*) Development (of building land).
loto, *s.m. Games*: Lotto. *F*: **Yeux en boules**
de loto, goggle eyes.
lotus [-tyːs], *s.m.* **1.** *Bot*: Lotus. **2.** *Gr.Myth*:
Lotus. *F*: **Manger du lotus,** to live in a
state of dreamy content.
louable, *a.* Laudable, praiseworthy; commendable (*de*, for).
louablement, *adv.* Laudably, commend-
ably.
louage, *s.m.* **1.** Letting out, hiring out.
2. Hiring, hire **Voiture de louage,** hackney-
carriage.
louange [lwãːʒ], *s.f.* Praise; laudation.
Chanter ses propres louanges, to blow one's
own trumpet.
louche, *a.* **1.** Cross-eyed, squint-eyed.
2. *F*: (*a*) Ambiguous. (*b*) Shady, suspicious.
loucher, *v.i.* To squint. *L. de l'œil gauche,*
to have a cast in the left eye.
louer[1], *v.tr.* **1.** To hire out, let (out). **Maison**
à louer, house to let. **2.** To hire; to rent
(*à*, from). *L. une place d'avance,* to reserve
a seat.
louer[2], *v.tr.* To praise, laud, commend. *Le*
ciel en soit loué! F: thank Heaven (for that)!
se louer. *Se l. de qch.,* to be pleased with
sth.
loueur, -euse, *s.* Hirer out; letter.
lougre, *s.m. Nau*: Lugger.
Louis. *Pr.n.m.* Lewis; Louis.
Louise. *Pr.n.f.* Louisa, Louise.
loup, *s.m.* (*a*) Wolf. **Marcher à pas de loup,**
to walk stealthily. **Il fait un froid de loup,**
it is bitterly cold. **Se jeter dans la gueule**
du loup, to rush into the lion's mouth.
Tenir le loup par les oreilles, to be in a fix.
Prov: **Quand on parle du loup on en voit**
la queue, talk of the devil and he will appear.
Les loups ne se mangent pas entre eux, dog
won't eat dog. (*b*) **Loup de mer,** *F*: sea-dog,
jack-tar.
loup-cervier, *s.m. Z*: Lynx. *pl. Des loups-*
cerviers.

loupe, *s.f.* **1.** (*a*) *Med*: Wen. (*b*) Excrescence (on tree). **2.** Lens, magnifying-glass.
loup-garou, *s.m.* (*a*) *Myth*: Wer(e)wolf.
(*b*) *F*: Bugaboo. *pl. Des loups-garous.*
lourd, *a.* (*a*) Heavy; ungainly; ponderous.
adv. **Peser lourd,** to weigh heavy. (*b*) Clumsy;
dull; dull-witted. (*c*) *Incident l. de consé-*
quences, incident big with consequences.
(*d*) Close, sultry.
lourdaud. **1.** *a.* (*a*) Loutish; lumpish,
clumsy. (*b*) Dull-witted. **2.** *s.* (*a*) Lout.
(*b*) Dullard.
lourdement, *adv.* Heavily, awkwardly,
clumsily.
lourdeur, *s.f.* Heaviness; clumsiness;
dullness; sultriness.
loutre, *s.f. Z*: Otter.
louve, *s.f. Z*: She-wolf.
louveteau, *s.m.* Wolf-cub.
louvoyer, *v.i.* (je louvoie) (*a*) *Nau*: To tack.
(*b*) *F*: To scheme, manœuvre.
loyal, -aux, *a.* **1.** Honest, fair. **2.** Loyal,
faithful; true (friend).
loyalement, *adv.* **1.** Honestly, fairly.
2. Loyally.
loyauté, *s.f.* **1.** Honesty, uprightness.
2. Loyalty, fidelity.
loyer, *s.m.* Rent.
lu. See LIRE.
lubie, *s.f.* Whim, fad, freak, crotchet.
lubricité, *s.f.* Lubricity, lewdness.
lubrifiant. **1.** *a.* Lubricating. **2.** *s.m.*
Lubricant.
lubrification, *s.f.* Lubrication, greasing.
lubrifier, *v.tr.* To lubricate; to grease or oil.
lubrique, *a.* Libidinous, lustful.
Luc [lyk]. *Pr.n.m.* Luke.
lucarne, *s.f.* (*a*) Dormer-window, attic
window. (*b*) Skylight.
lucide, *a.* Lucid, clear (mind).
lucidement, *adv.* Lucidly, clearly.
lucidité, *s.f.* Lucidity, clearness.
luciole, *s.f. Ent*: Fire-fly, glow-worm.
Lucques. *Pr.n. Geog*: Lucca.
lucratif, *a.* Lucrative, profitable.
lucrativement, *adv.* Lucratively, profitably.
lucre, *s.m.* Lucre, profit.
lueur [lɥ-], *s.f.* **1.** Gleam, glimmer. **A la lueur**
des étoiles, by starlight. **2.** *L. momentanée,*
flash; blink of light.
luge, *s.f.* Luge; Swiss toboggan.
lugubre, *a.* **1.** Lugubrious, dismal. **2.** Ominous, dire.
lugubrement, *adv.* **1.** Lugubriously, dismally. **2.** Ominously.
lui[1], *pl.* **leur,** *pers. pron. m. & f.* (To) him,
her, it, them. (*a*) (Unstressed) *Donnez-lui-en,*
give him some. *Cette maison leur appartient,*
this house belongs to them. (*b*) (Stressed in
imp.) *Montrez-le-leur,* show it to them.
lui[2], *pl.* **eux,** *stressed pers. pron. m.* (*a*) He, it,
they. *C'est lui,* it is he. *Ce sont eux,* *F*: *c'est*
eux, it is they. *Lui et sa femme,* he and his

wife. (b) Him, it, them. *J'accuse son frère et lui*, I accuse him and his brother. *Ce livre est à eux*, this book is theirs. (c) (Refl.) Him(self), it(self), them(selves). *Ils ne pensent qu'à eux*, they think of nobody but themselves.

ui². See LUIRE.

uire, v.i. (*pr.p.* luisant; *p.p.* lui (no *f.*); *p.h.* il luisit is rare) To shine. *Le jour luit*, day is breaking.

uis-ait, -ent, etc. See LUIRE.

uisant. 1. *a.* Shining, bright; shiny, glossy; gleaming. **2.** *s.m.* Gloss, sheen.

umière, s.f. Light. *Mettre en l. les défauts de . . .*, to bring out the faults of. . . . *Faire la lumière sur une affaire*, to clear up a business.

uminaire, s.m. (a) Luminary, light; star, sun. (b) *Coll:* Lights, lighting.

umineux, a. Luminous.

unaire, a. Lunar.

unatique, a. & s. Whimsical, capricious.

une, s.f. **1.** Moon. *Lune de miel*, honeymoon. *Être dans la lune*, to be wool-gathering. **2.** *En forme de l.*, crescent-shaped. **3.** Pierre de lune, moonstone.

unetier, s.m. Spectacle-maker; optician.

unette, s.f. **1.** Lunette (d'approche), telescope; field-glass. **2.** *pl.* (Paire de) lunettes, (pair of) spectacles; goggles. *Serpent à lunettes*, Indian cobra. **3.** *Cu:* Merrythought, wish(ing)-bone (of fowl). **4.** *Fort:* Lunette.

upin, s.m. *Bot:* Lupin(e).

u-s, -t. See LIRE.

ustre¹, s.m. **1.** Lustre, polish, gloss. **2.** Chandelier. *L. électrique*, electrolier.

ustre², s.m. Lustrum; period of five years.

lustrer, v.tr. To glaze, polish (up). *Le poil lustré du chat*, the cat's glossy coat.

luth, s.m. *Mus:* Lute.

luthérien, -ienne, a. & s. *Rel.H:* Lutheran.

lutin. 1. s.m. Mischievous sprite; imp. **2.** a. Mischievous, impish.

lutrin, s.m. *Ecc:* Lectern.

lutte, s.f. **1.** Wrestling. **2.** (a) Contest, struggle, tussle. *L. à mort*, life-and-death struggle. *Sp:* Lutte à la corde de traction, tug-of-war. (b) Strife.

lutter, v.i. **1.** To wrestle. **2.** To struggle, contend, compete. *L. de vitesse avec qn*, to race s.o.

lutteur, -euse, s. **1.** Wrestler. **2.** Fighter.

luxe, s.m. Luxury. (a) Train de luxe, first-class and Pullman train. (b) Abundance, profusion.

luxueusement, adv. Luxuriously, sumptuously.

luxueux, a. Luxurious; rich; sumptuous.

luxure, s.f. Lewdness.

luxurieux, a. Lewd, lustful.

luzerne, s.f. Lucern(e); purple medick.

lycée, s.m. (In Fr.) Secondary school; *lycée*.

lycéen, -éenne, s. Pupil at a *lycée*; schoolboy, -girl.

lymphatique, a. & s. Lymphatic.

lymphe, s.f. Lymph.

lynx [lɛ̃ks], s.m. Lynx.

Lyon. *Pr.n. Geog:* Lyons.

lyonnais, a. & s. *Geog:* (Native) of Lyons.

lyre, s.f. **1.** *Mus:* Lyre. **2.** Oiseau lyre, lyre-bird.

lyrique, a. Lyric(al).

lyrisme, s.m. **1.** Lyricism. **2.** Poetic enthusiasm.

M

M, m [ɛm], s.m. (The letter) M, m.

m'. See ME.

ma, *poss.a.f.* See MON.

macabre, a. (a) La Danse macabre, the dance of Death. (b) Macabre; gruesome; grim.

macaque, s.m. *Z:* Macaque.

macareux, s.m. *Orn:* Puffin.

macaron, s.m. *Cu:* Macaroon.

macaroni, s.m. Macaroni.

Mac(c)habée. 1. *Pr.n.m.* Maccabeus. **2.** s.m. *P:* Corpse.

Macédoine. 1. *Pr.n.f.* Macedonia. **2.** s.f. (a) M. de fruits, fruit salad. (b) Medley.

macédonien, -ienne, a. & s. Macedonian.

macération, s.f. Maceration.

macérer, v.tr. (je macère; je macérerai) To macerate; to steep, soak.

mâchefer, s.m. Clinker, slag.

mâcher, v.tr. To chew, masticate. *M. le mors*, to champ the bit. *Je ne vais pas lui mâcher les mots*, I shall not mince words with him.

Machiavel [mak-]. *Pr.n.m.* Machiavelli.

machiavélique, a. Machiavellian.

machin, s.m. Gadget; thing(amy).

machinal, -aux, a. Mechanical, unconscious (action).

machinalement, adv. Mechanically, unconsciously.

machination, s.f. Machination; plot.

machine, s.f. **1.** Machine. (a) Écriture à la machine, typewriting, typing. *pl.* Les machines, the machinery. (b) Bicycle. (c) *F:* Thing, gadget, contraption. **2.** Engine. (a) Machine à vapeur, steam-engine. (b) *Rail:* Locomotive.

machine-outil, *s.f.* Machine-tool. *pl Des machines-outils.*

machiner, *v.tr.* To scheme, plot, machinate.

mâchoire, *s.f.* **1.** (*a*) Jaw. (*b*) Jaw-bone. **2.** *Mâchoires d'un étau,* jaws of a vice.

mâchonner, *v.tr.* **1.** To chew; to munch. **2.** To mumble.

macis, *s.m.* *Cu:* Mace.

maçon, *s.m.* Mason. *M. en briques,* brick-layer.

maçonnerie, *s.f.* Masonry; stonework or bricklaying.

macule, *s.f.* Stain, spot, blemish.

maculer, *v.tr.* To stain, maculate, spot. **maculé,** *a.* *Z:* Spotted.

madame, *pl.***mesdames,** *s.f.* **1.** (*a*) *Madame, Mme, Dupont,* Mrs Dupont. *Madame la marquise de . . .,* the Marchioness of. . . . *Comment va madame votre mère?* how is your mother? (*b*) (Used alone) (*pl.* **ces dames**) *Voici le chapeau de madame,* here is Mrs X's hat. *Ces dames n'y sont pas,* the ladies are not at home. **2.** (*a*) (In address) Madam. *Entrez, mesdames,* come in, ladies. (*b*) (In letter writing) *Madame* (always written in full), Dear Madam. (Implying previous acquaintance) *Chère Madame,* Dear Mrs X.

Madeleine. 1. *Pr.n.f.* (*a*) Magdalen(e). (*b*) Madeline. **2.** *s.f.* Sponge-cake.

mademoiselle, *pl.* **mesdemoiselles,** *s.f.* **1.** Miss. *Mademoiselle Mlle, Smith,* Miss Smith. *Mesdemoiselles Smith,* the Misses Smith. *Voici le chapeau de mademoiselle,* here is Miss X's hat. *Comment va mademoiselle votre cousine?* how is your cousin? **2.** (*a*) (In address) *Merci, mademoiselle,* thank you, Miss X. (*b*) (*pl.* **ces demoiselles**) *Que prendront ces demoiselles?* what can I offer you, ladies? (*c*) (In letter writing) *Mademoiselle* (always written in full), Dear Madam. (Implying previous acquaintance) *Chère Mademoiselle,* Dear Miss X.

Madère. 1. *Pr.n.f.* *Geog:* Madeira. **2.** *s.m.* Madeira (wine).

madone, *s.f.* Madonna.

madrier, *s.m.* (Piece of) timber; beam; joist; thick board.

madrigal, -aux, *s.m.* Madrigal.

madrilène, *a. & s.* Of Madrid.

magasin, *s.m.* **1.** (*a*) (Large) shop; emporium, stores. **Commis, demoiselle, de magasin,** shop-assistant. (*b*) Store, warehouse. **2.** Magazine (of rifle).

magazine, *s.m.* (Illustrated) magazine.

mage, *s.m.* **Les trois Mages,** the Three Magi, the Three Wise Men.

magenta, *a.inv.* Magenta (colour).

magicien, -ienne, *s.* Magician, wizard, sorcerer; *f.* sorceress.

magie, *s.f.* Magic, wizardry.

magique, *a.* Magic(al).

magiquement, *adv.* Magically.

magistral, -aux, *a.* Magisterial, authoritative; *F:* pompous; masterful.

magistrat, *s.m.* Magistrate; justice; judge.

magistrature, *s.f.* Magistrature.

magnanime, *a.* Magnanimous.

magnanimement, *adv.* Magnanimously.

magnanimité, *s.f.* Magnanimity.

magnésie, *s.f.* **1.** *Ch:* Magnesia. **2.** *Pharm:* Sulfate de magnésie, Epsom salts.

magnésium [-zjɔm], *s.m.* *Ch:* Magnesium.

magnétique, *a.* Magnetic.

magnétiser, *v.tr.* To magnetize.

magnétisme, *s.m.* Magnetism.

magnéto, *s.f.* *I.C.E:* Magneto.

magnificence, *s.f.* Magnificence, splendour.

magnifier [-gni-], *v.tr.* To magnify, glorify.

magnifique, *a.* Magnificent, grand; gorgeous.

magnifiquement, *adv.* Magnificently, grandly.

magnolia, *s.m.* *Bot:* Magnolia.

magot[1], *s.m.* *F:* Hoard (of money); savings.

magot[2], *s.m.* **1.** Barbary ape. **2.** (*a*) Chinese grotesque porcelain figure. (*b*) *F:* (*f.* magotte) Ugly person.

magyar, *a. & s.* *Ethn:* Magyar.

mahari, *s.m.* Racing dromedary.

Mahomet. *Pr.n.m.* Mohammed, Mahomet.

mahométan, *a. & s.* Mahometan.

mai, *s.m.* **1.** May. **Le premier mai,** May-day. **2.** Maypole.

maigre. 1. *a.* (*a*) Thin, skinny, lean. *Homme grand et m.,* tall spare man. (*b*) Lean (meat); scanty; poor (land). **Maigre repas,** frugal meal. **Jour maigre,** fast-day. **2.** *s.m.* Lean (part of meat).

maigreur, *s.f.* **1.** Thinness, leanness. **2.** Poorness, meagreness.

maigrir. 1. *v.i.* To grow thin, lean; to lose flesh. *J'ai maigri de vingt livres,* I have lost twenty pounds. **2.** *v.tr.* To make thinner.

mail [maːj], *s.m.* **1.** Avenue, promenade. **2.** Sledge-hammer.

maille[1] [maːj], *s.f.* **1.** (*a*) Stitch in (knitting). (*b*) Link (of chain). **2.** Mesh (of net).

maille[2], *s.f.* Avoir maille à partir avec qn, to have a bone to pick with s.o.

maillet [majɛ], *s.m.* *Tls:* Mallet; beetle.

maillon [mɑjɔ̃], *s.m.* **1.** Link (of a chain). **2.** *Nau:* M. de liaison, Shackle.

maillot[1] [majo], *s.m.* Swaddling-clothes.

maillot[2], *s.m.* (*a*) *Th:* Tights. (*b*) *M. de bain,* bathing costume.

main, *s.f.* **1.** Hand. (*a*) Soin des mains, manicure. **Se donner la main,** to shake hands. **Prêter la main à qn,** to lend s.o. a helping hand. **Porter la main sur qn,** to lay a hand on s.o. *F:* **Je n'en mettrais pas la main au feu,** I shouldn't like to swear to it. **En venir aux mains,** to come to blows. **N'y pas aller de main morte,** to put one's back into it. *F:* **Faire main basse sur les vivres,** to make a clean sweep of the victuals. **Haut les mains!** hands up! **A bas les mains!** hands off! **Donner un coup de main à qn,** to lend s.o. a helping hand. (b) (Hand used for gripping sth.) **Donner de l'argent à pleine(s) main(s),** to ladle out money by the handful. **Avoir sans cesse l'argent à la main,** to be constantly paying out money. **Tenir le succès entre ses mains,** to have success within one's grasp. **Mettre la m. sur qch.,** to lay hands on sth. (c) **Faire qch. en un tour de main,** to do sth. in a twinkling. **Mettre la main à l'œuvre,** F: to put one's hand to the plough. **Se faire la main,** to get one's hand in. **Il a perdu la main,** he is out of practice. (d) *Equit:* **Rendre la main à son cheval,** to give one's horse its head. F: **Homme à toute main,** man ready to do anything. *Être sous la m. de qn,* to be under s.o.'s thumb. **Avoir la haute main sur . . .,** to have supreme control over. . . . **Gagner haut la main,** to win hands down. (e) *Adv.phr.* **De longue main,** for a long time (past). **2.** Hand(writing). **3.** *Cards:* Hand. **4.** **Mains de caoutchouc,** rubber gloves. **5.** **Main de papier,** quire. **6.** **Main courante,** hand-rail.

main-d'œuvre, s.f. Labour; man-power.

maint, a. *Lit:* Many (a . . .). **Maintes et maintes fois, à maintes reprises,** many a time.

maintenant, adv. Now. *A vous m.,* your turn next.

maintenir, v.tr. (Conj. like TENIR) To maintain. **1.** (a) To keep, hold, (sth.) in position. (b) *M. sa famille par son travail,* to support one's family by one's work. (c) To uphold, keep (the law). **2.** To hold down (a lunatic). **se maintenir. 1.** To last well. **2.** To hold on. *Les prix se maintiennent,* prices are keeping up. **3.** To be maintained, to continue.

maintien, s.m. **1.** Maintenance, upholding, keeping. **2.** Bearing, carriage. **Perdre son maintien,** to lose countenance.

maire, s.m. Mayor.

mairesse, s.f. F: Mayoress.

mairie, s.f. Town-hall; municipal buildings.

mais. 1. adv. (a) **N'en pouvoir mais,** to be at the end of one's tether. (b) (Emphatic) **Mais oui!** why, certainly! **Mais non!** not at all! **Mais qu'avez-vous donc?** why, what is the matter? **2.** *conj.* But.

maïs [mais], s.m. Maize, Indian corn. **Farine de maïs,** cornflour.

maison, s.f. **1.** House. (a) *M. d'éducation,* educational establishment. *M. de jeu,* gambling-house. (b) **Maison de commerce,** business house; firm. (c) Home. **A la maison,** at home. **Trouver maison nette,** to find the house empty. **2.** Family. (a) **Être de la maison,** to be one of the family. (b) Dynasty. (c) Household, staff. **Faire maison nette,** to make a clean sweep of all the servants.

maître, -esse, s. **1.** (a) Master, f. mistress. **Parler à qn en maître,** to speak authoritatively to s.o. **Devenir maître de qch.,** to become the owner of sth. *Prov:* **Tel maître, tel valet,**

like master, like man. (b) **Maître d'école,** schoolmaster. *M. d'armes,* fencing-master. *M. de chapelle,* choir-master. (c) **Maître charpentier,** master carpenter. *C'est fait de main de m.,* it is a masterpiece. **Coup de maître,** master stroke. (d) Works owner. (e) Employee in charge. **Maître de poste,** postmaster. **Maître d'équipage,** boatswain. **Maître d'hôtel,** (i) butler; (ii) head waiter; (iii) *Nau:* chief steward. (f) (Title applied to notaries and advocates) Maître. **2.** *Attrib.* (a) **Maîtresse femme,** managing woman. *M. filou,* arrant knave. (b) Chief, principal. **Maîtresse poutre,** main girder. **3.** *s.f.* **Maîtresse,** mistress.

maîtrise, s.f. **1.** (a) Mastership. (b) Choir school. **2.** Mastery. *M. de soi,* self-control.

maîtriser, v.tr. To master; to subdue; to get under control.

majesté, s.f. **1.** Majesty. **2.** (a) Stateliness. (b) Grandeur.

majestueusement, adv. Majestically.

majestueux, a. Majestic.

majeur, a. (a) Major, greater. **En majeure partie,** for the most part. *Geog:* **Le lac Majeur,** Lake Maggiore. (b) **Être absent pour raison majeure,** to be unavoidably absent. **Cas de force majeure,** case of absolute necessity. (c) *Jur:* Of full age. *Devenir m.,* to come of age.

majolique, s.f. *Cer:* Majolica.

major, s.m. (Médecin) major, medical officer; M.O.

majoration, s.f. **1.** Additional charge (on bill). **2.** Increase (in price).

majorer, v.tr. **1.** To make an additional charge on (bill). **2.** To raise the price of (sth.).

majorité, s.f. **1.** Majority. **2.** *Jur:* Atteindre sa majorité, to come of age.

Majorque. Pr.n.f. *Geog:* Majorca.

majuscule, a. & s.f. Capital (letter).

mal¹, a. **Bon gré, mal gré,** willy-nilly.

mal², pl. **maux,** s.m. **1.** Evil. (a) Hurt, harm. **Faire du mal,** to do harm. *Vouloir du mal à qn,* to wish s.o. evil. **Il n'y a pas grand mal!** there's no great harm done! **Mal lui en a pris,** he has had cause to rue it. (b) **Prendre qch. en mal,** to take sth. amiss. **Tourner qch. en mal,** to put the worst interpretation on sth. (c) Wrong(doing). **Le bien et le mal,** right and wrong, good and evil. **Il ne songe pas à mal,** he doesn't mean any harm. **2.** (a) Disorder; malady; ailment; pain. *Vous allez prendre du mal,* you will catch your death of cold. **Mal de tête,** headache. **Mal de mer,** seasickness. **Mal de gorge,** sore throat. **Vous me faites (du) mal,** you are hurting me. **Avoir le mal du pays,** to be homesick. (b) **Se donner du mal pour faire qch.,** to take pains to do sth.

mal³, adv. **1.** (a) Badly, ill. *Faire qch. tant bien que mal,* to do sth. after a fashion. **S'y mal prendre,** to go the wrong way to work. *Vous ne trouvez pas mal . . .?* you do not mind . . . ? (b) **Aller, se porter, mal**, to be ill. **Être au plus mal**, to be dangerously ill. (c) F: **Pas mal** (de qch.), a fair amount (of sth.). *Pas mal de gens*, a good many people. **2.** (With adj. function) (a) Not right. (b) Uncomfortable; badly off. *Nous ne sommes pas mal ici*, we are quite comfortable here. (c) **Ils sont mal ensemble**, they are on bad terms. (d) (Of health) **Se trouver mal**, to faint. (e) F: **Pas mal**, of good appearance, quality.

malade. 1. a. Ill, sick, unwell. **Dent m.**, aching tooth. **Jambe m.**, bad leg. **Esprit m.**, disordered mind. **2.** s. Sick person; invalid. *Med:* Patient.

maladie, s.f. Illness, sickness, disease. *Vet:* **Maladie des chiens**, distemper.

maladif, a. Sickly; morbid.

maladresse, s.f. **1.** (a) Clumsiness, awkwardness. (b) Maladroitness. **2.** Blunder.

maladroit. 1. a. (a) Unskilful, clumsy, awkward. (b) Blundering. **2.** s. Blunderer.

maladroitement, adv. Clumsily, awkwardly.

malais, a. & s. Malay(an).

malaise, s.m. **1.** Uneasiness, discomfort. **2.** Indisposition.

malaisé, a. Difficult.

Malaisie. Pr.n.f. The Malay Archipelago.

malandrin, s.m. F: Brigand, robber; marauder.

malaria, s.f. Malaria, marsh-fever.

malavisé, a. Ill-advised; injudicious.

malchance, s.f. Bad luck, ill luck. **Par malchance**, as ill luck would have it.

malchanceux, a. Unfortunate, unlucky.

mâle, a. & s.m. **1.** Male; cock (bird). (Of animals) He-. **Un ours m.**, a he-bear. **2.** *Courage m.*, manly courage. *Style m.*, virile style.

malédiction, s.f. Malediction, curse. *Int:* **Malédiction!** curse it!

maléfice, s.m. Malefice; evil spell.

maléfique, a. Maleficent; baleful, evil.

malencontreux, a. **1.** Untoward. **2.** Unlucky.

malentendu, s.m. Misunderstanding.

malfaisance, s.f. Maleficence, evil-mindedness.

malfaisant, a. Maleficent; evil-minded; harmful; evil.

malfaiteur, -trice, s. Malefactor, evil-doer.

malgache, a. & s. Malagasy, Madagascan.

malgré, prep. In spite of; notwithstanding. **M. tout**, for all that.

malhabile, a. Unskilful; clumsy, awkward.

malhabilement, adv. Unskilfully, clumsily.

malheur, s.m. Misfortune. **1.** Untoward occurrence; calamity, accident. F: **Faire un malheur**, to do something desperate. **2.** Bad luck, ill luck. **Messager de malheur**, bird of ill omen. **Malheur à vous!** woe betide you! **Par malheur**, unfortunately. **Jouer de malheur**, to be unlucky. *C'est jouer de m.*, it is most unfortunate. *Prov:* A

quelque chose malheur est bon, it's an ill wind that blows nobody good.

malheureusement, adv. Unfortunately unluckily.

malheureux, a. (a) Unfortunate, unhappy badly off; woeful. **Le malheureux!** (the poor man! **Malheureux!** wretch! (b) Unlucky. *C'est bien m. pour vous!* it is hard lines on you! *Le voila enfin, ce n'est pas m.*, here he comes at last, and a good job too (c) F: Paltry, wretched.

malhonnête, a. (a) Dishonest. (b) Rude, impolite. (c) Improper.

malhonnêteté, s.f. **1.** (a) Dishonesty. (b) Dishonest action. **2.** Rudeness, incivility.

malice, s.f. **1.** (a) Malice, maliciousness, spitefulness. **Ne pas voir malice à qch.**, to see no harm in sth. (b) Mischievousness roguishness. **2.** Smart remark; dig.

malicieusement, adv. (a) Mischievously. (b) Archly, shyly.

malicieux, a. (a) Mischievous, naughty. (b) Waggish, sly, arch.

maligne. See MALIN.

malignement, adv. **1.** Malignantly, spitefully. **2.** Mischievously, slyly, archly.

malignité, s.f. (a) Malignity, malignancy. (b) Spite(fulness).

malin, -igne, a. **1.** Malignant. (a) Evil(-minded), wicked. (b) Malicious. (c) *Tumeur maligne*, malignant tumour. **2.** F Shrewd, cunning. s. **C'est un malin**, F: he knows a thing or two. *Prov:* A malin malin et demi, diamond cut diamond.

Malines. 1. Pr.n.f. Geog: Malines, Mechlin. **2.** s.f. Mechlin lace.

malingre, a. Sickly, puny.

malintentionné, a. & s. Ill-intentioned (person).

malle, s.f. Trunk, box. **Faire sa malle**, to pack.

malléable, a. (a) Malleable. (b) F: Plastic, soft, pliable.

mallette, s.f. (a) Small case. **M. de camping**, tea-basket. (b) Attaché case.

malmener, v.tr. (Conj. like MENER) (a) To maltreat, ill-treat. (b) To abuse.

malodorant, a. Evil-smelling, malodorous.

malouin, a. & s. (Native) of Saint-Malo.

malpeigné, a. Unkempt, tousled.

malpropre, a. (a) Dirty, grubby; slovenly, untidy. (b) F: Dirty, unsavoury.

malpropreté, s.f. (a) Dirtiness. (b) Indecency; unsavouriness.

malsain, a. **1.** (a) Unhealthy. (b) Nau: Dangerous (coast). **2.** Unwholesome.

malséance, s.f. Unseemliness.

malséant, a. Unseemly; unbecoming.

malt [malt], s.m. Brew: Malt.

maltais, a. & s. Maltese.

Malte. Pr.n.f. Geog: Malta.

maltraiter, v.tr. To maltreat, ill-treat.

malveillance [-vɛjɑ̃ːs], s.f. (a) Malevolence, ill-will. (b) Foul play.

malveillant [-vɛjã], *a.* (*a*) Malevolent, ill-willed; malicious. (*b*) Spiteful.

maman, *s.f.* F: Mam(m)a, mum(my).

mamelle, *s.f.* Breast; udder.

mamelon, *s.m.* **1.** *Anat:* (*a*) Nipple, teat. (*b*) Dug (of animal). **2.** Mamelon; rounded hillock.

mammifère. 1. *a.* Mammalian. **2.** *s.m.* Mammal.

mammouth, *s.m.* Mammoth.

manant, *s.m.* F: Churl, boor.

manche¹, *s.f.* **1.** Sleeve. (*a*) F: **Avoir qn dans sa manche,** to have s.o.'s services at command. **Ça, c'est une autre paire de manches!** that's quite another matter. **Avoir la manche large,** to be easy-going. (*b*) *M. d'incendie,* fire-hose. **Manche à air,** air-shaft. **2.** (*a*) *Cards:* Hand (played); single game. **Nous sommes manche à manche,** we are game all. (*b*) *Sp:* Heat. (*c*) *Ten:* Set. **3.** *Geog:* Strait, channel. **La Manche,** the (English) Channel.

manche², *s.m.* Handle; haft. **Manche à balai,** (i) broomstick; (ii) *Av:* F: direction-stick, F: joy-stick.

manchette, *s.f.* (*a*) Cuff. (*b*) Gauntlet (of glove). (*c*) Wristband (of shirt-sleeve).

manchon, *s.m.* **1.** Muff. **2.** (*a*) *Aut:* M. d'embrayage, clutch. (*b*) Gas-mantle.

manchot. 1. *a. & s.* One-armed, one-handed (person). **2.** *s.m. Orn:* Penguin.

mandarin, *s.m.* (Chinese) mandarin.

mandarine, *s.f.* Tangerine (orange).

mandat, *s.m.* **1.** Mandate; commission. **2.** Warrant. **3.** Order (to pay); money order; draft.

mandataire, *s.m. & f.* **1.** Mandatory. **2.** Proxy. **3.** *Jur:* Authorized agent; attorney. **4.** Trustee.

mandat-poste, *s.m. Post:* Money order. *pl. Des mandats-poste.*

mandchou [mãt-], *a. & s. Ethn:* Manchu, Manchurian.

Mandchourie [mãt-]. *Pr.n.ₗ.* Manchuria.

mander, *v.tr.* **1.** *Journ: On mande de . . .,* it is reported from. . . . **2.** *M. à qn de faire qch.,* to instruct s.o., to do sth. **3.** To summon.

mandibule, *s.f. Z:* Mandible.

mandoline, *s.f. Mus:* Mandolin(e).

mandragore, *s.f. Bot:* Mandragora, F: mandrake.

mandrill, *s.m. Z:* Mandrill.

mandrin, *s.m.* F: Bandit, ruffian.

manège, *s.m.* **1.** (*a*) Horsemanship. (*b*) (Salle de) **manège,** riding-school. (*c*) **Manège de chevaux de bois,** merry-go-round; round-about. **2.** F: Wile, stratagem, trick.

manette, *s.f.* (*a*) Handle, hand-lever. (*b*) *Nau:* Spoke (of the wheel).

manganèse, *s.m.* Manganese.

mangeable, *a.* Edible, eatable.

mangeaille [-ʒaːj], *s.f. F:* Victuals, F: grub.

mangeoire, *s.f.* **1.** Manger. **2.** Feeding trough.

manger. I. *v.tr.* (n. mangeons) **1.** To eat. **Salle à manger,** dining-room. **Donner à m. aux poules,** to feed the fowls. **Manger à son appétit, à sa faim,** to eat one's fill. **Manger ses mots,** to clip one's words. **2.** *M. son argent,* to squander one's money. **II. manger,** *s.m.* Food.

mangeur, *s.* Eater. *M. d'argent,* spendthrift.

manglier, *s.m. Bot:* Mangrove(-tree).

mangouste, *s.f. Z:* Mongoose.

mangue [mãːg], *s.f.* Mango (fruit).

manguier [-gje], *s.m. Bot:* Mango(-tree).

maniable, *a.* Manageable; easy to handle; handy (tool).

maniaque, *a. & s.* **1.** Maniac; raving mad(man, -woman). **2.** Finical. *s.* Faddist.

manie, *s.f.* **1.** Mania. (*a*) Mental derangement. (*b*) F: Craze. **2.** Idiosyncrasy. *Il a ses petites manies,* he has his little ways.

manier, *v.tr.* **1.** To feel (cloth); to handle (tool). **2.** To handle; to wield. *M. les avirons,* to ply the oars.

manière, *s.f.* **1.** Manner, way. **Laissez-moi faire à ma manière,** let me do it my own way. **De cette manière,** thus; in this way. **De manière ou d'autre,** somehow or other. **En quelque manière,** in a way. **De (telle) manière que,** so that. **2.** *pl.* Manners. F: **Faire des manières,** to affect reluctance.

maniéré, *a.* Affected, finical; mincing, genteel.

maniérisme, *s.m.* Mannerism.

manifestant, *s.* (Political) demonstrator.

manifestation, *s.f.* (*a*) Manifestation. (*b*) (Political) demonstration.

manifeste¹, *a.* Manifest, evident.

manifeste², *s.m.* Manifesto, proclamation.

manifestement, *adv.* Manifestly, clearly.

manifester, *v.tr.* **1.** To manifest; to evince (opinion); to show (confusion). **2.** *Abs.* To demonstrate.

    se manifester, to appear; to show itself.

manigance, *s.f.* F: (*a*) Intrigue. (*b*) *pl.* Underhand practices; wire-pulling.

manigancer, *v.tr.* (n. manigançons) F: To scheme, to plot.

Manille [-niːj]. *Pr.n. Geog:* Manilla.

manipulateur, -trice, *s.* Manipulator; handler (of money).

manipulation, *s.f.* Manipulation; handling.

manipuler, *v.tr.* To manipulate; to handle, operate.

manivelle, *s.f.* **1.** (*a*) Crank. (*b*) Pedal-crank (of bicycle). **2.** Crank-handle.

manne¹, *s.f.* B: Manna.

manne², *s.f.* Basket, hamper; crate.

mannequin, *s.m.* **1.** (*a*) *Art:* Lay figure. (*b*) *Dressm:* Dummy. **2.** *Occ. f.* Mannequin.

manœuvre. 1. *s.f.* (*a*) Working, driving (of machine). (*b*) *Nau:* Handling (of ship). **Maître de manœuvre,** boatswain. (*c*) Drill, exercise; tactical exercise; manœuvre. (d) Shunting (of trains). (e) F: Scheme, manœuvre. (f) pl. Scheming. **2.** s.f. Nau: Rope; rigging. **3.** s.m. Labourer.

manœuvrer. I. v.tr. (a) To work, operate. (b) To handle (ship). (c) Rail: To shunt. **2.** v.i. (a) Mil: To manœuvre. (b) F: To scheme, manœuvre.

manoir, s.m. (a) Manor-house. (b) F: Country-house, country-seat.

manquant. I. a. (a) Missing. (b) Wanting, lacking. **2.** s. Absentee; defaulter.

manque, s.m. Lack, want; deficiency. M. de parole, breach of faith.

manquement, s.m. Failure, shortcoming, lapse. M. au devoir, breach of duty.

manquer. I. v.i. **I.** (a) M. de qch., to lack, be short of, sth. (b) Il a manqué (de) tomber, he nearly fell. (c) Impers. Il s'en manque de beaucoup, far from it. **2.** To fail. (a) To be wanting, deficient. Les vivres commencent à m., provisions are running short. F: Il ne manquait plus que cela! that's the last straw! (b) To give way. Son cœur lui manqua, his heart failed him. (c) To be absent, missing. Manquer à qn, to be missed by s.o. (d) To fall short. M. à sa parole, to break one's word. M. à une règle, to violate a rule. M. à qn, to be disrespectful to s.o. Abs. Le coup a manqué, the attempt miscarried. (e) Ne manquez pas de nous écrire, be sure to write to us.

II. manquer, v.tr. **I.** To miss (train). Il l'a manqué belle, he missed a splendid chance. **2.** M. sa vie, to make a failure of one's life.

manqué, a. **I.** Missed; unsuccessful. Coup manqué, (i) miss; (ii) failure. Vie manquée, wasted life. **2.** F: C'est un garçon m., she's a regular tomboy.

mansarde, s.f. Arch: **I.** (Fenêtre en) mansarde, dormer-window. **2.** Attic, garret.

manteau, s.m. **I.** Cloak, mantle, wrap. **2.** Manteau de cheminée, mantelpiece.

mantelet, s.m. **I.** Cost: Tippet. **2.** (Carriage-)apron. **3.** Shutter; Nau: dead-light.

mantille [-tiːj], s.f. Cost: Mantilla.

manucure, s.m. & f. Manicurist.

manuel, -elle. I. a. Manual (labour). **2.** s.m. Manual, handbook.

manufacture, s.f. (Manu)factory; mill; works.

manufacturer, v.tr. To manufacture.

manufacturier. I. a. Manufacturing. **2.** s.m. Manufacturer; mill-owner.

manuscrit, a. & s.m. Manuscript.

manutention, s.f. **I.** Management, administration. **2.** Handling (of stores).

maori, a. & s. Ethn: Maori.

mappemonde, s.f. Map of the world in two hemispheres. M. céleste, planisphere.

maquereau, s.m. Mackerel.

maquignon, -onne, s. **I.** Horse-dealer; coper. **2.** (Shady) go-between.

maquillage [-kij-], s.m. Th: (a) Making up. (b) Make-up.

maquiller [-kije], v.tr. Th: To make up (face).

maquis, s.m. Scrub, bush (in Corsica); underground forces; prendre le m., to go underground, to take to the maquis.

maquisard, s.m. Man of the maquis.

maraîchage, s.m. Market-gardening.

maraîcher, s. Market-gardener.

marais, s.m. Marsh(land); bog, fen.

marâtre, s.f. (Cruel) stepmother or mother.

maraude, s.f. (a) Marauding, plundering. (b) F: Taxi en m., cruising taxi.

marauder, v.i. (a) To maraud, plunder. (b) F: (Of taxicabs) To cruise (in search of fares).

maraudeur, -euse, s. Marauder, plunderer.

marbre, s.m. (a) Marble. (b) Marble (statue).

marbrer, v.tr. To marble; to mottle; to vein.

marbré, a. Marbled; mottled; veined.

marbrure, s.f. Marbling, veining. Mottling (of the skin).

marc [maːr], s.m. **I.** Marc (of grapes). **2.** (Used) tea-leaves; coffee-grounds.

marcassin, s.m. Young wild boar.

marchand. I. s. Dealer, shopkeeper, merchant; tradesman. M. de poisson, fishmonger. M. de tabac, tobacconist. M. des quatre saisons, costermonger; hawker (of fruit and vegetables). **2.** a. (a) Saleable, marketable. (b) Trading. Place marchande, shopping centre. Navire marchand, merchant ship.

marchander, v.tr. (a) To haggle. (b) Il ne marchande pas sa peine, he spares no pains.

marchandise, s.f. Merchandise, goods, wares.

marche, s.f. **I.** (a) Step, stair. La m. du bas, the bottom stair. (b) Treadle (of lathe). **2.** (a) Walking. Aimer la m., to be fond of walking. Ralentir sa marche, to slacken one's pace. Se mettre en marche, to set out, start off. (b) March. (i) Ouvrir la marche, to lead the way. (ii) Mus: M. funèbre, dead march. **3.** (a) Running (of trains); sailing (of ships). (b) Entrer dans le garage en m. arrière, to back into the garage. **4.** (a) Running, going, working (of machine). (b) Course (of events); march (of time).

marché, s.m. **I.** (a) Dealing, buying. (b) Deal, bargain. C'est marché fait, it is a bargain; F: done! Par-dessus le marché, into the bargain. (c) Bon marché, cheapness. A meilleur m., cheaper. Articles bon m., low-priced goods, F: bargains. (d) Marché noir, black market. **2.** Market.

marchepied, s.m. (a) Step (of carriage). (b) Veh: Footboard. Aut: Running-board.

marcher, v.i. **I.** To tread. **2.** (a) To walk, go. Deux choses qui marchent toujours ensemble, two things that always go together. (b) F: To obey orders. Faire marcher qn, (i) to

rder s.o. ʀbout; (ii) to pull s.o.'s leg. (c)
ʹo march. **En avant, marche!** quick
ʹarch! **3.** (a) (Of trains) To move,
ʹavel, go; (of ships) to sail. *Le temps marche,*
ʹme goes on. *Les affaires marchent,* business
s brisk. *Est-ce que ça marche?* are you getting
long all right? (b) (Of machine) To work,
ʹun, go.

archeur, -euse. I. s. Walker. **2.** a. Walk-
ʹng (animal). *Navire bon m.,* good sailer.

ardi, s.m. Tuesday. **Mardi gras,** Shrove
ʹuesday.

are, s.f. (Stagnant) pool; pond.

arécage, s.m. (a) Fen, marshland. (b) Bog,
ʹlough, swamp.

arécageux, a. Boggy, marshy, swampy.

aréchal, -aux, s.m. **I. Maréchal ferrant,**
ʹhoeing-smith; farrier. **2.** Marshal. **3.** *Mil:*
ʹa) Field-marshal. (b) **Maréchal des logis,**
ʹcavalry) sergeant.

arée, s.f. **I.** Tide. *Port de m.,* tidal harbour.
2. Fresh (sea-water) fish. **Train de marée,**
F: boat-train. *F:* **Arriver comme marée**
en carême, to arrive in the nick of time.

arelle, s.f. *Games:* Hopscotch.

argarine, s.f. Margarine.

arge, s.f. (a) Border, edge. (b) Margin (of
ʹbook). **Note en marge,** marginal note.

argelle, s.f. Curb(-stone) (of a well).

arginal, -aux, a. Marginal.

arguerite. I. *Pr.n.f.* Margaret. **2.** s.f.
Bot: **(Petite) marguerite,** daisy. **Grande**
ʹmarguerite, ox-eye daisy, marguerite.

arguillier [-gije], s.m. Churchwarden.

ari, s.m. Husband.

ariable, a. Marriageable.

ariage, s.m. Marriage. (a) Wedlock,
ʹmatrimony. (b) Wedding, nuptials

ʹarie. *Pr.n.f.* Mary, Maria.

arier, v.tr. **I.** To marry. (a) (Of priest)
ʹTo join in marriage. (b) To give in marriage.
2. To join, unite. *M. des couleurs,* to blend
ʹcolours.

se marier. (a) To marry, to get married.
Se m. à, avec, qn, to marry s.o. (b) (Of colour)
Se m. avec qch., to go with sth.

marié, a. & s. **I.** Married (person).
Nouvelle mariée, f. bride. **2.** s.m. Bride-
ʹgroom, s.f. bride (about to be married).

arieur, -euse, s. Matchmaker.

arin. I. a. Marine. *Carte marine,* sea-
ʹchart. **Mille marin,** nautical mile. *F:* **Avoir**
le pied marin, to be a good sailor. **2.** s.m.
ʹSailor, seaman. **Se faire marin,** to go to sea.

marine, s.f. **I.** *Terme de m.,* nautical
ʹterm. **2.** The sea service. **La marine mar-**
chande, the mercantile marine. **La marine**
de guerre, the Navy.

arinier. I. a. Marine, naval. **2.** s.m.
ʹWaterman, bargeman.

arionnette, s.f. (a) Marionette, puppet.
(b) *F:* (Of pers.) Puppet, tool.

arital, -aux, a. Marital.

maritime, a. Maritime. *Courtier m.,* ship-
broker. *Arsenal m.,* naval dockyard. *Rail:*
Gare maritime, harbour station.

marjolaine, s.f. (Sweet) marjoram.

marmaille [-ma:j], s.f. *Coll: F:* Brats.

marmelade, s.f. (a) Compote (of fruit).
M. de pommes, stewed apples. (b) *F:* **Mettre**
qn en marmelade, to pound s.o. to a jelly.

marmite, s.f. **I.** (a) (Cooking-)pot; pan.
M. à conserves, preserving-pan. *F:* **Faire**
bouillir la marmite, to keep the pot boiling.
(b) Dixy, camp-kettle. **2.** *Mil: P:* Heavy
shell.

marmiton, s.m. Cook's boy.

marmonner, v.tr. To mumble, mutter.

marmot, s.m. Child, brat.

marmotte, s.f. *Z:* Marmot.

marmotter, v.tr. To mumble, mutter.

Maroc (le) [-rɔk]. *Pr.n.m.* Morocco.

marocain, a. & s. Moroccan.

maroquin, s.m. Morocco(-leather).

marotte, s.f. **I.** (Court fool's) bauble; **cap**
and bells. **2.** *F:* Fad, hobby, fancy.

marquant, a. **I.** Prominent, outstanding.
2. *Carte marquante,* s.f. **marquante,** card that
counts.

marque, s.f. Mark. **Marque de fabrique,**
trade-mark; brand. *F:* **Personnages de m.,**
distinguished people. **Porter la m. du génie,**
to bear the stamp of genius. *Marques d'amitié,*
tokens of friendship.

marquer, v.tr. To mark. (a) To put a
mark on (sth.). (b) To record, note. *Games:*
M. les points, to keep the score. (c) To indicate, show. *La pendule marque dix heures,*
the clock points to ten o'clock. **Marquer le**
pas, to mark time. **2.** v.i. To stand out, make
a mark.

marqué, a. **I.** Marked (card). **2.**
Marked, decided.

marqueterie, s.f. Inlaid-work, marquetry.

marqueur, -euse, s. Marker.

marquis, s.m. Marquis, marquess.

marquise, s.f. **I.** Marchioness. **2.** (a)
Awning. (b) Marquee (tent).

marraine, s.f. Godmother; sponsor.

marron, s.m. **I.** (a) (Large edible) chestnut.
(b) **Marron d'Inde,** horse-chestnut. **2.** *Pyr:*
Maroon. **3.** a. inv. in f. Chestnut(-colour);
maroon.

marronnier, s.m. Chestnut-tree. **Marronnier**
d'Inde, horse-chestnut tree.

Mars [mars]. **I.** *Pr.n.m. Astr:* Mars. *Mil:*
Champ de Mars, parade-ground. **2.** s.m.
March. *F:* **Arriver comme mars en carême,**
to come round as regularly as clock-work.

marseillais [-sejɛ], a. & s. *Geog:* Marseillais.
La Marseillaise, the Marseillaise.

Marseille [-sɛ:j]. *Pr.n. Geog:* Marseilles.

marsouin, s.m. *Z:* Porpoise.

marsupial, -aux, a. & s.m. *Z:* Marsupial.

marteau, s.m. (a) Hammer. (b) (Auctioneer's) hammer. (c) Knocker (of door).

marteler, v.tr. (je martèle) To hammer.

F: Marteler le cerveau à qn, to torment s.o.
martial, -aux, *a.* **1.** Martial; warlike.
2. Loi martiale, martial law.
martinet, *s.m. Orn:* Swift.
martin-pêcheur, *s.m. Orn:* Kingfisher.
pl. Des martins-pêcheurs.
martre, *s.f. Z:* Marten. **Martre zibeline,**
sable.
martyr, *s.* Martyr.
martyre, *s.m.* Martyrdom.
martyriser, *v.tr.* To make a martyr of.
marxiste. 1. *a.* Marxian. **2.** *s.* Marxist.
mascarade, *s.f.* Masquerade.
mascaret, *s.m.* Bore, tidal wave.
mascotte, *s.f.* Mascot, charm.
masculin, *a.* **1.** Male. **2.** Masculine.
masque, *s.m.* **1.** Mask. **2.** (a) *Th:* Masque.
(b) Masquerader, mummer.
masquer, *v.tr.* To mask. (a) *Se m.,* to put
on a mask. (b) To hide, screen. *Mil:*
Masquer une batterie, to conceal a battery.
Nau: Naviguer à feux masqués, to steam
without lights.
massacrante, *a.f.* Être d'une humeur
massacrante, to be in a very bad temper.
massacre, *s.m.* (a) Massacre, slaughter.
(b) Jeu de massacre, Aunt Sally.
massacrer, *v.tr.* **1.** To massacre, slaughter.
2. *F:* To bungle, spoil; to murder (music);
to ruin (clothes).
massage, *s.m.* Massage.
masse, *s.f.* Mass. (a) *Tomber comme une m.,*
to fall like a log. (b) Émouvoir les masses, to
move the masses. **En masse,** in a body.
massepain, *s.m.* Marzipan.
masser[1], *v.tr.* To mass.
se masser, to mass; to form a crowd.
masser[2], *v.tr.* To massage.
massette, *s.f. Bot:* Bulrush, reed-mace.
masseur, -euse, *s.* Masseur, *f.* masseuse.
massif. 1. *a.* (a) Massive, bulky. (b) *Argent
m.,* solid silver. **2.** *s.m.* (a) Clump (of shrubs).
(b) *Geog:* Mountain mass.
massivement, *adv.* Massively, ponderously.
massue, *s.f.* Club, bludgeon.
mastic [-tik], *s.m.* **1.** Mastic (resin). **2.**
M. à vitres, (glazier's) putty.
mastication, *s.f.* Mastication; chewing.
mastiquer, *v.tr.* To masticate, chew.
masure, *s.f* Tumbledown cottage; hovel,
shanty.
mat[1] [mat], *a.* Mat, unpolished, dull. *Son
mat,* dull sound; thud.
mat[2] [mat]. *s.m.* (Check)mate.
mât [mɑ], *s.m.* Mast, pole. **Mât de cocagne,**
greasy pole.
matamore, *s.m.* Braggart; swashbuckler.
matelas, *s.m.* Mattress *M. à eau,* water-
bed.
matelasser, *v.tr.* To pad, cushion.
matelot, *s.m.* Sailor, seaman.
mater, *v.tr.* (a) *Chess:* To (check)mate.
(b) *F:* Mater qn, to bring s.o. to heel.
mâter, *v.tr. M. les avirons,* to toss oars.

matérialiser, *v.tr.* To materialize.
matérialiste. 1. *a.* Materialistic. **2.**
Materialist.
matériaux, *s.m.pl.* Materials.
matériel, -elle. 1. *a.* (a) Material, physi
(b) Materialistic, gross, sensual. (c) *Bes*
matériels, bodily needs. **2.** *s.m.* Plant, imp
ments; material. *Rail:* **Matériel** roula
rolling-stock.
matériellement, *adv.* (a) Materially. *Ch*
m. impossible, thing physically impossit
(b) Materialistically, sensually.
maternel, -elle, *a.* Maternal. **1.** Mother
2. (a) Aïeul m., maternal grandmoth
(b) Langue maternelle, mother tongue.
maternellement, *adv.* Maternally.
maternité, *s.f.* Maternity, motherhood.
mathématicien, -ienne, *s.* Mathematici
mathématique. 1. *a.* Mathematical. **2.**
Usu. *pl.* Mathematics.
mathurin, *s.m. F:* Jack Tar.
matière, *s.f.* **1.** Material. **2.** Matter, su
stance. **3.** Subject; topic, theme. **Ta**
des matières, table of contents. Entrer
matière, to broach the subject.
matin. 1. *s.m.* Morning. **De grand mat**
early in the morning. **Un de ces** (quat
matins, one of these (fine) days. **2.** *a*
Se lever très m., to get up very early.
mâtin, *s.m.* **1.** (a) Mastiff. (b) *F:* Watch-d
2. *F:* (f. mâtine) Sacré mâtin! you sly d
you! *Petite mâtine!* you little minx! i
Mâtin! by Jove!
matinal, -aux, *a.* **1.** Morning. *A ce*
heure matinale, at this early hour. **2.** Com
tu es m! you are down very early!
matinée, *s.f.* **1.** Morning, forenoon. *Da*
la m., in the course of the morning. *F:* Fai
la grasse matinée, to lie late abed. **2.** Matiné
afternoon performance.
matines, *s.f.pl. Ecc:* Matins.
matois. 1. *a.* (a) Sly, cunning, crafty. **2.** *s. F*
matois, sly fox.
matou, *s.m.* Tom-cat.
matraque, *s.f.* Bludgeon.
matriarcal, -aux, *a.* Matriarchal.
matrice, *s.f.* Matrix. (a) *Anat:* Wom
(b) *Metalw:* Die.
matricule. 1. *s.f.* Roll, register, li
2. Numéro m., *s.m.* matricule, (regiment
number.
matrimonial, -aux, *a.* Matrimonial.
matrone, *s.f.* Matron (= married woman)
Matthieu. *Pr.n.m.* Matthew.
mâture, *s.f.* Masts; masts and spars. Da
la mâture, aloft.
maturité, *s.f.* Maturity, ripeness.
matutinal, -aux, *a.* Matutinal.
maudire, *v.tr.* (*pr.p.* maudissant; *p.*
maudit; *pr.sub.* je maudisse; *p.h.* je maudi
To curse.
maudit. *a.* (a) (Ac)cursed. (b) *Quel r*
temps! what damnable weather!
maudissement, *s.m.* Cursing.

maugréer, v.i. To curse, fume; to grumble.

Maure. Ethn: s.m. Moor.

mauresque. 1. a. Moorish. 2. s.f. Moorish woman.

Maurice. Pr.n.m. Maurice. **L'île Maurice,** Mauritius.

mausolée, s.m. Mausoleum.

maussade, a. (a) Surly, sullen; peevish. (b) Temps m., dull, cheerless, weather.

maussadement, adv. Sullenly, peevishly.

maussaderie, s.f. Sullenness, peevishness.

mauvais, a. (a) Evil, ill; bad, wicked. Né sous une mauvaise étoile, born under an unlucky star. (b) Ill-natured. C'est une mauvaise langue, she has a venomous tongue. (c) Nasty, unpleasant. Mauvais pas, dangerous situation. Mer mauvaise, rough sea. Trouver qch. mauvais, to dislike sth. Prendre qch. en mauvaise part, to take exception to sth. Adv. Sentir mauvais, to smell bad. Il fait mauvais, the weather is bad. (d) M. pour la santé, bad for the health. (e) Mauvaise santé, poor health. Faire de mauvaises affaires, to be doing badly. (f) Wrong; due to a mistake. Rire au m. endroit, to laugh in the wrong place.

mauvaisement, adv. Evilly, wickedly; ill-naturedly.

mauve. 1. s.f. Bot: Mallow. 2. a. & s.m. Mauve, purple.

mauviette, s.f. Cu: Lark. F: Manger comme une mauviette, to eat very little.

maxime, s.f. Maxim.

maximum [-mɔm]. Maximum. pl. Des maxima, des maximums.

mazagran, s.m. Glass of black coffee.

mazout, s.m. Fuel oil, oil fuel.

me, before a vowel sound m', pers.pron. (a) (Acc.) Me. Me voici, here I am. (b) (Dat.) (To) me. Donnez-m'en, give me some. (c) Myself. Je me lave, I wash myself. (d) Je me dis que . . ., I said to myself that. . . .

méandre, s.m. Meander, sinuosity, winding.

mécanicien, -ienne. 1. s.m. (a) Mechanic. (b) Mechanician. (c) Rail: Engine-driver. Nau: Engineer. 2. s.f. **Mécanicienne,** machinist; sewing-woman.

mécanique. 1. a. Mechanical. 2. s.f. (a) Mechanics. (b) Piece of machinery.

mécaniquement, adv. Mechanically.

mécanisme, s.m. 1. Mechanism, machinery; works. 2. Working, technique.

méchamment, adv. 1. Naughtily, wickedly. 2. Spitefully, ill-naturedly.

méchanceté, s.f. (a) Wickedness, mischievousness. (b) Unkindness, spitefulness. Faire qch. par méchanceté, to do sth. out of malice.

méchant, a. 1. (a) Miserable, wretched, sorry. (b) Unpleasant, disagreeable. Être de méchante humeur, to be out of temper. 2. (a) Wicked, evil; naughty. s. Oh, le m.! oh, the naughty boy! (b) Spiteful; vicious. s. Ne faites donc pas le méchant, don't be nasty.

mèche, s.f. 1. (a) Wick. (b) Match (for firing explosives); fuse (of mine). F: Vendre la mèche, to give the show away. 2. Lock (of hair). 3. Tls: Bit, drill.

mécompte [-kɔ̃:t], s.m. 1. Miscalculation, error. 2. Mistaken judgment; disappointment.

méconnaissable, a. Hardly recognizable, unrecognizable.

méconnaître, v.tr. (Conj. like CONNAÎTRE) To fail to recognize. (a) To misappreciate; to disregard. M. les faits, to ignore the facts. (b) To disown, disavow.

méconnu, a. Unrecognized, misappreciated, unappreciated; misunderstood.

mécontent. 1. a. (a) Discontented, displeased, dissatisfied. (b) Disaffected. 2. s. Malcontent.

mécontentement, s.m. Dissatisfaction (de, with); displeasure (de, at); disaffection.

mécontenter, v.tr. To dissatisfy, displease.

Mecque (la). Pr.n.f. Geog: Mecca.

mécréant. 1. a. Misbelieving. 2. s. Misbeliever.

médaille [-da:j], s.f. 1. Medal. Le revers de la médaille, F: the other side of the picture. 2. (Porter's) badge. 3. Arch: Medallion.

médaillon [-dajɔ̃], s.m. 1. Medallion. 2. Locket.

médecin, s.m. Medical man, doctor, physician. M. chirurgien, general practitioner.

médecine, s.f. 1. (Art of) medicine. 2. (Dose of) medicine.

médiateur, -trice. 1. a. Mediating. 2. s. Mediator; intermediary.

médiation, s.f. Mediation.

médical, -aux, a. Medical.

médicament, s.m. Medicament. F: medicine.

médicinal, -aux, a. Medicinal.

médiéval, -aux, a. Medi(a)eval.

médiocre, a. Mediocre; indifferent.

médiocrité, s.f. Mediocrity.

médire, v.i. (Conj. like DIRE, except pr.ind. and imp. médisez) M de qn, to speak ill of s.o.; to slander, vilify, s.o.

médisance, s.f. Slander, backbiting.

médisant. 1. a. Backbiting. 2. s. Slanderer, backbiter.

méditatif, a. Meditative.

méditation, s.f. Meditation; musing.

méditer. 1. v.i. To meditate, to muse. 2. v.tr. To contemplate (a journey); to have (sth.) in mind.

méditerrané, a. Inland, landlocked. La Méditerranée, the Mediterranean.

méditerranéen, -enne, a. Mediterranean.

médium [-djɔm], s.m. Psychics: Medium.

médoc [-dɔk], s.m. (Also **vin de Médoc**) Medoc (claret).

médullaire, a. Medullary.

Méduse. 1. Pr.n.f. Gr.Myth: Medusa. 2. s.f. Coel: Medusa, jelly-fish.

méduser, v.tr. F: To petrify; to paralyse with fear or astonishment.

méfait, s.m. Misdeed, ill deed.

méfiance, s.f. Distrust, mistrust.

méfiant, a. Distrustful, mistrustful, suspicious.

méfier (se), v.pr. Se m. de qn, to distrust, mistrust, s.o. Méfiez-vous des voleurs, beware of pickpockets.

mégalomane, s.m. & f. Megalomaniac.

mégaphone, s.m. Megaphone.

mégarde (par), adv.phr Inadvertently; through carelessness.

mégère, s.f. Shrew, termagant, scold.

mégot, s.m. F: Fag-end (of cigarette).

méhari, s.m. Fast dromedary; racing camel. pl. Des méhara.

meilleur [-jœːr], a. I. Better. De meilleure heure, earlier. adv. Il fait meilleur, the weather is better. 2. Le meilleur, (i) the better (of two); (ii) the best. s. Le m. est de s'en aller, it is best to go away.

mélancolie, s.f. Melancholy, dejection.

mélancolique, a. Melancholy, gloomy.

mélancoliquement, adv Mournfully, gloomily.

Mélanésie. Pr.n.f. Geog: Melanesia.

mélange, s.m. I. Mixing; blending. 2. Mixture; blend. Lit: Mélanges en prose, prose miscellany.

mélanger, v.tr. (n. mélangeons) To mix, to mingle; to blend (teas).

mélasse, s.f. Molasses, F: treacle. M. raffinée, golden syrup.

mêlée, s.f. (a) Conflict, mêlée. (b) F: Scuffle, free fight. (c) Scrimmage.

mêler, v.tr. To mix, mingle, blend. (a) Il est mêlé à tout, F: he has a finger in every pie. (b) To put out of order. Mêler les cartes, to shuffle the cards.

se mêler, to mix, mingle, blend. F: Le diable s'en mêle! the devil's in it! Se mêler de politique, to dabble in politics.

mêlé, a. Tangled; tousled; involved (business).

mélèze, s.m. Larch(-tree or -wood).

melliflu, a. Mellifluous, honeyed.

mélodie, s.f. I. Melody, tune. 2. Melodiousness.

mélodieusement, adv. Melodiously, tunefully.

mélodieux, a. Melodious, tuneful.

mélodramatique, a. Melodramatic.

mélodrame, s.m. Melodrama.

melon, s.m. I. Bot: Melon. 2. P: Simpleton. 3. (Chapeau) melon, bowler (hat).

membrane, s.f. Membrane.

membraneux, a. Membranous.

membre, s.m. Member. I. (a) Limb. (b) Member or fellow. 2. Constituent part.

membrure, s.f. (a) Coll. Limbs. Homme à forte m., powerfully built man. (b) Frame(-work).

même. I. a. (a) Same. En même temps, at the same time; at once. Pron.neut. Cela revient au même, it comes to the same thing. (b) (Following the noun). Very. C'est cela même, that's the very thing. (c) Self Elle est la bonté même, she is kindness itself. Moi-même, myself. Vous-même, yourself. Vous-mêmes, yourselves. 2. adv. Even. M. si je le savais, even if I knew. 3. De même, in the same way; likewise. De même que, (just) as, like. Tout de même, all the same; for all that. Boire à même la bouteille, to drink straight out of the bottle. Des maisons bâties à m. le trottoir, houses built flush with the pavement. Escalier taillé à m. la pierre, steps cut out of the solid rock. Être à même de faire qch., to be able to do sth.; to be in a position to do sth.

mémento, s.m. (a) Memorandum, note. (b) Memento, reminder.

mémo, s.m. F: = MÉMORANDUM.

mémoire[1], s.f. Memory. (a) Si j'ai bonne mémoire, if I remember rightly. (b) Recollection, remembrance. Garder la m. de qch., to keep sth. in mind.

mémoire[2], s.m. I. (a) Memorial; (written) statement. (b) Memoir, thesis. 2. Account; bill. 3. pl Memoirs.

mémorable, a. Memorable; eventful.

mémorandum [-dɔm], s.m. I. Memorandum, note. 2. Note-book.

mémorial, -aux, s.m. Memorial; memoirs.

menaçant, a. Menacing, threatening.

menace, s.f. Threat, menace.

menacer, v.tr. (n. menaçons) To threaten, menace. Menacer qn du poing, to shake one's fist at s.o.

ménage, s.m. I. (a) Housekeeping. (b) Faire le ménage, to do the housework. Femme de ménage, charwoman. 2. Household goods. 3. Household, family. (a) Jeune ménage, young married couple. Se mettre en ménage, to set up house. (b) Faire bon ménage (ensemble), to live happily together.

ménagement, s.m. Caution, care, consideration. Parler sans ménagement(s), to speak bluntly.

ménager[1], v.tr. (n. ménageons) I. (a) To save; to be sparing of (sth.). M. ses ressources, to husband one's resources. M. son cheval, to spare one's horse. M. qn, to deal tactfully with s.o. Ne le ménagez pas, don't spare him. (b) Sans ménager ses termes, without mincing one's words. 2. To contrive, arrange. M. une surprise à qn, to prepare a surprise for s.o.

ménager[2]. I. a. (a) Travaux ménagers, housework (b) Thrifty, sparing. s. Être m. de ses éloges, to be sparing of praise. 2. s.f. Ménagère, housekeeper, housewife.

ménagerie, s.f Menagerie.

mendiant. I. a. Mendicant, begging. 2. s. Mendicant; beggar Les quatre mendiants, F: almonds, raisins, nuts and figs.

mendicité, s.f. Mendicity, begging.

mendier. I. v.i. To beg. 2. v.tr M. son pain, to beg (for) one's bread.

menée, *s.f.* Underhand manœuvre, intrigue. *pl.* Schemings. *Déjouer les menées de qn,* to thwart s.o.

mener, *v.tr.* (Je **mène**) **1.** To lead. (*a*) *M. qn à sa chambre,* to take s.o. to his room. (*b*) To be or go ahead (of). *M. le deuil,* to be chief mourner. *Games: M. par huit points,* to lead by eight points. (*c*) *Cela nous mène à croire que . . .,* that leads us to believe that. . . . (*d*) To control, manage. *Mari mené par sa femme,* hen-pecked husband. **2.** To drive; to ride; to steer. **3.** To manage, conduct (business).

ménestrel, *s.m.* Minstrel.

ménétrier, *s.m.* (Strolling) fiddler.

meneur, -euse, *s.* (*a*) Leader. (*b*) Ringleader. (*c*) Driver (of machine). (*d*) *M. de bœufs,* cattle-drover.

menhir, *s.m.* Menhir; standing stone.

méningite, *s.f. Med:* Meningitis.

menotte, *s.f.* **1.** *F:* (Child's) little hand. **2.** *pl.* Handcuffs.

men-s, -t. See MENTIR.

mensonge, *s.m.* (*a*) Lie, untruth, falsehood. (*b*) Error, fallacy.

mensonger, *a.* Lying, untrue; deceitful; illusory.

mensuel, -elle, *a* Monthly.

mensuellement, *adv* Monthly; each month.

mental, -aux, *a.* Mental.

mentalement, *adv.* Mentally.

mentalité, *s.f.* Mentality.

menteur, -euse. 1. *a.* (*a*) Lying, mendacious; given to lying. (*b*) False, deceptive. **2.** *s.* Liar.

menteusement, *adv.* Falsely.

menthe, *s.f. Bot:* Mint. *M. verte,* spearmint, garden mint. *M. poivrée,* peppermint. *Pastilles de m.,* peppermint lozenges.

mention, *s.f.* (*a*) Mention. (*b*) *Post:* Endorsement. *M. "inconnu,"* endorsed 'not known.' (*c*) Reference (at head of letter).

mentionner, *v.tr.* To mention.

mentir, *v.i.* (*pr.p.* **mentant;** *pr.ind.* **je mens**) To lie; to tell lies, stories. **Sans mentir!** honour bright !

menton, *s.m.* Chin.

mentor, *s.m.* Mentor.

menu. 1. *a.* Small. (*a*) Fine (gravel); slender, slight (figure); tiny. **Menue monnaie,** small change. (*b*) Trifling. *Menus détails,* minute details. *Menus frais,* petty expenses. **2.** *adv.* Small, fine. **Hacher menu,** to chop up small; to mince. **3.** *s.m.* (*a*) Raconter qch. par le menu, to relate sth. in detail. (*b*) Bill of fare, menu.

menuet, *s.m.* Minuet.

menuiserie, *s.f.* **1.** Joinery, woodwork, carpentry. **2.** Joiner's shop.

menuisier, *s.m.* Joiner. *M. en bâtiments,* carpenter

méphitique, *a* Mephitic, foul, noisome.

méprendre (se), *v.pr.* (Conj. like PRENDRE)

To be mistaken, to make a mistake. **Il n'y a pas à s'y méprendre,** there can be no mistake about it.

mépris, *s.m.* Contempt, scorn.

méprisable, *a.* Contemptible, despicable.

méprisant, *a.* Contemptuous, scornful.

méprise, *s.f.* Mistake, misapprehension.

mépriser, *v.tr.* To despise, scorn; to hold in contempt.

mer, *s.f.* Sea. (*a*) **Le bord de la mer,** the seaside. **Il y a de la mer,** there is a heavy sea. **Essuyer un coup de mer,** to be struck by a heavy sea. **Un homme à la mer!** man overboard ! **Sur mer,** afloat. **Prendre la mer,** to put (out) to sea. *Mettre une embarcation à la mer,* to lower a boat. (*b*) **Basse mer,** low water.

mercantile, *a.* Mercantile; commercial.

mercenaire. 1. *a.* Mercenary, venal. **2.** *s.m. Mil:* Mercenary.

mercerie, *s.f.* Haberdashery.

merci. 1. *s.f.* (*a*) *F:* **Dieu merci,** thank God. (*b*) **A merci,** at pleasure. (*c*) Mercy. **2.** *adv.* (*a*) Thank you. (*b*) No, thank you. *Prenez-vous du thé?—Merci!* Will you have some tea?—No, thank you !

mercier, *s.* Haberdasher.

mercredi, *s.m.* Wednesday.

Mercure. 1. *Pr.n.m.* Mercury. **2.** *s.m. Ch:* Mercury, quicksilver.

mère, *s.f.* **1.** (*a*) Mother. (*b*) *F:* **La mère Dupont,** old Mrs Dupont. (*c*) *Ecc:* **Mère supérieure,** mother superior. **2.** Source, origin.

méridien, *s.m* Meridian.

méridional, -aux. 1. *a.* (*a*) Meridional. (*b*) South(ern). **2.** *s.* Southerner.

meringue, *s.f. Cu:* Meringue.

mérinos [-nɔs], *s.m.* Merino (sheep, cloth).

merise, *s.f.* Wild cherry; gean.

merisier, *s.m.* Wild cherry(-tree).

mérite, *s.m.* Merit. (*a*) *M:* Desert, worth. (*b*) Excellence, talent.

mériter, *v.tr.* **1.** To deserve, merit. *Cela mérite d'être vu,* it is worth seeing. **2.** To earn

méritoire, *a.* Meritorious, deserving.

merlan, *s.m. Ich:* Whiting.

merle, *s.m. Orn:* Blackbird. **Merle blanc,** *F:* rara avis.

merluche, *s.f.* **1.** *Ich:* Hake. **2.** Dried cod.

merveille [-vɛːj], *s.f* Marvel, wonder. **Crier merveille,** to exclaim in admiration. **A merveille,** excellently *Se porter à m.,* to be in excellent health.

merveilleusement |-vɛj-], *adv.* Marvellously, wonderfully.

merveilleux [-vɛjø] *a.* Marvellous, wonderful.

mes. See MON

mésalliance, *s.f.* Misalliance *Faire une m.,* to marry beneath one.

mésange, *s.f. Orn:* Tit(mouse)

mésaventure, *s.f.* Misadventure, mishap.

mesdames, -demoiselles. See MADAME, MADEMOISELLE

mésentente, *s.f.* Misunderstanding, disagreement.

mésestime, *s.f.* Disesteem, low esteem.

mésestimer, *v.tr.* **1.** To undervalue, underrate. **2.** To hold in low esteem.

mésintelligence, *s.f.* Disagreement.

mésinterprétation, *s.f.* Misinterpretation.

mésinterpréter, *v.tr.* (Conj. like INTER-PRÉTER) To misinterpret, misconstrue.

mesmérique, *a.* Mesmeric.

Mésopotamie. *Pr.n.f.* Mesopotamia.

mesquin, *a.* (*a*) Mean, shabby; paltry, petty. (*b*) Mean, stingy.

mesquinement, *adv.* Meanly, shabbily; pettily.

mesquinerie, *s.f.* **1.** Meanness. (*a*) Pettiness. (*b*) Niggardliness. **2.** Shabby action.

message, *s.m.* Message.

messager, *s.* **1.** Messenger. **2.** *s.m.* Carrier.

messagerie, *s.f.* Carrying trade. **Service de messageries,** parcel delivery.

messe, *s.f. Ecc :* Mass.

messeigneurs. See MONSEIGNEUR.

Messie. *Pr.n.m.* Messiah.

messieurs. See MONSIEUR.

mesurage, *s.m.* Measuring, measurement.

mesure, *s.f.* Measure. **1.** (*a*) **Prendre la mesure de qn,** (i) to take s.o.'s measurements, (ii) *F :* to size s.o. up. **Dans une certaine mesure,** in some degree. *Adv.phr.* **A mesure,** in proportion; successively; one by one. **A mesure que,** (in proportion) as. *A m. que je reculais il s'avançait,* as (fast as) I retired he advanced. (*b*) **Prendre des mesures,** to take action. *Prendre ses mesures,* to make one's arrangements. **2.** (*a*) Gauge, standard. *Poids et mesures,* weights and measures. (*b*) (Quantity measured out) *Une m. de vin,* a measure of wine. **3.** Standard size or amount. *F :* **Garder la mesure,** to keep within bounds. **Être en mesure de faire qch.,** to be in a position to do sth. **4.** *Mus :* (*a*) Bar. (*b*) Time. **Battre la mesure,** to beat time.

mesurer, *v.tr.* **1.** (*a*) To measure. **Mesurer qn des yeux,** to eye s.o. up and down. (*b*) *Colonne qui mesure vingt pieds,* column that measures twenty feet. (*c*) **Mesurer la nourriture à qn,** to grudge s.o. his food. **2.** To calculate; to weigh (one's words).

　　se mesurer *avec, contre, qn,* to measure one's strength against s.o.

　　mesuré, *a.* Measured (tread); temperate, restrained.

métairie, *s.f.* Small farm.

métal, -aux, *s.m.* Metal.

métallique, *a.* Metallic.

métallurgie, *s.f.* Metallurgy.

métallurgiste, *s.m.* Metallurgist.

métamorphose, *s.f.* Metamorphosis, transformation.

métamorphoser, *v.tr.* To metamorphose, transform.

　　se métamorphoser, to change completely.

métaphore, *s.f.* Metaphor; figure of speech.

métaphorique, *a.* Metaphorical; figurative.

métaphoriquement, *adv.* Metaphorically, figuratively.

métaphysicien, -ienne, *s.* Metaphysician.

métaphysique. **1.** *a.* Metaphysical; *F :* abstract, abstruse. **2.** *s.f.* Metaphysics.

métapsychique, *s.f.* Psychics.

métayage, *s.m. Husb :* Métayage system (by which farmer pays rent in kind).

métayer, *s.* (*a*) Farmer who pays rent in kind. (*b*) *F :* Farmer.

métempsyc(h)ose [ko:z], *s.f.* Metempsychosis ; transmigration of souls.

météore, *s.m.* Atmospheric phenomenon; meteor.

météorique, *a.* Meteoric.

météorite, *s.m. or f.* Meteorite.

météorologie, *s.f.* Meteorology.

météorologique, *a.* Meteorological. *Bulletin m.,* weather report.

méthode, *s.f.* Method, system.

méthodique, *a.* Methodical, systematic.

méthodiquement, *adv.* Methodically, systematically.

méticuleusement, *adv.* Meticulously, punctiliously.

méticuleux, *a.* Meticulous, punctilious.

métier, *s.m.* **1.** Trade, profession, craft. *M. manuel,* handicraft. **Gens de métier,** professionals. **Tours de métier,** tricks of the trade. **Parler métier,** to talk shop. *F :* **Quel métier !** what a life ! **2.** *Tex :* **Métier à tisser,** loom.

métis, -isse. **1.** *a.* Half-bred; mongrel; hybrid. **2.** *s.* Half-breed; mongrel.

mètre[1], *s.m. Pros :* Metre.

mètre[2], *s.m.* **1.** *Meas :* Metre. **2.** (Metre) rule. *M. à ruban,* tape-measure.

métrique[1]. **1.** *a.* Metrical. **2.** *s.f.* Prosody.

métrique[2], *a.* Metric.

Métro (le), *s.m. F :* The Underground (railway) (in Paris).

métropole, *s.f.* Metropolis.

métropolitain, *a.* Metropolitan.

mets[1] [me], *s.m.* (Article of prepared) food; viand; dish (of food).

mets[2]. See METTRE.

mettre, *v.tr.* (*p.p.* **mis**; *pr.ind.* **je mets, il met**; *p.h.* **je mis**) **1.** (*a*) To put, lay, place. **Mettre qn à la porte,** to turn s.o. out. *J'y mettrai tous mes soins,* I will give the matter every care. *M. du temps à faire qch.,* to take time over sth. (*b*) To put (clothes) on. *M. ses gants,* to draw on one's gloves. **2.** To set, put (in a condition). *M. une machine en mouvement,* to set a machine going. *M. qn à la torture,* to put s.o. to torture. **3.** (*a*) To admit, grant. *Mettons que vous ayez raison,* suppose you are right. *Mettons cent francs,* let's say a hundred francs. (*b*) *Mettez que je n'ai rien dit,* consider that unsaid.

se mettre. I. (a) To go, get. *Se m. au lit*, to go to bed. *Se m. d'une société*, to join an association. (b) To begin, to set about (sth.). *Se m. à l'œuvre*, to set to work. (c) Se mettre à faire qch., to begin to do sth. **2.** To dress. *Se m. en smoking*, to put on a dinner-jacket. **Être bien mis**, to be well dressed. **3.** *Se m. en route*, to start on one's way. **4.** *Le temps se met au beau*, the weather is turning out fine.

ieuble. I. a. Movable. **2.** s.m. Piece of furniture. **Être dans ses meubles**, to have a home of one's own.

ieubler, v.tr. To furnish; to stock (farm).

meublé. I. a. Furnished. **Cave bien meublée**, well-stocked cellar **2.** s.m. Furnished apartment(s).

ieugler, v.i. (Of cow) To low; F: to moo.

ieule, s.f. **I.** (a) Millstone. (b) *M. à aiguiser*, grindstone. **2.** Stack, rick (of hay).

ieunier, s. Miller.

ieur-e, -s, -t. See MOURIR.

ieurtre, s.m. *Jur:* Murder. **Au meurtre!** murder!

ieurtrier. I. a. Murderous; deadly (weapon). **2.** s. Murderer, f. murderess. **3.** s.f. Fort: **Meurtrière**, loop-hole.

ieurtrir, v.tr. To bruise.

meurtri, a. Bruised. **Être tout meurtri**, to be black and blue all over

ieurtrissure, s.f. Bruise.

ieu-s, -t. See MOUVOIR.

ieute, s.f. (a) *Ven:* Pack (of hounds). (b) F: Crowd, mob (of people).

ieuv-e, -ent. See MOUVOIR.

iexicain, a. & s. Mexican.

iexique (le). Pr.n.m. Mexico.

ii¹, adv. Half, mid, semi-. *La mi-avril*, mid-April. *A mi-hauteur*, half-way up.

ii², s.m.inv. *Mus:* (The note) E.

iiaou, s.m. Miaow, mew (of cat).

ii-août [miu], s.f.inv. Mid-August.

iiasme, s.m. Miasma.

iiauler, v.i. To mew; to caterwaul.

iica, s.m. *Miner:* Mica.

ii-carême, s.f. Mid-Lent.

iiche, s.f. Round loaf.

iichel. Pr.n.m. Michael. **La Saint-Michel**, Michaelmas.

iichel-Ange. Pr.n.m. Michelangelo.

iicheline, s.f. Rail-car.

ii-chemin (à), adv.phr. Half-way.

ii-clos, adj. Half-closed.

ii-corps (à), adv.phr. To the waist. *Saisi à mi-c.*, caught round the waist.

ii-côte (à), adv.phr. Half-way up the hill.

iicro, s.m. F: = MICROPHONE. *W.Tel:* Le micro, F: the mike.

iicrobe, s.m. Microbe, F: germ.

iicrocosme, s.m. Microcosm.

iicromètre, s.m. Micrometer.

iicrophone, s.m. Microphone; mouth-piece (of telephone); *W.Tel:* F: mike.

microphoniste, s.m. & f. *W.Tel:* Announcer.

microscope, s.m. Microscope.

microscopique, a. Microscopic(al).

midi, s.m. No pl. **I.** Midday, noon, twelve o'clock. **Arriver sur le midi**, F: sur les midi, to arrive about noon. **Avant midi**, a.m. **Après midi**, p.m. **M. et demi**, half-past twelve. F: **Chercher midi à quatorze heures**, to look for difficulties where there are none. **2.** (a) South. *Chambre au m.*, room facing south. (b) **Le Midi** (de la France), the South of France.

mi-distance, s.f. Middle distance.

mie, s.f. **I.** Crumb (of loaf). **2.** Ne . . . mie, not at all.

miel, s.m. Honey.

mielleusement, adv. With honeyed words.

mielleux, a. **I.** *Goût m.*, taste of honey. **2.** F: Honeyed, sugary; soft-spoken.

mien, mienne. I. poss.a. Mine. **Un mien ami**, a friend of mine. **2.** (a) poss.pron. Le mien, la mienne, les miens, les miennes, mine. (b) s.m. (i) My own (property); mine. Le mien et le tien, mine and thine. (ii) s.m.pl. *J'ai été renié par les miens*, I have been disowned by my own people. (c) s.f.pl. On dit que j'ai encore fait des miennes, they say I've been up to my old tricks again.

miette, s.f. (a) Crumb (of broken bread). (b) F: Morsel.

mieux, adv. **I.** *Comp.* Better. (a) *Ça va m.*, things are improving. *Pour mieux dire . . .*, to be more exact. . . Adv.phr. **Faire qch. à qui mieux mieux**, to vie with one another in doing sth. (b) (With adj. function) (i) C'est on ne peut mieux, it couldn't be better. (ii) *Vous serez m. dans ce fauteuil*, you will be more comfortable in this armchair. (c) s.neut. Le mieux est l'ennemi du bien, leave well alone. **Faute de mieux**, for want of something better. **Je ne demande pas mieux**, I shall be delighted. **2.** *Sup.* Le mieux, (the) best. (a) *La femme le m. habillée de Paris*, the best-dressed woman in Paris. (b) (With adj. function) (i) *C'est tout ce qu'il y a de m.*, there is absolutely nothing better. (ii) **Être le mieux du monde avec qn**, to be on the best of terms with s.o. (c) s.neut. **Faire de son mieux**, to do one's best.

mièvre, a. (a) Fragile, delicate. (b) Finical, affected.

mignard, a. Affected, mincing.

mignarder, v.tr. To pat, caress, fondle.

mignardise, s.f. Affectation; mincing manners.

mignon, -onne. I. a. Dainty, tiny, delicate. **2.** s. Pet, darling, favourite.

migraine, s.f. Sick headache; migraine.

migrateur, -trice, a. Migrating; migrant.

migration, s.f. Migration.

mijaurée, s.f. Conceited, affected, woman.

mijoter, v.tr. To let (sth.) simmer. F:

Mijoter un projet, to turn a scheme over in one's mind.

mil [mil], *a.* (Used only in legal documents in writing out dates A.D.) Thousand.

milan, *s.m. Orn:* Kite.

milice, *s.f.* Militia.

milicien, *s.m.* Militiaman.

milieu, -eux, *s.m.* **1.** Middle, midst. **Au milieu de,** amid(st). **Au beau milieu de la rue,** right in the middle of the street. **2.** (*a*) *Ph:* Medium. (*b*) Surroundings, environment; (social) sphere. *Dans les milieux autorisés,* in responsible quarters. **3.** Middle course; mean. **Le juste milieu,** the happy medium.

militaire. 1. *a.* Military. **2.** *s.m.* Soldier. *Les militaires,* the military.

militant, *a.* Militant.

militarisme, *s.m.* Militarism.

militer, *v.i.* To militate. *Cela milite en sa faveur,* that tells in his favour.

mille¹, *num.a.inv. & s.m.inv.* Thousand. *M. hommes,* a thousand men. *M. un,* a thousand and one. (But) **Les Mille et une Nuits,** the Arabian Nights. **Il a des mille et des cents,** he has tons of money.

mille², *s.m.* Mile.

millénaire. 1. *a.* Millennial. **2.** *s.m.* Thousand years; millennium.

millénium [-jɔm], *s.m.* Millennium.

mille-pattes, *s.m.inv.* Centipede.

mille-pertuis, *s.m.inv. Bot:* St John's wort.

millésime, *s.m.* Date (on coin).

millet [mijɛ], *s.m. Bot:* Millet. **(Grains de) millet,** canary-seed.

milliard, *s.m.* Milliard; one thousand million(s).

milliardaire, *a. & s.m.* Multi-millionaire.

millième. 1. *num.a. & s.* Thousandth. **2.** *s.m.* (One-)thousandth (part).

millier, *s.m.* (About a) thousand; *F:* a thousand or so. *Des milliers,* thousands.

million, *s.m.* Million.

millionnaire, *a. & s.* Millionaire (in French currency).

mime, *s.m.* Mimic.

mimer, *v.tr.* To mimic, to ape (s.o.).

mimique. 1. *a.* Mimic. **2.** *s.f.* (*a*) Mimicry. (*b*) *F:* Dumb show.

mimosa, *s.m. Bot:* Mimosa.

minable, *a. F:* Seedy-looking (person); shabby (appearance).

minaret, *s.m.* Minaret.

minauder, *v.i.* To simper, smirk.

minauderie, *s.f.* Simpering, smirking.

mince. 1. *a.* Thin; slender, slim (person); *F:* scanty (income). **2.** *int. P:* **Mince alors!** well I never!

minceur, *s.f.* Thinness; slenderness, slimness.

mine¹, *s.f.* **1.** Mine. (*a*) **M. de houille,** coal-mine. (*b*) **M. flottante,** floating mine. **2. Mine de plomb,** graphite, black-lead.

mine², *s.f.* Appearance, look, mien. (*a*) Av de la mine, to be good-looking. **Il ne pa pas de mine,** his appearance is against hi (*b*) (Of health) **Avoir bonne mine,** to look we (*c*) **Faire bonne mine à mauvais jeu, to g** and bear it. **Faire grise mine,** to look an thing but pleased. **Faire la mine,** to lo sulky. **Faire des mines,** to simper.

miner, *v.tr.* To mine, undermine. *Miné p l'envie,* consumed with envy.

minerai, *s.m.* Ore.

minéral, -aux. 1. *a.* Mineral. *Sour minérale,* spa. **2.** *s.m.* Mineral.

minet, -ette, *s.* Puss(y); *f.* tabby; *F:* p darling.

mineur¹, -euse. 1. *a.* Burrowing. **2.** *s.* (*a*) Miner. (*b*) *Mil:* Sapper.

mineur², -eure. 1. *a.* (*a*) Minor, lesse (*b*) *Jur:* Under age. **2.** *s.* Minor.

miniature, *s.f.* Miniature.

minier, *a.* Mining.

minime, *a.* Small; trivial; trifling.

minimum [-mɔm]. Minimum. **1.** *s.* **Thermomètre à minima,** minimum therm meter. *pl.* **Des minima, des minimums. 2.** *La largeur, les largeurs, minimum* or *minim* the minimum width(s).

ministère, *s.m.* **1.** (*a*) Agency. (*b*) *Ec* **Le saint ministère,** the ministry. **2.** *Adm* Ministry. (*a*) Office. (*b*) *Former un m.,* form a ministry, a government. (*c*) Gover ment department.

ministériel, -elle, *a.* Ministerial. *Cri ministérielle,* cabinet crisis.

ministre, *s.m.* **1.** *Ecc:* (Protestant) minister clergyman. **2.** Minister; Secretary of Stat

minois, *s.m. F:* Pretty face (of child).

minorité, *s.f.* Minority.

Minorque. *Pr.n.m. Geog:* Minorca.

minoterie, *s.f.* (Large) flour-mill.

minuit, *s.m.* Midnight. *M. et demi,* half-pa twelve at night.

minuscule, *a.* (*a*) Small, minute, tiny (*b*) **Lettre minuscule,** *s.f.* **minuscule,** sma letter.

minute, *s.f.* **1.** Minute. **Réparations à l minute,** repairs while you wait. **2.** (*a*) Minut draft. (*b*) Record (of deed).

minutie, *s.f.* Minute detail; trifle.

minutieusement, *adv.* Thoroughly, min utely.

minutieux, *a.* Scrupulously careful; minute detailed.

mioche, *s.m. & f. F:* Small child; urchin.

mi-parti, *a.* Parti-coloured.

miracle, *s.m.* Miracle. **Fait à miracle,** mar vellously well done.

miraculeusement, *adv.* Miraculously *F:* marvellously.

miraculeux, *a.* Miraculous; *F:* marvellous

mirage, *s.m.* Mirage.

mire, *s.f.* Aiming (of fire-arm). **Ligne de mire** line of sight. **Point de m.,** aim. *F:* **Point d mire de tous les yeux,** cynosure of all eyes.

mirer, *v.tr* (*a*) To aim at (*b*) *Surv:* To take a sight on
se mirer, to look at, admire, oneself.
mirifique, *a. F:* Wonderful.
miroir, *s.m* Mirror, looking-glass.
miroitant, *a* Flashing; shimmering
miroitement, *s.m* Flashing; glistening; shimmer
miroiter, *v.i.* To flash; to shimmer; to sparkle
mis, -e. See METTRE.
misanthrope. 1. *s.m* Misanthrope. **2.** *a.* Misanthropic(al).
misanthropie, *s.f.* Misanthropy
mise, *f* **1.** (*a*) Placing; putting. **Mise à l'eau,** launching (*b*) Setting. **M. en liberté,** release **Mise en retraite,** pensioning (off) **Mise en marche,** starting (of engine). **2.** Dress, attire **3.** (*a*) *Gaming:* Stake. (*b*) Bid (a sale)
misérable. 1. *a.* Miserable. (*a*) Unhappy, unfortunate; wretched. (*b*) Despicable, mean **2.** *s* (*a*) Poor wretch (*b*) Scoundrel, wretch.
misérablement, *adv.* Miserably.
misère, *s f.* **1.** (*a*) Misery (*b*) Trouble, ill. *Misères domestiques,* domestic worries **2.** Extreme poverty; destitution. **Crier misère,** to make a poor mouth. **3.** *F:* Trifle *Cent francs?* **Une misère!** a hundred francs? a mere nothing! **4.** *Cards:* Misère.
miséreux, *a. & s.* Poverty-stricken.
miséricorde, *s.f.* **1.** Mercy, mercifulness. **Crier miséricorde,** to cry for mercy **2.** *int.* Goodness gracious!
miséricordieux, *a. & s.* Merciful
misogame, *s.m & f.* Misogamist.
misogyne, *s.m* Misogynist, woman-hater
missel, *s.m.* Missal; (altar) mass-book
mission, *s.f.* Mission.
missionnaire, *s.m.* Missionary.
missive, *s.f.* Missive; letter.
mistral, *s.m.* Mistral.
mitaine, *s.f.* Mitten. **F: Dire qch. sans mitaines,** to tell sth. bluntly.
mite, *s.f.* **1.** Mite. **M. du fromage,** cheese-mite. **2.** Clothes-moth.
mité, *a.* Moth-eaten.
mitigation, *s.f* Mitigation.
mitiger, *v.tr.* (n. mitigeons) **1.** To mitigate. **2.** To relax (rule)
mitoyen, -enne, *a.* Intermediate *Mur m.,* party wall
mitraille [-ra:j], *s.f* Grape-shot
mitrailler [-raje], *v.tr* To rake with machine-gun fire.
mitraillette [-raj-], *s.f.* Sub machine-gun.
mitrailleur [-raj-], *s.m.* Machine-gunner. *a.* **Fusil mitrailleur,** automatic rifle.
mitrailleuse [-raj-], *s.f.* Machine-gun.
mitre, *s.f.* Mitre (of bishop).
mi-vitesse (à), *adv.phr.* At half-speed.
mi-voix (à), *adv.phr.* In an undertone, under one's breath, in a subdued voice.

mixte, *a.* **1.** Mixed. *Commission m,* joint commission. *s.m. Ten:* **Mixte double,** mixed doubles **2.** Serving a double purpose *Train m.,* composite train
mobile. 1. *a.* (*a*) Mobile, movable. (*b*) Unstable, changeable, fickle (nature). (*c*) Detachable. (*d*) Moving; changing (expression) *Mil: Colonne m.,* flying column. **2.** *s.m.* (*a*) Moving body. (*b*) Driving power. (i) *Premier m. dans un complot,* prime mover in a plot. (ii) *M. d'un crime,* motive of a crime.
mobilier. 1. *a. Jur:* Movable, personal. **2.** *s.m.* (*a*) Furniture. (*b*) Suite of furniture
mobilisation, *s.f* Mobilization: liberation (of capital).
mobiliser, *v.tr.* To mobilize; to liberate (capital)
mobilité, *s.f.* **1.** Mobility, movableness. **2.** Changeableness, instability
mocassin, *s.m.* Moccasin.
mode[1], *s.f.* **1.** Fancy, fashion. **Être de mode, à la mode,** to be in fashion, in vogue. **A la mode de . . .,** after the style of. . . . **2.** *pl Com:* (*a*) Ladies' dresses fashions. (*b*) **(Articles de) modes,** millinery.
mode[2], *s.m* **1.** *Gram:* Mood. **2.** Method, mode. **"Mode d'emploi,"** 'directions for use.'
modèle. 1. *s.m.* (*a*) Model, pattern. (*b*) *Cost:* Model frock or hat. **2.** *s.m.* (Artist's) model. **3.** *a. Un époux m.,* a model husband.
modeler *v.tr* (je modèle) To model; to mould.
modérateur, -trice. 1. *a.* Moderating, restraining. **2.** *s.* Moderator. **3.** *s.m.* Regulator.
modération, *s.f.* Moderation, restraint.
modérément, *adv.* Moderately.
modérer, *v.tr.* (je modère; je modérerai) **1.** To moderate, restrain; *M. son impatience,* to curb one's impatience **2.** To reduce.
se modérer. 1. To control oneself **2.** To abate.
modéré, *a.* Moderate; temperate; reasonable (price).
moderne, *a.* Modern
moderniser, *v.tr.* To modernize.
modeste, *a.* Modest; unassuming; quiet (dress).
modestement, *adv.* Modestly, unpretentiously.
modestie, *s.f.* Modesty; unpretentiousness.
modicité, *s.f.* Moderateness; slenderness (of means); reasonableness (of price).
modificateur, -trice, *a.* Modifying.
modification, *s.f.* Modification, alteration.
modifier, *v.tr.* **1.** To modify; to alter, change. **2.** *Gram:* To qualify, modify (the verb).
modique, *a.* Moderate, reasonable (cost); slender (income).
modiste, *s.f.,* occ. *m.* Milliner, modiste.
modulation, *s.f.* Modulation, inflexion.
moduler, *v.tr.* To modulate.

7

moelle [mwal], *s.f.* **1.** Marrow (of bone). *Corrompu jusqu'à la m.*, rotten to the core. *Discours plein de m.*, pithy discourse. **2.** *Bot:* Pith.

moelleusement [mwal-], *adv.* Softly, luxuriously.

moelleux [mwalø], *a.* **1.** (*a*) Marrowy (bone). (*b*) *Bot:* Pithy. **2.** (*a*) Soft, velvety; mellow. (*b*) *s.m.* Softness; mellowness.

mœurs [mœrs], *s.f.pl.* Morals or manners (of people); customs (of country); habits (of animals). **Gens sans mœurs,** unprincipled people.

moi. **1.** Stressed *pers.pron.* (*a*) (Subject) I. *Elle est invitée et moi aussi*, she is invited and so am I. *Moi, je veux bien*, for my part, I am willing. (*b*) (Object) Me. **A moi,** help! *De vous à moi*, between you and me. *Ce livre est à moi*, this book is mine. (*c*) (After imp.) (i) (acc.) *Laissez-moi tranquille*, leave me alone. (ii) (dat.) *Donnez-le-moi*, give it (to) me. **2.** *s.m.* Ego, self.

moignon, *s.m.* Stump (of amputated limb).

moindre, *a.* **1.** *Comp.* Less(er). **2.** *Sup.* **Le, la, moindre,** the least. *s.* **Le moindre d'entre nous,** the least of us.

moine, *s.m.* Monk, friar.

moineau, *s.m.* *Orn:* Sparrow.

moins. **1.** *adv.* (*a*) *Comp.* Less. *M. de dix francs*, less than ten francs. *F: Trois voitures, pas moins!* three cars, no less! *En m. de dix minutes*, within, under, ten minutes. **Dix francs de moins,** (i) ten francs less; (ii) ten francs short. *Prep.phr.* **A moins de,** unless, barring. *A m. d'avis contraire*, unless I hear to the contrary. **A moins que** + *sub.*, unless. *A m. que vous (ne) l'ordonniez*, unless you order it. **Rien moins que,** (ambiguous) (i) anything but; (ii) nothing less than. **Non moins que,** as well as; quite as much as. (*b*) *Sup.* **Le moins,** least. *Les élèves les m. appliqués*, the least industrious pupils. **Pas le moins du monde,** not in the least (degree); by no means. *s.neut.* **C'est bien le moins** (*qu'il puisse faire*), it is the least he can do. *Adv.phr.* **Du moins,** at least, that is to say, at all events. **Au moins,** at least (= not less than). **Vous compterez cela en moins,** you may deduct that. **2.** (*a*) *prep.* Minus, less. *Une heure m. cinq*, five minutes to one. (*b*) *s.m. Mth:* Minus sign.

moire, *s.f.* Moire; watered material.

moiré, *a.* *Tex:* Watered, moiré (silk).

mois, *s.m.* Month. *Du m. prochain*, proximo. *Du m. dernier*, ultimo. *De ce m.*, instant.

Moïse. *Pr.n.m. B.Hist:* Moses.

moisir, *v.i. & pr.* To mildew; to go mouldy.

moisi. **1.** *a.* Mouldy, mildewy; musty. **2.** *s.m.* Mould, mildew. **Sentir le moisi,** to smell musty.

moisissure, *s.f.* **1.** Mildew; mould. **2.** Mouldiness, mustiness.

moisson, *s.f.* **1.** (*a*) Harvest(ing) (of cereals). (*b*) Harvest-time. **2.** (Cereal) crop.

moissonner, *v.tr.* To reap; to harvest, gather.

moissonneur, -euse, *s.* **1.** Harvester, reaper. **2.** *s.f.* Moissonneuse, reaping-machine.

moite, *a.* Moist (brow). (**Froid et**) **moite,** clammy.

moiteur, *s.f.* Moistness (of hands). *M. froide*, clamminess.

moitié. **1.** *s.f.* Half. **Couper qch. par (la) moitié,** to cut something into halves. **Moitié plus,** half as much again. *Être de m. avec qn*, to take share and share alike. *Adv.phr.* **A moitié,** half. *A m. mort*, half-dead. **2.** *adv.* *M. l'un, m. l'autre*, half and half.

moitir, *v.tr.* To moisten.

Moka. **1.** *Pr.n.* Mocha. **2.** *s.m.* Mocha (coffee).

mol. See MOU.

molaire, *a. & s.f.* Molar (tooth); *F:* grinder.

môle, *s.m.* Mole; (harbour) breakwater.

moléculaire, *a.* Molecular.

molécule, *s.f.* Molecule.

molestation, *s.f.* Molestation.

molester, *v.tr.* To molest.

molle. See MOU.

mollement, *adv.* (*a*) Softly. (*b*) Slackly, feebly; indolently.

mollesse, *s.f.* (*a*) Softness; flabbiness. (*b*) Slackness, lifelessness. (*c*) Indolence.

mollet, *s.m.* Calf (of leg).

molletière, *a. & s.f.* (**Bandes**) **molletières,** puttees.

mollir. **1.** *v.i.* (*a*) To soften; to become soft. (*b*) To slacken; to abate. **2.** *v.tr.* To slacken (rope).

mollusque, *s.m.* Mollusc.

molosse, *s.m.* Watch-dog; mastiff.

moment, *s.m.* Moment. *Le m. venu . . .*, when the time had come. *. . . J'ai répondu sur le moment*, I answered on the spur of the moment. **Arriver au bon moment,** to arrive in the nick of time. **Par moments,** at times, now and again. **A tout moment, à tous moments,** constantly. **Au m. donné,** at the appointed time. *Conj.phr.* **Du moment que . . .,** seeing that. . . .

momentané, *a.* Momentary; temporary.

momentanément, *adv.* Momentarily; temporarily.

momie, *s.f.* Mummy.

momifier, *v.tr.* To mummify.

mon, ma, mes, *poss.a.* (*Mon* is used instead of *ma* before *f.* words beginning with vowel or *h* 'mute.') My. *Mon ami, mon amie*, my friend. *Un de mes amis*, a friend of mine. *Non, mon colonel*, no, sir.

monarchie, *s.f.* Monarchy.

monarchique, *a.* Monarchic(al).

monarchiste, *a. & s.* Monarchist.

monarque, *s.m.* Monarch.

monastère, *s.m.* Monastery; convent.

monastique, *a.* Monastic.

nonceau, *s.m.* Heap, pile.

nondain, *a.* **I.** Mundane, worldly. *s.* Worldling. **2.** Fashionable. *s.* Un mondain, a man about town. Une mondaine, a society woman.

nonde, *s.m.* **I.** World. (*a*) Il est encore de ce monde, he is still alive. Pour rien au monde, not for the world, not on any account. Être le mieux du monde avec qn, to be on the best of terms with s.o. Vieux comme le monde, (as) old as the hills. (*b*) Society. Le beau monde, (fashionable) society. Le grand monde, high society. Homme du monde, man of the world. **2.** People. (*a*) Avoir du monde à dîner, to have company to dinner. Il connaît son monde, he knows the people he has to deal with. Tout le monde, everybody, everyone. (*b*) Servants.

nondial, -aux, *a.* World-wide.

nonégasque, *a. & s.* (Native) of Monaco.

nonétaire, *a.* Monetary.

nongol, *a. & s. Ethn:* Mongol, Mongolian.

nongolique, *a.* Mongolian.

noniteur, -trice, *s. Sch:* Monitor.

nonnaie, *s.f.* **I.** Money. Pièce de monnaie, coin. M. *légale,* legal tender. (Hôtel de) la Monnaie, the Mint. *F:* Payer qn en monnaie de singe, to let s.o. whistle for his money. **2.** Change. *F:* Rendre à qn la monnaie de sa pièce, to pay s.o. (back) in his own coin.

nonnayer, *v.tr.* (je monnaie, je monnaye) To coin, mint.

nonnayeur, *s.m.* Coiner, minter. Faux monnayeur, coiner, counterfeiter.

nonochrome, *a.* Monochrome

nonocle, *s.m.* Monocle.

nonocotylédone, *Bot:* **I.** *a.* Monocotyledonous. **2.** *s.f.* Monocotyledon.

nonogamie, *s.f.* Monogamy.

nonogramme, *s.m.* Monogram.

nonographie, *s.f.* Monograph.

nonolithe. **I.** *a* Monolithic. **2.** *s.m.* Monolith.

nonologue, *s.m.* Monologue.

nonologuer, *v.i.* To soliloquize.

nonomane, monomaniaque. **I.** *a.* Monomaniac(al). **2.** *s.* Monomaniac, person of one idea.

nonomanie, *s.f.* Monomania, obsession.

nonoplace, *a. & s.m.* Single-seater.

nonoplan, *s.m. Av:* Monoplane.

nonopole, *s.m.* Monopoly.

nonopoliser, *v.tr.* To monopolize.

nonosyllabe. **I.** *a.* Monosyllabic. **2.** *s.m.* Monosyllable.

nonosyllabique, *a.* Monosyllabic.

nonotone, *a.* Monotonous ; *F:* humdrum, dull (life).

nonotonie, *s.f.* Monotony.

nonseigneur, *s.m.* **I.** (*a*) His Royal Highness ; his Eminence ; his Grace ; his Lordship. *pl. Nosseigneurs.* (*b*) Your Royal Highness ; your Eminence ; your Grace ; your Lordship. *pl. Messeigneurs.* **2.** *F;* Pince monseigneur (*inv.*), (burglar's) jemmy.

monsieur, *pl.* **messieurs** [m(ə)sjø, mesjø], *s.m.* **I.** (*a*) *Monsieur, M., Jules Durand,* Mr Jules Durand. *Messieurs, MM., Durand et Cie,* Messrs Durand and Co. *M. le duc de,* the Duke of. *Comment va monsieur votre oncle?* how is your uncle ? (*b*) *Monsieur Jean,* Master John. (*c*) (Used alone) *Voici le chapeau de monsieur,* here is Mr X's hat. *Monsieur n'y est pas,* Mr X is not at home. **2.** (*a*) (In address) Sir. *Bonsoir, messieurs,* good evening, gentlemen. *M. a sonné?* did you ring, sir? *Que prendront ces messieurs?* what will you have, gentlemen ? (*b*) (In letter writing) (i) (To stranger) *Monsieur* (always written in full), Dear Sir. (ii) (Implying some friendship) *Cher Monsieur,* Dear Mr Durand. **3.** Gentleman.

monstre. **I.** *s.m.* (*a*) Monster, monstrosity. (*b*) Monster. *Les monstres marins,* the monsters of the deep. **2.** *a.* Huge ; colossal ; monster.

monstrueusement, *adv.* Monstrously ; colossally.

monstrueux, *a.* Monstrous. **I.** Unnatural. **2.** Huge, colossal. **3.** Shocking, scandalous.

mont, *s.m.* Mount, mountain. *F:* Promettre monts et merveilles à qn, to promise s.o. wonders.

montagnard. **I.** *a.* Mountain, highland. **2.** *s.* Mountaineer, highlander.

montagne, *s.f.* (*a*) Mountain. **Montagnes** russes, switchback. (*b*) Mountain region. (*c*) Montagne de glace, iceberg.

montagneux, *a.* Mountainous, hilly.

montant. **I.** *a.* Rising ; ascending. *Chemin m.,* uphill road. *Rail:* Train montant, up train. **2.** *s.m.* (*a*) Upright (of ladder). (*b*) Total amount (of account).

monte, *s.f.* Rising, mounting.

monténégrin, *a. & s. Geog:* Montenegrin.

monter. **I.** *v.i.* (Aux. usu. *être,* occ. *avoir*) **I.** (*a*) To climb (up), mount, ascend ; to go upstairs. *M. se coucher,* to go (up) to bed. (*b*) To climb on, into (sth.). Monter à cheval, (i) to mount, (ii) to ride. M. *à bord,* to go on board (a ship). **2.** (*a*) To rise, to go up. *Frais montant à mille francs,* expenses amounting to one thousand francs. Faire monter les prix, to raise the prices. *Le sang lui monte à la tête,* the blood rushes to his head. *F:* Monter comme une soupe au lait, to flare up. (*b*) (Of road) To ascend, to climb. (*c*) (Of pers.) *M. dans l'estime de qn,* to rise in s.o.'s estimation.

II. **monter,** *v.tr.* **I.** To mount. (*a*) To climb (up), go up, ascend. (*b*) *Mil:* M. la garde, to mount guard. (*c*) To ride (horse). **2.** *Nau:* To man (boat). **3.** (*a*) To raise, take up. (*b*) *F:* Se monter la tête, to get excited. **4.** (*a*) To set, mount (jewel) ; to fit on (tyre) ; to erect (apparatus) ; to equip. M. un magasin, to open a shop. M. un complot, to hatch a plot.

se monter, to amount.

monté, *a.* **1.** Mounted. *F:* Il était, monté, il avait la tête montée, his blood was up. **2.** *F:* Coup monté, plot; *F:* put-up job.

montée, *s.f.* **1.** Rise. (*a*) Rising. *Mouvement de m.*, up motion. (*b*) Uphill pull; climb. **2.** (*a*) Ascent, gradient, acclivity. (*b*) Step (of stair).

monticule, *s.m.* (*a*) Hillock. (*b*) Hummock.

montre, *s.f.* **1.** (*a*) Show, display. (*b*) Shop-window. **2.** Watch.

montrer, *v.tr.* To show. (*a*) To display, exhibit. (*b*) To point out. (*c*) *M. à qn à faire qch.*, to show s.o. how to do sth.

se montrer. (*a*) *Se m. au bon moment*, to appear at the right moment. (*b*) *Pred.* *Il se montra prudent*, he showed prudence.

montueux, *a.* Hilly.

monture, *s.f.* **1.** Mount (horse, etc.). **2.** Setting (of jewel); mount(ing) (of picture). *Lunettes sans monture*, rimless spectacles.

monument, *s.m.* **1.** Monument, memorial. **2.** Public or historic building.

monumental, -aux, *a.* Monumental.

moquer (se), *v.pr.* *Se m. de qn*, to make fun of s.o. *Vous vous moquez*, you're joking. *C'est se m. du monde!* it is the height of impertinence!

moquerie, *s.f.* Mockery; derision.

moqueur, -euse. **1.** *a.* (*a*) Mocking, scoffing. (*b*) Given to mockery. **2.** *s.* Mocker, scoffer. **3.** *s.m.* Mocking-bird.

moraine, *s.f.* *Geol:* Moraine.

moral, -aux. **1.** *a.* (*a*) Moral; ethical. (*b*) Mental, intellectual. *Courage m.*, moral courage. **2.** *s.m.* (State of) mind; morale. *Relever le m. de, à, qn*, to raise s.o.'s spirits.

moralement, *adv.* Morally.

morale, *s.f.* **1.** (*a*) Morals. (*b*) Ethics; moral science. *F:* Faire de la morale à qn, to read s.o. a lecture. **2.** Moral (of story).

moraliser. **1.** *v.i.* To moralize. **2.** *v.tr.* To lecture, sermonize (s.o.).

moraliste, *s.m. & f.* Moralist.

moralité, *s.f.* **1.** (*a*) Morality; (good) moral conduct. (*b*) Morals; honesty. **2.** Moral lesson.

morbide, *a.* Morbid.

morbidement, *adv.* Morbidly.

morbidité, *s.f.* Morbidity, morbidness.

morceau, *s.m.* **1.** Morsel, piece (of food). Aimer les bons morceaux, to like good things (to eat). *F:* Manger un morceau, to have a snack. *F:* Gober le morceau, to swallow the bait. **2.** Piece (of soap); bit, scrap; lump (of sugar).

morceler, *v.tr.* (je morcelle) To cut up (sth.) into small pieces. *M. une propriété*, to parcel out an estate.

morcellement, *s.m.* Breaking up; parcelling out.

mordant. **1.** *a.* (*a*) Eating away; corrosive. *Lime mordante*, file that has plenty of bite. (*b*) Mordant, biting, caustic. **2.** *s.m.* (*a*)

Corrosiveness; bite (of file). (*b*) Mordancy pungency.

mordoré, *a. & s.m.* Bronze (colour)

mordre, *v.tr. & ind.tr.* To bite. (*a*) *F* Que chien l'a mordu? what's bitten him? Il s'e mord les pouces, he bitterly repents it. S mordre les poings d'impatience, to gnaw one' fingers with impatience. (*b*) *M. à, dans, un pomme*, to take a bite out of an apple. *Fish Ça mord*, I've got a bite. (*c*) (Of cog-wheels To catch, engage.

morfondre, *v.tr.* To chill to the bone.

se morfondre, to be bored to death.

morganatique, *a.* Morganatic.

morgue, *s.f.* **1.** Pride, arrogance. **2.** Mor tuary, morgue.

moribond, *a.* Moribund, at death's door.

moricaud. **1.** *a.* Dark-skinned, dusky swarthy. **2.** *s.* Blackamoor.

morigéner, *v.tr.* (je morigène; je mori génerai) To lecture; to talk seriously to.

mormon, -on(n)e, *a. & s.* Mormon.

mormonisme, *s.m.* Mormonism.

morne, *a.* Dejected; gloomy; dull; dreary

mornement, *adv.* Gloomily, dismally.

morose, *a.* Morose, moody; gloomy.

morphine, *s.f.* Morphia.

morphologie, *s.f.* Morphology.

mors, *s.m.* **1.** *Tls:* Jaw (of vice). **2.** *Harn* Bit. Ronger son mors, (i) (of horse) to champ the bit; (ii) *F:* (of pers.) to fret.

morse¹, *s.m.* *Z:* Walrus, morse.

Morse². *Pr.n.m.* *Tg:* Morse.

morsure, *s.f.* **1.** Bite. **2.** *Engr:* Biting.

mort¹, morte. See MOURIR.

mort², *s.f.* **1.** Death. A mort les traîtres death to the traitors! Se donner la mort, to take one's life. Mourir de sa belle mort, to die a natural death. Il avait la mort dans l'âme, he was sick at heart. **2.** (*a*) *Bot:* Mort au(x) loup(s), wolf's-bane. Mort aux poules, henbane. (*b*) Mort aux rats, rat-poison.

mortaise, *s.f.* Slot. *Carp:* Mortise.

mortalité, *s.f.* Mortality.

morte-eau, *s.f.,* **mortes-eaux,** *s.f.pl.* Neap tide(s); neaps.

mortel, -elle, *a.* Mortal. (*a*) Destined to die. *s.* Un m., une mortelle, a mortal. (*b*) Fatal (wound). (*c*) *F:* Je l'ai attendu deux mortelles heures, I waited two mortal hours for him. (*d*) Deadly. *Ennemi m.*, mortal foe.

mortellement, *adv.* Mortally, fatally. *Pécher m.*, to commit a mortal sin. *F:* S'ennuyer m., to be bored to death.

mortier, *s.m.* Mortar. **1.** (*a*) *Pilon et m.*, pestle and mortar. (*b*) *Artil:* M. de tranchée, trench-mortar. **2.** *Const:* M. ordinaire, lime mortar. *F:* Bâti à chaux et à mortier, built to last for ever.

mortifiant, *a.* Mortifying.

mortification, *s.f.* Mortification.

mortifier, *v.tr.* (*a*) To mortify (one's passions). (*b*) To mortify; to hurt (s.o.'s) feelings.

mort-né, *a.* (*a*) Still-born. (*b*) *Projet m.-né,* abortive plan. *pl. Mort-nés.*

mortuaire, *a.* Mortuary. **Drap mortuaire,** pall. *Chambre m.,* death-chamber.

morue, *s.f. Ich:* Cod.

morveux, *a. Prov:* **Qui se sent morveux se mouche,** if the cap fits wear it.

mosaïque¹, *a. B.Hist:* Mosaic (law).

mosaïque², *s.f. Art:* Mosaic.

Moscou. *Pr.n. Geog:* Moscow.

moscovite, *a. & s. Geog:* Muscovite.

mosquée, *s.f.* Mosque.

mot, *s.m.* Word. **Prendre qn au mot,** to take s.o. at his word. **Qui ne dit mot consent,** silence gives consent. **Dire deux mots à qn,** to have a word with s.o. **Ignorer le premier mot de la chimie,** not to know the first thing about chemistry. **Au bas mot,** at the lowest estimate. **Gros mot,** coarse expression. *Le mot de l'énigme,* the key to the enigma. **Voilà le fin mot de l'affaire!** so that's what's at the bottom of it! **Faire comprendre qch. à qn à mots couverts,** to give s.o. a hint of sth. **Écrire un mot à qn,** to drop s.o. a line. **Tranchons le mot,** *vous refusez,* to put it bluntly, you refuse. **Bon mot,** witty remark. **Avoir le mot pour rire,** to be fond of a joke.

moteur, -trice. I. *a.* Motive, propulsive, driving (power). **2.** *s.m.* Motor, engine.

motif. I. *a.* Motive. **2.** *s.m.* (*a*) Motive, incentive; reason. **Soupçons sans motif,** groundless suspicions. (*b*) (i) *Art:* Motif. (ii) *Needlew:* Design (iii) *Mus:* Theme, motto, figure.

motion, *s.f.* Motion, proposal.

motiver, *v.tr.* **1.** To state the reason for. *M. une décision sur qch.,* to base a decision on sth. **2.** To justify, warrant. *Refus motivé,* justifiable refusal.

moto, *s.f. F:* Motor bike.

motocyclette, *s.f.* Motor (bi)cycle.

motocycliste, *s.* Motor cyclist.

motoglisseur, *s.m.* Speed-boat.

motrice. See MOTEUR.

motte, *s.f.* **1.** Mound. **2.** Clod, lump (of earth). *M. de gazon,* sod, turf.

mou¹**, mol,** *f.* **molle. I.** *a.* (The masc. form *mol* is used before vowel or h 'mute') Soft; slack; weak, flabby. **2.** *s.m.* Slack (of rope).

mou², *s.m.* Lights, lungs (of animal).

mouchard, *s.m. F:* Sneak, informer; police-spy.

mouche, *s.f.* **1.** Fly. *M. commune,* house-fly. *M. bleue,* bluebottle. *M. à miel,* honey-bee. **On aurait entendu voler une mouche,** you could have heard a pin drop. **Prendre la mouche,** to take offence. **Quelle mouche vous pique?** what is the matter with you? **C'est une fine mouche,** he's a knowing card. **2.** (*a*) Spot, speck; stain. (*b*) Bull's-eye (of target). **Faire mouche,** to score a bull. **3.** River steamer (on the Seine).

moucher, *v.tr.* **1.** (*a*) To wipe (child's) nose. (*b*) *F:* To snub. **2.** To snuff (candle).

se moucher, to wipe, blow, one's nose. *F:* **Il ne se mouche pas du pied,** he thinks no small beer of himself.

moucheron, *s.m.* Midge.

moucheter, *v.tr.* (je mouchette) To spot, speckle. *Mer mouchetée d'écume,* foam-flecked sea.

moucheture, *s.f.* Spot, speck, fleck.

mouchoir, *s.m. M. de poche,* pocket hand-kerchief. *M. de tête,* kerchief.

moudre, *v.tr.* (*pr.p.* moulant; *p.p.* moulu) To grind.

moulu, *a.* (*a*) Ground, powdered. (*b*) *F:* Dead-beat, fagged-out.

moue, *s.f.* Pout. **Faire la moue,** to purse one's lips, to pout, to look sulky.

mouette, *s.f. Orn:* Gull, seamew.

mouf(f)ette, *s.f. Z:* Skunk.

mouflon, *s.m. Z:* Moufflon, wild sheep.

mouillage [-ja:ʒ], *s.m.* **1.** Moistening, damping. **2.** *Nau:* (*a*) Anchoring. (*b*) Lay-ing (of mine). **3.** Anchorage. **Être au mouillage,** to ride at anchor.

mouiller [muje], *v.tr.* **1.** To wet, moisten, damp. **2.** (*a*) *M. l'ancre,* to drop anchor. *M. un vaisseau,* to bring a ship to anchor. (*b*) To lay (mine).

mouillé, *a.* **1.** Moist, damp, wet. *F: M. jusqu'aux os,* wet through. *F:* **Poule mouillée,** milksop. **2.** At anchor.

mouilleur [mujœ:r], *s.m. Navy:* **Mouilleur de mines,** mine-layer.

moul-ant, etc. See MOUDRE and MOULER.

moule¹, *s.m.* Mould; matrix.

moule², *s.f. Moll:* Mussel.

mouler, *v.tr.* (*a*) To cast (statue). (*b*) To mould.

moulin, *s.m.* Mill. (*a*) *M. à vent,* windmill. *F:* **Faire venir l'eau au moulin,** to bring grist to the mill. (*b*) *F:* **Moulin à paroles,** chatterbox.

moulinet, *s.m.* **1.** *Fish:* Reel. **2.** **Faire des moulinets** (*avec sa canne*), to twirl one's stick.

moulu, -s, -t, etc. See MOUDRE.

moulure, *s.f.* (Ornamental) moulding.

mourant. I. *a.* Dying. *D'une voix mourante,* faintly. **2.** *s.* Dying man or woman.

mourir, *v.i.* (*pr.p.* mourant; *p.p.* mort; *pr.ind.* je meurs, ils meurent; *pr.sub.* je meure, nous mourions; *p.h.* il mourut; *fu.* je mourrai. Aux. *être*) To die. *Il est mort hier,* he died yesterday. *M. de faim,* (i) to die of starvation; (ii) *F:* to be starving. **Faire mourir qn,** to put s.o. to death. *F: Il me fera m.,* he will be the death of me. **Mourir d'envie de faire qch.,** to be dying to do sth.

mort. I. *a.* (*a*) Dead. *Prov:* **Morte la bête, mort le venin,** dead men tell no tales. (*b*) *Art:* Nature morte, still life. (*c*) *Balle morte,* spent bullet. **2.** *s.* Dead person; deceased. *Ecc:* **Jour des Morts,** All Souls' day. *L'office des morts,* the burial service. **Faire le mort,** (i) to sham dead; (ii) *F:* To

lie low. **Tête de mort**, death's head; skull.
3. *s.m. Cards:* Dummy.

mouron, *s.m.* Pimpernel.

mousquet, *s.m. A:* Musket.

mousquetaire, *s.m.* Musketeer.

mousse[1], *s.f.* **I.** Moss. **2.** Froth, foam; lather.

mousse[2], *s.m.* Ship's boy.

mousseline, *s.f. Tex:* Muslin.

mousser, *v.i.* To froth, foam; to lather. *F:* **Faire mousser qn**, to puff s.o.

mousseux, *a.* **I.** Mossy. **2.** (a) Frothy, foaming. (b) Sparkling (wine).

mousson, *s.f. Meteor:* Monsoon.

moustache, *s.f.* (a) Moustache. (b) Whiskers (of cat).

moustiquaire, *s.f.* Mosquito-net.

moustique, *s.m. Ent:* (a) Mosquito. (b) Gnat.

moutard, *s.m. F:* (a) Urchin. (b) Brat.

moutarde, *s.f.* Mustard. **La moutarde lui est montée au nez**, he lost his temper.

mouton, *s.m.* **I.** Sheep. *F:* **Revenons à nos moutons**, let us get back to the point. **Saut de mouton**, (of horse) buck. **2.** *Cu:* Mutton. **3.** *Civ.E:* Ram. **4.** *pl.* White horses (on sea).

moutonné, *a.* Fleecy (sky). **Mer moutonnée**, sea with white horses. **Tête moutonnée**, frizzy head of hair.

moutonneux, *a.* **I.** (Of the sea) Foam-flecked. **2.** (Of the sky) Fleecy.

mouvant, *a.* (a) Mobile. (b) *F:* Unstable, changeable. **Sables mouvants**, quicksand.

mouvement, *s.m.* Movement. **I.** Motion. **Se mettre en mouvement**, to start off. *Mec:* **Quantité de mouvement**, momentum. *Mus:* **Presser le m.**, to quicken the time. **2.** (a) Change, modification. **M. de terrain**, undulation in the ground. **Être dans le mouvement**, to be in the swim, up to date. (b) *M. d'humeur*, outburst of temper. (c) Agitation, emotion. **M. populaire**, rising of the people. **3.** Traffic. *Rail:* **Mouvements des trains**, train arrivals and departures. *Journ:* **Mouvements des navires**, shipping intelligence. **4.** Works, action, movement. **M. d'horlogerie**, clockwork.

mouvementé, *a.* **I.** Animated, lively; full of incident. **2.** *Terrain m.*, undulating ground.

mouvoir, *v.tr.* (*pr.p.* **mouvant**; *p.p.* **mû**, **mue**; *pr.ind.* **je meus, ils meuvent**; *pr.sub.* **je meuve, n. mouvions, ils meuvent**) **I.** **M. qch. de sa place**, to move sth. from its place. **2.** To drive; to propel. **Mû par la colère**, moved by anger.

 se mouvoir, to move, stir.

moyen[1], **-enne**. **I.** *a.* (a) Middle. **Le moyen âge**, the Middle Ages. (b) Average, mean. (c) Medium. **De taille moyenne**, medium-sized, middle-sized. **2.** *s.f.* **Moyenne**, average. **En moyenne**, on an average.

moyen[2], *s.m.* Means. (a) **Employer les grands moyens**, to take extreme measures. **Y a-t-il moyen de le faire?** is it possible to

do it? **Il n'y a pas moyen**, it can't be don **Dans la (pleine) mesure de mes moyens**, the utmost of my ability. (b) *Vivre au de de ses moyens*, to live beyond one's means.

moyennant, *prep.* On (a certain) conditio **Faire qch. moyennant finances**, to do st for a consideration. **Moyennant quoi,** consideration of which.

moyeu, -eux, *s.m.* Hub.

mû. See MOUVOIR.

muable, *a.* Changeable, mutable.

mucilage, *s.m.* Mucilage, gum.

mucilagineux, *a.* Mucilaginous, viscous.

mue, *s.f.* **I.** (a) Moulting (of birds); she ding of the antlers; changing of ski (b) Moulting-time. (c) Feathers moulted antlers, etc., shed. **2.** Breaking of the voi (at puberty).

muer. **I.** *v.tr. Le cerf mue sa tête*, the sta casts its antlers. **2.** *v.i.* (a) (Of bird) T moult; to shed the skin or antlers. (b) (C voice) To break (at puberty).

muet, -ette. **I.** *a.* Dumb, mute. (a) Unabl to speak. **M. de colère**, speechless with ange (b) Unwilling to speak. **Rester muet, t** remain silent. (c) Without word or soun *Th:* **Rôle m.**, silent part. *Gram:* **Lettr muette**, silent letter. **2.** *s.* Dumb perso **3.** *s.f. Gram:* **Muette**, mute letter.

muézin, *s.m.* Muezzin.

mufle, *s.m.* Muzzle (of ox); snout (of lion

muflier, *s.m. Bot:* Antirrhinum, snap dragon.

mugir, *v.i.* (a) To low; to bellow. (b) (O wind) To roar; to boom.

mugissement, *s.m.* (a) Lowing; bellowing (b) Roaring, booming, howling (of wind).

muguet [-gɛ], *s.m. Bot:* Lily of the valley.

mulâtre, *a. & s.* Mulatto, half-caste.

mule[1], *s.f.* (She-)mule.

mule[2], *s.f.* Bedroom slipper; mule.

mulet[1], *s.m.* (He-)mule.

mulet[2], *s.m. Ich:* Grey mullet.

muletier, *s.m.* Mule-driver, muleteer.

mulot, *s.m.* Field-mouse.

multicolore, *a.* Multi-coloured.

multiple. **I.** *a.* Multiple, manifold; multi farious. **2.** *s.m.* Multiple.

multiplicateur, -trice. **I.** *a.* Multiplying **2.** *s.m.* Multiplier.

multiplication, *s.f.* **I.** Multiplication **2.** *Mec.E:* **Grande m.**, high gear.

multiplicité, *s.f.* Multiplicity.

multiplier, *v.tr. & i.* To multiply.

 se multiplier. (a) To multiply. (b) T be here, there, and everywhere.

multiplié, *a.* Multiple; manifold.

multitude, *s.f.* Multitude; crowd; multi plicity.

municipal, -aux, *a.* Municipal.

municipalité, *s.f.* Municipality.

munificence, *s.f.* Munificence; bounty.

munificent, *a.* Munificent; bountiful.

munir, *v.tr.* To furnish, equip, provide.
munitions, *s.f. pl.* Stores, supplies.
mur, *s.m.* Wall. **Mettre qn au pied du mur,** to drive s.o. into a corner. **Donner de la tête contre un mur,** to run one's head against a brick wall.
mûr, *a.* Ripe ; mellow ; mature.
muraille [-raːj], *s.f.* **1.** (High defensive) wall. **2.** Side (of ship).
mural, -aux, *a.* Mural. *Pendule murale,* wall-clock.
mûre, *s.f.* **1.** Mulberry. **2.** *M. (de ronce),* blackberry.
mûrement, *adv.* With mature consideration.
murer, *v.tr.* To wall in ; to wall up, brick up.
mûrier, *s.m. Bot :* **1.** Mulberry(-tree). **2.** *M. sauvage,* bramble, blackberry-bush.
mûrir. 1. *v.tr.* To ripen, mature. **2.** *v.i. & occ. pr.* To ripen ; to mature.
murmure, *s.m.* Murmur, murmuring.
murmurer, *v.tr. & i.* (*a*) To murmur. (*b*) To grumble. *M. entre ses dents,* to mutter.
mu-s, -t, etc. See MOUVOIR.
musaraigne, *s.f.* Shrew-mouse.
musard. 1. *a.* Dawdling. **2.** *s.* Dawdler.
musc [mysk], *s.m.* **1.** Musk. **2.** *Z :* Musk-deer.
muscade, *s.f.* (**Noix**) **muscade,** nutmeg
muscadier, *s.m. Bot :* Nutmeg-tree.
muscat, *a. & s.m. Vit :* (**Raisin**) **muscat,** muscat grape. (**Vin**) **muscat,** muscatel.
muscle, *s.m.* Muscle.
musclé, *a.* Muscular ; sinewy, brawny.
musculaire, *a.* Muscular (system).
musculeux, *a.* Muscular, brawny.
Muse, *s.f.* Muse.
museau, *s.m.* (*a*) Muzzle, snout. (*b*) *F :* *Vilain m.,* ugly mug.
musée, *s.m.* (*a*) Museum. (*b*) **Musée de peinture,** picture-gallery.
museler, *v.tr.* (je **muselle**) To muzzle.
muselière, *s.f.* Dog muzzle.
musette, *s.f.* Haversack.
musical, -aux, *a.* Musical.
musicalement, *adv.* Musically.
musicien, -ienne, *a. & s.* **1.** Musician. **Elle est bonne musicienne,** she is very musical. **2.** Bandsman.
musique, *s.f.* **1.** Music. **Mettre des paroles**

en musique, to set words to music. **2.** Band. **Chef de musique,** bandmaster.
musoir, *s.m.* Pier-head.
musqué, *a.* **1.** (*a*) Musky. (*b*) Affected, effeminate (poet, style, etc.). **2. Bœuf musqué,** musk-ox.
mustang, *s.m.* Mustang.
musulman, *a. & s.* Mussulman, Mohammedan, Moslem.
mutabilité, *s.f.* Mutability.
mutable, *a.* Changeable, mutable.
mutation, *s.f.* Change, alteration.
mutilation, *s.f.* (*a*) Mutilation, maiming. (*b*) Defacement.
mutiler, *v.tr.* (*a*) To mutilate, maim. (*b*) To deface.
mutilé, *a. & s.* **Mutilés de guerre,** disabled ex-service men. *Il est m. du bras,* he has lost an arm.
mutin, *a. & s.* **1.** (*a*) Insubordinate ; disobedient, unruly. (*b*) Roguish, pert, saucy. **2.** *s.m.* Mutineer.
mutiner (se), *v.pr.* To rise in revolt ; to mutiny, to rebel ; to be unruly.
mutisme, *s.m.* Dumbness, muteness. **Se renfermer dans le mutisme,** to maintain a stubborn silence.
mutuel, -elle, *a.* Mutual.
mutuellement, *adv.* Mutually.
myope, *a. & s.* Short-sighted (person).
myopie, *s.f.* Myopia ; short-sightedness.
myosotis [-tis], *s.m. Bot :* Forget-me-not.
myriade, *s.f.* Myriad.
myrrhe, *s.f.* Myrrh.
myrte, *s.m. Bot :* Myrtle.
myrtille [mirtil, mirtiːj], *s.f.* Bilberry.
mystère, *s.m.* Mystery.
mystérieusement, *adv.* Mysteriously.
mystérieux, *a.* Mysterious ; uncanny.
mysticisme, *s.m.* Mysticism.
mystificateur, -trice. 1. *a.* Mystifying. **2.** *s.* Hoaxer, mystifier.
mystification, *s.f.* (*a*) Mystification. (*b*) Hoax.
mystifier, *v.tr.* (*a*) To mystify. (*b*) To hoax.
mystique. 1. *a.* Mystic(al). **2.** *s.* Mystic.
mythe, *s.m.* Myth, legend.
mythique, *a.* Mythical.
mythologie, *s.f.* Mythology.
mythologique, *a.* Mythological.

N

N, n [ɛn], *s.f.* (The letter) N, n.
n'. See NE.
nabab [-bab], *s.m.* Nabob.
Nabuchodonosor [-byk-]. *Pr.n.m.* Nebuchadnezzar.
nacelle, *s.f.* **1.** Skiff, wherry, dinghy.

2. *Aer :* Cockpit (of aeroplane).
nacre, *s.f.* Mother of pearl.
nacré, *a.* Nacreous, pearly.
nage, *s.f.* **1.** Rowing, sculling. **Chef de nage,** stroke oarsman. **2.** (*a*) Swimming. *Traverser une rivière à la n.,* to swim across a river

F: Être en nage, to be bathed in perspiration. (b) Stroke (in swimming)

nageoire, *s.f.* Fin (of fish).

nager, *v.i.* (n. nageons) **I.** *Nau:* To row; to scull. **2.** To swim. (a) Nager entre deux eaux, (i) to swim under water; (ii) *F:* to run with the hare and hunt with the hounds. (b) *Le bois nage sur l'eau,* wood floats on water. *N dans l'abondance,* to be rolling in luxury.

nageur, -euse. I. *a.* Swimming **2.** *s.* (a) Swimmer. (b) Oarsman.

naguère [-gɛːr], *adv* Not long since, a short time ago.

naïade, *s.f.* Naiad, water-nymph.

naïf, *a.* **I.** Artless, ingenuous, naive. **2.** Simple-minded

nain. I. s Dwarf **2.** *a* Dwarf(ish).

naissance, *s.f* Birth. (a) Anniversaire de naissance, birthday. (b) Descent, extraction. *De haute n.,* high-born. (c) Donner naissance à une rumeur, to give rise to a rumour

naiss-ant[1], -ais, -e, etc. See NAÎTRE.

naissant[2], *a.* New-born; nascent (beauty).

naître, *v.i.* (pr.p. naissant; p.p. né; pr ind. je nais, ils naissent; p.h. je naquis. Aux. être) (a) To be born *F:* Être né pour qch., to be cut out for sth *F:* Je ne suis pas né d'hier, I was not born yesterday (b) (Of hopes, fears) To be born, to spring up. *Faire n. un sourire,* to provoke a smile. (c) (Of vegetation) To spring up, come up (d) (Of river) To originate, rise.

naïvement, *adv.* Artlessly, ingenuously; naively.

naïveté, *s.f.* **I.** (a) Artlessness, simplicity, naivety. (b) Guilelessness. **2.** Ingenuous remark.

Nankin. I. *Pr.n. Geog:* Nanking. **2.** *s.m. & a.inv.* Nankeen.

nantir, *v.tr F:* N qn de qch., to provide s.o. with sth.

naphte, *s.m.* Naphtha; mineral oil.

Napoléon. *Pr.n.m* Napoleon.

napolitain, *a. & s* Neapolitan.

nappe, *s.f.* **I.** (a) Table-cloth. (b) Cloth, cover **2.** Sheet (of ice).

naqui-s, -t, etc. See NAÎTRE

Narcisse. I. *Pr.n.m.* Narcissus. **2.** *s.m. Bot:* Narcissus.

narcotique, *a. & s.m. Med:* Narcotic.

narguer, *v.tr* To flout; to snap one's fingers at.

narguilé [-gile], *s.m.* Hookah.

narine, *s.f.* Nostril.

narquois, *a.* Quizzing, bantering.

narrateur, -trice, *s.* Narrator.

narratif, *a* Narrative.

narration. *s.f* **I.** Narrating, narration. **2.** Narrative.

narrer, *v.tr.* To narrate, relate.

nasal, -als, -aux. I. *a* Nasal. **2.** *s.f. Ling:* Nasale, nasal.

nasalement, *adv.* Nasally.

naseau, *s.m.* Nostril (of horse).

nasillard [-zij-], *a Ton n.,* (nasal) twang; snuffle.

nasiller [-zije], *v.t.* To speak with a twang; to snuffle.

natal, -als, -aux, *a.* **I.** Native. *Ville natale,* birth-place. **2.** Jour natal, birthday.

natalité, *s.f.* Birth-rate.

natation, *s.f.* Swimming, natation.

natif. I. *a.* Native. (a) *Je suis n. de Londres,* I am London born. (b) Natural, inborn. *Bon sens n.,* mother wit. **2.** *s.m.pl.* Natifs, natives

nation, *s.f.* Nation.

national, -aux. I. *a.* National. **2.** *s.m.pl.* Nationaux, nationals.

nationaliste, *s.m. & f.* Nationalist.

nationalité, *s.f.* Nationality.

natte, *s.f.* **I.** Mat, matting (of straw). **2.** Plait, braid (of hair).

naturalisation, *s.f.* Naturalization.

naturaliser, *v.tr.* To naturalize

naturaliste, *s.* Naturalist.

nature, *s.f.* Nature. **I.** *Plus grand que n.,* larger than life. Nature morte, still-life (painting). **2.** (a) Kind, character. *N. du sol,* nature of the soil. (b) Character, disposition, temperament Il est timide de nature, he is naturally shy. **3.** Kind. Payer en nature, to pay in kind. **4.** *a.inv.* Pommes nature, plain boiled potatoes. Café nature, plain black coffee.

naturel, -elle. I. *a.* Natural. (a) De grandeur naturelle, life-size. (b) *Don n.,* natural gift. (c) Natural, unaffected. **2.** *s.m* Native (of country). **3.** *s.m.* Nature, character, disposition *Prov:* Chassez le naturel, il revient au galop, what's bred in the bone will come out in the flesh.

naturellement, *adv.* Naturally. **I.** By nature; by birth. **2.** Without affectation; unaffectedly **3.** *Vous lui avez répondu?—Naturellement,* you answered him?—Of course (I did).

naufrage, *s.m.* (Ship)wreck.

naufragé. I. *a* (Ship)wrecked; castaway. **2.** *s.* Castaway

naufrageur, *s.m.* Wrecker

nauséabond, *a.* Nauseous, nauseating; evil smelling.

nausée, *s.f.* (a) Nausea. (b) Avoir des nausées, to feel squeamish, sick.

nautique, *a.* Nautical. Sports nautiques, aquatic sports.

naval, -als, *a.* Naval, nautical.

navarin, *s.m.* Mutton stew; haricot mutton.

navet, *s.m.* Turnip.

navette, *s.f.* Shuttle. *F:* Faire la navette, to ply (to and fro).

navigabilité, *s.f.* **I.** Navigability **2.** Sea-worthiness; airworthiness.

navigable, *a.* **I.** Navigable **2.** Seaworthy; airworthy

navigateur, *s.m.* Navigator.

navigation, *s.f.* Navigation. Compagnie de navigation, shipping company.

naviguer. 1. *v.i.* To sail, navigate 2. *v.tr.* To navigate.

navire, *s.m.* Ship, vessel.

navrant, *a.* Heart-rending, heart-breaking.

navrer, *v.tr.* To grieve most deeply; to cut to the heart.
  navré, *a.* Heart-broken; woe-begone; dreadfully sorry.

nazi, *s. Pol:* Nazi.

nazisme, *s.m. Pol:* Naziism.

ne, n', *neg.adv.* Not. 1. Used alone (*i.e.* with omission of *pas*) with *cesser, oser, pouvoir, savoir, importer Je ne saurais vous le dire,* I cannot tell you. Always used without *pas* in the phr. **N'importe,** never mind, it doesn't matter. 2. In the following constructions: (*a*) *Que ne ferait-il pour vous?* what would he not do for you? (*b*) *Si je ne me trompe . . .,* unless I am mistaken. . . . *Voilà six mois que je ne l'ai vu,* it is now six months since I saw him. *Qu'à cela ne tienne!* by all means! *Je n'ai que faire de votre aide,* I don't need your help. 3. Used with a vague negative connotation. (*a*) (Expressions of fear) *Je crains qu'il (ne) prenne froid,* I am afraid he may catch cold. (*b*) *Évitez, prenez garde, qu'on (ne) vous voie,* avoid being seen; take care not to be seen. *Peu s'en fallut qu'il ne tombât,* he nearly came a cropper. *A moins qu'on (ne) vous appelle,* unless they call you. (*c*) (Comparison) *Il est plus vigoureux qu'il (ne) paraît,* he is stronger than he looks.

né. See NAÎTRE.

néanmoins, *adv.* Nevertheless, none the less; for all that; yet; still.

néant, *s.m.* Nothingness, nought, naught. *Sortir du néant,* to rise from obscurity.

nébulaire, *a. Astr:* Nebular.

nébuleusement, *adv.* Nebulously, obscurely.

nébuleux. 1. *a.* Nebulous (*a*) Cloudy, hazy. (*b*) Turbid, cloudy. (*c*) Gloomy, clouded. (*d*) Unintelligible, obscure. 2. *s.f. Astr:* Nébuleuse, nebula.

nécessaire. 1. *a.* Necessary, needful; requisite. *s.* **Faire le nécessaire,** to play the busybody. 2. *s.m.* (*a*) Necessaries, the needful. **Faire le nécessaire,** to do the needful. (*b*) Outfit. *N. d ouvrage,* housewife. *N. de toilette,* dressing-case.

nécessairement, *adv.* 1. Necessarily; of necessity. 2. Inevitably, infallibly.

nécessité, *s.f.* Necessity. *Il est de toute n. de (faire qch.),* it is essential to (do sth.). *Denrées de première n.,* essential foodstuffs. *Selon les nécessités,* as circumstances (may) require. *Être dans la n.,* to be in want.

nécessiter, *v.tr.* To necessitate, entail.

nécessiteux, *a.* Needy, in want, necessitous.

nécrologie, *s.f.* Obituary notice.

nécromancie, *s.f.* Necromancy.

nécromancien, -ienne, *s.* Necromancer.

nécropole, *s.f.* Necropolis.

nectaire, *s.m. Bot:* Nectary, honey-cup.

nectar, *s.m.* Nectar

néerlandais. 1. *a.* Dutch. 2. *s.* Netherlander, Dutchman, Dutchwoman.

nef [nɛf], *s.f.* Nave. *Nef latérale,* aisle.

néfaste, *a.* Luckless, ill-omened; baneful.

nèfle, *s.f.* Medlar (fruit).

néflier, *s.m.* Medlar(-tree).

négatif. 1. *a.* Negative. *s.m. Phot:* **Négatif,** negative. 2. *s.f.* **Negative,** negative.

négation, *s.f.* 1. Negation, denial. 2. *Gram:* Negative.

négativement, *adv.* Negatively.

négligeable, *a.* Negligible.

négligemment, *adv.* 1. Negligently, carelessly. 2. Casually.

négligence, *s.f.* Negligence; neglect; carelessness, want of care.

négligent, *a.* 1. Negligent, careless; neglectful. 2. Indifferent, casual (tone).

négliger, *v.tr.* (n. négligeons) To neglect. 1. To take no care of; to be neglectful of; to be careless of. 2. (*a*) To disregard. (*b*) *N. de faire qch.,* to leave sth. undone.
  se négliger, to neglect one's person.
  négligé. 1. *a.* (*a*) Neglected, unheeded. (*b*) Careless, slovenly. 2. *s.m.* Undress; dishabille.

négoce, *s.m.* Trade, trading, business.

négociabilité, *s.f.* Negotiability.

négociable, *a.* Negotiable, transferable.

négociant, *s.* (Wholesale) merchant; trader.

négociateur, -trice, *s.* Negotiator.

négociation, *s.f.* 1. Negotiation, negotiating. 2. Transaction.

négocier, *v.tr.* To negotiate.

nègre, négresse. 1. *s.* (*a*) Negro, *f.* negress; black. (*b*) *F:* Devil; ghost (of literary man). 2. *a.* (*f.* nègre) *La race nègre,* the negro race.

négrier, *s.m.* 1. Slave-trader. 2. Slave-ship.

négrillon, -onne [-rij-], *s.* (Little) nigger -boy, -girl; *F:* piccaninny.

neige, *s.f.* Snow. **Neige fondue,** (i) sleet, (ii) slush.

neiger, *v.impers.* (il neigeait) To snow.

neigeux, *a.* Snowy; snow-covered.

ne m'oubliez pas, *s.m.inv. F:* Forget-me-not.

nénuphar, *s.m. Bot:* Water-lily.

néolithique, *a.* Neolithic.

néon, *s.m. Ch:* Neon. *Tube au néon,* neon tube.

néophyte, *s.m.* (*a*) Neophyte. (*b*) Beginner, tyro.

néo-Zélandais. 1. *a.* New Zealand. 2. *s.* New Zealander.

népotisme, *s.m.* Nepotism.

néréide, *s.f.* Nereid; sea-nymph.

nerf [nɛːr, nɛrf, *pl.* always nɛːr], *s.m.* 1. Nerve. *Attaque de nerfs,* (fit of) hysterics. **Porter sur les nerfs à qn,** to get on s.o.'s nerves.

2. *F:* Sinew, tendon, ligament. **Nerfs d'acier,** thews of steel. *Manquer de n.,* to lack energy.

nerveusement, *adv.* **1.** Energetically. **2.** Impatiently, irritably.

nerveux, *a.* **1.** Nervous (system). **2.** Sinewy, wiry; vigorous. *Moteur n.,* responsive engine. **3.** Excitable, highly-strung.

nervosité, *s.f.* Irritability, state of nerves.

nervure, *s.f.* (*a*) Nervure, rib, vein (of leaf). (*b*) Branch (of mountain-group).

n'est-ce pas, *adv.phr.* (Inviting assent) *Vous venez, n'est-ce pas?* you are coming, aren't you? *Vous ne venez pas, n'est-ce pas?* you are not coming, are you?

net, nette, [nɛt], *a.* **1.** Clean, spotless; clear. *F:* **J'ai les mains nettes,** my hands are clean; I had nothing to do with it. **Maison nette comme un sou neuf,** house as clean as a new pin. **2.** (*a*) Clear; distinct; plain. *Contours nets,* sharp outlines. (*b*) *Poids net,* net weight. **3.** *adv.* (*a*) Plainly, flatly, outright. **Refuser net,** to refuse point-blank. *S'arrêter net,* to stop dead. (*b*) *Voir net,* to see distinctly.

nettement, *adv.* **1.** (*a*) Cleanly. (*b*) Clearly. **2.** Plainly.

netteté, *s.f.* **1.** Cleanness; cleanliness. **2.** (*a*) Clearness; distinctness; sharpness (of image). (*b*) Flatness (of refusal).

nettoiement, *s.m.* Cleaning.

nettoyage, *s.m.* Cleaning.

nettoyer, *v.tr.* (je nettoie) To clean; to scour.

nettoyeur, -euse. 1. *a.* Cleaning. **2.** *s.* Cleaner.

neuf[1], *num. a. inv. & s.m. inv.* Nine. **1.** *Card. a.* (At the end of the word-group [nœf]; before *ans* and *heures* [nœv]; otherwise before vowel sounds [nœf]; before a noun or adj. beginning with a consonant usu. [nœ], often [nœf]) *Neuf francs,* nine francs. **2.** Ordinal uses, etc. (Always [nœf]) *Le neuf mai,* the ninth of May.

neuf[2] [nœf]. **1.** *a.* (*a*) New. **A l'état (de) neuf,** in new condition. (*b*) *Pays n.,* new country. (*c*) *F:* **Qu'est-ce qu'il y a de neuf?** what is the news? **2.** *s.m.* **Habillé de neuf,** dressed in new clothes. **Meublé de neuf,** newly refurnished. **Il y a du neuf,** I have news for you. *Adv.phr.* **A neuf,** anew.

neurotique, *a. Med:* Neurotic.

neutraliser, *v.tr.* To neutralize.

neutralité, *s.f.* Neutrality.

neutre, *a.* **1.** Neuter. **2.** Neutral. *s.m. Droits des neutres,* rights of neutrals.

neutron, *s.m. El:* Neutron.

neuve. See NEUF[2].

neuvième. 1. *num. a. & s.* Ninth. **2.** *s.m.* Ninth (part).

neveu, -eux, *s.m.* Nephew.

névralgie, *s.f.* Neuralgia.

névralgique, *a.* Neuralgic.

névrite, *s.f.* Neuritis.

névrosé, *a. & s. Med:* Neurotic.

nez, *s.m.* **1.** Nose. (*a*) **Parler du nez,** t speak through one's nose. **Faire un pied d nez à qn,** to make a long nose at s.o. (*b*) Sens of smell; (of dogs) scent. **Avoir bon ne** to be shrewd, far-seeing. (*c*) *F:* **Nez** nez, face to face. **Regardez donc quel ne il fait,** do look at the face he's pullin **Regarder qn sous le nez,** to look defiantly s.o. **Rire au nez de qn,** to laugh in s.o.'s fac **2.** Bow, nose, head (of ship).

ni, *conj.* (*Ne* is either expressed or implied Nor, or. (*a*) *Ni moi (non plus),* neither do *Sans argent ni bagages,* without money luggage. (*b*) *Il ne mange ni ne boit,* he neith eats nor drinks. (*c*) **Ni . . . ni,** neithe . . . nor.

niable, *a.* Deniable.

niais. 1. *a.* Simple, foolish. **2.** *s.* Foo simpleton. *Petite niaise!* you little silly !

niaisement, *adv.* Foolishly.

niaiserie, *s.f.* **1.** Silliness, foolishnes **2.** *Dire des niaiseries,* to talk nonsense.

niche[1], *s.f.* **1.** Niche, nook, recess (in wa etc.). **2.** *N. à chien,* dog-kennel.

niche[2], *s.f. F:* Trick, prank.

nichée, *s.f.* Nest(ful) (of birds); brood.

nicher. 1. *v.i.* (Of bird) To build a nest to nest. **2.** *v.tr.* To put, lodge.

se nicher. (*a*) *Maisonnette nichée dar un bois,* cottage nestling in a wood. (*b*) T ensconce oneself (*dans,* in).

nickel, *s.m. Ch:* Nickel.

niçois, *a. & s.* (Native) of Nice.

Nicolas. *Pr.n.m.* Nicholas.

nicotine, *s.f. Ch:* Nicotine.

nid, *s.m.* **1.** Nest. *F:* **Trouver le ni vide,** to find the bird flown. *Nid de brigand* robbers' den. **2.** (*a*) *Nid de mitrailleuse.* nest of machine-guns. (*b*) *Nau:* **Nid de pi** crow's-nest.

nièce, *s.f.* Niece.

nier, *v.tr.* To deny. **Il n'y a pas à le nie** there is no denying it.

nigaud. (*a*) *s.* Simpleton, booby. (*b*) *a.* El *est un peu nigaude,* she is rather simple.

nihilisme, *s.m. Pol:* Nihilism.

nihiliste. 1. *a.* Nihilist(ic). **2.** *s.* Nihilist

Nil (le) [lənil]. *Pr.n.m.* The (river) Nile.

nimbe, *s.m.* Nimbus, halo.

nimbus [-byːs], *s.m.* Nimbus; rain-cloud.

nippes, *s.f.pl.* **1.** Garments. **2.** Old clothe

nippon, -one, *a.* Japanese.

nique, *s.f.* **Faire la nique à qn,** to make long nose at s.o.

nitouche, *s.f. F:* **Sainte nitouche,** littl hypocrite. *Un petit air de sainte n.,* a demur look.

nitrate, *s.m. Ch:* Nitrate.

nitre, *s.m.* Nitre, saltpetre.

nitreux, *a. Ch:* Nitrous.

nitrique, *a. Ch:* Nitric.

niveau, *s.m.* Level. **1.** (Instrument) *N. bulle d'air,* air-, spirit-level. **2.** (*a*) *N. d* *hautes eaux*, high water mark. (*b*) **Niveau de vie**, standard of living. **Être au niveau de qch.**, to be on a par with sth.

niveler, *v.tr.* (je **nivelle**) To level, to even up.

nivellement, *s.m.* Levelling.

noble. 1. *a.* Noble. **2.** *s.* Noble(-man), noblewoman.

noblement, *adv.* Nobly.

noblesse, *s.f.* Nobility.

noce, *s.f.* **1.** (*a*) Wedding; wedding festivities. (*b*) Wedding-party. (*c*) Épouser qn en secondes noces, to marry for the second time. **2.** *F:* **Faire la noce**, to go on the spree.

noceur, -euse, *s.* *F:* (*a*) Reveller. (*b*) Fast liver.

nocif, *a.* Injurious, noxious.

noctambule, *s.* (*a*) Somnambulist, sleepwalker. (*b*) *F:* Night-prowler.

nocturne. 1. *a.* Nocturnal. *Bot:* Night-flowering. *Attaque n.*, night attack. **2.** *s.m. Mus:* Nocturne.

nocturnement, *adv.* By night.

Noé. *Pr.n.m. B.Hist:* Noah.

Noël, *s.m.* **1.** Christmas. **A Noël**, at Christmas. *La nuit de N.*, Christmas Eve. **2. Un noël**, a Christmas carol.

nœud, *s.m.* **1.** (*a*) Knot. *F: Les nœuds de l'amitié*, the ties of friendship. (*b*) *Le n. de la question*, the crux of the matter. (*c*) *Cost:* Bow. *Faire un n.*, to tie a bow. **2.** (*a*) Knot (in timber). (*b*) Node, joint (in stem of grass). **3.** *N. de voies ferrées*, railway junction. **4.** *Nau.Meas:* Knot.

noir. 1. *a.* Black. (*a*) *Race noire*, negro race. (*b*) Dark, swarthy. (*c*) Dark; gloomy. **Il fait déjà noir**, it is dark already. **Ma bête noire**, my pet aversion. **Misère noire**, dire poverty. (*d*) Dirty, grimy. (*e*) Base, black. **2.** *s.* Black man, woman. **3.** *s.m.* (*a*) **Voir tout en noir**, to look at the dark side of everything. **Broyer du noir**, to be in the dumps. (*b*) Bull's-eye (of target). *F:* **Mettre dans le noir**, to hit the mark. (*c*) *Avoir des noirs*, to have bruises. (*d*) *N. de fumée*, lamp-black. **4.** *s.f.* **Noire**. (*a*) (At roulette). Black. (*b*) (In balloting) Black ball.

noirâtre, *a.* Blackish, darkish.

noiraud, *a.* Swarthy.

noirceur, *s.f.* **1.** Blackness; gloominess; baseness. **2.** Black spot; smut. **3.** Atrocity; base action.

noircir. 1. *v.i.* To become black; to darken. **2.** *v.tr.* (*a*) To blacken. *F:* **Noircir du papier**, to scribble. (*b*) To smut, grime, sully.

noircissement, *s.m.* Blackening.

noise, *s.f.* **Chercher noise à qn**, to try to pick a quarrel with s.o.

noisetier, *s.m.* Hazel(-tree, -bush).

noisette. 1. *s.f.* Hazel-nut. **2.** *a.inv.* Hazel.

noix, *s.f.* **1.** Walnut. **2.** Nut. *N. vomique*, nux vomica.

nom, *s.m.* **1.** Name. *Nom de famille*, surname. **Nom de guerre**, assumed name; pen-name. *Nom et prénoms*, full name. *Ça n'a pas de*

nom! it is unspeakable! **Nom de nom!** by jingo! **Fait en mon nom**, done by my authority. **2.** *Gram:* Noun, substantive.

nomade. 1. *a.* Nomadic; migratory; roving. **2.** *s.m.pl.* **Nomades**, nomads.

nombre, *s.m.* Number. **1.** (*a*) *N. entier*, whole number; integer. (*b*) **Nombre de . . .**, a good many. . . . **Ils ont vaincu par le nombre**, they conquered by force of numbers. **Tout fait nombre**, every little helps. **Mettre qn au nombre de ses intimes**, to number s.o. among one's friends. **2.** *Gram:* Number.

nombrer, *v.tr.* To number, reckon.

nombreux, *a.* (*a*) Numerous. (*b*) Multifarious, manifold.

nombril [-bri], *s.m.* Navel.

nomenclature, *s.f.* Nomenclature.

nominal, -aux, *a.* (*a*) **Appel nominal**, roll-call. (*b*) Nominal. **Valeur nominale**, face value.

nominalement, *adv.* Nominally. **1.** By name. **2.** In name.

nominateur, *s.m.* Nominator.

nominatif. 1. *a.* **État nominatif**, list of names. **2.** *a. & s.m. Gram:* Nominative (case).

nomination, *s.f.* **1.** Nomination. **2.** Appointment.

nommer, *v.tr.* **1.** To name. *Jur: Le nommé Dupont*, the man Dupont. **2.** (*a*) To mention by name. (*b*) **Nommer un jour**, to appoint a day. **3.** To appoint. *Être nommé au grade de . . .*, to be promoted to the rank of. . . .

se nommer. 1. To state one's name. **2.** To be called, named.

non, *adv.* No; not. **1.** *Fumez-vous?—Non*, do you smoke?—No, I don't. **Mais non!** no indeed! **Non pas!** not at all! **Je pense que non**, I think not. **Faire signe que non**, to shake one's head. **Non (pas) que je le craigne**, not that I fear him. *s.m.inv. Les non l'emportent*, the noes have it. **2.** *Non loin de la ville*, not far from the town.

nonagénaire, *a. & s.* Nonagenarian.

nonce, *s.m. N. du Pape*, Papal Nuncio.

nonchalamment, *adv.* Nonchalantly.

nonchalance, *s.f.* Nonchalance, unconcern.

nonchalant, *a.* Nonchalant, unconcerned.

non-combattant, *a. & s.m.* Non-combatant.

non-conducteur, -trice. *Ph:* **1.** *a.* Non-conducting. **2.** *s.m.* Non-conductor.

non-existant, *a.* Non-existent.

non-lieu, *s.m. Jur:* No ground for prosecution.

nonne, *s.f.* Nun.

nonobstant. 1. *prep.* Notwithstanding. **2.** *adv.* Nevertheless.

nonpareil, -eille [-re:j]. *a.* Peerless, matchless.

non-sens [-sã:s]. *s.m.inv.* Meaningless sentence or action.

non-valeur, *s.f.* **1.** Object of no value. **2.** Inefficient employee. *pl. Des non-valeurs.*

nord, *s.m.* No *pl.* **I.** North. **La mer du Nord,** the North Sea. **L'Amérique du Nord,** North America. *F:* **Perdre le nord,** to lose one's bearings. **2.** *a.inv.* North, northern. **Le pôle nord,** the North Pole.

nord-est, *s.m.* North-east.

nord-ouest, *s.m.* North-west.

normal, -aux. I. *a.* (*a*) Normal. **École normale,** teachers' training college. (*b*) *Poids n.,* standard weight. **2.** *s.f.* **Normale.** (*a*) *Geom:* Perpendicular. (*b*) *Au-dessus de la normale,* above (the) normal.

normalement, *adv.* Normally.

normalité, *s.f.* Normality.

normand, *a. & s.* **I.** Norman; of Normandy. **Les îles Normandes,** the Channel Islands. *F:* **Réponse normande,** non-committal answer. **2.** *Hist:* **Les Normands,** the Norsemen.

Normandie. *Pr.n.f.* Normandy.

norme, *s.f.* Norm, standard.

Norvège. *Pr.n.f.* Norway.

norvégien, -ienne. I. *a. & s.* Norwegian. **2.** *s.m. Ling:* Norwegian.

nos. See NOTRE.

nostalgie, *s.f.* Nostalgia; home-sickness.

notabilité, *s.f.* Notability.

notable, *a.* Notable. *s.m.* Person of standing.

notablement, *adv.* Notably; appreciably.

notaire, *s.m.* Notary. *F:* **C'est comme si le notaire y avait passé,** his word is as good as his bond.

notamment, *adv.* (*a*) More particularly; especially. (*b*) Among others. . . .

notation, *s.f.* Notation.

note, *s.f.* **I.** Note, memorandum, minute. **2.** Annotation. **3.** *Sch:* Mark. **Bonne n.,** good mark. **4.** *Mus:* Note. *F:* **Changer de note,** to change one's tune. **5.** **Un homme de note,** a man of note. **6.** Bill, account.

noter, *v.tr.* **I.** To note; to take notice of. **Chose à noter,** thing worthy of notice. *F:* **Notez bien!** mark! mind you! **2.** To put down, jot down.

noté, *a.* **Mal n.,** of bad reputation.

notice, *s.f.* **I.** Notice, account. **2.** Review.

notification, *s.f.* Notification, intimation.

notifier, *v.tr.* To notify; to intimate. **N. son consentement,** to signify one's consent.

notion, *s.f.* Notion, idea. **Perdre la n. du temps,** to lose count of time.

notoire, *a.* Well-known; of common knowledge; manifest.

notoirement, *adv.* (*a*) Manifestly. (*b*) Notoriously.

notoriété, *s.f.* Notoriety; repute.

notre, *pl.* **nos,** *poss.a.* Our. **Nos père et mère,** our father and mother.

nôtre. I. *poss.pron.* Ours; our own. **2.** *s.m.* (i) Our own. (ii) *pl.* **Est-il des nôtres?** is he one of us?

nouer, *v.tr.* **I.** To tie, knot. **2.** *L'âge lui a noué les membres,* age has stiffened his joints.

3. Nouer conversation avec qn, to enter into conversation with s.o.

noué, *a.* **Articulations nouées,** stiff joints.

noueux, *a.* Knotty; gnarled.

nougat, *s.m.* Nougat.

nouilles [nu:j], *s.f.pl. Cu:* Noodle(s).

nourrice, *s.f.* **I.** (Wet-)nurse. **Conte de nourrice,** nursery tale. **2.** **Mettre un enfant en nourrice,** to put out a child to nurse. **Enfant changé en nourrice,** changeling.

nourricier. I. *a.* Nutritious. **2.** *s.m.* (Père) **nourricier,** foster-father. *s.f.* (Mère) **nourricière,** foster-mother.

nourrir, *v.tr.* To nourish. **I.** (*a*) To nurse (infant). (*b*) To bring up, nurture. **2.** To feed; to maintain (one's family). **3.** To harbour (thoughts); to cherish (hope).

se nourrir. I. *Se n. de lait,* to live on milk. **2.** To keep oneself.

nourri, *a.* **I.** Nourished, fed. **2.** Rich, copious (style); full (tone). **Acclamations nourries,** sustained applause.

nourrissant, *a.* Nourishing, nutritive.

nourrisson, -onne, *s.* **I.** Baby at the breast; infant. **2.** Nurs(e)ling, foster-child.

nourriture, *s.f.* **I.** Food, nourishment, sustenance. **2.** Board, keep.

nous, *pers.pron.* **I.** (*a*) (Subject) We. (*b*) (Object) Us; to us. **Lisez-le-nous,** read it to us. (*c*) (Reflexive) *Nous nous chauffons,* we are warming ourselves. (*d*) (Reciprocal) *Nous nous connaissons,* we know each other. **2.** *Nous autres Anglais,* we English. *Nous l'avons fait nous-mêmes,* we did it ourselves. *Ce livre est à nous,* that book is ours. **Entre nous soit dit,** this is between ourselves. *F:* **Ce que c'est que de nous!** such is life!

nouveau, -el, -elle, -eaux, *a.* (The form *nouvel* is used before m. sing. nouns beginning with a vowel or h 'mute'; also occ. before *et.*) **I.** New. **Il n'y a rien de nouveau,** there is no news. *Sch:* **Les nouveaux (élèves),** the new boys. *s.m.* **J'ai appris du nouveau,** I have some news. **2.** (*a*) New, recent, fresh. (*b*) (With adj. function) Newly, recently. *Le nouvel arrivé,* the newcomer. **Nouveau riche,** upstart. **3.** Another, fresh, further. *Jusqu'à nouvel ordre,* till further orders. **Le nouvel an,** the new year. **4.** **De nouveau,** again, afresh. **A nouveau,** anew, afresh.

nouveau-né, *a. & s.* New-born (child). *pl.* (Des) **nouveau-nés, nées.**

nouveauté, *s.f.* **I.** Newness, novelty. **Costume de haute nouveauté,** costume in the latest style. **2.** Change, innovation. **3.** New invention, new publication, etc. **4.** *pl. Com:* Fancy goods. **Marchand de nouveautés,** linen-draper.

nouvel, -elle[1]. See NOUVEAU.

nouvelle[2], *s.f.* **I.** (*a*) (Piece of) news. *Journ:* **Dernières nouvelles,** latest intelligence. (*b*) *pl.* Tidings, news. **Envoyez-moi de vos nouvelles,** let me hear from you. *F:* **Vous m'en direz des nouvelles,** you will be delighted with it. **2.** *Lit:* Novelette; short story.

Nouvelle-Écosse. *Pr.n.f.* Nova Scotia.

Nouvelle-Galles du Sud. *Pr.n.f.* New South Wales.

Nouvelle-Guinée. *Pr.n.f.* New Guinea.

nouvellement, *adv.* Newly, lately, recently.

Nouvelle-Orléans (la). *Pr.n.f.* New Orleans.

Nouvelle-Zélande. *Pr.n.f.* New Zealand.

novateur, -trice. I. *a.* Innovating. **2.** *s.* Innovator.

novembre, *s.m.* November.

novice, *s.m. & f.* Novice; probationer; tyro.

noyade, *s.f.* Drowning (fatality).

noyau, -aux, *s.m.* **1.** Stone (of fruit); kernel. **2.** Nucleus. *Pol:* Noyau communiste, communist cell. **3.** Newel (of stairs).

noyer¹, *s.m. Bot:* Walnut(-tree or -wood). *N. (blanc) d'Amérique,* hickory.

noyer², *v.tr.* (je noie) To drown; to swamp, deluge. *Yeux noyés de larmes,* eyes suffused with tears.

se noyer. *(a)* To drown oneself. *(b)* To be drowned. *Un homme qui se noie,* a drowning man.

noyé, *a.* (i) Drowned, (ii) drowning. *Secours aux noyés,* first aid for the drowned.

nu. **I.** *a.* Unclothed; naked; bare. *Art:* Nude. Nu comme un ver, stark naked. NOTE. *Nu* before the noun that it qualifies is invariable and is joined to the noun by a hyphen. **Aller les pieds nus, aller nu-pieds,** to go bare-footed. *(b)* Uncovered, plain, undisguised. *(c)* Bare (room). **2.** *s.m. Art:* (The) nude. **3.** Mettre qch. à nu, to lay bare, expose sth.

nuage, *s.m.* Cloud. *(a) Nuages pommelés,* mackerel sky. *Ciel couvert de nuages,* overcast sky. *(b)* Haze, mist (before the eyes). *(c)* Gloom, shadow. **Être dans les nuages,** to be in a brown study.

nuageux, *a.* *(a)* Cloudy; overcast (sky). *(b)* Hazy (thought).

nuance, *s.f.* Shade (of colour); hue. *Une n. de regret,* a touch of regret. *Il y a une n.,* there is a slight difference of meaning.

nubile, *a.* Marriageable, nubile.

nubilité, *s.f.* Nubility.

nudisme, *s.m.* Nudism.

nudiste, *s.m. & f.* Nudist.

nudité, *s.f.* *(a)* Nudity, nakedness. *(b)* Bareness.

nues, *s.f. pl.* Skies. *F:* **Porter qn (jusqu')aux nues,** to praise s.o. to the skies. **Tomber des nues,** (i) to arrive unexpectedly; (ii) **to be thunderstruck.**

nuée, *s.f.* *(a)* (Large) cloud, storm-cloud. *(b) Une n. d'insectes,* a cloud of insects.

nuire, *v.ind.tr.* (*p.p.* nui, otherwise conj. like CONDUIRE) *N. à qn,* to be hurtful, injurious, to s.o. Cela ne nuira en rien, that will do no harm. *N. aux intérêts de qn,* to prejudice s.o.'s interests.

nuisibilité, *s.f.* Harmfulness, injuriousness.

nuisible, *a.* Hurtful, harmful, noxious, detrimental.

nuisiblement, *adv.* Harmfully, injuriously.

nuit, *s.f.* Night. *(a)* Cette n., (i) to-night; (ii) last night. **Partir de nuit,** to depart by night. **Je n'ai pas dormi de la nuit,** I did not close my eyes all night. *(b)* Darkness. Il se fait nuit, night is falling; it is growing dark. **A la nuit tombante,** at nightfall. **A (la) nuit close,** after dark.

nuitamment, *adv.* By night.

nul, nulle. **1.** (With *ne* expressed or understood) *(a) indef. a.* No; not one. *Nul espoir,* no hope. *Sans nulle vanité,* without any conceit. *(b) indef.pron.* No one; nobody. *Nul ne le sait,* no one knows. **2.** *a.* *(a)* Worthless. *(b) Jur:* Nul et de nul effet, null and void. *Sp:* **Partie nulle,** drawn game; draw; (in racing) dead heat. *(c)* Nonexistent.

nullement, *adv.* (With *ne* expressed or understood) Not at all. *Il n'est n. sot,* he is by no means a fool.

nullifier, *v.tr.* To nullify, neutralize.

nullité, *s.f.* **1.** Nullity, invalidity. **2.** *(a)* Nothingness; non-existence. *(b)* Incompetence; incapacity. **3.** Nonentity.

nûment, *adv.* Frankly; without embellishments.

numéral, -aux, *a. & s.m.* Numeral.

numérateur, *s.m. Mth:* Numerator.

numération, *s.f. Ar:* Numeration.

numérique, *a.* Numerical.

numériquement, *adv.* Numerically.

numéro, *s.m.* *(a)* Number. *La chambre n.* 20, room number 20. *Le dernier n. du programme,* the last item on the programme. *(b)* Size (of stock sizes).

numéroter, *v.tr.* To number (street); to page (book).

numismatique. **1.** *a.* Numismatic. **2.** *s.f.* Numismatics.

nuptial, -aux, *a.* Nuptial, bridal. **Marche nuptiale,** wedding-march.

nuque, *s.f.* Nape of the neck.

nutria, *s.m. Com:* Nutria (fur).

nutritif, *a.* Nutritious, nourishing. **Valeur nutritive,** food-value.

nutrition, *s.f.* Nutrition.

nymphe, *s.f.* Nymph.

O, o [o], *s.m.* (The letter) O, o.

ô, *int.* (Address or invocation) O! oh!

oasis, *s.f.* Oasis.

obéir, *v.ind.tr.* To obey. (₵) *O. à qn*, to obey s.o. *v.tr.* **Se faire obéir**, to compel, enforce, obedience. (*b*) *O. à un ordre*, to comply with an order. *O. à la force*, to yield to force.

obéissance, *s.f.* (*a*) Obedience. (*b*) Dutifulness; submission.

obéissant, *a.* Obedient, dutiful, submissive.

obélisque, *s.m. Archeol:* Obelisk.

obèse, *a.* Obese, fat, corpulent, stout.

obésité, *s.f.* Obesity, corpulence.

objecter, *v.tr. On a objecté que . . .*, the objection has been raised that. . . .

objectif. **I.** *a.* Objective. **2.** *s.m.* Aim, object(ive), end. **3.** *s.m.* (*a*) *Opt:* Objectglass. (*b*) *Phot:* Lens.

objection, *s.f.* Objection.

objet, *s.m.* **I.** (*a*) Object, thing. (*b*) *Gram:* Object, complement. **2.** Subject, (subject-)matter. **3.** Object, aim, purpose. **Remplir son objet**, to attain one's end.

oblation, *s.f. Ecc:* Oblation, offering.

obligation, *s.f.* **I.** (*a*) (Moral) obligation; duty. (*b*) *O. du service militaire*, liability to military service. **2.** *Jur:* Recognizance, bond. **3.** Bond, debenture. **4.** Obligation, favour.

obligatoire, *a.* Obligatory; compulsory, binding.

obligeamment, *adv.* Obligingly.

obligeance, *s.f.* Obligingness.

obligeant, *a.* Obliging; kind, civil.

obliger, *v.tr.* (n. obligeons) **I.** To oblige, constrain, bind, compel. *Être obligé de faire qch.*, to be obliged to do sth. **2.** *O. qn*, to oblige s.o.

    s'obliger *à faire qch.*, to bind oneself, to undertake, to do sth.

    obligé, *a.* (*a*) Obliged, bound, compelled. (*b*) Indispensable, necessary. (*c*) Inevitable. (*d*) Obliged; grateful.

oblique, *a.* Oblique. **Regard oblique**, sideglance.

obliquement, *adv.* Obliquely, aslant.

oblitération, *s.f.* Obliteration; cancelling (of stamps).

oblitérer, *v.tr.* (j'oblitère; j'oblitérerai) **I.** To obliterate. **2.** To cancel (stamp).

oblong, -ongue, *a.* Oblong.

obscène [ɔp-], *a.* Obscene; lewd.

obscénité [ɔp-], *s.f.* Obscenity; lewdness.

obscur [ɔp-], *a.* **I.** Dark; gloomy. **2.** Obscure. (*a*) Difficult to understand. (*b*) Indistinct. (*c*) Unknown.

obscurcir [ɔp-], *v.tr.* To obscure. (*a*) To darken, cloud. (*b*) To dim (the sight).

    s'obscurcir, to grow dark; to become dim.

obscurcissement [ɔp-], *s.m.* Darkening; growing dimness.

obscurément [ɔp-], *adv.* Obscurely, dimly.

obscurité [ɔp-], *s.f.* Obscurity. (*a*) Darkness. (*b*) Unintelligibility. (*c*) Dimness. (*d*) *Vivre dans l'o.*, to live in obscurity.

obsédant [ɔp-], *a.* Haunting; obsessing.

obséder [ɔp-], *v.tr.* (j'obsède; j'obséderai) (*a*) To beset. (*b*) To obsess.

obsèques [ɔp-], *s.f.pl.* Obsequies; funeral.

obséquieusement [ɔp-], *adv.* Obsequiously.

obséquieux [ɔp-], *a.* Obsequious.

observance [ɔp-], *s.f.* Observance; (i) observing, keeping (of rule); (ii) rule observed.

observateur, -trice [ɔp-]. **I.** *s.* Observer. **2.** *a.* Observant, observing.

observation [ɔp-], *s.f.* **I.** Observance, keeping (of laws). **2.** Observation. (*a*) *Poste d'o.*, look-out post. **Être en observation**, to be on the look-out. (*b*) Remark.

observatoire [ɔp-], *s.m. Astr:* Observatory.

observer [ɔp-], *v.tr.* To observe. (*a*) To keep (to), to comply with. (*b*) To watch. *On nous observe*, we are being watched. (*c*) To note, notice. **Faire observer qch. à qn**, to draw s.o.'s attention to sth.

    s'observer, to be circumspect.

obsession [ɔp-], *s.f.* Obsession.

obstacle [ɔp-], *s.m.* Obstacle (*à*, to); impediment, hindrance. **Faire obstacle à qch.**, to stand in the way of sth.

obstination [ɔp-], *s.f* Obstinacy, stubbornness.

obstinément [ɔp-], *adv.* Obstinately, stubbornly.

obstiner (s') [ɔp-], *v.pr.* To show obstinacy. *S'o. à qch.*, to persist in sth.

    obstiné, *a.* Stubborn, self-willed, obstinate, dogged; persistent.

obstructif [ɔp-], *a.* Obstructive.

obstruction [ɔp-], *s.f.* Obstruction.

obstruer [ɔp-], *v.tr.* To obstruct; to choke (outlet).

obtenir [ɔp-], *v.tr.* (Conj. like TENIR) To obtain, get; to gain, procure. *Où cela s'obtient-il?* where is it obtainable?

obturer [ɔp-], *v.tr.* To stop (tooth).

obtus [ɔp-], *a.* **I.** Blunt(ed). **2.** Dull, obtuse. **3.** *Geom:* Obtuse (angle).

obus [ɔby(:s)], *s.m. Artil:* Shell. *O. à balles*, shrapnel.

obusier, *s.m. Artil:* Howitzer.

obvier, *v.ind.tr. O. à qch.*, to obviate sth.

occasion, *s.f.* **I.** (*a*) Opportunity, occasion, chance. **Saisir l'occasion aux cheveux**, to take time by the forelock. **Suivant l'occasion**, as occasion arises. **A l'occasion**, when the opportunity offers. (*b*) Bargain. **Vente d'occasion**, (bargain) sale. **Marchandises**

d'occasion, job-lot. Livre d'occasion, second-hand book. **2.** Occasion, juncture. Pour l'occasion, for the nonce. A l'occasion, in case of need. **3.** Motive, reason, occasion.

ccasionnel, -elle, a. Occasional.

●ccasionnellement, adv. Occasionally.

●ccasionner, v.tr. To occasion, cause.

●ccident, s.m. West, occident.

●ccidental, -aux, a. West(ern); occidental.

●cculte, a. Occult; hidden (cause).

●ccupant, a. Occupying. s. Occupier.

●ccupation, s.f. Occupation. **I.** Occupancy. **2.** (a) Business, employment. **Cela me donne de l'occupation,** it gives me something to do. (b) Pursuit, profession.

●ccuper, v.tr. To occupy. **I.** (a) To inhabit. (b) Mil: To hold. (c) To fill, take up (time). (d) O. un poste important, to hold an important post. **2.** To give occupation to. O. qn, to give s.o. something to do.

s'occuper. I. To keep oneself busy. **2.** S'o. de qch., to busy oneself with sth. Je m'en occuperai, I shall see to it. Qui s'occupe de ce qu'il dit? who minds what he says?

occupé, a. **I.** Busy, engaged. **2.** Cette place est occupée, this seat is taken.

●ccurrence, s.f. Occurrence, event; emergency. En l'occurrence, in the circumstances.

●céan, s.m. Ocean.

●céanie (l'). Pr.n.f. Geog: The South Sea Islands.

●céanique, a. Oceanic.

●celot, s.m. Ocelot; tiger-cat.

●cre, s.f. Ochre.

●ctave, s.f. Mus: etc: Octave.

●ctobre, s.m. October.

●ctogénaire, a. & s. Octogenarian.

●ctogonal, -aux, a. Octagonal.

●ctogone. Geom: **I.** a. = OCTOGONAL. **2.** s.m. Octagon.

●ctroi, s.m. **I.** Concession, grant(ing). **2.** (a) Town dues. (b) Toll-house.

●ctroyer, v.tr. (j'octroie) To grant, concede.

●culaire. I. a. Ocular. **Témoin oculaire,** eyewitness. **2.** s.m. Opt: Eye-piece.

●culiste, s.m. Oculist.

●dalisque, s.f. Odalisque.

●de, s.f. Lit: Ode.

●deur, s.f. **I.** Odour, smell. **2.** Toil: Perfume, scent.

●dieusement, adv. Odiously, hatefully.

●dieux. I. a. Odious; hateful. **2.** s.m. Odiousness.

●dorant, a. Odorous, sweet-smelling.

●dorat, s.m. (Sense of) smell.

●dyssée, s.f. (a) Gr.Lit: L'O., the Odyssey. (b) F: Odyssey, wanderings.

Œdipe. Pr.n.m. Gr.Lit: Œdipus.

●eil [œːj], pl. yeux, s.m. **I.** Eye. Je n'ai pas fermé l'œil de la nuit, I didn't sleep a wink all night. Fermer les yeux sur qch., to wink at sth. Ouvrir de grands yeux, to open one's eyes wide. Ouvrir les yeux à qn to open

s.o.'s eyes. Il avait les yeux hors de la tête, his eyes were starting from his head. Regarder qn dans le blanc des yeux, to look s.o. full in the face. Il ne travaille pour les beaux yeux de personne, he doesn't do anything for love. Cela saute aux yeux, it is obvious. Payer les yeux de la tête, to pay an exorbitant price. **2.** Sight, look, eye. Cela charme les yeux, it delights the eye. Chercher qn des yeux, to look about for s.o. Mesurer qch. à l'œil, to measure sth. by eye. Prov: Loin des yeux, loin du cœur, out of sight, out of mind. Avoir l'œil, to be observant, sharp-eyed. Se consulter de l'œil, to exchange glances. A vue d'œil, visibly. Coup d'œil, (i) view; (ii) glance. Regarder qn d'un bon œil, to look favourably upon s.o. Voir du même œil que qn, to see eye to eye with s.o. Faire les yeux doux à qn, to make sheep's eyes at s.o. Faire les gros yeux à qn, to look sternly at s.o. Être très sur l'œil, to be very strict. **3.** Eye (of needle). **4.** Nau: L'œil du vent, the wind's eye.

œillade [œjad], s.f. Glance, ogle, leer.

œillet [œjɛ], s.m. **I.** Eyelet. **2.** Bot: Pink. O. de poète, sweet-william.

œuf [œf], pl. œufs [ø], s.m. (a) Egg. Cu: Œuf mollet, soft-boiled egg. Œuf sur le plat, fried egg. Œufs au lait, custard. En œuf, egg-shaped. F: Marcher sur des œufs, to tread on delicate ground. F: Tuer qch. dans l'œuf, to nip sth. in the bud. (b) pl. Spawn; (hard) roe.

œuvre, s.f. **I.** (a) Work, working. **Faire œuvre d'ami,** to behave like a friend. Exécuteur des hautes œuvres, executioner. Il est fils de ses œuvres, he is a self-made man. (b) Œuvre de bienfaisance, charitable institution. **2.** (Finished) work, production. Œuvres d'un écrivain, works of a writer. **3.** s.m. In sg. only. L'o. de Molière, the works of Molière (as a whole).

offensant, a. Offensive, insulting.

offense, s.f. **I.** Offence. **2.** Sin, trespass. **3.** Jur: Offense à la Cour, contempt of Court.

offenser, v.tr. **I.** To offend, to give offence to. **2.** (a) To be detrimental to, to injure. (b) To offend; to shock.

s'offenser, to take offence (de, at).

offensif. I. a. Offensive. **2.** s.f. Mil: L'offensive, the offensive.

offensivement, adv. Offensively.

offert, -erte. See OFFRIR.

offertoire, s.m. Ecc: Offertory.

office. I. s.m. (a) Office, functions, duty. **Faire office de secrétaire,** to act as secretary. Adv.phr. D'office, (i) officially; (ii) as a matter of course. (b) Service. (c) Divine Service. (d) Bureau, office. **2.** s.f. (a) (Butler's) pantry. (b) Servants' hall.

officiant, a. Officiating (priest).

officiel, -elle, a. Official; formal.

officiellement, adv. Officially.

officier[1], *v.i.* To officiate

officier[2], *s.m.* Officer.

officieusement, *adv.* **1.** Officiously. **2.** Unofficially.

officieux, **1.** *a.* (*a*) Officious; over-obliging. (*b*) Unofficial. (*c*) Kindly-meant. **2.** *s.* Busybody.

offrande, *s.f. Ecc:* Offering.

offrant, *a. & s.m.* Le plus offrant (et dernier enchérisseur), the highest bidder.

offre, *s.f.* Offer, proposal; tender. **L'offre et la demande**, supply and demand.

offrir, *v.tr.* (Conj. like OUVRIR) To offer; to offer up. *O. dix francs d'un objet*, to offer ten francs for an object.

    s'offrir. **1.** (Of pers.) To offer oneself. **2.** (Of thg) To offer itself, to present itself.

offusquer, *v.tr.* To offend, shock.

    s'offusquer, to take offence (*de*, at).

ogival, -aux, *a.* Pointed, ogival.

ogive, *s.f.* Ogive; pointed arch.

ogre, ogresse, *s.* Ogre, ogress.

oh, *int* Oh! O!

ohé, *int.* Hi! *Ohé du navire!* ship ahoy.

ohm [o:m], *s.m. El.Meas:* Ohm.

oie, *s.f.* Goose. **Pas de l'oie,** goose-step.

oign-ais, -is, etc See OINDRE.

oignon [ɔɲɔ̃], *s.m.* **1.** (*a*) Onion **En rang d'oignons,** in a row. (*b*) Bulb (of tulip). **2.** Bunion.

oindre, *v.tr.* (Conj. like JOINDRE) To anoint (king). **L'Oint du Seigneur,** the Lord's Anointed

oiseau, *s.m.* **1.** Bird. *Drôle d'o.*, queer customer. **2.** (Bricklayer's) hod.

oiseau-mouche, *s.m. Orn:* Hummingbird. *pl. Des oiseaux-mouches.*

oiseleur, *s.m.* Fowler, bird-catcher.

oiselier, *s.m.* Bird-fancier.

oiseusement, *adv.* Idly; unnecessarily.

oiseux, *a.* **1.** Idle, lazy. **2.** Idle (question).

oisif. **1.** *a.* Idle; lazy. **2.** *s.* Idler.

oisillon [-zijɔ̃], *s.m.* Fledgling.

oisivement, *adv.* Idly.

oisiveté, *s.f.* Idleness.

oison, *s.m.* Gosling.

oléagineux, *a.* Oleaginous; oily.

olfactif, *a.* Olfactory.

oligarchie, *s.f.* Oligarchy.

olivâtre, *a.* Olive-hued; sallow.

olive, *s.f.* (*a*) Olive. (*b*) *a.inv.* Olive-green.

olivier[1], *s.m.* Olive-tree.

Olivier[2]. *Pr.n.m.* Oliver.

Olympe. *Pr.n.m.* (Mount) Olympus.

olympien, -ienne, *a.* Olympian.

olympique, *a.* Olympic.

ombelle, *s.f. Bot:* Umbel.

ombellifère. *Bot:* **1.** *a.* Umbelliferous. **2.** *s.f.pl.* Umbelliferae, umbellifers.

ombrage, *s.m.* **1.** Shade. **2. Prendre ombrage de qch.,** (i) (of horse) to shy at sth.; (ii) *F:* to take umbrage at sth.

ombrager, *v.tr.* (Il ombrageait) (*a*) To shade. (*b*) To overshadow.

ombragé, *a.* Shaded, shady.

ombrageusement, *adv.* Distrustfully.

ombrageux, *a.* **1.** Shy, skittish (horse **2.** Easily offended; touchy.

ombre[1], *s.f.* **1.** Shadow. **2.** Shade. Fair ombre à qn, to put s.o. in the shade. **3.** Darkness. **4.** (*a*) Ghost, shade, shadowy figure N'être plus que l'ombre de soi-même, to b merely the shadow of one's former sel (*b*) *Vous n'avez pas l'o. d'une chance,* you hav not the ghost of a chance. Lâcher la pro pour l'ombre, to drop the substance for th shadow.

ombre[2], *s.f.* **Terre d'ombre,** umber.

ombrelle, *s.f.* Parasol, sunshade.

Ombrie. *Pr.n.f. Geog:* Umbria.

omelette, *s.f. Cu:* Omelet(te) *O. aux fine herbes,* savoury omelet.

omettre, *v.tr.* (Conj. like METTRE) To omit to leave out.

omi-s, -t, etc. See OMETTRE.

omission, *s.f.* Omission. *Typ:* Sign d'omission, caret.

omnibus [-by:s]. **1.** *s.m.* Omnibus. **2.** *a.ine* Train omnibus, slow train.

omnipotence, *s.f.* Omnipotence.

omnipotent, *a.* Omnipotent.

omnivore, *a.* Omnivorous.

omoplate, *s.f.* Shoulder-blade.

on, *indef.pron.* (Often l'on, esp. after a vow sound) One, people, they, we, etc *On ne sa jamais,* one never can tell *On dit, it i* said. *On frappe,* there is a knock at th door. *On demande une bonne cuisinièr* wanted, a good cook. NOTE: A pred. nou or adj. following *on* is fem. or pl. as the sens requires. *Ici on est égaux,* here we are all equa

once[1], *s.f. Meas:* Ounce.

once[2], *s.f. Z:* Ounce, snow-leopard.

oncle, *s.m.* Uncle.

onction, *s.f.* Unction. (*a*) Anointing (*b*) Unctuousness.

onctueusement, *adv.* Unctuously.

onctueux, *a.* (*a*) Unctuous. (*b*) *Pej:* Oily.

onctuosité, *s.f.* Unctuousness.

onde, *s.f.* **1.** *Lit:* Wave. **2.** (*a*) Wavy line (*b*) Corrugation. **3.** *Ph:* Wave. *Grande ondes,* long waves.

ondé, *a.* Undulating, wavy; waved (hair).

ondée, *s.f.* Heavy shower.

on-dit, *s.m.inv.* Rumour, hearsay.

ondoiement, *s.m.* Undulation; wavy motior

ondoyant, *a.* Undulating, wavy; swayir (crowd). *Blé o.,* waving corn.

ondoyer, *v.i.* (j'ondoie) To undulate wave, ripple.

ondulant, *a.* Undulating (landscape); wav ing (corn); flowing (mane, drapery).

ondulation, *s.f.* **1.** Undulation. (l *Région à ondulations,* rolling country. **2** *Hairdr:* Wave.

onduler. **1.** *v.i.* To undulate, rippl **2.** *v.tr.* To wave (the hair). **Se faire ondule** to have one's hair waved.

ondulé. *a.* Undulating; wavy (hair); corrugated.

onduleux, *a.* Wavy, sinuous.

onéreusemen., *adv.* Onerously.

onéreux, *a.* Onerous; burdensome.

ongle, *s.m.* (Finger-)nail; claw. **Coup d'ongle.** scratch. **Se faire les ongles,** to trim one's nails. **F:** **Rogner les ongles à qn,** to cut s.o.'s claws. **Se ronger les ongles,** *F:* to be impatient. **Français jusqu'au bout des ongles,** French to the finger-tips.

onglée, *s.f.* Tingling, aching (of finger-ends).

onguent [ɔ̃gã], *s.m.* Ointment, unguent, salve.

ont. See AVOIR.

onyx [ɔniks], *s.m.* *Miner:* Onyx.

onze, *num. a. inv. & s.m. inv.* (The *e* of *le, de,* is not, as a rule, elided before *onze* and its derivatives) Eleven. *Le onze avril,* the eleventh of April. *P:* **Prendre le train onze,** to go on Shanks's mare.

onzième. 1. *num. a. & s.* Eleventh. **2.** *s.m.* Eleventh (part).

opacité, *s.f.* Opacity.

opale. 1. *s.f.* Opal. **2.** *a.inv.* Opalescent.

opalescence, *s.f.* Opalescence.

opalescent, *a.* Opalescent.

opaque, *a.* Opaque.

opéra, *s.m.* **1.** Opera. **2.** Opera-house.

opérateur, -trice, *s.* Operator.

opératif, *a.* Operative.

opération, *s.f.* **1.** Operation; working; process. **2.** *Opérations militaires,* military operations. **3.** Transaction; deal.

opérer, *v.tr.* (j'opère; j'opérerai) To operate. **1.** To bring about, to effect. **2.** (*a*) To carry out, perform. (*b*) *O. un malade,* to operate on a patient. **Se faire opérer,** to undergo an operation. **3.** *Abs.* (Of remedy) To work, act. **s'opérer,** to be wrought, to take place.

opéré, *s.* Patient (operated upon).

opérette, *s.f.* Operetta; musical comedy.

ophidien, *s.m.* Ophidian

ophtalmie, *s.f.* Ophthalmia.

opiat, *s.m.* Opiate, narcotic.

opiner, *v.i.* To opine; to be of opinion (*que,* that).

opiniâtre, *a.* Obstinate. (*a*) Self-opinionated. (*b*) Self-willed; stubborn. (*c*) Persistent. *Résistance o.,* dogged resistance.

opiniâtrement, *adv.* Obstinately; doggedly.

opiniâtrer (s'), *v.pr. S'o. à faire qch.,* to persist stubbornly in doing sth.

opiniâtreté, *s.f.* Obstinacy, stubbornness.

opinion, *s.f.* Opinion; view, judgment. **Donner bonne opinion de sa capacité,** to make a good impression.

opium [-ɔm], *s.m.* Opium.

opossum [-sɔm], *s.m.* *Z:* Opossum

opportun, *a.* (*a*) Opportune, timely. (*b*) Expedient, advisable.

opportunément, *adv.* Opportunely, seasonably.

opportunisme, *s.m.* Opportunism.

opportuniste. 1. *a.* Time-serving. **2.** *s.* Opportunist; time-server.

opportunité, *s.f.* **1.** (*a*) Opportuneness, seasonableness (*b*) Expediency, advisability. **2.** Favourable occasion; opportunity.

opposer, *v.tr.* **1.** To oppose. *O. une vigoureuse résistance,* to offer a vigorous resistance. **2.** To compare, to contrast (*à,* with). **s'opposer** *à qch.,* to oppose sth.; to be opposed to sth.

opposé. 1. *a.* Opposed, opposing; opposite (side). *Tons opposés,* contrasting colours. **2.** *s.m.* Contrary, reverse, opposite.

opposition, *s.f.* **1.** Opposition. **2.** Contrast. **Par opposition à qch.,** as opposed to sth.

oppresser, *v.tr.* To oppress. (*a*) To weigh down; to lie heavy on. (*b*) To deject, depress.

oppresseur, *s.m.* Oppressor.

oppressif, *a.* Oppressive.

oppression, *s.f.* Oppression.

oppressivement, *adv.* Oppressively.

opprimer, *v.tr.* To oppress, crush (down).

opprimé, *a.* Oppressed, down-trodden.

opprobre, *s.m.* Disgrace, opprobrium.

opter, *v.i. O. pour qch.,* to decide in favour of sth.

opticien, *s.m.* Optician.

optimisme, *s.m.* Optimism.

optimiste. 1. *a.* Optimistic; sanguine. **2.** *s.* Optimist.

option, *s.f.* Option, choice.

optique. 1. *a.* Optic; optical. **2.** *s.f.* Optics.

opulence, *s.f.* Opulence, affluence.

opulent, *a.* Opulent, rich; affluent.

or¹, *s.m.* Gold.

or², *conj.* Now. **Or donc,** well then.

oracle, *s.m.* Oracle.

orage, *s.m.* (Thunder-)storm.

orageusement, *adv.* Stormily.

orageux, *a.* **1.** Stormy. *Discussion orageuse,* stormy discussion. **2.** Threatening, thundery (weather); lowering (sky).

oraison, *s.f.* **1.** **Oraison funèbre,** funeral oration. **2.** Orison, prayer.

oral, -aux. **1.** *a.* Oral; verbal. **2.** *s.m.* Oral examination, viva voce examination.

oralement, *adv.* Orally, by word of mouth.

orange, *s.f.* **1.** Orange. *O. amère,* Seville orange. **2.** *s.m.* Orange (colour).

oranger, *s.m.* Orange-tree.

orang-outan(g) [ɔrãutã], *s.m.* *Z:* Orangoutang. *pl. Des orangs-outan(g)s.*

orateur, *s.m.* Orator, speaker.

oratoire¹, *a.* Oratorical. *L'art o.,* oratory.

oratoire², *s.m.* Oratory; chapel.

oratorio, *s.m.* *Mus:* Oratorio.

orbe, *s.m.* Orb; globe; sphere.

orbite, *s.m.* or *f.* **1.** Orbit (of planet). **2.** Socket (of the eye).

Orcades (les). *Pr.n.f.pl.* The Orkneys.

orchestral, -aux [-kɛs-], *a.* Orchestral.

orchestre [-kɛs-], *s.m.* Orchestra.

orchidée [-ki-], *s.f.* Orchid.

orchis [·kis], *s.m. Bot:* Orchis; wild orchid.
ordinaire. 1. *a.* Ordinary, usual, common.
Fractions ordinaires, vulgar fractions. Vin
ordinaire, table wine. **2.** *s.m.* (*a*) Wont,
custom, usual practice. D'ordinaire, usually,
as a rule. Comme d'ordinaire, as usual.
(*b*) Cela sort de l'o., it is out of the ordinary.
ordinairement, *adv.* Ordinarily, as a rule,
usually.
ordinal, -aux, *a.* Ordinal.
ordination, *s.f. Ecc:* Ordination.
ordonnance, *s.f.* **1.** Order, (general) arrangement. **2.** Enactment, order. **3.** Officier
d'ordonnance, aide-de-camp; *Navy:* flag-
lieutenant. **4.** *Mil:* (*a*) Orderly. (*b*) Occ.
m. Officer's servant; batman. **5.** *Med:*
Prescription.
ordonner, *v.tr.* **1.** To arrange (sth.). **2.** To
order, command. *O. un remède à qn,* to
prescribe a remedy for s.o. **3.** To ordain
(priest)
 ordonné, *a.* (*a*) Orderly, well-ordered.
(*b*) Of regular habits; tidy.
ordre, *s.m.* Order. **1.** Homme d'ordre,
orderly, methodical, man. Mettre (bon) ordre
à un abus, to put an abuse right. **2.** A
l'ordre! order! chair! *Jur:* Ordre public,
law and order. *Délit contre l'o. public,* breach
of the peace. **3.** Ordre du jour, (i) agenda
(of meeting); (ii) *Mil:* order of the day.
Mil: Cité à l'ordre (du jour), mentioned in
despatches. **4.** (*a*) Order (of architecture);
class, division, category. De premier ordre,
first-rate. *Renseignements d'o. privé,* enquiries
of a private nature. De l'ordre de . . .,
ranging about. . . (*b*) Ordre religieux,
monastic order. (*c*) *pl. Ecc:* Holy Orders.
Recevoir les ordres, to be ordained. (*d*) Decoration. L'Ordre de la Jarretière, the Order of
the Garter. **5.** (*a*) Command; warrant.
O. d'exécution, death-warrant. "Toujours à
vos ordres," 'yours obediently.' (*b*) Billet à
ordre, promissory note.
ordure, *s.f.* **1.** (*a*) Dirt, filth. (*b*) Excrement,
dung. (*c*) Filthiness. **2.** *pl.* Sweepings, refuse.
oréade, *s.f. Myth:* Oread.
orée, *s.f.* Edge, verge, skirt (of a wood).
oreille [ɔrɛːj], *s.f.* Ear. **1.** Baisser l'oreille,
to be crestfallen. (Of horse) Coucher les
oreilles, to lay its ears back. *F:* Il s'est fait
tirer l'oreille, he took a lot of coaxing. Montrer le bout de l'oreille, to show the cloven
hoof. **2.** N'écouter que d'une oreille, to
listen absent-mindedly. *Souffler qch. à l'o.
de qn,* to whisper sth. to s.o. *F:* Dresser
l'oreille, to prick up one's ears. Faire la
sourde oreille, to turn a deaf ear. **3.** Bergère
à oreilles, grandfather chair.
oreiller [ɔrɛje], *s.m.* Pillow. Prendre conseil
de son oreiller, to sleep over it.
orfèvre, *s.m.* Goldsmith.
orfèvrerie, *s.f.* **1.** (*a*) Goldsmith's craft.
(*b*) Goldsmith's shop. **2.** (Gold) plate.
orfraie, *s.f.* Osprey, sea-eagle, sea-hawk.

organe, *s.m.* **1.** Organ (of sight). **2.** Agent,
means, medium.
organique, *a.* Organic.
organiquement, *adv.* Organically.
organisateur, -trice, *s.* Organizer.
organisation, *s.f.* **1.** Organizing. **2.** Organization.
organiser, *v.tr.* To organize; to arrange.
 organisé, *a.* **1.** Organic (body). **2.** Or-
ganized, constituted.
organisme, *s.m.* Organism. *Anat:* (The)
system.
organiste, *s.m. & f. Mus:* Organist.
orge, *s.* Barley. **1.** *s.f.* Grain d'o., barleycorn. **2.** *s.m.* Orge perlé, pearl-barley.
orgelet, *s.m.* Sty(e) (on the eye).
orgie, *s.f.* (*a*) Orgy; drunken feast. (*b*) *F:*
Profusion; riot (of colour).
orgue [ɔrg], *s.m. Mus:* Organ. **2.** Orgue
de Barbarie, barrel-organ.
orgueil [-gœːj], *s.m.* Pride, arrogance.
orgueilleusement [-gœj-], *adv.* Proudly.
orgueilleux [-gœj-], *a.* Proud, arrogant.
orient, *s.m.* **1.** Orient, East. **2.** Water,
orient (of pearl).
oriental, -aux. *a.* Eastern, oriental.
orientation, *s.f.* **1.** Orientation. Perdre le
sens de l'orientation, to lose one's bearings.
2. *O. d'une maison,* aspect of a house.
orienter, *v.tr.* **1.** (*a*) *O. des voiles,* to trim
sails. *Navy: O. un canon,* to train a gun.
(*b*) To direct, guide. **2.** *Surv:* To take the
bearings of (spot).
 s'orienter, to take, find, one's bearings.
orifice, *s.m.* Aperture, opening, orifice.
originaire, *a.* **1.** Originating; native. **2.**
Original.
originairement, *adv.* Originally.
original, -aux, *a. & s.* **1.** Original. Copier
qch. sur l'original, to copy sth. from the
original. **2.** (*a*) Original; novel, fresh.
(*b*) *F:* Odd, queer. C'est un original, he's
a character.
originalité, *s.f.* (*a*) Originality. (*b*) Eccentricity, oddity.
origine, *s.f.* Origin. **1.** Beginning. **2.** (*a*)
Extraction (of person). (*b*) Nationality.
3. Source, derivation. Mots de même origine,
cognate words. *Post:* Bureau d'origine,
(postal) office of dispatch.
originel, -elle, *a.* Primordial, original.
originellement, *adv.* Originally.
orignac [-nak], *s.m., Z:* Moose.
oripeau, *s.m.* **1.** Tinsel, foil. **2.** *pl.* Tawdry
finery.
ormaie, *s.f.* Elm-grove.
orme, *s.m.* Elm(-tree, -wood). *O. de montagne,* wych-e m.
ormeau, *s.m. Bot:* (Young) elm.
ornement, *s.m.* Ornament, adornment,
embellishment.
ornemental. -aux *a* Ornamental decorative
ornementation, *s.f.* Ornamentation.

ornementer, *v.tr.* To ornament.

orner, *v.tr.* To ornament, adorn, decorate. **orné,** *a.* Ornate.

ornière, *s.f.* Rut.

ornithologie, *s.f.* Ornithology.

ornithologiste, *s.m.* Ornithologist.

ornithorynque, *s.m.* *Z:* Ornithorhynchus, duck-billed platypus.

Orphée. *Pr.n.m.* *Gr.Myth:* Orpheus.

orphelin, *s.* Orphan; *a.* orphan(ed).

orphelinat, *s.m.* Orphanage; orphan-home.

orpin, *s.m.* *Bot:* Stonecrop.

orteil [-tɛːj], *s.m.* Toe. **Gros orteil,** big toe.

orthodoxe, *a.* Orthodox.

orthodoxie, *s.f.* Orthodoxy.

orthographe, *s.f.* Orthography, spelling.

orthographier, *v.tr.* To spell.

ortie, *s.f.* Nettle. *O. brûlante* stinging nettle.

ortolan, *s.m.* *Orn:* Ortolan (bunting).

orvet, *s.m.* Slow-worm, blind-worm.

os [ɔs; *pl.* o], *s.m.* Bone. **Trempé jusqu'aux os,** wet through. **Il y laissera ses os,** he'll die there.

oscillant, *a.* Oscillating; rocking.

oscillation, *s.f.* Oscillation. (*a*) Swing (of pendulum). (*b*) Rocking (*c*) Vibration.

osciller [ɔsije, ɔsile], *v.i* To oscillate. **I.** To swing; to sway; to rock. **2.** To waver

oseille [ozɛːj, o-], *s.f.* *Bot:* Sorrel.

oser, *v.tr.* To dare, venture **osé,** *a.* Bold, daring.

oseraie, *s.f.* Osier-bed.

osier, *s.m.* Osier, water-willow. **Brin d'osier,** withe. **Panier d'osier,** wicker-basket.

osmium [-jɔm], *s.m.* *Ch:* Osmium.

ossature, *s.f.* **I.** Frame, skeleton. **2.** Frame-(work).

osselet, *s.m.* Knuckle-bone.

ossements, *s.m.pl* Bones, remains.

osseux, *a.* Bony; osseous.

ossuaire, *s.m.* Ossuary, charnel-house.

ostensible, *a.* Fit to be seen; patent to all

ostensiblement, *adv.* Openly publicly.

ostentation, *s.f.* Ostentation, show.

ostraciser, *v.tr.* To ostracize.

ostracisme, *s.m* Ostracism.

•tage, *s.m.* Hostage.

•tarie, *s.f.* Sea-lion.

•ter, *v.tr.* To remove take away (*a*) *O son chapeau à qn,* to raise one's hat to s.o. (*b*) *O. qch. à qn,* to take sth. away from s.o. (*c*) *O. qch. de qch.,* to take sth. away from sth.

•ttoman. I. *a. & s.* Ottoman. **2.** *s.f.* **Ottomane,** divan, ottoman.

•u, *conj.* Or. **I.** *Entrez ou sortez,* either come in or go out **2. Ou . . ou . . .,** either or

•ù, *adv.* **I.** *Interr.* Where? *Où en êtes-vous?* how far have you got with it? **D'où?** whence? *D'où vient que . . ?* how does it happen that . ? **Jusqu'où?** how far? *Déposez-le* **n'importe où,** put it down anywhere. **2.** *Rel:* (*a*) Where **Partout où** *il va,* wher-

ever he goes. **Là où,** (there) where. (*b*) When. *Dans le temps où il était jeune,* in the days when he was young. (*c*) *La maison où il demeure,* the house he lives in. **3.** (Concessive) *Où que vous soyez,* wherever you may be.

ouaille [waːj], *s.f. Le pasteur et ses ouailles,* the minister and his flock.

ouate, *s.f.* (Usu. *la ouate*) (*a*) Wadding. (*b*) Cotton-wool.

ouater, *v.tr.* To pad; to quilt. **ouaté,** *a.* **I.** Padded; quilted. **2.** *F:* Fleecy (cloud); soft (footstep).

oubli, *s.m.* **I.** (*a*) Forgetting; forgetfulness. (*b*) **Tomber dans l'oubli,** to sink into oblivion **2.** Omission, oversight.

oublier, *v.tr.* To forget. (*a*) **Faire oublier son passé,** to live down one's past. *On ne nous le laissera pas o.,* we shall never hear the last of it. (*b*) To overlook, neglect. **s'oublier,** to forget one's manners.

oublieux, *a.* Forgetful.

Ouessant. *Pr.n.m. Geog:* Ushant.

ouest [west]. **I.** *s.m.* No *pl.* West. **2.** *a.inv.* *Côté o.,* western, west, side.

ouf [uf], *int.* **I.** (Sigh of relief) Ah ! ha ! **2.** (Indicating oppression) Phew !

oui. Yes. **I.** *adv.* **Je crois que oui,** I think so. *Faire signe que oui,* to nod assent. **Oui-dà!** yes, rather ! *Nau: Oui, commandant!* aye, aye, sir ! **2.** *s.m. inv.* *Deux cents oui,* two hundred ayes.

ouï. See OUÏR.

ouiche, *int.* (Denotes incredulity) *Ah o.!* pooh ! don't you believe it !

oui-dire, *s.m.inv* Hearsay

ouïe, *s.f.* **I.** (Sense of) hearing. *Avoir l'o. fine,* to be sharp of hearing **2.** *pl.* Gills (of fish).

ouïr, *v.tr.* (Used in the *inf & in p.p.* **ouï**) To hear.

ouistiti, *s.m.* *Z:* Marmoset.

ouragan, *s.m.* Hurricane.

Oural (l'). *Pr.n. Geog:* The Ural (river).

ourdir, *v.tr.* *F:* To hatch (plot).

ourler, *v.tr.* To hem

ourlet, *s.m.* Hem.

ours [urs], *s.* **I.** *Z:* Bear. *F:* **Ours mal léché,** unlicked cub. **2.** *Astr:* **La Grande Ourse,** the Great Bear.

oursin, *s.m.* Sea-urchin, sea-hedgehog.

ourson, *s.m.* Bear's cub.

outarde, *s.f.* *Orn:* Bustard.

outil [uti], *s.m.* Tool, implement.

outillage [-jaːʒ], *s.m.* Gear, plant, equipment.

outiller [-je], *v.tr.* To equip, supply.

outrage, *s.m.* Outrage.

outrageant, *a.* Insulting; outrageous.

outrager, *v.tr.* (n. outrageons) **I.** To insult. **2.** To outrage.

outrageusement, *adv.* Outrageously.

outrageux, *a.* Insulting, outrageous.

outrance, *s.f* *A outrance,* to the bitter end. **Guerre à outrance,** war to the knife.

outre[1], *s.f.* Goatskin bottle; water-skin.

outre². **I.** *prep.* (*a*) Beyond. (*b*) In addition to. (*c*) *Pref.* Ultra-. *Outremarin*, ultramarine. **2.** *adv.* (*a*) **Passer outre,** to go on, proceed further. *Passer o. à la loi*, to set the law at defiance. (*b*) **En outre,** besides, moreover; over and above. (*c*) *Conj.phr.* **Outre que** + *ind.*, apart from the fact that. . .

outrecuidance, *s.f* Presumptuousness, bumptiousness.

outrecuidant, *a.* Presumptuous, bumptious.

outre-Manche, *adv.phr.* On the other side of, across, the Channel.

outremer, *s.m.* (**Bleu d')outremer,** ultramarine.

outre-mer, *adv.phr.* Overseas.

outrepasser, *v.tr.* To go beyond; to exceed.

outrer, *v.tr.* **I.** To carry to excess; to overdo. **2.** To tire out. **3.** To provoke beyond measure.

outré, *a.* *O. de colère*, beside oneself with anger.

outre-tombe (**d'**), *adv.phr.* From beyond the grave.

ouvertement, *adv.* Openly, frankly.

ouverture, *s.f.* **I.** (*a*) Opening (of door). *O. d'hostilités*, outbreak of hostilities. (*b*) **Faire des ouvertures à qn,** to make overtures to s.o. (*c*) *Mus:* Overture. (*d*) *Heures d'o.*, business hours (of shop); visiting hours (of museum). **2.** Opening, aperture.

ouvrable, *a.* **I.** Workable, tractable. **2.** **Jour ouvrable,** working day.

ouvrage, *s.m.* Work. **I.** (*a*) **Se mettre à l'ouvrage,** to set to work. (*b*) Workmanship. **2.** Piece of work; product. **Boîte à ouvrage,** work-box.

ouvré, *a.* Worked (timber); wrought (iron).

ouvre-boîtes, *s.m.inv.* Tin-opener.

ouvreuse, *s.f.* Usherette.

ouvrier. **I.** *s.* (*a*) Worker; workman, work-woman. *O. de ferme*, farm-labourer. (*b*) *Première ouvrière*, forewoman. **2.** *a.* *Les classes ouvrières*, the working classes. *Le parti o.* the labour party. *Train o.*, workmen's train

ouvrir, *v.* (*pr.p.* ouvrant; *p.p.* ouvert *pr.ind.* **j'ouvre**) **I.** *v.tr.* To open. (*a*) *O. ur robinet*, to turn on a tap. **Ouvrir à qn,** to let s.o. in. (*b*) To cut through, open up. *S'o. un chemin à travers la foule*, to push one's way through the crowd. (*c*) To begin *O. un débat*, to open a debate. *O. une liste*, to head a list. **Ouvrir boutique,** to set up shop. **2.** *v.i. La scène ouvre par un chœur* the scene opens with a chorus.

s'ouvrir, to open. **S'ouvrir à qn,** tc unbosom oneself to s.o.

ouvert, *a.* Open. (*a*) **Accueillir qn à bras ouverts,** to receive s.o. with open arms. (*b*) **Ville ouverte,** open, unfortified, town (*c*) **Ouvert la nuit,** open all night. (*d*) *Caractère o.*, frank, open, nature.

ovaire, *s.m.* Ovary.

ovale. **I.** *a.* Oval, egg-shaped. **2.** *s.m.* Oval.

ovation, *s.f.* Ovation.

ové, *a.* Egg-shaped, ovate (fruit).

oviforme, *a.* Oviform, egg-shaped.

ovipare, *a.* *Z:* Oviparous.

ovoïde, *a.* Ovoid, egg-shaped.

oxalique, *a.* *Ch:* Oxalic (acid).

oxhydrique, *a.* **Lumière oxhydrique,** lime-light.

oxydation, *s.f.* *Ch:* Oxidation.

oxyde, *s.m.* *Ch:* Oxide.

oxyder, *v.tr.* *Ch:* To oxidize.

oxygène, *s.m* *Ch:* Oxygen.

oxygéné, *a.* **Eau oxygénée,** peroxide of hydrogen.

ozone, *s.m.* *Ch:* Ozone.

P

P, p [pe], *s.m.* (The letter) P, p.

pacha, *s.m.* Pasha, pacha.

pachyderme. *Z:* **I.** *a.* Pachydermatous, thick-skinned. **2.** *s.m.* Pachyderm

pacificateur, -trice. **I.** *a.* Pacifying; peace-making. **2.** *s.* Peacemaker.

pacification, *s.f.* Pacification.

pacifier, *v.tr* To pacify; to appease. **se pacifier,** to calm down.

pacifique, *a.* (*a*) Pacific, peaceable (*b*) Peaceful, quiet.

pacifiquement, *adv.* Peaceably, quietly.

pacifisme, *s.m.* *Pol:* Pacifism.

pacifiste, *s.m. & f.* *Pol:* Pacifist.

pacotille [-ti:j], *s.f.* **Marchandises de pacotille,** shoddy goods.

pacte, *s.m.* Compact, pact, agreement.

pactiser, *v.i.* *P. avec l'ennemi*, to treat with the enemy.

pagaie, *s.f.* Paddle (for canoe).

paganisme, *s.m.* Paganism.

pagayer, *v.tr. & i.* (je pagaie) To paddle.

page¹, *s.f.* Page (of book). *F:* **Être à la page,** to be up to date.

page², *s.m.* Page(-boy).

pagne, *s.m.* Loin-cloth.

pagode, *s.f.* Pagoda.

paie, *s.f.* = PAYE.

paiement, *s.m.* = PAYEMENT.

païen, -ïenne, *a. & s.* Pagan, heathen.

paillard [-ja:r], *a.* Ribald.

paillasse. **I.** *s.f.* Straw mattress palliasse. **2.** *s.m.* Clown, buffoon.

paillasson [-jas-], *s.m.* Mat; door-mat.

aille [pɑːj], *s.f.* **1.** Straw. *(a)* **Feu de paille,** flash in the pan. **Être sur la paille,** to be reduced to beggary. **Tirer à la courte paille,** to draw lots. *(b) a.inv.* Straw-coloured. **2. Paille hachée,** chaff.

ailleter [pajte], *v.tr.* (je paillette) To spangle.
  pailleté, *a* Spangled.

aillette [-jɛt], *s.f.* Spangle, paillette.

ain, *s.m.* **1.** Bread. **P. grillé,** toast. *F:* **Acheter qch. pour une bouchée de pain,** to buy sth. for a song. **Il ne vaut pas le pain qu'il mange,** he is not worth his salt. **2.** Loaf. *(a)* **Petit pain,** (French) roll. *(b)* **Pain de sucre,** sugar-loaf. **P. de savon,** cake of soap **3.** **Pain à cacheter,** (sealing) wafer.

air. **I.** *a.* *(a)* **Equal De pair,** on a par. **Marcher de pair avec qn,** to keep pace with s.o. *(b) Ar:* **Nombres pairs,** even numbers. *Rail:* **Voie paire,** up line. **2.** *s.m.* (*a*) Equal, peer. *(b) Les pairs du royaume,* the peers of the realm. **3.** *s.m.* (State of) equality; par. **Au pair,** with board and lodging but no salary.

aire, *s.f.* Pair; brace.

airesse, *s.f.* Peeress.

airie, *s.f.* Peerage.

aisible, *a.* Peaceful, peaceable, quiet.

aisiblement, *adv.* Peacefully, quietly.

aître, *v.* (*pr.p.* paissant; *pr.ind.* je pais) **I.** *v.tr.* *(a)* To graze (cattle). *(b)* To feed upon; to crop. **2.** *v.i.* To feed; to graze, browse; to pasture. **Allez paître!** go to Jericho !

aix, *s.f.* Peace. **Laissez-moi en paix,** leave me alone.

al, pals, paux, *s.m.* **1.** Pale, stake. **Le supplice du pal,** impalement. **2.** *Her:* Pale.

alabre, *s.f.* Palaver.

alabrer, *v.i.* To palaver.

alace, *s.m.* Sumptuous hotel or cinema.

aladin, *s.m.* Paladin.

alais¹, *s.m.* **1.** Palace. **2. Palais de Justice,** law-courts.

alais², *s.m.* Palate. *(a)* Roof of the mouth. *(b)* (Sense of) taste.

alanque, *s.f.* Timber stockade.

alanquin, *s.m.* Palankeen, palanquin.

alatal, -aux, *a* Palatal. *s.f.* **Palatale,** palatal.

ale, *s.f.* **1.** Stake, paling. **2.** Blade (of oar).

âle, *a.* Pale. **Un sourire p.,** a wan smile.

alefrenier, *s.m.* Groom, stableman, ostler.

alet, *s.m.* *Games:* Quoit.

aletot, *s.m.* **1.** Overcoat, greatcoat. **2.** Coat.

alette, *s.f* **1.** (Table-tennis) bat. **2.** *Roue à palettes,* paddle-wheel. **3.** (Painter's) palette.

alétuvier, *s.m.* *Bot:* Mangrove.

âleur, *s.f.* Pallor, paleness.

alier, *s.m.* **1.** *(a)* Landing (of stairs). *(b)* Stage, degree. **2.** *Aut:* Level stretch.

alindrome, *s.m.* Palindrome.

âlir, *v.i.* To become pale; to grow dim; to fade.

pâli, *a.* Wan, blanched.

palissade, *s.f.* *(a)* Palisade, fence, paling. *(b)* Stockade. *(c)* (Street) hoarding.

palissader, *v.tr.* To palisade; to fence in.

palissandre, *s.m.* Rosewood.

palliatif, *a. & s.m* Palliative.

pallier, *v.tr.* To palliate.

palmarès [-rɛːs], *s.m. Sch :* Prize-list, honours list

palme, *s.f* **1.** *Huile de p ,* palm-oil. **2.** Palm (-branch). **Remporter la palme,** to bear the palm.

palmé, *a.* **1.** Palmate (leaf). **2.** Web-footed.

palmeraie, *s. f.* Palm-grove.

palmier, *s.m.* Palm-tree.

palombe, *s.f.* Ring-dove, wood-pigeon.

pâlot, -otte, *a F:* Palish , peaky (look).

palourde, *s.f. Moll:* Clam.

palpable, *a.* Palpable. **1.** Tangible. **2.** Obvious ; palpable (error).

palpablement, *adv.* Palpably.

palper, *v.tr.* To feel; to examine by feeling.

palpitant, *a.* Palpitating, throbbing, quivering. *Roman p. d'intérêt,* thrilling novel.

palpitation, *s.f.* Palpitation.

palpiter, *v.i.* To palpitate. *(a)* To flutter; to quiver. *(b)* To throb. *(c)* To thrill.

pâmer, *v.i. & pr.* To swoon; to faint (away). *F:* **(Se) pâmer de rire,** to die with laughter. **Se pâmer de joie,** to be overjoyed.
  pâmé, *a.* In a swoon.

pâmoison, *s.f.* Swoon; fainting fit.

pampas, *s.m.pl.* Pampas.

pamplemousse, *s.m. or f.* Grape-fruit.

pan¹, *s.m.* **1.** Skirt, flap; tail (of coat). **2.** *Pan de mur,* bare wall, piece of wall. *F: Pan de ciel,* patch of sky. **3.** Face side (of building).

Pan². *Pr.n.m.* **Flûte de Pan,** Pan's pipes.

pan³, *int.* Bang ! bif(f) !

panacée, *s.f.* Panacea.

panache, *s.m.* *(a)* Plume. **P. de fumée,** wreath of smoke. *(b) F:* **Faire panache,** *F:* to take a header. *(c) F:* **Il a du panache,** he has an air about him.

panais, *s.m.* Parsnip.

Panama. **1.** *Pr.n.m.* Panama. **2.** *s.m.* Panama hat.

panaris, *s.m. Med:* Whitlow.

panca, *s.m.* Punkah.

pancarte, *s.f.* **1.** Placard, bill; (show-)card. **2.** Jacket (for documents).

pancréas [-reɑːs], *s.m. Anat:* Pancreas.

panda, *s.m. Z:* Panda.

pandit, *s.m.* Pundit.

Pandore. *Pr.n.f. Gr.Myth:* Pandora

panégyrique. **1.** *s.m.* Panegyric, encomium. **2.** *a.* Panegyric(al).

panicule, *s.f. Bot:* Panicle.

panier, *s.m.* **1.** Basket. *Rail:* **Panier-repas,** luncheon-basket. *P:* **Panier à salade,** Black Maria. *F:* **C'est un panier percé,** he is a spendthrift. **2.** Pony-carriage.

panique. **1.** *a.* Panic. **2.** *s.f.* Panic, scare; stampede. **Semeur de panique,** scaremonger.

panne, *s.f.* **1.** *Nau:* En panne, hove to. **2.** Breakdown, mishap; hold-up. **Panne sèche,** failure of engine through shortage of petrol.

panneau, *s.m.* **1.** Panel. **2.** P. *à affiches,* advertisement hoarding. *Nau: Fermer le p.,* to close down the hatch.

panoplie, *s.f.* **1.** Panoply. **2.** (Wall-)trophy.

panorama, *s.m.* Panorama.

panoramique, *a.* Panoramic.

panse, *s.f.* **1.** (*a*) *F:* Belly. (*b*) Paunch (of ruminant). **2.** Belly, bulge (of bottle).

pansement, *s.m.* *Med:* **1.** Dressing (a wound). **Trousse de pansement,** first-aid outfit. **2.** Dressing

panser, *v.tr.* **1.** To rub down (horse). **2.** To dress (wound).

pantalon, *s.m.* (*a*) (Pair of) trousers. (*b*) Knickers.

pantelant, *a.* (*a*) Panting (*b*) *Corps encore pantelants,* bodies still quivering, still warm.

panteler, *v.i.* (il pantelle) To pant.

panthéisme, *s m.* Pantheism.

panthéon, *s.m.* Pantheon.

panthère, *s.f.* *Z:* Panther.

pantin, *s.m.* (*a*) *Toys:* Jumping-jack. (*b*) *F:* Nonentity; puppet.

pantomime, *s.f* (*a*) Pantomime. (*b*) Dumb show; significant play of features.

pantoufle, *s.f* Slipper.

paon [pã], *s.m.* Peacock

paonne [pan], *s.f.* *Orn:* Peahen

papa, *s.m* *F:* Papa dad(dy). **Bon papa,** grandpapa.

papal, -aux, *a.* Papal.

papauté, *s.f.* Papacy.

pape, *s.m.* *Ecc:* Pope

paperasse, *s.f* Usu *pl* Official papers; old archives.

paperasserie, *s.f.* **1.** Accumulation of old papers. **2.** *F:* Red tape.

papeterie, *s.f.* Stationer's shop.

papetier, *s.* (*a*) Paper-maker. (*b*) Stationer.

papier, *s.m.* Paper. **1.** (*a*) *P gris,* brown paper. (*b*) **Papier à lettres,** note-paper. *F:* Figure de papier mâché, washed-out face. **2.** Document. paper. (*a*) **Être bien dans les papiers de qn,** to be in s.o.'s good books. *Vieux papiers,* waste paper. (*b*) *P timbré,* stamped paper. (*c*) *Com:* Bill(s). (*d*) *pl.* *Adm:* Papers. *Papiers de bord,* ship's papers. **3.** Papier d'étain, tinfoil.

papillon [-pij-], *s.m.* **1.** Butterfly. **Papillon de nuit,** moth. *F:* **Papillons noirs,** gloomy thoughts. **2.** Inset (in book).

papillote [-pij-], *s.f.* **1.** Curl-paper. **2.** Twist of paper; frill.

papillotement [-pij-], *s.m.* Flickering.

papilloter [-pij-], *v.i.* To blink; to twinkle; to flicker

papiste. **1.** *s.m. & f.* Papist. **2.** *a.* Papist-ic(al).

papyrus [-ry:s], *s.m.* Papyrus.

pâque. **1.** *s.f.* (Jewish) Passover. **2.** (*a*) *s.m.* Usu. spelt **Pâques,** Easter. (*b*) **Pâques,** *s.f.pl.*

Faire ses pâques, to take the Sacrament at Easter.

paquebot, *s.m.* Liner.

pâquerette, *s.f.* *Bot:* Daisy.

paquet, *s.m.* **1.** Parcel, package, packet *F:* **Faire ses paquets,** to pack up. Donn son paquet à qn, to give s.o. the sac Paquet de sottises, pack of nonsense. **2.** *Nau* Paquet de mer, heavy sea.

paquetage, *s.m.* **1.** Parcelling; balin **2.** (Soldier's) pack.

paqueter, *v.tr.* (je paquette) To parcel u

par, *prep.* **1.** (*a*) *Regarder par la fenêtre,* look out of the window. **Par mer et par ter** by land and sea. Il court par les rues, h runs about the streets. Par tout le pays, a over the country. **Venez par ici,** come th way. (*b*) Par un jour d'hiver, on a winter day. *Par le froid qu'il fait,* in this cold weathe **2.** (*a*) *Il a été puni par son père,* he w punished by his father. **Faire qch. p** soi-même, to do sth. unaided. (*b*) *Réussir p* *l'intrigue,* to succeed through intrigue. *E voyer qch. par la poste,* to send sth. by pos *Remarquable par sa beauté,* remarkable fo her beauty. (*c*) *Vous êtes par trop aimabl* you are far too kind. **3.** *J'ai fait cela p* *amitié,* I did it out of friendship. **Par piti** for pity's sake! **4.** *Par ordre alphabétique,* alphabetical order. *Trois fois par jour,* thr times a day. **5.** *Par + inf* Commencer pa *aire qch.,* to begin by doing sth. **6.** De p le Roi, by order of the King.

parabole, *s.f.* **1.** Parable. **2.** *Geom* Parabola.

parachute, *s.m.* Parachute

parachuter, *v.tr* To land by parachute.

parachutiste, *s.m. & f* Parachutist.

parade[1], *s.f.* **1.** *Mil:* Parade. **2.** Parad show. Faire parade de ses bijoux, to sho off one's jewels.

parade[2], *s.f.* *Fenc:* Parry.

parader, *v.i.* **1.** *Mil:* To parade. **2.** T make a display.

paradigme, *s.m.* *Gram:* Paradigm.

paradis, *s.m* Paradise *Th: F:* Le paradi the gallery, the gods. *Orn:* Oiseau paradis, bird of paradise.

paradoxal, -aux, *a.* Paradoxical

paradoxalement, *adv.* Paradoxically.

paradoxe, *s.m.* Paradox.

parafer, *v.tr* To initial (document).

paraffine, *s.f.* *Ch:* Paraffin. *Pharm:* Hui de paraffine, liquid paraffin.

parages, *s.m.pl.* *Nau:* Localities (of th ocean); latitudes, regions.

paragraphe, *s.m.* Paragraph

paraître, *v.i.* (Conj. like CONNAÎTRE) appear. **1.** (*a*) To make one's appearance to come in sight. (*b*) (Of book) To be pu lished. "Vient de paraître," 'just published **2.** (*a*) To be visible, apparent. **Laiss** paraître ses sentiments, to show one's feeling (*b*) *Impers.* Il y paraît, that is quite apparen

3. To seem, to look. (*a*) *Il paraît triste*, he looks sad. (*b*) *Impers. Il paraît qu'elle fait des vers*, it seems she writes poetry. **A ce qu'il paraît**, as it would appear.

parallèle. 1. *a. & s.f. Geom:* Parallel. **2.** *s.m.* (*a*) Parallel, comparison. (*b*) *Geog:* Parallel (of latitude).

paralysant, *a.* Paralysing.

paralyser, *v.tr.* To paralyse.

paralysie, *s.f. Med:* Paralysis. **Tomber en paralysie**, to have a paralytic stroke.

paralytique, *a. & s. Med:* Paralytic.

parangon, *s.m.* Paragon; pattern, model.

parapet, *s.m.* Parapet; breastwork.

paraphrase, *s.f.* Paraphrase.

paraphraser, *v.tr.* To paraphrase.

parapluie, *s.m.* Umbrella.

parasite. 1. *s.m.* (*a*) Parasite, hanger-on, sponger. (*b*) *Biol:* Parasite. **2.** *a.* Parasitic. *W.Tel:* **Bruits parasites,** *s.m.pl.* parasites, interference.

parasitique, *a.* Parasitical.

parasol, *s.m.* Parasol, sunshade.

paratonnerre, *s.m.* Lightning-conductor.

paravent, *s.m.* Draught-screen.

parbleu, *int.* Why, of course!

parc [park], *s.m.* **1.** Park. **2.** *P. pour autos*, car-park, parking-place. *P. à moutons*, sheep-fold. *Mil: P. des prisonniers*, prisoners' cage.

parcage, *s.m.* Parking (of cars); folding (of sheep). *Aut:* "*P. interdit,*" 'no parking.'

parcelle, *s.f.* Small fragment; particle (of gold); plot, patch (of land).

parceller, *v.tr.* To divide into lots; to portion out (inheritance).

parce que, *conj.phr.* Because.

parchemin, *s.m.* Parchment.

par-ci par-là, *adv.* Here and there.

parcimonie, *s.f.* Parsimony, stinginess.

parcimonieux, *a.* Parsimonious; stingy.

parcourir, *v.tr.* (Conj. like COURIR) **1.** To travel through, go over, traverse. *P. les mers*, to sail the seas. **2.** To examine (cursorily). *P. un livre*, to glance through a book. *Son regard parcourut l'horizon*, his eyes swept the horizon.

parcours, *s.m.* **1.** (*a*) Distance covered; length. (*b*) Route (of omnibus); course (of river). **2.** Run, trip (of locomotive).

par-dessous, *prep. & adv.* Under, beneath, underneath.

par-dessus, *prep. & adv.* Over (the top of). **Par-dessus le marché**, into the bargain.

pardessus, *s.m.* Overcoat, greatcoat, top-coat.

pardon, *s.m.* Pardon. (*a*) Forgiveness. **Je vous demande pardon**, I beg your pardon. **Pardon?** I beg your pardon? (*b*) *Jur:* Remission of a sentence. (*c*) *Ecc:* Pardon pilgrimage.

pardonner, *v.tr.* To pardon, forgive. (*a*) *Pardonnez la liberté que je prends*, pardon the liberty I am taking. (*b*) *P. à qn*, to pardon s.o. **Pardonnez-moi**, excuse me.

pare-boue, *s.m.inv.* Dash-board; mud-guard (of motor-car, bicycle).

pare-brise, *s.m.inv. Aut:* Wind-screen.

pare-choc(s), *s.m.inv Aut:* Fender; bumper.

parégorique, *a. & s.m. Pharm:* Paregoric.

pareil, -eille [-rɛːj]. **1.** *a.* (*a*) Like, alike; similar. (*b*) Same, identical. **L'an dernier à pareil jour**, this day last year (*c*) Such; like that. **En pareil cas**, in such cases. **2.** *s.* (*a*) *Lui et ses pareils*, he and his like. (*b*) Equal, fellow, match. **3.** *s.f.* **La pareille**, the like. **Rendre la pareille à qn**, to give s.o. tit for tat.

pareillement [-rɛj-], *adv.* **1.** In like manner. **2.** Also; likewise.

parement, *s.m.* **1.** Adorning. **2.** (*a*) Ornament, adornment. (*b*) *pl.* Facings (of uniform).

parent, *s.* **1.** *s.m.pl.* (*a*) Parents. (*b*) Forefathers. **2.** Relative, connection; relation.

parentage, *s.m.* **1.** Parentage, birth. **2.** *Coll:* Kindred.

parenté, *s.f.* **1.** Kinship, relationship. **2.** *Coll.* Kindred.

parenthèse, *s.f.* Parenthesis; (i) digression; (ii) *Typ:* bracket.

parer[1], *v.tr.* **1.** To prepare; to dress trim. **2.** To adorn, embellish. **se parer**, to adorn oneself. **paré,** *a.* Adorned, bedecked.

parer[2]. **1.** *v.tr.* (*a*) To avoid, ward off. *P. un cap*, to clear, double, a headland. (*b*) To parry, ward off. **2.** *v.ind.tr. P. à qch.*, to provide, guard, against sth. **On ne peut pas parer à tout**, accidents will happen.

paresse, *s.f.* (*a*) Laziness, idleness. (*b*) Sluggishness.

paresseusement, *adv.* Idly, lazily.

paresseux. 1. *a.* (*a*) Lazy, idle, slothful. (*b*) Sluggish; slow-acting. **2.** *s.* Lazy person; sluggard. **3.** *s.m. Z:* Sloth.

pare-torpilles, *s.m. & a.inv.* (Filet) pare-torpilles, torpedo-net.

parfaire, *v.tr.* (Conj. like FAIRE) To finish off, perfect, round off.

parfait. 1. *a.* Perfect. (*a*) Faultless; flawless. *En ordre p., F:* in apple-pie order. *F: C'est parfait!* excellent! (*b*) Complete, thorough. **2.** *s.m. Gram:* Perfect.

parfaitement, *adv.* **1.** (*a*) Perfectly; to perfection. (*b*) Completely, thoroughly. **2.** Quite so; certainly; exactly.

parfois, *adv.* Sometimes, at times.

parfum, *s.m.* Perfume. **1.** Fragrance, scent. **2.** *Toil:* Scent.

parfumer, *v.tr.* To scent (one's handkerchief). *L'air parfumé du soir*, the balmy evening air.

parfumerie, *s.f.* Perfumery.

parfumeur, -euse, *s.* Perfumer.

pari, *s.m.* **1.** Bet, wager. **2.** Betting.

paria, *s.m.* Pariah.

parier, *v.tr.* To bet, to wager. *P. pour un*

cheval, to back a horse Il y a (gros) à parier
que . . ., it is long odds that
parieur, -euse, s. Better, punter ; backer.
Paris. *Pr.n.m. Geog:* Paris **Articles de
Paris,** fancy goods.
parisien, -ienne, *a. & s.* Parisian.
parité, *s.f.* Parity ; equality.
parjure[1]*, s.m* Perjury
parjure[2]. **1.** *a.* Perjured **2.** *s.* Perjurer.
parjurer (se), *v.pr* To forswear oneself,
to perjure oneself
parlant, *a.* Speaking ; talking. *F: Portrait
p.,* speaking likeness.
parlement, *s.m.* Parliament.
parlementaire[1]*, a.* Parliamentary.
parlementaire[2]. **1.** *s.m.* Bearer of a flag
of truce. **2.** *a* **Drapeau parlementaire,** flag
of truce.
parlementer, *v.i.* To parley.
parler. I. *v.i.* To speak, talk. **1.** *(a)* S'enrouer
à force de parler, to talk oneself hoarse.
(b) Parler pour parler, to talk for talking's
sake. *Parlons peu et parlons bien,* let us be
brief but to the point **Parler pour ne rien
dire,** *F:* to talk through one's hat. **Pour
parler franc . .,** to put it bluntly
Savoir ce que parler veut dire, to be able
to take a hint. **Faire parler qn,** to loosen
s.o.'s tongue. **Voilà ce qui s'appelle parler!**
now you're talking ! *(c) P. à qn,* to talk to,
to converse with, s.o. **Elle a trouvé à qui
parler,** she has met her match. *(d) Il n'en
parle jamais,* he never refers to it. *Est-ce de
moi que vous parlez?* do you mean me?
Cela ne vaut pas la peine d'en parler, it isn't
worth mentioning. **Entendre parler de qch.,**
to hear of sth. **Faire parler de soi,** to get
talked about. *On ne parle que de cela,* it is
the talk of the town. *P de choses et d'autres,*
to alk on indifferent matters **2.** **Parler
français,** to speak French.
II. parler, .*m* (Way of) speaking ;
speech, language
parlé. 1. *a.* Spoken **2.** *s.m* Patter (in
song) ; spoken part (in opera).
parleur, -euse, s. Talker, speaker.
parloir, *s.m* Parlour (of convent).
parmi, *prep.* Among(st), amid(st).
Parnasse (le). *Pr.n* Parnassus.
parodie, *s.f* Parody ; skit.
parodier, *v.tr* To parody.
paroi, *s.f.* **1.** *(a)* Partition-wall (between
rooms). *(b)* Wall (of rock). **2.** Lining (of
tunnel).
paroisse, *s.f* Parish.
paroissial, -aux, *a.* Parochial. *L'église
paroissiale,* the parish church.
paroissien, -ienne, s Parishioner s.m.
Prayer-book
parole, *s.f* **1.** (Spoken) word ; remark.
Perdre le temps en paroles, to waste time
talking. *Cette p. le piqua,* this remark went
home. **2.** Promise, word ; *Mil:* parole.

Croire qn sur parole, to take a person's word.
3. Speech, speaking *(a)* Delivery. **Perdre
la parole,** to lose the power of speech
(b) **Adresser la parole à qn,** to speak to s.o.
Prendre la parole, to begin to speak. **Demander la parole,** to request leave to speak.
paroxysme, *s.m.* Paroxysm. **Être au
paroxysme de la colère,** to be in a towering
rage.
parquer, *v.ti* To old (sheep) ; to park
(motor cars).
parquet, *s.m* **1.** *Jur:* Well of the court.
Déposer une plainte au parquet, to lodge a
complaint in court.
parrain, *s.m.* *(a)* Godfather *(b)* Proposer
pars. See PARTIR.
parsemer, *v.tr* (Conj. ike SEMER) To strew,
sprinkle *Ciel parsemé d'étoiles* sky studded
with stars.
parsi, *a. & s.* *Rel.H:* Parsee.
part[1]*, s.f.* **1.** Share, part, portion. *(a)* **Mettre
qn de part à demi,** to go half-shares with s.o.
(b) **Pour ma part,** as for me. *(c)* **Prendre qch.
en bonne part,** to take sth. in good part.
2. Share, participation **Avoir part à qch.,**
to have a hand in sth. **Faire part de qch. à
qn,** to inform s.o of sth **Billet de faire part,**
intimation (of wedding). **Faire la part de
qch.,** to take sth. into consideration. **3.** **Nulle
part,** nowhere **Autre part,** somewhere else.
Faire des concessions de part et d'autre, to
make concessions on both sides. **De part
en part,** through and through. **D'une part,**
on the one hand *Dites-lui de ma part,* tell
him from me **4.** **A part,** apart, separately
Prendre qn à p., to take s.o. aside. *Mettre de
l'argent à p.,* to put money by. *Plaisanterie
à p.,* joking apart. **A part quelques exceptions,**
with a few exceptions
part[2]. See PARTIR.
partage, *s.m.* **1.** Division. *(a)* Sharing,
apportionment *(b)* **Il y a partage d'opinions,**
opinions are divided. *Geog:* **Ligne de
partage des eaux,** watershed. **2.** Share,
portion, lot.
partager, *v.tr.* (n. partageons) **1.** To divide.
(a) To share out *(b)* **Partager le différend,**
to split the difference. **2.** *Ils se partagent
les bénéfices,* they share the profits between
them. *P. les idées de qn,* to agree with s.o.'s
views. **3.** **Être bien partagé,** to be well
provided for
   se partager, to divide.
partance, *s.f. Nau:* Departure. **Pavillon
de partance,** Blue Peter. **En partance pour,**
bound for.
partant[1]*, adv.* Consequently, therefore.
partant[2]*, a* Departing.
partenaire, *s.m. Games:* Partner.
parterre, *s.m.* **1.** Flower-bed **2.** *Th:* Pit.
parthe, *a. & s.* Parthian.
parti, *s.m.* **1.** Party. **Prendre parti pour qn,**
to side with s.o. **2.** **Un bon parti,** a good
match. **3.** Decision, choice. **Prendre (un**

) **arti,** to make up one's mind. **En prendre son**)'**arti,** to make the best of it **Parti pris, (i) set purpose**; (ii) bias **4.** Advantage, profit.

partial, -aux, *a.* Partial; bias(s)ed

partialité, *s.f.* Partiality; bias.

participant, *s.* Participant.

participation, *s.f.* **I.** Participation. **2.** *Com:* Share, interest. *P aux bénéfices,* profit-sharing.

participe, *s.m.* *Gram:* Participle.

participer, *v.i* **I.** Participer à qch. *(a)* To participate, have a share in. *(b)* To take a hand in. **2.** Participer de, to partake of, have some of the characteristics of.

participial, -aux, *a.* Participial

particulariser, *v.tr* **I.** To particularize. **2.** To specify; to give particulars of.

se particulariser, to distinguish one-self from others.

particularité, *s.f.* **I.** Detail, particular. **2.** Peculiarity.

particule, *s.f* **I.** Particle, atom **2.** *Gram:* Particle.

particulier. I. *a.* *(a)* Particular, special. *(b)* Peculiar, characteristic. *(c)* Unusual, uncommon *(d)* Private; personal. **2.** *s.* Private person, private individual. **3.** *s.m.* En particulier, particularly. Recevoir qn en particulier, to receive s.o. privately

particulièrement, *adv.* *(a)* Particularly, (e)specially *(b)* Peculiarly *(c)* In detail

partie, *s.f.* **I.** Part (of a whole). En grande partie, to a great extent. Vendre qch. par parties, to sell sth. in lots. **Tenue des livres en partie double,** double entry book-keeping. **2.** *(a)* Party **Voulez-vous être de la partie?** will you join us? *(b)* Game, match. *F:* Vous avez la partie belle, now's your chance! **3.** *Jur* Party (to dispute). *F:* Avoir affaire à forte partie, to have a powerful opponent to deal with. *F:* Prendre qn à partie, to take s.o. to task.

partiel, -elle, *a.* Partial, incomplete.

partiellement, *adv* Partially, in part.

partir, *v.* (Conj. like MENTIR) **I.** *v.i.* (Aux. *être)* *(a)* To depart, leave, start; to set out; to go away. *Sp:* Partez! go! *P. au galop,* to gallop away. **Nous voilà partis!** now we're off! *(b)* To part, to give way; (of gun) to go off. *P. de rire,* to burst out laughing. *(c)* To emanate, spring (from). *(d)* A partir d'aujourd'hui, from to-day.

partisan. I. *s.* Partisan, follower. **2.** *s.m. Mil:* Guer(r)illa soldier.

partitif, *a.* *Gram:* Partitive

partition, *s.f* *Mus:* Score.

partout, *adv* *(a)* Everywhere; on all sides *(b)* All; all together *Ten·* Quatre jeux p., four all

paru, -s, -t, etc. See PARAÎTRE.

parure, *s.f.* **I.** Ornamenting, adorning. **2.** *(a)* Dress, finery. *(b)* Ornament.

parvenir, *v.i.* (Conj. like VENIR) Aux. *être)*

I. To arrive. *Votre lettre m'est parvenue,* your letter has reached me. **2.** *(a)* To attain, reach; to succeed *P. à faire qch.,* to manage to do sth *(b)* *Abs* To succeed in life.

parvenu, *s* Parvenu, upstart.

parvis, *s.m.* Square (in front of a church).

pas , *s.m* **I.** Step, pace stride. *(a)* **Mesurer une distance au pas,** to pace off a distance. **Allonger le pas,** to step out. **J'y vais de ce pas,** I am going at once. **Marcher à grands pas,** to stride along **Faux pas,** (i) slip, stumble; (ii) blunder. **Avoir le pas sur qn,** to have precedence of s.o *(b)* **Au pas,** at a walking pace. **Avancer au pas gymnastique,** to advance at the double. **Marquer le pas,** to mark time. **2.** Footprint. **3.** Step (of stair); threshold. *Le pas de la porte,* the door-step. **4.** Passage; (mountain) pass; strait. **Le Pas de Calais,** the Straits of Dover. **Mauvais pas,** tight corner. **Sauter le pas,** to take the plunge. **5.** Thread (of screw).

pas², *neg.adv.* **I.** Not. *Je ne sais pas,* I don't know. *Nous marchons peu ou pas,* we walk little or not at all. *F: Pas (vrai)?* = N'EST-CE PAS? *Non pas!* not at all! **2.** Pas un. *(a) Pas un mot ne fut dit,* not a word was spoken. *(b) Il connaît Paris mieux que pas un,* he knows Paris better than anyone.

passable, *a.* Passable, tolerable; so so.

passablement, *adv.* Passably, tolerably.

passage, *s.m.* Passage **I.** Crossing (of sth.); passing over; going past. *(a)* **Guetter le passage de qn,** to lie in wait for s.o. **Livrer passage à qn,** to allow s.o. to pass. *P. de Vénus,* transit of Venus. **Droit de passage,** right of way. **"Passage interdit au public,"** 'no thoroughfare.' **Être de passage dans une ville,** to be only passing through a town. *(b) Nau: Payer son p.,* to pay for one's passage. *(c) P. du jour à la nuit,* transition from day to night. **2.** *(a)* Way, way through. *Nau:* Channel. *(b)* Arcade. *(c) Rail:* **Passage à niveau,** level crossing **3.** Passage (in book).

passager. I. *a.* *(a) Oiseau p.,* bird of passage. *(b)* Fleeting, transitory. **2.** *s.* Passenger.

passant, *s.* Passer-by.

passe, *s.f.* **I.** Permit; pass. **2.** *(a) Fenc:* Pass, thrust. *(b)* **Passe d'armes,** passage of arms. **3.** *Nau:* Pass, fairway. **Être en mauvaise passe,** to be in a tight corner.

passe-lacet, *s.m.* Bodkin *pl. Des passe-lacets.*

passementerie, *s.f.* Passementerie; trimmings.

passe-montagne, *s.m.* Balaclava helmet. *pl. Des passe-montagnes.*

passe-partout, *s.m.inv* Master-key

passe-passe, *s.m.* No *pl* **Tour de passe-passe,** conjuring trick

passeport, *s.m* Passport

passer. I. *v.i.* **I.** (Aux. *avoir* or *être)* To pass; to go past; to proceed. *P. sur un pont,* to cross a bridge. *Je ne peux pas p.,* I can't

get by. "**Laissez passer**," 'admit bearer.'
En passant, by the way. *Dire qch. en passant*,
to mention sth. casually. **Passer son chemin**,
to go one's way. **2.** (Aux. *être*) *P. chez qn*,
to call on s.o. **3.** (Aux. *avoir*) To undergo,
pass through. **Il a dû en passer par là**, he
had to put up with it. **4.** (Aux. *avoir*) To
pass away. (*a*) To disappear, to cease. *P. de
mode*, to pass out of fashion. *Couleurs qui
passent*, colours that fade. (*b*) To elapse, to
go by. *Comme le temps passe (vite)!* how
(quickly) time flies! **Faire passer le temps**,
to pass the time. **5.** (Aux. *avoir* or *être*) To
die. **6.** Pred. (*a*) (Aux. *avoir* or *être*) To
become. *P. capitaine*, to be promoted captain. (*b*) (Aux. *avoir*) To be considered, to
pass for. **Se faire passer pour**, to pass oneself
off for. **7.** (Aux. *avoir*) To be accepted.
Qu'il revienne demain, **passe encore**, if he
returns to-morrow, well and good. **Cela ne
passe pas**, that won't do. **Enfin, passe pour
lui!** well, that's all right as far as he is
concerned.
   II. passer, *v.tr.* **1.** To pass, cross. **2.** (*a*)
To carry across. *P. des marchandises en
fraude*, to smuggle in goods. (*b*) *P. qch. à qn*,
to hand sth. to s.o. (*c*) *P. sa tête par la fenêtre*,
to put one's head in at the window. *P. une
chemise*, to slip on a shirt. **3.** To pass, spend.
F: **Se la passer douce**, to take it easy. **4.** To
pass, go beyond. *Cela passe ma capacité*, that
is beyond my powers. *Cela passe la mesure*,
that is going too far. *F:* **Cela me passe**,
it passes my comprehension. **5.** To pass
over. (*a*) To excuse, pardon. **Je vous passe
cela**, I grant you that. (*b*) To omit, leave out.
Passer qch. sous silence, to pass over sth. in
silence. **6.** (*a*) *P. une loi*, to pass a law. (*b*)
P. un examen, to pass an examination. **7.** To
strain (liquid).
   se passer. 1. To happen; to take place.
2. (*a*) To pass away. **Il faut que jeunesse se
passe**, youth will have its fling. **Cela ne se
passera pas ainsi**, I shall not let it rest at this.
(*b*) To fade. **3.** Se passer de qch., to do
without sth.
   passé. 1. *a.* (*a*) Past; gone by. (*b*) Faded.
2. *s.m.* **Le passé**. The past. **Oublions le
passé**, let bygones be bygones. **3.** *prep.*
Passé, beyond. **Il est passé quatre heures**,
it is, has, gone four.
passereau, *s.m.* Sparrow.
passerelle, *s.f.* **1.** Foot-bridge. **2.** *Nau:*
La passerelle (de commandement), the bridge.
passe-temps, *s.m.inv.* Pastime, diversion.
passeur, -euse, *s.* Ferryman, ferrywoman.
passible, *a.* Liable (*de*, to, for).
passif. 1. *a.* Passive. **2.** *s.m.* (*a*) *Gram:*
Passive. (*b*) *Com:* Liabilities.
passion, *s.f.* **1. La Passion**, the Passion.
2. *P. pour la musique*, passion for music.
La p. de la vérité, a passion for truth.
passionnant, *a.* Entrancing, thrilling.
passionnel, -elle, *a.* Pertaining to the

passions. **Crime passionnel**, crime due to
jealousy.
passionnément, *adv.* Passionately.
passionner, *v.tr.* To impassion. *Livre qui
passionne*, book that grips you.
   passionné, *a.* Passionate, impassioned,
ardent.
passivement, *adv.* Passively.
pastel, *s.m.* Pastel. **1.** *Bot:* Woad. **2.** *Art:*
Crayon.
pastèque, *s.f.* Water-melon.
pasteur, *s.m.* Pastor.
pastille [-tiːj], *s.f.* Lozenge, jujube.
pastoral, -aux, *a.* Pastoral.
pat [pat], *s.m.inv.* Chess: Stalemate.
patate, *s.f.* **1.** Sweet potato. **2.** *P:* Potato;
P: spud.
patati. *F:* **Et patati et patata**, and so on.
patatras, *int. F:* Crash!
pataud, *a. & s.* Clumsy (person).
patauger, *v.i.* (n. pataugeons) (*a*) To flounder
(in the mud). (*b*) To paddle (in sea).
pâte, *s.f.* **1.** Paste. (*a*) *P.* (*à pain*), dough.
C'est une bonne pâte (d'homme), he's a good
sort. (*b*) *Toil:* *P. d'amandes*, almond-cream.
2. **Vivre comme un coq en pâte**, to live like
a fighting-cock.
pâté, *s.m.* **1.** (Meat) pie. **2.** Block (of houses).
3. Blot, blob (of ink).
patelle, *s.f.* Limpet.
patenôtre, *s.f.* Paternoster.
patent, *a.* (*a*) Patent. **Lettres patentes**,
(letters) patent. (*b*) Obvious, evident.
patente, *s.f.* **1.** Licence (to exercise a trade).
2. *Nau:* **Patente de santé**, bill of health
patenter, *v.tr.* To license.
   patenté, *s.* Licensee; licensed dealer.
pater [-tɛːr], *s.m.inv.* The Lord's prayer;
paternoster.
patère, *s.f.* Hat-peg, coat-peg.
paternel, -elle, *a.* Paternal.
paternellement, *adv.* Paternally.
paternité, *s.f.* Paternity, fatherhood.
pâteux, *a.* (*a*) Pasty, clammy. (*b*) Thick
(voice); muddy (ink).
pathétique. 1. *a.* Pathetic, moving, touching. **2.** *s.m.* Pathos.
pathétiquement, *adv.* Pathetically.
pathologie, *s.f.* Pathology.
pathologique, *a.* Pathological.
pathologiste, *s.m.* Pathologist.
pathos [-tɔs], *s.m.* Affected pathos.
patibulaire, *a.* Relating to the gallows.
Une mine patibulaire, a hang-dog look.
patiemment, *adv.* Patiently.
patience, *s.f.* Patience, long-suffering. **Jeu
de patience**, puzzle; esp. jig-saw puzzle.
patient. 1. *a.* Patient. (*a*) Long-suffering.
(*b*) Forbearing. **2.** *s.* Condemned man.
patienter, *v.i.* To exercise patience.
patin, *s.m.* (*a*) Skate. (*b*) Runner (of sledge);
skid (of aeroplane).
patinage, *s.m.* Skating.
patine, *s.f.* Patina.

patiner, *v.i.* **1.** To skate. **2.** (Of wheel)
To skid; (of belt) to slip.

patinette, *s.f.* Scooter.

patineur, -euse, *s.* Skater.

pâtir, *v.i.* To suffer (for others).

pâtisserie, *s.f.* **1.** (*a*) Pastry. (*b*) *pl.* Cakes.
2. Pastry-making. **3.** Tea-rooms.

pâtissier, *s.* Pastry-cook.

patois, *s.m.* (*a*) Patois. (*b*) *F:* Jargon.

pâtre, *s.m.* Herdsman; shepherd.

patriarcal, -aux, *a.* Patriarchal.

patriarche, *s.m.* Patriarch.

patricien, -ienne, *a. & s.* Patrician.

patrie, *s.f.* Fatherland. **Mère patrie,** mother
country.

patrimoine, *s.m.* Patrimony.

patrimonial, -aux, *a.* Patrimonial.

patriote. 1. *a.* Patriotic. **2.** *s.* Patriot.

patriotique, *a.* Patriotic.

patriotiquement, *adv.* Patriotically.

patriotisme, *s.m.* Patriotism.

patron, -onne, *s.* **1.** Patron, patroness.
2. (*a*) Employer; head (of firm); proprietor.
(*b*) *Nau:* Skipper **3.** *s.m.* Pattern (for dress);
model.

patronage, *s.m.* Patronage, support.

patronner, *v.tr.* To patronize, support.

patronymique, *a.* Patronymic.

patrouille [-ru:j], *s.f.* Patrol.

patrouiller [-ruje], *v.i.* To patrol.

patte, *s.f.* **1.** Paw; foot (of bird); leg (of
insect). *F:* **Pattes de mouche,** scrawl.
Marcher à quatre pattes, to go on all fours.
Faire patte de velours, (of cat) to draw in its
claws. **Tomber sous la patte de qn,** to fall
into s.o.'s clutches. **2.** Foot (of wine-glass).
3. Flap (of pocket). **4.** Fluke (of anchor).
5. Tab, strap (on garment).

patte-d'oie, *s.f.* **1.** Road junction. **2.**
Crow's-foot (wrinkle). *pl.* **Des pattes-d'oie.**

pâturage, *s.m.* **1.** Grazing. **2.** (*a*) Pasture.
(*b*) *pl.* Pasture-land.

pâture, *s.f.* **1.** Food, feed, fodder. **2.** Pasture.

pâturer, *v.i.* To graze, to feed.

paume, *s.f.* **1.** Palm (of hand). **2.** (Jeu de)
paume. (i) Tennis. (*N.B.* Not lawn-tennis.)
(ii) Tennis-court.

paupérisme, *s.m.* Pauperism.

paupière, *s.f.* Eyelid.

pause, *s.f.* Pause.

pauvre. 1. *a.* Poor. (*a*) Needy, in want.
Un homme p., a poor man. (*b*) Unfortunate.
Le p. homme! poor fellow! *P. de moi!* poor
me! (*c*) Wretched; shabby. **2.** *s.* (*a*) Poor
man, poor woman; pauper. (*b*) Beggar.

pauvrement, *adv.* Poorly, wretchedly.

pauvresse, *s.f.* (*a*) Poor woman; pauper.
(*b*) Beggar-woman.

pauvreté, *s.f.* Poverty, indigence, want.

pavage, *s.m.* **1.** Paving. **2.** Pavement.

pavaner (se , *v.pr.* To strut (about)

paver, *v.tr.* To pave.

pavé, *s.m.* **1.** Paving-stone. **2.** (*a*) Pave-

ment. (*b*) Paved road. **Prendre le haut du
pavé,** *F:* to lord it. (*c*) *F:* **Battre le pavé,**
to tramp the streets.

pavillon [-vijɔ̃], *s.m.* **1.** Pavilion. *P.* (*de
jardin*), summer-house. *P. de chasse,* shooting-
lodge. **2.** *Nau:* Flag, colours. *P. de poupe,*
ensign.

pavois, *s.m.* *Nau:* (*a*) Bulwark. (*b*) *Coll.*
Flags (for dressing ship).

pavoiser, *v.tr.* *F:* To deck with flags.

pavot, *s.m. Bot:* Poppy.

paye, *s.f.* **1.** Pay; wages. **2.** Payment.

payement, *s.m.* Payment. *P. contre livraison,*
cash on delivery.

payer, *v.tr.* (je paye, je paie) **Payer qn de
paroles,** to put s.o. off with fine words. **Payer
de sa personne,** to risk one's own skin. **Payer
d'audace,** to take the risk. **Payer d'effronterie,** to put a bold face on it. (*b*) To pay,
settle (debt). **Payer rubis sur l'ongle,** to pay
on the nail. (*c*) To pay for (sth.). *P. qch. à qn,*
to pay s.o. for sth. *P. un dîner à qn,* to stand
s.o. a dinner. *Je me suis payé une glace,* I
treated myself to an ice. **Se payer la tête
de qn,** to take a rise out of s.o. **Cela ne se
paie pas,** money cannot buy it. **Vous me le
paierez!** you shall smart for this!

payeur, -euse, *s.* Payer; paymaster.

pays[1] [pe(j)i], *s.m.* Country. (*a*) Land.
Battre du pays, to roam about. (*b*) Region,
district. **Pays perdu,** out-of-the-way place.
F: **Être en pays de connaissance,** to be
among friends. (*c*) Native land; home.
Avoir le mal du pays, to be homesick.

pays[2], *s.* *Nous sommes p.,* we are from the
same parts.

paysage, *s.m.* Landscape; scenery.

paysan, -anne, *s. & a.* Peasant, rustic.

Pays-Bas (les). *Pr.n.m.* The Netherlands.

péage, *s.m.* **1.** Toll. **2.** Toll-house.

péan, *s.m.* Paean; song of triumph.

peau, *s.f.* **1.** Skin. *A même la p.,* next to the
skin. *A fleur de peau,* skin-deep. *Prendre par
la p. du cou,* to take by the scruff of the neck.
Sauver sa peau, to save one's bacon. **Avoir qn
dans la peau,** to be infatuated with s.o. **2.**
Pelt, fur; hide. **3.** Peel, skin (of fruit). **4.**
Coating; film, skin.

Peau-Rouge, *s.m.* Red Indian, redskin.
pl. **Des Peaux-Rouges.**

pécari, *s.m.* *Z:* Peccary; Mexican hog.

peccadille [-di:j], *s.f.* Peccadillo.

pêche[1], *s.f.* Peach.

pêche[2], *s.f.* **1.** Fishing. *P. à la ligne,* angling.
2. Catch (of fish). **3.** Fishery.

péché, *s.m.* Sin; transgression. *Les péchés
capitaux,* the deadly sins. *Son p. mignon,*
his besetting sin. *Péchés de jeunesse,* indis-
cretions of youth.

pécher, *v.i.* (je pèche; je pécherai) To sin.
P. par excès, to exceed what is required

pêcher[1], *s.m.* Peach-tree.

pêcher[2], *v.tr.* **1.** To fish for. *P. à la ligne,*
to angle. *P. la baleine,* to hunt whales.

2. *P. une truite,* to catch a trout. *F:* Où avez-vous pêché cela? where did you get hold of that?

pécheresse. See PÉCHEUR.

pécheur, pécheresse. 1. *s.* Sinner, offender, transgressor. **2.** *a.* Sinning.

pêcheur, -euse, *s.* Fisher ; fisherman, -woman. *P. à la ligne,* angler.

pectoral, -aux, *a.* Pectoral *Pastille pectorale,* cough-lozenge.

péculat, *s.m.* Peculation, embezzlement.

péculateur, *s.m.* Peculator ; embezzler.

pécule, *s.m.* Savings ; nest-egg.

pécuniaire, *a.* Pecuniary.

pédagogue, *s.m. & f.* Pedagogue.

pédale, *s.f.* Pedal ; treadle.

pédaler, *v.i.* To pedal.

pédant. 1. *s.* Pedant. **2.** *a.* Pedantic.

pédestre, *a.* Pedestrian.

pédicure, *s.m. & f.* Chiropodist.

Pégase. *Pr.n.m.* Pegasus.

peigne, *s.m.* **1.** Comb. **2.** Card (for wool).

peign-e, -ons. See PEINDRE and PEIGNER.

peigner, *v.tr.* To comb (out).

   se peigner, to comb one's hair.

   peigné, *a* *Mal p.,* unkempt, slatternly

peignoir, *s.m.* (Lady's) dressing-gown.

peindre, *v.tr* (*pr.p.* peignant ; *p.p.* peint ; *pr.ind.* je peins ; *p.h* je peignis) To paint. **1.** *P une carte,* to colour a map. *Papiers peints,* wall-papers. **2.** *P. un coucher de soleil,* to paint a sunset. *F:* Elle est à peindre, she is a perfect picture. *Cette action le peint bien,* that action is typical of him.

peine, *s.f.* **1.** Punishment, penalty. *Errer comme une âme en peine,* to wander about like a lost soul. **2.** (*a*) Sorrow, affliction. *Faire de la peine à qn,* to distress s.o. *Cela fait peine à voir,* it is painful to behold. *Être en peine de qn,* to be uneasy about s.o. (*b*) *Être dans la peine,* to be in want, in distress. **3.** Pains, trouble. *Donnez-vous la peine de vous asseoir,* pray take a seat. *En être pour sa peine* to have one's labour for one's pains. *Iron:* C'était bien la peine de venir! we might as well have stayed at home! *Homme de peine,* common labourer. **4.** Difficulty. **5.** A peine, hardly, barely, scarcely.

peiner. 1. *v.tr.* To pain, vex, distress. **2.** *v.i.* To toil, labour.

pein-s, -t. See PEINDRE.

peintre, *s.m.* Painter. **1.** (*Artiste*) *p.,* artist. **2.** *P. en bâtiment(s),* house-painter.

peinture, *s.f.* **1.** Painting. *Faire de la peinture,* to paint. **2.** Picture, painting. **3.** Paint, colour. "Attention à la peinture!" wet paint.

Pékin. 1. *Pr.n.m. Geog:* Pekin(g) **2.** *s.m. Mil: F:* Civilian *Être en pékin,* to be in mufti.

pelage, *s.m.* Coat, wool, fur (of animal).

pelé, *a.* Bald ; bare, hairless.

pêle-mêle. 1. *adv.* Pell-mell. **2.** *s.m.inv* jumble, medley, confusion.

peler, *v.* (je pèle) **1.** *v.tr.* To peel, skin **2.** *v.i. & pr.* To peel.

pèlerin. 1. *s.* Pilgrim. **2.** *s.f.* Pèlerine hooded cape.

pèlerinage, *s.m.* **1.** Pilgrimage. **2.** Place of pilgrimage.

pélican, *s.m. Orn:* Pelican.

pelle, *s.f.* **1.** Shovel, scoop. *Ramasser une pelle,* to come a cropper. **2.** (Child's) spade. **3.** Blade (of oar).

pelletée, *s.f.* Shovelful, spadeful.

pelleterie, *s.f.* **1.** Fur ; peltry. **2.** Fur-trade, furriery.

pelletier, *s.* Furrier.

pellicule, *s.f.* **1.** (*a*) Pellicle ; thin skin ; film. (*b*) *Phot:* Film. **2.** *pl.* Scurf.

pellucide, *a.* Pellucid, limpid.

pelote, *s.f.* Ball (of wool). *P. à épingles,* pincushion. *F:* Faire sa (petite) pelote, to make one's pile.

peloton, *s.m.* **1.** Ball (of wool). **2.** *Mil:* Squad, party.

pelouse, *s.f.* Lawn ; grass-plot ; green (sward). *Golf: P. d'arrivée,* (putting-)green.

peluche, *s.f. Tex:* Plush.

pelure, *s.f.* Peel, skin ; paring ; rind.

pénal, -als, -aux, *a* Penal.

pénalité, *s.f* Penalty

penaud, *a.* Crestfallen, chapfallen.

penchant. 1. *a* Sloping, inclined, leaning. **2.** *s.m* (*a*) Slope, declivity (*b*) *P à qch.,* leaning towards sth.

pencher, *v.* To incline, bend, lean **1.** *v.tr. P. la tête en avant,* to lean forward. **2.** *v.i.* To lean (over) ; to incline *Faire pencher la balance,* to turn the scale.

   se pencher, to incline, bend, stoop, lean.

   penché, *a.* **1.** Leaning. **2.** Stooping.

pendaison, *s.f.* (Death by) hanging

pendant. I. *a.* **1.** Hanging, pendent *Joues pendantes,* flabby cheeks. **2.** Pending ; in suspense, in abeyance.

   II. **pendant,** *s.m.* **1.** Pendant. **2.** Match, fellow. *Ces deux tableaux (se) font pendant,* these two pictures make a pair.

   III **pendant,** *prep.* During. *Conj. phr.* Pendant que, while, whilst.

pendard, *s. F:* Rascal, gallows-bird.

pendeloque, *s.f.* Pendant ; drop.

pendre. 1. *v.tr* (*a*) To hang up. (*b*) To hang (on the gallows). **2.** *v.i.* To hang (down).

pendu. 1. *a.* Hanged, hung ; hanging. **2.** *s.* One who has been hanged.

pendule. 1. *s.m.* Pendulum. **2.** *s.f.* Clock.

pêne, *s.m.* Bolt (of lock) ; latch.

pénétrabilité, *s.f.* Penetrability.

pénétrable, *a.* Penetrable.

pénétrant, *a.* Penetrating ; sharp ; piercing ; searching ; shrewd.

pénétration, *s.f.* (*a*) Penetration (of bullet). (*b*) Penetration, insight ; acuteness ; acumen.

pénétrer, *v.* (je pénètre ; je pénétrerai) To

penetrate. **I.** *v.i.* To enter. *L'eau avait pénétré partout*, the water had got in everywhere. **2.** *v.tr.* (*a*) *P. la pensée de qn*, to see through s.o. (*b*) *Votre lettre m'a pénétré de douleur*, your letter has filled me with grief.

se pénétrer, to become imbued. *D'un air pénétré*, with an earnest air.

pénible, *a.* **I.** Laborious, toilsome; laboured; arduous. **2.** Painful, distressing.

péniblement, *adv.* Laboriously, painfully.

péniche, *s.f.* Coal-barge; lighter.

pénicilline, *s.f. Med:* Penicillin.

péninsulaire, *a.* Peninsular.

péninsule, *s.f.* Peninsula.

pénitence, *s.f.* **I.** Penitence, repentance. **2.** Penance. *F:* **Mettre un enfant en pénitence,** to put a child in the corner.

pénitencier, *s.m.* Penitentiary; reformatory

pénitent, *a. & s.* Penitent.

penne, *s.f.* (*a*) Quill(-feather). (*b*) Feather (of arrow).

pennon, *s.m* Pennon.

pénombre, *s.f.* Half-light, semi-darkness.

pensant, *a.* Thinking. **Bien pensant,** orthodox, righ -thinking.

pensée[1], *s.f. Bot:* Pansy.

penser, *v.* To think. **I.** *v.ind.tr* **Penser à qn, à qch.,** to think of s.o., sth. **Je l'ai fait sans y penser,** I did it withou thinking. **(Y) pensez-vous!** you don't mean it! **Vous n'y pensez pas!** you don't mean it! **Ah, j'y pense!** by the way! **Rien que d'y penser,** the mere thought (of it). **Faire penser qn à qch.,** to remind s.o. of sth **2.** *v.i.* **Manière de penser,** attitude of mind. **Pensez donc!** just fancy! **3.** *v.tr* (*a*) **Je le pensais bien,** I thought as much. (*b*) *Pred:* **Je le pense fou,** I consider him crazy. (*c*) *P. du bien de qn*, to think well of s.o. (*d*) *Je pense le voir demain*, I expect to see him to-morrow. *J'ai pensé mourir de rire*, I nearly died with laughter.

pensée[2], *s.f.* **I.** Thought. **Il me vint dans la pensée,** the thought occurred to me. **2.** Intention

penseur, -euse, *s.* Thinker.

pensif, *a.* Thoughtful, pensive.

pension, *s.f.* **I.** Pension, allowance. **2.** (*a*) Payment for board (and lodging). **Être en pension chez qn,** to board with s.o (*b*) **Pension de famille,** residential hotel; boarding-house. **3.** (*a*) Boarding-school fees. (*b*) (Private) boarding-school.

pensionnaire, *s.m. &* **I.** Pensioner. **2.** Boarder.

pensionnat, *s.m.* (Private) boarding-school.

pensionner, *v.tr.* To pension.

pensivement, *adv.* Pensively, thoughtfully.

pensum [-sɔm], *s.m. Sch:* Imposition.

pentagonal, -aux, *a.* Pentagonal.

pentagone. I. *a.* Pentagonal **2.** *s.m.* Pentagon.

Pentateuque (le), *s.m.* The Pentateuch

pente, *s.f.* (*a*) Slope, incline, gradient.

P. d'un toit, pitch of a roof. *Rail:* **Lignes à forte pente,** steep gradients. (*b*) Bent, inclination, propensity.

Pentecôte, *s.f.* Whitsun(tide); Pentecost; **Dimanche de la Pentecôte,** Whit-Sunday.

pénultième, *a. & s.f.* Penultimate; last but one.

pénurie, *s.f* (*a*) Scarcity, shortage; lack. (*b*) Poverty.

pépier, *v.i.* To cheep, chirp.

pépin, *s.m.* Pip (of apple); stone (of grape).

pépinière, *s.f. Hort:* Seed-bed; nursery.

pépiniériste, *s.m.* Nurseryman.

pépite, *s.f.* Nugget (of gold).

pérambulation, *s.f.* Perambulation.

perçant, *a.* Piercing, penetrating; keen; shrill.

perce-neige, *s.m. or f.inv. Bot:* Snowdrop.

perce-oreille, *s.m. Ent:* Earwig. *pl. Des perce-oreilles.*

percepteur, -trice. I. *a.* Perceiving, discerning. **2.** *s.* (*a*) Tax-collector (*b*) Bus or tram conductor.

perceptible, *a.* Perceptible; discernible.

perceptiblement, *adv.* Perceptibly.

perceptif, *a.* Perceptive.

perception, *s.f.* **I.** Perception. **2.** Collection, receipt (of taxes).

percer, *v.* (n. *perçons*) **I.** *v.tr.* (*a*) To pierce, to go through. *P. le cœur à qn*, to cut s.o. to the heart. (*b*) To perforate; to make a hole, an opening, in. *P. une porte dans un mur*, to make a door in a wall. (*c*) *P. un trou*, to bore a hole. **2.** *v.i.* To pierce; to come through.

percé, *a.* (*a*) Pierced; holed. (*b*) (Of garment) In holes.

percée, *s.f.* **I.** Cutting (in a forest); break (in hedge); glade; vista. **2.** *Mil:* Break-through.

percevoir, *v.tr.* (Conj. like RECEVOIR) **I.** To perceive, discern. **2.** To collect (taxes).

perche[1], *s.f.* (Thin) pole.

perche[2], *s.f. Ich:* Perch.

percher, *v.i.* To perch, roost.

se percher. (Of bird) *Se p. sur une branche,* to alight, perch, on a branch.

perchoir, *s.m.* (Bird's) perch, roost.

perclus, *a* Stiff-jointed. *F: P. de rhumatismes*, crippled with rheumatism.

perçoi-s, -t, -ve, etc. See PERCEVOIR

percolateur, *s.m* Percolator

perçu, -s, -t, etc. See PERCEVOIR.

percussion, *s.f.* Percussion, impact.

perdant. I. *a.* Losing. **Billet perdant,** blank (ticket, at lottery). **2.** *s.* Loser.

perdition, *s.f. Ecc:* Perdition.

perdre, *v.tr* **I.** To ruin, destroy. **2.** To lose. **Vous ne perdrez rien pour attendre,** you will lose nothing by waiting. **Perdre son temps,** to waste (one's) time. **3.** *Abs.* (*a*) **Vous n'y perdrez pas,** you won't lose by it. (*b*) *P. sur ses concurrents,* to fall behind.

se perdre. I. To be lost. **2.** To lose

one's way. *F:* **Je m'y perds,** I can't make head or tail of it.

perdu, *a.* **I.** Ruined. **2.** Lost. **A mes heures perdues,** in my spare time. *Sentinelle perdue,* advanced sentry. **3. A corps perdu,** recklessly.

perdreau, *s.m.* Young partridge.

perdrix, *s.f.* Partridge. *P. des neiges,* ptarmigan.

père, *s.m.* **I.** Father. **M. Dupont père,** Mr Dupont senior. **Valeurs de père de famille,** gilt-edged securities. *Th:* **Père noble,** heavy father. **Nos pères,** our forefathers. **2.** *Ecc:* Father.

pérégrination, *s.f.* Peregrination.

péremptoire, *a.* **I.** (*a*) Peremptory. (*b*) Unanswerable, decisive.

péremptoirement, *adv.* Peremptorily.

perfection, *s.f.* Perfection.

perfectionnement, *s.m.* **I.** Perfecting; improving. **2.** Improvement.

perfectionner, *v.tr.* **I.** To perfect. **2.** To improve.

perfide, *a.* Treacherous; perfidious.

perfidie, *s.f.* **I.** Treachery, perfidy, perfidiousness. **2.** Treacherous act.

perforation, *s.f.* Perforation.

perforer, *v.tr.* **I.** To perforate; to bore (through), to drill. **2.** To puncture (tyre)

péri, *s.m. & f.* (Oriental) peri; fairy.

périclitant, *a.* Unsound, shaky.

péricliter, *v.i.* (Of undertaking) To be in danger, in jeopardy.

péril [-ril], *s.m.* Peril, danger; risk, hazard.

périlleusement [-rij-], *adv.* Perilously.

périlleux [-rij-], *a.* Perilous, hazardous.

périmer, *v.i. Jur:* To lapse.

périmé, *a.* Out-of-date; expired (bill); (ticket) no longer available; lapsed.

périmètre, *s.m.* Perimeter.

période, *s.f.* (*a*) Period (of recurring phenomenon). (*b*) Period of time; age, era. (*c*) *Rh:* Period; complete sentence.

périodique. **I.** *a.* Periodical; recurring; intermittent. **2.** *s.m.* Periodical (publication).

périodiquement, *adv.* Periodically.

péripétie, *s.f.* **I.** Sudden change of fortune. **2.** *pl. F:* Vicissitudes; ups and downs.

périphérie, *s.f.* **I.** Periphery; circumference. **2.** Outskirts (of town).

périr, *v.i.* (Aux *avoir*) To perish; to be destroyed.

périscope, *s.m.* Periscope.

périssable, *a.* Perishable.

périssoire, *s.f.* (Single-seater) canoe.

péristyle, *s.m. Arch:* Peristyle. *Ecc:* Cloisters.

perle, *s.f.* **I.** Pearl. **2.** Bead (of glass).

perler, *v.i.* To form in beads.

permanence, *s.f.* **I.** Permanence. **2.** Building always open to the public.

permanent. **I.** *a.* Permanent; standing

(army). *Cin:* **Spectacle permanent,** continuous performance. **2.** *s.f. Hairdr* **Permanente,** permanent wave.

perméable, *a.* Permeable; porous.

permettre, *v.tr.* (Conj. like METTRE) T permit, allow. *S'il est permis de s'exprime ainsi,* if one may say so. **Permis à vous de n pas me croire,** you are at liberty to believ me or not. **Permettez!** excuse me! allov me! **Vous permettez?** may I? *Se p. de fair qch.,* to make bold to do sth.

permis. **I.** *a.* Allowed, permitted, per missible. **2.** *s.m.* Permit, permission. *P. d chasse,* game-licence. *Aut:* P. de conduire driving-licence. *P. de circulation,* car-licence

permission, *s.f.* (*a*) Permission, leave (*b*) Leave of absence.

permissionnaire, *s.m.* Soldier on leave *Navy:* liberty man.

permutation, *s.f.* **I.** Exchange of posts **2.** *Mth:* Permutation.

permuter, *v.tr.* To exchange (post). *Abs* To exchange posts.

pernicieusement, *adv.* Perniciously.

pernicieux, *a.* Pernicious, injurious

péroraison, *s.f.* Peroration.

pérorer, *v.i.* To hold forth; to speechify.

Pérou (le). *Pr.n.m. Geog:* Peru. *F:* Ce **n'est pas le Pérou,** it is not highly paid.

peroxyde, *s.m. Ch:* Peroxide.

perpendiculaire, *a. & s.* Perpendicular.

perpétration, *s.f.* Perpetration.

perpétrer, *v.tr.* (**je perpètre; je perpétrerai** To perpetrate.

perpétuation, *s.f.* Perpetuation.

perpétuel, -elle, *a.* (*a*) Perpetual, everlasting; (imprisonment) for life (*b*) F Constant.

perpétuellement, *adv.* (*a*) Perpetually. (*b*) Constantly.

perpétuer, *v.tr.* To perpetuate.

se perpétuer, to endure, to become established.

perpétuité, *s.f.* Perpetuity. **A perpétuité,** in perpetuity; (penal servitude) for life.

perplexe, *a.* **I.** Perplexed, puzzled **2.** Perplexing (situation).

perplexité, *s.f.* Perplexity.

perquisition, *s.f.* Thorough inquiry **Mandat de perquisition,** search-warrant.

perquisitionner. *v.i. Jur:* To make a search.

perron, *s.m.* (Flight of) steps (before building).

perroquet, *s.m.* **I.** Parrot. **2.** *Nau:* Mât **de perroquet,** topgallant mast.

perruche, *s.f. Orn:* (*a*) Parakeet (*b*) Henparrot.

perruque, *s.f.* Wig. **Tête à perruque,** barber's block.

perruquier, *s.* Wig-maker.

persan. **I.** *a & s.* Persian. **2.** *s.m. Ling:* Persian.

Perse. *Pr.n.f.* Persia.

persécuter, *v.tr.* To persecute.
persécuteur, -trice, *s.* Persecutor.
persécution, *s.f.* Persecution.
persévérance, *s.f.* Perseverance.
persévérant, *a.* Persevering; dogged.
persévérer, *v.i.* (je persévère; je persé-
vérerai) **1.** To persevere. **2.** *La fièvre persévère,* the fever persists.
persiflage, *s.m.* Banter; persiflage.
persifler, *v.tr.* To banter, rally.
persil, *s.m.* *Bot:* Parsley.
persique, *a.* *Geog:* Le Golfe Persique, the
Persian Gulf.
persistance, *s.f.* Persistence, persistency.
1. Doggedness. **2.** Continuance (of fever).
persistant, *a.* Persistent. **1.** Dogged.
2. Lasting, enduring.
persister, *v.i.* To persist.
personnage, *s.m.* (a) Personage. (b) Character (in play).
personnalité, *s.f.* Personality. **1.** Individuality. **2.** Person, personage. **3.** *pl.* Dire
des personnalités, to make personal remarks.
personne. 1. *s.f.* Person. (a) Individual.
Les grandes personnes, the grown-ups. (b) En
personne, in person; personally. *Il est la bonté
en p.,* he is kindness itself. (c) *Elle est bien faite
de sa p.,* she is a fine figure of a woman.
(d) *Gram:* Écrire à la troisième p., to write in
the third person. **2.** *pron.indef.m.inv.* (a)
Anyone, anybody (with vaguely implied
negation). *Il travaille plus fort que p.,* he
works harder than anyone. (b) (With *ne*
expressed or understood) No one; nobody.
Qui est là?—Personne, who is there?—No
one. *Il n'y a p. de blessé,* there is no one
wounded. *Sans nommer p.,* without mentioning any names.
personnel, -elle. 1. *a.* Personal. *Strictement p.,* not transferable. **2.** *s.m.* (a) Personnel, staff; hands. (b) *Navy:* Complement.
personnellement, *adv.* Personally, in
person.
personnification, *s.f.* (a) Personification.
(b) Impersonation.
personnifier, *v.tr.* (a) To personify. (b) To
impersonate.
perspectif. 1. *a.* Perspective. **2.** *s.f.*
Perspective. (a) *Art:* Perspective. (b) Outlook, view, prospect. Avoir qch. en perspective, to have sth. in view. (c) *Une longue
perspective de hêtres,* a long vista of beech-
trees.
perspicace, *a.* Perspicacious, shrewd.
perspicacité, *s.f.* Perspicacity, shrewdness.
persuader, *v.tr.* **1.** *P. qch. à qn,* to persuade
s.o. of sth. **2.** *P. qn,* to persuade, convince,
s.o. **3.** *P. à qn de faire qch.,* to induce s.o.
to do sth.
  persuadé, *a.* Persuaded, convinced.
persuasif, *a.* Persuasive; convincing.
persuasion, *s.f.* **1.** Persuasion. **2.** Conviction, belief.

perte, *s.f.* **1.** Ruin, destruction. **2.** Loss.
Courir à perte d'haleine, to run oneself out
of breath. Parler en pure perte, to talk to
no purpose. **3.** Loss, leakage.
pertinemment, *adv.* Pertinently.
pertinence, *s.f.* Pertinence, relevance.
pertinent, *a.* Pertinent; relevant.
perturbateur, -trice. 1. *a.* Disturbing,
upsetting. **2.** *s.* Disturber.
perturbation, *s.f.* (a) Perturbation. (b) Per-
turbations atmosphériques, *W Tel:* atmospherics.
pervenche, *s.f.* *Bot:* Periwinkle.
pervers, *a.* Perverse, depraved.
perversement, *adv.* Perversely.
perversion, *s.f.* Perversion.
perversité, *s.f.* Perversity.
pervertir, *v.tr.* To pervert, to corrupt.
  se pervertir, to become depraved.
pesage, *s.m.* **1.** Weighing. **2.** *Turf:* Weighing in.
pesamment, *adv.* Heavily; clumsily.
pesant. 1. *a.* Heavy, weighty; ponderous,
clumsy. **2.** *s.m.* Cela vaut son pesant d'or, it
is worth its weight in gold.
pesanteur, *s.f.* **1.** Weight. **2.** (a) Heaviness.
(b) Dullness (of mind).
pesée, *s.f.* Weighing.
pèse-lettres, *s.m.inv.* Letter-balance.
peser, *v.* (je pèse) **1.** *v.tr.* To weigh. **2.** *v.i.*
(a) To weigh; to be heavy. Le temps lui pèse,
time hangs on his hands. (b) *P. sur un mot,*
to lay stress on a word.
peson, *s.m.* *P. à ressort,* spring-balance.
pessimisme, *s.m.* Pessimism.
pessimiste. 1. *a.* Pessimistic. **2.** *s.* Pessimist.
peste, *s.f.* Plague, pestilence. Peste! bless
my soul!
pester, *v.i.* *F:* P. contre qn, to storm at s.o.
pestifère, *a.* Pestiferous, pestilential.
pestiféré, *a. & s.* Plague-stricken.
pestilentiel, -elle, *a.* Pestilential.
pétale, *s.m.* *Bot:* Petal.
pétard, *s.m.* (a) *Rail:* Fog-signal. (b) (Firework) cracker.
pétillant [-tijă], *a.* Crackling (fire); sparkling.
pétillement [-tij-], *s.m.* Crackling; sparkling; bubbling.
pétiller [-tije], *v.i.* To crackle; to sparkle,
bubble.
petit, *a.* Small, little. **1.** (a) En petit, in
miniature. (b) Les petits prophètes, the minor
prophets. *Petite guerre,* sham fight. *Com:*
Petite caisse, petty cash. **2.** Insignificant,
unimportant, petty. *Les petites gens, s.* les
petits, common folk. **3.** Mean, petty, paltry.
4. (a) P. enfant, infant. Les petits Dupont,
the Dupont children. (b) *s. Pauvre petit(e),*
poor little chap, poor little thing. (c) *s.m. Les
petits des animaux,* the young of animals.
petite-fille, *s.f.* Grand-daughter. *pl. Des
petites-filles.*

petitesse, *s.f.* **1.** (*a*) Smallness, diminutiveness. (*b*) Meanness, pettiness. **2.** *Faire des petitesses,* to do shabby things.

petit-fils, *s.m.* Grandson. *pl. Des petits-fils.*

pétition, *s.f.* (*a*) Petition, memorial. (*b*) *Faire une p. de principe,* to beg the question.

pétitionnaire, *s.m. & f.* Petitioner.

pétitionner, *v.i.* To petition.

petit-lait, *s.m.* Whey.

petits-enfants, *s.m.pl.* Grand-children.

pétoncle, *s.m. Moll:* Scallop.

pétrel, *s.m. Orn:* Petrel.

pétrification, *s.f.* Petrifaction.

pétrifier, *v.tr.* To petrify.

pétrin, *s.m.* Kneading-trough. *F:* Être dans le pétrin, to be in the soup.

pétrir, *v.tr.* To knead; to mould, shape.

pétrole, *s.m.* Petroleum; mineral oil. *P. lampant,* paraffin oil.

pétrolifère, *a.* Oil-bearing. *Gisement pétrolifère,* oil-field.

pétulance, *s.f.* Liveliness, irrepressibleness (of spirits); friskiness (of horse).

pétulant, *a.* Lively, irrepressible; frisky.

pétunia, *s.m. Bot:* Petunia.

peu. 1. *adv.* (*a*) Little. *Ce n'est pas peu dire,* that's saying a good deal. *Quelque peu surpris,* somewhat surprised. *Pour si peu de chose,* for so small a matter. (*b*) Few. *Peu d'entre eux,* few of them. (*c*) Not very. *Peu honnête,* dishonest. *Peu abondant,* scarce. **2.** *s.m.* (*a*) Little, bit. *Donnez-m'en si peu que rien,* give me the least little bit. *Son peu d'éducation,* his lack of learning. *F:* Ça, c'est un peu fort! that's rather too much of a good thing! *Pour un peu on eût crié,* we very nearly shouted. *Écoutez un peu,* just listen. (*b*) Peu après, shortly after. **Sous peu,** before long. *Depuis peu,* lately.

peuh, *int.* Pooh!

peuplade, *s.f.* Small tribe.

peuple, *s.m.* People. **1.** Nation. **2.** Le peuple, the masses. **Les gens du peuple,** the lower classes.

peuplement, *s.m.* Peopling.

peupler, *v.tr.* To people, populate. *Rues peuplées de monde,* streets thronged with people.

peuplier, *s.m.* Poplar.

peur, *s.f.* Fear, fright, dread. **N'ayez pas peur!** do not be afraid. **J'ai peur qu'il (ne) soit en retard,** I fear he may be late. **Prendre peur,** to take fright. *F:* Avoir une peur bleue, to be in a blue funk. **Être laide à faire peur,** to be frightfully ugly.

peureusement, *adv.* Timorously.

peureux, *a.* Timorous; easily frightened; timid (nature).

peut. See POUVOIR.

peut-être, *adv.* Perhaps, maybe, possibly. *P.-ê que oui,* perhaps so. *P.-ê. bien qu'il viendra,* he will very possibly come.

peuvent, peux. See POUVOIR.

phalange, *s.f.* **1.** *Mil:* Phalanx. **2.** *Anat:* Finger-joint, toe-joint.

phantasme, *s.m. Med:* Phantasm.

pharaon, *s.m.* **1.** Pharaoh. **2.** *Cards:* Faro.

phare, *s.m* **1.** Lighthouse **2.** *Aut:* Headlight.

pharisaïque, *a.* Pharisaic(al).

pharisien, *s.m* Pharisee.

pharmaceutique. 1. *a.* Pharmaceutic(al). **2.** *s.f.* Pharmaceutics.

pharmacie, *s.f.* **1.** (*a*) Pharmacy; chemist's and druggist's shop. (*b*) Dispensary. **2.** (Armoire à) pharmacie, medicine-chest.

pharmacien, -ienne, *s* Chemist; druggist.

pharmacopée, *s.f.* Pharmacopoeia.

pharynx [-rɛːks], *s.m. Anat:* Pharynx.

phase, *s.f.* Phase.

Phénicie. *Pr.n.f Geog:* Phoenicia.

phénicien, -ienne, *a. & s.* Phoenician.

phénique, *a.* Carbolic (acid).

phénix [-niks], *s.m. Myth:* Phoenix.

phénol, *s.m. Com:* Carbolic acid.

phénoménal, -aux, *a.* Phenomenal.

phénoménalement, *adv.* Phenomenally.

philanthrope, *s.m.* Philanthropist.

philatélie, *s.f.* Philately.

philatélique, *a.* Philatelic.

philatéliste, *s.m. & f.* Philatelist.

Philippe. *Pr.n.m.* Philip.

philistin, *a. & s.* Philistine.

philologue, *s.m.* Philologist.

philosophe. 1. *s.m. & f.* Philosopher, sage. **2.** *a.* Philosophical.

philtre, *s.m.* Philtre.

phonétique. 1. *a.* Phonetic. **2.** *s.f.* Phonetics.

phonétiquement, *adv.* Phonetically.

phonographe, *s.m.* Phonograph.

phoque, *s.m. Z:* Seal.

phosphate, *s.m. Ch:* Phosphate.

phosphore, *s.m. Ch:* Phosphorus.

phosphorescence, *s.f.* Phosphorescence.

phosphorescent, *a.* Phosphorescent.

photographe, *s.m* Photographer.

photographie, *s.f.* **1.** Photography. **2.** Photograph.

photographier, *v.tr.* To photograph.

photographique, *a.* Photographic.

phrase, *s.f.* **1.** Sentence. *F:* Faire des phrases, to speak in flowery language. **Parler sans phrase,** to speak straight out. **2.** *Mus:* Phrase.

phraséologie, *s.f.* Phraseology.

phrénologie, *s.f.* Phrenology.

phrénologique, *a.* Phrenological.

phrénologiste, *s.m.* Phrenologist.

phrygien, -ienne, *a. & s.* Bonnet phrygien, Phrygian cap (emblem of liberty).

phtisie, *s.f. Med:* Phthisis; consumption.

phtisique, *a. & s. Med:* Consumptive.

phylactère, *s.m.* Phylactery.

phylloxéra, *s.m. Ent:* Phylloxera.
physicien, -ienne, *s.* Physicist.
physiologie, *s.f.* Physiology.
physiologique, *a.* Physiological.
physiologiste, *s.m.* Physiologist.
physionomie, *s.f.* Physiognomy; face, countenance; (of thg) appearance, aspect. Jeu de physionomie, play of features.
physique. 1. *a.* Physical. *Douleur p.,* bodily pain. 2. *s.f.* Physics. 3. *s.m.* Physique (of person).
physiquement, *adv.* Physically, materially.
piaffer, *v.i.* (Of horse) (*a*) To paw the ground. (*b*) To prance.
piailler [pjɑje], *v.i.* (Of small birds) To cheep; (of children) to squall, squeal.
pianiste, *s.m. & f.* Pianist.
piano¹, *s.m.* Piano, pianoforte. *P. à queue,* grand piano. *P. droit,* upright piano.
piano², *adv. Mus:* Piano, softly.
pianola, *s.m.* Pianola.
piastre, *s.f. Num:* Piastre.
piauler, *v.i.* (Of chicks) To peep, cheep; (of children) to whine, whimper.
pic¹ [pik], *s.m.* 1. Pick, pickaxe. 2. (Mountain-)peak. *Adv.phr.* A pic, perpendicular(ly), sheer. *Sentier à pic,* precipitous path. *F:* Arriver, tomber, à pic, to come in the nick of time. 3. L'ancre est à pic, the anchor is apeak.
pic², *s.m. Orn:* Woodpecker.
picard, *a. & s.* (Native) of Picardy.
Picardie. *Pr.n.f. Geog:* Picardy.
picorer. 1. *v.i.* (Of bird) To forage; to pick, scratch about, for food.
picotement, *s.m.* Pricking, tingling.
picoter, *v.tr.* 1. (*a*) (Of bird) To peck. (*b*) *Fumée qui picote les yeux,* smoke that makes the eyes smart. 2. *v.i.* To smart, tingle.
Pictes, *s.m.pl. Ethn:* Picts.
pic-vert [pivɛːr], *s.m. Orn:* Green woodpecker. *pl. Des pics-verts.*
pie. 1. *s.f. Orn:* Magpie. 2. *a.,* often *inv.* Piebald.
pièce, *s.f.* 1. Piece (as a whole). (*a*) Pièce de gibier, head of game. *P. de blé,* corn-field. *P. d'eau,* sheet of water. *Ils coûtent mille francs p.,* they cost a thousand francs apiece. Travail à la pièce, aux pièces, piece-work. (*b*) *Jur:* Pièces d'un procès, documents in a case. (*c*) Pièce de théâtre, play. 2. Piece (as part of a whole). (*a*) *P. de bœuf,* joint of beef. *Pièces d'une machine,* parts of a machine. Être armé de toutes pièces, to be armed at all points. *F:* Créer une armée de toutes pièces, to create an army out of nothing. (*b*) *Games:* (Chess-)piece; (draughts)man. (*c*) Room (in house). (*d*) Patch. *Mettre une p. à un vêtement,* to patch a garment. 3. Fragment, bit.
pied, *s.m.* 1. (*a*) Foot. *Frapper du p.,* to stamp one's foot. Mettre pied à terre, to alight; to dismount; to step ashore. Marcher sur les pieds de qn, to tread on s.o.'s toes.

Avoir bon pied, bon œil, to be hale and hearty. Faire qch. au pied levé, to do sth. off-hand, at a moment's notice. Coup de pied, kick. A pied, on foot, walking. Aller à pied, to walk. Sur pied, afoot, standing, on one's legs. Récolte sur pied, standing crop. *Remettre qn sur p.,* (i) to restore s.o. to health; (ii) to set s.o. on his feet again. Portrait en pied, full-length portrait. *Mil:* L'arme au pied, with arms at the order. (*b*) Footing, foothold. Perdre pied, to lose one's foothold; to get out of one's depth. Le pied me manqua, I lost my footing. Tenir pied, to stand fast. Payer qn sur le pied de . . ., to pay s.o. at the rate of. . . . 2. (*a*) Foot; base. (*b*) Leg (of chair); stem, foot (of glass). (*c*) *P. de céleri,* head of celery. (*d*) Stand, rest. 3. *Meas:* Foot. 4. *Pros:* (Metrical) foot.
pied-à-terre [-tatɛːr], *s.m.inv.* (Small) occasional lodging, shooting-box.
pied-d'alouette, *s.m.* Larkspur, delphinium. *pl. Des pieds-d'alouette.*
piédestal, -aux, *s.m.* Pedestal.
piège, *s.m.* Trap, snare. *P. à loups,* man-trap.
pierraille [-rɑːj], *s.f.* Rubble; ballast; road metal.
pierre¹, *s.f.* Stone. Poser la première pierre, to lay the foundation stone. *P. à aiguiser,* whetstone. C'est une pierre dans votre jardin, that's a dig at you. Faire d'une pierre deux coups, to kill two birds with one stone.
Pierre². *Pr.n.m.* Peter.
pierreries, *s.f.pl.* Precious stones, jewels, gems.
pierreux, *a.* Stony.
Pierrot, *s.m. Th:* Pierrot, clown.
piété, *s.f.* (*a*) Affectionate devotion. (*b*) Piety.
piétinement, *s.m.* Stamping, trampling.
piétiner. 1. *v.tr.* To trample, stamp, on; to tread under foot. 2. *v.i. P. de rage,* to dance with rage.
piéton, *s.m.* Pedestrian.
piètre, *a. F:* Wretched, poor; paltry.
pieu, -eux, *s.m.* Stake, post.
pieusement, *adv.* Piously, reverently.
pieuvre, *s.f.* Octopus, devil-fish, poulpe.
pieux, *a.* (*a*) Reverent. (*b*) Pious, godly.
pif, *int.* Pif, paf! bang, bang!
pigeon, -onne, *s.* 1. Pigeon. *P. voyageur,* carrier-pigeon. 2. *F:* Greenhorn, gull.
pigment, *s.m.* Pigment.
pignon, *s.m.* 1. Gable, gable-end. *F:* Avoir pignon sur rue, to have a house of one's own. 2. *Mec.E:* Pinion.
pile¹, *s.f.* 1. Pile; heap. 2. Pier (of bridge). 3. *El:* Battery. *P. de rechange* refill (for torch).
pile², *s.f.* Reverse (of coin). Pile ou face, heads or tails.
piler, *v.tr.* To pound; to crush.
pilier, *s.m.* Pillar, column, post.
pillage [-jaːʒ], *s.m.* Pillage, looting.
pillard [pijaːr], *a.* 1. *a.* Thieving. 2. *s.* Pillager, looter.

piller [pije], *v.tr.* **1.** To pillage, loot, sack. **2.** (Of dog) To attack. **Pille! pille!** at him!

pilon, *s.m.* **1.** Pestle. **2.** *F:* (*a*) Drumstick (of fowl). (*b*) Wooden leg.

pilonner, *v.tr.* To pound; to ram; to stamp.

pilori, *s.m.* Pillory.

pilorier, *v.tr.* To pillory.

pilotage, *s.m.* Pilotage, piloting.

pilote, *s.m.* Pilot.

piloter, *v.tr.* To pilot.

pilule, *s.f. Pharm:* Pill.

piment, *s.m.* Pimento, capsicum. *Cu:* Red pepper.

pimpant, *a.* Smart, spruce.

pin, *s.m.* Pine(-tree), fir(-tree).

pinacle, *s.m.* Pinnacle; ridge ornament.

pince, *s.f.* **1.** Grip, hold. **2.** Holder, gripper. (*a*) Pincers, pliers. *Surg:* Forceps. *P. à sucre,* sugar-tongs. (*b*) Clip. *P. à linge,* clothes-peg. (*c*) Crowbar. **3.** Claw, nipper.

pinceau, *s.m.* (Artist's) paint-brush.

pincement, *s.m.* Pinching, nipping.

pince-nez, *s.m.inv.* Eye-glasses, pince-nez.

pincer, *v.tr.* (n. **pinçons**) **1.** To pinch, nip. **2.** To grip, hold fast. **Se faire pincer,** to get nabbed.

    pincé, *a.* Affected, prim. *Sourire p.,* tight-lipped smile; wry smile.

    pincée, *s.f.* Pinch (of snuff).

pince-sans-rire, *s.m.inv. F:* Man of dry humour.

pincette, *s.f.* Usu. *pl.* (*a*) Tweezers, nippers. (*b*) (Fire-)tongs; pair of tongs.

pingouin, *s.m. Orn:* Auk.

pinson, *s.m. Orn:* Chaffinch.

pintade, *s.f.* Guinea-fowl.

pinte, *s.f.* (French) pint = half a litre. *F: Se faire une pinte de bon sang,* to laugh loud and long.

pioche, *s.f.* Pickaxe, pick.

piocher, *v.tr.* (*a*) To dig (with a pick). (*b*) *F:* To grind, swot, at (sth.)

piolet, *s.m.* Piolet; ice-axe.

pion, *s.m.* **1.** *F:* Usher; junior master. **2.** (*a*) Pawn. (*b*) *Draughts:* Piece, man.

pionnier, *s.m.* Pioneer.

pipe, *s.f.* Pipe. **1.** Tube. **2.** Tobacco-pipe.

pipeau, *s.m. Mus:* (Reed-)pipe. *P. de chasse,* bird-call.

piper, *v.tr.* (*a*) To lure (birds). (*b*) *P. les dés,* to load dice.

piquant. **1.** *a.* Pungent; tart, biting; piquant. **2.** *s.m.* Point, pith (of story); pungency. **3.** *s.m.* Prickle; quill (of porcupine); spike.

pique¹. **1.** *s.f.* Pike. *Bois de pique,* pikestaff. **2.** *s.m. Cards:* Spade(s).

pique², *s.f.* Pique, ill-feeling.

pique-nique, *s.m.* Picnic. *pl. Des pique-niques.*

piquer, *v.tr.* **1.** (*a*) To prick, sting. **Piquer des deux,** to clap spurs to one's horse. *La fumée pique les yeux,* the smoke makes the eyes smart. (*b*) To nettle, pique. *P. la jalousie de qn,* to arouse s.o.'s jealousy. **2.** To prick, puncture. **3.** To stick, insert. **4.** **Piquer une tête,** to take a header.

    se piquer. **1.** To prick oneself. **2.** To take offence. **3.** **Se piquer de qch.,** to pride oneself on sth. **4.** **Se piquer au jeu,** to get excited over the game.

    piqué, *a.* **1.** (*a*) Quilted; padded (door). (*b*) *s.m.* Quilting, piqué. **2.** *P. des mouches,* fly-spotted. **3.** *Av: Descente piquée, s.m.* **piqué,** nose-dive.

piquet¹, *s.m.* **1.** Peg, stake, post. **2.** *Mil:* Picket.

piquet², *s.m. Cards:* Piquet.

piqûre, *s.f.* **1.** (*a*) Prick, sting, bite. (*b*) Hypodermic injection. **2.** Puncture.

pirate, *s.m.* Pirate.

piraterie, *s.f.* **1.** Piracy **2.** Act of piracy.

pire, *a.* **1.** *Comp.* Worse. **2.** *Sup. a.* **Le pire,** the worst. *Quand les choses sont au pire,* when things are at their worst.

Pirée (le). *Pr.n.m. Geog:* The Piraeus.

pirouette, *s.f.* Pirouette.

pis¹, *s.m.* Udder.

pis², *adv.* **1.** *Comp.* Worse. **Pour ne pas dire pis,** to say no more. **2.** *Sup. a.* **Le pis,** (the) worst. *s.m.* **Mettre les choses au pis,** to suppose the worst. **3.** **Pis aller,** *s.m. inv.* Last resource; makeshift.

piscine, *s.f.* Swimming-bath.

pissenlit, *s.m. Bot:* Dandelion.

pistache, *s.f.* Pistachio(-nut).

piste, *s.f.* **1.** (*a*) Running-track; race-track. **Piste cavalière,** bridle-path. (*b*) *Av:* **Piste d'envol,** runway. *P. d'atterrissage,* landing strip. **2.** *Ven:* Track, trail, scent.

pistil, [-til], *s.m. Bot:* Pistil.

pistolet, *s.m.* Pistol.

piston, *s.m.* **1.** *Mch:* Piston. **2.** *Mus: Cornet à pistons,* cornet.

pitance, *s.f. F: Se faire une maigre pitance,* to eke out a living.

piteusement, *adv.* Piteously, woefully.

piteux, *a.* Piteous, woeful, pitiable.

pitié, *s.f.* Pity, compassion. **Regarder qn d'un œil de pitié,** to look compassionately at s.o. **Faire pitié,** to arouse pity.

pitoyable, *a.* (*a*) Pitiable, pitiful. (*b*) Paltry, despicable.

pitoyablement, *adv.* Pitifully, woefully.

pittoresque. **1.** *a.* (*a*) Picturesque, quaint. (*b*) Pictorial. **2.** *s.m.* Picturesqueness.

pivert, *s.m.* Green woodpecker.

pivoine, *s.f.* Peony.

pivot, *s.m.* Pivot, pin, axis; swivel.

pivotement, *s.m.* Pivoting, swivelling.

pivoter, *v.i.* **1.** To pivot; to turn; to swivel, revolve. **2.** (Of troops) To wheel.

placage, *s.m.* **1.** Veneering. **2.** Plating (of metal).

placard, *s.m.* **1.** Wall-cupboard. **2.** Poster, bill, placard.

placarder, *v.tr.* To stick (a bill) on a wall.

place, *s.f.* Place. **I.** (a) Position. **Il ne peut pas rester en place,** he can't keep still. (b) Stead. **A votre place,** if I were you. (c) **Faire place à qn,** to make room, make way, for s.o. **(Faites) place!** stand aside! make way! **Place aux dames!** ladies first! **2.** (a) Seat. *Prix des places,* (i) fares; (ii) prices of admission. (b) Situation, office, post. **3.** Locality, spot. **Place publique,** public square, market-place. **Place d'armes,** parade-ground. **Automobile de place,** motor car plying for hire. **Sur place,** on the spot. **Rester sur place,** to be left on the field.

placement, *s.m.* **I.** (a) Placing; investing (of money). **Bureau de placement,** employment bureau. (b) Sale, disposal (of goods). **2.** Investment.

placer, *v.tr.* (n. plaçons) To place. **I.** (a) To put, set (in a certain place); to find a place for. (b) To find a situation for. *Gens bien placés,* people of good position. (c) To invest (money). **2.** To sell, dispose of (goods). **se placer. I.** To take one's seat, one's place. **2.** To obtain a situation.

placide, *a.* Placid; calm; unruffled.

placidement, *adv.* Placidly, calmly.

placidité, *s.f.* Placidity.

plafond, *s.m.* **I.** Ceiling. **2.** Maximum attainable or permissible; ceiling (of aeroplane).

plage, *s.f.* (a) Beach, shore. (b) Seaside resort.

plagiat, *s.m.* Plagiarism.

plaid, *s.m.* Travelling-rug.

plaider, *v.tr.* To plead (a cause).

plaideur, -euse, *s.* Litigant, suitor.

plaidoirie, *s.f.* Counsel's speech.

plaidoyer, *s.m.* *Jur:* Address to the Court; speech for the defence.

plaie, *s.f.* **I.** Wound, sore. **2.** Affliction, evil.

plaignant, *s.* Plaintiff.

plaign-e, -es, etc. See PLAINDRE.

plaindre, *v.tr.* (Conj. like CRAINDRE) To pity. **se plaindre,** to complain.

plaine, *s.f.* Plain; flat open country.

plain-pied, *s.m.* **I.** Suite of rooms on one floor. **2.** *Adv.phr.* **De plain-pied,** on one floor, on a level.

plain-s, -t. See PLAINDRE.

plainte, *s.f.* **I.** Moan, groan. **2.** (a) Complaint. (b) *Jur:* Indictment, complaint.

plaintif, *a.* (a) Plaintive, doleful (tone). (b) Querulous.

plaintivement, *adv.* (a) Plaintively. (b) Querulously.

plaire, *v.ind.tr.* (pr.p. plaisant; p.p. plu; pr.ind. il plaît) *P. à qn,* to please s.o. **Cela vous plaît à dire,** you are joking. *Impers.* **S'il vous plaît,** (if you) please. **Plaît-il?** I beg your pardon? what did you say? **A Dieu ne plaise,** God forbid. **Plût au ciel,** would to heaven. **se plaire,** to take pleasure; to be pleased, be happy.

plaisamment, *adv.* (a) Drolly, amusingly. (b) Ludicrously.

plaisance, *s.f.* **Bateau de plaisance,** pleasure-boat.

plaisant. I. See PLAIRE. **2.** *a.* (a) Funny, amusing. (b) (Always before the noun) Ridiculous, absurd. **3.** *s.m.* Wag, joker. *Des mauvais plaisants,* practical jokers.

plaisanter. I. *v.i.* To joke, jest. **Je ne plaisante pas,** I am in earnest. **2.** *v.tr.* To chaff, banter.

plaisanterie, *s.f.* Joke, jest; joking, jesting. *Une mauvaise p.,* a silly joke. **Tourner une chose en plaisanterie,** to laugh a thing off. **Entendre la plaisanterie,** to know how to take a joke.

plaisir, *s.m.* Pleasure. **I.** Delight. **Cela fait plaisir à voir,** it is pleasant to see. **Au plaisir de vous revoir,** good-bye; I hope we shall meet again. **A votre bon plaisir,** at your convenience. **A plaisir,** ad lib. **2.** (a) Amusement, enjoyment. **Train de plaisir,** excursion train. (b) *Vie de plaisirs,* gay life.

plan¹. I. *a.* Even, level, flat. **2.** *s.m.* (a) Plane. (b) **Premier plan,** (i) *Art:* foreground; (ii) *Th:* down-stage.

plan², *s.m.* Plan. (a) Drawing; draft. **Lever les plans d'une région,** to survey a district. (b) Scheme, project, design.

planche, *s.f.* **I.** (a) Board, plank. *Nau:* **P. de débarquement,** gang-plank. (b) Shelf (of cupboard). **2.** *Engr:* (Printed) plate, engraving.

plancher, *s.m.* (Boarded) floor.

planer, *v.i.* (a) To soar; to hover. (b) *Av:* To glide. **plané,** *a. & s.m.* *Av:* Gliding. **Vol plané,** glide.

planétaire, *a.* Planetary.

planète, *s.f.* *Astr:* Planet.

planquer (se), *v.pr.* To lie flat.

plantation, *s.f.* Plantation.

plante¹, *s.f.* Sole (of the foot).

plante², *s.f.* Plant. **Le Jardin des Plantes,** the Botanical Gardens.

planter, *v.tr.* **I.** To plant, set. **2.** To fix, set (up). *F:* **Planter là qn,** to leave s.o. in the lurch. **se planter,** to stand, take one's stand. *Se p. sur ses jambes,* to take a firm stand.

planteur, *s.m.* Planter.

planton, *s.m.* *Mil:* Orderly.

plantureusement, *adv.* Copiously, abundantly.

plantureux, *a.* **I.** Copious, abundant; lavish. **2.** Rich, fertile.

plaque, *s.f.* **I.** (a) Plate, sheet (of metal); slab (of marble). (b) **P. tournante,** turn-table. (c) **Plaque photographique,** photographic plate. **2.** (a) (Ornamental) plaque. **P. commemorative,** (votive) tablet. (b) **P. de porte,** door-plate. **3.** Badge. **P. d'un ordre,** star of an order. *Aut:* **P. matricule, p. de police,** number plate.

plaquemine, s.f. Bot: Persimmon.

plaquer, v.tr. To veneer. Plaqué de sang, caked with blood.

se plaquer. Se p. contre le sol, to lie flat on the ground.

plastique. 1. a. Plastic. **2.** s.f. Plastic art. **3.** s.m. (Usu. in pl.) Plastics.

plastron, s.m. **1.** Breast-plate. **2.** P. de chemise, (man's) shirt-front.

plat. 1. a. (a) Flat, level. Calme p., dead calm. (b) Dull, insipid, tame. (c) A plat, flat. Tomber à plat (ventre), to fall flat on one's face. **2.** s.m. (a) Flat (part); blade (of oar). (b) Cu: Dish (container or contents). F: Mettre les petits plats dans les grands, to make a great spread. Mettre les pieds dans le plat, to put one's foot in it. (c) Cu: Course (at dinner).

platane, s.m. Bot: Plane-tree.

plat-bord, s.m. Gunwale. pl. Des plats-bords.

plateau, s.m. **1.** (a) Tray. (b) Pan, scale (of balance). **2.** Geog: Plateau, table-land. **3.** Platform. **4.** Disc, plate.

plate-bande, s.f. (a) Grass border. (b) Flower-bed. pl. Des plates-bandes.

plate-forme, s.f. Platform (of motor bus); flat roof (of house); foot-plate (of locomotive). pl. Des plates-formes.

platine[1], s.f. Lock (of fire-arm).

platine[2], s.m. Platinum.

platitude, s.f. **1.** (a) Flatness, dullness. (b) Contemptibleness (of conduct). **2.** Commonplace remark; platitude.

Platon. Pr.n.m. Plato.

platonique, a. Platonic (love).

plâtrage, s.m. Plastering; plaster-work.

plâtras, s.m. Debris; rubbish.

plâtre, s.m. Plaster. P de moulage, plaster of Paris.

plâtrer, v.tr. To plaster.

plausibilité, s.f. Plausibility.

plausible, a. Plausible.

plausiblement, adv. Plausibly.

plèbe, s.f. The common people.

plébéien, -ienne, a. & s. Plebeian.

plébiscite, s.m. Plebiscite; referendum.

plein. 1. a. Full. (a) Filled, replete. Th: Salle pleine à étouffer, house crammed to suffocation. J'ai le cœur p., my heart is full. (b) Complete, entire, whole. Pleine lune, full moon. De plein gré, of one's own free will. (c) Solid. Table en acajou p., solid mahogany table. (d) En plein visage, full in the face. En p. hiver, in the depth of winter. En p. air, in the open. En p. jour, in broad daylight. (e) Respirer à pleins poumons, to breathe deep. (f) adv. Il avait des larmes plein les yeux, his eyes were full of tears. **2.** s.m. (a) Fully occupied space. Aut: Faire le p. d'essence, to fill up with petrol. (b) Full (extent). La lune est dans son p., the moon is at the full. F: La saison bat son p., the season is in full swing. (c) En plein dans le centre, right in the middle.

pleinement, adv. Fully, entirely, quite.

plénipotentiaire, a. & s.m. (a) Plenipotentiary. (b) s.m. Authorized agent.

plénitude, s.f. Plenitude, fullness (of power).

pléthore, s.f. F: Superabundance, plethora.

pleurer. 1. v.tr. To weep, mourn, for (s.o.). **2.** v.i. (a) To weep, to shed tears, to cry. (b) (Of the eyes) To water, to run.

pleurésie, s.f. Med: Pleurisy.

pleureur, -euse. 1. s. Mute; hired mourner. **2.** a. Weeping.

pleurnicher, v.i. To whimper, snivel.

pleuvoir, v. (p.p. plu; pr.ind. il pleut, ils pleuvent; fu. il pleuvra) To rain. **1.** v.impers. Il pleut à petites gouttes, it is drizzling. F: Il pleuvait des coups, blows fell thick and fast. **2.** Les invitations lui pleuvent de tous les côtés, invitations are pouring in on him.

pli, s.m. **1.** (a) Fold, pleat; tuck. Hairdr: Mise en plis, setting (the hair). (b) Wrinkle, pucker. Pli de terrain, fold of the ground. (c) Crease. **2.** Bend (of the arm). **3.** Cover, envelope (of letter). Nous vous l'envoyons sous ce pli, we send it you herewith.

pliable, a. Pliable, flexible.

pliant. 1. a. (a) Pliant, flexible. (b) Folding (chair); collapsible **2.** s.m. Folding chair; camp-stool.

plie, s.f. Ich: Plaice.

plier. 1. v.tr. (a) To fold, fold up; to strike (tent). (b) To bend. **2.** v.i. (a) To bend. (b) To submit, yield.

se plier aux circonstances, to bow to circumstances.

Pline. Pr.n.m. Lt.Lit: Pliny.

plinthe, s.f. **1.** Plinth (of column). **2.** Skirting-board (of room); plinth.

plissement, s.m. **1.** Pleating; corrugation. **2.** Crumpling; crinkling.

plisser. 1. v.tr. (a) To pleat (skirt). (b) To crease, crumple. P. les yeux, to screw up one's eyes. **2.** v.i. & pr. To crease, crumple.

ploiement, s.m. Folding, bending.

plomb, s.m. **1.** Lead. F: Sommeil de plomb, heavy sleep. **2.** Ven: Shot. **3.** Fil à plomb, plumb-line. A plomb, upright, vertical(ly). **4.** El.E: Plomb de sûreté, fuse, cut-out. Faire sauter les plombs, to blow the fuses.

plombagine, s.f. Graphite, plumbago.

plomber, v.tr. (a) To cover with lead. (b) To weight with lead.

se plomber, (of sky) to take on a leaden hue.

plombé, a. **1.** Leaded; lead-covered (roof). **2.** Leaden (sky); livid (complexion).

plomberie, s.f. Plumbing.

plombier, s.m. Plumber.

plongeoir, s.m. Diving-board.

plongeon, s.m. **1.** Orn: Diver, loon. **2.** Plunge, dive. Faire le plongeon, (i) to dive; (ii) F: to take the plunge.

plonger, v. (n. plongeons) **1.** v.i. To plunge. (a) To dive; to take a header. (b) To become

immersed; (of submarine) to submerge.
2. *v.tr.* To plunge, immerse. *P. la main dans sa poche*, to thrust one's hand into one's pocket.
  se plonger, to immerse oneself.
  plongée, *s.f.* **1.** (*a*) Plunge, dive. (*b*) Submergence (of submarine). **2.** Dip, slope (of ground).
plongeur, -euse. 1. *a.* Diving (bird). **2.** *s.m.* (*a*) Diver. (*b*) Washer-up (in restaurant). (*c*) *Orn:* Diving-bird. (*d*) Plunger (of pump).
ploutocrate, *s.m.* Plutocrat.
ploutocratie, *s.f.* Plutocracy.
ployable, *a.* Pliable, flexible.
ployer, *v.* (je ploie) **1.** *v.tr.* To bend. **2.** *v.i.* To bow (under burden).
plu. See PLAIRE and PLEUVOIR.
pluie, *s.f.* Rain. (*a*) Le temps est à la pluie, it looks like rain. "Craint la pluie," 'to be kept dry.' Parler de la pluie et du beau temps, to talk about the weather, of nothing in particular. *Prov:* Après la pluie le beau temps, every cloud has a silver lining. *F:* Faire la pluie et le beau temps, to rule the roost. (*b*) Douche en pluie, shower-bath.
plumage, *s.m.* Plumage, feathers.
plume, *s.f.* **1.** Feather. Oiseau sans plumes, callow, unfledged, bird. **2.** Pen. *P. d'oie*, quill (pen). *P. d'acier*, steel nib. Dessin à la plume, pen and ink drawing.
plumeau, *s.m.* Feather-duster; whisk.
plumer, *v.tr.* To pluck (poultry); *F:* to fleece (s.o.).
plumet, *s.m.* Plume (of helmet).
plupart (la), *s.f.* The most; the greater part. *La p. d'entre eux*, most of them. La plupart du temps, most of the time; in most cases; generally.
plural, -aux, *a.* Plural.
pluriel, -elle, *a. & s.m. Gram:* Plural.
plus¹. 1. *adv.* (*a*) More. *Il est plus grand que moi*, he is taller than I. *Deux fois plus grand*, twice as large. *Plus de dix hommes*, more than ten men. Plus loin, farther on. Plus tôt, sooner. Pour ne pas dire plus, to say the least. Plus on est de fous plus on rit, the more the merrier. Il y en a tant et plus, there is any amount of it. (*b*) (Le) plus, most. Une ascension des plus hasardeuses, a most perilous ascent. C'est tout ce qu'il y a de plus simple, nothing could be simpler. (*c*) (With negative expressed or understood), Ne . . . plus, no more, no longer. Plus de doute, there is no more doubt about it. Plus rien, nothing more. Plus que dix minutes! only ten minutes left! (*d*) Non plus, (not) either. Ni moi non plus, neither do I. (*e*) (Often [plys]) Plus, also, besides, in addition. (*f*) De plus, more. *Rien de plus, merci*, nothing else, thank you. De plus en plus, more and more. En plus, in addition; (i) into the bargain, (ii) extra. *Le vin est en plus*, wine is extra. **2.** *s.m.* (*a*) More.

(*b*) Most. Tout au plus, at (the very) most. (*c*) *Alg:* Plus (sign).
plus². See PLAIRE.
plusieurs, *a. & pron.pl.* Several.
plus-que-parfait, *s.m. Gram:* Pluperfect.
pluss-e, -es, etc. See PLAIRE.
plus-value, *s.f.* **1.** Increase in value; appreciation. **2.** Extra payment. *pl. Des plus-values.*
plut, plût. See PLAIRE and PLEUVOIR.
plutôt, *adv.* (*a*) Rather, sooner. (*b*) Rather; on the whole. *Il faisait p. froid*, the weather was cold if anything.
pluvial, -aux, *a.* Pluvial; rainy (season).
pluvier, *s.m. Orn:* Plover.
pluvieux, *a.* Rainy; wet (weather).
pluviomètre, *s.m.* Rain-gauge.
pneu, *s.m. F:* **1.** (Pneumatic) tyre. **2.** = PNEUMATIQUE 2 (*b*). *pl. Des pneus.*
pneumatique. 1. *a.* Pneumatic. **2.** *s.m.* (*a*) Pneumatic tyre. (*b*) Express letter (transmitted by pneumatic tube).
pneumonie, *s.f.* Pneumonia.
poche, *s.f.* **1.** Pocket. J'y suis de ma poche, I am out of pocket by it. *F:* Mettez ça dans votre poche (et votre mouchoir dessus), put that in your pipe and smoke it. Connaître qch. comme le 'ond de sa poche, to know sth. through and through. Il n'a pas sa langue dans sa poche, he has plenty to say for himself. **2.** (*a*) Bag, pouch, sack. *Av:* Poche d'air, air-pocket. (*b*) *Biol:* Sac. **3.** *pl.* Pouches (under the eyes).
pocher. 1. *v.tr. Cu:* To poach (eggs). *F:* Œil poché, black eye. **2.** *v.i.* (Of clothes) To get baggy.
pochette, *s.f.* (*a*) Small pocket; pouch; hand-bag. (*b*) Pocket-case (of instruments). (*c*) P. d'allumettes, book of matches.
pochoir, *s.m.* Stencil(-plate).
podagre, *s.f.* Gout (in the feet).
poêle¹ [pwɑːl, pwal], *s.f.* Frying-pan.
poêle², *s.m.* **1.** *Ecc:* Canopy. **2.** (Funeral-) pall.
poêle³, *s.m.* Stove.
poème, *s.m.* Poem.
poésie, *s.f.* **1.** Poetry. **2.** Poem.
poète. 1. *s.m.* Poet. **2.** *a. Femme p.*, *s.f.* poétesse, woman poet; poetess.
poétique, *a.* (*a*) Poetic (licence). (*b*) Poetical (works).
poétiquement, *adv.* Poetically.
poids [pwɑ], *s.m.* Weight. **1.** (*a*) Heaviness. Vendre au poids, to sell by weight. *Le p. n'y est pas*, this is short weight. (*b*) Importance. Gens de poids, people of weight, of consequence. **2.** *F:* Avoir deux poids et deux mesures, to have one law for the rich and another for the poor. **3.** Load, burden.
poignant, *a.* Poignant.
poignard, *s.m.* (*a*) Dagger. (*b*) Dirk.
poignarder, *v.tr.* To stab.

poigne, *s.f.* Grip, grasp. **Montrer de la poigne,** to show energy.

poignée, *s.f.* **I.** (*a*) Handful. (*b*) **Poignée de main,** handshake. **2.** Handle (of door).

poignet, *s.m.* **I.** Wrist. · **Faire qch. à la force du poignet,** to do sth. by sheer hard work. **2.** (*a*) Wristband. (*b*) Cuff (of garment).

poil [pwal], *s.m.* **I.** (*a*) Hair, fur. **Monter à poil,** to ride bareback. (*b*) Coat (of animals). (*c*) Nap (of cloth); pile (of velvet). (*d*) *Poils d'une brosse,* bristles of a brush. **2.** (Of pers.) Hair (on the body).

poilu. I. *a.* Hairy, shaggy. **2.** *s.m. F:* Man of mettle; French soldier.

poinçon, *s.m.* **I.** Bradawl. **2.** (*a*) (Perforating) punch. (*b*) *P. de contrôle,* hall-mark.

poinçonner, *v.tr.* **I.** To prick, bore. **2.** (*a*) To punch, clip (ticket). (*b*) To stamp, to hall-mark.

poindre, *v.i.* (Conj. like JOINDRE) (Of daylight) To dawn, break.

poing, *s.m.* Fist. **Sabre au poing,** sword in hand. **Dormir à poings fermés,** to sleep soundly.

point[1], *s.m.* **I.** Hole (in strap). **2.** (*a*) Stitch. (*b*) **Point de côté,** stitch in one's side. **3.** Point. (*a*) **Le point du jour,** daybreak. **Arriver à point nommé,** to arrive in the nick of time. *Prov:* **Tout vient à point à qui sait attendre,** all things come to him who waits. (*b*) *Mec:* **Point d'appui,** fulcrum (of lever); purchase. *Opt:* **Au point,** in focus. **Mettre un article au p.,** to put an article into shape. **4.** (*a*) Point, dot; punctuation mark. **Point** (final), full stop. **Deux points,** colon. **Point et virgule,** semicolon. *P. d'exclamation,* note of exclamation. (*b*) *Games:* Point, score. *Marquer les points,* to keep the score. (*c*) *Sch:* Mark. (*d*) Speck, spot, dot. **5.** (*a*) Point, stage, degree. **A ce point,** so much so. **Au dernier point,** in the last degree. (*b*) **En bon point,** in good condition. (*c*) **A point,** in the right condition. *Viande cuite à p.,* meat done to a turn. **6.** Point, particular. **Mettre son point d'honneur à ne pas céder,** to make it a point of honour not to yield.

point[2], *adv.* Not. **Peu ou point,** little or not at all.

pointe, *s.f.* **I.** (*a*) Point (of pin); head (of arrow); toe (of shoe). **Coup de pointe,** thrust. **En pointe,** tapering; pointed. **Sur la pointe des pieds,** on tiptoe. *Rail:* **Heures de pointe,** rush hours. (*b*) **Pointe du jour,** daybreak. *P. d'ironie,* touch of irony. *Sp:* **Pointe de vitesse,** spurt, sprint. **2.** *Geog:* **Pointe de terre,** foreland, head(land); spit, tongue (of land). **3.** **Pointe de Paris,** wire nail, French nail.

pointer[1], *v.tr.* **I.** To check, tick off (names on list). **2.** To point, level (telescope); to aim (gun).

pointer[2]. **I.** *v.tr.* To thrust, prick, stab. **2.** *v.i.* To appear; (of plant) to sprout; to jut upwards.

pointeur, *s.m.* **I.** Checker; tallyman. **2.** Gun-layer.

pointiller [-tije], *v.tr.* **I.** To dot. **2.** *Engr:* To stipple.

pointillé, *a.* Dotted (line); stippled (engraving).

pointilleux [-tijø], *a.* **I.** Captious. **2.** (*a*) Particular; fastidious. (*b*) Finical.

pointu, *a.* Sharp-pointed.

pointure, *s.f.* Size (in boots).

poire, *s.f.* **I.** Pear. **Couper la poire en deux,** to split the difference. **2.** (Pear-shaped) bulb (of horn). *P. à poudre,* powder-flask.

poireau, *s.m.* Leek.

poirier, *s.m.* Pear-tree.

pois, *s.m.* **I.** Pea. *P. de senteur,* sweet pea. **2.** *Cu:* **Petits pois,** green peas. **3.** *Étoffe à p.,* spotted material.

poison, *s.m.* Poison.

poissard. I. *a.* Vulgar, low. **2.** *s.f.* **Poissarde,** fishwife. **Langage de poissarde,** billingsgate.

poisson, *s.m.* Fish. *P. rouge,* gold-fish.

poitevin, *a. & s. Geog:* (Native) of (i) Poitou, (ii) Poitiers.

poitrail [-ra:j], *s.m.* Breast (of horse).

poitrinaire, *a. & s.* Consumptive.

poitrine, *s.f.* (*a*) Breast, chest; bosom. (*b*) *Cu:* Brisket (of beef).

poivre, *s.m.* Pepper. **Grain de p.,** pepper-corn.

poivrer, *v.tr.* To pepper.

poivré, *a.* Peppery (food); pungent (smell); stiff (price).

poivrier, *s.m.* Pepper-plant.

poivrière, *s.f.* Pepper-castor.

poix, *s.f.* Pitch; cobbler's wax.

polaire, *a.* Polar. **L'étoile polaire,** *s.* **la polaire,** the pole-star.

pôle, *s.m.* Pole.

police[1], *s.f.* **I.** Policing. **Faire la police,** to keep order. **Tribunal de simple police,** police-court. **2.** Police. **Remettre qn entre les mains de la police,** to give s.o. in charge.

police[2], *s.f.* (Insurance) policy.

policer, *v.tr.* (n. **poliçons**) To bring under orderly government.

polichinelle, *s.m.* Punch, punchinello. *F:* **Secret de polichinelle,** open secret.

policier, *a. Ordonnance policière,* police regulation. **Roman policier,** detective novel.

poliment, *adv.* Politely, civilly.

polir, *v.tr.* **I.** To polish; to burnish. **2.** To polish, refine.

poli. I. *a.* (*a*) Polished; bright; sleek. (*b*) Polished, elegant. (*c*) Polite, urbane. **2.** *s.m.* Polish, gloss.

polisseur, -euse, *s.* Polisher.

polisson, -onne, *s.* Naughty child; scamp.

politesse, *s.f.* Politeness; civility, urbanity. **Brûler la politesse à qn,** to fail to keep an appointment with s.o. *Aut: P. de la route,* road manners.

politicien, -ienne, *s.* Politician.
politique. 1. *a.* (*a*) Political. (*b*) Politic, prudent; diplomatic. **2.** *s.f.* (*a*) Policy. (*b*) Politics.
politiquement, *adv.* (*a*) Politically. (*b*) Shrewdly, prudently.
polka, *s.f. Danc:* Polka.
pollen [-lɛn], *s.m. Bot:* Pollen.
polluer, *v.tr.* To pollute, defile.
pollution, *s.f.* Pollution, defilement.
Pologne. *Pr.n.f.* Poland.
polonais. 1. (*a*) *a.* Polish. (*b*) *s.* Pole. **2.** *s.m. Ling:* Polish. **3.** *s.f. Danc:* Polonaise, polonaise.
poltron, -onne. 1. *a.* Easily frightened; timid. **2.** *s.* Poltroon, milksop.
polycopier, *v.tr.* To manifold.
polygame. 1. *a.* Polygamous. **2.** *s.* Polygamist.
polyglotte, *a. & s.* Polyglot.
Polynésie. *Pr.n.f. Geog:* Polynesia.
polynésien, -ienne, *a. & s.* Polynesian.
polysyllabe, *s.m.* Polysyllable.
polysyllabique, *a.* Polysyllabic.
polytechnique, *a.* Polytechnic.
pommade, *s.f.* Pomade, pomatum.
pomme, *s.f.* **1.** (*a*) Apple. *P. sauvage,* crab-apple. (*b*) **Pomme de terre,** potato. **Bifteck aux pommes,** steak and chips. (*c*) **Pomme épineuse,** thorn-apple. **Pomme de pin,** fir-cone, pine-cone. **2.** Knob (of walking-stick); head (of cabbage). **Pomme d'arrosoir,** rose of a watering-can.
pommeau, *s.m.* Pommel.
pommelé, *a.* Dappled, mottled. *Ciel p.,* mackerel sky.
pommeraie, *s.f.* Apple-orchard.
pommette, *s.f.* Cheek-bone.
pommier, *s.m.* Apple-tree.
pompe[1], *s.f.* Pomp, ceremony, display. **Entrepreneur de pompes funèbres,** undertaker.
pompe[2], *s.f.* Pump. **Pompe à incendie,** fire-engine.
pomper, *v.tr.* To pump.
pompeusement, *adv.* Pompously.
pompeux, *a.* Pompous.
pompier, *s.m.* Fireman.
pompon, *s.m.* **1.** Pompon; tuft. **2.** Powder-puff.
ponce, *s.f.* **1.** (**Pierre**) **ponce,** pumice-stone. **2.** *Draw:* Pounce.
ponceau[1], *s.m.* Culvert.
ponceau[2], *s.m. & a.inv.* Poppy-red.
Ponce Pilate. *Pr.n.m.* Pontius Pilate.
ponctualité, *s.f.* Punctuality.
ponctuation, *s.f.* Punctuation.
ponctuel, -elle, *a.* Punctual.
ponctuellement, *adv.* Punctually.
ponctuer, *v.tr.* To punctuate.
pondeur, -euse, *a. & s.* **Poule pondeuse,** laying hen. **Bonne pondeuse,** good layer.

pondre, *v.tr.* To lay (eggs); *abs.* to lay.
poney [pɔnɛ], *s.m.* Pony.
pont, *s.m.* **1.** (*a*) Bridge. *P. tournant,* swing-bridge. *P. à bascule,* weigh-bridge. *Adm:* **Les ponts et chaussées,** the Highways Department. (*b*) *Ind:* Platform, stage, bridge. **2.** Deck (of ship).
ponte[1], *s.f.* Laying (of eggs).
ponte[2], *s.m. Gaming:* Punter.
ponté, *a.* Decked (boat).
pontife, *s.m.* Pontiff.
pontifical, -aux, *a. & s.m.* Pontifical.
pont-levis, *s.m.* Drawbridge. *pl. Des ponts-levis.*
ponton, *s.m.* **1.** *Mil:* Section of pontoon-bridge. **2.** *Nau:* Hulk.
pope, *s.m.* Pope (of the Greek church).
popote, *s.f. F: Faire p. ensemble,* to mess together.
populace, *s.f.* Populace, rabble, riff-raff.
populaire, *a.* Popular. (*a*) *Places populaires,* cheap seats. (*b*) *Expression p.,* vulgar, popular, expression. *Chanson p.,* folk-song. (*c*) *Se rendre p.,* to make oneself popular.
populairement, *adv.* Popularly.
populariser, *v.tr.* To popularize, to make popular.
popularité, *s.f.* Popularity.
population, *s.f.* Population.
populeux, *a.* Populous.
porc, *s.m.* **1.** Pig. **2.** *Cu:* Pork.
porcelaine, *s.f.* Porcelain, china(ware).
porcelet, *s.m.* Young pig; piglet.
porc-épic, *s.m.* Porcupine. *pl. Des porcs-épics.*
porche, *s.m.* Porch.
porcher, *s.* Swine-herd.
porcherie, *s.f.* Piggery; pigsty.
porcine, *a.f.* Porcine.
pore, *s.m.* Pore.
poreux, *a.* Porous.
porosité, *s.f.* Porosity, porousness.
porphyre, *s.m.* Porphyry.
port[1], *s.m.* **1.** Harbour, haven, port. **Arriver à bon port,** to arrive safely. **Capitaine de port,** harbour-master. **2.** Port. *P. de guerre,* naval base.
port[2], *s.m.* **1.** (*a*) (Act of) carrying. (*b*) Wearing. **2.** Cost of transport; postage. **En port dû,** carriage forward. **3.** Bearing, gait, carriage (of person).
portable, *a.* Portable.
portage, *s.m.* (*a*) Porterage, conveyance, transport. (*b*) Portage.
portail [-ta:j], *s.m.* Portal. *pl. Des portails.*
portant. 1. *a.* **Être bien portant,** to be in good health. **2.** *s.m.* Supporter, stay.
portatif, *a.* Portable; easily carried.
porte, *s.f.* **1.** Gate(way), doorway, entrance. *P. cochère,* carriage entrance. **2.** Door. *F:* **Agir à portes ouvertes,** to act publicly. *Trouver porte close,* to find nobody at home. **Demander la porte,** to call to the concierge to open the door. **Écouter aux portes,** to

eavesdrop. **3.** Eye (of hook and eye). **4.** *pl.* Gorge, defile, pass.
porte-adresse, *s.m.inv.* Luggage-label holder.
porte-affiches, *s.m.inv.* Notice-board.
porte-aiguilles, *s.m.inv.* Needle-case.
porte-allumettes, *s.m.inv.* Match-holder.
porte-amarre, *s.m.inv.* Life-saving (rocket) apparatus.
porte-avions, *s.m.inv.* Aircraft carrier.
porte-bagages, *s.m.inv.* (a) Luggage-rack. (b) *Aut:* Luggage-carrier.
porte-bijoux, *s.m.inv.* Jewel-stand.
porte-billets, *s.m.inv.* (Bank-)note case.
porte-cigare, *s.m.* Cigar-holder. *pl. Des porte-cigares.*
porte-cigares, *s.m.inv.* Cigar-case.
porte-cigarette, *s.m.* Cigarette-holder. *pl. Des porte-cigarettes.*
porte-cigarettes, *s.m.inv.* Cigarette-case.
porte-clefs, *s.m.inv.* Turnkey.
porte-crayon, *s.m.inv.* Pencil-case.
portefaix, *s.m.* Porter; (i) street-porter, (ii) dock hand.
porte-fenêtre, *s.f.* French window. *pl. Des portes-fenêtres.*
portefeuille [-fœ:j], *s.m.* **I.** Portfolio. **2.** Pocket-book; letter-case. *F:* **Lit en portefeuille,** apple-pie bed
portemanteau, *s.m.* Coat(-and-hat)-rack, -stand.
porte-mine, *s.m.inv.* Pencil-case.
porte-monnaie, *s.m.inv.* Purse.
porte-parapluies, *s.m.inv.* Umbrella-stand.
porte-parole, *s.m.inv.* Spokesman.
porte-plume, *s.m.inv.* Penholder; pen. *P.-p. (à) réservoir,* fountain-pen.
porter. I. *v.tr.* To carry. (a) To bear, support. (b) To wear. *P. un nom illustre,* to bear an illustrious name. *F:* **Le porter haut,** to think no small beer of oneself. *Mil:* **Portez armes!** shoulder arms! (c) To carry, convey, take. *Il porta le verre à ses lèvres,* he lifted the glass to his lips. (d) **Porter un coup à qn,** to strike s.o. *P. ses regards sur qn,* to cast one's eye on s.o. *P. une accusation contre qn,* to bring a charge against s.o. (e) To inscribe, enter. *Portez cela à mon compte,* put that down to me. **Se faire porter malade,** to report sick. (f) To induce, incline, prompt. *Tout me porte à croire,* everything leads me to believe. (g) To produce, bring forth. *Argent qui porte intérêt,* money that bears interest. *Prov:* **La nuit porte conseil,** sleep on it. (h) *P. la production au maximum,* to raise production to a maximum. (i) *Par la tendresse que je vous porte,* by the love I bear you. (j) **Porter témoignage,** to bear witness. **2.** *v.i.* (a) To rest, bear. (b) To hit, reach. *Aucun des coups de feu ne porta,* none of the shots took effect. *Sa voix porte bien,* his voice carries well.
se porter. I. To betake oneself, proceed (to a place). **2. Se porter à merveille,** to

enjoy the best of health. **3.** *Se p. caution,* to offer oneself as surety.
porté, *a.* Inclined, disposed. *Être p. à la colère,* to be prone to anger.
portée, *s.f.* **I.** Span (of bridge). **2.** (a) Litter, brood. (b) *Mus:* Stave. **3.** (a) Reach (of arm); range (of gun); scope. *À p. de la voix,* within call. **Hors de portée,** out of reach; out of range. (b) Bearing, full significance (of a statement). *Affirmation d'une grande p.,* weighty statement.
porte-serviette(s), *s.m.inv.* Towel-rail.
porteur, -euse, *s.* Porter, carrier, bearer. *P. d'actions,* shareholder.
porte-vêtement(s), *s.m.inv.* Coat-, skirt-, dress-hanger.
porte-voix, *s.m.inv.* **I.** Speaking-tube. **2.** Speaking-trumpet; megaphone.
portier, *s.* (a) Porter, door-keeper, janitor. (b) Gate-keeper.
portière, *s.f.* Door (of carriage).
portion, *s.f.* Portion, share, part.
portionner, *v.tr.* To portion out.
portique, *s.m.* Portico, porch.
Porto. I. *Pr.n. Geog:* Oporto. **2.** *s.m.* (Vin de) Porto. Port (wine).
portrait, *s.m.* Portrait, likeness.
portraitiste, *s.m.* Portrait-painter.
portugais. I. *a. & s.* Portuguese. **2.** *s.m. Ling:* Portuguese.
pose, *s.f.* **I.** *P. de câbles sous-marins,* cable-laying. **2.** (a) Pose, attitude, posture. *Golf: P. d'une balle* lie of a ball. (b) Posing, affectation. **3.** *Phot:* (Time of) exposure.
poser. I. *v.i.* (a) To rest, lie (on sth.). (b) To pose (as artist's model); to sit (for one's portrait). (c) *F:* To pose; *F:* to put on side. **2.** *v.tr.* (a) To place, put, set. *P. les armes,* to lay down one's arms. *P. un chiffre,* to put down a number. **Poser une question à qn,** to put a question to s.o. (b) To put up, fix (up). (c) To suppose, grant.
se poser, (of bird) to settle, alight.
posé, *a.* Staid, grave; steady.
poseur, -euse. I. *s. Rail: P. de voie,* plate-layer. *Navy: P. de mines,* mine-layer. **2.** *a. & s.* (Person) who poses.
positif, *a.* (a) Positive, actual, real. *C'est positif,* that's so. (b) Positive (pole). (c) Practical, matter-of-fact.
position, *s.f.* Position. **I.** (a) Situation, site. (b) Posture, attitude. *Golf:* Stance. (c) Tactical position. (d) Condition, circumstances. **2.** Post, situation.
positivement, *adv* Positively.
posséder, *v.tr* (je possède; je posséderai) To be in possession of (sth.). (a) To possess, own. *P. un titre,* to hold a title. (b) To be master of (subject). (c) To curb, control (one's tongue). (d) *Quel démon le possède?* what devil possesses him?
se posséder, to possess oneself; to contain oneself.

possesseur]   233   [poupon

possédé. 1. *a.* Possessed; infatuated, dominated. 2. *s.* Person possessed; madman.
possesseur, *s.m.* Possessor, owner.
possessif, *a. & s.m. Gram:* Possessive.
possession, *s.f.* 1. Possession. *Prov:* Possession vaut titre, possession is nine points of the law. 2. Property; in *pl.* possessions.
possibilité, *s.f.* Possibility; feasibility.
possible. 1. *a.* Possible. C'est bien possible, it is quite likely. Pas possible! you don't say so! 2. *s.m.* Dans la mesure du possible, as far as possible.
postal, -aux, *a.* Postal.
poste¹, *s.f.* (a) Post. Les Postes et Télégraphes, the Postal and Telegraph Service. Mettre une lettre à la poste, to post a letter. Directeur des Postes, Postmaster General. (b) Post office. Bureau de(s) poste(s), post office.
poste², *s.m.* 1. Post, station. (a) *P. d'amarrage,* mooring berth; moorings. *Navy: Postes de combat,* action stations. (b) *Navy: P. d'équipage,* forecastle. (c) *P. d'incendie,* fire-station. Poste de police, (i) police station; (ii) *Mil:* guard-room. Conduire qn au poste, to run s.o. in. (d) *W.Tel: P. émetteur,* broadcasting station. "Ici poste de Toulouse," 'Toulouse calling.' (e) *W.Tel: P. de T.S.F.,* wireless set. 2. Post, place, appointment.
poster, *v.tr.* To post (sentry); to station (men).
postérieur. 1. *a.* Posterior. (a) Subsequent; later. (b) Hinder, hind. 2. *s.m. F:* Posterior(s), buttocks.
postérieurement, *adv.* Subsequently.
postérité, *s.f.* Posterity.
posthume, *a.* Posthumous.
posthumement, *adv.* Posthumously.
postiche, *a.* False (hair). Canon p., dummy gun.
postillon [-tijɔ̃], *s.m.* Postilion.
post-scriptum [-tɔm], *s.m.inv.* Postscript.
postulant, *s.* Candidate, applicant.
postulat, *s.m.* Postulate, assumption.
posture, *s.f.* 1. Posture, attitude. 2. Position.
pot, *s.m.* Pot, jug, can, jar. Pot à fleurs, flower-pot. *F:* Payer les pots cassés, to stand the racket. Dîner à la fortune du pot, to take pot-luck.
potable, *a.* Drinkable; fit to drink. Eau potable, drinking water.
potage, *s.m.* Soup.
potager, *a.* Herbes potagères, pot-herbs. Plante potagère, vegetable. Jardin potager, kitchen-garden.
potasse, *s.f. Ch:* Potash.
potassium [-jɔm], *s.m. Ch:* Potassium.
pot-au-feu, *s.m.inv.* 1. Soup-pot, stock-pot. 2. Boiled beef with vegetables. 3. *a.inv.* Plain, homely.
pot-de-vin, *s.m. F:* 1. Douceur, gratuity. 2. Bribe. *pl.* Des pots-de-vin.
poteau, *s.m.* Post, pole, stake.

potelé, *a.* Plump and dimpled (arm).
potence, *s.f.* 1. Gallows, gibbet. 2. Support, arm, cross-piece, bracket.
potentat, *s.m.* Potentate.
potentiel, -elle. 1. *a.* Potential. 2. *s.m.* Potentialities (of a country, etc.).
potentiellement, *adv.* Potentially.
poterie, *s.f.* 1. Pottery works. 2. Pottery.
poterne, *s.f.* Postern (gate).
potiche, *s.f.* (Large) vase.
potier, *s.* Potter.
potin, *s.m. F:* (a) Piece of gossip. (b) *pl.* Gossip, tittle-tattle.
potion, *s.f. Med:* Potion, draught.
potiron, *s.m.* Pumpkin.
pou, *pl.* **poux,** *s.m.* Louse.
pouah, *int.* Faugh! ugh!
poubelle, *s.f.* Dustbin.
pouce, *s.m.* Thumb. *F:* Donner un coup de pouce à qch., to shove sth. on. Manger sur le pouce, to take a snack. Mettre les pouces, to knuckle under. Et le pouce, and a bit over.
Poucet. *Pr.n.m.* Le Petit Poucet, Hop-o'-my-thumb, Tom Thumb.
poucettes, *s.f.pl. A:* Thumb-screw. Mettre les poucettes à qn, to put on the screw.
pouding, *s.m.* Pudding.
poudre, *s.f.* 1. *Jeter de la p. aux yeux de qn,* to throw dust in s.o.'s eyes. 2. Powder. P. d'or, gold-dust. P. à lever, baking-powder. 3. P. à canon, gunpowder. La nouvelle se répandit comme une traînée de p., the news spread like wildfire.
poudrer, *v.tr.* To powder; to sprinkle with powder; to dust on.
poudreux, *a.* Dusty.
poudrier, *s.m.* Powder-box; compact.
poudrière, *s.f.* Powder-magazine.
pouf [puf]. 1. *int.* (a) Plop! (b) Phew! 2. *s.m.* Puff; inflated advertisement.
pouffer, *v.i. & pr.* (Se) p. (de rire), to burst out laughing, to guffaw.
pouilleux [pujø], *a.* Lousy, verminous.
poulailler [-laje], *s.m.* (a) Hen-house, hen-roost. (b) *Th: F:* Gallery; 'the gods.'
poulain, *s.m.* Colt, foal.
poularde, *s.f. Cu:* (Table-)fowl.
poule, *s.f.* 1. (a) Hen; *Cu:* fowl. Poule au pot, boiled fowl. Ma petite poule! my dear! Lait de poule, (non-alcoholic) egg-flip. egg-nog. *F:* Quand les poules auront des dents, when pigs fly. (b) P. d'eau, moor-hen. 2. (a) (At games) Pool. (b) Sweepstake.
poulet, *s.m.* Chicken.
pouliche, *s.f.* Filly.
poulie, *s.f.* Pulley.
poulpe, *s.m. Moll:* Octopus.
pouls [pu], *s.m. Physiol:* Pulse.
poumon, *s.m.* Lung. Respirer à pleins poumons, to draw a deep breath.
poupe, *s.f. Nau:* Stern, poop.
poupée, *s.f.* 1. Doll. 2. *F:* Bandaged finger.
poupon, -onne, *s. F:* Baby.

pour. I. *prep.* For. **1.** (*a*) Instead of. *Allez-y pour moi*, go in my stead. (*b*) *Laisser qn pour mort*, to leave s.o. for dead. *F:* **C'est pour de bon**, I am in earnest. (*c*) *Je pars pour la France*, I am starting for France. *Bon pour les pauvres*, good to the poor. (*d*) (i) *Pour toujours*, for ever. *Il sera ici pour quatre heures*, he will be here by four o'clock. (ii) *J'en ai pour huit jours*, it will take me a week. *Être pour beaucoup*, to count for much. (*e*) *Je suis ici pour mes affaires*, I am here on business. (*f*) Because of, for the sake of. *Pour la forme*, for form's sake. (*g*) *Parler pour qn*, to speak in favour of s.o. *Moi, je suis pour*, I am in favour of it. (*h*) With regard to. *Pour* (*ce qui est de*) *moi*, for my part. (*i*) For lack of. (*j*) *Dix pour cent*, ten per cent. **2.** *Pour + inf.* (*a*) (In order) to. **Pour ainsi dire**, so to speak. (*b*) Although. *Pour être petit il n'en est pas moins brave*, though small he is none the less brave. *Nous ne perdrons rien pour attendre*, we shall lose nothing by waiting. (*c*) Because of. *Je le sais pour l'avoir vu*, I know it through having seen it. (*d*) Of a nature to. *Cela n'est pas pour me surprendre*, that does not come as a surprise to me. **3.** (*a*) **Pour que + sub.**, in order that. *Il est trop tard pour qu'elle sorte*, it is too late for her to go out. (*b*) **Pour** (+ *adj.* or *sb.*) **que** + *sub.*, however, although. *Cette situation, pour terrible qu'elle soit*, this situation, terrible though it may be. (*c*) **Pour peu que** + *sub.*, if only, if ever. *Pour peu que vous hésitiez*, if you hesitate at all.
II. **pour**, *s.m.* **Peser le pour et le contre**, to weigh the pros and cons.

pourboire, *s.m.* Tip, gratuity.

pourceau, *s.m.* Hog, pig, swine.

pour-cent, *s.m.* Percentage; rate per cent.

pourcentage, *s.m.* Percentage; rate (of interest).

pourchasser, *v.tr.* To pursue. *P. un débiteur*, to dun a debtor.

pourlécher, *v.tr.* (je pourlèche; je pourlécherai) Se pourlécher les babines, to lick one's chops.

pourparlers, *s.m.pl.* (*a*) *Mil:* Parley. (*b*) Diplomatic conversation; pourparlers.

pourpre. **1.** *s.f.* (*a*) Purple (dye) (of the ancients). (*b*) Royal or imperial dignity. **2.** *s.m.* Crimson; rich red. **3.** *a.* Crimson.

pourquoi, *adv. & conj.* Why? **Pourquoi faire?** what for? **Pourquoi cela?** why so? *Mais p. donc?* what on earth for?

pourrir. **1.** *v.i.* To rot, decay; to go bad. **2.** *v.tr.* To rot.
se pourrir, to go bad; (of egg) to addle.
pourri, *a.* Rotten; putrid (flesh). *P. d'orgueil*, eaten up with self-conceit.

pourriture, *s.f.* **1.** Rot, decay. **2.** Rottenness.

poursuite, *s.f.* **1.** Pursuit; chase. **2.** Usu. pl. *Jur:* Lawsuit, action.

poursuivant, *s.* Plaintiff, prosecutor.

poursuivre, *v.tr.* (Conj. like SUIVRE) **1.** To pursue; to chase. *Poursuivi par la guigne*,

dogged by ill-luck. **2.** *P. qn en justice*, to proceed against s.o. **3.** To pursue, continue. *P. un avantage*, to follow up an advantage. *Abs.* **Poursuivez**, go on; continue.

pourtant, *adv.* Nevertheless, however.

pourtour, *s.m.* Periphery; circumference.

pourvoir, *v.* (*pr.p.* pourvoyant; *p.p.* pourvu; *pr.ind.* je pourvois, *pr.sub.* je pourvoie) To provide. **1.** *v.ind.tr. P. aux frais*, to defray the cost. **2.** *v.tr.* (*a*) *P. qn de qch.*, to supply s.o. with sth. *Se p. d'argent*, to provide oneself with money. (*b*) To equip, fit.
pourvu que, *conj.phr.* Provided (that); so long as.

pourvoyeur, -euse, *s.* Purveyor; caterer.

pousse, *s.f.* **1.** Growth (of hair). **2.** Young shoot, sprout.

pousse-pousse, *s.m.inv.* Jinricksha, rickshaw.

pousser. **1.** *v.tr.* (*a*) To push, shove, thrust. *P. qn du coude*, to nudge s.o. *P. le verrou*, to shoot the bolt. *P. la porte*, to push the door to. (*b*) To drive, impel. (*c*) To push on. *P. un cheval*, to urge on a horse. (*d*) To put forth, shoot out (leaves). (*e*) To utter (cry). **2.** *v.i.* (*a*) To push. *P. à la roue*, to put one's shoulder to the wheel. (*b*) To push on, make one's way (to a place). (*c*) (Of plants) To grow. **Laisser pousser sa barbe**, to grow a beard.
se pousser, to push oneself forward.

poussée, *s.f.* **1.** (*a*) Thrust. (*b*) *P. du vent*, wind-pressure. **2.** Pushing, pressure. **3.** Push, shove. **4.** (*a*) Sprouting, growth. (*b*) *P. de la sève*, rising of the sap.

poussière, *s.f.* **1.** Dust. **2.** **Poussière d'eau**, (fine) spray; spindrift.

poussiéreux, *a.* Dusty.

poussif, *a.* *F:* Wheezy, short-winded.

poussin, *s.m.* (*a*) Chick. (*b*) *Cu:* Spring chicken.

poutre, *s.f.* **1.** (Wooden) beam; balk. **2.** Girder.

poutrelle, *s.f.* Small beam or girder.

pouvoir. I. *v.tr.* (*pr.p.* pouvant; *p.p.* pu; *pr.ind.* je puis or je peux (always puis-je), tu peux, il peut, ils peuvent; *pr.sub.* je puisse; *fu.* je pourrai) **1.** To be able; 'can.' *Comment a-t-il pu dire cela?* how could he say that? *Il aurait pu le faire s'il avait voulu*, he could have done it if he had wanted to. *On n'y peut rien*, it can't be helped. *Il travaille on ne peut mieux*, he could not work better. *N'en plus pouvoir*, to be tired out, exhausted. *Sauve qui peut*, every man for himself. *v.pr. Si cela se peut*, if possible. **2.** 'May.' (*a*) To be allowed. *Vous pouvez partir*, you may go. (*b*) *Puissiez-vous dire vrai!* may what you say be true! **3.** To be possible, probable. *Il pouvait avoir dix ans*, he may have been ten. *Advienne que pourra*, come what may. *v.pr.* **Il peut se faire que** + *sub.*, it may be that.
II. **pouvoir**, *s.m.* Power. **1.** Force, means. **2.** Influence, sway. **Être au pouvoir**

de qn, to be in s.o.'s power. **3.** (a) *P. paternel*, paternal authority. (b) Competency, warrant, power. **En dehors de mes pouvoirs**, not within my competence. (c) **Le parti au pouvoir**, the party in power. **4.** *Jur:* Power of attorney; procuration. **Avoir plein(s) pouvoir(s) pour agir**, to have full powers to act.

prairie, *s.f.* (a) Meadow. (b) Grass-land.

praline, *s.f.* Burnt almond; praline.

praticabilité, *s.f.* Practicability.

praticable, *a.* Practicable. (a) Feasible. (b) Passable, negotiable (road).

praticien, *s.m.* (a) Practitioner. (b) Practical man; expert.

pratique¹, *a.* Practical, useful.

pratique², *s.f.* **1.** Practice; application (of theory). **C'est de pratique courante**, it is the usual practice. **2.** (a) Practice, experience. **Perdre la pratique de qch.**, to get out of practice. (b) *Jur:* Practice (of the law). (c) *Avoir des pratiques avec l'ennemi*, to have dealings with the enemy. **3.** *Pratiques religieuses*, religious observances. **4.** Custom, business. *Donner sa p. à qn*, to give s.o. one's custom. **5.** Customer. **6.** *Nau:* Avoir libre pratique, to be out of quarantine.

pratiquement, *adv.* **1.** Practically. **2.** In actual fact.

pratiquer, *v.tr.* **1.** To practise; to employ, use. **2.** *P. une ouverture dans un mur*, to make an opening in a wall. **3.** To frequent; to associate with.

pré, *s.m.* Meadow.

préalable. 1. *a.* (a) Previous. (b) Preliminary. **2.** *s.m.* Au préalable, as a preliminary.

préambule, *s.m.* Preamble.

préau, *s.m.* Courtyard; playground (of school).

prébendier, *s.m.* *Ecc:* Prebendary.

précaire, *a.* Precarious.

précairement, *adv.* Precariously.

précaution, *s.f.* **1.** Precaution. **2.** Caution, wariness; care.

précédemment, *adv.* Previously, before.

précédence, *s.f.* Precedence; priority.

précédent. 1. *a.* Preceding, previous, former. **2.** *s.m.* Precedent.

précéder, *v.tr.* (Conj. like CÉDER) **1.** To precede; to go before. **2.** *P. qn*, to have precedence of s.o.

précepte, *s.m.* Precept.

précepteur, -trice, *s.* Family tutor; (private) teacher; *f.* governess.

prêcher, *v.tr.* **1.** To preach. **2.** To preach to; to exhort.

précieusement, *adv.* Preciously. **1.** Very carefully. **2.** Affectedly.

précieux, *a.* (a) Precious. (b) Valuable. (c) Affected.

précipice, *s.m.* Precipice.

précipitamment, *adv.* Precipitately, headlong.

précipitation, *s.f.* **1.** Precipitancy, violent hurry. **Sortir avec précipitation**, to hurry out. **2.** *Ch:* Precipitation.

précipiter, *v.tr.* **1.** To precipitate; to throw down. **2.** To hurry, hasten, precipitate.

se précipiter, to dash, to rush headlong.

précipité. 1. *a.* Precipitate; hasty; headlong. **2.** *s.m. Ch: etc:* Precipitate.

précis. 1. *a.* Precise, exact, definite. *A deux heures précises*, at two o'clock precisely. *En termes p.*, in distinct terms. **2.** *s.m.* Abstract, summary; epitome.

précisément, *adv.* Precisely, exactly.

préciser, *v.tr.* (a) To specify; to state precisely. **Sans rien préciser**, without going into details. (b) *Abs.* To be precise, explicit.

précision, *s.f.* **1.** Precision, exactness, accuracy. **2.** *pl.* Precise details; full particulars.

précoce, *a.* Precocious; early, forward.

précocité, *s.f.* Precocity; forwardness.

préconiser, *v.tr.* To (re)commend, praise; to advocate.

précurseur. 1. *s.m.* Precursor, forerunner. **2.** *a.m.* Precursory; premonitory.

prédécesseur, *s.m.* Predecessor.

prédestination, *s.f.* Predestination.

prédicat, *s.m.* *Gram:* Predicate.

prédicateur, *s.m.* Preacher.

prédicatif, *a.* *Gram:* Predicative.

prédiction, *s.f.* Prediction.

prédilection, *s.f.* Predilection, partiality.

prédire, *v.tr.* (Conj. like DIRE except *pr. ind. & imp.* (v.) prédisez) To predict.

prédisposer, *v.tr.* To predispose.

prédisposition, *s.f.* Predisposition.

prédominance, *s.f.* Predominance, prevalence.

prédominant, *a.* Predominant, prevalent.

prédominer, *v.i.* To predominate, prevail.

prééminence, *s.f.* Pre-eminence.

prééminent, *a.* Pre-eminent.

préemptif, *a.* Pre-emptive.

préemption, *s.f.* Pre-emption.

préfabriqué, *a.* Prefabricated.

préface, *s.f.* Preface, foreword.

préfectoral, -aux, *a.* Prefector(i)al.

préfecture, *s.f.* **1.** *Fr.Adm:* Prefecture. **2. La Préfecture de police**, the headquarters of the (Paris) police.

préférable, *a.* Preferable; better.

préférablement, *adv.* Preferably.

préférence, *s.f.* Preference. **De préférence à**, in preference to.

préférer, *v.tr.* (je préfère; je préférerai) To prefer; to like better.

préféré, *a. & s.* Favourite.

préfet, *s.m.* **1.** *Fr.Adm:* Prefect. **2. Le préfet de police**, the prefect of police.

préfète, *s.f.* *F:* The prefect's wife.
préfixe, *s.m.* *Gram:* Prefix.
préhensile, *a.* Prehensile.
préhistorique, *a.* Prehistoric.
préjudice, *s.m.* Prejudice, detriment.
préjudiciable, *a.* Prejudicial, detrimental.
préjudicier, *v.i.* To be detrimental.
préjuger, *v.tr.* (Conj. like JUGER) To prejudge.

    préjugé, *s.m.* **1.** *Jur:* Precedent. **2.** *Les préjugés sont contre lui,* appearances are against him. **3.** Prejudice, preconception.
prélart, *s.m.* *Nau:* Tarpaulin.
prélasser (se), *v.pr.* *F:* *Se p. dans un fauteuil,* to loll in an arm-chair.
prélat, *s.m.* Prelate.
prélature, *s.f.* Prelature, prelacy.
prélèvement, *s.m.* **1.** Deduction in advance; setting apart. **2.** (*a*) Sample. (*b*) Amount deducted.
prélever, *v.tr.* (Conj. like LEVER) To deduct, set apart, in advance.
préliminaire. **1.** *a.* Preliminary. **2.** *s.m.pl.* Preliminaries.
prélude, *s.m.* Prelude.
préluder, *v.i.* **1.** *Mus:* To prelude. **2.** *F:* Préluder à qch., to serve as prelude to sth.
prématuré, *a.* Premature, untimely
prématurément, *adv.* Prematurely.
préméditation, *s.f.* Premeditation. **Avec préméditation,** deliberately.
préméditer, *v.tr.* To premeditate **De dessein prémédité,** of set purpose.
prémices, *s.f.pl.* First fruits.
premier, *a.* First. **1.** (*a*) *Le p. janvier,* the first of January. **Dans les premiers temps,** at first. **En premier (lieu),** in the first place; firstly. **Du premier coup,** at the first attempt. *F:* **Le premier venu vous dira cela,** anyone will tell you that. *Nau:* **P. voyage,** maiden trip (of ship). *Aut:* **Première vitesse,** bottom gear. (*b*) **Sens p. d'un mot,** original meaning of a word. *Com:* **Matières premières,** raw materials. **2. Demeurer au premier,** to live on the first floor. **3. Le tout premier,** the foremost. **Premier ministre,** Prime Minister, Premier. **Monter en première,** to travel first (class). *Mth:* **Nombres premiers,** prime numbers. **Première danseuse,** leader of the ballet. **4.** *Sch:* (**Classe de**) **première,** sixth form.
première, *s.f.* **1.** *Dressm:* Forewoman. **2.** *Th:* First-night.
premièrement, *adv.* First, firstly, in the first place.
premier-né, *a. & s.* First-born
prémisse, *s.f.* *Log:* Premise.
prémonition, *s.f.* Premonition.
prémunir (se), *v.pr.* To provide oneself (*de*), with.
prendre, *v.* (*pr.p.* prenant; *p.p.* pris; *pr.ind.* ils prennent; *pr.sub.* je prenne; *p.h.* je pris) I. *v.tr.* To take. **1.** To take (up),

to take hold of. (*a*) *P. les armes,* to take up arms. *F:* **Je sais comment le prendre,** I know how to manage him. *P. qch. sur la table,* to take sth. from the table. *F:* **Où avez-vous pris cela?** where did you get that idea? (*b*) *P. des pensionnaires,* to take in boarders. *Vous avez mal pris mes paroles,* you took me up wrong. (*c*) **Prendre qch. à qn,** to take sth. from s.o. (*d*) **C'est à prendre ou à laisser,** take it or leave it. **A tout prendre,** (up)on the whole; everything considered. **A bien prendre les choses,** rightly speaking. *F:* **En prendre à son aise,** to take it easy. **Le prendre de haut,** to put on airs. **2.** To take, capture. (*a*) *P. un poisson,* to catch a fish. *P. qn à mentir,* to catch s.o. in a lie. **Que je vous y prenne!** let me catch you at it! **On ne m'y prendra pas!** I know better! (*b*) *L'envie lui prend de partir,* he is seized with a desire to go away. **Qu'est-ce qui lui prend?** what's up with him now? **Bien lui en prit,** it was lucky for him that he did. **3.** (*a*) *Je passerai vous p. à votre hôtel,* I shall call for you at your hotel. *P. des voyageurs,* to take up passengers. (*b*) *P. une chambre,* to take a room. *P. un ouvrier,* to engage a workman. (*c*) *P. qn pour exemple,* to take s.o. as an example. (*d*) *P. une personne pour une autre,* to take one person for another. (*e*) *P. un bain,* to take a bath. (*f*) *P. des habitudes,* to acquire habits. (*g*) *P. un air innocent,* to put on an innocent air. *P. du poids,* to put on weight. (*h*) **Prendre de l'âge,** to be getting on in years. **4.** *P. le train,* to take the train. *P. à travers champs,* to strike across the fields. *Abs.* **"Prendre à gauche,"** 'bear left.' *Nau:* **Prendre le large,** to take to the open sea.

    II. **prendre,** *v.i.* **1.** (*a*) To set; to congeal. (*b*) To freeze. (*c*) To seize, to jam. (*d*) *Cu:* To catch (in the pan). **2.** *Le feu a pris,* the fire has caught **Ça ne prend pas!** it won't wash!

    se prendre. **1.** (*a*) To catch, to be caught. (*b*) **Se prendre d'amitié pour qn,** to take a liking for s.o. **2. Se prendre à qch.,** to cling to sth. **3. Se prendre à rire,** to begin to laugh. **4. S'en prendre à qn,** to lay the blame on s.o. **5.** *Il sait comment s'y p.,* he knows how to set about it.

    pris, *a.* **1.** Engaged, occupied. **2. Être bien pris,** to be well set up. **3. Pris de boisson,** the worse for drink. **Pris de colère,** in a passion.
preneur, -euse, *s.* Taker. (*a*) *P. de tabac,* snuff taker. (*b*) Buyer, purchaser. (*c*) Lessee, leaseholder.
prénom, *s.m.* First name; Christian name.
préoccupation, *s.f.* Preoccupation.
préoccuper, *v.tr* To preoccupy. *Elle a quelque chose qui la préoccupe,* she has something on her mind.
préparateur, -trice, *s.* **1.** Preparer. **2.** Assistant (in laboratory); demonstrator. **3.** Tutor; *F:* Coach.

préparatifs, *s.m.pl.* Preparations.
préparation, *s.f.* **1.** Preparation, preparing. **2.** *P. anatomique,* anatomical preparation; specimen.
préparatoire, *a.* Preparatory.
préparer, *v.tr.* **1.** To prepare; to get ready. **2.** *P. un examen,* to prepare for an examination.
se préparer. 1. *Il se prépare quelque chose,* there is something afoot. **2.** *Se p. à partir,* to make ready to depart.
prépondérance, *s.f.* Preponderance.
prépondérant, *a.* Preponderant. **Voix prépondérante,** casting vote.
préposer, *v.tr.* *P. qn à une fonction,* to appoint s.o. to an office.
préposé, *s.* Official in charge. *Rail: La préposée (à la librairie),* the bookstall-keeper.
préposition, *s.f.* *Gram:* Preposition.
prérogative, *s.f.* Prerogative.
près. 1. *adv.* Near. **2.** *Adv.phr.* A . . . près. *A cela près,* with that exception. **A cela près que,** except that. **A peu près,** nearly, about. *Il était à peu près certain,* it was fairly certain. *Le mieux équipé* **à beaucoup près,** by far the best equipped. **Au plus près,** to the nearest point. **De près,** close, near; from close to. *Tirer de près,* to fire at close range. *Rasé de près,* close-shaved. **Il n'y regarde pas de si près,** he is not so particular as all that. **3.** *Prep.phr.* **Près de qn,** near, close to, s.o. *Assis tout près du feu,* seated close by the fire. *Près de partir,* about to start.
présage, *s.m.* Presage, portent, foreboding, omen.
présager, *v.tr.* (n. présageons) To presage. **1.** To portend, betoken. **2.** To predict, to augur.
presbytère, *s.m.* Presbytery.
prescience, *s.f.* Prescience, foreknowledge.
prescription, *s.f.* *(a) Med:* Direction(s) (for treatment). *(b)* Regulation(s).
prescrire, *v.tr.* (Conj. like ÉCRIRE) To prescribe, lay down; to stipulate for.
préséance, *s.f.* Precedence; priority.
présence, *s.f.* Presence. *(a) Sch: Régularité de p.,* regular attendance. **En présence,** face to face. *(b)* **Présence d'esprit,** presence of mind.
présent¹, *a.* Present. *(a)* **A présent,** just now. **Jusqu'à présent,** as yet. **Dès à présent,** henceforth. **A présent que,** now that. *(b)* **Esprit présent,** alert mind; ready wit.
présent², *s.m.* Present, gift.
présentable, *a.* *F:* Presentable.
présentation, *s.f.* **1.** Presentation. **2.** (Formal) introduction.
présentement, *adv.* At present.
présenter, *v.tr.* **1.** To present, offer. *(a) P. une excuse à qn,* to offer an apology to s.o. *P. un revolver à qn,* to point a revolver at s.o. *(b) P. des conclusions,* to submit conclusions. *P. un projet de loi,* to introduce a bill. **2.** **Présenter qn à qn,** to present, introduce, s.o. to s.o.

se présenter. 1. *Une occasion se présente,* an opportunity offers. *Si le cas se présente,* if the case arises. **2.** To present oneself. *Se p. aux élections,* to stand at the elections.
préservatif, *a. & s.m.* Preservative; preventive.
préservation, *s.f.* Preservation.
préserver, *v.tr.* To preserve.
présidence, *s.f.* *(a)* Presidency. *(b)* Chairmanship.
président, *s.* **1.** President. **2.** Chairman.
présidentiel, -elle, *a.* Presidential.
présider, *v.tr. & i.* *(a) P. un conseil,* to preside over a council. *(b)* To preside, to be in the chair.
présomptif, *a.* Presumptive. *Heritier p.,* heir apparent.
présomption, *s.f.* Presumption.
présomptueux, *a.* Presumptuous, presuming.
presque, *adv.* **1.** Almost, nearly. **2.** (With negative) Scarcely, hardly. **Presque jamais,** hardly ever.
presqu'île, *s.f.* Peninsula.
pressant, *a.* Pressing, urgent.
presse, *s.f.* **1.** Press, pressing-machine. *P. à imprimer,* printing-press. **2.** Press, newspapers. **3.** Pressure; press, crowd. **4.** *(a)* Haste, urgency. *(b) P. des affaires,* pressure of business.
pressentiment, *s.m.* Presentiment, foreboding.
pressentir, *v.tr.* (Conj. like MENTIR) **1.** To have a presentiment, a foreboding, of. *Faire p. qch. à qn,* to give s.o. an inkling of sth. **2.** *P. qn (sur qch.),* to sound s.o. (on sth.).
presse-papiers, *s.m.inv.* Paper-weight.
presser, *v.tr.* To press. **1.** To squeeze. **2.** To press (upon); to beset. *P. qn de questions,* to ply s.o. with questions. **3.** To hurry, push, (s.o.) on. *P. le pas,* to hasten one's steps. *Qu'est-ce qui vous presse?* why are you in such a hurry? *Abs. L'affaire presse,* the matter is urgent. **Il n'y a rien qui presse,** there is no hurry.
se presser. 1. To press, crowd, throng. **2.** To hurry, make haste.
pressé, *a.* **1.** *(a)* Pressed, crowded, close together. *(b)* Compressed. **2.** *(a)* Pressed; in a hurry. *(b) P. d'argent,* pressed for money. *(c)* Pressing, urgent.
pression, *s.f.* Pressure. *Exercer une p. sur qn,* to bring pressure to bear on s.o.
pressoir, *s.m.* Wine-press, cider-press.
pressurer, *v.tr* *(a)* To press (grapes for wine). *(b)* To press out (the juice).
prestance, *s.f.* *Avoir une belle p.,* to have a fine presence.
preste, *a.* Quick, nimble; alert.
prestement, *adv.* Quickly, nimbly.
prestesse, *s.f.* Quickness, alertness.
prestidigitateur, *s.m.* Conjurer.
prestidigitation, *s.f.* Conjuring, legerdemain, sleight of hand.

prestige, *s.m.* **1.** Glamour (of a name). **2.** Prestige; high reputation.

prestigieux, *a.* Marvellous, wondrous.

présumer, *v.tr.* To presume. **1.** Il est à présumer, the presumption is. **2.** (*a*) *P. de faire qch.,* to presume to do sth. (*b*) *Trop présumer de soi,* to presume too much. *Trop p. de ses forces,* to over-estimate one's strength.

présupposer, *v.tr.* To presuppose; to take (sth.) for granted.

présure, *s.f.* Rennet.

prêt¹, *a.* Ready, prepared.

prêt², *s.m.* **1.** Loan. **2.** Advance (on wages).

prétendant, *s.* **1.** Applicant, candidate; claimant; pretender. **2.** *s.m.* Suitor.

prétendre, *v.tr.* **1.** To claim; to require. **2.** To maintain, assert; to mean. **3.** *v.ind.tr.* Prétendre à qch., to lay claim to sth. *P. aux honneurs,* to aspire to honours.

prétendu. 1. *a.* Alleged, would-be. **2.** *s.* Intended.

prétentieusement, *adv.* Pretentiously.

prétentieux, *a.* Pretentious, showy.

prétention, *s.f.* (*a*) Pretension, claim. (*b*) Homme à prétentions, pretentious man.

prêter, *v.tr.* **1.** To lend. (*a*) *P. qch. à qn,* to lend sth. to s.o. (*b*) Prêter attention, to pay attention. **Prêter serment,** to take the oath; to be sworn. **2.** To attribute, ascribe. **3.** *v.ind.tr. Privilège qui prête aux abus,* privilege that lends itself to abuses.

se prêter. 1. To lend oneself, to be a party. **2.** *Se p. au plaisir,* to indulge in pleasure.

prêté, *s.m* Un prêté pour un rendu, tit for tat.

prêteur, -euse, *s* Lender. **Prêteur sur gages,** pawnbroker.

prétexte, *s.m.* Pretext, excuse. *Ce n'était qu'un p.,* it was only a blind. **Sous aucun prétexte,** not on any account.

prétexter, *v.tr.* To pretext. *P. la fatigue,* to plead fatigue.

prêtre, *s.m.* Priest. **Grand prêtre,** high priest.

prêtresse, *s.f.* Priestess.

prêtrise, *s.f.* Priesthood.

preuve, *s.f.* Proof, evidence. **Faire preuve d'intelligence,** to show intelligence. **Faire ses preuves,** to prove oneself; to show one's mettle.

prévaloir, *v.i.* (Conj. like VALOIR, except *pr.sub.* je prévale) To prevail. **Faire prévaloir son droit,** to make good one's right.

se prévaloir *de qch.* (*a*) To avail oneself of sth. (*b*) To presume on.

prévarication, *s.f.* Breach of trust; mal-administration; jobbery.

prévariquer, *v.i.* To betray one's trust.

prévenance, *s.f.* (Kind) attention; kindness.

prévenant, *a.* **1.** Kind, attentive, considerate. **2.** Pleasing, prepossessing.

prévenir, *v.tr.* (Conj. like VENIR) **1.** (*a*) To forestall, anticipate. (*b*) To prevent, ward off. **2.** To predispose, to bias. *P. qn contre qn,* to prejudice s.o. against s.o. **3.** To inform, forewarn. *P. qn de qch.,* to give s.o. notice of sth.

prévenu. 1. *a.* Prejudiced, bias(s)ed. **2.** *s.* Le prévenu, la prévenue, the accused.

préventif, *a.* **1.** Preventive. **2.** *Jur:* Détention préventive, detention on suspicion.

prévention, *s.f.* **1.** Prepossession; prejudice, bias. **2.** *Jur:* Imprisonment on suspicion.

prévi-s, -t, etc. See PRÉVOIR.

prévision, *s.f.* Forecasting or forecast. **Selon toute prévision,** in all likelihood. **En prévision de qch.,** in anticipation of sth.

prévoir, *v.tr.* (Conj. like VOIR except *fu.* and *condit.* je prévoirai, je prévoirais) **1.** To foresee, forecast. **Faire prévoir qch.,** to foreshadow sth. **2.** To take measures beforehand; to provide for. *Chiffre prévu pour les dépenses,* estimate of expenditure.

prévôt, *s.m.* (*a*) Provost. (*b*) Grand prévôt, Provost-marshal.

prévoyance, *s.f.* Foresight, precaution. **Société de prévoyance,** provident society.

prévoyant, *a.* Provident; far-sighted.

prier, *v.tr.* **1.** To pray. **2.** To ask, beg, beseech. **Je vous en prie!** oh do! I do, please! **Se faire prier,** to require much pressing. **3.** *P. qn à dîner,* to invite s.o. to dinner.

prière, *s.f.* **1.** Prayer. **2.** Request, entreaty.

prieur, *s. Ecc:* Prior; *f.,* prioress.

prieuré, *s.m.* Priory.

primaire, *a.* Primary.

primat, *s.m. Ecc:* Primate.

primauté, *s.f.* Primacy.

prime¹, *a.* **De prime abord,** to begin with; at first. **De prime saut,** on the first impulse.

prime², *s.f.* **1.** Premium. **Faire prime,** to be at a premium. **2.** Bounty, subsidy, bonus.

primer, *v.tr.* To excel, surpass.

prime-sautier, *a.* Impulsive, spontaneous.

primeur, *s.f.* **1.** Newness, freshness. **2.** *Cultiver des primeurs,* to grow early vegetables.

primevère, *s.f. Bot:* Primrose.

primitif, *a.* **1.** Primitive. **1.** (*a*) Primeval, original. *Opt: Couleurs primitives,* primary colours. (*b*) First, original. **2.** Primitive, crude.

primitivement, *adv.* Primitively.

primogéniture, *s.f.* Primogeniture.

primordial, -aux, *a.* (*a*) Primordial. (*b*) Primeval.

prince, *s.m.* Prince.

princeps [-sɛps], *a.inv.* Édition princeps, first edition.

princesse, *s.f.* Princess.

princier, *a.* Princely.

principal, -aux. 1. *a.* Principal, chief, leading. **2.** *s.m.* (*a*) Principal, chief; headmaster. (*b*) Principal thing, main point. (*c*) *Com:* Principal; capital sum.

principauté, *s.f.* Principality.

principe, *s.m.* Principle; rule of conduct. **En principe,** as a rule.

printanier, *a.* Spring (flowers).

printemps [-tã], *s.m.* Spring, springtime.

priorité, *s.f.* Priority. **Actions de priorité,** preference shares. *Aut:* **Route de priorité,** major road.

pri-s, -t, etc. See PRENDRE.

prise, *s.f.* **1.** Hold, grasp, grip. (*a*) **Trouver prise à qch.,** to get a grip of sth. **Lâcher prise,** to let go. (*b*) **Mettre les gens aux prises,** to set people by the ears. (*c*) *Mec.E:* **En prise,** in gear, engaged. **2.** Congealing, setting. **3.** (*a*) Taking; capture. (*b*) *P. de colis à domicile,* collection of parcels. (*c*) **Prise de vues,** taking of photographs. (*d*) *Nau:* Prize. **Part de prise,** prize-money. **4.** (*a*) *P. de poisson,* catch of fish. (*b*) **Prise de tabac,** pinch of snuff.

priser¹, *v.tr.* To snuff (sth.) up. *Abs.* To take snuff. **Tabac à priser,** snuff.

priser², *v.tr.* (*a*) To appraise, value. (*b*) To set a (high) value on; to prize.

prismatique, *a.* Prismatic.

prisme, *s.m.* Prism.

prison, *s.f.* **1.** Prison, gaol. **Aller en prison,** to go to prison, to jail. **2.** Imprisonment.

prisonnier. 1. *s.* Prisoner. **Se constituer prisonnier,** to give oneself up. **2.** *a.* Imprisoned, captive.

privation, *s.f.* **1.** Deprivation. **2.** Privation, hardship.

privé, *a.* (*a*) Private. (*b*) **Le Conseil privé,** the Privy Council.

priver, *v.tr.* To deprive.

se priver, to deny oneself.

privilège, *s.m.* **1.** Privilege. **2.** Preferential right; preference.

privilégier, *v.tr.* To privilege; to license. **privilégié,** *a.* (*a*) Privileged. (*b*) Licensed. (*c*) *Créancier p.,* preferential creditor.

prix, *s.m.* **1.** (*a*) Value, worth, cost. **Faire qch. à prix d'argent,** to do sth. for money. **Se vendre à prix d'or,** to fetch huge prices. **A aucun prix,** not at any price. **Tenir qch. en haut prix,** to prize sth. highly. (*b*) Price. **Articles de prix,** expensive goods. **C'est hors de prix,** the price is prohibitive. **N'avoir pas de prix,** to be priceless. (*c*) Charge. *P. du voyage,* fare. **2.** Reward, prize.

probabilité, *s.f.* Probability, likelihood.

probable, *a.* Probable, likely.

probablement, *adv.* Probably.

probe, *a.* Honest, upright.

probité, *s.f.* Probity, integrity.

problématique, *a.* Problematical.

problème, *s.m.* Problem. *Sch:* **Faire des problèmes,** to do sums.

procédé, *s.m.* **1.** Proceeding, dealing, conduct. **2.** Process; method.

procéder¹, *v.i.* (Conj. like CÉDER) To proceed.

procéder², *v.i.* To proceed (*de,* from); to originate (*de,* in).

procédure, *s.f. Jur:* **1.** Procedure. **2.** Proceedings.

procès, *s.m.* **Procès civil,** lawsuit. **Procès criminel,** (criminal) trial. **Intenter un procès à qn,** to prosecute s.o.

procession, *s.f.* Procession.

procès-verbal, *s.m.* **1.** (Official) report; minute(s). **2.** Policeman's report (against s.o.). *pl.* **Des procès-verbaux.**

prochain. 1. *a.* (*a*) Nearest. **Cause prochaine,** immediate cause. (*b*) Next. **Fin prochain,** at the end of next month. (*c*) Near at hand. *Dans un avenir p.,* in the near future. **2.** *s.m.* Neighbour, fellow-creature.

prochainement, *adv.* Shortly, soon.

proche. 1. *adv.* Near. **Tout proche,** close at hand. **2.** *a.* Near, neighbouring. **Ses proches (parents),** his near relations; his next of kin.

proclamation, *s.f.* Proclamation.

proclamer, *v.tr.* To proclaim, declare.

procréer, *v.tr.* To procreate, to beget.

procurable, *a.* Procurable, obtainable.

procuration, *s.f.* Procuration, proxy, power of attorney.

procurer, *v.tr. P. qch. à qn,* to procure sth. for s.o. *Se p. de l'argent,* to raise money.

procureur, procuratrice, *s.* **1.** Procurator, proxy. **2.** *Jur:* Attorney (at law). **Procureur de la République** = public prosecutor.

prodigalité, *s.f.* Prodigality, lavishness.

prodige, *s.m.* Prodigy, wonder, marvel.

prodigieusement, *adv.* Prodigiously.

prodigieux, *a.* Prodigious, stupendous.

prodigue, *a.* (*a*) Prodigal, lavish. (*b*) Prodigal, wasteful.

prodiguer, *v.tr.* **1.** To be prodigal, lavish, of (sth.). **2.** To waste, squander.

se prodiguer. *Se p. en éloges,* to be lavish of praise.

producteur, -trice. 1. *a.* Productive; producing. **2.** *s.* Producer.

productif, *a.* Productive.

production, *s.f.* **1.** Production. **2.** (*a*) Product. (*b*) Yield; output.

produire, *v.tr.* (Conj. like CONDUIRE) **1.** To produce, bring forward. **2.** To produce, yield. **3.** To produce, bring about.

se produire, to occur, happen; to take place.

produit, *s.m.* (*a*) Product. (*b*) *P. d'une vente,* proceeds of a sale.

proéminence, *s.f.* Prominence.

proéminent, *a.* Prominent.

profanateur, -trice, *s.* Desecrator.

profanation, *s.f.* Profanation, desecration.

profane. 1. *a.* Profane. (*a*) Secular. (*b*) Unhallowed. **2.** *s.* Uninitiated person; layman.

profaner, *v.tr.* To profane; to desecrate; to violate (a grave).

proférer, *v.tr.* (je profère; je proférerai) To utter.

professer, *v.tr.* **1.** To profess (opinion). **2.** To teach; to exercise (a calling).

professeur, *s.m.* Professor; teacher.

profession, *s.f.* **1.** *P. de foi,* profession of faith. **2.** Occupation, calling, business, profession.

professionnel, -elle, *a.* Professional.

profil [-fil], *s.m.* **1.** Profile, side-face. **2.** Contour, outline; section.

profiler, *v.tr.* **1.** To profile. **2.** To shape.   **se profiler,** to be outlined.

profit, *s.m.* Profit, benefit. **Mettre qch. à profit,** to turn sth. to account.

profitable, *a.* Profitable, advantageous.

profitablement, *adv.* Profitably.

profiter, *v.i.* **1.** (*a*) *P. de qch.,* to profit by sth.; to turn sth. to account. *P. de l'occasion,* to improve the occasion. (*b*) *P. sur une vente,* to make a profit on a sale. **2.** *P à qn,* to profit s.o.

profiteur, *s.m.* *F:* Profiteer.

profond. 1. *a.* (*a*) Deep. (*b*) Deep-seated. (*c*) Profound; deep (sleep). **2.** *s.m.* Au plus profond de mon cœur, in the depths of my heart.

profondément, *adv.* Profoundly, deeply.

profondeur, *s.f.* Depth.

profus, *a.* Profuse.

profusément, *adv.* Profusely.

profusion, *s.f.* Profusion, profuseness.

progéniture, *s.f.* Progeny, offspring.

programme, *s.m.* Programme; syllabus. *Sch: P. d'études,* curriculum.

progrès, *s.m.* Progress.

progresser, *v.i.* (*a*) To progress, advance; to make headway. (*b*) To improve.

progressif, *a.* Progressive.

progression, *s.f.* Progress(ion); advancement.

progressivement, *adv.* Progressively.

prohiber, *v.tr.* To prohibit, forbid.

prohibitif, *a.* Prohibitive.

prohibition, *s.f.* Prohibition.

proie, *s.f.* Prey; *Ven:* quarry.

projecteur, *s.m.* Searchlight, projector.

projectile, *a. & s.m.* Projectile; missile.

projection, *s.f.* Projection.

projet, *s.m.* (*a*) Project, plan; scheme. (*b*) Plan (of building).

projeter, *v.tr.* (Conj. like JETER) To project. **1.** To throw; to cast. **2.** To plan, contemplate.   **se projeter,** to project, stand out.

prolétariat, *s.m. Coll.* The proletariate.

prolifique, *a.* Prolific.

prolixe, *a.* Prolix, verbose, wordy.

prolixité, *s.f.* Prolixity; verbosity.

prologue, *s.m.* Prologue.

prolongation, *s.f.* Prolongation; protraction.

prolongement, *s.m.* Lengthening, extension.

prolonger, *v.tr.* (n. prolongeons) To prolong; to protract, extend.   **se prolonger,** to be prolonged; to continue, extend.

prolongé, *a.* Long(-continued); prolonged; long-drawn.

promenade, *s.f.* **1.** (*a*) Walking (as exercise). (*b*) Stroll, outing. **Faire une promenade (à pied),** to go for a walk. **Faire une promenade à cheval,** to go for a ride (on horseback). *P. en bateau,* row, sail. *P. en auto,* motor run. **2.** Promenade, (public) walk.

promener, *v.tr.* (je promène) **1.** (*a*) To take for a walk, for a drive, etc. (*b*) To take, lead, about. **2.** *P. sa main sur qch.,* to pass one's hand over sth.   **se promener,** to walk; to go for a walk, for a drive, etc. **Allez vous promener!** away with you!

promeneur, -euse, *s.* (*a*) Walker, pedestrian. (*b*) Promenader.

promesse, *s.f.* Promise, assurance.

promettre, *v.tr.* (Conj. like METTRE) To promise. **1.** (*a*) *P. qch. à qn,* to promise s.o. sth. (*b*) *Se p. qch.,* to promise oneself sth. **2.** *Le temps promet de la chaleur,* it promises to be warm.

promiscuité, *s.f. Pej:* Promiscuity.

promontoire, *s.m.* Promontory; headland.

promoteur, -trice, *s.* Promoter, originator.

promotion, *s.f.* Promotion, preferment.

prompt [pr5], *a.* Prompt, quick, ready.

promptement [pr5t-], *adv.* Promptly.

promptitude [pr5t-], *s.f.* Promptitude; quickness. *Avec toute la p. possible,* with all possible dispatch.

promu, *a.* Promoted, raised.

promulgation, *s.f.* Promulgation.

promulguer, *v.tr.* To promulgate.

prône, *s.m. Ecc:* Sermon, homily.

pronom, *s.m. Gram:* Pronoun.

pronominal, -aux, *a. Gram:* Pronominal.

prononcer, *v.tr.* (n. prononçons) To pronounce. **1.** (*a*) *Sans p. un mot,* without a word. (*b*) *P. un discours,* to deliver a speech. *Abs. P. en faveur de qn,* to declare in favour of s.o. **2.** *Mot difficile à p.,* word hard to pronounce.   **se prononcer,** to express one's opinion; to make a decision.

prononcé, *a.* Pronounced, decided. *Courbe prononcée,* sharp curve.

prononciation, *s.f.* **1.** Delivery (of speech); passing (of sentence). **2.** Pronunciation.

pronostic [-tik], *s.m.* Prognostic(ation). *P. du temps,* weather forecast.

pronostiquer, *v.tr.* To forecast.

propagande, *s.f.* Propaganda; publicity.

propagation, *s.f.* Spread(ing), propagation.

propager, *v.tr.* (n. propageons) To propagate; to spread.   **se propager. 1.** To spread. **2.** To propagate, reproduce.

propension, *s.f.* Propensity, tendency.
prophète, prophétesse, *s.* Prophet, seer *f.* prophetess.
prophétie, *s.f.* Prophecy.
prophétique, *a.* Prophetic(al).
prophétiquement, *adv.* Prophetically.
prophétiser, *v.tr* (*a*) To prophesy. (*b*) To foretell.
propice, *a.* Propitious; auspicious; favourable.
propitiation, *s.f.* Propitiation.
propitiatoire, *a.* Propitiatory.
proportion, *s.f.* **I.** Proportion, ratio. Toute(s) proportion(s) gardée(s), due allowance being made. **2.** *pl.* Size.
proportionné, *a. Bien p.*, well-proportioned. **2.** Proportionate, suited.
proportionnel, -elle, *a.* Proportional.
proportionnellement, *adv.* Proportionately.
propos, *s.m.* **I.** Purpose, resolution. **2.** Subject, matter. **A ce propos,** in this connection. **A tout propos,** at every turn. *Dire qch. à propos,* to say sth. to the point. *Arriver fort à p.,* to arrive in the nick of time. **A propos, *avez-vous lu ce livre?*** by the way, have you read this book? *pl.* talk, gossip. **Changer de propos,** to change the subject
proposer, *v.tr.* To propose; to propound. **se proposer. I.** To offer oneself, to come forward. **2.** Se proposer qch. to have sth. in view.
proposition, *s.f.* **I.** Proposal, proposition. **2.** (*a*) *Mth:* Proposition. (*b*) *Gram:* Clause.
propre. I. *a.* (*a*) Proper. **Aller en propre personne,** to go in person. (*b*) Peculiar (*à,* to). (*c*) Own. *Ses idées lui sont propres,* his ideas are his own. (*d*) Appropriate, proper. **Propre à tout,** fit for anything (*e*) Neat, clean. *F:* **Nous voilà propres!** we're in a nice mess! **2.** *s.m.* (*a*) Property, attribute. (*b*) **En propre,** in one's own right
proprement, *adv.* **I.** Properly, appropriately. **2.** Cleanly, neatly.
propret, -ette, *a. F:* Neat, tidy
propreté, *s.f.* Cleanliness; neatness.
propriétaire, *s.m. & f.* **I.** Proprietor, proprietress; owner. **2.** Landlord, landlady.
propriété, *s.f.* **I.** (*a*) Proprietorship, ownership. (*b*) Property, estate, **2.** Property, characteristic. **3.** Propriety, correctness.
propulser, *v.tr.* To propel.
propulsif, *a.* Propulsive, propelling.
propulsion, *s.f.* Propulsion, propelling.
prorogation, *s.f.* Prorogation.
proroger, *v.tr.* (n. **prorogeons**) **I.** To prorogue. **2.** To extend (time-limit).
prosaïque, *a.* Prosaic(al)
prosaïquement, *adv.* Prosaically.
prosateur, -trice, *s.* Prose-writer.
proscription, *s.f.* Proscription; outlawry.
proscrire, *v.tr.* (Conj. like ÉCRIRE) (*a*) To proscribe, outlaw. (*b*) *F:* To taboo.
proscrit. I. *a.* Proscribed. **2.** *s.* Outlaw.

prose, *s.f.* Prose.
prosélyte, *s.m. & f.* Proselyte.
prosodie, *s.f.* Prosody.
prospecter, *v.tr. Min:* To prospect.
prospecteur, *s.m.* Prospector.
prospectus [-ty:s], *s.m.* **I.** Prospectus. **2.** Handbill.
prospère, *a.* **I.** Favourable. **2.** Prosperous, thriving, flourishing.
prospérer, *v.i.* (je prospère; je prospérerai) To prosper, thrive.
prospérité, *s.f.* Prosperity.
prosterner (se), *v.pr.* (*a*) To prostrate oneself; to bow down. (*b*) *F:* To grovel. **prosterné,** *a.* Prostrate, prone.
prostituer, *v.tr.* To prostitute.
prostituée, *s.f.* Prostitute.
prostitution, *s.f.* Prostitution.
prostration, *s.f.* Prostration. **I.** Lying prone. **2.** Exhaustion
protecteur, -trice. I. *s.* (*a*) Protector. (*b*) Patron. **2.** *a.* (*a*) Protecting. (*b*) Patronizing (tone).
protection, *s.f.* **I.** Protection. **2.** Patronage, influence. **Avoir de la protection,** to have a friend at court.
protectorat, *s.m.* Protectorate.
protéger, *v.tr.* (jo **protège,** n. **protégeons:** je **protégerai**) To protect. **I.** To shelter, guard. **2.** To patronize.
protégé, *s.* (*a*) Protégé, *f.* protégée. (*b*) Dependant.
protestant, *a. & s.* Protestant.
protestation, *s.f.* **I.** Protestation, asseveration. **2.** Protest. **Réunion de protestation,** indignation meeting.
protester. I. *v.tr.* To protest, asseverate. **2.** *v.i.* (*a*) *P. de son innocence,* to protest one's innocence. (*b*) *P. contre qch.,* to protest against sth.; to challenge (a statement).
protubérance, *s.f.* Protuberance; knob (on stick).
protubérant, *a.* Protuberant.
proue, *s.f.* Prow, stem, bows (of ship).
prouesse, *s.f.* **I.** Prowess, valour. **2.** Doughty deed.
prouver, *v.tr.* **I.** To prove. **2.** *P. sa capacité,* to give proof of (one's capacity).
provenance, *s.f.* **I.** Source, origin. *Train en p du Midi,* train from the South. **2.** Produce, product(ion).
provençal, -aux. I. *a. & s.* Provençal; of Provence. **2.** *s.m. Ling:* Provençal
provende, *s.f.* Provender, fodder.
provenir, *v.i.* (Conj. like VENIR) To proceed, come; to originate.
proverbe, *s.m.* Proverb.
proverbial, -aux, *a.* Proverbial.
proverbialement, *adv.* Proverbially.
providence, *s.f.* Providence.
providentiel, -elle, *a.* Providential.
providentiellement, *adv.* Providentially.
province, *s.f.* **I.** Province **2.** **Vivre en province,** to live in the country.

provincial, -aux, *a. & s.* Provincial.

proviseur, *s.m.* Head-master (of a *lycée*).

provision, *s.f.* **1.** Provision, store, supply. *Aller aux provisions,* to go marketing. **2.** *Com:* Funds, reserve.

provisoire, *a.* Provisional; acting; temporary *Dividende p.,* interim dividend.

provisoirement, *adv.* Provisionally; temporarily.

provocant, *a.* Provocative. **1.** Aggressive. **2.** Tantalizing.

provocateur, -trice. 1. *a.* Provocative. **2.** *s.* (*a*) Aggressor. (*b*) Instigator.

provocatif, *a.* Provocative.

provocation, *s.f.* **1.** Provocation. *Lancer des provocations à qn,* to hurl defiance at s.o. **2.** Instigation.

provoquer, *v.tr.* **1.** To provoke. *P. qn en duel,* to challenge s.o. to a duel. **2.** To induce, instigate. **3.** To cause, bring about.

proximité, *s.f.* Proximity, nearness. *A proximité,* near at hand, close by.

prude. 1. *a.* Prudish. **2.** *s.f.* Prude.

prudemment, *adv.* Prudently; carefully.

prudence, *s.f.* Prudence, carefulness.

prudent, *a.* Prudent, discreet; advisable.

pruderie, *s.f.* Prudery, prudishness.

prune, *s.f.* Plum. *P. de damas,* damson.

pruneau, *s.m.* Prune, dried plum.

prunelle, *s.f* **1.** *Bot:* Sloe. **2.** Pupil (of the eye).

prunellier, *s.m.* Blackthorn, sloe-tree.

prunier, *s.m.* Plum-tree.

Prusse. *Pr.n.f. Geog:* Prussia.

prussien, -ienne, *a. & s.* Prussian.

prussique, *a. Ch:* Prussic (acid).

psalmodie, *s.f.* (*a*) *Ecc:* Intoning. (*b*) *F:* Singsong.

psalmodier, *v.i.* To intone, to chant.

psaume, *s.m.* Psalm.

pseudonyme. 1. *a.* Pseudonymous. **2.** *s.m.* Pseudonym.

psitt [pst], *int.* Hist! here!

Psyché. 1. *Pr.n.f. Gr.Myth:* Psyche. **2.** *s.f.* Cheval-glass, swing-mirror.

psychique, *a.* Psychic(al).

psychologie [-kɔl-], *s.f.* Psychology.

psychologique [-kɔl-], *a.* Psychological.

psychologiquement [-kɔl-], *adv* Psychologically

psychologue [-kɔl-], *s.m.* Psychologist.

pu. See POUVOIR.

puant, *a.* Stinking, ill-smelling, noisome.

puanteur, *s.f.* Stench; foul smell.

puberté, *s.f.* Puberty.

pubescent, *a.* Pubescent, downy.

public, -ique [-lik]. **1.** *a.* Public. *La chose publique,* the public welfare. *La Dette publique,* the National Debt. *Adm:* *Le Ministère public,* the public prosecutor. **2.** *s.m.* Le public, the public, the people. *Le grand p.,* the general public.

publication, *s.f.* Publication.

publicité, *s.f.* Publicity, advertising. *Agent de publicité,* advertising agent.

publier, *v.tr.* To publish.

publiquement, *adv.* Publicly; openly.

puce. 1. *s.f.* Flea. *F:* Avoir la puce a l'oreille, to be suspicious. **2.** *a.inv.* Puce(-coloured).

pucelle, *s.f.* Maid(en), virgin.

pudeur, *s.f.* Modesty; sense of decency. *Rougir de pudeur,* to blush for shame.

pudibond, *a.* Easily shocked; prudish.

pudique, *a.* Modest; chaste.

pudiquement, *adv.* Modestly.

puer, *v.i.* To stink, smell. *Puer l'ail,* to smell of garlic.

puéril [-ril], *a.* Puerile, childish.

puérilement, *adv.* Childishly.

puérilité, *s.f.* Puerility.

puffin, *s.m. Orn:* Shearwater.

pugilat, *s.m.* Pugilism, boxing.

pugiliste, *s.m.* Pugilist, boxer.

puîné, *a.* Younger (brother or sister).

puis¹, puisse. See POUVOIR.

puis², *adv.* (*a*) Then, afterwards, next. (*b*) Besides. *Et puis après?* what then?

puiser, *v.tr.* To draw (water). *Abs.* Puiser à la source, to go to the fountain-head

puisette, *s.f.* Ladle, scoop.

puisque, *conj.* Since, as, seeing that. *F:* Puisque je te dis que je l'ai vu! but I tell you I saw it!

puissamment, *adv.* (*a*) Powerfully. (*b*) Extremely.

puissance, *s.f.* Power. **1.** Force; strength. **2.** Sway, authority. **3.** *Les puissances européennes,* the European Powers.

puissant, *a.* (*a*) Powerful, mighty (*b*) *Remède p.,* potent remedy.

puits [pyi], *s.m.* **1.** Well, hole. **2.** Shaft, pit (of mine).

pulluler, *v.i.* To be found in profusion; to swarm.

pulmonaire, *a.* Pulmonary.

pulpe, *s.f.* Pulp.

pulper, *v.tr* To pulp.

pulpeux, *a.* Pulpy; pulpous.

pulsation, *s.f.* Pulsation. **1.** Throbbing; beating **2.** Throb; (heart-)beat.

pulvérisation, *s.f.* (*a*) Pulverization, crushing (*b*) Spraying.

pulvériser, *v.tr.* (*a*) To pulverize; to grind. (*b*) To spray.

puma, *s.m. Z:* Puma, cougar.

pûmes. See POUVOIR.

punaise, *s.f* **1.** *Ent:* Bug. **2.** Drawing-pin.

punique, *a.* Foi punique, treachery.

punir, *v.tr.* To punish; to avenge.

punition, *s.f.* Punishment.

pupille¹ [-pil], *s.m. & f. Jur:* Ward.

pupille², *s.f.* Pupil (of the eye).

pupitre, *s.m* Desk. *P à musique,* music-stand.

pur, *a.* Pure. **1.** *Pur hasard,* pure chance,

mere chance. *La pure vérité,* the simple truth.
2. *Ciel pur,* clear sky.
purée, *s.f. Cu:* (*a*) *P. de pommes de terre,* mashed potatoes. (*b*) Thick soup.
purent. See POUVOIR.
pureté, *s.f.* Purity ; pureness.
purgatif, *a. & s.m. Med:* Purgative.
purgatoire, *s.m. Theol:* Purgatory.
purge, *s.f.* **1.** Purge. **2.** *Mch:* Draining. **3.** Paying off, redemption.
purger, *v.tr.* (n. purgeons) To purge, cleanse, clear. *P. une hypothèque,* to redeem, pay off, a mortgage.
purification, *s.f.* Purification ; cleansing.
purifier, *v.tr.* To purify cleanse.
puriste, *s.m.* Purist.
puritain, *s.* Puritan.
puritanisme, *s.m.* Puritanism.
pur-sang, *s.m.inv.* Thoroughbred.
pus. See POUVOIR.
pusillanime, *a.* Pusillanimous.
pusillanimité, *s.f.* Pusillanimity.

puss-e, -ent, put. See POUVOIR.
putatif, *a.* Putative, supposed, presumed.
pûtes. See POUVOIR.
putois, *s.m.* Polecat.
putréfaction, *s.f.* Putrefaction.
putréfier, *v.tr.* To putrefy.
putrescent, *a.* Putrescent.
putride, *a.* Putrid, tainted.
pygmée, *s.m. & f.* Pygmy.
pyjama, *s.m.* Pyjamas.
pylône, *s.m.* Pylon(e) ; lattice-mast.
pyramidal, -aux, *a.* Pyramidal.
pyramide, *s.f.* Pyramid.
pyrénéen, -enne, *a.* Pyrenean.
Pyrénées (les). *Pr.n.f.pl.* The Pyrenees.
pyrite, *s.f.* Pyrites.
pyrotechnie [-tɛk-], *s.f.* Pyrotechnics.
pyrotechnique [-tɛk-], *a.* Pyrotechnic(al).
Pythagore. *Pr.n.m. Gr.Phil:* Pythagoras.
python, *s.m.* Python.
pythonisse, *s.f.* Pythoness.

Q

Q, q [ky], *s.m.* (The letter) Q, q.
quadragénaire [kwad-], *a. & s.* Quadragenarian.
quadrant, *s.m.* Quadrant.
quadratique [kwad-], *a. Mth:* Quadratic.
quadrilatéral, -aux [kwad-], *a.* Quadrilateral.
quadrilatère [kwad-], *s.m.* Quadrilateral.
quadrille [-ri:j], *s.m.* Quadrille.
quadrillé [-rije], *a.* Squared, cross-ruled ; chequered.
quadrimoteur, -trice [kwad-], *a. Av:* Four-engined.
quadrupède [kwad-]. **1.** *a.* Four-footed. **2.** *s.m.* Quadruped.
quadruple [kwad-], *a. & s.m.* Quadruple, fourfold.
quai, *s.m.* (*a*) Quay, wharf, pier. **Propriétaire de quai,** wharfinger. **A quai,** alongside the quay. (*b*) Embankment. (*c*) *Rail:* Platform. **Le train est à quai,** the train is in.
qualificatif, *a.* Qualifying.
qualification, *s.f.* **1.** Qualifying. **2.** Designation, name, title.
qualifier, *v.tr.* **1.** To style, term, qualify. *F: Q. qn de menteur,* to call s.o. a liar. **2.** *Gram:* To qualify.
  se qualifier. 1. *Se q. colonel,* to call, style, oneself colonel. **2.** *Se q. pour une fonction,* to qualify for an office.
  qualifié, *a. Q. pour faire qch.,* qualified to do sth.
qualité, *s.f.* **1.** Quality. **2.** Quality, property

(of sth.). **3.** Qualification, capacity, profession, occupation. *Servir* **en qualité de page,** to serve as a page. **Avoir qualité pour agir,** to be qualified to act. **4.** Title, rank. **Gens de qualité,** people of quality.
quand. When. **I.** *conj.* (*a*) *F:* **Quand je vous le disais!** didn't I tell you so ! (*b*) **Quand (même).** (i) Even if, even though, although. (ii) **Je le ferai quand même,** I'll do it all the same. **2.** *adv. Q. viendra-t-il?* when will he come? *A quand la noce?* when is the wedding to be?
quant, *adv.* **Quant à,** as to, as for, as regards.
quantième, *s.m.* Day of the month.
quantité, *s.f.* Quantity. **Quantité de gens,** a lot of people.
quarantaine, *s.f.* **1.** (About) forty, some forty. **Approcher de la quarantaine,** to be getting on for forty. **2.** Quarantine. **Mettre en quarantaine,** to send to Coventry.
quarante, *num.a.inv. & s.m.inv.* Forty. *F:* **Je m'en fiche comme de l'an quarante,** I don't care a rap.
quart, *s.m.* **1.** Quarter, fourth part. *F:* **Dans un petit quart d'heure,** in a few minutes. **Pour le quart d'heure,** for the moment. *F:* **Passer un mauvais quart d'heure,** to have a trying moment. **Il est deux heures et quart,** it is a quarter past two. **Quart de cercle,** quadrant. **2.** *Nau:* **Quart de vent,** point of the compass (= 11° 15'). **3.** *Nau:* Watch. **Petit quart,** dog-watch. **Être de quart,** to be on watch.

quarteron, -onne, *a. & s. Ethn:* Quadroon.
quartier, *s.m.* Quarter. **1.** Fourth part. *Q. de la lune,* quarter of the moon. **2.** Part, portion. *Mettre qch. en quartiers,* to tear sth. to pieces. **3.** (*a*) District, neighbourhood. (*b*) *Nau: De quel q. vient le vent?* from what quarter is the wind blowing? (*c*) *Mil:* *Rentrer au q.,* to return to quarters. **Quartier général,** headquarters. **4.** *Demander q.,* to ask for quarter.

quartz [kwarts], *s.m.* Quartz, rock-crystal.

quasi, *adv.* Quasi, almost.

quasiment, *adv. F:* Almost, as it were. *Q. guéri,* as good as cured.

quatorze, *num.a.inv. & s.m.inv.* Fourteen.

quatrain, *s.m. Pros:* Quatrain.

quatre, *num.a.inv. & s.m.inv.* Four. *Pain de q. livres,* quartern loaf. *Il se mettrait en quatre pour vous,* he would do anything for you

Quatre-Cantons. *Pr.n.* **Le lac des Quatre-Cantons,** the Lake of Lucerne.

quatre-vingt-dix, *num.a. & s.m.* Ninety.

quatre-vingts, *num.a. & s.m.* (Omits the final *s* when followed by a *num.a.* or when used as an ordinal) Eighty.

quatrième. 1. *num.a. & s.* Fourth. **2.** *s.m.* Fourth (part).

quatuor [kwatɥɔːr], *s.m.* Quartet.

que¹, *rel.pron.* That; whom; which; what. **1.** *Advienne que pourra,* come what may. **2.** *Menteur que tu es!* you liar! *Couvert qu'il était de poussière,* covered with dust as he was. *Purs mensonges que tout cela!* that's all a pack of lies! *C'est une belle maison que la vôtre,* yours is a fine house. **3.** *Les livres que vous avez achetés,* the books you have bought. **4.** *Les jours qu'il fait chaud,* on (the) days when it is warm.

que², *interr. pron. neut.* What? **1.** *Que voulez-vous?* what do you want? *Que dire?* what could I say? **2.** (*a*) *Qu'est-il arrivé?* what has happened? (*b*) *Que devenir?* what was to become of us? **3.** (*a*) *Que ne le disiez-vous?* why didn't you say so? (*b*) *Qu'il est beau!* how handsome he is! *Que de gens!* what a lot of people!

que³, *conj.* That; but (that); lest. **1.** *Je désire qu'il vienne,* I want him to come. *Je pense que non,* I think not. **2.** (*a*) *Qu'elle entre!* let her come in! *Que je vous y reprenne!* let me catch you at it again! (*b*) (i) *Qu'il pleuve ou qu'il fasse du vent,* whether it rains or blows. (ii) *Que tu le veuilles ou non,* whether you wish it or not. **3.** *Il l'affirmerait que je ne le croirais pas,* even though he affirmed it, I would not believe it. **4.** *Approchez qu'on vous entende,* come nearer that we may hear you. *Il y a trois jours que je ne l'ai vu,* it is three days since I saw him. **5.** *Quand il entrera et qu'il vous trouvera ici,* when he comes in and finds you here. **6.** *À ce que, de ce que. Je ne m'attendais pas à ce qu'on entrât,* I did not expect anyone to enter.

On s'alarmait de ce qu'il ne reparaissait pas, alarm was felt at his failure to appear again. **7.** *Aussi grand que moi,* as tall as I (am). **8.** (*a*) *Ne . . . que,* only. *Je n'ai fait que le toucher,* I only touched it. *Il ne fait que de sortir,* he has only just gone out. (*b*) *Ne . . . que, J'étais sans ami que mon chien,* I had no friend but my dog. (*c*) *Ne . . . pas que,* not only. (*d*) *Il ne me reste plus que vingt francs,* I have only twenty francs left. *Plus que dix minutes!* only ten minutes left! (*e*) *À peine était-il rentré que le téléphone retentit,* he had scarcely come in when the telephone bell rang. **9.** *F: Ah! que non!* ah! surely not!

quel, quelle, *a. & pron.* What, which. **1.** *Quel que soit le résultat, je le ferai,* whatever the result may be, I will do it. *Quels que soient ces hommes,* whoever these men may be. **2.** *Quelle heure est-il?* what is the time? *Quels sont ces messieurs?* who are these gentlemen? **3.** *Quel homme!* what a man!

quelconque, *a.* **1.** Any (whatever). **2.** *Répondre d'une façon q.,* to make some sort of reply.

quelque. 1. *a.* (*a*) Some, any. *Adressez-vous à q. autre,* apply to someone else. (*b*) Some, a few. *Il y a quelques jours,* a few days ago. *Cent et quelques mètres,* a hundred odd yards. (*c*) *Quelque . . . qui, que,* whatever, whatsoever. **Quelque chose qu'il vous ait dite,** whatever (thing) he said to you. **2.** *adv.* (*a*) Some, about. *Quelque dix ans,* some ten years. (*b*) **Quelque . . . que,** however. *Q. grandes que soient ses fautes,* however great his faults may be.

quelque chose, *indef. pron. m. inv.* Something, anything. *Quelque chose de nouveau,* something new. **Il y a quelque chose,** there's something up.

quelquefois, *adv.* Sometimes; now and then.

quelque part, *adv.* **1.** Somewhere. **2.** *Quelque part qu'il fouillât,* wherever he rummaged.

quelques-uns. See QUELQU'UN I.

quelqu'un, *indef. pron.* **1.** *m. & f.* One (or other). *Quelques-un(e)s d'entre nous,* a few of us. **2.** *m.* Someone, somebody; anyone, anybody. *Com: Quelqu'un!* shop! *Quelqu'un d'autre,* someone else.

quémander. 1. *v.i.* To beg. **2.** *v.tr. Q. qch. à qn,* to beg for sth. from s.o.

quenouille [-nuːj], *s.f.* Distaff.

querelle, *s.f.* Quarrel, dispute.

quereller, *v.tr. Q. qn,* to quarrel with s.o. **se quereller,** to quarrel, wrangle.

querelleur, -euse. 1. *s.* Quarreller. **2.** *a.* Quarrelsome.

quérir, quérir, *v.tr. Aller q. qn,* to go and fetch s.o.

qu'est-ce que, *interr. pron.* What? **Qu'est-ce que c'est que ça?** what's that?

qu'est-ce qui, *interr. pron.* What?

question, *s.f.* **1.** (a) Question, query. *Son adhésion ne fait pas question,* there is no question of his adherence. **Mettre qch. en question,** to question sth. (b) Question, matter, point, issue. *Sortir de la q.,* to wander from the point. **2.** *Hist:* Question; judicial torture; the rack.

questionner, *v.tr.* To question.

quête, *s.f.* **1.** (a) Quest, search. (b) *Ven:* Tracking. **2.** Collection. **Faire la quête,** to take up the collection; to pass round the hat.

quêter, *v.tr.* To collect (alms).

queue, *s.f.* **1.** Tail. *Cheval à q. écourtée,* bobtail (horse). *Q. de renard,* fox's brush. *Finir en queue de poisson,* to fizzle out. **2.** Tail (of comet); handle (of pan); pin (of brooch); pigtail. **Habit à queue,** swallow-tail coat. **3.** (Tail-)end, fag-end. **Venir en queue,** to bring up the rear. *Être à la q. de la classe,* to be at the bottom of the class. **4.** Queue. **Faire (la) queue,** to queue up. **5.** *Bill:* Cue.

queue-d'aronde, *s.f. Carp:* Dovetail. *pl. Des queues-d'aronde.*

qui¹, *rel.pron.* **1.** Who, that, which. *Je le vois qui vient,* I see him coming. **2.** (a) *Qui vivra verra,* he who lives will see. *Sauve qui peut,* every man for himself. (b) *Qui plus est,* what is more. **3.** Whom; which. (a) *Voilà l'homme à qui je pensais,* there is the man of whom I was thinking. (b) *On se dispersa qui d'un côté, qui d'un autre,* we scattered, some going one way, some the other. **4.** (a) **Qui que,** who(so)ever, whom(so)ever. (b) **Qui que ce soit,** anyone (whatever).

qui², *interr.pron.m.sg.* **1.** Who? whom? (a) *Qui a dit cela?* who said that? *Qui désirez-vous voir?* whom do you wish to see? *À qui est ce canif?* whose is this knife? *C'était à qui l'aiderait,* they vied with each other in helping him. *F: Il est là.—Qui ça? Qui donc?* he is there.—Who? (b) *Qui des deux a raison?* which of the two is right? **2.** *Qui t'amène si matin?* what brings you so early?

Quichotte, Don. *Pr.n.m* Don Quixote. *Agir en Don Q.,* to act quixotically.

quiconque, *indef. pron. m. sg.* **1.** Who(so)ever; anyone who. **2.** *Pas un mot de cela à q.,* not a word of that to anybody.

qui est-ce que, *interr.pron* Whom?

qui est-ce qui, *interr.pron* Who?

quiétude, *s.f* Quietude.

quille¹ [ki:j], *s.f.* Ninepin, skittle. **Jeu de quilles,** (i) set of ninepins, of skittles; (ii) skittle-alley.

quille², *s.f.* Keel.

quincaillerie [-kɑj-], *s.f.* Hardware, iron-mongery.

quincaillier [-kɑje], *s.m.* Ironmonger.

quinine, *s.f.* Quinine.

quinquennal, -aux [kɥ̃ɛkɥɛ-], *a.* Quin-quennial; five-year.

quinquet, *s.m.* (Argand) lamp.

quinquina, *s.m.* Cinchona; Peruvian bark.

quinte, *s.f.* **1.** *Mus:* Fifth, quint. **2. Quinte de toux,** fit of coughing.

quintessence, *s.f.* Quintessence.

quintuple, *a. & s.m.* Quintuple, fivefold.

quinzaine, *s.f.* **1.** (About) fifteen, some fifteen. **2.** Fortnight.

quinze, *num.a.inv. & s.m.inv.* **1.** Fifteen. **2. Quinze jours,** a fortnight.

quiproquo, *s.m.* Mistake (taking of one thing for another); misunderstanding.

quittance, *s.f.* Receipt, discharge.

quitte, *a.* **1.** Free, quit. *Être q. de dettes,* to be out of debt. *Nous sommes quittes,* I am quits with you. *Il en a été q. pour la peur,* he got off with a fright. **2.** *Inv.* **Je le ferai quitte à être grondé,** I'll do it even if I am scolded.

quitter, *v.tr.* **1.** **Quitter la partie,** to throw up the sponge. **2.** To leave, quit. *Q. ses habits,* to take off one's clothes. *Tp:* **Ne quittez pas (l'écoute)!** hold the line!

qui-vive, *s.m.inv.* Sentry's challenge. *F: Être sur le qui-vive,* to be on the alert.

quoi¹, *rel.pron.* What **1.** (a) *C'est en quoi vous vous trompez,* that is where you are wrong. (b) *Il a bien autre chose à quoi penser!* he has something else to think about! **2. De quoi.** *Il a de quoi vivre,* he has enough to live on. *Il y a de quoi vous faire enrager,* it's enough to drive you mad. **Il n'y a pas de quoi,** pray don't mention it. **3. Sans quoi,** otherwise. **4. Quoi qui, quoi que.** (a) *Quoi qui survienne,* whatever comes of it. **Quoi qu'il en soit,** be that as it may. (b) **Quoi que ce soit,** anything (whatever).

quoi², *interr.pron.* What? (a) *Quoi de nouveau?* what news? *Eh bien! quoi?* well, what about it? (b) *Vous désirez quoi?* what is it you want? **Un je ne sais quoi,** an indescribable something. (c) *À quoi bon,* what's the use?

quoique, *conj* Usu. + *sub.* (Al)though.

quolibet, *s.m* Gibe.

quote-part, *s f.* Share, quota portion. *pl. Des quotes-parts.*

quotidien, -ienne. 1. *a.* Daily, everyday. **2.** *s.m.* **Les quotidiens,** the daily papers.

quotidiennement, *adv.* Daily.

quotient, *s.m. Mth:* Quotient.

R, r [ɛːr], *s.f.* (The letter) R, r.

rabâcher, *v.tr.* *Ils rabâchent toujours la même chose,* they are for ever harping on the same string

rabais, *s.m.* Rebate, discount. **Vendre qch. au rabais,** to sell sth. at a reduced price.

rabaisser, *v.tr.* **1.** To lower; to reduce. **2.** (*a*) To depreciate, belittle. (*b*) To humble.

rabat-joie, *s.m.* & *f.inv.* Kill-joy spoil-sport.

rabatteur, *s.m.* *Ven:* Beater.

rabattre, *v.tr.* (Conj. like BATTRE) **1.** To fold back; to bring down; to lower. *Le vent rabat la fumée,* the wind beats down the smoke. **2.** To reduce, lessen. (*a*) *Com: R. tant du prix,* to take so much off the price. (*b*) *R. l'orgueil de qn,* to take down s.o.'s pride. **3.** *R. les flammes,* to beat back the flames.

rabbin, *s.m.* *Jew.Rel:* Rabbi.

rabot, *s.m.* *Tls:* Plane.

raboter, *v.tr.* To plane (wood).

rabougri, *a.* Stunted, ill-thriven.

rabrouer, *v.tr.* To scold, snub.

racaille [-kɑːj], *s.f.* **1.** Rabble, riff-raff. **2.** Trash, rubbish.

raccommodage, *s.m.* **1.** Mending, repairing; darning. **2.** Mend, repair, darn.

raccommodement, *s.m.* Reconciliation.

raccommoder, *v.tr.* **1.** To mend, repair; to darn. **2.** To reconcile.

raccorder, *v.tr.* To join, connect, to link up.

raccourcir. 1. *v.tr.* (*a*) To shorten. **Raccourcir son bras,** to draw up one's arm. (*b*) To abridge, curtail; to cut short. **2.** *v.i.* & *pr.* To grow shorter; to shrink.

raccourci. 1. *a.* Shortened; short, squat; abridged. **2.** *s.m.* (*a*) Abridgment, epitome. (*b*) Short cut (to a place).

raccourcissement, *s.m.* **1.** Shortening. **2.** Growing shorter; shrinking.

raccrocher, *v.tr.* To hang up again. *Tp: R.* (*l'appareil*), to hang up the receiver; to ring off.

race, *s.f.* Race. **1.** Strain. **Minorités de race,** racial minorities. **2.** Stock, breed. **Chien de (pure) race,** pedigree dog. *Prov:* **Bon chien chasse de race,** what's bred in the bone comes out in the flesh.

racème, *s.m.* *Bot:* Raceme.

rachat, *s.m.* Repurchase, buying back; redemption.

racheter, *v.tr.* (Conj. like ACHETER) (*a*) To repurchase; to buy back. (*b*) To redeem. (*c*) To ransom.

racine, *s.f.* (*a*) Root. (*b*) *Mth:* **Racine carrée,** square root.

racler, *v.tr.* To scrape. *Se r. la gorge,* to clear one's throat.

raclée, *s.f.* *F:* Hiding, drubbing.

racloir, *s.m.* Scraper, scraping-tool.

raconter, *v.tr.* To tell, relate, narrate. *Il vous en raconte,* he is drawing the long bow.

raconteur, -euse, *s.* (Story-)teller, narrator.

radar, *s.m.*, Radar.

rade, *s.f.* *Nau:* Roadstead, roads.

radeau, *s.m.* Raft.

radiateur, -trice. 1. *a.* Radiating. **2.** *s.m.* Radiator.

radiation, *s.f.* *Ph:* Radiation.

radical, -aux, *a.* & *s.m.* Radical.

radicalement, *adv.* Radically.

radieux, *a.* Radiant; beaming.

radio. 1. *s.m.* *F:* Wireless message; radio. **2.** *s.f.* *F:* Wireless telegraphy or telephony; wireless.

radioactif, *a.* *Ph:* Radio-active.

radiodiffuser, *v.tr.* *W.Tel:* To broadcast.

radiodiffusion, *s.f.* *W.Tel:* Broadcasting.

radioémission, *s.f.* **1.** Broadcasting. **2.** Broadcast.

radiogoniomètre, *s.m.* *W.Tel:* Direction-finder.

radiogoniométrie, *s.f.* *W.Tel:* Direction-finding (by wireless)

radiogramme, *s.m.* Radiogram.

radiotéléphone, *s.m.* Radiotelephone.

radis, *s.m.* Radish.

radium [-jɔm], *s.m.* Radium.

radotage, *s.m.* Drivel. *Tomber dans le r.,* to fall into one's dotage.

radoter, *v.i.* To drivel

radoteur, -euse, *s.* Dotard.

radoub, *s.m.* *Nau:* Repair, refitting. **Bassin de radoub,** dry dock.

radoucir, *v.tr.* To calm, soften; to mollify. **se radoucir. 1.** To grow softer. **2.** (Of weather) To grow milder.

radoucissement, *s.m.* (*a*) Softening (*b*) Getting milder.

rafale, *s.f.* (*a*) Squall; strong gust, blast (of wind). (*b*) Burst of gun-fire.

raffermir, *v.tr.* **1.** To make firm(er). **2.** To confirm, strengthen. **se raffermir. 1.** To harden. **2.** *Son autorité se raffermit,* he is recovering his authority.

raffermissement, *s.m.* **1.** Making firmer. **2.** Strengthening.

raffinage, *s.m.* Refining.

raffinement, *s.m.* **1.** = RAFFINAGE. **2.** (Over-)refinement; affectedness.

raffiner, *v.tr.* To refine. **se raffiner,** to become refined. **raffiné,** *a.* (*a*) Refined. (*b*) Subtle. (*c*) Refined, delicate.

raffinerie, *s.f.* (Sugar-)refinery.

raffolement, *s.m.* Doting; infatuation.

raffoler, *v.i.* R. *de qch.*, to be excessively fond of sth.

rafistoler, *v.tr.* F: To patch up.

rafle, *s.f.* (a) (i) Clean sweep. (ii) Swag. (b) Comb-out.

rafraîchir, *v.tr.* 1. To cool, refresh; to air (a room). 2. (a) To freshen up. (b) R. *la mémoire à qn*, to refresh s.o.'s memory. **se rafraîchir.** 1. To grow cooler. 2. To refresh oneself.

rafraîchissant, *a.* Refreshing, cooling.

rafraîchissement, *s.m.* 1. (a) Cooling. (b) Freshening up. (c) Refreshing. 2. *pl.* Refreshments.

ragaillardir [-gaja-], *v.tr.* F: To cheer up.

rage, *s.f.* 1. (Canine) madness; rabies. 2. Rage, fury. F: Cela fait rage, it is all the rage. R. *d'écrire*, mania for writing.

rager, *v.i.* (n. rageons) F: To rage; to be in a rage.

rageur, -euse, *a.* Passionate, choleric.

rageusement, *adv.* Passionately; angrily.

ragoût, *s.m.* Stew, ragout.

raid [rɛd], *s.m.* 1. *Mil:* Raid. 2. Long-distance run or flight.

raide. 1. *a.* (a) Stiff; tight, taut. *Cheveux raides*, straight and wiry hair. (b) Stiff, starchy; inflexible, unbending. (c) Steep; abrupt. (d) F: Ça, c'est un peu raide! that's a bit thick! Il en a vu de raides, he's had some queer experiences. 2. *adv.* (a) Frapper r., to strike hard. (b) Tomber raide mort, to fall stone-dead.

raidement, *adv.* Stiffly; tensely.

raideur, *s.f.* 1. Stiffness; tightness. 2. Stiffness, starchiness; inflexibility. 3. Steepness, abruptness.

raidillon [-dijɔ̃], *s.m.* (Steep) rise; abrupt path.

raidir, *v.tr.* To stiffen; to tighten. **se raidir.** 1. To stiffen, to grow stiff. 2. *Se r. contre le malheur,* to steel oneself against misfortune.

raie¹, *s.f.* 1. Line, stroke (on paper). 2. Streak, stripe. 3. Parting (of the hair).

raie², *s.f. Ich:* Ray, skate.

raifort, *s.m.* Horse-radish.

rail [rɑːj], *s.m.* Rail.

railler [rɑje], *v.tr.* To laugh at, jeer at. **se railler** *de qn,* to make game of s.o.

raillerie [rɑjri], *s.f.* Raillery, chaff. Il n'entend pas raillerie, he cannot take a joke.

railleur, -euse [rɑjœ-]. 1. *a.* Bantering, scoffing, mocking. 2. *s.* Banterer, scoffer.

rainure, *s.f.* Groove, channel, furrow.

raisin, *s.m.* Le raisin, du raisin, grapes. Grappe de raisin, bunch of grapes. Grain de raisin, grape. Raisins secs, raisins. *Raisins de Smyrne,* sultanas.

raison, *s.f.* 1. Reason, motive, ground. Pas tant de raisons! don't argue so much! Raison de plus, all the more reason. Raison d'être, reason, object, justification. 2. Reason.

Ramener qn à la raison, to bring s.o. to his senses. Parler raison, to talk sense. Rendre raison de qch., to explain sth. 3. Reason, justification. Avoir raison, to be right. Se faire une raison, to accept the inevitable. Comme de raison, as one might expect. 4. Satisfaction, reparation. Demander raison d'un affront, to demand satisfaction for an insult. Se faire raison à soi-même, to take the law into one's own hands. Avoir raison de qn, to get the better of s.o. 5. Com: Raison sociale, name, style (of a firm). 6. *Mth:* Raison géométrique, geometrical ratio. A raison de, at the rate of.

raisonnable, *a.* Reasonable.

raisonnablement, *adv.* Reasonably.

raisonnement, *s.m.* (a) Reasoning. (b) Pas de raisonnements! don't argue!

raisonner. 1. *v.i.* To reason; to argue. 2. *v.tr.* R. qn, to reason with s.o. **raisonné,** *a.* Reasoned. Com: Catalogue raisonné, descriptive catalogue.

raisonneur, -euse. 1. *a.* (a) Reasoning, rational. (b) Argumentative. 2. *s.* Reasoner, arguer.

rajeunir. 1. *v.tr.* To rejuvenate. 2. *v.i.* To grow young again.

rajeunissement, *s.m.* Rejuvenation.

rajustement, *s.m.* Readjustment.

rajuster, *v.tr.* To readjust; to set to rights. **se rajuster,** to put one's clothes straight.

râle¹, *s.m. Orn:* Rail.

râle², *s.m.* Rattle (in the throat). Le râle (de la mort), the death-rattle.

ralentir, *v.tr. & i.* To slacken, slow down. "Ralentir!" 'drive slowly!'
ralenti. 1. *a.* Slow(er). 2. *s.m.* Slow motion. *Aut:* (Of engine) Prendre le r., to slow down.

ralentissement, *s.m.* Slackening; slowing down.

râler, *v.i.* To rattle (in one's throat).

ralliement, *s.m.* Rally(ing), assembly.

rallier, *v.tr.* 1. (a) To rally, assemble. (b) To rejoin (ship). (c) Nau: R. la terre, to stand in for land. 2. To rally, to win over.

rallonge, *s.f.* (a) Extension-piece. (b) Extra leaf (of table).

rallonger, *v.tr.* (n. rallongeons) To lengthen; to make longer.

rallumer, *v.tr.* To relight; to rekindle.

ramage, *s.m.* Song, warbling (of birds).

ramasse-poussière, *s.m.inv.* Dust-pan.

ramasser, *v.tr.* 1. To gather together. 2. To collect, gather. 3. R. son mouchoir, to pick up one's handkerchief. F: Ramasser une bûche, to come a cropper. **se ramasser.** 1. To collect, gather. 2. To gather oneself (for an effort); to crouch. 3. To pick oneself up.

rame¹, *s.f.* Oar, scull.

rame², *s.f.* 1. Ream (of paper). 2. String (of barges).

rameau, *s.m.* 1. (a) (Small) branch, bough,

twig. (b) **Le dimanche des Rameaux,** Palm
Sunday **2.** Branch, subdivision.
ramener, *v.tr.* (Conj. like MENER) To bring
back (again). *R. ses pensées en arrière,* to cast
one's thoughts back.
ramer, *v.i.* To row.
rameux, *a.* Ramose, branched.
ramier, *a.m. & s.m. Orn:* (Pigeon) **ramier,**
ring-dove, wood-pigeon.
ramification, *s.f.* Ramification.
ramifier (se), *v.pr.* To ramify, branch out.
ramollir, *v.tr.* To soften.
ramoner, *v.tr* To sweep (chimney).
ramoneur, *s.m.* Chimney-sweep.
rampant, *a.* (a) Creeping; crawling.
(b) Grovelling, cringing.
rampe, *s.f.* **I.** (a) Slope, rise, incline. (b) *Civ.E:*
Gradient, up grade. **2.** Banisters, hand-rail.
3. *Th:* Footlights.
ramper, *v.i.* To creep, crawl.
ramure, *s.f.* Branches, boughs, foliage.
rancart, *s.m.* **Mettre qch. au rancart,** to
cast sth. aside.
rance, *a.* Rancid, rank.
rancidité, *s.f* Rancidity, rancidness.
rancœur, *s.f.* Rancour; bitterness.
rançon, *s.f.* Ransom.
rançonner, *v.tr* To hold to ransom; to
ransom.
rancune, *s.f.* Rancour, spite, malice. **Garder
rancune à qn,** to bear s.o. a grudge.
rancunier, *a.* Vindictive, rancorous, spiteful.
randonnée, *s.f.* Outing, run, trip, excursion.
rang, *s.m.* **I.** (a) Row, line. (b) *Mil:* **Former
les rangs,** to fall in. **Rompre les rangs,**
to dismiss. **Sortir du rang,** to rise from
the ranks. (c) **Se mettre sur les rangs,**
to enter the lists. **2.** (a) Rank; station.
F: **De premier rang,** first-class. **Arriver
au premier rang,** to come to the front. **Par
rang d'âge,** according to age. (b) **Rang social,**
social status.
ranger, *v.tr.* (n. rangeons) **I.** To arrange;
to draw up (troops). **2.** (a) To put away.
(b) *R. la foule,* to keep the crowd back.
3. To arrange, tidy.
　se ranger. I. To draw up, line up.
2. *Se r. du côté de qn,* to side with s.o. **3.** *Se r.
(de côté),* to get out of the way **4.** *Il s'est
rangé,* he has settled down.
　rangé, *a.* **I.** *Bataille rangée,* pitched
battle **2.** Orderly **3.** Steady (person).
　rangée, *s.f.* Row, line; tier (of seats).
ranimer, *v.tr* To revive *R. la colère de qn,*
to reawaken s.o.'s anger. *R. l'assemblée,* to
put fresh life into the meeting.
　se ranimer, to revive.
Raoul [-ul], *Pr.n.m* Ralph.
rapace, *a.* Rapacious.
rapacité, *s.f.* Rapacity.
rapatriement, *s.m.* Repatriation.
rapatrier, *v.tr.* To repatriate.
râpe, *s.f.* Rasp; grater.
râper, *v.tr.* To rasp; to grate.
　râpé, *a.* ( ) Grated. (b) Threadbare.

rapetisser. I. *v.tr.* To make (sth.) smaller;
to shrink (stuff). **2.** *v.i. & pr* To shorten;
to shrink.
raphia, *s.m* Raphia(-grass), raffia.
rapide. I. *a.* (a) Rapid, swift, fast. (b) Steep,
rapid. **2.** *s.m.* (a) Rapid (in river). (b) Express; fast train.
rapidement, *adv.* (a) Rapidly. (b) Steeply.
rapidité, *s.f.* (a) Rapidity, swiftness.
(b) Steepness.
rapiécer, *v.tr.* (**je rapièce; je rapiécerai**)
To piece, patch (garment).
rapière, *s.f.* Rapier.
rapine, *s.f.* Rapine, pillage.
rappel, *s.m.* **I.** (a) Recall. (b) **R. à l'ordre,**
call(ing) to order. **2.** *Mil:* **Battre le rappel,**
to call to arms
rappeler, *v.tr.* (Conj. like APPELER) **I.** (a) To
recall; to call back. (b) **Rappeler qn à l'ordre,**
to call s.o. to order. **2.** To call back to mind.
Vous me rappelez mon oncle, you remind me
of my uncle. **Rappelez-moi à son bon
souvenir,** remember me kindly to him.
　se rappeler qch., to recall, remember,
sth.; to call sth. to mind.
rappliquer, *v.tr.* To re-apply.
rapport, *s.m.* **I. I.** Return, yield. **Maison
de rapport,** block of flats; tenement. **2.** (a)
Official) report. (b) Report, account.
　II. rapport. I. Relation, connection.
En rapport avec qch., in keeping with sth.
Par rapport à qch., in comparison with sth.
Sous tous les rapports, in every respect.
2. *Mth:* Ratio, proportion. **3.** Relations,
intercourse. **Avoir des rapports avec qn,** to
be in touch with s.o.
rapporter, *v.tr.* **I.** To bring back. **2.** To
bring in, yield. *Cela ne rapporte rien* it
doesn't pay **3.** (a) *R. un fait,* to report,
relate, a fact. (b) *F:* To tell tales. **4.** *R. qch.
à une cause,* to ascribe sth. to a cause. **5.** To
revoke (decree)
　se rapporter. I. To agree, tally. **2.** To
refer relate. **3.** **S'en rapporter à qn,** to rely
on s.o.
rapporteur, -euse, *s.* **I.** Tale-bearer,
sneak. **2.** *s.m.* Reporter, recorder **3.** *s.m.*
Geom: Protractor.
rapprochement, *s.m.* **I.** Bringing together;
reconciling; comparing. **2.** Nearness.
3. Coming together; reconciliation.
rapprocher, *v.tr.* **I.** (a) To bring closer
together *R. une chaise du feu,* to draw up a
chair to the fire (b) To bring together
2. *R. des faits,* to compare facts.
　se rapprocher *de qch.* to draw near(er)
to sth
　　rapproché, *a.* Near. *Yeux rapprochés,*
close-set eyes.
rapsodie, *s.f.* Rhapsody.
rapt [rapt], *s.m. Jur:* Abduction.
raquette, *s.f.* **I.** *Games:* Racket, racquet.
2. Snow-shoe.
rare, *a.* **I.** Rare. **Se faire rare,** to be seldom

seen. **2.** (*a*) Rare, uncommon. (*b*) Unusual.
3. Thin, sparse, scanty.

raréfaction, *s.f.* Rarefaction.

rarement, *adv.* Rarely, seldom.

rareté, *s.f.* **I.** (*a*) Scarceness, scarcity. (*b*) Singularity, unusualness. **2.** (*a*) *Cabinet de raretés,* cabinet of rarities. (*b*) Rare occurrence.

ras. I. *a.* (*a*) Close-cropped. **A poil ras,** short-haired. (*b*) Bare, blank. **En rase campagne,** in the open country. **Faire table rase,** to make a clean sweep. **2.** *s.m.* A, au, ras de, (on a) level with, flush with.

rasade, *s.f.* Brim-full glass; bumper

rasant, *a. F:* Boring, tiresome.

rase-mottes, *s.m. Av:* Vol à rase-mottes, hedge-hopping.

raser, *v.tr.* **I.** (*a*) To shave. (*b*) *F:* To bore (s.o.). **2.** To raze to the ground. **3.** (*a*) To graze, brush, skim (over). (*b*) Raser la côte, to hug the shore.
    se raser, to shave.

raseur, -euse, *s. F:* Bore.

rasoir, *s.m.* Razor.

rassasier, *v.tr.* **I.** To satisfy (hunger). **2.** To sate, satiate.
    se rassasier, to eat one's fill.

rassemblement, *s.m.* **I.** Assembling, gathering. **2.** Assemblage, crowd.

rassembler, *v.tr.* To assemble; to gather together. *R. toutes ses forces,* to summon up all one s strength.
    se rassembler, to assemble to come together *Mil:* To fall in

rasseoir, *v.tr.* (Conj. like ASSEOIR) To settle, compose (one's ideas)
    se rasseoir, to resume one's seat
    rassis, *a.* (*a*) Settled, staid, sedate. (*b*) Pain rassis, stale bread

rasséréner (se), *v.pr.* (je me rassérène; je me rassérénerai) **I.** To clear (up). **2.** To recover one' equanimity; to brighten up.

rassied, rassis. Se RASSEOIR

rassurer, *v.tr.* To reassure, cheer.
    se rassurer, to feel reassured. *Rassurez-vous,* make yourself easy

rat, *s.m.* Rat. **Mort aux rats,** rat-poison

rataplan, *s.m.* Rat-tat, rub-a-dub.

ratatiner, *v.tr. & pr.* To shrivel (up): to shrink *Ratatiné,* wizened.

rate[1], *s.f. Anat:* Spleen. *F:* **Ne pas se fouler la rate,** to take things easy.

rate[2], *s.f* She-rat.

râteau, *s.m Tls:* Rake.

râtelier, *s.m.* **I.** Rack (in a stable). **2.** *R. d pipes,* pipe-rack. **3.** (*a*) Row of teeth. (*b*) *F:* Set of false teeth.

rater. I. *v.i.* (*a*) To miss fire, misfire. (*b*) To fail; to miscarry. **2.** *v.tr* (*a*) R. son *coup,* to miss the mark. (*b*) *F:* R. une affaire, to fail in an affair.

raté. I. *a.* Miscarried, ineffectual. *Av: Atterrissage r.,* bad landing. **2.** *s.* (Of pers.) Failure. **3.** *s.m.* Misfire.

ratière, *s.f.* Rat-trap.

ratification, *s.f.* Ratification, approval.

ratifier, *v.tr.* To ratify; to approve.

ration, *s.f.* Ration(s), allowance.

rationaliser, *v.tr.* To rationalize.

rationnel, -elle, *a.* Rational.

rationnellement, *adv.* Rationally.

rationnement, *s.m.* Rationing.

rationner, *v.tr.* To ration.

ratisser, *v.tr.* To rake.

rattacher, *v.tr.* **I.** To refasten, retie. **2.** (*a*) To bind. (*b*) To link up, connect.
    se rattacher *à qch.* **I.** To be fastened to sth. **2.** To be connected with sth.

rattraper, *v.tr.* **I.** To recapture; to catch again. **Je vous rattraperai!** I'll get my own back on you! **2.** To overtake; to catch up. **3.** To recover.
    se rattraper. *Se r. de ses pertes,* to make good one's losses; to recoup oneself.

raturer, *v.tr.* To erase, scratch out; cross out.

rauque, *a.* Hoarse, raucous, harsh.

ravage, *s.m.* Havoc, devastation, ravages.

ravager, *v.tr.* (n. ravageons) To ravage, devastate; to make havoc of.

ravaler, *v.tr.* **I.** To swallow down. **2.** To disparage; depreciate.
    se ravaler, to lower oneself.

ravaudage, *s.m.* **I.** Mending; darning. **2.** Mend; darn

ravauder, *v.tr.* To mend. patch; to darn.

ravin, *s.m.* Ravine, gully.

raviner, *v.tr.* To hollow out; to cut up (roads).

ravir, *v.tr.* **I.** To ravish, carry off. **2.** To ravish, enrapture.
    ravi, *a.* **I.** Entranced, enraptured. **2.** *F:* Delighted; overjoyed.

raviser (se), *v.pr.* To change one's mind.

ravissamment, *adv* Ravishingly; delight-fully

ravissant, *a.* Entrancing; delightful.

ravissement, *s.m.* **I.** Carrying off, ravishing. **2.** Rapture, ecstasy, delight.

ravisseur, *s.m.* Ravisher; kidnapper.

ravitaillement [-taj-], *s.m.* Revictualling.

ravitailler [-taj-], *v.tr.* To revictual.

raviver, *v.tr.* **I.** To revive. **2.** To brighten up. Raviver une plaie, to re-open an old sore.

ravoir, *v.tr.* (Used only in the inf.) To get back again; to recover.

rayer, *v.tr.* (je raie, je raye) **I.** (*a*) To scratch; to score. (*b*) To rule, line (paper). (*c*) To stripe. **2.** To strike out (word)

rayon[1], *s.m.* **I.** Ray; beam. *R. de lune,* moonbeam. **2.** Radius. **3.** Spoke, arm (of wheel)

rayon[2], *s.m.* **I. Rayon de miel,** honeycomb. **2.** (*a*) Shelf (of cupboard). (*b*) Department (in shop).

rayonnant, *a.* (*a*) *Ph:* Radiating. (*b*) Radiant, beaming.

rayonne, *s.f. Tex:* Rayon; artificial silk.

rayonnement, *s.m.* (*a*) *Ph:* Radiation. (*b*) Radiance, effulgence.

rayonner, *v.i.* (*a*) *Ph:* To radiate. (*b*) To beam, shine.

rayure, *s.f.* **1.** (*a*) Stripe, streak. (*b*) Scratch. (*c*) Groove. *Sm.a:* Rifling. **2.** Erasure.

raz [rɑ], *s.m.* Strong current; race. **Raz de marée,** (i) tide-race; (ii) tidal wave.

razzia, *s.f.* Incursion, raid, foray.

ré, *s.m.inv. Mus:* (The note) D.

réactif. 1. *a. Ch:* Reactive. **Papier réactif,** test-paper. **2.** *s.m. Ch:* Reagent.

réaction, *s.f.* Reaction. **Avion à réaction,** Jet plane, jet-propelled aircraft.

réactionnaire, *a. & s.* Reactionary.

réagir, *v.i.* To react.

réalisable, *a.* Realizable; workable.

réalisation, *s.f.* Realization; carrying into effect, carrying out.

réaliser, *v.tr.* To realize. **1.** To effect, carry into effect. **2.** To realize (one's assets). **se réaliser,** to materialize; to come true.

réalisme, *s.m.* Realism.

réaliste. 1. *a.* Realistic **2.** *s.* Realist.

réalité, *s.f.* Reality.

réapparition *s.f.* Reappearance.

réarmement, *s.m.* **1.** *Mil:* Rearming. **2.** *Nau:* Refit(ment).

réarmer, *v.tr.* **1.** *Mil:* To rearm. **2.** *Nau:* To refit, recommission.

rébarbatif, *a.* Grim, forbidding.

rebâtir, *v.tr.* To rebuild.

rebattre, *v.tr.* (Conj. like BATTRE) **1.** (*a*) To beat again. (*b*) To reshuffle (cards). **2.** *F:* **Rebattre les oreilles à qn de qch.,** to din sth. into s.o.'s ears.

rebattu, *a.* (*a*) **Sentier rebattu,** the beaten track. (*b*) Hackneyed.

rebelle. 1. *a.* Rebellious; tubborn, obstinate. *Minerai r.,* refractory ore. **2.** *s.* Rebel.

rebeller (se), *v.pr* To rebel, to rise, to revolt.

rébellion, *s.f.* Rebellion, rising, revolt.

rebiffer (se), *v.pr. F:* To bridle up **Faire rebiffer qn,** to get s.o.'s back up.

reboisement, *s.m.* (Re)afforestation.

reboiser, *v.tr.* To (re)afforest.

rebond, *s.m.* Rebound, bounce (of ball).

rebondi, *a.* Rounded, chubby (cheeks); plump (body).

rebondir, *v.i.* To rebound; to bounce.

rebondissement, *s.m.* Rebound(ing).

rebord, *s.m.* **1.** Edge, border. **2.** Flange.

rebours, *s.m.* Wrong way (of the grain), contrary, reverse. *Adv.phr.* **A rebours,** against the grain, the wrong way **A, au, rebours de,** contrary to.

rebouteur, *s.m.* Bone-setter.

reboutonner, *v.tr.* To rebutton.

rebrousse-poil (à), *adv.phr. Brosser un chapeau à r.-p.,* to brush a hat the wrong way.

rebrousser, *v.tr* **Rebrousser chemin,** to turn back.

rebuffade, *s.f.* Rebuff; snub.

rébus [-by:s], *s.m.* Picture puzzle; rebus.

rebut, *s.m.* (*a*) Casting out, scrapping (*b*) Thing scrapped. **Papier de rebut,** waste paper. *Marchandises de r.,* trash. **Mettr** qch. au rebut, to throw sth. away. *Post* **Bureau des rebuts,** dead-letter office.

rebuter, *v.tr.* **1.** To rebuff. **2.** To dis hearten, discourage. **se rebuter,** to become disheartened.

récalcitrance, *s.f.* Recalcitrance.

récalcitrant, *a.* Recalcitrant, refractory.

recaler, *v.tr. F:* To plough, pluck (s.o. i an examination).

récapitulation, *s.f.* Recapitulation.

récapituler, *v.tr.* To recapitulate; to sun up.

recéler, *v.tr.* (**je recèle; je recèlerai**) *Jur* **1.** To receive (stolen goods). **2.** To conceal

receleur, -euse, ˹. *Jur:* Receiver; F fence.

récemment, *adv.* Recently, lately.

recensement, *s.m.* (*a*) *Adm:* Census (*b*) Counting (of votes).

recenser, *v.tr.* (*a*) To take the census of (*b*) To count (votes).

récent, *a.* Recent, late.

récépissé, *s.m.* (Acknowledgment of) receipt

réceptacle, *s.m.* Receptacle; repository.

récepteur, -trice. 1. *a.* Receiving. *W.Tel* **Poste récepteur,** receiving set. **2.** *s.m. Tp* **Décrocher le r.,** to lift the receiver.

réception, *s.f.* **1.** (*a*) Receipt (of letter) (*b*) Taking delivery; acceptance. **2.** (*a*) Welcome. (*b*) Reception; levee, drawing-room (at court). (*c*) At-home. **3.** *W.Tel: Apparei de r.,* receiving set. **4.** (Hotel) receiving desk

recette, *s.f.* **1.** Receipts, returns. **2.** Receiving; receipt (of stores). **3.** *Cu:* Recipe.

receveur, -euse, *s.* **1.** Receiver. **2.** (*a*) R *des postes,* postmaster. (*b*) Conductor (of bus)

recevoir, *v.tr.* (*pr.p.* **recevant;** *p.p.* **reçu;** *pr.ind.* **je reçois, ils reçoivent;** *pr.sub.* **je reçoive;** *fu.* **je recevrai**) **1.** To receive (letter) **2.** (*a*) To receive, welcome. (*b*) To receive, entertain. *Abs. Elle ne reçoit pas aujourd'hui,* she is not at home to-day. (*c*) *Elle reçoit des pensionnaires,* she takes in boarders. (*d*) **Être reçu à un examen,** to pass an examination. *Être reçu médecin,* to qualify as (a) doctor. **3.** (*a*) *Il reçut la balle dans sa main,* he caught the ball in his hand. (*b*) To accept, admit (excuse). *"Recevez mes respects,"* 'respectfully yours.'

reçu. 1. *a.* Received, accepted, recognized. **2.** *s.m.* (*a*) Receipt, voucher. (*b*) **Au reçu de votre lettre,** on receipt of your letter.

rechange, *s.m.* Replacement **Pièces de rechange,** spare parts, spares.

réchapper, *v.i.* (Aux. *avoir* or *être*) *R. d'un péril,* to escape from a peril *Il n'en réchappera pas,* it is all up with him.

rechargement, *s.m.* (*a*) Recharging. (*b*) Re loading.

echarger, *v.tr.* (Conj. like CHARGER) (*a*) To recharge. (*b*) To reload.

échaud, *s.m.* (*a*) Small portable stove. Réchaud-four, gas-cooker. (*b*) Hot-plate.

échauffer, *v.tr.* **I.** To warm up again. *Voilà qui vous réchauffera,* that will warm you up. **2.** R. le zèle de qn, to rekindle s.o.'s zeal. *F:* R. le cœur à qn, to comfort s.o.
    se réchauffer, to warm oneself.

réchauffé, *s.m.* (*a*) Warmed-up food. (*b*) *F:* Stale news.

echausser (se), *v.pr.* To put one's shoes on again.

êclu, a. Harsh, rough.

echerche, s.f. (*a*) Quest, search, pursuit. (*b*) Research. (*c*) Searching.

echercher, *v.tr.* (*a*) To search for, inquire into. (*b*) To seek (after), to try to obtain.
    recherché, a. I. Article très r., article in great request. **2.** Choice, select. **3.** Studied, strained.

echignement, *s.m.* Crabbedness, sourness.

echigner, *v.i. F:* Faire qch. en rechignant, to do sth. with a bad grace. R. à faire qch., to jib at doing something.
    rechigné, a Sour-tempered, sour-faced.

echute, *s.f.* Relapse, set-back.

écidive, *s.f.* Repetition of an offence; relapse (into crime).

écidiviste, *s.m. & t.* Habitual criminal.

écif, *s.m.* Reef.

écipient, *s.m.* Container, vessel, receptacle.

éciprocité, *s.f.* Reciprocity.

éciproque. I. *a.* Reciprocal, mutual. **2.** *s.f.* (*a*) Rendre la réciproque à qn, to be even with s.o.

éciproquement, *adv* Reciprocally.

écit, *s.m* Narration narrative; account.

écitateur, -trice, *s.* Reciter.

écitation, *s.f.* Recitation, reciting.

éciter, *v.tr* To recite.

éclamation, *s.f* (*a*) Complaint; objection, protest. (*b*) *Jur:* C aim, demand.

éclame, *s.f* (*a*) Advertising; publicity. (*b*) (Puffing) advertisement.

éclamer. I. *v.i.* To complain; to lodge a complaint. **2.** *v.tr.* (*a*) To lay claim to; to claim. (*b*) To claim back. (*c*) To crave, beg, for. (*d*) To call for. R. qch. à grands cris, o clamour for sth. (*e*) R. qch de qn, to require sth. of s.o.

eclus, *s* Recluse.

ecoin, *s.m.* Nook, recess. Coins et recoins, nooks and corners.

eçoi-s, -t, -vent. See RECEVOIR.

écolte, *s.f.* **I.** (*a*) Harvesting. (*b*) Collecting, gathering. **2.** Harvest, crop(s).

écolter, *v.tr.* **I.** To harvest; o gather in. **2.** To collect, gather.

ecommandable, *a.* **I.** Worthy of commendation. **2.** Advisable.

ecommandation, *s.f.* **I.** Recommendation. (Lettre de) recommandation, (i) letter

of introduction; (ii) testimonial. **2.** Advice, injunction. **3.** Registration (of letter).

recommander, *v.tr.* **I.** R. qn à ses amis, to (re)commend s.o. to one's friends. **2.** R. la prudence à qn, to enjoin prudence on s.o. Je vous recommande de, I strongly advise you to. **3.** To register (letter).

recommencer, *v.* (n. recommençons) **I.** *v.tr.* To recommence; to begin (over) again. R. sa vie, to start life afresh. **2.** *v.i.* To do it again; to start afresh. Le voilà qui recommence! he's at it again!

récompense, *s.f.* Recompense, reward.

récompenser, *v.tr.* To reward, recompense.

réconciliable, *a.* Reconcilable.

réconciliation, *s.f.* Reconciliation.

réconcilier, *v.tr.* To reconcile.
    se réconcilier. I. Se r. à, avec, qn, to make it up with s.o. **2.** *F:* To make it up.

reconduire, *v.tr.* (Conj. like CONDUIRE) (*a*) To see home; to take back. (*b*) To accompany to the door.

réconfort, *s.m.* Consolation.

réconfortant. I. *a.* (*a*) Strengthening, stimulating. (*b*) Comforting, cheering. **2.** *s.m.* Tonic.

reconnaissable, *a.* Recognizable.

reconnaissance, *s.f.* **I.** Recognition. **2.** (*a*) Recognition, acknowledgment. (*b*) Donner une reconnaissance à qn, to give s.o. an I.O.U. Reconnaissance de dépôt de gage, pawn-ticket. **3.** (*a*) Reconnoitring. R. du littoral, charting of the coast. (*b*) Reconnaissance. **4.** Gratitude.

reconnaissant, a. (*a*) Grateful   *b*) Thankful

reconnaître, *v.tr.* (Conj. like CONNAÎTRE) **I.** To recognize; to know again. Se faire reconnaître de qn, to make oneself known to s.o. **2.** (*a*) To recognize, acknowledge; to admit. Reconnu pour incorrect, admittedly incorrect. (*b*) To own, acknowledge. **3.** To reconnoitre, explore. **4.** R. une faveur, to be grateful for a favour.
    se reconnaître. I. Se r. vaincu, to own oneself beaten. **2.** (*a*) To collect oneself. (*b*) To get one's bearings. Je ne m'y reconnais plus, I am quite at sea.

reconquérir, *v.tr.* (Conj. like ACQUÉRIR) To regain, recover.

reconstituer, *v.tr.* To reconstitute; to restore.

reconstitution, *s.f.* Reconstitution.

reconstruction, *s.f.* Reconstruction.

reconstruire, *v.tr.* (Conj. like CONDUIRE) To reconstruct, rebuild.

recopier, *v.tr.* To recopy.

recoucher (se), *v.pr.* To go back to bed.

recourber, *v.tr.* To bend back.
    recourbé, a. Bent, curved.

recourir, *v.i.* (Conj. like COURIR) **I.** To run again. **2.** R. à qn, to have recourse to s.o.

recours, *s.m.* Recourse, resort, resource.

recouvrement[1], *s.m.* Recovery.

recouvrement², s.m. I. Re-covering. 2. (a) Covering. (b) Overlapping.
recouvrer, v.tr. To recover.
recouvrir, v.tr. (Conj. like OUVRIR) I. To re-cover. 2. (a) To cover (over). (b) To cover, hide (faults).
se recouvrir, to become overcast.
récréatif, a. Entertaining, amusing.
récréation, s.f. Recreation.
recréer, v.tr. To recreate.
récréer, v.tr. I. To enliven, refresh; to please (the eye). 2. To entertain.
récrier (se), v.pr. I. Se r. d'admiration, to cry out in admiration. 2. Se r. contre qch., to cry out against sth.
récrimination, s.f. Recrimination.
récriminer, v.i. To recriminate.
récrire, v.tr. (Conj. like ÉCRIRE) To rewrite.
recroqueviller (se), v.pr. To shrivel (up) (with the heat); to wilt.
    recroquevillé, a. Shrivelled, curled up.
recrudescence, s.f. Recrudescence.
recrue, s.f. Recruit.
recrutement, s.m. Recruiting.
recruter, v.tr. To recruit.
recruteur, a. Sergent recruteur, recruiting sergeant.
rectangle. I. a. Right-angled. 2. s.m. Rectangle.
rectangulaire, a. Rectangular.
rectificatif, a. Rectifying.
rectification, s.f. Rectification.
rectifier, v.tr. To rectify, correct.
rectiligne, a. Rectilinear.
rectitude, s.f. I. Straightness. 2. Rectitude.
reçu. See RECEVOIR.
recueil [-kœ:j], s.m. Collection, compilation.
recueillement [-kœj-], s.m. Self-communion, meditation, contemplation.
recueillir [-kœj-], v.tr. (Conj. like CUEILLIR) I. To collect, gather. 2. To garner, get in (crops). 3. To take in, to shelter. R. un orphelin, to give an orphan a home.
    se recueillir, to collect oneself, one's thoughts; to commune with oneself.
    recueilli, a. Collected, meditative.
recul, s.m. I. Retirement; backing (of horse); set-back. Mouvement de recul, backward movement. 2. Recoil (of cannon); kick (of rifle).
reculement, s.m. I. Backing. 2. Moving back; postponement.
reculer. I. v.i. To move back, recede; to retreat; (of gun) to recoil; (of rifle) to kick. Il n'y a plus moyen de reculer, there is no going back. Ne reculer devant rien, to shrink from nothing. 2. v.tr. (a) To move back. R. un cheval, to back a horse. (b) To postpone, defer.
    se reculer, to draw back; to move back.
    reculé, a. Distant, remote.
reculons (à), adv.phr. Backwards.

récupération, s.f. I. Recuperation, re-covery. 2. Recoupment (of losses).
récupérer, v.tr. (je récupère; je récupérera) I. To recover. 2. To recoup.
    se récupérer, to recuperate.
récurrence, s.f. Recurrence.
récurrent, a. Recurrent.
récuser, v.tr. To challenge (witness).
rédacteur, -trice, s. I. Writer, drafte 2. Member of the staff (of a newspaper Rédacteur en chef, editor.
rédaction, s.f. I. (a) Drafting, drawing u (of deed). (b) Editing. 2. Editorial staff.
reddition, s.f. Surrender (of town).
rédempteur, -trice. I. a. Redeeming 2. s. Redeemer.
rédemption, s.f. Redemption, redeeming.
redescendre. I. v.i. To come, go, dow again. 2. v.tr. To take down again.
redevable, a. Être r. de qch. à qn, to b indebted to s.o. for sth.
redevance, s.f. (a) Dues. (b) Royalties.
redevenir, v.i. (Conj. like VENIR) R. jeune to grow young again.
rédiger, v.tr. (n. rédigeons) I. To draw up draft (agreement); to write (article). 2. T edit.
redingote, s.f. Frock-coat.
redire, v.tr. (Conj. like DIRE) I. To tell say, again; to repeat. 2. Trouver à redir à qch., to take exception to sth.
redondance, s.f. Redundancy.
redondant, a. Redundant.
redonder, v.i. (a) To be redundant. (b) T be in excess; to superabound.
redonner, v.tr. To give again.
redoublement, s.m. Redoubling.
redoubler, v.tr. & v.i. To redouble.
redoutable, a. Redoubtable, formidable.
redoute, s.f. Fort: Redoubt.
redouter, v.tr. To dread, fear; to hold i awe.
redressement, s.m. I. (a) Re-erecting (b) Righting (of a boat). 2. (a) Straight ening. R. économique, economic recovery (b) Rectification, righting.
redresser, v.tr. I. (a) To re-erect. (b) T right (boat). 2. (a) To straighten (out) (b) R. la tête, to hold up one's head (c) T redress, to right; to rectify.
    se redresser. I. (a) Se r. sur son seant to sit up again. (b) (Of boat) To right. 2. T draw oneself up.
réducteur, -trice. I. a. Reducing. 2. s.m Reducer; reducing agent.
réductible, a. Reducible.
réduction, s.f. I. (a) Reduction; cutting down. (b) Conquest; reduction (of a town) 2. Réductions de salaires, cuts in wages.
réduire, v.tr. (Conj. like CONDUIRE) I. T reduce. 2. (a) R. qn à la misère, to reduc s.o. to poverty. (b) R. une ville, to reduce town.
    se réduire. I. Se r. au strict nécessaire

:o confine oneself to what is strictly necessary.
2. *Se r. en poussière*, to crumble into dust.
:duit, *s.m.* Retreat; nook.
:el, -elle, *a.* Real, actual.
:élire, *v.tr.* (Conj. like LIRE) To re-elect.
:ellement, *adv.* Really, in reality, actually.
:expédier, *v.tr.* To send on, to forward.
:faire, *v.tr.* (Conj. like FAIRE) **1.** To remake; to do again. *C'est à r.*, it will have
to be done (over) again. **2.** To repair;
recover (one's health) **3.** To dupe; to
take in.
　se refaire. 1. (*a*) To recuperate. (*b*) To
refresh the inner man. **2.** To retrieve one's
losses.
:fasse, etc. See REFAIRE.
:fection, *s.f.* Remaking; repairing; restoration.
:fectoire, *s.m.* Refectory.
:férence, *s.f.* **1.** Reference, referring.
2. Reference; recommendation.
:ferendum [-dɔm], *s.m.* Referendum.
:érer, *v.* (je **réfère**; je **réfèrerai**) *v.tr.* To
refer, ascribe.
　se référer. 1. *Se r. à qch.*, to refer to
sth. **2.** *Se r. à qn*, to ask s.o.'s opinion. *S'en*
r. à qn, to refer the matter to s.o.
:fermer, *v.tr.* To reclose; to shut again.
　se refermer, to close again.
:fi-s, -t, etc. See REFAIRE.
:fléchir. 1. *v.tr.* To reflect; to reverberate.
2. *v.i. R. sur, à, qch.*, to reflect on sth.
Réfléchissez donc! do consider! Donner à
réfléchir à qn, to give s.o. food for thought.
Parler sans réfléchir, to speak without
thinking.
　se réfléchir, to be reflected, to
reverberate.
réfléchi, *a.* **1.** Reflective, thoughtful;
deliberate. **2.** Reflexive.
:flecteur. 1. *a.m.* Reflecting (mirror).
2. *s.m.* Reflector.
:flet, *s.m.* Reflection; reflected light.
Chevelure à reflets d'or, hair with glints of
gold.
:fléter, *v.tr.* (il **reflète**; il **reflétera**) To
reflect (light).
:fleurir, *v.i.* **1.** To flower, blossom, again.
2. To flourish anew.
:flexe, *a.* Reflex (action).
:flexion, *s.f.* **1.** Reflection, reflexion (of
light). **2.** Reflection, thought. (Toute)
réflexion faite, everything carefully considered.
:fluer, *v.i.* To flow back; to ebb.
:flux [-fly], *s.m.* Reflux, flowing back; ebb.
Le flux et le reflux, the ebb and flow.
:fondre, *v.tr.* To remelt; to recast.
:formateur, -trice. 1. *a.* Reforming.
2. *s.* Reformer.
:formation, *s.f.* Reformation.
:forme, *s.f.* **1.** Reformation, reform.
2. (*a*) Discharge; invaliding out of the
service. (*b*) *Ind:* R. du matériel, scrapping of
the plant.

reformer, *v.tr.* To form again, to re-form.
réformer, *v.tr.* **1.** To reform, amend.
2. (*a*) To discharge (soldier) as unfit; to
retire (officer). (*b*) *Ind:* To scrap (the plant).
　se réformer, to reform.
réformé, *s.* Man invalided out of the
service.
refoulement, *s.m.* **1.** Driving back, forcing
back. **2.** *Psy:* Suppression (of desires).
refouler, *v.tr.* To drive back, force back.
R. ses sentiments, to repress one's feelings.
réfractaire, *a.* Refractory, insubordinate.
réfracter, *v.tr.* To refract, bend (rays).
réfraction, *s.f. Ph:* Refraction.
refrain, *s.m.* **1.** Refrain, burden (of a song).
2. Refrain en chœur, chorus.
refrènement, *s.m.* Curbing (of instincts).
refréner, *v.tr.* (je refrène; je refrénerai) To
curb, bridle, restrain.
réfrigérant. 1. *a.* Refrigerating; freezing.
2. *s.m.* Refrigerator.
réfrigérateur, *s.m.* Refrigerator.
réfrigération, *s.f.* Refrigeration.
réfrigérer, *v.tr.* (je réfrigère; je réfrigérerai)
To refrigerate, cool.
refroidir. 1. *v.tr.* To cool, chill; to damp.
2. *v.i. & pr.* To grow cold; to cool down.
refroidissement, *s.m.* **1.** Cooling (down).
2. *Med:* Attraper un refroidissement, to
catch a chill.
refuge, *s.m.* Refuge; shelter.
réfugier (se), *v.pr.* To take refuge.
　réfugié, *s.* Refugee.
refus, *s.m.* Refusal. Ce n'est pas de refus,
I can't say no to that.
refuser, *v.tr.* **1.** (*a*) To refuse, decline.
R. tout talent à qn, to deny that s.o. has any
talent. *R. la porte à qn*, to deny s.o. admittance. (*b*) (Of horse) To refuse, to ba(u)lk.
2. To reject. *Sch:* Être refusé, to fail.
　se refuser *à qch.*, to object to, set one's
face against sth. *Se r. à l'évidence*, to shut
one's eyes to the evidence.
réfutation, *s.f.* Refutation.
réfuter, *v.tr.* To refute; to disprove.
regagner, *v.tr.* **1.** To regain, recover.
2. To get back to; to regain.
regain, *s.m.* **1.** *Agr:* Aftermath. **2.** Renewal
(of youth).
régal, -als, *s.m.* (*a*) Feast. (*b*) Treat.
régaler, *v.tr.* To entertain, feast. *C'est moi*
qui régale, I'm standing treat.
　se régaler, to feast; to treat oneself.
regard, *s.m.* Look, glance, gaze. Yeux sans
regard, lack-lustre eyes. Chercher qn du
regard, to look round for s.o. Détourner le r.,
to look away. *R. appuyé*, stare. Attirer le(s)
regard(s), to draw the eye. En regard de qch.,
facing sth. Au regard de qch., compared
with sth.
regarder, *v.tr.* **1.** (*a*) To regard, consider.
(*b*) *Ne r. que ses intérêts*, to consider only one's
interest. (*c*) *v.ind.tr. R. à qch.*, to pay attention to sth. *Je n'y regarde pas de si près*, I

am not so very particular. (*d*) To concern, regard. Cela me regarde, that is my business. En ce qui regarde, as regards. **2.** To look at. *R. qn fixement*, to stare at s.o. Se faire regarder, to attract attention. *R. à la fenêtre*, to look in at the window. *R. par la fenêtre*, to look out of the window. **3.** To look on to; to face.

régate, *s.f.* Regatta.

régence, *s.f.* Regency.

régénérateur, -trice. I. *a.* Regenerating. **2.** *s.* Regenerator.

régénération, *s.f,* Regeneration.

régénérer, *v.tr.* (je régénère; je régénérerai) To regenerate

régent, *s.* Regent.

régicide, *s.m.* Regicide.

régie, *s.f.* **I.** Administration, stewardship; management, control. **2.** Excise-office. *Employé de la r.*, exciseman.

regimber, *v.i.* To kick; to jib, to ba(u)lk.

régime, *s.m.* **I.** Regime. *Le r. du travail,* the organization of labour. *Le r. actuel,* the present order of things. **2.** *Med:* Regimen, diet. **3.** *Gram:* Object. **4.** Bunch, cluster.

régiment, *s.m.* Regiment.

régimentaire, *a.* Regimental.

région, *s.f.* Region, territory, area.

régional, -aux. I. *a.* Regional, local.**2.** *s.f.* Régionale, provincial branch.

régir, *v.tr.* To govern, rule.

régisseur, *s.m.* Steward; (farm) bailiff.

registre, *s.m.* **I.** Register; account-book; minute-book. **2.** *Mus:* Register; (i) compass, (ii) tone quality. **3.** *R. de cheminée,* register, damper.

réglable, *a.* Adjustable.

réglage, *s.m.* (*a*) Regulating, adjusting. (*b*) *W.Tel:* Tuning.

règle, *s.f.* **I.** Rule, ruler. *R. à calcul,* slide-rule. **2.** Rule (of conduct). Tout est en règle, everything is in order. *F:* Bataille en règle, stand-up fight. **3.** Prendre qn pour règle, to take s.o. as an example.

règlement, *s.m.* **I.** Settlement, adjustment. **2.** Regulation(s); statutes. **3.** Se faire un r. de vie, to adopt a rule of life.

réglementaire, *a.* Regular, prescribed.

réglementation, *s.f.* **I.** Making of rules. **2.** Regulating, regulation.

réglementer, *v.tr.* To regulate.

régler, *v.tr.* (je règle; je réglerai) **I.** To rule (paper). **2.** (*a*) To regulate, order. (*b*) To regulate, adjust. *R. sa montre,* to set one's watch right. **3.** (*a*) To settle (account). (*b*) *R. ses affaires,* to set one's affairs in order. **se régler** *sur qn,* to take s.o. as an example.

réglé, *a.* **I.** Ruled (paper). **2.** Regular; steady. *A des heures réglées,* at stated hours.

réglisse, *s.f.* Liquorice.

règne, *s.m.* **I.** (Animal) kingdom. **2.** Reign (of a king); sway (of fashion).

régner, *v.i.* (je règne; je régnerai) To reign,

rule; to be prevalent. *Le calme règne,* ca prevails.

regorgeant, *a.* Overflowing, abounding.

regorger, *v.i.* (n. regorgeons) (*a*) overflow, run over. (*b*) To abound; to glutted. *Les trains regorgent de gens,* t trains are packed with people.

regratter, *v.i.* To huckster.

regrattier, *s.* Huckster.

régressif, *a.* Regressive.

régression, *s.f.* Regression.

regret, *s.m.* Regret. Faire qch. à regre to do sth. reluctantly.

regrettable, *a.* Regrettable; unfortunate.

regrettablement, *adv.* Regrettably.

regretter, *v.tr.* **I.** To regret. Je regrett (I'm) sorry! **2.** *R. un absent,* to miss a absent friend.

régularisation, *s.f.* Regularization.

régulariser, *v.tr.* To regularize.

régularité, *s.f.* (*a*) Regularity. (*b*) Stead ness, evenness. (*c*) Equability.

régulateur, -trice. I. *a.* Regulating **2.** *s.m.* Regulator.

régulier. I. *a.* (*a*) Regular. (*b*) Steady even; orderly. (*c*) *Humeur régulière,* equab temper. **2.** *a. &* *s.m.* Regular.

régulièrement, *adv.* (*a*) Regularly (Steadily, evenly.

régurgiter, *v.tr* To regurgitate.

réhabilitation, *s.f.* Rehabilitation.

réhabiliter, *v.tr.* To rehabilitate.

rehausser, *v.tr.* **I.** To raise; to mak higher. **2.** To heighten, enhance.

réimprimer, *v.tr.* To reprint.

Reims [rɛ̃:s]. *Pr.n.m* *Geog:* Rheims.

rein, *s.m.* **I.** *Anat:* Kidney. **2.** *pl.* Loin back. La chute des reins, the small of th back. Il a les reins solides, he is a sturd fellow.

reine, *s.f.* (*a*) Queen. (*b*) *R des abeille,* queen-bee.

reine-Claude, *s.f.* Greengage. *pl. D reines-Claude.*

réintégration, *s.f.* Reinstatement, restora tion.

réintégrer, *v.tr.* (je réintègre; je réintégrera **I.** *R. qn,* to reinstate s.o. **2.** *R. son domicile* to return to one's home.

réitération, *s.f.* Reiteration.

réitérer, *v.tr.* (je réitère· ie réitérerai) T reiterate, repeat.

rejet, *s.m.* **I.** (*a*) Throwing out. (*b*) Materi thrown out. **2.** Rejection.

rejeter, *v.tr.* (Conj. like JETER) **I.** (*a*) T throw back; to return. (*b*) To throw up **2.** To transfer. *R. la faute sur d'autres,* t lay the blame on others. **3.** To reject. *R. u projet de loi,* to throw out a bill. **se rejeter. I.** *Se r. sur les circonstances* to lay the blame on circumstances. **2.** *Se r en arrière,* to leap, dart, spring, back(wards).

rejeton, *s.m.* **I.** Shoot, sucker (of plant, **2.** Scion, descendant, offspring.

rejoindre, *v.tr.* (Conj. like JOINDRE) **1.** To rejoin, reunite. **2.** To rejoin, overtake.

se rejoindre. 1. To meet. **2.** To meet again.

rejouer, *v.tr.* To replay

réjouir, *v.tr.* (*a*) To delight, gladden. (*b*) *R. la compagnie,* to amuse the company.

se réjouir. 1. To rejoice; to be glad; to be delighted. **2.** To make merry.

réjoui, *a.* Jolly, joyous, cheerful.

réjouissance, *s.f.* Rejoicing.

réjouissant, *a.* **1.** Cheering, heartening. **2.** Mirth-provoking, diverting.

relâchant, *a.* Relaxing.

relâche. 1. *s.m.* (*a*) Slackening. (*b*) Relaxation, respite; breathing space. (*c*) *Th:* "Relâche," 'Closed.' **2.** *s.f. Nau:* (*a*) Call; putting in. **Faire une relâche,** to call at a port. (*b*) Port of call.

relâchement, *s.m.* (*a* Relaxing, slackening. (*b*) Falling off; abatement. (*c*) Relaxation.

relâcher. 1. *v.tr.* (*a*) To loosen, slacken. (*b*) To relax; to abate. **2.** *v.tr. R. un prisonnier,* to release a prisoner. **3.** *v.i. Nau:* To put into port.

se relâcher, to slacken; to get loose; to flag, to abate.

relâché, *a* Relaxed; slack.

relai(s), *s.m.* (*a*) Relay; shift. (*b*) Stage. *Aut: R. d'essence,* (re)filling station.

relancer, *v.tr.* (Conj. like LANCER) **1.** To throw back. *Ten:* To return (the ball). **2.** *Aut: R. le moteur,* to restart the engine.

relaps [-laps], *s.* Backslider.

relater, *v.tr.* To relate, state (facts).

relatif, *a.* (*a*) Relative (*b*) *Questions relatives à un sujet,* questions relating to a matter.

relation, *s.f.* Relation. **1.** *Les relations humaines,* human intercourse. *Être en r. avec qn,* to be in touch with s.o. *Tp: Être mis en r. avec qn,* to be put through to s.o. *R. étroite entre deux faits,* close connection between two facts. *Relations directes,* through connections. **2.** Account, narrative.

relativement, *adv.* (*a*) Relatively. (*b*) Comparatively.

relativité, *s.f.* Relativity.

relaxation, *s.f.* (*a*) Reduction (of a sentence). (*b*) Release, discharge (of prisoner).

relaxer, *v.tr. Jur:* To release.

relayer, *v.* (je relaie, je relaye) **1.** *v.i.* To change horses. **2.** *v.tr.* (*a*) To relay, relieve, take turns. (*b*) To relay (telephonic message).

reléguer, *v.tr.* (Conj. like LÉGUER) To relegate.

relent, *s.m.* Musty smell or taste.

relevant, *a.* Dependent; within the jurisdiction.

relève, *s.f.* Relief; changing (of the guard).

relèvement, *s.m.* **1.** (*a*) Raising up. (*b*) Picking up; *Mil:* collection (of the wounded). (*c*) Re-establishment, restoration; increase. **2.** *Nau:* Bearing. **3.** Rise (in temperature).

relever, *v.* (Conj. like LEVER) I. *v.tr.* **1.** (*a*)

To raise, lift, set up again. (*b*) To pick up. (*c*) To raise; to turn up. *R. la tête,* to look up. *R. les salaires,* to raise wages. **2.** (*a*) To call attention to (sth.). (*b*) *R. qn,* to take s.o. up sharply. **3.** To bring into relief; to enhance, heighten. **4.** To relieve; to take s.o.'s place. **5.** *R. qn de ses fonctions,* to relieve s.o. of his office. **6.** *Nau:* To take the bearing(s) of (land). *Surv: R. un terrain,* to survey, plot, land.

II. **relever,** *v.i.* **1.** *R. de maladie,* to have just recovered from an illness. **2.** *R. de qn,* to be dependent on s.o.

se relever. 1. To rise to one's feet (again). **2.** *Les affaires se relèvent,* business is looking up. **3.** (*a*) To rise again. (*b*) *Se r. de qch.,* to recover from sth.

relevé. 1. *a.* (*a*) Raised, erect; turned up. (*b*) Exalted, high. (*c*) Highly-seasoned. **2.** *s.m.* (*a*) Abstract, summary, statement. (*b*) Survey.

relief [-jef], *s.m. Sculp:* Relief.

relier, *v.tr.* **1.** To tie again. **2.** (*a*) To connect, join. (*b*) To bind (book).

relieur, *s.m.* (Book)binder.

religieusement, *adv.* Religiously. **1.** Piously. **2.** Scrupulously.

religieux. 1. *a.* Religious; scrupulous. **2.** *s.* Monk, friar. **Religieuse,** nun.

religion, *s.f.* (*a*) Religion. (*b*) *Se faire une religion de qch.,* to make a religion of sth.

reliquaire, *s.m.* Reliquary, shrine.

relique, *s.f.* Relic.

relire, *v.tr.* (Conj. like LIRE) To re-read; to read (over) again.

reliure, *s.f.* **1.** Bookbinding. **2.** Binding.

reluire, *v.i.* (Conj. like CONDUIRE) To shine; to glitter.

reluisant, *a.* Shining, glittering; glossy.

remâcher, *v.tr. F:* To ruminate over.

remaniement, *s.m.* **1.** Altering, changing. **2.** Alteration, modification, change.

remanier, *v.tr.* (*a*) To rehandle (material). (*b*) To recast, alter, adapt.

remarier (se), *v.pr.* To remarry; to marry again.

remarquable, *a.* (*a*) Remarkable, noteworthy; distinguished. (*b*) Strange, astonishing.

remarquablement, *adv.* Remarkably.

remarque, *s.f.* **1.** Remark. **2.** *Nau:* Landmark.

remarquer, *v.tr.* (*a*) To remark, notice, observe. **Faire remarquer qch. à qn,** to point sth. out to s.o. (*b*) **Se faire remarquer,** to attract attention.

remballer, *v.tr.* To repack.

rembarquer. 1. *v.tr.* To re-embark. **2.** *v.i. & pr.* To re-embark, to go on board again.

remblai, *s.m.* Embankment, bank.

remblayer, *v.tr.* (je remblaie, je remblaye) To embank, to bank (up).

rembourrer, *v.tr.* To stuff, upholster.

remboursement, *s.m.* Reimbursement, re-payment, refunding.

rembourser, *v.tr.* **1.** To repay, refund. **2.** *R. qn de qch.,* to reimburse s.o. for sth.

rembrunir, *v.tr.* **1.** To make dark(er). **2.** To cast a gloom over.

  se rembrunir, to cloud over, to grow dark.

remède, *s.m.* Remedy, cure. **C'est sans remède,** it can't be helped.

remédiable, *a.* Remediable.

remédier, *v.ind.tr.* **R.** *à qch.,* to remedy sth.

remerciement, *s.m.* Thanks, acknowledgment.

remercier, *v.tr.* **1.** (*a*) *R. qn de qch.,* to thank s.o. for sth. (*b*) To decline. *Du café? —Je vous remercie,* have some coffee?—No, thank you. **2.** To dismiss (employee).

remettre, *v.tr.* (Conj. like METTRE) **1.** To put back (again). (*a*) *R. son chapeau,* to put one's hat on again. **Remettre un os,** to set a bone. *R. en état,* to repair. (*b*) *R. l'esprit de qn,* to calm, compose, s.o.'s mind. (*c*) (**Se**) **remettre qn,** to recall s.o. **2.** (*a*) *R. une dépêche à qn,* to hand a telegram to s.o. (*b*) *R. une charge,* to hand over one's duties. **3.** *R. une peine,* to remit a penalty. **4.** To postpone.

  se remettre. 1. (*a*) *Se r. au lit,* to go back to bed. (*b*) *Se r. au travail,* to start work again. **2.** *Se r. d'une maladie,* to recover from an illness. **Remettez-vous!** calm yourself! **3.** **S'en remettre à qn,** to leave it to s.o.

réminiscence, *s.f.* Reminiscence.

remise, *s.f.* **1.** (*a*) Putting back. (*b*) *R. en état,* repairing. **2.** (*a*) Delivery (of letter). (*b*) Remission. **3.** *Com:* (*a*) Remittance. (*b*) Discount, allowance. **4.** Coach-house.

remiser, *v.tr.* To put up (vehicle).

rémission, *s.f.* Remission.

remmener, *v.tr.* (Conj. like MENER) To lead away (again).

remontant, *a.* (*a*) Ascending. (*b*) Stimulating, tonic.

remonter. 1. *v.i.* (Aux. usu. *être*) (*a*) To go up (again). *R. à cheval,* to remount one's horse. (*b*) To go back. *R. plus haut,* to go further back. **2.** *v.tr.* (*a*) To re-ascend; to climb up again. *R. la rue,* to go up the street. (*b*) To take, carry, raise up. *R. ses chaussettes,* to pull up one's socks. (*c*) To wind (up) (clock). *R. le courage de qn, F:* **remonter qn,** to revive s.o.'s courage. (*d*) *R. sa garde-robe,* to replenish one's wardrobe.

remontrance, *s.f.* Remonstrance.

remontrer, *v.tr.* To show again.

remordre, *v.tr.* To bite again.

remords [-mɔːr], *s.m.* Remorse, self-reproach. *Un r.,* a twinge of remorse. **Pris de remords,** conscience-stricken.

remorquage, *s.m.* Towage, haulage.

remorque, *s.f.* **1.** Towing. **2.** Tow-line. **3.** (*a*) Tow; vessel towed. (*b*) *Veh:* Trailer.

remorquer, *v.tr.* To tow; to haul.

remorqueur, *s.m.* Tug-boat; tug.

rémouleur, *s.m.* (Knife-)grinder.

remous, *s.m.* Eddy; wash (of ship); swi (of the tide); backwash.

rempailleur, -euse [-paj-|, *s.* Chair-mende

rempart, *s.m.* Rampart.

remplaçable, *a.* Replaceable.

remplaçant, *s.* Substitute; locum tenens.

remplacement, *s.m.* Replacing, substitu tion. **De remplacement,** refill.

remplacer, *v.tr.* (Conj. like PLACER) **1.** T take, fill, the place of. **2.** (*a*) To replace *R. qch. par qch.,* to replace sth. by sth. (*b*) T supersede.

remplir, *v.tr.* **1.** To fill up or refill. *R. un place,* to fill a situation. **2.** *R. l'air de ses cris* to fill the air with one's cries. **3.** To fill up fill in (a form). **4.** To fulfil. *Th: R. un rôle* to fill a part.

  se remplir, to fill.

remplissage, *s.m.* Filling up; refilling.

remporter, *v.tr.* **1.** To take back or away **2.** To carry off, bear away; to achiev (success); to win (victory).

remuant, *a.* Restless, bustling.

remue-ménage, *s.m.inv.* Stir, bustle.

remuer. 1. *v.tr.* To move; to shift; to stir to turn over (the ground). *R. les masses,* t stir up the masses. **2.** *v.i.* To move, stir budge.

  se remuer, to move, stir; to besti oneself.

rémunérateur, -trice, *a.* Remunerative.

rémunération, *s.f* Remuneration, pay-ment.

rémunérer, *v.tr.* (je rémunère; je rémuné-rerai) To remunerate.

renâcler, *v.i.* (*a*) To snort. (*b*) *F:* To show reluctance; to hang back.

renaissance, *s.f.* (*a*) Rebirth. (*b*) *R. de lettres,* revival of letters.

renaissant, *a.* Renascent; reviving.

renaître, *v.i.* (Conj. like NAÎTRE) **1.** To be born again. *R. à la vie,* to take on a new lease of life. **2.** To reappear; to revive.

renaqui-s, -t. See RENAÎTRE.

renard, *s.m.* (*a*) Fox. (*b*) *Ind:* Blackleg.

renarde, *s.f.* *Z:* Vixen, she-fox.

renardeau, *s.m.* Fox-cub.

renchérir, *v.i.* (*a*) To get dearer; to ad-vance in price. (*b*) *R. sur qn,* to outdo s.o.

renchérissement, *s.m.* Rise in price.

rencontre, *s.f.* **1.** (*a*) Meeting, encounter. **Aller, venir, à la rencontre de qn,** to go to meet s.o. *Connaissance de r.,* chance acquaint-ance. (*b*) *R. de deux automobiles,* collision of two motor cars. **2.** Encounter; skirmish. **3.** Occasion, conjuncture.

rencontrer, *v.tr.* To meet, to fall n with. *R. l'ennemi,* to encounter the enemy. *Abs.* **Vous avez rencontré juste,** you have guessed right.

  se rencontrer. 1. (*a*) To meet. (*b*) To

collide. (*e*) To occur. **Comme cela se ren-contre!** how things do happen! **2.** (Of ideas) To agree.

rendement, *s.m.* (*a*) Produce, yield; return, profit. (*b*) Output.

rendez-vous, *s.m.inv.* Rendezvous. **I.** Appointment. **2.** Place of meeting; resort, haunt.

rendormir, *v.tr.* (Conj. like DORMIR) To send to sleep again.

   se rendormir, to go to sleep again.

rendre, *v.tr.* **I.** (*a*) To give back, return, restore; to repay. **F: Je le lui rendrai!** I'll be even with him! (*b*) To render, give. **Rendre la justice,** to administer justice. (*c*) To yield; to give, produce. **2.** To convey, deliver. **3.** (*a*) To bring up (food). **Rendre l'âme,** to give up the ghost. (*b*) *Jur:* **R. un jugement,** to deliver a judgment. **4.** To give up, surrender. **5.** To reproduce, render, express. **6.** *Pred. Il se rend ridicule,* he is making himself ridiculous.

   se rendre. I. *Se r. dans un lieu,* to make one's way to a place. **Se rendre à une assignation,** to keep an appointment. **2.** (*a*) To surrender; to give in. **Rendez-vous!** hands up! (*b*) **Se rendre à la raison,** to yield to reason.

   rendu, *a.* **Rendu (de fatigue),** exhausted.

rêne, *s.f.* Usu. *pl.* Rein.

renégat, *s.* Renegade, turncoat.

renfermer, *v.tr.* **I.** To shut up again. **2.** (*a*) To shut up. (*b*) *Se r. dans ses instructions,* to confine oneself to one's instructions. **3.** To contain, comprise.

   renfermé. I. *a.* Uncommunicative. **2.** *s.m.* **Sentir le renfermé,** to smell stuffy.

renflement, *s.m.* **I.** Swelling, bulging. **2.** Bulge.

renfler, *v.tr. & i.* To swell (out).

renfoncement, *s.m.* **I.** Driving in deeper. **2.** Hollow, recess.

renfoncer, *v.tr.* (Conj. like ENFONCER) To knock in, drive in. **Renfoncer son chapeau,** to pull down one's hat.

renforcer, *v.tr.* (Conj. like FORCER) (*a*) To reinforce. (*b*) To strengthen. (*c*) To intensify.

   se renforcer, to gather strength.

   renforcé, *a.* Stout; reinforced.

renfort, *s.m.* **I.** Reinforcement(s). **En renfort,** in support. **2.** Strengthening piece; backing.

renfrogné, *a.* Frowning; sullen; glum.

renfrogner (se), *v.pr.* To frown, scowl.

rengager, *v.tr.* (Conj. like ENGAGER) (*a*) To re-engage; to renew. (*b*) *v.i.* To re-enlist.

   se rengager, to re-enlist, rejoin.

rengaine, *s.f.* **F: Vieille rengaine,** old story; threadbare story.

rengainer, *v.tr.* To sheathe.

rengorgement, *s.m.* Strut; swagger.

rengorger (se), *v.pr.* (Conj. like ENGORGER) To strut, swagger.

reniement, *s.m.* **I.** Disowning; repudiation. **2.** (*a*) Disavowal. (*b*) Abjuration.

renier, *v.tr.* **I.** To disown; to repudiate. **2.** (*a*) To disavow. (*b*) To abjure.

reniflement, *s.m.* **I.** (*a*) Sniffing, snuffling. (*b*) Snivelling. **2.** Sniff, snort.

renifler. I. *v.i.* (*a*) To sniff, snort. (*b*) To snivel. **2.** *v.tr.* (*a*) To sniff (up). (*b*) To sniff, smell.

renne, *s.m.* *Z:* Reindeer.

renom, *s.m.* Renown, fame.

renommer, *v.tr.* To reappoint.

   renommé, *a.* Renowned, famed.

   renommée, *s.f.* (*a*) Renown, fame; good name. (*b*) *Connaître qn de r.,* to know s.o. by repute.

renoncement, *s.m.* **I.** Renouncing. **2.** (*a*) Self-denial. (*b*) Renunciation.

renoncer, *v.* (n. renonçons) **I.** *v.ind.tr.* (*a*) **R. à qch.,** to renounce, give up, forgo, sth. **Y renoncer,** to give it up. (*b*) (At cards) To revoke. **2.** *v.tr.* **R. sa foi,** to renounce one's faith.

renonciation, *s.f.* Renunciation, abnegation.

renouer, *v.tr.* To renew, resume.

renouveau, *s.m.* **F: R. de jeunesse,** renewal of youth.

renouvelable, *a.* Renewable.

renouveler, *v.tr.* (je renouvelle) **I.** (*a*) To renew, to renovate. (*b*) **R. son personnel,** to renew one's staff. (*c*) **R. la face du pays,** to alter the appearance of the country. **2.** To renew; to revive. **Com: R. une commande,** to repeat an order. **3.** **R. de zèle,** to act with renewed zeal.

   se renouveler. I. To be renewed. **2.** To recur; to happen again.

renouvellement, *s.m.* **I.** (*a*) Renovation. (*b*) Complete change. **2.** Renewal.

rénovateur, -trice. I. *a.* Renovating. **2.** *s.* Renovator, restorer.

rénovation, *s.f.* **I.** Renovation, restoration. **2.** Renewing, renewal.

renseignement, *s.m.* (Piece of) information, (piece of) intelligence. **Aller aux renseignements,** to make inquiries. *Mil:* **Service de(s) renseignements,** intelligence.

renseigner, *v.tr.* **R. qn sur qch.,** to give s.o. information about sth. *On vous a mal renseigné,* you have been misinformed.

   se renseigner *sur qch.,* to make inquiries, find out, about sth.

rente, *s.f.* **I.** *Pol.Ec:* Revenue, rent. **2.** Usu. *pl.* (Unearned) income. **Vivre de ses rentes,** to live on one's private means. **3.** Annuity, pension, allowance. **4.** **Rente (s) (sur l'État),** (government) stock(s).

rentier, *s.* **I.** (*a*) *Fin:* Stockholder, fund-holder. (*b*) Annuitant. **2.** *F:* Person of independent means.

rentrer. I. *v.i.* (Aux. *être*) **I.** (*a*) To re-enter; to go in again. *R. dans ses droits,* to recover one's rights. (*b*) To return home. (*c*) To re-open, to resume. (*d*) **Faire rentrer ses fonds,** to call in one's money. **2.** (*a*) To

enter, go in. *R. en soi-même,* to retire within oneself. (*b*) *F:* **Les jambes me rentrent dans le corps,** I am too tired to stand. (*c*) *Cela ne rentre pas dans mes fonctions,* that does not fall within my province.
II. **rentrer,** *v.tr.* To take in, bring in. *R. la récolte,* to gather in the harvest.

rentrée, *s.f.* **1.** (*a*) Return, home-coming. (*b*) Re-opening (of schools). **La rentrée des classes,** the beginning of term. **2.** (*a*) Taking in (of money). (*b*) Getting in (of crops). **3.** Coming in.

renverse, *s.f.* **Tomber à la renverse,** to fall backwards.

renversement, *s.m.* **1.** Reversal, inversion. **2.** Overthrow.

renverser. 1. *v.tr.* (*a*) To reverse, invert. *F:* **Renverser les rôles,** to turn the tables. (*b*) To turn upside down. *Com:* **"Ne pas renverser,"** 'this side up.' (*c*) To knock over; to overturn, upset; to spill. (*d*) To overthrow. (*e*) *F:* To astonish. **2.** *v.i.* To overturn, upset.
se renverser, to fall over; to upset. **Se renverser sur la chaise,** to lean back in one's chair.

renversé, *a.* **1.** Inverted, reversed. **2. Il avait le visage renversé,** he looked very much upset.

renvoi, *s.m.* **1.** Return(ing), sending back. **2.** Dismissal (of servant). **3.** Putting off, postponement. **4.** Referring, reference.

renvoyer, *v.tr.* (Conj. like ENVOYER) **1.** To send back; to return. *F:* **Être renvoyé de Caïphe à Pilate,** to be driven from pillar to post. **2.** (*a*) To send away. (*b*) To dismiss. **3.** To put off, postpone. **4.** To refer.

réorganisation, *s.f.* Reorganization.

réorganiser, *v.tr.* To reorganize.

réouverture, *s.f.* Reopening; resumption.

repaire, *s.m.* Den; lair; haunt.

repaître, *v.tr.* (Conj. like CONNAÎTRE) (*a*) To feed (animal). (*b*) *R. ses yeux de qch.,* to feast one's eyes on sth.
se repaître. (*a*) To eat one's fill. (*b*) *Se r. de qch.,* to feed on sth.

repu, *a.* Satiated, full; sated.

répandre, *v.tr.* **1.** To pour out; to spill, shed. **2.** To spread, scatter; to give off (scent). **3.** To scatter, distribute.
se répandre. (*a*) To spill; to run over. (*b*) To spread. *Sa chevelure se répandit sur ses épaules,* her hair came down over her shoulders.

répandu, *a.* Wide-spread, prevalent.

reparaître, *v.i.* (Conj. like CONNAÎTRE. Aux. usu. *avoir*) To reappear.

réparateur, -trice. 1. *a.* Repairing, restoring. **2.** *s.* Repairer, mender.

réparation, *s.f.* Reparation. **1.** Repairing. **Être en réparation,** to be under repair. **2.** Atonement, amends.

réparer, *v.tr.* **1.** To repair, mend. *R. ses*

pertes, to make good one's losses. **2.** To make amends; to put right.

reparler, *v.i.* To speak again.

repartir, *v.i.* (Conj. like MENTIR) **1.** (Aux. *être*) To set out again. **2.** (Aux. *avoir*) To retort, reply.
repartie, *s.f.* Retort, rejoinder.

répartir, *v.tr.* (Conj. regular) **1.** To distribute, divide, share out. **2.** To apportion; to allot.

répartition, *s.f.* **1.** Distribution; dividing up; sharing out. **2.** Apportionment; allotment.

repas, *s.m.* Meal, repast.

repasser. 1. *v.i.* (Aux. usu. *être*) To repass. *R. chez qn,* to call on s.o. again. **2.** *v.tr.* (*a*) To repass; to cross (over) again. (*b*) *R. qch. dans son esprit,* to go over sth. in one's mind. (*c*) *Le batelier nous repassera,* the boatman will take us back. (*d*) To sharpen, grind. (*e*) To iron (clothes). **Fer à repasser,** flat-iron.

repêcher, *v.tr.* (*a*) To fish up (again), out (again). (*b*) *F:* To rescue. *F:* to fish out (drowning man).

repeindre, *v.tr.* (Conj. like PEINDRE) To repaint.

repenser, *v.i. Je n'y ai pas repensé,* I did not give it another thought.

repentant, *a.* Repentant.

repentir (se). 1. *v.pr.* (Conj. like MENTIR) *Se r. de qch.,* to repent sth.; to be sorry for sth.
II. **repentir,** *s.m.* Repentance.

répercussion, *s.f.* Repercussion; reverberation.

répercuter, *v.tr.* To reverberate.
se répercuter. 1. To reverberate. **2.** To have repercussions.

reperdre, *v.tr.* To lose again.

repère, *s.m.* **Point de repère,** guide mark; landmark.

repérer, *v.tr.* (je repère; je repérerai) *Artil:* To locate, *F:* to spot.

répertoire, *s.m.* **1.** List, catalogue. **2.** Repertory, repository. **3.** *Th:* Repertoire.

répéter, *v.tr.* (je répète; je répéterai) (*a*) To repeat; to say (over) again. **Je ne me le ferai pas répéter,** I shall not require to be told twice. (*b*) *Th:* To rehearse.
se répéter. 1. To repeat oneself. **2.** To repeat, recur.

répétiteur, -trice, *a. & s.* (*a*) (Maître) répétiteur, (maîtresse) répétitrice, assistant-master, assistant-mistress. (*b*) Private tutor; coach.

répétition, *s.f.* **1.** (*a*) Repetition. **Fusil à répétition,** repeating rifle. (*b*) Reproduction, replica. **2.** *Th:* Rehearsal. **3.** *Sch:* Donner des répétitions, to give private lessons.

repeuplement, *s.m.* Repeopling; restocking.

repeupler, *v.tr.* To repeople; to restock.

répit, *s.m.* Respite; breathing-space.

replacer, *v.tr.* (Conj. like PLACER) To replace; to put (sth.) back in its place.

replanter, *v.tr.* To replant.

replet, -ète, *a.* Stoutish, F: podgy.

réplétion, *s.f.* **1.** (*a*) Repletion. (*b*) Surfeit. **2.** Corpulence.

repli, *s.m.* **1.** Fold, crease. **2.** Winding, bend (of river). **3.** *Mil:* Falling back.

replier, *v.tr.* To fold up (again); to tuck in (edge). *R. un parapluie,* to close an umbrella.
se replier. 1. (*a*) To fold up, turn back. (*b*) To wind, turn, bend. **2.** *Se r. sur soi-même,* to retire within oneself. **3.** *Mil:* To withdraw.

réplique, *s.f* **1.** Retort, rejoinder. Avoir la réplique prompte, to be ready with an answer. **2.** *Th:* Cue. **3.** *Art:* Replica.

répliquer, *v.i.* To retort, rejoin.

replonger, *v.* (Conj. like PLONGER) **1.** *v.tr.* To replunge. **2.** *v.i.* To dive in again.

repolir, *v.tr.* To repolish.

répondre. 1. *v.tr.* To answer, reply, respond. **2.** *v.ind.tr. R. à une question,* to answer a question. *R. à une demande,* to comply with a request. *R. à l'attente,* to fall short of expectation. **4.** *v.i. R. de qn,* to answer for s.o. *F: Je vous en réponds!* rather !

réponse, *s.f.* (*a*) Answer, reply. (*b*) Response (to an appeal). (*c*) Responsiveness, response.

reportage, *s.m. Journ:* **1.** Reporting. **2.** Report. **3.** *W.Tel:* Running commentary.

reporter, *v.tr.* **1.** To take back. **2.** (*a*) *R. qch. à plus tard,* to postpone sth. until later. (*b*) *Com:* To carry forward (total).

repos, *s.m.* **1.** (*a*) Rest, repose. En repos, at rest. (*b*) Pause, rest. **2.** Peace, tranquillity. Valeur de tout repos, gilt-edged security.

reposant, *a.* Restful.

reposer. I. *v.tr.* **1.** To put back; to replace. **2.** (*a*) *R. ses regards sur qch.,* to let one's glance rest on sth. (*b*) *R. l'esprit,* to rest the mind.
II. reposer, *v.i.* To lie, rest. *Bruit qui ne repose sur rien,* unfounded report.
se reposer. 1. To alight, settle, again. **2.** (*a*) To rest, repose. (*b*) *Se r. sur qn,* to rely upon s.o.

repoussant, *a.* Repulsive, repellent.

repousser. 1. *v.tr.* (*a*) To push back, thrust aside, repulse. *R. une accusation,* to deny a charge. *R. une mesure,* to reject a measure. (*b*) To be repellent to; to repel. **2.** *v.tr.* To shoot (up) again.

repoussoir, *s.m.* Set-off, foil.

répréhensible, *a.* Reprehensible.

répréhensiblement, *adv.* Reprehensibly.

répréhension, *s.f.* Reprehension.

reprendre, *v.* (Conj. like PRENDRE) **1.** *v.tr.* (*a*) To take again, retake. (*b*) *R. sa place,* to resume one's seat. (*c*) To take back. (*d*) To resume, take up again. **Reprendre la mer,** to put out to sea again. *R. des forces,* to regain strength. *Abs. Oui, madame, reprit-il,* yes, madam, he replied. (*e*) To reprove, admonish. **2.** *v.i.* (*a*) To recommence,

return. *Les affaires reprennent,* business is improving. (*b*) (Of liquid) To freeze, set, again.
se reprendre. 1. To recover oneself, to pull oneself together. **2.** To correct oneself. **3.** *Se r. à espérer,* to begin to hope again. **4.** S'y reprendre à plusieurs fois, to make several attempts.

repris, *s.* Repris de justice, habitual criminal; old offender.

reprise, *s.f.* **1.** Retaking, recapture. **2.** (*a*) Resumption, renewal. (*b*) *R. du froid,* new spell of cold. (*c*) *Box:* Round. *Fenc:* Bout. **A plusieurs reprises,** on several occasions. (*d*) Chanson à reprises, catch (song). **3.** (i) Darning, mending; (ii) darn.

représailles [-za:j], *s.f.pl.* Reprisals, retaliation.

représentant, *s.* Representative.

représentatif, *a.* Representative.

représentation, *s.f.* **1.** (*a*) *Pol:* Representation. (*b*) *Com:* Agency. **2.** *Th:* Performance. **3.** Remonstrance, protest. *Faire des représentations à qn,* to make representations to s.o.

représenter, *v.tr.* **1.** To present again. **2.** To represent. (*a*) To depict, portray. *Représentez-vous mon étonnement,* picture my astonishment. (*b*) To represent, stand for. **3.** *Th:* (*a*) To perform, act. (*b*) To act, personate. **4.** *R. qch. à qn,* to represent, point out, sth. to s.o.
se représenter. *Se r. comme officier,* to represent oneself as an officer.

répressif, *a.* Repressive.

répression, *s.f.* Repression.

réprimande, *s.f.* Reprimand, reproof.

réprimander, *v.tr.* To reprimand, reprove.

réprimer, *v.tr.* To repress.

repris, reprise. See REPRENDRE.

repriser, *v.tr.* To mend, darn.

reprit. See REPRENDRE.

réprobateur, -trice, *a.* Reproachful; reproving.

réprobation, *s.f.* Reprobation.

reproche, *s.m.* Reproach. Vie sans reproche, blameless life.

reprocher, *v.tr.* **1.** To reproach. Je n'ai rien à me reprocher, I have nothing to blame myself for. **2.** *R. un plaisir à qn,* to grudge s.o. a pleasure.

reproducteur, -trice, *a.* Reproductive.

reproductif, *a.* Reproductive.

reproduction, *s.f.* **1.** Reproduction. **2.** Copy.

reproduire, *v.tr.* (Conj. like CONDUIRE) To reproduce.
se reproduire. 1. To recur; to happen again. **2.** To breed, multiply.

réprouver, *v.tr.* To reprobate; to disapprove of.

réprouvé, *s.* Outcast; reprobate.

reptile, *s.m.* Reptile.

repu, -s, -t, etc. See REPAÎTRE.

républicain, *a. & s.* Republican.
republier, *v.tr.* To republish.
république, *s.f.* (*a*) Republic. (*b*) Commonwealth, community.
répudiation, *s.f.* **1.** Repudiation. **2.** Renunciation.
répudier, *v.tr.* **1.** To repudiate (wife, opinion). **2.** To renounce.
répugnance, *s.f.* **1.** Repugnance. (*a*) Dislike; aversion. (*b*) Loathing. **2.** *R. à faire qch.*, reluctance to do sth.
répugnant, *a.* Repugnant,l oathsome.
répugner, *v.i.* **1.** *R. à qch.*, to feel repugnance to sth. *R. à faire qch.*, to feel reluctant to do sth. **2.** *R. à qn*, to be repugnant to s.o. *Impers. Il me répugne de le faire*, I am reluctant to do it.
répulsif, *a.* Repulsive.
répulsion, *s.f.* Repulsion.
réputation, *s.f.* Reputation, repute. **Jouir d'une bonne réputation,** to bear a good character. **Se faire une réputation,** to make a name for oneself. **Perdre qn de réputation,** to ruin s.o.'s character.
réputer, *v.tr.* To repute, consider, think.
réputé, *a.* Well-known; of repute.
requérir, *v.tr.* (Conj. like ACQUÉRIR) **1.** To ask for; to solicit. **2.** *R. qn de faire qch.*, to call upon s.o. to do sth.
requis, *a.* Required, requisite.
requête, *s.f.* Request, suit, petition.
requin, *s.m.* *Ich:* Shark. **Peau de requin,** shagreen. **2.** *F:* Shark, swindler.
requis. See REQUÉRIR.
réquisition, *s.f.* (*a*) Requisitioning, commandeering. (*b*) Requisition.
réquisitionner, *v.tr.* To requisition; to commandeer.
réquisitoire, *s.m.* Charge, indictment.
rescapé, *a. & s.* (Person) rescued; survivor.
rescinder, *v.tr.* To rescind, annul.
rescision, *s.f.* Rescission, annulment.
rescousse, *s.f.* **Aller à la rescousse de qn,** to go to s.o.'s rescue.
réseau, *s.m.* (*a*) Network, system (of roads). (*b*) *Mil:* *Réseau(x) de fil de fer*, wire entanglements.
réséda, *s.m.* *Bot:* Mignonette.
réservation, *s.f.* Reservation. **Réservation faite de . . . ,** without prejudice to . . .
réserve, *s.f.* **1.** (*a*) Reserving, reservation. (*b*) Reserve. **En réserve,** in reserve. **Pièces de réserve,** spare parts. **2.** (*a*) **Sous (la) réserve de qch.,** subject to sth. (*b*) Reserve, caution; coyness. **3.** (*a*) Reserve (of provisions). (*b*) *Ven:* Preserve.
réserver, *v.tr.* (*a*) To reserve; to save up; to keep back. **Pêche réservée,** fishing preserve. (*b*) To set apart.
se réserver *pour qch.*, to reserve oneself, save oneself, hold back, wait, for sth.
réservé, *a.* Reserved. (*a*) Guarded. (*b*) Shy. (*c*) Stand-offish.
réserviste, *s.m.* *Mil:* Reservist.

réservoir, *s.m.* **1.** Reservoir. **2.** Tank, cistern.
résidence, *s.f.* Residence. **1.** Residing. **2.** Dwelling-place, abode.
résident, *s.m.* *Adm:* Resident.
résider, *v.i.* **1.** To reside, dwell, live. **2.** *La difficulté réside en ceci*, the difficulty lies in this.
résidu, *s.m.* Residue.
résignation, *s.f.* Resignation.
résigner, *v.tr.* To resign; to give up.
se résigner *à qch.*, to resign oneself to sth.
résigné, *a.* Resigned; meek.
résiliation, *s.f.* Cancellation.
résilience, *s.f.* *Mec:* Resilience.
résilier, *v.tr.* To annul, cancel.
résine, *s.f.* Resin.
résineux, *a.* Resinous.
résistance, *s.f.* Resistance. **1.** Opposition. **2.** (*a*) Strength, toughness. (*b*) Staying power, stamina, endurance. **Pièce de résistance,** principal feature.
résistant, *a.* Resistant; strong, stout.
résister, *v.ind.tr.* To resist. (*a*) *R. à qn*, to offer resistance to s.o. (*b*) *R. à qch.*, to withstand; to hold out against.
résolu, -s, -t, etc. See RÉSOUDRE.
résoluble, *a.* **1.** Solvable. **2.** Terminable.
résolument, *adv.* Resolutely.
résolution, *s.f.* **1.** (*a*) Solution (of problem). (*b*) Termination (of agreement). **2.** Resolution, determination. (*a*) Resolve. (*b*) Resoluteness. (*c*) **Adopter une résolution,** to adopt a resolution.
résonance, *s.f.* Resonance.
résonner, *v.i.* To resound.
résoudre, *v.tr.* (*pr.p.* résolvant; *p.p.* (i) résolu, (ii) *Ph:* résous, -oute; *pr.ind.* je résous) **1.** (*a*) *R. qch. en qch.*, to resolve sth. into sth. (*b*) *Jur:* To annul, terminate. **2.** To resolve, clear up; to solve; to settle. **3.** *R. de partir*, to resolve on going.
se résoudre. 1. *Se r. en qch.*, to resolve into sth. **2.** *Se r. à faire qch.*, to make up one's mind to do sth.
résolu, *a.* Resolute, determined.
respect [-spε], *s.m.* Respect, regard. **Respect de soi,** self-respect. **Respect humain,** common decency. **Tenir qn en respect,** to keep s.o. at a respectful distance. **Sauf votre respect,** saving your presence.
respectabilité, *s.f.* Respectability.
respectable, *a.* **1.** Respectable; worthy of respect. **2.** *F:* *Nombre r.*, fair number.
respectablement, *adv.* Respectably.
respecter, *v.tr.* To respect, have regard for.
respectif, *a.* Respective.
respectivement, *adv.* Respectively.
respectueusement, *adv.* Respectfully.
respectueux, *a.* Respectful; dutiful.
respirateur, *s.m.* Respirator.
respiration, *s.f.* Respiration, breathing. **Couper la respiration à qn,** to take s.o.'s breath away.

respiratoire, *a.* Respiratory.
respirer. **1.** *v.i.* To breathe. *R. longuement*, to draw a long breath. *Laissez-moi r.*, let me take breath. **2.** *v.tr.* (*a*) To breathe (in); to inhale. (*b*) *R. la vengeance*, to breathe (out) vengeance.
resplendir, *v.i.* To be resplendent, to shine.
resplendissant, *a.* Resplendent; dazzling.
responsabilité, *s.f.* Responsibility; liability.
responsable, *a.* Responsible, answerable.
ressac [-sak], *s.m.* *Nau:* **1.** Undertow. **2.** Surf.
ressaisir, *v.tr.* To seize again; to recapture.
  se ressaisir, to regain one's self-control.
ressemblance, *s.f.* Resemblance, likeness.
ressemblant, *a.* Like, alike.
ressembler, *v.ind.tr.* *R. à qn*, to resemble, to be like, s.o. *Cela ne vous ressemble pas du tout, F:* it isn't a bit like you.
  se ressembler, to be (a)like.
ressentiment, *s.m.* Resentment.
ressentir, *v.tr.* (Conj. like MENTIR) (*a*) To feel. (*b*) To resent. (*c*) To feel, experience.
  se ressentir *d'un accident*, to feel the effects of an accident.
resserrement, *s.m.* **1.** Contracting, contraction, tightening. **2.** Tightness; heaviness, oppression.
resserrer, *v.tr.* **1.** To contract, confine, close up. **2.** To tie (up) again; to tighten.
  se resserrer. **1.** To contract, shrink. **2.** To retrench; to curtail one's expenses.
resserré, *a.* Confined, cramped.
ressort[1], *s.m.* **1.** (*a*) Elasticity, springiness. (*b*) Spring. *Grand r.*, mainspring. *L'intérêt est un puissant r.*, interest is a powerful motive. **2.** *Jur:* (*a*) Province, scope, competence. (*b*) **En dernier ressort,** (i) without appeal; (ii) *F:* in the last resort.
ressort[2]. See RESSORTIR.
ressortir, *v.i.* (Conj. like MENTIR) **1.** (*a*) (Aux. *être*) To come, go, out again. (*b*) *v.tr.* To bring out again. **2.** (Aux. usu. *être*) (*a*) *Faire r. un fait*, to emphasize a fact. (*b*) To result, follow.
ressource, *s.f.* Resource. **1.** (*a*) Resourcefulness. (*b*) *Être ruiné sans ressource*, to be irretrievably ruined. **2.** Expedient, shift. **En dernière ressource,** in the last resort. **3.** *pl.* Resources, means. **4.** *Av:* Flattening out.
ressusciter. **1.** *v.tr* (*a*) To resuscitate; to restore to life. (*b*) *F:* To revive **2.** *v.i.* To resuscitate, revive.
restant. **1.** *a.* (*a*) Remaining, left. (*b*) *Poste restante,* 'to be called for.' **2.** *s.m.* Remainder, rest.
restaurant. **1.** *a.* Restoring, restorative. **2.** *s.m.* (*a*) Restorative. (*b*) Restaurant.
restaurateur, *s.m.* Keeper of a restaurant.
restauration, *s.f.* Restoration; restoring.
restaurer, *v.tr.* (*a*) To restore; to re-establish. (*b*) To refresh.
  se restaurer, to take refreshment.

reste, *s.m.* **1.** Rest, remainder, remains. **Être en reste,** to be behindhand. **Et le reste,** and so on. **De reste,** over and above. **Au reste, du reste,** besides, moreover. **2.** *pl.* (*a*) Remnants, remains; leavings. (*b*) **Restes** mortels, mortal remains.
rester, *v.i.* (Aux. *être*) To remain. **1.** To be left. (Il) **reste à savoir,** it remains to be seen. **2.** (*a*) To stay, remain (behind). **En rester là,** to stop at that point. (*b*) *Pred.* *R. tranquille,* to keep still. **3.** (Aux. may be *avoir*) To stay, dwell.
restituer, *v.tr.* **1.** (*a*) To restore (building). (*b*) *Jur:* To reinstate. **2.** To restore; to return; to make restitution of.
restitution, *s.f.* Restoration.
restreindre, *v.tr.* (Conj. like PEINDRE) To restrict; to curtail.
  se restreindre, to cut down expenses; to retrench.
restreint, *a.* Restricted, limited.
restrictif, *a.* Restrictive.
restriction, *s.f.* Restriction, limitation. **Restriction mentale,** mental reservation.
résultant, *a.* Resultant; resulting; consequent.
résultat, *s.m.* Result, outcome.
résulter, *v.i.* (Used only in the third pers. Aux. usu. *être*) To result, follow.
résumer, *v.tr.* To summarize; to sum up.
  résumé, *s.m.* Summary, abstract, résumé. **En résumé,** to sum up.
résurrection, *s.f.* Resurrection.
rétablir, *v.tr.* To re-establish, restore.
  se rétablir. **1.** (*a*) To recover; to get well again. (*b*) *L'ordre se rétablit,* order is being restored. **2.** To re-establish oneself.
rétablissement, *s.m.* **1.** Re-establishment; restoration; reinstatement. **2.** Recovery (after illness).
rétameur, *s.m.* Tinker.
retard, *s.m.* Delay, slowness; backwardness. **Le train a du retard,** the train is behind time. **En retard,** late, behindhand. *Votre montre a dix minutes de r.*, your watch is ten minutes slow.
retardataire. **1.** *a.* (*a*) Late, behind time; behindhand. (*b*) Backward. **2.** *s.* (*a*) Latecomer. (*b*) Loiterer; laggard.
retardateur, -trice, *a.* Retarding.
retarder. **1.** *v.tr.* (*a*) To retard, delay; to make late (*b*) To delay, put off. (*c*) *R. la pendule,* to put back the clock **2.** *v.i.* To be late, slow.
retenir, *v.tr.* (Conj. like TENIR) **1.** (*a*) To hold back; to detain. *R. l'attention,* to hold the attention. **Retenir qn prisonnier,** to keep s.o. prisoner. *Nau: Retenu par les glaces,* ice-bound. (*b*) To hold in position; to secure. **2.** To retain. (*a*) *R. son accent anglais,* to retain one's English accent. (*b*) To engage (a servant); to reserve (a seat). **3.** To restrain, check. *R. un cri,* to stifle ⸫ cry. *R. son haleine,* to hold one's breath.
  se retenir. **1.** *Se r. à qch.,* to cling to sth.

2. To hold oneself in. *Se r. de faire qch.*, to refrain from doing sth.
retenu, *a.* Prudent, circumspect.
retenue, *s.f.* **1.** (*a*) Withholding, deduction. (*b*) Sum kept back. **2.** *Sch:* Detention. **3.** Reserve, discretion. **4.** (*a*) Holding back. (*b*) Holding up.
retentir, *v.i.* To (re)sound, echo, ring.
retentissant, *a.* Resounding, ringing.
retentissement, *s.m.* Resounding sound. *Avoir peu de r.*, to create little stir.
réticence, *s.f.* Reticence, reserve.
réticulation, *s.f.* Reticulation.
réticule, *s.m.* Reticule, hand-bag.
réticulé, *a.* Reticulate(d).
rétif, *a.* Restive, stubborn.
rétine, *s.f. Anat:* Retina.
retirer, *v.tr.* **1.** (*a*) To pull out; to withdraw. *R. son habit*, to take off one's coat. (*b*) *R. un profit de qch.*, to derive a profit from sth. **2.** *R. qch. à qn*, to withdraw sth. from s.o.; to take sth. back from s.o. *R. sa main*, to draw one's hand away.
   se retirer. 1. To retire, withdraw. **2.** (Of waters) To subside; (of sea) to recede.
   retiré, *a.* Retired, remote.
retomber, *v.i.* (Aux. usu. *être*) **1.** To fall (down) again. **2.** To fall (back). *R. sur sa chaise*, to sink back into one's chair. *Faire r. la faute sur qn*, to lay the blame on s.o. **3.** To hang down.
retordre, *v.tr. F:* Il vous donnera du fil à retordre, you have your work cut out with him.
retors, *a.* Crafty, wily, intriguing.
retouche, *s.f.* Slight alteration; retouching.
retoucher, *v.tr.* To retouch, touch up.
retour, *s.m.* **1.** (*a*) Twisting, winding. *Tours et retours*, twists and turns. (*b*) Turn, vicissitude. (*c*) Recurrence. **2.** Return. *Dès mon retour*, as soon as I am back. *Voyage de retour*, return journey. *Être de retour*, to be back (again). *Être sur le retour*, to be past middle age. *Être perdu sans retour*, to be irretrievably lost. **3.** Return (for a service). *Payer qch. de retour*, to requite sth.
retourner. 1. *v.tr.* (*a*) To turn inside out. (*b*) To turn over. *R. une carte*, to turn up a card. *F: Cela m'a retourné les sangs*, it gave me quite a turn. (*c*) To turn round. *R. la tête*, to turn one's head. *R. une situation*, to reverse a situation. **2.** *v.tr. R. qch. à qn*, to return sth. to s.o. **3.** *v.i.* (Aux. *être*) (*a*) To return; to go back. (*b*) *R. sur qn*, to recoil upon s.o. **4.** *Impers. De quoi retourne-t-il? F:* what is it all about?
   se retourner. (*a*) To turn (round); to turn over. *F: Avoir le temps de se retourner*, to have time to look round. (*b*) To look round. (*c*) To round (*contre qn*, on s.o.).
retracer, *v.tr.* (Conj. like TRACER) To retrace.

rétracter[1], *v.tr.* To retract, to draw in (claws).
rétracter[2], *v.tr.* To retract; to withdraw, recant.
retrait, *s.m.* **1.** Shrinkage, shrinking. **2.** (*a*) Withdrawal; cancelling. (*b*) Redemption, repurchase. **3.** Recess (in wall). *En retrait*, recessed; set back.
retraite, *s.f.* **1.** Retreat, retirement. **2.** Tattoo. *Battre la retraite*, to beat the tattoo. *Navy:* Coup de canon de retraite, evening gun. **3.** (*a*) Retirement (from active life). *Caisse de retraite*, superannuation fund. *Retraite de vieillesse*, old-age pension. (*b*) *Vivre dans la retraite*, to live in retirement. **4.** (*a*) Retreat; place of retirement. (*b*) (Place of) shelter; refuge; lair.
retraiter, *v.tr.* To pension.
retranchement, *s.m.* **1.** Cutting off; stopping; excision. **2.** *Mil:* Entrenchment.
retrancher, *v.tr.* **1.** (*a*) *R. qch. de qch.*, to cut off sth. from sth. (*b*) *R. qch. à qn*, to dock s.o. of sth. **2.** To entrench.
   se retrancher, to retrench; to curtail one's expenses.
rétrécir. 1. *v.tr.* To narrow; to contract; to shrink. **2.** *v.i. & pr.* To contract; to grow narrow.
   rétréci, *a.* Narrow, contracted.
rétrécissement, *s.m.* **1.** (*a*) Contracting. (*b*) Shrinking. **2.** Narrow part, neck.
rétribuer, *v.tr.* To remunerate, pay.
rétribution, *s.f.* Remuneration; salary.
rétroactif, *a.* Retrospective.
rétrograde, *a.* Retrograde, backward.
rétrograder. 1. *v.i.* To retrogress; to go back. **2.** *v.tr.* To reduce to a lower rank.
rétrogressif, *a.* Retrogressive.
rétrogression, *s.f.* Retrogression.
rétrospectif, *a.* Retrospective.
rétrospectivement, *adv.* Retrospectively.
retrousser, *v.tr.* To turn up, roll up.
retrouver, *v.tr.* (*a*) To find (again); to meet (with) again. (*b*) *Aller retrouver qn*, to go and join s.o.
   se retrouver. 1. To find one's bearings. *Je ne puis m'y retrouver!* I can't make it out! **2.** To recover oneself. **3.** To meet again.
réunion, *s.f.* Reunion. **1.** Bringing together, reuniting. **2.** (*a*) Coming together. *Salle de réunion*, assembly room. (*b*) Assembly, gathering, meeting.
réunir, *v.tr.* To (re)unite; to join together.
   se réunir. (*a*) To meet; to gather together. (*b*) To join together.
réussir. 1. *v.i.* (*a*) *Cela lui a mal réussi*, it turned out badly for him. (*b*) *R. dans qch.*, to succeed in sth. (*c*) *La pièce a réussi*, the play is a success. **2.** *v.tr.* To make a success of.
   réussi, *a.* Successful.
réussite, *s.f.* **1.** Issue, result, upshot. **2.** Success. **3.** *Cards:* Patience.
revaloir, *v.tr.* (Conj. like VALOIR) To return,

pay back in kind. **Je vous revaudrai cela!** I'll be even with you!

revanche, *s.f.* I. Revenge. **Jouer la revanche,** to play the return game. 2. Requital; return service. **En revanche,** on the other hand.

rêvasser, *v.i.* To muse; to be wool-gathering.

rêvasserie, *s.f.* I. Musing, day-dreaming. 2. *pl.* Day-dreams, idle musings.

rêve, *s.m.* I. Dream. 2. Day-dream. **C'est le rêve!** it is ideal.

revêche, *a.* I. Harsh, rough. 2. Crabbed, cross-grained, cantankerous.

réveil [-vɛːj], *s.m.* I. (*a*) Waking, awakening. (*b*) *Mil:* **Sonner le réveil,** to sound reveille. 2. Alar(u)m(-clock).

réveille-matin [-vɛj-] *s.m.inv.* = RÉVEIL 2.

réveiller [-vɛje], *v.tr.* I. To awake; to wake up; to rouse. 2. To awaken, stir up, rouse. **se réveiller.** I. To wake (up). 2. (Of feelings) To be awakened.

réveillon [-vɛjɔ̃], *s.m.* Midnight supper.

réveillonner [-vɛjɔ-], *v.i.* To see the New Year in.

révélateur, -trice. I. *a.* Revealing, tell-tale. 2. *s.* Revealer. 3. *s.m. Phot:* Developer.

révélation, *s.f.* Revelation, disclosure.

révéler, *v.tr.* (je révèle; je révélerai) (*a*) To reveal, disclose. (*b*) To show; to betray, reveal. **se révéler.** I. To reveal oneself. 2. To be revealed; to come to light.

revenant. I. *a.* Pleasing, prepossessing. 2. *s.m.* Ghost.

revendication, *s.f.* Claim, demand.

revendiquer, *v.tr.* To claim, demand; to assert (one's rights).

revendre, *v.tr.* To resell.

revenir, *v.i.* (Conj. like VENIR. Aux. *être*) I. To return; to come back. **Esprit qui revient,** ghost that walks. **Revenir sur ses pas,** to retrace one's steps. **Revenir sur une promesse,** to go back on a promise. 2. **Revenir à qn,** (*a*) To return, come back to s.o. *A chacun ce qui lui revient,* to each one his due. (*b*) *Son visage me revient,* I am beginning to recall his face. (*c*) **Son visage ne me revient pas,** I don't like his looks. 3. *R. d'une maladie,* to get over an illness. *R. d'une erreur,* to realize one's mistake. **Je n'en reviens pas!** I can't get over it! **Revenir à soi,** to recover consciousness. 4. **En revenir à qch.,** *y revenir,* to revert to sth. 5. (*a*) To cost. (*b*) *Cela revient au même,* it comes to the same thing.

revenu, *s.m.* I. Income; revenue. 2. *Com:* (i) Yield (of investment); (ii) *pl.* incomings.

rêver. I. *v.i.* To dream. (*a*) *R. de qch.,* to dream about sth. (*b*) *R. à qch.,* to ponder over sth. (*c*) **Rêver tout éveillé,** to be full of idle fancies. 2. *v.tr.* To dream. *F:* **Vous l'avez rêvé!** you must have dreamt it!

réverbération, *s.f.* Reverberation.

réverbère, *s.m.* Street-lamp.

réverbérer, *v.* (il réverbère; il réverbérera) To reverberate.

révéremment, *adv.* Reverently.

révérence, *s.f.* I. Reverence. 2. Bow; curtsey.

révérenciel, -elle, *a.* Reverential.

révérencieux, *a.* Over-polite; ceremonious.

révérend, *a. Ecc:* Reverend.

révérer, *v.tr.* (je révère; je révérerai) To revere; to reverence.

rêverie, *s.f.* Reverie; dreaming, musing.

reverr-ai, -as, etc. See REVOIR.

revers, *s.m.* I. (*a*) Reverse (of coin); wrong side (of stuff); other side (of page). (*b*) Facing, lapel (of coat). **Bottes à revers,** top-boots. 2. Reverse (of fortune).

réversible, *a.* Reversible.

réversion, *s.f.* Reversion.

revêtement, *s.m.* Facing, coating.

revêtir, *v.tr.* (Conj. like VÊTIR) I. To clothe again; to reclothe. 2. (*a*) To clothe, dress; to invest. *Revêtu de verdure,* verdure-clad. (*b*) *Const:* To face, coat, case. 3. *R. un habit,* to put on a coat. *R. la forme humaine,* to assume human shape. **se revêtir.** I. To put on one's clothes again. 2. *Se r. de qch.,* to put on sth.; to assume (a dignity).

rêveur, -euse, *a.* Dreaming, dreamy.

rêveusement, *adv.* Dreamily.

revien-s, -t, etc. See REVENIR.

revient, *s.m.* (Prix de) **revient,** cost price.

revin-s, -t, etc. See REVENIR.

revirement, *s.m.* Sudden change; revulsion (of feeling).

revi-s, -t, etc. See REVIVRE and REVOIR.

reviser, réviser, *v.tr.* I. To revise. 2. To examine (again); to overhaul.

reviseur, réviseur, *s.m.* Reviser, examiner.

revision, révision, *s.f.* I. Revision. 2. Inspection, testing; overhaul(ing).

revivre, *v.i.* (Conj. like VIVRE) To live again; to revive.

révocable, *a.* Revocable.

révocation, *s.f.* I. Revocation, rescinding. 2. Removal, dismissal.

revoir, *v.tr.* (Conj. like VOIR) I. To see again. *s.m.inv.* **Au revoir,** good-bye. 2. To revise, re-examine.

revue, *s.f.* I. Review, survey, inspection. 2. (*a*) Review, magazine. (*b*) *Th:* Revue.

révoltant, *a.* Revolting; outrageous.

révolte, *s.f.* Revolt, rebellion; mutiny.

révolter, *v.tr.* To arouse indignation; to revolt. **se révolter,** to revolt, rebel.

révolté, *s.* Rebel, insurgent.

révolu, *a.* (Of time) Completed. *Quand le temps sera r.,* in the fullness of time.

révolution, *s.f.* Revolution; upheaval.

révolutionnaire. (*a*) *a. & s.* Revolutionary. (*b*) *s.* Revolutionist.

revolver [-vɛːr], *s.m.* Revolver.
révoquer, *v.tr.* **1.** To revoke; to counter-mand. **2.** To dismiss (official).
revu, revue. See REVOIR.
rez-de-chaussée, *s.m.inv.* (*a*) Ground level; street level. (*b*) Ground-floor.
rhabiller [-bije], *v.tr.* **1.** To repair, overhaul, mend. **2.** To reclothe.
   se rhabiller, to dress again.
rhénan, *a.* Rhenish; (of the) Rhine.
rhétorique, *s.f.* Rhetoric.
Rhin (le). *Pr.n.m. Geog:* The Rhine.
rhinocéros [-rɔs], *s.m.* Rhinoceros.
rhododendron [-dɛd-], *s.m. Bot:* Rhodo-dendron.
rhombe, *s.m. Geom:* Rhombus.
rhubarbe, *s.f. Bot:* Rhubarb.
rhum [rɔm], *s.m.* Rum.
rhumatisant, *a. & s.* Rheumatic (subject).
rhumatismal, -aux, *a.* Rheumatic.
rhumatisme, *s.m.* Rheumatism.
rhume, *s.m. Med:* Cold.
ri. See RIRE.
riant, *a.* **1.** Smiling. **2.** Cheerful, pleasant.
ricanement, *s.m.* Sneering, derisive, laugh. *pl.* Derisive laughter.
ricaner, *v.i.* To laugh unpleasantly, deri-sively.
ricaneur, -euse, *a.* Derisive.
riche, *a.* **1.** Rich, wealthy, well-off. **2.** Valu-able; handsome (gift). **3.** *F: Une r. idée,* a topping idea.
richement, *adv.* Richly. (*a*) Abundantly. (*b*) Sumptuously.
richesse, *s.f.* **1.** Wealth; riches. **2.** Rich-ness; fertility.
ricin, *s.m.* Huile de ricin, castor oil.
ricocher, *v.i.* (*a*) To rebound; to glance off. (*b*) To ricochet.
ricochet, *s.m.* (*a*) Rebound. (*b*) Ricochet.
rictus [-tyːs], *s.m.* Grin.
ride, *s.f.* **1.** Wrinkle. **2.** Ripple (on water).
rideau, *s.m.* **1.** Screen, curtain. **2.** (*a*) Cur-tain. (*b*) *Th:* (Drop-)curtain.
rider, *v.tr.* **1.** (*a*) To wrinkle, line. (*b*) To corrugate. **2.** To ripple.
   se rider. **1.** To wrinkle; to become lined. **2.** To ripple.
   ridé, *a.* **1.** Wrinkled. **2.** Ribbed, corru-gated, fluted.
ridicule. **1.** *a.* Ridiculous, laughable, ludicrous. **2.** *s.m.* (*a*) Ridiculousness, absurdity. (*b*) Ridicule.
ridiculement, *adv.* Ridiculously.
ridiculiser, *v.tr.* To ridicule.
rien. I. *pron. indef. m.* **1.** Anything. (In questions *rien* is preferred to *quelque chose* when a negative answer is expected) *Y a-t-il rien de plus triste?* is there anything more depressing? **2.** Nothing, not anything. (*a*) Il n'y a rien à faire, there is nothing to be done. *Il ne vous faut rien d'autre?* do you require anything else? **Cela ne fait rien,** that doesn't matter. **Comme si de rien**

n'était, as if nothing had happened. **Il n'en est rien!** nothing of the kind! **N'être pou** rien dans une affaire, to have no hand in a matter. (*b*) *Que faites-vous?*—Rien, what d** you do?—Nothing. **Parler pour rien, t** waste one's breath. *Merci, madame.*—D** rien, *monsieur,* thank you, madam.—Please don't mention it. **En moins de rien,** in less than no time. (*c*) **Rien que,** nothing but only, merely. *Il tremblait rien qu'en l** racontant,* only to tell of it made him tremble (*d*) *On ne peut pas vivre de rien,* you can't live on nothing. **Ce n'est pas rien!** that's some-thing! *Ce n'est pas pour rien,* it is not without good reason.
   II. **rien,** *s.m.* **1.** Trifle; mere nothing. *Il le fera en un rien de temps,* he'll do it in no time. **2.** Just a little.
rieur, -euse. **1.** *a.* Laughing; fond of laughter. **2.** *s.* Laugher.
rigide, *a.* Rigid; tense; fixed.
rigidement, *adv.* Rigidly; tensely.
rigidité, *s.f.* Rigidity; stiffness; tenseness.
rigole, *s.f.* Drain, gutter, channel.
rigoler, *v.i. P:* (*a*) To laugh. (*b*) To have some fun, to enjoy oneself.
rigoureusement, *adv.* Rigorously. (*a*) Severely. (*b*) Strictly.
rigoureux, *a.* Rigorous. **1.** Severe, harsh. **2.** Strict.
rigueur, *s.f.* **1.** Rigour, harshness, severity. **2.** Strictness. **Être de rigueur,** to be com-pulsory. **A la rigueur,** if need be.
rime, *s.f. Pros:* Rhyme.
rimer. **1.** *v.tr.* To versify; to put into rhyme. **2.** *v.i.* (*a*) To rhyme (*avec,* with). *F: Cela ne rime à rien,* there's no sense in it. (*b*) To write verse.
rincer, *v.tr.* (n. rinçons) To rinse; to rinse out.
ripaille [-paːj], *s.f. F:* Feasting, carousal.
riposte, *s.f.* Riposte. **1.** *Box:* Counter. **2.** (*a*) Retort. (*b*) Counterstroke.
riposter, *v.i.* **1.** *Box:* To riposte, counter. **2.** To retort.
rire. I. *v.i.* (*p.p.* ri) **1.** To laugh. **Se tenir les côtes de rire,** to shake with laughter. *R. bruyamment,* to guffaw. **Il n'y a pas de quoi rire,** it is no laughing matter. **Rire de qn,** laugh at s.o. **2.** To jest, joke. **Vous voulez rire!** you are joking! *Prendre qch. en riant,* to laugh sth. off. **Pour rire,** for fun. *Soldats pour r.,* make-believe soldiers. **3.** (*a*) *R. à qn,* to greet s.o. with a smile. (*b*) To be favour-able. *La fortune lui rit,* fortune smiles on him.
   se rire. (*a*) **Se rire de qn,** to laugh at s.o. (*b*) *Se r. de qch.,* to make light of sth.
   II. **rire,** *s.m.* (*a*) Laughter, laughing. **Avoir un accès de fou rire,** to be overcome with uncontrollable laughter. (*b*) **Un rire,** a laugh.
ris[1], *s.m. Nau:* Reef (in sail).
ris[2], *s.m. Cu:* Ris de veau, sweetbread.

risée, *s.f.* (*a*) Jeer, mockery. (*b*) Laughing-stock, butt.

risible, *a.* Ludicrous, laughable.

risque, *s.m.* Risk. **A tout risque,** at all hazards.

risquer, *v.tr.* To risk, venture, chance. **Risquer le coup,** to chance it.
se risquer, to take a risk. *Se r. à faire qch.,* to venture to do sth.
risqué, *a.* Risky.

rissole, *s.f. Cu:* Rissole.

ristourne, *s.f.* Refund.

ristourner, *v.tr.* To refund.

rit, rite [rit], *s.m.* (*pl.* always *rites*) Rite.

ritualiste. 1. *a.* Ritualistic. **2.** *s.* Ritualist.

rituel, -elle. 1. *a.* Ritual. **2.** *s.m.* Ritual.

rivage, *s.m.* Bank; shore; strand.

rival, -aux, *a. & s.* Rival.

rivaliser, *v.i. R. avec qn,* (i) to rival s.o.; (ii) to vie with s.o.

rivalité, *s.f.* Rivalry, emulation.

rive, *s.f.* Bank; shore.

river, *v.tr.* (*a*) To rivet. (*b*) To clinch (nail). *F:* River son clou à qn, to settle s.o.'s hash.

riverain. 1. *a.* Riverside, waterside. **2.** *s.* Riverside resident.

rivet, *s.m.* Rivet.

rivetage, *s.m.* Riveting.

riveter, *v.tr.* (je rivette) To rivet.

rivière, *s.f.* **1.** River, stream. **2. Rivière de diamants,** diamond rivière.

rivure, *s.f.* Riveting.

rixe, *s.f.* Brawl, scuffle, affray.

riz [ri], *s.m.* Rice.

rizière, *s.f.* Rice-plantation.

robe, *s.f.* **1.** (*a*) Dress, gown, frock. (*b*) **Robe de chambre,** dressing-gown; wrapper. (*c*) Robe, gown. **Les gens de robe; la robe,** the legal profession. **2.** (*a*) Skin (of sausage). (*b*) Coat (of horse).

robinet, *s.m.* (Stop-)cock; tap, faucet, spigot. **Fermer le r.,** to turn off the tap.

robre, *s.m. Cards:* Rubber.

robuste, *a.* Robust; strong; sturdy; hardy.

robustement, *adv.* Robustly, stoutly.

robustesse, *s.f.* Robustness, sturdiness, hardiness; strength.

roc [rɔk], *s.m.* Rock.

rocailleux [-kaj-], *a.* Rocky, stony.

roche, *s.f.* Rock, boulder. **Roche de fond,** bed-rock.

rocher, *s.m.* Rock; crag.

rocheux, *a.* Rocky, stony. **Les montagnes Rocheuses,** the Rocky Mountains.

roder, *v.tr.* To grind; to polish (gem).

rôder, *v.i.* To prowl; to loiter.

rôdeur, -euse. 1. *a.* Prowling. **2.** *s.* Prowler.

rodomontade, *s.f.* Rodomontade; *pl.* bluster.

rogner, *v.tr.* To clip, trim, pare.

rognon, *s.m. Cu:* Kidney.

rogue, *a.* Arrogant, haughty.

roi, *s.m.* King. **Jour des Rois,** Twelfth-day.

roide, *a.,* **roideur,** *s.f.,* **roidir,** *v.tr.* See RAIDE, RAIDEUR, RAIDIR.

roitelet, *s.m. Orn:* Wren.

rôle, *s.m.* **1.** Roll; list; register. **A tour de rôle,** by turns. **2.** *Th:* Part, rôle. **Distribution des rôles,** cast (of the play). **Sortir de son rôle,** to take too much upon oneself.

romain. 1. *a. & s.* Roman. **2.** *s.f.* **Romaine,** cos lettuce.

romaine, *s.f.* Steelyard.

roman¹, *s.m.* **1.** (*a*) Novel. (*b*) **Les romans,** fiction. **2.** *Mediev.Lit:* Romance.

roman², *a. & s.m.* **1.** *Ling:* Romance. **2.** *Arch:* Romanesque; (in Eng.) Norman.

romance, *s.f. Mus:* (Sentimental) song.

romancier, *s.* Novelist.

romanesque, *a.* Romantic.

romanichel, -elle, *s.* Gipsy, romany.

romantique, *a. Lit:* Romantic.

romantisme, *s.m. Lit.Hist:* Romanticism.

romarin, *s.m. Bot:* Rosemary.

Rome. *Pr.n.f. Geog:* Rome.

rompre, *v.* (*pr. ind.* **il rompt**) **1.** *v.tr.* To break. (*a*) To break in two. (*b*) (Of stream) *R. ses digues,* to burst its banks. *F:* **Rompre la tête, les oreilles, à qn,** to drive s.o. crazy. **Se rompre la tête,** to cudgel one's brains. *Mil:* **Rompez!** dismiss! (*c*) *R. le silence,* to break the silence. (*d*) *R. un choc,* to deaden a shock. (*e*) *R. un mariage,* to break off an engagement. (*f*) *R. l'équilibre,* to upset the balance. (*g*) *R. un cheval,* to break in a horse. *R. qn à la fatigue,* to inure s.o. to fatigue. **2.** *v.i. R. avec qn,* to break with s.o.
se rompre. To break; to snap, break off. **rompu,** *a.* (*a*) Broken. **Rompu de fatigue,** worn out. (*b*) Broken in.

romsteck [-tɛk], *s.m. Cu:* Rump-steak.

ronce, *s.f.* **1.** *Bot:* Bramble; blackberry-bush. **2.** *F:* Thorns.

ronchonner, *v.i. F:* To grumble, grouse.

rond. I. 1. *a.* (*a*) Round; rounded; plump. (*b*) *Voix ronde,* full voice. **2.** *s.m.* (*a*) Round, ring, circle. **Le chat se met en rond,** the cat curls up. (*b*) Disc. *Mec.E:* Washer. *R. de pain,* round of bread. *R. de beurre,* pat of butter.
II. ronde, *s.f.* **1.** (*a*) Round (dance). (*b*) Round(s); (of policeman) beat. **2. A la ronde,** around.

rond-de-cuir, *s.m. F:* (*a*) Clerk. (*b*) Bureaucrat. *pl. Des ronds-de-cuir.*

rondelet, -ette, *a.* Roundish, plumpish.

rondelle, *s.f.* **1.** Small round; disc; slice. **2.** (*a*) Ring. (*b*) Washer.

rondement, *adv.* (*a*) Roundly, briskly, smartly. (*b*) *Il nous a dit r.,* he told us straight.

rondeur, *s.f.* **1.** Roundness, rotundity. *pl.* rounded forms. **2.** Outspokenness.

rondin, *s.m.* (Round) billet; log.

rond-point, *s.m.* Circus (where several roads meet). *pl. Des ronds-points.*

ronflant, *a.* **1.** Snoring. **2.** Rumbling, booming, humming.

ronflement, *s.m.* **1.** (*a*) Snoring. (*b*) Snore. **2.** Rumbling, booming, whirring.

ronfler, *v.i.* **1.** To snore. **2.** (Of wind) To roar; to boom.

rongeant, *a.* (*a*) Corroding. (*b*) Gnawing.

ronger, *v.tr.* (n. rongeons) **1.** To gnaw. **Se ronger le cœur,** to fret one's heart out. **2.** To corrode; to eat away.

rongeur, -euse. 1. *a.* Rodent, gnawing. **2.** *s.m. Z :* Rodent.

ronronnement, *s.m.* (*a*) Purring. (*b*) Humming.

ronronner, *v.i.* (*a*) To purr. (*b*) To hum.

roquet, *s.m.* (*a*) Pug-dog. (*b*) Cur, mongrel.

rosace, *s.f.* Rose(-window).

rosaire, *s.m. Ecc :* Rosary.

rosâtre, *a.* Pinkish.

rosbif [-bif], *s.m.* Roast beef.

rose. 1. *s.f Bot :* Rose. (*a*) *R. mousseuse,* moss rose. **Essence de roses,** attar of roses. **Découvrir le pot aux roses,** to find out the secret. (*b*) **Rose trémière,** hollyhock. **2.** (*a*) *a.* Pink; rosy. (*Inv.* in compounds) *Des rubans rose pivoine,* peony-red ribbons. (*b*) *s.m.* Rose; pink. **3.** *s.f.* (*a*) *Arch :* Rose-window. (*b*) *Nau :* **Rose des vents,** compass-card.

rosé, *a.* Roseate, rosy.

roseau, *s.m. Bot :* Reed.

rosée, *s.f.* Dew.

roséole, *s.f.* German measles.

rosette, *s.f.* (*a*) Bow (of ribbon). (*b*) Rosette.

rosier, *s.m.* Rose-tree, rose-bush.

rosir, *v.i.* To become rosy; to go pink.

rosse, *s.f. F :* Sorry steed; screw.

rosser, *v.tr. F :* To give (s.o.) a beating. **rossée,** *s.f. P :* Beating, thrashing.

rossignol, *s.m.* **1.** Nightingale. **2.** Pick-lock.

rotatif, *a.* Rotary.

rotation, *s.f.* Rotation.

rotin, *s.m. Bot :* Rattan.

rôtir. 1. *v.tr.* (*a*) To roast; to toast. *Pain rôti,* toast. (*b*) *F :* To scorch. **2.** *v.i.* To roast.

rôti, *s.m.* Roast.

rôtie, *s.f.* Round of toast.

rôtissage, *s.m.* Roasting.

rotonde, *s.f.* Rotunda; circular hall.

rotondité, *s.f.* Rotundity.

rotule, *s.f.* Knee-cap.

roturier, *s.* (*a*) Commoner. (*b*) Self-made man.

rouage, *s.m.* **1.** Wheels; works (of a watch). **2.** (Toothed) wheel.

rouan, -anne, *a.* Roan.

roublard, *a. & s.* Wily (person).

rouble, *s.m. Num :* Rouble.

roucoulement, *s.m.* Cooing.

roucouler, *v.i.* To coo.

roue, *s.f.* Wheel. **Pousser à la roue,** to put one's shoulder to the wheel. **Faire la roue,** to turn cartwheels.

rouer, *v.tr. F :* **Rouer de coups,** to beat black and blue.

roué. 1. *s.m.* Rake, profligate. **2.** *a. & s.* Cunning, artful (person).

rouerie, *s.f.* Piece of trickery, of knavery.

rouet, *s.m.* Spinning-wheel.

rouge. 1. *a.* Red. (*a*) **Fer rouge,** red-hot iron. *adv.* **Se fâcher tout rouge,** to lose one's temper completely. (*b*) (*Inv.* in compounds) *Des rubans rouge cerise,* cherry-red ribbons. **2.** *s.m.* (*a*) Red. (*b*) Rouge. **Bâton de rouge,** lipstick.

rougeâtre, *a.* Reddish.

rougeaud, *a. & s.* Red-faced (person).

rouge-gorge, *s.m.* (Robin) redbreast. *pl. Des rouges-gorges.*

rougeole, *s f. Med :* Measles.

rougeoyer, *v.i.* (il rougeoie) (*a*) To turn red. (*b*) To glow.

rougeur, *s.f.* **1.** Redness. **2.** Blush, flush.

rougir. 1. *v.tr.* (*a*) To redden; to turn red. (*b*) To bring to a red heat. (*c*) To flush. **2.** *v.i.* (*a*) To redden, to turn red. (*b*) To turn red; to blush; to flush (up). *R. de qch.,* to be ashamed of sth.

rouille [ru:j], *s.f.* **1.** Rust. **2.** *Agr :* Rust, mildew, blight.

rouiller [ruje], *v.tr.* To rust. **se rouiller,** to rust (up).

rouillé, *a.* Rusted, rusty.

roulade, *s.f. Mus :* Roulade, run.

roulant, *a.* Rolling; sliding (door); moving.

rouleau, *s.m.* **1.** Roller. **2.** (*a*) Roll; coil (of rope). *F :* **Je suis au bout de mon rouleau,** I am at the end of my tether. (*b*) Roller-blind.

roulement, *s.m.* **1.** Rolling. **Bande de roulement,** tread (of tyre). **2.** Rumbling; roll(ing) (of drum). **3.** *Mec.E :* Bearing.

rouler. 1. *v.tr.* (*a*) To roll (along). *Golf :* **Coup roulé,** putt. (*b*) *F :* **Rouler qn,** to take s.o. in. (*c*) To roll (the lawn). (*d*) To roll, wrap (up). **2.** *v.i.* (*a*) To roll. *R. en voiture,* to bowl along, in a carriage. *Av :* *R. sur le sol,* to taxi. *Tout roule sur lui,* everything turns upon him. *R. par le monde,* to knock about the world. (*b*) To roll, rumble. (*c*) *Auto qui roule bien,* car that runs well. (*d*) *Nau :* To roll.

se rouler. (*a*) To roll. (*b*) To roll up (into a ball).

roulette, *s.f.* **1.** Caster; roller; small wheel. **Patins à roulettes,** roller-skates. **2.** (Game of) roulette.

roulier, *s.m.* Carter, waggoner; carrier.

roulis, *s.m. Nau :* Rolling.

roulotte, *s.f.* House on wheels; caravan.

roumain, *a. & s.* Rumanian.

Roumanie, *Pr.n.f. Geog :* Rumania.

roupie, *s.f. Num :* Rupee.

roussâtre, *a.* Reddish.

rousse. See ROUX.

rousseur, *s.f.* Redness. **Tache de rousseur,** freckle.

roussir. I. *v.tr.* (*a*) To redden. *Cu:* To brown. (*b*) To scorch, singe. **2.** *v.i.* (*a*) To turn brown; to redden. (*b*) To singe; to get scorched.

   roussi. I. *a.* Browned; scorched. **2.** *s.m.* Cela sent le roussi, there is a smell of something burning.

route, *s.f.* **I.** Road(way), path, track. Grande route, route nationale, main road, high-road, highway. *R. départementale*, secondary road. **2.** Route, course, way. Se mettre en route, to set out. Frais de route, travelling expenses. En route! let us be off!

routier, *a. & s.* Carte routière, road-map.

routine, *s.f.* Routine.

routinier, *a.* Routine.

rouvrir, *v.tr. & i.* (Conj. like OUVRIR) To reopen.

   se rouvrir, to open again; to reopen.

roux, rousse. I. (*a*) *a.* (Russet-)red, (reddish-)brown; (of hair) red. (*Inv.* in compounds) *Chevelure blond roux*, sandy hair. (*b*) *s.* Red-haired person. **2.** *s.m.* Russet, reddish-brown.

royal, -aux, *a.* Royal, regal, kingly.

royalement, *adv.* Royally, regally.

royalisme, *s.m.* Royalism.

royaliste, *a. & s.* Royalist.

royaume, *s.m.* Kingdom, realm.

royauté, *s.f.* Royalty; kingship.

ruade, *s.f.* Lashing out, fling out.

ruban, *s.m.* **I.** (*a*) Ribbon, band. (*b*) *R. de fil*, tape. Mètre à ruban, measuring-tape. **2.** Metal strip. *R. d'acier*, steel band.

rubicond, *a.* Rubicund, florid.

rubis, *s.m.* Ruby. Montée sur rubis, jewelled (watch).

rubrique, *s.f.* (*a*) *Ecc:* Rubric. (*b*) *Journ:* Heading.

ruche, *s.f.* (Bee-)hive.

rucher, *s.m.* Apiary.

rude, *a.* **I.** (*a*) Uncouth, unpolished. (*b*) Rough; stiff, hard; harsh; rugged. **2.** (*a*) Hard, arduous. *R. épreuve*, severe trial. (*b*) Gruff, ungracious, brusque. **3.** *F:* R. appétit, hearty appetite. *R. adversaire*, tough opponent.

rudement, *adv.* **I.** (*a*) Roughly, harshly, severely. (*b*) Roughly, coarsely. **2.** *F:* Je suis r. fatigué, I am awfully tired.

rudesse, *s.f.* **I.** Uncouthness, primitiveness. **2.** Roughness, ruggedness. **3.** (*a*) Severity. (*b*) Abruptness, bluntness.

rudiment, *s.m.* **I.** *Biol:* Rudiment. **2.** *pl.* Rudiments.

rudimentaire, *a.* Rudimentary.

rudoiement, *s.m.* Rough treatment.

rudoyer, *v.tr.* (je rudoie) To treat roughly.

rue[1], *s.f.* Street, thoroughfare. La grande rue, la grand'rue, the high street. Courir les rues, to be common talk.

rue[2], *s.f. Bot:* Rue.

ruelle, *s.f.* Lane, by-street, alley.

ruer, *v.i.* To kick, to lash out.

   se ruer *sur qn*, to hurl oneself at s.o.

   ruée, *s.f.* Rush, onrush.

rugir, *v.i.* To roar; to howl.

rugissement, *s.m.* **I.** Roaring; howling. **2.** Roar.

rugosité, *s.f.* **I.** Rugosity, ruggedness, roughness. **2.** Wrinkle, corrugation.

rugueux, *a.* (*a*) Rugged, rough; gnarled. (*b*) Wrinkled.

ruine, *s.f.* Ruin. **I.** Downfall; decay. **2.** (Usu. in *pl.*) Ruins.

ruiner, *v.tr.* To ruin, destroy.

ruineux, *a.* Ruinous.

ruisseau, *s.m.* **I.** Brook; (small) stream. **2.** (Street) gutter, runnel.

ruisseler, *v.i.* (il ruisselle) **I.** To stream (down), run (down). **2.** (Of surface) To run, to drip.

ruissellement, *s.m.* Streaming, running.

rumeur, *s.f.* **I.** (*a*) Hum (of traffic). (*b*) Din, clamour. **2.** Rumour, report.

ruminant, *a. & s.m. Z:* Ruminant.

rumination, *s.f.* Rumination, ruminating.

ruminer, *v.tr.* **I.** *Abs.* To ruminate; to chew the cud. **2.** *F:* R. une idée, to ruminate about an idea.

runes, *s.f.pl.* Runes.

runique, *a.* Runic (letters, verse).

rupture, *s.f.* Breaking, rupture. (*a*) Breaking down; bursting. (*b*) Breaking (in two); rupture; fracture. (*c*) Breaking up. (*d*) Breaking off; discontinuance.

rural, -aux, *a.* Rural.

ruse, *s.f.* Ruse, trick, wile, dodge.

rusé, *a. & s.* Artful, crafty, sly, astute.

russe, *a. & s.* Russian.

Russie. *Pr.n.f. Geog:* Russia.

rustaud. I. *a.* Boorish, uncouth. **2.** *s.* Boor.

rustique. I. *a.* (*a*) Rustic. (*b*) Hardy (plant).

rustre. I. *a.* Boorish. **2.** *s.m.* Boor, churl, lout.

rutabaga, *s.m.* Swedish turnip; swede.

Ruthène, *s. & a.* Ruthenian.

rutiler, *v.i.* To glow; to gleam red.

rythme, *s.m.* Rhythm.

rythmique, *a.* Rhythmic(al).

S, s [ɛs], *s.f.* (The letter) S, **s.**

s'. See SE.

sa, *a.poss.f.* See SON¹.

sabbat, *s.m.* **I.** (Jewish) Sabbath. **2.** (Witches') sabbath, midnight revels.

sabin, *a. & s. A.Hist:* Sabine.

sable¹, *s.m.* **I.** Sand. *Sables mouvants,* quicksands.

sable², *s.m.* **I.** Sable (fur). **2.** Sable, black.

sablier, *s.m.* Hour-glass. *Cu:* Egg-timer.

sablière, *s.f.* Sand-pit, gravel-pit.

sablonneux, *a.* Sandy.

sablonnière, *s.f.* Sand-pit.

sabord, *s.m. Nau:* Port(-hole).

saborder, *v.tr.* To scuttle (ship).

sabot, *s.m.* **I.** Wooden shoe; clog, sabot. *Baignoire en sabot,* slipper-bath. **2.** Hoof. **3.** Drag, skid (of wheel). **4.** Whip(ping)-top.

sabotage, *s.m.* (*a*) Scamping (of work). (*b*) Sabotage, malicious destruction.

saboter, *v.tr.* To botch; to do wilful damage to; to sabotage.

sabre, *s.m.* Sabre; sword. **Sabre au clair,** with drawn swords.

sabrer, *v.tr.* To sabre.

sac¹ [sak], *s.m.* Sack, bag, pouch. *Sac de nuit,* travelling-bag. *Sac de couchage,* sleeping-bag. **Homme de sac et de corde,** thorough-paced scoundrel. **Vider son sac,** to unbosom oneself. **L'affaire est dans le sac,** it's as good as settled.

sac², *s.m.* Sacking, pillage.

saccade, *s.f.* Jerk, start, jolt.

saccadé, *a.* Jerky, abrupt.

saccager, *v.tr.* (**n. saccageons**) To sack, pillage; to ransack.

saccharine [-kar-], *s.f.* Saccharin(e).

sacerdoce, *s.m.* **I.** Priesthood; ministry. **2.** *Coll.* The priesthood.

sacerdotal, -aux, *a.* Sacerdotal; priestly.

sach-e, -es, etc. See SAVOIR.

sachet, *s.m.* Sachet.

sacoche, *s.f.* **I.** (*a*) Satchel, wallet. (*b*) *Mil:* Saddlebag. **2.** *Aut:* Tool-bag.

sacramentel, -elle, *a. Ecc:* Sacramental.

sacre, *s.m.* Anointing; consecration.

sacrement, *s.m. Ecc:* (*a*) Sacrament. (*b*) *F:* The marriage tie.

sacrer, **I.** *v.tr.* To anoint; to consecrate. **2.** *v.i. F:* To curse and swear.

sacré, *a.* **I.** Holy; sacred, consecrated. **2.** Sacred, inviolable. **3.** Confounded, damned.

sacrifice, *s.m.* Sacrifice.

sacrifier, *v.tr.* (*a*) To sacrifice; to offer in sacrifice. (*b*) To sacrifice, give up.

sacrilège¹, *s.m.* Sacrilege.

sacrilège², *a. & s.* Sacrilegious (person).

sacristain, *s.m.* Sacristan; sexton.

sacristie, *s.f. Ecc:* Sacristy, vestry.

sacro-saint, *a.* Sacrosanct.

sadique, *a.* Sadistic.

sadisme, *s.m.* Sadism.

sadiste, *s.m. & f.* Sadist.

saducéen, *s.m. Rel.H:* Sadducee.

safran, *s.m. Bot:* Saffron, crocus.

saga, *s.f. Scand.Lit:* Saga.

sagace, *a.* Sagacious, shrewd.

sagacement, *adv.* Sagaciously, shrewdly.

sagacité, *s.f.* Sagacity, shrewdness.

sagaie, *s.f.* Assegai.

sage, *a.* **I.** Wise. **2.** Judicious, discreet. **3.** Well-behaved; good (child). **Sage comme une image,** as good as gold.

sage-femme, *s.f.* Midwife. *pl. Des sages-femmes.*

sagement, *adv.* **I.** Wisely, prudently. **2.** Steadily, soberly.

sagesse, *s.f.* **I.** (*a*) Wisdom. (*b*) Prudence, discretion. **2.** Steadiness, good behaviour.

sagou, *s.m.* Sago.

saignant, *a.* **I.** Bleeding, raw. **2.** *Cu:* Raw, underdone, red (meat).

saigner. **I.** *v.i.* To bleed. **2.** *v.tr.* (*a*) To bleed. (*b*) To tap (gum-tree).

saignée, *s.f. Med:* Bleeding, bloodletting. *F:* Drain (on one's resources).

saillant [sajɑ̃], **I.** *a.* (*a*) Projecting. (*b*) Salient, outstanding. **2.** *s.m. Mil:* Salient.

saillir [sajiːr], *v.i.* **I.** To gush out, spurt out; to (make a) sally. **2.** (Used only in *pr.p.* **saillant;** *p.p.* **sailli;** *pr.ind.* **il saille, ils saillent;** *fu.* **il saillera**) To jut out, stand out.

saillie, *s.f.* **I.** (*a*) Spurt; spring, bound. (*b*) *Mil:* Sally. (*c*) *F:* Sally; flash of wit. **2.** Protrusion; projection.

sain, *a.* (*a*) Healthy, hale; sound; sane. (*b*) *Nau:* Clear, safe.

saindoux, *s.m.* Lard.

sainement, *adv.* **I.** Healthily, wholesomely. **2.** Sanely.

saint. **I.** *a.* Holy. (*a*) *Les Saintes Écritures,* Holy Writ. (*b*) Saintly, godly. (*c*) Hallowed, consecrated. **2.** *s.* Saint. **A chaque saint sa chandelle,** honour where honour is due.

saint-bernard, *s.m.inv.* St Bernard (dog).

Sainte-Hélène. *Pr.n. Geog:* Saint Helena.

Saint-Elme. *Pr.n.m.* **Feu de Saint-Elme,** corposant, Saint-Elmo's fire.

Saint-Esprit. *Pr.n.m.* **Le Saint-Esprit,** the Holy Ghost.

sainteté, *s.f.* Holiness, saintliness; sanctity. *Ecc:* **Sa Sainteté,** His Holiness.

Saint-Jean (la), *s.f.* Midsummer Day.

Saint-Jean d'Acre. *Pr.n. Geog:* Acre.

Saint-Laurent (le). *Pr.n.m. Geog:* The Saint Lawrence (river).
Saint-Martin (la), *s.f.* Martinmas.
Saint-Michel (la), *s.f.* Michaelmas.
Saint-Père (le), *s.m.* The Holy Father.
Saint-Siège (le), *s.m.* The Holy See.
sais. See SAVOIR.
saisir, *v.tr.* To seize. (*a*) To grasp; to take hold of. *Être saisi (d'étonnement),* to be startled. (*b*) To perceive, apprehend. *Je ne saisis pas,* I don't quite get the idea.
se saisir *de qch.,* to lay hands on sth.
saisie, *s.f.* (*a*) Seizure. (*b*) *Jur:* Distraint. *Nau:* Embargo.
saisissant, *a.* (*a*) Piercing (cold). (*b*) Striking (resemblance); thrilling (spectacle).
saisissement, *s.m.* Seizure. (*a*) Surprise, thrill. (*b*) Shock.
saison, *s.f.* Season. *La saison bat son plein,* it is the height of the season. *De saison,* in season. *Propos hors de saison,* ill-timed remarks.
sait. See SAVOIR.
salade, *s.f.* Salad.
salaire, *s.m.* Wage(s). **1.** Pay. **2.** Reward, recompense, retribution.
salaison, *s.f.* Salting; curing.
salamandre, *s.f.* **1.** (*a*) Salamander. (*b*) *S. aquatique,* newt. **2.** Slow-combustion stove.
salarié. 1. *a.* (*a*) Wage-earning. (*b*) Paid (work). **2.** *s.* Wage-earner.
salaud, *s. P:* Dirty dog; skunk.
sale, *a.* Dirty. **1.** (*a*) Unclean, filthy; soiled (linen). (*b*) Offensive, nasty. **2.** *F: S. temps,* beastly weather.
saler, *v.tr.* To salt. **1.** (*a*) To season with salt. (*b*) *F: S. la note,* to stick it on (to the bill). **2.** To salt, pickle; to cure.
salé, *a.* **1.** Salt; salted. *s.m. Petit salé,* pickled pork. **2.** *F:* Exorbitant, stiff.
saleté, *s.f.* **1.** (*a*) Dirtiness, filthiness. (*b*) Dirt, filth. **2.** (*a*) Nastiness. (*b*) Nasty, coarse, remark.
salière, *s.f.* Salt-cellar.
salin, *a.* Saline, briny; salty.
salir, *v.tr.* To dirty, soil. *S. sa réputation,* to sully one's good name.
salive, *s.f.* Saliva, spittle. *F: Perdre sa salive,* to waste one's breath.
salle, *s.f.* **1.** Hall; (large) room. **2.** *Th:* Auditorium. *Toute la s. applaudit,* the whole house applauded.
Salomon. *Pr.n.m.* Solomon.
salon, *s.m.* (*a*) Drawing-room. (*b*) Saloon, cabin (in ship). (*c*) *S. de thé,* tea-room(s). *S. de modiste,* milliner's showroom. (*d*) *Le S. de l'automobile,* the Motor Show.
salpêtre, *s.m.* Saltpetre, nitre.
salsepareille [-rɛːj], *s.f. Bot:* Sarsaparilla.
saltimbanque, *s.m.* Mountebank.
salubre, *a.* Salubrious; wholesome.
salubrité, *s.f.* Salubrity; wholesomeness.
saluer, *v.tr.* (*a*) To salute; to bow to. *S. qn de la main,* to wave to s.o. (*b*) To greet,

to hail. *Saluez-le de ma part,* give him my kind regards.
salut, *s.m.* **1.** (*a*) Safety. *Le salut public,* public welfare. *Port de salut,* haven of refuge. (*b*) Salvation. **2.** (*a*) Bow, salutation, greeting. (*b*) *Mil:* Salute.
salutaire, *a.* Salutary, wholesome.
salutation, *s.f.* Salutation, greeting. *"Salutations à votre famille,"* 'kind regards to your family.'
salve, *s.f.* Salvo.
samedi, *s.m.* Saturday.
samovar, *s.m.* Samovar.
sampan, *s.m.* Sampan.
sanatorium [-jɔm], *s.m.* Sanatorium.
sanctification, *s.f.* Sanctification.
sanctifier, *v.tr.* To sanctify; to hallow.
sanction, *s.f.* Sanction. **1.** Approbation. *S. royale,* royal assent. **2.** Sanction (pénale), penalty.
sanctionner, *v.tr.* To sanction. **1.** To approve, ratify. **2.** To penalize.
sanctuaire, *s.m.* (*a*) Sanctuary. (*b*) *F:* Sanctum, den.
sandale, *s.f.* Sandal.
sandwich [-witʃ], *s.m.* Sandwich.
sang, *s.m.* **1.** Blood. *Coup de sang,* apoplectic fit; *F:* stroke. *Se faire du mauvais sang,* to worry. *Suer sang et eau,* to toil and moil. **2.** (*a*) Blood, race, lineage. *Cheval pur sang,* thoroughbred (horse). (*b*) Blood, kinship. *Son propre s.,* one's own flesh and blood.
sang-froid, *s.m.* No *pl.* Coolness, composure. *De sang-froid,* deliberately.
sanglant, *a.* **1.** Bloody; blood-stained. **2.** (*a*) Cutting; scathing. (*b*) Deadly (affront).
sangle, *s.f.* Strap, band, webbing. *Lit de sangle,* camp-bed.
sangler, *v.tr.* **1.** To girth (horse); to strap (parcel). **2.** To thrash, lash.
sanglier, *s.m.* Wild boar.
sanglot, *s.m.* Sob.
sangloter, *v.i.* To sob.
sangsue, *s.f.* Leech.
sanguin [-gɛ̃], *a.* Full-blooded.
sanguinaire, *a.* Sanguinary; blood-thirsty.
sanitaire, *a.* Sanitary. *Matériel s.,* medical stores. *Train s.,* hospital train.
sans, *prep.* **1.** (*a*) Without. *Cela va sans dire,* (it is a matter of course). *Vous n'êtes pas sans le connaître,* you cannot but know him. *Conj.phr. Sans que* + *sub.,* without + *ger. Sans que nous le sachions,* without our knowing it. (*b*) -less, -lessly. *Agir sans peur,* to act fearlessly. *Être sans le sou,* to be penniless. (*c*) Un-. *Plaintes sans fin,* unending complaints. **2.** But for. *Sans cela, sans quoi,* otherwise, else.
sanscrit, *a. & s.m. Ling:* Sanskrit.
sans-façon. 1. *s.m.* (*a*) Homeliness, straight-forwardness. (*b*) = SANS-GÊNE 1. **2.** *a.inv.* Homely. **3.** = SANS-GÊNE 2.

sans-fil, *s.inv.* **1.** *s.f.* Wireless. **2.** *s.m.* (Dépêche par) sans-fil, wireless message.

sans-gêne. 1. *s.m.* Off-handedness. **2.** *a.inv.* Unceremonious.

sans-souci, *s.inv.* **1.** *s.m.* **&** *f.* Care-free individual. **2.** *s.m.* Unconcern.

santal, -als, -aux, *s.m.* Sandal(wood).

santé, *s.f.* Health; well-being. Respirer la santé, to look the picture of health. *Mil:* Le service de (la) santé, the medical service. *F:* A votre santé! good health!

saoul [su] = soûl.

sape, *s.f.* Undermining.

saper, *v.tr.* To sap, undermine.

sapeur, *s.m. Mil:* Sapper; pioneer.

sapeur-pompier, *s.m.* Fireman. *Les sapeurs-pompiers,* the fire-brigade.

sapin, *s.m.* **1.** (*a*) Fir(-tree). (*b*) (Bois de) sapin, deal. **2.** *P:* Coffin. Toux qui sent le sapin, churchyard cough.

sapinière, *s.f.* Fir-plantation.

saponacé, *a.* Saponaceous, soapy.

sarabande, *s.f. Danc:* Saraband.

sarbacane, *s.f.* Blow-pipe; pea-shooter.

sarcasme, *s.m.* (Piece of) sarcasm; gibe.

sarcastique, *a.* Sarcastic.

sarcelle, *s.f. Orn:* Teal.

sarcler, *v.tr.* To weed (garden); to hoe.

sarcloir, *s.m.* (Weeding-)hoe; spud.

sarcophage, *s.m.* Sarcophagus.

Sardaigne, *Pr.n.f. Geog:* Sardinia.

sarde, *a. & s. Geog:* Sardinian.

sardine, *s.f.* (*a*) *Ich:* Pilchard. (*b*) *Com:* Sardine.

sardonique, *a.* Sardonic.

sargasse, *s.f. Geog:* **La mer des Sargasses,** the Sargasso Sea.

sarment, *s.m.* Vine-shoot.

sarrasin. 1. *Hist:* s. Saracen. **2.** *s.m. Agr:* Buckwheat.

sarrau, *pl.* **-s, -x,** *s.m.* Overall, smock.

Sarre (la), *Pr.n.f. Geog:* The Saar.

sas¹ [sɑ], *s.m.* Sieve, screen, riddle.

sas², *s.m.* (*a*) *Hyd.E:* Lock-chamber. (*b*) Lock.

sasser, *v.tr.* To sift, bolt, screen.

Satan. *Pr.n.m.* Satan.

satané, *a. F:* Devilish, confounded. *S. temps!* beastly weather!

satanique, *a.* Satanic; fiendish.

satellite, *s.m.* Satellite.

satiété, *s.f.* Satiety; surfeit.

satin, *s.m. Tex:* Satin.

satire, *s.f.* Satire.

satirique, *a.* Satiric(al).

satiriquement, *adv.* Satirically.

satiriser, *v.tr.* To satirize.

satisfaction, *s.f.* **1.** Satisfaction, gratification. **2.** Reparation, amends.

satisfaire, *v.* (Conj. like FAIRE) To satisfy. **1.** *v.tr.* (*a*) To content; to give satisfaction to. *S. l'attente de qn,* to come up to s.o.'s expectations. (*b*) To make amends to. **2.** *v.ind.tr.* Satisfaire à qch., to satisfy

(honour); to answer, meet (condition); to fulfil (duty).

satisfait, *a.* Satisfied, contented

satisfaisant, *a.* Satisfying, satisfactory.

saturation, *s.f.* Saturation.

saturer, *v.tr.* To saturate.

se saturer, to become saturated.

saturnin, *a.* Saturnine.

satyre, *s.m.* Satyr.

sauce, *s.f.* Sauce.

saucière, *s.f.* Sauce-boat.

saucisse, *s.f.* ('Fresh') sausage.

saucisson, *s.m.* (Large 'dry') sausage.

sauf¹ [sof], **sauve,** *a.* Safe, unhurt. S'en tirer la vie sauve, to get off with a whole skin.

sauf², *prep.* Save, but, except. Sauf correction, subject to correction. Je consens, sauf à revenir sur ma décision, I consent, reserving the right to reconsider my decision. *Conj.phr.* Sauf que + *ind.,* except that.

sauf-conduit, *s.m.* Safe-conduct; pass. *pl.* Des sauf-conduits.

sauge, *s.f. Bot:* Sage.

saugrenu, *a.* Absurd, preposterous.

saule, *s.m. Bot:* Willow. S. pleureur, weeping willow.

saumâtre, *a.* Brackish, briny.

saumon, *s.m.* **1.** Salmon. *a.inv.* Rubans saumon, salmon-pink ribbons. **2.** Ingot.

saumoné, *a.* Truite saumonée, salmon-trout.

saumure, *s.f.* Pickling brine; pickle.

saupoudrer, *v.tr.* To sprinkle, powder.

saupoudroir, *s.m.* Dredger, castor.

saur [sɔːr], *a.m.* Hareng saur, red herring.

saur-ai, -as, etc. See SAVOIR.

saurien [sɔr-], *a. & s.m. Rept:* Saurian.

saut, *s.m.* **1.** (*a*) Leap, jump, vault. Au saut du lit, on getting out of bed. Saut périlleux, somersault. (*b*) S. de température, sudden rise, jump, of temperature. **2.** Saut de loup, ha-ha, sunk fence.

saut-de-lit, *s.m.* **1.** (Bedside) rug. **2.** Morning wrap. *pl.* Des sauts-de-lit.

saute, *s.f.* Jump. Esp *Nau:* Saute de vent, shift, change, of wind.

saute-mouton, *s.m. Games:* Leap-frog.

sauter. 1. *v.i.* (Aux. *avoir*) (*a*) To jump, leap, skip. S. à terre, to dismount. S. à la gorge de qn, to fly at s.o.'s throat. S. au cou de qn, to fling one's arms round s.o.'s neck. *F:* Sauter au plafond, to jump out of one's skin. (*b*) To explode; to blow up; to go smash; to come off, fly off. (*c*) *Nau:* (Of wind) To change, shift. **2.** *v.tr.* To jump (over); leap over, clear.

sauterelle, *s.f.* Grasshopper. Grande sauterelle d'Orient, locust.

sauterie, *s.f.* Hop.

sautiller [-tije], *v.i.* To hop; to skip, jump (about).

sautoir, *s.m.* (*a*) St Andrew's Cross; *Her:* saltire. En sautoir, crosswise. (*b*) Long neck chain. (*c*) Kerchief (worn over the shoulders).

sauvage. 1. *a.* (*a*) Savage, uncivilized; wild,

untamed; barbarous. (b) Averse to society; unsociable; shy; coy. **2.** s. (With f. **sauvage** or F: **sauvagesse**) (a) Savage. (b) Unsociable person.

sauvagement, adv. Wildly, savagely.

sauvagerie, s.f. **I.** (State of) savagery, savageness. **2.** Unsociability.

sauvagesse. See SAUVAGE 2.

sauvegarde, s.f. **I.** Safeguard, safe-keeping. **2.** Safe-conduct. **3.** Nau: Life-line.

sauvegarder, v.tr. To safeguard, protect.

sauve-qui-peut, s.m.inv. Stampede, head-long flight.

sauver, v.tr. (a) To save, rescue, deliver. (b) To salve.

se **sauver. I.** Se s. d'un péril, to escape from a danger. **2.** To run away, to be off.

sauvetage, s.m. (a) Life-saving; rescue. Canot de sauvetage, lifeboat. Echelle de sauvetage, fire-escape. (b) Salvage, salving.

sauveur, s.m. Saver, preserver, deliverer.

savamment, adv. (a) Learnedly. (b) Knowingly, wittingly.

savane, s.f. Savanna(h).

savant. I. a. (a) Learned, scholarly. (b) Skilful. Chien savant, performing dog. (c) Knowing. **2.** s. Scientist; scholar.

savate, s.f. **I.** En savates, down at heel; slipshod. **2.** Foot boxing.

savetier, s.m. **I.** Cobbler. **2.** F: Botcher.

saveur, s.f. **I.** Savour, taste, flavour. **2.** Pungency (of style).

Savoie. Pr.n.f. Geog: Savoy.

savoir. I. v.tr. (pr.p. sachant; p.p. su; pr.ind. je sais, n. savons, ils savent; p.d. je savais; fu. je saurai) To know. **I.** Il en sait plus d'une, he knows a thing or two. **2.** To be aware of. (a) Savez-vous qu'il est midi? are you aware that it is twelve o'clock? Je (le) sais bien! I know! Ce n'est pas bien, tu sais! it isn't right, you know! Vous ne savez pas! nous allons nous cacher, I'll tell you what, let us hide. Vous en savez plus long que moi, you know more (about it) than I do. Sans le savoir, unconsciously. Pas que je sache, not that I am aware of. (b) Je ne sache pas l'avoir froissée, I am not aware of having offended her. (c) Je vous savais à Paris, I knew you were in Paris. (d) Je lui savais une grande fortune, I knew him to be wealthy. (e) Ne savoir que faire, to be at a loss what to do. **3.** (a) Il n'en a rien su, he never knew of it. C'est à savoir, that remains to be seen. (b) Faire savoir qch. à qn, to inform s.o. of sth. (c) (A) savoir, to wit, namely. **4.** To know how, to be able. Savez-vous nager? can you swim? Je ne saurais permettre cela, I cannot allow that. **5.** Des robes, des chapeaux, que sais-je! dresses, hats, and goodness knows what else!

II. savoir, s.m. Knowledge, learning.

su, s.m. Knowledge. Au su de, to the knowledge of.

savoir-faire, s.m. Ability, tact.

savoir-vivre, s.m. Good manners, good-breeding, knowledge of the world.

savon, s.m. Soap. Pain de savon, cake of soap. Eau de savon, soapsuds. F: Recevoir un s., to catch it.

savonner, v.tr. To soap. Se s. le menton, to lather one's chin.

savonnette, s.f. **I.** Cake of toilet-soap. **2.** (Montre à) savonnette, hunter (watch).

savonneux, a. Soapy.

savourer, v.tr. To relish, enjoy.

savoureux, a. Savoury, tasty.

savoyard, a. & s. Savoyard; of Savoy.

Saxe. Pr.n.f. Saxony. Porcelaine de Saxe, Dresden china.

saxifrage, s.f. Bot: Saxifrage.

saxophone, s.m. Saxophone.

saynète, s.f. Th: Playlet, sketch.

sbire, s.m. F: Myrmidon (of the law).

scabreux, a. **I.** Difficult, risky, ticklish. **2.** Indelicate; improper.

scaferlati, s.m. Cut tobacco.

scalène, a. Scalene (triangle).

scalpe, s.m. Scalp (as a war trophy).

scalpel, s.m. Surg: Scalpel.

scalper, v.tr. To scalp (an enemy).

scandale, s.m. Scandal; (cause of) shame. C'est un s., it's disgraceful.

scandaleusement, adv. Scandalously, disgracefully.

scandaleux, a. Scandalous, shameful, disgraceful.

scandaliser, v.tr. To scandalize.

se **scandaliser,** to be scandalized.

scander, v.tr. To scan (verse). Marche scandée, measured tread.

scandinave, a. & s. Scandinavian.

Scandinavie. Pr.n.f. Scandinavia.

scansion, s.f. Scansion, scanning.

scaphandre, s.m. Diving-suit.

scaphandrier, s.m. Diver (in diving-suit).

scarabée, s.m. **I.** Beetle. **2.** Scarab.

scarlatine, a. & s.f. (Fièvre) scarlatine, scarlet fever, scarlatina.

sceau, s.m. Seal. S. du génie, stamp of genius.

scélérat. I. a. Villainous. **2.** s. Scoundrel.

scélératesse, s.f. **I.** Wickedness, villainy. **2.** Wicked action.

sceller, v.tr. **I.** (a) To seal; to seal up. Signé et scellé par moi, given under my hand and seal. (b) F: To ratify, confirm; to seal. **2.** Const: To fix, fasten.

scellé. I. a. Sealed; under seal. **2.** s.m. (Imprint of official) seal. Lever les scellés, to remove the seals.

scénario, s.m. Th: Scenario.

scène, s.f. **I.** Stage. Entrer en scène, to come on. Mettre en scène, to stage. Metteur en scène, producer. **2.** Scene. (a) Scene of action. (b) Troisième s. du second acte, scene three of act two. (c) Ce fut une s. pénible, it was a painful scene. (d) F: Angry discussion; row.

scénique, a. Scenic; theatrical. Indications scéniques, stage directions.

scepticisme, s.m. Scepticism.

sceptique. 1. *a.* Sceptical. **2.** *s.* Sceptic.
sceptiquement, *adv.* Sceptically.
sceptre, *s.m.* Sceptre.
schah, *s.m.* Shah.
schako, *s.m.* Shako.
schampooing, *s.m.* Hair-wash, shampoo.
schelling, *s.m.* Shilling.
schéma [ʃema, skɛ-], *s.m.* Diagram.
schibboleth, *s.m. F:* Shibboleth.
schismatique, *a. & s.* Schismatic.
schisme, *s.m.* Schism.
schiste, *s.m. Geol:* Schist, shale.
sciant, *a. P:* Boring, tiresome.
sciatique. 1. *a.* Sciatic. **2.** *s.f. Med:* Sciatica.
scie, *s.f.* **1.** Saw. *S. à découper,* fret-saw. *Bot:* En dents de scie, serrate. **2.** *Ich:* Scie de mer, saw-fish. **3.** *P:* (a) Bore, nuisance. (b) Catchword, gag.
sciemment, *adv.* Knowingly, wittingly.
science, *s.f.* **1.** Knowledge, learning, skill. **2.** Science.
scientifique, *a.* Scientific.
scientifiquement, *adv.* Scientifically.
scientiste, *s.m.* Scientistes chrétiens, Christian scientists.
scier¹, *v.tr.* **1.** To saw. *F:* Scier le dos à qn, to bore s.o. stiff. **2.** To saw off.
scier², *v.i.* To back water, back the oars.
scierie, *s.f.* Saw-mill, saw-yard.
scieur, *s.m.* Sawyer.
scinder, *v.tr.* To divide, split up.
scintillant [-tijɑ̃, -tillɑ̃], *a.* Scintillating; twinkling (star, *Nau:* light); sparkling (wit).
scintillation [-tij-, -tilla-], *s.f.* Scintillation; twinkling. *Cin:* Flicker(ing).
scintiller [-tije, -tille], *v.i.* To scintillate; to twinkle. *Cin:* To flicker.
scion, *s.m. Hort:* Scion, shoot.
scission, *s.f.* Scission, cleavage, split.
sciure, *s.f.* Sciure de bois, sawdust.
scolaire, *a. Vie s.,* school life.
scolastique, *s.m.* Schoolman, scholastic.
scolopendre¹, *s.f. Myr:* Centipede.
scolopendre², *s.f. Bot:* Hart's-tongue.
sconse, *s.m. Com:* Skunk (fur).
scorbut, *s.m. Med:* Scurvy.
scorie, *s.f.* Usu. *pl.* Slag, cinders.
scorpion, *s.m.* Scorpion.
scriptural, -aux, *a.* Scriptural.
scrofule, *s.f.* Usu. *pl. Med:* Scrofula.
scrofuleux, *a.* Scrofulous.
scrupule, *s.m.* **1.** Scruple (weight). **2.** Scruple, (conscientious) doubt. **Exact jusqu'au scrupule,** scrupulously accurate.
scrupuleusement, *adv.* Scrupulously.
scrupuleux, *a.* Scrupulous.
scrutateur, -trice. 1. *a.* Searching; scrutinizing. **2.** *s.* (a) Scrutinizer. (b) Teller, scrutineer.
scruter, *v.tr.* To scrutinize; to scan. *S. qn du regard,* to give s.o. a searching look.
scrutin, *s.m.* **1.** Poll. *Dépouiller le s.,* to count the votes. **2. Voter au scrutin,** to ballot.

3. Voting. **Procéder au scrutin,** to take the vote.
sculpter, *v.tr.* To sculpture, to carve.
sculpteur, *s.m.* Sculptor. *S. sur bois,* wood-carver.
sculpture, *s.f.* Sculpture. *S. sur bois,* wood-carving.
scythe, *a. & s. A.Geog:* Scythian.
se, before a vowel sound **s',** *pers.pron.acc. & dat.* **1.** (a) (Reflexive) Oneself; himself, herself, itself, themselves. *Se flatter,* to flatter oneself. (b) Each other, one another. *Il est dur de se quitter,* it is hard to part. **2.** *La clef s'est retrouvée,* the key has been found. *Cet article se vend partout,* this article is sold everywhere. **3.** (In purely pronom. conjugation) See S'EN ALLER, etc. NOTE. *Se* is often omitted before an infinitive dependent on *faire, laisser, mener, envoyer, voir.* E.g. *Faire taire les enfants.* Envoyer coucher les enfants. *Nous avons vu lever le soleil.*
séance, *s.f.* **1.** Sitting, session, meeting. **Déclarer la séance ouverte,** to open the meeting. **2.** Performance. **Séance de spiritisme,** seance. **3.** Sitting (for one's portrait).
séant. I. See SEOIR.
   II. séant, *a.* **1.** (a) Sitting; in session. (b) *s.m.* Se dresser sur son séant, to sit up (in bed). *Tomber sur son s., F:* to fall on one's behind. **2.** Becoming; fitting, seemly.
seau, *s.m.* Pail, bucket. *S. à charbon,* coal-scuttle.
sébile, *s.f.* Wooden bowl. **Tendre la sébile,** to beg.
sec [sɛk], **sèche,** *a.* **1.** (a) Dry. **Avoir la gorge sèche,** to be thirsty. (b) Dried; seasoned (wood); dry (wine). (c) **Perte sèche,** dead loss. **2.** (a) Spare, gaunt; lean. **Sec et nerveux,** wiry. (b) Sharp, dry, curt; incisive. **Donner un coup sec à qch.,** to give sth. a sharp blow or tap. **Un merci tout sec,** a bare thank you. (c) Unsympathetic. *Adv.* **Rire sec,** to give a harsh, dry, laugh. (d) Barren; dry, bald (narrative). (e) *F:* **Faire qch. en cinq sec,** to do sth. in a jiffy. **3.** *Adv.phr.* **A sec,** (i) dry, (ii) dried up, (iii) *P:* hard-up. **Mettre une mare à sec,** to drain a pond. **Navire à sec,** ship high and dry.
sécession, *s.f.* Secession.
sèche. See SEC.
sèchement, *adv.* Curtly, tartly.
sécher, *v.* (je sèche; je sécherai) **1.** *v.tr.* To dry (up). **2.** *v.i.* To dry. **Sécher sur pied,** to wilt.
sécheresse, *s.f.* **1.** (a) Dryness. (b) Drought. **2.** (a) Leanness, spareness. (b) Curtness. (c) Coldness, unfeelingness.
séchoir, *s.m.* Clothes-horse, towel-rail.
second. 1. *a.* Second. **Habiter au second (étage),** to live on the second floor. **2.** *s.m.* Principal assistant; second (in command). *Nau:* First mate, first officer. *Navy:* Second

maître, petty officer. **3.** *s.f.* **Seconde.**
(*a*) *Rail:* **Voyager en seconde,** to travel
second (class). (*b*) Second (of time).

secondaire, *a.* **1.** Secondary. **2.** Subordinate; of minor importance.

seconder, *v.tr.* **1.** To second, back up.
2. To forward, promote.

secouer, *v.tr* **1.** (*a*) To shake. (*b*) *F:* To
shake up, rouse. **2.** (*a*) To shake down (fruit).
(*b*) **Secouer le joug,** to shake off the yoke.
     se secouer (*a*) To shake oneself. (*b*) To
bestir oneself.

secourable, *a.* Helpful; willing to help.
Tendre une main s. à qn, to lend s.o. a helping
hand.

secourir, *v.tr.* (Conj. like COURIR) To
succour, help, aid.

secours, *s.m.* Help, succour, relief, aid. **Au
secours!** help! **Premiers secours,** first aid.
S. à domicile, outdoor relief. **Le secours aux
enfants,** child-welfare work. **Société de
secours mutuels,** friendly society. **Sortie de
secours,** emergency exit. *Rail:* **Convoi de
secours,** break-down train.

secousse, *s.f.* Shake, shaking; jolt, jerk.
Se dégager d'une s., to shake oneself free.

secret¹, -ète, *a.* Secret; hidden.

secret², *s.m.* **1.** Secret. **Garder le secret au
sujet de qch.,** to keep sth. secret. **2.** Secrecy,
privacy.

secrétaire. 1. *s.m. & f.* Secretary. *S. de la
mairie,* town clerk **2.** *s.m.* *Orn:* Secretary-
bird.

secrètement, *adv.* Secretly; in secret.

sécrétion, *s.f. Physiol:* Secretion.

sectaire, *s.m. & f.* Sectary, sectarian.

sectateur, -trice, *s.* Follower, votary,
member (of a sect).

secte, *s.f.* Sect.

secteur, *s.m.* Sector.

section, *s.f.* **1.** Section, cutting. **2.** Section;
branch. **3.** Stage (on bus route).

séculaire, *a.* **1.** Occurring once in a hundred
years; secular. **2.** Century-old.

séculier. 1. *a.* (*a*) Secular. (*b*) Laic. **2.** *s.*
Layman.

sécurité, *s.f.* **1.** Security. **2.** Safety.

sédatif, *a. & s.m. Med:* Sedative.

sédentaire, *a.* Sedentary.

sédiment, *s.m.* Sediment, deposit.

séditieusement, *adv.* Seditiously.

séditieux, *a.* (*a*) Seditious. (*b*) Mutinous.

sédition, *s.f.* Sedition; mutiny.

séducteur, -trice. 1. *s.* (*a*) Tempter,
enticer. (*b*) *s.m.* Seducer. **2.** *a.* Tempting,
seductive.

séduction, *s.f.* **1.** Seduction; enticement.
2. Charm, seductiveness.

séduire, *v.tr.* (Conj. like CONDUIRE) **1.** To
seduce; to lead astray; to suborn. **2.** To
fascinate, captivate.

séduisant, *a.* **1.** Seductive, tempting.
2. Fascinating, taking, attractive.

segment, *s.m.* Segment.

ségrégation, *s.f.* Segregation; isolation.

seiche, *s.f.* Cuttle-fish.

seigle, *s.m.* Rye.

seigneur, *s.m.* **1.** Lord. **2. Le Seigneur,** God;
the Lord.

sein, *s.m.* Breast, bosom.

seine, *s.f. Fish:* Seine; draw-net.

seize, *num.a.inv. & s.m.inv.* Sixteen.

séjour, *s.m.* **1.** Stay, sojourn **2.** (Place of)
abode; residence.

séjourner, *v.i.* To stay, stop, sojourn.

sel, *s.m.* **1.** Salt. **2.** *F:* Piquancy, wit.

sélection, *s.f* Selection, choice.

selle, *s.f.* **1.** Saddle. **Être bien en selle**
to be firmly established. **2.** *Cu:* **Selle de
mouton,** saddle of mutton.

seller, *v.tr.* To saddle.

sellerie, *s.f.* **1.** Saddlery. **2.** Harness-room.

sellier, *s.m.* Saddler, harness-maker.

selon, *prep.* According to. *S. moi,* in my
opinion. **C'est selon,** that is as may be; it
all depends.

seltz [sɛls], *s.m.* **Eau de seltz,** seltzer-water;
soda-water.

semailles [-maːj], *s.f.pl.* Sowing.

semaine, *s.f.* (*a*) Week. (*b*) Working week.
(*c*) Week's pay.

sémaphore, *s.m.* Semaphore.

semblable. 1. *a.* (*a*) Alike; similar; like.
(*b*) Such. **Je n'ai rien dit de semblable,** I
said no such thing. **2.** *s.* (*a*) *Vous ne trouverez
pas son s.,* you will not find his like. (*b*) **Nos
semblables,** our fellow-men.

semblablement, *adv.* Similarly, likewise.

semblant, *s.m.* Semblance, appearance;
(outward) show. **Faire semblant de faire qch.**
to pretend to be doing sth.

sembler, *v.i.* (Aux. *avoir*) (*a*) To seem, to
appear. (*b*) *Impers.* **A ce qu'il me semble,**
as it strikes me; I fancy. **Faites comme bon
vous semble(ra),** do as you think fit. **Que
vous en semble?** what do you think of it?

semelle, *s.f.* **1.** Sole (of shoe). *F:* **Ne pas
reculer d'une semelle,** not to give way an
inch. **Battre la semelle,** to be on the tramp.
2. Tread (of tyre).

semence, *s.f.* **1.** Seed. **2.** (*a*) **Semence de
perles,** seed pearls. (*b*) (Tin)tacks.

semer, *v.tr.* (je sème) **1.** To sow. *S. à la
volée,* to sow broadcast. **2.** To spread, strew,
scatter. *Ciel semé d'étoiles,* star-spangled sky.

semestre, *s.m.* **1.** Half-year. **2.** Six months'
pay. **3.** *Sch:* Term (of six months).

semestriel, -elle, *a.* Half-yearly.

semeur, -euse, *s.* (*a*) Sower. (*b*) Disseminator, spreader.

semi-circulaire, *a.* Semicircular.

sémillant [-mijã], *a.* Sprightly, bright.

séminaire, *s.m.* Seminary.

semis, *s.m.* **1.** Sowing. **2.** Seedlings.

sémitique, *a.* Semitic.

semonce, *s.f.* Reprimand, scolding. *Verte
s.,* good talking-to.

semoule, *s.f.* Semolina.
sénat, *s.m.* **1.** Senate. **2.** Senate-house.
sénateur, *s.m.* Senator.
sénatorial, -aux, *a.* Senatorial.
séné, *s.m.* Senna.
Sénégal. *Pr.n.m. Geog:* Senegal.
sénégalais, *a. & s.* Senegalese.
Sénèque. *Pr.n.m. Lt.Lit:* Seneca.
sénile, *a.* Senile.
sénilité, *s.f.* Senility.
sens [sāːs], *s.m.* **1.** Sense. Perdre ses sens, to lose consciousness. **2.** Sense, judgment, intelligence. A mon sens, as I think, in my opinion. **3.** Sense, meaning. S'exprimer dans le même sens, to express oneself to the same effect. **4.** Direction, way. Retourner qch. dans tous les sens, to turn sth. over and over. *Rue à sens unique,* one-way street. "Sens interdit," 'no entry.' Sens dessus dessous, topsy-turvy.
sensation, *s.f.* Sensation. **1.** Feeling. **2.** Excitement.
sensationnel, -elle, *a.* Sensational.
sensé, *a.* Sensible, judicious.
sensibilité, *s.f.* Sensibility. **1.** Sensitiveness. **2.** Feeling, compassion, pity.
sensible, *a.* **1.** (*a*) Sensitive, susceptible. *Être s. au froid,* to feel the cold. *F:* Toucher la corde sensible, to appeal to the emotions. (*b*) Sympathetic. (*c*) Sensitive. *Phot:* Papier *s.,* sensitized paper. (*d*) Sensitive, tender. L'endroit sensible, the sore point. **2.** Sensible ; perceptible.
sensiblement, *adv.* Appreciably, perceptibly.
sensiblerie, *s.f.* Sentiment(ality).
sensitif, *a.* Sensitive ; having feeling.
sensualiste. 1. *s.m.* Sensualist. **2.** *a.* Sensual.
sensualité, *s.f.* Sensuality.
sensuel, -elle, *a.* Sensual.
sente, *s.f.* Footpath ; track.
sentence, *s.f.* (*a*) Sentence, judgment. (*b*) *Rendre une s. arbitrale,* to make an award.
sentencieusement, *adv.* Sententiously.
sentencieux, *a.* Sententious.
senteur, *s.f.* Scent, perfume.
sentier, *s.m.* (Foot)path.
sentiment, *s.m.* **1.** Feeling. (*a*) Sensation. (*b*) Sense, consciousness. (*c*) *Ses sentiments vis-à-vis de moi,* his feelings towards me. **2.** Opinion.
sentimental, -aux, *a.* Sentimental.
sentimentalité, *s.f.* Sentimentality.
sentinelle, *s.f. Mil:* Sentry ; sentinel.
sentir, *v.* (Conj. like MENTIR) **1.** *v.tr.* (*a*) To feel. Sentir quelque chose pour qn, to feel drawn to s.o. (*b*) To be conscious, sensible, of. L'effet se fera sentir, the effect will be felt. (*c*) To smell. *F:* Je ne peux pas le sentir, I can't stand him. **2.** *v.i.* (*a*) To taste of, smell of. *La pièce sent l'humidité,* the room smells damp. (*b*) Sentir bon, to smell good. (*c*) To smell, to stink.

se sentir. 1. *Je me sens fatigué,* I feel tired. **2.** Il ne se sent pas de joie, he is beside himself for joy.
senti, *a. Paroles bien senties,* heartfelt words.
seoir [swaːr], *v.i.* **1.** (In *p.p.* sis) *Jur:* To be situated. **2.** (Used only in *pr.p.* seyant, séant ; *pr.ind.* il sied, ils siéent ; *pr.sub.* il siée ; *p.d.* il seyait, ils seyaient ; *fu.* il siéra) To suit, become. *Cette robe vous sied,* that dress suits you. *Il lui sied mal,* it ill becomes him.
sépale, *s.m. Bot:* Sepal.
séparable, *a.* Separable.
séparation, *s.f.* **1.** Separation, parting. **2.** Breaking up, dispersal.
séparément, *adv.* Separately. *Vivre s.,* to live apart.
séparer, *v.tr.* To separate. **1.** To disunite, part. **2.** To divide, keep apart.
se séparer. 1. To separate, part ; to part company. **2.** To divide, branch off. **3.** To break up, disperse.
séparé, *a.* **1.** Separate, different, distinct. **2.** Separated, apart.
sépia, *s.f.* Sepia (colour).
sept [sɛ(t)], *num.a.inv. & s.m.inv.* Seven. (As *card. adj.* before a noun or adj. beginning with a consonant sound [sɛ] ; otherwise [sɛt]) Bottes de sept lieues, [sɛljø] seven-league boots.
septembre, *s.m* September.
septentrional, -aux, *a.* Northern.
septième [sɛtjɛm]. **1.** *num.a. & s.* Seventh. **2.** *s.m.* Seventh (part).
septique, *a. Med:* Septic.
septuagénaire, *a. & s.* Septuagenarian
sépulcral, -aux, *a.* Sepulchral.
sépulcre, *s.m.* Sepulchre.
sépulture, *s.f.* **1.** Burial, sepulture, interment. **2.** Burial-place.
séquence, *s.f.* Sequence.
séquestrer, *v.tr* To sequester, sequestrate.
sequin, *s.m. Cost:* Sequin.
ser-ai, -as, -ons, etc. See ÊTRE.
sérail [-raːj], *s.m.* Seraglio.
séraphin, *s.m.* Seraph.
séraphique, *a.* Seraphic, angelic.
serbe, *a. & s. Geog:* Serb, Serbian.
Serbie. *Pr.n.f. Geog:* Serbia
serbo-croate, *a & s Geog:* Serbo-Croat(ian).
Sercq. *Pr.n. Geog:* (The island of) Sark.
serein[1], *a.* Serene, calm.
serein[2], *s.m.* Evening dew.
sérénade, *s.f.* Serenade.
sérénité, *s.f.* Serenity, calmness.
serf [sɛrf], **serve. 1.** *s.* Bond(s)man, bond(s)-woman ; serf. **2.** *a.* In bondage.
serge, *s.m. Tex:* (Woollen) serge.
sergent, *s.m.* Sergeant. (*a*) Sergent de ville, policeman. (*b*) *Mil:* Sergeant. Sergent major, quartermaster-sergeant.

série, *s.f.* **1.** (*a*) Series; succession. *Faire une s. de visites,* to go on a round of visits. *F:* **Série noire,** chapter of accidents. *Ind:* **Fabrication en (grande) série,** mass production. **Voiture de série,** car of standard model. *Com:* **Fin de série,** remnant. (*b*) Break (at billiards). **2.** Set (of tools).

sérieusement, *adv.* Seriously. (*a*) Solemnly. (*b*) Earnestly.

sérieux. 1. *a.* Serious. (*a*) Grave, sober. (*b*) Serious-minded. (*c*) Earnest, genuine. *Êtes-vous s.?* do you mean it? *Acheteur s.,* genuine purchaser. (*d*) Grave, weighty, important. **2.** *s.m.* Seriousness, gravity.

serin, *s.m.* (*a*) *Orn:* Canary. (*b*) *F:* Noodle, muff.

seringue, *s.f.* Syringe, squirt.

seringuer, *v.tr.* (*a*) To syringe. (*b*) To squirt.

serment, *s.m.* (Solemn) oath. **Prêter serment,** to take an oath. **Faire un faux serment,** to commit perjury.

sermon, *s.m.* Sermon.

sermonner. *F:* **1.** *v.i.* To sermonize. **2.** *v.tr.* To lecture; to give a talking-to.

serpe, *s.f.* Bill-hook, hedging-bill.

serpent, *s.m.* Serpent, snake.

serpentement, *s.m.* Winding, meandering.

serpenter, *v.i.* To wind, meander.

serpentin. 1. *a.* Serpentine. **2.** *s.m.* (Paper) streamer.

serpolet, *s.m. Bot:* Wild thyme.

serrage, *s.m.* Tightening; screwing tight.

serre, *s.f.* **1.** Greenhouse, conservatory, glass-house. **Serre chaude** hothouse. **2.** (*a*) Grip. (*b*) Claw, talon.

serrement, *s.m.* Squeezing, pressure. **Serrement de cœur,** pang.

serrer, *v.tr.* **1.** To put away, stow away. **2.** To press, squeeze, clasp. **Serrer le cou à qn,** to strangle s.o. *Cela me serre le cœur,* it wrings my heart. **3.** To tighten; to screw up. *S. les freins,* to put on the brakes. *S. qch. dans un étau,* to grip sth. in a vice. *S. les dents,* to clench one's teeth. **4.** To close, close up. *Mil:* *S. les rangs,* to close the ranks. **5.** To keep close to. *S. la muraille,* to skirt the wall. **se serrer. 1.** To stand, sit, close together; to crowd. **2.** To tighten.

serré. *a.* (*a*) Tight; close; compact, serried. **Avoir le cœur serré,** to be sad at heart. (*b*) Close-fisted.

serrure, *s.f.* Lock. **Trou de la serrure,** key-hole.

serrurier, *s.m.* Locksmith.

servage, *s.m.* Bondage, thraldom.

servant. 1. *a.* Serving. **2.** *s.m.* (*a*) *Artil:* *Les servants,* the gun crew. (*b*) *Ten:* Server. **3.** *s.f.* Servante, (maid-)servant.

serve, *s.f.* See SERF.

serviable, *a.* Obliging; willing to help.

service, *s.m.* **1.** (*a*) Service. **Escalier de service,** backstairs. (*b*) Department; administrative authority **Chef de service,** depart-

mental head. (*c*) Service (of trains). **2.** (*a*) Duty. **Officier de service,** orderly officer. (*b*) Attendance. (*c*) Divine service. (*d*) *Ten:* Service. **3. A votre service,** at your service. **4.** (*a*) Course (of a meal). (*b*) *Rail:* **Premier service,** first lunch or dinner. **5.** Set (of utensils).

serviette, *s.f.* **1.** (*a*) (Table-)napkin. (*b*) *S. de toilette,* towel. **2.** Portfolio (carried under the arm).

servile, *a.* Servile.

servilité, *s.f.* Servility; cringing.

servir, *v.* (*pr.p.* **servant;** *pr.ind.* **je sers**) To serve. **1.** *v.i.* (*a*) To serve. (*b*) *Servir à qch.,* to be useful for sth. *Cela ne sert à rien de pleurer,* it's no good crying. (*c*) *Servir de,* to serve as, be used as. *S. de prétexte,* to serve as a pretext. **2.** *v.tr.* (*a*) To be a servant to; to serve. (*b*) *Abs.* To serve (in army). (*c*) To serve, wait on. *Madame est servie,* dinner is served, madam. (*d*) To serve up, dish up. (*e*) To help, be of service to. (*f*) *Ten:* To serve. **se servir. 1.** *Se s. chez qn,* to buy one's provisions at a shop. **2.** *Se s. de qch.,* to use sth.

serviteur, *s.m.* Servant. "**Votre serviteur,**" 'your obedient servant.'

servitude, *s.f.* Servitude.

ses [se sɛ], *poss.a.* See SON[1].

session, *s.f.* Session, sitting.

seuil [sœːj], *s.m.* Threshold; door-step.

seul, *a.* **1.** (*Seul* preceding the noun) (*a*) Only, sole, single. **Avancer comme un seul homme,** to advance as one man. *Son s. souci,* his one, only, care. **Pas un seul,** not a single one. (*b*) *La seule pensée m'effraie,* the bare thought frightens me. **2.** (*Seul* following the noun or used predicatively) *Un homme seul,* a man by himself. *Rail:* *Compartiment de dames seules,* carriage for ladies only. *Je l'ai fait tout seul,* I did it (by) myself. **3.** *Seul un homme pourrait l'entreprendre,* only a man could undertake it.

seulement, *adv.* **1.** (*a*) Only. (*b*) Solely, merely. **2.** Even. **Si seulement il m'avait regardé!** if only he had looked at me!

sève, *s.f.* (*a*) Sap. (*b*) *F:* Vigour.

sévère, *a.* Severe. **1.** Stern, harsh. **2.** Strict, rigid.

sévèrement, *adv.* **1.** Severely, sternly. **2.** Strictly.

sévérité, *s.f.* Severity; sternness.

sévir, *v.i.* (Of pestilence) To rage.

sevrer, *v.tr.* (je sèvre) To wean.

sexagénaire, *a. & s.* Sexagenarian.

sexe, *s.m.* Sex.

sextuor, *s.m. Mus:* Sextet(te).

sexuel, -elle, *a.* Sexual.

sey-ait, -ant[1]. See SEOIR.

seyant[2], *a.* Becoming.

si[1], *conj.* (By elision **s'** before *il, ils*) **1.** If. (*a*) *Si j'avais su,* had I but known. *Si ce n'était mon rhumatisme,* were it not for my rheumatism. **Si tant est que** + *sub.*, if so it be that. (*b*) *S'il fut sévère, il fut juste*, if severe, he was just. **2.** Whether. *Je me demande si c'est vrai*, I wonder whether it is true. *F: Vous connaissez Paris?—Si je connais Paris!* you know Paris?—Of course, I know Paris! **3.** How; how much. *Vous savez si je vous aime*, you know how I love you. **4.** What if; suppose. *Et si elle l'apprend?* and what if she hears of it?

si², *adv.* **1.** So; so much. (*a*) *Un si bon dîner*, such a good dinner. (*b*) *Il n'est pas si beau que vous*, he is not as handsome as you. (*c*) *Si bien que*, with the result that. **2.** *Si peu que ce soit*, however little it may be. **3.** (In answer to a neg. question) Yes. **Si fait**, yes indeed. *Il n'est pas parti?—Si*, he hasn't gone?—Yes (, he has). *Il ne s'en remettra pas.—Que si!* he will not get over it. Yes, he will!

si³, *s.m.inv. Mus:* (The note) B.

siamois, *a. & s.* Siamese.

Sibérie. *Pr.n.f. Geog:* Siberia.

sibérien, -ienne, *a. & s.* Siberian.

sibilant, *a.* Sibilant, hissing.

sibylle, *s.f.* Sibyl.

Sicile. *Pr.n.f. Geog:* Sicily.

sicilien, -ienne, *a. & s.* Sicilian.

sicle, *s.m. B:* Shekel.

sidecar, *s.m. Mot:* Side-car.

sidéral, -aux, *a.* Sidereal.

siècle, *s.m.* **1.** Century. **2.** Age, period.

sied, sié-e, -ent, etc. See SEOIR.

siège, *s.m.* **1.** Seat, centre. **Siège social**, registered offices. **2.** *Mil:* Siege. **3.** Seat, chair. *Le s. du juge*, the judge's bench. **4.** Bottom (of chair).

siéger, *v.i.* (*Je siège*, n. *siégeons; je siégerai*) **1.** (Of company) To have its head office, (of malady) to be seated. **2.** (Of assembly) To sit.

sien, sienne¹. His, hers, its, one's. **1.** *poss.a. Mes intérêts sont siens*, my interests are his. **2.** *Le sien, la sienne, les siens, les siennes.* (*a*) *poss.pron. Ma sœur est plus jolie que la sienne*, my sister is prettier than his. (*b*) *s.m.* (i) *A chacun le sien*, to each one his own. **Y mettre du sien**, to contribute to an undertaking. (ii) *pl.* His own, her own, one's own (friends). *F: Il a encore fait des siennes*, he's been up to his old tricks.

Sienne². *Pr.n.f. Geog:* Sienna.

siér-a, -ont, etc. See SEOIR.

sieste, *s.f.* Siesta, *F:* nap.

sifflant. 1. *a.* Hissing; whistling; sibilant. **2.** *s.f. Ling:* Sifflante, sibilant.

sifflement, *s.m.* Whistling, whistle; hissing; whizz.

siffler. 1. *v.i.* (*a*) To whistle; to hiss; to whizz. (*b*) To blow a whistle. **2.** *v.tr.* (*a*) To whistle. (*b*) To whistle for. (*c*) *Th:* To hiss.

sifflet, *s.m.* Whistle.

siffleur, -euse. 1. *s.* Whistler. **2.** *a.* Whistling, hissing.

siffloter, *v.i.* To whistle to oneself.

signal, -aux, *s.m.* Signal. *Aut: Signaux de route*, road warnings.

signalement, *s.m.* Description; particulars.

signaler, *v.tr.* **1.** (*a*) To make conspicuous. (*b*) *S. qch. à l'attention de qn*, to draw s.o.'s attention to sth. (*c*) To report to the police. **2.** To signal. **3.** To give a description of. **se signaler**, to distinguish oneself.

signaleur, *s.m.* Signaller; signalman.

signataire, *s.m. & f.* Signatory, subscriber.

signature, *s.f.* **1.** Signing. **2.** Signature.

signe, *s.m.* Sign. **1.** Indication; symptom; mark, token. **2.** Symbol, mark. **3.** Gesture, motion. **Signe de tête**, nod. **Faire signe à qn**, to beckon to s.o

signer, *v.tr.* To sign. **se signer**, to cross oneself.

significatif, *a.* Significant.

signification, *s.f.* Meaning, signification, sense, import.

significativement, *adv.* Significantly.

signifier, *v.tr.* **1.** To mean, signify. *F: Qu'est-ce que cela signifie?* what's the meaning of this? **2.** To intimate clearly.

silence, *s.m.* **1.** Silence. **Faire silence**, to stop talking. **Passer qch. sous silence**, to pass over sth. in silence. **2.** *Mus:* Rest.

silencieusement, *adv.* Silently.

silencieux, *a.* Silent. (*a*) Taciturn. (*b*) Noiseless. (*c*) Still, peaceful.

silex [-lɛks], *s.m.* Silex, flint.

silhouette, *s.f.* (*a*) Silhouette. (*b*) Outline.

silhouetter, *v.tr.* To silhouette. **se silhouetter**, to show up.

silice, *s.f. Ch:* Silica

siliceux, *a* Siliceous.

silique, *s.f. Bot:* Siliqua, silique; pod.

sillage [sija:ʒ], *s.m.* (*a*) Wake, wash (of ship). (*b*) *Av:* Slip-stream.

sillon [sijɔ̃], *s.m.* (*a*) Furrow (*b*) Line, wrinkle.

sillonner [sijɔ-], *v.tr* (*a*) To furrow. (*b*) To streak (the heavens).

simagrée, *s.f.* (*a*) Pretence. (*b*) *pl.* Affected airs; grimaces; affectation.

simien, -ienne, *a. Z:* Simian.

simiesque, *a.* Monkey-like, apish.

similaire, *a.* Similar; like.

similairement, *adv.* Similarly.

similarité, *s.f.* Similarity, likeness.

simili, *s.m. F:* Imitation.

similicuir, *s.m.* Imitation leather.

similitude, *s.f.* Similitude; resemblance, likeness; similarity.

simoun [-mun], *s.m* Simoon; sand-storm.

simple, *a.* Simple. **1.** (*a*) Single (*b*) Not compound. *Avoir une chance s.*, to have even chances. *Ch:* **Corps simple**, element. **2.** (*a*) Ordinary, common. **Simple soldat**, private (soldier). (*b*) *Croire qn sur sa s. parole*, to believe s.o. on his word alone. (*c*) *Gens simples*, plain people. (*d*) Easy. **3.** (*a*) Simple-minded, unsophisticated. (*b*) Half-witted.

(c) Ingenuous. **4.** *s.m.pl.* **Simples,** simples, medicinal herbs.

simplement, *adv.* Simply.

simplicité, *s.f.* **I.** Simplicity; plainness. **2.** Artlessness, simpleness.

simplificateur, -trice, *a.* Simplifying.

simplification, *s.f.* Simplification.

simplifier, *v.tr.* To simplify.

simulacre, *s.m.* (a) Simulacrum, image. (b) Semblance.

simulation, *s.f.* Simulation, feint.

simuler, *v.tr.* To simulate, feign. **simulé,** *a.* Feigned; sham.

simultané, *a.* Simultaneous.

simultanément, *adv.* Simultaneously.

sinapisme, *s.m. Med:* Mustard plaster.

sincère, *a.* Sincere. **I.** Frank, candid. **2.** (a) Genuine, true-hearted (person). (b) Genuine, unfeigned.

sincèrement, *adv.* Sincerely.

sincérité, *s.f.* (a) Sincerity, frankness, candour. (b) Genuineness.

sinécure, *s.f.* Sinecure.

Singapour. *Pr.n.m. Geog:* Singapore.

singe, *s.m.* (a) Monkey, ape. (b) *F:* Ape, imitator.

singer, *v.tr.* (n. singeons) To ape, mimic.

singerie, *s.f.* (a) Grimace. (b) Affectation.

singularité, *s.f.* Singularity. **I.** Peculiarity, special feature. **2.** Oddness, oddity.

singulier, *a.* Singular. **I.** Peculiar (d, to). **2.** Peculiar, remarkable. **3.** (a) Odd, curious. (b) Conspicuous.

singulièrement, *adv.* **I.** Singularly **2.** Oddly, strangely.

sinistre. I. *a.* Sinister, ominous. **2.** *s.m.* Disaster, catastrophe.

sinon, *conj.* **I.** Otherwise, (or) else, if not. **2.** Except.

sinueux, *a.* Sinuous; winding.

sinuosité, *s.f.* (a) Sinuosity, winding. (b) Bend (of river).

siphon, *.m.* Siphon.

sirène, *s.f.* **I.** (a) Siren, mermaid. (b) *F:* Charmer. **2.** (a) Siren, hooter. (b) Fog-horn.

sirocco, *s.m.* Sirocco.

sirop, *s.m.* Syrup.

siroter, *v.tr. F:* To sip.

sis. See SEOIR.

sismique, *a.* Seismic (movement).

sitôt, *adv.* (a) = AUSSITÔT Sitôt que, as soon as (b) Vous ne le reverrez pas de sitôt, it will be long before you see him again

situation, *s.f.* Situation **I.** Position site. **2.** State, condition *S. sociale,* station in life. *S. difficile,* predicament. **3.** *Il a une belle s.,* he has a first-rate position.

situer, *v.tr* To place, situate, locate.

six, *num.a.inv. & s.m.* Six. **I.** *card.a.* (At the end of the word-group [sis]; before a noun or adj. beginning with a vowel sound [siz]; before a noun or adj. beginning with a consonant [si]) *J'en ai six,* I have six. **2.** (Always [sis]) *Six et demi,* six and a half.

sixième [siz-]. **I.** *num.a. & s.* Sixth. **2.** *s.m.* Sixth (part).

ski, *s.m.* **I.** Ski. **2.** Skiing.

slave. I. *a.* Slav, Slavonic. **2.** *s.* Slav.

sleeping [-piŋ], *s.m.* Rail: *F:* Sleeping-car.

sloop [slup], *s.m. Nau:* Sloop.

slovaque, *a. & s.* Slovak.

smoking [-kiŋ], *s.m.* Dinner-jacket.

snob [snɔb], *s.m.* Pretentious fellow.

sobre, *a.* Temperate, abstemious.

sobrement, *adv.* Soberly.

sobriété, *s.f.* **I.** Temperateness, sobriety, moderation. **2.** Quietness (in dress).

sobriquet, *s.m.* Nickname.

soc [sɔk], *s.m.* Ploughshare.

sociabilité, *s.f.* Sociability.

sociable, *a.* Sociable, companionable.

social, -aux, *a.* Social. (a) L'ordre social, the social order. (b) *Com:* Capital social, registered capital.

socialisme, *s.m.* Socialism.

socialiste. I. *a.* Socialistic; socialist. **2.** *s.* Socialist.

société, *s.f.* Society. **I.** (a) Community. (b) Company. **2.** (a) Association, fellowship. (b) *Com:* Company. **3.** (a) Companionship (of one's fellows). (b) *Fréquenter la bonne s.,* to move in good society.

sociologue, *s.m.* Sociologist.

socle, *s.m* Base, pedestal, plinth.

socque, *s.m.* Clog, patten.

Socrate. *Pr.n.m.* Socrates.

sodium [-jɔm], *s.m. Ch:* Sodium.

sœur, *s.f.* **I.** Sister. **2.** *Ecc:* Sister (of charity); nun.

sofa, *s.m.* Sofa, settee.

soi, *pers.pron.* Oneself; himself, herself, itself, etc. *Chacun pour soi,* everyone for himself. *Petits services qu'on se rend entre soi,* small services that we do one another.

soi-disant. I. *a.inv.* (a) Self-styled, would-be. (b) So-called. **2.** *adv.* Supposedly, ostensibly.

soie, *s.f.* **I.** Bristle. **2.** Silk. Papier de soie, tissue paper.

soient. See ÊTRE.

soierie, *s.f.* **I.** Silk goods; silks. **2.** Silk trade.

soif [swaf], *s.f.* Thirst Boire à sa soif, to drink one's fill.

soigner, *v.tr* To look after, take care of, attend to. **soigné,** *a* Well finished, carefully done. *Repas s.,* carefully cooked meal.

soigneusement, *adv.* Carefully, with care.

soigneux, *a.* Careful; painstaking.

soi-même, *pers.pron.* Oneself. Faire qch. de soi-même, to do sth. of one's own accord.

soin, *s.m.* Care. (a) *Le s. des enfants,* the care of the children. Prendre soin de qch., to look after sth. (On letters) "Aux (bons) soins de . . .," 'care of. . . .' (b) Attention, trouble. Avoir soin, to take care. (c) Avec soin, carefully; with care. (d) *pl.* Attentions, solicitude. **Être aux petits soins pour qn,** to wait on s.o. hand and foot.

soir, *s.m.* (a) Evening. *A dix heures du s.,* at ten (o'clock) p.m. (b) Afternoon.

soirée, *s.f.* I. (Duration of) evening. 2. (a) (Evening) party. **Donner une s. dansante,** to give a dance. **Habit de soirée,** dress-suit. (b) *Th:* **Représentation de soirée,** evening performance.

sois. See ÊTRE.

soit [swat, (before a consonant) swa] (Third pers. of *pr.sub.* of *être*) I. **Soit!** all right! 2. (a) *conj.* **Soit** *l'un* **soit** *l'autre,* either one or the other. (b) **Soit qu'il vienne ou qu'il ne vienne pas,** whether he comes or not.

soixantaine [swasã-], *s.f.* About sixty. **Avoir passé la soixantaine,** to be in the sixties.

soixante [swasã:t], *num.a.inv.* & *s.m.inv.* Sixty.

soixante-dix, *num.a.inv.* & *s.m.inv.* Seventy.

sol¹ [sɔl], *s.m.* (a) Ground, earth. *F:* **Rester cloué au sol,** to stand rooted to the spot. (b) *Agr:* Soil.

sol², *s.m.inv. Mus:* (The note) G.

solaire, *a.* Solar.

soldat, *s.m.* Soldier. *S. de première classe,* lance-corporal. **Se faire soldat** to go into the army.

solde¹, *s.f.* Pay.

solde², *s.m. Com:* I. Balance. "**Pour solde,**" 'in settlement.' 2. (a) Surplus stock, job lot. (b) **Vente de soldes,** clearance sale.

sole, *s.f. Ich:* Sole.

solécisme, *s.m.* Solecism.

soleil [-lɛ:j], *s.m.* I. Sun. 2. Sunshine. **Il fait du soleil,** the sun is shining. **Avoir du bien au soleil,** to have landed property. **Coup de soleil,** touch of sunstroke. 3. *Bot:* Sunflower. 4. *Pyr:* Catherine-wheel.

solennel, -elle, *a.* Solemn.

solennellement, *adv.* I. With ceremony. 2. Impressively, solemnly.

solenniser, *v.tr.* To solemnize; to celebrate.

solennité, *s.f.* (a) Solemnity; awfulness. (b) Solemn ceremony.

solfège, *s.m. Mus:* Solfeggio; sol-fa.

solidaire, *a.* I. *Jur:* Jointly responsible. *Être s. des actes de qn,* to be responsible for s.o.'s acts. 2. Interdependent.

solidairement, *adv.* Jointly.

solidarité, *s.f.* I. Joint responsibility. 2. (a) Interdependence. (b) Fellowship, solidarity. **Grève de solidarité,** sympathetic strike.

solide. I. *a.* (a) Solid. (b) Solid, strong. *Com:* Sound, solvent. 2. *s.m.* Solid (body).

solidement, *adv.* Solidly, firmly.

solidification, *s.f.* Solidification.

solidifier, *v.tr.* To solidify.

solidité, *s.f.* Solidity; strength.

soliloque, *s.m.* Soliloquy.

soliste, *s.m.* & *f.* Soloist.

solitaire. I. *a* Solitary, lonely, lonesome.

2. *s.m.* (a) Hermit, recluse. (b) Solitaire (diamond).

solitude, *s.f.* I. Solitude, loneliness 2. Lonely spot; wilderness; solitude.

solive, *s.f. Const:* Joist, beam, balk.

sollicitation, *s.f.* Solicitation, entreaty.

solliciter, *v.tr.* To solicit; to beg for *S. des voix,* to canvass for votes.

solliciteur, -euse, *s.* Petitioner; applicant

sollicitude, *s.f.* (a) Solicitude, (tender) care. (b) Anxiety, concern.

solo, *s.m. Mus:* Solo.

solstice, *s.m.* Solstice.

solubilité, *s.f.* Solubility.

soluble, *a.* Soluble.

solution, *s.f.* I. **Solution de continuité,** gap; solution of continuity. 2. Solution (of solid in liquid). 3. Solution; answer.

solvabilité, *s.f.* Solvency.

solvable, *a.* Solvent (financially).

Somalie. *Pr.n.f. Geog:* Somaliland.

sombre, *a.* Dark, sombre, gloomy.

sombrement, *adv.* Gloomily, sombrely.

sombrer, *v.i.* To founder; to sink. *Sa raison sombra complètement,* his mind entirely gave way.

sommaire. I. *a.* (a) Summary, succinct, concise. (b) Summary, hasty. 2. *s.m.* Summary, abstract, synopsis.

sommairement, *adv.* I. Summarily. 2. Hastily.

sommation, *s.f. Jur:* Summons; notice.

somme¹, *s.f.* **Bête de somme,** beast of burden.

somme², *s.f.* Sum, amount; sum of money. **Tout fait somme,** everything counts **Somme toute,** upon the whole. **En somme,** in short.

somme³, *s.m.* Nap; short sleep.

sommeil [-mɛ:j], *s.m.* I. Sleep, slumber. **Avoir le sommeil dur,** to be hard to wake. 2. Drowsiness, sleepiness. **Avoir sommeil,** to be sleepy

sommeiller [-mɛje], *v.i.* To doze, nod; to sleep lightly; to slumber.

sommelier, *s.m.* Wine-waiter

sommer, *v.tr* To summon.

sommes. See ÊTRE.

sommet, *s.m.* Top, summit (of hill); apex.

sommier, *s.m.* I. Pack-horse. 2. *S. élastique,* spring-mattress.

somnambule, *s.* Somnambulist.

somnambulisme, *s.m.* Somnambulism.

somnolence, *s.f* Somnolence, sleepiness, drowsiness.

somnolent, *a.* Somnolent, sleepy, drowsy.

somnoler, *v.i.* To drowse, doze.

somptueusement, *adv.* Sumptuously.

somptueux, *a.* Sumptuous.

somptuosité, *s.f.* Sumptuousness.

son¹, sa, ses, *poss.a.* (*Son* is used instead of *sa* before fem. nouns beginning with a vowel or h 'mute.') His, her, its, one's. *Un de ses amis,* a friend of his, of hers. *Ses père et mère,* his father and mother.

son², *s.m.* Sound. *Son d'une cloche*, ringing of a bell.

son³, *s.m.* Bran.

sonate, *s.f. Mus:* Sonata.

sondage, *s.m.* (*a*) *Nau:* Sounding. *Min:* Boring. (*b*) *Med:* Probing.

sonde, *s.f.* **1.** *Nau:* (*a*) Sounding-line, plummet. **Jeter la sonde**, to heave the lead. (*b*) (Of whale) **Faire la sonde**, to sound. **2.** *Surg:* Probe. **3.** *Min:* Borer.

sonder, *v.tr.* **1.** (*a*) *Nau:* To sound. *F:* On *n'a jamais sondé ce mystère*, this mystery has never been fathomed. (*b*) *v.i.* (Of whale) To sound. **2.** To probe, examine. **Sonder le terrain**, *F:* to see how the land lies. **3.** *Surg:* To probe.

songe, *s.m.* Dream.

songe-creux, *s.m.inv.* Dreamer, visionary.

songer, *v.i.* (n. songeons) **1.** (*a*) To dream. (*b*) To muse; to day-dream. *Je songeais en moi-même*, I thought to myself. **2.** (*a*) Songer **à qch.**, to think of sth. *Il ne faut pas y s.*, that's quite out of the question. (*b*) To imagine. *Songez donc!* just fancy! (*c*) To remember. *Songez à lui*, bear him in mind.

songerie, *s.f.* (Day-)dreaming.

songeur, -euse, *a.* (*a*) Dreamy. (*b*) Pensive, thoughtful.

sonnant, *a.* **1.** Striking. **A dix heures sonnant(es)**, on the stroke of ten. **2.** Resounding. **Monnaie sonnante**, hard cash.

sonner. **1.** *v.i.* To sound; to strike; to ring. **2.** *v.tr.* (*a*) To sound. *S. la cloche*, to ring the bell. *Abs. On sonne*, there is a ring at the door. (*b*) To ring for.

sonné, *a. Il est dix heures sonnées*, it is past ten.

sonnerie, *s.f.* **1.** (*a*) Ringing (of bells). (*b*) Set of bells; chimes. **2.** (*a*) **Montre à sonnerie**, repeater. (*b*) **S. électrique**, electric bell. **3.** *Mil:* (Trumpet-, bugle-) call. *S. aux morts*, last post.

sonnet, *s.m.* Sonnet.

sonnette, *s.f.* **1.** (*a*) Small bell. (*b*) Handbell. (*c*) House-bell. **Cordon de sonnette**, bell-pull. **Coup de sonnette**, ring (at the door). **2.** **Serpent à sonnettes**, rattlesnake.

sonneur, *s.m.* Bell-ringer.

sonore, *a.* Sonorous. **1.** Loud-sounding; resonant; resounding. *Ph:* **Onde sonore**, sound-wave. **2.** Deep-toned, ringing.

sont. See ÊTRE.

sophisme, *s.m.* Sophism.

sophiste, *s.m.* Sophist.

sophisterie, *s.f.* Sophistry.

sophistique. **1.** *a.* Sophistic(al). **2.** *s.f.* Sophistry.

soporatif. **1.** *a.* Sleep-inducing, soporific. **2.** *s.m.* Soporific.

soporifique = SOPORATIF **Potion soporifique**, sleeping-draught.

soprano, *s.m. & f.* Soprano.

sorbet, *s.m.* Sorbet; water-ice.

sorcellerie, *s.f.* Witchcraft, sorcery.

sorcier, *s.* Sorcerer, *f.* sorceress; wizard, *f.* witch. *F:* **Vieille sorcière**, old hag.

sordide, *a.* Sordid, squalid. **1.** Filthy, dirty. **2.** Mean, base.

Sorlingues (les). *Pr.n.f.pl.* The Scilly Islands.

sornettes, *s.f.pl.* Nonsense; idle talk.

sor-s, -t¹. See SORTIR.

sort², *s.m.* **1.** Lot (in life). **2.** Destiny, fate. **3.** Chance, fortune, lot. **Tirer au sort**, to draw lots. **Le sort en est jeté**, the die is cast. **4.** Spell, charm.

sortant, *a.* Coming out. *Foule sortante*, outgoing crowd.

sorte, *s.f.* **1.** Manner, way. **Ne parlez pas de la sorte**, don't talk like that. **En quelque sorte**, in a way. **Parlez de sorte qu'on vous comprenne**, speak so as to be understood. **En sorte que** + *sub.*, so that, in such a manner that. **2.** Sort, kind.

sortilège, *s.m.* Spell, charm.

sortir, *v.* (Conj. like MENTIR) **I.** *v.i.* **1.** (*a*) To go or come out. *Ne le laissez pas s.*, don't let him out. *Th:* **Macbeth sort**, exit Macbeth. *S. d'un emploi*, to leave a situation. (*b*) To ride out; to drive out; to sail out. (*c*) *S. en courant*, to run out. (*d*) To have just come out. *Je sors de table*, I have just risen from table. (*e*) *S. de son sujet*, to wander from one's subject. **2.** To go out, go from home. *Madame est sortie*, Mrs X is out. **3.** To get out, extricate oneself. *Il sortit vainqueur*, he came off victorious. **4.** To spring, descend (from). *Officier sorti des rangs*, officer who has risen from the ranks. **5.** To stand out, project. *Yeux qui sortent de la tête*, protruding eyes.

II. sortir, *v.tr.* To take out, bring out.

III. sortir, *s.m.* **Au sortir du théâtre**, on coming out of the theatre.

sortie, *s.f.* **1.** (*a*) Going out, coming out, departure, exit. *A la s. des ateliers*, when the men leave work. (*b*) Leaving (for good). **A ma sortie d'école**, on (my) leaving school. (*c*) *Com:* **Droit de sortie**, export duty. **2.** Trip, excursion. **3.** (*a*) *Mil:* Sortie. (*b*) *F:* Outburst, tirade. **4.** Exit; way out. **Par ici la sortie**, this way out. **5.** *Cost:* **Sortie de théâtre**, evening wrap, opera-cloak.

sosie, *s.m.* *F:* Double, counterpart.

sot, sotte. **1.** *a.* (*a*) Silly, stupid, foolish. (*b*) Embarrassed, disconcerted. **2.** *s.* Fool, dolt.

sottement, *adv.* Stupidly, foolishly.

sottise, *s.f.* **1.** Stupidity, folly. **2.** (*a*) Foolish act or word. (*b*) Offensive remark.

sou, *s.m.* Sou (= five centimes). *A:* **Gros sou**, penny(-piece). **Il n'a pas pour deux sous de courage**, he hasn't a ha'p'orth of pluck.

soubresaut, *s.m.* (*a*) Sudden start; bound, leap; jolt. (*b*) Sudden emotion; gasp.

souche, *s.f.* **1.** (*a*) Stump, stub (of tree). (*b*) *F:* Blockhead, dolt. **2.** **Faire souche** to,

found a family. *Famille de vieille s.*, an old family. **3.** *Com:* Counterfoil.
souci[1], *s.m. Bot:* Marigold.
souci[2], *s.m.* Care. **1.** Solicitude. *S. de la vérité*, regard for truth. **2.** Anxiety, worry. **Être en souci de qch.**, to worry about sth.
soucier (se), *v.pr.* To trouble oneself, concern oneself; to care; to mind.
soucieux, *a.* (*a*) Anxious, concerned. (*b*) Full of care; worried.
soucoupe, *s.f.* Saucer.
soudain. 1. *a.* Sudden, unexpected. **2.** *adv.* Suddenly; all of a sudden.
soudainement, *adv.* Suddenly, unexpectedly.
soudaineté, *s.f.* Suddenness.
soude, *s.f.* Soda.
souder, *v.tr.* (*a*) To solder. (*b*) To weld. **se souder. 1.** To weld. **2.** (Of bone) To knit.
soudure, *s.f.* **1.** (*a*) Soldering. (*b*) Welding. **2.** Solder.
souffle, *s.m.* Breath. **1.** Puff, blast. **2.** Respiration, breathing. **Retenir son souffle**, to hold one's breath. **Couper le souffle à qn**, to take s.o.'s breath away. **Être à bout de souffle**, to be out of breath.
souffler. 1. *v.i.* (*a*) To blow. (*b*) To recover one's breath. (*c*) To pant; to puff. (*d*) *Le vent souffle en tempête*, it is blowing a gale. **2.** *v.tr.* (*a*) To blow up (the fire); to blow out (a candle). (*b*) To breathe, utter. (*c*) To prompt (an actor). (*d*) *Draughts:* To huff.
soufflet, *s.m.* **1.** (Pair of) bellows. **2.** (*a*) *Malle à soufflets*, portmanteau with expanding sides. (*b*) *Rail:* 'Concertina' vestibule. **3.** (*a*) Box on the ear, slap in the face. (*b*) Affront.
souffleter, *v.tr.* (**je soufflette**) **Souffleter qn**, to box s.o.'s ears, to slap s.o.'s face.
souffleur, -euse, *s. Th:* Prompter.
souffrance, *s.f.* **1. En souffrance**, in suspense, in abeyance. **3.** Suffering, pain.
souffrant, *a.* (*a*) Suffering; in pain. (*b*) Unwell, poorly, ailing.
souffreteux, *a.* **1.** Destitute, needy. **2.** Sickly, peaky, half-starved.
souffrir, *v.* (Conj. like OUVRIR) To suffer. **1.** *v.tr.* (*a*) To endure, undergo, put up with. (*b*) To permit, allow. **2.** *v.i.* (*a*) To feel pain. *Mon bras me fait s.*, my arm pains me. *Je souffre de le voir si changé*, it pains me to see him so changed. (*b*) To suffer injury.
soufre, *s.m.* Sulphur.
souhait, *s.m.* Wish, desire. *Présenter ses souhaits à qn*, to offer s.o. one's good wishes. **A souhait**, to one's liking.
souhaitable, *a.* Desirable.
souhaiter, *v.tr.* To wish. *S. les richesses*, to desire wealth.
souiller [-je], *v.tr.* **1.** To soil, dirty. **2.** To pollute. **3.** To tarnish, sully.
souillure [-jy:r], *s.f.* **1.** Spot (of dirt); stain. **2.** Blot, blemish.
soûl [su]. *F:* **1.** *a.* (*a*) Glutted, gorged. (*b*)

Drunk, tipsy. **2.** *s.m.* **Manger tout son soûl**, to eat one's fill. *Dormir tout son s.*, to have one's sleep out.
soulagement, *s.m.* Relief, alleviation; solace.
soulager, *v.tr.* (n. **soulageons**) To ease; to relieve, alleviate. **se soulager. 1.** To ease oneself. **2.** To relieve one's feelings.
soulèvement, *s.m.* (*a*) Rising, heaving. **Soulèvement de cœur**, nausea. (*b*) *Geol:* Upheaval. (*c*) Revolt, rising. (*d*) Burst of indignation.
soulever, *v.tr.* (**je soulève**) **1.** (*a*) To raise; to lift (up). (*b*) To raise slightly. (*c*) *S. une objection*, to raise an objection. **2.** To rouse, stir up. **se soulever. 1.** To rise. *La mer se soulève*, the sea heaves. **2.** (*a*) To raise oneself. (*b*) To revolt.
soulier, *s.m.* Shoe.
soulignement, *s.m.* (*a*) Underlining. (*b*) Stressing.
souligner, *v.tr.* (*a*) To underline. (*b*) To emphasize, lay stress on.
soumettre, *v.tr.* (Conj. like METTRE) **1.** To subdue. **2.** To submit, refer. **3.** *S. qch. à un examen*, to subject sth. to an examination. **se soumettre**, to submit, yield.
soumis, *a.* **1.** Submissive, obedient. **2.** Subject, amenable.
soumission, *s.f.* **1.** (*a*) Submission. **Faire (sa) soumission**, to surrender, yield. (*b*) Profession of allegiance. (*c*) Obedience, submissiveness. **2.** *Com:* Tender.
soupape, *s.f.* Valve.
soupçon, *s.m.* Suspicion. **1.** *J'en avais le s.!* I suspected as much! **2.** Surmise, conjecture. **3.** *F:* Slight flavour, small quantity, dash.
soupçonner, *v.tr.* **1.** To suspect. **2.** To surmise, conjecture.
soupçonneusement, *adv.* Suspiciously, distrustfully.
soupçonneux, *a.* Suspicious, distrustful.
soupe, *s.f.* **1.** Sop. *S. au lait*, bread and milk. **2.** Soup.
soupente, *s.f.* Loft, garret.
souper. I. *v.i.* To have supper; to sup. *F:* **J'en ai soupé**, I have had enough of it. **II. souper**, *s.m.* Supper.
soupeser, *v.tr.* (**je soupèse**) To feel, try, the weight of.
soupière, *s.f.* Soup-tureen.
soupir, *s.m.* Sigh. **Rendre le dernier soupir**, to breathe one's last.
soupirant, *s.m. F:* Suitor, wooer.
soupirer, *v.i.* (*a*) To sigh. (*b*) *S. après qch.*, to long for sth.
souple, *a.* (*a*) Supple, pliant; flexible, lithe. *Esprit s.*, versatile mind. (*b*) Docile.
souplement, *adv.* Supply, lithely.
souplesse, *s.f.* **1.** Suppleness, flexibility, pliability, litheness. *S. d'esprit*, versatility. **2.** Pliability (of character).

source, *s.f.* Source. **1.** Spring(-head), fountain(-head), well. **Eau de source,** spring water. **2.** Origin. *Aller à la s. du mal,* to get to the root of the evil. **Je le tiens de bonne source,** I have it on good authority.

sourcil [-si], *s.m.* Eyebrow.

sourciller [-sije], *v.i.* **1.** To knit one's brows. **2.** To flinch. **Sans sourciller,** *F:* without turning a hair.

sourcilleux [-sij-], *a.* Supercilious.

sourd, *a.* **1.** (a) Deaf. (b) *s.* Deaf person. *F:* **Taper comme un sourd,** to lay about one. **2.** Dull; muffled. *Cela tomba avec un coup s.,* it fell with a thud. **Lanterne sourde,** dark-lantern. *Hostilité sourde,* veiled hostility.

sourdement, *adv.* With a dull, hollow, sound.

sourdine, *s.f.* **1.** *Mus:* Mute. **2. A la sourdine,** in secret, on the sly.

sourd-muet, sourde-muette. 1. *a.* Deaf-and-dumb. **2.** *s.* Deaf-mute. *pl. Des sourd(e)s-muet(te)s.*

sourdre, *v.i.* (Used only in third pers. **il sourd, ils sourdent,** and in inf.) To spring, to well (up).

souriant, *a.* Smiling.

souricière, *s.f.* (a) Mouse-trap. (b) *F:* Trap, snare.

sourire. I. *v.i.* (Conj. like RIRE) **1.** To smile. **2.** To prove attractive to.
  II. **sourire,** *s.m.* Smile. *S. affecté,* smirk. **Garder le sourire,** to keep smiling.

souris, *s.f.* Mouse.

sournois. 1. *a.* Artful, sly, crafty; under-hand. **2.** *s.* Sneak.

sournoisement, *adv.* Cunningly; slyly.

sous, *prep.* **1.** Under(neath), beneath, below. *Sous clef,* under lock and key. *Sous le vent,* under the lee. *Sous les tropiques,* in the tropics. **2. Sous-,** *pref.* Sub-, under-.

NOTE. Compound nouns and adjectives of which the first element is *sous* vary in the plural.

sous-bois, *s.m.* Underwood, undergrowth.

sous-chef, *s.m.* **1.** Deputy chief clerk. **2.** Assistant manager.

souscripteur, *s.m.* Subscriber.

souscription, *s.f.* **1.** (a) Execution, signing (of deed) (b) Subscription, signature. **2.** Subscription, application **3.** Subscription, contribution

souscrire, *v.tr.* (Conj. like ÉCRIRE) **1.** To sign, execute (deed). **2.** *S. un abonnement,* to take out a subscription *S mille francs,* to subscribe a thousand francs. **3.** *Abs. S. à une opinion,* to subscribe to an opinion.

sous-entendre, *v.tr.* To understand; not to express; to imply.
  sous-entendu, *s.m.* Thing understood; implication.

sous-entente, *s.f.* Mental reservation.

sous-estimer, *v.tr.* To under-estimate, underrate.

sous-exposer, *v.tr.* *Phot:* To under-expose.

sous-exposition, *s.f.* *Phot:* Under-exposure.

sous-jacent, *a.* Subjacent, underlying.

Sous-le-vent. *Pr.n. Geog:* Les îles Sous-le-vent, the Leeward Islands.

sous-lieutenant, *s.m.* Second-lieutenant, sub-lieutenant. *Av:* Pilot officer.

sous-locataire, *s.m. & f.* Subtenant.

sous-location, *s.f.* **1.** Sub-letting, under-letting. **2.** Under-tenancy, sub-lease.

sous-louer, *v.tr.* To sub-let, sub-lease.

sous-main, *s.m.* Blotting-pad, writing-pad.

sous-maître, -maîtresse, *s. Sch:* Assistant master, assistant mistress.

sous-marin. 1. *a.* Submarine; submerged. **2.** *s.m.* Submarine.

sous-mentionné, *a.* Undermentioned.

sous-off, *s.m. F:* N.C.O., non-com.

sous-officier, *s.m.* **1.** Non-commissioned officer. **2.** *Navy:* Petty officer.

sous-préfecture, *s.f.* Sub-prefecture.

sous-préfet, *s.m. Adm:* Sub-prefect.

sous-principal, *s.m. Sch:* Vice-principal.

sous-production, *s.f.* Under-production.

sous-produit, *s.m. Ind:* By-product.

sous-secrétaire, *s.m. & f.* Under-secretary.

sous-seing [-sɛ̃], *s.m.* Private contract.

sous-sel, *s.m. Ch:* Subsalt; basic salt.

soussigner, *v.tr.* To sign, undersign.
  soussigné, *a. & s.* Undersigned.

sous-sol, *s.m.* **1.** *Geol:* Subsoil. **2.** *Const:* Basement; basement-flat.

sous-tendre, *v.tr. Geom:* To subtend.

sous-titre, *s.m.* **1.** Sub-title. **2.** *Cin:* Caption.

soustraction, *s.f.* (a) Removal, abstraction. (b) *Mth:* Subtraction.

soustraire, *v.tr* (Conj. like TRAIRE) **1.** To take away, abstract. **2.** To screen, shield. **3.** *Mth:* To subtract.
  se soustraire à qch., to avoid, escape, sth. *Se s. aux regards,* to retire from sight.

sous-vêtement, *s.m.* Undergarment.

soutane, *s.f.* Cassock, soutane. *F:* **Prendre la soutane,** to become a priest.

soute, *s.f. Nau:* Store-room. *S. à charbon,* coal-bunker. *Soutes à mazout,* oil(-fuel) tanks. *S. à munitions,* magazine

soutenable, *a.* Tenable.

soutenant, *a.* Sustaining.

soutenir, *v.tr.* (Conj. like TENIR) To sustain, support **1.** (a) To hold up, prop up. (b) To keep, maintain (family). (c) To back (up); to stand up for. (d) To maintain, uphold (opinion); to affirm. (e) To keep up, sustain. **2.** To sustain, withstand
  se soutenir. 1. To support, maintain, oneself; to hold up, keep up. **2.** To last, continue.
  soutenu, *a.* Sustained.

souterrain. 1. *a.* Underground, subterranean. **Passage souterrain,** subway. **2.** *s.m.* Underground passage; subway.

soutien, *s.m.* (*a*) Support, prop. (*b*) Supporter, upholder.

soutirer, *v.tr.* To draw off; to tap.

souvenir. I. *v.impers.* (Conj. like VENIR. Aux. *être*) To occur to the mind. **Autant qu'il m'en souvienne,** to the best of my recollection.
se souvenir de qch., to remember sth. **Faire souvenir qn de qch.,** to remind s.o. of sth.
II. **souvenir,** *s.m.* I. Remembrance, recollection, memory. **Veuillez me rappeler à son bon souvenir,** please remember me kindly to him. **2.** Memorial, memento. **3.** Keepsake, souvenir.

souvent, *adv.* Often. **Le plus souvent,** more often than not.

souverain. I. *a.* Sovereign; supreme. **2.** *s.* Sovereign.

souveraineté, *s.f.* Sovereignty.

soviet [-vjɛt], *s.m.* Soviet.

soviétique, *a.* Soviet.

soya [sɔja], *s.m. Bot :* Soya-bean, soy.

soyeux, *a.* Silky.

soy-ons, -ez. See ÊTRE.

spacieux, *a.* Spacious, roomy.

spadassin, *s.m.* Bully, bravo.

spaghetti, *s.m.pl.* Spaghetti.

spahi, *s.m. Mil :* Spahi (Algerian trooper).

sparte[1], *s.m. Bot :* Esparto (grass).

Sparte[2]. *Pr.n.f. A.Geog :* Sparta.

spartiate, *a. & s. A.Geog :* Spartan.

spasme, *s.m.* Spasm.

spath, *s.m. Miner :* Spar.

spathe, *s.f. Bot :* Spathe.

spatule, *s.f.* I. Spatula. **Doigts en spatule,** spatulate fingers. **2.** *Orn :* Spoonbill.

spécial, -aux, *a.* Special, especial.

spécialement, *adv.* (E)specially, particularly.

spécialisation, *s.f.* Specialization

spécialiser, *v.tr.* To specialize.

spécialiste, *s.m. & f.* Specialist, expert.

spécialité, *s.f.* Speciality, special feature.

spécieusement, *adv.* Speciously, plausibly.

spécieux, *a.* Specious; plausible.

spécification, *s.f.* Specification.

spécifier, *v.tr.* To specify. *S.* que, to lay down that.

spécifique. I. *a.* Specific. **2.** *s.m Med :* Specific (remedy).

spécifiquement, *adv.* Specifically.

spécimen [-mɛn], *s.m.* Specimen.

spectacle, *s.m.* I. Spectacle, sight. *F :* **Se donner en spectacle,** to make an exhibition of oneself. **2.** *Th :* Play entertainment. **3.** Show, display.

spectaculaire, *a.* Spectacular.

spectateur, -trice, *s.* Spectator, onlooker, bystander.

spectral, -aux, *a.* Spectral. I. Ghostly, ghostlike. **2.** *Opt : Couleurs spectrales,* colours of the spectrum.

spectre, *s.m.* I. Spectre, ghost, apparition **2.** *Opt :* (Solar) spectrum.

spectroscope, *s.m. Opt :* Spectroscope.

spéculateur, -trice, *s.* I. Speculator theorizer. **2.** *Fin :* Speculator.

spéculatif, *a.* Speculative.

spéculation, *s.f.* Speculation. I. (*a*) Cogitation. (*b*) Theory, conjecture. **2.** *Pure s.* pure gamble.

spéculer, *v.i.* I. To speculate, cogitate **2.** *Fin :* To speculate.

spermaceti [-seti], *s.m.* Spermaceti. **Huile de spermaceti,** sperm oil.

sphère, *s.f.* Sphere. I. Globe, orb. **2.** *F.* Circuit, orbit.

sphérique, *a.* Spherical.

sphinx [sfɛ̃ks], *s.m. Myth :* Sphinx.

spicule, *s.m.* Spicule, spikelet.

spinal, -aux, *a. Anat :* Spinal.

spiral, -aux. I. *a.* Spiral. **2.** *s.m.* Hairspring (of watch). **3.** *s.f.* **Spirale,** spiral.

spirite. I. *a.* Spiritualistic. **2.** *s.* Spiritualist.

spiritisme, *s.m.* Spiritualism.

spirituel, -elle, *a.* I. Spiritual. **2.** Witty humorous.

spirituellement, *adv.* I. Spiritually. **2.** Wittily.

spiritueux. I. *a.* Spirituous. **2.** *.m* Spirituous liquor. *Les spiritueux,* spirits.

spleen [-lin], *s.m.* Spleen; lowness of spirits.

splendeur, *s.f.* Splendour. (*a*) Brilliance, brightness. (*b*) Magnificence.

splendide, *a.* Splendid.

splendidement, *adv.* Splendidly.

spoliateur, -trice. I. *s.* Despoiler. **2.** *a.* Despoiling.

spoliation, *s.f.* Spoliation; despoiling.

spolier, *v.tr.* To despoil, rob.

spondée, *s.m. Pros :* Spondee.

spongieux, *a.* Spongy.

spontané, *a.* Spontaneous.

spontanéité, *s.f.* Spontaneity.

spontanément, *adv.* Spontaneously.

sporadique, *a.* Sporadic.

sporadiquement, *adv.* Sporadically.

spore, *s.f. Biol :* Spore.

sport, *s.m.* Sports; games.

sportif. I. *a.* (*a*) Sporting; (of) sport. *Ils n'ont pas l'esprit s.,* they are no sportsmen. (*b*) *Biol :* Variation sportive, sport, *F :* freak (of nature). **2.** *s.* Devotee of outdoor games.

square [skwa:r], *s.m.* (Public) square (with garden).

squelette, *s.m.* (*a*) Skeleton. (*b*) Carcass, skeleton, frame-work.

st, *int.* Here ! you there !

stabilisation, *s.f.* Stabilization; steadying.

stabiliser, *v.tr.* To stabilize; to steady.
se stabiliser, to become stable, steady.

stabilité, *s.f.* Stability, firmness; steadiness.

stable, *a.* Stable. I. Firm, steady. **2.** Durable; lasting.

stade, *s.m.* Stadium, sports ground

stagnant [stagnɑ̃], *a.* Stagnant.

stagnation [stagn-], *s.f.* Stagnation; dullness (of trade).

stalactite, *s.f. Geol:* Stalactite.

stalagmite, *s.f. Geol:* Stalagmite.

stalle, *s.f.* **1.** Stall (in cathedral); (numbered) seat (in theatre). **2.** Stall, box (in stable).

stance, *s.f.* Stanza.

stand [stãd], *s.m.* **1.** Stand (on racecourse). **2.** (*a*) Shooting-gallery. (*b*) Rifle-range.

standardiser, *v.tr. Ind:* To standardize.

tation, *s.f.* Station. **1.** (*a*) (Action of) standing. **En station derrière un arbre,** stationed behind a tree. (*b*) Position. **2.** Break of journey; (short) halt. **3.** (*a*) (Railway) station; stage (on bus route); taxi-rank. (*b*) **Station d'été,** summer resort. **Station balnéaire,** watering-place; spa; seaside resort. (*c*) Post, station.

stationnaire. **1.** *a.* Stationary. **2.** *s.m.* Guardship.

stationnement, *s.m.* (*a*) Stopping, standing. "*S. interdit,*" 'no parking.' (*b*) *Mil:* Stationing, quartering.

stationner, *v.i.* **1.** To stop; to take up one's position; to halt. **2.** To stand; to park. "**Défense de stationner,**" 'no parking here.'

statique. **1.** *a.* Static. **2.** *s.f.* Statics.

statisticien, *s.m.* Statistician.

statistique. **1.** *a.* Statistical. **2.** *s.f.* Statistics.

statuaire. **1.** *s.* Sculptor, sculptress. **2.** *s.f.* (Art of) statuary.

statue, *s.f.* Statue.

statuer, *v.tr.* **1.** To decree, enact, ordain. **2.** *Abs: S. sur un litige,* to settle a dispute.

stature, *s.f.* Stature, height.

statut, *s.m.* Statute, ordinance.

statutaire, *a.* Statutory.

stéatite, *s.f. Miner:* Steatite, soapstone.

stèle, *s.f.* Stele (bearing inscription).

stellaire, *a.* Stellar.

ténodactylographe, *s.m. & f.* Shorthand-typist.

ténographe, *s.m. & f* Stenographer; shorthand writer.

sténographie, *s.f.* Stenography; shorthand.

sténographier, *v.tr.* To take down in shorthand.

steppe, *s.m. or f.* Steppe.

stère, *s.m. Meas:* Stere, cubic metre.

stéréoscope, *s.m. Opt:* Stereoscope.

stéréoscopique, *a.* Stereoscopic.

stéréotyper, *v.tr. Typ:* To stereotype.

stérile, *a.* Sterile, unfruitful; barren.

stérilisation, *s.f.* Sterilization.

stériliser, *v.tr.* To sterilize.

stérilité, *s.f.* Sterility, barrenness.

stertoreux, *a. Med:* Stertorous (breathing).

stéthoscope, *s.m. Med:* Stethoscope.

stigmate, *s.m. F:* Stigma, brand of infamy, stain (on character).

stigmatiser, *v.tr. F:* To stigmatize; to brand with infamy.

stimulant. **1.** *a.* Stimulating, stimulative. **2.** *s.m.* (*a*) Stimulant. (*b*) Stimulus, incentive.

stimulateur, -trice, *a.* Stimulative.

stimulation, *s.f.* Stimulation.

stimuler, *v.tr.* To stimulate. **1.** To incite; to spur on. **2.** To stimulate; to give a stimulus to.

stipulation, *s.f.* Stipulation, provision.

stipuler, *v.tr.* To stipulate; to lay down.

stock, *s.m. Com:* Stock (of goods).

stoïcien, -ienne. **1.** *a.* Stoical. **2.** *s.* Stoic.

stoïcisme, *s.m.* Stoicism.

stoïque. **1.** *a.* Stoic, stoical. **2.** *s.* Stoic.

stoïquement, *adv.* Stoically.

stop [stɔp], *int.* Stop!

stopper. **1.** *v.i.* (Of ship) To stop; to come to a stop. **2.** *v.tr.* To stop (train); to check (cable).

store, *s.m.* (Window-)blind; carriage-blind.

strabisme, *s.m.* Squinting.

strangulation, *s.f.* Strangulation.

strapontin, *s.m.* Flap-seat, folding seat.

strass, *s.m.* Strass; paste (jewellery).

stratagème, *s.m.* Stratagem.

stratégie, *s.f.* Strategy; generalship.

stratégique, *a.* Strategic(al).

stratégiquement, *adv.* Strategically.

stratégiste, *s.m.* Strategist.

stratosphère, *s.f. Meteor:* Stratosphere.

strict [-rikt], *a.* Strict. (*a*) *Le s. nécessaire,* no more than is necessary. (*b*) Severe, exact.

strictement, *adv.* Strictly.

stridemment, *adv.* Stridently.

stridence, *s.f.* Harshness; stridency.

strident, *a.* Strident, harsh.

strider, *v.i.* To chirr, to stridulate.

strie, *s.f.* **1.** Score, scratch. **2.** (*a*) Rib, ridge. (*b*) Streak.

strier, *v.tr.* **1.** To score, scratch. **2.** (*a*) To flute, groove. (*b*) To streak.

  strié, *a.* **1.** Scored, scratched. **2.** (*a*) Fluted, grooved. (*b*) Streaked.

strontium [-sjɔm], *s.m. Ch:* Strontium.

strophe, *s.f. Pros:* Stanza, verse.

structural, -aux, *a.* Structural.

structure, *s.f.* Structure.

strychnine, [-ik-] *s.f.* Strychnin(e).

stuc [styk], *s.m. Const:* Stucco.

studieusement, *adv.* Studiously.

studieux, *a.* Studious.

stupéfaction, *s.f.* Stupefaction, amazement.

stupéfait, *a.* Stupefied, amazed, astounded.

stupéfiant. **1.** *a.* (*a*) *Med:* Stupefying. (*b*) Amazing, astounding. **2.** *s.m. Med:* Narcotic; *F:* drug.

stupéfier, *v.tr.* (*a*) To bemuse. *Med:* To stupefy. (*b*) To astound, amaze.

stupeur, *s.f.* Stupor. **1.** Dazed state. **2.** Amazement. **Muet de stupeur,** dumbfounded.

stupide, *a.* Stupid. (*a*) Bemused. (*b*) Dull-witted. (*c*) Silly; foolish.

stupidement, *adv.* Stupidly.

stupidité, *s.f.* **I.** Stupidity; foolishness. **2.** Piece of stupidity.

style, *s.m. Lit:* Style. **Robe de style,** period dress.

stylet, *s.m.* Stiletto, stylet.

stylo, *s.m. F:* = STYLOGRAPHE.

stylographe, *s.m.* (*a*) Stylograph (pen). (*b*) Fountain-pen.

su. See SAVOIR.

suaire, *s.m.* Winding-sheet; shroud.

suave, *a.* (*a*) Sweet, pleasant. (*b*) Suave, bland.

suavement, *adv.* (*a*) Sweetly, pleasantly. (*b*) Suavely, blandly.

suavité, *s.f.* (*a*) Sweetness. (*b*) Suavity, blandness.

subalterne. **I.** *a.* Subordinate, minor. **2.** *s.m.* Underling, subaltern.

subdiviser, *v.tr.* To subdivide, to split up.

subdivision, *s.f.* Subdivision.

subir, *v.tr.* To undergo, go through; to suffer, sustain; to submit to.

subit, *a.* Sudden, unexpected.

subitement, *adv.* Suddenly; all at once.

subjonctif. *Gram: a. & s.m.* Subjunctive.

subjugation, *s.f.* Subjugation.

subjuguer, *v.tr.* To subjugate, subdue.

sublime, *a.* Sublime; lofty, exalted.

sublimité, *s.f.* Sublimity.

submerger, *v.tr.* (n. submergeons) **I.** To submerge. (*a*) To flood. (*b*) To swamp. (*c*) To immerse. **2.** *F:* To overwhelm.

submersion, *s.f.* Submersion. **I.** Immersion. **Mort par submersion,** death by drowning. **2.** Flooding.

subordination, *s.f.* Subordination.

subordonner, *v.tr.* To subordinate. subordonné, *a.* Subordinate.

suborner, *v.tr* To suborn, to tamper with (witness).

subrécargue, *s.m. Nau:* Supercargo.

subreptice, *a.* Surreptitious; clandestine.

subrepticement, *adv.* Surreptitiously.

subrogation. *s f Jur:* Delegation (of powers)

subséquemment [syp-], *adv.* Subsequently

subséquent ⌜syp-⌝, *a* Subsequent

subside ⌊syp-⌋, *s.m* Subsidy

subsidence [syp-], *s.f* Subsidence

subsidiaire [syp-], *a* Subsidiary, auxiliary

subsistance [syp-], *s.f* **I.** Subsistence, sustenance, maintenance. **2.** *pl* Provisions

subsistant [syp-], *a* Subsisting, existing

subsister [syp-]. *v.i.* To subsist.

substance, *s.f.* **I.** Substance **2.** Matter, material, stuff.

substantiel, -elle, *a.* Substantial.

substantiellement, *adv.* Substantially.

substantif. **I.** *a.* Substantive. **2.** *s.m. Gram:* Substantive, noun.

substituer, *v.tr.* **I.** To substitute. **2.** *Jur:* To entail (an estate).
se substituer *à* qn, to take the place of s.o.

substitut, *s.m.* Assistant; deputy.

substitution, *s.f.* **I.** Substitution. **2.** *Jur:* Entail.

subterfuge [syp-], *s.m.* Subterfuge, shift.

subtil [syptil], *a.* Subtle. **I.** (*a*) Tenuous, thin. (*b*) Pervasive. **2.** (*a*) Acute; discerning, shrewd. (*b*) Delicate, fine (distinction).

subtilement [syp-], *adv.* (*a*) Subtly. (*b*) Craftily.

subtilité [syp-], *s.f.* **I.** Subtlety (of poison). **2.** (*a*) Acuteness, shrewdness. (*b*) Subtlety (of argument).

suburbain, *a.* Suburban.

subvenir, *v.ind.tr.* (Conj. like VENIR Aux. *avoir*) *S. aux besoins de qn* to provide for the needs of s.o.

subvention, *s.f.* Subsidy, subvention.

subventionner, *v.tr.* To subsidize.

subversif, *a.* Subversive.

subversion, *s.f.* Subversion.

subvertir, *v.tr.* To subvert.

suc [syk], *s.m.* Juice. *Bot:* Sap.

succéder, *v.ind.tr.* (je succède; je succéderai) *S à qn,* to succeed, follow after, s.o *S à une fortune,* to inherit a fortune.

succès, *s.m.* **I.** Result, issue. **2.** Success; favourable result. *Th:* **Pièce à succès,** hit.

successeur, *s.m.* Successor

successif, *a.* Successive.

succession, *s.f.* Succession. **I.** (*a*) Series, sequence. (*b*) *S. à la couronne,* succession to the crown. **2.** *Jur:* Inheritance. (*a*) Inheriting. (*b*) Estate.

successivement, *adv.* Successively.

succinct [-sɛ̃, -sɛ̃kt], *a.* Succinct, brief, concise.

succinctement [-sɛ̃tmã], *adv.* Succinctly, briefly

succion, *s.f.* Suction; sucking

succomber, *v.i.* To succumb. **I.** To sink (under the burden of sth.). **2.** (*a*) To be worsted. (*b*) To yield. *S. à l'émotion,* to be overcome by emotion. (*c*) To die.

succulence, *s.f.* Succulence; juiciness.

succulent, *a.* Succulent, juicy; tasty

succursale, *s.f.* Branch (establishment).

sucer, *v.tr* (n. suçons) To suck.

sucre, *s.m.* Sugar. *S. en poudre,* castor sugar *S. cristallisé* granulated sugar *S. en morceaux,* lump sugar

sucrer, *v tr* To sugar; to sweeten.
sucré, *a* **I.** Sugared, sweetened; sweet **2.** *F:* Sugary (words)

sucrerie, *s.f.* **I.** Sugar-refinery **2.** *pl* Sweetmeats, sweets, confectionery

sucrier, *s.m.* Sugar-basin.

sud [syd]. **I.** *s.m.* No *pl.* South. **2.** *a.inv* South, southerly; southern.

sud-africain, *a. & s. Geog:* South-African

sud-est. **I.** *s.m.* No *pl.* South-east. **2.** *a.inv* South-easterly; south-eastern

ud-ouest. 1. *s.m.* No *pl.* South-west.
2. *a.inv.* South-westerly ; south-western.

Suède. *Pr.n.f.* Sweden.

Suédois. 1. *a.* Swedish. **2.** *s* Swede.
3. *s.m. Ling:* Swedish.

suer, *v.i.* To sweat **1.** *(a)* To perspire.
(b) (Of walls) To ooze, weep. **2.** (With cogn.
acc.) *(a)* To exude (poison) *(b) S du sang,*
to sweat blood.

sueur, *s.f.* Sweat, perspiration.

suffire, *v.i.* (*pr.p.* suffisant ; *p.p.* suffi) *(a)* To
suffice ; to be sufficient. *Cela ne me suffit pas,*
that won't do for me. *F: (Il) suffit!* enough !
(b) S. à qch., to be equal to sth. *Il ne peut
pas s. à tout,* he cannot cope with everything.

suffisamment, *adv.* Sufficiently, enough.

suffisance, *s.f.* **1.** Sufficiency adequacy.
2. Self-complacency ; self-conceit.

suffisant, *a.* **1.** Sufficient, adequate, enough.
2. Self-satisfied, conceited.

suffixe, *s.m. Ling:* Suffix.

suffocant, *a.* Suffocating, stifling.

suffocation, *s.f.* Suffocation, choking.

suffoquer. 1. *v.tr.* To suffocate, stifle.
2. *v.i. S. de colère,* to choke with anger.

suffrage, *s.m.* Suffrage, vote. *S universel,*
universal franchise.

suffusion, *s.f. Med:* Suffusion ; flush.

suggérer, *v.tr.* (je suggère ; je suggérerai)
To suggest.

suggestif, *a.* Suggestive.

suggestion, *..f.* Suggestion.

suicide[1], *s.m* Suicide, self-murder.

suicide[2]. 1. *s.m.* = SUICIDÉ. **2.** *a.* Suicidal.

suicider (se), *v.pr.* To commit suicide.
suicidé, *s.* Suicide, self-murderer.

suie, *s.f.* Soot

suif [suif], *s.m* Tallow ; *F:* candle-grease

suinter, *v.i.* To ooze, seep, sweat.

suis[1, 2]. See ÊTRE and SUIVRE.

Suisse[1]. *Pr.n.f.* Switzerland.

suisse[2]. 1. *a.* Swiss **2.** *s.m. (a)* Un Suisse,
a Swiss. *(b) Hist:* Swiss mercenary *(c)*
Church officer or hall porter. *(d)* **Petit
suisse,** small cream cheese.

Suissesse, *s.f.* Swiss (woman).

suite, *s.f.* **1.** *(a)* Continuation **Donner suite
à une décision,** to give effect to a decision.
A la suite les uns des autres, one after another.
A la s. de la décision prise, following the
decision arrived at. **Dix carrosses de suite,**
ten carriages in succession. **Et ainsi de suite,**
and so on. **Tout de suite,** *F:* **de suite,** at
once, immediately. **Dans la suite,** subsequently, in process of time. **Par la suite,**
later on, afterwards. *(b)* Sequel "**Suite au
prochain numéro,**" 'to be continued in our
next.' *(c)* Coherence, consistency. **2.** Suite,
retinue, train. **3.** *(a)* Series, sequence,
succession. *(b) Mus:* **Suite d'orchestre,**
orchestral suite. **4.** Consequence, result.
Par suite de, in consequence of.

suivant[1], *prep.* According to, in accordance
with.

suivant[2]. 1. *a.* Next, following. **2.** *s.m.*
Follower, attendant.

suivre, *v.tr.* (*p.p.* suivi ; *pr.ind.* je suis, il suit)
To follow. **1.** *(a)* To go behind. "**Prière de
faire suivre,**" 'please forward.' "**A suivre,**"
'to be continued.' *(b)* To escort, attend,
accompany. *(c)* To pursue. *(d)* To pay heed
to, be attentive to. *(e)* To watch (over),
observe. *(f) S. une piste,* to follow up a clue.
2. *(a)* To succeed ; to come after. *(b)* To
result from. **3.** *(a)* To go, proceed, along.
S. son chemin, to pursue one's way. *(b)* To
obey, conform to ; to act upon. **4.** *(a) S. des
conférences,* to attend lectures. *(b)* To practise, exercise.
suivi, *a.* Connected ; sustained, close.

sujet[1], -ette. 1. *a.* Subject. *(a)* Dependent.
(b) Liable, prone, exposed. **2.** *s.* Subject (of a
state).

sujet[2], *s.m.* **1.** Subject. *(a)* Cause, reason,
ground. *(b)* Subject-matter ; topic. *(c) Gram:*
Subject. **2.** Individual, fellow **Mauvais
sujet,** bad lot.

sujétion, *s.f.* **1.** Subjection ; servitude.
2. Constraint, obligation.

sulfate, *s.m. Ch:* Sulphate.

sulfure, *s.m. Ch:* Sulphide.

sulfureux, *a.* *(a)* Sulphureous. *(b) Ch:*
Sulphurous

sulfurique, *a. Ch:* Sulphuric.

sultan, *s.m.* Sultan

sultane, *s.f* Sultana, sultaness.

superbe, *a* *(a)* Superb ; stately *(b) F:*
Magnificent ; splendid, first-rate

superbement, *adv.* Superbly, magnificently.

supercherie, *s.f* Deceit ; fraud ; swindle.

superficie, *s.f* *(a)* Superficies, surface.
(b) Area.

superficiel, -elle, *a.* Superficial ; skin-deep
(wound) ; shallow (mind). *Eau superficielle,*
surface water

superficiellement, *adv* Superficially.

superfin, *a.* Superfine.

superflu. 1. *a.* *(a)* Superfluous, unnecessary.
(b) Regrets superflus, vain, useless, regrets.
2. *s.m.* Donner de son *s.,* to give of one's
superfluity.

superfluité, *s.f.* Superfluity, superabundance.

supérieur, -eure. 1. *a.* *(a)* Upper. *(b)* Superior. *Se montrer s. aux événements,* to rise
above events *(c)* Higher, upper. *(d) Com:*
Of superior quality **2.** *s.* Superior. *(a)* One's
better. *(b)* Head (of convent). **La Mère
supérieure,** the Mother Superior.

supérieurement, *adv.* Superlatively well.

supériorité, *s.f.* Superiority. *S. d'âge,*
seniority.

superlatif, *a.* Superlative.

superposer, *v.tr.* To superpose.

superstitieusement, *adv.* Superstitiously.

superstitieux, *a.* Superstitious.

superstition, *s.f.* Superstition.

supplanter, *v.tr.* To supplant; to supersede.

suppléant. I. *s.* Substitute; deputy. **2.** *a.* Acting, temporary.

suppléer. I. *v.tr.* (*a*) To supply, make up. (*b*) To take the place of, act as deputy for. **Se faire suppléer,** to find a substitute. **2.** *v.i.* *S. à qch.,* to make up for. *S. à une vacance,* to fill a vacant post.

supplément, *s.m.* (*a*) Supplement, addition. (*b*) Extra or additional payment; *Rail:* excess fare. (*c*) Supplement (to book).

supplémentaire, *a.* Supplementary, additional, extra. *Ind:* **Heures supplémentaires** (de travail), overtime.

suppliant. I. *a.* Supplicating, imploring, pleading. **2.** *s.* Suppliant, supplicant.

supplication, *s.f.* Supplication, beseeching, entreaty.

supplice, *s m.* (*a*) (Severe corporal) punishment; torture. **Le dernier supplice,** capital punishment. (*b*) Torment, anguish, agony. **Être au supplice,** to be on the rack, on thorns.

supplier, *v.tr.* To beseech, implore.

supplique, *s.f.* Petition.

support, *s.m.* **I.** Support, prop, stay. **2.** Rest; stand.

supportable, *a.* Bearable, tolerable.

supporter, *v.tr.* To support. **I.** To prop, hold up; to support, back up. **2.** (*a*) To endure, suffer, bear. (*b*) To tolerate, put up with.

supposer, *v.tr.* **I.** To suppose, assume, imagine. *On le supposait riche,* he was thought to be wealthy. **2.** To presuppose, imply. *Cela lui suppose du courage,* it implies courage on his part.

   supposé. I. *a.* Supposed, alleged; assumed. *Conj.phr.* **Supposé que** + *sub.,* supposing that. . . .

supposition, *s.f.* Supposition. **Si par supposition il revenait,** supposing he came back.

suppôt, *s.m.* Tool, instrument (of another); myrmidon. *F:* **Suppôt de Satan,** hell-hound.

suppression, *s.f.* Suppression; discontinuance; quelling.

supprimer, *v.tr.* **I.** To suppress; to abolish; to omit, cut out (word); to remove (difficulty); to quell. *F:* **Supprimer qn,** to make away with s.o. **2.** *S. qch à qn,* to deprive s.o. of sth.

supputation, *s.f.* Computation, calculation.

supputer, *v.tr.* To compute, calculate.

suprématie, *s.f.* Supremacy.

suprême, *a.* (*a*) Supreme; highest; paramount. (*b*) Last (honours). **L'heure suprême,** the hour of death.

suprêmement, *adv.* Supremely, in the highest degree.

sur[1], *prep.* **I.** (*a*) On, upon. **Sur toute la ligne,** all along the line. (*b*) Towards. *Tirer sur l'âge,* to be growing old. (*c*) Over, above. **Sur toute(s) chose(s),** above all (things). (*d*) About, concerning. **2.** (*a*) About, towards. *Sur le soir,* towards evening. (*b*) **Sur quoi,**

whereupon. **3.** Out of. (*a*) *Un jour sur quatre* one day out of four. (*b*) *Vous vous payerez su le surplus,* you will pay yourself out of wha remains over. **4.** *Huit pieds sur six, eigh* foot by six.

sur[2], *a.* Sour; tart.

sûr, *a.* Sure. **I.** (*a*) Safe, secure. **Jouer a plus sûr,** to play for safety. **Pour le plus sûr** to be on the safe side. (*b*) Trustworthy reliable; trusty. **2.** Certain. *Remède sû* infallible remedy. **A coup sûr,** for certain without fail. *F:* **Bien sûr!** to be sure! **Bie sûr?** honour bright?

surabondamment, *adv.* Superabundant ly.

surabondance, *s.f.* Superabundance.

surabondant, *a.* Superabundant.

suraigu, -uë, *a.* Overshrill, high-pitched.

suranné, *a.* Antiquated, old-fashioned.

surcharge, *s.f.* **I.** Overloading. **2.** (*a*) Over load; additional burden. (*b*) Excess weigh (of luggage). **3.** Additional charge.

surcharger, *v.tr.* (n. **surchargeons**) (*a*) T overburden, overload. (*b*) To overtax, over charge.

surchauffer, *v.tr.* To overheat.

surclasser, *v.tr.* To outclass.

surcontrer, *v.tr.* *Cards:* To redouble.

surcouper, *v.tr.* *Cards:* To overtrump.

surcroît, *s.m.* Addition, increase. **Par su croît,** into the bargain. *Pour s. de malheur,* t make matters worse.

surdité, *s.f.* Deafness.

sureau, *s.m.* Elder(-tree).

sûrement, *adv.* **I.** Steadily, confidently **2.** Surely, certainly. **3.** Securely, safely.

surenchérir, *v.i.* (*a*) To, overbid (*b*) T rise higher in price.

surestimation, *s.f.* Over-estimate, over valuation.

surestimer, *v.tr.* To over-estimate, over value.

sûreté, *s.f.* **I.** Safety, security **Agent de** sûreté, detective. **La Sûreté,** the Crimina Investigation Department, *F:* the C.I.D **2.** Sureness; unerringness, soundnes: **3.** *Com:* Surety, security.

surexcitation, *s.f.* Excitement; over excitement.

surexciter, *v.tr.* (*a*) To over-stimulate. (*b* To excite.

surexposition, *s.f.* *Phot:* Over-exposure.

surface, *s.f.* Surface. (*a*) Outside. (*b*) Are:

surfaire, *v.tr.* (Conj. like FAIRE) (*a*) T overcharge. (*b*) To over-estimate, overrate.

surfin, *a.* *Com:* Superfine.

surgir, *v.i.* (Aux. *avoir,* occ. *être*) To rise to come into view; to loom (up).

surhomme, *s.m.* Superman, overman.

surhumain, *a.* Superhuman.

surintendant, *s.m.* Superintendent, ove seer, steward.

sur-le-champ, *adv.* At once

surlendemain, *s.m.* Next day but one.

surmener, *v.tr.* (Conj. like MENER) To overwork.

se surmener, to overwork; to over-exert oneself; to work too hard.

surmené, *a.* Jaded; *F:* fagged.

surmonter, *v.tr.* **1.** To surmount; to (over-)top; to rise above. **2.** To overcome, surmount.

surnager, *v.i.* (n. surnageons) (*a*) To float on the surface. (*b*) To remain afloat.

surnaturel, -elle, *a.* Supernatural.

surnom, *s.m.* Nickname.

surnommer, *v.tr.* To nickname.

surnuméraire, *a. & s.m.* Supernumerary.

surpasser, *v.tr.* To surpass. **1.** To be higher than; to overtop. **2.** To go beyond, to exceed; to outdo. *F: Cela me surpasse*, that beats me.

surpeuplé, *a.* Over-populated.

surpeuplement, *s.m.* Overcrowding.

surplis, *s.m. Ecc:* Surplice.

surplomber. 1. *v.i.* To overhang; to jut out. **2.** *v.tr.* To overhang, hang over.

surplus, *s.m.* Surplus, overplus, excess. *Au surplus*, besides, after all; moreover.

surpoids [-pwɑ], *s.m.* Overweight.

surprenant, *a.* Surprising, astonishing.

surprendre, *v.tr.* (Conj. like PRENDRE) To surprise. **1.** (*a*) To come upon unexpectedly; to catch unawares. *La nuit nous surprit*, night overtook us. (*b*) To intercept (glance); to overhear. **2.** To astonish.

surpris, *a.* Surprised.

surprise, *s.f.* Surprise.

sursaut, *s.m.* Start, jump. *Se réveiller en s.*, to wake up with a start.

sursauter, *v.i.* To start; to give a jump.

sursis, *s.m. Jur:* Delay; respite; reprieve.

surtaxe, *s.f. S. d'une lettre*, extra postage on a letter.

surtout, *adv.* Particularly, especially, principally, above all.

survécu, -s, -t, etc. See SURVIVRᴇ.

surveillance [-vɛj-], *s.f.* Supervision, surveillance.

surveillant [-vɛj-], *s.* **1.** Supervisor, superintendent, overseer. **2.** Guardian, watchman.

surveiller [-vɛj-], *v.tr.* **1.** To supervise, oversee, superintend. **2.** To watch (over), observe, look after.

survenant, *a.* Coming unexpectedly; supervening.

survenir, *v.i.* (Conj. like VENIR. Aux. *être*) To supervene, happen; to arise; to arrive unexpectedly.

survivance, *s.f.* (*a*) Survival, outliving. (*b*) Reversion (of estate).

survivant. 1. *a.* Surviving. **2.** *s.* Survivor.

survivre, *v.ind.tr.* (Conj. like VIVRE. Aux. *avoir*) To survive, outlive.

survoler, *v.tr. Av:* To fly over.

sus [sy(s)]. **1. En sus**, in addition, extra. **2.** *int.* Come on! now then! *Sus à l'ennemi!* at them!

susceptibilité, *s.f.* **1.** Susceptibility, sensitiveness. **2.** Touchiness, irritability.

susceptible, *a.* Susceptible. **1.** *Les documents susceptibles de vous intéresser*, the documents likely to interest you. **2.** (*a*) Sensitive, delicate. (*b*) Touchy, easily offended.

susciter, *v.tr.* **1.** (*a*) To raise up. (*b*) To create; to give rise to. **2.** To (a)rouse; to instigate.

suscription, *s.f.* Superscription, address.

susdit, *a. & s.* Aforesaid, above-mentioned.

susmentionné, *a. & s* Above-mentioned, aforesaid.

susnommé, *a. & s.* Above-named.

suspect [-pɛ(kt)]. **1.** *a.* Suspicious, doubtful, suspect. *Devenir s.*, to arouse suspicion. *Être s. à qn de qch.*, to be suspected by s.o. of sth. **2.** *s.m.* Suspect.

suspecter, *v.tr.* To suspect; to doubt.

suspendre, *v.tr.* **1.** To suspend. **1.** To hang up. **2.** (*a*) To defer, stay; to stop (payment). (*b*) *S. un fonctionnaire*, to suspend an official.

suspendu, *a.* Suspended; hanging.

suspens (en), *adv.phr* In suspense; (i) in uncertainty; (ii) in abeyance.

suspension, *s.f.* Suspension. **1.** Hanging (up). **2.** (*a*) (Temporary) discontinuance, interruption. *Gram:* **Points de suspension**, points of suspension. (*b*) *S. d'un fonctionnaire*, suspension of an official.

suspicion, *s.f.* Suspicion *Être en suspicion*, to be suspected.

susurrer, *v.i.* To murmur, whisper.

suzerain. 1. *a.* Paramount, suzerain. **2.** *s.* Suzerain, *f.* suzeraine.

suzeraineté, *s.f.* Suzerainty; lordship.

svastika, *s.m.* Swastika.

svelte, *a.* Slender, slim.

sveltesse, *s.f.* Slenderness, slimness.

sybarite, *a. & s.* Sybarite; voluptuary.

sybaritique, *a.* Sybaritic.

sycomore, *s.m. Bot:* Sycamore.

sycophante. 1. *s.m.* Sycophant. **2.** *a.* Sycophantic.

sycophantisme, *s.m.* Sycophancy.

syllabaire, *s.m.* Spelling-book.

syllabe, *s.f.* Syllable.

syllabique, *a.* Syllabic.

sylphe, *s.m.*, **sylphide**, *s.f.* Sylph.

sylvestre, *a.* Woodland; sylvan.

sylviculture, *s.f.* Forestry

symbole, *s.m.* (*a*) Symbol. (*b*) Conventional sign. (*c*) *Ecc:* Creed.

symbolique, *a.* Symbolic(al).

symboliquement, *adv.* Symbolically.

symboliser, *v.tr.* To symbolize.

symbolisme, *s.m.* Symbolism.

symétrie, *s.f.* Symmetry.

symétrique, *a.* Symmetrical.

symétriquement, *adv.* Symmetrically.

sympathie, *s.f.* Sympathy. (*a*) Instinctive attraction. *Se prendre de sympathie pour qn*, to take a liking to s.o (*b*) *Idées qui ne sont pas en s.* ideas that do not go together.

sympathique, *a.* **1.** Sympathetic. **2.** Likable, attractive. *Il me fut tout de suite s.*, I took to him at once. *Entourage s.*, congenial surroundings.

sympathiquement, *adv.* Sympathetically.

sympathiser, *v.i.* To sympathize.

symphonie, *s.f.* Symphony.

symphonique, *a.* Symphonic.

symptôme, *s.m.* Symptom.

synagogue, *s.f.* Synagogue.

synchroniser [-krɔn-], *v.tr.* To synchronize.

syncope, *s.f.* **1.** *Med:* Syncope; swoon. *S. mortelle*, heart-failure. **2.** *Mus:* (a) Syncopation. (b) Syncopated note.

syndicalisme, *s.m.* Syndicalism. **Syndicalisme ouvrier**, trade-unionism.

syndicaliste, *s.m.* Trade-unionist.

syndicat, *s.m.* Syndicate. **Syndicat ouvrier**, trade-union.

synode, *s.m.* *Ecc:* Synod.

synonyme. **1.** *a.* Synonymous. **2.** *s.m.* Synonym.

syntaxe, *s.f.* *Gram:* Syntax.

synthèse, *s.f.* Synthesis.

synthétique, *a.* Synthetic(al).

synthétiquement, *adv.* Synthetically.

Syrie. *Pr.n.f.* *Geog:* Syria.

syrien, -ienne, *a. & s.* Syrian.

systématique, *a.* Systematic.

systématiquement, *adv.* Systematically.

système, *s.m.* System.

T

T, t [te], *s.m.* (The letter) T, t.

t'. See TE.

ta, *poss.a.f.* See TON[1].

ta ta ta, *int.* Hoity-toity!

tabac [taba], *s.m.* *Bot:* Tobacco(-plant). **Prendre du tabac**, to take snuff.

tabatière, *s.f.* Snuff-box.

tabernacle, *s.m.* Tabernacle.

table, *s.f.* Table. **1. Tenir table ouverte**, to keep an open board. **Avoir table et logement chez qn**, to board and lodge with s.o. *T. d'officiers*, officers' mess. **2.** (a) Slab; tablet. (b) List, catalogue.

tableau, *s.m.* **1.** (a) Board. *El.E:* **Tableau de distribution**, switchboard. (b) (In hotel) Key-rack, -board. **2.** (a) Picture, painting. (b) *Th:* Tableau. **3.** (a) List, table. (b) *Être rayé du t.*, to be struck off the rolls.

tablette, *s.f.* **1.** (a) Shelf (of bookcase). (b) Flat slab. **2.** Cake, slab (of chocolate). *Pharm:* Tablet, lozenge.

tablier, *s.m.* **1.** Apron. *T. d'enfant*, pinafore. **2.** *Veh:* Apron. *Aut:* Dashboard.

tabou. **1.** *s.m.* Taboo. **2.** *a.* Taboo(ed).

tabouret, *s.m.* (a) High stool. (b) Footstool.

tac [tak], *s.m.* Click; clack.

tache, *s.f.* Stain, spot; flaw, blemish. *T. d'encre*, blot.

tâche, *s.f.* Task. **Travail à la tâche**, piecework. **Prendre à tâche de faire qch.**, to undertake to do sth.

tacher, *v.tr.* To stain, spot; to sully.

tâcher, *v.i.* To try, endeavour.

tacheter, *v.tr.* (je tachette) To mark with spots; to speckle, fleck.

tacite, *a.* Tacit; implied.

tacitement, *adv.* Tacitly.

taciturne, *a.* Taciturn, uncommunicative. **Guillaume le Taciturne**, William the Silent.

taciturnité, *s.f.* Taciturnity.

tact [takt], *s.m.* **1.** (Sense of) touch. **2.** Tact.

tacticien, *s.m.* Tactician.

tactile, *a.* Tactile.

tactique. **1.** *a.* Tactical. **2.** *s.f.* Tactics.

taffetas, *s.m.* (a) *Tex:* Taffeta. (b) *Med:* **Taffetas gommé**, sticking-plaster. *T imperméable*, oiled silk.

taïcoun [-kun], *s.m.* Tycoon (of Japan).

taie, *s.f.* **Taie d'oreiller**, pillow-case.

taillade [tajad], *s.f.* Cut, slash, gash.

taillader [tajade], *v.tr.* To slash, gash.

taille [ta:j, ta:j], *s.f.* **1.** Cutting; pruning; trimming. **2.** Method of cutting; cut (of garment). **3.** Edge (of sword). **Coup de taille**, cut, slash. **4.** (a) Stature, height; dimensions. **Par rang de taille**, in order of height. *F:* **Il est de taille à se défendre**, he is big enough to look after himself. (b) Figure, waist. **Tour de taille**, waist measurement. **Être bien pris de taille**, to have an elegant figure.

taille-crayons, *s.m.inv.* Pencil-sharpener.

tailler [taje], *v.tr.* (a) To cut; to hew; to prune; to trim. *T. un crayon*, to sharpen a pencil. (b) *Complet bien taillé*, well-cut suit.

　　taillé, *a.* *Il est t. pour commander*, he is cut out for a leader.

tailleur, -euse [taj-], *s.* **1.** (a) Cutter; hewer. (b) Tailor, tailoress. **2.** *s.m.* (Costume) **tailleur**, tailor-made costume.

taillis [taji], *s.m.* Copse, coppice. *a.* **Bois taillis**, brushwood.

tain, *s.m.* Silvering (for mirrors). **Glace sans tain**, plate-glass.

taire, *v.tr.* (pr.p. *taisant*; p.p. *tu*) To say nothing about. *Une dame dont je tairai le nom*, a lady who shall be nameless.

　　se taire, to hold one's tongue, to be silent.

Tais-toi! be quiet!

Taïti. *Pr.n.* *Geog:* Tahiti.

talc [talk], *s.m.* Talc; French chalk. *Toil:* (Poudre) de talc, talcum powder.

talent, *s.m.* **1.** *Gr.Ant:* Talent. **2.** Talent, faculty, gift.

talion, *s.m.* Talion, retaliation.

talisman, *s.m.* Talisman.

taloche, *s.f. F:* Cuff; clout on the head.

talocher, *v.tr.* To cuff; to clout on the head.

talon, *s.m.* **1.** Heel. **2.** (*a*) (At cards) Stock (not yet dealt out); talon. (*b*) Fag-end, remnant. (*c*) **Talon de souche,** counterfoil.

talonner, *v.tr.* (*a*) To follow closely. (*b*) To spur on, urge.

talus, *s.m.* **1.** Slope. **2.** Bank, embankment, ramp.

tamarin, *s.m. Bot:* Tamarind.

tambour, *s.m.* **1.** Drum. **Tambour de basque,** tambourine. **Sans tambour ni trompette,** quietly, without fuss. **2.** Drummer. **Tambour de ville,** town-crier. **3.** Drum (of oil). *Mec.E:* Barrel (of capstan). **4.** (*a*) Tambour (of vestibule); revolving door (*b*) *T. d'une roue à aubes,* paddle-box.

tambouriner, *v.i.* (*a*) To beat a drum. (*b*) *F:* To drum, thrum (with the fingers).

tambour-major, *s.m.* Drum-major. *pl. Des tambours-majors.*

tamis, *s.m.* Sieve, sifter; strainer.

Tamise (la). *Pr.n.* The Thames.

tamiser, *v.tr.* To pass through a sieve; to sift, screen; to strain.

tampon, *s.m.* **1.** Plug, stopper. **2.** (*a*) (Inking-)pad. (*b*) Rubber stamp. **3.** **Tampon (de choc),** buffer.

tamponner, *v.tr.* **1.** To plug. **2.** To dab. *Se t. le front,* to mop one's brow.

tam-tam [tamtam], *s.m.* Tom-tom.

tan, *s.m.* Tan; (tanner's) bark.

tancer, *v.tr.* (n. tançons) To rate, scold.

tanche, *s.f. Ich:* Tench.

tandem [-dɛm], *s.m. Veh:* Tandem.

tandis que, *conj.phr.* (*a*) Whereas. (*b*) While, whilst.

tangage, *s.m.* Pitching (of ship).

tangente, *s.f.* Tangent. *F:* **S'échapper par la tangente,** to fly off at a tangent.

tangentiel, -elle, *a.* Tangential.

Tanger. *Pr.n. Geog:* Tangier(s).

tangible, *a.* Tangible.

tango, *s.m. Danc:* Tango.

tanguer, *v.i.* (Of ship) To pitch.

tanière, *s.f.* Den, lair.

tanin, *s.m. Ch:* Tannin.

tanner, *v.tr.* To tan.

tannerie, *s.f.* Tannery, tan-yard.

tanneur, *s.m.* Tanner.

tant, *adv.* **1.** (*a*) So much. **Si vous faites tant que de,** if you decide to. **Pour tant faire,** if it comes to that. **Il a tant et plus d'argent,** he has any amount of money. **Faire tant et si bien que,** to work to such good purpose that. **Tant s'en faut,** far from it. **Tant soit peu,** ever so little. **Tant (il) y a que** + *ind.,* the fact remains that. **Si tant est qu'il le**

fasse, if indeed he does it at all. (*b*) So many; as many. (*c*) So; to such a degree. **En tant que,** in so far as. (*d*) Tant aimable qu'il soit, however pleasant he may be. (*e*) Tant mieux, so much the better; good! **Tant pis!** so much the worse; it can't be helped! **2.** (*a*) As much, as well (as). (*b*) As long, as far (as).

Tantale. *Pr.n.m. Myth:* Tantalus.

tantaliser, *v.tr.* To tantalize, tease.

tante, *s.f.* Aunt. **Chez ma tante,** at the pawnbroker's.

tantième, *s.m.* Percentage, share, quota.

tantôt, *adv.* **1.** Soon, presently. **A tantôt,** good-bye for the present. **2.** Just now; a little while ago. **3.** *T. triste, t. gai,* now sad, now gay.

taon [tã], *s.m.* Gad-fly, horse-fly, cleg.

tapage, *s.m.* Din, uproar; row.

tapageur, -euse. **1.** *a.* Noisy; rowdy, uproarious. **2.** *s.* Roisterer, rowdy.

tape, *s.f.* Tap, rap, pat, slap.

taper, *v.tr. F:* To tap, strike, hit. *Abs. T. sur qch.,* to tap, bang, on sth.

tapioca, *s.m.* Tapioca.

tapir¹, *s.m. Z:* Tapir.

tapir² (se), *v.pr.* To squat, cower.

tapis, *s.m.* **1.** Cloth, cover. **Tapis vert,** gaming table. **Mettre qch. sur le tapis,** to bring sth. up for discussion. **2.** Carpet.

tapisser, *v.tr.* **1.** To hang with tapestry. **2.** To paper (room).

tapisserie, *s.f.* **1.** Tapestry, hangings. **Faire tapisserie,** to be a wall-flower. **2.** Tapestry-work.

tapissier, *s.* **1.** Upholsterer. **2.** *s.f.* **Tapissière,** delivery-van.

tapoter, *v.tr. F:* To pat. *T. un air,* to strum a tune.

taquin. **1.** *a.* (Given to) teasing. **2.** *s.* Tease.

taquinage, *s.m.* Teasing.

taquiner, *v.tr.* To tease; to worry.

tarbouch(e), *s.m. Cost:* Tarboosh.

tard, *adv.* Late. **Plus t.,** later on. **Pas plus t. qu'hier,** only yesterday. *s.m.* **Sur le tard,** late in the day.

tarder, *v.i.* **1.** To delay. **Sans tarder,** without delay. **2.** *Impers. Il lui tarde de partir,* he is longing to get away.

tardif, *a.* Tardy, belated; backward.

tardivement, *adv.* Tardily, belatedly.

tardiveté, *s.f.* Lateness, backwardness.

tare, *s.f.* **1.** (*a*) *Com:* Depreciation, loss in value. (*b*) Defect, blemish; taint. **2.** Tare; allowance for weight.

tarentelle, *s.f. Danc:* Tarantella.

tarentule, *s.f. Arach:* Tarantula.

tarer, *v.tr.* To spoil, damage.

targuer (se), *v.pr. Se t. de qch.,* to plume oneself on sth.

tarière, *s.f. Tls:* Auger.

tarif [-rif], *s.m.* (*a*) Tariff, price-list. (*b*) Scale of charges. *T. télégraphique,* telegraph rates. *Rail:* Billet à demi-tarif, half-fare ticket.

tarir. **1.** *v.tr.* (*a*) To dry up. (*b*) To exhaust. **2.** *v.i.* To dry up, run dry.

tarissement, *s.m.* Drying up; exhausting.
tarmac [-mak], *s.m. Civ.E:* Tarmac.
tartan, *s.m.* Tartan.
tartare, *a. & s. Ethn:* Ta(r)tar.
tarte, *s.f. Cu:* (Open) tart; flan.
tartelette, *s.f. Cu:* Tartlet.
tartine, *s.f.* Slice of bread and butter, bread and jam.
tartre, *s.m. Ch:* Tartar.
tartrique, *a. Ch:* Tartaric.
tas [tɑ], *s.m.* (*a*) Heap, pile. (*b*) *F:* Lot, crew, gang; heaps, lots.
tasse¹, *s.f.* Cup. *F:* **La grande tasse,** the sea, Davy Jones's locker.
Tasse² (**le**). *Pr.n.m. Lit:* Tasso.
tasser, *v.tr.* To compress, squeeze, together; to ram, pack.
　　se tasser. 1. (*a*) To settle, set. (*b*) To sink, subside. **2.** To crowd (up) together; to huddle together. **Tassez-vous un peu,** squeeze up a bit.
tâter, *v.tr.* To feel, touch; to finger, handle. **Tâter le terrain,** to explore the ground. **Avancer en tâtant,** to grope one's way down, forward.
tâtonnement, *s.m.* **1.** Groping. **2.** Tentative effort.
tâtonner, *v.i.* To grope; to feel one's way.
tâtons (**à**), *adv.phr.* Gropingly.
tatou, *s.m. Z:* Armadillo, tatu.
tatouage, *s.m.* Tattooing.
tatouer, *v.tr.* To tattoo.
taudis, *s.m.* Miserable room; hovel.
taupe, *s.f. Z:* Mole.
taupier, *s.m.* Mole-catcher.
taupinière, *s.f.* Mole-hill.
taureau, *s.m.* **1.** Bull. **2.** *Astr:* **Le Taureau,** Taurus, the Bull.
tautologie, *s.f.* Tautology, redundancy.
tautologique, *a.* Tautological.
taux, *s.m.* Rate (of discount); established price. *T. de pension,* scale of pension. *T. du change,* rate of exchange.
taverne, *s.f.* Tavern; public house.
taxation, *s.f.* **1.** Fixing of prices. **2.** *Adm:* Taxation.
taxe, *s.f.* **1.** (*a*) Fixed price; fixed rate. (*b*) Charge; rate. **2.** Tax, duty.
taxer, *v.tr.* **1.** To regulate the price of. **2.** To tax, impose a tax on. **3.** To accuse.
taxi, *s.m.* Taxi(-cab).
taxidermie, *s.f.* Taxidermy.
taxidermiste, *s.m.* Taxidermist.
taximètre, *s.m.* Taximeter.
Tchad (**le**) [-ʃad], *Pr.n.m.* Lake Chad.
tchécoslovaque, *a. & s.* Czecho-Slovak.
Tchécoslovaquie. *Pr.n.f.* Czecho-Slovakia.
tchèque, *a. & s.* Czech.
te, before a vowel sound **t',** *pers.pron. sg.,* unstressed. **1.** (*a*) (Acc.) You. (*b*) (Dat.) (To) you. (*c*) (With pr.vbs) *Tu te fatigues,* you are tiring yourself. **2.** Thee, thyself.
technicien [tɛk-] *s.m.* Technician.
technique [tɛk-]. **1.** *a.* Technical. **2.** *s.f.* (*a*) Technique. (*b*) Technics.

techniquement [tɛk-], *adv.* Technically.
technologie [tɛk-], *s.f.* Technology
te(c)k [tɛk], *s.m.* Teak.
teign-e, -es, etc. See TEINDRE.
teindre, *v.tr.* (Conj. like PEINDRE) **1.** To dye. **2.** To stain, tinge, colour.
teint, *s.m.* **1.** Dye, colour.˙ **Bon teint,** fast dye. **2.** Complexion, colour.
teinte, *s.f.* Tint, shade, hue.
teinter, *v.tr.* To tint.
teinture, *s.f.* **1.** Dyeing. **2.** (*a*) Dye (*b*) Colour, hue, tinge. **3.** *Pharm:* Tincture
teinturerie, *s.f.* **1.** Dyeing. **2.** Dye-works
teinturier, *s.* Dyer.
tel, telle, *a.* **1.** Such. (*a*) *Un tel homme* such a man. (*b*) *En tel lieu,* in such and such a place. *Je sais telle maison où . . . ,* I could mention a house where. . . . (*c*) *A tel point* to such an extent. **2.** (*a*) Like; as. **Tel père,** **tel fils,** like father, like son. (*b*) **Tel que,** such as, like. (*c*) **Tel quel.** (i) *Je vous achète la maison telle quelle,* I'll buy the house from you just as it stands. (ii) *C'est un homme tel quel,* he's just an ordinary person. **3.** *pron* Such a one. *Tel l'en blâmait, tel l'en excusait,* one would blame him, another would excuse him. **Tel qui,** he who, many a one who. *s.* **Un tel, une telle,** so-and-so.
télégramme, *s.m.* Telegram.
télégraphe, *s.m.* Telegraph.
télégraphie, *s.f.* Telegraphy.
télégraphier, *v.tr. & i.* To telegraph, to wire.
télégraphique, *a.* Telegraphic.
télégraphiste, *s.* Telegraphist. *Facteur t.,* telegraph-messenger.
télémètre, *s.m.* Range-finder.
télémétrie, *s.f.* Range-finding.
télépathie, *s.f.* Telepathy.
télépathique, *a.* Telepathic.
téléphone, *s.m.* Telephone.
téléphoner, *v.tr. & i.* To telephone.
téléphonie, *s.f.* Telephony.
téléphonique, *a.* Telephonic. **Cabine téléphonique,** telephone box. *Appel t.,* telephone call.
téléphoniste, *s.m. & f.* Telephonist; telephone operator
télescope, *s.m.* Reflecting telescope.
télescoper, *v.i., tr. & pr.* To telescope; to crumple up.
télescopique, *a.* Telescopic.
télévision, *s.f.* Television.
tellement, *adv.* **1.** In such a manner; so. **2.** To such a degree; so.
tellière, *a.inv. & s.m.* Foolscap (paper).
téméraire, *a.* Rash, reckless.
témérairement, *adv.* Rashly, recklessly.
témérité, *s.f.* **1.** Temerity, rashness, recklessness, foolhardiness. **2.** Rash deed.
témoignage, *s.m.* **1.** Testimony, evidence. **2.** *Jur:* Hearing (of witness). **3.** **En témoignage d'estime,** as a token of esteem.
témoigner. 1. *v.i.* To testify; **to bear**

witness ; to give evidence. **2.** *v.tr. or ind.tr.* T. (*de*) *qch.*, to show, prove, sth. ; to testify to sth.

témoin, *s.m.* **I.** Witness. (*a*) *Être t. d'un accident,* to witness an accident. (*b*) **Appeler qn à témoin,** to call s.o. to witness. (*c*) Second (in duel). **2.** (*a*) Boundary mark. (*b*) *El.E : Ind :* **Lampe témoin,** tell-tale lamp.

tempe, *s.f. Anat :* Temple.

tempérament, *s.m.* (*a*) Constitution, temperament. **Paresseux par tempérament,** constitutionally lazy. (*b*) *T. placide* placid temper.

tempérance, *s.f.* Temperance, moderation.

tempérant, *a.* Temperate, moderate.

température, *s.f.* Temperature.

tempérer, *v.tr.* (je **tempère ; je tempérerai**) To temper, moderate.

tempéré, *a.* Temperate, moderate.

tempête, *s.f.* Storm ; tempest.

tempêter, *v.i. F :* To storm ; to rage.

tempétueusement, *adv.* Tempestuously ; stormily.

tempétueux, *a.* Tempestuous ; stormy.

temple, *s.m.* **I.** Temple. **2.** Church ; chapel.

templier, *s.m. Hist :* (Knight) Templar.

temporaire, *a.* Temporary ; provisional.

temporairement, *adv* Temporarily ; provisionally.

temporel, -elle, *a.* Temporal. *Puissance temporelle,* temporal power.

temporisation, *s.f.* Temporization.

temporiser, *v.i.* To temporize.

temps [tã], *s.m.* **I.** Time. (*a*) **Vous avez (tout) le temps voulu,** you have plenty of time. (*b*) (i) While, period. **Il y a peu de temps,** a little while ago. **Entre temps,** meanwhile. **Temps d'arrêt,** pause, halt. **Marquer un temps,** to pause. (ii) Term. (*c*) Age, days, times. **Le bon vieux temps,** the good old days. **Au temps jadis,** in times past. **Dans la suite des temps,** in the course of ages. **Par le temps qui court,** in these days. **Être de son temps,** to be up to date. (*d*) Hour. **En temps voulu,** in due time. **Il n'est plus temps,** it is too late. **En temps et lieu,** in due course. **2.** Weather. **Par tous les temps,** in all weathers. **3.** *Gram :* Tense. **4.** *Mus :* Beat ; time.

tenable, *a.* Tenable, defensible.

tenace, *a.* Tenacious ; clinging ; tough ; dogged ; retentive.

ténacité, *s.f.* Tenacity ; toughness ; retentiveness.

tenaille [-na:j], *s.f.* Pincers ; tongs.

tenailler [-nɑje], *v.tr. F :* **Tenaillé par le remords,** tortured by remorse.

tenant, *a.* **Séance tenante,** forthwith, then and there.

tendance, *s.f.* Tendency, propensity, trend.

tendon, *s.m.* Tendon, sinew.

tendre[1], *a.* Tender. (*a*) Soft ; delicate ; early (age). (*b*) Fond, affectionate.

tendre[2]. **I.** *v.tr.* (*a*) To stretch. *T. un ressort,* to set a spring. (*b*) To fix up (tent) ; to

spread (sail) ; to lay (carpet) ; to hang (wall-paper). (*c*) To stretch out, hold out. **Tendre la main,** to hold out one's hand. (*d*) To (over)strain. **2.** *v.i.* To tend, lead.

se tendre, to become taut ; to become strained.

tendu, *a.* Tense, taut, tight. *Situation tendue,* tense situation.

tendresse, *s.f.* Tenderness ; fondness ; love.

ténèbres, *s.f.pl.* Darkness, gloom.

ténébreux, *a.* **I.** Gloomy, dark, sombre. **2.** Mysterious, sinister.

teneur[1], **-euse,** *s.* **Teneur de livres,** bookkeeper.

teneur[2], *s.f.* Tenor, purport.

tenir, *v.* (*pr.p.* **tenant ;** *p.p.* **tenu ;** *pr.ind.* **je tiens, ils tiennent ;** *pr. sub.* **je tienne ;** *p.h.* **je tins ;** *fu.* **je tiendrai**) **I.** *v.tr.* **I.** To hold. (*a*) *T. qch. à la main,* to hold sth. in one's hand. **Tiens! tenez!** look here ! here ! (*b*) To contain. *v.i. Tout ça tient en deux mots,* all that can be said in a couple of words. (*c*) *Baril qui tient l'eau,* barrel that holds water. (*d*) **Tenir de,** to have, derive, from. (*e*) To keep, stock. **2. T. un magasin,** to keep a shop. *T. la caisse,* to have charge of the cash. *Mlle X tenait le piano,* Miss X was at the piano. **3.** (*a*) To hold, maintain ; to keep (one's word). (*b*) *T. de grands discours,* to hold forth at great length. (*c*) **Tenir son rang,** to keep up one's position. (*d*) *T. qn en grand respect,* to hold s.o. in great respect. **4.** To hold back, restrain. **5.** (*a*) To hold, keep. *T. qch. en état,* to keep sth. in good order. **Tenez votre gauche,** keep to the left. (*b*) **Tenir la chambre,** to be confined to one's room. **6.** To occupy, take up (space). **7.** *Pred.* **T. qn captif,** to keep s.o. prisoner. **Tenez-vous-le pour dit,** I shall not tell you again.

II. tenir, *v.i.* **I.** (*a*) To hold ; to adhere. *Cela tient comme poix,* it sticks like pitch. (*b*) *Sa terre tient à la mienne,* his estate borders on mine. (*c*) To bide, remain. *Il ne tient plus sur ses jambes,* he is ready to drop. **2.** (*a*) **Tenir (bon),** to hold out, to stand fast. **Je n'y tiens plus,** I can't stand it any longer. (*b*) To last, endure. **3. Tenir pour,** to hold for, be in favour of. **4. Tenir à qch.** (*a*) To value, prize, sth. **Tenir à faire qch.,** to be bent on doing sth. (*b*) To depend on, result from, sth. *A quoi cela tient-il?* what's the reason for it? *Impers. Il ne tient qu'à vous de le faire,* it rests entirely with you to do it. **Qu'à cela ne tienne,** never mind that. **5. Tenir de qn,** to,take after s.o. *Cela tient du miracle,* it sounds like a miracle.

se tenir. I. (*a*) To keep, be, remain. *Tenez-vous là!* stay where you are ! **Se tenir tranquille,** to keep quiet. **Tiens-toi,** behave yourself. (*b*) *Se t. à qch.,* to hold on to sth. **2.** To contain oneself. **3. Se tenir à qch.,** to keep to sth. ; to abide by sth. **S'en tenir à qch.,** to confine oneself to sth. ; to be satisfied with sth. **Je ne sais pas à quoi m'en tenir,** I don't know what to believe.

tenu. *a.* (*a*) **Bien tenu,** well-kept. (*b*) **Être tenu de, à, faire qch.,** to be obliged to do sth.

tenue, *s.f.* **1.** (*a*) Session, holding (of an assembly). (*b*) Keeping, managing (of shop). **2.** Bearing, behaviour, carriage. *Arthur,* **de la tenue!** Arthur, behave yourself! **3.** Dress. *En grande t.,* in full dress (uniform).

tennis [-nis], *s.m.* **1.** Lawn tennis. **2.** (Lawn-) tennis court.

ténor, *s.m. Mus:* Tenor.

tension, *s.f.* Tension. **1.** (*a*) Stretching; tightening. (*b*) Strain, stress. **2.** Tightness; tenseness. **3.** Pressure.

tentacule, *s.m. Z:* Tentacle, feeler.

tentant, *a.* Tempting, alluring, enticing.

tentateur, -trice. 1. *s.* Tempter, temptress. **2.** *a.* Tempting.

tentatif. 1. *a.* Tentative. **2.** *s.f.* Tentative, attempt, endeavour.

tentation, *s.f.* Temptation.

tente, *s.f.* (*a*) Tent. (*b*) *Nau:* Awning.

tenter, *v.tr.* **1.** *F:* T. **la chance,** to try one's luck. **2.** To tempt. **3.** To attempt, try.

tenture, *s.f.* Hangings, tapestry.

ténu, *a.* Tenuous, thin; slender, fine; subtle.

ténuité, *s.f.* Tenuity, tenuousness; slenderness; fineness.

tenure, *s.f. Jur:* Tenure.

tercet, *s.m. Pros:* Tercet. *Mus:* Triplet.

térébenthine, *s.f.* Turpentine.

terme[1], *s.m.* **1.** Term, end, limit. **Mener qch. à bon terme,** to carry sth. through. **2.** (Appointed) time. *Mil:* **Engagement à long terme,** long service. **3.** (*a*) Quarter (of rent); term. (*b*) Quarter's rent. (*c*) Quarter day.

terme[2], *s.m.* **1.** Term, expression. *Il m'a dit en termes propres,* he told me in so many words. **2.** *pl.* Wording; terms, conditions. **3.** *pl.* Terms, footing. **Être en bons termes avec qn,** to be on good terms with s.o.

terminaison, *s.f.* Termination, ending.

terminer, *v.tr.* To terminate. **1.** To bound, limit. **2.** (*a*) To end, finish; to conclude; to complete. (*b*) *v.i. Il faut en t.,* we must make an end.

se terminer, to end; to come to an end.

terminus [-nyːs], *s.m.* (Railway) terminus.

termite, *s.m. Ent:* Termite, white ant.

terne, *a.* Dull, lustreless, leaden. *Voix t.,* flat voice.

ternir, *v.tr.* To tarnish, dull, dim.

se ternir, to tarnish; to grow dull.

ternissement, *s.m.* Tarnishing.

terrain, *s.m.* Ground. (*a*) Piece of ground, plot of land. (*b*) Land. *T. mou,* soft soil. (*c*) Duelling ground; football field; golf course. **Aller sur le terrain,** to fight a duel. *Mil:* **Gagner du terrain,** to gain ground. *F:* **Être sur son terrain,** to be on familiar ground.

terrasse, *s.f.* (*a*) Terrace; bank. (*b*) Pavement (in front of a café).

terrassement, *s.m.* **1.** Banking, digging. **Travaux de terrassement,** navvying. **2.** Earthwork, embankment.

terrasser, *v.tr.* **1.** To embank. **2.** (*a*) To lay low; to throw. (*b*) *F:* To overwhelm, crush.

terre, *s.f.* **1.** Earth. (*a*) The world. (*b*) Ground, land. **Tomber par terre,** to fall down (from standing position). **Tomber à terre,** to fall down (from height). (Of ship) **Être à terre,** to be aground. **Descendre à terre,** to land, disembark. *F:* **Être terre à terre,** to be matter-of-fact. **2.** Soil, land. **3.** (*a*) Estate, property. (*b*) *Terres étrangères,* foreign lands. *Geog:* **La Terre de Feu,** Tierra del Fuego. **4.** Loam, clay. *Parquet en t. battue,* mud floor. **Terre cuite,** terra cotta.

Terre-Neuve. 1. *Pr.n.f.* Newfoundland. **2.** *s.m.inv.* Newfoundland dog.

terre-neuvien, -ienne. (*a*) *a.* (Of) Newfoundland. (*b*) *s.* Newfoundlander.

terre-plein, *s.m.* Earth platform; terrace. *pl. Des terre-pleins.*

terrestre, *a.* Terrestrial; earthly, worldly.

terreur, *s.f.* Terror; dread.

terreux, *a.* (*a*) Earthy. (*b*) Grubby, dirty (hands). (*c*) Dull (colour); sickly (face).

terrible, *a.* Terrible, frightful, dreadful.

terriblement, *adv.* Terribly; dreadfully.

terrier[1], *s.m.* Burrow, hole; earth (of fox).

terrier[2], *a.m. & s.m.* (Chien) terrier, terrier.

terrifiant, *a.* Terrifying, awe-inspiring.

terrifier, *v.tr.* To terrify.

terrine, *s.f.* (Earthenware) pot.

territoire, *s.m.* Territory.

territorial, -aux, *a.* Territorial.

terroir, *s.m. Agr:* Soil. **Sentir le terroir,** to smack of the soil.

terroriser, *v.tr.* To terrorize.

terrorisme, *s.m.* Terrorism.

terroriste, *s.m.* Terrorist.

tertre, *s.m.* Hillock, mound, knoll.

tes, *a.poss.* See TON[1].

tesson, *s.m.* Potsherd. *T. de bouteille,* broken bottle end.

testacé, *s.m.* Shell-fish; testacean.

testament[1], *s.m.* Will, testament.

testament[2], *s.m. B:* **L'ancien Testament,** the Old Testament.

testamentaire, *a.* Testamentary.

testateur, -trice, *s.* Testator, testatrix.

tétanos [-nɔs], *s.m. Med:* Tetanus, lock-jaw.

têtard, *s.m.* **1.** Tadpole. **2.** *Arb:* Pollard.

tête, *s.f.* Head. **1.** (*a*) **Tenir tête à qn,** to stand up to s.o. **J'en ai par-dessus la tête,** I can't stand it any longer. **Ne (pas) savoir où donner de la tête,** not to know which way to turn. **Dîner tête à tête,** to dine alone together. **Signe de tête,** nod. (*b*) Face, appearance. *F:* **Faire une tête,** to pull a long face. **Il a une bonne tête,** he looks a decent fellow. **2.** Headpiece, brains, mind.

C'est une femme de tête, she is a capable woman. **Mauvaise tête**, unruly boy, workman. **En faire à sa tête**, to have one's way. **3.** (*a*) Leader. (*b*) Summit, crown, top. (*c*) Head (of pin). (*d*) Front. *Rail:* **Voiture de tête**, front carriage. *Rac:* **Prendre la tête**, to take the lead. **Tête de ligne**, rail-head.

tête-à-tête, *s.m.inv.* Private interview; tête-à-tête.

teter, *v.tr.* (il tette) To suck.

tétras [-trɑ(s)], *s.m. Orn:* Grouse.

têtu, *a.* Stubborn, obstinate; mulish.

teuton, -onne. 1. *a.* Teuton(ic). **2.** *s.* Teuton.

teutonique, *a.* Teutonic.

texte, *s.m.* (*a*) Text. *Bookb:* **Gravure hors texte**, plate; full-page engraving. (*b*) Letterpress.

textile, *a. & s.m.* Textile.

textuel, -elle, *a.* Textual.

texture, *s.f.* Texture.

thé, *s.m.* **1.** Tea. **2.** Tea-party.

théâtral, -aux, *a.* Theatrical.

théâtralement, *adv.* Theatrically.

théâtre, *s.m.* **1.** Theatre. **2.** Stage. *Le t. français*, the French stage. **3.** (*a*) Dramatic art. **Pièce de théâtre**, play. **Faire du théâtre**, to be on the stage. **Coup de théâtre**, dramatic turn (to events). (*b*) Plays, dramatic works. **Le théâtre anglais** the English drama.

théière, *s.f.* Teapot.

théiste. 1. *a.* Theistic. **2.** *s.* Theist.

thème, *s.m.* (*a*) Theme, topic; subject. (*b*) *Sch:* Composition exercise.

théodolite, *s.m. Surv:* Theodolite.

théologal, -aux, *a.* Relating to theology.

théologie, *s.f.* Theology. **Docteur en théologie**, doctor of divinity; D.D.

théologien, *s.m.* Theologian; divine.

théologique, *a.* Theological.

théorème, *s.m.* Theorem.

théorie, *s.f.* Theory.

théorique, *a.* Theoretic(al).

théoriquement, *adv.* Theoretically.

théoriser, *v.tr. & i.* To theorize.

théosophie, *s.f.* Theosophy.

thérapeutique, *s.f.* Therapeutics.

thermal, -aux, *a.* Thermal.

thermomètre, *s.m.* Thermometer.

thésauriser, *v.tr* To hoard, pile up (money); *abs.* to hoard.

thèse, *s.f.* Thesis, proposition, argument. **Pièce à thèse**, problem play. **En thèse générale**, generally speaking. **Changer de thèse**, to change the subject.

thon, *s.m. Ich:* Tunny(-fish).

thorax [-aks], *s.m.* Thorax, chest.

thym, *s.m. Bot:* Thyme.

thyroïde, *a. Anat:* Thyroid.

tiare, *s.f.* Tiara.

Tibère, *Pr.n.m. Rom.Hist:* Tiberius.

tibétain, *a. & s.* Tibetan.

tibia, *s.m. Anat:* Tibia, shin-bone.

Tibre (le). *Pr.n.m.* The (river) Tiber.

tic [tik], *s.m.* (*a*) *Med:* Tic; twitching. (*b*) *F:* Habit; trick (of doing sth.).

ticket, *s.m.* Numbered slip, check. *T. de place*, reserved-seat ticket. *T. de quai*, platform ticket. *T. de pain*, bread coupon.

tic-tac [-tak], *s.m.* Tick-tack; ticking; pit-a-pat.

tiède, *a.* Tepid; lukewarm.

tièdement, *adv.* Lukewarmly.

tiédeur, *s.f.* Tepidity, lukewarmness. **Agir avec tiédeur**, to act half-heartedly.

tien, tienne[1]. Yours; thine. **1.** *Occ. poss. a. pred.* Mes intérêts sont tiens, my interests are yours. **2. Le tien, la tienne, les tiens, les tiennes.** (*a*) *poss.pron.* Ma sœur se promène avec la tienne, my sister is out walking with yours. (*b*) *s.m.* (i) Your own; yours. **Il faut y mettre du tien**, you must contribute your share. (ii) *pl.* Your own (people). (iii) *F:* **Tu as encore fait des tiennes**, you have been up to your old tricks.

tien-drai, -ne[2], **-s**[1], **-t**, etc. See TENIR.

tiens[2], *int.* **1.** Hullo! **2.** To be sure! **3. Tiens, Tiens!** indeed? well, well!

tierce. See TIERS.

tiers, *f.* tierce, *s.* (*a*) Third (part). (*b*) Third person, third party.

tige, *s.f.* **1.** (*a*) Stem, stalk (of plant). (*b*) Trunk, bole (of tree). **2.** (*a*) Shaft (of column); shank (of key). (*b*) Rod. *Mch:* *T. du piston*, piston-rod.

tignasse, *s.f.* Shock, mop (of hair).

tigre[1], **tigresse**, *s. Z:* Tiger, tigress.

Tigre[2] **(le)**. *Pr.n.m.* The (river) Tigris.

tigré, *a.* Striped. **Lis tigré**, tiger-lily.

tillac [tijac], *s.m. Nau:* Deck.

tilleul [tijœl], *s.m.* Lime-tree, linden-tree.

timbale, *s.f.* **1.** *Mus:* Kettledrum. **2.** Metal drinking-cup. **3.** *Cu:* Pie-dish.

timbre, *s.m.* **1.** (*a*) Bell; gong. **Timbre électrique**, electric bell. *F:* **Avoir le timbre fêlé**, to have a screw loose. (*b*) Timbre, quality in tone. **2.** Stamp (on document). **Timbre de la poste**, post-mark.

timbre-poste, *s.m.* Postage stamp. *pl. Des timbres-poste.*

timbre-quittance, *s.m.* Receipt stamp. *pl. Des timbres-quittance.*

timbrer, *v.tr.* To stamp.

timbré, *a.* **1.** Sonorous. **2.** *F:* Cracked (person). **3.** Stamped.

timide, *a.* Timid. (*a*) Timorous, apprehensive. (*b*) Shy, bashful; diffident.

timidement, *adv.* Timidly. (*a*) Timorously. (*b*) Shyly, bashfully; diffidently.

timidité, *s.f.* Timidity. (*a*) Timorousness. (*b*) Shyness, bashfulness.

timon, *s.m.* Pole (of vehicle).

timonerie, *s.f.* **1.** (*a*) Steering (of ship). (*b*) (Naval) signalling. **Maître de timonerie** quartermaster. **2.** *Aut:* Steering-gear.

timonier, *s.m.* **1.** *Nau:* (*a*) Quartermaster. (*b*) Signalman. **2.** *Veh:* Wheel-horse.

timoré, *a.* Timorous, fearful.

tinctorial, -aux, *a.* Tinctorial. *Matières tinctoriales,* dye-stuffs.

tin-s, -t, etc. See TENIR. .

tintamarre, *s.m.* F: Din, racket, noise.

tintement, *s.m.* **I.** Ringing; tolling. **2.** Tinkling; jingling. **3.** Buzzing.

tinter. I. *v.tr.* To ring, toll. **2.** *v.i.* (a) To ring, toll; to tinkle; to jingle; to clink. (b) (Of the ears) To buzz, tingle. **Les oreilles ont dû vous tinter hier soir,** your ears must have burned last night.

tipule, *s.f.* Ent: Tipula; F: Daddy-long-legs.

tique, *s.f.* Arach: Tick, cattle-tick.

tir, *s.m.* **I.** Shooting; musketry; gunnery. **2.** Fire, firing. **A tir rapide,** quick-firing. **3.** Rifle-range.

tirade, *s.f.* (a) Th: Declamatory speech. (b) Tirade; vituperative speech.

tirage, *s.m.* **I.** Pulling, hauling. **2.** Draught. *T. forcé,* forced draught. **3.** Drawing (of lottery). **4.** *Typ:* Printing (off).

tiraillement [-raj-], *s.m.* **I.** Tugging. **2.** Tiraillements d'estomac, pangs of hunger.

tirailler [-raje], *v.tr.* **I.** To pull about. *F: Tiraillé entre deux émotions,* torn between two emotions. **2.** *Abs.* To blaze away.

tirailleur [-raj-], *s.m.* Mil: Skirmisher, sharp-shooter, tirailleur.

tirant, *s.m.* **Tirant d'eau,** (ship's) draught.

tire, *s.f.* **Voleur à la tire,** pickpocket.

NOTE. In the following compounds TIRE is inv., the noun takes the plural.

tire-botte, *s.m.* Boot-jack.

tire-bouchon, *s.m.* Corkscrew.

tire-bouton, *s.m.* Buttonhook.

tire-d'aile (à), *adv.phr.* **S'envoler à tire-d'aile,** to fly swiftly away.

tire-ligne, *s.m.* **I.** Drawing-pen. **2.** *Tls:* Scriber, scribing-awl.

tirelire, *s.f.* Money-box.

tirer. I. *v.tr.* **I.** To pull out; stretch. **2.** To pull, tug, draw. *T. la jambe,* to limp. *F:* **Être tiré à quatre,** to be worried on every side. **3.** (a) To pull off, draw off. (b) Tirer son chapeau à qn, to raise one's hat to s.o. **4.** To pull out, take out, extract. *T. de l'eau,* to draw water. **Tirer les cartes,** to tell fortunes by cards. **Tirer plaisir de qch.,** to derive pleasure from sth. **5.** To draw. **6.** (a) To shoot, fire. *T. un lièvre,* to shoot at a hare. *T. à blanc,* to fire blank (cartridge). (b) **Tirer (des armes),** to fence. **7.** Nau: To draw.

II. **tirer,** *v.i.* **I.** To pull. **2.** (a) To incline (to); to verge (on). *Bleu tirant sur le vert,* blue tending to green. **Le jour tire à sa fin,** the day is drawing to its close. (b) *T. sur la gauche,* to incline to the left.

se tirer. Se tirer d'affaire, to get out of trouble.

tiré, *a.* (a) Drawn, worn-out, haggard. (b) Tiré par les cheveux, far-fetched.

tiret, *s.m.* Typ: (a) Hyphen. (b) Dash.

tireur, -euse, *s.* **I.** One who draws; drawer. **2.** (a) Shooter; marksman. (b) Tireur (d'armes), fencer.

tiroir, *s.m.* Drawer (of table).

tisane, *s.f.* Infusion (of herbs).

tison, *s.m.* **I.** (Fire-)brand.' F: **Un tison arraché du feu,** a brand from the burning. **2.** Fusee (match).

tisonner, *v.tr.* To poke, stir (the fire).

tisonnier, *s.m.* Poker.

tissage, *s.m.* Weaving.

tisser, *v.tr.* To weave.

tisserand, *s.* Weaver.

tissu, *s.m.* **I.** (a) Texture. (b) Fabric, tissue.

titan, *s.m.* Titan.

titanesque, titanique, *a.* Titanic.

Tite-Live. *Pr.n.m.* Lt.Lit: Livy.

titillation, *s.f.* Titillation, tickling.

titiller, *v.tr.* To titillate; to tickle.

titrage, *s.m.* Assaying (of ore).

titre, *s.m.* **I.** (a) Title. (b) *Adj.phr.* **En titre,** titular; on the regular staff. **2.** (a) Diploma, certificate. (b) Title-deed. (c) *Fin:* Warrant, bond, certificate; *pl.* stocks and shares, securities. **3.** Title, claim, right. **A titre de,** by virtue of. *A t. d'office,* ex officio. *A t. d'essai,* on approval. **A quel titre?** by what right? **4.** (a) Title (of book). (b) Heading (of chapter). **5.** Grade (of ore); fineness (of coinage).

titrer, *v.tr.* To assay (ore).

titré, *a.* **I.** Titled. **2.** Certificated.

tituber, *v.i.* To reel (about); to lurch; to stagger.

titulaire. I. *a.* Titular. **2.** *s.* Holder (of right); bearer (of passport).

toast [tost], *s.m.* Toast. **Porter un toast,** to propose a toast.

toaster [tɔs-], *v.tr* To toast; to drink (s.o.'s) health.

toboggan, *s.m.* Toboggan.

toc [tɔk]. **I.** (a) *int.* **Toc toc!** tap, tap! (b) *s.m.* Tap, rap. **2.** *s.m.* F: *Bijoux en toc,* imitation jewellery.

tocsin, *s.m.* Tocsin; alarm-bell.

toge, *s.f.* (a) Rom.Ant: Toga. (b) Gown, robe.

tohu-bohu, *s.m.* F: Confusion; hubbub.

toi, stressed *pers. pron.* (Familiar form of address) (a) You. *C'est toi,* it is you. *Ce livre est à toi,* this book is yours. *Tais-toi,* hold your tongue. (b) Thou, thee.

toile, *s.f.* **I.** (a) Linen, linen cloth. (b) Cloth. **Toile cirée,** (i) oilcloth; (ii) *Nau:* oilskin. (c) Canvas. (d) *T. métallique,* wire gauze. (e) Toile d'araignée, cobweb; spider's web. **2.** Oil painting; canvas. **3.** *Nau:* Sail.

toilette, *s.f.* **I.** Wash-stand. **2.** Faire sa toilette, to make one's toilet; to dress. **3.** Lavatory. **4.** (Woman's) dress, costume.

toi-même, *pers.pron.* Thyself; yourself.

toiser, *v.tr.* **I.** To measure. **2.** To eye from head to foot.

toison, *s.f.* **1.** Fleece. **2.** *F:* Mop, shock (of hair).

toit, *s.m.* **1.** Roof; house-top. **2.** *F:* Le t. *paternel,* the home.

toiture, *s.f.* Roofing, roof.

tôle, *s.f.* Sheet-metal. *T. ondulée,* corrugated iron.

tolérable, *a.* Bearable, tolerable.

tolérablement, *adv.* Tolerably; bearably.

tolérance, *s.f.* Tolerance. **Par tolérance,** on sufferance.

tolérant, *a.* Tolerant.

tolérer, *v.tr.* (je tolère; je tolérerai) (*a*) To tolerate. (*b*) To allow tacitly, wink at.

tomahawk [tɔmaɔk], *s.m.* Tomahawk.

tomate, *s.f.* Tomato.

tombal, -aux, *a.* **Pierre tombale,** tombstone.

tombant, *a.* Falling. *A la nuit tombante,* at nightfall.

tombe, *s.f.* (*a*) Tomb, grave. (*b*) Tombstone.

tombeau, *s.m.* Tomb; monument.

tomber. I. *v.i.* (Aux. usu. *être*) **1.** To fall, fall down, drop down. *Impers. Il tombe de la neige,* it is snowing. **Faire tomber qch.,** to knock over sth. **Laisser tomber qch.,** to drop sth. **Fruits tombés,** windfalls. **2.** To drop, abate, subside. **3.** *T. en disgrâce,* to fall into disgrace. **4. Tomber sur l'ennemi,** to attack, fall on, the enemy. **5.** *T. sur qch.,* to fall in with, come across, sth. **Tomber juste,** to occur opportunely; to come at the right moment. **6.** To fail. **7.** To fall, hang down. **8. Tomber amoureux de qn,** to fall in love with s.o.
II. **tomber,** *s.m.* **Au tomber du jour,** at nightfall.

tombée, *s.f.* Fall. **A la tombée de la nuit,** at nightfall.

tombereau, *s.m.* Tip-cart; tumbril.

Tombouctou. *Pr.n.m.* Timbuctoo.

tome, *s.m.* (Heavy) volume; tome.

tom-pouce [tɔm-], *s.m.* **1.** Tom Thumb, midget. **2.** Stumpy umbrella. *pl. Des tompouces.*

ton[1], **ta, tes,** *poss.a.* (*Ton* is used instead of *ta* before fem. words beginning with a vowel or h 'mute.') (*a*) Your. *Un de tes amis,* a friend of yours. *Tes père et mère,* your father and mother. (*b*) Thy.

ton[2], *s.m.* **1.** (*a*) Tone, intonation. **Faire baisser le ton à qn,** to make s.o. sing small. *Elle le prend sur ce ton?* is that how she speaks to you? (*b*) Tone, manners, breeding. *Le bon ton,* good form. **2.** *Mus:* (*a*) (Hauteur du) ton, pitch. (*b*) Key. **3.** *Ling:* Pitch accent. **4.** Tone, tint, colour.

tondeur, -euse. 1. *s.* Shearer, clipper. **2.** *s.f.* **Tondeuse,** (*a*) Clippers. (*b*) Lawn-mower.

tondre, *v.tr.* To shear, to clip. *T. le gazon,* to mow the lawn. *F:* Il tondrait (sur) un œuf, he would skin a flint.

tonique, *a.* **1.** *Med:* **Médicament t.,** *s.m.* **tonique,** tonic. **2.** *Ling:* Tonic; accented. **3.** *Mus:* **Note t.,** *s.f.* **tonique,** key-note.

tonitruant, *a.* Like thunder; stentorian

Tonkin (le). *Pr.n. Geog:* Tonkin.

tonnage, *s.m. Nau:* Tonnage.

tonne, *s.f.* **1.** Tun; (large) cask. **2.** *Meas:* Metric ton (= 1000 kilograms).

tonneau, *s.m.* **1.** Cask, barrel. **Bière au tonneau,** draught beer. **2.** *Nau:* Ton. **3.** Governess-cart.

tonnelet, *s.m.* Small cask; keg.

tonnelle, *s.f.* Arbour, bower.

tonner, *v.i.* To thunder.

tonnerre, *s.m.* Thunder.

tonsure, *s.f.* Tonsure.

tonte, *s.f.* (*a*) Sheep-shearing; clipping. (*b*) Clip. (*c*) Shearing-time.

top [tɔp], *s.m. W.Tel:* **Les tops,** the pips.

topaze, *s.f.* Topaz.

toper, *v.i.* *F:* To agree, consent; to shake hands on it. **Tope là!** done! agreed!

topinambour, *s.m.* *Bot:* Jerusalem artichoke.

topographie, *s.f.* Topography.

topographique, *a.* Topographic(al).

toque, *s.f. Cost:* (*a*) Cap. (*b*) Toque.

toqué, *a.* *F:* **1.** Crazy, cracked. **2.** Infatuated.

torche, *s.f.* Torch.

torchis, *s.m.* *Mur en t.,* mud wall.

torchon. 1. *s.m.* Floor-cloth; dish-cloth; duster. **2.** *a.inv.* **Dentelle torchon,** torchon lace.

tordant, *a.* *P:* Screamingly funny.

tordre, *v.tr.* To twist; to wring. **Tordre la bouche,** to make a wry mouth.
se tordre, to writhe, twist. *F:* **Se tordre (de rire),** to split one's sides with laughter.

toréador, *s.m.* Toreador, bull-fighter.

tornade, *s.f.* Tornado.

torpédo, *s.m. or f. Aut:* Open touring-car.

torpeur, *s.f.* Torpor.

torpille [-piːj], *s.f.* Torpedo.

torpiller [-pije], *v.tr.* To torpedo.

torpilleur [tɔrpijœːr], *s.m. Navy:* **1.** Torpedo man. **2.** (Small) destroyer; torpedo-boat.

torréfier, *v.tr.* To roast (coffee); to scorch.

torrent, *s.m.* Torrent.

torrentiel, -elle, *a.* Torrential.

torrentiellement, *adv.* Torrentially.

torride, *a.* Torrid, *F:* scorching.

tors, *a.* Twisted.

torse, *s.m.* Torso (of statue, *F:* of person).

torsion, *s.f.* Torsion; twisting.

tort, *s.m.* Wrong. **1.** Error, fault. **Être dans son tort,** to be in the wrong. **Donner tort à qn,** to decide against s.o. **A tort ou à raison,** rightly or wrongly. **A tort et à travers,** at random. **2.** Injury, harm.

torticolis, *s.m.* Crick in the neck; stiff neck.

tortiller [-tije]. *v.tr.* To twist (up), to twirl.
se tortiller. 1. To wriggle, twist. **2.** To writhe, squirm.

tortue, *s.f.* Tortoise. *T. de mer,* turtle.

tortueusement, *adv.* Crookedly; tortuously.

tortueux, *a.* Tortuous, winding; twisted; crooked, underhand.

torture, *s.f.* Torture.

torturer, *v.tr.* **1.** To torture. **2.** *F:* To strain, twist, pervert.

toscan, *a. & s.* Tuscan.

Toscane. *Pr.n.f. Geog:* Tuscany.

tôt, *adv.* (*a*) Soon. **Tôt ou tard,** sooner or later. (*b*) *Se lever tôt,* to rise early.

total, -aux. 1. *a.* Total, complete, entire, whole. **2.** *s.m.* Whole, total.

totalement, *adv.* Totally, entirely.

totalitaire, *a.* Totalitarian.

totalitarisme, *s.m.* Totalitarianism.

totalité, *s.f.* Totality, whole.

totem [-tɛm], *s.m.* Totem.

totémisme, *s.m.* Totemism.

toton, *s.m.* Teetotum.

touage, *s.m.* Towing; warping.

toucan, *s.m. Orn:* Toucan.

touchant. 1. *a.* Touching, moving, affecting. **2.** *prep.* Touching, concerning.

touche, *s.f.* **1.** Touch, touching. **Pierre de touche,** touchstone, test. **2.** Key (of typewriter).

touche-à-tout, *s.m. & f. inv.* Meddler.

toucher. I. *v.* To touch. **1.** *v.tr.* (*a*) *T. le but,* to hit the mark. *T. ses appointements,* *Abs.* **toucher,** to be paid. *Mil: T. des rations,* to draw rations. (*b*) To move, affect. *T. qn jusqu'aux larmes,* to move s.o. to tears. (*c*) To concern, affect. **2.** (*a*) *v.tr.* To touch on, deal with; allude to. (*b*) *v.ind.tr.* To meddle, interfere. **Ne pas toucher à un plat,** to leave a dish untasted. *F:* **Sans avoir l'air d'y toucher,** in a detached manner. **3.** *v.i.* (*a*) *T. à qch.,* to be in touch, in contact, with sth.; to be near to sth.; to border on sth. (*b*) *Cela touche de très près à mes intérêts,* it closely affects my interests.

se toucher, to touch, adjoin.

II. toucher, *s.m.* Touch.

touer, *v.tr. Nau:* (*a*) To warp. (*b*) To tow.

touffe, *s.f.* Tuft; wisp; clump, cluster.

touffu, *a.* Bushy (beard); thick (wood).

toujours, *adv.* **1.** Always, ever. **2.** Still. *Cherchez t.,* go on looking. **3.** Nevertheless, all the same. *Je peux t. essayer,* anyhow I can try.

toundra, *s.f. Geog:* Tundra.

toupet, *s.m.* **1.** (*a*) Tuft of hair. (*b*) Forelock. **2.** *F:* Cheek, impudence, effrontery.

toupie, *s.f.* Top; peg-top, spinning-top.

tour[1] [tuːr], *s.f.* **1.** Tower. **2.** *Chess:* Castle, rook.

tour[2], *s.m.* **1.** (*a*) (Turning-)lathe. (*b*) *T. de potier,* potter's wheel. **2.** (*a*) Circumference, circuit. **Faire le tour du monde,** to go round the world. *Sp:* **Tour de piste,** lap. **Tour de poitrine,** chest measurement. (*b*) **Tour de lit,** bed-valance. *Cost:* **Tour de cou,** necklet (of fur). (*c*) **Tours et retours d'un** chemin, twists and turns of a road. (*d*) Turn (of phrase); shape, contour (of face); course, direction (of business affair). **3.** (*a*) Round, revolution, turn. **Frapper à tour de bras,** to strike with all one's might. **Son sang n'a fait qu'un tour,** it gave him a dreadful shock. (*b*) Stroll. (*c*) Trip, tour. **4.** Rotation, turn. **Chacun à son tour,** each one in his turn. **A tour de rôle,** in turn. **5.** Trick, feat. **Tour de main,** knack. **Tour d'adresse,** (i) piece of sleight of hand; (ii) feat of acrobatics. **Tour de force,** feat of strength.

tourangeau, -elle, *a. & s.* (Native, inhabitant) (i) of Tours, (ii) of Touraine.

tourbe, *s.f.* Peat, turf.

tourbeux, *a.* Peaty, boggy.

tourbier. 1. *a.* Peaty. **2.** *s.f.* **Tourbière,** peat-bog.

tourbillon [-bijɔ̃], *s.m.* **1.** Whirlwind; swirl (of dust). **2.** (*a*) Whirlpool. (*b*) Eddy. (*c*) *F:* Whirl, bustle.

tourbillonnement [-bij-], *s.m.* Whirling, eddying.

tourbillonner [-bij-], *v.i.* To whirl (round); to eddy, swirl.

tourelle, *s.f.* Turret.

tourie, *s.f.* Carboy.

tourillon [-rijɔ̃], *s.m.* Pivot(-pin), swivel-pin.

tourisme, *s.m.* Touring. **Bureau de tourisme,** tourist agency.

touriste, *s.m. & f.* Tourist.

tourment, *s.m.* (*a*) Torment, torture. (*b*) Anguish, pain.

tourmente, *s.f.* Gale, storm, tempest. **Tourmente de neige,** blizzard.

tourmenter, *v.tr.* **1.** To torture, torment. **2.** (*a*) To harass, worry. (*b*) To plague, pester. **se tourmenter,** to fret, worry. **tourmenté,** *a.* (*a*) Distorted. (*b*) Tormented, tortured. (*c*) Agitated; turbulent.

tournant. 1. *a.* (*a*) Turning; revolving. **Pont tournant,** swing-bridge. (*b*) Winding (road); spiral (staircase). **2.** *s.m.* Turning, bend; street corner. *Aut: T. brusque,* dangerous corner.

tourne-à-gauche, *s.m.inv. Tls:* Wrench.

tournedos, *s.m. Cu:* Fillet steak.

tournemain, *s.m.* **En un tournemain,** in a trice, in the twinkling of an eye.

tourner, *v.* To turn. **I.** *v.tr.* (*a*) To fashion, shape, on a lathe. (*b*) To revolve, turn round, rotate. **Tourner le dos à qn,** to turn one's back on s.o. **Tourner bride,** to turn one's horse's head. (*c*) To change, convert. *T. tout en mal,* to put a bad complexion upon everything. **Tourner qn en ridicule,** to hold s.o. up to ridicule. (*d*) To turn over. (*e*) To get round; to evade. **2.** *v.i.* (*a*) To revolve; to go round. **Tourner autour du pot,** to beat about the bush. **Le pied lui a tourné,** he twisted his ankle. (*b*) To change in direction. *Tournez à gauche,* turn to the left. (*c*) To turn out, result. **Mal tourner,** to go to the bad. (*d*) *Abs. Lait qui tourne*, milk that is curdling.

se tourner. (*a*) *Se t. vers qn*, to turn towards s.o. (*b*) To turn round.

tourné, *a.* **1.** *Jeune fille bien tournée*, well set up girl. **2.** *Esprit t. aux plaisirs*, mind disposed to enjoyment. **3.** (*a*) Sour (milk). (*b*) Avoir la tête tournée, to have one's head turned.

tournée, *s.f.* Round, tour.

tournesol [-sɔl], *s.m.* **1.** *Bot:* Sunflower. **2.** Papier (de) tournesol, litmus paper.

tournevis [-vis], *s.m.* *Tls:* Screw-driver.

tourniquet, *s.m.* **1.** Tourniquet (-compteur), turnstile. **2.** *Surg:* Tourniquet.

tournoi, *s.m.* Tournament; (whist) drive.

tournoiement, *s.m.* **1.** Whirling; wheeling. **2.** Giddiness, dizziness.

tournoyer, *v.i.* (je tournoie) To turn round and round; to whirl; to eddy, swirl.

tournure, *s.f.* **1.** Turn, course (of events). **2.** Shape, form, figure. **Tournure d'esprit,** turn of mind.

tourte, *s.f.* Raised pie; (covered) tart.

tourtereau, *s.m.* Young turtle-dove. *F:* Faire les tourtereaux, to bill and coo.

tourterelle, *s.f.* Turtle-dove.

tous. See TOUT.

Toussaint (la). *Pr.n.f.* All Saints' day; All-Hallows. *La veille de la T.,* Hallowe'en.

tousser, *v.i.* To cough.

tout, toute, *pl.* **tous, toutes.** (When *tous* is a pronoun it is pronounced [tus]) All. **I.** *a.* **1.** Any, every, all. **Tout autre que vous,** anybody but you. *J'ai toute raison de croire,* I have every reason to believe. **2.** *De toute force il nous faut,* we absolutely must. **A toute vitesse,** at full speed. **Tout à vous,** entirely yours. **3.** The whole; all. *Pendant tout l'hiver,* throughout the winter. **4.** All, every. **Tous les jours,** every day. **5.** **Tous (les) deux,** both. **Tous les deux jours,** every other day. **6.** C'est toute une histoire, it's a long story.

II. tout, *pron.* **1.** *sg.neut.* All, everything. **C'est tout ce qu'il y a de plus beau,** it is most beautiful. **C'est tout dire,** I needn't say more. **En tout et pour tout,** first and last. **2.** *pl.* **Tous à la fois,** all together.

III. tout, *s.m.* **Le tout,** the whole. **Du tout au tout,** entirely. **Pas du tout,** *F:* du tout, not at all.

IV. tout, *adv.* (Before a fem. adj. beginning with a consonant or *h* 'aspirate' *tout* becomes *toute*) **1.** Quite, entirely. *Tout nouveau(x), toute(s) nouvelle(s),* quite new. *Tout de noir vêtue, toute vêtue de noir,* dressed all in black. **Des lutteurs de tout premier ordre,** wrestlers of the very first order. **Vêtement tout fait,** ready-made garment. *Tout au bout,* right at the end. **Tout doux!** gently! **Tout à fait,** quite, entirely. **Tout au plus,** at the very most. **Tout à vous,** yours very truly. **2.** **Tout en parlant,** while

speaking. **3.** **Tout ignorant qu'il est, qu'il soit,** ignorant though he may be. **4.** Être tout oreilles, to be all ears.

toutefois, *adv.* Yet, nevertheless, however.

toute-puissance, *s.f.* Omnipotence.

toutou, *s.m.* Doggie, bow-wow. *pl. Des toutous.*

tout-puissant, *f.* **toute-puissante,** *a* Almighty, omnipotent. *pl. Tout-puissants toutes-puissantes.*

toux, *s.f.* Cough.

toxicologie, *s.f.* Toxicology.

toxicomane, *s.m. & f.* Drug addict.

toxique, *a.* Toxic. **Gaz toxique,** poison gas.

tracas, *s.m.* Worry, trouble, bother.

tracasser, *v.tr.* To worry, bother.

se tracasser, to worry.

tracasserie, *s.f.* Worry, fuss.

tracassier, *a.* (*a*) Vexatious. (*b*) Pestering, interfering.

trace, *s.f.* Trace. (*a*) Trail, track; footprint(s). *F: Marcher sur les traces de qn,* to tread in s.o.'s footsteps. (*b*) Weal, scar, mark. (*c*) (Slight) trace.

tracer, *v.tr.* (n. traçons) To trace. (*a*) To lay out (road); to map out (route). (*b*) To draw (a line); to outline (plan).

tracé, *s.m.* **1.** (*a*) Tracing, sketching. **2.** Outline, sketch.

traceur, -euse, *a.* Tracer. **Balle traceuse,** tracer-bullet.

trachée-artère, *s.f.* Trachea, windpipe.

tract [trakt], *s.m.* Tract.

tracteur, *s.m.* Tractor, traction-engine.

traction, *s.f.* Traction. (*a*) Pulling. (*b*) Draught. *T. automobile,* motor traction. (*c*) *Aut:* T. avant, (car with) front-wheel drive.

tradition, *s.f.* (*a*) Tradition. (*b*) Folklore.

traditionnel, -elle, *a.* Traditional.

traditionnellement, *adv.* Traditionally.

traducteur, -trice, *s.* Translator.

traduction, *s.f.* **1.** Translating. **2.** Translation.

traduire, *v.tr.* (Conj. like CONDUIRE) **1.** *Jur:* T. qn en justice, to sue s.o. **2.** (*a*) To translate. (*b*) To decode (a cable). (*c*) To interpret, explain; express.

trafic [-fik], *s.m.* Traffic. **1.** Trading, trade. **Faire trafic de son influence,** to trade on one's influence. **2.** *T. de chemin de fer,* railway traffic.

trafiquant, *s.m.* Trader, trafficker.

trafiquer, *v.i.* To traffic, deal, trade.

tragédie, *s.f.* Tragedy.

tragédien, -ienne, *s.* Tragedian.

tragique. 1. (*a*) *a.* Tragic (play); tragic(al). (*b*) *s.m.* Cela tourne au tragique, the thing is becoming tragic. **2.** *s.m.* Tragic poet. **3.** *s.m.* Le tragique, the tragic art; tragedy.

tragiquement, *adv.* Tragically.

trahir, *v.tr.* To betray. **1.** To reveal, disclose. **2.** *T. qn,* to play s.o. false.

trahison, *s.f.* **1.** (*a*) Treachery, perfidy. (*b*) *Jur:* Treason. **2.** Betrayal, betraying.

train, *s.m.* **1.** (a) Train, string, line. *T. de bois,* timber raft. (b) (Railway-)train. (c) *Mil:* Train (of transport). (d) Suite, attendants. (e) Quarters (of horse). *T. de derrière,* hind quarters. (f) *Av:* **Train d'atterrissage,** under-carriage. **2.** Movement. (a) Pace, rate. **A fond de train,** at top speed. (b) **Mettre qch. en train,** to set sth. going. *Il est en t. de travailler,* he is at work. **Les choses vont leur train,** things are proceeding as usual. (c) **Mener grand train,** to live on a grand scale. **3.** Mood. **Être en train,** to be in good form.

traînant, *a.* **1.** Dragging, trailing. **2.** Languid, listless; drawling.

traînard, *s.m.* (a) *Mil:* Straggler. (b) *F:* Slow-coach; dawdler.

traîneau, *s.m.* Sledge, sleigh.

traîner. 1. *v.tr.* To drag, pull, draw, along; to spin out; to drawl. **Traîner la jambe,** to be lame. **Traîner le pied,** to lag behind. **2.** *v.i.* (a) To lag behind; to straggle. (b) To linger. **Traîner la rue,** to loaf. (c) To lie about. (d) To flag, languish. **Traîner en longueur,** to drag (on).

se traîner. 1. To crawl (along). **2.** To trail along.

traînée, *s.f.* Trail. **Se répandre comme une traînée de poudre,** to spread like wildfire.

train-poste, *s.m.* Mail-train. *pl. Des trains-poste(s).*

traire, *v.pr.* (*pr.p.* **trayant;** *p.p.* **trait;** *pr.ind.* **ils traient,** no *p.h.*) To milk (a cow).

trait, *s.m.* **1.** (a) Pulling. **Tout d'un trait,** at one stretch. **Cheval de trait,** draught-horse. (b) Trace (of harness). **2.** (a) Throwing, shooting (of missile). (b) Arrow, dart. *F:* **Partir comme un trait,** to be off like a shot. *T. de satire,* gibe. (c) Beam (of light). (d) **Trait d'esprit,** flash of wit. **3.** Draught, gulp. **D'un (seul) trait,** at one gulp. **4.** (a) Stroke, line. *Tg:* **Points et traits,** dots and dashes. (b) **Trait d'union,** hyphen. **5.** (a) Feature, lineament. (b) Trait. **6.** Act, deed. **Trait de génie,** stroke of genius.

traitable, *a.* Tractable, manageable.

traite, *s.f.* **1.** Stretch (of road); stage (of journey). **(Tout) d'une traite,** at a stretch. **2.** Transport; trading. *La t. des noirs,* *Abs.* **la traite,** the slave-trade. **3.** *Com:* Bill (of exchange). **4.** Milking.

traitement, *s.m.* **1.** Treatment. **2.** Salary; pay.

traiter, *v.tr.* To treat. **1.** (a) *T. qn de haut en bas,* to put on airs with s.o. (b) *T. qn de lâche,* to call s.o. a coward. (c) *T. un malade,* to treat a patient. (d) To entertain. **2.** (a) To negotiate; to handle. (b) To discuss, deal with. **3.** *v.i.* (a) *T. de la paix,* to treat for peace. (b) *T. d'un sujet,* to deal with a subject.

traité, *s.m.* **1.** Treatise. **2.** Treaty.

traître, traîtresse. 1. *a.* Treacherous, traitorous. **2.** *s.* Traitor, traitress.

traîtreusement, *adv.* Treacherously.

traîtrise, *s.f.* Treachery.

trajectoire, *s.f.* Trajectory.

trajet, *s.m.* (a) Journey; passage. *J'ai fait une partie du t. en avion,* I flew part of the way. (b) Path (of projectile).

trame, *s.f.* **1.** *Tex:* Woof, weft. *F: La t. de la vie,* the web, thread of life. **2.** Plot, conspiracy.

tramontane, *s.f.* Tramontana, north wind

tramway [tramwɛ], *s.m.* **1.** Tramway. **2.** Tram(car).

tranchant. 1. *a.* (a) Cutting, sharp; keen. (b) Trenchant; peremptory. **2.** *s.m.* Edge (of knife).

tranche, *s.f.* **1.** (a) Slice; rasher. (b) Block, portion. **2.** Slab. **3.** Edge. **Livre doré sur tranche,** gilt-edged book.

trancher. 1. *v.tr.* (a) To slice; to cut. (b) To cut short; to settle out of hand. **Trancher le mot,** to speak plainly. (c) To decide, settle. **2.** *v.i.* To contrast strongly; to stand out clearly.

tranchée, *s.f.* **1.** Trench; drain; cutting. **2.** *pl.* Colic, gripes.

tranchoir, *s.m.* *Cu:* Cutting-board.

tranquille [-kil], *a.* Tranquil. (a) Calm, still, quiet. (b) Quiet, peaceful. (c) Undisturbed. *Laissez-moi t.,* leave me alone.

tranquillement [-kil-], *adv.* Tranquilly, calmly, quietly.

tranquilliser [-kil-], *v.tr.* To tranquillize; to reassure; to set at rest, to soothe.

se tranquilliser. 1. To calm down. **2.** To set one's mind at rest.

tranquillité [-kil-], *s.f.* **1.** Tranquillity, calm(ness), quiet. **2.** *T. d'esprit,* peace of mind.

transaction, *s.f.* (a) Transaction; *pl.* dealings, deals. (b) Compromise.

transalpin, *a.* Transalpine.

transatlantique. 1. *a.* Transatlantic. **2.** *s.m.* (a) (Atlantic) liner. (b) Deck-chair.

transbordement, *s.m.* Trans-shipment.

transborder, *v.tr.* **1.** To trans-ship. **2.** To convey across (river).

transcendance, *s.f.* Transcendency.

transcendant, *a.* Transcendent.

transcripteur, *s.m.* Transcriber.

transcription, *s.f.* **1.** Transcription, transcribing. **2.** Transcript, copy.

transcrire, *v.tr.* (Conj. like ÉCRIRE) To transcribe.

transe, *s.f.* **1.** Usu. *pl.* Fright, fear. **2.** (Hypnotic) trance.

transept [-sɛpt], *s.m.* *Ecc.Arch:* Transept.

transférable, *a.* Transferable.

transférer, *v.tr.* (je **transfère;** je **transférerai**) (a) To transfer. (b) *T. une propriété,* to convey an estate.

transfert, *s.m.* **1.** Transference. **2.** Making over; transfer.

transfiguration, *s.f.* Transfiguration.

transfigurer, *v.tr.* To transfigure.
se transfigurer, to be, become, transfigured.
transformateur, -trice. *El.E:* **1.** *a.* Transforming. **2.** *s.m.* Transformer.
transformation, *s.f.* Transformation.
transformer, *v.tr.* To transform, change.
se transformer, to change, turn.
transgresser, *v.tr.* To transgress, break.
transgression, *s.f.* Transgression.
transiger, *v.i.* (n. transigeons) To compound, compromise.
transir, *v.tr.* To chill, benumb.
transi, *a.* Perished with cold.
transitif, *a. Gram:* Transitive.
transition, *s.f.* Transition.
transitoire, *a.* Transitory, transient.
translation, *s.f. Jur:* Transferring, conveyance.
translucide, *a.* Translucent.
transmettre, *v.tr.* (Conj. like METTRE) **1.** To transmit; to pass on, convey. **2.** *Jur:* To transfer, convey.
transmi-s, -t, etc. See TRANSMETTRE.
transmissible, *a.* Transferable.
transmission, *s.f.* **1.** Transmission; *Tg:* sending (of message). **2.** *Jur:* Transfer(ence), conveyance.
transmuer, *v.tr.* To transmute.
transmutation, *s.f.* Transmutation.
transparaître, *v.i.* (Conj. like CONNAÎTRE) To show through.
transparence, *s.f.* Transparency.
transparent, *a.* Transparent.
transpercer, *v.tr.* (n. transperçons) To (trans)pierce; to transfix.
transpiration, *s.f.* **1.** (*a*) Perspiring. (*b*) Transpiring. **2.** Sweat, perspiration.
transpirer, *v.i.* **1.** To perspire. **2.** (Aux. *avoir* or *être*) To transpire; to leak out.
transplanter, *v.tr.* To transplant.
transport, *s.m.* **1.** Transport, conveyance, carriage. **2.** Transport(-ship); troopship. **3.** Transport, rapture.
transportation, *s.f.* **1.** Conveyance (of goods). **2.** Transportation (of convicts).
transporter, *v.tr.* **1.** To transport, convey, remove. **2.** To transport, to enrapture.
transposer, *v.tr.* To transpose.
transposition, *s.f.* Transposition.
transvaser, *v.tr.* To decant.
transversal, -aux, *a.* Transverse, transversal.
transversalement, *adv.* Transversely, crosswise, athwart.
trapèze, *s.m. Gym:* Trapeze.
trappe, *s.f.* **1.** *Ven:* Trap, pitfall. **2.** Trapdoor.
trappeur, *s.m.* Trapper.
trappiste, *a. & s.m.* Trappist (monk).
trapu, *a.* Thick-set, squat, stocky.
traquenard, *s.m.* Trap, deadfall.
traquer, *v.tr.* (*a*) To enclose, surround, hem in. (*b*) To hunt down, run to earth.

traqueur, *s.m. Ven:* Tracker.
travail [-vaɪj], **aux,** *s.m.* Work. **1.** (*a*) Labour, toil. Travaux forcés, transportation with hard labour. (*b*) Working, operation. (*c*) Occupation, employment. **Les sanstravail,** the unemployed. **2.** (*a*) Piece of work. (*b*) (Literary) work. **3.** *D'un beau t.,* of fine workmanship.
travailler [-vaje]. **1.** *v.tr.* (*a*) To torment. Se travailler l'esprit, to worry. (*b*) To work upon; to bring pressure to bear upon. (*c*) To work, fashion, shape. **2.** *v.i.* To work, labour, toil.
se travailler, to labour, to strain.
travaillé, *a.* (*a*) Worked, wrought. (*b*) Laboured, elaborate.
travailleur, -euse [-vaj-]. **1.** *a.* Industrious, hard-working. **2.** *s.* Worker, workman.
travailliste [-vaj-]. *Pol:* a. Parti t., Labour party.
travée, *s.f.* **1.** *Const:* Bay. **2.** Span (of bridge).
travers, *s.m.* **1.** (*a*) Breadth. En travers, across, crosswise. En travers de, across. A travers qch., au travers de qch., through sth. (*b*) *Nau:* Beam, broadside. De travers, askew, awry, the wrong way, amiss. Regarder qn de travers, to look askance at s.o.
traverse, *s.f.* **1.** (Chemin de) traverse, cross-road, short cut. **2.** (Barre de) traverse, cross-bar, cross-piece. *Rail:* Sleeper.
traverser, *v.tr.* **1.** To traverse; to cross; to go through. *T. qch. de part en part,* to go clean through sth. **2.** To cross, thwart.
traversée, *s.f.* **1.** Passage, crossing. **2.** *Rail:* Traversée de voie, railway crossing.
traversin, *s.m.* Bolster (of bed).
travestir, *v.tr.* **1.** To disguise. *T. un homme en femme,* to disguise a man as a woman. Bal travesti, fancy-dress ball. **2.** To travesty, parody, burlesque.
travestissement, *s.m.* **1.** (*a*) Disguising. (*b*) Disguise. **2.** Travesty.
tray-ant, -ais, etc. See TRAIRE.
trébucher, *v.i.* To stumble, totter. Faire trébucher qn, to trip s.o. up.
trèfle, *s.m.* **1.** *Bot:* Trefoil, clover. **2.** *Arch:* Trefoil. **3.** *Cards:* Clubs.
tréfonds [-fɔ̃], *s.m.* Subsoil.
treillage [trɛjaːʒ], *s.m.* Trellis(-work); latticework.
treille [trɛːj], *s.f.* Vine-arbour.
treillis [trɛji], *s.m.* Trellis(-work); lattice.
treize, *num.a.inv. & s.m.inv.* Thirteen.
treizième, *num.a. & s.* Thirteenth.
tréma, *s.m.* Diaeresis.
tremblant, *a.* Trembling; quivering; quaking; unsteady.
tremble, *s.m.* Aspen.
tremblement, *s.m.* **1.** Trembling, shaking; quivering. **2.** Tremor. **Tremblement de terre,** earthquake.
trembler, *v.i.* (*a*) To tremble, shake; to quake; to quiver, flicker; to quaver. *T. de*

froid, to shiver with cold. (*b*) To tremble, quake, with fear.

trembleur, -euse, *s.* **1.** Timid person. **2.** *Tp:* Buzzer, ticker.

trembloter, *v.i.* To quiver; to quaver; to flicker.

trémoussement, *s.m.* Fluttering, flutter.

trémousser, *v.i.* To flutter.

trempe, *s.f.* **1.** (*a*) Steeping, dipping, soaking. (*b*) *Metall:* Tempering. **2.** (*a*) Temper (of steel). (*b*) *F:* Quality. *Les hommes de sa t.*, men of his stamp.

tremper. 1. *v.tr.* (*a*) To mix, dilute, with water. (*b*) To soak, steep. *T. sa plume dans l'encre*, to dip one's pen in the ink. (*c*) *Metall:* To temper. **2.** *v.i.* (*a*) To soak. (*b*) *F:* **Tremper dans un complot,** to have a hand in a plot.

trempé, *a.* (*a*) Wet, soaked. **Trempé jusqu'aux os,** wet through. (*b*) Tempered; hardened.

tremplin, *s.m.* Spring-board; (spring) diving-board.

trentaine, *s.f.* (About) thirty, some thirty.

trente, *num.a.inv. & s.m.inv.* Thirty.

trente-six [for rules of pronunciation see SIX], *num.a.inv. & s.m.inv.* Thirty-six. *F:* **Voir trente-six chandelles,** to see stars. **Je le vois tous les trente-six du mois,** I see him once in a blue moon.

trentième. 1. *num.a. & s.* Thirtieth. **2.** *s.m.* Thirtieth (part).

trépaner, *v.tr. Surg:* To trepan; to trephine.

trépas, *s.m.* Death, decease.

trépasser, *v.i.* (Aux. *avoir*, occ. *être*) To die; to depart this life.

trépassé, *a. & s.* Dead, deceased. **Les trépassés,** the dead, the departed.

trépidation, *s.f.* **1.** Tremor; trepidation. **2.** Trepidation; agitation.

trépied, *s.m.* Tripod. (*a*) Three-legged stool. (*b*) *Cu:* Trivet.

trépignement, *s.m.* Stamping (with the feet).

trépigner. 1. *v.i. T. de colère*, to dance with rage. **2.** *v.tr.* To trample down.

très, *adv.* Very, most; (very) much.

trésor, *s.m.* **1.** Treasure. **2.** *pl. Entasser des trésors*, to accumulate riches. **3. Le Trésor (public),** the (French) Treasury.

trésorerie, *s.f.* Treasury.

trésorier, *s.* Treasurer; paymaster.

tressaillement [-saj-], *s.m.* Start (of surprise); quiver; thrill.

tressaillir [-saj-], *v.i.* (Conj. like CUEILLIR) To start; to give a start; to quiver. *T. de douleur*, to wince. **Faire tressaillir qn,** to startle s.o.

tressaut, *s.m.* Start, jump.

tressauter, *v.i.* To start, jump.

tresse, *s.f.* Plait, tress.

tresser, *v.tr.* To plait; to braid; to weave.

tréteau, *s.m.* Trestle, support, stand.

treuil [trœːj], *s.m.* Winch, windlass.

trêve, *s.f.* (*a*) Truce. (*b*) Respite, intermission.

triade, *s.f.* Triad.

triage, *s.m.* Sorting.

triangle, *s.m.* Triangle.

triangulaire, *a.* Triangular.

tribord, *s.m. Nau:* Starboard.

tribu, *s.f.* Tribe.

tribulation, *s.f.* Tribulation; trial.

tribun, *s.m.* Tribune.

tribunal, -aux, *s.m.* Tribunal. (*a*) Judge's seat, bench. (*b*) Court of justice.

tribune, *s.f.* **1.** Tribune, rostrum, platform. **2.** (*a*) Gallery. *Parl: La t. publique*, the strangers' gallery. (*b*) Grand stand. (*c*) *T. de l'orgue*, organ-loft.

tribut, *s.m.* Tribute.

tributaire, *a. & s.m.* Tributary.

tricher, *v.i. & tr.* To cheat; to trick.

tricherie, *s.f.* Cheating; trickery.

tricheur, -euse. 1. *a.* Given to cheating. **2.** *s.* Cheat; trickster.

tricolore, *a.* Tricolour(ed).

tricorne, *s.m.* Three-cornered hat.

tricot, *s.m.* **1.** Knitting. **2.** (*a*) (Knitted) jersey. (*b*) (Under)vest.

tricoter, *v.tr.* To knit.

tricoteur, -euse, *s.* Knitter.

trictrac [-trak], *s.m.* **1.** Click, rattle. **2.** *Games:* Backgammon.

tricycle, *s.m.* Tricycle.

trident, *s.m.* Trident.

triennal, -aux, *a.* Triennial.

trier, *v.tr.* (*a*) To sort. (*b*) To pick out, sort out.

trieur, -euse, *s.* Sorter.

trigonométrie, *s.f.* Trigonometry.

trigonométrique, *a.* Trigonometric(al).

trille [triːj], *s.m. Mus:* Trill, shake.

trilogie, *s.f. Lit:* Trilogy.

trimer, *v.i.* To drudge; to fag.

trimestre, *s.m.* **1.** Quarter; three months. *Sch:* Term. **2.** Quarter's salary, quarter's rent. *Sch:* Term's fees.

trimestriel, -elle, *a.* Quarterly.

tringle, *s.f.* Rod. *T. de rideau*, curtain-rod.

trinité, *s.f.* **1.** *Theol:* Trinity. **2.** *Geog:* (Ile de) la Trinité, Trinidad.

trinquer, *v.i.* To clink glasses.

trio, *s.m. Mus: etc:* Trio.

triolet, *s.m.* **1.** *Pros:* Triolet. **2.** *Mus:* Triplet.

triomphal, -aux, *a.* Triumphal.

triomphalement, *adv.* Triumphantly.

triomphant, *a.* Triumphant.

triomphe, *s.m.* Triumph. **Porter en triomphe,** to carry shoulder high; to chair. **Arc de triomphe,** triumphal arch.

triompher, *v.i.* **1.** To triumph. *T. d'une difficulté*, to overcome a difficulty. **2.** To exult, glory.

tripe, *s.f.* Usu. *pl.* (*a*) *F:* Intestines. (*b*) *Cu:* Tripe.

triphtongue, *s.f. Ling:* Triphthong.

tripier, *s.* Tripe-dealer.

triple, *a. & s.m.* Treble, threefold, triple.

triplement, *adv.* Trebly; threefold.

tripler, *v.tr. & i.* To treble, triple.

tripot, *s.m.* Gambling-den.

tripotage, *s.m.* **1.** (*a*) Fiddling about. (*b*) Odd jobs. **2.** Intrigue; jobbery.

tripoter. 1. *v.i.* (*a*) To fiddle about. (*b*) To engage in shady business. **2.** *v.tr.* (*a*) To finger, handle; to meddle with. (*b*) To deal shadily with (money).

tripoteur, -euse, *s.* Schemer.

trique, *s.f.* F: Cudgel; heavy stick.

tris(s)yllabe, *s.m.* Trisyllable.

tris(s)yllabique, *a.* Trisyllabic.

Tristan. *Pr.n.m. Mediev.Lit:* Tristram.

triste, *a.* Sad. **1.** (*a*) Sorrowful, doleful, melancholy. (*b*) Dreary, dismal. **Faire triste figure,** to pull a long face. **2.** Unfortunate, painful. **C'est une triste affaire,** it's a bad job. **3.** F: Poor, sorry, wretched. **Faire triste figure,** to look sadly out of place.

tristement, *adv.* **1.** Sadly, mournfully. **2.** Gloomily. **3.** Poorly, wretchedly.

tristesse, *s.f.* (*a*) Sadness; melancholy, gloom. (*b*) Dullness, dreariness.

Triton. 1. *Pr.n.m.* Triton. **2.** *s.m. Amph:* Triton, F: newt, eft.

triturer, *v.tr.* To triturate, grind.

triumvirat [-ɔm-], *s.m.* Triumvirate.

trivial, -als, *a.* Vulgar, low, coarse.

trivialement, *adv.* Vulgarly, coarsely.

trivialité, *s.f.* Vulgarity, coarseness.

troc [trɔk], *s.m.* Truck; exchange; barter.

troène, *s.m. Bot:* Privet.

troglodyte, *s.m.* **1.** Troglodyte; cave-dweller. **2.** *Orn:* Wren.

trognon, *s.m.* Core; stump.

Troie. *Pr.n.f. A.Geog:* Troy. **La guerre de Troie,** the Trojan War.

trois, *num.a.inv. & s.m.* Three. *F:* **Les trois quarts du temps,** most of the time.

troisième, *num.a. & s.* Third. **Demeurer au troisième (étage),** to live on the third floor. *Rail:* **Voyager en troisième,** to travel third(-class).

trois-mâts, *s.m.* Three-masted ship.

trois-pièces, *s.m.* (Lady's) three-piece suit.

troll, *s.m. Norse Myth:* Troll.

trombe, *s.f.* **1.** Waterspout. **2.** Whirlwind.

tromblon, *s.m.* Blunderbuss.

trombone, *s.m.* Trombone.

trompe, *s.f.* **1.** (*a*) Trump, horn. (*b*) Hooter. **2.** Proboscis; trunk.

trompe-l'œil, *s.m.inv.* Deceptive appearance; illusion; eye-wash; piece of bluff.

tromper, *v.tr.* To deceive. **1.** (*a*) To cheat; to impose upon. (*b*) To betray, be unfaithful to. **2.** (*a*) *T. les espérances de qn,* to disappoint s.o.'s hopes. (*b*) To outwit, baffle. (*c*) To beguile; to while away.

se tromper, to be mistaken; to be wrong. **Il n'y a pas à s'y tromper,** there is no doubt about it.

tromperie, *s.f.* **1.** (*a*) Deceit, deception, fraud. (*b*) Illusion. **2.** Piece of deceit.

trompette. 1. *s.f.* Trumpet. **2.** *s.m. Mil:* Trumpeter.

trompeur, -euse. 1. *a.* (*a*) Deceitful. (*b*) Deceptive, misleading. **2.** *s.* Deceiver, cheat. **Le trompeur trompé,** the biter bit.

trompeusement, *adv.* (*a*) Deceitfully. (*b*) Deceptively.

tronc [trɔ̃], *s.m.* **1.** (*a*) Trunk; stem. (*b*) Parent stock (of family). **2.** Collecting-box.

tronçon, *s.m.* (Broken) piece, end, stump.

tronçonner, *v.tr.* To cut into sections, into lengths; to cut up.

trône, *s.m.* Throne.

trôner, *v.i.* (*a*) To sit enthroned. (*b*) F: To occupy a place of honour; F: to lord it.

tronquer, *v.tr.* (*a*) To truncate; to mutilate (statue). (*b*) F: To curtail, cut down.

trop. 1. *adv.* Too. (*a*) (With adj.) Too, over-. *Trop fatigué,* over-tired. (*b*) (With vb) Too much, unduly, over-. *Trop travailler,* to over-work, to work too hard. **Je ne sais trop que dire,** I hardly know what to say. **2.** *s.m.* Too much, too many. **Être de trop,** to be in the way, unwelcome. **Par trop,** (altogether) too (much).

trophée, *s.m.* Trophy.

tropical, -aux, *a.* Tropical.

tropique, *s.m. Geog:* Tropic.

trop-plein, *s.m.* Overflow. *pl. Des trop-pleins.*

troquer, *v.tr.* To exchange, barter.

trot, *s.m.* Trot.

trotte-menu, *a.inv.* Pitter-patter.

trotter, *v.i.* To trot; to scamper.

trottiner, *v.i.* **1.** F: To jog along. **2.** F: To trot about; to toddle.

trottinette, *s.f.* Scooter.

trottoir, *s.m.* (*a*) Footway, footpath, pavement. **Bordure du trottoir,** kerb. (*b*) Rail: Platform.

trou, *s.m.* Hole. *Av:* **Trou d'air,** air-pocket.

troubadour, *s.m. Lit.Hist:* Troubadour.

troublant, *a.* Disturbing. **1.** Disquieting, disconcerting. **2.** Perturbing.

trouble¹, *a.* **1.** Turbid, cloudy; dim; murky. **Avoir la vue trouble,** to be dim-sighted. **2.** Confused.

trouble², *s.m.* (*a*) Confusion, disorder. (*b*) Agitation, perturbation. (*c*) *pl.* Public disturbances.

troubler, *v.tr.* **1.** To make cloudy, thick, muddy. **2.** To disturb; to interfere with. **Troubler le repos,** to make a disturbance. **3.** To perturb. (*a*) To confuse, upset, discompose. (*b*) To agitate, excite, stir.

se troubler. 1. To become overcast,

to cloud over; to become blurred; to grow dim. **2.** To falter; to get confused.

trouer, *v.tr.* To make a hole in; to perforate. **Troué aux coudes,** out at elbows. **se trouer. 1.** To wear into holes. **2.** To open up; to show an opening.

trouée, *s.f.* Gap, opening, breach.

troupe, *s.f.* **1.** (*a*) Troop, band; gang, set. (*b*) *Th:* Troupe. (*c*) Herd; flock. **2.** *Mil:* (*a*) Troop. (*b*) **Officiers et troupe,** officers and other ranks. (*c*) *pl.* Troops, forces.

troupeau, *s.m.* Herd, drove; flock.

trousse, *s.f.* **1.** Bundle, package; truss. **2.** *pl.* *F:* **Être aux trousses de qn,** to be after s.o. **3.** Case, kit (of instruments).

trousseau, *s.m.* **1.** **Trousseau de clefs,** bunch of keys. **2.** (*a*) Outfit (of clothing). (*b*) (Bride's) trousseau.

trousser, *v.tr.* *Cu:* To truss (fowl).

trouvaille [-va:j], *s.f.* Find, windfall.

trouver, *v.tr.* To find. **1.** (*a*) *Je lui trouve d'excellentes qualités,* I find in him excellent qualities. **Aller trouver qn,** to go and see s.o. (*b*) To discover, invent. **2.** *T. par hasard,* to discover, hit upon, come across. **C'est bien trouvé!** happy thought! **3.** To think, deem. **Vous trouvez?** you think so? **se trouver. 1.** (*a*) To be. *Je me trouvais alors à Paris,* I was then in Paris. (*b*) To feel. **Se trouver bien de qch.,** to feel all the better for sth. **2.** To happen; to turn out.

troyen, -enne, *a. & s.* Trojan.

truc [tryk], *s.m.* *F:* **1.** (*a*) Knack. (*b*) Trick, dodge. **2.** Contraption, gadget.

trucage, *s.m.* **1.** Faking. **2.** Fake.

truculence, *s.f.* Truculence.

truculent, *a.* Truculent.

truelle, *s.f.* **1.** Trowel. **2.** *T. à poisson,* fish-slice.

truffe, *s.f.* Truffle.

truie, *s.f.* Sow. **Peau de truie,** pigskin.

truisme, *s.m.* Truism.

truite, *s.f.* *Ich:* Trout.

trumeau, *s.m.* (*a*) *Arch:* Pier. (*b*) *Furn:* Pier-glass.

truquage, *s.m.* = TRUCAGE.

truquer, *v.tr.* To fake.

tsar, *s.m.* Czar, tsar.

tsarévitch, *s.m.* Czarevitch, tsarevitch.

tsarine, *s.f.* Czarina, tsarina.

tsé-tsé, tsétsé, *s.f.* *Ent:* Tsetse(-fly).

tu¹, *pers.pron.nom.* (Familiar form of address) (*a*) You. *Qui es-tu, toi?* who are you? *F:* **Être à tu et à toi avec qn,** to be on familiar terms with s.o. (*b*) Thou.

tu². See TAIRE.

tube, *s.m.* Tube, pipe.

tubercule, *s.m.* **1.** *Bot:* Tuber. **2.** *Med:* Tubercle.

tuberculeux. *a.* (*a*) *Bot:* Tubercular (root). (*b*) *Med:* Tuberculous.

tuberculose, *s.f.* Tuberculosis.

tubéreux. *Bot:* **1.** *a.* Tuberous, tuberose. **2.** *s.f.* Tubéreuse, tuberose.

tubulaire, *a.* Tubular.

tudesque, *a.* Teutonic, Germanic.

tuer, *v.tr.* To kill. **1.** To slaughter, butcher. **2.** To slay, make away with. **Tuer qn raide,** to kill s.o. on the spot. **Se faire tuer,** to get killed. **Tué à l'ennemi,** killed in action. **se tuer. 1.** (*a*) To kill oneself. (*b*) To get killed. **2.** *Je me tue à vous le dire,* I am sick and tired of telling you.

tuerie, *s.f.* Slaughter, butchery, carnage.

tue-tête (à), *adv.phr.* At the top of one's voice. **Crier à t.-t.,** to bawl, yell.

tueur, *s.m.* Killer, slayer.

tuile, *s.f.* (Roofing) tile.

tulipe, *s.f.* Tulip.

tumeur, *s.f.* *Med:* Tumour.

tumulte, *s.m.* Tumult, hubbub, uproar.

tumultueusement, *adv.* Tumultuously; boisterously.

tumultueux, *a.* Tumultuous, noisy.

tumulus [-ly:s], *s.m.* Tumulus, barrow; sepulchral mound. *pl.* *Des tumulus, des tumuli.*

tungstène [tœk-], *s.m.* *Ch:* Tungsten.

tunique, *s.f.* *Cost:* Tunic.

Tunisie. *Pr.n.f.* *Geog:* Tunisia.

tunnel, *s.m.* Tunnel.

turban, *s.m.* Turban.

turbidité, *s.f.* Turbidity, cloudiness.

turbine, *s.f.* Turbine.

turbot, *s.m.* *Ich:* Turbot.

turbulence, *s.f.* Turbulence.

turbulent, *a.* Turbulent.

turc, *f.* **turque** [tyrk]. **1.** *a.* Turkish. **2.** *s.* (*a*) Turk. (*b*) *a.m. Ling:* Turkish.

turcoman, *s.m.* *Ethn:* Turcoman.

turlututu, *int.* Fiddlesticks! fiddle-de-dee!

turpitude, *s.f.* **1.** Turpitude. **I.** Depravity, baseness. **2.** Scurvy trick.

turque, *a. & s.f.* See TURC.

Turquie. *Pr.n.f.* *Geog:* Turkey.

turquoise. 1. *s.f.* Turquoise. **2.** *a.inv. & s.m.inv.* Turquoise (blue).

tu-s, -t, etc. See TAIRE.

tutélaire, *a.* Tutelary; guardian (angel).

tutelle, *s.f.* **1.** *Jur:* Tutelage, guardianship. **2.** *F:* Protection.

tuteur, -trice. **1.** *s.* (*a*) Guardian. (*b*) *F:* Protector. **2.** *s.m.* *Hort:* Prop, stake.

tutoiement, *s.m.* Use of *tu* and *toi.*

tutoyer, *v.tr.* (je tutoie) To address as *tu* and *toi;* to be on familiar terms with.

tuyau, -aux, *s.m.* **1.** (*a*) Pipe, tube. **Tuyau d'incendie,** fire-hose. **T. d'arrosage,** garden-hose. **Tuyau de cheminée,** chimney-flue. (*b*) Stem (of pipe). **2.** *F:* Tip; wrinkle, hint. **Avoir des tuyaux,** to be in the know.

tympan, *s.m.* Drum (of ear).

type, *s.m.* **1.** Type. **Com:** Pattern. **2.** (*a*) *F:* Personality. **Drôle de type,** queer chap. (*b*) *P:* Fellow, chap, bloke. **3.** *Typ:* Type.

typhoïde, *a.* **Fièvre typhoïde,** typhoid (fever); enteric fever.

typhon, *s.m. Meteor:* Typhoon.
typhus [-fy:s], *s.m. Med:* Typhus (fever).
typifié, *a.* Typical; standardized.
typique, *a.* Typical. **1.** Symbolical. **2.** True to type.
typographe, *s.m.* Typographer, printer.
typographie, *s.f.* Typography.

typographique, *a.* Typographic(al). **Erreur typographique,** misprint.
tyran, *s.m.* Tyrant.
tyrannie, *s.f.* Tyranny.
tyrannique, *a.* Tyrannical, tyrannous.
tyranniquement, *adv.* Tyrannically.
tyranniser, *v.tr.* To tyrannize over.
tyrolien, -ienne, *a. & s.* Tyrolese.

U

U, u [y], *s.m.* (The letter) U, u.
ubiquité, *s.f.* Ubiquity.
uhlan, *s.m.* Uhlan.
ukase, *s.m.* Ukase, edict.
ulcère, *s.m.* Ulcer.
ultérieur, -eure, *a.* Ulterior. **1.** *Geog:* Further. **2.** Subsequent; later.
ultérieurement, *adv.* Subsequently, hereafter.
ultimatum [-tɔm], *s.m.* Ultimatum.
ultime, *a.* Ultimate, final, last.
ululation, *s.f.,* **ululement,** *s.m.* Ululation (of owls); hoot(ing).
ululer, *v.i.* (Of owl) To ululate; to hoot.
Ulysse. *Pr.n.m.* Ulysses.
un, une. 1. *num.a. & s.* (a) One. **Une heure,** one o'clock. *Page un,* page one. *Th:* **Le un,** the first act. *F:* **En savoir plus d'une,** to know a thing or two. **Une, deux, trois, partez!** one, two, three, go! (b) **C'est tout un,** it's all one. **2.** *Indef.pron.* One. (**L'**)**un d'entre nous,** one of us. **Les uns disent,** some say. **3.** *Indef.art.* (pl. **des**) A, an (pl. some). (a) *Venez me voir un lundi,* come and see me some Monday. **Pour une raison ou pour une autre,** for some reason or other. (b) Such a one as. (c) *Tu m'as fait une peur!* you gave me such a fright!
unanime, *a.* Unanimous; of one mind.
unanimement, *adv.* Unanimously.
unanimité, *s.f.* Unanimity. **A l'unanimité,** unanimously.
unième, *num.a.* (Used only in compounds) First. *Trente et unième,* thirty-first.
unifier, *v.tr.* To unify (ideas); to amalgamate (industries).
uniforme 1. *a.* Uniform, unvarying. **2.** *s.m.* Uniform.
uniformément, *adv.* Uniformly, consistently.
uniformité, *s.f.* Uniformity.
unilatéral, -aux, *a.* Unilateral; one-sided.
union, *s.f.* Union. **1.** Coming together. **2.** Society, association. **3.** Marriage. **4.** *F:* Unity, agreement.
uniprix, *a.inv.* **Magasin uniprix,** one-price store.

unique, *a.* **1.** Sole, only, single. **2.** Unique, unrivalled.
uniquement, *adv.* Solely, uniquely.
unir, *v.tr.* **1.** To unite, join. **2.** To smooth, level.
  s'unir. 1. To unite, join. **2.** To become smooth, even.
uni, *a.* **1.** United, harmonious. **2.** Smooth, level, even. **3.** Plain (material).
unisson, *s.m. Mus:* Unison. **A l'unisson,** (i) in unison; (ii) in keeping.
unité, *s.f.* **1.** (a) Unit (of measure). (b) *Mth:* Unity, one. **2.** Unity.
univers, *s.m.* Universe. **Par tout l'univers,** all over the world.
universel, -elle, *a.* Universal. *Réputation universelle,* world-wide reputation. *F:* **Hommes universels,** all-rounders. **Légataire universel,** residuary legatee.
universellement, *adv.* Universally.
universitaire. 1. *a.* University. **2.** *s.* Member of the teaching profession.
université, *s.f.* University.
upas [ypɑs], *s.m.* Upas(-tree).
uranium [-njɔm], *s.m. Ch:* Uranium.
urbain. 1. *a.* Urban; town. **2.** *s.m.* Town-dweller.
urbanisme, *s.m.* Town-planning.
urbanité, *s.f.* Urbanity.
urgemment, *adv.* Urgently.
urgence, *s.f.* Urgency. **En cas d'urgence,** in case of emergency.
urgent, *a.* Urgent, pressing.
urine, *s.f.* Urine.
urinoir, *s.m.* (Public) urinal.
urne, *s.f.* (a) Urn. (b) **Urne de scrutin,** ballot-box.
urticaire, *s.f. Med:* Nettle-rash.
us [y:s], *s.m.pl.* **Les us et coutumes** *d'un pays,* the ways and customs of a country.
usage, *s.m.* **1.** (a) Use, using, employment. *Pharm:* "Pour l'usage externe," 'for external application.' **Article à mon usage,** article for my personal use. **Article d'usage,** article for everyday use. (b) Wear, service. **Garanti à l'usage,** warranted to wear well. **2.** (a) Usage;

custom. **Phrases d'usage,** conversational commonplaces. **Comme d'usage,** as usual. (b) Practice, experience. **L'usage du monde,** good breeding.

user. 1. *v.ind.tr.* **User de qch.,** to use sth., make use of sth. **En bien user aveo qn,** to treat s.o. well. **2.** *v.tr.* (a) To use (up), consume. (b) To wear (out).
   s'user, to wear (away).
   usé, *a.* Worn.

usine, *s.f.* Works, (manu)factory, mill.

usinier, *s.m.* Mill-owner.

usité, *a.* Used ; in use ; current.

ustensile, *s.m.* Utensil, implement.

usuel, -elle, *a.* Usual, customary, habitual, common. *Connaissances usuelles,* knowledge of everyday things.

usuellement, *adv.* Usually, habitually.

usuraire, *a.* Usurious.

usure¹, *s.f.* Usury. *F:* **Rendre un bienfait aveo usure,** to repay a service with interest.

usure², *s.f.* Wear (and tear). *Mil:* **Guerre d'usure,** war of attrition.

usurier. 1. *s.* Usurer. **2.** *a.* Usurious.

usurpateur, -trice. 1. *s.* Usurper. **2.** *a.* (a) Usurping. (b) Encroaching.

usurpation, *s.f.* (a) Usurpation. (b) Encroaching, encroachment.

usurper. 1. *v.tr.* To usurp. **2.** *v.i.* U. **sur** *les droits de qn,* to encroach on s.o.'s rights.

ut [yt], *s.m.inv.* *Mus:* (The note) C.

utile, *a.* Useful, serviceable. *Puis-je être u. en rien?* can I be of any use? **En temps utile,** in (good) time.

utilement, *adv.* Usefully ; profitably.

utiliser, *v.tr.* To utilize ; to make use of ; to turn (sth.) to account.

utilité, *s.f.* Utility, use(fulness) ; service. *Articles d'u sociale,* utility goods.

utopie, *s.f.* Utopia.

utopique, *a.* Utopian.

utopiste. 1. *s.* Utopian. **2.** *a.* Utopian.

uvule, *s.f.* *Anat:* Uvula.

V

V, v [ve], *s.m.* (The letter) V, v.

va. See ALLER.

vacance, *s.f.* **1.** Vacancy ; vacant post. **2.** *pl.* Vacation, holidays. *Sch:* **Les grandes** *vacances,* the summer holidays ; the long vacation.

vacant, *a.* Vacant, unoccupied.

vacarme, *s.m.* *F:* Uproar, din, hubbub.

vacation, *s.f.* **1.** (a) Sitting (of officials). (b) *pl.* Fees. **2.** *pl. Jur:* Vacation, recess.

vaccin, *s.m.* *Med:* Vaccine, lymph.

vaccination, *s.f.* *Med:* Vaccination.

vacciner, *v.tr.* *Med:* To vaccinate.

vache, *s.f.* Cow. **Parler français comme une vache espagnole,** to murder the French language. **Manger de la vache enragée,** to have a rough time of it.

vacher, *s.* Cowherd.

vacherie, *s.f.* Cow-house.

vacillant [-sillã, -sijã], *a.* **1.** Unsteady ; flickering ; uncertain. **2.** Vacillating ; wavering.

vacillation [-silla-,-sija-], *s.f.* **1.** Unsteadiness, flickering. **2.** Vacillation ; wavering.

vacillement [-sij-], *s.m.* = VACILLATION 1.

vaciller [-sille, -sije], *v.i.* **1.** (a) To be unsteady. **Entrer en vacillant,** to stagger in. (b) To flicker. **2.** To vacillate, waver.

vacuité, *s.f.* Vacuity, emptiness.

vacuum, [-om], *s.m.* Vacuum.

va-et-vient, *s.m.inv.* (a) Movement to and fro. (b) Coming and going.

vagabond. 1. *a.* Vagabond ; roving. **2.** *s.* Vagabond ; vagrant.

vagabondage, *s.m.* Vagrancy, vagabondage.

vagabonder, *v.i.* V. **par le monde,** to rove about the world ; to roam.

vagissement, *s.m.* Cry, wail(ing) (of newborn infant).

vague¹, *s.f.* Wave. **Grosse vague,** billow, sea. *V. de fond,* tidal wave.

vague². 1. *a.* (a) Vague, indefinite ; dim. **2.** *s.m.* Vagueness, indefiniteness.

vague³. 1. *a.* **Regard vague,** vacant stare. **Terrains vagues,** waste ground. **2.** *s.m.* Empty space.

vaguement, *adv.* Vaguely ; dimly ; indefinitely.

vaguemestre, *s.m.* (a) *Mil:* Post orderly. (b) *Navy:* Postman.

vaguer, *v.i.* To wander, ramble (about).

vaillamment [vaj-], *adv.* Valiantly ; bravely.

vaillance [vaj-], *s.f.* Valour, bravery.

vaillant [vajã]. **1.** *a.* (a) Valiant, brave. (b) *F:* **Être vaillant,** to be in good health. **2.** *adv.* **N'avoir pas un sou v.,** to be penniless.

vaill-e, -es, etc. See VALOIR.

vain, *a.* **1.** Vain. (a) Sham, unreal, empty. *Vaine gloire,* vainglory. *Vaines promesses,* hollow promises. (b) Ineffectual, useless. **2.** Vain, conceited.

vaincre, *v.tr.* (*pr.p.* **vainquant** ; *pr.ind.* il **vaino** ; *p.h.* **je vainquis**) **1.** (a) To vanquish, defeat. (b) *Sp:* To beat. **2.** To overcome, conquer.

vainement, *adv.* Vainly ; to no purpose.

vainqu-e, etc. See VAINCRE.

vainqueur. 1. *s.m.* (a) Victor, conqueror.

(b) *Sp :* Winner. **2.** *a.m.* Vanquishing, conquering.
vais. See ALLER.
vaisseau, *s.m.* **I.** Vessel, receptacle. **2.** Ship, vessel. *V. amiral,* flagship. **3.** *Anat :* Vessel, canal, duct.
vaisseau-école, *s.m.* Training-ship. *pl. Des vaisseaux-écoles.*
vaisselle, *s.f.* Table-service; plates and dishes. **Vaisselle plate,** silver plate. **Laver la vaisselle,** to wash up. **Eau de vaisselle,** dish-water.
val, *s.m.* Valley, vale. The *pl.* is usu. **vals,** except in the phr. **Par monts et par vaux,** up hill and down dale.
valable, *a.* Valid, good. *Billet v. pour un mois,* ticket available for a month.
valence, *s.f. Ch :* Valence, valency.
valenciennes, *s.f.* Valenciennes lace.
valériane, *s.f. Bot :* Valerian, all-heal.
valet, *s.m.* **I.** *Cards :* Knave, jack. **2.** *V. de chambre,* valet, man-servant. *V. de pied,* footman. *V. d'écurie,* groom. *V. de ferme,* farm-hand.
valeur, *s.f.* **I.** (a) Value, worth. **Mettre une terre en valeur,** to develop land. (b) Import, weight, value. **Mettre un mot en valeur,** to emphasize a word. **2.** *Fin :* (a) Asset. (b) *pl.* Bills, shares, securities. **3.** Valour, gallantry.
valeureusement, *adv.* Valorously, gallantly.
valeureux, *a.* Valorous, brave, gallant.
valide, *a.* **I.** Valid. **2.** *Mil : etc :* Fit for service; able-bodied.
validité, *s.f.* Validity.
valise, *s.f.* (a) Valise. (b) Suit-case. (c) *V. diplomatique,* embassy dispatch-bag.
vallée, *s.f.* Valley.
vallon, *s.m.* Small valley; dale; glen.
valoir, *v.tr. & i.* (*pr.p.* **valant;** *p.p.* **valu;** *pr.ind.* **je vaux, il vaut;** *pr.sub.* **je vaille;** *fu.* **je vaudrai) I.** (a) To be worth. **A valoir,** on account. **Ce n'est rien qui vaille,** it is not worth having. (b) To be equivalent to. *C'est une façon qui en vaut une autre,* it is as good a way as any other. (c) **Il vaut mieux qu'il en soit ainsi,** (it is) better that it should be so. **Autant vaut rester ici,** we may as well stay here. (d) **Faire valoir qch.,** to make the most of sth. *Faire v. ses droits,* to assert one's claims. **Se faire valoir,** to push oneself forward. **2.** To be worth, to deserve, merit. **3. Valoir qch.** (a) To bring in, yield, fetch. **Vaille que vaille,** come what may. (b) To obtain, win, gain. *Cette action lui a valu la croix,* this act won him the cross.
valse, *s.f.* Waltz.
valser, *v.i.* To waltz. **Faire valser qn,** (i) to dance with s.o.; (ii) to lead s.o. a dance.
valve, *s.f.* Valve.
vampire, *s.m.* Vampire.
vandale, *s.m. & a.* Vandal.
vandalisme, *s.m.* Vandalism.
vanille [-niːj] *s.f.* Vanilla.

vanité, *s.f.* Vanity. **I.** Futility. **2.** Conceit, vainglory.
vaniteux, *a.* Vain, conceited, vainglorious.
vannage, *s.m.* Winnowing.
vanne, *s.f.* Sluice(-gate), water-gate.
vanneau, *s.m. Orn :* Lapwing, peewit.
vanner, *v.tr.* To winnow.
vannerie, *s.f.* **I.** Basket-making. **2.** Basket-work, wicker-work.
vanneur, -euse, *s.* Winnower.
vannier, *s.m.* Basket-maker.
vantail [tɑːj], **-aux,** *s.m.* Leaf (of door).
vantard. I. *a.* Boasting, boastful, bragging. **2.** *s.* Braggart, boaster.
vantardise, *s.f.* **I.** Bragging, boastfulness. **2.** Boast.
vanter, *v.tr.* To praise up.
se vanter, to boast, brag; **.o** pride oneself.
vanterie, *s.f.* **I.** Bragging, boasting. **2.** Boast.
va-nu-pieds, *s.m. & f.inv.* Tatterdemalion; barefoot tramp.
vapeur[1], *s.f.* Vapour; haze; fumes. **Vapeur (d'eau),** steam. **Bateau à vapeur,** steamer, steamship.
vapeur[2], *s.m.* Steamer, steamship.
vaporeux, *a.* (a) Vaporous, vapoury; steamy. (b) *F :* Filmy, hazy (ideas).
vaporisateur, *s.m.* a. Atomizer; sprayer. (b) Scent-spray.
vaporiser, *v.tr.* To atomize, spray (liquid).
vaquer, *v.i.* **Vaquer à qch.,** to attend to sth.; to concern oneself with sth.
varec(h) [-rɛk], *s.m.* Wrack, seaweed, kelp.
vareuse, *s.f.* **I.** *Nau :* (a) (Sailor's) jersey, jumper. (b) Pilot-coat. **2.** *Mil :* Field-service tunic.
variable, *a.* (a) Variable. (b) Changeable, altering.
variation, *s.f.* Variation.
varier. I. *v.tr.* To vary; to diversify. **2.** *v.i.* To vary, change.
varié, *a.* Varied; varying; chequered (existence).
variété, *s.f.* **I.** Variety; diversity. **2.** *Nat. Hist :* Variety.
variole, *s.f. Med :* Smallpox.
Varsovie. *Pr.n.f. Geog :* Warsaw.
vas. See ALLER.
vase[1], *s.m.* Vase, vessel, receptacle.
vase[2], *s.f* Mud, silt, slime, ooze.
vaseline, *s.f.* Vaseline. [Marque déposée].
vaseux, *a.* Muddy, slimy.
vasistas [-tɑːs], *s.m.* Fanlight (over door).
vasque, *s.f.* Basin (of fountain).
vassal, -aux, *s. & a.* Vassal.
vaste, *a.* Vast, immense, spacious.
vastement, *adv.* Vastly, spaciously.
vastitude, *s.f.* Vastitude.
vau (à), *adv.phr.* **A vau-l'eau,** with the stream. *F :* **Tout va à vau-l'eau,** everything is going to rack and ruin.
vaudeville, *s.m.* Vaudeville, light comedy.

vaudr-ai, -as, etc. See VALOIR.
vaurien, -ienne, *s.* (*a*) Waster, rotter, bad lot. (*b*) *F:* *Petit v.!* you little rascal.
vaut. See VALOIR.
vautour, *s.m. Orn:* Vulture.
vautrer (se), *v.pr.* (*a*) To wallow. (*b*) *F:* To sprawl on one's stomach.
vaux. See VALOIR.
veau, *s.m.* **1.** (*a*) Calf. *F:* **Pleurer comme un veau,** to blubber. (*b*) **Veau marin,** seal. (*c*) *F:* Lumpish fellow, clod. **2.** *Cu:* Veal. **Côtelette de v.,** veal cutlet. **3.** Calf(-leather).
vécu. See VIVRE.
vedette, *s.f.* **1.** *Mil:* Vedette; mounted sentry. **2.** (*a*) *Navy:* Vedette-boat; picket-boat. **V. lance-torpille,** motor torpedo-boat. (*b*) Small steamer, motor boat. **3.** (*a*) **Mots en vedette,** words displayed in bold type. (*b*) *Th:* Star.
végétal, -aux. 1. *a.* Plant; vegetable. **2.** *s.m.* Plant.
végétarien, -ienne, *a. & s.* Vegetarian.
végétarisme, *s.m.* Vegetarianism.
végétation, *s.f.* **1.** Vegetation. **2.** *pl. Med:* Vegetations. **Végétations adénoïdes,** adenoid growths; *F:* adenoids.
végéter, *v.i.* (je végète; je végéterai) To vegetate.
véhémence, *s.f.* Vehemence.
véhément, *a.* Vehement, violent.
véhémentement, *adv.* Vehemently, violently.
véhiculaire, *a.* Vehicular.
véhicule, *s.m.* Vehicle.
veille [vɛːj], *s.f.* **1.** (*a*) Sitting up (at night); watching (by night). (*b*) Vigil. (*c*) *Mil:* (Night) watch. *Nau:* Look-out. **Ancre de veille,** sheet-anchor. (*d*) Wakefulness. **Entre la veille et le sommeil,** between waking and sleeping. **2.** (*a*) Eve; preceding day. **La veille au soir,** the night before. (*b*) **Être à la veille de la ruine,** to be on the brink of ruin.
veiller [vɛje]. **1.** *v.i.* (*a*) To sit up, keep awake. (*b*) To watch, be on the look-out. (*c*) *V. sur qn,* to look after s.o. (*d*) *V. à qch.,* see to sth. *F:* **Veiller au grain,** to look out for squalls. **2.** *v.tr.* To sit up with, watch over.
  veillée, *s.f.* **1.** Night-nursing; watching, vigil. **2.** Evening (spent in company).
veilleur, -euse [vɛj-]. **1.** *s.* Watcher (by night); keeper of a vigil. **2.** *s.f.* Veilleuse. Night-light. **Lumière en veilleuse,** light turned low. *Aut:* **Mettre les phares en v.,** to dim the head-lights.
veinard, *a. & s. F:* Lucky. *C'est un v.,* he has all the luck.
veine, *s.f.* **1.** Vein. **2.** (*a*) *Geol:* Vein; lode; seam. (*b*) Vein, humour. *F:* **Être en veine de faire qch.,** to be in the mood to do sth. (*c*) *F:* Luck. **Porter veine à qn,** to bring s.o. good luck. **Coup de veine,** (i) stroke of luck, (ii) fluke.
veineux, *a.* Venous (system).

vélin, *s.m.* **1.** Vellum. **2.** (Papier) vélin, wove paper.
velléitaire, *a.* Impulsive, erratic.
velléité, *s.f.* Slight desire or inclination.
vélo, *s.m. F:* Bike, push-bike. **Aller à vélo,** to cycle.
vélocité, *s.f.* Speed, velocity, swiftness.
vélodrome, *s.m.* Cycle-racing track.
velours, *s.m.* Velvet.
velouté. 1. *a.* Velvety; soft as velvet; downy. **2.** *s.m.* Softness (of material); bloom (of peach).
velu, *a.* Hairy.
vélum [velɔm], *s.m.* Awning.
venaison, ..*f. Cu:* Venison.
vénal, -als, -aux, *a.* **1.** Venal, purchasable. *Com:* **Valeur vénale,** market value. **2.** Venal, mercenary, corrupt.
vénalité, *s.f.* Venality.
venant. 1. *a.* Thriving. **2.** *s.m.* **A tout venant, à tous venants,** to all comers.
vendable, *a.* Saleable, marketable.
vendange, *s.f.* **1.** Vintage. **2.** (*a*) Vintaging; grape-gathering. (*b*) The grapes.
vendanger, *v.tr. & i.* (n. vendangeons) To vintage ; to gather (the grapes).
vendangeur, -euse, *s.* Vintager; wine-harvester.
vendéen, -enne, *a. & s. Geog:* Vendean; of Vendée.
vendetta, *s.f.* Vendetta.
vendeur, -euse, *s.* **1.** *Com:* Seller; salesman, saleswoman. **2.** *Jur:* (*f.* venderesse) Vendor.
vendre, *v.tr.* **1.** To sell. *V. un objet trois francs,* to sell an object for three francs. **Maison à vendre,** house for sale. **L'art de vendre,** salesmanship. **2. Vendre qn,** to betray s.o.
vendredi, *s.m.* Friday. **Le vendredi saint,** Good Friday.
vénéneux, *a.* Poisonous (plant).
vénérabilité, *s.f.* Venerability.
vénérable, *a.* Venerable.
vénération, *s.f.* Veneration, reverence.
vénérer, *v.tr.* (je vénère; je vénérerai) To venerate, reverence, revere.
vénerie, *s.f.* Venery; hunting.
vengeance, *s.f.* **1.** Revenge. **Tirer vengeance d'une injure,** to be revenged for an insult. **2.** Vengeance, retribution, requital.
venger, *v.tr.* (nous vengeons) To avenge. **se venger,** to be revenged; to have one's revenge.
vengeur, -eresse. 1. *s.* Avenger, revenger. **2.** *a.* Avenging, vengeful.
véniel, -elle, *a.* Venial (sin).
venimeux, *a.* Venomous. (*a*) Poisonous (serpent). (*b*) *F:* Spiteful.
venin, *s.m.* Venom. (*a*) Poison. (*b*) *F:* Spite, malice.
venir, *v.i.* (*pr.p.* venant; *p.p.* venu; *pr.ind.* je viens; ils viennent; *pr.sub.* je vienne; *p.h.* je vins; *fu.* je viendrai. *Aux. être*) To

come. **1.** (a) *Je viens!* I'm coming! **Ne faire qu'aller et venir,** to be always on the go. **Je ne ferai qu'aller et venir,** I shall come straight back. **Il vint sur moi,** he advanced on me. *Vienne un peu de soleil et tout le monde est gai,* the minute the sun comes out everyone is cheerful. **Faire venir qn,** to send for, fetch, s.o. *F:* **Je vous vois venir!** I see what you are getting at. **Être bien venu,** to be welcome. *Il est venu deux lettres pour vous,* two letters have come for you. (b) *Venez me trouver à quatre heures,* come and see me at four o'clock. (c) **Venir de faire qch.** (pr. & p.d. only), to have (only) just done sth. *Il vient de sortir,* he has just gone out. **2.** (a) *Il vient d'Amérique,* he hails from America. *Mot qui vient du latin,* word derived from Latin. **Tout cela vient de ce que,** all this is the result of. (b) **D'où vient(-il) que?** how is it that? **3.** (a) To occur, to come. **Le premier exemple venu,** the first instance that comes to hand. (b) **Venir à faire qch.,** to happen to do sth. **4.** (a) To attain, reach. *L'eau leur venait aux genoux,* the water was up to their knees. (b) **Venir à bien,** to succeed. (c) *En v. aux mains,* to come to blows. **Les choses en sont-elles venues là?** have things come to such a pass? **5.** To grow, grow up. **Bien venir,** to thrive.
    venu, *s.* Comer.

venue, *s.f.* Coming, arrival.

Venise. *Pr.n.f.* Venice.

vénitien, -ienne, *a. & s.* Venetian.

vent, *s.m.* **1.** (a) Wind. *Nau:* **V. frais,** strong breeze. **Coup de vent,** gust of wind; gale. **Il fait du vent,** it is windy (weather). **Aller vent arrière,** to run before the wind. **Sous le vent,** to leeward. *Au v. de,* to windward of. **Côté du vent,** weather-side. (b) **Aire de vent,** point of the compass. (c) Air. **Mettre qch. au vent,** to hang sth. out to air. (d) Blast (of gun). (e) Wind, breath. **2.** *Ven:* Scent. *F:* **Avoir vent de qch.,** to get wind of sth.

vente, *s.f.* Sale. **Salle des ventes,** auction-room.

venter, *v.impers.* To blow, to be windy.

ventilateur, *s.m.* Ventilator.

ventilation, *s.f.* Ventilation.

ventiler, *v.tr.* To ventilate, air (room).

ventre, *s.m.* **1.** (a) Abdomen, belly. **Ventre à terre,** at full speed. (b) Stomach, paunch. **2.** *Tchn:* Bulge, swell; belly.

ventricule, *s.m.* *Anat:* Ventricle.

ventriloque, *s.* Ventriloquist.

ventriloquie, *s.f.* Ventriloquy, ventriloquism.

ventru, *a.* Corpulent, portly.

vêpres, *s.f.pl. Ecc:* Vespers; evensong.

ver, *s.m.* **1.** Worm. *Med:* **Ver solitaire,** tapeworm. **2.** (a) Grub, larva, maggot. *F:* **Tirer les vers du nez de qn,** to worm secrets out of s.o. (b) **Ver luisant,** glow-worm. (c) **Ver à soie,** silk-worm.

véracité, *s.f.* Veracity.

véranda, *s.f.* Veranda(h).

verbal, -aux, *a.* Verbal.

verbalement, *adv.* Verbally, by word of mouth.

verbaliser, *v.i. Jur:* To draw up an official report (of an offence).

verbe, *s.m.* **1.** **Avoir le verbe haut,** to be loud of speech. **2.** *Gram:* Verb.

verbeux, *a.* Verbose, long-winded; prosy.

verbiage, *s.m.* Verbiage.

verbosité, *s.f.* Verbosity, wordiness.

verdâtre, *a.* Greenish.

verdeur, *s.f.* **1.** Greenness. **2.** *F:* Vigour; greenness (of old age).

verdict [-dikt], *s.m.* Finding of the jury; verdict.

verdier, *s.m.* Greenfinch.

verdir. 1. *v.tr.* To make or paint green. **2.** *v.i.* To become, turn, green.

verdoyant, *a.* Verdant, green.

verdure, *s.f.* **1.** (a) Greenness. (b) Verdure, greenery. **2.** *Cu:* Green-stuff, greens.

véreux, *a.* **1.** Maggoty. **2.** *F:* Of dubious character; fishy.

verge, *s.f.* (a) Rod, wand, switch. (b) (*Poignée de*) *verges,* birch-rod, birch.

vergé, *a.* Laid (paper). *s.m.* **V. blanc,** cream-laid paper.

verger, *s.m.* Orchard.

verglas, *s.m.* Glazed frost.

vergogne, *s.f.* **Sans vergogne,** shameless(ly).

vergue, *s.f. Nau:* Yard. **Bout de vergue,** yard-arm.

véridique, *a.* Veracious.

véridiquement, *adv.* Veraciously.

vérificateur, *s.m.* **1.** Verifier, examiner. **Vérificateur de comptes,** auditor. **2.** Testing device.

vérification, *s.f.* Verification; checking. **Vérification de comptes,** audit(ing) of accounts.

vérifier, *v.tr.* **1.** To verify; to check; to audit. **2.** To verify, confirm.

vérin, *s.m. Tchn:* Jack.

véritable, *a.* **1.** True. **2.** Real, genuine, veritable.

vérité, *s.f.* **1.** Truth. **En vérité,** really, actually. **2.** Fact, truth. *F:* **C'est la vérité vraie,** it's the honest truth. **Dire à qn ses quatre vérités,** to tell s.o. a few home truths.

verjus, *s.m.* Verjuice.

vermeil, -eille [-mɛːj]. **1.** *a.* Vermilion; ruby (lips); rosy (cheeks). **2.** *s.m.* Silver-gilt.

vermicel(le), *s.m. Cu:* Vermicelli.

vermillon[-mijɔ̃], *s.m.* Vermilion; bright red.

vermine, *s.f.* Vermin.

vermoulu, *a.* (a) Worm-eaten. (b) *F:* Out-of-date; decrepit.

vermout(h) [-mut], *s.m.* Vermouth.

vernal, -aux, *a.* Vernal.

vernir, *v.tr.* To varnish; to polish; to japan.   **verni,** *a.* Varnished. **Cuir verni,** patent leather.

vernis, *s.m.* Varnish, polish, glaze, gloss.

vernissage, *s.m.* Varnishing, glazing.

vernisser, *v.tr.* To glaze (pottery).

vernissure, *s.f.* **1.** (*a*) Varnishing. (*b*) *Cer:* Glazing. **2.** (*a*) Varnish. (*b*) Glaze.

vérole, *s.f. Med:* **Petite vérole,** smallpox.

verr-ai, -as, etc. See VOIR.

verrat, *s.m. Breed:* Boar.

verre, *s.m.* **1.** Glass. *V. de couleur,* stained glass. **Papier de verre,** sand-paper. **2.** (Object made of glass) *V. grossissant,* magnifying glass. *V. ardent,* burning glass. *Nau: V. de hublot,* bull's-eye. **3.** (*a*) **Verre à boire,** (drinking-)glass. (*b*) Glass(ful). **Plein verre,** bumper. **Boire un petit verre,** to have a drop of spirits. *F:* **Tempête dans un verre d'eau,** storm in a tea-cup. **4. Verre soluble,** water-glass.

verrerie, *s.f.* Glassware.

verrou, *s.m.* Bolt, bar. **Sous les verrous,** under lock and key, in safe custody.

verrouiller [-ruje], *v.tr.* To bolt.

verrue, *s.f.* Wart.

vers[1], *s.m.* Verse, line (of poetry). **Faire des vers,** to write poetry. *Méchants vers,* doggerel.

vers[2], *prep.* **1.** Toward(s), to. **2.** (*a*) Toward(s). (*b*) About. *Venez vers* (*les*) *trois heures,* come about three.

versant, *s.m.* Slope, side; bank.

versatile, *a.* Changeable, inconstant.

versatilité, *s.f.* Inconstancy.

verse, *s.f.* **A verse,** in torrents.

versé, *a.* Versed, experienced, practised.

versement, *s.m.* **1.** Pouring (out). **2.** *Fin:* Payment.

verser, *v.tr.* (*a*) To overturn, upset. (*b*) To pour (out). (*c*) To shed. (*d*) To pay (in), to deposit (money).

   se verser, (of river) to flow.

verset, *s.m.* Verse (of Bible).

versification, *s.f.* Versification.

version, *s.f.* **1.** *Sch:* Translation. **2.** Version, account.

verso, *s.m.* Verso, back. "**Voir au verso,**" 'see overleaf.'

vert. 1. *a.* (*a*) Green. **Légumes verts,** greens. (*b*) *Fruits verts,* unripe fruit. *Prov:* **Ils sont trop verts,** the grapes are sour. (*c*) *Verte vieillesse,* green old age. (*d*) Sharp (reprimand); severe (punishment). (*e*) **Langue verte,** slang. **2.** *s.m.* (*a*) (The colour) green. **Des rubans vert bouteille,** bottle-green ribbons. (*b*) **Mettre un cheval au vert,** to turn a horse out to grass. *F:* **Prendre qn sans vert,** to catch s.o. napping.

vert-de-gris, *s.m.* Verdigris.

vertébral, -aux, *a.* Vertebral. *Colonne vertébrale,* spine.

vertèbre, *s.f. Anat:* Vertebra.

vertébré, *a. & s.m. Z:* Vertebrate.

vertement, *adv. F:* **Tancer qn vertement,** to reprimand s.o. sharply.

vertical, -aux. 1. *a.* Vertical; perpendicular; upright. **2.** *s.f.* **Verticale,** vertical

verticalement, *adv.* Vertically.

vertige, *s.m.* Dizziness, giddiness. *Avoir le v.,* to feel dizzy.

vertigineux, *a.* Vertiginous; dizzy, giddy (height).

vertu, *s.f.* **1.** Virtue. **2.** Chastity. **3.** Quality, property. **En vertu de,** by virtue of.

vertueux, *a.* **1.** Virtuous. **2.** Chaste.

verve, *s.f.* Animation, zest, verve. **Être en verve,** to be in capital form.

verveine, *s.f. Bot:* Vervain, verbena.

vesce, *s.f. Bot:* Vetch, tare.

vésicule, *s.f. V. biliaire,* gall-bladder.

vessie, *s.f.* Bladder.

vestale, *s.f. Rom.Ant:* Vestal (virgin).

veste, *s.f. Cost:* (Short) jacket.

vestiaire, *s.m.* (*a*) Cloakroom. (*b*) Changing-room; robing-room.

vestibule, *s.m.* Vestibule, (entrance-)hall.

vestige, *s.m.* **1.** Mark, trace. **2.** *F:* Vestige, remains, trace.

veston, *s.m.* (Man's) jacket; lounge-coat. **Complet veston,** lounge suit.

Vésuve. *Pr.n.m. Geog:* Vesuvius.

vêtement, *s.m.* Garment. *pl.* Clothes, clothing. **Vêtements sacerdotaux,** canonicals. *Vêtements de dessous,* underwear, under-clothing.

vétéran, *s.m.* Veteran; old campaigner

vétérinaire. 1. *a.* Veterinary. **2.** *s.m.* Veterinary surgeon.

vétille [-ti:j], *s.f.* Bagatelle, trifle.

vétilleux [-tij-], *a.* **1.** Delicate, ticklish (business). **2.** Finicky (person).

vêtir, *v.tr.* (*pr.p.* vêtant; *p.p.* vêtu; *pr.ind.* je vêts.) To clothe; to dress, attire. *Chaudement vêtu,* warmly clad.

   se vêtir, to dress; to clothe oneself.

veto [veto], *s.m.* Veto. **Mettre son veto à qch.,** to veto sth.

vétusté, *s.f.* Decay, decrepitude.

veuf [vœf]. **1.** *a.* Widowed. **2.** *s.* Widower, *f.* widow.

veuill-e, -es, etc. [vœ:j]. See VOULOIR.

veule, *a.* Weak, feeble, flabby.

veulent. See VOULOIR.

veulerie, *s.f.* Inertia listlessness.

veut. See VOULOIR.

veuvage, *s.m.* Widowhood or widowerhood.

veuve. See VEUF.

veux. See VOULOIR.

vexant, *a.* Vexing, provoking, annoying.

vexateur, -trice, *a.* Vexatious.

vexation, *s.f.* **1.** Harassing. **2.** Vexatious measure.

vexatoire, *a.* Vexatious.

vexer, *v.tr.* To vex. **1.** To plague, harass. **2.** To annoy, provoke.

viabilité, *s.f.* Traffic condition (of road).

viable, *a.* (Road) fit for traffic.

viaduc [-dyk], *s.m.* Viaduct.

viager. *a.* For life. **Rente viagère,** life annuity.

viande, *s.f.* Meat; flesh.

vibrant, *a.* **1.** Vibrating, vibrant. **2.** (*a*) Ringing (voice). (*b*) Stirring (speech).

vibrateur, *s.m. El.E:* Buzzer.

vibration, *s.f.* **1.** Vibration. **2.** Resonance.

vibratoire, *a.* Vibratory.

vibrer, *v.i.* To vibrate. *Faire v. le cœur de qn,* to thrill s.o.

vicaire, *s.m.* Curate (of parish).

vice, *s.m.* **1.** (*a*) Vice, depravity. (*b*) Vice; moral failing. **2.** Fault, defect, blemish. *Vice propre,* inherent defect.

NOTE. In the following compounds VICE is inv.; the noun takes the plural.

vice-amiral, -aux, *s.m.* Vice-admiral.

vice-chancelier, *s.m.* Vice-chancellor.

vice-consul, *s.m.* Vice-consul.

vice-président, *s.m.* (*a*) Vice-president. (*b*) Vice-chairman.

vice-roi, *s.m.* Viceroy.

viciateur, -trice, *a.* Vitiating, contaminating.

viciation, *s.f.* Vitiation; corruption.

vicier, *v.tr.* To vitiate, corrupt, spoil. *V. l'air,* to taint the air.

　　vicié, *a.* Vitiated, corrupt; tainted.

vicieux, *a.* Vicious. **1.** Depraved. **2.** Defective, faulty. **3.** Bad-tempered (horse).

vicinal, -aux, *a* Chemin vicinal, by-road, local road.

vicissitude, *s.f.* Vicissitude.

vicomte, *s.m.* Viscount.

vicomtesse, *s.f.* Viscountess.

victime, *s.f.* Victim. *Être la v. d'une illusion,* to labour under a delusion.

victoire, *s.f.* **1.** Victory. *F: Chanter victoire,* to crow. **2.** *Pr.n.f.* Victoria.

victorieusement, *adv.* Victoriously.

victorieux, *a.* Victorious. *Être v. de qn,* to be victorious over s.o.

victuailles [-tцa:j], *s.f.pl.* Victuals, eatables.

vidange, *s.f.* **1.** Draining, emptying. **2.** Usu. *pl.* (*a*) Night-soil. (*b*) Sediment, sludge.

vidangeur, *s.m.* Scavenger.

vide. 1. *a.* Empty; blank; unoccupied. *Vide de sens,* devoid of meaning. **2.** *s.m.* (*a*) Empty space; void; blank. *Combler les vides,* to fill up the gaps. (*b*) *Ph:* Vacuum. *Nettoyage par le vide,* vacuum cleaning. (*c*) Emptiness. *Regarder dans le v.,* to stare into vacancy.

vider, *v.tr.* **1.** To empty; to clear out. *Vider les lieux,* to vacate the premises. **2.** To clean (fish); to draw (fowl). **3.** To settle (question).

　　se vider, to empty; to become empty.

viduité, *s.f.* Widowhood.

vie, *s.f.* Life. **1.** *Être en vie,* to be alive. *Avoir la vie dure,* to die hard. *Il y va de la vie,* it's a case of life and death. *F: Sur ma vie!* as I live! *Musique pleine de vie,* music full of go. **2.** Lifetime. *Entre eux c'est à la*

vie à la mort, they are sworn friends. *Nommé à vie,* appointed for life. **3.** Existence, mode of life. *C'est la vie!* such is life! *Changer de vie,* to mend one's ways. *Mauvaise vie,* loose living. **4.** Living, livelihood.

vieil, vieille. See VIEUX.

vieillard [-εja:r], *s.m.* (*f.* usu. **vieille**) Old man. *Les vieillards,* the aged; old people.

vieillesse [-εjɛs], *s.f.* (Old) age; oldness.

vieillir [-εji:r]. **1.** *v.i.* (*a*) To grow old. (*b*) To age. (*c*) To become obsolete. **2.** *v.tr.* To age; to make (s.o.) look older.

vieillissement [-εjis-], *s.m.* Ageing.

vielle, *s.f.* Hurdy-gurdy.

viendr-ai, vienn-e, vien-s, -t. See VENIR.

vierge. 1. *s.f.* (*a*) Virgin, maid(en). (*b*) *Astr:* La Vierge, Virgo. **2.** *a.* Virgin, virginal; pure. *Page v.,* blank page.

vieux, vieil, *f.* **vieille** [vjø, vjε(:)j], *a.* (The form *vieil* is used before masc. nouns beginning with a vowel or *h* 'mute,' but *vieux* also occurs in this position) **1.** Old. (*a*) *Se faire vieux,* to be getting on in years. *F: Eh bien, mon vieux!* well, old chap! *Mes vieux,* my old people. (*b*) Of long standing. *Un vieil ami,* an old friend. *Une vieille fille,* an old maid. *s. F: Un vieux de la vieille,* a veteran. **2.** (*a*) Old, ancient; worn, shabby. *V. papiers,* waste paper. *Adj.phr.inv.* Vieux jeu, old-fashioned. *Doctrines v. jeu,* antiquated doctrines. (*b*) *inv.* Des rubans viei' or, old-gold ribbons.

vif. 1. *a.* (*a*) Alive, living. *De vive force,* by main force. *De vive voix,* by word of mouth. *Eau vive,* running water. *Vives eaux,* springtide. (*b*) Lively, animated; fast. *Vive allure,* rapid gait, brisk pace. (*c*) Sharp (wind). *Vive arête,* sharp edge. *adv.* Il gèle vif, it is freezing hard. (*d*) Keen, quick. (*e*) *Couleurs vives,* bright colours. **2.** *s.m. Jur:* Living person. **3.** *s.m.* Living flesh; quick. *F: Blessé au vif,* stung to the quick.

vif-argent, *s.m.* Quicksilver, mercury.

vigie, *s.f. Nau:* Look-out.

vigilamment, *adv.* Vigilantly; watchfully.

vigilance, *s.f.* Vigilance; watchfulness.

vigilant, *a.* Vigilant, watchful, alert.

vigile, *s.f. Ecc:* Vigil(s).

vigne, *s.f.* **1.** *Vit:* (*a*) Vine. (*b*) Vineyard. **2.** *Bot:* Vigne vierge, Virginia creeper.

vigneron, -onne, *s.* Vine-grower.

vignette, *s.f.* Vignette. *Typ:* Text illustration; head-; tail-piece; ornamental border.

vignoble, *s.m.* Vineyard.

vigoureusement, *adv.* Vigorously.

vigoureux, *a.* Vigorous, strong, sturdy.

vigueur, *s.f.* **1.** Vigour, strength. **2.** *Entrer en vigueur,* to come into force, into operation.

vil, *a.* **1.** Cheap, low-priced. *Vendre qch. à vil prix,* to sell sth. dirt cheap. **2.** Low(ly) (origin); base (metal). **3.** Vile, base.

vilain. 1. *s.* (*a*) Scurvy fellow. (*b*) *F: Oh, la vilaine!* for shame, you naughty girl!

2. *a.* (*a*) Nasty, bad, unpleasant. *Un v. tour*, a mean trick. (*b*) Ugly; shabby; sordid, wretched. (*c*) Mean; stingy.

vilainage, *s.m. Hist:* Villeinage.

vilebrequin, *s.m. Tls:* Brace and bit.

vilement, *adv.* Vilely, basely.

vilenie, *s.f.* **1.** Meanness, stinginess. **2.** (*a*) Mean action; foul deed. (*b*) *Dire des vilenies à qn*, to hurl foul abuse at s.o.

vilipender, *v.tr.* To vilify, abuse; to run down.

villa [vil-], *s.f.* Villa; suburban residence.

'illage [vil-], *s.m.* Village. *F:* Il est bien de son village, he is still very green.

villageois [vil-]. **1.** *s.* Villager; countryman. **2.** *a.* Rustic, country.

ville [vil], Town. **Être en ville**, to be in town, not at home. "En ville," (on letters) 'local.' **Toilette de ville,** out-door dress. **Hôtel, maison, de ville,** town-hall.

villégiature [vil-], *s.f.* (*a*) Stay in the country. (*b*) **En villégiature**, on holiday.

villégiaturiste [vil-], *s.m. & f.* Holidaymaker.

vin, *s.m.* Wine. *Vin ordinaire*, dinner wine. **Offrir un vin d'honneur à qn**, to hold an official reception in honour of s.o.

vinaigre, *s.m.* Vinegar.

vinaigrier, *s.m.* Vinegar-cruet.

vindas, *s.m.* Windlass, winch.

vindicatif, *a.* Vindictive, spiteful, revengeful.

vindicativement, *adv.* Vindictively, spitefully.

vineux, *a.* Vinous (flavour).

vingt [vɛ̃], *num.a.inv. & s.m.inv.* Twenty; a score.

vingtaine [vɛ̃tɛn], *s.f.* (About) twenty; a score.

vingtième [vɛ̃tjɛm]. **1.** *num. a. & s.* Twentieth. **2.** *s.m.* Twentieth (part).

vinicole, *a.* Wine-growing (district).

vin-s, -t, vinss-e, etc. See VENIR.

Vintimille [-mijɔ]. *Pr.n. Geog:* Ventimiglia.

viol, *s.m. Jur:* Rape.

violacé, *a.* Purplish-blue.

violateur, -trice, *s.* Violator; transgressor.

violation, *s.f.* Violation, infringement, breach.

violâtre, *a.* Purplish.

violemment, *adv.* Violently.

violence, *s.f.* Violence, force. **Se faire violence**, to do violence to one's feelings.

violent, *a.* Violent.

violenter, *v.tr.* To do violence to.

violer, *v.tr.* To violate; to transgress; to break.

violet, -ette[1], *a.* Violet, purple. *s.m.* (The colour) violet.

violette[2], *s.f. Bot:* Violet.

violon, *s.m.* **1.** (*a*) Violin. (*b*) Violin (player). *F:* **Payer les violons**, to pay the piper. **2.** *P:* **Le violon**, the cells, the lock-up. **3.** *Nau:* *Violons de mer*, fiddles (for the tables).

violoncelle, *s.m.* Violoncello, 'cello.

violoniste, *s.m. & f.* Violinist.

viorne, *s.f. Bot:* Viburnum.

vipère, *s.f.* Viper, adder. *F:* **Langue de vipère**, viperish, venomous, tongue.

virage, *s.m.* **1.** Turning, sweeping round. *Nau:* Tacking. **2.** *Aut:* (Sharp) turn, corner, bend. **3.** *Phot:* Toning.

virago, *s.f.* Virago, termagant.

virer. **1.** *v.i.* To turn; to sweep round. (*a*) *Aut:* To take a bend or a corner. (*b*) To slew round, swing about. (*c*) *Nau:* **Virer de bord**, to tack. **2.** *v.tr.* (*a*) To turn over. **Virer une crêpe**, to toss a pancake. (*b*) *Phot:* To tone.

virevolter, *v.i.* To spin round.

virginal, -aux, *a.* Virginal; maiden(ly).

virginité, *s.f.* Virginity; maidenhood.

virgule, *s.f.* (*a*) *Gram:* Comma. (*b*) *Mth:* = Decimal point. **Trois virgule cinq** $(3,5)$ = three point five (3.5).

viril [-ril], *a.* Virile. (*a*) Male. (*b*) Manly. **L'âge viril**, man's estate; manhood.

virilité, *s.f.* Virility, manliness.

virole, *s.f.* Ferrule.

virtuel, -elle, *a.* Virtual.

virtuellement, *adv.* Virtually.

virtuose, *s.m. & f.* Virtuoso.

virtuosité, *s.f.* Virtuosity.

virulence, *s.f.* Virulence.

virulent, *a.* Virulent.

virus [-ryːs], *s.m. Med:* Virus.

vis [vis], *s.f.* Screw. *Vis à droite*, right-handed screw or thread. *F:* **Serrer la vis à qn**, to put the screw on s.o. **Escalier à vis**, spiral staircase.

vi-s, -t, etc. See VOIR and VIVRE.

visa, *s.m.* Visa.

visage, *s.m.* Face, countenance, visage. **Faire son visage**, to make one's face up. **A deux visages**, double-faced. **Avoir bon visage**, to look well. **Faire bon visage à qn**, to smile on s.o. *F:* **Trouver visage de bois**, to find nobody at home.

vis-à-vis. **1.** *Adv.phr.* Opposite. *Assis v.-à-v.*, sitting face to face. **2.** *Prep.phr.* **Vis-à-vis de.** (*a*) Opposite, facing. (*b*) Towards, with respect to, with regard to. **3.** *s.m.* Person opposite. *Cards:* Partner.

viscosité, *s.f.* Viscosity; stickiness.

viser[1]. **1.** *v.i.* To aim. *V. à faire qch.*, to aim at doing sth. **2.** *v.tr.* (*a*) To aim, take aim, at. *Golf:* *V. la balle*, to address the ball. (*b*) *Surv:* To sight; to take a sight on. (*c*) To have (sth.) in view. (*d*) To allude to.

visée, *s.f.* **1.** Aim. *Mil:* Aiming, sighting. **Ligne de visée**, line of sight. **Point de visée**, point aimed at. **2.** *pl.* Aims, designs.

viser[2], *v.tr. Adm:* To visa; to countersign.

viseur, -euse. **1.** *s.* Aimer. **2.** *s.m.* (*a*) *Phot:* View-finder. (*b*) *Av:* *V. de lancement*, bomb-sights.

visibilité, *s.f.* Visibility.

visible, *a.* **1.** (*a*) Visible, perceptible.

(b) F: Obvious, manifest, evident. **2.** (a) At home. (b) Disengaged. (c) Accessible, open, to the public.

visiblement, *adv.* **1.** Visibly, perceptibly. **2.** Obviously, evidently.

visière, *s.f.* (a) Vizor. F: **Rompre en visière à qn,** to take an opposite view to that of s.o. (b) Peak (of cap). (c) Eye-shade.

vision, *s.f.* Vision. **1.** (a) Eyesight. (b) Sight. *V. momentanée,* glimpse. **2.** *Les visions d'un poète,* a poet's visions.

visionnaire, *a. & s.* Visionary; dreamer.

visite, *s.f.* Visit. **1.** (a) (Social) call. *Faire une petite v. à qn,* to drop in on s.o. *Carte de visite,* visiting-card. (b) Caller, visitor. **2.** Attendance (of doctor). **3.** (a) Inspection; overhauling; survey. *V. médicale,* medical examination. *V. de la douane,* customs examination. (b) Search (of ship).

visiter, *v.tr.* **1.** To visit; attend. **2.** (a) To examine, inspect, view. (b) To visit, search.

visiteur, -euse. **1.** *s.* (a) Caller, visitor. (b) Inspector. **2.** *a.* Visiting.

vison, *s.m.* Z: Mink.

visqueux, *a.* Viscous, sticky; thick (oil); slimy (secretion).

visser, *v.tr.* To screw, screw on, screw down.

visuel, -elle, *a.* Visual. **Champ visuel,** field of vision.

vit. See VIVRE and VOIR.

vital, -aux, *a.* Vital. *Parties vitales,* vitals.

vitalité, *s.f.* Vitality.

vitamine, *s.f.* Bio-Ch: Vitamin(e).

vite. **1.** *a.* Swift, rapid, speedy. **2.** *adv.* Quickly, fast, swiftly. **Faites vite!** make haste! look sharp! *Allons, et plus v. que cela!* now then, be quick about it! **Au plus vite,** as quickly as possible.

vitesse, *s.f.* Speed, swiftness, rapidity; velocity; rate. F: **En vitesse,** with all speed. **Vitesse folle,** breakneck speed. **Gagner qn de vitesse,** to outstrip s.o. **Prendre de la vitesse,** to gather pace. *Aut:* **Faire de la vitesse,** to speed. **Indicateur de vitesse,** speedometer. *V. acquise,* impetus. *Aut:* **Boîte de vitesses,** gear-box. **Première vitesse,** bottom gear.

viticulture, *s.f.* Vine-growing.

vitrage, *s.m.* **1.** Glazing. **2.** Glass partition or door.

vitrail [-ra:j], **-aux,** *s.m.* Leaded glass window; stained glass window.

vitre, *s.f.* Pane; window-pane.

vitrer, *v.tr.* To glaze.
  vitré, *a.* **1.** Glazed. **2.** Vitreous, glassy.

vitreux, *a.* Vitreous; glassy. **Yeux vitreux,** glassy, glazed, eyes.

vitrier, *s.m.* Glazier.

vitrine, *s.f.* **1.** Shop-window. **2.** Glass case, glass cabinet. *Com:* Show-case.

vitriol, *s.m.* Vitriol.

vitupération, *s.f.* Vituperation.

vivace, *a.* (a) Long-lived. (b) Bot: Hardy. (c) Bot: Perennial. (d) F: *Haine v.,* undying, inveterate, hatred.

vivacité, *s.f.* **1.** *V. à agir,* promptness to act. **2.** Hastiness; petulance. **3.** (a) Acuteness (of feeling); heat (of a discussion); intensity. (b) Vividness, brilliancy. **4.** Vivacity, vivaciousness, liveliness.

vivandière, *s.f.* Vivandière, canteen-keeper.

vivant. **1.** *a.* (a) Alive, living. **Être le portrait vivant de qn,** to be the very image of s.o. **Langue vivante,** modern language. (b) Lively, animated. (c) Vivid, live. **2.** *s.m.* (a) Living being. (b) **Bon vivant,** man who enjoys life. **3.** *s.m.* **De son vivant,** during his lifetime.

vive¹. See VIF.

vive², *int.* See VIVRE I.

vivement, *adv.* **1.** (a) Briskly, sharply, smartly. (b) *Répondre v.,* to answer sharply. **2.** (a) Keenly, deeply. (b) (To thank s.o.) warmly.

vivier, *s.m.* Fish-pond.

vivifiant, *a.* Vivifying; invigorating, bracing.

vivifier, *v.tr.* To vivify; to endue with life; to invigorate.

vivipare, *a.* Viviparous.

vivisection, *s.f.* Vivisection.

vivre. I. *v.i* (p.p. vécu; *pr.ind.* je vis) To live. **1.** To be alive. **Vive le roi!** long live the King! *Mil:* **Qui vive?** who goes there? **Ne rencontrer âme qui vive,** to meet no one. *Prov:* **Qui vivra verra,** time will tell. **2.** To spend one's life. **Savoir vivre,** to know how to behave. **3.** To subsist. **Il fait cher vivre ici,** living is dear here. **Avoir de quoi vivre,** to have enough to live on.
  II. **vivre,** *s.m.* (a) Living. (b) Food. (c) *pl.* Provisions, supplies, victuals.

vécu, *a.* **1.** Choses vécues, actual experiences. **2.** True to life.

vizir, *s.m.* Vizier.

vlan, v'lan, *int.* Slap(-bang)! whack!

vocable, *s.m.* Vocable, word.

vocabulaire, *s.m.* Vocabulary.

vocal, -aux, *a.* Vocal.

vocalement, *adv.* Vocally.

vocation, *s.f.* Vocation. **1.** (Divine) call. **2.** Calling, bent, inclination.

vociférations, *s.f.pl.* Vociferation(s).

vociférer, *v.i.* (je vocifère; je vociférerai) To vociferate; to shout, bawl, yell.

vœu, -x, *s.m.* **1.** Vow. **2.** Wish. **Tous mes vœux!** all good wishes!

vogue, *s.f.* Fashion, vogue. **Être en vogue,** to be popular.

voguer, *v.i.* Nau: To sail. **Voguer à pleines voiles,** to forge ahead.

voici, *prep.* **1.** Here is, are. **La voici qui vient,** here she comes. **Mon ami que voici vous le dira,** my friend here will tell you. **La petite histoire que voici,** the following little story. **2.** *Je l'ai vu v. trois ans,* I saw him three years ago.

voie¹, *s.f.* **1.** (a) Way, road, route, track. **Par voie de terre,** by land; overland. (b) *Ven:* (Often *pl.*) Tracks (of game). F: **Mettre qn**

sur la v., to put s.o. on the right track. (c) *Rail:* **Voie ferrée,** railway track; railway line. **V. de garage,** siding. (d) *Nau:* **Voie d'eau,** leak. (e) *Anat:* Passage, duct. **2. Way. Voies et moyens,** ways and means. **Par voie diplomatique,** through the channels of diplomacy. **Affaire en bonne voie,** affair going well. **En voie de formation,** in process of formation. **Voies de fait,** acts of violence. *En venir aux voies de fait,* to come to blows.

voie². See VOIR.

voilà, *prep.* **1.** (a) There is, are. **En voilà assez!** that's enough (of it)! that will do! **En voilà une idée!** what an idea! **Voilà tout,** that's all. **Le voilà qui entre,** there he is coming in. (b) *F:* Often = VOICI. **Me voilà!** here I am! **2.** *V. dix ans que je le connais,* I've known him these ten years.

voile. I. *s.f.* Sail. **Grande voile,** mainsail. **Toutes voiles dehors,** all sails set.
II. **voile,** *s.m.* (a) Veil. *F:* **Sous le voile de la religion,** under the cloak of religion. (b) *Tex:* Voile.

voiler, *v.tr.* (a) To veil. (b) To veil, obscure, dim; to muffle. (c) *Phot:* To fog.
se voiler, to become overcast, to cloud over.
voilé, *a.* (a) Veiled, dim; obscure (meaning); muffled (drum). (b) Fogged (print).

voilette, *s.f.* (Hat-)veil.

voilier, *s.m.* **1.** Sailing-ship; *F:* windjammer. **2.** Sail-maker.

voilure, *s.f.* Sails (of ship).

voir, *v.tr.* (*pr.p.* voyant; *p.p.* vu; *pr.ind.* ils voient; *pr.sub.* je voie; *p.h.* je vis; *fu.* je verrai) To see. **1.** To set eyes upon; to sight. **A le voir,** to judge by his looks. *Monument qui se voit de loin,* monument that can be seen from afar. **Voir trouble,** to see things through a mist. **Voyez vous-même!** see for yourself! *Iron:* **Voyez un peu!** behold him! **Faire voir qch. à qn,** to show sth. to s.o. **Faites voir!** let me see it! **2. Voir** + *inf.* (a) *V. venir qn,* to see s.o. coming. (b) *V. faire qch. à qn,* to see s.o. do sth. **3.** (a) To visit. **Aller voir qn,** to go to see s.o. **Voir du pays,** to travel. (b) *Il ne voit personne,* he receives no one. **4.** (a) To understand. *F:* **Ni vu ni connu,** nobody is any the wiser for it. (b) To perceive, observe. **Cela se voit,** that is obvious. *Vous voyez ça d'ici,* you can imagine what it was like. **5.** (a) *C'est ce que nous verrons!* that remains to be seen. **Il n'a rien à voir là-dedans,** it is nothing to do with him. (b) *Voyez à nous loger,* see that we are housed. (c) *int.* **Voyons!** (i) let us see; (ii) come! come! **6. Être bien vu de tous,** to be highly esteemed by all. *F:* **Je ne peux pas le voir,** I can't bear the sight of him.

vu. I. *s.m.* **Au vu de tous,** openly, publicly. **Au vu et au su de tous,** as everyone knows. **2.** *prep.* Considering, seeing. **Vu que,** seeing that.

vue, *s.f.* **1.** Sight. **Avoir la vue basse,** to be short-sighted. **A perte de vue,** as far as the eye can reach. **Personnes les plus en vue,** people most in the public eye. **A vue d'œil,** visibly. **2.** (a) View. **Vues saines,** sound views. (b) View, survey. **3. A première vue,** at first sight, off-hand. **4.** View. (a) Prospect, outlook. *Voir qch. sous un autre point de vue,* to see sth. in another light. (b) Intention, purpose, design. *Entrer dans les vues de qn,* to agree with s.o.'s views. *Prep.phr.* **En vue de,** with a view to.

voire, *adv.* Nay. **Voire même,** and even. *J'en suis ahuri, v. révolté,* I am astounded, nay, disgusted.

voirie, *s.f.* **1. La grande voirie,** the high roads. **2.** Refuse-dump.

voisin. 1. *a.* Neighbouring, adjoining. *Émotion voisine de la terreur,* emotion bordering on terror. **2.** *s.* Neighbour.

voisinage, *s.m.* **1.** Proximity, vicinity, nearness. **2.** Neighbourhood.

voisiner, *v.i.* To be placed side by side; to adjoin.

voiture, *s.f.* (a) Conveyance, vehicle, carriage, motor car. **Aller en voiture,** to drive. (b) Cart, van. **V. d'enfant,** perambulator. **V. cellulaire,** prison-van. **Voiture de chemin de fer,** railway coach, carriage. **"En voiture!"** 'take your seats!'

voiturier, *s.m.* Carter, carrier.

voix, *s.f.* **1.** Voice. **Parler à voix basse,** to speak in a low voice, under one's breath. **Donner de la voix,** to bark, to give tongue. **2.** Demeurer sans voix, to remain speechless. **D'une commune voix,** by common consent. **Mettre une question aux voix,** to put a question to the vote. *La Chambre alla aux v.,* the House divided. *F:* **Avoir voix au chapitre,** to have a say in the matter.

vol¹, *s.m.* **1.** (a) Flying, flight. **Prendre son vol,** to take wing. **Au vol,** on the wing. **V. d'oiseau,** as the crow flies. **Vue à vol d'oiseau,** bird's-eye view. (b) *Av:* **Vol piqué,** dive. **2.** Flock, flight.

vol², *s.m.* Theft; stealing, robbery. **Vol à l'étalage,** shop-lifting. **Vol à l'américaine,** confidence trick.

volage, *a.* Fickle, inconstant, flighty.

volaille [-la:j], *s.f.* Poultry, fowls.

volant. I. *a.* **1.** Flying; fluttering. **2.** Loose; movable. **Feuille volante,** loose leaf.
II. **volant,** *s.m.* **1.** *Games:* Shuttlecock. **2.** Fly-wheel. **3.** Hand-wheel. *Aut:* **Volant de direction,** steering-wheel. **4.** *Dressm:* Flounce.

volatil, *a.* Volatile.

volatile, *s.m. or f.* Winged creature; bird.

volatilisation, *s.f.* Volatilization.

volatiliser, *v.tr. Ch:* To volatilize.
se volatiliser, to volatilize.

vol-au-vent, *s.m.inv. Cu:* Puff-pie; vol-au-vent.

volcan, *s.m.* Volcano.

volcanique, *a.* Volcanic.

voler[1], *v.i.* To fly. (*a*) *F:* **On aurait entendu voler une mouche**, you could have heard a pin drop. (*b*) *F:* To travel fast; to move with speed. *Le temps vole*, time flies.

volée, *s.f.* **I.** Flight (of bird). **Prendre sa volée**, to take wing. *Agr: Semer à la v.*, to broadcast. **2.** Flock, flight. **3.** (*a*) Volley (of missiles). (*b*) *V. de coups de bâton*, shower of blows. (*c*) *V. de cloches*, full peal of bells. **Sonner à toute volée**, to set all the bells a-ringing. **4. Volée d'escalier**, flight of stairs.

voler[2], *v.tr.* **I.** To steal. *F:* **Il ne l'a pas volé**, he richly deserves it. **2.** (*a*) To rob. (*b*) *F:* To swindle, cheat.

volet, *s.m.* **I.** *F:* **Trié sur le volet**, very select. **2.** Shutter.

voleter, *v.i.* (il volette) To flutter; to flit.

volettement, *s.m.* (*a*) Fluttering, flutter. (*b*) Flitting (hither and thither).

voleur, -euse. I. *s.* Thief, robber, burglar. *Voleuse à l'étalage*, shop-lifter. **Au voleur!** stop thief! **2.** *a.* Thieving, thievish.

volière, *s.f.* Aviary.

volition, *s.f.* Volition.

volontaire, *a.* **I.** Voluntary; spontaneous. *Mil: Engagé v.*, *s.m.* **volontaire**, volunteer. **2.** Self-willed, wilful, headstrong. *Menton v.*, firm chin.

volontairement, *adv.* **I.** Voluntarily, willingly. **2.** Obstinately, wilfully.

volonté, *s.f.* **I.** Will. (*a*) *Ne pas avoir de v.*, to have no will of one's own. (*b*) *Faire qch. de bonne v.*, to do sth. of one's own free will. (*c*) **Suivre sa volonté** to have one's own way. **A volonté**, at will, at pleasure, ad lib. **2.** *pl.* (*a*) **Les dernières volontés de**, the last will and testament of. (*b*) Whims, caprices. **Elle fait ses quatre volontés**, she does just what she pleases.

volontiers [-tje], *adv.* (*a*) Willingly, gladly. *Il cause v.*, he is fond of talking. (*b*) Readily.

volt [vɔlt], *s.m. El.Meas:* Volt.

voltage, *s.m. El:* Voltage.

volte-face, *s.f.inv.* Turning round; volte-face; wheel round; face-about.

voltigement, *s.m.* Fluttering, flitting.

voltiger, *v.i.* (n. voltigeons) To fly about; to flit; to flutter, flap.

volubilis [-lis], *s.m. Bot:* Convolvulus.

volubilité, *s.f.* Volubility.

volume, *s.m.* **I.** Volume, tome. **2.** (*a*) Volume, bulk, mass. (*b*) Volume (of sound).

volumineux, *a.* **I.** Voluminous, bulky, large. **2.** Voluminous (writer).

volupté, *s.f.* (Sensual) pleasure or delight.

voluptueusement, *adv.* Voluptuously.

voluptueux. I. *a.* Voluptuous. **2.** *s.* Voluptuary, sensualist.

volute, *s.f.* (*a*) Volute, helix; scroll. *V. de fumée*, wreath of smoke. (*b*) *Conch:* Whorl.

vomir, *v.tr.* (*a*) To vomit. (*b*) To vomit, belch forth (smoke).

vomissement, *s.m.* **I.** Vomiting. **2.** Vomit.

vont. See ALLER.

vorace, *a.* Voracious.

voracement, *adv.* Voraciously.

voracité, *s.f.* Voracity, voraciousness.

vortex [-tɛks], *s.m.* (*a*) Whorl. (*b*) Vortex-ring.

vos. See VOTRE.

votant, *s.* Voter.

votation, *s.f.* Voting.

vote, *s.m.* **I.** (*a*) Vote. (*b*) Voting, ballot(ing), poll. **Droit de vote**, franchise. **2. Vote d'une loi**, passing of a bill.

voter. I. *v.i.* To vote. **2.** *v.tr.* (*a*) To pass, carry (a bill). (*b*) To vote (money).

votif, *a.* Votive (offering).

votre, *pl.* **vos**, *poss.a.* Your. *Vos père et mère*, your father and mother.

vôtre. I. Occ. *poss.a.* Yours. *Je suis tout vôtre*, I am entirely at your service. **2. Le vôtre, la vôtre, les vôtres.** Yours; your own. *F:* **A la vôtre!** here's to you! (*b*) *s.m.* (i) **Il faut y mettre du vôtre**, you must do your share. (ii) *pl.* Your own (folk). (iii) *F:* **Vous avez encore fait des vôtres**, you've been up to some of your tricks again.

voudr-ai, etc. See VOULOIR.

vouer, *v.tr.* To vow, dedicate, consecrate. *V. sa vie à l'étude*, to devote one's life to study.

vouloir. I. *v.tr.* (*pr.p.* voulant; *p.p.* voulu; *pr.ind.* je veux, il veut, ils veulent; *pr.sub.* je veuille, ils veuillent; *imp.* tu veux, otherwise veuille, veuillez; *fu.* je voudrai) **I.** To will; to be determined on. **Dieu le veuille!** please God! *Prov:* **Vouloir, c'est pouvoir**, where there's a will there's a way. **Vous l'avez voulu!** you have only yourself to blame! **2.** (*a*) To want, to wish (for), to desire. **Faites comme vous voudrez**, do as you please. **Qu'il le veuille ou non**, whether he chooses or not. **Je ne le veux pas!** I will not have it! *F:* **Que voulez-vous!** well, well! *Ils ne veulent pas de moi*, they won't have me. *Adv.phr.* **En veux-tu, en voilà**, as much as ever you like. (*b*) *Pred.* *Je te veux heureuse*, I want you to be happy. (*c*) **En vouloir à qn**, to bear s.o. a grudge. *Ne m'en veuillez pas*, don't be vexed with me. **A qui en voulez-vous?** what ails you? **3.** Vouloir + *inf.*, vouloir que + *sub.* (*a*) To will, to require, to demand. *Le mauvais sort voulut qu'il arrivât trop tard*, ill-luck would have it that he should get there too late. *Je veux être obéi*, I mean to be obeyed. **Vouloir absolument faire qch.**, to insist upon doing sth. (*b*) To want, wish. *Il voulait me frapper*, he wanted to hit me. *Que voulez-vous que je fasse?* what would you have me do? *Rentrons, voulez-vous?* let us go in, shall we? (*c*) To try to. *Il voulut arrêter le coup*, he tried to stop the blow. (*d*) To mean, intend. **Faire qch. sans le vouloir**, to do sth. unintentionally. (*e*) **Vouloir bien faire qch.**, to consent, be willing, to do sth. *Veuillez (bien) vous asseoir*, kindly sit down. (*f*) **Voulez-vous**

bien vous taire! *will* you be silent! **4.** To be convinced, to insist. *Il veut absolument que je me sois trompé*, he will have it that I was mistaken. **5.** To require, need, demand. *La vigne veut un terrain crayeux*, vines require a chalky soil.
 II. **vouloir**, *s.m.* Will. **Bon vouloir**, goodwill.
 voulu, *a.* **1.** Required, requisite. **2.** Deliberate, intentional.

vous, *pers.pron. sg. & pl.* **1.** (*a*) (Subject) You. (*b*) (Object) You, to you. (*c*) (Refl.) *Vous vous êtes donné bien de la peine*, you have given yourself much trouble (*d*) (Reciprocal) *Vous vous connaissez*, you know one another. **2.** (Stressed) (*a*) (Subject) You. *Vous et votre femme*, you and your wife. *Vous autres Anglais*, you English. *Faites-le vous-même*, do it yourself. (*b*) (Object) *C'est à vous de jouer*, it is your turn to play.

vous-même(s), *pers.pron.* See VOUS and MÊME.

voûte, *s.f.* Vault, arch.

voûter, *v.tr.* To arch, vault.
 se voûter, to become bent, bowed.
 voûté, *a.* (*a*) Vaulted, arched. (*b*) Stooping, bent. **Dos voûté**, bent back.

voyage, *s.m.* Journey, voyage. *Aimer les voyages*, to be fond of travel. **Petit voyage d'agrément**, pleasure trip. **Il est en voyage**, he is travelling. **Compagnon de voyage**, fellow-traveller. **Bon voyage!** pleasant journey!

voyager, *v.i.* (n. **voyageons**) (*a*) To travel; to make a journey. (*b*) *Com:* To travel. *V. pour les vins*, to travel in wine.

voyageur, -euse. 1. *s.* (*a*) Traveller, (in train) passenger; (in cab) fare. (*b*) Esp. *Hist:* Voyager, explorer. (*c*) **Voyageur de commerce**, commercial traveller. **2.** *a.* (*a*) Travelling. **Commis voyageur**, commercial

traveller. (*b*) **Pigeon voyageur**, carrier pigeon.

voyant, *a.* Gaudy, loud (colour); showy, conspicuous (monument).

voyelle, *s.f.* Vowel.

voy-ez, -ons, etc. See VOIR.

voyou, -oute, *s. F:* (Young) loafer, hooligan.

vrac [vrak], *s.m.* **En vrac**, loose, in bulk.

vrai. 1. *a.* (*a*) True, truthful. **C'est (bien) vrai!** true! *F:* (**Pour) de vrai**, really, in earnest. (*b*) True, real, genuine. (*c*) Downright, arrant, regular. **2.** *adv.* Truly, really, indeed. **A vrai dire**, if the truth must be told. *F: Tu m'aimes*, **vrai?** you *do* love me? *Vous m'écrirez*, **pas vrai?** you *will* write to me, won't you? **3.** *s.m.* Truth.

vraiment, *adv.* Really, truly, in truth. **Vraiment?** indeed? is that so?

vraisemblable. 1. *a.* Probable, likely. **2.** *s.m.* What is probable, likely.

vraisemblablement, *adv.* Probably, very likely.

vraisemblance, *s.f.* Probability, likelihood.

vrille [vriːj], *s.f.* **1.** *Bot:* Tendril. **2.** *Tls:* Gimlet. **3.** *Av:* Spin.

vriller [vrije], *v.tr.* To bore (with a gimlet).

vrombir, *v.i.* To buzz; to hum; to throb.

vrombissement, *s.m.* Buzzing; humming; throbbing.

vu, vue. See VOIR.

vulcaniser, *v.tr. Ind:* To vulcanize.

vulcanite, *s.f.* Vulcanite, ebonite.

vulgaire. 1. *a.* Vulgar. (*a*) Common, everyday. (*b*) Low, unrefined, coarse. **2.** *s.m.* **Le vulgaire**, the common people.

vulgarisation, *s.f.* Popularization.

vulgariser, *v.tr.* **1.** To popularize. **2.** To coarsen, vulgarize.
 se vulgariser, to grow vulgar.

vulgarité, *s.f.* Vulgarity.

vulnérabilité, *s.f.* Vulnerability.

vulnérable, *a.* Vulnerable.

W

W, w [dubləve], *s.m.* (The letter) W, w.

wagon [vagɔ̃], *s.m. Rail:* Carriage, coach; waggon, truck. **Monter en wagon**, to get into the train.

 NOTE. In the following compounds both nouns vary in the plural.

wagon-frein, *s.m.* Brake-van.

wagon-lit, *s.m.* Sleeping-car; *F:* sleeper.

wagon-restaurant, *s.m.* Restaurant-car; dining-car.

wagon-salon, *s.m.* Saloon(-car, -carriage).

Walkyrie [val-], *s.f. Myth:* Valkyrie.

wallon, -onne [val-], *a. & s. Ethn:* Walloon.

wapiti, *s.m. Z:* Wapiti.

water-closet [-tɛrklɔzɛt], *s.m.* Water-closet, w.-c. *pl. Des water-closets.*

waterproof [-pruf], *s.m.* Waterproof (coat).

watt, *s.m. El.Meas:* Watt.

whist, *s.m.* Whist.

wisigoth [vi-], *s. Hist:* Visigoth.

wolfram [vɔlfram], *s.m. Miner:* Wolfram.

X, x [iks], *s.m.* (The letter) X, x. *Ph:* Rayons X, X rays.
Xérès [kerɛs, gzerɛs]. **1.** *Pr.n. Geog:* Jerez. **2.** *s.m.* (Also **vin de Xérès**) Sherry.
xylonite, *s.f.* Xylonite, celluloid.
xylophone, *s.m. Mus:* Xylophone.

Y

Y, y¹ [igrɛk], *s.m.* (The letter) Y, y.
y², *adv. & pron.* **1.** *adv.* There; here; thither. *F: J'y suis, j'y reste!* here I am and here I stay! **Madame y est-elle?** is Mrs X at home? *F:* **Ah, j'y suis!** ah, now I understand! *Pendant que vous y êtes,* while you are about it. **2.** *pron.inv.* (*a*) *J'y gagnerai,* I shall gain by it. *Je m'y attendais,* I expected as much. (*b*) *Je n'y manquerai pas,* I shall not fail to do so. (*c*) *Pensez-vous à lui?—Oui, j'y pense,* do you think of him?—Yes, I do. **3.** **Je vous y prends!** I have caught you (in the act)! **Ça y est!** (i) it's done!

that's it! (ii) all right! done! **Il y est pour quelque chose,** he has a hand in it.
yacht [jak(t), jat, jɔt], *s.m. Nau:* Yacht.
ya(c)k [jak], *s.m. Z:* Yak.
yatagan, *s.m.* Yataghan.
yeuse, *s.f. Bot:* Ilex, holm-oak.
yeux. See ŒIL.
yole, *s.f. Nau:* Gig, yawl. **Y. d'amiral,** galley.
yougoslave, *a. & s. Geog:* Jugo-Slav.
Yougoslavie (la). *Pr.n.f. Geog:* Jugoslavia.
youyou, *s.m. Nau:* Dinghy. *pl. Des youyous.*
ypérite, *s.f. Ch:* Yperite; mustard-gas.

Z

Z, z [zɛd], *s.m.* (The letter) Z, z.
zagaie, *s.f.* Assegai.
Zambèze (le). *Pr.n.* The Zambezi (river).
zèbre, *s.m.* Zebra.
zébrer, *v.tr.* (je zèbre; je zébrerai) To mark with stripes; to streak.
　zébré, *a.* Striped (*de,* with); stripy.
zébrure, *s.f.* **1.** Stripe. **2.** (Series of) stripes; zebra markings.
zébu, *s.m. Z:* Zebu; humped ox.
Zélande. *Pr.n.f.* Zealand.
zélateur, -trice, *s.* Zealot.
zèle, *s.m.* Zeal, ardour.
zélé, *a. & s.* Zealous.
zélote, *s.m. B.Hist:* Zealot.
zénana, *s.m.* Zenana.
zénith, *s.m.* Zenith.
zéphire, zéphyr(e), *s.m.* Balmy breeze; zephyr.
zéro, *s.m.* **1.** Cipher, nought. *Ten:* **Trois à zéro,** three love. **2.** Starting point, zero. *El.E:* **"Zéro,"** 'off' (on electric stove).
zeste, *s.m. Cu:* Peel (of lemon). *Z. confit,* candied peel.
Zeus [zøːs]. *Pr.n.m. Myth:* Zeus.

zézaiement, zézayement, *s.m.* Lisping, lisp.
zézayer, *v.i. & tr.* (je zézaie, je zézaye) To lisp.
zibeline, *s.f.* **1.** *Z:* (Martre) zibeline, sable. **2.** *Cost:* Sable (fur).
zigzag [-zag], *s.m.* Zigzag. **Éclair en zigzag,** forked lightning.
zigzaguer, *v.i.* To zigzag.
zinc [zɛ̃ːg], *s.m.* Zinc. *Com:* Spelter.
zodiacal, -aux, *a. Astr:* Zodiacal.
zodiaque, *s.m.* Zodiac.
zonal, -aux, *a.* Zonal.
zone, *s.f.* Zone. (*a*) *Geog:* **Z. houillère,** coal-belt. (*b*) *Adm:* **Z. postale,** postal area.
zoologie [zɔɔlɔʒi], *s.f.* Zoology.
zoologique [zɔɔ-], *a.* Zoological.
zoologiste [zɔɔ-], *s.m.* Zoologist.
zoophytes [zɔɔ-], *s.m.pl. Biol:* Zoophytes.
zouave, *s.m. Mil:* Zouave.
zoulou, *a. & s.* Zulu. *pl. Des zoulous.*
Zoulouland. *Pr.n. Geog:* Zululand.
zut [zyt], *int. P:* (*a*) Botheration! dash (it)! (*b*) Rats! shut up!
Zuyderzée (le). *Pr.n. Geog:* The Zuyder Zee.

PART TWO
ENGLISH—FRENCH

PART TWO
ENGLISH-FRENCH

CONCISE
FRENCH AND ENGLISH DICTIONARY

PART TWO

ENGLISH—FRENCH

A

A, a¹. I. (La lettre) A, a *m*. **AI,** *F:* de première qualité. **2.** *Mus:* La *m*
a², *before a vowel* **an,** *indef. art.* **I.** Un, une. *A man and woman,* un homme et une femme. **2.** (*a*) *To have a big mouth,* avoir la bouche grande. (*b*) *To have a taste for sth.,* avoir le goût de qch. (*c*) (*Generalizing use*) *A woman takes life too seriously,* les femmes prennent la vie trop au sérieux. **3.** (*Distributive use*) *Fivepence a pound,* cinq pence la livre. *Five francs a head,* cinq francs par tête. *Three times a week,* trois fois par semaine. **4.** (*a*) (= *A certain, a particular*) *I know a Doctor Smith,* je connais un certain docteur Smith. (*b*) (= *The same; with 'at', 'of'*) *To eat two at a time,* en manger deux à la fois. *To be of a size,* être de la même grandeur, de (la) même taille. (*c*) (= *A single*) *I haven't understood a word,* je n'ai pas compris un seul mot. **5.** (*Omitted in Fr.*) (*a*) (*Before unqualified pred. nouns*) *He is an Englishman,* il est Anglais. (*But* C'est un Anglais de passage.) (*b*) (*Before nouns in apposition*) *Caen, a large town in Normandy,* Caen, grande ville de Normandie. (*c*) (*In many verb-phrases*) *To make a fortune,* faire fortune. (*d*) *What a pity!* quel dommage! (*e*) *In a cab,* en fiacre. *To live like a prince,* vivre en prince.
aback, *adv. F:* **To be taken aback,** être déconcerté, interdit; se déconcerter.
abandon¹, *s.* (*a*) Abandon *m*; laisser-aller *m*. (*b*) Entrain *m*.
abandon², *v.tr.* Abandonner; délaisser (sa famille); renoncer à (un plan). *To a. oneself to despair,* s'abandonner au désespoir. **abandoned,** *a.* Dévergondé; dépravé.
abandonment, *s.* Abandon *m*, abandonnement *m* (de qn, de qch.).
abase, *v.tr.* Abaisser; *F:* ravaler (qn).
abasement, *s.* Abaissement *m*.
abash, *v.tr.* Confondre, décontenancer, déconcerter, interdire.
abate. I. *v.tr.* Diminuer (l'orgueil); affaiblir (le courage); relâcher (son activité). **2.** *v.i.* (*Of storm*) Diminuer, s'affaiblir; (*of pain*)

s'apaiser; se modérer; (*of flood*) baisser. *The wind abated,* le vent tomba.
abatement, *s.* **I.** Diminution *f*; apaisement *m* (de la tempête); relâchement *m* (du temps); baisse *f* (des eaux). **2.** *Com:* Rabais *m* (sur le prix).
abbess, *s.* Abbesse *f*.
abbey, *s.* **I.** Abbaye *f*. **2.** Église abbatiale.
abbot, *s.* Abbé *m* (d'un monastère).
abbreviate, *v.tr.* Abréger.
abbreviation, *s.* Abréviation *f*.
abdicate, *v.tr.* **I.** Abdiquer (un trône); renoncer à (un droit). **2.** *Abs.* Abdiquer.
abdication, *s.* Abdication *f*; renonciation *f*; démission *f*.
abduct, *v.tr. Jur:* Enlever (qn).
abduction, *s. Jur:* Enlèvement *m* (de qn).
abed, *adv.* Au lit; couché.
aberration, *s.* **I.** Aberration *f*, déviation *f*. **2. Mental aberration,** égarement *m* d'esprit; aberration.
abet, *v.tr.* **To abet s.o. in a crime,** encourager qn in un crime. **To aid and abet s.o.,** être le complice de qn. **abetting,** *s.* (**Aiding and**) **abetting,** complicité *f*.
abeyance, *s.* Suspension *f* (d'une loi). *The matter is still in a.,* la question est toujours pendante.
abhor, *v.tr.* Abhorrer.
abhorrence, *s.* Horreur *f* (*of,* de); extrême aversion *f* (*of,* pour, de).
abhorrent, *a.* **To be abhorrent to s.o.,** être répugnant, en horreur, à qn.
abide, *v.* **I.** *v.i.* (*a*) *A. & Lit:* Rester. *To a. at a place,* habiter un lieu. (*b*) *To abide by a promise,* rester fidèle à une promesse. **2.** *v.tr. I can't a. him,* je ne peux pas le sentir.
ability, *s.* **I.** Capacité *f*, pouvoir *m* (*to do sth.,* de faire qch.). **2.** Habileté *f*., capacité, intelligence *f*. **To do sth. to the best of one's ability,** faire qch. de son mieux.
abject, *a.* **I.** Abject, misérable. **2.** (*a*) Bas, vil. (*b*) Servile. **-ly,** *adv.* Abjectement.
abjection, *s.* Abjection, *f*, misère *f*.

abjure, *v.tr.* Abjurer (sa foi); renier (sa religion).

ablative, *a. & s. Gram:* Ablatif (*m*).

ablaze, *adv. & pred.a.* En feu, en flammes. *To be a.,* flamber.

able, *a.* **1.** (*a*) Capable, compétent, habile. (*b*) **To be able to do sth.,** (i) savoir, être capable de, faire qch.; (ii) (*as infinitive to the vb.* CAN) pouvoir, être à même de, être en état de, faire qch. *A. to pay,* en mesure de payer. **2.** *A. piece of work,* travail bien fait. **ably,** *adv.* Habilement. **able-bodied,** *a.* Fort, robuste.

abnegation, *s.* **1.** Abnégation *f*; renoncement *m*. **2.** Désaveu *m* (d'une doctrine).

abnormal, *a.* Anormal, -aux. **-ally,** *adv.* Anormalement.

aboard. **1.** *adv.* A bord. *To go aboard,* aller à bord; **s'embarquer. 2.** *prep.* Aboard (a) *ship,* à bord d'un navire.

abode, *s.* **1.** Demeure *f*, habitation *f*, résidence *f*. **2.** (Lieu *m* de) séjour *m*. **To take up one's abode in the country,** s'installer à la campagne. **Place of abode,** domicile *m*.

abolish, *v.tr.* Abolir, supprimer.

abolition, *s.* Abolissement *m*, abolition *f*.

abominable, *a.* Abominable; odieux. **-ably,** *adv.* Abominablement.

abominate, *v.tr.* Abominer; avoir en horreur.

abomination, *s.* Abomination *f*.

aboriginal, *a.* Indigène, aborigène.

aborigines, *s.pl.* Aborigènes *m*, indigènes *m*.

abortive, *a.* (*Of plan*) Avorté, manqué.

abound, *v.i.* Abonder (*in, with,* en); foisonner. **abounding,** *a.* Abondant.

about, *adv. & prep.* **1.** (*a*) Autour (de). (*b*) De côté et d'autre. *Don't leave those papers lying a.,* ne laissez pas traîner ces papiers. **About here,** par ici. (*c*) **There's something about a horse that . . . ,** il y a chez le cheval un je ne sais quoi qui. . . . (*d*) *To do sth.* **turn (and turn) about,** faire qch. à tour de rôle. **2. To turn sth. about,** retourner qch. *Mil:* **About turn!** demi-tour! **3.** Environ, presque. *There are a. thirty,* il y en a une trentaine. *That's about right,* c'est à peu près cela. *It is about time,* (i) il est presque temps; (ii) *Iron:* il est grand temps! *He came a. three o'clock,* il est venu vers trois heures. **4.** Au sujet de. **Much ado about nothing,** beaucoup de bruit pour rien. **About that,** là-dessus, à ce sujet. **What is it all about?** de quoi s'agit-il? *To speak a. sth.,* parler de qch. *F: What a. my bath?* et mon bain? **5.** (*a*) **To be about to do sth.,** être sur le point de faire qch. (*b*) **To go about one's task,** faire sa besogne. *This is how I go a. it,* voici comment je m'y prends. *What are you a.?* qu'est-ce que vous faites là? *You haven't been long a. it,* il ne vous a pas fallu longtemps (pour le faire). *While you are a. it,* pendant que vous y êtes.

above, *adv. & prep.* **1.** Au-dessus (de). (*a*) *The water reached a. their knees,* l'eau leur montait jusqu'au-dessus des genoux. (*b*) *To hover a. the town,* planer au-dessus de la ville. **A voice from above,** une voix d'en haut. (*c*) *His voice was heard a. the din,* on entendait sa voix par-dessus le tumulte. *The Seine basin a. Paris,* le bassin de la Seine à l'amont de Paris. (*d*) *You must show yourself a. prejudice,* il faut vous montrer supérieur aux préjugés. **Above all . . . ,** surtout . . . , par-dessus tout. . . . **2.** (*In book*) Ci-dessus. **As above,** comme ci-dessus. **3.** (*Of pers.*) *To be a.* (*all*) *suspicion,* être au-dessus de tout soupçon. **4.** *A. twenty,* plus de vingt. **above-board,** *a. His conduct was a.-b.,* sa conduite a été franche et ouverte. **above-mentioned, above-named,** *a.* Sus-mentionné, susnommé, susdit.

abrade, *v.tr.* User (qch.) par le frottement; écorcher (la peau).

abrasion, *s.* (Usure *f* par le) frottement *m*.

abreast, *adv.* (*a*) De front; sur la même ligne. (*b*) (*Of pers.*) *To walk a.,* marcher côte à côte. **To be abreast of the times,** être de son temps.

abridge, *v.tr.* Abréger.

abridg(e)ment, *s.* **1.** Diminution *f*; restriction *f*. **2.** Abrégé *m*, précis *m*, résumé *m*.

abroad, *adv.* **1.** A l'étranger. *From a.,* de l'étranger. **2.** Au loin. *Scattered a.,* éparpillé de tous côtés. *The news got a.,* la nouvelle se répandit.

abrogate, *v.tr.* Abroger (une loi).

abrogation, *s.* Abrogation *f*.

abrupt, *a.* **1.** (Personne) brusque; (départ) brusqué, précipité; (ton) cassant; (style) heurté, saccadé. **2.** *A. mountain,* montagne abrupte, escarpée. **-ly,** *adv.* **1.** Brusquement. **2.** Abruptement, à pic.

abruptness, *s.* **1.** (*a*) Brusquerie *f*. (*b*) Précipitation *f*. **2.** Raideur *f* (d'un sentier).

abscess, *s.* Abcès *m*.

abscond, *v.i.* Se soustraire à la justice; s'enfuir, s'évader.

absence, *s.* **1.** Absence *f*, éloignement *m*. **2. In the absence of definite information,** faute de, à défaut de, renseignements précis. **3.** Absence of mind, distraction *f*.

absent[1], *a.* (*a*) Absent. (*b*) Manquant. **absent-minded,** *a.* Distrait. **-ly,** *adv.* Distraitement; d'un air distrait. **absent-mindedness,** *s.* Distraction *f*.

absent[2], *v.pr. To a.* oneself, s'absenter.

absentee, *s.* (*a*) Absent *m*. (*b*) Manquant *m* (à l'appel).

absolute, *a.* (*a*) Absolu. *A. power,* pouvoir absolu, illimité. (*b*) Autoritaire; (ton) absolu. (*c*) *F: An a. knave,* un coquin achevé. *It's an a. scandal,* c'est un véritable scandale. **-ly,** *adv.* Absolument.

absolution, *s. Ecc:* Absolution *f*.

absolve, *v.tr.* **1.** Absoudre (qn d'un péché). **2.** Affranchir (qn d'un vœu).

absorb, *v.tr.* **1.** (*a*) Absorber (un liquide).

(b) *To a. a shock*, amortir un choc. **2.** *His business absorbs him*, ses affaires l'absorbent.

absorbing, *a.* Absorbant.

absorbent, *a. & s.* Absorbant (*m.*).

absorption, *s.* **1.** Absorption *f* (de chaleur). **2.** Absorbement *m* (de l'esprit).

abstain, *v.i.* S'abstenir (*from sth.*, de qch.).

abstainer, *s.* Buveur d'eau.

abstemious, *a.* Sobre, tempérant. **-ly,** *adv.* Frugalement.

abstemiousness, *s.* Sobriété *f*, tempérance *f.*

abstention, *s.* Abstention *f*, abstinence *f.*

abstinence, *s.* Abstinence *f.*

abstract[1]. **1.** *a.* Abstrait. **2.** *s.* **The abstract,** l'abstrait *m.*

abstract[2], *s.* Résumé *m*, abrégé *m.*

abstract[3], *v.tr.* **1.** Soustraire, dérober (*sth. from s.o.*, qch. à qn.). **2.** *Ch:* Extraire (par distillation). **abstracted,** *a.* Distrait; rêveur. **-ly,** *adv.* Distraitement.

abstraction, *s.* **1.** Soustraction *f* (de papiers); détournement *m.* **2.** (*a*) *Phil:* Abstraction *f.* (*b*) Idée abstraite. **3.** *A. of mind*, distraction *f*, préoccupation *f.*

abstruse, *a.* Abstrus.

absurd, *a.* Absurde: déraisonnable. **-ly,** *adv.* Absurdement.

absurdity, *s.* Absurdité *f.*

abundance, *:.* Abondance *f*, affluence *f.* *In abundance*, en abondance, *F:* à foison.

abundant, *a.* Abondant; copieux. **-ly,** *adv.* Abondamment; copieusement.

abuse[1], *s.* **1.** (*a*) Abus *m.* (*b*) *To remedy an a.,* redresser un abus. (*c*) Emploi abusif (d'un terme). **2.** Insultes *fpl*, injures *fpl.*

abuse[2], *v.tr.* **1.** Abuser (de son autorité); mésuser (de son pouvoir). **2.** (*a*) Médire de (qn); dénigrer (qn). (*b*) Injurier; dire des injures à (qn).

abusive, *a.* (Propos) injurieux; (homme) grossier. **-ly,** *adv.* Injurieusement.

abut, *v.i. & tr.* **1.** *Our fields a.,* nos champs sont attenants. **2.** *Const: To a. on, against* (*a wall*), s'appuyer, buter, contre (une paroi).

abutting, *a.* Aboutissant, attenant (*on*, à).

abutment, *s* (*a*) Arc-boutant *m*; contrefort *m.* (*b*) Butée *f*, culée *f* (d'un pont).

abysmal, *a.* Sans fond; insondable.

abyss, *s.* Abîme *m.*, gouffre *m*

Abyssinia. *Pr.n.* L'Éthiopie *f*; 'Abyssinie *f.*

Abyssinian, *a & s.* Éthiopien abyssinien

acacia, *s Bot:* Acacia *m*

academic, *a.* Académique. (*a*) *A. discussion,* discussion abstraite (*b*) (Carrière) universitaire

academical, *a.* Universitaire

academician, *s.* Académicien *m.*

academy, *s* **1.** *Gr.Phil:* L'Académie *f* (de Platon). **2.** (*a*) Académie. *Fencing a.,* salle *f* d'escrime. (*b*) **Military Academy,** École *f* militaire.

acanthus, *s.* Acanthe *f.*

accede, *v.i.* **1.** *To a. to the throne,* monter sur le trône. **2.** *To a. to a request,* accueillir une demande.

accelerate. **1.** *v.tr.* Accélérer (la marche); précipiter (les événements); activer (un travail). **2.** *v.i.* (*Of motion*) S'accélérer.

accelerating, *a.* Accélérateur, -trice.

acceleration, *s.* Accélération *f.*

accelerator, *a. & s.* Accélérateur, -trice.

accent[1], *s.* Accent *m.* **1.** (*a*) *To have a German a.,* avoir l'accent allemand. (*b*) *In broken accents,* d'une voix brisée. **2.** *Grammatical accents,* accents grammaticaux.

accent[2], *v.tr.* Accentuer (une syllabe); appuyer sur (une syllabe).

accentuate, *v.tr.* Accentuer, appuyer sur (un détail). **accentuated,** *a.* Accentué.

accentuation, *s.* Accentuation *f.*

accept, *v.tr. & ind.tr.* Accepter (un cadeau); agréer (les prières de qn); admettre (les excuses de qn). *The accepted custom,* l'usage admis.

acceptable, *a.* Acceptable, agréable.

acceptance, *s.* Acceptation *f*; consentement *m* à recevoir (qch.). *A. of a proposal,* agrément donné à une proposition.

acceptation, *s.* Acception *f.* (d'un mot).

access, *s.* **1.** Accès *m*, abord *m.* **Difficult of access,** d'un accès difficile. **Easy of access,** abordable. **To have access to s.o.,** avoir accès auprès de qn. **2.** *A. of fever,* accès de fièvre.

accessible, *a.* **1.** (Endroit) accessible, approchable. **2.** (*Of pers.*) Accueillant.

accession, *s.* **1.** *A. of light,* admission *f* de lumière. **2.** (*a*) *A. to one's income,* augmentation *f* de revenus. (*b*) Adhésion *f* (à un parti). **3.** *A. to power,* accession *f* au pouvoir. *A. to the throne,* avènement *m* au trône.

accessory. **1.** *a.* Accessoire, subsidiaire (*to,* à). **2.** *s.* Accessoire *m* (d'une machine). *Toilet accessories,* objets *m*, ustensiles *m*, de toilette. **3.** *s. & pred. a. A. to a crime,* complice *m* d'un crime.

accidence, *s.* *Gram:* Morphologie *f.*

accident, *s.* (*a*) Accident *m.* **By accident,** accidentellement. **By a mere accident,** par pur hasard. (*b*) *Serious a.,* accident grave.

accidental. **1.** *a.* (*a*) Accidentel, fortuit. (*b*) Accessoire. **2.** *s. Mus:* Accident *m.* **-ally,** *adv* Accidentellement; par hasard, fortuitement.

acclaim, *v.tr* Acclamer.

acclamation, *s.* Acclamation *f.*

acclimatization, *s* Acclimatation *f.*

acclimatize, *v.tr* Acclimater. **To become acclimatized,** s'acclimater.

acclivity, *s.* Montée *f*, côte *f*; rampe *f.*

accommodate, *v.tr.* **1.** (*a*) Accommoder, approprier. *To a. oneself to circumstances,* s'accommoder aux circonstances. (*b*) Ajuster, adapter (qch. à qch.). **2. To accommodate s.o,** accommoder, servir, obliger, qn. **3.** Loger, recevoir (tant de personnes).

accommodating, *a.* Complaisant, serviable, accommodant.

accommodation, *s.* **1.** (*a*) Ajustement *m*, adaptation *f* (*to,* à). (*b*) Accommodement *m*,

ajustement (d'une dispute). **2.** (*a*) Commodité *f*, facilités *fpl*. (*b*) Logement *m*. (*c*) Avance *f*, prêt *m* (d'argent).
accompaniment, *s*. (*a*) Accompagnement *m*; accessoires *mpl*. (*b*) *Mus:* Accompagnement (au piano).
accompanist, *s*. *Mus:* Accompagnateur, -trice.
accompany, *v.tr.* Accompagner.
accomplice, *s.* Complice *mf*.
accomplish, *v.tr.* Accomplir, achever (qch.). *To a. one's object,* atteindre son but. **accomplished,** *a.* (*a*) (Musicien) accompli, achevé. (*b*) Qui possède de nombreux talents.
accomplishment, *s.* **1.** Accomplissement *m*, consommation *f* (d'une tâche). **Difficult of accomplishment,** difficile à réaliser. **2.** *Usu.pl.* Art(s) *m* d'agrément.
accord[1], *s.* **1.** Accord *m*, consentement *m*. **With one accord,** d'un commun accord. **2. To do sth. of one's own accord,** faire qch. de son plein gré.
accord[2]. **1.** *v.i.* S'accorder, être d'accord (*with*, avec). **2.** *v.tr.* Accorder, concéder.
according, *adv.* **1.** *Conj.phr.* **According as,** selon que, suivant que, + *ind.* **2.** *Prep.phr.* (*a*) **According to the orders,** selon les ordres. *A. to age,* par rang d'âge. (*b*) **According to him,** d'après lui; à l'en croire. **According to that,** d'après cela. **-ly,** *adv.* **1. To act accordingly,** agir en conséquence. **2.** (*Therefore*) *A. I wrote to him,* je lui ai donc écrit.
accordance, *s.* Accord *m*, conformité *f*.
accordion, *s.* Accordéon *m*.
accost, *v.tr.* Accoster, aborder.
account[1], *s.* **1.** (*a*) Compte *m*, note *f*. **Current account,** compte courant. *My bank a.,* mon compte en banque. **To keep the accounts,** tenir les livres, les comptes. *To pay a sum on account,* payer un acompte. (*b*) Exposé *m*, état *m*, note. (*c*) **To turn sth. to account,** tirer parti de qch.; faire valoir qch. (*d*) **To call s.o. to account,** demander une explication à qn; prendre qn à partie (d'avoir fait qch.). *F: He gave quite a good a. of himself,* il s'est bien acquitté. **2.** (*a*) (*Person*) **of some account,** (personne) qui compte. **To make much account of sth.,** faire grand cas de qch. **To be of some a.,** être (tenu) en grande estime. **To take sth. into account,** tenir compte de qch. (*b*) **On account of s.o.,** à cause de qn. *I was nervous on his a.,* j'avais peur pour lui. **On account of sth.,** à cause de qch. **On every account,** sous tous les rapports. **On no account, not on any account,** dans aucun cas, pour rien au monde. (*c*) **To act on one's own account,** agir de sa propre initiative. **3. To give an account of sth.,** faire le récit de qch. **By all accounts,** au dire de tout le monde.
account[2], *v.tr. & ind.tr.* **1.** *Pred.* **To account oneself lucky,** s'estimer heureux. **2.** (*a*) **To account for (sth.),** rendre raison de, justifier (de) (sa conduite); expliquer (une circonstance). (*b*) *I can't a. for it,* je n'y comprends

rien. (*c*) *F:* **To account for** (= *kill*) s.o., faire son affaire à qn.
accountable, *a.* *To be a. for a sum of money,* être redevable d'une somme d'argent. *Not a. for one's actions,* irresponsable.
accountancy, *s.* **1.** Comptabilité *f*. **2.** Tenue *f* des livres.
accountant, *s.* Comptable *m*.
accoutrement(s), *s.(pl.)* Équipement *m* (du soldat).
accredit, *v.tr.* Accréditer (qn, qch.).
accredited, *a.* *A.* opinions, opinions reçues.
accretion, *s.* (*a*) Accroissement *m* organique. (*b*) Accroissement par addition.
accrue, *v.i.* **1.** (*a*) Provenir, dériver (*from*, de). (*b*) *To a. to s.o.,* revenir à qn. **2.** (*Of interest*) S'accumuler.
accumulate. **1.** *v.tr.* Accumuler, amasser. **2.** *v.i.* S'accumuler, s'amonceler.
accumulation, *s.* **1.** Accumulation *f*, amoncellement *m*. **2.** Amas *m*, monceau *m*.
accumulator, *s.* Accumulateur *m*.
accuracy, *s.* Exactitude *f*; précision *f*.
accurate, *a.* Exact, juste, précis. *To take a. aim,* viser juste. **-ly,** *adv.* Exactement, avec précision.
accursed, *a.* *Lit:* **1.** Maudit. **2.** *F:* Maudit, exécrable, détestable.
accusation, *s.* Accusation *f*.
accusative, *a. & s.* (Cas) accusatif *m*.
accuse, *v.tr.* Accuser (*s.o. of sth.,* qn de qch.).
accused, *s.* *Jur:* **The accused,** le, la, prévenu(e).
accuser, *s.* Accusateur, -trice.
accustom, *v.tr.* Accoutumer, habituer (*s.o. to sth.,* qn à qch.). *To a. oneself to discipline,* se faire à la discipline. **accustomed,** *a.* **1.** Accoutumé, habitué (*to*, à). **To get accustomed to sth.,** s'accoutumer à qch.; se faire à qch. **2.** Habituel, coutumier.
ace, *s.* As *m*. *F:* **Within an ace of sth.,** à deux doigts de qch.
acerbity, *s.* Acerbité *f*; âpreté *f* (de ton).
acetate, *s.* *Ch:* Acétate *m*.
acetic, *a.* *Ch:* Acétique.
acetylene, *s.* *Ch:* Acétylène *m*.
ache[1], *s.* Mal *m*, douleur *f*. *Headache,* mal de tête. *I have a headache,* j'ai mal à la tête.
ache[2], *v.i.* **My head aches,** j'ai mal à la tête. **It makes my heart ache,** cela me serre le cœur. **aching,** *a.* Douloureux, endolori.
achieve, *v.tr.* **1.** Accomplir (un exploit); réaliser (une entreprise). **2.** Acquérir (de l'honneur). **3.** Atteindre (à) (un but). *To a. victory,* remporter la victoire. *He will never a. anything,* il n'arrivera jamais à rien.
achievement, *s.* **1.** Accomplissement *m*, réalisation *f* (d'un projet). **2.** Exploit *m*, (haut) fait.
Achilles. *Pr.n.m.* Achille.
acid. **1.** *a.* (*a*) Acide. **Acid drops,** bonbons acidulés. (*b*) Revêche, aigre. **2.** *s.* Acide *m*.
acidity, *s.* Acidité *f*.
acknowledge, *v.tr.* **1.** Reconnaître, avouer

(qch.); reconnaître (qn). *He was acknowledged as king*, il fut reconnu pour roi. *To a. oneself beaten*, s'avouer vaincu. **2.** Répondre à (un salut). **To acknowledge (receipt of) a letter**, accuser réception d'une lettre.

acknowledg(e)ment, *s.* **1.** (*a*) Reconnaissance *f* (d'un bienfait). Reçu *m* (d'un payement). **Acknowledgement of receipt**, accusé *m* de réception (d'une lettre). (*b*) Aveu *m* (d'une faute). **2. Acknowledgements**, remerciements *mpl.*

acme, *s.* Plus haut point (de la perfection); sommet *m*, apogée *m* (de la puissance).

acolyte, *s. Ecc. & F:* Acolyte *m.*

aconite, *s. Bot:* Aconit *m.*

acorn, *s. Bot:* Gland *m* (du chêne).

acoustic(al), *a.* Acoustique.

acoustics, *s.pl.* Acoustique *f.*

acquaint, *v.tr.* **1. To acquaint s.o. with sth.**, of a fact, informer qn de qch.; faire savoir qch. à qn. **2.** (*a*) **To be acquainted with s.o.**, connaître qn. (*b*) **To become acquainted with s.o.**, lier connaissance avec qn.

acquaintance, *s.* **1.** Connaissance *f* (*with*, de). (*a*) *His a. with the classical tongues*, sa connaissance des langues classiques. (*b*) *To make a. with s.o.*, faire connaissance avec qn. *He improves upon acquaintance*, il gagne à être connu. **2.** (*Pers.*) Connaissance. **To have a wide circle of acquaintances**, avoir des relations très étendues.

acquaintanceship, *s.* Relations *fpl*, rapports *mpl.*

acquiesce, *v.i.* Acquiescer (à une demande); donner son assentiment (*in*, à).

acquiescence, *s.* **1.** Acquiescement *m* (*in*, à); assentiment *m.* **2.** Soumission *f* (*in*, à).

acquiescent, *a.* Disposé à acquiescer; consentant.

acquire, *v.tr.* Acquérir (qch.). *To a. a habit*, prendre une habitude.

acquirement, *s.* **1.** Acquisition *f.* **2.** (*a*) Talent (acquis). (*b*) *pl.* Connaissances *f pl.*

acquisition, *s.* Acquisition *f.*

acquisitive, *a.* Apre au gain.

acquit, *v.tr.* **1.** Acquitter (un accusé). **To acquit s.o. of sth.**, absoudre qn de qch. **2.** *To a. oneself of a duty*, s'acquitter d'un devoir.

acquittal, *s.* **1.** Acquittement *m* (d'un accusé). **2.** Exécution *f* (d'un devoir).

acre, *s. Meas:* Acre *f.*

acrid, *a.* **1.** (Goût) âcre. **2.** (Style) mordant; (critique) acerbe. **-ly,** *adv.* Avec âcreté; avec acerbité.

acridity, *s.* Acreté *f.*

acrimonious, *a.* Acrimonieux, atrabilaire. **-ly,** *adv.* Avec acrimonie.

acrimony, *s.* Acrimonie *f*; aigreur *f*

acrobat, *s.* Acrobate *mf.*

acrobatic, *a.* Acrobatique.

across, *adv. & prep.* En travers (de). **1.** (*a*) **To walk across (a street)**, traverser (une rue). *To go a. a bridge*, franchir un pont.

(*b*) **To lay sth. across (sth.)**, mettre qch. en travers (de qch.). (*c*) **To come across a person**, rencontrer (par hasard) une personne. **2.** (*a*) **The distance across**, la distance en largeur. *The river is a mile a.*, le fleuve a un mille de large. (*b*) **He lives across the street**, il demeure de l'autre côté de la rue.

acrostic, *a. & s.* Acrostiche (*m*).

act[1]**,** *s.* **1.** Acte *m.* (*a*) **Act of kindness**, acte de bonté. (*b*) **Act of Parliament**, loi *f*, décret *m.* **2.** Action *f. An act of folly*, une folie. **To catch s.o. in the act**, prendre qn sur le fait. **3.** *Th:* Acte (d'une pièce).

act[2]**. 1.** *v.tr.* (*a*) **To act a play**, jouer une pièce. *To act a part*, remplir un rôle. *To act the ass*, faire l'imbécile. (*b*) **He was only acting**, il faisait semblant. (*c*) **To act the part of an honest man**, agir en honnête homme. **2.** *v.i.* Agir. (*a*) **He did not know how to act**, il ne savait quel parti prendre. *I acted for the best*, j'ai fait pour le mieux. **To act for s.o.**, représenter qn. *To act upon advice*, suivre un avis. (*b*) **The pump is not acting well**, la pompe ne marche pas bien. *The engine acts as a brake*, le moteur fait fonction de frein. (*c*) **To act (up)on the brain**, agir sur le cerveau. (*d*) *Th: Cin:* Jouer. **acting**[1]**,** *a.* Remplissant les fonctions de. . . . *Lieutenant a. captain*, lieutenant faisant fonction de capitaine. **acting**[2]**,** *s.* **1.** Action *f.* **2.** (*a*) Jeu *m* (d'un acteur); production *f* (d'une pièce de théâtre). (*b*) *To go in for a.*, faire du théâtre. (*c*) *F:* **It is mere acting**, c'est de la comédie.

actinic, *a. Ph:* Actinique.

action, *s.* **1.** Action *f* (d'une personne). **To take action**, agir; prendre des mesures. **To suit the action to the word**, joindre le geste à la parole. **To come into action**, entrer en action, en jeu. **Out of action**, hors de service. **To put (sth.) out of action**, détraquer, mettre en panne (une machine). **2.** (*Deed*) Action, acte *m*, fait *m.* **3.** *Th:* Action (d'une pièce). **4.** (*a*) Action, gestes *mpl* (d'un joueur). (*b*) Mécanisme *m* (d'une montre). **5.** *Jur:* **To bring an action against s.o.**, intenter une action, un procès, à, contre, qn. **6.** Action, combat *m.* **To go into action**, engager le combat; donner. **Killed in action**, tué à l'ennemi.

active, *a.* **1.** Actif; agile, alerte. *A. volcano*, volcan en activité. *A. brain*, cerveau éveillé. *A. imagination*, imagination vive. **2.** *Gram:* Verb in the active voice, verbe à l'actif. **3. To take an active part in sth.**, prendre une part active à qch. **4.** *Mil:* **To be on the active list**, être en activité. *On a. service*, en campagne.

activity, *s.* Activité *f.*

actor, *s.* Acteur *m.*

actress, *s.* Actrice *f.*

actual, *a.* **1.** Réel, véritable. *It's an a. fact*, c'est un fait positif. **2.** (*Present*) Actuel, présent. **-ally,** *adv.* **1.** (*a*) Réellement, véritablement, positivement. *He a. swore*, il alla (même) jusqu'à lâcher un juron. **2.** Actuellement, à présent.

actuality, *s.* (*a*) Réalité *f.* (*b*) Actualité *f.*

actuary, *s.* *Ins:* Actuaire *m.*

actuate, *v.tr.* **1.** Mettre en action, actionner (une machine). **2.** *Actuated by jealousy*, poussé par la jalousie.

acumen, *s.* Pénétration *f*, finesse *f* (d'esprit).

acute, *a.* **1.** (Angle) aigu. **2.** (Son) aigu ; (douleur) aiguë, intense ; vif. **3.** (*a*) *Acute ear*, oreille fine, ouïe fine. *A. sight*, vue perçante. (*b*) (Esprit) fin, pénétrant. **-ly,** *adv.* Vivement ; intensément.

acuteness, *s.* **1.** Aiguité *f* (d'un angle). **2.** Acuité *f* (d'une douleur). **3.** (*a*) Finesse *f* (d'ouïe) ; acuité (de la vision). (*b*) Pénétration *f*, perspicacité *f* (de l'esprit).

adage, *s.* Adage *m* ; maxime *f.*

Adam. *Pr.n.m.* Adam. **Adam's apple,** pomme *f* d'Adam.

adamant, *s.* **1.** Aimant *m.* **2.** *On this point he is a.*, sur ce point il ne transige pas.

adapt, *v.tr.* Adapter, ajuster, approprier (*sth. to sth.*, qch. à qch.). **adapted,** *a.* *A. to sth.*, approprié à, fait pour, qch.

adaptability, *s.* Faculté *f* d'adaptation.

adaptable, *a.* **1.** (*a*) Adaptable, ajustable. (*b*) Susceptible d'être utilisé. **2.** *A. person*, personne qui s'accommode à toutes les circonstances.

adaptation, *s.* Adaptation *f.*

adapter, *s.* **1.** Auteur *m* d'une adaptation. **2.** *El:* Raccord *m* (de lampe).

add, *v.tr.* **1.** (*a*) Ajouter, joindre (*to*, à). *This news adds to our joy*, cette nouvelle augmente notre joie. *Added to which . . .*, en outre de quoi. . . (*b*) (*Say besides*) Ajouter. *He added that . . .*, il ajouta que. . . . **2.** *Ar:* *To add (together) ten numbers*, additionner dix nombres. **adding-machine,** *s.* Additionneuse *f* ; totalisateur *m.*

adder, *s.* Vipère *f.* *Young a.*, vipereau *m.*

addict[1]**,** *s.* Personne adonnée à (l'opium). *Morphia addict*, morphinomane.

addict[2]**,** *v.tr.* *To be addicted to drink*, s'adonner, se livrer à la boisson.

addiction, *s.* *A. to study, good*, attachement *m* à l'étude, penchant *m* au bien.

addition, *s.* **1.** Addition *f. A welcome a. to my salary*, un heureux surcroît d'appointements. *In addition*, en outre, de plus, par surcroît. **2.** *Mth:* Addition.

additional, *a.* Additionnel, supplémentaire. *A. reason*, raison de plus. **-ally,** *adv.* En outre (*to*, de).

addle[1]**,** *a.* **1.** (Œuf) pourri, gâté, couvi. **2.** *F:* (Cerveau) brouillé. **Addle-pate,** *s.* (homme) écervelé.

addle[2]**.** *v.tr.* (*a*) Pourrir, gâter (un œuf). (*b*) *F:* Troubler, brouiller (le cerveau).

address[1]**,** *s.* **1.** Adresse *f*, habileté *f.* **2.** Adresse (d'une lettre). **3.** (*a*) Abord *m. Young man of good a.*, jeune homme qui se présente bien. (*b*) **To pay one's addresses to a lady,** faire la cour à une femme. **4.** Discours *m.* **5.** Form of address, titre *m.*

address[2]**,** *v.tr.* **1.** (*a*) *To a. a letter to s.o.*, adresser une lettre à qn. (*b*) **To address a letter,** mettre, écrire, l'adresse sur une lettre. **2. To address s.o.**, (i) aborder, accoster, qn ; (ii) adresser la parole à qn. **3.** *Golf:* Viser (la balle). **4. To address oneself to a task,** se mettre à une tâche.

addressee, *s.* Destinataire *mf.*

adduce, *v.tr.* Alléguer, apporter (des preuves) ; citer (une autorité).

adenoids, *s.pl.* Végétations *f* adénoïdes.

adept. **1.** *a.* *To be a. in sth.*, être expert, habile, à qch. **2.** *s.* Adepte *mf* ; expert *m* (*in*, en).

adequacy, *s.* Suffisance *f* ; justesse *f.*

adequate, *a.* **1.** Suffisant. *A. reward*, juste récompense. *A. help*, aide efficace. **2.** *He is a. to the task*, il est à la hauteur de la tâche. **-ly,** *adv.* Suffisamment, en juste proportion.

adhere, *v.i.* **1.** (*Of thg*) Adhérer, se coller. **2.** (*Of pers.*) (*a*) **To adhere to a proposal,** adhérer à une proposition. (*b*) **To adhere to one's decision,** persister dans sa décision.

adherence, *s.* **1.** (*Of thg*) Adhérence *f*, adhésion *f.* **2.** (*Of pers.*) Attachement *m* (à un parti).

adherent. **1.** *a.* Adhérent. **2.** *s.* Adhérent, -e, partisan, -e.

adhesion, *s.* Adhésion *f* ; approbation *f* (d'un projet).

adhesive, *a.* **1.** Adhésif, collant. **2.** *Mec:* *A. capacity*, pouvoir adhérent.

adieu. **1.** *int.* Adieu ! **2.** *s.* **To bid s.o. adieu,** dire adieu, faire ses adieux, à qn.

adipose, *a.* Adipeux.

adjacent, *a.* (Angle, terrain) adjacent ; attenant.

adjectival, *a.* *Gram:* Adjectif. **-ally,** *adv.* Adjectivement.

adjective, *s.* Adjectif *m.*

adjoin. **1.** *v.tr.* Avoisiner (un lieu) ; toucher à (qch.). **2.** *v.i.* *The two houses adjoin*, les deux maisons se touchent. **adjoining,** *a.* (*a*) Contigu, -uë ; avoisinant. (*b*) *The a. room*, la pièce voisine.

adjourn. **1.** *v.tr.* *To a. sth. for a week*, ajourner, renvoyer, qch. à huitaine. **2.** *v.i.* (*Of meeting*) S'ajourner (*until*, à).

adjournment, *s.* (*a*) Ajournement *m*, suspension *f* (d'une séance). (*b*) Renvoi *m*, remise *f* (d'une affaire).

adjudge, *v.tr.* **1.** Prononcer sur, juger (une querelle). **2.** *Pred.* *To adjudge s.o. guilty*, déclarer qn coupable. **3.** *To adjudge a prize to s.o.*, décerner une récompense à qn.

adjudicate, *v.tr. & i.* Juger, décider (une affaire).

adjudication, *s.* Jugement *m*, arrêt *m.*

adjudicator, *s.* Arbitre *m* ; juge *m.*

adjunct, *s.* **1.** (*Pers.*) Adjoint *m* (*to*, de) ; auxiliaire *mf.* (*b*) (*Thg*) Accessoire *m.* **2.** *Gram:* Complément *m.*

adjure, *v.tr.* To a. s.o. to do sth., adjurer, conjurer qn de faire qch.

adjust, *v.tr.* **1.** Arranger (une affaire). **2.** (a) Ajuster (qch. à qch.). To a. oneself to new conditions, s'adapter aux conditions nouvelles. (b) Régler (une montre). (c) Ajuster, arranger (son chapeau).

adjustable, *a.* Mec.E: Ajustable, réglable.

adjustment, *s.* **1.** Ajustement *m* (d'un différend) ; arrangement *m* (d'une affaire). **2.** Ajustement (d'une balance) ; réglage *m* (d'un mécanisme).

adjutant, *s.* Mil: Adjudant major.

administer, *v.tr.* (a) Administrer, régir (un pays) ; gérer (des biens). To administer justice, dispenser la justice. (b) Administrer (un médicament). To administer an oath to s.o., assermenter qn.

administration, *s.* (a) Administration *f*, gestion *f* (d'une fortune). (b) Administration (de la justice).

administrative, *a.* Administratif.

administrator, *s.* Administrateur *m* ; gestionnaire *m*.

admirable, *a.* Admirable. **-ably,** *adv.* Admirablement.

admiral, *s.* Amiral *m*, pl. -aux.

admiralty, *s.* The Admiralty, l'Amirauté *f* ; le Ministère de la Marine.

admiration, *s.* Admiration *f*.

admire, *v.tr.* Admirer. **admiring,** *a.* (Regard) admiratif. **-ly,** *adv.* Avec admiration.

admirer, *s.* (a) Admirateur, -trice. (b) Adorateur, -trice, soupirant *m* (d'une femme).

admissible, *a.* (Idée) admissible.

admission, *s.* **1.** Admission *f*, accès *m* (à un emploi). Admission free, entrée libre. **2.** (a) Admission (d'une preuve). (b) Confession *f* (d'un crime) ; aveu *m*.

admit, *v.* **1.** *v.tr.* (a) Admettre (qn à qch.) ; laisser entrer ; livrer passage à (qn). 'Admit bearer,' "laissez passer." (b) Admettre (des excuses) ; reconnaître (sa faute). To a. one's guilt, s'avouer coupable. Let it be admitted, avouons-le ! (c) To a. a claim, accueillir une réclamation. **2.** v.ind.tr. It admits of no doubt, cela ne permet aucun doute.

admitted, *a.* A. custom, usage admis. **-ly,** *adv.* A. incorrect, reconnu (pour) incorrect.

admittance, *s.* Entrée *f* (to, dans) ; accès *m* (to, à, auprès de). No admittance, entrée interdite.

admixture, *s.* Mélange *m*.

admonish, *v.tr.* (a) Admonester, reprendre (qn). (b) Exhorter (qn à faire qch.).

admonition, *s.* Remontrance *f*, admonestation *f*.

admonitory, *a.* (Lettre) de remontrances.

ado, *s.* **1.** Agitation *f* ; bruit *m*. Without (any) more ado, sans plus de façons. **2.** Difficulté *f*, peine *f*.

adolescence, *s.* Adolescence *f*.

adolescent, *a.* & *s.* Adolescent, -te.

adopt, *v.tr.* **1.** Adopter (un enfant). **2.** Adopter (une ligne de conduite) ; choisir (une carrière). **adopted,** *a.* A. son, fils adoptif.

adoption, *s.* Adoption *f* (d'un enfant) ; choix *m* (d'une carrière).

adorable, *a.* Adorable. **-ably,** *adv.* Adorablement.

adoration, *s.* Adoration *f*.

adore, *v.tr.* Adorer.

adorer, *s.* Adorateur, -trice.

adorn, *v.tr.* Orner, parer (with, de).

adornment, *s.* Ornement *m*, parure *f*.

Adriatic, *a.* & *s.* (La mer) Adriatique.

adrift, *adv.* Nau: A la dérive. F: To turn s.o. adrift, mettre qn sur le pavé. To cut a boat adrift, couper l'amarre.

adroit, *a.* Adroit ; habile. **-ly,** *adv.* Adroitement.

adroitness, *s.* Adresse *f*, dextérité *f*.

adulation, *s.* Adulation *f*, flatterie *f*.

adult, *a.* & *s.* Adulte (mf).

adulterate, *v.tr.* Adultérer (une substance) ; frelater (du vin).

adulteration, *s.* Adultération *f* ; frelatage *m* (des boissons).

adulterer, *s.* Adultère *mf*.

adultery, *s.* Adultère *m*.

advance[1], *s.* **1.** (a) Marche *f* en avant ; mouvement *m* en avant. To make an advance, avancer. Mil: Advance guard, avant-garde *f*. (b) To arrive in a., arriver en avance. To pay in a., payer d'avance. **2.** Avancement *m*, progrès *m* (des sciences). **3.** To make advances to s.o., faire des avances *f* à, auprès de qn. **4.** Com: Avance (de fonds). (b) Augmentation *f* (de prix) ; hausse *f*.

advance[2]. **I.** *v.tr.* **1.** (a) Avancer (le pied). (b) Avancer (l'heure d'un payement). (c) Avancer (une opinion). **2.** (a) Faire avancer (les sciences). **3.** Augmenter, hausser. **4.** To a. s.o. money, avancer de l'argent à qn. **II. advance,** *v.i.* **1.** S'avancer (of troops) se porter en avant. **2.** (a) The work is advancing, l'ouvrage avance. (b) (Of officers) Recevoir de l'avancement. **3.** Augmenter de prix ; hausser. **advanced,** *a.* (a) (Poste) avancé. (b) A. mathematics, mathématiques supérieures

advancement, *s.* Avancement *m* ; progrès *m*.

advantage, *s.* Avantage *m*. To have the advantage of numbers, avoir l'avantage du nombre. To take advantage of sth. profiter de qch. To take a. of s.o., exploiter qn. To turn sth. to advantage, tirer parti de qch. To show off sth. to advantage, faire valoir qch.

advantageous, *a.* Avantageux (to, pour) ; profitable. **-ly,** *adv.* Avantageusement.

advent, *s.* **1.** Ecc: Avent *m*. **2.** Arrivée *f* ; venue *f*.

adventitious, *a.* Adventice. (a) (Fait) accessoire. (b) Accidentel, fortuit.

adventure[1], *s.* Aventure *f.* (*a*) Entreprise hasardeuse. (*b*) Événement *m* (qui arrive à qn).

adventure[2], *v.tr.* Aventurer, hasarder.

adventurer, *s.* Aventurier *m.* *Pej:* Chevalier *m* d'industrie.

adventuress, *s.* Aventurière *f*; intrigante *f.*

adventurous, *a.* Aventureux.

adverb, *s.* *Gram:* Adverbe *m.*

adverbial, *a.* *Gram:* Adverbial, -aux.

adversary, *s.* Adversaire *m.*

adverse, *a.* Adverse. (*a*) Contraire, opposé. *A. wind*, vent contraire. (*b*) Ennemi (*to*, de); hostile (*to*, à, envers). (*c*) Défavorable. **-ly**, *adv.* (*a*) *To act a. to s.o.*, agir (tout) au contraire de qn. (*b*) *To influence s.o. a.*, exercer une influence défavorable sur qn.

adversity, *s.* Adversité *f*, infortune *f.*

advert, *v.i.* *To a. to sth.*, faire allusion à qch.

advertise, *v.tr. & i.* (*a*) (i) (Faire) annoncer, (un événement); (ii) afficher (une vente). (*b*) Faire de la réclame, de la publicité pour (un produit). *Abs.* Faire de la réclame.

advertising, *s.* Publicité *f*, réclame *f.*

advertisement, *s.* **1.** Publicité *f.* **2.** (*a*) (*In newspaper*) Annonce *f.* (*b*) (*On a wall*) Affiche *f.*

advertiser, *s.* Auteur *m* de l'annonce.

advice, *s.* **1.** Conseil(s) *m(pl)*, avis *m.* **Piece of advice**, conseil. **To ask for advice**, demander des conseils. **2.** Avis.

advisability, *s.* Opportunité *f.*

advisable, *a.* **1.** (Démarche) recommandable, judicieuse. **2.** Opportun; convenable. *It might be a. to . . .*, peut-être conviendrait-il de. . . .

advise, *v.tr.* **1.** (*a*) *To a. s.o.*, conseiller qn. *To a. s.o. to do sth.*, conseiller à qn de faire qch. (*b*) *To a. sth.*, recommander qch. (à qn). **2. To advise s.o. on a question**, renseigner qn sur une question. **3. To advise s.o. of sth.**, avertir, instruire, qn de qch.

advisedly, *adv.* De propos délibéré; à dessein.

adviser, *s.* Conseiller *m.*

advisory, *a.* Consultatif.

advocacy, *s.* *A. of a cause*, appui donné à une cause.

advocate[1], *s.* **1.** *Jur:* Avocat *m.* **2.** Défenseur *m* (d'une doctrine).

advocate[2], *v.tr.* Préconiser.

adze, *s.* *Tls:* (H)erminette *f*; doloire *f.*

Aegean, *a. & s.* *Geog:* (La mer) Égée.

aegis, *s.* Égide *f.*

Aeolian, *a.* Aeolian harp, harpe éolienne.

aeon, *s.* Durée *f* (de l'univers); éternité *f.*

aerate, *v.tr.* **1.** Aérer. **2.** Gazéifier (`l'eau). **aerated**, *a.* (*a*) (Pain) aéré. (*b*) (Eau) gazeuse.

aeration, *s.* Aération *f.*

aerial. **1.** *a.* Aérien. **2.** *s.* *W.Tel:* Antenne *f.*

aerodrome, *s.* Aérodrome *m.*

aerolite, aerolith, *s.* Aérolithe *m.*

aeronaut, *s.* Aéronaute *m.*

aeronautic(al), *a.* Aéronautique.

aeroplane, *s.* Aéroplane *m*; avion *m.*

Aesop. *Pr.n.m.* *Gr.Lit:* Ésope.

aesthete, *s.* Esthète *mf.*

aesthetic(al), *a.* **1.** Esthétique. **2.** *F:* De bon goût.

afar, *adv.* From afar, de loin: **Afar off**, au loin; éloigné.

affability, *s.* Affabilité *f*; aménité *f.*

affable, *a.* Affable, courtois (*to*, envers). **-ably**, *adv.* Avec affabilité.

affair, *s.* Affaire *f.* **That is my affair**, ça, c'est mon affaire. *The affairs of this world*, les choses *f* de ce monde.

affect[1], *v.tr.* **1.** (*a*) Affecter (une forme). (*b*) Affecter (une manière). (*c*) Simuler (la piété). *To a. stupidity*, faire la bête. **2.** (*Of animals*) Fréquenter (une région). **affected**[1], *a.* (*a*) Affecté, maniéré. (*b*) Simulé. **-ly**, *adv.* Avec affectation.

affect[2], *v.tr.* **1.** Atteindre, attaquer (qn); affecter (un organe); influer sur (qch.). *The climate has affected his health*, le climat a altéré sa santé. **It affects me personally**, cela me touche personnellement. **2.** Affecter, affliger, toucher (qn). **3.** Toucher, concerner (qn, qch.). *That does not a. the matter*, cela ne fait rien à l'affaire. **affected**[2], *a.* (*a*) *To be well a. towards s.o.*, être bien disposé pour qn. (*b*) *The lung is a.*, le poumon est atteint. (*c*) Ému, touché. **affecting**, *a.* Touchant, attendrissant.

affectation, *s.* **1.** *A. of interest*, affectation *f*, simulation *f*, d'intérêt. **2.** Affectation (de langage).

affection, *s.* **1.** Impression (ressentie). **2.** Affection *f*; attachement *m.* **To win s.o.'s affection**, se faire aimer de qn. **3.** *Med:* Affection (de poitrine).

affectionate, *a.* Affectueux. *Your a. son*, votre fils affectionné. **-ly**, *adv.* Affectueusement.

affidavit, *s.* *Jur:* Déclaration *f.* sous serment.

affiliate, *v.tr.* Affilier.

affiliation, *s.* Affiliation *f* (à une société).

affinity, *s.* (*a*) Affinité *f.* (*b*) Conformité *f* de caractère. (*c*) *Ch:* **Affinity for a body**, affinité pour un corps.

affirm, *v.tr.* **1.** Affirmer, soutenir (*that*, que). **2.** *Jur:* Confirmer (un jugement).

affirmation, *s.* **1.** (*a*) Affirmation *f*, assertion *f.* (*b*) *Jur:* Déclaration solennelle. **2.** *Jur:* Confirmation *f* (d'un jugement).

affirmative. **1.** *a.* Affirmatif. *To make an a. sign*, faire signe que oui. **2.** *s.* *The answer is in the a.*, la réponse est oui.

affix, *v.tr.* Attacher (*sth. to sth.*, qch. à qch.). *To a. a seal*, apposer un sceau.

afflict, *v.tr.* Affliger; désoler. **afflicting**, *a.* Affligeant.

affliction, *s.* **1.** Affliction *f.* **2.** Calamité *f*, revers *m.*

affluence, *s.* Abondance *f*, richesse *f.*

affluent[1], *a.* Opulent, riche. *In a. circumstances*, dans l'aisance.

affluent[2], *s. Geog:* Affluent *m* (d'une rivière).

afflux, *s.* Concours *m* (de gens).

afford, *v.tr.* **1.** (*a*) Avoir les moyens (de faire qch.); être en mesure (de faire qch.). *I can't afford it*, mes moyens ne le permettent pas. (*b*) **I can afford to wait**, je peux attendre. **2.** Fournir, offrir.

afforestation, *s.* Boisement *m*, afforestation *f.*

affranchise, *v.tr.* Affranchir.

affranchisement, *s.* Affranchissement *m.*

affray, *s.* Bagarre *f*, échauffourée *f.*

affront[1], *s.* Affront *m*, offense *f.*

affront[2], *v.tr.* (*a*) Insulter; faire affront à (qn). (*b*) Faire honte à (qn).

afield, *adv. F:* **To go far afield**, aller très loin.

afire, *adv. & pred.a.* En feu.

aflame, *adv. & pred. a.* En flammes. *To be a. with curiosity*, brûler de curiosité.

afloat, *adv. & pred. a.* **1.** A flot; sur l'eau. **2.** (*Of rumour*) *To be a.*, courir, circuler.

afoot, *adv.* **1.** *To be a.*, être à pied. **2.** **To be afoot**, être sur pied, en mouvement. **3.** *There's something afoot*, il se prépare quelque chose.

aforesaid, *a.* Susmentionné, susdit.

afraid, *pred. a.* Pris de peur. **To be afraid**, avoir peur (de qch.); craindre (qch.). *To make s.o. a.*, faire peur à qn; effrayer qn. *I am a. he will die*, je crains qu'il ne meure. *I'm afraid it is so!* j'en ai (bien) peur! *F: I'm a. he is out*, je crois bien qu'il est sorti.

afresh, *adv.* De nouveau, à nouveau.

Africa. *Pr.n. Geog:* L'Afrique *f.*

African, *a. & s. Geog:* Africain, -e.

aft, *adv. Nau:* Sur, à, vers, l'arrière.

after. **I.** *adv.* Après. **1.** (*Place, order*) **To come after**, venir après, venir à la suite. **2.** (*Time*) *I never spoke to him a.*, je ne lui ai jamais parlé après. *I heard of it a.*, je l'ai appris plus tard. *The week a.*, la semaine d'après. **II.** *after, prep.* Après. **1.** (*Place*) (*a*) *To walk a. s.o.*, marcher après qn. (*b*) *To run a. s.o.*, courir après qn. *The police are a. you*, la police est à vos trousses. *The boys are a. your fruit*, les gamins en veulent à vos fruits. *What is he after?* (i) qu'est-ce qu'il a en tête? (ii) qu'est-ce qu'il cherche? *I see what you're a.*, je vois où vous voulez en venir. **2.** (*Time*) *To reign a. s.o.*, régner après qn. **After all (said and done)**, au bout du compte; enfin. *The day a. the battle*, le lendemain de la bataille. **The day after to-morrow**, après-demain. *It is a. five (o'clock)*, il est cinq heures passées. *He read page a. page*, il lut page sur page. **Time after time**, maintes fois. **3.** (*Order*) 'After you, sir,' "après vous, monsieur." **4.** (*Manner*) **After a pattern**, d'après, suivant, un modèle. *Landscape a. Turner*, paysage d'après Turner.

III. after, *conj.* Après que + *ind. I come a. he goes*, je viens après qu'il est parti. **IV. after-**, *a.* **1.** Après. **2.** A venir. **3.** Arrière. **after-effect(s)**, *s.(pl.)* Suites *fpl*, contre-coup *m* (d'un événement). **after-life**, *s.* **1.** La vie future. **2.** *In after-life*, plus tard dans la vie. **after-mentioned**, *a.* Mentionné ci-après. **after-taste**, *s.* Arrière-goût *m.*

aftermath, *s.* **1.** *Agr:* Regain *m.* **2.** Suites *fpl.* (d'un événement).

afternoon, *s.* Après-midi *m or f*, après-dîner *m. At half past two in the a.*, à deux heures et demie de l'après-midi. **Good afternoon!** bonjour!

afterthought, *s.* Réflexion *f* après coup.

afterwards, *adv.* Après, plus tard, ensuite.

again, *adv. With a vb. often rendered by the pref.* re-: *to begin a.*, recommencer; *to bring a.*, ramener, rapporter. **1.** (*a*) De nouveau, encore. **Once again**, encore une fois. **Here we are again!** *F:* nous revoilà! *Don't do it a.!* ne recommencez pas! **Again and again**, à plusieurs reprises. **Now and again**, de temps en temps. *As large a.*, deux fois aussi grand. (*b*) (*Back*) *To send sth. back a.*, renvoyer qch. **2.** (*a*) De plus, d'ailleurs, en outre. (*b*) (**Then**) again, d'autre part.

against, *prep.* Contre. **1.** (*a*) *I have nothing to say a. it.*, je n'ai rien à dire là-contre. *I did it a. my will*, je l'ai fait à contre-cœur. *Action that is a. the rules*, action contraire aux règlements. *To brush a hat against the nap*, brosser un chapeau à contre-poil. (*b*) *Warned a. s.o.*, mis en garde contre qn. (*c*) *To dash a. the wall*, donner contre le mur. *F: To run up a. s.o.*, rencontrer qn par hasard. (*d*) *Leaning a. the wall*, appuyé contre le mur. (*e*) A l'encontre de. **2.** (*a*) *My rights (as)* a. *the Government*, mes droits vis-à-vis du Gouvernement. (*b*) **Over against the school**, en face de l'école. **3.** *To show up a. a background*, se détacher sur un fond. **4.** *To make preparation a. his return*, faire des préparatifs pour son retour.

agaric, *s. Fung:* Agaric *m.*

agate, *s.* Agate *f.*

age[1], *s.* **1.** Age *m.* (*a*) **Middle age**, âge mûr. **To be past middle age**, être sur le retour. **What age are you?** quel âge avez-vous? **To be under age**, être mineur. **To come of age**, atteindre sa majorité. **To be of an age to marry**, être en âge de se marier. (*b*) (**Old**) **age**, vieillesse *f.* **2.** (*a*) Age, époque *f*, siècle *m. Hist:* **The Middle Ages**, le moyen âge. (*b*) *F: It is an age since I saw him*, il y a une éternité que je ne l'ai vu.

age[2], *v.* **1.** *v.i.* Vieillir; prendre de l'âge. **2.** *v.tr.* Vieillir. **aged**, *a.* **1.** Agé, vieux. **2.** (*a*) *A. twenty years*, âgé de vingt ans. (*b*) *I found him greatly a.*, je le trouvai bien vieilli. **ageing**[1], *a.* Vieillissant. **ageing**[2], *s.* Vieillissement *m.*

agency, *s.* **1.** (*a*) Action *f*, opération *f.*

Through the a. of water, par l'action de l'eau. (*b*) Agent *m. Natural agencies*, agents naturels. (*c*) Entremise *f. Through s.o.'s a.*, par l'entremise de qn. **2.** *Com:* Agence *f*, bureau *m*.

agent, *s.* (*a*) Agent *m.* **To be a free agent,** avoir son libre arbitre. (*b*) Régisseur *m. Com:* Agent.

agglomeration, *s.* Agglomération *f*.

aggrandize, *v.tr.* Agrandir; exagérer.

aggrandizement, *s.* Agrandissement *m*.

aggravate, *v.tr.* **I.** (*a*) Aggraver; envenimer (une querelle). (*b*) Augmenter. **2.** *F:* Agacer, exaspérer.

aggravating, *a.* **I.** *A. circumstance*, circonstance aggravante. **2.** Exaspérant.

aggravation, *s.* **I.** (*a*) Aggravation *f*; envenimement *m* (d'une querelle). (*b*) *F:* Agacement *m*, exaspération *f*. **2.** Circonstance aggravante.

aggregate¹. I. *a.* Collectif. *Ind:* *A. output*, rendement global. **2.** *s.* (*a*) Ensemble *m*, total *m.* (*b*) Masse *f*, assemblage *m.* **In the aggregate,** en somme.

aggregate². I. *v.tr. Ph:* Agréger. **2.** *v.i.* (*a*) S'élever à. (*b*) *Ph:* S'agréger.

aggregation, *s. Ph:* Agrégation *f*.

aggression, *s.* Agression *f*.

aggressive, *a.* Agressif. **-ly,** *adv.* D'une manière agressive; d'un ton agressif.

aggressor, *s.* Agresseur *m*.

aggrieve, *v.tr.* Chagriner, blesser.

aghast, *pred. a.* Consterné (*at*, de).

agile, *a.* Agile, leste **-ly,** *adv.* Agilement.

agility, *s.* Agilité *f*.

agitate, *v.tr.* **I.** Agiter, remuer (qch.). **2.** Agiter, troubler (qn). **3.** *Abs. To a. against sth.*, faire de l'agitation contre qch. **agitated,** *a.* Agité; troublé. **agitating,** *a.* Émotionnant; troublant.

agitation, *s* **I.** Agitation *f*; mouvement *m.* **2.** (*a*) Agitation, émotion *f*, trouble *m.* (*b*) Agitation; troubles

agitator, *s.* Agitateur *m*.

aglow, *adv. & pred. a.* **I.** (*Of thg*) Enflammé, embrasé. **2.** (*Of pers.*) *I was all a.*, (l'exercice) m'avait fouetté le sang.

agnostic, *a. & s.* Agnostique (*mf*).

ago. I. *a. Ten years ago*, il y a dix ans. *A little while ago*, tout à l'heure; tantôt. **2.** *adv* **Long ago**, il y a longtemps *No longer ago than last week.* pas plus tard que la semaine dernière.

agog, *adv. & pred. a.* **To be** (all) **agog to do sth.**, être impatient de faire qch. *The whole town was a.*, toute la ville était en émoi. **To set s.o.** (all) **agog**, mettre qn en train, en émoi.

agonize, *v.tr.* Torturer. **agonized,** *a.* **I.** (Cri) d'angoisse. **2.** *I was a.*, j'étais angoissé. **agonizing,** *a.* Atroce. *A. cry*, cri déchirant.

agony, *s.* **I.** Angoisse *f.* **To suffer agonies,** être au supplice. *Journ:* **Agony column,** annonces personnelles. **2. To be in the death agony**, être à l'agonie.

agrarian, *a.* (Loi) agraire.

agree, *v.i. & tr.* **I.** Consentir (*to*, à); faire droit (à une requête). *I a. that he was mistaken*, j'admets qu'il s'est trompé. *They have agreed about the prices*, ils sont convenus des prix. *To a. to sth. being done*, accepter que qch. se fasse. **Unless otherwise agreed,** sauf arrangement contraire. **2.** (*Of pers.*) (*a*) *Être d'accord*; tomber d'accord. (*b*) *To a. with s.o. on, in, a matter*, s'accorder avec qn sur une question. *I quite a. with you*, je suis tout à fait de votre avis. (*c*) *"That is so,"* he agreed, "c'est vrai," acquiesça-t-il. **3.** (*Of thgs*) (*a*) S'accorder (ensemble). (*b*) *Gram:* S'accorder. (*c*) Convenir (*with*, à). *The climate does not a. with him*, le climat ne lui convient pas. **agreed,** *a.* **I.** *We are a. about the prices*, nous sommes convenus des prix. **2. Agreed upon, convenu. (That is) agreed!** c'est convenu! d'accord! **Agreed unanimously,** adopté à l'unanimité.

agreeable, *a.* **I.** Agréable (*to*, à); (*of pers.*) aimable (*to*, envers). *If that is a. to you*, si cela vous convient. **2.** *Pred. F: To be a. to sth.*, consentir à qch. *I am* (quite) *a.*, je veux bien. **-ably,** *adv.* **I.** Agréablement. **2.** Conformément (*to, with*, à).

agreement, *s.* **I.** Convention *f*, acte *m*, contrat *m.* **2.** Accord *m. To be in a. with a decision*, approuver une décision. **To come to an agreement**, tomber d'accord. **By mutual agreement**, de gré à gré. **3.** (*a*) Conformité *f*, concordance *f.* (*b*) *Gram:* Accord (*with*, avec).

agricultural, *a.* Agricole.

agriculture, *s.* Agriculture *f*.

agriculturist, *s.* Agriculteur *m*.

aground, *adv. Nau:* Échoué; au sec. **To run aground,** échouer.

ague, *s.* Fièvre intermittente.

ah, *int.* Ah! heu!

aha, *int.* Haha!

ahead, *adv.* **I.** *The ship was right a.*, le navire était droit devant. **To draw ahead of s.o.**, dépasser qn. **To go ahead,** avancer. **2.** *F: To go on ahead*, prendre les devants. *Ahead of s.o.* en avant de qn. **To be two hours ahead of s.o.**, avoir deux heures d'avance sur qn. **To look ahead.** penser à l'avenir.

ahem, *int.* Hum!

aid¹, *s.* **I.** Aide *f*, assistance *f*, secours *m*, appui *m.* **In aid of**, au profit de. **2.** (*Pers.*) Aide *mf*; auxiliaire *m*.

aid², *v.tr.* **I.** Aider, assister, secourir; venir à l'aide de. *To aid one another*, s'entr'aider. **2.** Soutenir (une entreprise). **aiding,** *s.* Aide *f*.

aide-de-camp, *s.* Officier *m* d'ordonnance.

ail, *v.tr.* Faire souffrir (qn). *What ails you?*

qu'est-ce que vous avez? **ailing,** *a.* Souffrant, malade.

ailment, *s.* Mal *m*; maladie (légère).

aim¹, *s.* I. (*a*) Action *f* de viser. **To miss one's aim,** manquer son but. **To take aim at s.o.,** viser qn. (*b*) But *m*. 2. But, objet *m*; visées *fpl.* **With the aim of doing sth,** dans le dessein de faire qch.

aim². I. *v.tr.* (*a*) **To aim a blow at s.o.,** allonger un coup à qn. (*b*) Viser. **To aim a gun at s.o.,** viser qn. (*c*) *Measures aimed against our trade,* mesures dirigées contre notre commerce. 2. *v.ind.tr.* (*a*) **To aim at s.o.** (with a gun), coucher qn en joue. (*b*) **What are you aiming at?** quel but poursuivez-vous?

aimless, *a.* Sans but, sans objet. **-ly,** *adv.* Sans but.

air¹, *s.* I. Air *m.* (*a*) *Breath of air,* souffle *m* (d'air). *F:* **I can't live on air,** je ne peux pas vivre de l'air du temps. *To carry goods by air,* transporter des marchandises par la voie des airs. *To throw sth. into the air,* jeter qch. en l'air. *F:* **To walk on air,** ne pas se sentir de joie. **There is something in the air,** il se prépare quelque chose. *All that money has vanished into thin air,* tout cet argent a passé au bleu. (*b*) *Attrib.* **Air raid,** raid aérien. (*c*) *W.Tel: F:* **To be on the air,** parler à la radio. II. **air.** *Mus:* Air. III. **air.** Air, mine *f,* apparence *f.* **To put on airs,** se donner des airs. *To put on airs with s.o.,* traiter qn de haut. **air-borne,** *a.* Aéroporté. **airborne troops,** troupes aéroportées. **aircushion,** *s.* Coussin *m* à air, pneumatique. **air-fleet,** *s.* Flotte aérienne. **air-force,** *s.* Aviation *f.* (de guerre); armée *f* de l'air. **air-gun,** *s.* Carabine *f* à air comprimé. **air-landing,** *s.* Atterrissage. **air-landing strip,** piste d'atterrissage. **air-line,** *s.* Service *m* de transports aériens. **air-liner,** *s.* Grand avion de transport. **air-mail,** *s.* Poste aérienne. **By air-mail,** par avion. **airpilot,** *s.m.* Pilote aviateur. **air-pocket,** *s. Av:* Trou *m* d'air. **air-port,** *s.* Aéroport *m.* **air-pressure,** *s.* Pression *f* atmosphérique. **air-pump,** *s.* Pompe *f* à air. **air-screw,** *s. Av:* Hélice *f.* **air-station,** *s.* Aéroport *m;* centre *m* d'aviation. **airtight,** *a.* Étanche (à l'air).

air², *v.tr.* I. (*a*) *To air a room,* aérer, rafraîchir, une chambre. (*b*) **The question needs to be aired,** la question demande à être ventilée. 2. **To air one's opinions,** faire parade de ses opinions. **airing,** *s.* I. (*a*) Ventilation *f*; aérage *m.* (*b*) Exposition *f* à l'air. 2. (Petite) promenade.

aircraft, *s. Coll.* Aéronefs *mpl* or *fpl* et avions *mpl.*

airiness, *s.* I. Situation aérée. 2. Légèreté *f* (d'esprit); désinvolture *f.*

airless, *a.* Privé d'air; renfermé.

airman, *s.* Aviateur *m.*

airship, *s.* (Ballon) dirigeable *m.*

airworthy, *a. Aer:* Navigable.

airy, *a.* I. Bien aéré; ouvert à l'air. 2. *Poet:* Élevé, aérien. 3. (*Of material*) Léger. 4. (*a*) (*Of conduct*) Léger, insouciant. (*b*) *A. promises,* promesses en l'air. **-ily,** *adv.* Légèrement.

aisle, *s. Ecc.Arch:* Nef latérale.

ajar, *adv. & pred. a.* Entrebâillé.

a-kimbo, *adv.* With arms a-kimbo, les (deux) poings sur les hanches.

akin, *adv. & pred. a.* I. *A.* **to s.o.,** parent de qn; apparenté à, avec, qn. 2. **To be akin to sth.,** ressembler à qch.

alabaster, *s.* Albâtre *m.*

alacrity, *s.* Empressement *m,* alacrité *f.*

alarm¹, *s.* I. Alarme *f,* alerte *f.* **To raise the alarm,** donner l'éveil. **To take (the) alarm,** prendre l'alarme; s'alarmer. **False alarm,** fausse alerte. 2. Avertisseur *m,* signal *m.* **alarm (-clock),** *s.* Réveille-matin *m inv.*; réveil *m.*

alarm², *v.tr.* I. (*a*) Alarmer, donner l'alarme à. (*b*) Alerter (des troupes). 2. (*Frighten*) Alarmer, effrayer. **To be alarmed at sth.,** s'alarmer de qch. **alarming,** *a.* Alarmant. **-ly,** *adv.* D'une manière alarmante.

alarum, *s.* Réveille-matin *m inv.*

alas, *int.* Hélas !

Albania. *Pr.n. Geog:* L'Albanie *f.*

albatross, *s.* Albatros *m.*

Albert. *Pr.n.* Albert *m.*

albino, *s.* Albinos *mf.*

album, *s.* Album *m.*

albumen, *s.* Albumine *f.*

alchemist, *s.* Alchimiste *m.*

alchemy, *s.* Alchimie *f.*

alcohol, *s.* Alcool *m.*

alcoholic, *a.* Alcoolique.

alcove, *s.* I. Alcôve *f* (de chambre). 2. Niche *f,* enfoncement *m* (dans un mur).

alder, *s. Bot:* Aune *m.*

alderman, *s.* Alderman *m.*

Alderney. *Pr.n. Geog:* Aurigny *m.*

ale, *s.* Ale *f.* **Pale ale,** bière blanche.

Alec(k). *Pr.n.* Alexandre *m. F:* **A smart Aleck,** un finaud; un monsieur je-sais-tout.

alee, *adv. Nau:* Sous le vent.

alert. I. *a.* (*a*) Alerte, vigilant. (*b*) Actif, vif. 2. *s.* Alerte *f.* **To be on the alert,** être sur le qui-vive. **-ly,** *adv.* D'une manière alerte; prestement.

alertness, *s.* I. Vigilance *f.* 2. Vivacité *f,* prestesse *f.*

Alexander. *Pr.n.* Alexandre *m.*

alfa(-grass), *s. Bot:* Alfa *m.*

alfresco, *a. & adv.* En plein air.

algebra, *s.* Algèbre *f.*

algebraic(al), *a.* Algébrique.

Algeria. *Pr.n. Geog:* L'Algérie *f.*

Algerian, *a. & s.* Algérien, -ienne.

Algiers. *Pr.n. Geog:* Alger *m.*

alias. 1. *adv.* Autrement dit. **2.** *s.* Nom *m.* d'emprunt.

alibi, *s.* Alibi *m.*

alien. 1. *a. & s.* Étranger, -ère. **2.** *a. A. to* *sth.,* contraire, opposé, à qch.

alienate, *v.tr.* **1.** *Jur:* Aliéner. **2.** Détacher, éloigner, (s')aliéner (qn).

alienation, *s.* Aliénation *f.*

alight¹, *v.i.* Descendre. **1.** *To a. from horseback,* descendre de cheval; mettre pied à terre. **2.** (*a*) (*Of birds*) S'abattre, se poser. (*b*) *To a. on one's feet,* tomber debout.

alight², *pred. a.* Allumé; en feu. **To set** **sth. alight,** mettre le feu à qch.

align. 1. *v.tr.* Aligner; mettre en ligne. **2.** *v.i.* S'aligner; se mettre en ligne.

alignment, *s.* Alignement *m.*

alike. 1. *pred. a.* Semblable, pareil, ressemblant. **You are all alike!** vous vous ressemblez tous! *All things are a. to him,* tout lui est égal. **2.** *adv.* Pareillement; de même. *Dressed a.,* habillés de même. *Winter and summer a.,* été comme hiver.

aliment, *s.* Aliment *m.*

alimentary, *a.* Alimentaire.

alimentation, *s.* Alimentation *f.*

alimony, *s.* *Jur:* Pension *f* alimentaire.

aliquot, *a. & s. Mth:* A. (*part*), (partie *f*) aliquote (*f*).

alive, *a.* **1.** (*a*) Vivant, en vie. *To be burnt alive,* être brûlé vif. *It's good to be alive!* il fait bon vivre! *Dead or alive,* mort ou vif. *F:* **Man alive!** par exemple! (*b*) *To keep a.,* entretenir. **2. To be alive to an impression,** ressentir une impression. *To be a. to . . .,* se rendre compte de. . . . **3.** *He is very much alive,* il est très remuant. *Look alive!* dépêchez-vous! **4.** *The street was a. with people,* la rue fourmillait de monde.

alkali, *s. Ch:* Alcali *m.*

alkaline, *a. Ch:* Alcalin.

alkaloid, *a. & s.* Alcaloïde (*m*).

all. I. *a., pron., & adv.* **1.** Tout, tous. (*a*) **All day,** (pendant) toute la journée. **All** **men,** tous les hommes. **All the way, tout** le long du chemin. **For all his wealth . . .,** malgré sa fortune. . . . **With all speed,** au plus vite, à toute vitesse. **At all hours,** à toute heure. **You are not as ill as all that,** vous n'êtes pas malade à ce point-là. (*b*) **All** **of us,** nous tous. **All together,** tous, toutes, à la fois, ensemble. (*c*) *We all love him,* nous l'aimons tous. *Take it all,* prenez le tout. *Ten: Fifteen all,* quinze à. (*d*) *neut. Almost all,* presque tout. **All is lost,** tout est perdu. **For all he may say,** quoi qu'il en dise. **That's all,** c'est tout, voilà tout. *If that is all (the difficulty),* s'il ne tient qu'à cela. **All's well,** tout va bien. **When all is said and done,** somme toute; quand tout est dit. **2.** (*a*) **Once for all,** une fois pour toutes. **For all** **I know,** autant que je sache. (*b*) *Most of all,* surtout; le plus. (*The*) *best of all would be to . . .,* le mieux serait de. . . . (*c*) **At all.**

(i) *Do you know him at all?* le connaissez-vous aucunement? **Not at all,** pas du tout; *F:* du tout l' (ii) *If you hesitate at all,* pour peu que vous hésitiez. (*d*) **All but.** *All but* *impossible,* presque impossible. *I all but fell,* j'ai failli tomber. (*e*) **All in all.** *Taking it all in all,* à tout prendre. *They were all in all to each other,* ils étaient dévoués l'un à l'autre. **3.** *adv.* Tout. *She is all alone,* elle est toute seule. *To be (dressed) all in black,* être habillé tout de noir. **She is all ears,** elle est tout oreilles. **All the better,** tant mieux. *You will* *be all the better for it,* vous vous en trouverez mieux. *The hour came all too soon,* l'heure n'arriva que trop tôt. **All at once,** (i) (*suddenly*) tout à coup; (ii) (*at one time*) tout d'un coup, tous à la fois. **II. all,** *s.* Tout *m,* totalité *f.* **To lose one's all,** perdre tout son avoir. **All Fools' Day,** *s.* Le premier avril.

all-important, *a.* De la plus haute importance; de toute importance. **all-powerful,** *a.* Tout-puissant, toute-puissante. **all-round,** *a. F:* Complet. *An a.-r. man,* un homme universel. **All Saints'** **Day,** *s.* (Le jour de) la Toussaint. **All** **Souls' Day,** *s.* Le jour, la fête, des Morts.

allay, *v.tr.* Apaiser, calmer. **allaying,** *s.* Apaisement *m,* soulagement *m.*

allegation, *s.* Allégation *f.*

allege, *v.tr.* Alléguer, prétendre (*that,* que + *ind.*) **alleged,** *a. The a. thief,* le voleur présumé.

allegiance, *s.* Fidélité *f,* obéissance *f* (*to,* à).

allegoric(al), *a.* Allégorique.

allegory, *s.* Allégorie *f.*

alleviate, *v.tr.* Alléger, soulager (la douleur); adoucir (le chagrin).

alleviation, *s.* Allègement *m;* soulagement *m,* adoucissement *m.*

alley, *s.* (*In garden*) Allée *f;* (*in town*) ruelle *f,* passage *m.*

alliance, *s.* **1.** Alliance *f.* **To enter into an** **alliance,** s'allier (*with,* avec). **2.** *A. by marriage,* alliance; apparentage *m.*

alligator, *s. Rept:* Alligator *m.*

alliteration, *s.* Allitération *f.*

allocate, *v.tr.* Allouer, assigner.

allocation, *s.* **1.** (*a*) Allocation *f.* (*b*) Attribution *f* (de fonctions). **2.** Part assignée.

allot, *v.tr.* **1.** *To a. sth. to s.o.,* attribuer, assigner, qch. à qn. **2.** Répartir, distribuer.

allotment, *s.* **1.** (*a*) Attribution *f* (de qch. à qn). (*b*) Partage *m,* répartition *f;* distribution *f.* **2.** (*a*) Portion *f,* part *f,* lot *m.* (*b*) Lopin *m* de terre. **Allotments,** jardins ouvriers.

allow, *v.tr.* **1.** *To a. a claim,* admettre une requête. **2.** (*a*) (*Permit*) Permettre, souffrir. **To allow s.o. to do sth.,** permettre à qn de faire qch. **Allow me!** permettez(-moi)! (*b*) *To a. oneself to be deceived,* se laisser tromper. **3.** (*a*) **To allow a debtor time to pay,** accorder un délai à un débiteur. (*b*)

Com: To allow s.o. a discount, consentir une remise à qn. (c) *ind.tr.* To allow for sth., tenir compte de qch.; faire la part de qch. After allowing for . . ., déduction faite de. . . . Allowing for the circumstances, eu égard aux circonstances.

allowable, *a.* Admissible, légitime.

allowance, *s.* 1. (a) Pension *f* alimentaire; rente *f.* (b) *Adm:* Allocation *f.* (c) *Travelling a.,* frais *mpl* de voyage. (d) (*Of food*) Ration *f.* To put s.o. on (short) allowance, mettre qn à la ration; rationner qn. 2. *Com:* Remise *f,* rabais *m.* 3. To make allowance(s) for sth., tenir compte de, faire la part de, qch.

alloy¹, *s.* Alliage *m.*

alloy², *v.tr.* Allier. *F:* Altérer, diminuer (le bonheur).

allude, *v.ind.tr.* To a. to sth., (*of pers.*) faire allusion à qch.; (*of phrase*) avoir trait à qch.

allure, *v.tr.* Attirer, séduire. **alluring,** *a.* Attrayant, séduisant.

allurement, *s.* Attrait *m*; appât *m.*

allusion, *s.* Allusion *f.*

alluvial, *a. Geol:* (Terrain) alluvial, d'alluvion.

ally¹, *s.* Allié,-e.

ally², 1. *v.tr.* Allier (to, with, à, avec). 2. *v.i.* S'allier (to, with, à, avec). **allied,** *a.* 1. Allié. 2. *Biol:* Nearly a. species, espèces voisines.

almanac, *s.* 1. Almanach *m.* 2. Annuaire *m.*

almighty, *a. & s.* Tout-puissant.

almond, *s.* 1. Amande *f.* Burnt almonds, amandes grillées; pralines *f.* Almond (-shaped) eyes, yeux (taillés) en amande. 2. Almond(-tree), amandier *m.*

almoner, *s.* Aumônier *m.*

almost, *adv.* Presque; à peu près. It is a. noon, il est près de midi. He a. fell, il faillit tomber.

alms, *s.sg. or pl.* Aumône *f.* To give a. to s.o., faire l'aumône à qn. **alms-giving,** *s.* L'aumône *f.* **alms-house,** *s.* Asile *m* (de vieillards).

aloe, *s.* 1. *Bot:* Aloès *m.* 2. *pl. Pharm:* Bitter aloes, amer *m* d'aloès.

aloft, *adv.* (a) *Nau:* En haut. (b) *F:* Caps were thrown a., on jetait les casquettes en l'air.

alone, *pred.a.* 1. Seul. I did it alone, je l'ai fait à moi seul. I want to speak to you a., je voudrais vous parler seul à seul. His silence a. is sufficient proof against him, rien que son silence le condamne. 2. (a) To leave s.o. alone, (i) laisser qn tranquille; (ii) laisser qn faire. *Prov:* Let well alone, le mieux est l'ennemi du bien. (b) *F:* Let alone . . , sans parler de . . .

along. 1. *prep.* Le long de. (a) To go a. a street, suivre une rue. (b) Trees a. the river, arbres qui bordent la rivière. 2. *adv* (a) To move along, avancer. Come along! arrivez donc! venez donc! (b) I knew that all along je le savais dès le commencement. (c) *F:* Along with, avec.

alongside, *adv. & prep.* To come a., accoster, aborder. A. the quay, le long du quai.

aloof, *adv. & pred. a.* To keep aloof, se tenir à l'écart, éloigné. To stand aloof, s'abstenir. He kept very much a., il s'est montré très distant.

aloofness, *s.* Attitude distante; réserve *f* (from, à l'égard de).

aloud, *adv.* A haute voix; (tout) haut.

alp, *s.* Alpe *f*; pâturage *m* de montagne. *Geog:* The Alps, les Alpes.

alpaca, *s.* 1. *Z:* Alpaca *m.* 2. *Tex:* Alpaga *m.*

alpenstock, *s.* Alpenstock *m*; bâton ferré.

alphabet, *s.* Alphabet *m.*

alphabetical, *a.* Alphabétique. **-ally,** *adv.* Alphabétiquement.

alpine, *a.* (Club) alpin; (site) alpestre.

already, *adv.* Déjà.

Alsatian, *a. & s. Geog:* Alsacien, -ienne. Alsatian wolf-hound, chien-loup *m.*

also, *adv.* Aussi. He saw it a., il l'a vu également.

altar, *s.* Autel *m.*

alter. 1. *v.tr.* (a) Retoucher (un dessin); changer de (plans). To a. one's mind, changer d'avis. That alters matters, voilà qui change les choses. (b) Fausser (les faits). 2. *v.i.* He has greatly altered, il a bien changé.

alteration, *s.* Remaniement *m,* retouche *f*; changement *m.*

altercation, *s.* Altercation *f,* dispute *f.*

alternate¹, *a.* Alternatif, alterné, alternant. To come on a. days, venir tous les deux jours. 2. *Geom:* (Angles) alternes. 3. *Pros:* (Rimes) croisées. **-ly,** *adv.* Alternativement; tour à tour.

alternate², 1. *v.tr.* Faire alterner. 2. *v.i.* Alterner (with, avec); se succéder (tour à tour). **alternating,** *a.* Alternant, alterné.

alternation, *s.* Alternance *f.*

alternative. 1. *a.* Alternatif. 2. *s.* Alternative *f.* To have no alternative, n'avoir pas le choix. **-ly,** *adv.* 1. Alternativement; tour à tour. 2. Avec l'alternative de.

although, *conj.* = THOUGH I. 1.

altitude, *s.* 1. Altitude *f,* élévation *f.* 2. *Usu.pl.* Hauteur(s) *f.*

alto, *s. Mus:* 1. Alto *m.* 2. (a) (*Male*) Haute-contre *f.* (b) (*Female*) Contralto *m.*

altogether, *adv.* (a) (*Wholly*) Entièrement, tout à fait. (b) (*On the whole*) Somme toute. Taking things a., à tout prendre. (c) How much a.? combien en tout?

altruism, *s.* Altruisme *m.*

altruist, *s.* Altruiste *mf.*

altruistic, *a.* Altruiste.

alum, *s.* Alun *m.*

aluminium, *s.* Aluminium *m.*

always, *adv.* Toujours.

amalgam, *s.* Amalgame *m.*

amalgamate. 1. *v.tr.* Amalgamer (des idées); fusionner (des sociétés). 2. *v.i.* (*Of*

metals) S'amalgamer ; (*of companies*) fusionner.

amalgamation, *s.* **I.** Amalgamation *f* (des métaux). **2.** Fusion *f* (de sociétés).

amass, *v.tr.* Amasser, accumuler.

amateur, *s.* Amateur *m.*

amateurish, *a.* D'amateur. **-ly,** *adv.* En amateur.

amaze, *v.tr.* Confondre, stupéfier, frapper de stupeur. **amazed,** *a.* Confondu, stupéfait. **amazing,** *a.* Stupéfiant. **-ly,** *adv.* Étonnamment.

amazement, *s.* Stupéfaction *f*; stupeur *f.*

Amazon. I. *s.* *F:* Amazone *f.* **2.** *Pr.n.* The river Amazon, le fleuve des Amazones.

ambassador, *s.* Ambassadeur *m.*

amber, *s.* Ambre *m.* **Amber light,** feu jaune. **amber-coloured,** *a.* Ambré

ambergris, *s.* Ambre gris.

ambidextrous, *a.* Ambidextre.

ambient, *a.* Ambiant.

ambiguity, *s.* **I.** Ambiguïté *f.* **2.** Équivoque *f.*

ambiguous, *a.* **I.** Ambigu, *f.* -uë; équivoque. **2.** Incertain. **-ly,** *adv.* Avec ambiguïté ; d'une manière équivoque.

ambit, *s.* **I.** Circuit *m,* tour *m* (d'une ville). **2.** Étendue *f,* portée *f* (d'une action).

ambition, *s.* Ambition *f.*

ambitious, *a.* Ambitieux. *To be a. to do sth.,* ambitionner de faire qch. **-ly,** *adv.* Ambitieusement.

ambitiousness, *s.* **I.** Ambition *f.* **2.** Caractère ambitieux.

amble¹, *s.* **I.** *Equit:* Amble *m,* entrepas *m.* **2.** (*Of pers.*) Pas *m* tranquille.

amble², *v.i.* **I.** *Equit:* Aller (à) l'amble. **2.** *F:* (*Of pers.*) *To a. along,* marcher d'un pas tranquille.

Ambrose. *Pr.n.* Ambroise *m.*

ambulance, *s.* Ambulance *f.*

ambuscade, *s.* = AMBUSH¹.

ambush¹, *s.* Embuscade *f.* **Troops in ambush,** troupes embusquées.

ambush². *v.tr.* *To a. the enemy,* attirer l'ennemi dans un piège.

ameer, *s.* Émir *m.*

ameliorate. I. *v.tr.* Améliorer. **2.** *v.i.* S'améliorer, s'amender.

amelioration, *s.* Amélioration *f.*

amen, *int.* Amen ; ainsi soit-il.

amenable, *a.* Soumis (à la discipline) ; docile (aux conseils). **Amenable to reason,** raisonnable.

amend. I. *v.tr.* (*a*) Amender (un projet de loi) ; corriger (un texte). (*b*) Réformer (sa vie). *To a. one's ways,* s'amender. **2.** *v.i.* S'amender, se corriger. **amending,** *a.* Correctif.

amendment, *s.* (*a*) Modification *f*; rectification *f.* (*b*) *Parl:* Amendement *m.*

amends, *s.pl.* Réparation *f,* dédommagement *m,* compensation *f.*

amenity, *s.* **I.** Aménité *f,* charme *m* (d'un

lieu). **2.** Aménité, affabilité *f.* **3.** *pl.* The amenities of life, les commodités *f* de l'existence.

America. *Pr.n.* L'Amérique *f.* *North A.,* l'Amérique du Nord.

American, *a.* & *s.* Américain, -aine.

amethyst, *s.* Améthyste *f.*

amiability, *s.* Amabilité *f* (*to,* envers).

amiable, *a.* Aimable (*to,* envers). **-ably,** *adv.* Aimablement.

amicable, *a.* (*Of manner*) Amical ; (*of pers.*) bien disposé. **-ably,** *adv.* (i) Amicalement ; (ii) à l'amiable.

amid(st), *prep.* Au milieu de ; parmi.

amidships, *adv.* Au milieu du navire.

amiss, *adv.* & *pred.a.* **I.** *To judge a.,* mal juger. **To take sth. amiss,** prendre qch. en mauvaise part. **2.** Mal à propos. *Something is a.,* il y a quelque chose qui cloche.

ammonia, *s.* *Ch:* Ammoniaque *f*; gaz ammoniac.

ammonium, *s.* *Ch:* Ammonium *m.*

ammunition, *s.* **I.** Munitions *fpl* de guerre. **2.** *Attrib.* D'ordonnance. **ammunition-wagon,** *s.* *Artil:* Caisson *m.*

amnesty, *s.* Amnistie *f.*

amok, *adv.* = AMUCK.

among(st), *prep.* Parmi, entre. (*a*) *Sitting a. her children,* assise au milieu de ses enfants. (*b*) *We are a. friends,* nous sommes entre amis. (*c*) *To count s.o. a. one's friends,* compter qn au nombre de ses amis. (*d*) *Do it a. you,* faites-le entre vous.

amorous, *a.* Amoureux (*of s.o.,* de qn). **-ly,** *adv.* Amoureusement.

amorphous, *a.* Amorphe.

amount¹, *s.* **I.** *Com:* Somme *f,* montant *m,* total *m. Have you the right a.?* avez-vous votre compte? **2.** Quantité *f.* *F:* **To spend any amount of money,** dépenser énormément d'argent.

amount², *v.i.* **I.** S'élever, (se) monter (*to,* à). *I don't know what my debts a. to,* j'ignore le montant de mes dettes. **2.** Équivaloir, revenir (*to,* à). *It amounts to the same thing,* cela revient au même. **3.** *F:* He will never amount to much, il ne sera jamais grand'chose.

amphibian, *a.* & *s.* Amphibie (*m*).

amphibious, *a.* *Z.* & *F:* Amphibie.

amphitheatre, *s.* Amphithéâtre *m.*

ample, *a.* Ample. **I.** *A. resources,* d'abondantes ressources. **2.** *To make a. apologies,* faire d'amples excuses. **-ply,** *adv.* Amplement, grandement.

amplify, *v.tr.* **I.** Amplifier (une idée). **2.** Exagérer (une nouvelle).

amplitude, *s.* **I.** Amplitude *f.* **2.** Abondance *f,* ampleur *f* (de style).

amputate, *v.tr.* Amputer. *His leg was amputated,* il fut amputé de la jambe.

amputation, *s.* Amputation *f.*

amuck, *adv.* **To run amuck. I.** Tomber dans la folie furieuse des Malais. **2.** *F:* Faire les cent coups.

amulet, s. Amulette f.

amuse, v.tr. Amuser, divertir. *To be amused by sth.,* être amusé de qch.; s'amuser de qch.

amusing, a. Amusant, divertissant. *The a. thing about it is that . . .,* le plaisant de l'affaire c'est que. . . . **-ly,** adv. D'une manière amusante.

amusement, s. Amusement m; divertissement m.

Amy. Pr.n. Aimée f.

an. See A².

anachronism, s. Anachronisme m.

anaemia, s. Anémie f.

anaemic, a. Anémique.

anaesthetic, a. & s. Anesthésique (m).

anagram, s. Anagramme f.

analogical, a. Analogique. **-ally,** adv. Analogiquement; par analogie.

analogous, a. Analogue (to, with, à).

analogy, s. Analogie f (to, with, avec).

analyse, v.tr. Analyser; faire l'analyse de.

analysis, s. Analyse f. *Gram: A. of a sentence,* analyse logique d'une phrase.

analyst, s. *Ch:* Analyste m.

analytic(al), a. Analytique.

anarchist, s. Anarchiste mf.

anarchy, s. Anarchie f.

anathema, s. Anathème m.

anathematize, v.tr. (a) Anathématiser (qn). (b) F: Maudire (qn).

anatomical, a. Anatomique.

anatomy, s. Anatomie f.

ancestor, s. Ancêtre m; aïeul m, pl. aïeux.

ancestral, a. Héréditaire; de famille. *His a. castle,* le château de ses ancêtres.

ancestry, s. **1.** Lignage m; longue suite d'ancêtres; ascendance f. **2.** *Coll.* Ancêtres mpl; aïeux mpl.

anchor¹, s. Ancre f. **To come to anchor,** s'ancrer, mouiller.

anchor². **1.** v.tr. Ancrer (un navire). **2.** v.i. Jeter l'ancre; mouiller. **anchored,** a. Ancré, mouillé; à l'ancre.

anchorage, s. Ancrage m, mouillage m.

anchorite, s. Anachorète m.

anchovy, s. Anchois m.

ancient, a. Ancien. (a) De vieille date. (b) *The a. world,* le monde antique. s. **The ancients,** les anciens.

and, conj. Et. **1.** (a) *A knife and fork,* un couteau et une fourchette. (b) (*With numerals*) *Two hundred and two,* deux cent deux. *Four and a half,* quatre et demi. *Four and three quarters,* quatre trois quarts. *An hour and twenty minutes,* une heure vingt minutes. (c) **Carriage and pair,** voiture à deux chevaux. **To walk two and two,** marcher deux à deux. (d) (*After 'without'*) Ni. *He had come without pencils and pens,* il était venu sans plumes ni crayons. (e) (*Intensive repetition*) *For miles and miles,* pendant des milles et des milles. *Better and better,* de mieux en mieux. **2.** (*Connecting clauses*) (a) *He sang and danced,* il chantait et dansait. (b) *F:* **Wait and see,**

attendez voir. *Try and help me,* tâchez de m'aider.

Andes. Pr.n. **The Andes,** les Andes f.

Andrew. Pr.n. André m.

anecdote, s. Anecdote f.

anemone, s. *Bot:* Anémone f.

anew, adv. (*Once more*) De nouveau. *To begin a.,* recommencer.

angel, s. Ange m.

angelic, a. Angélique.

angelica, s. *Bot: Cu:* Angélique f.

anger¹, s. Colère f; emportement m. *To act in a.,* agir sous le coup de la colère.

anger², v.tr. Irriter, mettre (qn) en colère.

angered, a. Irrité, furieux.

angle¹, s. (a) Angle m. **At an angle of . . .,** sous un angle de. . . . **At an angle,** en biais. (b) (*Corner*) Coin m.

angle², v.i. Pêcher à la ligne. **angling,** s. Pêche f à la ligne.

angler, s. Pêcheur m à la ligne.

Anglo-Indian, a. & s. Anglo-Indien, -ienne.

Anglo-Saxon. **1.** a. & s. Anglo-Saxon, -onne. **2.** s. *Ling:* L'anglo-saxon m.

angry, a. Fâché, irrité, courroucé (*with s.o. about sth.,* contre qn de qch.). *To get a. with s.o.,* se fâcher contre qn. *To make s.o. a.,* fâcher qn; mettre qn en colère. *A. voices,* voix irritées. *A. sky,* ciel à l'orage. **-ily,** adv. En colère, avec colère.

anguish, s. Angoisse f; douleur f. *To be in a.,* être au supplice.

angular, a. (*Visage*) anguleux. *F:* (*Of pers.*) Décharné.

aniline, s. *Dy:* Aniline f.

animal, s. Animal m.

animate¹, a. Animé; doué de vie.

animate², v.tr. (a) Animer. (b) Encourager, stimuler. **animated,** a. Animé.

animation, s. **1.** Animation f; vivacité f; feu m. **2.** Stimulation f, encouragement m.

animosity, s. Animosité f.

aniseed, s. (Graine f d')anis m.

ankle, s. Cheville f (du pied).

anklet, s. **1.** Bracelet m de cheville. **2.** Molletière f cycliste.

annals, s.pl. Annales f.

Anne. Pr.n. Anne f.

annex¹, v.tr. **1.** Annexer. **2.** *To a. a province,* annexer une province.

annex(e)², s. Annexe f (d'un hôtel).

annexation, s. Annexion f.

annihilate, v.tr. Anéantir (une flotte); annihiler (le temps, etc.).

annihilation, s. Anéantissement m; annihilation f.

anniversary, s. Anniversaire m.

annotate, v.tr. Annoter.

announce, v.tr. Annoncer.

announcement, s. Annonce f, avis m.

announcer, s. *W.Tel:* Microphoniste mf.

annoy, v.tr. **1.** (*Vex*) Contrarier. **2.** (*Inconvenience*) Gêner, ennuyer, importuner.

annoyed, *a.* Contrarié, ennuyé. **annoying,** *a.* Contrariant, ennuyeux, ennuyant.

annoyance, *s.* **1.** Contrariété *f*, chagrin *m.* **2.** Désagrément *m*, ennui *m.*

annual. 1. *a.* Annuel. **2.** *s.* (*a*) *Bot:* Plante annuelle. (*b*) Annuaire *m.* **-ally,** *adv.* Annuellement; tous les ans.

annuitant, *s.* **1.** Pensionnaire *mf.* **2.** Rentier, -ière (en viager).

annuity, *s.* Rente (annuelle). **Life annuity,** rente viagère.

annul, *v.tr.* Annuler; abroger (une loi).

anoint, *v.tr.* Oindre. **anointing,** *s.* **1.** Onction *f.* **2.** Sacre *m* (d'un roi).

anomalous, *a.* **1.** Anomal, -aux. **2.** *F:* Anormal, -aux. **-ly,** *adv.* Irrégulièrement.

anomaly, *s.* Anomalie *f.*

anon, *adv.* Tout à l'heure, bientôt.

anonymity, *s.* Anonyme *m*, anonymat *m.*

anonymous, *a.* Anonyme. *A. writer,* anonyme *m.* **-ly,** *adv.* Anonymement.

another, *a. & pron.* **1.** (*An additional*) Encore (un). *In a. ten years,* dans dix ans d'ici. *Without a. word,* sans un mot de plus. **2.** (*A similar*) Un(e) autre, un(e) second(e). *Such another,* un autre du même genre. **3.** (*a*) (*A different*) Un(e) autre. *That is* (quite) *another matter,* c'est tout autre chose. (*b*) *She now has a. husband,* elle a maintenant un nouvel époux. **4.** (*a*) (Taking) *one year with another,* bon an mal an. *Taking one* (*thing*) *with a.,* l'un dans l'autre. (*b*) (*Reciprocal pron.*) *One another,* l'un l'autre, les uns les autres. *Near one a.,* l'un près de l'autre. *To help one a.,* s'entr'aider.

answer¹, *s.* **1.** Réponse *f* (à une question); réplique *f* (à une critique). *He has an a. to everything,* il a réponse à tout. *I could find no a.,* je n'ai rien trouvé à répondre. 'An answer will oblige,' "réponse, s'il vous plaît." **2.** Solution *f* (d'un problème).

answer², *v.tr. & i.* **1.** Répondre. (*a*) *To a. s.o.,* répondre à qn. (*b*) *To a. a question,* répondre à une question. (*c*) *To answer the bell,* répondre à un coup de sonnette. *To answer the door,* aller ouvrir. (*d*) (*Of ship*) *To answer the helm,* obéir à la barre. (*e*) *To a. a charge,* répondre à une accusation. (*f*) *To a. a description,* répondre à un signalement. (*g*) *To a. a prayer,* exaucer une prière. **2. To answer the purpose,** remplir le but. *That will a. my purpose,* cela fera mon affaire. *His scheme didn't a.,* son projet n'a pas réussi. **3. To answer** (= *vouch*) **for s.o.,** répondre de qn. *He has a lot to answer for,* il est responsable de bien des choses. **answering,** *a. An a. cry,* un cri jeté en réponse.

answerable, *a.* Garant, responsable (*to s.o. for sth.,* envers qn de qch.).

ant, *s.* Fourmi *f.* **White ant,** fourmi blanche; termite *m.* **ant-bear,** *s.* *Z:* Tamanoir *m.* **ant-eater,** *s.* *Z:* Fourmilier *m.* **ant-hill,** *s.* Fourmilière *f.*

antagonism, *s.* Antagonisme *m*, opposition *f.*

antagonistic, *a.* Opposé, contraire (*to,* à).

antagonize, *v.tr.* Éveiller l'antagonisme, l'hostilité, de (qn).

antarctic. *à.* Antarctique.

antecedent. 1. *a.* Antécédent,-e; antérieur,-e (*to,* à). **2.** *s.* Antécédent *m.*

antediluvian, *a. & s.* Antédiluvien, -ienne.

antelope, *s.* *Z:* Antilope *f.*

ante meridiem. *Lt.phr.* Avant midi. *Five a.m.,* cinq heures du matin.

antenna, *s.* *Ent:* Antenne *f.*

antepenultimate, *a.* Antépénultième.

anterior, *a.* Antérieur,-e (*to,* à).

anthem, *s.* **1.** *Ecc.Mus:* Motet *m.* **2.** National anthem, hymne national.

anther, *s.* *Bot:* Anthère *f.*

anthology, *s.* Anthologie *f*, florilège *m.*

Anthony. *Pr.n.* Antoine *m.*

anthracite, *s.* *Min:* Anthracite *m.*

anthropoid, *a. & s.* Anthropoïde (*m*).

anthropological, *a.* Anthropologique.

anthropologist, *s.* Anthropologiste *m*, anthropologue *m.*

anthropology, *s.* Anthropologie *f.*

anti-aircraft, *a.* **Anti-aircraft gun,** canon anti-aérien, contre-avion(s).

antic, *s.* (*Usu. pl.*) (*a*) Bouffonnerie *f.* **To play one's antics,** faire le bouffon, faire des singeries. (*b*) *pl.* Gambades *f*, cabrioles *f.*

antichrist, *s.* Antéchrist *m.*

anticipate, *v.tr.* **1.** (*a*) *To a. events,* anticiper sur les événements. (*b*) Escompter (un résultat). **2.** *To a. s.o.,* prévenir, devancer, qn. **3.** Anticiper, avancer (un payement). **4.** Prévoir, envisager; se promettre (un plaisir).

anticipation, *s.* Anticipation *f.* **1.** Action *f* d'escompter (un résultat). *Com:* 'Thanking you in anticipation," "avec mes remercîments anticipés." **2.** Prévision *f.* **3.** Attente *f.*

antidote, *s.* Antidote *m*, contre-poison *m.*

Antilles (the). *Pr.n. Geog:* Les Antilles *f.*

antimacassar, *s.* Têtière *f*, voile *m* (de fauteuil).

antimony, *s.* Antimoine *m.*

antipathetic(al), *a.* Antipathique (*to,* à).

antipathy, *s.* Antipathie *f* (*to,* pour).

antipodes, *s.pl.* **The antipodes,** les antipodes *m.*

antiquarian. 1. *a.* Archéologique. **2.** *s.* = ANTIQUARY.

antiquary, *s.* Archéologue *m*; amateur *m* d'antiquités.

antiquated, *a.* Vieilli; désuet, -ète; (*of pers.*) vieux jeu. *A. dress,* habit démodé.

antique. 1. *a.* Antique; suranné. **2.** *s.* (*a*) *Art:* The antique, l'antique *m.* (*b*) Objet *m* antique. **Antique dealer,** antiquaire *m.*

antiquity, *s.* **1.** (*a*) Ancienneté *f.* (*b*) L'antiquité (grecque). **2.** *pl.* Antiquités.

antirrhinum, *s.* *Bot:* Muflier *m*, gueule-de-loup *f.*

anti-Semitism, *s.* Antisémitisme *m*,

antiseptic, *a. & s. Med:* Antiseptique (*m*).
anti-tank, *attrib. a.* (Canon) antichars.
antithesis, *s.* **1.** Antithèse *f* (*to, of,* de).
2. Opposé *m*, contraire *m* (de).
antithetic(al), *a.* Antithétique. **-ally,** *adv.*
Par antithèse.
antitoxin, *s. Med:* Antitoxine *f.*
antler, *s.* Andouiller *m.* **The antlers,** le bois,
les bois.
Antony. *Pr.n.* Antoine *m.*
antonym, *s.* Antonyme *m.*
Antwerp. *Pr.n. Geog:* Anvers *m.*
anvil, *s. Metalw:* Enclume *f.*
anxiety, *s.* (*a*) Inquiétude *f. Deep a.,* anxiété
f. (*b*) *A. for s.o.'s safety,* sollicitude *f* pour la
sûreté de qn. (*c*) *A. for knowledge,* désir *m*
de savoir.
anxious, *a.* **1.** (*a*) Inquiet, soucieux (*about,*
sur, de, au sujet de). (*b*) Inquiétant. *An a.
moment,* un moment d'anxiété. **2.** Désireux.
To be a. for sth., désirer vivement qch.
-ly, *adv.* **1.** (*a*) Avec inquiétude. (*b*)
Anxieusement. **2.** Avec sollicitude. **3.** Avec
impatience.
any. I. *a. & pron.* **1.** (*Some(one)*) *Is there
any Englishman who . . .?* y a-t-il un Anglais
qui . . .? *Have you any milk?* avez-vous
du lait? *If any of them should see him,* si
aucun d'entre eux le voyait. *There are few
if any,* il y en a peu, si tant est qu'il y en ait
du tout. *He knows English if any man does,*
il sait l'anglais comme pas un. **2.** (*a*) *Not
any,* ne . . . aucun, nul. *I can't find any,*
je n'en trouve pas. (*b*) (*With implied negation*)
The impossibility of giving him any education,
l'impossibilité de lui donner aucune éducation. **3.** (*a*) (*No matter which*) N'importe
(le)quel. *Come any day (you like),* venez
n'importe quel jour. *Any but he would have
refused,* tout autre que lui aurait refusé.
That may happen any day, cela peut arriver
d'un jour à l'autre. *Draw any two cards,*
tirez deux cartes quelconques. (*b*) (*Any and
every*) *At any hour of the day,* à toute heure
de la journée. II. **any,** *adv.* (*Not translated*)
I cannot go any further, je ne peux aller plus
loin.
anybody, anyone, *s. & pron.* **1.** Quelqu'un ;
(*with implied negation*) personne. *Do you see
a. over there?* voyez-vous quelqu'un là-bas?
Does a. dare to say so? y a-t-il personne qui
ose le dire? **2.** Not anybody, not anyone,
ne . . . personne. **3.** (*No matter who*)
N'importe qui ; tout le monde. *A. will tell
you so,* le premier venu vous le dira. *A. would
think him mad,* on le croirait fou. *A. who
had seen him at that time,* quiconque
l'aurait vu alors. **Anyone but he,** tout
autre que lui.
anyhow. **1.** *adv.* **To do sth. anyhow,** faire
qch. tant bien que mal. **2.** *conj.* En tout
cas, de toute façon. *A. you can try,* vous
pouvez toujours essayer.
anything, *pron. & s.* **1.** Quelque chose ;

(*with implied negation*) rien. **Can I do anything for you?** puis-je vous être utile à
quelque chose? *Is there a. more pleasant
than . . .?* est-il rien de plus agréable que
. . .? **If anything should happen to him,**
s'il lui arrivait quelque malheur. **2.** Not
anything, ne . . . rien. *Hardly a.,* presque
rien. **3.** (*No matter what*) N'importe quoi ;
tout. *Anything you like,* tout ce que vous
voudrez. **He is anything but mad,** il n'est
rien moins que fou. **4.** *Adv.phr.* (*Intensive*)
F: **Like anything,** avec acharnement. *It is
raining like a.,* il pleut tant qu'il peut.
anyway, *adv. & conj.* = ANYHOW.
anywhere, *adv.* **1.** N'importe où. *Can you
see it a.?* peux-tu le voir quelque part?
Anywhere else, partout ailleurs. **2. Not . . .
anywhere,** nulle part ; en aucun endroit.
anywise, *adv.* **1.** D'une manière quelconque.
2. En aucune façon ; d'aucune façon.
aorta, *s. Anat:* Aorte *f.*
apace, *adv. Lit:* A grands pas ; vite.
Apache, *s.* Apache *m.*
apart, *adv.* A part. **1.** (*Aside*) De côté.
2. (*Separate*) **To get two things apart,**
séparer deux choses. **To come apart,** se
détacher, se défaire. *To stand with one's feet
wide apart,* se tenir les jambes écartées.
3. (*a*) (*Distant*) *They are a mile a.,* ils sont à
un mille l'un de l'autre. (*b*) **Apart from the
fact that . . .,** hormis que . . ., outre
que. . . . *Joking apart,* plaisanterie à part.
apartment, *s.* (*a*) Salle *f*, chambre *f* ; pièce
f. (*b*) (*Usu. pl.*) Logement *m* ; appartement
m. **To let furnished apartments,** louer en
meublé.
apathetic, *a.* Apathique, indifférent. **-ally,**
adv. Apathiquement ; nonchalamment.
apathy, *s.* Apathie *f*, nonchalance *f.*
ape[1], *s.* (*a*) *Z:* (Grand) singe (sans queue).
(*b*) *F:* Singe. **To play the ape,** faire le singe.
ape[2], *v.tr.* Singer ; imiter ; mimer.
aperient, *a. & s. Med:* Laxatif (*m*).
aperture, *s.* Ouverture *f*, orifice *m.*
apex, *s.* Sommet *m* (d'un triangle). *F:* Point
culminant (d'une carrière).
aphis, *s. Ent:* Aphidé *m* ; puceron *m.*
aphorism, *s.* Aphorisme *m.*
apiary, *s.* Rucher *m.*
apiece, *adv.* Chacun. *To cost a penny a.,*
coûter un penny (la) pièce.
apish, *a.* **1.** Simiesque. *A. trick,* singerie *f.*
2. Imitateur, -trice.
apishness, *s.* Singeries *fpl* ; sotte imitation.
apocalypse, *s.* Apocalypse *f.*
apocalyptic, *a.* Apocalyptique.
Apocrypha (the), *s.pl. B.Lit:* Les Apo-
cryphes *m.*
apocryphal, *a.* Apocryphe.
apogee, *s.* Apogée *m.*
Apollo. *Pr.n. Myth:* Apollon *m.*
apologetic, *a.* (Ton) d'excuse. **-ally,** *adv.*
En manière d'excuse ; en s'excusant.
apologist, *s.* Apologiste *m.*

apologize, *v.i.* To apologize to s.o. for sth., s'excuser de qch. auprès de qn.
apologue, *s.* Apologue *m.*
apology, *s.* **I.** (*a*) Excuses *fpl.* **To make an apology,** faire des excuses. (*b*) *F:* An a. for a dinner, un semblant de dîner. **2.** Apologie *f* (*for*, de) ; justification *f.*
apoplectic, *a.* Apoplectique ; d'apoplexie.
apoplexy, *s.* *Med:* Apoplexie *f.*
apostasy, *s.* Apostasie *f.*
apostate, *a. & s.* Apostat (*m*).
apostle, *s.* Apôtre *m.*
apostolic(al), *a.* Apostolique.
apostrophe, *s.* Apostrophe *f.*
apostrophize, *v.tr.* Apostropher.
apothecary, *s.* Apothicaire *m.*
apotheosis, *s.* Apothéose *f.*
appal, *v.tr.* Consterner ; épouvanter. **appalling,** *a.* Épouvantable, effroyable. **-ly,** *adv.* Épouvantablement, effroyablement.
apparatus, *s.* Appareil *m,* dispositif *m.*
apparel, *s.* Vêtement(s) *m,* habillement *m.*
apparent, *a.* Apparent, manifeste, évident. **-ly,** *adv.* **I.** Évidemment, manifestement. **2.** Apparemment *This is a. true,* il paraît que c'est vrai.
apparition, *s.* **I.** Apparition *f.* **2.** Fantôme *m,* revenant *m.*
appeal¹, *s.* **I.** Appel *m,* recours *m.* **2.** *To make an a. to s.o.'s generosity,* faire appel à la générosité de qn. **3.** Prière *f,* supplication *f.*
appeal², *v.i.* **I.** (*a*) To appeal to the law, invoquer l'aide de la justice. *To a. to the country,* en appeler au pays. (*b*) *Abs.* Interjeter appel. **2.** *To a. to s.o. for help,* faire appel à qn. **3.** *To a. to s.o.'s imagination,* s'adresser à l'imagination de qn. **The plan appeals to me,** le projet me sourit. **That doesn't appeal to me,** cela ne me dit rien.
appealing, *a.* **I.** (Regard) suppliant. **2.** (Ton) émouvant. **-ly,** *adv.* D'un ton, d'un regard, suppliant.
appear, *v.i.* **I.** (*Become visible*) Paraître, apparaître ; se montrer. *A ghost appeared to him,* un spectre lui apparut. **2.** (*Present oneself publicly*) (*a*) Se présenter. *Jur:* To a. before a court, comparaître devant un tribunal. **To appear for s.o.,** représenter qn. (*b*) **To appear on the stage,** entrer en scène. (*c*) (*Of book*) Paraître. **3.** (*a*) (*Seem*) To a. sad, paraître triste. **So it appears,** il paraît que oui. (*b*) (*Be manifest*) As will presently a., comme on le verra bientôt.
appearance, *s.* **I.** (*a*) Apparition *f* ; entrée *f.* **To make one's appearance,** paraître, se montrer, se présenter. **To make one's first appearance,** débuter ; faire ses débuts. (*b*) Comparution *f* (devant un tribunal). **2.** (*a*) (*Look, aspect*) Apparence *f,* air *m,* mine *f.* **To have a good a.,** faire bonne figure. **At first appearance,** à première vue ; au premier abord. (*b*) (*Semblance*) Apparence. **By all appearance(s),** selon toute apparence. **For the sake of appearances,** pour sauver les apparences.

appease, *v.tr.* Apaiser.
appeasement, *s.* Apaisement *m.*
appellation, *s.* Appellation *f,* nom *m,* désignation *f.*
append, *v.tr.* Attacher, joindre (qch. à qch.).
appendage, *s.* Accessoire *m,* apanage *m* (*to,* de).
appendicitis, *s.* Appendicite *f.*
appendix, *s.* Appendice *m.*
appertain, *v.i.* **I.** Appartenir (*to,* à). **2.** Se rapporter (*to,* à).
appetite, *s.* (*a*) Appétit *m.* *To have a good a.,* avoir bon appétit. **To spoil s.o.'s appetite,** gâter l'appétit à qn. (*b*) **Appetite for revenge,** soif *f* de vengeance.
appetizer, *s.* Apéritif *m.*
appetizing, *a.* Appétissant, alléchant.
applaud, *v.tr.* **I.** Applaudir (qn). **2.** *To a. s.o.'s efforts,* applaudir aux efforts de qn.
applause, *s.* **I.** Applaudissements *mpl.* *To be greeted with a.,* être applaudi. **2.** Approbation *f.*
apple, *s.* **I.** Pomme *f.* **2.** Apple of the eye, prunelle *f* de l'œil. **apple-cart,** *s.* *F:* To upset s.o.'s apple-cart, bouleverser les plans de qn. **apple-green,** *a. & s.* Vert pomme *m. inv.* **apple-orchard,** *s.* Pommeraie *f.* **apple-pie,** *s.* Tourte *f* aux pommes. *F:* In apple-pie order, en ordre parfait. Apple-pie bed, lit *m* en portefeuille. **applesauce,** *s.* Compote *f* de pommes. **apple-tart,** *s.* Tourte *f* aux pommes. **apple-tree,** *s.* Pommier *m.*
appliance, *s.* (*a*) Appareil *m,* instrument *m,* dispositif *m.* (*b*) *pl.* Accessoires *m* ; attirail *m.*
applicable, *a.* **I.** Applicable (*to,* à). **2.** Approprié (*to,* à).
applicant, *s.* *A. for a place,* candidat *m* à une place ; solliciteur *m* d'une place.
application, *s.* **I.** (*a*) Application *f* (*of sth. to sth.,* de qch. à, sur, qch.). *Pharm:* 'For external application,' "pour l'usage externe." (*b*) (*Thing applied*) Application ; enduit *m.* (*c*) Application (d'une découverte). **2.** Assiduité *f,* application **3.** Demande *f,* sollicitation *f.*
apply, *v.tr. & i.* **I.** (*a*) Appliquer (sth. to sth., qch. sur qch.) ; faire l'application de (qch. à qch.). (*b*) *This applies to my case,* ceci s'applique à mon propre cas. (*c*) To a. one's mind to sth., s'appliquer à qch. **2.** *To a. to s.o.,* s'adresser, recourir, à qn. *To a. for a post,* solliciter un emploi. **applied,** *a.* The applied sciences, les sciences appliquées. Applied arts, arts industriels.
appoint, *v.tr.* **I.** Nommer. (*a*) *Pred.* To a. s.o. mayor, nommer qn maire. (*b*) To a. s.o. to sth., nommer qn à qch. **2.** Fixer, arrêter (un jour). **appointed,** *a.* **I.** Désigné. *At the a. time,* à l'heure dite. **2.** Équipé, monté. Well-appointed house, maison bien installée.
appointment, *s.* **I.** Rendez-vous *m.* **2.** (*a*) *A. of s.o. to a post,* nomination *f* de qn à un emploi. *Purveyor by appointment to His*

Majesty, fournisseur breveté, attitré, de sa Majesté. (b) Place f, charge f, emploi m. **3.** pl. Équipement m (d'une auto).

apportion, v.tr. Répartir (les frais); lotir (une propriété).

apportionment, s. Partage m, répartition f.

apposite, a. Juste; approprié (to, à); (fait) à propos. **-ly,** adv. À propos.

appraise, v.tr. Priser, évaluer (qch.) (at so much, à tant); faire l'expertise de.

appraisement, s. Évaluation f, estimation f.

appraiser, s. Estimateur m, priseur m.

appreciable, a. Appréciable; sensible. **-ably,** adv. Sensiblement.

appreciate. I. v.tr. Apprécier; faire cas de (qch.). I fully appreciate that . . ., je me rends clairement compte que. . . . **2.** v.i. Augmenter de valeur; hausser de prix.

appreciation, s. **I.** (a) Appréciation f (d'un service); estimation f (de la valeur de qch.). (b) To write an a., faire la critique (of, de). **2.** Accroissement m, hausse f, de valeur.

appreciative, a. **I.** (Jugement) élogieux. **2.** To be appreciative of music, apprécier la musique. **-ively,** adv. (a) Favorablement. (b) Avec satisfaction.

apprehend, v.tr. **I.** Arrêter (qn); appréhender (qn). **2.** Comprendre. **3.** Appréhender, redouter.

apprehension, s. **I.** Arrestation f. **2.** Compréhension f. **3.** Appréhension f, crainte f.

apprehensive, a. Timide, craintif. To be apprehensive of danger, redouter le danger.

apprentice¹, s. Apprenti, -ie.

apprentice², v.tr. To apprentice s.o., placer qn en apprentissage (to, chez).

apprenticeship, s. Apprentissage m.

apprise, v.tr. To apprise s.o. of sth., prévenir qn de qch.

approach¹, s. Approche f. **I.** (a) The a. of death, l'approche de la mort. (b) Easy of approach, d'un abord facile. (c) To make approaches to s.o., faire des avances à qn. **2.** Voie f d'accès. **3.** Rapprochement m.

approach². **I.** v.i. Approcher, s'approcher. To a. to perfection, approcher de la perfection. **2.** v.tr. (a) We are approaching London, nous approchons de Londres. (b) S'approcher de; aborder, approcher. To be easy to approach, avoir l'abord facile. (c) To a. a question, aborder, s'attaquer à, une question. **approaching,** a. His a. death, sa mort prochaine.

approbation, s. Approbation f.

appropriate¹, a. **I.** Approprié. **2.** Propre, convenable (to, for, à). **-ly,** adv. Convenablement, proprement; à propos.

appropriate², v.tr. **I.** S'approprier; s'emparer de. **2.** Approprier, affecter (qch. à une destination).

appropriateness, s. Convenance f, justesse f, à-propos m, applicabilité f.

appropriation, s. **I.** Appropriation f. (of, de). **2.** Affectation f (de qch. à un usage).

approval, s. **I.** Approbation f, agrément m. To nod approval, approuver de la tête. **2.** Adm: Ratification f. **3.** Com: On approval, à condition.

approve. **I.** v.tr. (a) The old approved methods, les méthodes classiques. (b) Approuver (une action); ratifier (une décision). **2.** v.ind.tr. To approve of sth., approuver qch. I don't a. of your friends, vos amis ne me plaisent pas. **approving,** a. Approbateur, -trice. **-ly,** adv. D'un air approbateur.

approximate¹, a. (Calcul) approximatif. **-ly,** adv. Approximativement.

approximate². **I.** v.tr. Rapprocher (deux cas). **2.** v.i. To a. to the truth, approcher, se rapprocher, de la vérité.

approximation, s. **I.** Rapprochement m. **2.** Approximation f.

appurtenance, s. **I.** Jur: Appartenance f. **2.** pl. Accessoires m.

apricot, s. **I.** Abricot m. **2.** Apricot(-tree), abricotier m.

April, s. Avril m. **April-fool-day,** le premier avril. To make an April-fool of s.o., faire un poisson d'avril à qn.

apron, s. Tablier m. **apron-strings,** s.pl. F: To be tied to one's mother's apron-strings être pendu aux jupes de sa mère.

apse, s. Ecc.Arch: Abside f, apside f.

apt, a. **I.** (Mot) juste, fin. **2.** Apt to do sth. (a) (Of pers.) Enclin, porté, à faire qch. (b) (Of thg) Sujet à, susceptible de, faire qch. **3.** (Élève) intelligent. To be apt at sth., être habile à qch. **-ly,** adv. **I.** Avec justesse; convenablement. **2.** Adroitement.

aptitude, s. Aptitude f (for, à, pour); disposition(s) f (for, pour).

aptness, s. **I.** Justesse f, à-propos m. **2.** Penchant m (to do sth., à faire qch.).

aquamarine, s. Aigue-marine f.

aquarium, s. Aquarium m.

aquatic, a. **I.** Aquatique. **2.** Aquatic sports, sports nautiques.

aqueduct, s. Aqueduc m.

aquiline, a. Aquilin.

Arab, a. & s. Arabe (mf).

Arabia. Pr.n. L'Arabie f.

Arabian. **I.** a. Arabe, d'Arabie. The Arabian Gulf, le golfe Arabique. The Arabian Nights, les Mille et une Nuits. **2.** s. Arabe mf.

Arabic. **I.** a. (Gomme) arabique; (langue) arabe. **2.** s. Ling: L'arabe m.

arable, a. (Terre) arable, labourable.

arbiter, s. Arbitre m.

arbitrary, a. Arbitraire. **-ily,** adv. Arbitrairement.

arbitrate. I. v.tr. Arbitrer, juger. **2.** v.i. Décider en qualité d'arbitre; arbitrer.

arbitration, s. Arbitrage m.

arbitrator, s. Arbitre m.

arbour, s. Berceau m de verdure; tonnelle f.

arc, s. Arc m.

arcade, s. (a) Arcade(s) f; galeries fpl. (b) Passage m (à boutiques).

arch[1], s. **1.** Voûte f, arc m; cintre m. **Centre arch,** voûte maîtresse. A. of a vault, arceau m. **2.** Arche f (d'un pont). **Railway arch,** pont m de chemin de fer.

arch[2]. **1.** v.tr. Arquer; cambrer. **2.** v.i. Se voûter, former voûte. **arched,** a. (a) A arc, en voûte; voûté. (b) Arqué, cintré; cambré.

arch[3], a. Espiègle; malicieux. **-ly,** adv. D'un air espiègle.

archaeologic(al), a. Archéologique.

archaeologist, s. Archéologue m.

archaeology, s. Archéologie f.

archaic, a. Archaïque.

archaism, s. Archaïsme m.

archangel, s. Archange m.

archbishop, s. Archevêque m.

archdeacon, s. Archidiacre m.

archer, s. Archer m.

archery, s. Tir m à l'arc.

arch-fiend, s. The a.-f., Satan m.

archipelago, s. Archipel m. **The Indian Archipelago,** l'Insulinde f.

architect, s. Architecte m.

architecture, s. Architecture f.

archives, s.pl. Archives f.

archness, s. Malice f, espièglerie f.

archpriest, s. Archiprêtre m.

archway, s. Passage voûté; portail m.

arctic, a. Arctique.

ardent, a. Ardent. **-ly,** adv. Ardemment; avec ardeur.

ardour, s. Ardeur f.

arduous, a. (Travail) ardu; (chemin) escarpé. **-ly,** adv. Péniblement.

arduousness, s. Arduité f, difficulté f.

area, s. **1.** Cour f d'entrée en sous-sol. **2.** Aire f, superficie f **3.** Étendue f (de pays); région f. **Postal area,** zone postale.

areca, s. Bot: Arec m. **Areca palm,** aréquier m. **Areca-nut,** (noix f d')arec.

arena, s. (a) Arène f. (b) Champ m (d'une activité).

Argentina. Pr.n. Geog: L'Argentine f.

Argentine, a. Geog: **The Argentine Republic,** la République Argentine.

argillaceous, a. Argileux.

Argonaut, s. Gr.Myth: Argonaute m.

arguable, a. Discutable, soutenable.

argue. 1. v.tr. (a) Prouver, indiquer, démontrer. (b) Discuter, débattre. **2.** v.i. (a) Argumenter (about sth., sur qch.). **To argue from sth.,** tirer argument de qch. (b) Discuter, (se) disputer, raisonner (with s.o. about sth., avec qn sur qch.); plaider (for, against, sth., pour, contre, qch.).

argument, s. **1.** Argument m (for, against, en faveur de, contre). To follow s.o.'s (line of) a., suivre le raisonnement de qn For the sake of a., à titre d'exemple. **2.** Discussion f, dispute f, débat m.

argumentative, a. Raisonneur, -euse.

argumentativeness, s. Esprit raisonneur.

aria, s. Mus: Aria f.

arid, a. Aride.

aridity, aridness, s. Aridité f.

aright, adv. Bien, juste, correctement.

Ariosto. Pr.n. Lit.Hist: L'Arioste m.

arise, v.i. **1.** A prophet arose, un prophète surgit. **2.** (a) S'élever, survenir, se présenter. A storm arose, il survint une tempête. **Should the occasion arise,** le cas échéant. (b) Émaner, provenir, résulter (from, de).

aristocracy, s. Aristocratie f.

aristocrat, s. Aristocrate mf.

aristocratic, a. Aristocratique.

Aristophanes. Pr.n. Aristophane m.

Aristotle. Pr.n. Aristote m.

arithmetic, s. Arithmétique f, calcul m.

arithmetical, a. Arithmétique. **-ally,** adv. Arithmétiquement.

ark, s. Arche f.

arm[1], s. **1.** Bras m. **Arm-in-arm,** bras dessus bras dessous. She took my arm, elle me prit le bras. **To put one's arm round s.o.,** prendre qn par la taille. **At arm's length,** à bout de bras. F: **To keep s.o. at arm's length,** tenir qn à distance. **2.** Bras de fauteuil; fléau m (de balance). **arm-chair,** s. Fauteuil m.

arm-rest, s. Veh: Accoudoir m, accotoir m.

arm[2], s. Usu. pl. **1.** Arme f. (a) **To take up arms,** prendre les armes (against, contre). **To lay down one's arms,** mettre bas les armes. (b) Mil: (Branch of service) Arme. **2.** pl. Her: Armoiries f, armes.

arm[3]. **1.** v.tr. Armer. **2.** v.i. S'armer; prendre les armes. **armed,** a. Armé (with, de). **arming,** s. Nau: Suif m (de la grande sonde).

armada, s. F: Grande flotte de guerre.

armadillo, s. Z: Tatou m.

armament, s. **1.** Armement m. **2.** Forces fpl; armée f, flotte navale.

Armenia. Pr.n. L'Arménie f.

Armenian, a. & s. Arménien, -ienne.

armful, s. Brassée f. In armfuls, à pleins bras.

armistice, s. Armistice m.

armlet, s. Brassard m.

armorial, a. A. bearings, armoiries fpl.

armour, s. **1.** Armure f Suit of armour, armure complète. **In full armour,** armé de pied en cap. **2.** (a) Blindage m. (b) N.Arch: Cuirasse f, blindage. **armour-plate,** s. N.Arch: Plaque f de cuirasse, de blindage.

armour-plated, a. Cuirassé; blindé.

armourer, s. Armurier m.

armoury, s. Magasin m d'armes.

armpit, s. Aisselle f.

army, s. **1.** Armée f. **To join the army,** se faire soldat. **Standing army, regular army,** armée permanente **2.** F: Foule f, multitude

f. **army-corps,** *s.inv.* Corps *m* d'armée.
Army-list, *s.* L'Annuaire *m* militaire.
arnica, *s.* Arnica *f.*
aroma, *s.* Arome *m*; bouquet *m* (d'un vin).
aromatic, *a.* Aromatique; (parfum) balsamique.
around. 1. *adv.* Autour, à l'entour. *The woods a.*, les bois d'alentour. **2.** *prep* Autour de.
arouse, *v.tr.* **1.** (*a*) Réveiller, éveiller. (*b*) Secouer (qn) (de sa paresse); stimuler (qn). **2.** Exciter, susciter (un sentiment).
arraign, *v.tr.* (*a*) Mettre en accusation; accuser (*for*, de). (*b*) Attaquer, s'en prendre à.
arraignment, *s.* **1.** (*a*) Mise *f* en accusation. (*b*) Acte *m* d'accusation. **2.** Censure *f.*
arrange, *v.tr.* Arranger, aménager. **1.** (*a*) (*Set in order*) Disposer, ranger. (*b*) Adapter, arranger (pour piano). **2.** (*Plan beforehand*) Arranger. *To a. to do sth.*, s'arranger pour faire qch. *To a. a time*, fixer une heure. *It was arranged that . . .*, il fut convenu que. . . . **3.** (*Settle*) Ajuster, arranger.
arranging, *s.* Arrangement *m*, règlement *m*, ajustement *m.*
arrangement, *s.* **1.** Arrangement *m*, disposition *f.* **To make arrangements to do sth.,** prendre des dispositions pour faire qch. **2.** Accommodement *m*; entente *f.*
arrant, *a.* Insigne, achevé.
array¹, *s.* (*a*) Rangs *mpl.* (*b*) Étalage *m.*
array², *v.tr.* Ranger, mettre en ordre; disposer.
arrear(s), *s.* Arriéré *m.* **Rent in arrear,** loyer arriéré. **To get into arrears,** se mettre en retard; s'arriérer.
arrest¹, *s.* **1.** Arrestation *f.* **2.** Arrêt *m*, suspension *f* (d'un mouvement).
arrest², *v.tr.* **1.** Arrêter (un mouvement). **2.** Arrêter (un malfaiteur). **3.** Arrêter, fixer, retenir (l'attention). **arresting,** *a.* Attachant, frappant.
arrival, *s.* **1.** (*a*) Arrivée *f.* **On arrival,** à l'arrivée. (*b*) *Com:* Arrivage *m* (de marchandises). (*c*) *Nau:* Entrée *f* (d'un vaisseau). **2. A new arrival,** un nouveau venu.
arrive, *v.i.* **1.** Arriver (*at, in*, à, dans). *We arrived at three o'clock*, nous sommes arrivés à trois heures. *To a. unexpectedly*, survenir. **2.** *To a. at a conclusion*, arriver à une conclusion. *To a. at a price*, fixer un prix.
arrogance, *s.* Arrogance *f*; morgue *f.*
-ly, *adv.* Avec arrogance.
arrogate, *v.tr.* **To arrogate sth. to oneself,** s'arroger qch., s'attribuer qch.
arrow, *s.* Flèche *f.* *To shoot, let fly, an a.*, lancer, décocher, une flèche. *Adm:* **Broad arrow** = marque *f* de l'État. **arrow-head,** *s.* Tête *f*, fer *m*, pointe *f*, de flèche.
arsenal, *s.* Arsenal *m*, -aux.
arsenic, *s.* Arsenic *m.*
arson, *s.* Incendie *m* volontaire.
art, *s.* **1.** Art *m.* (*a*) The (fine) arts, les

beaux-arts. (*b*) **The black art,** la magie noire. **2.** Adresse *f*, habileté *f.* *To use every art,* user de tous les artifices. **art-school,** *s.* École *f* de dessin.
arterial, *a.* **1.** *Anat:* Artériel. **2. Arterial road,** grande voie de communication.
artery, *s.* *Anat:* Artère *f.*
artful, *a.* (*a*) Adroit, ingénieux. (*b*) Rusé, artificieux. **-fully,** *adv.* **1.** Adroitement. **2.** Artificieusement.
artfulness, *s.* **1.** Art *m*, adresse *f*, habileté *f*, ingéniosité *f.* **2.** Astuce *f.*
artichoke, *s.* **1.** Artichaut *m.* **2. Jerusalem artichoke,** topinambour *m.*
article¹, *s.* **1.** (*a*) Article *m*, clause *f* (d'un contrat). **Articles of partnership,** contrat *m* de société. *Mil:* **Articles of war,** code *m* (de justice) militaire. (*b*) **Article of faith,** article de foi. **2.** Article (de journal). **3.** (*a*) Article, objet *m.* (*b*) *A. of clothing,* pièce *f* d'habillement. **4.** *Gram:* Article.
article², *v.tr.* *To a. s.o.,* placer qn (comme élève) (*to*, chez). **Articled clerk,** clerc d'avoué.
articulate¹, *a.* (*a*) *A. speech,* langage articulé. (*b*) (*Of utterance*) Net, distinct.
articulate², *v.tr. & i.* **1.** *Anat:* Articuler. **2.** Articuler, énoncer (un mot).
artifice, *s.* **1.** Artifice *m*, ruse *f*; combinaison *f.* **2.** Art *m*, habileté *f*, adresse *f.*
artificer, *s.* Artisan *m*, ouvrier *m.* *Navy:* Engine-room artificer, mécanicien *m.*
artificial, *a.* **1.** Artificiel. **2.** Factice, simulé. **-ally,** *adv.* Artificiellement.
artillery, *s.* Artillerie *f.*
artilleryman, *s.* Artilleur *m.*
artisan, *s.* Artisan *m*, ouvrier *m.*
artist, *s.* (*a*) Artiste *mf.* (*b*) Artiste peintre *mf. He is an a.,* il est peintre.
artiste, *s.* *Th:* Artiste *mf.*
artistic(al), *a.* Artistique; (style) artiste. **-ally,** *adv.* Artistement, avec art, artistiquement.
artless, *a.* **1.** Naturel; sans artifice. **2.** Naïf, ingénu. **-ly,** *adv.* **1.** Naturellement, simplement. **2.** Naïvement.
artlessness, *s.* **1.** Naturel *m*, simplicité *f.* **2.** Naïveté *f*, ingénuité *f.*
arum, *s.* *Bot:* Arum *m.* **Arum lily,** arum.
Aryan, *a. & s.* *Ethn:* Aryen, -enne.
as. I. *adv.* **1.** Aussi, si. *I am as tall as you,* je suis aussi grand que vous. **2.** *I worked as hard as I could,* j'ai travaillé tant que j'ai pu. **3.** *As to that,* quant à cela. *To entertain fears as to sth.,* éprouver des craintes au sujet de qch. **II.** *As, conj. & rel. adv.* **1.** (*Degree*) (*a*) Que. *You are as tall as he,* vous êtes aussi grand que lui. (*b*) Comme. *As pale as death,* pâle comme un mort. **2.** *Ignorant as he is,* tout ignorant qu'il est. *Be that as it may,* quoi qu'il en soit. **3.** (*Manner*) (*a*) Comme. *Do as you like,* faites comme vous voudrez. *Leave it as it is,* laissez-le tel qu'il est. *As it is,* les choses étant ainsi. (*b*) *As . . ., so. . . . As the parents do, so*

will the children, tel font les parents, tel feront les enfants. (*c*) *To treat s.o. as a stranger*, traiter qn en étranger. *He was often ill as a child*, il fut souvent malade dans son enfance. **4.** (*Time*) (*a*) *One day as I was sitting . . .*, un jour que j'étais assis. . . . (*b*) *He grew more charitable as he grew older*, il devenait plus charitable en vieillissant. **5.** (*Reason*) *As you are not ready we cannot go*, comme, puisque, vous n'êtes pas prêt, nous ne pouvons pas partir. **6.** (*Result*) *Be so good as to come*, soyez assez bon pour venir. III. **as**, *rel. pron. Beasts of prey*, (such) *as the lion*, les bêtes fauves, telles que, comme, le lion.

asbestos, *s.* Asbeste *m*, amiante *m*.

ascend. I. *v.i.* Monter, s'élever. **2.** *v.tr.* (*a*) *To ascend the throne*, monter sur le trône. (*b*) *To a. a hill*, gravir une colline. (*c*) *To a. a river*, remonter un fleuve. **ascending,** *a.* **I.** *Mth:* Ascendant. **2.** (*Sentier*) montant.

ascendancy, -ency, *s.* Ascendant *m*, influence *f* (*over s.o.*, sur qn).

ascendant, -ent, *s.* *To be in the ascendant*, (i) être à l'ascendant *m*; (ii) avoir le dessus.

ascent, *s.* **I.** Ascension *f*. **2.** Montée *f*, pente *f*, rampe *f*.

ascertain, *v.tr.* Constater; s'assurer de (la vérité de qch.).

ascertainment, *s.* Constatation *f*.

ascetic. I. *a.* Ascétique. **2.** *s.* Ascète *mf*.

asceticism, *s.* Ascétisme *m*.

ascribable, *a.* Attribuable, imputable (*to*, à).

ascribe, *v.tr.* Attribuer, imputer (*to*, à).

ash[1]**,** *s.* *Bot:* Frêne *m*.

ash[2]**,** *s.* **I.** (*a*) Cendre(s) *f(pl)*. *Cigar ash*, cendre de cigare. *To reduce to ashes*, réduire en cendres. **2.** Cendres (des morts). **ash-bin,** *s.* Cendrier *m*. **ash-pan,** *s.* Cendrier *m* (de poêle). **ash-tray,** *s.* Cendrier *m* (de fumeur). **Ash Wednesday,** *s.* Le mercredi des Cendres.

ashamed, *a.* Honteux, confus. *To be ashamed of s.o.*, avoir honte de qn. *I am a. of you*, vous me faites honte. *You ought to be ashamed of yourself*, vous devriez avoir honte.

ashen[1]**,** *a.* De frêne, en frêne.

ashen[2]**,** *a.* Cendré; couleur de cendres; (*of face*) pâle comme la mort.

ashore, *adv.* *Nau:* **I.** A terre. *To put* (*passengers*) *a.*, débarquer (des passagers). **2.** Échoué.

ashy, *a.* **I.** Cendreux; couvert de cendres. **2.** *He went ashy pale*, il devint blême.

Asia. *Pr.n.* *Geog:* L'Asie *f*. **Asia Minor,** l'Asie Mineure.

Asiatic, *a. & s.* Asiatique (*mf*); d'Asie.

aside. I. *adv.* De côté; à l'écart; à part. *To stand aside*, se ranger. *Putting that a. . . .*, à part cela. . . . *I took him a.*, je le pris à part. *Th: Words spoken a.*, paroles dites en aparté. **2.** *s.* *Th:* Aparté *m*. *In an aside*, en aparté.

asinine, *a.* *F:* Stupide, sot.

ask, *v.tr. & i.* Demander. **I.** (*Inquire*) *To ask s.o. sth.*, demander qch. à qn. *To ask s.o. a question*, faire une question à qn. *Ask the policeman*, adressez-vous à l'agent de police. **2.** (*a*) *To ask a favour of s.o.*, demander une faveur à qn. (*b*) *To ask six francs for sth.*, demander six francs pour qch. **3.** (*a*) *To ask to do sth.*, demander à faire qch. *He asked to be admitted*, il demanda qu'on le laissât entrer. (*b*) *To ask s.o. to do sth.*, demander à qn de faire qch. **4.** (*a*) *To ask about sth.*, se renseigner sur qch. *To ask s.o. about sth.*, interroger qn sur qch. (*b*) *To ask after s.o.*, demander des nouvelles de qn. **5.** (*a*) *To ask for s.o.*, demander à voir qn. (*b*) *To ask for sth.*, demander qch.; solliciter qch. **6.** *To ask s.o. to lunch*, inviter qn à déjeuner. **asking,** *s.* *It is yours for the asking*, il n'y a qu'à (le) demander.

askance, *adv.* *To look askance at s.o.*, regarder qn de travers, avec méfiance.

askew, *adv.* De biais, de côté.

aslant, *adv.* Obliquement, de biais.

asleep, *adv. & pred.a.* Endormi. **I.** *To be a.*, dormir, sommeiller. *To fall asleep*, s'endormir. **2.** *My foot is asleep*, j'ai le pied engourdi, endormi.

asp, *s.* Aspic *m*.

asparagus, *s.* *Coll.* Asperges *fpl*.

aspect, *s.* **I.** Exposition *f*, vue *f*; orientation *f*. **2.** Aspect *m*, air *m*. *To see sth. in its true aspect*, voir qch. sous son vrai jour.

aspen, *s.* *Bot:* (Peuplier *m*) tremble *m*.

asperity, *s.* **I.** (*a*) Apreté *f*. (*b*) Rigueur *f*, sévérité *f*. **2.** (*Rough excrescence*) Aspérité *f*.

asperse, *v.tr.* Calomnier, diffamer, dénigrer.

aspersion, *s.* Calomnie *f*. *To cast aspersions upon s.o.*, répandre des calomnies sur qn.

asphalt, *s.* Asphalte *m*.

asphodel, *s.* *Bot:* Asphodèle *m*.

asphyxia, *s.* Asphyxie *f*.

asphyxiate, *v.tr.* Asphyxier.

aspirant, *s.* Aspirant, -ante (*to, after*, à); candidat, -e.

aspirate[1]**. I.** *a.* *Ling:* Aspiré. **2.** *s.* (*a*) (Lettre) aspirée *f*. (*b*) (La lettre) h.

aspirate[2]**,** *v.tr.* Aspirer.

aspiration, *s.* Aspiration *f*.

aspire, *v.i.* Aspirer. *To a. to sth.*, aspirer à qch.; ambitionner qch. **aspiring,** *a.* Ambitieux.

aspirin, *s.* *Pharm:* Aspirine *f*. *F: Take an a.*, prenez un comprimé d'aspirine.

ass, *s.* **I.** Ane *f*, ânesse *f*. **2.** *F:* Sot, *f.* sotte; âne. *He is a perfect ass*, c'est un âne bâté. *To make an ass of oneself*, agir d'une manière idiote.

assail, *v.tr.* **I.** Assaillir, attaquer. **2.** *To a. the ear*, frapper l'oreille.

assailant, *s.* Assaillant *m*.

assassin, *s.* Assassin *m*.

assassinate, *v.tr.* Assassiner.

assassination, *s.* Assassinat *m*.

assault[1], *s.* **I.** (*a*) Assaut *m.* **To take by assault,** prendre d'assaut. (*b*) Attaque (brusquée). **2.** *Jur:* Assault and battery, Voies *fpl* de fait ; coups *mpl* et blessures *fpl.*

assault[2], *v.tr.* **I.** Donner l'assaut à (une ville). **2.** Attaquer (qn).

assay[1], *s.* Essai *m.*

assay[2], *v.tr.* Essayer, titrer.

assegai, *s.* Zagaie *f*, sagaie *f.*

assemblage, *s.* **I.** Assemblage *m.* **2.** (*a*) Réunion *f* (de personnes). (*b*) Collection *f* (d'objets).

assemble. **I.** *v.tr.* Assembler. **2.** *v.i.* S'assembler ; se rassembler.

assembly, *s.* **I.** (*a*) Assemblée *f.* (*b*) *Mil:* (Sonnerie *f* du) rassemblement *m.* **2.** Assemblement *m*, réunion *f.*

assent[1], *s.* Assentiment *m*, consentement *m.*

assent[2], *v.i.* Accéder, acquiescer (*to*, à).

assert, *v.tr.* **I.** (*a*) **To assert one's rights,** revendiquer, faire valoir, ses droits. (*b*) **To assert oneself,** soutenir ses droits ; s'imposer. **2.** Affirmer.

assertion, *s.* **I.** *A. of one's rights*, revendication *f* de ses droits. **2.** Affirmation *f.*

assertive, *a.* (Ton) péremptoire, cassant.

assertiveness, *s.* Assurance *f.*

assess, *v.tr.* **I.** (*a*) Répartir, établir (un impôt). (*b*) Estimer, évaluer. **2.** *Adm:* To *a. s.o. at so much*, taxer qn à tant.

assessment, *s.* **I.** (*a*) Évaluation *f* (de dégâts). (*b*) Imposition *f* (d'un immeuble). (*c*) Cotisation *f* (du contribuable). **2.** (*Amount*) Cote *f.*

assessor, *s.* Assesseur *m.*

asset, *s.* **I.** Possession *f* ; avoir *m.* **II.** **assets,** *s.pl.* **I.** Biens *m* meubles. **2.** *Com:* Actif *m.*

asseverate, *v.tr.* Affirmer (solennellement) (*that*, que + *ind.*).

asseveration, *s.* Affirmation (solennelle).

assiduity, *s.* Assiduité *f*, diligence *f* (*in doing sth.*, à faire qch.).

assiduous, *a.* Assidu. **-ly,** *adv.* Assidûment.

assign, *v.tr.* **I.** Assigner (*to*, à). (*a*) Donner (qch.) en partage (à qn). (*b*) **To assign a reason for sth.,** donner la raison de qch. **2.** Céder, transférer.

assignable, *a.* Assignable, attribuable (*to*, à).

assignation, *s.* Rendez-vous *m.*

assignment, *s.* **I.** Cession *f*, transfert *m.* **2.** Tâche assignée.

assimilate, *v.tr.* **I.** (*a*) Assimiler, comparer (*to*, à). (*b*) *v.i.* S'assimiler. **2.** *To a. food*, assimiler des aliments.

assimilation, *s.* **I.** Assimilation *f* (*to, with*, à). **2.** Assimilation (des aliments).

assist. **I.** *v.tr.* (*a*) Aider. (*b*) *To a. s.o. in misfortune*, secourir, assister, qn dans le malheur. **2.** *v.i. To a. at a ceremony*, prendre part à une cérémonie.

assistance, *s.* Aide *f*, secours *m*, assistance *f.*

To be of assistance to s.o., aider qn, être utile à qn.

assistant. **I.** *a.* Qui aide ; auxiliaire ; adjoint. **Assistant-master,** sous-maître *m.* **2.** *s.* Aide *mf* ; auxiliaire *mf.* *Com:* Commis *m* ; demoiselle *f* de magasin.

assizes, *s.pl.* Assises *fpl.*

associate[1], *s.* (*a*) Associé *m*, adjoint *m.* (*b*) Compagnon *m*, camarade *mf.*

associate[2]. **I.** *v.tr.* Associer (à qch.). **2.** *v.i.* (*a*) *To a. with s.o. in doing sth.*, s'associer avec qn pour faire qch. (*b*) *To a. with s.o.*, fréquenter qn.

association, *s.* **I.** (*a*) Association *f* (d'idées). *Land full of historic associations*, pays fertile en souvenirs historiques. (*b*) Fréquentation *f* (*with s.o.*, de qn). **2.** Association, société *f.*

assort. **I.** *v.tr.* (*a*) Assortir (*with*, à). (*b*) Classer, ranger (*with*, parmi). **2.** *v.i. To a. well with sth.*, (s')assortir bien avec qch.

assortment, *s.* **I.** Assortiment *m.* **2.** Classement *m*, classification *f.*

assuage, *v.tr.* Apaiser, soulager ; satisfaire.

assume, *v.tr.* **I.** Prendre (un air) ; affecter, revêtir (une forme). **2.** (*a*) Prendre sur soi, assumer (une charge) ; se charger (d'un devoir). (*b*) *To a. power*, prendre possession du pouvoir. **3.** S'attribuer, s'approprier (un droit). **To assume a name,** adopter un nom. **4.** Simuler, affecter (une vertu). **5.** Présumer, supposer (qch.) ; tenir (qch.) comme établi. *Let us a. that such is the case*, mettons qu'il en soit ainsi. **assumed,** *a.* Supposé, feint, faux. **Assumed name,** pseudonyme *m.*

assuming, *a.* Présomptueux, prétentieux.

assumption, *s.* **I.** (*a*) Action *f* de prendre (une forme). (*b*) *A. of office*, entrée *f* en fonctions. **2.** (*a*) Affectation *f* (de vertu). (*b*) Arrogance *f*, prétention(s) *f.* **3.** Supposition *f*, hypothèse *f.*

assurance, *s.* **I.** (*a*) (*Certainty*) Assurance *f.* **To make assurance double sure,** pour surcroît de sûreté. (*b*) Promesse (formelle). (*c*) Affirmation *f.* **2.** *Com:* Assurance (sur la vie). **3.** (*a*) Assurance, fermeté *f.* (*b*) Hardiesse *f*, présomption *f.*

assure, *v.tr.* (*a*) (*Make safe*) *To a. s.o. against* sth., assurer qn contre qch. (*b*) (*Make certain*) *To a. the peace of s.o.*, assurer la paix de qn. (*c*) (*Affirm*) *To a. s.o. of sth.*, assurer qn de qch. *He will do it*, **I assure you!** il le fera, je vous en réponds ! **Be assured that . . .,** soyez certain que. . . .

assuredly, *adv.* Assurément ; à coup sûr.

Assyria. *Pr.n.* *A.Geog:* L'Assyrie *f.*

aster, *s.* *Bot:* Aster *m.*

asterisk, *s.* Astérisque *m.*

astern, *adv.* (*a*) A l'arrière, sur l'arrière. (*b*) *To go astern*, marcher en arrière. (*c*) *To have the wind a.*, avoir le vent en arrière.

asteroid, *s.* Astéroïde *m.*

asthma, *s.* Asthme *m.*

asthmatic, *a. & s.* Asthmatique (*mf*).

astir, *adv. & pred. a.* **I.** Actif ; en mouvement. **2.** Debout, levé. **3.** Agité.

astonish, *v.tr.* Étonner, surprendre. *To be astonished at seeing sth.,* s'étonner de voir qch.

astonishing, *a.* Étonnant, surprenant. **-ly,** *adv.* Étonnamment.

astonishment, *s.* Étonnement *m,* surprise *f. My a. at seeing him,* mon étonnement de le voir. *A look of blank a.,* un air ébahi.

astound, *v.tr.* Confondre; stupéfier **astounding,** *a.* Abasourdissant.

Astrak(h)an. *Pr.n. Geog:* Astrakan *m.*

astral, *a.* Astral, -aux.

astray, *adv. & pred. a.* (i) Égaré; (ii) *Pej:* dévoyé. *To go astray* (i) s'égarer; (ii) *Pej:* se dévoyer. *To lead s.o. astray,* dévoyer qn.

astride, *adv., pred.a., & prep.* A califourchon. *To sit a. sth.,* être à cheval sur qch.

astringent, *a. & s.* Astringent (*m*).

astrologer, *s.* Astrologue *m.*

astrological, *a.* Astrologique.

astrology, *s.* Astrologie *f.*

astronomer, *s.* Astronome *m.*

astronomic(al), *a.* Astronomique.

astronomy, *s.* Astronomie *f.*

astute, *a.* **1.** Fin, avisé. **2.** *Pej:* Astucieux, rusé. **-ly,** *adv.* **1.** Avec finesse. **2.** Astucieusement.

astuteness, *s.* **1.** Finesse *f,* sagacité *f;* pénétration *f.* **2.** *Pej:* Astuce *f.*

asunder, *adv.* **1.** Éloignés, écartés. **2.** To **come asunder,** se désunir.

asylum, *s.* **1.** Asile *m,* (lieu *m* de) refuge *m.* **2.** Hospice *m.*

at, *prep.* A. **1.** (*a*) *At table, at school,* à table, à l'école. *The dog was at his heels,* le chien marchait sur ses talons. *At hand,* sous la main. *At sea,* en mer (*b*) *At home,* à la maison, chez soi. *At the tailor's,* chez le tailleur. (*c*) *To sit at the window,* se tenir (au)près de la fenêtre. *He came in at the window,* il entra par la fenêtre. **2.** *At present,* à présent. *Two at a time,* deux à la fois. *At night,* la nuit. **3.** *At two francs a pound,* à deux francs la livre. **4.** *At my request,* sur ma demande. *At all events,* en tout cas. **5.** *Good at games,* habile aux jeux. **6.** (*a*) *To look at sth.,* regarder qch. *To be surprised at sth.,* être étonné de qch. *To catch at sth.,* s'accrocher à qch. (*b*) *To laugh at s.o.,* se moquer de qn. *To swear at s.o.,* jurer contre qn. (*c*) *To be at work,* être au travail. *To be at sth.,* être occupé à faire qch. *She's at it again,* voilà qu'elle recommence! *While we are at it,* pendant que nous y sommes. (*d*) *To be at s.o.,* être acharné contre qn.

atavism, *s.* Atavisme *m.*

atheism, *s.* Athéisme *m.*

atheist, *s.* Athée *mf.*

Athenian, *a. & s.* Athénien, -ienne.

Athens. *Pr.n.* Athènes *f.*

athirst, *pred. a.* Altéré, assoiffé (*for,* de).

athlete, *s.* Athlète *m.*

athletic, *a.* Athlétique.

athletics, *s.pl.* Sports *m* (athlétiques); culture *f* physique.

athwart. 1. *adv.* En travers. **2.** *prep.* En travers de.

Atlantic, *a. & s.* The Atlantic (Ocean), (l'océan) Atlantique *m.*

Atlas. 1. *Pr.n. Gr.Myth:* Atlas *m.* **2.** *s.* Atlas.

atmosphere, *s.* Atmosphère *f.* *F: A. of vice,* ambiance *f* de vice.

atmospheric(al). 1. *a.* Atmosphérique. **2.** *s.pl. W.Tel:* Atmospherics, parasites *m.*

atoll, *s.* Atoll *m*; île *f* de corail.

atom, *s.* Atome *m.* *Smashed to atoms,* réduit en miettes.

atomic(al), *a.* Atomique.

atone, *v.tr. or ind.tr.* *To atone (for) a fault,* expier une faute.

atonement, *s.* Expiation *f,* réparation *f* (*for,* de). *To make atonement for a fault,* réparer une faute.

atrocious, *a.* **1.** (*Crime*) atroce. **2.** *F:* Exécrable. **-ly,** *adv.* **1.** Atrocement. **2.** *F:* Exécrablement.

atrocity, *s.* Atrocité *f.*

atrophy. 1. *v.tr.* Atrophier. **2.** *v.i.* S'atrophier.

attach. 1. *v.tr.* (*a*) Attacher, lier, fixer (*sth. to sth.,* qch. à qch.). (*b*) *To attach credence to sth.,* ajouter foi à qch. **2.** *v.i.* S'attacher.

attached, *a.* (*a*) Attaché (*to,* à); adjoint (à un personnel). *Salary a. to a post,* traitement afférent à un emploi. (*b*) *To be deeply a. to s.o.,* être fortement attaché à qn.

attaché, *s. Dipl:* Attaché *m.* **attaché-case,** *s.* Mallette *f.*

attachment, *s.* **1.** Accessoire *m.* **2.** (*Affection*) Attachement *m* (*of s.o. for s.o.,* de qn pour qn).

attack¹, *s.* **1.** Attaque *f,* assaut *m.* *To make an attack upon s.o.,* attaquer qn. *To return to the attack,* revenir à la charge. **2.** Attaque, crise *f.* *A. of fever,* accès *m* de fièvre.

attack², *v.tr.* Attaquer. *To a. s.o.,* attaquer qn; s'attaquer à qn.

attacker, *s.* Attaquant *m*; agresseur *m.*

attain. 1. *v.tr.* Atteindre, arriver à. *To attain knowledge,* acquérir des connaissances. **2.** *v.ind.tr.* *To a. to perfection,* atteindre à la perfection.

attainable, *a.* Accessible; à la portée (*by,* de).

attainment, *s.* **1.** Arrivée *f* (à ses fins); réalisation *f.* *Easy of attainment,* facile à atteindre. **2.** Connaissance(s) *f*; savoir *m.*

attempt¹, *s.* **1.** Tentative *f,* essai *m,* effort *m.* *To make an a. at sth.,* essayer, tâcher, de faire qch. *No attempt will be made to . . .,* on n'essaiera pas de . . . *First attempt,* coup *m* d'essai. *To be successful at the first a.,* réussir du premier coup. *To give up the attempt,* y renoncer. **2.** *Attempt on s.o.'s life,* attentat *m* contre la vie de qn.

attempt², *v.tr.* **1.** (*a*) *To a. to do sth.,* essayer, tenter, tâcher, de faire qch. (*b*) *To a. resistance,* essayer de résister. *To attempt impossibilities,* tenter l'impossible. *Attempted* murder, tentative *f* d'assassinat. **2.** To attempt s.o.'s life, attenter à la vie de qn.

attend. I. *v.ind.tr.* (*a*) To a. to sth., faire attention à qch. (*b*) *To a. to s.o.*, écouter qn. (*c*) *To a. to sth.*, s'occuper de qch. (*d*) *To a. to a customer*, servir un client. **2.** *v.tr.* Soigner (un malade). **3.** *v.tr. & ind.tr.* (*a*) *To a. on, upon, s.o.*, servir qn. (*b*) *Method attended by great difficulties*, méthode qui comporte de grandes difficultés. **4.** *v.tr.* To attend school, aller à l'école. To attend a meeting, assister à une réunion.

attendance, *s.* **I.** (*a*) (*In shop*) Service *m.* (*b*) (*Of doctor*) *A. on s.o.*, soins *mpl* pour qn. (*c*) To be in attendance (up)on the king, être de service auprès du roi. **2.** *A. at a meeting*, présence *f* à une réunion. **3.** *There was a good a.*, il y avait une nombreuse assistance.

attendant. I. *a.* (*a*) *A. on s.o.*, qui suit, qui sert, qn. (*b*) *The a. crowd*, la foule qui y assistait. **2.** *s.* (*a*) Serviteur *m*, domestique *mf.* (*In museum*) gardien, -ienne ; (*in theatre*) ouvreuse *f.* (*b*) (*Usu. pl.*) Suivants *m*, gens *m* ; personnel *m* de service.

attention, *s.* **I.** (*a*) Attention *f* (*to*, à) To turn one's attention to sth., diriger son attention vers qch. *To pay a. to s.o.*, prêter (son) attention à qn. **Pay attention!** faites attention ! *To attract a.*, se faire remarquer. (*b*) Soins *mpl*, entretien *m.* **2.** Attention(s), soins, prévenance(s) *f.* *F:* To pay one's attentions to a lady, faire la cour à une dame. **3.** *Mil:* Attention ! garde à vous !

attentive, *a.* **I.** Attentif (*to*, à) ; soigneux, soucieux (*to*, de). **2.** *A. to s.o.*, empressé auprès de qn ; prévenant pour qn. **-ly,** *adv.* Attentivement.

attentiveness, *s.* **I.** Attention *f.* **2.** Prévenances *fpl* (*to s.o.*, pour qn).

attenuate, *v.tr.* Atténuer.

attest, *v.tr.* (*a*) Attester, certifier (un fait). (*b*) Affirmer sous serment. *To a. a signature*, légaliser une signature. (*c*) *v.ind.tr.* To a. to sth., témoigner de qch.

attic, *s.* Mansarde *f.*

attire, *s.* Vêtement(s) *m* ; costume *m.*

attitude, *s.* (*a*) Attitude *f*, pose *f* (de la tête). (*b*) *To maintain a firm a.*, rester ferme.

attorney¹, *s.* Mandataire *m* ; fondé *m* de pouvoir(s).

attorney², *s.* **Power of attorney,** procuration *f.*

attract, *v.tr.* **I.** Attirer (*to*, à, vers). **2.** Séduire, attirer

attraction, *s.* **I.** Attraction *f* (*to*, *towards*, vers). **2.** Séduction *f* ; attractions, attraits *mpl.* **3.** The chief attraction, le clou.

attractive, *a.* Attrayant, séduisant ; alléchant. **-ly,** *adv.* D'une manière attrayante.

attractiveness, *s.* Attrait *m*, charme *m.*

attributable, *a.* Attribuable, imputable.

attribute¹, *s.* **I.** Attribut *m*, qualité *f.* **2.** Symbole *m*, attribut. **3.** *Gram:* Épithète *f.*

attribute², *v.tr.* Attribuer, imputer (*to*, à).

attribution, *s.* Attribution *f* (*to*, à).

attrition, *s.* Attrition *f* ; usure *f* par le frottement. **War of attrition,** guerre d'usure.

auburn, *a.* *A.* hair, cheveux blond ardent, châtain roux.

auction¹, *s.* (**Sale by**) auction, auction-sale, vente *f* aux enchères *fpl.* **To put sth. up to** auction, mettre qch. aux enchères.

auction², *v.tr.* Vendre aux enchères.

auctioneer, *s.* **I.** Commissaire-priseur *m.* **2.** Directeur *m* de la vente.

audacious, *a.* **I.** Audacieux, hardi, intrépide. **2.** *Pej:* Effronté, hardi, cynique.

audacity, *s.* **I.** Audace *f.* **I.** Intrépidité *f*, hardiesse *f.* **2.** *Pej:* Effronterie *f.*

audibility, *s.* Perceptibilité *f* (d'un son).

audible, *a.* Perceptible (à l'oreille) ; distinct, intelligible. *He was scarcely a.*, on l'entendait à peine. **-ibly,** *adv.* Distinctement, intelligiblement.

audience, *s.* **I.** Audience *f.* **2.** Assistance *f*, auditoire *m.*

audit¹, *s.* Vérification *f* (de comptes).

audit², *v.tr.* Vérifier (des comptes).

auditor, *s.* **I.** Auditeur *m.* **2.** Expert *m* comptable.

auger, *s.* *Tls:* Tarière *f.*

aught, *s.* Quelque chose *m.* **For aught I** know, (pour) autant que je sache.

augment. I. *v.tr.* Augmenter, accroître (*by*, de). **2.** *v.i.* Augmenter, s'accroître.

augmentation, *s.* Augmentation *f*, accroissement *m.*

augur¹, *s. Rom.Ant:* Augure *m.*

augur², *v.tr. & i.* Augurer, présager. It augurs well, cela est de bon augure.

augury, *s.* Augure *m* ; *F:* présage *m.*

august¹, *a.* Auguste ; majestueux.

August², *s.* Août *m.*

Augustus. *Pr.n.* Auguste *m.*

auk, *s.* *Orn:* Pingouin *m.*

aunt, *s.* **I.** Tante *f.* **2.** *F:* Aunt Sally = jeu *m* de massacre.

aureole, *s.* *Art:* Auréole *f.*

auricular, *a.* Auriculaire.

auriferous, *a.* Aurifère.

Aurora. I. *Pr.n.* Aurore *f.* **2.** *s.* Aurore. Aurora borealis, aurore boréale.

auspices, *s.pl.* Auspices *m.*

auspicious, *a.* **I.** (*a*) Propice, favorable. (*b*) De bon augure. **2.** Heureux, prospère. **-ly,** *adv.* Favorablement.

auspiciousness, *s.* Aspect *m* favorable.

austere, *a.* Austère. **-ly,** *adv.* Austèrement.

austerity, *s.* Austérité *f*

austral, *a.* Austral, -als, -aux.

Australia. *Pr.n.* L'Australie *f.*

Australian, *a. & s.* Australien, -ienne.

Austria. *Pr.n.* L'Autriche *f.*

Austrian, *a. & s.* Autrichien, -ienne.

authentic, *a.* Authentique ; digne de foi. **-ally,** *adv.* Authentiquement.

authenticate, *v.tr.* **I.** Certifier. **2.** Établir l'authenticité de ; vérifier

authenticated, *a.* D'une authenticité établie.
authentication, *s.* Certification *f.*
authenticity, *s.* Authenticité *f.*
author, *s.* Auteur *m.*
authoress, *s.* Femme *f* auteur.
authoritative, *a.* **1.** (Caractère) autoritaire ; (ton) péremptoire. **2.** Revêtu d'autorité. **-ly,** *adv.* **1.** Autoritairement ; péremptoirement. **2.** Avec autorité.
authority, *s.* Autorité *f.* **1.** To have authority over s.o., avoir une autorité sur qn. Who is in authority here? qui est-ce qui commande ici ? **2.** Autorisation *f*, mandat *m.* To have authority to act, avoir qualité *f* pour agir. **3.** (*a*) To be an authority on sth., faire autorité en matière de qch. (*b*) To have sth. on good authority, tenir qch. de bonne source. **4.** *Adm:* The authorities, l'administration *f* ; les autorités.
authorization, *s.* Autorisation *f* (to do sth., de faire qch.)
authorize, *v.tr.* Autoriser (qch.). **authorized,** *a.* Autorisé.
authorship, *s.* **1.** Profession *f* ou qualité *f* d'auteur. **2.** Paternité *f.*
autobiographic(al), *a.* Autobiographique.
autobiography, *s.* Autobiographie *f.*
autocracy, *s.* Autocratie *f.*
autocrat, *s.* Autocrate *m.*
autocratic(al), *a* Autocratique.
autograph, *s.* (*a*) Autographe *m.* (*b*) Reproduction autographiée.
automatic, *a.* Automatique. **Automatic machine,** distributeur *m* automatique. *Sm.a :* Automatic pistol, automatique *m.* **-ally,** *adv.* **1.** Automatiquement. **2.** Machinalement.
automaton, *s.* Automate *m.*
autonomous, *a.* Autonome.
autonomy, *s.* Autonomie *f.*
autopsy, *s.* Autopsie *f.*
autumn, *s.* Automne *m.*
autumnal, *a.* Automnal ; d'automne.
auxiliary, *a. & s.* Auxiliaire *mf.*
avail[1], *s.* Avantage *m*, utilité *f. It is of no a.,* cela ne sert à rien **Without avail,** inutile (ment).
avail[2], *v.tr. & i.* **1.** Servir ; être efficace. **2.** To avail oneself of sth., se servir de qch.
availability, *s.* **1.** Disponibilité *f.* **2.** Validité *f.*
available, *a* **1.** (*a*) Disponible *To try every a. means,* essayer de tous les moyens dont on dispose. (*b*) Accessible. **2.** Valable, bon.
avalanche, *s.* Avalanche *f.*
avarice, *s.* Avarice *f.*
avaricious, *a.* Avare, avaricieux. **-ly,** *adv.* Avaricieusement.
avariciousness, *s.* Avarice *f.*
avenge, *v.tr.* Venger (qn). **avenging,** *a.* Vengeur, *f.* -eresse.
avenger, *s.* Vengeur, -eresse.
avenue, *s.* (*a*) Avenue *f.* (*b*) Chemin *m* d'accès. *To explore every a.,* explorer toutes les voies.

aver, *v.tr.* Avérer, déclarer, affirmer (que).
average[1], *s.* Moyenne *f.* **On an average,** en moyenne.
average[2], *a.* Moyen. *Man of a. abilities,* homme ordinaire.
average[3], *v.tr. & i.* **1.** Faire la moyenne de. **2.** To average so much, donner, atteindre, une moyenne de tant.
averse, *a. To be a. to sth.,* répugner à qch. ; être opposé à qch. **He is not averse to a glass of beer,** il prend volontiers un verre de bière.
aversion, *s.* **1.** Aversion *f*, répugnance *f.* To have an a. to s.o., avoir qn en aversion. **2.** *F:* Objet *m* d'aversion *F: My pet aversion,* ma bête noire.
avert, *v.tr.* **1.** Détourner (les yeux) (*from,* de). **2.** Écarter (un danger) ; détourner (un coup).
aviary, *s* Volière *f.*
aviation, *s.* Aviation *f.*
aviator, *s.* Aviateur, -trice.
avid, *a.* Avide (*of, for,* de). **-ly,** *adv.* Avidement, avec avidité.
avidity, *s.* Avidité *f* (*for,* de, pour).
avocation, *s.* (*a*) Occupation *f.* (*b*) Vocation *f*, profession *f.*
avoid, *v.tr.* **1.** Éviter. *To a. doing sth.,* éviter de faire qch. **2.** Se soustraire à. **To avoid notice,** se dérober aux regards.
avoidable, *a.* Évitable.
avoidance, *s.* Action *f* d'éviter. *For the a. of ill,* pour éviter le malheur.
avow, *v.tr* **1.** Reconnaître. **2.** Déclarer. **3.** Avouer, admettre (une faute). **avowed,** *a.* (Ennemi) avéré.
avowal, *s.* Aveu *m.*
avowedly, *adv.* Ouvertement, franchement.
await, *v.tr.* **1.** Attendre. *Com:* Awaiting your orders, dans l'attente de vos ordres. **2.** *The fate that awaits him,* le sort qui l'attend.
awake[1], *v.* **1.** *v.i.* (*a*) S'éveiller, se réveiller. (*b*) To awake to the danger, prendre conscience du danger. **2.** *v.tr.* Éveiller, réveiller.
awake[2], *pred.a.* **1.** Éveillé *I was a.,* je ne dormais pas. **Wide awake,** (i) bien éveillé ; (ii) *F:* averti, malin, -igne. *He's wide a.!* il a l'œil ouvert ! **2.** To be awake to a danger, avoir conscience d'un danger.
awaken, *v.tr. & i.* **1.** *To a. s.o. to a sense of his position,* ouvrir les yeux à qn sur sa position. **2.** = AWAKE[1]. **awakening,** *s.* (*a*) Réveil *m.* (*b*) *F: A rude a.,* un amer désillusionnement.
award[1], *s.* **1.** *Jur:* Arbitrage *m* ; adjudication *f.* **2.** (*a*) *Jur:* Dommages-intérêts *mpl.* (*b*) *Sch:* Récompense *f.*
award[2], *v.tr.* Adjuger, décerner (sth. to s.o., qch. à qn). **awarding,** *s.* Décernement *s.* (d'un prix).
aware, *a.* Avisé, informé, instruit (*of sth.,* de qch.). **To be aware of sth.,** savoir, ne pas ignorer, qch. **Not that I am aware of,** pas que je sache. **To become aware of sth.,** apprendre qch.

away, *adv.* Loin; au loin. **1.** (*a*) *To go a.,* partir, s'en aller. *The ball rolled a.,* la balle roula plus loin. (*b*) *To run a.,* s'enfuir. *To take s.o. a.,* emmener qn. *To carry away,* emporter. **2. Away with you!** allez-vous-en! *A. with it!* emportez-le! **Away with fear!** bannissons la crainte! **One, two, three, and away!** un, deux, trois, partez! **3.** *Sing a.!* continuez à chanter! **4.** Loin. (*a*) *Far away,* dans le lointain; au loin. *Five paces a.,* à cinq pas de là. (*b*) *To hold sth. away from sth.,* tenir qch. éloigné de qch. (*c*) *When he is a.,* lorsqu'il n'est pas là. *When I have to be a.,* lorsque je dois m'absenter.

awe, *s.* Crainte *f,* terreur *f;* respect *m.* **To stand in awe of s.o.,** (i) craindre, redouter, qn; (ii) avoir une crainte respectueuse de qn. **awe-inspiring,** *a.* Terrifiant, imposant. **awe-struck,** *a.* **1.** Frappé d'une terreur mystérieuse. **2.** Intimidé.

awesome, *a.* = AWE-INSPIRING.

awful, *a.* **1.** Terrible, redoutable, effroyable. **2.** (*a*) Terrifiant. (*b*) Imposant. **3.** (*Intensive*) *F: An a. hat,* un chapeau affreux. *What a. weather!* quel chien de temps! **-fully,** *adv.* **1.** Terriblement, effroyablement. **2.** Solennellement. **3.** *F:* (*Intensive*) *I am a. sorry,* je regrette infiniment. *A. ugly,* affreusement laid. **Thanks awfully!** merci mille fois!

awhile, *adv.* Pendant quelque temps; un moment. *Wait a.,* attendez un peu.

awkward, *a.* **1.** (*Clumsy*) Gauche, maladroit, disgracieux. *The awkward age,* l'âge ingrat. *F: The awkward squad,* le peloton des arriérés. **2.** (*Ill at ease*) Embarrassé, gêné.

3. Fâcheux, gênant. *An a. situation,* un mauvais pas. **4.** Incommode, peu commode. *A. corner,* virage difficile. **-ly,** *adv.* **1.** Gauchement, maladroitement. **2.** D'une manière embarrassée. **3.** D'une façon gênante. *To be a. situated,* se trouver dans une situation embarrassante.

awkwardness, *s.* **1.** (*a*) Gaucherie *f;* maladresse *f.* (*b*) Manque *m* de grâce. **2.** Embarras *m.* **3.** (*Of situation*) Inconvénient *m.*

awl, *s.* *Tls:* Alène *f.*

awn, *s.* *Bot:* Barbe *f.*

awning, *s.* Tente *f,* vélum *m;* banne *f* (de boutique).

awry, *adv. & pred.a.* De travers; de guingois. *To go all awry,* aller tout de travers.

ax, axe, *s.* Hache *f;* cognée *f* (de bûcheron). *F: To have an axe to grind,* avoir un intérêt personnel à servir. **axe-head,** *s.* Fer *m* de hache.

axiom, *s.* Axiome *m.*

axiomatic(al), *a.* (*a*) Axiomatique. (*b*) *F:* Évident.

axis, *s.* **1.** Axe *m.* **2.** *Pol:* Axe.

axle, *s.* **1.** Axle(-tree), essieu *m.* **2.** Arbre *m,* axe *m* (d'une roue).

ay(e). **1.** *adv. & int.* *Nau:* Ay(e), ay(e), sir! bien, capitaine! **2.** *s.* Ayes and noes, voix *f* pour et contre.

ayah, *s.* Ayah *f.*

azalea, *s.* *Bot:* Azalée *f.*

Azores (the). *Pr.n.pl.* Les Açores *f.*

Aztec, *a. & s.* *Ethn:* Aztèque (*mf*).

azure. **1.** *s.* Azur *m.* **2.** *Attrib. An a. sky,* un ciel d'azur.

B

B, b. **1.** (La lettre) B, b *m.* **2.** *Mus:* Si *m.*

baa¹, *s.* Bêlement *m.* *Baa!* bê!

baa², *v.i.* Bêler.

babble¹, *s.* **1.** Babil *m,* babillage *m.* **2.** Bavardage *m.* **3.** Murmure *m* (d'un ruisseau).

babble². **1.** *v.i.* (*a*) Babiller. (*b*) Bavarder, jaser. (*c*) (*Of stream*) Murmurer. **2.** *v.tr.* *To b. nonsense,* débiter des sottises **babbling,** *a.* Babillard, bavard, jaseur.

babbler, *s.* **1.** Babillard, -e; bavard, -e. **2.** Jaseur, -euse.

babe, *s.* Enfant *m* (en bas âge).

Babel, *s.* *It was an absolute B.,* c'était un vacarme à ne pas s'entendre.

baboon, *s.* *Z:* Babouin *m.*

baby, *s.* **1.** Bébé *m.* **2.** *Attrib.* (*a*) D'enfant, de bébé. *Baby talk,* babil enfantin. (*b*) *F:* De petites dimensions. *Baby grand,* piano *m* (à) demi-queue; crapaud *m.* *Aut:* *Baby car,* voiturette *f.* **baby-linen,** *s.* Layette *f.*

babyhood, *s.* Première enfance; bas âge.

babyish, *a.* *F:* De bébé; puéril.

bacchante, *s.* Bacchante *f,* ménade *f.*

bachelor, *s.* **1.** Célibataire *m,* garçon *m.* **2.** *Sch:* Bachelier, -ière. **Bachelor of Arts,** *approx.* = licencié ès lettres.

bacillus, *s.* *Biol:* Bacille *m.*

back¹. **1.** *s.* **1.** (*a*) Dos *m.* *To fall on one's b.,* tomber à la renverse. *To be at the back of s.o.,* soutenir qn. *To do sth. behind s.o.'s back,* faire qch. à l'insu de qn. *To be glad to see the back of s.o.,* être content de voir partir qn. *F: To put s.o.'s back up,* mettre qn en colère. *To make a back for s.o.,* faire la courte échelle à qn. *Back to back,* dos à dos; adossés. *Back to front,* sens devant derrière. *With one's back to the wall,* acculé; aux abois. *F: To put one's back into sth.,* s'appliquer à qch. (*b*) Les reins *m;* *F:* l'échine *f.* *To break one's back,* se casser les

reins. **2.** (*a*) Dossier *m* (d'une chaise).
(*b*) **The back of the hand,** le revers de la main.
(*c*) Derrière *m* (de la tête); arrière *m* (d'une
voiture). *The frock fastens at the b.,* la robe
s'agrafe dans le dos. **Idea at the back of one's
mind,** arrière-pensée *f.* **3.** Fond *m* (d'une
salle). *Th:* **The back of the stage,** l'arrière-
scène *f.* II. **back,** *a.* Arrière, de derrière. **The
back streets of a town,** les derrières *m* d'une
ville. **Back wheel,** roue arrière. III. **back,**
adv. **1.** (*a*) En arrière. **Stand back!** rangez-
vous! *House standing back from the road,* maison en retrait. (*b*) **To hit back,** rendre coup
pour coup. **To call s.o. back,** rappeler qn. **To
come back,** revenir. **To make one's way back,**
s'en retourner. (*c*) *As soon as I get b.,* dès
mon retour. **2.** **Some few years back,** il y a
quelques années. **back-answer,** *s.* *F:*
Réplique impertinente. **back-breaking,** *a.*
Éreintant. **back-fire**[1], *s.* *I.C.E:* Contre-
allumage *m.* **back-fire**[2], *v.i.* *I.C.E:*
Pétarder. **back-garden,** *s.* Jardin *m* de
derrière. **back-handed,** *a.* Back-handed
blow, coup déloyal. *B.-h. compliment,* compliment *m* équivoque. **back-hander,** *s.* *F:*
Coup *m* du revers de la main. **back-
number,** *s.* Vieux numéro (d'un journal).
back-pay, *s.* *Mil: Navy:* Arriéré *m* de
solde. **back-pedal,** *v.i.* Contre-pédaler.
back-seat, *s.* Siège *m* de derrière. **To take
a back-seat,** *F:* céder le pas à d'autres.
back-sight, *s.* *Sm.a.:* Hausse *f.* **back-
yard,** *s.* Arrière-cour *f.*

back[2], I. *v.tr.* **1.** (*a*) Renforcer (un mur).
(*b*) **To back (up),** soutenir, appuyer. *Sp:*
To back a horse, parier sur un cheval.
2. Faire (re)culer (un cheval). *Rail:* Refouler (un train). II. **back,** *v.i.* **1.** Aller en
arrière. **To back out,** *v.i.* **1.** Sortir à reculons.
2. *F:* Retirer sa promesse. **back up,** *v.tr.*
Soutenir. **backing,** *s.* **1.** (*a*) Renforcement
m (d'un mur) (*b*) *Sp:* B. *of a horse,* paris
mpl sur un cheval. **2.** Renfort *m,* support *m.*
3. Recul *m* (d'une charrette); refoulement *m*
(d'un train).

backbite, *v.tr.* Médire de (qn). **backbiting,** *s.* Médisance *f.*

backbiter, *s.* Médisant, -e.

backbone, *s.* Épine dorsale, échine *f.* *F:*
English to the backbone, anglais jusqu'à la
moelle des os. **He has got backbone,** il a du
caractère.

backer, *s.* **1.** *Sp:* Parieur, -euse **2.** Partisan *m.*

backgammon, *s* (Jeu *m* de) trictrac *m.*

background, *s.* Fond *m,* arrière-plan *m.*
F: **To keep (oneself) in the background,**
s'effacer.

backslide, *v.i* Retomber dans l'erreur.

backsliding, *s.* Rechute *f* dans le péché

backslider, *s.* Relaps, *f* relapse.

backstair(s), *s.* (i) Escalier *m* de service;
(ii) escalier dérobé. *F:* **Backstair influence,**
menées secrètes.

backward. **1.** *a.* (*a*) B. *glance,* regard en
arrière. (*b*) *B. harvest,* moisson en retard.
B. child, enfant arriéré. **2.** *adv.* = BACK-
WARDS.

backwardness, *s.* **1.** Retard *m.* **2.** B. in
doing sth., lenteur *f* à faire qch

backwards, *adv.* En arrière. *To walk b.,*
marcher à reculons. *To fall b.,* tomber à la
renverse. *To walk b. and forwards,* se promener de long en large.

backwash, *s.* Remous *m.*

backwater, *s.* Bras *m* de décharge (d'une
rivière).

backwoodsman, *s.* Colon *m* des forêts.

bacon, *s.* Lard *m.* *F:* **To save one's bacon,**
sauver sa peau.

bacteriology, *s.* Bactériologie *f.*

bacterium, *s.* Bactérie *f.*

bad. I. *a.* Mauvais. **1.** (*a*) (*Inferior*) *Bad air,*
air vicié. *Bad meat,* viande gâtée. *Bad coin,*
pièce fausse. (*Of food*) **To go bad,** se gâter,
s'avarier. (*b*) (*Incorrect*) *Bad translation,*
mauvaise traduction. *Bad shot,* coup mal
visé. **To be bad at,** s'entendre mal à. *F:* **It
isn't half bad,** ce n'est pas mal du tout.
(*c*) (*Unfortunate*) **To be in a bad way,** être
en mauvais état. **He will come to a bad end,**
il finira mal. **It would not be a bad thing to,**
on ne ferait pas mal de. **From bad to worse,**
de mal en pis. **2.** (*a*) (*Wicked*) *Bad man,*
méchant homme. *Bad book,* mauvais livre.
Don't call people bad names, n'injuriez pas
les gens. **He's a bad lot,** c'est un vilain
personnage. (*b*) (*Unpleasant*) *Bad news,*
mauvaise nouvelle. *To have a bad cold,* avoir
un gros rhume. **To be on bad terms with
s.o.,** être mal avec qn. **That's too bad!** c'est
(par) trop fort! (*c*) *Bad accident,* grave
accident. *Bad mistake,* lourde méprise. **To
be bad for sth.,** ne rien valoir pour qch.
(*d*) *F:* (*Ill*) *She is very bad to-day,* elle est
très mal aujourd'hui. *She has a bad finger,*
elle a mal au doigt. *My bad leg,* ma jambe
malade. **-ly,** *adv.* **1.** Mal. **To do badly,**
mal réussir. **To be doing badly,** faire de
mauvaises affaires. **2.** **Badly wounded,**
grièvement blessé. *B. beaten,* battu à plate
couture. **3.** **To want sth. badly,** avoir grand
besoin de qch. II. **bad,** *s.* (*a*) **To take the
bad with the good,** accepter la mauvaise
fortune aussi bien que la bonne. (*b*) **To go
to the bad,** mal tourner. (*c*) *I am 500 francs
to the bad,* je suis en perte de 500 francs.

bad-looking, *a.* *F:* *He is not b.-l.,* il n'est
pas mal (de sa personne) **bad-tempered,**
a Acariâtre.

badge, *s* **1.** Insigne *m;* plaque *f* (de cocher);
Mil: brassard *m* **2.** Symbole *m:* signe
distinctif.

badger[1], *s.* *Z:* Blaireau *m*

badger[2], *v.tr.* Harceler, tourmenter, tracasser, importuner (qn).

badness, *s.* **1.** Mauvaise qualité; mauvais
état. **2.** (*Of pers.*) Méchanceté *f.*

baffle, *v.tr.* (a) Confondre, déconcerter. (b) Déjouer; frustrer. *To b. definition,* échapper à toute définition.

bag¹, *s.* **I.** Sac *m.* *Travelling bag,* sac de voyage. **2.** (a) *Nat.Hist:* Sac, poche *f.* (b) *F:* *Bags under the eyes,* poches sous les yeux. **3.** *Ven:* **The bag,** le tableau. *To secure a good bag,* faire bonne chasse. **4.** *pl. F:* Pantalon *m.*

bag², *v.* **I.** *v.tr.* (a) Mettre en sac; ensacher. (b) *F:* Empocher; s'emparer de. **2.** *v.i.* Bouffer, avoir trop d'ampleur.

bagatelle, *s.* **I.** Bagatelle *f.* **2.** Billard anglais.

bagful, *s.* Sac plein; plein sac.

baggage, *s. Mil:* Bagage *m.*

baggy, *a.* (Vêtement) trop ample.

bagpipe(s), *s.* Cornemuse *f.*

Bahama. *Pr.n.* **The Bahama Islands,** *F:* the Bahamas, les Lucayes *f.*

bail¹, *s. Jur:* Caution *f,* garant *m.* **To go bail for s.o.,** se porter garant de qn.

bail², *v.tr.* **To bail s.o. out,** se porter caution pour obtenir l'élargissement de qn.

bail³, *v.tr.* **To bail out the water,** écoper l'eau d'une embarcation.

bailiff, *s.* **I.** Huissier *m.* **2.** Régisseur *m,* intendant *m* (d'un domaine). **3.** *Hist:* Bailli *m.*

bait¹, *s.* (a) *Fish:* Amorce *f.* (b) *F:* Appât *m,* leurre *m.*

bait², **I.** *v.tr.* Harceler. **2.** *v.tr.* Faire manger (un cheval). **3.** *v.tr.* Amorcer, appâter. **baiting,** *s.* **I.** Harcelage *m.* **2.** Amorçage *m.,* amorcement *m.*

baize, *s.* Serge *f,* reps *m.* **Green baize,** tapis vert.

bake. **I.** *v.tr.* Cuire, faire cuire. **2.** *v.i.* Cuire (au four). *F:* **We are baking in the heat,** nous brûlons par cette chaleur. **baking,** *s.* Cuisson *f.* **baking-powder,** *s. Cu:* Poudre *f* à lever.

bakehouse, *s.* Fournil *m,* boulangerie *f.*

bakelite, *s.* Bakélite *f.*

baker, *s.* Boulanger, -ère. **Baker's shop,** boulangerie *f.*

bakery, *s.* Boulangerie *f.*

Balaclava. *Pr.n. Geog:* Balaklava. **Balaclava helmet,** passe-montagne *m*

balance¹, *s.* **I.** Balance *f.* *F:* **To hang in the balance,** rester en balance. **2.** Équilibre *m,* aplomb *m.* **To keep one's balance,** se tenir en équilibre **3.** *Com:* (a) **Balance in hand,** solde créditeur. (b) **To strike a balance,** dresser le bilan. **On balance,** à tout prendre **balance-sheet,** *s.* Bilan *m.*

balance². **I.** *v.tr.* (a) Balancer, peser (les conséquences). (b) Mettre en équilibre; équilibrer; faire contrepoids à (qch.). (c) *Com:* **To balance the budget,** équilibrer le budget. **2.** *v.i.* (a) Se faire contrepoids. (Of accounts) Se balancer. (b) Osciller, balancer. **balanced,** *a.* Équilibré; compensé. **balancing¹,** *a.* Compensateur,

-trice. **balancing²,** *s.* **I.** Balancement *m* (entre deux choses). **2.** (a) Mise *f* en équilibre. (b) *B. of accounts,* règlement *m,* solde *m* des comptes. **3.** Ajustement *m* (de deux choses); compensation *f.*

balcony, *s.* Balcon *m.*

bald, *a.* **I.** Chauve. **2.** (Of style) Décharné. **-ly,** *adv.* Nûment, platement. **bald-headed,** *a.* (A la tête) chauve. *F:* **To go at it bald-headed,** y aller tête baissée.

baldness, *s.* **I.** (a) Calvitie *f.* (b) Nudité *f* (d'une montagne). **2.** Platitude *f* (du style).

bale¹, *s. Com:* Balle *f,* ballot *m.*

bale², *v.tr.* Emballotter, paqueter.

bale³, *v.i.* *Av:* **To bale out,** se lancer en parachute.

Balearic, *a. Geog:* **The Balearic Islands,** les îles Baléares.

baleful, *a. Lit:* Sinistre, funeste.

balk¹, *s.* **I.** Obstacle *m.* **2.** *Const:* Poutre *f,* solive *f.*

balk². **I.** *v.tr.* Contrarier. (a) *To b. s.o. of his prey,* frustrer qn de sa proie. (b) Entraver (qn). **2.** *v.i.* (Of horse) Refuser. *F:* **To balk at sth.,** reculer devant qch.

Balkan, *a. Geog:* Balkanique.

ball¹, *s.* **I.** Boule *f* (de neige); balle *f* (de tennis); ballon *m* (de football); bille *f* (billard); pelote *f* (de laine). *F:* **To keep the ball rolling,** soutenir la conversation. **To have the ball at one's feet,** avoir la partie belle. **2.** Globe *m* (de l'œil). **ball-bearing(s),** *s.(pl.) Mec.E:* Roulement *m* à billes. **ball-cartridge,** *s.* Cartouche *f* à balle.

ball², *s. Danc:* Bal *m, pl.* bals. **To open the ball,** ouvrir le bal. **ball-room,** *s.* Salle *f* de bal.

ballad, *s.* **I.** *Mus:* Romance *f.* **2.** *Lit:* Ballade *f.*

ballast, *s.* **I.** *Nau:* Lest *m.* **2.** *Rail:* Ballast *m.*

ballet, *s.* Ballet *m.* **ballet-dancer,** *s.* Danseur, -euse, d'opéra; *f* ballerine.

ballistics, *s.pl.* Balistique *f.*

balloon, *s. Aer:* Ballon *m,* aérostat *m.* **balloon-tyre,** *s.* Pneu *m* ballon.

ballot¹, *s.* (a) Tour *m* de scrutin. **To vote by ballot,** voter au scrutin. (b) Scrutin *m,* vote *m.* **ballot-box,** *s.* Urne *f* de scrutin.

ballot², *v.i.* (a) Voter au scrutin. (b) Tirer au sort. **balloting,** *s.* **I.** Élection *f* au scrutin. **2.** Tirage *m* au sort.

balm, *s.* Baume *m.*

balmy, *a.* **I.** (a) Embaumé, parfumé. (b) *Lit:* Calmant. **2.** *P:* Toqué.

balsam, *s.* Baume *m*

Baltic, *a. & s.* **I.** **The Baltic (Sea),** la (mer) Baltique. **2.** **Baltic port,** port *m* balte.

baluster, *s.* **I.** Balustre *m.* **2.** *pl.* = BANISTER.

balustrade, *s.* (a) Balustrade *f.* (b) Accoudoir *m,* appui *m* (de fenêtre).

bamboo, *s.* Bambou *m.*

bamboozle, *v.tr.* *F:* Mystifier, enjôler, embobeliner.

ban[1], *s.* (a) Ban *m*, bannissement *m*, proscription *f.* (b) *Ecc:* Interdit *m.*

ban[2], *v.tr.* Interdire.

banal, *a.* Banal, -aux.

banality, *s.* Banalité *f.*

banana, *s.* Banane *f.* **Banana-tree,** bananier *m.*

band[1], *s.* **I.** (a) Lien *m*; cercle *m*; ruban *m* (d'un chapeau). *Elastic b., F:* élastique *m.* *Aut:* **Brake band,** ruban de frein. *Mil:* **Cap-band,** bandeau *m.* (b) Bande *f.* **Paper band,** bande de papier. **2.** *Mec.E:* Bande, courroie *f.* **band-saw,** *s.* Scie *f* à ruban.

band[2], *v.tr.* Bander.

band[3], *s.* **I.** (a) Bande *f*, troupe *f.* (b) Compagnie *f.* **2.** *Mus:* (a) Orchestre *m.* (b) *Mil:* Musique *f.* **Brass band,** fanfare *f.*

band[4], *v.i.* To band (together), se bander.

bandage[1], *s.* *Med:* Bandage *m*; bandeau *m.*

bandage[2], *v.tr.* Bander (un bras cassé); poser un appareil, mettre un pansement, sur.

bandbox, *s.* Carton *m* à chapeau(x).

banderol(e), *s.* Banderole *f.*

bandit, *s.* Bandit *m*, brigand *m.*

bandmaster, *s.* Chef *m* de musique.

bandolier, *s.* Bandoulière *f.*

bandsman, *s.* Musicien *m.*

bandstand, *s.* Kiosque *m* à musique.

bandy[1], *v.tr.* (Se) renvoyer (des paroles); échanger (des plaisanteries).

bandy[2], *a.* **Bandy legs,** jambes bancales. **bandy-legged,** *a.* Bancal, -als.

bane, *s.* Fléau *m*, peste *f.*

baneful, *a.* Funeste; pernicieux. **-fully,** *adv.* Pernicieusement.

bang[1], *s.* Coup (violent); détonation *f.*

bang[2]. **I.** *v.i.* (a) Frapper avec bruit. (b) Claquer, battre. **2.** *v.tr.* (a) Frapper (violemment). (b) To bang the door, (faire) claquer la porte. **banging,** *s.* (a) Coups violents; claquement *m.* (b) Détonations *fpl.*

bang[3]. **I.** *int.* Pan! v'lan! boum! **2.** *adv.* *F:* To go bang, éclater.

bang[4], *s.* Coiffure *f* à la chien.

bangle, *s.* Bracelet *m.*

banian, *s.* *Bot:* Banian(-tree), banian *m*; figuier *m* de l'Inde.

banish, *v.tr.* Bannir exiler.

banishment, *s.* Bannissement *m*, proscription *f*, exil *m.*

banister, *s.* (*Usu. in pl.*) Balustres *m*; rampe *f* (d'escalier).

banjo, *s.* *Mus:* Banjo *m.*

bank[1], *s.* **I.** (a) Talus *m.* *Civ.E:* Remblai *m.* *Rail:* Rampe *f.* (b) Banc *m* (de sable). (c) Digue *f.* **2.** Berge *f*, rive *f* (d'une rivière).

bank[2]. **I.** *v.tr.* To bank up, remblayer. (b) *Mch:* To bank (up) fires, couvrir les feux. **2.** *v.i.* (Of clouds) S'entasser, s'amonceler. **3.** *v.i.* *Av:* Pencher l'avion.

bank[3], *s.* **I.** (a) Banque *f.* **Bank account,** compte en banque. (b) Bureau *m* de banque. **Branch bank,** succursale *f.* **2.** *Gaming:*

Banque. **bank-book,** *s.* Livret *m* de banque. **bank-holiday,** *s.* (Jour *m* de) fête légale. **bank-note,** *s.* Billet *m* de banque.

bank[4], *v.tr.* & *i.* Mettre (de l'argent) en banque. *F:* To bank on sth., compter sur qch. **banking,** *s.* (Opérations *fpl* de) banque. **Banking house,** maison *f* de banque.

banker, *s.* Banquier *m.*

bankrupt, *a.* & *s.* Failli, -e; banqueroutier, -ère. **To go bankrupt,** faire faillite.

bankruptcy, *s.* **I.** Faillite *f*; banqueroute *f.* **2.** *F:* Ruine *f.*

banner, *s.* Bannière *f*, étendard *m.*

banns, *s.pl.* Bans *m* (de mariage).

banquet[1], *s.* Banquet *m.*

banquet[2]. **I.** *v.tr.* Offrir un banquet. **2.** *v.i.* *F:* Banqueter; faire festin.

bantam, *s.* Coq *m*, poule *f*, (de) Bantam.

banter[1], *s.* (a) Badinage *m.* (b) Ironie *f.*

banter[2], *v.tr.* & *i.* (a) Badiner. (b) Gouailler, railler. **bantering,** *a.* Railleur, -euse.

baptism, *s.* Baptême *m.*

baptize, *v.tr.* Baptiser.

bar[1], *s.* **I.** (a) Barre *f.* (b) *pl.* Barreaux *m* (d'une cage). (c) Barre (de sable). **2.** Empêchement *m*, obstacle *m.* **3.** *Jur:* (a) Barre (des accusés). **The prisoner at the bar,** l'accusé. (b) Barreau (des avocats). **To be called to the bar,** être reçu avocat. **4.** Bar *m.* *Rail:* Buvette *f.* **5.** (a) Barre, ligne *f*, trait *m.* (b) *Mus:* Mesure *f.*

bar[2], *v.tr.* **I.** Barrer; bâcler. **To bar oneself in,** se barricader. **2.** To bar s.o.'s way, barrer la route à qn. **3.** (a) Défendre, prohiber. (b) *F:* Ne pas supporter. **4.** Rayer (de lignes); barrer. **barred,** *a.* Barré; muni de barreaux. *B.* **window,** fenêtre grillée.

bar[3], *barring,* *prep.* *F:* Excepté, sauf. **Barring accidents,** sauf accident.

barb[1], *s.* Barbillon *m.*

barb[2], *v.tr.* Garnir de barbillons. **barbed,** *a.* **Barbed wire,** fil de fer barbelé.

Barbado(e)s. *Pr.n.* La Barbade.

barbarian, *a.* & *s.* Barbare (*mf*)

barbaric, *a.* Barbare.

barbarism, *s.* **I.** *Gram:* Barbarisme *m.* **2.** Barbarie *f.*

barbarity, *s.* Barbarie *f*, cruauté *f.*

barbarous, *a.* **I.** Barbare. **2.** Cruel, barbare, inhumain. **-ly,** *adv.* Cruellement.

Barbary. *Pr.n.* *Geog:* La Barbarie.

barber, *s.* Barbier *m*, coiffeur *m.* **Barber's pole,** enseigne *f* de barbier.

barbican, *s.* *Archeol:* Barbacane *f.*

bard, *s.* **I.** Barde *m.* **2.** *F:* Poète *m.*

bare[1], *a.* **I.** (a) Nu; dénudé. **The trees are already b.,** les arbres sont déjà dépouillés. **To lay bare,** mettre à nu, exposer. *Nau:* **Under bare poles,** à sec (de toiles). *Cards:* **Ace bare,** as sec. **2.** To earn a bare living, gagner tout juste de quoi vivre. *B.* **majority,** faible majorité. **-ly,** *adv.* A peine, tout

juste. **bare-headed**, *a. & adv.* Nu-tête, (la) tête nue.
bare², *v.tr.* Mettre (qch.) à nu.
bareback, *adv.* To ride bareback, monter à poil.
barefaced, *a.* Éhonté, cynique.
barefoot, *adv.* Nu-pieds; (à) pieds nus.
barefooted, *a.* Aux pieds nus; les pieds nus.
bareness, *s* Nudité *f*, dénuement *m*.
bargain¹, *s.* **1.** Marché *m*, affaire *f*. A real b., une véritable occasion. Into the bargain, par-dessus le marché. It's a bargain! c'est entendu! **2.** Bargain sale, vente de soldes.
bargain², *v.i.* (*a*) Entrer en négociations, négocier (*with s.o.*, avec qn). F: I didn't bargain for that, je ne m'attendais pas à cela. (*b*) To b. *over*, marchander.
barge, *s.* (*a*) Chaland *m*, péniche *f*. (*b*) Admiral's barge, canot *m* de l'amiral.
bargee, *s.* F: Batelier *m*, marinier *m*.
baritone, *s. Mus:* Baryton *m*.
barium, *s. Ch:* Baryum *m*.
bark¹, *s.* Écorce *f*. Peruvian bark, quinquina *m*.
bark², *v.tr.* (*a*) Écorcer (un arbre). (*b*) F: To bark one's shins, s'érafler les tibias.
bark³, *s.* (*a*) Aboiement *m*, aboi *m*. F: His bark is worse than his bite, il aboie plus qu'il ne mord. (*b*) (*Of fox*) Glapissement *m*.
bark⁴, *v.i.* (*a*) Aboyer (*at*, après, contre). To bark up the wrong tree, suivre une fausse piste. (*b*) (*Of fox*) Glapir. **barking¹**, *a.* Aboyeur. **barking²**, *s.* (*a*) Aboiement *m*. (*b*) (*Of fox*) Glapissement *m*.
bark⁵, *s. Nau:* Trois-mâts barque *m*.
barley, *s.* Orge *f*. **barley-sugar**, *s.* Sucre *m* d'orge.
barleycorn, *s.* Grain *m* d'orge.
barmaid, *s* Demoiselle *f* de comptoir.
barman, *s.* Garçon *m* de comptoir.
barn, *s.* Grange *f*. **barn-door**, *s.* Porte *f* de grange. **barn-owl**, *s. Orn:* Effraie *f*.
barnacle, *s.* **1.** *Orn:* **Barnacle (goose)**, bernacle *f*, bernache *f*. **2.** *Crust:* Bernacle, bernacle.
barometer, *s.* Baromètre *m*.
baron, *s.* **1.** Baron *m*. **2.** Baron of beef, double aloyau *m*.
baronage, *s.* Baronnage *m*.
baroness, *s.* Baronne *f*.
baronet, *s.* Baronnet *m*.
baronetcy, *s.* Dignité *f* de baronnet.
barrack(s)¹, *s. Mil:* Caserne *f*; (*of cavalry*) quartier *m*. To be confined to barracks, être consigné. **barrack room**, *s.* Chambrée *f*.
barrack², *v.tr. P:* Conspuer, huer.
barrage, *s. Mil:* Tir *m* de barrage.
barrel, *s.* **1.** Tonneau *m*, barrique *f*, futaille *f*, fût *m* (de vin); caque *f*. **2.** Cylindre *m*; partie *f* cylindrique; canon *m* (de fusil).
barrel-organ, *s.* Orgue *m* de Barbarie.
barren, *a.* Stérile, improductif; aride.
barrenness, *s.* Stérilité *f*.

barricade¹, *s.* Barricade *f*.
barricade², *v.tr.* Barricader.
barrier, *s.* Barrière *f*. B. *to progress*, obstacle *m* au progrès.
barring, *prep.* See BAR³.
barrister, *s.* Barrister(-at-law), avocat *m*.
barrow¹, *s.* **1.** (Wheel-)barrow, brouette *f*. **2.** Charrette *f* à bras; civière *f*. **3.** *Hawker's b.*, baladeuse *f*; voiture *f* à bras.
barrow², *s. Archeol:* Tumulus *m*.
barrowful, *s.* Brouettée *f*.
barter¹, *s.* Échange *m*; troc *m*.
barter², *v.tr.* To b. sth. for sth., échanger, troquer, qch. contre qch. **barter away**, *v.tr.* Vendre, faire trafic de.
Bartholomew. *Pr.n.* Barthélemy *m*.
barytes, *s.* Barytine *f*.
basal, *a.* Fondamental, -aux.
basalt, *s.* Basalte *m*.
base¹, *s.* **1.** Base *f*. **2.** (*a*) Partie inférieure; fondement *m*; base.
base², *v.tr.* Baser, fonder (*on*, sur).
base³, *a.* (*a*) Bas, vil. B. *action*, action ignoble. Base metals, métaux vils. (*b*) Base coin(age), fausse monnaie. **-ly**, *adv.* Basement, vilement **base-born**, *a.* De basse naissance.
Basel. *Pr.n. Geog:* Bâle *f*.
baseless, *a.* Sans base, sans fondement.
basement, *s.* Sous-sol *m*.
baseness, *s.* Bassesse *f*.
bash¹, *s. F:* Coup *m*, enfoncement *m*.
bash², *v.tr. F:* Cogner. To bash (in), défoncer. To bash s.o. about, houspiller qn.
bashful, *a.* (*a*) Timide. (*b*) Modeste, pudique. **-fully**, *adv.* (*a*) Timidement. (*b*) Pudiquement.
bashfulness, *s.* Timidité *f*; fausse honte.
basic, *a.* **1.** Fondamental. *Ling:* Basic vocabulary, vocabulaire de base. **2.** *Ch:* Basique. **-ally**, *adv.* Fondamentalement.
basilica, *s.* Basilique *f*.
basilisk, *s. Myth:* Basilic *m*.
basin, *s.* **1.** (*a*) Bassin *m*; (*for soup*) écuelle *f*, bol *m*. (*b*) (Wash-hand-)basin, cuvette *f*; lavabo *m*. **2.** *Geog:* Bassin (d'un fleuve).
basis, *s.* Base *f*; fondement *m*.
bask, *v.i.* To b. *in the sun*, se chauffer (au soleil); prendre le soleil.
basket, *s.* (*Without a handle*) Corbeille *f*; (*with a handle*) panier *m*; (*carried on the back*) hotte *f*. **basket-maker**, *s.* Vannier *m*. **basket-work**, *s.* Vannerie *f*.
basketful, *s.* Plein panier; panerée *f*.
Basle. *Pr.n. Geog:* Bâle *f*.
Basque, *a. & s. Ethn:* Basque (*mf*).
bas-relief, *s.* Bas-relief *m*.
bass¹, *s. Ich:* **1.** Perche *f*. **2.** Bar(s) *m*.
bass², *s.* **1.** Tille *f*, filasse *f*. **2.** Bass(-mat), paillasson *m* en tille.
bass³, *a. & s. Mus:* Basse *f*. Bass voice, voix de basse.
bassoon, *s.* Basson *m*.
bastard. **1.** *a. & s.* Bâtard, -e. **2.** *a.* Faux, *f.* fausse.

bastardy, s. Bâtardise f.

baste[1], v.tr. Needlw: Bâtir, faufiler.

baste[2], v.tr. **1.** Cu: Arroser (un rôti). **2.** F: Bâtonner (qn). **basting,** s. **1.** Arrosement m. **2.** F: Bastonnade f.

bastinado, s. Bastonnade f.

bastion, s. Fort: Bastion m.

bat[1], s. Z: Chauve-souris f, pl. chauves-souris.

bat[2], s. **1.** Batte f (de cricket). F: Off one's own bat, de son (propre) chef. **2.** Palette f (de ping-pong); battoir m (de blanchisseuse).

bat[3], v.i. Cr: Être au guichet.

batch, s. **1.** Fournée f (de pain). **2.** Lot m.

bate, v.tr. To speak with bated breath, parler en baissant la voix.

bath[1], s. **1.** Bain m. Turkish baths, hammam m. The Order of the Bath, l'Ordre du Bain. **2.** (a) Baignoire f. (b) Phot: Cuvette f. **bath-mat,** s. Descente f de bain. **bath-room,** s. Salle f de bain(s). **bath-tub,** s. Baignoire f.

bath[2]. **1.** v.tr Baigner. **2.** v.i. Prendre un bain.

Bath[3]. Pr.n. Geog: Bath. **Bath-chair,** s. Voiture f de malade.

bathe[1], s. Bain m; baignade f.

bathe[2]. **1.** v.tr. (a) Baigner. (b) Laver (une plaie). **2.** v.i. Se baigner. **bathing,** s. **1.** Bains mpl. **2.** Bassinage m (d'une plaie).

bathing-costume, s. Costume m de bain(s). **bathing-drawers,** s.pl. Caleçon m de bain.

bather, s. Baigneur, -euse.

bathos, s. Affectation f ridicule du sublime.

batman, s. Mil: Ordonnance m or f.

baton, s. Bâton m.

batrachian, a. & s. Batracien (m).

batsman, s. Cr: Batteur m.

battalion, s. Mil: Bataillon m.

batten[1], s. **1.** Nau: Barre f, latte f, tringle f. **2.** Planche f.

batten[2], v.tr. Nau: To batten down the hatches, coincer les panneaux.

batten[3], v.i. S'engraisser, se repaître (on, de).

batter[1], s. Cu: Pâte f lisse.

batter[2]. **1.** v.tr. Battre. **2.** v.i. To batter at the door, frapper avec violence à la porte. **battered,** a. Délabré, bossué. **battering-ram,** s. Bélier m.

battery, s. **1.** Jur: Voie f de fait. **2.** Artil: Batterie f. **3.** (a) El: Pile f ou batterie. (b) El: (Storage-)battery, accumulateur m, F: accu m.

battle[1], s. Bataille f, combat m. To give battle, livrer bataille. That's half the battle, c'est bataille à moitié gagnée. F: To fight s.o.'s battles, prendre le parti de qn. Battle royal, bataille en règle. **battle-axe,** s. Hache f d'armes. **battle-cruiser,** s. Nau: Croiseur m de combat. **battle-cry,** s. Cri m de guerre. **battle-field,** s. Champ m de bataille.

battle[2], v.i. Se battre, lutter.

battledore, s. Sp: Raquette f. To play at battledore and shuttlecock, jouer au volant.

battlements, s.pl. (a) Créneaux m. (b) Parapet m, rempart m.

battleship, s. Cuirassé m (de ligne).

bauble, s. Babiole f.

baulk s.[1],[2], & v. = BALK[1],[2].

bauxite, s. Miner: Bauxite f.

Bavaria. Pr.n. La Bavière.

Bavarian, a. & s. Bavarois, -e.

bawdy, a. Obscène, impudique.

bawl, v.tr. & i. Brailler; crier à tue-tête; F: beugler.

bay[1], s. Bot: Laurier m. Bay-tree, laurier.

bay[2], s. Geog: Baie f.

bay[3], s. **1.** (Of bridge) Travée f. **2.** Enfoncement m; baie f. bay-window, s. Fenêtre f en saillie.

bay[4], s. Aboi m, aboiement m. To be at bay, être aux abois.

bay[5], v.i. Aboyer. **baying,** s. Aboiement m, clabaudage m.

bay[6], a. & s. (Cheval) bai (m).

bayonet[1], s. Mil: Baïonnette f. To fix bayonets, mettre baïonnette au canon.

bayonet[2], v.tr. Percer d'un coup de baïonnette.

bazaar, s. **1.** Bazar m (oriental). **2.** Vente f de charité.

be, v.i. Être. **1.** (a) Mary is pretty, Marie est jolie. Seeing is believing, voir c'est croire. Isn't he lucky? n'est-ce pas qu'il a de la chance? (b) He is an Englishman, il est Anglais, c'est un Anglais. If I were you, si j'étais (que) de vous. (c) Unity is strength, l'union fait la force. Three and two are five, trois et deux font cinq. **2.** (a) Don't be long, ne tardez pas (à revenir). To be in danger, se trouver en danger. I was at the meeting, j'ai assisté à la réunion. I don't know where I am, F: je ne sais pas où j'en suis. Here I am, me voici. (b) How are you? comment allez-vous? (c) How much is that? combien cela coûte-t-il? How far is it to London? combien y a-t-il d'ici à Londres? When is the concert? quand le concert aura-t-il lieu? Christmas is on a Sunday this year, Noël tombe un dimanche cette année. To-morrow is Friday, c'est demain vendredi. **3.** (a) To be (= feel) cold, avoir froid. (b) To be twenty (years old), avoir vingt ans. **4.** (a) That may be, cela se peut. Well, be it so! eh bien, soit! Everything must remain just as it is, tout doit rester tel quel. However that may be, quoi qu'il en soit. How is it that? comment se fait-il que + sub. (b) Impers. There is, there are. (i) Il y a. What is there to see? qu'est-ce qu'il y a à voir? There will be dancing, on dansera. There were a dozen of us, nous étions une douzaine. (ii) Il est. There are men on whom Fortune always smiles, il est des hommes à qui tout sourit. (iii) There was once a princess, il était une fois une princesse. **5.** He had been and inspected the land, il était allé inspecter le terrain. *I have been into every room*, j'ai visité toutes les pièces. *Where have you been?* d'où venez-vous? *Has anyone been?* est-il venu quelqu'un? **6.** *Impers.* (a) *It is late*, il est tard. *It is a fortnight since I saw him*, il y a quinze jours que je ne l'ai vu. (b) *It is fine*, il fait beau (temps). (c) *It is said that*, on dit que. *It is for you to decide*, c'est à vous à décider. *What is it?* (i) que voulez-vous? (ii) qu'est-ce qu'il y a? *As it were*, pour ainsi dire. *Were it only to please me*, ne fût-ce que pour me plaire. *Had it not been for the rain*, n'eût été la pluie. **7.** (*Auxiliary uses*) (a) *I am doing sth.*, je fais qch. *They are always laughing*, ils sont toujours à rire. *I have* (*just*) *been writing*, je viens d'écrire. *I have been waiting for a long time*, j'attends depuis longtemps. (b) *The sun is set*, le soleil est couché. (c) (*Forming passive voice*) (i) *He was killed*, il fut tué. *He is allowed to smoke*, on lui permet de fumer. (ii) *He is to be pitied*, il est à plaindre. *What is to be done?* que faire? (d) *I am to see him to-morrow*, je dois le voir demain. *I was to have come*, je devais venir. (e) *Am I to do it?* faut-il que je le fasse? **8.** (a) *The bride to-be*, la future. (b) *To be for s.o.*, tenir pour qn. (c) *The battle is to the strong*, la victoire est aux forts. **9.** *Are you happy?* —*I am*, êtes-vous heureux?—Oui, je le suis, or mais oui! *He is back.*—*Is he?* il est de retour.—Vraiment? *So you are back, are you?* alors vous voilà de retour? **being**[1], *a.* For the time being, pour le moment. **being**[2], *s.* **1.** Existence *f*, être *m.* **2.** Être. (a) *All my being*, tout mon être. (b) *A human being*, un être humain. *Human beings*, le genre humain.

beach[1], *s.* Plage *f*, grève *f*, rivage *m.* **beach-comber**, *s.* *F:* Batteur de grève.

beach[2], *v.tr.* Échouer (un navire).

beacon, *s.* **1.** Feu *m* d'alarme. **2.** *Nau:* Beacon (-light), fanal *m*, phare *m.* **3.** *Nau:* Balise *f.*

bead[1], *s.* **1.** (String of) beads chapelet *m.* To tell one's beads, dire son chapelet. **2.** (a) Perle *f.* (String of) beads, collier *m.* (b) Goutte *f*, perle. Beads of dew, perles de rosée. **3.** Guidon *m*, mire *f* (de fusil); *F:* To draw a bead on s.o., ajuster qn.

bead[2], *v.tr.* Couvrir de perles. **beading**, *s.* Garniture *f* de perles.

beadle, *s.* Bedeau *m.*

beagle, *s.* (Chien *m*) bigle *m.*

beak[1], *s.* Bec *m*; *F:* nez crochu.

beak[2], *s.* *P:* Magistrat *m.*

beaker, *s.* Gobelet *m*; coupe *f.*

beam[1], *s.* **1.** (a) Poutre *f*; solive *f*, (b) Fléau *m* (d'une balance). **2.** *N.Arch:* Bau *m.* (Breadth of) beam, largeur *f* (d'un navire). **3.** Rayon *m* (de lumière). **beam-ends**, *s.pl.* (Of ship) To be on her beam-ends, être engagé. *F:* (Of pers.) To be on one's beam-ends, être à bout de ressources.

beam[2], *v.i.* Rayonner. **beaming**, *a.* Rayonnant; radieux.

bean, *s.* Fève *f.* French beans, haricots verts. *F:* To be full of beans, être plein d'entrain. To give s.o. beans, laver la tête à qn. He hasn't a bean, il n'a pas le sou. **bean-feast**, *s.* *F:* Partie *f* de plaisir; noce *f.*

bear[1], *s.* **1.** (a) Ours *m.* She-bear, ourse *f.* Bear's cub, ourson *m.* Polar bear, ours blanc. *F:* What a bear! quel ours! (b) *Astr:* The Great Bear, la Grande Ourse. **2.** *St.Exch:* Baissier *m.* **bear-garden**, *s.* To turn the place into a bear-garden, mettre le désordre partout. **bear-leader**, *s.* *F:* Précepteur *m* qui accompagne son élève en voyage.

bear[2], *v.tr. & i.* (a) Porter. To bear oneself well, se bien comporter. (b) Supporter, soutenir. He could bear it no longer, il ne pouvait plus y tenir. I cannot bear the sight of him, je ne peux pas le sentir. I cannot bear to see it, je ne peux pas en supporter la vue. To bear with s.o., être indulgent pour qn. (c) We were borne backwards, nous fûmes refoulés. It was borne in upon him, il se laissa persuader. To bear to the right, appuyer à droite. That does not b. on the question, cela n'a aucun trait à la question. To bear on a lever, peser sur un levier. (d) Bring to bear. To bring all one's strength to b., peser (de toutes ses forces). To bring one's mind to bear on sth., porter son attention sur qch. To bring a telescope to bear on sth., braquer une lunette sur qch. (e) To bear a child, donner naissance à un enfant. She has borne him three sons, elle lui a donné trois fils. **bear down. 1.** *v.tr.* To bear down all resistance, briser toute résistance. **2.** *v.i.* *Nau:* To b. down on the enemy, foncer sur l'ennemi. **bear out**, *v.tr.* To bear out a statement, confirmer une assertion. To bear s.o. out, corroborer le dire de qn. **bear up. 1.** *v.tr.* Soutenir. **2.** *v.i.* To bear up against misfortune, faire face au malheur. Bear up! tenez bon! **bearing**, *s.* **1.** (a) Port *m* (d'armes). (b) Port, maintien *m.* Soldierly b., allure martiale. (c) *pl.* *Her:* (Armorial) bearings, armoiries *f*, blason *m.* **2.** (a) Beyond (all) bearing, insupportable. (b) (Appareil *m* d')appui *m.* (c) *Nau:* Relèvement *m.* To take the ship's bearings, faire le point. *F:* To take one's bearings, s'orienter. To lose one's bearings, perdre le nord. (d) Portée *f* (d'une question). Bearing on a question, rapport *m* avec une question. **3.** (Of tree) To be in full bearing, être en plein rapport.

bearable, *a.* Supportable.

beard[1], *s.* (a) Barbe *f.* Man with a b., homme barbu. (b) *Bot:* Arête *f* (d'épi).

beard[2], *v.tr.* Braver, défier, narguer (qn).

bearded, *a.* Barbu. Black-bearded man, homme à barbe noire.

beardless, *a.* Imberbe; sans barbe.

bearer, *s.* **1.** (a) Porteur, -euse. (b) Bearer of a passport, titulaire *mf* d'un passeport.

2. (*Of tree*) To be a good bearer, être de bon rapport.

bearish, *a.* Bourru.

beast, *s.* **1.** Bête *f.* *The brute beasts,* les brutes *f.* **2.** *pl.* *Husb:* Bétail *m,* bestiaux *mpl.* **3.** *F:* To make a beast of oneself, s'abrutir. *What a b.!* quel animal!

beastliness, *s.* **1.** Bestialité *f,* brutalité *f.* **2.** *F:* Saleté *f* (d'esprit).

beastly, *a.* (*a*) Bestial, -aux, brutal -aux. (*b*) *F:* Sale, dégoûtant, infect.

beat[1], *s.* **1.** (*a*) Battement *m* (du cœur); batterie *f* (de tambour). (*b*) *Mus:* Mesure *f,* temps *m.* **2.** Ronde *f* (d'un agent de police).

beat[2], *v.tr. & i.* Battre. **I.** (*a*) To b. on the door, frapper à la porte. To b. a drum, battre du tambour. To beat a retreat, *F:* se retirer. To beat time, battre la mesure. *F:* To beat about the bush, tourner autour du pot. *Nau:* To beat to windward, louvoyer. (*b*) (*Of bird*) To b. its wings, battre de l'aile. **2.** (*a*) To b. the enemy, battre l'ennemi. *F:* That beats me! ça me dépasse! That beats everything! ça c'est le comble! (*b*) To beat the record, battre le record. **beat back,** *v.tr.* Repousser, refouler. **beat down.** **I.** *v.tr.* (*a*) To b. sth. down, (r)abattre qch. (*b*) To beat s.o. down, marchander (avec) qn. **2.** *v.i.* The sun beats down upon our heads, le soleil donne sur nos têtes. **beat in,** *v.tr.* Enfoncer, défoncer. **beat off,** *v.tr* To b. off an attack, repousser un assaut. **beaten,** *a.* The beaten track, le chemin battu.

beating, *s.* **1.** Battement *m* (du cœur). **2.** (*a*) Coups *mpl*; rossée *f.* (*b*) Défaite *f.*

beater, *s.* *Ven:* Rabatteur *m,* traqueur *m.*

beatitude, *s.* Béatitude *f.*

beau, *s.* **1.** Élégant *m.* **2.** Prétendant *m* (d'une jeune fille); galant *m.*

beautiful, *a.* **1.** Beau, belle. **2.** *F:* Magnifique; admirable. **3.** *s.* The beautiful, le beau. **-fully,** *adv.* Admirablement.

beautify, *v.tr.* Embellir, enjoliver.

beauty, *s.* Beauté *f.* **1.** That's the beauty of it! c'est là le plus beau de l'affaire! **2.** *F:* You're a beauty! tu es encore un drôle de type, toi! The Sleeping Beauty, la Belle au bois dormant.

beaver, *s.* Castor *m.*

becalm, *v.tr.* To be becalmed, être accalminé.

because. **1.** *conj.* Parce que. **2.** *Prep.phr.* Because of sth., à cause de qch.

beck, *s.* To be at s.o.'s beck and call, obéir à qn au doigt et à l'œil.

beckon, *v.tr. & i.* Faire signe (*to s.o.,* à qn); appeler (qn) de la main, d'un geste.

become, *v.* **I.** *v.i.* Devenir; se faire. (*a*) To b. old, vieillir. To b. a priest, se faire prêtre. To b. accustomed, s'accoutumer. (*b*) What has become of X? qu'est devenu X? **2.** *v.tr.* Convenir à, aller (bien) à. **becoming,** *a.* **I.** Convenable, bienséant. **2.** Qui sied (à); qui va bien (à). **-ly,** *adv.* Convenablement.

bed[1], *s.* Lit *m.* **I.** (*a*) Single bed, lit à u[n] place, pour une personne Spare bed, [lit] d'ami. To go to bed, se coucher. To ta[ke] to one's bed, s'aliter. To keep to one's be[d] garder le lit. To get into bed, se mettre au l[it] To get out of bed, se lever. *To make the bed* faire les lits. (*b*) = BEDSTEAD. (*c*) Spring-be[d] sommier *m* élastique. **2.** (*a*) Lit (d'un rivière); banc *m* (d'huitres). (Flower-)be[d] parterre *m.* (*b*) *Geol:* Assise *f*; couche *Miner:* Gisement *m.* **bed-clothes,** s.p[l] Couvertures *f* (de lit). **bed-cover,** s. Dessus *m* de lit. **bed-post,** *s.* Colonne de lit. **bed-ridden,** *a.* Cloué au li[t] **bed-rock,** *s. F:* To get down to bed-rock descendre au fond des choses. **Bed-roc[k]** price, dernier prix.

bed[2]. *v.tr.* To bed (out) plants, dépoter de[s] plantes. **bedding,** *s.* **I.** *Hort:* Bedding out, dépotage *m.* **2.** Literie *f*; fournitur[e] *fpl* (d'un lit).

bedaub, *v.tr.* Barbouiller (de peinture).

bedfellow, *s.* Camarade *mf* de lit.

bedizen, *v.tr.* Attifer, chamarrer.

Bedlam, *s.* *F:* (*a*) Maison *f* de fous (*b*) Charivari *m,* tohu-bohu *m.*

Bedouin, *a. & s.* Bédouin, -ine.

bedroom, *s.* Chambre *f* à coucher. Spar[e] bedroom, chambre d'ami.

bedside, *s.* Chevet *m*; bord *m* du lit. **Bedsid[e]** rug, descente *f* de lit.

bedstead, *s.* Bois *m* de lit, lit *m.*

bedtime, *s.* Heure *f* du coucher.

bee, *s.* Abeille *f.* To keep bees, élever de[s] abeilles. *F:* To have a bee in one's bonnet avoir une araignée au plafond. **bee-keeper,** *s.* Apiculteur *m.* **bee-line,** *s. F:* To mak[e] a bee-line for sth. aller droit vers qch.

beech, *s.* Hêtre *m.* **beech-nut,** *s.* Faîne *f.*

beef, *s.* *Cu:* Bœuf *m.* Roast beef, rôti *m* de bœuf; rosbif *m.* Corned beef, bœuf de conserve. **beef-steak,** *s. Cu:* Bifteck *m* tournedos *m.* **beef-tea,** *s.* Bouillon *m.*

beehive, *s.* *Ap:* Ruche *f.*

Beelzebub. *Pr.n. B.Lit:* Belzébuth *m.*

beer, *s.* Bière *f.* *F:* To think no small beer of oneself, ne pas se prendre pour de la petite bière.

beeswax, *s.* Cire *f* d'abeilles.

beet, *s.* Betterave *f.*

beetle, *s.* *Ent:* Coléoptère *m*; scarabée *m.*

beetling, *a.* Surplombant, menaçant.

beetroot, *s.* Betterave *f.*

befall, *v.tr. & i.* **I.** So befell that, il arriva que.

befitting, *a.* Convenable, seyant.

before. **I.** *adv.* (*a*) En avant; devant. To go on before, marcher en avant, prendre les devants. *This page and the one before,* cette page et la précédente. (*b*) Auparavant, avant. The day before, le jour précédent; la veille. The year before, l'année d'auparavant. *I have seen him b.,* je l'ai déjà vu. **2.** *prep.* (*a*) Devant. To stand before s.o., se tenir devant qn. Before my eyes, sous mes yeux. (*b*) **Avant. Before long,** avant (qu'il soit) longtemps. **It ought to have been done before now,** ce devrait être déjà fait. *We are b. our time,* nous sommes en avance. *B. answering,* avant de répondre. (*c*) **Before everything else,** avant tout. **3.** *conj.* *Come and see me b. you leave,* venez me voir avant que vous (ne) partiez, avant de partir.

beforehand, *adv.* Préalablement; d'avance. *To pay b.,* payer d'avance.

befriend, *v.tr.* Secourir; se montrer l'ami de.

beg, *v.tr. & i.* **1.** Mendier. **2. To beg a favour of** s.o., solliciter une faveur de qn. *I beg (of) you!* je vous en prie! **To beg the question,** supposer vrai ce qui est en question.

begging, *s.* **1.** Mendicité *f.* **2. Begging the question,** pétition *f* de principe.

beget, *v.tr.* **1.** Engendrer, procréer. **2.** Causer, susciter.

beggar¹, *s.* **1. Beggar(-man, -woman,)** mendiant, -e, gueux, -euse, pauvre, -esse. **2.** *F:* Individu *m.* **Poor beggar!** pauvre diable! **Lucky beggar!** veinard!

beggar², *v.tr.* **1.** Réduire à la mendicité. **2.** *F:* **To beggar description,** défier toute description.

beggarly, *a.* Chétif, misérable, mesquin.

beggary, *s.* Mendicité *f,* misère *f.*

begin, *v.tr. & i.* Commencer. *The day began well,* la journée s'annonça bien. **To begin to do sth.,** commencer à, de, faire qch. *To b. to laugh,* se mettre à rire. **To begin with,** tout d'abord; pour commencer. **To begin again,** recommencer. **beginning,** *s.* Commencement *m;* début *m* (d'une carrière); origine *f.* **In the beginning,** au commencement, au début. **To make a beginning,** commencer, débuter.

beginner, *s.* **1.** Auteur *m* (d'une querelle). **2.** Commençant, -e, débutant, -e.

begrudge, *v.tr.* Donner à contre-cœur. *To b. s.o. sth.,* envier qch. à qn.

begrudgingly, *adv.* A contre-cœur.

beguile, *v.tr.* **1.** Enjôler, séduire, tromper. **2.** Distraire, amuser.

behalf, *s.* **1. On behalf of s.o.,** au nom de qn; *I come on behalf of Mr X,* je viens de la part de M. X. **2.** *To plead in s.o's b.,* plaider en faveur de qn.

behave, *v.i.* *To b. well,* se conduire, se comporter, bien. *To b. well to s.o.,* bien agir envers qn. **To know how to behave,** savoir vivre. (*To child*) **Behave yourself!** sois sage!

behaviour, *s.* **1.** Tenue *f,* maintien *m;* conduite *f* (*to, towards,* s.o., avec, envers, qn). *To be on one's best b.,* se surveiller. **2.** Allure *f* (d'une machine).

behead, *v.tr.* Décapiter. *He was beheaded,* on lui coupa le cou.

behest, *s.* Ordre *m.* **At s.o.'s behest,** sur l'ordre de qn.

behind. 1. *adv.* Derrière; par derrière. (*a*) *To come b.,* venir derrière; suivre. **To**

remain behind, rester en arrière. (*b*) **To be behind with one's work,** être en retard dans son travail. **2.** *prep.* (*a*) Derrière **What is behind all this?** qu'y a-t-il derrière tout cela? **To be behind** (= *to support*) s.o., soutenir qn. (*b*) En arrière de, en retard sur. *Country b. its neighbours,* pays en arrière de ses voisins. **3.** *s.* *F:* Derrière *m.*

behindhand, *adv. & pred. a.* En arrière; en retard; attardé.

behold, *v.tr.* Voir; apercevoir.

behoof, *s.* **To, for, on, s.o.'s behoof,** à l'avantage, au profit, de qn.

belabour, *v.tr.* Rouer de coups.

belated, *a.* **1.** (Voyageur) attardé. **2.** (Repentir) tardif.

belch¹, *s.* Éructation *f.*

belch². **1.** *v.i.* Éructer. **2.** *v.tr.* **To belch (forth) flames,** vomir des flammes.

beleaguer, *v.tr.* Assiéger.

belfry, *s.* Beffroi *m,* clocher *m.*

Belgian, *a. & s.* Belge (*mf*); de Belgique.

Belgium, *Pr.n.* La Belgique.

belie, *v.tr.* Donner un démenti à; démentir.

belief, *s.* **1.** Croyance *f,* conviction *f.* **To the best of my belief,** à ce que je crois. **2.** *B. in* s.o., confiance *f* en qn.

believe. 1. *v.tr.* (*a*) Croire; ajouter foi à (une rumeur). *I b.* (*that*) *I am right,* je crois avoir raison. *Seeing is believing,* voir c'est croire. *To make s.o. b. that,* faire accroire à qn que. (*b*) **To believe** s.o., croire qn. *If he is to be believed,* à l'en croire. **2.** *v.i.* (*a*) **To believe in God,** croire en Dieu. (*b*) **To believe in s.o.'s word,** croire à la parole de qn. **3.** *To make believe to do sth.,* faire semblant de faire qch.

believer, *s.* **1.** Croyant, -e. **2. A believer in,** un partisan de.

belittle, *v.tr.* Rabaisser, déprécier.

bell, *s.* **1.** (*a*) (Clapper-)bell cloche *f;* (*smaller*) clochette *f;* (*in house*) sonnette *f;* (*fixed bell*) timbre *m.* **Sleigh-bell,** grelot *m.* **Electric bell,** sonnerie *f* (électrique). **Chime of bells,** carillon *m.* **To ring the bell,** sonner. (*b*) *Nau:* **To strike eight bells,** piquer midi. **2.** *Hort:* Cloche. **bell-pull,** *s.* Cordon *m* de sonnette. **bell-push,** *s* Bouton *m.* **bell-ringer,** *s.* Sonneur *m.* **bell-tower,** *s.* Clocher *m.*

belladonna, *s.* Belladone *f.*

belle, *s.* Beauté *f.*

bellicose, *a.* Belliqueux.

belligerent, *a. & s.* Belligérant (*m*).

bellow¹, *s.* (*a*) Beuglement *m,* mugissement *m.* (*b*) *F:* Hurlement *m* (de douleur).

bellow². *v.i.* Beugler, mugir; *F:* hurler.

bellows, *s.pl.* **1.** Soufflet *m.* **A pair of bellows,** un soufflet. **2.** Soufflerie *f* (d'une forge).

belly, *s.* Ventre *m.* **belly-ache,** *s.* *F:* Mal *m* de ventre; colique *f.*

belong, *v.i.* **1.** Appartenir, être (*to,* à). *That book belongs to me,* ce livre m'appartient,

12

est à moi. (*Of land*) To b. to the Crown, dépendre de la Couronne. **2.** (*Be appropriate*) Être propre (à qch.). **3.** To belong to a society, faire partie d'une société. I belong here, je suis d'ici.

belongings, *s.pl.* Affaires *f*, effets *m*. Personal belongings, objets personnels.

beloved. 1. *p.p. & pred. a.* B. by all, aimé de tous. **2.** *a. & s.* Bien-aimé(e).

below. 1. *adv.* (*a*) En bas, (au-)dessous. Here below, ici-bas. (*b*) The passage quoted below, le passage cité ci-dessous. **2.** *prep.* Au-dessous de. (*a*) B. the knee, au-dessous du genou. (*b*) Below the average, au-dessous de la moyenne. (*c*) Below the surface, sous la surface. (*d*) Below the bridge, en aval du pont.

belt¹, *s.* **1.** (Waist-)belt, ceinture *f*, *Mil:* ceinturon *m*. (Shoulder-)belt, baudrier *m*. *F:* To hit s.o. below the belt, donner à qn un coup en traître. **2.** *Mec.E:* Courroie *f* (de transmission). **3.** Coal belt, zone houillère.

belt², *v.tr.* **1.** Ceinturer, ceindre. **2.** Entourer d'une ceinture. **belted,** *a.* Ceinturé; à ceinture.

bemoan, *v.tr.* Pleurer, déplorer (qch.).

bemuse, *v.tr.* Stupéfier.

bench, *s.* **1.** (*a*) Banc *m*; banquette *f*; gradin *m* (d'amphithéâtre). (*b*) *Jur:* The Bench, (i) la magistrature; (ii) la Cour. **2.** Établi *m* (de menuisier).

bend¹, *s.* Courbure *f*; courbe *f*; (*of road*) coude *m*; virage *m*; (*of river*) méandre *m*.

bend², *v.tr. & i.* **1.** Courber (le corps); plier (le coude); fléchir (le genou); baisser (la tête). To b. beneath a burden, plier, fléchir, sous un fardeau. **2.** *v.tr.* To b. a rod out of shape, forcer, fausser, une barre de fer. **3.** Tendre, bander (un ressort). **4.** To bend one's steps towards a place, diriger ses pas vers un endroit. **bend down.** *v.i.* Se courber, se baisser. **bend forward,** *v.i.* Se pencher en avant. **bent,** *a.* **1.** (*a*) Courbé, plié, arqué. B. back, dos voûté. (*b*) Faussé, fléchi. **2.** Résolu, décidé (*on doing sth.*, à faire qch.).

beneath. 1. *adv.* Dessous, au-dessous, en bas. **2.** *prep.* Au-dessous de; sous. *F:* It is beneath him, il est indigne de lui.

Benedict. *Pr.n.* Benoît *m*.

benedictine. 1. *Ecc: a. & s.* Bénédictin, -e. **2.** *s.* Bénédictine *f*.

benediction, *s.* **1.** Bénédiction *f*. **2.** (*At meals*) Bénédicité *m*.

benefaction, *s.* Bienfait *m*.

benefactor, *s.* Bienfaiteur, -trice.

benefice, *s.* *Ecc:* Bénéfice *m*.

beneficence, *s.* Bienfaisance *f*.

beneficent, *a.* **1.** Bienfaisant. **2.** Salutaire.

beneficial, *a.* Salutaire, profitable, avantageux. **-ally,** *adv.* Avantageusement.

beneficiary, *a. & s.* *Jur:* Bénéficier, -ère; bénéficiaire *m*.

benefit¹, *s.* **1.** Avantage *m*, profit *m*. *Jur:* Benefit of the doubt, bénéfice *m* du doute. **2.** *Adm:* Indemnité *f*, allocation *f*. Unemployment benefit, indemnité de chômage.

benefit². **1.** *v.tr.* Faire du bien, être avantageux, profiter, à (qn). **2.** *v.i.* To benefit by sth., profiter de qch.

benevolence, *s.* Bienveillance *f*, bonté *f*.

benevolent, *a.* **1.** Bienveillant (*to*, envers). **2.** Benevolent society, association de bienfaisance. **-ly,** *adv.* Avec bienveillance.

Bengal. *Pr.n. Geog:* Le Bengale.

benighted, *a.* **1.** Anuité; surpris par la nuit. **2.** Plongé dans les ténèbres de l'ignorance.

benign, *a.* Bénin, *f.* bénigne; doux, *f.* douce; favorable.

benignant, *a.* Bénin *f.* bénigne; bienveillant. **-ly,** *adv.* Avec bienveillance.

benignity, *s.* Bienveillance *f*, bonté *f*.

bent, *s.* Penchant *m*, inclination *f*, disposition *f* (*for*, pour).

benumb, *v.tr.* Engourdir, transir.

bequeath, *v.tr.* Léguer (*to*, à).

bequest, *s.* Legs *m*.

bereave, *v.tr.* **1.** Priver, déposséder. **2.** *s.pl.* The bereaved, la famille du mort; les affligés.

bereavement, *s.* Perte *f* (d'un parent); deuil *m*.

beret, *s.* *Cost:* Béret *m*.

bergamot, *s.* Bergamote *f*.

Bermudas (the). *Pr.n. Geog:* Les Bermudes *f*.

berry, *s.* *Bot:* Baie *f*.

berth¹, *s.* **1.** (*a*) *F:* To give s.o. a wide berth, éviter qn. (*b*) (Anchoring) berth, poste *m* de mouillage, d'amarrage. **2.** Couchette *f* (de voyageur). **3.** *F:* Place *f*, emploi *m*.

berth², *v.i.* (*a*) Aborder à quai. (*b*) To berth forward, coucher à l'avant.

beryl, *s.* *Miner:* Béryl *m*.

beseech, *v.tr.* Supplier, adjurer, conjurer (*s.o. to do sth.*, qn de faire qch.). **beseeching,** *a.* Suppliant.

beset, *v.tr.* **1.** Beset with difficulties, entouré de difficultés. **2.** Assiéger (un endroit). **3.** (*Of misfortunes*) Assaillir (qn). **besetting,** *a.* Besetting sin, péché d'habitude.

beside, *prep.* **1.** A côté, auprès, de. **2.** (*a*) Beside the point, en dehors du sujet. (*b*) To be beside oneself, être hors de soi; (*with joy*) être transporté de joie.

besides. 1. *adv.* (*a*) En outre, en plus. Nothing besides, rien de plus. (*b*) It is too late; b., I am tired, il est trop tard; d'ailleurs je suis fatigué. **2.** *prep.* Others b. him, d'autres que lui.

besiege, *v.tr.* Assiéger.

besmirch, *v.tr.* Salir, tacher, souiller (qch.).

besotted, *a.* Abruti.

bespatter, *v.tr.* Éclabousser.

bespeak, *v.tr.* **1.** Commander (des souliers); retenir (une place). **2.** Accuser, annoncer.

bespoke, *a.* Bespoke garment, vêtement (fait) sur mesure.

best[1]. **1.** *a. & s.* (*a*) (Le) meilleur, (la) meilleure ; le mieux. **Best man** (*at a wedding*), garçon d'honneur. **We drank of the best,** nous avons bu du meilleur. (Dressed) in one's best (clothes), endimanché. **The best of it,** le plus beau de l'affaire. **To know what is best for s.o.,** savoir ce qui convient le mieux à qn. *It would be b. to,* le mieux serait de. **To do one's best,** faire de son mieux. *He did his b. to smile,* il s'efforça de sourire. **To be at one's best,** être en train. **To get, have, the best of it,** l'emporter ; avoir le dessus. **To make the best of a bad bargain,** faire bonne mine à mauvais jeu. (*b*) *Adv.phr.* **At (the) best,** pour dire le mieux. **To act for the best,** agir pour le mieux. **To the best of my belief,** à ce que je crois. **2.** *adv.* (*a*) He does it (the) best, c'est lui qui le fait le mieux. **I comforted her as best I could,** je la consolai de mon mieux. *Do as you think b.,* faites comme bon vous semble(ra). (*b*) *The b. dressed man,* l'homme le mieux habillé.

best-seller, *s. F:* Livre *m* à succès.

best[2], *v.tr. F:* L'emporter sur (qn).

bestial, *a.* Bestial, -aux.

bestir, *v.pr. To b. oneself,* se remuer.

bestow, *v.tr.* Accorder, octroyer, donner (*sth. upon s.o.,* qch. à qn).

bet[1], *s.* Pari *m,* gageure *f.* **To make a bet,** parier, faire un pari.

bet[2], *v.tr.* Parier. *To bet ten to one,* parier à dix contre un. **To bet on sth.,** parier sur qch.

betting, *s.* Les paris *m.*

betake, *v.pr. To b. oneself to a place,* se rendre dans, à, un endroit.

betel, *s.* Bétel *m.* Betel-nut, (noix *f* d')arec *m*

bethink, *v.pr.* **1.** *To b. oneself,* réfléchir, considérer. **2.** Se rappeler (*that,* que).

betide, *v.* **1.** *v.i.* Whate'er betide, advienne que pourra. **2.** *v.tr.* Woe betide him, malheur à lui.

betimes, *adv. Lit:* De bonne heure.

betoken, *v.tr.* **1.** Être signe de (qch.) ; accuser, dénoter, révéler. **2.** Présager, annoncer.

betray, *v.tr.* **1.** Trahir ; vendre (qn). **2.** Révéler, montrer, laisser voir ; trahir.

betrayal, *s.* Action *f* de trahir ; trahison *f.*

betrothal, *s.* Fiançailles *fpl* (*to,* avec).

betrothed, *a. & s.* Fiancé(e).

better[1]. **1.** *a. & s.* Meilleur. *F:* **They have seen better days,** ils ont eu des malheurs. *He's a b. man than you,* il vaut plus que vous. (*At games*) *You are b. than I,* vous êtes plus fort que moi. **The respect due to your betters,** le respect dû à vos supérieurs. *I had hoped for b. things,* j'avais espéré mieux. *The b. part of the day,* la plus grande partie du jour. **2.** Mieux. (*a*) *That's better,* voilà qui est mieux. *Nothing could be b.,* c'est on ne peut mieux. **So much the better,** tant mieux. **To get better,** (i) (*of thgs*) s'améliorer ; (ii) (*of pers.*) guérir, se remettre. **The weather** is better, il fait meilleur. **To be better** (*in health*), aller mieux. **To get the better of** s.o., l'emporter sur qn. **To go one better than** s.o., (r)enchérir sur qn. (*b*) **Better so,** il vaut mieux qu'il en soit ainsi. **3.** *adv.* (*a*) Mieux. **Better and better,** de mieux en mieux. **To think better of it,** se raviser. **Better still,** (i) mieux encore, (ii) qui mieux est. (*b*) **B. known,** plus connu.

better[2], *v.tr.* (*a*) Améliorer ; rendre meilleur (*b*) Surpasser (un exploit).

between, *prep.* Entre. (*a*) **No one can come between us,** personne ne peut nous séparer. (*b*) **B. now and Monday,** d'ici à lundi. **B. twenty and thirty,** de vingt à trente. (*c*) **Between ourselves,** entre nous.

betwixt. **1.** *rep.* Entre. **2.** *adv. F:* **Betwixt and between,** entre les deux.

bevel[1], *s.* Angle *m* oblique. Biseau *m,* biais *m,*

bevel[2], *v.tr.* Biseauter, chanfreiner. **bevelled**, *a.* (Bord) biseauté, en biseau, en chanfrein.

beverage, *s.* Breuvage *m,* boisson *f.*

bevy, *s.* Bande *f,* troupe *f.*

bewail, *v.tr.* Pleurer.

beware, *v.ind.tr.* Beware! prenez garde ! 'Beware of pickpockets,' "se méfier des pickpockets."

bewilder, *v.tr.* Désorienter, égarer ; *F:* ahurir. **bewildered**, *a.* Désorienté ; *F:* ahuri. **I am bewildered,** j'y perds la tête

bewildering, *a.* Déroutant.

bewilderment, *s.* Désorientation *f* ; trouble *m* ; *F:* ahurissement *m.*

bewitch, *v.tr.* Ensorceler. **bewitching**, *a* Ensorcelant, ravissant.

beyond. **1.** *adv.* Au delà, par delà, plus loin. **2.** *prep.* Au delà de, par delà. (*a*) **Beyond the seas,** outre-mer. (*b*) **To stay beyond one's time,** rester trop longtemps. (*c*) **Beyond all praise,** au-dessus de tout éloge. **It is beyond me,** cela me dépasse. **Beyond doubt,** hors de doute. **Beyond belief,** incroyable(ment) **That is (going) beyond a joke,** cela dépasse les bornes de la plaisanterie.

bezique, *s. Cards:* Bésigue *m.*

bias[1], *s.* **1.** *Bowls:* (*a*) Fort *m* (de la boule). (*b*) Déviation *f.* **2.** Prévention *f* ; parti pris

bias[2], *v.tr.* Rendre (qn) partial ; prédisposer

biased, *a.* Partial, -aux. **To be b.,** avoir une prévention.

bib, *s.* Bavette *f* (d'enfant).

Bible, *s.* Bible *f.*

biblical, *a.* Biblique.

bibliographer, *s.* Bibliographe *m.*

bibliography, *s.* Bibliographie *f.*

bibliophile, *s.* Bibliophile *m.*

bibulous, *a.* Adonné à la boisson.

bicarbonate, *s.* Bicarbonate *m.*

biceps, *s. Anat:* Biceps *m.*

bicker, *v.i.* Se quereller, se chamailler.

bickering, *s.* Chamailleries *fpl*

bicycle, *s.* Bicyclette *f.*

bid¹, s. (a) Enchère f, offre f, mise f. *Higher bid,* surenchère f. *F: To make a bid for power,* viser au pouvoir. (b) *Cards:* Appel m.
bid², v.tr. & i. **1.** Commander, ordonner (*s.o.* (*to*) *do sth.,* à qn de faire qch.). *Do as you are bid,* faites ce qu'on vous dit. **2.** (a) To bid s.o. welcome, souhaiter la bienvenue à qn. (b) **The weather bids fair to be fine,** le temps s'annonce beau. **3.** (a) To bid for sth., mettre une enchère sur qch. (b) *Cards:* Demander, appeler. **bidding,** s. **1.** Commandement m, ordre m. **2.** Enchères fpl, mises fpl.
bidder, s. Enchérisseur m. **The highest bidder,** le plus offrant.
bide, v.tr. To bide one's time, attendre l'heure.
biennial, a. & s. *Bot:* Biennial (plant), plante bisannuelle.
bier, s. (a) Civière f.
bifurcate, v.i. (Se) bifurquer.
bifurcation, s. Bifurcation f.
big. 1. a. (a) (*Large*) Grand; (*bulky*) gros. *Big hotel,* grand hôtel. *Big man,* (i) homme de grande taille, (ii) gros homme, (iii) homme marquant. To grow big(ger), (i) grandir; (ii) grossir. (b) **Big with consequences,** lourd de conséquences. **2.** adv. To talk big, faire l'important.
bigamist, s. Bigame mf.
bigamous, a. Bigame.
bigamy, s. Bigamie f.
bigot, s. Fanatique mf.
bigoted, a. Fanatique.
bigotry, s. Fanatisme m.
bigwig, s. *F:* Gros bonnet.
bike, s. *F:* (= BICYCLE) Vélo m, bécane f.
bilberry, s. *Bot:* Airelle f.
bile, s. *Physiol:* Bile f.
bilge, s. *Nau:* Bilge(-water), eau f de cale.
bilingual, a. Bilingue.
bilious, a. Bilieux.
biliousness, s. Attaque f de bile.
bill¹, s. **1.** Bec m (d'oiseau). **2.** *Geog:* Bec, promontoire m.
bill², v.i. To bill and coo, faire les tourtereaux.
bill³, s. **1.** *Com:* Note f, facture f, mémoire m; (*in restaurant*) addition f. **2.** Bill of exchange, lettre f de change; traite f. **3.** Affiche f, placard m, écriteau m. Stick no bills! défense d'afficher. **4.** (a) Bill of fare, carte f du jour; menu m. (b) *Nau:* Bill of lading, connaissement m. **5.** Projet m de loi. **bill-poster, -sticker,** s. Afficheur m.
billet¹, s. **1.** *Mil:* Logement m **2.** *F:* Place f, emploi m.
billet², v.tr. *Mil:* To billet troops on s.o., loger des troupes chez qn.
billiards, s.pl. (Jeu m de) billard m. **Billiard-ball,** bille f de billard. **billiard-room,** s. (Salle f de) billard m. **billiard-table,** s. Billard m.

billion, s. Trillion m.
billow, s. Grande vague; lame f.
billy-goat, s. Bouc m.
bin, s. Coffre m, huche f.
bind, v.tr. Attacher, lier. **1.** (a) Bound hand and foot, pieds et poings liés. (b) To bind sth. (down) to sth., attacher, fixer, qch. à qch. (c) To bind a bargain, confirmer un marché. **2.** To bind (up) a wound, bander une blessure. **3.** (a) To bind (up) a sheaf, lier une gerbe. (b) Relier (un livre). Bound in paper, broché. Bound in boards, cartonné. **4.** Lier, engager (qn). *To b. oneself to do sth.,* s'engager à faire qch. **bound,** a. **1.** Lié. **2.** (a) To be bound to do sth., être obligé, tenu, de faire qch. To be in honour bound to do sth., être engagé d'honneur à faire qch. (b) *It's b. to happen,* c'est fatal. *We are b. to be successful,* nous réussirons à coup sûr. (c) *F: He'll come,* I'll be bound, il viendra, j'en suis sûr!
binding¹, a. Obligatoire (*upon s.o.,* pour qn). **binding²,** s. Reliure f (d'un livre).
binnacle, s. *Nau:* Habitacle m.
binocular, s.pl. Binoculars, jumelle(s) f.
binomial. *Mth:* a. Binôme. **The binomial theorem,** le théorème de Newton.
biographer, s. Biographe m.
biographic(al), a. Biographique.
biography, s. Biographie f.
biologist, s. Biologiste m. biologue m.
biology, s. Biologie f.
biped, a. & s. Bipède (m).
biplane, s. Avion biplan; biplan m.
birch¹, s. **1.** *Bot:* Bouleau m. **2.** Birch(-rod), verge f, poignée f de verges.
birch², v.tr. Donner les verges à (qn).
bird, s. Oiseau m. *F:* A little bird told me so, mon petit doigt me l'a dit. To give s.o. the bird, envoyer promener qn. A bird in the hand is worth two in the bush, un 'tiens' vaut mieux que deux 'tu l'auras.' **bird-cage,** s. Cage f d'oiseau. **bird-catcher,** s. Oiseleur m. **bird-lime,** s. Glu f. **bird's-eye,** s. Bird's-eye view, vue à vol d'oiseau.
biretta, s. *Ecc.Cost:* Barrette f.
birth, s. Naissance f. Irish by birth, Irlandais de naissance. **birth-certificate,** s. Acte m de naissance. **birth-place,** s. Lieu m de naissance. **birth-rate,** s. Natalité f.
birthday, s. Anniversaire m de naissance.
birthright, s. Droit m d'aînesse.
Biscay. *Pr.n. Geog:* **The Bay of Biscay,** le golfe de Gascogne.
biscuit, s. Biscuit m. Fancy biscuits, petits fours. *P: That takes the biscuit!* ça, c'est fort!
bisect, v.tr. Couper, diviser.
bishop, s. **1.** *Ecc:* Évêque m. **2.** *Chess:* Fou m.
bishopric, s. Évêché m.
bismuth, s. *Miner:* Bismuth m.

bison, s. Bison m.

bit¹, s. **1.** Harn: Mors m. F: To take the bit between one's teeth, prendre le mors aux dents ; s'emballer. **2.** Tls: Mèche f.

bit², s. F: (a) Morceau m. (b) Bout m, brin m. Bit of paper, bout de papier. (c) F: (Coin) Pièce f. **2.** A bit (of), un peu (de). He is a bit jealous, il est quelque peu jaloux. He is a bit of a liar, il est tant soit peu menteur. Wait a bit! attendez un peu. A good bit older, sensiblement plus âgé. Bit by bit, peu à peu. Not a bit (of it)! n'en croyez rien ! It's not a bit of use, cela ne sert absolument à rien.

bitch, s. Chienne f.

bite¹, s. **1.** (a) Coup m de dent. (b) Fish: Touche f. F: Got a bite? ça mord? **2.** (a) (Wound) Morsure f. (b) Piqûre f (d'un insecte). **3.** F: Bouchée f, morceau m.

bite², v.tr. Mordre. **1.** Donner un coup de dent à (qch.) ; (of insect) piquer. Prov: Once bitten, twice shy, chat échaudé craint l'eau froide. To be bitten with a desire to do sth., brûler de faire qch. **2.** The wind bites the face, le vent coupe le visage. **bite off,** v.tr. Enlever d'un coup de dent(s). F: To bite s.o.'s head off, rembarrer qn. **biting,** a. Mordant ; (of cold) cuisant ; (of wind) cinglant.

biter, s. F: The biter bit, le trompeur trompé.

bitter, a. **1.** (Goût) amer ; (vent) piquant ; (ennemi) implacable ; (ton) âpre. B. remorse, remords cuisants. B. experience, expérience cruelle. **2.** s. pl. Bitters, amer(s) m. **-ly,** adv. Amèrement, avec amertume. It was b. cold, il faisait un froid de loup.

bitter-end, s. To the bitter-end, à outrance ; jusqu'au bout.

bittern, s. Orn: Butor m.

bitterness, s. (a) Amertume f. (b) Rigueur f (du temps) ; aigreur f (de paroles).

bitumen, s. Bitume m.

bivalve, a. & s. Moll: Bivalve (m).

bivouac¹, s. Mil: Bivouac m.

bivouac², v.i. Bivouaquer.

bizarre, a. Bizarre.

blab, v. Jaser, bavarder.

black¹. I. a. Noir. **1.** (a) As black as ebony, d'un noir d'ébène. To be black in the face, avoir le visage tout congestionné. To look black, faire une vilaine figure. To beat s.o. black and blue, rosser qn de coups. Black eye, œil poché. (b) Black woman, négresse f. (c) His hands were b., il avait les mains toutes noires. **2.** B. despair, sombre désespoir. II. **black,** s. Noir m. **1.** Brunswick black, laque f à l'asphalte. **2.** (a) She always wears b., elle est toujours en noir. (b) Black-and-white artist, dessinateur à l'encre. To set sth. down in black and white, coucher qch. par écrit. **black-beetle,** s. Blatte f, cafard m. **black-cock,** s. Petit coq de bruyère. **black-lead,** s. **1.** Mine f de plomb. **2.** Crayon m de mine de plomb. **black-pudding,** s. Cu: Boudin m.

black², v.tr. **1.** Noircir. To b. boots, cirer des chaussures. F: To black s.o.'s eye, pocher l'œil à qn. **2.** To black out, obscurcir (une ville), F: blackouter. **blacking,** s. Cirage m (de ou pour chaussures). **black-ing-brush,** s. Brosse f à cirer. **black-out,** s. Blackout m.

blackamoor, s. Noir ; moricaud, -e.

blackball, v.tr. Blackbouler.

blackberry, s. Mûre f (de ronce).

blackbird, s. Orn: Merle m.

blackboard, s. Tableau noir.

blacken. I. v.tr. Noircir ; obscurcir (le ciel). **2.** v.i. (Se) noircir ; devenir noir.

blackguard¹, s. Gouape f, vaurien m.

blackguard², v.tr. Lancer des injures à.

blackguardly, a. Ignoble, canaille.

blackish, a. Noirâtre.

blackleg, s. Ind: Renard m ; jaune m.

blackmail¹, s. F: Chantage m.

blackmail², v.tr. F: faire chanter (qn).

blackmailer, s. Maître-chanteur m.

blackness, s. Noirceur f ; obscurité f.

blacksmith, s. Forgeron m.

blackthorn, s. **1.** Bot: Épine noire. **2.** Gourdin m (d'épine).

bladder, s. Vessie f.

blade, s. **1.** Brin m (d'herbe). **2.** (a) Lame f (de couteau). (b) F: Sabre m, épée f. **3.** Pelle f, pale f (d'aviron).

blame¹, s. **1.** Reproches mpl ; condamnation f. **2.** Responsabilité f ; faute f. To put the blame upon s.o., rejeter le blâme sur qn.

blame², v.tr. Blâmer, condamner (qn). To b. s.o. for sth., blâmer qn de qch. To have only oneself to blame, s'en prendre qu'à soi-même. He is to blame, il y a de sa faute.

blameless, a. Innocent, irréprochable.

blameworthy, a. Blâmable.

blanch. I. v.tr. Blanchir **2.** v.i. Blêmir, pâlir.

blancmange, s. Blanc-manger m.

bland, a. Doux, f. douce ; affable ; débonnaire. **-ly,** adv. Avec affabilité.

blandishment, s. Flatterie f ; cajoleries fpl.

blandness, s. Douceur f, suavité f, affabilité f.

blank. I. a. **1.** (a) B. page, page blanche. (b) Blank cheque, chèque en blanc. (c) Blank verse, vers blancs. **2.** (a) B. look, regard sans expression. (b) To look blank, avoir l'air confondu. (c) B. despair, profond découragement. **-ly,** adv. To look b. at s.o., regarder qn (i) d'un air confondu, (ii) sans expression. II. **blank,** s. **1.** Blanc m, vide m. F: His mind is a blank, sa mémoire est une table rase. **2.** Billet blanc, billet perdant.

blanket, s. Couverture f.

blare¹, s. Sonnerie f, accents cuivrés.

blare². 1. v.i. Mus: Cuivrer le son. **2.** v.tr. The band blared (out) a quickstep, la fanfare fit retentir une marche.

blarney¹, s. F: Eau bénite de cour.

blarney², *v.tr.* Cajoler, enjôler (qn).

blaspheme, *v.i. & tr.* Blasphémer.

blasphemer, *s.* Blasphémateur, -trice.

blasphemous, *a.* Blasphématoire, impie.

blasphemy, *s.* Blasphème *m.*

blast¹, *s.* **1.** Coup *m* de vent; rafale *f.* **2.** B. on the whistle, coup de sifflet. B. on the trumpet, sonnerie *f* de trompette. **3.** Metall: Air *m*, vent *m.* To be in full blast, être en pleine activité. **4.** (a) Ball: Souffle *m.* (b) Min: (i) Coup de mine. (ii) Charge *f* d'explosif. **blast-furnace**, *s.* Haut-fourneau.

blast². *v.tr.* (a) Min: Faire sauter. (b) Ruiner; détruire. (c) (Of lightning) Foudroyer. **blasting**, *s.* (a) Travail *m* aux explosifs. (b) Anéantissement *m*; ruine *f.* (c) Foudroiement *m.*

blatant, *a.* **1.** D'une vulgarité criarde. **2.** (Injustice) criante. **-ly**, *adv.* Avec une vulgarité criarde.

blaze¹, *s.* **1.** Flamme(s) *f*, flambée *f.* In a blaze, en flammes. **2.** Flamboiement *m* (du soleil); éclat *m* (des couleurs). **3.** *pl.* F: To work like blazes, travailler furieusement.

blaze², *v.i.* (a) Flamber; flamboyer. (b) F: To blaze with anger, être enflammé de colère. **blaze away**, *v.i.* Tirer sans désemparer; travailler ferme. **blaze down**, *v.i.* Darder ses rayons (on, sur). **blaze up**, *v.i.* **1.** S'embraser, s'enflammer. **2.** S'emporter. **blazing**, *a.* (a) En feu; enflammé; embrasé. (b) (Soleil) flambant.

blazer, *s.* Cost: Blazer *m.*

blazon¹, *s.* Her: Blason *m.*

blazon², *v.tr.* Publier, proclamer.

bleach, *v.tr. & i.* Blanchir. To b. the hair, décolorer les cheveux. **bleaching**, *s.* Blanchiment *m.*

bleak, *a.* **1.** (Terrain) exposé au vent. **2.** (Temps) triste; (vent) froid. **3.** B. prospects, avenir morne. B. smile, sourire pâle.

blear-eyed, *a.* Aux yeux troubles, larmoyants.

bleat¹, *s.* Bêlement *m.*

bleat², *v.i.* Bêler. **bleating**, *s.* Bêlement *m.*

bleed, *v.* **1.** *v.tr.* Saigner. To b. oneself white, se saigner aux quatre veines. **2.** *v.i.* Saigner; perdre du sang. His nose is bleeding, il saigne du nez. To b. for one's country, verser son sang pour sa patrie. **bleeding¹**, *a.* Saignant. With a b. heart, le cœur navré de douleur. **bleeding²**, *s.* (a) Écoulement *m* de sang. B. at the nose, saignement *m* de nez. (b) Surg: Saignée *f.*

blemish¹, *s.* **1.** Défaut *m*; imperfection *f.* **2.** Souillure *f*, tache *f*, tare *f.*

blemish², *v.tr.* Tacher, entacher, souiller.

blench¹, *v.i.* Sourciller, broncher.

blench², *v.i.* Pâlir, blêmir.

blend¹, *s.* Mélange *m.*

blend², *v.* **1.** *v.tr.* Mélanger. **2.** *v.i.* Se mêler, se mélanger, se confondre (into, en); (of

colours) s'allier, se marier; (of parties) fusionner. **blending**, *s.* Mélange *m*; alliance *f* (de deux qualités).

bless, *v.tr.* Bénir. God bless you! que (le bon) Dieu vous bénisse! F: To be blessed with sth., jouir de qch. God bless me! miséricorde! Bless my soul! tiens, tiens, tiens! Well, I'm blest! que, par exemple!

blessed, *a.* (a) The Blessed Virgin, la Sainte Vierge. (b) R.C.Ch: Bienheureux. (c) P: The whole b. day, toute la sainte journée. **blessing**, *s.* Bénédiction *f.* To ask a blessing, dire le bénédicité. The blessings of civilization, les avantages *m* de la civilisation.

blight¹, *s.* **1.** Rouille *f*, brûlure *f.* **2.** F: Influence *f* néfaste; fléau *m.*

blight², *v.tr.* Rouiller, nieller. F: To blight s.o.'s hopes, flétrir les espérances de qn.

blind¹, *a.* Aveugle. (a) Blind in one eye, borgne. F: To turn a blind eye to sth., refuser de voir qch. Blind man's holiday, entre chien et loup. (b) To be blind to one's interests, ne pas voir ses propres intérêts. (c) *adv.* Av: To fly blind, voler à l'aveuglette. Blind alley, cul-de-sac *m*, impasse *f.* **-ly**, *adv.* Aveuglément; en aveugle; à l'aveuglette. **blind-man's-buff**, *s.* Colin-maillard *m.* **blind-worm**, *s.* Orvet *m.*

blind², *v.tr.* Aveugler. (a) Rendre (qn) aveugle. (b) Éblouir.

blind³, *s.* **1.** (Awning-)blind, (outside sun-)blind, store *m* (à l'italienne). Roller blind, store sur rouleau. Venetian blind, jalousie *f.* **2.** Masque *m*, feinte *f.*

blindfold¹, *a. & adv.* **1.** Les yeux bandés. **2.** Aveuglément.

blindfold², *v.tr.* Bander les yeux à, de (qn).

blindness, *s.* **1.** Cécité *f.* **2.** (Ignorance, folly) Aveuglement *m.*

blink, **1.** *v.i.* (a) Battre des paupières; cligner des paupières; clignoter. (b) (Of light) Papilloter. **2.** Fermer les yeux à demi. *v.tr.* To blink the facts, fermer les yeux sur la vérité. **blinking**, *s.* (a) Clignotement *m.* (b) Papillotage *m.*

blinkers, *s.pl.* Harn: Œillères *f.*

bliss, *s.* Béatitude *f*, félicité *f.*

blissful, *a.* (Bien)heureux.

blister¹, *s.* (a) Ampoule *f*, bulle *f.* (b) Cloque *f*, boursouflure *f* (de la peinture).

blister². **1.** *v.tr.* Faire venir les ampoules à. **2.** *v.i.* Se couvrir d'ampoules.

blithe(some), *a.* Joyeux, folâtre.

blithely, *adv.* Joyeusement.

blizzard, *s.* Tempête *f*, rafale *f*, de neige.

bloated, *a.* Boursouflé, gonflé, bouffi.

bloater, *s.* Hareng bouffi.

blob, *s.* Tache *f* (de couleur); pâté *m* (d'encre).

block¹, *s.* **1.** (a) Bloc *m* (de marbre); bille *f*, tronçon *m* (de bois); tête *f* à perruque. (b) (Chopping-)block, billot *m.* **2.** Pâté *m*, îlot *m* (de maisons). **3.** Encombrement *m* (de voitures).

block², *v.tr.* Bloquer, obstruer. *To b. progress,* arrêter le progrès. **block up,** *v.tr.* (*a*) Boucher, bloquer (un trou); condamner, murer (une porte). (*b*) Obstruer (un tuyau).

blockade¹, *s.* Blocus *m.* To run the blockade, forcer le blocus. **blockade-runner,** *s.* Forceur *m* de blocus.

blockade², *v.tr.* Bloquer (un port).

blockhead, *s.* *F:* Lourdaud *m*; sot *m.*

blond, *a. & s.* **1.** Blond, -e. **2.** *F:* Blondin, -e.

blood, *s.* Sang *m.* (*a*) *Without shedding of b.,* sans effusion de sang. To draw blood, faire saigner qn. The blood stream, le cours du sang. It makes my blood boil, cela me fait bouillir le sang. His blood was up, il était monté. His blood ran cold, son sang se glaça. In cold blood, de sang-froid. There is bad blood between them, il y a de vieilles rancunes entre eux. *The committee needs new b.,* le comité a besoin d'être rajeuni. (*b*) It runs in the blood, c'est dans le sang. *Prov:* Blood will tell, bon sang ne peut mentir. Blood horse, (cheval) pur-sang *m.* **blood-curdling,** *a.* A vous tourner les sangs. **blood-orange,** *s.* (Orange) sanguine *f.* **blood-poisoning,** *s.* *Med:* Empoisonnement *m* du sang. **blood-relation,** *s.* Parent(e) par le sang. **blood-stain,** *s.* Tache *f* de sang. **blood-stained,** *a.* Taché de sang. **blood-sucker,** *s.* *F:* Sangsue *f,* vampire *m.* **blood-vessel,** *s.* Vaisseau sanguin.

bloodhound, *s.* Limier *m.*

bloodless, *a.* **1.** Exsangue, anémié. **2.** Sans effusion de sang.

bloodshed, *s.* **1.** Effusion *f* de sang. **2.** Carnage *m.*

bloodshot, *a.* Injecté de sang.

bloodthirsty, *a.* Sanguinaire; altéré de sang.

bloody, *a.* Sanglant, ensanglanté; (tyran) sanguinaire.

bloom¹, *s.* **1.** (i) Fleur *f*; (ii) floraison *f,* épanouissement *m.* In full bloom, épanoui; en pleine fleur. *F: In the b. of youth,* à, dans, la fleur de l'âge. **2.** Velouté *m,* duvet *m* (d'une pêche).

bloom², *v.i.* Fleurir; être en fleur. **blooming,** *a.* Fleurissant; en fleur.

bloomer, *s.* *P:* Bévue *f,* gaffe *f.*

blossom¹, *s.* Fleur *f.* Orange blossom, fleur d'oranger.

blossom², *v.i.* Fleurir. To blossom (out) into sth., devenir qch. (de beau). **blossom out,** *v.i.* S'épanouir.

blot¹, *s.* Tache *f*; (*of ink*) pâté *m.*

blot², *v.tr.* **1.** Tacher, souiller. **2.** Sécher l'encre. **blot out,** *v.tr.* **1.** Effacer. **2.** Exterminer. **blotting-pad,** *s.* (Bloc) buvard *m*; sous-main *m.* **blotting-paper,** *s.* Papier buvard.

blotch, *s.* Tache *f,* éclaboussure *f.*

blotchy, *a.* **1.** (Teint) brouillé, couperosé. **2.** Tacheté.

blotter, *s.* Buvard *m*; bloc buvard.

blouse, *s.* Blouse *f.*

blow¹, *s.* **1.** Coup *m* de vent. **2.** Souffle *m.*

blow², *v.* I. *v.i.* Souffler. **1.** *It is blowing,* il fait du vent. It was blowing great guns, il faisait un vent à (d)écorner les bœufs. **2.** (*Of whale*) Rejeter l'eau par les évents. II. **blow,** *v.tr.* **1.** *The wind blows the rain against the windows,* le vent chasse la pluie contre les vitres. **2.** (*a*) *To b. the organ,* souffler l'orgue. (*b*) To blow one's nose, se moucher. *To b. the horn,* sonner du cor. *F:* To blow one's own trumpet, chanter ses propres louanges. To blow glass, souffler le verre. **3.** Essouffler (un cheval). **4.** *El:* To blow a fuse, faire sauter les plombs. **blow about.** **1.** *v.i.* Voler çà et là. **2.** *v.tr.* Faire voler çà et là. **blow away,** *v.tr.* Emporter. **blow down,** *v.tr.* Abattre, renverser. **blow in.** **1.** *v.tr.* Enfoncer. **2.** *v.i.* *The wind blows in at the window,* le vent entre par la fenêtre. **blow off.** **1.** *v.tr.* (*a*) Emporter. *To b. the dust off,* souffler la poussière. (*b*) *Mch:* To blow off steam, purger de la vapeur. **2.** *v.i.* S'envoler. **blow out,** *v.tr.* (*a*) Souffler, éteindre (une bougie). (*b*) *To b. out one's cheeks,* gonfler les joues. **blow over.** **1.** *v.tr.* ⚌ BLOW DOWN. **2.** *v.i.* The scandal soon blew over, le scandale fut bientôt oublié. **blow up.** **1.** *v.i.* (*a*) Éclater, sauter. (*b*) *Nau:* It is blowing up for a gale, il vente grand frais. **2.** *v.tr.* (*a*) Faire sauter. (*b*) Gonfler (un pneu). (*c*) *F:* Semoncer. **blow-fly,** *s.* Mouche *f* à viande. **blow-lamp,** *s.* Chalumeau *m.* **blow-pipe,** *s.* **1.** Sarbacane *f.* **2.** *Ch:* Chalumeau *m.*

blow³, *s.* **1.** Coup *m.* Without striking a blow, sans coup férir. To come to blows, en venir aux mains. B. to s.o.'s credit, atteinte *f* au crédit de qn. **2.** Coup (du sort).

blubber¹, *s.* Graisse *f,* lard *m,* de baleine.

blubber², *v.* *F:* **1.** *v.i.* (*a*) Pleurer bruyamment. (*b*) Pleurnicher. **2.** *v.tr.* To blubber out sth., dire qch. en pleurant.

bludgeon¹, *s.* Gourdin *m,* matraque *f.*

bludgeon², *v.tr.* Asséner un coup de gourdin, de matraque, à.

blue¹. I. *a.* (*a*) Bleu, azuré. B. spectacles, lunettes bleutées. (*b*) (*Of pers.*) To go blue, prendre une teinte violacée. (*c*) To feel blow, avoir le cafard. II. **blue,** *s.* **1.** Bleu *m,* azur *m.* Dark blue socks, des chaussettes bleu foncé. Navy blue, bleu marine *inv.* Out of the blue, soudainement. **2.** *Pol:* A true blue, un patriote. **3.** (Washing-)blue, indigo *m*; bleu (d'empois). **4.** *s.pl.* To have (a fit of) the blues, avoir des idées noires; avoir le cafard. **blue-bell,** *s.* **1.** Jacinthe *f* des bois. **2.** Campanule *f.* **blue-black,** *a.* Noir tirant sur le bleu. **blue-eyed,** *a.* Aux yeux bleus. **blue jacket,** *s.* Marin *m,* matelot *m,* de l'État; col-bleu *m.* **blue-stocking,** *s.* Bas-bleu *m.*

blue², *v.tr.* *F:* To blue one's money, gaspiller son argent.

Bluebeard. *Pr.n.* Barbe-bleue *m.*
bluebottle, *s.* **1.** *Bot:* Bluet *m*, bleuet *m.*
2. Mouche *f* à viande.
bluff[1]**.** I. *a.* *(a)* Accore, escarpé, à pic. *(b)*
Brusque; un peu bourru. II. **bluff,** *s.*
Geog: Cap *m* à pic; à-pic *m.*
bluff[2]**,** *s.* *F:* Bluff *m*, battage *m.* To call s.o.'s
bluff, *F:* relever un défi.
bluff[3]**,** *v.tr.* *Abs.* Faire du bluff.
bluffness, *s.* Brusquerie *f*; franc-parler *m.*
bluish, *a.* Bleuâtre; bleuté.
blunder[1]**,** *s.* Bévue *f*, maladresse *f*, erreur *f.*
F: gaffe *f*, impair *m.*
blunder[2]**,** *v.i.* & *tr.* **1.** Faire une bévue, une
gaffe, une maladresse. **2.** To blunder against
s.o., se heurter contre qn. He managed to
blunder through, il s'en est tiré tant bien
que mal. **blundering,** *a.* Brouillon,
maladroit.
blunderbuss, *s.* Tromblon *m*, espingole *f.*
blunderer, *s.* Maladroit, -e; gaffeur, -euse.
blunt[1]**,** *a.* **1.** Émoussé; (instrument) conton-
dant. **2.** Brusque, carré. The blunt fact,
le fait brutal. **-ly,** *adv.* Brusquement,
carrément.
blunt[2]**,** *v.tr.* Émousser.
bluntness, *s.* **1.** Manque *m* de tranchant.
2. Brusquerie *f*, franchise *f.*
blur[1]**,** *s.* **1.** Tache *f.* **2.** Apparence confuse;
brouillard *m.*
blur[2]**,** *v.tr.* **1.** Barbouiller. **2.** Brouiller.
Eyes blurred with tears, yeux voilés de larmes.
blurt, *v.tr.* To blurt out a secret, laisser
échapper un secret.
blush[1]**,** *s.* **1.** Aspect *m.* At the first blush,
au premier abord. **2.** *(a)* Rougeur *f.* To put
s.o. to the blush, faire honte à qn. *(b)* Incarnat *m* (des roses).
blush[2]**,** *v.i.* Rougir. I blush for you, vous
me faites rougir. **blushing,** *a.* Rougissant;
timide.
bluster[1]**,** *s.* *(a)* Fureur *f*, fracas *m* (de l'orage).
(b) Bravacherie *f*, rodomontades *fpl.*
bluster[2]**,** *v.i.* *(a)* Souffler en rafales. *(b)* *(Of
pers.)* Faire du fracas; parler haut; faire
le rodomont. **blustering,** *a.* *(a)* (Vent)
violent. *(b)* Bravache, tonitruant.
blusterer, *s.* Bravache, rodomont *m.*
boa, *s.* Boa *m.*
boar, *s.* Verrat *m.* Wild boar, sanglier *m.*
board[1]**,** *s.* **1.** *(a)* Planche *f*, ais *m.* *(b)* *pl.* *Th:*
The boards, la scène, le théâtre. *(c)* Carton
m. **2.** *(a)* Table *f.* The festive board, la table
du festin. *(b)* Table, nourriture *f*, pension *f.*
Board and lodging, pension et chambre(s).
Partial b., demi-pension *f.* With b. and
lodging, nourri et logé. *(c)* (Gaming) board,
table de jeu. **3.** *(a)* Board of enquiry, commission *f* d'enquête. *(b)* *Com:* Board of
directors, (conseil *m* d')administration *f.*
Board meeting, réunion du conseil. **4.** *Nau:*
Bord *m.* On board (ship), à bord d'un navire.
To go on board, monter à bord; s'embarquer.
To go by the board, s'en aller par-dessus bord.
board-room, *s.* Salle *f* du conseil.

board-wages, *s.pl.* Indemnité *f* de
nourriture.
board[2]**.** **1.** *v.tr.* Planchéier. **2.** *(a)* *v.i.*
Être en pension. *(b)* *v.tr.* Nourrir. **3.** *v.tr.*
Nau: *(a)* Aborder, accoster. *(b)* Aller,
monter, à bord. *(c)* *Navy:* Aborder.
boarding, *s.* **1.** *Const:* Planchéiage *m.*
2. *(a)* *Nau:* Accostage *m.* *(b)* *Navy:*
Abordage *m.* **3.** *Coll:* Planches *fpl.*
boarding-house, *s.* Pension *f* de famille.
boarding-school, *s.* Pensionnat *m*, internat *m.*
boarder, *s.* Pensionnaire *mf*; *(in schools)*
interne *mf.*
boast[1]**,** *s.* Vanterie *f.*
boast[2]**.** **1.** *v.i.* Se vanter. To b. that one
can do sth., se vanter de pouvoir faire qch.
That's nothing to boast of, il n'y a pas là de
quoi être fier. Without wishing to boast,
sans vanité. **2.** *v.tr.* The school boasts a fine
library, l'école possède une belle bibliothèque.
boasting, *s.* Vantardise *f.*
boaster, *s.* Vantard *m*, fanfaron *m.*
boastful, *a.* Vantard. **-fully,** *adv.* Avec
vanterie, avec jactance.
boastfulness, *s.* Vantardise *f*, jactance *f.*
boat[1]**,** *s.* Bateau *m*; (i) canot *m*; barque *f*
(de pêcheur); embarcation *f*; (ii) navire
(marchand). Ship's b., embarcation de bord.
To go by boat, prendre le bateau. *F:* To be
all in the same boat, être tous logés à la même
enseigne. To burn one's boats, brûler ses
vaisseaux. **boat-builder,** *s.* Constructeur
m de canots. **boat-hook,** *s.* *Nau:* Gaffe *f.*
boat-house, *s.* Hangar *m* à bateaux.
boat-race, *s.* Course *f* de bateaux; match
m d'aviron. **boat-train,** *s.* *Rail:* Train *m*
du bateau.
boat[2]**,** *v.i.* Aller, se promener, en bateau.
boating, *s.* Canotage *m.*
boatman, *s.* **1.** Batelier *m.* **2.** Loueur *m* de
canots.
boatswain, *s.* *Nau:* Maître *m* d'équipage.
bob[1]**,** *s.* *(a)* Bob of hair, chignon *m.* *(b)*
Coiffure *f* à la Ninon.
bob[2]**,** *v.tr.* To bob one's hair, se faire couper
les cheveux à la nuque.
bob[3]**,** *v.i.* Se mouvoir de haut en bas et de
bas en haut; s'agiter. To bob up and down
in the water, danser sur l'eau. bob down,
v.i. Baisser brusquement la tête. bob up,
v.i. Surgir brusquement.
Bob[4]**.** *Pr.n.* Robert *m.*
bob[5]**,** *s.inv.* *P:* Shilling *m.*
bobbin, *s.* Bobine *f.*
Boccaccio. *Pr.n.* Boccace *m.*
bode, *v.tr.* & *i.* Présager. To bode ill, être
de mauvais augure.
bodice, *s.* Corsage *m.*
bodiless, *a.* Sans corps.
bodily, *a* Corporel, physique. To go about
in bodily fear, craindre pour sa sûreté personnelle.

bodkin, *s.* (a) Passe-lacet *m.* (b) *Needlw :* Poinçon *m.*

body, *s.* Corps *m.* **1.** (a) To keep body and soul together, vivre tout juste. (b) (Dead) body, corps (mort); cadavre *m.* (c) Sève *f,* générosité *f* (d'un vin). (d) Consistance *f.* **2.** (a) Legislative body, corps législatif. (b) Large body of people, nombreuse société. To come in a body, venir en masse, en corps. **3.** *F:* A queer body, un drôle de corps. **4.** (a) Corps (de document). (b) *Veh:* Bâti *m,* corps, caisse *f.* **5.** Heavenly body, astre *m;* corps céleste. **body-guard,** *s.* Garde *f* du corps. **body-snatcher,** *s.* Déterreur *m* (de cadavres).

bog¹, *s.* Fondrière *f;* marécage *m.*

bog², *v.tr.* Embourber, enliser. To get bogged, s'embourber, s'enliser.

bogey, *s.* **1.** Épouvantail *m.* **2.** *Golf:* (Colonel) Bogey, la normale du parcours. **bogey-man,** *s.* Croque-mitaine *m;* le Père Fouettard (des enfants).

boggle, *v.i.* Rechigner (*at* sth., devant qch.; *at doing* sth., à faire qch.).

boggy, *a.* Marécageux, tourbeux.

bogus, *a.* Faux, *f.* fausse; feint, simulé.

bogy, *s.* = BOGEY 1.

Bohemia. *Pr.n. Geog:* La Bohême.

Bohemian. 1. *a. & s. Geog:* Bohémien, -ienne. **2.** *a.* B. life, vie de bohème. B. habits, mœurs débraillées.

boil¹, *s. Med:* Furoncle *m, F:* clou *m.*

boil², *s.* To come to the boil, commencer à bouillir. The water is on the boil, l'eau bout.

boil³. 1. *v.i.* Bouillir. To keep the pot boiling, (i) faire bouillir la marmite; (ii) *F:* pourvoir aux besoins du ménage. **2.** *v.tr.* Faire bouillir. *Cu:* Cuire, faire cuire, à l'eau. Boiled egg, œuf à la coque. **boil over,** *v.i.* S'en aller, se sauver. *F:* To boil over with rage, bouillir de colère. **boiling¹,** *a.* Bouillant, bouillonnant. *adv.* Boiling hot, tout bouillant. **boiling²,** *s.* Bouillonnement *m,* ébullition *f.* **boiling-point,** *s.* Point *m* d'ébullition.

boiler, *s.* Chaudière *f.* **boiler-house,** *s. Ind:* Salle *f,* bâtiment *m,* des chaudières.

boisterous, *a.* Bruyant, turbulent; tapageur; (*of wind*) violent; (*of sea*) tumultueux. **-ly,** *adv.* (a) Bruyamment. (b) Tempétueusement.

boisterousness, *s.* Turbulence *f;* violence *f* (du vent); agitation *f* (de la mer).

bold, *a.* **1.** Hardi; audacieux; (regard) assuré, confiant. Bold stroke, coup d'audace. To make (so) bold (as) to do sth., se permettre de faire qch. To put a bold face on the matter, payer d'audace. **2.** Impudent, effronté. **3.** B. cliff, falaise escarpée. **-ly,** *adv.* **1.** Hardiment; audacieusement. To assert sth. b., affirmer qch. avec confiance. **2.** Effrontément.

boldness, *s.* **1.** Hardiesse *f;* audace *f.* **2.** Effronterie *f.*

bole, *s.* Fût *m,* tronc *m.*

Bolshevik, *a. & s.* Bolcheviste (*mf*).

Bolshevism, *s.* Bolchevisme *m.*

bolster¹, *s.* Traversin *m.*

bolster², *v.tr. F:* To bolster s.o. up, appuyer, soutenir, qn (qui a tort).

bolt¹, *s.* **1.** *F:* Bolt from the blue, événement imprévu. **2.** (Sliding) bolt, verrou *m.* **3.** *Mec.E:* Boulon *m;* cheville *f.* **4.** Pièce *f* (de toile).

bolt². **1.** *v.i.* (a) *F:* Décamper, déguerpir. (b) (*Of horse*) S'emballer, s'emporter. **2.** *v.tr.* Gober; avaler sans mâcher. **3.** *v.tr.* Verrouiller. To bolt the door, mettre les verrous.

bolt³, *adv.* Bolt upright, tout droit; droit comme un piquet.

bolt⁴, *s. F:* To make a bolt for it, décamper, déguerpir, filer.

bomb¹, *s.* Bombe (explosive). To release a b., lâcher, larguer, une bombe. **bomb-crater,** *s. Mil:* Entonnoir *m.* **bomb-proof,** *a.* A l'épreuve des bombes. **bomb-shell,** *s. F:* This was a b.-s. to us, cette nouvelle nous consterna. **bomb-sight,** *s. Av:* Viseur *m.*

bomb², *v.tr. Av:* Lancer des bombes sur. **bombing,** *s.* Bombardement *m.* Bombing plane, avion de bombardement.

bombard, *v.tr.* Bombarder.

bombardment, *s.* Bombardement *m.*

bombast, *s.* Emphase *f;* grandiloquence *f.*

bombastic, *a.* Ampoulé; emphatique.

bomber, *s.* Avion *m* de bombardement.

bona fide, *a. & adv.* De bonne foi. B. f. offer, offre sérieuse.

bona fides, *Lt.s.* Bonne foi.

bond, *s.* Lien *m;* attache *f.* **1.** *pl.* Fers *m,* liens, chaînes *f.* **2.** *F:* Bonds of friendship, liens d'amitié. **3.** (a) Engagement *m,* contrat *m;* obligation *f.* (b) *Fin:* Bon *m.* (c) *Jur:* Caution *f.* **4.** *Com:* To be in bond, être à l'entrepôt.

bondage, *s.* Esclavage *m,* servitude *f.*

bone¹, *s.* **1.** Os *m.* (Fish-)bone, arête *f.* He won't make old bones, il ne fera pas de vieux os. I feel it in my bones, j'en ai le pressentiment. To make no bones about doing sth., ne pas se gêner pour faire qch. **2.** *pl.* (Of the dead) Ossements *m.* **bone-black,** *s.* Noir *m* animal. **bone-dry,** *a.* Sec à l'absolu. **bone-setter,** *s.* Rebouteur *m.*

bone², *v.tr.* **1.** Désosser; ôter les arêtes (du poisson). **2.** *P:* Chiper, voler (qch.)

bonfire, *s.* Feu *m* de joie.

bonnet, *s.* **1.** *Cost:* Chapeau *m* à brides; capote *f;* béguin *m* (d'enfant). **2.** *Aut:* Capot *m.*

bonus, *s.* Surpaye *f,* boni *m;* prime *f.* B. on shares, bonification *f* sur les actions.

bony, *a.* **1.** Osseux. **2.** (Visage) décharné. **3.** Plein d'os; (*of fish*) plein d'arêtes.

boo¹. 1. *int.* Hou! **2.** *s.* Huée *f.*

boo², *v.tr. & i.* To boo (at) s.o., huer, conspuer, qn. **booing,** *s.* Huées *fpl.*

booby, s. **1.** Nigaud, -e, benêt m. **2.** Orn: F: Fou m. **booby-trap,** s. Attrape-nigaud m.
book¹, s. **1.** (a) Livre m. Old books, vieux bouquins. To speak by the book, citer ses autorités. Class book, livre classique, de classe. (b) Livret m (d'un opéra). (c) Bible f. **2.** Registre m. (a) Account book, livre de comptes. F: To be in s.o.'s good books, être en faveur auprès de qn. To bring s.o. to book for sth. forcer qn à rendre compte de qch. (b) F: That just suits my book, ça fait mon beurre. B. of tickets, carnet m de billets. (c) The telephone book, l'annuaire m du téléphone. **book-keeper,** s. Teneur m de livres; comptable m. **book-keeping,** s. Tenue f des livres; comptabilité f. **book-learning,** s. Savoir acquis dans les livres. **book-maker,** s. Turf: Bookmaker m. **book-mark(er),** s. Signet m. **book-plate,** s. Ex-libris m. **book-post,** s. Service postal des imprimés. **book-shelf,** s. Rayon m; planche réservée aux livres. **book-worm,** s. F: Dévoreur, -euse, de livres; bouquineur m.
book², v.tr. **1.** Inscrire, enregistrer. **2.** Retenir, réserver (une place). **3.** Rail: To book, prendre son billet. **booking,** s. Enregistrement m. Th: B. of tickets, location f de billets. Rail: B. of seats, réservation f des places. **booking-clerk,** s. Rail: Préposé m à la distribution des billets. **booking-office,** s. Rail: Guichet m.
bookbinder, s. Relieur m.
bookbinding, s. Reliure f.
bookcase, s. Bibliothèque f.
booklet, s. Livret m; opuscule m.
booklover, s. Bibliophile m.
bookseller, s. Libraire mf. Second-hand bookseller, bouquiniste m.
bookshop, s. Librairie f.
bookstall, s. Bibliothèque f (de gare).
boom¹, s. (Pannes fpl de) barrage m; chaîne f (de fermeture); barre f.
boom², s. Grondement m (du canon); mugissement m (du vent).
boom³, v.i. Retentir, gronder, mugir.
boom⁴, s. Com: **1.** Hausse f rapide. **2.** Vague f de prospérité.
boom⁵. **1.** v.tr. Faire une grosse publicité en faveur de (qch.). **2.** v.i. Être en hausse.
boomerang, s. Boumerang m.
boon¹, s. **1.** Don m, faveur f. **2.** Bienfait m, avantage m.
boon², a. Boon companion, gai compagnon; bon vivant.
boor, s. Rustre m, rustaud m.
boorish, a. Rustre, rustaud, grossier.
boorishness, s. Grossièreté f.
boost, v.tr. F: Faire de la réclame pour.
boot¹, s. Chaussure f, bottine f; (high b.) botte f. Boot and shoe manufacturer, fabricant de chaussures. To put on one's boots, se chausser. To take off one's boots, se déchausser. F: The boot is on the other leg,

c'est tout (juste) le contraire. **boot-black,** s. Décrotteur m, cireur m (de chaussures).
boot-maker, s. Bottier m, cordonnier m.
boot-polish, s. Crème f à chaussures.
boot², s. To boot, par surcroît, en sus.
booth, s. Baraque f, tente f.
bootlace, s. Lacet m (de chaussure).
boots, s. Garçon m d'étage.
booty, s. Butin m.
boracic, a. Ch: Borique. Boracic ointment, pommade à l'acide borique. Boracic powder, poudre boriquée.
borax, s. Borax m.
border¹, s. **1.** Bord m (d'un lac); lisière f, bordure f (d'un bois); marge f (d'un chemin); frontière f (d'un pays). Border town, ville frontière. **2.** Galon m, bordé m (d'un habit); bordure (d'un tableau, d'un tapis, etc.); encadrement m (d'un panneau). **border-land,** s. (a) Pays m frontière, limitrophe; marche f. (b) Les confins m de l'au-delà. **border-line,** s. **1.** Ligne f de séparation; frontière f (entre deux états). **2.** Border-line case, cas limite.
border². **1.** v.tr. (a) Border (un habit); encadrer. (b) Border; confiner à (un pays). **2.** v.i. To border on (sth.). (a) Toucher, confiner, à (un autre pays). (b) To border on insanity, être voisin de la folie. **bordering,** a. (a) Contigu, -uë, aboutissant (on, à); limitrophe (on, de). (b) Statement b. on untruth, déclaration qui frise le mensonge.
bore¹, s. Calibre m.
bore², v.tr. & i. To bore (out), creuser. To bore through sth., percer, perforer, qch. Min: To bore for water, sonder pour trouver de l'eau. **boring¹,** s. Percement m.
bore³, s. F: (a) (Of pers.) Fâcheux, -euse; raseur, -euse. (b) (Of thg) Ennui m, scie f, corvée f.
bore⁴, v.tr. F: Ennuyer; F: raser, assommer (qn). To be bored to death, s'ennuyer à mourir. **boring²,** a. Ennuyeux, F: assommant, rasant.
bore⁵, s. Mascaret m; raz m de marée.
boredom, s. Ennui m.
boric, a. Ch: Borique.
born. **1.** p.p. To be born, naître; venir au monde. He was b. in 1870, il naquit, il est né, en 1870. Confidence is b. of knowledge, la confiance vient du savoir. **2.** a. He is a born poet, il est né poète. F: Born fool, parfait idiot.
boron, s. Ch: Bore m.
borough, s. (a) Ville f (avec municipalité). (b) Circonscription électorale.
borrow, v.tr. Emprunter (from, of, à). Borrowed feathers, plumes d'emprunt.
borrower, s. Emprunteur, -euse.
bosh, s. & int. F: Bêtises fpl, blague f.
bosom, s. **1.** (a) Giron m, sein m. (b) In the bosom of one's family, au sein de sa famille. **2.** Poitrine f.
Bosphorus. Pr.n. Geog: The Bosphorus, le Bosphore.

boss¹, s. Protubérance f, renflement m.
boss², s. F: (a) The boss, le patron, le chef. (b) Ind: Contremaître m.
boss³, v.tr. F: Mener, diriger. **To boss the show,** contrôler toute l'affaire.
bossy, a. F: Autoritaire.
botanic(al), a. Botanique.
botanist, s. Botaniste mf.
botany, s. Botanique f.
botch¹, s. F: To make a b. of sth., saboter un travail.
botch², v.tr. F: 1. Bousiller, saboter. 2. To botch up, réparer grossièrement.
both. 1. a. & pron. Tous (les) deux, toutes (les) deux; l'un(e) et l'autre. **In both hands,** tenir qch. à deux mains. **Both alike,** l'un comme l'autre. 2. adv. **Both you and I,** (et) vous et moi. She b. attracts and repels me, elle m'attire et me repousse à la fois. I am fond of music b. ancient and modern, j'aime la musique tant ancienne que moderne.
bother¹, s. Ennui m, F: embêtement m, tracas m. **Bother! zut!**
bother². 1. v.tr. Gêner, ennuyer, tourmenter (qn). Don't b. me! laissez-moi tranquille! F: I can't be bothered, ça m'embête. **Bother it! zut!** 2. v.i. He doesn't bother about anything, il ne s'inquiète de rien. **bothered,** a. Inquiet, -ète; embarrassé.
bottle¹, s. 1. Bouteille f; (small) flacon m; (wide-mouthed) bocal m. **Cider in bottle,** cidre bouché. 2. Feeding bottle, biberon m. **bottle-brush,** s. Goupillon m. **bottle-green,** a. & s. Vert bouteille (m) inv. **bottle-neck,** s. Étranglement m, embouteillage m (dans une rue). **bottle-washer,** s. F: Head cook and bottle-washer, homme qui mène toute l'affaire.
bottle², v.tr. Mettre en bouteilles; mettre (des fruits) en bocal. **bottle up,** v.tr. 1. Emboutiller. 2. F: To b. up one's feelings, étouffer ses sentiments. **bottling,** s. Mise f en bouteille(s), en bocal.
bottom, s. 1. (a) Bas m. (b) Fond m. At the b. of the garden, au fond du jardin. (Of ship) To go to the bottom, couler à fond. From the very bottom of the heart, du fond du cœur. To be at the bottom of sth., être l'instigateur de qch. 2. Bas-fond m (de terrain). 3. F: To knock the bottom out of an argument, démolir un argument. 4. F: Derrière m, postérieur m. 5. Nau: (a) Carène f, fond (d'un navire). (b) Navire m. **In British bottoms,** sous pavillon anglais. 6. B. boy of the class, dernier élève de la classe.
bottomless, a. Sans fond.
bough, s. Branche f, rameau m.
boulder, s Gros galet.
bounce¹, s. 1. To take the ball on the bounce, prendre la balle au bond. 2. F: Jactance f, vantardise f.
bounce². 1. v.i. (a) Rebondir. (b) To bounce in, entrer en coup de vent. (c) F: Faire

l'important. 2. v.tr. Faire rebondir (une balle).
bound¹, s. (Usu. pl.) Limite(s) f, bornes fpl. Sch: To put out of bounds, consigner. **To go beyond all bounds,** dépasser toutes les bornes. **To keep within bounds,** rester dans la juste mesure.
bound², v.tr. Borner, limiter.
bound³, s. Bond m, saut m.
bound⁴, v.i. Bondir, sauter.
bound⁵, a. Nau: Bound for, en partance pour, en route pour.
boundary, s. Limite f, bornes fpl. **Boundary (line),** ligne f de démarcation. **Boundary post,** borne.
bounder, s. F: Homme mal élevé.
boundless, a. Sans bornes; illimité.
bounteous, a. 1. Libéral, -aux; généreux. 2. B. harvest, moisson abondante.
bountiful, a. 1. Bienfaisant. 2. Généreux.
bounty, s. 1. Générosité f, munificence f. 2. (a) Don m, gratification f (à un employé, etc.). (b) Adm: Indemnité f; prime f (d'exportation).
bouquet, s. Bouquet m.
bout, s. 1. Tour m, reprise f. 2. Accès m (de fièvre).
bovine, a. (a) Bovin. (b) F: (Esprit) lourd.
bow¹, s. 1. Arc m. To have two strings to one's bow, avoir deux cordes à son arc. 2. Mus: Archet m (de violon). 3. Nœud m (de ruban). 4. Harn: (Saddle-)bow, arçon m, pontet m. **bow-legged,** a. Bancal, -als. **bow-window,** s. Fenêtre f en saillie.
bow², s. Salut m; (i) révérence f; (ii) inclination f de tête. With a bow, en saluant, en s'inclinant.
bow³. 1. v.i. (a) (i) S'incliner; baisser la tête; (ii) faire une génuflexion. **To bow to s.o.,** saluer qn. To bow low to s.o., faire un grand salut à qn. To bow and scrape to s.o., faire force révérences à qn. **To bow (down) before s.o.,** se prosterner devant qn. (b) To bow to the inevitable, s'incliner devant les faits. 2. v.tr. (a) Incliner, baisser (la tête); fléchir (le genou). (b) Courber, voûter (le dos). **bow down,** v.i. Se baisser.
bow⁴, s. Nau: Avant m, étrave f.
bowel, s. Anat: (a) Intestin m. (b) pl. Intestins, entrailles f. (c) Bowels of compassion, sentiment m de compassion; F: entrailles.
bower, s. Berceau m de verdure.
bowl¹, s. 1. Bol m, jatte f; coupe f (de cristal). 2. Fourneau m (de pipe).
bowl², s. Boule f. (Game of) bowls, (jeu m de) boules.
bowl³, v.tr. (a) Rouler, faire courir (un cerceau). (b) Bowls: Lancer, rouler. (c) Cr: Servir (la balle). **bowl along,** v.i. Rouler rapidement. **bowl over,** v.tr. Renverser.
bowling, s. 1. Jeu m de boules. 2. Cr: Lancement m de la balle. **bowling-alley,**

s. Jeu *m* de boules. **bowling-green,** *s.* (Terrain *m* pour) jeu *m* de boules.

bowler¹, *s.* **1.** Joueur *m* de boules. **2.** *Cr:* Serveur *m.*

bowler², *s.* Bowler (hat), chapeau *m* melon.

bowman, *s.* Archer *m.*

bowsprit, *s. Nau:* Beaupré *m.*

bowstring, *s.* **1.** Corde *f* d'arc. **2.** (*As mode of execution*) Lacet *m*, cordon *m.*

bow-wow. 1. *int.* Ouâ-ouâ! **2.** *s. F:* Toutou *m.*

box¹, *s. Bot:* Buis *m.*

box², *s.* **1.** (*a*) Boîte *f*; (*small*) coffret *m*; (*large wooden*) caisse *f*; (*of cardboard*) carton *m. F:* To find oneself in the wrong box, s'être trompé; s'être fourvoyé. (*b*) *Ecc:* (*For alms*) Tronc *m.* **2.** *Veh:* Siège *m* (du cocher). **3.** (*a*) *Th:* Loge *f.* (*b*) (*In stable*) Stalle *f.* **box-bed,** *s.* Lit clos. **box-kite,** *s.* Cerf-volant *m* cellulaire. **box-office,** *s. Th:* Bureau *m* de location. **box-room,** *s.* Chambre *f* de débarras. **box-seat,** *s.* Place *f* à côté du siège du cocher. **box-spanner,** *s. Tls:* Clef *f* à douille.

box³, *v.tr.* Emboîter, encaisser, encartonner (qch.). **boxed,** *a. Com:* En boîte. Boxed in, encaissé; sans issue.

box⁴, *s.* Box on the ear, gifle *f*, claque *f.*

box⁵. 1. *v.tr.* To box s.o.'s ears, gifler qn. **2.** *v.i. Sp:* Boxer; faire de la boxe. **boxing,** *s.* La boxe, le pugilat. **boxing-gloves,** *s.pl.* Gants de boxe. **boxing-match,** *s.* Match *m* de boxe.

box-calf, *s. Leath:* Veau chromé.

boxer, *s.* Boxeur *m*, pugiliste *m.*

boxful, *s.* Pleine boîte, pleine caisse.

boxing-day, *s.* Le lendemain de Noël.

boxwood, *s.* Buis *m.*

boy, *s.* **1.** (*a*) Garçon *m.* When I was a boy, quand j'étais petit. I have known him from a boy, je le connais depuis sa jeunesse. Boys will be boys, il faut que jeunesse se passe. *F:* My dear boy! mon cher (ami)! mon bon! Old boy! mon vieux! The old boy, (i) le paternel; (ii) le patron. (*b*) *Sch:* Élève *m.* An old boy, un ancien élève. (*c*) *F:* One of the boys, un joyeux vivant. **2.** (*a*) Domestique *m* ou ouvrier *m* indigène. (*b*) The grocer's boy, le garçon épicier.

boycott¹, *s.* Mise *f* en interdit.

boycott², *v.tr.* Boycotter.

boyhood, *s.* Enfance *f*, première jeunesse, ou adolescence *f* (d'un garçon).

boyish, *a.* Puéril, enfantin, d'enfant.

boylike, *adv.* En vrai(s) garçon(s).

brace¹, *s.* **1.** *Const:* Attache *f*, lien *m*; croisillon *m.* **2.** *pl. Cost:* Bretelles *f.* **3.** *inv.* Couple *f.* **4.** *Tls:* Brace (and bit), vilebrequin *m.*

brace², *v.tr.* **1.** *Const:* Ancrer, amarrer. **2.** Fortifier. To brace s.o. up, retremper qn. To b. oneself (up) to do sth., raidir ses forces

pour faire qch. **bracing¹,** *a.* (Air) fortifiant, tonifiant. **bracing²,** *s.* **1.** Ancrage *m*; renforcement *m.* **2.** Retrempe *f* (du corps).

bracelet, *s.* Bracelet *m.*

bracken, *s.* Fougère *f.*

bracket¹, *s.* Support *m.* (*a*) Console *f. Arch:* Corbeau *m.* (*b*) Tasseau *m.*

bracket², *v.tr.* **1.** Mettre entre crochets. **2.** Réunir (des mots) par une accolade.

brackish, *a.* Saumâtre.

brad, *s.* Pointe *f*; clou *m* à tête perdue.

bradawl, *s. Tls:* Alène plate; poinçon *m.*

Bradshaw, *s.* Indicateur *m* des chemins de fer britanniques.

brag¹, *s.* **1.** (Piece of) brag, vanterie *f*, vantardise *f.* **2.** Fanfaron *m*; vantard *m.*

brag², *v.i.* Hâbler; se vanter; fanfaronner.

bragging¹, *a.* Vantard. **bragging²,** *s.* Vantardise *f.*

braggadocio, *s.* Fanfaronnade *f.*

braggart, *s.* Fanfaron *m*, vantard *m.*

brahmin, *s.* Brahmane *m*, brame *m.*

braid¹, *s.* **1.** Tresse *f* (de cheveux). **2.** Galon *m*, ganse *f*, tresse. Gold braid, galon.

braid², *v.tr.* **1.** Tresser, natter. **2.** Galonner, soutacher. **braiding,** *s.* **1.** Tressage *m.* **2.** (Garniture *f* de) galon *m*; soutache *f.*

brain¹, *s.* **1.** Cerveau *m. F:* To turn s.o.'s brain, tourner la tête à qn. To get sth. on the b., être hanté par la pensée de qch. **2.** *pl.* Brains, cervelle *f.* (*a*) Matière cérébrale. To blow s.o.'s brains out, brûler la cervelle à qn. (*b*) To rack one's brains, se creuser la cervelle, le cerveau. He has brains, il est intelligent. **brain-fag,** *s.* Épuisement cérébral. **brain-fever,** *s. Med:* Fièvre cérébrale. **brain-wave,** *s. F:* Inspiration *f*, bonne idée. **brain-work,** *s.* Travail *m* de tête.

brain², *v.tr.* Casser la tête à; assommer.

brainless, *a. F:* Sans cervelle; stupide.

brainy, *a. F:* Intelligent, débrouillard.

braise, *v.tr. Cu:* Braiser. Braised beef, bœuf en daube.

brake¹, *s.* Fourré *m*, hallier *m.*

brake², *s. Veh:* Frein *m.* To put on the brake, serrer le frein.

brake³, *v.tr.* Appliquer le frein sur. *Abs.* Serrer le frein; freiner; enrayer.

bramble, *s.* Ronce *f.* **bramble-berry,** *s.* Mûre *f* sauvage.

bran, *s. Mill:* Son *m.*

branch¹, *s.* **1.** Branche *f*, rameau *m* (d'un arbre). **2.** (*a*) Branche, bras *m* (d'un fleuve); embranchement *m* (d'une route). (*b*) Branche (d'une famille). (*c*) Succursale *f*, filiale *f* (d'une société). **branch-line,** *s. Rail:* Embranchement *m*; ligne *f* d'intérêt local.

branch². 1. *v.i.* To branch (forth), pousser des branches. To branch (out), se ramifier. **2.** *v.i.* To branch (off), (se) bifurquer, s'embrancher (*from*, sur).

brand¹, *s.* **1.** Brandon *m*, tison *m. F:* A brand from the burning, un tison arraché au feu ; un nouveau converti. **2.** (a) Fer chaud. (b) Marque (faite avec un fer chaud) ; flétrissure f. **3.** Com: (a) Marque (de fabrique). (b) F: Sorte f, qualité f. **brand-new**, a. Tout (battant) neuf, tout flambant neuf.

brand², v.tr. **1.** To b. with a hot iron, marquer au fer chaud ; flétrir. **2.** F: To b. sth. on s.o.'s memory, graver qch. dans la mémoire de qn. **branding**, s. Impression f au fer chaud. **branding-iron**, s. Fer m à marquer.

brandish, v.tr. Brandir. **brandishing**, s. Brandissement m.

brandy, s. Eau-de-vie f, cognac m. Liqueur brandy, fine champagne.

brass, s. **1.** Cuivre m jaune ; laiton m. Brass plate, plaque de cuivre. F: Brass-hat, officier m d'état-major. **2.** Mus: The brass, les cuivres. **3.** P: Argent m, pépète f, galette f. **4.** P: (Cheek) Toupet m, culot m.

brassy¹, s. Golf: Brassie m.

brassy², a. (Son) cuivré, claironnant.

brat, s. Marmot m, mioche mf.

bravado, s. Bravade f.

brave¹. a. Courageux, brave. **2.** s. Brave m. **-ly**, adv. Courageusement.

brave², v.tr. Braver, défier. To brave it out, ne pas se laisser démonter.

bravery, s. Bravoure f, vaillance f.

bravo¹, s. Bravo m, pl. bravi ; spadassin m.

bravo², int. Bravo !

brawl¹, s. Rixe f, bagarre f.

brawl², v.i. **1.** (Of pers.) Brailler. **2.** (Of streams) Murmurer. **brawling¹**, a. **1.** Braillard. **2.** Murmurant. **brawling²**, s. **1.** Braillement m. **2.** Murmure m.

brawler, s. Braillard, -e.

brawn, s. **1.** Muscles mpl. **2.** Cu: Fromage m de cochon.

brawny, a. Musclé.

bray, v.i. Braire.

brazen¹, a. **1.** D'airain. **2.** F: Brazen (-faced), au front d'airain ; effronté.

brazen², v.tr. To brazen it out, payer d'effronterie, de toupet.

Brazil, Pr.n. Geog: Le Brésil. **Brazilnut**, s. Noix f du Brésil.

Brazilian, a. & s. Brésilien, -ienne.

breach¹, s. **1.** Infraction f. B. of rules, infraction aux règles. B. of faith, violation f de foi. Breach of trust, abus m de confiance. Breach of the peace, attentat m contre l'ordre public. Breach of promise, violation de promesse de mariage. **2.** Brouille f, rupture f (entre deux amis, etc.). **3.** Brèche f (dans un mur).

breach², v.tr. Ouvrir une brèche dans.

bread, s. Pain m. Brown b., pain bis. A loaf of bread, un pain, une miche. Bread and butter, (i) pain beurré ; (ii) F: moyens m de subsistance. Slice of b. and butter, tartine f de beurre. He knows on which side his bread is buttered, il sait où est son avantage. Bread

and milk, panade f au lait ; soupe f au lait. To take the bread out of s.o.'s mouth, ôter le pain à qn. **bread-crumb**, s. Miette f (de pain). Cu: Bread-crumbs, chapelure f ; (when cooked) gratin m. **bread-fruit**, s. Bot: Fruit m à pain. Bread-fruit tree, arbre m à pain ; jaquier m. **bread-knife**, s. Couteau m, scie f, à pain. **bread-poultice**, s. Cataplasme m à la mie de pain. **bread-sauce**, s. Sauce f à la mie de pain. **bread-winner**, s. Gagne-pain m inv.

breadth, s. **1.** Largeur f. The table is three feet in breadth, la table a trois pieds de large. **2.** Largeur (de pensée).

break¹, s. **1.** Rupture f. (a) Brisure f, cassure f, fracture f ; brèche f ; ouverture f ; éclaircie f (à travers les nuages) ; lacune f (dans une succession). Break in the voice, altération f de la voix. B. in a journey, arrêt m. To work without a break, travailler sans interruption. (b) Break in the weather, changement m de temps. (c) B. between two friends, rupture, brouille f, entre deux amis. **2.** (a) (Moment m de) repos m, répit m. (b) Sch: Intervalle m ; récréation f. **3.** Break of day, point m du jour. **4.** Bill: Série f, suite f.

break², v. **I.** v.tr. **1.** (a) Casser, briser, rompre. To b. one's arm, se casser le bras. To b. the skin, entamer la peau. F: To break (new) ground, faire œuvre de pionnier. (b) To break (the) silence, rompre le silence. To break one's journey, interrompre son voyage. **2.** To break s.o. of a bad habit, faire perdre à qn une mauvaise habitude. **3.** To break bounds, violer la consigne. **4.** To break s.o.'s heart, briser, crever, le cœur à qn. Equit: To break a horse, rompre un cheval. **5.** To break a fall, amortir une chute. **6.** (a) To break s.o., ruiner qn. To break the bank, faire sauter la banque. (b) Mil: Casser (un officier). **7.** To break the peace, troubler, violer, l'ordre public. To break one's word, manquer de parole. **II.** break, v.i. **1.** (Se) casser, se rompre, se briser ; (of wave) déferler. **2.** (Of heart) Se briser ; se fendre, crever ; (of weather) changer. **3.** To break with s.o., rompre avec qn. **4.** To break into a laugh, éclater de rire. To break into a trot, prendre le trot. **5.** Day was beginning to break, le jour commençait à poindre. **break away. 1.** v.tr. Détacher (from, de). **2.** v.i. Se détacher (from, de) ; s'échapper, s'évader. **break down. 1.** v.tr. Abattre, démolir, renverser. To b. down all opposition, vaincre toute opposition. **2.** v.i. (a) (Of health) S'altérer ; (of plan) échouer ; (of bridge) s'effondrer. (b) (Of pers.) (i) S'arrêter tout court ; (ii) éclater en sanglots ; (iii) tomber malade. (c) (Of motor car) Rester en panne. **break-down**, s. **1.** Arrêt complet. **2.** Nervous break-down, épuisement nerveux. **3.** Aut: Panne f. **broken down**, a. Cassé ; brisé ; en panne ; détraqué. **break in. 1.** v.tr. (a) Enfoncer ;

défoncer. (b) To b. oneself in to sth., se rompre à qch. 2. v.i. (a) To break in (up)on s.o., interrompre qn. Abs. To break in, intervenir. (b) S'introduire par effraction. **break loose,** v.i. 1. Se dégager de ses liens ; s'évader, s'échapper. 2. His fury broke loose, sa fureur se déchaîna. **break off.** 1. v.tr. (a) Casser, rompre. (b) Interrompre, abandonner. The engagement is broken off, le mariage est rompu. 2. v.i. (a) Se détacher (from sth., de qch.). (b) Discontinuer. (c) To break off with s.o., rompre avec qn. **break open,** v.tr. Enfoncer, forcer. **break out,** v.i. 1. (a) Éclater. (b) To b. out into a sweat, se mettre à transpirer. 2. S'échapper, s'évader. **break through,** v.tr. To b. through a barrier, abs. to break through, se frayer un passage. The sun breaks through (the clouds), le soleil perce les nuages. **break up.** 1. v.tr. Mettre en morceaux ; démolir ; disperser (la foule) ; rompre (une conférence). 2. v.i. (Of ship) Se démembrer ; (of crowd) se disperser. F: He is beginning to b. up, il commence à se casser. (b) Se séparer. (c) Sch: Entrer en vacances. (d) (Of weather) Se gâter, se brouiller. **breaking up,** s. 1. Démolition f ; dispersion f (d'une foule). 2. (a) Séparation f. On the b. up of the meeting, au sortir de la réunion. (b) Sch: Entrée f en vacances. (c) Débâcle f (des glaces). **broken,** a. (a) Cassé, brisé, rompu. His spirit is b., il est abattu. (b) (Terrain) accidenté ; (sommeil) interrompu ; (temps) incertain. B. water, brisants mpl. In a broken voice, d'une voix entrecoupée. In broken French, en mauvais français. **-ly,** adv. Sans suite ; par à-coups ; (parler) à mots entrecoupés. **broken-hearted,** a. Au cœur brisé. **breaking,** s. (a) Rupture f. (b) Breaking into a house, entrée f par effraction dans une maison. **break-neck,** a. It was a b.-n. path, le sentier était un véritable casse-cou.

breakable. 1. a. Cassant, fragile. 2. s.pl. Breakables, objets m fragiles.

breakage, s. Casse f.

breaker, s. Nau: Brisant m ; vague déferlante.

breakfast¹, s. (Petit) déjeuner. To have breakfast, déjeuner.

breakfast², v.i. Déjeuner (le matin).

breakwater, s. Brise-lames m inv. ; môle m.

bream, s. Ich: Brème f.

breast¹, s. 1. Sein m, mamelle f. 2. Poitrine f ; poitrail m (de cheval). Cu: Blanc m (de volaille). To press s.o. to one's b., serrer qn sur son cœur. F: To make a clean breast of it, tout avouer. **breast-plate,** s. Plastron m ; cuirasse f. **breast-pocket,** s. Poche f de poitrine.

breast², v.tr. Affronter, faire front à.

breastbone, s. Anat: Sternum m.

breath, s. Haleine f, souffle m, respiration f. To draw breath, respirer. All in the same breath, tout d'une haleine. To hold one's breath, retenir son souffle. To gasp for breath, haleter. He caught his breath, il eut un sursaut. To lose one's breath, perdre haleine. To waste one's breath, perdre ses paroles. Out of breath, hors d'haleine ; essoufflé. To take s.o.'s breath away, couper la respiration à qn ; interloquer qn. To speak below one's breath, parler à (de)mi-voix.

breathe. I. v.i. Respirer, souffler. II. **breathe,** v.tr. 1. Respirer. To breathe in, breathe out, the air, aspirer, exhaler, l'air. 2. (a) To breathe one's last, rendre le dernier soupir. Don't breathe a word of it! n'en soufflez pas un mot ! (b) To breathe out threats, proférer des menaces. 3. Laisser souffler (un cheval). **breathing,** s. Respiration f ; souffle m. **breathing-space,** s. Le temps de souffler ; répit m.

breathless, a. 1. Hors d'haleine ; essoufflé. 2. Breathless suspense, attente fiévreuse. **-ly,** adv. 1. En haletant. 2. En retenant son haleine.

breech, s. 1. (Pair of) breeches, culotte f. 2. Artil: Culasse f. **breeches-buoy,** s. Nau: Bouée f culotte.

breed¹, s. Race f ; lignée f. Prov: Breed will tell, bon sang ne peut mentir.

breed², v. I. v.tr. 1. Produire, engendrer ; faire naître, donner naissance à. 2. (a) Élever (du bétail, etc.). (b) Country-bred, élevé à la campagne. II. breed, v.i. Multiplier ; se reproduire. **breeding,** s. 1. (a) Reproduction f. (b) Élevage m. Silkworm breeding, éducation f des vers à soie. 2. (a) Éducation. (b) (Good) breeding, bonnes manières ; savoir-vivre m.

breeder, s. Éleveur m.

breeze, s. Vent assez fort ; brise f.

breezy, a. 1. Venteux. 2. F: Jovial ; désinvolte.

Bremen. Pr.n. Geog: Brême m.

Breton. 1. a. & s. Breton, -onne. 2. s. Ling: Le breton.

breviary, s. Ecc: Bréviaire m.

brevity, s. Brièveté f.

brew. 1. v.tr. (a) Brasser. (b) Abs. Brasser ; faire de la bière. 2. v.i. (a) S'infuser. (b) F: There is a storm brewing, un orage couve, se prépare. There is something brewing, il se trame quelque chose.

brewer, s. Brasseur m.

brewery, s. Brasserie f.

briar, s. (a) Églantier m. (b) F: Briars, ronces f. **briar-rose,** s. Églantine f.

bribe¹, s. Payement m illicite ; F: pot-de-vin m. To take a b., se laisser corrompre.

bribe², v.tr. Corrompre, soudoyer.

bribery, s. Corruption f.

brick, s. 1. (a) Brique f. F: To drop a brick, faire une boulette, une gaffe. F: Box of bricks, boîte de constructions. 2. F: He's a brick! c'est un chic type. **brick-field,** s. Briqueterie f.

brickbat, *s.* Fragment *m* de brique.
bricklayer, *s.* Maçon *m*.
bridal, *a.* Nuptial, -aux, de noce(s). **Bridal wreath**, couronne de mariée.
bride, *s.* Épousée *f*; (nouvelle) mariée. **The bride and bridegroom**, les nouveaux mariés.
bridegroom, *s.* (Nouveau) marié.
bridesmaid, *s.* Demoiselle *f* d'honneur.
bridge[1], *s.* **1.** Pont *m*. **2.** *Nau:* Passerelle *f* (de commandement). **3.** Dos *m*, arête *f* (du nez). **bridge-head**, *s.* *Mil:* Tête *f* de pont.
bridge[2], *v.tr.* To bridge (over) a river, jeter un pont sur un fleuve. *F:* To bridge a gap, combler une lacune.
bridge[3], *s.* *Cards:* Bridge *m*.
bridle[1], *s.* (*a*) *Harn:* Bride *f*. (*b*) *F: To put a b. on one's passions*, mettre un frein à ses passions. **bridle-path**, *s.* Sentier *m* pour cavaliers.
bridle[2]. **1.** *v.tr.* Maîtriser, brider, mettre un frein à (ses passions). **2.** *v.i.* To bridle (up), (i) se rengorger; (ii) se rebiffer.
brief[1], *a.* Bref; court. In brief, en raccourci. To be brief, bref. **-ly**, *adv.* Brièvement; en peu de mots.
brief[2], *s.* *Jur:* Dossier *m*. To hold a brief, être chargé d'une cause.
brief[3], *v.tr.* To brief a barrister, confier une cause à un avocat.
brier, *s.* Brier (pipe), pipe *f* en bruyère.
brig, *s.* *Nau:* Brick *m*.
brigade, *s.* **1.** Brigade *f*. **2.** Corps organisé.
brigadier, *s.* *Mil:* Général *m* de brigade.
brigand, *s.* Brigand *m*, bandit *m*.
brigandage, *s.* Brigandage *m*.
bright, *a.* **1.** Lumineux. (*a*) B. light, lumière vive. B. eyes, yeux brillants, lumineux. (*b*) (Of weather) Clair. (*c*) Vif, éclatant. Bright red, rouge vif. (*d*) To see the bright side of things, prendre les choses par le bon côté. **2.** (*a*) Vif, animé. (*b*) F: Bright lad, garçon éveillé. A. b. idea, une idée lumineuse. **-ly**, *adv.* Brillamment; avec éclat.
brighten. 1. *v.tr.* To brighten sth. (up), faire briller qch.; égayer (la conversation). **2.** *v.i.* To brighten (up), s'éclaircir. His eyes brightened, ses yeux s'allumèrent.
brightness, *s.* Éclat *m* (du soleil); clarté *f* (du jour); vivacité *f*.
brilliance, brilliancy, *s.* Éclat *m*, brillant *m*, lustre *m*.
brilliant[1], *a.* Brillant, éclatant. **-ly**, *adv.* Brillamment; avec éclat.
brilliant[2], *s.* *Lap:* Brillant *m*.
brim[1], *s.* Bord *m*. **brim-full**, *a.* Plein jusqu'au bord; débordant.
brim[2], *v.i.* To brim over (with sth.), déborder, regorger (de qch.).
brimful, *a.* *F:* Débordant.
brine, *s.* Eau salée; saumure *f*.
bring, *v.tr.* (*a*) Amener (qn); apporter (qch.). (*b*) To bring tears (in)to s.o.'s eyes, faire

venir les larmes aux yeux de qn. *To b. s.o. luck*, porter bonheur à qn. You have brought it on yourself, vous vous l'êtes attiré vous-même. (*c*) To bring an action against s.o., intenter un procès à qn. (*d*) To bring sth. into question, mettre qch. en question. (*e*) To bring s.o. to beggary, réduire qn à la mendicité. To bring sth. to perfection, porter qch. à la perfection. (*f*) To bring sth. to pass, amener, faire arriver, qch. (*g*) To bring oneself to do sth., se résoudre à faire qch. **bring about**, *v.tr.* (*a*) Amener, causer, déterminer, occasionner. (*b*) Effectuer, accomplir, opérer. **bring along**, *v.tr.* Amener (qn); apporter (qch.). **bring away** *v.tr.* Emmener (qn); emporter (qch.). **bring back**, *v.tr.* Rapporter (qch.); ramener (qn). **bring down**, *v.tr.* **1.** Abattre; faire tomber; faire crouler; terrasser (un adversaire). *Th: F:* To bring down the house, faire crouler la salle. **2.** (*a*) Faire descendre. (*b*) Descendre. **3.** Abaisser. **bring forth**, *v.tr.* Produire. **bring forward**, *v.tr.* Avancer. **bring in**, *v.tr.* **1.** Introduire. **2.** To bring in interest, rapporter; porter intérêt. **3.** (*a*) Déposer, présenter (un projet de loi). (*b*) To bring in a verdict, rendre un verdict. To bring s.o. in guilty, déclarer qn coupable. **bring off**, *v.tr.* Réussir, conduire à bien (une affaire). **bring on**, *v.tr.* **1.** Produire, occasionner. **2.** Introduire (un sujet de discussion). **bring out**, *v.tr.* **1.** Sortir. **2.** Faire ressortir, mettre en relief; faire valoir (une couleur). **3.** Publier, faire paraître. **bring over**, *v.tr.* **1.** Transporter, amener (from, de). **2.** To bring s.o. over to a cause, gagner qn à une cause. **bring round**, *v.tr.* **1.** (*a*) Rappeler à la vie. (*b*) Remettre de bonne humeur. **2.** (R)amener (la conversation sur un sujet). **bring through**, *v.tr.* To b. a patient through, sauver un malade. **bring to**, *v.tr.* To bring s.o. to, faire reprendre connaissance à qn. **bring together**, *v.tr.* Réunir; mettre en contact. *To b. persons together again*, réconcilier des personnes. **bring up**, *v.tr.* **1.** (*a*) Monter. (*b*) To bring up one's food, vomir. **2.** B. up your chair to the fire, approchez votre chaise du feu. **3.** Élever (des enfants). **4.** To b. s.o. up before the court, citer qn en justice. **5.** Arrêter. **6.** To bring up a subject, mettre une question sur le tapis. **bringing up**, *s.* Éducation *f* (des enfants).
brink, *s.* Bord *m*. *To be on the b. of tears*, avoir peine à retenir ses larmes.
briny, *a.* Saumâtre, salé.
brisk, *a.* Vif, actif, alerte. At a brisk pace, à vive allure. Brisk trade, commerce actif. **-ly**, *adv.* Vivement; avec entrain.
briskness, *s.* (*a*) Vivacité *f*, animation *f*, entrain *m*. (*b*) Activité *f*.
bristle[1], *s.* Soie *f*; poil *m* raide.
bristle[2], *v.i.* (*a*) To bristle (up), se hérisser.

(b) *F:* **To bristle with difficulties,** être hérissé de difficultés. **bristling,** *a.* Hérissé (*with,* de).

bristly, *a.* Couvert de poils raides. **Bristly** moustache, moustache hérissée.

Britain. *Pr.n. Geog:* **Great Britain,** la Grande-Bretagne.

British, *a.* Britannique; de la Grande-Bretagne; anglais, d'Angleterre. *s.pl.* **The British,** les Anglais *m.*

Briton, *s. F:* Anglais, -aise.

Brittany. *Pr.n.* La Bretagne.

brittle, *a.* Fragile, cassant.

brittleness, *s.* Fragilité *f.*

broach[1], *v.tr.* **I.** *Coop:* Percer, entamer (un fût). **2.** *F:* Entamer, aborder (une question).

broach[2], *v.i. Nau:* To broach (to), venir en travers.

broad. **I.** *a.* (a) Large. **B. grin,** sourire épanoui. **In broad daylight,** en plein jour. *F:* **It is as broad as it is long,** cela revient au même. (b) **The broad facts,** les faits tout simples. (c) **B. views,** idées larges. **2.** *s.* **The broad of the back,** le milieu du dos. **-ly,** *adv.* Largement. **Broadly speaking,** généralement parlant. **broad-brimmed,** *a.* A larges bords. **broad-minded,** *a.* **To be b.-m.,** avoir l'esprit large. **broad-mindedness,** *s.* Largeur *f* d'esprit. **broad-shouldered,** *a.* Large d'épaules, trapu.

broadcast[1]. **I.** *adv. Agr:* To sow broadcast, semer à la volée. **Scattered b.,** répandu à profusion. **2.** *a. W.Tel:* (Omni)diffusé. **Broadcast announcement,** radio-émission *f.*

broadcast[2]. **I.** *v.tr.* **I.** (a) *Agr:* Semer à la volée. (b) *F:* Faire savoir (qch.) partout. **2.** *W.Tel:* Radiodiffuser. **II. broadcast,** *s. W.Tel:* Radio-émission *f.*

broadcloth, *s. Tex:* Drap noir fin.

broaden. **I.** *v.tr.* Élargir. **2.** *v.i.* S'élargir.

broadside, *s.* (a) Flanc *m,* travers *m* (du navire). (b) **To fire a broadside,** tirer une bordée.

broadsword, *s.* Sabre *m;* latte *f.*

brocade, *s. Tex:* Brocart *m.*

brogue[1], *s.* Soulier *m* de golf.

brogue[2], *s.* (a) Accent *m* de terroir. (b) Accent irlandais.

broil[1], *s.* Querelle *f;* bagarre *f;* rixe *f.*

broil[2], *v.tr. & i.* Griller. **broiling,** *a. F:* Ardent, brûlant.

broke, *a. P:* **To be (stony) broke,** être sans le sou.

broker, *s.* (a) Courtier *m.* (b) **(Stock-)broker,** agent *m* de change.

brokerage, *s.* Courtage *m.*

bromine, *s. Ch:* Brome *m.*

bronchial, *a. Anat:* Bronchial, -aux.

bronchitis, *s. Med:* Bronchite *f.*

bronze[1]. **I.** *s.* Bronze *m.* **2.** *Attrib.* **B. statue,** statue de, en, bronze. (Cuir) bronzé, mordoré.

bronze[2]. **I.** *v.tr.* Bronzer. *F:* **Bronzed skin,** peau bronzée. **2.** *v.i.* Se bronzer.

brooch, *s. Cost:* Broche *f.*

brood[1], *s.* **I.** Couvée *f.* **2.** *F:* Enfants *mpl.*

brood[2], *v.i. F:* Broyer du noir; rêver noir. **To brood on, over, sth.,** songer sombrement à qch. **To b. over the fire,** couver le feu.

broody, *a.* (a) *B. hen,* poule couveuse. (b) *F:* Distrait, rêveur, -euse.

brook[1], *s.* Ruisseau *m.*

brook[2], *v.tr.* **The matter brooks no delay,** l'affaire ne souffre pas de retard.

broom, *s.* **I.** *Bot:* Genêt *m.* **2.** Balai *m.*

broomstick, *s.* Manche *m* à balai.

broth, *s.* Bouillon *m,* potage *m.*

brother, *s.tr.* **I.** Frère *m.* **2.** (a) Frère. (b) Confrère *m* (d'un corps de métier.) **3.** *Ecc.* Frère.

brother-in-law, *s.* Beau-frère *m.* *pl.* beaux-frères.

brotherhood, *s.* **I.** Fraternité *f.* **2.** Confraternité *f;* (*religious*) confrérie *f.*

brotherly, *a.* De frère; fraternel.

brow, *s.* **I.** Sourcil *m.* **To pucker one's brows,** froncer les sourcils. **2.** Front *m.* **3.** *F:* Front, croupe *f* (de colline); bord *m* (de précipice).

browbeat, *v.tr.* Intimider, rudoyer.

brown[1]. **I.** *a.* (a) Brun. **Light-brown hair,** cheveux châtain clair. **Brown boots,** chaussures jaunes. (b) Bruni par le soleil. **2.** *s.* Brun *m.*

brown[2]. **I.** *v.tr.* Brunir. **2.** *v.i.* (Se) brunir.

brownie, *s.* Farfadet *m.*

brownish, *a.* Brunâtre.

browse, *v.tr. & i.* Brouter.

bruise[1], *s.* Meurtrissure *f;* contusion *f.*

bruise[2], *v.tr.* Meurtrir, contusionner.

brunette, *a. & s.* Brune *f.*

brunt, *s.* Choc *m.* **To bear the b.,** payer de sa personne.

brush[1], *s.* **I.** = BRUSHWOOD. **2.** (a) Brosse *f.* (b) (Paint-)brush, pinceau *m.* **Flat brush,** queue-de-morue *f.* (c) *Ven:* Queue *f* (de renard). **3.** Coup *m* de brosse. **4.** Rencontre *f,* échauffourée *f. F:* **At the first brush,** au premier abord.

brush[2]. **I.** *v.tr.* (a) Brosser. **To b. one's hair,** se brosser les cheveux. (b) Effleurer, frôler. **2.** *v.i.* **To brush against,** froisser, frôler, en passant. **brush aside,** *v.tr.* Écarter. **brush down,** *v.tr.* Donner un coup de brosse à. **brush up,** *v.tr.* Donner un coup de brosse à. *F:* **To brush up a subject,** se remettre à un sujet.

brushwood, *s.* Broussailles *fpl;* fourré *m.*

brusque, *a.* Brusque; (ton) rude, bourru. **-ly,** *adv.* Avec brusquerie.

brusqueness, *s.* Brusquerie *f,* rudesse *f.*

Brussels. *Pr.n. Geog:* Bruxelles *f.*

brutal, *a.* Brutal, -aux; (instinct) de brute. **-ally,** *adv.* Brutalement.

brutality, *s.* Brutalité *f* (to, envers).

brutalize, *v.tr.* Abrutir.

brute. **I.** *s.* Brute *f;* bête *f* brute. **2.** *a.* (a) **Brute beast,** bête brute. (b) **By brute force,** de vive force.

brutish, *a.* **1.** De brute; bestial. **2.** Abruti.
brutishness, *s.* **1.** Bestialité *f.* **2.** Abrutissement *m.*
bubble¹, *s.* **1.** Bulle *f.* **2.** Projet *m* chimérique.
bubble², *v.i.* Bouillonner; dégager des bulles; (*of wine*) pétiller **bubble over,** *v.i.* Déborder
buccaneer, *s* *F:* Boucanier *m,* flibustier *m*; pirate *m.*
buck¹, *s.* **1.** (*a*) Daim *m* ou chevreuil *m.* (*b*) Mâle *m* (du lapin). **2.** *Equit:* = BUCK-JUMP¹. **buck-jump¹,** *s.* Saut *m* de mouton.
buck-jump², *v.i.* Faire le saut de mouton.
buck-shot, *s.* *Ven:* Chevrotine *f.*
buck², *v.i.* = BUCK-JUMP².
buck³. **1.** *v.tr.* To buck s.o. up, remonter le courage de qn. **2.** *v.i.* To buck up, (i) reprendre courage; (ii) se hâter.
bucket, *s.* Seau *m.* **bucket-shop,** *s.* *Fin:* Bureau *m* d'un courtier marron.
bucketful, *s.* Plein seau.
buckle¹, *s.* Boucle *f,* agrafe *f.*
buckle². **1.** *v.tr.* Boucler (un soulier); serrer (une ceinture). **To buckle on** *one's sword,* ceindre son épée. **2.** *v.i.* *F:* To buckle to, s'y atteler; s'y mettre. **3.** *v.i.* To buckle (up), se déformer, gauchir. **buckling,** *s.* **1.** Agrafage *m.* **2.** Déformation *f,* flambage *m.*
buckram, *s.* *Tex:* Bougran *m.*
buckthorn, *s* *Bot:* Nerprun *m.*
buckwheat, *s.* Sarrasin *m*; blé noir.
bucolic, *a.* & *s.* Bucolique (*f*).
bud¹, *s.* **1.** Bourgeon *m*; œil *m* (d'une plante). To be in bud, bourgeonner. **2.** *Bot:* Bouton *m* (de fleur).
bud², *v.i.* (*Of flower*) Boutonner. **budding,** *a.* *F:* Budding artist, artiste en herbe.
Buddha, *s.* (Le) Bouddha.
Buddhist. **1.** *s.* Bouddhiste *mf.* **2.** *a.* Bouddhique.
budge, *v.i.* (*a*) Bouger, céder; reculer. (*b*) Bouger, remuer.
budget, *s.* **1.** Tas *m,* collection *f* (de papiers). **2.** Budget *m.*
buff, *s.* **1.** Buff-leather, buffle *m.* **2.** Couleur *f* chamois; jaune clair *inv.*
buffalo, *s.* *Z:* Buffle *m.*
buffer, *s.* Appareil *m* de choc; amortisseur *m.* *Rail:* Tampon *m* (de choc).
buffet¹, *s.* Coup *m* (de poing).
buffet², *v.tr.* & *i.* (*a*) Bourrer de coups. (*b*) To buffet (with) the waves, lutter contre les vagues. *Buffeted by the wind,* secoué par le vent. **buffeting,** *s.* Succession *f* de coups, de chocs.
buffet³, *s.* Buffet *m.*
buffoon, *s.* Bouffon *m,* paillasse *m.*
buffoonery, *s.* Bouffonneries *fpl.*
bug, *s.* **1.** Punaise *f.* **2.** *F:* Big bug, gros bonnet.
bugbear, *s.* (*a*) Objet *m* d'épouvante. (*b*) *F:* Cauchemar *m.*
bugle, *s.* Clairon *m.* **Bugle band,** fanfare *f.*
bugler, *s.* Clairon *m.*

build¹, *s.* **1.** Construction *f*; façons *fpl* (d'un navire). **2.** Carrure *f,* taille *f,* conformation *f* (d'une personne).
build², *v.tr.* **1.** Bâtir (une maison); construire (un vaisseau). *F:* I'm built that way, je suis comme ça. **2.** To build vain hopes on sth., fonder de vaines espérances sur qch. **build up,** *v.tr.* (*a*) Affermir (la santé). (*b*) Built-up area, agglomération (urbaine).
built, *a.* British built, de construction anglaise. *F:* Well-built man, homme bien bâti. **building,** *s.* **1.** Construction *f.* Building land, terrain *m* à bâtir. **2.** Bâtiment *m*; maison *f.* Public building, édifice public.
builder, *s.* Entrepreneur *m* (en bâtiments); *F:* créateur, -trice (d'un empire).
bulb, *s.* **1.** *Bot:* Bulbe *m,* oignon *m.* **2.** *El:* Ampoule *f*; lampe *f.* **3.** *Ph:* Boule *f,* ampoule (de thermomètre).
bulbous, *a.* Bulbeux.
Bulgaria. *Pr.n.* La Bulgarie.
Bulgarian, *a.* & *s.* Bulgare (*mf*).
bulge¹, *s.* Bombement *m,* ventre *m.*
bulge², *v.tr.* & *i.* To bulge (out), bomber, ballonner; faire saillie. **bulging,** *a.* Bombé. B. eyes, yeux protubérants.
bulk, *s.* **1.** *Com:* In bulk, en bloc, globalement; en gros. **2.** Grandeur *f,* grosseur *f,* volume *m.* **3.** *The* (great) b., la masse, la plupart.
bulkhead, *s.* *N.Arch:* Cloison *f.*
bulky, *a.* **1.** Volumineux. **2.** Gros, *f.* grosse.
bull¹, *s.* **1.** (*a*) Taureau *m.* (*b*) Bull elephant, éléphant *m* mâle. (*c*) *Astr:* The Bull, le Taureau. **2.** *St.Exch:* Haussier *m.* **3.** *F:* = BULL'S-EYE. **bull-dog,** *s.* Bouledogue *m.* **bull-fight,** *s.* Course *f,* combat *m,* de taureaux. **bull-fighter,** *s.* Toréador *m.* **bull-frog,** *s.* Grenouille mugissante. **bull-ring,** *s.* Arène *f* (pour les courses de taureaux). **bull's-eye,** *s.* **1.** Bull's-eye lantern, lanterne sourde. **2.** Noir *m,* mouche *f* (d'une cible) To make a bull's-eye, mettre dans le noir. **bull-terrier,** *s.* (Chien) bull-terrier *m.*
bull², *s.* *Ecc:* Bulle *f.*
bull³, *s* Irish bull, inconséquence *f*; coq-à-l'âne *m.*
bullet, *s.* Balle *f.* **bullet-headed,** *a.* A tête ronde. **bullet-proof,** *a.* A l'épreuve des balles.
bulletin, *s.* Bulletin *m,* communiqué *m.* News bulletin, bulletin d'actualités.
bullfinch, *s.* *Orn:* Bouvreuil *m.*
bullion, *s.* Or *m* argent *m,* en lingot(s).
bullock, *s.* Bœuf *m.*
bully¹, *s.* *F:* Brute *f,* tyran *m.*
bully², *v.tr.* Intimider, malmener, brutaliser. **bullying¹,** *a.* Brutal, -aux. **bullying²,** *s.* Intimidation *f,* brutalité *f.*
bully³, *s.* *F:* Bully (beef), bœuf *m* de conserve.
bulrush, *s.* *Bot:* Massette *f,* quenouille *f.*

bulwark, *s. pl. Nau:* Pavois *m*, bastingage *m*.
bumble-bee, *s. Ent:* Bourdon *m*.
bumboat, *s.* Bateau *m* à provisions.
bump¹, *s.* **1.** Choc (sourd); secousse *f*, heurt *m*; cahot *m*. **2.** Bosse *f*.
bump², **1.** *v.tr.* Cogner, frapper. *To b. one's head against sth.*, se cogner la tête contre qch. **2.** *v.i.* Se cogner, se heurter, buter (*into*, *against*, *sth.*, contre qch.). **bumping,** *s.* Heurtement *m*, cahotement *m*.
bump³, *adv. & int.* Pan! boum!
bumper, *s.* **1.** Rasade *f* (de champagne). *F:* **Bumper crop,** récolte magnifique. **2.** *Aut:* Pare-choc(s) *m inv.*
bumpkin, *s.* Rustre *m*, lourdaud *m*.
bumptious, *a.* Présomptueux, suffisant. **-ly,** *adv.* D'un air suffisant.
bumptiousness, *s.* Suffisance *f*.
bumpy, *a.* (Chemin) cahoteux.
bun, *s. Cu:* Petit pain au lait.
bunch¹, *s.* (*a*) Botte *f* (de radis); bouquet *m* (de fleurs); grappe *f* (de raisin); trousseau *m* (de clefs). (*b*) *F:* **He's the best of the bunch,** c'est lui le meilleur (de la bande).
bunch², *v.i.* To bunch (**together**), se presser en foule; se serrer.
bundle¹, *s.* Paquet *m* (de linge); ballot *m* (de marchandises); liasse *f* (de papiers); fagot *m* (de bois).
bundle², *v.tr.* (*a*) To bundle (**up**), empaqueter; mettre (des documents) en liasse. (*b*) *F:* To bundle s.o. **out of the house,** flanquer qn à la porte.
bung¹, *s.* Bondon *m* (de fût). **bung-hole,** *s.* Bonde *f*.
bung², *v.tr.* To bung (**up**), boucher. *F: Eyes bunged up,* yeux pochés.
bungalow, *s.* **1.** (*In India*) Bungalow *m*. **2.** *F:* Maison *f* sans étage.
bungle¹, *s.* To make a bungle of sth., bousiller, gâcher, qch.
bungle², *v.tr.* Bousiller, gâcher; rater (une affaire). **bungling¹,** *a.* Maladroit. **bungling²,** *s.* Maladresse *f*.
bungler, *s.* (*a*) Bousilleur, -euse (de travail); gâcheur, -euse. (*b*) Maladroit, -e.
bunion, *s. Med: F:* Oignon *m*.
bunk, *s. Nau:* Couchette *f*.
bunker¹, *s.* **1.** *Nau:* Soute *f*. **2.** *Golf:* Banquette *f*.
bunker², *v.tr.* To be bunkered, *F:* se trouver dans une impasse.
bunkum, *s. F:* Blague *f*, bêtises *fpl*.
bunny, *s. F:* Jeannot lapin *m*.
bunting¹, *s. Orn:* Bruant *m*.
bunting², *s. Coll.* Drapeaux *m*, pavillons *m*.
buoy¹, *s. Nau:* Bouée *f*; balise flottante.
buoy², *v.tr.* **1.** *F:* To buoy s.o. **up,** soutenir qn. **2.** Baliser (un chenal).
buoyancy, *s.* **1.** Flottabilité *f*. **2.** *F:* Entrain *m*; élasticité *f* de caractère.
buoyant, *a.* **1.** Flottable; léger. **2.** *F:* Plein d'entrain. *B. step,* pas élastique.
bur, *s. Bot:* Teigne *f*.
burden¹, *s.* **1.** Fardeau *m*, charge *f*. *To be*

a b. to s.o., être à charge à qn. *To make s.o.'s life a b.*, rendre la vie dure à qn. **Beast of burden,** bête de somme. **2.** (*a*) Refrain *m* (d'une chanson). (*b*) Substance *f*, fond *m* (d'un discours).
burden², *v.tr.* Charger (*with sth.*, de qch.).
burdensome, *a.* Onéreux (*to*, à); fâcheux.
bureau, *s.* **1.** *Furn:* Bureau *m*; secrétaire *m*. **2.** (*Office*) Bureau.
bureaucracy, *s.* Bureaucratie *f*.
bureaucrat, *s.* Bureaucrate *m*.
burgher, *s. Hist:* Bourgeois *m*, citoyen *m*.
burglar, *s.* Cambrioleur *m*.
burglary, *s. F:* Vol avec effraction; cambriolage *m*.
burgle, *v.tr. F:* Cambrioler, dévaliser.
Burgundian, *a. & s Geog:* Bourguignon, -onne.
Burgundy. **1.** *Pr.n.* La Bourgogne. **2.** *s.* (Vin *m* de) bourgogne *m*.
burial, *s.* Enterrement *m*, inhumation *f*. **burial-ground,** *s.* Cimetière *m*. **burial-service,** *s.* Office des morts.
burke, *v.tr.* Étouffer, étrangler.
burlesque¹, *a. & s.* Burlesque (*m*).
burlesque², *v.tr.* Travestir, parodier.
burly, *a.* Solidement bâti.
Burma(h). *Pr.n.* La Birmanie
Burmese, *a. & s.* Birman, -e.
burn¹, *s.* Brûlure *f*.
burn², *v.* **1.** *v.tr.* (*a*) Brûler. *To b. sth. to ashes,* réduire qch. en cendres. *To b. one's fingers,* se brûler les doigts. *F:* He's the best of burnt his fingers over it, il lui en a cuit. To be burnt to death, être carbonisé. (*b*) *Ind:* Cuire (des briques). **2.** *v.i.* Brûler. *To burn like matchwood,* flamber comme une allumette. *My wound was burning,* ma blessure cuisait. *To burn with desire,* brûler de désir. **burn away.** **1.** *v.tr.* Brûler, consumer. **2.** *v.i.* Se consumer. **burn down.** *v.tr.* Brûler, incendier. **burn out.** **1.** *v.tr.* *El:* Griller (une lampe). **2.** *v.i.* Se consumer; brûler; (*of electric lamp*) griller. **burn up.** **1.** *v.tr.* Brûler (entièrement); consumer. **2.** *v.i.* (*Of fire*) Se ranimer, flamber. **burnt,** *a.* (*a*) Brûlé, carbonisé. (*b*) Face b. by the sun, figure bronzée par le soleil. **burning¹,** *a.* Brûlant, ardent. **Burning question,** question brûlante. **burning-hot,** *a.* Brûlant. **burning²,** *s.* Brûlage *m*; incendie *m*. There is a smell of burning, ça sent le brûlé.
burn³, *s.* Ruisseau *m*.
burner, *s* Bec *m* (de gaz).
burnish, *v.tr.* Brunir; polir.
burr, *s.* = BUR.
burrow¹, *s.* Terrier *m*.
burrow², *v.i.* (i) Fouir la terre; (ii) (se) terrer. *F: To b. into,* fouiller dans.
bursar, *s.* Économe *m*.
burst¹, *s.* **1.** Éclatement *m*, explosion *f*. **2.** Jet *m* (de flamme); coup *m* (de tonnerre); éclat *m* (de rire); salve *f* (d'applaudissements).
burst², *v.* **1.** *v.i.* (*a*) Éclater, faire explosion;

(*of tyre*) crever; (*of bud*) éclore. To burst in pieces, voler en éclats. (*b*) *To be bursting with laughter*, crever de rire. (*c*) A cry burst from his lips, un cri s'échappa de ses lèvres. (*d*) To burst into bloom, fleurir, s'épanouir. The horses burst into a gallop, les chevaux prirent le galop. To burst into tears, se mettre à pleurer. (*e*) To burst into a room, entrer dans une chambre en coup de vent. (*Of sun*) *To b. through a cloud*, percer un nuage. 2. *v.tr.* Faire éclater; crever (un ballon); rompre (ses liens). To burst a door open, enfoncer une porte. burst asunder. I. *v.tr.* Rompre (ses liens). 2. *v.i.* Se rompre. burst in. I. *v.tr.* Enfoncer. 2. *v.i.* Faire irruption. burst open. I. *v.tr.* Enfoncer. 2. *v.i.* S'ouvrir tout d'un coup. burst out, *v.i.* S'écrier, s'exclamer. To burst out laughing, éclater de rire.

bury, *v.tr.* Enterrer, inhumer, ensevelir (un mort). Buried treasure, trésor enterré, enfoui. To bury one's face in one's hands, se couvrir la figure de ses mains. burying, *s.* I. Enterrement *m*; ensevelissement *m*. 2. Enfouissement *m*.

bus, *s.* Omnibus *m*. (Motor-)bus, autobus *m*.

bush, *s.* I. (*a*) Buisson *m*. (*b*) Fourré *m*, taillis *m*. 2. The bush, la brousse.

bushel, *s.* Boisseau *m*.

bushman, *s.* *Ethn:* Boschiman *m*.

bushy, *a.* Touffu; buissonneux.

business, *s.* I. Affaire *f*, besogne *f*, occupation *f*. To make it one's business to do sth., se faire un devoir de faire qch. To have business with s.o., avoir affaire avec qn. It is my business to, c'est à moi de. It's none of your business, cela ne vous regarde pas. *F:* To send s.o. about his business, envoyer promener qn. 2. (*a*) Les affaires *f*. Business is business, les affaires sont les affaires. To set up in business as a grocer, s'établir épicier. To go into business, entrer dans les affaires. To do business with s.o., faire des affaires avec qn. To mean business, avoir des intentions sérieuses. *Attrib.* Business hours, heures d'ouverture. Business house, maison de commerce. Business man, homme d'affaires. (*b*) Fonds *m* de commerce.

business-like, *a.* I. (*Of pers.*) Capable; pratique. 2. (*Of manner*) sérieux, carré.

bust, *s.* I. *Sculp:* Buste *m*. 2. Buste, gorge *f*, poitrine *f*.

bustard, *s.* *Orn:* Outarde *f*.

bustle[1], *s.* Remue-ménage *m*.

bustle[2]. I. *v.i.* To bustle (about), se remuer, faire l'empressé. 2. *v.tr.* Faire dépêcher (qn).

bustling, *a.* Affairé; empressé.

busy[1], *a.* Affairé, occupé; actif. B. day, jour chargé. To keep oneself busy, s'activer. *F:* To get busy, s'y mettre. -ily, *adv.* Activement; avec empressement.

busy[2], *v.tr.* & *pr.* *To b. oneself with sth.*, s'occuper à qch.

busybody, *s.* Officieux, -euse; important *m*.

but. I. *conj.* (*a*) Mais. *F:* But I tell you I saw it! (mais) puisque je vous dis que je l'ai vu! But yet, néanmoins. (*b*) *I never pass there but I think of you*, je ne passe jamais par là sans penser à vous. I cannot but believe that, il m'est impossible de ne pas croire que. 2. *adv.* Ne . . . que; seulement. *He talks but little*, il parle assez peu. But yesterday, pas plus tard qu'hier. Had I but known! si j'avais su! 3. *conj. or prep.* (*a*) All but he, tous excepté lui. None but he, personne d'autre que lui. *Anything but that*, tout plutôt que cela. He is anything but a hero, il n'est rien moins qu'un héros. There is nothing for it but to obey, il n'y a qu'à obéir. (*b*) But for, sans. But for that, à part cela.

butcher[1], *s.* (*a*) Boucher *m*. Butcher's shop, boucherie *f*. (*b*) *F:* Boucher, massacreur *m*.

butcher[2], *v.tr.* Égorger, massacrer.

butchery, *s.* *F:* Tuerie *f*, boucherie *f*, massacre *m*.

butler, *s.* Maître *m* d'hôtel.

butt[1], *s.* (*a*) Barrique *f*, futaille *f*. (*b*) Tonneau *m* (pour l'eau de pluie).

butt[2], *s.* I. Bout *m*; souche *f* (d'arbre). 2. Gros bout, talon *m*. 3. Crosse *f* (de fusil). butt-end, *s.* I. Extrémité inférieure; gros bout. 2. Couche *f* (d'un fusil).

butt[3], *s.* I. *Mil:* The butts, le champ de tir. 2. *F:* To be a butt for s.o.'s jokes, servir de plastron à qn.

butt[4], *s.* Coup *m* de tête; coup de corne.

butt[5], *v.i.* & *tr.* To butt (into) sth., donner du front, buter, contre qch. *To b. s.o.*, donner un coup de corne à qn. *F:* To butt in, intervenir sans façon.

butter[1], *s.* Beurre *m*. butter-bean, *s.* *Hort:* Haricot *m* beurre. butter-dish, *s.* Beurrier *m*. butter-fingered, *a.* Maladroit. butter-scotch, *s.* Caramel *m* au beurre.

butter[2], *v.tr.* Beurrer (du pain). *F:* To butter s.o. up, flatter, pateliner, qn.

buttercup, *s.* *Bot:* Bouton *m* d'or.

butterfly, *s.* Papillon *m*.

buttock, *s.* I. Fesse *f*. 2. *pl.* Croupe *f* (de cheval).

button[1], *s.* I. Bouton *m*. *F:* Buttons, chasseur *m*; groom *m*. 2. (*a*) Bouton (-pressoir) *m*. (*b*) Bouton, mouche *f* (de fleuret). button-hole[1], *s.* Boutonnière *f*. *F:* To wear a button-hole, porter une fleur à sa boutonnière. button-hole[2], *v.tr.* *F:* To b.-h. s.o., retenir, accrocher, qn (au passage). button-hook, *s.* Tire-bouton *m*.

button[2], *v.tr.* (*a*) To button (up) sth., boutonner qch. (*b*) *Dress that buttons behind*, robe qui se boutonne par derrière.

buttress[1], *s.* *Const:* Contrefort *m*, contre-boutant *m*.

buttress[2], *v.tr.* *Const:* Arc-bouter, étayer.

buxom, *a.* Aux formes plastiques.

buy, *v.tr.* Acheter (*sth. from*, *of*, *s.o.*, qch. à qn). *Money cannot buy it*, cela ne se paie pas.

A dear-bought advantage, un avantage chère-ment payé. **buy back,** *v.tr.* Racheter. **buy out,** *v.tr.* Désintéresser (un associé). **buy over,** *v.tr.* Corrompre, acheter (qn). **buy up,** *v.tr.* Rafler, accaparer. **buyer,** *s.* **1.** Acheteur, -euse ; acquéreur *m.* **2.** *Com :* Chef *m* de rayon. **buzz**[1], *s.* Bourdonnement *m* (d'un insecte) ; brouhaha *m* (de conversations). **buzz**[2], *v.i.* Bourdonner. **buzzing,** *s.* = BUZZ[1]. Buzzing in the ears, tintement *m* des oreilles. **buzzard,** *s.* *Orn :* Buse *f,* busard *m.* **buzzer,** *s.* (*a*) Sirène *f.* (*b*) *El.E :* Vibreur *m,* vibrateur *m.* **by.** I. *prep.* **1.** (*a*) (Au)près de, à côté de. *By the sea,* au bord de la mer. By oneself, seul ; à l'écart. (*b*) *North by East,* Nord quart nord-est. **2.** Par. By land and sea, par terre et par mer. **3.** (*a*) Par, de. *To be punished by s.o.,* être puni par qn. Made by hand, fait à la main. Known by the name of X, connu sous le nom d'X. By force, de force. By (an) error, par suite d'une erreur. Three feet by two, trois pieds sur deux. (*b*) *By doing that you will offend him,* en faisant cela vous l'offenserez. *We shall lose nothing by waiting,* nous ne perdrons rien pour attendre. **4.** By right, de droit. By rights, à la rigueur. *To judge by appearances,* juger sur l'apparence. To sell sth. by the pound, vendre qch. à la livre. **5.** By degrees, par degrés. By turn(s), tour à tour. One by one, un à un. **6.** By

day, de jour, le jour. **7.** *By Monday,* d'ici lundi. *He ought to be here* by now, il devrait être déjà ici. **8.** By far, de beaucoup. **9.** I know him by sight, je le connais de vue. *He is a grocer by trade,* il est épicier de son métier. To do one's duty by s.o., faire son devoir envers qn. II. **by,** *adv.* **1.** Près. Close by, tout près. *F :* Taking it by and large, à tout prendre. **2.** To put sth. by, mettre qch. de côté. **3.** (*Past*) To pass by, passer. **4.** *Adv.phr.* By and by, tout à l'heure, bientôt. By the by(e), à propos. III. **by(e),** *a.* Secondaire. **by-election,** *s.* *Parl :* Élection *f* de remplacement. **by-pass**[1], *s.* *Aut :* By-pass (road), route *f* d'évitement, de contournement. **by-pass**[2], *v.tr.* Contourner, éviter (une ville). **by-path,** *s.* Sentier écarté, détourné. **by-play,** *s.* *Th :* Jeu *m* acces-soire ; aparté mimé. **by-product,** *s.* *Ind :* Sous-produit *m.* **by-road,** *s.* Chemin détourné. **by-way,** *s.* Chemin détourné, voie indirecte. **by-word,** *s.* **1.** Proverbe *m,* dicton *m.* **2.** To be the by-word of the village, être la fable, la risée, du village. **bye-bye,** *int.* *F :* Adieu ! au revoir ! **by(e)-law,** *s.* Statut *m* émanant d'une autorité locale ; arrêté municipal. **bygone.** **1.** *a.* Passé, d'autrefois. *In b. days,* dans l'ancien temps. **2.** *s.pl.* Let bygones be bygones, oublions le passé. **byre,** *s.* Vacherie *f* ; étable *f* à vaches. **bystander,** *s.* Assistant *m* ; spectateur, -trice.

C

C, c. **1.** (La lettre) C, c *m.* **2.** *Mus :* Ut *m,* do *m.* **cab,** *s.* **1.** Voiture *f* de place. (*a*) Fiacre *m.* (*b*) Taxi *m* (automobile). **2.** Abri *m* (de locomotive). **cab-driver,** *s.* = CABMAN. **cab-rank,** *s.* Station *f* de fiacres. **cabal,** *s.* **1.** Cabale *f,* brigue *f.* **2.** Coterie *f.* **cabbage,** *s.* Chou *m, pl.* choux. **cabbage-lettuce,** *s.* Laitue pommée. **cabin,** *s.* **1.** Cabane *f,* case *f.* **2.** (*a*) *Nau :* Cabine *f.* (*b*) *Av :* Carlingue *f.* **cabin-boy,** *s.* Mousse *m.* **cabinet,** *s.* **1.** (*a*) Meuble *m* à tiroirs. (*b*) Glass cabinet, vitrine *f.* **2.** *Pol :* Cabinet *m,* ministère *m.* Cabinet minister, ministre *m* d'État. **cabinet-maker,** *s.* Ébéniste *m.* **cable**[1], *s.* **1.** Câble *m.* **2.** *Nau :* Chaîne *f* (d'ancre). **3.** = CABLEGRAM. **cable**[2], *v.tr. & i.* Câbler. **cablegram,** *s.* Câblogramme *m.* **cabman,** *s.* Cocher *m* de fiacre. **caboose,** *s.* *Nau :* Cuisine *f.* **cachalot,** *s.* *Z :* Cachalot *m.*

cache[1], *s.* Cache *f,* cachette *f* (d'explorateur). **cache**[2], *v.tr.* Mettre dans une cache. **cachou,** *s.* Cachou *m.* **cackle**[1], *s.* **1.** Caquet *m.* **2.** Ricanement *m.* **cackle**[2], *v.i.* **1.** Caqueter. **2.** Ricaner. **cactus,** *s.* *Bot :* Cactus *m.* **cad,** *s* Goujat *m,* pleutre *m,* cuistre *m.* **cadaverous,** *a.* Cadavéreux. **caddie,** *s.* *Golf :* Cadet *m,* caddie *m.* **caddish,** *a.* *F :* Voyou, arsouille. **caddishness,** *s.* Goujaterie *f.* **caddy,** *s.* (Tea-)caddy, boîte *f* à thé. **cadence,** *s.* **1.** Cadence *f,* rythme *m,* batte-ment *m.* **2.** *Mus :* Cadence. **cadet,** *s.* (*a*) Élève *m* d'une école militaire. (*b*) *Sch :* Cadet corps, bataillon *m* scolaire. **cadge,** *v.tr. & i.* Écornifler, chiner. **cadger,** *s.* Écornifleur, -euse ; chineur, -euse. **Cadiz.** *Pr.n. Geog :* Cadix. **Caesar.** *Pr.n.* Julius Caesar, Jules César *m.* **caesura,** *s.* *Pros :* Césure *f.* **café,** *s.* Café(-restaurant) *m.*

cage¹, *s.* **1.** Cage *f.* **2.** Cabine *f* (d'ascenseur). **cage-bird,** *s.* Oiseau *m* de volière.

cage², *v.tr.* Encager; mettre en cage.

Cain. *Pr.n.* Cain *m.* *F:* To raise Cain, faire une scène.

cairn, *s.* Cairn *m.*

Cairo. *Pr.n. Geog:* Le Caire.

cajole, *v.tr.* Cajoler; enjôler.

cajolery, *s.* Cajolerie(s) *f(pl)*; enjôlement *m.*

cake¹, *s.* **1.** Gâteau *m.* *F:* To take the cake, remporter la palme. **2.** Pain *m* (de savon); tablette *f* (de chocolat). **3.** Masse *f*, croûte *f* (de sang coagulé). **cake-shop,** *s.* Pâtisserie *f.*

cake², *v.i.* (*a*) Former une croûte. (*b*) (*Of blood*) se cailler. Caked with mud, plaqué de boue.

calamitous, *a.* Calamiteux, désastreux.

calamity, *s.* **1.** Calamité *f*, infortune *f*, malheur *m.* **2.** Désastre *m*; sinistre *m.*

calcareous, *a.* *Miner:* Calcaire.

calcine, *v.tr.* Calciner.

calcium, *s.* *Ch:* Calcium *m.*

calculate, *v.tr. & i.* (*a*) Calculer; estimer (une distance). *Abs.* Faire un calcul; compter. (*b*) To c. upon sth., compter sur qch.

calculated, *a.* (*a*) *C.* insolence, insolence délibérée, calculée. (*b*) Words c. to reassure us, paroles propres à nous rassurer. **calculating¹,** *a.* Calculateur, -trice. **calculating²,** *s.* Calcul *m.* **Calculating machine,** machine *f* à calculer.

calculation, *s.* Calcul *m.*

calendar, *s.* **1.** Calendrier *m.* **2.** *Jur:* Liste *f* des accusés; rôle *m* des assises.

calf¹, *s.* **1.** (*a*) Veau *m.* *Attrib.* Calf love, amours enfantines. (*b*) *Leath:* Veau. **2.** Petit *m* (de certains animaux). **calf's-foot,** *s.* *Cu:* Pied *m* de veau.

calf², *s.* Mollet *m* (de la jambe).

calfskin, *s.* (Cuir *m* de) veau *m.*

calibre, *s.* (*a*) Calibre *m*, alésage *m.* (*b*) *F:* A man of his c., un homme de son calibre.

calico, *s.* *Tex:* Calicot *m.*

California. *Pr.n.* La Californie.

Californian, *a. & s.* Californien, -ienne.

caliph, *s.* Calife *m.*

call¹, *s.* **1.** (*a*) Appel *m*, cri *m.* (*b*) Cri (d'un oiseau). **2.** (*a*) Appel. To come at s.o.'s call, venir à l'appel de qn. To be within call, être à portée de voix. To give s.o. a call, appeler qn You have no call to do so, vous n'avez aucune raison de le faire. (*b*) *Tp:* Telephone call, appel téléphonique; coup *m* de téléphone. (*c*) *Th:* Rappel *m* (d'un acteur). **3.** Visite *f.* *Nau:* Port of call, port d'escale, de relâche. **4.** Demande *f* (d'argent). **call-box,** *s.* *Tp:* Cabine *f*, guérite *f* (téléphonique). **call-boy,** *s.* *Th:* Avertisseur *m.*

call², **I.** *v.tr* **1.** (*a*) Appeler (qn) (qch.). To call a halt, faire halte. *W.Tel:* London calling! ici (poste de) Londres! (*b*) To call to s.o. to do sth., crier à qn de faire qch. **2.** (*a*) Appeler (qn); héler (un taxi); con-

voquer (une assemblée). *Mil:* To call to arms, battre la générale. To call into play, faire appel à. (*b*) To call me at six o'clock, réveillez-moi à six heures. **3.** He is called John, il s'appelle Jean. To call s.o. names, injurier qn. To c. s.o. a liar, traiter qn de menteur. **4.** *Cards:* Appeler, déclarer. **5.** To call a strike, décréter une grève. **II. call,** *v.i.* (*a*) To c. at s.o.'s house, (i) faire une visite chez qn; (ii) passer chez qn. Has anyone called? est-il venu quelqu'un? (*b*) The train calls at every station, le train s'arrête à toutes les gares. To call at a port, faire escale à un port. **call back. 1.** *v.tr.* Rappeler (qn). **2.** *v.i.* I shall call back for it, je repasserai le prendre. **call for,** *v.ind.tr.* (*a*) To c. for help, crier au secours. (*b*) Venir prendre, venir chercher. (*c*) To call for an explanation, demander une explication. **call forth,** *v.tr.* Produire, faire naître. **call in,** *v.tr.* **1.** Faire entrer. **2.** Retirer de la circulation. **3.** To c. in a specialist, faire appel à un spécialiste. **call off,** *v.tr.* To call off a strike, décommander une grève. **call on,** *v.i.* **1.** Faire visite chez (qn); passer chez (qn). **2.** = CALL UPON. **call out. 1.** *v.tr.* (*a*) To c. out the military, faire intervenir la force armée. (*b*) Provoquer (qn) en duel. **2.** *v.i.* Appeler; appeler au secours. **call up,** *v.tr.* **1.** Évoquer (un souvenir). **2.** Appeler au téléphone. **3.** Appeler (qn) sous les armes. **call upon,** *v.i.* (*a*) Invoquer. (*b*) To c. upon s.o. for sth., demander qch. à qn. I now call upon Mr S., la parole est à M. S. **calling,** *s.* **1.** (*a*) Appel *m*, cri *m.* **2.** Convocation *f.* **3.** Visite *f* (on, à). **3.** Vocation *f*, état *m*, métier *m.*

caller, *s.* Visiteur, -euse.

cal(l)iper, *s.* Calliper compasses, (pair of) callipers, compas *m* à calibrer.

callous, *a.* Insensible, endurci. **-ly,** *adv.* Sans pitié, sans cœur.

callow, *a.* Sans plumes. *F:* A c. youth, un blanc-bec.

calm¹, *s.* Calme *m*; tranquillité *f.*

calm², *a.* Calme, tranquille. **-ly,** *adv.* Avec calme; tranquillement.

calm³. **1.** *v.tr.* Calmer, apaiser. Calm yourself, remettez-vous! To calm s.o. down, pacifier qn. **2.** *v.i.* To calm down, se calmer, s'apaiser.

calmness, *s.* Tranquillité *f*, calme *m.*

calumniate, *v.tr.* Calomnier.

calumniator, *s.* Calomniateur, -trice.

calumny, *s.* Calomnie *f.*

calve, *v.i.* Vêler.

calyx, *s.* *Bot:* Calice *m*; vase *m.*

camber¹, *s.* Courbure *f*; bombement *m.*

camber², *v.tr.* Bomber (une chaussée).

cambered, *a.* Arqué, courbé.

cambric, *s.* *Tex:* Batiste *f.*

camel, *s.* Chameau *m.* She-camel, chamelle *f.* **camel-driver,** *s.* Chamelier *m.*

camellia, *s.* *Bot:* Camélia *m.*

cameo, s. Camée m.

camera, s. **1.** *Phot:* Appareil m. **2.** *Jur:* In camera, à huis clos.

Cameroons (the). *Pr.n.pl. Geog:* Le Cameroun.

camomile, s. *Bot:* Camomille f.

camouflage¹, s. Camouflage m.

camouflage², v.tr. Camoufler.

camp¹, s. Camp m; campement m. To pitch a camp, établir un camp. To strike camp, lever le camp. **camp-bed,** s. Lit m de sangle. **camp-chair,** s. Chaise pliante. **camp-stool,** s. Pliant m.

camp², v.i. To camp (out), camper.

campaign¹, s. Campagne f.

campaign², v.i. Faire (une) campagne. **campaigning,** s. Campagnes fpl.

campaigner, s. Old campaigner, vieux soldat; vieux routier.

campanile, s. *Arch:* Campanile m.

campanula, s. *Bot:* Campanule f.

camphor, s. Camphre m.

camphorated, a. Camphorated oil, huile camphrée.

can¹, s. (a) Bidon m, broc m. (b) *Ind:* Burette f (à huile).

can², modal aux. v. **1.** Pouvoir. I can do it, je peux, je puis, le faire. I cannot allow that, je ne saurais permettre cela. As soon as I can, aussitôt que je pourrai. F: I will help you all I can, je vous aiderai de mon mieux. That cannot be, cela ne se peut pas. What can it be? qu'est-ce que cela peut bien être? Mr. X? what can he want? M. X? qu'est-ce qu'il peut bien me vouloir? She is as pleased as can be, elle est on ne peut plus contente. **2.** Savoir. I can swim, je sais nager. **3.** When can I move in? quand pourrai-je emménager? **4.** I could have wished it otherwise, j'aurais préféré qu'il en fût autrement. **5.** You can but try, vous pouvez toujours essayer.

Canada. *Pr.n. Geog:* Le Canada.

Canadian, a. & s. Canadien, -ienne.

canal, s. Canal m, -aux.

Canary. 1. *Pr.n. Geog:* The Canary Islands, les îles Canaries. **2.** s. *Orn:* Serin m.

cancel, v.tr. Annuler; résilier, résoudre; biffer (un mot).

cancellation, s. Annulation f; résiliation f; résolution f.

cancer, s. **1.** Cancer m. **2.** *Astr:* Le Cancer.

candelabrum, s. Candélabre m.

candid, a. Franc, f. franche; sincère. **-ly,** adv. Franchement, sincèrement, de bonne foi.

candidate, s. Candidat, -e, aspirant, -e, prétendant, -e, (for sth.), à qch.).

candle, s. **1.** Wax candle, bougie f. Tallow candle, chandelle f. F: To burn the candle at both ends, brûler la chandelle par les deux bouts. He cannot hold a candle to you, il vous est très inférieur. **2.** *Pyr:* Roman candle, chandelle romaine. **candle-grease,**

s. Suif m. **candle-power,** s. Bougie f.

Candlemas, s. *Ecc:* La Chandeleur.

candlestick, s. Chandelier m. Flat candlestick, bougeoir m.

candour, s. Franchise f, bonne foi, sincérité f.

candy, v.tr. Faire candir. **candied,** a. Candi; confit.

cane¹, s. (a) Canne f, jonc m. Raspberry cane, tige f de framboisier. (b) (Walking-stick) Canne. Malacca cane, (canne de) jonc. (c) (For chastisement) Canne. To get the cane, être fouetté. **cane(-bottomed) chair,** s. Chaise cannée. **cane-sugar,** s. Sucre m de canne.

cane², v.tr. **1.** Battre, frapper, (qn) à coups de canne. **2.** Canner (une chaise). **caning,** s. *Sch:* Correction f.

canine. 1. a. Canin; de chien. **2.** s. Canine (tooth), canine f.

canister, s. Boîte f (en fer blanc).

canker¹, s. **1.** Chancre m. **2.** F: Influence corruptrice; plaie f.

canker², v.tr. (a) Ronger. (b) Corrompre (une âme). **cankered,** a. Atteint par le chancre; rongé.

cannibal, s. & a. Cannibale (mf); anthropophage (mf).

cannibalism, s. Cannibalisme m, anthropophagie f.

cannon¹, s. **1.** Canon m; pièce f d'artillerie. **2.** *Bill:* Carambolage m. **cannon-ball,** s. Boulet m. **cannon-fodder,** s F: Chair f à canon.

cannon², v.i. **1.** *Bill:* Caramboler. **2.** To cannon into s.o., heurter violemment qn.

cannonade, s. Canonnade f.

canny, a. Prudent, finaud.

canoe, s. **1.** *Sp:* Périssoire f. **2.** (Of savages) Pirogue f.

canon¹, s. **1.** (a) Canon law, droit canon. (b) Règle f, critère m. **2.** *Mus:* Canon.

canon², s. *Ecc:* Chanoine m.

canonize, v.tr. *Ecc:* Canoniser.

canopy, s. Dais m; baldaquin m (de lit); (over doorway) auvent m, marquise f. F: The canopy of heaven, la voûte du ciel.

cant¹, s. (a) Inclinaison f, dévers m. (b) To have a c., pencher.

cant². 1. v.tr. Incliner. **2.** v.i. (a) S'incliner. (b) Pencher.

cant³. 1. s. (a) Jargon m. (b) Langage m hypocrite. **2.** a. Cant phrase, cliché m.

cantankerous, a. Revêche, acariâtre.

cantankerousness, s Humeur f revêche, acariâtre.

cantata, s. *Mus:* Cantate f

canteen, s. **1.** Cantine f. **2.** *Mil:* Bidon m. **3.** Canteen of cutlery, service m de table en coffre.

canter¹, s. *Equit:* Petit galop. *Rac:* To win in a canter, arriver bon premier.

canter², v.i. Aller au petit galop.

Canterbury. *Pr.n.* Cantorbéry m. Canterbury bell, campanule f à grosses fleurs

canticle, *s.* Cantique *m.*

canting, *a.* Hypocrite.

canto, *s.* Chant *m.*

canton, *s.* Canton *m.*

cantonment, *s.* Cantonnement *m.*

canvas, *s.* **1.** *Tex:* (Grosse) toile; toile à voiles, toile de tente. *Mil:* **Under canvas,** sous la tente. **2.** *Art:* A fine *c.*, une belle toile.

canvass¹, *s.* Sollicitation *f* de suffrages.

canvass², *v.tr.* Solliciter (des suffrages).

canvassing, *s.* Sollicitation *f* (de suffrages).

canvasser, *s.* *Com:* Placier *m* (de marchandises). *Pol:* Courtier électoral.

canyon, *s.* Cañon *m*; gorge profonde.

caoutchouc, *s.* Caoutchouc *m.*

cap¹, *s.* **1.** Bonnet *m*; (*with peak*) casquette *f*; toque *f* (de jockey); képi *m* (de militaire). **Skull cap,** calotte *f.* **Cap of liberty,** bonnet phrygien. **Cap and bells,** marotte *f.* *F:* **To come cap in hand,** se présenter le bonnet à la main. *F:* **To set one's cap at a man,** entreprendre la conquête d'un homme. **If the cap fits, wear it!** qui se sent morveux se mouche! **2.** *Tchn:* Chapeau *m* (de protection); capuchon *m* (de porte-plume à réservoir). **3.** *Exp:* Amorce *f.*

cap², *v.tr.* **1.** Coiffer. **2.** Coiffer, couronner (*sth. with sth.,* qch. de qch.). **3.** *F:* **To cap it all,** pour comble.

capability, *s.* Capacité *f* (pour faire qch.); faculté *f* (de faire qch.).

capable, *a.* **1.** Capable (*of sth.,* de qch.). **2.** Susceptible (d'amélioration). **-ably,** *adv.* Avec compétence.

capacious, *a.* Vaste, spacieux; ample.

capaciousness, *s.* Amples proportions *fpl.*

capacity, *s.* **1.** (*a*) Contenance *f* (d'un tonneau). (*b*) Rendement *m* (d'une locomotive). **Seating capacity,** nombre *m* de places. **House filled to capacity,** salle comble. **2.** Capacité (*for,* pour). *C.* **for doing sth.,** aptitude *f* à faire qch.

cape¹, *s.* *Cost:* Pèlerine *f*, cape *f.*

cape², *s.* Cap *m*, promontoire *m.* **Cape Colony,** la colonie du Cap.

caper¹, *s.* *Bot:* Câpre *f.*

caper², *s.* Entrechat *m*, cabriole *f*, gambade *f.*

caper³, *v.i.* **To caper** (about), faire des entrechats, des cabrioles; gambader.

capillary, *a.* Capillaire.

capital¹, *s.* *Arch:* Chapiteau *m.*

capital². **I.** *a.* **1.** Capital, -aux. **Capital letter,** *s.* **capital,** (lettre) capitale, (lettre) majuscule (*f*). **Capital town,** *s.* **capital,** (ville) capitale (*f*). **2.** *Jur:* *C.* **punishment,** peine capitale. **3.** It is **of capital importance,** c'est de la plus haute importance. **4.** **Capital!** fameux! **-ally,** *adv.* Admirablement (bien). **II. capital,** *s.* *Fin:* Capital *m*, capitaux *mpl*, fonds *mpl.* **To make capital out of sth.,** profiter de qch.

capitalism, *s.* Capitalisme *m.*

capitalist, *s.* Capitaliste *mf.*

capitalize, *v.tr.* Capitaliser.

capitulate, *v.i.* Capituler.

capitulation, *s.* Capitulation *f*, reddition *f.*

capon, *s.* *Cu:* Chapon *m*, poulet *m.*

caprice, *s.* **1.** Caprice *m*, lubie *f.* **2.** *Mus:* Caprice.

capricious, *a.* Capricieux. **-ly,** *adv.* Capricieusement.

capriciousness, *s.* Humeur capricieuse, inégale.

Capricorn, *s.* *Astr:* Le Capricorne.

capsicum, *s.* *Cu:* Piment *m*, poivron *m.*

capsize. **1.** *v.i.* Chavirer. **2.** *v.tr.* Faire chavirer. **capsizing,** *s.* Chavirement *m.*

capstan, *s.* Cabestan *m.*

capsule, *s.* Capsule *f.*

captain¹, *s.* **1.** (*a*) Chef *m*, capitaine *m.* (*b*) *Sp:* Chef d'équipe. **2.** (*Rank*) Capitaine *m.* **Group captain,** colonel *m.*

captain², *v.tr.* *Sp:* **To** *c.* **a team,** mener une équipe.

captaincy, *s.* Grade *m* de capitaine. **To obtain one's captaincy,** passer capitaine.

caption, *s.* (*In book*) En-tête *m.* *Cin:* Sous-titre *m.* *Journ:* Rubrique *f.*

captious, *a.* **1.** Captieux, insidieux. **2.** (*Of pers.*) Pointilleux, chicaneur, -euse, vétilleux. **-ly,** *adv.* Pointilleusement.

captivate, *v.tr.* Charmer, captiver. **captivating,** *a.* Séduisant; captivant.

captivation, *s.* Séduction *f.*

captive. **1.** *a.* Captif. **2.** *s.* Captif, -ive, prisonnier, -ière.

captivity, *s.* Captivité *f.*

captor, *s.* Celui qui s'est emparé de qn.

capture¹, *s.* Capture *f*, prise *f.*

capture², *v.tr.* Capturer; prendre (*from,* sur).

Capuchin, *s.* *Ecc:* Capucin, -e.

car, *s.* **1.** *Lit:* Char *m.* **2.** (Motor) car, automobile *f.*

carafe, *s.* Carafe *f.*

caramel, *s.* **1.** Caramel *m.* **2.** Bonbon *m* au caramel.

carapace, *s.* *Crust:* Carapace *f*; bouclier *m.*

carat, *s.* *Meas:* Carat *m.* **Eighteen-carat gold,** or au titre 750.

caravan, *s.* **1.** Caravane *f.* **2.** *Veh:* Roulotte *f.*

caravanserai, *s.* Caravansérail *m.*

caraway, *s.* *Bot:* Carvi *m.*

carbide, *s.* *Ch:* Carbure *m.*

carbine, *s.* Carabine *f.*

carbolic, *a.* *Ch:* Phénique. *Com:* **Carbolic acid,** phénol *m.*

carbon, *s.* **1.** *Ch:* Carbone *m.* **2.** *Typewr:* (*a*) Papier *m* carbone. (*b*) = CARBON-COPY.

carbon-copy, *s.* *Typewr:* Copie *f*, double *m*, au (papier) carbone. **carbon paper,** *s.* *Typewr:* Papier *m* carbone.

carbonate, *s.* *Ch:* Carbonate *m.*

carbonic, *a.* *Ch:* Carbonique. **Carbonic acid gas,** anhydride *m* carbonique.

carbonize, *v.tr.* Carboniser; *I.C.E:* carburer.

carboy, *s.* Tourie *f*; bonbonne *f*.

carbuncle, *s.* **1.** *Lap:* Escarboucle *f*. **2.** *Med:* Anthrax *m*; bourgeon *m*.

carburettor, *s.* *I.C.E:* Carburateur *m*.

carcase, *s.* *F:* (i) Cadavre *m*; (ii) corps *m*. *F:* To save one's carcase, sauver sa peau.

card¹, *s.* **1.** (Playing-)oard, carte *f* (à jouer). *F:* To play one's cards well, bien jouer son jeu. To lay one's cards on the table, mettre cartes sur table. To have a card up one's sleeve, avoir encore une ressource. It is (quite) on the cards that, il est bien possible que. He's a queer card, c'est un drôle de type. He's a knowing card, c'est une fine mouche. He's a card, c'est un original. **2.** (*a*) (Visiting-)oard, carte (de visite). (*b*) Admission card, carte, billet *m*, d'entrée. (*c*) *Com:* (Index-)oard, (carte-)fiche *f*. **card-case,** *s.* Porte-cartes *m* *inv.* **card index¹,** *s.* Fichier *m*; classeur *m*. **card-index²,** *v.tr.* Mettre sur fiches. **card-sharper,** *s.* Tricheur *m*; bonneteur *m*. **card-table,** *s.* Table *f* de jeu.

card², *v.tr.* Mettre (des notes) sur fiche.

cardboard, *s.* Carton *m*.

cardiac, *a.* *Med:* Cardiaque.

cardigan, *s.* Gilet *m* de tricot.

cardinal, I. *a.* Cardinal, -aux. The cardinal numbers, les nombres cardinaux. II **cardinal,** *s.* Cardinal *m*.

care¹, *s.* **1.** Souci *m*, inquiétude *f.* **2.** Soin(s) *m(pl)*, attention *f*, ménagement *m*. To take care in doing sth., apporter du soin à faire qch. To take care not to do sth., se garder, prendre garde, de faire qch. Take care! faites attention! prenez garde! *To take c. of one's health,* ménager sa santé. That matter will take care of itself, cela s'arrangera tout seul. **3.** Soin(s), charge *f*, tenue *f*. Care of Mrs X, c/o Mrs X, aux bons soins de Mme X. Want of care, incurie *f*, négligence *f*. **care-free,** *a.* Libre de soucis; insouciant; sans souci. **care-taker,** *s.* Concierge *mf* (de maison); gardien *m* (d'un musée). **care-worn,** *a.* Rongé par le chagrin.

care², *v.i.* Se soucier, s'inquiéter, se préoccuper (*for, about,* de). *I don't c. what he says,* peu m'importe ce qu'il dit. Not that I care, non pas que ça me fasse quelque chose. For all I care, pour (tout) ce que ça me fait. I don't care! ça m'est égal! **2.** To care for invalids, soigner les malades. **3.** To care for s.o., aimer qn. *He doesn't c. for her,* elle ne lui plaît pas. If you care to, si le cœur vous en dit.

careen. **1.** *v.tr.* (*a*) Abattre en carène. (*b*) Caréner (un navire); nettoyer la carène (d'un navire). **2.** *v.i.* Donner de la bande.

career¹, *s.* **1.** Course *f*. To stop in mid career, rester en (beau) chemin. **2.** Carrière *f*.

career², *v.i.* To career along, être en pleine course.

careful, *a.* **1.** Soigneux (*of*, de); attentif (*of*, à). *Be c. of it!* ayez-en soin! Be careful! prenez garde! faites attention! **2.** Prudent, circonspect. **-fully,** *adv.* **1.** Soigneusement; attentivement. **2.** Prudemment.

carefulness, *s.* **1.** Soin *m*, attention *f*. **2.** Prudence *f*.

careless, *a.* **1.** (*a*) Insouciant (*of, about,* de); nonchalant. (*b*) *C. mistake,* faute d'inattention. **2.** Négligent; sans soin. **-ly,** *adv.* Avec insouciance; négligemment; sans soin.

carelessness, *s.* **1.** (*a*) Insouciance *f*. (*b*) Inattention *f*. **2.** Manque *m* de soin; négligence *f*.

caress¹, *s.* Caresse *f*.

caress², *v.tr.* Caresser. **caressing,** *a.* Caressant.

caret, *s.* *Typ:* Signe *m* d'omission.

cargo, *s.* *Nau:* Cargaison *f*, chargement *m*. **cargo-boat,** *s.* Cargo *m*.

Caribbean, *a.* Caribbean Sea, mer des Caraïbes

caribou, *s.* *Z:* Caribou *m*, *pl.* -ous.

caricature¹, *s.* Caricature *f*, charge *f*.

caricature², *v.tr.* Caricaturer. *Th:* To caricature a part, charger un rôle.

caricaturist, *s.* Caricaturiste *m*.

carillon, *s.* *Mus:* Carillon *m*.

carking, *a.* Carking care, soucis rongeurs.

carman, *s.* Camionneur *m*, charretier *m*.

Carmelite, *s.* Carme *m*; carmélite *f*.

carmine. **1.** *s.* Carmin *m*. **2.** *a.* Carminé; carmin *inv*.

carnage, *s.* Carnage *m*.

carnal, *a.* **1.** Charnel. **2.** Mondain.

carnation¹. (*a*) *s.* Incarnat *m*. (*b*) *a.* (Teint) incarnat, incarnadin.

carnation², *s.* *Bot:* Œillet *m*.

carnival, *s.* Carnaval *m*, *pl.* -als

carnivora, *s.pl.* *Z:* Carnassiers *m*.

carnivorous, *a.* **1.** (*Of animal*) Carnassier. **2.** (*Of plant*) Carnivore

carol¹, *s.* (*a*) Chant *m*. Christmas carol, noël *m*. (*b*) Tire-lire *m* (de l'alouette)

carol², *v.i. & tr.* (*a*) Chanter (joyeusement). (*b*) (*Of lark*) Tire-lirer.

carotid, *a. & s.* *Anat:* Carotide (*f*).

carousal, *s.* B(e)uverie *f*; *F:* bombe *f*

carouse, *v.i.* Faire la fête, *F:* la bombe.

carp¹, *s.* *Ich:* Carpe *f*.

carp², *v.i.* To c. at sth., trouver à redire à qch. **carping¹,** *a.* Chicanier. **carping²,** *s.* Critique (malveillante).

carpenter, *s.* Charpentier *m*; menuisier *m* en bâtiments.

carpentry, *s.* **1.** Charpenterie *f*. **2.** Charpente *f*

carpet¹, *s.* Tapis *m*. Brussels carpet, moquette *f* de Bruxelles. *F:* To be on the carpet, être sur la .ellette **carpet-slippers,** *s.pl.* Pantoufles *f* en tapisserie. **carpet-sweeper,** *s.* Balai *m* mécanique.

carpet², *v.tr.* Recouvrir d'un tapis. **carpeted,** *a.* Couvert d'un tapis. *Slope c. with*

flowers, pente tapissée de fleurs. **carpeting,** s. F: Semonce f.
carriage, s. **I.** Port m, transport m. *Com:* Carriage free, franc de port; franco. Carriage forward, (en) port dû. **2.** Port, maintien m. **3.** (a) *Veh:* Voiture f; équipage m, attelage m. Carriage and pair, voiture à deux chevaux. (b) *Rail:* Voiture, wagon m. **4.** *Artil:* (Gun-)carriage, affût m. **carriage-builder,** s. Carrossier m. **carriage-drive,** s. Avenue f pour voitures; grande avenue. **carriage-entrance,** s. Porte cochère. **carriage-window,** s. Glace f (de voiture).
carrier, s. **I.** (a) Porteur, -euse. (b) *Com:* Camionneur m, roulier m. **2.** (Luggage-)carrier, porte-bagages m. inv. **3.** *Navy:* Aircraft carrier, (navire m) porte-avions m inv, **carrier-pigeon,** pigeon voyageur.
carrion, s. Charogne f.
carrot, s. *Hort:* Carotte f
carroty, a. F: Roux, f. rousse.
carry, v.tr. **I.** Porter; transporter, camionner. **2.** Conduire (le son); amener (l'eau). **3.** *Liberty carried to the point of effrontery,* licence poussée jusqu'au cynisme. To carry sth. into effect, mettre qch. à exécution. **4.** Emporter (une position) d'assaut. To carry all before one, vaincre toutes les résistances. To carry one's hearers with one, entraîner son auditoire. To carry one's point, imposer sa manière de voir. **5.** (i) Adopter, (ii) faire adopter (une proposition). **6.** Porter sur soi. To carry authority, avoir de l'autorité. **7.** Porter, supporter. **8.** *Abs. His voice carries well*, il a une voix qui porte bien. **carry along,** v.tr. Emporter, entraîner. **carry away,** v.tr. **I.** = CARRY OFF **I. 2.** *Carried away by his feelings*, entraîné par ses émotions. **carry off,** v.tr. **I.** Emporter (qch.); emmener, enlever (qn). **2.** To c. off the prize, remporter le prix. **3.** F: To carry it off, faire passer la chose. **carry on. I.** v.tr. Poursuivre; continuer; exercer (un commerce); entretenir (une correspondance); soutenir (une conversation). **2.** v.i. (a) F: Se comporter. (b) F: She carried on dreadfully, elle nous a fait une scène terrible. **carry out,** v.tr. Mettre à exécution; effectuer. **carry through.** Mener à bonne fin. **carrying,** s. **I.** Port m, transport m. **2.** Adoption f, vote m.
cart¹, s. Charrette f. F: To put the cart before the horse, mettre la charrue devant les bœufs. P: To be in the cart, être dans de beaux draps. **cart-horse,** s. Cheval m de (gros) trait. **cart-load,** s. Charretée f, voiturée f (of, de). **cart-shed,** s. Remise f. **cart-wheel,** s. Roue f de charrette.
cart², v.tr. Charrier, charroyer.
cartage, s. Charroi m, charriage m.
carter, s. Charretier m, roulier m.
cartful, s. Charretée f.
Carthusian, a. & s. Chartreux, -euse.
cartilage, s. Cartilage m.

cartilaginous, a. Cartilagineux.
carton, s. Carton m.
cartoon, s. **I.** *Art:* Carton m. **2.** *Journ:* Dessin m (humoristique ou satirique).
cartridge, s. Cartouche f. To fire blank cartridge, tirer à blanc. **cartridge-belt,** s. Ceinture-cartouchière f **cartridge-paper,** s. Papier fort.
carve, v.tr. **I.** Sculpter, graver, ciseler. To carve one's way, se tailler un chemin. **2.** Découper (la viande). **carving,** s. **I.** *Art:* Sculpture f, gravure f, ciselure f. **2.** Découpage m de la viande. **carving-fork,** s. Fourchette f à découper. **carving-knife,** s. Couteau m à découper.
cascade¹, s. Chute f d'eau; cascade f.
cascade², v.i. Tomber en cascade; cascader.
case¹, s. **I.** Cas m. *Jur:* A case in point, un cas d'espèce. *If that is the c.,* s'il en est ainsi. *That is often the c.*, cela arrive souvent. It is a case for the doctor, c'est affaire f au médecin. In any case, en tout cas; dans tous les cas. Just in case, à tout hasard. In most cases, en général. **2.** *Med:* (a) Cas. (b) F: Malade mf; blessé, -e. **3.** *Jur:* (a) Cause f, affaire f; réclamation f. **4.** *Gram:* Cas.
case², s. **I.** Case of goods, caisse f de marchandises; colis m. **2.** (a) Étui m; écrin m (pour bijoux). (b) (Display) case, vitrine f.
case-hardened, a. F: Endurci.
casement, s. Châssis m de fenêtre à deux battants. **casement-window,** s. Croisée f.
cash¹, s. Espèces fpl; argent comptant. To be out of cash, n'être pas en fonds; F: être à sec. Hard cash espèces sonnantes. Cash down, argent (au) comptant. Cash price, prix au comptant. Cash with order, payable à la commande. **cash-book,** s. Livre m de caisse. **cash-box,** s. Caisse f. **cash-desk,** s. Caisse f. **cash-register,** s. Caisse enregistreuse.
cash², v.tr. Toucher (un chèque).
cashier¹, s. Caissier, -ière. Cashier's desk, caisse f.
cashier², v.tr. Casser (un officier).
Cashmere. I. *Pr.n.* Le Cachemire. **2.** s. *Tex:* Cachemire m.
casino, s. Casino m.
cask, s. Barrique f, fût m, tonneau m.
casket, s. Coffret m, cassette f.
Caspian, a. The Caspian Sea, la mer Caspienne.
cassava, s. Cassave f, manioc m.
cassock, s. *Ecc:* Soutane f.
cassowary, s. *Orn:* Casoar m.
cast¹, s. **I.** (a) Jet m (d'une pierre); coup m (de dés); lancer m (du filet). (b) *Fish:* Bas m de ligne. **2.** Plaster cast, moulage m au plâtre. To take a c. of sth., mouler qch. **3.** Cast of mind, tournure f d'esprit. Cast of features, physionomie f. **4.** To have a cast in one's eye, avoir une tendance à loucher. **5.** Addition f (de chiffres). **6.** *Th:* Distribution f (des rôles); la troupe.

cast², *v.tr.* **I.** (*a*) Jeter, lancer (une pierre); projeter (une ombre). **2.** *Fish:* To c. the line, lancer la ligne. **3.** Donner (un suffrage). **4.** To cast (up) figures, additionner des chiffres. **5.** *Th:* To cast a play, distribuer les rôles d'une pièce. To c. s.o. for a part, assigner un rôle à qn. **cast aside,** *v.tr.* Se défaire de (qch.); mettre (qch.) de côté. **cast away,** *v.tr.* (*a*) Jeter au loin; rejeter. (*b*) *Nau:* To be cast away, faire naufrage. **cast down,** *v.tr.* (*a*) Baisser (les yeux). (*b*) To be cast down, être abattu, déprimé. **cast in,** *v.tr.* To cast in one's lot with s.o., partager le sort de qn. **cast off.** *v.tr.* (*a*) Rejeter. (*b*) Cast-off clothing, vêtements *mpl* de rebut; défroque *f*. **cast up,** *v.tr.* **I.** To cast sth. up to s.o., reprocher qch. à qn. **2.** Flotsam cast up on the shore, épaves rejetées sur le rivage. **cast³,** *a.* Cast iron, fonte *f* de fer; (fer de) fonte. **casting¹,** *a.* The chairman has the c. vote, la voix du président est prépondérante. **casting²,** *s.* *Metall:* Pièce *f* de fonte.

castanets, *s.pl.* Castagnettes *f*.

castaway, *s.* Naufragé, -e.

caste, *s.* Caste *f*. *F:* To lose caste, déroger (à son rang).

castellated, *a.* Crénelé.

castigate, *v.tr.* Châtier, corriger.

castigation, *s.* Châtiment *m*, correction *f*.

Castile. *Pr.n.* *Geog:* La Castille. *Com:* Castile soap, savon blanc.

Castilian, *a. & s.* Castillan, -e.

castle¹, *s.* **I.** Château (fort). *F:* To build castles in the air, bâtir des châteaux en Espagne. **2.** *Chess:* Tour *f*.

castle², *v.tr.* *Chess:* Roquer.

castor, *s.* **I.** Saupoudroir *m*. **2.** Roulette *f* (de fauteuil).

castor oil, *s.* Huile *f* de ricin.

casual, *a.* (*a*) Fortuit, accidentel. Casual labourer, homme à l'heure. (*b*) *F:* Insouciant. **-ally,** *adv.* (*a*) Fortuitement, en passant. (*b*) Négligemment.

casualty, *s.* **I.** Accident *m*. Casualty ward, salle des accidentés. **2.** Mort, -e; blessé, -e.

casuistry, *s.* Casuistique *f*.

cat, *s.* **I.** (*a*) Chat, *f*. chatte. Tom cat, matou *m*. *F:* To be like a cat on hot bricks, être sur des épines. To let the cat out of the bag, éventer la mèche. They quarrel like cat and dog, ils s'accordent comme chien et chat. It would make a cat laugh, c'est à mourir de rire. *Prov:* A cat may look at a king, un chien regarde bien un évêque. When the cat's away the mice will play, le chat parti les souris dansent. (*b*) *F:* An old cat, une vieille chipie. **2.** *Z:* The (great) cats, les grands félins. **3.** = CAT-O'-NINE-TAILS. **cat-burglar,** *s.* *F:* Monte-en-l'air *m inv*. **cat-o'-nine-tails,** *s.* *Nau:* Chat *m* à neuf queues. **cat's-eye,** *s.* *Lap:* Œil-de-chat *m*. **cat's-meat,** *s.* Mou *m*, tripes *fpl*, abats *mpl*. **cat's-paw,** *s.* **I.** Petite bouffée de vent.

2. *F:* To be made a c.-p. of, tirer les marrons du feu (pour qn).

cataclysm, *s.* Cataclysme *m*.

catacombs, *s.pl.* Catacombes *f*.

catalepsy, *s.* *Med:* Catalepsie *f*.

cataleptic, *a. & s.* *Med:* Cataleptique (*mf*)

catalogue¹, *s.* Catalogue *m*, liste *f*. Subjec catalogue, catalogue raisonné.

catalogue², *v.tr.* Cataloguer.

catalysis, *s.* *Ch:* Catalyse *f*.

cataplasm, *s.* *Med:* Cataplasme *m*.

catapult¹, *s.* **I.** Fronde *f*. **2.** *Av:* Catapult *f* (de lancement).

catapult², *v.tr.* *Av:* Lancer (un avion).

cataract, *s.* Cataracte *f*.

catarrh, *s.* *Med:* Catarrhe *m*.

catastrophe, *s.* Catastrophe *f*; désastre *m*.

catastrophic, *a.* Désastreux.

catcall, *s.* *Th:* (Coup *m* de) sifflet *m*.

catch¹, *s.* **I.** Prise *f*. **2.** (*a*) *Fish:* Prise, pêche *f*. To have a good c., faire (une) bonne pêche. (*b*) *F:* It's no great catch, ce n'est pas le Pérou. **3.** (*On door*) Loquet *m*. **4.** There's a catch in it, c'est une attrape. **5.** *Mus:* Chant *m* à reprises; canon *m*.

catch², *v.* **I.** *v.tr.* **I.** (*a*) Attraper, prendre. *Fish:* To catch nothing, revenir bredouille. (*b*) *F:* Catch me (doing such a thing)! il n'y a pas de danger! (*c*) We were caught in the storm, l'orage nous a surpris. **2.** (*a*) Saisir (des sons); rencontrer (le regard de qn). (*b*) I didn't quite c. that, pardon? plaît-il? (*c*) Accrocher, happer. **3.** Attraper (une maladie); contracter (une habitude). **4.** You'll catch it! votre affaire est bonne! **5.** *F:* (*Entrap*) Attraper. II. **catch,** *v.i.* **I.** To catch at sth., s'accrocher à qch. **2.** (*a*) (*Of cog-wheel*) Mordre; (*of door-bolt*) s'engager. (*b*) (*Of fire*) Prendre. **3.** *Cu:* To catch in the pan, attacher. **catch on,** *v.i.* *F:* Prendre, réussir. **catch out,** *v.tr.* *F:* Prendre (qn) sur le fait. **catch up,** *v.tr.* To catch s.o. up, *v.i.* To catch up with s.o., rattraper qn. **catching,** *a.* Contagieux, infectieux.

catchpenny, *s.* Attrape-sou *m*.

catchword, *s.* *F:* Scie *f*, rengaine *f*.

catchy, *a.* Entraînant.

catechism, *s.* Catéchisme *m*.

catechize, *v.tr.* **I.** Catéchiser. **2.** *F:* Poser une série de questions à.

categoric(al), *a.* Catégorique. **-ally,** *adv.* Catégoriquement.

category, *s.* Catégorie *f*.

cater, *v.i.* To c. for s.o., approvisionner qn. To cater for all tastes, pourvoir à tous les goûts. **catering,** *s.* Approvisionnement *m*.

caterer, *s.* Approvisionneur; pourvoyeur.

caterpillar, *s.* Chenille *f*.

caterwaul, *v.i.* **I.** Miauler. **2.** *F:* Faire un vrai sabbat. **caterwauling,** *s.* **I.** Miaulements *mpl*. **2.** *F:* Sabbat *m* de chats.

catgut, *s.* Corde *f* de boyau.

cathedral, s. Cathédrale f. **Cathedral town,** ville épiscopale.

Catherine. Pr.n. Catherine f. Pyr: **Catherine wheel,** soleil m; roue f à feu.

catholic. 1. a. (a) Universel. (b) Tolérant. C. taste, goûts éclectiques. 2. a. & s. Ecc: Catholique (mf).

catholicism, s. Catholicisme m.

catkin, s. Bot: Chaton m.

cattle, s. Coll. inv. 1. Bétail m; bestiaux mpl. 2. F: Chevaux mpl. **cattle-shed,** s. Étable f. **cattle-show,** s. Comice m agricole. **cattle-truck,** s. Fourgon m à bestiaux.

cauldron, s. Chaudron m.

cauliflower, s. Chou-fleur m.

caulk, v.tr. Calfater. **caulking,** s. Calfatage m.

cause[1], s. 1. Cause f. 2. Raison f, motif m, sujet m. To have good cause for doing sth., faire qch. à bon droit. 3. (a) Jur: Cause; procès m. (b) F: To take up s.o.'s c., épouser la querelle de qn.

cause[2], v.tr. 1. Causer, occasionner. 2. To cause s.o. to do sth., faire faire qch. à qn.

causeway, s. (a) Chaussée f. (b) Levée f, digue f.

caustic. 1. a. Caustique. C. wit, esprit mordant. 2. s. Pharm: Caustique m. **-ally,** adv. D'un ton mordant.

cauterize, v.tr. Cautériser.

caution[1], s. 1. Précaution f, prévoyance f, prudence f, circonspection f. 2. (a) Avis m, avertissement m. Caution! attention! (b) Réprimande f.

caution[2], v.tr. 1. Avertir; mettre sur ses gardes. 2. Menacer de poursuites à la prochaine occasion.

cautious, a. Circonspect, prudent. **-ly,** adv. Avec circonspection; prudemment.

cautiousness, s. Prudence f.

cavalcade, s. Cavalcade f.

cavalier. 1. s. Cavalier m. 2. a. Cavalier, désinvolte. **-ly,** adv. Cavalièrement.

cavalry, s. Cavalerie f.

cave[1], s. Caverne f, antre m. **cave-man,** s. 1. Anthr: Troglodyte m. 2. F: Homme m à la manière forte.

cave[2], v.i. To cave in. 1. S'effondrer. 2. Céder.

cavern, s. Caverne f.

cavernous, a. Caverneux.

caviar(e), s. Caviar m.

cavil, v.i. Chicaner, ergoter. To c. at sth., pointiller sur qch. **cavilling,** a. Argutieux; chicaneur,-euse.

cavity, s. Cavité f; creux m.

caw[1], s. Croassement m.

caw[2], v.i. Croasser. **cawing,** s. Croassement m.

cayman, s. Rept: Caïman m.

cease[1], s. Without cease, sans cesse.

cease[2], v.tr. & i. 1. Cesser ((from) doing sth., de faire qch.). 2. To cease work, cesser le

travail. **ceasing,** s. Cessation f. Without ceasing, sans arrêt.

ceaseless, a. Incessant; sans arrêt. **-ly,** adv. Sans cesse, sans arrêt.

cedar, s. Bot: Cèdre m.

cede, v.tr. Céder.

cedilla, s. Cédille f.

ceiling, s. Plafond m.

celebrate, v.tr. Célébrer (la mémoire de qn); commémorer (un événement). **celebrated,** a. Célèbre (for, par).

celebration, s. Célébration f, commémoration f.

celebrity, s. Célébrité f.

celerity, s. Célérité f.

celery, s. Hort: Céleri m. Head of celery, pied m de céleri.

celestial. 1. a. Céleste. 2. s. Chinois,-e.

celibacy, s. Célibat m.

celibate. 1. a. (Personne) célibataire; (vie) de célibataire. 2. s. Célibataire mf.

cell, s. 1. Cellule f. 2. El: Élément m (de pile). Dry cell, pile sèche.

cellar, s. Cave f.

'cello, s. Violoncelle m.

cellular, a. Cellulaire.

celluloid, s. Celluloïd(e) m.

cellulose, s. Cellulose f.

Celt, s. Ethn: Celte mf.

Celtic. 1. a. Celtique; celte. 2. s. Ling: Le celtique.

cement[1], s. Ciment m.

cement[2], v.tr. Cimenter.

cemetery, s. Cimetière m.

cenotaph, s. Cénotaphe m.

censer, s. Ecc: Encensoir m.

censor[1], s. Adm: Censeur m. Banned by the c., interdit par la censure.

censor[2], v.tr. To be censored, (of play) passer par la censure; (of letter) passer par le contrôle.

censorious, a. Porté à censurer; sévère (of, upon, pour).

censorship, s. Adm: The Censorship, la censure.

censure[1], s. Censure f, blâme m.

censure[2], v.tr. Censurer.

census, s. Recensement m.

cent, s. 1. I haven't got a red cent, je n'ai pas le sou. 2. Com: Per cent, pour cent.

centaur, s. Myth: Centaure m.

centenarian, a. & s. Centenaire (mf).

centenary, a. & s. (Anniversaire) centenaire (m).

centigrade, a. Centigrade.

centipede, s. Centipède m; F: mille-pattes m inv.

central, a. Central, -aux. **-ally,** adv. Centralement.

centralize, v.tr. Centraliser.

centre[1], s. 1. Centre m; milieu m. In the centre, au centre. Centre of attraction, F: clou m. 2. Attrib. Central, -aux. The centre arch, l'arche centrale.

centre², *v.tr.* Placer au centre. **To centre one's affections on s.o.**, concentrer toute son affection sur qn.

centrifugal, *a.* Centrifuge.

centripetal, *a.* Centripète.

centuple¹, *a. & s.* Centuple (*m*).

centuple², *v.tr.* Centupler.

century, *s.* **1.** Siècle *m.* **In the twentieth century**, au vingtième siècle. **2.** *Cr :* Centaine *f.*

ceramics, *s.pl.* La céramique.

Cerberus. *Pr.n. Myth :* Cerbère *m.*

cereal, *a. & s.* Céréale (*f*).

cerebral, *a.* Cérébral, -aux.

ceremonial. 1. *a.* De cérémonie. **2.** *s.* Cérémonial *m.* **-ally**, *adv.* En grande cérémonie.

ceremonious, *a.* Cérémonieux. **-ly**, *adv.* Cérémonieusement.

ceremony, *s.* Cérémonie *f* **To stand (up)on ceremony**, faire des façons.

cerise, *a. & s.* (*Colour*) Cerise (*m*) *inv.*

certain, *a.* Certain. **1.** (*a*) **This much is certain, that . . .**, ce qu'il y a de certain, c'est que. (*b*) **To be certain of sth.**, être certain, sûr, de qch. **I am almost c. of it**, j'en ai la presque certitude. (*c*) **To know sth. for certain**, être bien sûr de qch. (*d*) **To make certain of sth.**, (i) s'assurer de qch. ; (ii) s'assurer qch. **2. There are c. things**, il y a certaines choses. **C. people**, (de) certaines gens ; certains *mpl.* **-ly**, *adv.* (*a*) Certainement ; certes ; assurément ; à coup sûr. (*b*) (*Assent*) Assurément ; parfaitement.

certainty, *s.* (*a*) Certitude *f* ; chose certaine. **Of a certainty**, à coup sûr. **To bet on a certainty**, parier à coup sûr. (*b*) Certitude (morale) ; conviction *f.*

certificate¹, *s.* **1.** Certificat *m*, attestation *f.* *Fin :* Titre *m* (d'actions). **2. Certificate (of competency)**, certificat ; diplôme *m*, brevet *m.* **3.** Acte *m.* **Birth certificate**, acte de naissance. **4. Savings certificate**, bon *m.* d'épargne.

certificate², *v.tr.* Diplômer, breveter. **certificated**, *a.* Diplômé, titré.

certify, *v.tr.* **1.** (*a*) Certifier, déclarer, attester. **To c. a death**, constater un décès. (*b*) Authentiquer (un document). (*c*) Diplômer, breveter. **2.** *v.ind.tr.* **To certify to sth.**, attester qch.

certitude, *s.* Certitude *f.*

cessation, *s.* Cessation *f*, arrêt *m.*

cession, *s* Cession *f* ; abandon *m.*

cesspool, *s.* Fosse *f* d'aisance. *F :* **A cesspool of iniquity**, un cloaque de vice.

cetacean, *a. & s.* Cétacé (*m*).

Ceylon. *Pr.n. Geog :* Ceylan *m.*

chafe. 1. *v.tr.* (*a*) Frictionner, dégourdir (les membres). (*b*) User, échauffer, par le frottement ; écorcher (la peau). **2.** *v.i.* (*a*) S'user par le frottement ; (*of rope*) s'érailler, raguer. (*b*) *F :* **To chafe at sth.**, s'énerver de qch.

chafing, *s.* **1.** Friction *f.* **2.** (*a*) Écorchement *m* (de la peau). (*b*) Usure *f*, frottement

m (d'une corde). **chafing-dish**, *s Cu :* Réchaud *m* (de table).

chaff¹, *s.* **1.** (*a*) Balle(s) *f* (du grain). (*b*) *Husb :* Paille hachée. **2.** *F :* Raillerie *f* ; persiflage *m.*

chaff², *v.tr.* Railler, taquiner ; persifler.

chaffer, *v.i.* Marchander, barguigner.

chaffinch, *s.* *Orn :* Pinson *m.*

chagrin¹, *s.* Chagrin *m*, dépit *m.*

chagrin², *v.tr.* Chagriner, dépiter.

chain¹, *s.* (*a*) Chaîne *f* ; chaînette *f.* (*b*) Chaîne (de montagnes). **chain-armour**, *s. Archeol :* Cotte *f* de mailles. **chain-stores**, *s.* Grand magasin à succursales.

chain², *v.tr.* **1. To chain sth. to sth.**, attacher qch. à qch. par une chaîne. **2. To chain sth. down**, retenir qch. par une chaîne. **To chain s.o. (down)**, enchaîner qn. **Chained up**, à la chaîne. **3.** Fermer (un port, etc.) avec des chaînes. **4.** *Surv :* Chaîner (un champ).

chair¹, *s.* (*a*) Chaise *f*, siège *m.* **To take a chair**, s'asseoir. (*b*) *Sch :* Chaire *f.* (*c*) **To be in the chair**, occuper le fauteuil présidentiel ; présider. **To take the chair**, prendre la présidence. **Chair! Chair!** à l'ordre ! à l'ordre ! **chair-back**, *s* Dossier *m* de chaise.

chair², *v.tr.* Porter (qn) en triomphe.

chairman, *s.* Président, -ente.

chairmanship, *s.* Présidence *f.*

chalcedony, *s.* *Lap :* Calcédoine *f.*

Chaldea. *Pr.n. A.Geog :* La Chaldée.

chalice, *s.* *Ecc :* Calice *m.*

chalk¹, *s.* **1.** Craie *f.* **French chalk**, stéatite *f.* **2.** *F :* **Not by a long chalk**, tant s'en faut.

chalk², *v.tr.* Marquer (qch.) à la craie.

chalky, *a.* **1.** Crayeux. **2.** (Teint) pâle.

challenge¹, *s.* **1.** (*a*) Défi *m* ; provocation *f.* (*b*) Interpellation *f.* sommation *f* (par une sentinelle) ; qui-vive *m inv.* **2.** Récusation *f* (du jury).

challenge², *v.tr.* **1.** (*a*) **To c. s.o. to fight**, défier qn à un combat ; provoquer qn en duel. **To c. s.o. to do sth.**, défier qn de faire qch. (*b*) *Mil :* **To challenge s.o.**, interpeller qn. **2.** (*a*) Disputer, relever (une affirmation). (*b*) Récuser (un juré). **3.** Provoquer (l'admiration). **challenging**, *a.* Provocateur, -trice.

challenger, *s.* Provocateur, -trice.

chamber, *s.* **1.** (Bed-)chamber, chambre *f* (à coucher). **2. Chamber of Commerce**, chambre de commerce. **3.** *Tchn :* Chambre. **chamber-music**, *s.* Musique *f* de chambre.

chamberlain, *s.* Chambellan *m.*

chambermaid, *s.* Femme *f* de chambre.

chameleon, *s.* *Rept :* Caméléon *m.*

chamois, *s.* Chamois *m.* **chamois-leather**, *s.* (Peau *f* de) chamois *m.*

champ, *v.tr.* Mâcher bruyamment ; ronger (le mors).

Champagne. 1. *Pr.n. Geog :* La Champagne. **2.** *s.* Vin *m* de Champagne ; champagne *m.*

champion[1], *s.* Champion *m.*

champion[2], *v.tr.* Soutenir, défendre.

championship, *s.* **1.** *Sp:* Championnat *m.* **2.** Défense *f* (d'une cause).

chance[1], *s.* **1.** (*a*) Chance *f*, hasard *m*, sort *m.* By (mere) **chance**, par hasard. *Shall we see you there* **by any chance?** est-ce qu'on vous y verra par extraordinaire? **The chances are that**, il y a fort à parier que. **To do sth. on the off chance**, faire qch. à tout hasard. (*b*) **To have an eye to the main chance**, s'attacher au solide. **2.** Occasion *f.* **Now's your chance!** vous avez beau jeu! **To stand a chance**, avoir des chances de succès. **To take one's chance**, risquer les chances. **3. To take a chance**, encourir un risque. **4.** *Attrib.* Fortuit, accidentel. **Chance comer**, survenant *m.*

chance[2]. **1.** *v.i.* (*a*) *To c. to do sth.*, faire qch. par hasard. *If I c. to find it*, si je viens à le trouver. (*b*) *To chance upon sth.*, trouver qch. par hasard. **2.** *v.tr.* **To chance it**, risquer le coup.

chancel, *s.* *Ecc.Arch:* **1.** Sanctuaire *m.* **2.** Chœur *m.*

chancellor, *s.* Chancelier *m.*

chancery, *s.* **1.** *Jur:* (Court of) Chancery, cour *f* de la chancellerie. **2.** *Box:* Hold in chancery, cravate *f.*

chandelier, *s.* Lustre *m.*

change[1], *s.* **1.** Changement *m*; retour *m* (de la marée); revirement *m* (d'opinion). **To make a change**, effectuer un changement (*in*, à). **For a change**, comme distraction *f*; pour changer. **Change of front**, *F:* volte-face *f inv.* **2.** (*a*) **Change of clothes**, vêtements *mpl* de rechange. (*b*) **Change of horses**, relais *m.* **3.** (*Exchange*) Change *m.* **4.** Monnaie *f.* **Small change**, petite monnaie. *P:* He won't get much change out of me, il perdra ses peines avec moi. **5.** *F:* **To ring the changes** *on a subject*, ressasser un sujet.

change[2]. **1.** *v.tr.* Changer. (*a*) Modifier (ses plans). *F:* **To change one's tune**, changer de ton. **To change the subject**, changer de sujet. (*b*) **To change one's clothes**, *abs.* to change, changer de vêtements; se changer. (*c*) *Rail:* *To c. trains*, *abs.* to change, changer de train. **All change!** tout le monde descend! (*d*) *To c. one thing for another*, échanger une chose contre une autre. **2.** *v.i.* (Se) changer (*into*, en); se modifier. *To c. for the better*, changer en mieux; (*of weather*) tourner au beau. **change about**, *v.i.* Faire volte-face.

changing, *a.* Changeant. **changing-room**, *s.* Vestiaire *m.*

changeable, *a.* (*Of pers.*) Changeant; (*of weather*) variable, inconstant.

changeling, *s.* Enfant changé en nourrice.

channel, *s.* **1.** Lit *m* (d'une rivière). **2.** (*a*) Passe *f*, chenal *m* (d'un port). (*b*) *Geog:* Détroit *m*, canal *m.* **The (English) Channel**, la Manche. **The Channel Islands**, les îles Anglo-normandes. **3.** Canal, conduit *m.* **4.** Voie *f.*

chant[1], *s.* *Mus:* Chant *m.*

chant[2], *v.tr.* *Ecc:* Psalmodier.

chanty, *s.* (Sea-)chanty, chanson *f* de bord.

chaos, *s.* Chaos *m.*

chaotic, *a* Chaotique, désorganisé. **-ally**, *adv.* Sans ordre.

chap[1], *s.* Gerçure *f*, crevasse *f.*

chap[2], *v.tr.* Gercer, crevasser.

chap[3], *s.* Bajoue(s) *f* (d'un cochon). **chap-fallen**, *a.* Penaud, décontenancé.

chap[4], *s.* *F:* Garçon *m*, type *m*, individu *m.* **Old chap**, mon vieux. *A queer c.*, un drôle de corps.

chapel, *s.* (*a*) Chapelle *f.* (*b*) Temple (dissident).

chaperon[1], *s.* Chaperon *m.*

chaperon[2], *v.tr.* Chaperonner.

chaplain, *s.* *Ecc:* Aumônier *m.*

chaplet, *s.* *Ecc:* Chapelet *m.*

chapter, *s.* Chapitre *m.* *F:* **To give chapter and verse**, citer ses autorités. *F:* **A chapter of accidents**, une suite de malheurs.

char[1], *v.i.* *F:* *To go out charring*, aller en journée; faire des ménages.

char[2]. **1.** *v.tr.* Carboniser. **2.** *v.i.* Se carboniser.

char-à-banc, *s.* Autocar *m.*

character, *s.* **1.** *Typ:* Caractère *m*, lettre *f.* **2.** Caractère; marque distinctive. **To be in character with**, s'harmoniser avec. **In his character of**, en (sa) qualité de. **3. Man of (strong) character**, homme de caractère, de volonté. **4.** (*a*) *Of bad c.*, de mauvaise réputation; mal famé. (*b*) *F:* **To give s.o. a good character**, dire du bien de qn. **5.** (*a*) Personnage *m.* (*b*) **A public character**, une personnalité. **A bad character**, un mauvais sujet. *F:* **He's a character**, c'est un type, un original.

characteristic. **1.** *a.* Caractéristique. **2.** *s.* Trait *m*, signe *m*, de caractère, particularité *f.* **-ally**, *adv.* D'une manière caractéristique.

charade, *s.* Charade *f.*

charcoal, *s.* Charbon *m* (de bois). **charcoal-burner**, *s.* Charbonnier *m.*

charge[1], *s.* **1.** (*a*) Charge *f* (d'une cartouche). (*b*) *El:* Charge. **2.** (*a*) Frais *mpl*, prix *m.* **Charge for admittance**, prix des places. *No c. for admission*, entrée gratuite. (*b*) **To be a charge on s.o.**, être à la charge de qn. **3.** (*a*) Commission *f*, devoir *m.* (*b*) Charge; emploi *m*; fonction *f*; (*of clergy*) cure *f.* **4.** (*a*) Garde *f*, soin *m.* **Nurse in charge of a child**, bonne commise à la garde d'un enfant. **To be in charge of sth.**, être préposé à la garde de qch. *Jur:* **To give s.o. in charge**, faire arrêter qn. (*b*) Personne confiée à la garde de qn. **5.** Recommandation *f*, exhortation *f*; résumé *m* (du juge). **6.** *Jur:* Charge; chef *m* d'accusation. **To bring a charge against s.o.**, porter une accusation contre qn. **On a charge of**, sous l'inculpation de. **7.** *Mil:* Charge, attaque *f.*

charge², *v.tr.* **1.** Charger (*with*, de). **2.** To charge s.o. with a crime, imputer un crime à qn. **3.** (*a*) *Com:* Charger. *C. it on the bill*, portez-le sur la note. (*b*) *To c. s.o. a price for sth.*, prendre, demander, un prix à qn pour qch. **4.** *v.tr. & i.* Charger (l'ennemi).

chargeable, *a.* **1.** A la charge (*to*, de). **2.** Imputable (à une cause).

charger, *s.* Cheval *m* de bataille.

chariot, *s.* Char *m.*

charitable, *a.* **1.** Charitable. **2.** De bienfaisance, de charité. **-ably**, *adv.* Charitablement.

charity, *s.* **1.** Charité *f.* *Out of charity*, par charité. **2.** (*a*) Acte *m* de charité. (*b*) Charité, aumônes *fpl.* **3.** Œuvre *f* de bienfaisance, de charité.

charlatan, *s.* Charlatan *m.*

Charles, *Pr.n.* Charles *m.*

charm¹, *s.* **1.** Charme *m* (*against*, contre); sortilège *m*, sort *m.* **2.** (*a*) Amulette *f*, fétiche *m.* (*b*) Breloque *f*; porte-bonheur *m inv.* **3.** Charme, agrément *m.*

charm², *v.tr.* Charmer, enchanter. *He bears a charmed life*, sa vie est sous un charme.

charming, *a.* Charmant, ravissant.

charmer, *s.* Charmeur, -euse.

charnel-house, *s.* Charnier *m*, ossuaire *m.*

chart¹, *s.* **1.** *Nau:* Carte *f* (marine). **2.** (*Of statistics*) Graphique *m*, diagramme *m.*

chart², *v.tr.* *Nau:* Porter sur une carte.

charter¹, *s.* **1.** Charte *f* (d'une ville). **2.** *Nau:* Affrètement *m.*

charter², *v.tr.* *Nau:* Affréter, fréter. **chartered**, *a.* (Compagnie) à charte. *F:* Chartered libertine, fantasque à qui l'on permet tout.

charwoman, *s.* Femme *f* de journée, femme de ménage.

chary, *a.* **1.** Prudent, circonspect. *To be c. of, in, doing sth.*, hésiter à faire qch. **2.** Chary of praise, avare de louanges.

chase¹, *s.* Chasse *f*, poursuite *f.* *To give chase to s.o.*, donner la chasse à qn. *F:* Wild goose chase, poursuite vaine.

chase², *v.tr.* Poursuivre; donner la chasse à.

chase³, *v.tr.* Ciseler. **chasing**, *s.* Ciselure *f.*

chasm, *s.* Gouffre béant.

chassis, *s.* *Aut:* Châssis *m.*

chaste, *a.* Chaste, pudique.

chasten, *v.tr.* (*a*) Châtier, éprouver. (*b*) Rabattre l'orgueil de (qn). **chastened**, *a.* Assagi; radouci.

chastise, *v.tr.* Châtier; infliger une correction à (qn); corriger (un enfant).

chastisement, *s.* Châtiment *m.*

chastity, *s.* Chasteté *f.*

chat¹, *s.* Causerie *f*, causette *f.*

chat², *v.i.* Causer, bavarder.

chattel, *s.* *Jur:* (*a*) Bien *m* meuble. (*b*) *pl.* Objets mobiliers. *F:* Goods and chattels, biens et effets *m.*

chatter¹, *s.* Caquet(age) *m*, jacasserie *f*; bavardage *m.*

chatter², *v.i.* **1.** (*Of birds*) Caqueter; (*of pers.*) bavarder, caqueter. *magpie*, jaser comme une pie. **2.** (*Of teeth*) Claquer. **chattering**, *s.* **1.** = CHATTER¹. **2.** Claquement *m* (des dents).

chatterbox, *s.* Babillard, -arde; grand(e) bavard(e).

chauffeur, *s.* Chauffeur, -euse; conducteur, -trice (d'une auto).

cheap. **1.** *a.* (*a*) (A) bon marché. Cheaper, (à) meilleur marché, moins cher. Dirt cheap, à vil prix; pour rien. *To do sth. on the cheap*, faire qch. à peu de frais. (*b*) De peu de valeur. *F:* To feel cheap, être honteux. *To make oneself cheap*, déroger; se déprécier. **2.** *adv. F:* = CHEAPLY. **-ly**, *adv.* (A) bon marché; à peu de frais. *F:* He got off cheap(ly), il en est quitte à bon compte.

cheapen, *v.tr.* **1.** Diminuer la valeur de (qch.). **2.** *v.i.* Diminuer de prix.

cheapness, *s.* Bon marché; bas prix.

cheat¹, *s.* (*a*) Trompeur, -euse. escroc *m.* (*b*) (*At games*) Tricheur, -euse.

cheat², *v.tr.* **1.** Tromper; frauder. *To cheat s.o. out of sth.*, frustrer qn de qch. **2.** (*At games*) Tricher. **cheating**, *s.* **1.** Tromperie *f*; fourberie *f.* **2.** *Cards:* Tricherie *f.*

check¹, *s.* **1.** (*a*) *Chess:* Échec *m.* 'Check!' "échec au roi!" (*b*) Revers *m*, échec. **2.** Arrêt *m*, pause *f*, anicroche *f.* **3.** Frein *m.* **4.** Contrôle *m.*

check². **1.** *v.tr.* (*a*) *Chess:* Mettre (le roi) en échec. (*b*) Faire échec à; arrêter (une attaque). (*c*) Refouler, retenir. (*d*) Réprimander. (*e*) Vérifier (un compte). **To check (off)**, pointer (des noms sur une liste). **To check (up)** *information*, contrôler des renseignements. **2.** *v.i.* Hésiter, s'arrêter (*at*, devant). **checking**, *s.* **1.** Répression *f.* **2.** Contrôle *m*; vérification *f.*

check³, *s.* *Tex:* Carreau *m*; à carreaux.

checked, *a.* A carreaux; quadrillé.

checkmate¹, *s.* *Chess:* Échec *m* et mat *m.*

checkmate², *v.tr.* **1.** *F:* Faire échec et mat à. **2.** *F:* Déjouer (les projets de qn).

cheek¹, *s.* **1.** Joue *f.* Cheek by jowl with s.o., côte à côte avec qn. **2.** *F:* (*a*) Toupet *m*, effronterie *f*, impudence *f.* (*b*) Impertinences *fpl.* **cheek-bone**, *s.* Pommette *f.*

cheek², *v.tr.* *F:* Faire l'insolent avec.

cheekiness, *s.* *F:* Effronterie *f.*

cheeky, *a.* *F:* Effronté. **-ily**, *adv.* *F:* D'un ton effronté.

cheep¹, *s.* Piaulement *m.*

cheep², *v.i.* Piauler.

cheer¹, *s.* Hourra *m*; *pl.* acclamations *f*, bravos *m.*

cheer². **1.** *v.tr.* (*a*) To cheer s.o. (up), égayer, ragaillardir, qn. (*b*) Acclamer, applaudir. **2.** *v.i.* (*a*) To cheer up, reprendre sa gaieté. Cheer up! courage! (*b*) Pousser des hourras; applaudir. **cheering¹**, *a.* Encourageant, réjouissant. **cheering²**, *s.* Acclamation *f*; applaudissements *mpl.*

cheerful, *a.* Gai; de bonne humeur; (*of room*) d'aspect agréable, riant; (*of news*) réconfortant. **-fully,** *adv.* **1.** Gaiement, allégrement. **2.** De bon cœur; volontiers.

cheerfulness, *s.* (*a*) Gaieté *f*, belle humeur; contentement *m.* (*b*) Air *m* agréable.

cheerio, *int.* P: **1.** A bientôt! **2.** A la vôtre!

cheerless, *a.* Morne, triste, sombre.

cheery, *a.* Joyeux, gai. **-ily,** *adv.* Gaiement.

cheese, *s.* Fromage *m.* **cheese-biscuit,** *s.* Biscuit non sucré. **cheese-paring,** *s.* Parcimonie *f.*

cheesemonger, *s.* Marchand, -e, de fromage.

cheetah, *s.* Z: Guépard *m.*

chef, *s.* Chef *m* de cuisine.

chemical. 1. *a.* Chimique. **2.** *s.pl.* Chemicals, produits *m* chimiques. Com: Drogues *f.*

chemise, *s.* Chemise *f* (de femme).

chemist, *s.* **1.** Pharmacien, -ienne. Chemist's shop, pharmacie *f.* **2.** Chimiste *m.*

chemistry, *s.* Chimie *f.* Inorganic c., chimie minérale.

cheque, *s.* Com: Chèque *m.* **chequebook,** *s.* Carnet *m* de chèques.

chequered, *a.* Chequered career, vie accidentée.

cherish, *v.tr.* **1.** Chérir. **2.** Bercer, caresser (un espoir).

cherry. I. *s.* Cerise *f.* Black-heart cherry, guigne noire. White-heart cherry, bigarreau *m.* Wild cherry, merise *f.* F: Not to make two bites at a cherry, ne pas s'y prendre à deux fois. **2.** *s.* Cherry(-tree), cerisier *m.* **3.** *a.* Cherry(-red), cerise *inv.* **cherry-orchard,** *s.* Cerisaie *f.* **cherry-pie,** *s.* Tourte *f* aux cerises. **cherry-stone,** *s.* Noyau *m* de cerise.

cherub, *s.* Chérubin *m.*

cherubic, *a.* Chérubique.

chess, *s.* Jeu *m* d'échecs. To play c., jouer aux échecs. **chess-board,** *s.* Échiquier *m.* **chess-men,** *s.pl.* Pièces *f* (du jeu d'échecs).

chest, *s.* **1.** Coffre *m*, caisse *f*, boîte *f.* **2.** Anat: Poitrine *f.* To throw out one's chest, bomber la poitrine. F: To get it off one's chest, dire ce qu'on a sur le cœur.

chestnut. I. *s.* (*a*) Châtaigne *f*; marron *m.* (*b*) Chestnut(-tree), châtaignier *m*; marronnier *m.* (*c*) F: Plaisanterie usée. **2.** Attrib. Châtain; (cheval) alezan.

chevron, *s.* Her: Mil: Chevron *m.*

chew, *v.tr.* Mâcher, mastiquer.

chicanery, *s.* Chicanerie *f*, chicane *f*, tracasserie *f.*

chick, *s.* Poussin *m.*

chicken, *s.* **1.** Poulet *m.* Orn: F: Mother Car(e)y's chicken, pétrel *m* de tempête. **2.** Cu: Poulet. Spring chicken, poussin *m.* **chicken-hearted,** *a.* Poltron. **chicken-pox,** *s.* Med: Varicelle *f.*

chickweed, *s.* Bot: Mouron *m* des oiseaux.

chicory, *s.* Bot: Chicorée *f.*

chide, *v.tr. & i.* Réprimander, gronder.

chief. I. *s.* (*a*) Chef *m.* (*b*) In chief, en chef. **II. chief,** *a.* Principal, -aux; premier; (en) chef. **-ly,** *adv.* **1.** Surtout, avant tout. **2.** Principalement.

chieftain, *s.* Chef *m* (de clan).

chiffon, *s.* Tex: Chiffon *m*, gaze *f.*

chilblain, *s.* Engelure *f.*

child, *s.* Enfant *mf.* Be a good child! sois sage! From a child, dès son enfance. **childbirth,** *s.* Enfantement *m*; couches *fpl.*

childhood, *s.* Enfance *f.*

child's-play, *s.* Jeu *m* d'enfant.

childish, *a.* **1.** Enfantin, d'enfant, d'enfance. **2.** Don't be so childish, ne faites pas l'enfant. **3.** To grow childish, retomber en enfance. **-ly,** *adv.* Comme un enfant; puérilement.

childishness, *s.* Enfantillage *m*, puérilité *f.*

childless, *a.* Sans enfant(s).

childlike, *a.* Enfantin; naïf.

chill[1], *s.* **1.** (*a*) To catch a chill, prendre froid. (*b*) Chill of fear, frisson *m* de crainte. **2.** (*a*) To take the chill off, (faire) tiédir. (*b*) To cast a chill over the company, jeter un froid sur l'assemblée.

chill[2], *a.* Froid, glacé.

chill[3], *v.tr.* (*a*) Refroidir, glacer; faire frissonner. F: Chilled to the bone, morfondu; transi de froid. (*b*) Réfrigérer (la viande).

chilli, *s.* Cu: Piment *m.*

chilliness, *s.* (*a*) Froid *m*, froideur *f*, fraîcheur *f.* (*b*) Froideur (d'un accueil).

chilly, *a.* **1.** (*a*) Frileux. (*b*) To feel c., avoir froid. **2.** (Of weather) Froid. **3.** Froid. Chilly politeness, politesse glaciale.

chime[1], *s.* Carillon *m.*

chime[2]. 1. *v.i.* Carillonner. F: To chime in with s.o.'s ideas, tomber d'accord avec les idées de qn. F: To chime in, placer son mot, intervenir. **2.** *v.tr.* To c. the hour, carillonner l'heure. **chiming,** *a.* Chiming clock, pendule à carillon.

chimera, *s.* Chimère *f.*

chimerical, *a.* Chimérique.

chimney, *s.* Cheminée *f.* Lamp chimney, verre *m* de lampe. **chimney-corner,** *s.* Coin *m* du feu. **chimney-piece,** *s.* Chambranle *m* de cheminée; F: la cheminée. **chimney-pot,** *s.* **1.** Mitre *f*; pot *m* de cheminée. **2.** F: Chimney-pot (hat), F: tube *m*; huit-reflets *m.* **chimney-stack,** *s.* Cheminée *f* d'usine. **chimney-sweep,** *s.* Ramoneur *m.*

chimpanzee, *s.* Chimpanzé *m.*

chin, *s.* Menton *m.* **chin-strap,** *s.* Mil: Jugulaire *f*, (sous-)mentonnière *f.*

China. 1. Pr.n. Geog: La Chine. **2.** *s.* (i) Porcelaine *f*; faïence fine; (ii) vaisselle *f* de porcelaine.

Chinaman, *s.* Chinois *m.*

Chinese. I. *a. & s.* Chinois, -e. **2.** *s.* Ling: Le chinois.

chink,[1] *s.* Fente *f*, crevasse *f* (dans un mur); entre-bâillement *m* (de la porte).

chink², **1**. *v.tr.* Faire sonner (son argent); faire tinter (des verres). **2**. *v.i.* Sonner (sec).
chintz, *s.* *Tex:* Perse *f*, indienne *f*.
chip¹, *s.* **1**. Éclat *m*, copeau *m* (de bois); écaille *f*, éclat (de marbre). *F:* He is a chip of the old block, c'est bien le fils de son père. **2**. Brisure *f*, écornure *f* (d'assiette). **3**. *Cu:* Chip potatoes, chips, pommes de terre frites.
chip², *v.tr.* **1**. Tailler par éclats. **2**. (*a*) Ébrécher; écorner (un meuble). To c. a piece off sth., enlever un morceau à qch. **chip in**, *v.i.* *F:* Intervenir; placer son mot.
chiropodist, *s.* Pédicure *mf*.
chiropody, *s.* Chirurgie *f* pédicure.
chirp¹, *s.* Pépiement *m*, gazouillement *m*; cri *m* (du grillon).
chirp², *v.i.* Pépier, gazouiller; (*of grasshopper*) crier.
chirrup, *s. & v.i.* = CHIRP¹, ².
chisel¹, *s.* Ciseau *m*.
chisel², *v.tr.* Ciseler.
chit-chat, *s.* *F:* Bavardages *mpl*, commérages *mpl*.
chivalrous, *a.* Chevaleresque; courtois. **-ly**, *adv.* Chevaleresquement.
chivalry, *s.* Conduite *f* chevaleresque; courtoisie *f*.
chlorate, *s.* *Ch:* Chlorate *m*.
chloride, *s.* *Ch:* Chlorure *m*.
chlorine, *s.* *Ch:* Chlore *m*.
chloroform¹, *s.* *Med:* Chloroforme *m*.
chloroform², *v.tr.* Chloroformer.
chock, *s.* Cale *f*; tin *m*, coin *m*.
chock-a-block, *a.* *F:* = CHOCK-FULL.
chock-full, *a.* *F:* Plein comme un œuf.
chocolate, **1**. *s.* Chocolat *m*. Cake of c., tablette *f* de chocolat. *F:* A chocolate, une crotte de chocolat. **2**. *a.* Chocolat *inv.*
choice¹, *s.* **1**. Choix *m*. (*a*) Préférence *f*. For choice, de préférence. (*b*) Alternative *f*. You have no c. in the matter, vous n'avez pas le choix. **2**. Assortiment *m*, choix.
choice², *a.* **1**. Bien choisi. **2**. *Com:* C. article, article de choix; article surfin.
choir, *s.* Chœur *m*. **choir-boy**, *s.* *Ecc:* Enfant *m* de chœur. **choir-master**, *s.* Maître *m* de chapelle.
choke, *v.* **1**. *v.tr.* Étouffer, suffoquer. To choke (up) a pipe, obstruer, boucher, un tuyau (*with*, de). **2**. *v.i.* (*a*) Étouffer, étrangler (*with*, de). To c. with laughter, suffoquer de rire. (*b*) S'engorger, s'obstruer (*with*, de). **choke back**, *v.tr.* Refouler. **choke off**, *v.tr.* *F:* (*a*) To c. s.o. off from doing sth., dissuader qn de faire qch. (*b*) Se débarrasser de. **choking**, *s.* **1**. Étouffement *m*, suffocation *f*, étranglement *m*. **2**. Engorgement *m*, obstruction *f*.
cholera, *s.* Choléra *m*.
choleric, *a.* Colérique, irascible.
choose, *v.tr.* **1**. (*a*) Choisir; faire choix de. (*b*) He cannot choose but obey, il ne peut faire autrement qu'obéir. (*c*) There is nothing to choose between them, l'un vaut

l'autre. **2**. I do not choose to do so, il ne me plaît pas de le faire. When I choose, quand je voudrai. **chosen**, *a.* Choisi. *s.* The chosen, les élus. **choosing**, *s.* Choix *m*. The difficulty of choosing, l'embarras du choix.
chop¹, *s.* **1**. Coup *m* de hache, de couperet. **2**. *Cu:* Côtelette *f*. **3**. Clapotis *m* (de la mer).
chop², *v.* **1**. *v.tr.* Couper, fendre. To c. to pieces, hacher qch. en morceaux. **2**. *v.i.* (*Of sea*) Clapoter. **chop down**, *v.tr.* Abattre (un arbre). **chop off**, *v.tr.* Trancher. **chop up**, *v.tr.* Couper (qch.) en morceaux.
chop³, *v.i.* To chop and change, manquer de suite; girouetter.
chopper, *s.* Couperet *m*, hachoir *m*.
choppy, *a.* *Nau:* Clapoteux. C. sea, mer hachée; lame courte.
chop-sticks, *s.pl.* Bâtonnets *m*, baguettes *f*.
choral, *a.* *Mus:* **1**. Choral (*no m.pl.*). **2**. Chanté en chœur.
chord¹, *s.* Corde *f*. *F:* To touch the right chord, faire vibrer la corde sensible.
chord², *s.* *Mus:* Accord *m*.
chorister, *s.* Choriste *m*; *Ecc:* chantre *m* ou enfant *m* de chœur.
chortle, *v.i.* *F:* Glousser de joie.
chorus, *s.* **1**. Chœur *m*. Chorus of praise, concert *m* de louanges. **2**. Refrain *m* (d'une chanson). To join in the chorus, faire chœur.
chrestomathy, *s.* Chrestomathie *f*.
Christ. *Pr.n.* Le Christ; Jésus-Christ *m*.
christen, *v.tr.* Baptiser. **christening**, *s.* Baptême *m*.
Christendom, *s.* La chrétienté.
Christian, *a. & s.* Chrétien, -ienne.
Christianity, *s.* Christianisme *m*.
Christmas, *s.* Noël *m*. At C., à Noël, à la Noël. A merry Christmas! joyeux Noël! Father Christmas, le Bonhomme Noël. **Christmas-box**, *s.* = Étrennes *fpl*; gratification *f*. **Christmas-card**, *s.* Carte *f* de Noël. **Christmas-carol**, *s.* Chant *m* de Noël; noël *m*. **Christmas-day**, *s.* Le jour de Noël. **Christmas-eve**, *s.* La veille de Noël. **Christmas-tree**, *s.* Arbre *m* de Noël.
chromate, *s.* *Ch:* Chromate *m*.
chromatic, *a.* Chromatique.
chrome, *s.* (*a*) Chrome leather, cuir chromé. (*b*) Chrome yellow, jaune de chrome.
chromium, *s.* *Ch:* Chrome *m*.
chronic, *a.* (*a*) *Med:* Chronique. (*b*) *F:* Constant, continuel.
chronicle¹, *s.* Chronique *f*.
chronicle², *v.tr.* To c. events, faire la chronique des événements; raconter les faits.
chronicler, *s.* Chroniqueur *m*.
chronological, *a.* Chronologique. In chronological order, par ordre de dates.
chronometer, *s.* Chronomètre *m*.
chrysalis, *s.* Chrysalide *f*.

chrysanthemum, s. Chrysanthème m.
chubby, a. Boulot, -otte; (of face) joufflu.
chubby-cheeked, a. Joufflu.
chuck¹, s. **I.** Petite tape (sous le menton).
2. F: To get the chuck, recevoir son congé.
chuck², v.tr. **I.** To chuck s.o. under the chin, relever le menton à qn. **2.** F: (a) Jeter, lancer. (b) Lâcher, plaquer (qn). (c) P: Chuck it! en voilà assez! **chuck out,** v.tr. Flanquer (qn) à la porte. **chuck up,** v.tr. F: Abandonner To chuck it up, y renoncer; quitter la partie.
chuckle¹, s. Rire étouffé; petit rire.
chuckle², v.i. Rire tout bas, en soi-même, sous cape (at, over, sth., de qch.).
chuckle-headed, a. F: Sans cervelle.
chum¹, s. F: Camarade mf: copain m, copine f.
chum², v.i. To chum (up) with s.o., se lier d'amitié avec qn.
chump, s. **I.** (a) Tronçon m (de bois). (b) Chump-chop, côtelette f de gigot. **2.** P: (a) Off one's chump, timbré. (b) A (silly) chump, un nigaud.
chunk, s. Gros morceau; quignon m (de pain).
church, s. **I.** Église f; (protestant) temple m. **2.** (a) The Church of England, l'Église anglicane. To go into the Church, entrer dans les ordres. (b) Church service, office m; service (divin). To go to church, aller à l'office.
churchwarden, s. **I.** Marguillier m. **2.** Longue pipe (en terre).
churchyard, s. Cimetière m.
churl, s. (a) Hist: Manant m. (b) F: Rustre m. (c) F: Grincheux m.
churlish, a. (a) Mal élevé; grossier. (b) Hargneux. **-ly,** adv. Avec mauvaise grâce.
churlishness, s. (a) Grossièreté f. (b) Tempérament hargneux.
churn¹, s. Baratte f.
churn², v.tr. Baratter (la crème); battre.
cicada, s. Ent: Cigale f.
cicatrice, s. Cicatrice f.
Cicero, Pr.n. Cicéron m.
cicerone, s. Cicerone m.
cider, s. Cidre m.
cigar, s. Cigare m. **cigar-case,** s. Étui m à cigares. **cigar-cutter,** s. Coupe-cigares m.inv.
cigarette, s. Cigarette f. **cigarette-case,** s. Étui m à cigarettes. **cigarette-holder,** s. Porte-cigarette m, pl. porte-cigarettes.
cinchona, s. Quinquina m.
cinder, s. **I.** Cendre f. **2.** pl. (Partly burnt coal) Escarbilles fpl. **cinder-track,** s. Piste f (en) cendrée.
Cinderella, Pr.n. Cendrillon f.
cine-camera, s. Cin: Camera f.
cinema, s. F: (a) Le cinéma, le ciné. (b) (Salle f de) cinéma.
cinnamon, s. Cinnamon(-bark), cannelle f.
cipher, s. **I.** Mth: Zéro m. F: He's a mere

cipher, c'est une nullité. **2.** (a) Chiffre m. To send a message in c., transmettre une dépêche en chiffre. (b) Message chiffré. **3.** (Monogram) Chiffre.
circle¹, s. **I.** Cercle m. **2.** Révolution f, orbite m or f (d'une planète). To come full circle, compléter son orbite. **3.** Inner circle, (chemin m de fer de) petite ceinture. **4.** Th: Upper circle, seconde galerie. **5.** Milieu m, coterie f The family c., le sein de la famille.
circle², v.tr. (a) Ceindre, entourer (with, de). (b) Faire le tour de.
circuit, s. **I.** Pourtour m (d'une ville). **2.** (a) Révolution f. (b) To make the c. of the town, faire le tour de la ville. (c) Tournée f, circuit m. To go on circuit, aller en tournée. **3.** Détour m. **4.** El: Circuit. Short circuit, court-circuit m.
circuitous, a. Détourné.
circular. I. a. Circulaire. Circular letter, lettre circulaire; circulaire f. **2.** s. = circular letter.
circularize, v.tr. Envoyer des circulaires à.
circulate. I. v.i. Circuler. **2.** v.tr. (a) Faire circuler. (b) Mettre en circulation.
circulation, s. Circulation f (du sang); tirage m (d'un journal). To restore the c. in one's legs, se dégourdir les jambes.
circumcise, v.tr. Circoncire. **circumcised,** a. Circoncis.
circumcision, s. Circoncision f.
circumference, s. Circonférence f. On the circumference, à la circonférence.
circumflex, a. & s. Circumflex (accent), accent m circonflexe.
circumlocution, s. Circonlocution f, ambages fpl.
circumscribe, v.tr. **I.** Circonscrire. **2.** Limiter. **circumscribed,** a. **I.** Geom: Circonscrit. **2.** Restreint, limité.
circumscription, s. **I.** Restriction f. **2.** Région f, circonscription f (administrative).
circumspect, a. Circonspect; avisé. **-ly,** adv. Prudemment; avec circonspection.
circumspection, s. Circonspection f.
circumstance, s. **I.** pl. (a) Circonstances f. In the circumstances, dans ces circonstances; puisqu'il en est ainsi. That depends on circumstances, c'est selon. Circumstances alter cases, les cas changent avec les circonstances. (b) If his circumstances allow, si ses moyens le permettent. In easy circumstances, dans l'aisance. **2.** sing. Circonstance, détail m, fait m. Were it not for the c. that, n'était le fait que.
circumstanced, a. Well circumstanced, dans l'aisance.
circumstantial, a. **I.** Circonstanciel. C. evidence, preuves indirectes. **2.** Circonstancié, détaillé.
circumvent, v.tr. Circonvenir.
circus, s. **I.** (a) Cirque m. (b) (Of roads)

Rond-point *m.* **2.** Travelling circus, cirque forain.

Cistercian, *a. & s.* Cistercien, -ienne. The Cistercian Order, l'ordre de Cîteaux.

cistern, *s.* (*a*) Réservoir *m* à eau (sous les combles). (*b*) (*Underground*) Citerne *f.*

citadel, *s.* Citadelle *f.*

cite, *v.tr.* Citer.

citizen, *s.* Citoyen, -enne; bourgeois, -e.

citizenship, *s.* **1.** Droit *m* de cité, de bourgeoisie. **2.** Good citizenship, civisme *m.*

citrate, *s. Ch:* Citrate *m.*

citric, *a. Ch:* Citrique.

citron, *s.* Cédrat *m.*

city, *s.* **1.** (*a*) Grande ville. (*b*) Cité *f*, agglomération *f.* **2.** The City, la Cité de Londres.

civet, *s.* Civet(-cat), civette *f.*

civic, *a.* Civique. The c. authorities, les autorités municipales.

civil, *a.* **1.** Civil. Civil rights, droits civiques. In civil life, dans le civil. **2.** Civil defence, défense passive. **3.** Poli, honnête, courtois. **-illy,** *adv.* Civilement, poliment.

civilian, **1.** *s.* Bourgeois *m*; civil *m.* **2.** *a.* Civil. In civilian life, dans le civil.

civility, *s.* Civilité *f*; politesse *f.*

civilization, *s.* Civilisation *f.*

civilize, *v.tr.* Civiliser.

clack[1], *s.* **1.** Bruit sec; claquement *m.* **2.** *F:* = CHATTER[1].

clack[2], *v.i.* **1.** Claquer. **2.** *F:* Caqueter, bavarder, jacasser.

claim[1], *s.* **1.** Demande *f*; revendication *f*; réclamation *f.* **2.** Droit *m*, titre *m*, prétention *f* (to sth., à qch.). To lay claim to sth., s'attribuer qch. To put in a claim, faire valoir ses droits. **3.** Créance *f.* **4.** *Jur:* Réclamation. **5.** Concession (minière).

claim[2], *v.tr.* (*a*) Réclamer; revendiquer; demander. To claim one's due, faire valoir ses droits. (*b*) Prétendre, avancer, affirmer. To c. kinship with s.o., se prétendre parent de qn.

claimant, *s.* Prétendant, -ante; revendicateur *m.* Rightful claimant, ayant droit *m.*

clairvoyance, *s.* Lucidité *f* (somnambulique).

clairvoyant. **1.** *a.* Doué de seconde vue. **2.** *s.* Voyant, -ante; somnambule *mf* lucide.

clamber[1], *s.* Ascension *f* raide; escalade *f.*

clamber[2], *v.i.* Grimper (des pieds et des mains). To c. over a wall, escalader un mur.

clamminess, *s.* Moiteur froide.

clammy, *a.* **1.** (Froid et) moite. **2.** Gluant, collant.

clamorous, *a.* Bruyant, braillard.

clamour[1], *s.* Clameur *f*; cris *mpl.*

clamour[2], *v.i.* Vociférer; pousser des clameurs. To c. for sth., réclamer qch. à grands cris.

clamp[1], *s.* Crampon *m.*

clamp[2], *v.tr.* Agrafer.

clan, *s.* **1.** Clan *m.* The head of the clan, le chef de clan. **2.** (*a*) Tribu *f.* (*b*) *F:* Coterie *f.*

clandestine, *a.* Clandestin, subreptice. **-ly,** *adv.* Clandestinement; à la dérobée.

clang[1], *s.* Son *m* métallique; bruit strident.

clang[2], *v.i.* Retentir, résonner.

clank[1], *s.* Bruit sec (de fers); cliquetis *m.*

clank[2]. **1.** *v.i.* Rendre un bruit métallique. **2.** *v.tr.* The prisoners c. their chains, les prisonniers font sonner leurs fers.

clannish, *a.* Dévoué aux intérêts de sa coterie.

clannishness, *s.* Esprit *m* de corps.

clansman, *s.* Membre *m* d'un clan.

clap[1], *s.* **1.** (*a*) Battement *m* (de mains). To give s.o. a clap, applaudir qn. (*b*) Coup *m*, tape *f* (de la main). **2.** Clap of thunder, coup de tonnerre.

clap[2]. **1.** *v.tr.* (*a*) To clap one's hands, battre des mains. To clap s.o. on the back, donner à qn une tape dans le dos. To c. a performer, applaudir un artiste. (*b*) Battre (des ailes). (*c*) To c. s.o. in prison, fourrer qn en prison. To c. a pistol to s.o.'s head, appuyer brusquement un pistolet sur la tempe de qn. To clap on one's hat, camper son chapeau sur sa tête. *F:* To clap eyes on s.o., voir qn (tout à coup). **2.** *v.i.* Applaudir. **clapping,** *s.* Battement *m* des mains; applaudissements *mpl.*

clapper, *s.* Battant *m.*

claptrap, *s.* Boniment *m*; phrases *f* vides.

claret, *s.* Vin *m* de Bordeaux (rouge); bordeaux *m.*

clarify, *v.tr.* Clarifier (le beurre); éclaircir (l'esprit).

clarinet, *s.* Clarinette *f.*

clarion, *s.* Clairon *m.*

clarity, *s.* Clarté *f.*

clash[1], *s.* **1.** Fracas *m*; résonnement *m* (de cloches); cliquetis *m* (d'épées). **2.** (*a*) Conflit *m* (d'opinions); (between mobs) échauffourée *f.* (*b*) Disparate *f* (de couleurs).

clash[2]. **1.** *v.i.* (*a*) Résonner (bruyamment). (*b*) (Of colours) Jurer; faire disparate; (of opinions) s'opposer; (of interests) se heurter. **2.** *v.tr.* Faire résonner.

clasp[1], *s.* **1.** Agrafe *f* (de broche); fermeture *f* (de collier); fermoir *m* (de porte-monnaie). **2.** Étreinte *f.* **clasp-knife,** *s.* Couteau *m* à cran d'arrêt.

clasp[2], *v.tr.* **1.** Agrafer (un bracelet). **2.** (*a*) Serrer, étreindre (qn). (*b*) To c. s.o.'s hand, serrer la main à qn.

class[1], *s.* **1.** Classe *f.* **1.** The upper class, les gens du monde. The lower classes, le prolétariat. The middle class, la bourgeoisie. **2.** *Sch:* The French class, la classe de français. Evening classes, cours *m* du soir. **3.** Catégorie *f*, sorte *f*, genre *m.* **class-book,** *s. Sch:* Livre *m* de classe. **class-room,** *s. Sch:* (Salle *f* de) classe *f.*

class[2], *v.tr.* Classer; ranger par classes.

classic, *a. & s.* Classique *m.*

classical, *a.* Classique.

classification, *s.* Classification *f.*

classify, *v.tr.* Classifier, classer.

clatter¹, *s.* **1.** Bruit *m*, vacarme *m.* **2.** *F:* Brouhaha *m* (de conversation).

clatter², *v.i.* Faire du bruit; se choquer avec fracas.

clause, *s.* **1.** Clause *f*, article *m.* **2.** *Gram:* Membre *m* de phrase.

claw¹, *s.* Griffe *f* (de félin); serre *f* (d'oiseau de proie); pince *f* (d'une écrevisse). *F: To cut s.o.'s claws,* rogner les ongles à qn.

claw-hammer, *s.* Marteau *m* à panne fendue.

claw², **1.** *v.tr.* Griffer, égratigner; déchirer avec ses griffes. **2.** *v.i.* To claw at sth., s'accrocher à qch.; agripper qch.

clay, *s.* **1.** Argile *f*; (terre-)glaise *f.* **2.** Clay (-pipe), pipe *f* en terre.

clean¹. **I.** *a.* Propre, net. *F: As clean as a new pin,* propre comme un sou neuf. *To make sth. c.,* nettoyer qch. **Clean break,** cassure nette, franche. *Nau:* **Clean bill of health** patente nette. **Clean hands,** (i) mains propres; (ii) (*clean from crime*) mains nettes. **II. clean,** *adv.* **1.** *F:* Tout à fait. I **clean forgot,** j'ai absolument oublié. *They got c. away,* ils ont décampé sans laisser de traces. **2.** To cut clean through sth., couper qch. de part en part. **clean-handed,** *a.* Aux mains nettes. **clean-shaven,** *a.* Sans barbe ni moustache; (visage) glabre.

clean², *s.* Nettoyage *m.*

clean³, *v.tr.* Nettoyer; balayer (les rues); faire (une chambre); vider (le poisson). *To c. one's teeth,* se nettoyer les dents. *F: To clean oneself (up),* se débarbouiller. **clean up,** *v.tr.* **1.** Nettoyer. **2.** *Abs.* Faire le nettoyage. **clean-up,** *s.* Nettoyage *m.*

cleaning, *s.* Nettoyage *m.*

cleaner, *s.* Nettoyeur, -euse; décrotteur, -euse.

cleanliness, *s.* Propreté *f*; netteté *f.*

cleanly¹, *a.* Propre (par habitude).

cleanly², *adv.* Proprement, nettement.

cleanness, *s.* **1.** Propreté *f.* **2.** Netteté *f.*

cleanse, *v.tr.* **1.** Curer (un égout). **2.** Purifier (le sang). **cleansing¹,** *a.* Assainissant, purifiant. **cleansing²,** *s.* **1.** Curage *m* (d'un égout). **2.** Purification *f* (du sang).

clear¹. **I.** *a.* **1.** (*a*) Clair, limpide; net, *f.* nette. *On a c. day,* par temps clair. *As clear as day,* clair comme le jour. (*b*) *F: C. conscience,* conscience nette. (*c*) *C. voice,* voix claire, nette. **2.** *C. indication,* signe certain, évident. *C. case of bribery,* cas de corruption manifeste. **3.** *To make one's meaning c.,* se faire comprendre. *C. thinker,* esprit lucide. **4.** *To be clear about sth.,* être convaincu de qch. **5.** (*a*) **Clear profit,** bénéfice clair et net. **Clear loss,** perte sèche. **Clear majority,** majorité absolue. (*b*) *Jur:* **Three clear days,** trois jours francs. **6.** Libre, dégagé (*of,* de). *Mil:* 'All clear!' "fin d'alerte." *F:* The coast is clear, le champ est libre. **II. clear,** *a. or adv. To steer c. of a rock,* passer au large d'un

écueil. *F:* To steer clear of sth., éviter qch.; se garer de qch. **Stand clear of the doorway!** dégagez la porte! **-ly,** *adv.* Clairement, nettement. *To see c.,* voir clair. You must clearly understand that, il vous faut bien comprendre que. **clear-cut,** *a.* *C.-c. features,* traits nettement dessinés. **clear-headed,** *a.* Perspicace. **clear-sighted,** *a.* Clairvoyant; qui voit juste.

clear², *v.* **I.** *v.tr.* **1.** Éclaircir. To clear the air, (i) rafraîchir l'air; (ii) mettre les choses au point. **2.** To clear s.o. of a charge, innocenter qn d'une accusation. *To c. oneself,* se disculper. **3.** Dégager (une route); désencombrer (une salle). Clear the way! faites place! To clear the table, enlever le couvert. *Navy:* To clear (the decks) for action, faire le branle-bas de combat. 'Must be cleared,' "vente à tout prix." **4.** *To c. one's plate,* faire assiette nette. *To c. the letter-box,* lever les lettres. **5.** (*a*) *To c. a barrier,* franchir une barrière. (*b*) *Nau:* To clear the harbour, quitter le port. **6.** Acquitter (une dette); affranchir (une propriété); solder, liquider (un compte). **7.** To clear ten per cent, faire un bénéfice net de dix pour cent. **II. clear,** *v.i.* (*Of the weather*) To clear (up), s'éclaircir; se mettre au beau. (*Of mist*) To clear (away), se dissiper. **clear away,** *v.tr.* Enlever, ôter; écarter. **clear off,** *v.tr* S'acquitter de (ses dettes). **clear out.** **1.** *v.tr.* Nettoyer (une chambre). **2.** *v.i.* Clear out! filez! hors d'ici! **clear-out,** *s.* Nettoyage *m.* **clear up,** *v.tr.* Éclaircir, élucider (un mystère).

clearing, *s.* **1.** Clearing of s.o., désinculpation *f* de qn. **2.** Dégagement *m* (d'une voie). **3.** (*In forest*) Éclaircie *f*, clairière *f.*

clearance, *s.* **Clearance sale,** vente *f* de soldes.

clearness, *s.* **1.** Clarté *f* (de l'atmosphère). **2.** Netteté *f* (des idées).

cleavage, *s.* **1.** Fendage *m. Miner:* Clivage *m.* **2.** Scission *f* (dans un parti).

cleave, *v.tr.* (*a*) Fendre. *F:* To be in a cleft stick, se trouver dans une impasse. **Cloven hoof,** pied fourchu. (*b*) Fendre (l'air).

cleaver, *s.* Fendoir *m.*

clef, *s.* *Mus:* Clef *f.*

cleft, *s.* Fente *f*, fissure *f*, crevasse *f.*

clematis, *s.* *Bot:* Clématite *f.*

clemency, *s.* **1.** Clémence *f* (*to,* envers, pour). **2.** Douceur *f* (du temps).

clement, *a.* **1.** Clément, indulgent (*to,* envers, pour). **2.** (*Of weather*) Doux, *f.* douce.

clench, *v.tr.* Serrer. With clenched hands, les mains crispées.

clergy, *s.* **1.** *Coll.* Clergé *m.* **2.** Membres *m* du clergé.

clergyman, *s.* Ecclésiastique *m*; ministre *m.*

cleric, *s.* = CLERGYMAN.

clerical, *a.* **1.** Clérical, -aux; du clergé. **2.** Clerical error, faute de copiste.

clerk, *s.* **1.** (*a*) Employé, -ée, de bureau;

commis *m*; clerc *m* (d'avoué). *Chief c.*, chef
m de bureau. (*b*) *Jur:* Clerk of the court,
greffier *m*. 2. *Ecc:* Clerk (in holy orders),
clerc; ecclésiastique *m*.
clerkship, *s.* Emploi *m* ou place *f* de commis.
clever, *a.* 1. Habile, adroit. 2. (*a*) To be
clever, être intelligent. (*b*) *F: He was too c.
for us*, il nous a roulés. (*c*) *C. device*, dispositif
ingénieux. **-ly,** *adv.* Habilement, adroitement.
cleverness, *s.* 1. Habileté *f*, adresse *f*.
2. Intelligence *f*. 3. Ingéniosité *f*.
cliché, *s.* Cliché *m*.
click¹, *s.* 1. Bruit sec; clic *m*; cliquetis *m*
(d'épées). 2. Click (of the tongue), clappe-
ment *m* (de la langue).
click², *v.tr. & i.* Cliqueter; faire tic-tac.
To click one's heels, (faire) claquer les talons.
client, *s.* Client, -ente.
clientele, *s.* Clientèle *f*.
cliff, *s.* Falaise *f*.
climate, *s.* Climat *m*.
climax, *s.* *F:* Comble *m*, plus haut point.
This brought matters to a c., ce fut le comble.
climb¹, *s.* 1. Ascension *f*. 2. Montée *f*.
climb², *v.tr. & i.* 1. (*a*) Monter, gravir;
grimper à (un arbre); monter à (l'échelle);
escalader (une falaise). *To c. a mountain*,
faire l'ascension d'une montagne. **To climb
over** *the wall*, franchir le mur. (*b*) *The road
climbs*, la route va en montant. 2. To climb
to power, s'élever au pouvoir. 3. *Av:*
Prendre de l'altitude. **climb down,** *v.i.*
1. Descendre. 2. *F:* En rabattre. **climb-
down,** *s.* *F:* Défaite *f*. **climbing¹,** *a.*
Grimpant. **climbing²,** *s.* Escalade *f*;
montée *f*.
climber, *s.* 1. Ascension(n)iste *mf* (de montagne). 2. *F:* Arriviste *mf*.
clinch. 1. *v.tr.* (*a*) River. (*b*) Conclure (un
marché). 2. *v.i. Box:* Se prendre corps-à-
corps.
cling, *v.i.* (*a*) S'attacher, s'accrocher, se
cramponner (*to*, à). To cling close to s.o.,
se serrer contre qn. **To cling together,**
(i) rester étroitement unis; (ii) se tenir
étroitement enlacés. (*b*) Adhérer (*to*, à).
clinic, *s. Med:* Clinique *f*.
clinical, *a.* Clinique. **Clinical thermometer,**
thermomètre médical.
clink¹, *s.* Tintement *m*, choc *m*.
clink², 1. *v.i.* Tinter. 2. *v.tr.* Faire tinter,
faire résonner. **To clink glasses,** trinquer.
clip¹, *s.* Pince *f*, attache *f*.
clip², *v.tr.* Pincer, serrer.
clip³, *s.* Tonte *f*.
clip⁴, *v.tr.* 1. Tondre (un mouton); tailler
(une haie). *F:* **To clip** s.o.'s claws, rogner
les ongles à qn. 2. Poinçonner (un billet).
clipper, *s. Nau:* Fin voilier.
clique, *s.* Coterie *f*; petite chapelle.
cloak¹, *s.* Manteau *m*. **Under the cloak of**
night, sous le voile de la nuit. *Under the c.
of religion*, sous le manteau de la religion.

cloak-room, *s.* 1. *Th:* Vestiaire *m*.
2. *Rail:* Consigne *f*.
cloak², *v.tr.* (*a*) Couvrir d'un manteau.
(*b*) Masquer (ses projets).
clock, *s.* (*Large*) Horloge *f*; (*smaller*)
pendule *f*. **What o'clock is it?** quelle heure
est-il? **It is two o'clock,** il est deux heures.
F: Like one o'clock, fameusement.
clockwise, *a.* Dans le sens des aiguilles d'une
montre; à droite.
clockwork, *s.* Mouvement *m* d'horlogerie.
F: Everything is going like clockwork, tout
va comme sur des roulettes.
clod, *s.* Motte *f* (de terre). **clod-hopper,**
s. Rustre *m*.
clog¹, *s.* 1. Entrave *f*. 2. Socque *f*, galoche *f*.
clog², *v.tr.* (*a*) Boucher, obstruer (un tuyau).
(*b*) Entraver.
cloister, *s.* Cloître *m*.
close¹. I. *a.* 1. (*a*) Bien fermé; clos. (*b*) The
room smells close, ça sent le renfermé ici.
Close weather, temps lourd. (*c*) *C. secret*,
secret impénétrable. (*d*) *C. corporation*,
société exclusive. (*e*) *Ven:* Close season,
chasse fermée. 2. *C. connection*, rapport
étroit. Close friend, ami(e) intime. *To resemblance*, ressemblance exacte. *To keep c. watch
on* s.o., surveiller qn de près. *To cut hair c.*,
couper les cheveux ras. *Rac:* *C. finish*,
arrivée serrée. 3. Peu communicatif. To be
close about sth. être réservé à l'égard de qch.
4. Avare, regardant. **-ly,** *adv.* 1. (*a*)
Étroitement. (*b*) (Interroger qn) à fond.
2. *C. packed in a box*, serrés dans une boîte.
II. close, *adv.* 1. *C. shut*, étroitement
fermé. 2. Près, de près, auprès. *To follow c.
behind* s.o., suivre qn de près. *To stand c.
together*, se tenir serrés. 3. (*a*) Close at hand,
close by, tout près, tout proche. (*b*) Close
(up)on *nine o'clock*, tout près de neuf heures.
To be c. on fifty, friser la cinquantaine.
close-cropped, *a.* (*Of hair*) Coupé ras;
(*of grass*) tondu de près. **close-fisted,** *a.*
Ladre. **close-fitting,** *a.* Collant. **close-
up,** *s. Cin:* (Vue *f* de) premier plan.
close², *s.* 1. *Jur:* Clôture *f*. 2. (*a*) Clos *m*,
enclos *m*. (*b*) Enceinte *f* (de cathédrale).
close³, *s.* Fin *f*, conclusion *f*; bout *m*.
close⁴. I. *v.tr.* 1. Fermer. *Book-k:* To
close the books, régler les livres. 2. Conclure, terminer; clore, fermer (un débat).
3. To close the ranks, serrer les rangs.
II. close, *v.i.* 1. (Se) fermer; se refermer.
2. Finir; se terminer. 3. To close with s.o.,
(i) conclure le marché avec qn; (ii) se prendre
corps à corps avec qn. **close down.** 1. *v.tr.*
Fermer. 2. *v.i.* (*a*) Fermer; chômer.
(*b*) *W.Tel:* Terminer l'émission. **close in,**
v.i. (*a*) *The days are closing in*, les jours (se)
raccourcissent. (*b*) **To close in on** s.o., cerner
qn de près. **close up.** 1. *v.tr.* Boucher;
barrer. 2. *v.i.* (*a*) (*Of aperture*) S'obturer.
(*b*) Se serrer, se tasser. **closed,** *a.* Fermé;
(*of pipe*) obturé. *With c. eyes*, les yeux clos.

'Road closed,' "rue barrée." *Th:* 'Closed,' "relâche." **closing**¹, *a.* (*a*) Qui (se) ferme. (*b*) Dernier; final, -als. *The c. bid*, la dernière enchère. **closing**², *s.* **1.** Fermeture *f.* 'Closing time!' "on ferme!" **2.** Clôture *f* (d'un compte).

closeness, *s.* **1.** Rapprochement *m*, proximité *f.* **2.** Exactitude *f.* **3.** (*a*) Manque *m* d'air. (*b*) Lourdeur *f* (du temps). **4.** Réserve *f* (de qn). **5.** Ladrerie *f.*

closet, *s.* **1.** Cabinet *m.* **2.** Armoire *f*, placard *m.*

closure, *s.* Clôture *f*, fermeture *f.*

clot¹, *s.* Caillot *m.*

clot², *v.i.* (*Of milk*) Se cailler; (*of blood*) se figer.

cloth, *s.* **1.** *Tex:* (*a*) Étoffe *f* de laine; drap *m.* (*b*) (*Cotton*) Toile *f.* **2.** (*a*) Linge *m*; (*for cleaning*) torchon *m.* (*b*) (Table-)cloth, tapis *m* (de table); (*of linen*) nappe *f.* **3.** *F:* The cloth, le clergé.

clothe, *v.tr.* Vêtir, revêtir, habiller (*in, with,* de). *Warmly clad*, chaudement vêtu. **clothing,** *s.* Habillement *m*; vêtements *mpl.*

clothes, *s.pl.* Vêtements *m*, habits *m*, effets *m.* Suit of clothes, complet *m.* *In one's best c.,* dans ses habits de cérémonie; *F:* endimanché. **clothes-basket,** *s.* Panier *m* au linge sale. **clothes-horse,** *s.* Séchoir *m.* **clothes-line,** *s.* Corde *f* à linge; étendoir *m.* **clothes-peg,** *s.* Pince *f*; fichoir *m.* **clothes-prop,** *s.* Perche *f* d'étendoir.

clothier, *s.* (*a*) Drapier *m.* (*b*) Marchand *m* de confections.

cloud¹, *s.* **1.** Nuage *m.* To drop from the clouds, tomber des nues. *Prov:* Every cloud has a silver lining, après la pluie le beau temps. To be under a cloud, être l'objet de soupçons. **2.** Nuage, voile *m* (de fumée). **3.** Nuée *f* (de sauterelles). **cloudburst,** *s.* Trombe *f*; rafale *f* de pluie.

cloud². **1.** *v.tr.* Couvrir, voiler, obscurcir (le ciel); troubler (un liquide); couvrir (une vitre) de buée. **2.** *v.i.* To cloud (up, over), se couvrir de nuages. *His brow clouded* (*over*), son front s'assombrit. **clouded,** *a.* (Ciel) couvert (de nuages).

cloudiness, *s.* **1.** Aspect nuageux (du ciel). **2.** Turbidité *f* (d'un liquide).

cloudy, *a.* **1.** (Temps) couvert; (ciel) nuageux, assombri. **2.** (Liquide) trouble.

clout¹, *s.* **1.** Chiffon *m*, linge *m*, torchon *m.* **2.** *F:* Claque *f*, taloche *f.*

clout², *v.tr.* *F:* To clout s.o. on the head, flanquer une taloche à qn.

clove, *s.* **1.** Clou *m* de girofle. **2.** *Bot:* Clove-pink, œillet *m* des fleuristes.

cloven-footed, *a.* *Z:* Au pied fourchu.

clover, *s.* *Bot:* Trèfle *m.* *F:* To be in clover, être comme un coq en pâte.

clown, *s.* **1.** Rustre *m* manant *m.* **2.** *Th:* (*a*) Bouffon *m*, paillasse *m.* (*b*) Clown *m* (de cirque).

clownish, *a.* **1.** (*a*) Gauche, empoté. (*b*)

Grossier; mal élevé **2.** (Tour) de paillasse.

cloy, *v.tr.* Rassasier; écœurer. **cloying,** *a.* Rassasiant, affadissant.

club¹, *s.* **1.** (*a*) Massue *f*, gourdin *m.* (*b*) *Golf:* Crosse *f*, club *m.* **2.** *Cards:* Trèfle *m.* **3.** (*a*) Club, cercle *m.* (*b*) Association *f*, société *f.* **club-foot,** *s.* Pied bot *m.*

club², *v.* **1.** *v.tr.* Frapper avec une massue, avec un gourdin. **2.** *v.tr.* To c. one's resources, mettre ses ressources en commun. **3.** *v.i.* (*a*) Se réunir, s'associer. (*b*) To club together, se cotiser.

cluck, *v.i.* Glousser. **clucking,** *s.* Gloussement *m.*

clue, *s.* Indication *f*, indice *m.* To give s.o. a clue, mettre qn sur la voie, sur la piste. The clues of a cross-word puzzle, les définitions *f.*

clump, *s.* (*a*) Bloc *m*, masse *f.* (*b*) Groupe *m*, bouquet *m* (d'arbres).

clumsiness, *s.* Maladresse *f*, gaucherie *f.*

clumsy, *a.* **1.** Maladroit, gauche. **2.** (*Of shape*) Lourd, informe. **-ily,** *adv.* Maladroitement, gauchement.

cluster¹, *s.* Massif *m*, groupe *m* (d'arbres); grappe *f* (de raisins).

cluster², *v.i.* To cluster round s.o., se grouper, se rassembler, autour de qn.

clutch¹, *s.* **1.** (*a*) *F:* To be in s.o.'s clutches, être dans les griffes *f* de qn. (*b*) To make a clutch at sth., tâcher de saisir qch. **2.** *Mec.E:* (Manchon *m* d')embrayage *m.* To let in the clutch, embrayer.

clutch², *v.tr. & ind.tr.* Saisir, empoigner. To clutch at sth., se raccrocher à qch.

clutch³, *s.* Couvée *f* (d'œufs).

clutter¹, *s.* Encombrement *m*, confus on *f.*

clutter², *v.tr.* To clutter up a room, encombrer une chambre (*with*, de).

coach¹, *s.* **1.** *Rail:* Voiture *f*, wagon *m.* **2.** (*a*) *Sch:* Répétiteur *m.* (*b*) *Sp:* Entraîneur *m.* **coach-builder,** *s.* Carrossier *m.*

coach², *v.tr.* (*a*) Donner les leçons particulières à. *F:* To coach s.o. up, faire la leçon à qn. (*b*) *Sp:* Entraîner.

coachman, *s.* Cocher *m.*

coagulate. 1. *v.tr.* Coaguler, figer. **2.** *v.i.* Se coaguler, se figer.

coagulation, *s.* Coagulation *f*, figement *m.*

coal¹, *s.* (*a*) Charbon *m* (de terre); houille *f.* (*b*) Morceau *m* de charbon. To haul s.o. over the coals, réprimander, semoncer, qn. **coal-barge,** *s.* Chaland *m* à charbon. **coal-cellar,** *s.* Cave *f* au charbon. **coal-field,** *s.* *Min:* Bassin houiller. **coal-gas,** *s.* Gaz *m* de houille; gaz d'éclairage. **coal-merchant,** *s.* **1.** Négociant *m* en charbon. **2.** Marchand *m* de charbon. **coal-mine,** *s.* Mine *f* de houille; houillère *f.* **coal-miner,** *s.* (Ouvrier) mineur *m*, houilleur *m.* **coal-mining,** *s.* Exploitation *f* de la houille. **coal-owner,** *s.* Propriétaire *m* de mines de charbon. **coal-pit,** *s.* = COAL-MINE. **coal-scuttle,** *s.* Seau *m* à charbon.

coal-shovel, s. Pelle f à charbon. **coal-tar,** s. Goudron m de houille.

coal², v.tr. Approvisionner de charbon. To coal ship, abs. to coal, faire le charbon.

coaling, s. Nau: Charbonnage m.

coalesce, v.i. S'unir; se fondre (ensemble).

coalescence, s. Coalescence f, fusion f.

coalition, s. Coalition f.

coalman, s. Charbonnier m.

coarse, a. **1.** Grossier, vulgaire. **2.** Gros, grossier, rude. **-ly,** adv. Grossièrement. **coarse-grained,** a. A gros grain(s); (of wood) à gros fil.

coarseness, s. **1.** Grossièreté f, brutalité f (des manières). **2.** Grosseur f de fil (d'une étoffe).

coast¹, s. Côte f, rivage m. **coast-guard,** s. Garde-côte m, pl. gardes-côte.

coast², v.i. & tr. Nau: To coast (along), suivre la côte. **coasting,** s. Cabotage m.

coaster, s. Caboteur m.

coastline, s. Littoral m.

coat¹, s. **1.** (a) Habit m. Dress coat, habit (à queue); frac m. Morning-coat, jaquette f. (Over)coat, (top-)coat, pardessus m. Archeol: Coat of mail, cotte f de mailles. (b) Coat and skirt, costume m tailleur; F: tailleur m. (c) Her: Coat of arms, armes fpl, armoiries fpl. **2.** Robe f (d'un chien). **3.** Couche f (de peinture). **coat-hanger,** s. Cintre m; porte-vêtements m inv. **coat-hook,** s. Patère f.

coat², v.tr. Enduire (with, de). **coated,** a. Enduit, couvert (with, de). Coated tongue, langue chargée.

coax, v.tr. Cajoler, enjôler, câliner. **coaxing¹,** a. Câlin, cajoleur. **coaxing²,** s. Cajolerie f, enjôlement m.

cob, s. **1.** (Horse) Cob m, bidet m. **2.** Cob (-nut), grosse noisette.

cobalt, s. Ch: Cobalt m.

cobble¹, s. Cobble(-stone), galet m, caillou m (de chaussée).

cobble², v.tr. Paver en cailloutis.

cobble³, v.tr. Carreler (des souliers).

cobbler, s. Savetier m. **cobbler's wax,** s. Poix f de cordonnier.

cobra, s. Rept: Cobra m.

cobweb, s. Toile f d'araignée.

cocaine, s. Pharm: Cocaïne f.

Cochin-China. Pr.n. Geog: La Cochin-chine.

cochineal, s. Dy: Cochenille f.

cock¹, s. **1.** (a) Coq m. The cock of the walk, le coq du village. (b) Cock-bird, oiseau m mâle. **2.** (a) Robinet m. (b) Sm.a: Chien m (de fusil). At full cock, au cran d'armé.

cock-a-doodle-doo! Cocorico! **cock-a-hoop,** a. & adv. (En) jubilant; triomphant, exultant. **cock-and-bull,** attrib. a. Cock-and-bull story, histoire f de pure invention. **cock-crow,** s. At cock-crow, au (premier) chant du coq. **cock-fight,** s. Combat m de coqs. **cock-sure,** a. Sûr de soi; outrecuidant.

cock², v.tr. **1.** (a) To cock one's eye at s.o., lancer une œillade à qn. (b) To cock the ears, dresser les oreilles. **2.** To cock one's hat, mettre son chapeau de travers. Cocked hat, chapeau à cornes. F: To knock s.o. into a cocked hat, battre qn à plates coutures. **3.** To cock a gun, armer un fusil.

cockade, s. Cocarde f.

cockatoo, s. Orn: Cacatoès m, cacatois m.

cockatrice, s. Myth: Basilic m.

cockchafer, s. Ent: Hanneton m.

cockerel, s. Jeune coq m.

cockle¹, s. Moll: Bucarde f, clovisse f. **cockle-shell,** s. **1.** Bucarde f, coque f. **2.** F: (Boat) Coquille f de noix.

cockle², v.i. Se recroqueviller; (of paper) (se) gondoler; (of tissue) goder.

cockney, a. & s. Londonien, -ienne. C. accent, accent faubourien (de Londres).

cockpit, s. **1.** Arène f de combats de coqs. **2.** Navy: Poste m des blessés. **3.** Av: Carlingue f.

cockroach, s. Ent: Blatte f; F: cafard m.

cockscomb, s. Crête f de coq.

cockspur, s. Ergot m de coq.

cocktail, s. Cocktail m.

cocky, a. F: Suffisant, outrecuidant.

cocoa, s. Cacao m.

coco-nut, s. **1.** (i) (Noix f de) coco m; (ii) P: tête f, caboche f. Coco-nut shy, jeu m de massacre. **2.** Coco-nut palm, cocotier m.

cocoon, s. Cocon m.

cod, s. Cod(-fish), morue f. (Fresh) cod, cabillaud m. **cod-fisher,** s. Morutier m. **cod-fishing,** s. Pêche f de la morue. **cod-liver-oil,** s. Pharm: Huile f de foie de morue.

coddle, v.tr. Gâter, choyer. To coddle oneself, se dorloter.

code, s. **1.** Code m. The highway c., le code de la route. **2.** (a) Code word, mot convenu. (b) (Secret) Chiffre m.

codicil, s. Codicille m.

codify, v.tr. Codifier.

coefficient, s. Coefficient m.

coerce, v.tr. Forcer, contraindre (s.o. into doing sth., qn à faire qch.).

coercion, s. Coercition f, contrainte f.

coffee, s. Café m. Black coffee, café noir; café nature. F: White coffee, café au lait ou café crème. **coffee-bean,** s. Grain m de café. **coffee-cup,** s. Tasse f à café. **coffee-grounds,** s.pl. Marc m de café. **coffee-pot,** s. Cafetière f. **coffee-room,** s. Salle f des voyageurs. **coffee-stall,** s. Cantine f, de coin de rue.

coffer, s. Coffre m.

coffin, s. Cercueil m, bière f.

cog¹, s. Mec.E: Dent f (d'une roue dentée). **cog-rail,** s. Rail: Crémaillère f. **cog-wheel,** s. Mec.E: Roue dentée.

cog², v. **1.** v.tr. Denter, endenter (une roue). **2.** v.i. (Of wheels) S'engrener.

cogency, s. Force f, puissance f.

cogent, *a.* Puissant ; (raison) valable.

cogitate, *v.i.* Méditer, réfléchir (*upon, over,* sur).

cogitation, *s.* Réflexion *f,* délibération *f* (*upon, over,* sur).

cognate, *a. C.* (*with sth.*), qui a du rapport (avec qch.) ; analogue (à qch.).

cognizance, *s.* Connaissance *f.*

cognizant, *a.* To be c. of a fact, être instruit d'un fait.

cognomen, *s.* (*a*) Surnom *m,* sobriquet *m.* (*b*) Nom *m* de famille.

cohabit, *v.i.* Cohabiter.

cohere, *v.i.* Se tenir ensemble ; adhérer.

coherent, *a.* **I.** Cohérent. **2.** Conséquent, cohérent. **-ly,** *adv.* (Parler) avec cohérence.

cohesion, *s.* Cohésion *f* ; adhérence *f.*

cohesive, *a.* Cohésif.

coign, *s.* Coign of vantage, position avantageuse.

coil[1]**,** *s.* **I.** Rouleau *m* (de corde). *Coils of hair,* torsades *f* de cheveux. **2.** (*a*) Pli *m,* repli *m* (d'un cordage) ; anneau *m* (d'un serpent). (*b*) *Coils of smoke,* tourbillons *m* de fumée. **3.** *El :* Enroulement *m,* bobine *f.*

coil[2]**. I.** *v.tr.* (En)rouler (un cordage). To coil (itself) up, s'enrouler ; (*of cat*) se mettre en rond. **2.** *v.i.* Serpenter. **coiling,** *s.* Enroulement *m* ; bobinage *m.*

coin[1]**,** *s.* **I.** Pièce *f* de monnaie. **2.** *Coll.* Monnaie(s) *f,* espèces *fpl.*

coin[2]**,** *v.tr.* **I.** To c. money, (i) frapper de la monnaie ; (ii) faire des affaires d'or. **2.** Inventer (un mot nouveau).

coinage, *s.* (*a*) Système *m* monétaire. (*b*) Monnaie(s) *f* ; numéraire *m.*

coincide, *v.i.* **I.** Coïncider (*with,* avec). **2.** S'accorder, être d'accord (*with,* avec).

coincidence, *s.* Coïncidence *f.*

coiner, *s.* **I.** Monnayeur *m.* **2.** Faux monnayeur.

coke, *s.* Coke *m.*

colander, *s. Cu :* Passoire *f.*

colchicum, *s. Bot :* Colchique *m.*

cold[1]**,** *a.* Froid. **I.** (*a*) It is cold, il fait froid. To grow cold, se refroidir. Cold steel, l'arme blanche. *Com :* Cold storage, conservation par le froid. Cold store, entrepôt frigorifique. To give s.o. the cold shoulder, battre froid à qn. (*b*) To be cold, to feel cold, avoir froid. *My feet are* as cold as ice, j'ai les pieds glacés. **2.** A cold reception, un accueil froid. *F :* That leaves me cold, cela ne me fait ni chaud ni froid. **-ly,** *adv.* Froidement. **cold-blooded,** *a.* **I.** (Animal) à sang froid. **2.** (*Of pers.*) Froid, insensible ; (*of action*) délibéré. **cold-hearted,** *a.* Au cœur froid, sec. **cold-shoulder,** *v.tr.* Battre froid à.

cold[2]**,** *s.* **I.** Froid *m.* To leave s.o. out in the cold, laisser qn à l'écart. **2.** *Med :* Rhume *m.* To have a cold, être enrhumé. Cold in the head, rhume de cerveau. To catch (a) cold, attraper un rhume ; s'enrhumer.

coldness, *s.* Froideur *f.*

colic, *s. Med :* Colique *f.*

collaborate, *v.i.* Collaborer (*with,* avec).

collaboration, *s.* Collaboration *f.*

collaborator, *s.* Collaborateur, -trice.

collapse[1]**,** *s.* **I.** Écroulement *m,* effondrement *m* ; débâcle *f* (d'un pays). **2.** *Med :* Affaissement subit.

collapse[2]**,** *v.i.* **I.** S'affaisser, s'écrouler, s'effondrer. **2.** *Med :* S'affaisser (subitement).

collapsible, *a.* Pliant, repliable.

collar[1]**,** *s.* **I.** (*a*) Col *m* (de robe) ; collet *m* (de manteau) ; tour *m* de cou (en fourrure). Lace collar, collerette *f.* To seize s.o. by the collar, saisir qn au collet. (*b*) (Detachable) collar, faux col. Size in collars, encolure *f.* **2.** Collier *m* (de chien). **collar-bone,** *s.* Clavicule *f.*

collar[2]**,** *v.tr.* (*a*) Colleter ; saisir, prendre, au collet. (*b*) *Fb :* Arrêter. (*c*) *F :* Saisir, pincer.

collate, *v.tr.* Collationner.

collateral, *a.* Collatéral, -aux.

collation, *s.* Collation *f.*

colleague, *s.* Collègue *mf* ; confrère *m.*

collect[1]**,** *s. Ecc :* Collecte *f.*

collect[2]**. I.** *v.tr.* (*a*) Rassembler (la foule) ; assembler (des matériaux). To c. the letters, lever les lettres. (*b*) Collectionner (des timbres). (*c*) Percevoir, lever (les impôts) ; toucher (une traite). To collect a debt, faire rentrer une créance. (*d*) *F :* Recueillir, rassembler (ses idées) ; ramasser (ses forces). *To c. oneself,* se reprendre. *To c. one's thoughts,* se recueillir. **2.** *v.i.* S'assembler, se rassembler ; (*of thgs*) s'amasser. **collected,** *a.* (*a*) Recueilli. (*b*) (Plein) de sang-froid. **collecting-box,** *s.* tronc *m.*

collection, *s.* **I.** Rassemblement *m* ; recouvrement *m* (d'une somme) ; perception *f* (des impôts) ; levée *f* (des lettres). **2.** Quête *f,* collecte *f.* **3.** Amas *m,* assemblage *m.* **4.** Collection *f* (de timbres) ; recueil *m* (de proverbes).

collective, *a.* Collectif.

collector, *s.* (*a*) Quêteur, -euse (d'aumônes) ; collecteur, -trice (de cotisations). (*b*) Encaisseur (de la Compagnie du gaz). *Adm :* Percepteur *m.* (*c*) Collectionneur, -euse.

college, *s.* **I.** Collège *m.* **2.** École *f* (militaire). **3.** Collège ; école secondaire.

collide, *v.i.* Se rencontrer, se heurter. To c. with sth., heurter qch.

collie, *s.* Chien *m* de berger écossais.

collier, *s.* **I.** Houilleur *m* ; mineur *m* (de charbon). **2.** (Navire *m*) charbonnier *m.*

colliery, *s.* Houillère *f.*

collision, *s.* Collision *f,* rencontre *f* ; tamponnement *m* (de trains) ; abordage *m* (de navires).

colloquial, *a.* Familier ; de (la) conversation. **-ally,** *adv.* Familièrement.

colloquialism, *s.* Expression familière.

colloquy, *s.* Colloque *m*, entretien *m*.
collusion, *s.* Collusion *f*. *To act in c. with s.o.*, agir de complicité avec qn.
colon, *s.* Deux-points *m*.
colonel, *s.* Colonel *m*.
colonial, *a. & s.* Colonial *m*, -aux.
colonist, *s.* Colon *m*.
colonization, *s.* Colonisation *f*.
colonize, *v.tr.* Coloniser.
colony, *s.* Colonie *f*.
colossal, *a.* Colossal, -aux ; démesuré.
colossus, *s.* Colosse *m*.
colour¹, *s.* **I.** (*a*) Couleur ,. *What c. is it?* de quelle couleur est-ce ? (*b*) *Art :* Coloris *m*.
2. Matière colorante ; pigment *m*. **3.** Teint *m*, couleurs. *To change colour*, changer de visage. *High colour*, vivacité *f* de teint. *F :* *To be off colour*, n'être pas dans son assiette. **4.** *Usu. pl.* Couleurs (d'un parti). *Nau :* Pavillon *m*. (*Regimental*) *colours*, drapeau *m*. *To be with the colours*, être sous les drapeaux. *F :* *To pass with flying colours*, passer haut la main. *To sail under false colours, F :* se faire passer pour quelqu'un d'autre. *F :* *To stick to one's colours*, rester fidèle à ses principes. *To show oneself in one's true colours*, jeter le masque. *To nail one's colours to the mast*, clouer son pavillon. **5.** *To give colour to a story*, rendre une histoire vraisemblable. **colour-blind,** *a.* Daltonien. **colour-blindness,** *s.* Daltonisme *m*.
colour², *a.* **I.** *v.tr.* (*a*) Colorer ; colorier (une carte). *To c. sth. blue*, colorer qch. en bleu. (*b*) Donner de l'éclat à (une description). **2.** *v.i.* Rougir. **coloured,** *a.* Coloré ; (*of drawing*) colorié. *C. shirt*, chemise de couleur.
colouring, *s.* **I.** (*a*) *Art :* Coloris *m*. (*b*) Teint *m*. *People with high c.*, gens hauts en couleur. **2.** Apparence *f*.
colourless, *a.* Sans couleur ; incolore.
colt, *s.* Poulain *m*, pouliche *f*.
columbine¹, *s.* *Bot :* Ancolie *f*.
Columbine². *Pr.n.* *Th :* Colombine *f*.
Columbus. *Pr.n.* Christopher Columbus, Christophe Colomb *m*.
column, *s.* Colonne *f*.
coma, *s.* *Med :* Coma *m*.
comatose, *a.* *Med :* (État) comateux.
comb¹, *s.* **I.** Peigne *m*. **2.** Crête *f* (de coq).
comb², *v.tr.* Peigner. **comb out,** *v.tr.* **I.** Démêler (les cheveux). **2.** (*a*) (*Of police*) *To c. out a district*, faire une rafle (de suspects). (*b*) Éliminer les non-valeurs.
combat¹, *s.* Combat *m*.
combat². **I.** *v.i.* Combattre (*with*, *against*, contre). **2.** *v.tr.* Lutter contre, combattre.
combatant, *a. & s.* Combattant, -ante.
combative, *a.* Combatif ; batailleur, -euse.
comber, *s.* Longue lame déferlante.
combination, *s.* **I.** Combinaison *f*. **2.** Association *f*. **3.** *pl.* *Cost :* (A pair of) combinations, une combinaison-culotte.
combine. **I.** *v.tr.* Combiner ; allier (*with*,

à). *To combine business with pleasure*, joindre 'utile à l'agréable. **2.** *v.i.* (*a*) S'unir, s'associer (*against*, contre). (*b*) *Ch :* Se combiner. **combined,** *a.* *C. efforts*, efforts réunis.
combustible. **I.** *a.* Combustible. **2.** *s.* (*a*) Matière *f* inflammable. (*b*) Combustible *m*.
combustion, *s.* Combustion *f*. *Spontaneous c.*, inflammation spontanée.
come, *v.i.* **I.** Venir, arriver. (*a*) *He comes this way every week*, il passe par ici tous les huit jours. *Here he comes!* le voilà qui arrive ! *Coming!* voilà ! on y va ! *To come for sth.*, venir chercher qch. *F :* *You have come to the wrong person*, vous vous adressez mal. *F :* *What are things coming to?* où allons-nous ? *Come now!* allons ! voyons ! (*b*) *To come to oneself*, reprendre connaissance. **2.** (*a*) *Come what may*, advienne que pourra. (*b*) *Now that I come to think of it*, maintenant que j'y songe. **3.** (*a*) *What will come of it?* qu'en adviendra-t-il ? *That's what comes of . . .*, voilà ce qu'il en est de . . . . (*b*) *To come of a good family*, sortir d'une bonne famille. **4.** (*a*) *How much does it come to?* combien cela fait-il ? *It comes to this*, cela revient à ceci. (*b*) *It must come to that*, il faudra bien en arriver là. *What he knows does not come to much*, ce qu'il sait ce n'est pas grand'chose. (*c*) *That doesn't come within my duties*, cela ne rentre pas dans mes fonctions. **5.** (*a*) *That comes easy to him*, cela lui est facile. *To come expensive*, coûter cher. (*b*) *You come first*, vous venez en premier. **6.** *I have come to believe that*, j'en suis venu à croire que. **7.** *The time to come*, le temps à venir ; l'avenir *m*. *For three months to c.*, pendant trois mois encore.
come about, *v.i.* Arriver, se passer, se produire, avoir lieu. **come across,** *v.i.* Trouver, rencontrer, sur son chemin ; tomber sur. **come after,** *v.i.* **I.** (*a*) Suivre. (*b*) Succéder à. **2.** Suivre ; venir plus tard. **come again,** *v.i.* Revenir. **come against,** *v.i.* Heurter, frapper. **come along,** *v.i.* **I.** Arriver, venir. *Come along!* (i) amène-toi ! arrive ! (ii) allons-y ! allons-nous-en ! **2.** *F :* Survenir. **come apart,** *v.i.* (*a*) Se séparer, se défaire. (*b*) Se décoller. **come away,** *v.i.* **I.** Partir, s'en aller. **2.** Se détacher. **come back,** *v.i.* Revenir. **come before,** *v.i.* **I.** Précéder. **2.** Primer ; (*of pers.*) prendre le pas sur. **come between,** *v.i.* Intervenir, s'interposer, entre. **come by,** *v.i.* **I.** (*a*) *To come by the house*, passer par la maison. (*b*) Honestly come by, honnêtement acquis. **2.** *I heard him come by*, je l'ai entendu passer. **come down,** *v.i.* **I.** Descendre ; faire la descente de. **2.** (*a*) *F :* *To come down in the world*, déchoir. *Prices are coming down*, les prix baissent. (*b*) *F :* *To come down upon s.o.*, semoncer vertement qn. (*c*) *To come down.* (*Of horse*) S'abattre ; (*of structure*) s'écrouler. **come-down,** *s.* *F :* Humiliation *f* ; déchéance *f*. **come forward,** *v.i.*

1. S'avancer. **2.** *To c. forward as a candidate,* se présenter comme candidat. **come in,** *v.i.* **1.** Entrer. **2.** (*Of tide*) Monter; (*of year*) commencer; (*of fashion*) entrer en vogue. **3.** (*Of funds*) Rentrer. **4.** (*a*) To come in useful to s.o., for sth., servir à qn, à qch. (*b*) *Sp:* To come in first, arriver premier. **5.** To come in for sth., recevoir qch. *F:* And where do I come in? et moi, qu'est-ce que j'y gagne? **come into,** *v.i.* **1.** *To c. into s.o.'s mind,* se présenter à l'esprit de qn. **2.** To come into a property, entrer en possession d'un domaine. **come off,** *v.i.* **1.** *To c. off one's horse,* tomber de (son) cheval. **2.** (*a*) Se détacher; s'en aller. (*b*) (*Of event*) Avoir lieu; (*of attempt*) réussir, aboutir. (*c*) To come off badly, s'en mal tirer. *He came off victorious,* il en sortit vainqueur. **come on,** *v.i.* (*a*) S'avancer. Come on, let's have a game! allons! faisons une partie! (*b*) (Bien) venir; faire des progrès. (*c*) (*Of illness*) Survenir; (*of winter*) venir, arriver; (*of night*) tomber. (*d*) To come on for trial, venir devant la cour. (*e*) *Th:* Entrer en scène. **come out,** *v.i.* **1.** To come out of a place, sortir d'un lieu. **2.** (*a*) Sortir. *Ind:* To come out (on strike), se mettre en grève. (*b*) *Sch:* To c. out first, être reçu premier. (*c*) (*Of stars*) Paraître; (*of buds*) éclore. (*d*) (*Of stain*) S'enlever, s'effacer. (*e*) (*Of book*) Paraître. (*f*) (*Of problem*) Se résoudre. (*g*) *F:* To come out with a remark, lâcher une observation. **come over,** *v.i.* What has come over you? qu'est-ce qui vous prend? **come round,** *v.i.* (*a*) *F:* Come round and see me one day, venez me voir un de ces jours. (*b*) Reprendre connaissance; revenir à soi. (*c*) *To c. round to s.o.'s way of thinking,* se ranger à l'avis de qn. **come through,** *v.i.* **1.** *To c. through trials,* passer par des épreuves. *To c. through an illness,* surmonter une maladie. **2.** (*a*) *The water is coming through,* l'eau pénètre. (*b*) He came through without a scratch, il s'en est tiré indemne. **come to,** *v.i.* = COME ROUND (*b*). **come together,** *v.i.* S'assembler, se réunir. **come under,** *v.i.* **1.** To come under s.o.'s influence, tomber sous, subir, l'influence de qn. **2.** *To c. under a heading,* être compris sous un article. **come up,** *v.i.* (*a*) Come up to my rooms, montez chez moi. (*b*) To come up to s.o., s'approcher de qn. *Jur:* To come up before the Court, comparaître (devant le tribunal). (*c*) (*Of plants*) Sortir de terre; pousser. (*d*) To come up (for discussion), venir sur le tapis. (*e*) To come up to s.o.'s expectations, répondre à l'attente de qn. (*f*) Égaler. (*g*) To come up against sth., se heurter à, contre, qch. (*h*) To come up with s.o., rattraper, rejoindre, qn. **come upon,** *v.i.* To come upon s.o., rencontrer qn par hasard. **coming¹,** *a.* *The c.* year, l'année qui vient, l'année prochaine. The c. storm, l'orage qui approche. A coming man, un homme d'avenir. **coming²,** *s.* Venue *f*,

arrivée *f*; approche *f*. **Comings and goings,** allées *f* et venues.

comedian, *s.* Comédien, -ienne.

comedy, *s.* Comédie *f*.

comely, *a.* Avenant.

comer, *s.* **1.** Comers and goers, allants *m* et venants *m*. All comers, tout le monde. **2.** First comer, premier venu.

comet, *s.* Comète *f*.

comfort¹, *s.* **1.** Consolation *f*; soulagement *m*. That is cold comfort, c'est là une piètre consolation. **2.** Bien-être *m*. **3.** Confort *m*; confortable *m*; aisance *f*. To live in comfort, vivre dans l'aisance.

comfort², *v.tr* **1.** Consoler, soulager. **2.** Redonner du courage à. **comforting,** *a.* Réconfortant. *C. words,* paroles de consolation.

comfortable, *a.* **1.** Confortable; (*of dress*) commode, aisé; (*of warmth*) agréable. To make oneself comfortable, se mettre à son aise. **2.** Comfortable income, revenu suffisant. **3.** Sans inquiétude; tranquille. **-ably,** *adv.* Confortablement, commodément, agréablement. To be comfortably off, être à l'aise.

comforter, *s.* **1.** Consolateur, -trice. **2.** Cache-nez *m inv.*

comfortless, *a.* Incommode; sans commodité.

comic, *a.* Comique. Comic opera, opéra bouffe.

comical, *a.* Comique, risible.

comma, *s.* (*a*) Virgule *f*. (*b*) Inverted commas, guillemets *m*.

command¹, *s.* **1.** Ordre *m*, commandement *m*. Done at s.o.'s command, fait d'après les ordres de qn. Word of command, commandement *m*. By royal command, sur l'invitation du Roi. **2.** Commandement (*of*, de; *over,* sur); gouvernement *m*. Second in command, commandant *m* en second. **3.** (*a*) Connaissance *f*, maîtrise *f*. (*b*) Command over oneself, maîtrise de soi. (*c*) The money at my command, les fonds à ma disposition.

command², *v.tr.* **1.** Ordonner, commander (s.o. to do sth., à qn de faire qch.). **2.** Commander (un régiment). **3.** Avoir (qch.) à sa disposition. You may c. me, vous pouvez disposer de moi. **4.** To command attention, forcer l'attention. **5.** Commander, dominer. **commanding,** *a.* **1.** Commanding officer, officier commandant. **2.** (Ton) d'autorité, de commandement. **3.** *C.* presence, air, port, imposant.

commandant, *s.* Commandant *m*.

commandeer, *v.tr.* Réquisitionner.

commander, *s.* (*a*) *Mil:* Commandant *m*. Commander-in-chief, commandant en chef; généralissime *m*. (*b*) *Navy:* Capitaine *m* de frégate.

commandment, *s.* Commandement *m*.

commemorate, *v.tr.* Commémorer.

commence, *v.tr. & i.* Commencer. *To c. to do sth.,* commencer à, de, faire qch.

commencement, *s.* Commencement *m*, début *m*.

commend, *v.tr.* **I.** Recommander, confier (qch. à qn). **2.** (a) Louer. (b) *A course of action that did not c. itself to me,* une ligne de conduite qui n'était pas à mon goût.

commendable, *a.* Louable.

commendation, *s.* Éloge *m*, louange *f*.

commensurate, *a.* **I.** Coétendu (*with,* à). **2.** Proportionné (*to, with,* à). **-ly,** *adv.* Proportionnellement (*to, with,* à).

comment¹, *s.* Commentaire *m*. **No comments, please!** point d'observations, s'il vous plaît !

comment², *v.i.* **I.** *To c. on a text,* commenter un texte. **2.** *F: To c. on s.o.'s behaviour,* critiquer la conduite de qn. Faire des observations (*on,* sur).

commentary, *s.* Commentaire *m*.

commentator, *s.* Commentateur, -trice.

commerce, *s.* Le commerce ; les affaires *f*.

commercial. **I.** *a.* (a) Commercial, -aux. *C. car,* automobile industrielle. (b) (Esprit) mercantile. **2.** *s. F:* Commis voyageur. **-ally,** *adv.* Commercialement.

commingle. **I.** *v.tr.* Mêler ensemble ; mélanger. **2.** *v.i.* Se mêler (*with,* avec).

commiserate, *v.tr. & i.* **To commiserate** (with) s.o., s'apitoyer sur le sort de qn.

commiseration, *s.* Commisération *f*, compassion *f* (*with,* pour).

commissariat, *s. Mil:* Intendance *f*.

commissary, *s.* Commissaire *m*, délégué *m*.

commission¹, *s.* Commission *f*. **I.** Délégation *f* (d'autorité). **2.** Brevet *m. Mil: To get one's commission,* être nommé officier. *To resign one's c.,* démissionner. **3.** Ordre *m*, mandat *m. To carry out a c.,* s'acquitter d'une commission. **4.** *Nau:* Armement *m* (d'un navire). **To put a ship into commission,** armer un vaisseau. **5.** *Com:* Commission ; pourcentage *m*. **6.** Perpétration *f* (d'un crime). **commission-agent,** *s.* Commissionnaire *m* en marchandises.

commission², *v.tr.* **I.** (a) Commissionner. (b) Préposer, déléguer, à une fonction. (c) Commander (un tableau). **2.** *Nau:* Armer (un navire). **commissioned,** *a.* **I.** Muni de pouvoirs ; commissionné. **2. Commissioned officer,** officier *m*.

commissionaire, *s.* Commissionnaire *m*.

commissioner, *s.* Commissaire *m*. (a) Membre *m* d'une commission. (b) Délégué *m* d'une commission. **Commissioner of police** = préfet *m* de police.

commit, *v.tr.* **I.** Commettre, confier. **To commit sth. to writing,** coucher qch. par écrit. **2. To commit s.o. to prison,** *abs.* **to commit s.o.,** envoyer qn en prison. **To commit for trial,** renvoyer aux assises. **3. To commit oneself,** se compromettre. **Without committing myself,** sous toutes réserves. **4.** Commettre (un crime).

commitment, *s.* **I.** = COMMITTAL. **2.** Engagement financier.

committal, *s.* **I.** Délégation *f* (*to,* à). **2.** (a) *C. of a body to the earth,* mise *f* en terre d'un cadavre. (b) *Jur:* Mise en prison. **3.** Perpétration *f*. **4.** Engagement *m*.

committee, *s.* Comité *m*, commission *f*, conseil *m*. *C. of management,* conseil d'administration.

commode, *s. Furn:* Commode *f*.

commodious, *a.* Spacieux.

commodiousness, *s.* Amples dimensions *f*.

commodity, *s.* Marchandise *f*, denrée *f*, article *m*.

commodore, *s. Navy:* Chef *m* de division ; commodore *m*.

common¹, *a.* **I.** Commun (*to,* à). *The c. opinion,* l'opinion courante. **2.** (a) Ordinaire. *C. occurrence,* chose fréquente. *C. honesty,* la probité la plus élémentaire. **In common use,** d'usage courant. **In common parlance,** en langage ordinaire. **To be common talk,** courir les rues. **They are as common as blackberries,** les rues en sont pavées. (b) De peu de valeur. *The c. people,* les gens du peuple. **3.** Vulgaire. **-ly,** *adv.* **I.** Communément, ordinairement. **2.** Vulgairement.

common², *s.* **I.** Terrain, pré, communal. **2. To have sth. in common with s.o.,** avoir qch. en commun avec qn.

commoner, *s.* Homme *m* du peuple.

commonness, *s.* **I.** Fréquence *f*. **2.** Banalité *f* ; vulgarité *f*.

commonplace. **I.** *s.* (a) Lieu commun. (b) Banalité *f*. **2.** *a.* Banal, -aux.

commons, *s.* **I.** Le peuple. **The House of Commons,** la Chambre des Communes. **2.** *F: To be on short commons,* faire maigre chère.

commonwealth, *s.* État *m* ; république *f*.

commotion, *s.* **I.** Confusion *f*, agitation *f*, commotion *f*. **2.** Troubles *mpl*.

communal, *a.* Communal, -aux.

commune, *v.i.* Converser, s'entretenir. **To commune with oneself,** se recueillir.

communicable, *a.* Communicable.

communicant, *s.* **I.** Informateur, -trice. **2.** *Ecc:* Communiant, -e.

communicate. **I.** *v.tr. & i.* Communiquer. **2.** *Ecc: v.i.* Communier.

communication, *s.* **I.** Communication *f*. **2. To get into communication with s.o.,** communiquer avec qn. **3. Line of communication,** voie d'intercommunication.

communicative, *a.* Communicatif ; expansif.

communicativeness, *s.* Caractère expansif ; humeur bavarde.

communicator, *s.* Communicateur *m*.

communion, *s.* **I.** Relations *fpl*, rapports *mpl* (*with s.o.,* avec qn). **Self-communion,** recueillement *m*. **2.** *Ecc:* **The (Holy) Communion,** la communion, la (Sainte) Cène. **The Communion table,** la Sainte Table.

communism, *s.* Communisme *m.*

communist, *s.* Communiste *mf.*

community, *s.* 1. Communauté *f* (de biens). 2. *Ecc:* Communauté. 3. (*a*) The community, l'État *m*; le public. (*b*) Community singing, chant en commun.

commutable, *a.* Permutable; interchangeable.

commutation, *s.* Commutation *f.*

commute, *v.tr.* 1. Interchanger. 2. Échanger (*for, into*, pour, contre); racheter (une servitude).

compact¹, *s.* Convention *f*, pacte *m.*

compact², *a.* Compact; serré, tassé.

compact³, *s. Toil:* Poudrier *m.*

compactness, *s.* Compacité *f*; concision *f.*

companion, *s.* 1. (*a*) Compagnon, *f.* compagne. (*b*) (Lady-)companion, dame *f* de compagnie. 2. (*a*) Manuel *m.* (*b*) Lady's companion, nécessaire *m* à ouvrage.

companionable, *a.* D'une société agréable. -ably, *adv.* Sociablement.

companionship, *s.* (*a*) Compagnie *f.* (*b*) Camaraderie *f.*

company, *s.* 1. Compagnie *f.* To keep s.o. company, tenir compagnie à qn. To part company (with s.o.), se séparer (de qn). 2. (*a*) Assemblée *f*, compagnie; bande *f.* Present company excepted, les présents exceptés. (*b*) (Guests) Monde *m.* 3. (*Associates*) Compagnie, société *f.* F: He is very good company, il est fort amusant. 4. *Com:* (i) Compagnie; (ii) société (commerciale). *Gas c.*, compagnie du gaz. Joint stock company, société par actions. Limited (liability) company, société à responsabilité limitée. 5. (*a*) *Th:* Troupe *f.* Touring c., troupe ambulante. (*b*) *Nau:* The ship's company, l'équipage *m.* 6. *Mil:* Compagnie.

comparable, *a.* Comparable (*with, to*, avec, à). -ably, *adv.* Comparablement.

comparative, *a.* 1. Comparatif. 2. Relatif. *This would be c. wealth*, ce serait l'aisance relative. -ly, *adv.* 1. Comparativement, par comparaison (*to*, à). 2. Relativement.

compare¹, *s.* Beyond compare, sans pareil(le).

compare², 1. *v.tr.* Comparer (*to, with*, à, avec). (As) compared with, en comparaison de, auprès de. *To c. a copy with the original,* confronter une copie avec l'original. *F:* To compare notes, échanger ses impressions. 2. *v.i.* He can't c. with you, il ne vous est pas comparable. To compare favourably with sth., ne le céder en rien à qch. **comparing,** *s.* Comparaison *f.*

comparison, *s.* Comparaison *f.* In c. with, en comparaison de; auprès de.

compartment, *s.* 1. Compartiment *m.* *Rail:* Smoking c., compartiment fumeurs. 2. Case *f* (d'un tiroir).

compass¹, *s.* 1. (A pair of) compasses, un compas. 2. (*a*) Limite(s) *f(pl).* (*b*) Pourtour *m.* 3. (*a*) Étendue *f.* In small compass,

sous un volume restreint. (*b*) *Mus:* Étendue, registre *m.* 4. Boussole *f*; compas. Pocket compass, boussole de poche. Mariner's compass, compas (de mer). **compass-card,** *s. Nau:* Rose *f* des vents.

compass², *v.tr.* 1. Faire le tour de (qch.). 2. *Compassed about by, with*, entouré de. 3. Atteindre.

compassion, *s.* Compassion *f.* To have compassion on s.o., avoir compassion de qn. *To arouse c.*, faire pitié.

compassionate, *a.* Compatissant (*to, towards*, à, pour). -ly, *adv.* Avec compassion.

compatibility, *s.* Compatibilité *f.*

compatible, *a.* Compatible (*with*, avec).

compatriot, *s.* Compatriote *mf.*

compel, *v.tr.* To compel s.o. to do sth., contraindre, forcer, obliger, qn à faire qch. *He compels respect*, il impose le respect.

compelling, *a. C. force*, force compulsive.

compendious, *a.* Abrégé, succinct.

compendium, *s.* 1. Abrégé *m*, compendium *m inv.* 2. Pochette *f* (de papeterie).

compensate. 1. *v.tr.* (*a*) To compensate s.o. for sth., dédommager qn de qch. (*b*) Rémunérer (qn). (*c*) *Med:* Compenser. 2. *v.i.* To compensate for sth., (i) remplacer, racheter, qch.; (ii) compenser qch.

compensation, *s.* Compensation *f*; dédommagement *m*; indemnité *f. F:* In compensation, en revanche.

compete, *v.i.* 1. To compete with s.o., faire concurrence à qn. 2. To c. for a prize, concourir pour un prix. 3. To compete with s.o. in talent, le disputer en talent avec qn.

competence, competency, *s.* 1. Suffisance *f* de moyens d'existence. To enjoy a competency, avoir de quoi vivre. 2. Competence in a subject, compétence *f* en un sujet. 3. Attributions *fpl* (d'un fonctionnaire).

competent, *a.* 1. Capable. 2. Compétent. -ly, *adv.* 1. Avec compétence. 2. D'une manière suffisante.

competition, *s.* 1. Rivalité *f*, concurrence *f.* 2. Concours *m.* 3. *Com:* Concurrence.

competitive, *a. C. spirit*, esprit de concurrence.

competitor, *s.* Concurrent, -e.

compilation, *s.* Compilation *f.*

compile, *v.tr.* Compiler.

compiler, *s.* Compilateur, -trice.

complacence, complacency, *s.* 1. Satisfaction *f.* 2. Contentement *m* de soi-même; suffisance *f.*

complacent, *a.* Content de soi-même. *C. air*, air suffisant. -ly, *adv.* Avec satisfaction; avec suffisance.

complain, *v.i.* 1. Se plaindre (*of*, de). *I have nothing to c. of*, je n'ai pas à me plaindre. 2. What do you complain of? sur quoi porte votre plainte?

complainant, *s. Jur:* Plaignant, -e.

complaint, *s.* 1. (*a*) Grief *m.* I have no cause of complaint, je n'ai aucun sujet de plainte. (b) To lodge a complaint against s.o., porter plainte contre qn. 2. Maladie f, mal m.

complaisance, s. Complaisance f. obligeance f.

complaisant, a. Complaisant, obligeant. **-ly,** adv. Avec complaisance.

complement¹, s. I. (a) Plein m. (b) Navy: Effectif m. 2. Complément m.

complement², v.tr. Compléter.

complementary, a. Complémentaire.

complete¹, a. I. (a) Complet, -ète ; entier, total. (b) Terminé. 2. Parfait, achevé. **-ly,** adv. Complètement, totalement.

complete², v.tr. I. Compléter, achever. To complete the misfortune, pour comble de malheur. 2. To c. a form, remplir une formule.

completeness, s. État complet ; plénitude f.

completion, s. Achèvement m, complétement m.

complex. I. a. Complexe. 2. s. Psy: Complexe m. Inferiority complex, complexe d'infériorité.

complexion, s. I. Teint m. 2. Aspect m.

complexity, s. Complexité f.

compliance, s. I. Acquiescement m (with, à). In compliance with your wishes, en conformité de vos désirs. 2. Pej: (Base) compliance, soumission (abjecte).

compliant, a. Obligeant, accommodant.

complicated, a. Compliqué ; embrouillé.

complication, s. Complication f.

complicity, s. Complicité f (in, à).

compliment¹, s. Compliment m. To send one's compliments to s.o., se rappeler au bon souvenir de qn.

compliment², v.tr. Complimenter, féliciter (on, de).

complimentary, a. Flatteur, -euse.

comply, v.i. To c. with, se conformer à ; observer ; accéder à (une demande).

component. I. a. Component parts, parties constituantes. 2. s. Composant m ; partie composante.

comport, v.pr. To comport oneself, se comporter.

comportment, s. Conduite f, maintien m.

compose, v.tr. I. Composer. 2. Arranger, accommoder (un différend). 3. (a) To c. one's features, se composer le visage. (b) Compose yourself! calmez-vous ! **composed,** a. Calme, tranquille.

composedly, adv. Tranquillement ; avec calme.

composer, s. Compositeur, -trice.

composition, s. I. (a) Action f de composer ; composition f. (b) Composition, constitution f. 2. Mélange m, composé m. 3. (a) A musical composition, une composition musicale. (b) Sch: Thème m. 4. (a) Accommodement m, entente f. (b) Accommodement (avec des créanciers).

compositor, s. Typ: Compositeur m.

composure, s. Calme m, sang-froid m

compound¹. I. a. (a) Composé. Compound interest, intérêts composés. (b) Complexe. II. **compound,** s. (Corps m) composé m.

compound². I. v.tr. (a) Composer, mélanger. (b) Accommoder, arranger. (c) To compound a felony, pactiser avec un crime. 2. v.i. S'arranger, composer.

comprehend, v.tr. Comprendre. I. Se rendre compte de. 2. Englober.

comprehensible, a. Compréhensible, intelligible.

comprehension, s. Compréhension f.

comprehensive, a. Compréhensif. **-ly,** adv. Dans un sens très étendu.

comprehensiveness, s. Étendue f, portée f.

compress¹, s. Surg: Compresse f.

compress², v.tr I. Comprimer. 2. Condenser (un discours).

compressible, a. Compressible, comprimable.

compression, s. Compression f.

comprise, v.tr. Comprendre, renfermer.

compromise¹, s. Compromis m. To agree to a c., accepter une transaction ; transiger.

compromise². I. v.tr. (a) Compromettre. (b) Arranger. 2. v.i. Compromettre, transiger.

compromising, a. Compromettant.

comptroller, s. I. Administrateur m. 2. Contrôleur m ; vérificateur m.

compulsion, s. Contrainte f. Under compulsion, par contrainte.

compulsory, a. I. Obligatoire. 2. C. powers, pouvoirs coercitifs. **-ily,** adv. Obligatoirement.

compunction, s. Componction f ; remords m. F: Without compunction, sans scrupule.

computation, s. Calcul m, estimation f.

compute, v.tr. Computer, calculer, estimer.

comrade, s. Camarade m, compagnon m.

comradeship, s. Camaraderie f.

con¹, v.tr. Étudier (un rôle).

con², v.tr. Nau: Gouverner. **conning-tower,** s. Navy: Blockhaus m ; kiosque m (de sous-marin).

concave, a. Concave, incurvé.

concavity, s. Concavité f.

conceal, v.tr. Cacher ; celer, dissimuler ; tenir secret. To c. sth. from s.o., cacher qch. à qn ; taire qch. à qn. **concealed,** a. Caché, dissimulé. Concealed turning, virage masqué.

concealment, s. I. Dissimulation f. 2. Action f de cacher. A place of concealment, une cachette, une retraite.

concede, v.tr. Concéder.

conceit, s. I. Vanité f, suffisance f. 2. He has got a very good c. of himself, il est très satisfait de sa petite personne.

conceited, a. Suffisant, vaniteux. **-ly,** adv. Avec suffisance.

conceivable, a. Concevable, imaginable.

conceive, v.tr. I. Concevoir. To conceive a dislike for s.o., prendre qn en aversion. 2. v.i. To conceive of sth., (s')imaginer, comprendre, qch.

concentrate. 1. *v.tr.* Concentrer. **2.** *v.i.*
(*a*) Se concentrer. (*b*) To concentrate on sth.,
concentrer son attention sur qch.
concentration, *s.* Concentration *f.*
concentric, *a.* Concentrique.
conception, *s.* Conception *f. F:* **I haven't
the remotest conception,** je n'en ai pas la
moindre idée.
concern¹, *s.* **1.** (*a*) Rapport *m.* (*b*) Intérêt *m*
(*in*, dans) **It's no concern of mine,** cela ne
me regarde pas. **2.** Souci *m,* anxiété *f,* inquiétude *f* (*about*, à l'égard de). **He enquired
with concern,** il demanda avec sollicitude *f.*
3. (*a*) *Com:* Entreprise *f;* fonds *m* de
commerce. (*b*) *F:* Appareil *m,* machin *m.*
concern², *v.tr.* **1.** (*a*) Concerner, regarder,
intéresser; se rapporter à. **That does not
concern me,** cela ne me regarde pas. **It
concerns him to know,** il lui importe de
savoir. **As concerns,** quant à, pour ce qui
est de. (*b*) **To concern oneself with sth.,**
s'intéresser à, s'occuper de, se mêler de, qch.
2. (*a*) *His honour is concerned,* il s'agit de son
honneur. **The persons concerned,** les intéressés. **As far as I am concerned,** en ce qui
me concerne. (*b*) **To be concerned about sth.,**
s'inquiéter de qch. *He looked very much
concerned,* il avait l'air très soucieux. **concerning,** *prep.* Concernant, touchant, en
ce qui concerne.
concert¹, *s.* **1.** Concert *m,* accord *m.* **To act
in concert** (with s.o.), agir de concert (avec
qn). **2.** *Mus:* Concert; séance musicale.
Wireless concerts, auditions musicales. **con-
cert-hall,** *s.* Salle *f* de concert.
concert². **1.** *v.tr.* Concerter. **2.** *v.i.* Se
concerter (*with*, avec).
concertina, *s.* **1.** *Mus:* Accordéon *m.* **2.**
Rail: Concertina vestibule, soufflet *m.*
concession, *s.* Concession *f.*
conch, *s.* Conque *f.*
conciliate, *v.tr.* Concilier, réconcilier.
conciliation, *s.* Conciliation *f.*
conciliatory, *a.* Conciliant.
concise, *a.* Concis. **-ly,** *adv.* Avec concision.
conciseness, *s.* Concision *f.*
conclave, *s. F:* Assemblée *f,* réunion *f.*
conclude, *v.tr. & i.* **1.** Conclure; arranger,
régler. **2.** Terminer, conclure, achever.
3. From this I conclude that, de ceci je
conclus que. **concluding,** *a.* Final, -als.
conclusion, *s.* **1.** Conclusion *f* (d'un traité).
2. Fin *f,* conclusion (d'une lettre). **In conclusion,** pour conclure. **3.** Conclusions
arrived at, décisions prises. **To come to the
conclusion that,** conclure que. *It was a foregone c.,* c'était prévu. *F:* **To try conclusions
with s.o.,** se mesurer avec qn.
conclusive, *a.* Concluant, décisif. **-ly,** *adv.*
D'une manière concluante.
concoct, *v.tr.* **1.** Composer; confectionner.
2. Imaginer; tramer (un complot).
concoction, *s.* **1.** (*a*) Confectionnement *m.*

(*b*) Boisson *f,* potion *f.* **2.** Conception *f;*
machination *f* (d'un complot).
concord, *s.* **1.** Concorde *f,* harmonie *f.*
2. *Gram:* The concords, les règles *f* d'accord.
concordance, *s.* Concordance *f,* accord *m*
(*with*, avec); harmonie *f.*
concordant, *a.* **1.** Qui s'accorde, concordant (*with*, avec). **2.** *Mus:* Consonant.
concourse, *s.* Foule *f,* rassemblement *m,*
concours *m.*
concrete. 1. *a.* Concret, -ète. **2.** *s.* Béton *m*
(de ciment).
concretion, *s.* Concrétion *f.*
concubine, *s.* Concubine *f.*
concur, *v.i.* **1.** Concourir, coïncider. **2.** Être
d'accord (*with s.o.,* avec qn). *All c. in the
belief that,* tous s'accordent à croire que.
concurrence, *s.* **1.** (*a*) Concours *m* (de
circonstances); coopération *f* (de personnes).
(*b*) Simultanéité *f.* **2.** (*a*) Accord *m.* (*b*) Assentiment *m,* approbation *f.*
concurrent, *a.* Unanime, concordant.
-ly, *adv.* Concurremment (*with*, avec).
concussion, *s.* Secousse *f,* ébranlement *m.*
Med: Commotion (cérébrale).
condemn, *v.tr.* Condamner. **1.** Condemned
cell, cellule des condamnés. **2.** To c. stores,
condamner, réformer, du matériel. **3.** Déclarer coupable. **4.** Censurer, blâmer.
condemnation, *s.* (*a*) Condamnation *f.*
(*b*) Censure *f,* blâme *m.*
condensation, *s.* Condensation *f.*
condense. **1.** *v.tr.* Condenser; serrer (son
style); concentrer (un produit). **2.** *v.i.* Se
condenser.
condescend, *v.i.* **1.** Condescendre (à faire
qch.). **2.** Se montrer condescendant (envers
qn). **condescending,** *a.* Condescendant
(*to,* envers).
condescension, *s.* **1.** Condescendance *f*
(*to,* envers, pour). **2.** Complaisance *f.*
condign, *a.* Mérité, exemplaire.
condiment, *s.* Condiment *m.*
condition, *s.* Condition *f.* **1.** On condition
that, à (la) condition que. **2.** (*a*) État *m,* situation *f. To be in a c. to do sth.,* être à même,
en état, de faire qch. **To keep oneself in
condition,** se maintenir en forme. (*b*) État
civil. **To change one's condition,** changer
d'état; se marier.
conditional, *a.* Conditionnel. (*a*) *My
promise was c.,* ma promesse était soumise à
certaines réserves. (*b*) *Conditional* on sth.,
dépendant de qch. **-ally,** *adv.* Condition-
nellement; sous certaines conditions.
condole, *v.i.* To condole with s.o., exprimer
ses condoléances à qn.
condolence, *s.* Condoléance *f.*
condone, *v.tr.* Pardonner.
condor, *s. Orn:* Condor *m.*
conduce, *v.i.* Contribuer, tendre (*to,* à).
conducive, *a.* Qui contribue; favorable.
conduct¹, *s.* Conduite *f.* **1.** C. of affairs,
conduite, gestion *f,* des affaires. **2.** Allure *f;*
manière *f* de se conduire.

conduct², *v.tr.* **1.** Conduire, (a)mener. Conducted tours, excursions accompagnées. **2.** (*a*) Mener, gérer. *Jur:* To c. one's own case, plaider soi-même sa cause. (*b*) *Mus:* Diriger. **3.** To conduct oneself, se comporter, se conduire. **4.** *Ph:* Être conducteur de. **conducting,** *a.* Conducteur, -trice.

conduction, *s.* *Ph:* Conduction *f,* transmission *f.*

conductor, *s.* **1.** (*a*) Conducteur, -trice; accompagnateur *m* (de touristes). (*b*) Receveur, -euse (d'un tramway). (*c*) *Mus:* Chef *m* d'orchestre. **2.** Conducteur (de la chaleur, de l'électricité).

conduit, *s.* *Hyd.E:* Conduit(-pipe), conduit *m;* tuyau conducteur.

cone, *s.* **1.** Cône *m.* **2.** *Bot:* Pomme *f,* cône. **cone-bearing,** *a.* *Bot:* Conifère.

confection, *s.* Confection *f.*

confectioner, *s.* Confiseur *m.*

confectionery, *s.* Confiserie *f.*

confederacy, *s.* **1.** Confédération *f* (d'États). **2.** Conspiration *f.*

confederate. 1. *a.* Confédéré (*with,* avec). **2.** *s.* (*a*) Confédéré *m.* (*b*) *Jur:* Complice *mf.*

confederation, *s.* Confédération *f.*

confer, *v.* **1.** *v.tr.* Conférer. To c. a favour on s.o., accorder une faveur à qn. **2.** *v.i.* Conférer, entrer en consultation. **conferring,** *s.* **1.** = CONFERMENT. **2.** Consultation *f.*

conference, *s.* **1.** Conférence *f,* entretien *m,* consultation *f.*

conferment, *s.* **1.** Collation *f* (d'un titre). **2.** Octroi *m* (d'une faveur).

confess, *v.tr.* **1.** (*a*) Confesser, avouer. I was wrong, I confess, j'ai eu tort, je l'avoue. (*b*) *Abs.* Faire des aveux. (*c*) *v.ind.tr.* To confess to a crime, avouer un crime. **2.** *Ecc:* (*a*) To confess (oneself), se confesser. (*b*) Confesser (un pénitent). **confessed,** *a.* Confessé, avoué.

confession, *s.* **1.** Confession *f,* aveu *m.* **2.** *Ecc:* To go to confession, aller à confesse. To hear s.o.'s confession, confesser qn.

confessor, *s.* Confesseur *m.*

confidant, *f.* **confidante,** *s.* Confident, -ente.

confide. 1. *v.tr.* Confier. **2.** *v.i.* To confide in s.o., se confier à qn. **confiding,** *a.* Confiant; sans soupçons. **-ly,** *adv.* Avec confiance.

confidence, *s.* **1.** (*a*) Confiance *f* (*in,* en). To have every confidence in s.o., faire toute confiance à qn. (*b*) Assurance *f,* confiance, hardiesse *f.* **2.** Confidence *f.* In strict confidence, à titre essentiellement confidentiel. **3.** To make a confidence to s.o., faire une confidence à qn. **4.** Confidence-trick, vol *m* à l'américaine.

confident. 1. *a.* (*a*) Assuré, sûr (*of,* de); confiant. (*b*) Plein de hardiesse; effronté. **2.** *s.* Confident, -ente. **-ly,** *adv.* **1.** Avec confiance. **2.** Avec assurance.

confidential, *a.* **1.** Confidentiel. **2.** To be

c. with s.o., faire des confidences à qn. **3.** Confidential clerk, homme de confiance. **-ally,** *adv.* Confidentiellement.

configuration, *s.* Configuration *f.*

confine, *v.tr.* **1.** (R)enfermer To be confined to bed; être alité. (*b*) To confine oneself to doing sth., se borner à faire qch. To c. oneself to facts, s'en tenir aux faits. (*c*) Confined space, espace resserré, restreint.

confinement, *s.* **1.** Emprisonnement *m,* réclusion *f.* In solitary confinement, au secret; dans une réclusion rigoureuse. **2.** Couches *fpl.*

confines, *s.pl.* Confins *m.*

confirm, *v.tr.* **1.** (R)affermir (son pouvoir); confirmer (qn dans une opinion). **2.** Confirmer (un traité). **3.** Confirmer, corroborer. **confirmed,** *a.* Invétéré.

confirmation, *s* (R)affermissement *m;* confirmation *f* (d'un traité).

confiscate, *v.tr.* Confisquer.

confiscation, *s.* Confiscation *f.*

conflagration, *s.* (*a*) Conflagration *f,* embrasement *m.* (*b*) Incendie *m.*

conflict¹, *s.* Conflit *m,* lutte *f.*

conflict², *v.i.* Être en conflit, en contradiction (*with,* avec). **conflicting,** *a.* Opposé (*with,* à); incompatible (*with,* avec). C. evidence, témoignages discordants.

confluence, *s.* Confluent *m.*

conform, *v.i.* Se conformer (*to, with,* à). To c. to fashion, suivre la mode.

conformable, *a.* **1.** Conforme (*to,* à). **2.** Accommodant. **-ably,** *adv.* Conformably to, conformément à.

conformation, *s.* Conformation *f,* structure *f.*

conformity, *s.* Conformité *f* (*to, with,* à).

confound, *v.tr.* **1.** Confondre. **2.** Confound him! que le diable l'emporte! C. it! zut! **confounded,** *a.* *F:* Maudit, satané, sacré.

confront, *v.tr.* **1.** Affronter, faire face à. **2.** To c. s.o. with witnesses, confronter qn avec des témoins.

confuse, *v.tr.* **1.** Mêler, brouiller. **2.** To c. sth. with sth., confondre qch. avec qch. **3.** (*a*) Embrouiller. To get confused, s'embrouiller. (*b*) Bouleverser, troubler. To get confused, se troubler. **confused,** *a.* (*a*) Embrouillé. (*b*) Bouleversé, *F:* ahuri. (*c*) Confus. **confusing,** *a.* Embrouillant. It is very confusing, on s'y perd.

confusedly, *adv.* Confusément.

confusion, *s.* **1.** Confusion *f.* **2.** Désordre *m,* remue-ménage *m.* Everything was in confusion, tout était sens dessus dessous.

confutation, *s.* Réfutation *f.*

confute, *v.tr.* **1.** Convaincre d'erreur. **2.** Réfuter (un argument).

congeal, *v.* **1.** *v.tr.* Congeler, geler. **2.** *v.i.* (*a*) Se congeler; geler. (*b*) (*Of blood*) Se figer.

congenial, *a.* (*a*) We have c. tastes, nous avons des goûts en commun. (*b*) Congenial spirit, esprit sympathique, aimable. C. employment, travail agréable. **-ally,** *adv.* Agréablement.

conger, *s.* *Ich:* Conger(-eel), congre *m.*

congest. **I.** *v.tr.* Encombrer, embouteiller. **2.** *v.i.* S'embouteiller. **congested,** *a.* **I.** *Med:* Congestionné. **2.** Encombré, embouteillé *Congested area,* région surpeuplée.

congestion, *s.* **I.** *Med:* Congestion *f*; engorgement *m.* **2.** (*a*) Encombrement *m.* (*b*) Surpeuplement *m.*

conglomeration, *s.* Conglomération *f.*

congratulate, *v.tr.* Féliciter (qn de qch.).

congratulation, *s.* Félicitation *f.*

congregate. *v.i.* Se rassembler, s'assembler.

congregation, *s.* **I.** Rassemblement *m.* **2.** Assistance *f*; Paroissiens *m pl.*

congress, *s.* **I.** Réunion *f.* **2.** Congrès *m.*

conic(al), *a.* *Geom:* Conique.

coniferous, *a.* *Bot:* Conifère.

conjectural, *a.* Conjectural, -aux.

conjecture¹, *s.* Conjecture *f.*

conjecture², *v.tr.* Conjecturer.

conjoin, *v.i.* S'unir; s'associer. **conjoined,** *a.* Conjoint.

conjoint, *a.* Conjoint, associé. **-ly,** *adv.* Conjointement, ensemble.

conjugal, *a.* Conjugal, -aux.

conjugate, *v.tr.* Conjuguer.

conjugation, *s.* Conjugaison *f.*

conjunction, *s.* Conjonction *f.* In conjunction with s.o., de concert avec qn.

conjunctive, *a. & s. Gram:* Conjonctif (*m*).

conjuncture, *s.* Conjoncture *f*, circonstance *f*, occasion *f.*

conjure, *v.* **I.** *v.tr.* Conjurer (qn de faire qch.). **2.** (*a*) *v.tr.* Conjurer (un démon). To conjure up, évoquer. *F:* A name to conjure with, un nom tout-puissant. (*b*) *v.i.* Faire des tours de passe-passe. **conjuring,** *s.* **I.** Conjuring up, évocation *f.* **2.** Prestidigitation *f.*

conjuror, *s.* Prestidigitateur *m.*

conker, *s.* *F:* Marron *m* d'Inde.

connect. **I.** *v.tr.* (*a*) (Re)lier, (ré)unir; rattacher, joindre (*with, to,* à). (*b*) Associer (*with,* avec, à); relier (des idées). (*c*) To be connected with a family, être allié, à, avec, une famille. **2.** *v.i.* Se lier, se relier, se joindre, se réunir. *Rail:* To connect with a train, faire correspondance avec un train.

connected, *a.* **I.** (*a*) C. speech, discours suivi. (*b*) Two closely c. trades, deux métiers affins, connexes. **2.** To be well connected, être bien apparenté. **connecting,** *a.* Connecting wire, fil de connexion.

connection, *s.* **I.** Rapport *m*, liaison *f* (des choses); connexion *f*, suite *f* (des idées). In connection with, à propos de. In this connection, à ce propos. In another connection, d'autre part. **2.** To form a connection with s.o., établir des rapports, des relations *f*, avec qn. **3.** (*a*) Parenté *f*; liens *mpl* de famille. (*b*) He is a c. of mine, c'est un de mes parents. **4.** *Rail:* Correspondance *f.* **5.** *Mec.E:* Connexion; assemblage *m.*

Tp: Wrong connection, fausse communication. **6.** (*a*) Raccord *m.* (*b*) *El.E:* Contact *m*; prise *f* de courant.

connexion, *s.* = CONNECTION.

connivance, *s.* Connivence *f*; complicité *f* (*at, in,* dans).

connive, *v.i.* To connive at an abuse, fermer les yeux sur un abus.

connoisseur, *s.* Connaisseur, -euse.

connote, *v.tr.* *F:* Signifier; impliquer.

connubial, *a.* Conjugal, -aux.

conquer, *v.tr.* **I.** Conquérir. **2.** Vaincre.

conquering, *a.* **I.** Conquérant. **2.** Victorieux. *The c. hero,* le héros triomphant.

conqueror, *s.* **I.** Conquérant *m.* **2.** Vainqueur *m.*

conquest, *s.* Conquête *f.*

conscience, *s.* Conscience *f.* With a clear conscience, en (toute) sûreté de conscience. *For c. sake,* par acquit de conscience. In (all) conscience, en vérité, assurément, certes. **conscience-stricken,** *a.* Pris de remords.

conscientious, *a.* **I.** Consciencieux. **2.** Conscientious objector, objecteur *m* de conscience. **-ly,** *adv.* Consciencieusement.

conscientiousness, *s.* Conscience *f*; droiture *f.*

conscious, *a.* **I.** (*a*) To be conscious of sth., avoir conscience de qch. To become conscious of sth., s'apercevoir de qch. (*b*) Conscious movement, mouvement conscient. **2.** To become c., reprendre connaissance. **-ly,** *adv.* Consciemment.

consciousness, *s.* **I.** (*a*) Conscience *f*, sentiment *m* (*of, de*). (*b*) Sentiment intime. **2.** To lose consciousness, perdre connaissance *f.* To regain consciousness, revenir à soi.

conscript¹, *a. & s.* Conscrit (*m*).

conscript², *v.tr.* Enrôler, engager.

conscription, *s.* Conscription *f.*

consecrate, *v.tr.* Consacrer. **consecrated,** *a.* Consacré; (of bread) bénit.

consecration, *s.* **I.** Consécration *f.* **2.** The c. of a life, le dévouement d'une vie.

consecutive, *a.* Consécutif. On three c. days, trois jours de suite. **-ly,** *adv.* Consécutivement; de suite.

consensus, *s.* Consensus *m*, unanimité *f.*

consent¹, *s.* Consentement *m*, assentiment *m.* By common consent, d'une commune voix. With one consent, d'un commun accord.

consent², *v.i.* To consent to sth., consentir à qch. I consent, j'y consens; je veux bien.

consequence, *s.* **I.** Conséquence *f*; suites *fpl.* In consequence, par conséquent. In consequence of, par suite de. **2.** Importance *f*; *F:* conséquence. It is of no consequence, cela ne tire pas à conséquence; cela ne fait rien.

consequent, *a.* **I.** Résultant. **2.** Conséquent, logique. **-ly,** *adv. & con.* Par conséquent; conséquemment.

consequential, *a.* **I.** Conséquent, consécutif (*to,* à). **2.** Suffisant; plein d'importance.

conservation, *s.* Conservation *f.*

conservative. 1. *a. At a c. estimate,* au bas mot. **2.** *a. & s. Pol:* Conservateur, -trice.

conservator, *s.* Conservateur, -trice.

conservatory, *s. Hort:* Serre *f.*

conserve, *v.tr.* Conserver, préserver.

conserves, *s.pl. Cu:* Confiture(s) *f,* conserves *f.*

consider, *v.tr* **1.** *(a)* Considérer. *I will c. it,* j'y réfléchirai. **Considered opinion,** opinion réfléchie. **All things considered,** tout bien considéré. *(b)* Prendre en considération; étudier, examiner. **2. To consider s.o.'s feelings,** ménager qn. *To c. the expense,* regarder à la dépense. **3.** *(a) Pred. I c. him crazy,* je le considère comme fou. **Consider it as done,** tenez cela pour fait. *(b) We c. that he ought to do it,* à notre avis il doit le faire. **considering,** *prep.* Eu égard à. *C. his age,* étant donné son âge. *C. the circumstances,* vu les circonstances. *F: It is not so bad considering,* somme toute, ce n'est pas si mal.

considerable, *a.* Considérable. **-ably,** *adv.* Considérablement.

considerate, *a.* Prévenant, plein d'égards *(towards,* pour, envers). **-ly,** *adv.* Avec égards, avec prévenance.

consideration, *s.* **1.** Considération *f.* *(a) Taking all things into c.,* tout bien considéré. *After due consideration,* après mûre réflexion. *(b) On no consideration,* à aucun prix. **2.** Compensation *f,* rémunération *f.* *For a consideration,* contre espèces *fpl;* moyennant finance. **3. Out of consideration for s.o.,** par égard pour qn. *To treat s.o. with c.,* ménager qn. **4.** *Money is no c.,* l'argent n'entre pas en ligne de compte.

consign, *v.tr.* **1.** Consigner, expédier. **2. To consign sth. to oblivion,** ensevelir qch. dans l'oubli.

consignee, *s.* Consignataire *m.*

consignment, *s.* **1.** Envoi *m,* expédition *f.* **2.** Envoi, arrivage *m.*

consignor, *s. Com:* Consignateur *m,* expéditeur *m.*

consist, *v.i. To consist of sth.,* consister en, dans, se composer de, qch.

consistence, *s.* Consistance *f.*

consistency, *s.* **1.** = CONSISTENCE. **2.** Uniformité *f.*

consistent, *a.* **1.** Conséquent; logique. *Ideas that are not c.,* idées qui ne se tiennent pas. **2.** Compatible, d'accord *(with,* avec). **-ly,** *adv.* **1.** Conséquemment; avec conséquence. **2.** Conformément *(with,* à).

consolation, *s.* Consolation *f.*

console, *v.tr.* Consoler (qn d'une perte). **consoling,** *a.* Consolant; consolateur, -trice.

consolidate, *v.tr.* Consolider, (r)affermir.

consolidation, *s.* **1.** Consolidation *f,* (r)affermissement *m.* **2.** Unification *f* (des lois).

consonance, *s.* **1.** Consonance *f; Mus:* accord *m.* **2.** Accord, communion *f.*

consonant[1], *a.* Consonant with duty, qui s'accorde avec le devoir.

consonant[2], *s. Ling:* Consonne *f.*

consort[1], *s.* **1.** Époux, -ouse. **2. To sail in consort,** naviguer de conserve.

consort[2], *v.i.* **To consort with s.o.,** frayer avec qn; fréquenter qn.

conspicuous, *a.* **1.** *In a c. position,* bien en évidence. *To be c.,* attirer les regards. **2.** Frappant, marquant. **To make oneself conspicuous,** se faire remarquer. *C. gallantry,* bravoure insigne. **-ly,** *adv.* Manifestement; bien en évidence.

conspiracy, *s.* Conspiration *f,* conjuration *f.*

conspirator, *s.* Conspirateur, -trice; conjuré *m.*

conspire, *v.i. (a)* Conspirer *(against,* contre); agir de concert (avec qn). *(b)* Concourir, conspirer (*to,* à).

constable, *s.* **1.** *Hist:* Connétable *m.* **2. (Police) constable,** gardien *m* de la paix. **Chief constable** = commissaire *m* de police.

constabulary, *s.* Police.

constancy, *s.* **1.** Constance *f,* fermeté *f.* **2.** Constance; régularité *f.*

constant, *a. (a)* Constant; invariable. *(b)* Incessant, continuel. *(c)* (Ami) loyal, -aux. **-ly,** *adv.* Constamment, continuellement.

constellation, *s.* Constellation *f.*

consternation, *s.* Consternation *f;* atterrement *m.*

constituency, *s.* Circonscription électorale.

constituent. 1. *a.* Constituant, constitutif. **2.** *s.* Élément constitutif; composant *m.* **3.** *s.pl.* Mandants *m;* électeurs *m.*

constitute, *v.tr.* Constituer.

constitution, *s.* **1.** Constitution *f,* composition *f.* **2.** Complexion *f,* constitution (du corps). **3.** *Pol:* Constitution.

constitutional, *a.* Constitutionnel. **-ally,** *adv.* **1.** Constitutionnellement. **2.** Par tempérament.

constrain, *v.tr.* **1. To constrain s.o. to do sth.,** contraindre, forcer, qn à, de, faire qch. **2.** Retenir de force. **constrained,** *a.* (Sourire) forcé; (air) gêné.

constraint, *s.* **1.** Contrainte *f.* **To put s.o. under constraint,** retenir qn de force. **2.** *(a)* Gêne *f,* contrainte. *(b)* Retenue *f.*

constrict, *v.tr.* Resserrer, étrangler, rétrécir.

constriction, *s.* Resserrement *m,* étranglement *m.*

construct, *v.tr.* Construire; bâtir.

construction, *s.* **1.** *(a)* Construction *f,* établissement *m.* **In course of construction,** en construction. *(b)* Construction, édifice *m,* bâtiment *m.* **2.** *To put a wrong c. on sth.,* mésinterpréter qch.; entendre qch. de travers.

constructive, *a.* Constructif.

constructor, *s.* Constructeur *m.*

construe, *v.tr.* Interpréter; expliquer.

consul, s. Consul m.

consular, a. Consulaire.

consulate, s. Consulat m.

consult. I. v.tr. (a) Consulter (qn sur qch.). (b) To c. one's own interests, consulter ses intérêts. 2. v.i. Consulter (avec qn). To c. together, délibérer; se consulter. **consulting-hours**, s.pl. Heures f de consultation.

consultation, s. Consultation f.

consume, v.tr. (a) (Of fire) Consumer, dévorer. (b) Consommer (des vivres). (c) To be consumed with thirst, être consumé par la soif.

consumer, s. Consommateur, -trice. Consumers of gas, abonnés au gaz.

consummate[1], a. Consommé, achevé.

consummate[2], v.tr. Consommer.

consummation, s. I. Consommation f. 2. Fin f; but m; comble m.

consumption, s. I. (a) Consommation f. 2. Med: Phtisie f; consomption f.

consumptive, a. & s. Med: Poitrinaire (mf), phtisique (mf).

contact, s. Contact m. To be in contact with s.o., être en contact, en rapport, avec qn.

contagion, s. Contagion f.

contagious, a. Contagieux.

contain, v.t. I. (a) Contenir. (b) Contenir, renfermer; comprendre. 2. Contenir, maîtriser. He cannot c. himself for joy, il ne se sent pas de joie.

container, s. (a) Récipient m; réservoir m. (b) Com: Boîte f.

contaminate, v.tr. Contaminer; corrompre.

contamination, s. Contamination f.

contemplate, v.tr. I. (a) Contempler, considérer. (b) v.i. Se recueillir; méditer. 2. (a) Prévoir, envisager. (b) To contemplate sth., projeter, se proposer, qch.

contemplation, s. I. (a) Contemplation f. (b) Recueillement m, méditation f. 2. To have sth. in contemplation, projeter qch.

contemplative, a. Contemplatif, recueilli.

contemporaneous, a. Contemporain (with, de). **-ly**, adv. Contemporaneously with, à la même époque que.

contemporary, a. Contemporain (with, de). Contemporary events, événements actuels.

contempt, s. I. Mépris m; dédain m. Beneath contempt, tout ce qu'il y a de plus méprisable. 2. Jur: Contempt of court, outrage m à la Cour.

contemptible, a. Méprisable; indigne. **-ibly**, adv. D'une manière méprisable.

contemptuous, a. I. Dédaigneux (of, de). 2. (Air) méprisant; (geste) de mépris. **-ly**, adv. Avec mépris.

contend. I. v.i. Combattre, lutter (with, against, contre); disputer (avec qn sur qch.). To contend with s.o. for sth., contester qch. à qn. 2. v.tr. To contend that, prétendre, soutenir, que + ind. **contending**, a. C. parties, contestants m.

content[1], s. (a) Contenance f. (b) pl. Contents, contenu m. (Table of) contents, table f des matières.

content[2], s. Contentement m, satisfaction f.

content[3], a. Satisfait (with, de). To be c. with sth., se contenter de qch.

content[4], v.tr. I. Contenter, satisfaire. 2. To content oneself with (doing) sth., se contenter de (faire) qch. **contented**, a. Satisfait, content (with, de). **-ly**, adv. Sans se plaindre; (vivre) content.

contention, s. I. Dispute f, démêlé m, débat m. To be a bone of contention, être une pomme de discorde. 2. Affirmation f, prétention f.

contentious, a. Disputeur, -euse; disputailleur, -euse.

contentment, s. Contentement m de son sort.

contest[1], s. (a) Combat m, lutte f (with, avec, contre; between, entre). (b) Concours m.

contest[2]. I. v.tr. (a) Contester, débattre. (b) To contest a seat in Parliament, disputer un siège au Parlement. (c) Jur: Attaquer; contester. 2. v.i. Se disputer (with, against, avec).

contestant, s. I. Contestant, -ante. 2. Compétiteur, -trice.

context, s. Contexte m.

contiguity, s. Contiguïté f. In contiguity, contigu, -uë (with, à).

contiguous, a. Contiguous to sth., contigu, -uë, à qch., avec qch.; attenant à qch.

continence, s. Continence f, chasteté f.

continent[1], a. Continent, chaste.

continent[2], s. Geog: Continent m.

continental, a. Continental, -aux.

contingency, s. Éventualité f; cas imprévu. To provide for contingencies, parer à l'imprévu.

contingent. I. a. (a) Éventuel, fortuit, accidentel. (b) C. on sth., sous (la) réserve de qch. (Of event) To be c. upon sth., dépendre de qch. 2. s. Mil: Contingent m.

continual, a. Continuel. **-ally**, adv. Continuellement; sans cesse.

continuance, s. Continuation f.

continuation, s. I. Continuation f. 2. Prolongement m; suite f.

continue. I. v.tr. (a) Continuer; poursuivre; reprendre. Journ: 'To be continued,' "à suivre." (b) Perpétuer. (c) To continue to do sth., continuer à, de, faire qch. 2. v.i. (a) (Se) continuer; se prolonger. (b) To c. in office, garder sa charge.

continuity, s. Continuité f.

continuous, a. Continu. Cin: Continuous performance, spectacle permanent. **-ly**, adv. Continûment; sans interruption.

contort, v.tr. Tordre, contourner. **contorted**, a. Contorsionné, contourné.

contortion, s. Contorsion f.

contour, s. Contour m; profil m (du terrain). **contour-map**, s. I. Carte f en courbes de niveau. **2.** *Aut:* Carte des profils de la route.

contraband, *s.* Contrebande *f.*

contract¹, *s.* **I.** (*a*) Pacte *m*; contrat *m* (de mariage). (*b*) Acte *m* de vente. **2.** Entreprise *f*; soumission *f*; adjudication *f.* **To enter into a contract,** passer (un) contrat (*with,* avec). **Breach of contract,** rupture de contrat. **3.** *Cards:* Contrat.

contract², *v.* **I. I.** *v.tr.* Contracter; crisper (les traits). **2.** *v.i.* Se contracter, se resserrer, se rétrécir. **II. contract. I.** *v.tr.* (*a*) Contracter; prendre. *To c. a liking for sth.,* prendre goût à qch. (*b*) *Com:* **To contract to do sth.,** s'engager par traité à faire qch. **2.** *v.i.* **To contract for work,** entreprendre des travaux à forfait.

contraction, *s.* **I.** Contraction *f*; rétrécissement *m.* **2.** Prise *f* (d'une habitude).

contractor, *s.* Entrepreneur *m*, pourvoyeur *m*, fournisseur *m.*

contradict, *v.tr.* Contredire; dém ntir.

contradiction, *s.* Contradiction *f.* **I.** Démenti *m.* **2. In contradiction with,** en contradiction avec.

contradictory, *a.* Contradictoire; opposé (*to,* à).

contralto, *s.* *Mus:* Contralte *m.*

contrariety, *s.* Contrariété *f.*

contrariness, *s.* Esprit *m* de contradiction.

contrary. I. *a.* (*a*) Contraire (*to,* à); opposé (à), en opposition (avec). (*b*) *F:* Indocile; qui prend plaisir à contrarier. **2.** *s.* Contraire *m.* **On the contrary,** au contraire. **Unless you hear to the contrary,** à moins d'avis contraire. **3.** *adv.* Contrairement (*to,* à); en opposition (*to,* à, avec).

contrast¹, *s.* Contraste *m.* **In contrast with sth.,** par contraste avec qch.

contrast². **I.** *v.tr.* Faire contraster, mettre en contraste (*with,* avec). **2.** *v.i.* Contraster, faire contraste (*with,* avec).

contravene, *v.tr.* **I.** Transgresser, enfreindre. **To contravene the regulations,** contrevenir aux règlements. **2.** Aller à l'encontre de; opposer un démenti à.

contravention, *s.* C. *of a law,* contravention *f*, infraction *f*, à la loi.

contribute, *v.tr. & i.* **I.** *To c. a sum of money,* contribuer pour une somme. **To contribute to a charity,** contribuer à une bonne œuvre. **To contribute to the success,** aider au succès.

contribution, *s.* **I.** Contribution *f*; cotisation *f.* **2. Contribution to a newspaper,** article écrit pour un journal.

contributor, *s.* Collaborateur, -trice.

contrite, *a.* Contrit, pénitent, repentant.

contrition, *s.* Contrition *f*, pénitence *f.*

contrivance, *s.* **I.** Invention *f*; combinaison *f.* **2.** Invention; artifice *m.* **3.** Appareil *m*, dispositif *m.*

contrive, *v.tr.* (*a*) Inventer, combiner. (*b*) Pratiquer, ménager. **To contrive to do**

sth., trouver moyen de faire qch. (*c*) *Abs.* Se débrouiller; s'arranger.

control¹, *s.* (*a*) Autorité *f.* (*b*) Maîtrise *f.* **Circumstances beyond our control,** circonstances en dehors de notre action. **To lose control of oneself,** ne plus se maîtriser. (*c*) Gouverne *f*, manœuvre *f.* *The driver had lost c. of the train,* le mécanicien n'était plus maître du train. (*d*) Surveillance *f.* **Under government control,** assujetti au contrôle du gouvernement.

control², *v.tr.* **I.** Diriger; régler. **To control men,** commander aux hommes. *He cannot c. his boys,* il ne sait pas tenir ses élèves. *Adm:* *To c. the traffic,* réglementer la circulation. **2.** Maîtriser, gouverner. **To control oneself,** se maîtriser.

controller, *s.* **I.** Contrôleur, -euse. **2.** (Appareil) contrôleur *m*; commande *f.*

controversial, *a.* Controversable.

controversy, *s.* Polémique *f*; controverse *f.*

controvert, *v.tr.* **I.** Controverser. **2.** Disputer; mettre en doute.

contumacious, *a.* Rebelle, récalcitrant.

contumacy, *s.* Entêtement *m*, obstination *f.*

contumely, *s.* **I.** Insolence *f*; souverain mépris. **2.** Honte *f.*

contusion, *s.* Contusion *f.*

conundrum, *s.* **I.** Devinette *f.* **2.** Énigme *f.*

convalesce, *v.i.* *He is convalescing,* il est en convalescence (*at,* à).

convalescence, *s.* Convalescence *f.*

convalescent, *a. & s.* Convalescent.

convene. **I.** *v.tr.* Convoquer, réunir. **2.** *v.i.* S'assembler, se réunir.

convenience, *s.* **I.** Commodité *f*, convenance *f.* **At your earliest convenience,** le plus tôt (qu'il vous sera) possible. **2.** (Public) **convenience,** cabinets *m* d'aisances. **3.** *pl.* Commodités, agréments *m.* **All modern conveniences,** tout le confort moderne.

convenient, *a.* Commode. *If it is c. to you,* si cela ne vous dérange pas. **To make it convenient to do sth.,** s'arranger de manière à faire qch. **-ly,** *adv.* Commodément; sans inconvénient.

convent, *s.* Couvent *m* (de femmes).

convention, *s.* **I.** (*a*) Convention *f.* (*b*) Accord *m*, contrat *m.* **2.** *Usu. pl.* Convenances *fpl*, bienséances *fpl.*

conventional, *a.* **I.** Conventionnel; de convention. *Art:* *C. design,* dessin stylisé. **2.** Courant; normal, -aux.

converge, *v.i.* Converger (*on,* sur). **converging,** *a.* Convergent, concourant.

convergence, *s.* Convergence *f.*

convergent, *a.* Convergent.

conversant, *a.* Familier. **Conversant with sth.,** versé dans, au courant de, qch.

conversation, *s.* Conversation *f*, entretien *m.* **To hold a conversation with s.o.,** s'entretenir avec qn. **To be the subject of conversation,** faire les frais de la conversation.

conversational, *a*. **1.** De (la) conversation. **2.** Qui aime à causer.

converse, *v.i.* Causer. **To converse with s.o. on, about, sth.,** converser avec qn sur qch.

conversely, *adv.* Réciproquement.

conversion, *s*. **1.** Conversion *f* (de qn). **2.** *C. of water into steam*, conversion de l'eau en vapeur.

convert[1], *s*. Converti, -ie. **To become a convert to sth.,** se convertir à qch.

convert[2], *v.tr.* **1.** Convertir. **2.** Transformer, changer, convertir (qch. en qch.).

convertible, *a*. Convertible (*into*, en).

convex, *a*. Convexe.

convey, *v.tr.* **1.** Transporter, porter, conduire. **2.** Transmettre (le son). **To convey one's meaning,** communiquer sa pensée. **To convey to s.o. that,** faire comprendre à qn que. **3.** *Jur:* Transmettre, céder (un bien) (*to*, à).

conveyance, *s*. **1.** Transport *m*; moyens *m* de transport; transmission *f*. **2.** *Jur:* Transmission (de biens). **3.** Véhicule *m*; voiture *f*.

convict[1], *s*. Forçat *m*.

convict[2], *v.tr.* Convaincre. *He was convicted*, il fut déclaré coupable.

conviction, *s*. **1.** Condamnation *f*. **2.** **To be open to conviction**, être accessible à la persuasion. **3.** (*Belief*) Conviction *f*.

convince, *v.tr.* Convaincre, persuader (*s.o. of sth.*, qn de qch.). **convincing**, *a*. Convaincant. **-ly**, *adv*. D'une façon convaincante.

convivial, *a*. Joyeux, jovial, -aux.

convoke, *v.tr.* Convoquer.

convolution, *s*. Circonvolution *f*.

convolvulus, *s*. *Bot:* Volubilis *m*.

convoy[1], *s*. Convoi *m*. **To sail under convoy**, naviguer de conserve, en convoi.

convoy[2], *v.tr.* Convoyer, escorter.

convulse, *v.tr.* **1.** Bouleverser; ébranler. **2.** *F:* **To be convulsed with laughter**, se tordre de rire. *Face convulsed with terror*, visage décomposé par la terreur.

convulsion, *s*. **1.** *Med:* (*Usu. pl.*) Convulsions *f pl.* **2.** Bouleversement *m*, commotion *f*.

convulsive, *a*. Convulsif.

coo, *v.i.* Roucouler; (*of baby*) gazouiller. **cooing**, *s*. Roucoulement *m*.

cook[1], *s*. (*a*) Cuisinier, -ière. **Plain cook**, cuisinière bourgeoise. (*b*) *Nau:* Maître-coq *m*.

cook[2]. **1.** *v.tr.* (*a*) (Faire) cuire. *Abs.* Faire la cuisine; cuisiner. *F:* **To cook s.o.'s goose**, faire son affaire à qn. (*b*) *F:* **To cook accounts**, cuisiner, truquer, les comptes. **2.** *v.i.* Cuire. **cooking**, *s*. **1.** Cuisson *f*. **2.** Cuisine *f*. **Plain cooking**, cuisine bourgeoise. **Cooking utensils**, articles de cuisine. **3.** Cooking of accounts, trucage *m* des comptes. **cooking-range**, *s*. Fourneau *m* de cuisine.

cooker, *s*. Cuisinière *f*.

cookery, *s*. (L'art de la) cuisine.

cool[1]. **1.** *a.* (*a*) Frais, *f*, fraîche. *C. drink*, boisson rafraîchissante. *It is cool*, il fait frais. '*To be kept in a cool place*,' "craint la chaleur." (*b*) **To keep cool (and collected)**, garder son sang-froid. *F:* **As cool as a cucumber**, avec un sang-froid imperturbable. **Keep cool!** du calme! (*c*) **To give s.o. a cool reception**, faire un accueil froid à qn. (*d*) *F:* **He is a cool customer**, il ne se laisse pas démonter. **2.** **In the cool of the evening**, dans la fraîcheur du soir. **-lly**, *adv*. **1.** Fraîchement. **2.** De sang-froid. **3.** Froidement. **4.** Effrontément; sans gêne.

cool[2]. **1.** *v.tr.* Rafraîchir, refroidir. **2.** *v.i.* Se rafraîchir, (se) refroidir. **cool down**, *v.i.* Se rafraîchir; s'apaiser, se calmer. **cool off**, *v.i. F:* Se refroidir, tiédir. **cooling**[1], *a*. Rafraîchissant. **cooling**[2], *s*. Rafraîchissement *m*, refroidissement *m*.

coolness, *s*. **1.** Fraîcheur *f*. **2.** (*a*) Sang-froid *m*, flegme *m*. (*b*) *F:* Aplomb *m*. **3.** Froideur *f* (d'un accueil).

coop, *v.tr. F:* **To coop s.o. up**, tenir qn enfermé.

co-operate, *v.i.* Coopérer (avec qn à qch.); agir en commun.

co-operation, *s*. Coopération *f*, concours *m* (*in*, à).

co-operative, *a*. Coopératif.

co-ordinate, *v.tr.* Coordonner (*with*, à).

co-ordination, *s*. Coordination *f*.

coot, *s*. *Orn:* Foulque *f*.

cope[1], *s*. *Ecc:* Chape *f*. *F:* **Under the cope of night**, sous le manteau de la nuit.

cope[2], *v.i.* (*a*) *To c. with s.o.*, tenir tête à qn. (*b*) *To c. with a difficulty*, venir à bout d'une difficulté.

Copenhagen. *Pr.n.* Copenhague *f*.

copious, *a*. Copieux, abondant, ample. **-ly**, *adv*. Copieusement.

copper, *s*. **1.** Cuivre *m*. **2.** Cuve *f* à lessive. **3.** *Attrib.* De cuivre, en cuivre.

copperplate, *s*. **Copperplate engraving**, (gravure *f* en) taille-douce *f*. *F:* **Copperplate writing**, écriture moulée.

coppice, *s*. Taillis *m*, hallier *m*.

copse, *s*. = COPPICE.

copy[1], *s*. **1.** Copie *f*, reproduction *f*. **2.** (*a*) Copie, transcription *f*. **Rough copy**, brouillon *m*. **3.** Modèle *m*, exemple *m*. **4.** Exemplaire *m* (d'un livre); numéro *m* (d'un journal). **5.** *Journ:* Matière *f* à reportage. **copybook**, *s*. Cahier *m* d'écriture.

copy[2], *v.tr.* Copier. **1.** (*a*) Imiter, reproduire. (*b*) *To c. s.o.*, se modeler sur qn. **2. To copy (out)** *a letter*, copier, transcrire, une lettre. **copying**, *s*. Transcription *f*, imitation *f*.

copyright[1], *s*. Droit *m* d'auteur; propriété *f* littéraire.

copyright[2], *v.tr. Publ:* Déposer (un livre).

copyright[3], *a*. (Livre) qui est protégé par des droits d'auteur.

coquetry, *s*. Coquetterie *f*.

coquette[1], *s*. Coquette *f*.

coquette², *v.i.* Faire la coquette ; flirter.
coquettish, *a.* Provocant, *F:* aguichant.
coral, *s.* Corail *m*, -aux. **Coral island**, île corallienne, de corail
cord¹, *s.* (*a*) Corde *f* (mince) ; cordon *m* ; ficelle *f.* (*b*) *Anat:* **The spinal cord,** le cordon médullaire.
cord², *v.tr.* Corder ; lier avec une corde.
cordage, *s.* *Coll:* Cordages *m pl.*
cordial, **I.** *a.* Cordial, -aux ; chaleureux. **2.** *s.* Cordial *m.* **-ally**, *adv.* Cordialement.
cordiality, *s.* Cordialité *f.*
cordon, *s.* Cordon *m.*
Cordova. *Pr.n. Geog:* Cordoue *f.*
corduroy, *s. & a. Tex:* Velours côtelé, à côtes. *F:* **Corduroy road,** chemin de rondins.
core, *s.* **I.** Cœur *m* ; trognon *m.* **Selfish to the core,** d'un égoïsme foncier.
Corinth. *Pr.n. Geog:* Corinthe *f.*
cork¹, *s.* **I.** Liège *m.* **2.** Bouchon *m* (de liège). **To draw the cork of a bottle,** déboucher une bouteille. **cork-oak**, *s. Bot:* Chêne-liège *m*, *pl.* chênes-lièges.
cork², *v.tr.* **To cork a bottle,** boucher une bouteille.
corkscrew, *s.* Tire-bouchon *m*, *pl.* tire-bouchons.
cormorant, *s. Orn:* Cormoran *m.*
corn¹, *s.* **I.** Grain *m* (de poivre). **2.** Grains, blé(s) *m(pl).* **Corn crops,** céréales *f.* **3.** Indian corn, maïs *m.* **corn-cob**, *s.* Épi *m* de maïs.
corn-field, *s.* Champ *m* de blé.
corn², *s. Cor m. F:* **To tread on s.o.'s corns,** toucher qn à l'endroit sensible.
corncrake, *s. Orn:* Râle *m* des genêts.
corned, *a.* **Corned beef,** bœuf salé.
corner¹, *s.* **I.** Coin *m*, angle *m.* **2.** Coin ; encoignure *f.* **To drive s.o. into a corner,** *F:* mettre qn au pied du mur. **Corner seat,** place de coin. **3.** (*a*) **Corner house,** maison qui fait le coin, l'angle, de la rue. *F:* **To turn the corner,** passer le moment critique. (*b*) Tournant *m* ; *Aut:* virage *m.* **4.** *Com:* Monopole *m.* **corner-cupboard**, *s.* Encoignure *f.*
corner², *v.tr.* **I.** (*a*) Acculer. (*b*) *F:* Mettre (qn) au pied du mur. **2.** Accaparer (une denrée).
cornet, *s. Mus:* Cornet *m* à pistons.
cornflour, *s.* Farine *f* de maïs.
cornflower, *s. Bot:* Bluet *m.*
cornice, *s.* Corniche *f.*
Cornish, *a.* Cornouaillais.
Cornwall. *Pr.n.* (Le comté de) Cornouailles *f.*
corolla, *s. Bot:* Corolle *f.*
corollary, *s. Log: Mth:* Corollaire *m.*
coronation, *s.* Couronnement *m*, sacre *m.*
coronet, *s.* (*a*) (Petite) couronne. (*b*) Diadème *m*, bandeau *m.*
corporal¹, *a.* Corporel.
corporal², *s. Mil:* (*Of infantry*) Caporal *m*, -aux ; (*of cavalry*) brigadier *m.*
corporation, *s.* **I.** Corporation *f* ; corps

constitué. **2.** *Com:* Société enregistrée. **3.** **Municipal corporation,** conseil municipal.
corps, *s.* Corps *m.*
corpse, *s.* Cadavre *m* ; corps (mort).
corpulence, *s.* Corpulence *f.*
corpulent, *a.* Corpulent.
corpuscle, *s.* Corpuscule *m.* **Blood corpuscles,** globules sanguins.
corral, *s.* Corral *m*, *pl.* -als.
correct¹, *v.tr.* **I.** Relever les fautes ; corriger. **2.** Rectifier (une erreur) **3.** Reprendre (un enfant).
correct², *a.* **I.** Correct, exact ; (réponse) juste. **2.** Bienséant ; conforme à l'usage. **-ly**, *adv.* Correctement, exactement.
correction, *s.* **I.** Correction *f* ; rectification *f.* **Under correction,** sauf erreur. **2.** Correction, châtiment *m.*
correctness, *s.* Correction *f*, convenance *f* (de tenue) ; exactitude *f*, justesse *f.*
correspond, *v.i.* **I.** (*a*) Correspondre, être conforme (*with, to,* à). (*b*) Correspondre (*to,* avec). **2.** Correspondre (avec qn). **They correspond,** ils s'écrivent. **corresponding**, *a.* Correspondant. **-ly**, *adv.* Également ; à l'avenant.
correspondence, *s.* **I.** Correspondance *f* (*to,* avec). **2.** Correspondance, courrier *m.*
correspondent, *s* Correspondant *m.* *Journ:* **Answers to correspondents,** la petite poste. **From our special correspondent,** de notre envoyé spécial.
corridor, *s.* Couloir *m*, corridor *m.* *Rail:* **Corridor carriage,** wagon *m* à couloir.
corroborate, *v.tr.* Corroborer, confirmer.
corroboration, *s.* Corroboration *f*, confirmation *f.*
corrode, **I.** *v.tr.* Corroder ; ronger. **2.** *v.i.* Se corroder.
corrosion, *s.* Corrosion *f.*
corrosive, *a. & s.* Corrosif (*m*).
corrugate, *v.tr.* Onduler (la tôle) ; gaufrer (le papier). **corrugated**, *a.* Gaufré ; ondulé.
corrugation, *s.* Plissement *m*, ondulation *f.*
corrupt¹, *a.* Corrompu. **C. press,** presse vénale.
corrupt², *v.tr.* Corrompre, altérer ; suborner (un témoin) ; dépraver (la jeunesse).
corruption, *s.* **I.** (*a*) Corruption *f*, putréfaction *f.* (*b*) Dépravation *f.* **2.** *Jur:* **Bribery and corruption,** corruption, subornation.
corsair, *s.* Corsaire *m.*
corset, *s. Cost:* Corset *m.*
Corsica. *Pr.n. Geog:* La Corse.
Corsican, *a. & s.* Corse (*mf*).
cos, *s.* Cos (lettuce), (laitue) romaine *f.*
cosine, *s. Trig:* Cosinus *m.*
cosiness, *s.* Confortable *m.*
cosmetic, *a. & s.* Cosmétique (*m*).
cosmic, *a.* Cosmique.
cosmopolitan, *a. & s.* Cosmopolite (*mf*).
Cossack, *a. & s.* Cosaque (*mf*).
cost¹, *s.* **I.** Coût *m*, frais *mpl.* **Cost of living,**

coût de la vie. **At the cost of one's life,** au prix de sa vie. **At little cost,** à peu de frais. **At all costs,** à tout prix. *I learnt it to my cost,* je l'ai appris à mes dépens. **2.** *pl. Jur :* Frais d'instance ; dépens *mpl. They were ordered to pay costs,* ils furent condamnés aux frais.
cost², *v.i.* Coûter ; revenir à. **Cost what it may,** coûte que coûte.
coster(monger), *s.* Marchand ambulant ; marchand des quatre saisons.
costliness, *s.* **I.** Somptuosité *f.* **2.** Haut prix ; prix élevé.
costly, *a.* **I.** (a) Précieux ; de grand prix.(b) Riche, somptueux. **2.** Coûteux, dispendieux.
costume, *s.* Costume *m.*
cosy, *a.* Chaud, confortable ; (of pers.) bien au chaud. *It is c. here,* il fait bon ici. **-ily,** *adv.* Confortablement ; douillettement.
cot, *s.* Lit *m* d'enfant ; couchette *f.*
coterie, *s.* Coterie *f* ; cénacle *m.*
cotill(i)on, *s.* *Danc :* Cotillon *m.*
cottage, *s.* **I.** Chaumière *f.* **2.** Villa *f.*
cottager, *s.* Paysan, -anne.
cotton, *s.* **I.** (a) Cotton(plant), cotonnier *m.* (b) Coton *m.* **2.** (Sewing-)cotton, fil *m* à coudre ; fil d'Écosse. **3.** *Attrib.* (a) De, en, coton. (b) Cotonnier. **cotton-cake** *s. Husb:* Tourteau *m.* **cotton-mill,** *s.* Filature *f* de coton ; cotonnerie *f.* **cotton-planta-tion,** *s.* Cotonnerie *f.* **cotton-wool,** *s.* Ouate *f.*
coytledon, *s. Bot:* Cotylédon *m.*
couch¹, *s.* **I.** *Lit:* Lit *m,* couche *f.* **2.** *Furn:* Canapé *m,* divan *m.*
couch². **I.** *v.tr.* (a) Mettre en arrêt. (b) *Letter couched in these terms,* lettre ainsi conçue. **2.** *v.i.* (a) Se coucher. (b) *(Of dog)* Se tapir (devant qn) ; s'aplatir. (c) Se tenir embusqué.
cough¹, *s.* Toux *f.* **To have a cough,** tousser. **cough-lozenge,** Pastille pectorale.
cough², *v.i.* Tousser. **coughing,** *s.* Toux *f.*
council, *s.* **I.** Conseil *m.* **To hold council,** tenir conseil. **2.** *Ecc:* Concile *m.* **council-chamber,** *s.* Salle *f* du conseil.
councillor, *s.* Conseiller *m* ; membre *m* du conseil.
counsel¹, *s.* **I.** Délibération *f* ; consultation *f. To take c. together,* se consulter, se con-certer. **2.** Conseil *m,* avis *m. F:* **Counsel of perfection,** idéal *m* difficile à atteindre. **3.** Dessein *m,* intention *f.* **To keep one's (own) counsel,** observer le silence. **4.** *Jur:* Avocat *m* ; conseil.
counsel², *v.tr. To c. s.o. to do sth.,* conseiller, recommander, à qn de faire qch.
counsellor, *s.* Conseiller *m.*
count¹, *s.* **I.** (a) Compte *m,* calcul *m.* **To keep count of,** compter ; tenir le compte de. **To lose count,** perdre le compte. (b) Total, *m.* **2.** *Jur:* Chef *m* (d'accusation). **3.** *Box:* Compte.
count². **I.** *v.tr.* Compter ; dénombrer. **To count the cost,** compter, calculer, la dépense.

To count up sth., compter qch. **To count the votes,** dépouiller le scrutin. **Counting from to-morrow,** à compter de demain. **2.** *v.i.* **To count on s.o.,** compter sur qn. **To count on doing sth.,** compter faire qch. **3.** *v.i.* (a) *He doesn't c. for much,* il ne compte guère. (b) Avoir de l'importance. *Every minute counts,* il n'y a pas une minute à perdre. **count out,** *v.tr.* Compter pièce par pièce. **counting,** *s.* Compte *m,* calcul *m* ; dé-pouillement *m* (du scrutin) ; dénombrement *m* (de personnes). **counting-house,** *s.* (Bureau *m* de) la comptabilité.
count³, *s.* Comte *m.*
countenance¹, *s.* **I.** Expression *f* du visage ; visage, figure *f,* mine *f.* **To lose countenance,** se décontenancer ; perdre contenance. **To stare s.o. out of countenance,** dévisager qn. **2.** **To give countenance to sth.,** appuyer qch.
countenance², *v.tr.* **I.** Autoriser, approuver. **2.** Encourager, appuyer.
counter¹, *s.* **I.** *Games:* Fiche *f* ; jeton *m.* **2.** (a) *(In bank)* Guichets *mpl* ; caisse *f.* (b) *(In shop)* Comptoir *m.*
counter². **I.** *a.* (a) Contraire, opposé (to, à). (b) *In compounds often translated by* contre-. **2.** *adv.* En sens inverse ; à contre-sens. **To run counter to one's orders,** aller à l'encontre de ses instructions. **counter-attack,¹** *s.* Contre-attaque *f.* **counter-attack²,** *v.tr. & i.* Contre-attaquer. **counter-attrac-tion,** *s.* Attraction opposée.
counter³, *v.tr.* Aller à l'encontre de ; contre-carrer.
counteract, *v.tr.* Neutraliser ; parer à.
counterbalance¹, *s.* Contrepoids *m.*
counterbalance², *v.tr.* Contre-balancer ; compenser (une force, etc.).
countercharge, *s.* Contre-accusation *f.*
counterfeit¹. **I.** *a.* Contrefait ; faux. **Counterfeit coin,** fausse monnaie. **2.** *s.* Contrefaçon *f.*
counterfeit², *v.tr.* **I.** Contrefaire (la mon-naie). **2.** Simuler, feindre.
counterfoil, *s.* Souche *f,* talon *m.*
countermand, *v.tr.* Contremander ; ré-voquer, rappeler (un ordre).
countermarch, *s.* Contremarche *f.*
countermine, *v.tr. & i.* Contre-miner.
counterpane, *s.* Courtepointe *f* ; couvre-lit *m.*
counterpart, *s.* Contre-partie *f* ; duplicata *m,* double *m* (d'un document).
counterplot, *s.* Contre-ruse *f,* contre-trame *f.*
counterpoint, *s. Mus:* Contrepoint *m.*
counterpoise¹, *s.* **I.** Contrepoids *m.* **2.** Équilibre *m.*
counterpoise², *v.tr.* Contre-balancer.
countersign¹, *s.* Mot *m* d'ordre ; mot de ralliement.
countersign², *v.tr.* Contresigner, viser.
countervail, *v.i.* Prévaloir *(against,* contre).
counterweight, *s.* Contrepoids *m.*
countess, *s.* Comtesse *f.*

countless, *a.* Innombrable.

country, *s.* **1.** (*a*) Pays *m*, contrée *f*, région *f*. Open country, rase campagne. (*b*) (*Native country*) Patrie *f*. **2.** (*a*) Province *f*. Country cousin, cousin de province. (*b*) Campagne *f*. In the country, à la campagne. **country-house**, *s.* **1.** Maison *f* de campagne. **2.** Château *m*.

countryman, *s.* **1.** Compatriote *m*, concitoyen *m*. **2.** Paysan *m*, campagnard *m*.

countrywoman, *s.* **1.** Compatriote *f*, concitoyenne *f*. **2.** Paysanne *f*, campagnarde *f*.

county, *s.* Comté *m*. County town, chef-lieu *m* de comté, *pl.* chefs-lieux.

couple[1], *s.* **1.** Couple *f* (d'œufs). **2.** (*a*) *F:* To hunt in couples, être toujours ensemble. (*b*) Couple *m* (d'époux). The young c., les deux jeunes époux.

couple[2], *v.tr.* (*a*) Coupler, accoupler (des bœufs); associer (des noms). (*b*) *Rail:* To couple on *a carriage*, atteler, accrocher, un wagon. **coupling**, *s.* **1.** Accouplement *m* (de deux choses); association *f* (d'idées). **2.** *Rail:* Attelage *m*, accrochage *m* (des wagons).

couplet, *s.* *Pros:* Distique *m*.

coupon, *s.* Coupon *m*. Bread c., ticket *m* de pain.

courage, *s.* Courage *m*. To have courage, avoir du cœur. To have the courage of one's convictions, avoir le courage de ses opinions. To muster up courage, faire appel à tout son courage.

courageous, *a.* Courageux. **-ly**, *adv.* Courageusement.

courier, *s.* Courrier *m*, messager *m*.

course, *s.* **1.** (*a*) Cours *m*; marche *f* (des événements). In (the) course of time, avec le temps; à la longue. In the ordinary course of things, normalement. To do sth. in due course, faire qch. en temps voulu, en temps utile. Let things take their course, *F:* laissez faire. (*b*) Of course, bien entendu; naturellement. (*c*) As a matter of course, comme de juste, comme de raison. **2.** (*a*) *Sch:* Cours. To go through a course, suivre un cours. (*b*) *Med:* Traitement *m*, régime *m*. **3.** (*a*) Route *f*, direction *f*. To hold (on) one's course, suivre tout droit son chemin. (*b*) To take a course of action, adopter une ligne de conduite. To take one's own course, agir à sa guise. The best course, le parti le plus sûr. **4.** Service *m*, plat *m*. **5.** *Sp:* (*a*) Champ *m*, terrain *m* (de courses). (*b*) Piste *f*. **6.** Lit *m* (d'un cours d'eau). **7.** *Fin:* Course of exchange, cote *f* des changes.

courser, *s.* Coursier *m*.

court[1], *s.* **1.** (*a*) = COURTYARD. (*b*) Ruelle *f*. **2.** (*a*) Cour *f*. (*b*) To make, pay, court to s.o., faire la cour à qn **3.** *Jur:* Cour, tribunal *m*. Court-room, salle *f* d'audience. The Law Courts, le palais de justice. Police court, tribunal de simple police. **4.** Tennis *m*, court *m* (de tennis). **court-card**, *s.*

Cards: Figure *f*; carte peinte. **court-house**, *s.* Palais *m* de justice; tribunal *m*.

court-martial[1], *s.* Conseil *m* de guerre.

court-martial[2], *v.tr.* Faire passer (qn) en conseil de guerre.

court[2], *v.tr.* **1.** Courtiser; faire la cour à. **2.** Rechercher, solliciter. To 'court danger, aller au-devant du danger.

courteous, *a.* Courtois, poli (*to*, *towards*, envers). **-ly**, *adv.* Courtoisement.

courteousness, *s.* Courtoisie *f*, politesse *f*.

courtesy, *s.* Courtoisie *f*, politesse *f*. As a matter of courtesy, à titre gracieux. Exchange of courtesies, échange de bons procédés.

courtier, *s.* Courtisan *m*.

courtliness, *s.* **1.** Courtoisie *f*. **2.** Élégance *f*; grand air.

courtly, *a.* **1.** Courtois. **2.** Élégant.

courtship, *s.* Cour *f*.

courtyard, *s.* Cour *f* (de maison).

cousin, *s.* Cousin, -ine. First cousin, cousin(e) germain(e).

cove, *s.* *Ph.Geog:* Anse *f*; petite baie.

covenant[1], *s.* **1.** *Jur:* Convention *f*, contrat *m*. **2.** *Pol:* Pacte *m*, traité *m*.

covenant[2]. **1.** *v.tr.* (*a*) Promettre, accorder, par contrat. (*b*) Stipuler. (*c*) To c. to do sth., convenir de faire qch. **2.** *v.i.* To c. with s.o. for sth., convenir de qch. avec qn.

Coventry. *Pr.n.* *Geog:* *F:* To send s.o. to Coventry, mettre qn en quarantaine.

cover[1], *s.* **1.** Couverture *f*; tapis *m*. Loose cover, housse *f*. Outer cover *of tyre*, enveloppe *f* de pneu. **2.** Couvercle *m* (de marmite); cloche *f* (pour plat). **3.** Couverture (d'un livre). To read a book from cover to cover, lire un livre d'un bout à l'autre. **4.** *Post:* Enveloppe *f*. Under separate cover, sous pli séparé. **5.** (*a*) Abri *m*. To take cover, se mettre à l'abri. (*b*) *Ven:* Couvert *m*, fourré *m*. (*c*) *Mil:* To take c., s'embusquer. **6.** Voile *m*, masque *m*. Under the cover of darkness, sous le couvert de la nuit. **7.** *Covers were laid for four*, la table était de quatre couverts.

cover[2], *v.tr.* **1.** Couvrir (*with*, de). **2.** Couvrir, recouvrir, envelopper. **3.** To cover a distance, couvrir, franchir, une distance. **4.** Couvrir, dissimuler. **5.** To cover s.o. with a revolver, braquer un revolver sur qn. **6.** Comprendre, englober. **cover up**, *v.tr.* Couvrir entièrement; recouvrir; dissimuler (la vérité). **covering**, *s.* **1.** Recouvrement *m*. **2.** Couverture *f*, enveloppe *f*.

covert, *a.* Caché, voilé.

covet, *v.tr.* (*a*) Convoiter. (*b*) Ambitionner; aspirer à.

covetous, *a.* **1.** Avide. **2.** To be c. of sth., convoiter qch. **-ly**, *adv.* Avec convoitise; avidement.

covetousness, *s.* **1.** Cupidité *f*. **2.** Convoitise *f*.

cow[1], *s.* **1.** Vache *f*. **2.** (*Of elephant*) Femelle *f*. **cow-hide**, *s.* (Peau *f* de) vache *f*.

cow-house, *s.* Vacherie *f*, étable *f*. **cow-man,** *s.* Vacher *m*.

cow², *v.tr.* Intimider, dompter.

coward, *s. & a.* Lâche (*mf*).

cowardice, cowardliness, *s.* Lâcheté *f*.

cowardly, *a.* Lâche.

cowboy, *s.* Cowboy *m*.

cower, *v.i.* Se blottir, se tapir. **To cower before s.o.,** trembler devant qn.

cowherd, *s.* Vacher *m*; bouvier *m*.

cowl, *s.* **1.** (*a*) Capuchon *m*. **Penitent's cowl,** cagoule *f*. (*b*) Têtière *f* (d'un capuchon). **2.** Capuchon (de cheminée).

cowslip, *s. Bot:* (Fleur *f* de) coucou *m*.

coxcomb, *s.* Petit-maître *m, pl.* petits-maîtres.

coxswain, *s.* **1.** *Nau:* Patron *m* (d'une chaloupe). **2.** *Row:* Barreur *m*.

coy, *a.* Timide, modeste, farouche. **-ly,** *adv.* Modestement, timidement.

coyness, *s.* Timidité *f*, réserve *f*.

coyote, *s.* *Z:* Coyote *m*.

crab¹, *s. Crust:* Crabe *m*, cancre *m*. *F:* **To catch a crab,** engager un aviron.

crab², *s.* Crab(-apple), pomme *f* sauvage.

crabbed, *a.* **1.** Maussade, grincheux. **2.** *C. writing,* écriture illisible.

crack¹. I. *s.* **1.** (*a*) Claquement *m* (de fouet); détonation *f*, coup sec. (*b*) *F:* **Crack on the head,** coup violent sur la tête. **2.** (*a*) Fente *f*, fissure *f*; (*in pottery*) fêlure *f*. (*b*) Entre-bâillement *m* (d'une porte). II. **crack,** *a.* *F:* Fameux; d'élite; de première force. **Crack player,** *etc.*, as *m.* **crack-brained,** *a.* Au cerveau timbré, fêlé.

crack², *int.* Clac! crac! pan!

crack³. I. *v.tr.* **1.** Faire claquer (un fouet); faire craquer (ses doigts). **2.** (*a*) Fêler. (*b*) Casser (une noisette). **3. To crack a joke,** lâcher une plaisanterie. II. **crack,** *v.i.* **1.** Craquer; (*of whip*) claquer. *A rifle cracked,* un coup de fusil partit. **2.** Se fêler. **3.** (*Of voice*) Se casser, se fausser. **crack up,** *v.tr.* *F:* Vanter, prôner. **cracked,** *a.* **1.** Fêlé, fendu; (*of wall*) lézardé. **Cracked voice,** voix cassée. **2.** *F:* Timbré, toqué.

cracker, *s.* (*a*) Pétard *m*. **Jumping cracker,** crapaud *m*. (*b*) (**Christmas-**)**cracker,** diablotin *m*; papillote *f* à pétard.

crackle¹, *s.* Craquement *m*, crépitement *m*.

crackle², *v.i.* Craqueter; (*of fire*) pétiller.

crackling, *s.* Peau croquante (du porc rôti); couenne *f*.

cracksman, *s.* *F:* Cambrioleur *m*.

Cracow. *Pr.n.m.* *Geog:* Cracovie *f*.

cradle¹, *s.* Berceau *m*. **cradle-song,** *s.* Berceuse *f*.

cradle², *v.tr.* *F:* **Cradled in luxury,** bercé dans le luxe.

craft, *s.* **1.** Ruse *f*; fourberie *f*. **2.** (i) Métier manuel; (ii) profession *f*. **3.** *Coll.* *Nau:* Embarcations *f*; petits navires.

craftiness, *s.* Ruse *f*, astuce *f*.

craftsman, *s.* **1.** Artisan *m*, ouvrier *m*;

homme *m* de métier. **2.** Artiste *m* dans son métier.

crafty, *a.* Astucieux, rusé. **-ily,** *adv.* Astucieusement.

crag, *s.* Rocher escarpé.

cram¹, *s.* *F:* **1.** Presse *f* à étouffer, foule serrée. **2.** Mensonge *m*, craque *f*, blague *f*.

cram-full, *a.* Tout plein; bondé.

cram², *v.* **1.** *v.tr.* (*a*) Fourrer. *Th:* **The house was crammed,** la salle était bondée. (*b*) Bourrer. (*c*) *Husb:* Empâter, gaver. (*d*) *Sch:* Chauffer. **2.** *v.i.* *F:* (*a*) S'entasser (*into,* dans). (*b*) Se gorger de nourriture.

cramming, *s.* **1.** Entassement *m*. **2.** Gavage *m*. **3.** *Sch:* Chauffage *m*.

cramp¹, *s.* *Med:* Crampe *f*.

cramp², *v.tr.* **1.** Donner des crampes à. **Limbs cramped by the cold,** membres engourdis par le froid. **2.** Gêner. *F:* **To cramp s.o.'s style,** priver qn de ses moyens.

cramped, *a.* A l'étroit; gêné. **To feel cramped for room,** se sentir à l'étroit. **Cramped handwriting,** écriture gênée. *C. style,* style contraint.

cranberry, *s.* *Bot:* Airelle *f* coussinette.

crane¹, *s.* Grue *f*.

crane², *v.tr.* **To crane one's neck,** tendre, allonger, le cou.

cranium, *s.* Crâne *m*.

crank¹, *s.* *Mec.E:* Manivelle *f*.

crank², *v.tr.* **To crank up a car,** lancer une auto à la main.

crank³, *s.* *F:* Excentrique *mf*, original *m*.

crankiness, *s.* **1.** Humeur *f* difficile. **2.** État délabré.

cranky, *a.* D'humeur difficile.

crape, *s.* *Tex:* Crêpe noir.

crash¹, *s.* **1.** Fracas *m*. **2.** Catastrophe *f*, débâcle *f*. *Fin:* Krach *m*. **3.** Écrasement *m*; chute *f*. *Av:* Atterrissage brutal. **4.** *int.* Patatras!

crash², *v.i.* (*a*) Retentir; éclater avec fracas. (*b*) **To crash (down),** tomber avec fracas. s'abattre. (*c*) *Av:* S'écraser sur le sol.

crass, *a.* **Crass stupidity,** stupidité grossière. **Crass ignorance,** ignorance crasse.

crate, *s.* Caisse *f* à claire-voie.

crater, *s.* **1.** Cratère *m*. **2.** (*Shell-hole*) Entonnoir *m*.

crave, *v.tr. & i.* **1.** Implorer. **2. To crave for sth.,** désirer ardemment qch. **craving,** *s.* Désir ardent.

craven, *a. & s.* Poltron (*m*), lâche (*m*).

cravenness, *s.* Lâcheté *f*, couardise *f*.

crawfish, *s.* = CRAYFISH.

crawl¹, *s.* **1.** Rampement *m*. **2.** Mouvement traînant.

crawl², *v.i.* **1.** Ramper. **2.** (*a*) **To crawl (along),** se traîner. (*b*) Avancer lentement. **crawling,** *a.* **1.** Rampant. **2.** Grouillant (*with,* de).

crayfish, *s.* **1.** (**Fresh-water**) **crayfish,** écrevisse *f*. **2.** *F:* (= *spiny lobster*) Langouste *f*.

crayon, *s.* Pastel *m*.

craze, *s.* Manie *f*, toquade *f* (*for sth.*, de qch.).
craziness, *s.* Folie *f*, démence *f*.
crazy, *a.* **1.** Fou, *f.* folle (à lier); toqué. *C. with fear*, affolé (de terreur). **To drive s.o. crazy**, rendre qn fou; affoler qn. **2.** Délabré. *C. furniture*, meubles branlants. **3.** *Crazy paving*, dallage irrégulier. **-ily,** *adv.* Follement.
creak¹, *s.* Grincement *m*; craquement *m*.
creak², *v.i.* Crier, grincer; (*of shoes*) craquer.
cream¹, *s.* **1.** (*a*) Crème *f.* (*b*) *The cream of society*, la crème de la société. *The cream of the joke*, le plus beau de l'histoire. **2.** *Crème* (de beauté). **3.** *Attrib.* Cream(-coloured), crème *inv*; (cheval) isabelle *inv*.
cream-jug, *s.* Pot *m* à crème.
cream², *v.tr.* Écrémer.
creamy, *a.* Crémeux.
crease¹, *s.* (Faux) pli *m*.
crease², *v.tr.* (*a*) Plisser, faire des (faux) plis à. (*b*) Chiffonner, froisser (une robe).
create, *v.tr.* **1.** Créer. **2.** Créer, susciter (une difficulté); faire, produire (une impression).
creation, *s.* Création *f*.
creative, *a.* Créateur, -trice; créatif.
creator, *s.* Créateur, -trice.
creature, *s.* **1.** Créature *f*, être *m*. **2.** Animal *m*, bête *f*. *Dumb creatures*, les bêtes, les animaux. **3.** *Not a c. was to be seen*, on ne voyait âme qui vive. **4.** *Man is the creature of circumstances*, l'homme dépend des circonstances. **5.** *Attrib: Creature comforts*, l'aisance matérielle.
credence, *s.* Créance *f*, croyance *f*, foi *f*.
credentials, *s.pl.* **1.** Certificat *m*. **2.** Pièces justificatives d'identité.
credible, *a.* Croyable; digne de foi. **-ibly,** *adv.* *To be credibly informed of sth.*, tenir qch. de bonne source.
credit¹, *s.* **1.** Croyance *f*, créance *f*, foi *f*. *To give credit to a report*, ajouter foi à un bruit. **2.** Crédit *m*, influence *f*, réputation *f* (*with*, auprès de). *He has credit at court*, il est bien en cour. **3.** Mérite *m*, honneur *m*. *I gave him c. for more sense*, je lui croyais plus de jugement. *It does him credit*, cela lui fait honneur. **4.** (*a*) *Com:* Crédit. *To give s.o. credit*, faire crédit à qn. (*b*) *Book-k:* Credit side, avoir *m*.
credit², *v.tr.* **1.** Ajouter foi à, donner, accorder, créance à; croire. **2.** Attribuer, prêter (une qualité à qn) *I credited you with more sense*, je vous croyais plus de jugement. *To be credited with having done sth.*, passer pour avoir fait qch. **3.** *Com:* Créditer (*with*, de).
creditable, *a.* Estimable, honorable. **-ably,** *adv.* Honorablement.
creditor, *s.* Créancier, -ière.
credulity, *s.* Crédulité *f*.
credulous, *a.* Crédule. **-ly,** *adv.* Crédulement; avec crédulité.
credulousness, *s.* Crédulité *f*.

creed, *s.* **1.** *Theol:* Credo *m*, symbole *m*. **2.** Croyance *f*. **3.** *F:* Profession *f* de foi.
creek, *s.* Crique *f*, anse *f*.
creel, *s.* (*a*) Panier *m* de pêche. (*b*) Casier *m*.
creep, *v.i.* Ramper; (*of pers.*) se traîner, se glisser. *F: To c. into bed*, se glisser dans son lit. **creep on,** *v.i.* Avancer lentement.
creeping, *s.* Rampement *m*.
creeper, *s.* Plante rampante ou grimpante.
creeps, *s. pl. F:* *To give s.o. the creeps*, donner la chair de poule à qn.
creepy, *a. F: To feel creepy*, avoir la chair de poule.
cremate, *v.tr.* Incinérer.
cremation, *s.* Incinération *f*; crémation *f*.
creole, *a. & s.* Créole (*mf*).
creosote, *s. Ch:* Créosote *f*.
crêpe, *s.* **1.** *Tex:* Crêpe *m*. **2.** *Crêpe (-rubber) soles*, semelles *f* (de) crêpe.
crepitate, *v.i.* Crépiter.
crepitation, *s.* Crépitation *f*.
crescent, *s.* (*a*) Croissant *m*. (*b*) Rue *f* en arc de cercle.
cress, *s. Bot:* Cresson *m*.
crest, *s.* **1.** Crête *f* (de coq). **2.** Crête, sommet *m*, arête *f*. **3.** Armoiries *fpl*. **crest-fallen,** *a.* Abattu, découragé.
cretaceous, *a.* Crétacé, crayeux.
Cretan, *a. & s.* Crétois, -oise.
Crete. *Pr.n. Geog:* La Crète.
crevasse, *s.* Crevasse *f* (glaciaire).
crevice, *s.* Fente *f*; crevasse *f*, lézarde *f* (de mur); fissure *f* (de rocher).
crew, *s.* **1.** *Nau:* Équipage *m*; (*of rowing boat*) équipe *f*. **2.** *Artil:* Gun crew, servants *mpl* d'une pièce. **3.** Bande *f*, troupe *f*. *Sorry crew*! triste engeance *f*!
crib, *s.* **1.** Mangeoire *f*, râtelier *m*. **2.** Lit *m* d'enfant. **3.** *F: Sch:* Traduction *f* (d'auteur), corrigé *m* (de thèmes).
crick, *s.* **1.** *Crick in the neck*, torticolis *m*. **2.** *Crick in the back*, tour *m* de reins.
cricket¹, *s. Ent:* Grillon *m*, cricri *m*.
cricket², *s. Games:* Cricket *m*. *F: That's not cricket*, cela n'est pas loyal.
cricketer, *s.* Joueur *m* de cricket.
crime, *s.* (*a*) Crime *m*. (*b*) Délit *m*.
Crimea. *Pr.n. Geog:* La Crimée.
criminal. **1.** *a.* Criminel. *The Criminal Investigation Department, F:* the C.I.D., la Sûreté; la police secrète. **2.** *s.* (*a*) Criminel, -elle. (*b*) *F:* Le coupable. **-ally,** *adv.* Criminellement.
crimson, *a. & s.* Cramoisi (*m*); pourpre (*m*).
cringe, *v.i.* **1.** Se faire tout petit. **2.** S'humilier, ramper (*to, before, s.o.*, devant qn).
cringing, *a.* **1.** Craintif. **2.** Servile, obséquieux.
crinkle. **1.** *v.tr.* Froisser, chiffonner. *Crinkled paper*, papier ondulé, gaufré. **2.** *v.i.* Se froisser, se ratatiner.
cripple¹, *s.* Estropié, -ée; boiteux, -euse; infirme *mf*.
cripple², *v.tr.* (*a*) Estropier. (*b*) Disloquer; paralyser.

crisis, *s.* Crise *f.*

crisp, *a.* (*a*) (Biscuit) croquant, croustillant. (*b*) (Style) nerveux; (ton) tranchant. (*c*) (Air) vif.

crispness, *s.* **1.** Qualité croustillante. **2.** Netteté *f.* **3.** Froid vif (de l'air).

criterion, *s.* Critérium *m*, critère *m.*

critic, *s.* (*a*) Critique *m.* *F:* Armchair critic, critique en chambre. (*b*) Censeur *m.*

critical, *a.* Critique. **-ally,** *adv.* **1.** To look at sth. c., considérer qch. en critique. **2.** Critically ill, dangereusement malade.

criticism, *s.* Critique *f.*

criticize, *v.tr.* **1.** Critiquer, faire la critique de. **2.** Censurer, blâmer.

croak¹, *s.* Coassement *m* (de grenouille); croassement *m* (de corbeau).

croak², *v.i.* **1.** (*Of frog*) Coasser; (*of raven*) croasser. **2.** *F:* Grogner, ronchonner.

croaking, *s.* Coassement *m*; croassement *m.*

croaker, *s.* **1.** Ronchonneur, -euse; grognon *mf.* **2.** Prophète *m* de malheur.

crock¹, *s.* (*a*) Cruche *f.* (*b*) Pot *m* de terre.

crock², *s.* *P:* **1.** Vieille rosse. **2.** (*Of motor car*) Vieux clou; (*of pers.*) bonhomme fini.

crockery, *s.* Faïence *f*, poterie *f.*

crocodile, *s.* Crocodile *m.* Crocodile tears, larmes de crocodile.

crocus, *s.* *Bot:* Crocus *m.*

croft, *s.* **1.** Petit clos. **2.** Petite ferme.

crofter, *s.* Petit fermier.

crone, *s.* Vieille (femme); commère *f.*

crony, *s.* Compère *m*, commère *f.* An old crony, *F:* un vieux copain

crook¹, *s.* **1.** (*a*) Croc *m*, crochet *m.* (*b*) (*b*) Houlette *f* (de berger); crosse *f* (d'évêque). **2.** Angle *m*; coude *m.* **3.** *F:* Escroc *m*; chevalier *m* d'industrie. **crook-backed,** *a.* Bossu.

crook², *v.tr.* Courber, recourber. **crooked,** *a.* (*a*) Courbé; crochu; (*of path*) tortueux. (*b*) Malhonnête. **-ly,** *adv.* **1.** Tortueusement. **2.** De travers.

crookedness, *s.* **1.** Sinuosité *f.* **2.** (*a*) Perversité *f.* (*b*) Manque *m* de droiture.

croon, *v.tr.* Chantonner; fredonner.

crooner, *s.* Fredonneur, -euse.

crop¹, *s.* **1.** Jabot *m* (d'un oiseau). **2.** Récolte *f*, moisson *f.* The crops, la récolte. **3.** Coupe *f* (des cheveux). Eton crop. cheveux *mpl* à la garçonne.

crop², *v.tr.* (*a*) Tondre, tailler, couper. Hair cropped close, cheveux coupés ras. (*b*) Brouter, paître (l'herbe). **crop up,** *v.i.* *F:* Surgir.

cropper, *s.* *F:* To come a cropper, ramasser une bûche.

croquet, *s.* (Jeu *m* de) croquet *m.*

cross¹, *s.* **1.** Croix *f.* Maltese cross, croix de Malte. The Red Cross, la Croix rouge (de Genève). **2.** Contrariété *f*, ennui *m.* **3.** *Husb:* (*a*) Croisement *m.* (*b*) Métis, -isse.

cross². **1.** *v.tr.* (*a*) Croiser. (*b*) *Ecc:* To cross oneself, se signer. (*c*) Barrer (un chèque). (*d*) Traverser; franchir. To c. a bridge, passer (sur) un pont. To cross s.o.'s mind, passer par l'esprit de qn. (*e*) *F:* To cross s.o., contrecarrer qn. Crossed in love, contrarié dans ses amours. **2.** *v.i.* (*a*) Se croiser. (*b*) To cross (over), from Dover to Calais, faire la traversée de Douvres à Calais.

cross out, *v.tr.* Biffer, barrer, rayer.

cross over, *v.i.* Passer de l'autre côté.

crossing, *s.* **1.** Barrement *m* (d'un chèque). **2.** (*a*) Traversée *f* (de la mer); passage *m.* (*b*) Pedestrian c., passage pour piétons. **3.** Croisement *m*; intersection *f.* Rail: Level crossing, passage à niveau.

cross³. **1.** *a.* & *comb.fm.* (*a*) Transversal, -aux; oblique; mis en travers. (*b*) (Entre-)croisé. (*c*) Contraire, opposé (to, à). **2.** *a.* *F:* (Of pers.) Maussade, de mauvaise humeur, fâché. To be as cross as two sticks, être d'une humeur massacrante. **-ly,** *adv.* Avec (mauvaise) humeur. **cross-bones,** *s.pl.* Os *m* en croix. **cross-bow,** *s.* Arbalète *f.* **cross-breed,** *s.* *F:* Métis, -isse. **cross-country,** *attrib.* *a.* A travers champs. **cross-examination,** *s.* *Jur:* Interrogatoire *m* contradictoire. **cross-examine,** *v.tr.* *Jur:* Interroger contradictoirement; *F:* mettre sur la sellette. **cross-eyed,** *a.* Louche; qui louche. **cross-fire,** *s.* Feu croisé. **cross-grained,** *a.* *F:* (*a*) Revêche, grincheux. (*b*) Bourru, ronchonneur, -euse. **cross-legged,** *a.* Les jambes croisées. **cross-purposes,** *s.pl.* Malentendu *m*, quiproquo *m.* We are at cross-purposes, il y a malentendu. **cross-question,** *v.tr.* = CROSS-EXAMINE. **cross-road,** *s.* **1.** Chemin *m* de traverse. **2.** Cross-roads, carrefour *m*; croisée *f* de chemins. **cross-word,** *s.* Cross-word (puzzle), mots croisés.

crossbill, *s.* Bec-croisé *m*, *pl.* becs-croisés.

crosswise, *adv.* En croix, en travers.

crotch, *s.* Fourche *f*, enfourchure *f.*

crotchet, *s.* **1.** *Mus:* Noire *f.* **2.** *F:* (*a*) Lubie *f*, caprice *m.* (*b*) Idée *f* fixe.

crotchety, *a.* Sujet à des lubies; capricieux, fantasque; à l'humeur difficile.

crouch, *v.i.* Se blottir, se tapir, s'accroupir.

croupier, *s.* Croupier *m.*

crow¹, *s.* **1.** *Orn:* Corneille *f.* Carrion crow, corneille noire. *F:* As the crow flies, à vol d'oiseau. To have a crow to pluck with s.o., avoir maille à partir avec qn. **2.** *Tls:* Crow (-bar), pince *f* (à levier). **crow's-foot,** *s.* Patte *f* d'oie. **crow's-nest,** *s.* *Nau:* Nid *m* de pie.

crow², *s.* Chant *m* du coq.

crow³, *v.i.* **1.** Chanter. *F:* To crow over s.o., chanter victoire sur qn. **2.** (*Of infant*) Gazouiller. **crowing,** *s.* **1.** Chant *m.* **2.** Gazouillement *m.*

crowd¹, *s.* **1.** Foule *f*, affluence *f*, rassemblement *m.* **2.** *F:* Grande quantité, tas *m.*

crowd². **1.** *v.tr.* (*a*) Serrer, (en)tasser. (*b*) Remplir, bourrer. The hall was crowded *with people*, la salle était bondée. *The streets were crowded*, il y avait foule dans les rues. *Th:* Crowded house, salle comble. **2.** *v.i.* To crowd (together), se presser en foule; s'attrouper. **crowd out**, *v.tr.* Ne pas laisser de place à.

crown¹, *s.* **1.** Couronne *f.* Crown prince, prince héritier. **2.** Couronne. Half a crown, une demi-couronne. **3.** Sommet *m*, haut *m* (de la tête). **4.** Crown of a hat, calotte *f*, forme *f*, d'un chapeau.

crown², *v.tr.* **1.** Couronner. **2.** (*a*) Couronner, récompenser (les efforts de qn). (*b*) *F:* To crown all, pour y mettre le comble. **3.** Damer (un pion). **crowning¹**, *a.* Final, -als; suprême. **crowning²**, *s.* Couronnement *m.*

crozier, *s.* Crosse *f.*

crucial, *a.* Décisif, critique.

crucible, *s.* *Ind:* Creuset *m.*

crucifix, *s.* Crucifix *m*, christ *m.*

crucifixion, *s.* Crucifixion *f*; mise *f* en croix.

crucify, *v.tr.* Crucifier; mettre en croix.

crude, *a.* (*a*) (A l'état) brut. (*b*) (*Of colour*) cru. (*c*) Informe, grossier. **-ly**, *adv.* **1.** Crûment, grossièrement. **2.** D'une manière fruste.

crudeness, crudity, *s.* Crudité *f.*

cruel, *a.* Cruel. **-lly**, *adv.* Cruellement.

cruelty, *s.* Cruauté *f* (*to, towards*, envers).

cruet, *s.* Burette *f.*

cruise¹, *s.* Croisière *f.* Pleasure c., voyage *m* d'agrément.

cruise², *v.i.* *Nau:* Croiser.

cruiser, *s.* *Navy:* Croiseur *m.*

crumb, *s.* **1.** (*a*) Miette *f.* *F:* Crumb of comfort, brin *m* de consolation. (*b*) *Cu:* Bread crumbs, chapelure *f.* **2.** (*Opposed to crust*) Mie *f.*

crumble. **1.** *v.tr.* Émietter (du pain); effriter (les pierres). To crumble sth. up, réduire qch. en miettes. **2.** *v.i.* S'émietter; s'effriter; (*of masonry*) s'écrouler. **crumbling**, *s.* **1.** Émiettement *m*, effritement *m*, désagrégation *f.* **2.** Écroulement *m.*

crumple. **1.** *v.tr.* Friper, froisser. **2.** *v.i.* To crumple (up). Se friper, se froisser.

crunch¹, *s.* Bruit *m* de broiement.

crunch². **1.** *v.tr.* Croquer, broyer. **2.** *v.i.* Crier, craquer.

crusade, *s.* Croisade *f.*

crusader, *s.* Croisé *m.*

crush¹, *s.* Presse *f*, foule *f.*

crush². **1.** *v.tr.* (*a*) Écraser. *To c. sth. into a box*, fourrer qch. dans une boîte. (*b*) *F:* Crushed with grief, accablé de douleur. (*c*) Froisser (une robe). (*d*) *Min:* Broyer, concasser. **2.** *v.i.* Se presser en foule. **crushing¹**, *a.* Écrasant. **crushing²**, *s.* Aplatissage *m*, écrasement *m*; broyage *m.*

crust¹, *s.* **1.** (*a*) Croûte *f.* (*b*) Piece of crust, croûton *m.* **2.** Écorce *f*, croûte.

crust². **1.** *v.tr.* Encroûter. **2.** *v.i.* Se couvrir d'une croûte. **crusted**, *a.* Crusted over, couvert d'une croûte.

crustacean, *s.* Crustacé *m.*

crusty, *a.* **1.** (Pain) qui a une forte croûte. **2.** *F:* (*a*) Bourru. (*b*) Hargneux, irritable. *He's a c. fellow*, c'est un ours. **-ily**, *adv.* (*a*) D'un ton bourru. (*b*) Avec humeur.

crutch, *s.* Béquille *f.*

crux, *s.* Nœud *m.*

cry¹, *s.* **1.** Cri *m.* It is a far cry from here, il y a loin d'ici. **2.** Cri; plainte *f.* **3.** Action *f* de pleurer; pleurs *mpl.* To have a good cry, donner libre cours à ses larmes.

cry², *v.tr.* & *i.* **1.** Crier; pousser un cri, des cris. To cry for help, crier au secours. **2.** S'écrier. *"That is false!" he cried*, "c'est faux!" s'écria-t-il. **3.** Pleurer; verser des larmes. To cry for sth., demander qch. en pleurant. To cry one's eyes out, pleurer toutes les larmes de ses yeux. **cry down**, *v.tr.* Décrier. **cry off**, *v.i.* Se dédire. **cry out**. **1.** *v.tr.* Crier. **2.** *v.i.* (*a*) Pousser des cris; s'écrier. (*b*) *To cry out against s.o.*, se récrier contre qn. **crying¹**, *a.* **1.** Crying injustice, injustice criante. **2.** Pleurant; qui pleure. **crying²**, *s.* **1.** Cri(s) *m(pl)*; clameur *f.* **2.** Pleurs *mpl*, larmes *fpl.* Fit of crying, crise *f* de larmes. **cry-baby**, *s.* Pleurard, -arde.

crypt, *s.* Crypte *f.*

cryptic, *a.* Secret, occulte.

cryptogram, *s.* Cryptogramme *m.*

crystal, *s.* **1.** Cristal *m*, -aux. **2.** Crystal (-glass), cristal.

crystalline, *a.* Cristallin.

crystallization, *s.* Cristallisation *f.*

crystallize. **1.** *v.tr.* (*a*) Cristalliser. (*b*) Crystallized fruits, fruits candis. **2.** *v.i.* (Se) cristalliser.

cub, *s.* Petit *m.* *F:* Unlicked cub, ours mal léché.

cubby-hole, *s.* **1.** Retraite *f.* **2.** Placard *m.*

cube¹, *s.* Cube *m.* Cube root, racine cubique.

cube², *v.tr.* *Mth:* Cuber.

cubic, *a.* *Meas:* Cubic foot, pied cube. *C. capacity*, volume *m.*

cubical, *a.* Cubique; en (forme de) cube.

cubicle, *s.* Alcôve *f* (d'un dortoir).

cubism, *s.* *Art:* Cubisme *m.*

cuckoo, *s.* **1.** *Orn:* Coucou *m.* **2.** *F:* Niais, -e, benêt *m.* **cuckoo-clock**, *s.* (Pendule *f* à) coucou *m.* **cuckoo-pint**, *s.* *Bot:* Arum maculé.

cucumber, *s.* Concombre *m.*

cud, *s.* To chew the cud, ruminer.

cuddle¹, *s.* *F:* Étreinte *f*, embrassade *f.*

cuddle². *F:* **1.** *v.tr.* Serrer doucement dans ses bras. **2.** *v.i.* Se peloter. (*b*) To cuddle up to s.o., se pelotonner contre qn.

cudgel¹, *s.* Gourdin *m*, trique *f.* *F:* To take up the cudgels, prendre fait et cause (pour qn).

cudgel², *v.tr.* Bâtonner.

cue[1], *s.* (*a*) *Th:* Fin *f* de tirade ; réplique *f.* To take (up) one's cue, donner la réplique. (*b*) Avis *m*, mot *m*, indication *f.*

cue[2], *s.* Queue *f* (de billard).

cuff[1], *s.* **1.** Poignet *m* (de chemise) ; (*starched*) manchette *f.* **2.** (*Of coat*) Parement *m.* **cuff-links**, *s.pl.* Boutons *m* de manchettes jumelés.

cuff[2], *s.* Taloche *f*, calotte *f.*

cuff[3], *v.tr.* Talocher, calotter.

cuirass, *s.* Cuirasse *f.*

cuirassier, *s. Mil:* Cuirassier *m.*

culinary, *a.* Culinaire.

culminate, *v.i.* To culminate in sth, se terminer en qch. Culminating point, point culminant.

culmination, *s. F:* Point culminant.

culpability, *s.* Culpabilité *f.*

culpable, *a.* Coupable. **-ably**, *adv.* Coupablement.

culprit, *s.* Coupable *mf.*

cult, *s.* Culte *m* (*of*, de).

cultivate, *v.tr.* **1.** Cultiver, exploiter (la terre). **2.** To c. s.o.'s friendship, cultiver l'amitié de qn. **cultivated**, *a.* Cultivé.

cultivation, *s.* Culture *f.*

cultivator, *s. Agr:* Cultivateur *m.*

culture, *s.* Culture *f.*

cultured, *a.* Cultivé, lettré.

cumber, *v.tr.* Embarrasser, encombrer (*with*, de).

cumbersome, cumbrous, *a.* Encombrant, gênant, incommode.

cumulative, *a.* Cumulatif.

cunning[1], *s.* **1.** (*a*) Ruse *f*, finesse *f.* (*b*) Fourberie *f*, astuce *f.* **2.** Adresse *f*, habileté *f.*

cunning[2], *a.* Rusé ; malin, *f.* maligne ; astucieux. **-ly**, *adv.* Avec ruse ; astucieusement.

cup, *s.* **1.** Tasse *f.* **2.** (*Metal*) Gobelet *m*, timbale *f.* **3.** There's many a slip 'twixt the cup and the lip, il y a loin de la coupe aux lèvres. **4.** *Bot:* Calice *m* (d'une fleur). **cup-final**, *s. Fb:* Finale *f* du championnat. **cup-tie**, *s. Fb:* Match *m* éliminatoire.

cupboard, *s.* Armoire *f* ; (*in wall*) placard *m. F:* Cupboard love, amour intéressé.

cupful, *s.* Pleine tasse.

Cupid. *Pr.n.* Cupidon *m.*

cupidity, *s.* Cupidité *f.*

cupola, *s. Arch:* Coupole *f.*

cur, *s.* **1.** Roquet *m* ; chien *m* sans race. **2.** *F:* Homme *m* méprisable ; cuistre *m.*

curable, *a.* Guérissable ; curable.

curacy, *s. Ecc:* Vicariat *m*, vicairie *f.*

curate, *s.* Vicaire *m.*

curative, *a. & s.* Curatif (*m*).

curator, *s.* Conservateur *m.*

curb[1], *s.* **1.** *F:* To put a curb on one's passions, mettre un frein à ses passions. **2.** Curb(-stone), bordure *f* (de trottoir).

curb[2], *v.tr.* Réprimer, refréner.

curd, *s.* (Lait) caillé *m* ; caillebotte *f.* Curds and whey, lait caillé sucré.

curdle. **1.** *v.tr.* Cailler ; *F:* glacer, figer (le sang). **2.** *v.i.* Se cailler ; se figer.

cure[1], *s.* **1.** Guérison *f.* **2.** (*a*) To take a cure, suivre un traitement. (*b*) Remède *m.*

cure[2], *v.tr.* **1.** To c. s.o. of an illness, guérir qn d'une maladie. **2.** (*a*) Saler, fumer (la viande) ; saurer (des harengs). (*b*) *Leath:* Saler.

curing, *s.* **1.** Guérison *f.* **2.** Salaison *f.*

curfew, *s.* Couvre-feu *m inv.*

curio, *s.* Curiosité *f* ; bibelot *m.* **curio-dealer**, *s.* Marchand *m* de curiosités.

curiosity, *s.* **1.** Curiosité *f.* **2.** Old curiosities curiosités ; bibelots *m* antiques. Old curiosity shop, boutique *f* de bric-à-brac.

curious, *a.* **1.** (*a*) Curieux. (*b*) Curieux ; indiscret, -ète. **2.** Curieux, singulier. **-ly**, *adv.* **1.** Curieusement. **2.** Singulièrement.

curl[1], *s.* **1.** Boucle *f* (de cheveux) ; frisure *f.* **2.** (*a*) Curl of the lips, moue *f* de dédain. (*b*) In curl, bouclé, frisé. **curl-paper**, *s.* Papillote *f.*

curl[2]. **1.** *v.tr.* (*a*) Boucler, friser (les cheveux). (*b*) To curl one's lip, faire la moue. **2.** *v.i.* (*a*) Boucler, friser. (*b*) s'abaisser avec dédain. **curl up**. **1.** *v.tr.* To curl up one's lip, retrousser la lèvre. **2.** Se mettre en boule.

curlew, *s. Orn:* Courlis *m.*

curly, *a.* Bouclé, frisé.

curmudgeon, *s.* **1.** Bourru *m.* **2.** Grippe-sou *m* ; pingre *m.*

currant, *s.* **1.** Groseille *f* (à grappes). Black currant, cassis *m.* **2.** Raisin *m* de Corinthe. **currant-bush**, *s.* Groseillier *m.*

currency, *s.* **1.** Circulation *f*, cours *m.* **2.** Terme *m* d'échéance, échéance *f.* **3.** Unité *f* monétaire ; monnaie *f.*

current[1], *a.* Courant ; en cours. Current number, dernier numéro. C. reports, bruits qui courent. In current use, d'usage courant ; très usité. Current events, actualités *f.* **-ly**, *adv.* Couramment.

current[2], *s.* **1.** (*a*) Courant *m* ; fil *m* de l'eau. (*b*) The current of events, le cours des événements. **2.** Electric current, courant électrique.

curriculum, *s.* Programme *m* d'études.

curry[1], *s. Cu:* Cari *m.*

curry[2], *v.tr.* **1.** Étriller (un cheval). **2.** To curry favour with s.o., chercher à plaire à qn. **curry-comb**, *s.* Étrille *f.*

curse[1], *s.* **1.** (*a*) Malédiction *f*, anathème *m.* (*b*) Imprécation *f* ; juron *m* ; gros mot. **2.** Fléau *m*, calamité *f.*

curse[2]. **1.** *v.tr.* Maudire, anathématiser. **2.** *v.i.* Blasphémer ; sacrer, jurer. **cursed**, *a.* Maudit. **cursing**, *s.* **1.** Malédiction(s) *f(pl).* **2.** *F:* Jurons *mpl* ; gros mots *pl.*

cursory, *a.* Rapide, superficiel. **-ily**, *adv.* Rapidement ; à la hâte.

curt, *a.* Brusque ; sec, *f.* sèche. **-ly**, *adv.* Brusquement, sèchement.

curtail, *v.tr.* **1.** Raccourcir ; écourter. **2.** Diminuer (l'autorité de qn) ; restreindre (ses dépenses).

curtailment, *s.* Raccourcissement *m*; restriction *f*, diminution *f*.

curtain, *s.* **1.** Rideau *m*. **2.** *Th:* Rideau. The curtain rises at eight sharp, rideau à huit heures précises. **curtain-lecture,** *s.* Semonce conjugale. **curtain-raiser,** *s.* Lever *m* de rideau.

curtness, *s.* Brusquerie *f*.

curts(e)y¹, *s.* Révérence *f*.

curts(e)y², *v.i.* Faire une révérence (*to s.o.,* à qn); *F:* tirer sa révérence (à qn).

curvature, *s.* Courbure *f*.

curve¹, *s.* (*a*) Courbe *f*. *C. of an arch,* voussure *f* d'une voûte. (*b*) *C. in the road,* tournant *m*; *Aut:* virage *m*.

curve². **1.** *v.tr.* Courber, cintrer. **2.** *v.i.* Se courber; décrire une courbe. **curved,** *a.* Courbé, courbe.

cushion¹, *s.* **1.** Coussin *m*. **2.** *Bill:* Bande *f*. **3.** (*Pad*) Bourrelet *m*.

cushion², *v.tr.* **1.** (*a*) Garnir de coussins. (*b*) Rembourrer (un siège). **2.** Amortir (un coup).

custard, *s.* *Cu:* Crème *f* (au lait); œuf(s) *m* au lait. Baked custard, flan *m*.

custodian, *s.* Gardien, -ienne; (of museum) conservateur *m*.

custody, *s.* **1.** Garde *f*. In safe custody, en lieu sûr. **2.** Emprisonnement *m*; détention *f*. To take s.o. into custody, arrêter qn.

custom, *s.* **1.** Coutume *f*, usage *m*, habitude *f*. The manners and customs, les us *m* et coutumes. **2.** *pl. Adm:* Douane *f*. **Customs officer,** douanier *m*. **3.** *Com:* (*a*) Achalandage *m*; clientèle *f*. (*b*) Patronage *m* (du client). **custom-house,** *s.* (Bureau *m* de la) douane.

customary, *a.* Accoutumé, habituel, d'usage. It is customary to, il est de coutume, d'usage, de. **-ily,** *adv.* Ordinairement, habituellement.

customer, *s.* **1.** Client, -ente. **2.** *F:* A queer customer, un drôle de type *m*. Ugly customer, vilain bonhomme; sale type.

cut¹, *s.* **1.** (*a*) Coupe *f*. (*b*) Wage cuts, réductions *f* de salaires. (*c*) *Cards:* Coupe. Cut for partners, tirage *m* pour les places. (*d*) *Cr:* Coup tranchant. (*e*) *F:* To give s.o. the cut direct, passer près de qn sans le saluer. **2.** (*a*) Coup *m* (d'épée); taillade *f*. (*b*) *Cut with a whip,* coup de fouet. **3.** (*Wound*) Coupure *f*; entaille *f*. **4.** (*a*) Illustration *f*, gravure *f*. (*b*) Diagramme *m*. **5.** Coupe (d'un vêtement). **6.** *F:* To be a cut above s.o., être supérieur à qn. **7.** *Cu:* Cut off the joint, tranche *f* de rôti. *Prime cut,* morceau *m* de choix. **8.** Short cut, raccourci *m*.

cut², *v.tr. & i.* **1.** Couper, tailler. *To cut one's finger,* se couper au doigt. To have one's hair cut, se faire tailler les cheveux. *This remark cut him to the quick,* cette parole le piqua au vif. *F: That cuts both ways,* c'est un argument à deux tranchants. To cut and come again, revenir au plat. *Com:* To cut prices, faire des prix de concurrence. **To cut and run,** *F:* prendre ses jambes à son cou. **2.** (*a*) To cut sth. to ribbons, déchiqueter qch. (*b*) To cut sth. short, couper court à qch. *F:* Cut it short! abrégez! **3.** To cut into the conversation, intervenir dans la conversation. **4.** Couper (les cartes). To cut for deal, tirer pour la donne. **5.** *Cr:* Trancher, couper. **6.** To cut s.o. (dead), faire semblant de ne pas voir qn. **7.** *F:* To cut the whole concern, abandonner l'affaire. **cut away,** *v.tr.* Retrancher. **cut down,** *v.tr.* **1.** (*a*) Abattre (un arbre). (*b*) Sabrer (un adversaire). **2.** Rogner (des dépenses). *Ind:* Restreindre (la production). **cut off.** *v.tr.* (*a*) Couper, détacher. (*b*) *To cut off s.o.'s retreat,* couper la retraite à qn. (*c*) *Tp:* Don't cut me off, ne coupez pas. (*d*) *El:* To cut off the current, interrompre le courant. **cut out,** *v.tr.* **1.** (*a*) Couper, enlever; exciser. (*b*) *F:* To cut s.o. out, supplanter qn. **2.** Découper. *To cut out a garment,* tailler un vêtement. *F:* To be cut out for sth., être fait pour qch. **3.** Supprimer; retrancher. **cut up,** *v.tr.* **1.** Couper, débiter (le bois); découper, dépecer (une volaille). *To cut up the bread,* tailler le pain par morceaux. **2.** *F:* (*a*) Don't be so cut up about it, ne vous affligez pas ainsi. (*b*) *v.i.* To cut up rough, se fâcher **cut³,** *a.* **1.** Cut glass, cristal taillé. Cut and dried opinions, opinions toutes faites. **2.** Cut prices, prix réduits. **cutting¹,** *a.* **1.** Cutting edge, tranchant *m*. **2.** Cutting wind, vent cinglant. **3.** Cutting remark, réponse mordante. **cutting²,** *s.* **1.** (*a*) Coupe *f*, coupage *m*. (*b*) Taille *f* (d'un diamant). **2.** Coupon *m*, bout *m* (d'étoffe). *C. from a newspaper,* coupure prise dans un journal. **3.** *Civ.E:* Tranchée *f*.

cute, *a.* *F:* Malin, -igne; rusé.

cuteness, *s.* *F:* Intelligence *f*, finesse *f*.

cutlass, *s.* *Nau:* Sabre *m* d'abordage.

cutler, *s.* Coutelier *m*.

cutlery, *s.* Coutellerie *f*.

cutlet, *s.* Côtelette *f*; escalope *f* (de veau).

cutter, *s.* *Nau:* Canot *m*; patache *f* (de la douane).

cut-throat, *s.* Coupe-jarret *m*; *pl.* coupe-jarrets. **Cut-throat inn,** coupe-gorge *m inv.*

cuttle, *s.* *Moll:* Cuttle(-fish), seiche *f*.

cyanide, *s.* *Ch:* Cyanure *m*.

cycle¹, *s.* **1.** Cycle *m*; *Geol:* période *f*. **2.** = BICYCLE.

cycle², *v.i.* Faire de la bicyclette; aller à bicyclette. **cycling,** *s.* Cyclisme *m*.

cyclist, *s.* Cycliste *mf*.

cyclone, *s.* *Meteor:* Cyclone *m*.

cyclopaedia, *s.* = ENCYCLOPAEDIA.

Cyclops, *s.* *Myth:* Cyclope *m*.

cygnet, *s.* *Orn:* Jeune cygne *m*.

cylinder, *s.* Cylindre *m*.

cylindrical, *a.* Cylindrique.
cymbal, *s.* Cymbale *f.*
Cymric, *a.* Kymrique; gallois.
cynic, *s.* Censeur *m* caustique; railleur *m*; sceptique *m.*
cynical, *a.* Sarcastique; sceptique. **-ally,** *adv.* D'un ton sceptique; caustiquement.
cynicism, *s.* **1.** Scepticisme railleur **2.** Mot *m* caustique.
cynosure, *s.* Point *m* de mire.

cypher, *s.* = CIPHER.
cypress, *s.* *Bot:* Cyprès *m.*
Cyprus. *Pr.n.* L'île *f* de Chypre *f.*
czar, *s.* Tsar *m.*
czarevitch, *s.* Tsarévitch *m.*
czarina, *s.* Tsarine *f.*
Czech, *a. & s.* Tchèque (*mf*).
Czecho-Slovak, *s.* Tchécoslovaque *mf.*
Czecho-Slovakia. *Pr.n.* La Tchécoslovaquie.

D

D, d, *s.* **1.** (La lettre) D, d *m.* **2.** *Mus:* Ré *m.*
dab[1], *s.* **1.** Coup léger; tape *f.* **2.** Tache *f* (d'encre).
dab[2], *v.tr.* **1.** Lancer une tape à (qn). **2.** Tapoter. **To dab one's eyes with a handkerchief,** se tamponner les yeux.
dab[3], *s.* *Ich:* Limande *f*, carrelet *m.*
dab[4], *s.* *F:* **To be a dab at sth.,** s'entendre à qch.
dabble. 1. *v.tr.* Humecter, mouiller. **2.** *v.i.* (a) Barboter. (b) *F:* **To dabble in law,** s'occuper un peu de droit.
dace, *s.* *Ich:* Vandoise *f*; dard *m.*
dacoit, *s.* Dacoït *m.*
dad, *s.* *F:* Papa *m*; petit père.
daddy, *s.* = DAD. **daddy-long-legs,** *s. Ent:* *F:* Tipule *f.*
dado, *s.* Lambris *m.*
daffodil, *s.* *Bot:* Narcisse *m* des bois.
daft, *a.* **1.** Écervelé. **2.** Toqué.
dagger, *s.* **1.** Poignard *m*, dague *f.* *F:* **To be at daggers drawn,** être à couteaux tirés (*with,* avec). **To look daggers,** lancer un regard furibond (à qn). **2.** *Typ:* Croix *f.*
dahlia, *s.* *Bot:* Dahlia *m.*
daily. 1. *a.* Journalier, quotidien. **D. servant,** domestique à la journée. **2.** *adv.* Journellement, quotidiennement. **3.** *s. Journ:* Quotidien *m.*
daintiness, *s.* Délicatesse *f*, raffinement *m* (de goût).
dainty[1], *s.* Friandise *f.*
dainty[2], *a.* **1.** Friand, délicat. **2.** Délicat, exquis. **3.** **To be d.,** être délicat sur la nourriture. **-ily,** *adv.* Délicatement; d'une manière raffinée.
dairy, *s.* Laiterie *f.* **dairy-farm,** *s.* (Ferme *f*) vacherie *f.* **dairy-farming,** *s.* L'industrie laitière.
dairymaid, *s.* Fille *f* de laiterie.
dairyman, *s.* *Com:* Laitier *m*; crémier *m.*
dais, *s.* Estrade *f*; dais *m.*
daisy, *s.* *Bot:* Marguerite *f.* **Common daisy,** pâquerette *f.*
dale, *s.* Vallée *f*, vallon *m.*

dally, *v.i. Lit:* **1.** Badiner, flirter (*with,* avec). **2.** Tarder, baguenauder.
dam[1], *s.* *Hyd.E:* Barrage *m.*
dam[2], *v.tr.* Contenir, endiguer.
damage[1], *s.* **1.** Dommage(s) *m(pl)*, dégâts *mpl*; avarie(s) *f(pl).* *F:* **There's no great d. done,** il n'y a pas grand mal. **2.** Préjudice *m*, tort *m.* **3.** *pl. Jur:* Dommages-intérêts *m*, indemnité *f.*
damage[2], *v.tr.* **1.** Endommager; avarier; abîmer. **2.** Faire tort, nuire, à (qn). **damaged,** *a.* Avarié, endommagé. **damaging,** *a.* Préjudiciable, nuisible.
Damascus. *Pr.n. Geog:* Damas *m.*
damask, *a. & s. Tex:* Damas *m.*
dame, *s.* *F:* **An old d.,** une vieille dame.
damn[1], *s.* Juron *m.* **Not to be worth a damn,** ne pas valoir chipette.
damn[2], *v.tr.* (a) Condamner. (b) Perdre, ruiner (un projet). **2.** (a) *Theol:* Damner. (b) *F:* **Well, I'm damned!** ça c'est fort! **3.** *int.* Sacristi! sacrebleu! **Damn it!** zut!
damned, *a.* **1.** Damné. *F:* (a) Sacré, satané. (b) *adv.* Diablement, bigrement.
damning[1], *a.* Portant condamnation. **Damning evidence,** preuves accablantes. **damning**[2], *s.* **1.** Condamnation *f.* **2.** Damnation *f.*
damnation, *s.* Damnation *f.*
damp[1], *s.* Humidité *f.* **damp-proof,** *a.* Hydrofuge; imperméable.
damp[2], *v.tr.* **1.** Mouiller; humecter. **2.** Étouffer (le feu); assourdir (un son). **3.** Refroidir. **To damp s.o.'s spirits,** décourager qn.
damp[3], *a.* Humide; (*of skin*) moite.
damper, *s.* **1.** *F:* Événement déprimant. **To put a damper on the company,** jeter un froid sur la compagnie. **2.** Registre *m* (de foyer).
dampness, *s.* Humidité *f*; moiteur *f.*
damsel, *s.* Demoiselle *f*; jeune fille *f.*
damson, *s.* Prune *f* de Damas.
dance[1], *s.* **1.** (a) Danse *f.* *F:* **To lead s.o. a dance,** (i) donner du fil à retordre à qn; (ii) faire voir bien du chemin à qn. (b) (Air

m de) danse. **2.** Bal *m*, *pl.* bals ; soirée dansante. **dance-hall,** *s.* Bal public ; dancing *m*. **dance²**. **1.** *v.i.* (*a*) Danser. *To d. with s.o.*, faire danser qn. (*b*) To dance for joy, danser de joie. *To d. with rage*, trépigner de colère. **2.** *v.tr.* (*a*) Danser (une valse). (*b*) To dance attendance on s.o., faire l'empressé auprès de qn. **dancing¹,** *s.f.* **2.** Danse *f*. **dancing-girl,** *s.f.* Bayadère. **dancing²,** *s.* Danse *f*. **dancing-hall,** *s.* Salle *f* de danse ; dancing *m*. **dancing-master,** *s.* Maître *m* de danse.

dancer, *s.* Danseur, -euse.

dandelion, *s.* *Bot:* Pissenlit *m*.

dandy, *s.* Dandy *m*, gommeux *m*.

Dane, *s.* **1.** Danois, -oise. **2.** (Great) Dane, (grand) danois.

danger, *s.* Danger *m*, péril *m*. To be in danger, courir un danger. 'Danger, road up,' "attention aux travaux." **danger-signal,** *s.* *Rail:* Arrêt *m*.

dangerous, *a.* Dangereux, périlleux. *D. illness,* maladie grave. **-ly,** *adv.* Dangereusement.

dangle. 1. *v.i.* Pendiller, pendre. With one's legs dangling, les jambes ballantes. **2.** *v.tr.* Faire pendiller.

Danish. 1. *a.* Danois. **2.** *s.* *Ling:* Le danois.

dank, *a.* Humide.

dapper, *a.* **1.** Pimpant. **2.** Sémillant.

dappled, *a.* Pommelé.

dare, *v.* **1.** *Modal aux.* Oser. How dare you! vous avez cette audace ! I dare say, sans doute ; peut-être bien. **2.** *v.tr.* (*a*) *To d. to do sth.*, oser faire qch. (*b*) Braver, affronter. (*c*) To dare s.o. to do sth., défier qn de faire qch. **daring¹,** *a.* (i) Audacieux, hardi ; (ii) téméraire. **-ly,** *adv.* Audacieusement, témérairement. **daring²,** *s.* (i) Audace *f*, hardiesse *f* ; (ii) témérité *f*. **dare-devil. 1.** *s.* Casse-cou *m inv* ; cervelle brûlée. **2.** *a.* Qui ne craint ni Dieu ni diable.

dark¹, *a.* **1.** Sombre, obscur, noir. It is dark, il fait nuit, il fait noir. *The sky grew d.*, le ciel s'assombrit. **2.** Foncé, sombre. **3.** (*Of pers.*) Brun ; basané. **4.** (*a*) Sombre, triste. To look on the dark side of things, voir tout en noir. (*b*) Ténébreux, mauvais. **5.** *D. saying,* mot mystérieux. To keep sth. dark, tenir qch. secret. Dark horse, (cheval, homme) dont on ne sait rien. **6.** The Dark Ages, l'âge des ténèbres. **-ly,** *adv.* Obscurément. **dark-lantern,** *s.* Lanterne sourde. **dark-room,** *s.* *Phot:* Cabinet noir.

dark², *s.* **1.** Ténèbres *fpl*, obscurité *f*. After dark, à (la) nuit close. To be (kept) in the dark, être (laissé) dans l'ignorance.

darken. 1. *v.tr.* Obscurcir ; assombrir ; brunir (le teint). **2.** *v.i.* S'obscurcir ; (*of sky*) s'assombrir. **darkening,** *s.* Assombrissement *m*.

darkness, *s.* **1.** Obscurité *f*, ténèbres *fpl*. **2.** Teinte foncée.

darling, *s. & a.* Favori. -ite. **My darling** mon chéri ! ma chérie !

darn¹, *s.* Reprise *f*.

darn², *v.tr.* Repriser. **darning,** *s.* Reprise *f*. **darning-needle,** *s.* Aiguille *f* à repriser.

dart¹, *s.* **1.** (*a*) Dard *m*, trait *m*. (*b*) *Games:* Fléchette *f*. **2.** To make a dart on sth., foncer, se précipiter, sur qch.

dart². 1. *v.tr.* Darder. **2.** *v.i.* Se précipiter, s'élancer, foncer (*at, upon,* sur).

dash¹, *s.* **1.** Coup *m*, heurt *m*, choc *m*. **2.** Soupçon *m*, goutte *f*. **3.** Dash of colour, tache *f* de couleur. **4.** Trait *m*. *Typ:* Tiret *m*. **5.** (i) Attaque soudaine ; (ii) course *f* à toute vitesse ; élan *m* ; ruée *f*. To make a dash forward, s'élancer en avant. *To make a d. at sth.*, se précipiter sur qch. **6.** Élan, impétuosité *f*, fougue *f*. **7.** *F:* To cut a dash, faire figure. **dash-board,** *s.* *Aut:* Tablier *m*.

dash². 1. *v.tr.* (*a*) Lancer violemment (qch. contre qch.) ; jeter (qch. par terre). (*b*) Déconcerter (qn) ; anéantir (les espérances). To dash s.o.'s spirits, abattre le courage de qn. (*c*) *int. Euphemism for* DAMN² 3. **2.** *v.i.* (*a*) To dash against sth., se heurter, se jeter, contre qch. (*b*) To dash at s.o., se précipiter, s'élancer, sur qn. **dash along,** *v.i.* Avancer, filer, à fond de train. **dash away. 1.** *v.tr.* Écarter violemment (qch.). **2.** *v.i.* S'éloigner en coup de vent. **dash off. 1.** *v.tr.* Enlever (une lettre). **2.** *v.i.* = DASH AWAY 2. **dash out.** *v.tr.* To dash out one's brains, se fracasser la cervelle. **dashed,** *a. Euphemism for* DAMNED 2. **dashing,** *a.* Impétueux ; plein d'élan.

dastard, *s.* Lâche *m*.

dastardly, *a.* **1.** Lâche. **2.** (Crime) infâme.

data, *s. pl.* Données *f*.

date¹, *s.* Datte *f*. **date-palm,** *s.* Dattier *m*.

date², *s.* Date *f* ; (*on coins*) millésime *m*. To be up to date, *F:* être à la page. *To be up to d. with one's work*, être à jour dans son travail. To bring up to date, remettre au point. *Com:* Interest to date, intérêts à ce jour. *F:* To have a date with s.o., avoir rendez-vous avec qn.

date³, *v.tr. & i.* Dater.

dative, *a. & s.* *Gram:* Datif (*m*).

daub¹, *s.* **1.** Enduit *m*, barbouillage *m*. **2.** (*Picture*) Croûte *f*.

daub², *v.tr.* **1.** Barbouiller, enduire (*with,* de). **2.** *Art: F:* Peintur(lur)er, barbouiller.

daughter, *s.* Fille *f*. **daughter-in-law,** *s.* Belle-fille *f*, *pl.* belles-filles ; bru *f*.

daunt, *v.tr.* Intimider, décourager. Nothing daunted, aucunement intimidé.

dauntless, *a.* Intrépide. **-ly,** *adv.* Intrépidement.

davit, *s.* *Nau:* Bossoir *m*, davier *m*.

dawdle. 1. *v.i.* Flâner, musarder, lambiner. **2.** *v.tr.* To dawdle away one's time, passer son temps à flâner. **dawdling,** *s.* Flânerie *f*, musarderie *f*.

dawdler, s. Flâneur, -euse.

dawn¹, s. Aube f, aurore f. **At dawn, au point du jour.**

dawn², v.i. (Of day) Poindre ; naître. *Day is dawning,* le jour se lève. *At length it dawned on me that,* enfin il me vint à l'esprit que.

day, s. **I.** (a) Jour m ; journée f *It's a fine day,* il fait beau aujourd'hui. **All day (long),** toute la journée. **To work by the day,** travailler à la journée. **Twice a day,** deux fois par jour. **This day week,** (d')aujourd'hui en huit. **The day before sth.,** la veille de qch. **The day after (sth.),** le lendemain (de qch.). **Every other day,** tous les deux jours. **Day after day,** tous les jours. **Day in day out,** sans trêve. **Day by day,** jour par jour ; de jour en jour. **From day to day,** de jour en jour. (b) **To win the day,** gagner la journée. **2.** (a) **At break of day,** au point du jour. (b) *To travel by day,* voyager le jour. **3.** (a) **Day of the month,** quantième m du mois. *What is the day of the month?* c'est le combien aujourd'hui ? *He may arrive any day,* il peut arriver d'un jour à l'autre. **Day off,** jour de congé (d'un employé). *F:* **To name the day,** fixer le jour du mariage. (b) **Fête** f. **All Saints' Day,** la fête de la Toussaint. **Easter Day,** le jour de Pâques. **4.** The good old days, le bon vieux temps. **In our days,** de nos jours. *I was a student in those days,* j'étais étudiant à ce moment-là, à cette époque. **To this day,** encore aujourd'hui. **In days to come,** dans un temps futur. **To have had its day,** avoir fait son temps. **day-boarder,** s. *Sch:* Demi-pensionnaire mf. **day-boy,** s. *Sch:* Externe m. **day-break,** s. Point m du jour ; aube f. **day-dream,** s. Rêverie f. **day-labourer,** s. Journalier m ; ouvrier m à la journée. **day-time,** s. Le jour, la journée. In the day-time, pendant la journée.

daylight, s. **I.** Jour m ; lumière f du jour. **In broad daylight,** en plein jour. **2.** Espace m libre ; ouverture f ; jour. *F:* **To see daylight,** voir jour.

daze¹, s. Étourdissement m, stupéfaction f. **To be in a daze,** être hébété, stupéfait.

daze², v.tr. **I.** (a) (Of drug) Stupéfier, hébéter. (b) (Of blow) Étourdir. (c) *F:* Abasourdir, ahurir. **2.** = DAZZLE. **dazed,** a. (a) Stupéfié ; hébété. (b) Tout étourdi. (c) *F:* Abasourdi, ahuri.

dazzle, v.tr. Éblouir, aveugler. **dazzling,** a. Éblouissant, aveuglant.

deacon, s. *Ecc:* Diacre m.

dead. I. a. **I.** Mort. (a) *He is d.,* il est mort, décédé. **The dead man, woman,** le mort, la morte. *Prov:* **Dead men tell no tales,** morte la bête mort le venin. **To kill s.o.** (stone) **dead,** tuer qn raide. *F:* **Dead as a door-nail,** mort et bien mort. **To become a dead letter,** tomber en désuétude. *Post:* **Dead letters,** lettres tombées au rebut. (b) (Doigt) mort. (Of limb) **To go dead,** s'engourdir. **2. Dead**

season, morte-saison. **3.** *To come to a d. stop,* s'arrêter net. *Nau:* **Dead calm,** calme plat. **Dead silence,** silence de mort. **Dead secret,** profond secret. *D. level,* niveau parfait. **To be dead on time,** être à la minute. **Dead loss,** perte sèche. **To be in dead earnest,** être tout à fait sérieux. **He's a dead shot,** il ne manque jamais son coup. **II. dead,** s. **I.** pl. The dead, les morts m ; les trépassés m. **2.** At dead of night, au milieu de la nuit. **In the dead of winter,** au (plus) fort de l'hiver. **III. dead,** adv. (a) Absolument. **Dead drunk,** ivre mort. *D. tired,* mort de fatigue ; éreinté. **To go dead slow,** aller au grand ralenti. (b) **To stop dead,** s'arrêter net. (c) **To be dead against sth.,** être absolument opposé à qch. **dead(-and)-alive,** a. (Endroit) mort, sans animation. **dead-beat,** a. *P:* Épuisé, éreinté, fourbu. **dead-end,** s. Cul-de-sac m. **dead-lock,** s. Impasse f. **dead march,** s. *Mus:* Marche f funèbre. **dead-weight,** s. Poids mort ; *F:* poids accablant.

deaden, v.tr. Amortir (un coup) ; assourdir, étouffer (un son) ; émousser (les sens). *To d. one's footsteps,* ouater, feutrer, ses pas.

deadly. I. a. Mortel. **II.** adv. Mortellement. **Deadly pale,** d'une pâleur mortelle.

deaf, a. Sourd. **Deaf and dumb,** sourd-muet, f. sourde-muette. **To turn a deaf ear to s.o.,** faire la sourde oreille à ce que dit qn.

deafen, v.tr. Assourdir ; rendre sourd. **deafening,** a. Assourdissant.

deafness, s. Surdité f.

deal¹, s. A good deal, beaucoup. **That's saying a good deal,** ce n'est pas peu dire. adv. **He is a good deal better.** il va beaucoup mieux.

deal², s. **I.** *Cards:* La donne ; la main. **Whose deal is it?** à qui de faire, de donner ? **2.** *Com:* F: Affaire f, marché m.

deal³, v. **I.** v.tr. **I.** **To deal out gifts,** distribuer, répartir, des dons (to, among, entre). **2. To deal a blow,** donner, porter, un coup (at, à). **3.** Donner (les cartes). **II. deal,** v.i. **I.** (a) **To (have to) deal with s.o.,** avoir affaire à, avec, qn. (b) **To deal with a subject,** traiter, s'occuper, d'un sujet. **2.** (a) **To deal with a piece of business,** conclure une affaire. (b) **To deal with a culprit,** disposer d'un coupable. **3.** **To deal with s.o.,** traiter, négocier, avec qn. **4.** *Cards:* Faire la donne ; donner ; *F:* faire. **dealing,** s. **I.** Dealing (out), distribution f. **2.** pl. (a) **To have dealings with s.o.,** avoir des relations avec qn. (b) **Underhand dealings,** menées sourdes, sournoises. **3.** Conduite f, procédé m. **Fair dealing(s),** loyauté f, honnêteté f.

deal⁴, s. Bois m de pin ou de sapin.

dealer, s. **I.** *Cards:* Donneur m. **2.** *Com:* (a) Négociant m (in, en) ; distributeur m (in, de). (b) Marchand, -ande (in, de).

dean, s. *Ecc:* Doyen m.

dear. I. a. (a) Cher (to, à). *F:* **My dear**

fellow, mon cher. **Dear Madam,** Madame, Mademoiselle. **Dear Sir,** D. *Mr Smith,* Cher Monsieur. **To run for dear life,** courir de toutes ses forces. (*b*) Cher, coûteux. **-ly,** *adv.* **1.** Cher, chèrement. *You shall pay d. for this,* cela vous coûtera cher. **2. Dearly loved,** tendrement aimé(e), bien aimé(e). **II. dear,** *s.* Cher, *f.* chère. *My dear,* cher ami, chère amie, mon ami(e). **III. dear,** *adv.* (Vendre) cher. **IV. dear,** *int.* **Dear me!** mon Dieu! **Oh dear!** (i) oh là là! (ii) hélas!

dearth, *s.* Disette *f*, pénurie *f*.

death, *s.* **1.** Mort *f*. **To die a violent death,** mourir de mort violente. **Till death,** pour la vie. *F:* **He'll be the death of me,** (i) il me fera mourir; (ii) il me fait mourir de rire. **To be sick (un)to death,** être malade à mourir. **To drink oneself to death,** se tuer à force de boire. *F:* **To be in at the death,** être présent au bon moment. **2.** *Jur:* Décès *m*. *Journ:* **Deaths,** Nécrologie *f*. **3.** La mort. **To be at death's door,** être à l'article de la mort. **death-bed,** *s.* Lit *m* de mort. **death-blow,** *s.* Coup mortel, fatal. **death-chamber,** *s.* Chambre *f* mortuaire. **death-rate,** *s.* (Taux *m* de la) mortalité. **death-rattle,** *s.* Râle *m* (de la mort). **death's-head,** *s.* Tête *f* de mort. **death-trap,** *s.* Endroit dangereux pour la vie; casse-cou *m inv.* **death-warrant,** *s.* *Jur:* Ordre *m* d'exécution.

deathlike, *a.* De mort; cadavéreux.

deathly, *adv.* *D. pale,* d'une pâleur mortelle.

debar, *v.tr.* **To debar s.o. from sth.,** exclure qn de qch. **To debar s.o. from doing sth.,** défendre à qn de faire qch.

debase, *v.tr.* Avilir, dégrader. **debasing,** *a.* Avilissant.

debasement, *s.* Avilissement *m*, dégradation *f*.

debatable, *a.* Contestable, discutable.

debate¹, *s.* Débat *m*, discussion *f*.

debate². **1.** *v.tr.* Débattre, discuter. **2.** *v.i.* Discuter, disputer (*with s.o. on sth.,* avec qn sur qch.).

debauch¹, *s.* *To have a d.,* faire une débauche.

debauch², *v.tr.* Débaucher, corrompre.

debauched, *a.* Débauché, corrompu.

debauchery, *s.* Débauche *f*.

debility, *s.* *Med:* Débilité *f*.

debit¹, *s.* *Book-k:* Débit *m*, doit *m*.

debit², *v.tr.* *Book-k:* **To d. s.o. with a sum,** inscrire, porter, une somme au débit de qn.

debris, *s.* Débris *mpl*.

debt, *s.* Dette *f*; créance *f*. **Bad debts,** mauvaises créances. **To be in debt,** être endetté; avoir des dettes. **To be out of debt,** être quitte de dettes. **debt-collector,** *s.* *Com:* Agent *m* de recouvrements.

debtor, *s.* **1.** Débiteur, -trice. **2.** *Book-k:* Debtor side, débit *m*, doit *m*.

début, *s.* Début *m*.

decadence, *s.* Décadence *f*.

decadent, *a.* En décadence; décadent.

decamp, *v.i.* *F:* Décamper, filer.

decant, *v.tr.* Décanter.

decanter, *s.* Carafe *f*.

decapitate, *v.tr.* Décapiter; couper la tête à.

decapitation, *s.* Décapitation *f*.

decay¹, *s.* **1.** Décadence *f* (d'un pays); délabrement *m* (d'un bâtiment). **Senile decay,** affaiblissement *m* sénile. **To fall into decay,** tomber en ruine. **2.** (*a*) Pourriture *f*, corruption *f*. (*b*) Carie *f* (des dents).

decay², *v.i.* (*a*) Tomber en décadence; (*of building*) tomber en ruine; (*of race*) dépérir. (*b*) (*Of meat*) Se gâter, pourrir; (*of teeth*) se carier. **decayed,** *a.* **1.** Déchu. **2.** (Bois) pourri. **Decayed tooth,** dent gâtée.

decease¹, *s.* *Adm:* Décès *m*.

decease², *v.i.* *Adm:* Décéder. **deceased. 1.** *a.* Décédé. **Mary Smith, deceased,** feue Mary Smith. **2.** *s.* Défunt, défunte.

deceit, *s.* Tromperie *f*, duperie *f*.

deceitful, *a.* Trompeur, -euse; fourbe; faux, *f.* fausse. **-fully,** *adv.* **1.** Frauduleusement. **2.** Faussement.

deceitfulness, *s.* Nature trompeuse; fausseté *f*.

deceive, *v.tr.* Tromper, abuser; en imposer à. **deceiving,** *a.* Trompeur, -euse; décevant.

deceiver, *s.* Trompeur, -euse; fourbe *m*.

December, *s.* Décembre *m*. **In December,** au mois de décembre, en décembre.

decency, *s.* **1.** Décence *f*, bienséance *f* (de costume). **2.** Bienséance, convenance(s) *f(pl)*; décence.

decent, *a.* **1.** (*a*) Bienséant, convenable. (*b*) Décent, honnête, modeste. **2.** *F:* Passable; assez bon. **3.** *F:* **A very decent fellow,** un très bon garçon. **-ly,** *adv.* **1.** Décemment, convenablement. **2.** Passablement; assez bien.

deception, *s.* Tromperie *f*, duperie *f*; fraude *f*.

deceptive, *a.* Trompeur, -euse; décevant. **-ly,** *adv.* Trompeusement.

decide, **1.** *v.tr.* (*a*) Décider (une question); statuer sur (une affaire). (*b*) *To d. s.o.'s fate,* décider du sort de qn. *Nothing has been decided yet,* il n'y a encore rien de décidé. (*c*) **To decide to do sth.,** se décider à faire qch. *I have decided what I shall do,* mon parti est pris. **2.** *v.i.* **To decide (up)on sth.,** se décider à qch. *To d. upon a day,* fixer un jour. **decided,** *a.* **1.** (*Of opinion*) Arrêté; (*of manner*) décidé. *In a d. tone,* d'un ton net, résolu. *A d. refusal,* un refus catégorique. **2.** Incontestable. **A decided difference,** une différence marquée. **-ly,** *adv.* **1.** Résolument, avec décision. **2.** Incontestablement, décidément. **deciding,** *a.* Décisif.

decimal. **1.** *a.* Décimal, -aux. *s.* Décimale *f*. **Recurring decimal,** fraction *f* périodique.

decimate, *v.tr.* Décimer.

decipher, *v.tr.* Déchiffrer.

decision, *s.* **I.** (*a*) Décision *f* (d'une question). (*b*) Décision, jugement *m*, arrêt *m*. **2.** Décision, résolution *f*. **To come to a decision,** arriver à une décision. **3.** Résolution (de caractère); fermeté *f*, décision.

decisive, *a.* **I.** Décisif; (*of experiment*) concluant. **2.** (Ton) tranchant; net, nette. **-ly,** *adv.* Décisivement.

deck¹, *s.* *Nau:* Pont *m.* **deck-chair,** *s.* Transatlantique *m.*

deck², *v.tr.* Parer, orner (*with*, de). **To deck oneself out,** s'endimancher; se mettre sur son trente et un.

declaim. I. *v.i.* Déclamer (*against*, contre). **2.** *v.tr.* Déclamer.

declamation, *s.* Déclamation *f.*

declamatory, *a.* Déclamatoire, déclamateur.

declaration, *s.* (*a*) Déclaration *f.* (*b*) *Cards:* Annonce *f.*

declare. I. *v.tr.* (*a*) Déclarer (*sth. to s.o.*, qch. à qn). *He declared he had seen nothing,* il déclara n'avoir rien vu. **To declare war,** déclarer la guerre (*on, against,* à). *Have you anything to declare?* avez-vous quelque chose à déclarer? *F:* **Well, I declare!** par exemple! (*b*) *Pred. To d. s.o. guilty,* déclarer qn coupable. **2.** *v.i.* **To declare for sth.,** se déclarer pour qch. **declared,** *a.* Ouvert, avoué, déclaré.

declension, *s.* *Gram:* Déclinaison *f.*

decline¹, *s.* **I.** Déclin *m* (du jour); baisse *f* (de prix). **2. To go into a decline,** entrer en consomption.

decline². I. *v.tr.* **I.** (*a*) Refuser courtoisement; décliner (un honneur). *Abs:* S'excuser. (*b*) Refuser; repousser. *To d. to do sth.,* refuser de faire qch. **2.** *Gram:* Décliner. **II. decline,** *v.i.* (*a*) (*Of sun*) Décliner; (*of day*) tirer à sa fin. (*b*) (*Of health*) Décliner, baisser; (*of prices*) baisser. **declining,** *a.* **In one's declining years,** au déclin de la vie.

decompose. I. *v.tr.* Décomposer, corrompre. **2.** *v.i.* (*a*) Se décomposer. (*b*) Entrer en décomposition; pourrir.

decomposition, *s.* Décomposition *f.*

decorate, *v.tr.* **I.** Décorer, orner (*with*, de). **2.** Médailler, décorer.

decoration, *s.* **I.** (*a*) Décoration *f*; parement *m.* (*b*) Remise *f* d'une décoration (à qn). **2.** (*a*) Décor *m* (d'un appartement). (*b*) Décoration, médaille *f.*

decorative, *a.* Décoratif.

decorator, *s.* Décorateur *m.*

decorous, *a.* Bienséant, convenable; comme il faut.

decorum, *s.* Décorum *m*, bienséance *f.*

decoy¹, *s.* Appât *m*, piège *m*, leurre *m*, amorce *f.* **decoy-duck,** *s.* Canard privé.

decoy², *v.tr.* **I.** Piper, leurrer (des oiseaux). **2.** Leurrer, amorcer (qn).

decrease¹, *s.* Diminution *f*, décroissance *f.* *D. in speed,* ralentissement *m.*

decrease². I. *v.tr.* Diminuer, faire décroître, amoindrir. **2.** *v.i.* Diminuer; décroître;

s'amoindrir. **decreasing,** *a.* Décroissant, diminuant.

decree¹, *s.* **I.** *Adm:* Décret *m*, édit *m*, arrêté *m.* **2.** *Jur:* Décision *f*, arrêt *m*, jugement *m.* **Decree nisi,** jugement provisoire.

decree², *v.tr.* Décréter, ordonner.

decrepit, *a.* Décrépit; caduc, -uque.

decrepitude, *s.* Décrépitude *f*; caducité *f.*

decry, *v.tr.* Décrier, dénigrer.

dedicate, *v.tr.* **I.** Dédier, consacrer. **2.** Dédier (un livre) (*to*, à).

dedication, *s.* Dédicace *f.*

deduce, *v.tr.* Déduire (*from*, de).

deduct, *v.tr.* Déduire, retrancher (*from*, de).

deduction, *s.* **I.** Déduction *f* (*from*, sur). **2.** (*a*) Raisonnement déductif; déduction. (*b*) Déduction, conclusion *f* (*from*, tirée de).

deed, *s.* **I.** (*a*) Action *f*, acte *m.* (*b*) Deed of valour, haut fait. (*c*) **Foul deed,** forfait *m.* (*d*) Fait. **2.** *Jur:* Acte notarié.

deem, *v.tr.* Juger, estimer, croire.

deep. I. *a.* **I.** (*a*) Profond. **To be ten feet deep,** avoir dix pieds de profondeur. **Deep in study,** plongé dans l'étude. (*b*) *D. sigh,* profond soupir. **2.** (*a*) (*Of colour*) Foncé, sombre. (*b*) **In a deep voice,** d'une voix profonde. **3.** Rusé, malin, -igne, astucieux. **-ly,** *adv.* Profondément. *To go d. into sth.,* pénétrer fort avant dans qch. **II. deep,** *adv.* **I.** Profondément. *Prov:* **Still waters run deep,** il n'y a pire eau que l'eau qui dort. **2.** *D. into the night,* très avant dans la nuit. **III. deep,** *s.* **The deep.** (*a*) Les profondeurs *f*, l'abîme *m.* (*b*) L'océan *m.* **deep-laid,** *a.* (Complot) ténébreux. **deep-rooted,** *a.* Profondément enraciné. **deep-seated,** *a.* Profond, enraciné. **deep-set,** *a.* (Yeux) enfoncés, creux.

deepen. I. *v.tr.* (*a*) Approfondir, creuser. (*b*) Rendre plus intense. **2.** *v.i.* Devenir plus profond; s'approfondir.

deepness, *s.* **I.** Profondeur *f.* Gravité *f* (d'un son). **2.** Astuce *f.*

deer, *s.inv.* (Red) deer, cerf. **Fallow deer,** daim *m.* **deer-hound,** *s.* Limier *m*; lévrier *m* d'Écosse.

deerskin, *s.* Peau *f* de daim.

deface, *v.tr.* Défigurer; mutiler.

defacement, *s.* Défiguration *f*, mutilation *f.*

defalcation, *s.* Détournement *m* de fonds.

defame, *v.tr.* Diffamer.

default¹, *s.* **I.** Manquement *m.* **2.** *Jur:* Défaut *m.* **3.** *Prep.phr.* **In default of,** à, au, défaut de; faute de.

default², *v.i.* *Jur:* Faire défaut.

defaulter, *s.* **I.** Délinquant, -ante. **2.** *Mil:* Retardataire *m.* **3.** Auteur *m* de détournements de fonds.

defeat¹, *s.* **I.** Défaite *f.* **2.** Renversement *m*; insuccès *m.*

defeat², *v.tr.* **I.** Battre, défaire, vaincre. **2.** Renverser, faire échouer (un projet).

defect, s. **1.** Défaut m, insuffisance f, manque m (of, de). **2.** Défaut, imperfection f. *Physical defect,* défaut.

defective, a. Défectueux, imparfait. *D. child,* enfant anormal. *Defective brakes,* freins mauvais. **-ly,** adv. Défectueusement.

defence, s. **1.** Défense f, protection f. **2.** (a) Défense, justification f. (b) *Jur:* Défense. *Counsel for the defence,* défenseur m. *Witness for the defence,* témoin m à décharge.

defenceless, a. Sans défense. **1.** (a) Sans protection. (b) Incapable de se défendre. **2.** Désarmé.

defend, v.tr. **1.** Défendre, protéger (from, against, contre). **2.** (a) Faire l'apologie de (qn). (b) Défendre, justifier.

defendant, a. & s. *Jur:* Défendeur, -eresse.

defender, s. Défenseur m.

defensive. 1. a. Défensif. **2.** s. Défensive f. **-ly,** adv. Défensivement.

defer[1], v.tr. Différer, ajourner; reculer. *To d. doing sth.,* différer à, de, faire qch.

deferred, a. Différé.

defer[2], v.i. Déférer (to, à).

deference, s. Déférence f. *In, out of, deference to,* par déférence pour. *With all due deference to you,* sauf votre respect.

deferential, a. (Ton) de déférence.

deferment, s. Ajournement m, remise f.

defiance, s. Défi m. *To set s.o. at defiance,* défier qn.

defiant, a. (a) Provocant; (regard) de défi. (b) Qui repousse les avances; intraitable. **-ly,** adv. D'un air de défi.

deficiency, s. **1.** Manque m, insuffisance f, défaut m (of, de). **2.** Défaut, imperfection f. **3.** Déficit m.

deficient, a. Défectueux, insuffisant, incomplet. *To be d. in sth.,* manquer de qch.

deficit, s. *Fin:* Déficit m.

defile[1], s. Défilé m.

defile[2], v.i. Défiler.

defile[3], v.tr. Souiller, salir; polluer.

defilement, s. Souillure f; pollution f.

define, v.tr. **1.** Définir. **2.** Déterminer; délimiter. **3.** *Well-defined outlines,* contours nettement dessinés.

definite, a. **1.** Défini; bien déterminé. *D. answer,* réponse catégorique. **2.** *Gram:* *Definite article,* article défini. **-ly,** adv. D'une manière précise; décidément.

definition, s. Définition f.

deflate, v.tr. Dégonfler. *Deflated tyre,* pneu aplati, à plat.

deflation, s. Dégonflement m.

deflect. 1. v.tr. (Faire) dévier; détourner. **2.** v.i. (Se) dévier, se détourner.

deform, v.tr. Déformer. **deformed,** a. Contrefait, difforme.

deformation, s. Déformation f.

deformity, s. Difformité f.

defraud, v.tr. **1.** Frauder. **2.** *To defraud s.o. of sth.,* frustrer qn de qch.

defray, v.tr. *To defray s.o.'s expenses,* défrayer qn. *To defray the cost of sth.,* couvrir les frais de qch.

deft, a. Adroit, habile. **-ly,** adv. Adroitement, prestement.

deftness, s. Adresse f, habileté f, dextérité f.

defunct, a. Défunt; décédé. s. *The defunct,* le défunt, la défunte.

defy, v.tr. Défier; mettre au défi. *To defy description,* défier toute description.

degeneracy, s. Dégénération f.

degenerate[1], a. & s. Dégénéré, -ée.

degenerate[2], v.i. Dégénérer (from, de; into, en).

degeneration, s. Dégénérescence f, dégénération f.

degradation, s. **1.** Dégradation f (d'un officier). **2.** Avilissement m, dégradation.

degrade, v.tr. (a) Dégrader (un officier). (b) Avilir, dégrader. **degrading,** a. Avilissant, dégradant.

degree, s. **1.** (a) *To some degree,* à un certain degré. *In the highest degree,* au plus haut degré. *In some degree,* dans une certaine mesure. *F:* *To a degree,* au plus haut degré. *By degrees,* par degrés; petit à petit. (b) Degré. *Angle of 30 degrees,* angle de 30 degrés. *Twenty degrees west of Greenwich,* sous le méridien de vingt degrés à l'ouest de Greenwich. **2.** *Sch:* Grade m. *To take one's degree,* prendre ses grades.

de-ice, v.tr. Dégivrer. **de-icing,** s. Dégivrage m. **de-icer,** s. Dégivreur m.

deign, v.tr. *To deign to do sth.,* daigner faire qch.; condescendre à faire qch.

deity, s. Dieu m, déesse f; déité f, divinité f.

deject, v.tr. Abattre, décourager. **dejected,** a. Triste, abattu, déprimé.

dejection, s. Découragement m, tristesse f.

delay[1], s. **1.** Sursis m, remise f; délai m, retard m. *Without further delay,* sans plus tarder. **2.** Retardement m, arrêt m.

delay[2]. **1.** v.tr. (a) Différer, retarder, remettre. (b) Retenir, arrêter, retarder. **2.** v.i. (a) Tarder (à faire qch.). (b) S'attarder.

delegate[1], s. Délégué m.

delegate[2], v.tr. Déléguer.

delegation, s. Délégation f.

delete, v.tr. Effacer, rayer.

deleterious, a. Nuisible à la santé; délétère.

deletion, s. **1.** Rature f, suppression f. **2.** Passage supprimé.

deliberate[1], a. **1.** Délibéré, prémédité, voulu. **2.** (a) Réfléchi, avisé. (b) Lent; sans hâte. **-ly,** adv. **1.** De propos délibéré; à dessein; exprès. **2.** (Agir) posément, délibérément.

deliberate[2], v.tr. & i. Délibérer (on, de, sur).

deliberateness, s. **1.** Intention marquée. **2.** Sage lenteur f, mesure f.

deliberation, s. **1.** (a) Délibération f. (b) *The deliberations of an assembly,* les débats m d'une assemblée. **2.** (a) *To act with d.,* agir après réflexion. (b) Sage lenteur f.

delicacy, *s.* Délicatesse *f.* **1.** (*a*) Finesse *f.* (*b*) Délicatesse, faiblesse *f.* **2.** Table delicacies, délicatesses, friandises *f,* de table.

delicate, *a.* Délicat. **1.** (*a*) To have a delicate touch, avoir de la légèreté de touche, de doigté. (*b*) D. feelings, sentiments délicats, raffinés. **2.** D. situation, situation délicate, difficile. **3.** D. health, santé délicate, faible. **-ly,** *adv.* Délicatement; avec délicatesse.

delicious, *a.* Délicieux, exquis. **-ly,** *adv.* Délicieusement.

delight¹, *s.* **1.** Délices *fpl,* délice *m.* **2.** Joie *f.* **3.** To take delight in sth., se délecter à, dans, qch.

delight². **1.** *v.tr.* Enchanter, ravir, réjouir (qn). **2.** *v.i.* To delight in, se délecter à, dans. **delighted,** *a.* Enchanté, ravi (*with,* at, de). I shall be delighted, je ne demande pas mieux.

delightful, *a.* Délicieux, ravissant. **-fully,** *adv.* Délicieusement; à ravir.

delineate, *v.tr.* **1.** Tracer, décrire. **2.** Dessiner.

delineation, *s.* **1.** Délinéation *f.* **2.** Tracé *m,* dessin *m.*

delinquency, *s.* **1.** Culpabilité *f.* **2.** Délit *m,* faute *f;* écart *m* de conduite.

delinquent, *a. & s.* Délinquant, -ante; coupable (*mf*).

delirious, *a.* En délire, délirant. F: D. with joy, fou, délirant, de joie.

delirium, *s.* Délire *m.*

deliver, *v.tr.* **1.** Délivrer (qn de qch.). To deliver s.o. from captivity, (re)tirer qn de (la) captivité. **2.** To deliver oneself of an opinion, émettre, exprimer, une opinion. **3.** To deliver sth. to s.o., livrer, délivrer, qch. à qn. To deliver up, restituer, rendre (*to,* à). **4.** Remettre, délivrer (un paquet); livrer (des marchandises). To deliver a message, faire une commission. Com: Delivered free, rendu à domicile. **5.** Porter, donner (un coup); faire, lancer (une attaque); livrer (bataille). **6.** Faire, prononcer (un discours); prononcer, rendre (un jugement).

deliverance, *s.* Délivrance *f,* libération *f* (*from,* de).

deliverer, *s.* Libérateur, -trice; sauveur *m.*

delivery, *s.* **1.** (*a*) D. of a message, exécution *f* d'une commission. (*b*) Livraison *f,* délivrance *f,* remise *f.* Free delivery, livraison franco. To pay on delivery, payer sur livraison. **2.** (*a*) Delivery of a speech, prononciation *f* d'un discours. (*b*) Débit *m,* diction *f* (d'un orateur).

dell, *s.* Vallon *m,* combe *f.*

Delphi. *Pr.n. A.Geog:* Delphes *f.*

Delphic, *a.* The Delphic Oracle, l'Oracle *m* de Delphes.

delta, *s.* *Geog:* Delta *m.*

delude, *v.tr.* **1.** Abuser, tromper. To d. oneself, s'abuser; se faire illusion. **2.** Duper; en faire accroire à.

deluge¹, *s.* Déluge *m.*

deluge², *v.tr.* Inonder (*with,* de).

delusion, *s.* Illusion *f,* erreur *f.* To be under a delusion, se faire illusion; s'abuser.

delusive, *a.* Illusoire; trompeur, -euse. **-ly,** *adv.* Illusoirement; trompeusement

demagogue, *s.* Démagogue *m.*

demand¹, *s.* **1.** Demande *f,* réclamation *f,* revendication *f.* **2.** To be in demand, être demandé. **3.** *pl.* To make great demands upon s.o.'s energy, exiger de qn beaucoup d'énergie

demand², *v.tr.* **1.** To demand sth. of, from, s.o., réclamer qch. à qn; exiger qch. de qn. To d. that . . ., demander, exiger, que + *sub.* **2.** The matter demands great care, l'affaire demande, exige, beaucoup de soin.

demean, *v.pr.* To demean oneself, s'abaisser, se dégrader.

demeanour, *s.* Air *m,* tenue *f,* maintien *m.*

demented, *a.* Fou, *f.* folle; en démence.

demigod, *s.* Demi-dieu *m, pl.* demi-dieux.

demise, *s.* **1.** *Jur:* Cession *f,* transmission *f.* **2.** *F:* Décès *m,* mort *f.*

demobilization, *s.* Démobilisation *f.*

demobilize, *v.tr.* *Mil:* Démobiliser.

democracy, *s.* Démocratie *f.*

democrat, *s.* Démocrate *mf.*

democratic, *a.* Démocratique.

demolish, *v.tr.* **1.** Démolir. **2.** *F:* Avaler, dévorer.

demolition, *s.* Démolition *f.*

demon, *s.* Démon *m,* diable *m.*

demoniacal, *a.* Démoniaque, diabolique.

demonstrable, *a.* Démontrable. **-ably,** *adv.* Statement d. false, affirmation dont la fausseté peut être prouvée.

demonstrate. **1.** *v.tr.* (*a*) Démontrer. (*b*) Décrire, expliquer. **2.** *v.i.* Pol: Manifester.

demonstration, *s.* **1.** Démonstration *f.* **2.** *F:* Demonstrations of love, témoignages *m,* démonstrations, de tendresse. **3.** Manifestation *f.*

demonstrative, *a.* Démonstratif.

demonstrator, *s.* **1.** Démonstrateur *m.* **2.** Manifestant *m.*

demoralization, *s.* Démoralisation *f.*

demoralize, *v.tr.* **1.** Dépraver, corrompre. **2.** Démoraliser (les troupes).

demur¹, *s.* Hésitation *f.* To make no demur, ne faire aucune difficulté.

demur², *v.i.* Faire des difficultés; soulever des objections (*at, to,* contre).

demure, *a.* **1.** Posé, grave; réservé. **2.** D'une modestie affectée. **-ly,** *adv.* **1.** D'un air posé, modeste. **2.** Avec une modestie affectée.

demureness, *s.* **1.** Gravité *f* de maintien. **2.** Modestie affectée.

den, *s.* **1.** Tanière *f,* antre *m,* repaire *m.* Den of thieves, retraite *f* de voleurs. **2.** *F:* Cabinet *m* de travail. **3.** *F:* Bouge *m.*

denial, s. **I.** Déni m, refus m. **2.** Dénégation f, démenti m.

denizen, s. *Denizens of the forest*, hôtes m, habitants, -antes, des bois.

Denmark. *Pr.n.* Le Danemark.

denomination, s. **I.** Dénomination f. **2.** *Ecc:* Culte m, secte f, confession f. **3.** Catégorie f. *Coins of all denominations*, pièces de toutes valeurs.

denominational, a. Confessionnel, sectaire.

denote, *v.tr.* **I.** Dénoter. **2.** Signifier.

denounce, *v.tr.* **I.** (a) Dénoncer. (b) Démasquer (un imposteur). **2.** S'élever contre (un abus).

dense, a. **I.** Épais, -aisse. *D. crowd*, foule compacte. **2.** Stupide, bête.

denseness, s. = DENSITY 2, 3.

density, s. **I.** *Ph:* Densité f. **2.** Épaisseur f; densité. **3.** Stupidité f.

dent[1], s. **I.** Marque f de coup; bosselure f; renfoncement m.

dent[2], *v.tr.* Bosseler, bossuer.

dental, a. **I.** Dentaire. **Dental surgeon**, chirurgien dentiste. **2.** *Ling:* Dental, -aux.

dentifrice, s. Dentifrice m.

dentist, s. Dentiste m.

dentistry, s. Art m dentaire.

denude, *v.tr.* Dénuder.

denunciation, s. **I.** Dénonciation f. **2.** (a) Condamnation f. (b) Accusation publique.

deny, *v.tr.* **I.** Nier (un fait); démentir (une nouvelle). **I don't deny it**, je n'en disconviens pas. **There is no denying the fact**, c'est un fait indéniable. **2.** To deny s.o. sth., refuser qch. à qn. **He is not to be denied**, il n'acceptera pas de refus. **3.** (a) To deny oneself sth., se refuser qch.; se priver de qch. (b) **To deny oneself**, faire abnégation de soi-même.

depart, *v.i.* **I.** S'en aller, partir. *To d. from a place*, quitter un lieu. **2.** *To d. from a rule*, sortir d'une règle. **departed,** a. **I.** Passé, évanoui. **2.** Mort, défunt.

department, s. **I.** (a) *Adm:* Département m, service m. *Heads of departments*, chefs de service. (b) Rayon m, comptoir m. **2.** *Fr. Geog:* Département.

departmental, a. Départemental, -aux.

departure, s. **I.** Départ m. **To take one's departure,** s'en aller; partir. **2.** *D. from a principle*, déviation f d'un principe. **3. A new departure,** une nouvelle tendance.

depend, *v.i.* **I.** Dépendre (on, de). **That depends entirely on you**, cela ne tient qu'à vous. **That depends**, cela dépend; *F:* c'est selon. **2. To depend upon s.o.**, compter sur qn. *I can d. on him*, je suis sûr de lui. **(You may) depend upon it**, comptez là-dessus.

dependable, a. Digne de confiance.

dependant, s. Protégé, -ée.

dependence, s. **I.** *D. on s.o.*, dépendance f de qn. **2.** Confiance f (on, en). **To place dependence on s.o.**, se fier à qn.

dependent. I. a. (a) Dépendant (on, de). (b) *To be d. on s.o.*, être à la charge de qn. **2.** s. = DEPENDANT.

depict, *v.tr.* Peindre, dépeindre.

deplete, *v.tr.* Épuiser.

depletion, s. Épuisement m.

deplorable, a. Déplorable, lamentable. **-ably,** adv. Lamentablement.

deplore, *v.i.* Déplorer; regretter vivement.

depopulate, *v.tr.* Dépeupler.

depopulation, s. Dépopulation f.

deport. I. *v.tr.* Expulser. **2.** *v.pr.* To deport oneself, se comporter.

deportation, s. Expulsion f.

deportment, s. (a) Tenue f, maintien m. (b) Conduite f; manière f d'agir.

depose, *v.tr.* **I.** Déposer. **2.** *Jur:* Déposer, témoigner (that, que + ind.).

deposit[1], s. **I.** *Bank d.*, dépôt m en banque. **2. To pay a deposit**, verser une somme par provision. **3.** Dépôt(s); sédiment m. *To form a d.*, se déposer.

deposit[2], *v.tr.* Déposer.

deposition, s. **I.** Déposition f (d'un roi). **2.** Déposition, témoignage m.

depositor, s. *Bank:* Déposant, -ante.

depository, s. Dépôt m, entrepôt m.

depot, s. Dépôt m; entrepôt m. *Tramway d.*, garage m de(s) tramways.

depravation, s. Dépravation f.

deprave, *v.tr.* Dépraver.

depravity, s. Dépravation f; perversité f.

deprecate, *v.tr.* Désapprouver, déconseiller.

deprecating, a. Désapprobateur, -trice.

deprecation, s. Désapprobation f.

deprecatory, a. (Rire) qui va au-devant des reproches, de la critique.

depreciate. I. *v.tr.* (a) Déprécier; avilir. (b) Déprécier, dénigrer (qn). **2.** *v.i.* Se déprécier; diminuer de valeur.

depreciation, s. **I.** Dépréciation f; moins-value f. **2.** Dépréciation, dénigrement m.

depredation, s. Déprédation f.

depredator, s. Déprédateur, -trice.

depress, *v.tr.* **I.** Abaisser; baisser (qch.). **2.** (a) Faire languir (le commerce). (b) Attrister, décourager. **depressed,** a. **I.** *Com:* (Marché) languissant. **2.** Triste, abattu. *He is easily d.*, un rien l'abat. **depressing,** a. Attristant.

depression, s. **I.** Abaissement m. **2.** Dépression f, creux m (de terrain). **3.** *Com:* Affaissement m, marasme m. **4.** Découragement m, abattement m.

deprival, s. Privation f (of, de).

deprivation, s. **I.** Privation f, perte f (de droits). **2.** Dépossession f.

deprive, *v.tr.* *To d. s.o. of sth.*, priver qn de qch. **To deprive oneself,** s'infliger des privations.

depth, s. **I.** Profondeur f. **2.** Fond m, hauteur f (de l'eau). **To get out of one's depth,** (i) perdre fond; (ii) *F:* sortir de sa compétence. **3.** Hauteur (d'un faux col); épaisseur f (d'une couche). **4.** (a) Gravité f (d'un son). (b) Portée f (de l'intelligence). (c) Intensité f (de coloris). **5.** Fond (d'une forêt); milieu m (de la nuit). **In the depth of winter,** au plus fort de l'hiver. **6.** pl. **In the depths of despair,** dans le plus profond désespoir. **depth-charge,** s. Navy: Grenade sous-marine.

deputation, s. Députation f, délégation f.

depute, v.tr. **I.** Déléguer. **2.** To d. s.o. to do sth., députer, déléguer, qn pour faire qch.

deputize, v.i. To d. for s.o., faire l'intérim de qn; remplacer qn.

deputy, s. **I.** Délégué m. To act as d. for s.o., suppléer qn. **Deputy-chairman,** vice-président m. **Deputy-governor,** sous-gouverneur m. **2.** (a) Délégué. (b) Fr.Pol: Député m.

derail, v.tr. Faire dérailler (un train).

derange, v.tr. Déranger.

derangement, s. Dérangement m.

derelict. I. a. Abandonné, délaissé, à l'abandon. **2.** s. (a) Objet abandonné; navire abandonné; épave f. (b) Épave humaine.

dereliction, s. **I.** Abandon m. **2.** Dereliction of duty, manquement m au devoir.

deride, v.tr. Tourner en dérision; bafouer, railler, se moquer de.

derision, s. Dérision f. Object of derision, objet de risée f. To hold s.o. in derision, se moquer de qn.

derisive, a. **I.** Moqueur, -euse. **2.** D. offer, offre dérisoire. **-ly,** adv. D'un air moqueur.

derivation, s. Dérivation f.

derivative, a. & s. Dérivé (m).

derive, v.tr. & i. **I.** (a) To d. sth. from sth., tirer (son origine) de qch.; trouver (du plaisir) à qch. (b) Word derived from Latin, mot qui vient du latin. **2.** To be derived, v.i. to derive, dériver, (pro-)venir (from, de).

derogate, v.i. To d. (from one's dignity), déroger (à sa dignité).

derogatory, a. **I.** Dérogatoire (from, à). **2.** Dérogeant, qui déroge (to, à).

derrick, s. Mât m de charge.

dervish, s. Derviche m.

descant, v.i. Discourir, s'étendre (on, sur).

descend. I. v.i. (a) Descendre. (b) To descend on s.o., s'abattre, tomber, sur qn. (c) To descend to s.o.'s level, s'abaisser au niveau de qn. (d) To be descended from s.o., descendre de qn. **2.** v.tr. Descendre, dévaler.

descendant, -ent, s. Descendant, -ante. pl. Descendants, descendance f, postérité f.

descent, s. **I.** Descente f. **2.** (Lineage) Descendance f.

describe, v.tr. **I.** (a) Décrire, dépeindre. (b) Pred. To d. s.o. as, qualifier qn de. **2.** Décrire (une courbe).

description, s. **I.** (a) Description f. Beyond description, indescriptible. (b) (For police purposes) Signalement m. (c) Com: Désignation f. **2.** F: Sorte f, espèce f, genre m. People of this description, les gens de cette espèce.

descriptive, a. Descriptif.

descry, v.tr. Apercevoir, aviser.

desecrate, v.tr. Profaner.

desecration, s. Profanation f.

desecrator, s. Profanateur, -trice.

desert[1], s. Mérite m. To get one's deserts, avoir ce que l'on mérite.

desert[2]. **I.** a. Désert. **2.** s. Désert m.

desert[3], v.tr. (a) Déserter. (b) Abandonner, délaisser. **deserted,** a. Abandonné; (of place) désert.

deserter, s. Déserteur m.

desertion, s. **I.** Abandon m, délaissement m. **2.** Mil: Désertion f.

deserve, v.tr. Mériter. He richly deserves it! F: il ne l'a pas volé! **deserving,** a. (Of pers.) Méritant; (of action) méritoire. Deserving case, cas digne d'intérêt.

deservedly, adv. A juste titre; à bon droit.

desiccate, v.tr. Dessécher.

desiccation, s. Dessiccation f.

design[1], s. **I.** Dessein m, intention f, projet m. By design, à dessein. **2.** (Decorative) design, dessin m d'ornement. **3.** Dessin, modèle m. Car of the latest d., voiture dernier modèle.

design[2], v.tr. **I.** Destiner (for, à). **2.** Projeter, se proposer. **3.** (a) Préparer (un projet). (b) Créer (une robe); établir (un avion). Well designed premises, local bien agencé. **designing,** a. Artificieux, intrigant.

designate, v.tr. **I.** Désigner, nommer. **2.** Indiquer (qch.).

designation, s. **I.** Désignation f. **2.** D. to a post, nomination f à un emploi. **3.** Désignation, nom m.

designedly, adv. A dessein.

designer, s. Dessinateur, -trice. Th: Stage designer, décorateur m de théâtre.

desirability, s. Caractère m désirable; avantage m; attrait m.

desirable, a. Désirable; à désirer; souhaitable; avantageux. **-ably,** adv. Avantageusement.

desire[1], s. **I.** Désir m, souhait m. I feel no d. to, je n'éprouve aucune envie de. **2.** At s.o.'s desire, à la demande de qn.

desire[2], v.tr. **I.** Désirer; avoir envie de. Since you desire it, puisque vous y tenez. It leaves much to be desired, cela laisse beaucoup à désirer. **2.** (a) To d. sth. of s.o., demander qch. à qn. (b) To d. s.o. to do sth., prier qn de faire qch.

desirous, a. Désireux (of, de).

desist, v.i. **I.** Cesser (from doing sth., de faire qch.). **2.** To d. from sth., renoncer à qch.; se désister de qch.

desk, s. **I.** Pupitre m; (in office) bureau m; (schoolmaster's) chaire f. **2.** Pay at the desk! payez à la caisse!

desolate[1], a. **I.** (Lieu) désert. **2.** Affligé.

desolate[2], v.tr. Désoler. **I.** Ravager (un pays). **2.** Affliger (qn).

desolation, s. Désolation f.

despair[1], s. Désespoir m. To be in despair,

être au désespoir. **To drive s.o. to despair**, désespérer qn.
despair², v.i. (a) Désespérer (of, de). (b) Abs. Perdre espoir ; (se) désespérer. **despairing**, a. Désespéré. In a d. tone, d'un ton de désespoir. **-ly**, adv. En désespéré.
despatch, s. & v. = DISPATCH¹, ².
desperado, s. Homme m capable de tout ; cerveau brûlé ; risque-tout m inv.
desperate, a. 1. (a) Désespéré. (b) Desperate remedy, remède héroïque. 2. (a) A d. man, un désespéré. (b) D. conflict, combat acharné. **To do something desperate**, F: faire un malheur. **-ly**, adv. Désespérément, avec acharnement.
desperation, s. (Outrance f du) désespoir m. **To drive s.o. to desperation**, pousser qn à bout. **In desperation**, en désespoir de cause.
despicable, a. Méprisable. **-ably**, adv. Bassement.
despise, v.tr. (a) Mépriser ; faire mépris de. (b) Dédaigner.
despite, prep. & prep.phr. **Despite**, **in despite of** (sth.), en dépit de (qch.).
despoil, v.tr. Dépouiller, spolier (of, de).
despoiler, s. Spoliateur, -trice.
despond, v.i. Perdre courage.
despondency, s. Découragement m, abattement m.
despondent, a. Découragé, abattu.
despot, s. Despote m ; tyran m.
despotic, a. 1. (Pouvoir) despotique. 2. (Of pers.) Arbitraire, despote. **-ally**, adv. Despotiquement, arbitrairement.
despotism, s. Despotisme m.
dessert, s. Dessert m. **dessert-spoon**, s. Cuiller f à dessert.
destination, s. Destination f.
destine, v.tr. Destiner (for, à).
destiny, s. Destin m, destinée f ; le sort.
destitute, a. 1. Dépourvu, dénué (of, de). 2. Indigent ; sans ressources. **To be utterly d.**, manquer de tout.
destitution, s. Dénuement m, indigence f.
destroy, v.tr. 1. Détruire ; anéantir. 2. Tuer, abattre (une bête). **destroying**, a. Destructeur, -trice.
destroyer, s. 1. Destructeur, -trice. 2. Navy: Contre-torpilleur m.
destructible, a. Destructible.
destruction, s. Destruction f. The d. caused by the fire, les ravages m du feu.
destructive, a. Destructeur, -trice ; destructif.
destructiveness, s. 1. Effet destructeur, pouvoir destructeur (d'un explosif). 2. Penchant m à détruire.
destructor, s. Destructeur, -trice.
desultory, a. Décousu, sans suite. D. conversation, conversation à bâtons rompus.
detach, v.tr. Détacher, séparer (from, de) ; dételer (des wagons). **detached**, a. Détaché. 1. Séparé(from, de) ; à part. D. house, maison détachée. 2. (Of pers.) Désintéressé.

detachment, s. 1. (a) Séparation f (from, de). (b) Décollement m. 2. Détachement m.
detail¹, s. 1. Détail m, particularité f. **To go into all the details**, donner tous les détails. **In every detail**, de point en point. 2. Mil: Détachement m.
detail², v.tr. Détailler ; raconter en détail. To d. the facts, énumérer les faits.
detain, v.tr. 1. Détenir (en prison). 2. Retenir ; empêcher de partir.
detect, v.tr. 1. Découvrir. 2. Apercevoir.
detection, s. Découverte f.
detective, s. Détective m, agent m de la police secrète. **Detective novel**, roman policier.
detention, s. 1. (a) Détention f. (b) Sch: Retenue f. 2. Retard m (inévitable) ; arrêt m.
deter, v.tr. Détourner, décourager (s.o. from doing sth., qn de faire qch.).
deteriorate. 1. v.tr. Détériorer. 2. v.i. (a) (Se) détériorer. (b) Diminuer de valeur.
deterioration, s. (a) Détérioration f. (b) Diminution f de valeur.
determination, s. 1. (a) Détermination f (d'une date). (b) Délimitation f (d'une frontière). 2. Détermination, résolution f. **To come to a determination**, se décider. 3. Expiration f.
determine, v.tr. & i. 1. (a) Déterminer (une date). (b) Délimiter (une frontière). (c) Constater (la nature de qch.). 2. Décider (une question). 3. To d. to do sth., décider de faire qch. 4. v.tr. Résoudre. **determined**, a. 1. (Prix) déterminé. 2. Déterminé, résolu. 3. To be determined to do sth., être résolu de faire qch.
deterrent, s. To act as a d., exercer un effet préventif.
detest, v.tr. Détester.
detestable, a. Détestable. **-ably**, adv. Détestablement.
detestation, s. Détestation f (of, de). **To hold sth. in detestation**, détester qch.
dethrone, v.tr. Détrôner.
detonate. 1. v.tr. Faire détoner. 2. v.i. Détoner.
detonation, s. Détonation f, explosion f.
detonator, s. Détonateur m ; amorce f.
detour, s. Détour m.
detract, v.i. To detract from s.o.'s merit, rabaisser le mérite de qn.
detractor, s. Détracteur, -trice.
detriment, s. Détriment m, dommage m.
detrimental, a. Nuisible (to, à). It would be d. to my interests, cela desservirait mes intérêts. **-ally**, adv. Nuisiblement.
deuce¹, s. 1. Deux m. 2. Ten: A deux ; égalité f (à quarante).
deuce², s. F: Diantre m, diable m. **Go to the deuce!** allez vous promener ! va-t'en au diable ! **To play the deuce with sth.**, ruiner, gâcher, qch.
devastate, v.tr. Dévaster, ravager. **devastating**, a. Dévastateur, -trice.

devastation, *s.* Dévastation *f.*
develop, *v.* I. *v.tr.* **1.** Développer. **2.** *To
d. a district,* mettre en valeur une région.
3. *To d. heat,* engendrer de la chaleur.
4. *Phot:* Révéler, développer. II. **develop,**
v.i. **1.** Se développer. **2.** Se manifester.
developing, *s.* Développement *m.*
developer, *s.* *Phot:* Révélateur *m.*
development, *s.* **1.** Développement *m.* **2.**
Exploitation *f,* mise *f* en valeur. **3.** *Phot:*
Développement. **4.** *To await further develop-
ments,* attendre les événements.
deviate, *v.i.* Dévier, s'écarter (*from,* de).
deviation, *s.* Déviation *f* (*from,* de); écart *m.*
device, *s.* **1.** (*a*) Expédient *m,* moyen *m.*
To leave s.o. to his own devices, livrer qn à
lui-même. (*b*) Stratagème *m,* ruse *f.* **2.** Dispositif *m,* appareil *m.* **3.** Emblème *m,* devise *f.*
devil, *s.* **1.** (*a*) Diable *m.*   **Devil take it!**
que le diable l'emporte! *The devil's in it!*
le diable s'en mêle! (*b*) *F:* **What the devil
are you doing?** que diable faites-vous là?
To work like the devil, travailler avec acharnement. **There'll be the devil to pay,** les conséquences seront sérieuses. *A d. of a business,*
une diable d'affaire. **2.** Démon *m.* *F:* **To
raise the devil in s.o.,** évoquer les pires passions chez qn.
devilish. 1. *a.* (*a*) Diabolique. (*b*) *F:*
Maudit, satané. **2.** *adv.* *F:* *It's d. hot!* il
fait diablement chaud! **-ly,** *adv.* Diaboliquement.
devilry, *s.* **1.** Méchanceté *f.* **2.** *To be full
of d.,* avoir le diable au corps.
devious, *a.* Détourné, tortueux.
devise, *v.tr.* Combiner (un projet); inventer,
imaginer (un appareil).
devoid, *a.* Dénué, dépourvu (*of,* de).
devolve, *v.i.* Incomber (*on, upon,* à).
devote, *v.tr.* Vouer, consacrer; accorder (du
temps à qch.). **devoted,** *a.* Dévoué,
attaché (*to,* à). *D. to work,* assidu au travail.
-ly, *adv.* Avec dévouement.
devotion, *s.* **1.** Dévotion *f.* **2.** Dévouement
m (*to s.o.,* à, pour, qn). *D. to work,* assiduité
f au travail.
devour, *v.tr.* Dévorer. **devouring,** *a.*
Dévorateur, -trice.
devourer, *s.* Dévorateur, -trice.
devout, *a.* **1.** Dévot, pieux. **2.** (*Of wish*)
Fervent, sincère. **-ly,** *adv.* **1.** Dévotement.
2. Sincèrement.
dew, *s.* Rosée *f.*
dewdrop, *s.* Goutte *f* de rosée.
dexterity, *s.* Dextérité *f;* habileté *f.*
dexterous, *a.* Adroit, habile (*in doing sth.,*
à faire qch.). **-ly,** *adv.* Avec dextérité;
habilement.
diabolical, *a.* (Cruauté) diabolique; (complot) infernal, -aux. **-ally,** *adv.* Diaboliquement.
diadem, *s.* Diadème *m,* bandeau *m.*
diaeresis, *s.* *Gram:* Tréma *m.*
diagnose, *v.tr.* Diagnostiquer.
diagnosis, *s.* *Med:* Diagnostic *m.*

diagonal. 1. *a.* Diagonal, -aux. **2.** *s.*
Diagonale *f.* **-ally,** *adv.* Diagonalement.
diagram, *s.* Diagramme *m,* tracé *m,* schéma *m.*
dial¹, *s.* Cadran *m.*
dial², *v.tr.* *Tp:* To dial a number, composer
un numéro. **dialling,** *s.* **Dialling tone,**
signal *m* de numérotage.
dialect, *s.* Dialecte *m.* *Provincial d.,* patois *m.*
dialogue, *s.* Dialogue *m.*
diameter, *s.* Diamètre *m.*
diametrical, *a.* Diamétral, -aux. **-ally,**
adv. Diamétralement.
diamond, *s.* **1.** Diamant *m.* *F:* **He's a
rough diamond,** c'est un homme très capable
sous des dehors frustes. *F:* **Diamond cut
diamond,** à malin malin et demi. **2.** (*a*)
Losange *m.* **Diamond panes,** vitres en forme
de losange. (*b*) *Cards:* Carreau *m.* **dia-
mond-shaped,** *a.* En losange. **diamond-
wedding,** *s.* Noces *fpl* de diamant.
Diana. *Pr.n.* Diane *f.*
diaphanous, *a.* Diaphane.
diaphragm, *s.* Diaphragme *m,* membrane
diarrhoea, *s.* *Med:* Diarrhée *f.*
diary, *s.* **1.** Journal *m.* **2.** Agenda *m.*
diatribe, *s.* Diatribe *f.*
dice¹, *s.pl.* See DIE¹ I. **dice-box,** *s.* Cornet
m à dés.
dice², *v.i.* Jouer aux dés.
dickens, *s.* *F:* = DEVIL, DEUCE.
dicotyledon, *s.* *Bot:* Dicotylédone *f,* dicoty-
lédonée *f.*
dictate¹, *s.* Commandement *m.* **The dictates
of conscience,** la voix de la conscience.
dictate². 1. *v.tr.* Dicter. *Abs.* *F:* Faire la
loi. **2.** *v.i.* *F:* *I won't be dictated to,* je n'ai
pas d'ordres à recevoir.
dictation, *s.* **1.** Dictée *f.* *To write to s.o.'s d.,*
écrire sous la dictée de qn. **2.** Étalage *m*
d'autorité.
dictator, *s.* *Pol:* Dictateur *m.*
dictatorial, *a.* **1.** (Pouvoir) dictatorial, -aux.
2. (Ton) impérieux.
dictatorship, *s.* Dictature *f.*
diction, *s.* Style *m* (d'un orateur).
dictionary, *s.* Dictionnaire *m.*
dictum, *s.* **1.** Affirmation *f.* **2.** Maxime *f,*
dicton *m.*
die¹, *s.* I. Dé *m* (à jouer). **The die is cast,**
le sort en est jeté. II. **die. 1.** *Minting:*
Coin *m.* **2.** *Metalw:* Matrice *f.*
die², *v.i.* **1.** Mourir; (*of animals*) crever.
To be dying, être à l'agonie. *He died yesterday,*
il est mort hier. **To die a natural death,**
mourir de sa belle mort. **To die by one's
own hand,** périr de sa propre main. **To die
by inches,** mourir à petit feu. *This superstition
will die hard,* cette superstition aura la vie
dure. **Never say die!** tenez bon! **2.** *To die
of laughing,* mourir de rire. **To be dying to
do sth.,** mourir d'envie de faire qch. **3.** *His
secret died with him,* il emporta son secret
dans le tombeau. **My heart dies within me,**

le cœur me manque. **die away**, v.i. (*Of sound*) S'affaiblir ; (*of voice*) s'éteindre. **die down**, v.i. (*Of fire*) Baisser ; (*of wind*) s'apaiser ; (*of excitement*) se calmer. **die out**, v.i. S'éteindre ; (*of custom*) disparaître.

dying[1], a. Mourant, agonisant. **dying**[2], s. To one's dying day, jusqu'au dernier soupir.

die-hard, s. Jusqu'auboutiste m.

diet[1], s. **1.** Nourriture f. **2. To be on a diet**, être au régime.

diet[2], v.tr. Mettre au régime.

differ, v.i. **1.** Différer (*from*, de) ; être différent (de). **2. To differ about sth.**, ne pas s'accorder sur qch. **To agree to differ**, garder chacun son opinion.

difference, s. **1.** Différence f, écart m (*between*, entre). **Difference in age**, différence d'âge. **With a slight difference**, à peu de chose près. *It makes no d.*, cela ne fait rien. *That makes all the difference*, voilà qui change les choses du tout au tout. **2. To split the difference**, partager le différend. **3.** Dispute f, différend m.

different, a. **1.** Différent (*from*, *to*, de). *I feel a d. man*, je me sens tout autre. *To do sth. quite d.*, faire tout autre chose. *That's quite a different matter*, ça, c'est une autre affaire. **2.** Divers, différent. *At different times*, à diverses reprises. **-ly**, adv. **1.** Différemment. *He speaks d. from you*, il parle autrement que vous. **2.** Diversement.

differentiate, v.tr. Différencier (qch. de qch.). *Abs. To d. between two things*, faire la différence entre deux choses.

difficult, a. (a) Difficile, malaisé. *It is d. to believe that . . .*, on a peine à croire que + sub. (b) Difficile ; peu commode. **Person difficult to get on with**, personne difficile à vivre.

difficulty, s. Difficulté f. **1.** *Work of some d.*, travail assez difficile. *There will be no d. about that*, cela ne fera pas de difficulté. *With great d.*, à grand'peine. **2.** Obstacle m. *I see no d. about it*, je n'y vois pas d'inconvénient. **3.** Embarras m, ennui m. **To be in a difficulty**, être dans l'embarras. **To get out of one's difficulties**, se tirer d'affaire.

diffidence, s. Manque m d'assurance ; modestie excessive.

diffident, a. Qui manque d'assurance. *I was d. about speaking to him*, j'hésitais à lui parler. **-ly**, adv. Timidement ; en hésitant.

diffuse[1], a. Diffus. **-ly**, adv. Avec prolixité.

diffuse[2], v.tr. Répandre ; diffuser.

dig[1], s. F: (a) **To give s.o. a dig in the ribs**, enfoncer son doigt dans les côtes de qn. (b) *That's a dig at you*, c'est une pierre dans votre jardin.

dig[2], v.tr. **1.** (a) Bêcher. (b) Creuser (un trou). (c) *Abs.* Travailler la terre. **2.** Enfoncer (*sth. into sth.*, qch. dans qch.). *To dig one's spurs into one's horse*, piquer des deux. **dig in**, v.tr. (a) *Mil:* **To dig oneself in**, se terrer. (b) **To dig one's toes in**, s'assurer ; se tenir de pied ferme. **dig out**, v.tr.

Déterrer. **dig up**, v.tr. Déraciner ; mettre à jour (un trésor) ; piocher (la rue).

digging, s. **1.** Bêchage m. **2.** pl. **Diggings**, (a) *Min:* Placer m. (b) F: Logement m, garni m. **To live in diggings**, loger en garni.

digest[1], s. Sommaire m, abrégé m, résumé m.

digest[2], v.tr. **1.** (a) Mettre en ordre. (b) Résumer. **2.** Digérer.

digestible, a. Digestible.

digestion, s. Digestion f.

digestive, a. Digestif.

digit, s. **1.** (a) Doigt m. (b) Doigt de pied. **2.** *Mth:* Chiffre m.

dignify, v.tr. Donner de la dignité à.

dignified, a. Plein de dignité ; (air) digne.

dignitary, s. Dignitaire m.

dignity, s. **1.** Dignité f. **To stand on one's dignity**, se tenir sur son quant-à-soi. **2.** Dignité ; haut rang.

digress, v.i. Faire une digression (*from*, de).

digression, s. Digression f, écart m.

dike, s. (a) Digue f, levée f. (b) Chaussée surélevée.

dilapidated, a. Délabré, décrépit.

dilapidation, s. Délabrement m.

dilate, v.i. (a) Se dilater. (b) **To dilate (up)on a topic**, s'étendre sur un sujet.

dilation, s. Dilatation f.

dilatory, a. Lent (à agir) ; (*of action*) tardif.

dilemma, s. F: **To be in a dilemma**, être fort embarrassé.

diligence, s. Assiduité f, diligence f.

diligent, a. Assidu, diligent. **-ly**, adv. Avec assiduité ; diligemment.

dilly-dally, v.i. F: Lanterner.

dilute, v.tr. Diluer ; arroser (le vin).

dilution, s. Dilution f ; arrosement m (du vin).

dim[1], a. Faible ; pâle. **Eyes dim with tears**, yeux voilés de larmes. **To grow dim**, (*of light*) baisser ; (*of sight*) se troubler. **-ly**, adv. Faiblement, sans éclat.

dim[2], v.tr. (a) Obscurcir ; ternir. **Eyes dimmed with weeping**, yeux ternis de pleurs. (b) *Aut:* **To dim the head-lights**, baisser les phares.

dimension, s. Dimension f.

diminish. **1.** v.tr. Diminuer, réduire, amoindrir. **2.** v.i. Diminuer, décroître.

diminished, a. Diminué, amoindri.

diminution, s. Diminution f ; réduction. f.

diminutive. **1.** a. & s. *Gram:* Diminutif (m). **2.** a. F: Tout petit ; minuscule.

dimness, s. **1.** Faiblesse f (de la vue) ; obscurité f (d'une salle). **2.** Imprécision f.

dimple, s. Fossette f.

dimpled, a. A fossette(s).

din[1], s. Tapage m, fracas m, vacarme m.

din[2], v.tr. **To din sth. into s.o.'s ears**, corner qch. aux oreilles à qn.

dine, v.i. Dîner. **To dine out**, dîner en ville.

dining, s. Dîner m. **dining-car**, s. Wagon-restaurant m, pl. wagons-restaurants.

dining-room, s. Salle f à manger.

diner, *s.* Dîneur, -euse.

ding-dong. 1. *adv.* Digue-din-don. **2.** *s.* Tintement *m.* **3.** *a.* D.-d. *match,* partie durement disputée.

dinghy, *s.* *Nau:* Canot *m,* youyou *m.* Collapsible dinghy, berthon *m.*

dinginess, *s.* Aspect enfumé, manque *m* de fraîcheur.

dingle, *s.* Vallon (boisé).

dingo, *s.* Dingo *m.*

dingy, *a.* Qui manque de fraîcheur; défraîchi; (*of colour*) terne.

dinner, *s.* Dîner *m.* To go out to dinner, dîner (i) en ville, (ii) chez des amis. Public dinner, banquet *m.* **dinner-dance,** *s.* Dîner suivi de bal. **dinner-jacket,** *s.* (Veston *m*) smoking *m.* **dinner-service,** *s.* Service *m* de table. **dinner-time,** *s.* L'heure *f* du dîner.

dint, *s.* **1.** = DENT[1]. **2.** By dint of, à force de.

diocese, *s.* Diocèse *m.*

dip[1], *s.* **1.** Plongement *m,* immersion *f.* **2.** (*a*) Inclinaison *f* (de l'aiguille aimantée). (*b*) Plongée *f* (du terrain). **3.** Baignade *f.* *I'm going for a dip,* je vais me baigner.

dip[2], *v.* **I.** *v.tr.* **1.** Plonger, tremper. **2.** Immerger (un métal). **3.** Baisser subitement. *Aut:* To dip the head-lights, faire basculer les phares. *Nau:* To dip one's flag to a ship, saluer un vaisseau avec son pavillon. **4.** *He dipped his spoon into the pot,* il puisa dans la marmite avec sa cuiller. **II.** dip, *v.i.* **1.** Plonger. **2.** (*Of compass-needle*) Incliner; (*of scale*) pencher. *The road dips sharply,* la route plonge brusquement. **3.** To dip into a book, feuilleter un livre. **dipping,** *s.* Plongée *f,* immersion *f.*

diphtheria, *s.* *Med:* Diphtérie *f.*

diphthong, *s.* *Ling:* Diphtongue *f.*

diploma, *s.* Diplôme *m.*

diplomacy, *s.* Diplomatie *f.*

diplomat, *s.* Diplomate *m.*

diplomatic, *a.* **1.** Diplomatique. **2.** Adroit, prudent. **-ally,** *adv.* **1.** Diplomatiquement. **2.** Avec tact.

diplomatist, *s.* Diplomate *m.*

dire, *a.* Désastreux, affreux. Dire necessity, nécessité implacable. D. *poverty,* misère noire. D. *forebodings,* pressentiments lugubres.

direct[1], *v.tr.* **1.** Adresser (une lettre). **2.** Gouverner (sa conduite); gérer, régir (une entreprise). **3.** (*a*) To d. *s.o.'s attention to sth.,* attirer l'attention de qn sur qch. (*b*) To direct one's steps towards, diriger ses pas vers. **4.** To direct s.o. to the station, indiquer la gare à qn. **5.** (*a*) To direct s.o. to do sth., ordonner à qn de faire qch. As directed, selon les instructions. (*b*) To direct the jury, instruire le jury.

direct[2]. **1.** *a.* (*a*) Direct. Direct cause, cause immédiate. (*b*) Franc, *f.* franche. (*c*) Absolu, formel. D. *answer,* réponse catégorique. **2.** *adv.* (Aller) directement, tout droit. **-ly. 1.** *adv.* (*a*) (Aller) directement, tout

droit. To go d. to the point, aller droit au fait. (*b*) Absolument. D. *contrary,* diamétralement opposé (*to,* à). (*c*) Tout de suite, tout à l'heure. **2.** *conj.* F: Aussitôt que, dès que.

direction, *s.* **1.** Direction *f,* administration *f* (d'une société). **2.** Adresse *f* (d'une lettre). **3.** Direction, sens *m.* In every direction, en tous sens. **4.** (*Usu. pl.*) Instruction(s) *f(pl).* Stage direction, indication *f* scénique.

directness, *s.* Franchise *f* (d'une réponse).

director, *s.* Administrateur *m,* directeur *m.*

directorate, *s.* (Conseil *m* d')administration *f.*

directorship, *s.* Directorat *m.*

directory, *s.* **1.** Répertoire *m* d'adresses; (*in France*) le Bottin; annuaire *m* (des téléphones. **2.** *Fr.Hist:* The Directory, le Directoire.

direful, *a.* *Poet:* = DIRE.

dirge, *s.* Hymne *m* ou chant *m* funèbre.

dirk, *s.* Poignard *m.*

dirt, *s.* Saleté *f.* **1.** Boue *f,* crotte *f,* ordure *f.* *F:* To throw dirt at s.o., éclabousser la réputation de qn. To treat s.o. like dirt, traiter qn comme le dernier des derniers. **2.** Malpropreté *f.* **dirt-track,** *s.* *Sp:* Piste *f* en cendrée.

dirtiness, *s.* Saleté *f,* malpropreté *f.*

dirty[1], *a.* **1.** Sale, malpropre, crasseux; crotté. D. *hands,* mains sales. D. *shoes,* souliers crottés. D. *streets,* rues fangeuses. **2.** Dirty weather, mauvais temps; *Nau:* gros temps. **3.** To play s.o. a dirty trick, jouer un vilain tour à qn. It's a dirty business, c'est une sale affaire.

dirty[2], *v.tr.* Salir, crotter, encrasser. To d. one's hands, se salir les mains.

disability, *s.* (*a*) Incapacité *f.* (*b*) Physical disability, infirmité *f.*

disable, *v.tr.* Mettre hors de combat; estropier (qn); désemparer (un navire). Disabled ex-service-men, mutilés *m* de guerre.

disablement, *s.* **1.** Mise *f* hors de combat. **2.** Invalidité *f*; incapacité *f* de travail.

disabuse, *v.tr.* Désabuser (*of,* de).

disadvantage, *s.* Désavantage *m,* inconvénient *m.* To take s.o. at a disadvantage, prendre qn au dépourvu.

disadvantageous, *a.* Désavantageux, défavorable (*to,* à).

disaffected, *a.* Désaffectionné.

disaffection, *s.* Désaffection *f.*

disagree, *v.i.* **1.** (*a*) Être en désaccord (*with,* avec). (*b*) To d. with s.o., donner tort à qn. I disagree, je ne suis pas de cet avis. **2.** Se brouiller (*with,* avec). **3.** *Wine disagrees with him,* le vin lui est contraire.

disagreeable, *a.* (*a*) Désagréable (*to,* à); déplaisant (*to,* à). (*b*) (*Of pers.*) Désagréable, maussade. **-ably,** *adv.* Désagréablement; fâcheusement.

disagreeableness, *s.* **1.** Désagrément *m.* **2.** Mauvaise humeur.

disagreement, s. **1.** Différence f (*between,* entre). **2.** Désaccord m (avec qn sur qch.). **3.** (*a*) Différend m, querelle f. (*b*) Mésintelligence f, mésentente f (*between,* entre).

disallow, v.tr. Ne pas admettre.

disappear, v.i. Disparaître. *He disappeared from our sight,* il disparut à nos yeux.

disappearance, s. Disparition f.

disappoint, v.tr. (*a*) Désappointer. (*b*) Décevoir, chagriner. *Are you disappointed?* c'est une déception? *To be disappointed in love,* avoir des chagrins d'amour. (*c*) Décevoir (les espérances de qn); tromper (l'attente de qn).

disappointing, a. Décevant.

disappointment, s. Déception f, désappointement m; mécompte m.

disapprobation, s. Désapprobation f (*of,* de).

disapproval, s. Désapprobation f (*of,* de).

disapprove, v.i. *To disapprove of sth.,* désapprouver qch.

disarm, v.tr. & i. Désarmer.

disarmament, s. Désarmement m.

disarrange, v.tr. Déranger; mettre en désordre.

disarrangement, s. Dérangement m.

disaster, s. Désastre m; sinistre m.

disastrous, a. Désastreux; funeste. **-ly,** adv. Désastreusement.

disband. 1. v.tr. Licencier, congédier. **2.** v.i. Se débander.

disbelief, s. *Disbelief in sth.,* incrédulité f à l'égard de qch.

disbelieve. 1. v.tr. Ne pas croire; refuser créance à. **2.** v.i. *To d. in sth.,* ne pas croire à qch.

disbeliever, s. Incrédule mf.

disburden, v.tr. Décharger.

disburse, v.tr. Débourser.

disbursement, s. **1.** Déboursement m. **2.** pl. Disbursements, débours mpl.

disc, s. = DISK.

discard, v.tr. Mettre de côté; se défaire de.

discern, v.tr. Distinguer, discerner, apercevoir. **discerning,** a. (*Of pers.*) Judicieux; (*of intelligence*) pénétrant.

discernible, a. Perceptible.

discernment, s. Discernement m.

discharge[1], s. **1.** Déchargement m (d'un navire). **2.** Décharge f (d'artillerie). **3.** (*a*) Décharge; dégagement m (de gaz). (*b*) *El:* Décharge. **4.** (*a*) Renvoi m (d'un employé). (*b*) Libération f (d'un militaire). **5.** *Jur:* (*a*) Mise f en liberté, élargissement m. (*b*) Acquittement m. **6.** Accomplissement m. *In the discharge of his duties,* dans l'exercice m de ses fonctions. **7.** (*a*) Payement m (d'une dette). (*b*) Quittance f.

discharge[2], v.tr. **1.** Décharger (une cargaison). **2.** (*a*) Congédier. (*b*) Libérer du service militaire. *Navy:* Débarquer. (*c*) *To discharge a patient,* renvoyer un malade guéri. **3.** *Jur:* (*a*) Libérer. (*b*) Acquitter. **4.** (*a*)

Lancer (un projectile). (*b*) *River that discharges into a lake,* rivière qui se déverse dans un lac. **5.** (*a*) S'acquitter de (son devoir). (*b*) Acquitter (une dette).

disciple, s. Disciple m.

disciplinarian, s. Disciplinaire m.

discipline[1], s. Discipline f.

discipline[2], v.tr. Discipliner.

disclaim, v.tr. Désavouer. *To d. all responsibility,* dénier toute responsabilité.

disclose, v.tr. Découvrir, révéler; divulguer (un secret).

disclosure, s. Mise f à découvert; révélation f; divulgation f (d'un secret).

discolour, v.tr. Décolorer.

discolo(u)ration, s. Décoloration f.

discomfiture, s. **1.** Déconfiture f (d'une armée). **2.** Déconvenue f.

discomfort, s. (*a*) Manque m de confort. (*b*) Malaise m, gêne f.

discommode, v.tr. Incommoder.

discompose, v.tr. Troubler, agiter. **Discomposed countenance,** visage défait.

discomposure, s. Trouble m, agitation f; perturbation f (d'esprit).

disconcert, v.tr. Déconcerter, interloquer.

disconcerting, a. Déconcertant, troublant.

disconnect, v.tr. Désunir, disjoindre; décrocher (des wagons). **disconnected,** a. **1.** Détaché, isolé; déconnecté. **2.** (*Of speech*) Décousu. **-ly,** adv. Sans suite, à bâtons rompus.

disconsolate, a. Tout triste; inconsolable; désolé.

discontent, s. Mécontentement m.

discontented, a. Mécontent (*with,* de); peu satisfait.

discontinuance, s. Discontinuation f, cessation f.

discontinue. 1. v.tr. Discontinuer. *To d. one's visits,* cesser ses visites. **2.** v.i. Cesser.

discontinuous, a. Discontinu.

discord, s. **1.** Discorde f, désunion f. **2.** *Mus:* (i) Dissonance f; (ii) accord dissonant.

discordant, a. **1.** (*a*) Discordant; peu harmonieux. (*b*) *Mus:* Dissonant. **2.** D. opinions, opinions opposées.

discount[1], s. **1.** *Com:* Remise f, rabais m. *To sell sth. at a discount,* vendre qch. au rabais. **2.** *Fin:* Escompte m. *F: Politeness is at a d.,* on fait peu de cas de la politesse.

discount[2], v.tr. **1.** *Fin:* Escompter. **2.** (*a*) Ne pas tenir compte de. (*b*) *F:* Faire la part de l'exagération dans.

discountenance, v.tr. Décourager; désapprouver.

discourage, v.tr. Décourager, abattre. *To become discouraged,* se décourager. **discouraging,** a. Décourageant. **-ly,** adv. D'une manière décourageante.

discouragement, s. Découragement m.

discourse[1], s. *Lit:* Discours m; dissertation f (*on,* sur).

discourse², *v.i. Lit:* (*a*) Discourir (*on, of, sur*). (*b*) Causer, s'entretenir (de).
discourteous, *a.* Discourtois, impoli.
discourtesy, *s.* Impolitesse *f.*
discover, *v.tr.* Découvrir, trouver. (*a*) *To d. a new gas*, découvrir un gaz nouveau. (*b*) *I discovered too late that...*, je m'aperçus trop tard que...
discoverer, *s.* Découvreur, -euse.
discovery, *s.* Découverte *f.*
discredit¹, *s.* **1.** Doute *m.* **2.** Discrédit *m;* déconsidération *f.*
discredit², *v.tr.* **1.** Ne pas croire; mettre en doute. **2.** Discréditer; déconsidérer.
discreditable, *a.* Peu digne.
discreet, *a.* **1.** Avisé, sage. *A d. smile*, un petit sourire contenu. **2.** Discret, -ète. **-ly**, *adv.* Avec réserve. **2.** Discrètement.
discrepancy, *s.* Désaccord *m;* divergence *f.*
discretion, *s.* **1.** Discrétion *f.* *I shall use my own discretion*, je ferai comme bon me semblera. **2.** Sagesse *f*, jugement *m*, prudence *f.* *To use discretion*, agir avec discrétion. *To come to years of d.*, atteindre l'âge de raison. **3.** Discrétion; silence judicieux.
discriminate. **1.** *v.tr.* Distinguer (*from*, de, d'avec). **2.** *v.i.* (*a*) Distinguer, établir une distinction (*between*, entre). (*b*) Faire des distinctions. **discriminating**, *a.* Plein de discernement.
discrimination, *s.* **1.** Discernement *m.* **2.** Jugement *m.* **3.** Distinction *f*, préférence *f.*
discursive, *a.* Décousu, sans suite.
discuss, *v.tr.* Discuter, débattre; agiter (une question). *D. the matter with him*, concertez-vous avec lui là-dessus.
discussion, *s.* Discussion *f*; agitation *f* (d'une question). *Question under discussion*, question en discussion.
disdain¹, *s.* Dédain *m* (*of*, de).
disdain², *v.tr.* Dédaigner.
disdainful, *a.* Dédaigneux (*of*, de). **-fully**, *adv.* Dédaigneusement.
disease, *s.* Maladie *f*; mal *m*, affection *f.*
diseased, *a.* **1.** Malade. **2.** Morbide.
disembark, *v.tr. & i.* Débarquer.
disembarkation, *s.* Débarquement *m.*
disembarrass, *v.tr.* Débarrasser (*of*, de); dégager (*from*, de).
disembowel, *v.tr.* Éventrer; éviscérer.
disenchanted, *a.* Désenchanté.
disencumber, *v.tr.* Débarrasser (*of*, de); désencombrer (qn).
disengage. **1.** *v.tr.* Dégager (qch. de qch.). **2.** *v.i.* Se dégager. **disengaged**, *a.* Libre, inoccupé.
disentangle, *v.tr.* Démêler; débrouiller (une situation).
disentanglement, *s.* Débrouillement *m;* démêlage *m.*
disfavour, *s.* Défaveur *f. To fall into disfavour*, tomber en disgrâce.
disfigure, *v.tr.* Défigurer; enlaidir.

disfigurement, *s.* Défiguration *f.*
disgorge, *v.tr.* Dégorger, rendre.
disgrace¹, *s.* **1.** Disgrâce *f. To be in disgrace*, être dans la disgrâce. **2.** Honte *f*, déshonneur *m. To be a disgrace to one's family*, être la honte de sa famille.
disgrace², *v.tr.* **1.** Disgracier (un courtisan). **2.** Déshonorer.
disgraceful, *a.* Honteux, déshonorant, scandaleux. **-fully**, *adv.* Honteusement.
disgruntled, *a. F:* Contrarié (*at*, de).
disguise¹, *s.* **1.** Déguisement *m;* travestissement *m. In disguise*, déguisé. **2.** Feinte *f*; fausse apparence. *To throw off all disguise*, laisser tomber le masque.
disguise², *v.tr.* **1.** Déguiser, travestir. **2.** (*a*) Déguiser (sa pensée). (*b*) *There is no disguising the fact that*, il faut avouer que. (*c*) *To d. one's feelings*, dissimuler ses sentiments.
disgust¹, *s.* **1.** Dégoût (profond) (*at, for, pour*). **2.** Profond mécontentement.
disgust², *v.tr.* Dégoûter; écœurer. *To be disgusted at, with, by, sth.*, être profondément mécontent de qch. **disgusting**, *a.* Dégoûtant.
dish¹, *s.* **1.** Plat *m. Vegetable dish*, légumier *m.* **2.** *Cu:* Plat (de viande); mets *m. Dainty dish*, mets délicat. **3.** Récipient *m.*
dish-cloth, *s.* **1.** Torchon *m.* **2.** Lavette *f.*
dish-cover, *s.* **1.** Couvercle *m* (de plat). **2.** Cloche *f.* **dish-water**, *s.* Eau *f* de vaisselle.
dish², *v.tr. To dish (up) meat*, servir, dresser, la viande.
dishearten, *v.tr.* Décourager, abattre, démoraliser, rebuter. **disheartening**, *a.* Décourageant.
dishevel, *v.tr.* Ébouriffer. **dishevelled**, *a.* **1.** Échevelé, dépeigné; ébouriffé. **2.** Aux vêtements chiffonnés.
dishonest, *a.* Malhonnête; déloyal, -aux. **-ly**, *adv.* Malhonnêtement.
dishonesty, *s.* Improbité *f*, malhonnêteté *f.*
dishonour¹, *s.* Déshonneur *m.*
dishonour², *v.tr.* **1.** Déshonorer **2.** Dishonoured cheque, chèque impayé.
dishonourable, *a.* **1.** (*Of pers.*) Sans honneur. **2.** (*Of action*) Déshonorant, honteux. **-ably**, *adv.* D'une façon peu honorable.
disillusion, *v.tr.* Désillusionner, désabuser.
disillusionment, *s.* Désillusionnement *m.*
disinclination, *s.* Répugnance *f*, aversion *f* (*for, to*, pour).
disinclined, *a.* Peu disposé (*for, to*, à).
disinfect, *v.tr.* Désinfecter.
disinfectant, *a. & s.* Désinfectant (*m*).
disingenuous, *a.* Sans franchise; faux, *f.* fausse. **-ly**, *adv.* Sans franchise.
disingenuousness, *s.* Manque *m* de franchise; mauvaise foi.
disinherit, *v.tr.* Déshériter.
disintegrate. **1.** *v.tr.* Désagréger; effriter (la pierre). **2.** *v.i.* Se désagréger.

disintegration, s. Désagrégation f, effritement m.

disinter, v.tr. Déterrer, exhumer.

disinterested, a. Désintéressé.

disinterestedness, s. Désintéressement m.

disinterment, s. Déterrement m; exhumation f.

disjointed, a. Disjoint, disloqué; sans suite; (style) décousu.

disk, s. Disque m, rondelle f. Mil: Identity disk, plaque f d'identité.

dislike¹, s. Aversion f, répugnance f (to, of, for, pour). To take a dislike to s.o., prendre qn en grippe.

dislike², v.tr. Ne pas aimer; détester. He dislikes you, vous lui êtes antipathique.

dislocate, v.tr. (a) Désorganiser. (b) Luxer, déboîter (un membre).

dislocation, s. (a) Désorganisation f. (b) Luxation f, déboîtement m (d'un membre).

dislodge, v.tr. 1. Déloger. 2. Détacher.

disloyal, a. Infidèle; déloyal, -aux. **-ally,** adv. Infidèlement, déloyalement.

disloyalty, s. Infidélité f, déloyauté f.

dismal, a. Sombre, triste; lugubre. **-ally,** adv. Lugubrement, tristement.

dismantle, v.tr. Dégarnir (of, de).

dismast, v.tr. Démâter.

dismay¹, s. Consternation f; épouvante f.

dismay², v.tr. Consterner, épouvanter.

dismiss, v.tr. 1. Congédier; donner congé à; destituer. 2. (a) Congédier (aimablement). (b) Dissoudre (une assemblée). 3. To dismiss sth. from one's thoughts, bannir, chasser, qch. de ses pensées. 4. Let us dismiss the subject, n'en parlons plus; brisons là. 5. (a) Écarter (une proposition). (b) To dismiss the accused, acquitter l'inculpé. 6. Mil: Dismiss! rompez (les rangs)!

dismissal, s. Congédiement m, renvoi m (d'un employé); révocation f, destitution f (d'un fonctionnaire).

dismount. 1. v.i. Descendre (de cheval); mettre pied à terre. 2. v.tr. Démonter.

disobedience, s. Désobéissance f.

disobedient, a. Désobéissant. To be disobedient to s.o., désobéir à qn.

disobey, v.tr. Désobéir à.

disobliging, a. Désobligeant.

disorder¹, s. 1. Désordre m, confusion f. They fled in d., ils s'enfuirent à la débandade. 2. Désordre, tumulte m.

disorder², v.tr. Déranger; mettre le désordre, la confusion, dans. **disordered,** a. 1. Désordonné; en désordre. 2. Dérangé.

disorderliness, s. 1. Désordre m. 2. Turbulence f.

disorderly, a. 1. Qui manque d'ordre; désordonné; en désordre. 2. Turbulent. 3. Désordonné, déréglé.

disorganization, s. Désorganisation f.

disorganize, v.tr. Désorganiser.

disown, v.tr. Désavouer; renier.

disparage, v.tr. Déprécier, dénigrer. **disparaging,** a. 1. (Terme) de dénigrement; dépréciateur,-trice. 2. Peu flatteur,-euse. **-ly,** adv. To speak disparagingly of s.o., parler de qn en termes peu flatteurs.

disparagement, s. Dénigrement m, dépréciation f.

disparity, s. Inégalité f. Disparity of age, différence f d'âge.

dispassionate, a. 1. Sans passion; calme. 2. Impartial, -aux. **-ly,** adv. 1. Sans passion; avec calme. 2. Sans parti pris.

dispatch¹, s. 1. Expédition f; envoi m. 2. Mise f à mort. 3. (a) Expédition (d'une affaire). (b) Promptitude f, diligence f. 4. Dépêche f. Mil: To be mentioned in dispatches, être cité à l'ordre (du jour). 5. Nau: Dispatch(-boat), aviso m. **dispatch-box,** s. Valise f diplomatique.

dispatch², v.tr. 1. Expédier (des marchandises); envoyer (qn). 2. Tuer. 3. To d. current business, expédier les affaires courantes.

dispel, v.tr. Chasser, dissiper.

dispensary, s. 1. Dispensaire m, policlinique f. 2. Pharmacie f.

dispensation, s. 1. Décret m, arrêt m. 2. Dispensation from sth., fait m d'être dispensé de qch.

dispense. 1. v.tr. (a) Dispenser, distribuer. (b) Administrer (la justice). (c) To dispense a prescription, exécuter une ordonnance. 2. v.i. To dispense with sth., se passer de qch. **dispensing,** s. 1. Dispensation f, distribution f. 2. Pharm: Préparation f.

dispersal, s. Dispersion f.

disperse. 1. v.tr. Disperser; dissiper. 2. v.i. Se disperser.

dispersion, s. Dispersion f.

dispirit, v.tr. Décourager, abattre.

displace, v.tr. 1. Déplacer. 2. (a) Déplacer, destituer. (b) Remplacer (by, par).

displacement, s. Déplacement m; changement m de place.

display¹, s. 1. Étalage m; manifestation f (de colère). D. of courage, déploiement m de courage. 2. Étalage (de luxe); parade f, apparat m.

display², v.tr. 1. Exhiber, étaler, exposer. To display a notice, afficher un avis. 2. Montrer, manifester. 3. Étaler, afficher (son luxe). 4. Découvrir, révéler (son ignorance).

displease, v.tr. Déplaire à (qn); contrarier, mécontenter (qn). **displeasing,** a. Déplaisant, désagréable (to, à).

displeasure, s. Déplaisir m, mécontentement m.

disposal, s. 1. (a) The d. of one's money, ce qu'il faut faire de son argent. D. of a piece of business, expédition f d'une affaire. (b) At s.o.'s disposal, à la disposition de qn. The means at my disposal, les moyens dont je dispose. 2. For disposal, à vendre.

dispose, v.tr. & i. 1. Disposer, arranger. 2. To dispose of sth., se défaire de qch. To dispose of an opponent, vaincre un adversaire. *To d. of a matter,* régler une affaire. **3.** *Com:* **To dispose of goods,** écouler des marchandises. *To d. of one's business,* céder son fonds. **To be disposed of,** à vendre, à céder. **4.** Disposer, incliner, porter (qn à faire qch.). **disposed,** *a.* **1.** Intentionné, disposé. **If you feel so disposed,** si le cœur vous en dit. **2.** *I am d. to help you,* je suis disposé à vous aider.

disposition, *s.* **1.** Disposition *f*, agencement *m*. **2.** = DISPOSAL 1 (*b*). **3.** Caractère *m*, naturel *m.* **4.** (*a*) **Disposition to do sth.,** désir *m* de faire qch. (*b*) Penchant *m*, tendance *f* (*to*, à).

dispossess, *v.tr.* Déposséder (*of*, de).

disproportionate, *a.* Disproportionné (*to*, à), hors de proportion (*to*, avec).

disprove, *v.tr.* Réfuter (un dire); démontrer la fausseté de.

dispute¹, *s.* **1.** Contestation *f*, débat *m.* **The matter in dispute,** l'affaire dont il s'agit. **Beyond dispute,** incontestable. **2.** Querelle *f*, dispute *f.*

dispute². **1.** *v.i.* (*a*) **To dispute with s.o. about sth.,** débattre qch. avec qn. (*b*) Se disputer. **2.** *v.tr.* (*a*) Contester. (*b*) **To dispute sth. with s.o.,** disputer qch. à qn.

disqualification, *s.* **1.** Incapacité *f.* **2.** Cause *f* d'incapacité (*for*, à). **3.** Mise *f* en état d'incapacité.

disqualify, *v.tr.* **1.** Rendre incapable (*for sth.,* de faire qch.). **2.** *Sp:* Disqualifier.

disquiet, *v.tr.* Inquiéter; troubler. **disquieting,** *a.* Inquiétant.

disquietude, *s.* Inquiétude *f*, anxiété *f.*

disregard¹, *s.* Indifférence *f*, insouciance *f* (*of, for,* à l'égard de).

disregard², *v.tr.* Ne tenir aucun compte de.

disreputable, *a.* **1.** Déshonorant; honteux. **2.** De mauvaise réputation; taré. **3.** (*Of garments*) Minable.

disrepute, *s.* **To bring sth. into disrepute,** discréditer qch.

disrespect, *s.* Manque *m* d'égards, de respect (*for,* envers).

disrespectful, *a.* Irrespectueux, irrévérencieux. **-fully,** *adv.* **To speak disrespectfully,** parler avec irrévérence.

dissatisfaction, *s.* Mécontentement *m* (*with, at,* de).

dissatisfy, *v.tr.* Mécontenter. **dissatisfied,** *a.* Mécontent (*with, at,* de).

dissect, *v.tr.* Disséquer.

dissection, *s.* Dissection *f.*

dissemble, *v.tr.* Dissimuler; passer sous silence. *Abs.* User de dissimulation. **dissembling,** *s.* Dissimulation *f.*

dissension, *s.* Dissension *f.*

dissent¹, *s.* Dissentiment *m.*

dissent², *v.i.* **1.** Différer (*from s.o. about sth.,* de qn sur qch.). **2.** *Ecc:* Être dissident. **dissenting,** *a.* Dissident.

dissenter, *s.* Dissident, -ente.

dissentient, *a. & s.* Dissident, -ente.

dissertation, *s.* Dissertation *f.*

disservice, *s.* Mauvais service rendu. *To do s.o. a d.,* desservir qn.

dissimilar, *a.* Dissemblable (*to*, à, de); différent (*to*, de).

dissimulate, *v.tr.* (*a*) Dissimuler; cacher. (*b*) *Abs.* Feindre.

dissimulation, *s.* Dissimulation *f.*

dissipate. **1.** *v.tr.* Dissiper. **2.** *v.i.* Se dissiper. **dissipated,** *a.* Dissipé.

dissipation, *s.* Dissipation *f.*

dissociate, *v.tr.* Désassocier (*from*, de).

dissolute, *a.* Dissolu, débauché.

dissolution, *s.* Dissolution *f.*

dissolve. **1.** *v.tr.* Dissoudre, faire dissoudre. **2.** *v.i.* Se dissoudre; fondre.

dissuade, *v.tr.* **To dissuade s.o. from doing sth.,** dissuader qn de faire qch.

dissuasion, *s.* Dissuasion *f.*

distaff, *s.* Quenouille *f.*

distance, *s.* **1.** (*a*) Distance *f*, éloignement *m.* **Within speaking distance,** à portée de voix. *Seen from a d.,* vu de loin. (*b*) Lointain *m.* **Away in the distance,** dans le lointain. **2.** Distance, intervalle *m.* **To keep s.o. at a distance,** tenir qn à distance.

distant, *a.* **1.** (*a*) (Endroit) éloigné; (pays) lointain. **To have a distant view of sth.,** voir qch. de loin. **Distant likeness,** faible ressemblance. (*b*) Éloigné, reculé. *D. recollection,* souvenir lointain. **2.** Réservé, froid, distant. **-ly,** *adv.* **1.** De loin. **Distantly related,** d'une parenté éloignée. **2.** Avec réserve; froidement.

distaste, *s.* Dégoût *m* (*for*, de); aversion *f*, répugnance *f* (*for*, pour).

distasteful, *a.* Désagréable, déplaisant (*to*, à). *To be d. to s.o.,* répugner à qn.

distemper, *s.* Détrempe *f*, badigeon *m.*

distend. **1.** *v.tr.* Dilater, gonfler. **2.** *v.i.* (*a*) Se dilater, enfler. (*b*) Se distendre.

distension, *s.* Dilatation *f*, distension *f*, gonflement *m.*

distil, *v.tr.* Distiller.

distillery, *s.* Distillerie *f.*

distinct, *a.* **1.** Distinct, différent (*from*, de). **To keep two things d.,** distinguer entre deux choses. **2.** Distinct, net, *f.* nette. **D.** *promise,* promesse formelle. **3.** Caractérisé, marqué. **-ly,** *adv.* **1.** (*a*) Distinctement, clairement. (*b*) *I told him d.,* je le lui ai dit expressément. **2.** Indéniablement, décidément.

distinction, *s.* Distinction *f.* **To gain distinction,** se distinguer.

distinctive, *a.* Distinctif.

distinctness, *s.* Clarté *f*, netteté *f.*

distinguish. **1.** *v.tr.* (*a*) Distinguer, discerner. (*b*) Distinguer, différencier (*from*, de). (*c*) **To distinguish oneself by . . .,** se signaler, se faire remarquer, par. . . . **2.** *v.i.* Faire une distinction (*between*, entre). **distinguished,** *a.* Distingué.

distinguishable, *a.* **1.** Que l'on peut distinguer (*from*, de). **2.** Perceptible, reconnaissable.

distort, *v.tr.* (*a*) Tordre, contourner; décomposer. (*b*) Fausser, dénaturer (les faits). **distorted,** *a.* Tordu, contourné. *Face d. by rage,* visage convulsé par la fureur.

distortion, *s.* (*a*) Distorsion *f*; décomposition *f* (des traits). (*b*) Déformation *f* (des faits).

distract, *v.tr.* **1.** (*a*) Distraire, détourner. (*b*) Brouiller (l'esprit). **2.** Affoler (qn). **distracted,** *a.* Affolé, éperdu. *Like one d.,* comme un affolé.

distraction, *s.* **1.** Distraction *f.* **2.** Confusion *f.* **3.** Affolement *m.* *To drive s.o. to distraction,* mettre qn hors de soi. *To love s.o. to distraction,* aimer qn éperdument.

distraint, *s.* *Jur:* Saisie *f.*

distress[1], *s.* **1.** Détresse *f*, angoisse *f.* **2.** Misère *f*; gêne *f.* **3.** Détresse, embarras *m.* *Companions in distress,* compagnons d'infortune.

distress[2], *v.tr.* **1.** Affliger, angoisser, chagriner. **2.** Épuiser, excéder. **distressed,** *a.* Affligé, désolé. **distressing,** *a.* Affligeant, angoissant.

distribute, *v.tr.* Distribuer, répartir.

distribution, *s.* (Mise *f* en) distribution *f*; répartition *f.*

distributor, *s.* Distributeur, -trice.

district, *s.* **1.** Région *f*, contrée *f*, territoire *m*, district *m.* **2.** *Adm:* (*a*) District. (*b*) Quartier *m* (d'une ville).

distrust[1], *s.* Méfiance *f*, défiance *f.*

distrust[2], *v.tr.* Se méfier, se défier, de.

distrustful, *a.* Défiant, méfiant (*of*, de); soupçonneux.

disturb, *v.tr.* **1.** Déranger; troubler (le repos); agiter, remuer (une surface). *Please don't disturb yourself,* ne vous dérangez pas. **2.** Inquiéter, troubler (qn). **disturbing,** *a.* Perturbateur, -trice.

disturbance, *s.* **1.** Trouble *m*; dérangement *m.* **2.** Bruit *m*, tapage *m.* *To make a disturbance,* troubler l'ordre public. **3.** Agitation *f*, trouble.

disunite, *v.tr.* Désunir.

disuse, *s.* Désuétude *f.*

disused, *a.* Hors d'usage.

ditch, *s.* Fossé *m.*

ditto, *a. & s.* Idem; de même.

ditty, *s.* Chanson *f.*

divan, *s.* Divan *m.*

dive[1], *s.* (*a*) Plongeon *m.* *High dive,* plongeon de haut vol. (*b*) Plongée *f* (d'un sous-marin). (*c*) *Av:* Vol piqué; piqué *m.* *Dive-bombing,* attaque *f* en piqué.

dive[2], *v.i.* (*a*) Plonger (*into*, dans); piquer une tête. (*b*) *Av:* *To* (*nose-*)*dive,* piquer (du nez). (*c*) (*Of submarine*) Plonger.

diving-board, *s.* Plongeoir *m*, tremplin *m.*

diving-dress, *s.* Scaphandre *m.*

diver, *s.* (*a*) Plongeur *m.* (*b*) Scaphandrier *m.*

diverge, *v.i.* Diverger, s'écarter. **diverging,** *a.* Divergent.

divergence, *s.* Divergence *f.*

divergent, *a.* Divergent.

divers, *a.pl.* On divers occasions, en diverses occasions; à diverses reprises.

diverse, *a.* **1.** Divers, différent. **2.** Divers, varié. **-ly,** *adv.* Diversement.

diversify, *v.tr.* Diversifier.

diversion, *s.* **1.** Détournement *m* (de la circulation). **2.** (*a*) Diversion *f* (de l'esprit). *To create a diversion,* faire diversion. (*b*) Divertissement *m*, distraction *f*, jeu *m.*

diversity, *s.* Diversité *f.*

divert, *v.tr.* **1.** Détourner; écarter (un coup). *To d. s.o.'s attention,* distraire l'attention de qn. **2.** Divertir, amuser. **diverting,** *a.* Divertissant, amusant.

divest, *v.tr.* **1.** *To divest s.o. of his clothes,* dévêtir qn. **2.** Dépouiller, priver.

divide, **1.** *v.tr.* (*a*) Diviser. *Divided between hatred and pity,* partagé entre la haine et la pitié. *Parl:* *To divide the House,* aller aux voix. (*b*) Partager, répartir (*among*, entre). *We d. the work among us,* nous nous partageons le travail. (*c*) *Mth:* Diviser. (*d*) Séparer (*from*, de). (*e*) Désunir (une famille). (*f*) *Opinions are divided,* les avis sont partagés. **2.** *v.i.* (*a*) Se diviser, se partager (*into*, en); (*of road*) fourcher. (*b*) *Parl:* Aller aux voix.

dividend, *s.* Dividende *m.*

dividers, *s.pl.* Compas *m* à pointes sèches.

divination, *s.* Divination *f.*

divine[1]. **1.** *a.* (*a*) Divin. (*b*) *F:* Divin, admirable. **2.** *s.* Théologien *m.* **-ly,** *adv.* Divinement.

divine[2], *v.tr.* Deviner. **divining-rod,** *s.* Baguette *f* divinatoire.

divinity, *s.* (*a*) Divinité *f.* (*b*) Divinité, dieu *m.*

divisible, *a.* Divisible (*by*, par).

division, *s.* **1.** Division *f*, partage *m* (*into*, en); scission *f* (d'un parti). **2.** Répartition *f*, partage. **3.** Division, désunion *f.* **4.** *Mth:* Division. **5.** *Parl:* Vote *m.* **6.** **Parliamentary division,** circonscription électorale. **7.** Cloison *f.*

divisor, *s.* *Mth:* Diviseur *m.*

divorce[1], *s.* Divorce *m.*

divorce[2], *v.tr.* *Jur:* (*a*) Divorcer. (*b*) *To divorce s.o.,* divorcer d'avec qn. (*c*) *F:* Séparer (*from*, de).

divot, *s.* *Golf:* Motte *f* (de gazon).

divulge, *v.tr.* Divulguer.

dixie, *s.* *Mil:* *F:* Gamelle *f*; marmite *f.*

dizziness, *s.* Étourdissement *m*, vertige *m.*

dizzy, *a.* **1.** Pris d'étourdissement; pris de vertige. *To feel dizzy,* avoir le vertige. *To make s.o. d.,* étourdir qn. **2.** *F:* (*Of height*) Vertigineux.

do[1]. **I.** *v.tr.* **1.** (*a*) Faire. *To do good,* faire le bien. *To do right,* bien faire. *He did brilliantly at his examination,* il s'est acquitté brillamment à son examen. *The car was doing sixty,* l'auto faisait du soixante. *Are you doing anything to-morrow?* avez-vous quelque chose en vue pour demain? *F:* **It isn't done,** cela ne se fait pas. *Prov:* **What is done cannot be undone,** à chose faite point de remède. *I shall do nothing of the sort, no such thing,* je n'en ferai rien. *What is to be done?* que faire? *What can I do for you?* en quoi puis-je vous servir? *Do what we would,* malgré tous nos efforts. **Well done!** très bien! à la bonne heure! (b) *He came to see what was doing,* il est venu voir ce qui se faisait. *F:* **Nothing doing!** rien à faire! ça ne prend pas! **2.** (a) Faire (une chambre). (b) Cuire, faire cuire. **Done to a turn,** cuit à point. (c) *To do a sum,* faire un calcul. (d) *F:* Refaire, faire. **To do s.o. out of sth.,** soutirer qch. à qn. (e) *P:* **To do oneself well,** faire bonne chère. **3.** (a) **To have done,** avoir fini. **Have done!** finissez donc! (b) *P:* **To be done (to the world),** être éreinté, exténué. (c) **Done!** tope là! c'est marché fait! **4. How do you do?** comment vous portez-vous? comment allez-vous? *He is a lad who will do well,* c'est un garçon qui réussira. **5.** That will do, (i) c'est bien; (ii) en voilà assez! *This room will do for the office,* cette pièce ira bien pour le bureau. *That won't do here,* cela ne passe pas ici. *It would hardly have done to,* il n'aurait pas été convenable de. *I will make it do,* je m'en arrangerai. *That will do me,* cela fera mon affaire. **II. do,** *verb substitute.* **1.** *Why act as you do?* pourquoi agir comme vous le faites? *He writes better than I do,* il écrit mieux que moi. **2.** *May I open these letters?*—Please do, puis-je ouvrir ces lettres?—Faites donc! Je vous en prie! *Did you see him?*—*I did,* l'avez-vous vu?—Oui (,je l'ai vu). *I like coffee; do you?* j'aime le café; et vous? *You like him, don't you?* vous l'aimez, n'est-ce pas? *He said so, did he?* il a dit cela, ah vraiment? **Don't!** ne faites pas cela! finissez! **3.** *You like Paris?* so do I, vous aimez Paris? moi aussi. **III. do,** *v.aux.* **1.** *He did go, did I he then allé. Why don't you work?*—*I do work!* pourquoi ne travaillez-vous pas?—Mais si, je travaille! *Did he indeed?* non vraiment? **Do sit down,** asseyez-vous donc! *Do shut up!* voulez-vous bien vous taire! **2. Do you see him?** le voyez-vous? **We do not know,** nous ne le savons pas. **Don't do it!** n'en faites rien! **IV. do. 1.** *To do well by s.o.,* bien agir envers qn. *He has been hard done by,* il a été traité durement. **2.** *F:* **Do for.** (a) **To do for s.o.,** faire le ménage de qn. (b) Tuer; faire son affaire à. **I'm done for,** j'ai mon compte; je suis perdu. (c) Détruire, ruiner. **3.** (a) **To have to do with s.o.,** avoir affaire à qn. **To have to do with sth.,** être mêlé à qch; (of thg) avoir rapport à qch. *To have nothing to do with a matter,* n'être pour rien dans une affaire. *Jealousy has a lot to do with it,* la jalousie y est pour beaucoup. (b) **I cannot do with any noise,** je ne peux pas supporter le bruit. (c) **How many can you do with?** combien en désirez-vous? *I could do with a cup of tea,* je prendrais bien une tasse de thé. **4. Do without,** se passer de. **V. do,** *s. F:* Attrape *f,* fourberie. **do again,** *v.tr.* **1.** Refaire. **2.** *I won't do it again,* je ne le ferai plus. **do away,** *v.i.* **To do away with,** abolir; détruire. *F:* supprimer. **do out,** *v.tr.* Faire, nettoyer (une chambre). **do up,** *v.tr.* **1.** (a) Réparer; décorer. *F:* **To do oneself up,** faire toilette. (b) Blanchir (le linge). **2.** Faire, envelopper, ficeler (un paquet); boutonner, agrafer (un vêtement). **3.** *F:* **To be done up,** être éreinté, fourbu. **doing,** *s.* **1.** (a) *That requires some doing,* ce n'est pas facile. (b) *This is so-and-so's doing,* cela est du fait d'un tel. **2.** (*Usu. in pl.*) Ce qu'on fait. (a) Agissements *mpl.* *That's some of Tom's doings!* c'est encore Tom qui a fait des siennes! (b) Événements *mpl,* grande activité.

do², *s. Mus:* Do *m,* ut *m.*

docile, *a.* Docile. **-ely,** *adv.* Docilement.

docility, *s.* Docilité *f.*

dock¹, *v.tr.* Diminuer, rogner; supprimer.

dock², *s. Nau:* (a) Bassin *m.* **The docks,** les docks *m.* (b) **Dry dock,** cale sèche. (c) **Floating dock,** dock flottant.

dock³. 1. *v.tr.* Faire entrer au bassin. **2.** *v.i.* Entrer au bassin.

dock⁴, *s. Jur:* Banc *m* des prévenus.

docket, *s.* Étiquette *f,* fiche *f.*

dockyard, *s.* Chantier *m* de construction de navires; arsenal *m* maritime.

doctor¹, *s.* **1.** *Sch:* **Doctor of Divinity,** docteur *m* en théologie. **Doctor of Science,** docteur ès sciences. **2.** Docteur, médecin *m.* **Woman doctor,** docteur femme.

doctor², *v.tr.* **1.** (a) Soigner. (b) *Turf:* Droguer (un cheval). **2.** *F:* Réparer (un objet). **3.** *F:* Falsifier (des comptes).

doctrine, *s.* Doctrine *f.*

document, *s.* Document *m,* pièce *f,* titre *m.*

documentary, *a.* Documentaire.

dodder, *v.i.* Trembloter. **doddering,** *a.* Gaga *inv.*

dodderer, *s. F:* Vieux gaga.

dodge¹, *s.* **1.** Mouvement *m* de côté. **2.** (a) Ruse *f,* artifice *m.* (b) Truc *m,* ficelle *f.* **To be up to all the dodges,** connaître tous les trucs.

dodge². 1. *v.i.* (a) Se jeter de côté. (b) Biaiser; user d'artifices. **2.** *v.tr.* Esquiver (un coup); éviter (qn). **To dodge a question,** éluder une question.

dodger, *s. F:* **An artful dodger,** un malin, un fin matois, un roublard.

doe, *s. Z:* **1.** Daine *f.* **2.** (*Of rabbit*) Lapine *f;* (*of wild rabbit and hare*) hase *f.*

doer, *s.* Faiseur, -euse; auteur *m.*

doeskin, *s.* Peau *f* de daim.

doff, *v.tr.* Enlever, ôter.

dog¹, s. **1.** Chien m. **Sporting-dog,** chien de chasse. **Dog racing,** courses de lévriers. F: **To go to the dogs,** marcher à la ruine. **To lead a dog's life,** mener une vie de chien. Prov: **Every dog has his day,** à chacun son tour. **2.** F: **Sly dog,** rusé coquin, fin renard. **Lucky dog!** (le) veinard! P: **Dirty dog,** sale type m. **dog-biscuit,** s. Biscuit m de chien. **dog-cart,** s. Veh: Charrette anglaise. **dog-collar,** s. **1.** Collier m de chien. **2.** F: Faux col d'ecclésiastique. **dog-days,** s.pl. (La) canicule. **dog-fight,** s. **1.** Combat m de chiens. **2.** F: Mêlée générale. **dog-in-the-manger,** s. F: Chien m du jardinier. **dog-Latin,** s. Latin m de cuisine. **dog-rose,** s. Bot: **1.** Églantine f. **2.** Rosier m sauvage; églantier m. **dog's-ear¹,** s. Corne f. **dogs'-ear²,** v.tr. Corner. **dog-show,** s. Exposition canine. **dog-tired,** a. F: Éreinté, vanné, fourbu. **dog-watch,** s. Nau: Petit quart.

dog², v.tr. Suivre à la piste; filer. **To dog s.o.'s footsteps,** s'attacher aux pas de qn. **Dogged by ill fortune,** poursuivi par la guigne.

doge, s. Hist: Doge m.

dogged, a. Obstiné, résolu, tenace. **-ly,** adv. Avec ténacité; opiniâtrement.

doggedness, s. Courage m tenace; persévérance f.

doggerel, a. & s. (i) (Poésie f) burlesque; (ii) (vers mpl) de mirliton.

doggie, s. F: Toutou m.

dogma, s. Dogme m.

dogmatic, a. **1.** Dogmatique. **2.** F: Autoritaire, tranchant. **-ally,** adv. D'un ton autoritaire, tranchant.

dogmatize, v.i. Dogmatiser.

doldrums, s.pl. **The doldrums,** (i) le cafard; (ii) Nau: la zone des calmes. **To be in the doldrums,** avoir le cafard.

dole¹, s. (a) Aumône f. (b) Adm: F: **Unemployment dole,** secours m, allocation f, de chômage. **To go on the dole,** s'inscrire au chômage.

dole², v.tr. **To dole out sth.,** distribuer parcimonieusement qch.

doleful, a. Lugubre; (cri) dolent, douloureux. **-fully,** adv. Tristement, douloureusement.

doll, s. Poupée f. **Doll's house,** maison de poupée.

dollar, s. Num: **1.** U.S.: Dollar m. **2.** P: (Pièce f de) cinq shillings.

dollop, s. P: Morceau m (informe).

dolly, s. F: Poupée f.

dolmen, s. Archeol: Dolmen m.

dolorous, a. **1.** Douloureux. **2.** Triste, plaintif.

dolphin, s. (a) Z: Dauphin m. (b) Ich: Dorade f.

dolt, s. Sot m, benêt m; lourdaud m.

domain, s. Domaine m; terres fpl; propriété f.

dome, s. Dôme m.

domestic, a. **1.** Domestique. **Domestic quarrels,** scènes de ménage. **Domestic life,** la vie de famille. **Domestic servant,** s. domestic, domestique mf. **2.** **Domestic animal,** animal domestique.

domicile, s. Domicile m.

domiciled, a. Domicilié, demeurant (at, à).

dominant. 1. a. Dominant. **2.** s. Mus: Dominante f.

dominate, v.tr. & i. To dominate (over) s.o., dominer (sur) qn. The fortress dominates the town, la forteresse commande la ville. **dominating,** a. Dominant.

domination, s. Domination f.

domineer, v.i. **1.** Se montrer autoritaire. **2.** To domineer over s.o., tyranniser qn.

domineering, a. Autoritaire.

Dominican, a. & s. Dominicain, -aine.

dominion, s. **1.** Domination f, maîtrise f, autorité f. **To hold dominion over,** exercer son empire sur. **2.** Possessions fpl; dominion(s) m.

domino, s. **1.** Domino m (de bal masqué). **2.** To play (at) dominoes, jouer aux dominos.

don¹, s.m. Professeur (d'université).

don², v.tr. Revêtir; mettre.

donate, v.tr. Faire un don de (qch.).

donation, s. Donation f, don m.

donkey, s. **1.** Ane, f. ânesse; baudet m. **Donkey ride,** promenade à âne. **Donkey work,** travail de routine. **2.** F: Imbécile mf, âne m. **donkey-cart,** s. Charrette f à âne. **donkey-engine,** s. **1.** Mch: Petit-cheval m. **2.** Treuil m à vapeur.

donor, s. **1.** Donateur, -trice. **2.** Surg: Donor of blood, donneur, -euse, de sang.

doom¹, s. **1.** Destin m (funeste); sort (malheureux). **2.** Perte f, ruine f.

doom², v.tr. Doomed man, homme perdu. Attempt doomed to failure, tentative condamnée à l'insuccès.

doomsday, s. Le (jour du) jugement dernier. Till doomsday, jusqu'à la fin du monde.

door, s. **1.** Porte f. **Folding door,** porte à deux battants. **Sliding door,** porte à coulisse. **To show s.o. the door,** éconduire qn. **To turn s.o. out of doors,** mettre qn à la porte. F: **To open a door to abuses,** prêter aux abus. F: **To lay a charge at s.o.'s door,** imputer qch. à qn. **2.** Portière f (de wagon). **door-keeper,** s. Portier m; concierge mf. **door-mat,** s. Paillasson m; essuie-pieds m inv. **door-step,** s. Seuil m, pas m (de la porte). **doorway,** s. In the doorway, sous la porte.

dope¹, s. F: Stupéfiant m, narcotique m. **dope-fiend,** s. Toxicomane mf.

dope², v.tr. **1.** Administrer un narcotique à. **2.** Mêler un narcotique à (un verre de vin).

Doric, a. & s. Arch: Dorique (m).

dormant, a. Assoupi, endormi. **To lie dormant,** sommeiller, dormir.

dormer(-window), s. Lucarne f; (fenêtre f en) mansarde f.

dormitory, s. Dortoir m.

dormouse, s. Z: Loir m.

dose¹, s. Dose f (de médecine).

dose², v.tr. Médicamenter, droguer.

dot¹, s. I. Point m. He arrived on the dot, il est arrivé à l'heure tapante. 2. Mioche mf.

dot², v.tr. I. Mettre un point sur (un i). 2. Marquer avec des points; pointiller. Dotted line, ligne en pointillé. Hillside dotted with chalets, coteau parsemé de chalets.

dotage, s. Radotage m.

dotard, s. (Vieillard) radoteur.

dote, v.i. I. Radoter. 2. To dote (up)on s.o., aimer qn à la folie. **doting,** a. I. Radoteur, -euse. 2. Qui montre une tendresse ridicule.

dottle, s. F: Culot m (de pipe).

dotty, a. P: Toqué, piqué.

double¹. I. a. I. (a) Double. With a double meaning, à deux sens, à double sens. Double bedroom, chambre à deux personnes. To reach double figures, atteindre les deux chiffres. To play a double game, jouer double jeu; ménager la chèvre et le chou. (b) De grandeur ou de force double. 2. Bent double, courbé en deux. 3. Double the number, le double; deux fois autant. I am double your age, je suis deux fois plus âgé que vous. 4. Double time, pas redoublé. II. **double,** adv. I. Double as long as, deux fois plus long que. 2. To see double, voir double. III. **double,** s. I. Double m; deux fois autant. 2. (Of pers.) Double; F: sosie m. 3. Détour m (d'un animal poursuivi). 4. Mil: At the double, au pas de course; au pas gymnastique. 5. Ten: Men's doubles, double messieurs. **double-barrelled,** a. A deux coups. **double-bass,** s. Mus: Contrebasse f. **double-bedded,** a. (Chambre) à deux lits. **double-breasted,** a. (Gilet) croisé. **double-cross,** v.tr. F: Duper, tromper. **double-dealing,** s. Duplicité f, fourberie f. **double-dyed,** a. F: Double-dyed scoundrel, gredin fieffé. **double-edged,** a. (Argument) à deux tranchants. **double-faced,** a. (Homme) à deux visages, hypocrite. **double-quick,** a. & adv. In double-quick time, double-quick, F: en moins de rien. **double-width,** a. Double-width cloth, étoffe grande largeur.

double². I. v.tr. I. Doubler. Th: To double parts, jouer deux rôles. 2. Nau: To double a cape, doubler un cap. 3. To double (up) paper, plier en deux, replier, doubler, du papier. To double (up) one's fist, serrer le poing. 4. Cards: Contrer. II. **double,** v.i. I. Doubler, se doubler. 2. Prendre le pas gymnastique, le pas de course. 3. To double (back), faire un brusque crochet; doubler ses voies. **double up,** I. v.i. (a) Se

plier (en deux); se replier. To double up with laughter, se tordre de rire. 2. v.tr. Faire plier en deux.

doubly, adv. Doublement.

doubt¹, s. Doute m. To be in doubt, être en doute, dans le doute. To cast doubts on sth., mettre qch. en doute. To have one's doubts about sth., avoir des doutes sur, au sujet de qch. There is no room for doubt, le doute n'est pas permis. Beyond (a) doubt, sans le moindre doute; à n'en pas douter. No doubt he will come, sans doute qu'il viendra. Without (a) doubt, sans aucun doute. There is no doubt about it, cela ne fait point de doute.

doubt². I. v.tr. Douter. To doubt s.o.'s word, douter de la parole de qn. I d whether he will come, je doute qu'il vienne, s'il viendra. 2. v.i. He doubted no longer, il n'hésita plus.

doubtful, a. I. Douteux. 2. (Of pers.) (a) Indécis, incertain. (b) To be d. of sth., douter de qch. 3. (Caractère) équivoque, suspect; (question) discutable. Doubtful society, compagnie louche. **-fully,** adv. I. D'un air de doute. 2. En hésitant.

doubtfulness, s. I. Ambiguïté f. 2. Incertitude f (du temps). 3. Irrésolution f.

doubtless, adv. Sans doute; très probablement.

dough, s. Pâte f (à pain).

doughty, a. Doughty deeds, hauts faits.

douse, v.tr. F: Plonger, tremper, dans l'eau.

dove. I. s. Colombe f. 2. a. Dove(-coloured), gorge-de-pigeon inv.

dovecot(e), s. Colombier m, pigeonnier m.

Dover. Pr.n. Geog: Douvres m. The Straits of Dover, le Pas de Calais.

dovetail¹, s. Carp: Queue-d'aronde f.

dovetail². I. v.tr. Assembler à queue-d'aronde. 2. v.i. Se rejoindre, se raccorder.

dowager, s. Douairière f.

dowdiness, s. Manque m d'élégance.

dowdy, a. Peu élégante, sans élégance.

dower¹, s. Douaire m.

dower², v.tr. I. Assigner un douaire à (une veuve). 2. Doter (une jeune fille).

down¹, s. Dune f.

down², s. Duvet m.

down³. I. adv. I. Vers le bas. To go down, aller en bas; descendre. To fall down, tomber (i) à terre, (ii) par terre. Cash down, argent (au) comptant. Down with the traitors! à bas les traîtres! Down! à bas! couché! 2. Down below, en bas, en contrebas. Down there, là-bas. Down here, ici; dans ces parages. The blinds were down, les stores étaient baissés. Face down, face en dessous. Head down, la tête en bas. To hit a man when he is down, frapper un homme à terre. Down with fever, frappé par la fièvre. The sun is down, le soleil est couché. The tide is d., la mer est basse. Bread is down, le pain a baissé. Her hair is down, ses cheveux sont défaits. Your tyres are down, vos pneus sont dégonflés, à plat. *Cards:* To be two down, avoir deux de chute. Ship down by the head, navire enfoncé par l'avant. 3. Down to recent times, jusqu'à présent. *D.* to here, jusqu'ici. 4. To be down on s.o., en vouloir à qn. To be down in the mouth, être découragé, abattu. *F:* To be down and out, être ruiné, décavé. II. down, *prep.* Her hair is hanging down her back, les cheveux lui pendent dans le dos. To go down the street, descendre la rue. Down the river, en aval. To fall down the stairs, tomber en bas de l'escalier. Down town, en ville. III. down, *a.* 1. *Rail:* Down train, train descendant. 2. *Mus:* Down beat, temps fort. 3. *F:* = DOWN-HEARTED. IV. down, *s.* *P:* To have a down on s.o., en vouloir à qn. down-at-heel, *a.* (Soulier) éculé; (*of pers.*) râpé. down-hearted, *a.* Découragé; déprimé, abattu. down-stage, *adv. & a.* *Th:* Sur le devant (de la scène). down-stream. I. *adv.* En aval. 2. *a.* D'aval.

down⁴, *v.tr.* 1. To down s.o., terrasser, abattre, qn. 2. *Ind:* To down tools, mettre bas les outils.

downcast, *a.* 1. (*Of pers.*) Abattu, déprimé. 2. (*Of look*) Baissé (vers la terre).

downfall, *s.* Chute *f.*

downhill. I. *a.* En pente; incliné. 2. *adv.* To go downhill, (*of road*) aller en descendant; *F:* (*of pers.*) être sur le déclin.

downpour, *s.* Forte pluie; grosse averse.

downright. I. *adv.* (*a*) Tout à fait; complètement. (*b*) (Refuser) nettement, catégoriquement. 2. *a.* (*a*) Direct; franc, *f.* franche. (*b*) Absolu, véritable. Downright lie, mensonge éclatant.

downstairs, *adv.* En bas (de l'escalier). To come, go, downstairs, descendre (l'escalier).

downtrodden, *a.* Foulé aux pieds; (peuple) opprimé, tyrannisé.

downward. I. *a.* Descendant, de haut en bas. 2. *adv.* = DOWNWARDS.

downwards, *adv.* De haut en bas; en descendant. *Face d.*, face en dessous.

downy, *a.* 1. Duveteux; couvert de duvet. 2. *F:* A downy bird, un malin, un rusé.

dowry, *s.* Dot *f*

doze¹, *s.* Petit somme.

doze², *v.i.* Sommeiller; être assoupi. To doze off, s'assoupir.

dozen, *s.* Douzaine *f.* 1. *Half a d.*, une demi-douzaine. Six dozen bottles, six douzaines de bouteilles. 2. Dozens and dozens of times, maintes et maintes fois.

drab, *a. & s.* (*a*) Gris (*m*) ou brun (*m*). (*b*) *F:* Drab existence, existence terne.

drachm, *s.* *Pharm.Meas:* Drachme *f.*

draft¹, *s.* I. 1. *Mil:* Détachement *m.* 2. Traite *f*; lettre *f* de change. 3. Plan *m*, tracé *m*; ébauche *f.* 4. Brouillon *m* (de lettre). II. draft, *s.* = DRAUGHT I.

draft², *v.tr.* Rédiger (un acte); faire le brouillon (d'une lettre).

drag¹, *s.* 1. Araignée *f*; *Nau:* grappin *m* à main. 2. To be a drag on s.o., entraver qn; être un boulet au pied de qn.

drag², *v.* I. *v.tr.* (*a*) Traîner, tirer; entraîner. To drag one's feet, traîner les pieds. (*b*) *Nau:* To drag her anchor, chasser sur ses ancres. (*c*) Draguer (un étang). 2. *v.i.* (*a*) Traîner, rester en arrière; traîner en longueur; languir, s'éterniser. (*b*) Offrir de la résistance. drag along, *v.tr.* Traîner, entraîner. drag away, *v.tr.* (*a*) Entraîner, emmener, de force. (*b*) Arracher (qn) (*from*, à, de). drag down, *v.tr.* Tirer, entraîner, en bas. drag in, *v.tr.* Faire entrer de force. drag on, *v.i.* Traîner en longueur; s'éterniser. drag out, *v.tr.* 1. To drag s.o. out of bed, tirer qn de son lit. To drag the truth out of s.o., arracher la vérité à qn. 2. Faire traîner.

dragon, *s.* Dragon *m.* dragon-fly, *s.* Libellule *f*; *F:* demoiselle *f.*

dragoon¹, *s.* *Mil:* Dragon *m.*

dragoon², *v.tr.* To dragoon s.o. into doing sth., contraindre qn à faire qch.

drain¹, *s.* 1. Canal *m*, -aux (de décharge); tranchée *f*, rigole *f.* 2. Égout *m.* *F:* To throw money down the drain, jeter son argent par la fenêtre. 3. Tuyau *m* d'écoulement. 4. Perte *f*, fuite *f* (d'énergie). drain-pipe, *s.* Tuyau *m* d'écoulement.

drain². I. *v.tr.* (*a*) To drain water (off), évacuer, faire écouler, des eaux. (*b*) Boire jusqu'à la dernière goutte. (*c*) Assécher (un terrain). (*d*) Épuiser, *F:* saigner. To drain a country of money, épuiser l'argent d'un pays. *F:* To drain s.o. dry, saigner qn à blanc. 2. *v.i.* To drain (away), s'écouler.

draining, *s.* Écoulement *m* (des eaux); assèchement *m* (d'un marais).

drainage, *s.* 1. = DRAINING. 2. Système *m* d'écoulement des eaux.

drake, *s.* Canard *m* mâle.

dram, *s.* 1. = DRACHM. 2. *F:* Petit verre.

drama, *s.* 1. Drame *m.* 2. The drama, l'art *m* dramatique; le théâtre.

dramatic, *a.* Dramatique. The dramatic works of Corneille, le théâtre de Corneille. -ally, *adv.* Dramatiquement.

dramatist, *s.* Auteur *m* dramatique; dramaturge *m.*

dramatize, *v.tr.* Dramatiser.

drape, *v.tr* Draper, tendre (*with*, *in*, de).

draper, *s.* Marchand *m* d'étoffes, de nouveautés. Draper's shop, magasin *m* de nouveautés.

drapery, *s.* Draperie *f.* Drapery and fancy goods store, magasin *m* de nouveautés.

drastic, *a.* To take drastic measures, prendre des mesures énergiques, rigoureuses. -ally, *adv.* Énergiquement, rigoureusement.

draught, *s.* I. 1. Traction *f*, tirage *m.* Draught animal, bête de trait. 2. *Fish:* Coup *m* de filet; pêche *f.* 3. Trait *m*, gorgée *f.* At a draught, d'un seul trait. 4. *Med:* Potion *f*, breuvage *m.* 5. *Nau:* Tirant *m* d'eau.

6. *pl.* Draughts, (jeu *m* de) dames *fpl.*
7.Courant *m* d'air. **8. Beer on draught,** bière
au tonneau. **II. draught,** *s.* = DRAFT[1] I.
draught-board, damier *m.* **draught-
screen** *s.* Paravent *m.*
draughtsman, *s.* **I.** *Ind:* Dessinateur *m.*
2. *Games:* Pion *m.*
draughtsmanship, *s.* **I.** L'art *m* du dessin
industriel; *Ind:* le dessin. **2.** Talent *m* de
dessinateur.
draughty, *a.* **I.** Plein de courants d'air.
2. Exposé à tous les vents.
draw¹, *s.* **I.** Tirage *m.* **2.** (*a*) Tirage au sort.
(*b*) Loterie *f.* **3.** *F:* Attraction *f*; clou *m.*
(*Of play*) To be a draw, faire recette. **4.** *Sp:*
Partie nulle; résultat nul.
draw², *v.* **I.** *v.tr.* **I.** (*a*) Tirer. *To d. the*
blinds, baisser les stores. (*b*) Tirer, traîner.
2. (*a*) Tirer, aspirer. (*b*) **To draw a crowd,**
attirer une foule. **To feel drawn to s.o.,** se
sentir attiré vers qn. **3.** (*a*) Tirer, retirer,
ôter (*sth. from, out of, sth.,* qch. de qch.).
To draw (one's sword), tirer l'épée. **To draw**
(**lots**) **for sth.,** tirer qch. au sort. *The number*
drawn, le numéro sortant. (*b*) Arracher (un
clou). *F:* **To draw s.o.'s teeth,** mettre qn
hors d'état de nuire. (*c*) *To d. water from the*
river, puiser, tirer, de l'eau à la rivière. *To*
d. a conclusion from sth., tirer une conclusion
de qch. (*d*) Toucher (un salaire). *F:* **To**
draw upon one's memory, faire appel à sa
mémoire. (*e*) *F: To try to d. s.o.,* essayer de
faire parler qn. **4.** (*a*) Vider (une volaille).
(*b*) *Ven:* **To draw a covert,** battre un taillis.
5. To draw the tea, faire infuser le thé.
6. (*a*) Tracer (un plan); tirer, mener (une
ligne). (*b*) Dessiner. (*c*) Faire, établir (une
distinction). **7.** *Nau:* *To d. twenty feet of*
water, tirer, jauger, vingt pieds d'eau.
II. draw, *v.i.* **I.** (*a*) **To draw near to s.o.,**
se rapprocher de qn; s'approcher de qn.
The crowd drew to one side, la foule se
rangea (de côté). *The train drew into the*
station, le train entra en gare. **To draw**
round the table, s'assembler autour de la
table. (*b*) **To draw to an end,** tirer, toucher,
à sa fin. **2. To let the tea draw,** laisser infuser
le thé. **draw along,** *v.tr.* Traîner, entraîner. **draw aside. I.** *v.tr.* (*a*) Détourner, écarter. (*b*) Prendre à l'écart.
2. *v.i.* S'écarter; se ranger. **draw away.**
I. *v.tr.* (*a*) Entraîner. (*b*) Détourner. **2.** *v.i.*
S'éloigner. **draw back. I.** *v.tr.* (*a*) Tirer
en arrière; retirer. (*b*) Tirer, ouvrir (les
rideaux). **2.** *v.i.* (Se) reculer; se retirer en
arrière. **draw down,** *v.tr.* Faire descendre;
baisser (les stores). **draw in. I.** *v.tr.* (*a*)
Faire entrer (en tirant). (*b*) Aspirer (l'air).
2. *v.i.* The days are drawing in, les jours
diminuent. **draw off,** *v.tr.* (*a*) Retirer, ôter
(ses gants). (*b*) Détourner (l'attention).
(*c*) Soutirer (un liquide). **draw on,** *v.i.*
Evening was drawing on, la nuit approchait.
draw out, *v.tr.* **I.** Sortir, retirer (qch. de
qch.); arracher. **2.** Prolonger; tirer en

longueur; (faire) traîner. **draw up. I.** *v.tr.*
(*a*) Lever (un store); relever (ses manches).
To draw oneself up, se (re)dresser. (*b*) *To d.*
up a chair (*to the table*), approcher une chaise
(de la table). (*c*) Ranger, aligner (des troupes).
(*d*) Dresser, rédiger (un document); établir
(un compte). **2.** *v.i.* (*a*) *To d. up to the table,*
s'approcher de la table. (*b*) S'arrêter, stopper.
drawn, *a.* **I. With drawn curtains,** les
rideaux tirés. **2. With drawn swords,** sabre
au clair. **3. Drawn features,** traits tirés, contractés. **4. Drawn match,** partie égale, nulle.
drawing, *s.* **I.** Tirage *m*; puisage *m*; (*of*
teeth) extraction *f.* **2.** Dessin *m.* **drawing-
board,** *s.* Planche *f* à dessin. **drawing-
paper,** *s.* Papier *m* à dessin. **drawing-
pen,** *s.* Tire-ligne *m.* **drawing-pin,** *s.*
Punaise *f.*
drawback, *s.* Inconvénient *m,* désavantage *m.*
drawbridge, *s.* **I.** Pont-levis *m.* **2.** *Civ.E:*
Pont basculant.
drawer, *s.* **I.** Tireur, -euse. **2.** Tiroir *m.*
Chest of drawers, commode *f.* **3.** *pl.* (Pair
of) drawers, caleçon *m*; pantalon *m.*
drawing-room, *s.* **I.** Salon *m.* **2.** Réception *f.*
drawl¹, *s.* Voix traînante; débit traînant.
drawl². **I.** *v.i.* Parler d'une voix traînante.
2. *v.tr.* To drawl out sth., dire qch. avec une
nonchalance affectée.
dread¹, *s.* Crainte *f,* terreur *f,* épouvante *f.*
To stand in dread of s.o., craindre, redouter,
qn.
dread², *v.tr.* Redouter, craindre. **To dread**
that . . ., redouter que (ne) + *sub.*
dreadful, *a.* **I.** Terrible, redoutable.
2. Atroce, épouvantable. **It is something**
dreadful, c'est quelque chose d'affreux.
-fully, *adv.* Terriblement, affreusement.
dream¹, *s.* Rêve *m,* songe *m.* **To have a**
dream, faire un rêve, un songe.
dream², *v.tr. & i.* **I. To dream of, about,**
sth., rêver de qch. **2.** Laisser vaguer ses
pensées; rêvasser. **3.** I shouldn't dream of
doing it, jamais je ne m'aviserais de faire cela.
Little did I dream that, je ne songeais guère
que. **dreaming,** *s.* Rêves *mpl,* songes *mpl.*
dreamer, *s.* Rêveur, euse.
dreaminess, *s.* (État *m* de) rêverie *f.*
dreamy, *a.* Rêveur, -euse; songeur, -euse.
dreariness, *s.* Tristesse *f,* aspect *m* morne.
dreary, *a.* Triste, morne.
dredge, *v.tr. & i.* Draguer, dévaser. **To**
dredge for sth., draguer à la recherche de qch.
dredging, *s.* Dragage *m.*
dredger¹, *s.* Drague *f.*
dredger², *s.* Saupoudroir *m* (à sucre).
dreg, *s.* **To drink the cup to the dregs,** boire
la coupe jusqu'à la lie.
drench, *v.tr.* Tremper, mouiller (*with,* de).
Drenched to the skin, trempé jusqu'aux os.
drenching, *a.* **Drenching rain,** pluie
battante.
Dresden. *Pr.n. Geog:* Dresde *f.* **Dresden**
china, porcelaine *f* de Saxe.

dress¹, s. **1.** Habillement m; habits mpl; vêtements mpl. **In full dress,** en grande tenue. **Morning dress,** tenue de ville. **Evening dress,** tenue de soirée. **2.** Robe f, costume m, toilette f. **dress-circle,** s. Th: (Premier) balcon. **dress-coat,** s. Habit m (de soirée); frac m. **dress-suit,** s. Habit m.

dress², v.tr. **1.** (a) Habiller, vêtir. (b) v.pr. & i. To dress (oneself), s'habiller; faire sa toilette. **To dress (for dinner),** se mettre en habit. **2.** Orner, parer (with, de). **3.** Mil: Aligner. v.i. S'aligner. **Right dress!** à droite alignement! **4.** Med: Panser. **5.** (a) To dress s.o.'s hair, coiffer qn. (b) Cu: Apprêter, accommoder. **dress down,** v.tr. F: Chapitrer; laver la tête à. **dressing down,** s. F: Verte semonce. **dress up,** v.tr. Habiller, parer, F: attifer. **dressing,** s. **1.** (a) Habillement m, toilette f. (b) Arrangement m (des cheveux). (c) Pansement m (d'une blessure). **2.** Med: Pansement, appareil m. **dressing-case,** s. Nécessaire m, sac m (de voyage). **dressing-gown,** s. Robe f de chambre; (for women) peignoir m. **dressing-jacket,** s. Camisole f. **dressing-room,** s. **1.** Cabinet m de toilette. **2.** Th: Loge f (d'acteur). **dressing-station,** s. Mil: Poste m de secours. **dressing-table,** s. (Table f de) toilette f; coiffeuse f.

dresser¹, s. Furn: Buffet m; dressoir m.
dresser², s. Th: Habilleur, -euse.
dressmaker, s. (a) Couturière f. (b) Couturier m.
dressmaking, s. **1.** Couture f. **2.** Confections fpl pour dames; confection de robes.
dribble, v.i. (a) Dégoutter; tomber goutte à goutte. (b) (Of child) Baver.
driblet, s. Petite quantité; chiquet m. **To pay in driblets,** payer petit à petit.
drift¹, s. **1.** (a) Mouvement m. (b) Direction f, sens m. (c) Cours m, marche f (des événements). **2.** Nau: Dérive f. **3.** But m, tendance f. **4.** Amoncellement m (de neige).
drift-ice, s. Glaces flottantes; glaçons mpl en dérive. **driftwood,** s. Bois flottant, bois flotté.
drift², v.i. (a) Flotter; être charrié. Nau: Dériver, aller en dérive. **To drift with the current,** se laisser aller au fil de l'eau. (b) **To let things drift,** laisser aller les choses. (c) S'amonceler, s'amasser.
drifter, s. Nau: Chalutier m.
drill¹, s. **1.** Tls: Foret m, pointe f à forer, mèche f; perforateur m. **2.** Mil: etc: Exercice(s) m(pl), manœuvre(s) f(pl). **drill-sergeant,** s. Mil: Sergent instructeur.
drill², **1.** v.tr. Forer; perforer; percer. **2.** v.tr. Faire faire l'exercice à; instruire, faire manœuvrer. **3.** v.i. Faire l'exercice; manœuvrer.
drill³, s. Tex: Coutil m, treillis m.
drink¹, s. **1.** (a) Boire m. **Food and drink,** le boire et le manger. (b) **To give s.o. a drink,**

donner à boire à qn; faire boire qn. **To have a drink,** se désaltérer. (c) Consommation f. **To have a drink,** prendre quelque chose; boire un coup. **2.** Boisson f, breuvage m. **Strong drink,** liqueurs fortes; spiritueux mpl. **3.** Boisson; ivrognerie f. **To take to drink,** s'adonner à la boisson. **To be the worse for drink,** avoir trop bu.
drink², v.tr. Boire. **1.** Will you have something to drink? voulez-vous boire quelque chose? **2.** Abs. Être adonné à la boisson. **To drink like a fish,** boire comme une éponge. **drink in,** v.tr. F: Boire (les paroles de qn). **drink off,** v.tr. Boire (un verre) d'un coup, d'un trait. **drink up,** v.tr. Achever de boire; vider (un verre). **drunk.** Pred.a. (a) Ivre, gris; soûl (with, de). **To get drunk,** s'enivrer, se griser, se soûler. **Dead drunk,** ivre-mort, pl. ivres-morts. (b) Enivré, grisé (par le succès). **drinking,** s. Ivrognerie f, alcoolisme m. **drinking-bout,** s. Soûlerie f, ribote f. **drinking-fountain,** s. Fontaine publique. **drinking-song,** s. Chanson f à boire. **drinking-trough,** s. Abreuvoir, m. **drinking-water,** s. Eau f potable.
drinkable, a. (a) Buvable. (b) (Eau) potable.
drinker, s. Buveur, -euse.
drip¹, s. **1.** Dégouttement m; égouttement m. **2.** Goutte f.
drip², v.i. Dégoutter, s'égoutter; tomber goutte à goutte. **dripping¹,** a. Ruisselant; (robinet) qui pleure. **dripping²,** s. **1.** Dégouttement m, égouttement m. **2.** pl. Égoutture f (des arbres). **3.** Cu: Graisse f de rôti.
drive¹, s. **1.** Promenade f en voiture; course f. **2.** Ven: Battue f. **3.** Mec.E: (Mouvement m de) propulsion f. **4.** To have plenty of drive, avoir de l'énergie. **5.** (a) Avenue f (dans une forêt). (b) = CARRIAGE-DRIVE. **6.** Bridge drive, tournoi m de bridge
drive², v. **I.** v.tr. **1.** (a) Chasser, pousser. **To d. cattle,** conduire le bétail. F: **To drive sth. out of s.o.'s head,** faire oublier qch. à qn. **To be driven out of one's course,** être entraîné hors de sa route. (b) Ven: **To drive the game,** rabattre le gibier. **2.** (a) Faire marcher (une machine); conduire (un cheval). (b) **To drive s.o. to the station,** conduire qn à la gare. **3.** (a) Pousser (qn à une action); contraindre (qn à faire qch.). **He was driven to it,** on lui a forcé la main. (b) **To drive s.o. out of his senses,** rendre qn fou. **4.** Surcharger de travail. **5.** Enfoncer (un clou). **6.** Percer, forer, avancer (un tunnel). **7.** (a) **To drive a trade,** exercer un métier. (b) **To drive a bargain,** faire, conclure, un marché. **8.** Actionner, faire marcher (une machine). **II. drive,** v.i. **1.** (a) **To drive before the wind,** chasser, être charrié, devant le vent. **To let drive at s.o.,** décocher un coup à qn. (b) (Of snow) S'amonceler. **2.** **To drive along the road,** rouler sur la route. **To drive to a place,** se rendre en voiture à un endroit.

drive along. 1. *v.tr.* Chasser, pousser. **2.** *v.i.* Cheminer (en voiture); rouler. **drive at,** *v.i.* What are you driving at? à quoi voulez-vous en venir? **drive away.** (a) *v.tr.* Chasser, éloigner, repousser. (b) *v.i.* Partir, s'en aller, en voiture. **drive back. 1.** *v.tr.* Repousser, refouler. **2.** *v.i.* Rentrer, revenir en voiture. **drive in. 1.** *v.tr.* Enfoncer (un clou); visser (une vis). **2.** *v.i.* Entrer (en voiture). **drive off,** *v.tr. & i.* = DRIVE AWAY. **drive out,** *v.tr.* Chasser; faire sortir. **drive through. 1.** *v.tr.* To drive one's sword through s.o.'s body, passer son sabre à travers le corps à qn. **2.** *v.i.* Traverser, passer par, en voiture. **driving**[1], *a.* **1.** Driving force, force motrice. **2.** Driving rain, pluie battante. **driving**[2], *s.* Conduite *f* (d'une voiture). **driving-wheel,** *s.* Roue motrice.

drivel[1], *s.* F: Radotage *m*; balivernes *fpl*. To talk drivel, radoter.
drivel[2], *v.i.* **1.** Baver. **2.** F: Radoter.
driver, *s.* (a) Mécanicien *m* (de locomotive); conducteur, -trice, chauffeur, -euse (d'automobile); cocher *m* (de voiture). He is a good driver, il conduit bien. (b) Conducteur (de bestiaux).
drizzle[1], *s.* Bruine *f*, crachin *m*.
drizzle[2], *v.i.* Bruiner, crachiner.
droll, *a.* Drôle, bouffon, -onne, plaisant.
dromedary, *s.* Dromadaire *m*.
drone, *s.* **1.** (a) Ent: Abeille *f* mâle; faux-bourdon. (b) F: Fainéant *m*, parasite *m*. **2.** Bourdonnement *m* (des abeilles). *Av:* Drone of the engine, vrombissement *m*, du moteur.
droop. 1. *v.i.* (a) (Se) pencher; s'abaisser. (b) Pencher, languir (c) To revive s.o.'s drooping spirits, remonter le courage à qn. **2.** *v.tr.* Baisser, pencher (la tête); abaisser (les paupières); laisser pendre (les ailes).
drop[1], *s.* **1.** (a) Goutte *f.* Drop by drop, goutte à goutte. F: A drop of wine, une goutte, un doigt, de vin. F: To take a drop, boire la goutte. He has had a drop too much, il a bu un coup de trop. (b) Pendant *m*, pendeloque *f* (c) Peppermint drop, pastille *f* de menthe. **2.** Chute *f.* Drop in prices, chute, baisse *f*, de prix.
drop[2], *v.* I *v.i.* **1.** Tomber goutte à goutte, dégoutter (from, de). **2.** Tomber; se laisser tomber. I am ready to drop, je tombe de fatigue. **3.** Baisser; (of wind) tomber, se calmer. **4.** There the matter dropped, l'affaire en resta là. **5.** To drop across s.o., rencontrer qn par hasard. **6.** F: To drop (up)on s.o., attraper qn; rembarrer qn. II. **drop,** *v.tr.* **1.** Verser (une larme). **2.** (a) Laisser tomber; lâcher; (in knitting) sauter, laisser échapper (une maille). (b) Laisser échapper (une observation). To drop a word in s.o.'s ear, couler, glisser, un mot à l'oreille de qn. (c) F: To drop s.o. a line, a card, envoyer, écrire, un mot, une carte,

à qn. **3.** Perdre (de l'argent) (over sth., sur qch.). **4.** I shall drop you at your door, je vous déposerai chez vous en passant. **5.** (a) Omettre, supprimer. (b) Ne pas prononcer. **6.** Baisser. **7.** (a) Abandonner, délaisser. Let us drop the subject, laissons ce sujet. F: Drop it! finissez! en voilà assez! (b) F: To drop s.o., cesser ses relations avec qn. **drop in,** *v.i.* Entrer en passant. To drop in on s.o., faire une petite visite à qn. **drop off,** *v.i.* **1.** Tomber, se détacher. **2.** F: To drop off to sleep, s'assoupir, s'endormir. **drop out. 1.** *v.tr.* Omettre, supprimer. **2.** *v.i.* To drop out of a contest, se retirer. **dropping,** *s.* (a) Dégouttement *m.* (b) Descente *f*, chute *f*; baisse *f* (des prix); suppression *f* (d'un mot); abandon *m* (d'un projet).
dropsy, *s.* Med: Hydropisie *f.*
dross, *s.* (a) Impuretés *fpl*; déchet *m.* (b) F: Rebut *m.*
drought, *s.* (Période *f* de) sécheresse *f*; disette *f* d'eau.
drove, *s.* (a) Troupeau *m* en marche. (b) F: Multitude *f*, foule *f* (de personnes en marche).
drover, *s.* Conducteur *m* de bestiaux; toucheur *m.*
drown, *v.tr.* **1.** Noyer. To drown oneself, se noyer; se jeter à l'eau. To be drowned, *v.i.* to drown, se noyer. A drowning man, un homme qui se noie. **2.** Inonder, submerger. **3.** Étouffer, couvrir (un son).
drowned, *a.* Noyé.
drowse, *v.i.* Somnoler, s'assoupir.
drowsiness, *s.* Somnolence *f.*
drowsy, *a.* Assoupi, somnolent. To grow drowsy, s'assoupir. To be d., avoir sommeil.
drub, *v.tr.* Battre, rosser. **drubbing,** *s.* Volée *f* de coups; F: tripotée *f.*
drudge[1], *s.* Femme *f*, homme *f*, de peine.
drudge[2], *v.i.* Trimer, peiner.
drudgery, *s.* Travail pénible, ingrat.
drug[1], *s.* **1.** Drogue *f.* **2.** Narcotique *m*, stupéfiant *m.* **3.** F: To be a drug in the market, être invendable.
drug[2], *v.tr.* **1.** Donner un narcotique à. **2.** Mettre un narcotique à.
druggist, *s.* Pharmacien *m.*
Druid, *s.* Druide *m.*
Druidess, *s.* Druidesse *f.*
drum[1], *s.* **1.** Mus: Tambour *m*, caisse *f.* Big drum, grosse caisse. Mil: The drums, la batterie. With drums beating, tambour(s) battant(s). **2.** Tambourinage *m.* **3.** Anat: Tympan *m.* **4.** Tonneau *m*; tonnelet *m.*
drum-major, *s.* Tambour-major *m.*
drum[2], *v.* **1.** *v.i.* Tambouriner; battre du tambour. **2.** *v.tr.* To drum sth. into s.o.'s head, enfoncer qch. dans la tête de qn.
drumming, *s.* Tambourinage *m*; bruit *m* de tambour.
drummer, *s.* Tambour *m.* **drummerboy,** *s.m.* Petit tambour.

drumstick, s. **1.** Baguette f de tambour. **2.** Cu: Pilon m.

drunkard, s. Ivrogne, f. ivrognesse.

drunken, a. Ivrogne. **-ly,** adv. En ivrogne.

drunkenness, s. **1.** Ivresse f. **2.** Ivrognerie f.

dry¹, a. Sec, f. sèche. **1.** (a) (Of well) Tari, à sec; (of country) aride. **Dry land,** terre ferme. **To run dry,** se dessécher. (b) Dry bread, pain sec. 'To be kept dry,' "craint l'humidité." (c) F: (Of pers.) **To feel dry,** avoir le gosier sec; avoir soif. **Dry work,** travail qui donne soif. **2.** Aride; sans intérêt. **3.** (a) Dry smile, sourire teinté d'ironie. Dry humour, esprit caustique, mordant. (b) Dry reception, accueil peu cordial. **-ly,** adv. **1.** D'un ton sec; sèchement. **2.** Avec une pointe d'ironie contenue. **dry-cleaning,** s. Nettoyage m à sec. **dry-eyed,** a. To look on dry-eyed, regarder d'un œil sec. **dry-foot(ed),** a. & adv. A pied sec. **dry-rot,** s. Carie sèche. **dry-shod,** a. & adv. A pied sec.

dry², v. **1.** v.tr. Sécher; faire sécher. **To dry one's eyes,** s'essuyer les yeux. **To dry one's tears,** sécher ses larmes. **2.** v.i. Sécher, se dessécher. **To put sth. out to dry,** mettre qch. à sécher dehors. **dry up,** v.i. **1.** Se dessécher, tarir. Little dried-up man, petit homme sec. **2.** F: Cesser de parler; se taire.

dried, a. Séché, desséché. **Dried fruits,** fruits secs. **drying,** s. Séchage m; assèchement m, dessèchement m; (with a cloth) essuyage m.

dryad, s. Myth: Dryade f.

dryness, s. **1.** Sécheresse f; aridité f. **2.** Sécheresse, sévérité f (de ton); aridité (d'un discours); causticité f (de l'esprit).

dual, a. Double. Psy: Dual personality, dédoublement m de la personnalité.

dub, v.tr (a) To dub s.o. (a) knight, armer qn chevalier. (b) F: To dub s.o. a quack, qualifier qn de charlatan.

dubbin, s. Leath: Dégras m.

dubiety, s. (Sentiment m de) doute m.

dubious, a. **1.** Douteux. (a) Uncertain. (b) Équivoque, louche. **2.** Hésitant. Dubious expression, air de doute. **-ly,** adv. D'un air ou d'un ton de doute.

dubiousness, s. **1.** Incertitude f. **2.** Caractère douteux, équivoque f.

ducal, a. Ducal, -aux; de duc.

duchess, s. Duchesse f.

duchy, s. Duché m.

duck¹, s. **1.** Orn: (a) Cane f. (b) (Generic) Canard m. Wild duck, canard sauvage. Cu: Duck and green peas, canard aux petits pois. **To play ducks and drakes with one's money,** jeter son argent par les fenêtres. **2.** Cr: Duck, duck's egg, zéro m. **duck-boards,** s.pl. Caillebotis m. **duck-pond,** s. Canardière f.

duck², s. Tex: Coutil m. Duck trousers, pl. F: ducks, pantalon blanc; pantalon de coutil.

duck³, s. **1.** Plongeon m. **2.** Mouvement instinctif de la tête (pour se dérober).

duck⁴. 1. v.i. Baisser la tête, se baisser (subitement). **2.** v.tr. (a) Plonger dans l'eau; faire faire le plongeon à (qn). (b) Baisser subitement (la tête). **ducking,** s. Plongeon m (involontaire); bain forcé.

duckling, s. Orn: Caneton m.

duckweed, s. Bot: Lentille f d'eau.

ductile, a. Ductile.

dud, P: **1.** s.pl. Duds, frusques fpl; nippes fpl. **2.** s. & a. (a) Incapable. He's a dud, c'est un type nul. (b) Mauvais; P: moche.

dudgeon, s. Colère f, ressentiment m.

due¹. 1. a. (a) Exigible; échéant, échu. Bill due on 1st May, effet payable le premier mai. The balance due to us, le solde qui nous revient. **To fall due,** échoir. When due, à l'échéance. (b) Dû, f. due; juste, mérité. In due form, dans les formes voulues. After due consideration, après mûre réflexion. (c) Due to, dû à. What is it due to? à quoi cela tient-il? (d) The train is due at two o'clock, le train arrive à deux heures. **2.** adv. Due north, droit vers le nord.

due². 1. s. Dû m. To give s.o. his due, rendre justice à qn. **2.** pl. Droits mpl, frais mpl.

duel, s. Duel m. To fight a duel, se battre en duel.

duelling, s. Le duel.

duellist, s. Duelliste m.

duenna, s. Duègne f.

duet, s. Duo m; morceau m à quatre mains.

duffer, s. F: Sch: Cancre m, croûte f. An old duffer, un ganache.

dug-out, s. **1.** Canot creusé dans un tronc d'arbre. **2.** Mil: Abri (blindé).

duke, s. Duc m.

dukedom, s. Duché m.

dull¹, a. **1.** Lent, lourd; à l'esprit obtus. **2.** (a) A dull ache, une douleur sourde. (b) Sourd, étouffé, mat. **3.** The dull season, la morte-saison. **4.** Triste, morne. I feel dull, je m'ennuie. **5.** Triste, ennuyeux. As dull as ditch-water, ennuyeux comme un jour de pluie. A thoroughly dull evening, une soirée tout à fait assommante. **6.** Terne, mat. Dull eyes, yeux morts, sans éclat. **7.** (Of weather) Lourd, triste, sombre. **8.** (Of tool) Émoussé. **-lly,** adv. **1.** Lourdement; ennuyeusement. **2.** Sourdement, faiblement; sans éclat. **dull-witted,** a. A l'esprit lourd.

dull², v.tr. **1.** Alourdir, appesantir (l'esprit). **2.** Amortir (une douleur).

dullard, s. Lourdaud m. Sch: Cancre m.

dullness, s. **1.** Lenteur f, pesanteur f, de l'esprit; émoussement m (des sens). **2.** Matité f (d'un son). **3.** Ennui m; monotonie f. **4.** Com: Stagnation f, marasme m. **5.** Émoussement m (d'une pointe). **6.** Manque d'éclat; faiblesse f (d'un son).

duly, *adv.* **1.** Dûment, justement; convenablement. **2.** En temps voulu.

dumb, *a.* Muet, *f.* muette. **Dumb animals,** les bêtes, les animaux. **To strike s.o. dumb,** (i) frapper qn de mutisme; (ii) *F:* abasourdir qn. **Dumb show,** pantomime *f;* jeu muet. **-ly,** *adv.* Sans rien dire; en silence.

dumb-bell, *s.* Haltère *m.*

dumbfound, *v.tr.* Abasourdir, stupéfier.

dumbness, *s.* **1.** Mutisme *m.* **2.** Silence *m.*

dummy, *s.* **1.** Homme *m* de paille. **2.** (*a*) *Dressm:* Mannequin *m.* (*b*) Chose *f* factice; faux paquet. (*c*) (Baby's) dummy, sucette *f.* **3.** *Cards:* Mort *m.* **4.** *Attrib:* Postiche; faux, *f.* fausse.

dump¹, *s.* **1.** Tas *m,* amas *m.* **2.** Chantier *m* de dépôt. **3.** Dépôt *m.*

dump², *v.tr.* (*a*) Décharger, déverser. (*b*) **To dump (down),** déposer, jeter; laisser tomber lourdement. **dumping,** *s.* (*a*) Déversement *m,* versage *m.* (*b*) Dépôt *m.*

dumpling, *s.* *Cu:* Boulette *f.*

dumps, *s.pl.* *F:* Cafard *m;* idées noires. **To be (down) in the dumps,** broyer du noir.

dumpy, *a.* Trapu; boulot, -otte

dun¹, *a.* Brun foncé.

dun², *s.* Créancier importun.

dun³, *v.tr.* Importuner.

dunce, *s.* Ignorant, -ante; âne *m.*

dunderhead, *s.* *F:* (*a*) Lourdaud, -aude. (*b*) Imbécile *mf.*

dune, *s.* (Sand-)dune, dune *f.*

dung, *s.* **1.** Fiente *f;* bouse *f* (de vache); crottin *m* (de cheval). **2.** *Agr:* Fumier *m.*

dungarees, *s.* *pl.* *Ind:* Combinaison *f;* *F:* salopette *f.*

dungeon, *s.* Cachot *m.*

dunghill, *s.* Tas *m* de fumier; fumier *m.*

Dunkirk. *Pr.n. Geog:* Dunkerque *f.*

dunnage, *s.* *F:* Effets personnels; sac *m* (de marin).

dupe¹, *s.* Dupe *f.*

dupe², *v.tr.* Duper, tromper.

duplicate¹. **I.** *a.* Double. **D. parts,** pièces de rechange. **2.** Double *m,* répétition *f.* **In duplicate,** en double exemplaire.

duplicate², *v.tr.* Faire le double de. **duplicating,** *s.* **1.** Duplication *f.* **2.** Reproduction *f* à l'autocopiste. **duplicating-machine,** *s.* Duplicateur *m,* autocopiste *m.*

duplication, *s.* Duplication *f,* reproduction *f.*

duplicity, *s.* Duplicité *f;* mauvaise foi.

durability, *s.* Durabilité *f;* durée *f.*

durable, *a.* Durable; résistant.

duration, *s.* Durée *f;* étendue *f.*

duress, *s.* **1.** Emprisonnement *m.* **2.** **To act under duress,** agir à son corps défendant.

during, *prep.* Pendant, durant. **During the winter,** au cours de l'hiver.

dusk. **I.** *a.* **It is growing dusk,** la nuit tombe. **2.** *s.* (*a*) Obscurité. (*b*) Crépuscule *m.* **At dusk,** à la brune.

dusky, *a.* **1.** Sombre, obscur. **2.** (*a*) *Of complexion*) Bistré. (*b*) Noirâtre; (*of pers.*) noiraud.

dust¹, *s.* Poussière *f.* *F:* **To throw dust in s.o.'s eyes,** jeter de la poudre aux yeux de qn. **To kick up a dust,** faire une scène. **dust-cap,** *s.* *Cost:* Bonnet *m* anti-poussière.

dust-cart, *s.* Tombereau *m* aux ordures.

dust-coat, *s.* *Cost:* Cache-poussière *m inv.*

dust-colour(ed), *a.* Cendré. **dust-pan,** *s.* Pelle *f* à main; ramasse-poussière *m inv.*

dust², *v.tr.* **1.** Saupoudrer (*with,* de). **2.** Épousseter (un meuble). *F:* **To dust s.o.'s jacket,** flanquer une raclée à qn. **dusting,** *s.* **1.** Saupoudrage *m.* **2.** (*a*) Époussetage *m.* (*b*) *F:* Frottée *f,* raclée *f.* **dust-up,** *s.* *F:* Querelle *f.*

dustbin, *s.* Poubelle *f.*

duster, *s.* Chiffon *m* (à épousseter). **Feather duster,** plumeau *m,* époussette *f.*

dustman, *s.* Boueur *m,* boueux *m.*

dusty, *a.* **1.** Poussiéreux, poudreux; recouvert de poussière. **2.** *P:* **It's not so dusty,** c'est pas mal du tout.

Dutch. **I.** *a.* Hollandais; de Hollande. *F:* **Dutch courage,** bravoure après boire. **2.** *s.* (*a*) **The Dutch,** les Hollandais. (*b*) *Ling:* Le hollandais.

Dutchman, *s.* Hollandais *m.*

dutiable, *a.* Soumis aux droits de douane; taxable.

dutiful, *a.* Respectueux, soumis. **-fully,** *adv.* Avec soumission.

duty, *s.* **1.** Obéissance *f,* respect *m.* **2.** Devoir *m* (to, envers). **To do one's duty,** faire son devoir. **I shall make it my d. to help him,** je prendrai à tâche de l'aider. **As in duty bound,** comme il est de mon devoir. **From a sense of duty,** par devoir. **3.** Fonction(s) *f(pl).* **To take up one's duties,** entrer en fonctions. **To do duty for s.o.,** remplacer qn. **4.** Service *m.* **To be on duty,** être de service. **To be on sentry duty,** être en faction *f.* **5.** Droit *m.* **Customs duty,** droit(s) de douane.

dwarf¹, *s. & a.* Nain, -e.

dwarf², *v.tr.* Rapetisser (par contraste).

dwarfish, *a.* (De) nain; chétif.

dwell, *v.i.* **1.** **To dwell in a place,** habiter (dans) un lieu; demeurer, résider, dans un lieu. **2.** Rester; se fixer. **3.** **To dwell on sth.,** s'étendre sur, s'appesantir sur. **We will not dwell on that,** glissons là-dessus. **dwelling,** *s.* **1.** (*a*) Séjour *m,* résidence *f.* (*b*) Insistance *f* (sur un fait). **2.** Lieu *m* de séjour; demeure *f.* **dwelling-house,** *s.* Maison *f* d'habitation. **dwelling-place,** *s.* Demeure *f,* résidence *f.*

dweller, *s.* Habitant, -ante (*in, on,* de).

dwindle, *v.i.* **To dwindle (away),** diminuer, dépérir. **dwindling,** *s.* Diminution *f,* dépérissement *m.*

dye¹, *s.* **1.** (*a*) *Dy:* Teinture *f,* teint *m.* (*b*) Teinte *f.* **Villain of the deepest dye,** triple

coquin. **2.** Matière colorante; teinture, colorant *m.* **dye-works,** *s.* Teinturerie *f.*
dye², *v.tr.* Teindre. *To dye sth. black,* teindre qch. en noir. **dyeing,** *s.* (*a*) Teinture *f* (d'étoffes). (*b*) Teintage *m.*
dyer, *s.* Teinturier *m.*
dyke, *s.* = DIKE.
dynamic, *a.* Dynamique.
dynamics, *s.pl.* Dynamique *f.*

dynamite¹, *s.* Dynamite *f.*
dynamite², *v.tr.* Dynamiter.
dynamo, *s.* Dynamo *f.*
dynastic, *a.* Dynastique.
dynasty, *s.* Dynastie *f.*
dysentery, *s.* Dysenterie *f.*
dyspepsia, *s.* *Med:* Dyspepsie *f.*
dyspeptic, *a. & s.* Dyspepsique (*mf*) dyspeptique (*mf*).

E

E, e, *s.* **1.** (La lettre) E, e *m.* **2.** *Mus:* Mi *m.*
each. 1. *a.* Chaque. **Each one of us,** chacun, chacune, de nous. **2.** *pron.* (*a*) Chacun, -une. (*b*) **We each earn one pound,** nous gagnons une livre chacun. (*c*) **Each other,** l'un l'autre, les uns les autres. *Separated* **from each other,** séparés l'un de l'autre. **To fight each other,** s'entre-battre.
eager, *a.* (*a*) Ardent, passionné. **Eager for gain,** âpre au gain. **To be eager to do sth.,** désirer ardemment faire qch. (*b*) **Eager glance,** œillade avide. **-ly,** *adv.* Ardemment, passionnément, avidement.
eagerness, *s.* Ardeur *f*; impatience *f*; vif désir.
eagle, *s.* Aigle *mf.* **Golden eagle,** aigle royal.
eagle-eyed, *a.* Aux yeux d'aigle; au regard d'aigle.
eaglet, *s.* Aiglon *m.*
ear¹, *s.* Oreille *f.* **Your ears must have burned,** les oreilles ont dû vous corner. *F:* **To be over head and ears in work,** être débordé de travail **To set people by the ears,** brouiller les gens. *He went off with a flea in his ear,* il est parti l'oreille basse. **To have sharp ears,** avoir l'oreille, l'ouïe, fine. **To keep one's ears open,** se tenir aux écoutes. **To have s.o.'s ear,** avoir l'oreille de qn. **To give ear to s.o.,** prêter l'oreille à qn. **ear-ache,** *s.* **To have ear-ache,** avoir mal *m* à l'oreille, aux oreilles. **ear-mark,** *v.tr. To e.-m. funds for a purpose,* affecter des fonds à un projet. **ear-ring,** *s.* Boucle *f* d'oreille. **ear-shot,** *s.* **Within ear-shot,** à portée de voix, de l'ouïe. **ear-splitting,** *a* **Ear-splitting noise,** bruit à briser le tympan, à fendre la tête. **ear-trumpet,** *s.* Cornet *m* acoustique.
ear², *s.* Épi *m* (de blé).
earl, *s.* Comte *m.*
earldom, *s.* Comté *m.*
early. I. *a.* **1.** (*a*) **In the early morning,** de grand matin. **In early summer** au commencement de l'été. **To be an early riser,** se lever (de bon) matin. **To keep early hours,**

se coucher tôt. (*b*) *The earliest times,* les temps les plus reculés. (*c*) **Early youth,** première jeunesse. **2.** Précoce, hâtif. **Early death,** mort prématurée. **3.** Prochain, rapproché. **At an early date,** prochainement. **II. early,** *adv.* (*a*) De bonne heure; tôt. **Earlier,** de meilleure heure; plus tôt. **Too early,** trop tôt; de trop bonne heure. *To arrive five minutes too e.,* arriver avec cinq minutes d'avance. **Early in the morning,** le matin de bonne heure. **E. in the afternoon,** au commencement de l'après-midi. **As early as the tenth century,** dès le dixième siècle. **As early as possible,** aussitôt que possible. (*b*) **To die early,** mourir prématurément.
earn, *v.tr.* **1.** Gagner **2.** Mériter, gagner.
earnest¹. 1. *a.* (*a*) Sérieux. *E. worker,* ouvrier consciencieux. (*b*) **Earnest request,** demande pressante. *E. prayer,* prière fervente. **2.** *s.* **In earnest,** sérieusement. **To be in earnest,** être sérieux; ne pas plaisanter. **It is raining in real earnest,** il pleut pour (tout) de bon. **-ly,** *adv.* Sérieusement. **To entreat s.o. earnestly,** prier qn instamment.
earnest², *s.* **1. Earnest money,** arrhes *fpl.* **2.** Gage *m,* garantie *f.*
earnestness, *s.* Gravité *f,* sérieux *m.*
earnings, *s.pl.* **1.** Salaire *m,* gages *mpl.* **2.** Profits *mpl,* bénéfices *mpl.*
earth, *s* **1.** Terre *f.* (*a*) Le monde. **On earth,** sur terre. *F:* **Where on earth have you been?** où diable étiez-vous? (*b*) Le sol. *F:* **To come back to earth,** retomber des nues. **2.** Terrier *m,* tanière *f.* **To go to earth,** se terrer. **To run to earth,** dépister, dénicher
earthen, *a.* De terre.
earthenware, *s.* Poterie *f*; faïence *f.*
earthly, *a.* **1.** Terrestre. **2.** *F:* **For no earthly reason,** à propos de rien
earthquake, *s.* **1.** Tremblement *m* de terre. **2.** *F:* Convulsion *f,* bouleversement *m.*
earthworks, *s.pl.* *Civ.E:* Travaux *mpl* en terre.
earthworm, *s.* Lombric *m*; ver *m* de terre.
earthy, *a.* Terreux.

earwig, s. Perce-oreille m, pl. perce-oreilles.

ease¹, s. **1.** (a) Tranquillité f; repos m, bien-être m, aise f. **To be at one's ease,** être à son aise. **To set s.o.'s mind at ease,** tirer qn de son inquiétude. **To take one's ease,** prendre ses aises. *Mil:* **Stand at ease!** (en place,) repos! (b) **Ease from pain,** soulagement m. **2.** (a) Loisir m. (b) Oisiveté f. **3.** (a) Aisance f (de manières). (b) Simplicité f (de réglage); facilité f (de manœuvre). **With ease,** facilement; aisément; avec aisance.

ease², v.tr. **1.** (a) Adoucir, calmer; soulager. v.i. *The pain has eased,* la douleur s'est atténuée. (b) Calmer, tranquilliser. **2.** Débarrasser, délivrer (qn de qch.). **3.** Détendre, relâcher, soulager. **ease up,** v.i. (a) *F:* Se relâcher; moins travailler. (b) Diminuer la vitesse; ralentir.

easel, s. Chevalet m.

easiness, s. **1.** Bien-être m, commodité f. **2.** Aisance f, grâce f. **3.** Indifférence f, insouciance f. **4.** Facilité f (d'un travail).

east. 1. s. (a) Est m, orient m, levant m. **To the east,** à l'est (of, de). (b) **The East,** l'Orient, le Levant. **The Far, Middle, Near, East,** l'extrême, moyen, proche, Orient. **2.** adv. A l'est, à l'orient. **3.** adj. (Vent) d'est.

Easter, s. Pâques m. **Easter Day,** le jour de Pâques.

easterly. 1. a. **Easterly wind,** vent (d')est. **2.** adv. Vers l'est.

eastern, a. Est, de l'est; oriental, -aux.

eastward. 1. s. **To the eastward,** vers l'est m. **2.** a. (a) A l'est. (b) Du côté de l'est.

eastwards, adv. A l'est; vers l'est.

easy. I. a. **1.** (a) A l'aise. **To feel easier,** se sentir plus à son aise. (b) Tranquille; sans inquiétude. **2.** Aisé, libre. **Easy style,** style facile. **3.** (a) Easy task, travail facile, aisé. *That is easy to see,* cela se voit. **Within easy reach,** à distance commode. (b) Facile, accommodant, complaisant. **Easy to get on with,** d'un commerce facile. (c) **To travel by easy stages,** voyager à petites étapes. **To come in an easy first,** arriver bon premier. **-ily,** adv. **1.** Tranquillement; à son aise, paisiblement. **2.** Facilement, sans difficulté. **II. easy,** adv. *F:* **1.** Easier said than done, c'est plus facile à dire qu'à faire. **2.** To take things easy, prendre les choses en douceur. **Take it easy!** ne vous faites pas de bile! **To go easy with sth.,** ménager qch. **easy-chair,** s. Fauteuil m; bergère f. **easy-going,** a. (a) Qui prend les choses tranquillement; insouciant. (b) D'humeur facile.

eat, v.tr. Manger. *To ask for something to eat,* demander à manger. **To eat one's heart out,** se ronger le cœur. **To eat one's words,** se rétracter. **eat away,** v.tr. Ronger, éroder. **eat up,** v.tr. **1.** Achever de manger, dévorer. **Eat up your bread!** finis ton pain! **To eat up the miles,** dévorer la route. **2.** *F:* **To be eaten up (with sth.),** être dévoré (d'orgueil).

eating, s. Manger m. **eating-house,** s. Restaurant m.

eatable. 1. a. Mangeable; bon à manger. **2.** s.pl. Eatables, provisions f de bouche.

eaves, s.pl. *Const:* Avance f (du toit).

eavesdrop, v.i. Écouter aux portes.

eavesdropper, s. Écouteur, -euse, aux portes.

ebb¹, s. **1.** Reflux m, jusant m. **The ebb and flow,** le flux et le reflux. **2.** *F:* Déclin m. **At a low ebb,** très bas. **ebb-tide,** s. Marée descendante; jusant m; reflux m.

ebb², v.i. **1.** Baisser, refluer. **To ebb and flow,** monter et baisser. **2.** *F:* Décliner; être sur le déclin.

ebony, s. Ébène f; bois m d'ébène.

ebullient, a. *F:* Débordant, exubérant.

eccentric, a. & s. Excentrique (mf).

eccentricity, s. Excentricité f; originalité f.

ecclesiastic, a. & s. Ecclésiastique (m).

echo¹, s. Écho m. **To applaud to the echo,** applaudir à tout rompre.

echo². 1. v.tr. Répéter. **To echo s.o.'s opinions,** se faire l'écho des opinions de qn. **2.** v.i. (a) Faire écho. (b) Retentir.

eclipse¹, s. Éclipse f.

eclipse², v.tr. Éclipser.

economic, a. Qui se rapporte à l'économie politique; (problème) économique.

economical, a. (a) (Of pers.) Économe. (b) (Of method) Économique. **-ally,** adv. Économiquement.

economics, s.pl. L'économie f politique.

economist, s. Économiste m

economize, v.tr. Économiser, ménager. *Abs.* Faire des économies.

economy, s. Économie f.

ecstasy, s. **1.** Transport m (de joie); ravissement m. **To go into ecstasies over sth.,** s'extasier devant qch. **2.** Extase f.

ecstatic, a. Extatique.

Ecuador. Pr.n. Geog: (La République de) l'Équateur m.

eddy¹, s. Remous m; tourbillon m; tournoiement m.

eddy², v.i. (Of water) Faire des remous; (of wind) tourbillonner, tournoyer.

Eden. Pr.n. (The Garden of) Eden, l'Éden m.

edge¹, s. **1.** Fil m, tranchant m. *F:* **The thin edge of the wedge,** le premier pas. **To put an edge on a blade,** (re)donner du fil à, affiler, une lame. **To take the edge off sth.,** émousser (un couteau). **2.** Arête f, angle m (d'une pierre). **Sharp edge,** arête vive. **3.** Bord m, rebord m; tranche f (d'une planche) *Bookb:* **With gilt edges,** doré sur tranches. **On edge,** *F:* énervé. **It sets my teeth on edge,** cela m'agace les dents. **4.** Lisière f, bordure f (d'un bois); bord, rive f (d'une rivière); liséré m, bord (d'une étoffe).

edge², v.tr. & i. **To edge (one's way) into a

room, se faufiler dans une pièce. **edged,** *a.*
I. Tranchant, acéré. *F:* To play with edged
tools, jouer avec le feu. **2.** (*a*) A tranchant.
Two-edged sword, épée à deux tranchants.
(*b*) Gilt-edged, doré sur tranches.
edgeways, *adv.* (Placé) de champ. *F:* I
can't get a word in edgeways, impossible de
glisser un mot.
edible. I. *a.* Comestible; bon à manger.
2. *s.pl.* Edibles, comestibles *m.*
edict, *s. Hist:* Édit *m.*
edification, *s.* Édification *f*, instruction *f.*
edifice, *s.* Édifice *m.*
edify, *v.tr.* Édifier (qn).
Edinburgh. *Pr.n.* Édimbourg.
edit, *v.tr.* (*a*) Annoter, éditer. (*b*) Rédiger,
diriger.
edition, *s.* Édition *f.*
editor, *s.* **I.** Annotateur *m*, éditeur *m.*
2. (*a*) Surveillant *m* de la publication;
directeur *m.* (*b*) Rédacteur *m* en chef,
directeur (d'un journal).
editorial. I. *a.* Éditorial, -aux. **2.** *s.* Article
m de fond, de tête.
educate, *v.tr.* **I.** Donner de l'instruction à,
instruire. *He was educated in France*, il a fait
ses études en France. **2.** Educated man,
homme instruit.
education, *s.* **I.** Éducation *f.* **2.** Enseignement *m*, instruction *f. He has had a good e.*,
il a fait de fortes études.
educational, *a.* D'éducation, d'enseignement.
Edward. *Pr.n.* Édouard *m.*
eel, *s.* **I.** Anguille *f.* **2. Electric eel,** gymnote *m.*
eerie, *a.* Étrange, mystérieux.
efface, *v.tr.* Effacer; oblitérer.
effect[1]**,** *s.* **I.** (*a*) Effet *m*, influence *f*; résultat
m. To have an effect on s.o., produire de
l'effet sur qn. To have no effect, ne produire
aucun effet; rester sans action. Nothing has
any effect on it, rien n'y fait. To take effect,
(i) faire (son) effet; (ii) entrer en vigueur;
(iii) (*of drugs*) agir, opérer. To no effect, en
vain; sans résultat. To carry into effect,
mettre à exécution. (*b*) Sens *m*, teneur *f.*
2. (*a*) *Th:* **Stage effects,** effets scéniques.
(*b*) To do sth. for e., faire qch. pour se faire
remarquer. **3. In effect,** en fait, en réalité.
4. *pl.* **(Personal) effects,** effets.
effect[2]**,** *v.tr.* Effectuer, accomplir. To effect
one's purpose, atteindre son but. To effect
an entrance, forcer la porte.
effective. I. *a.* (*a*) Efficace. (*b*) *E. contrast,*
contraste frappant. *E. picture,* tableau qui
fait de l'effet. **2.** *s.pl. Mil:* **Effectives,**
effectifs *m.* **-ly,** *adv.* **I.** Avec effet; efficacement. **2.** Effectivement; en réalité. **3.** D'une
façon frappante.
effectual, *a.* Efficace. **-ally,** *adv.* Efficacement.
effeminacy, *s.* Caractère efféminé; mollesse *f.*

effeminate, *a. & s.* Efféminé (*m*).
effervesce, *v.i.* Être en effervescence
effervescence, *s.* Effervescence *f.*
effete, *a.* Caduc, -uque.
efficacious, *a.* Efficace. **-ly,** *adv.* Efficacement; avec efficacité.
efficacy, *s.* Efficacité *f.*
efficiency, *s.* **I.** Efficacité *f.* **2.** Capacité *f*;
valeur *f.*
efficient, *a.* (*a*) Effectif, efficace. (*b*) Capable,
compétent. **-ly,** *adv.* **I.** Efficacement.
2. *Work e. done,* travail exécuté avec compétence.
effigy, *s.* Effigie *f.*
effort, *s.* Effort *m. To make an e. to do sth.,*
faire (un) effort pour faire qch. He spares
no effort, il ne s'épargne pas.
effrontery, *s.* Effronterie *f.*
effulgence, *s.* Éclat *m*, splendeur *f.*
effulgent, *a.* Resplendissant, éclatant.
effusion, *s.* Effusion *f*, épanchement *m.*
effusive, *a.* Démonstratif, expansif. To be
effusive in one's thanks, se confondre en
remercîments. **-ly,** *adv.* Avec effusion, avec
expansion.
effusiveness, *s.* Effusion *f*; volubilité *f.*
egg[1]**,** *s.* Œuf *m. Hard-boiled egg,* œuf dur.
P: A bad egg, un bon à rien. **egg-cup,**
s. Coquetier *m.* **egg-shaped,** *a.* Ovoïde.
egg-shell, *s.* Coquille *f* d'œuf. **egg-
spoon,** *s.* Cuiller *f* à œufs.
egg[2]**,** *v.tr.* To egg s.o. on (to do sth.), pousser,
inciter, encourager, qn (à faire qch.).
egoism, *s.* Égoïsme *m.*
egoist, *s.* Égoïste *mf.*
egotism, *s.* Égotisme *m.*
egotist, *s.* Égotiste *mf.*
egregious, *a.* Insigne, fieffé.
egress, *s.* Sortie *f*, issue *f.*
egret, *s. Orn:* Aigrette *f.*
Egypt. *Pr.n.* L'Égypte *f.*
Egyptian, *a. & s.* Égyptien, -ienne.
eh, *int.* Eh! hé! hein?
eider(-duck), *s. Orn:* Eider *m.* **eider-
down,** *s.* **I.** Duvet *m* d'eider. **2. Eider-down
(quilt),** édredon piqué.
eight. I. *num. a. & s.* Huit (*m*). *P:* He's
had one over the eight, il a bu un coup de
trop. **2.** *s. Sp:* Équipe *f* de huit rameurs.
eighteen, *num. a. & s.* Dix-huit (*m*).
eighteenth, *num. a. & s.* (*a*) Dix-huitième.
(*b*) (*On*) the e., le dix-huit.
eighth, *num. a. & s.* (*a*) Huitième. (*b*) (On)
the eighth, le huit.
eighty, *num. a. & s.* Quatre-vingts (*m*).
Eighty-one, quatre-vingt-un. **Page eighty,**
page quatre-vingt.
either. I. *a. & pron.* (*a*) L'un(e) et l'autre.
On either side, de chaque côté; des deux
côtés. (*b*) L'un(e) ou l'autre. **Either of them,**
soit l'un(e), soit l'autre. *I don't believe e. of
you,* je ne vous crois ni l'un ni l'autre.

2. *conj. & adv.* (*a*) Either . . . or . . ., ou . . ., ou . . .; soit . . ., soit. . . . Either come in or go out, entrez ou sortez. (*b*) Not . . . either, ne . . non plus. Nor I either! ni moi non plus.

ejaculate, *v.tr.* *"What a misfortune!"* he *ejaculated,* "quel malheur!" s'écria-t-il.

ejaculation, *s.* Cri *m,* exclamation *f.*

eject, *v.tr.* **1.** Jeter, émettre. **2.** Expulser.

ejection, *s.* Éviction *f,* expulsion *f.*

eke, *v.tr.* To eke out, augmenter; ménager.

elaborate[1], *a.* Compliqué; (*of style*) travaillé; (*of inspection*) minutieux. **-ly,** *adv.* Avec soin; minutieusement.

elaborate[2], *v.tr.* Élaborer.

elapse, *v.i.* S'écouler; (se) passer.

elastic. **1.** *a.* Élastique. **2.** *s.* Élastique *m.*

elasticity, *s.* Élasticité *f*; ressort *m* (de caractère); souplesse *f* (de corps).

elate, *v.tr.* Exalter, transporter.

elation, *s.* **1.** Exaltation *f.* **2.** Joie *f,* gaîté *f.*

elbow[1], *s.* **1.** Coude *m.* To rest one's e. on *sth.,* s'accouder sur qch. To be out at elbow(s), (i) (*of coat*) être troué aux coudes; (ii) *F:* (*of pers.*) être déguenillé. **2.** Coude, tournant *m.* **elbow-grease,** *F:* Huile *f* de bras. **elbow-room,** *s.* To have elbow-room, avoir ses coudées franches.

elbow[2], *v.tr. & i.* (*a*) Coudoyer. To elbow s.o. aside, écarter qn d'un coup de coude. (*b*) To elbow (one's way) through the crowd, se frayer un passage à travers la foule.

elder[1]. **1.** *a.* Aîné, plus âgé. **2.** *s.* Aîné, -ée; plus âgé, -ée.

elder[2], *s.* *Bot:* Elder(-tree), sureau *m.* **elder-berry,** *s.* Baie *f* de sureau.

elderly, *a.* D'un certain âge; assez âgé.

eldest, *a.* Aîné.

elect[1], *a.* Élu.

elect[2], *v.tr.* **1.** To elect to do sth., choisir de faire qch. **2.** Élire.

election, *s.* Élection *f.*

elector, *s.* Électeur *m,* votant *m.*

electric, *a* Électrique.

electrical, *a.* Électrique. **-ally,** *adv.* Électriquement.

electrician, *s.* Électricien *m.*

electricity, *s.* Électricité *f.*

electrify, *v.tr.* **1.** Électriser (son auditoire). **2.** Électrifier (un chemin de fer).

electro-plate[1], *s.* Articles argentés; couverts *mpl* en ruolz.

electro-plate[2], *v.tr.* Argenter.

electrocute, *v.tr.* Électrocuter.

electrocution, *s.* Électrocution *f.*

electrode, *s.* Électrode *f.*

electrolysis, *s.* Électrolyse *f.*

electron, *s.* Électron *m.*

elegance, *s.* Élégance *f.*

elegant, *a.* Élégant. **-ly,** *adv.* Élégamment.

elegy, *s.* Élégie *f.*

element, *s.* Élément *m.* **1.** *F:* To be in

one's element, être dans son élément. **2.** Corps *m* simple. **3.** *pl.* Elements, rudiments *m.*

elementary, *a.* Élémentaire. Elementary school, école primaire. *Sch:* E. algebra, rudiments *mpl* d'algèbre.

elephant, *s.* (Bull) elephant, éléphant *m* (mâle). Cow elephant, éléphant femelle. *F:* White elephant, objet inutile et encombrant.

elephant-driver, *s.* Cornac *m.*

elephantine, *a.* **1.** Éléphantin. **2.** (*Of proportions*) Éléphantesque.

elevate, *v.tr.* Élever. **elevated,** *a.* Élevé. E. personage, personnage éminent. *F:* To be slightly elevated, être un peu gris. **elevating,** *a.* Qui élève l'esprit.

elevation, *s.* **1.** Élévation *f* (de qn). **2.** Élévation, éminence *f.* **3.** Élévation ,grandeur *f.*

eleven. **1.** *num. a. & s.* Onze (*m*). They are only e., ils ne sont que onze, *F:* qu'onze. **2.** *s. Sp: Cr:* Équipe *f* de onze joueurs.

eleventh, *num. a. & s.* Onzième. At the eleventh hour, *F:* au dernier moment. (On) the eleventh, le onze.

elf, *s.* Elfe *m*; lutin *m,* lutine *f.*

elfin, *a.* D'elfe, de lutin, de fée.

elfish, *a.* (*a*) Des elfes. (*b*) Espiègle.

elicit, *v.tr.* Faire jaillir; découvrir. To e. the facts, tirer les faits au clair. To e. a reply from s.o., tirer une réponse de qn.

elide, *v.tr.* Élider.

eligible, *a.* **1.** Éligible (*to,* à). **2.** E. for an occupation, admissible à un emploi. Eligible young man, jeune homme acceptable.

Elijah. *Pr.n.* *B.Hist:* Élie *m.*

eliminate, *v.tr.* Éliminer; supprimer, écarter.

elimination, *s.* Élimination *f.*

Elisha. *Pr.n.* *B.Hist:* Élisée *m.*

elision, *s.* Élision *f.*

elixir, *s.* Élixir *m.*

elk, *s.* *Z:* Élan *m.*

ell, *s.* Aune *f.*

ellipse, *s.* *Geom:* Ellipse *f.*

ellipsis, *s.* *Gram:* Ellipse *f.*

elliptic(al), *a.* Elliptique.

elm, *s.* Orme *m.*

elocution, *s.* Élocution *f,* diction *f.*

elongate, *v.tr.* Allonger, étendre.

elope, *v.i.* S'enfuir avec un amant. They eloped, ils ont pris la fuite.

elopement, *s.* Fuite *f*; enlèvement (consenti).

eloquence, *s.* Éloquence *f.*

eloquent, *a.* Éloquent. Eloquent look, regard qui en dit long. **-ly,** *adv.* Éloquemment.

else. **1.** *adv.* Autrement; ou bien. **2.** (*a*) *a. or adv.* Anyone else, (i) toute autre personne; tout autre. (ii) *Did you see anybody else?* avez-vous vu encore quelqu'un? Anything else, (i) n'importe quoi d'autre. (ii) *Anything else, madam?* et avec cela, madame? Someone else, quelqu'un d'autre, un autre.

Something else, autre chose *m*. **Nothing else,** rien *m* d'autre. *Nothing else, thank you,* plus rien, merci. *What else can I do?* que puis-je faire d'autre, de mieux? **Everything else,** tout le reste. (*b*) *adv.* **Everywhere else,** partout ailleurs. **Somewhere else,** autre part ; ailleurs.
elsewhere, *adv.* Ailleurs ; autre part.
elucidate, *v.tr.* Élucider, éclaircir.
elucidation, *s.* Élucidation *f* ; éclaircissement *m* (of, de).
elude, *v.tr.* Éluder (une question) ; tourner (la loi) ; échapper à (la poursuite).
elusive, *a.* Insaisissable, intangible. **Elusive reply,** réponse évasive.
elusory, *a.* Évasif.
emaciated, *a.* Émacié, amaigri, décharné.
emaciation, *s* Amaigrissement *m*, émaciation *f*.
emanate, *v.i.* Émaner (*from*, de).
emanation, *s.* Émanation *f*.
emancipate, *v.tr.* Émanciper.
emancipation, *s.* Émancipation *f*.
embalm, *v.tr.* **1.** Embaumer (un cadavre). **2.** Embaumer, parfumer (l'air). **embalming,** *s.* Embaumement *m*.
embankment, *s.* (*a*) Digue *f* ; levée *f* de terre. (*b*) Talus *m* ; remblai *m*. **River embankment,** berge *f*, quai *m*, d'un fleuve.
embargo, *s.* Embargo *m*, séquestre *m*.
embark. **1.** *v.tr.* Embarquer **2.** *v.i.* S'embarquer.
embarkation, *s.* Embarquement *m*.
embarrass, *v.tr.* Embarrasser, gêner ; déconcerter. **embarrassed,** *a.* Embarrassé ; gêné ; dans l'embarras.
embarrassment, *s.* Embarras *m*, gêne *f*.
embassy, *s.* Ambassade *f*.
embellish, *v.tr.* Embellir, orner.
embellishment, *s.* Embellissement *m*, ornement *m*, agrément *m*.
ember, *s.* (*Usu. pl.*) Braise *f* ; charbon (ardent) ; *pl.* cendres ardentes.
embezzle, *v.tr.* Détourner, s'approprier.
embezzlement, *s.* Détournement *m* de fonds.
embezzler, *s.* Détourneur *m* de fonds.
embitter, *v.tr.* Remplir d'amertume ; aigrir ; envenimer, aggraver. **embittered,** *a.* Aigri (*by*, par).
emblem, *s.* Emblème *m*, symbole *m*.
emblematic(al), *a.* Emblématique.
embodiment, *s.* Incorporation *f* ; incarnation *f* ; personnification *f*.
embody, *v.tr.* **1.** Incarner. **2.** Réaliser (une conception) ; personnifier (une qualité). **3.** Incorporer.
embolden, *v.tr.* Enhardir.
emboss, *v.tr.* Graver en relief ; repousser. **embossing,** *s* Bosselage *m* ; repoussage *m*.
embrace[1]**,** *s.* Étreinte *f*, embrassement *m*.
embrace[2]**,** *v.tr.* **1.** Embrasser, étreindre. **2.** Embrasser ; adopter (une cause) ; saisir (une occasion). **3.** Embrasser (*in*, dans) ;

contenir, renfermer (*in*, dans) ; comporter, comprendre.
embroider, *v.tr.* Broder.
embroidery, *s.* Broderie *f*.
embroil, *v.tr.* **1.** To embroil a nation in a war, entraîner une nation dans une guerre. **2.** To embroil s.o. with s.o., brouiller qn avec qn.
embryo, *s.* *Biol:* Embryon *m*. In embryo, *F:* (avocat) en herbe.
emend, *v.tr.* Corriger (un texte).
emendation, *s.* Émendation *f*.
emerald, *s.* Émeraude *f*. **emerald-green,** *a. & s.* Vert (*m*) d'émeraude.
emerge, *v.i.* **1.** Émerger (*from* de) ; surgir (de l'eau). **2.** Déboucher (*from*, de) ; sortir (d'un trou). **3.** (*Of difficulty*) Se dresser ; surgir.
emergency, *s.* Circonstance *f* critique ; cas urgent. To provide for emergencies, parer aux éventualités, à l'imprévu. In this emergency, en cette conjoncture. In case of emergency, au besoin. Emergency repairs, réparations d'urgence. Emergency-exit, sortie éventuelle, de secours.
emery, *s.* Émeri *m*.
emetic, *a. & s.* Émétique (*m*).
emigrant, *a. & s.* Émigrant, -ante.
emigrate, *v.i.* Émigrer.
emigration, *s.* Émigration *f*.
eminence, *s.* Éminence *f*. **1.** Élévation *f* ; monticule *m*. **2.** Grandeur *f*, distinction *f*. **3.** *Ecc:* Your E., votre Éminence.
eminent, *a.* Éminent. **-ly,** *adv.* Éminemment ; par excellence.
emir, *s.* Émir *m*.
emissary, *s.* Émissaire *m*.
emission, *s.* Émission *f*.
emit, *v.tr.* Dégager, émettre (de la chaleur) ; exhaler, répandre (une odeur) ; lancer (des étincelles) ; rendre (un son).
emollient, *a. & s.* Émollient (*m*).
emolument, *s.* (*Usu. pl.*) Émoluments *mpl*, appointements *mpl*, traitement *m*.
emotion, *s.* Émotion *f* ; trouble *m*, attendrissement *m*.
emperor, *s.* Empereur *m*.
emphasis, *s.* **1.** Force *f* ; (énergie *f* d')accentuation *f*. **2.** To lay emphasis on a fact, souligner un fait. **3.** *Ling:* Accent *m* d'insistance.
emphasize, *v.tr.* Accentuer, appuyer sur, souligner (un fait).
emphatic, *a.* Énergique ; (ton) autoritaire ; (refus) positif. **-ally,** *adv.* Énergiquement, positivement.
empire, *s.* Empire *m*.
empiric(al), *a.* Empirique. **-ally,** *adv.* Empiriquement.
emplane. **1.** *v.i.* Monter en avion. **2.** *v.tr.* Faire monter en avion.
employ[1]**,** *s.* Emploi *m*. To be in s.o.'s e., être au service de qn.

employ², *v.tr.* **1.** Employer; faire usage de (la force). **2.** To employ oneself (in doing sth.), s'occuper (à faire qch.).

employee, *s.* Employé, -ée.

employer, *s.* *Ind:* Patron, patronne; maître, maîtresse. *The employers of labour*, les employeurs de main-d'œuvre.

employment, *s.* **1.** Emploi *m* (de qch.). **2.** Emploi, travail *m*; place *f*, occupation *f*. To be out of employment, être sans emploi; chômer.

empower, *v.tr.* To e. s.o. to do sth., autoriser qn à faire qch.

empress, *s* Impératrice *f*.

emptiness, *s.* Vide *m*.

empty¹. **1.** *a.* Vide (*of*, de). (a) E. stomach, estomac creux. (b) E. words, vaines paroles. E. threats, menaces en l'air. **2.** *s.pl. Com:* Empties, caisses *f* vides. **empty-handed**, *a.* Les mains vides. **To return empty-handed**, *F:* revenir bredouille.

empty². **1.** *v.tr.* Vider; décharger. **2.** *v.i.* (a) Se décharger, se déverser (*into*, dans). (b) Se dégarnir, se vider.

emu, *s.* *Orn:* Émeu *m*.

emulate, *v.tr.* Être l'émule de; rivaliser avec, imiter.

emulation, *s.* Émulation *f*.

emulous, *a.* Émulateur, -trice (*of*, de).

emulsion, *s.* Émulsion *f*.

enable, *v.tr.* To enable s.o. to do sth., mettre qn à même de faire qch.

enact, *v.tr* **1.** Ordonner, décréter. **2.** *Lit:* Jouer, représenter; accomplir.

enactment, *s.* Loi *f*, ordonnance *f*; décret *m*.

enamel¹, *s.* Émail *m*, *pl.* émaux.

enamel², *v.tr.* Émailler. **Enamelled saucepan**, casserole en fer émaillé.

enamour, *v.tr.* To be enamoured of s.o., of sth., être amoureux de qn, féru de qch.

encampment, *s.* Campement *m*; camp *m*.

enchant, *v.tr.* **1.** Enchanter, ensorceler. **2.** Enchanter, charmer, ravir. **enchanting**, *a.* Enchanteur, -eresse; ravissant, charmant. **-ly**, *adv.* A ravir.

enchanter, *s.* Enchanteur *m*.

enchantment, *s.* Enchantement *m*. **1.** Ensorcellement *m*. **2.** Ravissement *m*.

enchantress, *s.* Enchanteresse *f*.

encircle, *v.tr.* Ceindre, encercler; envelopper. **encircling**, *s.* Encerclement *m*.

enclose, *v.tr.* **1.** Enclore, clôturer, enceindre (*with*, de). **2.** Inclure, renfermer, enfermer (*in*, dans). **Enclosed (herewith) please find**, veuillez trouver ci-inclus.

enclosure, *s.* **1.** (a) Renfermement *m*, clôture *f*. (b) Enceinte *f*, clôture. **2.** Enclos *m*, clos *m*. **3.** *Com:* Pièce annexée; annexe *f*.

encompass, *v.tr.* **1.** Entourer, environner, ceindre. **2.** Consommer (la mort de qn).

encore¹, *s. & int.* Bis *m*.

encore², *v.tr.* Bisser.

encounter¹, *s.* **1.** Rencontre *f*. **2.** Rencontre (hostile); combat *m*.

encounter², *v.tr.* Rencontrer (un obstacle);

éprouver, essuyer (des difficultés); affronter, aborder (l'ennemi).

encourage, *v.tr.* **1.** Encourager, enhardir. **2.** Encourager, inciter. **3.** Favoriser. **encouraging**, *a.* Encourageant. **-ly**, *adv.* D'une manière encourageante.

encouragement, *s.* Encouragement *m*.

encroach, *v.i.* To e. (*up*)on sth., empiéter sur (une terre). *To e. upon s.o.'s time*, abuser du temps de qn.

encroachment, *s.* Empiétement *m* (*on*, sur).

encumber, *v.tr.* **1.** Encombrer (*with*, de); embarrasser, gêner (qn). **2.** **Encumbered estate**, propriété grevée de dettes.

encumbrance, *s.* Embarras *m*, charge *f*. To be an e. to s.o., être à charge à qn.

encyclopaedia, *s.* Encyclopédie *f*.

encyclopaedic, *a.* Encyclopédique.

end¹, *s.* **1.** Bout *m*, extrémité *f*; fin *f*. The end house of the street, la dernière maison de la rue. *F:* To have hold of the wrong end of the stick, comprendre de travers. *F:* To keep one's end up, ne pas se laisser démonter; tenir bon *Adv.phrs.* End to end, bout à bout. From end to end, d'un bout à l'autre; de bout en bout. On end. (i) Debout; sur bout. (ii) Two hours on end, (pendant) deux heures de suite. **2.** Limite *f*, borne *f*. To the ends of the earth, jusqu'au bout du monde. **3.** Bout, fin (du mois); issue *f* (d'une réunion). We shall never hear the end of the matter, cela va être des commérages sans fin. And there's an end of it! et voilà tout! To make an end of sth., en finir avec qch. To come to an end, prendre fin; arriver à son terme. In the end, (i) à la longue, avec le temps; (ii) à la fin; enfin. *F:* No end, à n'en plus finir. No end of, infiniment de. It'll do you no end of good, ça vous fera énormément de bien. No end of books, des livres sans nombre. No end of money, un argent fou. To think no end of s.o., avoir une très haute idée de qn. To come to a bad end, mal finir. To meet one's end, trouver la mort. **4.** Fin, but *m*, dessein *m*. Private ends, intérêt(s) personnel(s). With this end in view, dans cette intention; à cet effet. To no end, en vain; vainement.

end². **1.** *v.tr.* Finir, achever, terminer; conclure, clore (un discours). In order to end the matter, pour en finir. **2.** *v.i.* Finir, se terminer. He ended by insulting me, il finit par m'injurier. To end in a point, se terminer en pointe. **ended**, *a.* Fini, terminé.

ending, *s.* **1.** Terminaison *f*, achèvement *m*. **2.** Fin *f*, conclusion *f*.

endanger, *v.tr.* Mettre en danger; exposer, hasarder, risquer.

endear, *v.tr.* Rendre cher (*to*, à). **endearing**, *a.* **1.** Qui inspire l'affection. **2.** (Mot) tendre, affectueux.

endeavour¹, *s.* Effort *m*, tentative *f*.

endeavour[2], *v.i.* *To e. to do sth.*, s'efforcer, essayer, tâcher, de faire qch.

endless, *a.* **1.** (*a*) Sans fin. (*b*) Sans bornes; infini. **2.** (*a*) Sans fin; éternel. *It is an e. task*, c'est à n'en plus finir. (*b*) Continuel, incessant. **-ly**, *adv.* Sans fin; sans cesse.

endorse, *v.tr.* **1.** Endosser. **2.** Appuyer; souscrire à.

endorsement, *s.* **1.** Endossement *m*. **2.** Approbation *f.*

endow, *v.tr.* Doter (*with*, de). *Endowed with great talents*, doué de grands talents.

endowment, *s.* **1.** (*a*) Dotation *f.* (*b*) Fondation *f.* **2.** Don (naturel).

endue, *v.tr.* *To be endued with a quality*, être doué d'une qualité.

endurance, *s.* **1.** Endurance *f* résistance *f. Beyond endurance*, insupportable, intolérable. **2.** Patience *f.*

endure. 1. *v.tr.* Supporter, endurer. **2.** *v.i.* Durer, rester. **enduring**, *a.* **1.** Durable, permanent. **2.** Patient, longanime, endurant.

enemy, *s.* (*a*) Ennemi, -e. *To be one's own (worst) enemy*, se desservir soi-même. (*b*) *Coll.* **The enemy**, l'ennemi, l'adversaire *m.*

energetic, *a.* Énergique. **-ally**, *adv.* Énergiquement.

energy, *s.* Énergie *f*, force *f*, vigueur *f.*

enervate, *v.tr.* Affaiblir, amollir, énerver.

enervation, *s.* **1.** Affaiblissement *m*, aveulissement *m.* **2.** Mollesse *f.*

enfeeble, *v.tr.* Affaiblir (qn).

enfold, *v.tr.* Envelopper (*in, with*, dans).

enforce, *v.tr.* **1.** Faire valoir; appuyer (une demande). **2.** Mettre en vigueur, exécuter. *To enforce one's rights*, faire valoir ses droits. *To enforce the law*, appliquer la loi. **3.** *To e. a rule*, faire observer un règlement. *To enforce obedience*, se faire obéir.

enforcement, *s.* *Jur:* Exécution *f*, mise *f* en vigueur, application *f.*

enfranchisement, *s.* Admission *f* au suffrage.

engage, *v.tr. & i.* **1.** Engager. *To engage to do sth.*, s'engager à faire qch. **2.** (*a*) Engager, prendre (un domestique). (*b*) Retenir, réserver (une chambre); louer (un taxi). **3.** Occuper. *To engage s.o. in conversation*, lier conversation avec qn. **4.** *To engage the enemy*, en venir aux prises avec, attaquer, l'ennemi. **engaged**, *a.* **1.** Engaged (*to be married*), fiancé. *To become e.*, se fiancer. **2.** Occupé, pris. *Are you engaged?* êtes-vous occupé? (*to taxi-driver*) êtes-vous libre? **3.** *This seat is engaged*, cette place est retenue, prise. *Tp:* 'Line engaged,' "ligne occupée." **engaging**, *a.* Engageant, attrayant, séduisant.

engagement, *s.* **1.** Engagement *m*, promesse *f*, obligation *f.* *To have an engagement*, être pris. **2.** (*a*) Engagement (de domestiques). (*b*) Poste *m*, situation *f* (de domestique). **3.** Fiançailles *fpl.* **4.** Combat *m*, action *f.*

engender, *v.tr.* Engendrer.

engine, *s.* **1.** Machine *f*, appareil *m.* **2.** (*a*) (Steam-)engine, machine à vapeur. (*b*) *Rail:* Locomotive *f.* **3.** Moteur *m.* **engine-driver**, *s.* Mécanicien *m.*

engineer[1], *s.* **1.** Ingénieur *m.* **Mining engineer**, ingénieur des mines. **Electrical engineer**, ingénieur électricien. **2.** *Nau:* Mécanicien *m.* **3.** *Mil:* Soldat *m* du génie. *The Engineers*, le génie.

engineer[2], *v.tr.* Machiner (un coup).

engineering, *s.* (i) Le génie; (ii) la construction mécanique.

England. *Pr.n.* L'Angleterre *f.*

English. 1. *a. & s.* Anglais, -aise. **2.** *s. Ling:* L'anglais *m*; la langue anglaise.

Englishman, *s.* Anglais *m.*

Englishwoman, *s.* Anglaise *f.*

engrave, *v.tr.* Graver. **engraving**, *s.* Gravure *f*; (*print*) estampe *f.*

engraver, *s.* Graveur *m.*

engross, *v.tr.* **1.** *Jur:* Rédiger. **2.** S'emparer de, accaparer. **3.** Absorber, occuper. *To become engrossed in sth.*, s'absorber dans qch.

engulf, *v.tr.* Engloutir, engouffrer.

enhance, *v.tr.* Rehausser; augmenter (le plaisir); relever (la beauté de qn).

enigma, *s.* Énigme *f.*

enigmatic(al), *a.* Énigmatique.

enjoin, *v.tr.* Enjoindre, prescrire, imposer. *To enjoin prudence (up)on s.o.*, recommander la prudence à qn.

enjoy, *v.tr.* **1.** Aimer, goûter; prendre plaisir à. *To enjoy one's dinner*, trouver le dîner bon. *To enjoy oneself*, s'amuser, se divertir. *To enjoy doing sth.*, prendre plaisir à faire qch. **2.** Jouir de, posséder.

enjoyable, *a.* Agréable. **-ably**, *adv.* Agréablement.

enjoyment, *s.* **1.** *Jur:* Jouissance *f.* **2.** Plaisir *m.*

enlarge. 1. *v.tr.* (*a*) Agrandir; élargir (un trou). (*b*) Développer; amplifier. **2.** *v.i. To enlarge upon*, s'étendre sur.

enlargement, *s.* Agrandissement *m.*

enlighten, *v.tr.* Éclairer. **enlightened**, *a.* Éclairé.

enlightenment, *s.* Éclaircissements *mpl* (*on*, sur).

enlist. 1. *v.tr.* (*a*) Enrôler. *To enlist the services of s.o.*, s'assurer le concours de qn. **2.** *v.i.* S'engager, s'enrôler.

enlistment, *s.* Engagement *m*, enrôlement *m.*

enliven, *v.tr.* (*a*) Animer; stimuler. (*b*) Égayer.

enmity, *s.* Inimitié *f*, hostilité *f.*

ennoble, *v.tr.* **1.** Anoblir. **2.** Ennoblir (le caractère).

enormity, *s.* Énormité *f.*

enormous, *a.* Énorme. **-ly**, *adv.* Énormément.

enough. 1. *a. & s.* Assez. *E. money*, assez d'argent. *F:* *I've had enough of it*, j'en ai assez. *That's e.*, (i) cela suffit ; (ii) en voilà assez ! **More than enough,** plus qu'il n'en faut. **Have you enough to pay the bill ?** avez-vous de quoi payer ? **Enough said !** assez parlé ! brisons là ! *It was e. to drive one crazy,* c'était à vous rendre fou. **2.** *adv.* (*a*) **Good enough,** assez bon. (*b*) **You know well enough what I mean,** vous savez très bien ce que je veux dire. **Curiously enough,** chose curieuse. **She sings well enough,** elle chante passablement.

enquire, *v.* = INQUIRE.

enquiry, *s.* = INQUIRY.

enrage, *v.tr.* Rendre furieux ; faire enrager.

enrapture, *v.tr.* Ravir, enchanter.

enrich, *v.tr.* Enrichir.

enrichment, *s.* Enrichissement *m.*

enrol(l), *v.tr.* Enrôler ; immatriculer (des étudiants).

ensconce, *v.tr.* **To ensconce oneself** *in an armchair,* se camper dans un fauteuil.

ensign, *s.* Étendard *m*, drapeau *m. Nau :* Pavillon national.

enslave, *v.tr.* Réduire à l'esclavage ; asservir.

enslavement, *s.* Asservissement *m.*

ensnare, *v.tr.* Prendre au piège.

ensue, *v.i.* S'ensuivre. **A long silence ensued,** il se fit un long silence. **ensuing,** *a.* Suivant ; subséquent.

ensure, *v.tr.* **1.** Assurer (*against, from,* contre) ; garantir (de). **2.** Assurer (le succès).

entail[1], *s. Jur :* Substitution *f.*

entail[2], *v.tr.* **1.** *Jur :* **To entail an estate,** substituer un bien. **2.** Amener, entraîner (des conséquences) ; occasionner (des dépenses).

entangle, *v.tr.* **1.** Empêtrer. **2.** Emmêler ; enchevêtrer.

entanglement, *s.* Embrouillement *m*, enchevêtrement *m.*

enter, *v.* **I.** *v.i.* Entrer (*into, through,* dans, par). **II. enter,** *v.tr.* **1.** Entrer, pénétrer, dans (une maison) ; monter dans (une voiture). **2. To enter the Army,** se faire soldat. **3.** (*a*) **To enter a name on a list,** inscrire un nom sur une liste. **To enter a horse for a race,** engager un cheval dans une course. *Abs.* **To enter for a race,** se faire inscrire pour une course. (*b*) **To enter an action against s.o.,** intenter un procès à qn. **To e. a protest,** protester formellement. **enter into,** *v.i.* **1. To enter into explanations,** fournir des explications ; s'expliquer. **2. To enter into s.o.'s feelings,** partager les sentiments de qn. **enter on, upon,** *v.i.* Entrer en (fonctions) ; entreprendre (une tâche) ; débuter dans (une carrière) ; entamer (des négociations).

enterprise, *s.* **1.** Entreprise *f.* **2.** Esprit entreprenant.

enterprising, *a.* Entreprenant.

entertain, *v.tr.* **1.** Amuser, divertir. **2.** Régaler, fêter. *Abs.* **They entertain a great deal,**

ils reçoivent beaucoup. **3.** Admettre, accueillir (une proposition). **4.** Concevoir (une idée) ; éprouver (des craintes) ; nourrir, caresser (un espoir). **entertaining,** *a.* Amusant, divertissant.

entertainer, *s.* Hôte *m*, hôtesse *f.*

entertainment, *s.* **1.** (*a*) Divertissement *m.* (*b*) *Th :* Spectacle *m.* **2.** Hospitalité *f.*

enthral(l), *v.tr.* Captiver, charmer, ensorceler.

enthrone, *v.tr.* Mettre sur le trône.

enthusiasm, *s.* Enthousiasme *m* (*for, about,* pour).

enthusiast, *s.* Enthousiaste *mf* (*for,* de). *Golf e.,* fervent(e) du golf.

enthusiastic, *a.* Enthousiaste. **To become e. over sth.,** s'enthousiasmer sur qch. **-ally,** *adv.* Avec enthousiasme.

entice, *v.tr.* Attirer, séduire. **enticing,** *a.* Séduisant, attrayant, alléchant.

enticement, *s.* **1.** Séduction *f.* **2.** Attrait *m*, charme *m.* **3.** Appât *m.*

entire, *a.* (*a*) Entier, tout. (*b*) Entier, complet. **-ly,** *adv.* Entièrement, tout à fait.

entirety, *s.* Intégralité *f.* **In its entirety,** en entier ; totalement.

entitle, *v.tr.* **1.** Intituler (un livre). **2.** *To e. s.o. to do sth.,* donner à qn le droit de faire qch. **entitled,** *a.* **To be entitled to sth.,** avoir droit à qch. **To be entitled to do sth.,** avoir qualité pour faire qch.

entity, *s.* Entité *f.*

entomb, *v.tr.* Mettre au tombeau ; enterrer, ensevelir.

entomological, *a.* Entomologique.

entomology, *s.* Entomologie *f.*

entrails, *s.pl.* Entrailles *f.*

entrance[1], *s.* **1.** Entrée *f.* (*a*) *To make one's e.,* faire son entrée. (*b*) Admission *f*, accès *m.* **2. Main entrance,** entrée principale. **entrance-fee,** *s.* (*a*) Prix *m* d'entrée. (*b*) Droit *m* d'inscription.

entrance[2], *v.tr.* Extasier, ravir, transporter. **entrancing,** *a.* Enchanteur, -eresse ; ravissant.

entrap, *v.tr.* Prendre au piège.

entreat, *v.tr.* **To entreat s.o. to do sth.,** prier, supplier, qn de faire qch. **entreating,** *a.* Suppliant.

entreaty, *s.* Prière *f*, supplication *f.* **Look of entreaty,** regard suppliant.

entrench, *v.tr.* Retrancher (un camp).

entrenchment, *s.* *Mil :* Retranchement *m.*

entrust, *v.tr.* **To entrust s.o. with sth.,** charger qn (d'une tâche). **To entrust sth. to s.o.,** confier (un enfant) à qn.

entry, *s.* **1.** (*a*) Entrée *f.* **'No entry,'** "sens interdit." (*b*) **To make one's entry,** faire son entrée. (*c*) Début *m.* **2.** (*a*) Enregistrement *m* ; inscription *f. Book-k :* **Double entry,** comptabilité *f* en partie double. **3.** *Sp :* Engagement *m*, inscription.

entwine. 1. *v.tr.* (*a*) Entrelacer. (*b*) Enlacer (*with,* de). **2.** *v.i.* S'entrelacer.

enumerate, *v.tr.* Énumérer, détailler.
enumeration, *s.* Énumération *f*, dénombrement *m*.
enunciate, *v.tr.* **1.** Énoncer, exprimer. **2.** Prononcer, articuler.
envelop, *v.tr.* Envelopper (*in*, dans, de).
envelope, *s.* Enveloppe *f*. *To put a letter in an e.*, mettre une lettre sous enveloppe.
envenom, *v.tr.* Envenimer, aigrir.
enviable, *a.* Enviable ; digne d'envie.
envious, *a.* Envieux. *E. looks*, regards d'envie. *To be e. of s.o.*, porter envie à qn. **-ly,** *adv.* Avec envie.
environment, *s.* Milieu *m*, entourage *m* ; ambiance *f*, environnement *m*.
environs, *s.pl.* Environs *m*, alentours *m*.
envisage, *v.tr.* Envisager.
envoy, *s.* Envoyé, -ée.
envy[1], *s.* **1.** Envie *f*. *To be green with envy*, être dévoré d'envie. **2.** *To be the envy of s.o.* faire envie à qn.
envy[2], *v.tr.* Envier, porter envie a. *To envy s.o. sth.*, envier qch. à qn.
epaulet(te), *s.* Épaulette *f*.
ephemeral, *a.* Éphémère.
epic. **1.** *a.* Épique. **2.** *s.* Poème *m* épique ; épopée *f*.
epicure, *s.* Gourmet *m*, gastronome *m*.
epicurean, *a. & s.* Épicurien, -ienne.
epidemic. **1.** *a.* Épidémique. **2.** *s.* Épidémie *f*.
epidermis, *s.* *Anat :* Épiderme *m*.
epigram, *s.* Épigramme *f*.
epilepsy, *s.* Épilepsie *f*.
epileptic, *a. & s.* Épileptique (*mf*). *Epileptic fit*, crise *f* d'épilepsie.
epilogue, *s.* Épilogue *m*.
Epiphany, *s.* *Ecc :* L'Épiphanie *f* ; *F :* le jour, la fête, des Rois.
episcopal, *a.* Épiscopal, -aux.
episode, *s.* Épisode *m*.
epistle, *s.* Épître *f*.
epitaph, *s.* Épitaphe *f*.
epithet, *s.* Épithète *f*.
epitome, *s.* Épitomé *m*, abrégé *m*, résumé *m* ; raccourci *m*.
epitomize, *v.tr.* Abréger, résumer.
epoch, *s.* Époque *f*, âge *m*.
Epsom. *Pr.n.* **Epsom salts,** sulfate *m* de magnésie.
equability, *s.* Uniformité *f* (de climat) ; égalité *f*, régularité *f* (d'humeur).
equable, *a.* Uniforme, régulier. **Equable temperament,** humeur égale.
equal[1]. **1.** *a.* (*a*) Égal, -aux (*to*, *with*, à). *To be on e. terms*, être sur un pied d'égalité. *All things being equal*, toutes choses égales. *F :* *To get equal with s.o.*, se venger de qn. (*b*) **To be equal to the occasion,** être à la hauteur de la situation. **To be equal to doing sth.**, être de force à faire qch. **2.** *s.* Égal, -ale ; pair *m*. **Your equals**, vos pareils, vos égaux.

To treat s.o. as an equal, traiter qn d'égal à égal. **-ally,** *adv.* Également, pareillement.
equal[2], *v.tr.* Égaler (*in*, en).
equality, *s.* Égalité *f*. **On an equality,** sur un pied d'égalité.
equalization, *s.* **1.** Égalisation *f*. **2.** Compensation *f* ; équilibrage *m*.
equalize, *v.tr.* (*a*) Égaliser (*b*) *Fb :* Compenser, équilibrer.
equanimity, *s.* Égalité *f* d'âme, de caractère ; tranquillité *f* d'esprit ; équanimité *f*.
equation, *s.* Équation *f*.
equator, *s.* Équateur *m*. *At the e.*, sous l'équateur.
equatorial, *a.* Équatorial, -aux.
equestrian. **1.** *a.* Équestre. **2.** *s.* Cavalier, -ière.
equilateral, *a.* Équilatéral, -aux.
equilibrium, *s.* Équilibre *m*, aplomb *m*.
equine, *a.* Équin ; de cheval.
equinoctial, *a.* Équinoxial, -aux.
equinox, *s.* Équinoxe *m*.
equip, *v.tr.* **1.** Équiper, armer. **2.** Meubler, monter (une maison). *To e. s.o. with sth.*, munir qn de qch.
equipage, *s.* Équipage *m*.
equipment, *s.* **1.** Équipement *m* (d'une expédition) ; outillage *m* (d'une usine) ; installation *f* (d'un laboratoire). **2.** Équipement ; équipage *m*. **Camping equipment,** matériel *m* de campement. *A soldier's e.*, les effets *m* d'un soldat.
equitable, *a.* Équitable, juste. **-ably,** *adv.* Équitablement ; avec justice.
equity, *s.* Équité *f*, justice *f*.
equivalence, *s.* Équivalence *f*.
equivalent, *a. & s.* Équivalent (*m*).
equivocal, *a.* Équivoque. (*a*) Ambigu, -uë. (*b*) Incertain, douteux. (*c*) Suspect, douteux ; louche. **-ally,** *adv.* D'une manière équivoque.
equivocate, *v.i.* User d'équivoque ; équivoquer.
equivocation, *s.* Équivocation *f*.
era, *s.* Ère *f*.
eradicate, *v.tr.* *F :* Extirper, déraciner.
eradication, *s.* *F :* Extirpation *f*.
erase, *v.tr.* Effacer.
eraser, *s.* (*a*) Grattoir *m*. (*b*) *Ink e.*, gomme *f* à encre
erasure, *s.* Rature *f* ; grattage *m*.
ere. **1.** *prep.* Avant. *Ere now*, auparavant, déjà. **2.** *conj.* Avant que + *sub.*
erect[1], *a.* (*Of pers.*) Droit. **With tail erect,** la queue levée. **With head e.,** la tête haute.
erect[2], *v.tr.* **1.** Dresser (un mât). **2.** Ériger, construire (un édifice) ; dresser (un échafaudage).
erection, *s.* **1.** (*a*) Dressage *m* (d'un mât). (*b*) Construction *f* (d'un édifice). **2.** Bâtisse *f*, construction.

ermine, *s.* **I.** *Z:* Hermine *f.* **2.** (*Fur*) Hermine.

erode, *v.tr.* Éroder ; ronger (la côte).

erosion, *s.* Érosion *f* ; affouillement *m.*

erotic, *a* Érotique.

err, *v.i.* (*a*) S'égarer, s'écarter (*from*, de). (*b*) Pécher. (*c*) Errer ; se tromper **erring,** *a.* Dévoyé, égaré.

errand, *s.* Commission *f*, course *f.* **errand-boy,** *s.* Garçon *m* de courses.

errant, *a.* Errant.

erratic, *a.* **I.** Irrégulier. **2.** (*Of pers.*) Excentrique, velléitaire. **-ally,** *adv.* Sans méthode, sans règle.

erroneous, *a.* Erroné ; faux, *f.* fausse. **-ly,** *adv.* Erronément ; par erreur.

error, *s.* **I.** Erreur *f*, faute *f*, méprise *f.* Printer's error, faute d'impression. Clerical error, erreur de plume. *It is an e. to suppose that . . .,* on aurait tort de le croire que. . . . **2.** To be in error, être dans l'erreur ; avoir tort. **3.** Écart *m* (de conduite).

erudite, *a.* Érudit, savant.

erudition, *s.* Érudition *f.*

erupt, *v.i.* Entrer en éruption ; faire éruption.

eruption, *s.* (*a*) Éruption *f.* (*b*) Éclat *m*, accès *m* (de colère).

escalade¹, *s.* Escalade *f.*

escalade², *v.tr.* Escalader.

escalator, *s.* Escalier roulant.

escapade, *s.* Escapade *f* ; *F:* frasque *f.*

escape¹, *s.* (*a*) Fuite *f*, évasion *f.* To make one's escape, s'échapper, se sauver. To have a narrow escape, l'échapper belle. Way of escape, issue *f.* (*b*) Échappement *m*, fuite.

escape², **I.** *v.i.* (*a*) (S')échapper (*from, out of*, de) ; prendre la fuite. *To e. from prison,* s'évader. (*b*) To escape by the skin of one's teeth, échapper tout juste (*c*) Se dégager ; s'échapper. **2.** *v.tr.* (*a*) Échapper à (un danger). He just escaped being killed, il a manqué (de) se faire tuer. (*b*) To escape notice, échapper à l'attention ; passer inaperçu.

eschew, *v.tr.* Éviter ; renoncer à.

escort¹, *s.* Escorte *f* ; *F:* (*to a lady*) cavalier *m.*

escort², *v.tr.* Escorter, faire escorte à ; servir de cavalier à (une dame).

Eskimo, *a. & s.* Esquimau (*m*), -aux. E. woman, femme esquimau.

esparto(-grass), *s.* Spart(e) *m* ; alfa *m.*

especial, *a.* Spécial, -aux ; particulier. In especial, surtout ; en particulier. **-ally,** *adv.* Surtout, particulièrement. (*More*) e. as, d'autant plus que.

espionage, *s.* Espionnage *m.*

esplanade, *s.* Esplanade *f.*

espousal, *s.* Espousal of a cause, adhésion *f* à une cause.

espouse, *v.tr.* Épouser.

espy, *v.tr.* Apercevoir, aviser.

esquire, *s.* W. *Smith, Esq.* = Monsieur W. Smith.

essay¹, **I.** Essai *m*, effort *m* ; tentative *f* (*at, de*) **2.** (*a*) *Lit:* Essai. (*b*) *Sch:* Dissertation *f* ; composition *f* (littéraire)

essay², *v.tr* Essayer (de faire qch.)

essence, *s.* Essence *f.* The essence of the matter, le fond de l'affaire.

essential. **I.** *a.* Essentiel, indispensable ; capital, -aux. It is essential that . . ., il est indispensable que + *sub.* **2.** *s.* L'essentiel. **-ally,** *adv.* Essentiellement.

establish, *v.tr.* **I.** Établir (un gouvernement) ; édifier (un système) ; fonder (une maison de commerce). **2.** Établir, constater (un fait) ; démontrer (l'identité de qn). **established** *a.* Établi ; (réputation) solide ; (fait) avéré, acquis.

establishment, *s.* **I.** (*a*) Constatation *f* (d'un fait). (*b*) Établissement *m* (d'une industrie) ; création *f* (d'un système) ; fondation *f* (d'une maison de commerce). **2.** Établissement, maison *f.* **3.** Personnel *m.*

estate, *s.* **I.** État *m*, condition *f.* **2.** Rang *m*, condition. **3.** (*a*) Bien *m*, domaine *m.* (*b*) Succession *f* (d'un défunt). **4.** (*a*) Terre *f*, propriété *f.* (*b*) Housing estate, cité *f.* **estate-agent,** *s.* Agent *m* de location.

esteem¹, *s.* Estime *f*, considération *f.*

esteem², *v.tr.* **I.** Estimer ; priser. *Com:* Your esteemed favour, votre honorée. **2.** Estimer, considérer (*as*, comme).

estimable, *a.* Estimable.

estimate¹, *s.* **I.** Appréciation *f*, évaluation *f.* *To form a correct e. of sth.,* se faire une idée exacte de qch. *At the lowest e.,* au bas mot. **2.** *Building e.,* devis *m* de construction. *E. of expenditure,* chiffre prévu pour les dépenses.

estimate², *v.tr.* Estimer, évaluer.

estimation, *s.* (*a*) Jugement *m.* In my estimation, à mon avis *m.* (*b*) Estime *f*, considération *f.*

estrange, *v.tr.* To become estranged from s.o., se détacher de qn

estrangement, *s.* Aliénation *f* ; éloignement *m* ; brouille *f* (*between*, entre).

estuary, *s.* Estuaire *m.*

etch, *v.tr.* Graver à l'eau-forte. **etching,** *s.* **I.** Gravure *f* à l'eau-forte. **2.** Eau-forte *f*, *pl.* eaux-fortes.

eternal, *a.* (*a*) Éternel. (*b*) *F:* Continuel ; sans fin. **-ally,** *adv.* Éternellement.

eternity, *s.* Éternité *f*

ether, *s.* Éther *m.*

ethereal, *a.* Éthéré ; impalpable ; qui n'est pas de ce monde.

ethic(al), *a.* Moral, -aux.

ethics, *s.pl.* Éthique *f*, morale *f.*

Ethiopia. *Pr.n.* L'Éthiopie *f.*

ethnology, *s.* Ethnologie *f.*

etiquette, *s.* Étiquette *f* ; convenances *f.*

etymological, *a.* Étymologique.

etymologist, *s.* Étymologiste *mf.*

etymology, s. Étymologie f.
eucalyptus, s. Eucalyptus m.
eucharist (the), s. *Ecc:* L'eucharistie f.
Euclid, s. *F:* Géométrie f (d'Euclide).
eulogist, s. Panégyriste m.
eulogistic(al), a. Élogieux.
eulogize, v.tr. Faire l'éloge de.
eulogy, s. Panégyrique m.
eunuch, s. Eunuque m.
euphemism, s. Euphémisme m.
euphemistic, a. Euphémique. **-ally,** adv. Euphémiquement.
euphony, s. Euphonie f.
Europe. Pr.n. L'Europe f.
European, a. & s. Européen, -enne.
evacuate, v.tr. Évacuer.
evacuation, s. Évacuation f.
evade, v.tr. **I.** Éviter (un coup); se soustraire à (un châtiment); tourner (une question); déjouer (la vigilance de qn). **2.** Échapper à (l'intelligence).
evanescent, a. Évanescent.
evaporate. I. v.tr. Faire évaporer. **2.** v.i. S'évaporer, se vaporiser.
evaporation, s. Évaporation f.
evasion, s. **I.** Évitement m; moyen m d'éluder (une question). **2.** Échappatoire f. *Without e.,* sans détours.
evasive, a. Évasif. **-ly,** adv. Évasivement.
Eve[1]. Pr.n. Ève f.
eve[2], s. Veille f. *On the eve of,* à la veille de.
even[1], a. **I.** Uni; plan; égal, -aux; uniforme. **To make even,** aplanir (une surface). **2.** (Souffle) égal, régulier, uniforme. *Even pace,* allure uniforme. **Even temper,** humeur égale. **3.** *Games:* **To be even,** être manche à manche. *F:* **To get even with s.o.,** rendre la pareille à qn. *I'll be even with him yet,* je le lui revaudrai. **4.** (a) Pair. **Odd or even,** pair ou impair. (b) **Even money,** compte rond. **5.** *Com:* **Of even date,** de même date. **-ly,** adv. **I.** Uniment. **2.** (a) Régulièrement; (diviser) également. (b) **Evenly matched,** de force égale.
even[2], adv. Même; (with comparative) encore; (with negative) seulement, même. *Even the children knew,* les enfants mêmes le savaient. **That would be even worse,** ce serait encore pis. *Without even speaking,* sans seulement parler. **Even so,** mais cependant, quand même, encore.
even[3], v.tr. **I.** Aplanir, égaliser. **2.** Rendre égal. *F:* **That will even things up,** cela rétablira l'équilibre.
evening, s. **I.** Soir m; soirée f. **In the evening,** le soir, au soir. *At nine o'clock in the e.,* à neuf heures du soir. *(On) the previous e.,* la veille au soir. *On the e. of the next day,* le lendemain soir. *One fine summer e.,* (par) un beau soir d'été. *All the e.,* toute la soirée. *Th:* **Evening performance,** représentation de soirée. **2. Musical evening,** soirée musicale.
evening-dress, s. **I.** Habit m (à queue);

tenue f de soirée. **2.** Robe f du soir. **In evening dress,** en toilette de soirée.
evenness, s. **I.** Égalité f; régularité f. **2.** Sérénité f, calme m (d'esprit).
event, s. **I.** Cas m. **In the event of** *his refusing,* au cas, dans le cas, où il refuserait. **2.** Événement m. (a) **In the course of events,** au cours des événements. (b) Issue f, résultat m. **In either event,** dans l'un ou l'autre cas. **Wise after the event,** sage après coup. **At all events,** dans tous les cas; en tout cas. **3.** *Sp:* Épreuve f.
eventful, a. Plein d'événements; mouvementé; (jour) mémorable.
eventual, a. **I.** Éventuel. **2.** Définitif; final, -aux. **-ally,** adv. En fin de compte, par la suite, dans la suite.
eventuality, s. Éventualité f.
ever, adv. **I.** Jamais. (a) *I read seldom if ever,* je ne lis jamais, ou rarement. *He is a liar if ever there was one,* c'est un menteur, s'il en fut jamais. *It started to rain faster than ever,* il se mit à pleuvoir de plus belle. *It is as warm as ever,* il fait toujours aussi chaud. (b) *They lived happy ever after,* depuis lors ils vécurent toujours heureux. (c) **Ever since,** dès lors, depuis (lors). (d) **Ever and again,** de temps en temps. **2.** (a) Toujours. *The river grows ever wider,* le fleuve va s'élargissant. *Corr:* **Yours ever,** à vous de cœur; bien cordialement à vous; tout(e) à vous. (b) **For ever,** pour toujours; à jamais. *Gone for ever,* parti sans retour. **For ever and ever,** à tout jamais. **Scotland for ever!** vive l'Écosse! *To live for ever,* vivre éternellement. **He is for ever grumbling,** il grogne sans cesse. **3.** (a) **As quick as ever you can,** du plus vite que vous pourrez. **Ever so difficult,** difficile au possible. *Ever so long ago,* il y a bien, bien longtemps. *I waited ever so long,* j'ai attendu un temps infini. *Ever so many times,* je ne sais combien de fois. **Thank you ever so much,** merci infiniment. (b) **How ever** *did you manage?* comment diable avez-vous fait? **What ever** *shall we do?* qu'est-ce que nous allons bien faire? *What ever's the matter with you?* mais qu'est-ce que vous avez donc? **Why ever not?** pourquoi pas, grand Dieu!
evergreen. I. a. Toujours vert. **2.** s. **Evergreens,** plantes vertes.
everlasting, a. (a) Éternel. (b) *F:* Perpétuel. *E. complaints,* plaintes sans fin.
every, a. (a) Chaque; tout. **Every day,** chaque jour, tous les jours. **Every other day,** tous les deux jours. **Every few minutes,** *F:* toutes les cinq minutes. *I expect him every minute,* je l'attends d'un instant à l'autre. (b) *F:* *He was every inch a republican,* il était républicain jusqu'au bout des ongles. (c) **Every one,** chacun, chacune; tout le monde. *E. one of us* tous tant que nous sommes.
everybody, indef.pron. = EVERYONE.

everyday, *a.* **1.** Journalier, quotidien. **Everyday life,** la vie quotidienne. **2.** *My e. clothes,* mes vêtements de tous les jours. **3.** Banal, -aux; ordinaire, commun. *Words in e. use,* mots d'usage courant.

everyone, *indef.pron.* Chacun; tout le monde; tous. *E. knows that,* le premier venu sait cela. **Everyone else knows it,** tous les autres le savent.

everything, *indef.pron.* (a) Tout. *E. in its place,* chaque chose *f* à sa place. (b) **Money is everything,** l'argent fait tout.

everywhere, *adv.* Partout; en tout lieu. **Everywhere you go,** partout où vous allez.

evict, *v.tr.* Évincer, expulser (*from,* de).

eviction, *s.* Éviction *f,* expulsion *f.*

evidence[1], *s.* **1.** Évidence *f. F: A man much in e.,* un homme très en vue. **2.** Signe *m,* marque *f.* **3.** (a) Preuve *f.* (b) *Jur:* Témoignage *m.* **To give evidence,** témoigner. **4.** *Jur:* **The evidence for the prosecution,** les témoins *m* à charge.

evidence[2], *v.tr.* Prouver, manifester, démontrer.

evident, *a.* Évident. **-ly,** *adv.* Évidemment, manifestement.

evil. 1. *a.* Mauvais. (a) **Of evil omen,** de mauvais présage. **To fall on evil days,** tomber dans l'infortune. (b) Méchant. *E. spirit,* esprit malfaisant, malin. *E. influence,* influence néfaste. **Evil eye,** mauvais œil. **2.** *s.* Mal *m, pl.* maux. *A social e.,* une plaie sociale. **To speak evil of s.o.,** dire du mal de qn. **evil-doer,** *s.* Malfaiteur, -trice. **evil-looking,** *a.* De mauvaise mine. **evil-minded,** *a.* Porté au mal; malintentionné, malveillant.

evince, *v.tr* Montrer, témoigner, faire preuve de.

evocation, *s.* Évocation *f.*

evoke, *v.tr.* Évoquer.

evolution, *s.* Évolution *f.*

evolve. 1. *v.tr.* Dérouler, développer. **2.** *v.i.* (a) Se dérouler. (b) Se développer.

ewe, *s.* Brebis *f.*

ewer, *s.* Pot *m* à eau.

ex-, *pref.* Ancien.

exact[1], *a.* Exact. **1.** (a) Précis. (b) **The exact word,** le mot juste. **2.** *To be e. in carrying out one's duties,* être exact à s'acquitter de ses devoirs. **-ly,** *adv.* Exactement; tout juste, justement. *Exactly!* précisément! **He is not exactly a scholar,** il n'est pas à proprement parler un savant.

exact[2], *v.tr.* (a) Exiger (*from, of,* de). (b) Extorquer. **exacting,** *a.* (*Of pers.*) Exigeant; (*of work*) astreignant.

exaction, *s.* Exaction *f,* demande exorbitante.

exactitude, *s.* Exactitude *f.*

exactness, *s.* Exactitude *f,* précision *f.*

exaggerate, *v.tr.* Exagérer; grandir. *Abs.* Exagérer. **exaggerated,** *a.* Exagéré.

exaggeration, *s.* Exagération *f.*

exalt, *v.tr.* **1.** Élever. **2.** Exalter, louer.

To exalt s.o. to the skies, porter qn jusqu'aux nues. **3.** Exciter, exalter. **exalted,** *a.* Élevé. **Exalted personage,** personnage haut placé.

exaltation, *s.* **1.** Élévation *f.* **2.** Exaltation *f.*

examination, *s.* Examen *m.* **1.** Inspection *f,* visite *f;* vérification *f* (de comptes). **Under examination,** à l'examen. **2.** *Sch:* **Entrance examination,** examen d'entrée. **Competitive examination,** concours *m.* **3.** *Jur:* Interrogatoire *m* (d'un accusé); audition *f* (de témoins).

examine, *v.tr.* Examiner. **1.** Inspecter (une machine); visiter (les bagages); vérifier (des comptes). *v.i. To e. into a matter,* faire une enquête sur une affaire. **2.** Interroger.

examiner, *s.* **1.** Inspecteur, -trice. **2.** *Sch:* Examinateur, -trice. **The examiners,** le jury (d'examen).

example, *s.* Exemple *m.* **1.** *To quote sth. as an e.,* citer qch. en exemple. **For example,** par exemple. **2.** Précédent *m.* **3.** **To set an example,** donner l'exemple. *To take s.o. as an e.,* prendre exemple sur qn.

exasperate, *v.tr.* **1.** Exaspérer, aggraver. **2.** Exaspérer, irriter. **exasperating,** *a.* Exaspérant, irritant.

exasperation, *s.* **1.** Exaspération *f,* aggravation *f.* **2.** Exaspération, irritation *f.* **To drive s.o. to exasperation,** pousser qn à bout.

excavate, *v.tr.* Excaver, creuser. *Abs.* Faire des fouilles.

excavation, *s.* Excavation *f.* **1.** Fouillement *m.* **2.** Terrain excavé; fouille *f.*

exceed, *v.tr.* (a) Excéder, dépasser. *To e. one's powers,* sortir de sa compétence. *Aut:* **To exceed the speed limit,** dépasser la vitesse légale. (b) Surpasser (*in,* en). **exceedingly,** *adv.* Très, extrêmement, excessivement.

excel, *v.* **1.** *v.i.* Exceller (*in, at, sth.,* à qch.). **2.** *v.tr.* Surpasser.

excellence, *s.* Excellence *f.* **1.** Perfection *f.* **2.** Mérite *m,* qualité *f* (de qn).

excellency, *s.* **Your Excellency,** votre Excellence *f.*

excellent, *a.* Excellent, parfait. **-ly,** *adv.* Excellemment.

except[1], *v.tr.* Excepter, exclure (*from,* de).

except[2], *prep.* (a) Excepté; à l'exception de; sauf. (b) **Except for . . .,** à part . . . *Conj.phr.* **Except that,** excepté que.

exception, *s.* **1.** Exception *f.* **With the exception of,** à l'exception de, exception faite de. **With certain exceptions,** sauf exceptions. **2.** Objection *f.* **To take exception to sth.,** (i) trouver à redire à qch.; (ii) s'offenser de qch.

exceptionable, *a.* Blâmable, répréhensible.

exceptional, *a.* Exceptionnel. **-ally,** *adv.* Exceptionnellement.

excess, *s.* **1.** Excès *m.* **In excess, to excess,** (jusqu')à l'excès. **Indulgence carried to excess,** indulgence poussée trop loin. **2.** Excédent *m.* **Excess weight,** surpoids *m.* *Rail:* **Excess fare,** supplément *m.*

excessive, a. Excessif; immodéré; extrême. **-ly,** adv. Excessivement.

exchange[1], s. **I.** Échange m. In **exchange** (for sth.), en échange (de qch.). **2.** Fin: Foreign **exchange,** change (extérieur). (Rate of) **exchange,** taux m du change. At the current rate of e., au change du jour. **3.** (a) Bourse f (des valeurs). (b) Telephone **exchange,** central m (téléphonique). 'Exchange, please!' "la ville, s'il vous plaît."

exchange[2], v.tr. To **exchange** sth. for sth., échanger, troquer, qch. contre, qch.

exchequer, s. The Exchequer, (i) la Trésorerie, le fisc; (ii) le Trésor public.

excise[1], s. Contributions indirectes.

excise[2], v.tr. Retrancher.

exciseman, s. Employé m de la régie.

excision, s. Excision f, coupure f.

excitability, s. Promptitude f à s'émouvoir.

excitable, a. Émotionnable, surexcitable.

excite, v.tr. **I.** Provoquer, exciter; susciter (de l'intérêt). To **excite** s.o.'s curiosity, piquer la curiosité de qn. **2.** (a) Exciter, enflammer (une passion). (b) Agiter, émouvoir, surexciter (qn). Easily **excited,** surexcitable, émotionnable. **excited,** a. Agité, surexcité. Don't get **excited!** ne vous montez pas la tête! **exciting,** a. Passionnant, émouvant.

excitement, s. Agitation f, surexcitation f. To **cause great excitement,** faire sensation f.

exclaim, v.i. S'écrier, s'exclamer.

exclamation, s. Exclamation f.

exclude, v.tr. (a) Exclure (from, de). **Excluding,** à l'exclusion de. (b) Écarter (le doute).

exclusion, s. **I.** Exclusion f (from, de). **2.** Refus m d'admission (from, à).

exclusive, a. **I.** Exclusif. **2.** (a) (Droit) exclusif. Cin: **Exclusive** film, film en exclusivité. (b) Seul, unique. (c) E. profession, profession très fermée. **3.** E. of wine, vin non compris. **-ly,** adv. Exclusivement.

excommunicate, v.tr. Excommunier.

excommunication, s. Excommunication f.

excrescence, s. Excroissance f.

excretion, s. Excrétion f.

excruciating, a. Atroce, affreux.

exculpate, v.tr. Disculper (from, de).

exculpation, s. Disculpation f.

excursion, s. Excursion f; voyage m d'agrément; partie f de plaisir.

excusable, a. Excusable, pardonnable. **-ably,** adv. Excusablement.

excuse[1], s. **I.** Excuse f. **2.** Excuse, prétexte m. To **make excuses,** s'excuser.

excuse[2], v.tr. (a) Excuser, pardonner. E. my being late, excusez-moi d'être en retard. **Excuse me!** (i) excusez-moi! (ii) pardon! (b) To **excuse** s.o. from doing sth., excuser, dispenser, qn de faire qch.

execrable, a. Exécrable, détestable. **-ably,** adv. Détestablement.

execrate, v.tr. Exécrer, détester.

execration, s. Exécration f.

execute, v.tr. **I.** (a) Exécuter. To e. a deed, souscrire un acte. (b) Exécuter, jouer (un morceau de musique). **2.** Exécuter (un criminel).

execution, s. **I.** (a) Exécution f. In the **execution** of one's duty, dans l'exercice de ses fonctions. (b) Jur: Souscription f (d'un acte). (c) (i) Exécution (d'un morceau de musique); (ii) jeu m (d'un musicien). **2.** Exécution (d'un criminel).

executioner, s. Bourreau m; exécuteur m des hautes œuvres.

executive. I. a. Exécutif. **2.** s. Pouvoir exécutif, exécutif m.

executor, s. Exécuteur m testamentaire.

executrix, s. Jur: Exécutrice f testamentaire.

exemplary, a. Exemplaire. **I.** An exemplary husband, un époux modèle. **2.** Infligé pour l'exemple.

exemplify, v.tr. **I.** Démontrer par des exemples. **2.** Servir d'exemple à (une règle).

exempt[1], a. Exempt, dispensé.

exempt[2], v.tr. Exempter, exonérer, dispenser.

exemption, s. Exemption f, dispense f.

exercise[1], s. Exercice m (d'une faculté).

exercise-book, s. Cahier m.

exercise[2], v.tr. **I.** Exercer (un droit); pratiquer (un métier). To e. a right, user d'un droit. **2.** (a) To **exercise** oneself, prendre de l'exercice. (b) v.i. S'entraîner. **3.** To e. s.o.'s patience, mettre à l'épreuve la patience de qn.

exert, v.tr. **I.** Employer; mettre en œuvre; exercer (une influence). **2.** To **exert** oneself, s'employer; se donner du mal.

exertion, s. **I.** Usage m, emploi m (de la force). **2.** Effort m, efforts.

exhalation, s. **I.** (a) Exhalation f. (b) Expiration f (du souffle). **2.** Effluve m, exhalaison f.

exhale, v.tr. Exhaler.

exhaust, v.tr. (a) Épuiser, tarir. (b) Épuiser, éreinter, exténuer. **exhausted,** a. Épuisé. I am e., je n'en peux plus.

exhausting, a. (Effort) épuisant.

exhaustion, s. Épuisement m. To be in a state of e., être à bout de forces.

exhaustive, a. E. enquiry, enquête approfondie. **-ly,** adv. To treat a subject e., traiter un sujet à fond.

exhibit[1], s. Objet exposé (à une exposition).

exhibit[2], v.tr. **I.** Exhiber, montrer (un objet); faire preuve de (courage). **2.** Offrir, présenter (qch. à la vue). **3.** To e. goods, exposer des marchandises.

exhibition, s. **I.** Exposition f, étalage m (de marchandises). F: To **make an exhibition** of oneself, se donner en spectacle. **2.** Exposition. **3.** Sch: Bourse f.

exhilarate, v.tr. Vivifier; F: émoustiller. **exhilarated,** a. Ragaillardi, émoustillé. **exhilarating,** a. Vivifiant, émoustillant.

exhilaration, s. Gaieté f; joie f de vivre.

exhort, *v.tr.* Exhorter, encourager (*s.o. to (do) sth.*, qn à (faire) qch.).

exhortation, *s.* Exhortation *f.*

exhume, *v.tr.* Exhumer.

exigency, *s.* **1.** Exigence *f*, nécessité *f.* **2.** Situation *f* critique ;' cas pressant.

exigent, *a.* **1.** Urgent. **2.** Exigeant.

exiguous, *a.* Exigu, -uë.

exile¹, *s.* Exil *m*, bannissement *m.*

exile², *s.* Exilé, -ée ; banni, -ie.

exile³, *v.tr.* Exiler, bannir (*from*, de).

exist, *v.i.* Exister. **existing,** *a.* Existant, actuel, présent. *In e. circumstances*, dans les circonstances actuelles.

existence, *s.* **1.** Existence *f.* *To come into existence*, naître. **2.** Existence, vie *f.*

existent, *a.* Existant.

exit¹, *s.* **1.** Sortie *f.* *To make one's exit*, quitter la scène. **2.** Sortie ; (porte *f* de) dégagement *m.*

exit², *v.i.* *Th:* Exit Macbeth, Macbeth sort.

exodus, *s.* The Book of Exodus, l'Exode *m.* *F:* There was a general exodus, il y eut une sortie générale.

ex(-)officio, *adv.phr.* A titre d'office.

exonerate, *v.tr.* **1.** Exonérer, dispenser (*from*, de). **2.** To exonerate s.o. (from blame), disculper qn.

exoneration, *s.* **1.** Exonération *f*, décharge *f*, dispense *f* (*from*, de). **2.** Exoneration from blame, disculpation *f.*

exorbitance, *s.* Exorbitance *f*, énormité *f*, extravagance *f.*

exorbitant, *a.* Exorbitant, extravagant.

exorcism, *s.* Exorcisme *m.*

exorcize, *v.tr.* Exorciser.

exotic, *a.* Exotique.

expand. **1.** *v.tr.* (*a*) Dilater (un gaz) ; développer (un abrégé) ; élargir (l'esprit). (*b*) Déployer (les ailes). **2.** *v.i.* Se dilater ; (*of chess*) se développer. **expanding,** *a.* Expanding trunk, malle à soufflets.

expanse, *s.* Étendue *f.*

expansion, *s.* Dilatation *f* (d'un gaz) ; développement *m* (de la poitrine).

expansive, *a.* **1.** Expansif, démonstratif. **2.** Large, étendu.

expansiveness, *s.* Expansibilité *f.*

expatiate, *v.i.* Discourir (longuement), s'étendre (*on, upon*, sur).

expatiation, *s.* Dissertation *f* ; long discours.

expatriate, *v.tr.* Expatrier

expatriation, *s.* Expatriation *f.*

expect, *v.tr.* **1.** Attendre ; s'attendre à (un événement) ; compter sur (l'arrivée de qn). *I knew what to e.*, je savais à quoi m'attendre. *As one might expect, F:* comme de raison. *It is hardly to be expected that* . . ., il y a peu de chances (pour) que + *sub.* *To e. to do sth.*, compter faire qch. **2.** To expect sth. from s.o., attendre, exiger, qch. de qn. *What do you e. me to do?* qu'attendez-vous de moi ?

How do you e. me to do it? comment voulez-vous que je le fasse ? **3.** *F:* I expect so, je pense que oui. **expected,** *a.* Attendu, espéré. *s.* It is not always the expected that happens, le vraisemblable n'arrive pas toujours.

expectancy, *s.* Attente *f.*

expectant, *a.* Qui attend ; expectant. **-ly,** *adv.* To gaze at s.o. e., regarder qn avec un air d'attente.

expectation, *s.* **1.** (*a*) Attente *f*, espérance *f*, prévision *f.* To come up to s.o.'s expectations, répondre à l'attente de qn. Contrary to all expectations, contre toute attente. (*b*) With eager e., avec une vive impatience. **2.** *pl.* Expectations, espérances. **3.** Probabilité *f.* (d'un événement).

expectorate, *v.tr.* Expectorer.

expediency, *s.* Convenance *f*, opportunité *f.*

expedient. **1.** *a.* Expédient, convenable, opportun. **2.** *s.* Expédient *m*, moyen *m.*

expedite, *v.tr.* **1.** Activer ; accélérer. **2.** Expédier, dépêcher.

expedition, *s.* **1.** (*a*) Expédition *f.* (*b*) Excursion *f.* **2.** Célérité *f*, promptitude *f.*

expeditious, *a.* (Procédé) expéditif ; rapide ; prompt. **-ly,** *adv.* Avec célérité ; promptement.

expel, *v.tr.* Expulser. *To e. a boy*, chasser un élève.

expend, *v.tr.* **1.** (*a*) To expend money, dépenser de l'argent. (*b*) To e. time, employer du temps. **2.** (*a*) Épuiser. (*b*) Consommer.

expenditure, *s.* **1.** Dépense *f* (d'argent) ; consommation *f.* **2.** Dépense(s).

expense, *s.* **1.** (*a*) Dépense *f*, frais *mpl.* (*b*) *pl.* Expenses, dépenses, frais. **2.** Dépens *mpl.* *A laugh* at my expense, un éclat de rire à mes dépens. **3.** To be a great expense to s.o., être une grande charge pour qn. **4.** *pl.* Expenses, indemnité *f* (pour débours). Travelling expenses, indemnité de voyage.

expensive, *a.* Coûteux, cher. Expensive car, voiture de luxe. *To be expensive*, coûter cher *inv.*

expensiveness, *s.* Cherté *f* ; prix élevé.

experience¹, *s.* Expérience *f.* **1.** Épreuve personnelle. **2.** He lacks experience, il manque de pratique *f.* *Facts within my experience*, faits à ma connaissance.

experience², *v.tr.* **1.** Éprouver ; faire l'expérience de. **2.** Apprendre (par expérience) (*that*, que), **experienced,** *a.* Qui a de l'expérience ; expérimenté ; (œil) exercé (*in*, à).

experiment¹, *s.* Expérience *f* ; essai *m.*

experiment², *v.i.* Expérimenter, faire des expériences (*on, with*, sur, avec).

expert¹, *a.* Habile, expert. **-ly,** *adv.* Habilement, expertement.

expert², *s.* Expert *m* ; spécialiste *m.*

expertness, *s.* Adresse *f*, habileté *f.*

expiate, *v.tr.* Expier.

expiation, *s.* Expiation *f.*

expiration, *s.* Expiration *f.* **1.** *E. of air from the lungs,* expiration de l'air des poumons. **2.** Cessation *f,* terme *m.*

expire, *v.i.* (*a*) Expirer, mourir ; (*of fire*) s'éteindre ; (*of hope*) s'évanouir. (*b*) Expirer, cesser.

expiry, *s.* Expiration *f,* terme *m.*

explain, *v.tr.* Expliquer, éclaircir. **explain away,** *v.tr.* Donner une explication satisfaisante de.

explanation, *s.* Explication *f.*

explanatory, *a.* Explicatif.

expletive, *s. F:* Juron *m.*

explicable, *a.* Explicable.

explicit, *a.* Explicite ; formel, catégorique. *To be more e. in one's statements,* préciser ses affirmations. **-ly,** *adv.* Explicitement ; catégoriquement.

explode. 1. *v.tr.* (*a*) Discréditer (une théorie). (*b*) Faire éclater (un obus) ; faire sauter (une mine). **2.** *v.i.* Faire explosion ; éclater ; sauter.

exploit¹, *s.* Exploit *m* ; haut fait.

exploit², *v.tr.* Exploiter.

exploitation, *s.* Exploitation *f.*

exploration, *s.* Exploration *f.*

explore, *v.tr.* Explorer.

explorer, *s.* Explorateur, -trice.

explosion, *s.* **1.** Explosion *f.* **2.** Détonation *f.*

explosive. 1. *a.* (Matière) explosible ; (mélange) explosif. **2.** *s.* Explosif *m,* détonant *m.* High explosive, explosif puissant.

exponent, *s.* Interprète *mf.*

export¹, *s.* **1.** *pl.* Exports, (i) articles *m* d'exportation ; (ii) exportations *f.* **2.** Export trade, commerce d'exportation.

export², *v.tr.* Exporter.

exportation, *s.* Exportation *f.*

exporter, *s.* Exportateur, -trice.

expose, *v.tr.* Exposer. **1.** (*a*) Laisser sans abri. (*b*) *To expose oneself to danger,* s'exposer au danger. (*c*) *Phot:* Exposer. **2.** (*a*) Mettre à découvert, à nu. To expose one's ignorance, afficher son ignorance. (*b*) *To e. goods,* exposer, étaler, des marchandises. **3.** Démasquer (un hypocrite) ; dévoiler (un crime). **exposed,** *a.* (*a*) Exposé. (*b*) (*Laid bare*) A nu.

exposition, *s.* Exposition *f.*

expostulate, *v.i. To e. with s.o.,* faire des remontrances à qn.

expostulation, *s.* (*a*) Remontrances *fpl.* (*b*) Remontrance.

exposure, *s.* **1.** (*a*) Exposition *f* (à l'air). (*b*) *Phot:* (Temps *m* de) pose *f.* **2.** Dévoilement *m* (d'un crime).

expound, *v.tr.* **1.** Exposer (une doctrine). **2.** Expliquer, interpréter.

express¹. 1. *a.* (*a*) Exprès, -esse, formel. *For this e. purpose,* pour ce but même. (*b*) Express train, (train) express *m,* rapide *m.* **2.** *s. Rail:* Express *m.* rapide *m.*

express², *v.tr.* **1.** Exprimer (*out of, from,* de). **2.** Énoncer ; exprimer. To express a wish,

formuler un souhait. **3.** To express oneself in French, s'exprimer en français.

expression, *s.* **1.** Expression *f.* Beyond expression, inexprimable. **2.** Expression, locution *f.* **3.** Expression (du visage).

expressive, *a.* Expressif ; plein d'expression.

expressly, *adv.* **1.** Expressément, formellement. **2.** *I did it e. to please you,* je l'ai fait avec le seul but de vous plaire.

expulsion, *s.* Expulsion *f.*

expunge, *v.tr.* Effacer, rayer.

expurgate, *v.tr.* Expurger.

expurgation, *s.* Expurgation *f.*

exquisite, *a.* (*a*) Exquis. (*b*) (*Of pleasure*) Vif. **Exquisite torture,** tourment atroce. **-ly,** *adv.* D'une manière exquise.

ex-service-man, *s.* Ancien combattant.

extant, *a.* Existant ; qui existe encore.

extemporaneous, *a.* Improvisé ; impromptu *inv.*

extempore. 1. *adv. To speak e.,* parler d'abondance, impromptu. **2.** *a.* Improvisé, impromptu *inv.*

extemporize. *v.tr. & i.* Improviser.

extend. I. *v.tr.* **1.** Étendre, allonger. **2.** Prolonger. **3.** Étendre, porter plus loin. **4.** Tendre (la main). **II. extend,** *v.i.* **1.** S'étendre, s'allonger. **2.** Se prolonger, continuer.

extension, *s.* **1.** Extension *f* (du bras) ; agrandissement *m.* **2.** Extension, accroissement *m* (des affaires). **3.** (R)allonge *f* (de table). **4.** Prolongation *f* (de congé). **To get an extension of time,** obtenir un délai.

extensive, *a.* Étendu, vaste, ample. *E. researches,* travaux approfondis. **-ly,** *adv.* To use sth. extensively, se servir beaucoup de qch.

extent, *s.* Étendue *f.* **Extent of the damage,** importance *f* du dommage. **To a certain extent,** jusqu'à un certain point ; dans une certaine mesure. **To such an extent that,** à tel point que. *To some slight e.,* quelque peu.

extenuating, *a.* Extenuating circumstance, circonstance atténuante.

extenuation, *s.* **1.** Exténuation *f,* affaiblissement *m* extrême. **2.** Atténuation *f* (d'une faute).

exterior. I. *a.* Extérieur (*to,* à) ; en dehors (*to,* de). **2.** *s.* Extérieur *m,* dehors *mpl.* On the exterior, à l'extérieur.

exterminate, *v.tr.* Exterminer.

extermination, *s.* Extermination *f.*

external. I. *a.* (*a*) Externe. (*b*) Extérieur ; du dehors. **2.** *s.* To judge by externals, juger les choses d'après les dehors. **-ally,** *adv.* Extérieurement ; à l'extérieur.

extinct, *a.* (*a*) Éteint. (*b*) (*Of race*) Disparu.

extinction, *s.* Extinction *f.*

extinguish, *v.tr.* Éteindre.

extinguisher, *s.* (*a*) (Appareil) extincteur *m.* (*b*) (*For candle*) Éteignoir *m.*

extirpate, *v.tr.* Extirper.

extirpation, *s.* Extirpation *f.*

extol, *v.tr.* Exalter, prôner. **To extol s.o. to the skies,** porter qn aux nues.

extort, *v.tr.* Extorquer (*from, out of, s.o.,* à qn). *To e. a promise from s.o.,* arracher une promesse à qn.

extortion, *s.* Extorsion *f,* exaction *f;* arrachement *m* (d'une promesse).

extortionate, *a.* Extorsionnaire, exorbitant.

extortioner, *s.* Extorqueur, -euse.

extra. I. *a.* (*a*) En sus, de plus; supplémentaire. *E. charge,* supplément *m* de prix. (*b*) De qualité supérieure; superfin. **2.** *adv.* (*a*) Plus que d'ordinaire; extra-. *E. smart,* ultra-chic. (*b*) En plus. *The wine is e.,* le vin est en plus. **3.** *s.* (*a*) Supplément *m* (de menu); édition spéciale (d'un journal). (*b*) *pl.* **Extras,** frais *m* ou dépenses *f* supplémentaires.

extract¹, *s.* Extrait *m.*

extract², *v.tr.* Extraire. *To e. a confession from s.o.,* arracher un aveu à qn.

extraction, *s.* Extraction *f.* **1.** Extraction of a tooth, arrachement *m,* extraction, d'une dent. **2.** Origine *f.*

extradition, *s.* Extradition *f.*

extraneous, *a.* Étranger (*to,* à).

extraordinary, *a.* Extraordinaire. (*a*) *To have e. ability,* avoir des talents remarquables. (*b*) *The e. thing is that . . .,* ce qu'il y a d'étrange, c'est que. . . . (*c*) *F:* Prodigieux. **-ily,** *adv.* Extraordinairement.

extravagance, *s.* **1.** Extravagance *f.* **2.** Folles dépenses; prodigalités *fpl.*

extravagant, *a.* **1.** Extravagant. **2.** Dépensier. *E. tastes,* goûts dispendieux. **3.** Exorbitant. **-ly,** *adv.* **1.** D'une façon extravagante. *To talk e.,* dire des folies. **2.** Excessivement; à l'excès.

extreme. I. *a.* Extrême. **The extreme penalty,** le dernier supplice. *R.C.Ch:* Extreme unction, extrême-onction. *E. youth,* grande jeunesse. *In an e. case,* un cas exceptionnel. **2.** *s.* **In the extreme,** à l'excès; au dernier degré. **Extremes meet,** les extrêmes se touchent. *To drive s.o. to extremes,* pousser qn à bout. **-ly,** *adv.* Extrêmement; au dernier point.

extremity, *s.* **1.** Extrémité *f;* point *m* extrême; bout *m.* **2.** *pl.* **The extremities,** les extrémités. **3.** *They are in great e.,* ils sont dans une grande gêne.

extricate, *v.tr.* Dégager. *To e. oneself from difficulties,* se débrouiller.

exuberance, *s.* Exubérance *f.*

exuberant, *a.* Exubérant. **-ly,** *adv.* Avec exubérance.

exude, *v.tr. & i.* Exsude..

exult, *v.i.* **1.** Exulter. **2.** *To e. over s.o.,* triompher de qn.

exultant, *a.* Triomphant, exultant. *To be e.,* exulter. **-ly,** *adv.* D'un air de triomphe.

exultation, *s.* Exultation *f.*

eye¹, *s.* **1.** Œil *m, pl.* yeux. (*a*) *To have blue eyes,* avoir les yeux bleus. *To open one's eyes wide,* ouvrir de grands yeux; écarquiller les yeux. *To do sth. with one's eyes open,* faire qch. en connaissance de cause. **To keep one's eyes open,** avoir l'œil ouvert. *Keep your eyes open!* ouvrez l'œil! ayez l'œil! **To open s.o.'s eyes,** éclairer, désabuser, qn. **To shut one's eyes to the faults of s.o.,** être aveugle sur les défauts de qn. **To be up to the eyes in work,** avoir du travail par-dessus la tête. **With tears in one's eyes,** les larmes aux yeux. (*b*) **To catch the eye,** frapper l'œil, les regards. *To catch s.o.'s eye,* attirer l'attention de qn. *To set eyes on sth.,* apercevoir, voir, qch. *Where are your eyes?* êtes-vous aveugle? (*c*) **To make eyes at s.o.** *F:* to give s.o. the glad eye, faire de l'œil à qn. **To see eye to eye with s.o.,** voir les choses du même œil que qn. *Mil:* Eyes right! tête (à) droite! **Eyes front!** fixe! (*d*) **To give an eye to sth.,** veiller à qch. *To keep a strict eye on s.o.,* surveiller qn de près. **To be all eyes,** être tout yeux. (*e*) **To have an eye for a horse,** s'y connaître en chevaux. (*f*) **To be very much in the public eye,** occuper une position très en vue. **2.** (*a*) Chas *m* (d'une aiguille). (*b*) Piton *m.* **3.** **In the eye of,** dans la direction opposée à. **eye-ball,** *s.* Globe *m* de l'œil. **eye-glass,** *s.* (*a*) Monocle *m.* (*b*) Eye-glasses, binocle *m,* lorgnon *m,* pince-nez *m inv.* **eye-lash,** *s.* Cil *m.* **eye-opener,** *s.* Révélation *f;* surprise *f.* **eye-wash,** *s.* *F:* That's all eye-wash, tout ça c'est du boniment.

eye², *v.tr.* Regarder, observer. **To eye s.o. from head to foot,** toiser qn.

eyebrow, *s.* Sourcil *m.*

eyelet, *s.* Œillet *m.*

eyelid, *s.* Paupière *f.*

eyepiece, *s.* Oculaire *m.*

eyeshot, *s.* Within eyeshot, à portée de la vue.

eyesight, *s.* Vue *f.* *To have good e.,* avoir la vue bonne.

eyesore, *s.* Ce qui blesse la vue.

eyewitness, *s.* Témoin *m* oculaire.

eyrie, *s.* Aire *f.*

F, f, s. **1.** (La lettre) F, f f. **2.** Mus: Fa m.
fable, s. Fable f, conte m.
fabled, a. Légendaire, fabuleux.
fabric, s. **1.** Édifice m, bâtiment m. **2.** Tex: Tissu m; étoffe f. **3.** Structure f, fabrique f (d'un édifice).
fabricate, v.tr. F: Inventer, fabriquer.
fabrication, s. **1.** F: Invention f. **2.** A pure f., une pure invention.
fabricator, s. F: Inventeur, -trice, fabricateur, -trice.
fabulous, a. **1.** Fabuleux; (personnage) légendaire, mythique. **2.** F: Prodigieux. **-ly,** adv. Fabuleusement; prodigieusement.
façade, s. Arch: Façade f.
face[1], s. **1.** Figure f, visage m, face f. **To strike s.o. in the face,** frapper qn au visage. I can never look him in the f. again, je me sentirai toujours honteux devant lui. **He won't show his face here again!** il ne se risquera pas à remettre les pieds ici! To bring the two parties f. to f., mettre les deux parties en présence. **To set one's face against sth.,** s'opposer résolument à qch. **In the face of danger,** en présence du danger. To fly in the f. of facts, aller contre l'évidence. I told him so to his f., F: je ne le lui ai pas envoyé dire. **2.** (a) Mine f, physionomie f. **To save (one's) face,** sauver la face. **To make faces** (at s.o.), faire des grimaces (à qn). **To keep a straight face,** garder son sérieux. **To put a good face on a bad business,** faire bonne mine à mauvais jeu. (b) Audace f, front m. **He had the face to tell me so,** il a eu l'aplomb, le toupet, de me le dire. **3.** Apparence f, aspect m. **On the face of things,** au premier aspect. **4.** Surface f. **5.** (a) Face (d'une pièce de monnaie). (b) Devant m, façade f (d'un bâtiment). (c) Cadran m (de montre).
face-ache, s. Névralgie faciale. **face-cream,** s. Toil: Crème f de beauté. **face-powder,** s. Poudre f de riz. **face-value,** s. Fin: Valeur nominale.
face[2], v.tr. **1.** Affronter, faire face à; envisager (les faits). F: **To face the music,** tenir tête à l'orage. **2.** (a) v.tr. Faire face à, se tenir devant. Facing each other, vis-à-vis l'un de l'autre. (b) v.i. The house faces north, la maison est exposée au nord. Face this way! tournez-vous de ce côté! **facing,** s. Revers m, parement m (d'un habit).
facet, s Facette f (d'un diamant).
facetious, a. Facétieux, plaisant; (style) bouffon **-ly,** adv. Facétieusement.
facial, a. Facial, -aux.
facilitate, v.tr. Faciliter.
facility, s. Facilité f. **1.** (a) F. in speaking, facilité à parler. (b) To enjoy facilities for

doing sth., avoir la facilité de faire qch. **2.** Souplesse f de caractère; complaisance f.
facsimile, s. Fac-similé m. **Facsimile signature,** signature autographiée.
fact, s. **1.** Fait m, action f. **2.** To look facts in the face, voir les choses telles qu'elles sont. **To stick to facts,** s'en tenir aux faits. It is a f. that, il est de fait que. **Apart from the fact that,** hormis que. **To know for a fact that,** savoir de science certaine que. **The fact is,** c'est que. **In fact,** de fait. **In point of fact,** par le fait.
faction, s. Faction f, cabale f.
factor, s. **1.** Mth: Facteur m, diviseur m. **2.** Facteur. **The human f.,** l'élément humain.
factory, s. Ind: Fabrique f, usine f.
factotum, s. Factotum m; homme m à tout faire.
faculty, s. (a) Faculté f. (b) Facilité f, talent m.
fad, s. Marotte f, dada m.
fade. **1.** v.i. (a) Se faner, se flétrir; (of colour) perdre son éclat. Guaranteed not to f., garanti bon teint. (b) **To fade away,** out, s'évanouir, s'affaiblir. **She was fading away,** elle dépérissait. **2.** v.tr. Faner, flétrir.
fag[1], s. **1.** F: (a) Fatigue f. **What a fag!** quelle corvée! (b) Surmenage m. **2.** Sch: "Petit" attaché au service d'un "grand." **3.** P: Cigarette f. **fag-end,** s. Bout m.
fag[2], v. **1.** (a) v.i. & pron. **To fag (oneself),** trimer. **To fag oneself out,** s'éreinter. (b) v.tr. Fatiguer, F: éreinter (qn). **2.** v.i. Sch: **To fag for a senior,** être au service d'un grand.
faggot, s. Fagot m.
Fahrenheit, a. Fahrenheit.
fail[1]. Adv.phr. **Without fail,** (i) sans faute, sans remise; (ii) à coup sûr.
fail[2]. **1.** v.i. (a) Manquer, faillir, faire défaut. **To fail in one's duty,** manquer, faillir, à son devoir. **To fail to do sth.,** faillir à faire qch. **To fail s.o.,** manquer à ses engagements envers qn. His heart failed him, le cœur lui manqua. (b) Rester en panne; flancher. (c) Baisser. Daylight is failing, le jour baisse, s'éteint. His memory is failing, sa mémoire baisse. He is failing, sa santé baisse. (d) Ne pas réussir; échouer; manquer son coup. I fail to see why, je ne vois pas pourquoi. (e) Com: Faire faillite. **2.** v.tr. Sch: Refuser, coller. **failing**[1], s. **1.** (a) Manquement m. (b) Affaiblissement m, défaillance f; baisse f. (c) Non-réussite f; échec m. **2.** (a) Faiblesse f. **failing**[2], prep. A défaut de; faute de.
failure, s. **1.** (a) Manque m, manquement m, défaut m. (b) Panne f, défaillance f.

2. (a) Insuccès m, non-réussite f. **To court failure** aller au-devant d'une défaite. (b) *Com:* Faillite f. **3.** (a) (*Of pers.*) Raté, -ée. (b) *The play was a f.*, la pièce a fait four.

faint[1], a. **1.** **Faint heart**, cœur pusillanime. **2.** (a) Faible, affaibli. (b) (*Of sound*) léger; (*of idea*) vague. *I haven't the faintest idea*, je n'en ai pas la moindre idée. **3.** **To feel faint**, se sentir mal. **-ly**, *adv.* **1.** Faiblement; d'une voix éteinte. **2.** Légèrement; un peu. **faint-hearted**, a. Pusillanime, timide.

faint[2], s. Évanouissement m, défaillance f.

faint[3], *v.i.* To faint (away), s'évanouir, défaillir. **fainting**, s. Évanouissement m, défaillance f.

faintness, s. **1.** Faiblesse f. **2.** Malaise m, faiblesse.

fair[1], s. Foire f. **fair-ground**, s. Champ m de foire.

fair[2]. I. a. **1.** Beau, f. belle. **The fair sex**, le beau sexe. **2.** Spécieux, plausible. **3.** Blond. **4.** Juste, équitable. **Fair play**, jeu loyal. *F: It's not fair!* ce n'est pas juste! **As is only fair**, comme de juste. **By fair means or foul**, d'une manière ou d'une autre; de gré ou de force. **5.** Passable; assez bon. **He has a fair chance of success**, il a des chances de réussir. **6.** (a) Propice, favorable. (b) **Fair weather**, beau temps. **-ly**, *adv.* **1.** Impartialement, équitablement. **2.** Honnêtement, loyalement. **3.** *F:* Complètement, absolument. **4.** Passablement; assez. II. **fair**, *adv.* **1.** *To speak* (s.o.) fair, parler courtoisement (à qn). **2.** *F:* (Agir) loyalement, de bonne foi. **To play fair**, jouer beau jeu. **fair and square**. I. a. Loyal, honnête. **It's all fair and square**, c'est de bonne guerre. **2.** *adv.* (a) Struck fair(ly) and square(ly), frappé au plein milieu. (b) Loyalement. **fair-haired**, a. Blond; aux cheveux blonds. **fair-minded**, a. Équitable; impartial, -iaux. **fair-sized**, a. Assez grand.

fairness, s. **1.** Couleur blonde; blancheur f. **2.** Équité f, honnêteté f, impartialité f.

fairy. **1.** s. Fée f. **2.** a. Féerique; de(s) fée(s). **Fairy godmother**, (i) marraine f fée; (ii) *F:* marraine gâteau. *F. footsteps*, pas légers. **fairy-like**, a. Féerique. **fairy-queen**, s. Reine f des fées. **fairy-tale**, s. **1.** Conte m de fées. **2.** *F:* (a) Conte invraisemblable. (b) Mensonge m.

fairyland, s. (a) Le royaume des fées. (b) Féerie f.

faith, s. Foi f. **1.** (a) Confiance f, croyance f. **To have faith in s.o.**, avoir confiance en qn. (b) **The Christian faith**, la foi chrétienne. **2.** (a) Fidélité f à ses engagements. **To keep faith with s.o.**, tenir ses engagements envers qn. (b) **Good faith**, bonne foi, loyauté f. *To do sth. in all good f.*, faire qch. en tout honneur. **Bad faith**, perfidie f, déloyauté f.

faithful, a. Fidèle. (a) Loyal, -aux. (b) Exact, juste, vrai. **-fully**, *adv.* **1.** Fidèlement, loyalement. *Corr:* **We remain yours**

faithfully, agréez nos meilleures salutations. **2.** Exactement, fidèlement.

faithfulness, s. Fidélité f. **1.** Loyauté f (to, envers). **2.** Exactitude f.

faithless, a. **1.** Infidèle; sans foi. **2.** Déloyal, -aux; perfide.

faithlessness, s. **1.** Infidélité f (to, à). **2.** Déloyauté f.

fake[1], s. *F:* Article truqué; maquillage m.

fake[2], *v.tr.* *F:* Truquer (des calculs); maquiller (un meuble). **fake up**, *v.tr.* Inventer.

falcon, s. *Orn:* Faucon m.

fall[1], s. **1.** (a) Chute f (d'un corps); descente f (d'un marteau). (b) *F:* **To try a fall with s.o.**, lutter avec qn. (c) *There has been a heavy f. of snow*, il est tombé beaucoup de neige. **2.** **The fall of day**, la chute du jour. **3.** Chute (d'eau); cascade f, cataracte f. **4.** Baisse f (des prix). **5.** Perte f, ruine f. **6.** Chute (d'une place forte).

fall[2], *v.i.* Tomber. **1.** (a) **To fall to the ground**, (*from on high*), tomber à terre. **To fall into a trap**, donner dans un piège. **To fall into s.o.'s hands**, tomber entre les mains de qn. (b) **Christmas falls on a Thursday**, Noël tombe un jeudi. **2.** (*From standing position*) (a) **To fall to the ground**, tomber par terre. (b) (*Of building*) Crouler, s'écrouler. **To fall to pieces**, tomber en morceaux. **3.** (a) (*Of barometer*) Descendre, baisser; (*of wind*) tomber; (*of sea*) (se) calmer; (*of price, etc.*) baisser. (b) Aller en pente; s'incliner; descendre. **Her eyes fell**, elle baissa les yeux. **His face fell**, sa figure s'allongea. (c) **To fall from one's position**, déchoir de sa position. **4.** (a) **A sound fell (up)on my ear**, un son frappa mon oreille. (b) **To fall upon s.o.'s neck**, se jeter au cou de qn. (c) (*Of river*) Déboucher, se jeter. **5.** (a) **To fall to s.o.'s share**, échoir (en partage) à qn. *The responsibility falls on me*, toute la responsabilité retombe sur moi. *It fell to me to . . .*, le devoir m'échut de. . . . (b) **To fall under suspicion**, devenir suspect. **To fall across s.o.**, rencontrer qn par hasard. (c) **To fall into a habit**, contracter une habitude. **6.** *Pred.* (a) **To fall sick**, devenir malade, tomber malade. **To fall vacant**, se trouver vacant. (b) **To fall a victim to**, devenir victime de. **fall back**, *v.i.* **1.** Tomber en arrière. **2.** *To f. back on lies*, avoir recours au mensonge. **fall behind**, *v.i.* Rester en arrière. **fall down**, *v.i.* **1.** Tomber à terre, par terre. **To fall down before s.o.**, se prosterner devant qn. **2.** (*Of building*) Crouler, s'écrouler, s'effondrer. **fall in**, *v.i.* **1.** S'écrouler, s'effondrer. **2.** *Mil:* Former les rangs. **Fall in!** à vos rangs! **3.** (*Of lease*) Expirer. **4.** (a) **To fall in with s.o.**, rencontrer qn. (b) **To fall in with s.o.'s opinion**, se ranger à l'avis de qn. *To f. in with a proposal*, accepter une proposition. (c) (*Of plan*) *To f. in with*, cadrer avec. **fall off**, *v.i.* **1.** *His hat fell off*, son

chapeau tomba. **2.** (*Of followers*) Faire
défection. **3.** Diminuer. **fall out,** *v.i.*
1. Tomber dehors. **2.** Se brouiller, se fâcher
(*with*, avec). **3.** *Things fell out well*, les choses
se sont bien passées. **fall over,** *v.i.* **1.** (*Of
pers.*) Tomber à la renverse ; (*of thg*) se
renverser, être renversé. **2.** To fall over an
obstacle, buter contre un obstacle et tomber.
fall through, *v.i.* Ne pas aboutir. **fall to,**
v.i. (*a*) Se mettre à l'œuvre. (*b*). Entamer la
lutte. (*c*) S'attaquer au repas. **fallen. 1.** *a.*
(*a*) *F. leaves*, feuilles tombées. (*b*) *Fallen
humanity*, l'humanité déchue. **2.** *s.* *The
fallen*, les morts *m*.

fallacious, *a.* Fallacieux, trompeur, -euse.

fallacy, *s.* *F:* A current fallacy, une erreur
courante.

fallible, *a.* Faillible.

fallow, *a.* To lie fallow, être en jachère ; être,
rester, en friche.

false, *a.* Faux, *f.* fausse. **1.** False report,
F: canard *m*. To be in a false position, se
trouver dans une position fausse. **2.** Perfide,
infidèle. To play s.o. false, trahir qn. **3.** Artificiel, postiche ; (*of coin*) contrefait. **-ly,** *adv.*
Faussement.

falsehood, *s.* Mensonge *m*. To tell a f.,
mentir.

falseness, *s.* Fausseté *f*.

falsification, *s.* Falsification *f*.

falsify, *v.tr.* Falsifier.

falsity, *s.* Fausseté *f*.

falter, *v.i.* (*a*) (*Of voice*) Hésiter, trembler.
(*b*) Vaciller, chanceler ; défaillir. **faltering,**
a. **1.** Hésitant, tremblant. **2.** Vacillant,
chancelant ; défaillant.

fame, *s.* Renom *m*, renommée *f*.

famed, *a.* Célèbre, renommé, fameux.

familiar, *a.* (*a*) Familier, intime. *You are
rather too f.*, vous prenez trop de privautés.
(*b*) Familier ; bien connu. *Amid f. surroundings*, en pays de connaissance. To be on
familiar ground, être sur son terrain. (*c*) To
be familiar with sth., être familier avec qch. ;
connaître qch. **-ly,** *adv.* Familièrement,
intimement.

familiarity, *s.* Familiarité *f*. **1.** Intimité *f*.
2. Connaissance *f* (*with*, de).

familiarize, *v.tr.* To familiarize s.o. with
sth., habituer qn à qch.

family, *s.* Famille *f*. To be one of the
family, être de la maison. Man of good
family, homme de famille. Family life, vie
familiale.

famine, *s.* (*a*) Famine *f*. (*b*) Disette *f*.

famished, *a.* Affamé.

famishing, *a.* Qui a grand'faim. *To be f.,
F:* avoir une faim de loup.

famous, *a.* Célèbre, renommé, fameux (*for*,
pour, par).

fan¹, *s.* **1.** Éventail *m*. **2.** Ventilateur (rotatif).

fan-light, *s.* Vasistas *m*.

fan², *v.tr.* Éventer.

fan³, *s.* *F:* Passionné, -ée, enragé, -ée.

fanatic, *a. & s.* Fanatique (*mf*).

fanatical, *a.* Fanatique. **-ally,** *adv.*
Fanatiquement.

fanaticism, *s.* Fanatisme *m*.

fanciful, *a.* **1.** Capricieux, fantasque.
2. (Projet) chimérique ; (conte) imaginaire.

fancy¹. I. *s.* **1.** (*a*) Imagination *f*, fantaisie *f*.
(*b*) *It's only f.!* c'est pure imagination !
(*c*) Idée *f*. I have a fancy that, j'ai idée que.
2. (*a*) Fantaisie, caprice *m*. *Just as the f.
takes me*, comme l'idée me prend. (*b*) Fantaisie, goût *m*. To take a fancy to sth.,
prendre goût à qch. To take a fancy to s.o.,
prendre qn en affection. **II. fancy,** *a.*
(Pain) de fantaisie. Fancy goods, nouveautés
f. Fancy dress, travesti *m*, déguisement *m*.
Fancy-dress ball, bal travesti.

fancy², *v.tr.* **1.** (*a*) S'imaginer, se figurer.
F: Fancy (that)! figurez-vous ça ! (*b*) Croire,
penser. **2.** (*a*) To fancy sth., se sentir attiré
vers qch. *I don't f. his offer*, son offre ne me
dit rien. *Let him eat anything he fancies*,
il peut manger tout ce qui lui dira. (*b*) To
fancy oneself, s'en faire accroire. **fancied,**
a. Imaginaire, imaginé.

fang, *s.* **1.** (*a*) Croc *m*. (*b*) Crochet *m* (de
vipère). **2.** Racine *f* (d'une dent).

fantastic, *a.* Fantasque, bizarre.

fantasy, *s.* **1.** Fantaisie *f*. **2.** Idée fantasque.

far¹, *adv.* Loin. **1.** (*a*) How far *is it from
. . . to . . .?* combien y a-t-il de . . . à
. . .? As far as the eye can reach, à perte
de vue. *To live far away*, far off, demeurer
au loin. Far and wide, de tous côtés ; partout.
(*b*) To go so far as to do sth., aller jusqu'à
faire qch. That is going too far, cela passe la
mesure, les bornes. As far as I know, autant
que je sache. As far as that goes, pour ce qui
est de cela. So far so good, c'est fort bien
jusque-là. In so far as, dans la mesure où.
To be far from believing sth., être à mille
lieues de croire qch. Far from it, tant s'en
faut ; loin de là. By far the best, de beaucoup
le meilleur. **2.** So far, jusqu'ici. As far as I
can see, autant que je puisse prévoir. Far
into the night, bien avant dans la nuit.
3. Beaucoup, bien, fort. It is far better,
c'est beaucoup mieux. *It is far more serious*
c'est bien autrement sérieux. Far and away
the best, de beaucoup le meilleur. **far-
away,** *a.* Lointain, éloigné. Far-away look
regard perdu dans le vague. **far-fetched,**
a. Forcé, outré. **far-off,** *a.* = FAR-AWAY.

far-reaching, *a.* De grande envergure,
d'une grande portée. **far-seeing,** *a.*
Prévoyant, clairvoyant, perspicace. **far-
sighted,** *a.* = FAR-SEEING. **far-sighted-
ness,** *s.* Prescience *f* ; perspicacité *f*.

far², *a.* **1.** Lointain, éloigné, reculé. **2.** *A
the far end of the street*, à l'autre bout de la rue

farce, *s.* *Th:* Farce *f*.

farcical, *a.* Risible, bouffon, grotesque.

fare¹, *s.* **1.** Prix *m* du voyage, de la place
prix de la course. **2.** Chère *f*, manger *m*.

fare², *v.i.* **1.** To fare well, aller bien. **2.** Manger, se nourrir.

farewell, *int. & s.* Adieu (*m*). To bid farewell to s.o., dire adieu, faire ses adieux à qn.

farinaceous, *a.* Farinacé.

farm¹, *s.* Ferme *f.* **farm-labourer**, *s.* Valet *m* de ferme. **farm-house**, *s.* (Maison *f* de) ferme *f.* **farm-yard**, *s.* Cour *f* de ferme; basse-cour *f.*

farm², *v.tr.* (*a*) Cultiver. (*b*) *Abs.* Être fermier. **farming**, *s.* **1.** Affermage *m.* **2.** Exploitation *f* agricole; agriculture *f.*

farmer, *s.* Fermier, -ière, cultivateur, -trice.

farrier, *s.* Maréchal (ferrant).

farther. 1. *adv.* (*a*) Plus loin (*than*, que). Farther off, plus éloigné. *F:* To wish s.o. farther, envoyer qn au diable. (*b*) Farther back, plus en arrière. **2.** *a.* Plus lointain, plus éloigné.

farthermost, *a.* Le plus lointain, le plus éloigné, le plus reculé.

farthest. 1. *a.* (*a*) Farthest (off), le plus lointain, le plus éloigné. (*b*) Le plus long. **2.** *adv.* Le plus loin.

farthing, *s.* Quart *m* d'un penny. Not to be worth a brass farthing, ne pas valoir un centime.

fascinate, *v.tr.* (*a*) Fasciner, charmer. (*b*) *F:* Fasciner, enchanter. **fascinating**, *a.* Enchanteur, -eresse; séduisant.

fascination, *s.* **1.** Fascination *f.* **2.** *F:* Fascination, charme, attrait *m.*

fashion¹, *s.* **1.** Façon *f* (d'un habit); manière *f* (de faire qch.). (*In the*) French f., à la française. After a fashion, tant bien que mal. **2.** Mode *f*, vogue *f.* In (the) fashion, à la mode, de mode, en vogue. Out of fashion, passé de mode; démodé. **fashion-plate**, *s.* Gravure *f* de modes.

fashion², *v.tr.* Façonner, former; confectionner.

fashionable, *a.* A la mode, élégant, en vogue. A. f. resort, un endroit mondain. **-ably**, *adv.* Élégamment; à la mode.

fast¹, *s.* Jeûne *m.*

fast², *v.i.* (*a*) Jeûner. (*b*) *Ecc:* Jeûner; faire maigre. **fasting**, *s.* Jeûne *m.*

fast³. I. *a.* **1.** (*a*) Ferme, fixe, solide. To hold a prisoner f., tenir ferme un prisonnier. Fast friends, des amis sûrs, solides. (*b*) *Nau:* Amarré. To make a boat f., amarrer un bateau. (*c*) (*Of door*) (Bien) assujetti; bien fermé. (*d*) (*Of colour*) Solide, résistant; bon teint *inv.* **2.** Rapide, vite. *Rail:* Fast train, rapide *m.* **3.** En avance. My watch is five minutes f., ma montre avance de cinq minutes. **4.** *F:* (*a*) Dissipé; de mœurs légères. The fast set, les viveurs *m.* (*b*) (Trop) émancipé. **II. fast**, *adv.* **1.** Ferme, solidement. To hold fast, tenir ferme; tenir bon. To stand fast, tenir bon. *F:* To play fast and loose, agir avec inconstance. **2.** Vite, rapidement. Not so fast! pas si vite! doucement! It is raining f., il pleut à verse.

fasten. 1. *v.tr.* (*a*) Attacher (*to*, *on*, à). To f. the responsibility on s.o., mettre la responsabilité sur le dos de qn. (*b*) Fixer, assurer, assujettir (la porte). To fasten (up) a parcel with string, lier un colis avec une ficelle. To f. (up) a garment, agrafer, boutonner, un vêtement. **2.** *v.i.* S'attacher, se fixer. He fastened on me, il s'attacha à moi. **fastening**, *s.* **1.** Attache *f*, attachement *m*; assujettissement *m*; agrafage *m.* **2.** = FASTENER.

fastener, *s.* Attache *f*; (of garment) agrafe *f*; (of window) fermeture *f.*

fastidious, *a.* Difficile (à satisfaire); délicat (about sth., sur qch.).

fastness, *s.* (*a*) Fermeté *f*, stabilité *f.* (*b*) Rapidité *f*, vitesse *f.* (*c*) Légèreté *f* de conduite.

fat¹, *a.* Gras, *f.* grasse. To get fat, engraisser.

fat-head, *s.* *F:* Imbécile *mf*, nigaud, -e.

fat-headed, *a.* *F:* A l'esprit bouché; sot, *f.* sotte.

fat², *s.* **1.** Graisse *f.* Mutton fat, suif *m* de mouton. *F:* The fat is in the fire, le feu est aux poudres! **2.** Gras *m* (de viande). *F:* To live on the fat of the land, vivre comme un coq en pâte.

fatal, *a.* Fatal, -als. Fatal blow, coup fatal, mortel. Fatal disease, maladie mortelle. (*b*) A f. mistake, une faute capitale. **-ally**, *adv.* **1.** Fatalement, inévitablement. **2.** Mortellement.

fatalism, *s.* Fatalisme *m.*

fatalist, *s.* Fataliste *mf.*

fatalistic, *a.* Fataliste.

fatality, *s.* Accident mortel; sinistre *m.*

fate, *s.* Destin *m*, sort *m.* *Myth:* The Fates, les Parques *f.* To leave s.o. to his fate, abandonner qn à son sort.

fated, *a.* **1.** Fatal, -als; inévitable. **2.** Destiné, condamné (to do sth., à faire qch.). **3.** Voué à la destruction.

fateful, *a.* **1.** Fateful word, parole fatidique. **2.** Décisif, fatal, -als.

father, *s.* **1.** Père *m.* Yes, Father, oui, (mon) père. **2.** *pl.* Our fathers, nos ancêtres *m*, nos pères. **3.** *F:* Père, fondateur *m*, créateur *m.* **4.** *Ecc:* (*a*) The Holy Father, le Saint-Père. Father confessor, père spirituel. (*b*) Father O'Malley, le Père O'Malley. **father-in-law**, *s.* Beau-père *m.*

fatherland, *s.* Patrie *f.*

fatherless, *a.* Sans père; orphelin, -ine, de père.

fatherly, *a.* Paternel.

fathom¹, *s.* *Nau:* Brasse *f.*

fathom², *v.tr.* *F:* To fathom the mystery, approfondir, sonder, le mystère.

fathomless, *a.* Sans fond, insondable.

fatigue¹, *s.* **1.** Fatigue *f.* **2.** *Mil:* Corvée *f.* **fatigue-cap**, *s.* *Mil:* Bonnet *m* de police.

fatigue², *v.tr.* Fatiguer, lasser. **fatiguing**, *a.* Fatigant, épuisant.

fatness, *s.* Embonpoint *m*, corpulence *f.*

fatten. 1. *v.tr.* To fatten (up), engraisser. **2.** *v.i.* Engraisser; devenir gras.

fatty, *a.* Graisseux, oléagineux.
fatuity, *s.* Sottise *f*; imbécillité *f*.
fatuous, *a.* Sot, *f*. sotte, imbécile, idiot. **-ly,** *adv.* Sottement.
fault, *s.* **1.** Défaut *m*, travers *m*; imperfection *f*. In spite of all his faults, malgré tous ses travers. Scrupulous to a fault, scrupuleux à l'excès. To find fault with s.o., trouver à redire contre qn. **2.** Faute *f*. To be in fault, être en défaut. Whose fault is it? à qui la faute? **3.** *Ten:* Faute. **4.** Memory at fault, mémoire en défaut. **5.** *Geol:* Faille *f*. **fault-finder,** *s.* Critiqueur, -euse; mécontent *m*. **fault-finding,** *s.* Disposition *f* à critiquer.
faultiness, *s.* Défectuosité *f*, imperfection *f*.
faultless, *a.* Sans défaut, sans faute; impeccable, irréprochable. **-ly,** *adv.* Parfaitement, irréprochablement.
faulty, *a.* Défectueux, imparfait; (*of reasoning, etc.*) erroné, inexact.
faun, *s.* *Myth:* Faune *m*.
fauna, *s.* Faune *f*.
favour[1], *s.* Faveur *f*. **1.** Approbation *f*; bonnes grâces. To be in favour with s.o., être en faveur auprès de qn. **2.** Grâce *f*, bonté *f*. To ask a favour of s.o., solliciter une grâce, une faveur, de qn. To do s.o. a favour, faire une faveur à qn; obliger qn. As a favour, à titre gracieux. **3.** (*a*) Partialité *f*, préférence *f*. (*b*) Appui *m*, protection *f*. **4.** *Prep.phr.* In favour of, en faveur de. To have everything in one's favour, avoir tout pour soi. To decide in f. of s.o., donner gain de cause à qn. To be in favour of sth., être partisan de qch.; tenir pour qch.
favour[2], *v.tr.* Favoriser. **1.** Approuver, préférer. To f. a scheme, approuver un projet. **2.** Gratifier, obliger; accorder une grâce à. To favour s.o. with an interview, accorder un rendez-vous à qn. **3.** (*a*) Avantager; montrer de la partialité pour. (*b*) Faciliter. Favoured by fortune, secondé par le sort.
favoured, *a.* **1.** Favorisé. *F:* The favoured few, les élus. **2.** Well-favoured, beau, *f*. belle.
favourable, *a.* Favorable; (*of weather*) propice; (*of reception*) bienveillant. **-ably,** *adv.* Favorablement, avantageusement.
favourite. **1.** *s.* Favori, *f*. favorite. **2.** *a.* Favori, préféré.
favouritism, *s.* Favoritisme *m*.
fawn[1]. **1.** *s.* *Z:* Faon *m*. **2.** *a.* Fawn (-coloured), fauve.
fawn[2], *v.ind.tr.* To fawn (up)on s.o., (i) (*of dog*) caresser qn; (ii) (*of pers.*) faire le chien couchant auprès de qn; ramper devant qn.
fawning, *a.* Caressant; *F:* servile.
fealty, *s.* Féauté *f*; fidélité *f*.
fear[1], *s.* Crainte *f*, peur *f*. To stand in fear of s.o., redouter, craindre, qn. To go in fear of one's life, craindre pour sa vie. For fear of mistakes, de crainte d'erreur. F: No fear! pas de danger!
fear[2], *v.tr.* **1.** Craindre, avoir peur de, redouter. **2.** Appréhender, craindre. To fear

for s.o., s'inquiéter au sujet de qn. I f. it is too late, j'ai peur, je crains, qu'il ne soit trop tard.
fearful, *a.* **1.** Affreux, effrayant. **2.** Peureux, craintif. **-fully,** *adv.* **1.** Affreusement, terriblement. **2.** Peureusement.
fearless, *a.* Intrépide, courageux; sans peur (of, de). **-ly,** *adv.* Intrépidement; sans peur.
fearlessness, *s.* Intrépidité *f*.
fearsome, *a.* Redoutable.
feasibility, *s.* Praticabilité *f*, possibilité *f*.
feasible, *a.* Faisable, possible.
feast[1], *s.* **1.** Fête *f*. **2.** Festin *m*, banquet *m*.
feast[2]. **1.** *v.i.* Faire festin; banqueter, se régaler. To f. (up)on sth., se régaler de qch. **2.** *v.tr.* Régaler, fêter. **feasting,** *s.* Festoiement *m*; bonne chère.
feat, *s.* **1.** Exploit *m*, haut fait. **2.** Tour *m* de force.
feather[1], *s.* **1.** Plume *f*. *F:* To show the white feather, laisser voir qu'on a peur. **2.** Plumage *m*. To be in high feather, être gai et dispos. *Prov:* Birds of a feather flock together, qui se ressemble s'assemble. **3.** *F:* That's a feather in his cap, c'est pour lui un titre de vanité. **feather-bed,** *s.* Lit *m* de plume. **feather-brained,** *a.* Écervelé, étourdi.
feather[2], *v.tr.* *F:* To feather one's nest, faire sa pelote.
feature, *s.* **1.** Trait *m*. The features, la physionomie. **2.** Trait, caractéristique *f*, particularité *f*. Main features, grands traits.
February, *s.* Février *m*. In F., au mois de février.
fecundity, *s.* Fécondité *f*.
federal, *a.* Fédéral, -aux.
federation, *s.* Fédération *f*.
fee, *s.* (*a*) Honoraires *mpl*. (*b*) School fees, rétribution *f* scolaire; frais *mpl* de scolarité. Examination fee, droit *m* d'examen. *Post:* Registration fee, droit de recommandation.
feeble, *a.* Faible, infirme, débile. **-bly,** *adv.* Faiblement. **feeble-minded,** *a.* D'esprit faible.
feebleness, *s.* Faiblesse *f*.
feed[1], *s.* (*a*) Alimentation *f*. (*b*) Nourriture *f*, pâture *f*. To give the horse a f., donner à manger au cheval. *F:* To be off one's feed, bouder sur la nourriture. (*c*) *F:* Repas *m*, festin *m*. To have a good feed, bien manger; faire bonne chère.
feed[2], *v.* **I.** *v.tr.* **1.** Nourrir; donner à manger à. To feed s.o. on, with, sth., nourrir qn de qch. **2.** Alimenter (une machine). **II.** *v.i.* Manger. (*Of cattle*) Paître. To feed (up)on sth., se nourrir de qch. **feed up,** *v.tr.* Engraisser (une bête); suralimenter (qn). *P:* To be fed up, en avoir assez.
feeding, *s.* Alimentation *f*. **feeding-bottle,** *s.* Biberon *m*.
feel[1], *s.* **1.** Toucher *m*, tact *m*. **2.** (*a*) Toucher, manier *m*, main *f*. To know sth. by the feel

of it, reconnaître qch. au toucher. (*b*) Sensation *f*.
eel², *v*. **1.** (*a*) *v.tr.* Toucher, palper; tâter (le pouls). (*b*) *v.tr. & i.* **To feel about in the dark,** tâtonner dans l'obscurité. **To feel one's way,** (i) aller à tâtons; (ii) *F:* sonder le terrain. **To feel in one's pockets for sth.,** fouiller dans ses poches pour trouver qch. **2.** (*a*) *v.tr.* Sentir. **I felt the floor tremble,** je sentis trembler le plancher. (*b*) *v.tr. & i.* (Res)sentir, éprouver. **To feel the cold,** être sensible au froid; être frileux. **To make one's authority felt,** affirmer son autorité. **To feel a kindly interest towards s.o.,** éprouver de la sympathie pour qn. **To feel for s.o.,** être plein de pitié pour qn. (*c*) *v.tr.* Avoir conscience de (qch.). **I felt it necessary to interfere,** j'ai jugé nécessaire d'intervenir. **3.** *v.i.* (*a*) *Pred.* **To feel cold,** avoir froid. **To feel ill,** se sentir malade. **To feel all the better for it,** s'en trouver mieux. **To feel certain that,** être certain que. (*b*) *I felt like crying,* j'avais envie de pleurer. **4.** *v.i.* **To feel hard,** être dur au toucher. **feeling¹,** *a.* **1.** Sensible. **2.** Ému. **feeling²,** *s.* **1.** Tâtage *m*; maniement *m*. **2. (Sense of) feeling,** toucher *m*, tact *m*. **To have no feeling in one's arm,** avoir le bras mort. **3.** Sensation *f*. **4.** Sentiment *m*. (*a*) *Public f.,* le sentiment populaire. (*b*) *I had a feeling of danger,* j'avais le sentiment d'être en danger. (*c*) Sensibilité *f*, émotion *f*.
eeler, *s.* **1.** Antenne *f*, palpe *f*. **2.** *F:* **To throw out a feeler,** lancer un ballon d'essai.
eign, *v.tr.* Feindre, simuler. **To feign surprise,** affecter la surprise. **feigned,** *a.* Feint, simulé.
eint, *s.* (*a*) *Mil:* Fausse attaque. (*b*) *Box:* Feinte *f*.
elicitations, *s.pl.* Félicitations *f*.
elicitous, *a.* Heureux.
elicity, *s.* Félicité *f*, bonheur *m*.
eline. **1.** *a.* Félin. **2.** *s.* Félin *m*.
ell, *v.tr.* Abattre; assommer.
ellow, *s.* **1.** Camarade *m*, compagnon *m*, confrère *m*, collègue *m*. **Fellow-sufferer,** compagnon de misère. **Fellow-being, fellow-creature,** semblable *m*. **Fellow-citizen,** concitoyen, -enne. **Fellow-countryman, -woman,** compatriote *mf*. **2.** (*Of pers.*) Semblable *m*, pareil *m*; (*of thg*) pendant *m*. **3.** Membre *m*, associé, -ée (d'une société savante). **4.** *F:* (*a*) Homme *m*, garçon *m*. **A good fellow,** un brave garçon, un brave type. *He's a queer f.,* c'est un drôle de type. *The poor little f.,* le pauvre petit. (*b*) Individu *m*. **fellow-feeling,** *s.* Sympathie *f*.
ellowship, *s.* **1.** Communion *f*, communauté *f*. **2.** Association *f*, corporation *f*, (con)fraternité *f*.
elon, *s.* *Jur:* Criminel, -elle.
elonious, *a.* *Jur:* Criminel.
elony, *s.* *Jur:* Crime *m*.
elt, *s.* Feutre *m*.

female. **1.** *a.* (*a*) Féminin; (de) femme. **Female child,** enfant du sexe féminin. (*b*) (*Of animals*) Femelle. **2.** *s.f.* (*a*) Femme. (*b*) (*Of animals*) Femelle.
feminine, *a.* Féminin.
fen, *s.* Marais *m*, marécage *m*.
fence¹, *s.* **1.** Clôture *f*, barrière *f*, palissade *f*. *F:* **To sit on the fence,** ménager la chèvre et le chou. **2.** *P:* Receleur, -euse.
fence². **1.** *v.i.* Faire de l'escrime. **2.** *v.tr.* **To fence (in),** clôturer, palissader (un terrain).
fencing, *s.* **1.** Escrime *f*. **2. Fencing (in),** clôture *f*, palissadement *m*. **3.** Clôture, barrière *f*, palissade *f*. **fencing-master,** *s.* Maître *m* d'escrime, d'armes. **fencing-match,** *s.* Assaut *m* d'armes.
fend. **1.** *v.tr.* **To fend off,** parer, détourner. **2.** *v.i.* **To fend for oneself,** se débrouiller.
fender, *s.* *Furn:* Galerie *f* de foyer; garde-feu *m inv*.
ferment¹, *s.* **1.** Ferment *m*. **2.** Fermentation *f*; *F:* agitation *f*.
ferment², *v.i.* Fermenter.
fermentation, *s.* Fermentation *f*.
fern, *s.* *Bot:* Fougère *f*.
ferocious, *a.* Féroce. **-ly,** *adv.* Avec férocité.
ferocity, *s.* Férocité *f*.
ferret¹, *s.* *Z:* Furet *m*.
ferret², *v.* **1.** *v.i.* Fureter; chasser au furet. **2.** *v.tr.* *F:* **To ferret out (sth.),** dénicher (qch.). **ferreting,** *s.* Furetage *m*; chasse *f* au furet.
ferrule, *s.* Bout ferré, embout *m*.
ferry¹, *s.* **1.** Endroit *m* où l'on peut passer la rivière en bac; passage *m*; *F:* le bac. **To cross the ferry,** passer le bac. **2.** = FERRY-BOAT. **Train ferry,** transbordeur *m* de trains. **ferry-boat,** *s.* Bac *m*; bateau *m* de passage.
ferry², *v.tr.* **To f. the car across the river,** passer la voiture en bac.
ferryman, *s.* Passeur *m*.
fertile, *a.* Fertile, fécond (*in,* en).
fertility, *s.* Fertilité *f*, fécondité *f*.
fertilization, *s.* Fertilisation *f*.
fertilize, *v.tr.* Fertiliser.
fervency, *s.* Ferveur *f*.
fervent, *a.* Ardent, fervent. **-ly,** *adv.* Avec ferveur.
fervid, *a.* Fervent.
fervour, *s.* Passion *f*, ferveur *f*.
fester, *v.i.* Suppurer. **festering,** *a.* Ulcéreux, suppurant.
festival, *s.* Fête *f*.
festive, *a.* (Jour) de fête; (table) du festin. **The festive season,** Noël *m*.
festivity, *s.* Fête *f*, réjouissance *f*.
festoon¹, *s.* Feston *m*, guirlande *f*.
festoon², *v.tr.* Festonner (*with,* de).
fetch, *v.tr.* **1.** (*a*) Aller chercher. **Go and f. him,** allez le chercher. **To f. water from the river,** aller puiser de l'eau à la rivière. (*b*) Apporter (qch.); amener (qn). **2.** Rapporter.

It fetched a high price, cela se vendit cher. **3.** *F: That'll fetch him!* voilà qui le séduira! **4. To fetch a sigh,** pousser un soupir. **5.** *F: To fetch s.o. a blow,* flanquer un coup à qn. **fetching,** *a.* Séduisant, attrayant.

fête¹, *s.* Fête *f.*

fête², *v.tr.* Fêter; faire fête à.

fetid, *a.* Fétide, puant.

fetidity, *s.* Fétidité *f*, puanteur *f.*

fetish, *s.* Fétiche *m.*

fetter¹, *s.* Lien *m*; *pl.* chaînes *f*, fers *m*; entrave *f* (d'un cheval).

fetter², *v.tr.* Enchaîner; charger de fers; entraver (un cheval).

feud, *s.* Inimitié *f. Family feuds,* dissensions *f* domestiques.

feudal, *a.* Féodal, -aux.

feudalism, *s.* Le régime féodal; la féodalité.

fever¹, *s. Med:* Fièvre *f. F: A fever of excitement,* une agitation fébrile.

fever², *v.tr.* Enfiévrer; donner la fièvre à.

fevered, *a.* Enfiévré, fiévreux.

feverish, *a.* Fiévreux, fébrile. **-ly,** *adv.* Fiévreusement, fébrilement.

feverishness, *s.* État fiévreux.

few, *a.* **I.** *(a)* Peu de. *He has (but) few friends,* il a peu d'amis. *With few exceptions,* à de rares exceptions près. *(b)* **A few,** quelques. *A few more,* encore quelques-uns. *In a few minutes,* dans quelques minutes. *(c)* Peu nombreux. *Such occasions are few,* de telles occasions sont rares. **2.** *(a)* Peu (de gens). *Few of them had travelled,* peu d'entre eux avaient voyagé. *There are very few of us,* nous sommes peu nombreux. *(b)* Quelques-uns, -unes. *A few thought otherwise,* quelques-uns pensaient autrement. *F: There were a good few of them,* il y en avait pas mal.

fewer, *a.* **I.** Moins (de). **2.** *(Pred. use)* Plus rares; moins nombreux.

fewest, *a.* Le moins (de).

fewness, *s.* Rareté *f*; petit nombre.

fiasco, *s.* Fiasco *m*; *F:* four *m.*

fiat, *s.* Décret *m*, ordre *m.*

fib¹, *s. F:* Petit mensonge; *F:* colle *f.*

fib², *v.i. F:* Blaguer, craquer.

fibre, *s.* **I.** Fibre *f*; filament *m.* **A man of coarse fibre,** un homme d'une trempe grossière. **2.** *Com:* **Fibre trunk,** malle en fibre.

fibrous, *a.* Fibreux.

fickle, *a.* Inconstant, volage.

fickleness, *s.* Inconstance *f.*

fiction, *s.* **I.** Fiction *f*; création *f* de l'imagination. **2.** (Works of) **fiction,** romans *m*; ouvrages *m* d'imagination.

fictitious, *a.* Fictif. *F. being,* être imaginaire.

fiddle¹, *s.* **I.** *F:* *(a)* Violon *m.* *(b) First f.,* premier violon. *F:* **To play second fiddle,** jouer un rôle secondaire. **2.** *Nau:* Violon de mer; fiche *f* de roulis.

fiddle², *v.i. F:* **I.** Jouer du violon. **2.** S'amuser à des niaiseries; tripoter, bricoler.

fiddling, *a. F:* Futile, insignifiant.

fiddler, *s.* Joueur *m* de violon.

fiddlestick, *s.* Archet *m* (de violon).

fidelity, *s.* Fidélité *f*, loyauté *f.*

fidget¹, *s.* **I. To have the fidgets,** ne p[tenir en place. **2. He's a fidget,** c'est u[énervé.

fidget², *v.i.* *(a)* To fidget (about), remu[continuellement; se trémousser. *(b)* S'in[quiéter, se tourmenter. **fidgeting,** Agitation nerveuse; nervosité *f.*

fidgety, *a.* **I.** Qui remue continuellemen[**2.** Nerveux, impatient.

fie, *int.* Fie (upon you)! fi (donc)!

field, *s.* **I.** Champ *m.* *(a) In the fields,* au[champs. *(b)* District *m*, région *f.* *(c) Mi[* Field of battle, champ de bataille. *To tak[* the field, entrer en campagne. **2.** Étendue espace *m.* **Field of ice,** banc *m* de glace banquise *f.* **3.** Théâtre *m*, champ; domai[*m* (d'une science). **To have a clear fiel[** before one, avoir le champ libre. **field-artillery,** *s.* Artillerie *f* de campagn[**field-day,** *s.* **I.** *Mil:* Jour *m* de grande[manœuvres. **2.** *F:* Grande occasion; gran[jour. **field-glass,** *s.* *(a)* Lunette *f* d'ap[proche. *(b) Usu. pl.* Jumelle(s) *f.* **field-marshal,** *s.* (Feld-)maréchal *m, pl.* -aux[**field-mouse,** *s.* Mulot *m.* **field-office[** *s. Mil:* Officier supérieur. **field-sports[** *s.pl.* Sports *m* au grand air.

fiend, *s.* *(a)* Démon *m*, diable *m.* *(b)* Monstre *n* **fiendish,** *a.* Diabolique, satanique. **-ly** *adv.* Diaboliquement.

fierce, *a.* Féroce; *(of battle)* acharné; *([wind)* furieux, violent. **-ly,** *adv.* **I.** Féroc[ment. **2.** Violemment; avec acharnement.

fierceness, *s.* Violence *f*; férocité *f* (d'u[animal); ardeur *f* (du feu); acharnement [(de la bataille).

fiery, *a.* **I.** Ardent, brûlant, enflamm[**2.** (i) Fougueux, emporté, impétueux[(ii) colérique.

fife, *s. Mus:* Fifre *m.*

fifteen, *num. a. & s.* Quinze (*m*).

fifteenth, *num. a. & s.* Quinzièm[**Louis the Fifteenth,** Louis Quinze. **2.** [Quinzième *m.*

fifth. **I.** *num. a. & s.* Cinquième. **Henr[** the Fifth, Henri Cinq. **2.** *s.* Cinquième *m.*

fifty, *num. a. & s.* Cinquante (*m*). **To g[** **fifty-fifty with s.o.,** se mettre de moitié ave[qn. *About f. books,* une cinquantaine de livre[

fig, *s.* Figue *f*, figues fraîche[*F: A fig for Smith!* zut pour Smith! F[(-tree), figuier *m.* **fig-leaf,** *s.* Feuille *f* d[figuier.

fight¹, *s.* **I.** *(a)* Combat *m*, bataille *f.* *(b)* Box[Assaut *m.* **Hand-to-hand fight,** corps-à-corp[*m.* **Fight to the death,** combat à outrance[**Free fight,** mêlée générale. **2.** *(a)* Lutte [*(b)* **To show fight,** résister. **There was n[** fight left in him, il n'avait plus de cœur à s[battre.

fight², *v.* **I.** *v.i.* Se battre; combattre[

lutter. *To f. against disease*, combattre la maladie. *F: To f. for one's own hand*, défendre ses propres intérêts. **To fight a battle**, livrer une bataille. **To fight one's way (out)**, se frayer un passage (pour sortir). **2.** *v.tr.* **To fight s.o.**, se battre avec, contre, qn; combattre qn. **fight down**, *v.tr.* Vaincre. **fight off**, *v.tr.* Résister à. **fighting**[1], *a.* Fighting men, combattants *m.* **fighting**[2], *s.* Combat *m.* **fighting-cock**, *s.* Coq *m* de combat.

fighter, *s.* **1.** Combattant *m.* **2.** *Av:* Chasseur *m.*

figurative, *a.* **1.** Figuratif, emblématique. **2.** (*Of language*) Figuré, métaphorique. **-ly**, *adv.* **1.** Figurativement. **2.** Au figuré.

figure[1], *s.* **1.** (*a*) Figure *f;* forme extérieure. (*b*) (*Of pers.*) Taille *f,* tournure *f.* **2.** (*a*) Personne *f,* être *m. What a f. of fun!* quelle caricature! (*b*) Personnage *m.* (*c*) Figure, apparence *f.* **3.** *Art:* Lay figure, mannequin *m.* **4.** Geometrical figure, figure géométrique. **5.** Chiffre *m. In round figures*, en chiffres ronds. *A mistake in the figures*, une erreur de calcul. *To fetch a high figure*, se vendre cher. *F: What's the figure?* ça coûte combien? **6.** Figure of speech, façon *f* de parler. **figure-head**, *s.* **1.** *N.Arch:* Figure *f* de proue. **2.** *F:* Personnage purement décoratif.

figure[2]. **1.** *v.tr.* (*a*) Figurer, représenter. (*b*) To figure sth. (to oneself), se représenter, se figurer, qch. **2.** *v.i.* (*a*) Chiffrer, calculer. (*b*) His name figures on the list, son nom figure, se trouve, sur la liste.

filament, *s.* **1.** Filament *m,* cil *m.* **2.** *El:* Fil *m,* filament.

filbert, *s.* Aveline *f.*

filch, *v.tr.* Chiper, filouter, escamoter.

file[1], *s.* *Tls:* Lime *f.*

file[2], *v.tr.* Limer. **filing**[1], *s.* **1.** Limage *m* **2.** *pl.* Filings, limaille *f.*

file[3], *s.* **1.** (*a*) Bill file, spike file, pique-notes *m inv.* (*b*) Classeur *m,* cartonnier *m.* Card-index file, fichier *m.* **2.** Collection *f,* liasse *f.* *Adm:* Dossier *m.*

file[4], *v.tr.* Enfiler; classer (des fiches); ranger (des lettres). *To f. a document*, joindre une pièce au dossier. **filing**[2], *s.* Classement *m.* Filing-case, cartonnier *m.* Filing-cabinet, classeur *m.*

file[5], *s.* File *f.* In single, Indian, file, en file indienne; *F:* à la queue leu leu.

file[6], *v.i.* To file off, défiler.

filial, *a.* Filial, -als, -aux.

filibuster, *s.* *Hist:* Flibustier *m.*

filigree, *s.* Filigrane *f.*

fill[1], *s.* To eat one's fill, manger à sa faim.

fill[2]. **I.** *v.tr.* **1.** (*a*) Remplir, emplir (*with*, de). To fill one's pipe, charger sa pipe. To fill the air with one's cries, remplir l'air de ses cris. **2.** (*a*) Combler. (*b*) To fill (up) a vacancy, suppléer, pourvoir, à une vacance.

3. Occuper. (*a*) *Th:* To fill a part, remplir un rôle. (*b*) *The thoughts that filled his mind*, les pensées qui occupaient son esprit. **II.** fill, *v.i.* **1.** Se remplir, s'emplir. **2.** (*Of sails*) S'enfler, porter. **fill in**, *v.tr.* Combler, remplir. **To fill in the date**, insérer la date. **fill out. 1.** *v.tr.* Enfler, gonfler. **2.** *v.i.* S'enfler, se gonfler. **fill up. 1.** *v.tr.* (*a*) Remplir jusqu'au bord; combler. *Abs.* To fill up with petrol, faire le plein d'essence. (*b*) Boucher. (*c*) Remplir (une formule); libeller (un chèque). **2.** *v.i.* Se remplir, s'emplir, se combler. **filling**[1], *a.* Rassasiant.

filling[2], *s.* **1.** (R)emplissage *m* (d'une mesure); chargement *m* (d'un wagon). **2.** Filling of a vacancy, nomination *f* de quelqu'un à un poste. **3.** Occupation *f* (d'un poste). **4.** Matière *f* de remplissage.

fillet, *s.* **1.** *Cost:* Filet *m,* bandelette *f.* **2.** *Cu:* (*a*) Filet (de bœuf). (*b*) Rouelle *f* (de veau).

filly, *s.* Pouliche *f.*

film, *s.* **1.** (*a*) Pellicule *f,* couche *f.* (*b*) *F:* Voile *m* (de brume). **2.** *Phot:* Pellicule. **3.** *Cin:* (*a*) Film *m,* bande *f.* (*b*) The films, le cinématographe; *F:* le ciné. **Film-star**, vedette *f* de l'écran, du ciné.

filter[1], *s.* Filtre *m.* **filter-paper**, *s.* Papier *m* filtre.

filter[2], *v.tr. & i.* Filtrer.

filth, *s.* **1.** Ordure *f;* immondices *mpl.* **2.** Corruption morale.

filthiness, *s.* **1.** Saleté *f.* **2.** Corruption morale.

filthy, *a.* Sale, immonde, dégoûtant. A filthy hovel, un taudis infect.

filtration, *s.* Filtration *f,* filtrage *m.*

fin, *s.* Nageoire *f* (d'un poisson); aileron *m* (d'un requin).

final, *a.* Final, -als. (*a*) Dernier. To put the final touches to sth., mettre la dernière main à qch. (*b*) Définitif, décisif. Am I to consider that as final? c'est votre dernier mot? **-ally**, *adv.* Finalement. **1.** Enfin. **2.** Définitivement. **3.** En somme, en définitive.

finale, *s.* **1.** *Mus:* Final(e) *m.* **2.** *F:* Conclusion *f.*

finality, *s.* Caractère définitif; finalité *f.*

finance[1], *s.* Finance *f.*

finance[2], *v.tr.* Financer, commanditer.

financial, *a.* Financier.

financier, *s.* Financier *m.*

finch, *s.* *Orn:* Pinson *m.*

find[1], *s.* **1.** Découverte *f.* **2.** Trouvaille *f.*

find[2], *v.tr.* Trouver. **1.** (*a*) Rencontrer, découvrir. **It is found everywhere**, cela se trouve partout. **To find some difficulty in doing sth.**, éprouver quelque difficulté à faire qch. (*b*) *I found myself crying*, je me surpris à pleurer. **2.** (*a*) The (lost) key has been found, la clef s'est retrouvée. To try to find sth., chercher qch. He is not to be found, il est introuvable. **To find a leak in a main,** localiser une fuite dans une conduite. **I can't find time** to, je n'ai pas le temps de. (*b*) Obtenir (une sûreté). **3.** (*a*) Constater. *I f. it is time to go,* je m'aperçois qu'il est temps de partir. (*b*) **They will find it easy,** cela leur sera facile. **4.** *Jur:* (*a*) **To find s.o. guilty,** déclarer qn coupable. (*b*) Rendre (un verdict). **5.** (*a*) **To find the money for an undertaking,** procurer les capitaux pour une entreprise. (*b*) **All found,** tout fourni. *To f. oneself in clothes,* se vêtir à ses frais. **find out,** *v.tr.* (*a*) Deviner; découvrir; constater (une erreur). *Abs.* **To find out about sth.,** se renseigner sur qch. (*b*) **To find s.o. out,** (i) découvrir le vrai caractère de qn; (ii) trouver qn en défaut. **finding,** *s.* **I.** Découverte *f.* **2.** Trouvaille *f.* **3.** Constatation *f.*

fine¹, *s.* **I. In fine,** enfin, finalement. **2.** *Jur:* Amende *f.*

fine², *v.tr.* Condamner à une amende; frapper d'une amende.

fine³, *a.* **I.** (*a*) Fin, pur. (*b*) Fin, subtil, raffiné. *F. distinction,* distinction subtile. **2.** Beau, bel, belle, beaux. (*a*) **The fine arts,** les beaux-arts *m.* (*b*) **To appeal to s.o.'s finer feelings,** faire appel aux sentiments élevés de qn. **3.** (*a*) *Of the finest quality,* de premier choix. (*b*) Excellent, magnifique. *F. display,* étalage superbe. **We had a fine time,** nous nous sommes bien amusés. **That's fine!** voilà qui est parfait. (*c*) **That's all very fine,** tout cela est bel et bon. **4.** Beau. *When the weather is f.,* quand il fait beau. *F:* **One of these fine days,** un de ces beaux jours. **5.** (*a*) (*Of texture*) Fin; (*of dust*) menu, subtil. (*b*) **Fine edge,** tranchant affilé. **Fine nib,** plume pointue. **6.** *F:* **To cut it fine,** faire qch. tout juste. **-ly,** *adv.* **I.** Finement; (*b*) Habilement; on ne peut mieux. (*b*) Délicatement, subtilement. **2.** Admirablement, magnifiquement.

fineness, *s.* **I.** Titre *m,* aloi *m* (de l'or). **2.** Qualité supérieure, excellence *f.* **3.** Finesse *f* (d'une étoffe); ténuité *f* (d'un fil).

finery, *s.* Parure *f;* fanfreluches *fpl.*

finesse, *s* Finesse *f.*

finger¹, *s.* Doigt *m* (de la main). **First finger,** index *m.* *F:* **I forbid you to lay a finger on him,** je vous défends de le toucher. **To point the finger of scorn at s.o.,** montrer qn au doigt. *He has a f. in every pie,* il est mêlé à tout. **He has the whole business at his fingers' ends,** il est au courant de toute l'affaire. **finger-nail,** *s.* Ongle *m* (de la main). **finger-print,** *s.* *Adm:* Empreinte digitale.

finger², *v.tr.* **I.** Manier, tâter. **2.** *Mus:* Doigter. **fingering,** *s.* **I.** Maniement *m.* **2.** *Mus:* Doigter *m,* doigté *m.*

finicky, *a.* Méticuleux, vétilleux; (*of pers.*) fignoleur, -euse.

finish¹, *s.* **I.** Fin *f. Sp:* Arrivée *f.* **To fight (it out) to a finish,** se battre jusqu'à une décision. **2.** (*a*) Fini *m,* achevé *m;* finesse *f* de l'exécution. (*b*) Apprêt *m* (d'un drap).

finish². **I.** *v.tr.* Finir; terminer, achever. **To finish off a wounded beast,** expédier une bête blessée. **2.** *v.i.* Finir. (*a*) Cesser, se terminer. (*b*) *Wait till I've finished with him!* attendez que je lui aie réglé son compte! **finished,** *a.* **I.** (*Article*) fini, apprêté. **2.** Soigné, parfait. **A finished speaker,** un orateur accompli.

finite, *a.* Fini, limité, borné.

Finland. *Pr.n. Geog:* La Finlande.

Finn, *s.* Finnois, -oise.

Finnish. **I.** *a.* Finlandais. **2.** *s. Ling:* Le finnois.

fiord, *s.* Fiord *m,* fjord *m.*

fir, *s.* **I.** Fir(-tree), sapin *m.* **Fir plantation,** sapinière *f.* **2.** (Bois *m* de) sapin. **fir-cone,** *s* Pomme *f,* cône *m,* de sapin; pigne *f.*

fire¹, *s.* **I.** Feu *m.* (*a*) **To light a fire,** faire du feu. **Electric fire,** radiateur *m* électrique. (*b*) Incendie *m,* sinistre *m. An outbreak of f. took place,* un incendie s'est déclaré. **Fire!** au feu! **To catch fire,** prendre feu; s'enflammer. **To set fire to sth.,** mettre le feu à qch. **On fire,** en feu, en flammes. *F:* **To get on like a house on fire,** avancer à pas de géant. *F:* **To add fuel to the fire,** jeter de l'huile sur le feu. (*c*) Lumière *f,* éclat *m.* **2.** *F:* Ardeur *f,* zèle *m.* **3.** *Mil:* Feu, tir *m.* **To be under fire,** essuyer le feu. **fire-alarm,** *s.* (Appareil) avertisseur *m* d'incendie. **fire-arm,** *s.* Arme *f* à feu. **fire-brand,** *s.* **I.** Tison *m,* brandon *m.* **2.** *F:* Brandon de discorde. **fire-brigade,** *s.* (Corps *m* de) sapeurs-pompiers *mpl; F:* les pompiers *m.* **fire-dog,** *s.* *Furn:* Chenet *m.* **fire-eater,** *s.* Matamore *m.* **fire-engine,** *s.* Pompe *f* à incendie. **fire-escape,** *s.* Échelle *f* de sauvetage. **fire-extinguisher,** *s.* Extincteur *m* d'incendie. **fire-fly,** *s.* *Ent:* Luciole *f; F:* mouche *f* à feu. **fire-guard,** *s.* Pare-étincelles *m inv;* garde-feu *m inv.* **fire-insurance,** *s.* Assurance *f* contre l'incendie. **fire-irons,** *s.pl.* Garniture *f* de foyer. **fire-lighter,** *s.* Allume-feu *m inv.* **fire-place,** *s.* Cheminée *f,* foyer *m.* **fire-proof,** *a.* (*a*) Incombustible, ignifuge. (*b*) *Cer:* Réfractaire. *F.-p. dish,* plat allant au feu. **fire-screen,** *s.* Devant *m* de cheminée. **fire-wood,** *s* Bois *m* de chauffage; bois à brûler.

fire², *v.* **I.** *v.tr.* **I.** (*a*) Mettre feu à, embraser. (*b*) Animer. **2.** (*a*) **To fire a torpedo,** lancer une torpille. (*b*) *Abs.* **To fire at, on, s.o.,** tirer sur qn. **To fire (off),** décharger (un canon). *Without firing a shot,* sans brûler une amorce. **3.** *F:* Renvoyer (un employé). **II. fire,** *v.i. The revolver failed to f.,* le revolver fit long feu. **fire away,** *v. F:* **Fire away!** allez-y! **fire up,** *v.i. F:* S'emporter. *To f. up in a moment,* monter comme une soupe au lait. **firing,** *s.* **I.** *Cer:* Cuite *f,* cuisson *f.* **2.** Chauffage *m,* chauffe *f.* **3.** *Mil:* Tir *m,* feu *m.* **Firing party,** peloton *m* d'exécution.

fireman, s. **1.** Chauffeur *m.* **2.** (Sapeur-) pompier *m.*

fireside, s. Foyer *m*; coin *m* du feu.

firework, s. **1.** Pièce *f* d'artifice. **2.** *pl.* Fireworks, feu *m* d'artifice.

firm[1], s. *Com:* **1.** Raison sociale; firme *f.* **2.** Maison *f* (de commerce).

firm[2], *a.* Ferme. **1.** (*Of substance*) Consistant, compact; (*of post*) solide; (*of touch*) vigoureux, assuré. As firm as a rock, inébranlable. **2.** (*Of friendship*) Constant; (*of intention*) résolu. **3.** *adv.* To stand firm, tenir bon; tenir ferme. **-ly,** *adv.* **1.** Fermement, solidement. **2.** D'un ton ferme.

firmament, s. Firmament *m.*

firmness, s. Fermeté *f*; solidité *f.*

first. I. *a.* Premier. (*a*) *The f. of April,* le premier avril. At first sight, de prime abord; au premier abord. In the first place, d'abord; en premier lieu. To fall head first, tomber la tête la première. *F:* First thing, en tout premier lieu. *Th:* First night, première *f.* *Typ:* First edition, édition princeps. (*b*) *To have got news at* first hand, tenir une nouvelle de première main. **-ly,** *adv.* Premièrement; en premier lieu. **II. first,** s. **1.** (Le) premier, (la) première. To come in an easy first, arriver bon premier. **2.** Commencement *m.* *From f. to last,* depuis le début jusqu'à la fin. From the first, dès le premier jour At first, au commencement; d'abord. **3.** I always travel first, je voyage toujours en première. **III. first,** *adv.* **1.** Premièrement, au commencement, d'abord. First of all, en premier lieu. First and last, en tout et pour tout. To say first one thing and then another, *F:* dire tantôt blanc tantôt noir. **2.** Pour la première fois. **3.** Plutôt. I'd die first, plutôt mourir. **4.** He arrived first, il arriva le premier. You go first! allez devant! First come first served les premiers vont devant. Ladies first! place aux dames! **first-aid,** s. Premiers secours.

first-born, *a. & s.* Premier-né, *pl.* premiersnés, *f.* première(s)-née(s). **first-class,** *a.* De première classe; de première qualité. *F.-c.* player, joueur de premier ordre. That's firstclass! à la bonne heure! **first-rate,** *a.* Excellent; de première classe.

fiscal, *a.* Fiscal, -aux.

fish[1], s. Poisson *m.* *F:* Like a fish out of water, comme un poisson sur la paille. All is fish that comes to his net, tout lui est bon. I've other fish to fry, j'ai d'autres chats à fouetter. *F:* He's a queer fish, c'est un drôle de corps. **fish-bone,** s. Arête *f* (de poisson). **fish-hook,** s. Hameçon *m.* **fishknife,** s. Couteau *m* à poisson.

fish[2]. **1.** *v.i.* Pêcher. To *f. for trout,* pêcher la truite. **2.** *v.tr.* To fish up a dead body, (re)pêcher un cadavre. **fishing,** s. La pêche. **fishing-boat,** s. Bateau *m* de pêche. **fishing-line,** s. Ligne *f* de pêche. **fishingnet,** s. Filet *m* de pêche. **fishing-rod,**

s. Canne *f* à pêche. **fishing-tackle,** s. Appareil *m,* attirail *m,* de pêche.

fisherman, s. Pêcheur *m.*

fishery, s. **1.** Pêche *f.* *Whale f.,* pêche à la baleine. **2.** Pêcherie *f.*

fishmonger, s. Marchand, -ande, de poisson.

fishpond, s. Vivier *m.*

fishwife, s. Marchande *f* de poisson.

fishy, *a.* **1.** (Odeur) de poisson. *F:* Fishy eyes, yeux ternes, vitreux. **2.** *F:* Véreux; louche.

fission, s. Fission *f.* *Atomic f.* Fission de l'atome.

fissure, s. Fissure *f,* fente *f,* crevasse *f.*

fist, s. Poing *m.* To shake one's fist at s.o., menacer qn du poing.

fisticuffs, *s.pl.* Coups *m* de poing.

fit[1], s. **1.** (*a*) Accès *m,* attaque *f.* **Fit of coughing,** quinte *f* de toux. (*b*) To frighten s.o. into fits, convulser qn. **2.** Accès, mouvement *m.* Fit of crying, crise *f* de larmes. To be in fits of laughter, avoir le fou rire. To work by fits and starts, travailler à bâtons rompus.

fit[2], *a.* **1.** Bon, propre, convenable (*for sth.,* à qch.). I am not fit to be seen, je ne suis pas présentable. To think fit to do sth., juger convenable de faire qch. **2.** (*a*) Capable. Fit for sth., en état de faire qch.; apte à qch. He is fit for nothing, il n'est propre à rien. (*b*) *F:* Disposé, prêt (à faire qch.). **3.** To be (bodily) fit, être en bonne santé. *F:* To be as fit as a fiddle, être en parfaite santé. **-ly,** *adv.* Convenablement.

fit[3], s. Ajustement *m.* Your coat is a perfect fit, votre pardessus est juste à votre taille.

fit[4], *v.* **I.** *v.tr.* **1.** Aller à (qn); être à la taille de (qn). It fits you like a glove, cela vous va comme un gant. **2.** (*a*) Adapter, ajuster, accommoder (*sth. to sth.,* qch. à qch.). (*b*) To fit parts (*together*), monter, assembler, des pièces. **3.** To fit s.o. for sth., préparer qn à qch. **4.** To fit sth. with sth., garnir, munir, qch. de qch. **II. fit,** *v.i.* (*a*) To fit (together), s'ajuster, s'adapter, se raccorder. (*b*) Your dress fits well, votre robe (vous) va bien. **fit in,** *v.i.* To fit in with sth., être en harmonie avec qch. **fit on,** *v.tr.* Essayer (un vêtement). **fit out,** *v.tr.* Équiper (*sth. with sth.,* qch. de qch.). **fitted,** *a.* **1.** Ajusté, monté. **2.** He is f. for the post, il est apte à occuper le poste. **fitting**[1], *a.* Convenable, bienséant; approprié (*to,* à). **-ly,** *adv.* Convenablement; à propos. **fitting**[2], s. **1.** (*a*) Ajustage *m.* (*b*) Fitting (on), essayage *m,* ajustage (de vêtements). **2.** *Usu. pl.* Agencements *m,* installations *f* (d'un atelier); garniture *f* (d'une chambre).

fitful, *a.* Irrégulier, capricieux. **-fully,** *adv.* Irrégulièrement; par à-coups.

fitness, s. **1.** Aptitude *f* (*for,* à, pour). **2.** (*a*) A-propos *m,* justesse *f.* (*b*) Convenance *f,* bienséance *f* **3.** Physical fitness, santé *f* physique.

five, *num. a. & s.* Cinq (*m*).

fix¹, s. F: Embarras m, difficulté f, mauvais pas. *To get into a fix,* se mettre dans le pétrin.

fix², v.tr. Fixer. **I.** Caler, monter; assurer. **2.** *Phot:* Fixer. **3.** (a) Fixer, établir (une limite); arrêter, nommer (un jour). **There is nothing fixed yet,** il n'y a encore rien d'assuré, rien d'arrêté. (b) **To fix (up)on sth.,** se décider pour qch. **fix up,** v.tr. F: Arranger (une affaire). *I've fixed it up,* j'ai conclu l'affaire. *It is all fixed up,* c'est une affaire réglée. **fixed,** a. Fixe, arrêté. *Com:* **Fixed prices,** prix fixes. F: *rule,* règle établie.

fixedly, adv. Fixement.

fixity, s. Fixité f.

fixture, s. **I.** Appareil m fixe; meuble m à demeure. **2.** *Sp:* Engagement m.

fizz¹, s. Pétillement m.

fizz², v.i. Pétiller.

fizzle, v.i. Pétiller. **fizzle out,** v.i. P: Ne pas aboutir; avorter.

fizzy, a. Gazeux, effervescent.

flabbergast, v.tr. F: Épater, abasourdir, ahurir.

flabbiness, s. Flaccidité f, manque m de fermeté; mollesse f (de caractère).

flabby, a. Flasque; mou, f. molle; (of cheeks) pendant.

flag¹, s. *Bot:* Iris m.

flag², s. (**Paving-)flag,** carreau m; dalle f.

flag³, s. **I.** (a) Drapeau m. **Flag of truce,** white flag, drapeau parlementaire. (b) *Nau:* Pavillon m. **To fly a flag,** (i) battre pavillon; (ii) arborer un pavillon. (c) **To deck a ship with flags,** pavoiser un vaisseau. **2.** Drapeau (de taximètre).

flag⁴, v.i. S'alanguir; (of conversation) traîner; (of zeal) se relâcher.

flagon, s. **I.** Flacon m. **2.** Grosse bouteille ventrue.

flagrancy, s. Énormité f.

flagrant, a. Flagrant, énorme. **-ly,** adv. Scandaleusement.

flagship, s. (Vaisseau m) amiral m.

flagstaff, s. **I.** (i) Mât m de drapeau; (ii) hampe f de drapeau. **2.** *Nau:* Mât de pavillon.

flagstone, s. = FLAG².

flail, s. *Husb:* Fléau m.

flair, s. Flair m, perspicacité f.

flake, s. (a) Flocon m (de neige, etc.). (b) Écaille f, éclat m.

flamboyant, a. Flamboyant.

flame¹, s. **I.** Flamme f. **In flames,** en flammes, en feu. **To burst into flame(s),** s'enflammer brusquement. **2.** F: Passion f, ardeur f, flamme.

flame², v.i. Flamber, jeter des flammes. **flame up,** v.i. (a) S'enflammer. (b) F: S'enflammer de colère; s'emporter. **flaming,** a. **I.** (Feu) flambant, flamboyant; (maison) en flammes. **2.** F: **Flaming red,** rouge feu inv.

flamingo, s. *Orn:* Flamant m.

Flanders. *Pr.n. Geog:* La Flandre.

flank, s. Flanc m.

flannel, s. Flanelle f.

flannelette, s. Flanelle f de coton.

flap¹, s. **I.** (a) Battement m, coup m (d'aile); clapotement m, claquement m (d'une voile). (b) Coup léger (de la main); tape f. **2.** (a) Patte f (d'une enveloppe). (b) Abattant m (de table).

flap², v. **I.** v.tr. (a) Battre (des ailes). (b) Frapper légèrement. **2.** v.i. (Of sail) Battre, fouetter, claquer; (of wings) battre.

flare¹, s. (a) Flamboiement irrégulier. (b) *Mil:* Artifice éclairant; fusée éclairante. *Av:* **Landing flare,** feu m d'atterrissage.

flare², v.i. Flamboyer, vaciller. **flare up,** v.i. (a) S'enflammer brusquement. (b) F: S'emporter; se mettre en colère. **flare-up,** s. F: Altercation f, scène f.

flash¹, s. **I.** Éclair m; éclat m (de flamme). F: **A flash in the pan,** un feu de paille. **Flash of wit,** saillie f, boutade f. **In a flash,** en un rien de temps.

flash². **I.** v.i. (a) Jeter des éclairs; (of diamonds) étinceler. (b) **To flash past,** passer comme un éclair. **It flashed upon me,** l'idée me vint tout d'un coup. **2.** v.tr. (a) Faire étinceler. (b) Projeter (un rayon de lumière). **flashing,** a. Éclatant, flamboyant.

flashiness, s. Éclat superficiel; faux brillant.

flashy, a. Voyant, éclatant, tapageur. **-ily,** adv. **Flashily-dressed,** à toilette tapageuse.

flask, s. Flacon m; gourde f.

flat¹, s. Appartement m.

flat². **I.** a. Plat. **I.** (a) Horizontal, -aux; posé à plat. (b) Étendu à plat. (c) Plat, uni. **Flat tyre,** pneu à plat. F: **As flat as a pancake,** plat comme une galette. **2.** F: Net, f. nette; positif. F: **That's flat,** voilà qui est net! **3.** (a) Monotone, ennuyeux. F: **To fall flat,** rater, manquer, son effet. (b) (Of drink) Éventé, plat. **4.** Invariable, uniforme. **Flat rate of pay,** taux uniforme de salaires. **5.** (a) (Son) sourd. (b) *Mus:* Bémol inv. **To sing flat,** chanter faux. **-ly,** adv. F: Nettement, carrément. II. **flat,** adv. F: Nettement, positivement. III. **flat,** s. **I.** Plat m (d'un sabre). **2.** Plaine f; bas-fond m; marécage m. **3.** *Mus:* Bémol m.

flatness, s. **I.** Égalité f (d'une surface); manque m de relief. **2.** F: Netteté f (d'un refus). **3.** F: Monotonie f (de l'existence).

flatten, v. **I.** v.tr. **To flatten (out),** aplatir. F: **To flatten oneself against a wall,** se plaquer contre un mur. **To flatten out (s.o.),** aplatir, écraser, qn. **2.** v.i. (a) S'aplatir, s'aplanir. (b) *Av:* **To flatten out,** se redresser.

flatter, v.tr. Flatter. **flattering,** a. Flatteur, -euse. **-ly,** adv. Flatteusement.

flatterer, s. Flatteur, -euse.

flattery, s. Flatterie f.

flaunt, v.tr. **To f. one's wealth,** faire étalage de son opulence. **To f. advanced opinions,** afficher des opinions avancées.

flavour¹, s. Saveur f, goût m.
flavour², v.tr. Assaisonner, parfumer. **flavouring**, s. Assaisonnement m, condiment m.
flavourless, a. Sans saveur; insipide.
flaw, s. Défaut m, défectuosité f, imperfection f. F. in a scheme, point m faible d'un projet.
flawless, a. Sans défaut; parfait; impeccable. **-ly**, adv. Parfaitement.
flax, s. Bot: Lin m.
flaxen, a. F: (Of hair) Blond filasse inv.
flaxen-haired, a. Blondasse.
flay, v.tr. (a) Écorcher. (b) F: Fouetter, rosser, étriller.
flea, s. Ent: Puce f. **flea-bite**, s. 1. Morsure f de puce. 2. F: Vétille f, bagatelle f, rien m.
fleck¹, s. 1. Petite tache; moucheture f. 2. Particule f.
fleck², v.tr. Tacheter, moucheter (with, de).
fledg(e)ling, s. 1. Oisillon m. 2. F: Béjaune m, novice mf.
flee, v. 1. v.i. Fuir, s'enfuir, se sauver. 2. v.tr. S'enfuir de; fuir, éviter.
fleece¹, s. Toison f.
fleece², v.tr. F: Tondre, écorcher, plumer.
fleecy, a. Floconneux; (of cloud) moutonné.
fleet¹, s. Flotte f.
fleet², a. Lit: **Fleet of foot**, au pied léger.
fleet-footed, a. Au pied léger.
fleeting, a. Fugitif, fugace; passager, éphémère.
fleetness, s. Vitesse f, rapidité f.
Fleming, s. Flamand, -ande.
Flemish. 1. a. Flamand. 2. s. Ling: Le flamand.
flesh, s. Chair f. 1. (a) To make s.o.'s flesh creep, donner la chair de poule à qn. (b) Occ. Viande f. (c) Chair (d'un fruit). 2. To mortify the flesh, mortifier son corps. In the flesh, en chair et en os. His own flesh and blood, la chair de sa chair; les siens.
flesh-eating, a. Z: Carnassier. **flesh-wound**, s. Blessure f dans les chairs.
fleshless, a. Décharné.
fleshy, a. Charnu.
flexibility, s. Flexibilité f; élasticité f; souplesse f.
flexible, a. Flexible, souple, pliant.
flexion, s. Flexion f, courbure f.
flick¹, s. Petit coup (de fouet); (with finger) chiquenaude f.
flick², v.tr. Effleurer (un cheval); (with finger) donner une chiquenaude.
flicker¹, s. Tremblotement m; battement m, clignement m (de paupière).
flicker², v.i. Trembloter, vaciller; (of light) clignoter. **flickering**, s. Tremblotement m, clignotement m.
flight¹, s. 1. (a) Vol m. Av: **Trial flight**, vol d'essai. (b) Course f (d'un projectile). The f. of time, le cours du temps. (c) Envol m (d'un oiseau). F: Flight of fancy, élan m, essor m, de l'imagination. (d) Migration f (d'oiseaux). 2. Volée f, distance parcourue. 3. **Flight of stairs**, volée d'escalier; escalier

m. 4. (a) Bande f, vol, volée (d'oiseaux). F: To be in the first flight, être parmi les premiers. (b) Av: Escadrille f (d'avions).
flight², s. Fuite f. **To take to flight**, prendre la fuite.
flightiness, s. Inconstance f; instabilité f; légèreté f, étourderie f.
flighty, a. Frivole, écervelé, étourdi.
flimsiness, s. Manque m de solidité. (a) Légèreté f. (b) Futilité f, faiblesse f (d'une excuse).
flimsy. 1. a. Sans solidité. (a) Léger; peu solide. (b) F: (Of excuse) Pauvre. 2. s. Papier m pellicule; papier pelure.
flinch, v.i. 1. Reculer, fléchir, défaillir. 2. Without flinching, sans broncher.
fling¹, s. 1. (a) Jet m. (b) F: Essai m, tentative f. 2. F: To have one's fling, jeter sa gourme.
fling², v.tr. Jeter; lancer. To f. one's arms round s.o.'s neck, se jeter au cou de qn. **fling about**, v.tr. Jeter de côté et d'autre. **fling aside**, v.tr. Rejeter; jeter de côté. **fling away**, v.tr. Jeter de côté. To f. away one's money, gaspiller son argent. **fling back**, v.tr. Repousser ou renvoyer violemment. **fling down**, v.tr. Jeter à terre. **fling out**, v.tr. (a) Jeter dehors; F: flanquer à la porte. (b) To fling out one's arm, étendre le bras.
flint, s. 1. Miner: Silex m. 2. Pierre f à briquet. F: To skin a flint, tondre (sur) un œuf.
flip, s. 1. Chiquenaude f. 2. Petite secousse vive.
flippancy, s. Légèreté f.
flippant, a. Léger, désinvolte. **-ly**, adv. Légèrement.
flirt¹, s. Flirteur m; (woman) coquette f.
flirt². v.i. Flirter. **flirting**, s. Flirt m.
flirtation, s. Flirt m.
flit, v.i. 1. To flit (away), partir. 2. To flit by, passer comme une ombre. To flit about, aller et venir sans bruit.
flitter, v.i. Voleter, voltiger.
float¹, s. 1. Flot m, train m (de bois). 2. Fish: Flotteur m.
float², v.i. (a) Flotter, nager; surnager. (b) Swim: Faire la planche. **floating**¹, a. 1. Flottant, à flot. 2. Libre, mobile. F: population, population flottante. **floating**², s. Flottement m.
flock¹, s. Bande f, troupe f; troupeau m (de moutons).
flock², v.i. To flock (together), s'attrouper, s'assembler.
flog, v.tr. Fustiger, flageller. **flogging**, s. Fustigation f, flagellation f.
flood¹, s. 1. Nau: Flot m, flux m; marée montante. 2. (a) Déluge m, inondation f. (b) Crue f (d'une rivière). **flood-gate**, s. Vanne f. **flood-light**, v.tr. Illuminer par projecteurs. **flood-lighting**, s. Éclairage diffusé. **flood-tide**, s. Marée montante; flux m.

flood². **1.** v.tr. Inonder, submerger. **2.** v.i. Déborder. **flooding**, s. **1.** Inondation f. **2.** Débordement m.

floor¹, s. **1.** Plancher m, parquet m. **2.** Étage m. **3.** Aire f (d'une grange).

floor², v.tr. (a) Terrasser (un adversaire). (b) F: Aplatir (qn).

flop¹, s. F: **1.** Coup mat. **2.** Four m, fiasco m.

flop², v.i. F: **1.** To flop (down), se laisser tomber; s'affaler. **2.** Faire four..

flora, s. Flore f.

floral, a. Floral, -aux.

florid, a. Fleuri; orné à l'excès; (of countenance) rubicond, fleuri.

florist, s. Fleuriste mf.

flotilla, s. Flotille f.

flotsam, s. Jur: Épave(s) flottante(s). **Flotsam and jetsam**, choses f de flot et de mer.

flounce¹, v.i. To flounce out, sortir dans un mouvement d'impatience.

flounce², s. Dressm: Volant m.

flounder¹, s. Ich: Flet m, carrelet m.

flounder², v.i. Patauger, barboter. **To flounder about in the water**, se débattre dans l'eau.

flour, s. Farine f. **flour-mill**, s. Moulin m à farine; (large) minoterie f.

flourish¹, s. **1.** Trait m de plume; (after signature) parafe m. **2.** Geste prétentieux; brandissement m (d'épée). **3.** Mus: (a) Fanfare f. (b) Fioriture f, ornement m.

flourish², v.i. (a) (Of plant) Bien venir. (b) Être florissant; prospérer. (c) Battre son plein; (of arts) fleurir. **2.** v.tr. Brandir (un bâton). **flourishing**, a. Florissant; prospère.

flout, v.tr. Faire fi de; se moquer de.

flow¹, s. **1.** (a) Coulement m; écoulement m. (b) Él: Passage m (du courant). (c) Courant, cours m, affluence f (d'eau). (d) Flow of the tide, flux m, flux m, de la marée. **2.** Volume m (de liquide débité). **3.** Flot, flux (de paroles). **To have a ready flow of language**, avoir de la faconde.

flow², v.i. **1.** (a) Couler, s'écouler. **To flow into the sea**, déboucher, se verser, dans la mer. (b) (Of tide) Monter, remonter. (c) (Of blood) Circuler. **2.** (Of tears) Se répandre; jaillir. **3.** Dériver, découler (from, de). **flowing**, a. **1.** Coulant; (of tide) montant. **2.** (Of draperies) Flottant.

flower¹, s. **1.** Fleur f. **Bunch of flowers**, bouquet m. **Flower show**, exposition f horticole. **2.** F: Fine fleur, élite f. **3.** Fleuraison f. **In flower**, en fleur. **In full f.**, en plein épanouissement. **To burst into flower**, fleurir. **flower-bed**, s. Parterre m. **flower-garden**, s. Jardin m d'agrément. **flower-girl**, s.f. Bouquetière. **flowerpot**, s. Pot m à fleurs.

flower², v.i. Fleurir. **flowering¹**, a. **1.** Fleuri; en fleur. **2.** Flowering plant, plante à fleurs. **flowering²**, s. Fleuraison f.

flowery, a. Fleuri.

fluctuate, v.i. Fluctuer. **fluctuating**, a. Variable.

fluctuation, s. Fluctuation f.

flue, s. Conduite f, tuyau m, de cheminée.

fluency, s. Facilité f (de parole).

fluent, a. Coulant, facile. To be a f. speaker, avoir la parole facile. **-ly**, adv Couramment.

fluff, s. **1.** Duvet m (d'étoffe); peluches fpl. **2.** Fourrure douce (d'un jeune animal).

fluffy, a. (Drap) pelucheux; (poussin) duveteux. F. hair, cheveux flous.

fluid, a. & s. (a) Fluide (m). (b) Liquide (m).

fluidity, s. Fluidité f.

fluke¹, s. **1.** Patte f (d'ancre). **2.** pl. Queue f (de baleine).

fluke², s. F: Coup de veine, de hasard.

flunkey, s. Laquais m, F: larbin m.

fluorine, s. Ch: Fluor m.

flurry¹, s. Agitation f, bouleversement m, émoi m. **All in a flurry**, tout effaré.

flurry², v.tr. Agiter, effarer (qn). **To get flurried**, perdre la tête.

flush¹, s. **1.** Chasse f (d'eau). **2.** F: Accès m, élan m. **In the first flush of victory**, dans l'ivresse de la victoire. **3.** (a) Éclat m. (b) Rougeur f, flux m de sang (au visage).

flush², v. **1.** v.tr. To flush (out), donner une chasse à. **2.** v.i. Rougir. His face flushed, he flushed up, le sang, le pourpre, lui monta au visage. **flushed**, a. Enfiévré, empourpré F. with success, ivre de succès.

flush³, a. **1.** To be flush (of money), être en fonds. **2.** Ras; de niveau. **To be flush with sth.**, être à fleur, au ras, de qch.

Flushing. Pr.n. Geog: Flessingue f.

fluster¹, s. Agitation f, trouble m. **In a fluster**, tout en émoi.

fluster², v.tr. Agiter, bouleverser. **To be flustered**, se troubler; être démonté, effaré.

flute, s. Flûte f.

flutter¹, s. **1.** Volètement m, voltigement m (d'un oiseau); battement m (des ailes); palpitation f (du cœur). **2.** Agitation f, trouble m, émoi m. **To be (all) in a flutter**, être tout en émoi.

flutter². **1.** v.i. Trémousser des ailes, battre des ailes; (of flag) flotter (au vent); (of heart) palpiter, battre. **2.** v.tr. (Of bird) To f. its wings, battre des ailes.

flux, s. Flux m; changement continuel.

fly¹, s. (a) Ent: Mouche f. There's a fly in the ointment, P: il y a un cheveu. There are no flies on him, il n'est pas bête. (b) Fish: Mouche. **To rise to the fly**, F: gober la mouche. **fly-paper**, s. Papier m attrape-mouche(s).

fly², s. **1.** Vol m. **On the fly**, en vol. **2.** pl. Th: The flies, les cintres m, les dessus m. **fly-leaf**, s. (Feuille f de) garde f **flywheel**, s. Mec.E: Volant m.

fly³, v. I. v.i. **1.** (a) Voler. F: To find the birds flown, trouver buisson creux. **To fly high**, F: avoir de hautes visées. (b) Av: Voler. **To fly to Paris**, se rendre à Paris en

avion. *To fly over London,* survoler Londres.
2. (*Of flag*) Flotter. **3.** (*a*) Courir, aller à
toute vitesse; (*of time*) fuir. **To fly at s.o.,**
(i) s'élancer sur qn; (ii) faire une algarade à
qn. **To fly into a rage,** s'emporter. **The
door flew open,** la porte s'ouvrit en coup de
vent. (*b*) (*Of sparks*) jaillir. *F:* **To make
the money fly,** prodiguer son argent. **To
fly off the handle,** *P:* s'emporter. *F:* **To
send s.o. flying,** envoyer rouler qn. (*c*) **To
fly in pieces,** voler en éclats. **4. To let fly,**
lancer. **To let fly at s.o.,** (i) tirer sur qn;
(ii) *F:* flanquer un coup à qn. **5.** (*a*) Fuir,
s'enfuir. *To fly from danger,* fuir le danger.
To fly for one's life, chercher son salut dans
la fuite. (*b*) *v.tr.* To fly the country, s'enfuir
du pays. II. **fly,** *v.tr.* **1.** *Nau:* To fly a
flag, battre (un) pavillon. **2.** To fly a kite,
faire voler un cerf-volant. **3.** *Av:* Piloter.
fly away, *v.i.* S'envoler; prendre son vol.
fly back, *v.i.* (*Of steel rod*) Faire ressort.
fly off, *v.i.* **1.** (*Of bird*) = FLY AWAY.
2. (*Of button*) Sauter. **flying**[1], *a.* **1.** Volant,
flottant. **2.** (*a*) *Mil:* Flying column, colonne *f*
mobile. (*b*) Court, passager. (*c*) *Sp:* Flying
start, départ lancé. **flying-fish,** *s. Ich:*
Poisson volant. **flying**[2], *s.* (*a*) Vol *m.*
(*b*) Aviation *f,* vol. Flying ground, terrain *m*
d'aviation. **flying-boat,** *s.* Hydravion *m*
à coque.
fly[4], *a. F:* Astucieux; *F:* ficelle.
flyer, *s.* Aviateur, -trice.
foal, *s.* Poulain *m.*
foam[1], *s.* Écume *f;* (*on beer*) mousse *f.*
foam[2], *v.i.* Écumer, moutonner. To foam at
the mouth, avoir l'écume aux lèvres. *F:* To
foam with rage, écumer.
fob, *v.tr.* To fob s.o. (off), tromper, duper,
qn. To fob sth. off on s.o., *F:* refiler qch.
à qn.
focus[1], *s.* Foyer *m.* In focus, au point.
focus[2], *v.tr.* **1.** Concentrer (*in, on,* dans, sur);
faire converger. *v.i. F:* **All eyes were
focused on him,** il était le point de mire de
tous les yeux. **2.** Mettre au point. **focus-
ing,** *s.* Mise *f* au point.
fodder, *s.* Fourrage *m.*
fog[1], *s.* Brouillard *m; Nau:* brume *f. F:*
I'm in a fog, je ne sais plus où j'en suis.
fog-horn, *s.* Corne *f,* trompe *f,* de brume;
sirène *f.* **fog-signal,** *s. Rail:* Pétard *m.*
fog[2], *v.tr. F:* Brouiller (les idées); embrouiller (qn).
foggy, *a.* **1.** Brumeux. On a f. day, par un
jour de brouillard. It is foggy, il fait du
brouillard. **2.** *F:* (*Of photograph*) Voilé;
(esprit) confus. **I haven't the foggiest (idea)!**
je n'en ai pas la moindre idée!
fogy, *s. F:* Old fogy, vieille baderne.
foible, *s.* Côté *m* faible, point *m* faible; faible
m (de qn).
foil[1], *s.* **1.** *Metalw:* Feuille *f,* lame *f;*
clinquant *m.* **2. To serve as a foil to,** servir
de repoussoir *m* à.

foil[2], *s. Fenc:* Fleuret *m.*
foil[3], *v.tr.* Faire échouer; déjouer.
foist, *v.tr.* Refiler (*sth. on s.o.,* qch. à qn).
To foist oneself on s.o., s'implanter chez qn.
fold[1], *s.* Pli *m,* repli *m;* accident *m* (de
terrain).
fold[2]. **I.** *v.tr.* (*a*) Plier. **To fold back,**
rabattre. (*b*) To fold s.o. in one's arms,
enlacer qn dans ses bras. (*c*) **To fold one's
arms,** (se) croiser les bras **2.** *v.i.* Se (re)plier,
se briser. **folding,** *a.* Pliant. **folding-
chair,** *s.* Chaise pliante.
foliage, *s.* Feuillage *m.*
folio, *s.* **1.** Folio *m,* feuille *f,* feuillet *m* (de
manuscrit). **2.** (Livre *m*) in-folio *m inv.*
folk, *s. pl.* Folk(s), gens *mf,* personnes *f.*
Country folk, campagnards *m.* My folk, les
miens, ma famille. **folk-lore**[2], *s.* Folklore
m; tradition *f.* **folk-song,** *s.* Chanson *f*
populaire.
follow. I. *v.tr.* **1.** Suivre. (*a*) To follow s.o.
about, suivre qn partout. **To follow the
hounds,** chasser à courre. *F:* **To follow
one's nose,** aller tout droit devant soi. (*b*) To
follow a road, suivre un chemin. (*c*) Succéder
à. **2.** Être le disciple, le partisan, de.
3. Suivre, se conformer à. **To follow s.o.'s
advice,** suivre le conseil de qn. **4.** Exercer,
suivre (une profession). **5.** (*a*) Prêter attention à, suivre. II. **follow,** *v.i.* **1.** To follow
(after), suivre. **As follows,** ainsi qu'il suit.
Our method is as follows, notre méthode est
la suivante. **2.** To follow in s.o.'s footsteps,
marcher sur les traces de qn. **To follow
close behind s.o.,** emboîter le pas à qn.
3. S'ensuivre, résulter (*from,* de). **follow
up,** *v.tr.* **1.** Suivre de près. **2.** Poursuivre
(avec énergie). **To follow up a clue,** s'attacher
à une indication. **following**[1], *a.* **1.** Qui
suit. **2.** (*a*) Suivant. On the following day,
le jour suivant; le lendemain. (*b*) *The f.
resolution,* la résolution que voici. (*c*) Two
days following, deux jours de suite. **following**[2], *s.* (*a*) Suite *f.* (*b*) *Pol:* Parti *m.*
follower, *s.* (*a*) Serviteur *m,* satellite *m.*
(*b*) Partisan *m,* disciple *mf.*
folly, *s.* Folie *f,* sottise *f.*
foment, *v.tr.* Fomenter.
fomentation, *s.* Fomentation *f.*
fond, *a.* **1.** (*a*) (Parent) follement dévoué,
trop indulgent. (*b*) Affectueux, tendre.
2. (*a*) To be fond of s.o., aimer, affectionner,
qn. They are f. of each other, ils s'aiment.
(*b*) *F:* To be fond of music, être amateur de
musique. F. of sweets, friand de sucreries.
-ly, *adv.* **1.** Crédulement. **2.** Tendrement,
affectueusement.
fondle, *v.tr.* Caresser, câliner.
fondness, *s.* **1.** Indulgence excessive.
2. Affection *f,* tendresse *f* (*for,* pour, envers).
3. Penchant *m,* prédilection *f.*
food, *s.* **1.** (*a*) Nourriture *f;* aliments *mpl;*
vivres *mpl.* Food and clothing, le vivre et le

vêtement. **Food-stuffs,** denrées *f.* (*b*) **To give s.o. food for thought,** donner à penser à qn. **2. Food and drink,** le boire et le manger.

fool¹, *s.* **1.** Imbécile *mf*; idiot, -ote; niais, -aise; sot, *f.* sotte. **To make a fool of oneself,** se rendre ridicule. **2.** Fou *m,* bouffon *m.* **3.** Dupe *f.* **To make a fool of s.o.,** berner qn, mystifier qn. **fool-proof,** *a.* A l'épreuve des imbéciles.

fool². **1.** *v.i.* Faire la bête. **2.** *v.tr.* Berner, mystifier, duper. **fooling,** *s.* **1.** Bouffonnerie *f.* **2.** Bernement *m,* duperie *f.*

foolery, *s.* Sottise *f,* bêtise *f.*

foolhardiness, *s.* Témérité *f,* imprudence *f.*

foolhardy, *a.* Téméraire, imprudent.

foolish, *a.* **1.** (*a*) Insensé; fou, *f.* folle; étourdi. (*b*) Sot, *f.* sotte; bête. **2.** Absurde, ridicule. **To look foolish,** avoir l'air penaud. **-ly,** *adv.* **1.** Follement, étourdiment. **2.** Sottement, bêtement.

foolishness, *s.* **1.** Folie *f,* étourderie *f.* **2.** Sottise *f,* bêtise *f.*

foolscap, *s.* Papier *m* ministre.

foot¹, *s.* **1.** Pied *m.* (*a*) **To knock s.o. off his feet,** faire perdre l'équilibre à qn; renverser qn. **To keep one's feet,** tenir pied, rester debout. **To be on one's feet,** se tenir debout. **To find one's feet,** voler de ses propres ailes; se débrouiller. **To put one's foot down,** faire acte d'autorité. **To get one's foot in,** s'implanter. **To put one's foot in it,** mettre les pieds dans le plat. *P:* **To have cold feet,** caner, capronner. (*b*) Marche *f,* allure *f.* **Swift of foot,** léger à la course. (*c*) *Adv.phr.* **On foot.** (i) A pied; pédestrement. (ii) Debout. (iii) Sur pied, en train. **To set a business on foot,** mettre sur pied une affaire. **2.** Pied (d'animaux à sabot); patte *f* (de chien). **3.** *Coll:* Infanterie *f.* **4.** (*a*) Pied, semelle *f* (d'un bas). (*b*) Bas bout (d'une table); pied (d'un lit). (*c*) Base *f* (de colonne); patte *f* (de verre à boire). **5.** (*a*) *Pros:* Pied. (*b*) *Meas:* Pied anglais. **footbridge,** *s.* Passerelle *f*; pont *m* pour piétons. **foot-hills,** *s.pl.* Contreforts *m.* **foot-note,** *s.* Note *f* au bas de la page. **foot-passenger,** *s.* Piéton *m.* **foot-rule,** *s.* Règle *f* (d'un pied). **foot-soldier,** *s.* Fantassin *m.* **foot-wear,** *s.* Chaussures *fpl.*

foot², *v.tr.* *F:* **To foot the bill,** payer la note.

footing, *s.* **1. To lose one's footing,** perdre pied. *I missed my f.,* le pied me manqua. **2.** (*a*) **To gain a footing,** s'implanter, prendre pied. (*b*) Position *f,* condition *f.* **On a war footing,** sur le pied de guerre. (*c*) **To pay one's footing,** payer sa bienvenue.

football, *s.* **1.** Ballon *m.* **2.** Le football. **Rugby football,** le rugby.

footballer, *s.* Joueur *m* de football.

footfall, *s.* (Bruit *m* de) pas *m.*

foothold, *s.* Assiette *f* de pied. **To get a foothold,** prendre pied.

footlights, *s.pl.* *Th:* Rampe *f.*

footman, *s.* Valet de pied *m*; laquais *m*

footpath, *s.* Sentier *m*; trottoir *m.*

footprint, *s.* Empreinte *f* de pas.

footsore, *a.* Aux pieds endoloris.

footstep, *s.* **1.** Pas *m.* **2. To follow in s.o.'s footsteps,** suivre les brisées de qn.

footstool, *s.* Tabouret *m.*

fop, *s.* *F:* Bellâtre *m,* fat *m.*

foppish, *a.* *F:* Bellâtre, fat.

foppishness, *s.* Élégance affectée.

for¹, *prep.* Pour. **I.** **1.** (*a*) (i) *Member for Liverpool,* député de Liverpool. (ii) *To act for s.o.,* agir pour qn. (*b*) *He wants her for his wife,* il la veut pour femme. (*c*) *To exchange one thing for another,* échanger une chose contre une autre. *To sell sth. for ten francs,* vendre qch. dix francs. **2.** *He is for free trade,* il est pour le libre-échange. **3.** (*a*) *What for?* pourquoi (faire)? *What's that gadget for?* à quoi sert ce truc-là? *For sale,* à vendre. *For example,* par exemple. (*b*) *To marry s.o. for his money,* épouser qn pour son argent. *To jump for joy,* sauter de joie. **4.** (*a*) *Ship bound for America,* vaisseau en partance pour l'Amérique. (*b*) *His feelings for you,* ses sentiments envers vous. **5.** (*a*) *I am going away for a fortnight,* je pars pour quinze jours. *He will be away for a year,* il sera absent pendant un an. (*b*) *He was away for a fortnight,* il fut absent pendant quinze jours. (*c*) *I have been here for three days,* je suis ici depuis trois jours. **6.** *This box is for you,* cette boîte est pour vous. *To make a name for oneself,* se faire un nom. *To write for the papers,* écrire dans les journaux. **7.** *To care for s.o.,* aimer qn. *Eager for praise,* avide d'éloges. *Fit for nothing,* bon à rien. *Now for it!* allons-y! **8.** (*a*) *As for him,* quant à lui. *See for yourself!* voyez par vous-même! (*b*) *For all that,* malgré tout. (*c*) *But for her,* n'eût été elle, sans elle. (*d*) *Translate word for word,* traduisez mot à mot. **II.** **for** *introducing an infinitive clause.* **1.** *It is easy for him to come,* il lui est facile de venir. **2.** *I have brought it for you to see,* je te l'ai apporté pour que vous le voyiez. *It is not for me to decide,* ce n'est pas à moi de décider. **3.** *It's no good for Mr X to talk,* M. X a beau dire. **4.** *He gave orders for the trunks to be packed,* il donna l'ordre de faire les malles. **5.** *To wait for sth. to be done,* attendre que qch. se fasse. **6.** *For you to back out now would be a disgrace,* vous retirer maintenant serait honteux.

for², *conj.* Car.

forage¹, *s.* Fourrage(s) *m(pl).* **forage-cap,** *s.* *Mil:* Bonnet *m* de police.

forage², *v.i.* Fourrager.

foray, *s.* Razzia *f,* incursion *f,* raid *m.*

forbear¹, *s.* Aïeul, -eux *m*; ancêtre *m.*

forbear², *v.i.* S'abstenir. **forbearing,** *a.* Patient, endurant.

forbearance, *s.* Patience *f,* longanimité *f.*

forbid, *v.tr.* **1.** Défendre, interdire. 'Smoking forbidden,' "défense de fumer." *Forbidden subjects*, sujets tabous. **To forbid s.o. to do sth.**, défendre à qn de faire qch. **2.** *F:* Empêcher. *My health forbids my coming*, ma santé m'empêche de venir. **God forbid** (*that . . .*)! à Dieu ne plaise (que + *sub.*)! **forbidding**, *a.* Sinistre, rébarbatif; (temps) sombre.

force¹, *s.* Force *f.* **1.** (*a*) Violence *f*, contrainte *f. The f. of circumstances*, la force, la contrainte, des circonstances. (*b*) Influence *f*, autorité *f. F. of example*, influence de l'exemple. **2.** (*a*) Énergie *f* (d'un coup); intensité *f* (du vent). (*b*) *Mec:* Force, effort *m. Force of gravity*, (force de la) pesanteur. **3.** Puissance *f*; force. **The police force**, la police. **In (full) force**, en force. **4.** (*a*) **There is force in what you say**, votre argument n'est pas sans valeur. (*b*) Signification *f* (d'un mot). **5.** (*Of law*) **To be in force**, être en vigueur.

force², *v.tr.* Forcer. **1.** (*a*) **To force s.o.'s hand**, forcer la main à qn. **To force the pace**, forcer l'allure. *She forced a smile*, elle eut un sourire contraint. (*b*) **To force one's way**, se frayer un chemin. **2.** (*a*) Contraindre, obliger. (*b*) **To force sth. from s.o.**, extorquer, arracher, (une promesse) à qn. **force back**, *v.tr.* **1.** Repousser; faire reculer. **2.** Refouler (l'air). **forced**, *a.* Forcé. **1.** Inévitable, obligatoire. **2.** Contraint **Forced laugh**, rire du bout des dents.

forceful, *a.* Plein de force; énergique. **-fully**, *adv.* Avec force.

forceps, *s. sg. & pl. Surg:* Pince *f. Dent:* Davier *m.*

forcible, *a.* **1.** (Entrée) de, par, force. **2.** (Langage) énergique, vigoureux. **-ibly**, *adv.* **1.** Par force, de force. **2.** Énergiquement.

ford¹, *s.* Gué *m.*

ford², *v.tr.* Guéer, traverser à gué.

fore¹. **I.** *a.* Antérieur, -eure; de devant. **II.** *fore*, *s.* (*a*) *Nau:* Avant *m.* (*b*) **To the fore**, en vue, en évidence. **fore-court**, *s.* Avant-cour *f.* **fore-foot**, *s.* Pied antérieur; patte *f* de devant.

fore², *int. Golf:* Attention, gare, devant!

forearm, *s.* Avant-bras *m inv.*

forearmed, *a. See* FOREWARN.

forebode, *v.tr.* Présager, augurer. **foreboding**, *s.* **1.** Mauvais augure; présage *m.* **2.** (Mauvais) pressentiment.

forecast¹, *s.* Prévision *f.*

forecast², *v.tr.* Calculer, prévoir.

forecastle, *s. Nau:* Poste *m* de l'équipage.

foredoomed, *a.* Condamné d'avance (*to*, à).

forefather, *s.* Aïeul *m*, ancêtre *m. Our forefathers*, nos aïeux.

forefinger, *s.* Index *m.*

forefront, *s. F:* Premier rang.

forego, *v.tr.* = FORGO.

foregoing, *a.* Précédent, antérieur, -euse. **The foregoing**, ce qui précède.

foregone, *a.* Décidé d'avance; prévu.

foreground, *s.* Premier plan; avant-plan *m.*

forehead, *s. Anat:* Front *m.*

foreign, *a.* Étranger. **1. Foreign to**, étranger à, éloigné de, sans rapport avec. **2.** (*a*) **Foreign countries**, foreign parts, pays étrangers; l'étranger *m.* (*b*) **Foreign trade**, commerce extérieur. **The Foreign Office**, = le Ministère des Affaires étrangères.

foreigner, *s.* Étranger, -ère.

foreland, *s.* Cap *m*, promontoire *m.*

foreleg, *s.* Jambe *f* de devant; patte *f* de devant.

forelock, *s.* Toupet *m. F:* **To take time by the forelock**, saisir l'occasion aux cheveux.

foreman, *s.* **1.** *Jur:* Chef *m* du jury. **2.** *Ind:* Contremaître *m*; chef d'équipe.

foremast, *s.* Mât *m* de misaine.

foremost. **1.** *a.* Premier; le plus avancé. **2.** *adv.* **First and foremost**, tout d'abord; d'abord et avant tout.

forenoon, *s.* Matinée *f.*

forerunner, *s.* Avant-coureur *m.*

foresee, *v.tr.* Prévoir, entrevoir. **foreseeing**, *a.* Prévoyant.

foreshadow, *v.tr.* Présager, annoncer.

foresight, *s.* (*a*) Prévision *f.* (*b*) Prévoyance *f.*

forest, *s.* Forêt *f.* **forest-tree**, *s* Arbre forestier; arbre de haute futaie.

forestall, *v.tr.* Anticiper, devancer.

forestry, *s* Sylviculture *f.*

foretaste, *s.* Avant-goût *m.*

foretell, *v.tr.* **1.** Prédire. **2.** Présager.

forethought, *s.* **1.** Préméditation *f.* **2.** Prévoyance *f.*

forewarn, *v.tr.* Prévenir, avertir. **Forewarned is forearmed**, un homme averti en vaut deux.

foreword, *s.* Avant-propos *m inv*, préface *f.*

forfeit¹, *s.* (*a*) Amende *f.* (*b*) *Games:* Gage *m*, punition *f.*

forfeit², *v.tr.* Perdre. **To f. one's life**, payer de sa vie.

forfeiture, *s.* Perte *f.*

forge¹, *s.* Forge *f.*

forge², *v.tr.* **1.** *Metall:* Forger. **2.** Contrefaire (une signature). *Abs.* Commettre un faux. **forged**, *a.* **1.** (Fer) forgé. **2.** Faux, *f.* fausse, contrefait. **forging**, *s.* **1.** Travail *m* de forge. **2.** Pièce forgée. **3.** Falsification *f.*

forge³, *v.i.* **To forge ahead**, gagner les devants.

forger, *s.* Faussaire *mf.*

forgery, *s.* **1.** Contrefaçon *f*; falsification *f* (de documents). **2.** Faux *m. The signature was a f.*, la signature était contrefaite.

forget, *v.tr.* Oublier. **1.** Perdre le souvenir, la mémoire, de (qch.). **Forget about it!** n'y pensez plus! *F:* **And don't you forget it!** faites-y bien attention! **Never to be forgotten**, inoubliable. **2.** (*a*) Omettre, oublier. **Don't forget to**, ne manquez pas de. (*b*) Oublier (son mouchoir). (*c*) Négliger (son devoir). **3.** *F:* **To forget oneself**, s'oublier.

forget-me-not, *s. Bot:* Myosotis *m*; *F:* ne m'oubliez pas *m inv.*

forgetful, *a.* **1.** Oublieux (*of*, de). **2.** Négligent.

forgetfulness, *s.* **1.** (*a*) Manque *m* de mémoire. (*b*) **A moment of forgetfulness,** un moment d'oubli *m.* **2.** Négligence *f.*

forgivable, *a.* Pardonnable.

forgive, *v.tr.* **1.** (*a*) Pardonner. (*b*) *To f. s.o. a debt,* faire grâce d'une dette à qn. **2.** *To f. s.o.,* pardonner à qn. **forgiving,** *a.* Indulgent; peu rancunier.

forgiveness, *s.* **1.** Pardon *m.* **2.** Indulgence *f*, clémence *f.*

forgo, *v.tr.* Renoncer à (qch.); s'abstenir de (qch.).

fork[1], *s.* **1.** *Agr:* Fourche *f.* **2.** Fourchette *f* (de table). **3.** *Arb:* Branche fourchue. **4.** Bifurcation *f*, fourche.

fork[2], *v.i.* Fourcher. **fork up,** *v.tr. P:* Allonger (de l'argent). *Abs.* S'exécuter. **forked,** *a.* Fourchu, bifurqué.

forlorn, *a.* (*a*) Abandonné, délaissé. (*b*) *F. appearance,* mine triste.

form[1], *s.* **1.** (*a*) Forme *f.* (*b*) Figure *f*, silhouette *f.* **In the form of a dog,** sous la forme d'un chien. **2.** (*a*) Forme, formalité *f.* **For form's sake,** pour la forme. *It is a mere matter of f.,* c'est une pure formalité. (*b*) It is bad form, c'est de mauvais ton. **3.** (*a*) Formule *f*, forme. (*b*) *Adm:* Formule. **4.** *Sp:* Forme; état *m*, condition *f.* **To be in form,** être en forme. **5.** *Sch:* Classe *f.* **6.** Banc *m*, banquette *f.* **7.** Gîte *m* (du lièvre). **form-room,** *s. Sch:* Salle *f* de classe; la classe.

form[2]. **I.** *v.tr.* **1.** Former, faire, façonner. **2.** (*a*) Former, organiser. (*b*) Former, arrêter (un plan). **3.** *To form part of sth.,* faire partie de qch. **II. form,** *v.i.* Prendre forme; se former.

formal, *a.* **1.** Formel, en règle; (*of order*) formel, positif. **2. Formal bow,** salut cérémonieux. **3.** Formaliste, cérémonieux. **-ally,** *adv.* **1.** Formellement. **2.** Cérémonieusement.

formality, *s.* **1.** Formalité *f.* **2.** Cérémonie *f*, formalité(s).

formation, *s.* Formation *f.*

former, *a.* **1.** Antérieur, -eure, précédent, ancien. *My f. pupils,* mes anciens élèves. *In f. times,* autrefois. **2. The former,** *pron.* Celui-là, celle-là, ceux-là, celles-là. **-ly,** *adv.* Autrefois, jadis.

formidable, *a.* Formidable, redoutable.

formula, *s.* Formule *f.*

formulate, *v.tr.* Formuler.

forsake, *v.tr.* **1.** Abandonner, délaisser. **2.** Renoncer à, abandonner.

fort, *s. Mil:* **1.** Fort *m.* **2.** Place fortifiée; forteresse *f.*

forth, *adv.* **1.** *To go forth,* sortir. **To stretch forth one's hand,** avancer la main. **2.** From this time forth, dès maintenant; désormais. **3.** And so forth et ainsi de suite.

forthcoming, *a.* **1.** (*a*) Qui arrive. (*b*) Prochain, à venir. **2. To be forthcoming,** ne pas se faire attendre.

forthwith, *adv.* Sur-le-champ; tout de suite.

fortification, *s.* Fortification *f.*

fortify, *v.tr.* Fortifier.

fortitude, *s.* Force *f* d'âme; courage *m.*

fortnight, *s.* Quinzaine *f*; quinze jours *m.*

fortnightly. 1. *a.* Bimensuel. **2.** *adv.* Tous les quinze jours.

fortress, *s.* Forteresse *f*; place forte.

fortuitous, *a.* Fortuit, imprévu. **-ly,** *adv.* Fortuitement; par hasard.

fortunate, *a.* **1.** Heureux, fortuné. **To be fortunate,** avoir de la chance. **2.** Propice, heureux. *How f.!* quelle chance! **-ly,** *adv.* **1.** Heureusement. **2.** Par bonheur.

fortune, *s.* Fortune *f.* **1.** (*a*) Hasard *m*, chance *f.* **By good fortune,** par bonheur. (*b*) Destinée *f*, sort *m.* **To tell fortunes,** dire la bonne aventure. **2.** (*a*) Bonne chance; bonheur *m.* (*b*) Prospérité *f*, richesse *f.* **A man of fortune,** un homme riche. (*c*) Richesses *fpl*, biens *mpl.* **To make a fortune,** faire fortune. **fortune-hunter,** *s.* Coureur *m* de dots. **fortune-teller,** *s.* Diseur, -euse, de bonne aventure. **fortune-telling,** *s.* La bonne aventure.

forty, *num. a. & s.* Quarante (*m*) *About f. guests,* une quarantaine d'invités.

forward[1]. **I.** *a.* **1.** (Mouvement) progressif, en avant. **2.** Avancé; précoce. **3.** Effronté. **II. forward,** *adv.* **1.** From that day forward, à partir de ce jour-là. **To look forward to sth.,** attendre qch. avec plaisir. **2.** (*a*) En avant. **To move forward,** avancer. **To go straight forward,** aller tout droit. **Forward!** en avant! (*b*) A l'avant. (*c*) *Com:* (Carried) forward, à reporter; report *m.* **3. To come forward,** se proposer, s'offrir. **To thrust oneself forward,** se mettre en évidence.

forward[2], *v.tr.* **1.** Avancer, favoriser. **2.** (*a*) Expédier, envoyer. (*b*) 'Please forward,' "prière de faire suivre." **forwarding,** *s.* **1.** Avancement *m.* **2.** Expédition *f*, envoi *m.*

forwardness, *s.* **1.** Avancement *m.* **2.** État avancé. **3.** Hardiesse *f*, effronterie *f.*

fossil. 1. *s.* Fossile *m. F:* **An old fossil,** une vieille baderne. **2.** *a.* Fossile.

foster, *v.tr.* **1.** Élever, nourrir. **2.** Entretenir, nourrir (une idée).

foster-brother, *s.* Frère *m* de lait.

foster-child, *s.* Nourrisson, -onne.

foster-mother, *s.* (Mère) nourricière.

foster-sister, *s.* Sœur *f* de lait.

foul[1]. **I.** *a.* **1.** (*a*) Infect, nauséabond. *F. air,* air vicié. (*b*) **Foul deed,** infamie *f.* (*c*) *F: What f. weather!* quel sale temps! **2.** (Linge) sale. **3.** (*a*) *F:* **To fall foul of,** se brouiller avec. (*b*) **Foul weather,** gros temps. **4.** *Sp:* Déloyal, -aux. **-lly,** *adv.* **1.** Salement.

2. Abominablement. **II. foul,** *s.* *Sp:* Faute *f*; coup illicite, déloyal. **foul-mouthed,** *a.* Mal embouché; grossier.

foul², *v.tr.* **1.** Salir, souiller. **2.** Embarrasser, obstruer. *Nau:* Engager (une ancre).

found, *v.tr.* (*a*) Fonder. (*b*) Baser, fonder (ses soupçons) (*on,* sur).

foundation, *s.* **1.** Fondation *f*. **2.** Fondement *m*, fondation (d'un édifice). *The foundations of a building,* les fondements d'un édifice. **3.** Fondement, base *f* (d'une théorie). **foundation-stone,** *s.* To lay the foundation-stone, poser la première pierre.

founder¹, *s.* Fondateur *m*; souche *f*.

founder², *v.i.* *Nau:* Sombrer.

foundling, *s.* Enfant trouvé, -ée.

foundry, *s.* *Metalw:* Fonderie *f*.

fount¹, *s.* Source *f*.

fount², *s.* *Typ:* Fonte *f*.

fountain, *s.* Fontaine *f*. **fountain-head,** *s.* Source *f*. **fountain-pen,** *s.* Porte-plume *m inv* (à) réservoir.

four, *num. a. & s.* Quatre (*m*). To run on all fours, courir à quatre pattes. **four-engined,** *a.* *Av:* Quadrimoteur. **four-footed,** *a.* Quadrupède; à quatre pattes. **four-poster,** *s.* Lit *m* à colonnes. **four-square,** *a. & adv.* Solide(ment). **four-wheel(ed),** *a.* (Véhicule) à quatre roues.

fourfold, **1.** *a.* Quadruple. **2.** *adv.* Quatre fois autant; au quadruple.

fourteen, *num. a. & s.* Quatorze (*m*).

fourteenth, *num. a. & s.* Quatorzième. Louis the Fourteenth, Louis Quatorze.

fourth. **1.** *num. a. & s.* Quatrième. (On) the fourth of June, le quatre juin. **2.** *s.* (*a*) (*Fractional*) Quart *m*. (*b*) *Mus:* Quarte *f*.

fowl, *s.* **1.** (*a*) *Lit:* Oiseau *m*; volatile *m*. (*b*) *Coll.* Oiseaux. Wild fowl, gibier *m* d'eau. **2.** Poule *f*, coq *m*; volaille *f*. To keep fowls, élever de la volaille. **fowl-house,** *s.* Poulailler *m*.

fowler, *s.* Oiseleur *m*.

fowling-piece, *s.* Fusil *m* de chasse.

fox¹, *s.* Renard *m*. *F:* A sly fox, un madré, un fin matois. **fox-cub,** *s.* Renardeau *m*. **fox-glove,** *s.* *Bot:* Digitale *f*. **fox-hound,** *s.* *Ven:* Chien courant. **fox-hunt,** *s.* Chasse *f* au renard. **fox-hunter,** *s.* Chasseur *m* de renards. **fox-hunting,** *s.* La chasse au renard. **fox-terrier,** *s.* *F:* Fox *m*.

fox². **1.** *v.tr.* (*a*) Maculer, piquer (une gravure). (*b*) *P:* Mystifier, tromper (qn). **2.** *v.i.* *F:* Feindre; ruser.

foxiness, *s.* Astuce *f*, roublardise *f*.

foxy, *a.* **1.** Rusé, madré. **2.** Roux, *f* rousse.

fraction, *s.* **1.** Petite portion; fragment *m*. **2.** Fraction *f*; nombre *m* fractionnaire.

fractional, *a.* Fractionnaire. *F part,* fraction *f*.

fractious, *a.* (*a*) Difficile de caractère; revêche. (*b*) Pleurnicheur, -euse.

fractiousness, *s.* Humeur hargneuse; (*of a baby*) pleurnicherie *f*.

fracture¹, *s.* Fracture *f*.

fracture², *v.tr.* Casser, briser.

fragile, *a.* Fragile; (*of pers.*) faible, mièvre.

fragility, *s.* Fragilité *f*.

fragment, *s.* Fragment *m*, morceau *m*; éclat *m* (d'obus).

fragmentary, *a.* Fragmentaire.

fragrance, *s.* Parfum *m*; odeur *f* suave.

fragrant, *a.* Parfumé, odorant.

frail, *a.* **1.** Fragile; frêle. **2.** (*Of pers.*) Faible, délicat.

frailty, *s.* Faiblesse morale; fragilité humaine.

frame¹, *s.* **1.** Construction *f*, structure *f*, forme *f*. Frame of mind, disposition *f* d'esprit. **2.** (*a*) Ossature *f* (d'un animal). *Man of gigantic f.,* homme d'une taille colossale. (*b*) Charpente *f* (d'un bâtiment); cadre *m* (d'une bicyclette); monture *f* (d'un parapluie). **3.** Cadre, encadrement *m* (d'un tableau).

frame², *v.tr.* **1.** Former, régler. **2.** (*a*) Projeter (un dessein). (*b*) Articuler (un mot). **3.** Imaginer (une idée). **4.** Encadrer (un tableau).

framework, *s.* Charpente *f*, ossature *f*, carcasse *f*.

France. *Pr.n.* *Geog:* La France.

franchise, *s.* *Pol:* Droit *m* de vote.

Francis. *Pr.n.* François *m*.

frank¹, *a.* Franc, *f.* franche; sincère. **-ly,** *adv.* Franchement; ouvertement.

frank², *s.* *Post:* Marque *f* d'affranchissement.

frank³, *v.tr.* *Post:* Affranchir (une lettre).

Frank⁴. *Pr.n.* François *m*.

frankness, *s.* Franchise *f*, sincérité *f*.

frantic, *a.* Frénétique, forcené. **Frantic efforts,** efforts effrénés. *It drives him f.,* cela le met hors de lui. **-ally,** *adv.* Frénétiquement.

fraternal, *a.* Fraternel. **-ally,** *adv.* Fraternellement.

fraternity, *s.* **1.** Fraternité *f*. **2.** Confrérie *f*.

fraternize, *v.i.* Fraterniser (*with,* avec).

fraud, *s.* **1.** (*a*) *Jur:* Fraude *f*. (*b*) Supercherie *f*, tromperie *f*. **2.** *F:* Imposteur *m*.

fraudulence, *s.* (*a*) Caractère frauduleux. (*b*) Infidélité *f*.

fraudulent, *a.* Frauduleux. **-ly,** *adv.* Frauduleusement.

fraught, *a.* Remarks *f.* with malice, observations pleines de méchanceté.

fray¹, *s.* Bagarre *f*, échauffourée *f*. Ready for the fray, prêt à se battre.

fray², *v.i.* S'érailler, s'effiler.

freak, *s.* **1.** Caprice *m*; *F:* lubie *f*. Freak of fortune, jeu *m* de la fortune. **2.** Freak (of nature), *F:* phénomène *m*, curiosité *f*.

freakish, *a.* Capricieux, fantasque, bizarre.

freckle¹, *s.* Tache *f* de rousseur.

freckle². **1.** *v.tr.* Marquer de taches de rousseur. **2.** *v.i.* Se couvrir de taches de rousseur. **freckled,** *a.* Taché de rousseur.

free¹, *a. & adv.* **1.** (*a*) Libre. (*b*) En liberté.

To set f. a prisoner, élargir un prisonnier. **2.** Libre. **Is this table free?** est-ce que cette table est libre? **3.** (*a*) **Free speech**, libre parole. **To have a free hand**, avoir ses coudées franches (*to*, pour). **You are f. to do so**, libre à vous de le faire. (*b*) Franc, franche; sans raideur; souple. (*c*) **Free from sth.**, débarrassé de qch. **To be f. from care**, être sans souci. (*d*) Franc (*of*, de). *Cust:* **Free of duty**, exempt de droits d'entrée. **4.** *Ch:* (A l'état) libre, non-combiné. **5.** (*a*) **Free choice**, choix arbitraire. **As a free gift**, en pur don. (*b*) Libéral, -aux, généreux. **To be free with one's money**, ne pas regarder à l'argent. **To be free with one's hands**, avoir la main leste. (*c*) Franc, ouvert, aisé. **Free and easy**, désinvolte; sans gêne. (*d*) **To make free with s.o.**, prendre des libertés avec qn. **To make free with sth.**, user librement de qch. **6.** Gratuit; franco *inv.* **Admission free**, entrée gratuite, gratis. **Post free**, franco de port. **7.** *adv.* Catalogue sent free on request, catalogue franco sur demande. **-ly**, *adv.* **1.** Librement, volontairement. **2.** (Parler) franchement, sans contrainte. **free-hand**, *a. & s.* Free-hand (drawing), dessin *m* à main levée. **free-handed**, *a.* Généreux. **free lance**, *s.* Journaliste ou politicien indépendant. **free-spoken**, *a.* Franc, *f.* franche; qui a son franc-parler. **free-thinker**, *s.* Libre penseur; esprit fort. **free trade**, *s.* Libre-échange *m.* **free will**, *s.* Libre arbitre *m.* **Of one's own free will**, de (son) propre gré.

free², *v.tr.* (*a*) Affranchir (un peuple); libérer, élargir (un prisonnier). *To f. oneself from s.o.'s grasp*, se dégager des mains de qn. (*b*) Débarrasser (*from, of*, de).

freedom, *s.* **1.** (*a*) Liberté *f*, indépendance *f.* (*b*) **Freedom of speech**, le franc-parler. **2.** (*a*) Franchise *f*, familiarité *f.* (*b*) Sans-gêne *m.* **3.** (*a*) Exemption *f*, immunité *f* (*from*, de). (*b*) **Freedom of the city**, droit *m* de cité.

freehold, **1.** *a.* Tenu en propriété perpétuelle et libre. **2.** *s.* Propriété foncière libre.

freemason, *s.* Franc-maçon, *m, pl.* francs-maçons.

freemasonry, *s.* Franc-maçonnerie *f.*

freeze, *v.* Geler. **1.** *v.i.* (*a*) *It is freezing hard*, il gèle à pierre fendre. (*b*) (Se) geler; se congeler; prendre. **The river is frozen**, la rivière est prise. **The smile froze on his lips**, le sourire se figea sur ses lèvres. (*c*) **To freeze to death**, mourir de froid. **2.** *v.tr.* Geler, congeler. **To freeze the blood (in one's veins)**, glacer le sang, le cœur. **frozen**, *a.* (*a*) Gelé, glacé. *F: I am f. to death*, je meurs de froid. (*b*) (*Of meat*) Congelé.

freight, *s.* **1.** (*a*) Fret *m.* (*b*) Transport *m.* **2.** Fret, cargaison *f.*

freighter, *s.* **1.** Affréteur *m.* **2.** Cargo *m.*

French, **I.** *a.* **1.** (*a*) Français. (*b*) *Sch:* **French lesson**, leçon de français. **2.** **To take French leave**, filer à l'anglaise. **II.** **French**,

s. **1.** Le français; la langue française. *To speak F.*, parler français. **2.** *pl.* **The French**, les Français. **French window**, *s.* Porte-fenêtre *f, pl.* portes-fenêtres.

Frenchman, *s.* Français *m.*

Frenchwoman, *s.* Française *f.*

frenzied, *a.* Affolé, forcené.

frenzy, *s.* Frénésie *f.* **Frenzy of joy**, transport *m* de joie.

frequent¹, *a.* **1.** Nombreux, abondant. **2.** Fréquent; qui arrive souvent. **-ly**, *adv.* Fréquemment.

frequent², *v.tr.* Fréquenter, hanter.

fresh. **I.** *a.* **1.** (*a*) Nouveau, -el, -elle. **To put fresh courage into s.o.**, ranimer le courage de qn. (*b*) Frais, *f.* fraîche; récent. *It is still f. in my memory*, j'en ai le souvenir tout frais. **2.** Inexpérimenté, novice. **3.** (*a*) (Beurre) frais. (*b*) **Fresh water**, eau douce. **In the fresh air**, au grand air, en plein air. **4.** (Teint) frais, fleuri. **As fresh as a daisy**, frais comme une rose. **-ly**, *adv.* Nouvellement. **II.** **fresh**, *adv.* Fraîchement, nouvellement, récemment.

freshen. **1.** *v.i.* (*Of wind*) Fraîchir. **2.** *v.tr.* Rafraîchir.

freshness, *s.* **1.** Caractère récent. **2.** Fraîcheur *f.* **3.** (*a*) Vigueur *f*, vivacité *f.* (*b*) Naïveté *f*, inexpérience *f.*

fret, *v.* **1.** *v.tr.* (*a*) Ronger. (*b*) Inquiéter, tracasser. **2.** *v.pr. & i.* To fret (oneself), se tourmenter; se faire du mauvais sang. *Child fretting for its mother*, enfant qui pleurniche après sa mère. **To fret and fume**, enrager; se faire du mauvais sang.

fretful, *a.* Chagrin; irritable. *F. baby*, bébé agité. **-fully**, *adv.* Chagrinement; avec irritation.

fretfulness, *s.* Irritabilité *f.*

fret-saw, *s.* Scie *f* à découper.

fretwork, *s. Woodw:* Travail ajouré.

friable, *a.* Friable.

friar, *s.* Moine *m*, frère *m*, religieux *m.*

friction, *s.* **1.** Frottement *m.* **2.** *F:* Désaccord *m.*

Friday, *s.* Vendredi *m. He is coming on F.*, il viendra vendredi. *He comes on Fridays*, il vient le vendredi. **Good Friday**, (le) Vendredi saint.

friend, *s.* **1.** Ami, *f.* amie. **Bosom friend**, un(e) ami(e) de cœur. **To make friends with s.o.**, se lier d'amitié avec qn. **2.** Connaissance *f. F:* **A friend at court**, un ami en haut lieu. **3.** (*a*) **Friend of the poor**, bienfaiteur, -trice, des pauvres. (*b*) Ami, partisan *m* (de l'ordre); patron, -onne (des arts).

friendless, *a.* Délaissé; sans amis.

friendliness, *s.* Bienveillance *f*, bonté *f* (*to, towards*, envers).

friendly, *a.* **1.** Amical, -aux; sympathique. *To be f. with s.o.*, être ami avec qn. *In a f. manner*, amicalement. **To be on friendly terms with s.o.**, être en bons rapports avec qn. **2.** Bienveillant, favorablement disposé.

3. Friendly society, association *f* de bien-faisance.

friendship, *s.* Amitié *f.*

frieze, *s.* **1.** *Arch:* Frise *f.* **2.** Bordure *f.*

frigate, *s. Navy:* Frégate *f.*

fright, *s.* **1.** Peur *f*, effroi *m.* To take fright, s'effrayer, s'effarer (*at*, de). To give s.o. a fright, faire peur à qn. **2.** *F:* Personne *f* laide, grotesque.

frighten, *v.tr.* Effrayer; faire peur à. *F:* To frighten s.o. out of his wits, faire une peur bleue à qn. **frightened,** *a.* Apeuré, épeuré. Easily frightened, peureux, poltron, -onne. To be frightened, avoir peur. To be frightened to death, mourir de peur. **frightening,** *a.* Effrayant.

frightful, *a.* Terrible, effroyable, affreux, épouvantable. **-fully,** *adv.* Terriblement, effroyablement, affreusement.

frightfulness, *s.* **1.** Horreur *f*, atrocité *f.* **2.** Terrorisme *m.*

frigid, *a.* Glacial, -als; (très) froid.

frigidity, *s.* Frigidité *f*; grande froideur.

frill, *s.* (*a*) *Cost:* Volant *m*, ruche *f. Cu:* Papillote *f.* (*b*) *pl. F:* To put on frills, faire des façons; poser.

fringe[1], *s.* **1.** *Tex:* Frange *f.* **2.** (*a*) Bordure *f*, bord *m.* (*b*) Cheveux *mpl* à la chien.

fringe[2], *v.tr.* Eyes fringed with black lashes, yeux bordés, frangés, de cils noirs.

frisk. 1. *v.i.* To frisk (about), s'ébattre; faire des cabrioles. **2.** *v.tr.* Frétiller (de la queue).

friskiness, *s.* Folâtrerie *f*, vivacité *f.*

frisky, *a.* Vif, folâtre; (cheval) fringant.

fritter[1], *s. Cu:* Beignet *m.*

fritter[2], *v.tr.* To f. away one's money, gaspiller son argent.

frivolity, *s.* Frivolité *f.*

frivolous, *a.* Frivole; vain, futile; (*of pers.*) baguenaudier, évaporé. **-ly,** *adv.* Frivolement.

frizzle, *v.i.* Grésiller.

frizzy, *a.* Crêpelé, frisotté.

frock, *s. Cost:* **1.** Robe *f.* **2.** Froc *m* (de moine). **frock-coat,** *s.* Redingote *f.*

frog, *s.* Grenouille *f.*

frogged, *a. Cost:* A brandebourgs

frolic[1], *s.* (*a*) Ébats *mpl*, gambades *fpl.* (*b*) Fredaine *f*, divertissement *m.*

frolic[2], *v.i.* Se divertir, s'ébattre, folâtrer.

frolicsome, *a.* Gai, joyeux, folâtre.

from, *prep.* **1.** De. *F: flower to flower*, de fleur en fleur. **2.** Depuis, dès, à partir de. As from, à partir de. *F. his childhood*, depuis son enfance. **3.** (*a*) De, à. *He stole a pound f. her*, il lui a volé une livre. *To dissuade s.o. f. doing sth.*, dissuader qn de faire qch. (*b*) To shelter f. the rain, s'abriter contre la pluie. **4.** (*a*) D'avec, de. *To distinguish the good f. the bad*, distinguer le bon d'avec le mauvais. (*b*) To pick s.o. out from the crowd, démêler qn parmi la

foule. *To drink f. the brook*, boire au ruisseau. **5.** (*a*) *He comes f. Manchester*, il est natif de Manchester. *A quotation f. Shakespeare*, une citation tirée de Shakespeare. *To write f. s.o.'s dictation*, écrire sous la dictée de qn. From your point of view, à votre point de vue. (*b*) Tell him that from me, dites-lui cela de ma part. (*c*) Painted from nature, peint d'après nature. **6.** To act from conviction, agir par conviction. From what I heard, d'après ce que j'ai entendu dire. From what I can see, à ce que je vois. **7.** From above, d'en haut. From henceforth, à partir d'aujourd'hui.

front[1]. **I.** *s.* **1.** (*a*) Front *m*, contenance *f.* To put a bold front on it, faire bonne contenance. (*b*) To have the front to do sth., avoir l'effronterie, le front, de faire qch. **2.** *Mil:* Front. **3.** (*a*) Devant *m*, partie antérieure; façade *f*, face *f* (d'un bâtiment); devant, plastron *m* (de chemise). *Carriage in the f. of the train*, voiture en tête du train. (*b*) = SEA-FRONT. **4.** *F:* To come to the front, arriver au premier rang. **5.** *Adv.phr.* In front, devant, en avant. In front of, (i) en face de; (ii) devant. **II. front,** *a.* Antérieur, -e, de devant, d'avant, de face. *F. seat*, siège au premier rang. Front rank, premier rang. **front-door,** *s.* Porte *f* sur la rue.

front[2], *v.tr. & i.* To front sth.; to front (up)on sth., faire face à qch.

frontage, *s.* (*a*) Étendue *f* du devant. (*b*) Façade *f.*

frontal, *a. Mil:* De front.

frontier, *s.* Frontière *f.*

frontispiece, *s. Typ:* Frontispice *m.*

frost[1], *s.* **1.** Gelée *f*, gel *m. F:* Jack Frost, le bonhomme Hiver. *Ten degrees of f.*, dix degrés de froid. **2.** *F:* Four *m*, fiasco *m.* **frost-bite,** *s.* Gelure *f.* **frost-bitten,** *a.* Gelé.

frost[2], *v.tr.* (*a*) Givrer. (*b*) Saupoudrer de sucre. **frosted,** *a.* **1.** Givré. **2.** (*Of glass*) Dépoli.

frostiness, *s.* Froid glacial.

frosty, *a.* **1.** Gelé; glacial, -als. *F. day*, jour de gelée. *F:* Frosty reception, accueil glacial. **2.** Couvert de givre. **-ily,** *adv. F:* Glacialement.

froth[1], *s.* **1.** Écume *f*; mousse *f* (de la bière). **2.** *F:* Futilités *fpl*; paroles creuses.

froth[2], *v.i.* Écumer, mousser.

frothy, *a.* Écumeux, écumant; mousseux.

frown[1], *s.* Froncement *m* de sourcils; regard sévère, désapprobateur.

frown[2], *v.i.* (*a*) Froncer les sourcils. To frown at s.o., regarder qn de travers, en fronçant les sourcils. *To f. upon a suggestion*, désapprouver une suggestion. (*b*) Avoir l'air menaçant. **frowning,** *a.* Renfrogné; (*of brow*) sourcilleux; (*of thgs*) menaçant.

frowzy, *a.* **1.** Qui sent le renfermé. **2.** Sale, mal tenu, peu soigné.

fructify, *v.i.* Fructifier.
frugal, *a.* **1.** Frugal, -aux; économe. **2.** Frugal, simple. **-ally,** *adv.* Frugalement, sobrement.
frugality, *s.* Frugalité *f.*
fruit, *s.* Fruit *m.* Dried fruit, fruits secs. Stewed fruit, compote *f* de fruits. **fruit-tree,** *s.* Arbre fruitier.
fruiterer, *s.* Fruitier, -ière.
fruitful, *a.* (*Of tree*) Fructueux; (*of soil*) fertile, fécond. *F:* Action fruitful in consequences, action fertile en conséquences. **-fully,** *adv.* Fructueusement, utilement.
fruitfulness, *s.* Fertilité *f.*
fruition, *s.* To come to fruition, fructifier.
fruitless, *a.* Fruitless efforts, vains efforts. **-ly,** *adv.* Vainement.
frustrate, *v.tr.* (*a*) Faire échouer. *To f. s.o.'s hopes,* frustrer l'espoir de qn. (*b*) Contrecarrer (qn).
frustration, *s.* Frustration *f.*
fry[1]**,** *s.* *Coll. Ich:* Frai *m,* fretin *m,* alevin *m.* Small fry, menu fretin.
fry[2]**,** *v.* **1.** *v.tr.* (Faire) frire. Fried eggs, œufs sur le plat. **2.** *v.i.* Frire. **frying-pan,** *s.* Poêle *f.* To jump out of the frying-pan into the fire, tomber d'un mal dans un pire.
fuddle, *v.tr.* *F:* (*a*) Soûler, griser. (*b*) Brouiller les idées de (qn). **fuddled,** *a. F:* **1.** Soûl; pris de vin. To get fuddled, s'enivrer. **2.** Brouillé.
fudge, *s.* Bêtise(s) *f,* sottise(s) *f.*
fuel[1]**,** *s.* Combustible *m,* comburant *m.* *F:* To add fuel to the flame, jeter de l'huile sur le feu.
fuel[2]**,** *v.tr.* Pourvoir de combustibles.
fugitive. 1. *a.* Fugitif. **2.** *s.* Fugitif, -ive.
fulcrum, *s. Mec:* Point *m* d'appui *m.*
fulfil, *v.tr.* (*a*) Répondre à, remplir. (*b*) Satisfaire. (*c*) Accomplir (une tâche). *To f. a duty,* s'acquitter d'un devoir.
fulfilment, *s.* (*a*) Accomplissement *m.* (*b*) Exaucement *m* (d'une prière). (*c*) Exécution *f* (d'une condition).
full. 1. *a.* **1.** Plein, rempli, comble. *F:* His heart was full, il avait le cœur gros. Look f. of gratitude, regard chargé de reconnaissance. **2.** Plein, complet, -ète. To be full up, avoir son plein. Full up! complet! Full house, salle *f* comble. **3.** Full particulars, tous les détails. **4.** Complet, entier. (*a*) Full pay, paye entière; solde entière. (*b*) In full flower, en pleine fleur. Roses in full bloom, roses larges épanouies In full uniform, en grande tenue In full flight, en pleine déroute. (*c*) I waited two full hours, j'ai attendu deux grandes heures. **5.** (*Of face*) Plein; (*of figure*) rond, replet, -ète. **-lly,** *adv.* **1.** Pleinement, entièrement, complètement, amplement. **2.** It takes fully two hours, cela prend bien, au moins, deux heures. II. **full,** *s.* **1.** The moon is at the full, la lune est dans son plein.

2. *adv.phr.* (*a*) In full. To publish a letter in f., publier une lettre intégralement. Name in full, nom en toutes lettres. (*b*) To the full, complètement, tout à fait. III. **full,** *adv.* **1.** I know it full well, je le sais bien, parfaitement. **2.** Précisément, justement, en plein. Hit f. in the face, atteint en pleine figure.
full-blown, *a.* Épanoui; en pleine fleur.
full stop, *s.* Point. *F: He came to a f. s.,* il est resté court. **full-time.** *Ind:* **1.** *a.* (Emploi) de toute la journée. **2.** *adv.* To work full time, travailler à pleines journées.
ful(l)ness, *s.* **1.** Plénitude *f,* totalité *f.* **2.** Ampleur *f;* abondance *f.*
fulminate, *v.i.* Fulminer.
fulsome, *a.* Écœurant, excessif. Fulsome flattery, flagornerie *f,* adulation *f.*
fulsomeness, *s.* Bassesse *f,* platitude *f.*
fumble, *v.i.* Fouiller; tâtonner To fumble with sth., manier qch. maladroitement.
fumbling, *a.* Maladroit, gauche.
fume[1]**,** *s.* **1.** Fumée *f,* vapeur *f,* exhalaison *f.* **2.** *F:* In a fume, hors de soi; en rage.
fume[2]**,** *v.i.* *F:* Rager; se faire du mauvais sang.
fumigate, *v.tr.* Fumiger.
fun, *s.* *F:* Amusement *m,* gaieté *f;* plaisanterie *f.* To make fun of s.o., se moquer de qn. For fun, in fun, pour rire; par plaisanterie. It was great fun, c'était fort amusant. To have fun, s'amuser, se divertir.
function[1]**,** *s.* **1.** Fonction *f.* **2.** (*a*) Fonction, charge *f.* (*b*) *pl.* To discharge one's functions, s'acquitter de ses fonctions. **3.** (*a*) Réception *f,* réunion *f.* (*b*) Cérémonie publique; solennité *f.*
function[2]**,** *v.i.* Fonctionner, marcher.
functionary, *s.* Fonctionnaire *m.*
fund, *s.* **1.** Fonds *m.* **2.** *Fin:* (*a*) Fonds, caisse *f.* To start a fund, lancer une souscription. (*b*) *pl.* Funds, fonds, masse *f;* ressources *f* pécuniaires. To be in funds, être en fonds.
fundamental, *a.* Fondamental, -aux; essentiel. **-ally,** *adv* Fondamentalement, foncièrement
funeral, *s.* (*a*) Funérailles *fpl;* obsèques *fpl.* (*b*) Convoi *m* funèbre; cortège *m* funèbre.
funereal, *a.* *F:* Lugubre, funèbre; (*of voice*) sépulcral, -aux.
fungus, *s.* Champignon *m.*
funk[1]**,** *s.* *P:* **1.** Frousse *f,* trac *m,* venette *f.* **2.** Froussard, -arde.
funk[2]**,** *v.tr. & i. P:* To funk (it), caner. To funk sth., avoir peur de qch.
funky, *a.* *P:* Froussard.
funnel, *s.* **1.** Entonnoir *m.* **2.** Cheminée *f.*
funny, *a.* Drôle. **1.** Comique, amusant, facétieux. He is trying to be funny, il veut faire de l'esprit. **2.** Curieux, bizarre. A funny idea, une drôle d'idée. **-ily,** *adv.* Drôlement. **1.** Comiquement. **2.** Curieusement. Funnily enough, chose curieuse.
funny-bone, *s.* *F:* Le petit juif.

fur¹, *s.* (*a*) Fourrure *f*, pelleterie *f.* (*b*) Poil *m*, pelage *m* (de lapin). *F:* **To make the fur fly,** se battre avec acharnement. (*c*) *pl.* **Furs,** peaux *fpl.*

fur², *v.tr.* Entartrer, incruster; *Med:* charger (la langue).

furbish, *v.tr.* **To furbish (up). 1.** Fourbir, polir. **2.** (Re)mettre à neuf, retaper.

furious, *a.* Furieux; (*of look*) furibond; (*of battle*) acharné. **To get furious, To be furious with s.o.,** être en fureur. **To be furious with s.o.,** être furieux contre qn. **Furious driving,** conduite folle. **-ly,** *adv.* Furieusement; avec acharnement.

furl, *v.tr.* Serrer, ferler (une voile).

furlough, *s. Mil:* Congé *m*, permission *f.*

furnace, *s.* **1.** (*a*) Fourneau *m*, four *m.* (*b*) **Fiery furnace,** fournaise ardente. **2.** (House-heating) **furnace,** calorifère *m.*

furnish, *v.tr.* **1.** (*a*) Fournir, donner; pourvoir. (*b*) **To furnish s.o. with sth.,** fournir, pourvoir, munir, qn de qch. **2.** Meubler, garnir. *To live in furnished apartments,* loger en garni, en meublé. **furnishings,** *s. pl.* Ameublement *m.*

furniture, *s.* Meubles *mpl*, ameublement *m*, mobilier *m.* **Piece of furniture,** meuble. **furniture-polish,** *s.* Encaustique *f.* **furniture-remover,** *s.* Déménageur *m*; entrepreneur *m* de déménagements. **furniture-shop,** *s.* Maison *f* d'ameublement. **furniture-van,** *s.* Voiture *f* de déménagement.

furrier, *s.* Pelletier, -ière; fourreur *m.*

furrow¹, *s.* **1.** *Agr:* Sillon *m.* **2.** Cannelure *f*, rainure *f.* **3.** Ride profonde; sillon.

furrow², *v.tr.* **1.** Labourer (la terre). **2.** Rider profondément, sillonner.

further¹. I. *adv.* **1.** = FARTHER 1. **2.** (*a*) Davantage, plus. **Until you hear further,** jusqu'à nouvel avis. (*b*) **To go further into sth.,** entrer plus avant dans qch. (*c*) **Further back,** à une période plus reculée. (*d*) D'ailleurs, en outre, de plus. **II. further,** *a.* **1.** = FARTHER 2. **2.** Nouveau, -el, -elle, -eaux, additionnel. **Without further loss of time,** *without f. ado,* sans plus de cérémonie; sans plus. **Upon further consideration,** après plus ample réflexion.

further², *v.tr.* Avancer, favoriser.

furthermore, *adv.* En outre, de plus.

furthermost, *a.* = FARTHERMOST.

furthest, *a. & adv.* = FARTHEST.

furtive, *a.* Furtif; (*of pers.*) sournois. **-ly,** *adv.* Furtivement.

fury, *s.* Furie *f*, fureur *f*, emportement *m*; acharnement *m* (d'un combat). *F:* **To work like fury,** travailler avec acharnement.

furze, *s. Bot:* Ajonc *m.*

fuse¹, *s.* Fusée *f* (d'obus); amorce *f. Min:* (Safety-)fuse, étoupille *f*, cordeau *m.*

fuse², *s. El.E:* Fusible *m*; (*in private house*) plomb *m.* **fuse-box,** *s.* Boîte *f* à fusibles.

fuse³. 1. *v.tr.* (*a*) Fondre, mettre en fusion. (*b*) *F:* Fusionner, amalgamer. **2.** *v.i.* Fondre. *F:* **The light has fused,** les plombs ont sauté.

fusee, *s.* Allumette-tison *f.*

fusible, *a.* Fusible.

fusilier, *s. Mil:* Fusilier *m.*

fusillade, *s. Mil:* Fusillade *f.*

fusion, *s.* Fusion *f.* **1.** Fondage *m*, fonte *f.* **2.** Fusionnement *m. Pol:* Fusion (de deux partis, etc.).

fuss¹, *s.* **1.** Bruit exagéré. *A lot of f. about nothing,* beaucoup de bruit pour rien. **To make a fuss,** faire un tas d'histoires. **2.** Embarras *mpl*; façons *fpl.* **To make a fuss,** faire des cérémonies. **To make a fuss of s.o.,** être aux petits soins pour qn

fuss². 1. *v.i.* Tatillonner; faire des embarras. **To fuss about,** faire l'affairé. **To fuss over s.o.,** être aux petits soins pour qn. **2.** *v.tr.* Tracasser, agiter.

fussiness, *s.* Tatillonnage *m*; façons *fpl.*

fussy, *a.* Tatillon, -onne; tracassier, méticuleux. **-ily,** *adv.* (*a*) D'une manière tatillonne. (*b*) D'un air important.

fustiness, *s.* **1.** Odeur *f* de renfermé. **2.** Caractère suranné, démodé.

fusty, *a.* **Fusty smell,** odeur de renfermé. *F:* **Fusty ideas,** idées surannées, démodées.

futile, *a.* **1.** Futile, vain. **2.** Puéril.

futility, *s.* **1.** Futilité *f.* **2.** Puérilité *f.*

future. I. *a.* (*a*) Futur; (*of events*) à venir; (*of prospects*) d'avenir. **My future wife,** ma future. (*b*) *Gram:* **Future tense,** temps futur. **2.** *s.* (*a*) Avenir *m.* **In (the) future,** à l'avenir. **In the near future,** dans un avenir peu éloigné; à brève échéance. (*b*) *Gram:* (Temps) futur *m.* (*c*) **To ruin one's future,** briser son avenir

fuzziness, *s.* Crêpelure *f.*

fuzzy, *a.* (i) Bouffant, flou; (ii) crêpelu, frisotté.

G, g, *s.* **1.** (La lettre) G, g *m*. **2.** *Mus:* Sol *m*.

gab, *s.* *F:* (*a*) Faconde *f.* (*b*) Bagou(t) *m*. To have the gift of the gab, avoir la langue bien pendue.

gabble¹, *s.* **1.** Bredouillement *m*. **2.** Caquet *m*, jacasserie *f*.

gabble², **1.** *v.i.* (*a*) Bredouiller. (*b*) Caqueter, jacasser. **2.** *v.tr.* **To gabble out a speech,** débiter un discours à toute vitesse.

gable, *s.* *Const:* Pignon *m*.

gad, *v.i.* **To gad (about),** courir la prétentaine.

gadabout, *s.* Coureur, -euse.

gad-fly, *s.* *Ent:* Taon *m*.

gadget, *s.* *P:* Chose *m*, machin *m*, truc *m*.

Gaelic. 1. *a.* Gaélique. **2.** *s.* Le gaélique.

gaff¹, *s.* *Fish:* Gaffe *f*.

gaff², *v.tr.* Gaffer.

gaff³, *s.* *P:* **To blow the gaff,** vendre la mèche.

gag¹, *s.* **1.** Bâillon *m*. **2.** *F:* Interpolation faite par l'acteur.

gag², *v.tr.* Bâillonner; mettre un bâillon à.

gage, *s.* Gage *m*, garantie *f*.

gaiety, *s.* Gaîté *f*, gaieté *f*.

gain¹, *s.* **1.** Gain *m*, profit *m*, avantage *m*, bénéfice *m*. **2.** Accroissement *m*, augmentation *f*.

gain², *v.tr.* Gagner. **1.** Acquérir. **You will gain nothing by it,** vous n'y gagnerez rien. **2.** *Sp:* **To gain on a competitor,** prendre de l'avance sur un concurrent. **A bad habit gains on one,** une mauvaise habitude s'impose peu à peu. **3.** **To gain five minutes a day,** avancer de cinq minutes par jour. *Abs.* **To gain,** avancer.

gainer, *s.* **To be the gainer by sth.,** gagner à qch.

gainsay, *v.tr.* Contredire, démentir. **Facts that cannot be gainsaid,** faits indéniables.

gait, *s.* Allure *f*, démarche *f*.

gaiter, *s.* Guêtre *f*.

gala, *s.* Fête *f*, gala *m*.

galantine, *s.* *Cu:* Galantine *f*.

galaxy, *s.* **1.** *Astr:* **The Galaxy,** la Voie lactée. **2.** *F:* Assemblée brillante.

gale, *s.* **1.** *Nau:* Coup *m* de vent; vent fort. **2.** Tempête *f*. **To blow a gale,** souffler en tempête; faire rage.

Galilee. *Pr.n.* La Galilée.

gall¹, *s.* Fiel *m*.

gall², *s.* Écorchure *f*, excoriation *f*.

gall³, *v.tr.* (*a*) Écorcher. (*b*) *F:* Irriter, exaspérer; froisser. **galling,** *a.* Irritant, exaspérant; blessant.

gallant, *a.* **1.** Brave, vaillant. **2.** Galant. **-ly,** *adv.* Galamment.

gallantry, *s.* **1.** Vaillance *f*, bravoure *f*. **2.** Galanterie *f*.

gallery, *s.* (*a*) Galerie *f*. (*b*) **The gallery,** *Th:* la (troisième) galerie; *F:* le poulailler, le paradis.

galley, *s.* **1.** *Nau:* (*a*) *A:* Galère *f*. (*b*) Yole *f*. **2.** *Nau:* Cuisine *f*. **galley-slave,** *s.* Galérien *m*.

Gallic, *a.* Gallique, gaulois.

gallivant, *v.i.* Courir la prétentaine.

gallop¹, *s.* Galop *m*. **(At) full gallop,** ventre à terre.

gallop², *v.* **1.** *v.i.* (*a*) Galoper. (*b*) **To gallop away,** partir, s'éloigner, au galop. **2.** *v.tr.* Galoper. **galloping,** *a.* Au galop.

gallows, *s.* Potence *f*, gibet *m*. **gallows-bird,** *s.* Gibier *m* de potence; pendard *m*.

galop, *s.* *Danc:* Galop *m*.

galore, *s. & adv.* *F:* **(In) galore,** en abondance, à foison, à profusion.

galosh, *s.* Caoutchouc *m*.

galvanic, *a.* Galvanique.

galvanization, *s.* Galvanisation *f*.

galvanize, *v.tr.* Galvaniser. **Galvanized iron,** tôle zinguée.

gamble¹, *s.* *F:* Jeu *m* de hasard.

gamble². 1. *v.i.* Jouer de l'argent. *F:* **You may gamble on that,** vous pouvez compter là-dessus. **2.** *v.tr.* **To gamble away,** perdre au jeu. **gambling,** *s.* Le jeu.

gambler, *s.* Joueur, -euse (pour de l'argent).

gamboge, *s.* Gomme-gutte *f*.

gambol¹, *s.* (*a*) Gambade *f*, cabriole *f*. (*b*) *pl.* F: Ébats *m*.

gambol², *v.i.* (*a*) Gambader, cabrioler; faire des gambades. (*b*) S'ébattre.

game¹, *s.* **1.** (*a*) Amusement *m*, divertissement *m*, jeu *m*. **To make game of s.o.,** se moquer de qn. (*b*) Jeu. **Game of skill,** jeu d'adresse. *F:* **It's all in the game,** c'est dans la règle du jeu. (*c*) **To play the game,** jouer franc jeu. **To beat s.o. at his own game,** battre qn avec ses propres armes. **Two can play at that game,** à bon chat bon rat. (*d*) *F:* **What's his game?** où veut-il en venir? **To spoil s.o.'s game,** déjouer les plans de qn. **The game's up,** l'affaire est dans l'eau. (*e*) Partie *f* (de cartes); manche *f* (d'une partie de cartes). **The odd game,** the deciding game, la belle. *F:* **To have the game in one's hands,** tenir le succès entre ses mains. **2.** (*a*) Gibier *m*. **Big game,** grands fauves. *F:* **He is fair game,** on a bien le droit de se moquer de lui. (*b*) *Cu:* Gibier. **game-bag,** *s.* Carnassière *f*, gibecière *f*. **game-cock,** *s.* Coq *m* de combat.

game², *v.tr.* **To game away a fortune,** dissiper une fortune au jeu. **gaming,** *s.* Jeu *m*. **gaming-table,** *s.* Table *f* de jeu.

game³, *a.* Courageux, résolu. **He is game for anything,** il est prêt à tout. **To die game,** mourir crânement.

gamekeeper, *s.* Garde-chasse *m*, *pl.* gardes-chasse(s).

gammon¹, *s.* (*a*) Quartier *m* de derrière (du porc). (*b*) Quartier de lard fumé.

gammon², *s.* *P:* Blague *f*.

gammon³, *v.tr.* *P:* Blaguer.

gamut, *s.* Gamme *f*.

gander, *s.* Jars *m*.

gang, *s.* (*a*) Groupe *m*, troupe *f* (de personnes); équipe *f* (d'ouvriers). (*b*) Bande *f*. **The whole gang,** toute la bande.

gangrene, *s.* *Med:* Gangrène *f*.

gangway, *s.* **I.** Passage *m*; couloir central. **2.** *Nau:* Passerelle *f* de service.

gannet, *s.* *Orn:* Gannet *m*, fou *m*.

gaol, *s.* Prison *f*; maison *f* d'arrêt. **gaol-bird,** *s.* *F:* Gibier *m* de potence

gaoler, *s.* Gardien *m* de prison.

gap, *s.* (*a*) Trou *m*; trouée *f*, ouverture *f*. (*b*) Interstice *m*; jour *m*; distance *f*, intervalle *m*. (*c*) Trou, lacune *f*, vide *m*.

gape, *v.i.* **I.** (*a*) Ouvrir la bouche toute grande; bâiller. (*b*) **To gape (open),** s'ouvrir (tout grand). **2.** Rester bouche bée. **To gape at s.o.,** regarder qn bouche bée. **gaping,** *a.* Béant.

garage¹, *s.* *Aut:* Garage *m*. **Garage keeper,** garagiste *m*.

garage², *v.tr.* (i) Garer, (ii) remiser.

garb¹, *s.* Vêtement *m*, costume *m*.

garb², *v.tr.* Habiller, vêtir (*in*, de).

garbage, *s.* Immondices *fpl*; ordures *fpl*.

garble, *v.tr.* Tronquer; dénaturer. **Garbled account,** compte rendu mensonger.

garden¹, *s.* (*a*) Jardin *m*. **Winter garden,** hall vitré. (*b*) *pl.* Jardin public. (*c*) *pl.* Rue avec jardins. **garden-city,** *s.* Cité-jardin *f*, *pl.* cités-jardins. **garden-party,** *s.* Réception en plein air.

garden², *v.i.* Jardiner. **gardening,** *s.* Jardinage *m*; horticulture *f*.

gardener, *s.* Jardinier, -ière.

gargle, *v.i.* Se gargariser.

gargoyle, *s.* *Arch:* Gargouille *f*.

garland, *s.* Guirlande *f*; couronne *f* (de fleurs).

garlic, *s.* *Bot:* Ail *m*.

garment, *s.* Vêtement *m*.

garnet, *s.* *Miner:* Grenat *m*.

garnish, *v.tr.* Garnir, orner, embellir (*with*, de). **garnishing,** *s.* Garniture *f*.

garret, *s.* Mansarde *f*, galetas *m*.

garrison¹, *s.* Garnison *f*.

garrison², *v.tr.* **To garrison a town,** mettre une garnison dans une ville.

garrulity, *s.* Loquacité *f*; garrulité *f*.

garrulous, *a.* Loquace, bavard.

garter, *s.* Jarretière *f*.

gas¹, *s.* **I.** Gaz *m*. *Dent:* **Laughing gas,** *F:* gaz, gaz hilarant. *F:* **To have gas,** se faire anesthésier. **2.** *P:* Verbiage *m*, bavardage *m*. **gas-attack,** *s.* *Mil:* Attaque *f*

par les gaz, aux gaz. **gas-bag,** *s.* *F:* Grand parleur. **gas-burner,** *s.* Bec *m* de gaz. **gas-fire,** *s.* Radiateur *m* à gaz. **gas-fitter,** *s.* Gazier *m*. **gas-lamp,** *s.* Bec *m* de gaz; réverbère *m*. **gas-light,** *s.* Lumière *f* du gaz. **gas-mantle,** *s.* Manchon *m* (de bec de gaz). **gas-mask,** *s.* Masque *m* à gaz, contre les gaz. **gas-meter,** *s.* Compteur *m* (à gaz). **gas-pipe,** *s.* Tuyau *m* à gaz; conduite *f* de, du, gaz. **gas-proof,** *a.* *Mil:* A l'épreuve des gaz. **gas-range,** *s.* *Cu:* Fourneau *m* à gaz. **gas-ring,** *s.* (Brûleur *m* à) couronne *f*. **gas-stove,** *s.* Fourneau *m* à gaz.

gas², *v* **I.** *v.tr.* Asphyxier, intoxiquer. *Mil:* Gazer. **2.** *v.i.* *P:* Jaser.

Gascon, *a.* & *s.* *Geog:* Gascon, -onne.

Gascony. *Pr.n.* *Geog:* La Gascogne.

gaseous, *a.* Gazeux.

gash¹, *s.* Coupure *f*, entaille *f*.

gash², *v.tr.* Entailler, couper.

gasometer, *s.* Gazomètre *m*; réservoir *m* à gaz.

gasp¹, *s.* Hoquet *m*. **To be at one's last gasp,** agoniser.

gasp², *v.i.* & *tr.* (*a*) Avoir un hoquet. **To gasp with astonishment,** sursauter. **To make s.o. gasp,** couper la respiration à qn. (*b*) **To gasp for breath,** haleter, suffoquer.

gastric, *a.* Gastrique.

gate, *s.* **I.** Porte *f*. **Main gates** (*of exhibition*), entrée principale. **2.** (**Wooden**) **gate,** barrière *f*; porte à claire-voie. **gate-keeper,** *s.* Portier, -ière. **gate-money,** *s.* *Sp:* Recette *f*; les entrées *f* **gate-post,** *s.* Montant *m* (de barrière).

gateway, *s.* Porte *f*, entrée *f*.

gather, I. *v.tr.* **I.** (*a*) Assembler, rassembler. **To gather one's thoughts,** recueillir ses esprits. (*b*) Ramasser (ses papiers). (*c*) Cueillir (des fleurs). **To gather (in) the harvest,** rentrer la récolte. **2.** **To gather speed,** prendre de la vitesse. **3.** Conclure. **So far as I can gather,** à ce que je comprends. II. **gather,** *v.i.* **I.** (*a*) Se réunir, se rassembler. (*b*) Affluer, s'attrouper. **2.** (*Of thgs*) S'accumuler. (*a*) **A storm is gathering,** un orage se prépare. (*b*) **In the growing darkness,** dans la nuit grandissante. **3.** *Med:* Abcéder. **gathering,** *s.* **I.** (*a*) Rassemblement *m*, attroupement *m*. (*b*) Cueillette *f* (des fruits). **2.** (*a*) Assemblée *f*, réunion *f*. (*b*) *Med:* Abcès *m*.

gaudiness, *s.* Ostentation *f*; clinquant *m*.

gaudy, *a.* Voyant, criard, éclatant. **-ily,** *adv.* De manière voyante.

gauge¹, *s.* **I.** Calibre *m*. **2.** (Appareil *m*) vérificateur *m*; calibre, jauge *f*. **3.** Indicateur *m*, contrôleur *m*. *Aut:* **Petrol gauge,** indicateur jauge d'essence.

gauge², *v.tr.* Jauger, mesurer (le vent, etc.). *F:* **To gauge s.o.'s capacities,** estimer, jauger, les capacités de qn.

gaunt, *a.* **I.** Maigre, décharné. **2.** Lugubre, désolé.

gauntlet[1], *s.* **1.** To throw down the gauntlet, jeter le gant. **2.** Gauntlet glove, gant à crispins, à manchette.

gauntlet[2], *s.* *Mil:* To run the gauntlet, passer par les bretelles, par les baguettes; *F:* soutenir un feu roulant de critiques adverses.

gauze, *s.* Gaze *f.*

gawki ıess, *s.* Gaucherie *f.*

gawky, *a.* Dégingandé, gauche.

gay, *a.* **1.** (*a*) Gai, allègre. (*b*) To lead a gay life, mener une vie de plaisir(s). **2.** Gai, splendide, brillant. **gaily**, *adv.* Gaiement, allégrement.

gaze[1], *s.* Regard *m* fixe.

gaze[2], *v.i.* Regarder fixement. To gaze into space, regarder dans le vide.

gazelle, *s.* *Z:* Gazelle *f.*

gazette, *s.* **1.** Journal officiel. **2.** *Cin:* Topical Gazette, actualités *fpl.*

gazetteer, *s.* Répertoire *m* géographique.

gear, *s.* **1.** (*a*) Effets (personnels). (*b*) Attirail *m*, appareil *m*; *Nau:* apparaux *mpl.* Fishing gear, attirail de pêche. **2.** (*a*) In gear, engrené, en prise. Out oì gear, (i) débrayé, désengrené; (ii) détraqué. (*b*) *Aut:* Vitesse *f.* High gear, grande vitesse. To change gear, changer de vitesse. **gear-box**, *s.* *Aut:* Boîte *f* de vitesses.

gelatine, *s.* Gélatine *j.*

gelatinous, *a.* Gélatineux.

gelding, *s.* Cheval *m* hongre.

gem, *s.* (*a*) Pierre précieuse; gemme *f*, joyau *m.* (*b*) *F:* The gem of the collection, le joyau de la collection.

gender, *s.* **1.** *Gram:* Genre *m.* **2.** *F:* Sexe *m.*

genealogical, *a.* Généalogique.

genealogist, *s.* Généalogiste *m.*

genealogy, *s.* Généalogie *f.*

general. I. *a.* Général, -aux. **1.** (*a*) General meeting, assemblée générale. (*b*) As a general rule, en règle générale. The general public, le grand public. (*c*) General servant, bonne *f* à tout faire. (*d*) General resemblance, ressemblance générale, vague. **2.** *adv.phr.* In general, en général; généralement. **-ally**, *adv.* **1.** Généralement, universellement. **2.** Généralement; en général. Generally speaking, (parlant) d'une manière générale; en général. II. **general,** *s.* *Mil:* Général *m.* General Smith, Monsieur le général Smith.

generalization, *s.* Généralisation *f.*

generalize, *v.tr.* Généraliser.

generate, *v.tr.* Générer, produire. **generating**, *a.* Générateur, -trice.

generation, *s.* Génération *f.*

generator, *s.* Générateur *m.*

generosity, *s.* Générosité *f.* (*a*) Magnanimité *f.* (*b*) Libéralité *f.*

generous, *a.* Généreux. (*a*) Magnanime. (*b*) Libéral, -aux. **-ly**, *adv.* Généreusement. **1.** Avec magnanimité. **2.** Libéralement.

genesis, *s.* Genèse *f*; origine *f.*

Geneva. *Pr.n. Geog:* Genève *f.* The Lake of Geneva, le lac Léman.

genial, *a.* (*a*) Doux, *f.* douce; clément. (*b*) Plein de bienveillance; plein de bonne humeur **-ally**, *adv.* Affablement, cordialement.

geniality, *s.* (*a*) Douceur *ĵ* (d'un climat). (*b*) Bienveillance *f*; bonne humeur

genie, *s. Myth:* Djinn *m*, génie *m.*

genitive, *a. & s. Gram:* Génitif (*m*).

genius, *s.* **1.** Génie *m*, djinn *m.* **2.** (*a*) Aptitudes naturelles. (*b*) Man of genius, homme de génie. **3.** To be a genius, être un génie.

Genoa. *Pr.n. Geog:* Gênes *f.*

Genoese, *a. & s. Geog:* Génois, -oise.

genteel, *a.* De bon ton; comme il faut. *G. tone of voice*, ton maniéré.

Gentile, *a. & s. B.Hist:* Gentil.

gentility, *s.* Prétention *f* à la distinction, au bon ton.

gentle, *a.* **1.** Bien né. Of gentle birth, de bonne naissance. **2.** Doux, *f.* douce. The gentle(r) sex, le sexe faible. **-tly**, *adv.* Doucement. Gently (does it)! allez-y doucement.

gentlefolk(s), *s.pl.* (*a*) Gens *m* comme il faut. (*b*) Personnes *f* de bonne famille.

gentleman, *s.m.* **1.** Galant homme; homme comme il faut. **2.** *F:* To be a gentleman of leisure, vivre de ses rentes. **3.** Monsieur *m.* Ladies and gentlemen! mesdames et messieurs! Young gentleman, jeune homme, jeune monsieur. *Com:* Gentlemen's hairdresser, coiffeur pour hommes. **4.** *Danc:* Cavalier *m.*

gentlemanly, *a.* Comme il faut; bien élevé.

gentleness, *s.* Douceur *f.*

gentry, *s. Coll.* (*a*) Petite noblesse. (*b*) *F:* The gentry, la gentilhommerie.

genuine, *a.* (*a*) Authentique, véritable. *G. coin*, pièce de bon aloi. (*b*) Véritable, sincère; franc, *f.* franche. **-ly**, *adv.* **1.** Authentiquement. **2.** Franchement, véritablement.

genuineness, *s.* **1.** Authenticité *f.* **2.** Sincérité *f*, loyauté *f.*

genus, *s.* (*a*) *Nat.Hist:* Genre *m.* (*b*) *F:* Genre, espèce *f.*

geographic(al), *a.* Géographique.

geography, *s.* Géographie *f.*

geological, *a.* Géologique.

geologist, *s.* Géologue *m.*

geology, *s.* Géologie *f.*

geometric(al), *a.* Géométrique.

geometrician, *s.* Géomètre *m.*

geometry, *s.* Géométrie *f.*

George. *Pr.n.* Georges *m.*

geranium, *s. Bot:* Géranium *m.*

germ, *s.* **1.** *Biol:* Germe *m.* **2.** *Med: F:* Germe, microbe *m.*

German, *a. & s.* **1.** *Geog:* Allemand, -ande. The German Ocean, la mer du Nord. **2.** *Ling:* L'allemand *m.*

germane, *a.* Approprié (*to,* à); en rapport (*to,* avec).

Germany. *Pr.n. Geog:* L'Allemagne *f.*

germinate, *v.i.* Germer.

germination, *s. Biol:* Germination *f.*

gerund, *s. Gram:* Gérondif *m.*

gesticulate. **I.** *v.i.* Gesticuler. **2.** *v.tr.* Exprimer, manifester, par des gestes.

gesticulation, *s.* Gesticulation *f.*

gesture[1], *s.* Geste *m,* signe *m.*

gesture[2], *v.i.* Faire des gestes.

get, *v.* **I.** *v.tr.* **I.** Procurer, obtenir. (*a*) To get sth. (for oneself), se procurer qch. To get sth. for s.o., procurer qch. à qn. *I got this horse cheap,* j'ai eu ce cheval à bon marché. (*b*) Acquérir, gagner. To get the prize, gagner, remporter, le prix. I will see what I can get for it, je verrai ce qu'on m'en donnera. *F:* Don't you wish you may get it! je vous en souhaite! (*c*) To get leave to do sth., obtenir la permission de faire qch. If I get the time, si j'ai le temps. **2.** (*a*) Recevoir. *He gets his timidity from his mother,* il tient sa timidité de sa mère, (*b*) Attraper (une maladie). **3.** Aller chercher (son chapeau). **4.** To get the breakfast (ready), préparer le déjeuner. **5.** (*a*) To get sth. done (*by s.o.*), faire faire qch. (à, par, qn). *To get oneself appointed,* se faire nommer. (*b*) To get one's work finished, finir son travail. **6.** (*a*) *I haven't got any,* je n'en ai pas. (*b*) *It has got to be done,* il faut que cela se fasse. **7.** *Min:* Exploiter, extraire. **II. get,** *v.i.* **I.** (*a*) To get old, devenir vieux, se faire vieux, vieillir. To get angry, se mettre en colère. (*b*) To get dressed, s'habiller. To get married, (i) se marier; (ii) se faire épouser. *To get killed,* se faire tuer. *To get drowned,* se noyer. **2.** (*a*) Aller, arriver, se rendre. *He'll get here to-morrow,* il arrivera (ici) demain. *F:* We're not getting anywhere, nous n'aboutissons à rien. (*b*) Se mettre. To get to work, se mettre à l'œuvre. (*c*) *To get to know sth.,* apprendre qch. **get about,** *v.i.* **I.** Circuler. **get along,** *v.i.* (*a*) S'avancer. *F:* Get along (with you)! allons donc! (*b*) Faire des progrès; faire son chemin. **get at,** *v.i.* **I.** Parvenir à, atteindre (un endroit). *F:* What are you getting at? où voulez-vous en venir? **2.** *F:* To get at a witness, suborner un témoin. **3.** *F:* Faire des sorties contre (qn). **get away.** **I.** *v.i.* (*a*) Partir, déloger. (*b*) S'échapper, se sauver. To get away from one's environment, échapper, se soustraire, à son entourage. *F:* There's no getting away from it, il n'y a pas à sortir de là. **2.** *v.tr.* Arracher (*sth. from s.o.,* qch. à qn). **get back.** **I.** *v.i.* (*a*) Reculer. (*b*) Revenir, retourner. **2.** *v.tr.* Se faire rendre; rentrer en possession de. *I got my money back,* on m'a remboursé. To get one's own back, *F:* prendre sa revanche. **get by,** *v.i.* Passer. **get down.** **I.** *v.i.* (*a*) Descendre (*from, off,* de). To get down on one's knees, se mettre à genoux. (*b*) *F:* To get down to

the facts, en venir aux faits. **2.** *v.tr.* Descendre; décrocher (son chapeau). **get in.** **I.** *v.i.* **I.** *F:* = GET INTO I (*a*). **2.** Entrer; monter (en wagon, en voiture). *If the train gets in to time,* si le train arrive à l'heure. **II. get in,** *v.tr* **I.** Rentrer. To get in the crops, rentrer la moisson **2.** To get a word in, placer un mot **3.** To get one's hand in, se faire la main. **get into.** **I.** *v.i.* (*a*) Entrer dans (une maison); monter dans (une voiture). (*b*) To get into a rage, se mettre en rage. **2.** *v.tr.* To get s.o. into the way of doing sth., faire prendre à qn l'habitude de faire qch. **get off.** **I.** *v.i.* **I.** (*a*) Descendre de. (*b*) To get off a duty, se faire exempter d'une tâche. **2.** (*a*) Se tirer d'affaire. To get off with a fine, en être quitte pour une amende. (*b*) To get off to sleep, s'endormir. **II. get off,** *v.tr.* **I.** To get off one's clothes, ôter ses vêtements. **2.** Expédier (un colis). **3.** To get sth. off one's hands, se débarrasser de qch. **4.** Renflouer, déséchouer (un navire). **get on.** **I.** *v.tr.* **I.** Mettre (ses souliers). **2.** Faire faire des progrès à (un élève). **II. get on,** *v.i.* **I.** Monter, se mettre, sur. **2.** (*a*) To be getting on for forty, approcher de la quarantaine. To be getting on (in years), prendre de l'âge; avancer en âge. (*b*) Faire des progrès. To get on in life, réussir dans la vie. *How to get on,* le moyen de parvenir. To get on with the job, pousser la besogne. How are you getting on? comment allez-vous? To get on without sth., se passer de qch. (*c*) To get on with s.o., s'accorder, s'entendre, avec qn. (*d*) *P:* Get on with you! allons donc! **get out.** **I.** *v.tr.* (*a*) Tirer, retirer (un bouchon). *F:* To get sth. out of it, y gagner qch. (*b*) To get out one's car, (faire) sortir sa voiture. To get out a scheme, préparer un devis. **2.** *v.i.* (*a*) To get out of sth., sortir de qch. *The lion got out of its cage,* le lion s'échappa de sa cage. To get out of s.o.'s way, faire place à qn. Get out (of here)! fichez-moi le camp! (*b*) To get out of a difficulty, se soustraire à une difficulté. To get out of doing sth., se faire exempter de faire qch. (*c*) To get out of the habit of doing sth., se désaccoutumer de faire qch. **get over.** **I.** *v.i.* (*a*) Franchir (un mur). (*b*) To get over an illness, se remettre d'une maladie. *To get over one's surprise,* revenir de sa surprise. (*c*) *F:* To get over s.o., enjôler qn. **2.** *v.tr.* (*a*) Faire passer par-dessus (un mur). (*b*) To get sth. over, en finir avec qch. **(c)** Tourner (une difficulté). *F:* To get round s.o., enjôler qn. **get through,** *v.i.* **I.** (*a*) Passer (par un trou). (*b*) Accomplir, arriver au bout de. To get through the day, faire passer la journée. **2.** (*a*) (*Of candidate*) Passer; être reçu. (*b*) *Tp:* To get through (to s.o.), obtenir la communication (avec qn). **get together.** **I.** *v.i.* Se réunir, se rassembler. **2.** *v.tr.* Rassembler. **get up. I.** *v.i.* **I.** To get up a ladder, monter à une

échelle. **2.** (*a*) Se mettre debout; se lever.
(*b*) **To get up to mischief,** faire des malices.
(*c*) (*Of wind*) Se lever, s'élever; (*of sea*)
grossir. II. **get up,** *v.tr.* (*a*) Monter (une
malle). (*b*) Faire lever (qn). (*c*) Organiser
(une fête). (*d*) Préparer, travailler (un sujet
d'examen). (*e*) **To get oneself up,** se faire
beau, belle. **To get oneself up as a woman,**
se déguiser en femme.
geyser, *s.* **1.** *Geol:* Geyser *m*. **2.** Chauffe-
bain(s) *m*, *pl.* chauffe-bains.
ghastliness, *s.* **1.** Horreur *f* (d'un crime).
2. Pâleur mortelle.
ghastly, *a.* (*a*) Horrible, effroyable, affreux.
(*b*) Blême.
Ghent. *Pr.n. Geog:* Gand *m*.
gherkin, *s.* Cornichon *m*
ghetto, *s.* Ghetto *m*.
ghost, *s.* **1. To give up the ghost,** rendre
l'âme *f*. **2. The Holy Ghost,** le Saint-Esprit.
3. (*a*) Fantôme *m*, spectre *m*; revenant *m*.
(*b*) *F:* **Not the ghost of a chance,** pas la
moindre chance. **ghost-story,** *s.* Histoire
f de revenants.
ghostlike, *a.* Spectral, -aux; de spectre.
ghostly, *a.* Spectral, -aux; de fantôme.
ghoul, *s.* *Myth:* Goule *f*, vampire *m*.
ghoulish, *a.* De goule; *F:* vampirique.
giant. 1. *s.* Géant *m*; *F:* colosse *m*. **2.** *a.*
Géant, gigantesque.
giantess, *s.f.* Géante.
gibber, *v.i.* (*a*) Produire des sons inarticulés.
(*b*) Baragouiner. **gibbering**[1], *a.* Gibbering
idiot, *F:* espèce *m* d'idiot. **gibbering**[2], *s.*
Baragouinage *m*.
gibberish, *s.* Baragouin *m*.
gibbet, *s.* Gibet *m*, potence *f*.
gibe[1], *s.* Raillerie *f*; moquerie *f*; sarcasme *m*.
gibe[2], *v.tr. & i.* **To gibe (at) s.o.,** railler qn.
gibing, *a.* Railleur, -euse, moqueur, -euse.
giblets, *s.pl.* Abatis *m* (de volaille).
giddiness, *s.* **1.** Étourdissement *m*, vertige
m. **2.** (*a*) Étourderie *f*. (*b*) Frivolité *f*.
giddy, *a.* **1.** (*a*) Étourdi. **To turn giddy,**
être pris de vertige. *I feel g.,* la tête me
tourne. (*b*) Vertigineux. **2.** Frivole, étourdi.
gift, *s.* Don *m*. (*a*) **To make a gift of sth. to
s.o.,** faire don de qch. à qn. (*b*) Cadeau *m*,
présent *m*. (*c*) **To have a gift for mathematics,**
avoir le don des mathématiques.
gifted, *a.* Bien doué; de valeur, de talent.
gig, *s.* **1.** Cabriolet *m*. **2.** *Nau:* Yole *f*.
gigantic, *a.* Géant, gigantesque.
giggle[1], *s.* Petit rire nerveux.
giggle[2], *v.i.* Pousser des petits rires. **gig-
gling,** *s.* Rires nerveux; petits rires bêtes.
gild, *v.tr.* Dorer. **gilded,** *a.* Doré. **gilt**[1], *a.*
Doré. **gilt**[2], *s.* Dorure *f*, doré *m*. **gilt-
edged,** *a.* **1.** Doré sur tranche. **2.** *Fin:*
Gilt-edged stock, valeurs de tout repos.
gilding, *s.* Dorure *f*.
gill, *s.* Usu. pl. Ouïe(s) *f*, branchie(s) *f*.

gimlet, *s.* *Tls:* Vrille *f*; foret *m*.
gin[1], *s.* *Ven:* Piège *m*, trébuchet *m*.
gin[2], *s.* Genièvre *m*.
ginger. 1. *s.* (*a*) Gingembre *m*. (*b*) *F:*
Entrain *m*, énergie *f*. **2.** *a.* (*Of hair*) Roux,
f. rousse.
gingerbread, *s.* Pain *m* d'épice.
gingerly, *adv.* Délicatement, avec précaution.
gipsy, *s.* Bohémien, -ienne; nomade *mf*.
giraffe, *s.* *Z:* Girafe *f*.
gird[1], *v.tr.* **1.** Ceindre. (*a*) *F:* **To gird
oneself for the fray,** se préparer à la lutte.
(*b*) **To gird (on) one's sword,** ceindre son
épée. **2.** Entourer, ceindre (*with*, de).
girt, *a.* Entouré, ceint (*with*, de).
gird[2], *v.i.* **To gird at s.o.,** railler qn.
girder, *s.* Support *m*. (*a*) *Const:* Solive *f*.
(*b*) Poutre *f*.
girdle, *s.* Ceinture *f*.
girl, *s.* **1.** Jeune fille *f*. (*a*) **Little girl,** fillette *f*.
Girl's name, prénom féminin. (*b*) (**School**)
girl, élève *f*, écolière *f*. **2.** Jeune personne *f*,
jeune fille. (*a*) (*Often best translated by*
jeune). *A French g.,* une jeune Française.
The Smith girls, les demoiselles *f* Smith.
Attrib. **Girl friend,** (jeune) amie. (*b*) **My dear
girl!** ma chère amie! (*c*) **My eldest girl,** ma
fille aînée. **3.** (**Shop-**)**girl,** demoiselle de magasin. (**Servant-**)**girl,** domestique *f*; bonne *f*.
Work-girl, (jeune) ouvrière *f*.
girlhood, *s.* Jeunesse *f* ou adolescence *f*
(d'une femme).
girlish, *a.* **1.** De petite fille ou de jeune fille.
2. (*Of boy*) Mou, efféminé.
girth, *s.* **1.** *Harn:* Sangle *f*. **2.** Circonférence *f*.
gist, *s.* Fond *m*, essence *f*; point essentiel
(d'une question).
give[1], *s.* Élasticité *f*.
give[2], *v.* I. *v.tr.* Donner. **1.** (*a*) **To give
alms,** faire l'aumône. *F:* **Give me the good
old days!** parlez-moi du bon vieux temps!
(*b*) **To give and take,** chacun doit y mettre chacun du
sien. **2.** (*a*) *To g. s.o. sth. to eat,* donner à
manger à qn. (*b*) **To give sth. into s.o.'s
hands,** remettre qch. entre les mains de qn.
(*c*) **To give one's compliments to s.o.,** présenter ses compliments à qn. (*d*) Engager.
To give one's word, donner sa parole.
3. What did you give for it? combien l'avez-
vous payé? **4.** *To g. oneself to study,* s'adonner
à l'étude. **5.** Faire (une action). **To give a
jump,** faire un saut; tressauter. *To g. a sigh,*
pousser un soupir. **To give s.o. a blow,**
porter un coup à qn. *To g. s.o. a smile,*
adresser un sourire à qn. **6.** (*a*) **To give
s.o. one's hand,** donner, tendre, la main à qn.
(*b*) **To give (one's) attention to s.o.,** faire
attention à qn. **7.** (*a*) *F:* **I'll give you best,**
je vous donne gagné. (*b*) **To give no sign(s)
of life,** ne donner aucun signe de vie. (*c*) **To
give a toast,** boire à la santé de qn. **8.** (*a*) **To
give pleasure,** faire, causer, du plaisir.

(b) To give s.o. to suppose sth., faire supposer qch. à qn. **(c)** Rendre. **9.** **(a)** *P:* To give it **(to)** s.o., semoncer vertement qn. **(b)** *F:* To give as good as one gets, rendre coup pour coup. **10.** To give way. **(a)** *(Also abs.* to give) Céder ; se casser ; *(of cable)* partir. *The ground gave way under our feet*, le sol s'affaissa sous nos pieds. **(b)** Lâcher pied. To give way to s.o., céder à qn. To give way to despair, s'abandonner (au désespoir). **II.** **give,** *v.i.* *(Of elastic)* Prêter, donner. **give away,** *v.tr.* **I.** Donner *(sth. to s.o., qch. à qn).* **2.** To give away the bride, conduire la mariée à l'autel. **3.** *F:* To give s.o. away, trahir qn. To give the show away, bavarder ; vendre la mèche. **give back,** *v.tr.* Rendre, restituer. **giving back,** *s.* Restitution *f.* **give in.** **I.** *v.tr.* **(a)** To give in one's name, donner son nom ; se faire inscrire. **(b)** *Com:* Given in, ajouté en supplément. **2.** *v.i.* Céder ; se rendre. **give off,** *v.tr.* Dégager, exhaler. **give out.** **I.** *v.tr.* **(a)** Distribuer. **(b)** = GIVE OFF. **(c)** Annoncer. **2.** *v.i.* Manquer ; faire défaut. *My strength was giving out*, j'étais à bout de forces. **give over,** *v.tr.* *F:* Cesser ; finir. **give up,** *v.tr.* **I.** Rendre (sa proie) ; abandonner (ses biens). To give up one's seat to s.o., céder sa place à qn. **2.** **(a)** Renoncer à ; abandonner. *(Of riddle)* I give it up, je donne ma langue au chat. To give it up (as a bad job), y renoncer. **(b)** To give s.o. up (for lost), considérer qn comme perdu. I had given you up! je ne vous espérais plus ! **3.** **(a)** Livrer ; faire arrêter. To give oneself up, se constituer prisonnier. **(b)** To give oneself up to sth., se livrer (à un vice) ; s'adonner (à l'étude). **given,** *a.* **I.** In a given time, dans un délai donné, convenu. **2.** Porté, enclin *(to,* à). Given to drink, adonné à la boisson.

giver, *s.* Donneur, -euse ; donateur, -trice.

gizzard, *s.* Gésier *m.*

glacial, *a.* Glacial, -als.

glacier, *s.* *Geol:* Glacier *m.*

glad, *a.* Heureux. **I.** Bien aise ; content. I'm very glad of it, j'en suis bien aise. **2.** Glad tidings, nouvelles joyeuses. **-ly,** *adv.* **(a)** Avec plaisir, volontiers. **(b)** Avec joie.

gladden, *v.tr.* Réjouir.

glade, *s.* Clairière *f*, éclaircie *f.*

gladiator, *s.* Gladiateur *m.*

gladiolus, *s.* *Bot:* Glaïeul *m.*

gladness, *s.* Joie *f*, allégresse *f.*

glamour, *s.* **I.** Enchantement *m*, charme *m.* To cast a glamour over s.o., ensorceler qn. **2.** Fascination *f*; prestige *m*; éclat *m.*

glance¹, *s.* Regard *m*; coup d'œil. At a glance, d'un coup d'œil.

glance², *v.i.* **I.** To glance off, dévier, ricocher. **2.** To glance at sth., jeter un regard sur qch. To glance through sth., parcourir (un livre).

gland, *s.* *Biol:* Glande *f.*

glare¹, *s.* **I.** **(a)** Éclat *m*, clarté *f.* In the full glare of the sun, au grand soleil. **(b)** Éblouissement *m*, aveuglement *m* (d'un phare). **2.** Regard fixe et irrité.

glare², *v.i.* **I.** Briller d'un éclat éblouissant. **2.** To glare at s.o., lancer un regard furieux à qn. **glaring,** *a.* **I.** Éblouissant, éclatant. **2.** Manifeste, patent.

glass, *s.* **I.** Verre *m.* Cut glass, cristal taillé. **2.** **(a)** Glass of wine, verre de vin. To have had a glass too many, avoir bu un coup de trop. **(b)** *Coll.* Table glass, verrerie *f* de table. **3.** (Looking-)glass, glace *f*, miroir *m.* **4.** *pl.* To wear glasses, porter des lunettes. **5.** The glass is falling, le baromètre baisse. **6.** *Attrib.* De, en, verre. Glass bottle, bouteille de, en, verre. Glass door, porte vitrée. **glass-case,** *s.* Vitrine *f.* To keep sth. in a glass-case, garder qch. sous verre. **glass-house,** *s* *Hort:* Serre *f.* **glass-partition,** *s.* Vitrage *m.* **glass-ware,** *s.* Articles *mpl* de verre ; verrerie *f.*

glassful, *s.* (Plein) verre.

glassy, *a.* Vitreux.

glaucous, *a.* Glauque.

glaze¹, *s.* *Cer:* Glaçure *f*, vernis (luisant).

glaze². **I.** *v.tr.* **I.** Vitrer (une fenêtre). **2.** **(a)** Glacer, lustrer (une étoffe). **(b)** *Cer:* Vernir, émailler. **II.** **glaze,** *v.i.* To glaze (over), devenir vitreux. **glazed,** *a.* **I.** Vitré. Framed and g., encadré et sous verre. **2.** **(a)** (Tissu) glacé, lustré. **(b)** *Cer:* Glacé, émaillé ; *(of brick)* vitrifié. **glazing,** *s.* **(a)** Pose *f* des vitres. **(b)** Vernissage *m.* *Cer:* Émaillage *m.*

glazier, *s.* Vitrier *m.*

gleam¹, *s.* **(a)** Rayon *m*, lueur *f.* Gleam of hope, lueur d'espoir. **(b)** Reflet *m* (d'un couteau).

gleam², *v.i.* Luire, reluire ; *(of water)* miroiter. **gleaming,** *a.* Luisant.

glean, *v.tr.* Glaner. **gleaning,** *s.* **I.** Glane *f.* **2.** *pl.* Gleanings, glanure(s) *f.*

gleaner, *s.* Glaneur, -euse.

glee, *s.* Joie *f*, allégresse *f.* In high glee, au comble de la joie.

gleeful, *a.* Joyeux, allègre. **-fully,** *adv.* Joyeusement ; allégrement.

glen, *s.* Vallée étroite ; vallon *m.*

glib, *a.* **(a)** Spécieux. **(b)** Qui a de la faconde. To have a glib tongue, avoir le débit facile. **-ly,** *adv.* **(a)** Spécieusement. **(b)** Avec aisance.

glibness, *s.* **I.** Spéciosité *f* (d'une excuse). **2.** Faconde *f*; bagout *m.*

glide, *v.i.* **(a)** (Se) glisser, couler. To glide past, passer tout doucement. **(b)** *Av:* Planer. **gliding,** *s.* **(a)** Glissement *m.* **(b)** Vol plané.

glider, *s.* *Av:* Planeur *m*, glisseur *m.*

glimmer¹, *s.* Faible lueur *f*; miroitement *m* (de l'eau).

glimmer², *v.i.* Jeter une faible lueur ; *(of water)* miroiter.

glimpse, *s.* Vision momentanée. To catch a glimpse of sth., entrevoir qch.

glint¹, s. Trait m, éclair m (de lumière); reflet m (d'un couteau).

glint², v.i. Entreluire, étinceler.

glisten, v.i. Étinceler, scintiller. **glistening,** a. Étincelant, scintillant.

glitter¹, s. Étincellement m, scintillement m.

glitter², v.i. Scintiller, étinceler. **glittering,** a. Brillant, étincelant, éclatant.

gloat, v.i. To gloat over sth., savourer (un spectacle). To g. over one's victim, couver du regard sa victime. **gloating,** a. (Œil avide; (sourire) d'exultation méchante.

globe, s. Globe m. (a) Sphère f. (b) (La) terre. (c) Globe (de lampe). (d) Bocal m, -aux. **globe-trotter,** s. Touriste mf qui court le monde.

globular, a. Globulaire, globuleux.

globule, s. Globule m, gouttelette f.

gloom, s. **1.** Obscurité f, ténèbres fpl. **2.** Assombrissement m, mélancolie f.

gloominess, s. Assombrissement m. (a) Obscurité f. (b) Tristesse f.

gloomy, a. **1.** Sombre, obscur, ténébreux. **2.** Lugubre, morne, sombre.

glorify, v.tr. Glorifier.

glorious, a. **1.** Glorieux. **2.** (a) Resplendissant, radieux. (b) F: Magnifique, superbe. **-ly,** adv. **1.** Glorieusement. **2.** Magnifiquement.

glory¹, s. Gloire f. **1.** (a) Honneur m, renommée f. (b) F: Glory (be)! grand Dieu! **2.** To be in one's glory, être dans son élément.

glory², v.i. To glory in sth., se glorifier de qch.

gloss¹, s. Lustre m, vernis m.

gloss², v.tr. F: To g. over s.o.'s faults, glisser sur les défauts de qn.

glossary, s. Glossaire m, lexique m.

glossy, a. Lustré, glacé, brillant.

glove¹, s. Gant m. (a) The glove counter, la ganterie. To take off one's gloves, se déganter. (b) F: To handle s.o. with the gloves off, traiter qn sans ménagement.

glove², v.tr. Ganter.

glover, s. Gantier, -ière.

glow¹, s. **1.** Lueur f rouge; incandescence f. **2.** (a) Sensation f de douce chaleur. F: The exercise had put me all in a glow, l'exercice m'avait fouetté le sang. (b) Ardeur f, chaleur f. **glow-worm,** s. Ent: (a) Ver luisant. (b) Luciole f.

glow², v.i. **1.** Rougeoyer. **2.** (a) Rayonner. (b) His cheeks glowed, il avait les joues en feu. **glowing,** a. **1.** Incandescent, rougeoyant. **2.** (Of coal) Embrasé. **3.** Rayonnant. Glowing cheeks, joues rouges. **4.** (Of description) Chaleureux.

glower, v.i. To glower at s.o., regarder qn d'un air menaçant.

glue¹, s. Colle (forte).

glue², v.tr. (a) Coller (to, on, à). (b) F: Her face was glued to the window, son visage était collé à la vitre.

glum, a. Renfrogné, maussade. To look glum, se renfrogner. **-ly,** adv. D'un air maussade.

glumness, s. Air m sombre.

glut¹, s. Com: (a) Encombrement m. (b) Surabondance f.

glut², v.tr. (a) To glut oneself, se rassasier, se gorger. (b) Com: Encombrer, inonder.

glutinous, a. Glutineux.

glutton, s. (a) Gourmand, -ande; glouton, -onne. (b) F: He's a glutton for work, c'est un cheval à l'ouvrage.

gluttonous, a. Glouton, -onne, goulu. **-ly,** adv. Gloutonnement.

gluttony, s. Gloutonnerie f, gourmandise f.

glycerin(e), s. Ch: Glycérine f.

gnarled, a. Noueux.

gnash, v.tr. To gnash one's teeth, grincer des dents.

gnat, s. Ent: Cousin m, moustique m.

gnaw, v.tr. & i. (a) To gnaw (at, into) sth., ronger qch. (b) Gnawed by hunger, tenaillé par la faim. **gnawing,** s. (a) Rongement m. (b) Gnawings of hunger, tiraillements m de la faim.

gnome, s. Myth: Gnome m.

gnu, s. Z: Gnou m.

go¹, s. **1.** Aller m. To be always on the go, être toujours à trotter. To keep s.o. on the go, faire trimer qn. **2.** To have plenty of go, être plein d'entrain m. **3.** Coup m, essai m. To have a go at sth., tenter l'aventure. At one go, d'un (seul) coup. **4.** P: Here's a pretty go! en voilà une farce! No go! bernique! **5.** P: It's all the go, c'est la grande vogue.

go², v.i. Aller. **1.** (a) To go to a place, aller, se rendre, à un endroit. To go to France, to Japan, aller en France, au Japon. To go to prison, être mis en prison. To come and go, aller et venir. To go to s.o. for sth., aller trouver qn pour avoir qch. To go (on) a journey, faire un voyage. Who goes there? qui va là? qui vive? To go (at) ten miles an hour, faire dix milles à l'heure. You go first! à vous d'abord. (b) Mountains that go from east to west, montagnes qui courent de l'est à l'ouest. (c) To go to sea, se faire marin. Wine that goes to the head, vin qui monte à la tête. (d) To go hungry, se serrer la ventre. (e) To go one's own way, faire à sa guise. (f) Promotion goes by seniority, l'avancement se fait à l'ancienneté. **2.** Marcher. (a) To set a machine going, mettre une machine en marche. To keep the fire going, entretenir le feu. To make things go, faire marcher rondement les choses. F: How goes it? ça va bien? comment ça va? To go (well), réussir. Things are not going well, cela ne marche pas. As things are going, du train dont vont les choses. (b) It has just gone twelve, midi vient de sonner. (c) This is how the chorus goes, voici les paroles du refrain. (d) Aboutir. I don't know how matters will go, je ne sais pas comment cela tournera. **3.** (a) Passer. F: How goes the time?

quelle heure est-il? (b) **As the saying goes,** selon l'adage. **As times go,** par le temps qui court. (c) **To go by a false name,** être connu sous un faux nom. (d) **That goes without saying,** cela va sans dire. 4. (a) Partir; s'en aller. *After I have gone,* après mon départ. (b) *A hundred employees to go,* cent employés vont recevoir leur congé. (c) Disparaître. *It has all gone,* il n'y en a plus. **Her sight is going,** sa vue baisse. (d) *The spring went,* le ressort s'est cassé. (e) *These spoons are going for ten francs each,* ces cuillers sont en vente à dix francs pièce. **Going! going! gone!** une fois! deux fois! adjugé! (f) *If I hear of any job going,* si j'apprends qu'une situation se présente. 5. (a) **To go and see s.o.,** aller trouver qn. (b) **To go to do sth.,** aller pour faire qch. (c) *I am going to have my own way,* je veux en faire à ma tête. (d) *I am going to tell you a story,* je vais vous raconter une histoire. (e) *To go fishing,* aller à la pêche. *F:* **There you go again!** vous voilà reparti! 6. (a) **To go to law,** avoir recours à la justice. **To go to war,** se mettre en guerre. (b) **To go one better,** renchérir. 7. (a) *Where does this book go?* où est la place de ce livre? (b) *Six into twelve goes twice,* douze divisé par six fait deux. 8. *His title will go to his eldest son,* son titre (de noblesse) passera à son fils aîné. 9. **To go to prove sth.,** servir à prouver qch. 10. S'étendre. 11. (a) Devenir. *To go mad,* devenir fou. *To go red,* rougir. (b) **To go to ruin,** tomber en ruine. His son has gone to the bad, son fils a mal tourné. 12. (a) **Let me go!** lâchez-moi! (b) **To let oneself go,** se laisser aller. (c) **Well, let it go at that!** passons! **go about,** v.i. 1. Aller çà et là; circuler. 2. Se mettre à (une tâche). *How to go about it,* comment s'y prendre. **go across,** v.i. Traverser; franchir (le pont). **go against,** v.i. It goes against my conscience to . . ., il me répugne de. . . . **go along,** v.i. 1. Passer par (une rue). 2. *F:* **Go along with you!** dites cela à d'autres! **go away,** v.i. *To go away on business,* s'absenter pour affaires. **go back,** v.i. 1. (a) *To go back to one's native land,* retourner dans sa patrie. (b) Rebrousser chemin; reculer. (c) *To go back to a subject,* revenir sur un sujet. 2. **To go back on a promise,** revenir sur sa promesse; se dédire. **go behind,** v.i. **To go behind s.o.'s back,** faire qch. à l'insu de qn. **go by,** v.i. 1. Passer. *You must not let this chance go by,* il ne faut pas manquer cette occasion. 2. *To go by the directions,* suivre les instructions. **To go by appearances,** juger d'après les apparences. *That is nothing to go by,* on ne peut fonder là-dessus. **go down,** v.i. 1. Descendre (l'escalier). 2. (a) Descendre. (b) That won't go down with me, ça ne prend pas avec moi. (c) (*Of sun*) Se coucher. (d) (*Of ship*) Couler à fond; sombrer. (e) Tomber. **To go down on one's knees,** se mettre à genoux. (f) (*Of temperature*) Baisser, s'abais-

ser. *The neighbourhood has gone down,* ce quartier a déchu. (g) Se dégonfler. (h) **To go down to posterity,** passer à la postérité. **go for,** v.i. 1. Aller chercher. 2. (a) *F:* Tomber sur. (b) *F:* S'en prendre à. **go forward,** v.i. 1. Avancer. 2. *What is going forward?* qu'est-ce qui se passe? **go in,** v.i. (a) Entrer, rentrer. (b) **To go in for (sth.),** s'occuper de (qch.). **To go in for an examination,** se présenter à un examen. *F:* **Go in and win!** bonne chance! **go into,** v.i. 1. (a) Entrer dans. (b) *To go into mourning,* prendre le deuil. *To go into fits of laughter,* éclater de rire. 2. Examiner, étudier (une question). **go off,** v.i. 1. (a) Partir, s'en aller. (b) (*Of gun*) Partir. (c) *Everything went off well,* tout s'est bien passé. 2. **To go off the rails,** dérailler. *F:* **To go off the beaten track,** s'écarter du chemin battu. **go on,** v.i. 1. (a) (i) *Time goes on,* le temps marche. (ii) Continuer sa route. (b) Continuer (de faire qch.); reprendre la parole. **If you go on like this,** si vous continuez. *I've got enough to go on with,* j'ai de quoi marcher. *F:* **Go on!** allons donc! (c) Marcher. *This has gone on for years,* cela dure depuis des années. **What is going on here?** qu'est-ce qui se passe ici? **How are you going on?** comment allez-vous? (d) *F:* Se conduire. (e) **To go on at s.o.,** gourmander qn. 2. *I went on that supposition,* je me suis fondé sur cette hypothèse. **goings-on,** s.pl. *F:* Conduite f; manège m. **go out,** v.i. 1. Sortir. **Out you go!** hors d'ici! **To go out (on strike),** se mettre en grève. *I am going out to dinner,* je dîne en ville. 2. **To go out of fashion,** passer de mode. 3. **To go out of one's way,** s'écarter de son chemin. 4. (*Of fire*) S'éteindre. 5. (*Of tide*) Baisser. **go over,** v.i. 1. (a) Traverser, passer. (b) Examiner (un compte). **To go over the ground,** reconnaître le terrain. (c) **To go over sth. in one's mind,** repasser qch. dans son esprit. **go round,** v.i. 1. (a) Faire un détour, un circuit. (b) Tourner. (c) Circuler, courir. (d) **There is not enough to go round,** il n'y en a pas pour tout le monde. 2. *To go round the town,* faire le tour de la ville. **go through,** v.i. 1. (a) Passer par; traverser. (b) *To go through one's apprenticeship,* faire son apprentissage. (c) Remplir, accomplir (des formalités); subir, essuyer. (d) Transpercer, percer. (e) Examiner en détail. (f) Manger (une fortune). 2. (a) *The bill has gone through,* la loi a passé. (b) **To go through with sth.,** aller jusqu'au bout (d'une épreuve). 3. Succomber, sombrer. **go up,** v.i. 1. (a) Monter; aller en haut. (b) **To go up to s.o.,** aborder qn. (c) Monter, hausser. 2. Monter. *To go up a ladder,* monter à une échelle. **go with,** v.i. 1. (a) Accompagner. (b) *To go with the times,* marcher avec son époque. 2. S'accorder avec. **go without,** v.i. 1. Se passer de. (b) Manquer de (qch.). **gone,** a. 1. Disparu, parti. **2.** *He is too far g. to speak,* il est trop bas pour parler. **3.** *F:* To be gone on s.o., être épris de qn. **going**[1], *a:* **1.** Qui marche. *The business is a g. concern,* la maison est en pleine activité. **2.** One of the best firms going, une des meilleures maisons qui soient. **going**[2], *s.* **1.** Départ *m.* **2.** Rough going, chemin rude. **go-ahead**, *a.* Plein d'allant; entreprenant. **go-between**, *s.* Intermédiaire *mf*; entremetteur, -euse.

goad[1], *s.* Aiguillon *m.*

goad[2], *v.tr.* Aiguillonner, piquer.

goal, *s.* But *m.* **goal-keeper**, *s. Fb:* Gardien *m* de but. **goal-post**, *s. Fb:* Montant *m* de but.

goat, *s.* Chèvre *f.* She-goat, bique *f*, chèvre. He-goat, bouc *m.*

goatee, *s.* Barbiche *f*, bouc *m*

goatherd, *s.* Chevrier, -ière.

goatsucker, *s. Orn:* Engoulevent *m.*

gobble, *v.tr.* To gobble (up) sth., avaler qch. goulûment.

goblet, *s.* Verre *m* à pied.

goblin, *s.* Gobelin *m*, lutin *m.*

god, *s.* **1.** (*a*) Dieu *m.* (*b*) *Th: P:* The gods, le poulailler, le paradis. **2.** God willing, s'il plaît à Dieu. Would to God, plût à Dieu. Thank God! Dieu merci! grâce au ciel! **god-child**, *s.* Filleul, *f.* filleule. **god-daughter**, *s.* Filleule *f.* **god-forsaken**, *a. F:* God-forsaken place, endroit perdu. **god-parent**, *s.* Parent spirituel.

goddess, *s.* Déesse *f.*

godfather, *s.* Parrain *m.*

godless, *a.* Athée, impie.

godlessness, *s.* Impiété *f.*

godliness, *s.* Piété *f.*

godly, *a.* Dévot, pieux, saint.

godmother, *s.* Marraine *f.*

godsend, *s.* Aubaine *f.*

godson, *s.* Filleul *m.*

goggle[1], *v.i.* Rouler de gros yeux.

goggle[2], *a.* (Yeux) à fleur de tête. **goggle-eyed**, *a.* Qui a des yeux à fleur de tête.

goggles, *s.pl.* Lunettes (protectrices).

gold, *s.* (*a*) Or *m.* (*b*) (Pièces *fpl* d')or. (*c*) Couleur *f* de l'or. Gold-beater's skin, baudruche *f.* **gold-digger**, *s* Chercheur *m* d'or. **gold-dust**, *s.* Poudre *f*, poussière *f*, d'or. **gold-field**, *s.* Champ *m* aurifère. *pl.* Gold-fields, districts *m* aurifères. **gold-fish**, *s.* Poisson *m* rouge. **gold-laced**, *a.* Galonné d'or; chamarré d'or. **gold-leaf**, *s.* Feuille *f* d'or; or *m* en feuille. **gold-mine**, *s.* Mine *f* d'or. *F:* A regular gold-mine, une affaire d'or. **gold plate**, *s.* Vaisselle *f* d'or. **gold-plated**, *a.* Doublé d'or. **gold-rimmed**, *a.* G.-r. spectacles, lunettes à monture d'or.

golden, *a.* D'or. (*a*) G. hair, cheveux d'or, d'un blond doré. (*b*) Golden rule, règle précieuse. **golden wedding**, *s.* Noces *fpl* d'or.

goldfinch, *s.* Chardonneret *m.*

goldsmith, *s.* Orfèvre *m.*

golf, *s.* Golf *m.* **golf-club**, *s.* **1.** Crosse *f* de golf. **2.** Club de golf. **golf-course**, *s.* Terrain *m* de golf.

golfer, *s.* Golfeur, -euse.

golosh, *s.* = GALOSH.

gondola, *s.* Gondole *f.*

gondolier, *s.* Gondolier *m.*

gong, *s.* Gong *m.*

good. **I.** *a.* Bon. **1.** (*a*) G. handwriting, belle écriture. G. story, bonne histoire. *F:* That's a good one! en voilà une bonne! Good to eat, bon à manger. To have g. sight, avoir de bons yeux. (*b*) G. reason, raison valable. (*c*) G. opportunity, bonne occasion. They are people of good position, ce sont des gens bien. I thought good to do so, il m'a semblé bon d'en faire ainsi. To make a good thing out of sth., tirer bon parti de qch. (*d*) Good (job)! that's a good thing! tant mieux! à la bonne heure! bon! Very good! très bien! (*e*) Good day! bonjour! Good evening! bonsoir! (*f*) Good for nothing, bon à rien. (*g*) *He is g. at all sports,* il excelle à tous les sports. **2.** (*a*) Good man, homme de bien. Good conduct, bonne conduite. G. old John! ce brave Jean! (*b*) (*Of children*) Sage. (*c*) Her good man, son mari. (*d*) Aimable. That's very good of you, c'est bien aimable à vous. He is a good sort, c'est un brave garçon. (*e*) *F:* Good Lord! Good Heavens! grand Dieu! **3.** A good long time, a good while, pas mal de temps. A good deal, beaucoup. **4.** As good as. *My family is as g. as his,* ma famille vaut bien la sienne. To give s.o. as good as one gets, rendre la pareille à qn. It is as good as new, c'est comme neuf. **5.** To make good. (*a*) Se rattraper de (ses pertes); remédier à (l'usure). (*b*) Justifier (une affirmation); remplir (sa promesse). (*c*) Effectuer (sa retraite). (*d*) Assurer (sa position); faire prévaloir (ses droits). **II.** **good**, *s.* **1.** Bien *m.* (*a*) To do good (in the world), faire du bien. He is up to no good, il prépare quelque mauvais coup. (*b*) I did it for your good, je l'ai fait pour votre bien. Much good may it do you! grand bien vous fasse! That won't be much g., ça ne servira pas à grand'chose. No good talking about it, inutile d'en parler. He will come to no good, il tournera mal. (*c*) It is all to the good, c'est autant de gagné; tant mieux. (*d*) *Adv.phr. He is gone* for good (and all), il est parti pour (tout) de bon. **2.** *pl.* Goods. (*a*) *Jur:* Biens, effets *m.* (*b*) Objets *m*, articles *m*; *Com:* marchandise(s) *f.* Goods train, train *m* de marchandises. To send sth. by goods train, envoyer qch. en petite vitesse. **good-class**, *a.* De choix. **good-feeling**, *s.* Bonne entente. **good-fellowship**, *s.* Camaraderie *f.* **good-for-nothing**. **1.** *a.* (*Of pers.*) Qui n'est bon à rien; (*of thg*) sans valeur. **2.** *s.* (*a*) Propre *mf* à rien. (*b*) Vaurien, -ienne. **good-hearted**, *a.* (Personne) qui a bon cœur. **good-humoured,** *a.* (Personne) d'un caractère facile, facile à vivre ; (sourire) de bonne humeur. **-ly,** *adv.* Avec bonhomie. **good-looking,** *a.* Bien de sa personne ; beau, -eaux, *f.* belle. **good-nature,** *s.* Bon naturel ; bonhomie *f.* **good-natured,** *a.* (*Of pers.*) Au bon naturel. *G.-n. smile,* sourire bon enfant. **-ly,** *adv.* Avec bonhomie. **good-tempered,** *a.* De caractère facile, égal ; facile à vivre.

good-bye, *int. & s.* Adieu (*m*). *G.-b. for the present,* à bientôt, à tantôt.

goodness, *s.* **1.** (*a*) Bonté *f.* (*b*) Bonne qualité. **2.** Goodness gracious! bonté divine! miséricorde! **My goodness!** mon Dieu! **Thank goodness!** Dieu merci!

goodwill, *s.* Bonne volonté ; bienveillance *f* (*towards,* pour, envers).

goose, *s.* **1.** Oie *f.* **2.** *F:* Niais, *f.* niaise.

goose-flesh, *s.* *F:* Chair *f* de poule.

goose-step, *s.* *Mil:* Pas *m* de l'oie.

gooseberry, *s.* (*a*) Groseille *f* à maquereau, groseille verte. (*b*) **Gooseberry (-bush),** groseillier *m* (à maquereau).

gore¹, *s.* **1.** Sang coagulé. **2.** Sang (versé).

gore², *v.tr.* Blesser avec les cornes.

gorge¹, *s.* **1.** My gorge rises at it, cela me soulève le cœur. **2.** *Geog:* Gorge *f,* défilé *m.*

gorge², *s.* Repas plantureux.

gorge³. **1.** *v.i.* To gorge (oneself), se gorger ; se rassasier. **2.** *v.tr.* Assouvir, gorger.

gorging, *s.* Rassasiement *m.*

gorgeous, *a.* (*a*) Magnifique, splendide. (*b*) *F:* Épatant, superbe. **-ly,** *adv.* Magnifiquement, splendidement.

gorgeousness, *s.* Splendeur *f,* magnificence *f,* faste *m.*

gorilla, *s.* *Z:* Gorille *m.*

gormandize, *v.i.* Bâfrer.

gorse, *s.* *Bot:* Ajonc(s) *m(pl).*

gory, *a.* Sanglant, ensanglanté.

gosling, *s.* Oison *m.*

gospel, *s.* Évangile *m.*

gossamer, *s.* (*a*) Fils *mpl* de la Vierge ; filandres *fpl.* (*b*) *Tex:* Gaze légère.

gossip¹, *s.* **1.** Bavard, -arde. **2.** (*a*) Causerie *f.* (*b*) Cancans *mpl* ; commérage(s) *m(pl).*

gossip², *v.i.* Bavarder.

Gothic. **1.** *a.* (Race) gothique. **Gothic architecture,** architecture gothique, ogivale. **2.** *s. Ling:* Le gothique.

gouge, *s.* *Tls:* Gouge *f.*

gourd, *s.* **1.** *Bot:* Courge *f,* gourde *f.* **2.** (*Bottle*) Gourde, calebasse *f.*

gourmand. **1.** *a.* Gourmand, glouton. **2.** *s.* Gourmet *m.*

gourmet, *s.* Gourmet *m.*

gout, *s.* *Med:* Goutte *f* ; (*of feet*) podagre *f.*

gouty, *a.* Goutteux.

govern, *v.tr.* **1.** Gouverner, régir (un État) ; administrer (une entreprise). *Abs.* **To govern,** gouverner. **2.** Maîtriser, gouverner (ses passions). **governing,** *a.* Gouvernant.

Governing body, conseil *m* d'administration.

governess, *s.* Institutrice *f.*

government, *s.* Gouvernement *m.* (*a*) **Form of government,** régime *m.* (*b*) **Government offices,** Ministères *m.*

governor, *s.* **1.** Gouvernant *m.* **2.** (*a*) Gouverneur *m* (d'une colonie). (*b*) *F:* Père *m* ; le vieux. (*c*) *F:* Patron *m.*

gown, *s.* Robe *f.*

grab¹, *s.* Mouvement vif de la main pour saisir qch.

grab², *v.tr. & i.* To grab (hold of) sth., saisir qch.

grace¹, *s.* Grâce *f.* **1.** To do sth. with a good grace, faire qch. avec bonne grâce. **2.** Act of grace, gracieuseté *f,* faveur *f.* **3.** Grace, (*before meal*) bénédicité *m* ; (*after meal*) grâces. **4.** Your Grace, votre Grandeur *f.*

grace², *v.tr.* Embellir, orner.

graceful, *a.* Gracieux. **-fully,** *adv.* Avec grâce ; avec élégance.

gracefulness, *s.* Grâce *f,* élégance *f.*

gracious, *a.* Gracieux, indulgent, bienveillant. **-ly,** *adv.* Avec bienveillance.

graciousness, *s.* **1.** Grâce *f.* **2.** Bienveillance *f* (*to, towards,* envers).

gradation, *s.* (*a*) Gradation *f.* (*b*) *Art:* (Dé)gradation *f* (des teintes).

grade, *s.* (*a*) Grade *m,* rang *m,* degré *m.* (*b*) Qualité *f* ; classe *f.*

gradient, *s.* *Civ.E:* Upward gradient, rampe *f.* **Downward gradient,** pente *f.*

gradual, *a.* Graduel ; progressif. **-ally,** *adv.* Graduellement ; peu à peu.

graduate¹, *s. Sch:* Gradué, -ée.

graduate², *v.tr.* Graduer.

graduation, *s.* Graduation *f.*

graft¹, *s. Arb:* Greffe *f.*

graft², *v.tr. Arb:* Greffer, enter. **grafting,** *s. Arb:* Greffe *f,* greffage *m.*

grain, *s.* **1.** Grain *m.* *F:* Grain of consolation, brin *m* de consolation. **2.** (*a*) Grain (du bois). *F:* Man of coarse grain, homme sans délicatesse. (*b*) Fil *m* (de la viande). **Against the grain,** à contre-fil. *F:* It goes against the grain for me to do it, c'est à contre-cœur que je le fais.

grammar, *s.* Grammaire *f.* **grammar-school,** *s.* École *f* secondaire.

grammatical, *a.* Grammatical, -aux. **-ally,** *adv.* Grammaticalement.

gramophone, *s.* Gramophone *m.*

grampus, *s.* *Z:* Épaulard *m,* orque *f.*

granary, *s.* Grenier *m.*

grand, *a.* **1.** (*In titles*) Grand. **2.** (*a*) Grand ; principal, -aux. *Sp:* **The grand stand,** la tribune. (*b*) **Grand total,** total global. **3.** Grandiose, magnifique. **4.** *F:* Excellent ; *F:* épatant. **-ly,** *adv.* (*a*) Grandement, magnifiquement. (*b*) Grandiosement. **grand-daughter,** *s.f.* Petite-fille *f,* petites-filles.

grandchild, *s.* Petit-fils *m* ou petite-fille *f,* *pl.* petits-enfants *m.*

grandeur, *s.* Grandeur *f.* (*a*) Noblesse *f,* éminence *f.* (*b*) Splendeur *f.*

grandfather, s. Grand-père m, pl. grands-pères.

grandiloquence, s. Grandiloquence f; emphase f.

grandiloquent, a. Grandiloquent.

grandiose, a. (a) Grandiose, magnifique. (b) Pompeux.

grandmother, s. Grand'mère f, pl. grand'-mères.

grandparent, s. Grand-père m, grand-mère f; pl. grands-parents m.

grandson, s. Petit-fils m, pl. petits-fils.

granite, s. Geol: Granit m.

grant¹, s. **1.** (a) Concession f, octroi m. (b) Jur: Don m, cession f. **2.** Aide f pécuniaire; subvention f.

grant², v.tr. **1.** (a) Accorder, concéder, octroyer. Heaven grant that . . ., fasse le ciel que. . . (b) Exaucer (une prière); accéder à (une requête). **2.** Granted that you are right, admettons, F: mettons, que vous ayez raison. To take sth. for granted, prendre qch. pour avéré. You take too much for granted, vous présumez trop.

granular, a. Granulaire, granuleux.

granulate, v.tr. Granuler. **granulated,** a. Granulé, grené.

grape, s. (a) Grain m de raisin. (b) pl. Bunch of grapes, grappe f de raisin. F: Sour grapes! ils sont trop verts! **grape-fruit,** s. Bot: Pamplemousse f.

graph, s. Abaque m; barème m graphique.

graphic, a. Pittoresque, vivant.

graphite, s. Graphite m; mine f de plomb.

grapnel, s. Nau: Grappin m.

grapple, v.i. To grapple with s.o., en venir aux prises avec qn.

grasp¹, s. (a) Poigne f. To have a strong grasp, avoir la serre bonne. (b) Prise f; étreinte f. To have sth. within one's grasp, avoir qch. à sa portée. (c) Compréhension f.

grasp², **1.** v.tr. (a) Saisir; empoigner; serrer dans sa main; étreindre. To grasp s.o.'s hand, serrer la main à qn. (b) S'emparer, se saisir, de. To grasp the opportunity, saisir l'occasion au vol. **2.** v.tr. Comprendre.

grasping, a. Apre au gain.

grass, s. Herbe f. **1.** Bot: The grasses, les graminées f. **2.** Gazon m. 'Please keep off the grass,' "défense de circuler sur le gazon." **grass-plot,** s. Pelouse f; carré m de gazon.

grass-snake, s. Rept: Serpent m d'eau.

grass widow, s. F: Femme f. dont le mari est absent. **grass-widower,** s. Mari m. dont la femme est absente.

grasshopper, s. Ent: Sauterelle f.

grassy, a. Herbu, herbeux.

grate¹, s. F: Foyer m, âtre m.

grate², **I.** v.tr. **1.** Râper. **2.** To grate one's teeth, grincer des dents. **II.** grate, v.i. To grate on the ear, choquer, écorcher, l'oreille. **grating¹,** a. Discordant, grinçant. G. sound, grincement m.

grateful, a. **1.** Reconnaissant. **2.** Agréable ;

réconfortant. **-fully,** adv. Avec reconnaissance.

gratefulness, s. Reconnaissance f.

grater, s. Râpe f.

gratification, s. **1.** Satisfaction f, plaisir m. **2.** Satisfaction, assouvissement m.

gratify, v.tr. **1.** Faire plaisir, être agréable, à. **2.** Satisfaire, contenter. **gratified,** a. Satisfait, content (with, de); flatté. **gratifying,** a. Agréable; flatteur, -euse.

grating², s. Grille f, grillage m.

gratis. **1.** a. Gratis, gratuit. **2.** adv. Gratis, gratuitement, à titre gratuit.

gratitude, s. Gratitude f, reconnaissance f (to, envers).

gratuitous, a. **1.** Gratuit. **2.** F: Gratuitous insult, insulte injustifiée, gratuite.

gratuity, s. **1.** Gratification f. 'No gratuities,' "défense de donner des pourboires." **2.** Prime f de démobilisation.

grave¹, s. (a) Tombe f, tombeau m, fosse f. To be in one's grave, être enterré. To have one foot in the grave, être au bord de la tombe. (b) From beyond the grave, d'outre-tombe. **grave-digger,** s. Fossoyeur m.

grave², a. (a) Grave, sérieux. To look grave, avoir l'air sévère. (b) To make a g. mistake, se tromper lourdement. G. symptoms, symptômes graves, inquiétants. **-ly,** adv. Gravement, sérieusement.

gravel¹, s. **1.** Gravier m. **gravel-path,** s. Allée sablée.

gravel², v.tr. **1.** Graveler; sabler. **2.** F: Mettre, réduire, à quia.

graveness, s. Gravité f.

gravestone, s. Pierre tombale.

graveyard, s. Cimetière m.

gravitate, v.i. Graviter (towards, vers; round, autour de).

gravitation, s. Gravitation f.

gravity, s. Gravité f. **1.** (a) To lose one's gravity, perdre son sérieux. (b) Gravité (d'une situation). **2.** Ph: Gravité, pesanteur f.

gravy, s. Cu: (a) Jus m. (b) Sauce f (au jus).

gray, a. & s. = GREY.

graze¹, **1.** v.i. Paître, brouter. **2.** v.tr. (a) Paître, faire paître. (b) Paître (l'herbe).

grazing, s. Pâturage m.

graze², s. Écorchure f, éraflure f.

graze³, v.tr. **1.** Écorcher, érafler. **2.** Effleurer, raser, frôler.

grease¹, s. Graisse f. **grease-paint,** s. Fard m

grease², v.tr. Graisser. **greasing,** s. Graissage m.

greasiness, s. Onctuosité f.

greasy, a. **1.** (a) Graisseux, huileux. (b) Taché d'huile, de graisse. **2.** Gras, f. grasse. Greasy pole, mât m de cocagne.

great, a. Grand. (a) To grow greater, augmenter, grandir. (b) A great deal, beaucoup (of, de). A great many, beaucoup (de + pl.). The greater part, la plupart (of, de). To a great extent, en grande partie.

Of g. antiquity, de haute antiquité. (c) (*The*) **great men**, les grands hommes. *F:* **Great Scott!** grands dieux! (d) **To be great on**, aimer beaucoup; être grand amateur de. **To be great at tennis**, être fort au tennis. (e) **It is no great matter**, ce n'est pas une grosse affaire. *To have no g. opinion of s.o.*, tenir qn en médiocre estime. **-ly**, *adv.* Grandement; beaucoup. *G. irritated*, très irrité; fortement irrité. **great-aunt**, *s.* Grand'tante f, *pl.* grand'tantes. **great-coat**, *s.* Pardessus m. **great-grand-child**, *s.* Arrière-petit-fils m, arrière-petite-fille f, *pl.* arrière-petits-enfants m. **great-grandfather**, *s.* Arrière-grand-père m, *pl.* arrière-grands-pères. **great-grandmother**, *s.* Arrière-grand'mère f, *pl.* arrière-grand'mères. **great-uncle**, *s.* Grand-oncle m, *pl.* grands-oncles.

greatness, *s.* Grandeur f.

Grecian, *a.* Grec, f. grecque.

Greece. *Pr.n. Geog:* La Grèce.

greed, *s.* Avidité f, cupidité f.

greediness, *s.* **1.** = GREED. **2.** Gourmandise f, gloutonnerie f.

greedy, *a.* **1.** Avide, cupide; âpre (au gain). **2.** Gourmand; glouton, -onne **-ily**, *adv.* **1.** Avidement, cupidement. **2.** Avec gourmandise, gloutonnement.

Greek. **1.** *a. & s.* Grec, f. grecque. **2.** *s. Ling: F:* Le grec. *F:* **It is all Greek to me**, c'est de l'hébreu pour moi.

green. **1.** *a.* Vert. (a) **As green as grass**, vert comme pré. **To grow green**, verdir. (b) **To keep s.o.'s memory green**, chérir la mémoire de qn. (c) **To turn green**, blêmir. (d) (i) Jeune, inexpérimenté. (ii) Naïf, f, naïve. **He's not so green**, il n'est pas né d'hier. **2.** *s.* (a) Vert m. (b) *pl.* **Greens**, légumes verts. (c) Pelouse f, gazon m. **Village green**, pelouse communale. *Golf:* **The (putting-)green**, la pelouse d'arrivée. **green-fly**, *s. Ent:* **1.** Puceron m; aphis m. **2.** *Coll.* Aphidés mpl. **green-room**, *s. Th:* Foyer m des artistes.

greenery, *s.* Verdure f, feuillage m.

greenfinch, *s. Orn:* Verdier m.

greengage, *s.* Reine-Claude f, *pl.* reines-Claude.

greengrocer, *s.* Marchand, -ande, de légumes; fruitier, -ière.

greenhorn, *s. F:* Blanc-bec m, *pl.* blancs-becs; *F:* bleu m, béjaune m.

greenhouse, *s. Hort:* Serre f.

greenish, *a.* Verdâtre.

Greenland. *Pr.n.* Le Groenland.

greenness, *s.* **1.** Verdeur f. (a) Couleur verte. (b) Immaturité f (d'un fruit). (c) Naïveté f. **2.** Verdure f (du paysage).

greensward, *s.* Pelouse f; gazon m.

greet, *v.tr.* (a) Saluer, aborder. (b) *F:* **To greet the eye**, s'offrir aux regards. **greeting**, *s.* Salutation f, salut m; *pl.* compliments m (du jour de l'an). **To send one's greetings to s.o.**, envoyer le bonjour à qn.

gregarious, *a.* Grégaire.

Gregory. *Pr.n.* Grégoire m.

grenade, *s.* Grenade f.

grenadier, *s. Mil:* Grenadier m.

grey. **1.** *a.* Gris. (a) **To go grey**, grisonner. (b) (*Of complexion*) (Ashen) grey, blême. **2.** *s.* Gris m. **grey-haired**, *a.* Aux cheveux gris.

greyhound, *s.* Lévrier m. **Greyhound racing**, courses de lévriers. *G.-racing track*, cynodrome m.

greyish, *a.* Grisâtre.

greyness, *s.* Teinte grise.

grid, *s.* **1.** Grille f, grillage m. **2.** *F:* The grid, le réseau électrique national.

gridiron, *s. Cu:* Gril m.

grief, *s.* Chagrin m, douleur f, peine f. **To come to grief**, avoir un accident.

grievance, *s.* **1.** Grief m. **To air one's grievances**, conter ses doléances. **2.** Injustice f.

grieve. **1.** *v.tr.* Chagriner, affliger. **2.** *v.i.* Se chagriner, s'affliger (*over, about, sth.*, de qch.). **grieved**, *a.* Chagriné, affligé (*at*, de). *Deeply g.*, navré.

grievous, *a.* **1.** Douloureux, pénible. **2.** (Erreur) grave, lamentable. **-ly**, *adv.* Gravement; grièvement (blessé).

griffin, *s. Myth:* Griffon m.

grill[1], *s. Cu:* Grillade f. **2.** **Grill(-room)**, grill-room m.

grill[2], *s. Dom.Ec:* Gril m.

grill[3], *v.tr. Cu:* Griller, brasiller.

grille, *s.* Grille f; judas m (de porte).

grim, *a.* Sinistre; (humour) macabre; (visage) sévère, rébarbatif. *F:* **To hold on like grim death**, se cramponner avec acharnement. *G. determination*, volonté inflexible. **-ly**, *adv.* Sinistrement, sévèrement; avec acharnement.

grimace[1], *s.* Grimace f. **To make a grimace**, faire la grimace.

grimace[2], *v.i.* Grimacer; faire la grimace.

grime, *s.* Saleté f.

grimness, *s.* Caractère m sinistre, aspect m redoutable.

grimy, *a.* Sale, encrassé, noirci.

grin[1], *s.* Large sourire; sourire épanoui. **To give a broad grin**, sourire à belles dents.

grin[2], *v.i.* Sourire à belles dents. **To grin and bear it**, faire bonne mine à mauvais jeu.

grind[1], *s. F:* Labeur monotone et continu. **The daily grind**, le boulot journalier.

grind[3], *v.* **1.** *v.tr.* (a) Moudre. **To grind sth. to dust**, réduire qch. en poudre. *To g. sth. between one's teeth*, broyer qch. entre ses dents. **To grind sth. under one's heel**, écraser qch. sous ses pieds. **To grind (down) the poor**, opprimer les pauvres. (b) Repasser (un couteau). (c) **To grind one's teeth**, grincer des dents. **2.** *v.i.* (a) Grincer, crisser. (b) *F:* **To grind for an exam**, potasser un examen. **ground**, *a.* Moulu, broyé, pilé. **grinding**[1], *a.* **1.** Grinding sound, grincement m, crissement m. **2.** Grinding poverty, la misère écrasante. **grinding²**, *s.* **I.** Mouture *f.* **2.** Oppression *f* (du peuple). **3.** Aiguisage *m*, repassage *m.* **4.** Grincement *m*, crissement *m.*

grinder, *s.* **I.** Rémouleur *m.* **2.** (*a*) (Dent) molaire *f.* (*b*) *pl. F:* **Grinders**, dents *f.*

grindstone, *s.* Meule *f* à aiguiser. *F:* To keep one's nose to the grindstone, travailler sans relâche.

grip¹, *s.* **I.** Prise *f*; serrement *m*; étreinte *f.* To have a strong grip, avoir la serre bonne. To come to grips, en venir aux mains (*with*, avec). To get a grip on sth., trouver prise à qch. To have a good g. of a subject, bien posséder un sujet. **2.** Poignée *f.*

grip², *v.tr.* Saisir, empoigner.

grisly, *a.* Effrayant, macabre.

gristle, *s.* Cartilage *m*, croquant *m.*

gristly, *a. F:* Cartilagineux.

grit¹, *s.* **I.** Grès *m*, sable *m.* **2.** *F:* Cran *m*, courage *m.*

grit², *v.tr.* To grit one's teeth, grincer des dents.

gritty, *a.* Sablonneux, cendreux.

grizzle, *v.i. P:* **I.** Ronchonner; grognonner. **2.** Pleurnicher, geindre.

grizzled, *a.* Grisonnant.

grizzly, *a. Z:* Grizzly (**bear**), ours grizzlé.

groan¹, *s.* Gémissement *m*, plainte *f.*

groan², *v.i.* Gémir; pousser un gémissement.

grocer, *s.* Épicier, -ière.

grocery, *s.* **I.** Épicerie *f.* **2.** *pl.* Groceries, (articles *m* d')épicerie.

grog, *s.* Grog *m.*

groggy, *a.* Chancelant, titubant. To feel groggy, être peu solide sur ses jambes.

groin, *s.* **I.** *Anat:* Aine *f.* **2.** *Arch:* (*a*) Arête *f* (de voûte). (*b*) Nervure *f* (d'arête).

groom¹, *s.* **I.** Palefrenier *m*; valet *m* d'écurie. **2.** = BRIDEGROOM.

groom², *v.tr.* Panser (un cheval). **groomed**, *a.* **Well-groomed**, *F:* bien soigné, bien peigné.

groove, *s.* **I.** Rainure *f. Gramophones:* **Sound groove**, sillon *m* sonore. **2.** *F:* To get into a groove, s'encroûter; devenir routinier.

grope, *v.i.* Tâtonner. To grope for sth., chercher qch. à tâtons. To grope one's way, avancer à tâtons. **groping**, *a.* Tâtonnant.

gross¹, *s.inv.* Douze douzaines *f*; grosse *f.*

gross², *a.* **I.** Gras, *f.* grasse; gros, *f.* grosse. **2.** Grossier. G. ignorance, ignorance crasse, grossière. G. injustice, injustice flagrante. **3.** (*Of amount*) Brut. **-ly**, *adv.* Grossièrement. G. exaggerated, exagéré outre mesure.

grossness, *s.* Grossièreté *f*; énormité *f.*

grotesque. **I.** *a. & s.* Grotesque (*m.*). **2.** *a. F:* Absurde; saugrenu.

grotto, *s.* Grotte *f.*

ground¹, *s.* **I.** Fond *m.* (*Of ship*) To touch ground, talonner. **2.** *pl.* Grounds, marc *m* (du café). **3.** (*a*) Raison *f*, cause *f*, sujet *m.* Ground for complaint, grief *m. Upon what grounds?* à quel titre? (*b*) *Jur:* Grounds for

divorce, motifs *m* de divorce. **4.** (*a*) Sol *m*, terre *f. To sit down on the g.,* s'asseoir par terre. To fall to the ground, (i) tomber à, par, terre; (ii) *F:* tomber dans l'eau. *F:* To dash s.o.'s hopes to the ground, anéantir les espérances de qn. Above ground, sur terre. Burnt down to the ground, brûlé de fond en comble. *F:* That suits me down to the ground, cela me va à merveille. *F:* To be on firm ground, connaître le terrain; être sûr de son fait. To cut the ground from under s.o.'s feet, couper l'herbe sous le pied à qn. (*b*) Terrain *m.* To shift one's ground, changer de terrain. To gain ground, gagner du terrain; (*of idea*) se répandre. To stand one's ground, tenir bon. (*c*) *pl.* Grounds, terrains, parc *m*, jardin *m.* **ground-floor**, *s.* Rez-de-chaussée *m inv.* **ground-swell**, *s. Nau:* Houle *f*, lame *f*, de fond.

ground², *v.tr.* Fonder, baser, appuyer (*on, in, sth.,* sur qch.).

groundless, *a.* (Soupçon, bruit) mal fondé, sans fondement.

groundwork, *s.* Fondement *m*; assise *f.*

group¹, *s.* Groupe *m.* In groups, par groupes. To form a group, se grouper.

group². **I.** *v.tr.* Grouper, disposer en groupes. **2.** *v.i.* Se grouper (*round*, autour de).

grouse¹, *s. inv. Orn:* Tétras *m.* (**Red**) grouse, lagopède *m* rouge d'Écosse.

grouse², *v.i.* Ronchonner, grogner (*at, about,* contre). **grousing**, *s.* Grognonnerie *f.*

grove, *s.* Bocage *m*, bosquet *m.*

grovel, *v.i.* Ramper. To g. in the dirt, se vautrer dans la boue. **grovelling**, *a.* Rampant.

grow, *v.* **I.** *v.i.* **I.** (*a*) (*Of plant*) Croître, pousser. (*b*) (*Of seeds*) Germer. This State grew out of a few small towns, cet État est né de quelques bourgades. **2.** (*Of pers.*) Grandir. To grow into a woman, passer femme. To grow up, grandir; atteindre l'âge d'homme. He will grow out of it, cela passera avec l'âge. **3.** (*a*) S'accroître, croître, augmenter, grandir. The crowd grew, la foule grossissait. (*b*) Habit that grows on one, habitude qui vous gagne. **4.** Devenir. To grow old, devenir vieux; se faire vieux; vieillir. To grow alarmed, s'alarmer. **II.** **grow**, *v.tr.* **I.** Cultiver; planter (des choux). **2.** Laisser pousser (sa barbe). **grown**, *a.* **I.** When you are g. up, quand tu seras grand. **2.** Wall grown over with ivy, mur couvert de lierre. **grown-up**, *s.* The grown-ups, les grands. **growing**, *a.* **I.** Croissant; qui pousse. Growing crops, récoltes sur pied. **2.** Grandissant. G. child, enfant en cours de croissance.

grower, *s.* Cultivateur, -trice.

growl¹, *s.* Grondement *m*, grognement *m.*

growl², *v.i. & tr.* Grogner; gronder.

growler, *s.* Grogneur, -euse; grognon *mf.*

growth, *s.* **I.** Croissance *f*, venue *f.* To

attain full growth, arriver à maturité. **2.** Accroissement *m*; augmentation *f*. **3.** (*a*) Yearly growth, pousse annuelle. (*b*) Poussée *f* (de cheveux).

grub[1], *s.* *Ent:* (*a*) Larve *f.* (*b*) *F:* Ver (blanc); asticot *m.*

grub[2], *v.i.* Fouiller (dans la terre). **grub up,** *v.tr.* Déraciner (une plante).

grubby, *a.* Sale, malpropre.

grudge[1], *s.* Rancune *f.* **To bear s.o. a grudge,** garder rancune à qn.

grudge[2], *v.tr.* **1.** Donner, accorder, à contrecœur. **2.** *To g. s.o. his pleasures,* voir d'un mauvais œil les plaisirs de qn. **grudging,** *a.* **1.** Donné à contre-cœur. **2.** *He is g. of praise,* il est avare de louanges. **-ly,** *adv.* A contre-cœur.

gruel, *s.* **1.** *Cu:* Gruau *m* (d'avoine). **2.** *P:* To take one's gruel, avaler sa médecine.

gruelling, *a.* Éreintant, épuisant.

gruesome, *a.* Macabre, affreux.

gruff, *a.* Bourru, revêche, rude. *G. voice,* grosse voix. **-ly,** *adv.* D'un ton bourru.

grumble[1], *s.* (*a*) Grommellement *m*, grognement *m.* (*b*) Murmure *m* (de mécontentement).

grumble[2], *v.i. & tr.* Grommeler, grogner, murmurer. **To grumble at s.o.,** grommeler, gronder, contre qn. **grumbling**[1], *a.* Grognon; grondeur, -euse. **-ly,** *adv.* En murmurant. **grumbling**[2], *s.* **1.** Grognonnerie *f.* **2.** Mécontentement *m.*

grumbler, *s.* **1.** Grognard, -arde, grognon *mf.* **2.** Mécontent, -ente.

grumpy, *a.* Maussade, renfrogné, grincheux. **-ily,** *adv.* Maussadement.

grunt[1], *s.* Grognement *m.*

grunt[2], *v.i.* Grogner, grognonner; pousser un grognement. **grunting,** *s.* Grognement(s) *m(pl).*

guano, *s.* Guano *m.*

guarantee[1], *s.* **1.** Garant, -ante; caution *f.* To go guarantee for s.o., se rendre garant, se porter caution, pour qn. **2.** Garantie *f.*

guarantee[2], *v.tr.* Garantir, cautionner; porter garant, caution, pour; garantir. **guaranteed,** *a.* Com: Avec garantie.

guard[1], *s.* **1.** Garde *f.* (*a*) *Box:* To take one's g., se mettre en garde. (*b*) **To be on one's guard,** être sur ses gardes. **To be caught off one's guard,** être pris au dépourvu. (*c*) **To be on guard (duty),** être en faction. **To keep guard,** faire la garde. **2.** *Coll.* (*a*) *Mil:* Garde *f.* Advanced g., avant-garde *f.* (*b*) **To set a guard on a house,** faire surveiller une maison. **3.** (*a*) *Rail:* Chef *m* de train. (*b*) *Mil:* The Guards, la Garde. **4.** Corps-de-garde *m inv.* **guard-room,** *s.* *Mil:* **1.** Corps-de-garde *m inv.* **2.** Poste *m* de police.

guard[2]. **I.** *v.tr.* (*a*) Garder. (*b*) *Ind:* Protéger. **2.** *v.i.* **To guard against sth.,** se garder de qch.; parer à qch. **guarded,** *a.* Prudent, mesuré. **To be guarded in one's speech,** surveiller ses paroles.

guardian, *s.* **1.** Gardien, -ienne. **2.** Tuteur, -trice, curateur, -trice (de mineur). **3.** *Attrib.* Guardian angel, ange gardien.

guardianship, *s.* **1.** Garde *f.* **2.** *Jur:* Gestion *f* tutélaire; tutelle *f.*

guardsman, *s.* Officier *m* de la Garde.

guava, *s.* *Bot:* Goyave *f.* Guava(-tree), goyavier *m.*

guelder rose, *s.* *Bot:* Boule-de-neige *f.*

Guernsey. *Pr.n. Geog:* Guernesey *m.*

guer(r)illa, *s.* *Mil:* **1.** Guérillero *m.* **2.** Guerilla (war), guerre *f* de guérillas.

guess[1], *s.* Conjecture *f,* estimation *f. I give you three guesses,* je vous le donne en trois. By guess(-work), au jugé.

guess[2], *v.tr. & i.* **1.** To guess at sth., deviner, conjecturer, qch. **To keep an opponent guessing,** mystifier un adversaire. **2.** To guess right, bien deviner. **To guess a riddle,** trouver le mot d'une énigme. **You've guessed it!** vous y êtes!

guest, *s.* **1.** Convive *mf*; invité, -ée; hôte, -esse. **2.** (i) Pensionnaire *mf*, (ii) client, -ente (d'un hôtel). **guest-house,** *s.* Pension *f* de famille.

guffaw[1], *s.* Gros rire (bruyant).

guffaw[2], *v.i.* Pouffer, s'épouffer, de rire.

Guiana. *Pr.n. Geog:* La Guyane.

guidance, *s.* Direction *f,* gouverne *f,* conduite *f.*

guide[1], *s.* **1.** (*a*) Guide *m.* **To take sth. as a guide,** prendre qch. pour règle. (*b*) Girl guide, guide *m* (de France). **2.** Guide(-book), (livret-)guide *m. G. to Switzerland,* guide de la Suisse. Railway guide, indicateur *m* des chemins de fer. **3.** Indication *f,* exemple *m.*

guide[2], *v.tr.* Guider, conduire, diriger. *All are guided by him,* tous se règlent sur lui. **guiding,** *a.* Qui sert de guide; directeur, -trice. Guiding star, guide *m.*

guile, *s.* Artifice *m,* ruse *f,* astuce *f.*

guileful, *a.* Astucieux, artificieux, rusé.

guileless, *a.* **1.** Franc, *f.* franche; sans malice. **2.** Candide, naïf. **-ly,** *adv.* **1.** Franchement. **2.** Candidement.

guilelessness, *s.* **1.** Franchise *f.* **2.** Candeur *f,* naïveté *f.*

guillemot, *s.* *Orn:* Guillemot *m.*

guillotine[1], *s.* Guillotine *f.*

guillotine[2], *v.tr.* Guillotiner.

guilt, *s.* Culpabilité *f.*

guiltless, *a.* Innocent (of sth., de qch.).

guiltlessness, *s.* Innocence *f.*

guilty, *a.* Coupable. (*a*) To find s.o. guilty, prononcer qn coupable. (*b*) Guilty conscience, conscience chargée. G. look, regard confus. **-ily,** *adv.* Comme un coupable; d'un air coupable.

Guinea. I. *Pr.n. Geog:* La Guinée. **2.** Guinée. **guinea-fowl,** *s.* Pintade *f.* **guinea-pig,** *s.* Cobaye *m*; cochon *m* d'Inde.

guise, *s.* *F:* In the guise of friendship, sous l'apparence *f* de l'amitié.

guitar, *s. Mus:* Guitare *f.*

gulf, *s.* **1.** *Geog:* Golfe *m.* **2.** Gouffre *m,* abîme *m.*

gull¹, *s. Orn:* Mouette *f,* goéland *m.*

gull², *s.* Gogo *m,* jobard *m,* gobeur *m.*

gull³, *v.tr.* Jobarder, flouer, rouler.

gullet, *s.* Œsophage *m; F:* gosier *m.*

gullibility, *s.* Jobarderie *f,* jobardise *f.*

gullible, *a.* Facile à duper; jobard.

gully, *s. Geol:* (Petit) ravin; couloir *m.*

gulp¹, *s.* Coup *m* de gosier. **At one gulp,** d'un coup.

gulp², *v.tr.* **To gulp sth. down,** avaler qch. à grosses bouchées. *He gulped it down,* il n'en fit qu'une bouchée; *(of drink)* il n'en fit qu'une gorgée.

gum¹, *s.* **1.** Gomme *f.* **2.** *(Mucilage)* Gomme, colle *f.* **3. Gum resin,** gomme-résine *f.* **4.** *(Sweetmeat)* Boule *f* de gomme. **5.** *Bot:* Gum(-tree), gommier *m. P:* **To be up a gum-tree,** être dans le pétrin. **gum-arabic,** *s.* Gomme *f* arabique.

gum², *v.tr.* *(a)* Gommer; encoller. *(b)* Coller (une page dans un livre).

gum³, *s.* Gencive *f.*

gumboil, *s.* Abcès *m* à la gencive.

gumption, *s. F:* Jugeotte *f,* gingin *m.*

gun, *s.* **1.** Canon *m. The big guns,* le gros canon. *Navy:* Naval gun, pièce *f* de bord. **2.** Fusil *m.* **gun-carriage,** *s. Artil:* Affût *m* (de canon). **gun-cotton,** *s.* Fulmicoton *m,* coton-poudre *m.* **gun-room,** *s. Navy:* Poste *m* des aspirants.

gunboat, *s.* (Chaloupe) canonnière *f.*

gunner, *s.* Artilleur *m,* canonnier *m.*

gunnery, *s.* Artillerie *f;* tir *m* au canon.

gunpowder, *s.* Poudre *f* (à canon).

gunshot, *s.* **1.** Coup *m* de fusil, de canon; coup *m* de feu. **2. Within gunshot,** à (une) portée de fusil.

gunwale, *s. Nau:* Plat-bord *m, pl.* plats-bords.

gurgle¹, *s.* *(a)* Glouglou *m.* *(b)* *F:* *(Of pers.)* Gloussement *m.*

gurgle². **1.** *v.i.* Glouglouter; faire glouglou. **2.** *v.i. & tr.* *(Of pers.)* Glousser.

gush¹, *s.* **1.** Jaillissement *m,* effusion *f.* **2.** Flot *m* (de sang). **3.** Débordement sentimental.

gush², *v.i.* *(a)* **To gush (forth, out),** jaillir, saillir, couler à flots. *(b)* Faire de la sensiblerie. **gushing,** *a.* **1.** Jaillissant. **2.** *(Of pers.)* Exubérant.

gust, *s.* **Gust of rain,** ondée *f,* giboulée *f.* **Gust of wind,** coup *m* de vent; rafale *f,* bourrasque *f, Nau:* grain *m.*

gusto, *s. F: To do sth. with g.,* faire qch. (i) avec plaisir, (ii) avec élan, avec entrain.

gusty, *a.* A rafales; de grand vent.

gut, *s.* **1.** *Anat:* Boyau *m.* **2.** *pl.* **Guts.** *(a)* Boyaux, intestins. *(b)* *F:* **To have guts,** avoir du cran. **3.** Corde *f* à, de, boyau.

gutta-percha, *s.* Gutta-percha *f.*

gutter¹, *s.* **1.** **(Eaves-)gutter,** gouttière *f.* **2.** Ruisseau *m* (de rue). *F:* **Born in the gutter,** né dans la crasse. **gutter-snipe,** *s.* Gamin, -ine, des rues.

gutter², *v.i.* *(Of candle)* Couler.

guttural. 1. *a.* Guttural, -aux. **2.** *s.* Gutturale *f.* **-ally,** *adv.* Gutturalement.

guy¹, *s.* Épouvantail *m.*

guy², *v.tr.* Se moquer de.

guy³, *s. Nau:* Hauban *m,* gui *m,* étai *m.* **guy-rope,** *s.* Cordon *m* (de tente).

guzzle, *v.tr. & i.* *(a)* Bâfrer, bouffer (la nourriture). *(b)* Boire avidement, lamper.

guzzler, *s.* *(a)* Bâfreur, -euse; goinfre *m.* *(b)* Pochard, -arde; sac *m* à vin.

gymnasium, *s.* Gymnase *m.*

gymnast, *s.* Gymnaste *m.*

gymnastic. 1. *a.* Gymnastique. **2.** *s.pl.* Gymnastics, gymnastique *f.*

gyrate, *v.i.* Tourner; tournoyer.

gyration, *s.* Giration *f,* gyration *f.*

gyroscope, *s.* Gyroscope *m.*

gyroscopic, *a.* Gyroscopique.

H

H, h, *s.* (La lettre) H, h *mf.* **To drop one's h's,** ne pas aspirer les h.

ha¹, *int.* Ha! ah!

ha², *v.i. See* HUM² 1.

haberdasher, *s.* **1.** Chemisier *m.* **2.** Mercier *m.*

haberdashery, *s.* **1.** Chemiserie *f.* **2.** Mercerie *f.*

habit, *s.* Habitude *f,* coutume *f.* **To be in the habit of doing sth.,** avoir coutume, avoir l'habitude de faire qch. *I don't make a h. of it,* ce n'est pas une habitude chez moi. *From force of h.,* par habitude.

habitable, *a.* Habitable.

habitation, *s.* **1. Fit for habitation,** en état d'être habité. **2.** Habitation *f,* demeure *f.*

habitual, *a.* Habituel, d'habitude. **-ally,** *adv.* Habituellement, d'habitude.

habituate, *v.tr.* **To habituate s.o. to sth.,** habituer qn à qch.

hack¹, *s.* Taillade *f,* entaille *f.* **hack-saw,** *s.* Scie *f* à métaux.

hack², *v.tr. & i.* Hacher. **To hack sth. to pieces,** tailler qch. en pièces. **hacking,** *a.* **Hacking cough,** toux sèche et pénible.

hack³, *s.* **1.** *(a)* Cheval *m* de louage. *(b)* *F:*

Rosse *f*, haridelle *f*. **2.** Homme *m* de peine. Literary hack, écrivain *m* à la tâche.
hackney-carriage, *s*. Voiture *f* de place, de louage.
hackneyed, *a*. Rebattu, usé. **Hackneyed phrase,** expression devenue banale ; cliché *m*.
haddock, *s*. *Ich :* Aiglefin *m*.
Hades, *s*. *Gr.Myth :* Les Enfers *m*.
haemorrhage, *s*. Hémorragie *f*.
haft, *s*. Manche *m*, poignée *f*.
hag, *s*. (Vieille) sorcière. *F :* **Old hag,** vieille fée.
haggard, *a*. (*a*) Hâve. (*b*) Égaré, hagard.
haggle, *v.i*. Marchander.
Hague (the). *Pr.n*. La Haye.
ha-ha, *int*. Ha, ha !
hail¹, *s*. Grêle *f*. **hail-stone,** *s*. Grêlon *m*. **hail-storm,** *s*. Orage accompagné de grêle.
hail², *v.i. & tr*. Grêler. *Impers :* **It is hailing,** il grêle.
hail³. 1. *int*. Salut ! **2.** *s*. Appel *m*. **Within hail,** à portée de (la voix). **To be hail-fellow-well-met with everyone,** traiter les gens de pair à compagnon.
hail⁴. 1. *v.tr*. (*a*) Saluer. (*b*) **To hail a taxi,** appeler, héler, un taxi. **Within hailing distance,** à portée de (la) voix. **2.** *v.i. Ship hailing from London,** navire en provenance de Londres.
hair, *s*. **1.** (*Of head*) (*a*) Cheveu *m*. *F :* **To split hairs,** couper un cheveu en quatre. (*b*) *Coll*. **The hair,** les cheveux, la chevelure. **Head of hair,** chevelure. **To do one's hair,** se coiffer. **It was enough to make your hair stand on end,** c'était à faire dresser les cheveux sur la tête. *P :* **Keep your hair on !** ne vous emballez pas ! **2.** (*a*) (*Of body*) Poil *m*. (*b*) *Coll*. (*Of animal*) Poil, pelage *m*. (*c*) Crin *m* (de cheval). **hair-cut,** *s*. Taille *f*, coupe *f*, de cheveux. **To have a h.-c.,** se faire couper les cheveux. **hair-raising,** *a*. Horripilant, horrifique. **hair-restorer,** *s*. Régénérateur *m* des cheveux. **hair's-breadth,** *s*. **To escape death by a h.-b.,** avoir été à deux doigts de la mort. **hair-splitting,** *s*. Ergotage *m* ; distinctions subtiles. **hair-spring,** *s*. *Clockm :* (Ressort) spiral *m*.
hairbreadth. 1. *s*. = HAIR'S-BREADTH. **2.** *Attrib*. **To have a hairbreadth escape,** l'échapper belle.
hairbrush, *s*. Brosse *f* à cheveux.
hairdresser, *s*. Coiffeur, -euse.
hairdressing, *s*. Coiffure *f*.
hairless, *a*. Sans cheveux ; chauve. *H. face*, visage glabre.
hairpin, *s*. Épingle *f* à cheveux. *F :* **Hairpin bend,** (*in road*), lacet *m*.
hairy, *a*. Velu, poilu.
hake, *s*. *Ich :* Merluche *f*.
halberd, halbert, *s*. Hallebarde *f*.
hale, *a*. Vigoureux. **To be hale and hearty,** avoir bon pied bon œil.
half. 1. *s*. (*a*) Moitié *f*. **Half (of) his men,**

la moitié de ses hommes. *F :* **More than half (of) the time,** les trois quarts du temps. **To cut sth. in half,** in halves, couper qch. par moitié, en deux. **To go halves with s.o.,** se mettre de moitié avec qn. *F :* **He is too clever by half,** il est beaucoup trop malin. **To do things by halves,** faire les choses à demi. (*b*) Demi *m*, demie *f*. **Three and a half,** trois et demi. (*c*) *F :* **My better half,** ma (chère) moitié. (*d*) *Rail :* **Return half** (*of ticket*), coupon *m* de retour. **2.** Demi. **Half an hour,** une demi-heure. *F :* **In h.** *a second*, en moins de rien. **3.** *adv*. (*a*) **He only h. understands,** il ne comprend qu'à moitié. **Half laughing, half crying,** moitié riant, moitié pleurant. **Half done,** à moitié fait. *F :* **It isn't half bad,** ce n'est pas mauvais du tout. **Not half !** un peu ! (*b*) **It is half past two,** il est deux heures et demie. (*c*) **Half as big,** moitié aussi grand. **Half as big again,** plus grand de moitié. **Half as much again,** moitié plus. **half-breed,** *s*. Métis, -isse. **half-brother,** *s*. Demi-frère *m*, *pl*. demi-frères. **half-caste,** *a*. & *s*. Métis, -isse. **half-closed,** *a*. Entre-clos ; entr'ouvert. **half-crown,** *s*. *Num :* Demi-couronne *f*. **half-dead,** *a*. A moitié mort ; à demi mort. **Half-dead with fright,** plus mort que vif. **half-dozen,** *s*. Demi-douzaine *f*. **half-dressed,** *a*. A moitié vêtu ; à demi vêtu. **half-empty,** *a*. A moitié vide. **half-fare,** *s*. *Rail :* Demi-place *f*. **half-hearted,** *a*. Tiède ; sans entrain. **-ly,** *adv*. Avec tiédeur. **half-holiday,** *s*. Après-midi *m* or *f* libre. **half-hour,** *s*. Demi-heure *f*. **half-mast,** *s*. **At half-mast,** en berne. **half-naked,** *a*. A demi nu. **half-pay,** *s*. Demi-solde *f*. **half-seas-over,** *a*. *F :* A moitié ivre. **half-sister,** *s*. Demi-sœur *f*, *pl*. demi-sœurs. **half-term,** *s*. *Sch :* Congé *m* de mi-trimestre. **half-way,** *adv*. A moitié chemin ; à mi-chemin. *F :* **To meet s.o. half-way,** faire la moitié des avances. **half-witted,** *a*. Faible d'esprit.
halfpenny, *s*. *F :* = Sou *m*.
halibut, *s*. *Ich :* Flétan *m*.
hall, *s*. **1.** Grande salle. (*a*) **The servants' hall,** l'office *f*. (*b*) **Concert hall,** salle de concert. **2.** Château *m*. **3.** (Entrance-)hall, vestibule *m*. **Hall porter,** concierge *m*.
hall-mark, *s*. (Cachet *m* de) contrôle *m*. *F :* **The hall-mark of genius,** le cachet du génie.
hallo, *int*. & *s*. Holà ! ohé !
halloo¹, *s*. Cri d'appel. *Ven :* Huée *f*.
halloo², *v.i*. (*a*) Crier, appeler. (*b*) *Ven :* Huer.
hallow, *v.tr*. Sanctifier, consacrer. **Hallowed ground,** terre sainte.
hallucination, *s*. Hallucination *f*.
halo, *s*. **1.** *Astr :* Halo *m* ; auréole *f*. **2.** Auréole, nimbe *m* (d'un saint).
halt¹, *s*. **1.** Halte *f*, arrêt *m*. **2.** *Rail :* Halte.

halt², *v.i.* Faire halte ; s'arrêter. Halt! halte !

halter, *s.* Licou *m*, longe *f*.

halting, *a.* (Discours) hésitant.

halve, *v.tr.* (*a*) Diviser en deux. (*b*) Réduire de moitié.

halyard, *s. Nau:* Drisse *f*.

ham, *s. Cu:* Jambon *m*. **Ham and eggs**, œufs au jambon.

hamlet, *s.* Hameau *m*.

hammer¹, *s.* **1.** *Tls:* Marteau *m*; (*heavy*) masse *f*. *F:* **To go at it hammer and tongs**, y aller de toutes ses forces. **2. To come under the hammer**, passer sous le marteau ; être mis aux enchères.

hammer². **1.** *|v.tr.* Marteler ; battre. **2.** *v.i.* Travailler avec le marteau. *F:* **To hammer at the door**, heurter à la porte à coups redoublés. **To hammer away at sth.**, travailler d'arrache-pied à qch. **hammer in,** *v.tr.* Enfoncer à coups de marteau. **hammer out,** *v.tr.* Étendre sous le marteau. **hammering,** *s.* **To give s.o. a good hammering,** bourrer qn de coups.

hammock, *s.* Hamac *m*.

hamper¹, *s.* Manne *f*, banne *f*.

hamper², *v.tr.* Embarrasser, gêner. *To h. oneself with luggage,* s'empêtrer de colis.

hamstring, *v.tr.* Couper les jarrets à.

hand¹, *s.* **1.** Main *f*. (*a*) **To go on one's hands and knees,** aller à quatre pattes. *To vote by show of hands,* voter à main levée. *To hold (sth.) in one's h.,* tenir (son chapeau) à la main, (des sous) dans la main, (le succès) entre les mains. **To take s.o.'s hand,** donner la main à qn. **To lay hands on sth.,** mettre la main sur qch. ; s'emparer de qch. **Hands off!** à bas les mains ! **Hands up!** haut les mains ! **To act with a high hand,** agir en despote, de haute main. (*b*) *To put one's h. to a task,* commencer un travail. **He can turn his hand to anything,** c'est un homme à toute main. **To have a hand in sth.,** se mêler de qch. ; tremper dans (un crime). *I had no h. in it,* je n'y suis pour rien. **To give s.o. a hand,** donner un coup de main à qn. (*c*) **To have one's hands full,** avoir fort à faire. **To have sth. on one's hands,** avoir qch. à sa charge, sur les bras. *Com:* **Goods left on our hands,** marchandises invendues. **To change hands,** changer de propriétaire, de mains. *To put oneself in s.o.'s hands,* s'en remettre à qn. **To have s.o. in the hollow of one's hand,** avoir qn sous sa coupe. **2.** *Adv.phrs.* (*a*) **To be (near) at hand,** être sous la main, à portée de la main. *Christmas was (close) at h.,* Noël était tout proche. (*b*) **Made by hand,** fait à la main. **To send a letter by hand,** envoyer une lettre par porteur. (*c*) **Hat in hand,** chapeau bas. *Revolver in h.,* revolver au poing. *To have so much money in h.,* avoir tant d'argent disponible. **The matter in hand,** la chose en question. *To take sth. in h.,* prendre qch. en main ; se charger de qch. **Situation well**

in hand, situation bien en main. *To keep oneself well in h.,* se contenir. (*d*) **Work on hand,** travail en cours. (*e*) **On the right hand,** du côté droit. **On all hands,** partout. **On the one hand,** d'une part. **On the other hand,** d'autre part ; par contre. (*f*) **To do sth. out of hand,** faire qch. sur-le-champ. **To get out of hand,** perdre toute discipline. (*g*) *Your parcel has come to hand,* votre envoi m'est parvenu. *F:* **The first excuse to hand,** le premier prétexte venu. (*h*) **To be hand and glove with s.o.,** être d'intelligence avec qn. (*i*) **Hand in hand,** la main dans la main. (*j*) **Hand over hand,** main sur main. *F: To make money h. over fist,* faire des affaires d'or. (*k*) **Hand to hand,** corps à corps. **Hand-to-hand fight,** corps-à-corps *m*. (*l*) **To live from hand to mouth,** vivre au jour le jour. (*m*) *Rac:* **To win hands down,** gagner haut la main. **3.** (*Pers.*) (*a*) Ouvrier, -ière ; manœuvre *m*. *Nau:* *The ship's hands,* l'équipage *m*. **All hands on deck!** tout le monde sur le pont ! **To be lost with all hands,** périr corps et biens. (*b*) **To be a good hand at doing sth.,** être adroit à faire qch. **4.** (*a*) Écriture *f*. *He writes a good h.,* il a une belle main. (*b*) **Under your hand and seal,** signé et scellé de votre propre main. **Note of hand,** billet à ordre. **5.** *Cards:* (*a*) Jeu *m*. (*b*) Partie *f*. **6.** Aiguille *f* (de montre). **7.** *Attrib.* **Hand luggage,** bagages à main.

hand-bag, *s.* Sac *m* à main ; pochette *f*.

hand-cart, *s.* Voiture *f* à bras, charrette *f* à bras. **hand-grenade,** *s. Mil:* Grenade *f* à main. **hand-made,** *a.* Fait, fabriqué, à la main. **hand-rail,** *s.* Garde-fou *m*, *pl.* garde-fous. **Garde-corps** *m inv*; rampe *f*. **hand-sewn,** *a.* Cousu à la main.

hand², *v.tr.* Passer, remettre (qch. à qn). **hand down,** *v.tr.* **1.** Descendre (qch.) (et le remettre à qn.). **2.** Transmettre. **hand in,** *v.tr.* Remettre. **hand on,** *v.tr.* Transmettre. **hand out,** *v.tr.* Tendre, remettre (qch. à qn). **hand over,** *v.tr.* Remettre (qch. à qn). **hand round,** *v.tr.* Passer, faire passer, à la ronde.

handbell, *s.* Sonnette *f*, clochette *f*.

handbill, *s.* Prospectus *m*; programme *m* (de spectacle).

handbook, *s.* **1.** *Sch:* Manuel *m*. **2.** Guide *m*; livret *m*.

handcuff, *v.tr.* Mettre les menottes à.

handcuffs, *s.pl.* Menottes *f*.

handful, *s.* **1.** Poignée *f*. **2.** *F:* That child is a handful, cet enfant-là me donne du fil à retordre.

handicap¹, *s.* (*a*) *Sp:* Handicap *m*. (*b*) *F:* Désavantage *m*.

handicap², *v.tr. Sp:* Handicaper. **handicapped,** *a.* **1.** Handicapé. **2.** Désavantagé (*by*, par suite de).

handicraft, *s.* **1.** Travail manuel ; habileté manuelle. **2.** Métier manuel.

handiness, *s.* Adresse *f*, dextérité *f*.

handiwork, *s.* (a) Travail manuel. (b) Ouvrage *m,* œuvre *f.*

handkerchief, *s.* (Pocket-)handkerchief, mouchoir *m* (de poche).

handle¹, *s.* (a) Manche *m*; balancier *m* (de pompe); bras *m* (de brouette); queue *f* (de poêle); poignée *f* (de porte). **To give a handle to calumny,** donner prise à la calomnie. (b) Anse *f* (de corbeille); portant *m* (de valise). **handle-bar,** *s.* Guidon *m.*

handle², *v.tr.* **1.** Tâter des mains. **2.** (a) Manier, manipuler. **To handle a ship,** manœuvrer, gouverner, un navire. **To handle (qn).** **He is hard to handle,** il n'est pas commode. **To handle a situation,** prendre en main une situation. (c) To h. a lot of money, remuer beaucoup d'argent. **handling,** *s.* (a) Maniement *m*; manœuvre *f* (d'un navire). (b) **Rough handling,** traitement brutal.

handshake, *s.* Poignée *f* de main; serrement *m* de main.

handsome, *a.* (a) Beau, bel, beaux, *f.* belle. (b) (Of conduct) Gracieux, généreux. (c) To make a handsome profit, réaliser de beaux bénéfices. **-ly,** *adv.* (a) Élégamment. (b) Généreusement.

handwriting, *s.* Écriture *f.*

handy, *a.* **1.** Handy at doing sth., adroit à faire qch. To be h. with a tool, savoir se servir d'un outil. **2.** (Of implement) Maniable. **3.** Commode. That would come in very handy, cela viendrait bien à point. **4.** A portée (de la main). **To keep sth. handy,** tenir qch. sous la main. **handy-man,** *s.* Homme *m* à tout faire.

hang¹, *s.* **1.** F: To get the hang of sth., saisir le sens de qch. **2.** F: I don't care a hang, je m'en moque.

hang², *v.* **I.** *v.tr.* **1.** Pendre, accrocher, suspendre (on, from, à). **2.** To hang (down) one's head, baisser la tête. **3.** F: To hang fire, traîner (en longueur). **4.** Pendre (un criminel). F: Hang the fellow! que le diable l'emporte! Hang it! sacristi! zut! Hang the expense! je me fiche pas mal de la dépense! **II.** **hang,** *v.i.* **1.** Pendre, être suspendu (on, from, à). **2.** The danger hanging over our heads, le danger suspendu sur nos têtes. A heavy silence hung over the meeting, un silence pesait sur l'assemblée. **3.** Her hair hangs down her back, ses cheveux lui tombent dans le dos. **4.** (Of criminal) Être pendu. **hang about,** *v.i.* Rôder, flâner. **hang back,** *v.i.* **1.** Rester en arrière. **2.** F: Hésiter. **hang down,** *v.i.* **1.** Pendre. **2.** Pencher. **hang on,** *v.i.* **1.** Se cramponner, s'accrocher (to, à). H. on to your job, ne lâchez pas votre situation. To hang on s.o.'s words, boire les paroles de qn. (b) Everything hangs on his answer, tout dépend de sa réponse. **hang out.** **1.** *v.tr.* Pendre (qch.) au dehors; étendre (le linge); arborer (un pavillon). (Of dog)

To hang out its tongue, tirer la langue. **2.** *v.i.* F: Where do you hang out? où nichez-vous? **hang up,** *v.tr.* (a) Accrocher, pendre. *Tp:* To hang up the receiver, raccrocher (l'appareil). (b) Remettre à plus tard. (c) To be hung up, être retardé. **hanging¹,** *a.* Suspendu; pendant. **hanging²,** *s.* **1.** (a) Suspension *f.* (b) Pendaison *f.* It's a hanging matter, c'est un cas pendable. **2.** *pl.* Hangings, tenture *f*; tapisserie *f.* **hang-dog,** *a.* Hang-dog look, mine *f* patibulaire.

hangar, *s.* *Av:* Hangar *m.*

hanger, *s.* **1.** Crochet *m* (de suspension). (Coat-)hanger, cintre *m*; porte-vêtements *m inv.* **2.** Hanger-on, (i) dépendant *m*; (ii) F: parasite *m.*

hangman, *s.m.* Bourreau.

hank, *s.* Écheveau *m* (de laine).

hanker, *v.i.* To hanker after sth., désirer ardemment qch. **hankering,** *s.* Vif désir, grande envie (after, for, de).

hanky-panky, *s.* F: Supercherie *f.* That's all hanky-panky, tout ça c'est du boniment.

Hannibal. *Pr.n.* *A.Hist:* Annibal *m.*

hansom(-cab), *s.* Cab (anglais).

haphazard. **1.** *s.* At haphazard, au hasard; au petit bonheur. **2.** *a.* H. arrangement, disposition fortuite. **3.** *adv.* To live haphazard, vivre à l'aventure.

hapless, *a.* Infortuné, malheureux.

happen, *v.i.* **1.** Arriver. (a) Se passer, se produire. Don't let it happen again! que cela n'arrive plus! Just as if nothing had happened, comme si de rien n'était. Whatever happens, quoi qu'il advienne; quoi qu'il arrive. Happen what may, advienne que pourra. It so happened that, le hasard a voulu que. As it happens, justement. (b) What has happened to him? (i) qu'est-ce qui lui est arrivé? (ii) qu'est-ce qu'il est devenu? **2.** A carriage happened to be passing, une voiture vint à passer. The house happened to be empty, la maison se trouvait vide. Do you h. to know whether? sauriez-vous par hasard si? **3.** To happen upon sth., tomber sur qch. **happening,** *s.* Événement *m.*

happiness, *s.* Bonheur *m,* félicité *f.*

happy, *a.* Heureux. **1.** (a) In a h. hour, à un moment propice. (b) H. party of children, bande joyeuse d'enfants. To be happy to do sth., être heureux, bien aise, content, de faire qch. **2.** Happy thought! bonne inspiration! **-ily,** *adv.* Heureusement. To live h., vivre heureux. She smiled h., elle eut un sourire de contentement.

happy-go-lucky, *attrib.a.* Sans souci; insouciant.

harangue¹, *s.* Harangue *f.*

harangue², *v.tr.* Haranguer.

harass, *v.tr.* Harasser, tracasser, tourmenter.

harassment, *s.* **1.** Harcèlement *m.* **2.** Tourment *m.*

harbour¹, *s.* *Nau:* Port *m.* **Outer harbour,**

avant-port *m*. **harbour-master**, *s*. Capitaine *m* de port.

harbour², *v.tr*. Héberger; donner asile à. *To h. suspicions*, entretenir des soupçons.

hard. I. *a*. **1**. Dur. **To get hard**, durcir. *F*: **To be as hard as nails**, (i) être en bonne forme; (ii) être impitoyable. **2**. Difficile; (tâche) pénible. **To be hard to please**, être exigeant, difficile. **To be hard of hearing**, être dur d'oreille. **3**. (*a*) Dur, sévère, rigoureux (*to, towards*, envers). **To be hard on s.o.**, être sévère envers qn. (*b*) **Hard fact**, fait brutal. **Times are hard**, les temps sont rudes, durs. **To have a hard time of it**, en voir de dures. *F*: **Hard lines!** pas de chance! **4**. **Hard work**, (i) travail assidu; (ii) travail ingrat. **Hard drinker**, grand buveur. **Hard fight**, rude combat. **To try one's hardest**, faire tout son possible. **5**. **Hard frost**, forte gelée. **Hard winter**, hiver rigoureux. **-ly**, *adv*. **1**. (*a*) Sévèrement. (*b*) *H. contested*, vivement, chaudement, contesté. (*c*) Péniblement. **2**. (*a*) A peine; ne . . . guère. (*b*) **You'll hardly believe it**, vous aurez (de la) peine à le croire. **I hardly know**, je n'en sais trop rien. **I need hardly say**, point besoin de dire. **Hardly anyone**, presque personne. (*b*) *He could h. have said that*, il n'aurait sûrement pas dit cela. II. **hard**, *adv*. **1**. (*a*) *Pull the bell h.*, tirez fort la sonnette. *As h. as one can*, de toutes ses forces. **To hit hard**, cogner dur; frapper raide. *To look h. at s.o.*, regarder fixement qn. **To think hard**, réfléchir profondément. **To be hard at work**, être en plein travail. **It is raining hard**, il pleut à verse. **To snow hard**, neiger dru. (*b*) **It will go hard with him if** . . ., il lui en cuira si. . . . (*c*) *F*: **To be hard up (for money)**, être à court (d'argent). **To be hard up for sth.**, avoir grand besoin de qch. **2**. Difficilement; avec peine. **Hard-earned wages**, salaire péniblement gagné. **3**. **Hard by**, tout près. **To follow hard (up)on s.o.**, suivre qn de près. *It was h. on twelve*, il était bientôt minuit. **hard and fast**, *a*. **To lay down a hard and fast rule**, poser une règle absolue.

hard-boiled, *a*. (Œuf) dur. **hard-fought**, *a*. Chaudement contesté; âprement disputé. **hard-headed**, *a*. Positif, pratique. **hard-hearted**, *a*. Insensible, impitoyable, au cœur dur. **hard-tack**. *s*. *Nau*: Biscuit *m* de mer; *F*: galette *f*. **hard-won**, *a*. *H.-w. trophy*, trophée chaudement disputé. **hard-working**, *a*. Laborieux; travailleur, -euse; assidu.

harden. **1**. *v.tr*. Durcir. **To harden s.o. to fatigue**, aguerrir qn à, contre, la fatigue. **2**. *v.i*. Durcir, s'affermir. **His voice hardened**, sa voix devint dure. **hardened**, *a*. Durci; (criminel) endurci.

hardihood, *s*. Hardiesse *f*.

hardness, *s*. **1**. Dureté *f*. **2**. (*a*) Difficulté *f*. (*b*) **Hardness of hearing**, dureté d'oreille. **3**. Sévérité *f*, rigueur *f*, dureté.

hardship, *s*. Privation *f*, fatigue *f*; (dure) épreuve.

hardware, *s*. Quincaillerie *f*.

hardy, *a*. **1**. Hardi; audacieux, intrépide. **2**. (*a*) Robuste; endurci. (*b*) **Hardy annual**, plante annuelle de pleine terre. **-ily**, *adv*. **1**. Hardiment, audacieusement. **2**. Vigoureusement.

hare, *s*. Lièvre *m*. *Cu*: Jugged hare, civet *m* de lièvre. **hare-brained**, *a*. Écervelé, étourdi.

harem, *s*. Harem *m*.

haricot, *s*. *Bot*: Haricot (bean), haricot blanc.

hark, *v.i*. **1**. Hark! écoutez! **2**. *F*: **To hark back to sth.**, en revenir à un sujet.

harlequin, *s*. *Th*: Arlequin *m*.

harlequinade, *s*. Arlequinade *f*.

harm¹, *s*. Mal *m*, tort *m*. **To do s.o. harm**, faire du tort à qn; nuire à qn. **You will come to harm**, il vous arrivera malheur. **Out of harm's way**, à l'abri du danger. *That won't do any h.*, cela ne nuira en rien.

harm², *v.tr*. Faire du mal, du tort, à; nuire à.

harmful, *a*. Malfaisant, pernicieux; nocif, nuisible (*to*, à).

harmfulness, *s*. Nocivité *f*.

harmless, *a*. (Animal) inoffensif; (homme) sans malice; (passe-temps) innocent.

harmonious, *a*. Harmonieux. **1**. En bon accord. **2**. Mélodieux. **-ly**, *adv*. Harmonieusement; en harmonie.

harmonize. **1**. *v.tr*. Harmoniser; concilier. **2**. *v.i*. S'harmoniser, s'allier; (*of facts*) s'accorder.

harmony, *s*. **1**. *Mus*: Harmonie *f*. **2**. Harmonie, accord *m*. **To live in perfect harmony**, vivre en parfaite intelligence.

harness¹, *s*. Harnais *m*, harnachement *m*. *F*: **To die in harness**, mourir à la besogne.

harness², *v.tr*. **1**. (*a*) Harnacher. (*b*) Atteler. **2**. Aménager (une chute d'eau).

harp¹, *s*. *Mus*: Harpe *f*.

harp², *v.i*. *F*: **To be always harping on the same string**, rabâcher toujours la même chose.

harpoon¹, *s*. Harpon *m*.

harpoon², *v.tr*. Harponner.

harpooner, *s*. Harponneur *m*.

harpy, *s*. *Myth*: Harpie *f*. *F*: **Old harpy**, vieille mégère.

harridan, *s*. *F*: Vieille mégère.

harrow¹, *s*. *Agr*: Herse *f*.

harrow², *v.tr*. *Agr*: Herser. *F*: **To harrow s.o.'s feelings**, déchirer le cœur à qn. **harrowing**, *a*. *F*: Poignant, navrant.

Harry¹, *Pr.n*. **1**. Henri *m*. **2**. *F*: **Old Harry**, le diable;

harry², *v.tr*. **1**. Dévaster. **2**. Harceler.

harsh, *a*. **1**. Dur, rêche, rude (au toucher); aigre, strident (à l'oreille). **Harsh voice**, voix rude. **2**. (Caractère) dur; (maître) rude. **-ly**, *adv*. Avec dureté.

harshness, *s*. **1**. Dureté *f*, rudesse *f* (au

harum-scarum]

toucher); aigreur *f* (d'un son). **2.** Sévérité *f*, rudesse.
harum-scarum, *a. & s. F:* Étourdi, écervelé.
harvest[1], *s.* **1.** Moisson *f.* **To get in the harvest,** faire la moisson. **2.** (Époque *f* de) la moisson.
harvest[2], *v.tr.* Moissonner. *Abs.* Rentrer, faire, la moisson.
harvester, *s.* **1.** Moissonneur, -euse. **2.** (*Machine*) Moissonneuse *f.*
hash[1], *s.* **1.** *Cu:* Hachis *m.* **2.** *F: To make a h. of it,* bousiller l'affaire. *F: To settle s.o.'s hash,* régler son compte à qn.
hash[2], *v.tr.* **To hash (up) meat,** hacher la viande.
hasp, *s.* (*a*) Loquet *m.* (*b*) Fermoir *m,* agrafe *f.*
haste, *s.* Hâte *f,* diligence *f.* **In hot haste,** en toute hâte. **Make haste!** dépêchez-vous! **More haste less speed,** hâtez-vous lentement.
hasten. **1.** *v.tr.* Accélérer, hâter, presser. **2.** *v.i.* Se hâter, se dépêcher.
hastiness, *s.* **1.** Précipitation *f,* hâte *f.* **2.** (*Of temper*) Emportement *m,* vivacité *f.*
hasty, *a.* **1.** (Départ) précipité; (repas) sommaire. **2.** Emporté, vif. **-ily,** *adv.* **1.** A la hâte; précipitamment. **2.** Sans réfléchir (juger) à la légère.
hat, *s.* Chapeau *m.* **Soft felt hat,** chapeau mou. **Paper hat,** coiffure *f* de cotillon. **To raise one's hat to s.o.,** saluer qn (d'un coup de chapeau). **To take off one's hat,** enlever son chapeau; (*of man*) se découvrir. **hat-peg,** *s.* Patère *f.* **hat-stand,** *s.* Porte-chapeaux *m inv.*
hatch[1], *s. Nau:* (*a*) Hatch(way), descente *f,* écoutille *f.* (*b*) Hatch(-cover), panneau *m* de descente. **Under hatches,** dans la cale.
hatch[2]. **1.** *v.tr.* Faire éclore. **To hatch out eggs,** incuber, (faire) couver, des œufs. *F:* **To hatch a plot,** ourdir un complot. **2.** *v.i.* **To hatch (out),** éclore.
hatchet, *s.* Hachette *f,* cognée *f. F:* **To bury the hatchet,** faire la paix. **hatchet-faced,** *a.* Au visage en lame de couteau.
hate[1], *s. Lit:* = HATRED.
hate[2], *v.tr.* **1.** Haïr, détester, exécrer. **2.** **To hate to do sth.,** détester (de) faire qch. **I should hate to be late,** cela m'ennuierait fort d'être en retard.
hateful, *a.* Odieux, détestable.
hatred, *s.* Haine *f* (*of,* de, contre). **Out of hatred of sth.,** en haine de qch.
hatter, *s.* Chapelier, -ière.
haughtiness, *s.* Hauteur *f,* morgue *f.*
haughty, *a.* Hautain, altier, sourcilleux. **-ily,** *adv.* Hautainement; avec hauteur.
haul[1], *s. Fish:* Prise *f,* pêche *f.* **To make a good haul,** ramener un fameux coup de filet.
haul[2]. **1.** *v.tr.* Tirer; traîner; remorquer. **2.** *v.i. Nau:* **To haul on a rope,** haler sur une manœuvre. **hauling,** *s.* Traction *f.*
haunch, *s.* (*a*) *Anat:* Hanche *f.* (*b*) *Cu:* Cuissot *m,* quartier *m.* (*c*) *pl.* **Haunches,**

arrière-train *m. Dog sitting on his haunches,* chien assis sur son derrière.
haunt[1], *s.* Lieu fréquenté; repaire *m.*
haunt[2], *v.tr.* (*a*) Fréquenter, hanter. (*b*) Hanter. **This place is haunted,** il y a des revenants ici. (*c*) Obséder. **haunting,** *a.* Qui vous hante; (doute) obsédant.
Havana. *Pr.n.* La Havane.
have[1], *s. P:* Attrape *f.*
have[2], *v.tr.* **1.** (*a*) Avoir, posséder. **All I have,** tout ce que je possède, tout mon avoir. **I have it!** j'y suis! (*b*) **We don't have many visitors,** nous ne recevons pas beaucoup de visites. **2. To have a child,** avoir un enfant. **3.** (*a*) *There was no work to be had,* on ne pouvait pas obtenir de travail. **It is to be had at the chemist's,** cela se trouve chez le pharmacien. (*b*) **To have news from s.o.,** recevoir des nouvelles de qn. (*c*) *I must h. them by to-morrow,* il me les faut pour demain. **Let me have your keys,** donnez-moi vos clefs. *Let me h. an early reply,* répondez-moi sans retard. **4. To have tea with s.o.,** prendre le thé avec qn. *He is having his dinner,* il est en train de dîner. *P:* **I'm not having any!** on ne me la fait pas! **5.** (*a*) **To have an idea,** avoir une idée. **To have a right to sth.,** avoir droit à qch. (*b*) **To have a dream,** faire un rêve. **To have a game,** faire une partie. (*c*) **To have a lesson,** prendre une leçon. (*d*) **To have a pleasant evening,** passer une soirée agréable. **I didn't have any trouble at all,** cela ne m'a donné aucune peine. **We had a rather strange adventure,** il nous est arrivé une aventure assez étrange. **6.** (*a*) **He will have it that . . .,** il soutient que . . . . (*b*) **As Plato has it,** comme dit Platon. (*c*) **He will not have it that . . .,** il n'admet pas que . . . . **7.** (*a*) **You have me there!** voilà où vous me prenez en défaut! (*b*) *F:* Avoir, attraper. **You've been had!** on vous a eu! **8.** (*a*) **To have sth. done,** faire faire qch. (*b*) **He had his leg broken,** il s'est cassé la jambe. **9.** (*a*) **Which one will you have?** lequel voulez-vous? **She won't have him,** elle ne veut pas de lui. *What more would you h.?* que vous faut-il de plus? (*b*) **What would you have me do?** que voulez-vous que je fasse? (*c*) *I won't h. him teased,* je ne veux pas qu'on le taquine. **10. To have to do sth.,** devoir faire qch.; être obligé de faire qch.; être forcé de faire qch. *We shall h to walk faster,* il nous faudra marcher plus vite. **11.** (*a*) **To have been,** avoir été. **To have come, to have hurt oneself,** être venu, s'être blessé. **I have lived in London for three years,** voilà trois ans que j'habite Londres. *Well, you have grown!* ce que tu as grandi! (*b*) *You h. forgotten your gloves.* —So I have! vous avez oublié vos gants.— En effet! Tiens, c'est vrai! *You haven't swept the room.*—I have! vous n'avez pas balayé la chambre.—Si! Mais si! Si fait! *You h. been in prison before.*—I haven't! vous avez déjà fait de la prison.—C'est faux!

12. I had better say nothing, je ferai mieux de ne rien dire. I had as soon stay here, j'aimerais autant rester ici. **have in,** v.tr. *I had them in for a cup of tea,* je les ai fait entrer pour prendre une tasse de thé. *F:* I had the doctor in, j'ai fait venir le médecin. **have out,** v.tr. **1.** To have a tooth out, se faire arracher une dent. **2.** *F:* To have it out with s.o., vider une querelle avec qn. **have up,** v.tr. *F:* Citer en justice.

haven, s. (a) Havre m, port m. (b) *F:* Abri m, asile m.

haversack, s. **1.** *Mil:* Musette f. **2.** Havresac m (de tourisme).

havoc, s. Ravage m, dégâts mpl.

haw¹, s. *Bot:* Cenelle f.

haw², v.i. *See* HUM² **1.**

Hawaiian, a. & s. Hawaïen, -ienne.

hawfinch, s. Gros-bec m, pl. gros-becs.

haw-haw¹, s. **1.** Rire bruyant; gros rire. **2.** Prononciation affectée.

haw-haw², v.i. Rire bruyamment, bêtement.

hawk¹, s. *Orn:* Faucon m. *F:* To have eyes like a hawk, avoir des yeux d'aigle. **hawk-eyed,** a. Au regard d'aigle.

hawk², v.i. Chasser au faucon. **hawking,** s. Chasse f au faucon; fauconnerie f.

hawk³, v.tr. Colporter, cameloter.

hawker, s. (a) Colporteur m. (b) (Of vegetables) Marchand des quatre saisons.

hawser, s. *Nau:* Haussière f, aussière f.

hawthorn, s. Aubépine f.

hay, s. Foin m. To make hay, faire les foins; faner. To make hay while the sun shines, battre le fer pendant qu'il est chaud. **hayfork,** s. Fourche f à foin.

haycock, s. Meulette f de foin.

hayloft, s. Fenil m; grenier m à foin.

haymaker, s. Faneur, -euse.

haymaking, s. Fenaison f.

hayrick, haystack, s. Meule f de foin.

hazard¹, s. **1.** (a) Hasard m. (b) Risque m, péril m. At all hazards, quoi qu'il en coûte. **2.** *Golf:* Accident m de terrain.

hazard², v.tr. Hasarder, risquer, aventurer.

hazardous, a. Hasardeux, risqué, périlleux.

haze, s. Brume légère.

hazel, s. Hazel(-tree), noisetier m, coudrier m. Hazel eyes, yeux couleur (de) noisette. **hazel-nut,** s. Noisette f.

haziness, s. État brumeux, nébuleux.

hazy, a. **1.** Brumeux, embrumé. **2.** Nébuleux, fumeux, vague. **-ily,** adv. Vaguement.

he, pers.pron.nom.m. **1.** Il. (a) *What did he say?* qu'a-t-il dit? (b) *Here he comes,* le voici qui vient. *He is an honest man,* c'est un honnête homme. **2.** (a) Lui. *He and I,* lui et moi. *I am as tall as he,* je suis aussi grand que lui. *It is he,* c'est lui. *He knows nothing about it,* il n'en sait rien, lui. (b) (i) Celui. He that believes, celui qui croit. (ii) It is he who said so, c'est lui qui l'a dit. **3.** (As substantive) Mâle. *Attrib:* **He-bear,** ours mâle. **He-goat,** bouc.

head¹, s. **1.** Tête f. To walk with one's head in the air, marcher le front haut. He gives orders over my head, il donne des ordres sans me consulter. Head down, la tête baissée. Head downwards, la tête en bas. Head first, head foremost, la tête la première. To fall head over heels in love with s.o., devenir éperdument amoureux de qn. *Turf:* To win by a head, gagner d'une tête. His guilt be on his own head, puisse son crime retomber sur lui. *F:* To talk s.o.'s head off, étourdir qn. A fine head of hair, une belle chevelure. **2.** To have a good head for business, s'entendre aux affaires. To take it into one's head to do sth., s'aviser, se mettre en tête, de faire qch. To put ideas into s.o.'s head, donner des idées à qn. We put our heads together, nous avons conféré ensemble. To be over the heads of the audience, dépasser l'entendement de l'auditoire. To keep one's head, conserver sa tête. He is off his head, il est timbré. To go off one's head, devenir fou. Weak in the head, faible d'esprit. **3.** (a) Tête (d'arbre); pomme f (de chou); pied m (de céleri). (b) Tête (d'épingle); pomme (de canne). (c) Haut m (de page). (d) Chevet m, tête (de lit); haut bout (de la table). (e) To come to a head, aboutir. **4.** On this head, sur ce chapitre. Under separate heads, sous des rubriques différentes. **5.** (a) Nez m, avant m, cap m (de navire). Ship (down) by the head, vaisseau sur le nez. (b) = HEADLAND. **6.** (a) To be at the head of the list, venir en tête de liste. (b) Chef m; directeur, -trice (d'une école). (c) *Attrib:* **Head clerk,** premier commis; chef de bureau. **H.** gardener, jardinier en chef. **Head office,** bureau principal. **7.** To pay so much per head, so much a head, payer tant par tête, par personne. **8.** Head of a coin, face f. To toss heads or tails, jouer à pile ou face. *F:* I can't make head or tail of this, je n'y comprends rien. **9.** *Mch:* Head of steam, volant m de vapeur. To gather head, augmenter, gagner de la force.

head-dress, s. **1.** (Hairdressing) Coiffure f. **2.** Garniture f de tête; coiffure; chapeau m. **head-light,** s. Phare m. **head-line,** s. Titre m (de rubrique). **head-master,** s. Principal m; proviseur m (d'un lycée). **head-mistress,** s. Directrice f. **head-on,** a. De front. Head-on collision, collision frontale. **head-quarters,** s.pl. **1.** *Mil:* Quartier général; état-major m. **2.** Centre m, siège social, bureau principal. **head-wind,** s. *Nau:* Vent m contraire. **head-work,** s. Travail m de tête.

head², v.tr. & i. **1.** Conduire, mener (un cortège); être à la tête (d'un parti). To head the poll, venir en tête du scrutin. **2.** The State is heading for ruin, l'État marche à la ruine. **head off,** v.tr. Barrer la route à; détourner, intercepter. **heading,** s. Intitulé

m (d'un chapitre); rubrique *f* (d'un article); en-tête *m*, *pl.* en-têtes. **To come under the heading of,** ressortir à.
headache, *s.* Mal *m*, *pl.* maux, de tête.
header, *s.* **To take a header,** piquer une tête.
headland, *s. Geog:* Cap *m*, promontoire *m.*
headlong. 1. *adv.* **To fall headlong,** tomber la tête la première. **To rush headlong into the fight,** se jeter tête baissée dans la mêlée. **2.** *a.* (*a*) *H. fall,* chute *f* la tête la première. (*b*) Précipité, irréfléchi, impétueux.
headman, *s.* Chef *m* (d'une tribu).
headstone, *s.* Pierre tombale.
headstrong, *a.* Volontaire, têtu.
headway, *s.* Progrès *m. Nau:* Erre *f;* marche *f* avant.
heady, *a.* Capiteux.
heal. 1. *v.tr.* Guérir. **2.** *v.i.* To heal (up), (se) guérir. **healing,** *s.* Guérison *f.*
health, *s.* Santé *f.* **1.** (*a*) **To restore s.o. to health,** rendre la santé à qn. (*b*) **To be in good health,** être en bonne santé; se bien porter. **Health insurance,** assurance *f* maladie. **2. To drink (to) the health of s.o.,** boire à la santé de qn.
healthiness, *s.* Salubrité *f.*
healthy, *a.* **1.** (*a*) Sain; en bonne santé; bien portant. (*b*) Salubre. **2.** *H. appetite,* appétit robuste.
heap[1], *s.* (*a*) Tas *m*, monceau *m*, amas *m.* **In a heap,** en tas. *F:* (*Of pers.*) **To fall in a heap,** s'affaisser. **To be struck all of a heap,** en rester abasourdi. (*b*) *F:* Heaps of times, bien des fois. **Heaps of time,** grandement le temps.
heap[2], *v.tr.* **1.** (*a*) **To heap (up),** entasser, amonceler; amasser. (*b*) **To heap insults on s.o.,** accabler qn d'injures. **2.** *She heaped my plate with cherries,* elle a rempli mon assiette de cerises.
hear, *v.tr.* **1.** Entendre. *A groan was heard,* un gémissement se fit entendre. *To h. s.o. speak,* entendre parler qn. **To hear sth. said to s.o.,** entendre dire qch. à qn. **To hear s.o. say sth.,** entendre dire qch. à qn, par qn. **2.** Écouter. **Hear me out,** écoutez-moi, entendez-moi, jusqu'au bout. **Hear! hear!** très bien ! très bien ! **3. To hear a piece of news,** apprendre une nouvelle. **4.** (*a*) **To hear from s.o.,** recevoir des nouvelles de qn. **Hoping to hear from you,** dans l'attente de vous lire. (*b*) **To hear of, about, s.o.,** avoir des nouvelles de qn. **I never heard of such a thing !** a-t-on jamais entendu une chose pareille ! **I hear of nothing else,** j'en ai les oreilles rebattues. **Father won't hear of it,** mon père ne veut pas en entendre parler.
hearing, *s.* **1.** Audition *f,* audience *f.* **Give me a hearing !** veuillez m'entendre ! **2.** Ouïe *f.* **To be quick of hearing,** avoir l'oreille, l'ouïe, fine. **Within hearing,** à portée d'oreille, de la voix. **It was said in my hearing,** on l'a dit en ma présence.
hearer, *s.* Auditeur, -trice.

hearsay, *s.* Ouï-dire *m inv.*
hearse, *s.* Corbillard *m;* char *m* funèbre.
heart, *s.* Cœur *m.* **1. With beating heart,** le cœur battant. **Heart failure,** défaillance *f* cardiaque. *F:* **To have one's heart in one's mouth,** avoir un serrement de cœur. **To have one's heart in one's boots,** avoir une peur bleue. **To clasp s.o. to one's heart,** serrer qn sur son cœur. **To break s.o.'s heart,** briser le cœur à qn. **He died of a broken heart,** il est mort de chagrin. **2.** (*a*) **To wear one's heart on one's sleeve,** avoir le cœur sur la main. **Set your heart at rest,** soyez tranquille. *His h. was full,* il avait le cœur gros. *With a heavy h.,* le cœur serré. **In my heart of hearts,** au plus profond de mon cœur. **From the bottom of my heart,** de tout mon cœur. **At heart** *he is not a bad fellow,* au fond ce n'est pas un mauvais garçon. (*b*) **To love s.o. with all one's heart,** aimer qn de tout son cœur. (*c*) **To have set one's heart on sth.,** avoir qch. à cœur. **To one's heart's content,** à cœur joie. (*d*) **To have one's heart in one's work,** avoir le cœur à l'ouvrage. **With all my heart,** de tout mon cœur. (*e*) **To lose heart,** perdre courage. **3. The heart of the matter,** le vif de l'affaire. **In the heart of,** au cœur de. **4.** *Cards:* **Queen of hearts,** dame *f* de cœur. **heartbreaking,** *a.* Navrant. *It was h.-b.,* c'était à fendre l'âme. **heart-broken,** *a.* **To be heart-broken,** avoir le cœur brisé. **heart-disease,** *s.* Maladie *f* de cœur. **heart-failure,** *s.* Arrêt *m* du cœur. **heart-felt,** *a.* Sincère; qui vient du cœur. **heart-rending,** *a.* A fendre le cœur; navrant. *H.-r. cries,* cris déchirants. **heart's-ease,** *s. Bot:* Pensée *f* sauvage. **heart to heart,** *a. & adv.phr.* **Heart-to-heart talk,** conversation intime.
hearten, *v.tr.* **To hearten s.o. (up),** ranimer le courage de qn.
hearth, *s.* Foyer *m,* âtre *m.* **hearth-rug,** *s.* Tapis *m* de foyer; devant *m* de foyer.
heartiness, *s.* Cordialité *f,* chaleur *f.*
heartless, *a.* Sans cœur, sans pitié; dur.
heartlessness, *s.* Manque *m* de cœur.
hearty, *a.* **1.** Cordial, -aux. **2.** (*a*) Vigoureux, robuste. (*b*) (Repas) copieux, abondant. **-ily,** *adv.* **1.** Cordialement; sincèrement. **2.** (Dîner) copieusement; (manger) de bon appétit.
heat[1], *s.* **1.** (*a*) Chaleur *f;* ardeur *f. The h. and the cold should be avoided,* le chaud et le froid sont à éviter. (*b*) **Red heat,** chaude rouge. **2. To reply with some heat,** répondre avec une certaine vivacité. **In the heat of the moment,** dans la chaleur du moment. **3.** *Sp:* Épreuve *f,* manche *f.* **Dead heat,** manche nulle; course nulle. *Meteor:* Vague *f* de chaleur.
heat[2], *v.tr.* (*a*) Chauffer. (*b*) Échauffer (le sang). **heated,** *a.* **1.** Chaud, chauffé. **2. To get heated,** s'échauffer. **Heated**

debate, discussion chaude, animée. **-ly,**
adv. Avec chaleur, avec emportement.
heating, *s.* Central heating, chauffage
central.
heater, *s.* Electric heater, radiateur *m* électrique.
heath, *s.* **I.** Bruyère *f*, lande *f*. **2.** *Bot:*
Bruyère.
heathen, *a. & s.* Païen, -ïenne.
heather, *s. Bot:* Bruyère *f*, brande *f*.
heave¹, *s.* Soulèvement *m*.
heave², *v.* I. *v.tr.* **I.** Lever, soulever. *Nau:*
To heave (up) the anchor, *abs.* to heave up,
déraper ; lever l'ancre. **2.** Pousser (un
soupir). **3.** Lancer, jeter (*sth. at s.o.*, qch.
contre qn). *Nau:* To heave the lead, jeter
la sonde. II. **heave,** *v.i.* **I.** (Se) gonfler,
se soulever ; (*of bosom*) palpiter. **2.** *Nau:*
To heave at a rope, haler sur une manœuvre.
3. *Nau:* To heave in sight, paraître. **heave
to,** *v.tr. & i. Nau:* (Se) mettre en panne.
heaven, *s.* Ciel *m, pl.* cieux. In heaven, au
ciel. To go to heaven, aller au ciel. Good
Heavens! juste ciel! Thank Heaven! Dieu
merci! For Heaven's sake! pour l'amour
de Dieu! **heaven-sent,** *a.* Providentiel.
heavenly, *a.* Céleste. Heavenly body,
astre *m*.
heaviness, *s.* (*a*) Lourdeur, *f*, pesanteur *f*.
(*b*) Engourdissement *m*, lassitude *f*.
heavy, *a.* **I.** Lourd. (*a*) Heavy blow, (i) coup
violent ; (ii) rude coup (du sort). (*b*) Heavy
tread, pas pesant, lourd. **2.** (*a*) Heavy
baggage, gros bagages. Heavy guns, artillerie
lourde. Heavy cavalry, grosse cavalerie.
(*b*) Heavy features, gros traits. (*c*) *Mil:*
Heavy fire, feu .nourri. *H. shower,* grosse
averse. **3.** *Air h. with scent,* air chargé de
parfums. **4.** Heavy eyes, yeux battus.
5. (*a*) (Travail) pénible, laborieux. Heavy
day, journée chargée. (*b*) Heavy weather,
gros temps. Heavy sea, forte mer, grosse mer.
6. Heavy eater, gros mangeur. To be a
heavy sleeper, avoir le sommeil dur. **-ily,**
adv. **I.** Lourdement. Time hangs heavily
on his hands, le temps lui pèse. **2.** *H. under-
lined,* fortement souligné. To lose heavily,
perdre une forte somme. **3.** To sleep heavily,
dormir profondément. **heavy-eyed,** *a.*
Aux yeux battus. **heavy-handed,** *a.* A
la main lourde.
Hebrew. (*a*) *a. & s.* Hébreu, *f*. hébraïque.
(*b*) (The) Hebrew (language), l'hébreu *m*.
hecatomb, *s.* Hécatombe *f*.
hectic, *a.* **I.** *Med:* Hectique. **2.** *F:* Agité,
fiévreux.
hector, *v.tr. & i.* Intimider, rudoyer (qn).
hectoring, *a.* Autoritaire, impérieux.
hedge¹, *s.* Haie *f.* **hedge-hopping,** *s.*
Av: F: Vol *m* à ras de terre ; rase-mottes
m inv.
hedge². **I.** *v.tr.* Hedged in with difficulties,
entouré de difficultés. **2.** *v.i. F:* Chercher
des échappatoires ; se réserver.

hedgehog, *s.* Hérisson *m*.
hedgerow, *s.* Bordure *f* de haies.
heed¹, *s.* Attention *f*, garde *f*, soin *m*. To
take heed, prendre garde. To take no heed
of sth., ne tenir aucun compte de qch.
heed², *v.tr.* Faire attention à, prendre garde
à, tenir compte de.
heedful, *a.* Vigilant, prudent.
heedless, *a.* Étourdi, insouciant, imprudent.
-ly, *adv.* Étourdiment.
heedlessness, *s.* Inattention *f* (*of*, à) ; étourderie *f*, insouciance *f*.
hee-haw¹, *s.* Hi-han *m* ; braiment *m*.
hee-haw², *v.i.* Braire ; faire hi-han.
heel¹, *s.* (*a*) Talon *m*. To tread on s.o.'s
heels, marcher sur les talons de qn. To
take to one's heels, prendre la fuite. To lay
s.o. by the heels, arrêter qn. To cool one's
heels, croquer le marmot ; faire le pied de
grue. To come to heel, *F:* se soumettre.
(*b*) Talon (d'un soulier) Out at heels, (bas)
troués aux talons. To be down at heel, être
dans la dèche. (*c*) (*Of horse*) To fling out its
heels, ruer.
heel², *v.i. Nau:* To heel (over), avoir,
donner, de la bande.
hefty, *a. F:* Fort, solide.
heifer, *s.* Génisse *f*.
height, *s.* **I.** (*a*) Hauteur *f*, élévation *f*.
Wall six feet in height, mur qui a six pieds
de haut. (*b*) Taille *f*, grandeur *f*, stature *f*
(de qn). **2. Height above sea level,** altitude *f*
au-dessus du niveau de la mer. **3.** Hauteur ;
éminence *f* (de terrain) ; colline *f*. **4.** Apogée
m (de la fortune) ; comble *m* (de la folie).
At the height of the storm, au (plus) fort de
l'orage. In the height of summer, au cœur,
au fort, de l'été ; en plein été. In the height
of fashion, à la dernière mode.
heighten, **I.** *v.tr.* (*a*) Surélever, surhausser,
rehausser (un mur). (*b*) Accroître, augmenter
(un plaisir) ; accentuer (un contraste).
2. *v.i.* S'élever ; se rehausser ; augmenter.
heinous, *a.* Odieux, atroce.
heinousness, *s.* Énormité *f*, atrocité *f*.
heir, *s.* Héritier *m. Jur:* Heir apparent,
héritier présomptif.
heiress, *s.* Héritière *f*.
heirloom, *s.* Meuble *m* ou bijou *m* de
famille.
Helen. *Pr.n.* Hélène *f*.
heliograph, *s.* Héliographe *m*.
heliotrope. **I.** *s. Bot:* Héliotrope *m*.
2. *a.* Héliotrope *inv.*
hell, *s.* L'enfer *m*. To ride hell for leather,
galoper à bride abattue.
hellebore, *s. Bot:* Ellébore *m*.
hellish, *a.* Infernal, -aux ; diabolique.
-ly, *adv.* D'une manière diabolique.
hello, *int.* (*a*) *H. there!* holà! (*b*) (*On the
telephone*) Allô! (*c*) *H., is that you?* tiens!
c'est vous!
helm, *s. Nau:* Barre *f* (du gouvernail) ;
gouvernail *m*, timon *m*.

helmet, s. Casque m.

helmsman, s. Nau: Homme m de barre; timonier m.

help¹, s. **I.** Aide f, assistance f, secours m. With the h. of a rope, à l'aide, au moyen, d'une corde. With God's h., Dieu aidant. To cry for help, crier au secours. **2.** There's no help for it, il n'y a rien à faire. **3.** Aide mf.

help², v.tr. **I.** (a) Aider, secourir, assister; venir en aide à; venir à l'aide de. That will not h. you, cela ne vous servira à rien. I got a friend to h. me, je me suis fait aider par un ami. Help! au secours! (b) Faciliter (le progrès). To help s.o. down, aider qn à descendre. **2.** Servir. To help s.o. to soup, servir du potage à qn. Help yourself, servez-vous. **3.** (a) Empêcher. Things we cannot help, choses qu'on ne saurait empêcher. I can't help it, je n'y peux rien. It can't be helped, tant pis ! (b) S'empêcher, se défendre (de faire qch.). I can't help it, c'est plus fort que moi. **helping¹,** a. To lend a helping hand, prêter son aide. **helping²,** s. Portion f (de nourriture).

helper, s. Aide mf.

helpful, a. **I.** (Personne) secourable, serviable. **2.** (Livre) utile. **-fully,** adv. Utilement; salutairement.

helpless, a. **I.** Sans ressource, sans appui. **2.** Faible, impuissant. I am h. in the matter, je n'y puis rien. **-ly,** adv. **I.** Sans ressource. **2.** Faiblement.

helplessness, s. **I.** Abandon m, délaissement m. **2.** Faiblesse f.

helpmate, s. Compagnon m ou compagne f; épouse f.

helter-skelter. I. adv. Pêle-mêle, à la débandade. **2.** a. Helter-skelter flight, fuite désordonnée.

hem¹, s. **I.** Bord m (d'un vêtement). **2.** Ourlet m (d'un mouchoir).

hem², v.tr. **I.** Ourler. **2.** To hem in, entourer, cerner.

hem³, v.i. Faire hem, hum.

hemisphere, s. Hémisphère m.

hemispheric(al), a. Hémisphérique.

hemlock, s. Bot: Ciguë f.

hemorrhage, s. Hémorragie f.

hemp, s. (a) Bot: Chanvre m. (b) Tex: Chanvre, filasse f.

hen, s. **I.** Poule f. **2.** Femelle f (d'oiseau).

hen-coop, s. Cage f à poules; mue f.

hen-house, s. Poulailler m. **hen-pecked,** a. Hen-pecked husband, mari dont la femme porte la culotte. **hen-roost,** s. (a) Juchoir m, perchoir m. (b) F: Poulailler m.

hence, adv. **I.** (From) hence, d'ici. **2.** Dorénavant, désormais. Five years hence, dans cinq ans (d'ici). **3.** Hence his anger, de là sa fureur.

henceforth, adv. Désormais, dorénavant.

henna, s. Henné m.

Henrietta. Pr.n. Henriette f.

Henry. Pr.n. Henri m.

heptagon, s. Heptagone m.

heptagonal, a. Heptagone; heptagonal, -aux.

heptameter, s. Pros: Heptamètre m.

her¹, pers. pron. object. **I.** (a) (Direct) La, (before vowel sound) l'; (indirect) lui. Have you seen her? l'avez-vous vue? I obey her, je lui obéis. Look at her, regardez-la. Tell her, dites-lui. (b) I am thinking of her, je pense à elle. I remember her, je me souviens d'elle. **2.** Elle. Her I can never forgive, je ne lui pardonnerai jamais à elle. **3.** F: It's her, c'est elle. That's her! la voilà !

her², poss.a. Son, f. sa, pl. ses. Her friend, her friends, son ami, f. son amie ; ses amis, f. ses amies. She has hurt her hand, elle s'est fait mal à la main.

herald¹, s. (a) Héraut m. (b) F: Avant-coureur m, pl. avant-coureurs, précurseur m.

herald², v.tr. Annoncer, proclamer.

heraldic, a. Héraldique.

heraldry, s. L'art m, la science, héraldique ; le blason.

herb, s. Bot: (a) Herbe f. (b) Sweet herbs, fines herbes.

herbaceous, a. Bot: Herbacé.

herbal. I. s. Herbier m. **2.** a. (Tisane) d'herbes.

herbalist, s. Herboriste mf.

herbivorous, a. Z: Herbivore.

Herculean, a. (Travail) herculéen ; (taille) d'Hercule.

Hercules. I. Pr.n. Hercule m. **2.** s. F: Homme m d'une grande force ; hercule.

herd¹, s. (a) Troupeau m ; troupe f, bande f (de chevaux). (b) F: Troupeau, foule f (de gens). The vulgar herd, le commun des hommes. **herd-boy,** s. Jeune pâtre m ; aide m de bouvier.

herd², v.i. To herd together, s'assembler en troupeau.

herd³, s. Pâtre m, gardien m.

herdsman, s. Bouvier m, pâtre m.

here, adv. **I.** (a) Ici. In here, ici. Come in h., please, venez par ici, s'il vous plaît. Up to here, down to here, jusqu'ici. About here, par ici. Between h. and London, d'ici à Londres. Christmas is h.! voici Noël ! Here and now, sur-le-champ, séance tenante. Here goes! allons-y ! (b) Here lies, ci-gît. (c) (At roll-call) Présent ! (d) Here below, ici-bas. **2.** Here's your hat, voici votre chapeau. Here you are! (i) vous voici ! (ii) tenez! (ceci est pour vous). **3.** Here's to you! à votre santé ! **4.** My friend here will tell you, mon ami que voici vous le dira. **5.** Here! I want you! pst ! venez ici ! **6.** (a) Here and there, par-ci par-là ; çà et là. (b) Here, there, and everywhere, un peu partout. (c) F: That's neither here nor there, cela ne fait rien (à l'affaire).

hereabout(s), adv. Près d'ici, par ici, dans ces parages.

hereafter. I. adv. (a) Dorénavant, à l'avenir.

(b) Dans la vie à venir. **2. s.** L'au-delà *m*; l'autre monde *m*.

hereby, *adv.* (a) Par ceci. (b) *Jur:* Par ces présentes.

hereditary, *a.* Héréditaire.

heredity, *s.* Hérédité *f.*

herein, *adv.* **1.** Ici, dans ce livre. *The letter enclosed h.,* la lettre ci-incluse. **2.** En ceci, sur ce point.

heresy, *s.* Hérésie *f.*

heretic, *s.* Hérétique *mf.*

heretical, *a.* Hérétique.

heretofore, *adv.* Jadis, autrefois; jusqu'ici. *As heretofore,* comme auparavant.

hereupon, *adv.* Là-dessus; sur ce.

herewith, *adv.* Avec ceci.

heritage, *s.* Héritage *m*, patrimoine *m.*

hermetic, *a.* Hermétique. **-ally,** *adv.* (Scellé) hermétiquement.

hermit, *s.* Ermite *m.*

hermitage, *s.* Ermitage *m.*

hero, *s.* Héros *m.* *To die like a hero,* se faire tuer en brave, en héros. **hero-worship,** *s.* Culte *m* des héros.

Herod. *Pr.n. Hist:* Hérode *m.*

heroic(al). 1. *a.* Héroïque. **2.** *s. F:* Heroics, déclamation *f* de sentiments outrés; grandiloquence *f.* **-ally,** *adv.* Héroïquement.

heroine, *s.* Héroïne *f.*

heroism, *s.* Héroïsme *m.*

heron, *s. Orn:* Héron *m.*

herring, *s. Ich:* Hareng *m.* **Red herring,** hareng saur; *F:* sujet pour faire diversion.

hers, *poss.pron.* Le sien, la sienne, les siens, les siennes. *She took my pen and h.,* elle prit ma plume et la sienne. *This book is h.,* ce livre est à elle. *A friend of hers,* un(e) de ses ami(e)s; un(e) ami(e) à elle.

herself, *pers.pron. See* SELF 3.

hesitant, *a.* Hésitant, irrésolu.

hesitate, *v.i.* Hésiter. *To hesitate to do sth.,* hésiter à faire qch. **hesitating,** *a.* Hésitant, incertain. **-ly,** *adv.* Avec hésitation; en hésitant.

hesitation, *s.* Hésitation *f.*

heterodox, *a.* Hétérodoxe.

heterodoxy, *s.* Hétérodoxie *f.*

heterogeneous, *a.* Hétérogène.

hew, *v.tr.* Couper, tailler. *To hew one's way,* se frayer, se tailler, un passage.

hexagon, *s. Geom:* Hexagone *m.*

hexagonal, *a.* Hexagone, hexagonal, -aux.

hexameter, *s. Pros:* Hexamètre *m.*

hey, *int.* Hé! holà!

heyday, *s.* Apogée *m*, beaux jours. *To be in the heyday of life,* être dans la fleur de l'âge.

hi, *int.* Hé, là-bas! ohé!

hiatus, *s.* **1.** Lacune *f.* **2.** *Gram:* Hiatus *m.*

hibernate, *v.i.* Hiberner.

Hibernian, *a. & s.* Hibernien, -ienne; irlandais, -aise.

hiccough[1], *s.* Hoquet *m.*

hiccough[2], *v.i.* Avoir le hoquet; hoqueter.

hide[1], *v.* **1.** *v.tr.* (a) Cacher (*from,* à). To

hide one's face, se cacher la figure, se voiler la face. *I did not know where to hide my head,* je ne savais où me fourrer. *To hide (away) a treasure,* mettre un trésor dans une cache. (b) To hide sth. from sight, dérober, soustraire, qch. aux regards. *Clouds hid the sun,* des nuages voilaient le soleil. **2.** *v.i.* Se cacher. **hiding**[1], *s.* To go into hiding, se cacher. *To be in hiding,* se tenir caché.

hiding-place, *s.* Cachette *f*; retraite *f.*

hide-and-seek, *s. Games:* Cache-cache *m.*

hide[2], *s.* Peau *f*, dépouille *f. Com:* Cuir *m.* *F:* To save one's hide, sauver sa peau.

hide-bound, *a. F:* Aux vues étroites.

hideous, *a.* **1.** Hideux, affreux, effroyable. **2.** D'une laideur repoussante. **-ly,** *adv.* Hideusement, affreusement.

hideousness, *s.* Hideur *f*, horreur *f.*

hiding[2], *s.* Raclée *f.*

hierarchy, *s.* Hiérarchie *f.*

hieroglyphics, *s.pl.* Hiéroglyphes *m*; signes *m* hiéroglyphiques.

higgle, *v.i.* Marchander.

higgledy-piggledy, *adv.* Sans ordre, en pagaïe, pêle-mêle.

high. I. *a.* Haut. **1.** *H. mountain,* haute montagne. *Wall six feet high,* mur haut de six pieds. *How h. is that tree?* quelle est la hauteur de cet arbre? **2.** Élevé. (a) To hold one's head high, porter la tête haute. (b) *To be high in office,* avoir un poste élevé. *H. official,* haut fonctionnaire. *F:* To be high and mighty, le prendre de haut. *s.* High and low, les grands et les petits. (c) *H. rate of interest,* taux élevé. *It fetches a h. price,* cela se vend cher. *To set a high value on sth.,* estimer qch. haut. *To play for high stakes,* jouer gros (jeu). *High speed,* grande vitesse. (d) In the highest degree, au plus haut degré; par excellence. *High fever,* forte fièvre. *High wind,* vent fort, violent. (e) High voice, (i) voix élevée, haute; (ii) voix grêle. **3.** *Sch:* The higher forms, les classes supérieures. **4.** The High Street, la Grand'rue, la Grande rue. **5.** (a) High noon, plein midi. *It is high time he went to school,* il est grand temps, grandement temps, qu'il aille à l'école. (b) *Cu:* (Of meat) Avancé, gâté; (of game) faisandé. **6.** *Nau:* High and dry, (échoué) à sec. *F:* To leave s.o. high and dry, laisser qn en plan. **7.** On high, en haut; dans le ciel. **-ly,** *adv.* **1.** To think highly of s.o., avoir une haute opinion de qn. **2.** Fort, très, bien. Highly amusing, fort, très, amusant. **II. high,** *adv.* **1.** Haut; en haut. *Higher and higher,* de plus en plus haut. *To aim high,* viser haut. *F:* To hunt high and low for sth., chercher qch. de haut en bas. **2.** To go as high as £2000, aller jusqu'à 2000 livres. **3.** Fort, fortement, très. *To run high,* (i) (of the sea) être grosse, houleuse; (ii) (of feeling) s'échauffer; (iii) (of prices) être élevé. **highborn,** *a.* De haute naissance. **high-class,**

a. *F:* De premier ordre, de première qualité.
high-coloured, a. Haut en couleur.
high-handed, a. Arbitraire ; tyrannique.
high-minded, a. A l'esprit élevé. **high-pitched,** a. (*Of sound*) Aigu, -uë. **high-power(ed),** a. (Auto) de haute puissance. **high-priced,** a. De grand prix ; cher. **high-priest,** s. Grand-prêtre, *pl.* grands-prêtres. **high-sounding,** a. Pompeux, prétentieux. **high-spirited,** a. Intrépide ; plein d'ardeur, de feu ; (cheval) fougueux. **high-strung,** a Nerveux, exalté.

highbrow, s. *F:* Intellectuel, -elle.
highland. 1. *s.pl.* Highlands, hautes terres. **2.** *Attrib.a.* Montagnard.
highlander, s. **1.** Montagnard *m.* **2.** A Highlander, un montagnard écossais.
highness, s. Altesse *f.*
highway, s. Chemin *m* de grande communication. Highways and by-ways, chemins et sentiers.
highwayman, s. Voleur *m* de grand chemin.
hike¹, s. *F:* Excursion *f* à pied.
hike², v.i. *F:* Faire du tourisme à pied. To hike it, faire le trajet à pied. **hiking,** s. Excursions *fpl* à pied.
hiker, s. Excursionniste *mf* à pied.
hilarious, a. Gai, joyeux, hilare. **-ly,** adv. Gaiement, joyeusement.
hilarity, s. Hilarité *f,* gaieté *f.*
hill, s. **1.** (a) Colline *f,* coteau *m.* Up hill and down dale, par monts et par vaux. Hill-country, pays de montagne(s). (b) Éminence *f ;* monticule *m.* **2.** (*On road*) Côte *f.*
hill-side, s. Flanc *m* de coteau ; coteau *m.*
hillock, s. Petite colline ; butte *f.*
hilly, a. **1.** Montagneux ; (terrain) accidenté. **2.** (Chemin) montueux, à fortes pentes.
hilt, s. Poignée *f,* garde *f.* Up to the hilt, jusqu'à la garde. To prove an assertion up to the hilt, démontrer surabondamment une assertion.
him, *pers. pron. object.* **1.** (a) (*Direct*) Le, (*before a vowel sound*) l' ; (*indirect*) lui. Do you love him? l'aimez-vous ? I obey him, je lui obéis. (b) (*Refl.*) Lui, soi. He took his luggage with him, il prit ses bagages avec lui. **2.** (a) Lui. Him I admire, lui je l'admire. (b) The prize goes to him who comes in first, le prix est pour celui qui arrivera le premier. **3.** *F: It's him,* c'est lui. *That's him!* le voilà !
himself, *pers.pron.* See SELF 3.
hind¹, s. Biche *f.*
hind², hinder¹, a. **1.** Hinder part, partie postérieure. **2.** Hind legs, jambes de derrière. Hind quarters, arrière-train *m.*
hinder², v.tr. **1.** Gêner, embarrasser ; retarder, entraver. **2.** Empêcher, retenir (*s.o. from doing sth.,* qn de faire qch.).
hindmost, a. Dernier.
hindrance, s. Empêchement *m,* obstacle *m.*
Hindu, a. & s. *Ethn:* Hindou, -oue.

hinge¹, s. **1.** Gond *m* (de porte). **2.** Charnière *f.*
hinge², v.i. (a) Tourner, pivoter (*on,* autour de). (b) *F:* Everything hinges on *his answer,* tout dépend de sa réponse. **hinged,** a. A charnière(s).
hint¹, s. **1.** (a) Insinuation *f ;* allusion indirecte. Broad hint, avis peu voilé. To give s.o. a hint, toucher un mot à qn. To throw out a hint, donner à entendre. To know how to take a hint, entendre (qn) à demi-mot. (b) Signe *m,* indication *f.* Not the slightest hint of, pas le moindre soupçon de. **2.** Hints for housewives, conseils *m* aux ménagères.
hint², v.tr. & i. Insinuer ; dire à mots couverts. To hint at sth., laisser entendre qch.
hip¹, s. *Anat:* Hanche *f.* **hip-bath,** s. Bain *m* de siège.
hip², s. *Bot: F:* Gratte-cul *m inv.*
hip³, int. Hip! hip! hip! hurrah! hip! hip! hip! hourra!
hippodrome, s. Hippodrome *m.*
hippopotamus, s. *Z:* Hippopotame *m.*
hire¹, s. **1.** Louage *m.* To let sth. (out) on hire, louer qch. **2.** Salaire *m,* gages *mpl.*
hire-purchase, s. Location-vente *f.*
hire², v.tr. **1.** Louer. Hired assassin, assassin à gages. **2.** To hire out, louer.
his¹, *poss.a.* Son, *f.* sa, *pl.* ses. One of his friends, un de ses amis. He fell on his back, il tomba sur le dos. His idea would be to . ., son idée à lui serait de . . . .
his², *poss.pron.* Le sien, la sienne, les siens, les siennes. He took my pen and his, il prit ma plume et la sienne. This book is his, ce livre est à lui. A friend of his, un de ses amis.
hiss¹, s. (a) Sifflement *m.* (b) *Th:* Sifflet *m.*
hiss². 1. v.i. Siffler. **2.** v.tr. To hiss an actor, siffler un acteur.
historian, s. Historien *m.*
historic, a. Historique ; (événement) marquant.
historical, a. **1.** Historique, de l'histoire. **2.** *H. painting,* tableau d'histoire. *H. novel,* roman historique. **-ally,** adv. Historiquement.
history, s. **1.** L'histoire *f.* *F: That's ancient history,* c'est une vieille histoire. **2.** Natural history, histoire naturelle.
hit¹, s. **1.** (a) Coup *m.* *F: That's a hit at you,* c'est une pierre dans votre jardin. (b) *Fenc:* Touché *f.* To score a hit, toucher. **2.** (a) Coup réussi ; succès *m.* Lucky hit, (i) coup heureux ; (ii) trouvaille *f.* To make a hit, réussir. (b) *Th:* Pièce *f* à succès.
hit². 1. v.tr. (a) Frapper. To hit s.o. a blow, porter, donner, un coup à qn. (b) v.i. To hit against sth., se cogner contre qch. (c) Atteindre. *Fenc:* Toucher. To hit the mark, atteindre le but. *F:* To be hard hit, être gravement atteint. (d) adj. & adv.phr. Hit or miss, au hasard. **2.** v.tr. & i. To hit (up)on sth., découvrir, trouver. You've hit it! vous y êtes ! **hit back,** v.tr. & i.

Se défendre ; rendre coup pour coup (à qn).
hit off, *v.tr.* **I.** To hit off a likeness,
attraper une ressemblance. **2.** To hit it
off with s.o., s'accorder avec qn. **hit out,**
v.i. To hit out at s.o., décocher un coup
à qn.
hitch[1], *s.* **I.** Saccade *f*, secousse *f*. **2.** Anicroche *f*, contretemps *m*. **There is a hitch
somewhere,** il y a quelque chose qui cloche.
Without a hitch, sans à-coup.
hitch[2], *v.tr.* **I.** Remuer (qch.) par saccades.
To hitch (up) one's trousers, remonter son
pantalon. **2.** Accrocher, attacher, fixer.
hither, *adv* Ici. Hither and thither, çà et
là.
hitherto, *adv.* Jusqu'ici. **As hitherto,**
comme par le passé.
hive, *s.* Ruche *f*.
ho, *int.* **I.** Ho ! **2.** (*To attract attention*)
Hé ! ohé !
hoar, *s.* Hoar(-frost), gelée blanche ; givre *m*.
hoard[1], *s.* Amas *m*, accumulation secrète.
hoard[2], *v.tr.* Amasser ; accumuler. **hoarding**[1], *s.* Resserre *f*, amassage *m*.
hoarder, *s.* Amasseur, -euse.
hoarding[2], *s.* Palissade *f*.
hoarse, *a.* Enroué, rauque. **To shout
oneself hoarse,** s'enrouer à force de crier.
-ly, *adv.* D'une voix rauque, enrouée.
hoarseness, *s.* Enrouement *m*.
hoary, *a.* **I.** Blanchi, chenu. **2.** Vénérable,
séculaire.
hoax[1], *s.* Mystification *f*. **To play a hoax on
s.o.,** mystifier qn.
hoax[2], *v.tr.* Mystifier, attraper. **hoaxing,**
s. Mystification *f*.
hobble[1], *s* **I.** Boitillement *m*, clochement *m*.
2. Entrave *f*.
hobble[2]. **I.** *v.i.* Boitiller, clocher, clopiner.
To hobble along, avancer clopin-clopant.
2. *v.tr.* Entraver.
hobby, *s.* (*a*) Marotte *f*, dada *m*. (*b*) Passe-
temps favori.
hobgoblin, *s.* Lutin *m*, farfadet *m*.
hobnail, *s.* Caboche *f* ; clou *m* à ferrer.
hobnailed, *a* (Soulier) ferré, à gros clous.
hobnob, *v.i.* To hobnob with s.o., être de
pair à compagnon avec qn.
hock[1], *s.* Jarret *m* (de quadrupède).
hock[2], *s.* Vin *m* du Rhin.
hockey, *s.* (Jeu *m* de) hockey *m*.
hocus-pocus, *s.* Tromperie *f*, supercherie *f*.
hod, *s.* Oiseau *m*, auge *f*, hotte *f*.
hoe[1], *s* *Hort :* Houe *f*, binette *f*.
hoe[2], *v.tr* Houer, biner (le sol) ; sarcler (les
mauvaises herbes) *F :* **A hard row to hoe,**
une tâche difficile, ingrate.
hog, *s.* **I.** Porc *m*, cochon *m*, pourceau *m*.
F : To go the whole hog, aller jusqu'au bout.
2. (*Pers.*) *F :* Goinfre *m* glouton *m* ; *F :*
pourceau.
hoggish, *a.* *F :* Glouton, grossier.
hogshead, *s.* Tonneau *m*, barrique *f*.
hoist[1], *s.* **I.** To give s.o. a hoist (up), aider

qn à monter. **2.** (*a*) Appareil *m* de levage,
treuil *m*. (*b*) Ascenseur *m*.
hoist[2], *v.tr.* To hoist (up), hisser, guinder.
hold[1], *s.* **I.** (*a*) Prise *f*, étreinte *f*. **To have
hold of sth.,** tenir qch. To take hold of sth.,
saisir, empoigner, qch. **To keep hold of
sth.,** ne pas lâcher qch. **To keep tight hold
of sth.,** tenir qch. serré. **To let go one's
hold,** lâcher prise. (*b*) To have a hold over
s.o., avoir prise sur qn. **2.** Soutien *m* ;
point *m* d'appui.
hold[2], *v.* I. *v.tr.* **I.** Tenir. **To hold sth.
tight,** serrer qch. **To hold s.o. fast,** tenir
solidement qn. **2.** **To hold oneself in
readiness,** se tenir prêt. **To hold s.o. to his
promise,** contraindre qn à tenir sa promesse.
3. **To hold one's ground,** tenir bon, tenir
ferme. **To hold one's own,** maintenir sa
position. *Tp :* **Hold the line!** ne quittez
pas ! **4.** **To hold one's head high,** porter
la tête haute. *To h. oneself upright,* se tenir
droit. **5.** (*a*) Contenir, renfermer. (*b*) *What
the future holds,* ce que l'avenir nous réserve.
6. Tenir (une séance) ; célébrer (une fête).
7. Retenir, arrêter, empêcher. (*a*) **To hold
(in) one's breath,** retenir son haleine. **There
was no holding him,** il n'y avait pas moyen
de l'arrêter. *Abs.* Hold (hard)! arrêtez !
halte là ! (*b*) *F :* **To hold water,** tenir debout.
(*c*) *Mil :* **To hold the enemy,** contenir
l'ennemi. **8.** Avoir, posséder. **9.** (*a*) **To
hold s.o. responsible,** tenir qn responsable.
(*b*) Avoir, professer (une opinion). II. **hold,**
v.i. **I.** Tenir (bon). **To hold fast,** tenir
ferme. **2.** (*a*) Durer ; continuer ; (*of
weather*) se maintenir. (*b*) **To hold on one's
way,** suivre son chemin. **3.** **To hold (good),**
être vrai, valable. *The objection holds,* cette
objection subsiste. **4.** **To hold to one's
opinion,** adhérer à son opinion. **hold back.**
I. *v.tr.* (*a*) Retenir. (*b*) Cacher, dissimuler
(la vérité). **2.** *v.i.* Rester en arrière ; hésiter.
hold down, *v.tr.* **I.** Baisser (la tête).
2. Opprimer. **hold forth,** *v.i.* Disserter,
pérorer. **hold in,** *v.tr.* **To hold oneself
in,** se contenir. **hold off. I.** *v.tr.* Tenir à
distance. **2.** *v.i.* Se tenir à distance (*from,
de*). **hold on. I.** *v.tr.* Maintenir. **2.** *v.i.*
(*a*) To hold on to sth., (i) S'accrocher à qch.
(ii) Ne pas lâcher qch. Hold on! (i) tenez
bon ! (ii) *Tp :* ne quittez pas ! (iii) (attendez)
un instant ! (*b*) *F :* Hold on (a bit)! pas si
vite ! **hold out. I.** *v.tr.* Tendre, offrir.
2. *v.i.* Durer. *To h. out to the end,* tenir
jusqu'au bout. **hold over,** *v.tr.* Remettre.
hold together *v.i.* Tenir (ensemble).
We must h. together, il faut rester unis.
F : The story won't h. together, l'histoire ne
tient pas debout. **hold up. I.** *v.tr.* (*a*) Soutenir. (*b*) Lever (en l'air). (*c*) **To hold s.o.
up as a model,** citer qn comme modèle.
To hold s.o. up to ridicule, tourner qn en
ridicule. (*d*) Arrêter ; entraver, gêner. **2.** *v.i.*
(*a*) Se soutenir. (*b*) (*Of weather*) Se maintenir.
(*c*) Ne pas tomber. **hold-up,** *s.* **I.** (*a*) Arrêt

m, embarras *m*; suspension *f*. (*b*) Panne *f*.
2. Coup à main armée. **hold with,** *v.i.* To hold with s.o., tenir pour qn. **holding,** *s.*
I. Tenue *f*. **2.** (*a*) *Agr:* Terre affermée ; **Small holdings,** lopins *m* de terre. (*b*) *Fin:* Avoir *m* (en actions).
hold³, *s. Nau:* Cale *f*.
holder, *s.* **I.** Titulaire *mf* (d'un droit) ; propriétaire *mf* (d'une terre). **Small holder,** petit propriétaire. **2.** Support *m*, monture *f*. **3.** Récipient *m*.
hole¹, *s.* Trou *m*. **I.** (*a*) Creux *m*, cavité *f*. *F:* **To find oneself in a hole,** se trouver dans l'embarras. (*b*) Terrier *m* (de lapin). (*c*) *F:* **Dead and alive hole,** petit trou mort. **2.** Orifice *m*, ouverture *f*. *Holes in a strap,* points *m* d'une courroie. **To wear a hole in a garment,** trouer un vêtement. **hole-and-corner,** *attrib.a.* Clandestin, secret.
hole², **I.** *v.tr.* (*a*) Trouer, percer. (*b*) *Golf:* **To h. the ball,** *abs.* to hole (out), poter (la balle). **2.** *v.i.* Se trouer, se percer.
holiday, *s.* (*a*) (Jour *m* de) fête *f* ; jour férié. (*b*) **To take a holiday,** prendre un congé. (*c*) **The holidays,** les vacances. **A month's holiday,** un mois de vacances. **To be on one's holidays,** (i) être en congé, en vacance(s) ; (ii) être en villégiature. **holiday-maker,** *s.*
I. Fêteur, -euse. **2.** Villégiateur *m*.
holiness, *s.* Sainteté *f*.
Holland. *Pr.n.* La Hollande.
hollow¹. **I.** *a.* **I.** Creux, caverneux, évidé. **2.** (Son) sourd. **In a hollow voice,** d'une voix caverneuse. **3.** *F:* Faux, *f* fausse ; trompeur, -euse. **II.** **hollow,** *adv.* **I.** **To sound hollow,** sonner creux. **2.** **To beat s.o. hollow,** battre qn à plate couture. **III.** **hollow,** *s.* (*a*) Creux *m* (de la main) ; cavité *f* (d'une dent) ; excavation *f*. (*b*) Enfoncement *m*. **hollow-cheeked,** *a.* Aux joues creuses. **hollow-eyed,** *a.* Aux yeux caves, enfoncés.
hollow², *v.tr.* **To hollow (out),** creuser, évider.
hollowness, *s.* **I.** Creux *m*, concavité *f*. **2.** *F:* Manque *m* de sincérité.
holly, *s. Bot:* Houx *m*.
hollyhock, *s.* Rose trémière.
holocaust, *s.* Holocauste *m*.
holster, *s.* Fonte *f* (de selle) ; étui *m* de revolver.
holy, *a.* (*a*) Saint, sacré. **The Holy Ghost,** le Saint-Esprit. **Holy water,** eau bénite. **To swear by all that is holy** jurer ses grands dieux. (*b*) Saint, pieux.
homage, *s.* Hommage *m*
home. **I.** *s.* **I.** (*a*) Chez-soi *m inv :* foyer *m*. **To have a home of one's own,** avoir un chez-soi. **To give s.o. a home,** recevoir qn chez soi. **It's a home from home,** c'est un second chez-soi. (*b*) Le chez-soi, la maison, le foyer. **At home,** à la maison, chez soi. *To stay at h.,* garder la maison. **Is Mr X at home?** M. X est-il chez lui? est-ce que

monsieur y est? *Mrs X is not at h.,* Mme X ne reçoit pas. **To feel at home with s.o.,** se sentir à l'aise avec qn. **He is at home with any topic,** tous les sujets lui sont familiers. **To make oneself at home,** faire comme chez soi. **2.** Patrie *f*; pays (natal). **3.** Asile *m*, refuge *m*. **Home for the blind,** hospice *m* d'aveugles. **II.** **home,** *adv.* **I.** A la maison ; chez soi. **To go, come, home,** rentrer (à la maison). **2.** (*a*) *The reproach went h.,* le reproche le toucha au vif ; le reproche porta (coup). **To strike home,** frapper juste ; porter coup. **To bring sth. home to s.o.,** faire sentir qch. à qn. **To bring a charge home to s.o.,** prouver une accusation contre qn. (*b*) **To screw a piece home,** visser une pièce à fond. **III.** **home,** *attrib.a.* **I.** **Home circle,** cercle de famille. **Home address,** adresse personnelle. **The Home Office,** = le Ministère de l'Intérieur. **home-coming,** *s.* Retour *m* au foyer, à la maison. **home-made,** *a.* Fait à la maison ; (pain) de ménage. **home-thrust,** *s.* *F:* Pointe *f*, critique *f*, qui va droit au but. **home-work,** *s.* *Sch:* Devoirs *mpl* du soir.
homeless, *a.* Sans foyer ; sans feu ni lieu.
homeliness, *s.* **I.** Simplicité *f* (de manières). **2.** Manque *m* de beauté.
homely, *a.* **I.** (Nourriture) simple, ordinaire ; (gens) tout à fait simples. **2.** (*Of pers.*) Sans beauté.
Homer. *Pr.n.* Homère *m*.
homesick, *a.* Qui a le mal du pays.
homesickness, *s.* Mal *m* du pays ; nostalgie *f*.
homestead, *s.* Ferme *f*.
homeward-bound, *a.* Sur le retour.
homewards, *adv.* Vers sa demeure ; vers son pays. *To hasten h.,* se presser de rentrer.
homicidal, *a.* Homicide.
homicide, *s.* Homicide *mf*.
homily, *s.* Homélie *f*. *F:* **To read s.o. a homily,** sermonner qn.
homoeopathic, *a.* (Traitement) homéopathique ; (médecin) homéopathe.
homogeneous, *a.* Homogène.
hone, *s.* Pierre *f* à aiguiser.
honest, *a.* (*a*) Honnête, probe ; loyal, -aux. (*b*) Vrai, sincère. **The honest truth,** la pure vérité. **-ly,** *adv.* (*a*) Honnêtement, loyalement. (*b*) Sincèrement.
honesty, *s.* (*a*) Honnêteté *f*, probité *f* ; intégrité *f*. (*b*) Véracité *f*, sincérité *f*.
honey, *s.* **I.** Miel *m*. **He was all honey,** il a été tout sucre et tout miel. **2.** *F:* Chéri, *f.* chérie. **honey-bee,** *s. Ent:* Abeille *f* domestique ; *F:* mouche *f* à miel.
honeycomb¹, *s.* Rayon *m* de miel.
honeycomb², *v.tr* Cribler.
honeyed, *a.* *F:* **Honeyed words,** paroles doucereuses, mielleuses.
honeymoon, *s.* Lune *f* de miel. **Honeymoon trip,** voyage *m* de noces.
honeysuckle, *s.* Chèvrefeuille *m*.
honorarium, *s.* Honoraires *mpl*.

honorary, *a.* (*a*) Honoraire; non rétribué, bénévole. (*b*) **Honorary degree,** grade honorifique.

honour[1], *s.* Honneur *m.* **1.** **The seat of honour,** la place d'honneur. **All honour to him!** honneur à lui! **2.** **To consider it an honour to do sth.,** tenir à honneur de faire qch. **3.** **To make (it) a point of honour to do sth.,** se piquer d'honneur de faire qch. **To be in honour bound to,** être obligé par l'honneur à. **He is the soul of honour,** il est l'honneur incarné. **To be on one's honour,** être engagé d'honneur. **4.** Distinction *f* honorifique. **To carry off the honours,** remporter la palme. **5.** **To do the honours,** faire les honneurs. **6.** (*a*) **To be an honour to one's country,** faire honneur à sa patrie. (*b*) **Your Honour,** Monsieur le juge.

honour[2], *v.tr.* **1.** Honorer. **2.** *Com:* **To honour a bill,** faire honneur à un effet.

honoured, *a.* Honoré.

honourable, *a.* Honorable. **-ably,** *adv.* Honorablement.

hood, *s.* **1.** *Cost:* (*a*) Capuchon *m*; capeline *f* (de femme). (*b*) Capuchon (de cobra). **2.** *Veh:* Capote *f.*

hooded, *a.* Encapuchonné.

hoodwink, *v.tr.* *F:* Tromper, donner le change à.

hoof, *s.* Sabot *m.*

hoofed, *a.* *Z:* Ongulé; à sabots.

hook[1], *s.* **1.** Crochet *m*, croc *m.* (*a*) **Hat and coat hook,** patère *f.* (*b*) *F:* **By hook or (by) crook,** d'une manière ou d'une autre. (*c*) *Cost:* Agrafe *f.* **Hook and eye,** agrafe et œillet *m.* **2.** (**Fish-)hook,** hameçon *m.* *F:* **To do sth. on one's own hook,** faire qch. pour son propre compte. **3.** *P:* **To take one's hook,** décamper; plier bagage.

hook[2], *v.tr.* Prendre (un poisson) à l'hameçon; accrocher (un poisson). **hooked,** *a.* Crochu, recourbé.

hookah, *s.* Narguilé *m.*

hooligan, *s.* Voyou *m*; gouape *f.*

hooliganism, *s.* Voyouterie *f.*

hoop, *s.* **1.** Cercle *m* (de tonneau). **2.** Cerceau *m* (d'enfant). **3.** *Croquet:* Arceau *m*, arche *f.*

hoopoe, *s.* *Orn:* Huppe *f.*

hoot[1], *s.* **1.** Ululation *f* (de hibou). **2.** (*Of pers.*) Huée *f.* **3.** Cornement *m* (de trompe d'automobile).

hoot[2]. **1.** *v.i.* (*a*) (*Of owl*) (H)ululer, huer. (*b*) (*Of pers.*) Huer. (*c*) *Aut:* Corner, klaxonner. (*d*) (*Of siren*) Mugir. **2.** *v.tr.* Huer, conspuer; siffler (une pièce de théâtre). **To hoot s.o. down,** faire taire qn (par des huées).

hooter, *s.* **1.** Sirène *f*; sifflet *m.* **2.** Trompe *f* (d'auto).

hop[1], *s.* *Bot:* Houblon *m.* **hop-field,** *s.* Houblonnière *f.* **hop-kiln,** *s.* Four *m* à houblon. **hop-picker,** *s.* Cueilleur, -euse, de houblon. **hop-picking,** *s.* Cueillette *f*

du houblon. **hop-pole,** *s.* Perche *f* à houblon.

hop[2], *s.* **1.** (*a*) Petit saut; sautillement *m.* (*b*) Saut à cloche-pied. *F:* *He went off* with a hop, skip and a jump, il s'en alla en gambadant. **To catch s.o. on the hop,** prendre qn au pied levé. **2.** *F:* Sauterie *f.*

hop[3]. **1.** *v.i.* Sauter, sautiller. **2.** *v.tr.* *P:* **To hop it,** filer; ficher le camp. **Hop-o'-my-thumb.** *Pr.n.* Le Petit Poucet.

hope[1], *s.* **1.** (*a*) Espérance *f*, espoir *m.* **To be full of h.,** avoir bon espoir. **Past all hope,** perdu sans espoir. *Geog:* **The Cape of Good Hope,** le cap de Bonne Espérance. (*b*) **To live in hope of doing sth.,** avoir l'espoir de faire qch. **2.** **My last hope,** ma dernière planche de salut. **To have hopes of sth.,** avoir qch. en vue.

hope[2]. **1.** *v.i.* Espérer. **We must hope against hope,** il faut espérer quand même. **To hope for sth.,** espérer qch. **2.** *v.tr.* I **hope you may get it!** je vous en souhaite! *Corr:* **Hoping to hear from you,** dans l'espoir de vous lire.

hopeful, *a.* **1.** Plein d'espoir. **2.** (*a*) Qui promet. (*b*) **The situation looks more hopeful,** la situation s'annonce meilleure. **-fully,** *adv.* Avec bon espoir.

hopefulness, *s.* Bon espoir; confiance *f.*

hopeless, *a.* Sans espoir; désespéré. **-ly,** *adv.* **1.** Sans espoir; avec désespoir. **2.** (Vaincu) irrémédiablement.

hopelessness, *s.* État désespéré.

hopscotch, *s.* *Games:* La marelle.

horde, *s.* Horde *f.*

horehound, *s.* *Bot:* Marrube *m.*

horizon, *s.* Horizon *m.* **On the horizon,** à l'horizon.

horizontal, *a.* Horizontal, -aux. **-ally,** *adv.* Horizontalement.

horn, *s.* **1.** (*a*) Corne *f.* **Horns of a stag,** bois *m* d'un cerf. (*b*) *Nat.Hist:* Antenne *f*; corne. *F:* **To draw in one's horns,** rentrer les cornes. (*c*) *F:* **On the horns of a dilemma,** enfermé dans un dilemme. **2.** **Horn comb,** peigne en corne. **3.** *Mus:* Cor *m.* **French horn,** cor d'harmonie. **Hunting horn,** cor, trompe *f* de chasse. **Coach horn,** buccin *m* de mail-coach. **4.** *Aut:* Trompe. **horn-rimmed,** *a.* (Lunettes) à monture en corne.

hornbeam, *s.* *Bot:* Charme *m.*

hornbill, *s.* *Orn:* Calao *m.*

horned, *a.* A cornes, cornu.

hornet, *s.* *Ent:* Frelon *m.*

hornpipe, *s.* *Danc:* Matelote *f.*

horny, *a.* (*a*) Corné; en corne. (*b*) (*Of hand*) Calleux.

horoscope, *s.* Horoscope *m.*

horrible, *a.* Horrible, affreux. **-ibly,** *adv.* Horriblement, affreusement.

horrid, *a.* **1.** Horrible, affreux. **2.** *F:* **To be horrid to s.o.,** être méchant envers qn.

horrify, *v.tr.* (*a*) Horrifier; faire horreur à. (*b*) *F:* Scandaliser.

horror, *s.* **1.** Horreur *f.* To have a horror of sth., avoir horreur de qch. **2.** (*a*) Chose horrible, affreuse; horreur. (*b*) *F:* It gives me the horrors, cela me donne le frisson. **horror-struck,** *a.* Saisi d'horreur.

horse, *s.* **1.** Cheval *m*, -aux. (*a*) To mount, get on, a horse, monter, enfourcher, un cheval. *F:* To get on one's high horse, monter sur ses grands chevaux. (*b*) *Nau:* White horses, moutons *m.* **2.** *Coll. Mil:* Cavalerie *f*; troupes montées. Light horse, cavalerie légère. **horse-artillery,** *s.* Artillerie montée. **horse-chestnut,** *s.* **1.** Marron *m* d'Inde. **2.** (*Tree*) Marronnier *m* d'Inde. **horse-dealer,** *s.* Maquignon *m.* **horse-drawn,** *a.* (Véhicule) hippomobile. **Horse Guards,** *s.pl.* The (Royal) Horse Guards, la Garde du corps (à cheval). **horse-laugh,** *s.* Gros rire bruyant. **horse-play,** *s.* Jeu brutal, jeu de main(s). **horse-pond,** *s.* Abreuvoir *m.* **horse-power,** *s.* *Meas:* Cheval-vapeur *m*, *pl.* chevaux-vapeur. A forty horse-power car, une automobile de quarante chevaux; *F:* une quarante chevaux. **horse-race,** *s.* Course *f* de chevaux. **horse-racing,** *s.* Hippisme *m*; courses *fpl* de chevaux. **horse-radish,** *s.* *Bot:* Raifort *m.* **horse-show,** *s.* Exposition chevaline; concours *m* hippique.

horseback, *s.* On horseback, à (dos de) cheval.

horsehair, *s.* Crin *m.*

horseman, *s.* Cavalier *m*, écuyer *m.*

horsemanship, *s.* Équitation *f.*

horseshoe, *s.* Fer *m* à cheval.

horsewhip[1]**,** *s.* Cravache *f.*

horsewhip[2]**,** *v.tr.* Cravacher, sangler. **horse-whipping,** *s.* Cravachée *f.*

horsewoman, *s.* Amazone *f*, cavalière *f*, écuyère *f.*

horticulture, *s.* Horticulture *f.*

hose, *s.* **1.** *Com:* Bas *mpl.* **2.** Manche *f* à eau; tuyau *m.*

hosier, *s.* Bonnetier, -ière.

hosiery, *s.* Bonneterie *f.*

hospitable, *a.* Hospitalier. **-ably,** *adv.* Hospitalièrement.

hospital, *s.* Hôpital *m*, -aux. Hospital nurse, infirmière *f.* Hospital train, train sanitaire. Hospital ship, vaisseau hôpital.

hospitality, *s.* Hospitalité *f.*

host[1]**,** *s.* *F:* A (whole) host, (toute) une foule, (toute) une armée.

host[2]**,** *s.* (*a*) Hôte *m.* (*b*) Hôtelier *m*, aubergiste *m.*

hostage, *s.* Otage *m.*

hostel, *s.* (*a*) Pension *f*, foyer *m.* (*b*) Youth hostels, auberges *f* de la jeunesse.

hostess, *s.* (*a*) Hôtesse *f.* (*b*) Hôtelière *f*, aubergiste *f.*

hostile, *a.* (*a*) Hostile, adverse, ennemi. (*b*) Hostile, opposé (*to*, à); ennemi (*to*, de).

hostility, *s.* **1.** Hostilité *f* (*to*, contre); animosité *f.* **2.** *pl.* Hostilities, hostilités.

hot, *a.* **1.** (*a*) Chaud. Boiling hot, (tout) bouillant. To be very hot, (*of thg*) être très chaud; (*of pers.*) avoir très chaud; (*of weather*) faire très chaud. *F:* To get into hot water, se créer des ennuis. It was hot work, on s'y échauffait. (*b*) Brûlant, cuisant. (*c*) (Moutarde) piquante; (assaisonnement) épicé. **2.** To be hot on the scent, être sur la bonne piste. *Games:* You are getting hot, tu brûles. **3.** (*a*) Violent. To have a hot temper, s'emporter facilement. (*b*) Acharné. Hot contest, chaude dispute. To be in hot pursuit of s.o., presser qn de près. *Adv.phr.* They went at it hot and strong, ils y allaient avec acharnement. *Turf:* Hot favourite, grand favori. **4.** *F:* To make things too hot for s.o., rendre la vie intolérable à qn. To give it s.o. hot, laver la tête à qn. We are going to have a hot time, ça va chauffer. **-ly,** *adv.* **1.** (Répondre) vivement, avec chaleur. **2.** (Poursuivi) avec acharnement. **hot-blooded,** *a.* Emporté, ardent, passionné. **hot-foot,** *adv.* À toute vitesse, en (toute) hâte. **hot-head,** *s.* Tête chaude; impétueux *m.* **hot-headed,** *a.* **1.** Exalté, impétueux. **2.** Emporté, violent. **hot-tempered,** *a.* Colérique; emporté, vif. **hot-water bottle,** *s.* Bouillotte *f.*

hotbed, *s.* *F:* Hotbed of corruption, foyer *m* de corruption.

hotchpotch, *s.* *F:* Mélange confus.

hotel, *s.* Hôtel *m* (pour voyageurs). Private hotel, hôtel de famille. Residential hotel, pension *f* de famille. **Hotel-keeper,** hôtelier, -ière.

hothouse, *s.* Serre chaude.

hound[1]**,** *s.* Chien *m* de meute, chien courant. The (pack of) hounds, la meute. Master of hounds, maître d'équipage. To ride to hounds, chasser à courre. *F:* You miserable hound! misérable!

hound[2]**,** *v.tr.* To hound s.o. down, poursuivre qn avec acharnement.

hour, *s.* Heure *f.* **1.** An hour and a half, une heure et demie. Half an hour, une demi-heure. A quarter of an hour, un quart d'heure. Hour by hour, d'une heure à l'autre. To pay s.o. by the hour, payer qn à l'heure. Five miles an hour, cinq milles à l'heure. Office hours, heures de bureau. After hours, après l'heure de fermeture. **2.** (*a*) In the hour of need, à l'heure du besoin. The hour has come, le moment est venu; il est l'heure. (*b*) In the small hours (of the morning), fort avant dans la nuit. **hour-glass,** *s.* Sablier *m.* **hour-hand,** *s.* Petite aiguille.

hourly. **1.** *a.* (*a*) De toutes les heures; à chaque heure. (*b*) (Rendement) à l'heure. (*c*) De chaque instant. **2.** *adv.* Toutes les heures; d'heure en heure.

house[1]**,** *s.* **1.** Maison *f*, logis *m*, demeure *f.* Town house, hôtel (particulier). Country house, château *m*; maison de campagne. *Small h.*, maisonnette *f.* At, to, in, my house, chez moi. **To keep house for s.o.,** tenir le ménage de qn. **To set up house,** se mettre en ménage. *Attrib:* House work, travaux domestiques, de ménage. **2.** (*a*) **The House of Commons,** la Chambre des Communes. (*b*) **Business house,** maison de commerce. **3. The House of Bourbon,** les Bourbons *m*, la Maison des Bourbons. **4.** *Th:* Auditoire *m*, assistance *f*. **A good house,** une salle pleine. **house-agent,** *s.* Agent *m* de location. **house-dog,** *s.* Chien de garde. **house-fly,** *s.* Mouche *f* domestique. **house-property,** *s.* Immeubles *mpl.* **house-room,** *s.* Place *f*; logement *m.* **house-surgeon,** *s.* Interne *m* en chirurgie. **house-top,** *s.* Toit *m.* **house-warming,** *s.* **To have a house-warming,** pendre la crémaillère.

house², *v.tr.* Loger, héberger. **housing,** *s.* Logement *m.* **The housing problem,** la crise du logement.

housebreaker, *s.* Cambrioleur *m.*

housebreaking, *s.* Cambriolage *m.*

houseful, *s.* Maisonnée *f*; pleine maison.

household, *s.* **1.** (Membres *mpl* de) la maison; le ménage; la famille. **Household expenses,** frais de ménage. **Household word,** mot d'usage courant. **2.** Les domestiques.

householder, *s* Chef *m* de famille, de maison.

housekeeper, *s.* **1.** Concierge *mf.* **2.** Femme *f* de charge. **3.** *My wife is a good h.,* ma femme est bonne ménagère.

housekeeping, *s.* **1.** Le ménage. **2.** Économie *f* domestique; les soins *m* du ménage.

housemaid, *s.* Bonne *f*; femme *f* de chambre.

housewife. 1. *s.* Maîtresse *f* de maison; ménagère *f.* **2.** *s.* Trousse *f* de couture; nécessaire *m* à ouvrage.

hovel, *s.* Taudis *m*, bouge *m*, masure *f.*

hover, *v.i.* Planer. *F:* **A smile hovered over her lips,** un sourire errait sur ses lèvres.

how, *adv.* **1.** Comment. **How are you?** comment allez-vous? **How is it that?** comment se fait-il que? **How so? how's that?** comment ça? *I see how it is,* je vois ce qui en est. **To learn how to do sth.,** apprendre à faire qch. **2.** (*a*) **How much, how many,** combien (de). *You see how little he cares,* vous voyez combien peu il s'en soucie. *You can imagine how angry I was,* songez si j'étais furieux! *How long is this room?* quelle est la longueur de cette pièce? **How old are you?** quel âge avez-vous? (*b*) *How pretty she is!* comme elle est jolie! qu'elle est jolie! **How I wish I could!** si seulement je pouvais!

however, *adv.* **1.** (*a*) **However he may do it,** de quelque manière qu'il le fasse. **However that may be,** quoi qu'il en soit. (*b*) *H. good his work is,* quelque excellent que soit son ouvrage. **However little,** si peu que ce soit. **2.** Toutefois, cependant, pourtant.

howitzer, *s.* *Artil:* Obusier *m.*

howl¹, *s.* (*a*) Hurlement *m*; mugissement *m.* (*b*) Huée *f.*

howl², *v.i. & tr.* Hurler; pousser des hurlements; (*of wind*) mugir. **howling,** *s.* Hurlement *m*; mugissement *m.*

howler, *s.* *F:* Grosse gaffe, bourde *f* énorme.

howsoever, *adv.* = HOWEVER 1.

hub, *s.* **1.** Moyeu *m.* **2.** *F:* Centre *m* d'activité.

hubbub, *s.* Remue-ménage *m*, vacarme *m*, tohu-bohu *m.* *H. of voices,* brouhaha *m* de voix.

huddle, *v.tr. & i.* **1.** Entasser pêle-mêle, sans ordre. **To h. together,** se tasser; se serrer les uns contre les autres. **2.** *Huddled* (*up*) *in bed,* couché en chien de fusil. *Huddled* (*up*) *in a corner,* blotti dans un coin.

hue¹, *s.* Teinte *f*, nuance *f.*

hue² and cry, *s.* Clameur *f* de haro. **To raise a hue and cry against s.o.,** crier haro sur qn.

huff¹, *s.* **1. To be in a huff,** être froissé. **To take (the) huff,** s'offusquer; prendre la mouche. **2.** *Draughts:* Soufflage *m.*

huff², *v.tr.* (*a*) Froisser. (*b*) *Draughts:* Souffler.

huffiness, *s.* **1.** Susceptibilité *f.* **2.** Mauvaise humeur.

huffy, *a.* **1.** Susceptible. **2.** Fâché, vexé. **-ily,** *adv.* Avec (mauvaise) humeur.

hug¹, *s.* Étreinte *f.* **To give s.o. a hug,** étreindre qn.

hug², *v.tr.* **1.** (*a*) Étreindre, embrasser. (*b*) (*Of bear*) Étouffer, enserrer. (*c*) Chérir (ses défauts). **2.** *Nau:* **To hug the shore,** serrer la terre.

huge, *a.* Énorme, vaste; (succès) immense, *F:* formidable. **-ly,** *adv.* Énormément; immensément.

hulk, *s.* **1.** *Nau:* Carcasse *f* de navire; ponton *m.* **2.** *F:* (*Of pers.*) Gros pataud.

hulking, *a.* Gros, lourd.

hull, *s.* **1.** Cosse *f*, gousse *f* (de pois); coquille *f*, écale *f* (de noix). **2.** Coque *f* (de navire). *Nau:* **Hull down,** coque noyée.

hullabaloo, *s.* Tintamarre *m*, vacarme *m.*

hullo(a), *int.* (*a*) Ohé! holà! **Hullo you!** hé, là-bas! (*b*) *H., old chap!* tiens, c'est toi, mon vieux! (*c*) **Hullo everybody!** salut à tous! (*d*) *Tp:* Allô!

hum¹, *s.* Bourdonnement *m*; ronflement *m* (de machine); ronron *m* (d'un moteur). *Hum of conversation,* brouhaha *m* de conversation.

hum², *v.* **1.** *v.i.* (*Of insect*) Bourdonner; (*of top*) ronfler. *F:* **To make things hum,** faire marcher rondement les choses. **2.** *v.tr.* Fredonner. **humming-bird,** *s.* Oiseau-mouche *m*, pl. oiseaux-mouches; colibri *m.*

human. 1. *a.* Humain. **Human nature,** la nature humaine. **2.** *s.* Être humain. **-ly,** *adv.* **Humanly speaking,** humainement parlant.

humane, *a.* (*a*) Humain, compatissant. (*b*)

Clément. **-ly,** *adv.* Humainement; avec humanité.

humanitarian, *a. & s.* Humanitaire (*mf*).

humanity, *s.* Humanité *f.* **1.** (*a*) Nature humaine. (*b*) Le genre humain. **2. To treat s.o. with humanity,** traiter qn avec humanité.

humble¹, *a.* Humble. **1.** In my humb e opinion, à mon humble avis. **2.** Modeste. **-bly,** *adv.* **1.** Humblement, avec humilité. **2.** (*Vivre*) modestement.

humble², *v.tr.* Humilier, mortifier. **To humble oneself,** s'abaisser.

humble-bee, *s. Ent:* Bourdon *m.*

humbug¹, *s.* **1.** Charlatanisme *m*; *F:* blagues *fpl.* (That's all) humbug! tout cela c'est de la blague! **2.** (*a*) Charlatan *m*; blagueur *m.* (*b*) Enjôleur, -euse.

humbug², *v.tr.* Conter des blagues à; enjôler.

humdrum, *a.* Monotone; peu intéressant, ennuyeux.

humid, *a.* Humide.

humidity, *s.* Humidité *f.*

humiliate, *v.tr.* Humilier, mortifier.

humiliation, *s.* Humiliation *f,* affront *m,* mortification *f.*

humility, *s.* Humilité *f.* **With all humility,** en toute humilité.

humorist, *s.* **1.** Farceur *m,* plaisant *m.* **2.** (*At concert*) Comique *m.* **3.** Écrivain *m* humoristique.

humorous, *a.* Plein d'humour; drôle; (*of writer*) humoriste.

humour¹, *s.* **1.** Humeur *f,* disposition *f.* **To be in the humour to do sth.,** être en humeur de faire qch. **To be in a good humour,** être de bonne humeur. **2.** (*a*) Humour *m.* (*b*) The humour of the situation, le comique de la situation.

humour², *v.tr.* To humour s.o., ménager qn.

hump¹, *s.* **1.** Bosse *f.* **2.** *F:* To have the hump, avoir le cafard; broyer du noir.

hump², *v.tr.* To hump the back, arquer, bomber, le dos. **humped,** *a.* Bossu.

humpback, *s.* Bossu, -ue.

humpbacked, *a.* Bossu.

hunch¹, *s.* Gros morceau. **Hunch of bread,** quignon *m* de pain.

hunch², *v.tr.* Arrondir (le dos); voûter (les épaules).

hunchback, *s.* = HUMPBACK.

hundred, *num. a. & s.* Cent (*m*). *About a h. houses,* une centaine de maisons. *Two h. apples,* deux cents pommes. *Two h. and one pounds,* deux cent une livres. **In nineteen hundred,** en dix-neuf cent. *To live to be a h.,* atteindre la centaine.

hundredfold. **1.** *a.* Centuple. **2.** *adv.phr.* A hundredfold, cent fois autant.

Hungarian, *a. & s.* Hongrois, -oise.

Hungary. *Pr.n. Geog:* La Hongrie.

hunger¹, *s.* Faim *f.* **Hunger is the best sauce,** il n'est sauce que d'appétit. **hunger-strike,** *s.* Grève *f* de la faim

hunger², *v.i.* (*a*) Avoir faim. (*b*) To hunger after sth., être affamé de qch.; désirer ardemment qch. **hungering,** *s.* Faim *f (after,* de).

hungry, *a.* **1.** Affamé. **To be hungry,** avoir faim. **To go hungry,** souffrir de la faim. **To look hungry,** avoir l'air famélique. **2.** (*Regard*) avide. **-ily,** *adv.* Avidement, voracement; d'un œil avide.

hunk, *s.* = HUNCH¹.

hunt¹, *s.* **1.** (*a*) Chasse *f.* (*b*) Équipage *m* de chasse. **2.** Recherche *f.*

hunt². **1.** *v.i.* (*a*) *Ven:* Chasser à courre. (*b*) To hunt for sth., chercher qch. **2.** *v.tr.* (*a*) Chasser. (*b*) To hunt a thief, poursuivre un voleur. **hunt down,** *v.tr.* Traquer; *F:* mettre aux abois. **hunt out,** *v.tr.* *F:* Déterrer, dénicher. **hunt up,** *v.tr.* Déterrer (des faits). **hunting,** *s.* Chasse *f* (à courre). **hunting-box,** *s.* Pavillon *m* de chasse. **hunting-horn,** *s.* Cor *m* de chasse. **hunt-the-slipper,** *s.* *Games:* Jeu *m* du furet.

hunter, *s.* **1.** Chasseur *m.* **2.** Cheval *m* de chasse.

huntsman, *s.* **1.** Chasseur *m* (à courre). **2.** Veneur *m,* piqueur *m.*

hurdle, *s.* **1.** Claie *f.* **2.** *Sp:* Barrière *f.*

hurl, *v.tr.* Lancer avec violence (*at,* contre). **To hurl oneself at s.o.,** se ruer sur qn. *F:* **To hurl reproaches at s.o.,** accabler qn de reproches.

hurly-burly, *s.* Tohu-bohu *m.*

hurrah¹, *int. & s.* Hourra (*m*).

hurrah², *v.i.* Pousser un hourra, des hourras.

hurricane, *s.* Ouragan *m*; *Nau:* tempête *f.*

hurry¹, *s.* Hâte *f,* précipitation *f.* **To be in a hurry,** être pressé. *F: I shan't do it again in a h.,* on ne m'y reprendra pas de sitôt.

hurry². **1.** *v.tr.* Hâter, presser. **2.** *v.i.* (*a*) Se hâter, se presser; se dépêcher. (*b*) Presser le pas. *To h. to a place,* se rendre en toute hâte à un endroit. **hurry away,** *v.i.* Partir précipitamment. *I must h. away,* il faut que je me sauve. **hurry on.** **1.** *v.tr.* Activer, pousser (la besogne). **2.** *v.i.* Presser le pas; continuer sa route à vive allure. **hurry up,** *v.i.* *F:* Se dépêcher, se hâter.

hurried, *a.* Pressé, précipité; fait à la hâte. **-ly,** *adv.* A la hâte, en toute hâte; précipitamment.

hurt¹, *s.* Mal *m.* **1.** Blessure *f.* **2.** Tort *m,* dommage *m.*

hurt², *v.tr.* **1.** Faire (du) mal à, blesser. *To h. one's foot,* se blesser au pied. **2.** Faire de la peine à. **To hurt s.o.'s feelings,** blesser, peiner, qn. **3.** Nuire à.

hurtful, *a.* **1.** (*a*) Nuisible, nocif. (*b*) Préjudiciable (*to,* à). **2.** Hurtful to the feelings, froissant, blessant.

hurtle, *v.i.* Se précipiter, s'élancer.

husband¹, *s.* Mari *m,* époux *m.* *H. and wife,* les (deux) époux.

husband², *v.tr.* Ménager économiser.

husbandman, *s.* **I.** Cultivateur *m.* **2.** Laboureur *m.*

hush[1]**,** *s.* Silence *m*, calme *m.*

hush[2]**. I.** *v.tr.* Apaiser, faire taire; imposer silence à. **2.** *v.i.* Se taire; faire silence. **hush up,** *v.tr.* Étouffer (un scandale).

hush[3]**,** *int.* Chut l silence l **hush-hush,** *a.* *F:* Secret, -ète.

husk, *s.* Cosse *f*, gousse *f* (de pois, etc.); brou *m*, écale *f* (de noix). **Rice in the husk,** riz non décortiqué.

huskiness, *s.* Enrouement *m*, empâtement *m.*

husky[1]**,** *a.* **Husky voice,** (i) voix enrouée, voilée; (ii) voix altérée.

husky[2]**,** *s.* Chien *m* esquimau.

hussar, *s.* *Mil:* Hussard *m.*

hussy, *s.* *F:* **I.** Coquine *f*, friponne *f.* **2.** Drôlesse *f*, garce *f.*

hustle. I. *v.tr.* Bousculer; pousser, presser. **To hustle things on,** pousser le travail. **2.** *v.i.* Se dépêcher, se presser.

hut, *s.* Hutte *f*, cabane *f.*

hutch, *s.* **I.** Coffre *m*, huche *f.* **2.** (Rabbit-) **hutch,** clapier *m.*

hyacinth, *s.* *Bot:* Jacinthe *f.*

hybrid, *a. & s.* *Biol:* Hybride (*m*).

hydrant, *s.* Prise *f* d'eau; bouche *f* d'eau.

hydrate, *s.* *Ch:* Hydrate *m.*

hydraulic, *a.* Hydraulique.

hydro, *s.* *F:* = HYDROPATHIC 2.

hydrochloric, *a.* *Ch:* Chlorhydrique.

hydrocyanic, *a.* *Ch:* Cyanhydrique.

hydro-electric, *a.* Hydroélectrique.

hydrogen, *s.* *Ch:* Hydrogène *m.*

hydrographic(al), *a.* Hydrographique.

hydrography, *s.* Hydrographie *f.*

hydropathic. *Med:* **I.** *a.* (*a*) Hydro-
thérapique. (*b*) (Médecin) hydropathe. **2.** *s.* Établissement *m* thermal.

hydrophobia, *s.* *Med:* Hydrophobie *f*; *F:* la rage.

hydroplane, *s.* *Av:* Hydravion *m.*

hydrostatics, *s.pl.* Hydrostatique *f.*

hyena, *s.* *Z:* Hyène *f.*

hygiene, *s.* Hygiène *f.*

hygienic, *a.* Hygiénique. **-ally,** *adv.* Hygiéniquement.

hymn, *s.* *Ecc:* Hymne *f*, cantique *m.*

hyperbola, *s.* *Geom:* Hyperbole *f.*

hyperbole, *s.* *Rh:* Hyperbole *f.*

hyperbolic(al), *a.* Hyperbolique.

hyphen, *s.* Trait *m* d'union.

hyphenate, *v.tr.* Mettre un trait d'union à.

hypnotic, *a.* Hypnotique.

hypnotism, *s.* Hypnotisme *m.*

hypnotist, *s.* Hypnotiste *mf.*

hypnotize, *v.tr.* Hypnotiser.

hypochondria, *s.* Hypocondrie *f.*

hypochondriac, *a. & s.* Hypocondriaque (*mf*); *s.* hypocondre *mf.*

hypocrisy, *s.* Hypocrisie *f.*

hypocrite, *s.* Hypocrite *mf.*

hypocritical, *a.* Hypocrite. **-ally,** *adv.* Hypocritement.

hypodermic, *a.* *Med:* Hypodermique.

hypotenuse, *s.* *Geom:* Hypoténuse *f.*

hypothesis, *s.* Hypothèse *f.*

hypothetic(al), *a.* Hypothétique, supposé. **-ally,** *adv.* Par hypothèse.

hysteria, *s.* *Med:* Hystérie *f.*

hysterical, *a.* **I.** *Med:* Hystérique. **2.** (*a*) Sujet à des attaques de nerfs. (*b*) **To become hysterical,** avoir une attaque de nerfs. **-ally,** *adv.* **To weep h.,** avoir une crise de larmes. **To laugh h.,** rire nerveusement.

hysterics, *s.pl.* Attaque *f* de nerfs; crise *f* de nerfs.

I

I[1]**, i,** *s.* (La lettre) I, i *m.*

I[2]**,** *pers. pron.* (*a*) Je, j'. **I sing,** je chante. **I accuse,** j'accuse. **Here I am,** me voici. (*b*) Moi *mf.* **It is I,** c'est moi.

iambic. *Pros:* **I.** *a.* Iambique. **2.** *s.* Vers *m* ïambique; ïambe *m.*

ibex, *s.* *Z:* Bouquetin *m*, ibex *m.*

ibis, *s.* *Orn:* Ibis *m.*

ice[1]**,** *s.* Glace *f.* **I. The ice age,** la période glaciaire. **My feet are like ice,** j'ai les pieds glacés. *F:* **To break the ice,** rompre la glace. *F:* **To skate over thin ice,** toucher à un sujet délicat. **2.** *Cu:* **Strawberry ice,** glace à la fraise. **ice-axe,** *s.* Piolet *m.* **ice-bound,** *a.* (i) Retenu par les glaces; (ii) (port) fermé par les glaces. **ice-cream,** *s.* *Cu:*
(Crème *f* à la) glace. **ice-field,** *s.* Champ *m* de glace. **ice-floe,** *s.* Banquise *f*; banc *m* de glace. **ice-pudding,** *s.* *Cu:* Bombe glacée.

ice[2]**,** *v.tr.* **I.** Congeler, geler. **2.** Rafraîchir avec de la glace; frapper. **3.** Glacer (un gâteau).

iceberg, *s.* Iceberg *m*; montagne *f* de glace.

Iceland. *Pr.n.* *Geog:* L'Islande *f.*

Icelander, *s.* Islandais, -aise.

Icelandic. I. *a.* Islandais; d'Islande. **2.** *s.* *Ling:* L'islandais *m.*

icicle, *s.* Petit glaçon; chandelle *f* de glace.

iciness, *s.* **I.** Froid glacial. **2.** Froideur glaciale (d'un accueil).

icon, *s.* *Ecc:* Icone *f.*

iconoclast, *s.* Iconoclaste *mf.*

icy, *a.* **1.** Couvert de glace; glacial, -als. **2.** Glacial. **Icy hands,** mains glacées. **-ily,** *adv.* D'un air glacial.

idea, *s.* Idée *f.* **What a funny idea!** quelle drôle d'idée! *To give a general i. of a book,* donner un aperçu d'un livre. **I have an idea that,** j'ai idée que. **To get ideas into one's head,** se faire des idées. *F:* **The idea!** quelle idée! par exemple!

ideal. **1.** *a.* Idéal, -aux. *F:* **It is ideal!** c'est le rêve! **2.** *s.* Idéal *m,* -aux, -als. **-ally,** *adv.* Idéalement.

idealist, *s.* Idéaliste *mf.*

idealize, *v.tr.* Idéaliser.

identical, *a.* Identique (*with,* à). **-ally,** *adv.* Identiquement.

identification, *s.* Identification *f.* **Identification papers,** carte *f* d'identité.

identify, *v.tr.* **1.** Identifier (*sth. with sth.,* qch. avec qch.). **2.** To identify s.o., constater, établir, l'identité de qn.

identity, *s.* Identité *f.* **Identity card,** carte *f* d'identité. **Mistaken identity,** erreur *f* sur la personne.

idiocy, *s.* Idiotie *f.*

idiom, *s.* **1.** (*a*) Dialecte *m;* idiome *m* (d'une région). (*b*) Langue *f,* idiome (d'un pays). **2.** Idiotisme *m,* locution *f.*

idiomatic(al), *a.* **1.** Idiomatique. *I. phrase,* idiotisme *m.* **2.** Qui appartient à la langue courante. **-ally,** *adv.* D'une façon idiomatique.

idiosyncrasy, *s.* **1.** Idiosyncrasie *f.* **2.** *F:* Petite manie; particularité *f.*

idiot, *s.* (*a*) *Med:* Idiot, -ote. **The village idiot,** l'innocent *m* du village. (*b*) *F:* Imbécile *mf.* **You idiot!** espèce d'imbécile.

idiotic, *a.* *F:* Bête. *That's i.,* c'est stupide. **-ally,** *adv.* Bêtement.

idle¹, *a.* **1.** (*a*) Inoccupé, oisif. (*b*) (*Of machinery*) Qui chôme, en chômage. *Capital lying i.,* fonds dormants. **2.** Paresseux, fainéant. **The idle rich,** les riches désœuvrés. **3.** Inutile, oiseux, futile. *I. threats,* menaces en l'air. **Out of idle curiosity,** par curiosité désœuvrée. **idly,** *adv.* **1.** Sans travailler. *To stand i. by,* rester là à ne rien faire. **2.** Inutilement; (parler) en l'air. **3.** Paresseusement.

idle², *v.i.* Fainéanter; paresser. *v.tr.* To idle one's time away, perdre son temps à ne rien faire.

idleness, *s.* **1.** (*a*) Oisiveté *f,* désœuvrement *m.* (*b*) Chômage *m.* **2.** Futilité *f.* **3.** Paresse *f,* fainéantise *f.* **To live in idleness,** vivre dans l'oisiveté.

idler, *s.* (*a*) Oisif, -ive; désœuvré, -ée; flâneur, -euse. (*b*) Fainéant, -ante; paresseux, -euse.

idol, *s.* Idole *f.*

idolatrous, *a.* Idolâtre.

idolatry, *s.* Idolâtrie *f.*

idolize, *v.tr.* Idolâtrer, adorer.

idyll, *s.* Idylle *f.*

idyllic, *a.* Idyllique.

if, *conj.* Si. **1.** (*a*) *If I wanted him, I rang,* si j'avais besoin de lui, je sonnais. (*b*) *If he does it, he will be punished,* s'il le fait, il sera puni. *If it is fine, and (if it is) not too windy,* s'il fait beau et qu'il ne fasse pas trop de vent. *If they are to be believed,* à les en croire. *If you hesitate (at all),* pour peu que vous hésitiez. **It (it be) so,** s'il en est ainsi. *If the water was warm, if anything,* l'eau était plutôt tiède. *He will give you a shilling for it, if that,* il vous en donnera un shilling, et encore! **If not,** sinon; si ce n'est. *Go and see him, if only to please me,* allez le voir, ne fût-ce, ne serait-ce, que pour me faire plaisir. (*c*) **Even if he did say so,** quand même il l'aurait dit. (*d*) *If only he comes in time!* pourvu qu'il vienne à temps! (*e*) **As if,** comme si; comme. **As if by chance,** comme par hasard. **2.** *F:* *Pleasant weather, if rather cold,* temps agréable, bien qu'un peu froid. **3.** *Do you know if he is at home?* savez-vous s'il est chez lui?

igloo, *s.* Hutte *f* d'Esquimau; igloo *m.*

ignite. **1.** *v.tr.* Mettre le feu à; enflammer. **2.** *v.i.* Prendre feu; s'enflammer.

ignition, *s.* **1.** Ignition *f,* inflammation *f.* **2.** *I.C.E:* Allumage *m.*

ignoble, *a.* Ignoble; infâme, vil, indigne.

ignominious, *a.* Ignominieux; honteux. **-ly,** *adv.* Ignominieusement; avec ignominie.

ignominy, *s.* Ignominie *f,* honte *f.*

ignoramus, *s.* Ignorant, -ante; ignare *mf.*

ignorance, *s.* Ignorance *f.* **To keep s.o. in ignorance of sth.,** laisser ignorer qch. à qn.

ignorant, *a.* (*a*) Ignorant. **To be ignorant of a fact,** ignorer un fait. (*b*) *An i. question,* une question qui trahit l'ignorance.

ignore, *v.tr.* Ne tenir aucun compte de; passer sous silence. **To ignore s.o.,** ne pas vouloir reconnaître qn. **To ignore the facts,** méconnaître les faits. *To i. a prohibition,* passer outre à une interdiction.

iguana, *s.* *Rept:* Iguane *m.*

ill. **I.** *a.* **1.** (*a*) Mauvais. **Ill effects,** effets pernicieux. **To do s.o. an ill turn,** desservir qn. (*b*) Méchant, mauvais. *Ill deed,* mauvaise action. **2.** Malade, souffrant. **II. ill,** *s.* **1.** Mal *m.* **To speak ill of s.o.,** dire du mal de qn. **2.** Dommage *m,* tort *m.* **III. ill,** *adv.* Mal. **1.** To take sth. ill, prendre qch. en mauvaise part. **It will go ill with them,** il leur en cuira. **2.** *I can ill afford the expense,* je peux difficilement supporter cette dépense. **It ill becomes you to,** il vous sied mal. **3. To be ill at ease,** (i) être mal à l'aise; (ii) être inquiet. **ill-advised,** *a.* **1.** Malavisé. **2.** (*Of action*) Peu judicieux. **illassorted,** *a.* Mal assorti; disparate. **ill-bred,** *a.* Mal élevé. **ill-breeding,** *s.* Manque *m* de savoir-vivre. **ill-considered,** *a.* Peu réfléchi. **ill-deserved,** *a.* Peu mérité. **ill-disposed,** *a.* Malintentionné, malveillant. **ill-fated,** *a.* Infortuné. **ill-favoured,** *a.* Laid; de mauvaise mine. **ill-feeling,** *s.* Ressentiment *m,* rancune *f.* *F:* **No ill-feeling!** sans rancune! **ill-founded,** *a.* Mal fondé. **ill-health,** *s.* Mauvaise santé. **ill-humoured,** *a.* De mauvaise humeur; maussade, grincheux, **ill-informed,** *a.* **1.** Mal renseigné. **2.** Peu instruit. **ill-judged,** *a.* Malavisé. **ill(-)luck,** *s.* Mauvaise fortune; *F:* guigne *f.* By ill-luck, par malheur. **ill-mannered,** *a.* Malhonnête, grossier. **ill-natured,** *a.* Méchant; désagréable. **-ly,** *adv.* Méchamment. **ill-omened,** *a.* De mauvais présage. **ill-pleased,** *a.* Mécontent. **ill(-)temper,** *s.* Mauvais caractère. **ill-tempered,** *a.* De mauvais caractère; maussade. **ill-timed,** *a.* Mal à propos. *Ill-t. arrival,* arrivée inopportune. **ill-treat,** *v.tr.* Maltraiter, brutaliser. **ill-treatment, ill-usage,** *s.* Mauvais traitements. **ill-use,** *v.tr.* Maltraiter; malmener. **ill-will,** *s.* Mauvais vouloir; malveillance *f,* rancune*f.*

illegal, *a.* Illégal, -aux. **-ally,** *adv.* Illégalement.

illegality, *s.* Illégalité *f.*

illegible, *a.* Illisible. **-ibly,** *adv.* Illisiblement.

illegitimate, *a.* Illégitime.

illicit, *a.* Illicite.

illiteracy, *s.* Manque *m* d'instruction.

illiterate, *a. & s.* Illettré, -ée.

illness, *s.* Maladie *f.*

illogical, *a.* Illogique; peu logique. **-ally,** *adv.* Illogiquement.

illuminate, *v.tr.* Éclairer.

illumination, *s.* **1.** Éclairage *m.* **2.** To go out and see the illuminations, sortir voir les illuminations.

illusion, *s.* Illusion *f;* tromperie *f.* To be under an illusion, être le jouet d'une illusion.

illusive, *a.* Illusoire, trompeur, mensonger.

illusory, *a.* Illusoire; sans effet.

illustrate, *v.tr.* **1.** Éclairer, expliquer. **2.** Illustrer; orner de gravures.

illustration, *s.* **1.** Explication *f,* exemple *m.* **2.** Illustration *f,* gravure *f,* image *f.*

illustrative, *a.* Qui sert à éclaircir ou à expliquer.

illustrious, *a.* Illustre, célèbre.

image, *s.* Image *f.* **1.** Image sculptée; représentation *f* (d'un dieu); idole *f.* **2. He is the living image of his father,** c'est le portrait vivant de son père.

imaginable, *a.* Imaginable.

imaginary, *a.* Imaginaire.

imagination, *s.* Imagination *f.* *F:* **It's your imagination!** vous l'avez rêvé!

imaginative, *a.* Imaginatif.

imagine, *v.tr* (a) Imaginer, concevoir; se figurer, se représenter. *I. yourself in Paris,* supposez-vous à Paris. **As may (well) be imagined,** comme on peut (se) l'imaginer.

You can imagine *how angry I was!* pensez si j'étais furieux! (b) *I i.* them to be fairly *rich,* je les crois assez riches.

imbecile. 1. *a.* Imbécile; faible d'esprit. **2.** *s.* Imbécile *mf.*

imbecility, *s.* Imbécillité *f.*

imbibe, *v.tr.* (a) Absorber, s'assimiler. (b) Boire, avaler.

imbrue, *v.tr.* Tremper.

imbue, *v.tr.* To imbue s.o. with an idea, pénétrer qn d'une idée.

imitate, *v.tr.* (a) Imiter, copier. (b) Contrefaire (le cri d'un oiseau).

imitation, *s.* **1.** Imitation *f.* In imitation of sth., à l'imitation de qch. **2.** (a) Copie *f,* imitation. *Com:* **Beware of imitations,** méfiez-vous des contrefaçons *f.* (b) *Attrib.* Factice. **Imitation jewellery,** bijouterie fausse; bijoux *mpl* en toc.

imitative, *a.* Imitatif.

imitator, *s.* Imitateur, -trice.

immaculate, *a.* **1.** Immaculé; sans tache. **2.** *F:* (Of dress) Irréprochable. **-ly,** *adv.* **1.** Sans défaut. **2.** (Vêtu) irréprochablement.

immaterial, *a.* **1.** (Esprit) immatériel. **2.** Peu important. That is quite immaterial to me, cela m'est indifférent.

immature, *a.* Pas mûr.

immeasurable, *a.* Incommensurable. *F:* To my i. delight, à ma joie infinie. **-ably,** *adv.* Démesurément; outre mesure.

immediate, *a.* Immédiat. **1.** (a) Sans intermédiaire; direct. **My immediate object,** mon premier but. The immediate future, l'avenir prochain. (b) **In the immediate vicinity,** dans le voisinage immédiat. **2.** Instantané; sans retard. **3.** Pressant, urgent. **-ly,** *adv.* Immédiatement. (a) *It does not affect me i.,* cela ne me touche pas directement. (b) Tout de suite. **Immediately on his return,** dès son retour. Immediately after, aussitôt après. **2.** *conj.* Immediately he received the money, dès qu'il eut reçu l'argent.

immemorial, *a.* Immémorial, -aux. From time immemorial, *F:* de toute éternité.

immense, *a.* Immense, vaste. **-ly,** *adv.* Immensément. *F:* **To enjoy oneself immensely,** s'amuser énormément.

immensity, *s.* Immensité *f.*

immerse, *v.tr.* **1.** Immerger, submerger. **2. To be immersed in one's work,** être absorbé dans son travail.

immersion, *s.* Immersion *f,* submersion *f.*

immigrant, *a. & s* Immigrant, -ante; immigré, -ée.

immigrate, *v.i.* Immigrer.

immigration, *s.* Immigration *f.*

imminence, *s.* Imminence *f,* proximité *f* (of, de).

imminent, *a.* Imminent.

immobility, *s.* Immobilité *f.*

immoderate, *a.* Immodéré, intempéré. **-ly,** *adv.* Immodérément.

immodest, *a.* Immodeste, impudique.

immodesty, *s.* Immodestie *f*, impudeur *f*.
immoral, *a.* Immoral, -aux. (*Of pers.*)
Dissolu. **-ally,** *adv.* Immoralement.
immorality, *s.* Immoralité *f*.
immortal, *a. & s.* Immortel (*m*).
immortality, *s.* Immortalité *f*.
immovable, *a.* **1.** Fixe ; à demeure.
2. (Volonté) inébranlable. **3.** (Visage) impassible. **-ably,** *adv.* **1.** Sans bouger.
2. Immuablement. **3.** Sans s'émouvoir.
immune, *a.* *Med :* Immune from contagion, à l'abri de la contagion.
immunity, *s.* Exemption *f* (*from*, de).
immutable, *a.* Immuable ; inaltérable.
-ably, *adv.* Immuablement.
imp, *s.* (*a*) Diablotin *m*, lutin *m*. (*b*) *F :* (*Of child*) Petit(e) espiègle.
impact, *s.* *Mec.E :* Choc *m*, impact *m*.
impair, *v.tr.* Affaiblir ; altérer, abîmer (la santé) ; diminuer (les forces).
impale, *v.tr.* Empaler.
impalpable, *a.* Impalpable.
impart, *v.tr.* (*a*) Communiquer (*to*, à).
(*b*) *Body that imparts heat*, corps qui transmet de la chaleur.
impartial, *a.* Impartial, -aux. **-ally,** *adv.* Impartialement.
impartiality, *s.* Impartialité *f*.
impassable, *a.* Infranchissable.
impassioned, *a.* Passionné, exalté.
impassive, *a.* Impassible ; (visage) composé. **-ly,** *adv.* Sans s'émouvoir.
impatience, *s.* Impatience *f*.
impatient, *a.* (*a*) Impatient. (*b*) To be impatient of advice, souffrir difficilement les conseils. (*c*) To be impatient to do sth., être impatient de faire qch. **-ly,** *adv.* Avec impatience ; impatiemment.
impeach, *v.tr.* **1** Attaquer, mettre en doute.
2. *Jur :* To impeach s.o. for high treason, accuser qn de haute trahison.
impeachment, *s.* Accusation *f*.
impeccable, *a.* Impeccable. **-ably,** *adv.* De façon irréprochable.
impecunious, *a.* Impécunieux, besogneux.
impede, *v.tr.* Mettre obstacle à, empêcher, entraver.
impediment, *s.* (*a*) Entrave *f*, empêchement *m*, obstacle *m* (*to*, à). (*b*) Impediment of speech, empêchement de la langue.
impedimenta, *s.pl.* Impedimenta *mpl* ; *F :* bagages *m*.
impel, *v.tr.* **1.** Pousser, forcer (*s.o. to do sth.*, qn à faire qch.). **2.** Pousser (en avant).
impend, *v.i.* **1.** Être suspendu (*over* sur).
2. *War was impending*, la guerre était imminente. **impending,** *a.* Imminent.
impenetrability, *s.* Impénétrabilité *f*.
impenetrable, *a.* Impénétrable (*to, by*, à).
I. mystery, mystère insondable. **-ably,** *adv.* Impénétrablement.
impenitent, *a.* Impénitent.
imperative. 1. *a. & s. Gram :* Impératif (*m*). **2.** *a.* (*a*) Impérieux, péremptoire.

(*b*) Urgent, impérieux. **-ly,** *adv.* Impérativement ; impérieusement.
imperceptible, *a.* Imperceptible ; (bruit) insaisissable. **-ibly,** *adv.* Imperceptiblement, insensiblement.
imperfect. 1. *a.* Imparfait, incomplet, défectueux. **2.** *a. & s. Gram :* Imperfect (tense), (temps) imparfait *m*. **-ly,** *adv.* Imparfaitement.
imperfection, *s.* Imperfection *f*.
imperial, *a.* (*a*) Impérial, -aux. (*b*) *F :* Majestueux, auguste. **-ally,** *adv.* Impérialement ; *F :* majestueusement.
imperil, *v.tr.* Mettre en péril, en danger.
imperious, *a.* **1.** Impérieux, arrogant.
2. Urgent. *I. necessity*, besoin impératif. **-ly,** *adv.* Impérieusement.
imperishable, *a.* Impérissable.
impermeable, *a.* Imperméable.
impersonal, *a.* Impersonnel. **-ally,** *adv.* Impersonnellement.
impersonate, *v.tr.* (*a*) *Th :* Représenter. (*b*) Se faire passer pour.
impersonation, *s. Th :* Création *f*, interprétation *f*.
impertinence, *s.* (*a*) Impertinence *f*, nsolence *f*. (*b*) A piece of impertinence, une impertinence.
impertinent, *a.* Impertinent, insolent.
-ly, *adv.* Avec impertinence ; d'un ton insolent.
imperturbability, *s.* Imperturbabilité *f*.
imperturbable, *a.* Imperturbable. **-ably,** *adv.* Imperturbablement.
impervious, *a.* Person impervious to reason, personne inaccessible à la raison.
impetuosity, *s.* Impétuosité *f*.
impetuous, *a.* Impétueux. **-ly,** *adv.* Impétueusement.
impetus, *s.* To give an impetus to sth., donner l'impulsion à qch.
impiety, *s.* Impiété *f*.
impinge, *v.ind.tr.* To impinge on sth., entrer en collision avec qch. ; se heurter à qch.
impious, *a.* Impie. **-ly,** *adv.* Avec impiété.
impish, *a.* De petit diable. *I. laugh..er*, rire espiègle. **-ly,** *adv.* En espiègle.
impishness, *s.* Espièglerie *f*.
implacability, *s.* Implacabilité *f*.
implacable, *a.* Implacable (*towards*, à, pour). **-ably,** *adv.* Implacablement.
implant, *v.tr.* Implanter (*an idea in s.o.*, une idée dans la tête de qn).
implement, *s.* Outil *m*, nstrument *m*, ustensile *m*.
implicate, *v.tr.* Impliquer.
implication, *s.* Implication *f*. By implication, implicitement.
implicit, *a.* Implicit faith, confiance aveugle (*in*, dans). Implicit obedience, obéissance absolue. **-ly,** *adv.* To obey implicitly, obéir aveuglément.
implore, *v.tr.* Implorer. *To i. s.o. to do sth.,*

conjurer, supplier, qn de faire qch. **imploring,** *a.* Suppliant.

imply, *v.tr.* **1.** Impliquer. **2.** *You seem to i. that . . .,* ce que vous dites fait supposer que. . . . **implied,** *a.* Implicite, tacite.

impolite, *a.* Impoli (*to, towards,* envers). **-ly,** *adv.* Impoliment.

impoliteness, *s.* Impolitesse *f.*

import¹, *s.* **1.** Sens *m*, signification *f.* **2.** *Matter* of great import, affaire de haute importance. **3.** *Com:* Imports, importations *f.* Import duty, droit *m* d'entrée.

import², *v.tr.* **1.** *Com:* Importer. **2.** Indiquer.

importance, *s.* (*a*) Importance *f. It is of no great i.,* cela importe peu. *To attach the greatest i. to a fact,* tenir le plus grand compte d'un fait. (*b*) Importance, *F:* conséquence *f.* **People of importance,** personnages importants.

important, *a.* (*a*) Important. *It is i. for you to know that . . .,* il importe que vous sachiez que. . . . (*b*) *F:* Important. **To look important,** prendre des airs d'importance.

importation, *s.* Importation *f.*

importer, *s.* Importateur, -trice.

importunate, *a.* Importun; (visiteur) ennuyeux.

importune, *v.tr.* Importuner.

importunity, *s.* Importunité *f.*

impose. **1.** *v.tr.* (*a*) **To impose conditions** (up)on s.o., imposer des conditions à qn. (*b*) *To i. a tax on sugar,* imposer, taxer, le sucre. *To i. a penalty on s.o.,* infliger une peine à qn. **2.** *v.i.* **To impose** (up)on s.o., en imposer à qn; abuser de l'amabilité de qn.

imposing, *a.* (Air) imposant; (spectacle) grandiose.

imposition, *s.* **1.** Imposition *f* (d'une tâche). **2.** Abus *m* de la bonne volonté de qn. **3.** *Sch:* Pensum *m*.

impossibility, *s.* **1.** Impossibilité *f.* **2.** Chose *f* impossible. **Physical impossibility,** chose matériellement impossible.

impossible, *a.* (*a*) Impossible. *To make it i. for s.o. to do sth.,* mettre qn dans l'impossibilité de faire qch. (*b*) (Histoire) invraisemblable.

impostor, *s.* Imposteur *m*.

imposture, *s.* Imposture *f.*

impotence, *s.* (*a*) Impuissance *f.* (*b*) Impotence *f.*

impotent, *a.* (*a*) Impuissant. (*b*) Impotent. **-ly,** *adv.* Sans force; en vain.

impoverish, *v.tr.* Appauvrir.

impoverishment, *s.* Appauvrissement *m*.

impracticability, *s.* Impraticabilité *f.*

impracticable, *a.* Infaisable, impraticable.

imprecation, *s.* Imprécation *f.*

impregnable, *a.* Imprenable, inexpugnable.

impregnate, *v.tr.* Imprégner, imbiber (*sth. with sth.,* qch. de qch.).

impress¹, *s.* (*a*) Impression *f*, empreinte *f.* (*b*) Marque distinctive; cachet *m*.

impress², *v.tr.* **1.** Imprimer. **2. To impress sth. upon s.o.,** faire bien comprendre qch. à qn. **3.** *He impressed me favourably,* il m'a fait une impression favorable.

impression, *s.* **1.** Empreinte *f*, impression *f.* **2.** (*a*) **To make a good impression on s.o.,** faire une bonne impression sur qn. (*b*) **I am under the impression,** j'ai l'impression.

impressionable, *a.* Impressionnable, sensible.

impressive, *a.* Impressionnant. **-ly,** *adv.* D'une manière impressionnante.

imprint¹, *s.* Empreinte *f.*

imprint², *v.tr.* Imprimer.

imprison, *v.tr.* Emprisonner.

imprisonment, *s.* Emprisonnement *m*.

improbability, *s.* Improbabilité *f*; invraisemblance *f.*

improbable, *a.* Improbable; invraisemblable.

impromptu. **1.** *adv.* Impromptu. **2.** *a.* Impromptu *inv.* **3.** *s.* *Mus:* Impromptu *m*.

improper, *a.* **1.** (Expression) impropre. **2.** Malhonnête, inconvenant. **3.** Déplacé. **-ly,** *adv.* **1.** Word i. used, mot employé abusivement. **2.** Malhonnêtement.

impropriety, *s.* (*a*) Impropriété *f.* (*b*) Inconvenance *f* (de conduite).

improve. **1.** *v.tr.* (*a*) Améliorer; perfectionner. *To i. the appearance of sth.,* embellir qch. (*b*) **To improve the occasion,** tirer parti de l'occasion. (*c*) *v.ind.tr.* **To improve** (up)on sth., améliorer qch. **2.** *v.i.* S'améliorer. *He has greatly improved,* il a fait de grands progrès. *Business is improving,* les affaires reprennent.

improving, *a.* **1.** Édifiant. **2.** (Santé) en voie de rétablissement.

improvement, *s.* **1.** Amélioration *f* (de la situation); perfectionnement *m* (d'une invention). **2. To be an improvement on sth.,** surpasser qch.

improvidence, *s.* Imprévoyance *f.*

improvident, *a.* (*a*) Imprévoyant. (*b*) Prodigue. **-ly,** *adv.* Sans prévoyance.

improvise, *v.tr.* Improviser.

imprudence, *s.* Imprudence *f.*

imprudent, *a.* Imprudent. **-ly,** *adv.* Imprudemment.

impudence, *s.* Impudence *f*, effronterie *f*, audace *f.*

impudent, *a.* Effronté, insolent. **-ly,** *adv.* Effrontément.

impugn, *v.tr.* Attaquer; mettre en doute.

impulse, *s.* **1.** Impulsion *f*; poussée motrice. **2.** Impulsion; mouvement spontané: élan *m*. *Sudden i.,* coup *m* de tête.

impulsive, *a.* Impulsif, velléitaire. *I. action,* coup *m* de tête. **-ly,** *adv.* Par impulsion.

impunity, *s.* Impunité *f.* **With impunity,** impunément.

impure, *a.* Impur.

impurity, *s.* Impureté *f.*

imputation, *s.* Imputation *f.* (*a*) Attribution *f* (d'un crime à qn). (*b*) Chose imputée.

impute, *v.tr.* Imputer.

in, I. *prep.* **1.** *(a)* En, à, dans. In Europe, en Europe. *In Japan,* au Japon. *In such a latitude,* sous telle ou telle latitude. In Paris, à Paris. The streets in Paris, les rues de Paris. In the country, à la campagne. In the press, sous presse. In school, à l'école. In bed, au lit. *In one's house,* chez soi. *My fate is in your hands,* mon sort est entre vos mains. In the distance, au loin. *(b)* In the crowd, dans la foule. He is in the sixties, il a passé la soixantaine. **2.** Blind in one eye, aveugle d'un œil. Two feet in length, long de deux pieds. **3.** One in ten, un sur dix. Once in ten years, une fois tous les dix ans. **4.** *(a) In those days,* en ce temps-là. At four o'clock in the afternoon, à quatre heures de l'après-midi. In the evening, le soir, pendant la soirée. In summer, autumn, winter, en été, en automne, en hiver. In spring, au printemps. In August, au mois d'août. *In the future,* à l'avenir. *In the past,* par le passé. Never in my life, jamais de ma vie. *(b)* To do sth. in three hours, faire qch. en trois heures. He'll be here in three hours, il sera là dans trois heures. In a little while, sous peu. **5.** In tears, en larmes. In despair, au désespoir. **6.** *In his shirt,* en chemise. *Dressed in white,* habillé de blanc. **7.** To go out in the rain, sortir par la pluie. To work in the rain, travailler sous la pluie. In the sun, au soleil. **8.** In my opinion, à mon avis. **9.** *(a) In a gentle voice,* d'une voix douce. To be in (the) fashion, être à la mode. *(b)* To write in French, écrire en français. To write in ink, écrire à l'encre. In writing, par écrit. *(c)* In alphabetical order, par ordre alphabétique. *(d)* In the form of, sous forme de. **10.** *(a) A peculiarity in young people,* une particularité chez les jeunes gens. *(b) You are not in it,* vous n'avez aucune chance. II. **in,** *adv.* **1.** *(a)* A la maison, chez soi. *Mr Smith is in, F:* M. Smith y est. *(b) The harvest is in,* la moisson est rentrée. *(c) The train is in,* le train est en gare. *(d) Is the fire still in?* est-ce que le feu brûle encore? **2.** *(a)* Strawberries are in, c'est la saison des fraises. *(b)* My hand is in, je suis bien en train. *(c)* To be (well) in with s.o., être en bons termes avec qn. *(d)* My luck is in, je suis en veine. **3.** He is in for it! son affaire est bonne ! **4.** *(a)* Day in, day out, sans trêve. *(b)* All in. (i) Tout compris. (ii) *F:* I'm all in, je suis éreinté. III. **in,** *s. F:* The ins and outs of a matter, les coins *m* et recoins *m* d'une affaire.

inability, *s.* Incapacité *f* (de faire qch.); impuissance *f* (à faire qch.).
inaccessibility, *s.* Inaccessibilité *f.*
inaccessible, *a.* Inaccessible (to, à).
inaccuracy, *s.* Inexactitude *f.*
inaccurate, *a.* Inexact. **-ly,** *adv.* Inexactement.
inaction, *s.* Inaction *f.*
inactive, *a.* Inactif.

inadequacy, *s.* Insuffisance *f.*
inadequate, *a.* Inadéquat, insuffisant. **-ly,** *adv.* Insuffisamment.
inadmissibility, *s.* Inadmissibilité *f.*
inadmissible, *a.* Inadmissible.
inadvertence, *s.* Inadvertance *f.*
inadvertent, *a.* Commis par inadvertance. **-ly,** *adv.* Par inadvertance.
inadvisability, *s.* Imprudence *f,* inopportunité *f.*
inane, *a.* Inepte, stupide. **-ly,** *adv.* Bêtement, stupidement.
inanimate, *a.* Inanimé.
inapplicable, *a.* Inapplicable (to, à).
inappropriate, *a.* Qui ne convient pas (to, à); (of words) impropre. **-ly,** *adv.* D'une façon impropre.
inapt, *a.* Inapte. **-ly,** *adv.* Improprement.
inaptitude, *s.* Inaptitude *f (for,* à).
inarticulate, *a.* *(a)* (Son) inarticulé. *(b)* Muet, -ette; incapable de parler. Inarticulate with rage, bégayant de colère. **-ly,** *adv.* Indistinctement.
inartistic, *a.* Peu artistique.
inasmuch as, *conj.phr.* Attendu que, vu que.
inattentive, *a.* **1.** Inattentif, distrait; *Sch:* dissipé. **2.** Négligent (to, de). **-ly,** *adv.* Distraitement.
inaudible, *a.* Imperceptible. *I. voice,* voix faible.
inaugurate, *v.tr.* Inaugurer.
inauguration, *s.* Inauguration *f.*
inauspicious, *a.* Peu propice.
inborn, *a.* Inné, infus.
inbred, *a.* Inné, naturel.
incalculable, *a.* Incalculable. **-ably,** *adv.* Incalculablement.
incandescence, *s.* Incandescence *f.*
incandescent, *a.* Incandescent.
incantation, *s.* Incantation *f,* conjuration *f.*
incapability, *s.* Incapacité *f.*
incapable, *a.* **1.** Incapable (of, de). Incapable of speech, incapable de parler. **2.** Incapable, incompétent.
incapacitate, *v.tr.* Rendre (qn) incapable (from, for, de).
incapacity, *s.* Incapacité *f,* incompétence *f.*
incarcerate, *v.tr.* Incarcérer.
incarceration, *s.* Incarcération *f.*
incarnate, *a.* Incarné.
incarnation, *s.* **1.** Incarnation *f.* **2.** To be the incarnation of wisdom, être la sagesse incarnée.
incautious, *a.* Imprudent; inconsidéré. **-ly,** *adv.* Imprudemment.
incendiary, *s.* Incendiaire *m.*
incense[1], *s.* Encens *m.*
incense[2], *v.tr.* Exaspérer, courroucer. **incensed,** *a.* Enflammé de colère ; courroucé.
incentive, *s.* Stimulant *m,* aiguillon *m.*
inception, *s.* Commencement *m,* début *m.*
incessant, *a.* Incessant, continuel. **-ly,** *adv.* Sans cesse ; incessamment.
inch, *s. Meas:* Pouce *m. F: A man of your*

inches, un homme de votre taille *f*. Not to give way an inch, ne pas reculer d'une semelle. By inches, peu à peu.

inchoate, *a.* **I.** Rudimentaire, fruste. **2.** Incomplet, -ète, imparfait.

incidence, *s.* Incidence *f*.

incident[1], *s.* Incident *m*.

incident[2], *a.* Qui appartient, qui tient (*to*, à).

incidental. I. *a.* (*a*) Fortuit, accidentel; (*of observation*) incident. **Incidental expenses,** faux frais. (*b*) **Incidental to sth.,** qui est inséparable de qch. *Fatigues i. to a journey*, fatigues que comporte un voyage. **2.** *s.* Chose fortuite; éventualité *f*. **-ally,** *adv.* **I.** Accessoirement. **2.** *Be it said i.*, soit dit en passant.

incinerator, *s.* Incinérateur *m*.

incipient, *a.* Naissant; qui commence.

incision, *s.* Incision *f*, entaille *f*.

incisive, *a.* Incisif, tranchant; (ton) mordant; (esprit) pénétrant. **-ly,** *adv.* Incisivement.

incisor, *s.* (Dent) incisive *f*.

incite, *v.tr.* Inciter, aiguillonner, pousser (*to sth.*, à qch.).

incitement, *s.* **I.** Incitation *f*, excitation *f* (*to*, à). **2.** Stimulant *m*, aiguillon *m*.

incivility, *s.* Incivilité *f*, malhonnêteté *f*.

inclemency, *s.* Inclémence *f*, rigueur *f*. *I. of the weather*, intempérie *f*.

inclement, *a.* Rigoureux, rude.

inclination, *s.* **I.** Inclination *f* (de la tête). **2.** Inclinaison *f*, pente *f*. **3.** (*a*) Inclination, penchant *m* (*to, for*, à, pour). (*b*) **Inclination to stoutness,** tendance *f* à l'embonpoint.

incline[1], *s.* Pente *f*, déclivité *f*, inclinaison *f*. *Civ.E:* (*Acclivity*) Rampe *f*.

incline[2], *v.* **I.** *v.tr.* Pencher (la tête). **2.** *v.i.* (*a*) Incliner, pencher (*to, towards*, à, vers). (*b*) Avoir un penchant (*to*, pour qch., à faire qch.); être enclin, porté (*to*, à). (*c*) **To incline to the left,** obliquer à gauche.

inclined, *a.* **I.** (Plan) incliné. **2.** Enclin, porté (*to*, à). **To be inclined to do sth.,** avoir de l'inclination à faire qch. *If you feel inclined*, si le cœur vous en dit. *He is that way inclined*, il penche dans ce sens.

include, *v.tr.* Comprendre, renfermer, embrasser. *We were six including our host*, nous étions six y compris notre hôte. *Up to and including* **31st December,** jusqu'au 31 décembre inclus.

inclusion, *s.* Inclusion *f*.

inclusive, *a.* Qui comprend, qui renferme. **Inclusive sum,** somme globale. **Inclusive terms, conditions,** tout compris. **-ly,** *adv.* Inclusivement.

incoherence, *s.* Incohérence *f*.

incoherent, *a.* Incohérent. **-ly,** *adv.* Sans cohérence, sans suite.

incombustible, *a.* Incombustible.

income, *s.* Revenu *m*, revenus *mpl*. **Private income,** rente(s) *f(pl)*. **income-tax,** *s.* Impôt *m* sur le revenu.

incoming[1], *a.* Qui arrive; (locataire) entrant. **Incoming tide,** marée montante.

incoming[2], *s.* **I.** Entrée *f*, arrivée *f*. **2.** *pl.* **Incomings,** recettes *f*, revenus *m*.

incommode, *v.tr.* Incommoder, gêner.

incommunicable, *a.* Incommunicable.

incomparable, *a.* Incomparable (*to, with*, à). *I. artist*, artiste hors ligne. **-ably,** *adv.* Incomparablement.

incompatibility, *s.* Incompatibilité *f*. **Incompatibility of temper,** opposition *f* d'humeur.

incompatible, *a.* Incompatible (*with*, avec).

incompetence, *s.* Incompétence *f*; manque *m* de capacité.

incompetent, *a.* Incapable.

incomplete, *a.* Incomplet, -ète; inachevé. **-ly,** *adv.* Incomplètement.

incompleteness, *s.* Imperfection *f*, inachèvement *m*.

incomprehensible, *a.* Incompréhensible. **-ibly,** *adv.* Incompréhensiblement.

inconceivable, *a.* Inconcevable.

inconclusive, *a.* Peu concluant. **-ly,** *adv.* D'une manière peu concluante.

incongruity, *s.* **I.** Désaccord *m*. **2.** Absurdité *f*, incongruité *f*.

incongruous, *a.* **I.** Inassociable (*with*, avec). **2.** (*Of remark*) Incongru, déplacé. **-ly,** *adv.* Sans harmonie; incongrûment.

inconsequence, *s.* Inconséquence *f*.

inconsequent, *a.* Inconséquent, illogique. **-ly,** *adv.* Inconséquemment.

inconsiderable, *a.* Peu considérable; insignifiant.

inconsiderate, *a.* Sans égards pour les autres. *It was most i. of you*, vous avez manqué d'égards. **-ly,** *adv.* **To behave inconsiderately to s.o.,** manquer d'égards envers qn.

inconsistency, *s.* **I.** Inconsistance *f*. **2.** Inconséquence *f*, illogisme *m*.

inconsistent, *a.* **I.** Incompatible (*with*, avec); contradictoire (*with*, à). **2.** Inconstant, inconséquent.

inconsolable, *a.* Inconsolable. **-ably,** *adv.* Inconsolablement.

inconspicuous, *a.* Peu en vue; peu apparent.

inconstancy, *s.* Inconstance *f*.

inconstant, *a.* Inconstant, volage.

incontestable, *a.* Incontestable, indéniable. **-ably,** *adv.* Incontestablement.

incontrovertible, *a.* Incontestable. **-ibly,** *adv.* Sans contredit.

inconvenience[1], *s.* Incommodité *f*, contretemps *m*. *I am putting you to a lot of inconvenience*, je vous donne beaucoup de dérangement *m*. *Without the slightest inconvenience*, sans le moindre inconvénient.

inconvenience[2], *v.tr.* Déranger, gêner.

inconvenient, *a.* Incommode; (*of time*) inopportun. *It is very i.*, c'est très gênant. **-ly,** *adv.* Incommodément.

incorporate, *v.tr.* Incorporer, unir (*with,* à, avec). **incorporated,** *a.* Incorporé.

incorrect, *a.* **1.** Inexact. **2.** (*Of behaviour*) Incorrect. **-ly,** *adv.* **1.** Inexactement. **2.** Incorrectement.

incorrigible, *a.* Incorrigible.

incorruptible, *a.* Incorruptible.

increase¹, *s.* (*a*) Augmentation *f* (de prix); accroissement *m* (de vitesse); redoublement *m* (d'efforts). (*b*) *Adv. phr.* *To be* on the **increase,** être en augmentation; aller croissant.

increase². **1.** *v.i.* (*a*) Augmenter; grandir; s'agrandir; croître, s'accroître. *To i. in price,* renchérir. *To go on increasing,* aller toujours croissant. (*b*) Se multiplier. **2.** *v.tr.* Augmenter; accroître (sa fortune). *To increase* **speed,** forcer la vitesse. *To i. one's vigilance,* redoubler de vigilance. **Increased cost of living,** renchérissement *m* de la vie. **increasing,** *a.* Croissant. **-ly,** *adv.* De plus en plus.

incredible, *a.* Incroyable. **-ibly,** *adv.* Incroyablement.

incredulity, *s.* Incrédulité *f*.

incredulous, *a.* Incrédule.

increment, *s.* Augmentation *f*.

incriminate, *v.tr.* **1.** Incriminer. **2.** Impliquer. **Incriminating documents,** pièces *f* à conviction.

incrimination, *s.* Incrimination *f*, accusation *f*.

incrustation, *s.* Incrustation *f*.

incubate, *v.tr.* Couver (des œufs).

incubation, *s.* Incubation *f*.

incubator, *s.* Couveuse artificielle.

incubus, *s.* (*a*) *To be an* **incubus on s.o.,** être un cauchemar pour qn. (*b*) Fardeau *m*.

inculcate, *v.tr.* Inculquer.

inculpate, *v.tr.* Inculper, incriminer.

inculpation, *s.* Inculpation *f*.

incumbency, *s.* *Ecc:* (*a*) Possession *f* d'un bénéfice. (*b*) Charge *f*.

incumbent¹, *s.* *Ecc:* Bénéficier *m*; titulaire *m* (d'une charge).

incumbent², *a.* *To be* **incumbent on s.o.** *to do sth.,* incomber à qn de faire qch.

incumbrance, *s.* = ENCUMBRANCE.

incur, *v.tr.* Courir (un risque); encourir (un blâme); s'attirer (le courroux de qn); contracter (des dettes).

incurable, *a. & s.* Incurable. **-ably,** *adv.* *To be* **incurably lazy,** être d'une paresse incurable.

incursion, *s* Incursion *f*.

indebted, *a.* **1.** Endetté. **2.** Redevable (*to s.o. for sth.,* à qn de qch.).

indebtedness, *s.* Dette(s) *f(pl)*.

indecency, *s.* Indécence *f*, inconvenance *f*.

indecent, *a.* Peu décent, indécent, inconvenant. **-ly,** *adv.* Indécemment.

indecipherable, *a.* Indéchiffrable.

indecision, *s.* Indécision *f*, irrésolution *f*.

indecisive, *a.* (*Of argument*) Indécisif, peu concluant; (*of battle*) indécis.

indecorous, *a.* Inconvenant.

indeed, *adv.* **1.** (*a*) En effet; vraiment. *One may i. say so,* on peut bien le dire. *I am* **very glad indeed,** je suis très très content. *Thank you very much i.,* merci infiniment. (*b*) *I may i. be wrong,* il se peut toutefois que j'aie tort. **2.** Même; à vrai dire. **If indeed,** si tant est que. **3.** (*a*) **Yes indeed!** (i) mais certainement! (ii) (*contradicting*) si fait! (*b*) *I have lived in* **Paris.—Indeed?** j'ai vécu à Paris.—Vraiment?

indefatigable, *a.* Infatigable, inlassable. **-ably,** *adv.* Infatigablement.

indefensible, *a.* Indéfendable; (*argument*) insoutenable. **-ibly,** *adv.* D'une manière inexcusable.

indefinable, *a.* Indéfinissable.

indefinite, *a.* Indéfini. **1.** (Idée) vague **2.** (Nombre) indéterminé. **-ly,** *adv.* **1.** Vaguement. **2.** *To postpone sth.* **indefinitely** remettre qch. indéfiniment.

indelible, *a.* Indélébile, ineffaçable. **-ibly** *adv.* Ineffaçablement.

indelicacy, *s.* (*a*) Indélicatesse *f*; manque *m* de délicatesse. (*b*) Inconvenance *f*.

indelicate, *a.* Indélicat; peu délicat.

indemnification, *s.* **1.** Indemnisation *f* (*for,* de). **2.** Indemnité *f*.

indemnify, *v.tr.* **1.** Garantir (*from, against,* contre). **2.** Indemniser, dédommager (*for a loss,* d'une perte).

indemnity, *s.* **1.** Garantie *f*, assurance *f*. **2.** Indemnité *f*. dédommagement *m*.

indentation, *s.* **1.** Impression *f*, foulage *m*. **2.** Dentelure *f*; découpure *f*; échancrure (du littoral). **3.** Empreinte creuse.

indentures, *s.pl.* Contrat *m* d'apprentissage.

independence, *s.* Indépendance *f* (*of,* à l'égard de). *To show i.,* faire preuve d'indépendance.

independent, *a.* (*a*) Indépendant. (*b*) **A man of independent means,** un rentier. *To be i.,* vivre de ses rentes. **-ly,** *adv.* **1.** Indépendamment (*of,* de). **2.** Avec indépendance.

indescribable, *a.* Indescriptible; (joie) indicible. **-ably,** *adv.* Indescriptiblement, indiciblement.

indestructible, *a.* Indestructible.

index, *s.* **1.** Indice *m*; signe (indicateur). **2.** Index *m*, table *f* alphabétique.

India. *Pr.n.* L'Inde *f*. **india-rubber,** *s.* Caoutchouc *m*.

Indian. **1.** (*a*) *a.* De l'Inde; des Indes; indien. (*b*) *s.* Indien, -ienne. **2. Red Indians,** (les) Peaux-Rouges *m*.

indicate, *v.tr.* **1.** Indiquer, montrer. **2.** Indiquer, dénoter.

indication, *s.* Indice *m*, signe *m*.

indicative, *a.* Indicatif (*of,* de).

indicator, *s.* (*a*) Index *m*, aiguille *f* (de baromètre). (*b*) **Train indicator,** tableau indicateur du service des quais

indict, *v.tr.* Accuser, inculper (*for*, de); traduire en justice (*for*, pour).

indictment, *s. Jur:* Accusation *f.*

Indies (the). *Pr.n.pl.* Les Indes *f.* The East Indies, les Indes (orientales). The West Indies, les Antilles *f.*

indifference, *s.* Indifférence *f*, manque *m* d'intérêt (*to, towards, sth., s.o.*, pour qch., à l'égard de qn).

indifferent, *a.* 1. Indifférent (*to*, à). *He is i. to everything*, tout lui est indifférent, égal. 2. Médiocre, passable. 3. *To converse on i. topics*, causer de choses sans importance. **-ly,** *adv.* 1. Indifféremment; avec indifférence. 2. Médiocrement.

indigence, *s.* Indigence *f*, pauvreté *f.*

indigent, *a & s.* Indigent, pauvre.

indigestible, *a.* Indigeste.

indigestion, *s.* Dyspepsie *f.* An attack of indigestion, une indigestion.

indignant, *a.* (Air) indigné; (cri) d'indignation. To feel indignant at sth., s'indigner de qch. To make s.o. indignant, indigner qn. **-ly,** *adv.* Avec indignation.

indignation, *s.* Indignation *f.* **Indignation meeting,** meeting *m* de protestation.

indignity, *s.* Indignité *f*, affront *m.*

indigo, *s. Dy:* Indigo *m.* **indigo-blue,** *a. & s.* (Bleu) indigo *m inv.*

indirect, *a.* 1. Indirect. 2. Détourné, oblique. **-ly,** *adv.* Indirectement.

indiscreet, *a.* 1. Indiscret, -ète. 2. Peu judicieux; imprudent. **-ly,** *adv.* 1. Indiscrètement. 2. Imprudemment.

indiscretion, *s.* 1. (*a*) Manque *m* de discrétion. (*b*) Indiscrétion *f.* 2. Action inconsidérée; imprudence *f.*

indiscriminate, *a.* 1. *blows*, coups frappés à tort et à travers. **-ly,** *adv.* Sans faire de distinction; au hasard.

indispensable, *a.* Indispensable, de première nécessité. **-ably,** *adv.* Indispensablement.

indisposed, *a.* 1. Peu enclin, peu disposé (*to do sth.*, à faire qch.). 2. **To be indisposed,** être indisposé, souffrant.

indisposition, *s.* Indisposition *f*, malaise *m.*

indisputable, *a.* Incontestable, indiscutable.

indistinct, *a.* Indistinct; (bruit) confus; (souvenir) vague. **-ly,** *adv.* Indistinctement.

indistinguishable, *a.* Indistinguible (*from*, de).

individual. 1. *a.* (*a*) Individuel. (*b*) Particulier. 2. *s.* Individu *m.* **A private individual,** un simple particulier. **-ally,** *adv.* Individuellement.

individuality, *s.* Individualité *f.*

indivisibility, . Indivisibilité *f.*

indivisible, *a.* Indivisible, insécable. **-ibly,** *adv.* Indivisiblement.

Indo-China. *Pr.n.* L'Indochine *f.*

Indo-European, *a. & s. Ethn:* Indoeuropéen, -enne; aryen, -enne.

indolence, *s.* Indolence *f*, paresse *f.*

indolent, *a.* Indolent, paresseux. **-ly,** *adv.* Indolemment, paresseusement.

indomitable, *a.* Indomptable. **-ably,** *adv.* Indomptablement.

indoor, *a.* D'intérieur.

indoors, *adv.* A la maison. To keep indoors, garder la maison.

indubitable, *a.* Indubitable. **-ably,** *adv.* Indubitablement.

induce, *v.tr.* 1. To induce s.o. to do sth., persuader à qn de faire qch. 2. Amener, produire, occasionner. To induce sleep, provoquer le sommeil.

inducement, *s.* Motif *m*, raison *f*, qui encourage qn à faire qch. *The inducements of a large town,* les attraits *m* d'une grande ville.

indulge. 1. *v.tr.* (*a*) Avoir trop d'indulgence pour (qn); gâter (qn). To indulge s.o. in sth., permettre qch. à qn. (*b*) S'abandonner à. 2. *v.i.* To indulge in a practice, s'adonner à une habitude.

indulgence, *s.* Indulgence *f*, complaisance *f* (*to*, envers).

indulgent, *a.* 1. Indulgent (*to s.o.*, envers, pour, à qn). 2. Indulgent, faible. **-ly,** *adv.* Avec indulgence.

industrial, *a.* Industriel.

industrialization, *s.* Industrialisation *f.*

industrious, *a.* Travailleur, -euse, assidu, industrieux. **-ly,** *adv.* Industrieusement, assidûment.

industry, *s.* 1. Application *f*; assiduité *f* au travail; diligence *f.* 2. Industrie *f.*

inebriate, *v.tr.* Enivrer, griser. **inebriated,** *a.* Ivre, gris.

ineffaceable, *a.* Ineffaçable. **-ably,** *adv.* Ineffaçablement.

ineffective, *a.* 1. Inefficace, sans effet. 2. Incapable. **-ly,** *adv.* Inefficacement, vainement.

ineffectual, *a.* 1. Inefficace. 2. *I. person,* personne incapable. **-ally,** *adv.* Inefficacement.

inefficacious, *a.* Inefficace, sans effet.

inefficacy, *s.* Inefficacité *f.*

inefficiency, *s.* Incapacité *f*; incompétence *f*, insuffisance *f.*

inefficient, *a.* Incapable, incompétent. **-ly,** *adv.* Sans compétence.

inelegant, *a.* 1. Inélégant. 2. Peu délicat, fruste. **-ly,** *adv.* Sans élégance.

ineligible, *a.* (*a*) Inéligible. (*b*) Indigne d'être choisi.

inept, *a.* 1. Déplacé; mal à propos. 2. (*Of remark*) Inepte, absurde. **-ly,** *adv.* Ineptement; stupidement.

ineptitude, *s.* 1. Manque *m* de justesse, d'à-propos. 2. **Ineptitude for sth.,** inaptitude *f* à qch. 3. Ineptie *f*, sottise *f.*

inequality, *s.* 1. Inégalité *f.* 2. Irrégularité *f.*

inequitable, *a.* Inéquitable. **-ably,** *adv.* Inéquitablement, injustement.

ineradicable, *a.* Indéracinable
inert, *a.* Inerte.
inertia, *s.* Inertie *f.*
inescapable, *a.* Inéluctable.
inestimable, *a.* Inestimable, incalculable.
inevitable, *a.* (*a*) Inévitable. (*b*) Fatal, -als; obligé. **-ably,** *adv.* Inévitablement; fatalement.
inexact, *a.* Inexact. **-ly,** *adv.* Inexactement.
inexactitude, *s.* **1.** Inexactitude *f.* **2.** Erreur *f.*
inexcusable, *a.* Inexcusable; impardonnable. **-ably,** *adv.* Inexcusablement.
inexhaustible, *a.* Inépuisable.
inexorable, *a.* Inexorable. **-ably,** *adv.* Inexorablement.
inexpedient, *a.* Inopportun, malavisé.
inexpensive, *a.* Peu coûteux; bon marché; pas cher.
inexperienced, *a.* **1.** Inexpérimenté. **2.** Inaverti. *I. eye,* œil inexercé.
inexplicable, *a.* Inexplicable. **-ably,** *adv.* Inexplicablement.
inexpressible, *a.* Inexprimable; (charme) indicible. **-ibly,** *adv.* Indiciblement.
inextricable, *a.* Inextricable. **-ably,** *adv.* Inextricablement.
infallibility, *s.* Infaillibilité *f.*
infallible, *a.* Infaillible. **-ibly,** *adv.* Infailliblement.
infamous, *a.* Infâme; abominable.
infamy, *s.* Infamie *f.*
infancy, *s.* (*a*) Première enfance; bas âge. (*b*) *F:* Débuts *mpl*, enfance.
infant, *s.* Enfant *mf* en bas âge; tout(e) petit(e) enfant.
infantile, *a.* **1.** D'enfant; (raisonnement) enfantin. **2.** (Maladie) infantile.
infantry, *s.* Infanterie *f.*
infantryman, *s.* Fantassin *m.*
infatuate, *v.tr.* Infatuer, affoler. **infatuated,** *a.* Infatué, entiché.
infatuation, *s.* Infatuation *f,* engouement *m.*
infect, *v.tr.* **1.** Infecter, corrompre. **2.** *Med:* *Infected with the plague,* atteint de la peste.
infection, *s.* Infection *f,* contagion *f.*
infectious, *a.* (*a*) Infectieux. (*b*) *F:* *I. laughter,* rire contagieux.
infectiousness, *s.* Nature infectieuse; *F:* contagion *f* (du rire).
infer, *v.tr.* **1.** *To infer sth. from sth.,* inférer qch. de qch. *It is inferred that,* on suppose que. **2.** Impliquer.
inference, *s.* Déduction *f,* conclusion *f.*
inferior. 1. *a.* Inférieur, -e. *To be in no way inferior to s.o.,* ne le céder en rien à qn. **2.** *s.* (*a*) Inférieur, -e. (*b*) *Adm:* Subordonné, -ée; subalterne *mf.*
inferiority, *s.* Infériorité *f* (*to,* par rapport à).
infernal, *a.* **1.** Infernal, -aux; des enfers. **2.** *F:* (*a*) Infernal, abominable, diabolique. (*b*) **Infernal row,** bruit infernal. **-ally,** *adv.* *F: It is i. hot.,* il fait une chaleur d'enfer.

inferno, *s.* Enfer *m.*
infest, *v.tr.* Infester.
infidel, *a. & s.* **1.** *Hist:* Infidèle (*mf*). **2.** Incroyant, -ante.
infidelity, *s.* Infidélité *f.*
infiltration, *s.* Infiltration *f* (*through,* à travers).
infinite. 1. *a.* Infini. (*a*) Illimité; sans bornes. (*b*) *To have i. trouble in doing sth.,* avoir une peine infinie à faire qch. **2.** *s.* The Infinite, l'infini *m.* **-ly,** *adv.* Infiniment.
infinitesimal, *a.* Infinitésimal, -aux.
infinitive, *a. & s. Gram:* Infinitif (*m*).
infinity, *s.* **1.** Infinité *f,* infinitude *f.* **2.** *Mth:* Infini *m.*
infirm, *a.* **1.** Infirme, débile. **2.** (Esprit) irrésolu. *To be infirm of purpose,* avoir une volonté flottante.
infirmary, *s.* **1.** Infirmerie *f* (d'une école). **2.** Hôpital *m,* -aux.
infirmity, *s.* **1.** (*a*) Infirmité *f,* débilité *f.* (*b*) Infirmité; affection particulière. **2.** Infirmity of purpose, irrésolution *f.*
inflame. 1. *v.tr.* Mettre le feu à, enflammer; allumer. **2.** *v.i.* S'enflammer; prendre feu.
inflammability, *s.* Inflammabilité *f.*
inflammable, *a.* (*a*) Inflammable. (*b*) (*Of pers.*) Prompt à s'échauffer.
inflammation, *s.* Inflammation *f.*
inflate, *v.tr.* **1.** Gonfler. **2.** Hausser, faire monter (les prix). **inflated,** *a.* Gonflé. *Inflated with pride,* bouffi, gonflé, d'orgueil.
inflation, *s.* (*a*) Gonflement *m.* (*b*) Hausse *f* (des prix).
inflexibility, *s.* Inflexibilité *f.*
inflexible, *a.* Inflexible. **-ibly,** *adv.* Inflexiblement.
inflexion, *s.* **1.** Inflexion *f;* fléchissement *m.* **2.** *Gram:* Inflexion, flexion *f.* **3.** Inflexion (de la voix).
inflict, *v.tr.* *To i. suffering on s.o.,* faire subir du chagrin à qn. *Jur:* *To inflict a punishment on s.o.,* infliger une punition à qn. *F:* *To inflict oneself on s.o.,* imposer sa compagnie à qn.
infliction, *s.* **1.** *Jur:* Infliction *f* (d'une peine). **2.** Peine infligée; châtiment *m.*
influence¹, *s.* (*a*) Influence *f* (*upon,* sur). *To have great influence over s.o.,* avoir beaucoup d'influence sur qn. *To have an influence on sth.,* agir, influer, sur qch. *Under the influence of fear,* sous le coup de la peur. *Jur:* *Undue influence,* intimidation *f.* (*b*) *To have influence,* avoir de l'influence, de l'autorité.
influence², *v.tr.* Influencer; influer sur.
influential, *a.* Influent.
influenza, *s. Med:* Grippe *f.*
influx, *s.* Entrée *f,* affluence *f.*
inform. 1. *v.tr.* (*a*) *To inform s.o. of sth.,* informer, avertir, qn de qch.; faire part de qch. à qn. *To keep s.o. informed,* tenir qn au courant. *To i. the police,* avertir la police. (*b*) *To inform s.o. about sth.,* renseigner qn

sur qch. **2.** *v.i* *Jur:* To inform against s.o., dénoncer qn.

informal, *a.* **1.** Officieux. **2.** Sans cérémonie, en famille. **-ally,** *adv.* **1.** A titre non-officiel. **2.** Sans cérémonie; sans formalités.

informant, *s.* Informateur, -trice.

information, *s.* **1.** Renseignements *mpl*, informations *fpl.* To get information about sth., se renseigner sur qch. Piece of information, *f,* renseignement. Information bureau, bureau de renseignements. **2.** Instruction *f,* savoir *m,* connaissances *fpl.* **3.** Dénonciation *f* (*against s.o.,* contre qn).

informative, *a.* Instructif.

informer, *s.* Dénonciateur, -trice.

infra dig, *adj.phr.* *F:* Au-dessous de la dignité de; au-dessous de soi.

infrequent, *a.* Rare; peu fréquent. **-ly,** *adv.* Rarement.

infringe. **1.** *v.tr.* Enfreindre, violer. **2.** *v.ind.tr.* To infringe upon s.o.'s rights, empiéter sur les droits de qn.

infringement, *s.* Infraction *f;* violation *f.*

infuriate, *v.tr.* Rendre furieux. **infuriated,** *a.* Furieux; en fureur.

infuse, *v.tr.* **1.** To infuse courage into s.o., infuser du courage à qn. **2.** Infuser, faire infuser.

infusion, *s.* Tisane *f,* infusé *m;* infusion *f.*

ingenious, *a.* Ingénieux. **-ly,** *adv.* Ingénieusement.

ingenuity, *s.* Ingéniosité *f.*

ingenuous, *a.* **1.** Franc, *f.* franche; sincère. **2.** Ingénu, candide; naïf, *f.* naïve. **-ly,** *adv.* **1.** Franchement, sincèrement. **2.** Ingénument, naïvement.

ingenuousness, *s.* Ingénuité *f,* naïveté *f,* candeur *f.*

ingot, *s.* Lingot *m.*

ingratiate, *v.tr.* To ingratiate oneself with s.o., s'insinuer dans les bonnes grâces de qn. **ingratiating,** *a.* Insinuant.

ingratitude, *s.* Ingratitude *f.*

ingredient, *s.* Ingrédient *m;* élément *m.*

inhabit, *v.tr.* Habiter, habiter dans.

inhabitable, *a.* Habitable.

inhabitant, *s.* Habitant, -ante.

inhale, *v.tr.* Aspirer, humer.

inherent, *a.* Inhérent, naturel (*in,* à). *I.* defect, vice propre **-ly,** *adv.* Par inhérence. *I. lazy,* né paresseux

inherit, *v.tr.* (*a*) Hériter de (qch.); succéder à (une fortune). (*b*) *To i. sth. from s.o.,* hériter qch. de qn.

inheritance, *s.* **1.** Succession *t.* **2.** Patrimoine *m,* héritage *m.*

inhibition, *s.* Défense expresse; prohibition *f.*

inhospitable, *a.* Inhospitalier.

inhuman, *a.* Inhumain; brutal, -aux. **-ly,** *adv.* Inhumainement.

inhumanity, *s.* Inhumanité *f,* cruauté *f.*

inimical, *a.* (*a*) Ennemi, hostile. (*b*) Défavorable, contraire (*to,* à).

inimitable, *a.* Inimitable.

iniquitous, *a.* Inique. **-ly,** *adv.* Iniquement.

iniquity, *s.* Iniquité *f.*

initial[1]. **1.** *a.* Initial, -aux; premier. **2.** *s.* (*Usu. pl.*) Initials, initiales *f;* parafe *m.* **-ally,** *adv.* Au commencement; au début.

initial[2], *v.tr.* Parafer.

initiate[1], *a. & s.* Initié, -ée.

initiate[2], *v.tr.* **1.** Commencer, ouvrir. *To i. a reform,* prendre l'initiative d'une réforme. *Jur:* To initiate proceedings against s.o., instituer des poursuites contre qn. **2.** Initier.

initiation, *s.* **1.** Commencement(s) *m,* début(s) *m.* **2.** Initiation *f* (*into,* à).

initiative, *s.* Initiative *f.* To take the initiative in doing sth., prendre l'initiative pour faire qch. To do sth. on one's own initiative, faire qch. de sa propre initiative.

inject, *v.tr.* Injecter.

injection, *s.* Injection *f.*

injudicious, *a.* Peu judicieux; malavisé.

injunction, *s.* **1.** Injonction *f,* ordre *m.* To give s.o. strict injunctions to do sth., enjoindre strictement à qn de faire qch. **2.** *Jur:* Arrêt *m* de suspension.

injure, *v.tr.* **1.** Nuire à, faire tort à. *To i. s.o.'s interests,* compromettre, léser, les intérêts de qn. **2.** (*a*) Blesser; faire mal à. (*b*) Endommager, gâter. *To i. one's eyes,* se gâter la vue. **injured,** *a.* **1.** The injured party, l'offensé, -ée. In an injured tone (of voice), d'une voix offensée. **2.** (Bras, etc.) blessé ou estropié. *s.* The injured, les blessés *m;* (*from accident*) les accidentés *m.*

injurious, *a.* **1.** Nuisible, pernicieux (*to,* à). **2.** (Langage) injurieux.

injury, *s.* **1.** Tort *m,* mal *m.* To do s.o. an injury, faire du tort à qn. To the injury of s.o., au détriment de qn. **2.** (*a*) Blessure *f.* To do oneself an injury, se blesser; se faire du mal. (*b*) Dommage *m,* dégât *m;* *Mch:* avarie *f.*

injustice, *s.* **1.** Injustice *f.* **2.** *You do him an i.,* vous êtes injuste envers lui.

ink[1], *s* Encre *f.* Indian ink, encre de Chine. Written in ink, écrit à l'encre. **ink-bottle,** *s.* Bouteille *f* à encre. **ink-well,** *s.* Encrier *m.*

ink[2], *v.tr.* Noircir d'encre; .acher d'encre.

inkling, *s.* Soupçon *m.* He had an i. of the truth, il entrevit la vérité.

inkpot, *s.* Encrier *m.*

inkstand, *s.* Encrier *m*

inky, *a* **1.** Taché d'encre; (doigt) barbouillé d'encre. **2.** Noir comme (de) l'encre.

inland. **1.** *s.* (L')intérieur *m* (d'un pays). **2.** *Attrib.* Intérieur, -e. The Inland Revenue, le fisc. **3.** *adv.* To go i., pénétrer dans les terres.

inlay, *v.tr.* Incruster (*with,* de). *Metalw:* Damasquiner.

inlet, s. (a) Orifice m d'admission. (b) *Inlets into a lake,* débouchés m d'un lac.

inmate, s. (a) Habitant, -ante. (b) Pensionnaire mf (d'un asile).

inn, s. Auberge f; (*in town*) hôtellerie f.

innate, a. Inné, infus; foncier, naturel.

inner, a. Intérieur, -e; interne, de dedans. **Inner meaning,** sens intime. *To belong to the i. circle,* compter parmi les initiés.

innings, s. Cr: Tour m de batte. **He had a long innings,** F: il a fourni une longue carrière.

innkeeper, s. Aubergiste mf; hôtelier, -ière.

innocence, s. (a) Innocence f (d'un accusé). (b) Naïveté f, innocence, candeur f.

innocent, a. 1. (a) Innocent; pas coupable. (b) F: Dépourvu (*of,* de). 2. (a) Pur; innocent. (b) Naïf, f. naïve; innocent. **-ly,** adv. Innocemment.

innocuous, a. Inoffensif.

innovation, s. Innovation f, changement m.

innuendo, s. Allusion (malveillante).

innumerable, a. Innombrable; sans nombre.

inoculate, v.tr. Med: Inoculer, vacciner.

inoculation, s. Med: Inoculation f.

inoffensive, a. 1. Inoffensif. 2. (Odeur) sans rien de désagréable; (observation) qui n'a rien d'offensant.

inopportune, a. Inopportun; intempestif; hors de saison. **-ly,** adv. Inopportunément; mal à propos.

inordinate, a. Démesuré, excessif, immodéré. **-ly,** adv. Démesurément.

inorganic, a. Inorganique.

inquest, s. Enquête f.

inquire, v.tr. & i. 1. *To i. the price of sth.,* s'informer du prix de qch. *To i. the way of s.o.,* demander son chemin à qn. 'Inquire within,' ''s'adresser ici.'' 2. *To inquire about sth.,* s'enquérir de, se renseigner sur, qch. *To inquire for s.o.,* demander qn. *To inquire into sth.,* faire des recherches sur qch. **inquiring,** a. Investigateur, -trice; curieux.

inquiry, s. 1. Enquête f. *To hold an inquiry,* procéder à une enquête. 2. Demande f de renseignements. *To make inquiries about s.o.,* s'informer de, se renseigner sur, qn. *To make inquiries after s.o.,* s'enquérir de qn. **Inquiry office,** bureau m de renseignements.

inquisition, s. (a) Recherche f. (b) The Inquisition, l'Inquisition f.

inquisitive, a. Curieux; questionneur, -euse. **-ly,** adv. Avec curiosité.

inquisitiveness, s. Curiosité indiscrète.

inroad, s. (a) Mil: Incursion f. (b) *To make inroads upon one's capital,* entamer son capital.

inrush, s. Irruption f.

insane, a. 1. Fou, f. folle. 2. F: (Désir) insensé, fou. **-ly,** adv. Follement.

insanity, s. Med: Folie f, démence f.

insatiable, a. Insatiable. **-ably,** adv. Insatiablement.

inscribe, v.tr. 1. Inscrire. 2. Dédier.

inscription, s. 1. Inscription f; légende f (d'une pièce de monnaie). 2. Dédicace f (d'un livre, etc.).

inscrutable, a. (Dessein) impénétrable, inscrutable; (visage) fermé.

insect, s. Insecte m. **insect-powder,** s. Poudre f insecticide.

insecure, a. 1. Peu sûr; peu solide; mal affermi. 2. Exposé au danger. **-ly,** adv. Peu solidement; sans sécurité.

insecurity, s. Insécurité f.

insensate, a. (Désir) insensé.

insensibility, s. 1. Défaillance f. 2. Insensibilité f (*to,* à); indifférence f (*to,* pour).

insensible, a. 1. Insensible, imperceptible. 2. Sans connaissance. *To become i.,* perdre connaissance. 3. Insensible, indifférent. **-ibly,** adv. Insensiblement, imperceptiblement.

insensitive, a. Insensible (*to,* à).

inseparable, a. Inséparable (*from,* de).

insert, v.tr. 1. Insérer. 2. Introduire, enfoncer.

insertion, s. Insertion f, introduction f.

inside. 1. s. (a) Dedans m, intérieur m. **On the inside,** en dedans, au dedans. F: *To know the inside of an affair,* connaître les dessous d'une affaire. F: *To turn everything inside out,* mettre tout sens dessus dessous. F: *To know sth. inside out,* savoir qch. à fond. (b) Intérieur (d'une maison). 2. a. Intérieur, -eure, d'intérieur. F: **Inside information,** renseignements privés. 3. adv. Intérieurement; en dedans. 4. prep. A l'intérieur de; dans l'intérieur de; dans.

insidious, a. Insidieux; (raisonnement) captieux, astucieux. **-ly,** adv. Insidieusement.

insight, s. 1. Perspicacité f; pénétration f. 2. Aperçu m. *To get an insight into sth.,* prendre un aperçu de qch.

insignificance, s. Insignifiance f.

insignificant, a. Insignifiant; de peu d'importance; sans importance.

insincere, a. (a) Peu sincère. (b) Faux, f. fausse. **-ly,** adv. Sans sincérité.

insincerity, s. Manque m de sincérité.

insinuate, v.tr. Insinuer. 1. S'insinuer (dans les bonnes grâces de qn). 2. Donner adroitement à entendre. **insinuating,** a. Insinuant.

insinuation, s. Insinuation f.

insipid, a. Insipide, fade. **-ly,** adv. Insipidement, fadement.

insipidity, s. Insipidité f; fadeur f.

insist, v.i. Insister. 1. *He insisted that it was so,* il soutenait qu'il en était ainsi. 2. *To insist on doing sth.,* insister pour faire qch. *He insists on your coming,* il insiste pour que vous veniez. *I insist upon it,* je le veux absolument.

insistence, *s.* Insistance *f.*

insistent, *a.* Qui insiste; importun. **-ly,** *adv.* Instamment; avec insistance.

insobriety, *s.* Insobriété *f.*

insolence, *s.* Insolence *f* (*to*, envers).

insolent, *a.* Insolent (*to*, envers). **-ly,** *adv.* Insolemment.

insolubility, *s.* Insolubilité *f.*

insoluble, *a.* Insoluble.

insolvency, *s.* (*a*) Insolvabilité *f.* (*b*) Déconfiture *f*, faillite *f.*

insolvent, *a.* Insolvable. **To become insolvent,** faire faillite.

insomnia, *s.* Insomnie *f.*

inspect, *v.tr.* **I.** Examiner de près; inspecter; contrôler (les livres d'un négociant). **2.** Faire l'inspection (d'un régiment).

inspection, *s.* **I.** Inspection *f*; vérification *f*; contrôle *m* (de billets). **2.** *Mil:* Revue *f.*

inspector, *s.* Inspecteur, -trice.

inspiration, *s.* **I.** Aspiration *f*, inspiration *f* (d'air). **2. To have a sudden inspiration,** avoir une inspiration subite.

inspire, *v.tr.* **I.** Aspirer, inspirer (l'air). **2. To inspire s.o. with confidence,** inspirer (de la) confiance à qn.

inspirit, *v.tr.* Animer, encourager. **inspiriting,** *a.* Encourageant; (musique) entraînante.

instability, *s.* Instabilité *f*

install, *v.tr.* Installer.

installation, *s.* Installation *f.*

instalment, *s.* Acompte *m*; versement partiel. **To pay by instalments,** échelonner les payements.

instance[1], *s.* **I.** Exemple *m*, cas *m*. **2. For instance,** par exemple. **3. In the first instance,** en (tout) premier lieu. *In the present i., in this i.,* dans le cas actuel; dans cette circonstance.

instance[2], *v.tr.* Citer en exemple.

instant[1], *a.* **I.** Instant, pressant, urgent. **2.** Courant; de ce mois. **3.** (*a*) Immédiat. (*b*) Imminent. **-ly,** *adv.* Tout de suite; sur-le-champ.

instant[2], *s.* Instant *m*, moment *m.*

instantaneous, *a.* Instantané. **-ly,** *adv.* Instantanément.

instead. I. *Prep.phr.* **Instead of sth.,** au lieu de qch. **Instead of s.o.,** à la place de qn. **2.** *adv.* Au lieu de cela. *If he can't come, take me instead,* s'il ne peut pas venir, prenez-moi à sa place.

instep, *s.* Cou-de-pied *m.*

instigate, *v.tr.* Instiguer, inciter, provoquer (*to do sth.*, à faire qch. de mal).

instigation, *s.* Instigation *f*, incitation *f.*

instigator, *s.* **I.** Instigateur, -trice. **2.** Fauteur *m*, auteur *m* (de troubles).

instil(l), *v.tr.* **I.** Instiller (un liquide) (*into*, dans). **2. To instil an idea into s.o.,** infiltrer une idée dans l'esprit de qn.

instinct, *s.* Instinct *m*

instinctive, *a.* Instinctif. **-ly,** *adv.* D'instinct; instinctivement.

institute[1], *s.* Institut *m.*

institute[2], *v.tr.* **I.** Instituer, établir. **2.** *Jur:* To institute (legal) proceedings against s.o., intenter un procès à qn.

institution, *s.* **I.** Institution *f*, établissement *m.* **2.** Institution; chose établie. **3. Charitable institution,** institution, établissement, de charité.

instruct, *v.tr.* **I.** Instruire. **2.** (*a*) **To instruct s.o. of a fact,** instruire qn d'un fait. (*b*) *Jur:* **To instruct a solicitor,** donner ses instructions à un avoué. **3. To instruct s.o. to do sth.,** charger qn de faire qch.

instruction, *s.* **I.** Instruction *f*, enseignement *m.* **2.** *Usu. pl.* Indications *f*, instructions, ordres *m*; (*to sentry*) consigne *f.* *To go beyond one's instructions,* aller au delà des ordres reçus.

instructive, *a.* Instructif. **-ly,** *adv.* D'une manière instructive.

instructor, *s* Maître (enseignant). *Mil:* Instructeur *m.*

instrument, *s.* (*a*) Instrument *m*, appareil *m*, mécanisme *m.* (*b*) **Musical instrument,** instrument de musique.

instrumental, *a.* **I.** Contributif (*to*, à). **2. Instrumental music,** musique instrumentale.

instrumentality, *s.* **Through the instrumentality of s.o.,** par l'intermédiaire de qn.

insubordinate, *a.* Insubordonné.

insubordination, *s.* Insubordination *f.*

insubstantial, *a.* Insubstantiel. **I.** Imaginaire. **2.** (*a*) Immatériel. (*b*) *I. food,* aliments creux.

insufferable, *a.* Insupportable, intolérable. **-ably,** *adv.* Insupportablement.

insufficiency, *s.* Insuffisance *f.*

insufficient, *a.* Insuffisant. **-ly,** *adv.* Insuffisamment.

insulate, *v.tr.* *El:* Isoler. **insulating,** *a.* *El:* Isolant.

insulation, *s.* *El:* Isolement *m*, isolation *f.*

insulator, *s.* *El:* (*a*) (*Material*) Isolant *m.* (*b*) (*Device*) Isolateur *m*, isoloir *m.*

insult[1], *s.* Insulte *f*, affront *m.* **To pocket an insult,** boire un affront. **To add insult to injury,** doubler ses torts d'un affront.

insult[2], *v.tr.* Insulter. **insulting,** *a.* Offensant, injurieux.

insuperable, *a.* Insurmontable.

insurance, *s.* **I.** (*a*) Assurance *f.* **Life insurance,** assurance sur la vie; assurance-vie *f.* **Third-party insurance,** assurance au tiers. **To take out an insurance,** se faire assurer, s'assurer (*against*, contre). **Insurance company,** compagnie *f* d'assurance(s). (*b*) *F:* Prime *f* d'assurance. **2.** *Adm:* State insurance, prévoyance sociale; assurances sociales.

insure, *v.tr.* **I.** (i) Assurer, (ii) faire assurer. **To insure one's life,** s'assurer, se faire assurer, sur la vie. **2.** Garantir, assurer.

insurgent, *a. & s.* Insurgé, -ée.
insurmountable, *a.* Insurmontable.
insurrection, *s.* Insurrection *f*, soulèvement *m*, émeute *f*.
intact, *a.* Intact.
intaglio, *s.* *Lap:* Intaille *f*.
intangible, *a.* Intangible, impalpable.
integer, *s.* *Mth:* Nombre entier.
integral, *a.* Intégrant. **To be an integral part of sth.,** faire corps avec qch. **-ally,** *adv.* Intégralement.
integrity, *s.* Intégrité *f*. **1. In its integrity,** en entier. **2.** Honnêteté *f*, probité *f*.
intellect, *s.* Intelligence *f*, esprit *m*.
intellectual, *a. & s.* Intellectuel, -elle. **-ally,** *adv.* Intellectuellement.
intelligence, *s.* **1.** Intelligence *f*. (*a*) Entendement *m*, sagacité *f*. (*b*) **To exchange a look of intelligence,** échanger un regard d'intelligence. **2.** Renseignement(s) *m*(*pl*), nouvelle(s) *f*(*pl*).
intelligent, *a.* Intelligent; avisé. **-ly,** *adv.* Intelligemment; avec intelligence.
intelligible, *a.* Intelligible. **-ibly,** *adv.* Intelligiblement.
intemperance, *s.* **1.** Intempérance *f*. **2.** Alcoolisme *m*.
intemperate, *a.* **1.** Intempérant, immodéré. **2.** Adonné à la boisson.
intend, *v.tr.* **1.** (*a*) **To intend to do sth.,** avoir l'intention de faire qch. **Was that intended?** était-ce fait avec intention? (*b*) **I i. to be obeyed,** je veux être obéi. **2. To intend sth. for sth.,** destiner qch. à qch. **3.** Vouloir dire; entendre. **intended,** *a.* **1.** (*a*) Projeté. **My i. husband,** *F:* **my intended,** mon fiancé, mon prétendu. (*b*) **The intended effect,** l'effet voulu. **2.** Intentionnel.
intense, *a.* (*a*) Vif, *f.* vive; fort, intense. (*b*) **I. expression,** expression d'intérêt profond. **-ly,** *adv.* Excessivement. **To hate s.o. i.,** haïr qn profondément.
intensify. **1.** *v.tr.* Intensifier, augmenter; rendre plus fort, plus vif; renforcer. **2.** *v.i.* Devenir plus intense.
intensity, *s.* Intensité *f*; violence *f*; force *f*.
intensive, *a.* Intensif.
intent[1], *s.* Intention *f*, dessein *m*. **With intent to defraud,** dans l'intention de frauder. **To all intents and purposes,** virtuellement; en fait.
intent[2], *a.* **1.** (*a*) **To be intent on sth.,** être tout entier à qch. **To be intent on doing sth.,** être résolu à faire qch. (*b*) Attentif. **2. Mind i. on learning,** esprit acharné à l'étude. **Intent gaze,** regard fixe, profond. **-ly,** *adv.* Attentivement; (regarder) fixement.
intention, *s.* Intention *f*. (*a*) Dessein *m*. **To do sth. with the best (of) intentions,** faire qch. dans la meilleure intention. (*b*) But *m*.
intentional, *a.* Intentionnel, voulu. **-ally,** *adv.* A dessein; exprès; intentionnellement.
intentness, *s.* Contention *f* d'esprit; attention soutenue (du regard).

inter, *v.tr.* Enterrer, ensevelir.
intercede, *v.i.* To intercede (with s.o.) for s.o., intercéder (auprès de qn) en faveur de qn.
intercept, *v.tr.* Intercepter; arrêter (qn) au passage.
intercession, *s.* Intercession *f*.
interchangeable, *a.* Interchangeable.
intercourse, *s.* Commerce *m*, relations *fpl*, rapports *mpl*. **Human i.,** commerce du monde; relations humaines.
interdiction, *s.* Interdiction *f*.
interest[1], *s.* Intérêt *m*. **1.** *Com:* (*a*) Participation *f*. **To have an interest in the profits,** participer aux bénéfices. **To have a financial interest in sth.,** avoir des capitaux, être intéressé, dans qch. (*b*) **The landed interest,** les propriétaires terriens. **2.** Avantage *m*, profit *m*. **To act in one's own interest(s),** agir dans son intérêt. **3. To take an interest in s.c.,** s'intéresser à qn. **Questions of public interest,** questions qui agitent le grand public. **4.** **To bear interest,** porter intérêt. *F:* **To repay an injury with interest,** rendre le mal avec usure.
interest[2], *v.tr.* **1.** Intéresser. **2.** Éveiller l'intérêt de. **To be interested in s.o.,** s'intéresser à qn. **To be interested in painting,** s'occuper de peinture. **interested,** *a.* **1. The interested parties,** les parties intéressées; les intéressés *m*. **2. With an i. look,** d'un air intéressé. **interesting,** *a.* Intéressant.
interfere, *v.i.* (*a*) S'ingérer, intervenir (dans une affaire); s'interposer (dans une querelle). (*b*) Toucher (*with*, à). **Don't i.** (*with it*)! n'y touchez pas! (*c*) **To interfere with (sth.),** gêner **It interferes with my plans,** cela dérange mes plans. **interfering,** *a.* Importun, tracassier.
interference, *s.* **1.** Intervention *f*; intrusion *f* (*in*, dans). **2.** *W.Tel:* Effet *m* parasitaire.
interim. **1.** *s.* Intérim *m*. **In the interim,** dans l'intérim. **2.** *a.* Intérimaire.
interior. **1.** *a.* Intérieur, -e. **2.** *s.* Intérieur *m*.
interject, *v.tr.* **To i. a remark,** lancer une remarque.
interjection, *s.* Interjection *f*.
interlace. **1.** *v.tr.* Entrelacer; entrecroiser (des fils). **2.** *v.i.* S'entrelacer, s'entrecroiser.
interlocutor, *s.* Interlocuteur, -trice.
interloper, *s.* Intrus, -use.
interlude, *s.* Intermède *m*.
intermediary, *a. & s.* Intermédiaire (*m*).
intermediate, *a. & s.* Intermédiaire (*m*).
interment, *s.* Enterrement *m*, inhumation *f*.
interminable, *a.* Interminable; sans fin. **-ably,** *adv.* Interminablement; sans fin.
intermingle, *v.i.* S'entremêler, se mêler (*with*, avec).
intermission, *s.* Interruption *f*, trêve *f*.
intermittent, *a.* Intermittent. **-ly,** *adv.* Par intervalles, par intermittence.
intern, *v.tr.* Interner.

internal, *a.* **1.** Intérieur, -e. **2.** *A prey to i. wars,* en proie aux guerres intestines. **-ally,** *adv.* Intérieurement.

international, *a.* International, -aux.

internment, *s.* Internement *m.*

interplay, *s.* Effet *m* réciproque.

interpolate, *v.tr.* Interpoler, intercaler.

interpolation, *s.* Interpolation *f.*

interpose. 1. *v.tr.* Interposer. **2.** *v.i.* S'interposer, intervenir.

interposition, *s.* **1.** Interposition *f.* **2.** Intervention *f.*

interpret, *v.tr.* **1.** Interpréter, expliquer. **2.** *Th:* Interpréter (un rôle). **3.** Interpréter, traduire.

interpretation, *s.* Interprétation *f.*

interpreter, *s.* Interprète *mf.*

interregnum, *s.* Interrègne *m.*

interrogate, *v.tr.* Interroger, questionner.

interrogation, *s.* Interrogation *f*; interrogatoire *m* (d'un prévenu).

interrogative, *a.* Interrogateur, -trice. **-ly,** *adv.* D'un air interrogateur.

interrogatory. 1. *a.* Interrogateur, -trice. **2.** *s. Jur:* Interrogatoire *m.*

interrupt, *v.tr.* Interrompre.

interrupter, *s.* Interrupteur, -trice.

interruption, *s.* Interruption *f*; dérangement *m.*

intersect. 1. *v.tr.* Entrecouper, intersecter, entrecroiser *(with, by,* de). **2.** *v.i.* Se couper, s'intersecter, se croiser.

intersperse, *v.tr.* Entremêler *(between, among,* parmi; *with,* de).

interstice, *s.* Interstice *m.*

intertwine, *v.i.* S'entrelacer, s'accoler.

interval, *s.* Intervalle *m.* **1.** *(a)* At intervals, par intervalles; par à-coups. *Meetings held at short intervals,* séances très rapprochées. *(b) Sch:* Récréation *f.* *(c) Th:* Entr'acte *m.* **2.** Écartement *m.* *To place objects at regular intervals,* échelonner des objets.

intervene, *v.i.* **1.** Intervenir, s'interposer. **2.** *(Of event)* Survenir, arriver. **intervening,** *a.* Intermédiaire.

intervention, *s.* Intervention *f.*

interview[1], *s.* **1.** Entrevue *f.* **2.** *Journ:* Interview *m* or *f.*

interview[2], *v.tr.* **1.** Avoir une entrevue avec. **2.** *Journ:* Interviewer.

intestine, *s. Anat:* Intestin *m.*

intimacy, *s.* Intimité *f.*

intimate[1]. **1.** *a.* Intime. *(a)* To become intimate with s.o., se lier (d'amitié) avec qn. *(b)* To have an intimate knowledge of sth., avoir une connaissance approfondie de qch. **2.** *s.* His intimates, ses intimes *mf,* ses familiers *m.* **-ly,** *adv.* Intimement; à fond.

intimate[2], *v.tr.* **1.** To intimate sth. to s.o., signifier, notifier, qch. à qn. **2.** Donner à entendre, indiquer.

intimation, *s.* **1.** Avis *m.* **2.** Avis à mots couverts; suggestion *f.*

intimidate, *v.tr.* Intimider. **intimidating,** *a.* Intimidateur, -trice; intimidant.

intimidation, *s.* Intimidation *f.*

intimity, *s.* **1.** (Sentiment *m* d')intimité *f.* **2.** La vie privée; le privé.

into, *prep.* Dans, en. **1.** *To go into a house,* entrer dans une maison. *To fall into the hands of the enemy,* tomber entre les mains de l'ennemi. **2.** To change sth. into sth., changer qch. en qch. *To grow into a man,* devenir un homme. *To burst into tears,* fondre en larmes.

intolerable, *a.* Intolérable, insupportable. **-ably,** *adv.* Insupportablement.

intolerance, *s.* Intolérance *f (of,* de).

intolerant, *a.* Intolérant. **-ly,** *adv.* Avec intolérance.

intonation, *s.* Intonation *f,* ton *m.*

intoxicant. 1. *a.* Enivrant, grisant. **2.** *s.* Boisson *f* alcoolique.

intoxicate, *v.tr.* Enivrer, griser. **intoxicated,** *a.* Ivre; gris. *F:* Intoxicated with praise,* grisé d'éloges. **intoxicating,** *a.* Enivrant, grisant. Intoxicating liquors, boissons *f* alcooliques.

intoxication, *s. (a)* Ivresse *f. (b) F:* Griserie *f,* enivrement *m.*

intractable, *a.* Intraitable, insoumis.

intransitive, *a. Gram:* Intransitif.

intrepid, *a.* Intrépide. **-ly,** *adv.* Intrépidement.

intrepidity, *s.* Intrépidité *f.*

intricacy, *s.* Complexité *f.*

intricate, *a. (a)* Compliqué. *(b) (Of statements)* Embrouillé, confus.

intrigue[1], *s.* Intrigue *f.*

intrigue[2]. **1.** *v.i.* Intriguer; mener des intrigues. *To intrigue against s.o.,* travailler contre qn. **2.** *v.tr. F:* Intriguer; éveiller la curiosité de. **intriguing**[1], *a.* **1.** Intrigant. **2.** *F:* All this is very intriguing, tout cela nous intrigue beaucoup. **intriguing**[2], *s.* Machinations *fpl,* intrigues *fpl.*

intrinsic, *a.* Intrinsèque. **-ally,** *adv.* Intrinsèquement.

introduce, *v.tr.* **1.** Introduire. *(a)* Faire entrer. *To i. a subject,* amener un sujet. *(b)* Établir, faire adopter. **2.** To introduce s.o. to s.o., présenter qn à qn.

introduction, *s.* **1.** Introduction *f.* **2.** Présentation *f. To give s.o. an introduction to s.o.,* donner à qn une lettre de recommandation auprès de qn. **3.** Avant-propos *m inv*; introduction. **4.** Manuel *m* élémentaire; introduction *(to,* à).

introductory, *a.* Introductoire.

introspection, *s.* Introspection *f.*

introspective, *a.* Introspectif.

intrude, *v.i.* Faire intrusion *(on s.o.,* auprès de qn). I am afraid of intruding, je crains de vous être importun. *To i. on s.o.'s privacy,* empiéter sur la solitude de qn.

intruder, *s.* Intrus, -use; *F: (at reception)* resquilleur, -euse.

intrusion, *s.* Intrusion *f.*
intrusive, *a.* Importun, indiscret. **-ly,** *adv.*
Importunément; en importun.
intuition, *s.* Intuition *f.*
intuitive, *a.* Intuitif.
inundate, *v.tr.* Inonder (*with,* de).
inundation, *s.* Inondation *f.*
inure, *v.tr.* Accoutumer, habituer, rompre,
endurcir (*to,* à).
invade, *v.tr.* **1.** Envahir. **2.** Empiéter sur.
invader, *s.* Envahisseur *m.*
invalid[1], *a.* *Jur:* (Mariage) invalide; (arrêt)
nul et non avenu.
invalid[2], *a. & s.* Malade (*mf*); infirme (*mf*).
invalidate, *v.tr.* *Jur:* Invalider, rendre nul.
invaluable, *a.* Inestimable; d'un prix
incalculable.
invariable, *a.* Invariable. **-ably,** *adv.*
Invariablement, immanquablement.
invasion, *s.* Invasion *f,* envahissement *m.*
invective, *s.* Invective *f.*
inveigh, *v.i.* Invectiver, tonner, fulminer.
inveigle, *v.tr.* Attirer, séduire, enjôler.
invent, *v.tr.* Inventer.
invention, *s.* Invention *f.* **A story of his
own invention,** une histoire de son cru.
inventive, *a.* Inventif.
inventiveness, *s.* Fécondité *f* d'invention;
don *m* d'invention; imagination *f.*
inventor, *s.* Inventeur, -trice.
inventory, *s.* Inventaire *m.*
inverse. **1.** *a.* Inverse. **2.** *s.* Inverse *m,*
contraire *m* (*of,* de). **-ly,** *adv.* Inversement.
inversion, *s.* **1.** Renversement *m.* **2.** *Gram:*
Inversion *f.*
invert, *v.tr.* Renverser, retourner.
invertebrate, *a. & s.* *Z:* Invertébré (*m*).
invest, *v.tr.* **1.** Revêtir (*with, in,* de). **To
invest a subject with interest,** rendre un sujet
intéressant. **2. To invest s.o. with an office,**
investir qn d'une fonction. **3.** *Mil:* Investir,
cerner. **4.** *Fin:* Placer, investir. **To invest
money,** faire des placements. *F: To i. in a
new suite of furniture,* se payer un nouveau
mobilier.
investigate, *v.tr.* Examiner, étudier (une
question). *To i. a crime,* faire une enquête
sur un crime.
investigation, *s.* Investigation *f;* enquête *f*
(*of,* sur). **Question under investigation,**
question à l'étude.
investigator, *s.* Investigateur, -trice.
investiture, *s.* (*a*) Investiture *f.* (*b*) Remise
f de décorations.
investment, *s.* **1.** *Mil:* Investissement *m.*
2. *Fin:* Placement *m.*
investor, *s.* Actionnaire *mf,* capitaliste *mf.*
inveterate, *a.* (*a*) Invétéré. (*b*) (*Of smoker*)
Obstiné, acharné. **Inveterate hatred,** haine
implacable.
invidious, *a.* **1.** Haïssable, odieux. *I. task,*
tâche ingrate. **2. Invidious comparison,**
comparaison désobligeante. **-ly,** *adv.* Odieusement, désobligeamment.

invigorate, *v.tr.* (*a*) Fortifier; (*b*) Vivifier,
tonifier.
invincibility, *s.* Invincibilité *f.*
invincible, *a.* Invincible. **-ibly,** *adv.*
Invinciblement.
inviolable, *a.* Inviolable.
invisibility, *s.* Invisibilité *f.*
invisible, *a.* Invisible. **Invisible ink,** encre
sympathique.
invitation, *s.* Invitation *f* (*to do sth.,* à faire
qch.). **To come at s.o.'s invitation,** venir sur
l'invitation de qn.
invite, *v.tr.* **1.** Inviter; convier. **To invite
s.o. in,** prier qn d'entrer. **2.** Engager, inviter
(*s.o. to do sth.,* qn à faire qch.). **3.** Provoquer
(la critique). **inviting,** *a.* Invitant, attrayant; (mets) appétissant.
invocation, *s.* Invocation *f.*
invoice[1], *s.* *Com:* Facture *f.*
invoice[2], *v.tr.* Facturer.
invoke, *v.tr.* **1.** (*a*) Invoquer. (*b*) **To invoke
s.o.'s aid,** appeler qn à son secours. **2.**
Évoquer par des incantations.
involuntary, *a.* Involontaire. **-ily,** *adv.*
Involontairement.
involve, *v.tr.* **1.** (*a*) Envelopper, entortiller.
(*b*) Compliquer. **2. To involve s.o. in a
quarrel,** engager qn dans une querelle. **He
is involved in the plot,** il est compromis dans
le complot. **His honour is involved,** son
honneur est engagé. **The forces involved,**
les forces en jeu. **3.** Comporter, entraîner.
To involve much expense, nécessiter de
grands frais. **involved,** *a.* **1.** Embrouillé,
compliqué. **2.** Grevé de dettes. **To be in
involved circumstances,** être dans la gêne.
invulnerable, *a.* Invulnérable.
inward. **1.** *a.* (*a*) Intérieur, -e, interne. (*b*)
Vers l'intérieur. **2.** *adv.* = INWARDS. **-ly,**
adv. En dedans; intérieurement.
inwards, *adv.* Vers l'intérieur; en dedans.
iodide, *s.* *Ch:* Iodure *m.*
iodine, *s.* Iode *m.*
iodoform, *s.* *Pharm:* Iodoforme *m.*
Ionic, *a.* *Arch:* Ionique.
iota, *s.* *F:* Not one iota, pas un iota.
I.O.U., *s.* Reconnaissance *f* (de dette).
ipecacuanha, *s.* *Bot:* Ipécacuana *m.*
Iraq. *Pr.n.* *Geog:* L'Irak *m.*
Iraqi, *a. & s.* *Geog:* Irakien, -ienne.
irascibility, *s.* Irascibilité *f.*
irascible, *a.* (Homme) irascible, coléreux.
irate, *a.* Courroucé; en colère.
ire, *s.* Courroux *m,* colère *f.*
Ireland. *Pr.n.* L'Irlande *f.*
iridescence, *s.* Irisation *f,* iridescence *f.*
iridescent, *a.* Irisé, iridescent.
iridium, *s.* *Ch:* Iridium *m.*
iris. **1.** *s.* *Anat:* Iris *m* (de l'œil). **2.** *s.* *Bot:*
Iris *m.*
Irish. **1.** *a.* Irlandais; d'Irlande. **2.** *s.* (*a*)
Ling: L'irlandais *m.* (*b*) *pl.* **The Irish,** les
Irlandais *m.*
Irishman, *s.* Irlandais *m.*

Irishwoman, *s.* Irlandaise *f.*
irksome, *a.* Ennuyeux, ingrat.
irksomeness, *s.* Caractère ennuyeux, ingrat.
iron¹, *s.* **1.** Fer *m.* Cast iron, fonte *f.* Corrugated iron, tôle ondulée. Old iron, ferraille *f.* Iron ore, minerai de fer. *F:* Iron will, volonté de fer. **2.** *F:* To have too many irons in the fire, mener trop d'affaires de front. **3.** *Dom. Ec:* (Flat-)iron, fer à repasser. **4.** *pl.* Fers, chaînes *f. Nau: etc:* To put a man in irons, mettre un homme aux fers.
iron-bound, *a.* Cerclé de fer. **iron-filings,** *s.pl.* Limaille *f* de fer. **iron-foundry,** *s.* Fonderie *f* de fonte. **iron-shod,** *a.* Ferré.
iron², *v.tr.* Repasser. **ironing,** *s.* Repassage *m.*
ironic(al), *a.* Ironique. **-ally,** *adv.* Ironiquement; par ironie.
ironmonger, *s.* Quincaillier *m.*
ironmongery, ironware, *s.* Quincaillerie *f.*
ironwork, *s.* **1.** Serrurerie *f.* **2.** *pl.* Ironworks, forges *fpl.*
irony, *s.* Ironie *f.*
irradiate, *v.tr.* Illuminer.
irrational, *a.* (a) Dépourvu de raison. (b) Déraisonnable, absurde. **-ally,** *adv.* Déraisonnablement.
irreclaimable, *a.* Incorrigible.
irreconcilable, *a.* **1.** (Ennemi) irréconciliable; (haine) implacable. **2.** Incompatible, inconciliable (*with,* avec).
irrecoverable, *a.* Irrécouvrable.
irredeemable, *a.* Incorrigible. **-ably,** *adv.* (Condamné) sans recours.
irreducible, *a.* Irréductible.
irrefutable, *a.* Irréfutable. **-ably,** *adv.* Irréfutablement.
irregular, *a.* Irrégulier. **1.** Contraire aux règles. *I. life,* vie déréglée. **2.** Asymétrique; (*of surface*) inégal, -aux. **-ly,** *adv.* Irrégulièrement.
irregularity, *s.* **1.** Irrégularité *f.* **2.** Irregularity of ground, accidents *mpl.* de terrain.
irrelevance, *s.* **1.** Inapplicabilité *f* (*to,* à). **2.** Manque *m* d'à-propos.
irrelevant, *a.* Non pertinent; hors de propos. *That is i.,* cela n'a rien à voir avec la question. **-ly,** *adv.* Mal à propos.
irreligious, *a.* Irréligieux, indévot.
irremediable, *a.* Irrémédiable. **-ably,** *adv.* Irrémédiablement.
irreparable, *a.* Irréparable; (perte) irrémédiable. **-ably,** *adv.* Irréparablement.
irrepressible, *a.* Irrésistible, irréprimable. **-ibly,** *adv.* Irrésistiblement.
irreproachable, *a.* Irréprochable. **-ably,** *adv.* Irréprochablement.
irresistible, *a.* Irrésistible. **-ibly,** *adv.* Irrésistiblement.
irresolute, *a.* **1.** Indécis. **2.** (Caractère) irrésolu. **-ly,** *adv.* Irrésolument.
irrespective. 1. *a.* Indépendant (*of,* de).

2. *adv.* Irrespective of sth., indépendamment, sans tenir compte, de qch.
irresponsibility, *s.* Étourderie *f*; manque *m* de sérieux.
irresponsible, *a.* Étourdi, irréfléchi; évaporé. **-ibly,** *adv.* Étourdiment.
irresponsive, *a.* Flegmatique, froid.
irretrievable, *a.* Irréparable, irrémédiable. **-ably,** *adv.* Irréparablement, irrémédiablement.
irreverence, *s.* Irrévérence *f*; manque *m* de respect (*towards,* envers, pour).
irreverent, *a.* Irrévérencieux. **-ly,** *adv.* Irrévérencieusement.
irrevocable, *a.* Irrévocable. **-ably,** *adv.* Irrévocablement.
irrigate, *v.tr.* (a) *Ag:* Irriguer. (b) (*Of river*) Arroser.
irrigation, *s.* Irrigation *f.*
irritability, *s.* Irritabilité *f.*
irritable, *a.* Irritable, irascible.
irritate, *v.tr.* Irriter, agacer. **irritating,** *a.* Irritant, agaçant.
irritation, *s.* Irritation *f.*
irruption, *s.* Irruption *f.*
Isaiah. *Pr.n. B.Hist:* Isaïe *m.*
isinglass, *s.* (a) Colle *f* de poisson. (b) Gélatine *f.*
island, *s.* Ile *f. Small i.,* îlot *m.*
islander, *s.* Insulaire *mf.*
isle, *s.* Ile *f.*
islet, *s.* Ilot *m.*
isolate, *v.tr.* (a) Isoler (*from,* de, d'avec). (b) *F:* Faire le vide autour de. **isolated,** *a.* Isolé, écarté.
isolation, *s.* **1.** Isolement *m.* **2.** Isolement, solitude *f.*
isosceles, *a.* (Triangle) iso(s)cèle.
Israel. *Pr.n. B.Hist:* Israël *m.*
Israelite, *a. & s.* Israélite (*mf*).
issue¹, *s.* **1.** Écoulement *m.* **2.** Issue *f*, sortie *f*, débouché *m* (*out of,* de). **3.** Issue, résultat *m*, dénouement *m.* **To bring a matter to an issue,** faire aboutir une question. **4.** Progéniture *f*, descendance *f.* **5.** *F:* To join issue with s.o. about sth., discuter l'opinion de qn au sujet de qch. **The point at issue,** la question pendante, en litige. **6.** (a) *Fin:* Émission *f.* (b) Publication *f.* (c) Délivrance *f* (de billets). (d) *Mil:* Distribution *f*, versement *m.* **7.** Édition *f.*
issue². 1. *v.i.* (a) Jaillir, s'écouler. (b) Provenir, dériver. **2.** *v.tr.* (a) Émettre. (b) Publier. *Mil:* To issue an order, publier, donner, un ordre. (c) Verser, distribuer; délivrer.
Istanbul. *Pr.n. Geog:* Istamboul *m.*
isthmus, *s. Geog:* Isthme *m.*
it, *pers.pron.* **1.** (a) (Nom.) Il, *f.* elle. (b) (Acc.) Le, *f.* la. He took her hand and pressed it, il lui prit la main et la serra. (c) (Dat.) Lui *mf. Bring the child and give it a drink,* amenez l'enfant et donnez-lui à boire. (d) This book is absolutely it! c'est un livre épatant!

2. Hang it! zut ! *Now for it!* et maintenant allons-y ! **There is nothing for it but to run,** il n'y a qu'une chose à faire, c'est de filer. **To have a bad time of it,** en voir de dures. **The worst of it is,** le plus mauvais de la chose c'est. **3.** Ce, cela, il. *Who is it?* qui est-ce ? *That's it,* (i) c'est ça ; (ii) ça y est ! *It doesn't matter,* cela ne fait rien. *It is Monday,* c'est aujourd'hui lundi. **4.** *It's nonsense talking like that,* c'est absurde de parler comme ça. *It makes one shudder to look down,* cela vous fait frémir de regarder en bas. **How is it that?** d'où vient que ? *It is said that,* on dit que. *I thought it well to warn you,* j'ai jugé bon de vous avertir. **5. At it,** in it, to it, y. *To consent to it,* y consentir. *To fall in it,* y tomber. **Above it,** over it, au-dessus ; dessus. **For it,** en ; pour lui, pour elle, pour cela. *I feel the better for it,* je m'en trouve mieux. **From it,** en. **Far from it,** tant s'en faut, il s'en faut. **Of it,** en. **On it,** y, dessus.

Italian. 1. *a.* Italien, d'Italie. **2.** *s.* (a) Italien, -ienne. (b) *Ling:* L'italien *m.*

italic, *s. Typ:* **To print in italic(s),** imprimer en italique *m.*

Italy. *Pr.n.* L'Italie *f.*

itch¹, *s.* Démangeaison *f.*

itch², *v.i.* **1.** Démanger ; (of pers.) éprouver des démangeaisons. *My hand itches,* la main me démange. **2.** *F:* **To itch to do sth.,** brûler, griller d'envie, de faire qch. **itching,** *s.* Démangeaison *f.*

item. 1. *adv.* Item. **2.** *s.* Article *m* ; détail *m.* **News items,** faits divers. **The last item on the programme,** le dernier numéro du programme.

iterate, *v.tr.* Réitérer.

iteration, *s.* (Ré)itération *f.*

itinerant, *a.* Ambulant.

itinerary, *a. & s.* Itinéraire (*m*).

its, *poss.a.* Son ; *f.* sa, *(before vowel sound* son) ; *pl.* ses. *I cut off its head,* je lui ai coupé la tête.

itself, *pers.pron.* See SELF 3.

ivory, *s.* **1.** (a) Ivoire *m.* *F:* **The black ivory trade,** la traite des noirs. (b) (Objet *m* d')ivoire. **2.** *Attrib.* D'ivoire, en ivoire.

ivy, *s. Bot:* Lierre *m.*

izard, *s. Z:* Isard *m*, izard *m.*

J

J, j, *s.* (La lettre) J, j *m.*

jab¹, *s.* Coup *m* de pointe.

jab², *v.tr. & i.* **To jab (at) s.o. with sth.,** piquer qn du bout de qch.

jabber¹, *s.* **1.** Baragouin *m*, baragouinage *m.* **2.** Bavardage *m*, jacasserie *f.*

jabber². **1.** *v.i.* (a) Bredouiller, baragouiner. (b) Jacasser. **2.** *v.tr.* Baragouiner (le français).

Jack¹. I. *Pr.n.* **1.** Jean, *m.* **2.** Le marin. II. **jack,** *s.* **1. Cheap Jack,** camelot *m.* **Jack in office,** bureaucrate *m* (qui fait l'important). **Jack of all trades,** maître Jacques. **2.** *Cards:* Valet *m.* **3.** *Clockm:* Jaquemart *m.* **4.** *Ich:* Brochet *m.* III. **jack,** *s.* **1.** Cric *m*, vérin *m.* **2.** (At bowls) Cochonnet *m.* **jackboots,** *s.pl.* Bottes *f* de cavalier. **Jack-in-the-box,** *s. Toys:* Diable *m* (à ressort). **jack-knife,** *s.* Couteau *m* de poche ; couteau pliant. **jack-o'-lantern,** *s.* Feu follet. **jack-tar,** *s.* Marin *m* ; *F:* mathurin *m.*

jack² **up,** *v.tr.* Soulever avec un cric.

jackal, *s.* Chacal *m*, -als.

jackanapes, *s. F:* Impertinent *m*, fat *m.*

jackass, *s.* **1.** (a) *Z:* Ane (mâle) *m.* (b) *F:* Idiot *m*, imbécile *m.* **2.** *Orn:* **Laughing jackass,** martin-pêcheur *m* d'Australie.

jackdaw, *s.* Choucas *m* ; corneille *f* d'église.

jacket, *s.* **1.** (a) *Cost:* Veston *m* (d'homme) ; jaquette *f* (de femme) ; casaque *f* (de jockey).

(b) Robe *f* (d'un animal). **2.** (a) Chemise *f* (de documents). (b) Couverture *f* (mobile) (de livre).

Jacob. *Pr.n.* Jacob *m.*

jade¹, *s.* **1.** (Of horse) Rosse *f*, haridelle *f.* **2.** (Of woman) Drôlesse *f.*

jade², *s. Miner:* Jade *m.*

jaded, *a.* (a) (Of horse) Surmené, éreinté, excédé. (b) (Of pers.) Fatigué, excédé. **Jaded palate,** goût blasé.

jagged, *a.* Déchiqueté, dentelé, ébréché. **Jagged stone,** pierre aux arêtes vives.

jaguar, *s.* Jaguar *m.*

jail, *s.,* **jailer,** *s.* = GAOL, GAOLER.

jam¹, *s.* (a) Foule *f*, presse *f.* (b) Embouteillage *m* (de la circulation).

jam², *v.* **1.** *v.tr.* (a) Serrer, presser. (b) *To get one's finger jammed,* avoir le doigt coincé. **To jam one's hat on one's head,** enfoncer son chapeau sur sa tête. **To jam on the brakes,** freiner brusquement. (c) Coincer, caler (une machine). **2.** *v.i.* (Se) coincer, s'engager.

jam³, *s.* Confiture(s) *f(pl).* **jam-jar,** *s.* Pot *m* à confitures.

Jamaica. *Pr.n.* La Jamaïque.

jamb, *s.* Jambage *m*, montant *m.*

James. *Pr.n.* Jacques *m.*

Jane. *Pr.n.* Jeanne *f.*

Janet. *Pr.n.* Jeannette *f.*

jangle¹, *s.* Sons discordants; cliquetis *m.*
jangle², **I.** *v.i.* Cliqueter; s'entre-choquer.
2. *v.tr.* Faire entre-choquer. *F:* Jangled
nerves, nerfs ébranlés. **jangling,** *a.* Aux
sons discordants.
January, *s.* Janvier *m.* In January, en
janvier.
Japan¹. **I.** *Pr.n.* Le Japon. *In J.,* au Japon.
2. *s.* Laque *m* (de Chine).
japan², *v.tr.* Laquer.
Japanese. **I.** *a. & s.* Japonais, -aise, nippon,
-one. **2.** *s.* *Ling:* Le japonais.
jar¹, *s.* (*a*) Ébranlement *m* ; choc *m* ; secousse
f. *His fall gave him* a nasty jar, sa chute l'a
fortement ébranlé. (*b*) Manque *m* d'accord ;
choc (d'intérêts).
jar², *v.* **I.** *v.i.* (*a*) Heurter, cogner. To jar
on s.o.'s feelings, froisser les sentiments de
qn. The noise jarred on my nerves, le bruit
m'agaçait les nerfs. (*b*) Être en désaccord
(*with sth.,* avec qch.). Colours that jar,
couleurs qui jurent (*with,* avec). (*c*) *Mus:*
(*Of note*) Détonner. **2.** *v.tr.* Faire vibrer.
jarring, *a.* **I.** Discordant, dur. **2.** En
désaccord ; opposé.
jar³, *s.* **I.** Récipient *m* ; pot *m.* **2.** *El:*
Leyden jar, bouteille *f* de Leyde.
jargon, *s.* **I.** Jargon *m,* langage *m.* **2.** Baragouin *m.*
jasmin(e), *s.* *Bot:* Jasmin *m.*
jasper, *s.* *Miner:* Jaspe *m.*
jaundice, *s.* *Med:* Jaunisse *f.*
jaundiced, *a.* *F:* (Œil) jaloux, envieux.
jaunt, *s.* Petite excursion, randonnée *f.*
jauntiness, *s.* Désinvolture *f,* insouciance *f.*
jaunty, *a.* **I.** Insouciant, désinvolte. **2.** Enjoué, vif. Jaunty gait, démarche vive. **-ily,**
adv. Avec insouciance ; cavalièrement.
Javanese, *a. & s.* Javanais, -aise.
javelin, *s.* Javelot *m,* javeline *f.*
jaw¹, *s.* **I.** Mâchoire *f.* *F:* Jaws of a chasm,
gueule *f* d'un gouffre. **2.** *P:* (*a*) Caquet *m,*
bavardage *m.* (*b*) Causette *f.* (*c*) Sermon *m,*
semonce *f.* **jaw-bone,** *s.* Os *m* maxillaire ;
mâchoire *f.*
jaw², **I.** *v.i.* *P:* Caqueter, bavarder, jaser.
2. *v.tr.* *P:* Sermonner, chapitrer.
jay, *s.* **I.** *Orn:* Geai *m.* **2.** *P:* Jobard *m.*
jazz¹, *s.* Jazz *m.* **jazz-band,** *s.* Jazz-band *m.*
jazz², *v.i.* Danser le jazz.
jealous, *a.* Jaloux (*of,* de). **-ly,** *adv.*
Jalousement.
jealousy, *s.* Jalousie *f.*
jeer¹, *s.* **I.** Raillerie *f,* gausserie *f.* **2.** Huée *f.*
jeer², *v.i.* To jeer at sth., se moquer de qch.
jeering¹, *a.* Railleur, -euse, moqueur, -euse.
jeering², *s.* Raillerie *f,* moquerie *f.*
jelly, *s.* *Cu:* Gelée *f.* *F:* To pound s.o. to
a jelly, réduire qn en marmelade. **jelly-
fish,** *s.* *Coel:* Méduse *f.*
jemmy, *s.* Pince *f* monseigneur.
Jenny. **I.** *Pr.n.* Jeannette *f.* **2.** *s.* Jenny
wren, roitelet *m.*

jeopardize, *v.tr.* Exposer au danger ; mettre
en péril.
jeopardy, *s.* Danger *m,* péril *m.*
Jeremiah. **I.** *Pr.n.* Jérémie *m.* **2.** *s.* *F:*
Prophète *m* de malheur.
Jericho. *Pr.n.* Jéricho *m.* *F:* To send s.o.
to Jericho, envoyer promener qn. Go to
Jericho! va t'asseoir !
jerk¹, *s.* Saccade *f,* secousse *f.*
jerk². **I.** *v.tr.* (*a*) Donner une secousse, une
saccade, à. He jerked himself free, il se
dégagea d'une secousse. (*b*) Lancer brusquement. **2.** *v.i.* Se mouvoir soudainement, par
saccades.
jerky, *a.* Saccadé. **-ily,** *adv.* Par saccades ;
par à-coups.
Jerry. *Pr.n.* Jérémie *m.* **jerry(-built),** *a.*
Jerry(-built) house, maison de pacotille.
jersey, *s.* *Cost:* Jersey *m.* Sailor's jersey,
vareuse *f.* Football jersey, maillot *m.*
jest¹, *s.* **I.** Raillerie *f,* plaisanterie *f,* badinage
m. To say sth. in jest, dire qch. en plaisantant.
2. Bon mot ; facétie *f.*
jest², *v.i.* Plaisanter (*about sth.,* sur qch.) ;
badiner. **jesting,** *s.* Raillerie *f,* badinage *m.*
jester, *s.* *Hist:* Bouffon *m.*
Jesuit, *s.* Jésuite *m.*
Jesus. *Pr.n.* Jésus *m.*
jet¹, *s.* *Miner:* Jais *m.* **jet-black,** *a.* Noir
comme du jais.
jet². *s.* **I.** Jet *m.* **jet plane,** avion, appareil,
à réaction. **2.** (*a*) Ajutage *m,* jet (de tuyau
d'arrosage). (*b*) Brûleur *m.* **jet-propelled,**
a. (Avion) à réaction.
jetsam, *s.* *Jur:* **I.** Marchandise jetée à la
mer. **2.** Épaves jetées à la côte.
jettison, *v.tr.* *Nau:* To jettison the cargo,
jeter la cargaison à la mer.
jetty, *s.* Jetée *f,* digue *f.*
Jew, *s.* Juif *m*
jewel, *s.* (*a*) Bijou *m,* joyau *m.* (*b*) *pl.* Pierres
précieuses ; pierreries *f.* **jewel-case,** *s.*
Coffret *m* à bijoux ; écrin *m.*
jeweller, *s.* Bijoutier *m,* joaillier *m.*
jewellery, *s.* Bijouterie *f,* joaillerie *f.*
Jewess, *s.* Juive *f.*
Jewish, *a.* Juif, *f.* juive.
jib¹, *s.* *Nau:* Foc *m.*
jib², *v.i.* (*a*) (*Of horse*) Refuser ; se dérober.
(*b*) *F:* (*Of pers.*) Regimber. To jib at doing
sth., rechigner à faire qch.
jiffy, *s.* *F:* In a jiffy, en, dans, un instant.
jig¹, *s.* *Danc:* Gigue *f.*
jig², *v.i.* (*a*) Danser la gigue. (*b*) *F:* To
jig up and down, se trémousser (en dansant).
jig-saw, *s.* *Games:* Jig-saw puzzle, (jeu
m de) patience *f.*
jilt¹, *s.* Coquette *f* (qui plaque ses amoureux).
jilt², *v.tr.* *F:* Planter (là) (un amoureux).
jingle¹, *s.* Tintement *m* ; cliquetis *m.*
jingle². **I.** *v.i.* Tinter ; (*of keys*) cliqueter.
2. *v.tr.* Faire tinter ; faire sonner. **jingling,**
s. Tintement *m* ; cliquetis *m* (de clefs).

jingo. 1. *int.* By jingo! nom de nom !
2. *s.* Chauvin, -ine.

jinricksha, *s.* Pousse-pousse *m inv.*

job, *s.* **1.** (*a*) Tâche *f,* besogne *f,* travail *m.*
F: To be on the job, travailler avec acharne-
ment. Odd jobs, petits travaux. To do odd
jobs, bricoler. Odd-job man, homme à tout
faire. To work by the job, travailler à la
tâche, à la pièce. *F:* To make a (good) job
of sth., réussir qch. That's a good job!
ce n'est pas malheureux ! à la bonne heure !
To give sth. up as a bad job, y renoncer.
(*b*) Tâche difficile; corvée *f.* I had a job
to do it, j'ai eu du mal à le faire. **2.** *F:*
Emploi *m.* To be out of a job, être sans
ouvrage. He knows his job, il connaît son
affaire. **3.** Intrigue *f,* tripotage *m.* **job lot,**
s. Com: (Lot *m* de) soldes *mpl.*

jobbery, *s.* Tripotages *mpl;* prévarication *f.*

jobbing, *a.* Jobbing gardener, jardinier à la
journée.

jockey, *s.* Jockey *m.*

jocose, *a.* Facétieux; goguenard.

jocular, *a.* Facétieux. **-ly,** *adv.* Facétieusement.

jocularity, *s.* Jovialité *f.*

jog¹, *s.* (*a*) Coup *m* (de coude). *F:* To give
s.o.'s memory a jog, rafraîchir la mémoire
de qn. (*b*) Secousse *f,* cahot *m.* **jog-trot,**
s. At a jog-trot, au petit trot.

jog², *v.* **1.** *v.tr.* To jog s.o.'s elbow, pousser le
coude à qn. To jog s.o.'s memory, rafraîchir
la mémoire à qn. **2.** *v.i.* To jog along, aller
son petit bonhomme de chemin.

John. *Pr.n.* Jean *m.*

Johnny. 1. *Pr.n.* Jeannot *m.* **2.** *s.* P: Type
m, individu *m.*

join¹, *s.* Joint *m,* jointure *f;* ligne *f* de
jonction.

join². **I.** *v.tr.* **1.** (*a*) Joindre, unir, réunir.
To join forces with s.o., se joindre à qn.
(*b*) Ajouter. (*c*) The road that joins Paris to
Trouville, la route qui relie Paris et Trouville.
2. (*a*) Se joindre à, s'unir à; rejoindre.
Will you join us? voulez-vous vous mettre
des nôtres ? To j. the procession, se mêler au
cortège. (*b*) *Mil:* To join one's unit, rallier
son unité. (*c*) Entrer dans (un club). To j.
a party, s'affilier à un parti. **3.** Se joindre,
s'unir, à. The footpath joins the road, le
sentier rejoint la route. **II. join,** *v.i.* Se
(re)joindre, s'unir (*with,* à). To join together,
se réunir. **join in,** *v.i.* **1.** To j. in the
protests, prendre part aux protestations.
2. Se mettre de la partie. **join up. 1.** *v.tr.*
Assembler (deux choses). **2.** *v.i. Mil: F:*
S'engager; entrer au service.

joiner, *s.* Menuisier *m.*

joinery, *s.* Menuiserie *f.*

joint¹, *s.* **1.** (*a*) Joint *m,* jointure *f.* (*b*) *Carp:*
Assemblage *m.* **2.** *Anat:* Joint, jointure.
Out of joint, (bras) disloqué, déboîté. **3.** (*a*)
Partie *f* entre deux articulations; phalange *f*

(du doigt). (*b*) *Cu:* Morceau *m,* quartier *m,*
pièce *f,* de viande. Cut off the joint, tranche
f de rôti.

joint², *a.* **1.** (En) commun; combiné. Joint
action, action collective. **2.** Joint heir, co-
héritier. **-ly,** *adv.* Ensemble, conjointement.

jointed, *a.* Articulé.

jointure, *s.* Douaire *m.*

joist, *s. Const:* Solive *f,* poutre *f.*

joke¹, *s.* (*a*) Plaisanterie *f,* farce *f, F:* blague
f. I did it for a j., je l'ai fait histoire de rire.
The joke is that, le comique de l'histoire,
c'est que. *F:* Practical joke, mystification *f,*
farce. That's a good j.! en voilà une bonne !
He knows how to take a j., il entend la plaisanterie. (*b*) Bon mot; facétie *f,* plaisanterie.
He must have his little j., il aime à plaisanter.

joke², *v.i.* Plaisanter, badiner. To joke at,
about, sth., plaisanter de qch. I was only
joking, je l'ai dit histoire de rire. **joking¹,**
a. Moqueur, -euse, de plaisanterie. **-ly,** *adv.*
En plaisantant; pour rire. **joking²,** *s.* Plaisanterie *f,* badinage *m, F:* blague *f.*

joker, *s.* **1.** Farceur, -euse; plaisant *m.*
Practical joker, mauvais plaisant. **2.** *P:* Type
m, individu *m.* **3.** *Cards:* Joker *m.*

jollity, *s.* **1.** Gaieté *f.* **2.** Réjouissance *f.*

jolly. 1. *a.* (*a*) Joyeux, gai, gaillard. (*b*) *F:*
Éméché; légèrement pris de boisson. (*c*) *F.*
little room, gentille petite chambre. **2.** *adv.*
P: Rudement, fameusement. Jolly glad,
rudement content.

jolt¹, *s.* Cahot *m,* secousse *f.*

jolt². 1. *v.tr.* Cahoter, secouer. **2.** *v.i.*
Cahoter, tressauter.

Jonah. 1. *Pr.n.* Jonas *m.* **2.** *s. F:* Guignard
m. A Jonah, un porte-malheur *inv.*

jonquil, *s. Bot:* Jonquille *f.*

Jordan. *Pr.n.* Le Jourdain. *F:* This side
of Jordan, de ce côté de la tombe.

Joshua. *Pr.n.* B.Hist: Josué *m.*

jostle. 1. *v.i.* Jouer des coudes. **2.** *v.tr.*
Bousculer, coudoyer. **jostling,** *s.* Bousculade *f.*

jot¹, *s. F:* Not a jot, pas un iota.

jot², *v.tr.* To jot sth. down, noter qch.;
prendre note de qch. **jotting,** *s.* **1.** Jotting
down, prise *f* (d'une note). **2.** *pl.* Jottings,
notes *f.*

journal, *s.* Journal *m,* -aux.

journalism, *s.* Journalisme *m.*

journalist, *s.* Journaliste *mf.*

journey¹, *s.* Voyage *m;* trajet *m.* On a
journey, en voyage. Pleasant journey! bon
voyage !

journey², *v.i.* Voyager.

Jove. *Pr.n.* Jupiter *m. F:* By Jove! mâtin !

jovial, *a.* Jovial, -aux. **-ally,** *adv.* Jovialement.

joviality, *s.* Jovialité *f,* gaîté *f.*

jowl, *s.* (*a*) Mâchoire *f.* (*b*) Joue *f,* bajoue *f.*

joy, *s.* Joie *f,* allégresse *f.* To leap for joy,
sauter de joie. **joy-ride,** *s.* **1.** Balade en

auto. **2.** *Av:* Vol *m* de plaisir. **joy-stick,** *s.* *Av:* **F:** Levier *m* de commande ; **F:** manche *m* à balai.

joyful, *a.* Joyeux, heureux. **-fully,** *adv.* Joyeusement.

joyfulness, *s.* Joie *f*, allégresse *f*.

joyous, *a.* Joyeux. **-ly,** *adv.* Joyeusement.

joyousness, *s.* Joie *f*, allégresse *f*.

jubilant, *a.* (a) Réjoui (*at sth.*, de qch.). (b) (Cri) joyeux. *J. face*, visage épanoui. **-ly,** *adv.* Avec joie.

jubilation, *s.* Joie *f*, allégresse *f* ; **F:** jubilation *f*.

jubilee, *s.* Jubilé *m* ; cinquantième anniversaire *m*.

Judas. *Pr.n.* Judas *m*.

judge¹, *s.* **1.** Juge *m*. **2.** *Sp:* Arbitre *m*, juge. **3.** Connaisseur, -euse.

judge², *v.tr.* **1.** (a) Juger. (b) *To j. others by oneself*, mesurer les autres à son aune. *Judging by,* à en juger par. (c) Arbitrer. **2.** Apprécier, estimer. **3.** *v.ind.tr.* *Judge of my surprise!* jugez de ma surprise !

judg(e)ment, *s.* Jugement *m.* **1.** (a) **F:** *To sit in judgment on s.o.*, se poser en juge de qn. (b) Décision *f* judiciaire ; arrêt *m.* **F:** *It is a judgment on you*, c'est un châtiment de Dieu. **2.** Opinion *f*, avis *m.* **3.** Bon sens ; discernement *m.* *To have good judgment,* avoir le jugement sain. **judg(e)ment-day,** *s.* (Jour *m* du) jugement dernier.

judicial, *a.* **1.** Juridique. *Judicial enquiry,* enquête judiciaire. **2.** *Judicial faculty,* faculté judiciaire ; sens critique. **-ally,** *adv.* **1.** Judiciairement. **2.** Impartialement.

judicious, *a.* Judicieux. **-ly,** *adv.* Judicieusement.

judiciousness, *s.* Discernement *m* ; bon sens.

jug¹, *s.* Cruche *f*, broc *m* ; (*for milk*) pot *m.* *Small jug,* cruchon *m*.

jug², *v.tr.* *Cu:* Jugged hare, civet *m* de lièvre.

juggins, *s.* **F:** Niais *m*, jobard *m*.

juggle, *v.i.* (a) Jongler. (b) Faire des tours de passe-passe. **juggling,** *s.* = JUGGLERY.

juggler, *s.* (a) Jongleur, -euse. (b) Escamoteur, -euse ; prestidigitateur *m*.

jugglery, *s.* (a) Jonglerie *f*. (b) Tours *mpl* de passe-passe ; escamotage *m*.

Jugoslav, *a. & s.* Yougoslave (*mf*).

Jugoslavia. *Pr.n.* La Yougoslavie.

jugular, *a. & s.* *Anat:* Jugulaire (*f*).

juice, *s.* Jus *m*, suc *m*.

juiciness, *s.* Succulence *f*.

juicy, *a.* Succulent, juteux ; plein de jus.

jujube, *s.* Boule *f* de gomme.

July, *s.* Juillet *m.* **In July, in the month of July,** en juillet, au mois de juillet.

jumble¹, *s.* Méli-mélo *m*, fouillis *m*.

jumble², *v.tr.* Brouiller, mêler. *To j. everything up,* **F:** tout mettre en salade.

jump¹, *s.* **1.** Saut *m*, bond *m.* *Sp:* High jump, saut en hauteur. **F:** Jump in prices,

saute *f* dans les prix. **2.** Sursaut *m*, haut-le-corps *m* *inv.* *That gave me a jump*, cela m'a fait sursauter. **F:** *To keep s.o. on the jump*, ne pas laisser le temps de souffler à qn. **3.** *Equit:* Obstacle *m*.

jump², **I.** *v.i.* **1.** Sauter, bondir. *To jump off a wall*, sauter à bas d'un mur. **F:** *To jump down s.o.'s throat*, rembarrer qn. **F:** *To jump at an offer*, s'empresser d'accepter une offre. *To jump to a conclusion*, conclure à la légère. **2.** Sursaut, tressauter. **II.** **jump**, *v.tr.* Franchir, sauter. *Rail:* Jump the metals, sortir des rails. **jump about,** *v.i.* Sautiller. **jump across,** *v.tr.* Franchir d'un bond. **jump in,** *v.i.* **1.** Entrer d'un bond. *Rail:* Jump in! montez vite ! **2.** Se jeter à l'eau. **jump out,** *v.i.* Sortir d'un bond. *To jump out of bed*, sauter à bas du lit. **F:** *I nearly jumped out of my skin*, cela m'a fait sursauter. **jump up,** *v.i.* **1.** Sauter sur ses pieds. **2.** Bondir.

jumping-off place, *s.* Base avancée.

jumper, *s.* Casaquin *m*, casaque *f*. *Knitted j.*, tricot *m*.

jumpiness, *s.* Nervosité *f*, agitation *f*.

jumpy, *a.* **F:** Agité, nerveux.

junction, *s.* **1.** Jonction *f*, confluent *m* ; raccordement *m* (de tuyaux). **2.** (a) (Point *m* de) jonction ; (em)branchement *m*, bifurcation *f*. (b) *Rail:* Gare *f* de bifurcation, d'embranchement.

juncture, *s.* Conjoncture *f*.

June, *s.* Juin *m.* **In June, in the month of June,** en juin, au mois de juin.

jungle, *s.* Jungle *f*, fourré *m*, brousse *f*.

junior, *a. & s.* **1.** Cadet, -ette ; plus jeune. *W. Smith Junior,* W. Smith (i) le jeune (ii) fils. *Sch:* The junior school, les petits. **2.** Moins ancien ; subalterne (*m*).

juniper, *s.* *Bot:* Genévrier *m*, genièvre *m*.

junk¹, *s.* Vieux cordages ; vieux filin ; étoupe *f*.

junk², *s.* *Nau:* Jonque *f*.

junket, *s.* *Cu:* Lait caillé.

Juno. *Pr.n.* *Myth:* Junon *f*.

Jupiter. *Pr.n.* *Myth:* Jupiter *m*.

jurisdiction, *s.* Juridiction *f*. *This matter does not come within our j.*, cette matière n'est pas de notre compétence.

juror, *s.* Juré *m* ; membre *m* du jury.

jury, *s.* Jury *m* ; jurés *mpl.* *To serve on the jury*, être du jury. **jury-box,** *s* Banc(s) *m*(*pl*) du jury.

juryman, *s.* = JUROR.

just. **I.** *a.* Juste, équitable. *It is only just*, ce n'est que justice. *As was only just*, comme de juste. *To show just cause for*, donner une raison valable de. **-ly,** *adv.* Justement. **1.** Avec justice. *To deal j. with s.o.*, faire justice à qn. **2.** Avec justesse. **II.** **just**, *adv.* **1.** (a) Juste, justement. *J. by the gate*, tout près de la porte. **Not ready just yet**, pas encore tout à fait prêt. **Just how many are there?** combien y en a-t-il au juste ? **That's

just it, (i) c'est bien cela; (ii) justement!
Just so! c'est bien cela! parfaitement! **It's
just the same,** c'est tout un. *He did it j. for
a joke,* il l'a fait simplement histoire de rire.
(b) **Just as.** (i) *I can do it j. as well as he,* je
peux le faire tout aussi bien que lui. *It
would be just as well if he came,* il y aurait
avantage à ce qu'il vienne. **Just as you please!**
comme vous voudrez! à votre aise! *Leave
my things j. as they are,* laissez mes affaires
telles quelles. (ii) *Just as he was starting out,*
au moment où il partait. (c) **Just now.**
(i) *Business is bad j. now,* actuellement les
affaires vont mal. (ii) *I can't do it j. now,* je
ne peux pas le faire pour le moment. (iii) *I
saw him j. now,* je l'ai vu tout à l'heure.
(d) *You remember?*—**Don't I just!** vous vous en
souvenez?—Si je m'en souviens! **2.** (a) *Just
before I came,* immédiatement avant mon
arrivée. (b) *He has just written to you,* il
vient de vous écrire. *He has j. come,* il ne
fait que de paraître. (*Of book*) **Just out,** vient
de paraître. **3.** *I am j. coming!* j'arrive!
He is j. going out, il est sur le point de sortir.
4. He just managed to do it, c'est à peine s'il
a pu le faire. *I was only j. saved from drowning,* j'ai failli me noyer. *I've got only j. enough
to live on,* j'ai tout juste de quoi vivre. You

are just in time to . . ., vous arrivez juste
à temps pour. . . . **5.** (a) Seulement. **Just
once,** rien qu'une fois. **Just one,** un seul.
Just a little bit, un tout petit peu. (b) *F:
J. listen!* écoutez donc!

justice, *s.* **I.** Justice *f.* (a) **Poetical justice,**
justice idéale. *F:* To do justice to a meal,
faire honneur à un repas. (b) **To bring s.o.
to justice,** traduire qn en justice. **2.** Magistrat *m.* (a) Juge *m.* (b) The Justices, les
magistrats.

justifiable, *a.* (Crime) justifiable; (colère)
légitime. *J. refusal,* refus motivé. **-ably,**
adv. Justifiablement, légitimement.

justification, *s.* Justification *f.*

justify, *v.tr.* Justifier; motiver (une action).
justified, *a.* Justifié.

justness, *s.* **I.** Justice *f.* **2.** Justesse *f* (d'une
observation).

jut, *v.i.* To jut (out), être en saillie, faire
saillie. *To jut out over sth.,* surplomber qch.

juvenile. **I.** *a.* Juvénile. *J. books,* livres
pour la jeunesse. *J. offender,* accusé(e)
mineur(e). **2.** *s.* Jeune *mf.*

juxtaposed, *a.* Juxtaposé; en juxtaposition.
juxtaposition, *s.* Juxtaposition *f.* *To be in
j.,* se juxtaposer.

K

K, k, *s.* (La lettre) K, k *m.*
Kaffir, *a. & s. Ethn:* Cafre (*mf*).
kale, *s.* Curly kale, chou frisé.
kangaroo, *s. Z:* Kangourou *m.*
Kashmir. *Pr.n.* Le Cachemire.
Kate. *Pr.n.* Catherine *f.*
Katherine. *Pr.n.* Catherine *f.*
keel, *s. N.Arch:* Quille *f.* On an even keel,
sans différence de calaison.
keen, *a.* **I.** Affilé, aiguisé. *K. edge,* fil tranchant. **2.** (Vent) vif, perçant. **3.** *K. appetite,*
appétit vorace. **4.** (a) Ardent, zélé. *K. golfer,*
enragé *m* de golf. *F:* He is as keen as
mustard, il brûle de zèle. *F:* To be keen
on sth., être emballé pour qch. *He is not k.
on it,* il n'y tient pas beaucoup. (b) Keen
competition, concurrence acharnée. **5.** (Œil)
perçant, vif. To have a keen ear, avoir l'ouïe
fine. **6.** (Esprit) fin, pénétrant. **-ly,** *adv.*
Aprement, vivement.
keenness, *s.* **I.** Finesse *f*, acuité *f.* **2.** Apreté
f (du froid). **3.** Ardeur *f*, zèle *m.* **4.** Keenness of sight, acuité de la vision.
keep¹, *s.* **I.** *Hist:* Donjon *m* (du château
fort). **2.** Nourriture *f*; frais *mpl* de subsistance. *Ten francs a day and his k.,* dix
francs par jour logé et nourri. **3.** *F:* For
keeps, pour de bon.

keep², *v.* **I.** *v.tr.* **I.** Observer, suivre (une
règle); tenir (une promesse). To keep an
appointment, ne pas manquer à un rendez-
vous. **2.** Célébrer (une fête). **3.** Préserver
(*s.o. from evil,* qn du mal). **4.** (a) Garder
(des moutons). (b) *Badly kept road,* route
mal entretenue. (c) Tenir (un journal).
(d) *He has his parents to k.,* il a ses parents à
sa charge. To keep s.o. in clothes, fournir
le vêtement à qn. (e) Avoir (une voiture);
élever (de la volaille). (f) Tenir (une boutique). **5.** Maintenir (l'ordre); garder (le
silence). **6.** *To k. s.o. in prison,* retenir,
détenir, qn en prison. **7.** *The noise keeps him
from sleeping,* le bruit l'empêche de dormir.
8. Garder (des provisions). **9.** Conserver;
retenir (l'attention de qn). **10.** To keep sth.
from s.o., cacher, taire, qch. à qn. **11.** To
keep one's course, poursuivre sa route.
12. To keep one's bed, garder le lit. **13.** (a)
To keep sth. clean, tenir qch. propre. To
keep s.o. waiting, faire attendre qn. (b) To
keep one's eyes fixed on sth., fixer qch. du
regard. **II.** **keep,** *v.i.* **I.** Rester, se tenir.
To k. standing, se tenir debout. *How are you
keeping?* comment allez-vous? **2.** Continuer.
(a) To keep at work, continuer son travail.
F: To keep at it, travailler sans relâche.

To keep straight on, suivre tout droit. (b) **To keep doing sth.,** ne pas cesser de faire qch. **3.** (*Of food*) Se garder, se conserver. **keep away. 1.** *v.tr.* Éloigner; tenir éloigné. **2.** *v.i.* Se tenir à l'écart. **keep back. 1.** *v.tr.* (a) Arrêter; retenir (la foule). (b) Dissimuler (la vérité). **2.** *v.i.* Se tenir en arrière. **Keep back!** n'avancez pas! **keep down. 1.** *v.tr.* (a) Empêcher de monter. (b) *She kept her head down,* elle se tenait la tête baissée. **2.** *v.i.* Se tapir. **keep from,** (a) *v.i.* S'abstenir de (faire qch.). (b) *v.tr.* Empêcher de (faire qch.). **keep in. 1.** *v.tr.* (a) Retenir à la maison. *Sch :* To keep in, consigner. (b) Contenir. (c) Entretenir (le feu). (d) *F:* To keep one's hand in, s'entretenir la main. **2.** *v.i.* *F:* **To keep in with s.o.,** cultiver qn. **keep off. 1.** *v.tr.* (a) Keep your hands off! n'y touchez pas! (b) Éloigner. **2.** *v.i.* Se tenir éloigné. *If the rain keeps off,* si nous n'avons pas de pluie. **keep on. 1.** *v.tr.* (a) Garder. *K. your hat on,* restez couvert. (b) *I hope I'll be kept on,* j'espère garder ma place. **2.** *v.i.* (a) Avancer; aller toujours. (b) **To keep on doing sth.,** continuer de, à, faire qch. *He keeps on hoping,* il s'obstine à espérer. *F:* To keep on at s.o., harceler qn. **keep out. 1.** *v.tr.* (a) Empêcher d'entrer. (b) *v.i.* Se tenir dehors. **2. To keep out of.** (a) *v.tr.* frustrer de. (b) *v.i.* To k. out of a quarrel, ne pas se mêler d'une querelle. *To k. out of danger,* se tenir à l'abri du danger. **keep to,** (a) *v.tr.* To k.s.o. to his promise, obliger qn. à tenir sa promesse. (b) *v.i.* S'en tenir à. **To keep to one's bed,** garder le lit. **To keep to the left,** tenir la gauche. **keep together,** *v.i.* (a) Rester ensemble. (b) Rester unis. **keep under,** *v.tr.* Tenir dans la soumission; contenir (un incendie). **keep up. 1.** *v.tr.* (a) Entretenir; maintenir (une maison) en bon état. (b) *To k. up the pace,* conserver l'allure. *F:* Keep it up! allez toujours! continuez! (c) Soutenir (l'intérêt). **Keep up your courage!** haut les cœurs! **To keep up appearances,** sauver les apparences. (d) To keep s.o. up (at night), faire veiller qn. **2.** *v.i.* **To keep up with s.o.,** aller de pair avec qn. **To keep up with the times,** *F:* se maintenir à la page. **keeping,** *s.* **1.** (a) Observation *f* (d'une règle). (b) Célébration *f* (d'une fête). **2.** Garde *f*. **3. In keeping with,** en accord, en rapport, avec. **keeper,** *s.* (a) Garde *m*, gardien *m*; surveillant *m*; conservateur *m* (de musée). (b) = GAMEKEEPER. (c) **Boarding-house keeper,** patron, -onne, d'une pension de famille.
keepsake, *s.* Souvenir *m*.
keg, *s.* Caque *f* (de harengs); barillet *m*.
kelp, *s.* Varech *m*.
kennel, *s.* **1.** Chenil *m* (de chiens de chasse). **2.** Niche *f* (de chien de garde).
Kenya. *Pr.n. Geog:* Kenya *m*

kernel, *s.* **1.** Amande *f*. **2.** *F:* **The kernel of the matter,** l'essentiel *m* de l'affaire.
kestrel, *s. Orn:* Crécerelle *f*; émouchet *m*.
kettle, *s.* Bouilloire *f*. *F:* Here's a pretty **kettle of fish,** en voilà une jolie affaire.
kettle-drum, *s. Mus:* Timbale *f*.
key¹, *s.* **1.** Clef *f*, clé *f*. *To leave the key in the door,* laisser la clef sur la porte. **2.** (a) Clef (d'une énigme). (b) *Sch:* Corrigé *m*; solutions *fpl* (des problèmes). **3.** *Mus:* Major key, ton majeur. **4.** Touche *f* (de piano). **5.** Remontoir *m* (de pendule). **key-note,** *s.* (a) *Mus:* Tonique *f*. (b) *F:* Note dominante. **key-signature,** *s. Mus:* Armature *f* (de la clef).
key², *v.tr.* *F:* To key s.o. up, mettre du cœur au ventre à qn.
keyboard, *s.* **1.** Clavier *m* (de piano). **2.** (*In hotel*) Porte-clefs *m inv*; tableau *m*.
keyhole, *s.* Trou *m* de (la) serrure.
keystone, *s.* Clef *f* de voûte.
khaki. 1. *s. Tex:* Kaki *m*. **2.** *a.* Kaki *inv*.
kick¹, *s.* **1.** (a) Coup *m* de pied. (b) Ruade *f* (d'un cheval). **2.** *F:* He has no kick left in him, il est à plat. **3.** Recul *m*, réaction *f* (d'un fusil).
kick². 1. *v.i.* (a) Donner un coup de pied; (*of animals*) ruer. (b) (*Of pers.*) **To kick at sth.,** regimber contre qch. (c) (*Of gun*) Reculer, repousser. **2.** *v.tr.* (a) Donner un coup de pied à; (*of horse*) détacher un coup de sabot à (qn). **To kick s.o. downstairs,** faire dégringoler l'escalier à qn. *P:* To kick the bucket, mourir. (b) **To kick a goal,** marquer un but. **kick off,** *v.tr. Abs. Fb:* Donner le coup d'envoi. **kick-off,** *s. Fb:* Coup *m* d'envoi.
kid, *s.* **1.** (a) *Z:* Chevreau *m*, *f.* chevrette. (b) (Peau *f* de) chevreau. *F:* To handle s.o. with kid gloves, ménager qn. **2.** *F:* Mioche *mf*, gosse *mf*.
kidnap, *v.tr.* Enlever de vive force.
kidnapper, *s.* Auteur *m* d'un enlèvement.
kidney, *s.* **1.** (a) *Anat:* Rein *m*. (b) *F:* Of the same kidney, du même acabit. **2.** *Cu:* Rognon *m*.
kill, *v.tr.* **1.** (a) Tuer, faire mourir. To be hard to kill, avoir la vie dure. To kill two birds with one stone, faire d'une pierre deux coups. He was laughing fit to kill himself, il crevait de rire. (b) Abattre, tuer (un bœuf). **2. To kill time,** tuer le temps. **kill off,** *v.tr.* Exterminer. **kill-joy,** *s.* Rabat-joie *m inv*.
killer, *s.* Tueur, -euse; meurtrier *m*.
kiln, *s.* Four *m*.
kilogram(me), *s.* Kilogramme *m*, *F:* kilo *m*.
kilometre, *s.* Kilomètre *m*.
kilt, *s.* Kilt *m*.
kimono, *s. Cost:* Kimono *m*.
kin, *s.* (a) Parents *mpl*. (b) *To inform* the next of kin, prévenir la famille.
kind¹, *s.* **1.** (a) Genre *m*, espèce *f*, sorte *f*. *Of what k. is it?* de quelle sorte est-ce?

What k. of man is he? quel genre d'homme est-ce? **Nothing of the kind,** rien de la sorte. **In a kind of a way,** en quelque façon. *(b) F:* **These kind of men,** ce genre d'hommes. **2. Payment in kind,** paiement en nature. *F:* **To repay s.o. in kind,** payer qn de la même monnaie.

kind², a. Bon, aimable, bienveillant. **To be kind to s.o.,** se montrer bon pour, envers, qn. **It is very kind of you,** c'est bien aimable de votre part. **Be so kind as to,** soyez assez bon pour. **-ly,** *adv.* Avec bonté, avec bienveillance. **To be kindly disposed towards s.o.,** être plein de bienveillance pour qn. **Will you kindly?** voulez-vous avoir la bonté de?

kind-hearted, a. Bon, bienveillant.

kindergarten, s. Jardin *m* d'enfants; école maternelle.

kindle. 1. *v.tr.* Allumer; enflammer, embraser. **2.** *v.i.* S'allumer, s'enflammer, prendre feu.

kindliness, s. Bonté *f,* bienveillance *f.*

kindly, a. *(a)* Bon, bienveillant. *(b)* (Climat) doux.

kindness, s. 1. Bonté *f (towards s.o.,* pour qn); bienveillance *f.* **2. To do s.o. a kindness,** rendre service à qn.

kindred. 1. *s. (a)* Parenté *f. (b)* *Coll.* Parents *mpl.* **2.** *a.* De la même nature.

king, s. 1. Roi *m. (a) F:* **Dish fit for a king,** morceau *m* de roi. *(b) F:* **One of the oil kings,** un des rois du pétrole. **2.** *(a) (At chess, cards)* Roi. *(b) (At draughts)* Dame *f.*

kingdom, s. 1. Royaume *m.* **The United Kingdom,** le Royaume-Uni. **2.** *Biol:* Règne (animal).

kingfisher, s. *Orn:* Martin-pêcheur *m, pl.* martins-pêcheurs.

kingly, a. De roi; royal, -aux.

kink¹, s. 1. Nœud *m* (dans une corde); faux pli. **2.** *F:* Faux pli (dans l'esprit).

kink², v.i. *(Of rope)* Se nouer.

kinsfolk, *s.pl.* Parents et alliés *mpl*; famille *f.*

kinship, s. Parenté *f.*

kinsman, s. Parent *m*; *Jur:* affin *m.*

kinswoman, s. Parente *f.*

kiosk, s. Kiosque *m.*

kipper, s. Hareng légèrement salé et fumé.

kiss¹, s. 1. Baiser *m.* **2.** *Bill:* Contre-coup *m.* **kiss-curl, s.** Accroche-cœur *m.*

kiss². 1. *v.tr.* Donner un baiser à, embrasser; baiser (le front de qn). *They kissed (each other),* ils se sont embrassés. **2.** *v.i. Bill:* *(Of balls)* Se frapper par contre-coup.

kit, s. 1. *(a)* Petit équipement; fourniment *m. (b)* Sac *m* (de marin). *(c) F:* Effets *mpl* (de voyageur). **2.** *Tchn:* Trousseau *m,* trousse *f* (d'outils). *Repair kit,* nécessaire *m* de réparation. **kit-bag, s. 1.** Sac *m* (de voyage). **2.** *Mil:* Ballot *m,* musette *f.*

kitchen, s. Cuisine *f.* **kitchen-garden, s.** (Jardin *m*) potager *m.* **kitchen-gardener, s.** Maraîcher *m.* **kitchen-utensils, s.pl.** Batterie *f* de cuisine.

kite, s. 1. *Orn:* Milan *m.* **2.** Cerf-volant *m, pl.* cerfs-volants.

kith, s. Our **kith and kin,** nos amis et parents.

kitten, s. Chaton *m*; petit(e) chat(te).

kittenish, a. *(Of girl). (a)* Coquette, aguichante. *(b)* Enjouée.

kitty, s. *Cards:* Cagnotte *f.*

kiwi, s. *Orn:* Aptéryx *m.*

kleptomania, s. Kleptomanie *f.*

kleptomaniac, a. & s. Kleptomane *(mf).*

knack, s. Tour *m* de main; *F:* truc *m.* **To have the knack of doing sth.,** avoir le coup pour faire qch.

knapsack, s. *(a)* Havresac *m*; sac *m. (b)* *Mil:* Sac d'ordonnance.

knave, s. 1. Fripon *m,* coquin *m.* **2.** *Cards:* Valet *m.*

knavery, s. Friponnerie *f,* coquinerie *f.*

knavish, a. De fripon; fourbe, malin. *K. trick,* coquinerie *f,* friponnerie *f.*

knead, v.tr. Pétrir, malaxer, travailler.

knee, s. Genou *m,* -oux. **To bow the knee to s.o.,** mettre un genou en terre devant qn. **On one's (bended) knees,** à genoux. **To go down on one's knees,** s'agenouiller; se mettre à genoux. **To go down on one's knees to s.o.,** se jeter aux genoux de qn. **knee-breeches, s.pl.** Culotte courte. **knee-cap, s.** *Anat:* Rotule *f.* **knee-deep, a.** Jusqu'aux genoux.

kneel, v.i. **To kneel (down),** s'agenouiller; se mettre à genoux. **kneeling, a.** Agenouillé; à genoux.

knell, s. Glas *m.* **Death knell,** glas funèbre.

knickerbockers, s.pl. Culotte (bouffante).

knick-knack, s. Colifichet *m,* bibelot *m.*

knife¹, s. *(a)* Couteau *m. (b)* **War to the knife,** guerre à couteaux tirés. *F:* **To have one's knife in s.o.,** s'acharner contre qn. **knife-edge, s.** Arête *f* en lame de couteau. **knife-grinder, s.** Rémouleur *m*; repasseur *m* de couteaux.

knife², v.tr. Donner un coup de couteau à; poignarder.

knight¹, s. 1. Chevalier *m.* **2.** *(At chess)* Cavalier *m.* **knight-errant, s.** Chevalier errant.

knight², v.tr. Faire, créer, chevalier; donner l'accolade à (qn).

knighthood, s. 1. Chevalerie *f.* **2.** Titre *m* de chevalier.

knightly, a. Chevaleresque; de chevalier.

knit, v.tr. *(a)* Tricoter. *(b)* **To knit one's brows,** froncer les sourcils. *(c)* Joindre, unir, lier. **knitting, s. 1.** Tricotage *m.* **2.** Tricot *m.* **knitting-needle, s.** Aiguille *f* à tricoter.

knob, s. 1. *(a)* Bosse *f,* protubérance *f. (b)* Pomme *f* (de canne); bouton *m,* olive *f* (de porte, de tiroir). **2.** Morceau *m* (d) charbon).

knock¹, s. 1. Coup *m,* heurt *m,* choc *m.* **To get a nasty knock,** attraper un vilain coup.

2. There was a knock (at the door), on frappa à la porte.

knock². **I.** *v.tr.* Frapper, heurter, cogner. To knock one's head against sth., (i) se cogner la tête contre qch.; (ii) *F:* se heurter à un obstacle. To knock sth. out of s.o.'s hand, faire tomber qch. de la main de qn. **2.** *v.i.* (a) Frapper, heurter (*at*, à). (b) To knock against sth., se heurter contre qch. **knock about**, *v.tr.* Bousculer, maltraiter, malmener. **knock down**, *v.tr.* **I.** Renverser; jeter par terre; étendre par terre d'un coup de poing; abattre (une muraille). **2.** To knock sth. down to s.o., adjuger qch. à qn. **knock-down**, *attrib.a.* Knock-down blow, coup d'assommoir. **knock off**. I. *v.tr.* **I.** (a) *To k. the handle off the jug*, faire sauter l'anse de la cruche. (b) To knock something off the price, rabattre quelque chose du prix. **2.** Faire tomber (le chapeau de qn). II. **knock off**, *v.i.* Cesser le travail. **knock out**, *v.tr.* Faire sortir; chasser (un rivet). **knock up**. **I.** *v.tr.* (a) *To k. s.o.'s hand up*, faire sauter la main de qn. (b) Construire à la hâte. (c) Éreinter, épuiser, échiner. **2.** *v.i.* (a) To knock up against sth., se heurter contre qch. *F:* To knock up against s.o., rencontrer qn par hasard. (b) S'effondrer (de fatigue). **knocking**, *s.* Coups *mpl.* **knock-kneed**, *a.* Cagneux.

knocker, *s.* (Door-)knocker, marteau *m* (de porte); heurtoir *m.*

knoll, *s.* Tertre *m*, monticule *m*, butte *f.*

knot¹, *s.* **I.** (a) Nœud *m.* To tie a knot, faire un nœud. (b) Nœud (de rubans). (c) Knot of hair, chignon *m.* **2.** *Nau:* (a) Nœud, division *f*, de la ligne de loch. (b) To make ten knots, filer dix nœuds. **3.** Nœud (du bois). **4.** Groupe *m.*

knot², *v.tr.* Nouer.

knotty, *a.* **I.** Plein de nœuds. **2.** *F:* Knotty point, question difficile. **3.** (a) (*Of plank*) Noueux. (b) Knotty hands, mains noueuses.

know¹, *s.* *F:* To be in the know, avoir le mot de l'affaire.

know², *v.tr.* **I.** (a) Reconnaître. *I knew him by his walk*, je l'ai reconnu à sa démarche. (b) Distinguer (*from*, de, d'avec). To know good from evil, connaître le bien d'avec le mal. **2.** (a) Connaître. To get to know s.o., faire la connaissance de qn. To be in surroundings one knows, être en pays de connaissance. (b) *He knows no fear*, il ne sait pas ce que c'est que d'avoir peur. **3.** Connaître, fréquenter (qn). **4.** Savoir, connaître, posséder (un sujet). To know how to do sth., savoir faire qch. To know by heart, savoir par cœur. **5.** (a) I know that well enough, je ne le sais que trop. As far as I know, autant que je sache. *He doesn't seem to k. the value of time*, il semble ignorer le prix du temps. *Is his father rich?*—I don't know, son père est-il riche?—Je n'en sais rien.

How do I know? est-ce que je sais? As everyone knows, comme tout le monde le sait. I would have you know that . . ., sachez que. . . . I know not what, je ne sais quoi. (b) *I k. him to be a liar*, je sais que c'est un menteur. He had never been known to laugh, on ne l'avait jamais vu rire. **6.** To get to know sth., apprendre qch. Please let us know whether, veuillez nous faire savoir si. Everything gets known, tout se sait. **7.** *F:* Don't I know it! à qui le dites-vous! Not if I know it! pour rien au monde! **8.** To know better than to, se bien garder de. *He knows better than to do that*, il est trop fin pour faire cela. You know best, vous en êtes le meilleur juge. **know about**, *v.i.* To know about sth., être informé de qch. He knows all about it, il est renseigné. I know nothing about it, je n'en sais rien. I don't know about that! je n'en suis pas bien sûr! **know of**, *v.i.* To know of s.o., connaître qn de réputation. To get to know of sth., apprendre qch. **known**, *a.* Connu, reconnu, su. A known thief, un voleur avéré. To make sth. known to s.o., porter qch. à la connaissance de qn. To make one's wishes known, déclarer ses volontés. It is known to all that, il est notoire que. He is known to everyone, il est connu partout. Known as, connu sous le nom de. **knowing¹**, *a.* Fin, malin, -igne, rusé. A knowing smile, un sourire entendu. **knowing²**, *s.* There is no knowing, il n'y a pas moyen de savoir.

knowledge, *s.* **I.** (a) Connaissance *f.* I had no knowledge of it, je l'ignorais. Lack of knowledge, ignorance *f* (*of*, de). It is a matter of common knowledge, il est notoire. To the best of my knowledge, autant que je sache. To my certain knowledge, à mon vu et su. Not to my knowledge, pas que je sache. Without my knowledge, à mon insu. To speak with full knowledge (of the facts), parler en connaissance de cause. (b) He had grown out of all knowledge, il était tellement grandi qu'on ne le reconnaissait plus. **2.** Savoir *m*, science *f*, connaissances. To have a thorough knowledge of a subject, connaître un sujet à fond. Knowledge of the world, la science du monde. Knowledge is power, savoir c'est pouvoir.

knuckle¹, *s.* Articulation *f*, jointure *f*, du doigt. To rap s.o. over the knuckles, donner sur les ongles à qn. **knuckle-duster**, *s.* Coup-de-poing américain.

knuckle², *v.i.* To knuckle under, se soumettre.

Koran (the), *s.* Le Koran, e Coran.

Korea. *Pr.n. Geog:* La Corée.

kotow, *v.i.* *F:* To kotow to s.o., courber l'échine devant qn.

Krakow. *Pr.n. Geog:* Cracovie *f.*

kudos, *s.* *F:* La gloriole.

L, l, *s.* (La lettre) L, l *m or f.*
la, *s. Mus:* La *m.*
label¹, *s.* Étiquette *f.*
label², *v.tr.* Étiqueter.
labial. 1. *a.* Labial, -aux. **2.** *s. Ling:* Labiale *f.*
laboratory, *s.* Laboratoire *m.*
laborious, *a.* Laborieux. **1.** Travailleur, -euse. **2.** Pénible, fatigant. **-ly,** *adv.* Laborieusement, péniblement.
labour¹, *s.* **1.** (*a*) Travail *m*, labeur *m*, peine *f.* (*b*) Hard labour, réclusion *f* avec travail disciplinaire. **2.** (*a*) *Ind:* Main-d'œuvre *f*; travailleurs *mpl.* **Manual labour,** main-d'œuvre. **Skilled labour,** main-d'œuvre spécialisée. **Capital and labour,** le capital et le travail. (*b*) **The Labour party,** le parti travailliste. **3.** Labour of love, travail fait avec plaisir. **labour-exchange,** *s.* Bureau *m* de placement(s).
labour². 1. *v.i.* (*a*) Travailler, peiner. (*b*) To labour under a delusion, se faire illusion. **2.** *v.tr.* I will not labour the point, je ne m'étendrai pas là-dessus. **laboured,** *a.* **1.** (Style) travaillé. **2.** (Respiration) pénible. **labouring,** *a.* Labouring man, ouvrier *m.* The labouring class, la classe ouvrière.
labourer, *s.* (*a*) Travailleur. (*b*) *Ind:* Manœuvre *m*; homme *m* de peine. (*c*) Agricultural labourer, ouvrier *m* agricole.
laburnum, *s. Bot:* Cytise *m*; faux ébénier.
labyrinth, *s.* Labyrinthe *m*, dédale *m.*
lace¹, *s.* **1.** Lacet *m*; cordon *m* (de soulier). **2.** Gold lace, galon *m*, passement *m* d'or. **3.** Dentelle *f*, point *m.*
lace², *v.tr.* To lace (up) one's boots, lacer ses bottines. **Lace-up shoes,** chaussures à lacets.
lacerate, *v.tr.* Lacérer; *F:* déchirer.
laceration, *s.* Lacération *f*, déchirement *m.*
lachrymose, *a.* Larmoyant.
lack¹, *s.* Manque *m*, absence *f*, défaut *m* (*of*, de). For lack of, faute de.
lack², *v.tr. & i.* To lack (for) sth., manquer de qch.; ne pas avoir qch. **lacking,** *a.* Qui manque; manquant. He is lacking in courage, il manque de courage.
lackey, *s.* Laquais *m.*
laconic, *a.* Laconique. **-ally,** *adv.* Laconiquement.
lacquer¹, *s.* Vernis-laque *m inv*; laque *m.*
lacquer², *v.tr.* **1.** Laquer. **2.** *F:* Vernir.
lacrosse, *s. Games:* Crosse canadienne.
lad, *s.* (*a*) Jeune homme *m*; (jeune) garçon *m.* Now then, my lads! allons, les gars! (*b*) *F:* He's a regular lad! c'est un gaillard!
ladder¹, *s.* **1.** Échelle *f.* **2.** (*In silk stockings*) Maille partie; éraillure *f*, échelle.

ladder², *v.i.* (*Of stocking*) Se démailler.
laden, *a.* Chargé.
ladle¹, *s.* Cuiller *f* à pot. Soup ladle, cuiller à potage; louche *f.*
ladle², *v.tr.* To ladle (out) the soup, servir le potage (avec la louche).
lady, *s.* Dame *f.* **1.** (*a*) Femme bien élevée. (*b*) A lady and a gentleman, un monsieur et une dame. Young lady, demoiselle *f*, jeune fille *f.* **Ladies and gentlemen!** Mesdames, mesdemoiselles, messieurs! *F:* messieurs-dames! (*c*) Ladies' tailor, tailleur pour dames. **Lady doctor,** femme médecin; docteur *m* femme. **2.** My lady, madame *f* (la comtesse). **3.** *F:* My young lady, ma bonne amie.
lady-bird, *s. Ent:* Coccinelle *f*; *F:* bête *f* à bon Dieu. **Lady day,** *s. Ecc:* La fête de l'Annonciation. **lady-in-waiting,** *s.* Dame d'honneur.
ladylike, *a.* (Air) de dame; (*of pers.*) comme il faut.
ladyship, *s.* Her ladyship, madame *f* (la comtesse).
lag, *v.i.* To lag (behind), rester en arrière; traîner.
lager, *s.* Lager (beer), bière blonde allemande.
laggard. 1. *a.* Lent, paresseux. **2.** *s.* Traînard *m*; lambin, -ine.
lagoon, *s.* Lagune *f.*
lair, *s.* Tanière *f*, repaire *m.*
lake¹, *s* Lac *m.*
lake², *s. Paint:* Laque *f.*
lama, *s. Buddhist Rel:* Lama *m.*
lamb, *s.* Agneau *m.* Ewe lamb, agnelle *f.* *F:* He took it like a lamb, il s'est laissé faire.
lambent, *a.* Blafard.
lame¹, *a.* **1.** Boiteux. To be lame in one leg, boiter d'une jambe. To go lame, se mettre à boiter. **2.** Lame excuse, faible excuse.
lame², *v.tr.* (*a*) Rendre boiteux; écloper. (*b*) Estropier.
lameness, *s.* **1.** (*a*) Claudication *f*; boitement *m.* (*b*) Boiterie *f* (d'un cheval). **2.** Faiblesse *f* (d'une excuse).
lament¹, *s.* Lamentation *f.*
lament², *v.tr. & i.* To lament (over) sth., se lamenter sur qch.; pleurer qch. **lamented,** *a.* The late lamented, le regretté.
lamentable, *a.* Lamentable, déplorable. **-ably,** *adv.* Lamentablement, déplorablement.
lamentation, *s.* Lamentation *f.*
lamp, *s.* **1.** (*a*) Lampe *f.* Stable lamp, falot *m.* Pocket lamp, torche *f*; lanterne *f* de poche. (*b*) Lanterne (de voiture). Side lamps, feux *m* de côté. **2.** Standard lamp, torchère *f*; lampadaire *m.* **3.** *El:* Lampe, ampoule *f.*

lamp-black, *s.* Noir *m* de fumée. **lamp-post,** *s.* Réverbère *m.* **lamp-shade,** *s.* Abat-jour *m inv.*

lamplight, *s.* Lumière *f* de la lampe. **To work by lamplight,** travailler à la lampe.

lamplighter, *s.* Allumeur *m* de réverbères.

lampoon, *s.* Pasquinade *f,* libelle *m.*

lance, *s.* Lance *f.* **lance-corporal,** *s. Mil:* Soldat *m* de première classe.

lancer, *s.* **1.** *Mil:* Lancier *m.* **2.** *pl.* Lancers, (quadrille *m* des) lanciers.

lancet, *s. Med:* Lancette *f,* bistouri *m.*

land¹, *s.* **1.** *(a)* Terre *f.* **Dry land,** terre ferme. **To travel by land,** voyager par voie de terre. **By land and sea,** sur terre et sur mer. *F:* **To see how the land lies,** sonder, tâter, le terrain. *(b)* Terre, terrain *m,* sol *m.* **2.** Terre, pays *m,* contrée *f.* **3.** Terre(s) ; fonds *m* de terre ; terrain(s). **land-agent,** *s.* **1.** Intendant *m,* régisseur *m,* d'un domaine. **2.** Courtier *m* en immeubles. **land-lubber,** *s. F:* Marin *m* d'eau douce. **land-slide,** *s.* Éboulement *m* de terrain.

land². **1.** *v.tr.* *(a)* Mettre, faire descendre, à terre ; débarquer. **To land an aeroplane,** atterrir un avion. *(b)* **To land a fish,** amener un poisson à terre. *F:* **To land a prize,** remporter un prix. *(c)* Amener. *F:* **That will land you in prison,** cela vous vaudra de la prison. **2.** *v.i.* *(a)* Descendre à terre ; débarquer ; *(of aeroplane)* atterrir. *(b)* Tomber (à terre). *(c)* *F:* **He always lands on his feet,** il retombe toujours sur ses pattes. **landed,** *a.* **Landed property,** propriété foncière. **Landed proprietor,** propriétaire terrien. **landing¹,** *a.* **Landing force,** troupes *fpl* de débarquement. **landing²,** *s.* **1.** *(a)* *Nau:* Débarquement *m* ; mise *f* à terre. *(b)* *Mil:* Descente *f.* *(c)* *Av:* Atterrissage *m.* **To make a forced landing,** faire un atterrissage forcé. **2.** *Const:* Palier *m* (d'un escalier). **landing-ground,** *s.* *Av:* Terrain *m* d'atterrissage. **landing-net,** *s.* *Fish:* Épuisette *f.* **landing-stage,** *s.* Débarcadère *m* ; embarcadère *m* (flottant).

landfall, *s.* *Nau:* Arrivée *f* en vue de terre.

landlady, *s.* **1.** Propriétaire *f* (d'un immeuble). **2.** Logeuse *f* (en garni). **3.** Hôtelière *f,* hôtesse *f* ; *F:* patronne *f.*

landlocked, *a.* Enfermé entre les terres.

landlord, *s.* **1.** Propriétaire (foncier). **2.** Propriétaire (d'un immeuble) **3.** Aubergiste *m,* hôtelier *m,* hôte *m*

landmark, *s.* **1.** (Point *m* de) repère *m.* *Nau:* Amer *m.* **2.** Événement marquant.

landowner, *s.* Propriétaire foncier.

landscape, *s.* Paysage *m*

lane, *s.* *(In country)* Chemin vicinal, rural ; *(in town)* ruelle *f,* passage *m.*

language, *s.* **1.** Langue *f.* **2.** Langage *m.* **Bad language,** langage grossier ; gros mots.

languid, *a.* Languissant ; mou, *f.* molle. **-ly,** *adv.* Languissamment ; mollement.

languish, *v.i.* Languir. **languishing,** *a.* Languissant, langoureux.

languor, *s.* Langueur *f.*

lank, *a.* **1.** Maigre ; sec, *f.* sèche. **2.** **Lank hair,** cheveux plats.

lankiness, *s.* Taille grande et maigre.

lanky, *a.* Grand et maigre ; grand et sec.

lantern, *s.* *(a)* Lanterne *f,* falot *m.* *Nau:* Fanal *m,* -aux. **Dark lantern,** lanterne sourde. **Chinese lantern,** lanterne vénitienne. *(b)* **Magic lantern,** lanterne magique. **lantern-jawed,** *a.* Aux joues creuses.

lanyard, *s.* **1.** *Nau:* Amarrage *m.* **2.** *Artil:* (Cordon *m*) tire-feu *m inv.*

lap¹, *s.* **1.** Pan *m,* basque *f* (d'un vêtement). **2.** **To sit on s.o.'s lap,** s'asseoir sur les genoux de qn. **lap-dog,** *s.* Bichon *m* ; chien *m* de salon.

lap², *s.* *Sp:* Tour *m* (de piste) ; boucle *f,* circuit *m.*

lap³. **1.** *v.tr.* **To lap (up) milk,** laper du lait. **2.** *v.i.* Clapoter.

lapel, *s.* *Tail:* Revers *m* (d'un habit).

Lapland. *Pr.n.* La Laponie.

Laplander, *s.* Lapon, -one.

Lapp, *a. & s.* Lapon, -one.

lapse¹, *s.* **1.** *(a)* Erreur *f,* faute *f.* **Lapse of memory,** défaillance *f* de mémoire. *(b)* Faute ; faux pas ; écart *m* de conduite. **2.** Cours *m,* marche *f* (du temps) ; laps *m* de temps. *After a l. of three months,* après un délai de trois mois.

lapse², *v.i.* **1.** Déchoir. *To l. into silence,* rentrer dans le silence. **3.** *Jur:* (Se) périmer ; tomber en désuétude. *Ins:* Cesser d'être en vigueur. **lapsed,** *a.* **1.** Déchu. **2.** Périmé ; (contrat) caduc, *f.* caduque.

lapwing, *s.* *Orn:* Vanneau *m.*

larceny, *s.* *Jur:* Larcin *m* ; vol insignifiant. **Petty larceny,** vol simple.

larch, *s.* *Bot:* Mélèze *m.*

lard, *s.* Saindoux *m* ; graisse *f* de porc.

larder, *s.* Garde-manger *m inv.*

large. **I.** *a.* *(a)* De grandes dimensions ; grand ; gros, *f.* grosse, fort. *To grow l., larger,* grossir, grandir. *(b)* *A l. sum,* une grosse, forte, somme ; une somme considérable. *L. family,* famille nombreuse. **-ly,** *adv.* En grande partie ; pour une grande part. **II.** **large.** *(a)* **To set a prisoner at large,** élargir, relaxer, un prisonnier. **To be a! large,** être libre, en liberté. *(b)* **The people at large,** le grand public **large-sized.** *a* De grandes dimensions.

lariat, *s.* **1.** Corde *f* à piquet. **2.** Lasso *m.*

lark¹, *s.* *Orn:* Alouette *f* *F:* **To rise with the lark,** se lever au chant du coq

lark², *s.* *F:* Farce *f,* rigolade *f,* blague *f.* **For a lark,** histoire de rigoler.

lark³, *v.i.* *F:* Faire des farces ; rigoler.

larkspur, *s.* *Bot:* Pied-d'alouette *m.*

larva, *s.* Larve *f.*

larynx, *s.* *Anat:* Larynx *m.*

lascar, *s.* Lascar *m.*

lascivious, *a.* Lascif. **-ly,** *adv.* Lascivement.

lash¹, *s.* **I.** (*a*) Coup *m* de fouet; sanglade *f*, cinglon *m.* (*b*) Lanière *f* (de fouet). **2.** = EYE-LASH.

lash², *v.tr. & i.* (*a*) Fouailler, cingler. *F:* To lash oneself into a fury, entrer dans une violente colère. (*b*) (*Of animal*) To lash its tail, se battre les flancs avec la queue. **lash out,** *v.i.* **I.** (*Of horse*) Ruer. (*Of pers.*) To lash out at s.o., lancer un coup de langue à qn. **2.** To lash out into expenditure, se livrer à de folles dépenses. **lashing,** *s.* **I.** Fouettée *f.* **2.** *pl. F:* Lashings, profusion *f* (*of,* de).

lash³, *v.tr.* Lier, attacher.

lass, *s.* Jeune fille *f.*

lassitude, *s.* Lassitude *f.*

lasso¹, *s.* Lasso *m.*

lasso², *v.tr.* Prendre au lasso.

last¹, *s. Bootm:* Forme *f* (à chaussure).

last². **I.** *a.* Dernier. **I.** She was the last to arrive, elle arriva la dernière. The last but one, l'avant dernier. In the last resort, en dernier ressort. *F:* The last word in hats, chapeau dernier cri. Last thing at night, tard dans la soirée. **2.** Last week, la semaine dernière. This day last week, il y a aujourd'hui huit jours. This day last year, l'an dernier à pareil jour. **-ly,** *adv.* Pour finir . . .; en dernier lieu. **II. last,** *s.* **I.** This last, ce dernier, cette dernière. **2.** (*a*) We shall never hear the last of it, on ne nous le laissera pas oublier. *We haven't heard the l. of it,* tout n'est pas dit. *That is the l. I saw of him,* je ne l'ai pas revu depuis. (*b*) To, till, the last, jusqu'au bout, jusqu'à la fin. (*c*) At last, enfin. (*d*) To look one's last on sth., jeter un dernier regard sur qch. **III. last,** *adv.* (*a*) *When I saw him l.,* la dernière fois que je l'ai vu. (*b*) He came last, il est arrivé le dernier.

last³, *v.i.* Durer, se maintenir. It's too good to last, c'est trop beau pour durer. *The supplies will not last two months,* les vivres n'iront pas deux mois. *It will l. me a lifetime,* j'en ai pour la vie. *F:* He won't last long, il n'ira pas loin. **lasting,** *a.* Durable.

latch¹, *s.* (*a*) Loquet *m.* (*b*) Serrure *f* de sûreté. To leave the door on the latch, fermer la porte à demi-tour. **latch-key,** *s.* Clef *f* de maison.

latch², *v.tr* Fermer (la porte) à demi-tour.

late. **I.** *a.* **I.** (*a*) En retard. (*b*) Retardé. **2.** Tard. It is getting late, il se fait tard. *I was too l.,* je ne suis pas arrivé à temps. *F:* It is late in the day to change your mind, il est un peu tard pour changer d'avis. At a late hour (in the day), bien avant dans la journée. In the late afternoon, tard dans l'après-midi. In late summer, vers la fin de l'été. **3.** Tardif. Late frosts, gelées tardives. **4.** (*a*) Ancien, ex-. *The l. minister,* l'ancien ministre, l'ex-ministre. (*b*) My late father, feu mon père, mon père décédé. **5.** Récent,

dernier. Of late years, (dans) ces dernières années. Of late, dernièrement. That is the latest, c'est ce qu'il y a de plus nouveau. **-ly,** *adv.* Dernièrement, récemment. Till lately, jusqu'à ces derniers temps. As lately as yesterday, hier encore; pas plus tard qu'hier. **II. late,** *adv.* **I.** En retard. To arrive too late, arriver trop tard. *Prov:* Better late than never, mieux vaut tard que jamais. **2.** Early and late, à toute heure du jour; du matin au soir. To keep s.o. late, attarder qn. Very late at night, bien avant dans la nuit. Late in life, à un âge avancé. No later than yesterday, hier encore; pas plus tard qu'hier. A moment later, l'instant d'après. *F:* See you later! à plus tard! **3.** Late of London, dernièrement domicilié à Londres. **late-comer,** *s.* Retardataire *mf.*

lateness, *s.* **I.** Arrivée tardive. **2.** The lateness of the hour, l'heure avancée.

latent, *a.* Latent; caché.

lateral, *a.* Latéral, -aux. **-ally,** *adv.* Latéralement.

lath, *s. Const:* Latte *f.*

lathe, *s. Tls:* Tour *m.*

lather¹, *s.* **I.** Mousse *f* de savon. **2.** (*On horse*) Écume *f.*

lather². **I.** *v.tr.* (*a*) Savonner (le menton). (*b*) *F:* Rosser (qn); fouailler (un cheval). **2.** *v.i.* (*Of soap*) Mousser. **lathering,** *s.* **I.** Savonnage *m.* **2.** *F:* Rossée *f;* fouaillée *f.*

Latin. **I.** *a. & s.* Latin, -ine. **2.** *s. Ling:* Le latin.

latish, *a. & adv.* (*a*) Un peu en retard. (*b*) Un peu tard.

latitude, *s.* **I.** To allow s.o. the greatest latitude, laisser à qn la plus grande latitude. **2.** *Geog:* Latitude *f.* In these latitudes, sous ces latitudes.

latter, *a.* **I.** Dernier (des deux). The latter, ce, le, dernier, cette, la, dernière; celui-ci, ceux-ci, celle(s)-ci. **2.** The latter half of the story, la dernière moitié de l'histoire. **-ly,** *adv.* Dernièrement.

lattice, *s.* Treillis *m,* treillage *m.* **lattice-window,** *s.* Fenêtre treillagée.

Latvia. *Pr.n.* La Lettonie; la Latvie.

Latvian, *a. & s.* **I.** *Geog:* Letton, -one. **2.** *s. Ling:* Le lette.

laudable, *a.* Louable; digne d'éloges. **-ably,** *adv.* Louablement.

laudanum, *s.* Laudanum *m.*

laudatory, *a.* Élogieux.

laugh¹, *s.* Rire *m.* To burst into a laugh, éclater de rire. With a laugh, en riant. *F:* To have the laugh of s.o. mettre les rieurs de son côté.

laugh². **I.** *v.i.* Rire. (*a*) *To l. heartily,* rire de bon cœur. To laugh till one cries, rire (jusqu')aux larmes. To laugh to oneself, rire en soi-même. To laugh up one's sleeve, rire sous cape. (*b*) To laugh at sth., rire de qch. There is nothing to laugh at, il n'y a pas de quoi rire. To laugh at s.o., se moquer, (se) rire, de qn. **2.** *v.tr. We laughed him out*

of it, nous nous sommes tellement moqués de lui qu'il y a renoncé. **To laugh s.o. to scorn,** accabler qn de ridicule. **He laughed the matter off,** il tourna la chose en plaisanterie. **laughing¹,** *a.* Riant ; rieur, -euse. **-ly,** *adv.* En riant. **laughing²,** *s.* Rires *mpl.* **It is no laughing matter,** il n'y a pas de quoi rire. **laughing-stock,** *s.* **To make a laughing-stock of oneself,** se faire moquer de soi. **laughable,** *a.* Risible, ridicule. **-ably,** *adv.* Risiblement.
laughter, *s.* Rire(s) *m(pl).* **To be convulsed with laughter,** se tordre de rire. **To roar with laughter,** rire aux éclats.
launch¹, *s.* Chaloupe *f.* **Motor launch,** bateau *m* automobile ; vedette *f.*
launch², **1.** *v.tr.* (*a*) Lancer. (*b*) *Mil :* **To launch an offensive,** déclencher une offensive. **2.** *v.i.* **To launch out (into expense),** se lancer dans la dépense ; se mettre en frais.
launching, *s.* Lancement *m.*
laundress, *s.* Blanchisseuse *f.*
laundry, *s.* **1.** **Laundry(-works),** blanchisserie *f.* **2.** Linge blanchi ou à blanchir.
laureate, *a. & s.* Lauréat, -ate.
laurel, *s.* *Bot :* Laurier *m.* *F :* **To rest on one's laurels,** se reposer sur ses lauriers.
lava, *s.* Lave *f.*
lavatory, *s.* **1.** Cabinet *m* de toilette ; lavabo *m.* **2.** Water-closet *m*, cabinets *mpl.*
lavender. **1.** *s.* Lavande *f.* **2.** *a.* (*Colour*) Lavande *inv.* **lavender-water,** *s.* Eau *f* de lavande.
lavish¹, *a.* **1.** Prodigue (*in, of,* de). **To be lavish of praise,** prodiguer des louanges. **2.** Somptueux ; abondant. *L. expenditure,* dépenses folles. **-ly,** *adv.* Avec prodigalité.
lavish², *v.tr.* Prodiguer, répandre (son argent). **To lavish sth. on s.o.,** prodiguer qch. à qn.
lavishness, *s.* Prodigalité *f.*
law, *s.* **1.** Loi *f.* **Laws of a game,** règles *f* d'un jeu. **2. The law,** la loi. *F :* **His word is law,** sa parole fait loi. **To lay down the law,** faire la loi (*to s.o.,* à qn). **To take the law unto oneself,** n'en faire qu'à sa tête. **3.** Droit *m.* **To study law,** faire son droit. **Doctor of Laws,** docteur en droit. **4.** **Court of law,** cour *f* de justice ; tribunal *m*, -aux. **To go to law,** avoir recours à la justice. **To go to law with s.o.,** citer qn en justice. **To be at law,** être en procès. **To take the law into one's own hands,** se faire justice à soi-même.
law-abiding, *a.* Respectueux des lois ; ami de l'ordre. **law-breaker,** *s.* Violateur, -trice, de la loi.
lawful, *a.* Légal, -aux. **1.** Permis, licite ; loisible. **2.** (Droit) légitime. **-fully,** *adv.* Légalement, légitimement.
lawless, *a.* Déréglé, désordonné.
lawlessness, *s.* Dérèglement *m*, anarchie *f.*
lawn, *s.* Pelouse *f* ; (parterre *m* de) gazon *m.*
lawn-mower, *s.* Tondeuse *f* (de gazon).
lawn-tennis, *s.* (Lawn-)tennis, *m.*

Lawrence. *Pr.n.* Laurent *m.*
lawsuit, *s.* Procès *m* ; *F :* affaire *f.*
lawyer, *s.* **1.** Homme *m* de loi. **2.** = (i) SOLICITOR, (ii) BARRISTER.
lax, *a.* **1.** (*a*) (*Of conduct*) Relâché ; (*of pers.*) négligent ; (gouvernement) mou. (*b*) Vague ; peu exact. **2.** (*Limp*) Mou, *f.* molle ; flasque.
laxity, *s.* (*a*) Relâchement *m* (des mœurs) ; inexactitude *f* à remplir ses devoirs. (*b*) Vague *m*, imprécision *f* (de langage).
lay¹, *a.* Laïque, lai. *F :* **To the lay mind,** aux yeux du profane.
lay², *s.* **1.** *F :* Genre *m* d'affaires ; spécialité *f.* **2. Lay of the land,** configuration *f* du terrain.
lay³, *v.tr.* **1.** Coucher. **2.** (*a*) Abattre (la poussière). (*b*) Exorciser, conjurer (un esprit). **3.** Mettre, placer, poser (*sth. on sth.,* qch. sur qch.). **To have nowhere to lay one's head,** n'avoir pas où reposer la tête. **To lay s.o. to rest,** mettre qn au tombeau. **4.** Pondre (un œuf). **5.** Faire (un pari) ; parier (une somme). **6.** *Jur :* **To lay a complaint,** déposer une plainte ; porter plainte. **7.** (*a*) **To lay a tax on sth.,** mettre un impôt sur qch. ; frapper qch. d'un impôt. (*b*) **To lay a stick on s.o.'s back,** rosser qn. **To lay about one,** frapper de tous côtés. **8.** (*a*) Poser, asseoir (des fondements) ; ranger (des briques). **To lay the table, the cloth,** mettre le couvert. **To lay for three,** mettre trois couverts. **To lay a carpet,** poser un tapis. **To lay the fire,** préparer le feu. (*b*) Dresser, tendre (un piège). (*c*) *Th :* *The scene is laid in Paris,* la scène se passe à Paris. **lay aside,** *v.tr.* Mettre de côté. **lay by,** *v.tr.* Mettre de côté ; réserver. **lay down,** *v.tr.* **1.** (*a*) Déposer, poser. **To lay down one's arms,** mettre bas les armes. (*b*) Coucher, étendre. (*c*) **To lay down one's life,** donner sa vie (*for,* pour). **2.** Poser, établir (une règle) ; fixer (des conditions) ; stipuler. **lay in,** *v.tr.* Faire provision, s'approvisionner, de. **lay on,** *v.tr.* **1.** (*a*) *To lay on the lash,* appliquer le fouet. (*b*) *Abs.* He laid on with a will, il frappait, il y allait, de bon cœur. **2.** Installer (le gaz). **lay out,** *v.tr.* **1.** Arranger, disposer. **2.** *F :* Étendre d'un coup ; coucher par terre. **3.** Dépenser, débourser. **4.** Dessiner (un jardin). **5.** **To lay oneself out to please,** se mettre en frais pour plaire. **lay-out,** *s.* Tracé *m* ; dessin *m.* **lay up,** *v.tr.* **1.** **To lay up trouble for oneself,** s'apprêter bien des ennuis. **2.** **To lay up a car,** remiser une voiture. **3.** **To be laid up,** être alité, au lit.
layer, *s.* **1.** (*Of hen*) **Good layer,** bonne pondeuse **2.** Couche *f* (de peinture).
lay-figure, *s.* *Art :* Mannequin *m.*
laze, *v.tr. & i.* Paresser, fainéanter.
laziness, *s.* Paresse *f*, fainéantise *f.*
lazy, *a.* Paresseux, fainéant. **-ily,** *adv.* Paresseusement. **lazy-bones,** *s.* Paresseux, -euse ; fainéant, -ante.
lead¹, *s.* **1.** Plomb *m.* **White lead,** blanc *m*

de plomb; céruse f. Red lead, minium m. **2.** Mine f (de crayon). **3.** Nau: (Plomb de) sonde f. **lead-foil,** s. Papier m de plomb. **lead², s. I.** Conduite f. (a) **To follow s.o.'s lead,** se laisser conduire par qn; suivre l'exemple de qn. **To give the lead,** F: donner le ton. (b) **To take the lead,** (i) prendre la tête; (ii) prendre la direction. **2.** Cards: **Your lead!** à vous de jouer. **3.** Th: Premier rôle. **4.** (For dog) Laisse f. **On a lead,** en laisse.

lead³, v. **I.** v.tr. **I.** (a) Mener, conduire, guider. **To lead s.o. into temptation,** entraîner qn dans la tentation. (b) **To lead the way,** aller devant. **2.** Conduire; mener (un cheval). **He is easily led,** il va comme on le mène. **3.** (a) Mener (une vie heureuse). (b) **To lead s.o. a wretched life,** faire une vie d'enfer à qn. **4.** (a) Commander (une armée). (b) Mener (la danse). **5.** (In race) Abs. Tenir la tête. **6.** Cards: Abs. Ouvrir le jeu; jouer le premier. **II. lead,** v.i. **I.** (Of road) Mener, conduire (to, à). **2. To lead to a discovery,** conduire à une découverte. **To lead to nothing,** n'aboutir, ne mener, à rien. **lead away,** v.tr. **I.** Emmener. **2.** Entraîner, détourner (qn). **To be led away,** se laisser entraîner. **lead back,** v.tr. Ramener, reconduire. **lead on,** v.tr. Conduire, entraîner. **Lead on!** en avant! **To lead s.o. on to talk,** encourager qn à parler. **lead up,** v.i. **To lead up to a subject,** amener un sujet. **leading,** a. **I.** Jur: Leading question, question tendancieuse. **2.** Premier; principal, -aux. Leading article, Journ: = LEADER 2. Th: Leading man, lady, premier rôle; vedette f.

leaden, a. De plomb. **Leaden-eyed,** aux yeux ternes.

leader, s. **I.** (a) Conducteur, -trice; guide m. (b) Mil: Chef m. (c) Chef, directeur m (d'un parti); meneur m (d'une émeute). **2.** Journ: Article principal.

leadership, s. Conduite f.

leaf, s. **I.** Feuille f. **In leaf,** couvert de feuilles. **2.** Feuillet m (de livre). **To turn over the leaves of a book,** feuilleter un livre. F: **To turn over a new leaf,** changer de conduite. **To take a leaf out of s.o.'s book,** prendre exemple sur qn. **3.** Battant m (de porte).

leaflet, s. Feuillet m; papillon m (de publicité).

leafy, a. Feuillu; couvert de feuilles.

league¹, s. Meas: Lieue f.

league², s. Ligue f. **He was in league with them,** il était ligué avec eux.

league³, v.i. **To league (together),** se liguer.

leak¹, s. (a) Fuite f, écoulement m. (b) Nau: Voie f d'eau. **To spring a leak,** faire une voie d'eau.

leak², v.i. **I.** Avoir une fuite; fuir, couler. **2.** (Of ship) Faire eau. **leak out,** v.i. S'ébruiter, transpirer.

leakage, s. **I.** Fuite f. **2.** F: Leakage of official secrets, fuite de secrets officiels.

leaky, a. (a) (Tonneau) qui coule, qui perd, qui fuit. (b) (Bateau) qui fait eau.

lean¹. I. a. Maigre. (a) Amaigri, décharné; (of animal) efflanqué. (b) Lean meat, viande maigre. **2.** s. Maigre m (de la viande).

lean², v. **I.** v.i. (a) S'appuyer (against, on, sth., contre, sur, qch.). **To lean on one's elbow,** s'appuyer sur qn. (b) Se pencher (over, sur); (of wall), incliner, pencher. (c) To l. towards mercy, incliner vers la clémence. **2.** v.tr. To l. a ladder against the wall, appuyer une échelle contre le mur. **leaning¹,** a. Penché, penchant; hors d'aplomb. **leaning²,** s. Inclination f (towards, pour); tendance f (towards, à).

leanness, s. Maigreur f.

leap¹, s. Saut m, bond m. **To take a leap in the dark,** faire un saut dans l'inconnu. **To advance by leaps and bounds,** avancer par bonds et par sauts. **leap-frog,** s. Games: Saute-mouton m. **leap-year,** s. Année f bissextile.

leap², v. **I.** v.i. (a) Sauter, bondir. To l. over the ditch, sauter le fossé. F: **To leap at an offer,** sauter sur une offre. **To leap for joy,** sauter de joie. (b) (Of flame) To leap (up), jaillir. **2.** v.tr. Sauter.

learn, v.tr. **I.** Apprendre. F: **I have learnt better since then,** j'en sais plus long maintenant. **2.** Apprendre (une nouvelle).

learned, a. Savant, instruit. **-ly,** adv. Savamment. **learning,** s. **I.** Action f d'apprendre. The l. of the lessons, l'étude f des leçons. **2.** Science f, instruction f, érudition f.

learner, s. Élève mf, commençant, -ante, débutant, -ante.

lease¹, s. Jur: Bail m, pl. baux. F: **To take (on) a new lease of life,** se reprendre à la vie.

lease², v.tr. **I. To lease (out),** louer; donner à bail. **2.** Prendre à bail; louer. **leasing,** s. Location f à bail.

leasehold. a. Tenu à bail.

leaseholder, s. Locataire mf à bail.

leash, s. Laisse f, attache f.

least. I. a. (The) least, (le, la) moindre; (le, la) plus petit(e). **2.** s. (The) least, (le) moins. **To say the least (of it),** pour ne pas dire plus. **At least,** (tout) au moins. **I can at least try,** je peux toujours essayer. **Not in the least,** pas le moins du monde. **It does not matter in the least,** cela n'a pas la moindre importance. **3.** adv. (The) least, (le) moins. **He deserves it least of all,** il le mérite moins que personne.

leather¹, s. Cuir m. **Fancy leather-work,** maroquinerie f.

leather², v.tr. F: Étriller, rosser. **leathering,** s. F: **To give s.o. a leathering,** tanner le cuir à qn.

leave¹, s. **I.** Permission f, permis m. **By**

your leave, avec votre permission. **2.** (*a*) *Mil:* **Leave** (**of absence**), (*in months*) congé *m*; (*in days*) permission *f*. (*b*) **Release of prisoner on ticket of leave,** libération conditionnelle. **3.** **To take one's leave,** prendre congé; faire ses adieux. **To take French leave,** filer à l'anglaise.

leave², *v.tr.* **I.** Laisser. (*a*) *F:* **Take it or leave it,** c'est à prendre ou à laisser. (*b*) **To leave one's money to s.o.,** laisser, léguer, sa fortune à qn. (*c*) **To leave the door open,** laisser la porte ouverte. **Left to oneself,** livré à soi-même. **L. him to himself,** laissez-le faire. **Let us leave it at that,** demeurons-en là. (*d*) **To leave go of sth.,** lâcher qch. (*e*) *To l. one's bag in the cloak-room,* déposer sa valise à la consigne. **Left-luggage office,** consigne. (*f*) **Leave it to me,** remettez-vous-en à moi; laissez-moi faire. (*g*) **To be left,** rester. *There are three bottles left,* il reste trois bouteilles. **2.** (*a*) Quitter. *To l. the room,* sortir (de la salle). **To leave .he table,** se lever de table. **On leaving school,** au sortir du collège. **We leave to-morrow,** nous partons demain. (*b*) Abandonner. (*c*) (*Of train*) **To leave the rails,** dérailler. **leave about,** *v.tr.* Laisser traîner. **leave behind,** *v.tr.* Laisser (son parapluie). **leave off. I.** *v.tr* (*a*) Quitter (un vêtement). (*b*) **To leave off work,** cesser le travail. **2.** *v.i.* Cesser, s'arrêter. *Where did we l. off?* où en sommes-nous restés? **leave out,** *v.tr.* **I.** Exclure. **2.** (*a*) Omettre. (*b*) Oublier. **leave over,** *v.tr.* **I.** Remettre à plus tard. **2.** **To be left over,** rester. **leaving,** *s.* **I.** Départ *m.* **2.** *pl.* Leavings, restes *m.*

leaven¹, *s.* Levain *m.*

leaven², *v.tr. F:* Modifier (*with*, par).

Lebanon. *Pr.n. Geog:* Le Liban.

lecture¹, *s* **I.** Conférence *f* (*on*, sur); leçon *f* (*on*, de). **2.** *F:* Sermon *m*, semonce *f.*

lecture². **I.** *v.i.* Faire une conférence; faire un cours. **2.** *v.tr. F:* Sermonner, semoncer.

lecturer, *s.* Conférencier, -ière.

ledge, *s.* Rebord *m*; saillie *f*; (*on building*) corniche *f.*

ledger, *s. Book-k:* Grand livre.

lee, *s.* (*a*) *Nau:* Côté *m* sous le vent. **Under the lee of the land,** sous le vent de la terre. (*b*) Abri *m* (contre le vent). **lee-shore,** *s. Nau:* Terre *f* sous le vent.

leech, *s.* Sangsue *f.*

leek, *s* Poireau *m.*

leer¹, *s.* Œillade *t* en dessous; mauvais regard de côté.

leer², *v.i* To leer at s.o., (i) lorgner, guigner, qn d'un air méchant: (ii) lancer des œillades à qn.

leeward. *Nau:* **I.** *a. & adv.* Sous le vent. **2.** *s.* Côté *m* sous le vent.

leeway, *s. Nau:* Dérive *f. F:* **He has considerable leeway to make up,** il a un fort retard à rattraper.

left. I. *a.* Gauche. **On my left hand,** à ma

gauche. **2.** *adv. Mil:* **Eyes left!** tête (à) gauche! **3.** *s.* Gauche *f.* **On the left, to the left,** à gauche. **left-hand,** *attrib.a.* **On the left-hand side,** à gauche. **left-handed,** *a.* Gaucher.

leg, *s.* **I.** Jambe *f*; patte *f* (de chien). *F:* **To take to one's legs,** prendre ses jambes à son cou. **I ran as fast as my legs would carry me,** j'ai couru à toutes jambes. **To be on one's last legs,** tirer vers sa fin; être à bout de ressources. **To give s.o. a leg up,** (i) faire la courte échelle à qn; (ii) *F:* donner à qn un coup d'épaule. *F:* **To pull s.o.'s leg,** se payer la tête de qn. **2.** *Cu:* **Leg of chicken,** cuisse *f* de volaille. **Leg of mutton,** gigot *m.* **3.** Jambe (de pantalon); tige *f* (de bas). **4.** Pied *m* (de table). **leg-pull,** *s. F:* Mystification *f.*

legacy, *s.* Legs *m.* **To leave a legacy to s.o.,** faire un legs à qn.

legal, *a.* **I.** Légal, -aux; licite. **2.** Légal; judiciaire, juridique. **Legal document,** acte *m* authentique. **Legal practitioner,** homme de loi. **To take legal advice,** consulter un avocat. **-ally,** *adv.* Légalement.

legality, *s.* Légalité *f.*

legalize, *v.tr.* Rendre légal; légaliser.

legate, *s.* Légat *m.*

legatee, *s.* Légataire *mf.*

legation, *s.* Légation *f.*

legend, *s.* Légende *f*, fable *f.*

legendary, *a.* Légendaire.

legerdemain, *s.* (Tours *mpl* de) passe-passe *m*; tour d'adresse; escamotage *m.*

leggings, *s.pl. Cost:* Jambières *f*; guêtres *f.*

Leghorn. *Pr.n. Geog:* Livourne *f.*

legibility, *s.* Lisibilité *f*, netteté *f.*

legible, *a.* Lisible, net, *f.* nette. **-ibly,** *adv.* Lisiblement.

legion, *s.* Légion *f. F:* **Their name is Legion,** ils sont innombrables.

legislate, *v.i.* Faire les lois; légiférer.

legislation, *s.* Législation *f.*

legislative, *a.* Législatif.

legislator, *s.* Législateur *m.*

legislature, *s.* Législature *f.*

legitimacy, *s.* Légitimité *f.*

legitimate, *a.* Légitime. **-ly,** *adv.* Légitimement.

leisure, *s.* Loisir(s) *m(pl).* **To have leisure for reading,** avoir le loisir, le temps, de lire. **To be at leisure,** être de loisir. **In my leisure moments,** à mes moments perdus.

leisured, *a.* De loisir; désœuvré.

leisurely. I. *a.* Qui n'est jamais pressé. **Leisurely pace,** allure mesurée. **2.** *adv.* (*a*) A tête reposée. (*b*) Posément; sans se presser.

lemon. I. *s. Bot:* Citron *m*, limon *m.* **2.** *a.* Jaune citron *inv.* **lemon-squash,** *s.* Citron pressé; citronnade *f.* **lemon-squeezer,** *s.* Presse-citrons *m inv.* **lemon-tree,** *s. Bot:* Citronnier *m*, limonier *m.*

lemonade, *s.* Limonade *f.* **Still lemonade,** citronnade *f*; citron pressé.

lemur, *s. Z:* Lémur *m.*
lend, *v.tr.* **I.** Prêter. **2.** To lend an ear, prêter l'oreille. **3.** *v.pr. Spot that lends itself to meditation,* lieu propice à la méditation.
lending, *s.* Prêt *m.*
lender, *s.* Prêteur, -euse.
length, *s.* **I.** Longueur *f.* To be two feet in length, avoir deux pieds de longueur ; être long de deux pieds. *(Of ship)* To turn in its own length, virer sur place. *Row:* To win by a length, gagner d'une longueur. I fell my full length, je suis tombé de tout mon long. **2.** *Stay of some length,* séjour assez prolongé. **Length of service,** ancienneté *f. To recite sth. at length,* réciter qch. tout au long. *To speak at some length,* parler assez longuement. **At length,** enfin, à la fin. **3.** To go to the length of asserting, aller jusqu'à prétendre. To go to great lengths, pousser les choses bien loin. **4.** Morceau *m,* bout *m* (de ficelle). *Dressm:* Dress length, coupon *m* de robe.
lengthen. **I.** *v.tr.* Allonger, rallonger ; prolonger. **2.** *v.i.* S'allonger, se rallonger ; *(of days)* augmenter, croître. **lengthening,** *s.* **I.** Allongement *m,* rallongement *m ;* prolongation *f.* **2.** Augmentation *f* (des jours).
lengthiness, *s.* Longueurs *fpl ;* prolixité *f.*
lengthways, *adv.* En longueur ; en long.
lengthy, *a.* Assez long, prolixe. **-ily,** *adv.* Longuement, avec prolixité.
leniency, *s.* Clémence *f ;* douceur *f,* indulgence *f (to, towards,* pour).
lenient, *a.* Clément ; doux, *f.* douce ; indulgent *(to, towards,* envers, pour). **-ly,** *adv.* Avec clémence, avec douceur.
lens, *s. Opt:* *(a)* Lentille *f ;* verre *m.* *(b)* Loupe *f ;* verre grossissant.
Lent, *s. Ecc:* Le carême.
lentil, *s. Hort:* Lentille *f.*
leonine, *a.* De lion(s) ; léonin.
leopard, *s.* Léopard *m.*
leper, *s.* Lépreux, -euse.
leprosy, *s. Med:* Lèpre *f.*
leprous, *a.* Lépreux.
less. **I.** *a.* *(a)* Moindre. Quantities less than, quantités au-dessous de. To grow less, s'amoindrir. *(b)* Eat less meat, mangez moins de viande. **2.** *prep.* Moins. **3.** *s.* Moins *m.* In l. than an hour, en moins d'une heure. **4.** *adv.* *(a)* Less known, moins connu. One man less, un homme de moins. Less than six, moins de six. Less and less, de moins en moins. *He continued* none the less, il n'en continua pas moins. *None the less he came in first,* néanmoins il arriva premier. *(b)* He fears it no less than I, il ne le craint pas moins que moi.
lessee, *s* Locataire *mf* (à bail).
lessen. **I.** *v.i.* S'amoindrir, diminuer. **2.** *v.tr.* Amoindrir, diminuer.
lesson, *s.* Leçon *f.* To take lessons in French, prendre des leçons de français. *F:* Let that be a lesson to you! que cela vous serve d'exemple, de leçon !

lessor, *s.* Bailleur, -eresse.
lest, *conj.* **I.** Lest we forget, de peur que nous n'oubliions. **2.** *I feared l.* he should fall, je craignais qu'il (ne) tombât. *I feared l.* I should fall, j'avais peur de tomber.
let, *v.* **I.** *v.tr.* **I.** *(a)* Permettre ; laisser. *Let me tell you,* permettez-moi de vous dire. To let fall, slip, laisser échapper. He let go the rope, il lâcha la corde. *When can you let me have my coat?* quand pourrai-je avoir mon habit ? *(b)* To let s.o. know sth., about sth.,* faire savoir qch. à qn. *Let me hear the story,* racontez-moi l'histoire. **2.** House to let, maison à louer. **II.** **let,** *v.aux. Let us make haste!* dépêchons-nous ! Let there be no mistake about it! qu'on ne s'y trompe pas ! Let me see! voyons ! attendez un peu !
let down, *v.tr.* **I.** Baisser (un store) ; défaire (ses cheveux). **2.** *I won't let you down,* vous pouvez compter sur moi. **let in,** *v.tr.* **I.** Laisser entrer. *Shoes that let in water,* souliers qui prennent l'eau. **2.** *F:* *(a)* Mettre dedans ; rouler, duper. *(b)* *I did not know what I was letting myself in for,* je ne savais pas à quoi je m'engageais. **let into,** *v.tr.* To let s.o. into the house, laisser entrer qn dans la maison. To let s.o. into a secret, mettre qn dans le secret. **let off,** *v.tr.* **I.** Tirer, faire partir (un feu d'artifice). **2.** Lâcher, laisser échapper (de la vapeur). **3.** To let s.o. off, faire grâce à qn. To be let off with a fine, en être quitte pour une amende. **let on,** *v.i. & tr. F:* To let on about sth. to s.o., rapporter qch. à qn. **let out,** *v.tr.* **I.** Laisser sortir ; élargir (un prisonnier). *F:* To let out a yell, laisser échapper un cri. **2.** Louer. **letting,** *s.* Louage *m.*
lethal, *a.* Mortel. Lethal weapon, arme meurtrière, léthifère.
lethargic(al), *a.* Léthargique. **-ally,** *adv.* Lourdement, paresseusement.
lethargy, *s.* Léthargie *f.*
Lett, *s. Ethn:* Letton, -one.
letter[1]**,** *s.* **I.** Lettre *f,* caractère *m.* To the letter, au pied de la lettre. **2.** Lettre, missive *f.* To open the letters, dépouiller le courrier. **3.** *pl.* Letters, lettres ; belles-lettres ; littérature *f.* **letter-balance,** *s.* Pèse-lettres *m inv.* **letter-box,** *s* Boîte *f* aux lettres. **letter-card,** *s.* Carte-lettre *f, pl.* cartes-lettres. **letter-opener,** *s.* Ouvre-lettres *m inv.* **letter-paper,** *s.* Papier *m* à lettres.
letter[2]**,** *v.tr.* Marquer avec des lettres.
lettering, *s.* **I.** Lettrage *m.* **2.** Lettres *fpl ;* inscription *f.*
letterpress, *s.* **I.** *Typ:* Impression *f* typographique. **2.** Texte *m.*
Lettish. **I.** *a. Geog:* Letton, -one. **2.** *s. Ling:* Le lette, le letton.
lettuce, *s.* Laitue *f*
Levant[1]**.** *Geog: Pr.n.* The Levant, le Levant.
levant[2]**,** *v.i. F:* Partir sans payer.
Levantine, *a. & s. Geog:* Levantin, -ine.

level¹. I. *s.* **I.** *Tls:* Niveau *m.* **2.** Niveau (de la mer). **On a level with sth.,** à la hauteur de qch. *Drawing-room on a l. with the garden,* salon de plain-pied avec le jardin. **3.** *(a)* Surface *f* de niveau ; terrain *m* de niveau. *Rail:* Palier *m.* **On the level,** *F:* de bonne foi. *Aut:* **Speed on the level,** vitesse en palier. *(b) Min:* Niveau, étage *m.* II. **level,** *a.* **I.** *(a)* De niveau, à niveau ; en palier. *(b) (Flat)* Égal, -aux ; uni. *(c)* **Level with,** de niveau avec ; au niveau de ; à (la) hauteur de. **L. with the water,** à fleur de l'eau. *Sp :* **To draw level with,** arriver à (la) hauteur de. **2. To keep a level head,** garder sa tête, son sang-froid. *F:* **To do one's level best,** faire tout son possible. **level-headed,** *a.* Qui a la tête bien équilibrée.

level², *v.tr.* **I.** Niveler. **2.** Pointer (un fusil), diriger (une longue-vue) *(at, sur).* *F:* **To level accusations against s.o.,** lancer des accusations contre qn. **To level a blow at s.o.,** porter un coup à qn. **levelling,** *s.* **I.** Nivellement *m.* **2.** Pointage *m* (d'une arme à feu).

lever¹, *s. Mec:* Levier *m. Aut:* **Gear lever,** levier des vitesses.

lever², *v.tr.* **To lever sth. up,** soulever qch. au moyen d'un levier.

leverage, *s.* **I.** Force *f,* puissance *f,* de levier. **2.** Système *m* de leviers.

leveret, *s.* Levraut *m.*

levity, *s.* Légèreté *f ;* manque *m* de sérieux.

levy¹, *s.* **I.** Levée *f.* **2.** Impôt *m,* contribution *f.*

levy², *v.tr.* Lever, percevoir.

lewd, *a.* Impudique, lascif. **-ly,** *adv.* Impudiquement, lascivement.

lewdness, *s.* Impudicité *f,* lasciveté *f.*

Lewis. *Pr.n.* Louis *m.*

lexicon, *s.* Lexique *m.*

liability, *s.* **I.** *Jur:* Responsabilité *f.* **2.** *pl. Com:* **Liabilities,** ensemble *m* des dettes ; engagements *mpl,* obligations *fpl.* **Assets and liabilities,** actif *m* et passif *m.* **To meet one's liabilities,** faire face à ses engagements. **3.** *(a)* **Liability to a fine,** risque *m* d'amende. *(b)* Disposition *f,* tendance *f (to sth.,* à qch.). *(c) L. to explode,* danger *m* d'explosion.

liable, *a.* **I.** *Jur:* Responsable *(for,* de). **2. Liable to a fine,** passible d'une amende. *L. to military service,* astreint au service militaire. **3.** Sujet, -ette, apte, exposé *(to,* à). **4.** *Difficulties are l. to occur,* des difficultés sont susceptibles de se présenter.

liaison, *s.* Liaison *f.*

liana, *s. Bot:* Liane *f.*

liar, *s.* Menteur, -euse.

libel¹, *s.* Diffamation *f,* calomnie *f.*

libel², *v.tr. Jur:* Diffamer ; calomnier.

libellous, *a.* Diffamatoire, calomnieux.

liberal, *a.* **I.** *(a)* Libéral, -aux. *(b)* D'esprit large ; sans préjugés. *In the most l. sense of the word,* au sens le plus large du mot. **2.** *(a)* Libéral, généreux. **Liberal to s.o.,**

généreux envers qn. *(b)* Libéral, abondant. **3.** *a. & s. Pol:* Libéral *(m).* **-ally,** *adv.* Libéralement.

liberality, *s.* Libéralité *f.*

liberate, *v.tr.* Libérer ; mettre en liberté.

liberation, *s.* Libération *f ;* mise *f* en liberté.

liberator, *s.* Libérateur, -trice.

libertine, *a. & s.* Libertin *(m).*

liberty, *s.* Liberté *f.* *(a)* **To be at liberty to do sth.,** être libre de faire qch. *You are at l. to believe me or not,* libre à vous de ne pas me croire. *(b)* **To take the liberty of doing sth.,** se permettre de faire qch. *(c)* **To take liberties with s.o.,** prendre des libertés, se permettre des privautés *f,* avec qn.

librarian, *s.* Bibliothécaire *m.*

library, *s.* Bibliothèque *f.* **Lending library,** cabinet *m* de lecture. **Reference library,** salle *f* de lecture.

Libya. *Pr.n.* La Libye.

Libyan, *a. & s.* Libyen, -enne.

licence, *s.* **I.** *(a)* Permission *f,* autorisation *f.* *(b) Adm:* Permis *m,* autorisation. **Liquor licence,** patente *f* de débit de boissons. **Marriage licence,** dispense *f* de bans. **Gun licence,** permis de port d'armes. **To take out a licence,** se faire inscrire à la patente. *Aut:* **Driving licence,** permis de conduire. **2.** *(a)* Licence *f.* **Poetic licence,** licence poétique. *(b)* = LICENTIOUSNESS.

license, *v.tr.* Accorder un permis, une patente, à ; patenter (qn). **Licensed dealer,** patenté. **Licensed house,** débit *m* de boissons. *Av:* **Licensed pilot,** pilote breveté.

licensee, *s.* Patenté, -ée.

licentious, *a.* Licencieux, dévergondé.

licentiousness, *s.* Licence *f,* dérèglement *m,* dévergondage *m.*

lichen, *s.* Lichen *m.*

lick¹, *s.* Coup *m* de langue.

lick². **I.** *v.tr.* Lécher. **To lick one's lips,** se (pour)lécher les babines. *F:* **To lick s.o.'s boots,** lécher les bottes à qn. **To lick a recruit into shape,** dégrossir une recrue. **2.** *v.tr. F:* Battre, rosser. **This licks me,** ça me dépasse. **3.** *v.i. F:* **As hard as he could lick,** à toute vitesse. **licking,** *s.* *F:* *(a)* **To give s.o. a good licking,** rosser qn d'importance. *(b)* Défaite *f.*

lid, *s.* **I.** Couvercle *m.* *P:* **That puts the lid on it!** ça, c'est le comble ! **2.** = EYELID.

lie¹, *s.* *(a)* Mensonge *m.* **It's a pack of lies,** pure invention tout cela ! **To tell lies,** mentir. *(b)* **To give s.o. the lie (direct),** donner un démenti (formel) à qn.

lie², *v.i.* Mentir *(to s.o.,* à qn). **lying¹,** *a.* Menteur, -euse ; faux, *f.* fausse. **lying²,** *s.* Le mensonge.

lie³, *s.* **I.** Disposition *f.* **Lie of the land,** configuration *f,* disposition, du terrain. **2.** *Golf:* Position *f,* assiette *f.*

lie⁴, *v.i.* **I.** *(a)* Être couché. **To lie dead,** être étendu mort. **Here lies,** ci-gît. *(b)* Être, rester, se tenir. **To lie in ambush,** se tenir en embuscade. **To lie still,** rester tranquille. **To lie under suspicion,** être soupçonné. **2.** Être, se trouver. *His clothes were lying on the ground,* ses habits gisaient par terre. *The snow lies deep,* la neige est épaisse. *The snow never lies there,* la neige n'y séjourne jamais. **Time lies heavy on my hands,** le temps me pèse. *The onus of proof lies with them,* c'est à eux qu'incombe le soin de faire la preuve. **The difference lies in this,** la différence réside en ceci. **As far as in me lies,** autant qu'il m'est possible. **lie about,** *v.i.* Traîner. **lie back,** *v.i.* Se laisser retomber. **lie by,** *v.i. To have sth. lying by,* avoir qch. en réserve. **lie down,** *v.i.* **1.** Se coucher, s'étendre. **2.** *F: He won't take it lying down,* il ne se laissera pas faire. **lie over,** *v.i.* Rester en suspens. **lie up,** *v.i. F:* Garder le lit. **lying³,** *a.* Couché, étendu.

lien, *s.* Lien on goods, droit *m* de rétention de marchandises.

lieu, *s.* In lieu of, au lieu de.

lieutenant, *s.* Lieutenant *m.* *Navy:* Lieutenant de vaisseau. **Second lieutenant,** sous-lieutenant *m.* **lieutenant-colonel,** *s.* Lieutenant-colonel *m, pl.* lieutenants-colonels. **lieutenant-commander,** *s. Navy:* Capitaine *m* de corvette. **lieutenant-general,** *s.* Général *m* de corps d'armée.

life, *s.* **1.** Vie *f.* **It is a matter of life and death,** il y va de la vie. **Life-and-death struggle,** lutte désespérée. **To take s.o.'s life,** tuer qn. **To take one's own life,** se suicider. **To save s.o.'s life,** sauver la vie à qn. **To sell one's life dearly,** vendre cher sa peau. **He was carrying his life in his hands,** il risquait sa vie. **To escape with one's life,** s'en tirer la vie sauve. **To fly for one's life,** s'enfuir à toutes jambes. *F: I cannot for the life of me understand,* je ne comprends absolument pas. **Not on your life!** jamais de la vie! **To put new life into sth.,** ranimer (une entreprise). **He is the life and soul of the party,** c'est le boute-en-train de la compagnie. **Animal life,** la vie animale. **2.** *(a)* Vie, vivant *m.* **Never in (all) my life,** jamais de la vie. **At my time of life,** à mon âge. **Tired of life,** las de vivre. **Life annuity,** rente viagère. **Penal servitude for l.,** travaux forcés à perpétuité. *(b)* Biographie *f.* *(c)* Durée *f* (d'une lampe). **3. To depart this life,** mourir. *F: What a life!* quel métier! **Such is life!** c'est la vie! **He has seen life,** il a beaucoup vécu. **life-belt,** *s.* Ceinture *f* de sauvetage. **life-blood,** *s.* Sang *m.* **life-boat,** *s.* Canot *m* de sauvetage. **life-buoy,** *s.* Bouée *f* de sauvetage. **life-guard,** *s. Mil:* Garde *f* du corps. **life-preserver,** *s.* Casse-tête *m inv.* **life-saving,** *s.* Sauvetage *m.* **Life-saving apparatus,** engins *mpl* de sauvetage. **life-size,** *a.* De grandeur naturelle.

lifeless, *a.* Sans vie; inanimé.

lifelike, *a.* (Portrait) vivant.

lifelong, *a.* De toute la vie.

lifetime, *s.* Vie *f.* **In his lifetime,** de son vivant.

lift¹, *s.* **1.** Haussement *m*; levée *f.* *F: To give s.o. a lift,* faire monter qn avec soi (dans sa voiture). **To get a lift up in the world,** monter un degré de l'échelle sociale. **2.** Ascenseur *m.* **lift-attendant,** *s.* Liftier, -ière.

lift². I. *v.tr.* **1.** *(a)* Lever; soulever. **To lift one's hand against s.o.,** lever la main sur qn. **To lift up one's head,** redresser la tête. **To lift up one's voice,** élever la voix. **To lift sth. down,** descendre qch. *(b) The church lifts its spire to the skies,* l'église dresse sa flèche vers le ciel. **2.** *F:* Voler, lever. II. **lift,** *v.i.* *(Of fog)* S'élever. **lifting,** *s.* Levage *m,* relevage *m,* soulèvement *m.*

light¹, *s.* **1.** Lumière *f.* *(a)* By the light of the sun, à la lumière du soleil. *(b)* It is light, il fait jour. *F:* I was beginning to see light, le jour se faisait dans mon esprit. To come to light, se découvrir. To bring (sth.) to light, mettre au jour. *(c)* Éclairage *m.* Seated in one's own light, assis à contre-jour. To stand in s.o.'s light, cacher le jour à qn. *F:* To stand in one's own light, ne pas se faire valoir. I do not look upon it in that light, ce n'est pas ainsi que j'envisage la chose. *(d)* To throw light on sth., jeter le jour sur qch.; éclairer qch. To act according to one's lights, agir selon ses lumières. **2.** *(a)* Lumière, lampe *f,* bougie *f.* *F: One of the leading lights of the party,* une des lumières, un des hommes marquants, du parti. *(b)* The light, the lights, la lumière, l'éclairage *m.* *(c)* Feu *m,* phare *m.* *Mil:* Lights out, (sonnerie *f* de) l'extinction *f* des feux. *F:* To see the red light, se rendre compte du danger. *Adm:* (Traffic) lights, feux de circulation. *(d)* = LIGHTHOUSE. **3. Give me a light, please,** voudriez-vous bien me donner du feu? **4.** *Art:* Light and shade, les clairs *m* et les ombres *f.*

light². I. **1.** *v.tr.* *(a)* Allumer. *L. a fire in my room,* faites du feu dans ma chambre. *Abs.* To light up, allumer. *(b)* Éclairer, illuminer. *(c) A smile lighted (up) her face,* un sourire illumina son visage. **2.** *v.i.* *(a)* S'allumer; prendre feu. *(b)* S'éclairer, s'illuminer. *Her face lit up,* son visage s'éclaira. **lighting,** *s.* **1.** Allumage *m.* **2.** Éclairage *m.* *Adm:* Lighting-up time, heure *f* d'éclairage.

light³, *a.* **1.** Clair; (bien) éclairé. **2.** *(Of hair)* Blond; *(of colour)* clair. **Light blue,** bleu clair *inv.* **light-coloured,** *a.* Clair.

light⁴, *a.* **1.** *(a)* Léger. **Light as a feather,** aussi léger qu'une plume. **To be light on one's feet,** avoir le pas léger. *(b)* Light weight, poids faible. **2.** *(a)* To travel light, voyager avec peu de bagages. *(b)* To be a light sleeper, avoir le sommeil léger. **3.** *(a)* Light punishment, peine légère. (b) **Light task,** tâche facile ; travail peu fatigant. **4. Light reading,** lecture(s) amusante(s). *F:* To make light of sth., traiter qch. à la légère. **5.** *adv.* To sleep light, avoir le sommeil léger. **-ly,** *adv.* **1.** Lightly clad, vêtu légèrement. To touch lightly on a delicate matter, couler sur un point délicat. His responsibilities sit lightly upon him, ses responsabilités ne lui pèsent pas. **2.** To get off lightly, s'en tirer à bon compte. **3.** To speak lightly of sth., parler de qch. à la légère. **light-fingered,** *a.* Aux doigts agiles. **light-footed,** *a.* Agile, leste. **light-headed,** *a.* To be light-headed, avoir le délire. **light-hearted,** *a.* Au cœur léger ; allègre. **-ly,** *adv.* Gaiement ; de gaîté de cœur.

light⁵, *v.i.* (a) (Of bird) S'abattre, se poser. (b) To light on one's feet, retomber sur ses pieds. (c) To light (up)on sth., trouver qch. par hasard.

lighten. **1.** *v.tr.* Alléger ; réduire le poids de. **2.** *v.i.* My heart lightened, mon cœur fut soulagé.

lighter¹, *s.* *Nau:* Allège *f*, chaland *m*.

lighter², *s.* Allumeur *m.* (Petrol-)lighter, briquet *m* à essence.

lighthouse, *s.* *Nau:* Phare *m.* **light-house-keeper,** *s.* Gardien *m* de phare.

lightness, *s.* Légèreté *f.*

lightning, *s.* Éclairs *mpl*, foudre *f*. A flash of lightning, un éclair. Struck by lightning, frappé de, par, la foudre. As quick as lightning, aussi vite que l'éclair. *F:* Lightning progress, progrès foudroyants. **lightning-conductor,** *s.* Paratonnerre *m.*

lightship, *s.* Bateau-feu *m*, pl. bateaux-feux.

like¹. I. *a.* Semblable, pareil, tel. **1.** (a) Two plants of l. species, deux plantes de même espèce. *Prov:* Like master, like man, tel maître tel valet. (b) They are as like as two peas, ils se ressemblent comme deux gouttes d'eau. **2.** (a) I want to find one l. it, je veux trouver le pareil, la pareille. A critic l. you, un critique tel que vous. *Pej:* Fellows like you, des gens de votre sorte. What is he like? comment est-il? He was like a father to me, il m'a servi de père. Old people are like that, les vieilles gens sont ainsi faits. I never saw anything like that, je n'ai jamais rien vu de pareil. Something like ten pounds, quelque dix livres. That's something like! à la bonne heure ! There is nothing l. health, rien de tel que la santé. She is nothing like so pretty as you, elle est bien loin d'être aussi jolie que vous. (b) That's just like a woman! voilà bien les femmes ! II. **like** *prep.* Comme. *F:* He ran like mad, il courait comme un dératé. He stood there l. a statue, il se tenait debout telle une statue. To hate s.o. like poison, haïr qn à l'égal de la peste. III. **like,** *adv. F:* Like enough; (as) like as not, probablement, vraisemblablement. IV. **like,** *s.* Semblable *mf* ; pareil,

-eille. I never heard the like (of it), je n'ai jamais entendu chose pareille.

like², *s.* Likes and dislikes, sympathies *f* et antipathies *f.*

like³, *v.tr.* **1.** Aimer. I l. him, je l'aime bien ; il me plaît. I came to l. him, il me devint sympathique. I don't l. his looks, son visage ne me revient pas. How do you l. him? comment le trouvez-vous? As much as ever you like, tant que vous voudrez. Your father won't l. it, votre père ne sera pas content. Whether he likes it or not, qu'il le veuille ou non. *F:* I like that! en voilà une bonne ! par exemple ! **2.** (a) I l. to see them, j'aime à les voir. I l. to be obeyed, j'aime qu'on m'obéisse. (b) As you like, comme vous voudrez. He is free to act as he likes, il est libre d'agir comme il lui plaira. To do just as one likes, en faire à sa tête. He thinks he can do anything he likes, il se croit tout permis. People may say what they like, on a beau dire. **liking,** *s.* Goût *m*, penchant *m.* To one's liking, à souhait. I have taken a l. to it, j'y ai pris goût. I have taken a l. to him, il m'est devenu sympathique.

likeable, *a.* Agréable, sympathique.

likelihood, *s.* Vraisemblance *f*, probabilité *f.* In all likelihood, selon toute probabilité.

likely. I. *a.* **1.** Vraisemblable, probable. He is hardly l. to succeed, il a peu de chances de réussir. **2.** Incident l. to lead to a rupture, incident susceptible d'entraîner une rupture. The likeliest place for camping, l'endroit le plus propre au camping. II. **likely,** *adv.* Most likely, very likely, vraisemblablement ; très probablement. As likely as not, (pour) autant que je sache. He will succeed as l. as not, il se pourrait bien qu'il réussisse. *P:* Not likely! pas de danger !

likeness, *s.* **1.** Ressemblance *f* (to, à). **2.** Apparence *f.* **3.** Portrait *m*, image *f.* The picture is a good likeness, le portrait est très ressemblant.

likewise, *adv.* **1.** De plus, également, aussi. **2.** To do likewise, faire de même.

lilac. **1.** *s.* Lilas *m.* **2.** *a.* Lilas *inv.*

lilt, *s.* **1.** Chant (joyeux). **2.** Rythme *m*, cadence *f* (des vers).

lily, *s.* *Bot:* **1.** Lis *m* **2.** Lily of the valley, muguet *m.*

limb, *s.* **1.** Membre *m.* To tear an animal limb from limb, mettre un animal en pièces. **2.** (a) Limb of Satan, suppôt *m* de Satan. (b) *F:* Polisson *m.* **3.** (Grosse) branche (d'un arbre).

limber¹, *s.* *Artil:* Avant-train *m.*

limber², *v.tr. Artil: Abs.* To limber up, mettre l'avant-train.

limber³, *a.* Souple, agile.

lime¹, *s.* **1.** = BIRD-LIME. **2.** Chaux *f.* Slaked lime, chaux éteinte. **lime-kiln,** *s.* Four *m* à chaux. **lime-water,** *s.* Eau *f* de chaux.

lime², *v.tr.* Gluer (des ramilles). To l. birds, prendre des oiseaux à la glu.

lime[3], *s.* *Bot:* Lime *f.* **Sweet lime**, limette *f.* **Sour lime**, limon *m.* **lime-juice**, *s.* Jus *m* de limon.

lime[4], *s.* **Lime(-tree)**, tilleul *m.*

limelight, *s.* Lumière *f* oxhydrique. *F:* **In the limelight**, très en vue.

limestone, *s.* *Miner:* Pierre *f* à chaux. *Geol:* Calcaire *m.*

limit[1], *s.* Limite *f*, borne *f.* *Within a three-mile l.*, dans un rayon de trois milles. **Age limit**, limite d'âge. *F:* **That's the limit!** ça c'est le comble ! **He's the limit!** il est impayable !

limit[2], *v.tr.* Limiter, borner, restreindre. *Publ:* **Limited edition**, édition à tirage restreint.

limitation, *s.* **I.** Limitation *f*, restriction *f.* **2. He has his limitations**, ses capacités sont bornées.

limitless, *a.* Sans bornes ; illimité.

limp[1], *s.* Boitement *m*, clochement *m*, claudication *f.* **To walk with a limp**, boiter.

limp[2], *v.i.* Boiter, clocher, clopiner. **limping**, *a.* Boiteux.

limp[3], *a.* Mou, *f.* molle ; flasque. **-ly**, *adv.* **I.** Mollement, flasquement. **2.** Sans énergie.

limpet, *s.* *Moll:* Patelle *f.*

limpid, *a.* Limpide, clair.

limpidity, *s.* Limpidité *f*, clarté *f.*

limpness, *s.* Mollesse *f.*

linden(-tree), *s.* Tilleul *m.*

line[1], *s.* **I.** (*a*) Ligne *f*, corde *f.* (*b*) Ligne (de pêche). (*c*) *Tp:* Ligne, fil *m.* (*d*) *F:* **It's hard lines**, c'est dur. **2.** (*a*) Ligne, trait *m*, raie *f.* (*b*) *The lines on his forehead*, les rides *f* de son front. (*c*) *Geog:* **The line**, la ligne, l'équateur *m.* (*d*) *The hard lines of his face*, ses traits durs. **To be working on the right lines**, être en bonne voie. (*e*) *F:* **One must draw the line somewhere**, il y a une limite à tout. **I draw the line at lying**, je ne vais pas jusqu'à mentir. **3.** (*a*) Ligne, rangée *f.* *F:* **I must try to fall into line with your ideas**, je vais essayer de me conformer à vos idées. (*b*) File *f* ; queue *f.* (*c*) *F:* **To drop s.o. a line**, envoyer un (petit) mot à qn. **Line of poetry**, vers *m.* *F:* **Marriage lines**, acte *m* de mariage. **4.** Ligne, compagnie *f* (de paquebots). **Shipping line**, messageries *f* maritimes. **5.** Ligne de descendants. **In direct line**, en ligne directe. **6.** *Rail:* Voie *f*, ligne. **7.** *L. of thought*, suite *f* d'idées. *L. of argument*, raisonnement *m.* *The l. to be taken*, la conduite à tenir. **8.** Genre *m* d'affaires ; métier *m.* *F:* **That's not in my line**, ce n'est pas (de) mon métier.

line[2], *v.tr.* **I.** (*Of face*) **To become lined**, se rider. **2.** Border. *The troops lined the streets*, les troupes formaient la haie. **line up. I.** *v.tr.* Aligner ; mettre en ligne. **2.** *v.i.* S'aligner.

line[3], *v.tr.* **I.** Doubler (un vêtement) (*with*, de). **2.** *Nest lined with moss*, nid garni de mousse. **lined** *a.* (Habit) doublé ; (gant)

fourré. **lining**, *s.* Doublure *f* (de robe) ; coiffe *f* (de chapeau).

lineage, *s.* Lignée *f*, lignage *m.*

lineal, *a.* Linéal, -aux. **Lineal descendant**, descendant en ligne directe.

lineament, *s* Trait *m*, linéament *m.*

linear, *a.* Linéaire.

linen, *s* **I.** Toile *f* (de lin). **2.** Linge *m*, lingerie *f.* *F:* *Don't wash your dirty l. in public*, il faut laver son linge sale en famille

linen-draper, *s.* Marchand de blanc, de nouveautés.

liner, *s.* *Nau:* **(Ocean) liner**, paquebot *m.* **Atlantic l.**, transatlantique *m.*

ling[1], *s.* *Ich:* Morue longue.

ling[2], *s.* *Bot:* Bruyère commune.

linger, *v.i.* (*a*) Tarder, s'attarder. *A doubt still lingered in his mind*, un doute subsistait encore dans son esprit. (*b*) **To linger (on)**, traîner. **lingering**, *a.* **I. Lingering look**, regard prolongé. *L. doubt*, doute qui subsiste encore. **2. Lingering death**, mort lente.

lingo, *s.* *F:* (i) La langue du pays ; (ii) baragouin *m*, jargon *m.*

lingual, *a.* Lingual, -aux.

linguist, *s.* Linguiste *mf.*

linguistic, *a.* Linguistique.

liniment, *s.* Liniment *m.*

link[1], *s.* **I.** (*a*) Chaînon *m*, maillon *m*, anneau *m* (d'une chaîne). (*b*) **(Sleeve-, cuff-)links**, boutons jumelés, à chaînettes. **2.** Lien *m*, trait *m* d'union (*between*, entre). **Missing link**, (i) lacune *f* ; (ii) *Biol:* pithécanthrope *m.*

link[2]. **I.** *v.tr.* Enchaîner, (re)lier, attacher (*with*, *to*, à). **To link arms**, se donner le bras. **2.** *v.i.* **To link on to sth.**, s'attacher à qch.

links, *s.pl.* Terrain *m* de golf.

linnet, *s.* *Orn:* Linotte *f.*

linoleum, *s.* Linoléum incrusté.

linseed, *s.* Graine *f* de lin.

lint, *s.* *Med:* Charpie anglaise.

lintel, *s.* Linteau *m.*

lion, *s.* **I.** (*a*) Lion *m.* **Lion's cub**, lionceau *m.* *F:* **The lion's share**, la part du lion. (*b*) **Mountain lion**, puma *m*, couguar *m.* **2.** *F:* Personnage marquant ; lion. **3. The Gulf of Lions**, le golfe du Lion. **lion-hearted**, *a.* Au cœur de lion.

lioness, *s.* Lionne *f.*

lip, *s.* **I.** (*a*) Lèvre *f* ; babine *f* (d'un animal). *F:* **To keep a stiff upper lip**, ne pas se laisser abattre. **To bite one's lip(s)**, se mordre les lèvres. **To smack one's lips over sth.**, se lécher les babines. (*b*) *F:* Insolence *f.* **2.** (*a*) Bord *m*, rebord *m* (d'une tasse). (*b*) Rebord, saillie *f.* **lip-deep**, *a.* Peu profond.

lipstick, *s.* *Toil:* Bâton *m* de rouge ; *F:* raisin *m.*

liquefaction, *s.* Liquéfaction *f.*

liquefy. I. *v.tr.* Liquéfier. **2.** *v.i.* Se liquéfier.

liqueur, *s.* Liqueur *f* (de dessert). **Liqueur brandy**, fine champagne ; *F:* fine *f.*

liquid. 1. *a.* *(a)* Liquide. *(b)* (Œil) limpide. *(c)* (Son) doux. *(d)* *Fin:* Liquid assets, valeurs *f* disponibles. *(e)* *Ling:* (Consonne) liquide. **2.** *s.* Liquide *m.*
liquidate, *v.tr.* *Com:* Liquider.
liquidation, *s.* *Com:* Liquidation *f.*
liquor, *s.* Boisson *f* alcoolique. Spirituous liquors, spiritueux *m.*
liquorice, *s.* Réglisse *f.*
Lisbon. *Pr.n.* *Geog:* Lisbonne *f.*
lisle, *a.* Lisle thread, fil *m* d'Écosse.
lisp¹, *s.* Zézayement *m,* blèsement *m.* To speak with a lisp, zézayer.
lisp², *v.i.* *&* *tr.* Zézayer ; être blèse ; *F:* zozoter. **lisping,** *a.* Blèse.
lissom(e), *a.* Souple, agile, leste.
list¹, *s.* Liste *f,* rôle *m,* tableau *m,* état *m.* Alphabetical list, répertoire *m* alphabétique. List of names, état nominatif. Wine list, carte *f* des vins. To be on the danger list, être dans un état grave. *F:* *Person* on the black list, personne notée ; suspect *m.*
list², *s.* *Nau:* Faux bord ; bande *f.*
list³, *v.i.* *Nau:* Donner de la bande ; avoir un faux bord ; prendre de la gîte.
listen, *v.ind.tr.* **1.** Écouter. To listen to sth., écouter qch. To l. attentively, prêter une oreille attentive. **2.** Faire attention ; écouter. **listen in,** *v.i.* *W.Tel:* Se mettre à l'écoute. **listening,** *s.* Écoute *f.*
listener, *s.* Auditeur, -trice.
listless, *a.* Nonchalant, distrait ; apathique. **-ly,** *adv.* Nonchalamment.
listlessness, *s.* Nonchalance *f,* apathie *f;* indifférence *f.*
litany, *s.* *Ecc:* Litanies *fpl.*
literal, *a.* *(a)* Littéral, -aux. To take sth. in a l. sense, prendre qch. au pied de la lettre. *(b)* Positif ; sans imagination. **-ally,** *adv.* Littéralement.
literary, *a.* Littéraire.
literature, *s.* Littérature *f;* œuvres *f* littéraires. Light l., lectures amusantes.
lithe, *a.* Souple, agile.
lithograph, *s.* Lithographie *f;* image lithographiée.
lithographic, *a.* Lithographique.
lithography, *s.* Lithographie *f.*
Lithuania. *Pr.n.* La Lithuanie.
Lithuanian, *a.* *&* *s.* Lithuanien, -ienne.
litigant, *s.* Plaideur, -euse.
litigation, *s.* Litige *m.*
litigious, *a.* Litigieux.
litmus, *s.* Tournesol *m.*
litter¹, *s.* **1.** *Veh:* Litière *f.* **2.** *Husb:* Litière. **3.** Fouillis *m,* désordre *m.* **4.** Portée *f* (d'un animal).
litter², *v.tr.* Mettre en désordre. *Table* littered over *with papers,* table encombrée de papiers.
little. I. *a.* **1.** Petit. Little ones, enfants *m.* The little finger, le petit doigt. **2.** Peu (de). Little money, peu d'argent. A little money, un peu d'argent. Ever so little, un tout petit

peu (de). **3.** (Esprit) mesquin. **II. little,** *s.* **1.** Peu *m.* To eat little or nothing, manger peu ou point. He knows very l., il sait peu de chose. I see very l. of him, je ne le vois guère. To think little of sth., faire peu de cas de qch. Little by little, petit à petit ; peu à peu. *Prov:* Every little helps, tout fait nombre. **2.** A little more, encore un peu. For a little (while), pendant un certain temps. **III. little,** *adv.* Peu. L. more than an hour ago, il n'y a guère qu'une heure.
littleness, *s.* Petitesse *f.*
littoral, *s.* Littoral *m.*
liturgic(al), *a.* Liturgique.
liturgy, *s.* Liturgie *f.*
live¹, *a.* **1.** *(a)* Vivant ; en vie. *F:* A real live burglar, un cambrioleur en chair et en os. *(b)* Live coals, charbons ardents. **2.** *El.E:* Live wire, fil en charge. *F:* He's a (real) live wire, il est très entreprenant. **live-stock,** *s.* *Husb:* Bétail *m,* bestiaux *mpl.*
live². **1.** *v.i.* Vivre. *(a)* While my father lives, du vivant de mon père. He cannot live through the winter, il ne passera pas l'hiver. *Prov:* Live and learn, on apprend à tout âge. Live and let live, il faut que tout le monde vive. *(b)* To l. on vegetables, se nourrir de légumes. He earns enough to l. upon, il gagne de quoi vivre. To live on one's capital, manger son capital. He lives by his pen, il vit de sa plume. *(c)* To live in style, mener grand train. To live well, faire bonne chère. To l. up to one's reputation, faire honneur à sa réputation. *(d)* Where do you live? où demeurez-vous? I l. at number 36, Wilson Street, je demeure rue Wilson, numéro 36. House not fit to live in, maison inhabitable. *(e)* He is living with his grandparents, il habite chez ses grands-parents. **2.** *v.tr.* To live a happy life, mener, passer, une vie heureuse. **live down,** *v.tr.* To live down a scandal, faire oublier un scandale à la longue. **live in,** *v.i.* The employees l. in, les employés sont logés et nourris. **living¹,** *a.* Vivant, vif ; en vie. Not a living soul is to be seen, on ne rencontre pas âme qui vive. No living man could do better, personne au monde ne pourrait mieux faire. *s.* The living, les vivants. He is still in the land of the living, il est encore de ce monde. **living²,** *s.* **1.** Vie *f.* Style of living, train *m* de vie. **2.** To earn one's living, gagner sa vie. To work for one's living, travailler pour vivre. To make a living, gagner de quoi vivre. **3.** *Ecc:* Bénéfice *m,* cure *f.* **living-room,** *s.* Salle familiale.
livelihood, *s.* Vie *f;* moyens *mpl* d'existence ; gagne-pain *m.*
liveliness, *s.* Vivacité *f,* animation *f,* entrain *m,* vie *f.*
livelong, *a.* The livelong day, toute la (sainte) journée ; tout le long du jour.
lively, *a.* *(a)* Vif, animé ; plein d'entrain. *(b)* *F:* Things are getting l., ça chauffe. To

have a lively time of it, en voir de toutes les couleurs. (c) To take a lively interest in sth., s'intéresser vivement à qch.
liven. I. *v.tr.* To liven (up), animer, 2. *v.i.* To liven up, s'animer.
liver, *s.* *Anat:* Foie *m.*
livery, *s.* Livrée *f.*
livid, *a.* Livide, blême.
Livy. *Pr.n.* Tite-Live *m.*
lizard, *s.* Lézard *m.*
llama, *s.* *Z:* Lama *m.*
load¹, *s.* I. (a) Fardeau *m.* (b) Charretée *f.* 2. Charge *f* (d'une arme à feu). 3. To have a load on one's mind, avoir un fardeau, un poids, sur l'esprit. 4. *pl.* *F:* Loads of, des tas *m* de.
load², *v.tr.* (a) Charger. To load s.o. with sth., charger qn de qch. (b) To load s.o. with favours, combler qn de faveurs. (c) To load a gun with ball-cartridge, charger un fusil à balle. **loaded,** *a.* I. Chargé. 2. Loaded cane, canne plombée. Loaded dice, dés pipés. **loading,** *s.* Chargement *m.*
loadstone, *s.* Pierre *f* d'aimant.
loaf¹, *s.* Pain *m*; miche *f* (de pain). Cottage loaf, pain de ménage. **loaf-sugar,** *s.* Sucre *m* en pains.
loaf², *v.i.* To loaf (about), flâner, fainéanter.
loafing, *s.* Flânerie *f*, fainéantise *f.*
loafer, *s.* Flâneur *m.*
loam, *s.* *Agr:* Terre grasse, végétale.
loan, *s.* I. Prêt *m.* 2. Emprunt *m.* *Fin:* To raise a loan, contracter un emprunt.
loath, *a.* To be loath to do sth., faire qch. à contre-cœur. *He did it nothing loath,* il l'a fait très volontiers.
loathe, *v.tr.* Détester, exécrer. *I l. doing it,* il me répugne de le faire. **loathing,** *s.* Dégoût *m*, répugnance *f* (*for,* pour).
loathsome, *a.* Repoussant, écœurant, dégoûtant, répugnant.
lobby, *s.* Vestibule *m.*
lobe, *s.* *Nat.Hist:* Lobe *m.*
lobelia, *s.* *Bot:* Lobélie *f.*
lobster, *s.* Homard *m.* **lobster-pot,** *s.* Casier *m* à homards.
local, *a.* Local, régional; de la localité. Local government, administration décentralisée. **-ally,** *adv.* Localement. *He is well known l.,* il est bien connu dans la région.
locality, *s.* I. *F:* To have the bump of locality, avoir la bosse de l'orientation. 2. Localité *f*; endroit *m*, voisinage *m.* *In this l.,* *F:* dans ces parages.
locate, *v.tr.* I. Localiser; découvrir. 2. To be located in a place, être situé dans un endroit.
location, *s.* Situation *f*, emplacement *m.*
lock¹, *s.* Mèche *f*, boucle *f* (de cheveux).
lock², *s.* I. Serrure *f*, fermeture *f.* Under lock and key, sous clef. 2. Platine *f* (de fusil). *F:* Lock, stock, and barrel, tout sans exception. 3. *Hyd.E:* Écluse *f.* **lock-gate,** *s.*

Porte *f* d'écluse. **lock-keeper,** *s.* Gardien *m* d'écluse; éclusier *m.*
lock³, *v.tr.* I. Fermer à clef. 2. To be locked in a struggle, être engagés corps à corps dans une lutte. To be locked in each other's arms, se tenir étroitement embrassés. **lock in,** *v.tr.* Enfermer à clef; mettre sous clef. **lock out,** *v.tr.* Lock-outer (le personnel). **lock-out,** *s.* *Ind:* Lock-out *m.inv.* **lock up,** *v.tr.* (a) Mettre sous clef. (b) To lock s.o. up, enfermer qn; écrouer qn au dépôt. **lock-up,** *s.* *F:* Poste *m* de police.
locker, *s.* Armoire *f* ou coffre *m* (fermant à clef).
locket, *s.* Médaillon *m* (porté en parure).
locksmith, *s.* Serrurier *m.*
locomotion, *s.* Locomotion *f.*
locomotive. I. *a.* Locomotif, locomobile. 2. *s.* Locomotive *f.*
locum-tenens, *s.* Remplaçant, -ante; suppléant, -ante (d'un médecin).
locust, *s.* Grande sauterelle.
locution, *s.* Locution *f.*
lode, *s.* *Min:* Filon *m*, veine *f*, gisement *m.*
lodestone, *s.* = LOADSTONE.
lodge¹, *s.* I. Loge *f*; pavillon *m* d'entrée. 2. Shooting lodge, pavillon de chasse. 3. Loge, atelier *m* (des francs-maçons). **lodge-keeper,** *s.* Concierge *m.*
lodge². I. *v.tr.* I. Loger. 2. To lodge a complaint, porter plainte (*against,* contre). II. **lodge,** *v.i.* (Se) loger. To lodge with s.o., demeurer chez qn (comme locataire en garni). **lodging,** *s.* I. Hébergement *m.* 2. A night's lodging, le logement pour la nuit. 3. Logement, logis *m*, appartement meublé. To let lodgings, louer des chambres, des appartements. To let furnished lodgings, louer en garni. **lodging-house,** *s.* Hôtel garni; maison meublée.
lodger, *s.* Locataire *mf* (en meublé).
loft, *s.* I. Grenier *m*, soupente *f.* 2. Galerie *f*, tribune *f* (dans une église).
loftiness, *s.* I. Hauteur *f*, élévation *f.* 2. Élévation (des sentiments).
lofty, *a.* I. Haut, élevé. 2. (Air) condescendant. 3. Élevé, sublime.
log¹, *s.* I. Grosse bûche; tronçon *m* de bois. To fall like a log, tomber comme une masse. 2. *Nau:* Loch *m.* 3. *Nau:* = LOG-BOOK. **log-book,** *s.* I. *Nau:* (a) Livre *m* de loch. (b) Ship's log(-book), journal *m* de navigation. 2. *Av:* Livre de vol. **log-cabin,** *s.* Cabane *f* de bois.
log², *v.tr.* *Nau:* Porter au journal.
logarithm, *s.* Logarithme *m.*
loggerhead, *s.* To be at loggerheads with s.o., être en désaccord avec qn.
logic, *s.* Logique *f.*
logical, *a.* I. Logique. 2. Qui a de la logique. **-ally,** *adv.* Logiquement.
logician, *s.* Logicien, -ienne.
logwood, *s.* Bois *m* de Campêche.
loin, *s.* I. *pl.* Loins, reins *m.* 2. *Cu:* Filet *m.*

loiter, *v.i.* Flâner, traîner. **To loiter on the way,** s'attarder en route. **loitering**[1], *a.* Flâneur, -euse; traînard. **loitering**[2], *s.* Flânerie *f.*

loiterer, *s.* Flâneur, -euse.

loll, *v.i.* Être étendu. **To loll (back) in an arm-chair,** se renverser nonchalamment dans un fauteuil.

Lombardy. *Pr.n.* La Lombardie.

London. *Pr.n.* Londres *f.*

Londoner, *s.* Londonien, -ienne; habitant, -ante, de Londres.

lone, *a.* **1.** Solitaire, seul. **2.** To play a lone hand, *F:* agir tout seul.

loneliness, *s.* **1.** Solitude *f,* isolement *m.* **2.** Sentiment *m* d'abandon.

lonely, *a.* Solitaire, isolé. *To feel very l.,* se sentir bien seul.

lonesome, *a. F:* Solitaire, seul.

long[1]. I. *a.* Long, *f.* longue. **1.** To be six feet long, avoir six pieds de longueur; être long de six pieds. How long *is the table?* quelle est la longueur de la table? *The best by a long way,* de beaucoup le meilleur. To pull a long face, faire une tête. **2.** How long *are the holidays?* quelle est la durée des vacances? The days are getting longer, les jours croissent. It will take a long time, ce sera long. They are a long time (in) coming, ils se font attendre. A long time ago, il y a longtemps. It will not happen for a long time, cela ne se fera pas de longtemps. Three days at the longest, trois jours (tout) au plus. II. **long,** *s.* **1.** The long and the short of the matter, le fort et le fin de l'affaire. **2.** Before long, ere long, avant peu; sous peu. For long, pendant longtemps. III. **long,** *adv.* **1.** (*a*) Longtemps. *He has been gone* ever so long, il y a beau temps qu'il est parti. Long live the King! vive le roi! As long as I live, tant que je vivrai. *You may do as you like so l. as you leave me alone,* faites tout ce que vous voudrez pourvu que vous me laissiez tranquille. He was not long in setting up a ladder, il eut bientôt fait de dresser une échelle. You aren't long about it, vous allez vite en besogne. He won't be long, il ne tardera pas. Now we shan't be long! (i) nous n'en avons plus pour longtemps; (ii) *F:* voilà qui va bien! It is long since I saw him, il y a longtemps que je ne l'ai vu. *F:* So long! au revoir, à bientôt! (*b*) I have long been expecting him, je l'attends depuis longtemps. (*c*) How long? combien de temps? *How l. have you been here?* depuis combien de temps êtes-vous ici? *How l. does your leave last?* quelle est la durée de votre congé? **2.** Long before, longtemps avant. Not long before, peu de temps avant. *He died* long ago, il est mort depuis longtemps. **3.** All day long, toute la journée. **4.** *I could no* longer *see him,* je ne pouvais plus le voir. *I could not wait* any longer, je ne pouvais pas attendre plus

longtemps. **How much** longer *will it last?* combien (de temps) cela durera-t-il encore? **5.** Long felt want, besoin senti depuis longtemps. **long-armed,** *a.* Au(x) bras long(s). **long-bow,** *s. F:* To draw the long-bow, exagérer, hâbler. **long-distance,** *attrib.a.* A longue distance. **long-drawn(-out),** *a.* Long-drawn(-out) sigh, long soupir; soupir prolongé. **long-headed,** *a.* Perspicace, avisé. **long-legged,** *a.* A longues jambes. **long-lived,** *a.* Qui a la vie longue. **long-lost,** *a.* Perdu depuis longtemps. **long-sighted,** *a.* **1.** Presbyte. **2.** Prévoyant. **long-standing,** *attrib.a.* Ancien; de longue date. **long-suffering,** *a.* Patient, endurant. **long-winded,** *a.* **1.** (Histoire) interminable. **2.** Verbeux, intarissable.

long[2], *v.i.* To long for sth., désirer qch. ardemment; avoir grande envie de qch. To long for home, avoir la nostalgie du foyer. **longing,** *s.* Désir ardent, grande envie (*for, after,* de).

longitude, *s.* Longitude *f.*

longitudinal, *a.* Longitudinal, -aux.

look[1], *s.* **1.** Regard *m.* To have a look at sth., jeter un coup d'œil sur qch.; regarder qch. To take a look round the town, faire un tour de ville. **2.** (*a*) Aspect *m,* air *m,* apparence *f*; mine *f.* To judge by looks, juger d'après les apparences. I don't like the look of him, sa figure ne me revient pas. By the look(s) of it, d'après l'apparence. (*b*) *pl.* (Good) looks, belle mine, bonne mine, beauté *f.*

look[2], *v.i. & tr.* **1.** *v.i.* Regarder. (*a*) To look out of *the window,* regarder par la fenêtre. To look down a list, parcourir une liste. To look the other way, détourner les yeux. (*b*) Look where you are going, regardez où vous allez. **2.** *v.tr.* (*a*) To look s.o. (full) in the face, dévisager qn. *I can never l. him in the face again,* je me sentirai toujours honteux devant lui. To look s.o. up and down, toiser qn. (*b*) To look one's last on sth., jeter un dernier regard sur qch. **3.** *Pred.* Avoir l'air, paraître, sembler. He looks young for his age, il porte bien son âge. She looks her age, elle paraît son âge. Things are looking black, les choses prennent une mauvaise tournure. How does my hat look? quel effet fait mon chapeau? What does he look like? comment est-il? He looks a rascal, il porte la mine d'un coquin. He looks the part, il est fait pour ce rôle. It looks like it, cela en a l'air. It looks like rain, il a l'air de vouloir pleuvoir. **4.** *F:* Look here! écoutez donc! dites donc! **look about,** *v.i.* **1.** To look about one, regarder autour de soi. **2.** To look about for s.o., chercher qn des yeux. **look after,** *v.ind.tr.* Soigner; s'occuper de. He is able to look after himself, il sait se suffire; il peut marcher seul. To look after one's interests, veiller à ses intérêts. *I l. after the car myself,*

j'entretiens l'auto moi-même. **look at,**
v.ind.tr. **1.** Regarder, considérer. *Just look
at this!* voyez donc ! *To look at one's watch,*
regarder à sa montre. *To look at him,* à le
voir. *The hotel is* not much to look at, l'hôtel
ne paye pas de mine. **2.** *L. at the result,*
voyez, considérez, le résultat. *Way of looking
at things,* manière *f* de voir les choses.
look away, *v.i.* Détourner les yeux.
look back, *v.i.* (*a*) Regarder en arrière ;
se retourner, tourner la tête (*at sth.,* pour
regarder qch.). (*b*) *What a day to l. back to!*
quelle journée à se rappeler plus tard !
look down, *v.i.* Regarder en bas ; baisser
les yeux. *F :* *To look down on s.o.,* regarder
qn de haut en bas ; dédaigner qn. **look
for,** *v.ind.tr.* **1.** Chercher. *To go and look
for s.o.,* aller à la recherche de qn. **2.** S'attendre à. **look forward,** *v.i.* *To look
forward to sth.,* (i) s'attendre à qch. ; (ii) attendre qch. avec plaisir. **look in,** *v.i.* *To
look in* (up)on s.o., faire une petite visite à
qn. *I shall l. in again to-morrow,* je repasserai
demain. **look-in,** *s.* **1.** *To give s.o. a look-
in,* faire une petite visite à qn. **2.** *He won't
get a look-in,* il n'a pas la moindre chance.
look into, *v.ind.tr.* Examiner, étudier.
I will look into it, j'en prendrai connaissance.
look on, *v.i.* **1.** = LOOK UPON. Être
spectateur ; faire galerie. (*b*) *v.i.*
(*a*) Regarder au dehors. (*b*) *Room that looks
out on the yard,* pièce qui prend jour sur la
cour. (*c*) Veiller. *To look out for s.o.,* être
à la recherche de qn ; guetter qn. (*d*) *F :*
Prendre garde. *Look out!* attention ! prenez
garde ! **2.** *v.tr.* Chercher. **look-out,** *s.*
1. Guet *m,* surveillance *f ; Nau :* veille *f.*
To keep a sharp look-out, guetter d'un œil
attentif. *To be on the look-out for s.o.,*
guetter qn. **2.** *F :* *That's a bad look-out
for him,* c'est une triste perspective. *That's
his look-out!* ça c'est son affaire ! **look
over,** *v.tr.* Parcourir des yeux ; examiner.
To look over a house, visiter une maison.
To look s.o. all over, toiser qn. **look round,**
v.i. **1.** Regarder autour de soi. *To look
round for s.o.,* chercher qn du regard.
2. Tourner la tête. *Don't look round!* ne
regardez pas en arrière ! **look through,**
v.tr. **1.** Parcourir, examiner. **2.** *To look
s.o. through and through,* transpercer qn
du regard. **look to,** *v.i.* (*a*) *To look to
sth.,* s'occuper de qch. ; voir à qch. *Look
to it that . . .,* veillez, faites attention,
que + *sub.* *To look to the future,* envisager
l'avenir. (*b*) *To look to s.o. to do sth.,*
compter sur qn pour faire qch. **look up.**
1. *v.i.* (*a*) Regarder en haut ; lever les yeux.
(*b*) *F :* *To look up to s.o.,* respecter, considérer, qn. (*c*) *F :* *Things are looking up
with him,* ses affaires vont mieux. **2.** *v.tr.*
(*a*) *To look up the time-table,* consulter
l'indicateur. *To l. up a word in the dictionary,*
(re)chercher un mot dans le dictionnaire,
(*b*) *F :* *To look s.o. up,* aller voir qn. **look**

upon, *v.ind.tr.* **1.** Regarder. **2.** *To l. upon
s.o. favourably,* voir qn d'un œil favorable.
Look upon that as done, tenez cela pour fait.
looking-glass, *s.* Miroir *m,* glace *f.*
looker, *s.* Looker-on, spectateur, -trice (*at,*
de) ; assistant *m* (*at,* à). *To be a. l.-on,* faire
galerie.
loom[1], *s.* *Tex :* Métier *m* à tisser.
loom[2], *v.i.* Apparaître indistinctement. *A
ship loomed up out of the fog,* un vaisseau
surgit du brouillard. *F :* *To loom large,*
paraître imminent.
loop[1], *s.* **1.** Boucle *f.* **2.** (*a*) Méandre *m,*
boucle (de rivière). (*b*) *Rail :* Loop(-line),
(voie *f* de) dérivation *f.*
loop[2], *v.tr.* (*a*) Boucler. (*b*) *Av :* *To loop
the loop,* boucler la boucle.
loop-hole, *s.* **1.** *Fort :* Meurtrière *f,* créneau
m. **2.** *To find a loop-hole of escape,* trouver
une échappatoire.
loose[1], *a.* **1.** (*a*) Mal assujetti ; branlant ;
(*of page*) détaché ; (*of knot*) défait. *To come
loose,* se dégager. *To be loose in the handle,*
branler dans le manche. (*b*) Déchaîné,
échappé, lâché. *To let a dog loose,* lâcher,
détacher, un chien. (*c*) Non assujetti ;
mobile. *L. sheets,* feuilles volantes. *F :* *To
be at a loose end,* se trouver désœuvré.
To hang loose, pendre, flotter. (*d*) *The
money was loose in his pocket,* l'argent était
à même sa poche. *Loose cash,* menue monnaie. **2.** (*a*) *L. rope,* câble détendu. *L. knot,*
nœud lâche. *To come loose,* se relâcher.
(*b*) *Man of loose build,* homme dégingandé.
3. Vague, peu exact. **4.** Dissolu, débauché.
Loose living, mauvaise vie. **loose-fitting,**
a. Non ajusté ; (vêtement) ample. **loose-
leaf,** *attrib.a.* A feuilles mobiles. **loose-
limbed,** *a.* Démanché ; dégingandé.
loose[2], *v.tr.* **1.** Délier, détacher. *To loose
one's hold,* lâcher prise. **2.** Décocher (une
flèche).
loosen. **1.** *v.tr.* Relâcher (un nœud) ; desserrer (un écrou). *To l. one's grip,* relâcher
son étreinte. *F :* *To loosen s.o.'s tongue,*
délier la langue à qn. **2.** *v.i.* Se délier, se
défaire.
looseness, *s.* **1.** État branlant. **2.** Relâchement *m* (d'une corde) ; ampleur *f* (d'un
vêtement). **3.** (*a*) Vague *m* (d'une pensée).
(*b*) Relâchement (de la discipline). (*c*) Licence
f (de conduite).
loot[1], *s.* **1.** Pillage *m.* **2.** Butin *m.*
loot[2], *v.tr.* **1.** Piller, saccager. **2.** Voler (du
bétail). **looting,** *s.* Pillage *m* ; sac *m.*
lop[1], *v.tr.* Élaguer, tailler. *To lop off a
branch,* élaguer une branche.
lop[2], *v.i.* To lop (over), pendre flasque.
lop-eared, *a.* Aux oreilles pendantes.
lope[1], *s.* Pas de course allongé.
lope[2], *v.i.* *To lope along,* courir à petits
bonds.
lopsided, *a.* Qui penche trop d'un côté ;
déjeté, déversé ; de guingois.

loquacious, *a.* Loquace. **-ly**, *adv.* Avec loquacité.

loquacity, *s.* Loquacité *f.*

lord[1], *s.* **1.** Seigneur *m*, maître *m.* **2.** The Lord, le Seigneur; Dieu *m.* In the year of our Lord, en l'an de grâce. **3.** Lord *m.* *F:* To live like a lord, mener une vie de grand seigneur. My lord, monsieur (le baron).

lord[2], *v.i.* *F:* To lord it over s.o., vouloir dominer qn.

lordliness, *s.* **1.** (*a*) Dignité *f.* (*b*) Magnificence *f.* **2.** Hauteur *f.*

lordly, *a.* **1.** De grand seigneur; noble, majestueux; magnifique. **2.** Hautain, altier.

lordship, *s.* **1.** Suzeraineté *f* (*over*, de). **2.** Your lordship, votre Seigneurie *f*; monsieur (le comte).

lore, *s.* Science *f*, savoir *m.*

lorgnette, *s.* Face-à-main *m, pl.* faces-à-main.

lorry, *s.* *Veh:* Camion *m.*

lose, *v.tr.* **1.** (*a*) Perdre. The inc'dent did not lose in the telling, cet incident ne perdit rien de son importance à être raconté. To lose in value, perdre de sa valeur. (*b*) *He has lost an arm,* il lui manque un bras. To lose one's voice, avoir une extinction de voix. To lose one's character, se perdre de réputation. To lose strength, s'affaiblir. To lose weight, perdre de son poids. (*c*) To be lost at sea, périr en mer. **2.** To lose one's way, s'égarer. *Lost in amazement,* perdu d'étonnement. To lose sight of s.o., perdre qn de vue. **3.** Perdre (son temps). *F:* The joke was lost on him, il n'a pas saisi la plaisanterie. **4.** Clock that loses five minutes a day, pendule qui retarde de cinq minutes par jour. **5.** Manquer (le train). **6.** Perdre (une partie). The motion was lost, la motion a été rejetée. **7.** Faire perdre (qch. à qn). **lost**, *a.* Perdu. Lost property office, service *m* des objets trouvés. To give s.o. up for lost, abandonner tout espoir de retrouver qn. I gave myself up for lost, je me crus perdu. He looks lost, il a l'air dépaysé. To be lost to all sense of shame, avoir perdu tout sentiment de honte. **losing**, *a.* Perdant. Losing game, partie perdue d'avance.

loser, *s.* **1.** I am the loser by it, j'y perds. **2.** Perdant, -ante. To be a bad loser, être mauvais joueur.

loss, *s.* **1.** (*a*) Perte *f.* (*b*) Loss of voice, extinction *f* de voix. Without loss of time, sans perte de temps; sans tarder. **2.** To meet with a loss, subir une perte. Dead loss, perte sèche. *F:* To cut one's losses, faire la part du feu. The loss is hers, c'est elle qui y perd. He, it, is no loss, la perte n'est pas grande. **3.** Déperdition *f* (de chaleur). **4.** To be at a loss, être embarrassé, désorienté. To be at a loss what to do, ne savoir que faire. I am at a loss for words to express . . ., les mots me manquent pour exprimer.

lot, *s.* **1.** To draw lots for sth., tirer au sort pour qch.; tirer qch. au sort. To throw in one's lot with s.o., partager le sort, la fortune, de qn. **2.** (*a*) Sort, part *f*, partage *m.* To fall to s.o.'s lot, tomber en partage à qn. (*b*) Destin *m*, destinée *f.* **3.** (*a*) (*At auction*) Lot *m.* (*b*) *F:* A bad lot, un mauvais garnement. (*c*) *F:* The lot, le tout. That's the lot, c'est tout. The whole lot of you, tous tant que vous êtes. **4.** *F:* (*a*) Beaucoup. What a lot! en voilà-t-il! *What a lot of people!* que de monde! que de gens! Such a lot, tellement. *I have quite a lot,* j'en ai une quantité considérable. *He knows quite a lot about you,* il en sait long sur votre compte. *adv.* Times have changed a lot, les temps ont bien changé. (*b*) *pl.* Lots of good things, un tas de bonnes choses.

lotion, *s.* *Pharm:* Lotion *f.*

lottery, *s.* Loterie *f.*

lotus, *s.* *Bot:* Lotus *m.* **lotus-eater**, *s.* *Gr.Myth:* Lotophage *m*; *F:* rêveur *m.*

loud. **1.** *a.* (*a*) Bruyant, retentissant. *L. laugh,* gros rire In a loud voice, à haute voix. Loud cheers, vifs applaudissements. (*b*) (*Of colour*) Criard, voyant; (*of costume*) tapageur, -euse. **2.** *adv.* Haut, à haute voix. **-ly**, *adv.* (*Crier*) haut, fort, à voix haute; (*rire*) bruyamment. **loud-mouthed**, *a.* Au verbe haut. **loud-speaker**, *s.* *W.Tel:* Haut-parleur *m, pl.* haut-parleurs

loudness, *s.* Force *f* (d'un bruit); grand bruit.

lounge[1], *s.* **1.** Flânerie *f.* **2.** (*a*) Promenoir *m*; hall *m.* (*b*) Foyer *m.* **lounge-chair**, *s.* Chaise-longue *f., pl.* chaises-longues. **lounge-suit**, *s.* Complet veston *m.*

lounge[2], *v.i.* Flâner. To lounge along, avancer en se dandinant.

louring, *a.* **1.** Renfrogné; sombre. **2.** (Ciel) sombre, menaçant.

louse, *s.* Pou *m, pl.* poux.

lout, *s.* Rustre *m*, lourdaud *m.*

loutish, *a.* Rustre, lourdaud.

lovable, *a.* Aimable; sympathique.

love[1], *s.* **1.** Amour *m.* (*a*) Affection *f*, tendresse *f.* *F:* There is no love lost between them, ils ne peuvent pas se sentir. To play for love, jouer pour l'honneur. To work for love, travailler pour rien. Give my love to your parents, faites mes amitiés à vos parents. *F:* It cannot be had for love or money, on ne peut se le procurer à aucun prix. (*b*) Amour. To fall in love with s.o., s'éprendre, tomber amoureux, de qn. To make love to s.o., faire la cour à qn. To marry for love, faire un mariage d'inclination. **2.** My love, mon amour. **3.** *Pr.n.* L'Amour *m*, Cupidon *m.* **4.** (*At tennis*) Zéro *m*, rien *m.* Love all, égalité *f* à rien. Love game, jeu blanc. **love-letter**, *s.* Billet doux. **love-lorn**, *a.* Délaissé. **love-making**, *s.* Cour (amoureuse). **love-match**, *s.* Mariage *m* d'amour.

love[2], *v.tr.* **1.** (*a*) Aimer, affectionner. (*b*)

Aimer d'amour. **2.** Aimer. **As you love your life,** si vous tenez à la vie. *I l. music,* j'adore la musique. **I should love to,** je ne demande pas mieux. **loving,** *a.* Affectueux, affectionné, tendre. **-ly,** *adv.* Affectueusement, affectionnément.

loveliness, *s.* Beauté *f.*

lovely, *a.* Beau, *f.* belle; ravissant.

lover, *s.* **1.** *(a)* Amoureux *m,* prétendant *m.* *(b)* Fiancé *m.* *(c) They were lovers,* ils s'aimaient. **2. Her lover,** son amant, *F:* son bon ami. **3.** Amateur *m,* ami(e).

lovesick, *a.* Féru d'amour.

low[1]. I. *a.* **1.** Bas, *f.* basse. **Low relief,** bas-relief *m.* **Low dress,** robe décolletée. **Light turned low,** lumière en veilleuse. **2.** *(a) Low bow,* profonde révérence. *Geog:* **The Low Countries,** les Pays-Bas. *(b)* **To bring s.o. low,** humilier, abaisser qn. **To lie low,** *F:* se tenir coi. *(c)* **Lower part,** bas *m.* **The lower world,** les régions infernales. **The lower jaw,** la mâchoire inférieure. *(d) Ling:* **Low German,** le bas allemand. **3.** *(a)* **Low birth,** basse naissance. **The lower orders,** les basses classes. *(b)* **The lower animals,** les animaux inférieurs. *(c)* Bas, vil, canaille. **A low fellow,** un voyou. **The lowest of the low,** le dernier des derniers. **4.** **Low diet,** régime peu substantiel. **To be in low spirits,** être abattu. **5.** **Low price,** bas prix; prix faible. *The lowest price,* le dernier prix. **At the very lowest,** au bas mot. *Low speed,* petite vitesse. **6.** **Low note,** note basse. *In a low voice,* à voix basse, à mi-voix. **II. low,** *adv.* **1.** Bas. **To bow low,** s'incliner profondément. **2.** **The lowest paid employees,** les employés les moins payés. **3.** A voix basse. **low-born,** *a.* **1.** De basse naissance. **2.** D'humble naissance. **low-brow,** *s.* Bourgeois, -oise; philistin, -ine. **low-class,** *a.* Vulgaire, inférieur. **low-down,** *a.* Bas, *f.* basse, vil, ignoble. *L.-d. trick,* coup rosse. **low-lying,** *a.* Situé en bas; (terrain) enfoncé. **low-necked,** *a.* (Robe) décolletée. **low-pitched,** *a.* (Son) grave. **low-spirited,** *a.* Abattu, triste.

low[2], *v.i.* Meugler.

lower, *v.tr.* *(a)* Baisser (la tête); abaisser (les paupières). *(b)* **To lower a boat,** mettre une embarcation à la mer. *(c)* Abaisser; diminuer la hauteur de. *(d)* Baisser, rabaisser (un prix); réduire (la pression). *(e)* Baisser (la voix). *(f)* (R)abaisser. (r)abattre (l'orgueil). **To lower oneself,** s'abaisser, se rabaisser (*to,* à); s'avilir. **lowering**[1], *a.* Abaissant.

lowering[2], *s.* **1.** *(a)* Abaissement *m;* baissement *m.* *(b)* Mise *f* à la mer (d'une embarcation). **2.** Diminution *f* (des prix); réduction *f.* **lowering**[3], *a.* = LOURING.

lowliness, *s.* Humilité *f.*

lowly, *a.* Humble, modeste.

loyal, *a.* Fidèle, dévoué (*to,* à); loyal, -aux (*to,* envers). **-ally,** *adv.* Fidèlement.

loyalty, *s.* Fidélité *f.*

lozenge, *s.* **1.** *Geom:* Losange *m.* **2.** *Pharm:* Pastille *f,* tablette *f.*

lubber, *s.* *Nau:* Maladroit *m.*

lubberly, *a.* Lourdaud; empoté, gauche.

lubricant, *a. & s.* Lubrifiant (*m*).

lubricate, *v.tr.* Lubrifier; graisser.

lubrication, *s.* Lubrification *f.*

Lucerne. *Pr.n. Geog:* Lucerne *f.* **The Lake of Lucerne,** le lac des Quatre-Cantons.

lucid, *a.* **1.** Brillant, lumineux. **2.** *(a)* Lucide. *(b) Med:* **Lucid interval,** intervalle *m* de lucidité. *(c)* Clair, transparent. **-ly,** *adv.* Lucidement.

lucidity, *s.* **1.** *(a)* Luminosité *f.* *(b)* Transparence *f.* **2.** Lucidité *f.*

luck, *s.* **1.** Hasard *m,* chance *f,* fortune *f.* **Good luck,** bonne chance, bonheur *m.* **To be down on one's luck,** avoir de la déveine. **To try one's luck,** tenter la fortune, la chance. **To bring s.o. good luck,** porter bonheur à qn. **Better luck next time!** ça ira mieux une autre fois. **Worse luck!** tant pis! **Hard luck!** pas de chance! **As luck would have it . . .,** le hasard voulut que + *sub.* **2.** Bonheur *m,* (bonne) chance. **To keep sth. for luck,** garder qch. comme porte-bonheur. **Stroke of luck,** coup *m* de fortune, coup de veine. **To be in luck,** avoir de la chance. **To be out of luck,** jouer de malheur. **My luck's in!** quelle veine! **As luck would have it,** par bonheur.

luckless, *a.* Malheureux, infortuné.

lucky, *a.* *(a)* Heureux, fortuné. **To be lucky,** avoir de la chance; jouer de bonheur. *(b)* **Lucky hit,** coup de bonheur. *L. day,* jour de veine. **How lucky!** quelle chance! **-ily,** *adv.* Heureusement; par bonheur.

lucrative, *a.* Lucratif. **-ly,** *adv.* Lucrativement.

lucre, *s.* Lucre *m.*

ludicrous, *a.* Risible, grotesque. **-ly,** *adv.* Risiblement, grotesquement.

ludicrousness, *s.* Absurdité *f.*

lug[1], *s.* Traction violente, subite.

lug[2], *v.tr.* Traîner, tirer.

luggage, *s.* Bagage(s) *m(pl).* **luggage-carrier,** *s. Aut:* Porte-bagages *m inv.* **luggage-label,** *s.* Étiquette *f* à bagages. **luggage-van,** *s. Rail:* Fourgon *m* (aux bagages).

lugger, *s. Nau:* Lougre *m.*

lugubrious, *a.* Lugubre. **-ly,** *adv.* Lugubrement.

Luke. *Pr.n.* Luc *m.*

lukewarm, *a.* Tiède. **To become l.,** s'attiédir

lull[1], *s.* Moment *m* de calme. *Nau:* Accalmie *f.*

lull[2]. **1.** *v.tr.* Bercer, endormir. **2.** *v.i.* Se calmer, s'apaiser.

lullaby, *s. Mus:* Berceuse *f.*

lumber[1], *s.* **1.** Vieux meubles; fatras *m.* **2.** Bois *m* de charpente. **lumber-jack,** *s.* Bûcheron *m.* **lumber-room,** *s.* Cabinet *m,* chambre *f,* de débarras.

lumber², *v.tr.* Encombrer, embarrasser.
lumber³, *v.i.* To lumber along, avancer à pas pesants. **lumbering**, *a.* Lourd, pesant.
lumberman, *s.* Bûcheron *m*.
luminary, *s.* **I.** Corps lumineux; luminaire *m*. **2.** *F:* (*Of pers.*) Lumière *f*.
luminous, *a.* Lumineux.
lump¹, *s.* **I.** (*a*) Gros morceau, bloc *m*; motte *f* (d'argile); morceau (de sucre). Lump sum, somme grosse, globale. *F:* To have a lump in one's throat, se sentir le cœur gros. (*b*) Bosse *f* (au front). **2.** *F:* (*Of pers.*) Empoté, -ée, lourdaud, -e.
lump², *v.tr.* To lump things together, réunir des choses ensemble.
lump³, *v.tr.* *P:* If he doesn't like it, he may lump it, si cela ne lui plaît pas, qu'il s'arrange.
lunacy, *s.* Aliénation mentale; folie *f*.
lunar, *a.* Lunaire; de (la) lune.
lunatic. **I.** *a.* Fou, *f.* folle. **2.** *s.* Fou, *f.* folle; aliéné, -ée.
lunch¹, *s.* *F:* = LUNCHEON.
lunch², *v.i.* Déjeuner, luncher.
luncheon, *s.* Déjeuner *m* (à la fourchette); lunch *m*.
lung, *s.* Poumon *m*.
lunge¹, *s.* **I.** *Fenc:* Botte *f*; coup droit. **2.** Mouvement (précipité) en avant.
lunge², *v.i.* (*a*) *Fenc:* Se fendre. (*b*) To lunge out at s.o., allonger un coup de poing à qn.
lurch¹, *s.* To leave s.o. in the lurch, laisser qn le bec dans l'eau.
lurch², *s.* **I.** Embardée *f* (d'un navire). **2.** Pas titubant.
lurch³, *v.i.* **I.** (*Of carriage*) Embarder. **2.** To lurch along, marcher en titubant.
lurcher, *s.* Chien *m* de braconnier.
lure¹, *s.* **I.** Leurre *m*. **2.** *F:* (*a*) Piège *m*. (*b*) Attrait *m*.

lure², *v.tr.* Attirer, séduire. *To be lured on to destruction*, être entraîné à sa perte.
lurid, *a.* **I.** Blafard, fauve. **2.** Cuivré. *L. flames*, flammes rougeoyantes.
lurk, *v.i.* Se cacher; rester tapi. **lurking**, *a.* Caché; secret, -ète. A lurking suspicion, un vague soupçon.
luscious, *a.* Succulent, savoureux.
lush, *a.* (*Of grass*) Plein de sève.
lust¹, *s.* **I.** *Theol:* Appétit *m* (coupable); convoitise *f*. **2.** *Lit:* Soif *f* (du pouvoir).
lust², *v.ind.tr.* *Lit:* **I.** To l. after sth., convoiter qch. **2.** To l. for riches, avoir soif des richesses.
lustful, *a.* *Lit:* Lascif.
lustiness, *s.* Vigueur *f*.
lustre, *s.* **I.** Éclat *m*, brillant *m*, lustre *m*. **2.** Lustre (de plafond).
lustrous, *a.* Brillant, éclatant.
lusty, *a.* Vigoureux, fort, robuste. **-ily**, *adv.* Vigoureusement.
lute, *s.* *Mus:* Luth *m*.
luxuriance, *s.* Exubérance *f*, luxuriance *f*.
luxuriant, *a.* Exubérant, luxuriant. **-ly**, *adv.* Avec exubérance.
luxuriate, *v.i.* Se livrer avec délices (*in*, à); se complaire (*in*, à).
luxurious, *a.* Luxueux, somptueux. **-ly**, *adv.* Luxueusement.
luxuriousness, *s.* Luxe *m*; somptuosité *f*.
luxury, *s.* **I.** Luxe *m*. To live in (the lap of) luxury, vivre dans le luxe. **2.** (Objet *m* de) luxe. Table luxuries, friandises *f*.
lye, *s.* Lessive *f*.
lymphatic, *a.* Lymphatique.
lynch, *v.tr.* Lyncher. **lynching**, *s.* Lynchage *m*.
lynx, *s.* *Z:* Lynx *m*.
Lyons. *Pr.n.* *Geog:* Lyon *m*.
lyre, *s.* *Mus:* Lyre *f*. **lyre-bird**, *s.* *Orn:* Oiseau-lyre *m*, *pl.* oiseaux-lyres.
lyric. **I.** *a.* Lyrique. **2.** *s.* Poème *m* lyrique.
lyrical, *a.* Lyrique.

M

M, m, *s.* (La lettre) M, m *f*.
macaroni, *s.* *Cu:* Macaroni *m*.
macaroon, *s.* *Cu:* Macaron *m*.
mace¹, *s.* Masse *f*.
mace², *s.* *Cu:* Macis *m*; fleur *f* de muscade.
Macedonia. *Pr.n.* *Geog:* La Macédoine.
Macedonian, *a. & s.* *Geog:* Macédonien, -ienne.
macerate, *v.tr. & i.* Macérer.
maceration, *s.* Macération *f*.
Machiavelli. *Pr.n.* Machiavel *m*.
Machiavellian, *a.* Machiavélique.
machination, *s.* Machination *f*, complot *m*.

machine¹, *s.* Machine *f*. To be a mere machine, n'être qu'un automate. **machine-gun**, *s.* Mitrailleuse *f*. **machine-gunner**, *s.* Mitrailleur *m*.
machine², *v.tr.* *Dressm:* Coudre, piquer, à la machine.
machinery, *s.* **I.** Mécanisme *m*; machines *fpl*, machinerie *f*. **2.** *F:* The machinery of government, les rouages *m* du gouvernement.
mackerel, *s.* *Ich:* Maquereau *m*.
mackintosh, *s.* (Manteau *m* en) caoutchouc *m*; imperméable *m*.

mad, *a.* **1.** Fou, *f.* folle; aliéné. Raving mad, fou furieux. *F:* As mad as a hatter, fou à lier. To drive s.o. mad, rendre qn fou. *A mad gallop,* un galop furieux, effréné. *F:* Like mad, comme un enragé; follement. **2.** Mad for revenge, assoiffé de revanche. To be mad about sth., être fou de qch. **3.** *F:* To be mad with s.o., être furieux contre qn. **4.** Mad bull, taureau furieux. Mad dog, chien enragé. **-ly,** *adv.* **1.** Follement; en fou; comme un fou. **2.** (Aimer) à la folie, éperdument. **3.** Furieusement.

Madagascan, *a.* Malgache.

madam, *s.* Madame *f,* mademoiselle *f.* (*In letters*) Dear Madam, Madame, Mademoiselle.

madcap, *a. & s.* Écervelé, -ée.

madden, *v.tr.* Rendre fou, *f.* folle; exaspérer. **maddening,** *a.* A rendre fou, *f.* folle; exaspérant.

madder, *s. Bot:* Garance *f.*

Madeira. *Pr.n. Geog:* Madère *f.* Madeira cake, gâteau *m* de Savoie.

madman, *s.* Fou *m,* aliéné *m. To fight like a m.,* se battre comme un forcené.

madness, *s.* **1.** Folie *f.* **2.** (*Of dogs*) Rage *f.*

madonna, *s.* Madone *f.*

madrigal, *s.* Madrigal *m,* -aux.

Maelstrom, *s.* **1.** *Geog:* (Le) Maelström. **2.** *F:* Tourbillon *m.*

magazine, *s.* **1.** *Mil:* Magasin *m* (d'armes); dépôt *m* de munitions. **2.** Revue *f* périodique; magazine *m.*

Maggie. *Pr.n.* Margot *f.*

maggot, *s.* Ver *m,* asticot *m.*

maggoty, *a.* Plein de vers.

magic. 1. *s.* Magie *f,* enchantement *m.* **2.** *a.* Magique, enchanté. **magical,** *a.* Magique. **-ally,** *adv.* Magiquement; par magie.

magician, *s.* Magicien, -ienne.

magisterial, *a.* **1.** Magistral, -aux. **2.** De magistrat. **-ally,** *adv.* Magistralement.

magistracy, *s.* Magistrature *f.*

magistrate, *s.* Magistrat *m,* juge *m.* Police-court magistrate, juge de paix.

magnanimity, *s.* Magnanimité *f.*

magnanimous, *a.* Magnanime. **-ly,** *adv.* Magnanimement.

magnate, *s.* Magnat *m,* *F:* gros bonnet.

magnesia, *s. Ch:* Magnésie *f.*

magnesium, *s. Ch:* Magnésium *m.*

magnet, *s.* Aimant *m.*

magnetic, *a.* **1.** Magnétique; aimanté. **2.** (*Of pers.*) Magnétique, hypnotique. **-ally,** *adv.* Magnétiquement.

magnetism, *s.* Magnétisme *m.*

magnetize, *v.tr.* **1.** *F:* Magnétiser, attirer (qn). **2.** Aimanter.

magneto, *s. I.C.E.: etc:* Magnéto *f.*

magnificence, *s.* Magnificence *f.*

magnificent, *a.* Magnifique; (repas) somptueux. **-ly,** *adv.* Magnifiquement.

magnify, *v.tr.* Grossir, agrandir. Magnifying glass, loupe *f;* verre grossissant.

magnitude, *s.* Grandeur *f. Astr:* Magnitude *f.*

magnolia, *s. Bot:* Magnolia *m.*

magpie, *s. Orn:* Pie *f.*

Magyar, *a. & s. Ethn:* Magyar, -are.

mahogany, *s.* Acajou *m.*

Mahomet. *Pr.n. Rel.H:* Mahomet *m.*

Mahometan, *a. & s.* Mahométan, -ane.

mahout, *s.* Cornac *m,* mahout *m.*

maid, *s.* **1.** = MAIDEN 1 (*a*). **2.** = MAIDEN. 1 (*b*). The Maid (of Orleans), la Pucelle (d'Orléans). **3.** Old maid, vieille fille. **4.** Bonne *f,* domestique *f,* servante *f.* Lady's maid, femme *f* de chambre. **5.** Maid of honour, fille d'honneur. **maid-of-all-work,** *s.* Bonne *f* à tout faire.

maiden, *s.* **1.** (*a*) Jeune fille *f.* (*b*) Vierge *f.* **2.** *Attrib.* (*a*) Maiden aunt, tante non mariée. Maiden lady, demoiselle *f.* (*b*) Maiden modesty, modestie de jeune fille. Maiden name, nom de jeune fille. (*c*) Maiden voyage, premier voyage. Maiden speech, discours de début.

maidenhair, *s. Bot:* Maidenhair (fern), capillaire *m; F:* cheveux *mpl* de Vénus.

maidservant, *s.* Servante *f;* bonne *f.*

mail¹, *s. Archeol:* Mailles *fpl.*

mail², *s. Post:* **1.** Courrier *m.* **2.** La poste. **mail-bag,** *s.* Sac *m* de dépêches, sac de poste. **mail-boat,** *s.* Paquebot-poste *m,* *pl.* paquebots-poste. **mail-order,** *s. Com:* Commande faite par l'entremise de la poste. **mail-train,** *s.* Train-poste *m,* *pl.* trains-poste. **mail-van,** *s.* Wagon-poste *m,* *pl.* wagons-poste.

maim, *v.tr.* Estropier, mutiler.

main¹, *s.* **1.** With might and main, de toutes ses forces. **2.** In the main, en général, en somme. **3.** *Civ.E:* Canalisation maîtresse. *El:* Conducteur principal.

main², *a.* **1.** By main force, de vive force. **2.** Principal, -aux; premier. (*a*) The main body, le gros. *Agr:* Main crop, culture principale. (*b*) The main point, l'essentiel, le principal. (*c*) *Rail:* Main line, voie principale, grande ligne. **-ly,** *adv.* **1.** Principalement, surtout. **2.** En grande partie.

mainland, *s.* Continent *m;* terre *f* ferme.

mainmast, *s. Nau:* Grand mât.

mainspring, *s.* **1.** Grand ressort. **2.** *F:* Mobile essentiel, cheville ouvrière.

mainstay, *s. F:* Soutien principal.

maintain, *v.tr.* **1.** Maintenir (l'ordre); soutenir (la conversation); conserver (la santé). The improvement is maintained, le mieux se soutient. **2.** Entretenir, soutenir (une famille). **3.** Entretenir (une armée). **4.** Soutenir, défendre (une cause). **5.** Garder (un avantage).

maintenance, *s.* **1.** Maintien *m* (de l'ordre). **2.** Entretien *m* (d'une famille). **3.** *M. of one's rights,* défense *f* de ses droits.

maize, *s.* Maïs *m.*

majestic, *a.* Majestueux. **-ally,** *adv.* Majestueusement.

majesty, *s.* Majesté *f.* His Majesty, Sa Majesté.

major¹, *s.* *Mil:* Commandant *m.* **major-general,** *s.* Général *m* de division.

major². **I.** *a.* (*a*) The major portion, la majeure partie, la plus grande partie. *Mus:* Major key, ton majeur. *Aut:* Major road, route de priorité. (*b*) *Sch:* Smith major, Smith aîné. **2.** *s.* *Jur:* Majeur, -eure.

Majorca. *Pr.n.* *Geog:* Majorque *f.*

majority, *s.* **I.** Majorité *f.* (*a*) To be in a majority, être en majorité. (*b*) La plus grande partie, le plus grand nombre. *F:* To join the (great) majority, mourir. **2.** *Jur:* To attain one's majority, atteindre sa majorité; devenir majeur, -e.

make¹, *s.* **I.** (*a*) Façon *f,* fabrication *f.* (*b*) *Com:* Marque *f.* **2.** Taille *f* (de qn). **3.** *F:* To be on the make, poursuivre un but intéressé.

make², *v.* **I.** *v.tr.* **I.** Faire; construire (une machine); fabriquer (du papier); confectionner (des vêtements). You are made for the work, vous êtes fait pour ce travail. *F:* He's as cute as they make 'em, c'est un malin entre tous. What is it made of? en quoi est-ce? To make a friend of s.o., faire de qn son ami. I don't know what to make of it, je n'y comprends rien. To show what one is made of, donner sa mesure. To make the tea, faire le thé. *Cards:* To make the cards, battre les cartes. To make trouble, causer des désagréments. To make a noise, faire du bruit. To make peace, faire, conclure, la paix. To make one's escape, s'échapper, se sauver. **2.** Two and two make four, deux et deux font quatre. This book makes pleasant reading, ce livre est d'une lecture agréable. To make a good husband, se montrer bon époux. Will you make one (of the party)? voulez-vous être des nôtres? **3.** To make three pounds a week, gagner trois livres par semaine. What will you make by it? quel profit vous en reviendra-t-il? **4.** Faire la fortune de (qn). **5.** *Pred.* To make s.o. happy, rendre qn heureux. To m. s.o. hungry, donner faim à qn. To m. a dish hot, (faire) chauffer un plat. To m. s.o. a judge, nommer qn juge. He was made a knight, il fut créé chevalier. To make sth. known, faire connaître qch. To m. oneself comfortable, se mettre à l'aise. **6.** The climate is not so bad as you make it, le climat n'est pas si mauvais que vous le dites. What do you make the time? quelle heure avez-vous? **7.** You should make him do it, vous devriez le lui faire faire. What made you say that? pourquoi avez-vous dit cela? **II.** **make,** *v.i.* **I.** To make for a place se diriger vers un endroit. He made for me like a madman, il s'élança sur moi comme un fou. *Nau:* To make for, mettre le cap sur. To make

for the open sea, prendre le large. **2.** This fine weather makes for optimism, ce beau temps favorise l'optimisme. **3.** To make as though to do sth., faire semblant de faire qch. **make away,** *v.i.* (*a*) S'éloigner. (*b*) To make away with sth., enlever qch. **make off,** *v.i.* Se sauver; décamper, filer. **make out,** *v.tr.* **I.** Faire, dresser (une liste); faire, tirer (un chèque). **2.** (*a*) Établir, prouver (qch.). How do you make that out? comment arrivez-vous à ce résultat? (*b*) To make s.o. out to be richer than he is, faire qn plus riche qu'il ne l'est. **3.** (*a*) Comprendre (une énigme); déchiffrer (une écriture). I can't make it out, je n'y comprends rien. (*b*) Distinguer. **make over,** *v.tr.* Céder (*sth. to s.o.,* qch. à qn). **make up.** **I.** *v.tr.* **I.** Compléter (une somme); combler (un déficit). **2.** To make up lost ground, regagner le terrain perdu. To make it up to s.o. for sth., dédommager qn de qch. **3.** Faire (un paquet). *Pharm:* Composer (une ordonnance). **4.** (*a*) Faire, confectionner (des vêtements). (*b*) Dresser (une liste). (*c*) Régler, établir (un compte). (*d*) Inventer (une histoire). **5.** To make up the fire, ajouter du combustible au feu. **6.** Former, composer (un ensemble). **7.** To make (oneself) up, se farder, se maquiller. **8.** To make up one's mind, se décider; prendre son parti. **9.** Arranger, accommoder (un différend). To make it up (again), se réconcilier. **II.** **make up,** *v.i.* **I.** (*a*) To make up for lost time, rattraper le temps perdu. That makes up for it, c'est une compensation. (*b*) To make up for the want of sth., suppléer au manque de qch. **2.** To make up to s.o., *F:* faire des avances à qn. **make-up,** *s.* **I.** Composition *f.* **2.** Maquillage *m,* fard *m.* **3.** Invention *f.* **made-up,** *a.* Made-up story, histoire inventée de toutes pièces. **making up,** *s.* **I.** Compensation *f.* **2.** *Pharm:* Préparation *f.* **3.** (*a*) Confection *f* (de vêtements). (*b*) Dressage *m* (d'une liste). **made,** *a.* **I.** Fait, fabriqué, confectionné. **2.** *F:* He is a made man, sa fortune est faite. **making,** *s.* (*a*) Fabrication *f;* confection *f,* (de vêtements); construction *f* (d'un pont). This incident was the making of him, c'est à cet incident qu'il dut sa fortune. (*b*) I have not the makings of a hero, je n'ai rien du héros. **make-believe,** *s.* Semblant *m,* feinte *f,* trompe-l'œil *m.* **make-weight,** *s.* Complément *m* de poids.

maker, *s.* Faiseur, -euse. *Com:* Fabricant *m;* constructeur *m.*

makeshift, *s.* Pis aller *m inv,* expédient *m.*

maladministration, *s.* Mauvaise administration.

maladroit, *a.* Maladroit. **-ly,** *adv.* Maladroitement.

malady, *s.* Maladie *f,* mal *m.*

malaria, *s.* *Med:* Malaria *f.*

Malay. **I.** *a. & s.* *Geog:* Malais, -aise.

The Malay Archipelago, la Malaisie. **2.** *s.*
Ling : Le malais.
malcontent, *a. & s.* Mécontent, -ente.
male. I. *a.* Mâle. **Male sex,** sexe masculin.
2. *s.* Mâle *m.* **Male ward,** salle *f* pour
hommes.
malediction, *s.* Malédiction *f.*
malefactor, *s.* Malfaiteur, -trice.
malevolence, *s.* Malveillance *f (towards,*
envers).
malevolent, *a.* Malveillant. **-ly,** *adv.* Avec
malveillance.
malformation, *s.* Malformation *f.*
malice, *s.* **I.** Malice *f,* malveillance *f.* **Out**
of malice, par malice. **To bear s.o.** malice,
en vouloir à qn. **2.** *Jur :* Intention criminelle.
malicious, *a.* (*a*) Méchant, malveillant. (*b*)
Rancunier. **-ly,** *adv.* (*a*) Avec malveillance. (*b*) Par rancune.
malign¹, *a.* Pernicieux, nuisible.
malign², *v.tr.* Calomnier, diffamer.
malignancy, *s.* Malignité *f.*
malignant, *a.* Malin, *f.* maligne ; méchant.
-ly, *adv.* Avec malignité ; méchamment.
malignity, *s.* = MALIGNANCY.
malinger, *v.i.* Faire le malade. **malinger-**
ing, *s.* Simulation *f* (de maladie).
malingerer, *s.* Faux malade.
malleable, *a.* Malléable ; forgeable.
mallet, *s.* Maillet *m.*
mallow, *s. Bot :* Mauve *f.*
malodorous, *a.* Malodorant.
malt, *s.* Malt *m.* **Malt liquor,** bière *f.*
Malta. *Pr.n. Geog :* Malte *f.*
malted, *a.* **Malted milk,** farine lactée.
Maltese, *a. & s. Geog :* Maltais, -aise.
Maltese cross, croix *f* de Malte.
maltreat, *v.tr.* Maltraiter, malmener.
maltreatment, *s.* Mauvais traitement.
mamma, *s. F :* Maman *f.*
mammal, *s. Z :* Mammifère *m.*
mammoth. I. *s.* Mammouth *m.* **2.** *Attrib.*
a. F : Géant, monstre.
man¹, *s.* **I.** (*a*) Homme *m. Mil :* **No man's**
land, zone *f* neutre. *Solitude changes a man,*
la solitude, ça vous change. (*b*) L'homme.
Man proposes, God disposes, l'homme propose et Dieu dispose. (*c*) *F :* **To refresh the**
inner man, se refaire, se restaurer. **2.**
Homme. (*a*) **Between man and man,**
d'homme à homme. **They were killed to**
a man, ils furent tués jusqu'au dernier. **To**
show oneself a man, se montrer homme. **To**
bear sth. like a man, supporter qch. avec
courage. **He is not the man to** (*refuse*), il
n'est pas homme à (refuser). **I'm your man,**
cela me va ! **A man's man,** un vrai homme.
F : Come here, **my little man!** viens ici,
mon petit bonhomme ! **Good man!** bravo !
Good-bye, **old man!** adieu, mon vieux ! (*b*)
An old man, un vieillard. *The dead man,*
le mort. **The man Smith,** le nommé Smith.
3. (*a*) **Man and wife,** mari *m* et femme. (*b*)
P : **My young man,** mon bon ami. **4.** (*a*)

Domestique *m,* valet *m.* (*b*) *Com :* Employé
m, garçon *m.* (*c*) *Ind :* **The masters and**
the men, les patrons et les ouvriers *m.* (*d*)
Sp : Joueur *m.* **5.** (*At chess*) Pièce *f ;* (*at*
draughts) pion *m.* **man-eater,** *s.* Mangeur,
-euse, d'hommes. **man-eating,** *a.* Mangeur,
-euse, d'hommes. **man-handle,** *v.tr. F :*
Maltraiter. **man-hole,** *s.* Trou *m* de visite.
man-of-war, *s.* Vaisseau *m* de guerre.
man-power, *s.* **I.** *Mec.E :* La force des
bras. **2.** *Coll. Ind :* Main-d'œuvre *f.* **man-**
servant, *s.* Domestique *m ;* valet, *m* (de
chambre).
man², *v.tr.* Garnir d'hommes. (*a*) *To man a*
fort, garnir un fort. (*b*) *Nau :* Armer (un
canot). *To man the yards,* monter les vergues.
manacle¹, *s.* Menotte *f.*
manacle², *v.tr.* Mettre les menottes à (qn).
manage, *v.tr.* **I.** Conduire (une entreprise) ;
diriger, gérer (une affaire) ; mener (une
affaire). **2.** Gouverner ; tenir (des enfants) ;
maîtriser (un animal). **To know how to**
manage s.o., savoir prendre qn. **3.** Arranger,
conduire (une affaire). **To manage to do sth.,**
parvenir à faire qch. **I shall manage it,** j'en
viendrai à bout. *If you can m. to see him,* si
vous pouvez vous arranger pour le voir.
4. *Abs.* *She manages well,* elle est bonne
ménagère. **Manage as best you can,** arrangez-
vous comme vous pourrez. *He'll m. all right,*
il se débrouillera. **managing,** *a.* **I.** Directeur, -trice ; gérant. **Managing clerk,** commis
principal. **2.** **A managing woman,** une
maîtresse femme.
manageable, *a.* **I.** Maniable ; (canot)
manœuvrable. **2.** (*Of pers.*) Traitable.
management, *s.* **I.** (*a*) Maniement *m* (des
hommes). (*b*) Direction *f,* conduite *f* (d'une
affaire). **2.** Adresse *f ;* savoir-faire *m.*
3. *Coll :* L'administration *f.*
manager, *s.* **I.** Directeur *m,* administrateur
m ; gérant *m.* **2.** *She is a good m.,* elle est
bonne ménagère.
manageress, *s.* Directrice *f,* gérante *f.*
manatee, *s. Z :* Lamantin *m.*
Manchuria. *Pr.n.* La Mandchourie.
Manchurian, *a. & s.* Mandchou (*pl.* -ous),
-oue.
mandarin, *s.* Mandarin *m.*
mandarine, *s. Bot :* Mandarine *f.*
mandate¹, *s.* **I.** Commandement *m,* ordre *m.*
2. *Pol :* Mandat *m.*
mandate², *v.tr.* Attribuer sous mandat.
Mandated territories, territoires sous mandat.
mandolin(e), *s.* Mandoline *f.*
mandrake, *s. Bot :* Mandragore *f.*
mandrill, *s. Z :* Mandrill *m.*
mane, *s.* Crinière *f.*
manful, *a.* Vaillant, hardi, viril. **-fully,**
adv. Vaillamment, hardiment.
manganese, *s. Ch :* Manganèse *m.*
mange, *s.* Gale *f.*
manger, *s.* Mangeoire *f,* crèche *f.*
mangle¹, *s. Laund :* Calandreuse *f.*

mangle², *v.tr.* Calandrer. **mangling¹,** *s.* Calandrage *m.*

mangle³, *v.tr.* Déchirer, lacérer, mutiler. **mangling²,** *s.* Lacération *f* ; mutilation *f.*

mango, *s. Bot:* **I.** Mangue *f.* **2.** Mango (-tree), manguier *m.*

mangrove, *s. Bot:* Manglier *m.*

mangy, *a.* Galeux.

manhood, *s.* Age *m* d'homme ; virilité *f.*

mania, *s.* **I.** *Med:* Manie *f* ; folie *f.* **2.** *F:* To have a mania for sth., avoir la manie de qch.

maniac, *a. & s.* Fou furieux, folle furieuse.

maniacal, *a. Med:* Fou, *f.* folle.

manicure¹, *s.* **I.** Soin *m* des mains. **Manicure set,** trousse *f* de manucure. **2.** = MANICURIST.

manicure², *v.tr.* **I.** Soigner les mains de (qn.) **2.** Soigner (les mains).

manicurist, *s.* Manucure *mf.*

manifest¹, *a.* Manifeste, évident, clair. **-ly,** *adv.* Manifestement.

manifest², *v.tr.* (a) Manifester, témoigner (qch.). (b) **To manifest itself,** se manifester.

manifestation, *s.* Manifestation *f.*

manifesto, *s. Pol:* Manifeste *m.*

manifold, *a.* (a) Divers, varié. (b) Multiple, nombreux.

manikin, *s.* Homoncule *m,* nabot *m.*

Manila. *Pr.n. Geog:* Manille *f.*

manipulate, *v.tr.* **I.** Manipuler. **2.** *F:* **To manipulate accounts,** tripoter les comptes.

manipulation, *s.* **I.** Manipulation *f.* **2.** Tripotage *m.*

mankind, *s.inv.* **I.** Le genre humain ; l'homme *m.* **2.** Les hommes.

manliness, *s.* Caractère *m* mâle ; virilité *f.*

manly, *a.* D'homme ; mâle, viril.

manna, *s. B:* Manne *f.*

mannequin, *s.* Mannequin *m.*

manner, *s.* **I.** Manière *f,* façon *f.* **In this manner,** de cette manière ; ainsi. **The m. in which,** la manière dont. **In such a manner that,** de manière que. **In a manner (of speaking),** en quelque sorte ; pour ainsi dire. **It is a manner of speaking,** c'est une façon de parler. **2.** *pl.* Mœurs *f,* usages *m.* **3.** Maintien *m,* tenue *f,* air *m.* **4.** *pl.* (a) Manières. **Bad manners,** mauvaises manières. (b) (Good) **manners,** bonnes manières, politesse *f.* **To teach s.o. manners,** donner à qn une leçon de politesse. **To forget one's manners,** oublier les convenances. **5.** Espèce *f,* sorte *f.* **No manner of doubt,** aucun doute.

mannerism, *s.* Maniérisme *m,* affectation *f.*

mannerly, *a.* Poli ; courtois ; bien élevé.

manœuvre¹, *s.* **I.** Manœuvre *f.* **2.** *pl. F:* (Underhand) **manœuvres,** menées *f,* intrigues *f.*

manœuvre². **I.** *v.tr.* Manœuvrer, faire manœuvrer. **2.** *v.i.* Manœuvrer.

manor, *s. Hist:* Seigneurie *f.* **manor-house,** *s.* Château seigneurial ; manoir *m.*

manorial, *a.* Seigneurial, -aux.

mansion, *s.* **I.** (*In country*) Château *m* ; (*in town*) hôtel (particulier). **2.** *pl.* **Mansions,** maison *f* de rapport.

manslaughter, *s.* Homicide *m* involontaire.

mantelpiece, *s.* **I.** Manteau *m* de cheminée. **2.** Dessus *m* de cheminée.

mantilla, *s. Cost:* Mantille *f.*

mantle¹, *s.* **I.** (a) Manteau *m.* (b) Mante *f,* pèlerine *f* (de femme). **2.** Manteau (de neige) ; voile *m* (de brume). **3.** Manchon *m* (de bec de gaz).

mantle², *v.tr.* Couvrir, envelopper (*with,* de).

manual. **I.** *a.* (a) Manuel. (b) *Mil:* **Manual exercise,** maniement *m* des armes. **2.** *s.* Manuel *m* ; aide-mémoire *m inv.* **-ally,** *adv.* Manuellement ; à la main.

manufactory, *s.* Fabrique *f,* usine *f.*

manufacture¹, *s.* **I.** (a) Fabrication *f* ; confection *f* (de vêtements). (b) *The woollen m.,* l'industrie *f* de la laine. **2.** Produit manufacturé.

manufacture², *v.tr.* (a) Fabriquer, manufacturer ; confectionner (des vêtements). **Manufacturing town,** ville industrielle. (b) *F:* Forger, fabriquer.

manufacturer, *s.* Fabricant *m,* industriel *m,* manufacturier *m,* usinier *m.*

manure¹, *s.* Engrais *m.* (Farmyard) **manure,** fumier *m.* **Manure heap,** tas *m* de fumier ; *F:* fumier.

manure², *v.tr.* Fumer, engraisser.

manuscript. **I.** *s.* Manuscrit *m.* **2.** *a.* Manuscrit ; écrit à la main.

Manx, *a. Geog:* Mannois ; manxois. **Manx cat,** chat sans queue de l'île de Man.

many, *a. & s.* Un grand nombre (de) ; beaucoup (de) ; bien des ; plusieurs. **Many a time,** mainte(s) fois. **Many a man,** bien des gens. **Many's the time** *I've heard that song,* j'ai entendu cette chanson bien des fois. **Before many days have passed,** avant qu'il ne soit longtemps. **For many years,** pendant de longues années. **Ever so many times,** je ne sais combien de fois. **Many of us,** beaucoup d'entre nous. **Many have seen it,** beaucoup de personnes l'ont vu. **They were so many,** ils étaient si nombreux. **In so many words,** en propres termes. **Too many people,** trop de monde. **A card too many,** une carte de trop. **How many horses have you?** combien de chevaux avez-vous ? *I have* **as many books as you,** j'ai autant de livres que vous. **As many again, twice as many,** deux fois autant. **As many as ten people,** jusqu'à dix personnes. **There are a good many,** il y en a pas mal. **many-coloured,** *a.* Multicolore. **many-sided,** *a.* A plusieurs côtés, multilatère.

map¹, *s.* Carte *f* (géographique). **Map of the world,** mappemonde *f.* *F:* **On the map,** d'actualité.

map², *v.tr.* **To map out a route,** tracer un itinéraire.

maple, *s.* Érable *m.* **Maple sugar,** sucre *m* d'érable.

maquis, s. Maquis m. *Man of the m.,* maquisard m. To take to the m., prendre le maquis.

mar, v.tr. Gâter; troubler; déparer (la beauté de qn). F: To make or mar s.o., faire la fortune ou la ruine de qn.

maraud, v.i. & tr. Marauder. **marauding,** a. Maraudeur, -euse.

marauder, s. Maraudeur m.

marble, s. **1.** Marbre m. Marble quarry, marbrière f. **2.** *Games:* Bille f.

March¹, s. Mars m. In M., au mois de mars.

march², s. **1.** *Mil:* (a) Marche f. On the march, en marche. To do a day's march, faire une étape. March past, défilé m. (b) Pas m, allure f. Slow march, pas ordinaire. Quick march, pas cadencé, accéléré. **2.** Marche, progrès m. **3.** *Mus:* Marche.

march³. **1.** v.i. *Mil: etc:* Marcher. Quick march! en avant, marche! March at ease! pas de route! To march past (s.o.), défiler (devant qn). **2.** v.tr. F: He was marched off to gaol, il a été emmené en prison.

marching, s. *Mil:* Marching orders, feuille f de route. F: To give s.o. his marching orders, signifier son congé à qn.

marchioness, s. Marquise f.

mare, s. Jument f.

Margaret. Pr.n. Marguerite f.

margarine, s. *Com:* Margarine f.

margin, s. **1.** (a) Marge f. (b) Marge, écart m. To allow s.o. some margin, accorder quelque marge à qn. **2.** Marge, blanc m (d'une page).

marginal, a. Marginal, -aux; en marge.

marguerite, s. *Bot:* Grande marguerite.

Maria. Pr.n. Maria f. F: Black Maria, la voiture cellulaire.

marigold, s. *Bot:* Souci m.

marine. **1.** a. Marin. **2.** s. (a) Marine f. Mercantile marine, marine marchande. (b) Soldat m de l'infanterie de marine. F: Tell that to the marines! à d'autres!

mariner, s. *Nau:* Marin m.

marionette, s. Marionnette f.

marital, a. **1.** Marital, -aux. **2.** Matrimonial, -aux.

maritime, a. Maritime.

marjoram, s. *Bot:* Marjolaine f.

mark¹, s. **1.** But m, cible f. To be wide of the mark, être loin de la réalité. **2.** Marque f, preuve f, signe m. As a mark of my esteem, en témoignage de mon estime. **3.** (a) Marque f, tache f, signe, empreinte f. To make one's mark, se faire une réputation; arriver. (b) The mark of a foot, la marque, l'empreinte, d'un pied. **4.** (a) Marque, signe. Punctuation marks, signes de ponctuation. (b) *Sch:* Point m; note f d'appréciation. **5.** (a) Marque, repère m, trace f. (b) F: To be up to the mark, (i) (in ability) être à la hauteur; (ii) (in health) être dans son assiette.

mark², v.tr. **1.** Marquer, chiffrer. **2.** (a) To mark (the price of) an article, mettre le prix à un article. (b) *Sch:* To mark an exercise, coter un devoir. **3.** (a) Marquer, repérer, indiquer. To mark the points in a game, marquer les points du jeu. (b) Post marking the course, poteau indicateur de piste. (c) Indiquer. **4.** To mark time, F: piétiner sur place. To mark an era, faire époque. **5.** Observer, remarquer, noter. Mark my words! écoutez-moi bien! **mark off,** v.tr. To m. off a distance on the map, prendre, mesurer, une distance sur la carte. **marked,** a. Marqué. Marked improvement, amélioration sensible. Strongly marked features, traits fortement accusés. **marking,** s. **1.** Marquage m. **2.** pl. Markings, marques f; (on animal) taches f, rayures f. **marking-ink,** s. Encre f à marquer.

Mark³. Pr.n. Marc m.

markedly, adv. D'une façon marquée.

marker, s. (a) Bridge marker, carnet-bloc m, pl. carnets-blocs. (b) = BOOK-MARKER.

market¹, s. (a) Marché m. Covered market, halle f, halles fpl. In the market, au marché. (b) To be on the market, être mis en vente. To find a market for sth., trouver un débouché pour qch. To find a ready market, être d'un débit facile. (c) Black m., marché noir. **market-day,** s. Jour m de marché. **market-garden,** s. Jardin maraîcher. **market-gardener,** s. Maraîcher, -ère. **market-place,** s. Place f du marché. **market-price,** s. *Com:* Prix courant. **market-town,** s. Ville f où se tient un marché; bourg m, bourgade f.

market², v. (a) v.i. Faire son marché, faire ses emplettes. (b) Vendre (au marché).

marketable, a. D'un débit facile.

marksman, s. Bon tireur; tireur d'élite.

marksmanship, s. Adresse f, habileté f, au tir.

marmalade, s. *Cu:* Confiture f d'oranges.

marmoset, s. Ouistiti m, marmouset m.

marmot, s. *Z:* Marmotte f.

maroon¹. **1.** a. & s. Marron pourpré inv. **2.** s. *Pyr:* Marron m.

maroon², v.tr. Abandonner dans une île déserte.

marquee, s. (Tente-)marquise f.

marquess, marquis, s. Marquis m.

marriage, s. **1.** Mariage m. To take s.o. in marriage, épouser qn. Uncle by marriage, oncle par alliance. Marriage certificate, F: marriage lines, acte m de mariage. The marriage service, la bénédiction nuptiale. **2.** Mariage, union f.

marrow, s. **1.** Moelle f. **2.** *Hort:* Vegetable marrow, courge f à la moelle.

marry, v.tr. **1.** (Of priest) Marier. **2.** (a) Se marier avec; épouser. To marry money, faire un mariage d'argent. (b) Abs. To marry, se marier. To marry into a family, s'allier à une famille. To marry beneath one, faire une mésalliance.

Marseilles. Pr.n. Marseille f.

marsh, *s.* Marais *m*, marécage *m*. **marsh-mallow,** *s.* Guimauve *f*.

marshal[1], *s.* **1.** *Hist:* Maréchal *m*, -aux. **2.** Air Marshal, général *m*, *pl.* -aux, de corps aérien.

marshal[2], *v.tr.* (a) Placer en ordre. (b) To marshal s.o. in, introduire qn cérémonieusement. **marshalling,** *s.* Disposition *f* en ordre.

marshy, *a.* Marécageux.

marsupial, *s.* *Z:* Marsupial *m*, -aux.

marten, *s.* *Z:* Mart(r)e *f*.

martial, *a.* Martial, -aux; guerrier. Martial law, loi martiale.

martin, *s.* *Orn:* Martinet *m*.

martinet, *s.* Officier *m* à cheval sur la discipline.

martyr, *s.* Martyr, *f.* martyre. *F:* To be a martyr to gout, être torturé par la goutte.

martyrdom, *s.* Martyre *m*.

marvel[1], *s.* Merveille *f*.

marvel[2], *v.i.* S'émerveiller, s'étonner (*at*, de).

marvellous. 1. *a.* Merveilleux, étonnant. **2.** *s.* It savours of the marvellous, cela tient du prodige. **-ly,** *adv.* A merveille; merveilleusement.

Mary. *Pr.n.* Marie *f*.

marzipan, *s.* Massepain *m*.

mascot, *s.* Mascotte *f*; porte-bonheur *m inv*.

masculine, *a.* Masculin, mâle.

mash, *v.tr.* Brasser, broyer, écraser. *Cu:* Mashed potatoes, purée *f* de pommes de terre; pommes *f* mousseline.

mask[1], *s.* Masque *m*; (*velvet*) loup *m*. To throw off the mask, lever le masque; se démasquer.

mask[2], *v.tr.* Masquer. To mask one's face, se masquer.

mason, *s.* **1.** Maçon *m*. **2.** Franc-maçon *m*, *pl.* francs-maçons.

masonry, *s.* Maçonnerie *f*.

masquerade, *v.i.* Se masquer; aller en masque. To masquerade as, se déguiser en.

masquerader, *s.* (a) Personne déguisée. (b) Imposteur *m*.

mass[1], *s.* *Ecc:* Messe *f*. High mass, la grand'messe.

mass[2], *s.* **1.** Masse *f*, amas *m*. **2.** (a) A mass of people, une multitude de gens. *To gather in masses*, se masser. *He was a m. of bruises*, il était tout couvert de meurtrissures. Mass executions, exécutions *f* en masse. (b) The great mass of the people, la plus grande partie de la population. The masses, les masses; la foule. **mass meeting,** *s.* Réunion *f* en masse. **mass production,** *s.* Fabrication *f*, travail *m*, en série.

mass[3]. 1. *v.tr.* Masser; agglomérer. **2.** *v.i.* Se masser; (*of clouds*) s'amonceler.

massacre[1], *s.* Massacre *m*, tuerie *f*.

massacre[2], *v.tr.* Massacrer.

massage[1], *s.* Massage *m*.

massage[2], *v.tr.* *Med:* Masser.

masseur, *f.* **masseuse,** *s.* Masseur, -euse.

massive, *a.* Massif.

mast, *s.* **1.** *Nau:* Mât *m*. To sail before the mast, servir comme simple matelot. **2.** Pylône *m*. **mast-head,** *s.* *Nau:* Tête *f*, ton *m*, de mât. To be at the m.-h., être en vigie.

master[1], *s.* **1.** (a) Maître *m*. To be master in one's own house, être maître chez soi. To be one's own master, s'appartenir; ne dépendre que de soi. To meet one's master, trouver son maître. (b) Maître, patron *m*, chef *m*. (c) *Nau:* Patron, maître. (d) Master of Ceremonies, maître des cérémonies. **2.** *Sch:* (a) Maître; professeur *m*. (b) Fencing master, maître d'armes. (c) Master of Arts, maître ès arts = licencié ès lettres. **3.** To be master of a subject, posséder un sujet à fond. *Art:* An old master, un maître d'autrefois. **4.** Master John, Monsieur Jean. **5.** *Attrib.* (a) Master mariner, capitaine au long cours. (b) Master hand, main *f* de maître. (c) Master mind, esprit supérieur. **master-at-arms,** *s.* *Navy:* Capitaine *m* d'armes. **master-key,** *s.* Passe-partout *m inv*. **master-stroke,** *s.* Coup *m* de maître.

master[2], *v.tr.* **1.** Dompter, maîtriser. **2.** Maîtriser (ses passions); surmonter (sa colère); apprendre (un sujet) à fond.

masterful, *a.* Impérieux, autoritaire.

masterly, *a.* De maître; magistral, -aux. In a masterly manner, magistralement.

masterpiece, *s.* Chef-d'œuvre *m*, *pl.* chefs-d'œuvre.

mastery, *s.* Maîtrise *f* (*of*, de); domination *f*.

masticate, *v.tr.* Mâcher, mastiquer.

mastication, *s.* Mastication *f*.

mastiff, *s.* Mâtin *m*; dogue anglais.

mat[1], *s.* (a) Natte *f*. (b) Paillasson *m*.

mat[2], *v.tr.* (a) Natter, tresser. (b) Emmêler (les cheveux). (c) Matted hair, cheveux emmêlés. **matting,** *s.* Natte(s) *f(pl)*, paillassons *mpl*.

match[1], *s.* **1.** Égal, -ale; pareil, -eille. To meet one's match, trouver à qui parler. *To meet more than one's m.*, s'attaquer à plus fort que soi. To be a match for s.o., être de force à lutter avec qn. **2.** *Sp:* Lutte *f*, partie *f*, match *m*. Tennis match, partie de tennis. Football match, match de football. **3.** Mariage *m*, alliance *f*. To make a good match, se marier avantageusement. **match-maker,** *s.* Marieur, -euse. **match-making,** *s.* Manie *f* d'arranger des mariages.

match[2]. 1. *v.tr.* (a) Égaler; être l'égal de. *Pretty evenly matched*, à peu près de force égale. (b) Apparier (des gants); assortir (des couleurs). **2.** *v.i.* S'assortir; s'harmoniser. **matching,** *s.* Assortiment *m* (de couleurs); appariement *m* (d'objets).

match[3], *s.* Allumette *f*. Safety match, allumette de sûreté. To strike a match, frotter une allumette. **match-box,** *s.* Boîte *f* à allumettes.

matchless, *a*. Incomparable, inimitable.
mate[1], *s*. *Chess*: Échec *m* et mat *m*.
mate[2], *v.tr*. *Chess*: Faire échec et mat.
mate[3], *s*. **1.** Camarade *mf*; compagnon, *f*. compagne. **2.** (*Of birds*) Pair *m*; (*of persons*) époux, *f*. épouse. **3.** *Nau*: (*a*) (*On merchant vessel*) Officier *m*. **First mate**, second *m*. **Second mate**, lieutenant *m*. (*b*) *Navy*: Second maître.
mate[4]. *v.i*. (*a*) To mate with s.o., épouser qn. (*b*) (*Of birds*) S'accoupler.
material. I. *a*. **1.** (*a*) Matériel, grossier. *To be engrossed in m. things*, être enfoncé dans la matière. (*b*) **To have enough for one's material needs**, avoir de quoi vivre matériellement. **2.** (*a*) Important, essentiel (*to*, pour). (*b*) (*Fait*) pertinent. **-ally,** *adv*. **1.** Matériellement, essentiellement. **2.** Sensiblement. II. **material**, *s*. **1.** (*a*) Matière *f*, matériaux *mpl*. **Raw materials**, matières premières. *To provide m. for conversation*, fournir des sujets de conversation. (*b*) *pl*. **Materials**, fournitures *f*, accessoires *m*. **Writing materials**, de quoi écrire. **2.** *Tex*: Étoffe *f*, tissu *m*.
materialism, *s*. Matérialisme *m*.
materialist, *s*. Matérialiste *m*.
materialize, *v.i*. *F*: Se réaliser; (*of plans*) aboutir.
maternal, *a*. Maternel. **-ally,** *adv*. Maternellement.
maternity, *s*. Maternité *f*.
mathematical, *a*. Mathématique. **-ally,** *adv*. Mathématiquement.
mathematician, *s*. Mathématicien, -ienne.
mathematics, *s.pl*. Mathématiques *fpl*.
matinée, *s*. *Th*: Matinée *f*.
matins, *s.pl*. *Ecc*: Matines *f*.
matricide[1], *s*. Matricide *mf*.
matricide[2], *s*. (*Crime*) Matricide *m*.
matriculate, *v.i*. Passer l'examen d'entrée à l'université.
matriculation, *s*. Examen *m* de fin d'études secondaires.
matrimonial, *a*. Matrimonial, -aux.
matrimony, *s*. (Holy) matrimony, le mariage.
matrix, *s*. Matrice *f*.
matron, *s*. **1.** Matrone *f*; mère *f* de famille. **2.** (*a*) Intendante *f* (d'une institution). (*b*) Infirmière *f* en chef.
matter[1], *s*. **1.** Matière *f*; substance *f*. **Vegetable matter**, matières végétales. **2.** *Med*: Matière (purulente); pus *m*. **3.** Matière, sujet *m*. **Reading matter**, choses *f* à lire. **4.** It makes no matter, n'importe; cela ne fait rien. **5.** Affaire *f*, chose, cas *m*. **It is an easy matter**, c'est facile. **It is no great matter**, c'est peu de chose. **As matters stand**, au point où en sont les choses. **Business matters**, affaires. **In this matter**, à cet égard. **Matter of taste**, affaire de goût. **For that matter**, pour ce qui est de cela; d'ailleurs. **What is the matter?** qu'est-ce qu'il y a? qu'y a-t-il? *Something must be the m.*, il doit y avoir

quelque chose. *As if nothing was the m.*, comme si de rien n'était. **matter-of-fact**, *a*. Pratique, positif, prosaïque.
matter[2], *v.i*. Importer (*to* s.o., à qn); avoir de l'importance. *It does not m.*, n'importe; cela ne fait rien. *Nothing else matters*, tout le reste n'est rien.
Matterhorn (the). *Pr.n*. Le Mont Cervin.
Matthew. *Pr.n*. Mat(t)hieu *m*.
mattress, *s*. Matelas *m*.
mature[1], *a*. Mûr. **-ly,** *adv*. Mûrement.
mature[2], *v.i*. Mûrir.
maturity, *s*. Maturité *f*.
maudlin, *a*. Larmoyant, pleurard.
maul, *v.tr*. Meurtrir, malmener. **To be mauled by a tiger**, être écharpé par un tigre.
mauling, *s*. Tripotée *f*.
maunder, *v.i*. To maunder (on), divaguer, radoter. **Maunderings**, *s*. Divagations *f*.
Maundy Thursday, *s*. Le jeudi saint.
Mauritius. *Pr.n*. L'île *f* Maurice.
mausoleum, *s*. Mausolée *m*.
mauve, *a. & s*. Mauve (*m*).
maw, *s*. Gueule *f* (du lion).
mawkish, *a*. Fade, insipide.
maxim, *s*. Maxime *f*, dicton *m*.
maximum. **1.** *s*. Maximum *m*, *pl*. maximums, -a. **2.** *a*. Maximum, *f.occ*. maxima.
may[1], *v.aux*. **1.** (*a*) *With luck I may succeed*, avec de la chance je peux réussir. *He may not be hungry*, il n'a peut-être pas faim. *He may miss the train*, il se peut qu'il manque le train. (*b*) *How old might she be?* quel âge peut-elle bien avoir? *Might it not be well to warn him?* est-ce qu'on ne ferait pas bien de l'avertir? (*c*) *It may be that . . .*, il se peut bien que + *sub*. *That's as may be*, c'est selon. *As you may suppose*, comme vous (le) pensez bien. *Run as he might he could not overtake me*, il a eu beau courir, il n'a pas pu me rattraper. (*d*) *We may as well stay where we are*, autant vaut rester où nous sommes. (*e*) *I say, you might shut the door!* dites donc, vous pourriez bien fermer la porte! *He might have offered to help*, il aurait bien pu offrir son aide. **2.** *May I?* vous permettez? **May I come in?**—You may, puis-je entrer?—Mais parfaitement. **If I may say so**, si j'ose (le) dire. **3.** *I hope it may be true*, pourvu que cela soit vrai! *I hope he may succeed*, j'espère qu'il réussira. **4.** *May he rest in peace!* qu'il repose en paix! **Much good may it do you!** grand bien vous fasse! *Long may you live to enjoy it!* puissiez-vous vivre longtemps pour en jouir!
May[2], *s*. **1.** Mai *m*. *In (the month of) May*, en mai; au mois de mai. **2.** *Bot*: May(-tree), aubépine *f*. **May-day**, *s*. Le premier mai.
maybe, *adv*. Peut-être.
mayor, *s*. Maire *m*.
mayoress, *s*. Femme *f* du maire; mairesse *f*.
maypole, *s*. *To set up a m.*, planter un mai.
maze, *s*. Labyrinthe *m*, dédale *m*.

me, *pers.pron.* **1.** (a) Me, (*before a vowel sound*) m'; moi. *They see me,* ils me voient. *They hear me,* ils m'entendent. *Hear me!* écoutez-moi! *Give me some!* donnez-m'en! (b) Moi. *I will take it with me,* je le prendrai avec moi. **2.** Moi. *Come to me,* venez à moi. **3.** *F:* *It's me,* c'est moi. **4.** *Dear me!* mon Dieu! vraiment! par exemple!

meadow, s. Pré m, prairie f. **meadow-sweet,** s. *Bot:* Reine f des prés.

meagre, a. Maigre; peu copieux. **-ly** adv. Maigrement.

meal¹, s. Farine f.

meal², s. Repas m. **Square meal,** repas copieux. **To make a meal of it,** en faire son repas. **meal-time,** s. Heure f du repas.

mealy, a. **1.** Farineux. **2.** *F:* (Visage) terreux, farineux. **3.** **Mealy(-mouthed),** doucereux.

mean¹, s. **1.** (a) Milieu m; moyen terme. **The happy mean,** le juste milieu. (b) *Mth:* Moyenne f. **2.** pl. **Means,** moyen(s) m(pl), voie(s) f(pl). *There is no means of doing it,* il n'y a pas moyen. *He has been the means of,* c'est par lui que. **By all (manner of) means!** mais certainement! mais faites donc! *He is not by any means a hero,* il n'est rien moins qu'un héros. **By some means or other,** de manière ou d'autre. **By means of sth.,** au moyen, par le moyen, de qch. **3.** pl. Moyens (de vivre); ressources fpl. *He is a man of means,* il a une belle fortune.

mean², a. Moyen.

mean³, a. **1.** (a) Misérable, minable. *That ought to be clear to the meanest intelligence,* cela devrait être compris par l'esprit le plus borné. (b) *He had no mean opinion of himself,* il ne se croyait pas peu de chose. **2.** Bas, méprisable. *A mean trick,* un vilain tour. *To take a mean advantage of s.o.,* exploiter indignement qn. **3.** Avare, mesquin, chiche. **-ly,** adv. **1.** Misérablement, pauvrement. *To think meanly of sth.,* avoir une piètre opinion de qch. **2.** (Se conduire) bassement. **mean-spirited,** a. A l'âme basse; abject.

mean⁴, v.tr. **1.** (a) Avoir l'intention (*to do sth.,* de faire qch.); se proposer (de faire qch.). *What do you m. to do?* que comptez-vous faire? *He means no harm,* il n'y entend pas malice. *I mean him no harm,* je ne lui veux pas de mal. *He didn't mean (to do) it,* il ne l'a pas fait exprès. (b) *He means well,* il a de bonnes intentions. (c) *I mean to be obeyed,* j'entends qu'on m'obéisse. **2.** (a) *I meant this purse for you,* je vous destinais cette bourse. (b) *The remark was meant for you,* la remarque s'adressait à vous. (c) *Do you mean me?* est-ce de moi que vous parlez? **3.** (a) Vouloir dire; signifier. *The name means nothing to me,* ce nom ne me dit rien. (b) *What do you mean?* que voulez-vous dire? *What do you mean by that?* qu'entendez-vous par là? *You don't mean*

it! vous plaisantez! *I m. it,* c'est sérieux. (c) *Ten pounds means a lot to him!* dix livres, c'est une somme pour lui! *If you knew what it means to live alone!* si vous saviez ce que c'est que de vivre seul! **meaning¹,** a. (Regard) significatif. **-ly,** adv. D'un air significatif. **meaning²,** s. (a) Signification f, sens m, acception f. *What is the m. of that word?* que veut dire ce mot? *F:* **What's the meaning of this?** qu'est-ce que cela signifie? (b) *You mistake my m.,* vous me comprenez mal.

meander¹, s. Méandre m, repli m.

meander², v.i. Serpenter, se replier. **meandering,** a. Sinueux, serpentant.

meaningless, a. Dénué de sens.

meanness, s. **1.** Médiocrité f, pauvreté f. **2.** (a) Mesquinerie f, avarice f. (b) Vilenie f.

meantime, meanwhile, s. & adv. (In the) **meantime, (in the) meanwhile,** dans l'intervalle; en attendant.

measles, s.pl. Rougeole f. **German measles,** roséole f.

measurable, a. Mesurable.

measure¹, s. Mesure f. **1.** (a) **Cubic measure,** mesure de volume. (b) *F:* **To take the measure of a man,** prendre la mesure d'un homme. **Made to measure,** fait sur mesure. **2.** (a) Mesure. (b) Mètre m. **3.** Mesure, limite f. **Beyond measure,** outre mesure; démesurément. **In some measure,** en partie. **4.** (a) Mesure, démarche f. **To take extreme measures,** employer les grands moyens. (b) Projet m de loi. **5.** pl. *Geol:* **Coal measures,** gisements houillers.

measure², v.tr. **1.** (a) Mesurer; métrer. *To m. a piece of ground,* faire l'arpentage d'un terrain. *F:* **To measure one's length,** s'étaler par terre. (b) *Tail:* Mesurer; prendre la mesure de. (c) **To measure one's words,** mesurer, peser, ses paroles. **2.** *This book measures six inches by four,* ce livre a six pouces de long sur quatre de large. **measured,** a. **1.** Mesuré, déterminé. **2.** (a) (Pas) cadencé. (b) **With measured steps,** à pas comptés. **3.** **Measured language,** langage modéré.

measurement, s. **1.** Mesurage m. **2.** Mesure f, dimension f. **To take s.o.'s measurements,** prendre les mesures de qn.

meat, s. **1.** Viande f. **Meat diet,** régime carné. **2.** Aliment m, nourriture f. **Meat and drink,** le manger et le boire. *F:* **This was meat and drink to them,** ils en faisaient des gorges chaudes. **meat-safe,** s. Garde-manger m inv.

Mecca. *Pr.n. Geog:* La Mecque.

mechanic, s. **1.** Artisan m, ouvrier m. **2.** **Motor mechanic,** mécanicien m automobiliste.

mechanical, a. **1.** Mécanique. **2.** (*Of actions*) Machinal, -aux; automatique. **-ally,** adv. **1.** Mécaniquement. **2.** Machinalement.

mechanician, *s.* Mécanicien *m.*
mechanics, *s.pl.* La mécanique.
mechanism, *s.* Appareil *m,* dispositif *m*; mécanisme *m.*
mechanize, *v.tr.* Mécaniser.
medal, *s.* Médaille *f.*
medallion, *s* Médaillon *m.*
meddle, *v.i.* To meddle with sth., (i) se mêler de qch.; (ii) toucher à qch. **meddling,** *s.* Intervention *f,* ingérence *f* (dans une affaire).
meddler, *s.* Officieux, -euse; touche-à-tout *m inv.*
meddlesome, *a.* Officieux, intrigant.
mediaeval, *a.* Du moyen âge; médiéval, -aux.
mediate, *v.i.* S'entremettre, agir en médiateur.
mediation, *s.* Médiation *f*; intervention *f.*
mediator, *s.* Médiateur, -trice.
medical, *a.* Médical, -aux. **Medical student,** étudiant *m* en médecine; **Medical man,** médecin *m.* **Medical officer,** médecin *m* sanitaire. *Mil:* major *m.* **-ally,** *adv.* To be medically examined, subir un examen médical.
medicinal, *a.* Médicinal, -aux. **-ally,** *adv.* Médicinalement.
medicine, *s.* **1.** La médecine. **2.** Médicament *m,* médecine. **3.** (i) Sorcellerie *f*; (ii) charme *m.* **medicine-chest,** *s.* (Coffret *m* de) pharmacie *f.* **medicine-man,** *s.* (Sorcier) guérisseur *m.*
medieval = MEDIAEVAL.
mediocre, *a.* Médiocre.
mediocrity, *s.* Médiocrité *f.*
meditate. **I.** *v.tr.* Méditer. To meditate doing sth., méditer de faire qch. **2.** *v.i.* (a) Méditer (on, upon, sur). (b) Se recueillir.
meditation, *s.* Méditation *f* (upon, sur); recueillement *m.*
meditative, *a.* Méditatif, recueilli.
Mediterranean, *a.* The Mediterranean (Sea), la (mer) Méditerranée.
medium. **I.** *s.* **1.** Milieu *m*; moyen terme (between, entre). Happy medium, juste milieu. **2.** Milieu, véhicule *m.* **3.** Intermédiaire *m,* entremise *f.* Advertising medium, organe *m* de publicité. **4.** *Psychics:* Médium *m.* **II.** **medium,** *a.* Moyen. Medium-sized, de grandeur moyenne, de taille moyenne.
medlar, *s. Bot:* (a) Nèfle *f.* (b) Néflier *m.*
medley, *s.* Mélange *m*; bigarrure *f* (de couleurs). *Mus:* Pot pourri.
Medusa. *Pr.n. Gr.Myth:* Méduse *f.*
meed, *s. Poet:* Récompense *f.*
meek, *a.* Doux, *f.* douce; humble. **-ly,** *adv.* Avec douceur; humblement.
meekness, *s.* Douceur *f*; soumission *f.*
meerschaum, *s.* Écume *f* de mer.
meet¹, *a. Lit:* Convenable; séant.
meet², *s.* Rendez-vous *m* de chasse.
meet³, *v.* **I.** *v.tr.* **1.** Rencontrer; se rencontrer avec. To m. s.o. on the stairs, croiser qn dans l'escalier. **He met his death at . . .,** il trouva la mort à. . . . **2.** Faire face à (une difficulté). **3.** Rejoindre. To go to meet s.o., aller au-devant de qn; aller à la rencontre de qn. To arrange to meet s.o., donner rendez-vous à qn. **4.** Faire la connaissance de. **5.** What a scene met my eyes! quel spectacle frappa mes regards! *If this should m. the eye of,* si ceci tombe sous les yeux de. There is more in it than meets the eye, on ne voit pas le dessous des cartes. **6.** (a) To m. s.o.'s views, se conformer aux vues de qn. *F:* To meet s.o., faire des concessions à qn. (b) Satisfaire à (un besoin). **II.** **meet,** *v.i.* (a) Se rencontrer, se voir. *We have met before,* nous nous sommes déjà vus. (b) To meet (together), se réunir. (c) Se joindre. *Prov:* Extremes meet, les extrêmes se touchent. Our eyes met, nos regards se croisèrent. *F:* To make both ends meet, joindre les deux bouts. (d) To meet with sth., rencontrer, trouver, qch. To m. with a kindly reception, être accueilli avec bonté. To m. with difficulties, éprouver des difficultés. To m. with a refusal, essuyer un refus. He has met with an accident, il lui est arrivé un accident. **meeting,** *s.* **1.** Rencontre *f.* **2.** Assemblée *f,* réunion *f.* To address the meeting, prendre la parole.
megaphone, *s.* Porte-voix *m inv.*
melancholy. **1.** *s.* Mélancolie *f.* **2.** *a.* (a) Mélancolique; triste. (b) *M. news,* triste nouvelle.
mellifluous, *a.* Mielleux; doucereux.
mellow¹, *a.* **1.** (Fruit) fondant, mûr. **2.** Moelleux; doux, *f.* douce.
mellow², **I.** *v.tr.* (a) (Faire) mûrir. (b) Mûrir, adoucir. **2.** *v.i.* (a) Mûrir. (b) *(Of character)* S'adoucir.
mellowness, *s.* Maturité *f*; moelleux *m* (du vin); douceur *f* (du caractère).
melodious, *a.* Mélodieux, harmonieux. **-ly,** *adv.* Mélodieusement.
melodrama, *s.* Mélodrame *m.*
melodramatic, *a.* Mélodramatique.
melody, *s.* Mélodie *f,* air *m,* chant *m.*
melon, *s.* Melon *m.*
melt, *v.* **I.** *v.i.* **1.** Fondre; se fondre. **2.** His heart melted with pity, la pitié lui attendrissait le cœur. **II.** **melt,** *v.tr.* **1.** (Faire) fondre. **2.** Attendrir, émouvoir. **molten,** *a.* En fusion; fondu. **melting,** *a.* (a) *(Of snow)* Fondant. (b) *(Of voice)* Attendri. Melting mood, attendrissement *m.* **melting-pot,** *s.* Creuset *m.*
member, *s.* Membre *m.* **1.** *Nat.Hist:* Organe *m.* **2.** (a) *He is a m. of the family,* il fait partie de la famille. *M. of the audience,* assistant, -ante. (b) **Member of Parliament,** membre de la Chambre des Communes; *(in Fr.)* député *m.*
membership, *s.* **1.** Qualité *f* de membre. **2.** Nombre *m* des membres (d'une société).
membrane, *s.* Membrane *f.*

memento, *s.* Mémento *m*, souvenir *m*.

memoir, *s.* (a) Mémoire *m*, étude *f*. (b) Notice *f* biographique. (c) *pl.* **Memoirs,** mémoires.

memorable, *a.* Mémorable. **-ably,** *adv.* Mémorablement.

memorandum, *s.* Mémorandum *m*. **To make a memorandum of** sth., noter qch. **memorandum-book,** *s.* Carnet *m*, calepin *m*, agenda *m*.

memorial. **1.** *a.* Commémoratif. **2.** *s.* (a) Monument *m*. (b) Pétition *f*.

memory, *s.* **1.** Mémoire *f*. **To commit** sth. **to memory,** apprendre qch. par cœur. *I have a bad m. for names*, je n'ai pas la mémoire des noms. **To the best of my memory,** autant que je m'en souviens. *To play sth. from memory,* jouer qch. de mémoire. **2.** Mémoire, souvenir *m*. **Childhood memories,** souvenirs d'enfance.

menace¹, *s.* Menace *f*.

menace², *v.tr.* Menacer. **menacing,** *a.* Menaçant. **-ly,** *adv.* D'un air menaçant.

menagerie, *s.* Ménagerie *f*.

mend¹, *s.* **1.** Reprise *f*, raccommodage *m*. **2. On the mend,** en voie de guérison. *Trade is on the m.,* les affaires reprennent.

mend². I. *v.tr.* **1.** Racommoder. **2.** Rectifier, corriger. *To mend one's ways,* changer de conduite. **3.** (a) Réparer (une faute). (b) **To mend matters,** arranger les choses. (c) **To mend one's pace,** hâter le pas. II. **mend,** *v.i.* **1.** Se remettre. *The weather is mending,* le temps se remet au beau. **2.** S'amender, se corriger. **3.** S'améliorer. **mending,** *s.* Raccommodage *m*.

mendacious, *a.* Menteur, -euse, mensonger.

mendacity, *s.* **1.** Penchant *m* au mensonge. **2.** Fausseté *f*.

mendicancy, *s.* Mendicité *f*.

mendicant. **1.** *a.* Mendiant. **2.** *s.* Mendiant, -ante.

menial. **1.** *a.* Servile; bas, *f.* basse. **2.** *s.* Domestique *mf*; laquais *m*.

mental, *a.* Mental, -aux; de l'esprit. **Mental reservation,** restriction mentale. **Mental arithmetic,** calcul *m* de tête. **Mental home,** asile *m* d'aliénés. **-ally,** *adv.* Mentalement.

mentality, *s.* Mentalité *f*.

mention¹, *s.* Mention *f*.

mention², *v.tr.* Mentionner, citer. **I shall mention it to him,** je lui en toucherai un mot. *It must never be mentioned again,* il ne faut plus jamais en reparler. **It isn't worth mentioning,** cela est sans importance. **Not to mention,** sans parler de. *I heard my name ·mentioned,* j'entendis prononcer mon nom. **He mentioned no names,** il n'a nommé personne. *F:* **Don't mention it!** il n'y a pas de quoi !

mentor, *s.* Mentor *m*, guide *m*.

menu, *s.* Menu *m*.

mercantile, *a.* Mercantile, marchand.

mercenary. **1.** *a.* Mercenaire, intéressé. **2.** *s.* Mercenaire *m*.

merchandise, *s.* Marchandise(s) *f(pl)*.

merchant. **1.** *s.* Négociant *m* ; commerçant *m*. **2.** *a.* Marchand. **Merchant vessel,** navire marchand. **merchant-seaman,** *s.* Marin *m* du commerce. **merchant-service,** *s.* Marine marchande.

merchantman, *s.* Navire marchand.

merciful, *a.* Miséricordieux (*to,* pour); clément (*to,* envers). **-fully,** *adv.* Miséricordieusement ; avec clémence.

merciless, *a.* Impitoyable; sans pitié. **-ly,** *adv.* Impitoyablement ; sans merci.

mercilessness, *s.* Manque *m* de pitié.

mercurial, *a.* (a) Vif, éveillé. (b) Inconstant.

Mercury. I. *Pr.n.* Mercure *m*. II. **mercury,** *s. Ch:* Mercure *m*.

mercy, *s.* Miséricorde *f*, grâce *f*, merci *f*. (a) **To have mercy on** s.o., avoir pitié de qn. **To beg for mercy,** demander grâce. **To throw oneself on** s.o.'s **mercy,** s'abandonner à la merci de qn. *Int. F:* **Mercy** (on us)! grand Dieu ! miséricorde ! (b) **To be at** s.o.'s **mercy,** être à la merci de qn. **At the mercy of the waves,** au gré des flots. (c) **Thankful for small mercies,** reconnaissant des moindres bienfaits *m*. **What a mercy!** quel bonheur ! (d) **Sister of Mercy,** sœur de Charité.

mere¹, *s.* Lac *m*, étang *m*.

mere², *a.* Simple, pur, seul. **The m. sight of her,** sa seule vue. **I shudder at the m. thought of it,** je frissonne rien que d'y penser. **He's a m. boy,** ce n'est qu'un enfant. **-ly,** *adv.* Simplement, seulement. **He m. smiled,** il se contenta de sourire.

merge. **1.** *v.tr.* Fondre, fusionner. **2.** *v.i.* Se fondre, se perdre (*in, into,* dans) ; se confondre (*in, into,* avec).

meridian, *s.* (a) Méridien *m*. (b) Point culminant.

meringue, *s. Cu:* Meringue *f*.

merino, *s. Tex:* Mérinos *m*.

merit¹, *s.* **1.** (a) Mérite *m*. (b) **To treat** s.o. **according to his merits,** traiter qn selon ses mérites. (c) *To go into the merits of sth.,* discuter le pour et le contre de qch. **2.** Valeur *f*, mérite.

merit², *v.tr.* Mériter.

meritorious, *a.* Méritoire.

mermaid, *s.* Sirène *f*.

merman, *s.* Triton *m*.

merriment, *s.* Gaieté *f*, hilarité *f*.

merry, *a.* Joyeux, gai. **To make merry,** se réjouir. *To make m. over sth.,* se divertir de qch. **A merry Christmas!** joyeux Noël ! *Prov:* **The more the merrier,** plus on est de fous, plus on rit. **-ily,** *adv.* Gaiement, joyeusement. **merry-maker,** *s.* Noceur, -euse. **merry-making,** *s.* Réjouissances *fpl*.

mesh, *s.* Maille *f*.

mess¹, *s.* **1.** Saleté *f*. **To make a mess of the table-cloth,** salir la nappe. **2.** Fouillis *m*, gâchis *m*. *Everything is in a m.,* tout est en

désordre. What a mess! voilà du propre !
F: To get into a mess, se mettre dans le
pétrin. To make a mess of it, tout gâcher.
3. (For officers) Table f, mess m; (for men)
Mil: ordinaire m. Navy: plat m.
mess², v.tr. (a) Salir, souiller. (b) To mess
(up) a business, gâcher une affaire. **mess
about,** v.i. F: (a) Patauger. (b) Bricoler;
gaspiller son temps.
message, s. **I.** (a) Message m. (b) Communication f. **2.** Commission f, course f. To
run messages, faire les courses.
messenger, s. (a) Messager, -ère. (b) Commissionnaire m; garçon m de bureau. Hotel
messenger, chasseur m. Telegraph messenger, facteur m des télégraphes. (c) Courrier m.
Messiah. Pr.n. Messie m.
messmate, s. Camarade m de table.
Messrs, s.pl. Com: Messieurs m, abbr. MM.
messy, a. F: **I.** (a) Sale, malpropre. (b) En
désordre. **2.** Qui salit; salissant.
metal, s. **I.** Métal m, -aux. **2.** Civ.E: Road
metal, cailloutis m, pierraille f. **3.** pl. Rail:
To jump the metals, quitter les rails.
metallic, a. Métallique.
metallurgist, s. Métallurgiste m.
metallurgy, s. Métallurgie f.
metamorphose, v.tr. Métamorphoser, transformer (to, into, en).
metamorphosis, s. Métamorphose f.
metaphor, s. Métaphore f; image f. Mixed
metaphor, métaphore disparate.
metaphoric(al), a. Métaphorique. **-ally,**
adv. Métaphoriquement.
metaphysics, s.pl. La métaphysique.
mete, v.tr. Lit: To mete (out) punishments,
assigner des punitions.
meteor, s. Météore m.
meteoric, a. Météorique.
meteorology, s. Météorologie f.
meter, s. Compteur m. Electric meter,
compteur de courant.
method, s. (a) Méthode f; manière f (of
doing sth., de faire qch.); procédé m (pour
faire qch.). (b) Man of method, homme
d'ordre.
methodical, a. Méthodique. He is very m.,
il a beaucoup de méthode. **-ally,** adv.
Méthodiquement; avec méthode.
methylate, v.tr. Methylated spirit, alcool à
brûler.
meticulous, a. Méticuleux. **-ly,** adv.
Méticuleusement.
meticulousness, s. Méticulosité f.
metre¹, s. Pros: Mètre m, mesure f. In
metre, en vers.
metre², s. Meas: Mètre m.
metric¹, a. Meas: Métrique.
metric²(al), a. (Poésie) métrique.
metropolis, s. Métropole f.
metropolitan, a. Métropolitain.
mettle, s. **I.** Ardeur f, courage m, feu m;
(of horse) fougue f. To put s.o. on his mettle,

piquer qn d'honneur. **2.** Caractère m, tempérament m. To show one's mettle, faire
ses preuves.
mettlesome, a. Ardent, vif; (of horse) fougueux.
mew¹, s. Miaulement m.
mew², v.i. Miauler. **mewing,** s. Miaulement m.
mews, s. **I.** Écuries fpl. **2.** Impasse f (sur
laquelle donnaient des écuries).
Mexican, a. & s. Mexicain, -aine.
Mexico. Pr.n. Le Mexique.
miaow¹, s. Miaulement m, miaou m.
miaow², v.i. Miauler.
miasma, s. Miasme m.
mica, s. Mica m.
Michael. Pr.n. Michel m.
Michaelmas, s. **I.** La Saint-Michel. **2.** Bot:
Michaelmas daisy, marguerite f d'automne.
Michelangelo. Pr.n. Michel-Ange m.
microbe, s. Microbe m.
microcosm, s. Microcosme m.
micrometer, s. Micromètre m.
microphone, s. Microphone m.
microscope, s. Microscope m. Visible under
the microscope, visible au microscope.
microscopic(al), a. Microscopique.
mid, a. Du milieu; mi-, moyen. From mid
June to mid August, de la mi-juin à la mi-août.
In mid air, entre ciel et terre; au milieu des
airs. In mid channel, au milieu du chenal.
mid-season, s. Demi-saison f.
midday, s. Midi m.
middle. I. Attrib.a. Du milieu; central,
-aux; moyen, intermédiaire. To take a middle
course, prendre un parti moyen. Middle
size, grandeur moyenne. **2.** s. (a) Milieu,
centre m. In the middle of, au milieu de.
About the m. of August, à la mi-août. Right
in the middle of, au beau milieu de. (b) Taille
f, ceinture f. **middle-aged,** a. Entre deux
âges; d'un certain âge. **middle class,** s.
The middle class(es), la classe moyenne; la
bourgeoisie. **middle-sized,** a. De grandeur moyenne; de taille moyenne.
middleman, s. Com: Intermédiaire m.
middling. I. a. Médiocre. How are you?
—Middling, comment allez-vous?—Comme
ci comme ça. **2.** adv. Assez bien; passablement.
midge, s. Moucheron m; cousin m.
midget, s. **I.** Nain, f. naine. **2.** Attrib.
Minuscule.
midnight, s. Minuit m. To arrive about m.,
arriver sur les minuit.
midshipman, s. Nau: Aspirant m (de
marine).
midst, s. (a) In the midst of sth., au milieu
de, parmi. In the m. of winter, en plein hiver.
(b) In our midst, au milieu de nous; parmi
nous.
midstream, s. In midstream, au milieu du
courant.
midsummer, s. (a) Milieu m de l'été.
(b) Midsummer day, la Saint-Jean.

midway, *adv.* A mi-chemin, à moitié chemin.

midwife, *s.* Sage-femme *f*, *pl.* sages-femmes.

midwinter, *s.* Milieu *m* de l'hiver, fort *m* de l'hiver.

mien, *s.* Mine *f*, air *m*.

might, *s.* Puissance *f*, force(s) *f(pl)*. **To work with all one's might,** travailler de toute sa force. **Might is right,** la force prime le droit.

mighty. I. *a.* (*a*) Puissant, fort. (*b*) Grand, vaste. **-ily,** *adv.* I. Puissamment. 2. *F:* Extrêmement. II. **mighty,** *adv.* *F:* Fort, rudement.

mignonette, *s.* Réséda odorant.

migrate, *v.i.* Émigrer.

migration, *s.* Migration *f*.

migratory, *a.* Migrateur, -trice.

milch-cow, *s.* Vache laitière.

mild, *a.* I. Doux, *f.* douce. 2. Peu sévère, peu rigoureux. *M. punishment,* punition légère. 3. (Climat) doux. 4. (*a*) *F:* **Draw it mild!** tout doux! (*b*) **A mild form of measles,** une forme bénigne de la rougeole. **-ly,** *adv.* I. Doucement. 2. *F:* **To put it mildly,** pour m'exprimer avec modération.

mildew, *s.* Moisissure *f*; taches *fpl* d'humidité.

mildness, *s.* I. Douceur *f*, clémence *f*. 2. Bénignité *f* (d'une maladie).

mile, *s.* Mille *m*. *F:* **Not a hundred miles away,** tout près. **Nobody comes within miles of him,** personne ne lui monte à la cheville.

mileage, *s.* Distance *f* en milles.

milestone, *s.* I. Borne milliaire, routière. 2. *F:* *Milestones in s.o.'s life,* événements *m* qui jalonnent la vie de qn.

militant, *a.* Militant.

military. I. *a.* Militaire. **Of military age,** en âge de servir. 2. *s.pl. Coll.* **The military,** les militaires *m*.

militate, *v.i.* Militer.

militia, *s.* Milice *f*; garde nationale.

milk¹, *s.* I. Lait *m*. **Milk diet,** régime lacté. *Prov:* **It is no use crying over spilt milk,** à chose faite point de remède. 2. Lait, eau *f* (de noix de coco). **milk-and-water,** *a.* *F:* Fade, ins.pide. **milk-jug,** *s* Pot *m* à lait. **milk-tooth,** *s.* Dent *f* de lait. **milk-white,** *a.* D'une blancheur de lait.

milk², *v.tr.* I. Traire. 2. *F:* Dépouiller, exploiter (qn). **milking,** *s.* Traite *f*.

milkiness, *s.* Couleur laiteuse; lactescence *f*.

milkmaid, *s.* I. Laitière *f*. 2. Trayeuse *f*

milkman, *s.* Laitier *m*, crémier *m*.

milksop, *s.* *F:* Poule mouillée.

milky, *a.* Laiteux. *Astr:* **The Milky Way,** la Voie lactée.

mill, *s.* I. (Flour-)mill, moulin *m* (à farine). **Steam mill,** minoterie *f*. *F:* **To go through the mill,** passer par de dures épreuves. 2. Usine *f*; manufacture *f*. 3. *F:* Combat *m* à coups de poing. **mill-pond,** *s.* Réservoir *m* de moulin.

millboard, *s.* Carton-pâte *m inv*.

millennium, *s.* I. *Rel.H:* Millénium *m*. 2. Millénaire *m*; mille ans *m*.

miller, *s.* Meunier *m*.

millet, *s.* *Bot:* Millet *m*, mil *m*.

milliard, *s.* Milliard *m*.

milliner, *s.* Modiste *f*.

millinery, *s.* (Articles *mpl* de) modes *fpl*.

million, *s.* Million *m*.

millionaire, *a. & s.* Millionnaire (*mf*).

millstone, *s.* Meule *f*.

mimic¹. I. *a.* Mimique; imitateur, -trice. 2. *s.* (*a*) Mime *m*. (*b*) Imitateur, -trice.

mimic², *v.tr.* Imiter, mimer.

mimicry, *s.* Mimique *f*, imitation *f*.

minaret, *s.* Minaret *m*.

mince¹, *s.* *Cu:* Hachis *m*.

mince², *v.tr.* I. Hacher (menu). **Minced meat,** hachis *m*. 2. **Not to mince matters,** ne pas mâcher ses mots. **mincing,** *a.* (*a*) Affecté, minaudier. (*b*) **To take m. steps,** marcher à petits pas.

mincemeat, *s.* *F:* **To make mincemeat of s.o.,** réduire qn en chair à pâté.

mind¹, *s.* I. Souvenir *m*, mémoire *f*. **To keep sth. in mind,** (i) se souvenir de qch.; (ii) tenir compte de qch. **Bear him in m.,** songez à lui. **To bring sth. to s.o.'s mind,** rappeler qch. à la mémoire de qn. **To call sth. to mind,** évoquer le souvenir de qch. *He puts me in m. of his father,* il me fait penser à son père. **It went out of my mind,** cela m'est sorti de l'esprit. 2. (*a*) Pensée *f*, avis *m*, idée *f*. **To give s.o. a piece of one's mind,** dire son fait à qn. **To be of the same mind as s.o.,** être du même avis que qn. (*b*) **To know one's own mind,** savoir ce qu'on veut. **To make up one's mind,** prendre son parti; se décider. *To make up one's m. about sth.,* prendre une décision au sujet de qch. **To make up one's mind to sth.,** se résigner à qch. **To be in two minds about sth.,** être indécis sur qch. **I have a good mind to,** j'ai (grande) envie de. (*c*) **To let one's mind run upon sth.,** songer à qch. **To set one's mind on sth.,** désirer qch. ardemment. **To give one's mind to sth.,** s'adonner, s'appliquer, à qch. **To have sth. in mind,** avoir qch. en vue. **To find sth. to one's mind,** trouver qch. à son goût, à son gré. 3. Esprit *m*; âme *f*. **State of mind,** état *m* d'âme. **Turn of mind,** mentalité *f*. **Peace of mind,** tranquillité *f* d'esprit. 4. (*a*) Esprit, idée. **She has something on her mind,** elle a quelque chose qui la préoccupe. **To take s.o.'s mind off his sorrow,** distraire qn de son chagrin. **To be easy in one's mind,** avoir l'esprit tranquille. (*b*) **A noble m.,** une belle âme. *Prov:* **Great minds think alike,** les grands esprits se rencontrent. 5. **To be out of one's mind,** avoir perdu la raison. **To be in one's right mind,** être dans son bon sens.

mind², *v.tr.* I. Faire attention à. *Never m. that,* qu'à cela ne tienne. **Mind my words!** écoutez bien ce que je vous dis! **Mind you!**

remarquez bien ! **2.** S'occuper de, se mêler de. **Mind your own business!** occupez-vous, mêlez-vous, de ce qui vous regarde ! **3.** (a) *Would you m. shutting the door?* voudriez-vous bien fermer la porte? *You don't m. my smoking?* la fumée ne vous gêne pas? *You don't m. my mentioning it?* cela ne vous froisse pas que je vous le dise? **If you don't mind,** si cela vous est égal. **I shouldn't mind a cup of tea,** je prendrais volontiers une tasse de thé. (b) **Never mind!** (i) n'importe ! (ii) ne vous inquiétez pas ! *Who minds what he says?* qui s'occupe de ce qu'il dit? *He doesn't m. expense,* il ne regarde pas à la dépense. **I don't mind,** cela m'est égal. **4. Mind what you are about!** prenez garde à ce que vous faites ! **Mind you don't fall!** prenez garde de tomber ! *F:* **Mind and don't be late!** ayez soin de ne pas être en retard ! **Mind the step!** attention à la marche ! **Mind yourself!** méfiez-vous ! **5.** Soigner, avoir l'œil sur. **To mind the house,** garder la maison.

minded, a. Disposé, enclin (*to do sth.,* à faire qch.). **If you are so minded,** si le cœur vous en dit.

mindful, a. Attentif (*of one's health,* à sa santé) ; soigneux (*of,* de).

mine¹, s. **1.** Mine *f.* **2.** *Mil:* Mine. **mine field,** s. **1.** Région minière. **2.** *Navy:* Champ *m* de mines. **mine-layer,** s. *Navy:* Poseur *m,* mouilleur *m,* de mines. **mine-laying,** s. *Navy:* Pose *f,* mouillage *m,* de mines. **mine-shaft,** s. Puits *m* de mine. **mine-sweeper,** s. *Navy:* Dragueur *m* de mines.

mine², v.tr. & i. **1.** (a) *Mil:* Miner, saper. (b) *Navy:* **To mine a harbour,** miner un port. **2.** *Min:* **To mine (for) coal,** exploiter le charbon. **mining,** s. **1.** *Mil:* Sape *f.* **2.** *Navy:* Pose *f* de mines. **3.** *Min:* Exploitation minière ; l'industrie minière.

mine³, poss.pron. Le mien, la mienne, les miens, les miennes. (a) *Your country and m.,* votre patrie et la mienne. *This letter is m.,* cette lettre est à moi, m'appartient. **A friend of mine,** un(e) de mes ami(e)s. **It is no business of mine,** ce n'est pas mon affaire. **No effort of mine,** aucun effort de ma part. (b) *Be good to* **me and mine,** soyez gentil pour moi et les miens.

miner, s. *Min:* (Ouvrier *m*) mineur *m.*

mineral. 1. a. Minéral, -aux. **Mineral waters,** (i) eaux minérales ; (ii) boissons gazeuses. **2.** s. Minéral *m.*

mineralogist, s. Minéralogiste *m.*

mineralogy, s. Minéralogie *f.*

mingle. 1. v.tr. Mêler, mélanger. **2.** v.i. (a) Se mêler, se confondre (*with,* avec). (b) *To m. with the crowd,* se mêler à la foule.

miniature. 1. s. Miniature *f.* **2.** a. En miniature.

minimize, v.tr. Réduire au minimum.

minimum. 1. s. Minimum *m.* **2.** a. Minimum, *f.* occ. minima.

minion, s. The minions of the law, les recors *m* de la justice.

minister¹, s. **1.** *Adm:* Ministre *m.* **2.** *Ecc:* Ministre, pasteur *m.*

minister², v.i. **To minister to s.o.'s needs,** pourvoir aux besoins de qn. **ministering,** a. (Ange) secourable.

ministerial, a. **1.** *Ecc:* De ministre ; sacerdotal, -aux. **2.** *Pol:* Ministériel ; gouvernemental, -aux.

ministration, s. Service *m* ; ministère *m,* soins *mpl.*

ministry, s. **1.** (a) *Pol:* Ministère *m,* gouvernement *m.* (b) *Adm:* Ministère, département *m.* **2.** *Ecc:* The ministry, le saint ministère. **3.** Ministère, entremise *f* (*of,* de).

mink, s. *Z:* Vison *m.*

minnow, s. *Ich:* Vairon *m.*

minor. 1. a. (a) Petit, mineur, -e. (b) Petit, menu, peu important. **Minor poet,** poète de second ordre. *Of m. interest,* d'intérêt secondaire. *To play a* **m. part,** jouer un rôle subalterne. (c) *Mus:* In the minor (key), en mineur. (d) *Sch:* Jones minor, le plus jeune des deux Jones. **2.** s. *Jur:* Mineur, -eure.

Minorca. *Pr.n. Geog:* Minorque *f.*

minority, s. **1.** Minorité *f.* **To be in the minority,** être en minorité. **2.** *Jur:* Minorité (d'âge).

minster, s. Cathédrale *f.*

minstrel, s. (a) *Hist:* Ménestrel *m.* (b) *F:* Poète *m,* musicien *m,* chanteur *m.*

mint¹, s. **The Mint,** (l'Hôtel *m* de) la Monnaie. **Fresh from the Mint,** à fleur de coin. *F:* **To be worth a mint of money,** (i) rouler sur l'or ; (ii) valoir une somme fabuleuse.

mint², v.tr. Monnayer.

mint³, s. *Bot:* Menthe *f.* **mint-sauce,** s. *Cu:* Vinaigrette *f* à la menthe.

minuet, s. *Danc:* Menuet *m.*

minus. 1. prep. Moins. **2.** a. *Mth:* **Minus sign,** s. minus, moins *m.* **Minus quantity,** quantité négative.

minute¹, s. **1.** (a) Minute *f* **Ten minutes, past three,** trois heures dix. (b) *F:* **Wait a minute!** attendez un instant ! *I'll come* in a minute, j'arriverai dans un instant. **Punctual to a minute,** exact à une minute près. **I expect him every minute,** je l'attends à tout moment. **2.** Minute (de degré). **3.** (a) Note *f.* (b) *pl.* Minutes of a meeting, procès-verbal *m* d'une séance. **minute-hand,** s. Grande aiguille *f.*

minute², a. **1.** (a) Tout petit ; menu, minime. (b) *The minutest particulars,* les moindres détails. **2.** Minutieux ; en détail. **-ly,** adv. Minutieusement ; en détail.

minuteness, s. **1.** Petitesse *f,* exiguïté *f.* **2.** Minutie *f* ; exactitude minutieuse.

minx, s. Coquine *f* ; petite espiègle.

miracle, s. (a) Miracle *m.* **By a miracle,** par miracle. (b) *F:* Miracle, prodige *m.* **It is a miracle that . . .,** c'est (un) miracle que + sub.

miraculous, *a.* (*a*) Miraculeux. (*b*) *F:* Extraordinaire, merveilleux. **-ly,** *adv.* Miraculeusement; par miracle.

mirage, *s.* Mirage *m.*

mire, *s.* Boue *f,* bourbe *f,* fange *f.*

mirror, *s.* Miroir *m,* glace *f.* **Hand mirror,** glace à main. *Aut:* **Driving mirror,** (miroir) rétroviseur *m.*

mirth, *s.* Gaieté *f,* allégresse *f*; hilarité *f.*

mirthful, *a.* Gai, joyeux. **-fully,** *adv.* Gaiement, joyeusement.

mirthless, *a.* Sans gaieté; triste. **-ly,** *adv.* Sans gaieté; tristement.

miry, *a.* Fangeux, bourbeux; vaseux.

misadventure, *s.* Mésaventure *f,* contretemps *m.*

misanthrope, *s.* Misanthrope *mf.*

misanthropic(al), *a.* Misanthrope.

misanthropist, *s.* Misanthrope *m.*

misanthropy, *s.* Misanthropie *f.*

misapply, *v.tr.* **1.** Mal appliquer. **2.** Détourner (des fonds).

misapprehend, *v.tr.* Mal comprendre; se méprendre sur.

misapprehension, *s.* Malentendu *m,* méprise *f*; idée fausse (des faits).

misappropriate, *v.tr.* Détourner (des fonds).

misappropriation, *s.* Détournement *m* (de fonds).

misbecome, *v.tr.* Messeoir à. **misbecoming,** *a.* Malséant.

misbehave, *v.i. & pr.* To misbehave (oneself), se mal conduire.

misbehaviour, *s.* Mauvaise conduite.

miscalculate, *v.tr.* Mal calculer.

miscalculation, *s.* Faux calcul, calcul erroné; mécompte *m.*

miscarriage, *s.* Miscarriage of justice, erreur *f* judiciaire.

miscarry, *v.i.* **1.** (*Of letter*) S'égarer. **2.** (*Of scheme*) Avorter, échouer.

miscellaneous, *a.* Varié, mêlé, divers.

miscellany, *s.* Mélange *m.*

mischance, *s.* **1.** Mauvaise chance; malchance *f.* **2.** Malheur *m,* mésaventure *f.*

mischief, *s.* **1.** Mal *m,* tort *m,* dommage *m.* To mean mischief, méditer un mauvais coup. To make mischief, apporter le trouble. *To make m. between two people,* brouiller deux personnes. **2.** Malice *f.* Out of pure mischief, par pure malice. To be always getting into mischief, être toujours à faire des siennes. To keep s.o. out of mischief, empêcher qn de faire des sottises. **mischief-maker,** *s.* Brandon *m* de discorde.

mischievous, *a.* **1.** Méchant, malfaisant; mauvais, nuisible. **2.** (Enfant) espiègle. **-ly,** *adv.* **1.** Méchamment. **2.** Malicieusement; par espièglerie.

mischievousness, *s.* **1.** Méchanceté *f.* **2.** Malice *f,* espièglerie *f.*

misconception, *s.* **1.** Idée fausse. **2.** Malentendu *m.*

misconduct[1], *s.* Mauvaise conduite.

misconduct[2], *v.tr.* **1.** Mal diriger, mal gérer. **2.** To misconduct oneself, se mal conduire.

misconstruction, *s.* Fausse interprétation.

misconstrue, *v.tr.* Mal interpréter.

miscount[1], *s.* Erreur *f* d'addition.

miscount[2], *v.tr.* Mal compter.

miscreant, *s.* Scélérat *m,* misérable *m.*

misdeed, *s.* Méfait *m.*

misdemeanour, *s.* **1.** *Jur:* Délit contraventionnel. **2.** Écart *m* de conduite.

misdirect, *v.tr.* **1.** Mal adresser. **2.** Mal diriger (un coup). **3.** Mal renseigner, mal diriger.

misdoing, *s.* Méfait *m,* faute *f.*

miser, *s.* Avare *mf.*

miserable, *a.* **1.** Malheureux, triste. To make s.o.'s life miserable, rendre la vie dure à qn. **2.** Misérable, déplorable. **3.** Misérable, pauvre, piteux. **-ably,** *adv.* Misérablement.

miserliness, *s.* Avarice *f.*

miserly, *a.* **1.** Avare. **2.** (Of habits) D'avare; sordide.

misery, *s.* **1.** Souffrance(s) *f(pl),* supplice *m.* **2.** Misère *f,* détresse *f.*

misfire[1], *s.* Raté *m.*

misfire[2], *v.i.* Rater.

misfortune, *s.* Infortune *f,* malheur *m,* calamité *f.*

misgive, *v.tr.* My mind misgives me, j'ai de mauvais pressentiments. **misgiving,** *s.* Doute *m,* crainte *f.*

misguided, *a.* Peu judicieux; hors de propos; malencontreux.

mishap, *s.* Mésaventure *f,* contretemps *m.*

misinform, *v.tr.* Mal renseigner.

misinterpret, *v.tr.* Mal interpréter.

misinterpretation, *s.* Fausse interprétation.

misjudge, *v.tr.* Mal juger; méconnaître.

misjudged, *a.* Erroné; peu judicieux.

mislay, *v.tr.* Égarer.

mislead, *v.tr.* (*a*) Induire en erreur; tromper. (*b*) Égarer, fourvoyer. **misleading,** *a.* Trompeur, -euse; fallacieux.

mismanage, *v.tr.* Mal administrer.

mismanagement, *s.* Mauvaise administration.

misnomer, *s.* Faux nom; fausse appellation.

misogynist, *s.* Misogyne *m.*

misplace, *v.tr.* **1.** Placer à faux. **2.** Mal placer (sa confiance). **misplaced,** *a.* **1.** Mal placé. **2.** Hors de propos.

misprint, *s.* Faute *f* d'impression.

mispronounce, *v.tr.* Mal prononcer.

misquote, *v.tr.* Citer à faux.

misread, *v.tr.* Mal lire, mal interpréter.

misrepresent, *v.tr.* Mal représenter; dénaturer, travestir.

misrepresentation, *s.* Faux rapport.

miss[1], *s.* **1.** Coup manqué. **2.** *P:* He's no great miss, on peut se passer de lui.

miss[2], *v.tr.* **1.** (*a*) Manquer. *Abs.* He never

misses, il ne manque jamais son coup. **To miss the point,** répondre à côté. (b) **To miss one's way,** se tromper de route. **He missed his footing,** le pied lui manqua. (c) Ne pas trouver, ne pas rencontrer. (d) Manquer (un train). (e) Manquer, laisser échapper. **An opportunity not to be missed,** une occasion à saisir. (f) **You can't m. the house,** vous ne pouvez pas manquer de reconnaître la maison. **2. To miss (out) a word,** passer, sauter, un mot. **3.** (a) Remarquer l'absence de. **It will never be missed,** on ne s'apercevra pas que cela n'y est plus. (b) Regretter. **They will miss one another,** ils se manqueront. **missing,** a. Absent; perdu; disparu, manquant. *One man is m.,* un homme manque. *s.pl. Mil:* The missing, les disparus m.

miss³, s. Miss Smith, mademoiselle f Smith.

mis-shapen, a. Difforme.

missile, s. Projectile m.

mission, s. Mission f.

missionary. I. a. (Société) de missionnaires. **2.** s. Missionnaire m.

missive, s. Lettre f, missive f.

mis-spell, v.tr. Mal épeler. **nis-spelling,** s. Faute f d'orthographe.

mis-statement, s. Exposé inexact; erreur f de fait.

mist, s. **I.** Brume f. **Scotch mist,** bruine f, crachin m. **2.** Buée f (sur une glace); voile m (devant les yeux). **To see things through a mist,** voir trouble.

mistake¹, s. Erreur f, méprise f, faute f. **To make a mistake,** faire une faute; se méprendre, se tromper. *To do sth.* **by mistake,** faire qch. par erreur. **There is some mistake!** il y a erreur! *There is no m. about that,* il n'y a pas à s'y tromper. *F:* **And no mistake!** décidément!

mistake², v.tr. **I.** Comprendre mal; se méprendre sur. **To m. the way,** faire fausse route. **If I mistake not,** si je ne me trompe. **2. To mistake s.o. for s.o.,** confondre qn avec qn. **mistaken,** a. **I. To be mistaken,** être dans l'erreur; faire erreur. **If I am not mistaken,** si je ne me trompe. **2. Mistaken opinion,** opinion erronée. *M. zeal,* zèle mal entendu. **-ly,** adv. Par erreur, par méprise.

mister, s. Mr Smith, monsieur m Smith.

mistime, v.tr. **I.** Faire mal à propos. **2.** Mal calculer (un coup).

mistiness, s. État brumeux.

mistletoe, s. *Bot:* Gui m.

mistress, s. **I.** (a) Maîtresse f. **She is mistress of her subject,** elle possède son sujet à fond. (b) **Mistress of a household,** maîtresse de maison. *Is your m. at home?* madame y est-elle? (c) *Com:* Patronne f. (d) **The French m.,** la maîtresse de français, le professeur de français. **2.** (*Now always* **Mrs**) **Mrs Smith,** Madame f Smith.

mistrust, s. Méfiance f, défiance f (of, in, de).

misty, a. Brumeux, embrumé. *It is m.,* le temps est brumeux. *F:* **Misty outlines,** contours vagues.

misunderstand, v.tr. **I.** Mal comprendre; se méprendre sur. *If I have not misunderstood,* si j'ai bien compris. **2.** Méconnaître; se méprendre sur le compte de. **misunderstood,** a. **I.** Mal compris. **2.** (*Of pers.*) Incompris. **misunderstanding,** s. **I.** Malentendu m, quiproquo m. **2.** Mésintelligence f, mésentente f.

misuse¹, s. Abus m; mauvais usage.

misuse², v.tr **I.** Faire (un) mauvais usage, (un) mauvais emploi, de. **2.** Maltraiter, malmener.

mite, s. **I. The widow's mite,** le denier de la veuve. **2.** Mioche mf.

mitigate, v.tr. **I.** Adoucir, atténuer; amoindrir (un mal). **2.** Atténuer (une faute). **Mitigating circumstances,** circonstances atténuantes.

mitigation, s. Adoucissement m; amoindrissement m; atténuation f.

mitre, s. *Ecc:* Mitre f.

mix. I. v.tr. (a) Mêler, mélanger. (b) Composer (un breuvage). (c) Confondre (des faits). **2.** v.i. Se mêler, se mélanger (with, à, avec). **To mix with people,** fréquenter les gens. *To mix with the aristocracy,* frayer avec l'aristocratie. **mix up,** v.tr. **I.** Mêler, mélanger; embrouiller. **2.** *I was mixing you up with your brother,* je vous confondais avec votre frère. **3. To be mixed up in an affair,** être mêlé à une affaire. **4.** Embrouiller. **mix-up,** s. Confusion f, embrouillement m.

mixed, a. **I.** Mêlé, mélangé, mixte. *M. ice,* glace panachée. *M. company,* compagnie mêlée. *M. society,* société hétérogène. **Mixed feelings,** sentiments mixtes. **2. Mixed bathing,** bains m mixtes. **3. To get mixed,** s'embrouiller.

mixture, s. **I.** Mélange m. **2.** *Pharm:* Mixtion f, mixture f.

moan¹, s. Gémissement m plainte f.

moan², v.i. Gémir; pousser des gémissements; se lamenter. **moaning,** s. Gémissement m.

moat, s. Fossé m, douve f.

mob¹, s. **I. The mob,** la populace; le bas peuple. **2.** Foule f, cohue f, ameutement m.

mob², v.tr. (a) Houspiller. (b) Assiéger.

mobile, a. Mobile.

mobility, s. Mobilité f.

mobilization, s. Mobilisation f.

mobilize. I. v.tr. Mobiliser. **2.** v.i. Entrer en mobilisation.

moccasin, s. Mocassin m.

mock¹, *attrib.a.* D'imitation; feint, contrefait; faux, f. fausse. **Mock modesty,** modestie feinte. **mock turtle,** s. *Cu:* **Mock turtle soup,** potage m à la tête de veau.

mock², s. **To make a mock of s.o.,** se moquer de qn; tourner qn en ridicule.

mock³. I. v.tr. & i. **To mock (at) s.o.,** se moquer de qn; railler qn. **2.** v.tr. (a) Narguer. (b) Se jouer de, tromper. (c) Imiter, singer. **mocking¹,** a. Moqueur, -euse, railleur, -euse. **-ly,** adv. D'un ton moqueur, railleur. **mocking-bird,** s. Orn: Moqueur m. **mocking**[2], s. Moquerie f, raillerie f.

mocker, s. Moqueur, -euse.

mockery, s. **1.** Moquerie f, raillerie f. **2.** Semblant m, simulacre m (of, de).

mode, s. **1.** Mode m, méthode f, manière f. M. of life, façon f de vivre; train m de vie. **2.** (Fashion) Mode f.

model[1], s. **1.** Modèle m. Wax model, figurine f de cire. **2.** (a) To take s.o. as one's model, prendre modèle sur qn. (b) Art: Modèle mf. **3.** Dressm: Modèle m, patron m. **4.** Attrib. Model farm, ferme modèle.

model[2], v.tr. Modeler.

moderate[1], a. Modéré; moyen; médiocre. M. language, langage mesuré. Moderate price, prix modique. Moderate opinions, opinions modérées. M. meal, repas sobre, frugal. **-ly,** adv. Modérément; avec modération; sobrement.

moderate[2]. (a) v.tr. Modérer; tempérer. To m. one's pretensions, rabattre de ses prétentions. (b) v.i. Se modérer.

moderation, s. Modération f. mesure f; sobriété f (de langage). With moderation, mesurément. In moderation, modérément.

modern, a. Moderne. M. times, le temps présent, les temps modernes. Modern languages, langues vivantes.

modest, a. Modeste. (a) Pudique, honnête, chaste. (b) To be modest in one's requirements, être modéré dans ses demandes. M. fortune, fortune modeste. (c) Sans prétentions. **-ly,** adv. **1.** Modestement; avec modestie. **2.** Pudiquement, chastement. **3.** Modérément. **4.** Sans prétentions.

modesty, s. **1.** Modestie f. **2.** Pudeur f; honnêteté f. **3.** Absence f de prétention; simplicité f.

modicum, s. A (small) modicum, une petite portion.

modification, s. **1.** Modification f. **2.** Atténuation f.

modify, v.tr. (a) Modifier. (b) Mitiger, atténuer.

modulate, v.tr. Moduler.

modulation, s. Modulation f.

mohair, s. Tex: Mohair m.

Mohammedan, a. & s. Mahométan, -ane.

moiety, s. **1.** Moitié f. **2.** Part f, demi-portion f.

moist, a. Humide; (peau) moite. Eyes moist with tears, yeux mouillés de larmes.

moisten, v.tr (a) Humecter, mouiller; amoitir (la peau); arroser (la pâte). (b) To moisten a rag with . . ., imbiber un chiffon, une éponge, de. . . .

moistness, s. Humidité f.

moisture, s. Humidité f.

molar. 1. a. (Dent) molaire. **2.** s. Molaire f; grosse dent.

molasses, s.pl. Mélasse f.

mole[1], s. Grain m de beauté.

mole[2], s. Z: Taupe f. **mole-catcher,** s.

Taupier m; preneur m de taupes. **mole-hill,** s. Taupinière f.

mole[3], s. Môle m; brise-lames m inv.

molecular, a. Moléculaire.

molecule, s. Molécule f.

moleskin, s. (Peau f de) taupe f.

molest, v.tr. Rudoyer.

molestation, s. **1.** Molestation f. **2.** Voies fpl de fait.

mollification, s. Apaisement m.

mollify, v.tr. To mollify s.o., adoucir, apaiser, qn.

mollusc, s. Mollusque m.

Molucca, Pr.n. The Moluccas, les Moluques f.

moment, s. **1.** Moment m, instant m. Come this moment! venez à l'instant, tout de suite ! Wait a moment! un moment ! To expect s.o. every moment, attendre qn d'un moment à l'autre. To interrupt at every m., interrompre à tout propos. I have just this moment heard of it, je l'apprends à l'instant. At this moment, at the present moment, en ce moment; actuellement. I will come in a moment, je viendrai dans un instant. Not for a moment! jamais de la vie ! **2.** To be of moment, être important.

momentary, a. **1.** Momentané, passager. **2.** In momentary expectation of his arrival, attendant à chaque instant son arrivée. **-ily,** adv. **1.** Momentanément. **2.** D'un moment à l'autre.

momentous, a. Important. M. decision, décision capitale.

momentum, s. **1.** Mec: Force vive; quantité f de mouvement. **2.** F: Vitesse acquise.

monarch, s. Monarque m.

monarchic(al), a. Monarchique.

monarchist, s. Pol: Monarchiste m.

monarchy, s. Monarchie f.

monastery, s. Monastère m.

monastic, a. Monastique; monacal, -aux.

Monday, s. Lundi m.

monetary, a. Monétaire.

money, s. (a) Monnaie f; argent m. Paper money, papier-monnaie m. F: To throw good money after bad, s'enfoncer davantage dans une mauvaise affaire. Ready money, argent comptant. To pay in ready m., payer (au) comptant. (b) F: To be coining money, être en train de faire fortune. To come into money, hériter d'une fortune. To be made of money, être cousu d'or. To be rolling in money, rouler sur l'or. There is money in it, c'est une bonne affaire. You have had your money's worth, vous en avez eu pour votre argent. **money-box,** s. **1.** Tirelire f. **2.** Caisse f. **money-changer,** s. Changeur m, cambiste m. **money-grubber,** s. Grippe-sou m, pl. grippe-sous. **money-lender,** s. Prêteur m d'argent.

moneyed, a. Riche; qui a de l'argent. Moneyed man, richard m. The moneyed classes, les classes possédantes.

Mongol, *a. & s. Ethn:* Mongol, -ole.
Mongolia. *Pr.n.* La Mongolie.
mongoose, *s. Z:* Mangouste *f.*
mongrel, *s. & a.* Métis, -isse; (*of dog*) bâtard, -arde. **Mongrel cur,** roquet *m.*
monition, *s.* Avertissement *m.*
monitor, *s.* Moniteur, -trice.
monk, *s.* Moine *m*, religieux *m. To be a m.,* porter le froc. **monk's-hood,** *s. Bot:* (Aconit *m*) napel *m.*
monkey¹, *s. Z:* Singe *m.* **Female monkey,** guenon *f. F:* **You young monkey!** petit polisson! *F:* **To get one's monkey up,** se fâcher. **monkey-house,** *s.* Singerie *f*; pavillon *m* des singes. **monkey-jacket,** *s.* Veston court. **monkey-puzzle,** *s. Bot:* Araucaria *m.* **monkey-tricks,** *s.pl.* Singeries *f*, chinoiseries *f.* **monkey-wrench,** *s.* Clé anglaise.
monkey², *v.i. P:* **To monkey (about) with** sth., tripoter qch.
monochrome, *a. & s. Art:* Monochrome.
monocle, *s.* Monocle *m.*
monocotyledon, *s. Bot:* Monocotylédone *f.*
monogamist, *s.* Monogame *mf.*
monogamy, *s.* Monogamie *f.*
monogram, *s.* Monogramme *m*, chiffre *m.*
monograph, *s.* Monographie *f.*
monolith, *s.* Monolithe *m.*
monologue, *s.* Monologue *m.*
monomania, *s.* Monomanie *f.*
monomaniac, *s.* Monomane *mf.*
monoplane, *s. Av:* Monoplan *m.*
monopolize, *v.tr.* **1.** Monopoliser. **2.** *F:* Accaparer; s'emparer de.
monopoly, *s.* Monopole *m.*
monosyllabic, *a.* Monosyllabe, monosyllabique.
monosyllable, *s.* Monosyllabe *m.*
monotonous, *a.* Monotone; fastidieux. **-ly,** *adv.* Monotonement; fastidieusement.
monotony, *s.* Monotonie *f.*
monsoon, *s. Meteor:* Mousson *f.*
monster. **1.** *s.* Monstre *m.* **2.** *a. F:* Monstre; colossal, -aux; énorme.
monstrosity, *s.* Monstruosité *f.* **1.** Monstre *m.* **2.** Énormité *f* (d'un crime).
monstrous, *a.* Monstrueux.
month, *s.* Mois *m.* **Calendar month,** mois du calendrier. *In the m. of August,* au mois d'août. *At the end of the current m.,* fin courant. **What day of the month is this?** le quantième du mois avons-nous? *F:* le combien sommes-nous? **This day month,** dans un mois, jour pour jour. **By the month,** au mois. **Once a month,** une fois par mois; mensuellement.
monthly¹. **1.** *a.* Mensuel. **2.** *s. F:* Revue mensuelle.
monthly², *adv.* Mensuellement; une fois par mois; tous les mois.
monument, *s.* Monument *m.*
monumental, *a.* Monumental, -aux.
moo¹, *s.* Meuglement *m*, beuglement *m.*

moo², *v.i.* Meugler, beugler.
mood¹, *s. Gram:* Mode *m.*
mood², *s.* Humeur *f*, disposition *f.* **To be in the mood to write,** être en disposition d'écrire.
moodiness, *s.* Humeur chagrine; morosité *f.*
moody, *a.* **To be moody,** être maussade.
moon¹, *s.* Lune *f.* **Once in a blue moon,** tous les trente-six du mois.
moon², *v.i.* **To moon about,** musarder.
moonbeam, *s.* Rayon *m* de lune.
moonlight, *s.* Clair *m* de lune. **In the moonlight,** au clair de (la) lune.
moonshine, *s. F:* Balivernes *fpl*; contes *mpl* en l'air.
moonstone, *s. Lap:* Pierre *f* de lune.
moonstruck, *a. F:* Abasourdi, médusé.
moor¹, *s.* Lande *f*, bruyère *f.*
moor², *v.* *Nau:* **1.** *v.tr.* Amarrer; mouiller. **2.** *v.i.* S'amarrer. **mooring,** *s.* **1.** Amarrage *m.* **2.** *pl.* **Ship at her moorings,** navire sur ses amarres.
Moor³, *s.* Maure *m*, Mauresque *f.*
Moorish, *a.* Mauresque, moresque, maure.
moorland, *s.* = MOOR¹.
moose, *s. Z:* Élan *m*, orignac *m.*
moot¹, *a.* **Moot point,** point *m* de droit.
moot², *v.tr.* Soulever (une question).
mop¹, *s.* **1.** (*a*) Balai *m* à franges. (*b*) *Nau:* Faubert *m.* **2.** *F:* **Mop of hair,** tignasse *f.*
mop², *v.tr.* Éponger, essuyer. **mop up,** *v.tr.* (*a*) Éponger; essuyer. (*b*) Rafler, absorber (tous les bénéfices).
mope, *v.i.* Être triste; *F:* broyer du noir.
moraine, *s. Geol:* Moraine *f.*
moral. **I.** *a.* Moral, -aux. **1.** *To raise the m. standard,* relever les mœurs. **2.** Conforme aux bonnes mœurs. **3.** **Moral courage,** courage moral. **-ally,** *adv.* Moralement. **II** **moral,** *s.* **1.** Morale *f*, moralité *f.* **2.** *pl.* **Morals,** moralité, mœurs *fpl.*
morale, *s.* Moral *m* (d'une armée).
moralist, *s.* Moraliste *mf.*
morality, *s.* (*a*) Moralité *f*; principes moraux; sens moral. (*b*) Bonnes mœurs.
moralize, *v.i.* Moraliser.
morass, *s.* Marais *m*; fondrière *f.*
morbid, *a.* Morbide. **M. curiosity,** curiosité malsaine, maladive. **-ly,** *adv.* Morbidement, maladivement.
morbidity, *s.* (*a*) Morbidité *f*; état maladif. (*b*) Tristesse maladive.
mordant. **1.** *a.* Mordant, caustique. **2.** *s. Dy:* Mordant *m.*
more. **I.** *a.* Plus (de). **More than ten men,** plus de dix hommes. **One more,** un de plus; encore un. **One or more,** un ou plusieurs. (Some) **more bread,** *please!* encore du pain, s'il vous plaît! **Is there any more?** y en a-t-il encore? **As many more,** encore autant. **2.** *s.* or *indef. pron.* **I cannot give m.,** je ne peux donner davantage. **That's more than enough,** c'est plus qu'il n'en faut (*to,* pour). **What is more,** qui plus est. **3.** *adv.* (*a*) Plus,

davantage. **More and more,** de plus en plus. *He was* **more** surprised than annoyed, il était plutôt surpris que fâché. **More or less,** plus ou moins. (*b*) **Once more,** encore une fois, une fois de plus. **Never more,** jamais plus, plus jamais. **4.** **The more,** (*a*) *a.* (**The**) **more's the pity,** c'est d'autant plus malheureux. (*b*) *s.* **The more one has the more one wants,** plus on a, plus on désire avoir. (*c*) *adv.* **All the more . . .,** à plus forte raison, d'autant plus. . . . *It makes me all* **the** *m.* **proud,** je n'en suis que plus fier. **5. No more, not any more.** (*a*) *a.* *I have no m. money,* je n'ai plus d'argent. *No m. soup, thank you,* plus de potage, merci. (*b*) *s. I have no m.,* je n'en ai plus. **To say no more,** ne pas en dire davantage. (*c*) *adv.* (i) *I shall see her no m.,* je ne la verrai jamais plus. (ii) **He is no more a lord than I am,** il n'est pas plus (un) lord que moi.

moreover, *adv.* D'ailleurs; du reste; et qui plus est.

moribund, *a.* Moribond.

Mormon, *a.* & *s.* Mormon, -one.

morning, *s.* **1.** (*a*) Matin *m.* **To-morrow morning,** demain matin. **The morning before,** la veille au matin. **Every Monday morning,** tous les lundis matins. **Four o'clock in the morning,** quatre heures du matin. (**The**) **first thing in the morning,** dès le matin. **Early in the morning,** matinalement; de grand matin. *What do you do in the m.?* que faites-vous le matin? **Good morning,** bonjour. (*b*) Matinée *f.* **In the course of the morning,** dans la matinée. **2.** *Attrib.* Matinal, -aux; du matin. **morning-coat,** *s.* Jaquette *f.*

Moroccan, *a.* & *s.* Marocain, -aine.

Morocco. **1.** *Pr.n.* *Geog:* Le Maroc. **2.** *s.* **Morocco (leather),** maroquin *m.*

morose, *a.* Chagrin, morose. **-ly,** *adv.* D'un air chagrin, morose.

moroseness, *s.* Morosité *f*; humeur chagrine.

Morpheus. *Pr.n.* Morphée *m.*

morphia, *s.* Morphine *f.*

morphology, *s.* Morphologie *f.*

morrow, *s.* **On the morrow,** le lendemain.

Morse. *Pr.n.* *Tg:* **The Morse alphabet,** l'alphabet *m* Morse.

morsel, *s.* Petit morceau. *Not a m. of bread,* pas une bouchée de pain.

mortal, *a.* Mortel. **1. Mortal remains,** dépouille mortelle. **2.** Funeste; fatal, -als (*to*, à). *M. blow,* coup mortel. **3.** *Mortal enemy,* ennemi mortel. **Mortal combat,** combat à outrance. **4.** (*a*) *To be in m. fear of,* avoir une peur mortelle de. (*b*) *F:* **Two mortal hours,** deux mortelles heures. (*c*) *P:* **Any mortal thing,** n'importe quoi. **-ally,** *adv.* Mortellement. **Mortally wounded,** blessé à mort.

mortality, *s.* Mortalité *f.*

mortar, *s.* **1.** (*a*) Mortier *m* (pour piler). (*b*) *Artil:* Mortier, lance-bombes *m inv.* **2.** *Const:* Mortier.

mortgage[1], *s.* Hypothèque *f.*

mortgage[2], *v.tr.* Hypothéquer.

mortgagee, *s.* Créancier *m* hypothécaire.

mortgagor, *s.* Débiteur *m* hypothécaire.

mortification, *s.* Mortification *f.*

mortify. **1.** *v.tr.* Mortifier. **2.** *v.i.* *Med:* Se gangrener, se mortifier.

mortuary. **1.** *a.* Mortuaire. **2.** *s.* Morgue *f.*

mosaic. **1.** *a.* *M. flooring,* dallage *m* en mosaïque. **2.** *s.* Mosaïque *f.*

Moscow. *Pr.n.* Moscou *m.*

Moses. *Pr.n.* Moïse *m.*

Moslem, *a.* & *s.* Mahométan, -ane, musulman, -ane.

mosque, *s.* Mosquée *f.*

mosquito, *s.* *Ent:* Moustique *m.* **mosquito-net,** *s.* Moustiquaire *f.*

moss, *s.* *Bot:* Mousse *f.* **moss rose,** *s.* *Bot:* Rose moussue.

mossy, *a.* Moussu.

most. **1.** *a.* (*a*) Le plus (de). (*b*) **Most men,** la plupart des hommes. **2.** *s.* & *indef. pron.* (*a*) **At (the) most,** au plus. **To make the most of sth.,** tirer le meilleur parti possible de qch. (*b*) **Most of them** *have forgotten him,* la plupart d'entre eux l'ont oublié. **3.** *adv.* *What I desire most,* ce que je désire le plus. *The m. intelligent child,* l'enfant le plus intelligent. *The m. beautiful woman,* la plus belle femme. **4.** *adv.* Très, fort, bien. **Most likely,** très probablement. *He has been m. rude,* il a été on ne peut plus grossier. *It is m. remarkable,* c'est tout ce qu'il y a de plus remarquable. **-ly,** *adv.* **1.** Pour la plupart. **2.** Le plus souvent.

moth, *s.* *Ent:* **1.** (Clothes-)moth, mite *f.* **2.** Papillon *m* de nuit; phalène *f.* **moth-balls,** *s.pl.* Boules *f* de naphtaline. **moth-eaten,** *a.* Rongé des mites, mité.

mother[1], *s.* **1.** Mère *f.* *F:* *Every mother's son,* tous sans exception. **2. Mother Goose stories,** contes de ma mère l'Oie. **3.** *Ecc:* **The Mother Superior,** la Mère supérieure. **mother country,** *s.* Mère-patrie *f,* *pl.* mères-patries; métropole *f* (d'une colonie). **mother earth,** *s.* La terre nourricière. **mother-in-law,** *s.* Belle-mère *f.* **mother of pearl,** *s.* Nacre *f.* **mother tongue,** *s.* Langue maternelle.

mother[2], *v.tr.* (*a*) Donner des soins maternels à. (*b*) Dorloter.

motherhood, *s.* Maternité *f.*

motherless, *a.* Sans mère; orphelin (de mère).

motherly, *a.* Maternel.

motion[1], *s.* **1.** Mouvement *m,* déplacement *m.* **In motion,** en mouvement; en marche. **2.** Signe *m,* geste *m.* **3.** Motion *f,* proposition *f.* **To propose a motion,** faire une proposition.

motion[2] *v.tr.* & *i.* **To motion (to) s.o. to do sth.,** faire signe à qn de faire qch.

motionless, *a.* Sans mouvement.

motive. **1.** *a.* Moteur, -trice. **2.** *s.* (*a*) Motif *m.* (*b*) Mobile *m* (d'une action).

motley. **1.** *a.* (*a*) Bariolé, bigarré. (*b*) Divers, mêlé. **2.** *s.* Couleurs bigarrées; mélange *m.*
motor¹. **1.** *a.* Moteur, -trice. **2.** *s.* Moteur *m.* **motor boat,** *s.* Canot *m* automobile. **motor bus,** *s.* Autobus *m.* **motorcar,** *s.* Automobile *f, F:* auto *f,* voiture *f.* **motor coach,** *s.* Autocar *m.* **motor cycle,** *s.* Motocyclette *f, F:* moto *f.* **motor cyclist,** *s.* Motocycliste *mf.* **motor lorry,** *s.* Camion *m* automobile. **motor show,** *s.* Salon *m* de l'automobile. **motor torpedo boat,** Vedette *f* lance-torpille. **motor vehicle,** *s.* Voiture *f* automobile.
motor². **1.** *v.i.* Aller, voyager, en auto (mobile). **2.** *v.tr.* Conduire en auto(mobile).
motoring, *s.* To go in for motoring, faire de l'automobile.
motorist, *s.* Automobiliste *mf.*
mottle, *v.tr.* Tacheter, marbrer. **mottled,** *a.* Truité, marbré.
motto, *s.* Devise *f.*
mould¹, *s.* Terre végétale.
mould², *s.* Moule *m. Cu:* Jelly mould, moule à gelée.
mould³, *v.tr.* Mouler; *F:* pétrir, former. **moulding,** *s.* **1.** (*a*) Moulage *m.* (*b*) *F:* Formation *f* (du caractère). **2.** Moulure *f. Ind:* Mouldings, profilés *m.*
mould⁴, *s.* Moisi *m,* moisissure *f.*
moulder, *v.i.* Tomber en poussière; s'effriter.
mouldiness, *s.* État moisi; moisissure *f.*
mouldy, *a.* Moisi. To go mouldy, (se) moisir.
moult¹, *s.* Mue *f.*
moult², *v.i.* Muer. **moulting¹,** *a.* En mue. **moulting²,** *s.* Mue *f.* Moulting-time, mue.
mound, *s.* Tertre *m,* monticule *m,* butte *f.*
mount¹, *s.* Mont *m,* montagne *f.*
mount², *s.* **1.** (*a*) Montage *m,* support *m;* monture *f* (d'un éventail). (*b*) Picture mount, carton *m* de montage. (*c*) Stamp mount, charnière *f.* **2.** Monture (d'un cavalier).
mount³. I. *v.i.* Se mettre en selle; monter à cheval. II. **mount,** *v.tr. & i.* **1.** To mount (upon) a chair, monter sur une chaise. **2.** To mount (on, upon) a horse, monter sur un cheval. III. **mount,** *v.tr.* **1.** Monter, gravir. To m. a ladder, monter à une échelle. **2.** Mounted police, agents à cheval. **3.** To mount guard, monter la garde (*over,* auprès de). **4.** (*a*) Monter (un diamant). (*b*) *Th:* Mettre à la scène. **mount up,** *v.i.* Croître, monter, augmenter. **mounting,** *s.* **1.** (*a*) Entoilage *m,* encollage *m.* (*b*) *Th:* Mise *f* à la scène. **2.** Monture *f,* garniture *f* (de fusil).
mountain, *s.* Montagne *f.* To make mountains out of mole-hills, se fa re d'une mouche un éléphant. *M. scenery,* paysage montagneux. **mountain ash,** *s. Bot:* Sorbier *m* des oiseaux. **mountain range,** *s.* Chaîne *f* de montagnes.
mountaineer, *s.* **1.** Montagnard *m.* **2.** Alpiniste *mf,* ascensionniste *mf.*

mountaineering, *s.* Alpinisme *m.*
mountainous, *a.* Montagneux.
mountebank, *s.* (*a*) Saltimbanque *m,* bateleur *m.* (*b*) Charlatan *m.*
mourn, *v.i. & tr.* Pleurer, (se) lamenter, s'affliger. To mourn for s.o., pleurer qn.
mourning, *s.* **1.** Affliction *f,* deuil *m.* **2.** (*a*) House of mourning, maison endeuillée. (*b*) Habits *mpl* de deuil. To go into mourning, prendre le deuil.
mourner, *s.* **1.** Affligé, -ée. **2.** The mourners, le cortège funèbre.
mournful, *a.* Lugubre, mélancolique; *F:* (figure) d'enterrement; (voix) funèbre. **-fully,** *adv.* Lugubrement.
mouse, *s.* Souris *f.* **mouse-hole,** *s.* Trou *m* de souris.
mousetrap, *s.* Souricière *f.*
moustache, *s.* Moustache(s) *f(pl).* To wear a moustache, porter la moustache.
mouth, *s.* **1.** Bouche *f.* To make s.o.'s mouth water, faire venir l'eau à la bouche à qn. To make a poor mouth, crier famine. **2.** Bouche (de cheval); gueule *f* (de chien). **3.** (*a*) Bouche (de puits); goulot *m* (de bouteille); gueule (de canon); ouverture *f,* entrée *f* (de tunnel). (*b*) Embouchure *f* (de fleuve). **mouth-organ,** *s.* Harmonica *m.*
mouthful, *s.* Bouchée *f.*
mouthpiece, *s.* **1.** (*a*) Embouchure *f.* (*b*) *Mus:* Bec *m,* embouchure. (*c*) *Tp:* Embouchure, pavillon *m.* **2.** To be the mouthpiece of a party, être le porte-parole *inv* d'un parti.
movable. **1.** *a.* Mobile. **2.** *s.pl.* Movables, mobilier *m.*
move¹, *s.* **1.** (*a*) *Chess:* Coup *m.* To have first move, avoir le trait. To make a move, jouer. (*b*) Coup, démarche *f. He must make the first m.,* c'est à lui d'agir le premier. *F:* He is up to every move (in the game), il sait parer à tous les coups. **2.** Mouvement *m.* To be always on the move, être toujours en mouvement. *F:* To get a move on, se dépêcher. **3.** Déménagement *m.*
move². I. *v.tr.* **1.** (*a*) Déplacer. *To m. one's chair,* changer sa chaise de place. *Chess:* To move a piece, jouer une pièce. (*b*) To move house, *abs.* to move, déménager. **2.** (*a*) Remuer, bouger. Not to move a muscle, ne pas sourciller. (*b*) Mouvoir, animer; mettre en mouvement. **3.** (*a*) He is not to be moved, il est inébranlable. (*b*) To move s.o. to do sth., pousser qn à faire qch. (*c*) Émouvoir, toucher. To move s.o. to anger, provoquer la colère de qn. To move s.o. to tears, émouvoir qn jusqu'aux larmes. **4.** To move a resolution, proposer une motion. II. **move,** *v.i.* (*a*) Se mouvoir, se déplacer. Keep moving! circulez! To move in high society, fréquenter la haute société. (*b*) To move (about), faire un mouvement; bouger, (se) remuer. Don't move! ne bougez pas l (*c*) Marcher, aller; s'avancer. **move back.** **1.** *v.tr.* (*a*) Faire reculer. (*b*) Ramener en

arrière. **2.** *v.i.* (Se) reculer. **move forward. I.** *v.tr.* Avancer; faire avancer. **2.** *v.i.* (S')avancer; (*of troops*) se porter en avant. **move off,** *v.i.* S'éloigner, s'en aller; se mettre en marche; (*of motor car*) démarrer. **move on,** *v.i.* Avancer; continuer son chemin. Move on, please! circulez, s'il vous plaît! **moving,** *a.* **I.** (*a*) En mouvement; en marche. (*b*) Mobile. **2.** Moteur, -trice. The moving spirit, l'âme *f* (d'une entreprise). **3.** Émouvant, attendrissant.

movement, *s.* Mouvement *m*.

mover, *s.* **I.** Prime mover, premier moteur, premier mobile. **2.** Auteur *m* (d'une motion).

mow, *v.tr.* **I.** Faucher, moissonner. **2.** Tondre (le gazon).

Mr. *See* MISTER.

Mrs. *See* MISTRESS 2.

much. I. *a.* (*a*) Beaucoup (de); bien (du, de la, des). (*b*) How much bread? combien de pain? How much is it? c'est combien? **2.** *adv.* Beaucoup, bien. It doesn't matter much, cela ne fait pas grand'chose. Ever so much, infiniment. Much the largest, de beaucoup le plus grand. Much of an age, à peu près du même âge. Much to my astonishment, à mon grand étonnement. **3.** *s.* (*a*) Do you see much of one another? vous voyez-vous souvent? *F:* It is not up to much, cela ne vaut pas grand'chose. Not m. of a dinner, un dîner médiocre. (*b*) This much, autant que ceci. Cut that m. off, coupez-en long comme ça. This m. is certain, il y a ceci de certain. (*c*) To make much of s.o., faire fête à qn. I don't think much of it, j'en fais peu de cas. **4.** (*a*) Much as. *M. as I like him,* quelle que soit mon affection pour lui. (*b*) As much, autant (de). *F:* I thought as much, je m'y attendais; je m'en doutais bien. (*c*) As much as, autant que. *F: It is as m. as he can do to read,* c'est tout juste s'il sait lire. (*d*) As much (as), so much (as), tant (que), autant (que). (*e*) So much, tant (de), autant (de). So much the better, tant mieux. So much so, à tel point. *So m. for his friendship!* et voilà ce qu'il appelle l'amitié! (*f*) Too much, trop (de). Too much by half, trop de moitié. To make too much of sth., attacher trop d'importance à qch.

muck, *s.* Fange *f*; ordures *fpl*.

mucky, *a.* Sale, crotté, malpropre.

mud, *s.* Boue *f*, bourbe *f*. To throw mud at s.o., déblatérer contre qn.

muddied, *a.* Crotté; couvert de boue.

muddiness, *s.* **I.** État crotté; saleté *f*. **2.** Turbidité *f* (d'un liquide).

muddle¹, *s.* Confusion *f*, emmêlement *m*, fouillis *m*. To get into a muddle, s'embrouiller. **muddle-headed,** *a* A l'esprit confus; brouillon.

muddle², *v.tr.* (*a*) Embrouiller, brouiller. (*b*) Brouiller l'esprit à; embrouiller.

muddler, *s.* Brouillon, -onne.

muddy, *a.* **I.** (*a*) Boueux, fangeux, bourbeux. (*b*) (Vêtement) crotté, couvert de boue. **2.** (Liquide) trouble.

mudguard, *s.* *Veh:* Garde-boue *m inv*.

muff¹, *s.* Manchon *m*.

muff², *s.* *F:* Empoté, -ée.

muff³, *v.tr.* *F:* Rater, bousiller, louper.

muffle, *v.tr.* **I.** Emmitoufler (*in*, de). **2.** Assourdir (une cloche). Muffled drums, tambours voilés.

muffler, *s.* Cache-nez *m inv*.

mufti, *s.* *Mil: F:* In mufti, en civil, en bourgeois.

mug¹, *s.* (*For beer*) Chope *f*; (*for tea*) (grosse) tasse. Tin mug, timbale *f*

mug², *s.* *P:* Jobard *m*, nigaud, -e.

mug³, *v.tr.* *Sch: F:* To mug up a subject, bûcher un sujet.

mug⁴, *s.* *P:* Museau *m*.

muggy, *a.* **I.** Chaud et humide. **2.** (Salle) qui sent le renfermé.

mulatto, *s.* Mulâtre, -esse.

mulberry, *s.* *Bot:* **I.** Mûre *f*. **2.** Mulberry (-tree), mûrier *m*.

mulct, *v.tr.* Priver (*s.o. of sth.*, qn de qch.).

mule, *s.* **I.** (He-)mule, mulet *m*. (She-)mule, mule *f*. **2.** Métis, -isse; hybride *m*.

muleteer, *s.* Muletier *m*.

mulish, *a.* Entêté. **-ly,** *adv.* Avec entêtement.

mullet, *s.* *Ich:* **I.** Muge *m*. Grey mullet, mulet *m*. **2.** Red mullet, rouget *m*.

multi-colour(ed), *a.* Multicolore.

multifarious, *a.* Varié, divers; multiple.

multiple. I. *a.* Multiple. Multiple store, maison *f* à succursales (multiples). **2.** *s.* Multiple *m*.

multiplication, *s.* Multiplication *f*.

multiplicity, *s.* Multiplicité *f*.

multiply. I. *v.tr.* Multiplier. **2.** *v.i.* Se multiplier.

multitude, *s.* Multitude *f*; foule *f*.

multitudinous, *a.* Innombrable.

mum, *int. & a.* Mum's the word! motus! To keep mum (*about sth.*), ne pas souffler mot (de qch.).

mumble, *v.tr.* Marmotter, marmonner.

mummify, *v.tr.* Momifier.

mummy, *s.* Momie *f*.

mumps, *s.pl.* *Med:* Oreillons *mpl*.

munch, *v.tr.* Mâcher, mâchonner.

mundane, *a.* Mondain. **I.** Terrestre. **2.** Mundane pleasures, plaisirs mondains.

municipal, *a* Municipal, -aux. Municipal buildings, hôtel *m* de ville.

municipality, *s.* Municipalité *f*.

munificence, *s.* Munificence *f*.

munificent, *a.* Munificent, généreux.

munition, *s.* Munition(s) of war, munitions *f* de guerre.

mural, *a.* Mural, -aux.

murder¹, *s.* Meurtre *m*. Murder! à l'assassin!

murder², *v.tr.* **1.** Assassiner. **2.** *F:* Massacrer.

murderer, *s.* Meurtrier *m*, assassin *m*.

murderess, *s.* Meurtrière *f*, assassine *f*.

murderous, *a.* Meurtrier, assassin.

murkiness, *s.* Obscurité *f*.

murky, *a.* Ténébreux.

murmur¹, *s.* **1.** Murmure *m*; bruissement *m*. **2.** Murmure (d'approbation). **3.** *To converse in murmurs*, s'entretenir à voix basse.

murmur², *v.i. & tr.* **1.** Murmurer, susurrer; (*of brook*) bruire. **2.** To murmur at sth., murmurer contre qch.

muscatel, *s.* Muscatel raisins; muscatels, raisins secs de Malaga.

muscle, *s.* Muscle *m*.

muscular, *a.* **1.** (Force) musculaire. **2.** (Homme) musculeux, musclé.

muse¹, *s.* Muse *f*.

muse², *v.i.* Méditer, rêver, rêvasser. **musing¹**, *a.* Rêveur, -euse. **-ly**, *adv.* D'un air songeur. **musing²**, *s.* Rêverie *f* (*on*, à); méditation *f* (*on*, sur).

museum, *s.* Musée *m*.

mush, *s.* *F:* Bouillie *f*, panade *f*.

mushroom, *s.* Champignon *m*. *Cu:* Mushroom ketchup, sauce *f* aux champignons.

music, *s.* Musique *f*. **music-hall**, *s.* Music-hall *m*. **music-stand**, *s.* Pupitre *m* à musique.

musical, *a.* **1.** Musical, -aux. Musical instrument, instrument *m* de musique. **2.** Amateur, -trice, de bonne musique. **3.** Harmonieux, mélodieux, chantant.

musician, *s.* Musicien, -ienne.

musk, *s.* Musc *m*. **musk-ox**, *s.* *Z:* Bœuf musqué. **musk-rat**, *s.* *Z:* Rat musqué.

musket, *s.* *Sm.a:* Mousquet *m*.

musketeer, *s.* *A:* Mousquetaire *m*.

musky, *a.* Musqué. Musky smell, odeur de musc.

muslin, *s.* Mousseline *f*.

musquash, *s.* *Com:* Castor *m* du Canada.

mussel, *s.* *Moll:* Moule *f*.

Mussulman, *a. & s.* Musulman, -ane.

must, *modal aux. v.* **1.** (*a*) You m. hurry up, il faut vous dépêcher. They must have new clothes, il leur faut absolument de nouveaux habits. Do so if you must, faites-le s'il le faut. He is failing, I must say, il faut avouer qu'il baisse. (*b*) It must be the doctor, ce doit être le médecin I must have made a mistake, je me serai trompé. **2.** I saw that he m. have suspected something, je vis bien qu'il avait dû se douter de quelque chose.

mustang, *s.* *Z:* Mustang *m*.

mustard, *s.* Moutarde *f*. **mustard-gas**, *s.* *Mil:* Ypérite *f*; gaz *m* moutarde. **mustard-plaster**, *s.* *Med:* Sinapisme *m*. **mustard-pot**, *s.* Moutardier *m*.

muster¹, *s.* **1.** (*a*) Rassemblement *m*. (*b*) *Mil:* Revue *f*. *F:* To pass muster, passer; être passable. **2.** Assemblée *f*, réunion *f*.

muster². **1.** *v.tr.* (*a*) Rassembler. (*b*) To muster (up) one's strength, rassembler toutes ses forces. **2.** *v.i.* Se réunir, se rassembler.

mustiness, *s.* Relent *m*.

musty, *a.* **1.** To smell musty, sentir le moisi; (*of room*) sentir le renfermé. **2.** *F:* Suranné.

mutability, *s.* Mutabilité *f*.

mutable, *a.* Muable, variable.

mutation, *s.* Mutation *f*.

mute. **1.** *a.* Muet, -ette. **II. mute**, *s.* **1.** (*a*) Muet, -ette. (*b*) Employé *m* des pompes funèbres; croque-mort *m*, *pl.* croque-morts. **2.** *Mus:* Sourdine *f*.

mutilate, *v.tr.* Mutiler, estropier.

mutilation, *s.* Mutilation *f*.

mutineer, *s.* Révolté *m*, mutiné *m*, mutin *m*.

mutinous, *a.* Rebelle, mutiné, mutin.

mutiny¹, *s.* Révolte *f*, mutinerie *f*.

mutiny², *v.i.* Se révolter, se mutiner.

mutter, *v.tr. & i.* Marmonner, marmotter.

muttering, *s.* Marmottage *m*; murmures *mpl*; grondement *m*.

mutton, *s.* *Cu:* Mouton *m*. Leg of mutton, gigot *m*. **mutton-chop**, *s.* *Cu:* Côtelette *f* de mouton.

mutual, *a.* **1.** Mutuel, réciproque. **2.** *F:* Mutual friend, ami commun. **-ally**, *adv.* Mutuellement, réciproquement.

muzzle¹, *s.* **1.** Museau *m* (d'un animal). **2.** Bouche *f*, gueule *f* (d'une arme à feu). **3.** Muselière *f* (pour chiens).

muzzle², *v.tr.* Museler.

my, *poss.a.* Mon; *f.* ma, *pl.* mes. I have broken my arm, je me suis cassé le bras. My idea would be to . . ., mon idée à moi serait de. . . .

myopia, *s.* *Med:* Myopie *f*.

myopic, *a.* Myope.

myriad. **1.** *s.* Myriade *f*. **2.** *a.* Innombrable.

myrmidon, *s.* *F:* The myrmidons of the law, les sbires *m* de la police.

myrrh, *s.* Myrrhe *f*.

myrtle, *s.* *Bot:* Myrte *m*.

myself, *pers.pron.* See SELF 3.

mysterious, *a.* Mystérieux. A m. business, une ténébreuse affaire **-ly**, *adv.* Mystérieusement.

mystery, *s.* Mystère *m*.

mystic, *a.* **1.** (*a*) Ésotérique, mystique. (*b*) (*Of power*) Occulte. **2.** *a & s. Theol:* Mystique. (*mf*).

mystical, *a.* Mystique.

mysticism, *s.* Mysticisme *m*.

mystification, *s.* **1.** Mystification *f*. **2.** Embrouillement *m*.

mystify, *v.tr.* **1.** Mystifier. **2.** Embrouiller.

myth, *s.* Mythe *m*.

mythical, *a.* Mythique.

mythological, *a.* Mythologique.

mythology, *s.* Mythologie *f*.

N, n, s. (La lettre) N, n, m.
nab, v.tr. P: 1. Saisir, P: pincer. 2. Escamoter, chiper (qch.).
nabob, s. Nabab m.
nag¹, s. F: Petit cheval (de selle); bidet m.
nag², v.tr. & i. Chamailler; gronder sans cesse. **nagging,** a. 1. Grondeur, -euse, hargneux, -euse. 2. (Of pain) Agaçant, énervant.
naiad, s. Myth: Naïade f; nymphe f des eaux.
nail¹, s. 1. Ongle m. 2. Clou m, pl. clous. Brass-headed nail, clou doré. F: To hit the nail on the head, mettre le doigt dessus. 3. F: To pay on the nail, payer rubis sur l'ongle. **nail-brush,** s. Toil: Brosse f à ongles. **nail-file,** s. Toil: Lime f à ongles.
nail², v.tr. 1. Clouer. 2. P: Attraper, saisir. **nailed,** a. (a) Cloué. (b) Clouté; garni de clous.
naïve, a. Naïf, f. naïve; ingénu. **-ly,** adv. Naïvement, ingénument.
naïvety, s. Naïveté f.
naked, a. Nu. 1. (a) Sans vêtements. (b) (Dos) découvert, nu. (c) (Mur) nu; (pays) dénudé. 2. (a) Naked sword, épée nue. (b) Visible to the naked eye, visible à l'œil nu. (c) The naked truth, la vérité toute nue.
nakedness, s. Nudité f.
name¹, s. 1. Nom m. (a) Full name, nom et prénoms. Christian name, prénom m; nom de baptême. My name is, je m'appelle. Name of a ship, devise f d'un navire. To go by the name of, être connu sous le nom de. F: To mention no names, ne nommer personne. To put one's name down (for sth.), s'inscrire. A king in name only, un roi de nom seulement. (b) Terme m. 2. Réputation f, renommée f. He has a name for honesty, il passe pour honnête. To make a name for oneself, se faire un grand nom.
name², v.tr. 1. Nommer; dénommer. To name s.o. after s.o., donner à qn le nom de qn. 2. Désigner par son nom. 3. (a) Citer (un exemple). (b) Fixer (le jour).
nameless, a. 1. Sans nom; inconnu. 2. Anonyme. A lady who shall be nameless, une dame dont je tairai le nom. 3. Indicible, inexprimable.
namely, adv. (A) savoir; c'est-à-dire.
namesake, s. Homonyme m.
nanny-goat, s. F: Chèvre, bique.
nap¹, s. Petit somme. Afternoon nap, sieste f.
nap², v.i. Sommeiller. F: To catch s.o. napping, prendre qn au dépourvu.
nap³, s. Poil m.
nap⁴, s. Cards: Napoléon m; nap m.
nape, s. The nape of the neck, la nuque.

naphtha, s. (Huile f de) naphte m.
napkin, s. (Table-)napkin, serviette f (de table).
Napoleon. Pr.n. Napoléon m.
Napoleonic, a. Napoléonien.
narcissus, s. Bot: Narcisse m.
narcotic, a. & s. Narcotique (m).
narrate, v.tr. Narrer, raconter.
narration, s. Narration f.
narrative¹, s. Récit m, narration f.
narrative², a. Narratif.
narrator, s. Narrateur, -trice.
narrow¹, a. (a) Étroit. To grow narrow, se rétrécir. (b) De faibles dimensions; (esprit) étroit, borné. N. limits, limites restreintes. (c) (Examen) minutieux. (d) A narrow majority, une faible majorité. **-ly,** adv. 1. (a) Étroitement, rigoureusement. (b) (Examiner) minutieusement, de près. 2. Tout juste. He narrowly missed being run over, il faillit être écrasé. **narrow-minded,** a. Borné; à l'esprit étroit. **narrow-mindedness,** s. Étroitesse f, petitesse f, d'esprit.
narrow², 1. v.tr. (a) Resserrer. (b) Restreindre, limiter, borner. 2. v.i. Devenir plus étroit; se rétrécir.
narrowness, s. (a) Étroitesse f. (b) Petitesse f; limitation f.
nasal. 1. a. Nasal, -als, -aux. Nasal accent, accent nasillard. 2. s. Ling: Nasale f.
nasturtium, s. Hort: Capucine f.
nasty, a. 1. (a) Désagréable, dégoûtant. (b) Nasty weather, sale, vilain, temps. N. corner, tournant dangereux. 2. Méchant, désagréable; P: rosse. To turn nasty, prendre un air méchant.
natality, s. Natalité f.
nation, s. 1. Nation f. People of all nations, des gens de toutes les nationalités. 2. The whole n. rose in arms, tout le pays se souleva.
national, a. National, -aux; de l'État. **-ally,** adv. Nationalement; du point de vue national.
nationalist, s. Nationaliste mf.
nationality, s. Nationalité f.
native. I. s. 1. (a) Natif, -ive. (b) Indigène mf. 2. The elephant is a n. of Asia, l'éléphant est originaire de l'Asie. II. **native,** a. 1. Naturel, inné. 2. (a) Natal, -als, -aux; de naissance. Native language, langue maternelle. Native land, terre natale. (b) (Costume) du pays.
natty, a. 1. Pimpant; coquet, -ette. 2. To be natty with one's hands, être adroit de ses mains.
natural, a. Naturel. 1. Natural law, loi de la nature. 2. Natif, inné. It comes natural to him, c'est un don chez lui. (b) It is natural that . ., il est (bien) naturel

que + *sub.* **As is natural,** comme de raison. **-ally,** *adv.* Naturellement.
naturalist, *s.* Naturaliste *mf.*
naturalization, *s.* Naturalisation *f.*
naturalize, *v.tr.* Naturaliser.
naturalness, *s.* **1.** Caractère naturel. **2.** Naturel *m*; absence *f* d'affectation.
nature, *s.* Nature *f.* **1.** *(a)* Essence *f,* caractère *m.* **It is in the nature of things,** il est dans l'ordre des choses. *(b)* Naturel *m,* caractère. **It is not in his nature to,** il n'est pas de sa nature de. **By nature,** par tempérament *m*; naturellement. **2.** Espèce *f,* sorte *f,* genre *m.* **Of a nature to astonish us,** de nature à nous étonner. **3.** (La) nature.
naught, *s.* **1.** Rien *m,* néant *m.* **To come to naught,** échouer. **To set the law at naught,** ne tenir aucun compte de la loi. **2.** *Ar:* Zéro *m.*
naughty, *a.* Vilain, méchant. *You n. child!* petit méchant! **-ily,** *adv.* *To behave n.* ne pas être sage.
nausea, *s.* **1.** Nausée *f.* **2.** *F:* Dégoût *m,* nausée, écœurement *m.*
nauseate, *v.tr.* Écœurer, dégoûter. **nauseating,** *a.* Dégoûtant, écœurant.
nauseous, *a.* = NAUSEATING.
nautical, *a.* Nautique, marin.
naval, *a.* Naval, -als. *N. engagements,* combats en mer. **Naval base,** port *m* de guerre. **Naval officer,** officier de marine.
nave, *s.* Nef *f,* vaisseau *m* (d'église).
navigability, *s.* Navigabilité *f.*
navigable, *a.* Navigable.
navigate. **1.** *v.i.* Naviguer. **2.** *v.tr.* *(a)* Parcourir (les mers). *(b)* Gouverner, diriger.
navigation, *s.* Navigation *f*; conduite *f.*
navigator, *s.* Navigateur *m.*
navvy, *s.* Terrassier *m.*
navy, *s.* Marine *f* de guerre. *His son is in the n.,* son fils est dans la flotte. **The Royal Navy,** la marine de l'État. **navy blue,** *s.* Bleu *m* marine *inv.*
naze, *s.* Promontoire *m,* cap *m,* pointe *f.*
nazi, a. & *s.* *Pol:* Nazi, -ie.
nazi(i)sm, *s.* *Pol:* Nazisme *m.*
neap, *a.* & *s.* Neap tides, *F:* neaps, morteseaux *f*; marées de morte eau.
Neapolitan, *a.* & *s.* Napolitain, -aine.
near[1]. **I.** *adv.* **1.** *(a)* Près, proche. **To come near, draw near,** s'approcher (*to,* de). **Near at hand,** à proximité, tout près. **2.** *(a)* Those near and dear to him, ceux qui lui touchent de près. **2. As near as I can remember,** autant que je puisse m'en souvenir. **II. near,** *prep.* **1.** Près de, auprès de. *Bring your chair near(er) the fire,* (r)approchez votre chaise du feu. **2.** *N. death,* près de mourir. **To be near the end,** toucher à la fin. **III. near,** *a.* **1.** Proche; intime, cher. **Our near relations,** nos proches (parents). **2.** The hour is near, l'heure est proche. **3. To go by the nearest road,** prendre par le plus court. **4. It was a near thing,** nous l'avons échappé belle;

P: il était moins cinq. **5.** Chiche, parcimonieux. **-ly,** *adv.* **1.** (De) près. *We are n. related,* nous sommes proches parents. **2.** *(a)* Presque, à peu près, près de. *It is n. midnight,* il est bientôt minuit. **Very nearly,** peu s'en faut. *I n. fell,* je faillis tomber, j'ai manqué de tomber. *(b) She is not nearly so old as you,* elle n'est pas si âgée que vous à beaucoup près. **near by,** *adv.* & *prep.* Tout près (de), tout proche (de). **near-sighted,** *a.* Myope.
near[2], *v.tr.* (S')approcher de. *We are nearing the goal,* nous touchons au but.
nearness, *s.* **1.** Proximité *f.* **2.** Parcimonie *f.*
neat, *a.* **1.** Pur; sans eau. **2.** *(a)* Simple et de bon goût; bien rangé, en ordre; *N. handwriting,* écriture nette. *His n. attire,* sa mise soignée. **As neat as a new pin,** tiré à quatre épingles. *(b) (Of phrase)* bien tourné. **3.** Ordonné; qui a de l'ordre. **-ly,** *adv.* **1.** Avec ordre. *N. dressed,* habillé avec soin. **2.** Adroitement. *N. turned compliment,* compliment bien tourné.
neatness, *s.* **1.** Simplicité *f,* bon goût; apparence soignée; netteté *f* (d'écriture). **2.** *(a)* Ordre *m.* *(b)* Adresse *f,* dextérité *f.*
nebular, *a.* Nébulaire.
nebulous, *a.* Nébuleux.
necessary. **I.** *a.* *(a)* Nécessaire, indispensable (*to, for,* à). **It is necessary to** (do sth.), il faut (faire qch.). *It is n. for him to return,* il faut qu'il revienne. **To make all necessary arrangements,** prendre toutes dispositions utiles. **If necessary,** s'il le faut; au besoin. *(b)* Inévitable. **2.** *s.* *(a) Usu. pl.* **The necessaries of life,** les nécessités *f* de la vie. *Bare necessaries,* le strict nécessaire. *(b)* *F:* **To do the necessary,** faire le nécessaire. **-ily,** *adv.* Nécessairement, de (toute) nécessité.
necessitate, *v.tr.* Nécessiter; rendre nécessaire.
necessitous, *a.* Nécessiteux, besogneux.
necessity, *s.* **1.** Nécessité *f.* *(a)* Obligation *f,* contrainte *f.* **Of necessity,** de (toute) nécessité. **Case of absolute necessity,** cas de force majeure. *(b)* Besoin *m.* **In case of necessity,** au besoin, en cas de besoin. **2.** *A car is a necessity nowadays,* de nos jours une auto est indispensable. **3.** Nécessité, indigence *f.*
neck, *s.* **1.** *(a)* Cou *m.* **To have a stiff n.,** avoir un, le, torticolis. *F:* **To be up to one's neck in work,** avoir du travail par-dessus la tête. **To fling one's arms round s.o.'s neck,** se jeter au cou de qn. *Rac:* **To win by a neck,** gagner par une encolure. *To finish neck and neck,* arriver à égalité. *F:* **Neck and crop,** tout entier; à corps perdu. **It is neck or nothing,** il faut jouer le tout pour le tout. *(b)* Encolure *f* (de robe). **Low neck,** décolleté *m.* **2.** *(a)* Goulot *m* (de bouteille). *(b)* Langue *f* (de terre). **neck-tie,** *s.* Cravate *f.*
necklace, *s.* Collier *m.*
necklet, *s* Collier *m.* **Fur necklet,** tour *m* de cou (en fourrure).

necromancer, s. Nécromancien, -ienne.
necromancy, s. Nécromancie f.
necropolis, s. Nécropole f.
nectar, s. Nectar m.
nectarine, s. Brugnon m.
nectary, s. Bot: Nectaire m.
need¹, s. **1.** Besoin m. (a) If need(s) be, in case of need, en cas de besoin, au besoin; si besoin est. **There is no need to,** il n'est pas nécessaire de. **What need is there** to send for him? à quoi bon le faire venir? No n. to say, inutile de dire. (b) **To be in need of** sth., avoir besoin de qch. I have no n. of your assistance, je n'ai que faire de votre aide. **2.** (a) Adversité f; embarras m. **In times of need,** aux moments difficiles. (b) Besoin, indigence f. **To be in need,** être dans le besoin.
need². 1. v.tr. (a) Avoir besoin de; réclamer, exiger. This will n. some explanation, ceci demande à être expliqué. That needs no saying, cela va sans dire. **To need a lot of asking,** se faire prier. (b) **To need to do** sth., être obligé, avoir besoin, de faire qch. They n. to be told everything, il faut qu'on leur dise tout. You only needed to ask, vous n'aviez qu'à demander. **2.** Modal aux. **Need he go?** a-t-il besoin, est-il obligé, d'y aller? You n. not wait, inutile d'attendre. Why n. he bother us? qu'a-t-il besoin de nous déranger?
needful, a. Nécessaire (to, for, à, pour). s. F: **To do the needful,** faire le nécessaire.
needle, s. Aiguille f. **needle-case,** s. Étui m à aiguilles.
needless, a. Inutile, peu nécessaire, superflu.
needlewoman, s. Couturière f.
needlework, s. Travaux mpl à l'aiguille.
needs, adv. **If needs must,** s'il le faut.
needy, a. Nécessiteux, besogneux.
ne'er-do-well, a. & s. Propre mf à rien.
nefarious, a. Infâme, scélérat.
negation, s. Négation f.
negative¹. I. a. Négatif. **-ly,** adv. Négativement. **II. negative,** s. **1.** Négative f. Gram: Négation f. **2.** Phot: Négatif m, cliché m.
negative², v.tr. **1.** S'opposer à, rejeter. **2.** Réfuter; contredire, nier. **3.** Neutraliser.
neglect¹, s. **1.** (a) Manque m d'égards (of, envers, pour). (b) Manque m de soin(s). (c) Mauvais entretien. **2.** Négligence f, inattention f. **From neglect,** par négligence.
neglect², v.tr. **1.** (a) Manquer d'égards envers. (b) Manquer de soins pour. **2.** Négliger. **To n. an opportunity,** laisser échapper une occasion. **neglected,** a. Négligé.
neglectful, a. Négligent.
negligence, s. Négligence f. **Through negligence,** par négligence.
negligent, a. **1.** Négligent. **2.** Nonchalant, insouciant. **-ly,** adv. Négligemment; avec négligence.
negligible, a. Négligeable.

negotiable, a. **1.** Fin: Négociable. **2.** F: (Barrière) franchissable; (chemin) praticable.
negotiate. 1. v.tr. (a) Négocier. (b) F: Franchir (une haie). Aut: To n. a curve, prendre un virage. **2.** v.i. To n. for peace, entreprendre des pourparlers de paix.
negotiation, s. **1.** Négociation f. Under negotiation, en négociation. **To be in negotiation with** s.o., être en pourparler(s) avec qn. **2.** F: Franchissement m (d'un obstacle); prise f (d'un virage).
negotiator, s. Négociateur, -trice.
negress, s. Négresse f.
negro, a. & s. Nègre (m).
neigh¹, s. Hennissement m.
neigh², v.i. Hennir. **neighing,** s. Hennissement m.
neighbour, s. **1.** Voisin, -ine. **2.** Prochain m.
neighbourhood, s. **1.** Voisinage m, proximité f (of, de). **2.** Alentours mpl, environs mpl. **In the n. of the town,** aux alentours de la ville.
neighbouring, a. Avoisinant, voisin; proche.
neighbourly, a. **To act in a n. fashion,** agir en bon voisin.
neither. 1. adv. & conj. (a) He will n. eat nor drink, il ne veut ni manger ni boire. (b) Non plus. If you do not go, **neither shall I,** si vous n'y allez pas, je n'irai pas non plus. (c) = NOR 2. **2.** a. & pron. Ni l'un(e) ni l'autre; aucun(e). On n. side, ni d'un côté ni de l'autre.
neolithic, a. Néolithique.
neon, s. Ch: Néon m.
neophyte, s. Néophyte mf; F: débutant, -ante.
nephew, s. Neveu m.
Nereid, s. Myth: Néréide f.
Nero. Pr.n. Rom.Hist: Néron m.
nerve¹, s. **1.** (a) Anat: Nerf m. F: **To be in a state of nerves,** être énervé. **To get on** s.o.'s nerves, donner sur les nerfs à qn. (b) F: Courage m, assurance f. **To lose one's nerve,** perdre son sang-froid. (c) F: Audace f, aplomb m. P: You have got a nerve! tu en as un toupet! **2.** Bot: Nervure f. **3.** F: **To strain every nerve to do** sth., déployer tous ses efforts pour faire qch.
nerve-racking, a. Énervant, horripilant.
nerve², v.tr. **To nerve oneself to do** sth., s'armer de courage pour faire qch.
nerveless, s. Inertie f; manque m de force, d'énergie.
nerviness, s. Nervosité f; énervement m.
nervous, a. **1.** (a) Excitable, irritable. (b) Inquiet, -ète. (c) Timide, peureux. **To get nervous,** s'intimider. **2.** Anat: **The nervous system,** le système nerveux. **-ly,** adv. **1.** Timidement. **2.** Craintivement.
nervousness, s. (a) Nervosité f. (b) Timidité f.
nervy, a. F: (a) Énervé, irritable. She is n.,

elle est très nerveuse. (b) (Mouvement) nerveux, saccadé.

ness, s. Promontoire m, cap m.

nest¹, s. **1.** (a) Nid m. (b) Repaire m, nid (de brigands) **2.** Nichée f (d'oiseaux). **3.** Série f, jeu m (d'objets). Nest of tables, table f gigogne. **nest-egg,** s. **1.** Nichet m; œuf m en faïence. **2.** F: Argent mis de côté.

nest², v.i. (Se) nicher ; faire son nid.

nestle, v.i. Se nicher. To nestle close (up) to s.o., se serrer contre qn. Village nestling in a valley, village blotti dans une vallée.

nestling, s. Oisillon m; petit oiseau.

net¹, s. Filet m. Butterfly net, filet à papillons.

net², v.tr. Prendre au filet.

net³, a. Net, f. nette. 'Terms strictly net cash,' "sans déduction."

nether, a. Inférieur, -e, bas, f. basse. Nether garments, pantalon m. The nether regions, l'enfer m.

Netherlands (the). Pr.n.pl. Les Pays-Bas m.

nethermost, a. Le plus bas ; le plus profond.

nett, a. = NET³.

nettle¹, s. Ortie f. Stinging nettle, ortie brûlante. **nettle-rash,** s. Urticaire f.

nettle², v.tr. F: Piquer, irriter.

network, s Réseau m.

neuralgia, s. Névralgie f.

neuritis, s. Névrite f.

neurotic, a. Névrosé, neurotique.

neuter. 1. a. Neutre. **2.** s. Gram: (Genre) neutre m.

neutral. 1. a. (a) Pol: Neutre. To remain n., garder la neutralité. (b) Neutre ; moyen, indéterminé. **2.** s. Pol: Neutre m.

neutrality, s. Pol: Ch: Neutralité f.

neutralize, v.tr. Neutraliser.

never, adv. (a) (Ne . . .) jamais. I n. go there, je n'y vais jamais. He n. came back, il ne revint plus. Never, never, shall I forget it, jamais, au grand jamais, je ne l'oublierai. Never in (all) my life, jamais de la vie. (b) I n. expected him to come, je ne m'attendais aucunement à ce qu'il vînt. Never a one, pas un seul. Well I never! par exemple ! c'est formidable ! (c) Lit: Be he never so brave, quelque courageux qu'il soit. **never-ending,** a. Perpétuel, éternel ; qui n'en finit plus.

nevermore, adv. (Ne . . .) plus jamais ; (ne . . .) jamais plus.

nevertheless, adv. Néanmoins, quand même, toutefois, pourtant.

new, a. **1.** (a) Nouveau, -elle New ideas, idées nouvelles, idées neuves. New ground, terre vierge. That has made a new man of him, cela a fait de lui un autre homme. Sch: The new boys, les nouveaux. (b) To be new to business, être nouveau, neuf, aux affaires. **2.** Neuf, f. neuve ; non usagé. Com: As new, à l'état (de) neuf. To make

sth. like new, remettre qch. à neuf. The subject is quite new, ce sujet est neuf. **3.** (Pain) frais ; (vin) nouveau, jeune. New potatoes, pommes de terre nouvelles. **-ly,** adv. Récemment, nouvellement. The newly-elected members, les députés nouveaux élus. N.-painted wall, mur fraîchement peint. **new-born,** a. Nouveau-né. N.-b. children, enfants nouveau-nés. N.-b daughter, fille nouveau-née. **new-comer,** s. Nouveau venu, f. nouvelle venue. The new-comers, les nouveaux venus. **New Guinea.** Pr.n. La Nouvelle-Guinée. **new-laid,** a. (Œuf) frais pondu. **New Orleans.** Pr.n. La Nouvelle-Orléans. **New South Wales.** Pr.n. La Nouvelle-Galles du Sud. **New Year,** s. Nouvel an ; nouvelle année. New-Year's Day, le jour de l'an. To wish s.o. a happy New Year, souhaiter la bonne année à qn. New-Year's gift, étrennes fpl; cadeau m de jour de l'an. **New Zealand.** Pr.n. La Nouvelle-Zélande. **New Zealander,** s. Néo-Zélandais,-aise.

newfangled, a. D'une modernité outrée.

Newfoundland. 1. Pr.n. Geog: Terre-Neuve f. **2.** s. (Dog) Terre-neuve m inv.

Newfoundlander, s. Terre-neuvien,-ienne.

newness, s. **1.** (a) Nouveauté f. (b) Inexpérience f (d'un employé). **2.** État neuf.

news, s. Nouvelle(s) f. **1.** What (is the) news? quelles nouvelles? A sad piece of news, une triste nouvelle. To break the news to s.o., faire part d'une mauvaise nouvelle à qn. No news is good news, point de nouvelles, bonnes nouvelles. **2.** News film, reel, film m d'actualité. **news-agent,** s. Marchand m de journaux. **news-boy,** s. Vendeur m de journaux ; F: petit camelot.

newspaper, s. Journal m, -aux. Newspaper man, marchand m de journaux.

newt, s. Amph: Triton m ; salamandre f aquatique.

next. 1. a. **1.** Prochain ; le plus proche. The n. room, la chambre voisine. Her room is next to mine, sa chambre est contiguë à la mienne. Seated n. to me, assis à côté de moi. **2.** (a) Prochain, suivant. The next day, le lendemain. The next day but one, le surlendemain. The n. instant, l'instant d'après. Next year, l'année prochaine. By this time n. year, dans un an d'ici. (b) The n. chapter, le chapitre suivant. The next time I see him, la première fois que je le reverrai. F: What next! par exemple ! Who comes next? à qui le tour? The next best thing would be to, à défaut de cela, le mieux serait de. F: I got it for next to nothing, je l'ai eu pour presque rien. II. next, adv. **1.** Ensuite, après. What shall we do n.? qu'est-ce que nous allons faire maintenant? **2.** When next you are that way, la prochaine fois que vous passerez par là. III. next, prep. Auprès de, à côté de. next door. **1.** adv. phr.Ideas n. d. to madness, idées qui avoisinent,

qui frisent, la folie. **2.** *adv.* The people next door, les gens d'à côté. **3.** *Attrib.* Next-door neighbours, voisins de porte à porte, d'à côté.
nib, *s.* (Bec *m* de) plume *f.*
nibble¹, *s.* (*a*) Grignotement *m.* (*b*) *Fish:* Touche *f.*
nibble², *v.tr. & i.* Grignoter, mordiller. To nibble (at the bait), mordre à l'hameçon.
nice, *a.* **1.** *Lit:* (*a*) Délicat, exigeant; scrupuleux. (*b*) (*Of question*) Délicat; (*of distinction*) subtil, fin. That's a very n. point, voilà une question délicate. **2.** *F:* (*a*) Gentil, *f.* gentille; sympathique. To be nice to s.o., se montrer gentil avec qn. (*b*) Joli, bon. *N. car,* jolie auto. *It is n. here,* il fait bon ici. (*c*) Nice people, des gens bien. Not nice, pas tout à fait convenable. (*d*) We are in a nice mess! nous sommes dans de beaux draps! *That's a n. way to behave!* voilà une jolie conduite! **-ly,** *adv.* **1.** *Lit:* Scrupuleusement. **2.** Joliment, gentiment, bien. *Those will do n.,* ceux-là feront très bien l'affaire. *F:* How are you?—Nicely, comment allez-vous?—Bien.
nicety, *s.* **1.** (*a*) To a nicety, exactement, à la perfection, à merveille. (*b*) Subtilité *f,* délicatesse *f.* **2.** *pl.* Niceties, minuties *f.*
niche, *s.* Niche *f.*
Nicholas. *Pr.n.* Nicolas *m.*
Nick¹. *Pr.n.* Nicolas *m. F:* Old Nick, le diable.
nick², *s.* **1.** Entaille *f,* encoche *f,* cran *m.* **2.** (Just) in the nick of time, à point nommé; juste à temps.
nick³, *v.tr.* Entailler, encocher.
nickel, *s.* Nickel *m.*
nickname¹, *s.* Surnom *m*; sobriquet *m.*
nickname², *v.tr.* Surnommer; donner un sobriquet à.
nicotine, *s. Ch:* Nicotine *f.*
niece, *s.* Nièce *f.*
niggard, *s.* Grippe-sou *m,* pingre *m.*
niggardliness, *s.* Ladrerie *f,* pingrerie *f.*
niggardly, *a.* Chiche, ladre; mesquin.
nigger, *s. F:* Nègre *m, f.* négresse. *A little n. boy,* un négrillon.
niggle, *v.i.* Vétiller; tatillonner. **niggling,** *a.* Insignifiant; (*of work*) fignolé; (*of pers.*) tatillon, -onne.
night, *s.* **1.** (*a*) Nuit *f,* soir *m.* The night before, la veille (au soir). To-morrow night, demain soir. Ten o'clock at night, dix heures du soir. Good night! bonsoir! (*when retiring*) bonne nuit! At night, la nuit. In the night, (pendant) la nuit. By night, de nuit; nuitamment. Night attire, vêtement *m,* toilette *f,* de nuit. (*b*) *Th:* First night, première *f.* **2.** Obscurité *f,* ténèbres *fpl. N. is falling,* il commence à faire nuit. **night-cap,** *s.* **1.** Bonnet *m* de nuit (de femme); bonnet de coton (d'homme). **2.** *F:* Grog *m* (avant de se coucher). **night-club,** *s. F:* Boîte *f* de nuit. **night-dress, -gown,** *s.* Chemise *f* de nuit. **night-light,** *s.* Veilleuse *f.*

night-shift, *s. Ind:* Équipe *f* de nuit. To be on night-shift, être de nuit. **night-shirt,** *s.* Chemise *f* de nuit. **night-time,** *s.* La nuit. **night-watchman,** *s. Ind:* Veilleur *m,* gardien *m,* de nuit.
nightfall, *s.* Tombée *f* du jour, de la nuit. At nightfall, à la nuit tombante.
nightingale, *s. Orn:* Rossignol *m.*
nightjar, *s. Orn:* Engoulevent *m.*
nightly. **1.** *a.* (*a*) De nuit, de soir, nocturne. (*b*) Nightly performance, représentation (de) tous les soirs. **2.** *adv.* Tous les soirs, toutes les nuits.
nightmare, *s.* Cauchemar *m.*
nightshade, *s. Bot:* Woody nightshade, douce-amère *f.* Deadly nightshade, belladone *f.*
nihilism, *s.* Nihilisme *m.*
nihilist, *s.* Nihiliste *mf.*
nil, *s.* Rien *m. Sp:* Zéro *m.*
Nile (the). *Pr.n.* Le Nil.
nimble, *a.* Agile, leste, preste; (*of mind*) délié, prompt. Still nimble, encore ingambe. **-bly,** *adv.* Agilement; lestement, prestement. **nimble-footed,** *a.* Aux pieds agiles. **nimble-witted,** *a.* A l'esprit délié.
nimbus, *s.* **1.** *Art:* Nimbe *m,* auréole *f,* gloire *f.* **2.** *Meteor:* Nimbus *m.*
nincompoop, *s. F:* Benêt *m,* nigaud, -aude, niais, -aise.
nine, *num. a. & s.* Neuf (*m*). *Adv.phr. F:* To the nines, à la perfection.
ninepin, *s.* **1.** *pl.* Ninepins, (jeu *m* de) quilles *fpl.* **2.** Quille.
nineteen, *num. a. & s.* Dix-neuf (*m*).
nineteenth, *num. a. & s.* Dix-neuvième (*m*).
ninety, *num. a. & s.* Quatre-vingt-dix (*m*). Ninety-one, quatre-vingt-onze.
ninny, *s. F:* Niais, -aise.
ninth, *num. a. & s.* Neuvième (*m*).
nip¹, *s.* **1.** Pincement *m.* To give s.o. a nip, pincer qn. **2.** Morsure *f* (de la gelée). *There was a nip in the air,* l'air piquait.
nip², *v.* I. *v.tr.* **1.** Pincer. **2.** *F:* To nip in the bud, écraser dans l'œuf. **3.** (*Of cold*) Pincer, piquer, mordre. II. **nip,** *v.i. F: Just nip round to the baker's,* cours vite chez le boulanger.
nip³, *s. F:* Goutte *f,* doigt *m.* To take a nip, boire une goutte.
nipper, *s.* **1.** (Pair of) nippers (*a*) Pince(s) *f*(*pl*); tenaille(s) *f*(*pl*). (*b*) Cisaille(s) *f*(*pl*). **2.** *F:* Gamin *m,* gosse *m.*
nitrate, *s. Ch:* Nitrate *m,* azotate *m.*
nitre, *s.* Nitre *m,* salpêtre *m.*
nitric, *a. Ch:* Nitric acid, acide *m* nitrique, azotique; *Com:* eau-forte *f.*
nitrogen, *s. Ch:* Azote *m.*
nitrous, *a.* Nitreux, azoteux.
no. I. *a.* **1.** Nul, pas de, point de, aucun (*with ne expressed or understood*). To have no heart, n'avoir pas de cœur. He made no reply, il ne fit aucune réponse. It is no distance, ce n'est

pas loin. *No two men are alike,* il n'y a pas deux hommes qui se ressemblent. *Details of no interest,* détails sans intérêt. **No surrender!** on ne se rend pas! **No nonsense!** pas de bêtises! **No admittance,** entrée interdite. **No smoking,** défense de fumer. **2.** Peu; ne . . pas (du tout). *(a) The task is no easy one,* ce n'est pas une tâche facile. *(b) He is no artist,* il n'est pas artiste. *(c) There is no pleasing him,* il n'y a pas moyen de le satisfaire. **3. No one** = NOBODY I. II.

no, *adv.* **I.** *Whether or no,* que cela soit ou non; dans tous les cas. **2.** *I am no richer than he,* je ne suis pas plus riche que lui. *He is no longer here,* il n'est plus ici. III. **no.** **I.** *adv.* Non. *No, no, you are mistaken!* mais non, mais non, vous vous trompez! **2.** *s.* Non *m inv.* *Not to take (a) no for an answer,* ne pas admettre de refus.

Noah. *Pr.n. B.Hist:* Noé *m.*

nobility, *s.* **I.** Noblesse *f.* **2.** *Coll.* Noblesse; (la classe des) nobles *m.*

noble. **I.** *a.* *(a)* Noble. *(b)* (Sentiment) noble, sublime. **2.** *s.* Noble *m.* **-bly,** *adv.* **I.** Noblement. **2.** Magnifiquement, superbement.

nobleman, *s.* Noble *m*; gentilhomme *m, pl.* gentilshommes.

nobody. **I.** *pron.* Personne *m,* nul *m,* aucun *m* (with ne expressed or understood). *N. spoke to me,* personne ne m'a parlé. *N. is perfect,* nul n'est parfait. *There was nobody else on board,* personne (d')autre n'était à bord. *There was nobody about,* il n'y avait pas âme qui vive. **2.** *s.* Nullité *f,* zéro *m.*

nocturnal, *a.* Nocturne.

nocturne, *s. Mus:* Nocturne *m.*

nod¹, *s.* Inclination *f* de la tête. **I.** Signe de tête affirmatif. **2.** *He gave me a nod,* il me fit un petit signe de la tête.

nod², *v.tr. & i.* **I.** To nod (one's head), faire un signe de tête; incliner la tête. **2.** Dodeliner (de) la tête; somnoler, sommeiller.

noddle, *s. P:* Tête *f*; *P:* boule *f,* caboche *f.*

node, *s.* Nœud *m.*

noise¹, *s.* Bruit *m.* **I.** Tapage *m,* vacarme *m,* fracas *m.* *To make a noise,* faire du bruit, du tapage. *P:* **The big noise,** le grand manitou. **2.** Son *m.*

noise², *v.tr.* *To noise sth. abroad,* ébruiter, (une nouvelle); crier qch. sur les toits.

noiseless, *a.* Sans bruit; silencieux. **-ly,** *adv.* Silencieusement; sans bruit.

noisome, *a.* Fétide, infect.

noisy, *a.* Bruyant, tapageur, -euse. *To be n.,* faire du bruit, du tapage. **-ily,** *adv.* Bruyamment.

nomad, *a. & s.* Nomade (*mf*).

nomadic, *a.* Nomade.

nomenclature, *s.* Nomenclature *f.*

nominal, *a.* Nominal, -aux. *To be the nominal head,* n'être chef que de nom. *N. rent,* loyer purement nominal. **-ally,** *adv.* Nominalement; de nom.

nominate, *v.tr.* *(a)* Nommer, choisir, désigner. *(b)* Proposer, présenter.

nomination, *s.* **I.** Nomination *f.* **2.** Présentation *f* (d'un candidat).

nominative, *a. & s.* *Gram:* Nominatif (*m*).

nominee, *s.* Candidat désigné, choisi.

nonce, *s.* *For the nonce,* pour l'occasion.

nonchalance, *s.* Nonchalance *f.*

nonchalant, *a.* Nonchalant; indifférent. **-ly,** *adv.* Nonchalamment.

non-combatant, *a. & s.* Non-combattant (*m*).

non-commissioned, *a.* Sans brevet. **Non-commissioned officer** (above corporal), sous-officier *m*; gradé *m.*

non-committal, *a.* Qui n'engage à rien.

non-conducting, *a.* Non-conducteur, -trice. (heat) calorifuge; (electricity) isolant.

non-conductor, *s.* Non-conducteur *m*; (of heat) calorifuge *m* (of electricity) isolant *m.*

nonconformist, *s. & a. Ecc:* Dissident, -ente.

nondescript, *a.* Indéfinissable, inclassable; (costume) hétéroclite.

none. **I.** *pron.* *(a)* Aucun. **None of this** concerns me, rien de ceci ne me regarde. *Strawberries! there are none,* des fraises! il n'y en a pas. **None of your impudence!** pas d'insolences de votre part! *(b)* **None can tell,** nul ne le sait. *None but he knew of it,* lui seul le savait. **2.** *a.* Money I had none, d'argent je n'en avais point. **3.** *adv.* *(a)* I like him none the worse for that, je ne l'en aime pas moins. *(b)* He was none too soon, il arriva juste à temps.

nonentity, *s.* Personne insignifiante, de peu d'importance; non-valeur *f*; nullité *f.*

non-existent, *a.* Non-existant; inexistant.

non-freezing, *a.* Incongelable.

non-fulfilment, *s.* Non-exécution *f.*

non-inflammable, *a.* Ininflammable, ignifuge.

non-payment, *s.* Non-payement *m*; défaut *m* de payement.

non-performance, *s.* Non-exécution *f.*

nonplus, *v.tr.* Embarrasser, interdire, interloquer. *To be nonplussed,* être désemparé.

non-resident, *a. & s.* Non-résident (*m*).

nonsense, *s.* **I.** Non-sens *m.* **2.** Absurdité *f,* déraison *f.* *To talk nonsense,* dire des bêtises. **Nonsense!** pas possible! à d'autres! **Now, no nonsense!** allons, pas de bêtises!

nonsensical, *a.* Absurde.

non-stop. **I.** *Attrib.a.* **Non-stop train,** train faisant le trajet sans arrêt. *Av:* **Non-stop flight,** vol sans escale. **2.** *adv.* Sans arrêt; sans escale.

noodle, *s.* Niais, -aise, nigaud, -aude.

noodles, *s.pl. Cu:* Nouilles *f.*

nook, *s.* Coin *m,* recoin *m.* **Nooks and corners,** coins et recoins.

noon, *s.* Midi *m.*

noose, *s.* Nœud coulant; lacet *m,* lacs *m.*

nor, *conj.* **I.** (Ne, ni . . .) ni. **Neither you nor I,** ni vous ni moi. *He shall not go* **nor**

you either, il n'ira pas, ni vous non plus.
2. *I do not know, nor can I guess,* je n'en sais rien et je ne peux pas le deviner.

norm, *s.* Norme *f.*

normal. 1. *a.* Normal, -aux, régulier, ordinaire. **2.** *s.* Normale *f.* **-ally,** *adv.* Normalement.

Norman, *a. & s.* Normand, -ande.

Normandy. *Pr.n.* La Normandie.

Norse, *a.* (*a*) Norvégien. (*b*) *Hist:* Nordique.

Norseman, *s. Hist:* Norvégien *m.*

north. 1. *s.* Nord *m.* **On the north, to the north** (of), au nord (de). **2.** *adv.* Au nord. **To travel north,** voyager vers le nord. **3.** *a.* Nord *inv;* septentrional, -aux. **The north wind,** le vent du nord. **north-east. 1.** *s.* Nord-est *m.* **2.** *a.* (Du) nord-est *inv.* **3.** *adv.* Vers le nord-est. **North Sea (the),** *s.* La mer du Nord. **north-west. 1.** *s.* Nord-ouest *m.* **2.** *a.* (Du) nord-ouest *inv.* **3.** *adv.* Vers le nord-ouest.

northerly, *a.* Du nord; vers le nord. *N. aspect,* exposition au nord.

northern, *a.* (Du) nord; septentrional, -aux. **Northern lights,** aurore boréale.

northward. 1. *s.* **To the northward,** au nord. **2.** *a.* Au, du, nord.

northwards, *adv.* Vers le nord.

Norway. *Pr.n. Geog:* La Norvège.

Norwegian. 1. *a. & s.* Norvégien, -ienne. **2.** *s. Ling:* Le norvégien.

nose¹, *s.* **1.** Nez *m;* museau *m.* **To blow one's nose,** se moucher. **To hold one's nose,** se boucher le nez. **To speak through the nose,** nasiller; parler du nez. *I did it under his (very) nose,* je l'ai fait à son nez. **To lead s.o. by the nose,** mener qn par le bout du nez. **2.** Odorat *m.* **3.** *Navy:* Cône *m* de choc (d'une torpille). **nose-bag,** *s.* Musette *f.* **nose-dive¹,** *s. Av:* Vol piqué; piqué *m.* **nose-dive²,** *v.i. Av:* Piquer du nez; descendre en piqué.

nose², *v.i.* To nose about, fureter, fouiner. **nose out,** *v.tr.* To nose out the game, flairer le gibier. *F:* To nose out a secret, découvrir, éventer, un secret.

nosegay, *s.* Bouquet *m.*

nostalgia, *s.* Nostalgie *f.*

nostril, *s.* (*Of pers.*) Narine *f;* (*of horse*) naseau *m.*

nostrum, *s.* Drogue *f;* remède *m* de charlatan.

nosy, *a. P:* Fouinard; fureteur, -euse. **A Nosy Parker,** *F:* un fouinard.

not, *adv.* (Ne) pas, (ne) point. **1.** (*a*) He will not *come,* il ne viendra pas. *You understand, don't you?* vous comprenez, n'est-ce pas? (*b*) *Are you ill?—Not at all,* êtes-vous malade?—Pas du tout. *Thank you so much!—Not at all!* mille mercis!—De rien (monsieur)! **I think not,** je crois que non. **Not negotiable,** non-négociable. **2.** **Not including,** sans compter. *He begged me not to move,* il me pria de ne pas me déranger. **3.** *There*

were not a few *women amongst them,* il y avait pas mal de femmes parmi eux. **4.** Not **a murmur** *was heard,* pas un murmure ne se fit entendre.

notability, *s.* **1.** Notabilité *f,* notable *m.* **2.** Notabilité, caractère *m* notable.

notable, *a.* (*a*) Notable, insigne; (*of pers.*) éminent. (*b*) *s.* Notable *m.* **-ably,** *adv.* **1.** Notablement. **2.** Notamment, particulièrement.

notary, *s.* Notary (public), notaire *m.*

notation, *s.* Notation *f.*

notch¹, *s.* (*a*) Entaille *f,* encoche *f,* cran *m.* (*b*) Brèche *f* (dans une lame).

notch², *v.tr.* (*a*) Entailler, encocher. (*b*) Ébrécher (une lame).

note¹, *s.* **1.** (*a*) Note *f;* caractère *m* de musique. (*b*) Touche *f* (d'un piano). (*c*) Note, son *m.* **2.** Marque *f,* signe *m,* indice *m.* **Note of exclamation,** point *m* d'exclamation. **3.** (*a*) Note, mémorandum *m.* *To make a n. of sth.,* noter qch.; prendre note de qch. (*b*) Note, annotation *f.* (*c*) Billet *m;* petite lettre. **4.** *Com:* (*a*) **Note of hand,** reconnaissance *f.* (*b*) (**Bank**) **note,** billet (de banque). **5.** (*a*) **Man of note,** homme marquant. (*b*) **Nothing of note,** rien d'important. **To take note of sth.,** remarquer qch. **note-book,** *s.* Carnet *m,* calepin *m.* **note-case,** *s.* Porte-billets *m inv.* **note-paper,** *s.* Papier *m* à lettres, à écrire.

note², *v.tr.* **1.** Noter, constater, remarquer, prendre note de. **2.** **To note sth.** (down), écrire, inscrire, qch. **noted,** *a.* Distingué, éminent; (*of thg*) célèbre (*for sth.,* par qch.).

noteworthy, *a.* Remarquable; digne d'attention, de remarque.

nothing. I. *s. or pron.* Rien (*with* ne *expressed or understood*). (*a*) **Nothing could be simpler,** rien de plus simple. **To say nothing of,** sans parler de. **There's nothing in these rumours,** ces bruits sont sans fondement. *He was nothing if not discreet,* il était discret avant tout. *Out of n.,* de toutes pièces. (*b*) **Nothing new,** rien de nouveau. **Nothing much,** pas grand'chose. (*c*) *I have n. to do with it,* je n'y suis pour rien. *That is nothing to do with you,* cela ne vous regarde pas. **There is nothing to cry about,** il n'y a pas de quoi pleurer. (*d*) **He is nothing of a scholar,** ce n'est pas du tout un savant. (*e*) **Nothing else,** rien d'autre. **Nothing but the truth,** rien que la vérité. *He does n. but go in and out,* il ne fait qu'entrer et sortir. *There was n. for it but to wait,* force nous fut d'attendre. (*f*) **All that goes for nothing,** tout cela ne compte pas. (*g*) **She is nothing to him,** elle lui est indifférente. (*h*) **To think nothing of sth.,** ne faire aucun cas de qch. **II. nothing,** *s.* **1.** *Ar:* Zéro *m.* **2.** Néant *m;* rien *m.* **To come to nothing,** ne pas aboutir. **A mere nothing!** une misère! **III. nothing,** *adv.* Aucunement, nullement; pas du tout. **Nothing loath,** volontiers, sans

hésiter. **Nothing near** *so large*, loin d'être aussi grand. *It is nothing less than madness*, c'est de la folie ni pl s ni moins.
notice¹, *s.* **I.** (*a*) Avis *m*, notification *f*. (*b*) Avertissement *m*. **To give s.o. notice of sth.**, prévenir qn de qch. **Public notice**, avis au public. **Until further notice**, jusqu'à nouvel avis. (*c*) Avis formel, instructions formelles. **To give s.o. n. to do sth.**, aviser qn de faire qch. (*d*) **At short notice**, à court délai. **At a moment's notice**, à la minute. (*e*) **Notice to quit**, congé *m*. **To give notice to an employee**, donner son congé à un employé. **To give notice (to one's employer)**, donner sa démission. **2.** (*a*) Affiche *f*; indication *f*, avis. (*b*) (*In newspaper*) Annonce *f*. (*c*) Revue *f* (d'un ouvrage). **3.** **To take notice of sth.**, tenir compte, prendre connaissance, de qch. **To take no notice of sth.**, ne faire aucune attention à qch. **To come into notice**, commencer à être connu.
notice-board, *s.* Écriteau *m*; tableau *m* d'annonces.
notice², *v.tr.* Observer, remarquer, s'apercevoir de. *I have never noticed it*, je n'y ai jamais pris garde.
noticeable, *a.* Perceptible, sensible. **It is not noticeable**, cela ne se voit pas. **-ably,** *adv.* Perceptiblement, sensiblement.
notification, *s.* Avis *m*, notification *f*, annonce *f*; déclaration *f*.
notify, *v.tr.* Annoncer, notifier. **To notify the police of sth.**, signaler qch. à la police.
notion, *s* (*a*) Notion *f*, idée *f*. (*b*) Opinion *f*, pensée *f*. **I have a notion that**, j'ai dans l'idée que. (*c*) Caprice *m*. **As the notion takes him**, selon son caprice.
notoriety, *s.* **I.** Notoriété *f*. **To seek notoriety**, s'afficher. **2.** Notabilité *f*.
notorious, *a.* **I.** Notoire, bien connu. **2.** Insigne; (malfaiteur) reconnu notoire; (endroit) mal famé. **-ly,** *adv.* Notoirement.
notwithstanding. I. *prep.* Malgré; en dépit de. **This notwithstanding**, ce non-obstant. **2.** *adv.* Quand même, tout de même; néanmoins, pourtant.
nought, *s.* = NAUGHT.
noun, *s.* *Gram:* Substantif *m*, nom *m*.
nourish, *v.tr.* **I.** Nourrir; alimenter. **2.** *F:* Nourrir, entretenir. **nourishing,** *a.* Nourrissant, nutritif.
nourishment, *s.* **I.** Alimentation *f*, nourriture *f*. **2.** Nourriture, aliments *mpl*.
nous, *s.* *F:* Intelligence *f*.
Nova Scotia. *Pr.n.* *Geog:* La Nouvelle-Écosse.
novel¹, *s.* Roman *m*.
novel², *a.* Nouveau, -elle; original, -aux; singulier. *That's a n. idea!* voilà qui est original !
novelist, *s.* Romancier, -ière.
novelty, *s.* **I.** Chose nouvelle; innovation *f*. *Com:* (Article *m* de) nouveauté *f*. **2.** Nouveauté (de qch.).

November, *s.* Novembre *m*. *In N.*, au mois de novembre.
novice, *s.* **I.** *Ecc:* Novice *mf*. **2.** *F:* Novice, apprenti, -ie, débutant, -ante.
now. I. *adv.* **I.** Maintenant. (*a*) En ce moment, actuellement, à l'heure actuelle. (*b*) *He won't be long now*, il ne tardera plus guère. (*c*) Tout de suite. *Now I'm ready*, me voilà prêt. (*d*) (*In narrative*) Alors; à ce moment-là. *He was even now on his way*, il était déjà en route. (*e*) (Every) **now and then**, de temps en temps. **Now . . . now . ., tantôt . . . tantôt. . . . Even now**, même à cette heure tardive. **2.** (*a*) *Now Barabbas was a robber*, or Barabbas était un brigand. *Now this was little enough*, c'était déjà peu. (*b*) *Now what's the matter with you?* qu'avez-vous donc? **Come now!** voyons, voyons ! **Well now!** eh bien ! **Now then!** (i) attention ! (ii) voyons ! allons ! **II. now,** *conj.* Maintenant que, à présent que. **III. now,** *s.* **In three days from now**, d'ici trois jours. **By now**, à l'heure qu'il est. **Until now**, jusqu'ici. **From now (on)**, dès maintenant, dès à présent.
nowadays, *adv.* Aujourd'hui; de nos jours; par le temps qui court.
nowhere, *adv.* Nulle part; en aucun lieu.
noxious, *a.* Nuisible, nocif; malfaisant.
nozzle, *s.* Ajutage *m*; jet *m*, lance *f* (de tuyau); bec *m*, tuyau *m* (de soufflet).
nucleus, *s.* Noyau *m*.
nude. I. *a.* Nu. **2.** *s.* *Art:* Nudité *f*; figure nue. **To draw from the nude**, dessiner d'après le nu.
nudge¹, *s.* Coup *m* de coude.
nudge², *v.tr.* Pousser du coude.
nudist, *s.* Nudiste *mf*.
nudity, *s.* Nudité *f*.
nugget, *s.* Pépite *f* (d'or).
nuisance, *s.* *F:* *He is a perfect n.!*, il est assommant. *Go away, you're a n.!* va-t'en, tu m'embêtes ! *That's a nuisance!* voilà qui est bien ennuyeux ! *What a nuisance!* quel ennui !
null, *a.* **Null and void**, nul et de nul effet, nul et non avenu.
nullify, *v.tr.* Annuler, nullifier.
nullity, *s.* **I.** *Jur:* Nullité *f*, invalidité *f*. **2. A nullity**, une non-valeur; un homme nul.
numb¹, *a.* Engourdi.
numb², *v.tr.* Engourdir.
number¹, *s.* **I.** (*a*) *Ar:* Nombre *m*. (*b*) *They were six in number*, ils étaient au nombre de six. *Books without number*, des livres innombrables. (*c*) **A (large) number of men were killed**, nombre d'hommes furent tués. (*d*) *pl.* Numbers. *In small numbers*, en petit nombre. *To be overpowered by numbers*, succomber sous le nombre. (*e*) **One of their number**, (l')un d'entre eux. **2.** Chiffre *m*. *To write the n. on a page*, mettre le chiffre à une page. **3.** Numéro *m* (d'une maison). **I live at number forty**, je demeure au numéro

quarante. *F:* His number is up, son affaire
est faite. **4.** *Gram:* Nombre. **5.** *Publ:*
Numéro (d'un journal).
number², *v.tr.* **1.** Compter, dénombrer.
His days are numbered, ses jours sont
comptés. **2.** Numéroter (les maisons).
numbering-machine, *s.* Numéroteur *m.*
numberless, *a.* Innombrable ; sans nombre.
numbness, *s.* Engourdissement *m.*
numeral. **1.** *a.* Numéral, -aux. **2.** *s.* Chiffre
m, nombre *m.*
numerator, *s. Mth:* Numérateur *m.*
numerical, *a.* Numérique. **-ally,** *adv.*
Numériquement.
numerous, *a.* Nombreux.
numismatics, *s.pl.* La numismatique.
numismatist, *s.* Numismate *m.*
numskull, *s. F:* Nigaud, -aude.
nun, *s. Ecc:* Religieuse *f, F:* nonne *f.*
nunnery, *s.* Couvent *m* (de religieuses).
nuptial. **1.** *a.* Nuptial, -aux. **2.** *s.pl.* Nuptials, noces *f.*
nurse¹, *s.* **1.** (*a*) (Wet-)nurse, nourrice *f.*
(*b*) Bonne *f* (d'enfants). **2.** (Sick-)nurse,
garde-malade *f, pl.* gardes-malades. Hospital
nurse, infirmière *f.* Male nurse, garde-malade
m ; infirmier *m.*
nurse², *v.tr.* **1.** Soigner (un malade). **2.** Nourrir, entretenir (un chagrin). **3.** Bercer (un
enfant) ; tenir dans ses bras. **nursing,** *s.*

(*a*) Soins *mpl* (d'une garde-malade.) (*b*) Profession *f* de garde-malade. To go in for
nursing, se faire infirmière. **nursing home,**
s. Clinique *f* ; hôpital privé.
nursemaid, *s.* Bonne *f* d'enfants.
nursery, *s.* **1.** Chambre *f* des enfants ;
nursery *f.* Nursery rhyme, chanson *f* de
nourrice. **2.** Pépinière *f.* **nursery-gover-
ness,** *s.* Gouvernante *f* pour jeunes enfants.
nurseryman, *s.* Pépiniériste *m.*
nursling, *s.* Nourrisson *m.*
nurture, *v.tr.* **1.** Nourrir (on, de). **2.** Élever.
nut, *s.* **1.** (*a*) Noix *f. F:* Tough nut to
crack, (i) problème *m* difficile à résoudre ;
(ii) personne difficile. (*b*) *P:* Tête *f.* To
be off one's nut, être timbré. **2.** Écrou *m.*
nut-brown, *a.* (Couleur) noisette *inv.*
Nut-brown hair, cheveux châtains. **nut-
cracker,** *s.* (Pair of) nut-crackers, casse-
noisette(s) *m inv. F:* Nut-cracker chin,
menton en casse-noisette. **nut-tree,** *s.*
Noisetier *m.*
nutmeg, *s.* (Noix *f*) muscade *f.*
nutriment, *s.* Nourriture *f.*
nutrition, *s.* Nutrition *f.*
nutritious, *a.* Nutritif, nourrissant.
nutritive, *a.* Nutritif, nourrissant.
nutshell, *s.* Coquille *f* de noix. In a nutshell, en un mot.
nymph, *s. Myth:* Nymphe *f.*

O

O¹, o, *s.* **1.** (La lettre) O, o *m.* **2.** *Tp:*
Zéro *m.*
O², *int.* O, oh. O how tired I am! ah! que
je suis fatigué! O to be in England! que ne
suis-je en Angleterre!
oaf, *s.* Lourdaud *m.*
oafish, *a.* Lourdaud, stupide.
oak, *s.* (*a*) *Bot:* Oak(-tree), chêne *m.* Oak-
plantation, chênaie *f.* (*b*) (Bois *m* de) chêne.
(*c*) To sport one's oak, défendre sa porte.
oak-apple, *s.* Pomme *f* de chêne.
oakum, *s.* Étoupe *f*, filasse *f.*
oar, *s.* Aviron *m*, rame *f.* To rest on one's
oars, *F:* dormir sur ses lauriers. *F:* To
put in one's oar, intervenir.
oarsman, *s.* Rameur *m* ; tireur *m* d'aviron ;
Nau: nageur *m.*
oasis, *s.* Oasis *f.*
oat, *s.* Avoine *f. F:* To sow one's wild oats,
faire des fredaines.
oaten, *a.* D'avoine.
oath, *s.* **1.** Serment *m.* I'll take my oath on
it, j'en jurerais. On oath, sous (la foi du)
serment. **2.** Juron *m* ; gros mot.
oatmeal, *s.* Farine *f* d'avoine.

obduracy, *s.* (*a*) Endurcissement *m* ; opiniâtreté *f.* (*b*) Inflexibilité *f.*
obdurate, *a.* (*a*) Endurci ; têtu, opiniâtre.
(*b*) Inexorable, inflexible.
obedience, *s.* Obéissance *f* (to, à). To
compel obedience, se faire obéir. *Com:* In
obedience to your orders, conformément à
vos ordres.
obedient, *a.* Obéissant, soumis, docile. To
be o. to s.o., obéir à qn. **-ly,** *adv.* Avec
obéissance. *Corr:* Yours obediently, agréez,
Monsieur, mes salutations empressées.
obeisance, *s.* **1.** Salut *m*, révérence *f.* To
make (an) obeisance to s.o., s'incliner devant
qn. **2.** Obéissance *f*, hommage *m.*
obelisk, *s. Archeol:* Obélisque *m.*
obese, *a.* Obèse.
obesity, *s.* Obésité *f.*
obey, *v.tr.* Obéir à. He is obeyed, il est obéi.
obituary, *a. & s.* Nécrologe *m.* Obituary
notice, notice nécrologique.
object¹, *s.* (*a*) Objet *m*, chose *f.* (*b*) O. of
pity, objet ou sujet *m* de pitié. **2.** (*a*) But *m*,
objectif *m*, objet. With this object (in view),
à cette fin. There's no object in doing that,

cela ne sert à rien de faire cela. (b) F: **Expense is no object**, on ne regarde pas à la dépense. **3.** Gram: Complément m, régime m, objet. **object-lesson**, s. Sch: Leçon f de choses.

object², v.i. **To object to sth.**, faire objection, trouver à redire, à qch. Do you o. to my smoking? la fumée vous gêne-t-elle?

objection, s. **1.** Objection f. **To raise an objection**, soulever une objection. **To take objection to sth.**, se fâcher de qch. I have no o. to his doing so, je ne m'oppose pas à ce qu'il le fasse. **If you have no objection**, si cela ne vous fait rien. **2.** Obstacle m, inconvénient m.

objectionable, a. **1.** Répréhensible. **2.** Désagréable. Idea that is most o. to me, idée qui me répugne.

objective. 1. a. Gram: **Objective case**, cas régime, cas objectif. **2.** s. But m, objectif m.

oblate, a. Geom: Aplati (aux pôles).

oblation, s. Ecc: Oblation f.

obligation, s. Obligation f. (a) Dette f de reconnaissance. **To be under an obligation to s.o.**, devoir de la reconnaissance à qn. **To put s.o. under an obligation**, obliger qn. (b) **To meet one's obligations**, faire honneur à ses engagements.

obligatory, a. Obligatoire; de rigueur.

oblige, v.tr. **1.** Obliger, astreindre. **To be obliged to do sth.**, être obligé, tenu, de faire qch. **2.** (a) **To oblige a friend**, rendre service à un ami. Can you o. me with a light? auriez-vous l'amabilité de me donner du feu? In order to o. you, pour vous être agréable. (b) **To be obliged to s.o.**, être obligé à qn.

obliging, a. Obligeant, serviable. **-ly**, adv. Obligeamment.

obligingness, s. Obligeance f.

oblique, a. Oblique; de biais. **-ly**, adv. Obliquement, de biais.

obliterate, v.tr. (a) Faire disparaître, effacer. (b) Oblitérer (un timbre).

obliteration, s. **1.** (a) Effaçage m. (b) Rature f. **2.** Oblitération f (d'un timbre).

oblivion, s. (État m d')oubli m. **To sink into oblivion**, tomber dans l'oubli.

oblivious, a. **1.** Oublieux (of, de). **2.** F: To be totally o. of sth., ignorer tout à fait qch.

oblong. 1. a. Oblong, -ongue. **2.** s. Rectangle m.

obloquy, s. (a) Calomnie f. (b) Honte f, opprobre m.

obnoxious, a. (a) Odieux; antipathique (to s.o., à qn). (b) (Odeur) repoussante.

oboe, s. Hautbois m.

obscene, a. Obscène.

obscenity, s. Obscénité f.

obscure¹, a. **1.** Obscur, ténébreux, sombre. **2.** Obscur; peu clair. **3.** O. author, auteur peu connu. **-ly**, adv. Obscurément.

obscure², v.tr. Obscurcir. Clouds obscured the sun, des nuages voilaient le soleil.

obscurity, s. Obscurité f.

obsequies, s.pl. Obsèques f, funérailles f.

obsequious, a. Obséquieux. **-ly**, adv. Obséquieusement.

obsequiousness, s. Obséquiosité f.

observable, a. Visible; perceptible.

observance, s. **1.** Observation f, observance f. **2.** Religious observances, pratiques religieuses.

observant, a. **1.** Observateur, -trice. **2.** He is very o., rien ne lui échappe.

observation, s. Observation f. **1.** (a) To keep s.o. under observation, tenir qn en observation. **To escape observation**, se dérober aux regards. (b) Nau: **To take an observation**, faire le point. **2.** Remarque f.

observatory, s. Observatoire m.

observe, v.tr. **1.** Observer; se conformer à. **To observe silence**, observer le silence. **2.** Observer, regarder. **3.** Apercevoir, remarquer, noter. **4.** Dire.

observer, s. Observateur, -trice.

obsess, v.tr. Obséder.

obsession, s. Obsession f.

obsolete, a. Désuet, -ète; hors d'usage; tombé en désuétude; suranné.

obstacle, s. Obstacle m, empêchement m. Sp: **Obstacle-race**, course f d'obstacles.

obstinacy, s. Obstination f, entêtement m, opiniâtreté f. To show o., s'obstiner.

obstinate, a. Obstiné (in doing sth., à faire qch.); opiniâtre. **Obstinate as a mule**, entêté, têtu, comme un mulet. **-ly**, adv. Obstinément, opiniâtrement.

obstreperous, a. Bruyant, tapageur, -euse; turbulent.

obstruct, v.tr. (a) Obstruer; encombrer. **To obstruct the view**, gêner la vue. (b) Gêner, entraver (les mouvements de qn).

obstruction, s. **1.** (a) Engorgement m (d'un tuyau). (b) Empêchement m (de qn dans ses affaires). **2.** Encombrement m. Rail: An o. on the line, un obstacle sur la voie.

obstructive, a. Obstructif.

obtain. 1. v.tr. Obtenir; se procurer. **2.** v.i. Avoir cours; prévaloir. System now obtaining, régime actuellement en vigueur.

obtainable, a. Procurable.

obtrude, v.tr. & i. Mettre (qch.) en avant. To o. (oneself) on s.o., importuner qn.

obtrusion, s. Intrusion f; importunité f.

obtrusive, a. Importun; indiscret, -ète.

obtrusiveness, s. Importunité f.

obtuse, a. Obtus.

obviate, v.tr. Éviter, parer à, obvier à.

obvious, a. Évident, clair, manifeste. O. fact, fait patent. It was the obvious thing to do, c'était indiqué. **-ly**, adv. Évidemment, manifestement.

occasion¹, s. **1.** Cause f, occasion f. There's no o. to crow, il n'y a pas de quoi chanter victoire. **Should the occasion arise**, s'il y a lieu; le cas échéant. **2.** Occasion, occurrence f. **On the occasion of**, à l'occasion de; lors de. **On one occasion**, une fois. **On several**

occasions, à plusieurs reprises. **On occasion,** de temps à autre. **As occasion requires,** suivant l'occasion ; au besoin.
occasion², *v.tr.* Occasionner, donner lieu à.
occasional, *a. An o. visitor,* un visiteur qui vient de temps en temps. **Occasional showers,** averses éparses. **-ally,** *adv.* De temps en temps.
occident, *s.* Occident *m.*
occidental, *a.* Occidental, -aux.
occult, *a.* Occulte.
occupancy, *s.* Occupation *f,* habitation *f.*
occupant, *s.* Occupant, -ante.
occupation, *s.* Occupation *f.* **1. To be in occupation** *of a house,* occuper une maison. **2.** (*a*) **To give s.o. occupation,** donner de l'occupation à qn. (*b*) Métier *m,* emploi *m.*
occupier, *s.* Occupant, -ante ; locataire *mf* ; habitant, -ante (d'une maison).
occupy, *v.tr.* **1.** Occuper. (*a*) Habiter (une maison). (*b*) Garnir (une place de guerre). **2.** Remplir (un espace) ; occuper (l· temps). **3.** Occuper ; donner du travail à. **To keep one's mind occupied,** s'occuper l'esprit.
occur, *v.i.* **1.** Avoir lieu ; arriver ; se produire. *If another opportunity occurs,* si une autre occasion se présente. **Don't let it occur again!** que cela n'arrive plus ! **2.** Se rencontrer, se trouver. **3.** *It occurs to me that,* il me vient à l'idée que.
occurrence, *s.* **1. To be of frequent occurrence,** arriver souvent. **2.** Événement *m,* occurrence *f.*
ocean, *s.* Océan *m.* **Ocean currents,** courants océaniques.
Oceania. *Pr.n.* L'Océanie *f.*
oceanic, *a.* Océanique.
ocelot, *s.* *Z :* Ocelot *m.*
ochre, *s.* *Miner :* Ocre *f.* **Yellow ochre,** jaune *m* d'ocre.
o'clock, *adv.phr.* See CLOCK.
octagon, *s.* *Geom :* Octogone *m.*
octagonal, *a.* Octogonal, -aux.
octave, *s.* Octave *f.*
octavo, *a. & s.* *Typ :* In-octavo (*m*).
octet(te), *s.* *Mus :* Octuor *m.*
October, *s.* Octobre *m.* *In O.,* au mois d'octobre.
octogenarian, *a. & s.* Octogénaire (*mf*).
octopus, *s.* Poulpe *m* ; pieuvre *f.*
ocular, *a.* Oculaire.
oculist, *s.* Oculiste *m.*
odd, *a.* **1.** (*a*) Impair. (*b*) **Twenty pounds odd,** vingt livres et quelques shillings. *The odd three halfpence,* les trois sous de reste. **To be odd man,** rester en surnombre. **The odd game,** la belle. **2.** (*a*) Dépareillé. (*b*) **Odd moments,** moments de loisir, moments perdus. **At odd times,** par-ci par-là. **Odd man,** homme à tout faire. *Com :* **Odd lot,** solde *m.* **3.** Singulier, drôle ; (*of pers.*) excentrique. **Well, that's odd!** voilà qui est singulier ! **-ly,** *adv.* Bizarrement, singulièrement. **Oddly enough,** chose curieuse.

oddity, *s.* **1.** Singularité *f,* bizarrerie *f.* **2.** Personne *f* excentrique.
oddments, *s.pl.* *Com :* Fonds *m* de boutique.
oddness, *s.* **1.** Imparité *f.* **2.** Singularité *f,* bizarrerie *f.*
odds, *s.pl.* **1.** (*a*) Avantage *m* ; chances *fpl.* **The odds are against him,** les chances sont contre lui. **To fight against odds,** lutter contre des forces supérieures. (*b*) Différence *f.* **What's the odds?** qu'est-ce que ça fait? (*c*) *Turf :* Long odds, forte cote. **2. To be at odds with s.o.,** être brouillé avec qn. **3. Odds and ends,** petits bouts ; bribes *f* et morceaux *m.*
ode, *s.* *Lit :* Ode *f.*
odious, *a.* Odieux (*to,* à) ; détestable. **-ly,** *adv.* Odieusement, détestablement.
odiousness, *s.* Caractère odieux, l'odieux *m.*
odium, *s.* Réprobation *f* ; détestation *f.*
odoriferous, *a.* Odoriférant, parfumé.
odorous, *a.* Odorant.
odour, *s.* **1.** (*a*) Odeur *f.* (*b*) Parfum *m.* **2. To be in bad odour,** être en mauvaise odeur (*with s.o.,* auprès de qn).
odourless, *a.* Inodore ; sans odeur.
Odyssey, *s.* Odyssée *f.*
of, *prep.* De. **1.** (*a*) *South of,* au sud de. *Free of,* libre de. (*b*) (i) *To buy sth. of s.o.,* acheter qch. à, chez, qn. (ii) *Of necessity,* par nécessité. *The miracle came about of itself,* le miracle s'est accompli tout seul. **2.** *It is very kind of you,* c'est bien aimable de votre part. **3.** *Made of wood,* fait de, en, bois. **4.** (*a*) *Doctor of medicine,* docteur en médecine. (*b*) *F :* **Well, what of it?** eh bien, et après ? **5.** (*a*) (i) *Trees of my planting,* arbres que j'ai plantés moi-même. *People of foreign appearance,* gens à l'air étranger. (ii) *Swift of foot,* aux pieds légers. (b) *That fool of a sergeant,* cet imbécile de sergent. (*c*) *All of a tremble,* tout tremblant. **6.** (*a*) *How much of it do you want?* combien en voulez-vous ? *Two of them died,* deux d'entre eux moururent. *There were several of us,* nous étions plusieurs. *Of the twenty only one was bad,* sur les vingt un seul était mauvais. (*b*) *The best of men,* le meilleur des hommes. *The one he loved most of all,* celui qu'il aimait entre tous. (*c*) *The one thing of all others that I want,* ce que je désire par-dessus tout, avant tout. (*d*) *A fool of fools,* un triple sot. **7.** (*a*) *The first of June,* le premier juin. (*b*) *He is a friend of mine,* c'est un de mes amis. *It's no business of yours,* ce n'est pas votre affaire **8. What do you do of a Sunday?** que faites-vous le dimanche ?
off. **I.** *adv.* **1.** (*a*) *House a mile off,* maison à un mille de distance. *To keep s.o. off,* empêcher qn d'approcher. (*b*) **To go off,** s'en aller, partir. **Be off!** allez-vous-en ! filez ! **They're off!** les voilà partis ! **Off we go!** (i) en route ! (ii) nous voilà partis ! **To go off (to sleep),** s'endormir. (*c*) *Th :* 'Off,' à la cantonade. **2.** (*a*) **Hats off!** chapeaux bas !

Off with your boots! ôtez vos souliers! **Dish that is off,** plat qui est épuisé. **The concert is off,** le concert n'aura pas lieu. (b) *To finish off a piece of work,* parachever un travail. **3.** **To be badly off,** être dans la gêne. *He is better off where he is,* il est bien mieux où il est. **4.** *Adv.phr.* **Off and on,** par intervalles. **Right off,** immédiatement. II. **off,** *prep.* **1.** (a) *Usu.* De. *To fall off one's horse,* tomber à bas de son cheval. **To take sth. off a shelf,** prendre qch. sur une tablette. **To take sth. off the price,** rabattre qch. du prix. (b) Écarté de, éloigné de. *A yard off me,* à un mètre de moi. *Street off the main road,* rue qui donne sur la grande route. *Fb:* **Player off side,** joueur hors jeu. (c) **To be off one's food,** n'avoir pas d'appétit. **To have a day off,** avoir un jour de congé. **2.** *Nau:* **Off the Cape,** au large du Cap. *Off Calais,* devant Calais. III. **off,** *a.* Off day, jour de liberté. Off season, mortesaison *f.* **off-hand. 1.** *adv.* (a) Sans préparation; au pied levé. (b) Sans cérémonie, sans façon; d'un air dégagé. **2.** *a.* (a) Spontané. (b) Brusque, cavalier; désinvolte. **off-handed,** *a.* = OFF-HAND 2 (b). **-ly,** *adv.* = OFF-HAND 1 (b). **off-handedness,** *s.* Brusquerie *f*, sans-façon *m*, désinvolture *f.*

offal, *s.* Rebut *m*, déchets *mpl.*

offence, *s.* **1.** **To take offence (at sth.),** se froisser (de qch.); *F:* prendre la mouche. **To give offence to s.o.,** offenser, froisser, qn. **I meant no offence,** je ne voulais offenser personne. **2.** Offense *f*, faute *f.*

offend. 1. *v.i.* Pécher. **2.** *v.tr.* (a) Offenser, froisser. **To be offended at sth.,** se piquer de qch. **To be easily offended,** être très susceptible. (b) **To offend the eye,** choquer les regards. **offending,** *a.* Offensant, fautif.

offender, *s.* *Jur:* Délinquant, -ante. *The chief o.,* le grand coupable.

offensive. 1. *a.* (a) *Mil:* Offensif. (b) Offensant, choquant; (odeur) nauséabonde. (c) **To be offensive to s.o.,** dire des grossièretés à qn. **2.** *s.* *Mil:* **To take the offensive,** prendre l'offensive *f.* **-ly,** *adv.* **1.** *Mil:* Offensivement. **2.** Désagréablement.

offer¹, *s.* Offre *f.* **Offer of marriage,** demande *f* en mariage.

offer². 1. *v.tr.* (a) *To o. s.o. sth.,* offrir qch. à qn. **To offer battle,** inviter le combat. **To offer to do sth.,** offrir de, s'offrir à, faire qch. (b) **To offer a remark,** faire une remarque. (c) Présenter, offrir. (d) **To offer resistance,** faire (de la) résistance. **2.** *v.i.* S'offrir, se présenter. **offering,** *s.* **1.** (*Action*) Offre *f.* **2.** Offre; *Ecc:* offrande *f.* **Burnt offering,** holocauste *m.*

office, *s.* **1.** (a) Office *m*, service *m.* (b) Last offices, derniers devoirs. **2.** (a) Fonctions *fpl.* (b) Charge *f*, emploi *m.* **To be in office,** être au pouvoir. **3.** (a) Bureau *m*; (*lawyer's*) étude *f.* **Head office, registered offices,** bureau central; siège (social). (b) **Private**

office, cabinet particulier. (c) Government office, ministère *m.* **The War Office** = le ministère de la Guerre. (d) *pl.* **Offices** (*of a house*), communs *m* et dépendances *f.* **office-boy,** *s.* Saute-ruisseau *m inv.*

officer, *s.* **1.** Fonctionnaire *m*, officier *m.* **Police officer,** agent *m* de police. **2.** *Mil:* Officier. **Staff officer,** officier d'état-major. *Sch:* **Officers' training corps,** bataillon *m* scolaire.

official. 1. *a.* (a) Officiel. (b) **Official news,** nouvelles authentiques, officielles. **2.** *s.* Fonctionnaire *m.* **Railway official,** employé *m* des chemins de fer. **-ally,** *adv.* Officiellement.

officiate, *v.i.* **1.** *Ecc:* *To o. at a service,* officier à un office. **2.** *F:* **To officiate as host,** remplir les fonctions d'hôte.

officious, *a.* Empressé; trop zélé.

officiousness, *s.* Excès *m* de zèle.

offing, *s.* *Nau:* **In the offing,** au large.

offset¹, *s.* Compensation *f*, dédommagement *m.* *As an o. to my losses,* en compensation de mes pertes.

offset², *v.tr.* Compenser.

offshoot, *s.* Rejeton *m.*

offspring, *s.* **1.** *Coll.* Progéniture *f*, descendance *f*; descendants *mpl.* **2.** Descendant, rejeton *m.*

oft, *adv.* *Poet:* Souvent. **Many a time and oft,** mainte(s) et mainte(s) fois.

often, *adv.* Souvent, fréquemment, mainte(s) fois. **How often?** combien de fois? *F:* **As often as not, more often than not,** le plus souvent.

ogive, *s.* Ogive *f.*

ogle, *v.tr.* Lancer des œillades à.

ogre, *f.* **ogress,** *s.* Ogre, *f.* ogresse.

oh, *int.* = O².

oil¹, *s.* Huile *f.* **1.** *F:* **To burn the midnight oil,** travailler fort avant dans la nuit. **Painting in oil(s),** peinture à l'huile. **2.** **Paraffin oil,** pétrole (lampant). **Fuel oil,** mazout *m.* **3.** **Essential oil,** huile essentielle; essence *f.* **oil-can,** *s.* Burette *f* à huile. **oil-colour,** *s.* Couleur *f* à l'huile. **oil-field,** *s.* *Geol:* Gisement *m* pétrolifère. **oil-painting,** *s.* Tableau peint à l'huile. **oil-stove,** *s.* Fourneau *m* à pétrole. **oil-well,** *s.* Puits *m* pétrolifère; puits de, à, pétrole.

oil², *v.tr.* Huiler, graisser. **To oil the wheels,** *F:* faciliter les choses. **To oil s.o.'s palm,** graisser la patte à qn. **oiled,** *a.* (a) Graissé. (b) Oiled silk, taffetas *m* imperméable.

oiling, *s.* Graissage *m*, huilage *m.*

oilcloth, *s.* Linoléum imprimé.

oiliness, *s.* Aspect graisseux; onctuosité *f.*

oilman, *s.* Marchand *m* de couleurs; droguiste *m.*

oilskin, *s.* Toile cirée.

oilstone, *s.* *Tls:* Pierre *f* à huile.

oily, *a.* **1.** Huileux. **2.** *F:* Onctueux.

ointment, *s.* Onguent *m*, pommade *f.*

O.K.¹, *a.* *F:* (a) Très bien! d'accord! (b) *Everything is O.K.,* tout est en règle.

O.K.², *v.tr.* *F:* Passer, approuver.
old, *a.* **1.** (*a*) Vieux, *f.* vieille; âgé. *My old friend*, mon vieil ami. **To be growing old**, se faire vieux. **An old man**, un vieillard. **An old woman**, une vieille. **Old wives' tale**, conte de bonne femme. *s.pl.* **Old and young**, grands et petits. **Old age**, la vieillesse. *To die at a good old age*, mourir à un âge avancé. (*b*) *Old clothes*, vieux habits. **2. How old are you?** quel âge avez-vous? **To be five years old**, avoir cinq ans; être âgé de cinq ans. *He is older than I*, il est plus âgé que moi; il est mon aîné. **To be old enough to do sth.**, être d'âge à faire qch. **3.** (*a*) Vieux, ancien; (famille) de vieille souche. (*b*) **Old hand**, ouvrier expérimenté. *He's an old hand (at it)*, il possède la pratique du métier. **4.** Ancien. (*a*) **Old boy**, ancien élève. (*b*) **The Old World**, l'ancien monde. **The Old Country**, la mère-patrie. **5.** *F:* (*a*) **Any old thing**, la première chose venue; n'importe quoi. (*b*) **Old man, old chap;** mon vieux, mon brave. **6. Of old.** (*a*) *Adj.phr.* Ancien, d'autrefois. (*b*) *Adv.phr.* (i) Jadis, autrefois. (ii) **I know him of old**, je le connais depuis longtemps. **old-clothes-man,** *s.* Marchand *m* d'habits; fripier *m.* **old-established,** *a.* Ancien; établi depuis longtemps. **old-fashioned,** *a.* **1.** Démodé; suranné. **2.** Arriéré.
olden, *a.* In olden time(s), au temps jadis.
oldish, *a.* Vieillot, -otte.
oleaginous, *a.* Oléagineux, huileux.
oleander, *s.* Oléandre *m.*
olfactory, *a.* Olfactif.
oligarchy, *s.* Oligarchie *f.*
olive, *s.* **1.** Olive(-tree), olivier *m.* **2.** Olive *f.* **olive-branch,** *s.* *F:* To hold out the olive-branch, faire les premières avances (pour une réconciliation). **olive-oil,** *s.* Huile *f* d'olive.
Oliver. *Pr.n.* Olivier *m.*
Olympian, *a. & s.* Olympien, -ienne.
Olympus. *Pr.n.* L'Olympe *m.*
omelet(te), *s. Cu:* Omelette *f.*
omen, *s.* Présage *m*, augure *m.* **Bird of ill omen**, oiseau de sinistre présage; porte-malheur *m inv.*
ominous, *a.* De mauvais augure; sinistre; inquiétant. **-ly**, *adv.* Sinistrement.
omission, *s.* **1.** Omission *f.* **2.** Négligence *f.*
omit, *v.tr.* **1.** Omettre. **2. To omit to do sth.**, oublier, omettre, de faire qch.
omnibus, *s.* (Horse-)omnibus, omnibus *m.* (motor) omnibus, autobus *m.*
omnipotence, *s.* Omnipotence *f.*
omnipotent, *a.* Omnipotent.
omnivorous, *a.* Omnivore.
on. **I.** *prep.* **1.** (*a*) *Usu.* Sur. *Do not tread on it*, ne marchez pas dessus. *On the high seas*, en haute mer. (*b*) *On shore*, à terre. *On foot*, à pied. *On horseback*, à cheval. (*c*) **To be on the committee**, être membre du comité. *To be on the staff*, faire partie du personnel.

2. (*a*) *Hanging on the wall*, pendu au mur. *On the ceiling*, au plafond. **Have you any money on you?** avez-vous de l'argent (sur vous)? *On page four*, à la page quatre. (*b*) *Just on a year ago*, il y a près d'un an. **3.** (*a*) *On the right*, à droite. *On this side*, de ce côté. (*b*) **To smile on s.o.**, sourire à qn. (*c*) *To leave one's card on s.o.*, déposer une carte chez qn. **4.** *On good authority*, de source certaine. **On penalty of death**, sous peine de mort. *Dependent on circumstances*, qui dépend des circonstances. *On condition that*, à condition que. **5.** (*a*) **On Sundays**, le(s) dimanche(s). *On the following day*, le lendemain. **On April 3rd**, le trois avril. *On the evening of the first of June*, le premier juin au soir. (*b*) *On a warm day like this*, par une chaleur comme celle-ci. **On and after the fifteenth**, à partir du quinze. **On or about the twelfth**, vers le douze. *On that occasion*, à, dans, cette occasion. *On my arrival*, à mon arrivée. *On application*, sur demande. *On examination*, après examen. **6.** **On the cheap**, à bon marché. **On the sly**, en sourdine. **7. On sale**, en vente. **8.** *To congratulate s.o. on his success*, féliciter qn de son succès. **9.** *I am here on business*, je suis ici pour affaires. *On holiday*, en vacances. **10.** *To have pity on s.o.*, avoir pitié de qn. *Attack on s.o.*, attaque contre qn. **11. To live on one's private income**, vivre de ses rentes. **II. on**, *adv.* **1.** To have one's boots on, être chaussé. *What had he got on?* qu'est-ce qu'il portait? **On with your coat!** mettez votre veston! **2.** *To work on*, continuer son travail. *To talk on*, continuer à parler. **Go on!** continuez! allez toujours! *To toil on and on*, peiner sans fin. **And so on**, et ainsi de suite. **3.** Later on, plus tard. *From that day on*, à dater de ce jour. **Well on in April**, fort avant dans le mois d'avril. **Well on in years**, d'un âge avancé. **4.** *To turn on the tap*, ouvrir le robinet. 'On,' "ouvert"; (*of electric circuit*) "fermé." *The brakes are on*, les freins sont serrés. What is on (at the theatre) just now? qu'est-ce qui se joue actuellement? **5.** *F:* (*a*) **I'm on (for it)!** ça me va! (*b*) **He is always on at me**, il s'en prend toujours à moi.
once, *adv.* **1.** (*a*) Une fois. **Once only**, une seule fois. **Once a week**, tous les huit jours. **Once again**, encore une fois. **Once in a while**, une fois en passant. **Once (and) for all**, une (bonne) fois pour toutes. (*b*) *O. grasp this fact and everything becomes plain*, comprenez bien cela et tout s'éclaircit. **2.** Autrefois. **Once (upon a time) there was**, il était une fois. **I knew him once**, je l'ai connu autrefois. **3.** *At once.* (*a*) **Tout de suite;** à l'instant; sur-le-champ. (*b*) **Don't all speak at once**, ne parlez pas tous à la fois.
one. **I.** *num.a.* **1.** (*a*) Un. *Twenty-one apples*, vingt et une pommes. *A hundred and one*, cent un. (*b*) *F:* *That's one way of doing it*, c'est une manière comme une autre de le

faire. That's one comfort, c'est déjà une consolation. **2.** (*a*) Seul, unique. Like one man, comme un seul homme. (*b*) Même. *F:* It's all one, cela revient au même; c'est tout un. It's all one to me, cela m'est égal. II. **one,** *s.* **1.** *Eleven is written with two ones,* onze s'écrit avec deux un. *P:* To look after number one, mettre ses intérêts en premier lieu. **2.** (*a*) *There is only one left,* il n'en reste qu'un. The topmost stair but one, l'avant-dernière marche. To be at one with s.o., être d'accord avec qn. (*b*) One and sixpence, un shilling (et) six pence. One (o'clock), une heure. III. **one,** *dem.pron.* (*a*) *This one,* celui-ci, *f.* celle-ci. *Which one do you prefer?* lequel, laquelle, préférez-vous? *The one on the table,* celui, celle, qui est sur la table. *She is the one who helped Louise,* c'est elle qui a aidé Louise. (*b*) *To pick the ripe plums and leave the green ones,* cueillir les prunes mûres et laisser les vertes. That's a good one! celle-là est bonne! *He's a knowing one,* c'est un malin. *Our dear ones,* ceux qui nous sont chers. IV. **one,** *indef.a.* One day, un jour. *One stormy evening,* par une soirée orageuse. V. **one,** *indef.pron.* **1.** *I haven't a pencil, have you got one?* je n'ai pas de crayon, en avez-vous un? One of them, l'un d'eux. He is one of the family, il est de la famille. One and all, tous sans exception. One after the other, l'un après l'autre. One by one, un à un. **2.** Quelqu'un. *To one who can read between the lines,* à qui sait lire entre les lignes. I am not (the) one to, je ne suis pas de ceux qui. **3.** (*a*) On. (*b*) (*Acc.*) Vous. *It is enough to kill one,* il y a de quoi vous faire mourir. **4.** One's, son, *f.* sa, *pl.* ses; votre, *pl.* vos. *To give one's opinion,* donner son avis. *To cut one's finger,* se couper le doigt. **one-armed,** *a.* Manchot, -ote. **one-eyed,** *a.* Borgne. **one-legged,** *a.* Qui n'a qu'une jambe. **one-sided,** *a.* (*a*) (*Of bargain*) Inégal, -aux. (*b*) (*Of judgment*) Partial, -aux. **one-storied,** *a.* (Maison) sans étage. **one-way,** *attrib.a.* One-way street, rue à sens unique.

onerous, *a.* Onéreux; pénible.

oneself, *pron. See* SELF 3.

onion, *s.* Oignon *m.* Spring onion, ciboule *f.* **onion-sauce,** *s. Cu:* Sauce blanche à l'oignon.

onlooker, *s.* Spectateur, -trice. *The on-lookers,* les assistants *m.*

only. I. *a.* Seul, unique. His one and only hope, son seul et unique espoir. *His o. answer was to burst out laughing,* pour toute réponse il éclata de rire. II. **only,** *adv.* Seulement, ne . . . que. *I have o. three.—Only three?* je n'en ai que trois.—Que trois? *O. he can say,* lui seul saurait le dire. *I o. touched it,* je n'ai fait que le toucher. He has only to ask for it, il n'a qu'à le demander. *I will o. say,* je me bornerai à dire. Only to

think of it, rien que d'y penser. Only yesterday, hier encore; pas plus tard qu'hier. III. **only,** *conj.* Mais, seulement.

onset, *s.* Assaut *m,* attaque *f.*

onslaught, *s.* = ONSET.

onus, *s.* Responsabilité *f,* charge *f.*

onward. **1.** *adv.* = ONWARDS. **2.** *a.* En avant.

onwards, *adv.* (*a*) En avant. (*b*) From to-morrow onwards, à partir de demain. From this time onwards, désormais.

ooze[1], *s.* Vase *f,* limon *m.*

ooze[2], *v.i.* Suinter; dégoutter.

opal, *s. Lap:* Opale *f.*

opaque, *a.* Opaque.

open[1], *a.* Ouvert. **1.** (*a*) Half open, entr'ouvert, entrebâillé. To keep open house, tenir table ouverte. (*b*) (*Of box*) Ouvert; (*of bottle*) débouché. (*c*) Open to the public, ouvert, accessible, au public. (*d*) Open trial, jugement public. **2.** Sans limites; sans bornes. In the open air, *s.* in the open, au grand air, en plein air. Open country, pays découvert. *In the o. country,* en pleine campagne. The open sea, le large. **3.** (*a*) Open carriage, voiture découverte. Open light, feu nu. (*b*) *O. to every wind,* exposé à tous les vents. (*c*) To lay oneself open to criticism, donner prise à la critique. (*d*) To be open to conviction, être accessible à la conviction. **4.** (*a*) Manifeste; public, -ique. Open secret, secret de Polichinelle. (*b*) Franc. *O. admiration,* franche admiration. *O. enemy,* ennemi déclaré. To be open with s.o., parler franchement à qn; ne rien cacher à qn. **5.** Open wound, plaie béante. *Dress o. at the neck,* robe échancrée au col. **6.** Non serré. *Mil:* To attack in open order, attaquer en ordre dispersé. **7.** (*a*) Non obstrué. Open road, chemin libre. Open view, vue dégagée. (*b*) *The job is still o.,* la place est toujours vacante. *Two courses are o. to us,* deux moyens s'offrent à nous. It is open to you to object, il vous est permis de faire des objections. **8.** Non résolu. Open question, question discutable, indécise. To keep an open mind, rester sans parti pris. **-ly,** *adv.* Ouvertement, franchement, en toute franchise. **open-air,** *attrib.a.* Au grand air, en plein air. Open-air meeting, assemblée en plein vent. **open-handed,** *a.* Libéral, -aux; généreux. **open-hearted,** *a.* **1.** Franc, *f.* franche; expansif. **2.** Au cœur tendre, compatissant. **open-minded,** *a.* To be o.-m., n'avoir pas de parti pris. **open-mouthed,** *a.* Bouche bée.

open[2]. I. *v.tr.* **1.** (*a*) Ouvrir; baisser (une glace). (*b*) Déboucher (une bouteille); décacheter (une lettre); défaire (un paquet). To open the mail, dépouiller le courrier. (*c*) Inaugurer (une fête). **2.** Écarter (les jambes); ouvrir (la main). **3.** To open a road, ouvrir, frayer, un chemin. **4.** Découvrir, exposer, révéler. **5.** Commencer; entamer, engager (une conversation). II.

open, *v.i.* S'ouvrir. **I.** (*a*) *The exits o. on to the street*, les sorties donnent accès à la rue. (*b*) *As soon as the season opens*, dès l'ouverture de la saison. **2.** (*Of flower*) S'épanouir. **3.** Commencer. **open out. I.** *v.tr.* (*a*) Ouvrir, déplier. (*b*) Développer. **2.** *v.i.* (*Of view*) S'ouvrir, s'étendre. **open up,** *v.tr.* Ouvrir (une mine); exposer, révéler (une perspective); frayer, pratiquer (un chemin). **opening,** *s.* **I.** (*a*) Ouverture *f*; dépouillement *m* (du courrier). (*b*) *Formal opening*, inauguration *f.* **2.** Trou *m*, ouverture, orifice *m*; clairière *f* (dans un bois). **3.** Occasion *f* favorable. *Com:* Débouché *m*. *To give an adversary an opening*, prêter le flanc à un adversaire. **4.** *Attrib.* D'ouverture; inaugural, -aux. *O. sentence*, phrase de début.

openness, *s.* **I.** Situation exposée; aspect découvert. **2.** Franchise *f.*

opera, *s.* Opéra *m.* **Comic opera**, opéra bouffe. **opera-cloak,** *s.* Sortie *f* de théâtre.

opera-glass(es), *s.(pl.)* Jumelle(s) *f* (de théâtre).

operate. I. *v.i.* **I.** Opérer. **2.** *To operate on s.o.*, opérer qn. *To be operated (up)on*, subir une opération. **II. operate,** *v.tr.* Opérer, effectuer, accomplir.

operatic, *a.* D'opéra. **Operatic singer**, chanteur dramatique d'opéra.

operation, *s.* **I.** Fonctionnement *m*, action *f*. *To be in operation*, fonctionner, jouer. **2.** *Surg:* Opération *f.*

operative. I. *a.* Opératif, actif. *To become operative*, entrer en vigueur; prendre effet. **2.** *a. & s.* Ouvrier, -ière; artisan, -e.

operator, *s.* Opérateur, -trice. **Wireless operator**, sans-filiste *mf.*

operetta, *s. Mus:* Opérette *f.*

opiate, *s. Pharm:* Opiacé *m*, opiat *m.*

opinion, *s.* (*a*) Opinion *f*, avis *m.* *In my opinion*, à mon avis. *To be entirely of s.o.'s opinion*, abonder dans le sens de qn. *To give one's opinion*, dire son opinion. *To ask s.o.'s opinion*, se référer à qn; consulter qn. *What is your o. of him?* que pensez-vous de lui? *Public opinion*, l'opinion (publique). (*b*) Consultation *f* (de médecin).

opinionated, *a.* Opiniâtre.

opium, *s.* Opium *m.* **opium den**, *s.* Fumerie *f* d'opium. **opium-fiend**, *s. F:* Opiomane *mf.*

Oporto. *Pr.n. Geog:* Porto *m.*

opossum, *s. Z:* Opossum *m.*

opponent, *s.* Adversaire *m*, antagoniste *mf.*

opportune, *a.* Opportun, convenable, commode; à propos. *You have come at an o. moment*, vous tombez bien. **-ly**, *adv.* Opportunément. *It happens most o.*, cela arrive à point (nommé).

opportuneness, *s.* Opportunité *f*; à-propos *m.*

opportunism, *s.* Opportunisme *m.*

opportunist, *s.* Opportuniste *mf.*

opportunity, *s.* Occasion *f.* *When the o.*

offers, à l'occasion. *If I get an opportunity*, si l'occasion se présente.

oppose, *v.tr.* S'opposer à; résister à. *To oppose the motion*, soutenir la contre-partie.

opposed, *a.* Opposé, hostile. **opposing**, *a.* Opposé.

opposite. I. *a.* (*a*) Opposé (*to*, à); vis-à-vis (*to*, de); en face (*to*, de). *See the diagram on the o. page*, voir la figure ci-contre. (*b*) *The opposite sex*, l'autre sexe. *Magn:* **Opposite poles**, pôles contraires. *In the opposite direction*, en sens inverse. **2.** *s.* Opposé *m*; le contre-pied; l'opposite *m.* *Just the o. of what he says*, tout le contraire de ce qu'il dit. **3.** *adv.* Vis-à-vis; en face. **4.** *Prep.* En face de, vis-à-vis (de).

opposition, *s.* Opposition *f.* (*a*) *To act in o. to*, agir contrairement à. (*b*) Résistance *f.* (*c*) (*Le*) camp adverse. (*d*) *Com:* *To start in opposition to s.o.*, ouvrir un magasin en concurrence avec qn.

oppress, *v.tr.* (*a*) Opprimer. (*b*) Oppresser, accabler (l'esprit).

oppression, *s.* (*a*) Oppression *f.* (*b*) Accablement *m* (de l'esprit).

oppressive, *a.* **I.** Oppressif, opprimant. **2.** (*a*) Lourd, étouffant. (*b*) Accablant. **-ly**, *adv.* **I.** Tyranniquement. **2.** D'une manière accablante.

oppressiveness, *s.* **I.** Caractère oppressif. **2.** Lourdeur *f* (du temps).

oppressor, *s.* Oppresseur *m.*

opprobrious, *a.* Injurieux, outrageant. **-ly**, *adv.* Injurieusement.

opprobrium, *s.* Opprobre *m.*

optic, *a.* **Optic nerve**, nerf optique.

optical, *a.* **I.** Optique. **2.** **Optical illusion**, illusion d'optique.

optician, *s.* Opticien *m.*

optics, *s.pl.* L'optique *f.*

optimism, *s.* Optimisme *m.*

optimist, *s.* Optimiste *mf.*

optimistic, *a.* Optimiste. **-ally**, *adv.* Avec optimisme.

option, *s.* Option *f*, choix *m.*

optional, *a.* Facultatif.

opulence, *s.* Opulence *f*, richesse *f.*

opulent, *a.* Opulent. **-ly**, *adv.* Avec opulence.

or, *conj.* (*a*) Ou; (*with neg.*) ni. **Either one or the other**, soit l'un soit l'autre; l'un ou l'autre. *I cannot (either) read or write*, je ne sais ni lire ni écrire. *Without money or luggage*, sans argent ni bagages. *A mile or so*, environ un mille. (*b*) *Don't move, or I'll shoot*, ne bougez pas, sinon je tire.

oracle, *s.* Oracle *m.* *P:* *To work the oracle*, arriver à ses fins.

oracular, *a.* Équivoque, obscur. **-ly**, *adv.* En (style d')oracle.

oral, *a.* Oral, -aux. **-ally**, *adv.* Oralement; de vive voix.

orange, *s.* **I.** Orange *f.* **2.** **Orange(-tree)**, oranger *m.* **3.** *a. & s.* (*Colour*) Orangé (*m*);

orange (m) inv. **orange-blossom,** s.
Fleurs fpl d'oranger. **orange-lily,** s.
Bot: Lis orangé.
orang-(o)utang, s. Z: Orang-outang m,
pl. orangs-outan(g)s.
oration, s. Allocution f, discours m.
orator, s. Orateur m.
oratorical, a. (a) Oratoire. (b) Verbeux,
ampoulé.
oratorio, s. Mus: Oratorio m.
oratory¹, s. L'art m oratoire ; l'éloquence f.
oratory², s. Oratoire m ; chapelle privée.
orb, s. Orbe m ; globe m, sphère f.
orbit, s. Orbite f.
orchard, s. Verger m.
orchestra, s. Orchestre m.
orchestral, a. Orchestral, -aux.
orchid, s. Orchidée f.
ordain, v.tr. Ordonner. **I.** Ecc: To be
ordained, recevoir les ordres. **2.** (a) Destiner.
(b) Ordonner, fixer. (c) Prescrire, décréter
(une mesure).
ordeal, s. Épreuve f.
order¹, s. Ordre m. **I.** (a) The higher orders,
les classes supérieures. (b) pl. Ecc: Holy
orders, ordres sacrés. To be in holy orders,
être prêtre. (c) Monastic order, ordre religieux ; communauté f. Order of knighthood,
ordre de chevalerie. **2.** Succession f, suite f.
In alphabetical order, par ordre alphabétique.
Out of (its) order, hors de son rang. **3.** Mil :
In marching order, en tenue de route. **4.** The
old order of things, l'ancien régime. **5.** (a)
To set one's house in order, F : remettre de
l'ordre dans ses affaires. Is your passport
in order? votre passeport est-il en règle ?
Out of order, en mauvais état. To get out
of order, se dérégler, se détraquer. (b) Parl :
In order, dans les règles. To call s.o. to
order, rappeler qn à l'ordre. **6.** Law and
order, l'ordre public. **7.** In order to do sth.,
afin de, pour, faire qch. In order that . . .,
afin que, pour que, + sub. **8.** (a) Commandement m, instruction f. Mil : Consigne f.
He gave me orders to do it, il m'a donné
(l')ordre de le faire. Orders are orders, je ne
connais que la consigne. Until further orders,
jusqu'à nouvel ordre. (b) Com : Commande
f. Made to order, fabriqué sur commande.
Suit made to o., complet fait sur mesure.
P : That's a tall, large, order ! c'est demander
un peu trop ! **9.** (a) Arrêt m. Order of the
court, injonction f de la cour. Mil : Mention
in orders, citation f (à l'ordre du jour).
Navy : Sailing orders, instructions f pour
la marche. (b) Money order, mandat-poste m,
pl. mandats-poste. Postal order, bon m de
poste.
order², v.tr. **I.** Arranger, ranger ; régler (sa
vie). **2.** (a) To order s.o. to do sth., ordonner,
commander, à qn de faire qch. (b) Med :
Prescrire, ordonner. (c) Com : Commander.
order about, v.tr. F : Faire marcher, faire
aller.

orderliness, s. **I.** Bon ordre ; méthode f.
2. Habitudes fpl d'ordre. **3.** Discipline f.
orderly. I. a. (a) Ordonné, méthodique ;
réglé, rangé, régulier. (b) Tranquille, dis-
cipliné. (c) Mil : Orderly officer, officier m
de service. **2.** s. (a) Mil : Planton m. Hospital orderly, infirmier m, ambulancier m.
(b) Street orderly, balayeur m.
ordinal, a. & s. Ordinal, -aux.
ordinance, s. **I.** Ordonnance f, décret m,
règlement m. **2.** Ecc : Rite m, cérémonie f.
ordinary. I. a. **I.** Ordinaire ; coutumier ;
normal, -aux. **2.** A very ordinary kind of
man, un homme tout à fait quelconque.
-ily, adv. Ordinairement, normalement ;
d'ordinaire, d'habitude. II. **ordinary,** s.
Ordinaire m. Out of the ordinary, exceptionnel ; peu ordinaire.
ordination, s. Ecc : Ordination f.
ordnance, s. **I.** Artillerie f. **2.** Ordnance
Survey, service topographique.
ordure, s. Ordure f.
ore, s. Minerai m.
organ, s. **I.** Mus : (a) Orgue m, orgues fpl.
(b) Street organ, orgue de Barbarie. **2.** (a)
Organe m. The vocal organs, l'appareil vocal.
(b) Journal m, bulletin m, organe. **organ-
grinder,** s. Joueur m d'orgue de Barbarie.
organic, a. **I.** Organique. **2.** O. beings,
êtres organisés.
organism, s. Organisme m.
organist, s. Organiste mf.
organization, s. Organisation f.
organize, v.tr. Organiser.
organizer, s. Organisateur, -trice.
orgy, s. Orgie f.
orient, s. Orient m.
oriental. I. a. Oriental, -aux ; d'Orient.
2. s. Indigène mf de l'Orient ; Oriental, -ale.
orifice, s. Orifice m, ouverture f, trou m.
origin, s. Origine f.
original. I. a. (a) Originaire, primordial,
-aux, primitif. O. meaning of a word, sens
premier d'un mot. (b) (Ouvrage) original,
-aux. **2.** s. Original m (d'un tableau).
3. s. Personne originale ; original, -ale.
-ally, adv. **I.** (a) Originairement ; à
l'origine. (b) Originellement ; dès l'origine.
2. Originalement.
originality, s. Originalité f.
originate, v.i. Tirer son origine, dériver,
provenir (from, de) ; avoir son origine
(dans).
originator, s. Créateur, -trice ; auteur m.
oriole, s. Orn : Loriot m.
Orkneys (the). Pr.n.pl. Geog : Les Orcades f.
ornament¹, s. Ornement m.
ornament², v.tr. Orner, ornementer, décorer.
ornamental, a. Ornemental, -aux ; d'ornement.
ornamentation, s. **I.** Ornementation f,
décoration f. **2.** Les ornements m.
ornate, a. Orné.
ornithological, a. Ornithologique.

ornithologist, *s.* Ornithologue *m*, ornithologiste *m*.

ornithology, *s.* Ornithologie *f*.

orphan. 1. *s.* Orphelin, -ine. **2.** *a.* An orphan child, un(e) orphelin(e).

orphanage, *s.* Orphelinat *m*.

Orpheus. *Pr.n.* Orphée *m*.

orthodox, *a.* Orthodoxe.

orthodoxy, *s.* Orthodoxie *f*.

orthographic(al), *a.* *Gram:* Orthographique.

orthography, *s.* Orthographe *f*.

ortolan, *s.* *Orn:* Ortolan *m*.

oscillate. 1. *v.i.* Osciller. To o. *violently*, s'affoler. **2.** *v.tr.* Balancer; faire osciller.

oscillation, *s.* *Ph:* Oscillation *f*.

osier, *s.* Osier *m*. **osier-bed,** *s.* Oseraie *f*.

osprey, *s.* **1.** *Orn:* Orfraie *f*. **2.** *Cost:* Aigrette *f*.

osseous, *a.* Osseux.

ossify, *v.i.* S'ossifier.

ossuary, *s.* Ossuaire *m*.

Ostend. *Pr.n.* *Geog:* Ostende.

ostensible, *a.* Prétendu; qui sert de prétexte; soi-disant; feint. **-ibly,** *adv.* En apparence; *F:* censément.

ostentation, *s.* Ostentation *f*.

ostentatious, *a.* Fastueux; plein d'ostentation. **-ly,** *adv.* Avec ostentation.

ostler, *s.* Valet *m* d'écurie.

ostracism, *s.* Ostracisme *m*.

ostracize, *v.tr.* *F:* Ostraciser.

ostrich, *s.* Autruche *f*. **ostrich-feather,** *s.* Plume *f* d'autruche.

other. 1. *a.* Autre. (*a*) The other one, l'autre. (*b*) The other four, les quatre autres. Other things being equal, toutes choses égales (d'ailleurs). (*c*) Other people *have seen it*, d'autres l'ont vu. O. *people's property*, le bien d'autrui. **2.** *pron.* Autre. (*a*) One after the other, l'un après l'autre. (*b*) *pl.* The others, les autres, le reste. (*c*) Some . . . others . . . les uns . . . les autres. . . . I have no o., je n'en ai pas d'autre. One or other of us, l'un de nous. This day of all others, ce jour entre tous. (*d*) *pl.* Others, d'autres; autrui *m*. (*e*) I could not do other than, je n'ai pu faire autrement que. **3.** *adv.* Autrement.

otherwise, *adv.* **1.** Autrement (*than*, que). He could do no otherwise, il n'a pu faire autrement. If he is not otherwise engaged, s'il n'est pas occupé à autre chose. Except where otherwise stated, sauf indication contraire. **2.** Autrement; sans quoi, sans cela; dans le cas contraire. **3.** Sous d'autres rapports; par ailleurs. O. *he is quite sane*, *F:* à part ça, il est complètement sain d'esprit.

otter, *s.* *Z:* Loutre *f*.

Ottoman¹, *a. & s.* Ottoman, -ane; turc, *f.* turque.

ottoman², *s.* *Furn:* Divan *m*, ottomane *f*.

ought, *v.aux.* (*Parts of*) devoir, falloir. **1.** *One o. never to be unkind*, il ne faut, on ne doit, jamais être malveillant. To behave as one o., se conduire comme il convient. **2.** *You o. not to have waited*, vous n'auriez pas dû attendre. You ought to have seen it! il fallait voir ça! **3.** *That o. to do*, je crois que cela suffira.

ounce¹, *s.* *Meas:* Once *f*.

ounce², *s.* *Z:* Once *f*; léopard *m* des neiges.

our, *poss.a.* Notre, *pl.* nos. Our house and garden, notre maison et notre jardin. Our friends, nos ami(e)s. Let us look after our own, occupons-nous des nôtres.

ours, *poss.pron.* Le nôtre, la nôtre, les nôtres. This is ours, ceci est à nous; ceci nous appartient. A friend of ours, un(e) de nos ami(e)s.

ourselves, *pers.pron.pl.* See SELF 3.

oust, *v.tr.* **1.** Déloger. **2.** Évincer, supplanter (qn).

out. I. *adv.* **1.** Dehors. (*a*) To go out, sortir. Out you go! hors d'ici! The voyage out, l'aller *m*. (*b*) My father is out, mon père est sorti. He is out and about again, il est de nouveau sur pied. Day out, jour de sortie. The workmen are out, les ouvriers sont en grève. The troops are out, les troupes sont sur pied. Out at sea, au large. Out there, là-bas. The tide is out, la marée est basse. **2.** To lean out, se pencher au dehors. **3.** (*a*) Au clair; découvert, exposé. The sun is out, il fait du soleil. The book is just out, le livre vient de paraître. The secret is out, le secret est connu, éventé. (*b*) To pull out a revolver, tirer, sortir, un revolver. *F:* Out with it! achevez donc! allons, dites-le! (*c*) (*Of flower*) épanoui. The may is out, l'aubépine est en fleur. (*d*) *Aut:* All out, à toute vitesse. (*e*) Out loud, tout haut, à haute voix. To tell s.o. sth. straight out, dire qch. à qn carrément. **4.** Shoulder out (*of joint*), épaule luxée. My hand is out (*of practice*), je n'ai plus la main. The Tories are out (*of power*), les Tories ne sont plus au pouvoir. *Cr:* Out, hors jeu. **5.** To be out in one's calculations, être loin de compte. He is five pounds out, il a une erreur de cinq livres. I was not far out, je ne me trompais pas de beaucoup. **6.** *The fire is out*, le feu est éteint. **7.** (*a*) A bout; achevé. Before the week is out, avant la fin de la semaine. (*b*) Hear me out, écoutez-moi jusqu'au bout. To have one's sleep out, finir de dormir. **8.** Out of. (*a*) Hors de, au dehors de, en dehors de. That is out of our power, cela n'est pas en notre pouvoir. To be out of it, être laissé à l'écart. To feel out of it, se sentir dépaysé. (*b*) Out of season, hors de saison. Times out of number, maintes et maintes fois. To be out of one's mind, avoir perdu la raison. (*c*) To throw sth. out of the window, jeter qch. par la fenêtre. To turn s.o. out of the house, mettre qn à la porte. (*d*) Dans, à, par. To drink out of a glass, boire dans un verre. To drink out of the bottle, boire à (même) la bouteille. (e) Parmi, d'entre. *Choose one out of these ten,* choisissez-en un parmi les dix. *One out of three,* un sur trois. (f) *Hut made out of a few planks,* cabane faite de quelques planches. (g) **Out of respect for you,** par respect pour vous. (h) **To be out of tea,** ne plus avoir de thé. II. **out,** *attrib.a.* **1.** Extérieur, à l'extérieur. **2.** Hors de l'ordinaire. **out and out. 1.** *adv.phr.* Complètement, absolument. **2.** a. **Out-and-out** *liar,* menteur achevé. **out-building,** s. Bâtiment extérieur ; annexe f. Out-buildings, communs m, dépendances f. **out-of-date,** *adj.phr.* **1.** Suranné, vieilli ; passé de mode ; démodé. **2.** (Billet) périmé. **out-of-the-way,** a. **1.** Écarté. **2.** Peu ordinaire. **out-patient,** s. Malade qui vient consulter à la clinique. Out-patients' department, policlinique f, dispensaire m.

outbid, *v.tr.* (R)enchérir, surenchérir, sur.

outbreak, s. **1.** Éruption f ; début m, ouverture f (des hostilités). **2.** Révolte f, émeute f.

outburst, s. Éruption f, explosion f ; éclat m ; élan m (de générosité).

outcast, a. & s. Expulsé, -ée, proscrit, -ite.

outcome, s. Issue f ; dénouement m.

outcry, s. Réclamations indignées (*against,* contre).

outdistance, *v.tr.* Distancer, dépasser.

outdo, *v.tr.* Surpasser (*s.o. in sth.,* qn en qch.) ; l'emporter sur (qn).

outdoor, a. **1.** Extérieur, -eure ; au dehors ; (jeux) au grand air. Outdoor clothes, vêtements de ville. **2.** *Adm:* **Outdoor relief,** secours mpl à domicile.

outdoors, *adv.* Dehors ; hors de la maison ; en plein air.

outer, a. Extérieur, -eure ; externe. **Outer garments,** vêtements de dessus.

outfit, s. **1.** Équipement m, équipage m ; attirail m. O. of tools, jeu m d'outils. **Repairing outfit,** nécessaire m, trousse f, à réparations. **2.** Trousseau m ; effets mpl. *Mil:* Équipement m.

outfitter, s. *Com:* Fournisseur m d'articles d'habillement ; confectionneur m.

outflank, *v.tr. Mil:* Déborder.

outflow, s. Écoulement m, dépense f ; décharge f.

outgoing, a. Sortant. Outgoing tide, marée descendante.

outgoings, *s.pl.* Dépenses f, débours m ; sorties f de fonds.

outgrow, *v.tr.* Devenir trop grand pour (ses vêtements).

outhouse, s. (a) Dépendance f. **Outhouses,** communs m. (b) Appentis m.

outing, s. (a) Promenade f. (b) Excursion f, sortie f ; partie f de plaisir.

outlandish, a. (a) Baroque, bizarre ; (langage) barbare. (b) (*Of place*) Retiré.

outlast, *v.tr.* Durer plus longtemps que.

outlaw¹, s. Hors-la-loi m *inv* ; proscrit, -ite.

outlaw², *v.tr.* Mettre hors la loi ; proscrire.

outlawry, s. Mise f hors la loi ; proscription f.

outlay, s. Débours mpl, frais mpl, dépenses fpl.

outlet, s. Orifice m d'émission ; issue f.

outline¹, s. **1.** Outline(s), contour(s) m, profil m ; silhouette f (de qn). **2.** Dessin m au trait ; tracé m, argument m (d'un roman). **Main outlines of a scheme,** aperçu m d'un projet. **Outlines of astronomy,** éléments m d'astronomie.

outline², *v.tr.* **1.** Contourner, silhouetter. **2.** Exposer à grands traits ; esquisser ; ébaucher.

outlive, *v.tr.* Survivre à.

outlook, s. **1.** Guet m. **To be on the outlook for sth.,** guetter qch. **2.** Vue f, perspective f.

outlying, a. Éloigné, écarté.

outnumber, *v.tr.* L'emporter en nombre sur, être plus nombreux que.

outpost, s. Avant-poste m, pl. avant-postes, poste avancé.

output, s. Rendement m ; débit m (d'une pompe).

outrage¹, s. Outrage m, atteinte f.

outrage², *v.tr.* Outrager, faire outrage à.

outrageous, a. (a) Immodéré, indigne ; (*of price*) excessif. (b) Outrageux. **-ly,** *adv.* (a) Immodérément ; outre mesure. (b) D'une façon scandaleuse.

outright. I. *adv.* **1.** (a) Complètement. **To buy sth. outright,** acheter qch. comptant, à forfait. (b) Du premier coup ; sur le coup. **To kill s.o. outright,** tuer qn raide. **2.** Sans ménagement ; franchement, carrément. **To laugh outright,** éclater de rire. II. **outright,** a. Franc. f. franche ; carré.

outset, s. Commencement m. **From the outset,** dès le début, dès l'origine, dès l'abord.

outside. 1. s. (a) Extérieur m, dehors m. **On the outside of sth.,** à l'extérieur de qch. (b) **At the outside,** tout au plus ; au maximum. (c) *Impériale f* (d'un omnibus). **2.** *Attrib.a.* (a) Du dehors ; extérieur, -eure. (b) **Outside porter,** commissionnaire messager. **3.** *adv.* (a) Dehors, à l'extérieur, en dehors. *Seen from o.,* vu de dehors. (b) **Outside of,** hors de, à l'extérieur de, en dehors de. **4.** *prep.* En dehors de, hors de, à l'extérieur de.

outsider, s. *F:* **1.** Étranger, -ère ; profane mf. **He's a rank outsider,** c'est un pleutre. **2.** *Turf:* Cheval non classé ; outsider m.

outsize, s. **1.** Dimension f hors série ; taille exceptionnelle. **2.** *Attrib:* En taille exceptionnelle.

outskirts, *s.pl.* Abords m ; lisière f (d'une forêt) ; faubourgs m.

outspoken, a. Franc, f. franche ; carré, rond. *To be o.,* avoir son franc-parler. **-ly,** *adv.* Carrément, rondement.

outspread, a. Étendu, étalé. *With o. wings,* les ailes déployées.

outstanding, *a.* **1.** Saillant; marquant; hors ligne, éminent. **2.** (Affaire) en suspens; (compte) impayé, dû; (paiement) arriéré.

outstay, *v.tr.* To outstay one's welcome, lasser l'amabilité de ses hôtes.

outstretched, *a.* Déployé, étendu. With outstretched arms, les bras ouverts.

outstrip, *v.tr.* (a) Devancer, dépasser. (b) Surpasser.

outward. 1. *a.* (a) En dehors. *Rail:* Outward half (*of ticket*), billet *m* d'aller. (b) Extérieur,-e; de dehors. Outward form, extérieur *m*, dehors *m*. *Pharm:* For outward application, pour l'usage externe. **2.** *adv.* = OUTWARDS. **-ly,** *adv.* **1.** A l'extérieur, au dehors. **2.** En apparence. **outward-bound,** *a.* *Nau:* (Navire) en partance, sortant.

outwards, *adv.* Au dehors; vers l'extérieur.

outwit, *v.tr.* Circonvenir; duper.

oval. 1. *a.* Ovale; en ovale. **2.** *s.* Ovale *m.*

ovary, *s.* Ovaire *m.*

ovation, *s.* Ovation *f.*

oven, *s.* Four *m.* In the o., au four. Dutch oven, cuisinière *f*, rôtissoire *f.*

over. I. *prep.* **1.** (a) Sur, dessus, par-dessus. (b) Famous all over the world, célèbre par tout le monde. (c) Over (the top of) sth., par-dessus (qch.). *To throw sth. over the wall,* jeter qch. par-dessus le mur. *To fall over a cliff,* tomber du haut d'une falaise. **2.** (a) Jutting out over the street, faisant saillie sur la rue. *His name is over the door,* il a son nom au-dessus de la porte. To be over one's ankles in water, avoir de l'eau par-dessus la cheville. (b) To have an advantage over s.o., avoir un avantage sur qn. (c) *Bending over his work,* courbé sur son travail. Sitting over the fire, *F:* couvant le feu. **3.** (a) The house over the way, la maison d'en face. Over the border, au delà de la frontière. (b) The bridge over the river, le pont qui traverse la rivière. **4.** Over fifty pounds, plus de cinquante livres. Over five (years of age), au-dessus de cinq ans. He is over fifty, il a (dé)passé la cinquantaine. Over and above, en sus de. II. **over,** *adv.* **1.** (a) Sur toute la surface. To be all over dust, être tout couvert de poussière. To ache all over, avoir mal partout. (b) *To read a letter over,* lire une lettre en entier. *I have had to do it all over again,* j'ai dû le refaire d'un bout à l'autre. (c) Ten times over, dix fois de suite. *Twice over,* à deux reprises. Over and over (again), à plusieurs reprises; maintes et maintes fois. **2.** (a) Par-dessus. *The milk boiled over,* le lait s'est sauvé. (b) To lean over, (i) (*of pers.*) se pencher; (ii) (*of thg*) pencher. **3.** (a) To fall over, (i) (*of pers.*) tomber à la renverse; (ii) (*of thg*) se renverser; être renversé. To knock sth. over, renverser qch. Please turn over, voir au dos; tournez, s'il vous plaît. To turn sth. over and over, tourner et retourner qch. To bend sth. over, replier qch. **4.** To cross

over, (i) traverser; (ii) faire la traversée (de). Over there, over yonder, là-bas. Over here, ici; de ce côté. Over against sth., vis-à-vis de qch.; en face de qch. **5.** En plus, en excès. (a) Children of fourteen and over, les enfants qui ont quatorze ans et davantage, et au delà. *He is six foot and a bit over,* il a six pieds et le pouce. (b) *You will keep* what is (left) over, vous garderez le surplus. *I have a card over,* j'ai une carte de trop. Over and above, en outre. (c) To hold over a decision, ajourner une décision. *The question is held over,* la question est différée. (d) Trop; à l'excès. (e) Excès de. (f) Trop, sur-. **6.** Fini, achevé. *The storm is over,* l'orage est passé. It is all over, c'est fini; tout est fini. It is all over with me, c'en est fait de moi. III. **over,** *s.* *Cr:* Série *f.*

over-bold, *a.* **1.** Téméraire. **2.** Présomptueux. **over-confidence,** *s.* **1.** Confiance exagérée (in, en). **2.** Suffisance *f.* **over-confident,** *a.* **1.** Trop confiant (in s.o., en qn). **2.** Suffisant. **over-estimate,** *v.tr.* Surestimer; exagérer. **over-fatigue**[1], *s.* Surmenage *m.* **over-fatigue**[2], *v.tr.* Surmener. **over-indulgence,** *s.* **1.** Indulgence excessive. **2.** Abus *m* (du vin). **over-populated,** *a.* Surpeuplé. **over-ripe,** *a.* Trop mûr.

overall, *s.* (a) Blouse *f.* (b) Overalls, salopette *f*; combinaison *f*; *F:* bleus *mpl.*

overawe, *v.tr.* Intimider; en imposer à.

overbalance. 1. *v.i.* & *pr.* To overbalance (oneself), perdre l'équilibre. **2.** *v.i.* Se renverser; tomber.

overbearing, *a.* Arrogant, impérieux, autoritaire.

overbid, *v.tr.* Enchérir sur.

overboard, *adv.* To fall overboard, tomber à la mer.

overburden, *v.tr.* Surcharger, accabler (with, de).

overcast, *a.* (a) Obscurci, assombri, couvert (with, de). (b) Overcast sky, ciel couvert, sombre.

overcharge[1], *s.* Prix excessif; prix surfait.

overcharge[2], *v.tr.* To overcharge s.o., faire payer trop cher un article à qn; *F:* écorcher qn.

overcloud, *v.i.* Se couvrir de nuages.

overcoat, *s.* Pardessus *m.*

overcome, *v.tr.* Triompher de, vaincre; surmonter. **overcome,** *a.* To be overcome with, by (sth.), être accablé de. To be overcome by emotion, succomber à l'émotion.

overcrowded, *a.* (a) Trop rempli (with, de); bondé (with people, de monde). (b) (Ville) surpeuplée.

overdo, *v.tr.* **1.** Outrer. *F:* To overdo it, forcer la note; exagérer. **2.** *Cu:* Trop cuire.

overdose, *s.* Trop forte dose.

overdue, *a.* (a) Arriéré, en retard. (b) Train ten minutes overdue, train en retard de dix minutes.

overeat, *v.pr. & i.* **To overeat (oneself),** trop manger.

overexcite, *v.tr.* Surexciter.

overexcitement, *s.* Surexcitation *f.*

overexertion, *s.* Surmenage *m.*

overfed, *a.* **I.** Suralimenté. **2.** *F:* Pansu, ventru.

overflow[1], *s.* **I.** (*a*) Débordement *m*, épanchement *m.* (*b*) Inondation *f.* **2.** Trop-plein *m inv.* **3.** Overflow meeting, réunion *f* supplémentaire.

overflow[2]. **I.** *v.tr.* Déborder de. **2.** *v.i.* Déborder.

overgrown, *a.* Couvert (*with sth.*, de qch.). Garden overgrown with weeds, jardin envahi par les mauvaises herbes.

overgrowth, *s.* **I.** Surcroissance *f.* **2.** Couverture *f.*

overhang, *v.tr.* Surplomber. **overhanging**, *a.* Surplombant.

overhaul, *v.tr.* **I.** Examiner en détail; remettre en état. **2.** *Nau:* Rattraper, dépasser.

overhead. **I.** *adv.* Au-dessus (de la tête); en haut, en l'air. **2.** *Attrib.a.* (*a*) Overhead cable, câble aérien. (*b*) *Com:* Overhead expenses, *s.* frais généraux.

overhear, *v.tr.* Surprendre (une conversation).

overheat, *v.tr.* (*a*) Surchauffer. (*b*) **To overheat oneself,** s'échauffer (trop).

overjoyed, *a.* Transporté de joie. *To be o. to see s.o.,* être ravi de voir qn.

overladen, *a.* Surchargé (*with*, de).

overland. **I.** *adv.* Par voie de terre. **2.** *Attrib.a.* Overland route, voie *f* de terre.

overlap, *v.tr. & i.* **I.** **To overlap (one another),** chevaucher. **2.** Dépasser (l'extrémité de qch.).

overleaf, *adv.* Au dos, au verso.

overload, *v.tr.* Surcharger.

overlook, *v.tr.* **I.** Avoir vue sur; dominer, commander; donner sur (la rue). **2.** (*a*) Oublier, laisser passer. **I overlooked the fact**, ce fait m'a échappé. (*b*) Fermer les yeux sur. **Overlook it this time,** passez-le-moi cette fois. **3.** Surveiller.

overmastering, *a.* (*a*) (*Of will*) Dominateur, -trice. (*b*) (*Of passion*) Irrésistible.

overnight, *adv.* **I.** Pendant la nuit. **2.** Jusqu'au lendemain.

overpayment, *s.* **I.** Surpaye *f*; paiement *m* en trop. **2.** Rétribution excessive.

overpower, *v.tr.* Maîtriser, dominer, vaincre. Overpowered with grief, accablé de douleur. **overpowering**, *a.* (*Of desire*) irrésistible. Overpowering heat, chaleur accablante.

overproduction, *s.* Surproduction *f.*

overrate, *v.tr.* Surestimer.

overreach, *v.tr.* **I.** Tromper, duper. **2. To overreach oneself,** être victime de sa propre fourberie.

override, *v.tr.* (*a*) Outrepasser. (*b*) Avoir plus d'importance que; l'emporter sur.

overrule, *v.tr.* (*a*) Décider contre (l'avis de qn). (*b*) *Jur:* Annuler, casser.

overrun, *v.tr.* **I.** (*a*) Se répandre sur, envahir. (*b*) House overrun with mice, maison infestée de souris. **2.** Dépasser.

overseas, *adv.* **Visitors from overseas.** visiteurs d'outre-mer.

oversee, *v.tr.* Surveiller.

overseer, *s.* Surveillant, -ante; *Ind:* contremaître, -tresse.

overshadow, *v.tr.* **I.** Ombrager. **2.** Éclipser; surpasser en éclat.

overshoot, *v.tr.* Dépasser, outrepasser.

oversight, *s.* Oubli *m*, omission *f.*

oversleep, *v.i. & pron.* **To oversleep (oneself),** dormir trop longtemps.

overstatement, *s.* Exagération *f.*

overt, *a.* Patent, évident.

overtake, *v.tr.* **I.** (*a*) Rattraper, atteindre. (*b*) Doubler, dépasser. **2.** (*Of accident*) Arriver à. *Overtaken by a storm*, surpris par un orage.

overtax, *v.tr.* Trop exiger de. **To overtax one's strength,** se surmener.

overthrow[1], *s.* Renversement *m*; défaite *f.*

overthrow[2], *v.tr.* **I.** Renverser. **2.** Défaire, vaincre.

overtime. **I.** *s. Ind:* Heures *f* supplémentaires. **2.** *adv.* To work overtime, faire des heures supplémentaires.

overture, *s.* **I.** Ouverture *f*, offre *j.* **2.** *Mus:* Ouverture.

overturn. **I.** *v.tr.* Renverser; faire verser (une voiture); (faire) chavirer (un canot). **2.** *v.i.* Se renverser; (*of carriage*) verser; (*of boat*) chavirer.

overweening, *a.* Outrecuidant, présomptueux, suffisant.

overwhelm, *v.tr.* **I.** Ensevelir; submerger. **2.** (*a*) Écraser, accabler. (*b*) *To be overwhelmed with work*, être débordé de travail. (*c*) Combler (qn de bontés). *Overwhelmed with joy*, au comble de la joie. **overwhelming**, *a.* Irrésistible; accablant.

overwork. **I.** *v.tr.* Surmener; surcharger de travail. **2.** *v.i.* Se surmener.

overwrought, *a.* (*a*) Excédé; surmené. (*b*) O. senses, sens surexcités.

owe, *v.tr.* Devoir. **I. To owe s.o. sth.,** devoir qch. à qn. **2. To what do I owe this honour?** qu'est-ce qui me vaut cet honneur?

owing. **I.** *Pred.a.* Dû, *f.* due. **All the money owing to me,** tout l'argent qui m'est dû. **2.** Owing to, à cause de, par suite de.

owl, *s. Orn:* Hibou *m*, -oux. *The owl*, le hibou.

owlet, *s. Orn:* Jeune hibou *m.*

own[1], *v.tr.* **I.** Posséder. *Who owns this land?* quel est le propriétaire de cette terre? **2.** Reconnaître. (*a*) Dog nobody will own, chien que personne ne réclame. **To own s.o. as one's brother**, avouer qn pour frère. (*b*) Avouer; convenir de. **I own I was wrong**, j'ai eu tort, je l'avoue, j'en conviens.

To own oneself beaten, se reconnaître vaincu.
3. *v.ind.tr.* **To own to a mistake**, reconnaître, avouer, une erreur. **She owns (up) to (being) thirty**, elle accuse trente ans. **To own up to a crime**, faire l'aveu d'un crime.

own². I. *a.* (*a*) *Attrib.* Propre. **Own brother**, frère germain. **I do my own cooking**, je fais ma propre cuisine. (*b*) *Pred.* Le mien, le tien, etc.; à moi, à toi, etc. **My time is my own**, mon temps est à moi. **2.** *s.* **My own**, **his own**, *etc.* (*a*) Le mien, le sien, etc. **He has a copy of his own**, il a un exemplaire à lui, en propre. **For reasons of his own**, pour des raisons particulières. **May I have it for my (very) own?** est-ce que je peux l'avoir pour moi seul? **To come into one's own**, entrer en possession de son bien. (*b*) **To do sth. on one's own**, faire qch. de sa propre initiative. *F:* **I am (all) on my own to-day**, je suis seul aujourd'hui.

owner, *s.* Propriétaire *mf*, possesseur *m*; patron, -onne.

ownership, *s.* (Droit *m* de) propriété *f*; possession *f*.

ox, *s.* Bœuf *m*. **Wild oxen**, bovidés *m* sauvages.

ox-tail, *s.* *Cu:* Queue *f* de bœuf. **ox-tongue**, *s.* Langue *f* de bœuf.

oxalic, *a.* *Ch:* Oxalique.

oxide, *s.* *Ch:* Oxyde *m*.

oxidization, *s.* *Ch:* Oxydation *f*.

oxidize. I. *v.tr.* *Ch:* Oxyder. **2.** *v.i.* S'oxyder.

oxygen, *s.* *Ch:* Oxygène *m*.

oyster, *s.* Huître *f*. **Pearl oyster**, huître perlière, à perle. **oyster-bed**, *s.* Huîtrière *f*. **oyster-farm**, *s.* Parc *m* à huîtres. **oyster-shell**, *s.* Écaille *f* d'huître.

ozone, *s.* *Ch:* Ozone *m*.

P

P, p, s. (La lettre) P, p *m.* *F:* **To mind one's P's and Q's**, se surveiller.

pace¹, *s.* **I.** Pas *m.* **Ten paces off**, à dix pas de distance. **2.** (*a*) *F:* **To put s.o. through his paces**, mettre qn à l'épreuve. (*b*) Vitesse *f*, train *m*, allure *f*. **At a walking pace**, au pas. **To keep pace with s.o.**, marcher du même pas que qn. *F:* **To go the pace**, mener la vie à grandes guides.

pace², *v.i.* **To pace up and down**, faire les cent pas.

pacific, *a.* **I.** (*a*) Pacifique. (*b*) Paisible. **2.** *Geog:* **The Pacific (Ocean)**, l'océan *m* Pacifique.

pacifism, *s.* Pacifisme *m*.

pacifist, *s. & a.* Pacifiste (*mf*).

pacify, *v.tr.* Pacifier; apaiser, calmer.

pack¹, *s.* **I.** (*a*) Paquet *m*; ballot *m* (de colporteur). *Mil:* Paquetage *m.* (*b*) *F:* **Pack of lies**, tissu *m*, tas *m*, de mensonges. **2.** (*a*) Bande *f*. **P. of fools**, tas d'imbéciles. (*b*) *Ven:* **Pack of hounds**, meute *f*. **3.** Jeu *m* (de cartes). **pack-full**, *a.* Plein à déborder. **pack-horse**, *s.* Cheval *m* de bât. **pack-ice**, *s.* Glace *f* de banquise; pack *m*. **pack-saddle**, *s.* Bât *m*.

pack², *v.tr.* **I.** Emballer, empaqueter. *Abs.* **To pack (up)**, faire ses malles. **2.** Tasser; *F:* entasser, serrer. **Packed like herrings in a barrel**, serrés comme des harengs en caque. **3.** Remplir, bourrer (*sth. with sth.*, qch. de qch.). **To pack one's trunk**, faire sa malle. **The train was packed**, le train était bondé. *Packed hall*, salle comble. **4.** *F:* **To send s.o. packing**, envoyer promener qn. **packing**, *s.* **I.** Emballage *m*, empaquetage *m*.

To do one's packing, faire ses malles. **2.** Matière *f* pour emballage. **packing-case**, *s.* Caisse *f* d'emballage. **packing-paper**, *s.* Papier *m* d'emballage.

package, *s.* Paquet *m*, colis *m*, ballot *m*.

packer, *s.* Emballeur *m*.

packet, *s.* **I.** (*a*) Paquet *m*. (*b*) **Postal packet**, colis postal. **2.** **Packet(-boat)**, paquebot *m*.

pact, *s.* Pacte *m*, convention *f*, contrat *m*.

pad¹, *s.* **I.** (*a*) Bourrelet *m*, coussinet *m*. (*b*) Tampon *m*. **Stamp pad**, tampon à timbrer. **Inking pad**, tampon encreur. **2.** Bloc *m* (de papier).

pad², *v.tr.* Rembourrer. **Padded cell**, cellule matelassée. **padding**, *s.* **I.** Remplissage *m*, rembourrage *m*. **2.** Ouate *f*, bourre *f*.

paddle¹, *s.* Pagaie *f*. **paddle-steamer**, *s.* Vapeur *m* à aubes. **paddle-wheel**, *s.* Roue *f* à aubes, à palettes.

paddle², *v.tr.* Pagayer. *F:* **To paddle one's own canoe**, conduire seul sa barque.

paddle³, *v.i.* Barboter, *F:* grenouiller (dans l'eau).

paddler, *s.* Pagayeur, -euse.

paddock, *s.* Parc *m*, enclos *m* (pour chevaux).

padlock¹, *s.* Cadenas *m*.

padlock², *v.tr.* Cadenasser.

pagan, *a. & s.* Païen, -ïenne.

paganism, *s.* Paganisme *m*.

page¹, *s.* **I.** Page *m*. **2.** **Page(-boy)**, petit groom (d'hôtel); chasseur *m*.

page², *s.* Page *f*. **On page 6**, à la page 6.

pageant, *s.* **I.** Spectacle pompeux. **2.** **Air pageant**, fête *f* d'aviation.

pageantry, *s.* Apparat *m*, pompe *f*.

pagoda, *s.* Pagode *f*.

pail, s. Seau m.

pailful, s. (Plein) seau.

pain¹. 1. (a) Douleur f, souffrance f; (mental) peine f. To be in great pain, souffrir beaucoup. (b) To have a p. in one's head, souffrir de la tête. **2.** pl. Pains, peine. To take pains to do sth., se donner du mal pour faire qch. To take pains over sth., y mettre tous ses soins. **3.** On pain of death, sous peine de mort.

pain², v.tr. Faire souffrir; faire de la peine à; peiner, affliger. It pains me to say so, il m'en coûte de le dire. **pained,** a. Attristé, peiné (at, de).

painful, a. **1.** Douloureux. My knee was getting p., mon genou commençait à me faire mal. **2.** Pénible. It is p. to hear him, cela fait peine de l'entendre. **-fully,** adv. Douloureusement; péniblement.

painless, a. Sans douleur.

painstaking, a. Soigneux, assidu; (élève) travailleur, -euse, appliqué.

paint¹, s. Peinture f. (a) Coat of paint, couche f de peinture. 'Wet paint!' "attention à la peinture (fraîche)!" (b) Box of paints, boîte de couleurs. **paint-brush,** s. Pinceau m.

paint², v.tr. **1.** (a) Peindre (un portrait). (b) Abs. Faire de la peinture. **2.** Dépeindre. **3.** Enduire de peinture; peinturer. To p. a door green, peindre une porte en vert.

painting, s. Peinture f. **1.** To study p., étudier la peinture. **2.** Tableau m.

painter¹, s. **1.** Art: Peintre m. **2.** (House-) painter, peintre en bâtiments.

painter², s. Nau: Amarre f.

pair¹, s. (a) Paire f. The p. of you, vous deux. (b) A pair of trousers, of drawers, un pantalon, un caleçon. (c) Carriage and pair, voiture f à deux chevaux. (d) Couple m. The happy pair, les deux conjoints m. (e) These two pictures are a pair, ces deux tableaux se font pendant.

pair², v.i. S'accoupler, s'apparier.

pal, s. F: Camarade mf.

palace, s. Palais m.

palanquin, s. Palanquin m.

palatable, a. (a) Agréable au palais, au goût. (b) Agréable (to, à).

palate, s. Anat: Palais m.

palatial, a. Magnifique, grandiose.

palaver¹, s. **1.** Palabre f; conférence f (avec les indigènes). **2.** F: None of your p.! pas tant d'histoires !

palaver², v.i. Palabrer.

pale¹, s. Beyond the pale, au ban de la société.

pale², a. (a) Pâle, blême. Deadly pale, pâle comme la mort. To turn pale, pâlir. (b) Pale blue dress, robe bleu clair. By the p. light of the moon, à la lumière blafarde de la lune. **pale-face,** s. Blanc, f. blanche. **pale-faced,** a. Au visage pâle.

pale³, v.i. Pâlir, blêmir.

paleness, s. Pâleur f.

palette, s. Art: Palette f.

paling(s), s.(pl.). Clôture f à claire-voie; palissade f.

palisade, s. Palissade f.

palish, a. Un peu pâle; pâlot, -otte.

pall¹, s. **1.** Ecc: Poêle m. Drap m mortuaire. **2.** F: Manteau m (de neige); voile m (de fumée).

pall², v.i. S'affadir; devenir fade, insipide (on s.o., pour qn). It never palls on you, on ne s'en dégoûte jamais.

pallet, s. (a) Paillasse f. (b) Grabat m.

palliasse, s. Paillasse f.

palliate, v.tr. Pallier; atténuer.

palliation, s. Palliation f; atténuation f.

palliative, a. & s. Palliatif (m), lénitif (m).

pallid, a. (a) Pâle, décoloré. (b) (Of light) Blafard. (c) (Of face) Blême.

pallor, s. Pâleur f.

palm¹, s. **1.** Palmier m. **2.** Palm Sunday, le dimanche des Rameaux. F: To bear the palm, remporter la palme. **palm-oil,** s. Huile f de palme, de palmier.

palm², s. Paume f. P: To grease s.o.'s palm, graisser la patte de, à, qn.

palm³, v.tr. To palm a card, escamoter une carte. **palm off,** v.tr. Faire passer (sth. on s.o., qch. à qn).

palmist, s. Chiromancien, -ienne.

palmistry, s. Chiromancie f.

palmy, a. Palmy days, jours heureux.

palpable, a. **1.** Palpable; que l'on peut toucher. **2.** Palpable, F: manifeste, clair.

palpitate, v.tr. Palpiter.

palpitation, s. Palpitation f.

palsied, a. Paralysé, paralytique.

palter, v.i. To p. with one's honour, transiger sur, avec, l'honneur.

paltriness, s. Mesquinerie f.

paltry, a. Misérable, mesquin. P. excuses, plates excuses; pauvres excuses.

pampas, s.pl. Pampas f.pl. **pampas-grass,** s. Herbe f des pampas.

pamper, v.tr. Choyer, dorloter.

pamphlet, s. Brochure f.

pan¹, s. Cu: Casserole f, poêlon m.

Pan². Pr.n. Myth: (Le dieu) Pan m. Pan's pipes, flûte f de Pan.

panacea, s. Panacée f; remède universel.

Panama. 1. Pr.n. Geog: Le Panama. **2.** s. Panama (hat), panama m.

pancake¹, s. Cu: Crêpe f. Pancake day, mardi gras.

pancake², v.i. Av: To pancake, descendre à plat.

panda, s. Z: Panda m.

pandemonium, s. Pandémonium m. F: It's p., c'est une vraie tour de Babel.

pander, v.tr. & i. To pander to a vice, se prêter à un vice.

pane, s. Vitre f, carreau m.

panegyric, a. & s. Panégyrique (m).

panel¹, s. **1.** Panneau m (de porte). **2.** Tableau m, liste f. **3.** Commission f.

panel², *v.tr.* Diviser en panneaux. **panelled,** *a.* Boisé, lambrissé. **panelling,** *s.* **1.** Lambrissage *m.* **2.** Lambris *m,* boiserie *f.*

pang, *s.* Angoisse subite; douleur *f.* The pangs of death, les affres *fpl* de la mort. To feel the pangs of hunger, entendre crier ses entrailles.

panic¹, *a. & s.* Panic (terror), (terreur *f*) panique *f*; affolement *m. They fled in a p.,* pris de panique ils s'enfuirent. **panic-monger,** *s.* Semeur, -euse, de panique. **panic-stricken,** *a.* Pris de panique; affolé.

panic², *v.i.* Être pris de panique; s'affoler.

pannier, *s.* Panier *m.*

panoply, *s.* Panoplie *f.*

panorama, *s.* Panorama *m.*

panoramic, *a.* Panoramique.

pansy, *s. Bot:* Pensée *f.*

pant, *v.i.* **1.** *(a)* Panteler. *(b)* Haleter. To pant for breath, chercher à reprendre haleine. **2.** To pant for sth., soupirer après qch.

pantechnicon, *s.* Pantechnicon(-van), voiture *f* de déménagement.

pantheist, *s.* Panthéiste *m.*

panther, *s. Z:* Panthère *f.*

pantomime, *s. Th:* *(a) (Dumb show)* Pantomime *f.* *(b)* Revue-féerie *f.*

pantry, *s.* **1.** Garde-manger *m inv.* **2.** Butler's pantry, office *f.*

pants, *s.pl. Cost:* (Pair of) pants, caleçon *m.*

pap, *s.* Bouillie *f.*

papa, *s. F:* Papa *m*; peti. père.

papacy, *s.* Papauté *f.*

papal, *a.* Papal, -aux.

paper¹, *s.* **1.** Papier *m.* *(a)* Brown paper, papier gris. Cigarette paper, papier à cigarettes. *(b)* To put sth. down on paper, coucher qch. par écrit. **2.** (Morceau *m* de) papier. Paper of pins, carte *f* d'épingles. **3.** Écrit *m,* document *m,* pièce *f.* To send in one's papers, donner sa démission. Ship's papers, papiers du bord. **4.** Étude *f,* mémoire *m.* **5.** Journal *m,* -aux. Weekly paper, hebdomadaire *m.* **paper-chase,** *s. Sp:* Rallye-paper *m,* *pl.* rallye-papers. **paper-clip,** *s.* Attache-papiers *m inv.* **paper-fastener,** *s.* Attache *f* métallique. **paper-hanger,** *s.* Colleur *m* de papiers peints. **paper-hanging,** *s.* Collage *m* de papiers peints. **paper-knife,** *s.* Coupe-papier *m inv.* **paper-weight,** *s.* Presse-papiers *m inv.*

paper², *v.tr.* Tapisser.

papist, *s.* Papiste *mf.*

papyrus, *s.* Papyrus *m.*

par, *s.* Pair *m,* égalité *f.* *(a)* To be on a par with s.o., être au niveau de, aller de pair avec, qn. *(b) F:* To feel below par, n'être pas dans son assiette.

parable, *s.* Parabole *f.*

parabola, *s. Geom:* Parabole *f.*

parachute¹, *s. Aer:* Parachute *m. To land arms by p.,* parachuter des armes.

parachute², *v.i.* *Av:* To parachute down, descendre en parachute.

parachutist, *s.* Parachutiste *mf.*

parade¹, *s.* **1.** Parade *f.* **2.** *Mil:* *(a)* Rassemblement *m.* *(b)* Exercice *m.* On parade, à l'exercice. Parade-ground, terrain *m* de manœuvres; place *f* d'armes. **3.** Défilé *m.* **4.** Esplanade *f*; promenade publique.

parade². **1.** *v.tr.* *(a)* Faire parade, étalage, de. *To p. one's poverty,* afficher sa pauvreté. *(b) Mil:* Faire parader, faire défiler. **2.** *v.i. Mil:* Faire la parade; parader.

paradise, *s.* Paradis *m. F:* To live in a fool's paradise, se bercer d'un bonheur illusoire. Bird of paradise, oiseau *m* de paradis.

paradox, *s.* Paradoxe *m.*

paradoxical, *a.* Paradoxal, -aux. **-ally,** *adv.* Paradoxalement.

paraffin, *s.* **1.** *Ch:* Paraffine *f. Pharm:* Liquid paraffin, huile *f* de vaseline. **2.** *Com:* *F:* = PARAFFIN OIL. **paraffin lamp,** *s.* Lampe *f* à pétrole. **paraffin oil,** *s.* (Huile *f* de) pétrole *m*; pétrole lampant.

paragon, *s.* Parangon *m,* modèle *m.*

paragraph, *s.* **1.** Paragraphe *m* alinéa *m.* **2.** *Journ:* Entrefilet *m.*

parakeet, *s. Orn:* Perruche *f.*

parallel. **I.** *a.* Parallèle (*with, to,* à). **1.** *In a p.* direction with sth., parallèlement à qch. **2.** Pareil; (cas) analogue (*to, with,* à). **II. parallel,** *s.* **1.** *(a)* (Ligne *f*) parallèle *f.* *(b) Geog:* Parallèle *m* (de latitude). **2.** Parallèle *m,* comparaison *f.*

parallelogram, *s.* Parallélogramme *m.*

paralyse, *v.tr.* Paralyser. *F:* Paralysed with fear, transi de peur. **paralysing,** *a.* Paralysant; paralysateur, -trice.

paralysis, *s.* Paralysie *f.*

paralytic, *a. & s.* Paralytique *mf.*

paramount, *a.* **1.** Éminent, souverain. **2.** *Of p. importance,* d'une suprême importance.

parapet, *s.* Parapet *m*; garde-fou *m, pl.* garde-fous.

paraphernalia, *s.pl. F:* *(a)* Effets *m*; affaires *f.* *(b)* Attirail *m,* appareil *m.*

paraphrase¹, *s.* Paraphrase *f.*

paraphrase², *v.tr.* Paraphraser.

parasite, *s.* Parasite *m*; (*of pers.*) écornifleur, -euse; pique-assiette *m inv.*

parasitic, *a.* Parasite (*on,* de).

parasol, *s.* Ombrelle *f,* parasol *m.*

parcel, *s.* **1.** Morceau *m,* parcelle *f* (de terrain). **2.** Paquet *m,* colis *m.* Parcels office, bureau *m* de(s) messageries. **parcel post,** *s.* Service *m* des colis postaux; service de messageries.

parch, *v.tr.* *(a)* Rôtir, griller. *(b) F:* Grass parched (up) by the wind, herbe desséchée par le vent. To be parched with thirst, avoir une soif ardente.

parchment, *s.* Parchemin *m.*

pardon¹, *s.* **1.** Pardon *m.* I beg your pardon!

je vous demande pardon! **2.** *Ecc:* Indulgence *f.* **3.** *Jur:* **Free** pardon, grâce *f.* General pardon, amnistie *f.*

pardon², *v.tr.* **I.** Pardonner. **2.** *To p. s.o.,* pardonner à qn. **Pardon me!** faites excuse! **3.** *Jur:* Gracier, amnistier.

pardonable, *a.* Pardonnable, excusable.

pare, *v.tr.* **I.** Rogner. **2.** Éplucher; peler (un fruit). **paring**, *s.* *Usu.pl.* (a) Rognures *f.* (b) Épluchures *f,* pelures *f* (de légumes).

paregoric, *a.* & *s.* Parégorique (*m*).

parent, *s.* Père *m*, mère *f*; *pl.* parents *m*, les père et mère.

parentage, *s.* Parentage *m*, naissance *f.*

parental, *a.* Des parents, des père et mère ; (pouvoir) paternel.

parenthesis, *s.* Parenthèse *f.* **In parentheses**, entre parenthèses.

parenthetic(al), *a.* Entre parenthèses. **-ally**, *adv.* Par parenthèse.

pariah, *s.* Paria *m.* **pariah-dog**, *s.* Chien métis des Indes ; chien pariah.

Paris. *Pr.n. Geog:* Paris *m.*

parish, *s.* (a) *Ecc:* Paroisse *f.* **Parish church,** église paroissiale. (b) **Parish Council** = conseil municipal.

parishioner, *s.* Paroissien, -ienne.

Parisian, *a.* & *s.* Parisien, -ienne.

parity, *s.* Égalité *f* ; parité *f.*

park¹, *s.* **I.** (a) Parc *m.* (b) **Public park,** jardin public ; parc. **2.** Car park, parc de stationnement.

park², *v.tr.* *Aut:* Parquer, garer. *Abs.* stationner. **parking**, *s.* Parcage *m.* *Aut:* 'No parking,' "défense de stationner."

parlance, *s.* **In common parlance,** en langage ordinaire.

parley¹, *s.* Conférence *f.* *Mil:* Pourparlers *mpl.* **To hold a parley,** parlementer.

parley², *v.i.* Parlementer.

parliament, *s.* Le Parlement. **The Houses of Parliament,** le palais du Parlement. **In parliament,** au parlement.

parliamentarian, *a.* & *s.* Parlementaire *m.*

parliamentary, *a.* Parlementaire. **Parliamentary election,** élection législative.

parlour, *s.* Petit salon.

parlous, *a.* *Lit:* Périlleux, précaire.

Parnassus. *Pr.n.* Le Parnasse.

parochial, *a.* *Ecc:* Paroissial, -aux. *The p. hall,* la salle d'œuvres de la paroisse.

parody¹, *s.* Parodie *f,* pastiche *m.*

parody², *v.tr.* Parodier, pasticher.

parole, *s.* Parole *f.* **Prisoner on parole,** prisonnier sur parole.

paroxysm, *s.* (a) *Med:* Paroxysme *m.* (b) *F:* Crise *f* (de fou rire) ; accès *m* (de fureur).

parquet, *s.* **Parquet flooring.** parquetage *m.*

parricide¹, *s.* Parricide *mf.*

parricide², *s.* (Crime *m* de) parricide *m.*

parrot, *s.* *Orn:* Perroquet *m.*

parry, *v.tr.* Parer, détourner.

parse, *v.tr.* Faire l'analyse (grammaticale) de. **parsing**, *s.* Analyse grammaticale.

Parsee, *a.* & *s.* Parsi, -ie.

parsimonious, *a.* Parcimonieux. **-ly**, *adv.* Parcimonieusement.

parsimony, *s.* Parcimonie *f.*

parsley, *s.* *Bot:* Persil *m.*

parsnip, *s.* Panais *m.*

parson, *s.* *Ecc:* **I.** Titulaire *m* d'un bénéfice. **2.** *F:* Prêtre *m* ; pasteur *m.*

parsonage, *s.* Presbytère *m,* cure *f.*

part¹. **I.** *s.* **I.** Partie *f.* (a) Good in parts, bon en partie. *F:* **The funny part is,** le comique de l'histoire, c'est. **It is part and parcel of,** c'est une partie intégrante de. *To pay in part,* payer partiellement. *F:* **Three parts drunk,** aux trois quarts ivre. (b) *Ind:* Pièce *f,* organe *m.* **Machine part,** élément *m* de machine. **Spare parts,** pièces de rechange. (c) **Parts of speech,** parties du discours. (d) Fascicule *m,* livraison *f* (d'une œuvre littéraire). **2.** Part *f.* (a) To take part in sth., prendre part à qch. (b) *Th:* Rôle *m,* personnage *m.* *F:* He is playing a part, il joue la comédie. **To play one's part,** remplir son rôle. (c) **Orchestral parts,** parties d'orchestre. **3.** (a) *pl.* You don't belong to these parts? vous n'êtes pas de ces parages? (b) **To take s.o.'s part,** prendre le parti de qn. (c) *An indiscretion* on the part of, une indiscrétion de la part de. **For my part,** quant à moi, pour ma part. **4. To take sth. in good part,** prendre qch. en bonne part. **II. part,** *adv.* *P. eaten,* partiellement mangé ; mangé en partie. **part-owner**, *s.* Copropriétaire *mf.* **part-song**, *s.* Chant *m* à plusieurs parties, à plusieurs voix.

part². **I.** *v.tr.* (a) Séparer en deux ; fendre. **To part one's hair,** se faire une raie. (b) Séparer (*from,* de). (c) Rompre (une amarre). **2.** *v.i.* (a) Se diviser. (b) Se quitter, se séparer ; (*of roads*) diverger. (c) (Se) rompre ; partir, céder. **part with,** *v.i.* Céder ; se dessaisir, se défaire, de qch. **parting,** *s.* **I.** (a) Séparation *f.* *F:* To be at the parting of the ways, être au carrefour. (b) Départ *m.* **Parting kiss,** baiser d'adieu. *A few p. directions,* quelques dernières recommandations. **2.** Rupture *f* (d'un câble). **3.** (*Of the hair*) Raie *f.*

partake, *v.i.* **To partake of sth.,** prendre part, participer, à qch. *To p. of a meal,* prendre un repas.

partial, *a.* **I.** (a) Partial, -aux ; injuste. (b) *F:* **To be partial to sth.,** avoir un faible pour qch. *I am p. to a pipe,* je fume volontiers une pipe. **2.** Partiel ; en partie. *P. board,* demi-pension *f.* **-ally**, *adv.* **I.** Partialement ; avec partialité. **2.** Partiellement ; en partie.

partiality, *s.* **I.** Partialité *f* (*for, to,* pour, envers) ; injustice *f.* **2.** Prédilection *f.*

participate, *v.i.* **To participate in sth.,** prendre part, participer, s'associer, à qch.

participation, *s.* Participation *f* (*in*, à).
participator, *s.* Participant, -ante (*in*, de).
participle, *s.* *Gram:* Participe *m.*
particle, *s.* Particule *f*, parcelle *f.* *Not a p. of evidence,* pas la moindre preuve.
parti-coloured, *a.* **1.** Mi-parti. **2.** Bigarré, bariolé, panaché.
particular. I. *a.* **1.** Particulier; spécial, -aux. **For no particular reason,** sans raison précise. **In particular,** en particulier; notamment. **2.** Méticuleux, minutieux; pointilleux. **To be particular about one's food,** être difficile sur la nourriture. *To be p. about one's dress,* soigner sa mise. **3.** *F:* **I am not particular about it,** je n'y tiens pas plus que ça. **-ly,** *adv.* Particulièrement. *I p. asked him to be careful,* je l'ai prié instamment de faire attention. II. **particular,** *s.* Détail *m*, particularité *f.* *Alike in every particular,* semblables en tout point. **To give particulars of sth.,** donner les détails de qch. **For further particulars,** pour plus amples renseignements.
particularity, *s.* **1.** Particularité *f.* **2.** Méticulosité *f.*
partisan, *s.* Partisan *m.*
partition[1], *s.* **1.** Partage *m.* **2.** (*a*) Cloison *f.* **Glass partition,** vitrage *m.* (*b*) Compartiment *m.*
partition[2], *v.tr.* **1.** Morceler; partager. **2. To partition (off) a room,** cloisonner une pièce.
partitive, *a. & s.* *Gram:* Partitif (*m*).
partly, *adv.* Partiellement; en partie.
partner, *s.* (*a*) Associé, -ée. **Sleeping partner,** commanditaire *m.* (*b*) *Games:* Partenaire *mf.* (*c*) *Danc:* Cavalier *m*; dame *f.* **My partner,** mon danseur, ma danseuse.
partnership, *s.* **1.** (*a*) **P. in crime,** association *f* dans le crime. (*b*) *Com:* **To take s.o. into partnership,** prendre qn comme associé. *To give s.o. a p.,* intéresser qn (dans son commerce). **2.** *Com:* Société *f.*
partridge, *s.* (*a*) Perdrix *f.* (*b*) *Cu:* Perdreau *m.*
party, *s.* **1.** *Political parties,* partis *m* politiques. **2.** (*a*) **Pleasure party,** partie *f* de plaisir. (*b*) **Private party,** réunion *f* intime. **Evening party,** soirée *f.* **To give a party,** recevoir du monde. *To go to a p.,* aller en soirée. **3.** (*a*) Bande *f*, groupe *m.* (*b*) **Rescue party,** équipe de secours. (*c*) *Mil:* Détachement *m.* **4.** (*a*) **A third party,** un tiers, une tierce personne. **Third-party insurance,** assurance *f* au tiers. (*b*) **To be (a) party to a crime,** être complice d'un crime.
pasha, *s.* Pacha *m.*
pass[1], *s.* Col *m*, défilé *m.* *F:* **To sell the pass,** trahir son pays ou son parti.
pass[2], *s.* **1. To come to pass,** arriver, avoir lieu. **2.** Passe, permission *f.* **pass-book,** *s.* Carnet *m* de banque.
pass[3], *v.* I. *v.i.* Passer. **1.** (*a*) *Mil:* **Pass friend!** avance à l'ordre! (*b*) *Everyone smiles as he passes,* chacun sourit à son passage.

To let s.o. pass, livrer passage à qn. **Be it said in passing,** (ceci) soit dit en passant. **2. To pass (by),** (se) passer, s'écouler. *When five minutes had passed,* au bout de cinq minutes. **3. To pass (away),** disparaître. **4.** Arriver, avoir lieu. **5.** *She passes for a great beauty,* elle passe pour une beauté. **6.** *Jur:* Prononcer. II. **pass,** *v.tr.* **1.** (*a*) Passer devant, près de. *To p. s.o. on the stairs,* croiser qn dans l'escalier. (*b*) Passer, franchir (la frontière). (*c*) Dépasser (le but); outrepasser. *That passes my comprehension,* cela me dépasse. (*d*) Surpasser; gagner de vitesse; dépasser. (*e*) *To p. a test,* subir une épreuve avec succès. (*f*) **To pass an examination,** passer un examen; réussir à un examen. (*g*) *Abs.* *If the bill passes,* si le projet de loi est voté. (*h*) **To pass the censor,** être accepté par la censure. **2.** Approuver. (*a*) **To pass a dividend,** approuver un dividende. (*b*) *Sch:* **To pass a candidate,** recevoir un candidat. (*c*) *Parl:* **To pass a bill,** voter, adopter, un projet de loi. **3.** (*a*) *Trans*mettre, donner. (*b*) (Faire) passer, écouler (un faux billet de banque). **4. To pass (away) the time,** passer le temps. **5.** (*a*) **To pass sentence,** prononcer le jugement. (*b*) *F:* **To pass remarks on sth.,** faire des remarques sur qch. **pass away,** *v.i.* Trépasser. **pass off. 1.** *v.i.* (*a*) Se passer; disparaître. (*b*) *Everything passed off smoothly,* tout s'est bien passé. **2.** *v.tr.* (*a*) **To pass sth. off on s.o.,** repasser qch. à qn. (*b*) **To pass oneself off for an artist,** se faire passer pour artiste. **pass on. 1.** *v.i.* Passer son chemin; passer outre. **2.** *v.tr. Read this and p. it on,* lisez ceci et faites circuler. **pass over.** I. *v.i.* **1.** Passer (qch.) sous silence. **2.** Se dissiper, finir. II. **pass over,** *v.tr.* **1.** Donner, transmettre (qch. à qn). **2. To pass s.o. over,** passer par-dessus le dos à qn. **pass round,** *v.tr.* *To p. round the wine,* faire circuler le vin. **pass through,** *v.i.* Traverser. **passing,** *a.* (*a*) Passant. **P. remark,** remarque en passant. (*b*) Passager, éphémère.
passable, *a.* Passable; assez bon. **-ably,** *adv.* Passablement, assez.
passage, *s.* **1.** Passage *m.* **Bird of passage,** oiseau passager. **2.** (*a*) Couloir *m*, corridor *m.* (*b*) Passage, ruelle *f.* **3.** *F:* **Passage of arms,** passe *f* d'armes; échange *m* de mots vifs. **4.** Passage. **Selected passages,** morceaux choisis.
passenger, *s.* Voyageur, -euse; (*by sea or air*) passager, -ère. **passenger coach,** *s.* *Rail:* Wagon *m* à voyageurs. **passenger-pigeon,** *s.* Pigeon *m* de passage. **passenger train,** Train *m* de voyageurs. **By passenger train,** par grande vitesse.
passer(-by), *s.* Passant, -ante.
passion, *s.* **1.** Passion *f.* **Ruling passion,** passion dominante. **2.** Colère *f*, emportement *m.* **Fit of passion,** accès de colère. **To be in a passion,** être furieux. **3.** Amour *m*, passion.

passionate, *a.* **1.** Emporté ; véhément. **2.** Passionné. *P. embrace,* étreinte ardente. **-ly,** *adv.* **1.** Passionnément. **To be passionately fond of sth.,** être passionné de qch. **2.** Avec colère, avec emportement.

passive. 1. *a.* Passif. **2.** *a. & s. Gram:* The passive (voice), la voix passive ; le passif. **-ly,** *adv.* Passivement.

passover, *s.* La Pâque.

passport, *s.* Passeport *m.*

password, *s.* Mot *m* de passe.

past¹. 1. *a.* (*a*) Passé, ancien. **In times past,** autrefois. (*b*) *Gram:* Past participle, participe passé. (*c*) The p. *few years,* ces dernières années. **For some time past,** depuis quelque temps. **2.** *s.* Passé *m.* **In the past,** autrefois. **As in the past,** comme par le passé.

past². 1. *prep.* Au delà de. (*a*) To walk p. s.o., passer qn. **The train ran p. the signal,** le train brûla, dépassa, le signal. (*b*) Plus de. **A quarter past four,** quatre heures un quart. (*c*) Past all understanding, hors de toute compréhension. **Past endurance,** insupportable. **To be past one's work,** n'être plus en état de travailler. *F:* **I wouldn't put it past him,** je ne le croirais pas incapable de l'avoir fait. **2.** *adv.* To walk, go, past, passer. **To march past,** défiler.

paste¹, *s.* **1.** *Cu:* Pâte *f* (de pâtisserie). **2.** Pâte. **3.** *Lap:* Stras(s) *m* ; faux brillants ; *F:* du toc.

paste², *v.tr.* Coller.

pasteboard, *s.* Carton *m.* **Pasteboard box,** carton.

pastel, *s.* *Art:* Pastel *m.*

pastime, *s.* Passe-temps *m inv,* divertissement *m.*

pastor, *s.* *Ecc:* Pasteur *m,* ministre *m.*

pastoral, *a.* Pastoral, -aux.

pastry, *s.* **1.** Pâtisserie *f.* **2.** Pâte *f.* **pastrycook,** *s.* Pâtissier, -ière.

pasturage, *s.* **1.** Pâturage *m,* pacage *m.* **2.** = PASTURE¹ **1.**

pasture¹, *s.* **1.** Lieu *m* de pâture ; pâturage *m,* pacage *m.* **2.** = PASTURAGE **1.**

pasture². 1. *v.i.* Paître, pacager. **2.** *v.tr.* (Faire) paître. **pasturing,** *s.* Pacage *m.*

pasty¹, *a.* **1.** Pâteux. **2.** Pasty face, visage terreux.

pasty², *s.* *Cu:* Pâté *m.*

pat¹, *s.* **1.** (*a*) Coup léger ; petite tape. (*b*) Caresse *f.* *F:* **Pat on the back,** éloge *m* ; mot *m* d'encouragement. **2.** Rondelle *f,* pelote *f* (de beurre).

pat², *v.tr.* (*a*) Taper, tapoter. (*b*) Caresser. **To pat s.o. on the back,** encourager qn. **To pat oneself on the back over sth.,** s'applaudir de qch.

pat³. 1. *adv.* A propos. **2.** *a.* Apte ; à propos.

patch¹, *s.* **1.** Pièce *f* (pour raccommoder). *F:* **Not to be a patch on s.o.,** ne pas aller à la cheville de qn. **2.** *Aut:* (Rubber) patch, pastille *f.* **3.** Tache *f* (de couleur). **Patch** of blue sky, échappée *f* de ciel bleu. *P. of snow,* flaque *f* de neige. *F:* **To strike a bad patch,** être en guigne, en déveine. **4.** (*a*) Morceau *m,* parcelle *f* (de terre). (*b*) Carré *m,* plant *m* (de légumes).

patch², *v.tr.* Rapiécer, raccommoder. **patch up,** *v.tr.* Rapetasser (de vieux vêtemen.s) ; rafistoler (une machine).

patchwork, *s.* Ouvrage fait de pièces et de morceaux.

patchy, *a.* Inégal.

pate, *s.* *F:* Tête *f,* caboche *f.*

patent¹. I. *a.* **1.** Letters patent, lettres patentes. **2.** Breveté. **Patent medicine,** spécialité pharmaceutique. **Patent leather,** cuir verni. **3.** Patent, manifeste. **II.** patent, *s.* **1.** Patent of nobility, lettres de noblesse. **2.** (*a*) Brevet *m* d'invention. **Infringement of a patent,** contrefaçon *f.* (*b*) Invention brevetée.

patent², *v.tr.* Faire breveter.

paternal, *a.* Paternel. **-ally,** *adv.* Paternellement.

paternity, *s.* (*a*) Paternité *f.* (*b*) Origine *f.*

path, *s.* **1.** Chemin *m* ; sentier *m* ; (*in garden*) allée *f.* **The beaten path,** le chemin battu. **2.** Course *f* ; route *f.*

pathetic, *a.* Pathétique, attendrissant. **-ally,** *adv.* Pathétiquement.

pathless, *a.* Sans chemin frayé.

pathos, *s.* (*a*) Pathétique *m.* (*b*) Affected pathos, pathos *m.*

pathway, *s.* (*a*) Sentier *m.* (*b*) Trottoir *m.*

patience, *s.* **1.** Patience *f.* **To try s.o.'s patience,** exercer la patience de qn. **To have patience with s.o.,** prendre patience avec qn. **I have no patience with him,** il m'impatiente. **2.** *Cards:* Réussite *f.*

patient. I. *a.* Patient, endurant. *To be p.,* patienter. **-ly,** *adv.* Patiemment. **II.** **patient,** *s.* Malade *mf.* *A doctor's patients.* les clients *m* d'un médecin.

patriarch, *s.* Patriarche *m.*

patriarchal, *a.* Patriarcal, -aux.

patrician, *a. & s.* Patricien, -ienne.

Patrick. *Pr.n.* Patrice *m.*

patrimony, *s.* Patrimoine *m.*

patriot, *s.* Patriote *mf.*

patriotic, *a.* **1.** Patriote. **2.** (Chanson) patriotique. **-ally,** *adv.* Patriotiquement ; en patriote.

patriotism, *s.* Patriotisme *m.*

patrol¹, *s.* Patrouille *f.* **Patrol leader,** chef *m* de patrouille.

patrol². 1. *v.i.* Patrouiller ; faire une ronde. **2.** *v.tr.* Faire la patrouille dans.

patron. 1. *s.* (*a*) Protecteur *m* (des arts). (*b*) *Ecc:* Patron saint, patron, -onne. (*c*) Patron (d'un bénéfice). **2.** *s.m. & f.* *Com:* Client, -ente.

patronage, *s.* **1.** (*a*) Protection *f,* encouragement *m* ; patronage *m.* (*b*) Air protecteur (*of,* envers). **2.** Droit *m* de présentation (*of a living,* à un bénéfice).

patronize, *v.tr.* **1.** (*a*) Patronner, protéger. (*b*) Traiter d'un air protecteur. **2.** Accorder sa clientèle à. **patronizing,** *a.* (*a*) Protecteur, -trice. (*b*) Patronizing tone, ton de condescendance. **-ly,** *adv.* D'un air protecteur.

patter¹, *s.* **1.** Boniment *m* (de charlatan); bagout *m.* **2.** Parlé *m* (dans une chanson-nette).

patter², *s.* Petit bruit (de pas); fouettement *m* (de la pluie).

patter³, *v.i.* (*Of footsteps*) Sonner par petits coups; (*of rain*) fouetter.

pattern, *s.* **1.** Modèle *m,* type *m.* **2.** (*a*) Modèle, dessin *m.* (*b*) *Dressm:* Patron *m.* **3.** Échantillon *m.* **4.** Dessin, motif *m.*

patty, *s. Cu:* Petit pâté; bouchée *f* à la reine.

paucity, *s.* Manque *m,* disette *f*; rareté *f.*

Paul. *Pr.n.* Paul *m.*

paunch, *s.* Panse *f,* ventre *m.*

pauper, *s.* **1.** *Adm:* Indigent, -ente. **2.** Pauvre, -esse.

pause¹, *s.* (*a*) Pause *f,* arrêt *m.* (*b*) To give pause to s.o., faire hésiter qn.

pause², *v.i.* **1.** Faire une pause; s'arrêter un instant; marquer un temps. **2.** Hésiter.

pave, *v.tr.* Paver (une rue); carreler (une cour). *F:* To pave the way, préparer le terrain. **paving,** *s.* **1.** Pavage *m,* dallage *m,* carrelage *m.* **2.** Pavé *m,* dalles *fpl.* **paving-stone,** *s.* Pavé *m.*

pavement, *s.* (*a*) Pavé *m,* pavage *m,* dallage *m.* (*b*) Trottoir *m.*

pavilion, *s.* Pavillon *m.*

paw¹, *s.* Patte *f.*

paw², *v.tr.* (*Of horse*) To paw the ground, piaffer; gratter (la terre) du pied.

pawn¹, *s.* In pawn, en gage; *P:* chez ma tante. To put one's watch in pawn, engager sa montre. **pawn-ticket,** *s.* Reconnaissance *f* (de dépôt de gage).

pawn², *v.tr.* Engager; *P:* mettre chez ma tante. **pawning,** *s.* Mise *f* en gage.

pawn³, *s. Chess:* Pion *m. F:* To be s.o.'s pawn, être le jouet de qn.

pawnbroker, *s.* Prêteur, -euse, sur gage(s).

pawnshop, *s.* Bureau *m* de prêt sur gage(s)

pay¹, *s.* Paie *f,* salaire *m* (d'un employé); gages *mpl* (d'un domestique); traitement *m* (d'un fonctionnaire). *Mil:* Solde *f.* Unemployed pay, solde de non-activité. *Ind:* Holidays with pay, congés payés. To be in s.o.'s pay, être à la solde, aux gages, de qn. **pay-day,** *s.* Jour *m* de paie. **pay-desk,** *s.* Caisse *f.*

pay², *v.tr.* **1.** (*a*) To pay s.o ten francs, payer dix francs à qn. *Abs.* To pay cash down, payer (argent) comptant. To pay in advance, payer d'avance. *F:* To pay through the nose, payer un prix excessif. (*b*) Payer (un domestique); solder (des troupes); rétribuer (un employé). (*c*) To pay s.o. to do sth., payer qn pour faire qch. **2.** (*a*) Payer (une

dette) To pay a bill, solder, régler, un compte. 'Paid,' "pour acquit." (*b*) To pay honour to s.o., faire honneur à qn. To pay one's respects to s.o., présenter ses respects à qn. To pay s.o. a visit, faire une visite à qn. **3.** It will pay you, vous y gagnerez. *It doesn't pay,* on n'y trouve pas son compte. *Prov:* It pays to advertise, la publicité rapporte. **pay away,** *v.tr.* Dépenser. **pay back,** *v.tr.* **1.** Rendre. **2.** Rembourser. *F:* To pay s.o. back in his own coin, rendre la pareille à qn. **pay down,** *v.tr.* (*a*) Payer comptant. (*b*) To pay something down, verser une provision. **pay for,** *v.tr.* (*a*) To pay (s.o.) for sth., payer qch. (à qn). *What do you pay for tea?* combien payez-vous le thé? To pay s.o. for his trouble, dédommager qn de sa peine. (*b*) I'll make him pay for this! il me le paiera! **pay off,** *v.tr.* **1.** Solder, régler, acquitter. **2.** (*a*) Rembourser. (*b*) Congédier (un domestique); désarmer (un navire). **pay out,** *v.tr.* **1.** Payer, débourser. **2.** I'll pay you out for that! je vous revaudrai cela! **pay up,** *v.tr.* To pay up one's debts, *abs.* to pay up, se libérer (de ses dettes). Pay up! payez! **paid,** *a.* (Domestique) à gages; (employé) rétribué. **paying,** *a.* **1.** Payant. Paying guest, pensionnaire *mf.* **2.** (*Of business*) Rémunérateur, -trice; qui rapporte.

payable, *a.* Payable, acquittable. *To make a cheque p. to bearer,* souscrire un chèque au porteur.

paymaster, *s.* Payeur *m. Mil:* Trésorier *m. Navy:* Commissaire *m.*

payment, *s.* (*a*) Paiement *m*; versement *m.* On payment of ten francs, moyennant paiement de dix francs. Cash payment, paiement comptant. Payment on account, versement à compte; acompte *m.* (*b*) Rémunération *f.*

pea, *s.* **1.** *Hort:* Pois *m. Cu:* Green peas, petits pois. **2.** *Bot:* Sweet pea, pois de senteur. **pea-green,** *a. & s.* Vert feuille (*m*) *inv.* **pea-pod,** *s.* Cosse *f,* gousse *f,* de pois. **pea-shooter,** *s.* Petite sarbacane. **pea-soup,** *s.* Soupe *f* aux pois.

peace, *s.* **1.** (*a*) Paix *f.* At peace, en paix (with, avec). To make (one's) peace with s.o., faire la paix avec qn. (*b*) Traité *m* de paix. **2.** To keep the peace, (i) ne pas troubler l'ordre public; (ii) veiller à l'ordre public. Justice of the peace, juge *m* de paix. **3.** (*a*) Tranquillité *f* (de l'âme) To live in peace (and quietness), vivre en paix. *You may sleep in p.,* vous pouvez dormir tranquille. To give s.o. no peace, ne donner ni paix ni trêve à qn. (*b*) To hold one's peace, se taire; garder le silence.

peaceable, *a.* Pacifique **-ably,** *adv.* Pacifiquement.

peaceful, *a.* **1.** Paisible, calme, tranquille. **2.** Pacifique. **-fully,** *adv.* **1.** Paisiblement. **2.** Pacifiquement.

peacefulness, *s.* Tranquillité *f,* paix *f.*

peacemaker, *s.* Pacificateur, -trice.

peach¹, *s. Hort:* 1. Pêche *f.* 2. Peach(-tree), pêcher *m.*

peach², *v.i. P:* Cafarder, moucharder.

peacock, *s. Orn:* Paon *m.*

peafowl, *s.* Paon *m,* paonne *f.*

peahen, *s.* Paonne *f.*

peak, *s.* 1. Visière *f* (de casquette). 2. *(a)* Pic *m,* cime *f. The highest peaks,* les plus hauts sommets. *(b) Rail:* Peak hours, heures d'affluence.

peal¹, *s.* 1. Peal of bells, carillon *m.* 2. To ring a peal, carillonner. 3. Coup *m* (de tonnerre).

peal², *v.i. (a)* Carillonner. *(b)* Retentir, gronder.

peanut, *s. Bot:* Pistache *f* de terre ; arachide *f. Com:* Cacahouette *f.*

pear, *s.* 1. Poire *f.* 2. Pear(-tree), poirier *m.*

pearl, *s.* 1. Perle *f. String of pearls,* fil *m* de perles. 2. Nacre *f.* Pearl button, bouton de nacre. **pearl-barley,** *s.* Orge perlé. **pearl-diver,** *s.* Pêcheur *m* de perles. **pearl-fishery,** *s.* Pêcherie *f* de perles.

peasant, *s.* Paysan, -anne.

peasantry, *s. The peasantry,* les paysans *m.*

peat, *s. Coll:* Tourbe *f.*

pebble, *s.* 1. Caillou *m,* -oux ; *(on shore)* galet *m. F: You're not the only pebble on the beach,* vous n'êtes pas unique au monde. 2. *Opt:* Cristal *m* de roche.

pebbly, *a.* Caillouteux ; *(plage)* à galets.

peccadillo, *s.* Peccadille *f* ; vétille *f.*

peccary, *s. Z:* Pécari *m.*

peck¹, *s.* Coup *m* de bec.

peck², *v.tr.* 1. Picoter, becqueter ; donner un coup de bec à. 2. *v.ind.tr.* To Peck at, manger du bout des dents.

peck³, *s. Meas:* 1. *(a) Approx.* = Boisseau *m.* 2. *F: She's had a p. of trouble,* elle a eu bien des malheurs.

pecker, *s. To keep one's pecker up,* ne pas se laisser abattre.

peckish, *a. F: To feel peckish,* se sentir le ventre creux.

peculation, *s.* Péculat *m,* déprédation *f* ; détournement *m* de fonds ; prévarication *f.*

peculiar, *a. (a)* Particulier. *(b)* Spécial, -aux ; particulier. *Of p. interest,* d'un intérêt tout particulier. *(c) (Of thg)* Étrange ; *(of pers.)* bizarre, singulier. **-ly,** *adv. (a)* Particulièrement. *(b)* Étrangement ; singulièrement.

peculiarity, *s.* 1. Trait distinctif ; particularité *f.* 2. Bizarrerie *f,* singularité *f.*

pecuniary, *a.* Pécuniaire P *difficulties,* ennuis *m* d'argent

pedagogic(al), *a.* Pédagogique

pedagogue, *s. Pej:* Pédagogue *m.*

pedagogy, *s.* Pédagogie *f.*

pedal¹, *s.* Pédale *f.*

pedal², *v.i. Cy:* Pédaler.

pedant, *s.* Pédant, -ante.

pedantic, *a.* Pédant, pédantesque. **-ally,** *adv.* Pédantesquement ; en pédant.

pedantry, *s.* Pédantisme *m,* pédanterie *f.*

peddle. 1. *v.i.* Faire le colportage. 2. *v.tr.* Colporter. **peddling,** *s.* Colportage *m.*

pedestal, *s.* Piédestal *m,* -aux ; socle *m.*

pedestrian. 1. *a.* Pédestre. 2. *s.* Piéton *m.*

pedigree, *s.* 1. Arbre *m* généalogique. 2. *(a)* Ascendance *f,* généalogie *f. (b) Breed:* Certificat *m* d'origine. Pedigree dog, chien de race.

pedlar, *s.* Colporteur *m.*

peel¹, *s.* Pelure *f* ; écorce *f,* peau *f, Cu:* Candied peel, zeste confit.

peel², 1. *v.tr. (a)* Peler (un fruit) ; éplucher (des pommes de terre). *(b) Sp: F:* To peel, se dépouiller de ses vêtements. 2. *v.i. (a)* To peel (off), *(of paint)* s'écailler. *(b) (Of the nose)* Peler. **peeling,** *s.* 1. Épluchage *m* ; écorçage *m.* 2. *pl.* Peelings, épluchures *f.*

peep¹, *s.* 1. Coup *m* d'œil. To get a peep at sth., entrevoir qch. 2. At peep of day, au point du jour ; dès l'aube. **peep-bo,** *int.* Coucou !

peep², *v.i.* 1. To peep at sth., regarder qch. à la dérobée. 2. To peep (out), se laisser entrevoir, se montrer.

peer¹, *s.* 1. Pair *m* ; pareil, -eille. 2. Pair.

peer², *v.i. (a)* To peer at s.o., scruter qn du regard. *(b) To p. over the wall,* risquer un coup d'œil par-dessus le mur.

peerage, *s.* Pairie *f.*

peeress, *s.* Pairesse *f.*

peerless, *a.* Sans pareil, sans pair.

peevish, *a.* Irritable, geignard ; maussade. **-ly,** *adv.* Maussadement.

peevishness, *s.* Maussaderie *f.*

peg¹, *s. (a)* Cheville *f* ; fiche *f. (b)* (Hat-)peg, patère *f.* Peg to have a grievance on, prétexte *m* de plainte. **peg-top,** *s.* Toupie *f.*

peg², *v.tr.* 1. Cheviller. 2. *Games:* Marquer (des points). 3. *v.i. F:* To peg away, travailler ferme. **peg out,** 1. *v.tr.* To peg out a claim, piqueter une concession. 2. *F:* Mourir.

Pegasus. *Pr.n. Gr.Myth:* Pégase *m.*

Pekinese, *s.* (Épagneul *m)* pékinois *m.*

pelf, *s.* Richesses *fpl,* lucre *m.*

pelican, *s.* Pélican *m.*

pellet, *s. (a)* Boulette *f* (de papier) ; pelote *f* (d'argile). *(b)* Grain *m* de plomb.

pell-mell. 1. *adv.* Pêle-mêle. 2. *a.* Mis pêle-mêle ; en confusion.

pellucid, *a.* Pellucide, transparent.

pelt¹, *s.* Peau *f.*

pelt², *s. (At) full pelt,* à toute vitesse.

pelt³, 1. *v.tr.* To pelt s.o. with stones, lancer une volée de pierres à qn. 2. *v.i.* To pelt (down), tomber à verse. Pelting rain, pluie battante.

pen¹, *s.* Parc *m,* enclos *m.*

pen², *v.tr.* To pen (up, in), parquer ; (r)enfermer, confiner.

pen³, *s.* 1. Plume *f* (pour écrire). To put

one's pen to paper, mettre la main à la plume. **Pen-and-ink drawing,** dessin à la plume. **2. Pen(-nib),** (bec *m* de) plume. **Steel pen,** plume métallique. **pen-box,** *s.* Plumier *m.* **pen-wiper,** *s.* Essuie-plume(s) *m inv.*

pen[4], *v.tr.* Écrire (une lettre).

penal, *a.* Pénal, -aux. **Penal servitude,** travaux forcés.

penalize, *v.tr.* **1.** Sanctionner d'une peine. **2.** (*a*) Infliger une peine à. (*b*) *Games :* Pénaliser.

penalty, *s.* **1.** (*a*) Peine *f,* pénalité *f. Adm :* Sanction (pénale). **The death penalty,** la peine de mort. *F :* **To pay the penalty of one's foolishness,** être puni de sa sottise. (*b*) Désavantage *m.* **2.** *Sp :* Pénalisation *f,* pénalité.

penance, *s.* **To do penance** *for one's sins,* faire pénitence *f* de, pour, ses péchés.

pencil[1], *s.* Crayon *m.* (*a*) **Lead pencil,** crayon à mine de plomb. *Coloured p.,* crayon de couleur. **Propelling pencil,** porte-mine *m inv* à vis. **Written in pencil,** écrit au crayon. (*b*) **Slate pencil,** crayon d'ardoise. **pencil-box,** *s.* Plumier *m.* **pencil-case,** *s.* **1.** (*a*) Porte-crayon *m inv.* (*b*) Porte-mine *m inv.* **2.** Plumier *m.* **pencil-holder,** *s.* Porte-crayon *m inv.* **pencil-sharpener,** *s.* Taille-crayon *m inv.*

pencil[2], *v.tr.* (*a*) Marquer au crayon. (*b*) *Delicately pencilled eyebrows,* sourcils d'un tracé délicat.

pendant, *s.* Pendentif *m* (de collier) ; pendeloque *f* (de lustre).

pendent, *a.* Pendant ; retombant.

pending. **1.** *a. Jur :* Pendant. **2.** *prep.* (*a*) Pendant. (*b*) En attendant.

pendulum, *s.* Pendule *m,* balancier *m.*

penetrate. **1.** *v.tr.* Pénétrer, percer. **2.** *v.i.* Pénétrer. **penetrating,** *a.* **1.** (Vent) pénétrant ; (son) mordant. **2.** (Esprit) pénétrant.

penetration, *s.* (*a*) Pénétration *f.* (*b*) Pénétration ; perspicacité *f.*

penguin, *s. Orn :* Manchot *m.*

penholder, *s.* Porte-plume *m inv.*

penicillin, *s. Med :* Pénicilline *f.*

peninsula, *s.* Péninsule *f* ; presqu'île *f.*

peninsular, *a.* Péninsulaire. *Hist :* **The Peninsular War,** la guerre d'Espagne.

penitence, *s.* Pénitence *f,* contrition *f.*

penitent. **1.** *a.* Pénitent, contrit. **2.** *s.* Pénitent, -ente. **-ly,** *adv.* D'un air contrit.

penknife, *s.* Canif *m.*

penmanship, *s.* **1.** L'art *m* d'écrire. **2.** Calligraphie *f.*

pennant, *s. Nau :* Flamme *f,* guidon *m.*

penniless, *a.* Sans le sou ; sans ressources.

pennon, *s.* Flamme *f,* banderole *f.*

penny, *s.* **1.** Deux sous ; gros sou. **They haven't a penny,** ils n'ont pas le sou. **2. Nobody was a penny the worse,** cela n'a fait de tort à personne. **3. That will cost a pretty penny,** cela coûtera cher. **To earn an honest**

penny, gagner honnêtement de l'argent.

penny-piece, *s. F :* **I haven't a penny-piece,** je n'ai pas un sou vaillant. **penny-wise,** *a.* Qui fait des économies de bouts de chandelle.

pension[1], *s.* **1.** Pension *f,* retraite *f.* **Old age pension,** retraite de vieillesse. **Retiring pension,** pension de retraite. **To be discharged with a p.,** être mis à la retraite. **2.** Pension de famille.

pension[2], *v.tr.* Pensionner. **To pension s.o. off,** mettre qn à la retraite.

pensioner, *s.* Titulaire *mf* d'une pension. (**Army**) **pensioner,** (militaire) retraité.

pensive, *a.* Pensif, songeur, -euse. **-ly,** *adv.* Pensivement ; d'un air pensif.

pent, *a.* **1. Pent (in, up),** renfermé. **2. Pent up emotion,** émotion refoulée.

pentagon, *s.* Pentagone *m.*

pentameter, *s. Pros :* Pentamètre *m.*

Pentateuch (the), *s. B :* Le Pentateuque.

Pentecost, *s.* La Pentecôte.

penultimate. **1.** *a.* Pénultième ; avant-dernier. **2.** *s.* Pénultième *f.*

penurious, *a.* **1.** Pauvre. **2.** (*a*) Parcimonieux. (*b*) Mesquin. **-ly,** *adv.* **1.** Pauvrement. **2.** (*a*) Parcimonieusement. (*b*) Mesquinement.

penury, *s.* **1.** Pénurie *f.* **1.** Indigence *f.* **2.** Manque *m,* pauvreté *f* (*of,* de).

peony, *s. Bot :* Pivoine *f.*

people[1], *s.* **1.** Peuple *m,* nation *f.* **II. people, Coll :** **1.** (*a*) Peuple, habitants *mpl.* (*b*) **The King and his people,** le roi et ses sujets. (*c*) *F :* **Parents** *mpl.* **How are all your people?** comment va tout votre monde ? **2.** (*a*) *Pol :* **Citoyens** *mpl.* **Government by the people,** gouvernement par le peuple. (*b*) **The (common) people,** la populace. **3.** (*a*) **Gens** *mpl,* monde *m.* **Young people,** jeunes gens. **Fashionable people,** le beau monde. **What do you people think?** qu'en pensez-vous, vous autres ? (*b*) **Personnes** *fpl.* **One thousand people,** mille personnes. (*c*) (*Nom.*) On ; (*obl. cases*) vous. **People say,** on dit. *That's enough to alarm p.,* il y a de quoi vous alarmer.

people[2], *v.tr.* Peupler (*with,* de).

pepper[1], *s.* **1.** Poivre *m.* **2.** *Bot :* **Pepper (-tree),** poivrier *m.* **pepper-castor,** *s.* Poivrière *f.*

pepper[2], *v.tr.* **1.** Poivrer. **2.** *F :* Cribler (l'ennemi) de balles.

peppercorn, *s.* Grain *m* de poivre.

peppermint, *s.* **1.** Menthe poivrée. **2. Peppermint (-lozenge),** pastille *f* de menthe.

peppery, *a.* **1.** Poivré. **2.** Irascible.

per, *prep.* **1.** (*a*) Par. (*b*) **One franc per pound,** un franc la livre. **Sixty miles per hour,** soixante milles à l'heure. **2. Per annum,** par an. **Per cent,** pour cent.

perambulator, *s.* Voiture *f* d'enfant.

perceive, *v.tr.* **1.** S'apercevoir de. *He perceived that he was being watched,* il s'aperçut qu'on l'observait. **2. To p. s.o.,** apercevoir qn.

percentage, s. Pourcentage m.

perceptible, a. (a) Perceptible. *P. difference,* différence sensible. (b) *Perceptible to the eye,* visible. **-ibly,** adv. Sensiblement.

perception, s. (a) Perception f. (b) Sensibilité f.

perceptive, a. Perceptif

perch[1], s. Perchoir m. F: *To knock s.o. off his perch,* déjucher qn.

perch[2], v.i. (Se) percher (on, sur); jucher.

perch[3], s. Ich: Perche f.

percolation, s. 1. Infiltration f. 2. Filtration f.

percolator, s. Filtre m.

percussion, s. Percussion f; choc m. *Sm.a:* Percussion cap, capsule f de fulminate.

perdition, s. Perte f, ruine f.

peregrination, s. Pérégrination f.

peregrine, a. *Ven: Peregrine falcon,* faucon pèlerin.

peremptory, a. Péremptoire. (a) (*Of refusal*) Absolu. (b) (*Of tone*) Tranchant. **-ily,** adv. (a) Péremptoirement, absolument. (b) Impérieusement.

perennial. 1. a. (a) Éternel, perpétuel. (b) *Bot:* Vivace. 2. s. Plante f vivace. **-ally,** adv. A perpétuité.

perfect[1], a. 1. (a) Parfait; (ouvrage) achevé. *Perfect specimen,* spécimen parfait. *To have a p. knowledge of sth.,* savoir qch. à fond. (b) F: *She is a perfect fright,* c'est un véritable épouvantail. *He is a p. stranger to me,* il m'est parfaitement étranger. 2. *Gram:* The perfect tense, s. the perfect, le parfait. **-ly,** adv. Parfaitement.

perfect[2], v.tr. 1. Achever, parachever. 2. Rendre parfait, parfaire. **perfecting,** s. 1. Achèvement m. 2. Perfectionnement m.

perfection, s. Perfection f. 1. (a) Achèvement m, accomplissement m. (b) Perfectionnement m (d'un projet). 2. *To succeed to perfection,* réussir à souhait.

perfidious, a. Perfide; traître, -esse. **-ly,** adv. Perfidement, traîtreusement.

perfidy, s. Perfidie f, traîtrise f.

perforate. 1. v.tr. Perforer, percer, transpercer. 2. v.i. Pénétrer (into, dans). **perforated,** a. Perforé.

perforation, s. Perforation f. 1. Perçage m, percement m. 2. (a) Petit trou. (b) *Coll:* Trous mpl, perforation.

perform, v.tr. 1. Exécuter (un mouvement); accomplir (une tâche); s'acquitter de (son devoir). 2. (a) Jouer, représenter. (b) *Performing dogs,* chiens savants. **performing,** s. 1. Accomplissement m (of, de). 2. *Th:* Représentation f

performance, s. 1. Exécution f (d'un opéra); accomplissement m (d'une tâche). 2. Acte m, exploit m. 3. Représentation f (d'une pièce); séance f (de cinéma). *Evening performance,* soirée f. *Afternoon performance,* matinée f.

performer, s. Artiste mf. 1. *Mus:* Exécutant, -ante. 2. *Th:* Acteur, -trice.

perfume[1], s. Parfum m.

perfume[2], v.tr. Parfumer.

perfunctory, a. 1. *P. glance,* coup d'œil superficiel. *P. enquiry,* enquête peu poussée. 2. Négligent; peu zélé. **-ily,** adv. Superficiellement.

pergola, s. Tonnelle f.

perhaps, adv. Peut-être. *P. I have it,* il se peut que je l'aie.

peril, s. Péril m, danger m. *In peril of one's life,* en danger de mort. *Touch him at your p.,* gare à vous si vous le touchez.

perilous, a. Périlleux, dangereux. **-ly,** adv. Périlleusement, dangereusement.

perimeter, s. Périmètre m.

period, s. 1. Période f. 1. Durée f, délai m. 2. Époque f, âge m. 3. (a) *Rh:* Phrase f. *Well rounded periods,* phrases, périodes, bien tournées. (b) *Mus:* Phrase complète.

periodical. 1. a. Périodique. 2. s. Publication f périodique; périodique m. **-ally,** adv. Périodiquement.

periscope, s. Périscope m.

perish, v.i. (a) Périr, mourir. F: *I'm perishing with cold,* je meurs de froid. (b) (*Of rubber*) Se détériorer. **perished,** a. 1. (*Of rubber*) Détérioré. 2. F: *To be perished with cold,* être transi de froid.

perishable, a. Périssable; sujet à s'altérer.

periwinkle[1], s. *Bot:* Pervenche f.

periwinkle[2], s. *Moll:* Bigorneau m.

perjure, v.pr. *To perjure oneself,* violer son serment. **perjured,** a. Parjure.

perjurer, s. Parjure mf.

perjury, s. *Jur:* (a) *To commit perjury,* faire un faux serment. (b) Faux témoignage.

perk. 1. v.i. *To perk (up),* se ranimer. 2. v.tr. *To perk up one's head,* redresser la tête.

perkiness, s. 1. Allure(s) dégagée(s). 2. Air éveillé, alerte; ton guilleret.

perky, a. (a) Éveillé, alerte. (b) (*Ton*) dégagé, désinvolte. **-ily,** adv. (a) D'un air éveillé. (b) D'un air dégagé.

perm[1], s. *Hairdr:* (Ondulation) permanente f, indéfrisable f.

perm[2], v.tr. F: *To have one's hair permed,* se faire faire une indéfrisable.

permanence, s. Permanence f.

permanency, s. 1. = PERMANENCE. 2. Emploi permanent.

permanent, a. Permanent. *Permanent post,* place inamovible. *Permanent address,* résidence fixe. *Rail:* The permanent way, la superstructure; la voie ferrée. *Hairdr:* Permanent wave, ondulation permanente. **-ly,** adv. D'une façon permanente.

permeability, s. Perméabilité f.

permeable, a. Perméable.

permeate, v.tr. & i. *To permeate (through) sth.,* filtrer à travers qch.

permeation, s. Pénétration f, infiltration f.

permissible, *a.* Tolérable, permis.
permission, *s.* Permission *f* (*a*) *With your kind p.,* si vous voulez bien (me) le permettre. (*b*) Permis *m,* autorisation *f.*
permit¹, *s.* Permis *m,* autorisation *f.*
permit², *v.tr.* Permettre. *P. me to tell you the truth,* souffrez que je vous dise la vérité.
permute, *v.tr. Mth:* Permuter.
pernicious, *a.* Pernicieux. **-ly,** *adv.* Pernicieusement.
peroration, *s.* Péroration *f.*
peroxide, *s. Ch:* Peroxyde *m.* **Hydrogen peroxide,** eau oxygénée.
perpendicular. **I.** *a.* Perpendiculaire. **2.** *s.* (*a*) Fil *m* à plomb. (*b*) *Geom:* Perpendiculaire *f.* **-ly,** *adv.* Perpendiculairement ; verticalement.
perpetrate, *v.tr.* Commettre, perpétrer.
perpetration, *s.* Perpétration *f.*
perpetrator, *s.* Auteur *m.*
perpetual, *a.* (*a*) Perpétuel, éternel. (*b*) *F:* Sans fin ; continuel. **-ally,** *adv.* (*a*) Perpétuellement. (*b*) Sans cesse.
perpetuate, *v.tr.* Perpétuer, éterniser.
perpetuation, *s.* Perpétuation *f.*
perpetuity, *s.* Perpétuité *f.* **In, to, for, perpetuity,** à perpétuité.
perplex, *v.tr.* Embarrasser ; mettre dans la perplexité. **perplexed,** *a.* Perplexe, embarrassé. **perplexing,** *a.* Embarrassant, troublant.
perplexity, *s.* Perplexité *f,* embarras *m.*
perquisite, *s.* (*a*) Casuel *m.* (*b*) *F:* Pourboire (auquel l'on à droit).
persecute, *v.tr.* **I.** Persécuter. **2.** Tourmenter ; harceler.
persecution, *s.* Persécution *f.*
persecutor, *s.* Persécuteur, -trice.
perseverance, *s.* Persévérance *f.*
persevere, *v.i.* Persévérer (*with,* dans). **persevering,** *a.* Persévérant, assidu (*in doing sth.,* à faire qch.). **-ly,** *adv.* Avec persévérance.
Persia. *Pr.n. Geog:* La Perse.
Persian. **I.** *a. & s. Geog:* (i) Persan, -ane ; (ii) *A.Hist:* perse. (iii) **The Persian Gulf,** le Golfe Persique. *Com:* **Persian carpet,** tapis *m* de Perse. **2.** *s. Ling:* Le persan.
persimmon, *s. Bot:* Plaquemine *f.*
persist, *v.i.* Persister. **I.** *To persist in doing sth.,* persister, s'obstiner, à faire qch. **2.** Continuer.
persistency, *s.* Persistance *f.* **I.** Obstination *f.* **2.** Continuité *f.*
persistent, *a.* Persistant. **-ly,** *adv* Avec persistance.
person, *s.* Personne *f.* **I.** (*a*) Individu *m* ; *pl.* gens *m. Jur:* **Some person or persons unknown,** un certain quidam. (*b*) In (one's own) person, en (propre) personne. **2.** *Gram:* Personne.
personage, *s.* Personnage *m,* personne *f,* personnalité *f.*
personal, *a.* Personnel. **I.** (*a*) Personal

liberty, liberté individuelle. *This is p. to myself,* cela m'est propre. *Journ:* **Personal column,** petite correspondance. (*b*) *Don't be personal,* ne faites pas de personnalités. (*c*) *To make a p. application,* se présenter en personne. **2.** *Gram:* **Personal pronoun,** pronom personnel. **-ally,** *adv.* Personnellement. *P., I am willing,* moi, je veux bien. *Don't take that remark p.,* ne prenez pas cette remarque pour vous. *To deliver sth. to s.o. personally,* remettre qch. à qn en main(s) propre(s).
personality, *s.* **I.** (*a*) Personnalité *f,* personnage *m.* (*b*) Caractère *m* propre (de qn). **2.** *To indulge in personalities,* dire des personnalités.
personate, *v.tr. Th:* Jouer.
personation, *s. Th:* Représentation *f.*
personification, *s.* Personnification *f.*
personify, *v.tr.* Personnifier. *He is avarice personified,* il est, c'est, l'avarice même.
perspective, *s.* Perspective *f.*
perspicacious, *a.* Perspicace.
perspicacity, *s.* Perspicacité *f.*
perspicuity, *s.* Clarté *f,* netteté *f,* lucidité *f.*
perspicuous, *a.* Clair, lucide ; (*of reason*) évident.
perspiration, *s.* (*a*) Transpiration *f.* (*b*) Sueur *f.* **Bathed in perspiration,** trempé de sueur ; *F:* en nage.
perspire, *v.i.* Transpirer, suer. **perspiring,** *a.* En sueur.
persuade, *v.tr.* (*a*) *To persuade s.o. of sth.,* persuader qn de qch. (*b*) *To persuade s.o. to do sth.,* persuader à qn de faire qch. *P. your brother to come!* déterminez votre frère à venir ! (*c*) *He persuaded me not to,* il m'en a dissuadé.
persuasion, *s.* **I.** Persuasion *f.* (*a*) *The art of p.,* l'art de persuader. (*b*) Conviction *f.* **2.** (**Religious**) **persuasion,** religion *f,* confession *f.*
persuasive, *a.* Persuasif ; persuadant. **-ly,** *adv.* D'un ton persuasif.
pert, *a.* Mutin ; effronté, hardi. **-ly,** *adv.* Avec mutinerie ; d'un air effronté.
pertain, *v.i.* Appartenir (*to sth.,* à qch.).
pertinacious, *a.* Obstiné, entêté, opiniâtre. **-ly,** *adv.* Obstinément, opiniâtrement.
pertinacity, *s.* Obstination *f,* opiniâtreté *f,* entêtement *m* (*in doing sth.,* à faire qch.).
pertinence, *s.* Pertinence *f* (d'une raison) ; à-propos *m.* justesse *f* (d'une observation).
pertinent, *a.* Pertinent ; à propos, juste. **-ly,** *adv.* D'une manière pertinente ; à propos.
pertness, *s.* Mutinerie *f,* effronterie *f.*
perturb, *v.tr.* Troubler, inquiéter.
perturbation, *s.* Agitation *f,* inquiétude *f.*
Peru. *Pr.n. Geog:* Le Pérou.
perusal, *s.* Lecture *f.*
peruse, *v.tr.* Lire attentivement.
pervade, *v.tr.* S'infiltrer dans. **To become pervaded,** se pénétrer (*with,* de). (All-)

pervading, qui se répand partout ; dominant.
pervasive, *a.* Qui se répand partout ; pénétrant.
perverse, *a.* (*a*) Pervers, méchant. (*b*) Entêté dans le mal. (*c*) Contrariant. **-ly,** *adv.* Perversement.
perverseness, *s.* (*a*) Perversité *f.* (*b*) Esprit *m* contraire. (*c*) Caractère *m* revêche.
perversion, *s.* Perversion *f.* *A p. of the truth,* un travestissement de la vérité.
perversity, *s.* = PERVERSENESS.
pervert[1], *s.* (*a*) Perverti, -ie. (*b*) Apostat *m*.
pervert[2], *v.tr.* **I.** Détourner. **2.** Pervertir. **3.** Fausser (les faits).
perverter, *s.* Pervertisseur, -euse.
pervious, *a.* Perméable.
perviousness, *s.* Perméabilité *f* (*to,* à).
pessimism, *s.* Pessimisme *m*.
pessimist, *s.* Pessimiste *mf*.
pessimistic, *a.* Pessimiste. **-ally,** *adv.* Avec pessimisme.
pest, *s.* Peste *f,* fléau *m*.
pester, *v.tr.* Tourmenter, importuner.
pestiferous, *a.* (*a*) (*Of air*) Pestifère. (*b*) (*Of insects*) Nuisible.
pestilence, *s.* Peste *f*.
pestilent, *a.* Pestilentiel.
pestilential, *a.* Pestilentiel.
pestle, *s.* Pilon *m*.
pet[1]. **I.** *s.* (*a*) Animal familier, favori. **To make a pet of an animal,** choyer un animal. (*b*) *He is his mother's pet,* c'est l'enfant gâté de sa mère. **2.** *Attrib.* Choyé, favori. *He's on his pet subject again,* le revoilà sur son dada. **Pet name,** diminutif *m* ; nom *m* d'amitié.
pet[2], *v.tr.* Choyer, mignoter.
petal, *s.* *Bot:* Pétale *m*.
Peter[1]. **I.** *Pr.n.* Pierre *m*. **2.** *s. Nau:* Blue Peter, pavillon *m* de partance.
peter[2] **out,** *v.i. F:* **I.** *Min:* Mourir ; s'épuiser. **2.** (*Of scheme*) Tomber dans l'eau.
petition[1], *s.* (*a*) Prière *f* (à Dieu). (*b*) Pétition *f,* requête *f.* (*c*) *Jur:* **Petition for a reprieve,** recours *m* en grâce. **Petition for a divorce,** demande *f* en divorce.
petition[2], *v.tr.* Adresser, présenter, une pétition à.
petitioner, *s.* Pétitionnaire *mf*.
petrel, *s.* *Orn:* Pétrel *m*. **Stormy petrel,** (i) oiseau *m* des tempêtes ; (ii) *F:* émissaire *m* de discorde.
petrifaction, *s.* Pétrification *f*.
petrify, *v.tr.* (*a*) Pétrifier. (*b*) *F:* Pétrifier, méduser (qn de peur).
petrol, *s.* Essence *f* (de pétrole). **petrol-can,** *s.* Bidon *m* à essence.
petroleum, *s.* Pétrole *m*.
petticoat, *s.* (*a*) **Petticoat government,** régime *m* de cotillons. (*b*) Jupe *f* de dessous ; jupon *m*.
pettiness, *s.* Petitesse *f,* mesquinerie *f*.
pettish, *a.* De mauvaise humeur ; maussade ; irritable. **-ly,** *adv.* Avec humeur.
pettishness, *s.* Mauvaise humeur.

petty, *a.* **I.** (*a*) Petit, insignifiant, sans importance. (*b*) **Petty(-minded),** mesquin. **2.** *Com:* **Petty cash,** petite caisse. **3.** *Navy:* **Petty officer,** contremaître *m*.
petulance, *s.* Irritabilité *f.* vivacité *f*.
petulant, *a.* Irritable, susceptible, vif. **-ly,** *adv.* Avec irritation.
pew, *s.* Banc d'église (fermé).
pewit, *s. Orn:* Vanneau (huppé).
pewter, *s.* **I.** Étain *m,* potin *m.* **2.** Pot *m* d'étain.
phalanx, *s.* Phalange *f*.
phantasm, *s.* Chimère *f,* illusion *f*.
phantasmagoric, *a.* Fantasmagorique.
phantom, *s.* Fantôme *m,* spectre *m*.
Pharaoh, *s.* *A.Hist:* Pharaon *m*.
Pharisaic(al), *a.* Pharisaïque.
Pharisee, *s.* Pharisien *m*.
pharmaceutic(al), *a.* Pharmaceutique.
pharmacopœia, *s.* Pharmacopée *f* ; codex *m*.
pharmacy, *s.* Pharmacie *f*.
phase, *s.* Phase *f*.
pheasant, *s.* (**Cock-)pheasant,** (coq) faisan *m*. **Hen-pheasant,** faisane *f*.
phenacetin, *s.* Phénacétine *f*.
phenomenal, *a.* Phénoménal, -aux.
phenomenon, *s.* Phénomène *m* ; (*of pers.*) prodige *m*.
phew, *int.* **I.** Pouf ! **2.** (*Disgust*) Pouah !
phial, *s.* Fiole *f,* flacon *m*.
philanthropic(al), *a.* Philanthropique ; (*of pers.*) philanthrope.
philanthropist, *s.* Philanthrope *m*.
philanthropy, *s.* Philanthropie *f*.
philatelic, *a.* Philatélique, philatéliste.
philatelist, *s.* Philatéliste *mf*.
philately, *s.* Philatélie *f,* philatélisme *m*.
Philip. *Pr.n.* Philippe *m*.
Philistine, *s. F:* Philistin *m*.
philological, *a.* Philologique. **-ally,** *adv.* Philologiquement.
philologist, *s.* Philologue *m*.
philology, *s.* Philologie *f*.
philosopher, *s.* Philosophe *m*.
philosophical, *a.* **I.** Philosophique. **2.** (*Of pers.*) Philosophe, calme, modéré. **-ally,** *adv.* Philosophiquement.
philosophy, *s.* Philosophie *f*.
phlegm, *s.* Flegme *m*.
phlegmatic, *a.* Flegmatique. **-ally,** *adv.* Flegmatiquement.
phobia, *s.* Phobie *f*.
Phœnicia. *Pr.n.* *A.Geog:* La Phénicie.
Phœnician, *a. & s.* Phénicien, -ienne.
phœnix, *s.* Phénix *m*.
phone[1], *s. F:* Téléphone *m.* **He is not on the phone,** il n'a pas le téléphone.
phone[2], *v.tr. & i.* **To phone (up) s.o.,** téléphoner à qn. **To p. for sth.,** demander qch. par téléphone.
phonetic, *a.* Phonétique. **-ally,** *adv.* Phonétiquement.
phonetics, *s.pl.* Phonétique *f*.

phosphate, s. *Ch:* Phosphate m.
phosphide, s. *Ch:* Phosphure m.
phosphorescence, s. Phosphorescence f.
phosphorescent, a. Phosphorescent.
phosphorus, s. *Ch:* Phosphore m.
photograph[1], s. Photographie f. **To have
one's photograph taken,** se faire photographier.
photograph[2], v.tr. Photographier.
photographer, s. Photographe m.
photographic, a. Photographique.
photography, s. Photographie f. **Colour
photography,** héliochromie f.
phrase, s. **1.** Locution f, expression f.
2. *Mus:* Phrase f, période f.
phrenologist, s. Phrénologiste m.
phrenology, s. Phrénologie f.
phthisis, s. *Med:* Phtisie f.
physic[1], s. Médecine f, médicaments mpl.
physic[2], v.tr. *F:* Médicamenter.
physical, a. Physique. **1. Physical impossibility,** impossibilité matérielle. **2.** *P.* force,
force physique. **-ally,** adv. Physiquement.
Thing p. impossible, chose matériellement
impossible.
physician, s. Médecin m.
physics, s.pl. La physique.
physiognomy, s. Physionomie f.
physiological, a. Physiologique.
physiologist, s. Physiologiste m.
physiology, s. Physiologie f.
physique, s. **1.** Physique m. **2.** Structure f
du corps.
pianiste, s. Pianiste mf.
piano, pianoforte, s. *Mus:* Piano m.
(Concert) grand piano, piano à queue.
Baby-grand piano, *F:* crapaud m. **To play
(on) the piano,** jouer du piano.
piastre, s. *Num:* Piastre f.
Picardy. Pr.n. La Picardie.
pick[1], s. Choix m, élite f. *F:* **The pick of
the basket,** le dessus du panier.
pick[2], v.tr. **1.** (a) Piocher. (b) *F:* **To pick
holes in sth.,** trouver à redire à qch. **2. To
pick one's teeth,** se curer les dents. **3.** *F:*
To have a bone to pick with s.o., avoir maille
à partir avec qn. **4.** Picoter, becqueter.
F: **To pick (at) one's food,** manger du bout
des dents. **5.** Choisir. **To pick one's steps,**
marcher avec précaution. **To pick and
choose,** se montrer difficile. *Games:* **To
pick sides,** tirer les camps. **6.** (a) Cueillir.
(b) **To pick acquaintance with s.o.,** lier connaissance avec qn. **7.** (a) **To pick pockets,**
pratiquer le vol à la tire. (b) Crocheter (une
serrure). **To pick s.o.'s brains,** exploiter
l'intelligence de qn. **pick off,** v.tr. **1.** Enlever, ôter. **2.** *A sniper picked off the officers,*
un tireur descendit les officiers. **pick out,**
v.tr. (a) Extirper, enlever. (b) Choisir.
To pick s.o. out from the crowd, repérer qn
parmi la foule. **pick over,** v.tr. Trier.
pick up. I. v.tr. **1.** Ramasser. *To p. up*

shipwrecked men, recueillir des naufragés.
2. Apprendre. To pick up a language,
s'initier rapidement à une langue. **3.** Trouver,
retrouver. **To pick up sth. cheap,** acheter
qch. à bon marché. **To pick up a livelihood,**
gagner péniblement sa vie. **4.** (a) (*Of searchlight*) **To pick up an aeroplane,** repérer un
avion. (b) *W.Tel:* Capter (un message).
To p. up Paris, avoir Paris. **5. That will pick
you up,** voilà qui vous requinquera. **6. To
pick up strength,** reprendre des forces. II.
pick up, v.i. Retrouver ses forces;
se rétablir. **picking,** s. **1.** (a) Choix m (de
ses mots). (b) Cueillage m, cueillaison f (de
fruits). **2.** pl. **Pickings.** *F:* Bénéfices m.
pick-me-up, s. *F:* Cordial m, -aux.
pick-a-back, s. **To give s.o. a pick-a-back,**
porter qn sur le dos.
pickaxe, s. *Tls:* Pioche f.
picket, s. **1.** Piquet m. **2.** *Mil:* Piquet.
pickle[1], s. **1.** Marinade f; saumure f.
2. pl. **Pickles,** conserves f au vinaigre.
3. *F:* (a) **To be in a pickle,** être dans de
beaux draps. (b) Enfant mf terrible.
pickle[2], v.tr. Mariner; conserver (au vinaigre).
pickpocket, s. Voleur m à la tire; pickpocket m.
picnic[1], s. Partie f de plaisir; pique-nique m.
picnic[2], v.i. Faire un pique-nique.
pictorial, a. (a) En images. (b) Illustré.
-ally, adv. Au moyen d'illustrations.
picture[1], s. **1.** Image f; tableau m; peinture f; gravure f. **He is the picture of
health,** il respire la santé. **To be in the
picture,** compter. **2.** *Cin:* *F:* **The pictures,**
le ciné. **Sound picture,** film m sonore. **Talking
pictures,** le cinéma parlant. **picture-book,**
s. Livre m d'images. **picture-card,** s.
Cards: Figure f. **picture-palace,** s.
Cinéma m, *F:* ciné m.
picture[2], v.tr. **1.** Dépeindre, représenter.
2. To picture to oneself, se figurer.
picturesque, a. Pittoresque. **-ly,** adv.
Pittoresquement.
pie, s. (a) **Meat pie,** pâté m. **Shepherd's pie,**
hachis m aux pommes de terre. (b) **Fruit
pie,** tourte f. (c) *F:* **To eat humble pie,**
s'humilier. **pie-dish,** s. Terrine f (à
pâtés); tourtière f.
piebald, a. & s. (a) (Cheval) pie m. (b) *F:*
Bigarré, disparate.
piece[1], s. Pièce f. **1.** (a) Morceau m (de
pain); bout m (de ruban). (b) Fragment m.
To come to pieces, s'en aller en morceaux.
F: **He went to pieces,** il s'est écroulé. *F:* **To
pull s.o. to pieces,** critiquer qn sévèrement.
2. Partie f. **To take a machine to pieces,**
démonter une machine. **To take a dress to
pieces,** défaire une robe. **3.** *Com:* Pièce (de
drap). **4. All in one piece,** tout d'une pièce.
F: **They are all of a piece,** ils sont tous du
même acabit. **5.** (a) *A p. of my work,* un
échantillon de mon travail. **Piece of water,**
pièce d'eau. (b) **Piece of folly,** acte m de folie.

(c) A **piece** of advice, un conseil. A **piece** of news, une nouvelle. A **piece of furniture**, un meuble. A **piece of clothing**, un vêtement. **6.** (a) Pièce (d'artillerie). (b) Pièce (de monnaie). **7.** Morceau (de musique); pièce (de théâtre). **8.** Chess: Pièce. **piecework**, s. Travail m à la tâche.

piece², v.tr. Rapiécer, racommoder. **piece together**, v.tr. Joindre, unir.

piecemeal, adv. Par morceaux.

piecrust, s. Croûte f de pâté.

pied, a. Mi-parti; bariolé, bigarré.

pier, s. **I.** Jetée f, digue f. (Landing) **pier**, quai m. **2.** Civ.E: Pilier m.

pierce, v.tr. Percer, transpercer, pénétrer.

piercing, a. Aigu, perçant; (froid) pénétrant.

piety, s. Piété f.

piffle¹, s. F: Futilités fpl, balivernes fpl.

piffle², v.i. F: S'occuper à des futilités.

piffling, a. F: Futile.

pig, s. (a) Porc m, cochon m. F: To buy a pig in a poke, acheter chat en poche. (b) P: (i) Grossier personnage. (ii) To make a pig of oneself, manger gloutonnement. **pigiron**, s. Metall: Fer m en fonte, en gueuse.

pigeon, s. **I.** Pigeon m. **2.** F: Pigeon, dupe f. **pigeon-hole¹**, s. Case f. **pigeonhole²**, v.tr. Caser, classer. **pigeonhouse**, s. Colombier m, pigeonnier m.

piggish, a. (a) Sale, malpropre, grossier. (b) Goinfre. (c) Égoïste, désagréable.

piggishness, s. (a) Saleté f. (b) Goinfrerie f.

pigheaded, a. Obstiné, entêté.

pigheadedness, s. Obstination f, entêtement m.

pigment, s. **I.** Art: Matière colorante; colorant m. **2.** Physiol: Pigment m.

pigmy, s. = PYGMY.

pigskin, s. Peau f de porc.

pigsticking, s. **I.** Chasse f au sanglier. **2.** Égorgement m de porcs.

pigsty, s. **I.** Porcherie f; étable f à porcs. **2.** P: Bauge f.

pigtail, s. Queue f, natte f, de cheveux.

pike¹, s. Archeol: Pique f.

pike², s. Ich: Brochet m.

pikestaff, s. Bois m, hampe f, de pique.

pilchard, s. Ich: Sardine f.

pile¹, s. Pieu m. Built on piles, bâti sur pilotis.

pile², s. **I.** (a) Tas m, monceau m; pile f. (b) Mil: Faisceau m (d'armes). (c) F: Magot m. To make one's pile, faire fortune. **2.** Édifice m.

pile³. **I.** v.tr. (a) To pile (up), entasser, amasser F: Ship piled up on the rocks, vaisseau échoué sur les rochers. To pile on the agony, accumuler les détails pénibles. To pile it on, exagérer. (b) Mil: To pile arms, former les faisceaux. **2.** v.i. To pile up, s'amonceler, s'entasser.

pilfer, v.tr. Chaparder, chiper (sth. from s.o.

qch. à qn.). Abs. Grappiller. **pilfering**, s. Chapardage m.

pilferer, s. Chapardeur, -euse, chipeur, -euse.

pilgrim, s. Pèlerin, -ine.

pilgrimage, s. (a) Pèlerinage m. (b) F: Long voyage.

pill, s. Pilule f. F: It is a bitter pill, la dragée est amère. **pill-box**, s. **I.** Boîte f à pilules. **2.** Mil: Réduit m en béton.

pillage¹, s. Pillage m.

pillage², v.tr. Piller, saccager.

pillar, s. Pilier m; colonne f. To drive s.o. from pillar to post, renvoyer qn de Caïphe à Pilate. **pillar-box**, s. Borne postale.

pillion, s. Motor Cy: Pillion(-seat), siège m arrière. To ride pillion, monter derrière.

pillory¹, s. Pilori m.

pillory², v.tr. Mettre au pilori.

pillow, s. Oreiller m. **pillow-case**, s. Taie f d'oreiller.

pilot¹, s. (a) Pilote m. (b) F: Guide m, mentor m. (c) Av: Pilote (aviateur). **pilotengine**, s. Rail: Locomotive f estafette. **pilot-lamp**, s. lampe f témoin.

pilot², v.tr. (a) Piloter. (b) Mener, conduire.

piloting, s. Pilotage m.

pilotage, s. Pilotage m.

pimento, s. Bot: Cu: Piment m.

pimpernel, s. Bot: Mouron m. Scarlet pimpernel, mouron rouge.

pimple, s. Bouton m.

pin¹, s. **I.** (a) Épingle f. F: You could have heard a pin drop, ou aurait entendu trotter une souris. For two pins, pour un peu. To be on pins and needles, être sur des charbons. (b) Pins and needles, fourmillements m. **2.** Goupille f, cheville f. **3.** pl. F: Jambes fpl. **pin-hole**, s. Trou m d'épingle. **pin-money**, s. Argent de poche. **pin-prick**, s. F: Pin-pricks, coups m d'épingle.

pin², v.tr. **I.** Épingler; attacher avec une épingle. **2.** Fixer, clouer. To pin s.o.'s arms to his sides, coller les bras à qn. To pin s.o. (down) to facts, obliger qn à s'en tenir aux faits.

pinafore, s. Tablier m.

pincers, s.pl. (Pair of) pincers, pince f, tenaille(s) f(pl).

pinch¹, s. **I.** (a) Action f de pincer; pinçade f. To give s.o. a pinch, pincer qn. (b) F: The pinch of hunger, la morsure de la faim. (c) At a pinch, au besoin. **2.** Pincée f (de sel). To take a p. of snuff, humer une prise.

pinch², v.tr. **I.** Pincer. **2.** Serrer, gêner. To pinch oneself, abs. to pinch, se priver. **3.** P: (a) Chiper. (b) Arrêter (un malfaiteur).

pinched, a. **I.** (Of face) Tiré, hâve. **2.** Étroit. Pinched for money, dans la gêne.

pincushion, s. Pelote f à épingles.

pine¹, s. **I.** Pine(-tree), pin m. **2.** (Bois m de) pin. **pine-apple**, s. Ananas m. **pinecone**, s. Pomme f de pin. **pine-wood**, s. (Bois m de) pin m.

pine², *v.i.* **1.** To pine (away), languir, dépérir. **2.** To pine for s.o., languir pour, après, qn.

ping, *s.* Cinglement *m*, fouettement *m*.

pinion¹, *s.* **1.** (a) Aileron *m.* (b) *Poet:* Aile *f.* **2.** Penne *f*, rémige *f.*

pinion², *v.tr.* Lier les bras à, ligoter.

pink. 1. *s.* (a) *Bot:* Œillet *m.* (b) The pink of perfection, la perfection même. In the pink, en excellente condition. **2.** *a. & s.* Rose (*m*); couleur *f* de rose.

pinkish, *a.* Rosé, rosâtre.

pinkness, *s.* Couleur *f* rose ; rose *m.*

pinnace, *s.* *Navy:* Grand canot.

pinnacle, *s.* **1.** (a) Cime *f*; pic *m.* (b) Rock pinnacle, gendarme *m.* **2.** *F:* The pinnacle of glory, le faîte de la gloire.

pint, *s.* *Meas:* Pinte *f.*

pioneer, *s.* Pionnier *m.*

pious, *a.* (a) Pieux. (b) Pious deeds, œuvres *f* pies. **-ly**, *adv.* Pieusement.

pip¹, *s.* *F:* To give s.o. the pip, donner le cafard à qn.

pip², *s.* **1.** Point *m* (d'une carte). **2.** *Mil:* *F:* = STAR¹ 2 (b). **3.** *W.Tel:* *F:* Top *m.* The pips, le signal horaire.

pip³, *s.* Pépin *m* (de fruit).

pipe¹, *s.* **1.** Tuyau *m*, tube *m*, conduit *m.* **2.** (a) *Mus:* Pipeau *m*, chalumeau *m.* (Bag)pipes, cornemuse *f.* (b) *Nau:* Sifflet *m.* **3.** Pipe *f.* Pipe of peace, calumet *m* de paix. **pipe-clay**, *s.* Terre *f* de pipe. **pipe-lighter**, *s.* Briquet *m.* **pipe-line**, *s.* Conduite *f*, canalisation *f*; (*for petrol*) pipe-line *m*, *pl.* pipe-lines.

pipe², *v.tr.* **1.** (a) Jouer (un air). (b) *Navy:* Siffler (un commandement). **2.** *F:* To pipe one's eye(s), pleurer, pleurnicher. **pipe up**, *v.i.* *F:* Se faire entendre. **piping**, *a.* **1.** *Lit:* Piping times of peace, heureuse époque de paix. **2.** Piping hot, tout chaud, tout bouillant.

pipeful, *s.* Pipe *f* (de tabac).

piper, *s.* Joueur *m* de chalumeau, de cornemuse. *F:* To pay the piper, payer les violons.

pippin, *s.* (Pomme *f*) reinette *f.*

piquancy, *s.* **1.** Goût piquant. **2.** Sel *m*, piquant *m.*

piquant, *a.* Piquant.

pique¹, *s.* Pique *f*, ressentiment *m.*

pique², *v.tr.* **1.** Piquer, dépiter. **2.** Piquer, exciter. **3.** To pique oneself on sth., se piquer de qch.

piracy, *s.* **1.** Piraterie *f.* **2.** Contrefaçon *f* (d'un livre).

Piraeus (the). *Pr.n.* *Geog:* Le Pirée.

pirate¹, *s.* Pirate *m*, forban *m.*

pirate², *v.tr.* Contrefaire (un livre).

piratical, *a.* De pirate.

pistachio, *s.* Pistache *f.*

pistil, *s.* *Bot:* Pistil *m.*

pistol, *s.* *Sm.a:* Pistolet *m.* **pistol-shot**, *s.* Coup *m* de pistolet.

piston, *s.* Piston *m.*

pit¹, *s.* **1.** (a) Fosse *f*, trou *m.* (b) *F:* To dig a pit for s.o., tendre un piège à qn. (c) (i) Carrière *f* (à chaux). (ii) Mine *f* (de charbon). **2.** *Th:* Parterre *m.* **3.** Petite cavité, piqûre *f.* **4.** *Anat:* The pit of the stomach, le creux de l'estomac.

pit², *v.tr.* **1.** To pit oneself against s.o., mesurer contre qn. **2.** Grêler, marquer (le visage).

pit-(a-)pat, *adv.* To go pit-a-pat, (*of rain*) crépiter; (*of feet*) trottiner; (*of the heart*) battre, palpiter.

pitch¹, *s.* Poix *f*; brai *m.* **pitch-dark**, *a.* It is pitch-dark, il fait nuit noire.

pitch², *s.* **1.** (a) Place *f* habituelle (d'un camelot). (b) *Cr:* Terrain *m* entre les guichets. **2.** (a) Hauteur *f* (d'un son); diapason *m* (d'un instrument). (b) Degré *m.* To such a pitch that, à tel point que. **3.** Degré de pente (d'un toit).

pitch³. **I.** *v.tr.* **1.** Dresser (une tente). **2.** *Mus:* To pitch one's voice higher, hausser le ton de sa voix. **3.** Lancer; jeter. **II. pitch**, *v.i.* **1.** To pitch on one's head, tomber sur la tête. **2.** (*Of ship*) Tanguer. **3.** To pitch (up)on sth., arrêter son choix sur qch. **pitch in**, *v.i.* *P:* Se mettre à la besogne. **pitch into**, *v.i.* *F:* S'attaquer à. **pitched**, *a.* Pitched battle, bataille rangée. **pitch-and-toss**, *s.* Jeu *m* de pile ou face.

pitchblende, *s.* *Miner:* Pechblende *f.*

pitcher, *s.* Cruche *f*; broc *m.* **pitcher-plant**, *s.* Népenthès *m.*

pitchfork¹, *s.* Fourche *f.*

pitchfork², *v.tr.* **1.** Lancer avec la fourche. **2.** *F:* Bombarder (qn dans un poste).

piteous, *a.* Pitoyable, piteux. **-ly**, *adv.* Pitoyablement.

pitfall, *s.* Trappe *f*, fosse *f*; piège *m.*

pith, *s.* **1.** (a) Moelle *f.* (b) Peau blanche (d'une orange). **2.** (a) Vigueur *f*, sève *f*, ardeur *f.* (b) Moelle, essence *f.*

pithiness, *s.* Concision *f.*

pithy, *a.* (*Of style*) (i) Nerveux, concis; (ii) substantiel.

pitiable, *a.* Pitoyable, piteux. **-ably**, *adv.* Pitoyablement.

pitiful, *a.* **1.** Compatissant; plein de pitié. **2.** (a) Pitoyable, lamentable. It is p. to see him, il fait pitié. (b) Lamentable. **-fully**, *adv.* **1.** Avec compassion. **2.** Pitoyablement.

pitiless, *a.* Impitoyable; sans pitié; (froid) cruel. **-ly**, *adv.* Sans pitié.

pittance, *s.* Maigre salaire *m.*

pity¹, *s.* Pitié *f.* (a) Compassion *f*, apitoiement *m.* To take pity on s.o., prendre pitié de qn. To feel pity for s.o., s'apitoyer sur qn. For pity's sake, par pitié. (b) What a pity! quel dommage !

pity², *v.tr.* Plaindre; avoir pitié de, s'apitoyer sur. **pitying**, *a.* Compatissant.

pivot¹, *s.* Pivot *m*; axe *m*.
pivot², *v.i.* Pivoter, tourner.
pixy, *s.* (i) Lutin *m*, farfadet *m*; (ii) fée *f*.
placard¹, *s.* Écriteau *m*; affiche *f*.
placard², *v.tr.* 1. Couvrir d'affiches 2. Placarder, afficher (une annonce).
placate, *v.tr.* Apaiser, calmer.
place¹, *s.* 1. (*a*) Lieu *m*, endroit *m*, localité *f*. Place of refuge, lieu de refuge. Watering place, ville *f* d'eaux; station *f* balnéaire. *To move from p. to p.*, se déplacer souvent. Books all over the place, des livres dans tous les coins. In another place, autre part; ailleurs. This is no place for you, vous n'avez que faire ici. (*b*) Place of amusement, lieu de divertissement. Place of worship, édifice *m* du culte. Place of residence, demeure *f*. *At our p.*, chez nous. (*c*) Cour *f*, ruelle *f*. (*d*) Market place, place *f* du marché. 2. Place. To lay a place, mettre un couvert. To change places with s.o., changer de place avec qn. If I were in your place, à votre place. In (the) place of, au lieu de. Remark out of place, observation hors de propos, déplacée. To look out of place, avoir l'air dépaysé. To take place, avoir lieu; se passer; arriver. While this was taking place, sur ces entrefaites. 3. Place, rang *m*. To put s.o. in his place, remettre qn à sa place. To keep one's place, observer les distances. In the first place, d'abord. In the second place, en second lieu. In the next place, ensuite; puis. 4. Place, poste *m*, emploi *m*, situation *f*. It is not my place to do it, ce n'est pas à moi de le faire. 5. To find one's place (*in a book*), se retrouver. *To laugh at the right p.*, rire au bon endroit.
place-name, *s.* Nom *m* de lieu.
place², *v.tr.* 1. Placer, mettre. (*a*) To be awkwardly placed, se trouver dans une situation difficile. (*b*) Com: Difficult to place, de vente difficile. (*c*) To place a matter in s.o.'s hands, remettre une affaire entre les mains de qn. 2. Donner un rang à. To be well placed, avoir une bonne place. 3. *F: I can't p. you*, je ne vous remets pas.
placid, *a.* Placide, calme. tranquille. **-ly**, *adv.* Avec calme; tranquillement.
placidity, *s.* Placidité *f*, calme *m*.
plagiarist, *s.* Plagiaire *m*; démarqueur *m*.
plague¹, *s.* 1. Fléau *m*. 2. Peste *f*. **plague-spot**, *s.* Foyer *m* d'infection.
plague², *v.tr.* *F:* Tourmenter, harceler. To plague s.o. with questions, assommer qn de questions.
plaice, *s.* *Ich:* Carrelet *m*; plie *f*.
plain. I. *a.* 1. Clair, évident. *F:* It is as plain as daylight, cela saute aux yeux. In plain English, pour parler clairement. *Goods* marked in plain figures, articles marqués en chiffres connus. 2. (*a*) In plain clothes, en civil. Plain-clothes policeman, agent en bourgeois, en civil. (*b*) Uni, lisse. (*c*) Plain cooking, cuisine bourgeoise. (*d*) Plain truth,

vérité pure, simple. To be plain with s.o., être franc avec qn. 3. To be plain, manquer de beauté. **-ly**, *adv.* 1. Clairement, manifestement évidemment. *I can see it p.*, cela saute aux yeux. 2. (*a*) Simplement (*b*) Franchement, carrément. To put it plainly, pour parler clair. To speak plainly, user du franc-parler. II. **plain,** *adv.* Clairement, distinctement. III. **plain,** *s.* Plaine *f*.
plain-speaking, *s.* Franchise *f*; franc-parler *m*.
plainness, *s.* 1. Clarté *f*; netteté *f*. 2. (*a*) Simplicité *f*. (*b*) Franchise *f* (de langage). 3. Manque *m* de beauté.
plaint, *s.* *Poet:* Plainte, lamentation *f*.
plaintiff, *s.* *Jur:* Demandeur, -eresse; plaignant, -ante.
plaintive, *a.* Plaintif. **-ly**, *adv.* Plaintivement; d'un ton plaintif.
plait¹, *s.* Natte *f*, tresse *f* (de cheveux).
plait², *v.tr.* Natter, tresser.
plan¹, *s.* 1. (*a*) Plan *m* (d'une maison); cadre *m*. To draw a p., tracer un plan. (*b*) *Surv:* Levé *m* (d'un terrain). 2. Projet *m*, plan. Plan of campaign, plan de campagne. To change one's plans, prendre d'autres dispositions. Everything went according to plan, tout a marché selon les prévisions.
plan², *v.tr.* 1. Faire, tracer, le plan de. 2. Projeter, se proposer (un voyage); combiner (une attaque). To plan to do sth., se proposer de faire qch.
plane¹, *a.* Plan, uni; plat.
plane², *s.* 1. Plan *m*. Horizontal plane, plan horizontal. 2. *Mec:* Inclined plane, plan incliné. 3. *Av: F:* = AEROPLANE.
plane³, *s.* *Tls:* Rabot *m*.
plane⁴, *v.tr.* Raboter; aplanir, planer.
plane⁵, *s.* Plane(-tree), platane *m*.
planet, *s.* *Astr:* Planète *f*.
planetary, *a.* *Astr:* Planétaire.
plank¹, *s.* Planche *f*. *Nau: A:* To walk the plank, passer à la planche.
plank², *v.tr.* Planchéier. **plank down**, *v.tr.* *P:* Jeter, déposer. **planking**, *s.* 1. Planchéiage *m*. 2. Coll. Planches *fpl*.
plant¹, *s.* 1. Plante *f*. Plant life, (i) la vie végétale; (ii) flore *f* (d'une région). 2. *Ind:* Appareil(s) *m(pl)*; installation *f*. 3. *P:* Coup monté.
plant², *v.tr.* 1. Planter. 2. To plant oneself in front of s.o., se planter, se camper, devant qn.
plantain, *s.* 1. Banane *f* des Antilles. 2. Plantain(-tree), bananier *m* du paradis.
plantation, *s.* (*a*) *For:* Plantation *f* (d'arbres). (*b*) Plantation (de coton).
planter, *s.* Planteur *m*.
plaque, *s.* Plaque *f*.
plaster¹, *s.* 1. *Med:* Emplâtre *m*. Adhesive plaster, sparadrap *m*. Court plaster, taffetas gommé. 2. Plâtre *m*. Plaster of Paris, plâtre de moulage.
plaster², *v.tr.* Plâtrer (un mur). *F: To be*

20

plastered with mud, être tout couvert de boue.
Plastered with decorations, chamarré de
décorations.
plasterer, *s.* Plâtrier *m.*
plastic, *a.* **1.** (Art) plastique. **Plastic surgery,** chirurgie plastique. **2.** Plastique.
F : P. **mind,** esprit malléable. **3.** *s.pl.* **Plastics,** plastique(s) *m.*
plate[1], *s.* **1.** Plaque *f,* lame *f,* feuille *f* (de
métal). **2.** (*a*) *Cu :* **Hot plate,** plaque chauffante. (*b*) *Aut :* **Number plate,** plaque matricule. (*c*) *Dent :* Dentier *m.* **3.** *Phot :* Plaque.
4. *Engr :* Gravure *f,* estampe *f.* **Full-page
plate,** gravure hors texte. *Book of plates,*
atlas *m.* **5.** Orfèvrerie *f ;* vaisselle *f* d'or,
d'argent. **6.** Assiette *f.* **Dinner plate,** assiette
plate. **plate-armour,** *s.* (*a*) Plaque *f* de
blindage. (*b*) Blindage *m.* **plate-glass,** *s.*
Glace *f* sans tain ; glace de vitrage. **plate-
layer,** *s.* *Rail :* Ouvrier *m* de la voie.
plate-rack, *s.* *Dom.Ec :* Porte-assiettes *m
inv,* égouttoir *m.*
plate[2], *v.tr.* Plaquer. *To p. with gold.* dorer.
plated, *a.* Recouvert de plaques ; blindé.
Com : **Plated ware,** plaqué *m.*
plateau, *s.* *Ph.Geog :* Plateau *m.*
plateful, *s.* Assiettée *f.*
platform, *s.* **1.** Terrasse *f.* **2.** (*a*) Plateforme *f. Navy :* **Flying(-off) platform,** plateforme d'envol. (*b*) *Rail :* Quai *m,* trottoir *m.*
Departure platform, (quai de) départ *m ;*
embarcadère *m.* **Arrival platform,** débarcadère *m. From what p. does the train start?*
sur quel quai part le train? **3.** Estrade *f,*
tribune *f.*
platinum, *s.* Platine *m.*
platitude, *s.* **1.** Platitude *f.* insipidité *f.*
2. Platitude ; lieu commun.
Plato. *Pr.n.* Platon *m.*
Platonic, *a.* (Amour) platonique.
platoon, *s.* *Mil :* Section *f.*
platter, *s.* Plat *m* (de bois) ; écuelle *f.*
plaudits, *s.pl.* Applaudissements *mpl.*
plausibility, *s.* Plausibilité *f.*
plausible, *a.* (*a*) Plausible, vraisemblable.
(*b*) Spécieux. **2.** (*Of pers.*) Enjôleur, -euse.
-ibly, *adv.* Plausiblement.
play[1], *s.* **1.** (*a*) Jeu *m* (de lumière). (*b*) Jeu,
maniement *m* (d'armes). (*c*) Jeu, activité *f.*
To come into play, entrer en jeu. **To give
full play to sth.,** donner libre cours à qch.
In full play, en pleine activité. **2.** (*a*) Jeu,
amusement *m.* (*b*) **To say sth. in play,** dire
qch. pour plaisanter. **Play on words,** calembour *m,* équivoque *f.* **3.** (*a*) Jeu (de hasard).
The play runs high, on joue gros jeu. (*b*)
Games : **P. began at one o'clock,** la partie a
commencé à une heure. **4.** (*a*) Pièce *f* de
théâtre. *Shakespeare's plays,* le théâtre de
Shakespeare. (*b*) Spectacle *m.* **To go to the
play,** aller au spectacle, au théâtre. **play-
bill,** *s.* Affiche *f* (de théâtre) ; annonce *f* de
spectacle.
play[2]. **I.** *v.i.* **1.** Gambader, folâtrer. *The sun*

plays on the water, le soleil se joue sur l'eau.
2. (*a*) Jouer. (*b*) *The organ is playing,* les
orgues donnent. **3.** (*a*) Jouer, s'amuser, se
divertir. (*b*) **To play with fire,** jouer avec le
feu. **He's not a man to be played with,** ce
n'est pas un homme avec qui on plaisante.
II. play, *v.tr. or ind.tr.* **1. To play (at)
billiards,** jouer au billard. **To play fair,** jouer
franc jeu ; agir loyalement. **To play into
the hands of s.o.,** faire le jeu de qn. **2. To
play (on) the piano,** jouer du piano. *Won't
you p. for us?* voulez-vous nous faire un peu
de musique? **III. play,** *v.tr.* **1.** *Th :* **To
play a part,** jouer un rôle. *To p.* **Macbeth,**
tenir le rôle de Macbeth. *F :* **To play the
idiot,** faire l'imbécile. **To play the man,** se
conduire en homme. **2. To play a trick on
s.o.,** jouer un tour à qn. **3.** *Cards :* **To play
a card,** jouer une carte. **4.** (*a*) **To play a
game of tennis,** faire une partie de tennis.
To play a match, disputer un match. (*b*) **To
play s.o. at chess,** faire une partie d'échecs
avec qn. **5. To play s.o. false,** trahir qn.
6. To play a fish, épuiser un poisson. **7. To
play water on the fire,** diriger de l'eau sur
l'incendie. **To play on s.o.'s feelings,** agir
sur les sentiments de qn. **play out,** *v.tr.*
F : **To be played out,** être à bout de forces.
play up. I. *v.i.* (*a*) *F :* Faire de son mieux.
(*b*) **To play up to s.o.,** *F :* flatter, aduler, qn.
2. *v.tr. F :* **To play s.o. up,** agacer qn.
playing, *s.* Jeu *m.* **playing-card,** *s.*
Carte *f* à jouer.
player, *s.* Joueur, -euse. **1.** *Mus :* Exécutant,
-ante. **2.** *Th :* Acteur, -trice. **3.** *Sp :* Équipier *m.*
playfellow, *s.* Camarade *mf* de jeu.
playful, *a.* Enjoué, badin, folâtre. **-fully,**
adv. Gaiement ; en badinant.
playfulness, *s.* Enjouement *m,* badinage *m.*
playgoer, *s.* Habitué, -ée, des spectacles.
playground, *s.* *Sch :* Cour *f* de récréation.
playmate, *s.* = PLAYFELLOW.
plaything, *s.* Jouet *m.*
playtime, *s.* *Sch :* Récréation *f.*
playwright, *s.* Auteur *m* dramatique.
plea, *s.* **1.** Défense *f.* **2.** (*a*) Excuse *f,* prétexte *m.* (*b*) *P.* **for mercy,** appel *m* à la
clémence.
plead. I. *v.i.* Plaider (*for,* pour ; *against,*
contre). **To plead guilty,** s'avouer coupable.
To plead not guilty, nier sa culpabilité.
2. *v.tr.* (*a*) Plaider. *F :* **To plead s.o.'s
cause with s.o.,** intercéder pour qn auprès de
qn. (*b*) *F : To p.* **ignorance.** prétexter l'ignorance. **pleading,** *s.* **Special pleading,** arguments spécieux.
pleasant, *a.* **1.** Agréable, charmant, aimable.
2. Affable. **To make oneself pleasant (to
s.o.),** faire l'agréable (auprès de qn). **-ly,**
adv. **1.** Agréablement. **2.** Avec affabilité.
pleasantry, *s.* Plaisanterie *f.*
please, *v.tr.* **1.** (i) Plaire à ; faire plaisir à ;
(ii) contenter (qn). *To be easily pleased,*

s'arranger de tout. **There is no pleasing him,** il n'y a pas moyen de lui plaire. **He is hard to please,** il est difficile. **Please yourself!** faites à votre guise. **2.** (a) *Impers.* **Please God! plaise à Dieu!** (b) **(If you) please,** s'il vous plaît. *P. don't cry,* de grâce, ne pleurez pas. *P. tell me,* ayez la bonté de me dire. *May I?*—**Please do!** vous permettez? —Faites donc! **Please be seated,** veuillez (donc) vous asseoir. **3.** *Abs.* **To do as one pleases,** agir à sa guise. **Do as you please,** faites comme vous voudrez. *He will do just as he pleases,* il n'en fera qu'à sa tête. **pleased,** *a.* Satisfait, content. **To be pleased with sth.,** être satisfait de qch. **To be anything but pleased,** n'être pas du tout content. **pleasing,** *a.* Agréable. *P. countenance,* visage avenant, sympathique.

pleasurable, *a.* Agréable.

pleasure, *s.* **1.** Plaisir *m*. **To take (a) pleasure in doing sth.,** éprouver du plaisir à faire qch. **With pleasure,** avec plaisir; volontiers. **2.** Plaisir(s), jouissances *fpl.* **Pleasure trip,** voyage d'agrément. **3.** Volonté *f*; bon plaisir. **At s.o.'s pleasure,** au gré de qn. **pleasure-boat,** *s.* Bateau *m* de plaisance.

pleat[1], *s. Dressm: etc:* Pli *m*.

pleat[2], *v.tr.* Plisser.

plebeian, *a.* Plébéien; du peuple.

plebiscite, *s.* Plébiscite *m*.

pledge[1], *s.* **1.** Gage *m*, nantissement *m*. **2. Pledge of good faith,** garantie *f* de bonne foi. **3.** (a) Promesse *f*, vœu *m*. *I am under a pledge of secrecy,* j'ai fait vœu de garder le secret. (b) **To take the pledge,** faire vœu de tempérance. **4.** Toast *m*; santé *f*.

pledge[2], *v.tr.* **1.** Mettre en gage. **2.** Engager (sa parole). **To pledge one's allegiance,** vouer obéissance. **3.** Boire à la santé de.

plenipotentiary, *a. & s.* Plénipotentiaire (*m*).

plentiful, *a.* Abondant, copieux. **-fully,** *adv.* Abondamment; copieusement.

plenty, *s.* Abondance *f*. *He has p. of everything,* il a de tout en suffisance. *You have p. of time,* vous avez largement le temps. **To have plenty to live upon,** avoir grandement de quoi vivre.

pleurisy, *s. Med:* Pleurésie *f*.

pliability, *s.* (a) Flexibilité *f*. (b) Docilité *f*, souplesse *f*.

pliable, *a.* **1.** Flexible; souple. **2.** Docile, complaisant.

pliers, *s.pl. Tls:* Pince(s) *f*(*pl*), tenaille(s) *f*(*pl*).

plight[1], *s.* Condition *f*, état *m*. **To be in a sorry plight,** être dans un triste état.

plight[2], *v.tr. Lit:* **To plight one's troth,** engager sa foi.

plinth, *s. Arch:* Plinthe *f*; socle *m*.

plod, *v.i.* **1.** Marcher péniblement. **To plod along,** cheminer d'un pas pesant. **2. To plod (away),** travailler laborieusement (*at*, à).

plodding, *a.* (a) (Pas) pesant, lourd. (b) Persévérant.

plop[1], *s., adv., & int.* **1.** Flac (*m*), plouf (*m*). **2.** *He sits down p.,* pouf! il s'assoit.

plop[2], *v.i.* **1.** Faire flac, plouf. **2.** Tomber en faisant pouf.

plot[1], *s.* **1.** (Parcelle *f*, lot *m*, de) terrain *m*. **Building plot,** terrain à bâtir. **2.** Intrigue *f*, action *f*, plan *m*. **The plot thickens,** l'intrigue se noue. **3.** Complot *m*, conspiration *f*.

plot[2], *v.tr.* **1.** Relever (un terrain). **2.** (a) Comploter, conspirer, tramer. (b) *Abs.* Comploter, conspirer (*against s.o.,* contre qn). **plotting,** *s.* Complots *mpl*, machinations *fpl*.

plotter, *s.* Conspirateur, -trice.

plough[1], *s.* Charrue *f*. *F:* **To set one's hand to the plough,** mettre la main à la pâte. **plough-boy,** *s.* Valet *m* de charrue. **plough-horse,** *s.* Cheval, -aux *m*, de labour.

plough[2], *v.tr.* **1.** (a) Labourer (un champ); tracer, creuser (un sillon). *Abs.* **To plough,** labourer la terre. *Ploughed lands,* labours *m*. (b) (*Of ship*) Fendre, sillonner (les flots). **2.** *Sch: F:* **To be ploughed,** échouer. **plough through,** *v.tr. & i. F:* **To plough (one's way) through the mud,** avancer péniblement dans la boue.

ploughman, *s.* Laboureur *m*.

ploughshare, *s.* Soc *m* de charrue.

plover, *s. Orn:* Pluvier *m*.

pluck[1], *s. F:* Courage *m*, cran *m*.

pluck[2], *v.tr.* **1.** Arracher; cueillir (une fleur); épiler (les sourcils). **2. To pluck s.o. by the sleeve,** tirer qn par la manche. **3.** Plumer (une volaille). **pluck up,** *v.tr.* **To pluck up (one's) courage,** s'armer de courage.

plucky, *a.* Courageux. **-ily,** *adv.* Courageusement; sans se laisser abattre.

plug[1], *s.* **1.** Tampon *m*, bouchon *m*, bonde *f*. **2.** (a) Cheville *f. El:* Fiche *f* de connexion. **Wall plug,** prise *f* de courant. (b) *I.C.E:* **Sparking plug,** bougie *f*. **3.** Plug of tobacco, chique *f* de tabac.

plug[2], *v.* **I.** *v.tr.* Boucher, tamponner. **II.** **plug,** *v.i.* **To plug away,** persévérer, s'acharner.

plum, *s.* **1.** Prune *f*. **Plum(-tree),** prunier *m*. **2.** *F:* **The plums,** les meilleurs postes. **plum-cake,** *s.* Gâteau *m* aux raisins. **plum-duff,** *s.* Pudding *m* aux raisins.

plumage, *s.* Plumage *m*.

plumb[1], *s.* Plomb *m* (de fil à plomb). **plumb-line,** *s.* **1.** Fil *m* à plomb. **2.** *Nau:* Ligne *f* de sonde.

plumb[2], *v.tr.* Sonder. **plumbing,** *s.* **1.** Plomberie *f*. **2.** *Coll.* Tuyauterie *f*.

plumb[3], *adv. F:* **Plumb in the centre,** juste au milieu.

plumber, *s.* Plombier *m*.

plume[1], *s.* Panache *m*, aigrette *f*; plumet *m* (de casque).

plume[2], *v.pr.* (a) (*Of bird*) **To plume itself,** se lisser les plumes. (b) **To plume oneself on sth.,** se glorifier de qch.

plump¹, *a.* Rebondi, grassouillet, -ette, dodu ; (*of chicken*) bien en chair.

plump². **I**. *s.* Summer plump, ondée *f.* **2**. *adv.* To fall plump into the mud, tomber dans la boue avec un floc.

plump³. **I**. *v.tr.* Jeter brusquement ; flanquer. **2**. *v.i.* To plump for, être tout entier pour.

plumpness, *s.* Embonpoint *m*, rondeur *f.*

plunder¹, *s.* **I**. Pillage *m.* **2**. Butin *m.*

plunder², *v.tr.* Piller, dépouiller.

plunge¹, *s.* Plongeon *m.* F: To take the plunge, sauter le pas ; faire le plongeon.

plunge². **I**. *v.tr.* Plonger, immerger. **2**. *v.i.* (*a*) Plonger. F: piquer une tête (dans l'eau) ; s'enfoncer (dans un bois). (*b*) (*Of horse*) Ruer. (*c*) *Gaming :* Jouer sans compter.

pluperfect, *a. & s. Gram :* Plus-que-parfait (*m*).

plural, *a. & s. Gram :* Pluriel (*m*).

plus. **I**. *prep.* Plus. **2**. *s.* Plus *m*, signe *m* de l'addition. **plus-fours**, *s.pl. Cost :* Culotte *f* de golf.

plush, *s. Tex :* Peluche *f*, panne *f.*

plutocracy, *s.* Ploutocratie *f.*

plutocrat, *s.* Ploutocrate *m.*

ply. **I**. *v.tr.* (*a*) Manier vigoureusement. (*b*) To ply a trade, exercer un métier. (*c*) To ply s.o. with questions, presser qn de questions. **2**. *v.i.* (*a*) Faire le service, le va-et-vient. (*b*) *Car plying for hire*, automobile de place.

plywood, *s.* (Bois) contre-plaqué *m.*

pneumatic, *a.* Pneumatique. **Pneumatic tyre**, pneumatique *m*, F: pneu *m.*

pneumonia, *s. Med :* Pneumonie *f.*

poach¹, *v.tr. Cu :* Pocher (des œufs).

poach², *v.tr.* Braconner (le gibier). *Abs.* Braconner. F: To poach on s.o.'s preserves, empiéter sur les prérogatives de qn. **poaching**, *s.* Braconnage *m.*

poacher, *s.* Braconnier *m.*

pocket¹, *s.* **I**. (*a*) Poche *f.* F: To line one's pockets, faire sa pelote. F: To have s.o. in one's pocket, avoir qn dans sa manche. Pocket edition, édition de poche. (*b*) He always has his hand in his pocket, il est toujours à débourser. To be in pocket, être en bénéfice. I am out of pocket by it, j'y suis de ma poche. **2**. *Bill :* Blouse *f.* **3**. *Min :* Poche, sac *m.* **pocket-book**, *s.* (*a*) Carnet *m* de poche ; calepin *m.* (*b*) Portefeuille *m.* **pocket-handkerchief**, *s.* Mouchoir *m* de poche. **pocket-knife**, *s.* Couteau *m* de poche. **pocket-money**, *s.* Argent *m* de poche.

pocket², *v.tr.* **I**. Empocher ; mettre dans sa poche. **2**. Avaler (un affront). **3**. *Bill :* Blouser.

pocketful, *s.* Pleine poche ; pochée *f.*

pod, *s.* Cosse *f*, gousse *f.*

podgy, *a.* Boulot, -otte, replet, -ète.

poem, *s.* Poème *m* ; poésie *f.*

poet, *s.* Poète *m.*

poetic(al), *a.* Poétique. **-ally**, *adv.* Poétiquement.

poetry, *s.* Poésie *f.* To write poetry, écrire des vers. Piece of poetry, poésie.

poignancy, *s.* Violence *f* (d'une émotion) ; acuité *f* (d'une douleur).

poignant, *a.* Poignant, vif ; (*of thought*) angoissant. **-ly**, *adv.* D'une façon poignante.

point¹, *s.* **I**. Point *m.* **I**. Decimal point, virgule *f.* **2**. (*a*) Point of departure, point de départ. Armed at all points, armé de toutes pièces. (*b*) To consider sth. from all points of view, considérer qch. sous tous ses aspects. **3**. (*a*) Point, détail *m.* Figures that give point to his argument, chiffres qui ajoutent du poids à sa thèse. To make a point, faire ressortir un argument. Points to be remembered, considérations *f* à se rappeler. To make a point of doing sth., se faire un devoir de faire qch. In point of fact, par le fait. In point of numbers, sous le rapport du nombre. (*b*) Here is the point, voici ce dont il s'agit. Off the point, étranger à la question. On this point, à cet égard. *Your remark is not to the p.*, votre observation manque d'à-propos. Let us get back to the point, revenons à nos moutons. (*c*) What would be the point of (doing sth.)? à quoi bon (faire qch.)? (*d*) Point of interest, détail intéressant. To have one's good points, avoir ses qualités. **4**. (*a*) To be on the point of doing sth., être sur le point de faire qch. *I was on the p. of jumping*, j'allais sauter. (*b*) To come to the point, arriver au fait. Severe to the point of cruelty, sévère jusqu'à la cruauté. **5**. *Games :* Point. **II**. **point**, *s.* Pointe *f.* **I**. (*a*) Pointe, extrémité *f.* Point of a joke, piquant *m*, sel *m*, d'une plaisanterie. (*b*) *Geog :* Pointe, promontoire *m.* **2**. *Rail :* Points, aiguillage *m* ; aiguille *f.* **3**. Point of the compass, aire *f* de vent. **point-blank**. **I**. F: De but en blanc ; (refus) net. **2**. *adv.* To fire point-blank at s.o., tirer sur qn à bout portant. To refuse point-blank, refuser net.

point². **I**. *v.tr.* (*a*) Tailler en pointe. (*b*) To point a moral, inculquer une leçon. **II**. **point**, *v.i.* **I**. To point at s.o., montrer qn du doigt. **2**. (*a*) *The clock pointed to ten*, la pendule marquait dix heures. (*b*) *Everything points to him as the culprit*, tout indique que c'est lui le coupable. **point out**, *v.tr.* **I**. Montrer du doigt. **2**. To point out the mistakes, signaler les erreurs. **pointed**, *a.* **I**. Pointu ; à pointe. **2**. (*a*) (*Réplique*) mordante. (*b*) (Allusion) peu équivoque. **-ly**, *adv.* D'une manière marquée.

pointer, *s.* **I**. *Ven :* Chien *m* d'arrêt. **2**. (*a*) Aiguille *f*, index *m.* (*b*) *Sch :* Baguette *f.*

pointless, *a.* (*a*) Fade. (*b*) Qui ne rime à rien.

pointsman, *s. Rail :* Aiguilleur *m.*

poise¹, *s.* Équilibre *m*, aplomb *m.*

poise², *v.tr.* (*a*) Équilibrer. (*b*) Balancer.
poison¹, *s.* Poison *m*, toxique *m*. **To take poison**, s'empoisonner. **To die of poison**, mourir empoisonné. **poison-gas**, *s.* Gaz toxique.
poison², *v.tr.* (*a*) Empoisonner, intoxiquer. (*b*) Corrompre, pervertir (l'esprit). **poisoning**, *s.* Empoisonnement *m*; intoxication *f*.
poisoner, *s.* Empoisonneur, -euse.
poisonous, *a.* Toxique, intoxicant; empoisonné; (*of animal*) venimeux; (*of plant*) vénéneux.
poke¹, *s.* Poussée *f*. **To give s.o. a poke in the ribs**, enfoncer son doigt dans les côtes de qn.
poke². I. *v.tr.* **1.** Pousser. **To poke s.o. in the ribs**, donner une bourrade à qn. **2.** Tisonner (le feu). **3.** **To poke sth. up the chimney**, passer qch. dans la cheminée. **4.** **To poke fun at s.o.**, se moquer de qn. II. **poke**, *v.i.* **To poke (about) in every corner**, fouiller, farfouiller, dans tous les coins. **poke out**, *v.tr.* (*a*) **To poke s.o.'s eye out**, éborgner qn. (*b*) **To poke one's head out (of the window)**, passer la tête par la fenêtre.
poker¹, *s.* Tisonnier *m*.
poker², *s.* *Cards:* Poker *m*. **poker-face**, *s.* *F:* Visage impassible.
Poland. *Pr.n.* La Pologne.
polar, *a.* Polaire.
pole¹, *s.* **1.** (*a*) Perche *f*. **Tent pole**, mât, montant *m*, de tente. **Telegraph pole**, poteau *m* télégraphique. (*b*) Timon *m*, flèche *f* (de voiture). **2.** *Meas:* Perche.
pole², *s.* Pôle *m*. **South Pole**, Pôle sud. **The pole-star**, l'étoile polaire.
Pole³, *s.* *Geog:* Polonais, -aise.
pole-axe, *s.* Merlin *m*; assommoir *m*.
polecat, *s.* *Z:* Putois *m*.
police¹, *s.* Police *f* (de sûreté). (*a*) **Police inspector** = officier *m* de paix. **Police station**, poste *m* de police. (*b*) **The police**, la Sûreté. **police-van**, *s.* Voiture *f* cellulaire.
police², *v.tr.* Policer.
policeman, *s.* *F:* Agent *m* (de police), sergent *m* de ville.
policewoman, *s.* Femme-agent (de police), *pl.* femmes-agents.
policy¹, *s.* **1.** Politique *f*; ligne *f* de conduite. **Foreign policy**, politique extérieure. **2.** Diplomatie *f*.
policy², *s.* Police *f* (d'assurance(s)).
polish¹, *s.* **1.** Poli *m*, brillant *m*, lustre *m*. **To take the polish off sth.**, dépolir qch. **2.** **Stove polish**, pâte *f* pour fourneaux. **Nail polish**, vernis *m* pour les ongles. **3.** Politesse *f*; belles manières.
polish², *v.tr.* **1.** Polir; cirer (des chaussures); faire reluire (les meubles). **2.** Poli, civiliser. **polish off**, *v.tr.* (i) Terminer vite, expédier. (ii) En finir avec (qn).
polished, *a.* **1.** Poli, brillant. **2.** **Polished manners**, manières polies, distinguées.

Polish³, *a.* *Geog:* Polonais.
polite, *a.* Poli, courtois (*to s.o.*, envers, avec, qn). **-ly**, *adv.* Poliment; avec politesse.
politeness, *s.* Politesse *f*, civilité *f*.
politic, *a.* Politique, avisé.
political, *a.* Politique. **-ally**, *adv.* Politiquement.
politician, *s.* Homme *m* politique.
politics, *s.pl.* La politique.
polka, *s.* Polka *f*.
poll¹, *s.* Vote *m* (par bulletins); scrutin *m*. **To go to the poll**, prendre part au vote.
poll-tax, *s.* *Hist:* Capitation *f*.
poll². I. *v.tr.* Réunir (tant de voix). II. **poll**, *v.i.* Voter (à une élection). **polling**, *s.* Vote *m*; élections *fpl.* **polling-booth**, *s.* Bureau *m* de scrutin.
pollen, *s.* *Bot:* Pollen *m*.
pollute, *v.tr.* Polluer, souiller, corrompre.
pollution, *s.* Pollution *f*, souillure *f*.
polo, *s.* *Sp:* Polo *m*.
poltroon, *s.* Poltron *m*.
polygamist, *s.* Polygame *mf*.
polygamous, *a.* Polygame.
polygamy, *s.* Polygamie *f*.
polyglot, *a. & s.* Polyglotte (*mf*).
polygon, *s.* Polygone *m*.
polygonal, *a.* Polygonal, -aux.
Polynesia. *Pr.n.* La Polynésie.
Polynesian, *a. & s.* Polynésien, -ienne.
polysyllabic, *a.* Polysyllabe, polysyllabique.
polytechnic, **1.** *a.* Polytechnique. **2.** *s.* École professionnelle.
polytheism, *s.* Polythéisme *m*.
pomade, *s.* *Toil:* Pommade *f*.
pomegranate, *s.* *Bot:* Grenade *f*.
Pomeranian, *a. & s.* **Pomeranian (dog)**, loulou *n* de Poméranie.
pommel¹, *s.* Pommeau *m*.
pommel², *v.tr.* Bourrer de coups.
pomp, *s.* Pompe *f*, éclat *m*, splendeur *f*.
Pompeii. *Pr.n.* *A.Geog:* Pompéi *f*.
pom-pom, *s.* Canon-mitrailleuse *m*, *pl.* canons-mitrailleuses.
pompon, *s.* *Cost: etc:* Pompon *m*.
pomposity, *s.* Emphase *f*, suffisance *f*.
pompous, *a.* **1.** Pompeux, fastueux. **2.** **A pompous man**, un homme suffisant. **-ly**, *adv.* Pompeusement.
pond, *s.* Étang *m*; mare *f*.
ponder. **1.** *v.tr.* Réfléchir sur; ruminer. **2.** *v.i.* Méditer. **To ponder over sth.**, réfléchir à, méditer sur, qch.
ponderous, *a.* Lourd, pesant.
poniard¹, *s.* Poignard *m*.
poniard², *v.tr.* Poignarder.
pontiff, *s.* Pontife *m*. *Ecc:* Pape *m*; évêque *m*, prélat *m*.
pontifical, *a.* Pontifical, -aux.
Pontius Pilate. *Pr.n.* Ponce Pilate *m*.
pontoon, *s.* *Mil.E:* Ponton. **pontoon-bridge**, *s.* Pont *m* de bateaux.
pony, *s.* Poney *m*. **pony-carriage**, *s.* *Veh:* Panier *m*.

poodle, s. Caniche mf.
pooh, int. Bah ! peuh ! **Pooh, is that all!** la belle affaire !
pooh-pooh, v.tr. Traiter légèrement ; faire peu de cas de.
pool[1], s. **1.** Mare f. **2.** (In river) Trou m d'eau.
pool[2], s. Fonds communs ; masse commune.
pool[3], v.tr. Mettre en commun.
poop, s. Nau: Poupe f.
poor, a. Pauvre. **1.** (a) Besogneux, malheureux. **The poorer classes,** les classes pauvres. (b) s.pl. **The poor,** les pauvres m, les malheureux, les indigents. **2.** De piètre qualité. (a) **P. blood,** sang vicié. (b) **P. excuse,** piètre excuse. **Poor quality,** basse qualité. **P. health,** santé débile. **To have a poor opinion of** s.o., avoir une pauvre opinion de qn. **3. Poor fellow!** le pauvre homme ! le pauvre garçon ! **-ly. 1.** adv. Pauvrement, médiocrement, piètrement. **2.** pred.a. **To be poorly,** être indisposé.
poorness, s. **1.** Pauvreté f, insuffisance f. **2.** Infériorité f; peu m de valeur.
pop[1]. **1.** int. Crac ! pan ! **To go pop,** éclater, crever. **2.** s. Bruit sec. **pop-gun,** s. Toys: Canonnière f; pistolet m à bouchon.
pop[2], v. **1.** v.i. Faire entendre une petite explosion ; éclater, péter. **2.** (a) v.i. **To pop over to the grocer's,** faire un saut jusque chez l'épicier. (b) v.tr. **To pop sth. behind a screen,** fourrer qch. derrière un écran. **To pop one's head out of the window,** sortir sa tête par la fenêtre. **F: To pop the question,** faire la demande en mariage. **pop in,** v.i. **F:** Entrer en passant.
pope, s. Pape m.
popery, s. Pej: Papisme m.
popish, a. Papiste.
poplar, s. Bot: Peuplier m.
poppy, s. Pavot m. **Corn poppy,** coquelicot m.
populace, s. Populace f.
popular, a. Populaire. (a) **Popular phrase,** expression populaire. (b) À la mode, très couru. (c) Compréhensible pour tout le monde. (d) **Popular error,** erreur courante. **-ly,** adv. Populairement.
popularity, s. Popularité f.
popularize, v.tr. (a) Populariser. (b) Rendre populaire.
populate, v.tr. Peupler.
population, s. Population f.
populous, a. Populeux ; très peuplé.
porcelain, s. Porcelaine f.
porch, s. (a) Porche m, portique m. (b) Marquise f (d'hôtel).
porcupine, s. Z: Porc-épic m, pl. porcs-épics.
pore[1], s. Anat: Pore m.
pore[2], v.i **To pore over a book,** être plongé dans un livre.
pork, s. Cu: (Viande f de) porc m. **Salt pork,** petit salé. **Pork chop,** côtelette f de porc. **pork-butcher,** s. Charcutier, -ière.
pork-pie, s. Pâté m de porc (en croûte).

porosity, s. Porosité f.
porous, a. Poreux, perméable.
porphyry, s. Porphyre m.
porpoise, s. Z: Marsouin m.
porridge, s. Bouillie f d'avoine.
port[1], s. Port m **F: Any port in a storm,** nécessité n'a pas de loi.
port[2], s. Nau: Sabord m. **port-hole,** s. Nau: Sabord m, hublot m.
port[3], s. Nau: Bâbord m.
port[4](-wine), s. Vin m de Porto ; porto m.
portable, a. Portatif ; mobile. **Portable wireless set,** poste transportable.
portal, s. (a) Portail m (de cathédrale.) (b) Portique m.
portcullis, s. Fort: Herse f.
portend, v.tr. Présager, augurer.
portent, s. **1.** Présage m de malheur. **2.** Prodige m.
portentous, a. **1.** Menaçant. **2.** Prodigieux. **3.** Solennel. **-ly,** adv. **1.** Sinistrement. **2.** Prodigieusement. **3.** Solennellement.
porter[1], s. Portier m, concierge m. **Porter's lodge,** (i) loge f de concierge ; (ii) pavillon m, du portier.
porter[2], s. **1.** Portefaix m ; chasseur m, garçon m (d'hôtel) ; (at railway station) porteur m. **2.** Bière brune.
porterage, s. **1.** Transport m, manutention f. **2.** Prix m de transport.
portfolio, s. (a) Serviette f (pour documents). (b) Chemise f de carton. (c) **Minister's portfolio,** portefeuille m de ministre.
portico, s. Arch: Portique m.
portion[1], s. (a) Partie f ; part f. (b) Portion f, ration f. (c) (Marriage) portion, dot f.
portion[2], v.tr. **To portion (out),** partager ; distribuer.
portliness, s. **1.** Prestance f. **2.** Corpulence f, embonpoint m.
portly, a. **1.** Majestueux. **2.** Corpulent, ventru.
portmanteau, s. Valise f.
portrait, s. Portrait m.
portray, v.tr. Dépeindre, décrire. **To portray character,** peindre les caractères.
portrayal, s. Peinture f, description f.
portrayer, s. Peintre m.
Portugal. Pr.n. Le Portugal.
Portuguese. 1. a. & s.inv. Portugais, -aise. **2.** s. Ling: Le portugais.
pose[1], s. **1.** Pose f, attitude f. **2.** Pose, affectation f.
pose[2]. **I.** v.tr. Poser. **II. pose,** v.i. **1.** Poser. **2. To pose as a Frenchman,** se faire passer pour Français. **posing,** s. Pose f.
poser, s. Question embarrassante.
posh, a. **P:** Chic, bath.
position, s. **1.** Posture f, position f, attitude f. **2.** Position. (a) Place f ; situation f. **In position,** en place. (b) Nau: **Ship's position,** lieu m du navire. **To determine the ship's p.,** faire le point. (c) **To storm the**

enemy's positions, prendre d'assaut les positions de l'ennemi. **3.** (a) État m, condition f. **To be in a position to do sth.**, être en état, à même, de faire qch. (b) Rang social, **In a high position,** haut placé. (c) Sch: **Position in class,** place f dans la classe. **4.** Emploi m, place, situation. **Position of trust,** poste m de confiance.

positive, a. **I.** (a) Positif, affirmatif. (b) **It's a positive fact!** c'est un fait authentique. F: c'est positif! **2.** (a) Convaincu, assuré, sûr, certain (of, de). (b) **Positive tone of voice,** ton absolu, tranchant. **3.** Gram: **Positive (degree),** (degré) positif (m). **-ly,** adv. **I.** Positivement, affirmativement. **2.** Assurément. **I can't speak positively,** je ne puis rien affirmer.

positiveness, s. **I.** Certitude f, assurance f. **2.** Ton décisif, tranchant.

possess, v.tr. **I.** (a) Posséder. **All I possess,** tout mon avoir. (b) Avoir, posséder. **2. To possess oneself of sth.,** s'emparer de qch. **3. What possessed you to do that?** qu'est-ce qui vous a pris de faire cela? **To be possessed with an idea,** être obsédé d'une idée.

possession, s. **I.** Possession f, jouissance f (of, de). **To take possession of sth.,** s'emparer de qch. **In full possession of his faculties,** en pleine possession de toutes ses facultés. **Vacant possession,** libre possession. **2.** (a) Objet possédé; possession. (b) pl. **Possessions,** (i) possessions, biens m, avoir m; (ii) possessions, colonies f.

possessive, a. & s. Gram: Possessif (m).

possessor, s. Possesseur m; propriétaire mf.

possibility, s. **I.** Possibilité f. **By any possibility I am not there,** si par impossible je n'y étais pas. **Within the bounds of possibility,** dans la limite du possible. **2.** Événement m possible; éventualité f. **The subject is full of possibilities,** c'est un sujet qui prête. **The plan has possibilities,** ce projet offre des chances de succès.

possible. I. a. (a) Possible. **It is possible,** c'est possible; cela se peut bien. **To give as many details as possible,** donner le plus de détails possible. **As far as possible,** dans la mesure du possible. **As early as possible,** le plus tôt possible. (b) F: Tolérable, acceptable. **2.** s. **To do one's possible,** faire son possible (to, pour). **-ibly,** adv. **I.** I **cannot possibly do it,** il ne m'est pas possible de le faire. **It can't possibly be!** pas possible! **I'll do all I possibly can,** je ferai tout mon possible. **2.** Peut-être (bien). **Possibly!** c'est possible; cela se peut.

post¹, s. Poteau m, pieu m, montant m, pilier m.

post², v.tr. To post (up), placarder; afficher.

post³, s. **I.** Courrier m. **By return of post,** par retour du courrier. **The post has come,** le facteur est passé. Games: **General post,** chassé-croisé m. **2.** Poste f. **To send sth. by post,** envoyer qch. par la poste. **3.** = POST-OFFICE. **To take a letter to the post,** porter

une lettre à la poste. **post-chaise,** s. A: Chaise f de poste. **post-free,** attrib. a. Franc de port; en franchise; franco inv. **post-haste,** adv. En toute hâte. **post(-)office,** s. Bureau m de(s) poste(s); F: la poste. **The General Post Office,** la Grande Poste; les Postes et Télégraphes. **post-paid,** a. Affranchi; port payé.

post⁴, v.tr. (a) Mettre à la poste. **To post sth. to s.o.,** envoyer qch. à qn (par la poste). (b) Book-k: **To post an entry,** passer écriture d'un article. **To keep s.o. posted up,** tenir qn à jour.

post⁵, s. **I.** Poste m. **2.** Poste, situation f, emploi m.

post⁶, v.tr. **I.** Poster, mettre en faction. **2.** Navy: **To be posted to a ship,** être affecté à un navire.

post⁷, s. Mil: **Last post,** (i) la retraite (au clairon); (ii) la sonnerie aux morts.

postage, s. Port m, affranchissement m. **Postage paid,** port payé.

postal, a. Postal, -aux.

postcard, s. Carte postale. **Picture postcard,** carte postale illustrée.

poster, s. Affiche murale.

posterior, a. Postérieur, -eure (to, à).

posterity, s. Postérité f.

posthumous, a. Posthume. **-ly,** adv. Posthumement.

postil(l)ion, s. Postillon m.

postman, s. Facteur m.

postmark, s. Timbre m d'oblitération.

postmaster, s. Receveur m (des Postes). **The Postmaster General,** le ministre des Postes et Télégraphes.

post meridiem, Lt.phr. De l'après-midi, du soir. **At four p.m.,** à quatre heures de l'après-midi.

postmistress, s. Receveuse f des Postes.

post-mortem, attrib.a. & s. Après décès. **To hold a post-mortem (examination),** faire une autopsie.

postpone, v.tr. Remettre, ajourner, différer.

postponement, s. Remise f à plus tard; renvoi m; ajournement m.

postscript, s. Post-scriptum m inv.

postulate, v.tr. Poser en postulat; considérer comme établi.

posture¹, s. Posture f, pose f, attitude f.

posture², v.i. Prendre une posture, une pose.

post-war, attrib.a. D'après guerre.

posy, s. Bouquet m (de fleurs des champs).

pot¹, s. **I.** (a) Pot m. (b) Marmite f. **Pots and pans,** batterie f de cuisine. **2.** F: **Pots of money,** des tas m d'argent. **To make pots of money,** gagner gros. **3.** F: **A big pot,** un gros bonnet. **pot-hole,** s. F: Trou m (dans une route). **pot-house,** s. Cabaret m, taverne f. **pot-luck,** s. **Come and take p.-l. with us,** venez dîner chez nous sans cérémonie. **pot-shot,** s. F: **To take a pot-shot at sth.,** lâcher au petit bonheur un coup de fusil à qch.

pot², *v.tr.* **1.** *Bill:* Blouser (une bille). **2.** *F:* Tirer, tuer, abattre (du gibier).

potted, *a.* En pot, en terrine. **Potted foods,** conserves *fpl.*

potash, *s.* Potasse *f.*

potassium, *s.* *Ch:* Potassium *m.*

potato, *s.* **1.** Pomme *f* de terre. *Boiled potatoes,* pommes de terre à l'eau. *Baked potatoes,* pommes de terre au four. **2.** **Sweet potato,** patate *f.*

potency, *s.* Force *f,* puissance *f.*

potent, *a.* *(Of drug)* Efficace, puissant. *P. drink,* boisson très forte. *P. poison,* poison violent. **-ly,** *adv.* Puissamment.

potentate, *s.* Potentat *m.*

potential. *a.* *(a)* En puissance; virtuel; latent (danger). *(b)* Potentiel (ressources). **-ally,** *adv.* Potentiellement, virtuellement, en puissance.

potentiality, *s.* Potentialité *f.*

potion, *s.* Potion *f;* dose *f.*

potter¹, *s.* Potier *m.*

potter², *v.i.* **1.** S'occuper de bagatelles; s'amuser à des riens. **To potter about at odd jobs,** bricoler. **2.** **To potter about the house,** trottiner par la maison.

pottery, *s.* **1.** Poterie *f.* **2.** Vaisselle *f* de terre.

pouch¹, *s.* **1.** Petit sac; bourse *f.* **2.** *Nat. Hist:* Poche ventrale; abajoue *f* (de singe). **3.** Poche (sous les yeux).

pouch², *v.tr.* Empocher.

poulterer, *s.* Marchand *m* de volaille.

poultice¹, *s.* Cataplasme *m.*

poultice², *v.tr.* Mettre un cataplasme sur.

poultry, *s.* *Coll:* Volaille *f.* **poultry-yard,** *s.* Basse-cour *f,* pl. basses-cours.

pounce¹, *s.* **To make a pounce on sth.,** fondre, s'abattre, sur (sa proie).

pounce², *v.i.* *(a)* **To pounce on the prey,** fondre, s'abattre, sur la proie. *(b)* *F:* Se précipiter, se jeter *(on,* sur).

pound¹, *s.* **1.** Livre *f.* *To sell sugar by the pound,* vendre le sucre à la livre. **2.** **Pound sterling,** livre sterling. **Pound note,** billet *m* (de banque) d'une livre. **A question of pounds, shillings and pence,** une question de gros sous.

pound², *s.* Fourrière *f* (pour animaux).

pound³. **1.** *v.tr.* *(a)* Broyer, piler, concasser. *(b)* Bourrer de coups de poing. *(c)* **To pound sth. to atoms,** réduire qch. en miettes. **2.** *v.i.* **To pound away at sth.,** cogner dur, frapper ferme, sur qch.

pour. 1. *v.tr.* Verser *(into,* dans). **2.** *v.i.* Tomber à torrents, à verse. **It is pouring (with rain),** il pleut à verse. **pour out. 1.** *v.tr.* Verser (une tasse de thé). **2.** *v.i.* Sortir à flots. **pouring,** *a.* **Pouring rain,** pluie torrentielle; pluie battante.

pout¹, *s.* Moue *f.*

pout², *v.i.* *(a)* Faire la moue. *v.tr.* **To pout the lips,** faire la moue. *(b)* Bouder.

poverty, *s.* **1.** Pauvreté *f.* *To live in p.,*

vivre dans la gêne. **2.** Disette *f,* manque *m,* pénurie *f,* pauvreté. *P. of ideas,* dénuement *m* d'idées. **poverty-stricken,** *a.* Miséreux; dans la misère.

powder¹, *s.* Poudre *f.* *(a)* **To reduce sth. to powder,** réduire qch. en poudre. *(b)* (Gun-) powder, poudre (à canon). *It is not worth p. and shot,* le jeu n'en vaut pas la chandelle. **powder-magazine,** *s.* Poudrière *f.* **powder-puff,** *s.* Houppe *f.*

powder², *v.tr.* **1.** Saupoudrer *(with,* de). **2.** **To powder one's face,** *abs.* to powder, se poudrer le visage. **3.** Réduire en poudre.

powdery, *a.* *(a)* Poudreux. *(b)* Friable.

power, *s.* **1.** Pouvoir *m.* **As far as lies within my power,** dans la mesure où cela m'est possible. **It is beyond my power,** cela ne m'est pas possible. **2.** Faculté *f,* capacité *f.* **3.** Vigueur *f,* force *f.* **4.** *(a)* Puissance *f;* force. *(b)* Motive power, force motrice. **5.** *(a)* Pouvoir, influence *f,* autorité *f.* **To have s.o. in one's power,** avoir qn sous sa coupe. **To fall into s.o.'s power,** tomber au pouvoir de qn. **Power of life and death,** droit de vie et de mort. *(b)* **To act with full powers,** agir de pleine autorité. *(c)* *Jur:* Procuration *f,* mandat *m,* pouvoir. **6.** *(a)* **The powers that be,** les autorités constituées. *(b)* **The Great Powers,** les Grandes Puissances. **7.** *Mth:* Puissance. **power station,** *s.* Station génératrice.

powerful, *a.* *(a)* Puissant. *(b)* Fort, vigoureux. **-fully,** *adv.* Puissamment; fortement.

powerless, *a.* Impuissant. *They are p. in the matter,* ils n'y peuvent rien.

powerlessness, *s.* Impuissance *f.*

pow-wow, *s.* *F:* Conférence *f,* palabre *f.*

practicability, *s.* Praticabilité *f.*

practicable, *a.* Praticable.

practical, *a.* Pratique. *(a)* **Practical chemistry,** chimie appliquée. *(b)* **Practical proposal,** proposition d'ordre pratique. **-ally,** *adv.* **1.** Pratiquement, en pratique. **2.** Pour ainsi dire.

practice, *s.* **1.** Pratique *f.* *The p. of medicine,* l'exercice *m* de la médecine. **To put a principle into practice,** mettre un principe en action, en pratique. **2.** Habitude *f,* coutume *f,* usage *m.* **To make a practice of doing sth.,** se faire une habitude de faire qch. **3.** Exercice(s). *It can only be learnt by p.,* cela ne s'apprend que par l'usage. **Out of practice,** rouillé. **Choir practice,** répétition *f.* *Mil:* **Target practice,** exercices de tir. *Prov:* **Practice makes perfect,** c'est en forgeant qu'on devient forgeron. **4.** Pratique, clientèle *f* (de médecin). **5.** *Esp. in pl.* Pratiques, menées *fpl.*

practise, *v.tr.* **1.** Pratiquer; mettre en pratique, en action. **To practise what one preaches,** prêcher d'exemple. **2.** Pratiquer, exercer (une profession). **3.** *Abs. Mus:* Faire des exercices. **practised,** *a.* Exercé, expérimenté.

practitioner, *s.* Praticien *m.* **Medical practitioner,** médecin *m.* **General practitioner,** médecin et chirurgien.

prairie, *s.* Prairie *f.*

praise¹, *s.* (i) Éloge(s) *m(pl)*; (ii) louange(s) *f(pl)*. *To speak in p. of s.o.,* faire l'éloge de qn. *I have nothing but p. for him,* je n'ai qu'à me louer de lui. **Beyond all praise,** au-dessus de tout éloge.

praise², *v.tr.* Louer, faire l'éloge de.

praiseworthy, *a.* Digne d'éloges; méritoire.

prance, *v.i.* **I.** (*Of horse*) Fringuer; piaffer. **2.** (*Of pers.*) Se pavaner; se carrer.

prank, *s.* **I.** Escapade *f,* frasque *f,* fredaine *f.* *To play one's pranks,* faire des siennes. **2.** Tour *m,* farce *f.* **To play pranks on s.o.,** jouer des tours à qn.

prate, *v.i.* Dire des riens, des absurdités (d'un air important); jaser. **prating,** *a.* Babillard, bavard.

prattle¹, *s.* Babil *m,* babillage *m.*

prattle², *v.i.* Babiller.

prawn, *s.* Grande crevette; bouquet *m.*

pray, *v.tr. & i.* **I.** Prier, implorer, supplier (*s.o. to do sth.,* qn de faire qch.). **To pray (to) God,** prier Dieu. **He's past praying for,** *F:* il est incorrigible. **2.** *What good will that do,* **pray?** à quoi bon, je vous demande un peu? *P. take a seat,* veuillez (bien) vous asseoir.

prayer, *s.* **I.** Prière *f.* **The Lord's Prayer,** l'oraison dominicale; le Pater. **To say one's prayers,** faire ses dévotions. **2.** Demande instante. **prayer-book,** *s.* Livre *m* de prières.

preach, *v.* Prêcher. **I.** *v.i.* Prononcer le sermon. *F:* **To preach to s.o.,** sermonner qn. **2.** *v.tr.* (*a*) *To p. a sermon,* prononcer un sermon. (*b*) **To preach the gospel,** prêcher l'Évangile. **preaching,** *s.* **I.** Prédication *f.* **2.** Prêcherie *f.*

preacher, *s.* Prédicateur *m.*

preamble, *s.* Préambule *m.*

prebendary, *s.* Prébendier *m,* chanoine *m.*

precarious, *a.* Précaire, incertain. **-ly,** *adv.* Précairement.

precaution, *s.* Précaution *f.* **By way of precaution,** à tout événement.

precautionary, *a.* De précaution.

precede, *v.tr.* **I.** Précéder. **2.** Avoir le pas, la préséance, sur. **preceding,** *a.* Précédent. *The p. day,* la veille.

precedence, *s.* (*a*) Préséance *f;* priorité *f.* **To take precedence of s.o.,** prendre le pas sur qn. (*b*) Droit *m* de priorité.

precedent, *s.* Précédent *m.*

precept, *s.* Précepte *m.*

preceptor, *s.* Précepteur *m.*

precinct, *s.* (*a*) Enceinte *f,* enclos *m.* (*b*) *pl.* **Precincts,** pourtour *m.*

precious. I. *a.* (*a*) Précieux; de grand prix. **Precious stones,** pierres précieuses. (*b*) *F:* Fameux, fier. *A p. fool he is!* c'est un

fameux imbécile! (*c*) (Style) recherché, affecté **2.** *adv. F:* **To take precious good care,** prendre un soin particulier.

precipice, *s.* Précipice *m.* *To fall over a p.,* tomber dans un précipice.

precipitancy, *s.* Précipitation *f.*

precipitate¹, *a.* Précipité. **-ly,** *adv.* Précipitamment; avec précipitation.

precipitate², *v.tr.* (*a*) Précipiter (*into,* dans). (*b*) Accélérer, hâter, précipiter. *To p. matters,* brusquer les choses.

precipitation, *s.* Précipitation *f.*

precipitous, *a.* Escarpé, abrupt; à pic. **-ly,** *adv.* A pic.

précis, *s.* Précis *m,* résumé *m.*

precise, *a.* **I.** (*a*) Précis; exact. (*b*) *At the p. moment when,* au moment précis où. **2.** Formaliste; méticuleux. **-ly,** *adv.* **I.** (*a*) Avec précision. (*b*) *At six o'clock p.,* à six heures précises. **2.** *Precisely (so)!* précisément! parfaitement!

preciseness, *s.* **I.** Précision *f.* **2.** (*a*) Méticulosité *f.* (*b*) Formalisme *m.*

precision, *s.* Précision *f.*

preclude, *v.tr.* Empêcher, prévenir. **To be precluded from doing sth.,** être dans l'impossibilité de faire qch.

precocious, *a.* Précoce. **-ly,** *adv.* Précocement; avec précocité.

precociousness, *s.* Précocité *f.*

preconception, *s.* **I.** Préconception *f.* **2.** (*a*) Idée ou opinion préconçue. (*b*) Préjugé *m.*

preconcerted, *a.* Arrangé, concerté, d'avance.

precursor, *s.* Précurseur *m.*

predatory, *a.* **I.** (*a*) Rapace, pillard. (*b*) *P. animals,* bêtes de proie. **2.** *P. habits,* habitudes de pillage, de rapine.

predecease, *v.tr.* Mourir avant (qn).

predecessor, *s.* Prédécesseur *m;* devancier, -ière.

predicament, *s.* Situation difficile, fâcheuse. **We're in a fine predicament!** nous voilà dans de beaux draps!

predicate, *s. Gram:* Attribut *m.*

predict, *v.tr.* Prédire.

prediction, *s.* Prédiction *f.*

predilection, *s.* Prédilection *f (for,* pour). **To have a predilection for sth.,** affectionner, affecter, qch.

predispose, *v.tr.* Prédisposer (*to,* à).

predisposition, *s.* Prédisposition *f (to,* à).

predominant, *a.* Prédominant.

predominate, *v.i.* **I.** Prédominer. **2.** L'emporter par le nombre, par la quantité. **predominating,** *a.* Prédominant.

pre-eminence, *s.* Prééminence *f.*

pre-eminent, *a.* (*a*) Prééminent. (*b*) Remarquable (*in*, par). **-ly,** *adv.* A un degré prééminent.

pre-emption, *s.* (Droit *m* de) préemption *f.*

preen, *v.tr.* **I.** (*Of bird*) Lisser, nettoyer (ses plumes). **2. To preen oneself,** prendre un air avantageux.

prefabricated, *a.* Préfabriqué.
preface[1], *s.* **I.** Préface *f*; avant-propos *m inv.* **2.** Introduction *f*, préambule *m*.
preface[2], *v.tr.* Préluder à (un discours).
prefect, *s. Fr.Adm:* Préfet *m*.
prefer, *v.tr.* **I.** Nommer, élever (qn à une dignité). **2.** *To p. a complaint,* porter plainte. **3.** *To prefer sth. to sth.,* préférer qch. à qch. *I would p. to go without,* j'aimerais mieux m'en passer.
preferable, *a.* Préférable (*to,* à). **-ably,** *adv.* Préférablement.
preference, *s.* Préférence *f* (*for,* pour). In **preference,** préférablement (*to,* à).
preferential, *a.* Préférentiel; de faveur.
preferment, *s.* Avancement *m*; promotion *f*.
prefix[1], *s. Gram:* Préfixe *m*.
prefix[2], *v.tr.* **I.** Mettre comme introduction (à un livre). **2.** *Gram:* Préfixer.
pregnant, *a.* **Pregnant with consequences,** gros de conséquences.
prehensile, *a.* Préhensile.
prehistoric, *v.tr.* Préhistorique.
prejudge, *v.tr.* Préjuger.
prejudice[1], *s.* **I.** Préjudice *m*, tort *m*, dommage *m*. 'Without prejudice,' "sous toutes réserves." **2.** Préjugé *m*. **To have a prejudice against sth.,** être prévenu contre qch.
prejudice[2], *v.tr.* **I.** Nuire, porter préjudice, à. **2.** Prévenir, prédisposer. **prejudiced,** *a.* (i) Prévenu (*against,* contre); (ii) à préjugés. *To be p.,* avoir des préjugés.
prejudicial, *a.* Préjudiciable, nuisible (*to,* à).
prelate, *s.* Prélat *m*.
preliminary. I. *a.* Préliminaire, préalable. **2.** *s.* (*a*) Prélude *m*. (*b*) *pl.* **Preliminaries,** préliminaires *m*.
prelude[1], *s.* Prélude *m* (*to,* de).
prelude[2], *v.i.* Préluder.
premature, *a.* Prématuré. **-ly,** *adv.* Prématurément.
premeditate, *v.tr.* Préméditer. **premeditated,** *a.* Prémédité; (crime) réfléchi.
premeditation, *s.* Préméditation *f*.
premier. I. *a.* Premier. **2.** *s.* Premier ministre.
premise, *s.pl.* **The premises,** le local, les locaux. **On the premises,** sur les lieux.
premium, *s.* **I.** Prix *m*, récompense *f*. **To put a premium on,** donner une prime à. **2.** (*a*) Prix convenu, indemnité *f*. (*b*) *Insurance* **premium,** prime d'assurance. **3.** *To be at a premium,* faire prime.
premonition, *s.* Prémonition *f*; pressentiment *m*.
premonitory, *a.* Prémonitoire.
preoccupation, *s.* Préoccupation *f*.
preoccupy, *v.tr.* Préoccuper. **preoccupied,** *a.* Préoccupé.
preparation, *s.* **I.** Préparation *f*. **2.** *Usu.pl.* Préparatifs *mpl. To make preparations for sth.,* faire des préparatifs en vue de qch. **3.** *Sch:* Étude *f* (du soir).
preparative, *a.* Préparatoire.

preparatory. I. *a.* Préparatoire, préalable (*to,* à). **2.** *adv.* Préalablement (*to,* à).
prepare. I. *v.tr.* Préparer. *To p. the way for negotiations,* amorcer des négociations. **2.** *v.i.* Se préparer, se disposer (*for sth.,* à qch.). *To p. for departure,* faire ses préparatifs de départ. *To p. for an examination,* préparer un examen. **prepared,** *a. To be p. for anything,* être prêt, s'attendre, à toute éventualité.
prepay, *v.tr.* Payer d'avance; affranchir (une lettre). *Tg:* '**Answer prepaid,**' "réponse payée."
prepayment, *s.* Paiement *m* d'avance.
preponderance, *s.* Prépondérance *f* (*over,* sur).
preponderant, *a.* Prépondérant.
preponderate, *v.i.* Peser davantage; emporter la balance, l'emporter (*over,* sur).
preponderating, *a.* Prépondérant.
preposition, *s.* Préposition *f*.
prepossess, *v.tr.* **I.** Accaparer, posséder. **2.** Prévenir (*in favour of,* en faveur de). **prepossessed,** *a.* **I.** Imbu, imprégné (*with,* de); pénétré. **2.** Prévenu. **prepossessing,** *a.* Agréable, prévenant. **Of prepossessing appearance,** de bonne mine.
prepossession, *s.* Prévention *f*; préjugé *m*.
preposterous, *a.* Contraire au bon sens; absurde.
preposterousness, *s.* Absurdité *f*.
prerogative, *s.* Prérogative *f*, privilège *m*.
presage[1], *s.* (*a*) Présage *m*. (*b*) Pressentiment *m*.
presage[2], *v.tr.* Présager, annoncer.
prescribe, *v.tr.* Prescrire, ordonner. **Prescribed task,** tâche imposée. **In the prescribed time,** dans le délai prescrit.
prescription, *s.* Prescription *f*. (*a*) Ordre *m*, précepte *m*. (*b*) *Med:* Ordonnance *f*.
prescriptive, *a.* Consacré par l'usage.
presence, *s.* Présence *f*. **I.** (*a*) **In the presence of,** en présence de. (*b*) *F:* **Saving your presence,** sauf votre respect. **2. Presence of mind,** présence d'esprit. **3.** Air *m*, mine *f*. **To have a good presence,** avoir du maintien.
present[1]. **I.** *a.* (*a*) Présent. **To be present at a ceremony,** être présent, assister, à une cérémonie. *All p. heard it,* toute l'assistance l'a entendu. **2.** (*a*) Actuel. **At the present time,** à présent. (*b*) En question; que voici. **The present volume,** le volume en question, ce volume. (*c*) *Gram:* **The present tense,** *s.* **the present,** le (temps) présent. **-ly,** *adv.* Tout à l'heure; dans un instant. **II. present,** *s.* **The present,** le présent; le temps présent. **Up to the present,** jusqu'à présent. **At present,** à présent; actuellement. **For the present,** pour le moment. **present-day,** *attrib.a.* Actuel; d'aujourd'hui.
present[2], *s.* Don *m*, cadeau *m*, présent *m*. **To make s.o. a present of sth.,** faire cadeau de qch. à qn.
present[3], *v.tr.* Présenter. **I.** (*a*) *Th:* To

present a play, présenter une pièce. (*b*) **Affair that presents some difficulty**, affaire qui présente des difficultés. **A good opportunity presents itself**, une bonne occasion se présente (de faire qch.). **2.** (*a*) **To present sth. to s.o.**, donner qch. à qn. (*b*) **To present one's compliments**, présenter ses compliments. **3.** *Mil:* **To present arms**, présenter les armes.

presentable, *a.* Présentable.

presentation, *s.* **I.** (*a*) Présentation *f* (de qn à un poste). (*b*) Présentation, représentation *f* (d'une pièce à la scène). **2.** (*a*) Remise *f*, présentation (d'un cadeau à qn). (*b*) Souvenir (offert à un fonctionnaire).

presentiment, *s.* Pressentiment *m.*

preservation, *s.* **I.** Conservation *f.* **2.** Préservation *f* (*from*, de).

preservative. **I.** *a.* Préservatif; préservateur, -trice. **2.** *s.* Antiseptique *m*; agent *m* de conservation.

preserve[1], *s.* **I.** Confiture *f.* **2.** (*a*) *For:* Réserve *f.* (*b*) **Game preserve**, chasse gardée.

preserve[2], *v.tr.* **I.** Préserver, garantir (*from*, de). **2.** (*a*) Conserver. **To preserve appearances**, sauver les apparences. (*b*) Conserver; confire (des fruits). **3.** (*a*) Élever (du gibier) dans une réserve. (*b*) Garder (une chasse).

preserved, *a.* **I.** Conservé; (*of fruit*) confit. **Preserved food**, conserves *fpl.* **preserved meat**, conserve de viande. **2. Well preserved**, en bon état de conservation.

preserver, *s.* Préservateur, -trice (*from*, de); sauveur *m.*

preside, *v.i.* Présider. (*a*) **To preside at a meeting**, présider (à) une réunion. (*b*) *Abs.* Présider.

presidency, *s.* Présidence *f.*

president, *s.* Président, -ente.

presidential, *a.* Présidentiel.

press[1], *s.* **I. Press of business**, presse *f*, urgence *f*, des affaires. **2.** Presse. **Hydraulic press**, presse hydraulique. **3.** *Typ:* (*a*) *In time for p.*, à temps pour l'impression. (*b*) La presse, les journaux *m.* **press-cutting**, *s.* Coupure *f* de journal, de presse.

press[2]. **I.** *v.tr.* Presser. **I.** (*a*) Appuyer, peser, sur (qch.). **Press the button**, appuyez sur le bouton. (*b*) Serrer. **To press s.o. to one's heart**, presser, serrer, qn sur son cœur. **To press the juice out of a lemon**, exprimer le jus d'un citron. **2.** *Tail:* **To press a suit**, donner un coup de fer à un complet. **3.** (*a*) **Pressed by one's creditors**, pressé, harcelé, par ses créanciers. (*b*) *He did not need too much pressing*, il ne se fit pas trop prier. **To press for an answer**, insister pour avoir une réponse immédiate. (*c*) **To press a point**, insister sur un point. **To press one's advantage**, poursuivre son avantage. (*d*) **To press a gift on s.o.**, forcer qn à accepter un cadeau. **4.** *Abs.* **Time presses**, le temps presse. **II. press**, *v.i.* Se serrer, se presser. **press forward, press on. I.** *v.i.* Presser, forcer, le pas. **2.** *v.tr.* Activer, hâter. **pressed**, *a.*

I. Pressé, serré, comprimé. **2. To be hard pressed**, être aux abois. **Pressed for time**, très pressé; à court de temps. **pressing**, *a.* (*Danger*) pressant; (travail) pressé, urgent. **Pressing invitation**, invitation instante.

press[3], *v.tr.* *F:* **To press into service**, enrôler, faire appel à (qn); réquisitionner (qch.).

press-gang, *s.* (Détachement *m* de la) presse.

pressman, *s.* Journaliste.

pressure, *s.* **I.** (*a*) Pression *f*; poussée *f.* **High pressure**, haute pression. **Water pressure**, poussée de l'eau. **At full pressure**, sous toute pression. (*b*) *Med:* **Blood pressure**, tension artérielle (du sang). **2. To bring pressure to bear on s.o.**, exercer une pression sur qn. **Pressure of business**, presse *f*, urgence *f*, des affaires. **To work at high pressure**, travailler fiévreusement.

prestige, *s.* Prestige *m.*

presto, *int.* Hey presto! passez muscade!

presumably, *adv.* Probablement. *P. he will come*, il est à croire qu'il viendra.

presume. **I.** *v.tr.* (*a*) Présumer. *You are Mr X, I presume*, vous êtes M. X, je suppose. (*b*) **To presume to do sth.**, prendre la liberté, présumer, de faire qch. **2.** *v.i.* (*a*) **To presume too much**, trop présumer de soi. (*b*) *Abs.* Se montrer présomptueux. (*c*) **To presume on s.o.'s friendship**, abuser de l'amitié de qn. **presuming**, *a.* (*a*) Présomptueux. (*b*) Indiscret, -ète.

presumption, *s.* **I.** Présomption *f. The p. is that he is dead*, il est à présumer qu'il est mort. **2.** Présomption, arrogance *f. Pardon my p.*, excusez mon audace.

presumptuous, *a.* Présomptueux, outrecuidant.

pretence, *s.* **I.** (Faux) semblant; simulation *f*; prétexte *m.* **To obtain sth. by false pretences**, obtenir qch. par fraude *f.* **2.** Prétention *f*, vanité *f.*

pretend, *v.tr.* (*a*) Feindre, simuler. **To pretend to do sth.**, faire semblant, feindre, de faire qch. (*b*) Prétendre. **He does not pretend to be artistic**, il ne prétend pas être artiste.

pretender, *s.* **I.** Simulateur, -trice. **2.** Prétendant *m* (*to*, à).

pretension, *s.* **I.** Prétention *f* (*to*, à). **Man of no pretension**(s), homme sans prétentions. **To have pretensions to literary taste**, se piquer de littérature. **2.** Droit *m*, titre *m.*

pretentious, *a.* Prétentieux. **-ly**, *adv.* Prétentieusement.

pretentiousness, *s.* Prétention *f.*

preterit(e), *a. & s. Gram:* Preterite (tense), (temps) passé (*m*); prétérit *m.*

pretext[1], *s.* Prétexte *m. To find a p. for refusing*, trouver prétexte à un refus. **On the pretext** *of consulting me*, sous prétexte de me consulter.

pretext[2], *v.tr.* Alléguer comme prétexte; prétexter.

prettiness, s. Gentillesse f.
pretty. I. a. (a) Joli ; beau, f. belle ; gentil, -ille. (b) **This is a pretty state of affairs!** c'est du joli ! **2.** adv. Assez, passablement. I am pretty well, cela ne va pas trop mal. Pretty much the same, à peu près la même chose. **-ily,** adv. Joliment ; gentiment.
prevail, v.i. I. To prevail over s.o., prévaloir sur qn ; l'emporter sur qn. **2.** To prevail (up)on s.o. to do sth., amener, décider, qn à faire qch. He was prevailed upon by his friends, il se laissa persuader par ses amis (to, de). **3.** Prédominer, régner. **prevailing,** a. Prevailing winds, vents dominants. P. fashion, mode en vogue. The p. cold, le froid qui sévit en ce moment.
prevalence, s. Prédominance f. P. of bribery, généralité f de la corruption.
prevalent, a. (Pré)dominant, répandu, général.
prevaricate, v.i. I. Équivoquer, biaiser, tergiverser. **2.** Mentir ; altérer la vérité.
prevarication, s. I. Équivoques fpl ; tergiversation f. **2.** Mensonge m.
prevent, v.tr. I. Empêcher, mettre obstacle à. To be unavoidably prevented from doing sth., être dans l'impossibilité matérielle de faire qch. **2.** (a) Prévenir, détourner ; parer à (un accident). To p. any scandal, pour obvier à tout scandale. (b) Éviter.
prevention, s. Empêchement m. P. of accidents, précautions fpl contre les accidents.
preventive. I. a. Préventif. **2.** s. Empêchement m ; mesure préventive.
previous. I. a. Préalable ; antérieur, -e, antécédent (to, à). The p. day, le jour précédent ; la veille. Previous engagement, engagement antérieur. **2.** adv. Previous to my departure, avant mon départ. **-ly,** adv. Préalablement ; auparavant.
prevision, s. Prévision f.
pre-war, attrib.a. D'avant-guerre.
prey¹, s. Proie f. Birds of prey, oiseaux de proie. To be a prey to sth., être en proie à (la peur).
prey², v.i. To prey upon sth., faire sa proie de qch. F: Something is preying on his mind, il y a quelque chose qui le travaille.
price¹, s. Prix m. Cost price, prix de revient. Cash price, prix au comptant. At a reduced price, au rabais. Beyond price, sans prix. This must be done at any price, il faut que cela se fasse à tout prix. Not at any price, pour rien au monde. To set a high price on sth., faire grand cas de qch. **price-list,** s. Prix-courant m, pl. prix-courants.
price², v.tr. I. Mettre un prix à. **2.** Estimer, évaluer.
priceless, a. (a) Hors de prix ; inestimable. (b) P: Impayable.
prick¹, s. Piqûre f. F: Pricks of conscience, remords m de conscience.
prick², v.tr. (a) Piquer. F: His conscience pricks him, sa conscience l'aiguillonne. (b) To

prick a hole in sth., faire un trou d'épingle dans qch. **prick (up),** v.tr. To prick (up) one's ears, dresser l'oreille. **pricking,** s. I. Piquage m. **2.** Prickings of conscience, remords mpl (de conscience).
prickle, s. Piquant m ; épine f, aiguillon m.
prickly, a. I. Hérissé ; armé de piquants ; épineux. Bot: Prickly pear, figuier m de Barbarie. **2.** (Sensation) de picotement.
pride¹, s. Orgueil m. (a) Fierté f, morgue f. Puffed up with pride, bouffi d'orgueil. False pride, vanité f. (b) Proper pride, orgueil légitime ; amour-propre m. To take (a) pride in sth., être fier de qch.
pride², v.pr. To pride oneself (up)on sth., s'enorgueillir de qch.
priest, s. Prêtre m. The priests, le clergé.
priestess, s. Prêtresse f.
priesthood, s. Coll. The priesthood, le clergé.
priestly, a. Sacerdotal, -aux.
prig, s. Poseur m ; homme suffisant.
priggish, a. Poseur, suffisant.
priggishness, s. Pose f, suffisance f.
prim, a. Collet monté inv ; (of manner) guindé, compassé. **-ly,** adv. D'un air collet monté.
primacy, s. I. Primauté f. **2.** Ecc : Primatie f.
prima facie, adv. & a. De prime abord, à première vue.
primary, a. I. Premier, primitif, originel. Primary product, produit de base. P. colours, couleurs primaires. **2.** Premier, principal, -aux, essentiel.
primate, s. Ecc : Primat m ; archevêque m.
primates, s.pl. Z : Primates m.
prime¹, a. I. Premier ; principal, -aux ; de premier ordre. **2.** De première qualité. **3.** Premier, originel, primitif. Prime cause, cause première. **Prime Minister,** s. Premier ministre.
prime², s. I. (a) Perfection f. In the prime of life, dans la force de l'âge. To be past one's prime, F: être sur le retour. (b) Le choix, le meilleur. **2.** Premiers jours ; commencement m.
prime³, v.tr. F: Faire la leçon à.
primer, s. P. of geography, premier cours de géographie.
primeval, a. Primordial, -aux. Primeval forest, forêt vierge.
primitive, a. (a) Primitif. (b) (Of method) Primitif, rude, grossier.
primness, s. Air m collet monté.
primogeniture, s. Primogéniture f.
primrose, s. Bot : Primevère f. Evening primrose, onagre f ; herbe f aux ânes.
primula, s. Bot : Primevère f.
prince, s. Prince m.
princely, a. Princier ; royal, -aux. A p. gift, un cadeau royal, magnifique.
princess, s. Princesse f.
principal. I. a. Principal, -aux. P. clerk, commis en chef ; premier commis. **-ally,** adv. Principalement. II. **principal,** s.

1. (a) Directeur m, chef m, patron m. (b) (In transaction) Mandant m. (c) Principals in a duel, combattants m dans un duel. 2. Com: Capital m, principal m.

principality, s. Principauté f.

principle, s. Principe m. **1. To lay sth. down as a principle,** poser qch. en principe. **2. To have high principles,** avoir des principes. **To do sth. on principle,** faire qch. par principe.

print¹, s. **1.** Empreinte f, impression f. **2.** (a) **The book is in print,** le livre est en vente. **Out of print,** épuisé. (b) **Large print,** gros caractères. (c) Édition f, impression. **3.** Estampe f, gravure f, image f. **4.** Phot: (a) Épreuve f; copie f. (b) Ind: **Blue print,** dessin négatif; F: bleu m. **5.** Tex: Indienne f, cotonnade f.

print², v.tr. **1.** Empreindre; imprimer. **2.** Typ: Imprimer. Post: 'Printed matter,' "imprimés" mpl. **3.** Phot: **To print a negative,** tirer une épreuve d'un cliché.

printing, s. **1.** (a) Impression f, tirage m (d'un livre). (b) Imprimerie f, typographie f. **2.** Phot: Tirage. **printing-press,** s. Typ: Presse f d'imprimerie.

printer, s. Typ: Imprimeur m. **Printer's error,** faute f d'impression.

prior¹. 1. a. Préalable, précédent; antérieur, -e (to sth., à qch.). **To have a p. claim,** être le premier en date. **2.** adv. Antérieurement.

prior², s. Ecc.Hist: Prieur m.

prioress, s. Ecc.Hist: Prieure f.

priority, s. Priorité f, antériorité f. **To have priority over s.o.,** primer qn.

priory, s. Prieuré m.

prism, s. Prisme m.

prismatic, a. Prismatique.

prison, s. Prison f; maison f d'arrêt. **To send s.o. to prison,** mettre qn en prison.

prison-van, s. Voiture f cellulaire.

prisoner, s. Prisonnier, -ière.

pristine, a. Premier, primitif; d'antan.

privacy, s. **The privacy of one's home,** l'intimité f du foyer. **To live in privacy,** vivre dans la retraite.

private. I. a. Privé, particulier. **1. Private persons,** (simples) particuliers. **In private life,** dans le particulier, dans l'intimité f. **2.** Secret. **To keep a matter private,** tenir une affaire secrète. **3.** Private study, études particulières. **In my private opinion,** à mon avis personnel. **4. Private and confidential,** secret et confidentiel. P. conversation, conversation intime; aparté m. P. interview, entretien à huis clos. **5.** (a) Private house, maison particulière. (b) P. room, salon réservé. (c) P. theatricals, comédie de salon. **6.** Private property, propriété privée. 'Private,' "entrée interdite au public." Private income, rentes fpl; fortune personnelle. **-ly,** adv. **1.** Privément; en simple particulier. **2.** To speak to s.o. p., parler à qn en particulier. **II.** private, s. **1.** Adv.phr. In private.

To talk to s.o. in p., parler à qn sans témoins. **2.** Mil: Simple soldat m.

privateer, s. Corsaire m.

privation, s. Privation f.

privet, s. Bot: Troène m.

privilege¹, s. **1.** Privilège m, prérogative f. **2.** Parliamentary privilege, prérogative, immunité, parlementaire.

privilege², v.tr. Privilégier. **To be privileged to do sth.,** jouir du privilège de faire qch.

privy, a. **1. To be privy to sth.,** avoir connaissance de qch. **2.** Privé. **The Privy Council,** le Conseil privé (du Roi). **The Privy Purse,** la cassette du roi. **-ily,** adv. En secret.

prize¹, s. **1.** Prix m. **Prize ox,** bœuf primé. **2.** (In a lottery) Lot m. **To draw the first p.,** gagner le gros lot. **prize-book,** s. Livre m de prix. **prize-fighter,** s. Boxeur professionnel. **prize-fighting,** s. Boxe professionnelle. **prize-giving,** s. Distribution f de prix. **prize-list,** s. Palmarès m. **prize-winner,** s. Lauréat, -ate.

prize², v.tr. Évaluer, estimer, priser. **To prize sth. highly,** faire grand cas de qch.

prize³, s. Navy: Prise f, capture f. **prize-money,** s. Navy: Part f de prise.

prize⁴, v.tr. **To prize sth. up,** soulever qch. à l'aide d'un levier.

pro¹, Lt.prep. **1.** Pro forma, pour la forme. **2.** Pro rata, au prorata. **3.** Pro tempore, F: pro tem. Adv. phr. Temporairement. **4.** Pro and contra, F: The pros and cons, le pour et le contre.

pro², s. Sp: F: Professionnel, -elle.

probability, s. Probabilité f; vraisemblance f. **In all probability,** selon toute probabilité.

probable, a. **1.** Probable. **2.** P. story, histoire vraisemblable. **-ably,** adv. Probablement; vraisemblablement.

probation, s. Épreuve f, stage m. **To be on probation,** être à l'épreuve. **Period of p.,** période f stagiaire.

probationary, a. D'épreuve, de stage, stagiaire.

probationer, s. Stagiaire mf.

probe¹, s. Surg: Sonde f.

probe², v.tr. **1.** Med: Sonder, explorer. **2.** F: Approfondir, fouiller (un mystère). **3.** v.i. **To probe into the past,** sonder le passé.

probity, s. Probité f.

problem, s. Problème m. Th: Problem play, pièce à thèse.

problematic(al), a. Problématique; F: douteux, incertain.

proboscis, s. Trompe f.

procedure, s. **1.** Procédé m. The correct p., la (vraie) marche à suivre. **2.** (Mode m de) procédure f.

proceed, v.i. **1.** (a) To proceed (on one's way), continuer son chemin. Before we p. any farther, avant d'aller plus loin. (b) To proceed to(wards) a place, se rendre à un

endroit. (c) **How shall we proceed?** quelle
est la marche à suivre? (d) **To proceed to
do sth.**, se mettre à faire qch. **To proceed to
blows**, en venir aux coups. **2.** (a) (Se) continuer, se poursuivre. (b) *Things are proceeding as usual*, les choses vont leur train. (c) **To
proceed with sth.**, poursuivre, continuer (ses
études). **3. To proceed against s.o.**, procéder
contre qn ; intenter un procès à qn. **4.** Sortir,
provenir. **proceeding,** s. **1.** Façon f d'agir.
2. (a) Procédé m, action f. (b) pl. Débats m.
(c) *Jur:* **To take proceedings against s.o.**,
intenter un procès à qn.
proceeds, s.pl. Produit m, montant m.
process, s. **1.** (a) Processus m. *F:* **It's a
slow process**, c'est un travail long. (b) Cours
m, avancement m ; marche f. **To be in p. of
removal**, être en train de déménager. **2.**
Méthode f ; procédé m. **3.** *Jur:* Action f en
justice.
procession, s. Cortège m ; défilé m ; (religious) procession f.
proclaim, v.tr. Proclamer ; déclarer. *F:
His face proclaims his guilt*, son visage crie
sa culpabilité.
proclamation, s. Proclamation f ; déclaration f.
proclivity, s. Penchant m, tendance f,
inclination f (to sth., à qch.).
procrastinate, v.i. Remettre les affaires au
lendemain, à plus tard ; temporiser.
procrastination, s. Remise f des affaires
à plus tard ; temporisation f.
procrastinator, s. Remetteur, -euse, au
lendemain ; temporisateur, -trice.
procreate, v.tr. Procréer, engendrer.
procreation, s. Procréation f.
proctor, s. *Sch:* Membre exécutif du
conseil de discipline.
procurable, a. Procurable.
procuration, s. **1.** Procuration f. **2.** Acquisition f (de qch. pour qn).
procure, v.tr. Obtenir, procurer. **To p. sth.
for s.o.**, procurer qch. à qn.
prod¹, s. **To give s.o. a p. with a bayonet**,
donner un coup de baïonnette à qn. *F:*
Give him a prod, aiguillonnez-le un peu.
prod², v.tr. **1. To prod sth.**, pousser qch.
(du bout d'un bâton). **2.** *F:* Aiguillonner,
stimuler.
prodigal, a. & s. Prodigue (mf) ; gaspilleur,
-euse. **-ally,** adv. En prodigue.
prodigality, s. Prodigalité f.
prodigious, a. Prodigieux ; *F:* merveilleux.
prodigy, s. Prodige m ; *F:* merveille f.
produce¹, s. **1.** (a) Rendement m. (b) Produit
m. **2.** *Coll.* Denrées fpl, produits.
produce², v.tr. **1.** (a) Présenter, exhiber.
(b) *Th:* Mettre en scène. **2.** (a) Créer.
El: To p. a spark, faire jaillir une étincelle.
(b) *Ind:* Fabriquer. (c) Produire, éditer.
(d) Produire, causer, provoquer. **To produce
a sensation**, faire sensation. **3.** Rapporter,
rendre.

producer, s. Producteur, -trice. *Th:* Metteur m en scène.
product, s. Produit m.
production, s. **1.** (a) Production f, communication f ; présentation f (de son billet).
(b) *Th:* Mise f en scène. **2.** (a) Génération f ;
production. (b) Fabrication f. **Cost of
production**, prix m de fabrique. **3.** (a)
Produit m. *Productions of a country*, produits,
denrées f, d'un pays. (b) Production, œuvre f
(littéraire).
productive, a. Productif.
productivity, s. Productivité f.
profanation, s. Profanation f.
profane¹, a. Profane ; (langage) impie.
profane², v.tr. Profaner.
profanity, s. **1.** Impiété f. **2. To utter
profanities**, proférer des blasphèmes.
profess, v.tr. **1.** (a) Professer, faire profession
de. *To p. oneself satisfied*, se déclarer satisfait.
I do not p. to be a scholar, je ne prétends pas
être savant. **2.** Exercer (la médecine).
professed, a. (a) (Ennemi) déclaré. (b)
Prétendu, soi-disant.
professedly, adv. De son propre aveu ;
ouvertement.
profession, s. **1.** Profession f, déclaration f.
2. (a) Profession, métier m. **The** (learned)
professions, les carrières libérales. (b) **To
belong to the profession**, faire du théâtre.
professional. 1. a. Professionnel. (a) *P.
practices*, usages m du métier. (b) *P. diplomatist*, diplomate de carrière. **2.** s. (a) Expert
m. *Professionals*, gens m de métier. (b) *Sp:*
Professionnel, -elle.
professor, s. Professeur m.
professorship, s. Professorat m.
proffer, v.tr. Offrir, présenter.
proficiency, s. Capacité f, compétence f.
proficient, a. Capable, compétent ; versé.
profile, s. (i) Profil m ; (ii) silhouette f.
profit¹, s. Profit m, bénéfice m. (a) Avantage
m. **To turn sth. to profit**, tirer profit de qch.
(b) *Com:* **Net profit(s)**, bénéfice net. **To
make huge profits**, gagner gros. **Profit and
loss**, profits et pertes. **profit-sharing,** s.
Ind: Participation f aux bénéfices.
profit², v. **1.** v.tr. Profiter à ; être avantageux à. **2.** v.i. **To profit by sth.**, profiter,
bénéficier, de qch.
profitable, a. Profitable, avantageux. **-ably,**
adv. Profitablement, avantageusement.
profiteer¹, s. *F:* Profiteur, -euse ; mercanti m.
profiteer², v.i. Faire des bénéfices excessifs.
profiteering, s. Mercantilisme m.
profitless, a. Sans profit.
profligacy, s. **1.** Débauche f, libertinage m.
2. Prodigalité f.
profligate, a. & s. **1.** Débauché, -ée ;
libertin, -ine ; dévergondé, -ée. **2.** Prodigue
(mf).
profound, a. Profond. *P. secret*, secret
absolu. **-ly,** adv. Profondément.

profundity, s. Profondeur f.
profuse, a. **1. To be profuse in one's apologies,** se confondre en excuses. **2.** Profus, abondant. **-ly,** adv. Profusément. *To perspire* p., transpirer abondamment.
profuseness, s. Profusion f.
profusion, s. Profusion f; abondance f.
progenitor, s. Aïeul m, pl. aïeux ; ancêtre m.
progeny, s. **1.** Progéniture f. **2.** Descendants mpl, lignée f, postérité f.
prognostic, s. Pronostic m, présage m.
prognosticate, v.tr. Pronostiquer, présager.
program(me), s. Programme m.
progress¹, s. (a) Marche f en avant ; avancement m. *The progress of events,* le cours des événements. *Harvesting in full progress,* moisson qui bat son plein. (b) Progrès m. *To make progress in one's studies,* faire des progrès dans ses études.
progress², v.i. (a) S'avancer. *As the year progresses,* au cours de l'année. (b) *To progress with one's studies,* faire des progrès dans ses études.
progression, s. Progression f. *Mode of* p., mode m de locomotion.
progressive, a. Progressif. (a) **By progressive stages,** par degrés. (b) *To be* p., être ami du progrès. **-ly,** adv. Progressivement.
prohibit, v.tr. **1.** Prohiber, défendre, interdire. *To prohibit s.o. from doing sth.,* défendre, interdire, à qn de faire qch. **2.** Empêcher (*s.o. from doing sth.,* qn de faire qch.).
prohibition, s. Prohibition f, interdiction f, défense f.
prohibitive, a. **Prohibitive price,** prix prohibitif, inabordable.
project¹, s. Projet m.
project², I. v.tr. Projeter. **1.** *Projected buildings,* édifices en projet. **2.** Projeter, lancer, en avant. II. **project,** v.i. Faire saillie. **projecting,** a. Saillant, en saillie.
projectile, a. & s. Projectile (m).
projection, s. **1.** (a) Lancement m ; projection f. (b) Conception f (d'un projet). **2.** Saillie f.
projector, s. Projecteur m.
proletarian. **1.** a. Prolétarien, prolétaire. **2.** s. Prolétaire mf.
proletariat, s. Prolétariat m.
prolific, a. Prolifique ; fécond (*in, of,* en).
prolix, a. Prolixe, diffus.
prolixity, s. Prolixité f.
prologue, s. Prologue m (*to,* de).
prolong, v.tr. Prolonger.
prolongation, s. Prolongation f; délai accordé.
promenade¹, s. **1.** Promenade f. **2.** (a) (Lieu m de) promenade ; (*at seaside*) esplanade f. (b) *Th :* Promenoir m. **promenade concert,** s. Concert m où l'auditoire peut circuler librement. **promenade deck,** s. *Nau :* Pont-promenade m, pl. ponts-promenades.

promenade², v.i. Se promener, parader.
prominence, s. **1.** (a) Proéminence f; relief m. (b) Saillie f, protubérance f. **2.** Éminence f. *To give sth.* **prominence,** faire ressortir qch.
prominent, a. **1.** Saillant ; en saillie ; proéminent. **2.** (a) Saillant ; remarquable. *In a prominent position,* très en vue. *To play a p.* part, jouer un rôle important. (b) Éminent. **-ly,** adv. (a) Éminemment. (b) *Goods p. displayed,* marchandises bien en vue.
promiscuity, s. Promiscuité f.
promiscuous, a. **1.** Confus, mêlé. **2.** *P :* Casuel, fortuit. **-ly,** adv. **1.** Confusément, sans ordre ; en promiscuité. **2.** *P :* Casuellement, fortuitement.
promise¹, s. Promesse f. (a) *To release s.o. from his promise,* rendre sa parole à qn. (b) *To show great promise,* donner de belles espérances.
promise², v.tr. (a) *To promise s.o. sth.,* promettre qch. à qn. *To promise (s.o.) to do sth.,* promettre (à qn) de faire qch. (b) *Action that promises trouble,* action qui laisse prévoir des ennuis. *Abs. The scheme promises well,* le projet s'annonce bien.
promising, a. Plein de promesses. **Promising young man,** jeune homme qui promet.
promissory, a. **Promissory note,** billet m à ordre.
promontory, s. Promontoire m.
promote, v.tr. **1.** Donner de l'avancement à. *To be promoted,* être promu. **2.** (a) Encourager (les arts) ; favoriser (le succès) ; avancer (les intérêts de qn). (b) *To promote a company,* lancer une société anonyme.
promoter, s. Instigateur, -trice.
promotion, s. Promotion f, avancement m. *To get promotion,* obtenir de l'avancement.
prompt¹, a. Prompt. (a) Vif, rapide. (b) Immédiat. **Prompt delivery,** livraison immédiate. **-ly,** adv. Promptement. (a) Avec empressement. (b) Sur-le-champ, immédiatement.
prompt², v.tr. **1.** *To p. s.o. to do sth.,* inciter qn à faire qch. *To be prompted by a feeling of pity,* être animé par un sentiment de pitié. **2.** Souffler (un acteur). **prompting,** s. Suggestion f ; incitation f (*to do sth.,* à faire qch.).
prompter, s. Souffleur, -euse.
promptitude, s. Promptitude f, empressement m.
promulgate, v.tr. **1.** Promulguer. **2.** Disséminer, répandre.
promulgation, s. **1.** Promulgation f. **2.** Dissémination f.
prone, a. **1.** Couché sur le ventre. **2. To be prone to sth.,** être enclin à qch.
proneness, s. Disposition f, inclination f (*to,* à).
prong, s. Fourchon m, dent f, branche f.
pronged, a. A fourchons, à dents.
pronominal, a. *Gram :* Pronominal, -aux.

pronoun, s. *Gram:* Pronom m.

pronounce, v.tr. **1.** (a) Déclarer. (b) *Jur:* Prononcer. **2.** Prononcer; articuler. **pronounced,** a. Prononcé, marqué.

pronouncement, s. Déclaration f.

pronunciation, s. Prononciation f.

proof[1], s. **1.** Preuve f. **Positive proof,** preuve patente. *To give p. of one's gratitude,* témoigner sa reconnaissance. **This is proof that he is lying,** cela prouve qu'il ment. **To produce proof to the contrary,** fournir la preuve contraire. **2.** Épreuve f. **To put sth. to the proof,** mettre qch. à l'épreuve. **3.** *Typ:* Épreuve.

proof[2], a. **Proof against sth.,** résistant à qch.; à l'épreuve de qch. **To be proof against danger,** être à l'abri du danger. **Proof against flattery,** insensible à la flatterie.

prop[1], s. Appui m, support m, soutien m.

prop[2], v.tr. **To prop (up),** appuyer, soutenir.

propaganda, s. Propagande f.

propagate. 1. v.tr. (a) Propager. (b) **To propagate light,** propager, répandre, la lumière. **2.** v.pr. & i. Se propager, se reproduire.

propagation, s. Propagation f, reproduction f.

propel, v.tr. Propulser; pousser en avant. **Propelled by steam,** mû par la vapeur.

propelling, a. Propulsif.

propeller, s. **1.** Propulseur m. **2.** *Nau:* (Screw) propeller, (propulseur à) hélice f.

propensity, s. Propension f, penchant m, inclination f, tendance f.

proper, a. Propre. **1.** (a) **Proper to sth.,** propre, parti·ulier, à qch. (b) *To paint s.o. in his p. colour*, dépeindre qn sous son vrai jour. (c) *Gram:* **Proper noun,** nom propre. **2.** (a) Vrai, juste, approprié. **In a proper sense,** au sens propre. (b) *Mth:* **Proper fraction,** fraction moindre que l'unité. **3.** *P:* *To get a p. hiding,* recevoir une belle raclée. **4.** (a) Convenable. **At the proper time,** en temps opportun; en temps utile. **To deem it proper to,** juger bon de. *Do as you think p.,* faites comme bon vous semblera. **To do the proper thing by s.o.,** agir loyalement avec qn. *The p. way to do it,* la meilleure manière de le faire. *The p. tool to use,* le bon outil. **To keep sth. in proper condition,** tenir qch. en bon état. (b) Comme il faut; (*of language*) bienséant, correct. **-ly,** adv. **1.** (a) **Properly so called,** proprement dit. (b) Bien; de la bonne façon. **Do it properly or not at all,** faites-le comme il faut ou pas du tout. **2.** *F:* Absolument. **3.** (a) Convenablement. **To behave properly,** se conduire comme il faut. (b) *He very p. refused,* il a refusé, comme faire se devait.

property, s. **1.** (Droit m de) propriété f. **2.** (a) Propriété, biens mpl, avoir(s) m(pl). **That's my property,** cela m'appartient. *F:* **That's public property,** c'est un secret de Polichinelle. (b) Immeuble m, immeubles.

3. *Th:* Accessoire m. **4.** Propriété; qualité f (propre). **Inherent property,** attribut m.

prophecy, s. Prophétie f.

prophesy. 1. v.i. Parler en prophète; prophétiser. **2.** v.tr. Prophétiser, prédire (un événement).

prophet, s. Prophète m.

prophetess, s. Prophétesse f.

prophetic(al), a. Prophétique. **-ally,** adv. Prophétiquement.

propinquity, s. **1.** Proximité f; voisinage m. **2.** (Proche) parenté f.

propitiate, v.tr. **1.** Rendre propice, favorable. **2.** Apaiser; se faire pardonner par.

propitiation, s. **1.** Propitiation f. **2.** Apaisement m. **3.** Expiation f.

propitious, a. Propice, favorable. **-ly,** adv. D'une manière propice; favorablement.

proportion[1], s. **1.** Partie f; portion f; part f. **To divide expenses in equal proportions,** répartir les frais par parts égales. **2.** Rapport m, proportion f. (a) **In due proportion,** en proportions raisonnables. (b) **In proportion as,** à mesure que. (c) **Out of proportion,** mal proportionné. *F:* **To lose all sense of proportion,** ne garder aucune mesure. **3.** pl. **Proportions,** proportions (d'un édifice); dimensions f.

proportion[2], v.tr. Proportionner.

proportional, a. Proportionnel; en proportion (to, de); proportionné (to, à). **-ally,** adv. En proportion (to, de); proportionnellement (to, à).

proportionate, a. Proportionné (to, à). **-ly,** adv. = PROPORTIONALLY.

proposal, s. **1.** (a) Proposition f, offre f. (b) Demande f en mariage. **2.** Dessein m, projet m.

propose, v.tr. **1.** (a) **To propose a course of action,** proposer une ligne de conduite. (b) **To propose a motion,** proposer une motion. **To propose a toast,** porter un toast. (c) **To propose to do sth.,** se proposer de faire qch. *What do you p. to do now?* que comptez-vous faire maintenant? **2.** *Abs.* Faire la demande en mariage.

proposer, s. Proposeur, -euse.

proposition, s. (a) = PROPOSAL 1 (a). (b) *F:* Affaire f. **Paying proposition,** affaire qui rapporte.

propound, v.tr. Proposer (une énigme); émettre (une idée).

proprietary, a. (a) De propriété, de propriétaire. (b) *Com:* **Proprietary article,** spécialité f.

proprietor, s. Propriétaire mf. **Landed p.,** propriétaire foncier.

propriety, s. **1.** (a) Propriété f, justesse f, à-propos m; rectitude f (de conduite). (b) Opportunité f (d'une démarche). **2.** (a) Bienséance f, décence f. **Breach of propriety,** manque m de savoir-vivre. (b) **To observe the proprieties,** observer les convenances.

propulsion, s. Propulsion f.

propulsive, *a.* Propulsif.
prorogation, *s.* Prorogation *f.*
prorogue, *v.tr.* Proroger.
prosaic, *a.* Prosaïque. **-ally,** *adv.* Prosaïquement.
proscribe, *v.tr.* Proscrire. **1.** Mettre hors la loi ; bannir. **2.** Interdire, défendre.
proscript, *s.* Proscrit *m* ; hors-la-loi *m inv.*
proscription, *s.* Proscription *f.*
prose, *s.* **1.** Prose *f.* **2.** *Sch: Latin p.*, thème latin. **prose-writer,** *s.* Prosateur *m.*
prosecute, *v.tr.* **1.** (*a*) Poursuivre (en justice répressive). (*b*) **To prosecute a claim,** poursuivre une réclamation. **2.** (*a*) Effectuer. (*b*) Poursuivre (des études). (*c*) Exercer (un métier).
prosecution, *s.* **1.** *Jur:* (*a*) Poursuites *fpl.* (*b*) Accusation *f* ; action publique. (*c*) **Witness for the prosecution,** témoin à charge. **2.** (*a*) Continuation *f.* (*b*) Exercice *m* (d'un métier).
prosecutor, *s. Jur:* **1.** Plaignant, -e, demandeur, -eresse. **2. The Public Prosecutor,** le procureur du Roi.
proselyte, *s.* Prosélyte *mf.*
prosiness, *s.* Prosaïsme *m* (d'une conversation, etc.) ; terre à terre *m inv* (du style).
prosody, *s.* Prosodie *f* ; métrique *f.*
prospect¹, *s.* **1.** Vue *f* ; point *m* de vue ; perspective *f.* **Wide p.,** horizon très étendu. **2.** (*a*) Perspective, expectative *f.* **To have sth. in prospect,** avoir qch. en perspective. (*b*) **No p. of agreement,** aucune perspective d'accord. **3.** *pl.* Avenir *m,* espérances *fpl.*
prospect², *v.i. & tr. Min:* Prospecter.
prospective, *a.* En perspective ; à venir.
prospector, *s.* Chercheur *m* d'or ; prospecteur *m.*
prospectus, *s.* Prospectus *m.*
prosper. 1. *v.i.* Prospérer, réussir. **2.** *v.tr* Faire prospérer, faire réussir.
prosperity, *s.* Prospérité *f.*
prosperous, *a.* **1.** Prospère, florissant. **2.** Favorable, propice (*to,* à).
prosperousness, *s.* Prospérité *f.*
prostrate¹, *a.* **1.** Prosterné ; couché (à terre) ; étendu. **2.** Abattu, accablé.
prostrate², *v.tr.* **To prostrate oneself before s.o.,** se prosterner devant qn. *Prostrated by the heat,* accablé par la chaleur.
prostration, *s.* **1.** Prosternation *f,* prosternement *m.* **2.** Abattement *m.*
prosy, *a.* Prosaïque ; (*of pers.*) verbeux, ennuyeux. **-ily,** *adv.* Fastidieusement.
protagonist, *s.* Protagoniste *m.*
protect, *v.tr.* **1.** (*a*) Protéger. **To protect s.o. from sth.,** protéger qn contre qch. (*b*) Sauvegarder. **2.** Patronner ; tenir en tutelle. **protecting,** *a.* Protecteur, -trice ; de protection.
protection, *s.* **1.** (*a*) Protection *f,* défense *f* ; sauvegarde *f.* (*b*) **Under s.o.'s protection,** sous la sauvegarde de qn. (*c*) Patronage *m.*

2. *Pol.Ec :* Protectionnisme *m.* **3.** (*a*) Abri *m,* protection. (*b*) Blindage *m.*
protective, *a.* Protecteur, -trice ; préservatif.
protector, *s.* (*a*) Protecteur *m.* (*b*) Patron *m.*
protectorate, *s.* Protectorat *m.*
protest¹, *s.* Protestation *f* **To make a protest,** protester. **Under protest,** *F :* à son corps défendant, en protestant.
protest². **1.** *v.tr.* Protester. **To protest one's innocence,** protester de son innocence. **2.** *v.i.* Protester, réclamer (*against,* contre).
protestant, *a. & s.* Protestant, -ante.
protestation, *s.* Protestation *f.*
protoplasm, *s.* Protoplasme *m.*
prototype, *s.* Prototype *m,* archétype *m.*
protract, *v.tr.* Prolonger, allonger ; traîner en longueur.
protraction, *s.* Prolongation *f.*
protractor, *s. Geom:* Rapporteur *m.*
protrude. 1. *v.tr.* Faire sortir ; pousser en avant. **2.** *v.i.* S'avancer, faire saillie, déborder
protruding, *a.* En saillie ; saillant. *Protruding forehead,* front bombé. *P. eyes,* yeux qui sortent de la tête.
protrusion, *s.* **1.** Saillie *f.* **2.** Protubérance *f.*
protuberance, *s.* Protubérance *f.*
protuberant, *a.* Protubérant.
proud, *a.* (*a*) Fier, orgueilleux. (*b*) **To be proud of sth.,** être fier de qch. (*c*) **To be proud to do sth.,** se faire honneur de faire qch. *P :* **To do oneself proud,** ne se priver de rien. **-ly,** *adv.* Fièrement, orgueilleusement ; avec fierté.
prove. I. *v.tr.* **1.** (*a*) *Tchn:* Éprouver ; mettre à l'épreuve. *Proved remedy,* remède éprouvé. (*b*) *Ar:* Vérifier. **2.** (*a*) Prouver, démontrer. *It remains to be proved,* cela n'est pas encore prouvé. (*b*) *Jur:* Homologuer (un testament). (*c*) **To prove oneself,** faire ses preuves. **II. prove,** *v.i.* Se montrer. *To p. useful,* se trouver utile. *The news proved false,* la nouvelle s'est avérée fausse. *Their rashness proved fatal to them,* leur audace leur fut fatale.
provender, *s.* Fourrage *m,* provende *f.*
proverb, *s.* Proverbe *m.*
proverbial, *a.* Proverbial, -aux ; passé en proverbe. **-ally,** *adv.* Proverbialement.
provide. I. (*a*) *v.i.* **To provide against sth.,** se pourvoir contre (une attaque). *Expenses provided for in the budget,* dépenses prévues au budget. (*b*) *v.tr.* Stipuler. **2.** (*a*) *v.tr.* **To provide s.o. with sth.,** fournir qch. à qn. (*b*) *v.i.* **To provide for s.o.,** pourvoir à l'entretien de qn. **To provide for oneself,** se suffire. **To be provided for,** être à l'abri du besoin. (*c*) *v.i. He provided for everything,* il a subvenu à tout. **provided. I.** *a.* Pourvu, muni (*with,* de). **2.** *conj.* **Provided (that),** pourvu que + *sub.* ; à condition que + *ind. or sub.*
providence, *s.* **1.** Prévoyance *f,* prudence *f.* **2.** Providence (divine).

provident, *a.* Prévoyant. **Provident society,** société de prévoyance.
providential, *a.* Providentiel. **-ally,** *adv.* Providentiellement.
provider, *s.* Pourvoyeur, -euse; fournisseur, -euse.
province, *s.* **1.** Province *f.* In the provinces, en province. **2.** *F:* That is not (within) my province, ce n'est pas de mon ressort.
provincial, *a. & s.* Provincial, -ale, *pl.* -aux, -ales.
provision¹, *s.* **1.** (*a*) To make provision for sth., pourvoir à qch. To make provision for one's family, assurer l'avenir de sa famille. (*b*) Provision of the necessities of life, fourniture *f* des nécessités de la vie. **2.** (*a*) *Com:* Provision *f.* (*b*) **Provisions,** provisions (de bouche); vivres *m*, comestibles *m*. **Provision merchant,** marchand de comestibles. **3.** Article *m*; clause *f*, stipulation *f.* *F:* To come within the provisions of the law, tomber sous le coup de la loi.
provision², *v.tr.* Approvisionner; ravitailler.
provisional, *a.* Provisoire. **-ally,** *adv.* Provisoirement.
proviso, *s.* Clause conditionnelle.
provocation, *s.* Provocation *f.*
provocative, *a.* (*a*) Provocateur, -trice; provocant. (*b*) (Sourire) agaçant.
provoke, *v.tr.* **1.** (*a*) Provoquer, pousser, inciter (*s.o. to do sth.,* qn à faire qch.). To provoke s.o. to anger, mettre qn en colère. (*b*) Irriter, fâcher, agacer. **2.** Exciter (la curiosité). To provoke a smile, faire naître un sourire. **provoking,** *a.* Irritant, contrariant. How provoking! quel ennui! **-ly,** *adv.* D'une manière irritante, contrariante.
provost, *s.* Prévôt *m.* **provost-marshal,** *s.* Grand prévôt.
prow, *s.* Proue *f.*
prowess, *s.* Prouesse *f*, vaillance *f.*
prowl¹, *s.* *F:* To be for ever on the prowl, être toujours à rôder.
prowl², *v.i.* Rôder.
prowler, *s.* Rôdeur, -euse.
proximity, *s.* Proximité *f.* In the proximity of a town, à proximité d'une ville.
proximo, *adv.* (Du mois) prochain.
proxy, *s.* *Jur:* **1.** Procuration *f*; pouvoir *m*; mandat *m.* **2.** Mandataire *mf*; fondé *m* de pouvoir(s).
prude, *s.f.* Prude.
prudence, *s.* Prudence *f*, sagesse *f.*
prudent, *a.* Prudent, sage, judicieux. **-ly,** *adv.* Prudemment, sagement.
prudish, *a.* Prude.
prudishness, *s.* Pruderie *f.*
prune¹, *s.* Pruneau *m.*
prune², *v.tr.* (*a*) Tailler. (*b*) To prune (off) a branch, élaguer une branche. **pruning,** *s.* Taille *f.* **pruning-knife,** *s.* Serpette *f*
Prussia. *Pr.n.* La Prusse.
Prussian, *a. & s.* Prussien, -ienne. **Prussian blue,** bleu *m* de Prusse.

prussic, *a.* Prussic acid, acide *m* prussique.
pry¹, *v.i.* Fureter; fouiller; *F:* fourrer le nez (*into sth.,* dans qch.). **prying,** *a.* Curieux, indiscret, -ète; *F:* fureteur, -euse.
pry², *v.tr.* Soulever, mouvoir, à l'aide d'un levier. To pry open, exercer des pesées sur.
psalm, *s.* Psaume *m.*
psalmist, *s.* Psalmiste *m.*
pseudonym, *s.* Pseudonyme *m.*
pshaw¹, *int.* Fi! peuh! allons donc!
pshaw², *v.i.* Dire peuh.
Psyche. *Pr.n.* Psyché *f.*
psychiatrist, *s.* Psychiatre *mf.*
psychiatry, *s.* Psychiatrie *f.*
psychic(al), *a.* Psychique.
psychics, *s.pl.* La métapsychique.
psychological, *a.* Psychologique. **-ally,** *adv.* Psychologiquement.
psychologist, *s.* Psychologue *m.*
psychology, *s.* Psychologie *f.*
ptarmigan, *s.* *Orn:* Perdrix *f* des neiges.
ptomaine, *s.* *Ch:* Ptomaïne *f.* **Ptomaine poisoning,** intoxication *f* alimentaire.
public. **1.** *a.* Public, *f.* publique. (*a*) Public holiday, fête légale. (*b*) Public library, bibliothèque municipale. (*c*) To make a public protest, protester publiquement. (*d*) Public life, vie publique. Public spirit, patriotisme *m*, civisme *m.* **2.** *s.* (*a*) Public *m.* The general public, le grand public. (*b*) In public, en public; publiquement. **-ly,** *adv.* Publiquement; en public. **public house,** *s.* **1.** Auberge *f.* **2.** Débit *m* de boissons.
publican, *s.* (*a*) Aubergiste *mf.* (*b*) Débitant, -ante, d boissons.
publication, *s.* Publication *f.*
publicity, *s.* **1.** Publicité *f.* **2.** *Com:* Réclame *f.*
publish, *v.tr.* Publier. Just published, vient de paraître. **publishing,** *s.* Publication *f.* Publishing house, maison d'édition.
publisher, *s.* Éditeur *m.*
puce, *a. & s.* (Couleur) puce *m inv.*
pucker¹, *s.* Ride *f*, pli *m.*
pucker². **1.** *v.tr.* Rider; plisser. To pucker (up) one's lips, plisser les lèvres. **2.** *v.i.* To pucker (up), se froncer.
puckish, *a.* De lutin; espiègle.
pudding, *s.* *Cu:* (*a*) Pudding *m*, pouding *m.* (*b*) Rice pudding, riz *m* au lait. (*c*) Black pudding, boudin (noir).
puddle¹, *s.* Flaque *f* d'eau.
puddle², *v.i.* To puddle (about), patauger.
puerile, *a.* Puéril.
puerility, *s.* Puérilité *f.*
puff¹, *s.* **1.** Souffle *m* (d'air); bouffée *f* (de tabac). **2.** Réclame *f*; puff *m.* **puff-adder,** *s.* Vipère *f* clotho. **puff-ball,** *s.* *Fung:* Vesse-de-loup *f.* **puff-box,** *s.* Boîte *f* à houppe. **puff-pastry,** *s.* *Cu:* Pâte feuilletée.
puff². **1.** *v.i.* (*a*) Souffler. To puff and blow, haleter. (*b*) Lancer des bouffées (de fumée).

To puff (away), at one's pipe, tirer sur sa pipe.
2. *v.tr. F:* Prôner, vanter. **puff out,** *v.tr.*
(a) Gonfler. (b) Lancer. **puff up,** *v.tr.* To
puff oneself up, se rengorger. **puffed up,** *a.*
Puffed up with pride, gonflé d'orgueil.
puffed, *a. F:* Essoufflé; à bout de souffle.
puffin, *s. Orn:* Macareux *m.*
puffiness, *s.* Boursouflure *f*, enflure *f.*
puffy, *a.* Bouffi, boursouflé.
pug, *s.* Pug(-dog), carlin *m*; roquet *m.*
pug(-)nose, *s.* Nez épaté. **pug-nosed,** *a.*
Au nez épaté.
pugilism, *s.* Pugilat *m*; la boxe.
pugilist, *s.* Pugiliste *m*; boxeur *m.*
pugnacious, *a.* Querelleur, -euse.
pull¹, *s.* **I.** (a) Traction *f*, tirage *m.* To give
a pull, tirer. (b) Effort *m* de traction. (c)
Row: Coup *m* (d'aviron). **2.** Avantage *m.*
To have a pull, *F:* avoir du piston (*with s.o.,*
chez qn). **To have the pull of s.o.,** avoir
l'avantage sur qn.
pull², *v.tr.* **I.** (a) Tirer. To pull the trigger,
presser la détente. (b) *Row:* Manier (un
aviron). To pull a boat, *abs.* to pull, ramer.
(c) *v.i.* To pull at a rope, tirer sur un cordage.
To pull at one's pipe, tirer des bouffées de sa
pipe. **2.** Traîner, tirer. **3.** To pull a face,
faire une grimace. To pull a wry face, faire
la grimace. **pull about,** *v.tr. F:* Houspiller, malmener. **pull apart,** *v.tr.* Séparer; déchirer en deux. **pull down,** *v.tr.*
I. Baisser, faire descendre; rabattre (son
voile). **2.** Démolir, abattre (une maison).
pull in, *v.tr.* (a) Rentrer (un filet). (b) Retenir (son cheval). **pull off,** *v.tr.* (a) Retirer,
ôter. (b) *Sp:* Gagner, remporter. (c) Réussir
à faire (qch.). **pull on,** *v.tr.* Enfiler, mettre
(des bas). **pull out. I.** *v.tr.* (a) Sortir,
(re)tirer. (b) Arracher. **2.** *v.i.* Sortir de la
gare; démarrer. **pull over,** *v.tr.* (a) To
pull one's hat over one's eyes, ramener son
chapeau sur ses yeux. (b) Renverser. **pull-**
over, *s. Cost:* Pull-over *m.* **pull round.**
F: **I.** *v.tr.* (a) Ranimer. (b) Remettre sur
pied. **2.** *v.i.* (a) Se ranimer. (b) Se remettre.
pull through, *v.i.* Se tirer d'affaire.
He will never p. through, il ne guérira pas.
pull to, *v.tr.* Tirer, fermer (la porte).
pull together, *v.tr.* **I.** To pull oneself
together, se reprendre, se ressaisir. **2.** *Abs.*
Tirer ensemble. *They are not pulling together,*
ils ne s'entendent pas. **pull up. I.** *v.tr.*
(a) (Re)monter, hisser (qn, qch.). (b) Hausser,
lever; retrousser (sa jupe). To pull up one's
socks, *F:* Se dégourdir, s'activer. (c) Arracher, extirper. (d) Arrêter (un cheval). (e)
F: Réprimander. **2.** *v.i.* S'arrêter. **pulling,**
s. Tirage *m.*
pullet, *s.* Poulette *f.*
pulley, *s.* Poulie *f.*
Pullman. *Pr.n. Rail:* Pullman car, voiture
f Pullman.
pulp, *s.* Pulpe *f.* To reduce sth. to a pulp,
réduire en pulpe.

pulpit, *s.* Chaire *f.*
pulsate, *v.i.* (a) Battre. (b) Palpiter; vibrer.
pulsation, *s.* Pulsation *f*, battement *m.*
pulse, *s.* Pouls *m.* **To feel s.o.'s pulse,** tâter
le pouls à qn.
pulverization, *s.* Pulvérisation *f.*
pulverize, *v.tr.* Pulvériser; broyer.
puma, *s. Z:* Puma *m*, couguar *m.*
pumice, *s.* Pumice(-stone), (pierre *f*) ponce *f.*
pummel, *v.tr.* Bourrer de coups de poing.
pump¹, *s.* (a) Pompe *f.* Hand pump, pompe
à bras. (b) Bicycle pump, pompe à bicyclette.
pump-handle, *s.* Bras *m* de pompe.
pump². **I.** *v.tr.* (a) Pomper. (b) To pump
a well dry, assécher un puits. *F:* To pump
s.o., sonder qn. **2.** *v.i.* Pomper.
pump³, *s.* Escarpin *m.*
pumpkin, *s. Hort:* Potiron *m*, citrouille *f.*
pun¹, *s.* Calembour *m*; jeu *m* de mots.
pun², *v.i.* Faire des calembours, des jeux de
mots.
punch¹, *s.* **I.** *Tls:* (a) (Centre-)punch,
pointeau *m.* (b) Chasse-goupilles *m inv.*
(c) Perçoir *m.* (d) Étampe *f*, poinçon *m.*
2. Poinçon; pince *f* de contrôle.
punch², *s.* Coup *m* de poing; horion *m.*
punch³, *v.tr.* **I.** (a) Percer; découper;
poinçonner. (b) Poinçonner (un billet).
2. Donner un coup de poing à, cogner sur.
punch⁴, *s.* (Beverage) Punch *m.* **punch-**
bowl, *s.* Bol *m* à punch.
Punch⁵. *Pr.n.* = Polichinelle *m* ou Guignol *m.*
Punch and Judy Show, (théâtre *m* de)
Guignol *m.*
punctilio, *s.* **I.** Formalisme exagéré. **2.** To
stand upon punctilios, s'attacher à des
vétilles.
punctilious, *a.* Pointilleux, méticuleux.
-ly, *adv.* Pointilleusement; scrupuleusement.
punctiliousness, *s.* Pointillerie *f*; scrupule
m des détails.
punctual, *a.* Ponctuel, exact. **-ally,** *adv.*
Exactement, ponctuellement.
punctuality, *s.* Ponctualité *f*, exactitude *f.*
punctuate, *v.tr.* Ponctuer.
punctuation, *s.* Ponctuation *f.*
puncture¹, *s.* **I.** Crevaison *f.* **2.** Piqûre *f*,
perforation *f.*
puncture², *v.tr.* (a) Crever, perforer.
(b) (With passive force) Crever.
pungency, *s.* **I.** Goût piquant; odeur forte
(d'un parfum). **2.** Acreté *f*, aigreur *f* (de
paroles).
pungent, *a.* **I.** Mordant, caustique. **2.** Acre,
piquant, irritant. **-ly,** *adv.* D'une manière
piquante.
punish, *v.tr.* Punir; châtier. **To punish**
s.o. for sth., punir qn de qch.
punishable, *a.* Punissable.
punishment, *s.* Punition *f*, châtiment *m.*
Capital punishment, peine capitale. **As a**
punishment, par punition.
punitive, *a.* Punitif; répressif.

punt[1], *s.* Bachot *m.* **punt-pole,** *s.* Gaffe *f*, perche *f*.
punt[2], *v.tr.* Conduire à la perche.
puny, *a.* **1.** (*a*) Petit, menu. (*b*) Mesquin. **2.** (*Of pers.*) Chétif, faible, débile.
pup, *s.* **1.** Petit chien, jeune chien. *F:* To sell s.o. a pup, tromper qn. **2.** *F:* = PUPPY 2.
pupa, *s. Ent:* Nymphe *f*, chrysalide *f*.
pupil[1], *s. Sch:* Élève *mf*; écolier, -ière.
pupil[2], *s.* Pupille *f* (de l'œil).
puppet, *s.* Marionnette *f*. *F:* Mere puppet, pantin *m*.
puppy, *s.* **1.** Jeune chien *m*. **2.** (*Of pers.*) Freluquet *m*, fat *m*.
purblind, *a.* **1.** Myope. **2.** Obtus.
purchase[1], *s.* **1.** Achat *m*, acquisition *f*. **2.** (*a*) Force *f* mécanique. (*b*) Prise *f*. (*c*) Point *m* d'appui; appui *m*. **purchase-price,** *s.* Prix *m* d'achat.
purchase[2], *v.tr.* Acheter, acquérir.
purchaser, *s.* Acheteur, -euse.
pure, *a.* Pur. **-ly,** *adv.* Purement. **pure-bred,** *a.* (Chien) de race.
purgative, *a. & s.* Purgatif (*m*).
purgatory, *s. Theol:* Le purgatoire.
purge[1], *s.* Purgation *f*.
purge[2], *v.tr.* **1.** Purger. **2.** Purifier.
purification, *s.* Purification *f*; épuration *f*.
purify, *v.tr.* Purifier.
purist, *s.* Puriste *mf*.
Puritan, *a. & s.* Puritain, -aine.
puritanical, *a.* De puritain.
purity, *s.* Pureté *f*.
purlieu, *s.* **1.** Limites *fpl*, bornes *fpl*. **2.** *pl.* Purlieus, alentours *mpl*, environs *mpl*.
purloin, *v.tr.* Soustraire; voler.
purple. **I.** *a.* Violet; mauve. *F:* To get purple in the face, devenir cramoisi, pourpre. **II. purple,** *s.* Pourpre *f*.
purplish, *a.* Violacé, violâtre.
purport[1], *s.* (*a*) Sens *m*, signification *f*. (*b*) Portée *f*, valeur *f*, force *f*.
purport[2], *v.tr.* **1.** To purport to be sth., avoir la prétention d'être qch. **2.** Impliquer.
purpose[1], *s.* **1.** (*a*) Dessein *m*, objet *m*; but *m*, fin *f*, intention *f*. Fixed purpose, dessein bien arrêté. Novel with a purpose, roman à thèse. *To do sth.* on purpose, faire qch. exprès, à dessein. Of set purpose, de propos délibéré, de parti pris. (*b*) Résolution *f*. Infirmity of purpose, manque *m* de volonté. **2.** Destination *f*, fin. To answer the purpose, répondre au but. For this purpose, à cet effet. *For all necessary purposes,* pour tout ce qui est nécessaire. **3.** To speak to the purpose, parler à propos. **4.** *To work* to good purpose, travailler avec fruit. To some purpose, réussir.
purpose[2], *v.tr.* To purpose doing sth., se proposer, avoir l'intention, de faire qch.
purposeful, *a.* (*a*) Prémédité. (*b*) (*Of pers.*) Avisé. (*c*) Tenace. **-fully,** *adv.* Dans un but réfléchi.
purposeless, *a.* Sans but; inutile.

purposely, *adv.* **1.** A dessein. **2.** Exprès. *I came p. to see him,* je suis venu exprès pour le voir.
purr[1], *s.* Ronron *m* (de chat).
purr[2], *v.i.* Ronronner.
purse[1], *s.* (*a*) Bourse *f*, porte-monnaie *m inv.* Chain purse, aumônière *f*. *F:* Well-lined purse, bourse bien garnie. (*b*) The public purse, le Trésor. **purse-bearer,** *s.* Trésorier *m*. **purse-proud,** *a.* Orgueilleux de sa fortune. **purse-strings,** *s.pl.* Cordons *m*, tirants *m*, de bourse.
purse[2], *v.tr.* To (purse up) one's lips, pincer les lèvres; faire la moue.
purser, *s.* Commissaire *m*.
pursuance, *s.* In pursuance of, conformément à; suivant.
pursuant, *adv.* Pursuant to *your instructions,* conformément à vos instructions.
pursue, *v.tr.* **1.** (*a*) Poursuivre. (*b*) Rechercher. **2.** Continuer, suivre (son chemin).
pursuer, *s.* Poursuivant, -ante.
pursuit, *s.* **1.** (*a*) Poursuite *f*. *To set out in* pursuit of s.o., se mettre à la poursuite de qn. (*b*) In p. of happiness, à la recherche, en quête, du bonheur. **2.** (*a*) Carrière *f*, profession *f*. *His literary pursuits,* ses travaux *m* littéraires. (*b*) Occupation *f*.
purvey, *v.tr.* Fournir (des provisions).
purveyor, *s.* Fournisseur, -euse.
pus, *s. Med:* Pus *m*; sanie *f*.
push[1], *s.* **1.** Poussée *f*, impulsion *f*. *To give sth. a p.,* pousser qch. *P:* To give s.o. the push, donner son congé à qn. **2.** (*a*) Effort *m*. (*b*) To have plenty of push, avoir de l'entregent. **3.** At a push, dans une extrémité; au besoin. When it comes to the push, quand on en vient au fait. **push-bike,** *s. F:* Bicyclette *f*, *F:* bécane *f*. **push-cart,** *s.* Charrette *f* d'enfant.
push[2]. **I.** *v.tr.* Pousser. **1.** To push the button, appuyer sur le bouton. *To p. one's finger into s.o.'s eye,* fourrer le doigt dans l'œil de qn. **2.** (*a*) Don't push (me)! ne (me) bousculez pas! (*b*) To push oneself (forward), se mettre en avant. **3.** (*a*) Poursuivre (son avantage). (*b*) Pousser la vente de. **4.** I am pushed for time, le temps me manque. **II. push,** *v.i.* **1.** To push (one's way) through the crowd, se frayer un chemin à travers la foule. **2.** Pousser; exercer une pression. **push aside,** *v.tr.* Écarter (d'une poussée). **push back,** *v.tr.* Repousser; faire reculer. **push in.** **1.** *v.tr.* Enfoncer. **2.** *v.i.* Entrer à toute force. **push off,** *v.i. F:* Time to push off, il est temps de se mettre en route. **push on.** **1.** *v.tr.* Pousser en avant; faire avancer. **2.** *v.i.* (*a*) To push on to a place, pousser jusqu'à un endroit. (*b*) It's time to push on, il est temps de nous remettre en route. **push out,** *v.tr.* Pousser dehors; faire sortir. **pushing,** *a.* (*a*) Débrouillard, entreprenant. (*b*) A pushing man, un ambitieux. (*c*) Indiscret, -ète.
pusillanimity, *s.* Pusillanimité *f*.

pusillanimous, *a.* Pusillanime.
puss, *s.* **1.** Minet *m*, minette *f.* **Puss in Boots,** le Chat botté. **To play (at) puss in the corner,** jouer aux quatre coins. **2.** *F:* *You sly puss!* petite rusée!
pussy, *s.* Pussy(-cat) = PUSS 1.
put, *v.* I. *v.tr.* Mettre. **1.** (*a*) *To put milk in one's tea,* mettre du lait dans son thé. **To put s.o. in his place,** remettre qn à sa place. (*b*) **To put the matter right,** arranger l'affaire. **To put s.o. out of suspense,** tirer qn de doute. **To put the law into operation,** appliquer la loi. (*c*) **To put money into an undertaking,** verser des fonds dans une affaire. **2.** **To put a question to s.o.,** poser, faire, une question à qn. **I put it to you whether,** je vous demande un peu si. **Put it to him nicely,** présentez-lui la chose gentiment. **To put it bluntly,** pour parler franc. **If one may put it that way,** si l'on peut s'exprimer ainsi. **3.** *To put the population at* 10,000, estimer, évaluer, la population à 10,000. **4.** **To put a stop to sth.,** mettre fin à qch. **5.** (*a*) **To put s.o. to bed,** mettre qn au lit; coucher (un enfant). *F:* **To put s.o. through it,** faire passer un mauvais quart d'heure à qn. (*b*) *To put to flight,* mettre en déroute. **To put s.o. to sleep,** endormir qn. II. **put,** *v.i.* *Nau:* **To put (out) to sea,** prendre le large. **To put into port,** faire relâche. **put about,** *v.tr.* **1.** Faire circuler (une rumeur). **2.** Déranger. **3.** To put a ship about, virer de bord. **put away,** *v.tr.* **1.** (*a*) Serrer (qch. dans une armoire). *Put away your books,* rangez vos livres. (*b*) Mettre de côté. **2.** Écarter (une pensée). **put back.** **1.** *v.tr.* (*a*) Remettre à sa place. (*b*) Retarder (une horloge). **2.** *v.i.* *Nau:* Retourner. **put by,** *v.tr.* Mettre en réserve. **To put by for the future,** économiser pour l'avenir. **put down,** *v.tr.* **1.** Déposer, poser. **Put it down!** laissez cela! **2.** Supprimer. **3.** Fermer (un parapluie). **4.** (*a*) Noter (sur papier). **To put down one's name,** s'inscrire; se faire inscrire (*for,* pour). **Put it down to my account,** inscrivez-le, mettez-le, à mon compte. (*b*) **To put down a number,** poser un chiffre. (*c*) **I put him down for a Frenchman,** je jugeai qu'il était Français. (*d*) **To put down sth. to sth.,** attribuer qch. à qch. **put forward,** *v.tr.* **1.** (*a*) Émettre, avancer, proposer. (*b*) **To put oneself forward,** se mettre en avant. (*c*) *F:* **To put one's best foot forward,** se mettre en devoir de faire de son mieux. **2.** Avancer (la pendule). **put in.** **1.** *v.tr.* (*a*) *F:* **To put a word in,** placer un mot. **To put in a (good) word for s.o.,** dire un mot en faveur de qn. (*b*) **To put in an hour's work,** faire une heure de travail. **2.** *v.i.* (*a*) *To put in at a port,* faire escale dans un port. (*b*) **To put in for a post,** poser sa candidature à un poste. **put off.** **1.** *v.tr.* (*a*) Retirer, ôter. (*b*) Remettre, différer; ajourner. (*c*) **To put s.o. off with an excuse,** se débarrasser de qn avec une excuse.

(*d*) Déconcerter. **You put me off,** vous me faites tromper. **2.** *v.i.* *Nau:* Pousser au large; démarrer. **put on,** *v.tr.* **1.** (*a*) **To put the kettle on,** mettre chauffer de l'eau. **To put on a dish,** servir un plat. (*b*) **To put a play on,** monter une pièce de théâtre. **2.** (*a*) Mettre (ses vêtements); chausser (ses pantoufles). **Put on your hat,** couvrez-vous. **To put on one's shoes,** se chausser. (*b*) **To put on an innocent air,** prendre un air innocent. *F:* **To put it on,** poser. **3.** **To put on weight,** prendre du poids. **4.** Avancer (la pendule). **5.** **To put on the light,** mettre la lumière; allumer. **put out,** *v.tr.* **1.** Avancer (la main); étendre (le bras). **2.** (*a*) Mettre dehors. (*b*) *Nau:* **To put out a boat,** mettre un canot à l'eau. (*c*) **To put out one's tongue out,** tirer la langue. **3.** To put out (of joint), démettre, déboîter. **4.** (*a*) Éteindre. (*b*) **To put s.o.'s eyes out,** crever les yeux à qn. **5.** (*a*) Déconcerter. (*b*) Ennuyer, contrarier. (*c*) Incommoder, gêner. **To put oneself out for s.o.,** se déranger pour qn. **put through,** *v.tr.* **1.** Mener à bien. **2.** *Tp:* **To put s.o. through to s.o.,** mettre qn en communication avec qn. **put to,** *v.tr.* *He was hard put to it,* il a eu fort à faire (*to,* pour). **put together,** *v.tr.* **1.** Joindre; monter, assembler. **2.** Rapprocher (des faits). **put up,** *v.tr.* **1.** (*a*) Lever (une glace); ouvrir (un parapluie); dresser (une échelle); poser. **To put up one's hands,** mettre haut les mains. (*b*) Apposer, coller (une affiche). **2.** Augmenter. **3.** Offrir, faire (une prière); présenter (une pétition). **4.** **To put sth. up for sale,** mettre qch. en vente. **5.** **To put up a resistance,** se défendre. **6.** (*a*) Héberger. *v.i.* **To put up at a hotel,** loger à un hôtel. (*b*) Remiser (une voiture). **7.** *Abs.* **To put up with,** s'accommoder de; se résigner à; endurer. **8.** (*a*) **To put s.o. up to a thing,** mettre qn au courant de qch. (*b*) **To put s.o. up to sth.,** pousser qn à qch. **9.** Construire (une maison); ériger (un monument). **put-up,** *attrib.a.* *F:* **A put-up job,** un coup monté. **put upon,** *v.ind.tr.* *F:* **To put upon s.o.,** en imposer à qn.
putrefaction, *s.* Putréfaction *f.*
putrefy, *v.i.* Se putréfier, pourrir.
putrid, *a.* Putride; infect.
putt[1], *s.* *Golf:* Coup roulé.
putt[2], *v.tr.* *Golf:* Poter (la balle). **putting-green,** *s.* *Golf:* Pelouse *f* du trou.
puttee, *s.* Bande molletière.
putty, *s.* Mastic *m*, enduit *m.*
puzzle[1], *s.* **1.** Énigme *f.* **2.** (*a*) **Chinese puzzle,** casse-tête *m inv* chinois. (*b*) Devinette *f*, problème *m.*
puzzle[2]. **1.** *v.tr.* Embarrasser, intriguer. **2.** *v.i.* **To puzzle over sth.,** se creuser la tête pour comprendre qch. **puzzle out,** *v.tr.* Débrouiller, éclaircir. **puzzling,** *a.* Embarrassant, intriguant.

pygmy. 1. *s.* Pygmée *m.* **2.** *Attrib.* Pygméen.
pyjama, *s.* Pyjama suit, pyjamas, pyjama *m.*
pylon, *s.* Pylône *m.*
pyramid, *s.* Pyramide *f.*
pyre, *s.* Bûcher *m* (funéraire).

Pyrenean, *a.* Pyrénéen ; des Pyrénées.
Pyrenees (the). *Pr.n.* Les Pyrénées *f.*
pyrites, *s.* Pyrite *f.*
pyrotechnics, *s.pl.* Pyrotechnie *f.*
python, *s.* *Rept :* Python *m.*

Q

Q, q, *s.* (La lettre) Q, q *m.* *F :* On the strict
q.t., en secret.
quack¹, *s. & int.* Couin-couin (*m*).
quack², *v.i.* Crier ; faire couin-couin.
quack³, *s.* Quack (doctor), charlatan *m.*
quadrangle, *s.* **1.** *Geom :* Quadrilatère *m.*
2. Cour (carrée).
quadrangular, *a.* Quadrangulaire.
quadrant, *s.* *Astr :* Quart *m* de cercle ;
quadrant *m.*
quadratic, *a.* **Quadratic equation,** équation
du second degré.
quadrilateral. 1. *a.* Quadrilatéral, -aux ;
quadrilatère. **2.** *s.* Quadrilatère *m.*
quadrille, *s.* *Danc :* Quadrille *m.*
quadroon, *a. & s.* *Ethn :* Quarteron, -onne.
quadruped, *a. & s.* Quadrupède (*m*).
quaff, *v.tr.* (*a*) Boire à longs traits. (*b*) Vider
d'un trait ; *F :* lamper.
quagmire, *s.* Fondrière *f* ; marécage *m.*
quail¹, *s.* *Orn :* Caille *f.*
quail², *v.i.* Fléchir, faiblir (*before,* devant).
His heart quailed, son cœur défaillit.
quaint, *a.* Étrange, bizarre.
quaintness, *s.* Bizarrerie *f,* singularité *f.*
quake, *v.i.* Trembler (*with,* de). *F :* **To
quake in one's shoes,** trembler dans sa peau.
quaker, *s.* *Rel.H :* Quaker *m.*
qualification, *s.* **1.** Réserve *f,* restriction *f.*
2. *Qualifications for an appointment,* titres *m*
à un emploi. **To have the necessary qualifications,** avoir les qualités requises.
qualify. I. *v.tr.* **1. To qualify.** *Gram :*
Qualifier. **2. To qualify oneself for a job,**
acquérir les titres nécessaires pour remplir
un emploi. **3.** Apporter des réserves à ;
modifier. **II. qualify,** *v.i.* Acquérir les
connaissances requises, se qualifier (*for,*
pour). **To qualify as (a) doctor,** être reçu
médecin. **qualified,** *a.* **1.** (*a*) **To be
qualified to do sth.,** avoir les capacités pour
faire qch. (*b*) Autorisé. *To be q. to vote,*
avoir qualité d'électeur. **2.** Restreint, modéré.
qualitative, *a.* Qualitatif.
quality, *s.* Qualité *f.* **1.** *Of the best q.,* de
premier choix. **2.** Qualité. **He has many
good qualities,** il a beaucoup de qualités.
3. People of quality, gens de qualité. **The
quality,** la noblesse.
qualm, *s.* Scrupule *m,* remords *m.* **To have**

no **qualms about doing sth.,** ne pas se faire
le moindre scrupule de faire qch.
quandary, *s.* **To be in a quandary,** ne trop
savoir que faire.
quantity, *s.* **1.** Quantité *f.* **2.** *Mth :* Quantité. **Unknown quantity,** inconnue *f.*
quantum, *s.* Quantum *m.*
quarantine¹, *s.* Quarantaine *f.* **To be in
quarantine,** faire (la) quarantaine.
quarantine², *v.tr.* Mettre en quarantaine.
quarrel¹, *s.* (*a*) Querelle *f,* dispute *f.* **To
pick a quarrel with s.o.,** faire (une) querelle
à qn. (*b*) **I have no quarrel with him,** je
n'ai rien à lui reprocher. (*c*) **To take up s.o's
quarrel,** prendre fait et cause pour qn.
quarrel², *v.i.* **1.** Se quereller, se disputer ;
se brouiller. **2. To quarrel with s.o. for
doing sth.,** reprocher à qn de faire qch.
To quarrel with sth., trouver à redire à qch.
quarrelling, *s.* Querelle(s) *f(pl),* dispute(s)
f(pl).
quarrelsome, *a.* Querelleur, -euse.
quarry¹, *s.* *Ven :* Proie *f* ; gibier *m.*
quarry², *s.* Carrière *f.*
quarry³, *v.tr.* Extraire, tirer de la carrière.
quarryman, *s.* (Ouvrier *m*) carrier *m.*
quart, *s.* *Meas :* Deux pintes *f.*
quarter¹, *s.* **1.** (*a*) Quart *m.* **Bottle one
quarter full,** bouteille au quart pleine.
(*b*) *Cu :* Quartier *m.* **2.** (*a*) Trimestre *m* ;
terme *m* (de loyer). (*b*) **Moon at the first
quarter,** lune au premier quartier. (*c*) **A
quarter to six,** six heures moins le quart.
3. (*a*) **What quarter is the wind in?** de quel
côté souffle le vent? (*b*) **The four quarters
of the globe,** les quatre parties du globe.
From all quarters, de tous côtés. **In high
quarters,** en haut lieu. **4.** Quartier (d'une
ville). **5.** *pl.* (*a*) *To shift one's quarters,*
changer de résidence *f.* (*b*) *Mil :* Quartier,
logement *m.* **6.** *pl. Navy :* Postes de combat.
All hands to quarters! tout le monde à son
poste ! **7. To give quarter,** faire quartier.
quarter-day, *s.* Le jour du terme ; *F :*
le terme. **quarter-deck,** *s.* *Nau :* Gaillard
m (d')arrière. *Navy :* Plage *f* arrière.
quarter², *v.tr.* **1.** Diviser en quatre. **2.** *Mil :*
Cantonner, caserner.
quarterly. 1. *a.* Trimestriel. **2.** *s.* Publication trimestrielle. **3.** *adv.* Trimestriellement ;
par trimestre.

quartermaster, *s.* **I.** *Nau:* Maître *m* de timonerie. **2.** *Mil:* Quartermaster sergeant, (*cavalry*) = maréchal *m* des logis chef; (*infantry*) = sergent *m* chef

quartern, *s.* **I.** *Meas:* Quart *m* (de pinte). **2.** **Quartern loaf,** pain *m* de quatre livres.

quartet(te), *s.* *Mus:* Quatuor *m.*

quartz, *s.* *Miner:* Quartz *m.*

quash, *v.tr.* **I.** Casser, annuler. **2.** Étouffer.

quasi, *pref.* Quasi, presque.

quatrain, *s.* *Pros:* Quatrain *m.*

quaver¹, *s.* **I.** *Mus:* Croche *f.* **2.** (*a*) *Mus:* Trille *m*, tremolo *m.* (*b*) Tremblement *m*, chevrotement *m* (de la voix).

quaver², *v.i.* Chevroter, trembloter. **quavering,** *a.* *Q. voice,* voix tremblotante, chevrotante. **-ly,** *adv.* D'une voix mal assurée.

quay, *s.* Quai *m.*

queasy, *a.* To feel queasy, *F:* avoir le cœur fade.

queen, *s.* **I.** Reine *f.* **Queen Anne,** la reine Anne. **2.** (*a*) *Cards:* Dame *f.* (*b*) *Chess:* Dame, reine. **3.** *Ent:* Reine. **queen-bee,** *s.* Abeille *f* mère; reine *f.*

queenly, *a.* De reine; digne d'une reine.

queer¹, *a.* **I.** (*a*) Bizarre, étrange, singulier. *F:* To be in Queer Street, être dans une situation (financière) embarrassée. (*b*) Suspect. **2.** *F:* I feel very queer, je me sens tout chose. **-ly,** *adv.* Étrangement, bizarrement.

queer², *v.tr.* Déranger, détraquer. To queer s.o.'s pitch, contrecarrer qn.

queerness, *s.* Étrangeté *f*, bizarrerie *f.*

quell, *v.tr.* Calmer, apaiser; dompter, étouffer.

quench, *v.tr.* **I.** Éteindre. **2.** To quench one's thirst, apaiser sa soif; se désaltérer.

querulous, *a.* Plaintif et maussade.

query¹, *s.* Question *f*, interrogation *f.*

query², *v.tr.* Mettre en question, en doute.

quest, *s.* Recherche *f.* To go in quest of s.o., se mettre à la recherche de qn.

question¹, *s.* Question *f.* **I.** Mise *f* en doute. Without question, sans aucun doute. *To obey without q.,* obéir aveuglément. To call sth. in question, mettre qch. en question. **2.** (*a*) The matter in question, l'affaire en question. *There is no q. of his returning so soon,* il n'est pas question qu'il revienne si promptement. (*b*) That is not the question, il ne s'agit pas de cela. It is out of the question, il ne faut pas y songer. **3.** To ask s.o. a question, faire, adresser, une question à qn. **question-mark,** *s.* Point *m* d'interrogation.

question², *v.tr.* **I.** Questionner, interroger. **2.** Mettre en question, en doute. *I q. whether he will come,* je doute qu'il vienne. **questioning¹,** *a.* Interrogateur, -trice. **questioning²,** *s.* Questions *fpl*, interrogation *f.*

questionable, *a.* **I.** Contestable, discutable. **2.** Équivoque. *In q. taste,* d'un goût douteux.

questioner, *s.* Interrogateur, -trice.

queue¹, *s.* Queue *f.* To stand in a queue, faire (la) queue.

queue², *v.i.* To queue (up), faire queue.

quibble¹, *s.* Chicane *f* de mots; faux-fuyant *m*, *pl.* faux-fuyants.

quibble², *v.i.* Chicaner sur les mots. **quibbling,** *s.* Arguties *fpl*; chicane *f* de mots.

quibbler, *s.* Chicaneur, -euse.

quick. I. *a.* (*a*) Rapide. As quick as lightning, comme un éclair; en un clin d'œil. Be quick! faites vite! dépêchez-vous! (*b*) Quick wit, esprit prompt à la repartie. *Q. ear,* oreille fine. *She has a q. temper,* elle s'emporte facilement. **Quick to anger,** prompt, vif, à se fâcher. **Quick of foot,** agile. (*c*) *Mus:* Éveillé. 'Quicker,' "animez." (*d*) Quick hedge, haie vive. *s.* The quick and the dead, les vivants et les morts. **2.** *s.* Vif *m*; chair vive. *F:* To cut s.o. to the quick, blesser qn au vif. **3.** *adv.* Vite, rapidement. **-ly,** *adv.* Vite, rapidement, vivement. **quick-firing,** *a.* A tir rapide. **quick-lunch,** *attrib.a.* Quick-lunch bar, casse-croûte *m inv.* **quick-tempered,** *a.* Emporté, irascible. **quick-witted,** *a.* Vif, éveillé.

quicken, *v.tr.* (*a*) Exciter, stimuler. (*b*) Hâter, accélérer.

quicklime, *s.* Chaux vive.

quickness, *s.* **I.** Vitesse *f*, rapidité *f.* **2.** Acuité *f* (de vision); finesse *f* (d'oreille); promptitude *f* (d'esprit).

quicksand, *s.* Sable(s) mouvant(s). To get caught in a quicksand, s'enliser.

quickset, *a.* Quickset hedge, haie vive.

quicksilver, *s.* Vif-argent *m*, mercure *m.*

quid, *s.* Chique *f* (de tabac).

quid pro quo, *s.* Équivalent *m.*

quiescence, *s.* Repos *m*, quiétude *f.*

quiescent, *a.* En repos; tranquille.

quiet¹, *s.* Tranquillité *f*, repos *m.*

quiet², *a.* **I.** Tranquille, calme, silencieux. To keep quiet, rester tranquille. Be quiet! taisez-vous! laissez-moi tranquille! **2.** *Q. disposition,* caractère doux, calme. **3.** (*a*) Simple; sobre. To live in a quiet way, avoir un train modeste. (*b*) *s.* *F:* To do sth. on the quiet, faire qch. à la dérobée. **4.** Calme, tranquille, paisible. **-ly,** *adv.* (*a*) Tranquillement, doucement. (*b*) Silencieusement, sans bruit.

quiet³, *v.* **I.** *v.tr.* Apaiser, calmer. **2.** *v.i.* To quiet down, s'apaiser, se calmer.

quietness, *s.* **I.** Tranquillité *f*, repos *m*, calme *m.* **2.** Sobriété *f* (de tenue).

quietude, *s.* Quiétude *f.*

quietus, *s.* *F:* Coup *m* de grâce. To give s.o. his quietus, régler son compte à qn.

quill, *s.* **I.** (*a*) *Orn:* Tuyau *m* (de plume). (*b*) = QUILL-PEN. **2.** Piquant *m* (de porc-épic). **quill-pen,** *s.* Plume *f* d'oie.

quilt¹, *s.* Couverture piquée, ouatée.

quilt², *v.tr.* Piquer, ouater (un vêtement).

quince, *s.* **I.** Coing *m.* **2. Quince(-tree),** cognassier *m.*

quinine, *s.* *Ch:* Quinine *f.*

quinsy, *s.* *Med:* Esquinancie *f;* angine *f.*

quintessence, *s.* Quintessence *f.*

quintet(te), *s.* *Mus:* Quintette *m.*

quip, *s.* Sarcasme *m,* repartie *f.*

quire, *s.* Main *f* (de papier).

quirk, *s.* = QUIP.

quit[1], *a.* Quitte. **To be quit of s.o.,** être débarrassé de qn.

quit[2], *v.tr.* (*a*) Quitter. *Abs.* Vider les lieux. (*b*) **To quit one's job,** quitter son emploi.

quite, *adv.* **I.** Tout à fait; entièrement. *Q. new,* tout nouveau. *Q. recovered,* complètement rétabli. *It is q. five days ago,* il y a bien cinq jours de cela. **Quite as much,** tout autant. **Quite enough,** bien assez. **Quite right,** très bien. **Quite so!** *F:* quite! parfaitement! d'accord! *I do not q. know what he will do,* je ne sais pas trop ce qu'il fera. **2.** *His story is q. a romance,* son histoire est tout un roman. *It was q. a surprise,* ce fut une véritable surprise.

quits, *pred.a.* Quitte(s).

quiver[1], *s.* Carquois *m.*

quiver[2], *s.* Tremblement *m. With a q. in his voice,* d'une voix frémissante. *Q. of the eyelid,* battement *m* de paupière.

quiver[3], *v.i.* Trembler; frémir, tressaillir, frissonner; (*of voice*) trembloter. *Voice quivering with emotion,* voix vibrante d'émotion.

Quixote (Don). *Pr.n.* Don Quichotte *m.*

quixotic, *a.* (*a*) Exalté, visionnaire. (*b*) Par trop chevaleresque. **-ally,** *adv.* En Don Quichotte.

quiz, *v.tr.* **I.** Railler, persifler. **2.** Lorgner, reluquer.

quizzical, *a.* **I.** Risible, cocasse. **2.** Railleur, -euse; plaisant.

quoit, *s.* *Games:* Palet *m.*

quorum, *s.* Quorum *m;* nombre voulu.

quota, *s.* Quote-part *f, pl.* quotes-parts, quotité *f.*

quotation, *s.* **I.** Citation *f.* **2.** *St.Exch:* Cote *f,* cours *m,* prix *m.* **quotation-marks,** *s.pl.* Guillemets *m.*

quote, *v.tr.* **I.** (*a*) Citer. *Abs.* **To quote from an author,** tirer une citation d'un auteur. *To q. an instance of sth.,* fournir un exemple de qch. (*b*) *Com:* **In reply please quote this number,** prière de rappeler ce numéro. **2.** *Com:* Établir, faire (un prix).

quoth, *v.tr.* 'No,' quoth I, "non," dis-je.

quotient, *s.* *Mth:* Quotient *m.*

R

R, r, *s.* (La lettre) R, r *f.*

rabbi, *s.* *Jew.Rel:* Rabbin *m.*

rabbit, *s.* **I.** Lapin *m.* **Buck rabbit,** lapin mâle. **Doe rabbit,** lapine *f. Wild r.,* lapin de garenne. **2.** *Cu:* **Welsh rabbit,** fondue *f* au fromage sur canapé. **rabbit-hole,** *s.* Terrier *m* de lapin. **rabbit-hutch,** *s.* Clapier *m.* **rabbit-warren,** *s.* Garenne *f.*

rabble, *s.* **I.** Cohue *f;* foule *f* (en désordre). **2. The rabble,** la canaille.

rabid, *a.* **I.** (*a*) Furieux. (*b*) Outrancier. **2.** *Vet:* (Chien) enragé.

rabies, *s.* *Med:* Rage *f,* hydrophobie *f.*

race[1], *s.* **I.** Raz *m,* ras *m,* de courant. **2.** *Sp:* Course *f.* **To run a race,** disputer une course.

race-course, *s.* Champ *m* de courses.

race-horse, *s.* Cheval *m,* -aux, de course.

race[2]. **I.** *v.i.* (*a*) Lutter de vitesse (*with,* avec). (*b*) Aller à fond de train; filer à toute vitesse. **2.** *v.tr.* Lutter de vitesse avec. **racing,** *s.* Courses *fpl.* **Boat racing,** courses d'aviron. **Horse racing,** les courses (de chevaux); l'hippisme *m.*

race[3], *s.* Race *f.* **I. The human race,** la race humaine. **2.** (*a*) Descendance *f.* (*b*) Lignée *f.*

racer, *s.* Cheval *m,* -aux, de course.

racial, *a.* De (la) race.

rack[1], *s.* **To go to rack and ruin,** aller à la ruine.

rack[2], *s.* (*a*) *Husb:* Râtelier *m* (d'écurie). (*b*) *Av:* **Bomb rack,** lance-bombes *m inv. Rail:* **Luggage rack,** porte-bagages *m inv;* filet *m* (à bagages). **rack-railway,** *s.* Chemin *m* de fer à crémaillère.

rack[3], *s.* *Hist:* Chevalet *m* (de torture). *F:* **To be on the rack,** être à la torture.

rack[4], *v.tr.* Tourmenter, torturer. *Racked by remorse,* tenaillé par le remords.

racket[1], *s.* (*a*) Raquette *f.* (*b*) *pl. Games:* **Rackets,** la raquette.

racket[2], *s.* **I.** Tapage *m,* vacarme *m.* **To stand the racket,** subvenir aux dépenses. **2. To go on the racket,** faire la bombe. **3.** *P:* Affaire véreuse.

racketeer, *s.* Trafiquant *m.*

racoon, *s.* *Z:* Raton laveur.

racquet, *s.* = RACKET[1].

racy, *a.* Vif, piquant. **Racy style,** style plein de verve.

radar, *s.* Radar *m.*

radiance, *s.* Rayonnement *m,* splendeur *f.*

radiant, *a.* Radieux. *Face r. with smiles,* visage souriant et radieux. *R. eyes,* yeux rayonnants de joie. **-ly,** *adv.* D'un air radieux. *R. happy,* rayonnant de joie.

radiate. 1. *v.i.* Rayonner; irradier. *(a)* Émettre des rayons. *(b) (Of lines)* Partir d'un même centre. **2.** *v.tr.* Émettre, dégager.
radiation, *s.* Irradiation *f*; rayonnement *m*.
radiator, *s.* Radiateur *m*.
radical, *a.* Radical, -aux. *To make a r. alteration in sth.*, changer qch. radicalement. **-ally,** *adv.* Radicalement, foncièrement.
radio[1,2], *s. & v.tr.* = WIRELESS[1,2].
radio-active, *a. Ph:* Radio-actif.
radio-activity, *s. Ph:* Radio-activité *f*.
radiogram, *s. W.Tel:* Radiogramme *m*.
radiograph[1], *s.* Radiogramme *m*.
radiograph[2], *v.tr.* Radiographier.
radiographic, *a.* Radiographique.
radiography, *s. Med:* Radiographie *f*.
radiologist, *s. Med:* Radiologue *m*.
radiology, *s. Med:* Radiologie *f*.
radiotelephone, *s.* Radiotéléphone *m*.
radish, *s.* Radis *m*.
radium, *s.* Radium *m*.
radius, *s.* Rayon *m*.
raffia, *s. Bot:* Raphia *m*.
raffle[1], *s.* Tombola *f*.
raffle[2], *v.tr.* Mettre en tombola.
raft, *s.* Radeau *m*.
rag[1], *s.* **1.** Chiffon *m*; lambeau *m*. **2.** *pl.* Rags (and tatters), haillons *m*, guenilles *f*, loques *f*. **rag-and-bone,** *attrib.a.* Rag-and-bone man, chiffonnier *m*. **rag-tag,** *s. F:* The rag-tag (and bob-tail), la canaille. **rag-time,** *s.* Musique nègre syncopée.
rag[2], *s. Sch: F:* Brimade *f*; mauvais tour.
rag[3], *v.tr. F:* Brimer.
ragamuffin, *s.* **1.** *(a)* Gueux *m.* *(b)* Mauvais garnement. **2.** Gamin *m* des rues.
rage[1], *s.* **1.** Rage *f*, fureur *f*, emportement *m*. To be in a rage with s.o., être furieux contre qn. To fly into a rage, s'emporter. **2.** Manie *f*, toquade *f*. To be all the rage, faire fureur.
rage[2], *v.i.* **1.** To rage (and fume), être furieux; rager. **2.** *(Of wind)* Faire rage; *(of pestilence)* sévir. **raging**[1], *a.* Furieux; en fureur. To be in a raging temper, être furieux. R. sea, mer déchaînée. Raging fever, fièvre de cheval. R. thirst, soif ardente.
raging[2], *s.* Rage *f*, fureur *f*.
ragged, *a.* *(a)* En lambeaux, en loques. *(b) (Of pers.)* En haillons; déguenillé.
raggedness, *s.* Déguenillement *m*.
ragman, *s.* Marchand *m* de chiffons.
raid[1], *s.* *(a)* Razzia *f*. *(b)* Police raid, descente *f* de police. *(c) Mil:* Raid *m*. Air raid, raid aérien.
raid[2]. **1.** *v.t.* Faire une razzia. **2.** *v.tr.* Razzier (une tribu); *(of police)* faire une descente dans
raider, *s.* **1.** Maraudeur *m*; pillard *m*. **2.** *(a)* Avion *m* en raid. *(b)* Navire *m* de course.
rail[1], *s.* **1.** *(a)* Barre *f*, barreau *m*; bâton *m* (de chaise). *(b)* Barre d'appui; rampe *f* (d'escalier). **2.** *pl.* Grille *f*; palissade *f*.

3. *Rail:* *(a)* Rail *m*. Live rail, rail de contact. To leave the rails, dérailler. *(b)* To travel by rail, voyager en chemin de fer. **rail-car,** *s.* Micheline *f*.
rail[2], *v.tr.* To rail sth. round, entourer (une pelouse) d'une grille. **railed,** *a.* Railed(-in, -off) space, espace entouré d'une grille.
railing(s), *s.(pl.)* **1.** Grille *f*. **2.** Balustrade *f* (de balcon); rampe *f* (d'escalier).
rail[3], *v.i.* To rail at s.o., crier contre qn.
raillery, *s.* Raillerie *f*.
railway, *s.* Railway (line), (ligne *f* de) chemin *m* de fer; voie ferrée. Light railway, chemin de fer à voie étroite. Railway station, station *f* de chemin de fer; gare *f*. Railway rug, couverture *f* de voyage. **railway-cutting,** *s.* (Voie *f* en) déblai *m*; tranchée *f*. **railway-embankment,** *s.* Remblai *m*.
railwayman, *s.* Employé *m* des chemins de fer.
raiment, *s.* Habillement *m*; vêtement(s) *m(pl)*.
rain[1], *s.* Pluie *f*. It looks like rain, le temps est à la pluie. **rain-cloud,** *s.* Nimbus *m*. **rain-coat,** *s.* Imperméable *m*.
rain[2], *v.tr. & i.* **1.** Pleuvoir. *It is raining fast,* il pleut à verse. *F:* It is raining cats and dogs, il pleut des hallebardes. **2.** *F:* Blows rained upon him, les coups pleuvaient sur lui.
rainbow, *s.* Arc-en-ciel *m*, *pl.* arcs-en-ciel.
raindrop, *s.* Goutte *f* de pluie.
rainfall, *s.* **1.** Chute *f* de pluie. **2.** Averse *f*.
rainproof, *a.* Imperméable (à la pluie).
rainy, *a.* Pluvieux. To put something by for a rainy day, garder une poire pour la soif.
raise, *v.tr.* **1.** *(a)* Dresser, mettre debout (une échelle); relever (qch. qui est tombé). *(b)* To raise the people, soulever le peuple *(against,* contre). **2.** Ériger (une statue). **3.** Élever (une famille); cultiver (des légumes). **4.** *(a)* Produire. To raise a bump, faire une bosse. To raise a smile, provoquer un sourire. *(b)* To raise a hope, faire naître une espérance. *(b)* To raise a cry, pousser un cri. No one raised his voice, personne ne souffla mot. *(c)* To raise an objection, soulever une objection. **5.** *(a)* Lever (le bras); soulever (un poids). *(b)* Élever. To raise s.o. to power, élever qn au pouvoir. *(c)* To raise s.o.'s hopes, exalter l'espoir de qn. **6.** *(a)* Hausser, relever (un store). *(b)* To raise one's voice, élever, hausser, la voix. *(c)* To raise s.o.'s salary, augmenter (les appointements de) qn. **7.** *(a)* To raise an army, lever, mettre sur pied, une armée. *(b)* To raise money, se procurer de l'argent. *(c)* To raise a loan, émettre un emprunt. **8.** To raise a spirit, évoquer un esprit.
raisin, *s.* Raisin sec.
rajah, *s.* Rajah *m*.
rake[1], *s. Tls:* Râteau *m*.
rake[2], *v.tr.* **1.** Ratisser (les feuilles). **2.** *(a)* Râteler (le sol). *(b)* Gratter, racler (une

surface). **3.** **To rake a trench,** enfiler une
tranchée. **rake out,** *v.tr.* To rake out the
fire, retirer les cendres du feu. **rake up,**
v.tr. To rake up the past, revenir sur le passé.
raking, *a.* (Feu) d'enfilade.
rake³, *s.* Viveur *m*, roué *m*.
rakish, *a.* **1.** Libertin, dissolu. **2.** *R. appear-*
ance, air bravache.
rally¹, *s.* (*a*) Ralliement *m*. (*b*) **Boy scouts'**
rally, réunion *f* de boy-scouts.
rally², **1.** *v.tr.* Rallier (*round,* autour de).
2. *v.i.* (*a*) (*Of troops*) Se reformer. (*b*) Se
rallier (*to a party,* à un parti). (*c*) Reprendre
des forces. **To rally from an illness,** se
remettre d'une maladie.
rally³, *v.tr.* Railler (*s.o. on sth.,* qn de qch.).
Ralph. *Pr.n.* Raoul *m*, Rodolphe *m*.
ram¹, *s.* **1.** *Z:* Bélier *m*. **2.** (Battering-)ram,
bélier. **3.** *N.Arch:* Éperon *m*.
ram², *v.tr.* **1.** (*a*) Battre, tasser (le sol).
(*b*) *Min:* **To ram the charge home,** bourrer
la charge. *Nau:* Éperonner. **ram-rod,**
s. Baguette *f*.
ramble¹, *s.* Promenade *f*.
ramble², *v.i.* **1.** Errer à l'aventure. **2.** Parler
sans suite; (*in delirium*) battre la campagne.
rambling¹, *a.* **1.** Errant, vagabond.
2. (Discours) décousu. **rambling²,** *s.*
1. Promenades *fpl* à l'aventure. **2.** Divagations *fpl.*
ramification, *s.* Ramification *f*.
ramify, *v.i.* Se ramifier.
ramp¹, *s.* Rampe *f*; pente *f*, talus *m*.
ramp², *s.* *F:* Supercherie *f*.
rampage, *s.* *F:* To be on the rampage, ne
pas décolérer.
rampant, *a.* **1.** Violent, effréné. *Vice is r.,*
le vice s'étale. **2.** (*Of plant*) Exubérant.
rampart, *s.* *Fort:* Rempart *m*.
ramshackle, *a.* Délabré.
ranch, *s.* Ranch *m*.
rancher, *s.* Propriétaire *m* d'un ranch.
rancid, *a.* Rance.
rancidity, *s.* Rancidité *f*.
rancorous, *a.* Rancunier.
rancour, *s.* Rancune *f*, rancœur *f*.
random. **1.** *s.* At random, au hasard. *To*
hit out at r., lancer des coups à l'aveuglette.
2. *à.* *R. shot,* coup tiré au hasard.
ranee, *s.* Rani *f*.
range¹, *s.* **1.** (*a*) Rangée *f* (de bâtiments).
(*b*) Chaîne *f* (de montagnes). **2.** Direction *f*,
alignement *m*. **3.** Champ *m* libre. **4.** (*a*)
Étendue *f*, portée *f*. **Range of action,** champ
d'activité. (*b*) **Range of colours,** gamme *f* de
couleurs. **5.** *Ball:* (*a*) La distance. (*b*) Portée.
Within range, à portée de tir. **6.** *Dom.Ec:*
Fourneau *m* de cuisine. **range-finder,** *s.*
Télémètre *m*. **range-finding,** *s.* Télémétrie *f*.
range², **I.** *v.tr.* **1.** Ranger; classer. **2.** Parcourir (l'horizon). **II.** **range,** *v.i.* **1.** Courir,
errer. *Researches ranging over a wide field,*
recherches qui s'étendent sur un vaste terrain.
2. *Temperatures ranging from ten to thirty*

degrees, températures comprises entre dix et
trente degrés.
rank¹, *s.* **1.** *Mil:* (*a*) Rang *m*. **To close the**
ranks, serrer les rangs. (*b*) *pl.* **To rise from**
the ranks, sortir du rang. (*c*) **The rank and**
file, les hommes de troupe. **2.** (*a*) Rang
(social); classe *f*. (*b*) *Mil:* Grade *m*.
All ranks, officiers et troupe. **3.** (Taxi-)rank,
station *f* (de taxis).
rank², **1.** *v.tr.* Ranger, compter. **2.** *v.i.* Se
ranger, être classé (*among,* parmi). **To rank**
above s.o., occuper un rang supérieur à qn.
rank³, *a.* **1.** (Trop) luxuriant; exubérant.
2. (*a*) Rance; fétide. (*b*) Grossier, répugnant.
3. **Rank poison,** poison violent. *R. duffer,*
parfait imbécile. *R. injustice,* injustice criante.
rankle, *v.i.* To rankle in s.o.'s mind, rester
sur le cœur de qn. **rankling,** *a.* Envenimé.
rankness, *s.* **1.** Luxuriance *f*, exubérance *f*.
2. Goût fort et désagréable.
ransack, *v.tr.* **1.** Fouiller. **2.** Saccager,
piller.
ransom¹, *s.* **1.** Rachat *m*. **To hold s.o. to**
ransom, mettre qn à rançon. **2.** Rançon *f*.
ransom², *v.tr.* **1.** Payer la rançon de.
2. Mettre à rançon.
rant¹, *s.* Rodomontades *fpl.*
rant², *v.i.* Déclamer avec extravagance.
ranting, *a.* Déclamatoire.
ranter, *s.* Déclamateur, -trice.
rap¹, *s.* Petit coup sec et dur. *F:* **To give**
s.o. a rap on the knuckles, remettre qn à sa
place.
rap², *v.* **1.** *v.tr.* Frapper; donner un coup
sec à. **To rap s.o. on the knuckles,** donner
sur les doigts à qn. **2.** *v.i.* *To rap at the door,*
frapper un coup à la porte.
rap³, *s.* *F:* **I don't care a rap,** je m'en moque
comme de quatre sous.
rapacious, *a.* Rapace. **-ly,** *adv.* Avec
rapacité.
rapacity, *s.* Rapacité *f*.
rapid, *a. & s.* Rapide (*m*). **-ly,** *adv.* Rapidement; à grands pas.
rapidity, *s.* Rapidité *f*.
rapier, *s.* Rapière *f*.
rapine, *s.* Rapine *f*.
rapscallion, *s.* Homme *m* de rien; vaurien
m; propre *m* à rien.
rapt. **1.** *p.p.* (*a*) Ravi, extasié (*by,* par).
(*b*) Absorbé (*in,* dans). **2.** *a.* Profond.
rapture, *s.* Ravissement *m*, extase *m*. **To**
be in raptures, être ravi (*with, over,* de).
To go into raptures, s'extasier (*over,* sur).
rapturous, *a.* De ravissement, d'extase.
R. applause, applaudissements frénétiques.
-ly, *adv.* Avec transport, avec frénésie.
rare, *a.* **1.** Rare, peu dense. **2.** *R. occurrence,*
événement rare. **3.** *F:* *You gave me a r.*
fright, tu m'as fait une fière peur. **-ly,** *adv.*
Rarement.
rarebit, *s.* = RABBIT 2.
rarefied, *a.* (Air) raréfié
rareness, *s.* Rareté *f*.

rarity, *s.* **1.** = RARENESS. **2.** Objet *m* rare.
rascal, *s.* Coquin, -ine, fripon, -onne.
rascality, *s.* Coquinerie *f*, gredinerie *f*.
rascally, *a.* De coquin. *These r. servants!*
ces canailles de domestiques! **Rascally trick,**
méchant tour.
rash¹, *s.* *Med:* Éruption *f*.
rash², *a.* Téméraire. *R. words,* paroles
inconsidérées. **Rash act,** coup *m* de tête.
-ly, *adv.* Témérairement.
rasher, *s.* *Cu:* Tranche *f* (de lard).
rashness, *s.* Témérité *f*; étourderie *f*.
rasp¹, *s.* **1.** *Tls:* Râpe *f*. **2.** Grincement *m*.
rasp². **1.** *v.tr.* Râper. **2.** *v.i.* Grincer, crisser.
rasping, *a.* **Rasping voice,** voix âpre.
raspberry, *s.* Framboise *f*. **Raspberry bush,**
framboisier *m*.
rat¹, *s.* **1.** *Z:* Rat *m*. *F:* **To smell a rat,**
soupçonner anguille sous roche. **2.** *Ind:*
Jaune *m*; renard *m*. **rat-catcher,** *s.* Preneur
m de rats. **rat-poison,** *s.* Mort *f* aux rats.
rat-tail, *s.* **Rat-tail file,** queue-de-rat *f*.
rat-trap, *s.* Ratière *f*.
rat², *v.i.* *F:* (*a*) Tourner casaque. (*b*) *Ind:*
Faire le renard.
ratchet, *s.* **1.** Encliquetage *m* à dents.
2. Cliquet *m*, rochet *m*.
rate¹, *s.* **1.** Nombre proportionnel, quantité
proportionnelle. **Rate per cent,** pourcentage
m. **Birth rate,** (taux *m* de la) natalité. **2.** (*a*)
Taux, raison *f*. **Rate of speed,** degré *m* de
vitesse. (*b*) Allure *f*, vitesse *f*, train *m*.
(*c*) Taux, cours *m*. *R. of interest,* taux
d'intérêt. *To pay at the r. of,* payer sur le
pied de. **Rate of living,** train *m* de vie.
At that rate, sur ce pied-là; à ce compte-là.
At any rate, dans tous les cas, en tout cas.
3. *Adm:* Impôt local. **Rates and taxes,**
impôts et contributions. **4.** Estimation *f*,
évaluation *f*. *To value sth. at a low r.,* faire
peu de cas de qch. **rate-collector,** *s.*
Percepteur *m* des impôts locaux. **rate-**
payer, *s.* Contribuable *mf*.
rate². **1.** *v.tr.* (*a*) Estimer, évaluer. *To r.*
sth. high, faire grand cas de qch. (*b*) Considérer, regarder (*as,* comme). (*c*) *Nau:*
classer (un navire). **2.** *v.i.* Être classé (*as,*
comme). **rating¹,** *s.* **1.** (*a*) Estimation *f*,
évaluation *f*. (*b*) Classement *m*, classification
f. **2.** *pl.* **The ratings,** les matelots et gradés.
rate³, *v.tr.* Tancer, semoncer (*for doing sth.,*
d'avoir fait qch.). **rating²,** *s.* Semonce *f*;
verte réprimande.
rather, *adv.* **1.** Plutôt. **2.** Un peu; assez.
R. pretty, assez joli. *R. plain,* plutôt laid.
Rather a lot, *F:* un peu beaucoup. *I rather*
think you know him, je crois bien que vous
le connaissez. **3.** Plutôt (*than,* que). *I would*
r. be loved than feared, j'aime mieux être
aimé qu'être craint. *I would rather not,*
veuillez m'excuser. **4.** *F:* *Do you know him?*
—*Rather!* le connaissez-vous?—Pour sûr!
ratification, *s.* Ratification *f*.
ratify, *v.tr.* Ratifier.

ratio, *s.* Raison *f*, rapport *m*, proportion *f*.
In the ratio of, dans le rapport de.
ration¹, *s.* Ration *f*. *F:* **Iron ration,** vivres
m de réserve. **Ration book,** carnet *m* de
rations.
ration², *v.tr.* Rationner. **rationing,** *s.*
Rationnement *m*.
rational, *a.* (*a*) Raisonnable; doué de
raison. (*b*) Raisonné; conforme à la raison.
-ally, *adv.* Raisonnablement.
rat(t)an, *s.* *Bot:* Rotin *m*; jonc *m* d'Inde.
rat(-tat)-tat. Toc, toc.
rattle¹, *s.* **1.** (*a*) Hochet *m* (d'enfant).
(*b*) Crécelle *f* (d'alarme). (*c*) *pl.* *Rept:*
Rattles, sonnettes *f* (d'un crotale). **2.** (*a*)
Bruit *m*, fracas *m*; trictrac *m* (de dés).
(*b*) *Med:* Râle *m*. (*c*) Bavardage *m*.
rattle². **1.** *v.i.* (*a*) (*Of arms*) Cliqueter;
(*of window*) branler. *To make the windows r.,*
faire trembler les vitres. (*b*) *F:* Rattling along,
rouler à toute vitesse. (*c*) *Med:* Râler.
2. *v.tr.* (*a*) Agiter avec bruit; faire cliqueter
(des clefs). (*b*) Consterner, bouleverser.
He never gets rattled, il ne se laisse pas
démonter. **rattle off,** *v.tr.* Réciter rapidement; expédier (un travail). **rattle on,** *v.i.*
Continuer à bavarder. **rattling¹,** *a.*
1. Bruyant; crépitant. **2.** *F:* At a rattling
pace, au grand trot. **3.** *F:* Rattling (good),
excellent, épatant. **rattling²,** *s.* = RATTLE¹ 2.
rattlesnake, *s.* Serpent *m* à sonnettes;
crotale *m*.
rattletrap, *s.* Vieille guimbarde.
ratty, *a.* *F:* Fâché; en rogne.
raucous, *a.* Rauque. **-ly,** *adv.* D'une voix
rauque, éraillée.
ravage¹, *s.* Ravage *m*.
ravage², *v.tr.* Ravager, dévaster. **ravaging¹,**
a. Ravageur. **ravaging²,** *s.* Ravagement *m*.
ravager, *s.* Ravageur *m*, dévastateur *m*.
rave, *v.i.* (*a*) Être en délire; *F:* battre la
campagne. (*b*) **To rave at s.o.,** pester contre
qn. **Raving lunatic,** fou furieux. (*c*) (*Of*
wind) Être en furie. (*d*) *F:* **To rave about**
sth., s'extasier sur qch. **raving,** *s.* **1.** Délire
m, divagation *f*. **2.** *pl.* **Ravings,** paroles
incohérentes.
ravel, *v.* **1.** *v.tr.* Embrouiller, emmêler.
2. *v.i.* S'embrouiller.
raven, *s.* *Orn:* (Grand) corbeau. **Raven**
looks, boucles d'un noir de jais.
ravening, *a.* Vorace, rapace.
ravenous, *a.* **1.** Vorace. **2.** (*a*) *R. appetite,*
appétit vorace. (*b*) *F:* **To be ravenous,** avoir
une faim dévorante. **-ly,** *adv.* Voracement.
To eat r., manger gloutonnement.
ravine, *s.* Ravin *m*.
ravish, *v.tr.* **1.** Ravir; enlever de force.
2. Ravir; enchanter. **ravishing,** *a.*
Ravissant. **-ly,** *adv.* D'une manière ravis-
sante.
ravishment, *s.* Ravissement *m*.
raw. **I.** *a.* **1.** Cru. **Raw meat,** viande crue,
saignante. **2.** **Raw material,** matière(s) pre-
mière(s). **Raw hide,** cuir vert. **Raw silk,**

soie grège. **3.** Sans expérience. **A raw hand,** un novice. **Raw troops,** troupes non aguerries. **4.** A vif. **Raw wound,** plaie vive. **5.** Raw weather, temps gris et froid. II. **raw,** *s.* **To touch s.o. on the raw,** piquer qn au vif. **raw-boned,** *a.* Maigre, décharné; (cheval) efflanqué.

rawness, *s.* **I.** Crudité *f.* **2.** Inexpérience *f.* **3.** Froid *m* humide.

ray[1], *s.* *Ph:* Rayon *m.* *Ray of light,* rayon lumineux. *F:* **A ray of hope,** une lueur d'espoir.

ray[2], *Lt.* *Ich:* Raie *f.*

rayon, *s.* *Tex:* Rayonne *f.*

raze, *v.tr.* Raser. **To raze a building to the ground,** raser un édifice.

razor, *s.* Rasoir *m.* **Safety razor,** rasoir de sûreté.

re[1], *s.* *Mus:* Ré *m.*

re[2], *Lt.* *s.* *as prep. phr.* *F:* **Re your letter,** relativement à votre lettre.

reaccustom, *v.tr.* Rhabituer *(to,* à).

reach[1], *s.* **I.** Extension *f.* *Box:* Allonge *f.* **2.** *(a)* Portée *f,* atteinte *f.* **Within s.o.'s reach,** à la portée de qn. **Out of reach,** hors de portée. *Posts within the r. of all,* emplois accessibles à tous. *(b)* **Hotel within easy reach of the station,** hôtel à proximité de la gare. **3.** Partie droite (d'un fleuve) entre deux coudes; bief *m* (d'un canal).

reach[2]. I. *v.tr.* **I.** **To reach out,** étendre; tendre. **2.** Atteindre. **3.** *(a)* Arriver à, parvenir à. **To reach perfection,** atteindre à la perfection. **Your letter reached me to-day,** votre lettre m'est parvenue aujourd'hui. *(b)* Arriver à (une conclusion). **To reach an agreement,** aboutir à un accord. **4. Reach me (over) my gloves,** passez-moi mes gants. II. **reach,** *v.tr. & i.* Arriver, s'élever, monter, descendre (jusqu'à . . .). **To reach the bottom,** atteindre le fond; descendre jusqu'au fond. III. **reach,** *v.i.* **I.** S'étendre. **As far as the eye could reach,** à perte de vue. **2. To reach out for sth.,** tendre la main pour prendre qch. **reach-me-down,** *s.* *F:* Costume *m* de confection; un décrochez-moi-ça.

react, *v.i.* Réagir.

reaction, *s.* Réaction *f.*

reactionary, *a. & s.* Réactionnaire *(mf).*

read, *v.tr.* **I.** *(a)* Lire. *To teach s.o. to r.,* enseigner la lecture à qn. *(b)* *Typ:* **To read proofs,** corriger des épreuves. *(c)* **To read up a subject,** étudier un sujet. **2. To read sth. aloud,** lire qch. à haute voix. **To read to s.o.,** faire la lecture à qn. **3.** *(a)* Lire (la musique). *(b)* **To read s.o.'s thoughts,** lire dans la pensée de qn. **To read between the lines,** lire entre les lignes. **4.** *The clause reads both ways,* l'article peut s'interpréter dans les deux sens. **read out,** *v.tr.* Lire (qch.) à haute voix. **read through,** *v.tr.* **I.** Parcourir. **2.** Lire en entier. **reading**[1], *a.* **The reading public,** le public qui lit. **reading**[2], *s.* **I.** Lecture(s) *f(pl).* *To be fond of r.,* aimer la lecture.

2. *(a)* Lecture (d'un instrument de précision). *(b)* **Barometer reading,** hauteur *f* barométrique. **3.** *(a)* Façon *f* de lire. *(b)* Leçon *f,* variante *f* (d'un texte). **reading-book,** *s.* Livre *m* de lecture. **reading-desk,** *s.* Pupitre *m.* **reading-glass,** *s.* Loupe *f.* **reading-room,** *s.* Salle *f* de lecture.

readable, *a.* Lisible.

reader, *s.* **I.** Lecteur, -trice. **2.** *Sch:* Livre *m* de lecture.

readiness, *s.* **I.** *(a)* Empressement *m,* alacrité *f.* *(b)* Bonne volonté. **2.** Facilité *f* (d'esprit). **3. To be in readiness,** être prêt.

readjust, *v.tr.* Rajuster.

readjustment, *s.* Rajustement *m.*

ready. I. *a.* **I.** *(a)* Prêt. **Ready! go!** préparez-vous! partez! **To get ready,** se préparer *(to,* à). *(b)* **Ready to hand,** sous la main. **Ready money,** argent comptant. **2.** *(a)* Prêt, disposé (à faire qch.). *(b)* **Ready to die with hunger,** sur le point de mourir de faim. **3.** Prompt, facile. **To be ready with an answer,** avoir la réplique prompte. **-ily,** *adv.* **I.** Volontiers avec empressement. **2.** (Imaginer qch.) facilement. II. **ready,** *adv.* **Ready dressed,** tout habillé. **ready-made,** *a.* Tout fait. **Ready-made clothes,** vêtements de confection. **ready-reckoner,** *s.* Barème *m.* **ready-witted,** *a.* A l'esprit prompt.

reagent, *s.* *Ch:* Réactif *m.*

real, *a.* **I.** *(a)* Vrai. *R. silk,* soie naturelle. *(b)* Véritable, réel. *A r. friend,* un vrai ami, un véritable ami. **It is the real thing,** c'est authentique. **2.** *Jur:* **Real property,** propriété immobilière. **-lly,** *adv.* Vraiment; réellement; en effet. *You r. must go there,* il faut absolument que vous y alliez. *Is it r. true?* est-ce bien vrai? **Not really!** pas possible!

realism, *s.* Réalisme *m.*

realist, *a. & s.* Réaliste *(mf).*

realistic, *a.* Réaliste. **-ally,** *adv.* Avec réalisme.

reality, *s.* La réalité; le réel. **In reality,** en réalité.

realization, *s.* **I.** *(a)* Réalisation *f.* *(b)* Conversion *f* en espèces. **2.** Conception nette.

realize, *v.tr.* **I.** *(a)* Réaliser. *(b)* Convertir en espèces. **2.** Concevoir nettement; se rendre compte de.

realm, *s.* Royaume *m.*

ream, *s.* *Paperm:* Rame *f.*

reanimate, *v.tr.* Ranimer, réanimer.

reap, *v.tr.* *(a)* Moissonner. *(b)* Recueillir. **To reap profit from sth.,** tirer profit de qch.

reaping, *s.* Moisson *f.*

reaper, *s.* **I.** Moissonneur, -euse. **2.** *(Machine)* Moissonneuse *f.*

reappear, *v.i.* Reparaître.

reappearance, *s.* Réapparition *f.*

rear[1]. I. *s.* **I.** *Mil:* Arrière-garde *f.* **2.** *(a)* Arrière *m,* derrière *m.* *(b)* Dernier rang, queue *f.* II. **rear,** *a.* D'arrière, de queue;

postérieur, -eure. **rear-admiral,** s. Contre-amiral m, pl. contre-amiraux. **rear-guard,** s. Mil: Arrière-garde f, pl. arrière-gardes. **rear²,** **1.** v.tr. Élever; cultiver. **2.** v.i. (Of horse) Se cabrer.
rearm, v.tr. Réarmer.
rearmament, s. Réarmement m.
rearmost, a. Dernier; de queue.
re-arrange, v.tr. Arranger de nouveau.
re-arrangement, s. Nouvel arrangement.
reason¹, s. **1.** Raison f, cause f (for, de). For reasons best known to myself, pour des raisons de moi seul connues. For no reason at all, sans motif. The reason why, le pourquoi. You have reason to be glad, vous avez sujet à vous réjouir. I have reason to believe, j'ai lieu de croire. With (good) reason, à bon droit. All the more reason for going, raison de plus pour y aller. **2.** Raison; faculté f de raisonner. **3.** Raison; bon sens. To listen to reason, entendre raison. It stands to reason, c'est évident; cela va sans dire. Everything in reason, il y a mesure à tout.
reason², **1.** v.i. To reason with s.o., raisonner qn, avec qn. **2.** v.tr. (a) To r. that, arguer que. (b) To reason s.o. out of doing sth., faire entendre raison à qn. **reasoned,** a. **1.** Raisonné; motivé. **2.** Raisonnable. **reasoning¹,** a. Doué de raison. **reasoning²,** s. Raisonnement m.
reasonable, a. **1.** Raisonnable. You must try to be r., il faut vous raisonner. **2.** R. prices, prix modérés, raisonnables. **-ably,** adv. Raisonnablement.
reasonableness, s. **1.** Caractère m raisonnable; raison f. **2.** Modération f.
reasoner, s. Raisonneur, -euse.
reassemble. **1.** v.tr. Rassembler. **2.** v.i. Se rassembler.
reassure, v.tr. Rassurer, tranquilliser (on, about, sur). To feel reassured, se rassurer.
reassuring, a. Rassurant.
reawaken. **1.** v.tr. Réveiller. **2.** v.i. Se réveiller.
rebate, s. Rabais m, escompte m.
rebel¹. **1.** a. Insurgé. **2.** s. Rebelle mf.
rebel², v.i. Se rebeller (against, contre).
rebellion, s. Rébellion f, révolte f.
rebellious, a. Rebelle. **-ly,** adv. En rebelle.
rebelliousness, s. Esprit m de rébellion.
rebound¹, s. Rebondissement m; retour m brusque; ricochet m (d'une balle).
rebound², v.i. Rebondir.
rebuff¹, s. Rebuffade f; échec m.
rebuff², v.tr. Repousser, rebuter.
rebuild, v.tr. Rebâtir, reconstruire.
rebuke¹, s. Réprimande f, blâme m.
rebuke², v.tr. Réprimander, blâmer (qn).
rebut, v.tr. Réfuter.
recalcitrance, s. Récalcitrance f.
recalcitrant, a. & s. Récalcitrant, -ante.
recall¹, s. **1.** Rappel m. **2.** Rétractation f, révocation f. Beyond recall, irrévocablement.

recall², v.tr. **1.** Rappeler. **2.** (a) Rappeler (qch. à qn). (b) I don't r. his name, je ne me souviens pas de son nom. **3.** Rétracter.
recalling, s. **1.** Rappel m. **2.** Révocation f.
recant. **1.** v.tr. Rétracter; abjurer. **2.** v.i. Se rétracter.
recantation, s. Rétractation f, abjuration f.
recapitulate, v.tr. Récapituler.
recapitulation, s. Récapitulation f.
recapture¹, s. Reprise f.
recapture², v.tr. Reprendre, recapturer.
recede, v.i. (a) S'éloigner, reculer. (b) (Of forehead) Fuir. **receding,** a. (a) Qui s'éloigne. Receding tide, marée descendante. (b) Receding forehead, front fuyant.
receipt¹, s. **1.** = RECIPE. **2.** (a) Com: Recette f. (b) Perception f (des impôts). (c) Réception f. On receipt of this letter, au reçu de cette lettre. To pay on receipt, payer à la réception. **3.** Reçu m, quittance f. To give a receipt for sth., donner acquit de qch.
receipt², v.tr. Com: Acquitter (une facture).
receive, v.tr. **1.** (a) Recevoir. On receiving your letter, au reçu de votre lettre. Received with thanks, pour acquit. (b) Jur: To receive stolen goods, recéler (des objets volés). **2.** Recevoir (des invités). To receive s.o. with open arms, accueillir qn à bras ouverts.
receiving, s. Réception f; recel m (d'objets volés). **receiving-station,** s. W.Tel: Poste récepteur.
receiver, s. **1.** (a) Personne f qui reçoit. (b) Adm: Receveur m. (c) Receleur, -euse (d'objets volés). **2.** Récepteur m (de téléphone). To lift the receiver, décrocher le récepteur.
recent, a. Récent. **-ly,** adv. Récemment. As recently as yesterday, pas plus tard que d'hier. Until quite recently, jusque dans ces derniers temps.
receptacle, s. **1.** Réceptacle m. **2.** Récipient m.
reception, s. **1.** (a) Réception f. (b) Reception desk, la réception. **2.** Accueil m. **3.** Réception (officielle). **4.** W.Tel: Réception.
receptive, a. Réceptif.
recess, s. **1.** (a) Vacances fpl. (b) Sch: (L'heure f de) la récréation. **2.** (a) Recoin m. (b) Enfoncement m (de muraille); embrasure f (de fenêtre); niche f.
recipe, s. Cu: Recette f.
recipient. **1.** a. Réceptif. **2.** s. Personne f qui reçoit; donataire mf.
reciprocal, a. Réciproque, mutuel. **-ally,** adv. Réciproquement, mutuellement.
reciprocate. **1.** v.tr. (a) Se rendre mutuellement. (b) Payer de retour. To r. s.o.'s good wishes, souhaiter la pareille à qn. **2.** v.i. Retourner le compliment.
reciprocity, s. Réciprocité f.
recital, s. **1.** Récit m, narration f. **2.** Récitation f (d'une poésie). **3.** Mus: Audition f.

recitation, *s.* Récitation *f.*
recite, *v.tr.* (*a*) Réciter, déclamer. (*b*) *Abs.*
Réciter une pièce.
reckless, *a.* Insouciant (*of*, de); téméraire.
Aut: **Reckless driving,** conduite imprudente.
-ly, *adv.* Témérairement; avec insouciance.
He spends r., il dépense sans compter.
recklessness, *s.* Insouciance *f* (*of*, de);
imprudence *f*, témérité *f.*
reckon. **I.** *v.tr.* (*a*) Compter, calculer.
(*b*) Estimer, juger. (*c*) *To r. s.o. as*, regarder
qn comme. **2.** *v.i.* (*a*) Compter, calculer.
(*b*) **To reckon (up)on sth.**, compter sur qch.
reckon up, *v.tr.* Compter, calculer.
reckon with, *v.i.* **1. To reckon with s.o.**,
demander des comptes à qn. **2. To have to
reckon with s.o.**, avoir à compter avec qn.
reckoning, *s.* **1.** Compte *m*, calcul *m.*
To be out in one's reckoning, s'être trompé
dans son calcul. **Day of reckoning**, jour
d'expiation. **2.** Note *f*; addition *f.*
reclaim[1], *s.* Past reclaim, qui ne se corrigera
jamais.
reclaim[2], *v.tr.* (*a*) Réformer, corriger. **To
reclaim s.o. from vice**, tirer qn du vice.
(*b*) **Reclaimed land**, terrain amendé.
reclamation, *s.* **1.** Réforme *f.* **2.** Mise *f*
en valeur (des marais). **3.** Réclamation *f.*
recline. **I.** *v.tr.* Reposer, appuyer. **2.** *v.i.*
Être couché; reposer, être appuyé (*on*, sur).
Reclining on a couch, étendu sur un canapé.
reclothe, *v.tr.* Rhabiller.
recluse. **I.** *a.* Retiré du monde; reclus.
2. *s.* Reclus, -use; solitaire *mf.*
reclusion, *s.* Réclusion *f.*
recognition, *s.* Reconnaissance *f.*
recognizable, *a.* Reconnaissable.
recognizance, *s.* **To enter into recog-
nizances,** donner caution *f.*
recognize, *v.tr.* Reconnaître. (*a*) *I do not
r. you*, je ne vous remets pas. (*b*) *The duke
recognized me*, le duc me fit un signe de
connaissance. **recognized,** *a.* Reconnu,
admis, reçu. *The r. term*, le terme consacré.
recoil[1], *s.* **1.** (*a*) Rebondissement *m*, détente
f (d'un ressort). (*b*) Recul *m* (d'une arme
à feu). **2.** Mouvement *m* de recul.
recoil[2], *v.i.* **1.** (*a*) (*Of spring*) Se détendre.
(*b*) (*Of fire-arm*) Reculer. **2.** (*Of pers.*)
Reculer (*from*, devant). **3.** Retomber (*on*, sur).
recollect, *v.tr.* **1.** Se rappeler; se souvenir
de. *I don't recollect you*, je ne vous remets
pas. **2. To recollect oneself**, se recueillir.
recollection, *s.* Souvenir *m*, mémoire *f.*
To the best of my recollection, autant que
je m'en souviens.
recommence, *v.tr. & i.* Recommencer.
recommend, *v.tr.* Recommander.
recommendation, *s.* Recommandation *f.*
recompense[1], *s.* **1.** Récompense *f* (*for*, de).
2. Dédommagement *m* (*for*, de).
recompense[2], *v.tr.* **1.** Récompenser (*s.o.
for sth.*, qn de qch.). **2.** Dédommager (*s.o.
for sth.*, qn de qch.)

reconcilable, *a.* Conciliable (*with*, avec).
reconcile, *v.tr.* **1.** Réconcilier. **To become
reconciled,** se réconcilier. **2. To reconcile
oneself to sth.**, se résigner à qch. **3.** Concilier,
faire accorder (des faits).
reconciliation, *s.* **1.** Réconciliation *f*,
rapprochement *m.* **2.** Conciliation *f.*
recondite, *a.* Abstrus, profond.
recondition, *v.tr.* Rénover; remettre à
neuf, en état.
reconnaissance, *s.* Reconnaissance *f.*
reconnoitre, *v.tr.* Reconnaître (le terrain).
Abs. Faire une reconnaissance. **reconnoitring,** *s.* Reconnaissance *f.*
reconquer, *v.tr.* Reconquérir.
reconsider, *v.tr.* **1.** Considérer de nouveau.
2. Revenir sur (une décision).
reconsideration, *s.* Examen *m* à nouveau.
reconstruct, *v.tr.* **1.** Reconstruire (un
édifice). **2.** *To r. a crime*, reconstituer un
crime.
reconstruction, *s.* **1.** Reconstruction *f.*
2. Reconstitution *f* (d'un crime).
record[1], *s.* **1.** *Jur:* (*a*) **To be on record**, être
enregistré. (*b*) Minute *f* (d'un acte). **2.** (*a*)
Note *f*, mention *f.* (*b*) Registre *m.* **Record
of attendances,** registre de présence. **3.** *pl.*
Archives *f*, annales *f.* **4.** Monument *m*,
document *m*, souvenir *m.* **5.** Carrière *f*,
dossier *m.* **Service record**, état *m* de service.
His past record, sa conduite passée. **Police
record,** casier *m* judiciaire. **6.** *Sp:* Record
m. **At record speed**, à une vitesse record.
7. Disque *m* (de gramophone).
record[2], *v.tr.* (*a*) Enregistrer. (*b*) Narrer,
rapporter. (*c*) (*Of instrument*) Enregistrer,
marquer. **recording**[1], *a.* Enregistreur,
-euse. **recording**[2], *s.* (*a*) Enregistrement *m.*
(*b*) Narration *f*, relation *f.*
recorder, *s.* **1.** Archiviste *m.* **2.** Appareil
enregistreur.
recount[1], *v.tr.* Raconter.
recount[2], *v.tr.* Recompter.
recoup, *v.tr.* Dédommager. **To recoup
oneself for one's losses**, se dédommager de
ses pertes.
recourse, *s.* **1.** Recours *m.* **2.** Expédient *m.*
recover[1], *v.tr.* **1.** Recouvrer, retrouver. **To
recover one's breath**, reprendre haleine.
2. Regagner; rentrer en possession de. **To
recover lost time**, rattraper le temps perdu.
3. To recover one's health, *v.i.* to recover,
guérir. **To recover from an illness**, se
remettre d'une maladie. **To recover from
one's astonishment**, revenir, se remettre, de
son étonnement. **4. To recover oneself**, *abs.*
to recover, se remettre, se ressaisir.
recover[2], **re-cover**, *v.tr.* Recouvrir.
recovery, *s.* **1.** Recouvrement *m.* **2.** (*a*)
Rétablissement *m*, guérison *f.* **To be past
recovery,** être dans un état désespéré. (*b*) Redressement *m* (économique).
recreant. **I.** *a.* (*a*) Lâche. (*b*) Infidèle.
2. *s.* (*a*) Lâche *m.* (*b*) Apostat *m.*

recreation, *s.* Récréation *f*, divertissement *m*. recreation-ground, *s.* Terrain *m* de jeux.

recriminate, *v.i.* Récriminer.

recrimination, *s.* Récrimination *f*.

recriminatory, *a.* Récriminatoire.

recross, *v.tr.* Retraverser; repasser.

recrudescence, *s.* Recrudescence *f*.

recruit[1], *s.* Recrue *f*. A raw recruit, *F:* un bleu.

recruit[2], *v.tr.* I. Recruter (une armée); racoler (des hommes pour l'armée). 2. To recruit one's health, *abs.* to recruit, se restaurer, se remettre. recruiting, *s. Mil:* Recrutement *m*. Recruiting-sergeant, sergent recruteur; racoleur *m*.

rectangle, *s.* Rectangle *m*.

rectangular, *a.* Rectangulaire.

rectification, *s.* Rectification *f*.

rectify, *v.tr.* Rectifier, corriger.

rectitude, *s.* Rectitude *f*.

rector, *s.* I. Curé *m*. 2. Recteur *m* (d'une université).

rectory, *s. Ecc:* Presbytère *m*.

recumbent, *a.* Couché, étendu.

recuperate, *v.i.* Se remettre, se rétablir.

recuperation, *s.* Rétablissement *m*.

recur, *v.i.* I. Revenir (*to a subject*, sur un sujet). 2. (*a*) To r. to the memory, revenir à la mémoire. (*b*) Se reproduire, se renouveler.

recurring, *a.* Périodique.

recurrence, *s.* Réapparition *f*, renouvellement *m*, retour *m*. To be of frequent recurrence, revenir fréquemment.

recurrent, *a.* Périodique; qui revient souvent.

red. I. *a.* (*a*) Rouge; (*deep*) pourpre. Red lips, lèvres vermeilles. Red(-rimmed) eyes, yeux éraillés. To turn red, rougir. To see red, voir rouge. (*b*) (*Of hair*) Roux, *f.* rousse. (*c*) *Pol:* Rouge; de l'extrême gauche. 2. *s.* (*a*) Rouge *m*. (*b*) *Pol:* Rouge *mf*. (*c*) *Bill:* The red, la bille rouge. red-faced, *a.* Rougeaud, sanguin. red-haired, *a.* Roux, *f.* rousse. red-handed, *a.* To be caught red-handed, être pris sur le fait. red-hot, *a.* I. (Chauffé au) rouge. To make sth. red-hot, porter qch. au rouge. 2. *F:* Ardent. red lead, *s.* Minium *m*. red-letter, *attrib.a. F:* Red-letter day, jour mémorable. red tape, *s. F:* Bureaucratie *f*.

redbreast, *s. See* ROBIN 2.

redcoat, *s. Hist:* Soldat anglais.

redden. I. *v.tr.* Rougir. 2. *v.i.* Devenir rouge; rougir.

reddish, *a.* (*a*) Rougeâtre. (*b*) Roussâtre.

redeem, *v.tr.* I. Racheter (une obligation); amortir (une dette). To redeem one's watch (from pawn), retirer sa montre. 2. Tenir, accomplir (sa promesse). 3. Libérer, racheter. redeeming, *a.* Rédempteur, -trice. Redeeming feature, qualité *f* qui rachète les défauts.

redemption, *s.* I. Remboursement *m*, amortissement *m*. Redemption fund, caisse *f* d'amortissement. 2. Rachat *m*. *Theol:* Rédemption *f*.

redistribution, *s.* (*a*) Redistribution *f*. (*b*) Nouvelle répartition.

redness, *s.* I. Rougeur *f*. 2. Rousseur *f*.

redolence, *s.* I. Odeur *f* suave; parfum *m*. 2. Odeur forte (*of*, de).

redolent, *a.* I. Odorant, parfumé. 2. Qui a une forte odeur (*of*, de).

redouble. I. *v.tr.* Redoubler (ses cris). 2. *v.i.* Redoubler.

redoubt, *s. Fort:* Redoute *f*.

redoubtable, *a.* Redoutable, formidable.

redound, *v.i.* Contribuer (*to*, à). This will redound to your credit, votre réputation y gagnera.

redress[1], *s.* Redressement *m*, réparation *f*.

redress[2], *v.tr.* I. Rétablir. 2. Redresser, réparer.

redskin, *s. Ethn:* Peau-Rouge *m*, *pl.* Peaux-Rouges.

reduce, *v.tr.* I. (*a*) Réduire, rapetisser; (*in length*) raccourcir. (*b*) Réduire (la température); diminuer (le prix). To reduce speed, ralentir la marche. 2. (*a*) To reduce sth. to ashes, réduire qch. en cendres. (*b*) *To r.* everything to a single principle, tout ramener à un seul principe. (*c*) *To r.* bribery to a system, ériger la corruption en système. (*d*) To reduce sth. to writing, coucher qch. par écrit. 3. (*a*) To reduce s.o. to silence, faire taire qn. (*b*) Réduire (une ville). 4. He was reduced to begging, il en était réduit à mendier son pain. 5. (*a*) *To r.* s.o. to the level of beasts, ravaler qn au niveau des bêtes. (*b*) Réduire à un grade inférieur. reduced, *a.* I. Réduit. At (greatly) reduced prices, au (grand) rabais. 2. In reduced circumstances, dans l'indigence.

reduction, *s.* I. Rapetissement *m*. 2. (*a*) Réduction *f*, diminution *f*. (*b*) *Com:* Rabais *m*. 3. *Mil:* Réduction (d'une ville). 4. *Mil:* Rétrogradation *f* (d'un sous-officier).

redundancy, *s.* I. Redondance *f*. 2. Surabondance *f*. 3. Surplus *m*.

redundant, *a.* I. Redondant. 2. Surabondant.

reduplication, *s.* Redoublement *m*.

re-echo. I. *v.tr.* Répéter, renvoyer (un son). 2. *v.i.* Retentir, résonner.

reed, *s.* I. *Bot:* Roseau *m*; jonc *m* à balais. 2. *Poet:* Chalumeau *m*. 3. *Mus:* Anche *f*.

reedy, *a.* I. Couvert de roseaux 2. R. voice, voix flûtée.

reef[1], *s. Nau:* Ris *m*.

reef[2], *v.tr.* To reef a sail, prendre un ris dans une voile.

reef[3], *s.* I. Récif *m*. Coral reef, récif de corail. 2. *Gold-min:* Filon *m* de quartz aurifère.

reek[1], *s.* Odeur forte, âcre. R. of tobacco, relent *m* de tabac.

reek[2], *v.i.* Exhaler une mauvaise odeur. This room is reeking of tobacco, ça empoisonne le tabac ici.

reel¹, *s.* **1.** *Tex:* Dévidoir *m*, bobine *f.* **2.** Moulinet *m* (de canne à pêche). *F:* (Straight) **off the reel**, d'arrache-pied. **3.** Bobine (de coton).

reel², *v.tr.* (*a*) *F:* **To reel off**, réciter d'un trait (des vers). (*b*) **To reel in**, remonter.

reel³, *v.i.* **1.** Tournoyer. *My head reels,* la tête me tourne. **2.** Chanceler.

reel⁴, *s.* *Danc:* Branle *m.*

re-elect, *v.tr.* Réélire.

re-election, *s.* Réélection *f.*

re-eligible, *a.* Rééligible.

re-embark, *v.tr. & i.* Rembarquer.

re-embarkation, *s.* Rembarquement *m.*

re-enact, *v.tr.* Reconstituer, reproduire.

re-engage, *v.tr.* Rengager (des troupes); réintégrer (des employés).

re-enlist, *v.i.* Se rengager.

re-enter. **1.** *v.i.* Rentrer. **2.** *v.tr.* Rentrer dans.

re-establish, *v.tr.* Rétablir.

re-establishment, *s.* Rétablissement *m.*

re-examine, *v.tr.* Examiner de nouveau.

refasten, *v.tr.* Rattacher; ragrafer.

refectory, *s.* Réfectoire *m.*

refer, *v.* **1.** *v.tr.* (*a*) Rapporter, rattacher (un fait à une cause). (*b*) **To refer a matter to s.o.**, s'en référer à qn d'une question. (*c*) **To refer s.o. to s.o.**, renvoyer qn à qn. **2.** *v.i.* (*a*) Se référer. *Referring to your letter,* comme suite à votre lettre. (*b*) **To refer to sth.**, se rapporter, avoir rapport, à qch. (*c*) Faire allusion (à qn). *I am not referring to you,* ce n'est pas à vous que j'en ai. *To r. to a fact,* signaler un fait. *We will not r. to it again,* n'en reparlons plus.

referee, *s.* *Sp:* Arbitre *m.*

reference, *s.* **1.** (*a*) Renvoi *m*, référence *f.* (*b*) **Terms of reference** *of a commission*, mandat *m* d'une commission. **2.** **Work of reference**, ouvrage à consulter. **3.** Rapport *m.* **To have reference to sth.**, avoir rapport, se rapporter, à qch. **With reference to your letter**, en ce qui concerne votre lettre. **Without reference to**, sans tenir compte de. **4.** **To make reference to a fact**, signaler un fait. **5.** Renvoi (dans un livre). **6.** (*a*) **To take up s.o.'s references**, prendre des renseignements sur qn. *To have good references,* avoir de bonnes références. (*b*) Référence. *To give s.o. as a r.,* se recommander de qn.

referendum, *s.* Referendum *m.*

refill¹, *s.* Pile *f*, mine *f*, de rechange.

refill², *v.tr.* (*a*) Remplir (à nouveau). (*b*) *Abs.* Faire le plein (d'essence).

refine, *v.tr.* Raffiner; affiner. **refined**, *a.* **1.** (Or) fin, affiné; (sucre) raffiné. **2.** (Goût) raffiné; (homme) cultivé.

refinement, *s.* **1.** Raffinement *m* (de qn). *A person of r.,* un(e) raffiné(e). **2.** Raffinement, subtilité *f*

refit, *v.tr.* **1.** *Nau:* Réarmer (un vaisseau). **2.** Regarnir, remonter (une usine).

reflect. **1.** *v.tr.* (*a*) Réfléchir, refléter.

(*b*) **Action that reflects credit on s.o.**, action qui fait honneur à qn. **2.** *v.i.* (*a*) Méditer (*on, upon,* sur); réfléchir (à, sur). (*b*) **To reflect on s.o.**, adresser une critique à qn. (*c*) Faire du tort (*on s.o.,* à qn); nuire à la réputation de (qn).

reflection, *s.* **1.** Réfléchissement *m*, réflexion *f.* **2.** Réflexion, reflet *m*: image *f.* **3.** **To cast reflections on s.o.**, critiquer qn. **4.** On reflection, (toute) réflexion faite. *To do sth without due r.,* faire qch. sans avoir suffisamment réfléchi. **5.** *pl.* **Reflections**, considérations *f*, pensées *f.*

reflector, *s.* Réflecteur *m.*

reflexion, *s.* = REFLECTION.

reflexive, *a. & s.* *Gram:* Réfléchi.

refloat, *v.tr.* Renflouer, (re)mettre à flot.

reflux, *s.* Reflux *m.*

reform¹, *s.* Réforme *f.*

reform². **1.** *v.tr.* (*a*) Réformer; apporter des réformes à. (*b*) Réformer, corriger; ramener au bien. **2.** *v.i.* Se réformer, se corriger.

re(-)form, *v.i.* (*Of troops*) Se reformer.

reformation, *s.* Réformation *f*, réforme *f.*

reformatory, *s.* École *f* de réforme.

reformer, *s.* Réformateur, -trice.

refract, *v.tr.* *Ph:* Réfracter. *To be refracted,* se réfracter.

refraction, *s.* *Ph:* Réfraction *f.*

refractory, *a.* Réfractaire, indocile.

refrain¹, *s.* *Mus:* Refrain *m.*

refrain², *v.i.* Se retenir, s'abstenir (*from,* de). *He could not r. from smiling,* il ne put s'empêcher de sourire.

refresh, *v.tr.* (*a*) Rafraîchir. *F:* **To refresh the inner man**, se refaire, se restaurer. (*b*) Rafraîchir (la mémoire). **refreshing**, *a.* Rafraîchissant. *R. sleep,* sommeil reposant.

refreshment, *s.* **1.** Rafraîchissement *m.* *Rail:* **Refreshment room**, buffet *m.* **2.** *pl.* **Refreshments**, rafraîchissements.

refrigerate, *v.tr.* *Ind:* Réfrigérer, frigorifier. **refrigerating**, *s.* Réfrigération *f*, frigorification *f.*

refrigeration, *s.* Réfrigération *f*; frigorification *f.*

refrigerator, *s.* (*a*) Machine *f* frigorifique; congélateur *m.* (*b*) **(Cabinet-)refrigerator**, réfrigérateur *m.*

refuge, *s.* **1.** Refuge *m*, abri *m* (*from,* contre). **Place of refuge**, lieu *m* de refuge. **To take refuge**, se réfugier. **2.** Lieu de refuge, d'asile.

refugee, *s.* Réfugié, -ée.

refulgence, *s.* Splendeur *f*, éclat *m.*

refulgent, *a.* Resplendissant, éclatant.

refund¹, *s.* Remboursement *m.*

refund², *v.tr.* (*a*) Rembourser. (*b*) Restituer (de l'argent).

refurnish, *v.tr.* Meubler de neuf.

refusal, *s.* **1.** Refus *m.* **I will take no refusal,** je n'admets pas de refus. **2.** **To have the first refusal of sth.**, avoir la première offre de qch.

refuse¹. 1. *s.* Rebut *m*; déchets *mpl.* **Household refuse,** ordures ménagères. **2.** *a.* De rebut.

refuse², v.tr. 1. Refuser. **2.** (*a*) Rejeter, repousser. **To refuse s.o. sth.,** refuser qch. à qn. (*b*) **To refuse to do sth.,** refuser de faire qch. ; **se refuser à faire qch.**

refutation, *s.* Réfutation *f.*

refute, *v.tr.* Réfuter. *To r. a statement,* démontrer la fausseté d'un dire.

regain, *v.tr.* Regagner ; recouvrer (la liberté). **To regain possession of sth.,** rentrer en possession de qch. **To regain consciousness,** reprendre connaissance, revenir à soi.

regal, *a.* Royal, -aux. **-ally,** *adv.* Royalement ; en roi.

regale, *v.tr.* Régaler.

regalia, *s.pl.* Insignes *m* de la royauté ; joyaux *m* de la Couronne.

regard¹, *s.* **1. In this regard,** à cet égard. **With regard to,** quant à. **2.** Égard *m* (*to, for,* à, pour) ; attention *f* (*to, for,* à). *To have no r. for human life,* faire peu de cas de la vie humaine. **Having regard to,** si l'on tient compte de. **3.** (*a*) Égard, respect *m*, estime *f.* **To have (a) great regard for s.o.,** tenir qn en haute estime. **Out of regard for s.o.,** par égard pour qn. (*b*) *pl.* *Give my kind regards to your brother,* faites mes amitiés à votre frère.

regard², *v.tr.* **1.** Regarder (*fixedly,* fixement). **2.** Faire attention, prendre garde, à. **3. To regard sth. as a crime,** regarder qch. comme un crime. **4.** Concerner. *That does not regard me,* cela ne me regarde pas. **As regards,** pour ce qui regarde. *As far as regards you,* en ce qui vous touche. **regarding,** *prep.* A l'égard de ; concernant ; quant à.

regardful, *a.* **1.** Soigneux (*of,* de). **2.** Plein d'égards (*of s.o.,* pour qn).

regardless, *a.* Peu soigneux (*of,* de). **Regardless of expense,** sans regarder à la dépense. *P:* **He was got up regardless,** il s'était mis sur son trente et un.

regatta, *s.* Régate(s) *f(pl).*

regency, *s.* Régence *f.*

regenerate. 1. *v.tr.* Régénérer. **2.** *v.i.* Se régénérer.

regeneration, *s.* Régénération *f.*

regent, *a. & s.* Régent, -ente.

regime, *s.* Régime *m.*

regimen, *s.* *Med:* Régime *m.*

regiment, *s.* Régiment *m.*

regimental. 1. *a.* Du régiment, régimentaire. **2.** *s.pl.* **Regimentals,** uniforme *m.*

region, *s.* Région *f.* **The nether regions,** les enfers *m.*

register¹, *s.* **1.** Registre *m* ; matricule *f.* **2.** *Mus:* Registre ; étendue *f.*

register². 1. *v.tr.* (*a*) Enregistrer ; inscrire (un nom). **To register a birth,** déclarer une naissance. (*b*) **To register luggage,** enregistrer des bagages. **To register a letter,** recommander une lettre. (*c*) (*Of thermometer*) Marquer. **2.** *v.i.* S'inscrire sur le registre.

registrar, *s.* **1.** *Jur:* Greffier *m.* **2.** Officier *m* de l'état civil. **3.** Secrétaire *m* et archiviste *m* (d'une université).

registration, *s.* Enregistrement *m*, inscription *f.* **Registration of luggage,** inscription des bagages. (Hotel) **registration form,** fiche policière. *Aut:* **Registration plate,** plaque de contrôle, de police.

registry, *s.* **1.** Enregistrement *m.* **2.** **Registry (office).** (*a*) Bureau *m* d'enregistrement ; greffe *m.* (*b*) Bureau de l'état civil. **To be married at a registry (office),** se marier civilement. (*c*) Bureau, agence *f*, de placement.

regret¹, *s.* Regret *m.*

regret², *v.tr.* Regretter.

regretful, *a.* Plein de regrets. **-fully,** *adv.* Avec regret, à regret.

regrettable, *a.* Regrettable.

regular. I. *a.* Régulier. **1.** *F:* **As regular as clockwork,** exact comme une horloge. **My regular time for going to bed,** l'heure habituelle à laquelle je me couche. **To do sth. as a regular thing,** faire qch. régulièrement. **Regular staff,** employés permanents. **2.** Réglé, rangé. **Man of regular habits,** homme rangé dans ses habitudes. **3.** (*a*) Dans les règles ; réglementaire. (*b*) Ordinaire ; normal, -aux. (*c*) *Gram:* (Verbe) régulier. (*d*) *Regular troops,* troupes régulières. **Regular officer,** officier de carrière. **4.** *F:* Vrai, véritable. *R. rascal,* vrai coquin. **-ly,** *adv.* **1.** Régulièrement. **2.** *F:* Véritablement, franchement. **II. regular,** *s.* Soldat *m* de l'armée permanente. **Regulars,** troupes régulières.

regularity, *s.* Régularité *f.*

regularize, *v.tr.* Régulariser.

regulate, *v.tr.* **1.** Régler, ajuster. **2.** Régler, diriger.

regulation, *s.* **1.** (*a*) Réglage *m.* (*b*) Règlement *m*, réglementation *f* (des affaires). **2.** (*a*) Règlement, arrêté *m*, ordonnance *f.* (*b*) *Attrib.* Réglementaire.

regulator, *s.* Régulateur *m.*

rehabilitate, *v.tr.* Réhabiliter.

rehabilitation, *s.* Réhabilitation *f.*

rehearsal, *s.* **1.** Récit détaillé, relation *f.* **2.** *Th:* Répétition *f.* **The dress rehearsal,** la (répétition) générale.

rehearse, *v.tr.* **1.** Raconter tout au long ; énumérer (des faits). **2.** *Th:* Répéter.

reign¹, *s.* Règne *m.* **In the reign of,** sous le règne de.

reign², *v.i.* Régner (*over,* sur).

reimburse, *v.tr.* Rembourser.

reimbursement, *s.* Remboursement *m.*

rein¹, *s.* Rêne *f* (de cheval monté) ; guide (de cheval de voiture). **To give rein to one's anger,** lâcher la bride à sa colère. **To draw rein,** serrer la bride ; s'arrêter.

rein², *v.tr.* **To rein in a horse,** serrer la bride à un cheval. *Abs.* **To rein in,** ramener son cheval au pas.

21

reincarnation, *s.* Réincarnation *f.*
reindeer, *s.* *Z :* Renne *m.*
reinforce, *v.tr.* **1.** Renforcer (une armée); appuyer (une demande). **2.** Renforcer (un mur). **Reinforced concrete,** béton armé.
reinforcement, *s.* **1.** Renforcement *m.* **2.** *Mil :* (*Usu. pl.*) *To await reinforcements,* attendre des renforts *m.*
reinstate, *v.tr.* **1.** Réintégrer; rétablir (un fonctionnaire). **2.** Remettre, rétablir (qch.).
reinstatement, *s.* **1.** Réintégration *f.* **2.** Rétablissement *m* (de qch.).
reiterate, *v.tr.* Réitérer, répéter.
reiteration: *s.* Réitération *f*, répétition *f.*
reject, *v.tr.* Rejeter, repousser.
rejection, *s.* Rejet *m*; repoussement *m*; refus *m* (d'une offre).
rejoice. **1.** *v.tr.* Réjouir. **2.** *v.i.* (*a*) Se réjouir (*at, over,* de). (*b*) *F :* *To rejoice in* *sth.,* jouir de qch.; posséder qch. **rejoicing,** *s.* Réjouissance *f*, allégresse *f.*
rejoin[1], *v.i.* Répliquer, répondre.
rejoin[2], *v.tr.* Rejoindre (qn). *To rejoin one's ship,* rallier le bord.
rejoinder, *s.* Réplique *f*, repartie *f.*
rejuvenate, *v.tr. & i.* Rajeunir.
rejuvenation, *s.* Rajeunissement *m.*
rekindle. **1.** *v.tr.* Rallumer; ranimer. **2.** *v.i.* Se rallumer.
relapse, *s.* **1.** *R. into crime,* récidive *f.* **2.** *Med :* Rechute *f.*
relate. **1.** *v.tr.* Raconter, conter. *To r. one's adventures,* faire le récit de ses aventures. **Strange to relate !** chose étonnante à dire ! **2.** (*a*) *v.tr. Nat.Hist :* Rapporter, rattacher (une espèce à une famille); établir un rapport entre. (*b*) *v.i.* Se rapporter, avoir rapport (*to,* à). **related,** *a.* **1.** Ayant rapport (*to,* à). **2.** Apparenté (*to,* à); parent (*to,* de); (*by marriage*) allié (*to,* à). *They are nearly related,* ils sont proches parents. **relating,** *a.* **Relating to,** relatif à.
relation, *s.* **1.** Relation *f*, récit *m.* **2.** (*a*) Relation, rapport *m.* **In relation to,** relativement à; par rapport à. *That has no r. to the present situation,* cela n'a rien à faire avec la situation actuelle. (*b*) *pl.* **To enter into relations with s.o.,** entrer en rapport, en relations, avec qn. **3.** Parent, -ente. **Relation by marriage,** allié, -ée. **What relation is he to you?** quelle est sa parenté avec vous? **Is he any relation to you?** est-il de vos parents?
relationship, *s.* **1.** Rapport *m.* **2.** Parenté *f*; lien *m* de parenté. **Blood relationship,** proximité *f* de sang.
relative. **1.** *a.* (*a*) Relatif, qui se rapporte (*to,* à). (*b*) (*Of terms*) Relatif. (*c*) *Gram :* **Relative pronoun,** pronom relatif. **2.** *adv.* *F : I am writing relative to the rent,* je vous écris au sujet du loyer. **3.** *s.* = RELATION 3. **-ly,** *adv.* (*a*) Relativement (*to,* à); par rapport (à). (*b*) *F : She is r. happy,* somme toute elle est assez heureuse.

relativity, *s.* Relativité *f.*
relax. **1.** *v.tr.* (*a*) Relâcher (la discipline); détendre (l'esprit). *The serpent relaxed its hold,* le serpent desserra son étreinte. (*b*) Mitiger. **2.** *v.i.* (*a*) Se relâcher, se détendre. *His face relaxed into a smile,* son visage se détendit dans un sourire. (*b*) Se détendre.
relaxing, *a.* (Climat) énervant, débilitant.
relaxation, *s.* **1.** (*a*) Relâchement *m* (des muscles). (*b*) Mitigation *f.* **2.** Délassement *m*, repos *m*, détente *f.* *To take some relaxation,* se donner un peu de relâche; se délasser.
relay[1], *s.* Relais *m.* **To work in relays,** se relayer.
relay[2], *v.tr.* *W.Tel :* Relayer.
release[1], *s.* **1.** (*a*) Délivrance *f* (*from,* de); décharge *f*, libération *f.* (*b*) Élargissement *m*, mise *f* en liberté. **2.** *Av :* Lâchage *m* (d'une bombe); lancement *m* (d'un parachute). **3.** *Com :* Acquit *m*, quittance *f.*
release[2], *v.tr.* **1.** (*a*) Décharger, acquitter, libérer. **To release s.o. from his promise,** rendre sa parole à qn. (*b*) Libérer, élargir (un prisonnier). (*c*) Lâcher (des pigeons voyageurs). **2.** *Av :* Lâcher (une bombe); lancer (un parachute). **To release one's hold,** lâcher prise. *Phot :* **To release the shutter,** déclancher l'obturateur.
relegate, *v.tr.* Reléguer.
relent, *v.i.* Se laisser attendrir. *He would not r.* (*towards me*), il me tenait rigueur.
relentless, *a.* (*a*) Implacable, impitoyable. (*b*) *R. persecution,* persécution sans rémission. **-ly,** *adv.* (*a*) Implacablement, impitoyablement. (*b*) Sans rémission.
relentlessness, *s.* Inflexibilité *f*, implacabilité *f*; acharnement *m.*
relevance, *s.* Pertinence *f*, à-propos *m.*
relevant, *a.* Qui a rapport (*to,* à); pertinent (*to,* à); à propos (*to,* de). *All r. information,* tous renseignements utiles.
reliability, *s.* Sûreté *f*; honnêteté *f*; sécurité *f* du fonctionnement.
reliable, *a.* Sûr; (homme) sérieux. *R. firm,* maison de confiance.
reliance, *s.* Confiance *f.* **To place reliance in s.o.,** avoir confiance en qn.
reliant, *a.* **To be reliant on,** dépendre de.
relic, *s.* **1.** *Ecc :* Relique *f.* **2.** *pl.* Relics, restes *m.* (*a*) Dépouille mortelle. (*b*) *Relics of the past,* vestiges *m* du passé.
relief[1], *s.* **1.** (*a*) Soulagement *m*; allégement *m.* **To heave a sigh of relief,** pousser un soupir de soulagement. (*b*) Décharge *f.* **2.** (*a*) **To go to s.o.'s relief,** aller au secours de qn. **Relief fund,** caisse *f* de secours. (*b*) *Adm :* **Out(door) relief,** secours à domicile. **3.** *Mil :* (*a*) Dégagement *m* (d'une place forte). **Relief troops,** troupes de secours. (*b*) Relève *f* (d'une garde).
relief[2], *s.* *Art :* Relief *m*; modelé *m.* *To stand out in r.,* ressortir, se détacher (*against,* sur). **Relief map,** carte en relief.

relieve, *v.tr.* **1.** (*a*) Soulager, alléger. To relieve s.o.'s mind, tranquilliser l'esprit de qn. To relieve one's feelings, se décharger le cœur. (*b*) To r. the tedium of the journey, tromper, dissiper, l'ennui du voyage. (*c*) To relieve congestion, faciliter la circulation. **2.** Secourir, aider. **3.** To relieve s.o. of sth., soulager qn (d'un fardeau); débarrasser qn (de son manteau); dégager qn (d'une obligation); relever qn (de ses fonctions). *Relieved of anxiety,* hors d'inquiétude; allégé de souci. **4.** (*a*) *Mil:* Dégager (une ville). (*b*) Relever (une sentinelle). *Nau:* To relieve the watch, faire la relève.

relight, *v.tr.* Rallumer.

religion, *s.* Religion *f*; culte *m*.

religious, *a.* (*a*) Religieux, pieux, dévot. (*b*) (Ordre) religieux. (*c*) *F:* (Soin) religieux, scrupuleux. **-ly,** *adv.* Religieusement. (*a*) Pieusement. (*b*) *F:* Scrupuleusement.

relinquish, *v.tr.* **1.** Abandonner; renoncer à (un projet). **2.** Lâcher.

relinquishment, *s.* Abandon *m*; renonciation *f*.

reliquary, *s.* Reliquaire *m*.

relish[1], *s.* **1.** (*a*) Goût *m*, saveur *f*. (*b*) Assaisonnement *m*. **2.** To eat sth. with relish, manger qch. de bon appétit.

relish[2], *v.tr.* Goûter, savourer. *F: We did not r. the idea,* l'idée ne nous souriait pas.

reload, *v.tr.* Recharger.

reluctance, *s.* Répugnance *f* (*to do sth.,* à faire qch.). To do sth. with reluctance, faire qch. à regret, à contre-cœur.

reluctant, *a.* **1.** To be reluctant to do sth., être peu disposé à faire qch. *I feel r. to,* il me répugne de. **2.** (Consentement) accordé à contre-cœur. **-ly,** *adv.* A contre-cœur. *I say it r.,* il m'en coûte de le dire.

rely, *v.i.* To rely (up)on s.o., compter sur qn; se fier à qn.

remain, *v.i.* **1.** Rester. The fact remains, il n'en est pas moins vrai (*that,* que). It remains to be seen whether, reste à savoir si. **2.** Demeurer, rester. (*a*) To r. sitting, demeurer assis. (*b*) Let it r. as it is, laissez-le comme cela. **3.** (*a*) The weather remains fine, le temps se maintient au beau. (*b*) *Corr:* I remain, Sir, yours truly, agréez, Monsieur, mes salutations empressées. **remaining,** *a. I have four r.,* j'en ai quatre de reste. The r. travellers, le reste des voyageurs.

remainder, *s.* **1.** Reste *m*, restant *m*. **2.** *Coll.* The remainder, les autres *mf*.

remains, *s.pl.* Restes *m*; vestiges *m*. Mortal remains, dépouille mortelle.

remake, *v.tr.* Refaire. **remaking,** *s.* Réfection *f*.

remand[1], *s. Jur:* Renvoi *m* à une autre audience.

remand[2], *v.tr. Jur:* Renvoyer à une autre audience.

remark[1], *s.* **1.** Remarque *f*, attention *f*. Things worthy of remark, choses dignes d'attention. **2.** Remarque, observation *f*. To make a remark, faire une observation.

remark[2]. **1.** *v.tr.* (*a*) Remarquer, observer. *It may be remarked that,* constatons que. (*b*) Faire la remarque (que); faire observer (à qn). **2.** *v.i.* Faire une remarque, faire des remarques (*on,* sur).

remarkable, *a.* Remarquable; frappant. **-ably,** *adv.* Remarquablement.

remarry, *v.i.* Se remarier.

remedy[1], *s.* Remède *m*.

remedy[2], *v.tr.* Remédier à (qch.).

remember, *v.tr.* **1.** (*a*) Se souvenir de; se rappeler. If I remember aright, si j'ai bonne mémoire. As far as I remember, autant qu'il m'en souvient. Don't you remember me? est-ce que vous ne me remettez pas? It will be something to remember you by, ce sera un souvenir de vous. (*b*) That is worth remembering, cela est à noter. (*c*) He remembered me in his will, il ne m'a pas oublié dans son testament. (*d*) To remember oneself, se ressaisir. **2.** Remember me (kindly) to them, rappelez-moi à leur bon souvenir.

remembrance, *s.* Souvenir *m*, mémoire *f*. To the best of my remembrance, autant qu'il m'en souvienne.

remind, *v.tr.* To remind s.o. of sth., rappeler qch. à qn. That reminds me! à propos! Remind me to write to him, faites-moi penser à lui écrire.

reminder, *s.* (*a*) Mémento *m. As a r. that,* pour rappeler que. (*b*) I'll send him a r., je vais lui rafraîchir la mémoire.

reminiscence, *s.* **1.** Réminiscence *f*; souvenir *m* vague. **2.** To write one's reminiscences, écrire ses souvenirs.

reminiscent, *a.* **1.** Qui se souvient. **2.** Reminiscent of sth., qui rappelle qch.

remiss, *a.* Négligent, insouciant.

remission, *s.* **1.** Remission of sins, pardon *m*, rémission *f*, des péchés. **2.** Remise *f* (d'une peine).

remissness, *s.* Négligence *f*.

remit, *v.tr.* **1.** Remettre. **2.** Relâcher (son zèle). **3.** Renvoyer. **4.** *Com:* To remit a sum to s.o., remettre, envoyer, une somme à qn.

remittal, *s.* **1.** Remise *f*. **2.** *Jur:* Renvoi *m*.

remittance, *s. Com:* Remise *f*; envoi *m* de fonds.

remnant, *s.* **1.** Reste *m*, restant *m*. **2.** Vestige *m* (d'un usage). **3.** Coupon *m* (d'étoffe). Remnants, soldes *m*.

remodel, *v.tr.* Remanier (un ouvrage); transformer (une machine).

remonstrance, *s.* Remontrance *f*.

remonstrate, *v.i.* To remonstrate with s.o., faire des remontrances à qn. To remonstrate against sth., protester contre qch.

remorse, *s.* **1.** Remords *m. A feeling of remorse,* un remords. **2.** Without remorse, sans aucune componction; sans pitié.

remorseful, *a.* Plein de remords; repentant. **-fully,** *adv.* Avec remords.

remorseless, *a.* **1.** Sans remords. **2.** Sans pitié; impitoyable. **-ly,** *adv.* **1.** Sans remords. **2.** Sans pitié.

remote, *a.* **1.** Lointain; éloigné, écarté. **2.** *A r. resemblance,* une vague ressemblance. *Without the remotest chance of succeeding,* sans la moindre chance de réussir. **Remote prospect,** éventualité *f* peu probable. **-ly,** *adv.* **1.** Loin; au loin; dans le lointain. **2.** Vaguement.

remoteness, *s.* **1.** Éloignement *m.* **2.** *(a)* Degré éloigné. *(b)* Faible degré.

remount, *v.tr.* Remonter.

removable, *a.* **1.** Détachable; amovible. **2.** Transportable.

removal, *s.* **1.** *(a)* Enlèvement *m* (d'une tache); suppression *f* (d'un abus). *(b)* Révocation *f* (d'un fonctionnaire). **2.** Déplacement *m.* **3.** Déménagement *m. Adm:* **Removal expenses,** frais de déplacement.

remove, *v.tr.* **1.** *(a)* Enlever, ôter; écarter (un obstacle); supprimer (un abu:). *To r. s.o.'s name from a list,* rayer qn d'une liste. *(b)* Révoquer (un fonctionnaire). **2.** *(a)* Déplacer. *Abs.* **To remove,** déménager. *(b)* Éloigner (qch.). *(c)* Enlever, retirer (son chapeau). **removed,** *a.* Éloigné. **Far removed from,** bien loin de.

remunerate, *v.tr.* Rémunérer.

remuneration, *s.* Rémunération *f (for,* de).

remunerative, *a.* Rémunérateur, -trice.

renaissance, *s.* Renaissance *f.*

rend, *v.tr.* Déchirer. **A cry rent the air,** un cri fendit l'air.

render, *v.tr.* Rendre. **1.** *(a) To r. good for evil,* rendre le bien pour le mal. *(b)* **To render thanks to s.o.,** remercier qn. **2. To render a service to s.o.,** rendre un service à qn. **3. To render an account of sth.,** rendre compte de qch. **4.** Interpréter; rendre, traduire. **5.** Rendre; faire devenir.

rendezvous, *s.* Rendez-vous *m.*

renegade, *s.* Renégat, -ate.

renew, *v.tr.* *(a)* Renouveler. **To renew one's youth,** rajeunir. *To r. one's subscription,* se réabonner *(to,* à). *(b)* **To renew one's acquaintance with s.o.,** renouer connaissance avec qn. *To r. the combat,* rengager le combat.

renewal, *s.* *(a)* Renouvellement *m.* **Renewal of subscription,** réabonnement *m (to,* à). *(b)* **Renewal of acquaintance,** renouement *m* des relations. *R. of negotiations,* reprise *f* de négociations.

renounce, *v.tr.* **1.** Renoncer à, abandonner. **2.** Répudier (un traité). *To r. one's faith,* renoncer (à) sa foi.

renouncement, *s.* Renoncement *m (of,* à).

renovate, *v.tr.* **1.** Renouveler (l'air). **2.** Remettre à neuf.

renovation, *s.* Rénovation *f.*

renown, *s.* Renommée *f,* renom *m.*

renowned, *a.* Renommé *(for,* pour).

rent¹, *s.* **1.** Déchirure *f,* accroc *m.* **2.** Fissure *f* (de terrain).

rent², *s.* Loyer *m;* (prix *m* de) location *f. Quarter's r.,* terme *m.* **rent-collector,** *s.* Receveur *m* de loyers. **rent-day,** *s.* Jour *m* du terme.

rent³, *v.tr.* Louer.

rental, *s.* Loyer *m;* montan⁻ *m* du loyer. *Yearly r.,* redevance annuelle.

renunciation, *s.* **1.** Renoncement *m,* renonciation *f (of,* de). **2.** Reniement *m (of,* de).

reopen. **1.** *v.tr.* *(a)* Rouvrir. *F:* **To reopen an old sore,** raviver une plaie. *(b)* Reprendre (les hostilités). *(c) The question cannot be reopened,* il n'y a pas à y revenir. **2.** *v.i.* *(a) (Of wound)* Se rouvrir. *(b) (Of theatre)* Rouvrir; *(of school)* rentrer.

reorganization, *s.* Réorganisation *f.*

reorganize. **1.** *v.tr.* Réorganiser. **2.** *v.i.* Se réorganiser.

rep, *s. Tex:* Reps *m.*

repaint, *v.tr.* Repeindre.

repair¹, *v.i.* **To repair to a place,** aller, se rendre, à un endroit.

repair², *s.* **1.** Réparation *f.* **To be under repair,** subir des réparations. **2. To be in (good) repair,** être en bon état.

repair³, *v.tr.* Réparer, remettre en état; raccommoder (un vêtement). **repairing,** *s.* Réparation *f,* raccommodage *m.*

reparation, *s.* Réparation *f.*

repartee, *s.* Repartie *f.*

repast, *s.* Repas *m.*

repatriate, *v.tr.* Rapatrier.

repatriation, *s.* Rapatriement *m.*

repay, *v.tr.* **1.** Rendre. *To r. an obligation,* s'acquitter d'une obligation. **2.** (i) Rembourser; (ii) récompenser *(for,* de). *To r. s.o. with ingratitude,* payer qn d'ingratitude. *How can I r. you?* comment pourrai-je m'acquitter envers vous?

repayment, *s.* **1.** Remboursement *m.* **2.** Récompense *f.*

repeal¹, *s.* Abrogation *f;* rappel *m,* révocation *f* (d'un décret).

repeal², *v.tr.* Rapporter, abroger; révoquer.

repeat, *v.tr.* *(a)* Répéter; réitérer. *(b)* Rapporter. *(c)* Renouveler. **repeated,** *a.* Répété, réitéré, redoublé. **-ly,** *adv.* A plusieurs reprises. **repeating,** *a.* (Fusil) à répétition; (montre) à sonnerie.

repeater, *s.* *(a)* Montre *f* à répétition, à sonnerie. *(b)* Fusil *m* à répétition.

repel, *v.tr.* **1.** Repousser. **2.** Repousser (qn); répugner à. **repelling,** *a.* Répulsif.

repellent, *a.* Repoussant, répugnant.

repent. **1.** *v.i.* Se repentir *(of,* de). **2.** *v.tr.* **To repent having done sth.,** se repentir d'avoir fait qch.

repentance, *s.* Repentir *m.*

repentant, *a.* Repentant, repenti.

repeople, *v.tr.* Repeupler.

repercussion, *s.* Répercussion *f.*

repertoire, *s. Th:* Répertoire *m.*

repetition, *s.* **1.** *(a)* Répétition *f.* *(b) Sch:* Récitation *f.* **2.** Répétition, réitération *f;* renouvellement *m.*

repine, *v.i.* Être mécontent, se chagriner (*at, against*, de). **repining,** *a.* **1.** Disposé à se plaindre; mécontent. **2.** (Ton) dolent.

replace, *v.tr.* **1.** Replacer; remettre en place. *Tp:* To replace the receiver, raccrocher le récepteur; *F:* raccrocher. **2.** Remplacer. *To r.* coal by oil fuel, remplacer le charbon par le pétrole.

replaceable, *a.* Remplaçable.

replacement, *s.* **1.** Remise *f* en place. **2.** Remplacement *m*, substitution *f*.

replant, *v.tr.* Replanter.

replenish, *v.tr.* Remplir (*with*, de). *To r.* one's supplies, se réapprovisionner (*with*, de).

replenishment, *s.* Remplissage *m*.

replete, *a.* Rempli, plein (*with*, de).

repletion, *s.* Réplétion *f*.

replica, *s.* *Art:* Réplique *f*, double *m*.

reply¹, *s.* Réponse *f*. What have you to say in reply? qu'avez-vous à répondre? *Tg:* Reply paid, réponse payée.

reply², *v.i. & tr.* Répondre, répliquer.

report¹, *s.* **1.** (*a*) Rapport *m* (*on*, sur); compte rendu; exposé *m*. Policeman's report, procès-verbal. *Sch:* Terminal report, bulletin trimestriel. (*b*) Weather report, bulletin *m* météorologique. **2.** Bruit *m* qui court; rumeur *f*. To know of sth. by mere report, savoir qch. par ouï-dire. **3.** Réputation *f*, renommée *f*. **4.** Détonation *f* (d'une arme à feu); coup *m* (de fusil).

report². I. *v.tr.* **1.** (*a*) Rapporter; rendre compte de. To report progress, exposer l'état de l'affaire. (*b*) *Journ:* Faire le reportage de. (*c*) Rapporter, dire. *It is reported from Paris that*, on mande de Paris que. **2.** (*a*) *To r.* an accident to the police, signaler un accident à la police. (*b*) To report oneself to (s.o.), se présenter à, devant (un supérieur). II. **report,** *v.ind.tr.* To report (up)on sth., faire un rapport sur qch.; rendre compte de qch. **reporting,** *s.* Reportage *m*; comptes rendus.

reporter, *s.* Journaliste *m*, reporter *m*.

repose¹, *v.tr.* To repose one's trust in s.o., mettre sa confiance en qn.

repose², *s.* Repos *m*.

repose³, *v.i.* (*a*) Se reposer. (*b*) Reposer (*on, upon*, sur).

repository, *s.* Dépôt *m*, entrepôt *m*. Furniture repository, garde-meuble *m, pl.* garde-meubles.

repossess, *v.tr.* To r. oneself of sth., reprendre possession de qch.

reprehend, *v.tr.* Reprendre, blâmer, réprimander.

reprehensible, *a.* Répréhensible, blâmable. **-ibly,** *adv.* Répréhensiblement.

represent, *v.tr.* **1.** (*a*) Représenter. (*b*) *The flag represents the nation*, le drapeau symbolise la nation. **2.** Faire remarquer (*sth. to s.o.*, qch. à qn). **3.** *He represents himself as . . .*, il se donne pour. . . . **4.** Représenter (une maison de commerce).

representation, *s.* **1.** Représentation *f*. **2.** (i) Représentation; remontrance courtoise; (ii) exposé *m* des faits.

representative. **1.** *a.* (*a*) (Gouvernement) représentatif. (*b*) Qui représente. **2.** *s.* (*a*) Représentant, -ante; délégué, -ée. (*b*) *Pol:* Député *m*.

repress, *v.tr.* **1.** Réprimer (une sédition). **2.** Réprimer, retenir (ses désirs). **repressed,** *a.* Réprimé, contenu.

repression, *s.* Répression *f*.

repressive, *a.* Répressif, réprimant.

reprieve¹, *s.* **1.** (*a*) Commutation *f* de la peine capitale. (*b*) Lettre(s) *f(pl)* de grâce. **2.** Répit *m*, délai *m*.

reprieve², *v.tr.* *Jur:* Accorder (à un condamné) une commutation de la peine capitale.

reprimand¹, *s.* Réprimande *f*.

reprimand², *v.tr.* Réprimander.

reprint¹, *s.* Réimpression *f*.

reprint², *v.tr.* Réimprimer.

reprisal, *s.* *Usu.pl.* Représaille *f*.

reproach¹, *s.* **1.** (*a*) To be a reproach to, être la honte de. (*b*) Honte, opprobre *m*. **2.** Reproche *m*, blâme *m*. Beyond reproach, irréprochable.

reproach², *v.tr.* Faire des reproches à (qn) (*about*, au sujet de). To reproach s.o. with sth., reprocher qch. à qn.

reproachful, *a.* Réprobateur, -trice; plein de reproche(s) **-fully,** *adv.* D'un air de reproche.

reprobate, *s.* Chenapan *m*, vaurien, -ienne.

reprobation, *s.* Réprobation *f*.

reproduce. **1.** *v.tr.* Reproduire. (*a*) Copier. (*b*) Multiplier. **2.** *v.i.* Se reproduire, se multiplier.

reproduction, *s.* **1.** Reproduction *f*. **2.** Copie *f,* imitation *f*.

reproductive, *a.* Reproductif; reproducteur, -trice.

reproof, *s.* **1.** Reproche *m*. **2.** Réprimande *f*.

reprove, *v.tr.* Reprendre, réprimander.

reproving, *a.* Réprobateur, -trice. **-ly,** *adv.* D'un ton de reproche.

reptile, *s.* Reptile *m*.

republic, *s.* République *f*.

republican, *a. & s.* Républicain, -aine.

republicanism, *s.* Républicanisme *m*.

repudiate, *v.tr.* Répudier, désavouer.

repudiation, *s.* Répudiation *f*, désaveu *m*.

repugnance, *s.* Répugnance *f*, antipathie *f* (*to, against*, pour).

repugnant, *a.* **1.** Incompatible (*to, with*, avec); contraire (*to, with*, à). **2.** Répugnant (*to*, à). To be r. to s.o., répugner à qn.

repulse¹, *s.* **1.** Échec *m*; défaite *f* (de l'ennemi). **2.** Rebuffade *f*, refus *m*.

repulse², *v.tr.* **1.** Repousser (un assaut). **2.** Repousser (une demande); refuser, renvoyer (qn).

repulsion, *s.* Répulsion *f*, aversion *f*, répugnance *f*.

repulsive, *a.* Répulsif, repoussant. **-ly,** *adv.* R. ugly, d'une laideur repoussante.

repulsiveness, *s.* Caractère repoussant.
reputable, *a.* Honorable, estimé, estimable.
-ably, *adv.* Honorablement.
reputation, *s.* Réputation *f*, renom *m*.
To ruin s.o.'s r., perdre qn de réputation.
repute¹, *s.* Réputation *f*, renom *m*, renommée *f*. To know **s.o. by repute,** connaître qn de réputation. **Doctor of repute,** médecin réputé.
repute², *v.tr.* **To be reputed wealthy,** avoir la réputation d'être riche. **reputed,** *a.* Réputé, censé, supposé.
request¹, *s.* **I.** Demande *f*, requête *f*. *Earnest r.,* sollicitation *f*. *At the urgent r. of,* sur les instances pressantes de. **To sing sth. by request,** chanter qch. à la demande générale. 'Cars stop by request,' "arrêt facultatif." **2.** Recherche *f*, demande. **To be in request,** être recherché.
request², *v.tr.* **I.** To request sth. **of s.o.,** demander qch. à qn; solliciter q⌐h. de qn. **2.** To request **s.o. to do sth.,** prier qn de faire qch.
requiem, *s.* **I.** Requiem *m*; messe *f* des morts. **2.** *F:* Chant *m* funèbre.
require, *v.tr.* **I.** To require sth. **of s.o.,** demander, réclamer, qch. à qn. *What do you r. of me?* que prétendez-vous de moi? **To require s.o. to do sth.,** exiger de qn qu'il fasse qch. **2.** Exiger, réclamer. *Work that requires great precision,* travail qui nécessite une grande précision. *Have you got all you r.?* avez-vous tout ce qu'il vous faut? *You will not r. a coat,* vous n'aurez pas besoin d'un manteau. If required, s'il le faut; au besoin. *As occasion shall require,* selon les nécessités.
required, *a.* Exigé, demandé, voulu. *In the r. time,* dans le délai prescrit. *The qualities r. for this post,* les qualités requises pour ce poste.
requirement, *s.* **I.** Demande *f*, réclamation *f*. **2.** Exigence *f*, besoin *m*. **3.** Condition requise.
requisite. I. *a.* Requis (*to,* pour); nécessaire (*to,* à); voulu. **2.** *s.* (*a*) Condition requise (*for,* pour). (*b*) Chose *f* nécessaire. **Toilet requisites,** accessoires *m* de toilette. **Office requisites,** fournitures *f* de bureau. **Travelling requisites,** articles *m* de voyage.
requisition¹, *s.* **I.** Demande *f*. **2.** *Mil:* Réquisition *f*.
requisition², *v.tr.* Réquisitionner. *To r. s.o.'s services,* avoir recours aux services de qn.
requital, *s.* **I.** Récompense *f*, retour *m*. **In requital for,** en récompense, en retour, de. **2.** Revanche *f*, représailles *fpl*.
requite, *v.tr.* **I.** Récompenser, payer de retour. **Requited love,** amour partagé. **2.** To requite **s.o. for a service,** récompenser qn d'un service.
reredos, *s.* *Ecc:* Retable *m*.
rescind, *v.tr.* Rescinder (un acte); annuler (un vote); abroger (une loi).
rescission, *s.* Rescision *f*; annulation *f*.

rescue¹, *s.* Délivrance *f*; sauvetage *m*. **To the rescue!** au secours!
rescue², *v.tr.* Sauver, délivrer, secourir. **The rescued men,** les rescapés *m*.
rescuer, *s.* **I.** Secoureur, -euse; libérateur, -trice. **2.** (*From shipwreck*) Sauveteur *m*.
research, *s.* Recherche *f* (*after,* *for,* de).
resell, *v.tr.* Revendre.
resemblance, *s.* Ressemblance *f* (*to,* à, avec). **To bear a resemblance to sth.,** avoir de la ressemblance avec qch.
resemble, *v.tr.* Ressembler à.
resent, *v.tr.* **I.** Être offensé de; être irrité de. *You r. my being here,* ma présence vous déplaît. **2.** S'offenser de; ressentir.
resentful, *a.* **I.** Plein de ressentiment; rancunier. **2.** Froissé, irrité (*of,* de). **-fully,** *adv.* Avec ressentiment.
resentment, *s.* Ressentiment *m*.
reservation, *s.* **I.** Réserve *f* (des places). **2.** Réserve, restriction *f*. **With this reservation,** à cette restriction près. **3.** *U.S:* Terrain réservé.
reserve¹, *s.* **I.** (*a*) Réserve *f*. **Reserve fund,** fonds de réserve. (*b*) To have sth. in reserve, tenir qch. en réserve. **2.** *Mil:* The reserves, les réserves. **3.** Terrain réservé. *For:* Réserve. **4.** (*a*) Réserve, restriction *f*. (*b*) Reserve price, mise *f* à prix. **5.** Réserve, discrétion *f*.
reserve², *v.tr.* Réserver. **To reserve a seat for s.o.,** retenir une place pour qn. **To reserve the right to do sth.,** se réserver de faire qch. **reserved,** *a.* **I.** Réservé. **Reserved seats,** places réservées, louées. **2.** Réservé, renfermé; peu communicatif.
reservist, *s.* *Mil:* Réserviste *m*.
reservoir, *s.* Réservoir *m*.
reshuffle, *v.tr.* (*a*) Rebattre, remêler (les cartes). (*b*) *F:* Remanier (un personnel).
reside, *v.i.* Résider.
residence, *s.* **I.** Résidence *f*, demeure *f*, séjour *m*. **To take up one's residence somewhere,** établir sa demeure quelque part. **2.** Demeure, maison *f*, habitation *f*.
residency, *s.* Résidence du résident.
resident. I. *a.* Résidant; qui réside. **2.** *s.* (*a*) Habitant, -ante. (*b*) (Ministre) résident *m*.
residential, *a.* **Residential district,** quartier d'habitation.
residuary, *a.* *Jur:* **Residuary legatee,** légataire universel.
residue, *s.* **I.** *Ch:* Résidu *m*. **2.** Reste(s) *m(pl)*. **3.** *Jur:* Reliquat *m*.
resign, *v.tr.* **I.** (*a*) Résigner; donner sa démission de; *abs.* démissionner. (*b*) Abandonner; renoncer à (une tâche). **2.** To resign oneself to doing sth., se résigner à faire qch. **resigned,** *a.* Résigné (*to,* à).
resignation, *s.* **I.** (*a*) Démission *f*. (*b*) Abandon *m*. **2.** Résignation *f* (*to,* à); soumission *f*.
resignedly, *adv.* Avec résignation.
resilience, *s.* **I.** (*a*) *Mec:* Résilience *f*

(b) Élasticité *f* de tempérament. **2.** Rebondissement *m.*

resilient, *a.* Rebondissant, élastique. *F:* To be resilient, avoir du ressort.

resin, *s.* **1.** Résine *f.* **2.** Colophane *f.*

resinous, *a.* Résineux.

resist, *v.tr.* **1.** (*a*) Résister à. (*b*) *I couldn't r. telling him* . . ., je n'ai pas pu m'empêcher de lui dire. . . . **2.** (*a*) Résister à, s'opposer à. (*b*) Repousser (une suggestion).

resistance, *s.* **1.** Résistance *f. She made no r.,* elle s'est laissé faire. **Weary of resistance,** de guerre lasse. **2.** *F:* To take the line of least r. aller au plus facile.

resistless, *a.* Irrésistible.

resolute, *a.* Résolu, déterminé. **-ly,** *adv.* Résolument.

resoluteness, *s.* Résolution *f.*

resolution, *s.* **1.** Résolution *f*, délibération *f.* To put a resolution to the meeting, mettre une résolution aux voix. **2.** Résolution, détermination *f.* **3.** Résolution, fermeté *f*, décision *f.*

resolve¹, *s.* Résolution *f.*

resolve², **I.** *v.tr.* **1.** Résoudre. *The water resolves itself into vapour,* l'eau se résout en vapeur. **2.** Résoudre (un problème); dissiper (un doute). **3.** To resolve to do sth., prendre la résolution de faire qch. **II. resolve,** *v.i.* **1.** Se résoudre (en ses éléments). **2.** Se résoudre (*upon sth.,* à qch.); résoudre (*upon sth.,* de faire qch.). **resolved,** *a.* Résolu, décidé (*to do sth.,* à faire qch.).

resonance, *s.* Résonance *f. Mus:* Vibration *f.*

resonant, *a.* Résonnant. *R. voice,* voix sonore.

resort¹, *s.* **1.** (*a*) Ressource *f.* (*b*) Recours *m.* Without resort to compulsion, sans avoir recours à la force. **2.** (*a*) Lieu *m* de séjour, de rendez-vous. *R. of thieves,* repaire *m* de voleurs. (*b*) Health resort, station thermale. Holiday resort, (centre *m* de) villégiature *f.*

resort², *v.i.* **1.** Avoir recours, recourir (*to,* à); user (*to,* de). **To resort to force,** faire emploi de la force. **2.** To resort to a place, se rendre, affluer, dans un endroit.

resound, *v.i.* (*a*) Résonner; retentir (*with,* de). (*b*) Avoir du retentissement. **resounding,** *a.* Résonnant, retentissant; (rire) sonore.

resource, *s.* **1.** Ressource *f.* **2.** *pl.* To be at the end of one's resources, être au bout de ses ressources. **3.** Ressource *f.*

resourceful, *a.* Fertile en ressources.

resourcefulness, *s.* Ressource *f.*

respect¹, *s.* **1.** Rapport *m*, égard *m.* With respect to, en ce qui concerne. In some respects, sous quelques rapports. In this respect, à cet égard. **2.** Égard. Without respect of persons, sans acception de personnes. **3.** Respect *m.* To have respect for s.o., avoir du respect pour qn. Worthy of respect, respectable; digne d'estime. With

all due respect, sauf votre respect. **4.** *pl.* Respects, respects, hommages *m.* To pay one's respects to s.o., rendre ses respects à qn.

respect², *v.tr.* Respecter. **1.** Honorer; porter respect à. **2.** Avoir égard à. *To r. s.o.'s opinion,* respecter l'opinion de qn. **3.** Avoir rapport à; concerner. **As respects,** pour ce qui est de; quant à. **respecting,** *prep.* Relativement à; quant à; à l'égard de.

respectability, *s.* Respectabilité *f.*

respectable, *a.* Respectable. **1.** Digne de respect. **2.** Honorable, convenable. *Hardly r.,* peu honorable. **3.** Passable. **-ably,** *adv.* **1.** Respectablement, convenablement. **2.** Pas mal; passablement.

respecter, *s.* To be no respecter of persons, ne pas faire acception de personnes.

respectful, *a.* Respectueux (*to, envers, pour*). **-fully,** *adv.* Respectueusement; *Corr:* I remain yours respectfully, je vous prie d'agréer mes salutations très respectueuses.

respective, *a.* Respectif. **-ly,** *adv.* Respectivement.

respiration, *s.* Respiration *f.*

respirator, *s.* Respirateur *m*; masque *m* respiratoire; *Mil:* masque à gaz.

respire, *v.tr. & i.* *F:* Reprendre haleine; respirer.

respite, *s.* **1.** *Jur:* Sursis *m*, délai *m.* **2.** Répit *m*, relâche *m.*

resplendence, *s.* Splendeur *f*, resplendissement *m*, éclat *m.*

resplendent, *a.* Resplendissant.

respond, *v.i.* **1.** Répondre; faire une réponse. **2.** Répondre, être sensible; se prêter. (*Of plane*) To respond to the controls, obéir aux gouvernes.

response, *s.* **1.** Réponse *f*, réplique *f.* **2.** (*a*) Réponse (à un appel). (*b*) Réaction *f*, réponse.

responsibility, *s.* Responsabilité *f.* To accept responsibility for sth., prendre la responsabilité de qch. On one's own responsibility, de son chef.

responsible, *a.* **1.** (*a*) Chargé. Responsible to s.o., responsable devant qn. To be responsible to s.o. for sth., avoir à rendre compte à qn de qch. He is not responsible for his actions, il n'est pas maître de ses actes. (*b*) Responsable. To hold s.o. responsible (for sth.), tenir qn responsable (de qch.). **2.** Capable, compétent. In responsible quarters, dans les milieux autorisés. **3.** (Poste) plein de responsabilités.

responsive, *a.* Impressionnable; sensible (*to,* à). **-ly,** *adv.* Avec sympathie.

responsiveness, *s.* Émotion *f* sympathique; sensibilité *f.*

rest¹, *s.* **1.** (*a*) Repos *m.* To have a good night's rest, passer une bonne nuit. At rest, en repos. To set s.o.'s mind at rest, calmer l'esprit de qn. (*b*) To take a rest, se reposer. (*c*) To come to rest, s'arrêter, s'immobiliser. **2.** *Mus:* Pause *f*, silence *m.* **3.** Support *m.*

rest[2]. I. *v.i.* **1.** (*a*) Avoir du repos. (*b*) Se reposer. (*c*) So the matter rests, l'affaire en reste là. I shall not let it r. at that, cela ne se passera pas ainsi. **2.** Se poser, s'appuyer. A heavy responsibility rests upon them, une lourde responsabilité pèse sur eux. II. **rest**, *v.tr.* (*a*) Reposer, faire reposer. (*b*) Appuyer ; déposer. To rest sth. against sth., appuyer qch. contre qch. **resting**, *a.* Au repos.

resting-place, *s.* (Lieu *m* de) repos *m* ; gîte *m*, abri *m*.

rest[3], *s.* **1.** Reste *m*, restant *m*. For the rest, quant au reste ; d'ailleurs. **2.** The rest, les autres *mf*.

rest[4], *v.i.* **1.** Rester, demeurer. Rest assured that, soyez assuré que. **2.** It rests with you, (*to do sth.*), il dépend de vous (de faire qch.).

restaurant, *s.* Restaurant *m*. *Rail:* Restaurant-car, wagon-restaurant *m*, *pl.* wagons-restaurants.

restful, *a.* Qui repose ; paisible, tranquille. R. spot, endroit reposant. **-fully**, *adv.* Paisiblement, tranquillement.

restfulness, *s.* Tranquillité *f*.

restitution, *s.* Restitution *f*. To make restitution of sth., restituer qch.

restive, *a.* **1.** Rétif. **2.** Inquiet, -ète ; nerveux.

restiveness, *s.* **1.** Humeur rétive. **2.** Humeur inquiète ; nervosité *f*.

restless, *a.* **1.** Sans repos. To have a restless night, passer une nuit blanche. **2.** (*a*) Agité. To be restless in one's sleep, avoir le sommeil agité. (*b*) (Enfant) remuant. **3.** Inquiet, -ète, agité. The audience was getting restless, l'auditoire s'impatientait.

restlessness, *s.* **1.** (*a*) Inquiétude *f*, agitation *f*. (*b*) Turbulence *f* ; mouvement incessant. **2.** Nervosité *f*.

restoration, *s.* **1.** Restitution *f* ; remise *f*. **2.** Restauration *f* (d'un monument). **3.** (*a*) Réintégration *f*. (*b*) Rétablissement *m*.

restorative, *a. & s. Med:* **1.** Fortifiant (*m*). **2.** Cordial (*m*), -aux.

restore, *v.tr.* **1.** Restituer, rendre. **2.** Restaurer (un monument) ; réparer (un tableau). **3.** (*a*) To restore sth. to its place, remettre qch. en place. (*b*) Rétablir, réintégrer. (*c*) To restore s.o. to health, rétablir la santé de qn. To restore s.o. to life, ramener qn à la vie. **4.** (*a*) Rétablir (la liberté) ; ramener (la confiance). (*b*) To restore the circulation, réactiver la circulation.

restrain, *v.tr.* **1.** Retenir, empêcher (*from*, de). **2.** Contenir, refréner. To restrain oneself, se contraindre. **restrained**, *a.* Contenu.

restrainedly, *adv.* Avec retenue.

restraint, *s.* **1.** (*a*) Contrainte *f*, entrave *f*, frein *m*. (*b*) Contrainte ; réserve *f*. To put a restraint upon oneself, se contenir, se contraindre. Lack of restraint, abandon *m*. **2.** To keep s.o. under restraint, tenir qn emprisonné.

restrict, *v.tr.* Restreindre ; réduire. **restricted**, *a.* Restreint, limité.

restriction, *s.* Restriction *f*.

restrictive, *a.* Restrictif.

result[1], *s.* Résultat *m* (*of*, de) ; aboutissement *m*. As a result of, par suite de. Without result, sans résultat.

result[2], *v.i.* **1.** Résulter, provenir (*from*, de). **2.** It resulted in nothing, il n'en est rien résulté.

resultant, *a.* Résultant.

resume, *v.tr.* **1.** Reprendre, regagner. To resume one's seat, se rasseoir. **2.** Reprendre ; renouer (des relations). To resume work, se remettre au travail. **3.** Reprendre, récapituler.

résumé, *s.* Résumé *m*.

resumption, *s.* Reprise *f*.

resurrection, *s.* Résurrection *f*.

resuscitate, *v.tr. & i.* Ressusciter.

resuscitation, *s.* Ressuscitation *f*.

retail[1], *s. Com:* Détail *m* ; vente *f* au détail. Wholesale and retail, en gros et au détail.

retail[2], *v.tr.* **1.** Détailler, vendre au détail. **2.** *F:* Répéter, colporter.

retailer, *s.* **1.** Marchand *m* au détail. **2.** *F:* Retailer of news, colporteur *m* de nouvelles.

retain, *v.tr.* **1.** Retenir, maintenir. **2.** Engager, retenir (un domestique). **3.** Conserver, garder. To retain hold of sth., ne pas lâcher (prise de) qch. **4.** Garder en mémoire.

retainer, *s.* **1.** Serviteur *m*. **2.** Arrhes *fpl* ; avance *f*.

retake, *v.tr.* Reprendre ; rattraper.

retaliate, *v.i.* To retaliate on s.o., rendre la pareille (à qn).

retaliation, *s.* Revanche *f*, représailles *fpl*.

retaliatory, *a.* De représailles. Retaliatory measures, représailles *f*.

retard, *v.tr.* Retarder.

retell, *v.tr.* Raconter de nouveau.

retention, *s.* Conservation *f*.

retentive, *a.* (*a*) (Mémoire) tenace. (*b*) To be retentive of sth., retenir, garder, qch.

reticence, *s.* Réticence *f*.

reticent, *a.* Peu communicatif ; taciturne. **-ly**, *adv.* Avec réticence.

reticule, *s.* Réticule *m* ; sac *m* à main.

retina, *s. Anat:* Rétine *f* (de l'œil).

retinue, *s.* Suite *f*.

retire, *v.i.* **1.** (*a*) Se retirer (*to a place*, dans un endroit). To retire into oneself, se replier sur soi-même. (*b*) To retire for the night, aller se coucher. **2.** Se démettre. To retire from business, se retirer des affaires. To retire on a pension, prendre sa retraite. **3.** *Mil:* Reculer. **retired**, *a.* **1.** (*a*) Retiré. (*b*) (Endroit) retiré, peu fréquenté. In a retired spot, à l'écart. **2.** (*a*) Retraité. (*b*) Retired pay, pension *f* de retraite. **retiring**, *a.* **1.** Réservé ; farouche. **2.** (Président) sortant.

retirement, *s.* (*a*) *Adm:* La retraite. (*b*) To live in retirement, vivre retiré du monde.

retort¹, *s.* Réplique *f* (*to,* à); riposte *f.*

retort², *v.tr.* Répliquer, riposter, repartir.

retort³, *s. Ch: Ind:* Cornue *f.*

retrace, *v.tr.* To retrace one's steps, revenir sur ses pas.

retract, *v.tr.* Rétracter. *Abs.* To retract, se rétracter; se dédire.

retreat¹, *s.* 1. *Mil:* Retraite *f.* 2. Retraite recul *m.* 3. (*a*) Abri *m,* asile *m*; retraite. (*b*) Repaire *m* (de brigands).

retreat², *v.i.* (*a*) Se retirer. (*b*) *Mil:* Battre en retraite.

retrench, *v.tr.* Restreindre. *Abs.* To retrench, restreindre sa dépense.

retrenchment, *s.* Réduction *f* (des dépenses).

retribution, *s.* Châtiment *m*; jugement *m.*

retributive, *a.* Vengeur, *f.* vengeresse. Retributive punishment, punition justicière.

retrievable, *a.* 1. (Somme) recouvrable. 2. (Perte) réparable.

retrieval, *s.* 1. Recouvrement *m.* 2. Rétablissement *m.* 3. Réparation *f* (d'une erreur).

retrieve, *v.tr.* 1. (*a*) Rapporter (le gibier). (*b*) Recouvrer; retrouver. 2. Relever, rétablir. To r. one's honour, racheter son honneur. 3. Réparer (une erreur).

retriever, *s. Ven:* Chien rapporteur.

retrocede, *v.i.* Rétrograder, reculer.

retrocession, *s.* Recul *m.*

retrograde¹, *a.* Rétrograde.

retrograde², *v.i.* Rétrograder.

retrospect, *s.* Coup d'œil rétrospectif.

retrospection, *s.* Examen rétrospectif.

retrospective, *a.* Rétrospectif.

return¹, *s.* 1. Retour *m.* The return to school, la rentrée des classes. (Immediately) on my return, dès mon retour, à mon retour. On my r. home, de retour à la maison. Many happy returns (of the day)! mes meilleurs vœux pour votre anniversaire! *Rail:* Return ticket, *F:* return, billet d'aller et retour. Return journey, voyage de retour. *Com:* (*a*) *pl.* Returns, recettes *f.* Quick returns, un prompt débit. (*b*) Revenu *m,* profit *m*; rendement *m.* 3. (*a*) Retour *m,* retour. (*b*) Restitution *f.* (*c*) In return for which, moyennant quoi. 4. *Ten:* Renvoi; riposte *f.* 5. Récompense *f.* In return for this service, en retour de ce service. 6. (*a*) État *m,* exposé *m*; relèvement *m. Quarterly r.,* rapport trimestriel. (*b*) Return of income, déclaration *f* de revenu. 7. *Pol:* Élection *f.*

return². I. *v.i.* 1. (*Come back*) Revenir; (*go back*) retourner. To return home, rentrer (chez soi). They have returned, ils sont de retour. 2. To return to a task, reprendre une tâche. Let us return to the subject, *F:* revenons à nos moutons. II. return, *v.tr.* 1. (*a*) Rendre; restituer; renvoyer; rembourser. (*b*) To return a book to its place, remettre un livre à sa place. 2. (*a*) Rendre

(une visite). To return s.o.'s love, répondre à l'amour de qn. (*b*) Répondre, répliquer. (*c*) To return thanks to s.o., adresser des remerciements à qn. 3. Rapporter, donner (un bénéfice). 4. Déclarer, rapporter. 5. *Pol:* Élire.

reunion, *s.* Réunion *f,* assemblée *f.*

reunite. 1. *v.tr.* Unir de nouveau; réunir. 2. *v.i.* Se réunir.

reveal, *v.tr.* (*a*) Révéler, découvrir. To reveal one's identity, se faire connaître. (*b*) Laisser voir. (*c*) Révéler, découvrir (un objet caché); dévoiler (un mystère). **revealing,** *a.* Révélateur, -trice.

reveille, *s. Mil:* Le réveil; la diane.

revel¹, *s.* Often *pl.* (*a*) Divertissement(s) *m(pl)*; réjouissances *fpl.* (*b*) Bacchanale *f,* orgie *f.*

revel², *v.i.* To revel in sth., se délecter à qch.

revelation, *s.* 1. Révélation *f.* 2. *B:* Revelations, l'Apocalypse *f.*

reveller, *s.* (*a*) Joyeux convive. (*b*) Noceur, -euse.

revelry, *s.* (*a*) Divertissements *mpl,* ébats *mpl.* (*b*) Bacchanale *f,* orgie *f.*

revenge¹, *s.* 1. Vengeance *f.* To take revenge for sth. on s.o., se venger de qch. sur qn. In revenge, pour se venger (*for,* de). 2. *Sp:* Revanche *f.*

revenge², *v.tr.* 1. To revenge oneself, se venger (*on* s.o., sur qn). 2. Venger (une injure). 3. Venger (qn).

revengeful, *a.* 1. Vindicatif. 2. Vengeur, -eresse.

revenue, *s.* Revenu *m,* rentes *fpl.*

reverberate. 1. *v.tr.* (*a*) Renvoyer. (*b*) Réverbérer. 2. *v.i.* (*a*) (*Of sound*) Retentir, résonner. (*b*) (*Of light*) Réverbérer.

reverberation, *s.* (*a*) Renvoi *m* (d'un son). (*b*) Réverbération *f* (de la lumière).

revere, *v.tr.* Révérer, vénérer.

reverence¹, *s.* 1. Respect religieux; révérence *f,* vénération *f.* To pay reverence to s.o., rendre hommage à qn. 2. Your Reverence, monsieur l'abbé.

reverence², *v.tr.* Révérer.

reverend, *a.* 1. Vénérable. 2. *Ecc:* Révérend.

reverent, *a.* Respectueux; plein de vénération. -ly, *adv.* Avec respect.

reversal, *s.* 1. *Jur:* Réforme *f,* annulation *f.* 2. Reversal of opinion, revirement *m* d'opinion.

reverse¹, *a.* Inverse, contraire, opposé (*to,* à). The reverse side of a medal, le revers, l'envers *m,* d'une médaille.

reverse², *s.* 1. Inverse *m,* contraire *m,* opposé *m.* To be quite the reverse of s.o., être tout le contraire de qn. 2. Revers *m* (d'une médaille). 3. Reverse of fortune, revers de fortune. To suffer a reverse, essuyer un revers.

reverse³, *v.tr.* 1. Renverser. 2. (*a*) Invertir

(l'ordre). (b) *Aut:* To reverse one's car, *abs.* to reverse, faire marche arrière. 3. *Jur:* Réformer (un jugement). 4. *v.i. Danc:* Valser de gauche à droite. **reversed,** *a.* 1. Renversé. 2. Inverse, contraire, opposé. **reversion,** *s.* Retour *m. Biol:* Reversion to type, réversion *f* (au type primitif).

revert, *v.i.* (a) Revenir, retourner (*to,* à). (b) *Biol:* To revert to type, revenir au type primitif. (c) To revert to our subject, pour en revenir à notre sujet.

review[1], *s.* 1. *Mil:* Revue *f.* 2. Examen *m,* revue (du passé). 3. Compte rendu (d'un livre). 4. *Publ:* Revue.

review[2], *v.tr.* 1. Passer en revue. 2. To review a book, faire le compte rendu d'un livre.

reviewer, *s.* Critique *m* (littéraire).

revile, *v.tr.* Injurier; insulter à (qn).

revise, *v.tr.* 1. Revoir, relire; corriger, reviser. 2. Reviser (les lois).

revision, *s.* Revision *f.*

revisit, *v.tr.* Visiter de nouveau; revisiter; revenir voir (sa maison natale).

revival, *s.* 1. Renaissance *f* (des arts); reprise *f* (d'une pièce de théâtre). 2. Retour *m* à la vie; retour des forces. 3. Religious revival, renouveau religieux.

revive. 1. *v.i.* (a) Ressusciter; reprendre ses sens. (b) *His spirits revived,* son courage se ranima. (c) Reprendre; (*of arts*) renaître. *Industry is reviving,* l'industrie reprend. 2. *v.tr.* (a) Faire revivre; ressusciter. (b) Ranimer (les espérances); renouveler (un usage). *To r. s.o.'s courage,* remonter le courage de qn. (c) Remettre au théâtre; ressusciter.

revocable, *a.* Révocable.

revocation, *s.* Révocation *f;* abrogation *f.*

revoke[1], *s. Cards:* Fausse renonce.

revoke[2]. 1. *v.tr.* Révoquer (un ordre); rétracter (une promesse). 2. *v.i. Cards:* Faire une fausse renonce.

revolt[1], *s.* Révolte *f.*

revolt[2]. 1. *v.i.* Se révolter, se soulever (*from, against,* contre). 2. *v.tr.* Révolter, indigner.

revolting, *a.* Révoltant.

revolution, *s.* 1. (a) Rotation *f.* (b) Tour *m,* révolution *f.* 2. *Pol:* Révolution.

revolutionary, *a. & s.* Révolutionnaire (*mf*).

revolutionize, *v.tr.* Révolutionner.

revolve. 1. *v.tr.* (a) Retourner, ruminer. (b) Faire tourner. 2. *v.i.* Tourner. **revolving,** *a.* 1. En rotation. 2. R. bookcase, bibliothèque tournante.

revolver, *s.* Revolver *m.*

revue, *s Th:* Revue *f.*

revulsion, *s.* Revirement *m. R. from s.o.,* réaction *f* contre qn.

reward[1], *s.* Récompense *f.*

reward[2], *v.tr.* Récompenser, rémunérer (*s.o. for sth.,* qn de qch.).

rhapsodize, *v.i. F:* To rhapsodize over sth., s'extasier sur qch.

rhapsody, *s.* 1. Rapsodie *f.* 2. *F:* Transports *mpl.*

rhea, *s. Orn:* Rhée *f,* nandou *m.*

Rheims. *Pr.n. Geog:* Reims *m.*

rhetoric, *s.* Rhétorique *f,* éloquence *f.*

rhetorical, *a.* (a) De rhétorique. (b) (Style) ampoulé.

rheumatic, *a.* Rhumatismal, -aux. *R. person, s.* rheumatic, rhumatisant, -ante.

rheumatics, *s.pl. F:* Rhumatisme *m*

rheumatism, *s.* Rhumatisme *m.*

Rhine (the). *Pr.n.* Le Rhin.

rhinoceros, *s.* Rhinocéros *m.*

rhizome, *s. Bot:* Rhizome *m.*

Rhodesia. *Pr.n. Geog:* La Rhodésie *f.*

rhododendron, *s. Bot:* Rhododendron *m.*

rhombus, *s. Geom:* Losange *m;* rhombe *m.*

rhubarb, *s. Bot:* Rhubarbe *f.*

rhyme[1], *s.* 1. *Pros:* Rime *f. F: Without rhyme or reason,* sans rime ni raison. 2. *Usu. pl.* Vers (rimés); poésie *f.* In rhyme, en vers.

rhyme[2]. 1. *v.i.* (a) Rimer; faire des vers. (b) Rimer (*with,* avec). 2. *v.tr.* Faire rimer.

rhythm, *s.* Rythme *m,* cadence *f.*

rhythmic(al), *a.* Rythmique, cadencé. *R. tread,* marche scandée. **-ally,** *adv.* Avec rythme; avec cadence.

rib, *s.* 1. *Anat:* Côte *f.* 2. Nervure *f* (d'une feuille). 3. (a) Baleine *f* (de parapluie). (b) *N.Arch:* Membre *m,* membrure *f.*

ribald, *a.* Licencieux, impudique.

ribaldry, *s.* Paillardises *fpl.*

ribbon, *s.* 1. Ruban *m.* 2. Ruban (d'une décoration); cordon *m* (d'un ordre). 3. *pl.* To tear sth. to ribbons, mettre qch. en lambeaux.

rice, *s.* Riz *m.* Ground rice, farine *f* de riz.

rice-paper, *s.* Papier *m* de riz. **rice pudding,** *s. Cu:* Riz *m* au lait.

rich, *a.* 1. Riche. The newly rich, les nouveaux riches. To grow rich, s'enrichir. 2. *R.* in hope, riche d'espérances. 3. *F:* (*Of incident*) Très divertissant; impayable. **-ly,** *adv.* 1. Richement. 2. *F: He r. deserves it,* il l'a joliment bien mérité.

riches, *s.pl.* Richesse(s) *f(pl).*

richness, *s.* Richesse *f.*

rick, *s.* Meule *f.*

rickety, *a.* 1. *Med:* Rachitique. 2. *F:* Branlant.

rickshaw, *s.* Pousse-pousse *m inv.*

ricochet[1], *s.* Ricochet *m.*

ricochet[2], *v.i.* Ricocher.

rid, *v.tr.* Débarrasser, délivrer. To get rid of sth., se débarrasser de qch.

riddance, *s.* Débarras *m.* A good riddance! bon débarras!

riddle[1], *s.* Énigme *f,* devinette *f.*

riddle[2], *s.* Crible *m,* claie *f.*

riddle[3], *v.tr.* 1. Cribler; passer au crible. 2. *F:* To riddle s.o. with bullets, cribler qn de balles.

ride[1], *s.* (a) Course *f,* promenade *f* (à cheval). (b) Promenade, voyage *m* (en automobile).

To go for a ride in a carriage, aller se promener en voiture.
ride², *v.* I. *v.i.* **1.** (*a*) Chevaucher ; se promener, monter, à cheval. **To ride astride,** monter à califourchon. *He rides well,* il est bon cavalier. (*b*) *To r.* on an elephant, voyager à dos d'éléphant. **To ride on a bicycle,** se promener à bicyclette. **2.** Aller, se promener, en voiture ; aller en autobus. **3.** **To ride at** anchor, être mouillé. II. **ride,** *v.tr.* **1.** To ride a race, courir une course. **2.** (*a*) To ride a horse, monter un cheval. *To r.* an *elephant,* être monté à dos d'éléphant. **To ride a bicycle,** aller à bicyclette. (*b*) To ride one's horse at a fence, diriger son cheval sur une barrière. (*c*) Ridden by fear, hanté par la peur. **3.** *The ship rides the waves,* le navire vogue sur les flots. **ride away,** *v.i.* Partir, s'éloigner (à cheval). **ride back,** *v.i.* (S'en) retourner, s'en revenir (à cheval). **ride behind,** *v.i.* **1.** Monter en croupe. **2.** Suivre à cheval. **ride by,** *v.i.* Passer (à cheval). **ride down,** *v.tr.* Écraser, piétiner. **ride off,** *v.i.* Partir, s'éloigner (à cheval). **ride out.** **1.** *v.i.* Sortir (à cheval). **2.** *v.tr.* To ride out the storm, *Nau:* étaler la tempête.
riding, *s.* Équitation *f* ; exercice *m* à cheval. Riding costume, habit *m* de cavalier. **riding-boots,** *s.pl.* Bottes *f* (à l'écuyère). **riding-breeches,** *s.pl.* Culotte *f* de cheval. **riding-habit,** *s.* *Cost:* Amazone *f.* **riding-hood,** *s.* *A:* Capuchon *m.* Little Red Riding Hood, le petit Chaperon rouge. **riding-whip,** *s.* Cravache *f.*
rider, *s.* **1.** Cavalier, -ière ; (*in circus*) écuyer, -ère. **2.** Ajouté *m,* annexe *f.*
ridge, *s.* **1.** (*a*) Arête *f,* crête *f.* (*b*) Faîte *m,* crête (d'un comble). **2.** Chaîne *f,* rangée *f* (de coteaux). **3.** *Agr:* Billon *m,* butte *f.* **4.** Ride *f* (sur le sable).
ridicule¹, *s.* Moquerie *f,* raillerie *f,* dérision *f.* To hold up to ridicule, se moquer de.
ridicule², *v.tr.* Se moquer de, ridiculiser.
ridiculous, *a.* Ridicule. *It is perfectly r.,* c'est d'un ridicule achevé. **-ly,** *adv.* Ridiculement.
ridiculousness, *s.* Ridicule *m.*
rife, *pred.a.* To be rife, régner, sévir ; (*of rumour*) courir les rues.
riff-raff, *s.* *Coll.* Canaille *f,* racaille *f.*
rifle¹, *v.tr.* Piller.
rifle², *s.* **1.** Fusil (rayé). **Magazine rifle,** fusil à répétition. **2.** *pl.* Rifles, fusiliers *m,* fantassins *m.* **rifle-club,** *s.* Société *f* de tir. **rifle-range,** *s.* Champ *m* de tir. **rifle-shot,** *s.* **1.** Within rifle-shot, à portée de fusil. **2.** Coup *m* de fusil.
rifle³, *v.tr.* Rayer (une pièce à feu). **rifling,** *s.* **1.** Rayage *m* (d'un fusil). **2.** Rayure(s) *f.*
rifleman, *s.* Chasseur *m* à pied ; fusilier *m.*
rift, *s.* Fente *f* ; fissure *f.* R. *in the clouds,* éclaircie *f.*
rig¹, *s.* **1.** Gréement *m* (d'un navire). **2.** *F:* Rig(-out), toilette *f,* tenue *f.*

rig², *v.tr.* Gréer, équiper (un navire). **rig out,** *v.tr.* *F:* Attifer, accoutrer. **rig-out,** *s.* **1.** *See* RIG¹ 2. **2.** Trousseau *m,* équipement *m.* **rigging,** *s.* Gréement *m,* agrès *mpl.*
right¹. I. *a.* **1.** *Geom:* Right angle, angle droit. **To meet at right angles,** se croiser à angle droit. **2.** Bon, honnête, droit. **More than is right,** plus que de raison. **It is only** right, il n'est que justice (*to, de*). **I thought it right to...,** j'ai cru devoir.... **To take a right view of things,** voir juste. **3.** (*a*) Correct, juste, exact. **To give the r.** answer, répondre juste. *The sum is r.,* l'addition est exacte. **To put an error right,** corriger, rectifier, une erreur. **My watch is right,** ma montre est à l'heure. (*b*) **To be right,** avoir raison. (*c*) **The right word,** le mot juste. **Right side up,** à l'endroit *m.* *The plank is not the r.* width, la planche n'est pas de la largeur voulue. **To put s.o. right,** (i) mettre qn sur la voie ; (ii) détromper qn ; (iii) rectifier les dires de qn. (*d*) **In the right place,** (i) bien placé ; (ii) à sa place. *You came* at the right moment, vous êtes venu au bon moment. **The right thing to do,** ce qu'il y a de mieux à faire. **That's right!** c'est bien cela ! à la bonne heure ! **Quite right!** parfaitement ! *F:* **Right!** bon ! d'accord ! (*e*) **To get on the right side of s.o.,** s'insinuer dans les bonnes grâces de qn. **4.** (*a*) *F:* **As right as rain,** en parfait état. **To be in one's right mind,** avoir toute sa raison. **To set things right,** rétablir les choses. **Things will come right,** les affaires s'arrangeront. (*b*) **All right.** *Everything is all r.,* tout est très bien. **All** right ! c'est bon ! ça y est ! *I'm all r. again* now, je suis tout à fait remis maintenant. **He's all right!** c'est un bon type ! **5.** Droit. **On the right side,** à droite, sur la droite. **-ly,** *adv.* **1.** **To act r.,** bien agir. **2.** Correctement. **Rightly speaking,** à bien prendre les choses. **I cannot rightly say,** je ne saurais dire au juste. **Rightly or wrongly,** à tort ou à raison. II. **right,** *s.* **1.** Le droit ; la justice ; le bien. **Right and wrong,** le bien et le mal. **To be in the right,** avoir raison ; être dans son droit. **2.** (*a*) Droit, titre *m.* **To have a right to sth.,** avoir droit à qch. **He has no right to complain,** il est mal venu à se plaindre. **By what right?** de quel droit ? **In one's own right,** de son chef ; en propre. (*b*) *pl.* **Rights,** droits ; droit. **By rights,** en toute justice. **To be within one's rights,** être dans son droit. **3.** (*a*) **To set things to rights,** rétablir les choses. (*b*) **I want to know the** rights of it, je voudrais en avoir le cœur net. **4.** Droite *f* ; côté droit. **On the right,** à droite. III. **right,** *adv.* **1.** (*a*) Droit. **To go right on,** continuer tout droit. (*b*) *F:* **To do sth. right away,** faire qch. sur-le-champ. **Rail:** Right away! en route ! **2.** (*a*) **To sink right to the bottom,** couler droit au fond. (*b*) **Right at the top,** tout en haut. **Right in the middle,** au beau milieu. *He threw it r. in my face,* il me le jeta en

pleine figure. **3.** (a) To do right, bien faire ; bien agir. (b) (Répondre) correctement ; (deviner) juste. Nothing goes right with me, rien ne me réussit. *F :* He is coming right enough, il va venir sans aucun doute. **4.** A droite. He owes money right and left, il doit de l'argent de tous les côtés. *Mil :* Eyes right! tête à droite! **right-about. I.** *s. Mil :* Demi-tour *m* à droite. *F :* To send s.o. to the right-about, envoyer promener qn. **2.** *adv. Mil :* Right-about turn! demi-tour à droite! **right-angled,** *a.* A angle droit. **right-down.** *F :* **I.** *a.* Right-down thief, franc voleur. **2.** *adv.* He was right-down angry about it, il était tout à fait fâché. **right-hand,** *attrib.a.* (a) De la main droite. (b) On the right-hand side, à droite. Right-hand man, *F :* bras droit. **right-minded,** *a.* **I.** Bien pensant. **2.** *F :* Sain d'esprit.

right², *v.tr.* **I.** Redresser ; remettre d'aplomb. **2.** Redresser, réparer (un tort).

righteous, *a.* **I.** Droit, juste ; vertueux. **2.** Juste, justifié. *R. anger,* juste colère.

righteousness, *s.* Droiture *f,* vertu *f.*

rightful, *a.* Légitime, juste. **-fully,** *adv.* Légitimement ; à juste titre.

rightness, *s.* **I.** Rectitude *f,* droiture *f.* **2.** Justesse *f* (d'une décision).

rigid, *a.* **I.** Rigide, raide. **2.** Sévère, strict. **-ly,** *adv.* **I.** Rigidement. **2.** Sévèrement.

rigidity, *s.* **I.** Rigidité *f.* **2.** Sévérité *f.*

rigmarole, *s.* Discours *m* sans suite.

rigorous, *a.* Rigoureux. **-ly,** *adv.* Rigoureusement ; avec rigueur.

rigour, *s.* Rigueur *f,* sévérité *f.*

rile, *v.tr.* F : Agacer, exaspérer.

rill, *s.* Ruisselet *m* ; petit ruisseau.

rim, *s.* **I.** Jante *f.* **2.** Bord *m.* Spectacle rims, monture *f* de lunettes.

rime, *s.* Givre *m* ; gelée blanche.

rimmed, *a.* A bord ; bordé.

rind, *s.* Peau *f* ; pelure *f* ; couenne *f* (de lard).

ring¹, *s.* **I.** (Finger-)ring, anneau *m* ; (for adornment) bague *f.* Wedding ring, alliance *f.* **2.** Rond *m,* anneau. Napkin ring, rond de serviette. Split ring, anneau brisé. **3.** Anneau ; cerne *m* (autour des yeux) ; aréole *f* (autour de la lune). **4.** Cercle *m.* Sitting in a ring, assis en rond. **5.** (a) Groupe *m,* petite coterie (de personnes). (b) *Com :* Bande noire. **6.** Arène *f,* piste *f.* **7.** *Box :* Enceinte *f,* ring *m.* **ring-dove,** *s.* (Pigeon) ramier *m* ; palombe *f.*

ring², *s.* **I.** Son (clair) ; sonnerie *f* ; tintement *m* ; timbre *m* (de la voix). **2.** (a) Coup *m* de sonnette. There is a ring at the door, on sonne (à la porte). (b) Ring on the telephone, appel *m* téléphonique. I'll give you a ring (up), je vous téléphonerai.

ring³, *v.* **I.** *v.i.* (a) Sonner, tinter. (b) *F :* His answer did not r. true, sa réponse a sonné faux. (c) Résonner, retentir (*with,* de). (d) My ears are ringing, les oreilles me tintent. **2.** *v.tr.* Sonner, faire sonner. Ring the bell!

sonnez ! *Abs.* To ring for the maid, sonner la bonne. **ring off,** *v.tr. Tp : Abs.* To ring off, raccrocher (l'appareil). **ring out,** *v.i.* Sonner ; retentir. **ring up,** *v.tr.* To ring s.o. up, donner un coup de téléphone à qn. **ringing¹,** *a.* Sonore, retentissant. *In r. tones,* d'une voix vibrante. **ringing²,** *s.* **I.** Son *m,* tintement *m.* **2.** Tintement (dans les oreilles).

ringleader, *s.* Meneur *m* ; chef *m* d'émeute.

ringlet, *s.* Boucle *f* (de cheveux).

rinse, *v.tr.* Rincer.

riot¹, *s.* **I.** Émeute *f.* *F :* To read the Riot Act to s.o., semoncer qn d'importance. **2.** Orgie *f* (de couleurs). **3.** To run riot, se déchaîner ; (of plants) pulluler.

riot², *v.i.* S'ameuter. **rioting,** *s.* Émeutes *fpl* ; troubles *mpl.*

rioter, *s.* Émeutier *m,* séditieux *m.*

riotous, *a.* Tumultueux, turbulent. **-ly,** *adv.* Tumultueusement.

rip¹, *s.* Déchirure *f* ; fente *f.*

rip², *v.* **I.** *v.tr.* Fendre ; déchirer. To rip sth. open, ouvrir qch. en le déchirant. **2.** *v.i.* Se déchirer, se fendre. **rip off,** *v.tr.* Arracher. **rip out,** *v.tr.* Arracher. **ripping,** *a. P :* Épatant, fameux.

rip³, *s. F :* Mauvais garnement.

ripe, *a.* **I.** (a) Mûr. (b) A ripe old age, un bel âge. **2.** He is ripe for mischief, il est prêt à faire le mal.

ripen. I. *v.tr.* Mûrir ; faire mûrir. **2.** *v.i.* Mûrir ; venir à maturité.

ripeness, *s.* Maturité *f.*

riposte, *v.i.* Riposter.

ripple, *s.* **I.** (a) Ride *f* (sur l'eau) ; ondulation *f.* (b) Gazouillement *m* (d'un ruisseau). **2.** (In hair) Ondulation.

rise¹, *s.* **I.** (a) Ascension *f. Th :* Rise of the curtain, lever *m* du rideau. (b) *F :* To get a rise out of s.o., mystifier qn ; se payer la tête de qn. **2.** (a) Montée *f,* côte *f* (de route) ; rampe *f.* Rise in the ground, exhaussement *m* du terrain. (b) Éminence *f,* élévation *f.* **3.** (a) Crue *f* (des eaux) ; flot *m* (de la marée) ; hausse *f* (du baromètre) ; élévation (de température). (b) Augmentation *f,* hausse. **4.** Avancement *m* ; élévation. **5.** To give rise to sth., faire naître, engendrer, qch.

rise², *v.i.* **I.** (a) To rise (to one's feet), se lever ; se mettre debout. To rise (up) from table, se lever de table. The horse rose on its hind legs, le cheval se dressa sur ses pieds de derrière. (b) To rise early, se lever tôt. **2.** To rise (in revolt), se soulever (*against,* contre). **3.** Se lever ; monter, s'élever. **4.** (a) The barometer is rising, le baromètre est à la hausse. (b) In the distance rises a castle, au loin s'élève, se dresse, un château. (c) The wind is rising, le vent s'élève. (d) Everything has risen in price, tout a augmenté de prix. **5.** (a) To rise above vanity, être au-dessus de la vanité. (b) *F :* To rise to the occasion, se montrer à la hauteur de la situation. **6.** To rise in the world, faire son chemin. He rose from nothing, il est parti de rien. **7.** Prendre sa source (*at*, à; *in*, dans). **rising**[1], *a.* **1.** (Soleil) levant. **2.** (Route) qui monte; (baromètre) en hausse. Rising ground, élévation *f* de terrain. Rising tide, marée montante. **3.** (Vent) qui se lève; (colère) croissante. **4.** Rising man, homme d'avenir. **5.** The rising generation, la nouvelle génération. **rising**[2], *s.* **1.** Not to like early rising, ne pas aimer à se lever tôt. **2.** Ameutement *m*, soulèvement *m*. **3.** Lever *m* (d'un astre). **4.** Hausse *f* (du baromètre); crue *f* (des eaux); poussée *f* (de la sève).

riser, *s.* Early riser, personne matinale.

risk[1], *s.* Risque *m*, péril *m*. To take risks, courir des risques.

risk[2], *v.tr.* Risquer. (*a*) Aventurer, hasarder. *F:* To risk one's own skin, risquer sa peau. (*b*) I'll risk it, je vais risquer le coup.

risky, *a.* Hasardeux, chanceux.

rissole, *s. Cu:* Rissole *f.*

rite, *s.* Rite *m.*

ritual. **1.** *a.* Rituel; selon le rite. **2.** *s.* Rites *mpl.*

ritualism, *s. Ecc:* Ritualisme *m.*

ritualist, *s.* Ritualiste *mf.*

rival[1], *a. & s.* (*a*) Rival, -ale, *pl.* -aux, -ales; concurrent, -ente. (*b*) Émule *mf.*

rival[2], *v.tr.* (*a*) Rivaliser avec. (*b*) Être l'émule de.

rivalry, *s.* (*a*) Rivalité *f.* (*b*) Émulation *f.*

rive, *v.tr.* Fendre.

river, *s.* **1.** Cours *m* d'eau; (*main r.*) fleuve *m*; (*small r.*) rivière *f.* **2.** Coulée *f* (de lave).

riverside, *s.* Bord *m* de l'eau; rive *f.*

rivet[1], *s.* Rivet *m.*

rivet[2], *v.tr.* (*a*) River, riveter. (*b*) *F:* To rivet the attention, fixer l'attention.

Riviera (the). *Pr.n.* La Côte d'Azur.

rivulet, *s.* Ruisseau *m.*

roach, *s. Ich:* Gardon *m.*

road, *s.* **1.** Route *f*, chemin *m*, voie *f.* (*a*) High road, main road, grand chemin, grande route. Road transport, transports routiers. (*b*) To take the road, se mettre en route; partir. The road to success, la voie du succès. **2.** Chaussée *f.* **3.** *Nau:* Roads, rade *f.* **road-book**, *s.* Itinéraire *m*; guide routier. **road-house**, *s.* Auberge *f*, hôtel *m*; hôtellerie *f* en bord de route. **road-map**, *s.* Carte routière. **road-mender**, *s.* Cantonnier *m.*

roadside, *s.* Bord *m*, côté *m*, de la route, de la chaussée.

roadstead, *s. Nau:* Rade *f.*

roadway, *s.* Chaussée *f.*

roam, *v.i.* Errer, rôder. **roaming**[1], *a.* Errant, vagabond. **roaming**[2], *s.* Course errante.

roan, *a.* Rouan, -anne.

roar[1], *s.* **1.** (*a*) Hurlement *m*; rugissement *m.* Roars of laughter, grands éclats de rire.

(*b*) Rugissement (du lion). **2.** Grondement *m* (de canon); mugissement *m* (de la mer).

roar[2], *v.i.* (*a*) Hurler, rugir. (*b*) (*Of lion*) Rugir. (*c*) (*Of sea*) Mugir. **roaring**[1], *a.* **1.** (Lion) rugissant. **2.** To do a roaring trade, faire un gros commerce. **roaring**[2], *s.* = ROAR[1].

roast[1], *s. Cu:* Rôti *m.*

roast[2], *v.* **1.** *v.tr.* (*a*) Rôtir, faire rôtir. (*b*) Griller, torréfier (le café). (*c*) *F:* Railler, berner. **2.** *v.i.* Rôtir. **roast**[3], *a. R.* meat, viande rôtie. Roast beef, rôti *m* de bœuf; rosbif *m.*

rob, *v.tr.* Voler; piller (un verger); *abs. F:* brigander. To rob s.o. of sth., voler qch. à qn.

robber, *s.* Voleur, -euse.

robbery, *s.* Vol qualifié. *A:* Highway robbery, vol de grand chemin; brigandage *m.*

robe[1], *s.* **1.** Robe *f.* **2.** Vêtement *m.*

robe[2]. **1.** *v.tr.* Revêtir d'une robe d'office. **2.** *v.i.* Revêtir sa robe.

Robert. *Pr.n.* Robert *m.*

Robin. **1.** *Pr.n.* Robin Hood, Robin *m* des bois. **2.** *s.* (*a*) *Orn:* Robin (redbreast), rougegorge *m.* (*b*) *Bot:* Ragged robin, lychnide *f* des prés.

robot, *s.* Automate *m.*

robust, *a.* Robuste, vigoureux, solide.

rock[1], *s.* **1.** (*a*) Rocher *m*, roc *m.* (*b*) *Geol:* Roche *f.* **2.** A rock, un rocher, une roche. *Nau:* To run upon the rocks, donner sur les écueils. *F:* To see rocks ahead, voir des obstacles devant soi. *F:* To be on the rocks, être dans la débine. **rock-bottom**, *s. F:* Le fin fond. Rock-bottom price, prix le plus bas. **rock-crystal**, *s. Miner:* Cristal *m* de roche. **rock-garden**, *s.* Jardin *m* de rocaille. **rock-plant**, *s.* Plante *f* des rochers. **rock-salt**, *s.* Sel *m* gemme.

rock[2]. **1.** *v.tr.* (*a*) Bercer, balancer; basculer. To rock a cradle, balancer un berceau. (*b*) The earthquake rocks the house, le tremblement de terre ébranle la maison. **2.** *v.i.* The cradle rocks, le berceau balance. **rocking**[1], *a.* **1.** Oscillant. **2.** Branlant. **rocking-chair**, *s.* Fauteuil *m*, chaise *f*, à bascule. **rocking-horse**, *s.* Cheval *m*, -aux, à bascule. **rocking**[2], *s.* **1.** Balancement *m*, bercement *m*; oscillation *f.* **2.** Tremblement *m*, branlement *m.*

rockery, *s. Hort:* Rochers artificiels.

rocket, *s. Pyr:* Fusée *f.*

rockiness, *s.* Nature rocheuse, rocailleuse.

rocky, *a.* De roche; rocheux. The Rocky Mountains, les montagnes Rocheuses.

rod, *s.* **1.** Baguette *f.* **2.** Verge *f.* *F:* To make a rod for one's own back, se préparer des ennuis. To have a rod in pickle for s.o., avoir une dent contre qn. **3.** Verge (d'huissier). *F:* To rule s.o. with a rod of iron, mener qn à la baguette. **4.** Rod and line, ligne *f* de pêche. **5.** *Meas:* Perche *f.* **6.** Stair rod, tringle *f* d'escalier.

rodent, *s. Z:* Rongeur *m.*

roe¹, *s.* Z: Roe(-deer), chevreuil *m.*
roe², *s.* (*a*) (Hard) roe, œufs *mpl* (de poisson).
(*b*) Soft roe, laite *f*, laitance *f.*
roebuck, *s.* Chevreuil *m.*
Roger. *Pr.n.* Roger *m.* A: **The Jolly
Roger**, le pavillon noir (des pirates).
rogue, *s.* **1.** Coquin, -ine; fripon, -onne.
2. Malin, -igne; espiègle *mf.* **3.** (Éléphant)
solitaire *m.*
roguery, *s.* **1.** Coquinerie *f*, friponnerie *f*,
fourberie *f.* **2.** Malice *f*, espièglerie *f.*
roguish, *a.* **1.** Coquin, polisson, -onne; de
coquin(e). **2.** Malin, -igne, espiègle. **-ly**,
adv. **1.** En fripon(ne), en fourbe. **2.** Avec
espièglerie.
roguishness, *s.* = ROGUERY.
roisterer, *s.* Tapageur, -euse.
Roland. *Pr.n.* Roland *m.*
rôle, *s.* *Th. & F:* Rôle *m.*
roll¹, *s.* **1.** (*a*) Rouleau *m*; pièce *f* (d'étoffe).
(*b*) *Bak:* Roll of bread, petit pain. **2.** *Adm:*
Rôle *m*, contrôle *m*, liste *f.* **To call the roll**,
faire l'appel. *Jur:* **To strike off the rolls**,
rayer du tableau. **roll-call**, *s.* *Mil:* Appel
(nominal).
roll², *s.* **1.** *Nau:* Coup *m* de roulis. *F:* **To
walk with a roll**, se dandiner en marchant.
2. **To have a roll on the grass**, se rouler par
terre. **3.** Roulement *m* (de tambour).
roll³. I. *v.tr.* **1.** Rouler. **2.** **To roll one's
r's**, rouler les r; grasseyer. **3.** Rouler,
passer au rouleau. II. **roll**, *v.i.* Rouler.
1. (*a*) *The tears rolled down his cheeks*, les
larmes coulaient sur ses joues. (*b*) *His eyes
were rolling*, les yeux lui roulaient dans la
tête. **2.** *F:* **To be rolling in wealth**, rouler sur
l'or. **3.** Gronder, rouler. **roll over.** **1.**
v.tr. Retourner; culbuter. **2.** *v.i.* Se retourner
(en roulant). *To r. over and over*, rouler sur
soi-même. **roll up**, *v.tr.* (*a*) Rouler, enrouler (une carte); relever, retrousser (ses
manches). (*b*) Envelopper. **To roll oneself
up in a blanket**, s'enrouler dans une couverture. **rolling¹**, *a.* **1.** Roulant. **2.** **To have
a rolling gait**, se balancer en marchant. **3.**
Rolling country, contrée ondulée. **rolling-
stock**, *s.* *Rail:* Matériel roulant. **rolling²**,
s. **1.** Roulement *m.* **2.** Roulis *m* (d'un navire).
rolling-pin, *s.* *Cu:* Rouleau *m.*
roller, *s.* **1.** (*a*) Rouleau *m* (de pâtissier);
enrouleur *m* (de store). (*b*) (Rouleau) compresseur. Garden roller, rouleau de jardin.
2. *Nau:* Lame *f* de houle. **roller-skates**,
s.pl. Patins *m* à roulettes. **roller-towel**, *s.*
Essuie-main(s) *m* à rouleau.
rollicking, *a.* D'une gaieté exubérante.
Roman, *a. & s.* Romain, -aine. Roman
nose, nez busqué, aquilin. **Roman Catholic**, *a. & s.* Catholique (*mf*).
romance¹, *s.* **1.** The Romance languages,
les langues romanes. **2.** Histoire *f* romanesque. It's quite a romance, c'est tout un
roman. **3.** *Mus:* Romance *f.*
romance², *v.i.* Exagérer.

romantic, *a.* (*a*) Romanesque. (*b*) R. site,
site pittoresque. (*c*) *Lit:* Romantique.
Rome. *Pr.n.* Rome *f.* *Ecc:* The Church of
Rome, l'Église romaine.
romp¹, *s.* Gambades *fpl*; jeu turbulent.
romp², *v.i.* S'ébattre (bruyamment).
rondo, *s.* *Mus:* Rondeau *m.*
rood, *s.* *Meas:* Quart *m* d'arpent.
roof¹, *s.* **1.** Toit *m*, toiture *f*, comble *m.*
F: To lift the roof, applaudir à tout casser.
2. Roof of the mouth, dôme *m* du palais ;
le palais.
roof², *v.tr.* *Const:* Couvrir (une maison).
roofing, *s.* Toiture *f.*
rook¹, *s.* **1.** *Orn:* Freux *m.* **2.** *F:* Filou *m.*
rook², *v.tr.* *F:* Refaire, rouler.
rook³, *s.* *Chess:* Tour *f.*
rookery, *s.* Colonie *f* de freux.
room, *s.* **1.** (*a*) Place *f*, espace *m.* **To be
cramped for room**, être à l'étroit. **To make
room for s.o.**, faire place à qn. (*b*) **In s.o.'s
room**, au lieu de qn; à la place de qn.
2. That leaves no room for doubt, le doute
n'est plus permis. There is room for improvement, cela laisse à désirer. **3.** (*a*) Pièce
f; salle *f.* **(Bed)room**, chambre *f* (à coucher).
Reception rooms, appartements *m* de réception. **Private room**, cabinet particulier;
(*in hotel*) salon réservé. (*b*) *pl.* (Set of) rooms,
appartement *m.* **To live in rooms**, vivre en
garni.
roomy, *a.* Spacieux ; (vêtement) ample.
roost¹, *s.* Juchoir *m*, perchoir *m.* **To go to
roost**, (i) (*of hens*) se jucher; (ii) *F:* aller se
coucher. (*Of crime*) To come home to roost,
retourner sur son auteur.
roost², *v.i.* Se jucher. **roosting**, *a.* Perché,
juché.
rooster, *s.* Coq *m.*
root¹, *s.* **1.** Racine *f.* **2.** Source *f*, fondement
m. Root ideas, idées fondamentales. Root
cause, cause première. **3.** *Mth:* Square root,
racine carrée. **4.** *Ling:* Racine.
root². **1.** *v.tr.* Enraciner. *F:* **To remain
rooted to the spot**, rester cloué sur place.
2. *v.i.* S'enraciner; prendre racine. **root
out, up**, *v.tr.* Déraciner; extirper (un
abus). **rooted**, *a.* *F:* Enraciné, invétéré.
root³, *v.i.* (*a*) Fouiller avec le groin. (*b*) *F:*
To root among papers, fouiller dans des
paperasses.
rope¹, *s.* **1.** Corde *f*, cordage *m.* *Nau:* Filin
m. *F:* **To know the ropes**, connaître son
affaire. **To put s.o. up to the ropes**, mettre
qn au courant. **To give s.o. rope**, lâcher la
bride à qn. **2.** Grand collier (de perles).
rope-ladder, *s.* Échelle *f* de corde.
rope's-end, *s.* Bout *m* de corde.
rope², *v.tr.* **1.** Corder. **2.** *Climbers roped
together*, ascensionnistes en cordée.
rosary, *s.* Rosaire *m.*
rose, *s.* **1.** Rose *f.* *F:* Under the rose, en
cachette. **2.** Pomme *f* (d'arrosoir). **3.** (*Colour*)
Rose *m.* **rose-bush**, *s.* Rosier *m.* **rose-
coloured**, *a.* Rose, rosé; couleur de rose

inv. F : To see things through rose-coloured spectacles, voir tout en rose. **rose-leaf,** *s.* Feuille *f* de rose ; pétale *m* de rose. **rose-red,** *a.* Vermeil. **rosc-tree,** *s.* Rosier *m.* **rose-water,** *s.* Eau *f* de rose.

roseate, *a.* Couleur de rose *inv* ; rose, rosé.

rosebud, *s.* Bouton *m* de rose.

rosemary, *s. Bot :* Romarin *m.*

rosette, *s.* Chou *m,* -oux (de ruban) ; cocarde *f* ; rosette *f.*

rosewood, *s.* Palissandre *m.*

rosin, *s.* Colophane *f.*

rostrum, *s.* Tribune *f.*

rosy, *a.* De rose ; rose, rosé. *R. cheeks,* joues vermeilles. *A r. prospect,* une perspective souriante.

rot¹, *s.* **1.** Pourriture *f,* carie *f.* **2.** *F :* Blague *f,* bêtises *fpl.* **3.** Démoralisation *f.*

rot², *v.* **1.** *v.i.* (Se) pourrir ; se putréfier, se carier. **2.** *v.tr.* Pourrir, faire pourrir ; putréfier, carier.

rota, *s.* Liste *f* de roulement ; tableau *m.*

rotary, *a.* Rotatif, rotatoire. *R. motion,* mouvement de rotation.

rotate. 1. *v.i.* Tourner. **2.** *v.tr.* Faire tourner.

rotation, *s.* **1.** (Mouvement *m* de) rotation *f.* **2.** *(a)* Succession *f* tour à tour. In rotation, à tour de rôle. *(b) Agr :* Rotation of crops, assolement *m.* **3.** Rotation, tour *m.*

rotatory, *a.* Rotatoire ; de rotation.

rote, *s.* Routine *f.* To learn sth. by rote, apprendre qch. mécaniquement.

rotten, *a.* **1.** Pourri, carié. *F :* He is rotten to the core, il est pourri de vices. **2.** *P :* De mauvaise qualité ; *F :* lamentable ; *P :* moche. Rotten luck! quelle guigne !

rottenness, *s.* État *m* de pourriture.

rotter, *s.* Raté *m* ; propre *m* à rien.

rotund, *a.* Rond, arrondi.

rotunda, *s. Arch :* Rotonde *f.*

rotundity, *s.* Rondeur *f,* rotondité *f.*

rouble, *s. Num :* Rouble *m.*

rouge¹, *s. Toil :* Rouge *m,* fard *m,* carmin *m.*

rouge², *v.tr.* Mettre du rouge ; se farder.

rough¹. I. *a.* **1.** *(a)* Rêche, rugueux, rude. *(b) (Of road)* Raboteux, rude ; *(of ground)* inégal, accidenté. *(c)* In the rough state, à l'état brut. **2.** Grossier ; brutal, -aux. *R. sea,* mer agitée. *Nau :* Rough weather, gros temps. *To have a r. crossing,* faire une mauvaise traversée. Rough play, jeu brutal. *To give s.o. a r. handling,* malmener qn. **3.** Grossier ; bourru, rude. **4.** Approximatif. *R. translation,* traduction à peu près. Rough draft, brouillon *m.* Rough estimate, évaluation en gros. **5.** *(Of voice)* Rude. **-ly,** *adv.* **1.** Rudement, brutalement. *To treat s.o. r.,* malmener qn. **2.** Grossièrement. **3.** Approximativement ; à peu près ; en gros. Roughly speaking, en général. II. **rough,** *adv.* Rudement, grossièrement. III. **rough,** *s.* **1.** One must take the rough with the smooth, il faut prendre le bénéfice avec les charges. **2.** Voyou

m, bandit *m.* **rough-and-ready,** *a.* **1.** Exécuté grossièrement. *R.-and-r. installation,* installation de fortune. **2.** Cavalier ; sans façon. **rough-and-tumble,** *s.* Mêlée *f,* bousculade.

rough², *v.tr. F :* To rough it, en voir de dures.

roughen, *v.tr.* Rendre rude, rugueux.

roughness, *s.* **1.** Rudesse *f,* aspérité *f,* rugosité *f.* **2.** *(a)* Grossièreté *f* ; manières bourrues. *(b)* Agitation *f* (de la mer) ; rudesse (du temps). **3.** Rudesse (de la voix).

roughshod, *a. F :* To ride roughshod over s.o., traiter qn sans ménagement.

roulette, *s.* Roulette *f.*

round¹. I. *a.* **1.** Rond, circulaire. Round shoulders, épaules voûtées. **2.** Round dance, danse en rond ; ronde *f.* Round towel, essuie-main(s) à rouleau. **3.** *(a)* Round dozen, bonne douzaine. In round figures, en chiffres ronds. *(b)* To go at a good round pace, aller bon train. **-ly,** *adv.* Rondement, vivement. II. **round,** *s.* **1.** Cercle *m,* rond *m.* **2.** *Cu :* Round of beef, tranche grasse. *R. of toast,* rôtie *f.* **3.** *F :* The daily round, le train-train quotidien. **One** continual round of pleasures, une succession perpétuelle de plaisirs. **4.** *(a)* Tour *m.* To have a round of golf, faire une tournée de golf. *F :* The story went the round, l'histoire a passé de bouche en bouche. *(b)* Tournée *f.* (du facteur). *(c) Mil :* Ronde *f.* **5.** *Box :* Round *m,* reprise *f.* **6.** *(a) F :* Round of applause, salve *f* d'applaudissements. *(b) Mil :* Round of ammunition, cartouche *f.* **round-eyed,** *a.* To stare round-eyed, ouvrir de grands yeux étonnés. **round robin,** *s.* Pétition revêtue de signatures en rond. **round-shouldered,** *a.* Au dos voûté, bombé.

round². I. *adv.* **1.** *(a)* To go round, tourner. *To turn round and round,* tournoyer. To turn round (about), se retourner. *(b)* All the year round, (pendant) toute l'année. Winter came round, l'hiver arriva. **2.** *(a) Garden with a wall right round,* jardin avec un mur tout autour. To be six feet round, avoir six pieds de tour. *(b)* All the country round, tout le pays à l'entour. For a mile round, à un mille à la ronde. **3.** To hand round the cakes, faire circuler les gâteaux. There is not enough to go round, il n'y en a pas pour tout le monde. **4.** It's a long way round, cela fait un grand détour. II. **round,** *prep.* **1.** *(a)* Autour de. *(b) To row r. the island,* faire le tour de l'île à la rame. **2.** To go round an obstacle, contourner un obstacle.

round³. 1. *v.tr. Nau :* Doubler (un cap). **2.** *v.i. F :* To round on s.o., s'en prendre inopinément à qn. **round up,** *v.tr.* Rassembler (du bétail) ; cerner, rafler (des filous). **round-up,** *s.* *(a)* Rassemblement *m* (du bétail). *(b)* Rafle *f* (de filous).

rounded, *a.* Arrondi.

roundabout. I. *s.* **1.** (Manège *m* de) chevaux *mpl* de bois; carrousel *m*. **2.** *Aut:* Sens *m* gyro; circulation *f* giratoire. II.
roundabout, *a.* Détourné, indirect.
rounders, *s.pl.* *Games:* Balle *f* au camp.
Roundhead, *s.* *Hist:* Tête ronde.
roundish, *a.* Rondelet, -ette.
roundness, *s.* Rondeur *f.*
rouse. I. *v.tr.* **1.** (*a*) To rouse s.o. (from sleep), réveiller qn. *To r. the camp,* donner l'alerte au camp. **To rouse the masses,** remuer, activer, les masses. (*b*) Mettre en colère. *He is terrible when roused,* il est terrible quand il est monté. **2.** Susciter (l'admiration). II. **rouse,** *v.i.* To rouse (up), (i) se réveiller; (ii) se secouer. **rousing,** *a.* *R. cheers,* applaudissements chaleureux. *R. speech,* discours enlevant.
rout¹, *s.* *Mil:* Déroute *f*; débandade *f.*
rout², *v.tr.* *Mil:* Mettre en déroute.
routed, *a.* En déroute.
rout³, *v.tr.* *& i.* Fouiller. **rout out,** *v.tr.* Dénicher; tirer de son lit, etc.
route, *s.* Itinéraire *m*; route *f*, voie *f.*
route-march, *s.* *Mil:* Marche *f* d'entraînement.
routine, *s.* Routine *f.* **Routine work,** affaires courantes; *Adm:* service de détail.
rove. I. *v.i.* Rôder; vagabonder, errer. **2.** *v.tr.* Parcourir. **roving¹,** *a.* Vagabond, nomade. **roving²,** *s.* Vagabondage *m.*
rover¹, *s.* Coureur *m*; vagabond *m.*
rover², *s.* *Nau:* Écumeur *m* de mer.
row¹, *s.* **1.** Rang *m*, rangée *f*; ligne *f.* In a row, en rang, en ligne. In rows, par rangs. **2.** Rang (de chaises). **In the front row,** au premier rang.
row², *s.* **1.** Promenade *f* en canot. **2.** *It was a long row,* il a fallu ramer longtemps.
row³. I. *v.i.* (*a*) Ramer. *Nau:* Nager. *To row hard,* faire force de rames. **To row a race,** une course d'aviron. (*b*) Canoter. **2.** *v.tr.* Conduire à l'aviron. **rowing,** *s.* **1.** Conduite *f* à l'aviron. *Nau:* Nage *f. Sp:* Canotage *m.* **row(ing)-boat,** *s.* Bateau *m* à rames; canot *m* à l'aviron.
row⁴, *s.* **1.** Chahut *m*, tapage *m*, vacarme *m*. **To make a row,** faire du chahut; faire du tapage. **2.** Rixe *f*, dispute *f*; scène *f.* **3.** Réprimande *f*; *F:* savon *m.* **To get into a row,** se faire laver la tête.
row⁵. I. *v.tr.* *F:* Attraper, semoncer. **2.** *v.i.* Se quereller (*with s.o.,* avec qn).
rowdiness, *s.* Turbulence *f*; tapage *m.*
rowdy. I. *a.* Tapageur, -euse. **2.** *s.* Voyou *m.*
rowdyism, *s.* Chahutage *m*; désordre *m.*
rowel, *s.* Molette *f* (d'éperon).
rower, *s.* Rameur, -euse; canotier *m.*
rowlocks, *s.pl.* Dames *f* de nage.
royal, *a.* (*a*) Royal, -aux. *The R. household,* la maison du roi. (*b*) Royal, princier. **To have a (right) royal time,** s'amuser follement.
-ally, *adv.* Royalement.
royalist, *a.* *& s.* Royaliste (*mf*).

royalty, *s.* **1.** Royauté *f.* **2.** *pl.* Royalties, redevance *f*; droits *m* d'auteur.
rub¹, *s.* **1.** Frottement *m*; friction *f.* **2.** *F:* There's the rub, voilà le hic!
rub², *v.* **1.** *v.tr.* (*a*) Frotter. **To rub one's hands (together),** se frotter les mains. *F:* To rub shoulders with other people, se frotter au monde. **To rub s.o. (up) the wrong way,** contrarier qn. (*b*) To rub sth. dry, sécher qch. en le frottant. (*c*) *To rub sth. over a surface,* enduire une surface de qch. **2.** *v.i.* Frotter (*against,* contre); se frotter (contre). **rub along,** *v.i.* *F:* Se débrouiller. **rub down,** *v.tr.* (*a*) Panser (un cheval). (*b*) Frictionner (qn). **rub-down,** *s.* Friction *f.* To give s.o. a rub-down, frictionner qn. **rub in,** *v.tr.* *F:* Don't rub it in! n'insistez pas davantage. **rub out,** *v.tr.* Effacer. **rub up.** **1.** *v.tr.* Astiquer, frotter, fourbir. *F:* To rub up one's memory, rafraîchir sa mémoire. **2.** *v.i.* To rub up against other people, se frotter au monde. **rubbing,** *s.* Frottage *m.*
rub-a-dub, *s.* Rataplan *m.*
rubber¹, *s.* **1.** Frottoir *m.* **2.** (*a*) (India-) rubber, gomme *f* à effacer. (*b*) (India-) rubber, caoutchouc *m.* (India-)rubber band, élastique *m.*
rubber², *s.* *Cards:* Robre *m.* **The rubber game,** la belle.
rubbish, *s.* **1.** (*a*) Immondices *fpl*, détritus *mpl.* (*b*) Fatras *m*; choses *fpl* sans valeur. (*c*) Camelote *f.* **2.** To talk rubbish, dire des bêtises*f.* (**What**) rubbish! quelle blague!
rubbishy, *a.* Sans valeur; de camelote.
rubble, *s.* *Const:* Blocaille *f.*
rubicund, *a.* Rubicond; rougeaud.
ruby. **1.** *s.* *Miner:* Rubis *m.* **2.** *a.* *& s.* Couleur de rubis; rouge (*m*).
ruck, *s.* To get out of the ruck, sortir du rang.
rucksack, *s.* Sac *m* touriste.
ruction, *s.* *F:* Désordre *m*, scène *f.* **There will be ructions,** il va y avoir du grabuge.
rudder, *s.* Gouvernail *m.*
ruddiness, *s.* Coloration *f* du teint.
ruddy, *a.* (*a*) (Teint) coloré, haut en couleur. (*b*) Rougeâtre. *R. glow,* lueur rouge.
rude, *a.* **1.** (*a*) Primitif, rude. (*b*) Grossier, rudimentaire. **2.** Violent, brusque. **3.** *R. health,* santé robuste. **4.** Impoli; mal élevé. **To be rude to s.o.,** dire des grossièretés à qn.
-ly, *adv.* **1.** Primitivement; grossièrement. **2.** Violemment; brusquement. **3.** Impoliment, grossièrement.
rudeness, *s.* Impolitesse *f*, grossièreté *f.*
rudiment, *s.* **1.** *Biol:* Rudiment *m.* **2.** *pl.* Rudiments, éléments *m*, premières notions.
rudimentary, *a.* Rudimentaire.
rue¹, *v.tr.* Regretter amèrement; se repentir de.
rue², *s.* *Bot:* Rue *f.*
rueful, *a.* Triste, lugubre.
ruffian, *s.* Bandit *m*, brute *f.*
ruffianly, *a.* Brutal. *R. appearance,* allure *f* de brigand.

ruffle[1], *s.* (*a*) *Cost:* Manchette *f* en dentelle; (*at neck*) fraise *f.* (*b*) *Nat.Hist:* Collier *m*; cravate *f.*

ruffle[2], *v.tr.* Ébouriffer (les cheveux); troubler, rider To ruffle s.o.'s feelings, froisser qn

rug, *s.* **I.** Couverture *f.* Travelling rug, couverture de voyage; plaid *m* **2.** Carpette *f*; descente *f* de lit.

rugged, *a.* **1.** (*Of rock*) anfractueux; (*of bark*) rugueux. **2.** Rugged features, traits rudes, irréguliers. **3.** Bourru, rude.

ruggedness, *s.* **1.** Anfractuosités *fpl*; rugosité *f.* **2.** Rudesse *f* (de caractère).

ruin[1], *s.* **1.** Ruine *f.* To go to ruin, tomber en ruine. **2.** (*Often pl.*) Ruine(s). The building is a r., l'édifice est en ruines. **3.** To be the ruin of s.o., ruiner qn.

ruin[2], *v.tr.* Ruiner. **1.** (*a*) Abîmer (son chapeau). (*b*) To r. one's prospects, gâcher son avenir. To r. one's health, *F:* démolir sa santé. To ruin s.o.'s reputation, perdre qn de réputation. **2.** Her extravagance ruined him, ses folles dépenses l'ont ruiné. **ruined,** *a.* **1.** En ruines. **2.** Ruiné.

ruinous, *a.* **1.** (Tombé) en ruines; délabré; ruineux. **2.** R. expense, dépenses ruineuses.

rule[1], *s.* **1.** Règle *f.* (*a*) As a (general) rule, en règle générale. Rule of thumb, méthode *f* empirique. (*b*) To make it a rule to, se faire une règle de. Rules of conduct, directives *f*; normes *f* de conduite. (*c*) Rules and regulations, statuts *m* et règlements *m.* The rules of the game, les règles, les lois *f*, du jeu. **2.** Empire *m*, autorité *f.* **3.** *Carp:* Règle graduée; mètre *m.*

rule[2]. I. *v.tr.* **1.** Gouverner, régir. To rule one's passions, contenir ses passions. To be ruled by s.o., être sous la coupe de qn. **2.** Régler, rayer. To rule a line, tracer une ligne à la règle. II. **rule,** *v.i.* Prices are ruling high, les prix restent élevés. **rule out,** *v.tr.* **1.** Écarter, éliminer. **2.** Biffer, rayer. **ruling**[1], *a.* **1.** Souverain, dominant. **2.** Ruling price, prix *m* du jour. **ruling**[2], *s.* **1.** To give a ruling in favour of s.o., décider en faveur de qn. **2.** Réglage *m.*

ruler, *s.* **1.** Souverain, -aine (*of, over,* de). **2.** Règle *f*, mètre *m.*

rum[1], *s.* *Dist:* Rhum *m.*

rum[2], *a.* *F:* Drôle, bizarre.

Rumania. *Pr.n.* La Roumanie.

Rumanian, *a. & s.* Roumain, -aine.

rumble[1], *s.* Grondement *m*; roulement *m* (d'une charrette).

rumble[2], *v.i.* Gronder (sourdement); rouler, bruire.

ruminant, *a. & s.* *Z:* Ruminant (*m*).

ruminate, *v.i.tr.* Ruminer.

rumination, *s.* Rumination *f.*

ruminative, *a.* Méditatif.

rummage, *v.i.* Fouiller. To rummage about among old papers, fouiller, fourrager, dans de vieux documents.

rumour[1], *s.* Rumeur *f*, bruit *m*; on-dit *m inv.*

rumour[2], *v.tr.* It is rumoured, le bruit court.

rump, *s.* Croupe *f.* **rump-steak,** *s.* *Cu:* Romsteck *m.*

rumple, *v.tr.* Chiffonner, froisser; ébouriffer (les cheveux).

rumpus, *s.* *F:* Chahut *m*, vacarme *m.*

run[1], *s.* **1.** (*a*) Action *f* de courir. At a run, au pas de course. (*b*) Course *f.* To have a run for one's money, en avoir pour son argent. (*c*) Élan *m.* To make a run at s.o., s'élancer sur qn. (*d*) *Cr:* To make ten runs, faire dix courses. **2.** (*a*) Course, promenade *f*, tour *m.* (*b*) *Rail:* Trajet *m.* (*c*) *Nau:* Traversée *f*, parcours *m.* Day's run, distance parcourue. **3.** A run of luck, une suite d'heureuses chances. To have a run of luck, être en veine. In the long run, à la longue. **4.** There is a great run on that novel, on demande beaucoup ce roman. **5.** The common run of men, le commun des hommes. **6.** Libre accès *m.*

run[2], *v.* I. *v.i.* **1.** Courir. To run upstairs, monter l'escalier en toute hâte. To run a race, courir, disputer, une course. To run an errand, faire une course. To run the blockade, forcer le blocus. **2.** Fuir, s'enfuir, se sauver. Now we must run for it! main·tenant sauvons-nous! **3.** *F:* To run for office, se porter candidat. **4.** *Nau:* To run on the rocks, donner sur les roches. **5.** (*a*) Aller, marcher. Train running at fifty miles an hour, train qui marche à cinquante milles à l'heure. (*b*) Circuler. This train is not running to-day, ce train est supprimé aujourd'hui. **6.** (*a*) The thought keeps running through my head, cette idée me revient continuellement à l'esprit. It runs in the blood, cela est dans le sang. (*b*) The talk ran on this subject, la conversation a roulé sur ce sujet. (*c*) To run to, se monter, s'élever, à. (*d*) *F:* I can't run to that, c'est au-dessus de mes moyens. **7.** Fonctionner, marcher. **8.** (*Of colour*) Déteindre. **9.** (*a*) Couler. A heavy sea was running, la mer était grosse. Our stores are running low, nos provisions tirent à leur fin. (*b*) He was running with sweat, il était en nage. (*c*) Vessel that runs, vase qui coule. **10.** (*a*) A gallery runs round the room, une galerie fait le tour de la salle. To run north and south, être orienté du nord au sud. (*b*) So the story runs, c'est ainsi que l'histoire est racontée. II. **run,** *v.tr.* **1.** To run s.o. close, serrer qn de près. **2.** To run a boat ashore, atterrir une embarcation. To run one's head against the door, donner de la tête contre la porte. **3.** I can't afford to run a car, je n'ai pas les moyens d'entretenir une auto. **4.** Tenir (un hôtel). **5.** *F:* To run a candidate, appuyer un candidat. **6.** Passer; faire passer. To run a thorn into one's finger, s'enfoncer une épine dans le doigt. *To run one's eye over sth.*, parcourir qch. des yeux. **run across**, *v.i.* Rencontrer par hasard. **run against**, *v.i.* Se heurter contre. **run along**, *v.i.* **1.** *Road that runs along the river*, chemin qui longe la rivière. **2.** Run along! allez-vous-en! **run away**, *v.i.* (a) S'enfuir, se sauver. (b) (Of horse) S'emballer. (c) To run away with s.o., enlever qn. *F: Don't run away with the idea that*, n'allez pas vous imaginer que. *That runs away with a lot of money*, cela mange beaucoup d'argent. **run down**. I. *v.i.* **1.** *The sweat ran down his forehead*, la sueur lui coulait sur le front. **2.** (Of clock) s'arrêter. II. **run down**, *v.tr.* *F:* Dénigrer, déprécier. **run in**, *v.tr.* *F:* Conduire au poste (de police). **run into**, *v.i.* (a) To run into debt, s'endetter. (b) To run into sth., entrer en collision avec qch. **run off**. **1.** *v.i.* Fuir, s'enfuir, se sauver. *To run off with the cash*, filer avec l'argent. **2.** *v.tr.* Faire écouler (un liquide). **run on**, *v.i.* (a) Continuer sa course. (b) (Of time) S'écouler. (c) Continuer à parler. **run out**, *v.i.* (a) Sortir en courant. (b) *The tide is running out*, la mer se retire. (c) Couler, fuir. (d) Se terminer, expirer. (e) Venir à manquer; faire défaut. *We ran out of food*, les vivres vinrent à nous manquer. **run over**, *v.i.* **1.** (a) Parcourir du regard; passer en revue. (b) Passer sur le corps de, à (qn). *He has been run over*, il a été écrasé. **2.** Déborder. **run through**. **1.** *v.i.* (a) Traverser en courant. (b) Parcourir du regard. (c) To run through a fortune, dissiper une fortune. **2.** *v.tr.* To run s.o. through, transpercer qn. **run up**. **1.** *v.i.* (a) Accourir. *To come running up*, arriver en courant. *To run up against s.o.*, rencontrer qn par hasard. (b) Monter, s'élever. **2.** *v.tr.* (a) Laisser grossir (un compte); laisser accumuler. (b) To run up a flag, hisser un pavillon. **running**[1], *a.* **1.** *Sp:* Running jump, saut avec élan. **2.** Running water, eau courante. **3.** (a) Continu. Running accompaniment, accompagnement soutenu. (b) Consécutif; de suite. *Three days running*, trois jours de suite. **running**[2], *s.* **1.** Course(s) *f(pl)*. *F:* To take up the running, mener la course. *To be in the running*, avoir des chances d'arriver. **2.** (a) Marche *f*, fonctionnement *m*. In running order, prêt au service. (b) Direction *f* (d'un hôtel).

runaway, *attrib. a. & s.* (a) Fuyard, -arde, fugitif, -ive. (b) **Runaway horse**, cheval emballé.
rune, *s.* *Pal:* Rune *f*.
rung, *s.* Échelon *m*; bâton *m* (d'une chaise).
runner, *s.* **1.** Coureur, -euse. **2.** *Hort:* Scarlet runner, haricot *m* d'Espagne. **3.** Patin *m* (de traîneau).
runway, *s.* *Av:* Piste *f* d'envol.
rupee, *s.* *Num:* Roupie *f*.
rupture, *s.* Rupture *f*; brouille *f* (entre amis).
rural, *a.* Rural, -aux; champêtre.
ruse, *s.* Ruse *f*, stratagème *m*.
rush[1], *s.* Jonc *m*.
rush[2], *s.* **1.** (a) Course précipitée. To make a rush at s.o., se précipiter sur qn. (b) The rush hours, les heures d'affluence. **2.** Hâte *f*. Rush order, commande urgente. **3.** A rush of air, une chasse d'air. Rush of blood to the head, coup *m* de sang.
rush[3]. I. *v.i.* **1.** (a) Se précipiter; s'élancer. (b) To rush at s.o., fondre sur qn. **2.** *The blood rushed to his face*, le rouge lui monta au visage. II. **rush**, *v.tr.* **1.** (a) Pousser ou entraîner violemment. *They were rushed to hospital*, on les transporta d'urgence à l'hôpital. **I don't want to rush you**, je ne voudrais pas vous bousculer. (b) *F:* To rush s.o. for sth., faire payer à qn un prix exorbitant pour qch. **2.** Dépêcher; exécuter d'urgence. **3.** *Mil:* To rush a position, prendre d'assaut une position.
russet, *s.* *Hort:* Reinette grise. **2.** *a. & s.* (Couleur *f*) roussâtre.
Russia. *Pr.n.* La Russie.
Russian. **1.** *s.* (a) Russe *mf*. (b) *Ling:* Le russe. **2.** *a.* De Russie; russe.
rust[1], *s.* Rouille *f*.
rust[2]. **1.** *v.i.* Se rouiller. **2.** *v.tr.* Rouiller.
rustic. **1.** *a.* Rustique; agreste. **2.** *s.* Paysan, -anne; campagnard, -arde.
rustle[1], *s.* Bruissement *m*; frou-frou *m*.
rustle[2]. **1.** *v.i.* Bruire; (of garment) faire frou-frou. **2.** *v.tr.* Faire bruire.
rusty[1], *a.* Rouillé. To get rusty, se rouiller. *F:* My French is r., mon français est rouillé.
rusty[2], *a.* *F:* To cut up rusty, se rebiffer.
rut, *s.* Ornière *f*. *F:* To get out of the rut, sortir de l'ornière.
ruthless, *a.* Impitoyable; sans pitié. **-ly**, *adv.* Sans pitié.
ruthlessness, *s.* Nature *f* impitoyable.
rye, *s.* Seigle *m*.

S

S, s, *s.* (La lettre) S, s *f*.
Sabbath, *s.* (a) *Jew:* Sabbat *m*. (b) *Ecc:* Dimanche *m*.
sable[1], *s.* Zibeline *f*.

sable[2], *a.* Noir.
sabot, *s.* *Cost:* Sabot *m*.
sabotage[1], *s.* Sabotage *m*.
sabotage[2], *v.tr* Saboter

sabre[1], *s. Mil:* Sabre *m.* **Sabre out,** (i) coup *m* de sabre ; (ii) *(scar)* balafre *f.*
sabre[2], *v.tr.* Sabrer.
saccharin(e), *s.* Saccharine *f.*
sachet, *s. Toil:* Sachet *m.*
sack[1], *s.* **I.** (Grand) sac. **2.** *P:* **To give s.o. the sack,** congédier qn. **To get the sack,** recevoir son congé.
sack[2], *v.tr. P:* **To sack s.o.,** congédier qn.
sack[3], *s.* Sac *m*, pillage *m.*
sack[4], *v.tr.* Saccager, mettre à sac. **sacking,** *s.* Saccagement *m* ; sac *m.*
sackcloth, *s.* **I.** *Tex:* Toile *f* à sacs ; toile d'emballage. **2.** Sackcloth and ashes, le sac et la cendre.
sackful, *s.* Sachée *f*, plein sac.
sacrament, *s. Ecc:* Sacrement *m.* **To receive the sacrament,** s'approcher des sacrements ; communier.
sacred, *a.* **I.** (*a*) Sacré. (*b*) Sacred to the memory of, consacré à la mémoire de. **2.** (*a*) *Ecc:* Sacré, saint. (*b*) *S. music,* musique religieuse. **3.** Sacré, inviolable. *Nothing was s. to him,* il ne respectait rien.
sacredness, *s.* **I.** Caractère sacré. **2.** Inviolabilité *f.*
sacrifice[1], *s.* **I.** (*a*) Sacrifice *m*, immolation *f.* **To offer (up) sth. as a sacrifice,** offrir qch. en sacrifice (*to,* à). (*b*) Victime *f* ; offrande *f.* **2.** (*a*) Sacrifice, abnégation *f* (de qch.) ; renoncement *m* (à qch.). *He succeeded at the s. of his health,* il a réussi en sacrifiant sa santé. (*b*) *Com:* **To sell sth. at a sacrifice,** vendre qch. à perte.
sacrifice[2], *v.tr.* **I.** Sacrifier, immoler. *Abs.* **To sacrifice to idols,** offrir des sacrifices aux idoles. **2.** (*a*) Sacrifier, renoncer à. (*b*) *Com:* Sacrifier, vendre à perte.
sacrilege, *s.* Sacrilège *m.*
sacrilegious, *a.* Sacrilège.
sacristan, *s. Ecc:* Sacristain *m.*
sacristy, *s. Ecc:* Sacristie *f.*
sacrosanct, *a.* Sacro-saint.
sad, *a.* **I.** (*a*) Triste. **To make s.o. sad,** attrister qn. **To be sad at heart,** avoir le cœur gros. *F:* **A sadder and a wiser man,** un homme désillusionné. (*b*) *(Of news)* Affligeant ; *(of place)* morne, lugubre. **2.** *A sad mistake,* une erreur déplorable. **-ly,** *adv.* **I.** Tristement. **2.** Très ; beaucoup. *You are s. mistaken,* vous vous trompez fort.
sadden, *v.tr.* Attrister, affliger.
saddle[1], *s.* **I.** Selle *f.* **2.** Col *m* (de montagne). **3.** *Cu:* Selle (de mouton). **saddle-bag,** *s.* **I.** *Cy:* Sacoche *f* (de selle). **2.** *Furn:* Moquette *f.* **saddle-bow,** *s. Harn:* Pontet *m*, arçon *m.*
saddle[2], *v.tr.* (*a*) Seller. (*b*) *F:* **To saddle s.o. with sth.,** charger qn de qch.
saddler, *s.* Sellier *m* ; bourrelier *m.*
Sadducee, *s.* Saducéen, -enne.
sadism, *s.* Sadisme *m.*
sadist, *s.* Sadique *mf.*
sadistic, *a.* Sadique.

sadness, *s.* Tristesse *f*, mélancolie *f.*
safari, *s.* **On safari,** en expédition de chasse.
safe[1], *s.* Coffre-fort *m*, *pl.* coffres-forts.
safe[2], *a.* **I.** (*a*) En sûreté ; à l'abri. **Safe from sth.,** à l'abri de, en sûreté contre, qch. (*b*) Safe and sound, sain et sauf. His honour is safe, son honneur est à couvert. **2.** (*a*) Sans danger ; sûr. *To put sth. in a s. place,* mettre qch. en lieu sûr. (*b*) **Is it safe to leave him alone?** est-ce qu'il n'y a pas de danger à le laisser seul ? (*c*) **To be on the safe side,** être du bon côté. **It is safe to say,** on peut dire à coup sûr. **-ly,** *adv.* **I.** Sans accident. **To arrive safely,** arriver sain et sauf ; *(of ship)* arriver à bon port. **To put sth. safely away,** mettre qch. en lieu sûr. **2.** Sûrement, sans danger. **safe-conduct,** *s* Sauf-conduit *m*, *pl.* sauf-conduits. **safe-keeping,** *s.* Bonne garde.
safeguard[1], *s.* Sauvegarde *f*, garantie *f.*
safeguard[2], *v.tr.* Sauvegarder, protéger.
safeness, *s.* **I.** A feeling of safeness, un sentiment de sécurité *f.* **2.** Sûreté (d'un placement).
safety, *s.* Sûreté *f*, sécurité *f* ; salut *m.* For safety's sake, pour plus de sûreté. **In a place of safety,** en lieu sûr. **Safety first!** la sécurité d'abord ! **To play for safety,** jouer au plus sûr. **safety-pin,** *s.* Épingle anglaise ; épingle de nourrice, de sûreté. **safety-valve,** *s. Mch:* Soupape *f* de sûreté.
saffron, *s.* **I.** Safran *m.* **2.** *a. & s.* Jaune safran *inv.*
sag, *v.i.* S'affaisser, fléchir.
saga, *s. Lit:* Saga *f.*
sagacious, *a.* Sagace, avisé ; entendu. **-ly,** *adv.* Avec sagacité.
sagacity, *s.* Sagacité *f* ; sagesse *f* (d'une remarque).
sage[1]. **I.** *a. Lit:* Sage, prudent. **2.** *s.* Philosophe *m*, sage *m.*
sage[2], *s. Bot:* Sauge *f.* *a. & s.* Sage green, vert cendré *inv.*
sago, *s. Cu:* Sagou *m.* **Sago pudding,** sagou au lait. **sago-palm,** *s.* Sagoutier *m.*
Sahara (the). *Pr.n.* Le Sahara.
sail[1], *s.* **I.** *Nau:* (*a*) Voile *f.* (*b*) *Coll:* Voile(s), voilure *f*, toile *f.* **To set sail,** mettre à la voile ; prendre la mer. (*c*) **Sail ho!** navire en vue ! **2.** Aile *f*, volant *m* (de moulin).
sail[2], *s.* **I.** **To go for a sail,** faire une promenade à la voile. **2.** Voyage *m* sur mer.
sail[3]. **I.** *v.i.* (*a*) Aller à la voile ; naviguer ; faire route. **To sail (at) ten knots,** filer dix nœuds. (*b*) Partir, appareiller ; prendre la mer. **To be about to sail,** être en partance. **2.** *v.tr. & ind.tr.* **To sail (on, over) the seas,** parcourir les mers. **3.** *v.i.* Planer. *The clouds sailing by,* les nuages voguant dans le ciel. **sailing-ship,** *s.* Voilier *m.* **sailing,** *s.* **I.** (*a*) Navigation *f.* *F:* **It's (all) plain sailing,** cela va tout seul. (*b*) Marche *f*,

allure f (d'un navire). **2.** Départ m, appareillage m.

sailcloth, s. Toile f à voile(s).

sailor, s. (a) Marin m (officier ou matelot). (b) **To be a bad sailor,** être sujet au mal de mer. **To be a good sailor,** avoir le pied marin. **sailor-suit,** s. Costume marin.

saint. (a) s. Saint, -e. **Saint's day,** fête f de saint. **All Saints' (Day),** la Toussaint. (b) Attrib.a. Saint. Ellip. **St Peter's,** (l'église f) Saint-Pierre. **Saint Bernard,** s. (Chien m) saint-bernard inv. **Saint Helena.** Pr.n. Geog: Sainte-Hélène f. **Saint Lawrence.** Pr.n. Le (fleuve) Saint-Laurent.

saintliness, s. Sainteté f.

saintly, a. (De) saint.

sake, s. I forgive you for her s., je vous pardonne à cause d'elle. Do it for my sake, faites-le pour moi. For goodness sake, pour l'amour de Dieu. For old times' sake, en souvenir du passé. To talk for talking's sake, parler pour le plaisir de parler.

salaam[1], s. F: Salamalec m; salut m.

salaam[2], v.i. Faire des salamalecs, un salut.

salad, s. Salade f. **Mixed salad,** salade panachée. **Fruit salad,** macédoine f de fruits. **salad-bowl,** s. Saladier m. **salad-oil,** s. Huile f comestible.

Salamanca. Pr.n. Salamanque f.

salamander, s. Salamandre f.

salaried, a. **1.** (Personnel) aux appointements. **2.** (Of post) Rétribué.

salary, s. Traitement m, appointements mpl.

sale, s. **1.** Vente f. (a) Débit m, mise f en vente. **Cash sale,** vente au comptant. **House for sale,** maison à vendre. **On sale,** en vente. (b) **Sale by auction,** vente à l'enchère, aux enchères. **2.** Com: **Sale price,** prix de solde. **sale-room,** s. Salle f de(s) vente(s).

saleable, a. Vendable; de vente facile.

salesman, s. **1.** (Commis m) vendeur m. **2.** Courtier m de commerce.

salesmanship, s. L'art m de vendre.

saleswoman, s. Vendeuse f.

salient, a. **1.** (a) Saillant; en saillie. (b) s. Mil: Saillant m. **2.** Saillant, frappant.

saline, a. Salin, salé.

saliva, s. Salive f.

sallow, a. Jaunâtre, olivâtre.

sallowness, s. Ton m jaunâtre.

sally[1], s. **1.** Mil: Sortie f. **2.** Sally (of wit), saillie f (d'esprit).

sally[2], v.i. To sally forth, se mettre en route.

salmon. **1.** s. Saumon m. River full of salmon, rivière pleine de saumons. **2.** a. & s. (Colour) Saumon inv. **salmon-trout,** s. Truite saumonée.

salon, s. Salon m.

Salonika. Pr.n. Salonique f.

saloon, s. **1.** Salle f, salon m. **Billiard saloon,** salle de billard. **Hairdressing saloon,** salon de coiffure. **2.** Nau: Salon (de paquebot); la cabine. **Saloon deck,** pont de première classe. **3.** Rail: **Saloon(-car,**

-carriage), wagon-salon m, pl. wagons-salons. [s]alt[1]. **I.** s. **I.** (a) Cu: Sel (commun). F: To take a story with a grain of salt, croire à une histoire avec quelques réserves. He is not worth his salt, il ne vaut pas le pain qu'il mange. (b) F: Old salt, loup m de mer. **2.** Ch: Sel. Com: Spirit(s) of salts, esprit m de sel. **II.** salt, a. Salé. Salt water, eau salée; eau de mer **salt-cellar,** s Salière f. **salt-mine,** s. Mine f de sel. **salt-spoon,** s. Cuiller f à sel. **salt-water,** attrib.a. Salt-water fish, poisson de mer.

salt[2], v.tr. (a) To salt (down), saler. (b) Saupoudrer de sel. **salting,** s. Salaison f.

saltness, s. Salure f, salinité f.

saltpetre, s. Salpêtre m. Chile saltpetre, nitre m de Chili.

salty, a. Salé, saumâtre.

salubrious, a. Salubre, sain.

salubrity, s. Salubrité f.

salutary, a. Salutaire (to, à).

salutation, s. Salutation f.

salute[1], s. (a) Salut m, salutation f. (b) Mil: Salut. **To give a salute,** faire un salut. (c) Navy: To fire a salute, tirer une salve.

salute[2], v.tr. Saluer. **I.** To salute s.o. with a smile, accueillir qn par un sourire. **2.** To salute with the hand, saluer de la main. Abs. Mil: To salute, faire le salut militaire. To salute with twenty guns, saluer de vingt coups.

salvage[1], s. **1.** Indemnité f, prime f, de sauvetage. **2.** Sauvetage m; assistance f maritime. **3.** Objets sauvés.

salvage[2], v.tr. (a) = SALVE[3]. (b) Récupérer (une voiture).

salvation, s. Salut m.

salvationist, s. Salutiste mf.

salve[1], s. Pharm: Onguent m, baume m.

salve[2], v.tr. To do sth. to salve one's conscience, faire qch. par acquit de conscience.

salve[3], v.tr. Nau: Sauver, relever (un vaisseau); effectuer le sauvetage de.

salver, s. Plateau m.

salvo, s. Salve f. F: Salvo of applause, salve d'applaudissements.

Samaritan. a. & s. Samaritain, -aine.

same. **I.** a. & pron. (Le, la) même, (les) mêmes. They are sold the s. day as they come in, ils sont vendus le jour même de leur arrivée. Of the same kind, similaire. In the same way, de même. He got up and I did the same, il se leva et je fis de même. One and the same thing, une seule et même chose. At the same time, (i) en même temps; (ii) à la fois. It all comes to the same thing, tout cela revient au même. It's all the same, tout un. It is all the same to me, ça m'est égal. He is much about the s., il va à peu près de même. **2.** adv. To think the s., penser de même. All the same, malgré tout; quand même. All the s. it has cost us dear, n'empêche que cela nous a coûté cher. Things go on just the same, tout marche comme d'habitude.

sameness, s. **1.** (a) Identité f (with, avec). (b) Ressemblance f (with, à). **2.** Monotonie f.

samovar, s. Samovar m.

sampan, s. Nau: Sampan m.

sample¹, s. Échantillon m. F: **To give a sample of one's knowledge,** donner un exemple de son érudition.

sample², v.tr. (a) Com: Prendre des échantillons de. (b) F: Goûter; essayer. **sampling,** s. Prise f d'échantillons; échantillonnage m.

sanatorium, s. Sanatorium m.

sanctify, v.tr. Sanctifier; consacrer.

sanctimonious, a. Papelard, béat.

sanction¹, s. **1.** Jur: Sanction f. **2.** Sanction f, consentement m, approbation f.

sanction², v.tr. Sanctionner; autoriser. **Sanctioned by usage,** consacré par l'usage.

sanctity, s. **1.** Sainteté f. **2.** Caractère sacré; inviolabilité f.

sanctuary, s. **1.** Sanctuaire m. **2. To take sanctuary,** chercher asile.

sand¹, s. **1.** (a) Sable m. Choked up with s., ensablé. (b) sg. or pl. Banc m de sable. (c) Usu. pl. Grain(s) m(pl) de sable. **2.** pl. Sands, plage f, grève f. **sand-bank,** s. Banc m de sable. **sand-hill,** s. Dune f. **sand-martin,** s. Hirondelle f de rivage. **sand-shoes,** s.pl. Sandales f, espadrilles f. **sand-storm,** s. Simoun m; tempête f de sable.

sand², v.tr. Sabler.

sandal, s. Sandale f.

sandal(wood), s. (Bois m de) santal m.

sandbag¹, s. **1.** Fort: Sac m à terre. **2.** P: Assommoir m; boudin m.

sandbag², v.tr. Assommer (d'un coup de boudin).

sandpaper¹, s. Papier m de verre.

sandpaper², v.tr. Frotter au papier de verre.

sandstone, s. Geol: Grès m.

sandwich¹, s. Sandwich m. Ham sandwiches, sandwichs au jambon. **sandwich-board,** s. Panneau m. **sandwich-man,** s. Homme-sandwich, m, pl. hommes-sandwichs.

sandwich², v.tr. Serrer, intercaler.

sandy, a. **1.** Sableux, sablonneux; (of path) sablé. **2.** (Of hair) Roux pâle inv.

sane, a. Sain d'esprit; raisonnable, sensé. To be s., avoir toute sa raison. **-ly,** adv. Raisonnablement.

sanguinary, a. (a) Sanguinaire, sanglant. (b) Altéré de sang.

sanguine, a. (a) D'un rouge sanguin; rubicond. (b) (Of temperament) Sanguin. (c) Confiant, optimiste. **To feel sanguine about the future,** avoir confiance en l'avenir.

sanitary, a. Hygiénique, sanitaire. **Sanitary inspector,** inspecteur de la salubrité publique.

sanitation, s. **1.** Hygiène f; salubrité publique; système m sanitaire. **2.** F: Aménagements m sanitaires.

sanity, s. Santé f d'esprit; jugement sain.

Sanskrit, a. & s. Ling: (Le) sanscrit.

Santa Claus. Pr.n. Le Bonhomme Noël.

sap¹, s. Sève f. **sap-wood,** s. Aubier m.

sap², s. Mil: Sape f.

sap³, v.tr. & i. Mil: Saper.

sapling, s. Jeune arbre m; baliveau m.

sapper, s. Mil: Sapeur m. F: **The sappers,** le génie.

sapphire, s. Saphir m.

saraband, s. Danc: Sarabande f.

Saracen, a. & s. Hist: Sarrasin (m).

sarcasm, s. **1.** Ironie f; esprit m sarcastique. **2.** (Piece of) sarcasm, sarcasme m.

sarcastic, a. Sarcastique; mordant. **Sarcastic remark,** sarcasme m. **-ally,** adv. D'une manière sarcastique; ironiquement.

sarcophagus, s. Sarcophage m.

sardine, s. Ich: Sardine f.

Sardinia. Pr.n. La Sardaigne.

Sardinian, a. & s. Sarde (mf).

sardonic, a. Sardonique. **-ally,** adv. Sardoniquement.

Sark. Pr.n. Geog: Sercq m.

sarsaparilla, s. Salsepareille f.

sash¹, s. Cost: Écharpe f; ceinture f.

sash², s. Const: Châssis m mobile, cadre m.

Satan. Pr.n. Satan m.

satanic, a. Satanique, diabolique.

satchel, s. Sacoche f. Sch: Cartable m.

sate, v.tr. **1.** Assouvir; rassasier, satisfaire. **2.** = SATIATE. **sated,** a. **1.** Rassasié (with, de). **2. To become sated,** se blaser (with, de).

satellite, s. Satellite m.

satiate, v.tr. Rassasier jusqu'au dégoût (with, de); blaser (with, de). **satiated,** a. Rassasié.

satiety, s. Satiété f.

satin, s. Tex: Satin m.

satire, s. **1.** Lit: Satire f (on, upon, contre). **2.** Satire, sarcasme m.

satirical, a. **1.** Satirique. **2.** Sarcastique, ironique. **-ally,** adv. Satiriquement.

satisfaction, s. **1.** (a) Acquittement m, paiement m. (b) **Satisfaction for an offence,** réparation f, expiation f, d'une offense. (c) Assouvissement m. **2.** Satisfaction f, contentement m (at, with, de). **To give s.o. satisfaction,** satisfaire, contenter, qn. The work will be done to your s., le travail sera fait de manière à vous satisfaire. **3.** That is a great satisfaction, c'est un grand motif de contentement.

satisfactoriness, s. Caractère satisfaisant.

satisfactory, a. Satisfaisant. **To bring to a satisfactory conclusion,** mener à bien. **To give a satisfactory account of one's movements,** justifier de ses mouvements. **-ily,** adv. De façon satisfaisante.

satisfy, v.tr. **1.** (a) S'acquitter de; remplir (une condition). (b) Satisfaire; faire réparation à. To s. one's conscience, par acquit de conscience. **2.** (a) Satisfaire, contenter. (b) Satisfaire, assouvir. To s. all requirements, suffire à tous les besoins. Abs. Food that satisfies, nourriture qui satisfait. **3.** Convaincre, satisfaire. **I have satisfied myself**

that, je me suis assuré que. **satisfied,** a.
1. To be satisfied with sth., être content,
satisfait, de qch.; se louer de qch. **To rest
satisfied** with an explanation, se contenter
d'une explication. **2.** Convaincu. **satisfying,** a. Satisfaisant; qui contente; (of
food) nourrissant.
saturate, v.tr. Saturer, tremper (with, de).
saturation, s. **1.** Imprégnation f. **2.** Ch:
Saturation f.
Saturday, s. Samedi m.
Saturn. Pr.n. Astr: Myth: Saturne m.
saturnine, a. Taciturne, sombre.
satyr, s. Myth: Satyre m.
sauce¹, s. **1.** (a) Sauce f. (b) Assaisonnement
m; condiment m. **2.** P: Impertinence f,
insolence f. **sauce-boat,** s. Saucière f.
sauce², v.tr. P: Dire des impertinences à.
saucepan, s. Casserole f; poêlon m. **Double
saucepan,** bain-marie m, pl. bains-marie.
saucer, s. Soucoupe f.
sauciness, s. Impertinence f.
saucy, a. (a) Impertinent, effronté. (b) Fripon, -onne, gamin. S. smile, sourire aguichant.
-ily, adv. (a) D'un ton effronté. (b) D'un
air gamin.
Saul. Pr.n. B.Hist: Saül m.
saunter¹, s. Flânerie f.
saunter², v.i. To saunter (along), flâner; se
balader.
sausage, s. **1.** Cu: (a) Saucisse f. (b) (Hard,
dry) Saucisson m. **2.** Sausage (balloon),
ballon m d'observation; F: saucisse.
sausage-meat, s. Chair f à saucisse.
sausage-roll, s. Cu: Saucisse enrobée.
savage. 1. a. (a) Sauvage, barbare; non
civilisé. (b) Féroce. (c) F: Furieux; en
rage. **2.** s. Sauvage mf. **-ly,** adv. Sauvagement, férocement; furieusement.
savageness, s. Férocité f; brutalité f.
save¹, v.tr. **1.** (a) Sauver. To save s.o.'s life,
sauver la vie à qn. To save s.o. from death,
arracher qn à la mort. To s. s.o. from falling,
empêcher qn de tomber. (b) Sauver, protéger.
To save the situation, se montrer à la hauteur
de l'occasion. To save appearances, sauver,
sauvegarder, les apparences. **2.** (a) Mettre
de côté. (b) Économiser, épargner. I have
money saved, j'ai de l'argent de côté. Abs. To
save (up), économiser pour l'avenir. **3.** Ménager (ses vêtements); éviter (de la peine).
To save time, gagner du temps. I am saving
my strength, je me ménage. **4.** To save s.o.
sth., éviter, épargner, qch. à qn. **saving¹.**
I. a. **1.** (a) Qui sauve; qui protège.
(b) (Qualité) qui rachète des défauts.
2. Économe, ménager (of, de). **3.** Saving
clause, clause de sauvegarde; réservation f.
II. **saving. 1.** prep. & conj. = SAVE².
2. prep. Sauf; sans porter atteinte à.
saving², s. **1.** (a) Délivrance f, salut m.
This was the s. of him, cela a été son salut.
(b) Sauvetage m. (c) Protection f. **2.** (a)

Économie f, épargne f. (b) pl. **Savings,**
économies. **savings-bank,** s. Caisse f
d'épargne.
save². A. & Lit: prep. (a) Sauf, excepté,
hormis; à l'exception de. All, s. the doctor,
tous, à l'exception du docteur. (b) **Save for**
a grazed arm he is unhurt, il est indemne sauf
une écorchure au bras.
saveloy, s. Cu: Cervelas m.
saviour, s. Sauveur m.
savour¹, s. Saveur f, goût m, arome m.
savour², v.i. To savour of sth., sentir qch.;
tenir de qch.
savouriness, s. Saveur f, succulence f.
savoury. 1. a. (a) Savoureux, appétissant;
succulent. (b) **Savoury herbs,** plantes aroma-
tiques. **Savoury omelette,** omelette aux fines
herbes. **2.** s. Entremets non sucré.
Savoy. 1. Pr.n. Geog: La Savoie. **2.** s. Chou,
pl. -oux, frisé de Milan.
saw¹, s. Tls: Scie f. **saw-pit,** s. Fosse f
de scieur de long.
saw², v.tr. Scier. **To saw up wood,** débiter
du bois.
saw³, s. Adage m, maxime f; dicton m.
sawdust, s. Sciure f (de bois).
sawfish, s. Ich: Scie f (de mer).
sawmill, s. Scierie f.
saxifrage, s. Bot: Saxifrage f.
Saxon, a. & s. Saxon, -onne.
Saxony. Pr.n. Geog: La Saxe.
saxophone, s. Saxophone m.
say¹, s. Dire m, parole f, mot m. **To have
one's say,** dire son mot. I have no say in
the matter, F: je n'ai pas voix au chapitre.
say², v.tr. Dire. **1.** (a) F: To ask s.o. to
say a few words, prier qn de prendre la
parole. F: Who shall I say? qui dois-je
annoncer? **To say again,** répéter. What did
you say? plaît-il? **To say yes,** dire (que) oui.
What do you say to a drink? si on buvait
un verre? So he says! A l'en croire! "I
accept," said he, "j'accepte," fit-il. (b) All
that can be said in a couple of words, tout ça
tient en deux mots. So to say, pour ainsi dire.
As one might say, comme qui dirait. One
might as well say, autant dire. I must say,
j'avoue; franchement. That is to say, c'est-
à-dire; à savoir. The less said the better,
moins nous parlerons, mieux cela vaudra.
Say no more! n'en dites pas davantage!
To say nothing of, sans parler de. There is
something to be said on both sides, il y a du
pour et du contre. You don't say so! allons
donc! pas possible! (c) He is said to be rich,
on le dit riche. (d) Anyone would say that
he was asleep, on dirait qu'il dort. I should
say not, je ne crois pas; je crois que non.
Didn't I say so! quand je vous le disais!
(e) Well, say it were true, what then? eh bien,
mettons que ce soit vrai, alors quoi? (f) I
say! dites donc! **2.** Dire, réciter; faire (ses
prières)? **saying,** s. **1.** (a) Énonciation f;
récitation f. It goes without saying that, il

va de soi, cela va sans dire, que. (b) **There is no saying,** (il est) impossible de dire. **2. Dit** m. (Common) saying, adage m, dicton m. **As the saying goes,** comme dit le proverbe.
scab, s. Croûte f.
scabbard, s. Fourreau m.
scaffold, s. **I.** Échafaud m. **2.** Const: = SCAFFOLDING.
scaffolding, s. Échafaudage m. **scaffold-ing-pole,** s. Const: Écoperche f; perche f d'échafaudage.
scald[1], s. Échaudure f.
scald[2], v.tr. Échauder. **scalding,** a. Scalding hot, tout bouillant. F: Scalding tears, larmes brûlantes.
scale[1], s. Écaille f.
scale[2]. **I.** v.tr. Écailler. **II scale,** v.i. To scale (off), s'écailler.
scale[3], s. **I.** Plateau m, plat m (de balance). To turn the scale, emporter la balance. **2.** pl. (Pair of) scales, balance. **scale-pan,** s. = SCALE[3] I.
scale[4], s. **I.** Échelle f. (a) Graduation f, graduations (d'un thermomètre); série f, suite f (de nombres). Scale of salaries, échelle des traitements. (b) Cadran gradué. (c) Règle (divisée). (d) Échelle (d'une carte). To draw sth. to scale, dessiner qch. à l'échelle. On a large scale, en grand. (e) Envergure f; étendue f. To keep house on a small s., avoir un train de maison très simple. **2.** Mus: Gamme f.
scale[5], v.tr. Escalader. To s. a mountain, faire l'ascension d'une montagne. **scaling,** s. Escalade f. **scaling-ladder,** s. Échelle f d'escalade.
scallop, s. **I.** (a) Moll: Pétoncle m, coquille f (de) Saint-Jacques. (b) Cu: Coquille (de poisson au gratin). **2.** Needlw: Feston m, denteleure f.
scallywag, s. P: Propre m à rien.
scalp[1], s. **I.** (a) Anat: Épicrâne m. (b) Anat: Cuir chevelu. (c) Scalpe m. **scalp-hunter,** s. Chasseur m de chevelures.
scalp[2], v.tr. Scalper.
scalpel, s. Surg: Scalpel m.
scaly, a. Écailleux, squameux.
scamp[1], s. Vaurien, -enne; mauvais sujet; garnement m. Young scamp, petit galopin.
scamp[2], v.tr. F: Bâcler (un travail).
scamper[1], s. (a) Course f folâtre, allègre. (b) Course rapide.
scamper[2], v.i. (a) Courir allégrement, d'une manière folâtre. (b) To scamper off, se sauver à toutes jambes.
scan, v.tr. **I.** (a) Scander, mesurer (des vers). (b) v.i. (Of verse) Se scander. **2.** Examiner, scruter.
scandal, s. **I.** Scandale m; honte f. **2.** Médisance f; cancans mpl. To talk scandal, cancaner. **scandal-monger,** s. Cancanier, -ière; mauvaise langue.
scandalize, v.tr. Scandaliser.

scandalous, a. Scandaleux, infâme, honteux. **-ly,** adv. Scandaleusement.
Scandinavia. Pr.n. La Scandinavie.
Scandinavian, a. & s. Scandinave (mf).
scant, a. Insuffisant, peu abondant.
scantiness, s. Insuffisance f, rareté f. The s. of my resources, l'exiguïté f de mes ressources.
scanty, a. Insuffisant ou à peine suffisant; peu abondant; (of garment) étroit. S. hair, cheveux rares. In s. attire, en tenue (plutôt) sommaire. **-ily,** adv. Insuffisamment; peu abondamment.
scapegoat, s Bouc m émissaire.
scapegrace, s. Polisson, -onne; mauvais sujet.
scar[1], s. Cicatrice f.
scar[2], v. **I.** v.tr. Laisser une cicatrice sur. **2.** v.i. To scar (over), se cicatriser. **scarred,** a. Couturé (de cicatrices); balafré.
scarab, s. **I.** Ent: Scarabée sacré. **2.** Lap: Scarabée.
scarce. I. a. Rare; peu abondant. F: To make oneself scarce, s'esquiver, décamper. **2.** adv. = SCARCELY I. **-ly,** adv. **I.** A peine; presque pas. She could s. speak, c'est à peine si elle pouvait parler. **2.** Scarcely! j'en doute!
scarcity, s. Rareté f; manque m, pénurie f.
scare[1], s. Panique f, alarme f. F: You did give me a scare, vous m'avez fait rudement peur. **scare-monger,** s. Alarmiste mf.
scare[2], v.tr. Effrayer, effarer, alarmer. To scare away, effaroucher. **scared,** a. To be scared to death, avoir une peur bleue.
scarecrow, s. Épouvantail m.
scarf, s. **I.** Écharpe f, fichu m; cache-col m inv; (in silk) foulard m. **2.** Écharpe f (in dignitaire).
scarify, v.tr. Scarifier.
scarlet, a. & s. Écarlate (f). F: To blush scarlet, devenir cramoisi. **scarlet fever,** s. Med: (Fièvre) scarlatine f.
scatheless, a. Sans dommage; sain et sauf.
scathing, a. Acerbe, cinglant. **-ly,** adv. D'une manière acerbe; d'un ton cinglant.
scatter. I. v.tr. (a) Disperser, mettre en fuite. (b) Éparpiller. The region is scattered over with small towns, la région est parsemée de petites villes. **2.** v.i. (Of crowd) Se disperser; (of shot) s'éparpiller. **scattered,** a. Dispersé, éparpillé; épars. Thinly s. population, population clairsemée. **scattering,** s. **I.** Dispersion f; éparpillement m. **2.** Petit nombre; petite quantité. **scatter-brained,** a. F: Étourdi, écervelé.
scavenge, v.tr. Ébouer, balayer (les rues).
scavenging, s. Ébouage m, balayage m.
scavenger, s. Boueur m; balayeur m des rues.
scenario, s. Scénario m.
scene, s. **I.** Th: F: To appe·r on the scene, entrer en scène. **2.** (a) Th: Scène f. The scene is laid in London, l'action f se passe à Londres. (b) Théâtre m, lieu m The s. of

operations, le théâtre des opérations. **3.** (*a*) (*Sub-division of a play*) Scène. (*b*) Scène, incident *m*, spectacle *m*. *Distressing scenes*, des scènes affligeantes. **4.** (*a*) *Th:* (Set) scene, décor *m*. *Behind the scenes*, derrière la toile; *F:* dans la coulisse. *To know what is going on behind the scenes*, voir le dessous des cartes. (*b*) *The s. from the window*, la vue de la fenêtre. **5.** *F:* *To make a scene*, faire une scène. **scene-shifter**, *s.* *Th:* Machiniste *m*.

scenery, *s.* **1.** *Th:* Décors *mpl*; la mise en scène. **2.** Paysage *m*; vue *f*.

scent[1], *s.* **1.** (*a*) Parfum *m*, senteur *f*; odeur *f* agréable. (*b*) Bottle of scent, flacon *m* de parfum. **2.** *Ven:* (*a*) Fumet *m*. (*b*) Piste *f*, voie *f*. *F:* *To be on the right s.*, être sur la piste. **3.** Odorat *m*, flair *m*. **scent-bottle**, *s.* Flacon *m* de parfum; flacon à odeur.

scent[2], *v.tr.* **1.** *F:* *To scent trouble*, flairer des ennuis. **2.** Parfumer, embaumer.

scented, *a.* **1.** Parfumé (*with*, de); embaumé (*with*, de). **2.** Odorant.

sceptic, *s.* Sceptique *mf*.

sceptical, *a.* Sceptique. **-ally**, *adv.* Sceptiquement; avec scepticisme.

scepticism, *s.* Scepticisme *m.*

sceptre, *s.* Sceptre *m.*

schedule[1], *s.* **1.** (*a*) Annexe *f* (à une loi). (*b*) Bordereau *m*; note explicative. **2.** (*a*) Inventaire *m*; barème *m* (des prix). (*b*) *Adm:* Cédule *f* (d'impôts).

schedule[2], *v.tr.* Inscrire sur une liste, sur l'inventaire.

Scheldt (the). *Pr.n* L'Escaut *m.*

scheme[1], *s.* **1.** Arrangement *m*, combinaison *f*. *Colour scheme*, combinaison de(s) couleurs. **2.** Résumé *m*, exposé *m*; plan *m*. **3.** (*a*) Plan, projet *m*. (*b*) Machination *f*, intrigue *f*.

scheme[2]. **1.** *v.i.* Intriguer, ruser, comploter. **2.** *v.tr.* (*a*) Machiner, combiner. (*b*) Projeter (de faire qch.). **scheming**[1], *a.* Intrigant.

scheming[2], *s.* **1.** Plans *mpl*, projets *mpl*. **2.** Machinations *fpl*, intrigues *fpl*.

schemer, *s.* **1.** Faiseur de projets; homme à projets. **2.** Intrigant, -ante.

schism, *s.* Schisme *m.*

schismatic, *a. & s.* Schismatique (*mf*).

schist, *s.* Schiste *m.*

scholar, *s.* **1.** (*a*) Élève *mf*, écolier, -ière. (*b*) Personne *f* qui apprend. **2.** Savant, -ante, lettré, -ée. **3.** *Sch:* Boursier, -ière.

scholarly, *a.* Savant, érudit.

scholarship, *s.* **1.** Savoir *m*, science *f*; érudition *f*. **2.** *Sch:* Bourse *f* (d'études).

scholastic, *a.* (*a*) Scolaire. *The s. profession*, la carrière de l'enseignement. (*b*) Pédant.

school[1], *s.* **1.** (*a*) École *f*. *Infant school*, école maternelle. *Elementary school*, école primaire. *Secondary school*, établissement *m* d'enseignement secondaire. *Private school*, école libre. *Public school*, grande école d'enseignement secondaire. (*b*) The upper school,

les hautes, grandes, classes. **2.** *To go to school*, (i) aller en classe; (ii) aller à l'école. *To be in school*, être en classe. *School children*, écoliers *m*. **3.** École, institut *m*. *School of art*, école des beaux-arts. *School of dancing*, académie *f* de danse. *Evening school*, cours *mpl* du soir. **4.** (*In Universities*) Faculté *f*. *The Arts School*, la Faculté des lettres. **5.** (*a*) *Art:* The Flemish school, l'école flamande. (*b*) One of the old school, un homme de la vieille roche. **schoolbook**, *s.* Livre *m* classique; livre de classe.

school-day, *s.* **1.** Jour *m* de classe. **2.** *pl.* In my school-days, au temps où j'allais en classe. **school-house**, *s.* Maison *f* d'école; école *f*. **school-teacher**, *s.* Instituteur, -trice.

school[2], *v.tr.* **1.** Instruire; faire l'éducation de. **2.** Former; discipliner. *To school oneself to patience*, apprendre à patienter.

schooling, *s.* Instruction *f*, éducation *f*.

school[3], *s.* Banc *m* (de poissons); bande *f* (de marsouins).

schoolboy, *s.* Écolier *m*; élève *m.*

schoolfellow, *s.* Camarade *mf* de classe ou d'école; condisciple *m.*

schoolgirl, *s.* Écolière *f*; élève *f.*

schoolmaster, *s.* (*a*) (*In elementary school*) Instituteur *m*; maître *m* d'école; (*in secondary school*) professeur *m*. (*b*) Directeur *m*; chef *m* d'institution.

schoolmistress, *s.* (*a*) (*In elementary school*) Institutrice *f*; maîtresse *f* d'école; (*in secondary school*) professeur *m*. (*b*) Directrice *f.*

schoolroom, *s.* (Salle *f* de) classe *f.*

schooner, *s.* Schooner *m*; goélette *f.*

science, *s.* Science *f*. **science-master**, *s.* *Sch:* Professeur *m* de sciences.

scientific, *a.* Scientifique. *Scientific instruments*, instruments de précision. **-ally**, *adv.* Scientifiquement.

scientist, *s.* Savant, -ante; homme de science.

Scilly. *Pr.n.* The Scilly Isles, les Sorlingues *f.*

scimitar, *s.* Cimeterre *m.*

scintilla, *s.* Soupçon *m*, parcelle *f.*

scintillate, *v.i.* Scintiller, étinceler.

scintillation, *s.* Scintillation *f.*

scion, *s.* **1.** *Hort:* Scion *m*, ente *f*, greffon *m*. **2.** Descendant *m*. *Scion of a noble house*, rejeton *m* d'une famille noble.

scissor, *s.* (Pair of) scissors, ciseaux *mpl*. *Scissors-and-paste production*, ouvrage fait à coups de ciseaux.

scoff, *v.i.* Se moquer. *To scoff at s.o.*, se moquer de qn. *To be scoffed at*, recueillir des railleries. **scoffing**[1], *a.* Moqueur, -euse.

scoffing[2], *s.* Moquerie *f* raillerie *f.*

scoffer, *s.* Moqueur, -euse; railleur, -euse.

scold[1], *s.* (Femme *f*) criarde *f*; mégère *f.*

scold[2]. **1.** *v.i.* Gronder, ronchonner (*at s.o.*, contre qn). **2.** *v.tr.* Gronder, réprimander. **scolding**[1], *a.* Grondeur, -euse. **scolding**[2], *s.* **1.** Gronderie *f*, semonce *f*. To give s.o.

a good **scolding**, tancer qn. **2.** *Constant s.*, des criailleries *f* sans fin.

scone, *s.* Pain *m* au lait.

scoop[1], *s.* **1.** Pelle *f* à main. **2.** *Rail :* Cuiller *f.* **3.** (Coal) scoop, seau *m* à charbon.

scoop[2], *s.* (*a*) Coup *m* de pelle. (*b*) *Journ: F:* Primeur *f* d'une grosse nouvelle.

scoop[3], *v.tr.* To scoop (out), excaver ; évider. To scoop up, ramasser avec la pelle.

scooter, *s.* Trottinette *f*, patinette *f.*

scope, *s.* (*a*) Portée *f*, étendue *f.* That is outside my scope, cela n'est pas de ma compétence. To extend the s. of one's activities, élargir le champ de son activité. (*b*) Espace *m*, place *f.* To give full scope to, donner (libre) carrière à.

scorch. **I.** *v.tr.* Roussir, brûler légèrement ; (*of sun*) rôtir, flétrir. **2.** *v.i.* Roussir ; brûler légèrement. **3.** *v.i.* *F:* To scorch (along), brûler le pavé. **scorching**[1]. **I.** *a.* Brûlant, ardent. **2.** *adv.* Scorching hot, tout brûlant.

scorching[2], *s.* **1.** Roussissement *m* ; dessèchement *m.* **2.** *Aut: Cy:* Allure excessive.

score[1], *s.* **1.** Éraflure *f*, entaille *f.* **2.** *F:* To pay off old scores, régler de vieux comptes. **3.** (Nombre *m* de) points *m.* *Fb :* What's the score? où en est le jeu ? **4.** *Mus :* Partition *f.* **5.** (*a*) Vingt, vingtaine *f.* (*b*) *pl. F :* Scores, un grand nombre. Scores of people, une masse de gens. **6.** *Prn*, question *f*, sujet *m.* Have no fear on that score, n'ayez aucune crainte à cet égard. On the s. of ill-health, pour cause de santé.

score[2], *v.tr.* **1.** (*a*) Érafler ; strier ; rayer. (*b*) Souligner (un passage). **2.** *Games :* (*a*) Compter, marquer (les points). (*b*) Gagner (une partie). *Cr :* To score a century, faire une centaine. *Fb :* To score a goal, marquer un but. *F:* To score (a success), remporter un succès. **score off**, *v.i.* To score off s.o., *F:* river son clou à qn. **score out**, *v.tr.* Rayer, biffer. **scoring**, *s.* **1.** Éraflement *m* ; striation *f.* **2.** *Games :* Marque *f.* Bill: Scoring board, tableau *m*, boulier *m.*

scorer, *s.* *Games :* Marqueur *m.*

scorn[1], *s.* Dédain *m*, mépris *m.*

scorn[2], *v.tr.* Dédaigner, mépriser. **2.** To scorn to do sth., trouver indigne de soi de faire qch.

scornful, *a.* Dédaigneux, méprisant. **-fully,** *adv.* Dédaigneusement ; avec mépris.

scorpion, *s.* Scorpion *m.*

Scot,[1] *s.* Écossais, -aise

scot[2], *s.* Écot *m.* **scot-free,** *a* **1.** To get off scot-free, s'en tirer indemne. **2.** Sans frais.

Scotch. *a.* Écossais ; d'Écosse. Scotch terrier, terrier griffon.

Scotchman, *s.* Écossais *m.*

Scotchwoman, *s.* Écossaise *f.*

Scotland. *Pr.n.* L'Écosse *f.*

Scots, *a. & s.* = Scotch.

Scotsman, *s.* Écossais *m.*

Scotswoman, *s.* Écossaise *f*,

Scottish, *a. & s.* = Scotch. The Scottish Border, les marches *f* d'Écosse.

scoundrel, *s.* Chenapan *m*, coquin *m*, scélérat *m.* Regular scoundrel, franche canaille.

scoundrelly, *a.* Scélérat, vil, canaille.

scour[1], *s.* *F:* Nettoyage *m*, récurage *m.*

scour[2], *v.tr.* **1.** Nettoyer. To scour out a saucepan, récurer une casserole. **2.** Donner une chasse d'eau à.

scour[3]. **1.** *v.i.* To scour about, battre la campagne. **2.** *v.tr.* Parcourir, battre (la campagne) ; écumer (les mers). To scour a wood, fouiller un bois.

scourge[1], *s.* Fléau *m.*

scourge[2], *v.tr.* Châtier ; être un fléau pour.

scout[1], *s.* (*a*) *Mil :* Éclaireur *m.* (*b*) Boy scout, boy-scout *m*, *pl.* boy-scouts.

scout[2], *v.i.* Aller en reconnaissance.

scout[3], *v.tr.* Repousser avec mépris.

scoutmaster, *s.* Chef *m* éclaireur.

scowl[1], *s.* Air menaçant, re(n)frogné ; froncement *m* de(s) sourcils.

scowl[2], *v.i.* Se re(n)frogner ; froncer les sourcils. To scowl at s.o., regarder qn de travers. **scowling,** *a.* Re(n)frogné, menaçant.

scragginess, *s.* Décharnement *m.*

scraggy, *a.* Décharné, maigre.

scramble[1], *s.* **1.** Marche *f* difficile, à quatre pattes. **2.** Mêlée *f*, bousculade *f.*

scramble[2]. **1.** *v.i.* (*a*) To scramble up, monter à quatre pattes. (*b*) To scramble for sth., se bousculer pour avoir qch. **2.** *v.tr.* Scrambled eggs, œufs brouillés.

scrap[1], *s.* **1.** Petit morceau ; bout *m*, chiffon *m.* Not a s. of evidence, pas une parcelle de preuve. To catch scraps of conversation, saisir des bribes de conversation. Scrap of comfort, fiche *f*, brin *m*, de consolation. **2.** *pl.* Scraps, restes *m*, reliefs *m* (d'un repas). **scrap-book,** *s.* Album *m* (de découpures). **scrap-heap,** *s.* To throw sth. on the scrap-heap, mettre qch. au rebut. **scrap-iron,** *s.* Ferraille *f.*

scrap[2], *v.tr.* **1.** Mettre au rebut. **2.** *F:* Mettre au rancart.

scrap[3], *s.* *P:* Querelle *f*, rixe *f* ; bagarre *f.*

scrap[4], *v.i.* *P:* Se battre.

scrape[1], *s.* **1.** Coup *m* de grattoir. **2.** *F:* Mauvais pas. To get out of a scrape, se tirer d'affaire.

scrape[2]. **I.** *v.tr.* **1.** Érafler, écorcher. **2.** Racler, gratter. To scrape one's boots, s'essuyer les pieds. **3.** To scrape one's feet along the floor, frotter les pieds sur le plancher. **4.** (*a*) To scrape acquaintance with s.o. trouver moyen de lier connaissance avec qn. (*b*) To scrape (together, up) a sum of money, amasser petit à petit une somme d'argent. **II.** **scrape,** *v.i.* **1.** (*a*) Gratter. (*b*) Grincer. **2.** To scrape against the wall, raser le mur. **scrape away,** *v.tr.* Enlever en frottant, en raclant. **scrape off,** *v.tr.*

Enlever au racloir. **scrape through**, *v.i.*
F: To scrape through an examination,
passer tout juste.
scrappy, *a.* (*a*) Décousu. (*b*) Avec beaucoup
de lacunes; composé de bribes, de restes.
scratch[1], *s.* **I.** (*a*) Coup *m* d'ongle, de griffe.
(*b*) Égratignure *f*, éraflure *f. Without a s.*,
indemne, sans une égratignure. **2.** (*a*)
Grattement *m.* To give one's head a scratch,
se gratter la tête. (*b*) Grincement *m* (d'une
plume). **3.** *Sp:* To start (at) scratch, partir
scratch. To come up to scratch, *F:* se
montrer à la hauteur (de l'occasion). *F:* To
bring s.o. up to the scratch, amener qn à se
décider, à s'exécuter.
scratch[2]. **I.** *v.tr.* **I.** Égratigner, griffer;
donner un coup de griffe à. **2.** (*a*) To scratch
one's head, se gratter la tête. (*b*) To scratch
the surface, *F:* ne pas aller au fond. **3.** (*Of
animal*) Gratter (le sol). *v.i.* To scratch at
the door, gratter à la porte. **4.** To scratch,
s.o. off a list, rayer, biffer, qn d'une liste.
Sp: To scratch the race, *abs.* to scratch,
déclarer forfait. **II. scratch**, *v.i.* Grincer,
gratter. **scratch out**, *v.tr.* **I.** Rayer, biffer,
raturer. **2.** *F:* To scratch s.o.'s eyes out,
arracher les yeux à qn.
scratch[3], *a.* Improvisé, sommaire.
scratchy, *a.* **I.** Scratchy writing, pattes *f*
d'araignée. **2.** Qui gratte; qui grince.
scrawl[1], *s.* Griffonnage *m*, gribouillage *m.*
scrawl[2], *v.tr.* Griffonner, gribouiller.
scream[1], *s.* **I.** (*a*) Cri perçant. (*b*) Screams
of laughter, de grands éclats de rire. **2.** *P:*
It was a perfect scream, c'était à se tordre.
scream[2], *v.i.* (*a*) Pousser un cri perçant;
pousser des cris. (*b*) *F:* To scream with
laughter, rire aux éclats. *He made us s.*, il
nous a fait tordre. **screaming**, *a.* **I.**
Criard; perçant. **2.** *F:* Tordant. **-ly**, *adv.*
F: Screamingly funny, tordant.
scree, *s.* Éboulis *m.*
screech[1], *s.* Cri perçant; cri rauque.
screech[2], *v.i.* Pousser des cris perçants, des
cris rauques. **screech-owl**, *s. Orn:*
Effraie *f.*
screed, *s.* (*a*) Harangue *f.* (*b*) Longue
missive.
screen[1], *s.* **I.** (*a*) *Furn:* Écran *m.* (*b*) *S. of
trees*, rideau *m* d'arbres. *F:* Under screen of
night, à l'abri *m* de la nuit. **2.** *Cin:* Écran (de
projection). Screen star, vedette *f* de l'écran.
3. Crible *m*; sas *m.*
screen[2], *v.tr.* **I.** (*a*) Munir d'un écran.
(*b*) To screen sth. from view, cacher, dérober,
qch. aux regards. To screen oneself behind
sth., se cacher derrière qch. (*c*) Abriter,
protéger. To screen sth. from the wind,
garantir qch. du vent. **2.** Tamiser, cribler.
3. *Cin:* Mettre à l'écran.
screw[1], *s.* **I.** Vis *f.* (*a*) *F:* To have a screw
loose, avoir le timbre fêlé; être timbré.
There's a screw loose somewhere, il y a
quelque chose qui cloche. (*b*) To put the

screw on, forcer la main à (qn). **2.** Screw
(-propeller), hélice *f.* **3.** Coup *m* de tournevis.
4. Cornet *m* (de bonbons). **5.** *P:* Avare *m.*
6. *F:* Mauvais cheval. **7.** *P:* Gages *mpl*;
paye *f*, salaire *m.*
screw[2]. **I.** *v.tr.* **I.** Visser. *Screwed together*,
assemblé(s) à vis. **2.** To screw sth. tight,
visser qch. à bloc. **II. screw**, *v.i. F:* Faire
des économies; liarder. **screw down**, *v.tr.*
Visser; fermer à vis. **screw on**, *v.tr.*
Visser, fixer. *F:* His head is screwed on
the right way, il a de la tête. **screw up**,
v.tr. **I.** To screw up one's eyes, plisser les
yeux. To screw up one's lips, pincer les
lèvres. **2.** *F:* To screw up one's courage,
prendre son courage à deux mains.
screwdriver, *s.* Tournevis *m.*
scribble[1], *s.* **I.** Griffonnage *m.* **2.** *F:* Petit
billet. **3.** Écriture *f* illisible.
scribble[2], *v.tr.* Griffonner. **scribbling**, *s.*
Griffonnage *m.* Scribbling paper, papier à
brouillon. Scribbling block, bloc mémento.
scribbler, *s.* **I.** Griffonneur, -euse. **2.** *F:*
Écrivailleur, -euse.
scribe, *s.* Scribe *m.*
scrimmage, *s.* Mêlée *f*; bousculade *f.*
script, *s.* (*a*) Manuscrit *m.* (*b*) *Cin:* Scénario *m.*
scriptural, *a.* Scriptural, -aux.
scripture, *s.* **I.** Holy Scripture, l'Écriture
sainte.
scroll, *s.* Rouleau *m.*
scrounge, *P: v.tr.* Écornifler.
scrounger, *s. P:* Écornifleur *m.*
scrub[1], *s.* Broussailles *fpl*; brousse *f.*
scrub[2], *s.* Friction *f*; nettoyage *m. The
saucepan wants a s.*, la casserole a besoin
d'être récurée.
scrub[3], *v.tr.* Récurer (une casserole),
laver, frotter, (le plancher). **scrubbing-
brush**, *s.* Brosse *f* de chiendent.
scrubby, *a.* **I.** Rabougri. **2.** (*Of land*)
Couvert de broussailles. **3.** *F:* Insignifiant.
scruff, *s.* Nuque *f*; peau *f* de la nuque.
scrunch, *v.tr. & i.* = CRUNCH[2].
scruple[1], *s.* Scrupule *m.* To have no scruples
about doing sth., n'avoir aucun scrupule à
faire qch.
scruple[2], *v.i.* To scruple to do sth., avoir
des scrupules à faire qch.
scrupulous, *a.* **I.** Scrupuleux (*about, over,
as to*, sur). **2.** Scrupuleux, exact, méticuleux.
-ly, *adv.* **I.** Scrupuleusement. **2.** Méticuleusement.
scrutinize, *v.tr.* Scruter. **scrutinizing**,
a. Scrutateur, -trice.
scrutiny, *s.* Examen minutieux.
scud, *v.i. Nau:* To scud before the wind,
fuir vent arrière.
scuffle[1], *s.* Mêlée *f*, bousculade *f.*
scuffle[2], *v.i.* **I.** Se bousculer. **2.** Traîner les
pieds.
scull[1], *s.* **I.** Aviron *m*, rame *f.* **2.** Godille *f.*
scull[2], *v.i.* (*a*) Ramer, nager, en couple.
(*b*) Godiller. (*c*) *F:* Ramer.

scullery, *s.* Arrière-cuisine *f.* **scullery maid,** *s.* Laveuse *f* de vaisselle.
sculptor, *s.* Sculpteur *m.*
sculpture, *s.* Sculpture *f.*
scum, *s.* **1.** Écume *f.* **2.** *F:* The scum of society, le rebut de la société.
scupper[1], *s.* *Nau:* Dalot *m* (de pont).
scupper[2], *v.tr.* *F:* Couler à fond; saborder.
scurrility, *s.* Grossièreté *f.*
scurrilous, *a.* Grossier, injurieux.
scurry[1], *s.* **1.** Galopade *f*; débandade *f.* **2.** Tourbillon *m* (de neige).
scurry[2], *v.i.* Courir à pas précipités. To scurry through one's work, expédier son travail.
scurvy[1], *s.* *Med:* Scorbut *m.*
scurvy[2], *a.* Bas, *f.* basse, vil, vilain. *S.* trick, vilain tour.
scut, *s.* **1.** Couette *f* (de lapin). **2.** *P:* Mufle *m*; sale type *m.*
scutcheon, *s.* *Her:* Écu *m,* écusson *m.*
scuttle[1], *s.* Seau *m* à charbon.
scuttle[2], *s.* *Nau:* (a) Écoutillon *m*; descente *f.* (b) Hublot *m*; lentille *f* (de cabine).
scuttle[3], *v.tr.* *Nau:* Saborder.
scuttle[4], *v.i.* To scuttle off, déguerpir, filer.
scythe, *s.* *Tls:* Faux *f.*
sea, *s.* **1.** Mer *f.* (a) On land and sea, sur terre et sur mer. By the sea, au bord de la mer. By sea, par (voie de) mer. Beyond the sea(s), outre-mer. To go to sea, se faire marin. Sea trip, excursion *f* en mer. Sea battle, bataille navale. (b) The open sea, le large. On the high seas, en pleine mer. To put (out) to sea, prendre le large. Ship at sea, navire en mer. *F:* To be all at sea, être tout désorienté. (c) The seven seas, toutes les mers du monde. **2.** (a) Heavy sea, grosse mer. (b) Lame *f,* houle *f.* Head sea, mer debout. (c) Coup *m* de mer; paquet *m* de mer. To ship a sea, embarquer une lame. **3.** *F:* Océan *m,* multitude *f.* **sea-bathing,** *s.* Bains *mpl* de mer. **sea-borne,** *a.* Maritime; transporté par mer. **sea-breeze,** *s.* Brise *f* du large. **sea-chest,** *s.* Coffre *m* (de marin). **sea-coast,** *s.* Littoral *m,* -aux; côte *f.* **sea-dog,** *s.* *F:* An old sea-dog, un vieux loup de mer. **sea-eagle,** *s.* *Orn:* Orfraie *f.* **sea-fight,** *s.* Combat naval. **sea-front,** *s.* **1.** House on the sea-front, maison qui donne sur la mer. **2.** Digue *f,* esplanade *f.* **sea-going,** *a.* De haute mer. Sea-going ship, navire de long cours. **sea-green,** *s. & a.* Vert (*m*) de mer *inv*; glauque. **sea-gull,** *s.* *Orn:* Mouette *f,* goéland *m.* **sea legs,** *s.pl.* *F:* Pied marin. To get one's sea-legs, s'amariner. **sea-level,** *s.* Niveau *m* de la mer. **sea-lion,** *s.* *Z:* Otarie *f.* **sea-serpent,** *s.* Serpent *m* de mer. **sea-shell,** *s.* Coquille *f* de mer; coquillage *m.* **sea-shore,** *s.* (a) Rivage *m*; bord *m* de la mer. (b) Plage *f.* **sea-sick,** *a.* To be s.-s., avoir le mal de mer. **sea-sickness,** *s.* Mal *m* de mer. **sea-urchin,** *s.*

Echin: Oursin *m*; hérisson *m* de mer.
sea-wall, *s.* Digue *f.* **sea-water,** *s.* Eau *f* de mer.
seafarer, *s.* Homme *m* de mer; marin *m.*
seafaring[1], *a.* Seafaring man, marin *m.*
seafaring[2], *s.* Voyages *mpl* par mer.
seal[1], *s.* *Z:* Phoque *m.*
seal[2], *s.* **1.** (a) Sceau *m*; (on letter) cachet *m.* Given under my hand and seal, signé et scellé par moi. Under the seal of secrecy, sous le sceau du secret. (b) Cachet. *Jur:* To remove the seals, lever les scellés. *Com:* Lead seal, plomb *m.* **2.** (Instrument) Sceau, cachet.
seal[3], *v.tr.* **1.** (a) Sceller; cacheter (une lettre). *F:* His fate is sealed, son sort est réglé. (b) Cacheter (une bouteille); plomber (un colis). **2.** (a) To seal (up) a letter, fermer une lettre. (b) *F:* My lips are sealed, il m'est défendu de parler. **sealing-wax,** *s.* Cire *f* à cacheter.
sealskin, *s.* **1.** Peau *f* de phoque. **2.** *Com:* (Fourrure *f* en) loutre *f.*
seam[1], *s.* **1.** Couture *f.* **2.** (a) Fissure *f,* gerçure *f.* (b) *Min:* Couche *f,* gisement *m.*
seam[2], *v.tr.* Couturer.
seaman, *s.* **1.** Marin *m,* matelot *m.* Able (-bodied) seaman, *F:* A.B., matelot de deuxième classe. **2.** (a) Manœuvrier *m.* (b) Navigateur *m.*
seamanlike. **1.** *a.* De marin, d'un bon marin. **2.** *adv.* En bon marin.
seamanship, *s.* Manœuvre *f* et matelotage *m*; la manœuvre.
seamstress, *s.f.* Ouvrière couturière.
seamy, *a.* *F:* The seamy side of l' o, l envers *m* de la vie.
séance, *s.* Séance *f* de spiritisme.
seaplane, *s.* *Av:* Hydravion *m.*
seaport, *s.* Port *m* de mer.
sear, *v.tr.* Flétrir, dessécher.
search[1], *s.* **1.** Recherche(s) *f(pl).* In search of, à la recherche de. **2.** (a) *Cust:* Visite *f.* (b) *Jur:* Search warrant, mandat *m* de perquisition.
search[2]. **1.** *v.tr.* Inspecter; chercher dans; fouiller (un suspect), scruter (un visage). *Cust:* To search s.o.'s trunks, visiter les malles de qn. **2.** *v.i.* To search for sth., (re)chercher qch. **searching,** *a.* (Examen) minutieux; (regard) pénétrant. *S.* questions, questions qui vont au fond des choses.
searchlight, *s.* Projecteur *m.*
seaside, *s.* **1.** Bord *m* de la mer. **2.** *Attrib.* Seaside resort, station *f* balnéaire; plage *f.*
season[1], *s.* **1.** Saison *f.* Holiday season, saison des vacances. *Ven:* Close season, chasse (ou pêche) fermée. The dead season, la morte-saison. To be in season, être de saison. **2.** Période *f,* temps *m.* In due season, en temps voulu. Word in season, mot dit à propos. In season and out of season, à tout propos et hors de propos. **season-ticket,** *s.* Carte *f* d'abonnement. **Season-ticket holder,** abonné, -ée.

season², *v.tr.* (*a*) Assaisonner, relever. (*b*) Dessécher, étuver (le bois). (*c*) Acclimater, endurcir. (*d*) *F*: Tempérer, modérer. **seasoned**, *a.* **1.** Assaisonné. *Highly s.* dish, plat de haut goût. **2.** (*Of wood*) Sec, *f.* sèche. (*b*) To become seasoned, s'aguerrir. **seasoning**, *s.* **1.** (*a*) *Cu:* Assaisonnement *m.* (*b*) Séchage *m.* (*c*) Acclimatement *m.* **2.** *Cu:* Assaisonnement, condiment *m.* **seasonable**, *a.* **1.** De (la) saison. **2.** Opportun, à propos. **-ably**, *adv.* Opportunément, à propos.

seat¹, *s.* **1.** (*a*) Siège *m*; banquette *f.* Folding seat, pliant *m.* (*b*) To take a seat, s'asseoir. To keep one's seat, rester assis. (*c*) Place *f.* Rail: 'Take your seats!' "en voiture!" (*d*) He has a s. in the House, il siège au Parlement. **2.** (*a*) Siège, fond *m.* Rush s., siège en paille. (*b*) Fond (de culotte). **3.** Théâtre *m* (de la guerre); siège, centre *m.* **4.** *Equit:* Assiette *f*, assise *f.* To lose one's seat, être désarçonné.

seat², *v.tr.* **1.** (Faire) asseoir. Pray be seated, donnez-vous la peine de vous asseoir. **2.** Placer; trouver place pour. **3.** (Re-) mettre le siège à (une chaise). **seating**, *s.* (*a*) Allocation *f* des places. (*b*) Seating capacity, nombre *m* de places (assises).

seawards, *adv.* Vers la mer; vers le large. **seaweed**, *s.* Algue *f*, goémon *m.* **seaworthy**, *a.* Capable de tenir la mer. **secede**, *v.i.* Faire sécession (*from*, de); se séparer. **seceding**, *a.* Sécessionniste. **secession**, *s.* Sécession *f*; scission *f.* **seclude**, *v.tr.* Tenir retiré (*from*, de). **secluded**, *a.* Écarté, retiré. **seclusion**, *s.* Solitude *f*, retraite *f.* In seclusion, retiré du monde.

second¹, *s.* **1.** Seconde *f.* *F: I'll be back in a s.*, je reviens dans un instant. *F:* In a split second, en un rien de temps. **2.** Seconde (de degré). **second(s)-hand**, *s.* Aiguille *f* des secondes; trotteuse *f.*

second². I. *a.* **1.** Second, deuxième. (*a*) *The s. of January*, le deux janvier. To live on the second floor, habiter au deuxième (étage). Every second day, tous les deux jours. (*b*) The second largest, le plus grand sauf un. To travel second class, voyager en deuxième classe. *He is second to none*, il ne le cède à personne. **2.** Second; autre; nouveau, -elle. Second nature, seconde nature. **-ly**, *adv.* Deuxièmement; en second lieu. II. **second**, *s.* **1.** (Le) second, (la) seconde; (le, la) deuxième. **2.** (*a*) (*In duel*) Témoin *m.* (*b*) *Box:* Second *m.* **second-best.** **1.** *a.* *My s.-b. suit*, mon complet numéro deux. **2.** *adv* *F:* To come off second-best, être battu. **second-class**, *a.* (Wagon) de seconde (classe); de deuxième qualité. **second-hand.** **1.** *Adv.phr.* To buy sth. (at) second hand, acheter qch. de seconde main. **2.** *a.* Second-hand, d'occasion. *S.-h.* car, voiture usagée. Second-hand dealer,

brocanteur *m.* **second-rate**, *a.* Médiocre, inférieur, -e. **second sight**, *s.* *Psy:* Seconde vue; clairvoyance *f.*

second³, *v.tr.* **1.** (*a*) Seconder; appuyer. (*b*) To second a motion, appuyer une proposition. **2.** Mettre en disponibilité.

secondary, *a.* **1.** Secondaire. **2.** (Rôle) peu important.

secrecy, *s.* **1.** Discrétion *f.* **2.** In secrecy, en secret.

secret. **I.** *a.* (*a*) Secret, -ète; caché. The Secret Service, les agents secrets du gouvernement. (*b*) Discret, -ète; peu communicatif. (*c*) Secret, caché, retiré. **2.** *s.* (*a*) Secret *m.* *He can't keep a s.*, il ne peut pas garder le secret. I make no secret of it, je n'en fais pas mystère. Open secret, *F:* secret de Polichinelle. (*b*) In secret, en secret. **-ly**, *adv.* Secrètement; en secret.

secretarial, *a.* De secrétaire. **secretary**, *s.* **1.** Secrétaire *m*, occ. *f.* Private secretary, secrétaire particulier. (*b*) Secretary of State, ministre *m.*

secrete¹, *v.tr.* *Physiol:* Sécréter. **secrete**², *v.tr.* Soustraire à la vue; cacher **secretion**, *s.* *Physiol:* Sécrétion *f.* **secretive**, *a.* Réservé, dissimulé.

sect, *s.* Secte *f.* **sectarian**, *a.* & *s.* Sectaire (*m*).

section, *s.* **1.** Sectionnement *m*, section *f.* **2.** (*a*) Tranche *f.* (*b*) *Geom:* Conic sections, sections coniques. (*c*) Coupe *f*, profil *m.* **3.** Section; partie *f*, division *f.*

sectional, *a.* En sections. Sectional bookcase, bibliothèque démontable.

sector, *s.* Secteur *m.*

secular, *a.* Séculier; laïque. *S. music*, musique profane.

secure¹, *a.* **1.** Sûr; assuré. **2.** En sûreté; sauf. Secure against attack, à l'abri de toute attaque. **3.** Fixé, assujetti; solide; (*of foothold*) ferme, sûr. **-ly**, *adv.* **1.** (*a*) Sûrement; avec sécurité. (*b*) Avec confiance. **2.** Fermement, solidement.

secure², *v.tr.* **1.** (*a*) Mettre en sûreté, à l'abri. (*b*) Mettre en lieu sûr. **2.** Fixer, retenir. **3.** Obtenir, acquérir; se procurer. *To s. a room (in an hotel)*, retenir une chambre. To secure s.o.'s services, s'assurer de l'aide de qn.

security, *s.* **1.** (*a*) Sécurité *f*, sûreté *f.* (*b*) Solidité *f.* **2.** (Moyen *m* de) sécurité; sauvegarde *f.* **3.** *Com:* (*a*) Caution *f.* To give sth. as (a) security, donner qch. en gage. (*b*) (Donneur *m* de) caution; garant *m.* To stand security for s.o., se porter caution pour qn. (*c*) *pl.* Securities, titres *m*, valeurs *f.* *Government securities*, fonds *m* d'État.

sedate, *a.* Posé, reposé; (maintien) composé. **-ly**, *adv.* Posément.

sedative, *a.* & *s.* Sédatif (*m*); calmant (*m*).

sedentary, *a.* Sédentaire.

sedge, *s.* *Bot:* Laîche *f.*

sediment, *s.* Sédiment *m*, dépôt *m.*

sedition, s. Sédition f.
seditious, a. Séditieux.
seduce, v.tr. Séduire, corrompre.
seduction, s. **1.** Séduction f, corruption f. **2.** Attrait m, charme m.
seductive, a. Séduisant, attrayant.
sedulous, a. Assidu, appliqué. **-ly,** adv. Assidûment.
see¹, v.tr. **1.** Voir. (a) To see the sights of the town, visiter les monuments de la ville. To see s.o. in the distance, apercevoir qn dans le lointain. He is not fit to be seen, il n'est pas présentable. (b) Abs. As far as the eye can see, à perte de vue. It was too dark to see clearly, il faisait trop noir pour bien distinguer. (c) To see s.o. coming, voir venir qn. (d) I'll see you to the door, je vais vous accompagner jusqu'à la porte. **2.** (a) Comprendre, saisir. I don't see the point, je ne saisis pas la nuance. I see! je comprends! (b) Observer, remarquer; s'apercevoir de. I can see no fault in him, je ne lui connais pas de défaut. (c) To see, juger, apprécier. This is how I see it, voici comment j'envisage la chose. If you see fit to, si vous jugez convenable de. **3.** Examiner; regarder avec attention. Abs. I'll go and see, je vais y aller voir. Let me see, (i) attendez un peu; (ii) faites voir! **4.** To see (to it) that everything is in order, s'assurer que tout est en ordre. I will see you righted, je veillerai à ce qu'on vous fasse justice. **5.** (a) Fréquenter, avoir des rapports avec (qn). He sees a great deal of the Smiths, il fréquente beaucoup les Smith. F: See you on Thursday! à jeudi! (b) To go and see s.o., aller trouver qn. To see the doctor, consulter le médecin. (c) Recevoir (un visiteur). **see about,** v.ind.tr. S'occuper de; se charger de. I'll see about it, (i) je m'en occuperai; (ii) j'y réfléchirai. **see after,** v.ind.tr. = SEE TO. **see through.** **1.** v.i. (a) Voir à travers (qch.). (b) F: Pénétrer les intentions de; pénétrer (un mystère). **2.** v.tr. To see a business through, mener une affaire à bonne fin. F: To see it through, tenir jusqu'au bout. **see to,** v.ind.tr. S'occuper de; veiller à. To see to the house, vaquer aux soins du ménage. To see to everything, avoir l'œil à tout. It must be seen to, il faut y aviser. **seeing¹.** **1.** a. Voyant; qui voit. **2.** Conj.phr. Seeing (that), puisque, vu que. **seeing²,** s. Vue f; vision f. Seeing is believing, voir c'est croire. It is worth seeing, cela vaut la peine d'être vu.
see², s. Ecc: Siège épiscopal; évêché m.
seed¹, s. (a) Graine f. F: The seeds of discord, les germes m de discorde. (b) Coll. Semence f; graine(s). To run to seed, monter en graine. **seed-cake,** s. Cu: Gâteau m au carvi. **seed-pearls,** s.pl. Semence f de perles. **seed-potatoes,** s.pl. Pommes f de terre à semence.
seed², v.i. Monter en graine.
seedling, s. Hort: (Jeune) plant m.

seedy, a. **1.** F: (Vêtement) râpé, usé. Seedy-looking individuals, individus d'aspect minable. **2.** Mal en train.
seek, v.tr. **1.** Chercher; rechercher. To seek employment, être en quête d'un emploi. **2.** (a) To seek sth. from s.o., demander qch. à qn. (b) To seek to do sth., essayer de, chercher à, faire qch. **seek after,** v.ind.tr. Much sought after, très recherché, très couru. **seek for,** v.ind.tr. (Re)chercher (qch.).
seem, v.i. Sembler, paraître. **1.** (a) How does it seem to you? que vous en semble? It seems like a dream, on dirait un rêve. (b) I s. to have heard his name, il me semble avoir entendu son nom. **2.** Impers. It seems to me that you are right, il me semble que vous avez raison. It seemed as though, il semblait que + sub.; on aurait dit que + ind. So it seems, à ce qu'il paraît. **seeming,** a. Apparent; soi-disant inv. **-ly,** adv. Apparemment; en apparence.
seemliness, s. Décorum m.
seemly, a. Convenable, bienséant.
seep, v.i. Suinter; s'infiltrer.
seer, s. Prophète m.
see-saw¹, s. Bascule f, balançoire f.
see-saw², v.i. Basculer; osciller.
seethe, v.i. (a) Bouillonner. (b) F: S'agiter, grouiller. Country seething with discontent, pays en effervescence. To be seething with anger, bouillir de colère.
segment, s. Segment m.
segregate, v.tr. Isoler, mettre à part.
segregation, s. Ségrégation f; isolement m.
seigniory, s. Hist: Seigneurie f.
seignorial, a. Seigneurial, -aux.
seine, s. Fish: Seine f, senne f.
seize, v.tr. (a) Se saisir, s'emparer, de. (b) To seize (hold of) sth., saisir, s'emparer de qch. To s. s.o. by the throat, prendre qn à la gorge. (c) To seize the opportunity, saisir l'occasion. (d) v.ind.tr. To s. (up)on a pretext, saisir un prétexte, se saisir d'un prétexte.
seizure, s. **1.** Jur: (a) Appréhension f au corps. (b) Saisie f (de marchandises). **2.** Med: Attaque f.
seldom, adv. Rarement; peu souvent.
select¹, a. **1.** Choisi. **2.** De (premier) choix; d'élite. S. audience, public choisi.
select², v.tr. Choisir (from, parmi).
selection, s. **1.** Choix m, sélection f. **2.** To make a selection, faire un choix. Selections from Byron, morceaux choisis de Byron.
self. **1.** s. Le moi. One's better self, le meilleur côté de notre nature. He is quite his old self again, il est complètement rétabli. All by one's very self, absolument tout seul. **2.** pron. Com: Pay self, payez à moi-même. **3.** (In compound pronouns) (a) Myself, moi(-même); thyself, toi(-même); himself, herself, itself, oneself, lui(-même), elle(-même) soi(-même); yourself, vous(-même); ourselves, nous(-mêmes); yourselves, vous (-mêmes); themselves, eux(-mêmes) m,

elles(-mêmes) *f.* I, *myself, do not believe it,* (quant à) moi, pour ma part, je ne le crois pas. *They themselves continued to enjoy independence,* eux-mêmes continuèrent à jouir de l'indépendance. I am not (quite) myself to-day, je ne suis pas dans mon assiette aujourd'hui. I am quite myself again, je suis tout à fait rétabli. She is kindness itself, elle est la bonté même. (b) (*Reflexive*) Myself, me; thyself, te; himself, herself, itself, oneself, se; ourselves, nous; yourself, -selves, vous; themselves, se. (c) *To say sth. to oneself,* (se) dire qch. à part soi. *To speak of oneself,* parler de soi. To look after oneself, soigner son individu. **To keep oneself to oneself,** se tenir sur son quant-à-soi. *I am not speaking for myself,* je ne parle pas en mon nom. *He thinks for himself,* il pense de son chef. *See for yourselves,* voyez vous-mêmes. **Everyone for himself,** chacun pour soi. **To come to oneself,** revenir à soi. **The thing in itself,** la chose en elle-même. *They came and apologized of themselves,* ils sont venus de leur propre initiative nous faire des excuses. *She lived by herself,* elle vivait seule. **To do sth. (all) by oneself,** faire qch. tout seul. (d) *They whispered among themselves.* ils chuchotaient entre eux. **self-abasement,** *s.* Humiliation *f* de soi-même. **self-apparent,** *a.* Évident. **self-assertion,** *s.* Outrecuidance *f.* **self-assertive,** *a.* Outrecuidant. **self-assurance,** *s.* Confiance *f* en soi; assurance *f*; aplomb *m.* **self-centred,** *a.* Égocentrique. **self-command,** *s.* Maîtrise *f* de soi. **self-communion,** *s.* Recueillement *m.* **self-conceit,** *s.* Suffisance *f.* **self-confidence,** *s.* Confiance *f* en soi; assurance *f.* **self-confident,** *a.* Sûr de soi; plein d'assurance. **self-conscious,** *a.* Embarrassé, gêné. **self-consciousness,** *s.* Contrainte *f,* embarras *m,* gêne *f.* **self-contained,** *a.* **I.** Peu communicatif. **2.** Self-contained flat, appartement avec entrée particulière. **self-control,** *s.* Sang-froid *m*; maîtrise *f* de soi. **self-deception,** *s.* Illusion *f*; déception *f* de soi-même. **self-defence,** *s.* Défense personnelle. *Jur:* Légitime défense. **self-denial,** *s.* (a) Abnégation *f* de soi; renoncement(s) *m(pl).* (b) Frugalité *f.* **self-determination,** *s. Right of peoples to s.-d.,* droit des peuples de disposer d'eux-mêmes. **self-esteem,** *s.* Respect *m* de soi; amour-propre *m.* **self-evident,** *a.* Évident en soi. **self-explanatory,** *a.* Qui s'explique de soi-même. **self-importance,** *s.* Suffisance *f,* présomption *f.* **self-important,** *a.* Suffisant, présomptueux. **self-indulgence,** *s.* Satisfaction *f* égoïste de ses appétits. **self-indulgent,** *a.* Qui ne se refuse rien. **self-interest,** *s.* Intérêt personnel. **self-made,** *a.* (Homme) qui est arrivé par lui-même. **self-opinionated,** *a.* Suffisant. **self-possessed,** *a.* Maître de soi. **self-possession,** *s.* Aplomb *m,* sang-froid *m.*

self-preservation, *s.* Conservation *f* de soi-même. **self-reliance,** *s.* Indépendance *f.* **self-reliant,** *a.* Indépendant. **self-respect,** *s.* Respect *m* de soi; amour-propre *m.* **self-respecting,** *a.* Qui se respecte. **self-restraint,** *s.* Retenue *f*; modération *f.* *To exercise s.-r.,* se contenir. **self-righteous,** *a.* Pharisaïque. **self-sacrifice,** *s.* Abnégation *f* (de soi). **self-same,** *attrib. a.* Identique. **self-satisfaction,** *s.* Contentement *m* de soi; suffisance *f.* **self-satisfied,** *a.* Content de soi; suffisant. **self-seeking,** *a.* Égoïste, intéressé. **self-starter,** *s.* *Aut:* (Auto) démarreur *m.* **self-supporting,** *a.* Qui vit de son travail; (*of business*) qui couvre ses frais. **self-taught,** *a.* Autodidacte. **self-willed,** *a.* Opiniâtre, volontaire.

selfish, *a.* Égoïste, intéressé. **-ly,** *adv.* Égoïstement; en égoïste.

selfishness, *s.* Égoïsme *m.*

sell¹, *s.* *F:* Déception *f*; *F:* attrape *f.*

sell², *v.tr.* **I.** (a) Vendre (to, à). *He sold it me for ten shillings,* il me l'a vendu dix shillings. (b) *This book sells well,* ce livre est de bonne vente. Land to sell, terrain à vendre. **2.** (a) Vendre, trahir. (b) *F:* Duper, tromper. **You have been sold,** on vous a refait. **Sold again!** attrapé! **sell off,** *v.tr.* Solder; liquider (son écurie). **selling off,** *s.* Liquidation *f.* **sell out,** *v.tr.* We are sold out of this article, nous sommes démunis de cet article. **sell up,** *v.tr.* Vendre, faire saisir (un failli). **selling,** *s.* Vente *f*; écoulement *m,* placement *m.* Selling price, prix *m* de vente.

seller, *s.* (a) Vendeur, -euse. (b) Marchand, -ande; débitant, -ante (of, de).

seltzer, *s.* Seltzer(-water), eau *f* de seltz.

selvage, selvedge, *s.* *Tex:* Lisière *f.*

semaphore¹, *s.* Sémaphore *m.*

semaphore², *v.tr.* Transmettre par sémaphore.

semblance, *s.* Apparence *f,* semblant *m,* simulacre *m.* **To put on a semblance of** gaiety, faire semblant d'être gai.

semi-, *pref.* **I.** Semi-. **2.** Demi-. **3.** A moitié; à demi; mi-. **semi-conscious,** *a.* A demi conscient. **semi-detached,** *a.* Semi-detached house, maison jumelle.

semicircle, *s.* Demi-cercle *m, pl.* demi-cercles.

semicircular, *a.* Demi-circulaire, *pl.* demi-circulaires.

semicolon, *s.* Point *m* et virgule.

seminary, *s.* **I.** *R.C.Ch:* Séminaire *m.* **2.** *A:* Young ladies' seminary, pensionnat *m* de jeunes filles.

Semitic, *a.* Sémitique.

semolina, *s.* *Cu:* Semoule *f.*

sempstress, *s.f.* = SEAMSTRESS.

senate, *s.* Sénat *m.*

senator, *s.* Sénateur *m.*

send, *v.tr.* **I.** (a) Envoyer. **To send s.o. for** sth., envoyer qn chercher qch. (b) Envoyer;

expédier. **To send word to** s.o., faire savoir qch. à qn. **2.** *It sent a shiver down my spine*, cela m'a fait passer un frisson dans le dos. **3.** *Abs.* **To send for** s.o., envoyer chercher qn. I shall send for it, je vais l'envoyer prendre. **send away,** *v.tr.* (a) Renvoyer, congédier. (b) Expédier. **send back,** *v.tr.* Renvoyer. **send in,** *v.tr.* **1.** (a) Faire (r)entrer. (b) *To s. in one's name*, se faire annoncer. **2.** (a) Livrer, rendre (un compte); remettre (une demande). (b) **To send in one's resignation,** donner sa démission. **send off,** *v.tr.* (a) Envoyer. (b) Expédier (une lettre). **send on,** *v.tr.* (a) Faire suivre (une lettre). (b) Transmettre (un ordre). **send out,** *v.tr.* (a) Faire sortir. (b) Lancer (des circulaires). (c) Émettre. **send round,** *v.tr.* Faire circuler.

sender, *s* Envoyeur. -euse; expéditeur, -trice.

Senegal. *Pr.n.* Le Sénégal.

Senegalese, *a. & s.* Sénégalais, -aise.

seneschal, *s.* *Hist:* Sénéchal *m*, -aux.

senile, *a.* Sénile.

senility, *s.* Sénilité *f*.

senior. **1.** *a.* (a) Jones senior, Jones aîné. William Jones senior, William Jones père. (b) Senior in rank, de grade supérieur. The senior officer, le doyen des officiers. *My s. officer,* mon officier supérieur. **2.** *s.* (a) Aîné, -ée; doyen, -enne (d'âge). (b) (Le plus) ancien, (la plus) ancienne. *To be s.o.'s s.,* être l'ancien, le doyen, de qn.

seniority, *s.* **1.** Priorité *f* d'âge; supériorité *f* d'âge. **2.** Ancienneté *f* (de grade).

senna, *s.* Séné *m*.

sensation, *s.* **1.** Sensation *f*; sentiment *m*. *I had a s. of falling,* j'avais l'impression que je tombais. **2.** Sensation; effet sensationnel.

sensational, *a.* Sensationnel.

sense, *s.* **1.** Sens *m*. **To have a keen sense of smell,** avoir l'odorat fin. **2.** *pl.* (a) To be in one's senses, être sain d'esprit. Any man in his senses, tout homme jouissant de son bon sens. **To frighten** s.o. **out of his senses,** effrayer qn jusqu'à lui faire perdre la raison. **To come to one's senses,** revenir à la raison. (b) **To lose one's senses,** perdre connaissance *f*. **To come to one's senses,** revenir à soi. **3.** (a) Sensation *f*, sens. *To labour under a s. of injustice,* nourrir un sentiment d'injustice. (b) Sentiment, conscience *f*. *Keen* **sense of** humour, sentiment très vif de l'humour. **4.** Bon sens, intelligence *f*. **Common sense,** sens commun. **To talk sense,** parler raison. **5.** Sens, signification *f*. *I can't make* s. *of this passage,* je n'arrive pas à comprendre ce passage. **In the full sense of the word** dans toute l'acception du terme.

senseless, *a.* **1.** Sans connaissance; inanimé. **To knock** s.o. **senseless,** assommer qn. **2.** Insensé, stupide, déraisonnable. **-ly,** *adv.* Insensément, stupidement.

senselessness, *s.* Manque *m* de bon sens.

sensibility, *s.* Sensibilité *f*.

sensible, *a.* **1.** Sensible, perceptible. **2.** Sensible, appréciable. **3.** Conscient (*of,* de). *S. of an honour,* sensible à un honneur. **4.** Sensé, raisonnable. **-ibly,** *adv.* **1.** Sensiblement, perceptiblement. **2.** Sensément, raisonnablement.

sensitive, *a.* (a) Sensible, sensitif. (b) Susceptible; impressionnable. (c) **Sensitive scales,** balance sensible.

sensitiveness, *s.* Sensibilité *f*.

sensitize, *v.tr.* *Phot:* Sensibiliser. **sensitized,** *a.* Sensible, impressionnable.

sensual, *a.* Sensuel; voluptueux.

sensuality, *s.* Sensualité *f*.

sensuous, *a.* Sybaritique, voluptueux. **-ly,** *adv.* Avec volupté.

sentence[1], *s.* **1.** *Jur:* (a) Jugement *m*; sentence *f*, condamnation *f*. *Under s. of death,* condamné à mort. (b) Peine *f*. **2.** *Gram:* Phrase *f*.

sentence[2], *v.tr.* *Jur:* Condamner.

sententious, *a.* Sentencieux. **-ly,** *adv.* Sentencieusement.

sentient, *a.* Sentant, sensible.

sentiment, *s.* **1.** Sentiment *m*. (a) *Noble sentiments,* sentiments nobles. (b) Opinion *f*, avis *m*. **Those are my sentiments,** voilà mon sentiment. **2.** Sentimentalité *f*.

sentimental, *a.* (a) Sentimental, -aux. (b) D'une sensiblerie romanesque. **-ally,** *adv.* Sentimentalement.

sentimentality, *s.* Sentimentalité *f*, sensiblerie *f*.

sentinel, *s.* (i) (*Guard*) Factionnaire *m*; (ii) (*outpost*) sentinelle *f*.

sentry, *s.* **1.** (a) (*Guard*) Factionnaire *m*. **To relieve a sentry,** relever qn de faction. (b) (*Outpost*) Sentinelle *f*. **2.** Faction *f*. **To be on sentry(-go),** être de faction.

sentry-box, *s.* *Mil:* Guérite *f*.

sepal, *s.* *Bot:* Sépale *m*.

separate[1], *a.* (a) Séparé, détaché (*from,* de). (b) Distinct, indépendant. *Entered in a s. column,* inscrit dans une colonne à part. **-ly,** *adv.* Séparément; à part.

separate[2]. **1.** *v.tr.* Séparer. (a) Désunir, détacher (*from,* de). (b) Désunir (une famille). *He is separated from his wife,* il est séparé de sa femme. (c) *This river separates the two countries,* ce fleuve sépare les deux pays. **2.** *v.i.* (a) Se séparer, se détacher (*from,* de). (b) (*Of man and wife*) Se séparer de corps et de biens.

separation, *s.* **1.** Séparation *f*. **Separation from** s.o., séparation d'avec qn. *Mil:* **Separation allowances,** allocations faites aux femmes (des soldats). **2.** Écart *m*, distance *f*.

sepia, *s.* *Art:* Sépia *f*.

sepoy, *s.* Cipaye *m*.

September, *s.* Septembre *m*. *In S.,* au mois de septembre.

septet(te), *s.* *Mus:* Septuor *m*.

septic, *a.* *Med:* Septique.

septuagenarian] 672 [set

septuagenarian, s. & a. Septuagénaire (mf).
sepulchral, a. Sépulcral, -aux.
sepulchre, s. Sépulcre m, tombeau m.
sepulture, s. Sépulture f.
sequel, s. Suite f. **In the sequel,** par la suite.
sequence, s. **1.** (a) Succession f; ordre
naturel. **In sequence,** en série. (b) Suite f,
série f. (c) Gram: Sequence of tenses, concordance f des temps. **2.** Cards: Séquence f.
sequester, v.pr. To sequester oneself, se
retirer (du monde). **sequestered,** a. Retiré.
sequin, s. Sequin m.
seraglio, s. Sérail m, -ails.
seraph, s. Séraphin m.
seraphic, a. Séraphique.
Serb, a. & s. = SERBIAN.
Serbia. Pr.n. La Serbie.
Serbian. **1.** a. & s. Serbe (mf). **2.** s. Ling:
Le serbe.
sere, a. Poet: Flétri, desséché, fané.
serenade[1], s. Sérénade f.
serenade[2], v.tr. Donner une sérénade à (qn).
serene, a. **1.** Serein, calme, tranquille;
F: **All serene!** ça y est! c'est bien! **2.** His
Serene Highness, son Altesse sérénissime.
-ly, adv. Tranquillement; avec sérénité.
serenity, s. Sérénité f, calme m, tranquillité f.
serf, s. Serf, f. serve.
serfdom, s. Servage m.
serge, s. Tex: Serge f.
sergeant, s. (a) Mil: (Infantry) Sergent m;
(cavalry) = maréchal m des logis. (b) Police
sergeant, brigadier. **sergeant-major,** s.
Mil: **1.** (Infantry) Sergent m major ou adjudant m. (Mounted arms) Maréchal des logis
chef. **2.** Regimental sergeant-major = adjudant chef.
serial, a. **1.** Serial number, numéro de série.
2. Serial story, s. serial, feuilleton m.
1. Série f, suite f; échelle f,
gamme f. **2.** Adv.phr. In series, en série.
series, s.inv.
serious, a. Sérieux. **1.** S. wound, blessure
grave. **2.** (a) Serious promise, promesse
sérieuse, sincère. (b) Réfléchi. **I am serious,**
je ne plaisante pas. **-ly,** adv. Sérieusement.
1. Seriously ill, gravement malade. **2.** To
take sth. seriously, prendre qch. au sérieux.
seriousness, s. **1.** Gravité f. **2.** Sérieux m
(de maintien). **3.** In all seriousness, sérieusement.
sermon, s. **1.** Ecc: Sermon m; R.C.Ch:
prône m. **2.** F: Sermon, semonce f.
serpent, s. Serpent m.
serpentine, a. Serpentin; sinueux.
serrated, a. Dentelé.
serried, a. Lit: Serré.
serum, s. Physiol: Sérum m.
servant, s. **1.** (a) (Domestic) servant,
domestique mf; servante f, bonne f. **General
servant,** bonne à tout faire. Mil: Officer's
servant, ordonnance f. (b) Serviteur m,
servante. (c) Corr: Your obedient servant,
je vous prie d'agréer mes salutations empressées. **2.** Employé, -ée. Civil servant,

fonctionnaire mf. **servant-girl,** s. Domestique f; bonne f.
serve. **I.** v.tr. **1.** (a) Servir. Abs. To serve
at table, servir à table. Jur: To serve on
the jury, être du jury (b) To serve one's
apprenticeship, faire son apprentissage.
2. (a) Être utile à; suffire à. It will serve the
purpose, abs. it will serve, cela fera l'affaire.
(b) If my memory serves me right, si j'ai
bonne mémoire. **3.** Desservir (par un
chemin de fer). **4.** To serve s.o. with a
pound of butter, servir une livre de beurre
à qn. **5.** (a) To serve a dish, servir un mets.
(b) Ten: To serve the ball, abs. to serve,
servir (la balle). **6.** Traiter. It serves you
right! c'est bien fait! vous ne l'avez pas
volé! **II.** **serve,** v.i. **1.** To serve for sth.,
servir à qch. To serve as sth., servir de qch.
2. When occasion serves, lorsque l'occasion
est favorable. **serve out,** v.tr. **1.** Distribuer; servir à la ronde. **2.** F: To serve
s.o. out for sth., revaloir qch. à qn; se venger.
serving, a. Servant; au service.
service, s. **1.** Service m. Length of s.,
ancienneté f. To be on active service, être
en activité (de service). **2.** (a) Public services,
services publics. Army Service Corps
= service de l'Intendance. (b) Distribution
f, installation f (d'électricité). **3.** Emploi m.
To be in the civil service, être fonctionnaire.
4. (Domestic) service, service (domestique).
To take service with s.o., entrer au service
de qn. **5.** (a) To render s.o. a service, rendre
(un) service à qn. (b) I am at your service,
je suis à votre disposition f. (c) Utilité f.
To be of service to s.o., être utile à qn.
6. Ecc: Office m. **7.** Ten: Service.
serviceable, a. **1.** (Of pers.) Serviable.
2. (Of thg) Utilisable. (b) Utile; avantageux. (c) Pratique.
serviette, s. Serviette f de table.
servile, a. Servile. **-ly,** adv. Servilement.
servility, s. Servilité f.
servitude, s. **1.** Servitude f, esclavage m.
2. Jur: Penal servitude, travaux forcés.
session, s. **1.** Session f; séance f. Parl:
The House is now in session, la Chambre
siège actuellement. **2.** Jur: pl. Petty sessions,
session des juges de paix.
set[1], s. **1.** Ensemble m. (a) Jeu m (de
dominos); collection complète; service m
(de porcelaine). (b) Wireless set, poste m de
radio. (c) Ten: Manche f, set m. (d) Groupe m.
Set of thieves, bande f de voleurs. Literary
set, coterie f littéraire. The smart set, le
monde élégant. **2.** To make a set at, attaquer.
3. Direction f (du courant); Nau: lit m
(du vent).
set[2], v. **I.** v.tr. **1.** Asseoir, placer. **2.** Mettre,
poser. To set a dish on the table, servir un
plat. **3.** To set chairs, placer des chaises.
4. To set words to music, mettre des paroles
en musique. **5.** To set seeds, planter des
graines. **6.** To set the clock, régler la pendule.

To set the alarm for five o'clock, mettre le réveille-matin sur cinq heures. **7.** (a) To set a gem sertir, enchâsser, une pierre. Ring set with rubies, bague ornée de rubis. (b) Nau: To set a sail, déployer une voile. **8.** To set a snare, dresser, tendre, un piège. **9.** To set limits to sth., assigner des limites à qch. **10.** To set the fashion, fixer la mode. **11.** To set a bone, remettre un os. **12.** To set one's teeth, serrer les dents. **13.** (a) To set s.o. doing sth., mettre qn à faire qch. To set the dog barking, faire aboyer le chien. (b) To set sth. going, mettre qch. en train. **14.** To set a man to work, mettre un homme au travail. **15.** To set a good example, donner un bon exemple. To set a problem, donner un problème à résoudre. II. **set,** v.i. **1.** Se coucher. **2.** (Of broken bone) Se ressouder. **3.** (a) Se coaguler; (of jelly) prendre. **4.** (Of cement) Faire prise. **5.** Opinion is setting that way, le courant de l'opinion prend cette direction. **5.** To set to work, se mettre au travail, à l'œuvre. **set about. 1.** v.i. (a) To set about doing sth., se mettre à faire qch. I don't know how to set about it, je ne sais pas comment m'y prendre. (b) F: To set about s.o., attaquer qn. **2.** v.tr. To set a rumour about, donner cours à un bruit. **set against,** v.tr. (a) To set s.o. against s.o., prévenir qn contre qn. (b) To set one's face against sth., s'opposer résolument à qch. **set back,** v.tr. (Of horse) To set back its ears, coucher les oreilles. **set-back,** s. Déconvenue f; revers m de fortune. **set down,** v.tr. Poser, déposer. (Of train) To set down passengers, débarquer des voyageurs. **set forth. 1.** v.tr. Énoncer; exposer. **2.** v.i. Se mettre en route. **set in,** v.i. Commencer. Before winter sets in, avant le début de l'hiver. **set off. I.** v.tr. Faire ressortir, faire valoir. II. **set off,** v.i. Partir; se mettre en route. **set-off,** s. Contraste m. As a set-off, comme contraste. **set on,** v.tr. To set a dog on s.o., lancer un chien contre qn. I was set on by a dog, j'ai été attaqué par un chien. **set out. I.** v.tr. **1.** Équiper. **2.** Arranger, disposer. II. **set out,** v.i. Se mettre en route. **set to,** v.i. Se mettre au travail. We must set to! allons-y! **set-to,** s. **1.** Assaut m (de boxe). **2.** Lutte f, combat m. **set up¹. I.** v.tr. **1.** (a) Placer, fixer (un objet). (b) Élever, ériger. **2.** Exalter, élever. **3.** (a) Établir; fonder. (b) To set s.o. up in business, établir qn dans un commerce. (c) To set s.o. up as a model, proposer qn comme modèle. **4.** To set up a shout, pousser une clameur. **5.** Donner, rendre, de la vigueur à. **set up,** v.i. **1.** To set up in business, s'établir dans le commerce. **2.** v.i. & pr. To set (oneself) up as a critic, se poser en critique. **set up²,** a. Well set up fellow, gaillard bien campé. **set upon,** v.i. To set upon the enemy, attaquer l'ennemi. **set³,** a. **1.** (a) Set face, visage aux

traits rigides. Set smile, sourire figé. (b) (Ressort) bandé, tendu **2.** (a) Set time, heure fixée. Set purpose, ferme intention. (b) Set phrase, cliché m; expression consacrée. (c) Set task, tâche assignée. **3.** To be set on sth., être résolu, déterminé, à qch. To be dead set against s.o., s'acharner contre qn. **set square,** s. Équerre f. **setting¹,** a. Baissant, couchant. **setting²,** s. **1.** (a) Mise f, pose f. (b) Disposition f, arrangement m. (c) Réglage m; ajustage m. (d) Montage m (d'un spécimen); armement m (d'un piège). (e) Réduction f (d'une fracture). (f) Imposition f. **2.** (a) Coucher m (d'un astre). (b) Prise f; coagulation f. **3.** (a) Cadre m. Th: Mise en scène. (b) Monture f (d'un diamant). (c) Mus: (i) Ton m. (ii) Setting for piano, arrangement pour piano. **settee,** s. Canapé m, causeuse f. **setter,** s. Chien m d'arrêt. **settle¹,** s. Banc m à dossier. **settle². I.** v.tr. **1.** (a) Établir, installer. (b) Coloniser (un pays). **2.** To settle one's affairs, mettre à ses affaires. **3.** To s. s.o.'s doubts, dissiper les doutes de qn **4.** Concerter (son visage); calmer (les nerfs). **5.** Fixer, déterminer. It's all settled, c'est une affaire faite. **6.** (a) Résoudre, décider; vider (une querelle); arranger (une affaire). Settle it among yourselves, arrangez cela entre vous. (b) Conclure (une affaire); régler, solder (un compte); payer (une dette). Abs. To settle (up) with s.o., régler son compte avec qn. (c) To settle s.o., F: donner son reste à qn. **7.** To settle an annuity on s.o., constituer une annuité à qn. II. **settle,** v.i. **1.** v.i & pr. (a) To settle (down) in a locality, s'établir dans un lieu. (b) (Of bird) Se percher. (c) To settle (down) to work, se mettre sérieusement au travail. **2.** (Of liquid) Se clarifier; (of sediment) se précipiter. **3.** (a) (Of ground) Prendre son assiette; se tasser. (b) (Of ship) To settle (down), couler. **4.** (Of passion) S'apaiser, se calmer. The weather is settling, le temps se calme. **settle down,** v.i. **1.** See SETTLE² II. 1 (a), (c), 3 (b). **2.** (Of pers.) Se ranger. **3.** He is beginning to settle down at school, il commence à s'habituer à l'école. **settled,** a **1.** (a) Invariable, sûr; (of idea) fixe, enraciné. Settled intention, intention bien arrêtée. Settled weather, temps fait, fixe. (b) (Of pers.) Rangé. **2.** Arrangé, décidé. **3.** (Of pers.) Domicilié, établi; (of thg) bien assis. **4.** (Of country) Colonisé. **settlement,** s. **1.** (a) Établissement m; installation f. (b) Colonisation f (d'un pays). **2.** (a) Règlement m. (b) Com: Règlement, payement m. (c) Marriage settlement, contrat m de mariage. **3.** Colonie f. **settler,** s. Colon m. **seven,** num. a. & s. Sept (m). **seven-league(d),** attrib.a. Seven-league(d) boots, bottes de sept lieues. **seventeen,** num. a. & s. Dix-sept (m).

seventeenth, *num. a. & s.* Dix-septième (*m*). Louis the Seventeenth, Louis Dix-sept.

seventh, *num. a. & s.* Septième (*m*). (On) the seventh of May, mai sept.

seventy, *num. a. & s.* Soixante-dix (*m*). Seventy-one, -nine, soixante et onze, soixante-dix-neuf.

sever, *v.tr.* (*a*) Désunir, disjoindre ; rompre. (*b*) To s. s.o.'s leg, couper la jambe à qn.

several, *a.* **1.** Séparé ; différent. **2.** Plusieurs, divers ; quelques.

severance, *s.* Séparation / (*from,* de) ; rupture *f.*

severe, *a.* **1.** Sévère, strict, rigoureux (*with,* envers). A s. reprimand, une verte réprimande. **2.** (*a*) (Temps) rigoureux, dur. The cold was s., le froid sévissait. (*b*) Vif: rude. S. pain, vive douleur. **-ly,** *adv.* **1.** Sévèrement ; avec sévérité. **2.** Grièvement.

severity, *s.* **1.** Sévérité *f,* rigueur *f.* To use severity, sévir. **2.** (*a*) Rigueur, inclémence *f.* (*b*) Gravité *f* (d'une maladie).

sew, *v.tr.* Coudre. **sew on,** *v.tr.* Coudre, attacher. **sewing,** *s.* **1.** Couture *f.* Plain sewing, couture simple. Sewing needle, aiguille *f* à coudre. **2.** Ouvrage *m* (à l'aiguille).

sewing-cotton, *s.* Fil *m* à coudre. **sewing-machine,** *s.* Machine *f* à coudre.

sewage, *s.* Eau(x) *f(pl)* d'égout. Sewage farm, champs *mpl* d'épandage.

sewer, *s.* Civ.E: Égout *m.*

sex, *s.* Sexe *m.* (*a*) F: Sex appeal, attrait *m.* (*b*) The fair sex, le beau sexe.

sexagenarian, *a. & s.* Sexagénaire (*mf*).

sextant, *s.* Sextant *m.*

sextet, *s.* Mus: Sextuor *m.*

sexton, *s.* Ecc: (*a*) Sacristain *m.* (*b*) F: Sonneur *m.* (*c*) F: Fossoyeur *m.*

sexual, *a.* Sexuel.

sh, *int.* Chut !

shabbiness, *s.* **1.** État râpé ; état défraîchi ; apparence *f* pauvre. **2.** Mesquinerie / (de conduite).

shabby, *a.* **1.** Pauvre, minable. To look s., avoir l'air râpé. **2.** Mesquin. To do s.o. a shabby turn, faire une mesquinerie à qn. **-ily,** *adv.* **1.** Pauvrement. S. dressed, miteux. **2.** (Se conduire) mesquinement.

shackle¹, *s.* **1.** *pl.* Shackles, fers *m.* **2.** Maillon *m* de liaison (d'une chaîne).

shackle², *v.tr.* Mettre les fers à, entraver.

shade¹, *s.* **1.** Ombre *f.* F: To put s.o. in(to) the shade, éclipser qn. The shades of night, les ombres de la nuit ; les ténèbres *f.* **2.** Nuance *f ;* teinte *f.* **3.** (*a*) Pâle reflet *m,* ombre (de qch.). (*b*) Ombre, fantôme *m.* **4.** (*a*) (Lamp-)shade, abat-jour *m inv.* (*b*) Store *m* (de fenêtre).

shade², *v.tr.* **1.** (*a*) Ombrager ; couvrir d'ombre. To shade one's eyes with one's hand, mettre la main en abat-jour. (*b*) Obscurcir, assombrir. **2.** Ombrer (un dessin).

shadiness, *s.* Ombre *f,* ombrage *m.*

shadow¹, *s.* Ombre *f.* **1.** (*a*) Obscurité *f.*

(*b*) Noir *m* (d'un tableau). **2.** To cast a shadow, projeter une ombre ; faire ombre. **3.** (*a*) Compagnon, *f* compagne, inséparable. (*b*) Ombre (d'un mort). To wear oneself to a shadow, s'épuiser.

shadow², *v.tr.* **1.** Ombrager ; couvrir de son ombre. **2.** Filer (qn). **shadowing,** *s.* Filature *f* (d'une personne suspecte).

shadowy, *a.* Indécis, vague.

shady, *a.* **1.** (*a*) Qui donne de l'ombre ; ombreux. (*b*) Ombragé ; couvert d'ombre. S. walk, allée couverte. **2.** Louche. Shady-looking customer, individu *m* aux allures louches. The shady side, les dessous *m.*

shaft¹, *s.* **1.** Hampe *f,* bois *m.* **2.** Flèche *f,* trait *m.* **3.** Rayon *m* (de lumière). **4.** Tige *f.* **5.** Veh: Brancard *m* limon *m.*

shaft², *s.* Min: Puits *m.*

shaggy, *a.* Poilu ; à longs poils ; (sourcils) en broussailles.

shagreen, *s.* Leath: (Peau *f* de) chagrin *m.*

shah, *s.* Schah *m.*

shake¹, *s.* **1.** (*a*) Secousse *f.* To give sth. a good shake, bien secouer, bien agiter, qch. A shake of the head, un hochement de tête. Shake of the hand, poignée *f* de main. (*b*) Tremblement *m.* (*c*) Mus: Trille *m.* **2.** P: To be no great shakes, ne pas valoir grand'chose.

shake², *v.* **I.** *v.tr.* **1.** Secouer ; agiter. To shake one's head, faire non de la tête. To shake one's fist at s.o., menacer qn du poing. To shake hands with s.o., serrer la main à qn. They shook hands on it, ils ont topé. To shake oneself free, se dégager d'une secousse. **2.** Ébranler. To feel shaken after a fall, se ressentir d'une chute. **II.** *shake,* *v.i.* Trembler ; (of building) chanceler, branler ; (of voice) trembloter. To shake all over, trembler de tout son corps. F: To shake in one's shoes, trembler dans sa peau. **shake down,** *v.tr.* Secouer, faire tomber. **shake-down,** *s.* F: Lit improvisé. **shake off,** *v.tr.* F: Se débarrasser, se défaire, de. **shake up,** *v.tr.* **1.** Secouer, brasser. **2.** (*a*) Agiter. (*b*) F: Éveiller, secouer, stimuler. **shaking,** *s.* Secouement *m.* To give a good shaking, bien secouer.

shakiness, *s.* Manque *m* de stabilité ; tremblement *m ;* chevrotement *m* (de la voix).

shaky, *a.* Peu solide ; faible, chancelant. S. hand, main tremblante. S. voice, voix mal assurée.

shale, *s.* Schiste *m.*

shall, *modal aux. v.* **I.** **1.** (*a*) Ships shall carry three lights, les navires sont tenus de porter trois feux. All is as it should be, tout est très bien. (*b*) He shall not die! il ne faut pas qu'il meure ! He shall not do it, je défends qu'il le fasse. You shall do it! vous le ferez, je le veux ! (*c*) You should do it at once, vous devriez le faire tout de suite. It was an accident that should have been foreseen, c'était un accident à prévoir. F: You should have seen him, il fallait le voir! (d) *He should have arrived by this time*, il devrait être arrivé à l'heure qu'il est. **I should think so!** je crois bien! **2.** *Shall I open the window?* voulez-vous que j'ouvre la fenêtre? **3.** (a) *Why should you suspect me?* pourquoi me soupçonner (, moi)? **Whom should I meet but Jones!** voilà que je rencontre Jones! (b) *He ordered that they should be released*, il ordonna qu'on les relâchât. (c) *If he should come*, si par hasard il vient. *Should I be free*, si je suis libre. **Should the occasion arise**, le cas échéant. **In case he should not be there**, au cas où il n'y soit pas. **II. shall** *used as an auxiliary verb forming the future tenses*. **1.** *You shan't have any!* tu n'en auras pas! **2.** (a) *To-morrow I shall go and he will arrive*, demain, moi je partirai et lui arrivera. *Will you be there?—I shall*, y serez-vous?—Oui (, j'y serai). (b) *Shall you come to-morrow?* vous viendrez demain? **3.** *If he comes I shall speak to him*, s'il vient je lui parlerai. *We should come if we were invited*, nous viendrions si on nous invitait. **4.** *I should like a drink*, je prendrais bien quelque chose. *I shouldn't be surprised if* . . . , cela ne me surprendrait pas que. . . .

shallot, *s.* Échalote *f*.

shallow. I. *a.* (a) (*Of water*) Peu profond; (*of dish*) plat. *Nau:* **Shallow water**, hauts-fonds. (b) *F:* Superficiel, frivole. **2.** *s.* Bas-fond *m*, *pl.* bas-fonds, haut-fond *m*, *pl.* hauts-fonds.

shallowness, *s.* (a) (Le) peu de profondeur. (b) *F:* Caractère superficiel.

sham[1]. **I.** *a.* Simulé, feint; faux, *f.* fausse, postiche, en toc. *Sch:* **Sham fight**, bataille *f.* **II. sham**, *s.* **I.** Feinte *f*, *F:* trompe-l'œil *m inv.* **2.** **He's a sham**, c'est un imposteur.

sham[2], *v.tr.* Feindre, simuler. *To s. sleep*, faire semblant de dormir. **He is only shamming**, tout ça c'est de la frime.

shamble[1], *s.* Démarche traînante.

shamble[2], *v.i.* **To shamble (along)**, aller à pas traînants; s'avancer en traînant le pas.

shambles, *s.pl.* (a) Abattoir *m.* (b) Scène *f* de carnage.

shame[1], *s.* (a) Honte *f.* **To put s.o. to shame**, faire honte à qn. **Shame (up)on you!** honte à vous! **All the more shame to you!** c'est d'autant plus honteux à vous! **For shame!** fi! quelle honte! (b) *F:* **It's a (great) shame!** c'est honteux! **What a shame!** quel dommage! quelle pitié!

shame[2], *v.tr.* Faire honte à, humilier. **To be shamed into doing sth.**, faire qch. par amour-propre.

shamefaced, *a.* Honteux; penaud.

shamefacedly, *adv.* D'un air penaud.

shameful, *a.* Honteux, scandaleux. **-fully**, *adv.* Honteusement, scandaleusement.

shamefulness, *s.* Honte *f*, infamie *f.*

shameless, *a.* **1.** Éhonté, effronté. **2.** Honteux, scandaleux. **-ly**, *adv.* Effrontément. *To lie s.*, mentir impudemment.

shamelessness, *s.* **1.** Immodestie *f*, impudeur *f.* **2.** Effronterie *f*, impudence *f.*

shampoo[1], *s.* Schampooing *m.* **Dry shampoo**, friction *f.*

shampoo[2], *v.tr.* **To shampoo one's hair**, se dégraisser les cheveux. *To s. s.o.*, donner, faire, un schampooing à qn.

shamrock, *s.* Trèfle *m* d'Irlande.

shank, *s.* **I.** (a) **Shanks**, jambes *f.* (b) *Cu:* Manche *m* (de gigot de mouton). **2.** Queue *f* (d'un bouton).

shanty[1], *s.* Hutte *f*, cabane *f*, baraque *f.*

shanty[2], *s.* = CHANTY.

shape[1], *s.* **I.** (a) Forme *f*, configuration *f*; façon *f*, coupe *f* (d'un habit). **To get out of shape**, se déformer. **To put into shape**, mettre au point. (b) Taille *f*, tournure *f.* (c) Forme indistincte; apparition *f.* **2. To take shape**, prendre forme. **3. In any shape or form**, de n'importe quelle sorte. **4.** *Cu:* Moule *m.*

shape[2], *v.* **I.** *v.tr.* (a) Façonner; tailler. **To shape one's life**, régler sa vie. (b) **To shape one's course**, se diriger (*towards*, vers); *Nau:* faire route (*for*, sur). **2.** *v.i.* Se développer. **To shape well**, promettre. *The affair is shaping well*, l'affaire prend bonne tournure. **shaped**, *a.* Façonné, taillé.

shapeless, *a.* Informe; difforme.

shapelessness, *s.* Manque *m* de forme.

shapeliness, *s.* Beauté *f* de forme.

shapely, *a.* Bien fait, bien tourné.

share[1], *s.* Soc *m* (de charrue).

share[2], *s.* **I.** (a) Part *f*, portion *f.* *In equal shares*, par portions égales. **Share in profits**, participation *f* aux bénéfices. **To go shares**, partager (*with*, avec). **To go half-shares with s.o.**, mettre qn de part à demi. **Share and share alike**, en partageant également. (b) (Fair) share, portion juste; lot *m.* **2.** Contribution *f*, écot *m.* **To take a share in the conversation**, contribuer à la conversation. **To have a share in an undertaking**, avoir un intérêt dans une entreprise. **3.** *Com:* Action *f*, titre *m.*

share[3]. **I.** *v.tr.* Partager. **2.** *v.tr. & ind.tr* **To share (in) sth.**, prendre part à, participer à, qch. **To share (in) s.o.'s grief**, partager la douleur de qn. **share out**, *v.tr.* Partager, répartir. **sharing**, *s.* **I.** Partage *m.* **2.** Participation *f.*

shareholder, *s.* Actionnaire *mf.*

shark, *s.* **I.** *Ich:* Requin *m.* **2.** *F:* Escroc *m*; requin.

sharp. I. *a.* **1.** (a) Tranchant, aiguisé, affilé; (*of point*) aigu, -uë, pointu. (b) (*Of features*) Anguleux. **Sharp turn**, tournant brusque. (c) (*Of outline*) Net, *f.* nette. (d) **Sharp contrast**, contraste marqué. **2.** (a) Fin, éveillé; (*of hearing*) fin, subtil; (*of sight*) perçant; (*of glance*) pénétrant. **A sharp child**, un enfant vif, affûté. (b) Rusé, malin, -igne; peu scrupuleux. **Sharp practice(s)**, procédés peu honnêtes. **Too sharp for s.o.**, trop malin pour qn. **3.** (a) (Combat) vif, acharné. (b) (Orage) violent. *S. shower*, forte averse. (*c*) (Hiver) rigoureux; (vent) vif, perçant; (froid) pénétrant. *S. pain*, vive douleur. (*d*) Rapide; (trot) vif. (*e*) *S. rebuke*, verte réprimande. **Sharp tongue**, langue acérée. **In a sharp tone**, d'un ton acerbe, cassant. **4.** Piquant; (*of apple*) aigre, acide; (*of wine*) vert. **5.** (*a*) (*Of sound*) Pénétrant, aigu. (*b*) *Mus:* Dièse. **-ly**, *adv.* **I.** Nettement. **2.** *The road dips s.*, la route plonge brusquement. **3.** (*a*) *He looked s. at her*, il dirigea sur elle un regard pénétrant. (*b*) (Réprimander) sévèrement. **To answer sharply**, répondre avec brusquerie. II. **sharp**, *s.* **I.** *Mus:* Dièse *m.* **2.** = SHARPER. III. **sharp**, *adv.* **I.** (Tourner) brusquement. **2.** Ponctuellement, exactement. **At four o'clock sharp**, à quatre heures précises. **3.** *F:* **Look sharp!** faites vite! **sharp-edged**, *a.* Tranchant, affilé. **sharp-featured**, *a.* Aux traits tirés, amaigris. **sharp-set**, *a.* **To be sharp-set**, avoir l'estomac creux. **sharp-sighted**, *a.* A la vue perçante. **sharp-tongued**, *a.* Qui a la langue acérée. **sharp-witted**, *a.* Intelligent, éveillé.

sharpen, *v.tr.* **I.** (*a*) Affiler, affûter, aiguiser. (*b*) Tailler en pointe. **To sharpen a pencil**, tailler un crayon. **2.** *F:* **To sharpen (the wits of) s.o.**, dégourdir qn.

sharper, *s.* **I.** Aigrefin *m*; chevalier *m* d'industrie. **2.** (*At cards*) Tricheur *m.*

sharpness, *s.* **I.** (*a*) Acuité *f*, finesse *f.* (*b*) Netteté *f* (des contours). (*c*) Caractère marqué (d'un contraste). **2.** (*a*) *S. of sight*, acuité de la vue. (*b*) Intelligence *f.* **3.** Sévérité *f*, acerbité *f.*

sharpshooter, *s.* *Mil:* Tirailleur *m.*

shatter. **I.** *v.tr.* Fracasser; briser (en éclats). **2.** *v.i.* Se briser (en éclats); se fracasser. **shattering**, *a.* (Coup) écrasant.

shave[1], *s.* **I.** **To have a shave**, (i) se faire raser; (ii) se raser. *Hair-cut or s., sir?* les cheveux ou la barbe? **2.** *F:* **To have a close shave**, l'échapper belle.

shave[2], *v.tr.* **I.** (*a*) Raser; faire la barbe à. (*b*) **To shave (oneself)**, se raser, se faire la barbe. **2.** Friser, effleurer. **shaven**, *a.* Rasé. **shaving**, *s.* **I.** Action *f* de raser ou de se raser. **2.** Copeau *m* (de bois). *pl.* Shavings, copeaux. **shaving-brush**, *s.* Blaireau *m.* **shaving-glass**, *s.* Miroir *m* à barbe. **shaving-soap, -stick**, *s.* Savon *m* à barbe; bâton *m* de savon pour la barbe.

shaver, *s.* *F:* Young shaver, gosse *m.*

shawl, *s.* Châle *m.*

she, *pers. pron. nom.* **I.** Elle. (*a*) *What is she doing?* que fait-elle? *Here she comes*, la voici qui vient. (*b*) *F:* (*Of ships*) *She sails tomorrow*, il appareille demain. **2.** (*a*) Elle. *She and I*, elle et moi. *It is she*, c'est elle. *She knows nothing about it*, elle n'en sait rien, elle. (*b*) (i) Celle. **She who believes**, celle qui croit. (ii) **It is she who did it**, c'est elle qui l'a fait.

sheaf, *s.* **I.** Gerbe *f.* **2.** Liasse *f* (de papiers).

shear[1], *s.* (Pair of) **shears**, cisaille(s) *f(pl)*; (grands) ciseaux. **Garden shears**, cisailles à haie.

shear[2], *v.tr.* **I.** **To shear** (off), couper. **2.** Tondre. *F:* **To be shorn of sth.**, être dépouillé de qch. **shorn**, *a.* (Mouton) tondu. **shearing**, *s.* Coupage *m*; tonte *f*, tondaison *f.*

shearer, *s.* Tondeur *m* (de moutons).

sheath, *s.* Fourreau *m* (d'épée); gaine *f* (de couteau). **sheath-knife**, *s.* Couteau *m* à gaine.

sheathe, *v.tr.* (Re)mettre au fourreau, rengainer.

shed[1], *s.* Hangar *m.* **Lean-to shed**, appentis *m.* **Open shed**, auvent *m.*

shed[2], *v.tr.* **I.** (*a*) Perdre (ses feuilles); (*of animal*) jeter (sa peau). (*b*) *F:* Se défaire de (qn). (*c*) **To s. one's clothes**, se dévêtir. **2.** Répandre, verser. *F:* **To shed light on a matter**, éclairer une affaire.

sheen, *s.* Luisant *m*, lustre *m*; chatoiement *m.*

sheep, *s.* Mouton *m.* *F:* **The black sheep**, la brebis galeuse. **sheep-dog**, *s.* Chien *m* de berger.

sheepfold, *s.* Parc *m* à moutons; bercail *m.*

sheepish, *a.* **I.** Penaud; interdit. **2.** Timide; gauche. **-ly**, *adv.* **I.** D'un air penaud. **2.** D'un air timide.

sheepishness, *s.* **I.** Timidité *f*; fausse honte. **2.** Air penaud.

sheepskin, *s.* Peau *f* de mouton.

sheer[1], *v.i.* Embarder. **sheer off**, *v.i.* **I.** Larguer les amarres. **2.** *F:* S'écarter.

sheer[2] **I.** *a.* (*a*) Pur, véritable. *A s. impossibility*, une impossibilité absolue. (*b*) Perpendiculaire; à pic. **2.** *adv.* (*a*) Tout à fait. (*b*) A pic.

sheet, *s.* **I.** Drap *m* (de lit). **2.** (*a*) Feuille *f*, feuillet *m* (de papier). (*b*) *F:* Journal *m*, -aux; feuille. **3.** Feuille (de verre); tôle *f.* **4.** Nappe *f* (d'eau). **sheet-lightning**, *s.* Éclairs *mpl* diffus; éclairs en nappe(s).

sheet-anchor, *s.* *F:* **It is our sheet-anchor**, c'est notre ancre de salut.

sheik, *s.* Cheik *m*, scheik *m.*

shekel, *s.* **I.** Sicle *m.* **2.** *pl.* *F:* Shekels, argent *m.*

shelf, *s.* **I.** Tablette *f*; planche *f* (d'armoire); rayon *m* (de bibliothèque). **Set of shelves**, étagère *f.* *F:* **To be on the shelf**, être au rancart. **2.** Rebord *m*, corniche *f* (d'un rocher).

shell[1], *s.* **I.** (*a*) Coquille *f*; carapace *f* (de tortue); écaille *f* (d'huître). (*Empty*) *shells*, coquillages *m.* *F:* **To retire into one's shell**, rentrer dans sa coquille. (*b*) Coquille (d'œuf); coque *f* (d'œuf plein). (*c*) *F:* Forme *f* vide; simple apparence *f.* **2.** Carcasse *f*, coque (de navire). **3.** Cercueil *m* provisoire. **4.** *Artil:* Obus *m.* **High-explosive shell**, obus brisant. **shell-fire**, *s.* Tir *m* à obus. **To be under shell-fire, subir un bombardement. **shell-fish,** s. **I.** (a) Coquillage m. (b) Crustacé m. **2.** Coll. Mollusques m et crustacés. **shell-hole,** s. Trou m d'obus; cratère m; entonnoir m. **shell²,** v.tr **I.** Écaler (des noix); écosser (des pois). **2.** Mil: Bombarder. **shell out,** v.tr. F: To shell out one's money, abs. to shell out, payer la note; débourser. **shelling,** s. Mil: Bombardement m.

shelter¹, s. **I.** Lieu m de refuge; abri m; asile m. **2.** Under shelter, à l'abri, à couvert. To take shelter, s'abriter, se mettre à l'abri. **shelter².** **I.** v.tr. (a) Abriter. (b) Donner asile à. **2.** v.i. & pr. S'abriter, se mettre à l'abri (from, contre). To s. from the rain, se mettre à couvert. **sheltered,** a. Abrité (against, from, contre). **sheltering,** a. Protecteur, -trice.

shelve¹, v.tr. F: Ajourner; mettre au rancart. **shelving¹,** s. **I.** F: Enterrement m, ajournement m (d'une question). **2.** Rayons mpl; rayonnage m. **shelve²,** v.i. Aller en pente. **shelving,²** a. En pente; incliné.

shepherd¹, s. Berger m. **shepherd²,** v.tr. **I.** Garder, soigner. **2.** F: Piloter.

shepherdess, s. Bergère f.

sherbet, s. Sorbet m.

sheriff, s. **I.** Eng.Adm: Shériff m. **2.** U.S: Chef m de la police.

sherry, s. Vin m de Xérès; xérès m.

Shetland. Pr.n. The Shetland Islands, les îles Shetland. **Shetland pony,** s. Poney shetlandais.

shield¹, s. **I.** Bouclier m. **2.** Tchn: Tôle protectrice. **shield²,** v.tr. **I.** Protéger (from, against, contre). **2.** To shield one's eyes, se protéger les yeux.

shift¹, s. **I.** Changement m de position; renverse f (de la marée). To make a shift, changer de place. Shift of the wind, saute f du vent. **2.** Ind: Équipe f, poste m. To work in shifts, se relayer. **3.** Expédient m. To make shift to do sth., trouver moyen de faire qch. To make shift with sth., s'accommoder de qch. **shift².** **I.** v.tr. (a) Changer de place; déplacer. F: To shift the responsibility of sth. upon s.o., rejeter la responsabilité de qch. sur qn. (b) Changer. F: To shift one's quarters, changer de résidence. **II.** shift, v.i. **I.** (a) Changer de place; se déplacer. (b) Changer. The scene shifts, la scène change. The wind has shifted, le vent a tourné, sauté. **2.** F: To shift for oneself, se débrouiller. **shifting,** a. **I.** Qui se déplace. Shifting sand, sables mouvants. **2.** (Of scene) Changeant; (of wind) inégal, -aux.

shiftiness, s. Sournoiserie f; astuce f. **shiftless,** a. **I.** Paresseux; sans énergie. **2.** Peu débrouillard.

shiftlessness, s. **I.** Paresse f; manque m d'énergie. **2.** Manque de ressource.

shifty, a. Roublard, retors; (regard) chafouin, sournois. S. eyes, yeux fuyants.

shilling, s. Shilling m. F: To cut s.o. off with a shilling, déshériter qn.

shilly-shally¹, s. F: Barguignage m, vacillation f. **shilly-shally²,** v.i. F: Barguigner, vaciller.

shimmer¹, s. Lueur f; chatoiement m. **shimmer²,** v.i. Miroiter, luire, chatoyer.

shin¹, s. Anat: Le devant de la jambe. **shin²,** v.i. To shin up a tree, grimper à un arbre.

shindy, s. F: Tapage m, chahut m. To kick up a shindy, chahuter.

shine¹, s. **I.** Éclat m, lumière f. F: Rain or shine, par tous les temps. **2.** F: (On boots) Brillant m; (on material) luisant m. P: To take the shine out of s.o., éclipser qn. **shine²,** v.i. **I.** Briller; reluire. His face shone with happiness, sa figure rayonnait de bonheur. **2.** To shine on sth., illuminer qch. **shining,** a. Brillant, (re)luisant. Shining example, exemple insigne (of, de).

shingle¹, s. Hairdr: Coupe f à la garçonne. **shingle²,** v.tr. To shingle s.o.'s hair, couper les cheveux de qn à la garçonne. **shingle³,** s. Galets mpl; (gros) cailloux mp. **shingly,** a. Couvert de galets; caillouteux. **shiny,** a. (a) Brillant, luisant. (b) (Vêtements) lustrés.

ship¹, s. Navire (marchand); vaisseau m (de guerre); bâtiment m; F: bateau m. Convict ship, bagne flottant. The ship's company, l'équipage m. On board ship, à bord. To take ship, (s')embarquer. **ship('s) boy** s. Nau: Mousse m. **ship-mate,** s. Compagnon m, camarade m, de bord. **ship-owner,** s. Propriétaire m de navire; armateur m. **ship-shape.** F: a. Bien tenu; en bon ordre. **ship²,** v. **I.** v.tr. **I.** Embarquer. **2.** To ship a sea, embarquer une lame. **II.** ship, v.i. S'embarquer. **shipping,** s. **I.** Embarquement m. **2.** Coll: Navires mpl, vaisseaux mpl. **3.** Dangerous for shipping, dangereux pour la navigation.

shipbuilder, s. Constructeur m de navires. **shipbuilding,** s. Architecture navale; construction navale.

shipment, s. **I.** (a) Embarquement m. (b) Envoi m par mer. **2.** Chargement m.

shipwreck¹, s. Naufrage m. **shipwreck²,** v.tr. To be shipwrecked, faire naufrage. **shipwrecked,** a. Naufragé

shipyard, s. N.Arch: Chantier m de construction.

shire, s. Comté m.

shirk, v.tr. Manquer à, se dérober à; esquiver. Abs. Négliger son devoir.

shirker, s. Carotteur, -euse.

shirt, s. Chemise f. Soft shirt, chemise molle, souple. Dress shirt, starched shirt, chemise empesée, de soirée. *P:* **Keep your shirt on!** ne vous emballez pas ! ne vous fâchez pas ! **shirt-button,** *s.* Bouton *m* de chemise. **shirt-collar,** *s.* Col *m* de chemise. **shirt-front,** *s.* Plastron *m.* **shirt-sleeve,** *s.* Manche *f* de chemise. **To be in one's shirt-sleeves,** être en bras de chemise.

shiver[1]. **I.** *v.tr.* Fracasser ; briser en éclats. **2.** *v.i.* Voler en éclats.

shiver[2], *s.* Frisson *m.*

shiver[3], *v.i.* **To shiver (with cold),** frissonner, grelotter, trembler (de froid).

shoal[1]. **I.** *a.* **Shoal water,** eau peu profonde. **2.** *s.* Haut-fond *m, pl.* hauts-fonds, bas-fond *m, pl.* bas-fonds.

shoal[2], *s.* Banc voyageur (de poissons) ; *F:* grande quantité, tas *m* (de lettres).

shock[1], *s.* **Shock of hair,** tignasse *f*; *F:* toison *f.* **shock-headed,** *a.* A la tête ébouriffée.

shock[2], *s.* **I.** Choc *m,* heurt *m.* **2.** *(a)* Coup *m,* atteinte *f. It gave me a dreadful s.,* cela m'a porté un coup terrible. *The s. killed him,* il mourut de saisissement. *(b)* **Electric shock,** secousse *f* électrique. **shock troops,** *s.pl.* Troupes *f* d'assaut, de choc.

shock[3], *v.tr.* *(a)* Choquer, scandaliser. **Easily shocked,** pudibond. *(b)* Bouleverser. *(c)* **To shock the ear,** blesser l'oreille. **shocking,** *a.* **I.** Choquant ; révoltant ; affreux. *How s.!* quelle horreur ! **2.** *F:* Abominable. **-ly,** *adv.* Abominablement.

shoddy[1], *s.* Camelote *f,* pacotille *f.*

shoddy[2], *a.* De pacotille ; camelote.

shoe[1], *s.* **I.** Soulier *m.* **To put on one's shoes,** se chausser. **I should not like to be in his shoes,** je ne voudrais pas être à sa place. **2.** Fer *m* (de cheval). **shoe-buckle,** *s.* Boucle *f* de soulier. **shoe-horn,** *s.* Chausse-pied *m, pl.* chausse-pieds, corne *f.* **shoe-lace,** *s.* Lacet *m*; cordon *m* de soulier.

shoe[2], *v.tr.* **I.** Chausser. **2.** Ferrer (un cheval).

shoeblack, *s.* Décrotteur *m,* cireur *m.*

shoemaker, *s.* Cordonnier *m.*

shoo, *v.tr.* **To shoo (away),** chasser.

shoot[1], *s.* **I.** *Bot:* Pousse *f*; rejeton *m.* **2.** *Ind:* Couloir *m*; glissière *f.* **3.** Partie *f* de chasse.

shoot[2], *v.* **I.** *v.i.* **I.** Se précipiter. **To shoot ahead,** aller rapidement en avant. **2.** Lanciner. **II. shoot,** *v.tr.* **I.** Franchir (un rapide). **2.** *(a)* Précipiter, lancer ; pousser vivement (un verrou). *(b)* Verser, décharger. **3.** Darder, faire jaillir (des rayons). **4.** *(a)* Décocher (une flèche) ; tirer (une balle). **To shoot a glance at s.o.,** lancer, décocher, un regard à qn. *(b)* Décharger (un fusil). **To shoot straight,** bien viser. **To shoot at s.o.,** tirer, faire feu, sur qn. *(c)* **To shoot s.o. with a revolver,** atteindre qn d'un coup de revolver. *(d)* Tuer d'un coup de fusil ; fusiller. *To s. a deserter,* passer un déserteur

par les armes. *(e)* Chasser (le gibier). *To s. a partridge,* abattre une perdrix. **5.** *Cin:* **To shoot a film,** tourner un film. **shoot down,** *v.tr.* Abattre, descendre. **shoot up,** *v.i.* *(a)* Jaillir. *(b)* *(Of prices)* Augmenter rapidement. *(c)* *(Of plant)* Pousser. **shot**[1], *a.* Chatoyant. **Shot silk,** soie gorge-de-pigeon.

shooting[1], *a.* Qui s'élance ; jaillissant. **Shooting star,** étoile filante. **Shooting pains,** douleurs lancinantes. **shooting,**[2] *s.* **I.** Franchissement *m* (d'un rapide). **2.** *(a)* Décochement *m* (d'une flèche) ; action *f* de tirer. **Shooting affray,** bagarre *f* avec coups de feu. *(b)* Tir *m.* **Rabbit shooting,** chasse *f* aux lapins. **To go shooting,** aller à la chasse. **3.** *Cin:* **The shooting of the film,** la prise de vues. **shooting-box,** *s.* Pavillon *m* de chasse. **shooting-gallery,** *s.* Tir *m*; stand *m.* **shooting-party,** *s.* Partie *f* de chasse. **shooting-range,** *s.* Champ *m* de tir ; *F:* tir *m.*

shop[1], *s.* **I.** Magasin *m*; boutique *f.* *F:* **You have come to the wrong shop,** vous vous adressez mal. **Everything was all over the shop,** tout était en confusion. **2. To talk shop,** parler affaires. **shop-assistant,** *s.* Commis *m,* garçon *m,* demoiselle *f,* de magasin. **shop-front,** *s.* Devanture *f* de magasin. **shop-lifting,** *s.* Vol *m* à l'étalage. **shop-soiled,** *a.* Défraîchi. **shop-walker,** *s.* **I.** Chef *m* de rayon. **2.** Inspecteur, -trice (du magasin). **shop-window,** *s.* Vitrine *f*; devanture *f* (de magasin) ; étalage *m.*

shop[2], *v.i.* Faire des achats, des emplettes.

shopping, *s.* Achats *mpl,* emplettes *fpl.* **To go shopping,** faire ses emplettes ; courir les magasins. **Shopping centre,** quartier commerçant.

shopkeeper, *s.* Boutiquier, -ière ; marchand, -ande.

shopper, *s.* Acheteur, -euse.

shore[1], *s.* *(a)* Rivage *m,* littoral *m*; bord *m.* *(b)* *Nau:* On shore, à terre. **Off shore,** au large. *Nau:* **Shore clothes,** frusques *f* d'escale. *(c)* pl. **To return to one's native shores,** rentrer dans son pays natal.

shore[2], *v.tr.* **To shore (up),** étayer.

short. I. *a.* **I.** Court. **A short way off,** à peu de distance. *S. steps,* petits pas. *A s. man,* un homme de petite taille. **2.** Court, bref. *(a)* De peu de durée. **Days are getting shorter,** les jours raccourcissent. **For a short time,** pour peu de temps. **In a short time,** sous peu ; bientôt. **To make short work of it,** mener rondement les choses. *(b)* **Short story,** nouvelle *f,* conte *m.* **In short,** bref. *He is called Bob* **for short,** on l'appelle Bob pour abréger. *(c)* Brusque ; sec, *f.* sèche. **To be short with s.o.,** être sec, cassant, avec qn. **Short temper,** caractère brusque, vif. **3.** *(a)* Insuffisant. **To give short weight,** ne pas donner le poids. **I am twenty francs short,** il me manque vingt francs. **Not far short of it,** peu s'en faut. *It is little s. of folly,* cela confine à la folie. **Nothing short of violence would compel him,** la violence seule le contraindrait. (b) **To be short of sth.,** être à court de qch. **To be s. of hands,** manquer de main-d'œuvre. **To go short of sth.,** se priver de qch. **-ly,** adv. **1.** Brièvement, en peu de mots. **2.** (Répondre) brusquement, sèchement. **3.** Bientôt, prochainement; sous peu. **Shortly after(wards),** peu (de temps) après. II. **short,** s. (a) Voyelle brève. (b) pl. **Shorts,** culotte f de sport. III. **short,** adv. **1. To stop short,** s'arrêter court. **To cut s.o. short,** couper la parole à qn. **2.** F: **To fall short of sth.,** être au-dessous de qch. *S. of burning it,* à moins de le brûler. **To stop short of crime,** s'arrêter au seuil du crime. **short-circuit¹,** s. El: Court-circuit m. **short-circuit²,** v.tr. El: Court-circuiter. **short-handed,** a. A court de main-d'œuvre, de personnel. **short-lived,** a. Éphémère, de courte durée. **short-sighted,** a. **1.** Myope. **2.** F: Imprévoyant. **short-sightedness,** s. **1.** Myopie f. **2.** F: Imprévoyance f. **short-tempered,** a. Vif; d'un caractère emporté. **short-winded,** a. Poussif.

shortage, s. **1.** Insuffisance f, manque m. **2.** Crise f, disette f. **Food shortage,** disette.

shortbread, s. Cu: (Sorte de) sablé m.

shortcoming, s. Shortcomings, défauts m, imperfections f.

shorten. **1.** v.tr. (a) Raccourcir; abréger. (b) Nau: **To shorten sail,** diminuer de voile. **2.** v.i. Raccourcir, décroître.

shorthand, s. Sténographie f. **To take down in shorthand,** sténographier. **Shorthand typist,** sténodactylographe mf.

shortness, s. **1.** (a) Peu m de longueur. **Shortness of sight,** myopie f. (b) Brièveté f, courte durée. **Shortness of memory,** manque m de mémoire. (c) Brusquerie f (d'humeur). **2.** Manque, insuffisance f.

shot¹, s. **1.** Coll. Projectiles mpl. **2.** Ven: Plomb m. **3.** (a) Coup m de feu. Pistol shot, coup de pistolet. *Without firing a s.,* sans brûler une amorce. F: **To be off like a shot,** partir comme un trait. *He accepted like a s.,* il accepta avec empressement. (b) Tireur, -euse. Sp: **He's a good shot,** il est bon chasseur. **4.** Coup. (a) F: **I'll have a shot (at it),** je vais tenter à coup. (b) Cin: Prise f de vue. **shot-gun,** s. Fusil m de chasse.

should. See SHALL.

shoulder¹, s. (a) Épaule f. **Breadth of shoulders,** carrure f. **Slung across the shoulder,** en bandoulière. **To bring the gun to the shoulder,** épauler le fusil. *To stand s. to s.,* se soutenir les uns les autres. F: **To put one's shoulder to the wheel,** se mettre à l'œuvre. (b) Cu: Épaule (de mouton). (c) Épaulement m (de colline). **shoulder-blade,** s. Omoplate f. **shoulder-strap,**

s. **1.** Bretelle f; bandoulière f. **2.** Mil: Patte f d'épaule.

shoulder², v.tr. **1.** Pousser avec l'épaule. **2. To shoulder the responsibility,** endosser la responsabilité. **3.** Mil: **Shoulder arms!** portez armes !

shout¹, s. (a) Cri m. **Shouts of laughter,** éclats m de rire. (b) Clameur f. **Shouts of applause,** acclamations f.

shout². **1.** v.i. Crier; pousser des cris. v.pr. **To shout oneself hoarse,** s'enrouer à force de crier. **2.** v.tr. Crier; vociférer. **shout down,** v.tr. Huer. **shout out.** **1.** v.i. Crier, s'écrier. **2.** v.tr. Crier. **shouting,** s. Cris mpl; acclamations fpl.

shove¹, s. F: Coup m (d'épaule); poussée f. **shove²,** v.tr. F: Pousser. **To shove sth. into a drawer,** fourrer qch. dans un tiroir. **shove aside,** v.tr. Écarter d'une poussée; pousser de côté.

shovel¹, s. Pelle f. **shovel hat,** s. Chapeau m ecclésiastique.

shovel², v.tr. Pell(et)er.

shovelful, s. Pellée f, pelletée f.

show¹, s. **1.** Mise f en vue; étalage m. **Show of hands,** vote m à main(s) levée(s). **2.** (a) Exposition f; exhibition f; comice m. (b) Spectacle m. (c) Étalage. *Our furniture makes a poor s.,* notre mobilier fait triste figure. **3.** (a) Apparence f; semblant m. **With some show of reason,** avec quelque apparence de raison. **Show of resistance,** simulacre m de résistance. *To make a great s. of friendship,* faire de grandes démonstrations d'amitié. (b) Parade f, ostentation f. **To make a show of learning,** faire parade d'érudition. **To do sth. for show,** faire qch. pour faire parade. **4.** F: Affaire f. **To run the show,** diriger l'affaire. **show-case,** s. Com: Montre f, vitrine f. **show-ground,** s. Champ m de comice agricole.

show², v. I. v.tr. **1.** Montrer. (a) Faire voir, exhiber. **To show s.o. sth.,** montrer, faire voir, qch. à qn. F: **To show one's hand,** découvrir ses batteries. **To have sth. to show for one's money,** en avoir pour son argent. **He won't show his face here again,** il ne se montrera plus ici. **To show itself,** devenir visible; se révéler. (b) Représenter, figurer. (c) Indiquer. (Of watch) **To show the time,** indiquer, marquer, l'heure. **To show a profit,** faire ressortir un bénéfice. **2.** (a) **To show s.o. the way,** indiquer, tracer, le chemin à qn. (b) **To show s.o. to his room,** conduire qn à sa chambre. **To show s.o. into a room,** faire entrer qn dans une pièce. **3.** (a) **To s. intelligence,** faire preuve d'intelligence. **To show an interest in s.o.,** témoigner de l'intérêt à qn. **He shows his age,** il marque son âge. **To s. one's true character,** se démasquer. Abs. **Time will show,** qui vivra verra. (b) Révéler, montrer. (c) **To show s.o. to be a rascal,** prouver la coquinerie de qn. Abs. **I'll show you,** je vous apprendrai ! To show cause, exposer ses raisons. II. **show,** *v.i.* Se montrer, (ap)paraître ; se laisser voir. **show-down,** *s. If it comes to a s.-d.,* s'il faut en venir au fait et au prendre. **show off.** I. *v.tr.* (a) Faire valoir, mettre en valeur. (b) Faire parade, étalage, de. **2.** *v.i.* Parader, poser ; se pavaner. **show through,** *v.i.* Transparaître. **show up.** I. *v.tr.* Démasquer (un imposteur) ; dévoiler (une imposture) ; révélei (un défaut). II. **show up,** *v.i.* I. Se détacher, ressortir. **2.** *F:* Se présenter ; faire acte de présence. **showing,** *s.* Exposition *f,* mise *f* en vue. On your own showing, à ce que vous dites vous-même.

shower[1], *s.* (a) Averse *f.* Heavy shower, ondée *f.* Sudden shower, averse. (b) *F:* Shower of stones, volée *f* de pierres. *S. of sparks,* gerbe *f* d'étincelles. **shower-bath,** *s.* Douche *f.*

shower[2], *v.tr.* (a) Verser. (b) *F:* To shower blows, frapper dru. To shower invitations on s.o., accabler qn d'invitations.

showery, *a.* Pluvieux.

showman, *s.* (a) Directeur *m* (d'un spectacle de la foire). (b) Montreur *m* de curiosités.

showmanship, *s.* Art *m* de la mise en scène.

showroom, *s.* Salle *f,* salon *m* d'exposition.

showy, *a.* Prétentieux, voyant. **-ily,** *adv.* D'une façon prétentieuse.

shrapnel, *s.* Shrapnel *m* ; obus *m* à balles.

shred[1], *s.* Brin *m* ; lambeau *m,* fragment *m.* To tear sth. (in)to shreds, mettre qch. en lambeaux. *F:* There isn't a shred of evidence, il n'y a pas une parcelle d'évidence.

shred[2], *v.tr* Effilocher ; déchiqueter.

shrew[1](-mouse), *s. Z:* Musaraigne *f.*

shrew[2], *s.f.* Femme criarde, acariâtre ; mégère *f.*

shrewd, *a.* I. Sagace, perspicace. *S. reasoning,* raisonnement judicieux. **2.** I have a shrewd idea, je suis porté à croire. **-ly,** *adv.* Sagacement ; avec perspicacité.

shrewdness, *s.* Sagacité *f* ; finesse *f.*

shrewish, *a.* Acariâtre, criarde.

shrewishness, *s.* Humeur *f* acariâtre.

shriek[1], *s.* Cri déchirant ; cri perçant. Shrieks of laughter, grands éclats de rire.

shriek[2]. I. *v.i.* Pousser des cris aigus. To shriek with laughter, *F:* s'esclaffer (de rire). **2.** *v.tr.* To shriek out a warning, avertir qn d'un cri. **shrieking,** *s.* Cris stridents.

shrift, *s. F:* To give short shrift, expédier vite.

shrike, *s. Orn:* Pie-grièche *f, pl.* pies-grièches.

shrill, *a.* Aigu, -uë, strident. **-lly,** *adv.* D'un ton aigu, criard.

shrillness, *s.* Stridence *f.*

shrimp[1], *s* Crevette (grise). *F:* Gringalet *m.*

shrimp[2], *v.i.* Pêcher la crevette. **shrimping,** *s.* Pêche *f* à la crevette.

shrine, *s.* I. Châsse *f,* reliquaire *m.* **2.** Tombeau *m* de saint ou de sainte. **3.** Chapelle consacrée à un saint.

shrink, *v.* I. *v.i.* (a) Se contracter ; (se) rétrécir. (b) Faire un mouvement de recul. To shrink back from, reculer devant. To shrink from doing sth., répugner à faire qch. (c) *F:* To shrink into oneself, rentrer dans sa coquille. **2.** *v.tr.* (R)étrécir, faire rétrécir. **shrinking,** *a.* I. Qui se contracte. **2.** Timide, craintif. **-ly,** *adv.* Timidement.

shrinkage, *s.* Contraction *f* ; rétrécissement *m.*

shrivel, *v.* I. *v.tr.* To shrivel (up), rider, ratatiner ; (of sun) brûler. **2.** *v.i.* To shrivel (up), se rider, se ratatiner.

shroud[1], *s.* Linceul *m,* suaire *m.*

shroud[2], *s. Nau:* Hauban *m.*

shroud[3], *v.tr.* Envelopper, voiler. **shrouded,** *a.* (a) Enveloppé d'un suaire. (b) Enveloppé, voilé (in, de).

shrove. Shrove Tuesday, (le) mardi gras.

shrub, *s.* Arbrisseau *m,* arbuste *m.*

shrubbery, *s.* Bosquet *m* ; massif *m* d'arbustes.

shrug[1], *s.* Haussement *m* d'épaules.

shrug[2], *v.tr.* To shrug (one's shoulders), hausser les épaules.

shrunken, *a.* Contracté ; (of hands) ratatiné.

shudder[1], *s.* Frisson *m* ; frémissement *m.*

shudder[2], *v.i.* To shudder with horror, frissonner d'horreur ; frémir d'horreur.

shuffle[1], *s.* I. Marche traînante. **2.** Battement *m* (des cartes). **3.** (a) Tergiversation *f.* (b) Faux-fuyant *m, pl.* faux-fuyants.

shuffle[2]. I. *v.tr. & i.* To shuffle (one's feet), traîner les pieds. **2.** *v.tr.* (a) (Entre)mêler (des papiers). (b) Battre, mêler (les cartes). **3.** *v.i.* Équivoquer, tergiverser. **shuffling,** *a.* I. Traînant. **2.** (Of pers.) Tergiversateur, -trice ; (of conduct) équivoque.

shuffler, *s.* Tergiversateur, -trice.

shun, *v.tr.* Fuir, éviter.

shunt, *v.tr. Rail:* Manœuvrer. *F:* To shunt s.o., mettre qn au rancart. **shunting,** *s. Rail:* Manœuvre *f* ; aiguillage *m.*

shunter, *s. Rail:* Classeur *m* de trains.

shut, *v.* I. *v.tr.* (a) Fermer. To shut one's mouth, (i) fermer la bouche ; (ii) *F:* se taire. (b) To shut one's finger in the door, se pincer le doigt dans la porte. **2.** *v.i.* (Se) fermer. **shut down,** *v.tr.* (a) Rabattre. (b) *Ind:* Fermer (une usine). **shut in,** *v.tr.* (a) Enfermer. (b) Entourer, encercler. **shut off,** *v.tr.* I. Couper. **2.** Séparer, isoler (from, de). **shut out,** *v.tr.* (a) Exclure. The trees shut out the view, les arbres bouchent la vue. (b) To shut s.o. out (of doors), fermer la porte à qn. **shut to.** I. *v.tr.* Fermer. **2.** *v.i.* Se fermer. **shut up.** I. *v.tr.* (a) Enfermer. To shut oneself up, se renfermer. (b) Clore (une maison). To shut up shop, fermer boutique. (c) *P:* Réduire (qn) au silence. **2.** *v.i. P:* Se taire.

shutting, *s.* Fermeture *f.*

shutter, *s.* I. Volet *m.* Outside shutter, contrevent *m.* **2.** *Phot:* Obturateur *m.*

shuttle, *s.* I. Navette *f.* **2.** *Rail:* Shuttle service, navette*s.*

shuttlecock, *s. Games:* Volant *m.*
shy[1], *v.i.* Faire un écart; broncher. **To shy at** sth., prendre ombrage de qch.
shy[2], *a.* Sauvage, farouche, timide. **To fight shy** of sth., se défier de qch. *Don't pretend to be shy,* ne faites pas la réservée. **-ly,** *adv.* Timidement.
shy[3], *s. F:* **1.** Jet *m,* lancement *m.* **2.** Essai *m,* tentative *f.* **To have a shy at doing sth.,** s'essayer à faire qch.
shy[4], *v.tr.* Lancer.
shyness, *s.* Timidité *f;* sauvagerie *f.*
shyster. *s. F:* Homme d'affaires véreux.
Siamese, *a. & s.* Siamois, -oise.
Siberia. *Pr.n.* La Sibérie.
Siberian, *a. & s.* Sibérien, -ienne.
sibilant. 1. *a.* Sifflant. **2.** *s. Ling:* Sifflante *f.*
Sicilian, *a. & s.* Sicilien, -ienne.
Sicily. *Pr.n.* La Sicile.
sick, *a.* **1.** Malade. **2. To be sick,** vomir. **To feel sick,** avoir mal au cœur. **3. To be sick at heart,** être abattu. **He did look sick!** il en faisait une tête! **To be sick of** sth., être las, dégoûté, de qch. **sick-bed,** *s.* Lit *m* de douleur. **sick-headache,** *s.* Migraine *f.* **sick-leave,** *s.* Congé *m* de maladie, de réforme. **sick-list,** *s.* **To be on the sick-list,** *F:* être malade. **sick-nurse,** *s.* Garde-malade *mf, pl.* gardes-malades. **sick-room,** *s.* Chambre *f* de malade.
sicken. 1. *v.i.* (a) Tomber malade (*of, with,* de). (b) To sicken of sth., se lasser de qch. **2.** *v.tr.* (a) Rendre malade; donner mal au cœur à. (b) To sicken s.o. of sth., dégoûter qn de qch. **sickening,** *s.* Écœurant, navrant.
sickener, *s. F:* Déception *f.*
sickle, *s. Agr:* Faucille *f.*
sickliness, *s.* **1.** État maladif. **2.** Pâleur *f.* **3.** Fadeur *f.*
sickly, *a.* **1.** (a) Maladif, souffreteux. (b) Sickly smile, sourire pâle. **2.** Malsain, insalubre. **3.** (*Of taste*) Fade.
sickness, *s.* **1.** Maladie *f.* **2.** Mal *m,* maladie. Air sickness, mal des aviateurs. **3.** Mal de cœur.
side[1], *s.* Côté *m.* **1.** (a) Flanc *m.* By the side of s.o., à côté de qn. Side by side, côte à côte. *F:* To split one's sides (*with laughter*), se tenir les côtes de rire. (b) Side of bacon, flèche *f* de lard. **2.** Côté; flanc (d'une montagne); paroi *f* (d'un fossé). Side of a ship, bande *f*, bord *m.* **3.** (a) The right side, le bon côté; l'endroit *m* (d'une étoffe). Wrong side out, à l'envers. (b) *F:* The bright side of things, le bon côté des choses. The other side of the picture, le revers de la médaille. To be on the soft side of s.o., prendre qn par son endroit faible. To hear both sides, entendre le pour et le contre. The weather's on the cool side, il fait plutôt froid. **4.** (a) On this side, de ce côté-ci. On all sides, de tous côtés. To move to one side, se ranger. To put sth. on one side, mettre

qch. à l'écart. (b) *F:* To put on side, se donner des airs. **5.** (a) Parti *m.* **He is on our side,** il est de notre parti. **You have the law on your side,** vous avez la loi pour vous. (b) Section *f,* division *f.* The modern side, les classes modernes. (c) *Games:* Camp *m,* équipe *f.* To pick sides, tirer les camps. (d) On his mother's side, du côté maternel. **6.** *Attrib.* Latéral, de côté. Side entrance, entrée de côté. **Side door,** porte latérale. Side line, (i) *Rail:* voie *f* secondaire. (ii) *As a side line,* comme occupation secondaire. Side issue, question d'intérêt secondaire. **side-arms,** *s.pl.* Armes blanches. **side-face. 1.** *s.* Profil *m.* **2.** *adv.* Taken *s.-f.,* photographié de profil. **side-glance,** *s.* Regard *m* de côté. **side-road,** *s.* Chemin *m* de traverse. **side-saddle,** *s.* Selle *f* de dame. **side-slip,** *s.* **1.** *Cy:* Dérapage *m.* **2.** *Av:* Glissade *f* sur l'aile. **side-track**[1], *s. Rail:* Voie *f* secondaire. **side-track**[2], *v.tr.* (a) Garer (un train). (b) *F:* Reléguer au second plan. **side-view,** *s.* Vue *f* de profil, de côté. S.-v. of the hotel, l'hôtel vu de côté. **side-walk,** *s.* Trottoir *m.* **side-wind,** *s.* Vent *m* de côté. *F:* By a s.-w., indirectement.
side[2], *v.i.* **To side with s.o.,** se ranger du côté de qn. **siding,** *s. Rail:* (a) Voie *f* de garage. (b) Embranchement *m.*
sideboard, *s. Furn:* Buffet *m.*
sidelight, *s. F:* To throw a sidelight on a subject, donner un aperçu indirect sur un sujet.
sidelong. 1. *adv.* Obliquement, de côté. **2.** *a.* Oblique.
sideways. 1. *adv.* De côté; latéralement. **2.** *a.* Latéral, -aux; de côté.
sidle, *v.i.* **To sidle along,** s'avancer de guingois. **To sidle up to,** se couler auprès de.
siege, *s. Mil:* Siège *m.* **To lay siege to a town,** assiéger une ville.
Siena. *Pr.n. Geog:* Sienne *f.*
sienna, *s.* Terre *f* de Sienne. Raw, burnt, sienna, terre de Sienne naturelle, brûlée.
siesta, *s.* Sieste *f,* méridienne *f.*
sieve, *s.* Crible *m;* tamis *m.*
sift, *v.tr.* (a) Passer au tamis; tamiser. (b) *F:* Examiner minutieusement. **To sift a matter to the bottom,** éplucher une affaire.
sifting, *s.* (a) Tamisage *m.* (b) Examen minutieux.
sigh[1], *s.* Soupir *m.*
sigh[2], *v.i.* Soupirer. **sighing,** *s.* Soupirs *mpl.*
sight[1], *s.* **1.** Vue *f.* (a) Short sight, myopie *f.* To lose one's sight, perdre la vue. (b) To catch sight of, apercevoir. To lose sight of, perdre de vue. I can't bear the sight of him, je ne peux pas le sentir. *To shoot s.o. at s.,* faire feu sur qn à première vue. At first sight, au premier abord. To know s.o. by sight, connaître qn de vue. **2.** To come into sight, (ap)paraître. To be within sight, être à portée de la vue; être en vue. Land

in sight! terre ! Out of sight, caché aux regards. **3.** *Artil :* Visée *f.* **4.** Appareil *m* de visée. **5.** *(a)* Spectacle *m.* *It is a s. to see,* cela vaut la peine d'être vu. *(b)* F : *His face was a s.,* si vous aviez vu son visage ! *(c)* Chose digne d'être vue. **sight-seeing,** *s.* To go sight-seeing, visiter les monuments.

sight-seer, *s.* Curieux, -euse.

sight², *v.tr.* **I.** Apercevoir. *Nau :* To sight land, relever la terre. **2.** Pointer (un fusil).

sighting, *s.* **I.** Vue *f.* **2.** Visée *f,* pointage *m.*

sightliness, *s.* Grâce *f,* beauté *f.*

sightly, *a.* Agréable à voir ; avenant.

sign¹, *s.* **I.** Signe *m.* *To make an affirmative s.,* faire signe que oui. **2.** *(a)* Indice *m,* indication *f.* Sure sign, indice certain. *There is no s. of his coming,* rien n'annonce sa venue. *(b)* Trace *f.* To show no sign of life, ne donner aucun signe de vie. *There was no s. of him,* on ne l'a pas aperçu. **3.** *(a)* Enseigne *f.* *(b)* Sign of the Zodiac, signe du zodiaque. **4.** Symbole *m.* **5.** Sign of the cross, signe de la croix. **sign-board,** *s.* Enseigne *f.*

sign-language, *s.* Langage *m* mimique. **sign-post,** *s.* Poteau indicateur.

sign², *v.tr.* Signer. **signing,** *s.* Signature *f.*

signal¹, *s.* Signal, -aux *m.* **signal-box,** *s.* *Rail :* Cabine *f* à signaux ; cabine d'aiguillage.

signal², *v.* **I.** *v.i.* Donner un signal (to, à) ; signaler. **2.** *v.tr.* *(a)* Signaler. *(b)* To signal to s.o. to stop, faire signe à qn de s'arrêter.

signalling, *s.* Signalisation *f* ; transmission *f* de signaux. *Nau :* Timonerie *f.*

signal³, *a.* Signalé, insigne ; (succès) éclatant. **-ally,** *adv.* Remarquablement.

signalize, *v.tr.* Signaler, marquer.

signaller, *s.* Signaleur *m.*

signalman, *s.* **I.** *Rail :* Signaleur *m.* **2.** *Navy :* Timonier *m.*

signature, *s.* Signature *f.* **signature tune,** *s.* *W.Tel :* Indicatif musical.

signet, *s.* Sceau *m,* cachet *m.* **signet-ring,** *s.* (Bague *f*) chevalière *f.*

significance, *s.* **I.** Signification *f.* Look of deep significance, regard très significatif. **2.** Importance *f,* conséquence *f.*

significant, *a.* **I.** (Mot) significatif. **2.** Important, de grande portée. **-ly,** *adv.* (Regarder) d'une manière significative.

signification, *s.* Signification *f,* sens *m.*

significative, *a.* Significatif (of, de).

signify, **I.** *v.tr.* Signifier. *(a)* Être (le) signe de. *(b)* Vouloir dire. *(c)* Déclarer, faire connaître. **2.** *v.i.* Importer. It does not signify, cela ne fait rien.

Sikh, *a. & s. Ethn :* Sikh, -e.

silence¹, *s.* Silence *m.* *(a)* Dead silence, silence absolu. Silence gives consent, qui ne dit mot consent. *(b)* To pass over sth. in silence, passer qch. sous silence.

silence², *v.tr.* Réduire au silence ; faire taire.

silent, *a.* **I.** Silencieux. *(a)* To keep silent, se taire (*about,* sur). Be silent! taisez-vous ! *(b)* A silent man, un homme silencieux,

taciturne. **2.** *(a)* Silencieux, insonore. *(b)* *Ling :* Silent letter, lettre muette. **-ly,** *adv.* Silencieusement ; en silence.

silhouette¹, *s.* Silhouette *f.*

silhouette², *v.tr.* Silhouetter.

silk, *s.* Soie *f.* *(a)* Raw silk, soie grège. Sewing silk, soie à coudre. Silk stockings, bas de soie. *(b)* *Tex :* Oiled silk, taffetas *m* imperméable.

silken, *a.* Soyeux.

silkiness, *s.* **I.** Nature soyeuse (d'une étoffe). **2.** *F :* Moelleux *m* (de la voix).

silkworm, *s.* Ver *m* à soie.

silky, *a.* *(a)* Soyeux. *(b)* *S. voice,* voix moelleuse.

sill, *s.* (Window-)sill, tablette *f* de fenêtre.

silliness, *s.* Sottise *f,* niaiserie *f.*

silly, *a.* **I.** Sot, *f.* sotte ; niais. *S. answer,* réponse saugrenue. You silly boy! petit nigaud ! *s.* You little silly! petite niaise ! Silly ass! imbécile ! *To do a s. thing,* faire une bêtise. **2.** To knock s.o. silly, étourdir, assommer, qn. **-ily,** *adv.* Sottement, bêtement.

silt¹, *s.* Dépôt (vaseux) ; vase *f.*

silt², *v.* To silt (up), **I.** *v.tr.* Envaser, ensabler. **2.** *v.i.* S'envaser, s'ensabler.

silver¹, *s.* **I.** Argent *m.* **2.** *Attrib.* *(a)* D'argent, en argent. *S. spoon,* cuiller d'argent. *(b)* *S. hair,* cheveux argentés. **3.** Argent monnayé. Silver coin, pièce *f* d'argent. **4.** = SILVER-PLATE. **silver-haired,** *a.* Aux cheveux argentés. **silver-mounted,** *a.* Monté en argent. **silver-plate,** *s.* *Coll.* Argenterie *f* ; vaisselle *f* d'argent. **silver-plated,** *a.* Argenté. **silver wedding,** *s.* Noces *fpl* d'argent.

silver², *v.tr.* Argenter.

silversmith, *s.* Orfèvre *m.*

silvery, *a.* *(a)* (Nuage) argenté ; (écailles) d'argent. *(b)* (Rire) argentin.

similar, *a.* Semblable, pareil (to, à). **-ly,** *adv.* Pareillement, semblablement.

similarity, *s.* Ressemblance *f,* similarité *f*

simile, *s.* Comparaison *f,* image *f.*

similitude, *s.* Similitude *f.*

simmer, *v.i.* Mijoter, bouillotter. *(b)* *F :* Fermenter. To simmer down, s'apaiser peu à peu.

simoon, *s.* Simoun *m.*

simper¹, *s.* Sourire affecté, minaudier.

simper², *v.i.* Minauder, mignarder. **simpering¹,** *a.* Minaudier. **simpering²,** *s.* Minauderie(s) *f(pl)* ; grimaces *fpl.*

simple, **I.** *a.* *(a)* Simple, sans affectation. *S. folk,* les humbles. *(b)* Naïf, *f.* naïve ; crédule, niais. *(c)* *S. problem,* problème simple, peu difficile. *(d)* *Com :* Simple interest, intérêts simples. *(e)* *F :* It's simple robbery, c'est le vol pur et simple. **2.** *s. Med.Bot :* Simples, simples *m.* **-ply,** *adv.* **I.** Simplement. **2.** *(a)* Absolument. You simply must, il le faut absolument. *(b)* Uniquement ; tout simplement. **simple-minded,** *a.* Simple d'esprit ; naïf, *f.* naïve.

simple-mindedness, *s.* Simplicité *f* d'esprit; naïveté *f.*
simpleton, *s.* Nigaud, -aude; niais, -aise.
simplicity, *s.* **1.** (*a*) Candeur *f*, simplicité *f.* (*b*) Bêtise *f*, niaiserie *f.* **2.** (*a*) Simplicité. *F:* It is simplicity itself, c'est simple comme bonjour. (*b*) Absence *f* de recherche; simplicité.
simplification, *s.* Simplification *f.*
simplify, *v.tr.* Simplifier.
simulate, *v.tr.* Simuler, feindre.
simulation, *s.* Simulation *f*, feinte *f.*
simultaneous, *a.* Simultané. **-ly,** *adv.* (*a*) Simultanément. (*b*) En même temps (*with,* que).
sin[1], *s.* Péché *m.* To fall into sin, tomber dans le péché.
sin[2], *v.i.* (*a*) Pécher. (*b*) To sin against propriety, manquer aux convenances. **sinning,** *s.* Le péché.
since. 1. *adv.* Depuis. (*a*) Ever since, depuis (lors). (*b*) Many years since, il y a bien des années. **2.** *prep.* Depuis. He has been up s. dawn, il était levé dès l'aurore. Since when have you been here? depuis quand êtes-vous ici? Since then, depuis lors. **3.** *conj.* (*a*) Depuis que; que. (*b*) Puisque. S. he is not of age, puisqu'il est mineur.
sincere, *a.* (*a*) Sincère; franc, -che. (*b*) (Sentiment) sincère. **-ly,** *adv.* Sincèrement. Yours sincerely, cordialement à vous.
sincerity, *s.* Sincérité *f*; bonne foi. In all sincerity, de la meilleure foi du monde.
sine, *s. Mth:* Sinus *m.*
sinecure, *s.* Sinécure *f.*
sinew, *s.* **1.** Tendon *m.* **2.** *pl. F:* Sinews, nerf *m*, force *f.*
sinewy, *a.* **1.** Tendineux. **2.** *F:* (Bras) musclé, nerveux.
sinful, *a.* S. person, pécheur, *f.* pécheresse. S. world, monde de pécheurs. **-fully,** *adv.* D'une façon coupable.
sinfulness, *s.* **1.** Culpabilité *f.* **2.** Le péché.
sing, *v.* **1.** *v.tr.* Chanter. *F:* To sing small, filer doux. To sing s.o. to sleep, endormir qn en chantant. **2.** *v.i.* (Of the ears) Tinter, bourdonner. **singing**[1], *a.* (Oiseau) chanteur, *f.* -euse; chantant, qui chante. **singing**[2], *s.* **1.** Chant *m.* **2.** Bourdonnement *m*, tintement *m* (d'oreilles). **sing-song,** *s.* **1.** Chant *m* monotone. Sing-song accent, accent chantant. **2.** *F:* Concert improvisé.
Singapore. *Pr.n.* Singapour *m.*
singe, *v.tr.* **1.** Brûler légèrement; roussir. **2.** Passer à la flamme. *Hairdr:* Brûler, flamber.
singer, *s.* Chanteur; *f.* chanteuse, (professional) cantatrice.
single[1], *a.* **1.** (*a*) Seul, unique. Not a single one, pas un seul; pas un. I haven't seen a s. soul, je n'ai pas vu âme qui vive. (*b*) Individuel, particulier. **2.** (*a*) Single bed, lit pour une personne. Single bedroom, chambre à un lit. (*b*) Célibataire; non marié(e). To lead a single life, vivre dans

le célibat. **-gly,** *adv.* **1.** Séparément; un à un. **2.** Seul; sans aide. **single-barrelled,** *a.* (Fusil) à un coup. **single-handed,** *a.* Seul. sans aide. **single-seater,** *s. Av:* Monoplace *m.*
single[2], *v.tr.* To single out s.o., choisir qn.
singleness, *s.* **1.** With singleness of purpose, avec un seul but en vue. **2.** Célibat *m.*
singular, *a.* **1.** (*a*) *Gram:* Singulier. (*b*) All and singular, tous et chacun. **2.** Singulier, bizarre. **-ly,** *adv.* Singulièrement. (*a*) Remarquablement. (*b*) Bizarrement.
singularity, *s.* Singularité *f.*
sinister, *a.* Sinistre. A man of s. countenance, un homme de mauvaise mine.
sink[1], *s.* (*a*) Évier *m.* (*b*) *F:* Sink of iniquity, cloaque *m* de tous les vices.
sink[2], *v.* **I.** *v.i.* **1.** Tomber au fond; aller au fond; (of ship) couler bas; sombrer. **2.** (*a*) His words begin to sink in, ses paroles commencent à faire impression. (*b*) Tomber (dans le vice, dans l'oubli). To s. into insignificance, devenir insignifiant. **3.** (*a*) To sink (down), s'affaisser. (*b*) The fire is sinking, le feu baisse. (*c*) (Of pers.) To sink (down) into a chair, se laisser tomber dans un fauteuil. To sink on one's knees, (se laisser) tomber à genoux. His heart sank, le cœur lui manqua. His spirits sank, son courage s'abattit. **4.** Descendre; aller en descendant; s'abaisser. The sun is sinking, le soleil baisse. **5.** The patient is sinking, le malade baisse. **II.** sink, *v.tr.* **1.** Couler, faire sombrer. **2.** Baisser (la voix); enfoncer. **3.** Creuser (un puits). **4.** Supprimer. They sank their differences, ils ont fait table rase de leurs différends. **sunk,** *a.* (Navire) sombré, coulé; (terrain) submergé. *F:* Sunk in thought, plongé dans ses pensées. S. in the mud, embourbé. Sunk in debt, noyé de dettes. **sinking**[1], *a.* (Navire) qui coule; en perdition. With sinking heart, avec un serrement de cœur. **sinking**[2], *s.* **1.** Enfoncement *m*; engloutissement *m* (d'un navire). **2.** Affaissement *m*; oppression *f* (du cœur). **3.** Affaissement *m*, déclin *m* (des forces); abaissement *m* (de la voix). **4.** Creusage *m.*
sinker, *s.* Plomb *m* (d'une ligne de pêche).
sinner, *s.* Pécheur, *f.* pécheresse.
sinuous, *a.* **1.** Sinueux. **2.** Souple, agile.
sip[1], *s.* Petit coup; petite gorgée.
sip[2], *v.tr.* Boire à petits coups.
siphon, *s.* Siphon *m.*
sir, *s.* **1.** (*a*) Monsieur *m.* (*b*) Corr: Sir, (my) dear Sir. Monsieur. **2.** Sir.
sire, *s.* **1.** Père *m.* **2.** (In addressing sovereigns) Sire *m.*
siren, *s.* Sirène *f.*
sirloin, *s. Cu:* Aloyau *m.*
sirocco, *s. Meteor:* Siroc(co) *m.*
sister, *s.* **1.** Sœur *f.* **2.** (*a*) *Ecc:* Religieuse *f*; sœur. (*b*) (Ward-)sister, surveillante *f*; infirmière *f* en chef. **sister-in-law,** *s.* Belle-sœur *f*, *pl.* belles-sœurs.

sisterhood, *s.* Communauté religieuse.
sisterly, *a.* De sœur.
sit, *v.* I. *v.i.* **1.** (*a*) S'asseoir ; être assis. *To sit still,* rester tranquille. To sit at table, être à table. *F :* To sit tight, ne pas se laisser ébranler. **To sit on s.o.,** rabrouer qn. (*b*) **To sit for one's portrait,** poser pour son portrait. (*c*) **To sit in Parliament,** siéger au parlement. **2.** Siéger ; être en séance. **3.** To sit (on eggs), couver (des œufs). II. **sit,** *v.tr.* **1. To sit a horse,** se tenir à cheval. **2. To sit oneself down,** s'asseoir. **sit down,** *v.i.* S'asseoir ; prendre un siège. **To sit down to table,** se mettre à table. *F :* To sit down under an insult, avaler une insulte. **sit out,** *v.tr.* To sit out a dance, causer une danse. **sit up,** *v.i.* **1.** (*a*) Se redresser (sur sa chaise). *F :* To make s.o. sit up, étonner qn. (*b*) To sit up (in bed), se mettre sur son séant. **2.** To sit up late, veiller tard. **To sit up for s.o.,** (rester levé à) attendre qn. **sitting¹,** *a.* **1.** Assis. **2.** En séance. **3.** Sitting hen, poule en train de couver. **sitting²,** *s.* (*a*) *At one s.,* d'un seul jet, d'arrache-pied. (*b*) Séance *f.* **sitting-room,** *s.* Petit salon.
site, *s.* **1.** Emplacement *m.* **2.** Building site, terrain *m* à bâtir.
situate, *v.tr.* Situer. **situated,** *a.* **1.** Situé. **2.** *This is how I am s.,* voici la situation dans laquelle je me trouve.
situation, *s.* **1.** Situation *f.* **2.** Emploi *m,* place *f.* Situations vacant, offres *fpl* d'emplois.
six, *num. a. & s.* Six (*m*). *F :* It is six of one and half a dozen of the other, c'est bonnet blanc et blanc bonnet. **Everything is at sixes and sevens,** tout est en désordre.
sixpence, *s.* Six pence.
sixpenny, *attrib.a.* Sixpenny piece, bit, pièce *f* de six pence.
sixteen, *num. a. & s.* Seize (*m*). *She is s.,* elle a seize ans.
sixteenth, *num. a. & s.* Seizième. *Louis the S.,* Louis Seize. (On) the sixteenth (of August), le seize (août).
sixth, *num. a. & s.* Sixième (*m*). (On) the sixth of June, le six juin.
sixty, *num. a. & s.* Soixante (*m*). He is in the sixties, il a passé la soixantaine.
size¹, *s.* **1.** Grandeur *f,* dimension *f,* grosseur *f.* To take the size of sth., mesurer qch. All of a size, tous de même taille. Drawn full size, dessiné à grandeur naturelle. *P :* That's about the size of it, c'est à peu près cela. **2.** (*a*) Taille *f.* (*b*) Com : Numéro *m* (d'un article) ; taille (de vêtements) ; encolure *f* (de chemises) ; pointure *f* (de chaussures).
size², *v.tr.* Classer par grosseur. **size up,** *v.tr.* Jauger. *F :* To size s.o. up, classer, jauger, qn.
sizeable, *a.* *F :* D'une belle taille ; assez grand.
sizzle, *v.i.* Grésiller.

skate¹, *s.* *Ich :* Raie *f.*
skate², *s.* Patin *m.*
skate³, *v.i.* Patiner. **skating,** *s.* Patinage *m.* **skating-rink,** *s.* Skating *m.*
skater, *s.* Patineur, -euse.
skedaddle, *v.i.* *F :* (*a*) Déguerpir. (*b*) S'enfuir à la débandade.
skein, *s.* (*a*) Écheveau *m.* (*b*) *F :* Tangled skein, confusion *f.*
skeleton, *s.* **1.** Squelette *m,* ossature *f.* **2.** Charpente *f,* carcasse *f.* **Skeleton key,** fausse clef.
sketch¹, *s.* Croquis *m,* esquisse *f.* **sketch-book,** *s.* Cahier *m,* album *m,* de croquis.
sketch², *v.tr.* Esquisser ; faire le croquis de.
sketching, *s.* Prise *f* de croquis.
sketcher, *s.* Dessinateur, -trice.
sketchy, *a.* *F :* Qui manque de précision, de perfection. **-ily,** *adv.* D'une manière incomplète.
skewer¹, *s.* *Cu :* Brochette *f.*
skewer², *v.tr.* Brocheter.
ski¹, *s.* Ski *m.*
ski², *v.i.* Faire du ski. **skiing,** *s.* Le ski.
skid, *v.i.* *Aut :* Déraper, glisser, patiner.
skidding, *s.* Dérapage *m* ; patinage *m.*
skiff, *s.* **1.** *Nau :* Esquif *m.* **2.** *Row :* Skiff *m.*
skilful, *a.* Adroit, habile. **-fully,** *adv.* Habilement, adroitement.
skilfulness, *s.* Habileté *f,* adresse *f.*
skill, *s.* Habileté *f,* adresse *f,* dextérité *f.*
skilled, *a.* Habile.
skim, *v.tr. & i.* **1.** Écumer (le bouillon) ; écrémer (le lait). **2.** Effleurer, raser. To skim (through), parcourir rapidement.
skimp, *v.tr.* **1.** To skimp the food, lésiner sur la nourriture. To s. material, être parcimonieux d'étoffe. **2.** *F :* To skimp one's work, saboter son ouvrage.
skimpiness, *s.* Insuffisance *f,* manque *m.*
skimpy, *a.* Skimpy meal, maigre repas.
skin¹, *s.* **1.** Peau *f.* *F :* To have a thin skin, être susceptible. Next (to) one's skin, à même, sur, la peau. To come off with a whole skin, s'en tirer sain et sauf. **2.** Dépouille *f,* peau. **3.** Orange skin, peau d'orange. Banana skin, pelure *f* de banane. *Cu :* Potatoes boiled in their skins, pommes de terre en robe de chambre. **4.** Robe *f* (de saucisson). **5.** Pellicule *f* (sur le lait). **skin-deep,** *a.* Superficiel.
skin², *v.tr.* (*a*) Écorcher, dépouiller. (*b*) Peler, éplucher.
skinflint, *s.* *F :* Ladre *m.*
skinny, *a.* Décharné ; maigre.
skip¹, *s.* (Petit) saut ; gambade *f.*
skip², *v.* I. *v.i.* (*a*) Sauter, sautiller, gambader. (*b*) Sauter à la corde. **2.** *v.tr. & i.* Sauter, passer. **skipping-rope,** *s.* Corde *f* à sauter.
skipper, *s.* **1.** *Nau :* Patron *m.* **2.** *Sp :* *F :* Chef *m* d'équipe.
skirmish¹, *s.* *Mil :* Escarmouche *f.*
skirmish², *v.i.* Escarmoucher.

skirmisher, *s. Mil:* Tirailleur *m.*

skirt¹, *s.* **I.** *Cost:* Jupe *f.* **2.** *pl.* **Skirts,** bord *m*; lisière *f* (d'un bois).

skirt², *v.tr. & i.* Contourner; longer, serrer (le mur).

skit, *s. Lit:* Satire *f* (*on,* de).

skittish, *a.* **I.** (*a*) (Cheval) ombrageux. (*b*) (Femme) capricieuse. **2.** (Femme) folâtre. **-ly,** *adv.* D'un air espiègle.

skittle, *s.* **I.** Skittle(-pin), quille *f.* **2.** *pl.* (Game of) skittles, jeu *m* de quilles.

skulk, *v.i.* **I.** Se cacher; se tenir caché. **2.** Rôder furtivement. **3.** *P:* Se défiler; fainéanter.

skull, *s.* Crâne *m.* **Skull and cross bones,** tête *f* de mort et tibias. **skull-cap,** *s.* Calotte *f.*

skunk, *s.* **I.** *Z:* Mouffette *f.* **2.** (*Fur*) Skunks *m.* **3.** *F:* Mufle *m.*

sky¹, *s.* Ciel *m, pl.* cieux, ciels. *F:* To praise s.o. to the skies, élever qn aux nues. **sky-blue. I.** *s.* Bleu *m* céleste; bleu (de) ciel. **2.** *a.* Azuré. **sky-high,** *adv.* Jusqu'aux cieux, aux nues. **sky-line,** *s.* (Ligne *f* d')horizon *m.* **sky-rocket,** *s. Pyr:* Fusée volante. **sky-scraper,** *s. F:* Gratte-ciel *m inv.* **sky-sign,** *s.* Enseigne lumineuse. **sky-writing,** *s. Av:* Publicité aérienne.

sky², *v.tr. Cr:* Lancer (la balle) en chandelle.

skylark¹, *s. Orn:* Alouette *f.*

skylark², *v.i. F:* Rigoler; faire des farces. **skylarking,** *s. F:* Rigolade *f.*

skylight, *s.* Châssis vitré; lucarne *f.*

slab, *s.* Plaque *f,* tranche *f*; dalle *f* (de pierre).

slack¹, *s.* Mou *m,* ballant *m* (d'un câble).

slack², *a.* **I.** (*a*) Mou, *f* molle, lâche, flasque; dégonflé. (*b*) Faible, sans force. **2.** Négligent. To be slack at one's work, être mou au travail. **3.** Peu vif; faible. **Slack business,** affaires languissantes. **Slack time,** accalmie *f.* The slack season, la morte-saison, *pl.* mortes-saisons. **-ly,** *adv.* **I.** (Agir) négligemment; sans énergie. **2.** Mollement, lâchement.

slack³. I. *v.tr.* Détendre, relâcher. **2.** *v.i.* (*a*) Prendre du lâche, du mou. (*b*) Se relâcher. **slacking,** *s.* **I.** Relâchement *m.* **2.** *F:* Paresse *f.*

slacken. I. *v.tr.* (*a*) Ralentir. To slacken speed, diminuer de vitesse. (*b*) To slacken the reins, lâcher la bride. **2.** *v.i.* (*a*) To slacken off, se relâcher. (*b*) (*Of rope*) Prendre du mou. (*c*) (*Of speed*) Ralentir; (*of energy*) diminuer. **slackening,** *s.* Ralentissement *m*; diminution *f* (de zèle); relâchement *m* (d'un cordage).

slacker, *s. F:* Paresseux, -euse.

slackness, *s.* **I.** (*a*) Manque *m* d'énergie; négligence *f,* mollesse *f.* (*b*) Désœuvrement *m.* (*c*) Relâchement *m* (de la discipline). **2.** Mou *m* (d'un cordage). **3.** *Com:* Stagnation *f.*

slag, *s. Metall:* Scorie(s) *f*(*pl*).

slake, *v.tr.* (*a*) To slake one's thirst,

étancher sa soif; se désaltérer. (*b*) Éteindre (la chaux).

slam¹, *s.* Claquement *m.*

slam², *v.* **I.** *v.tr.* To slam a door, faire claquer une porte. **2.** *v.i.* Claquer.

slam³, *s. Cards:* Chelem *m.*

slander¹, *s.* Calomnie *f.*

slander², *v.tr.* Calomnier.

slanderer, *s.* Calomniateur, -trice.

slanderous, *a.* (Propos) calomnieux. **-ly,** *adv.* Calomnieusement.

slang¹, *s.* Argot *m.*

slang², *v.tr. F:* Injurier. **slanging,** *s. F:* Pluie *f* d'injures.

slant¹, *s.* **I.** Pente *f,* inclinaison *f.* **2.** Biais *m,* biseau *m.*

slant². I. *v.i.* (*a*) Être en pente; (s')incliner. (*b*) Être oblique. **2.** *v.tr.* Incliner. **slanting,** *a.* (*a*) En pente, incliné. (*b*) Oblique.

slantwise, *adv.* Obliquement; de biais; en écharpe.

slap¹. I. *s.* Claque *f,* tape *f.* **Slap in the face,** (i) soufflet *m,* gifle *f*; (ii) *F:* affront *m.* **II.** **slap,** *adv.* To run slap into sth., se heurter en plein contre qch. **slap-dash,** *a. & adv.* Sans soins. **slap-up,** *a. F:* Fameux, soigné, chic.

slap², *v.tr.* Frapper avec la main (ouverte). To slap s.o.'s face, gifler, souffleter, qn.

slapping, *s.* Fouettée *f,* fessée *f.*

slash¹, *s.* Estafilade *f,* entaille *f.*

slash², *v.tr.* Taillader; balafrer (le visage).

slashing, *a.* Mordant, cinglant.

slat, *s.* Lame *f,* lamelle *f.*

slate¹, *s.* **I.** (*a*) *Geol:* Ardoise *f.* (*b*) *Const:* (Feuille *f* d')ardoise. **2.** Ardoise (pour écrire). **slate-pencil,** *s.* Crayon *m* d'ardoise. **slate-quarry,** *s.* Ardoisière *f.*

slate², *v.tr.* Ardoiser (un toit).

slate³, *v.tr. F:* **I.** Tancer, réprimander vertement. **2.** Critiquer. **slating,** *s.* **I.** Verte réprimande. **2.** Dure critique.

slattern, *s.* Femme mal soignée.

slatternly, *a.* Mal soignée.

slaughter¹, *s.* **I.** (*a*) Abattage *m.* (*b*) Abattis *m* (de gibier). **2.** Tuerie *f,* carnage *m,* massacre *m.* **slaughter-house,** *s.* Abattoir *m.*

slaughter², *v.tr.* **I.** Abattre. **2.** Tuer, massacrer.

Slav, *a. & s. Ethn:* Slave (*mf*).

slave¹, *s.* Esclave *mf.* **slave-dealer,** *s.* Marchand *m* d'esclaves.

slave², *v.i.* Travailler comme un nègre; peiner. To slave away, s'échiner, s'éreinter.

slaver¹, *s.* Bave *f,* salive *f.*

slaver², *v.i.* Baver (*over,* sur).

slaver³, *s.* **I.** *Nau:* (Bâtiment) négrier *m.* **2.** = SLAVE-DEALER.

slavery, *s.* **I.** Esclavage *m.* **2.** *F:* Travail tuant.

slavish, *a.* D'esclave; servile. **-ly,** *adv.* En esclave; servilement.

Slavonic, *a. & s. Ling:* Slave (*m*).

slay, v.tr. Lit: Tuer; mettre à mort.
slaying, s. Tuerie f; massacre m.
sledge¹, s. Traîneau m.
sledge²(-hammer), s. Marteau m de forgeron; marteau à deux mains.
sleek, a. **1.** Lisse; luisant. **2.** F: (Of manner) Mielleux; onctueux.
sleekness, s. **1.** Luisant m. **2.** Onctuosité f (de ton).
sleep¹, s. **1.** Sommeil m. Short sleep, somme m. To go to sleep, s'endormir. To send s.o. to sleep, endormir qn. To have a good sleep, faire un bon somme. To walk in one's sleep, être somnambule. **2.** My foot has gone to sleep, j'ai le pied engourdi.
sleep², v.i. & tr. **1.** Dormir. (a) To sleep like a log, dormir à poings fermés. I have not slept a wink all night, je n'ai pas fermé l'œil de (toute) la nuit. To sleep on it, prendre conseil de son oreiller. (b) To sleep the sleep of the just, dormir du sommeil du juste. **2.** Coucher. To s. away from home, découcher. **sleep in,** v.i. (a) Être pensionnaire; être logé dans la maison. (b) Ne pas se réveiller à l'heure. **sleep off,** v.tr. Faire passer en dormant. **sleep out,** v.i. **1.** Découcher. **2.** Ne pas coucher à la maison.
sleeping¹, a. Dormant, endormi. Prov: Let sleeping dogs lie, ne réveillez pas le chat qui dort. **sleeping²,** s. Sommeil m. Sleeping accommodation, logement m. **sleeping apartments,** s.pl. Chambres f à coucher. **sleeping-bag,** s. Sac m de couchage. **sleeping-car,** s. Rail: Wagon-lit m, pl. wagons-lits. **sleeping draught,** s. Potion f soporifique. **sleeping-quarters,** s.pl. Dortoir m. **sleeping-suit,** s. Pyjama m.
sleeper, s. **1.** Dormeur, -euse. To be a light sleeper, avoir le sommeil léger. **2.** Rail: (Cross-)sleeper, traverse f. **3.** Rail: F: = SLEEPING-CAR.
sleepiness, s. **1.** Somnolence f. **2.** Indolence f, léthargie f.
sleepless, a. Sans sommeil. Sleepless night, nuit blanche.
sleeplessness, s. Insomnie f.
sleepy, a. **1.** (a) Somnolent. To feel sleepy, avoir sommeil. (b) Sleepy look, air endormi. **2.** Apathique, engourdi. **3.** (Of fruit) Blet, -ette, cotonneux. **-ily,** adv. D'un air endormi, somnolent.
sleet¹, s. Neige à moitié fondue.
sleet², v.impers. It is sleeting, il tombe de la neige fondue.
sleeve, s. Manche f. F: To have a plan up one's sleeve, avoir un expédient en réserve.
sleigh¹, s. Traîneau m.
sleigh², v.i. Aller en traîneau.
sleight, s. Sleight of hand, prestidigitation f; tours mpl de passe-passe.
slender, a. **1.** Mince, ténu; (of figure) svelte, élancé; (of finger) fuselé. **2.** Faible; (of income) exigu, -uë, mince. Our slender means, nos ressources exiguës.

slenderness, s. **1.** Minceur f, ténuité f; sveltesse f. **2.** Exiguïté f (d'une fortune); faiblesse f (des ressources).
sleuth(-hound), s. Limier m.
slice¹, s. Tranche f. Slice of bread and butter, tartine f de beurre.
slice², v.tr. Découper en tranches. **slice off,** v.tr. Trancher, couper.
slick, a. F: Habile, adroit.
slickness, s. F: Habileté f, dextérité f.
slide¹, s. **1.** Glissade f, glissement m. **2.** (On ice) Glissoire f, glissade. **3.** Phot: Dark slide, châssis m porte-plaques. **4.** Toil: (Hair-)slide, barrette f. **slide-rule,** s. Règle f à calcul.
slide², v. **1.** v.i. (a) Glisser, coulisser. (b) To slide (on ice), faire des glissades. (c) He slid on the floor, il glissa sur le parquet. (d) To let things slide, laisser tout aller à vau-l'eau. **2.** v.tr. (Faire) glisser. **sliding¹,** a. Glissant; coulissant. Sliding door, porte à glissières. On a sliding scale, suivant une échelle mobile. **sliding²,** s. (a) To go sliding, aller faire des glissades. (b) Coulissement m, glissement m.
slight¹, a. **1.** Mince, ténu; (of figure) frêle; menu. **2.** (Of pain) Léger. To some slight extent, quelque peu. Not the slightest danger, pas le moindre danger. Not in the slightest (degree), pas le moins du monde. **-ly,** adv. **1.** Slightly built, à la taille mince. **2.** Légèrement. I know him slightly, je le connais un peu.
slight², s. Manque m d'égards; affront m.
slight³, v.tr. Traiter sans considération; négliger (qn). **slighting,** a. (Air) de mépris. **-ly,** adv. Avec peu d'égards.
slightness, s. **1.** Minceur f; sveltesse f. **2.** Légèreté f; peu m d'importance.
slim, a. **1.** Svelte, élancé; mince. **2.** F: Rusé; malin, -igne.
slime, s. **1.** Limon m, vase f. **2.** Humeur visqueuse.
sliminess, s. (a) État vaseux. (b) Viscosité f.
slimness, s. **1.** Taille f mince; sveltesse f. **2.** F: Astuce f.
slimy, a. **1.** (a) Limoneux, vaseux. (b) Visqueux, gluant. **2.** Couvert de vase.
sling¹, s. **1.** Fronde f. **2.** (a) Med: Écharpe f. (b) Bandoulière f. (c) (For hoisting) Élingue f.
sling², v.tr. **1.** Lancer, jeter. **2.** Suspendre. To sling a hammock, suspendre un hamac. **3.** Élinguer (un fardeau).
slink, v.i. To slink off, partir furtivement.
slinking, a. Furtif.
slip¹, s. **1.** (a) Glissade f, glissement m, faux pas. (b) To give s.o. the slip, se dérober à qn. (c) Faute f d'inattention; inadvertance f. It was a s. of the tongue, la langue lui a fourché. (d) Écart m (de conduite); peccadille f. **2.** Taie f d'oreiller. **slip-carriage,** s. Rail: Voiture f remorque. **slip-knot,** s. Nœud coulant. **slip-way,** s. Cale f.

slip², v. I. v.i. **1.** (a) Glisser. To slip through s.o.'s fingers, glisser entre les doigts de qn. (b) Se glisser, se couler. (c) (Of bolt) To slip home, fermer à fond. **2.** (a) Faire une faute d'étourderie, une bévue. (b) Faire un écart de conduite. **3.** To let slip, laisser échapper. II. **slip**, v.tr. **1.** (a) Se dégager de. (b) F: Your name has slipped my memory, votre nom m'est sorti de la mémoire. **2.** (a) Ven: Lâcher (les chiens). (b) Rail: Décrocher (un wagon en marche). **3.** Pousser (un verrou); couler, glisser (qch. dans la main de qn). **slip on**, v.tr. Enfiler, passer (une chemise). **slip out**, v.i. (a) S'échapper. The secret slipped out, le secret se fit jour. (b) F: Sortir (à la dérobée).

slip³, s. **1.** (a) Hort: Bouture f, plant m. (b) F: Slip of a girl, jeune fille fluette. **2.** (a) Bande étroite. Slip of paper, bout m de papier. (b) F: Billet m, bordereau m.

slipper, s. Pantoufle f. **slipper-bath**, s. Baignoire f en sabot.

slipperiness, s. **1.** Nature glissante. **2.** Caractère rusé.

slippery, a. **1.** Glissant. **2.** Instable, incertain. **3.** Fin, rusé, matois. He's a slippery customer, on ne sait par où le prendre.

slippy, a. P: To look slippy, se dépêcher.

slipshod, a. Fait sans soin; négligé. Slipshod English, anglais peu correct.

slit¹, s. Fente f; fissure f. To have slits of eyes, avoir les yeux bridés.

slit², v.tr. (a) Fendre. To slit open a sack, éventrer un sac. (b) Faire une incision dans.

slither, v.i. Glisser.

sliver, s. Éclat m (de bois).

slobber, v.i. (a) Baver. (b) F: Larmoyer.

sloe, s. Bot: **1.** Prunelle f. **2.** Prunellier m.

slog, v. F: **1.** v.tr. Cogner violemment. **2.** v.i. (a) To slog away at sth., travailler avec acharnement à qch. (b) To slog along, marcher d'un pas lourd.

slogan, s. (a) Mot m d'ordre. (b) Com: Devise f.

sloop, s. **1.** Nau: Sloop m. **2.** Navy: Aviso m.

slop¹, s. **1.** Boue f. **2.** pl. Slops. (a) Boissons renversées. (b) Aliments m liquides. (c) Eaux ménagères. **slop-basin**, s. Vide-tasses m inv.

slop², v.i. To slop (over), déborder.

slope¹, s. **1.** Pente f, inclinaison f. **2.** Pente; talus m. Mountain slopes, versants m de montagne.

slope², v.i. (a) Être en pente; incliner, pencher. (b) Aller en pente. **sloping**, a. En pente; incliné. Sloping shoulders, épaules tombantes.

sloppy, a. **1.** Détrempé, bourbeux. **2.** (a) Mou, f. molle; flasque. (b) S. sentimentality, sensiblerie f.

slot, s. Entaille f, encoche f, rainure f. **slot-machine**, s. Distributeur m automatique.

sloth, s. **1.** Paresse f, fainéantise f. To become sunk in sloth, s'avachir. **2.** Z: (a) Paresseux m. (b) Sloth(-bear), ours jongleur.

slothful, a. Paresseux, fainéant; indolent. **-fully**, adv. Paresseusement.

slouch¹, s. **1.** (a) Lourdaud m. (b) Fainéant m. **2.** Démarche f mollasse. To walk with a slouch, traîner le pas. **slouch-hat**, s. Grand chapeau mou.

slouch², v.i. Se laisser aller en marchant; manquer de tenue. To slouch about, rôder. **slouching**, a. Mollasse.

slough¹, s. Bourbier m, fondrière f.

slough², s. Dépouille f, mue f.

slough³. **1.** v.i. (Of reptile) Se dépouiller; muer. **2.** v.tr. (Of reptile) To slough its skin, jeter sa dépouille.

Slovak, a. & s. Slovaque (mf).

sloven, s. Mal peigné, -ée; mal soigné, -ée.

Slovene, a. & s. Slovène (mf).

slovenliness, s. **1.** Négligence f (de mise); manque m de tenue. **2.** Manque de soin.

slovenly, a. **1.** Mal peigné, mal soigné. **2.** (a) Négligent; sans soin. (b) (Travail) négligé, bousillé.

slow¹. I. a. **1.** (a) Lent. At a s. trot, au trot ralenti. S. speed, petite vitesse; ralenti m. F: It is slow work, ça ne va pas vite. Slow and sure! hâtez-vous lentement! Rail: Slow train, train omnibus. (b) To be slow in starting sth., être lent à commencer qch. He was not slow to, il ne tarda pas à. Slow to anger, lent à la colère. (c) Slow (of wit), à l'esprit lourd. Slow child, enfant tardif, arriéré. (d) Ennuyeux, qui manque d'entrain. Business is slow, les affaires traînent. **2.** (Of clock) En retard. Your watch is five minutes slow, votre montre retarde de cinq minutes. **-ly**, adv. Lentement. Drive slowly! au pas! ralentir! II. **slow**, adv. Lentement. To go slow, ralentir sa marche. To go slow, F: ne pas agir à la hâte. **slow-coach**, s. F: Lambin, -ine. **slow-witted**, a. A l'esprit lent, lourd.

slow². **1.** v.i. To slow down, to slow up, ralentir (son allure); diminuer de vitesse. **2.** v.tr. To slow down, up, ralentir qch.

slowness, s. (a) Lenteur f. (b) Lourdeur f, lenteur (d'esprit).

slow-worm, s. Orvet m.

sludgy, a. Boueux.

slug¹, s. **1.** Limace f. **2.** Paresseux, -euse.

slug², s. Sm.a: Lingot m.

sluggard, s. Paresseux m, fainéant m.

sluggish, a. Paresseux, léthargique; (esprit) inerte. **-ly**, adv. **1.** Paresseusement. **2.** To flow s., couler lentement.

sluggishness, s. **1.** (a) Paresse f. (b) Lourdeur f (de l'esprit). **2.** Lenteur f (d'une rivière).

sluice¹, s. **1.** Hyd.E: (a) Écluse f. (b) Canal m, -aux, de décharge. **2.** F: To give (sth.) a sluice down, laver (le plancher) à grande eau. **sluice-gate**, s. Porte f d'écluse; vanne f.

sluice², *v.tr.* Laver à grande eau.
slum, *s.* Bas quartier.
slumber¹, *s.* Sommeil *m*; assoupissement *m*; somme *m*.
slumber², *v.i.* Sommeiller; être assoupi; dormir.
slump¹, *s. Com:* Baisse soudaine. *F:* The slump, la crise économique.
slump², *v.i. Com:* Baisser tout à coup.
slur¹, *s.* (*a*) Affront *m*. To cast a slur on s.o., infliger un affront à qn. (*b*) Tache *f*. To cast a slur on s.o.'s reputation, entamer la réputation de qn.
slur², *v.tr.* To s. a word, *v.i.* to slur over a word, bredouiller un mot. To slur (over) a fact, glisser sur un fait.
slush, *s.* (*a*) Neige à demi fondue. (*b*) Fange *f*, bourbe *f*.
slushy, *a.* (*a*) Boueux. (*b*) *F: S. sentimentality*, sentimentalité fadasse.
sly, *a.* **1.** (*a*) Matois, rusé. (*b*) Cauteleux, sournois. *F:* Sly dog, fin matois. (*c*) *s. F:* To do sth. on the sly, faire qch. furtivement. **2.** Malin, -igne. **-ly**, *adv.* **1.** (*a*) Avec finesse. (*b*) Sournoisement. **2.** D'une manière espiègle.
slyness, *s.* **1.** (*a*) Finesse *f*. (*b*) Sournoiserie *f*. **2.** Malice *f*, espièglerie *f*.
smack¹, *v.i.* To smack of sth., avoir un léger goût de qch.
smack², *s.* **1.** Claquement *m*. **2.** Claque *f*. Smack in the face, (i) gifle *f*; (ii) *F:* affront *m*. *F:* To have a smack at sth., essayer de faire qch. **II.** smack, *adv.* **1.** Smack went the whip, le fouet claqua. **2.** *F:* He fell smack on the floor, il est tombé paf! Smack in the middle, en plein milieu, vlan!
smack³, *v.tr.* (*a*) Faire claquer. To s. one's lips, *F:* se lécher les babines. (*b*) Frapper, taper. To smack s.o.'s face, donner une gifle à qn.
smack⁴, *s.* (Fishing-)smack, bateau pêcheur.
small. **I.** *a.* Petit. **1.** (*a*) Menu. Small stature, petite taille. To make oneself small, se faire tout petit. *Ven:* Small game, menu gibier. *Typ:* Small letters, minuscules *f*. (*b*) In small numbers, en petit nombre. **2.** (*a*) Small beer, petite bière. (*b*) Small voice, voix fluette. **3.** *S. income,* mince revenu. *S. harvest,* maigre récolte. **4.** Peu important; peu considérable. Small change, menue monnaie. In a small way, en petit. **5.** Mesquin, chétif. *S. mind,* petit esprit. To look small, avoir l'air penaud. To make s.o. look small, humilier qn. **II.** small, *s.* Small of the back, creux *m* des reins. **III.** small, *adv.* Menu, en petits morceaux.
small-arms, *s.pl.* Armes portatives.
small-minded, *a.* A l'esprit mesquin.
smallish, *a.* Assez petit; plutôt petit.
smallness, *s.* Petitesse *f*; exiguïté *f*.
smallpox, *s.* Petite vérole; variole *f*.
smarm, *v.tr. P:* To smarm one's hair down, s'aplatir les cheveux à la pommade.

smart¹, *s.* Douleur cuisante; cuisson *f* (d'une blessure).
smart², *v.i.* (*a*) Cuire, brûler. (*b*) To smart under an injustice, souffrir sous le coup d'une injustice. You shall s. for this, il vous en cuira.
smart³, *a.* **1.** Vif; prompt; alerte. **2.** (*a*) Habile; à l'esprit éveillé. *F:* He's a smart one, c'est une fine mouche. (*b*) Malin, -igne, madré. **3.** Élégant, distingué, chic. The smart set, le monde élégant. **-ly**, *adv.* **1.** Promptement, vivement. **2.** Habilement, adroitement. **3.** Élégamment.
smarten. **1.** *v.tr.* (*a*) To smarten s.o. up, dégourdir qn. (*b*) To smarten oneself up, se faire beau. **2.** *v.i.* To smarten up, (*a*) S'animer; (*b*) Se dégourdir.
smartness, *s.* **1.** (*a*) Vivacité *f*; esprit débrouillard. (*b*) A-propos *m* (d'une réponse). **2.** Habileté peu scrupuleuse. **3.** Élégance *f*; chic *m*.
smash¹. **I.** *s.* **1.** *F:* Coup écrasant. **2.** (*a*) Fracassement *m*. (*b*) Désastre *m*, sinistre *m* (de chemin de fer). **3.** Débâcle *f*; faillite (commerciale). **II.** smash, *adv.* To go smash, faire faillite.
smash². **I.** *v.tr.* (*a*) To smash sth. to pieces, briser qch. en morceaux. To s. the door open, enfoncer la porte. Smash-and-grab raid, rafle *f* après bris de devanture. (*b*) Détruire; écraser. **II.** smash, *v.i.* **1.** Se briser violemment (contre qch.). **2.** Éclater en morceaux. **3.** Faire faillite. smash up, *v.tr.* Briser en morceaux; fracasser. smash-up, *s.* Destruction complète. *Rail:* Collision *f*.
smashing, *a.* (Coup) écrasant, assommant.
smattering, *s.* Légère connaissance.
smear¹, *s.* Tache *f*, souillure *f*.
smear², *v.tr.* **1.** (*a*) Barbouiller, salir (with, de). (*b*) Enduire (with, de). **2.** Maculer, barbouiller.
smell¹, *s.* **1.** (Sense of) smell, odorat *m*; flair *m*. To have a keen sense of s., avoir l'odorat fin. **2.** (*a*) Odeur *f*; parfum *m*. Unpleasant s., relent *m*. (*b*) Mauvaise odeur.
smell². *v.* **1.** *v.tr. & ind.tr.* (*a*) Flairer; sentir (une fleur). (*b*) *Abs.* Avoir de l'odorat. (*c*) Sentir l'odeur de; sentir (une odeur). **2.** *v.i.* (*a*) To smell nice, sentir bon. (*b*) Sentir (mauvais); avoir une forte odeur.
smelling-bottle, *s.* Flacon *m* de sels.
smelling-salts, *s.pl.* Sels (volatils) anglais; *F:* sels.
smelt¹, *v.tr. Metall:* **1.** Fondre. **2.** Extraire par fusion. smelting, *s.* (*a*) Fonte *f*. (*b*) Extraction *f*.
smelt², *s. Ich:* Éperlan *m*.
smile¹, *s.* Sourire *m*. With a s. on his lips, le sourire aux lèvres. To be all smiles, être tout souriant.
smile², *v.i.* Sourire. To smile at s.o.'s endeavours, sourire des efforts de qn. *F:* To keep smiling, garder le sourire. smiling, *a.* Souriant.
smirch, *v.tr.* Tacher; salir, souiller.

smirk¹, s. Sourire affecté, minauder.
smirk², v.i. Sourire d'un air affecté; minauder. **smirking,** a. Affecté; minaudier.
smite, v.tr. Frapper. **I.** F: My conscience smote me, je fus frappé de remords. **2.** Smitten with, épris de.
smith, s. Forgeron m.
smithereens, s.pl. F: Morceaux m; miettes f.
smithy, s. Forge f.
smock, s. Smock(-frock), blouse f, sarrau m.
smoke¹, s. **I.** Fumée f. F: To end in smoke, s'en aller en fumée. **2.** Will you have a smoke? voulez-vous fumer? **smoke-dried,** a. Fumé **smoke-screen,** s. Navy: Rideau m de fumée.
smoke². I. v.i. Fumer. **2.** v.tr. (a) Fumer. (b) Noircir de fumée. (c) Fumer (du tabac). Abs. Do you smoke? êtes-vous fumeur? Do you mind if I s.? la fumée vous gêne-t-elle?
smoking¹, a. Fumant. **smoking²,** s. Habitude f de fumer (le tabac). No smoking (allowed), défense f de fumer. **smoking-compartment,** s. Rail: Compartiment m pour fumeurs.
smoker, s. **I.** Fumeur, -euse. **2.** F: = SMOKING-COMPARTMENT.
smokiness, s. Condition fumeuse.
smoky, a. **I.** Fumeux; (of room) plein de fumée. **2.** Smoky lamp, lampe qui fume.
smooth¹, a. (a) Lisse; uni, égal. Smooth as glass, poli comme la glace. Sea as smooth as a mill-pond, mer calme comme un lac. (b) (Menton) glabre. **2.** (a) Doux, f. douce; sans heurts. (b) S. voice, voix moelleuse. (c) Doucereux, mielleux. **-ly,** adv. **I.** Uniment; sans inégalités. **2.** (Marcher) doucement. **smooth-spoken,** a. Aux paroles doucereuses.
smooth², v.tr. Lisser (ses cheveux); égaliser (le terrain). F: To smooth the way for s.o., aplanir la voie pour qn.
smoothness, s. **I.** (a) Égalité f (d'une surface); satiné m (de la peau). (b) Calme m (de la mer). **2.** Douceur f (de la marche d'une machine). **3.** Air doucereux.
smother, v.tr. (a) Étouffer; suffoquer. (b) Recouvrir.
smoulder, v.i. (a) Brûler lentement. (b) Couver (sous la cendre). **smouldering,** a. Qui couve (sous la cendre).
smudge¹, s. Tache f; noircissure f.
smudge², v.tr. Salir, barbouiller.
smudgy, a. Taché; barbouillé.
smug, a. Suffisant; satisfait de soi-même. **-ly,** adv. D'un air suffisant.
smuggle, v.tr. (Faire) passer en contrebande, en fraude. Abs. Faire la contrebande. **smuggling,** s. Contrebande f.
smuggler, s. Contrebandier m.
smugness, s. Suffisance f; béatitude f.
smut, s. Parcelle f de suie.
smutty, a. Noirci; sali (de suie).
snack, s. Léger repas; casse-croûte m inv. To have a snack, manger sur le pouce.

snag, s. (a) Chicot m (d'arbre); souche f au ras d'eau. (b) F: Écueil m; obstacle caché. There's a snag, il y a un cheveu.
snail, s. Limaçon m, escargot m, colimaçon m. F: To go at a snail's pace, aller à pas de tortue.
snake, s. Serpent m. **snake-bite,** s. Morsure f de serpent. **snake-charmer,** s. Charmeur, -euse, de serpents.
snap¹. I. s. **I.** (a) Coup m de dents. (b) Coup sec, claquement m. **2.** Cassure f; rupture soudaine. **3.** Cold snap, courte période de temps froid. **4.** F: Énergie f. **5.** Snap (-fastener), fermoir m (de valise); bouton m (fermoir) à pression. **6.** Phot: = SNAPSHOT¹ 2. **II.** snap, attrib.a. Instantané, imprévu. **III.** snap, adv. Crac. To go snap, se casser net.
snap², v. **I.** v.i. **I.** To snap at s.o., chercher à mordre qn. **2.** Claquer; faire un bruit sec. **3.** To snap (asunder), se casser net. **II.** snap, v.tr. **I.** Happer. **2.** (a) To snap one's fingers, faire claquer ses doigts. F: To snap one's fingers at a threat, se moquer d'une menace. (b) Phot: To snap s.o., prendre un instantané de qn. **3.** Casser, rompre.
snap off. I. v.tr. (a) Enlever d'un coup de dents. (b) Casser. **2.** v.i. Se détacher brusquement. **snap up,** v.tr. Saisir, happer.
snappish, a. Irritable; hargneux.
snappishness, s. Humeur hargneuse; irritabilité f.
snappy, a. **I.** = SNAPPISH. **2.** Vif. **3.** P: Make it snappy! dépêchez-vous!
snapshot¹, s. **I.** Coup (de fusil) lâché sans viser. **2.** Phot: F: Instantané m.
snapshot², v.tr. Prendre un instantané de.
snare¹, s. (a) Ven: Lacet m, collet m. (b) F: Piège m.
snare², v.tr. Prendre au lacet; attraper.
snarl¹, s. Grondement m, grognement m.
snarl², v.i. Grogner, gronder. **snarling¹,** a. Hargneux. **snarling²,** s. Grondement m, grognement m.
snatch¹, s. **I.** To make a snatch at sth., chercher à saisir qch. **2.** (a) Courte période. Snatch of sleep, petit somme. (b) Snatches of song, fragments m de chanson.
snatch², v.tr. & i. **I.** Saisir, empoigner. To snatch a meal, manger un morceau sur le pouce. **2.** To snatch sth. out of s.o.'s hands, arracher qch. des mains de qn.
sneak¹, s. **I.** Pleutre m. **2.** Sch: Cafard, -arde; rapporteur, -euse.
sneak². I. v.i. (a) To sneak off, partir furtivement. (b) Sch: Moucharder, cafarder. **2.** v.tr. P: Chiper, chaparder. **sneaking,** a. (a) Furtif. (b) Sournois, dissimulé.
sneer¹, s. **I.** Sourire m de mépris; ricanement m. **2.** Sarcasme m.
sneer², v.i. Ricaner. To sneer at s.o., parler de qn d'un ton méprisant. **sneering,** a. Ricaneur, -euse; moqueur, -euse. **-ly,** adv. D'un air méprisant; en ricanant.

sneeze¹, *s.* Éternuement *m.*

sneeze², *v.i.* Éternuer. *F: That's not to be sneezed at,* cela n'est pas à dédaigner.

snick, *s.* Entaille *f,* encoche *f.*

sniff¹, *s.* Reniflement *m.*

sniff², *v.i. & tr.* Renifler.

sniffle, *v.i. F:* Renifler.

snigger¹, *s.* (*a*) Rire *m* en dessous; léger ricanement. (*b*) Petit rire grivois.

snigger², *v.i.* Rire sous cape. **sniggering**, *s.* Rires *mpl* en dessous.

snip¹, *s.* **I.** Morceau coupé. **2.** (*a*) Petite entaille. (*b*) Coup *m* de ciseaux. **3.** *P:* Affaire avantageuse.

snip², *v.tr.* Couper avec des ciseaux.

snipe¹, *s.* Bécassine *f.*

snipe², *v.i. & tr.* To snipe (at) the enemy, canarder l'ennemi. **sniping**, *s.* Tir *m* en canardeur.

sniper, *s. Mil:* Canardeur *m.*

snippet, *s.* Bout *m,* morceau *m.*

snivel¹, *s.* Reniflement larmoyant.

snivel², *v.i.* Pleurnicher, larmoyer. **sniveling**¹, *a.* Pleurnicheur, -euse; larmoyant.

snivelling², *s.* **I.** Reniflement *m.* **2.** Pleurnicherie *f.*

snob, *s.* Personne *f* qui admire les grands.

snobbery, *s.* Admiration *f* des grands.

snobbish, *a.* Admirateur, -trice, des grands.

snobbishness, *s.* = SNOBBERY.

snooze¹, *s. F:* Petit somme.

snooze², *v.i. F:* Sommeiller; faire un petit somme. **snoozing**, *s.* Endormi, assoupi.

snore¹, *s.* Ronflement *m.*

snore², *v.i.* Ronfler. **snoring**, *s.* Ronflement *m.*

snort¹, *s.* Reniflement *m*; ébrouement.

snort², *v.i.* Renifler fortement; (*of horse*) s'ébrouer.

snout, *s.* Museau *m*; groin *m* (de porc).

snow¹, *s.* Neige *f.* **snow-blind**, *a.* Atteint de la cécité des neiges. **snow-blindness**, *s.* Cécité *f* des neiges. **snow-capped**, *a.* Couronné, encapuchonné, de neige. **snow-drift**, *s.* Amoncellement *m* de neige. **snow-flake**, *s.* Flocon *m* de neige. **snow-line**, *s.* Limite *f* des neiges perpétuelles. **snow-man**, *s.* Bonhomme *m* de neige. **snow-plough**, *s.* Chasse-neige *m inv.* **snow-shoes**, *s.pl.* Raquettes *f.* **snow-storm**, *s.* Tempête *f* de neige. **snow-white**, *a.* D'un blanc de neige.

snow², **I.** *v. impers.* Neiger. *It is snowing,* il neige. **2.** To be snowed up, être retenu par la neige. *F:* Snowed under with work, submergé de besogne.

snowball¹, *s.* Boule *f* de neige.

snowball², *v.tr.* To snowball s.o., lancer des boules de neige à qn.

snowdrop, *s. Bot:* Perce-neige *m or f inv.*

snowy, *a.* Neigeux; de neige.

snub¹, *s.* Mortification *f,* rebuffade *f.*

snub², *v.tr.* Infliger un affront à.

snub³, *a.* (Nez) camus, retroussé. **snub-nosed**, *a.* (Au nez) camus.

snuff¹, *s.* Tabac *m* à priser. To take snuff, priser. A pinch of snuff, une prise. *P:* To be up to snuff, être à la hauteur. **snuff-box**, *s.* Tabatière *f.*

snuff², *v.tr.* Moucher.

snuffle¹, *s.* **I.** Reniflement *m.* **2.** Ton nasillard.

snuffle², *v.i.* **I.** Renifler. **2.** Nasiller. **snuffling**, *a.* **I.** Qui renifle. **2.** Nasillard.

snug, *a.* Confortable. To lie snug in bed, être bien au chaud dans son lit. **-ly**, *adv.* Confortablement, douillettement.

snuggle, *v.i.* To snuggle up to s.o., se pelotonner contre qn. To snuggle down in bed, se blottir dans son lit.

snugness, *s.* Confortable *m.*

so. I. *adv.* **I.** Si, tellement. I am not so sure of that, je n'en suis pas bien sûr. So true it is that, tant il est vrai que. He is not so feeble as he appears, il n'est pas aussi faible qu'il n'en a l'air. Would you be so kind as to? voudriez-vous avoir la bonté de? *What man would be so mean?* quel est l'homme assez mesquin? Ever so little, si peu que rien. So much, tellement, tant. *We enjoyed ourselves ever so much,* on s'est joliment bien amusés. **2.** (*a*) Ainsi; de cette manière. So it was that he became a soldier, c'est ainsi qu'il devint soldat. Why do you cry so? pourquoi pleurez-vous ainsi? So many men so many minds, autant de têtes autant d'avis. It so happened, le hasard a voulu. And so on, et ainsi de suite. So to speak, pour ainsi dire. So saying he departed, ce disant il partit. (*b*) I think so, je le crois. I fear so, j'en ai bien peur. So it seems, à ce qu'il paraît. I told you so! je vous l'avais bien dit! So much so that, à tel point que. Much more so, bien plus encore. Is that so? vraiment? It is not so, il n'en est rien. So be it! soit! (*c*) How so? comment cela? Perhaps so, cela se peut. Not so, pas du tout. Quite so! parfaitement! *A week or so,* une semaine environ. (*d*) He's right and so are you, il a raison et vous aussi. *He quickened his pace and so did I,* il hâta le pas et j'en fis autant. (*e*) *You're late.*—So I am! vous êtes en retard.—C'est vrai! **3.** *Conj.phr.* So that. (*a*) Pour que (je pusse entrer). (*b*) De (telle) sorte que. **4.** *Conj.phr.* So as to. (*a*) Afin de. (*b*) Speak so as to be understood, parlez de sorte qu'on vous comprenne. **II.** so, *conj.* **I.** Donc; c'est pourquoi. **2.** So there you are! vous voilà donc! *So you are not coming?* ainsi vous ne venez pas? **so-and-so**, *s. F:* Mr So-and-so, Monsieur un tel. **so-called**, *a.* **I.** Ainsi nommé. **2.** A so-called doctor, un soi-disant docteur. So-called improvements, prétendus progrès. **SO** so, **SO-SO**, *a. & adv.* Médiocre (ment), comme ci comme ça.

soak. I. *v.tr.* (*a*) Tremper, détremper. (*b*) To soak sth. in sth., tremper qch. dans qch. **2.** *v.i.* (*a*) Baigner, tremper (*in* sth., dans qch.). (*b*) S'infiltrer, s'imbiber (*into*, dans). **soaked,** *a.* Trempé. Soaked to the skin, trempé jusqu'aux os. **soaking**[1], *a.* Trempé. **soaking**[2], *s.* (*a*) Trempage *m*, trempe *f.* (*b*) Trempée *f.* F: To get a soaking, se faire tremper.

soap[1], *s.* Savon *m.* Cake of soap, (pain *m* de) savon; savonnette *f.* **soap-bubble,** *s.* Bulle *f* de savon. **soap-dish,** *s.* Plateau *m* à savon. **soap flakes,** *s.pl.* Savon *m* en paillettes. **soap-suds,** *s.pl.* Eau *f* de savon.

soap[2], *v.tr.* Savonner.

soapy, *a.* Savonneux; couvert de savon.

soar, *v.i.* Prendre son essor. Rents have soared, les loyers ont fait un bond. **soaring**[1], *a.* **1.** (*a*) Qui monte dans les airs. (*b*) Soaring flight, vol plané. **2.** (Ambition) sans bornes. **soaring**[2], *s.* **1.** (*a*) Essor *m.* (*b*) Hausse *f* (des prix). **2.** Planement *m* (d'un oiseau).

sob[1], *s.* Sanglot *m.*

sob[2], *v.* **1.** *v.i.* Sangloter. **2.** *v.tr.* (*a*) To sob (out) sth., dire qch. en sanglotant. (*b*) To sob one's heart out, pleurer à chaudes larmes.

sober[1], *a.* (*a*) Sobre, modéré, tempéré. (*b*) Calme, posé. In sober earnest, bien sérieusement. (*c*) In his sober senses, jouissant de son bon sens. **-ly,** *adv.* (*a*) Sobrement, modérément. (*b*) Avec calme; tranquillement. **sober-minded,** *a.* Sérieux; pondéré.

sober[2]. **1.** *v.tr.* Dégriser, dessouler. **2.** *v.i.* To sober down, s'assagir.

soberness, *s.* (*a*) Sobriété *f*, tempérance *f.* (*b*) Calme *m*, tranquillité *f.*

sobriety, *s.* = SOBERNESS.

sociability, *s.* Sociabilité *f.*

sociable, *a.* Sociable. **-ably,** *adv.* Sociablement, amicalement.

social, *a.* Social, -aux. (*a*) Social service, œuvres *fpl* d'amélioration sociale. (*b*) Social events, mondanités *f.* **-ally,** *adv.* Socialement.

socialism, *s.* Socialisme *m.*

socialist, *a. & s.* Socialiste (*mf*).

socialistic, *a.* Socialiste.

society, *s.* **1.** Société *f.* (*a*) Compagnie *f.* (*b*) Duties towards society, devoirs envers la société. (*c*) To go into society, aller dans le monde. Society woman, mondaine *f.* **2.** Société; association *f.*

sock, *s.* **1.** Chaussette *f.* **2.** Semelle intérieure.

socket, *s.* **1.** Emboîture *f*, douille *f.* El: Lamp socket, douille de lampe. **2.** *Anat:* (*a*) Alvéole *m or f* (de dent). (*b*) Orbite *f* (de l'œil). (*c*) Cavité *f* articulaire (d'un os).

Socrates. *Pr.n.* Socrate *m.*

sod, *s.* **1.** Gazon *m.* F: Under the sod, enterré. **2.** Motte *f* de gazon.

soda, *s.* **1.** (*a*) *Ch:* Soude *f.* Caustic soda, soude caustique. (*b*) Baking soda, bicarbonate *m* de soude. **2.** = SODA-WATER.

soda-water, *s.* Eau *f* de seltz; soda *m.*

sodden, *a.* (Dé)trempé.

sodium, *s.* *Ch:* Sodium *m.*

sofa, *s.* *Furn:* Sofa *m*, canapé *m.*

soft. **I.** *a.* **1.** Mou, *f.* molle. (*a*) Soft pencil, crayon tendre. Com: Soft fruit, fruits rouges. (*b*) Soft to the touch, mou, doux, au toucher. As soft as silk, doux comme du satin. **2.** Doux, *f.* douce. (*a*) Soft voice, voix douce. F: Soft job, emploi facile. To have a soft time of it, P: se la couler douce. (*b*) Soft heart, cœur tendre. **3.** *a. & s.* Soft (person), niais, -aise. **-ly,** *adv.* **I.** (*a*) Doucement. To tread s., marcher sans bruit. (*b*) Tendrement. **2.** Mollement. **II. soft,** *adv.* Doucement. **soft-boiled,** *a.* (Œuf) mollet. **soft-hearted,** *a.* Au cœur tendre. **soft-soap,** *s.* **1.** Savon vert, noir. **2.** F: Flatterie *f.* **soft-spoken,** *a.* Mielleux, doucereux.

soften. **1.** *v.tr.* (*a*) Amollir, ramollir. (*b*) Affaiblir, énerver. (*c*) Adoucir (sa voix). (*d*) Attendrir, émouvoir. **2.** *v.i.* (*a*) S'amollir, se ramollir. (*b*) S'attendrir. **softening,** *s.* (*a*) Amollissement *m.* (*b*) Attendrissement *m.*

softness, *s.* **1.** Douceur *f.* **2.** (*a*) Mollesse *f* (de caractère). (*b*) Flou *m* (des contours). **3.** Niaiserie *f*, simplicité *f.*

soggy, *a.* Détrempé; saturé d'eau.

soil[1], *s.* (*a*) Sol *m*, terrain *m*, terre *f.* (*b*) One's native soil, le sol natal.

soil[2], *v.tr.* Souiller, salir. **soiled,** *a.* Souillé, sali. Soiled linen, linge sale.

sojourn[1], *s.* Séjour *m.*

sojourn[2], *v.i.* Séjourner.

sol, *s.* *Mus:* Sol *m.* **sol-fa,** *s.* *Mus:* (*a*) Solmisation *f.* (*b*) Solfège *m.*

solace[1], *s.* Consolation *f*, soulagement *m.*

solace[2], *v.tr.* Consoler; soulager.

solar, *a.* (Système) solaire.

solder[1], *s.* Soudure *f.*

solder[2], *v.tr.* Souder; ressouder.

soldier, *s.* Soldat *m.* *Three soldiers and two civilians,* trois militaires *m* et deux civils. Private soldier, simple soldat. Tin soldier, soldat de plomb.

soldierly, *a.* Soldierly bearing, allure martiale.

sole[1], *s.* **1.** Plante *f* (du pied). **2.** Semelle *f* (de chaussure).

sole[2], *v.tr.* Ressemeler. **soling,** *s.* Ressemelage *m.*

sole[3], *s.* *Ich:* Sole *f.*

sole[4], *a.* Seul, unique. Sole agent, agent exclusif. **-ly,** *adv.* Uniquement.

solecism, *s.* Solécisme *m.*

solemn, *a.* **1.** Solennel. Solemn fact, réalité sérieuse. Solemn duty, devoir sacré. **2.** Grave, sérieux. To keep a s. face, composer son visage. **-ly,** *adv.* **1.** Solennellement. **2.** Gravement.

solemnity, *s.* Solennité *f.*

solemnization, *s.* Solennisation *f.*

solemnize, *v.tr.* Solenniser.

solicit, *v.tr.* Solliciter. To solicit s.o. for sth., solliciter qch. de qn.

solicitation, *s.* Sollicitation *f.*

solicitor, *s. Jur:* Avoué *m.*

solicitous, *a.* Soucieux, désireux (*of*, de). **Solicitous about** sth., préoccupé de qch. **To be solicitous of** sth., désirer qch. **-ly,** *adv.* Avec sollicitude.

solicitude, *s.* Sollicitude *f*, souci *m.*

solid. I. *a.* Solide. (*a*) **Solid food,** aliment solide. (*b*) **Steps cut in the solid rock,** escalier taillé dans la pierre vive. (*c*) Plein, massif. **Solid measures,** mesures de volume. *F:* **To sleep for nine solid hours,** dormir neuf heures d'affilée. **Solid vote,** vote unanime. (*d*) En une seule pièce. **2.** *s.* Solide *m.* **-ly,** *adv.* Solidement.

solidarity, *s.* Solidarité *f.*

solidify. I. *v.tr.* Solidifier. **2.** *v.i.* (i) Se solidifier ; (ii) se figer.

solidity, *s.* Solidité *f.*

soliloquize, *v.i.* Se parler à soi-même.

soliloquy, *s.* Soliloque *m.*

solitary, *a.* (*a*) Solitaire. *F:* **Not a solitary one,** pas un seul. (*b*) (Lieu) solitaire, retiré.

solitude, *s.* **I.** Solitude *f*, isolement *m.* **2.** (*a*) Lieu *m* solitaire. (*b*) Lieu inhabité.

solo, *s.* **I.** *Mus:* Solo *m.* **To play solo,** jouer en solo. **Violin solo,** solo de violon. **2.** *Cards :* **Solo whist,** whist *m* de Gand.

soloist, *s. Mus:* Soliste *mf.*

Solomon. *Pr.n.* Salomon *m.*

solstice, *s. Astr :* Solstice *m.*

solubility, *s.* Solubilité *f.*

soluble, *a.* Soluble.

solution, *s.* Solution *f.* **I.** Dissolution *f.* **2.** (*a*) (Ré)solution *f* (d'une équation). (*b*) (*Answer*) Solution.

solvable, *a.* (Problème) résoluble.

solve, *v.tr.* Résoudre (un problème). **To solve a riddle,** trouver le mot d'une énigme.

solvency, *s.* Solvabilité *f.*

solvent. I. *a. Com:* Solvable. **2.** *a. & s.* Dissolvant (*m*).

Somaliland. *Pr.n.* La Somalie.

sombre, *a.* Sombre, morne. **-ly,** *adv.* Sombrement.

some. **I.** *a.* **I.** Quelque, quelconque. (*a*) **He will arrive some day,** il arrivera un de ces jours. **Some way or another,** d'une manière ou d'une autre. **To make some sort of reply,** répondre d'une façon quelconque. (*b*) **S. . . . or other,** n'importe quel . . . . **S. experienced person,** quelqu'un qui a, qui ait, de l'expérience. **2.** (*Partitive*) De. **To drink some water,** boire de l'eau. **To eat s. fruit,** manger des fruits. **Can you give me s. lunch?** pouvez-vous me donner à déjeuner? **3.** (*a*) Quelque. **Some distance away,** à quelque distance de là. **After some time,** après un certain temps. **It takes some time,** cela prend pas mal de temps. **At some length,** assez longuement. (*b*) **There are some others,** il y en a d'autres. **4.** *P:* **It was some dinner,** c'était un chouette dîner. **II. some,** *pron.* **I.** Certains. **Some agree with us, and some disagree,** les uns

sont de notre avis, d'autres ne le sont pas. **Some one way, some another,** qui d'un côté, qui de l'autre. **2. I have some,** j'en ai. **Some of them,** quelques-uns d'entre eux. **III. some,** *adv.* (*a*) Environ, quelque *inv.* (*b*) **I waited some few minutes,** j'ai attendu quelques minutes.

somebody, someone, *s. or pron.* Quelqu'un. **I. Somebody is knocking,** on frappe. **Somebody or other,** je ne sais qui. **2. He's (a) somebody,** c'est un personnage.

somehow, *adv.* **I.** De façon ou d'autre, d'une manière ou d'une autre. **2. I never liked him somehow,** je ne sais pourquoi mais il ne m'a jamais été sympathique.

someone, *pron.* = SOMEBODY.

somersault, *s.* (*a*) **To turn a somersault,** faire la culbute. (*b*) *Gym :* Saut périlleux.

something. I. *s. or pron.* Quelque chose *m.* **I. Something or other,** une chose ou une autre. **S. or other went wrong,** je ne sais quoi a cloché. **Something to drink,** de quoi boire. **To ask for s. to drink,** demander à boire. **To give s.o. something for himself,** donner un pourboire à qn. **To give s.o. something to live for,** donner à qn une raison de vivre. **I have something else to do,** j'ai autre chose à faire. **2.** (*a*) **Perhaps we shall see s. of you now,** peut-être que maintenant on vous verra un peu. (*b*) **There's something in what you say,** il y a un fond de vérité dans ce que vous dites. **There's something in him,** il a du fond. **Well, that's something !** bon, c'est toujours quelque chose ! **II. something,** *adv.* Quelque peu, tant soit peu. **That's something like a cigar!** voilà un vrai cigare !

sometime, *adv.* Sometime (or other), tôt ou tard. **Sometime soon,** bientôt.

sometimes, *adv.* Quelquefois, parfois.

somewhat. I. *adv.* Quelque peu ; un peu ; tant soit peu. **To be somewhat surprised,** être passablement étonné. **2.** *s.* **He was somewhat of a coward,** il était quelque peu poltron.

somewhere, *adv.* Quelque part. **Somewhere in the world,** de par le monde. **Somewhere else,** ailleurs ; autre part. **Somewhere or other,** je ne sais où.

somnambulism, *s.* Somnambulisme *m.*

somnambulist, *s.* Somnambule *mf.*

somnolence, *s.* Somnolence *f.*

somnolent, *a.* Somnolent.

son, *s.* Fils *m.* **son-in-law,** *s.* Gendre *m.*

sonata, *s. Mus :* Sonate *f.*

song, *s.* **I.** Chant *m.* **To burst into song,** se mettre tout à coup à chanter. **2.** Chanson *f.* **Marching song,** chanson de route. *F:* **To buy sth. for a song,** acheter qch. à vil prix. **To make a song about sth.,** faire des embarras à propos de qch. **song-bird,** *s.* Oiseau chanteur. **song-thrush,** *s.* Grive chanteuse.

songster, *s.* (Oiseau *m*) chanteur *m.*

sonnet, *s. Pros:* Sonnet *m.*

sonorous, *a.* Sonore. **-ly,** *adv.* D'un ton sonore.

soon, *adv.* **I.** (a) Bientôt, tôt. *See you again soon!* à bientôt! *How s. can you be ready?* en combien de temps serez-vous prêt? *Too soon,* trop tôt; avant le temps. *None too soon,* juste à temps. (b) *As soon as,* aussitôt que, dès que. (c) *I would as soon stay,* j'aime autant rester. **2.** (a) *The sooner the better,* le plus tôt sera le mieux. *Sooner or later,* tôt ou tard. *No sooner said than done,* aussitôt dit, aussitôt fait. *No sooner had he finished,* à peine eut-il fini. (b) *I would sooner die,* j'aimerais mieux mourir; plutôt mourir!

soot, *s.* Suie *f.*

soothe, *v.tr.* Calmer, apaiser. **soothing,** *a.* Calmant, apaisant.

soothsayer, *s.* Devin *m, f.* devineresse.

soothsaying, *s.* *Lit:* Divination *f.*

sooty, *a.* Couvert de suie; noir de suie.

sop¹, *s.* **I.** Morceau de pain trempé. **2.** Pot-de-vin *m, pl.* pots-de-vin.

sop², *v.tr.* To sop up a liquid, éponger un liquide. **sopping,** *a.* **Sopping wet,** tout trempé.

sophism, *s.* Sophisme *m.*

sophist, *s.* Sophiste *m.*

sophistic(al), *a.* Sophistique.

sophisticated, *a.* Blasé.

sophistry, *s.* **1.** Sophistique *f.* **2.** Sophisme *m.*

soporific, *a. & s.* Soporifique (*m*).

soppy, *a.* **I.** Détrempé. **2.** (a) Mou, *f.* molle; flasque. (b) Fadasse; larmoyant.

soprano, *s.* *Mus:* Soprano *mf.*

sorcerer, *s.* Sorcier *m*; magicien *m.*

sorceress, *s.* Sorcière *f*; magicienne *f.*

sorcery, *s.* Sorcellerie *f.*

sordid, *a.* Sordide. (a) Sale, crasseux. (b) Bas, *f.* basse, vil. **-ly,** *adv.* Sordidement.

sordidness, *s.* Sordidité *f.* (a) Saleté *f.* (b) Bassesse *f.* (c) Avarice *f* sordide.

sore¹. **I.** *a.* **I.** (a) Douloureux, endolori. To be sore all over, avoir mal partout. (b) Enflammé, irrité. Sore throat, mal *m* de gorge. (c) *F:* To put one's finger on the sore place, mettre le doigt sur la plaie. (d) *F:* That's his sore spot, c'est son endroit sensible. **2.** Chagriné. **3.** To be in sore need of sth., avoir grandement besoin de qch. **-ly,** *adv.* Sorely tried, fort éprouvé. **II. sore,** *adv.* Sore distressed, dans une grande détresse.

sore², *s.* Plaie *f*; blessure *f,* écorchure *f.* *F:* To (re)open an old sore, raviver une ancienne plaie.

soreness, *s.* **I.** Endolorissement *m.* **2.** (a) Chagrin *m,* peine *f.* (b) Sentiment *m* de rancune.

sorrel¹, *s.* *Bot:* Oseille *f.*

sorrel², *a. & s.* (Cheval) alezan (*m*).

sorrow¹, *s.* Peine *f,* chagrin *m,* tristesse *f.* To my sorrow, à mon regret.

sorrow², *v.i.* S'affliger, être affligé (*over, at, about, sth.,* de qch.). **sorrowing,** *a.* Affligé.

sorrowful, *a.* Affligé, chagriné; triste; (*of news*) attristant, pénible. **-fully,** *adv.* Tristement; avec chagrin.

sorry, *a.* **I.** (a) Fâché, désolé, peiné. *F:* You will be sorry for it, il vous en cuira. *I am extremely s.,* je regrette infiniment. Sorry! pardon! je regrette! (b) I am sorry for him, je le plains. *F:* To look sorry for oneself, faire piteuse mine. **2.** Mauvais; misérable. *S. excuse,* piètre excuse. To cut a sorry figure, faire piteuse figure.

sort¹, *s.* **I.** (a) Sorte *f,* genre *m,* espèce *f.* *A strange s. of fellow,* un type bizarre. That's the sort of man he is, voilà comme il est. *F: He looks a good s.,* il a l'air bon garçon. Something of that sort, quelque chose dans ce genre-là. Nothing of the sort, pas du tout! *I shall do nothing of the s.,* je n'en ferai rien. *To make* some sort of excuse, faire des excuses quelconques. (b) We had coffee of a sort, on nous a donné du soi-disant café. (c) To be out of sorts, être indisposé. **2.** In some sort, à un certain degré.

sort², *v.tr.* (a) Trier, assortir; débrouiller (des papiers). *Post:* To sort the letters, trier les lettres. (b) *To s. out the bad ones,* trier les mauvais. **sorting,** *s.* Triage *m,* tri *m*; classement *m.*

sorter, *s.* Trieur, -euse; classeur, -euse.

sortie, *s.* *Mil:* Sortie *f.*

sot, *s.* Ivrogne *m.*

sotto voce, *adv.* (a) (Causer) tout bas, à demi-voix. (b) *Mus:* Sotto-voce.

soul, *s.* Ame *f.* **I.** (a) With all my soul, de toute mon âme. (b) *He is the s. of the enterprise,* c'est lui qui est le premier mobile de l'entreprise. **2.** (a) Ship lost with all souls, navire perdu corps et biens. Without meeting a living soul, sans rencontrer âme qui vive. (b) Poor soul! pauvre créature *f*!

soul-stirring, *a.* Émouvant.

sound¹, *s.* (a) Son *m,* bruit *m.* (b) *F:* I don't like the sound of it, cela ne me dit rien qui vaille. (c) (The science of) sound, l'acoustique *f.* **sound-wave,** *s.* Onde *f* sonore.

sound². **I.** *v.i.* **I.** Sonner, résonner; retentir. **2.** (a) To sound hollow, sonner creux. (b) Paraître, sembler. *Name that sounds French,* nom qui a une apparence française. *It sounded a long way off,* on aurait dit que cela venait de loin. That sounds well, cela fait bon effet. **II.** **sound,** *v.tr.* **I.** Sonner. *Aut:* To sound the horn, corner. **2.** Prononcer. *To sound one's r's,* faire sonner les r. **3.** *Med:* Ausculter. **sounding,** *a.* Sonore.

sound³. **I.** *v.tr.* (a) *Nau:* Sonder. *Abs.* Prendre le fond. (b) *F:* To sound s.o. (about sth.), sonder qn (relativement à qch.). **2.** *v.i.* (*Of whale*) Faire la sonde; foncer.

sound⁴, *s.* Détroit *m*; goulet *m.*

sound⁵. **I.** *a.* **I.** (a) Sain. Of sound mind, sain d'esprit. *F:* To be sound in wind and limb, avoir bon pied bon œil. (b) En bon état. **2.** (a) S. *financial position,* situation

financière solide. (b) (Argument) valide.
3. Sound sleep, sommeil profond. *To give
s.o. a s. thrashing,* rosser qn d'importance.
-ly, *adv.* **I.** Sainement; judicieusement.
2. To sleep soundly, dormir profondément.
To thrash **s.o.** soundly, rosser qn d'importance. **II. sound,** *adv.* **To sleep sound,**
dormir à poings fermés.

soundness, *s.* **I.** Bon état. **2.** Solidité *f.*

soup, *s.* Soupe *f,* potage *m.* **Thick soup,**
crème *f,* purée *f.* **Clear soup,** consommé *m.*
F: **To be in the soup,** être dans le pétrin.
soup-ladle, *s.* **soup-plate,** *s.*
Assiette creuse. **soup-tureen,** *s.* Soupière *f.*

sour¹, *a.* **I.** (a) Aigre, acide, sur. (b) To turn
sour, tourner à l'aigre. To turn sth. sour,
(faire) aigrir qch. **2.** (*Of pers.*) Revêche;
aigre. **-ly,** *adv.* Avec aigreur.

sour². **I.** *v.i.* Surir; (s')aigrir. **2.** *v.tr.* Aigrir.

source, *s.* Source *f. To trace a tradition back
to its s.,* remonter aux sources, à l'origine,
d'une tradition.

sourish, *a.* Aigrelet, -ette, suret, -ette.

sourness, *s.* **I.** Aigreur *f,* acidité *f.* **2.**
Aigreur; humeur *f* revêche.

souse, *v.tr.* Plonger, immerger (*in,* dans).

south. **I.** *s.* Sud *m,* midi *m.* On the south
(of), au sud (de). **The South of France,** le
Midi (de la France). **2.** *adv.* Au sud. To
travel south, voyager vers le sud. **3.** *a.* Sud
inv; (vent) du sud. **South Africa.** *Pr.n.*
L'Afrique australe. **The Union of South
Africa,** l'Union sud-africaine. **South-
African,** *a. & s.* Sud-africain, -aine.
south-east. **I.** *s.* Sud-est *m.* **2.** *adv.*
Vers le sud-est. **3.** *a.* Du sud-est. **south-
easterly,** *a.* Du sud-est. **south-eastern,**
a. Du sud-est. **South Sea (the).** *Pr.n.*
Le Pacifique sud. **The South Sea Islands,**
les îles *f* du Pacifique. **south-west.** **I.** *s.*
Sud-ouest *m.* **2.** *adv.* Vers le sud-ouest.
3. *a.* Du sud-ouest. **south-wester,** *s.*
I. Vent *m* de sud-ouest; le suroît. **2.** Chapeau *m* imperméable; suroît *m.* **south-
westerly,** *a.* Du sud-ouest. **south-
western,** *a.* Du sud-ouest.

southerly, *a.* (a) Du sud. (b) *S. aspect,*
exposition au midi.

southern, *a.* (Du) sud; du midi; méridional, -aux. *Astr:* **The Southern Cross,**
la Croix du Sud.

southerner, *s.* Habitant, -ante, du sud.

southward. **I.** *s.* To the southward, vers le
sud. **2.** *a.* Au du, sud; du côté du sud.

southwards, *adv.* Vers le sud.

souvenir, *s.* Souvenir *m,* mémento *m.*

sovereign. **I.** *a.* Souverain; suprême.
Sovereign rights, droits de souveraineté.
2. *s.* (a) Souverain, -aine. (b) *Num:* Souverain *m.*

sovereignty, *s.* Souveraineté *f.*

Soviet, *s.* Soviet *m.* **Soviet union,** union
soviétique.

sow¹, *v.tr.* Semer. To sow land with wheat,

ensemencer une terre en blé. *Abs.* **To sow
broadcast,** semer à la volée. **To sow discord,**
semer, répandre, la discorde. **sowing,** *s.*
Semailles *fpl,* semis *m.* **sowing-machine,**
s. Semoir *m.*

sow², *s.* (a) Truie *f.* (b) *Ven:* Laie *f.*

sower, *s.* Semeur, -euse.

sow-thistle, *s.* *Bot:* Laiteron *m.*

soya-bean, *s.* *Bot:* Soya *m*; pois chinois.

spa, *s.* Ville *f* d'eau; station thermale.

space¹, *s.* **I.** Espace *m,* intervalle *m* (de
temps). **2.** (a) L'espace. **Staring into space,**
le regard perdu dans l'espace. (b) **To take
up a lot of space,** occuper beaucoup de place.
(c) Étendue *f*; surface *f.* **3.** Espace libre;
espacement *m,* intervalle. **Space between
two things,** écartement *m* de deux choses.
Blank space, blanc *m.*

space², *v.tr.* **To space (out),** espacer.

spaced, *a.* Écarté; espacé. **spacing,** *s.*
Espacement *m,* écartement *m.*

spacious, *a.* (a) Spacieux, vaste. (b) Ample.

spaciousness, *s.* (a) Vaste étendue *f.*
(b) Logeabilité *f* (d'un appartement).

spade¹, *s.* *Tls:* Bêche *f*; (*child's*) pelle *f.*
F: **To call a spade a spade,** appeler les
choses par leur nom. **spade-work,** *s.*
F: Travaux *mpl* préliminaires.

spade², *s.* *Cards:* Pique *m.*

spadeful, *s.* Pleine bêche; pelletée *f.*

spaghetti, *s.* *Cu:* Spaghetti *mpl.*

Spain. *Pr.n.* L'Espagne *f.*

span¹, *s.* **I.** Empan *m* (de la main). **2.** (a)
Portée *f* (entre deux appuis); largeur *f* (d'une
arche). (b) Travée *f* (d'un pont).

span², *v.tr.* **I.** Mesurer à l'empan. **2.** Franchir, enjamber.

spangle¹, *s.* *Tex:* Paillette *f.* **Gold spangles,**
lamé *m* d'or.

spangle², *v.tr.* Pailleter (*with,* de). *Spangled
with silver,* lamé d'argent.

Spaniard, *s.* Espagnol, -ole.

spaniel, *s.* Épagneul *m.*

Spanish. **I.** *a.* Espagnol. **Spanish onion,**
oignon d'Espagne. **2.** *s.* *Ling:* L'espagnol
m. **Spanish-American,** *a.* Hispano-
américain.

spank¹, *v.tr.* Fesser (un enfant). **spanking¹,**
s. Fessée *f.*

spank², *v.i.* To spank along, aller bon train.
spanking², *a.* **I.** *F:* De premier ordre.
2. To go at a spanking pace, brûler le terrain.

spanner, *s.* Clef *f* (à écrous).

spar¹, *s.* *Nau:* (a) Espar *m.* (b) *pl.* **The
spars,** la mâture.

spar², *s.* *Miner:* Spath *m.*

spar³, *s.* (a) Assaut de boxe amical. (b) Assaut
de paroles.

spar⁴, *v.i.* **To spar up to s.o.,** se mettre en
posture de combat. **Sparring match,** assaut
de boxe amical. **Sparring partner,** partenaire
m (d'un boxeur).

spare¹, *a.* **I.** (a) *S. diet,* régime frugal.
(b) Sec, *f.* sèche; maigre, fluet, -ette. **2.** Spare

time, (i) temps disponible; (ii) moments perdus; loisir(s) *m(pl)*. **Spare bedroom,** chambre d'ami. **3.** Spare parts, *s.* spares, pièces *f* de rechange. *Aut:* Spare wheel, roue de secours. **-ly,** *adv. (a)* (Manger) frugalement. *(b)* Sparely built, sec, *f.* sèche; mince.

spare², *v.tr.* **I.** Épargner, ménager. **To spare no expense,** ne pas regarder à la dépense. **To spare no pains,** ne pas ménager sa peine. **2.** *(a)* Se passer de (qch.). **Can you spare it?** pouvez-vous vous en passer? **To have nothing to spare,** n'avoir que le strict nécessaire. **To have enough and to spare,** avoir plus qu'il n'en faut. **He has money and to spare,** il a de l'argent de reste. *(b)* **I cannot spare the time,** le temps me fait défaut. *I have a minute to s.,* je peux disposer d'un instant. *(c) Can you s. me a few moments?* voulez-vous m'accorder quelques minutes? **3.** *(a)* Faire grâce à. **To spare s.o.'s life,** épargner la vie de qn. **If he is spared,** s'il lui est donné de vivre. *Death spares no one,* la mort ne pardonne à personne. **To spare s.o.'s feelings,** ménager qn. *(b)* Ménager (son cheval). *(c) S. me this journey,* dispensez-moi de ce voyage. **sparing,** *a.* **I.** Ménager; *f* économe. **To be sparing with the butter,** ménager le beurre. **He is sparing of praise,** il est avare de louanges. **Sparing of words,** sobre de paroles. **2.** Sparing use of sth., emploi modéré de qch. **-ly,** *adv.* Frugalement; (manger) sobrement. *To use sth. s.,* ménager qch.

spark¹, *s. (a)* Étincelle *f.* **Spark of wit,** paillette *f* d'esprit. *F:* He hasn't a spark of generosity in him, il n'a pas pour deux sous de générosité. *(b) El:* Étincelle. *(c) Nau; F:* Sparks, le radio.

spark², *v.i.* Émettre des étincelles. **sparking,** *s. El:* **I.** Émission *f* d'étincelles. **2.** Allumage *m* par étincelle électrique. **sparking-plug,** *s. I.C.E:* Bougie *f* (d'allumage).

spark³, *s.* **I.** Élégant *m.* **2.** Gay spark, gaillard *m.*

sparkle¹, *s.* **I.** Brève lueur. **2.** Étincellement *m*; éclat *m*, pétillement *m* (des yeux); feux *mpl* (d'un diamant).

sparkle², *v.i. (a)* Étinceler, scintiller; *(of jewel)* chatoyer. *(b) (Of wine)* Pétiller. **sparkling¹,** *a. (a)* Étincelant, brillant. *(b)* (Vin) mousseux. **sparkling²,** *s.* **I.** Étincellement *m*; scintillement *m*, scintillation *f.* **2.** Pétillement *m.*

sparrow, *s.* Moineau *m*, passereau *m.* **sparrow-hawk,** *s. Orn:* Épervier *m.*

sparse, *a.* Clairsemé, épars. **-ly,** *adv.* Peu abondamment.

Sparta. *Pr.n. A.Geog:* Sparte *f.*

Spartan, *a. & s.* Spartiate *(mf). F:* To live a S. life, vivre en Spartiate.

spasm, *s.* Accès *m* (de toux). *F:* To work in spasms, travailler par à-coups.

spasmodic, *a.* **I.** Involontaire, convulsif. **2.** Fait par à-coups. **-ally,** *adv.* Par à-coups.

spat, *s.* Demi-guêtre *f*; guêtre *f* de ville.

spate, *s.* Crue *f.*

spathe, *s. Bot:* Spathe *f.*

spatter¹, *s.* Éclaboussure *f.*

spatter², *v.tr.* To spatter s.o. with mud, éclabousser qn de boue.

spatula, *s.* Spatule *f.*

spawn¹, *s.* Frai *m*; œufs *mpl* (de poisson).

spawn², *v.i.* Frayer. **spawning,** *s.* Le frai.

speak, *v.* **I.** *v.i.* **I.** *(a)* Parler. *Without speaking,* sans rien dire. *(b)* **To speak to s.o.,** parler à qn; s'adresser à qn. **I will speak to him about it,** je lui en toucherai un mot. **I know him to speak to,** je le connais pour lui avoir été présenté. **To speak with s.o.,** causer avec qn. **Speaking for myself,** pour ma part. **Roughly speaking,** approximativement. *(c)* **The facts speak for themselves,** ces faits se passent de commentaire. **2.** Faire un discours; prendre la parole. **II.** **speak,** *v.tr.* **I.** *(a)* Dire. **To speak the truth,** dire la vérité. *(b)* **To speak one's mind,** dire sa façon de penser. **2.** Parler. **Do you speak French?** parlez-vous français? **3.** *Nau:* Héler, arraisonner (un navire). **speak for,** *v.i. (a)* **To speak for s.o.,** parler pour qn. *(b)* **That speaks well for your courage,** cela en dit long sur votre courage. **speak of,** *v.i.* **I.** Parler de. **Speaking of,** à propos de. **She has no voice to speak of,** elle n'a pour ainsi dire pas de voix. **To speak well of s.o.,** dire du bien de qn. **2.** Être significatif de. *His features spoke of privation,* ses traits trahissaient les privations. **speak out,** *v.i. (a)* Parler à haute voix. *(b)* Parler franchement. **speak up,** *v.i.* **I.** Parler plus haut. **2.** **To speak up for s.o.,** parler en faveur de qn. **spoken,** *a.* **I.** The spoken word, la parole. *S. language,* langue parlée. **2.** A well-spoken man, un homme à la parole courtoise. **speaking¹,** *a.* Expressif, éloquent. *F:* A speaking likeness, un portrait parlant. **speaking²,** *s.* Parler *m*, discours *m*, parole *f.* **To be on speaking terms,** se connaître assez pour se parler. **speaking-trumpet,** *s.* Porte-voix *m inv.* **speaking-tube,** *s.* Tube *m* acoustique.

speaker, *s.* **I.** Parleur, -euse. **2.** *(In public)* Orateur *m.* **To be a fluent s.,** avoir la parole facile. **3.** *Parl:* The Speaker, le Président (des Communes).

spear¹, *s. (a)* Lance *f. (b) (For throwing)* Javelot *m*, javeline *f.* **spear-head,** *s.* Fer *m*, pointe *f*, de lance. **spear-shaft,** *s.* Bois *m*, hampe *f*, de lance. **spear-thrust,** *s.* Coup *m* de lance.

spear², *v.tr.* (Trans)percer d'un coup de lance.

special. **I.** *a. (a)* Spécial, -aux; particulier. *S. feature,* particularité *f. Com:* Special price, prix de faveur. *(b)* Special friend, ami intime. **I have nothing special to tell you,**

je n'ai rien de particulier à vous dire. **2.** *s.*
Train spécial. **-ally,** *adv.* Spécialement,
particulièrement ; surtout.
specialist, *s.* Spécialiste *mf.*
speciality, *s.* **1.** Spécialité *f.* **2.** Qualité
particulière ; particularité *f.*
specialize, *v.i.* Se spécialiser (*in,* dans).
To specialize in a subject, faire sa spécialité
d'un sujet.
specie, *s.* Espèces monnayées.
species, *s. inv.* **1.** (*a*) *Nat.Hist:* Espèce *f.*
(*b*) *Arb:* Essence *f.* **2.** Espèce, sorte *f.*
specific. 1. *a.* (*a*) Spécifique. *Ph:* **Specific
gravity,** poids *m* spécifique. (*b*) Explicite.
Specific aim, but déterminé. **2.** *s. Med:*
Spécifique *m* (*for,* contre). **-ally,** *adv.*
1. Spécifiquement. **2.** Précisément.
specification, *s.* Spécification *f.*
specify, *v.tr.* Spécifier, déterminer. **Unless
otherwise specified,** sauf indication contraire.
specimen, *s.* (*a*) Spécimen *m.* (*b*) Exemple
m, échantillon *m.* (*c*) *F:* **Queer specimen,**
drôle *m* de type.
specious, *a.* Spécieux.
speciousness, *s.* Spéciosité *f;* apparence
trompeuse.
speck, *s.* **1.** Petite tache ; point *m* ; moucheture *f.* **2.** Grain *m,* atome *m.* *S. on the
horizon,* point noir à l'horizon.
speckled, *a.* Tacheté, moucheté ; (*of
plumage*) grivelé.
spectacle, *s.* **1.** Spectacle *m.* **2.** *pl.* **Spectacles,** lunettes *f.* **spectacle-case,** *s.* Étui
m à lunettes.
spectacular, *a.* Spectaculaire.
spectator, *s.* Spectateur, -trice ; assistant,
-ante. *The spectators,* l'assistance *f.*
spectral, *a.* Spectral, -aux.
spectre, *s* Spectre *m,* fantôme *m.*
spectroscope, *s. Opt:* Spectroscope *m.*
spectrum, *s. Ph:* Spectre *m.* *The colours
of the s.,* les couleurs spectrales.
speculate, *v.i.* **1.** To speculate about sth.,
faire des conjectures sur qch. **2.** *Fin:*
Spéculer (*in,* sur).
speculation, *s* **1.** (*a*) Spéculation *f,* méditation *f* (*on,* sur). (*b*) Conjecture *f.* **2.** (*a*) *Fin:*
Spéculation. (*b*) Entreprise spéculative.
Good s., bonne affaire.
speculative, *a.* **1.** (*a*) Spéculatif, contemplatif. (*b*) Conjectural, -aux. **2.** *Fin:* Spéculatif.
speculator, *s.* Spéculateur *m.*
speech, *s.* **1.** (*a*) **(Faculty of) speech,** la
parole. **To lose the power of speech,** perdre
la parole. (*b*) **To be slow of speech,** parler
lentement. (*c*) **Figure of speech,** figure *f* de
rhétorique. *Gram:* **Parts of speech,** parties
f du discours. **2.** Langue *f* (d'un peuple) ;
parler *m.* **3.** Discours *m.* **speech-day,** *s.*
Sch: Distribution *f* de prix.
speechless, *a.* **1.** Incapable de parler.
2. Interdit, interloqué, ment, -elle. **Speechless
with surprise,** muet de surprise.
speed[1], *s.* Vitesse *f;* marche *f* (rapide) ;

rapidité *f.* **To do sth. with all speed,** faire
qch. au plus vite. **At full speed,** au plus vite ;
(*of car*) à toute vitesse. *Nau:* **Full speed
ahead !** en avant à toute vitesse ! **Maximum
speed,** vitesse limite. **speed-boat,** *s.* *Sp:*
Hors-bord *m.* **speed-indicator,** *s.*
Compteur *m* (de tours). **speed-way,** *s.*
Autostrade *f.*
speed[2], *v.i.* Se hâter, se presser ; aller vite.
speed[3], *v.* **1.** *v.tr.* **To speed (up) the work,**
accélérer les travaux. **2.** *v.i. Aut:* Faire de
la vitesse. **speeding,** *s.* **1.** *Aut:* Excès *m*
de vitesse. **2. Speeding (up),** accélération *f.*
speediness, *s.* Rapidité *f,* célérité *f.*
speedometer, *s.* *Aut:* Indicateur *m* de
vitesse ; compteur *m.*
speedy, *a.* Rapide, prompt. **-ily,** *adv.*
Vite ; promptement.
spell[1], *s.* **1.** Incantation *f*; formule *f*
magique. **2.** Charme *m,* maléfice *m.* **To cast
a spell over s.o.,** jeter un sort sur qn ; ensorceler qn. **Under a spell,** sous un charme ;
ensorcelé. **spell-bound,** *a.* *F:* figé sur
place. **To hold one's audience spell-bound,**
tenir ses auditeurs sous le charme.
spell[2], *v.tr.* **1.** Épeler ; (*in writing*) orthographier (un mot). **He can't spell,** il ne sait
pas l'orthographe. **To spell out sth.,** déchiffrer qch. péniblement. **How is it spelt?**
comment cela s'écrit-il ? **What do these
letters spell?** quel mot forment ces lettres ?
3. Signifier. *That would s. disaster !* ce
serait le désastre ! **spelling,** *s.* Épellation *f* ;
(*in writing*) orthographe *f.* **spelling-bee,** *s.*
Concours (oral) d'orthographe.
spell[3], *s.* **1.** Tour *m.* **To take spells at the
pumps,** se relayer aux pompes. **Three hours
at a spell,** trois heures de suite. **2.** (Courte)
période. **A spell of cold weather,** une période
de froid.
spend, *v.tr.* **1.** Dépenser. **To spend money
on s.o.,** faire des dépenses pour qn. **Without
spending a penny,** sans bourse délier. **2.** To
spend care on sth., consacrer du soin à qch.
3. Passer, employer (son temps). **4.** To
spend oneself, s'épuiser. **spent,** *a.* **1.** The
day was far spent, c'était tard dans la journée.
2. (*a*) Épuisé. *The horses are s.,* les chevaux
n'en peuvent plus. (*b*) *The storm is s.,* l'orage
est calmé. **Spent bullet,** balle morte. **Spent
cartridge,** cartouche vide. **spending,** *s.*
Dépense *f.*
spendthrift, *s.* Dépensier, -ière.
sperm, *s.* **Sperm(-whale),** cachalot *m.*
sperm oil, *s.* Huile *f* de baleine.
spermaceti, *s.* Spermaceti *m* ; blanc *m,*
sperme *m,* de baleine.
sphere, *s.* **1.** Sphère *f.* **2.** (*a*) Milieu *m,*
sphère. (*b*) *Limited s.,* cadre restreint. *That
does not come within my sphere,* cela ne
rentre pas dans ma compétence. **Sphere of
influence,** sphère, zone *f,* d'influence.
spherical, *a.* Sphérique.
sphinx, *s. Myth:* Sphinx *m.* **sphinx-like,**
a. (Sourire) de sphinx.

spice¹, s. **1.** Épice f, aromate m. **Mixed spice(s),** épices mélangées. **2.** Teinte f; nuance f; soupçon m.

spice², v.tr. Épicer.

spiciness, s. Goût épicé.

spick and span, adj.phr. Reluisant de propreté; (of pers.) tiré à quatre épingles.

spicy, a. **1.** Épicé; (goût) relevé. **2.** Aromatique, parfumé.

spider, s. Araignée f.

spidery, a. **Spidery handwriting,** pattes fpl d'araignée.

spigot, s. Fausset m, broche f.

spike¹, s. **1.** Pointe f; piquant m (de fil barbelé). **2.** Bot: Épi m.

spike², v.tr. (a) Clouer, cheviller. (b) Artil: Enclouer. F: **I spiked his guns for him,** je lui ai damé le pion. **spiked,** a. Garni de pointes; barbelé. **Spiked shoes,** chaussures à pointes.

spill¹, s. **To have a spill,** culbuter; (in motor car) faire panache.

spill², v. I. v.tr. Répandre, renverser; verser. II. **spill,** v.i. Se répandre; s'écouler.

spill³, s. Allume-feu m inv.

spin¹, s. **1.** (a) Tournoiement m. (b) Av: **To get into a spin,** descendre en vrille. **2.** **To go for a spin,** faire une randonnée.

spin², v. I. v.tr. (a) Filer (la laine). (b) **To spin a top,** faire aller une toupie. **To spin a coin,** jouer à pile ou face. **2.** v.i. Tourner. **To spin round and round,** tournoyer. **My head is spinning,** la tête me tourne. Blow that sent him spinning, coup qui l'a envoyé rouler. **spin out,** v.tr. Faire traîner en longueur. v.i. **To make one's money spin out,** ménager son argent. **spinning,** s. **1.** (a) Filage m. (b) Ind: Filature f. **2.** Tournoiement m; rotation f. **Spinning top,** toupie f. **spinning-wheel,** s. Rouet m.

spinach, s. Cu: Épinards mpl.

spinal, a. Spinal, -aux. **Spinal column,** colonne vertébrale.

spindle, s. Tex: Fuseau m. **spindle-shaped,** a. Fusiforme, fuselé.

spindrift, s. Embrun m.

spine, s. Anat: Épine dorsale; colonne vertébrale.

spineless, a. F: Mou, f. molle.

spinet, s. Mus: Épinette f.

spinner, s. Tex: Fileur, -euse.

spinney, s. Petit bois; bosquet m.

spinster, s. Fille non mariée.

spiny, a. Épineux.

spiraea, s. Bot: Spirée f.

spiral. 1. s. Spirale f, hélice f. **2.** a. Spiral, -aux; en spirale. S. curl of smoke, volute f de fumée. **-ally,** adv. En spirale, en hélice.

spire, s Aiguille f, flèche f (d'église).

spirit¹, s. **1.** Esprit m, âme f. **2.** **The Holy Spirit,** le Saint-Esprit **Evil spirit,** esprit malin, mauvais génie. **3.** The discontented spirits, les esprits factieux. **The leading**

spirit, l'âme, le chef (d'une entreprise). **4.** Esprit, disposition f. **In a spirit of mischief,** par espièglerie. **To enter into the spirit of sth.,** entrer de bon cœur dans (la partie). **5.** (a) Caractère m, cœur m, courage m. **To show spirit,** montrer du caractère, du courage. (b) Ardeur f, entrain m. (c) He is full of spirits, il est très remuant. **In high spirits,** en train, en verve. **In low spirits,** abattu, accablé. **To keep up one's spirits,** ne pas perdre courage. Their spirits rose, ils reprenaient courage. **6.** Usu. pl. (a) Spiritueux mpl; alcool m. (b) **Spirit(s) of salts,** esprit de sel. **spirit-lamp,** s. Lampe f à alcool, à esprit de vin. **spirit-level,** s. Niveau m à bulle d'air, à alcool. **spirit-stove,** s. Réchaud m à alcool.

spirit², v.tr. **To spirit s.o. away,** faire disparaître qn comme par enchantement. **To spirit sth. away,** F: escamoter qch.

spirited, a. **1.** (High-)spirited, vif, animé; (of horse) fougueux. **2.** To give a s. performance, jouer avec verve.

spiritedness, s. Ardeur f, fougue f.

spiritless, a. **1.** Sans vie; terne. **2.** Sans courage. **3.** Abattu. **4.** Sans force.

spiritual, a. (a) Spirituel; de l'esprit. (b) Spirituel, immatériel.

spiritualism, s. Spiritisme m.

spiritualist, s. & a. Psychics: Spirite (mf).

spirituous, a. Spiritueux, alcoolique.

spirt¹, s. **1.** Jaillissement m; jet m. **2.** = SPURT³.

spirt², v.i. **1.** **To spirt up,** jaillir. **To spirt out,** saillir, gicler. **2.** v.i. = SPURT⁴.

spit¹, s. **1.** Cu: Broche f. **2.** Ph.Geog: Langue f de sable; pointe f de terre.

spit², v.tr. Embrocher.

spit³, s. **1.** Crachat m. F: **He's the dead spit of his father,** c'est son père tout craché. P: **Spit and polish,** fourbissage m; astiquage m. **2.** Crachin m (de pluie).

spit⁴, v. I. v.i. Cracher. **It is spitting (with rain),** il crachine. **2.** v.tr. Cracher. **To spit sth. out,** cracher qch.

spite¹, s. **1.** (a) Rancune f. (b) Malveillance f. (c) Pique f, dépit m. **To have a spite against s.o.,** en vouloir à qn. **2.** Prep.phr. **In spite of,** en dépit de; malgré.

spite², v.tr. Vexer, contrarier.

spiteful, a. Rancunier, vindicatif. **-fully,** adv. **1.** Par dépit; par rancune; par méchanceté. **2.** Méchamment.

spitefulness, s. Méchanceté f; rancœur f.

spitfire, s. F: Rageur, -euse.

spittle, s. Salive f, crachat m.

spittoon, s. Crachoir m.

splash¹, s. **1.** Éclaboussement m; clapotis m. **To fall into the water with a splash,** tomber dans l'eau en faisant flac. F: **To make a splash,** faire de l'épate. **2.** (a) Éclaboussure f. (b) Tache f. (c) Flaque f (d'eau).

splash². I. v.tr. (a) Éclabousser (with, de).

(b) *F:* To splash one's money about, prodiguer son argent. **2.** *v.i.* (a) Rejaillir en éclaboussures; (*of waves*) clapoter. (b) Barboter; patauger. **To splash about in the water,** s'agiter dans l'eau.

spleen, *s.* **I.** *Anat:* Rate *f.* **2.** (a) Spleen *m*; humeur noire. (b) Mauvaise humeur. **To vent one's spleen (up)on s.o.,** décharger sa bile sur qn.

splendid, *a.* Splendide; superbe; magnifique. **That's splendid!** à la bonne heure! **-ly,** *adv.* Splendidement; magnifiquement.

splendour, *s.* Splendeur *f*; éclat *m.*

splice¹, *s.* Épissure *f.*

splice², *v.tr.* **I.** Épisser. **2.** *F:* **To get spliced,** se marier.

splint, *s.* *Surg:* Éclisse *f*, attelle *f.* **To put a limb in splints,** éclisser un membre.

splinter¹, *s.* Éclat *m.* *S. lodged under the skin,* écharde *f.*

splinter². **I.** *v.tr.* Briser en éclats. **2.** *v.i.* Éclater.

split¹, *s.* **I.** Fente *f*; fissure *f.* **2.** Division *f*; rupture *f.*

split². *v.* **I.** *v.tr.* (a) Fendre. *Ph:* **To split the atom,** désintégrer l'atome. (b) Diviser; partager. **2.** *v.i.* (a) Se fendre, se crevasser. **The ship split in two,** le navire s'est cassé en deux. **To split open,** se fendre largement. (b) *F:* **My head is splitting,** j'ai un mal de tête fou. (c) *F:* **To split on s.o.,** dénoncer qn.

split³, *a.* Fendu.

splotch, *s.* *F:* Tache *f.*

splutter¹, *s.* **I.** Bredouillement *m.* **2.** Crachement *m.*

splutter². **I.** *v.tr.* **To splutter (out) a threat,** bredouiller une menace. **2.** *v.i.* (a) Pen that *splutters,* plume qui crache. (b) Bredouiller.

spoil¹, *s.* (*Usu. pl.*) Dépouilles *fpl*; butin *m.*

spoil². *v.* **I.** *v.tr.* (a) Gâter, endommager, abîmer. **To s. a piece of work,** gâcher un travail. (b) Gâter (un enfant). **2.** *v.tr.* Piller, saccager (une ville). **3.** *v.i.* Se gâter. *F:* **To be spoiling for a fight,** brûler du désir de se battre. **spoil-sport,** *s.* *F:* Trouble-fête *m inv.*, rabat-joie *mf inv.*

spoke, *s.* **I.** (a) Rayon *m.* (b) *Nau:* Poignée *f* (de roue de gouvernail). **2.** (a) Échelon *m* (d'échelle). (b) *F:* **To put a spoke in the wheel,** mettre des bâtons dans les roues.

spokesman, *s.* Porte-parole *m inv.* **To act as spokesman,** porter la parole.

spoliation, *s.* (a) Spoliation *f*, dépouillement *m.* (b) Pillage *m.*

spondee, *s.* *Pros:* Spondée *m.*

sponge¹, *s.* **I.** Éponge *f.* *F:* **To throw up the sponge,** s'avouer vaincu; quitter la partie. **2.** = SPONGER. **sponge-cake,** *s.* *Cu:* **I.** Gâteau *m* mousseline. **2.** Madeleine *f.* **sponge-finger,** *s.* Biscuit *m* à la cuiller.

sponge², *s.* Coup *m* d'éponge.

sponge³. **I.** *v.tr.* (a) Éponger. (b) *F:* Écornifler. **2.** *v.i.* *F:* Écornifler. **To sponge**

on s.o., vivre aux crochets de qn. **sponging¹,** *a.* *F:* Parasite, écornifleur. **sponging²,** *s.* **I.** Nettoyage *m* à l'éponge. **2.** *F:* Écorniflage *m.*

sponger, *s.* *F:* Écornifleur, -euse.

spongy, *a.* Spongieux.

sponsor¹, *s.* **I.** Garant *m*, caution *f* (*for s.o.,* de qn). **2.** Parrain *m*, marraine *f.*

sponsor², *v.tr.* Être le garant de.

spontaneous, *a.* Spontané. **-ly,** *adv.* Spontanément.

spontaneousness, *s.* Spontanéité *f.*

spoof¹, *s.* *P:* Attrape *f*; mystification *f.*

spoof², *v.tr.* *P:* Mystifier, duper.

spook, *s.* *F:* Spectre *m*, revenant *m.*

spool, *s.* Bobine *f.*

spoon, *s.* Cuiller *f*, cuillère *f.* **Spoon and fork,** couvert *m.* **spoon-feed,** *v.tr.* Nourrir à la cuiller; *F:* mâcher les morceaux à.

spoonful, *s.* Cuillerée *f.*

spoor, *s.* *Ven:* Foulées *fpl*, erre *f.*

sporadic, *a.* Sporadique. **-ally,** *adv.* Sporadiquement.

spore, *s.* Spore *f.*

sporran, *s.* Sporran *m.*

sport¹, *s.* **I.** (a) Jeu *m*, divertissement *m.* **In sport,** par plaisanterie. **To make sport of,** se moquer de. (b) **To have good sport,** (*hunting*) faire bonne chasse. **2.** Sport *m.* *Aut:* **Sports model,** machine grand sport. **3. To be the sport of fortune,** être le jouet de la fortune. **4.** *Biol:* Variété anormale. **5.** *F:* **He's a (real) sport,** c'est un chic type. **Be a sport!** sois chic! **sports-ground,** *s.* Terrain *m* de jeux; stade *m.*

sport². **I.** *v.i.* Jouer; se divertir. **2.** *v.tr.* *F:* Exhiber (un manteau de fourrure).

sporting, *a.* Sporting man, amateur *m* de sport. **In a sporting spirit,** sportivement. *S. conduct,* conduite digne d'un sportsman.

sportive, *a.* Badin; folâtre. **-ly,** *adv.* En badinant; en plaisantant.

sportsman, *s.* **I.** Chasseur *m*; pêcheur *m.* **2.** Amateur *m* de sport. **3. He's a real sportsman,** il est animé de l'esprit sportif.

sportsmanlike, *a.* Digne d'un sportsman.

spot¹, *s.* **I.** (a) Endroit *m*, lieu *m.* (b) *Adv. phr:* **On the spot,** sur-le-champ; immédiatement. **To be killed on the spot,** être tué raide. (c) *Com:* **Spot cash,** argent comptant. (d) **To put one's finger on a weak spot,** mettre le doigt sur un point faible. **2.** Tache *f*, macule *f.* **3.** Pois *m.* *Blue tie with red spots,* cravate bleue à pois rouges. *A panther's spots,* la moucheture d'une panthère. *F:* **To knock spots off s.o.,** battre qn à plate(s) couture(s). **4.** (a) Goutte *f* (de pluie). (b) *F:* **A spot of trouble,** un petit ennui.

spot², *v.tr.* **I.** (a) Tacher, souiller. (b) Tacheter, moucheter. **2.** *F:* (a) Repérer; apercevoir. (b) Reconnaître. *Turf:* **To spot the winner,** prédire le gagnant. **spotted,** *a.* (a) Tacheté, moucheté. (b) *Tex:* À pois.

spotless, *a.* Sans tache; immaculé; pur.

S. *snow*, neige vierge. **-ly,** *adv.* Spotlessly clean, d'une propreté irréprochable.
spotlight, *s.* *Th:* (*a*) Feu *m* de projecteur. (*b*) Projecteur *m.*
spotter, *s.* *Av:* Avion *m* de réglage de tir.
spotty, *a.* Moucheté, tacheté.
spouse, *s.* *Lit:* Époux, *f.* épouse.
spout¹, *s.* **1.** (*a*) Rain-water spout, tuyau *m* de décharge. (*b*) Bec *m* (de théière); jet *m* (de pompe). **2.** *P:* (*a*) To put one's watch up the spout, mettre sa montre au clou. (*b*) (*Of pers.*) Up the s., raté.
spout², **1.** *v.i.* (*a*) Jaillir. (*b*) (*Of whale*) Souffler. **2.** *v.tr.* (*a*) Faire jaillir. (*b*) *P:* Dégoiser. *Abs.* To spout, parler à jet continu.
spouting, *s.* **1.** Jaillissement *m.* **2.** *F:* Déclamation *f.*
spouter, *s.* *F:* Déclamateur *m.*
sprain¹, *s.* Entorse *f,* foulure *f.*
sprain², *v.tr.* To sprain one's wrist, se fouler le poignet. To sprain one's ankle, se donner une entorse.
sprat, *s.* **1.** *Ich:* Sprat *m* harenguet *m.* **2.** *F:* Gringalet *m.*
sprawl, *v.i.* (*a*) S'étendre, s'étaler. (*b*) To go sprawling, s'étaler par terre. **sprawling,** *a.* **1.** Vautré. **2.** *S. handwriting,* grosse écriture informe.
spray¹, *s.* Spray of flowers, rameau fleuri.
spray², *s.* **1.** Embrun *m.* **2.** (*a*) Poussière *f* d'eau. (*b*) Jet pulvérisé (de parfum). **3.** Gicleur *m*; vaporisateur *m.*
spray³, *v.tr.* **1.** Pulvériser, vaporiser, atomiser (un liquide). **2.** Asperger, arroser.
spread¹, *s.* **1.** (*a*) Étendue *f.* (*b*) (*Of aeroplane*) Envergure *f.* **2.** Diffusion *f*; propagation *f*; expansion *f.* **3.** *F:* Régal *m, pl.* -als, festin *m.*
spread², *v.* **I.** *v.tr.* **1.** Étendre. To spread a net, tendre un filet. To s. oneself on a subject, se répandre sur un sujet. **2.** (*a*) Répandre. (*b*) Instalments spread over several months, versements échelonnés sur plusieurs mois. **3.** To spread butter, étendre du beurre. **II.** **spread,** *v.i.* **1.** S'étendre, s'étaler. **2.** Se disséminer; se répandre; (*of disease*) se propager. The fire is spreading, le feu gagne. **3.** (*Of small shot*) S'écarter, se disperser. **spread-eagle,** *v.tr.* Étaler.
spreading, *s.* **1.** (*a*) Déploiement *m,* développement *m.* (*b*) Propagation *f* (d'une maladie); diffusion *f.* **2.** (*a*) Extension *f.* (*b*) Dispersion *f.*
spree, *s.* *F:* Partie *f* de plaisir; bombe *f.* To go on the spree, faire la fête.
sprig, *s.* Brin *m,* brindille *f*; petite branche.
sprightliness, *s.* Vivacité *f,* enjouement *m.*
sprightly, *a.* Éveillé, enjoué.
spring¹, *s.* **1.** (*a*) Source *f* (d'eau). (*b*) Source, origine *f.* **2.** Printemps *m.* In (the) spring, au printemps. Spring flowers, fleurs printanières. **3.** Saut *m,* bond *m.* To take a spring, prendre son élan; faire un bond. **4.** Élasticité *f.* **5.** (*a*) Ressort *m.* (*b*) *pl.*

Springs, suspension *f.* **spring-balance,** *s.* Peson *m* à ressort. **spring-board,** *s.* *Gym:* Tremplin *m.* **spring-clean,** *v.tr.* Nettoyer à fond (au printemps). **spring-cleaning,** *s.* Grand nettoyage (fait au printemps). **spring-gun,** *s.* Piège *m* à fusil. **spring-mattress,** *s.* Sommier *m* élastique. **spring-tide,** *s.* Grande marée.
spring², *v.* **I.** *v.i.* **1.** (*a*) Bondir, sauter. To spring to one's feet, se dresser vivement sur ses pieds. To spring at s.o., s'élancer sur qn. *F:* Where did you spring from? d'où sortez-vous? (*b*) The lid sprang open, le couvercle se releva instantanément. **2.** (*a*) Jaillir, sourdre. (*b*) Hope springs eternal, l'espérance reste toujours vivace. (*c*) Sprung from the people, sorti du peuple. **II.** **spring,** *v.tr.* (*a*) Faire jouer (un piège); faire sauter (une mine). (*b*) *F:* To spring a surprise on s.o., prendre qn à l'improviste. **spring aside,** *v.i.* Faire un bond de côté. **spring back,** *v.i.* **1.** Faire un bond en arrière. **2.** Faire ressort. The branch sprang back, la branche se redressa. **spring up,** *v.i.* **1.** Se lever précipitamment. **2.** (*a*) (*Of plant*) Pousser. (*b*) A breeze sprang up, une brise se leva. An intimacy sprang up between them, l'intimité s'établit entre eux.
springiness, *s.* Élasticité *f.*
springlike, *a.* Printanier.
springtime, *s.* Printemps *m.*
springy, *a.* Élastique; flexible.
sprinkle, *v.tr.* (*a*) Répandre, jeter. (*b*) Asperger (*with water*, d'eau); saupoudrer (*with salt*, de sel). Lawn sprinkled with dew, gazon parsemé de rosée. **sprinkling,** *s.* **1.** Aspersion *f,* arrosage *m*; saupoudrage *m.* **2.** Petite quantité.
sprint¹, *s.* Pointe *f* de vitesse.
sprint², *v.i.* Faire une course de vitesse.
sprite, *s.* Lutin *m*; farfadet *m.*
sprout¹, *s.* *Bot:* **1.** (*a*) Jet *m,* rejeton *m,* pousse *f.* (*b*) Germe *m,* bourgeon *m.* **2.** Brussels sprouts, choux *m* de Bruxelles.
sprout², **1.** *v.i.* (*a*) Pousser, pointer. (*b*) (*Of seed*) Germer. **2.** *v.tr.* To sprout horns, pousser des cornes.
spruce¹, *a.* Pimpant; soigné; tiré à quatre épingles.
spruce², *v.tr.* To spruce oneself up, se faire beau, belle.
spruce³, *s.* Sapin *m,* épinette *f.*
spruceness, *s.* Mise pimpante.
spry, *a.* Vif, actif.
spud, *s.* *F:* Pomme *f* de terre.
spume, *s.* *Lit:* Écume *f.*
spunk, *s.* *F:* Courage *m,* cran *m.*
spur¹, *s.* **1.** Éperon *m.* To win one's spurs, faire ses preuves. To set spurs to one's horse, piquer des deux. **2.** Coup *m* d'éperon; stimulant *m.* The spur of necessity, l'aiguillon *m* de la nécessité. On the spur of the moment, sous l'impulsion du moment. **3.** Ergot *m* (de

coq). **4.** Éperon, contrefort *m* (d'une chaîne de montagnes).

spur², *v.tr.* **1.** Éperonner. **2.** To spur s.o. on, aiguillonner, stimuler, qn. **Spurred on** by desire, fouetté par le désir.

spurious, *a.* Faux, *f.* fausse ; contrefait.

spurn, *v.tr.* **1.** Repousser, écarter, du pied. **2.** Rejeter avec mépris ; traiter avec mépris.

spurt¹, ², *s. & v.* = SPIRT¹, ².

spurt³, *s.* *(a)* Effort soudain. *(b)* *Sp:* To put on a spurt, démarrer, emballer. **Final** spurt, pointe finale.

spurt⁴, *v.i.* *Sp:* Emballer, démarrer.

sputter. **1.** *v.tr.* Débiter en bredouillant. **2.** *v.i.* *(a)* Bredouiller. *(b)* *(Of pen)* Cracher. *(c)* Grésiller, crépiter. **sputtering,** *s.* **1.** Bredouillement *m.* **2.** Crachement *m* (d'une plume). **3.** Crépitement *m.*

spy¹, *s.* Espion, -onne ; *F:* mouchard *m.*

spy², *v.* **1.** *v.tr.* Apercevoir, remarquer. To spy out, explorer. **2.** *v.i.* Espionner. To spy (up)on s.o., espionner qn. **spying,** *s.* Espionnage *m.*

squabble¹, *s.* Querelle *f,* chamaillerie *f.*

squabble², *v.i.* Se chamailler, se quereller. **squabbling,** *s.* Chamaillerie *f* ; querelles *fpl.*

squad, *s.* **1.** Escouade *f.* **Firing squad,** peloton *m* d'exécution. **2.** Brigade *f* (de cheminots).

squadron, *s.* **1.** *(a)* *Mil:* Escadron *m.* *(b)* *Mil.Av:* Escadrille *f.* **Squadron leader,** commandant *m.* **2.** *Navy:* Escadre *f.*

squalid, *a.* Sale ; misérable.

squall¹, *s.* Cri *m* (rauque).

squall², *v.i.* Crier, brailler, piailler. **squalling,** *a.* Criard, braillard.

squall³, *s.* *Nau:* Grain *m* ; bourrasque *f.* *F:* **Look out for squalls!** veille au grain ! gare la bombe !

squally, *a.* (Temps) à grains, à rafales.

squalor, *s.* Saleté *f* ; misère *f.*

squander, *v.tr.* Gaspiller, prodiguer ; dissiper. **squandering,** *s.* Gaspillage *m.*

squanderer, *s.* Gaspilleur, -euse.

square¹. **I.** *s.* **1.** Carré *m.* *Mil:* To form square, former le carré. **2.** *(a)* Carreau *m* (de figure quadrillée) ; case *f* (d'échiquier). *(b)* Silk square, foulard *m.* **3.** *(Of town)* Place *f* ; *(with garden)* square *m.* **4.** Équerre *f.* T square, équerre en T. *F:* To act on the square, agir honnêtement. **5.** *Mth:* Carré. **II.** square, *a.* **1.** Carré. *(a)* Square game, partie à quatre. Square measure, mesure de surface. *(b)* Square shoulders, épaules carrées. **2.** *Mth:* Square root, racine carrée. **3.** To get things square, mettre tout en ordre. He always gives you a s. deal, il est toujours loyal en affaires. To be square with s.o., être quitte envers qn. **-ly,** *adv.* Carrément. **III.** square, *adv.* **1.** À angles droits (to, with, avec). **2.** *F:* Honnêtement.

square-jawed, *a.* Au menton carré.

square². **I.** *v.tr.* **1.** Carrer, équarrir. **2.** *(a)* Balancer, régler. To square matters, arranger les choses. *(b)* *F:* Graisser la patte à (qn). **3.** *Mth:* Élever au carré. **II.** square, *v.i.* S'accorder (with, avec). **square up.** **I.** *v.tr.* Abs. To square up with s.o., régler ses comptes avec qn. **2.** *v.i.* To square up to s.o., s'avancer vers qn en posture de combat.

squareness, *s.* **1.** Forme carrée. **2.** Honnêteté *f,* loyauté *f.*

squash¹, *s.* **1.** Écrasement *m,* aplatissement *m.* **2.** Cohue *f,* presse *f.*

squash². **1.** *v.tr.* *(a)* Écraser, aplatir. *(b)* *F:* Remettre à sa place. **2.** *v.i.* *(a)* S'écraser. *(b)* Se serrer, se presser.

squashy, *a.* Mou, *f.* molle, et humide.

squat¹, *v.i.* **1.** *(a)* To squat (down), s'accroupir. *(b)* *Ven:* Se tapir. **2.** To squat upon a piece of land, s'approprier un terrain. **squatting,** *a.* **1.** Accroupi. **2.** Qui occupe (un terrain) comme squatter.

squat², *a.* Ramassé, trapu.

squatter, *s.* Squatter *m.*

squaw, *s.* Femme *f* peau-rouge.

squawk¹, *s.* Cri *m* rauque.

squawk², *v.i.* Pousser des cris rauques.

squeak¹, *s.* Petit cri aigu ; crissement *m.* *F:* To have a narrow squeak, l'échapper belle.

squeak², *v.i.* Pousser des cris aigus ; *(of shoes)* crier. **squeaking,** *s.* Couics *mpl.*

squeal¹, *s.* Cri aigu ; cri perçant.

squeal². **1.** *v.i.* *(a)* Pousser des cris aigus. *(b)* *F:* Protester ; pousser les hauts cris. *(c)* *P:* Trahir ses complices. To squeal on s.o., dénoncer qn. **squealing¹,** *a.* Criard. **squealing²,** *s.* Cris aigus ; hauts cris.

squeamish, *a.* **1.** Sujet aux nausées. **To feel squeamish,** avoir mal au cœur. **2.** Difficile, délicat.

squeamishness, *s.* **1.** Disposition *f* aux nausées. **2.** Délicatesse exagérée.

squeeze¹, *s.* **1.** *(a)* Compression *f.* *(b)* Étreinte *f.* To give s.o. a squeeze, serrer qn dans ses bras. **2.** Presse *f,* cohue *f.* It was a tight squeeze, on tenait tout juste. **3.** A squeeze of lemon, quelques gouttes *f* de citron.

squeeze², *v.tr.* **1.** *(a)* Presser. To squeeze s.o.'s hand, serrer la main à qn. To s. one's finger, se pincer le doigt. *(b)* *F:* Embrasser, étreindre. **2.** Faire entrer de force. To squeeze the juice out of a lemon, exprimer le jus d'un citron. **3.** *(a)* Exercer une pression sur. *(b)* To squeeze money out of s.o., extorquer de l'argent à qn.

squelch. **1.** *v.tr.* *(a)* Écraser. *(b)* *F:* Aplatir (qn). **2.** *v.i.* The water squelched in his shoes, l'eau giclait dans ses chaussures.

squib, *s.* *Pyr:* Pétard *m,* serpenteau *m.* *F:* Damp squib, affaire ratée.

squint¹, *s.* **1.** Strabisme *m,* louchement *m.* **2.** Coup d'œil furtif. **3.** *F:* Regard *m* ; coup d'œil.

squint², *v.i.* **1.** Loucher. **2.** To squint at sth., regarder qch. de côté, furtivement.

squint³, *a.* **Squint eyes,** yeux louches. **squint-eyed,** *a.* Au regard louche; strabique.

squire, *s.* **1.** *Hist:* Écuyer. **2.** *F:* (*a*) Propriétaire terrien. (*b*) **The squire, le châtelain** (de l'endroit).

squirm, *v.i.* (*a*) Se tordre, se tortiller. (*b*) *F:* Ne savoir comment se tenir.

squirrel, *s.* Écureuil *m.*

squirt¹, *s.* **1.** Seringue *f*; (*toy*) clifoire *f.* **2.** Jet *m*, giclée *f.*

squirt². **1.** *v.tr.* Lancer en jet. **To squirt in oil,** injecter de l'huile. **2.** *v.i.* Jaillir, gicler.

stab¹, *s.* Coup *m* de poignard, de couteau. **Stab in the back,** *F:* attaque déloyale.

stab², *v.tr.* Poignarder. *F:* **To stab s.o. to the heart,** frapper qn au cœur.

stability, *s.* Stabilité *f*, solidité *f.*

stabilize, *v.tr.* Stabiliser.

stable¹, *s.* Écurie *f.* **stable-boy,** *s.* Valet *m*, garçon *m*, d'écurie.

stable², *v.tr.* Loger. **stabling,** *s.* **1.** Logement *m*, installation *f* (de chevaux). **2.** *Coll.* Écuries *fpl.*

stable³, *a.* **1.** Stable; solide, fixe. **2.** Constant, ferme.

stableman, *s.* Palefrenier *m.*

staccato, *a., adv., & s.* (*a*) *Mus:* Staccato (*m*). (*b*) **In a staccato voice,** d'une voix saccadée.

stack¹, *s.* **1.** (*a*) Meule *f* (de foin). (*b*) Pile *f*, tas *m.* **2.** Souche *f* (de cheminée).

stack², *v.tr.* **1.** Mettre en meule. **2.** To stack (up), empiler, entasser.

stadium, *s.* Stade *m.*

staff¹, *s.* **1.** (*a*) Bâton *m.* *F:* **Bread is the staff of life,** le pain est le soutien de la vie. (*b*) Hampe *f.* **2.** (*a*) *Mil:* État-major *m.* (*b*) Personnel *m.* **The domestic s.,** les domestiques *m.* **3.** *Mus:* Portée *f.* **staff officer,** *s.* Officier *m* d'état-major.

staff², *v.tr.* Pourvoir de personnel. **To be over-staffed,** avoir un personnel trop nombreux.

stag, *s.* Cerf *m.* **stag-beetle,** *s.* Cerf-volant *m*, *pl.* cerfs-volants. **stag-hunt(ing),** *s.* Chasse *f* (au cerf).

stage¹, *s.* **1.** Estrade *f*, échafaud *m.* **2.** (*a*) *Th:* Scène *f*; *F:* les planches *f.* **To come on the stage,** entrer en scène. **To go on the stage,** se faire acteur ou actrice. **Stage directions,** indications scéniques. (*b*) Champ *m* d'action. **3.** Phase *f*, période *f*, stade *m.* **To rise by successive stages,** monter par échelons. **4.** Étape *f.* **To travel by easy stages,** voyager à petites étapes. **stage-box,** *s.* Loge *f* d'avant-scène. **stage-coach,** *s.* Diligence *f.* **stage-door,** *s.* *Th:* Entrée *f* des artistes. **stage-effect,** *s.* *Th:* Effet *m* scénique. **stage-fright,** *s.* *Th:* Trac *m.* **stage-manager,** *s.* *Th:* Régisseur *m.* **stage-whisper,** *s.* *Th:* Aparté *m.* **In a stage-whisper,** en aparté.

stage², *v.tr.* (*a*) Monter (une pièce). (*b*) Organiser (une démonstration); monter (un coup). **staging,** *s.* Échafaud *m*, échafaudage *m.*

stager, *s.* *F:* **Old stager,** vieux routier.

stagger¹, *s.* (*a*) Titubation *f.* (*b*) Allure chancelante.

stagger². **1.** *v.i.* Chanceler, tituber. **To stagger to one's feet,** se lever en chancelant. **II.** **stagger,** *v.tr.* Confondre, consterner.

staggering¹, *a.* **1.** (Pas) chancelant, titubant. **2.** *F:* (*a*) **Staggering blow,** coup d'assommoir. (*b*) (*Of news*) Atterrant. **staggering²,** *s.* Titubation *f.*

staghound, *s.* Lévrier *m* d'Écosse.

stagnancy, *s.* Stagnation *f.*

stagnant, *a.* Stagnant; en stagnation.

stagnate, *v.i.* Être stagnant.

stagnation, *s.* Stagnation *f.*

staid, *a.* Posé, sérieux, sage. **-ly,** *adv.* Posément, sérieusement, sagement.

staidness, *s.* Caractère posé, sérieux.

stain¹, *s.* **1.** (*a*) Tache *f*, souillure *f.* (*b*) **To cast a stain on s.o.'s honour,** ternir l'honneur de qn. **2.** Couleur *f*, colorant *m.*

stain², *v.tr.* **1.** (*a*) Tacher; souiller (*with,* de). (*b*) Tacher, ternir. **2.** Teindre, teinter.

stainless, *a.* **1.** Sans tache; immaculé, pur. **2. Stainless steel,** acier inoxydable.

stair, *s.* **1.** Marche *f*, degré *m* (d'un escalier). **2.** (*Usu. pl.*) Escalier.

staircase, *s.* (i) Cage *f* d'escalier; (ii) escalier *m.* **Spiral staircase,** escalier tournant; escalier en vis.

stake¹, *s.* **1.** Pieu *m*, poteau *m.* *Hort:* Tuteur *m.* **2.** (Poteau du) bûcher. **To perish at the stake,** mourir sur le bûcher. **3.** *Gaming:* Mise *f*, enjeu *m.* *F:* **The interests are at stake,** les intérêts *m* en jeu. **To have a stake in sth.,** avoir des intérêts dans une affaire.

stake², *v.tr.* **1.** To stake (out), jalonner. **2.** Ramer (des haricots). **3.** Mettre en jeu; jouer (une somme). **To stake one's all,** jouer son va-tout.

stalactite, *s.* Stalactite *f.*

stalagmite, *s.* Stalagmite *f.*

stale, *a.* **1.** (*a*) (Pain) rassis. (*b*) (Œuf) qui n'est pas frais. (*c*) (Air) vicié. **2.** Vieux, *f.* vieille; passé.

stalemate¹, *s.* *Chess:* Pat *m.*

stalemate², *v.tr.* Faire pat (son adversaire).

staleness, *s.* **1.** État rassis (du pain). **2.** Manque *m* de fraîcheur (d'une nouvelle).

stalk¹, *s.* *Ven:* Chasse *f* d'affût en affût.

stalk². **1.** *v.i.* **To stalk (along),** marcher d'un pas majestueux. **2.** *v.tr.* (*a*) Traquer d'affût en affût. (*b*) *F:* **To stalk s.o.,** filer qn. **stalking,** *s.* *Ven:* = STALK¹. **stalking-horse,** *s.* *F:* Prétexte *m*, masque *m.*

stalk³, *s.* **1.** Tige *f* (de plante); queue *f* (de fruit); trognon *m* (de chou). **2.** Pied *m* (de verre à vin).

stalker, *s.* *Ven:* Chasseur *m* à l'affût.

stall¹, *s.* **1.** (*a*) Stalle *f* (d'écurie). (*b*) Étable *f.* **2.** Étalage *m*; échoppe *f.* **3.** (*a*) *Ecc:* Stalle; chaise *f* de chœur. (*b*) *Th:* (Orchestra) stalls, fauteuils *m* d'orchestre.

stall². **I.** *v.tr. Aut:* Caler (le moteur). **2.** *v.i.* (*a*) *Aut:* (Se) caler. (*b*) *Av:* Se mettre en perte de vitesse. **stalling,** *s.* (*a*) Calage *m.* (*b*) *Av:* Perte *f* de vitesse.

stallion, *s.* Étalon *m.*

stalwart, *a.* **I.** Robuste. **2.** Vaillant.

stamen, *s. Bot:* Étamine *f.*

stamina, *s.* Vigueur *f*, résistance *f.*

stammer¹, *s.* (*a*) Bégaiement *m.* (*b*) Balbutiement *m.*

stammer². **I.** *v.i.* (*a*) Bégayer. (*b*) Balbutier. **2.** *v.tr.* To stammer (out) sth., bégayer, balbutier, qch.

stammerer, *s.* Bègue *mf.*

stamp¹, *s.* **I.** Battement *m* de pied. With a stamp (of the foot), en frappant du pied. **2.** (*a*) Timbre *m*, empreinte *f.* Rubber stamp, tampon, *m.* (*b*) Découpoir *m.* (*c*) Étampe *f*, poinçon *m.* **3.** (*a*) Timbre; marque *f.* (*b*) Men of his s., les hommes de sa trempe. **4.** Adhesive stamp, timbre mobile. Embossed stamp, timbre à empreinte. Postage stamp, timbre(-poste) *m*, *pl.* timbres(-poste). **5.** *Min:* Pilon *m*; broyeuse *f.* **stamp-album,** *s.* Album *m* de timbresposte. **stamp-collector,** *s.* Collectionneur, -euse, de timbres-poste. **stamp-duty,** *s.* Impôt *m* du timbre. **stamp-machine,** *s.* Distributeur *m* automatique de timbresposte.

stamp², *v.tr.* **I.** (*a*) To stamp one's foot, frapper du pied. (*b*) *Abs.* To stamp (about), piétiner. To stamp on sth., fouler qch. aux pieds. **2.** Frapper, imprimer, une marque sur; frapper, estamper. **3.** Timbrer, affranchir (une lettre); estampiller (un document).

stamped, *a.* Stamped paper, papier timbré.

stamping, *s.* **I.** Piétinement *m.* **2.** Timbrage *m* (de documents).

stampede¹, *s.* **I.** Fuite précipitée; panique *f.* **2.** Ruée *f.*

stampede². **I.** *v.i.* (*a*) Fuir à la débandade. (*b*) Se ruer (*for, towards,* vers, sur). **2.** *v.tr.* Jeter la panique parmi.

stance, *s.* Position *f* des pieds; posture *f.*

stanch, *v.tr.* **I.** Étancher (le sang). **2.** Étancher le sang (d'une blessure).

stanchion, *s.* Étançon *m*, étai *m.*

stand¹, *s.* **I.** (*a*) To take a firm stand, se camper solidement sur ses jambes. (*b*) Arrêt *m*, halte *f.* To be brought to a stand, être forcé de s'arrêter. **2.** Résistance *f.* To make a stand against s.o., résister à qn. **3.** Situation *f*, position *f.* To take one's stand, (i) se placer (près de la porte); (ii) se fonder (sur un principe). **4.** Station *f*, stationnement *m* (de voitures). **5.** Support *m*, pied *m.* **6.** Étalage *m*, étal *m.* **7.** (*a*) *Sp:* Tribune *f*; stand *m.* (*b*) Estrade *f.*

stand², *v.* **I.** *v.i.* **I.** (*a*) Être debout; se

tenir debout. I could hardly stand, je pouvais à peine me tenir. *F:* To stand on one's own legs, ne dépendre que de soi. (*b*) To stand six feet high, avoir six pieds de haut. (*c*) Se lever. **2.** (*a*) Se trouver; être. The tears stood in his eyes, il avait les larmes aux yeux. To let sth. stand in the sun, laisser qch. exposé au soleil. To buy sth. as it stands, acheter qch. tel quel. Nothing stands between you and success, rien ne s'oppose à votre succès. (*b*) A man stood in the doorway, un homme se tenait à la porte. To stand talking, rester à causer. **3.** S'arrêter; faire halte. Stand! halte! halte là! **4.** Rester, durer. To stand fast, tenir (pied); tenir bon. **5.** The contract stands, le contrat tient. **6.** (*a*) To stand convicted, être déclaré coupable. To stand in need of, avoir besoin de. To stand to lose nothing, n'avoir rien à perdre. (*b*) To stand as security for a debt, assurer une créance. To stand as candidate, se porter candidat. (*c*) He stands first on the list, il vient en tête de la liste. The thermometer stood at 90°, le thermomètre marquait 90°. (*d*) The amount standing to your credit, votre solde créditeur. How do we stand? où en sont nos comptes? As matters stand, au point où en sont les choses. I don't know where I stand, j'ignore quelle est ma position. To stand well with s.o., être estimé de qn. **7.** I'll s. by the window, je me mettrai à la fenêtre. **8.** To allow a liquid to stand, laisser reposer un liquide. To let the tea stand, laisser infuser le thé. **II.** stand, *v.tr.* **I.** Mettre, poser. **2.** To stand one's ground, tenir bon. **3.** Supporter, subir. To s. a shock, soutenir un choc. We had to stand the loss, la perte a porté sur nous. *F:* I can't stand him, je ne peux pas le sentir. I can't s. it any longer, je n'y tiens plus. **4.** *F:* Payer, offrir. To stand s.o. a drink, payer à boire à qn.

stand aside, *v.i.* (*a*) Se tenir à l'écart. (*b*) S'écarter, se ranger. (*c*) Se désister (en faveur de qn). **stand back,** *v.i.* (i) Se tenir en arrière; (ii) reculer. House standing back from the road, maison en retrait (de la route). **stand by,** *v.i.* **I.** (*a*) Se tenir prêt. (*b*) Se tenir là (sans intervenir). **2.** (*a*) Se tenir près de. (*b*) Soutenir, défendre. (*c*) Rester fidèle à. I stand by what I said, j'en tiens pour ce que j'ai dit. **stand-by,** *s.* Ressource *f.* **stand for,** *v.ind.tr.* **I.** Défendre (une cause). **2.** Tenir lieu de. **3.** Signifier. **stand in,** *v.i.* **I.** To stand in with others, s'associer à d'autres. **2.** *Nau:* To stand in to land, rallier la terre. **stand off,** *v.i.* (*a*) Se tenir éloigné. (*b*) S'éloigner. *Nau:* Courir au large. (*c*) *Ind:* Chômer. **stand out,** *v.i.* **I.** Résister (*against,* à); tenir bon (*against,* contre). **2.** To stand out for sth., s'obstiner à demander qch. **3.** Faire saillie. To stand out against sth., faire contraste avec qch. **4.** *Nau:* To stand out to sea, gagner le large. **stand over,** *v.i.*

Rester en suspens. **stand to,** *v.i.* To stand to attention, se mettre au garde à vous. To stand to one's arms, se tenir sous les armes. **stand up,** *v.i.* **I.** (*a*) Se lever; se mettre debout. (*b*) Se dresser, se tenir droit. **2.** (*a*) To stand up against, résister à. (*b*) To stand up for s.o., défendre qn. (*c*) To stand up to s.o., affronter bravement qn. **standing**[1], *a.* **I.** (*a*) (Qui se tient) debout. (*b*) Standing crops, récoltes sur pied. **2.** Standing water, eau stagnante, dormante. **3.** Standing rule, règle fixe. Standing joke, plaisanterie courante. **standing**[2], *s.* **I.** Stationnement *m.* **2.** Durée *f.* Friend of long standing, ami de longue main. Officer of six months' standing, officier qui a six mois de service. **3.** Rang *m,* position *f.* Standing of a firm, importance *f* d'une maison. **standing room,** *s.* Place(s) *f(pl)* debout.

standard, *s.* **I.** Bannière *f.* Mil: Étendard *m. Nau:* Pavillon *m.* **2.** Étalon *m* (de poids). **3.** Modèle *m,* type *m.* Standard of living, niveau *m* de vie. Judged by that standard, à cette mesure. **4.** Degré *m*; qualité *f.* **5.** Of standard size, de taille courante. Car of standard model, voiture de série. The standard authors, les auteurs classiques. **stand-offish,** *a. F:* Peu accessible; distant. **stand-offishness,** *s. F:* Raideur *f,* réserve *f.* **standpoint,** *s.* Point *m* de vue. **standstill,** *s.* Arrêt *m,* immobilisation *f.* To come to a standstill, s'arrêter. *Trade is at a s.,* le commerce ne va plus. **stanza,** *s.* Stance *f,* strophe *f.* **staple**[1], *s.* Crampon *m* (à deux pointes). Wire staple, clou *m* à deux pointes. **staple**[2], *s.* (*a*) Produit principal (d'un pays). Staple industry, industrie principale. (*b*) Matière première, matière brute. **star**[1], *s.* **I.** Étoile *f*; astre *m. F:* To be born under a lucky star, naître sous une bonne étoile. *I thank my stars,* je bénis mon étoile (*that,* de ce que). To see stars, voir trente-six chandelles. **2.** (*a*) Star of an order, plaque *f* d'un ordre; décoration *f.* (*b*) *Mil:* Étoile. **3.** The stars and stripes, la bannière étoilée. **4.** Étoile, vedette *f. Th:* Star part, rôle de vedette. **star-fish,** *s. Echin:* Astérie *f*; étoile *f* de mer. **star-gazing,** *a.* Rêvasserie(s) *f(pl).* **star-lit,** *a. Star-lit night,* nuit étoilée. **star**[2], *v.* **I.** *v.tr.* Étoiler; (par)semer d'étoiles. **2.** *v.i. Th:* Être en vedette. **starboard,** *s. Nau:* Tribord *m.* **starch**[1], *s.* **I.** (*a*) Amidon *m.* (*b*) Starch (-paste), colle *f* d'amidon. **2.** *F:* To take the starch out of s.o., démonter qn. **starch**[2], *v.tr.* Empeser, amidonner. **starchy,** *a.* Empesé; guindé. **stare**[1], *s.* Regard fixe. Stony s., regard dur. *Vacant s.,* regard vague. **stare**[2]. **I.** *v.i.* (*a*) Regarder fixement. To stare in s.o.'s face, dévisager qn. (*b*) Écarquiller les yeux; ouvrir de grands yeux.

2. *v.ind.tr.* To stare at s.o., (i) regarder qn fixement; (ii) dévisager qn. **3.** *v.tr.* To stare s.o. in the face, dévisager qn. *F:* It's staring you in the face, ça vous crève les yeux. To stare s.o. out (of countenance), faire perdre contenance à qn. **staring,** *a.* **I.** *S.* eyes, yeux grands ouverts. **2.** Stark staring mad, complètement fou.

stark. I. *a. Lit:* (*a*) Raide, rigide. (*b*) *Poet:* Fort, vigoureux. **2.** *adv.* Stark naked, tout nu; nu comme un ver.

starlight, *s.* **I.** Lumière *f* des étoiles; lumière stellaire. In the starlight, à la lueur des étoiles. **2.** *Attrib.* A starlight night, une nuit étoilée.

starling, *s. Orn:* Étourneau *m.*

starry, *a.* (Ciel) étoilé, (par)semé d'étoiles.

start[1], *s.* **I.** (*a*) Tressaillement *m.* To wake with a start, se réveiller en sursaut. He gave a start, il sursauta. To give s.o. a start, faire tressaillir qn. (*b*) Saut *m*; mouvement *m* brusque. **2.** (*a*) Commencement *m,* début *m.* To make an early start, commencer de bonne heure. At the start, au début. From start to finish, du commencement à la fin. *F:* To give s.o. a start, lancer qn. To make a good start, bien commencer. To make a fresh start (in life), recommencer (sa vie). (*b*) Départ *m. Av:* Envol *m.* False start, faux départ. (*c*) To get the start of s.o., prendre les devants; devancer qn.

start[2]. **I.** *v.i.* **I.** (*a*) Tressaillir, tressauter, sursauter. (*b*) *Tears started from his eyes,* les larmes jaillirent de ses yeux. His eyes were starting out of his head, les yeux lui sortaient de la tête. **2.** (*Of rivets*) Se détacher; sauter. **3.** (*a*) Commencer; débuter. To start in life, débuter dans la vie. To start in business, se lancer dans les affaires. *To s. with,* en premier lieu. To start by doing sth., commencer par faire qch. (*b*) To start (off), partir; se mettre en route. (*c*) To start (off), (*of car*) démarrer; (*of train*) s'ébranler. **II. start,** *v.tr.* **I.** Commencer. To start (on) a fresh loaf, entamer un nouveau pain. *To s. life afresh,* recommencer sa vie. **2.** (*a*) To start (off) a horse at a gallop, faire partir un cheval au galop. (*b*) *Rac:* Donner le signal du départ à. (*c*) *Ven:* Lancer. **3.** (*a*) Lancer (une entreprise). (*b*) To start a fire, provoquer un incendie. **4.** Mettre en marche. **5.** To start s.o. on a career, lancer qn dans une carrière. Once you start him talking, quand on le met à causer. **starting,** *s.* **I.** Tressaillement *m*; sursaut *m,* soubresaut *m.* **2.** (*a*) Commencement *m,* début *m.* (*b*) Départ *m.* **3.** (*a*) Mise *f* en train. (*b*) Starting (up), mise en mouvement, mise en marche. **starting-handle,** *s.* Manivelle *f* de mise en marche. **starting-point,** *s.* Point *m* de départ; barrière *f.* **starting-post,** *s. Rac:* Poteau *m* de départ.

startle, *v.tr.* Effrayer, alarmer; faire tressaillir. To startle s.o. out of his sleep, éveiller qn en sursaut. **startling,** *a.* Effrayant, saisissant.

starvation, *s.* Privation *f* de nourriture; affamement *m.* To die of starvation, mourir de faim. Starvation wages, salaire de famine.

starve. I. *v.i.* (*a*) To starve to death, mourir de faim. (*b*) Manquer de nourriture. *F:* I am starving, je meurs de faim. **2.** *v.tr.* (*a*) Faire mourir de faim. (*b*) Priver de nourriture. **starved,** *a.* Affamé. **starving,** *a.* Mourant de faim.

state¹, *s.* **1.** (*a*) État *m,* condition *f.* Here's a pretty state of things, nous voilà bien! (*b*) *S.* of health, état de santé. State of mind, disposition *f* d'esprit. *F:* To be in a great state, être dans tous ses états. **2.** (*a*) Rang *m,* dignité *f.* (*b*) Pompe *f,* parade *f,* apparat *m.* To live in state, mener grand train. To lie in state, être exposé (sur un lit de parade). Lying in state, exposition *f* (d'un corps). *He was in his robes of state,* il était en costume d'apparat. (*c*) State coach, voiture d'apparat. State ball, grand bal officiel. State apartments, salons d'apparat. **3.** (*a*) The State, l'État. Secretary of State, secrétaire d'État. (*b*) État, nation *f.* The United States of America, les États-Unis d'Amérique. **stateroom,** *s.* **1.** Chambre *f* d'apparat. **2.** *Nau:* Cabine *f* (de luxe).

state², *v.tr.* **1.** (*a*) Énoncer, déclarer. As stated above, ainsi qu'il est dit plus haut. *I have seen it stated that,* j'ai lu quelque part que. (*b*) Exposer (une réclamation). *Jur:* To state the case, faire l'exposé des faits. **2.** Régler, arrêter, fixer. **stated,** *a.* At s. intervals, à des époques fixées.

stateliness, *s.* Majesté *f;* dignité *f.*

stately, *a.* **1.** Majestueux; imposant. **2.** Plein de dignité; noble, élevé.

statement, *s.* **1.** Exposition *f,* exposé *m;* rapport *m,* compte rendu. To make a statement, émettre une déclaration. **2.** *Com:* Statement of account, état *m* de compte.

statesman, *s.* Homme *m* d'État.

statesmanlike, *a.* D'homme d'État.

statesmanship, *s.* Science *f* du gouvernement.

statics, *s.pl.* *Mec:* La statique.

station¹, *s.* **1.** (*a*) Position *f,* place *f,* poste *m.* (*b*) Station *f,* poste. Coaling station, dépôt *m* de charbon. **2.** Position, condition *f;* rang *m.* Station in life, situation sociale. To marry below one's station, se mésallier. **3.** *Rail:* Gare *f.*

station², *v.tr.* (*a*) Placer, mettre. (*b*) To s. troops, poster des troupes.

stationary, *a.* Stationnaire; immobile.

stationer, *s.* Papetier, -ière. *Stationer's shop,* papeterie *f.*

stationery, *s.* Papeterie *f.* Office stationery, fournitures *fpl* de bureau.

stationmaster, *s.* Chef *m* de gare.

statistical, *a.* Statistique.

statistician, *s.* Statisticien, -ienne.

statistics, *s.pl.* La statistique.

statuary, *s.* Statues *fpl.*

statue, *s.* Statue *f.*

stature, *s.* Stature *f;* taille *f.*

status, *s.* (*a*) *Adm:* Civil status, état civil. (*b*) Condition *f,* position *f,* rang *m.* Social status, rang social.

statute, *s.* **1.** Acte *m* du Parlement; loi *f.* **2.** *pl.* Statuts *m,* règlements *m.* **statute-book,** *s.* Code *m* (des lois).

statutory, *a.* **1.** Établi, imposé, par la loi; réglementaire. **2.** Statutaire; conforme aux statuts.

staunch¹, *a.* Sûr, dévoué; ferme. **-ly,** *adv.* Avec fermeté; avec dévouement.

staunch², *v.tr.* = STANCH.

staunchness, *s.* Fermeté *f;* dévouement *m.*

stave¹, *s.* **1.** (*a*) *Coop:* Barrel staves, douves *f* pour tonneaux. (*b*) Bâton *m.* **2.** *Pros:* Stance *f,* strophe *f.*

stave², *v.tr.* = STAVE IN. **stave in,** *v.tr.* Défoncer, enfoncer. **stave off,** *v.tr.* Détourner, écarter; conjurer (un désastre). To stave off hunger, tromper la faim.

stay¹, *s.* **1.** Séjour *m.* **2.** *Jur:* Stay of proceedings, suspension *f* d'instance.

stay². I. *v.i.* **1.** Stay! attendez! **2.** (*a*) Rester; demeurer sur les lieux. To stay at home, rester à la maison. To stay in bed, garder le lit. To stay to dinner, rester à dîner. (*b*) To come to stay, venir pour rester définitivement. **3.** *Rac:* Soutenir l'allure. **II.** *v.tr.* **1.** Arrêter. To stay s.o.'s hand, retenir le bras de qn. **stay away,** *v.i.* Ne pas venir; s'absenter. **stay up,** *v.i.* Ne pas se coucher; veiller. **staying,** *s.* **1.** Séjour *m.* **2.** Staying power, résistance *f;* endurance *f.* **stay-athome,** *a.* & *s.* Casanier, -ière.

stay³, *s.* **1.** (*a*) Support *m,* soutien *m.* (*b*) *Const:* Support, appui *m,* étai *m.* **2.** *pl.* *Cost:* Stays, corset *m.*

stay⁴, *v.tr.* Étayer, arc-bouter.

stay⁵, *s.* Hauban *m.*

stead, *s.* **1.** To stand s.o. in good stead, être d'un grand secours à qn. **2.** In s.o.'s stead, à la place de qn.

steadfast, *a.* Ferme; constant. **-ly,** *adv.* Fermement; avec constance.

steadfastness, *s.* Fermeté *f;* constance *f.* Steadfastness of purpose, ténacité *f* de caractère.

steadiness, *s.* **1.** Fermeté *f.* **2.** Assiduité *f,* persévérance *f.* **3.** Stabilité *f.* **4.** Conduite rangée; sagesse *f.*

steady¹. I. *a.* (*a*) Ferme, solide; fixe, rigide. To keep steady, ne pas bouger; rester en place. To have a steady hand, avoir la main sûre. With a s. hand, d'une main assurée. (*b*) Continu, soutenu; persistant; régulier. *S.* progress, progrès ininterrompus, soutenus. *S.* pace, allure réglée. Steady barometer, baromètre stationnaire. *Com:* Steady demand, demande suivie. (*c*) Steady worker, travailleur assidu, régulier. (*d*) Rangé, posé;

sérieux. **2.** *adv.* **Steady!** ne bougez pas!
F: **Steady (on)!** doucement! **-ily,** *adv.*
1. Fermement. *To walk s.,* marcher d'un
pas ferme. **2.** (*a*) Régulièrement; sans arrêt.
(*b*) Uniment; sans à-coups. **3.** Assidûment.
4. D'une manière rangée; avec sagesse.
steady². **1.** *v.tr.* (*a*) Raffermir, affermir.
To steady oneself against sth., s'étayer contre
qch. *To s. the nerves,* raffermir les nerfs.
(*b*) Assagir. **2.** *v.i.* Se raffermir.
steak, *s. Cu:* (*a*) Tranche *f.* (*b*) Bifteck *m.*
Fillet steak, tournedos *m.*
steal, *v.* **1.** *v.tr.* (*a*) Voler, dérober, soustraire
(*sth. from s.o.,* qch. à qn). (*b*) **To steal a
glance at s.o.,** regarder qn à la dérobée.
(*c*) **To steal a march on s.o.,** devancer qn.
2. *v.i.* **To steal away,** s'en aller à la dérobée,
furtivement. *He stole away,* il s'esquiva.
He stole into the room, il se faufila, se glissa,
dans la chambre. **To steal along,** marcher à
pas de loup. **stealing,** *s.* Vol *m.*
stealth, *s.* **By stealth,** furtivement.
stealthiness, *s.* Caractère furtif.
stealthy, *a.* Furtif. *S. glance,* regard dérobé.
-ily, *adv.* A la dérobée; furtivement.
steam¹, *s.* (*a*) Vapeur *f*; buée *f.* **Room full
of s.,** salle remplie de buée. (*b*) **To get up
steam,** mettre (la chaudière) sous pression.
F: **To let off steam,** dépenser son superflu
d'énergie. **At full steam,** à toute vapeur.
Nau: **Full steam ahead!** en avant à toute
vapeur! **steam-engine,** *s.* Machine *f* à
vapeur. **steam-roller,** *s. Civ.E:* Rouleau
m compresseur.
steam². **1.** *v.tr.* (*a*) *Cu:* Cuire à la vapeur, à
l'étuvée. (*b*) **To steam open an envelope,**
décacheter une lettre à la vapeur. **2.** *v.i.* (*a*)
Fumer. (*b*) Marcher (à la vapeur). **The
train steamed off,** le train partit.
steamboat, *s.* Bateau *m,* navire *m,* à vapeur;
vapeur *m.*
steamer, *s.* **1.** ⚊ STEAMSHIP. **2.** *Cu:* Marmite *f* à vapeur.
steamship, *s.* Navire *m* à vapeur; vapeur *m.*
steed, *s. Lit:* Coursier *m.*
steel¹, *s.* **1.** *Metall:* Acier *m.* **Steel pen,**
plume métallique. **2.** *Lit:* Fer *m,* épée *f*;
lame *f. F:* **Cold steel,** l'arme blanche.
3. (*a*) (*For sharpening knives*) Fusil *m*; affiloir
m. (*b*) **Flint and steel,** briquet *m* à silex. **steel-
engraving,** *s.* Estampe *f* sur acier. **steel-
plate,** *s.* Tôle *f* d'acier. **steel-plated,**
a. Cuirassé.
steel², *v.tr. F:* **To steel oneself to do sth.,**
s'armer de courage pour faire qch. *Selfishness
had steeled his heart,* l'égoïsme lui avait bronzé
le cœur.
steep¹, *a.* (*a*) Escarpé; à pic; raide. (*b*) *F:*
That's a bit steep! c'est un peu fort! **Steep
price,** prix exorbitant. **-ly,** *adv.* En pente
rapide; à pic.
steep², *v.tr.* (*a*) *Ind:* Baigner, tremper.
(*b*) Saturer, imbiber (*sth. in sth.,* qch. de qch.).
Steeped in prejudice, imbibé de préjugés.

steeping, *s. Ind:* Trempage *m,* macération *f.*
steeple, *s.* (*a*) Clocher *m.* (*b*) Flèche *f* (de
clocher). **steeple-jack,** *s.* Réparateur *m*
de cheminées d'usines.
steeplechase, *s.* Steeple-chase *m.*
steepness, *s.* Raideur *f,* escarpement *m.*
steer¹, *v.tr.* Gouverner; diriger. *Abs.* To
steer, gouverner; *Row:* barrer. **To steer
clear of sth.,** éviter qch. **steering,** *s.*
1. Direction *f,* conduite *f.* **2.** *Nau:* Manœuvre *f* de la barre. **steering-gear,** *s.*
Appareil *m* à gouverner. **steering-wheel,**
s. (*a*) *Nau:* Roue *f* du gouvernail. (*b*) *Aut:*
Volant *m* (de direction).
steer², *s.* **1.** Jeune bœuf *m.* **2.** Bœuf *m.*
steerage, *s. Nau:* Entrepont *m.* **To travel
steerage,** faire la traversée en troisième classe.
steersman, *s. Nau:* Timonier *m.*
stellar, *a.* Stellaire.
stem¹ *s.* **1.** (*a*) *Bot:* Tige *f* (de plante);
queue *f* (de fruit); tronc *m,* souche *f*
(d'arbre). (*b*) Régime *m* (de bananes).
2. Pied *m,* patte *f* (de verre à boire); tuyau
m (de pipe de fumeur). **3.** (*a*) Souche (de
famille). (*b*) *Ling:* Thème *m,* radical *m.*
4. *N.Arch:* Étrave *f,* avant *m.* **From stem
to stern,** de l'avant à l'arrière.
stem², *v.tr.* **1.** Contenir, arrêter. **2.** Aller
contre, lutter contre (la marée); refouler,
remonter (le courant); (*of ship*) étaler (le
courant); refouler, résister à (une attaque).
F: **To stem the tide,** endiguer le flot.
stench, *s.* Odeur infecte; puanteur *f.*
stencil¹, *s.* Patron (ajouré). **Stencil-plate,**
pochoir *m.*
stencil², *v.tr.* Peindre, marquer, au patron.
Ind: Marquer (une caisse).
stenographer, *s.* Sténographe *mf.*
stenography, *s.* Sténographie *f.*
stentorian, *a.* (Voix) de Stentor.
step¹, *s.* **1.** Pas *m.* **To take a step,** faire un
pas. **To bend one's steps towards,** se diriger
vers. **Step by step,** pas à pas; petit à petit.
F: **To tread in the steps of s.o.,** marcher
sur les traces de qn. **2.** (*a*) Pas, cadence *f.*
Mus: **Quick step,** pas accéléré. **To keep
step,** marcher au pas. (*b*) **Waltz step,** pas de
valse. **3.** Démarche *f.* **To take the necessary
steps,** faire les démarches nécessaires. **To
take steps to do sth.,** se préparer à faire qch.
4. Marche *f,* degré *m,* pas (d'un escalier);
marchepied *m* (d'un véhicule). **Flight of
steps,** (i) escalier; (ii) perron *m.* **5.** (**Pair,
set, of**) **steps,** escabeau *m*; échelle *f* double.
Folding steps, échelle brisée. **step-dance,**
s. Danse *f* de caractère. **step-ladder,** *s.*
Escabeau *m*; échelle *f* double.
step², *v.i.* Faire un pas ou des pas; marcher
pas à pas. **Step this way,** venez par ici.
step aside, *v.i.* **1.** S'écarter, se ranger.
2. Se détourner de son chemin. **step in,**
v.i. **1.** Entrer; (*into carriage*) monter.
2. *F:* Intervenir; s'interposer. **step on,**

v.i. **1.** Mettre le pied sur, marcher sur. **2.** *Nau:* To step on board, monter à bord. **step out,** *v.i.* **1.** Sortir; descendre (de voiture). **2.** (a) Allonger le pas. (b) Marcher avec entrain. **step over,** *v.i.* **1.** Franchir; enjamber. **2.** To step over to s.o.'s house, faire un saut jusque chez qn. **stepping-stones,** *s.pl.* Pierres *f* de gué.

stepbrother, *s.* Demi-frère *m, pl.* demi-frères.

stepchild, *s.* Enfant *mf* d'un autre lit.

stepdaughter, *s.* Belle-fille *f, pl.* belles-filles.

stepfather, *s.* Beau-père *m, pl.* beaux-pères.

Stephen. *Pr.n.* Étienne *m.*

stepmother, *s.* Belle-mère *f, pl.* belles-mères.

steppe, *s.* *Ph.Geog:* Steppe *m or f.*

stepsister, *s.* Demi-sœur *f, pl.* demi-sœurs.

stepson, *s.* Beau-fils *m, pl.* beaux-fils.

stereoscope, *s.* *Opt:* Stéréoscope *m.*

stereoscopic, *a.* Stéréoscopique.

stereotype, *v.tr.* *Typ:* Stéréotyper, clicher.

stereotyped, *a.* *Typ:* Stéréotypé. *F:* Stereotyped phrase, cliché *m.*

sterile, *a.* Stérile.

sterility, *s.* Stérilité *f.*

sterilization, *s.* Stérilisation *f.*

sterilize, *v.tr.* Stériliser.

sterling, *a.* **1.** De bon aloi, d'aloi. **2.** Pound sterling, livre *f* sterling. **3.** *F:* De bon aloi, solide. Sterling qualities, qualités solides.

stern¹, *a.* Sévère, rigide, dur. The sterner sex, le sexe fort. **-ly,** *adv.* Sévèrement, durement.

stern², *s.* **1.** *Nau:* Arrière *m.* **2.** *F:* Derrière *m.* **stern-chase,** *s.* *Navy:* Chasse *f* dans les eaux du navire chassé.

sternmost, *a.* Le plus à l'arrière.

sternness, *s.* Sévérité *f*; austérité *f.*

stet, *Lt.imp.* *Typ:* Bon; à maintenir.

stethoscope, *s.* *Med:* Stéthoscope *m.*

stevedore, *s.* *Nau:* **1.** Arrimeur *m*; déchargeur *m.* **2.** Entrepreneur *m* de chargement et de déchargement.

stew¹, *s.* *Cu:* Ragoût *m*; civet *m.* (b) *F:* To be in a stew, être dans tous ses états.

stew², **1.** *v.tr.* *Cu:* Faire cuire en ragoût. To stew fruit, faire cuire des fruits en compote. **2.** *v.i.* *Cu:* Cuire à la casserole; mijoter. **stewed,** *a.* Stewed mutton, ragoût *m* de mouton. Stewed fruit, compote *f* de fruits. *S. prunes,* pruneaux au jus.

steward, *s.* **1.** Économe *m,* régisseur *m,* intendant *m.* **2.** *Nau:* (a) Commis *m* aux vivres. (b) Garçon *m* (de cabine); steward *m.* Chief steward, maître *m* d'hôtel. **3.** Commissaire *m* (d'un bal). **4.** *Ind:* Shop steward, délégué *m* d'atelier.

stewardess, *s.* *Nau:* Femme *f* de chambre (de bord); stewardess.

stick¹, *s.* **1.** (a) Bâton *m.* To get the stick, recevoir des coups de bâton. (b) Walking stick, canne *f.* (c) Manche *m* (à balai). (d) *Sp:* Crosse *f* (de hockey). (e) Morceau

m de bois. *To gather sticks,* ramasser du bois sec. Without a stick of furniture, sans un meuble. **2.** *F:* (a) Queer stick, drôle de type. (b) Personne *f* sans entrain, sans talent. **3.** Bâton (de cire à cacheter); barre *f* (de chocolat). **4.** Stick of celery, branche *f* de céleri. Stick of rhubarb, tige *f* de rhubarbe.

stick², *v.* I. *v.tr.* **1.** (a) Piquer, enfoncer (into, dans). To stick a dagger into s.o., percer qn d'un poignard. To stick a pin through sth., passer une épingle à travers qch. (b) To stick a pig, égorger, saigner, un porc. **2.** *F:* Mettre. To stick one's hat on one's head, planter son chapeau sur sa tête. Stick it in your pocket, fourrez-le dans votre poche. **3.** Coller. To stick photographs in an album, fixer, coller, des photographies dans un album. **4.** *F:* Supporter, souffrir. To stick it, tenir le coup; tenir. I can't stick him, je ne peux pas le sentir. II. **stick,** *v.i.* **1.** Se piquer, s'enfoncer, se ficher, se planter. **2.** (a) (Se) coller, adhérer (to, à). The vegetables have stuck to the pan, les légumes ont attaché. The name stuck to him, ce nom lui (en) est resté. It sticks like pitch, cela colle comme poix. To stick to a friend, ne pas abandonner un ami. To stick like glue (to s.o.), se cramponner (à qn). To stick to one's post, rester à son poste. Stick to it! persévérez! *F:* To stick to one's guns, ne pas en démordre. To stick to (the) facts, s'en tenir aux faits. (b) To stick to sth., garder qch. pour soi. (c) *He sticks to his room,* il ne sort pas de sa chambre. **3.** (a) To stick, to be stuck, être pris, engagé; (in mud) s'embourber, être embourbé. (b) It sticks in my throat, je ne peux pas avaler ça. **stick at,** *v.i.* **1.** To stick at a difficulty, s'arrêter devant une difficulté. To stick at nothing, ne reculer devant rien. **2.** S'acharner à. **stick down,** *v.tr.* To stick down an envelope, fermer, coller, une enveloppe. **stick out.** **1.** *v.tr.* (a) Faire dépasser; sortir. To stick out one's tongue, tirer la langue. (b) *F:* To stick it out, tenir jusqu'au bout. **2.** *v.i.* (a) Faire saillie; ressortir. To stick out beyond sth., dépasser qch. (b) *F:* To stick out for sth., s'obstiner à demander qch. **stick up.** **1.** *v.tr.* To stick up a notice, afficher un avis. **2.** *v.i.* (a) Se dresser; se tenir debout. (b) *F:* To stick up for s.o., prendre la défense de qn. (c) To stick up to s.o., tenir tête à qn. **stuck-up,** *a.* *F:* Prétentieux. **sticking-plaster,** *s.* *Pharm:* Taffetas gommé. **stick-in-the-mud,** *s.* *F:* Routinier, -ière.

sticker, *s.* *F:* Rude travailleur, -euse.

stickiness, *s.* Viscosité *f.*

stickleback, *s.* *Ich:* Épinoche *f.*

stickler, *s.* Rigoriste *mf (for sth.,* à l'égard de qch.). To be a stickler for etiquette, être à cheval sur l'étiquette.

sticky, *a.* **1.** Collant, gluant, visqueux, adhésif. To make one's hands s., s'engluer les

mains. *F:* **To have sticky fingers,** avoir de la poix aux mains. **2.** *P:* Peu accommodant.
stiff, *a.* **1.** (*a*) Raide, rigide, inflexible. **Stiff shirt-front,** plastron empesé. (*b*) **Stiff joint,** articulation ankylosée. *F:* **Stiff as a poker,** raide comme un piquet. (*c*) Raide, guindé. **Stiff bow,** salut contraint. (*d*) Inflexible, obstiné. **2.** (*a*) **The handle is stiff,** le bouton est dur. (*b*) Ferme. (*c*) *Nau:* **Stiff wind,** forte brise. **3.** (*a*) **Stiff climb,** montée rude, pénible. **Stiff examination,** examen difficile. (*b*) *F:* **Stiff price,** prix salé. **-ly,** *adv.* **1.** Raidement; avec raideur. **2.** D'un air guindé. **stiff-necked,** *a.* Obstiné, entêté.
stiffen. I. *v.tr.* (*a*) Raidir, renforcer. (*b*) Age has stiffened his joints, l'âge lui a noué les membres. (*c*) Raidir, rendre obstiné. **II. stiffen,** *v.i.* (Se) raidir; devenir raide.
stiffness, *s.* **1.** (*a*) Raideur *f*, rigidité *f*. (*b*) **Stiffness of manner,** raideur, contrainte *f*. (*c*) Obstination *f*, opiniâtreté *f*. **2.** Fermeté *f*, consistance *f*. **3.** Difficulté *f*.
stifle. 1. *v.tr.* (*a*) Étouffer, suffoquer. (*b*) Étouffer (un son). (*c*) Réprimer (une émotion). **2.** *v.i.* Suffoquer, étouffer. **stifling,** *a.* Étouffant, suffocant. **It is stifling here!** on étouffe ici !
stigma, *s.* Stigmate *m*, tache *f*.
stigmatize, *v.tr.* Stigmatiser, flétrir.
stile, *s.* Échalier *m*.
stiletto, *s.* Stylet *m*.
still¹, *a.* Tranquille. **(a)** Immobile. **To keep still,** ne pas bouger. *His heart stood s.,* son cœur cessa de battre. (*b*) Silencieux. **Still water,** eau tranquille. (*c*) **Still wines,** vins non mousseux. (*d*) *Art:* **Still life,** nature morte.
still², *v.tr.* Tranquilliser, calmer, apaiser. *To s. s.o.'s fears,* calmer les craintes de qn.
still³. 1. *adv.* (*a*) Encore. *I have s. five francs,* il me reste cinq francs. *I love him s.,* je l'aime toujours. (*b*) **Still more,** encore plus. **2.** *conj.* Cependant, pourtant, toutefois.
still⁴, *s.* Alambic *m*, cornue *f*.
stillness, *s.* Tranquillité *f*, calme *m*, silence *m*.
stilt, *s.* Échasse *f*.
stilted, *a.* Guindé, tendu.
stimulant. 1. *a. & s. Med:* Stimulant (*m*); remontant (*m*). **2.** *s.* Surexcitant *m*.
stimulate, *v.tr.* Stimuler; aiguillonner, activer, exciter (*to*, à).
stimulation, *s.* Stimulation *f*.
stimulus, *s.* Stimulant *m*; *F:* aiguillon *m*. **To give a stimulus to trade,** donner de l'impulsion *f* au commerce.
sting¹, *s.* **1.** (*a*) Dard *m*, aiguillon *m*. (*b*) Crochet venimeux (d'un serpent). **2.** (*a*) Piqûre *f*. (*b*) Douleur cuisante.
sting², *v.tr.* Piquer. **That reply stung him,** cette réponse l'a piqué. **stinging,** *a.* Piquant, cuisant.
stinginess, *s.* Mesquinerie *f*, ladrerie *f*.

stingy, *a.* Mesquin, chiche, ladre. **-ily,** *adv.* Chichement, mesquinement.
stink¹, *s.* Puanteur *f*; mauvaise odeur.
stink², *v.* **1.** *v.i.* Puer; sentir mauvais; *F:* empester. **To stink of garlic,** puer l'ail. **2.** *v.tr.* **To stink a room out,** empester une chambre. **stinking,** *a.* Puant, empesté, infect.
stint¹, *s.* Restriction *f*. **Without stint,** sans restriction; à discrétion.
stint², *v.tr.* Réduire à la portion congrue. **To stint oneself,** se refuser le nécessaire. **To stint s.o. of sth.,** priver qn de qch.
stipend, *s.* Traitement *m*, appointements *mpl*.
stipple, *s. Art:* Pointillé *m*.
stipulate. 1. *v.i.* **To stipulate for sth.,** stipuler, énoncer expressément (une condition obligatoire). **2.** *v.tr.* **To stipulate (in writing),** stipuler (par écrit).
stipulation, *s. Jur:* Stipulation *f*. **On the stipulation that,** à condition que.
stipule, *s. Bot:* Stipule *f*.
stir¹, *s.* **1.** Remuement *m*. **To give one's coffee a stir,** remuer son café. **2.** Mouvement *m*. **3.** (*a*) Remue-ménage *m inv.* (*b*) Agitation *f*, émoi *m*. **To make a stir,** faire du bruit; faire sensation.
stir², *v.* **1.** *v.tr.* (*a*) Remuer, mouvoir. **I will not stir a foot,** je ne bougerai pas d'ici. (*b*) Activer; agiter. **To stir one's tea,** remuer son thé. (*c*) Émouvoir, troubler. **2.** *v.i.* Bouger, remuer. *He did not stir out of the house,* il n'est pas sorti de la maison. **There is not a breath of air stirring,** on ne sent pas un souffle d'air. **stir up,** *v.tr.* **1.** Remuer, agiter; ranimer, activer (le feu). **2.** Fomenter (les dissensions); ameuter (le peuple). *To stir up hatred,* attiser les haines. **stirring,** *a.* **1.** Actif, remuant. **Stirring times,** époque mouvementée. **2.** Émouvant.
stirrup, *s.* Étrier *m*. **To put one's feet in the stirrups,** chausser les étriers. **stirrup-cup,** *s.* Coup *m* de l'étrier.
stitch¹, *s.* **1.** (*a*) *Needlw:* Point *m*, piqûre *f*. *Prov:* **A stitch in time saves nine,** un point à temps en épargne cent. *F:* **He has not a dry stitch on him,** il est complètement trempé. (*b*) (*In knitting*) Maille *f*. **To drop a stitch,** sauter, laisser échapper, une maille. **To put stitches in a wound,** suturer une plaie. **2.** *Med:* **Stitch (in the side),** point de côté.
stitch², *v.tr.* **1.** Coudre. **2.** *Surg:* Suturer.
stoat, *s. Z:* Hermine *f* d'été.
stock¹, *s.* **1.** (*a*) *Hort:* Sujet *m*, ente *f*. (*b*) Race *f*, famille *f*, lignée *f*. *Of good Puritan s.,* de bonne lignée puritaine. **2.** Fût *m*, bois *m* (de fusil). **3.** *pl. A:* **To put s.o. in the stocks,** mettre qn aux ceps. **4.** *pl. N.Arch:* Stocks, chantier *m*. *F:* **To have a piece of work on the stocks,** avoir un ouvrage sur le chantier. **5.** (*a*) Provision *f*, approvisionnement *m*. (*b*) *Com:* Marchandises *fpl;* stock *m*. **Surplus stock,** soldes *mpl*. **In stock,** en magasin, en stock, en dépôt. **To take**

stock, faire l'inventaire. *F:* To take stock of s.o., scruter, toiser, qn. **6.** *Fin:* Fonds *mpl,* valeurs *fpl.* Stocks and shares, valeurs mobilières. **7.** *Bot:* Stock(-gilly-flower), giroflée *f.* **8.** *Attrib.* (a) *Com:* Stock size, taille courante. (b) *Th:* Stock play, pièce du répertoire. Stock phrase, phrase toute faite; cliché *m.* **stock-broker,** *s. Fin:* Agent *m* de change. **stock exchange,** *s.* Bourse *f* (des valeurs). **stock-pot,** *s. Cu:* Pot *m* à bouillon; pot-au-feu *m inv.* **stock still,** *a.* To stand stock still, rester complètement immobile. **stock-taking,** *s. Com:* Inventaire *m.*

stock², *v.tr.* **1.** Garnir, stocker (un magasin) (with, de); monter (en); meubler de bétail. **2.** Tenir, garder, en magasin, en dépôt.

stockade, *s.* **1.** Palissade *f,* palanque *f.* **2.** Estacade *f.*

stocking, *s. Cost:* Bas *m. Open-work stockings,* bas à jours. *Ribbed stockings,* bas à côtes. *F:* A well-lined stocking, un bas de laine bien garni.

stocky, *a.* Trapu.

stodge, *v.i. & pr. F:* Se bourrer de nourriture.

stodgy, *a.* (Repas) lourd; (aliment) qui bourre.

stoic, *a. & s.* Stoïcien, -ienne; stoïque *mf.*
stoical, *a.* Stoïque. **-ally,** *adv.* Stoïquement.

stoicism, *s.* Stoïcisme *m.*

stoke, *v.tr.* **1.** Charger (un foyer); entretenir le feu. **2.** *Abs.* To stoke (up), pousser les feux.

stoker, *s. Nau:* Chauffeur *m.*

stole, *s.* **1.** *Ecc:* Étole *f.* **2.** *Cost:* Écharpe *f* (de fourrure).

stolid, *a.* Lourd, lent, impassible. **-ly,** *adv.* Avec flegme.

stolidity, *s.* Flegme *m.*

stomach¹, *s.* **1.** Estomac *m.* **2.** *F:* To crawl on one's s., ramper à plat ventre. **3.** Envie *f,* goût *m* (for, de); cœur *m,* courage *m* (pour faire qch.). **stomach-ache,** *s.* Douleurs *fpl* d'estomac.

stomach², *v.tr. F:* Endurer, supporter, tolérer; *F:* digérer (une insulte).

stone¹, *s.* **1.** Pierre *f.* (a) To leave no stone unturned (to . . .), ne rien négliger (pour . . .). To throw stones at s.o., (i) lancer des pierres à qn; (ii) *F:* jeter des pierres dans le jardin de qn. (b) Not to leave a stone standing, ne pas laisser pierre sur pierre. (c) Meule *f* (de moulin). **2.** Precious stones, pierres précieuses; pierreries *f.* **3.** Pierre (à bâtir). **4.** Noyau *m* (de fruit); pépin *m* (de raisin). **5.** *inv. Meas:* Stone *m.* **6.** *Attrib.* Stone jug, pot *m,* cruche *f,* de grès. **stone-blind,** *a.* Complètement aveugle. **stone-cold,** *a.* Complètement froid. **stone-dead,** *a.* Raide mort. **stone-deaf,** *a.* Complètement sourd. **stone-fruit,** *s.* Fruit *m* à noyau. **stone-quarry,** *s.* Carrière *f* de pierre. **stone's throw,** *s.*

F: Within a stone's throw, à quelques pas.
stone wall, *s.* (a) Mur *m* de, en, pierre. (b) Mur en pierre sèche.

stone², *v.tr.* **1.** To stone s.o. (to death), lapider qn. **2.** To stone fruit, enlever les noyaux des fruits; énoyauter, épépiner, les fruits.

stonecrop, *s. Bot:* Orpin *m.*

stonemason, *s.* Maçon *m.*

stoneware, *s.* Poterie *f* de grès.

stoniness, *s.* **1.** Nature pierreuse. **2.** Dureté *f* (de cœur).

stony, *a.* **1.** Pierreux; couvert de pierres. **2.** Dur comme la pierre. **3.** *S. heart,* cœur de roche. *S. look,* regard glacial. **4.** *P:* = STONY-BROKE. **-ily,** *adv.* D'un air glacial.
stony-broke, *a. F:* I'm s.-b., je n'ai pas le sou. **stony-hearted,** *a.* Au cœur de roche.

stool, *s.* (a) Tabouret *m.* Folding stool, pliant *m.* Stool of repentance, sellette *f. F:* To fall between two stools, demeurer entre deux selles. (b) (Wooden) Escabeau *m.*

stoop¹, *s.* Inclination *f* en avant. To walk with a stoop, marcher le dos voûté.

stoop², **1.** *v.i.* (a) Se pencher, se baisser. (b) S'abaisser, s'avilir, descendre (to do sth., à, jusqu'à, faire qch.). (c) Avoir le dos rond; être voûté. **2.** *v.tr.* Pencher, incliner, courber.

stooping, *a.* Penché, courbé; voûté.

stop¹, *s.* **1.** (a) Arrêt *m,* interruption *f.* To put a stop to sth., faire cesser qch.; mettre fin à qch. (b) Arrêt, halte *f,* pause *f.* To come to a stop, s'arrêter. (c) Bus stop, (point *m* d')arrêt d'autobus; halte. **2.** Signe *m* de ponctuation; point *m.* **3.** *Mus:* Jeu *m,* registre *m* (d'orgue). **4.** Dispositif *m* de blocage; arrêt, taquet *m,* butée *f.* **stop-gap,** *s.* Bouche-trou *m, pl.* bouche-trous.
stop-press, *attrib.a. Journ:* Stop-press news, informations de dernière heure. **stop-watch,** *s.* Montre *f* à arrêt.

stop², *v.* I. *v.tr.* **1.** Boucher, aveugler (une voie d'eau); plomber, obturer (une dent). To stop (up), boucher (un trou); obstruer (un tuyau). To stop one's ears, se boucher les oreilles. **2.** (a) Arrêter. Stop thief! au voleur! To stop s.o.'s breath, couper la respiration à qn. To stop a blow, parer un coup. (b) To stop sth. being done, empêcher que qch. (ne) se fasse. (c) Arrêter (une pendule). (d) Mettre fin à; enrayer (un abus). **3.** (a) Cesser. Stop it! assez! finissez! (b) *Impers.* It has stopped raining, il a cessé de pleuvoir; la pluie a cessé. **4.** To stop s.o.'s wages, retenir les gages de qn. To stop s.o.'s allowance, couper les vivres à qn. II. **stop,** *v.i.* **1.** (a) S'arrêter. *Nau:* To stop short, s'arrêter net. 'Cars stop by request,' "arrêt facultatif." 'All cars stop here,' "arrêt fixe, obligatoire." *Rail:* How long do we stop? combien d'arrêt? To pass a station without stopping, brûler une gare. *Nau:* To stop at a port, faire escale à un port. (b) Cesser. **My watch has stopped,** ma montre (s')est arrêtée. **Without stopping,** d'arrache-pied. **He did not stop at that,** il ne s'en tint pas là. **The matter will not stop there,** l'affaire n'en demeurera pas là. **2.** F: = STAY² I. 2. **stopping,** s. **1.** (a) Arrêt m. (b) Suspension f; cessation f. (c) Stopping (up), obturation f. **Stopping of a tooth,** plombage m, obturation, d'une dent. **2.** (a) Bouchon m, tampon m. (b) Dent: Plombage m, mastic m. **stopping-place,** s. (Point m d')arrêt m; halte f.

stopcock, s. Robinet m d'arrêt.

stoppage, s. **1.** Arrêt m; mise f au repos; suspension f. **2.** Obstruction f, engorgement m. **3.** Arrêt, pause f, halte f; interruption f.

stopper¹, s. **1.** (a) Bouchon m. **Screw stopper,** fermeture f à vis. (b) Obturateur m. **2.** F: **To put a stopper on s.o.'s activities,** enrayer les activités de qn.

stopper², v.tr. Boucher (un flacon).

storage, s. **1.** Emmagasinage m, emmagasinement m, entreposage m. **2.** Caves fpl, greniers mpl; entrepôts mpl; espace m disponible.

store¹, s. **1.** (a) Provision f, approvisionnement m. (b) Abondance f. **To lay in stores,** s'approvisionner. **What the future holds in s.,** ce que l'avenir nous réserve. **That is a treat in store,** c'est un plaisir à venir. **To set great store by sth.,** faire grand cas de qch. **2.** pl. Stores, provisions, approvisionnements, vivres m. **3.** (a) Entrepôt m, magasin m. (b) The **village stores,** l'épicerie f du village. (c) The (departmental) **stores,** les grands magasins.

store², v.tr. **1.** Pourvoir, munir, approvisionner (with, de). **2. To store sth. (up),** amasser, accumuler, qch. **3.** (a) Emmagasiner, mettre en dépôt. (b) Prendre en dépôt.

storehouse, s. Magasin m, entrepôt m. F: **He is a storehouse of information,** c'est une mine de renseignements.

storey, s. = STORY².

stork, s. Orn: Cigogne f.

storm¹, s. **1.** Orage m. F: **A storm in a tea-cup,** une tempête dans un verre d'eau. **To stir up a storm,** soulever une tempête. **2. Storm of abuse,** tempête d'injures. **3. To take by storm,** emporter, prendre d'assaut. F: **To take the audience by storm,** emporter l'auditoire. **storm-cloud,** s. (a) Nuée f (d'orage). (b) F: Nuage m à l'horizon; nuage menaçant. **storm-troops,** s.pl. Troupes f d'assaut.

storm², **1.** v.i. F: Tempêter. **2.** v.tr. Prendre d'assaut. **storming,** s. **1.** Violence f, emportements mpl. **2.** Mil: Prise f d'assaut. **storming party,** s. Mil: Troupes fpl d'assaut.

stormy, a. Tempétueux; orageux, d'orage. S. sea, mer démontée. F: **Stormy discussion,** discussion orageuse.

story¹, s. **1.** Histoire f, récit m, conte m. F: **That is quite another story,** ça c'est une

autre paire de manches. **It's the (same) old story,** c'est toujours la même rengaine, la même chanson. **It's a long story,** c'est toute une histoire. **These bruises tell their own story,** ces meurtrissures en disent long. **2.** Lit: Short story, nouvelle f, conte. **3.** Intrigue f (d'un roman). **4.** F: Conte; mensonge m. **story-book,** s. Livre m de contes; livre d'histoires. **story-teller,** s. **1.** Conteur, -euse. **2.** F: Menteur, -euse.

story², s. Étage m (d'une maison). **On the third story,** au troisième étage.

stout¹, a. **1.** (i) Fort, vigoureux; (ii) brave, vaillant; (iii) ferme, résolu. **To put up a stout resistance,** se défendre vaillamment. **Stout heart,** cœur vaillant. **2.** Fort, solide. **3.** Gros, f. grosse; corpulent. **-ly,** adv. **1.** Fortement, vigoureusement, vaillamment. **To deny sth. stoutly,** nier qch. (fort et) ferme. **2.** Stoutly built, solidement bâti. **stout-hearted,** a. Intrépide, vaillant.

stout², s. Stout m; bière noire forte.

stoutness, s. Embonpoint m, corpulence f.

stove, s. (a) Poêle m, fourneau m. **Slow-combustion stove,** calorifère m. (b) Fourneau de cuisine; cuisinière f. **stove-pipe,** s. Tuyau m de poêle.

stow, v.tr. **1. To stow (away),** mettre en place, ranger, serrer. P: **Stow it!** ferme ça! **2.** Nau: Arrimer. **To stow the cargo,** faire l'arrimage.

stowaway¹, s. Nau: Passager clandestin, passagère clandestine.

stowaway², v.i. S'embarquer clandestinement.

straddle, v.tr. Enfourcher; chevaucher.

straggle, v.i. **To straggle (along),** marcher sans ordre, à la débandade. **straggling,** a. Disséminé. S. village, village aux maisons éparses.

straggler, s. Traînard m.

straight. **I.** a. **1.** (a) Droit, rectiligne. **Straight line,** ligne droite; droite f. (b) En ligne droite. **2.** Juste, honnête; loyal, -aux. **Straight answer,** réponse franche, sans équivoque. **3.** Net, f. nette; tout simple. **4.** (a) Droit; d'aplomb. **To put sth. straight,** redresser, ajuster, qch. **Your tie isn't s.,** votre cravate est de travers. (b) En ordre. **To put things straight,** arranger les choses. **II. straight,** s. **To be out of the straight,** n'être pas d'aplomb; être de travers. **III. straight,** adv. **1.** Droit. **To shoot straight,** tirer juste. **Keep straight on,** continuez tout droit. **2.** Directement. **I shall come straight back,** je ne ferai qu'aller et (re)venir. **To go straight to the point,** aller droit au fait. **To drink straight from the bottle,** boire à même la bouteille. **To walk straight in,** entrer sans frapper. **Straight away,** immédiatement, aussitôt; tout de suite. **Straight off,** sur-le-champ; tout de suite; d'emblée. **3.** To **look s.o. straight in the face,** regarder qn bien en face. **I tell you straight,** je vous le dis tout net. **Straight out**, franchement ; sans détours.

straighten. I. v.tr. (a) Rendre droit ; (re)dresser. (b) To s. one's tie, arranger sa cravate. **To straighten (out) one's affairs**, mettre ses affaires en ordre. **2.** v.i. Se redresser ; devenir droit.

straightforward, a. Loyal, -aux ; franc, f. franche. **To give a straightforward answer**, répondre sans détours. **-ly**, adv. Avec droiture, loyalement ; (parler) carrément, franchement.

straightforwardness, s. Droiture f, franchise f.

straightness, s. Droiture f, rectitude f.

straightway, adv. Immédiatement, tout de suite, aussitôt.

strain[1], s. **1.** Tension f. The s. on the rope, la tension de la corde. It would be too great a s. on my purse, ce serait trop demander à ma bourse. **The strain of modern life**, la tension de la vie moderne. **Mental strain**, surmenage intellectuel. **2.** Med: Entorse f, foulure f. **3.** pl. Poet: **Sweet strains**, doux accords. **4.** Ton m, sens m (d'un discours).

strain[2]. **I.** v.tr. **1.** Tendre. **To strain one's ears**, tendre l'oreille. **To strain one's eyes**, s'abîmer les yeux. **To strain s.o.'s friendship**, exiger trop de l'amitié de qn. **To strain a point**, faire une exception. **2.** (a) To s. one's shoulder, se fouler l'épaule. (b) **To strain oneself**, se surmener. **3.** Lit: **To strain s.o. to one's bosom**, serrer qn sur son cœur. **4.** (a) Filtrer ; passer au tamis ; tamiser. (b) **To strain (off) the vegetables**, faire égoutter les légumes. **II. strain**, v.i. Faire un (grand) effort. **strained**, a. (a) **Strained relations**, rapports tendus. (b) **Strained ankle**, cheville foulée.

strain[3], s. **1.** Qualité héritée, inhérente ; tendance. A s. of weakness, un héritage, un fond, de faiblesse. **2.** Race f, lignée f ; trace f.

strainer, s. Filtre m ou tamis m. Cu: Passoire f.

strait. I. a. **Strait waistcoat**, camisole f de force. **2.** s. (a) Détroit m. **The Straits of Dover**, le Pas de Calais. (b) **To be in (great) straits**, être dans l'embarras. **strait-laced**, a. Prude ; collet monté inv.

straitened, a. **In straitened circumstances**, dans la gêne.

strand[1], s. Rive f, grève f.

trand[2]. **1.** v.tr. Échouer (un navire). **2.** v.i. Échouer. **stranded**, a. **1.** Échoué. **2.** F: **To leave s.o. stranded**, laisser qn en plan.

strand[3], s. **1.** Brin m. **2.** Fil m (de perles) ; tresse f (de cheveux).

strange, a. **1.** S. faces, visages nouveaux, inconnus. **2.** Singulier, bizarre, étrange. **Strange to say**, chose étrange (à dire). **3.** I am strange to the work, je suis nouveau dans le métier. **To feel strange**, se sentir dépaysé. **-ly**, adv. Étrangement, singulièrement.

strangeness, s. **1.** Étrangeté f, singularité f. **2.** Nouveauté f.

stranger, s. Étranger, -ère ; inconnu, -ue. I am a stranger here, je ne suis pas d'ici. **You are quite a stranger!** on ne vous voit plus ! **He is a stranger to fear**, il ne connaît pas la peur.

strangle, v.tr. Étrangler. **Strangled voice**, voix étranglée. **strangling**, s. Étranglement m.

stranglehold, s. **To have a stranglehold on s.o.**, tenir qn à la gorge.

strap[1], s. **1.** Courroie f. **Watch strap**, bracelet m en cuir pour montre. **2.** (a) Bande f, sangle f. (b) Cost: Bande. Bootm: Barrette f.

strap[2], v.tr. **1.** To strap sth. (up), lier qch. avec une courroie ; sangler (un paquet). **2.** Med: Mettre des bandelettes à (une blessure). **strapping**[1], a. F: **Strapping fellow**, grand gaillard. **strapping**[2], s. **1.** Correction (administrée avec une courroie). **2.** Med: Emplâtre adhésif.

straphanger, s. F: Voyageur, -euse, debout.

stratagem, s. Ruse f ; stratagème m.

strategic(al), a. Stratégique. **-ally**, adv. Stratégiquement.

strategist, s. Stratégiste m.

strategy, s. Stratégie f.

stratosphere, s. Stratosphère f.

stratum, s. Geol: Strate f, couche f, gisement m. F: **Social strata**, étages m de la société ; couches sociales.

straw, s. **1.** Paille f. F: **Man of straw**, homme de paille. **2.** Paille ; chalumeau m. F: **It is not worth a straw**, cela ne vaut pas un fétu. **It's the last straw!** c'est le comble ! **straw-board**, s. Carton m paille. **straw hat**, s. Chapeau m de paille. **straw mat**, s. Paillasson m. **straw mattress**, s. Paillasse f.

strawberry, s. (i) Fraise f ; (ii) (plant) fraisier m. **Wild strawberry**, (petite) fraise des bois. **Strawberry jam**, confiture de fraises. **Strawberry ice**, glace à la fraise.

stray[1]. **I.** s. Animal égaré ; bête perdue. **II. stray**, a. **1.** Égaré, errant. **2.** S. bullets, balles perdues. S. thoughts, pensées détachées.

stray[2], v.i. S'égarer, errer. **To let one's thoughts stray**, laisser vaguer ses pensées.

streak[1], s. **1.** Raie f, bande f ; trait m, filet m. **The first streak of dawn**, la première lueur du jour. **Like a streak of lightning**, comme un éclair. **2.** Trace f. There was a yellow streak in him, il y avait de la lâcheté dans sa nature.

streak[2]. **I.** v.tr. Rayer, strier, zébrer. **2.** v.i. F: Passer comme un éclair.

streaky, a. **1.** En raies. **2.** Rayé, strié, zébré. **3.** (Of bacon) Entrelardé.

stream[1], s. **1.** (a) Cours m d'eau ; fleuve m, rivière f. (b) Ruisseau m. (c) Flot m (d'eau). In a thin s., en mince filet. **2.** Coulée f (de

lave). *S. of abuse*, torrent *m* d'injures. **In one
continuous stream**, à jet continu. **3.** Courant
m. **With the stream**, au fil de l'eau. **Against
the stream**, à contre courant. **streamlined**, *a.* Caréné, fuselé, profilé.
stream², *v.i.* (*a*) Couler (à flots) ; ruisseler ;
aller à flot continu. (*b*) (*Of hair*) Flotter (au
vent). **streaming**, *a.* Ruisselant. **Face
streaming with tears**, visage inondé de larmes.
To be streaming with perspiration, être en
nage.
streamer, *s.* Banderole *f.* *Nau*: Flamme *f.*
(*Paper*) streamers, serpentins *m*.
street, *s.* Rue *f.* *F*: **To turn s.o. into the
streets**, mettre qn sur le pavé. **The man in
the street**, l'homme moyen. *F*: **Not to be
in the same street with s.o.**, n'être pas de
taille avec qn. **Street level**, rez-de-chaussée
m inv. **Street cries**, cris des marchands
ambulants. **Street musician**, musicien de
carrefour. **street-arab**, *s.* Gamin *m* des
rues. **street-door**, *s.* Porte *f* sur la rue ;
porte d'entrée.
strength, *s.* **I.** (*a*) Force(s) *f(pl).* **Strength
of mind**, fermeté *f* d'esprit. **Strength of will**,
résolution *f.* **By sheer strength**, de vive force.
On the strength of, sur la foi de. (*b*) Solidité
f. **2. To be present in great strength**, être
présents en grand nombre. **3.** *Mil*: Effectif(s)
m(pl) (d'un régiment).
strengthen, *v.tr.* Consolider ; renforcer ;
(r)affermir. **strengthening**, *s.* Renforcement *m* ; consolidation *f.*
strenuous, *a.* **I.** Actif, énergique. **2.** (Travail) acharné, ardu. *To offer s. opposition*,
faire une opposition vigoureuse (*to*, à).
-ly, *adv.* Vigoureusement ; énergiquement.
strenuousness, *s.* Ardeur *f*, vigueur *f.*
stress¹, *s.* **I.** Force *f*, contrainte *f.* **Stress
of weather**, gros temps. **Under stress of
poverty**, poussé par la misère. **2.** (*a*) *Mec*:
Effort (subi) ; tension *f.* (*b*) **Period of storm
and stress**, période de trouble et d'agitation.
3. (*a*) Insistance *f.* **To lay stress on a fact**,
insister sur un fait. *To lay s. on a syllable*,
appuyer sur une syllabe. (*b*) *Ling*: **Stress
(-accent)**, accent *m* (d'intensité) ; accent
tonique.
stress², *v.tr.* Appuyer, insister, sur ; accentuer.
stretch¹, *s.* **I.** (*a*) Allongement *m*, extension
f. *Rac*. **At full stretch**, à toute allure.
(*b*) Tension *f.* *F*: **By a stretch of the
imagination**, par un effort d'imagination.
(*c*) Étendue *f*, portée *f.* **Stretch of wing**,
envergure *f.* (*d*) Élasticité *f.* **2.** (*a*) Étendue
(de pays). (*b*) *F*: **At a stretch**, (tout) d'un
trait.
stretch². **I.** *v.tr.* (*a*) Tendre ; élargir (des
souliers). (*b*) **To stretch (oneself)**, s'étirer.
To stretch one's legs, se dégourdir les jambes.
Stretched on the ground, étendu de tout son
long par terre. (*c*) Forcer. *F*: **To stretch
a point**, faire une concession. **2.** *v.i.* (*a*)

S'élargir ou s'allonger ; (*of elastic*) s'étendre.
(*b*) S'étendre. **stretch out. I.** *v.tr.*
(*a*) Allonger (le bras). **To stretch s.o. out
(on the ground)**, assommer qn raide.
(*b*) Tendre, avancer (la main). **2.** *v.i.* S'étirer.
stretcher, *s.* Brancard *m*, civière *f.*
stretcher-bearer, *s.* Brancardier *m*,
ambulancier *m*.
strew, *v.tr.* **I. To strew sand over the floor**,
répandre du sable sur le plancher. **2. To
strew the floor with flowers**, joncher le
plancher de fleurs.
strict, *a.* **I.** Exact ; strict. (*a*) Précis.
(*b*) Rigoureux. **In strictest confidence**, à titre
tout à fait confidentiel. **2.** *S. orders*, ordres
formels. **Strict discipline**, discipline sévère.
3. Sévère. **To be strict with s.o.**, être sévère
avec, envers, pour, qn. **-ly**, *adv.* **I.** Exactement, rigoureusement. **Strictly speaking**, à
proprement parler. **2.** Étroitement ; strictement. **Smoking (is) strictly prohibited**,
défense expresse de fumer. *It is s. forbidden*,
c'est absolument défendu. **3.** Sévèrement ;
avec rigueur.
strictness, *s.* **I.** Exactitude rigoureuse,
précision *f.* **2.** Rigueur *f* ; sévérité *f.*
stricture, *s.* **To pass strictures (up)on sth.**,
trouver à redire à qch.
stride¹, *s.* (Grand) pas ; enjambée *f.* *F*: **To
make great strides**, faire de grands progrès.
To take sth. in one's stride, faire qch. sans
le moindre effort. **To get into one's stride**,
prendre son allure normale.
stride², *v.i.* (*a*) **To stride along**, avancer
à grandes enjambées. (*b*) **To stride over sth.**,
enjamber qch.
stridency, *s.* Stridence *f.*
strident, *a.* Strident.
strife, *s.* Lutte *f.*
strike¹, *s.* **I.** Coup (frappé). **2.** *Ind*: Grève
f. **To go on strike**, se mettre en grève.
3. *Min*: Rencontre *f.* *F*: **Lucky strike**,
coup de veine.
strike², *v.* **I.** *v.tr.* & *ind.tr.* **I.** (*a*) Frapper.
To strike at s.o., porter un coup à qn.
(*b*) Frapper (une monnaie). (*c*) **To strike a
chord**, plaquer un accord. (*d*) **To strike a
bargain**, faire, conclure, un marché. **2. To
strike a match**, frotter une allumette. **3.** (*a*)
Abs. (*Of serpent*) **To strike**, foncer. **To strike
terror into s.o.**, frapper qn de terreur. (*b*) *Fish*:
Ferrer, piquer. **4.** *Struck with terror*, saisi
d'effroi. **5.** Percer ; pénétrer. **6.** (*a*) **To strike
(against) sth.**, heurter contre qch. *His head
struck the pavement*, sa tête a porté sur le
trottoir. *To s. a mine*, heurter une mine.
The ship strikes (on) the rocks, le navire
donne sur les écueils. **A sound struck my
ear**, un bruit me frappa l'oreille. (*b*) **How
did she strike you?** quelle impression vous
a-t-elle faite ? *He strikes me as (being) sincere*,
il me paraît sincère. **It strikes me that**,
il me semble que. (*c*) Faire impression à ; impressionner ; frapper. **7.** Tomber sur, découvrir. **To strike oil**, (i) rencontrer le pétrole ;

(ii) *F:* faire une bonne affaire. **He has struck it rich,** il tient le filon. **8.** (*a*) *Nau:* **To strike one's flag,** amener, baisser, son pavillon. (*b*) **To strike tents,** abattre, plier, les tentes. **To strike camp,** lever le camp. **9.** *Ind:* **To strike work,** *abs.* **to strike,** se mettre en grève. **10. To strike an attitude,** poser. **11. To strike an average,** établir une moyenne. II. **strike,** *v.i.* **1.** Sonner. *The clock struck six,* six heures sonnèrent. **2. To strike across country,** prendre à travers champs. **strike off,** *v.tr.* **1.** Trancher, abattre. **2. To strike a name off a list,** rayer un nom d'une liste. **strike out. 1.** *v.tr.* (*a*) Rayer, biffer. (*b*) Faire jaillir (des étincelles). (*c*) Tracer, ouvrir (une route). **2.** *v.i.* (*a*) **To strike out at s.o.,** allonger un coup à qn. (*b*) S'élancer. (*c*) *F:* **To strike out for oneself,** voler de ses propres ailes. **strike through,** *v.tr.* (*a*) Rayer, biffer. (*b*) Percer. **strike up,** *v.tr.* **1.** Entonner (une chanson); commencer à jouer (un morceau). *Abs. The band struck up,* la fanfare attaqua un morceau. **2. To strike up an acquaintance with s.o.,** lier connaissance avec qn. **stricken,** *a.* Stricken with grief, accablé de douleur. *S. with fever,* atteint d'une fièvre. **striking¹,** *a.* **1.** Striking clock, pendule à sonnerie. **2.** Remarquable, frappant, saisissant. **striking²,** *s.* **1.** (*a*) Frappement *m*; coups *mpl.* Within striking distance, à portée. (*b*) Frappe *f* (de la monnaie). **2.** Striking camp, levée *f* du camp. **3.** Sonnerie *f* (d'une horloge).

striker, *s. Ind:* Gréviste *mf.*

string¹, *s.* **1.** (i) Ficelle *f* (ii) corde *f,* cordon *m. A ball of s.,* une pelote de ficelle. *F:* **To have s.o. on a string,** faire marcher qn. **To pull the strings,** tenir les fils, les ficelles. **2.** (*a*) *Mus:* Corde. (*b*) Corde (d'un arc). **3.** String of beads, (i) collier *m*; (ii) *Ecc:* chapelet *m.* String of onions, chapelet d'oignons. *S. of vehicles,* file *f* de véhicules. **string bag,** *s.* Filet *m* à provisions.

string², *v.tr.* **1.** Bander (un arc). **2.** Enfiler (des perles). **string up,** *v.tr.* **1.** Pendre haut et court. **2.** *F:* **To string oneself up to do sth.,** tendre toute sa volonté pour faire qch. **stringed,** *a.* (Instrument) à cordes.

stringency, *s.* Rigueur *f,* sévérité *f.*

stringent, *a.* Rigoureux, strict.

stringy, *a.* Fibreux, filandreux.

strip¹, *s.* Bande *f. S. of land,* bande, langue *f,* de terrain.

strip², *v.* I. *v.tr.* **1.** Mettre tout nu. Stripped to the waist, nu jusqu'à la ceinture. **2.** (*a*) **To strip s.o. of sth.,** dépouiller qn de qch. (*b*) Dégarnir (un lit). **3. To strip sth. off, from, sth.,** ôter, enlever, qch. de qch. II. **strip,** *v.i.* **1.** Se dépouiller de ses vêtements; se dévêtir. **To strip to the skin,** *F:* se mettre à poil. **2.** (*Of bark*) **To strip (off),** se détacher.

stripe¹, *s.* (*a*) Raie *f,* barre *f.* (*b*) Bande *f* (de pantalon). (*c*) *Mil:* Sergeant's stripes,

galons *m* de sergent. **Long-service stripe,** chevron *m.* **To lose one's stripes,** être dégradé.

stripe², *v.tr.* Rayer, barrer. **striped,** *a.* A raies, à barres. *Nat.Hist:* Zébré, rubané.

stripling, *s.* Tout jeune homme *m.*

strive, *v.i.* **1.** **To strive to do sth.,** tâcher, s'efforcer, de faire qch. *To s. after effect,* rechercher l'effet. **2. To strive with s.o.,** lutter, se débattre, contre qn.

stroke¹, *s.* Coup *m.* **1.** Finishing stroke, coup de grâce. **2.** (*a*) Coup (d'aviron). (*b*) *Swim:* Brassée *f.* (*c*) *Mec.E:* Mouvement *m,* course *f.* (*d*) *F:* He hasn't done a s. of work, il n'a pas fait œuvre de ses dix doigts. (*e*) **Stroke of good luck,** coup de bonheur. Stroke of genius, trait *m* de génie. A good stroke of business, une bonne affaire. **3.** Coup (d'horloge). On the stroke of nine, sur le coup de neuf heures. **4.** *F:* **To have a stroke,** tomber en apoplexie. **5.** With a stroke of the pen, d'un trait de plume. **6.** *Row:* (*a*) Chef *m* de nage. (*b*) **To row stroke,** donner la nage.

stroke², *s.* Caresse *f* de la main.

stroke³, *v.tr.* Passer la main sur, caresser de la main. *F:* **To stroke s.o. the wrong way,** prendre qn à contre-poil.

stroll¹, *s.* Petit tour; bout *m* de promenade. **To go for a stroll,** (aller) faire un tour.

stroll², *v.i.* Errer à l'aventure; flâner.

strolling, *a.* Vagabond, errant. **Strolling player,** comédien(ne) ambulant(e).

stroller, *s.* Promeneur, -euse.

strong, *a.* Fort. **1.** (*a*) Solide. (*b*) Strong constitution, tempérament robuste. **2.** (*a*) Strong voice, voix forte, puissante. **To be strong in the arm,** avoir le bras fort. Strong measures, mesures énergiques. Politeness is not his strong point, la politesse n'est pas son fort. Strong in numbers, en grand nombre. *S. argument,* argument puissant. Strong wind, grand vent. (*b*) Strong drink, liqueurs fortes. **3.** *adv. F:* Things are going strong, tout marche à merveille. Going strong? ça marche? **-ly,** *adv.* Fortement. **1.** Solidement, fermement. **2.** Vigoureusement, énergiquement. **strong-box,** *s.* Coffre-fort *m, pl.* coffres-forts. **strong-minded,** *a.* A l'esprit décidé. *S.-m. person,* forte tête. **strong room,** *s.* Chambre blindée; cave *f* des coffres-forts.

stronghold, *s.* Forteresse *f*; place forte.

strop¹, *s.* (Razor-)strop, cuir *m* (à rasoir).

strop², *v.tr.* Affiler, repasser sur le cuir.

structural, *a.* Structural, -aux.

structure, *s.* (*a*) Édifice *m,* structure *f,* bâtiment *m.* (*b*) *Civ.E:* Ouvrage *m* d'art. *F:* The social structure, l'édifice social.

struggle¹, *s.* Lutte *f. Desperate s.,* lutte désespérée; combat acharné. *He gave in without a struggle,* il n'a fait aucune résistance.

struggle², *v.i.* Lutter (*with, against,* avec,

contre); se débattre, se démener. *They s. for the prize,* ils se disputent le prix. *We struggled through,* nous avons surmonté tous les obstacles. **struggling,** *a.* (Artiste) qui vit péniblement.

struggler, *s.* Lutteur *m.*

strum, *v.tr.* To strum, *v.i.* to strum on the piano, taper sur le piano. *Abs.* To strum, pianoter. To strum a tune, tapoter un air (au piano).

strut¹, *s.* Démarche fière ; pas mesuré.

strut², *v.i.* To strut (about), se pavaner, se rengorger. To strut in, entrer d'un air important.

strut³, *s.* Entretoise *f*; support *m*, étai *m.*

strut⁴, *v.tr. Const:* Entretoiser, étayer.

strychnin(e), *s.* Strychnine *f.*

stub¹, *s.* **I.** Souche *f* (d'arbre); bout *m* (de crayon). **2.** Souche, talon *m* (de chèque).

stub², *v.tr.* **I.** To stub (up) roots, extirper des racines. **2.** To stub one's toe, se cogner le pied.

stubble, *s.* **I.** Chaume *m.* **2.** *F:* Barbe courte et raide.

stubbly, *a.* **I.** Couvert de chaume. **2.** *F:* Stubbly beard, barbe courte et raide.

stubborn, *a.* Obstiné, opiniâtre, entêté. **-ly,** *adv.* Obstinément, opiniâtrement.

stubbornness, *s.* Entêtement *m*, obstination *f*, opiniâtreté *f.*

stucco, *s. Const:* Stuc *m.*

stud¹, *s.* **I.** Clou *m* à grosse tête. **2.** Bouton *m* (de col, de plastron).

stud², *v.tr.* Garnir de clous; clouter.

studded, *a.* **I.** Garni de clous; clouté. **2.** Parsemé (*with,* de).

stud³, *s.* Écurie *f.* **stud-farm,** *s.* Haras *m.*

student, *s.* **I.** Étudiant, -ante. *Medical s.,* étudiant en médecine. **2.** He is a great student, il est très studieux.

studio, *s. Art:* Atelier *m. Cin:* Studio *m.* Broadcasting studio, studio d'émission.

studious, *a.* **I.** Studieux, appliqué. **2.** Studious to do sth., attentif à faire qch. **-ly,** *adv.* **I.** Studieusement. **2.** Avec empressement. He studiously avoided me, il s'étudiait à m'éviter.

study¹, *s.* **I.** Soin(s) *m(pl),* attention *f.* **2.** Brown study, rêverie *f.* **3.** Étude *f.* To make a study of sth., étudier qch. **4.** *Mus:* Étude. **5.** (*a*) Cabinet *m* de travail. (*b*) *Sch:* Salle *f* d'étude.

study², *v.tr.* **I.** Étudier; observer (les astres). To study for the bar, faire son droit. To study for an examination, préparer un examen. **2.** S'occuper de, se préoccuper de. **3.** S'étudier, chercher (*to do sth.,* à faire qch.).

studied, *a.* Étudié, recherché; calculé; voulu.

stuff¹, *s.* **I.** (*a*) Matière *f*, substance *f*, étoffe *f.* Garden stuff, légumes *mpl*, jardinage *m.* The stuff that heroes are made of, le bois, la pâte, dont on fait les héros. *F:* That's the stuff! c'est du bon ! *That's the s. to give him!* c'est comme ça qu'il faut le traiter. (*b*) *F:* Fatras *m.* Stuff and nonsense! quelle bêtise ! **2.** *Tex:* Étoffe *f*, tissu *m* (de laine).

stuff², *v.tr.* **I.** (*a*) Bourrer (*with,* de); rembourrer (un meuble). (*b*) *Cu:* Farcir. (*c*) *F:* To stuff for an exam, chauffer qn en vue d'un examen. (*d*) Empailler (un animal). **2.** *F:* To stuff s.o. (up), bourrer le crâne à qn. **3.** To stuff up a hole, boucher un trou. **4.** To stuff sth. into sth., fourrer qch. dans qch. **stuffing,** *s.* **I.** (*a*) Bourrage *m*, rembourrage *m.* (*b*) Empaillage *m.* **2.** (*a*) Bourre *f. F:* To knock the stuffing out of s.o., flanquer une tripotée à qn. (*b*) *Cu:* Farce *f.*

stuffiness, *s.* Odeur *f* de renfermé.

stuffy, *a.* **I.** Mal ventilé; mal aéré. *Room that smells s.,* pièce qui sent le renfermé. **2.** *F:* Collet monté *inv.*

stultify, *v.tr.* **I.** Enlever toute valeur à; rendre inutile. **2.** Rendre ridicule. To stultify oneself, se démentir.

stumble¹, *s.* Trébuchement *m*; faux pas.

stumble², *v.i.* **I.** Trébucher; faire un faux pas; (*of horse*) broncher. To stumble over sth., buter contre qch. **2.** To stumble in one's speech, hésiter en parlant. **3.** To stumble across s.o., rencontrer qn par hasard.

stumbling-block, *s.* Pierre *f* d'achoppement.

stumer, *s. F:* Chose qui ne vaut rien.

stump¹, *s.* **I.** Tronçon *m*, souche *f* (d'arbre); chicot *m* (de dent); moignon *m* (de bras); bout *m* (de crayon). **2.** *pl. F:* Jambes. You must stir your stumps, il faut vous remuer. **3.** Stump orator, harangueur *m.* **4.** *Cr:* Piquet *m.* To draw stumps, cesser la partie.

stump². **I.** *v.i.* To stump along, clopiner. **2.** *v.tr. F:* This fairly stumped me, cela m'a désarçonné. **stump up,** *v.i. F:* Payer, s'exécuter.

stumpy, *a.* Trapu, ramassé.

stun, *v.tr.* **I.** Étourdir, assommer. **2.** *F:* Renverser, abasourdir. **stunning,** *a.* **I.** (*a*) (Coup) étourdissant. (*b*) Accablant. **2.** *F:* Renversant, épatant.

stunner, *s. F:* Type épatant.

stunt¹, *v.tr.* Rabougrir. **stunted,** *a.* Rabougri, chétif.

stunt², *s. F:* **I.** Affaire *f* de pure réclame. **2.** Tour *m* de force.

stupefaction, *s.* Stupéfaction *f*; stupeur *f.*

stupefy, *v.tr.* **I.** Hébéter, abrutir. **2.** *F:* Abasourdir, stupéfier.

stupendous, *a.* Prodigieux; *F:* formidable. **-ly,** *adv.* Prodigieusement.

stupid, *a.* Stupide; sot, *f.* sotte; *F:* bête. *How s. of me!* que je suis bête ! **-ly,** *adv.* Stupidement, sottement; *F:* bêtement.

stupidity, *s.* Stupidité *f.* (*a*) Lourdeur *f* d'esprit. (*b*) Sottise *f*, niaiserie *f*, bêtise *f.*

stupor, *s.* Stupeur *f.*

sturdiness, s. **1.** Vigueur *f*, robustesse *f*. **2.** Résolution *f*, fermeté *f*.
sturdy, a. (a) Vigoureux, robuste. (b) Hardi, résolu, ferme. **-ily,** adv. **1.** Fortement. **2.** Hardiment, vigoureusement.
sturgeon, s. *Ich:* Esturgeon *m*.
stutter¹, s. Bégaiement *m*.
stutter², v.i. & tr. Bégayer, bredouiller.
stuttering¹, a. Bègue. **stuttering²,** s. Bégaiement *m*.
stutterer, s. Bègue *mf*.
sty, s. Étable *f* (à porcs); porcherie *f*.
stye, s. *Med:* Orgelet *m*; *F:* grain-d'orge *m*.
style¹, s. **1.** *Engr:* Style *m*. **2.** (a) Style, manière *f*, façon *f*. **To live in style,** mener grand train. **To win in fine style,** gagner haut la main. **That's the style!** bravo! à la bonne heure! (b) Style, genre *m*; modèle *m*. *Made in three styles,* fabriqué en trois genres, sur trois modèles. (c) **In the latest style,** de la dernière mode. **3.** Style; manière d'écrire. **4.** Ton *m*, chic *m*, cachet *m*. **5.** Titre *m*, nom *m*.
style², v.tr. Dénommer; appeler. **To style oneself Doctor,** se donner le titre de docteur.
stylet, s. Stylet *m*.
stylish, a. Élégant, chic *m* & *f*; coquet, -ette. **-ly,** adv. Élégamment; avec chic.
stylishness, s. Élégance *f*, chic *m*.
stylograph, s. Stylographe *m*.
suasion, s. Persuasion *f*.
suave, a. **1.** Suave; doux, *f*. douce. **2.** Suave manners, manières doucereuses. **-ly,** adv. **1.** Suavement. **2.** Doucereusement.
suavity, s. (a) Affabilité *f*. (b) Politesse mielleuse.
subaltern. 1. a. Subalterne, subordonné. **2.** s. Subalterne *mf*.
subconscious, a. *Psy:* Subconscient. **The subconscious self,** l'inconscient *m*. **-ly,** adv. Inconsciemment.
subdivide. 1. v.tr. Subdiviser. **2.** v.i. Se subdiviser.
subdivision, s. Subdivision *f*; sous-division *f*.
subdue, v.tr. **1.** Subjuguer, soumettre, assujettir; maîtriser (un incendie); dompter (ses passions). **2.** Adoucir (la voix). **subdued,** a. **1.** Vaincu, subjugué. **2.** Déprimé. **3.** Subdued light, demi-jour *m*. **In a s. voice,** à mi-voix.
subjacent, a. Sous-jacent, subjacent.
subject¹, s. **1.** Sujet, -ette. *British s.,* sujet britannique. **2.** *Gram:* Sujet. **3.** (a) Sujet (de conversation); objet *m* (de méditation). **Let us return to our subject,** revenons à nos moutons. **On the subject of,** au sujet de. **To change the subject,** changer de sujet. (b) *Sch: What subjects do you teach?* quelles matières enseignez-vous? **4.** *Good hypnotic subject,* sujet facile à hypnotiser. **subject-matter,** s. Sujet *m* (d'un livre); contenu *m* (d'une lettre).
subject², a. **1.** Assujetti, soumis (*to*, à);

sous la dépendance (*to*, de). **Subject to the laws of nature,** soumis aux lois de la nature. **2.** (a) Sujet, -ette, exposé. (b) **Subject to stamp duty,** passible du droit de timbre. *The plan is s. to modifications,* ce projet pourra subir des modifications. **3.** *S. to ratification,* sous réserve de ratification. **Subject to alteration,** sauf nouvel avis.
subject³, v.tr. **1.** Assujettir, subjuguer. **2. To subject sth. to an examination,** soumettre qch. à un examen. **To subject s.o. to criticism,** critiquer qn.
subjection, s. Sujétion *f*, soumission *f* (*to*, à). *To be in s. to s.o.,* être soumis à qn. **To bring into subjection,** assujettir.
subjective, a. *Phil:* Subjectif.
subjoin, v.tr. Ajouter, adjoindre.
subjugate, v.tr. Subjuguer, soumettre.
subjugation, s. Subjugation *f*.
subjunctive, a. & s. *Gram:* Subjonctif (*m*).
sub-let, v.tr. Sous-louer.
sub-lieutenant, s. Enseigne *m* (de vaisseau).
sublimation, s. Sublimation *f*.
sublime. 1. a. (a) Sublime. (b) *F:* Sublime indifference, suprême indifférence. **2.** s. **The sublime,** le sublime. **-ly,** adv. **1.** Sublimement. **2.** *F:* **To be sublimely unconscious,** être dans une ignorance absolue.
sublimity, s. Sublimité *f*.
sub-machine, a. Sub-machine gun, mitraillette *f*.
submarine. 1. a. Sous-marin. **2.** s. (Navire) sous-marin *m*.
submerge. 1. v.tr. (a) Submerger, immerger. (b) Inonder, noyer. **2.** v.i. (*Of submarine*) Plonger; effectuer sa plongée. **submerged,** a. (a) Submergé. (b) **Submerged reef,** écueil sous-marin.
submergence, s. Submersion *f*; plongée *f*.
submersible, a. Submersible.
submersion, s. Submersion *f*; plongée *f*.
submission, s. **1.** (a) Soumission *f*. **To starve s.o. into submission,** réduire qn par la famine. (b) Docilité *f*; humilité *f*. **2.** Soumission (d'une question à un arbitre).
submissive, a. Soumis, humble, résigné. **-ly,** adv. Avec docilité.
submissiveness, s. Soumission *f*, docilité *f*.
submit. 1. v.i. & *pr*. Se soumettre (*to*, à); se plier (à une nécessité). **2.** v.tr. (a) Soumettre. **To submit sth. to s.o.'s inspection,** soumettre qch. à l'inspection de qn. *To s. proofs of identity,* présenter des pièces d'identité. (b) Représenter, alléguer.
subordinate¹. 1. a. (a) Inférieur, -e, subalterne; (rôle) secondaire. (b) Subordonné (*to*, à). **2.** s. Subordonné, -ée.
subordinate², v.tr. Subordonner (*to*, à).
subordination, s. **1.** Subordination *f* (*to*, à). **2.** Soumission *f* (*to*, à).
suborn, v.tr. *Jur:* Suborner, corrompre.
subpoena¹, s. *Jur:* Citation *f*, assignation *f*.
subpoena², v.tr. **To subpoena s.o. to appear,** citer, assigner, qn à comparaître.

subscribe, *v.tr.* **I.** (*a*) Souscrire. (*b*) *Abs.* To subscribe to an opinion, souscrire à une opinion. **2.** (*a*) To subscribe ten pounds, souscrire pour (la somme de) dix livres. To s. to a loan, souscrire à un emprunt. (*b*) To subscribe to a newspaper, s'abonner à un journal.

subscriber, *s.* **I.** Signataire *mf*, souscripteur *m*. **2.** Abonné, -ée.

subscription, *s.* **I.** (*a*) Souscription *f*; signature *f*. (*b*) Adhésion *f* (*to*, à); approbation *f* (*to*, de). **2.** To pay a s., verser une cotisation. To get up a subscription, se cotiser. **Subscription list,** liste des souscripteurs. **3.** Abonnement *m*. **Subscription to a club,** cotisation à un cercle.

subsequent, *a.* Subséquent, qui suit. At a s. meeting, dans une séance ultérieure. **Subsequent to,** postérieur, -e, consécutif, à. **-ly,** *adv.* Plus tard; dans la suite; postérieurement (*to*, à).

subservience, *s.* **I.** Utilité *f* (*to*, à). **2.** Soumission *f*, servilité *f*.

subservient, *a.* **I.** Utile, qui aide (*to*, à). **2.** Subordonné (*to*, à). **3.** Obséquieux, servile.

subside, *v.i.* **I.** S'affaisser, s'enfoncer. *F:* To subside into an armchair, s'effondrer dans un fauteuil. **2.** Baisser. *The flood is subsiding,* la crue diminue. **3.** (*a*) S'apaiser, se calmer, tomber. (*b*) *F:* Se taire.

subsidence, *s.* (*a*) Affaissement *m*; effondrement *m*. (*b*) Décrue *f*, baisse *f* (d'une rivière).

subsidiary, *a.* Subsidiaire, auxiliaire.

subsidize, *v.tr.* Subventionner; primer. To be subsidized by the State, recevoir une subvention de l'État.

subsidy, *s.* Subvention *f*; *Ind:* prime *f*.

subsist, *v.i.* **I.** (*a*) Continuer d'être. (*b*) S'entretenir, vivre (*on*, de).

subsistence, *s.* **I.** Existence *f.* **2.** *Means of* s., moyens de subsistance *f*.

substance, *s.* **I.** Substance *f*, matière *f*. **2.** Substance, fond *m*, essentiel *m*. **3.** Solidité *f*. **Book of** s., livre solide. **4.** Avoir *m*, bien *m*, fortune *f*.

substantial, *a.* **I.** Substantiel, réel. **2.** Important. **Substantial reasons,** raisons sérieuses. A s. difference, une différence appréciable. **3.** (*a*) S. meal, repas solide. (*b*) Solide. **Man of** s. build, homme bien taillé. **4.** Cossu; (maison de commerce) bien assise. **-ally,** *adv.* Substantiellement. **I.** Réellement; en substance. **2.** Solidement. **3.** Fortement.

substantiate, *v.tr.* Établir, justifier. To substantiate a claim, établir le bien-fondé d'une réclamation.

substantive, **I.** *a.* Réel, indépendant. **2.** *s. Gram:* Substantif *m*, nom *m*. **-ly,** *adv.* Substantivement.

substitute¹, *s.* **I.** (*a*) Suppléant, -ante. To find a s., se faire suppléer. (*b*) Mandataire *mf*. **2.** (*a*) Succédané *m* (*for*, de). *Rubber* s., factice *m* de caoutchouc. (*b*) *Beware of substitutes,* se méfier des contrefaçons *f*.

substitute², *v.tr.* Substituer.

substitution, *s.* Substitution *f*, remplacement *m*.

substratum, *s.* Couche inférieure. *F:* A substratum of truth, un fond de vérité.

subterfuge, *s.* Subterfuge *m*; faux-fuyant *m, pl.* faux-fuyants.

subterranean, *a.* Souterrain.

subtle, *a.* Subtil. **I.** (*a*) (Parfum) pénétrant. (*b*) **Subtle distinction,** distinction subtile. **2.** (*a*) (Esprit) fin, raffiné; (*b*) Rusé, astucieux. **-tly,** *adv.* Subtilement; avec finesse.

subtlety, *s.* **I.** Subtilité *f.* (*a*) Raffinement *m*, finesse *f.* (*b*) Distinction subtile. **2.** Ruse *f*, astuce *f*.

subtract, *v.tr. Mth:* Soustraire, retrancher (*from*, de).

subtraction, *s. Mth:* Soustraction *f*.

suburb, *s.* Faubourg *m*. In the suburbs, dans la banlieue.

suburban, *a.* Suburbain; de banlieue.

subvention, *s.* Subvention *f*.

subversion, *s.* Subversion *f*; renversement *m*.

subversive, *a.* Subversif (*of*, de).

subvert, *v.tr.* Renverser, subvertir.

subway, *s.* Passage souterrain.

succeed, *v.tr. & i.* **I.** Succéder (à qn). To succeed to an estate, hériter d'une propriété. **2.** *v.i.* Réussir; venir à bien. How to succeed, le moyen de parvenir. To succeed in doing sth., réussir à faire qch. **succeeding,** *a.* **I.** Suivant, subséquent. **2.** A venir; futur. **3.** Successif.

success, *s.* (*a*) Succès *m*, réussite *f.* (*b*) (*Of venture*) To be a success, réussir. *The evening was a great* s., la soirée a été très réussie. To make a success of sth., réussir qch.

successful, *a.* Couronné de succès; réussi. S. play, pièce qui a du succès. To be s. in doing sth., réussir à faire qch. **Successful candidates,** (i) candidats élus; (ii) *Sch:* candidats reçus. **-fully,** *adv.* Avec succès.

succession, *s.* Succession *f.* **I.** (*a*) Suite *f.* In succession, successivement. In rapid succession, coup sur coup. (*b*) Série *f*, suite. **2.** (*a*) Succession (à la couronne). In succession to s.o., en remplacement de qn. (*b*) Héritage *m*. (*c*) Lignée *f*; descendants *mpl*.

successive, *a.* Successif, consécutif. **-ly,** *adv.* Successivement.

successor, *s.* Successeur *m* (*to*, *of*, de). To appoint a s. to s.o., remplacer qn.

succinct, *a.* Succinct, concis. **-ly,** *adv.* Succinctement; en peu de mots.

succour¹, *s.* Secours *m*; aide *f*.

succour², *v.tr.* Secourir, soulager.

succulence, *s.* Succulence *f*.

succulent, *a.* Succulent.

succumb, *v.i.* Succomber; céder. **To succumb to one's injuries,** succomber à, mourir de, ses blessures.

such. I. *a.* Tel, pareil, semblable. **I.** (*a*) S. men as he and I, des gens comme lui et moi. S. food is unwholesome, les aliments de cette nature sont malsains. **Such a man,** un tel homme. **Did you ever see such a thing!** a-t-on jamais vu chose pareille! **Some such plan,** un projet de ce genre. **There are no** *s.* *things as fairies,* les fées n'existent pas. *I said* **no** *s.* **thing,** je n'ai rien dit de la sorte. **No such thing!** il n'en est rien! pas du tout! *(b)* **S.** *is not the case,* il n'en est pas ainsi. **S.** *were his words,* tel fut son langage. *F:* **Such is the world!** ainsi va le monde! **2. In such (and such)** **a place,** en tel endroit. **Such a one,** un tel, une telle. **3. In such a way that,** de telle sorte que. **Until such time as,** jusqu'à ce que. **4. Such large houses,** de si grandes maisons. **S. courage,** un tel courage. **I had such a fright!** j'ai eu une de ces peurs! II. **such,** *pron.* I. *We know of* **no such,** nous n'en connaissons pas de cette espèce. **2.** *I* **will send you such as I have,** ce que j'en ai je vous les enverrai. **3. History as such,** l'histoire en tant que telle.

suchlike. I. *a. F:* Semblable, pareil; de ce genre. **2.** *pron. Usu. pl.* Beggars and suchlike, mendiants et autres gens de la sorte.

suck[1], *s.* Action *f* de sucer. **To have a suck at a sweet,** sucer un bonbon.

suck[2]. I. *v.tr.* Sucer. **To suck s.o.'s brains,** exploiter l'intelligence de qn. **2.** *v.i. (Of pers.)* **To suck at sth.,** sucer (un bonbon); sucer, tirer sur (une pipe). **suck down,** *v.tr.* Engloutir. **suck in,** *v.tr. (a)* Sucer, absorber. *(b)* Engloutir. **suck up,** *v.tr.* Sucer, aspirer, pomper; *(of sponge)* absorber. **sucking-pig,** *s.* Cochon de lait.

sucker, *s. Hort:* Rejeton *m*; drageon *m*.

suckle, *v.tr.* Allaiter.

suction, *s.* Succion *f*; aspiration *f*.

Sudan (the). *Pr.n.* Le Soudan.

sudden, *a. (a)* Soudain, subit. **S. shower,** averse inopinée. *(b)* **S. turning,** tournant brusque. *Adv.phr.* **All of a sudden,** subitement; tout à coup. **-ly,** *adv.* Soudain, soudainement; tout à coup.

suddenness, *s. (a)* Soudaineté *f*. *(b)* Brusquerie *f*.

suds, *s.pl.* (Soap-)suds, eau *f* de savon.

sue. I. *v.tr.* **To sue s.o. for damages,** poursuivre qn en dommages-intérêts. **2.** *v.i.* **To sue for sth.,** solliciter qch. **To sue for peace,** demander la paix.

suède, *s.* (i) *(For shoes)* Daim *m*. (ii) *(For gloves)* Peau *f* de suède; suède *m*.

suet, *s. Cu:* Graisse *f* de rognon.

Suez. *Pr.n.* Suez. **The Suez Canal,** le canal de Suez.

suffer. I. *v.tr.* I. Éprouver, souffrir; subir. **To suffer defeat,** essuyer, subir, une défaite. **To suffer death,** subir la peine de mort. **2.** Permettre, tolérer. II. **suffer,** *v.i.* I. Souffrir. **To suffer for one's misdeeds,** supporter la conséquence de ses méfaits. **2. To suffer from neglect,** pâtir d'un manque de soins. *Country suffering from labour troubles,* pays en proie à l'agitation ouvrière.

3. Subir une perte, un dommage. *The battalion suffered severely,* le bataillon a essuyé de fortes pertes. **suffering[1],** *a.* Souffrant; qui souffre. **suffering[2],** *s. (a)* Souffrance *f*. *(b) pl.* Sufferings, souffrances; douleurs *f*.

sufferance, *s.* Tolérance *f*, souffrance *f*. **On sufferance,** par tolérance.

sufferer, *s. (a)* Victime *f*. *(b)* Malade *mf*.

suffice. I. *v.i.* Suffire. **Suffice it to say,** qu'il (nous) suffise de dire. **2.** *v.tr.* Suffire à (qn).

sufficiency, *s. (a)* Suffisance *f*. *(b)* Fortune suffisante.

sufficient, *a. & s.* Assez; suffisant. *One lamp is s.,* il suffit d'une lampe. *F:* **Have you had sufficient?** avez-vous mangé à votre faim? **-ly,** *adv.* Suffisamment; assez.

suffix, *s. Gram:* Suffixe *m*.

suffocate. I. *v.tr.* Étouffer, suffoquer. **2.** *v.i.* Étouffer, suffoquer. **suffocating,** *a.* Suffocant, étouffant.

suffocation, *s.* Suffocation *f*; étouffement *m*.

suffrage, *s.* Suffrage *m*. *(a)* Vote *m*, voix *f*. *(b)* Droit *m* de vote.

suffuse, *v.tr.* Se répandre sur. *Eyes suffused with tears,* yeux baignés de larmes.

sugar[1], *s.* Sucre *m*. **Granulated s.,** sucre cristallisé. **Lump sugar,** sucre en morceaux. **Castor sugar,** sucre en poudre. **Brown sugar,** cassonade *f*. **sugar-almond,** *s.* Dragée *f*; amande lissée. **sugar-basin,** *s.* Sucrier *m*. **sugar-beet,** *s.* Betterave *f* à sucre. **sugar-candy,** *s.* Sucre candi. **sugar-cane,** *s.* Canne *f* à sucre. **sugar-loaf,** *s.* Pain *m* de sucre. *F:* **Sugar-loaf hat,** chapeau pointu. **sugar-tongs,** *s.pl.* Pince *f* à sucre.

sugar[2], *v.tr.* Sucrer; saupoudrer de sucre. *F:* **To sugar the pill,** dorer la pilule.

sugary, *a.* I. *(a)* Sucré. *(b)* Trop sucré. **2.** (Sourire) mielleux; (ton) doucereux.

suggest, *v.tr.* I. Suggérer, proposer. **A solution suggested itself to me,** une solution se présenta à mon esprit. **2.** Inspirer, faire naître. *Prudence suggests a retreat,* la prudence conseille la retraite. **3.** Insinuer. **4.** Évoquer.

suggestion, *s.* Suggestion *f*.

suggestive, *a.* Suggestif; évocateur, -trice.

suicidal, *a.* **S. tendencies,** tendances au suicide. *F:* **It would be** *s.* **to do so,** ce serait un véritable suicide que d'agir de la sorte.

suicide[1], *s.* Suicidé, -ée.

suicide[2], *s.* Suicide *m*. **To commit suicide,** se suicider.

suit[1], *s.* I. *Jur:* **To bring a suit against s.o.,** intenter un procès à qn. **2.** Prière *f*, demande *f*, requête *f*. **At the suit of s.o.,** à la requête de qn. **3.** Recherche *f*, demande, en mariage. **4.** *Cost:* Suit *(a)* of clothes, costume *m*, complet *m* (pour homme). *(b)* Ensemble *m* (pour femme). **5.** *Cards:* Couleur *f*. **To follow suit,** *F:* en faire autant, faire de même.

suit-case, *s.* Mallette *f*, valise *f*.

suit[2], *v.tr.* I. Accommoder, adapter, approprier *(to,* à). **They are suited to each other,** ils sont faits l'un pour l'autre. **2.** Convenir

à, aller à, accommoder. **That just suits me,** ça me va à merveille. *I shall do it when it suits me,* je le ferai quand cela me conviendra. **Suit yourself,** faites comme vous voudrez. *This hat suits you,* ce chapeau vous va.
suitability, *s.* Convenance *f*; à-propos *m*; accord *m. S. of a candidate for a post,* aptitude *f* d'un candidat à un poste.
suitable, *a.* **1.** Convenable, qui convient; approprié. *We have found nothing s.,* nous n'avons rien trouvé à notre convenance. **2. Suitable for sth.,** bon, *f.* bonne, à qch.; propre, approprié, à qch. **Suitable to the occasion,** qui convient à la circonstance. **-ably,** *adv.* Convenablement; à propos.
suite, *s.* **1.** Suite *f*, cortège *m.* **2.** (*a*) **Suite of rooms,** appartement *m.* (*b*) **Suite of furniture,** ameublement *m.* **3.** Orchestral suite, suite d'orchestre.
suitor, *s.* **1.** *Jur:* Plaideur, -euse. **2.** Prétendant *m*, soupirant *m.*
sulk[1], *s.* **To be in the sulks,** bouder.
sulk[2], *v.i.* Bouder; faire la mine.
sulkiness, *s.* Bouderie *f*, maussaderie *f.*
sulky, *a.* Boudeur, -euse, maussade. *To be s.,* bouder. *To look s.,* faire la mine. **-ily,** *adv.* En boudant.
sullen, *a.* Maussade, renfrogné, morose; (*of thg*) sombre, morne. **-ly,** *adv.* D'un air maussade.
sullenness, *s.* Maussaderie *f.*
sully, *v.tr.* Souiller, ternir; flétrir.
sulphate, *s. Ch:* Sulfate *m.*
sulphide, *s. Ch:* Sulfure *m.*
sulphite, *s. Ch:* Sulfite *m.*
sulphur, *s.* Soufre *m.* **sulphur mine,** *s.* Soufrière *f.*
sulphureous, *a.* Sulfureux.
sulphuretted, *a. Ch:* Sulfuré.
sulphuric, *a. Ch:* Sulfurique.
sulphurous, *a. Ch:* Sulfureux.
sultan, *s.* Sultan *m.*
sultana, *s.* **1.** Sultane *f.* **2.** Raisin sec de Smyrne.
sultriness, *s.* Chaleur étouffante.
sultry, *a.* Étouffant, suffocant.
sum[1], *s.* **1.** (*a*) Somme *f*, total *m*; montant *m.* (*b*) *F:* **The sum and substance of the matter,** le fond de l'affaire. **In sum,** en somme; somme toute. (*c*) **Sum of money,** somme d'argent. **2.** Problème *m* (d'arithmétique). **To do sums,** faire du calcul. **sum-total,** *s.* Somme totale, globale.
sum[2], *v.tr.* Additionner. **sum up,** *v.tr.* (*a*) Résumer, récapituler. **To sum up the matter,** *abs.* to sum up, en résumé. (*b*) *F:* **To sum s.o. up,** juger, classer, qn. **summing up,** *s.* (*a*) *Jur:* Résumé *m* des débats. (*b*) Évaluation *f.*
summarize, *v.tr.* Résumer sommairement.
summary. 1. *a.* Sommaire. *Jur:* **Summary proceedings,** affaire *f* sommaire. **2.** *s.* Sommaire *m*, résumé *m.* **-ily,** *adv.* Sommairement.

summer[1], *s.* Été *m.* **In summer,** en été. **Summer clothes,** habits d'été. **The summer holidays,** les grandes vacances. **summerhouse,** *s.* Pavillon *m*, kiosque *m.* **summertime,** *s.* **1.** L'été *m.* **2.** L'heure *f* d'été.
summer[2], *v.i.* Passer l'été, estiver.
summit, *s.* Sommet *m*, cime *f*, faîte *m.*
summon, *v.tr.* **1.** (*a*) Appeler, faire venir; mander; convoquer. (*b*) *Jur:* Sommer de comparaître. **2.** Sommer, requérir. **3.** To summon up one's courage, faire appel à tout son courage.
summons[1], *s.* **1.** Appel (fait d'autorité); convocation urgente. **2.** *Jur:* Citation *f. F:* procès-verbal *m*, *pl.* procès-verbaux. **To take out a summons against s.o.,** faire assigner qn. **3.** *Mil:* **Summons to surrender,** sommation *f.*
summons[2], *v.tr. Jur:* Citer à comparaître; assigner; appeler en justice.
sumptuous, *a.* Somptueux, fastueux. **-ly,** *adv.* Somptueusement.
sumptuousness, *s.* Somptuosité *f*, faste *m*; richesse *f.*
sun[1], *s.* (*a*) Soleil *m. The sun is shining,* il fait du soleil. (*b*) **To have one's place in the sun,** avoir sa place au soleil. **To take the sun,** s'insoler; prendre le soleil. **To get a touch of the sun,** prendre un coup de soleil. **sunbonnet,** *s.* Capeline *f.* **sun-dial,** *s.* Cadran *m* solaire. **sun-dried,** *a.* Séché au soleil. **sun-glasses,** *s.pl.* Lunettes *f* contre le soleil. **sun-spot,** *s.* *Astr:* Tache *f* solaire. **sun-up,** *s.* Lever *m* du soleil.
sun[2], *v.tr.* Exposer au soleil; insoler. **To sun oneself,** prendre le soleil; se chauffer au soleil.
sunbeam, *s.* Rayon *m* de soleil.
sunburn, *s.* Hâle *m.*
sunburned, *a.* Brûlé par le soleil; hâlé.
sundae, *s.* Glace *f* aux fruits.
Sunday, *s.* Dimanche *m.* **In one's Sunday best,** endimanché.
sunder, *v.tr.* (*a*) Séparer, disjoindre (*from*, de). (*b*) Couper, fendre, en deux.
sundew, *s. Bot:* Drosère *f*, rossolis *m.*
sundown, *s.* = SUNSET.
sundry. 1. *a.* Divers. *On s. occasions,* à différentes occasions. **2.** *s.* (*a*) **All and sundry,** tous sans exception. (*b*) *pl.* **Sundries,** (i) articles divers; (ii) frais divers.
sunflower, *s. Bot:* Tournesol *m*, soleil *m.*
sunken, *a.* (*a*) Noyé, submergé. (*b*) Affaissé, enfoncé. **Sunken cheeks,** joues creuses. (*c*) *S. road,* route encaissée.
sunlight, *s.* Lumière *f* du soleil. **In the sunlight,** au soleil.
sunny, *a.* **1.** (Journée) de soleil; (endroit) ensoleillé; (côté) exposé au soleil. **2.** (Visage) radieux, rayonnant; (caractère) heureux.
sunrise, *s.* Lever *m* du soleil.
sunset, *s.* Coucher *m* du soleil.
sunshade, *s.* **1.** Ombrelle *f.* **2.** *Aut:* Paresoleil *m inv.*

sunshine, s. (Clarté f, lumière f, du) soleil. In the sunshine, au soleil.

sunstroke, s. *Med:* Insolation f; coup m de soleil.

sup, v. **1.** v.tr. Prendre à petites gorgées. **2.** v.i. Souper (*off, on,* de).

superabundance, s. Surabondance f (*of,* de).

superabundant, a. Surabondant.

superannuate, v.tr. Mettre à la retraite; retraiter. **superannuated,** a. **1.** Suranné. **2.** En retraite; retraité.

superannuation, s. Retraite f par limite d'âge.

superb, a. Superbe, magnifique. **-ly,** adv. Superbement, magnifiquement.

supercargo, s. *Nau:* Subrécargue m.

supercilious, a. Sourcilleux, hautain; pincé, dédaigneux. **-ly,** adv. Avec une nuance de dédain.

superciliousness, s. Hauteur f; air dédaigneux.

superficial, a. Superficiel. *His knowledge is entirely s.,* son savoir est tout en superficie. **-ally,** adv. Superficiellement.

superficies, s.inv. Superficie f.

superfine, a. Superfin; *Com:* surfin.

superfluity, s. **1.** Superfluité f. **2.** Superflu m.

superfluous, a. Superflu.

superhuman, a. Surhumain.

superintend, v.tr. Diriger, surveiller.

superintendence, s. Direction f, surveillance f, contrôle m; conduite f.

superintendent, s. **1.** Directeur, -trice; surveillant, -ante. **2.** Police superintendent, officier m de paix.

superior. **1.** a. (a) Supérieur, -eure; d'une classe supérieure. To be superior to flattery, être au-dessus de la flatterie. (b) Sourcilleux, superbe. *With a s.* smile, avec un sourire suffisant. **2.** s. (a) Supérieur, -eure. (b) *Ecc:* The Father Superior, le père supérieur.

superiority, s. Supériorité f.

superlative. **1.** a. Suprême. **2.** a. & s. *Gram:* Superlatif (m). **-ly,** adv. *F:* Au suprême degré.

superman, s. Surhomme m.

supernatural, a. Surnaturel.

supernumerary. **1.** a. Surnuméraire. **2.** s. (a) Surnuméraire m. (b) *Th:* Figurant, -ante.

superpose, v.tr. Superposer (*upon, on,* à).

superposition, s. Superposition f.

superscribe, v.tr. **1.** Marquer d'une inscription. **2.** Mettre l'adresse sur.

superscription, s. Inscription f; (*on coin*) légende f; (*on letter*) adresse f, suscription f; (*on document*) en-tête m, pl. en-têtes.

supersede, v.tr. (a) Remplacer. (b) Prendre la place de; supplanter.

superstition, s. Superstition f.

superstitious, a. Superstitieux. **-ly,** adv. Superstitieusement.

supervene, v.i. Survenir.

supervise, v.tr. **1.** Avoir l'œil sur, surveiller. **2.** Diriger, conduire.

supervision, s. **1.** Surveillance f. **2.** Direction f.

supervisor, s. Surveillant, -ante; directeur, -trice.

supine, a. **1.** Couché, étendu, sur le dos. **2.** *F:* Mou, f. molle; indolent, inerte.

supineness, s. Mollesse f, inertie f.

supper, s. Souper m. To have supper, souper. The Last Supper, la (Sainte) Cène.

supper-time, s. Heure f du souper.

supplant, v.tr. Supplanter; prendre la place de; évincer.

supplanter, s. Supplantateur, -trice.

supple, a. Souple. **1.** Liant, pliable. **2.** Obséquieux, complaisant. **-ply,** adv. Souplement; avec souplesse.

supplement[1], s. Supplément m.

supplement[2], v.tr. Ajouter à. To supplement one's income, augmenter ses revenus.

supplementary, a. Supplémentaire (*to,* de); additionnel (*to,* à).

suppleness, s. **1.** Souplesse f, flexibilité f. **2.** Complaisance f, obséquiosité f.

suppliant, a. Suppliant.

supplicant, s. Suppliant, -ante.

supplicate, v.i. & tr. Supplier.

supplication, s. **1.** Supplication f. **2.** Supplique f.

supplier, s. Fournisseur, -euse; pourvoyeur, -euse (*of,* de).

supply[1], s. **1.** (a) Approvisionnement m, fourniture f. (b) *To hold a post* on supply, occuper une place par intérim. **2.** (a) Provision f. *To lay in* a supply of sth., se faire une provision de qch. *Pol.Ec:* Supply and demand, l'offre f et la demande. (b) pl. Supplies. Fournitures f. Food supplies, vivres m (c) Suppléant, -ante; *F:* intérim m.

supply[2], v.tr. **1.** (a) To supply s.o. with sth., fournir, pourvoir, qn de qch. *The tradesmen who s. us,* nos fournisseurs m. (b) To supply sth., fournir, apporter, qch. **2.** (a) Réparer (une omission); remplir (une vacance). To supply s.o.'s needs, fournir aux besoins de qn. (b) To supply s.o.'s place, remplacer qn.

support[1], s. **1.** (a) Appui m, soutien m. Moral support, appui moral. (b) *To be without means of support,* être sans ressources. **2.** (a) *The sole support of his old age,* son seul soutien dans sa vieillesse. (b) Appui, support m, soutien.

support[2], v.tr. **1.** Supporter, soutenir, appuyer, maintenir. **2.** Appuyer; soutenir (une théorie); patronner; faire une donation à. **3.** Entretenir. To support a family, faire vivre une famille. To support oneself, gagner sa vie. **4.** Supporter, tolérer.

supporter, s. **1.** Soutien m, support m. **2.** Défenseur m; partisan, -ane.

suppose, v.tr. Supposer. (a) Suppose you

are right, supposons, supposé, que vous ayez raison. *Supposing he came back*, si par supposition il revenait. *F:* **Suppose we change the subject**, si nous changions de sujet. *(b)* S'imaginer ; croire, penser. *You will do it*, I suppose, je suppose que vous le ferez. *I don't s. he will do it*, je ne suppose pas qu'il le fasse. *Will you go?*—I suppose so, irez-vous ?—Probablement ; sans doute. *I declined*, as you may suppose, vous pensez bien que j'ai refusé. **He is supposed to be wealthy**, il est censé être riche. **supposed**, *a.* Supposé, prétendu ; soi-disant.

supposedly, *adv.* Censément ; soi-disant.

supposition, *s.* Supposition *f*, hypothèse *f*.

suppress, *v.tr.* **1.** *(a)* Réprimer. *(b)* Supprimer. **2.** Étouffer ; faire taire (un interrupteur). **3.** Cacher, dissimuler. **suppressed**, *a.* *S. anger*, colère réprimée. *S. excitement*, agitation contenue. *In a s. voice*, en baissant la voix.

suppression, *s.* **1.** Répression *f* ; suppression *f*. **2.** Étouffement *m* ; refoulement *m* (des émotions). **3.** Dissimulation *f*.

supremacy, *s.* Suprématie *f* (*over*, sur).

supreme, *a.* Suprême. **To reign supreme**, régner en maître. *Jur:* Supreme court, cour souveraine. **To hold s.o. in supreme contempt**, avoir un souverain mépris pour qn. **-ly**, *adv.* Suprêmement ; au suprême degré.

surcharge¹, *s.* **1.** Droit *m* supplémentaire ; surtaxe *f*. **2.** Surcharge *f* (sur un timbre-poste).

surcharge², *v.tr.* **1.** (Sur)taxer. **2.** Surcharger (un timbre-poste).

sure. I. *a.* Sûr, certain. *(a)* *I am s. of it*, j'en ai la certitude. *F:* **I'm sure I don't know**, ma foi, je ne sais pas. **To make sure of a fact**, s'assurer d'un fait. *(b)* Infaillible ; (asile) assuré. *(c)* Indubitable. *F:* **Sure thing**, chose certaine. **To-morrow for sure**, demain sans faute. *(d)* **It is sure to be fine**, il fera sûrement beau. **He is sure to come**, il viendra sûrement. **Be sure to come early**, ne manquez pas d'arriver de bonne heure. **Be sure not to lose it**, prenez garde de le perdre. **(Yes,) to be sure!** certainement ! bien sûr ! **Well, to be sure!** tiens, tiens ! par exemple ! **2.** *adv.* **As sure as fate**, aussi sûr que deux et deux font quatre. **Sure enough**, *he was there*, il était bien là. **-ly**, *adv.* **1.** Sûrement. **2.** *(a)* *Lit:* Assurément. *(b)* *F:* **Surely you don't believe that!** vous ne croyez pas cela, voyons ! **sure-footed**, *a.* Au pied sûr.

sureness, *s.* **1.** Sûreté *f* (de pied). **2.** Certitude *f*.

surety, *s.* Caution *f* ; garant, -ante.

surf, *s.* Barre *f* de plage ; ressac *m* ; brisants *mpl* sur la plage. **surf-board**, *s.* *Sp:* Aquaplane *m*. **surf-boat**, *s.* Pirogue *f* de barre. **surf-rider**, *s.* *Sp:* Chevaucheur *m* de ressac. **surf-riding**, *s.* Sport *m* de l'aquaplane.

surface, *s.* **1.** *(a)* Surface *f*. *(b)* *F:* Extérieur *m*, dehors *m*. **On the surface** *everything was well*, tout allait bien en apparence. **2.** Aire *f*, étendue *f*, superficie *f*.

surfeit¹, *s.* **1.** Surabondance *f*. **2.** *(a)* Réplétion *f* ; satiété *f*. *(b)* Dégoût *m* ; nausée *f*.

surfeit², *v.tr.* **To surfeit oneself with sth.**, se gorger de qch. jusqu'à la nausée.

surge¹, *s.* *Nau:* Levée *f* de la lame ; houle *f*. *F: A s. of anger*, une vague de colère.

surge², *v.i.* *The crowd surged along the street*, la foule se répandit en flots dans la rue. *The blood surged to her cheeks*, le sang lui reflua au visage.

surgeon, *s.* **1.** Chirurgien, -ienne. **2.** *Navy:* Médecin.

surgery, *s.* **1.** Chirurgie *f* ; médecine *f* opératoire. **2.** Cabinet *m* de consultation ; dispensaire *m* (d'un hôpital) ; clinique *f*.

surgical, *a.* Chirurgical, -aux.

surliness, *s.* Air bourru ; maussaderie *f*.

surly, *a.* *(a)* Bourru. *(b)* Hargneux, maussade.

surmise¹, *s.* Conjecture *f*, supposition *f*.

surmise², *v.tr.* Conjecturer, deviner.

surmount, *v.tr.* Surmonter.

surname, *s.* Nom *m* de famille.

surpass, *v.tr.* **1.** Surpasser. *You have surpassed yourself*, vous avez été au-dessus de vous-même. **2.** *The result surpassed my hopes*, le résultat a excédé mes espérances. **surpassing**, *a.* Sans pareil. **-ly**, *adv.* Extrêmement, excessivement.

surplice, *s.* Surplis *m*.

surplus, *s.* **1.** Surplus *m*, excédent *m*. **To have a surplus of sth.**, avoir qch. en excès. **2.** *Attrib.* Sale of surplus stock, vente de soldes *m*.

surprise¹, *s.* Surprise *f*. **1.** **To take s.o. by surprise**, prendre qn à l'improviste, au dépourvu. **2.** **To give s.o. a surprise**, faire une surprise à qn. **3.** Étonnement *m*. **Much to my surprise**, à ma grande surprise.

surprise², *v.tr.* Surprendre. **1.** **To surprise s.o. in the act**, prendre qn sur le fait. **2.** Étonner. **To be surprised at sth.**, être surpris de qch. *I am surprised to see you*, je m'étonne de vous voir. *I am surprised at you!* vous m'étonnez ! **surprising**, *a.* Surprenant, étonnant.

surrender¹, *s.* **1.** *(a)* Reddition *f* (d'une forteresse). *(b)* **No surrender!** on ne se rend pas ! **2.** Abandon *m*, cession *f* (de biens) ; remise *f* (des armes à feu).

surrender². 1. *v.tr.* *(a)* Rendre, livrer. *(b)* Abandonner, céder. **2.** *v.pr. & i.* **To surrender (oneself)**, se rendre. **To surrender (oneself) to justice**, se livrer à la justice.

surreptitious, *a.* Subreptice, clandestin. **-ly**, *adv.* Subrepticement, clandestinement.

surround¹, *s.* Encadrement *m*, bordure *f*.

surround², *v.tr.* Entourer. *(a)* **Surrounded by dangers**, entouré de dangers. *(b)* *Mil:*

Entourer, cerner. **surrounding,** *a.* Entourant, environnant. **surroundings,** *s.pl.* **1.** Entourage *m*, milieu *m.* **2.** Environs *mpl*, alentours *mpl.*
surtax, *s.* Surtaxe *f.*
surveillance, *s.* Surveillance *f*, contrôle *m.*
survey[1]. *s.* **1.** (*a*) Aperçu *m*; vue générale. (*b*) Examen attentif; étude *f* (de la situation). **2.** *Surv:* (*a*) Levé *m* des plans; relevé. *m.* (*b*) Plan *m*, levé (du terrain). **3.** Inspection *f*, visite *f.*
survey[2], *v.tr.* **1.** (*a*) Regarder, contempler. (*b*) Mettre à l'étude; passer en revue. **2.** *Surv:* Relever; lever le(s) plan(s) de. **3.** Inspecter; visiter.
surveyor, *s.* **1.** (Land-)surveyor, arpenteur *m* (géomètre). **2.** *Adm:* Surveillant *m*, inspecteur *m.*
survival, *s.* Survivance *f.* Survival of the fittest, survivance des mieux adaptés.
survive. 1. *v.i.* Survivre; (*of custom*) subsister. **2.** *v.tr. To s. an injury,* survivre à une blessure.
survivor, *s.* Survivant, -ante. *The survivors of the disaster,* les rescapé(e)s.
Susan. *Pr.n.* Suzanne *f.*
susceptibility, *s.* **1.** Susceptibility to a disease, prédisposition *f* à une maladie. **2.** Sensibilité *f*, susceptibilité.
susceptible, *a.* **1.** (*a*) Susceptible of proof, susceptible d'être prouvé. (*b*) Susceptible to a disease, prédisposé à une maladie. **2.** (*a*) Sensible, impressionnable. (*b*) Qui se froisse facilement; susceptible.
suspect[1], *a. & s.* Suspect, -e.
suspect[2], *v.tr.* **1.** Soupçonner. To be suspected, être en suspicion. **2.** Soupçonner, s'imaginer. I suspected as much, je m'en doutais.
suspend, *v.tr.* Suspendre. **1.** Pendre. **2.** Suspendre (le travail). *Jur: To suspend judgment,* surseoir au jugement. **3.** Suspendre (un fonctionnaire). **suspended,** *a.* Suspendu. **1.** *S. particles,* particules en suspension. **2.** (*Of traffic*) Interrompu. Suspended animation, arrêt momentané des fonctions vitales.
suspender, *s.* (*a*) (Stocking) suspender, jarretelle *f.* (*b*) *pl.* Suspenders, bretelles *f.*
suspense, *s.* Suspens *m.* To keep s.o. in suspense, tenir qn en suspens.
suspension, *s.* **1.** Suspension *f* (de la circulation). **2.** Suspension (d'un fonctionnaire).
suspension-bridge, *s.* Pont suspendu.
suspicion, *s.* **1.** Soupçon *m.* With suspicion, avec défiance *f.* To have suspicions about s.o., avoir des doutes sur qn; soupçonner qn. To arouse suspicion, éveiller les soupçons. Above suspicion, au-dessus de tout soupçon. *Evidence not beyond s.,* témoignages sujets à caution. *Jur: To detain s.o. on suspicion,* détenir qn préventivement. **2.** *F: I had my suspicions about it,* je m'en doutais. **3.** Très petite quantité, soupçon (*of*, de).

suspicious, *a.* **1.** Soupçonnable, suspect; (*of conduct*) louche, équivoque. **2.** Méfiant, soupçonneux. *To be s. of s.o.,* avoir des soupçons à l'égard de qn. **-ly,** *adv.* **1.** D'une manière suspecte, équivoque, louche. **To look suspiciously like . . .,** avoir tout l'air d'être . . . . **2.** D'un air méfiant; soupçonneusement.
suspiciousness, *s.* **1.** Caractère suspect, louche (*of*, de). **2.** Méfiance *f.*
sustain, *v.tr.* Soutenir, supporter. **1.** Enough to sustain life, de quoi entretenir la vie. *Mus: To sustain a note,* soutenir, prolonger, une note. **2.** To sustain a loss, éprouver, subir, une perte. To sustain an injury, recevoir une blessure. **sustained,** *a.* Soutenu. *S. applause,* applaudissements prolongés, nourris. **sustaining,** *a.* Sustaining food, nourriture fortifiante.
sustenance, *s.* Aliments *mpl*, nourriture *f.*
suzerain, *s.* Suzerain *m.*
suzeraine, *s.* Suzeraine *f.*
suzerainty, *s.* Suzeraineté *f.*
swab[1], *s.* **1.** (*a*) Torchon *m.* (*b*) *Surg:* Swab of cotton wool, tampon *m* d'ouate. **2.** *P:* Lourdaud *m*, propre à rien.
swab[2], *v.tr.* Nettoyer, essuyer (avec un torchon).
swaddle, *v.tr.* Emmailloter (*with*, de).
swaddling-clothes, *s.pl.* Maillot *m.*
swag, *s. P:* (*a*) Rafle *f*, butin *m* (d'un cambrioleur). (*b*) Paquet *m* (de chemineau).
swagger[1], *a.* Élégant; ultra-chic.
swagger[2], *s.* **1.** (*a*) Air important. To walk with a swagger, marcher avec un air avantageux. (*b*) Air cavalier, désinvolte. **2.** Rodomontades *fpl.* **swagger-cane,** *s. Mil:* Jonc *m* de tenue de sortie.
swagger[3], *v.i.* (*a*) Crâner, se pavaner. (*b*) Fanfaronner. (*c*) To swagger in, entrer d'un air important. **swaggering,** *a.* Important, crâneur.
swaggerer, *s.* Crâneur, -euse.
swain, *s.* (*a*) *Poet:* Amoureux *m* (de pastorale). (*b*) *Hum:* Soupirant *m.*
swallow[1], *s.* **1.** Gosier *m.* **2.** Gorgée *f.*
swallow[2], *v.tr.* Avaler; gober. *F: To swallow one's tears,* dévorer ses larmes. To swallow one's pride, mettre son orgueil dans sa poche. **To swallow a story,** gober, avaler, une histoire. **swallow up,** *v.tr.* (i) Dévorer, avaler; (ii) engloutir, engouffrer.
swallow[3], *s.* Hirondelle *f.* **swallow-tail,** *s. Cost: F:* Queue-de-morue *f.* **swallow-tailed,** *a.* A queue fourchue.
swamp[1], *s.* Marais *m*, marécage *m.*
swamp[2], *v.tr.* **1.** Inonder, submerger. **2.** (*a*) Remplir d'eau. (*b*) *F: To be swamped with work,* être débordé de travail.
swampy, *a.* Marécageux.
swan, *s.* Cygne *m.* **swan-song,** *s.* Chant *m* du cygne.
swank[1], *s. F:* **1.** Prétention *f*, gloriole *f*, épate *f.* **2.** = SWANKER.

swank², *v.i.* *F:* Se donner des airs ; crâner.
swanker, *s.* *F:* Épateur, -euse ; crâneur, -euse.
swanky, *a.* *F:* Prétentieux, poseur, -euse.
swap¹, *s.* (*a*) Tróc *m*, échange *m*. (*b*) *pl.* (*In stamp-collecting*) Swaps, doubles *m*.
swap², *v.tr.* *F:* To swap sth. for sth., troquer qch. contre, pour, qch. To swap places with s.o., changer de place avec qn.
swapping, *s.* Échange *m*, troc *m*.
sward, *s.* Gazon *m* ; pelouse *f*.
swarm¹, *s.* Essaim *m*, jetée *f*. *F:* Swarm of children, essaim, troupe *f*, d'enfants.
swarm², *v.i.* **1.** (*a*) Essaimer. (*b*) *F:* Pulluler, grouiller. **2.** To swarm with, fourmiller, grouiller, de.
swarm³, *v.tr. & i.* To swarm (up) a tree, monter, grimper, à un arbre.
swarthiness, *s.* Teint basané, bistré.
swarthy, *a.* Basané, bistré, boucané.
swash, *s.* Clapotement *m*, clapotis *m*.
swashbuckler, *s.* Brétailleur *m*, matamore *m*.
swashbuckling¹, *a.* Brétailleur, fanfaron.
swashbuckling², *s.* Fanfaronnades *fpl.*
swastika, *s.* Svastika *m* ; croix gammée.
swat, *v.tr.* *P:* Frapper. *S. that fly!* écrasez donc cette mouche !
swath, *s.* *Husb:* Andain *m*, fauchée *f*.
swathe, *v.tr.* Emmailloter ; envelopper (*in*, de). **swathing**, *s.* Emmaillotement *m*, enveloppement *m*.
sway¹, *s.* **1.** Balancement *m*, oscillation *f*. **2.** Empire *m*, domination *f*. Under his sway, sous son influence *f*.
sway². **1.** *v.i.* (*a*) Se balancer ; osciller ; ballotter. (*b*) Rester indécis ; balancer. (*c*) Pencher ; incliner. **2.** *v.tr.* (*a*) Faire osciller ; balancer. (*b*) Gouverner, diriger, influencer.
swear¹, *s.* Jurons *mpl.* **swear-word**, *s.* *F:* Gros mot ; juron *m*.
swear², *v.* **I.** *v.tr.* (*a*) Jurer. To swear to do sth., jurer de faire qch. (*b*) To be sworn (in), prêter serment. To swear s.o. to secrecy, faire jurer le secret à qn. (*c*) Déclarer sous la foi du serment. **2.** *v.i.* Jurer ; proférer un juron. **swear at**, *v.ind.tr.* Maudire.
swear by, *v.i.* **1.** To swear by one's honour, jurer sa foi. **2.** Préconiser, vanter. **swear to**, *v.ind.tr.* Attester, certifier, sous serment. *I would s. to it*, j'en jurerais. **sworn**, *a.* **1.** Sworn official, fonctionnaire assermenté. Sworn enemies, ennemis jurés, acharnés. **2.** Sworn statement, déclaration sous serment.
swearing, *s.* **1.** (*a*) Attestation *f* sous serment. (*b*) Prestation *f* de serment. **2.** Jurons *mpl* ; gros mots.
sweat¹, *s.* Sueur *f*, transpiration *f*. By the sweat of one's brow, à la sueur de son front.
sweat². **I.** *v.i.* **1.** (*a*) Suer, transpirer. (*b*) (*Of worker*) Peiner. **2.** (*Of walls*) Suer, suinter. **II.** sweat, *v.tr.* (*a*) Suer. (*b*) Faire suer (qn). (*c*) Exploiter (la main-d'œuvre). **sweated**, *a.* (Travail) mal rétribué.

sweating, *s.* **1.** Transpiration *f*. **2.** Exploitation *f* (de la main-d'œuvre).
sweater, *s.* *Cost:* Chandail *m*.
Swede, *s.* **1.** Suédois, -oise. **2.** *Agr:* Rutabaga *m* ; navet *m* de Suède.
Sweden. *Pr.n.* La Suède.
Swedish. **1.** *a.* Suédois. **2.** *s.* *Ling:* Le suédois.
sweep¹, *s.* **1.** (*a*) Coup *m* de balai, de faux. At one sweep, d'un seul coup. (*b*) Balayage *m*. *F:* To make a clean sweep of sth., faire table rase de qch. **2.** Mouvement *m* circulaire (du bras). With a s. of the arm, d'un geste large. **3.** Course *f* rapide (d'un fleuve). **4.** (*a*) Courbe *f* ; boucle *f* (d'une rivière). (*b*) Fine sweep of grass, belle étendue de gazon. (*c*) Envergure *f*. **5.** Aviron *m* de queue. **6.** *Nau:* Câble balayeur ; drague *f* (pour mines). **7.** (Chimney-)sweep, ramoneur *m*. **8.** *F:* = SWEEPSTAKE.
sweep², *v.* **I.** *v.tr.* **1.** (*a*) Balayer ; ramoner (une cheminée). To sweep the horizon with a telescope, parcourir l'horizon avec une lunette. To sweep the board, faire table rase. (*b*) Draguer. *Abs.* To sweep for mines, draguer des mines. **2.** (*a*) Balayer (la poussière). (*b*) Emporter, entraîner. **II.** sweep, *v.i.* **1.** *The plain sweeps (away) towards the north*, la plaine s'étend vers le nord. **2.** *She swept into the room*, elle entra dans la salle d'un air majestueux. **sweep along**, *v.tr.* (*Of current*) Entraîner, emporter. **sweep aside**, *v.tr.* Écarter d'un geste large. **sweep away**, *v.tr.* Balayer ; supprimer, détruire. *Bridge swept away by the torrent*, pont emporté, balayé, par le torrent. **sweep down**, **1.** *v.tr.* *The current sweeps the logs down with it*, le courant entraîne, charrie, le bois. **2.** *v.i.* (*a*) *The enemy swept down upon us*, l'ennemi s'abattit sur nous. (*b*) *Hills sweeping down to the sea*, collines qui dévalent vers la mer. **sweep off**, *v.tr.* Enlever, emporter, avec violence. To sweep off one's feet, entraîner. **sweep on**, *v.i.* Continuer d'avancer (irrésistiblement). **sweep out**, *v.tr.* Balayer. **sweep up**, *v.tr.* Balayer, ramasser.
sweeping¹, *a.* **1.** Sweeping gesture, geste large. **2.** Sweeping statement, déclaration par trop générale. Sweeping reform, réforme complète. Sweeping changes, changement de fond en comble. **sweeping²**, *s.* **1.** Balayage *m* ; ramonage *m* (d'une cheminée). **2.** *pl.* Sweepings, balayures *f*. *F:* The sweepings of society, le rebut de la société.
sweeper, *s.* **1.** Balayeur, -euse. **2.** (*Machine*) Balayeuse *f* (mécanique).
sweepstake, *s.* Poule *f* ; sweepstake *m*.
sweet. **I.** *a.* Doux, *f.* douce. **1.** Sucré. As sweet as honey, doux comme (le) miel. Sweet stuff, bonbons *mpl*, friandises *fpl*. To have a sweet tooth, aimer les douceurs. *F:* Sweet morsel, morceau succulent. **2.** Sweet violet, violette odorante. To smell sweet, sentir bon. **3.** (Son) doux, mélodieux. **4.** (*a*)

Sweet temper, caractère doux, aimable. *Revenge is s* la vengeance est douce. (b) *F:* Charmant, gentil, *f.* gentille. **5.** *F:* To be sweet on s.o., être amoureux de qn. **-ly,** *adv.* **1.** (a) Doucement; avec douceur. (b) (Chanter) mélodieusement. **2.** Agréablement, *F:* gentiment. II. **sweet,** *s.* **1.** (a) Bonbon *m.* **Sweets,** sucreries *f.* (b) (*At dinner*) Entremets sucré. **2.** *pl.* **Sweets,** douceurs *f.* **sweet-smelling,** *a.* Qui sent bon, qui embaume; au parfum délicieux. **sweet-tempered,** *a.* Au caractère doux. **sweet-william,** *s.* *Bot:* Œillet *m* de poète. **sweetbread,** *s.* *Cu:* Ris *m* de veau, d'agneau. **sweeten,** *v.tr.* (a) Sucrer. (b) Purifier. (c) Adoucir (la vie). **sweetening,** *s.* **1.** Adoucissement *m*; sucrage *m.* **2.** Substance *f* pour sucrer.

sweetheart, *s.* Amoureux, -euse.

sweetish, *a.* Douceâtre.

sweetmeat, *s.* Bonbon *m.* **Sweetmeats,** sucreries *f.*

sweetness, *s.* **1.** Douceur *f.* **2.** *F:* Gentillesse *f*, charme *m.*

swell¹. I. *s.* **1.** (a) Bosse *f*; renflement *m.* (b) Swell of ground, éminence *f*, ondulation *f.* **2.** *Nau:* Houle *f.* **3.** (a) *F:* Élégant *m.* (b) *P:* Gros personnage. **The swells,** les gens chics. II. **swell,** *a.* Chic *m & f*, élégant.

swell², *v.* **I.** *v.tr.* (R)enfler, gonfler. *Eyes swollen with tears,* yeux gonflés de larmes. To swell the crowd, augmenter la foule. **2.** *v.i.* (a) To swell (up), (s')enfler, se gonfler; augmenter, grossir. (b) (*Of sea*) Se soulever. (c) To swell out, être bombé; bomber. **swollen,** *a.* Enflé, gonflé. **1.** (a) *The river is s.,* la rivière est en crue. (b) **To have a swollen face,** avoir une fluxion à la joue. **2.** *P:* To suffer from swelled head, être pénétré de sa propre importance. **swollen-headed,** *a.* *P:* Vaniteux, suffisant. **swelling,** *s.* **1.** Enflement *m*, gonflement *m.* **2.** *Med:* Tuméfaction *f*; boursouflement *m.* **3.** Bosse *f*, enflure *f* (au front); fluxion *f* (à la joue).

swelter, *v.i.* (a) Étouffer de chaleur. (b) Être en nage. **sweltering,** *a.* **1.** En nage. **2.** Sweltering heat, chaleur étouffante, accablante.

swerve¹, *s.* Écart *m*, déviation *f.*

swerve², *v.i.* Faire un écart, un crochet. (*of horse*) se dérober.

swift. I. *a.* (a) Rapide; vite. As swift as thought, rapide comme la pensée. (b) Prompt. **-ly,** *adv.* Vite, rapidement. II. **swift,** *adv.* Vite, rapidement. III. **swift,** *s.* *Orn:* Martinet. **swift-flowing,** *a.* (Rivière) au cours rapide. **swift-footed,** *a.* Au pied léger.

swiftness, *s.* **1.** Rapidité *f*, vitesse *f.* **2.** Promptitude *f.*

swig¹, *s.* *P:* Grand trait, lampée *f.*

swig², *v.tr.* *P:* Boire à grands traits.

swill, *v.tr.* Laver à grande eau.

swim¹, *s.* **1.** Action *f* de nager. To have a swim, faire un peu de nage. **2.** *F:* To be in the swim, être dans le mouvement. **swim²,** *v.* **I.** *v.i.* **1.** (a) Nager. To swim across a river, traverser une rivière à la nage. (b) To swim a stroke, faire une brasse. *F:* He can't swim a stroke, il nage comme un chien de plomb. (c) *Meat swimming in gravy,* viande noyée dans la sauce. (d) Surnager, flotter. **2.** Eyes swimming with tears, yeux inondés de larmes. **3.** (a) *My head is swimming,* la tête me tourne. (b) *Everything swam before my eyes,* tout semblait tourner autour de moi. II. **swim,** *v.tr.* **1.** Traverser, passer, à la nage. **2.** Faire nager (un cheval). **swimming¹,** *a.* **1.** Swimming eyes, yeux noyés de larmes. **2.** Swimming head, tête qui tourne. **-ly,** *adv.* *F:* Comme sur des roulettes; à merveille. **swimming²,** *s.* **1.** Nage *f*, natation *f.* **2.** Swimming of the head, vertige *m.* **swimming-bath,** *s.* Piscine *f.* **swimming-pool,** *s.* Piscine *f* (en plein air).

swimmer, *s.* Nageur, -euse.

swindle¹, *s.* **1.** Escroquerie *f*, filouterie *f.* **2.** *F:* Duperie *f.* **3.** *F:* Déception *f.*

swindle², *v.tr.* Escroquer, filouter. To swindle s.o. out of sth., escroquer qch. à qn.

swindler, *s.* Filou *m*, escroc *m.*

swine, *s.inv.* **1.** Cochon *m*, porc *m*; pourceau *m.* **2.** *P:* He's a s., c'est un salaud.

swing¹, *s.* **1.** Balancement *m.* **2.** (a) Oscillation *f.* To be in full swing, (*of fête*) battre son plein; (*of factory*) être en plein travail. Swing-to of the door, rabattement *m* de la porte. (b) To give a child a swing, balancer un enfant. **3.** (a) Amplitude *f* (d'une oscillation). (b) Évitage *m* (d'un navire à l'ancre). **4.** To walk with a swing, marcher d'un pas rythmé. Song that goes with a swing, chanson entraînante. *F:* Everything went with a swing, tout a très bien marché. *When you have got into the s. of things,* quand vous serez au courant. **5.** Escarpolette *f*, balançoire *f.*

swing-boat, *s.* Bateau *m* balançoire. **swing-bridge,** *s.* Pont tournant. **swing-door,** *s.* Porte battante.

swing², *v.* **I.** *v.i.* **1.** (a) To swing to and fro, se balancer; (*of bell*) branler; (*of pendulum*) osciller; *P:* être pendu. To set the bells swinging, mettre les cloches en branle. (b) Tourner, pivoter; basculer. (c) (*Of ship*) To swing (at anchor), éviter (sur l'ancre). (d) *Games:* Se balancer. **2.** Changer de direction. To swing round, faire volte-face. The car swung right round, la voiture a fait un tête-à-queue. **3.** To swing along, marcher d'un pas rythmé. II. **swing,** *v.tr.* **1.** (Faire) balancer; faire osciller. To s. one's arms, balancer les bras. **2.** (a) *Nau:* Boat swung out, embarcation parée au dehors. (b) Faire tourner. *Av:* To swing the propeller, lancer, brasser, l'hélice. **3.** *To s. a hammock,* pendre, (ac)crocher, un hamac. **4.** *v.pr. & i.* To

swing (oneself) into the saddle, monter vivement à cheval. **swing back**, *v.i.* **1.** Basculer; se rabattre. **2.** (*Of pendulum*) Revenir. **swinging**[1], *a.* **1.** Balançant, oscillant; (bras) ballants. **2.** *S. stride*, allure rythmée, cadencée. **swinging**[2], *s.* **1.** (*a*) Balancement *m*, oscillation *f.* (*b*) Mouvement *m* de bascule ou de rotation. **2.** *Av:* Lancement *m* (de l'hélice).
swinish, *a.* De cochon; sale.
swipe[1], *s.* **1.** *Cr:* Coup *m* à toute volée. **2.** *F:* Taloche *f.*
swipe[2], *v.tr. & ind.tr. Cr:* To swipe (at) the ball, frapper la balle à toute volée.
swirl[1], *s.* Remous *m* (de l'eau). *A s. of dust*, un tourbillon de poussière.
swirl[2], *v.i.* Tournoyer, tourbillonner.
swish[1], *s.* **1.** Bruissement *m* (de l'eau); froufrou *m* (d'une robe); sifflement *m* (d'un fouet). **2.** Coup *m* de fouet.
swish[2]. **1.** *v.i.* (*Of water*) Bruire. **2.** *v.tr.* (*a*) Fouetter. (*b*) Faire siffler (sa canne). (*c*) (*Of animal*) *To s. its tail*, battre l'air de sa queue.
Swiss. 1. *a.* Suisse. **2.** *s.* Suisse, -esse.
switch[1], *s.* **1.** (*a*) Badine *f*; houssine *f.* Riding switch, houssine. (*b*) Coup *m* de baguette. **2.** (*a*) *Rail:* Aiguille *f*; changement *m* de voie. (*b*) *El.E:* Interrupteur *m*; commutateur *m.*
switch[2], *v.tr.* **1.** (*a*) Donner un coup de badine à. (*b*) (*Of animal*) To switch its tail, battre l'air de sa queue. **2.** To switch a train, aiguiller, dériver, un train. **switch off**, *v.tr. El:* Interrompre, couper; *abs.* ouvrir le circuit. To switch off the light, couper la lumière. To switch off the wireless, *abs.* to switch off, arrêter la T.S.F. **switch on**, *v.tr. To s. on the current, abs.* to switch on, donner du courant. To switch on the light, allumer (l'électricité). To switch on the wireless, tourner le bouton.
switchback, *s.* Montagnes *f* russes.
switchboard, *s. El.E:* Tableau *m* de distribution.
Swithin. *Pr.n.* St Swithin's day, = la Saint-Médard.
Switzerland. *Pr.n.* La Suisse.
swivel[1], *s.* (*a*) Émerillon *m*; maillon tournant. (*b*) Pivot *m*; tourillon *m.*
swivel[2], *v.i.* Pivoter, tourner.
swizz(le), *s. P:* = SWINDLE[1].
swoon[1], *s.* Évanouissement *m*, défaillance *f.*
swoon[2], *v.i.* S'évanouir, défaillir. **swooning**, *a.* (*a*) Défaillant. (*b*) Évanoui.
swoop[1], *s.* Abat(t)ée*f* (*upon*, sur). *F:* At one (fell) swoop, d'un seul coup (fatal).
swoop[2], *v.i.* To swoop down upon sth., s'abattre, foncer, sur qch.
swop[1,2], *s. & v.tr.* = SWAP[1,2].
sword, *s.* (*a*) Épée *f.* To cross swords with s.o., *F:* mesurer ses forces avec qn. To put to (the edge of) the sword, passer au fil de l'épée. (*b*) Sabre *m.* With drawn sword,

sabre au clair. **sword-arm**, *s.* Le bras droit. **sword-belt**, *s.* Ceinturon *m.* **sword-cut**, *s.* Coup *m* de sabre; (*on face*) balafre *f.* **sword-fish**, *s. Ich:* Espadon *m.* **sword-play**, *s.* Maniement *m* de l'épée; escrime *f.* **sword-stick**, *s.* Canne *f* à épée. **sword-thrust**, *s.* Coup *m* de pointe; coup d'épée.
swordsman, *s.* Épéiste *m*; tireur *m* d'épée. *Fine s.*, fine lame.
swordsmanship, *s.* Maniement *m* de l'épée; escrime *f* (à l'épée).
swot[1], *s. P:* **1.** (*a*) *Sch:* Travail *m* intense. (*b*) Corvée *f.* **2.** (*Pers.*) Bûcheur, -euse.
swot[2], *v.tr. & i. Sch: P:* Bûcher, piocher. *To s. for an exam*, bûcher un examen.
sybarite, *a. & s.* Sybarite (*mf*).
sycamore, *s.* Sycomore *m*; faux platane.
sycophancy, *s.* Flagornerie *f.*
sycophant, *s.* Flagorneur, -euse.
syllabic(al), *a.* Syllabique.
syllable, *s.* Syllabe *f.*
syllabus, *s.* Programme *m.*
sylph, *s.* **1.** Sylphe *m*, sylphide *f.* **2.** *F:* (*Applied to a woman*) Sylphide. **sylph-like**, *a. F:* (Taille) de sylphide.
sylvan, *a.* Sylvestre.
symbol, *s.* **1.** Symbole *m*, emblème *m.* **2.** *Ch:* Symbole.
symbolic(al), *a.* Symbolique. **-ally**, *adv.* Symboliquement.
symmetrical, *a.* Symétrique. **-ally**, *adv.* Symétriquement.
symmetry, *s.* Symétrie *f.*
sympathetic, *a.* **1.** Sympathetic ink, encre sympathique. **2.** (*a*) *S. glance*, regard de sympathie. (*b*) *S. audience*, auditoire bien disposé. (*c*) Compatissant. **-ally**, *adv.* **1.** Sympathiquement. **2.** D'une manière compatissante.
sympathize, *v.i.* **1.** To sympathize with s.o., avoir de la compassion pour qn. **2.** To sympathize with s.o.'s point of view, comprendre le point de vue de qn. **sympathizing**, *a.* Compatissant.
sympathizer, *s.* **1.** *To be a s. in s.o.'s grief*, compatir au chagrin de qn. **2.** Partisan, -ane.
sympathy, *s.* **1.** Compassion *f. Accept my deep s.*, agréez mes condoléances. **2.** (*a*) Sympathie *f* (*for s.o.*, à l'égard de qn). Popular sympathy is on his side, il a l'opinion pour lui. *I know you are in s. with them*, je sais que vous êtes de leur côté. To strike in sympathy, se mettre en grève par solidarité. (*b*) Prices went up in sympathy, les prix sont montés par contre-coup.
symphonic, *a.* Symphonique.
symphony, *s.* Symphonie *f.* Symphony concert, concert *m* symphonique.
symposium, *s.* Recueil *m* d'articles.
symptom, *s.* Symptôme *m*; indice *m.* To show symptoms of, présenter des indices de.
synagogue, *s.* Synagogue *f.*
synchronism, *s.* Synchronisme *m.*

synchronize. 1. *v.tr.* Synchroniser. **2.** *v.i.* Arriver, avoir lieu, simultanément.
synchronous, *a.* Synchrone.
synchrony, *s.* Synchronisme *m.*
syncopate, *v.tr. Gram: Mus:* Syncoper.
syncopation, *s. Mus:* Syncope *f.*
syncope, *s. Med:* Syncope *f.*
syndic, *s.* Syndic *m.*
syndical, *a.* Syndical, -aux.
syndicate¹, *s. Com:* Syndicat *m.*
syndicate², *v.tr.* Syndiquer.
synod, *s. Ecc:* Synode *m,* concile *m.*
synonym, *s.* Synonyme *m.*
synonymous, *a.* Synonyme (*with,* de).
synopsis, *s.* Résumé *m,* sommaire *m.*
synoptic(al), *a.* Synoptique.
syntactic(al), *a.* Syntactique, syntaxique.
syntax, *s.* Syntaxe *f.*
synthesis, *s.* Synthèse *f.*

synthetic(al), *a.* Synthétique. **-ally,** *adv.* Synthétiquement.
Syria. *Pr.n.* La Syrie.
Syrian, *a. & s.* Syrien, -ienne.
syringa, *s. Bot:* Seringa *m.*
syringe¹, *s.* Seringue *f.*
syringe², *v.tr.* Seringuer.
syrup, *s.* **1.** Sirop *m.* **2.** Golden syrup, mélasse raffinée ; sirop de sucre.
syrupy, *a.* Sirupeux.
system, *s.* **1.** (*a*) Système *m. The feudal s.,* le régime féodal. *Anat:* **The digestive system,** l'appareil digestif. **The system,** l'organisme *m.* (*b*) Réseau. **2.** Méthode *f. To lack s.,* manquer de méthode, d'organisation.
systematic, *a.* Systématique, méthodique. *He is s.,* il a de l'ordre. **-ally,** *adv.* Systématiquement. *She does her work s.,* elle travaille avec méthode.

T

T, t, *s.* (La lettre) T, t *m.* *To cross one's t's,* *F:* mettre les points sur les i. *Adv.phr.* To a T, exactement. *That suits me to a T,* cela me va à merveille.
ta, *s. & int. F:* Merci (*m*).
tab, *s.* **1.** (*a*) Patte *f* (de vêtement). (*b*) Écusson *m,* insigne *m* (d'officier d'état-major). (*c*) Shoe-lace tab, ferret *m* de cordon de soulier. (*d*) (*For hanging up coat*) Attache *f.* **2.** Étiquette *f* (pour bagages).
tabby, *s.* **1.** Tabby (cat), *F:* chatte *f.* **2.** *F:* Vieille chipie.
tabernacle, *s.* Tabernacle *m.*
table, *s.* Table *f.* **1.** (*a*) Occasional table, guéridon *m.* Nest of tables, table gigogne. (*b*) To lay the table, mettre la table ; dresser le couvert. To clear the table, desservir. *Separate tables (at restaurant)* (service *m* par) petites tables. *Ecc:* The Communion table, la Sainte Table. **2.** *pl. F:* To turn the tables on s.o., renverser les rôles. **3.** Table, tableau *m.* Multiplication table, table de multiplication. **table-cover,** *s.* Tapis *m* de table. **table-fork,** *s.* Fourchette *f.* **table-knife,** *s.* Couteau *m* de table. **table-land,** *s. Ph.Geog:* Plateau (élevé). **table-linen,** *s.* Linge *m* de table. **table-spoon,** *s.* Cuiller *f* à soupe, à bouche. **table-talk,** *s.* Propos *mpl* de table. **table-tennis,** *s.* Tennis *m* de salon. **table-top,** *s.* Dessus *m* de table. **table-turning,** *s. Psychics:* Tables tournantes. **table-water,** *s.* Eau minérale.
tablespoonful, *s.* Cuillerée *f* à bouche.
tablet, *s.* **1.** Plaque commémorative. **2.** (*a*)

Pharm: Comprimé *m.* (*b*) **Tablet of soap,** pain *m* de savon.
taboo¹. 1. *s.* Tabou *m,* -ous. **2.** *Pred. a.* Interdit, proscrit.
taboo², *v.tr.* **1.** *Anthr:* Tabouer. **2.** *F:* Proscrire, interdire (qch.).
tabular, *a.* Tabulaire.
tabulate, *v.tr.* Disposer en forme de table(s) ; classifier ; cataloguer.
tacit, *a.* Tacite, implicite. **-ly,** *adv.* Tacitement.
taciturn, *a.* Taciturne.
taciturnity, *s.* Taciturnité *f.*
tack¹, *s.* **1.** Petit clou ; broquette *f;* pl. semence *f. F: To get down to brass tacks,* en venir au fait. **2.** *Needlw:* Long point ; point de bâti. **3.** *Nau:* To make a tack, courir un bord, une bordée. *F: To be on the right tack,* être sur la bonne voie.
tack². 1. *v.tr.* (*a*) To tack sth. (down), clouer qch. avec de la semence. *F: To tack sth.* (on) to sth., attacher qch. à qch. (*b*) *Needlw:* Faufiler, bâtir. **2.** *v.i. Nau:* To tack (about), (i) virer (de bord) ; (ii) tirer des bordées ; louvoyer. **tacking,** *s. Nau:* Virement *m* de bord.
tack³, *s.* Nourriture *f,* aliment *m.*
tackle¹, *s.* **1.** Attirail *m,* appareil *m,* engins *mpl.* **2.** Appareil de levage. **3.** *Fb:* Plaquage *m.*
tackle², *v.tr.* (*a*) Empoigner ; saisir à bras-le-corps ; s'attaquer à (une corvée). (*b*) *Fb:* Plaquer.
tact, *s.* Tact *m,* savoir-faire *m.*
tactful, *a.* De tact ; délicat. *To be t.,* avoir du tact. **-fully,** *adv.* Avec tact.

tactical, *a.* Tactique.
tactician, *s.* Tacticien *m.*
tactics, *s.pl.* Tactique *f.*
tactless, *a.* (*a*) Dépourvu de tact. (*b*) *T. question,* question indiscrète. **-ly,** *adv.* Sans tact.
tactlessness, *s.* Manque *m* de tact.
tadpole, *s.* *Amph:* Têtard *m.*
taffrail, *s.* *N.Arch:* (Lisse *f* de) couronnement *m* (de la poupe).
tag, *s.* **1.** (*a*) Morceau *m* (d'étoffe) qui pend. (*b*) Attache *f* (de botte). (*c*) Ferret *m* (de lacet). **2.** (*a*) Citation banale; cliché *m.* (*b*) Refrain *m.*
Tahiti. *Pr.n. Geog:* Taïti *m.*
tail¹, *s.* **1.** (*a*) Queue *f* (d'animal). (*Of peacock*) To spread its tail, faire la roue. With his tail between his legs, (i) (*of dog*) la queue entre les jambes; (ii) *F:* (*of pers.*) l'oreille basse. *F:* To keep one's tail up, ne pas se laisser abattre. To turn tail, s'enfuir. The sting is in the tail, à la queue gît le venin. (*b*) Empennage *m* (d'avion). Tail of a shirt, pan *m* de chemise. *pl.* Tails of a coat, basques *f,* pans, d'un habit. (*c*) Arrière *m* (d'une voiture). Tail of a procession, queue d'un défilé. **2.** (*Of coin*) Pile *f,* revers *m.* **tail-board,** *s.* *Veh:* Layon *m.* **tail-coat,** *s.* *Cost:* Habit *m* à queue. **tail-end,** *s.* Extrémité *f* arrière; queue *f* (d'un défilé); fin *f.*
tail², *v.i.* To tail after s.o., suivre qn à la queue leu leu. **tail off,** *v.i.* Se réduire en pointe; s'espacer; (*of voice*) s'éteindre.
tailed, *a.* A queue.
tailor¹, *s.* Tailleur *m.* Tailor-made costume, costume *m* tailleur; *F:* tailleur.
tailor², *v.tr.* Faire, façonner (un complet). *Tailored dress,* robe tailleur. **tailoring,** *s.* **1.** Métier *m* de tailleur. **2.** Ouvrage *m* de tailleur.
taint¹, *s.* **1.** (*a*) Corruption *f,* infection *f.* (*b*) The taint of sin, la tache du péché. **2.** Tare *f* héréditaire. **3.** Trace *f* (d'infection).
taint², *v.tr.* Infecter, vicier, gâter, corrompre.
tainted, *a.* Infecté, corrompu. Tainted meat, viande gâtée. Tainted heredity, hérédité chargée.
take, *v.* Prendre. I. *v.tr.* **1.** (*a*) To t. sth. on one's back, prendre, charger, qch. sur son dos. (*b*) To take sth. from s.o., enlever, prendre, qch. à qn. To t. sth. from the table, prendre qch. sur la table (*c*) To take (hold of) s.o., saisir, empoigner, qn. She took my arm, elle me prit le bras. To take an opportunity, saisir une occasion. (*d*) Prendre (une ville). To take s.o. prisoner, faire qn prisonnier. The deuce take him! que le diable l'emporte! To be taken ill, tomber malade. He was very much taken with the idea, l'idée lui souriait beaucoup. I was not taken with him, il ne m'a pas fait bonne impression. (*e*) To take a passage from a book, emprunter un passage à un livre. **2.** (*a*) Louer, prendre

(une maison). (*b*) To take tickets, prendre des billets. (*Of seat*) 'Taken,' "occupé." To take (in) a paper, acheter régulièrement un journal. (*c*) Prendre (le train). Take your seats! prenez vos places! Rail: en voiture! (*d*) T. the turning on the left, prenez à gauche. To take the wrong road, se tromper de chemin. (*e*) To take legal advice, consulter un avocat. (*f*) To take holy orders, recevoir les ordres. **3.** (*a*) Gagner, remporter (le prix). Cards: To take a trick, faire une levée. (*b*) To take one's degree, prendre ses diplômes. To take an examination, se présenter à un examen. **4.** Prendre (de la nourriture). To take a meal, faire un repas. **5.** (*a*) To take a walk, faire une promenade. To take a bath, prendre un bain. *Mr X is taking the sixth form,* M. X est chargé de la classe de première. To take breath, reprendre haleine. To take effect, produire son effet. (*b*) To take a photograph, faire une photographie. (*c*) To take sth. to pieces, démonter qch. **6.** (*a*) Prendre, recevoir. Take that (and that)! attrape (ça et ça)! To take no denial, ne pas accepter de refus. What will you take for it? combien en voulez-vous? To take a bet, tenir un pari. To take all responsibility, assumer toute la responsabilité. Taking one thing with another, l'un portant l'autre. *T. it from me!* croyez-m'en! *I wonder how he will t. it,* *F:* je me demande quelle tête il fera. (*b*) Bus that takes twenty passengers, autobus qui tient vingt voyageurs. **7.** (*a*) Prendre, *F:* attraper (un rhume). (*b*) To take a dislike to s.o., prendre qn en grippe. **8.** (*a*) How old do you t. him to be? quel âge lui donnez-vous? I take it that, je suppose que. (*b*) *I took you for an Englishman,* je vous croyais anglais. *F:* What do you take me for? pour qui me prenez-vous? **9.** (*a*) That will take some explaining, voilà qui va demander des explications. *The work took some doing,* le travail a été difficile, dur. The journey takes five days, le voyage prend, demande, cinq jours. It won't take long, ce sera tôt fait. *It took four men to hold him,* il a fallu le tenir à quatre. (*b*) *Gram:* Verb that takes a preposition, verbe qui veut la préposition. (*c*) *I t.* sixes (in gloves), j'ai six de pointure. **10.** (*a*) To take s.o. somewhere, mener, conduire, qn dans un endroit. (*b*) To take sth. to s.o., porter qch. à qn. To t. s.o. to the hospital, transporter qn à l'hôpital. II. **take,** *v.i.* (*a*) Avoir du succès; réussir; prendre. (*b*) *Med:* The vaccine has not taken, le vaccin n'a pas pris. **take after,** *v.i.* Tenir de (qn). **take away,** *v.tr.* **1.** Enlever, emporter; emmener (qn). **2.** (*a*) To take away a knife from a child, ôter un couteau à un enfant. (*b*) To take a child away from school, retirer un enfant du collège. **take back,** *v.tr.* **1.** (*a*) Reconduire. (*b*) *To take a book back,* reporter un livre. **2.** (*a*) Reprendre (un employé). (*b*) I take back what I said, je retire ce que j'ai dit.

take down, *v.tr.* **1.** (*a*) *To t. down a picture,* descendre un tableau. (*b*) *F:* To take s.o. down, remettre qn à sa place. **2.** Avaler. **3.** To take down a few notes, prendre quelques notes. *To t. down in shorthand,* sténographier. **take-down,** *s.* *F:* Mortification *f*, humiliation *f*. **take in,** *v.tr.* **1.** (*a*) *To t.* (*b*) To take in the harvest, rentrer la moisson. *Nau:* To take in water, faire de l'eau. (*Of boat*) To take in water, faire eau. (*c*) To take in lodgers, recevoir des locataires. **2.** To take in sail, diminuer de voile(s). **3.** Comprendre, inclure. **4.** (*a*) Comprendre. To take in the situation, se rendre compte de la situation. To take in everything at a glance, tout embrasser d'un coup d'œil. (*b*) *F:* He takes it all in, il prend tout ça pour argent comptant. (*c*) *F:* Mettre dedans; *F:* rouler. To be taken in, se laisser attraper. **take-in,** *s.* Duperie *f*; attrape *f*. **take into,** *v.tr.* **1.** To take s.o. into one's confidence, mettre qn dans sa confidence. **2.** To take it into one's head to do sth., se mettre dans la tête de faire qch. **take off.** I. *v.tr.* **1.** To take s.o.'s attention off sth., distraire l'attention de qn. To take one's eye off sth., quitter qch. des yeux. **2.** (*a*) Enlever, ôter. To take off one's clothes, quitter ses vêtements; se déshabiller. *Tp:* To take off the receiver, décrocher le récepteur. (*b*) Emmener. To take oneself off, s'en aller, s'éloigner. (*c*) To take so much off (the price of sth.), rabattre tant (sur le prix de qch.). (*d*) Imiter, singer. II. **take off,** *v.i.* Prendre son élan, s'élancer (*from,* de). *Av:* Décoller, s'envoler. **take-off,** *s.* (*a*) Élan *m*. (*b*) *Av:* Décollage *m*, envolée *f*. (*c*) Caricature *f*, charge *f*. **take on. 1.** *v.tr.* (*a*) Se charger de, entreprendre. (*b*) *I'll t. you on at billiards!* je vais vous faire une partie de billard! To take on a bet, accepter un pari. (*c*) Engager, embaucher (un ouvrier). (*d*) Prendre, revêtir (une qualité). (*e*) To take on passengers, prendre des voyageurs. (*f*) Mener plus loin. **2.** *v.i.* (*a*) *F:* Don't take on so! ne vous désolez pas comme ça! (*b*) *F:* Devenir populaire; réussir. **take out,** *v.tr.* **1.** (*a*) To take out one's pipe, sortir sa pipe. To take out a stain, enlever, ôter, une tache. (*b*) *F:* I'll take it out of him, je me vengerai. *The heat takes it out of me,* la chaleur m'épuise. **2.** He is going to take me out to dinner, il va m'emmener dîner. **3.** Prendre, obtenir. To take out an insurance policy, contracter une assurance. **4.** To take it out in goods, le payer en marchandises. **take over,** *v.tr.* **1.** To take over a business, prendre la suite des affaires. To take over the liabilities, prendre les dettes à sa charge. *Abs.* To take over from s.o., relever qn (dans ses fonctions). **2.** Transporter; passer. **take to,** *v.i.* **1.** To take to flight, prendre la fuite. *To t. to the woods,* gagner le taillis. **2.** To take

to drink, s'adonner à la boisson. **3.** (*a*) To take to s.o., prendre qn en amitié. (*b*) *I shall never t. to it,* je ne m'y ferai jamais. **take up.** I. *v.tr.* **1.** (*a*) To take up a carpet, enlever un tapis. (*b*) *Rail:* To take up passengers, embarquer des voyageurs. **2.** Absorber (de l'eau). **3.** (*a*) To take up a challenge, relever un défi. (*b*) To take up an idea, adopter une idée. **4.** (*a*) To take up a question, prendre une question en main. (*b*) Embrasser, s'adonner à (une carrière); épouser (une querelle). **5.** Arrêter. **6.** To take s.o. up sharply, reprendre qn vertement. To take s.o. up short, couper la parole à qn. **7.** To take s.o. up wrongly, mal comprendre les paroles de qn. **8.** Occuper. (*a*) To take up too much room, occuper trop de place. (*b*) To take up s.o.'s attention, absorber l'attention de qn. II. **take up,** *v.i.* To take up with, (i) se lier d'amitié avec; (ii) se mettre à fréquenter. **take upon,** *v.tr.* To take it upon oneself to do sth., prendre sur soi de faire qch. *He takes a good deal upon himself,* il se permet bien des choses. **taking¹,** *a.* Attrayant; (visage) séduisant. *T. manners,* manières engageantes. **taking²,** *s.* **1.** Prise *f.* **2.** *pl.* Takings, recette *f*, produit *m*.

talc, *s.* Talc *m*.

talcum, *s. Toil:* Talcum powder, (poudre de) talc *m*.

tale, *s.* **1.** Conte *m*. (*a*) Récit *m*, histoire *f.* Old wives' tales, contes de bonne femme. *F:* I've heard that tale before, je connais des paroles sur cet air-là. (*b*) *Lit:* Nouvelle *f*, conte. **2.** Rapport *m*, cafardage *m*. To tell tales, rapporter; cafarder.

talebearer, *s.* Rapporteur, -euse; cafard, -arde.

talent, *s.* **1.** (*a*) Talent *m*; aptitude *f*. (*b*) Man of talent, homme de talent. **2.** *Coll.* Gens *mpl* de talent.

talented, *a.* Qui a du talent; doué.

talisman, *s.* Talisman *m*.

talk¹, *s.* **1.** (*a*) Paroles *fpl.* He is all talk, ce n'est qu'un bavard. (*b*) Bruit *m*, dires *mpl*, racontages *mpl.* There is some talk of *his returning,* il est question qu'il revienne. It's all talk, ce ne sont que des on-dit. (*c*) Propos *mpl*; bavardage *m.* Idle talk, paroles en l'air. Small talk, menus propos. **2.** Entretien *m*; causerie *f.* To have a talk with s.o., causer, s'entretenir, avec qn. **3.** It is the talk of the town, on ne parle que de cela.

talk². I. *v.i.* **1.** (*a*) Parler. (*b*) Parler, discourir. To talk big, se vanter. *P:* To talk through one's hat, débiter des sottises. *P:* Now you're talking! voilà qui s'appelle parler! Talking of that, à propos de cela. He knows what he is talking about, il sait ce qu'il dit. *F:* Talk about luck! tu parles d'une chance! **2.** (*a*) To talk to s.o., causer, s'entretenir, avec qn. *To talk freely to s.o.,* s'ouvrir à qn. To talk to oneself, se parler à

soi-même. *F:* **Who do you think you are talking to! à qui croyez-vous donc parler?** (*b*) *F:* **I'll talk to him!** je vais lui dire son fait! **3.** (*a*) Jaser, bavarder. (*b*) **To get oneself talked about,** faire parler de soi. II. **talk,** *v.tr.* **I.** (*a*) *To t. French,* parler français. (*b*) **To talk sense,** parler raison. **2. To talk oneself hoarse,** s'enrouer à force de parler. **talk over,** *v.tr.* **I.** Discuter, débattre (une question). **2.** = TALK ROUND I. **talk round. I.** *v.tr.* Enjôler; amener à changer d'avis. *I talked them round at last,* j'ai fini par les persuader. **2.** *v.i.* **To talk round a question,** tourner autour du pot. **talking,** *s.* **I.** Discours *mpl,* propos *mpl.* **2.** (*a*) Conversation *f.* (*b*) Bavardage *m.* To do all the talking, faire tous les frais de la conversation. **No talking please!** pas de bavardage! **3. To give s.o. a good talking-to,** semoncer qn.
talkative, *a.* Causeur, -euse; jaseur, -euse.
talkativeness, *s.* Loquacité *f.*
talker, *s.* Causeur, -euse; parleur, -euse. **2. To be a great talker,** être bavard(e).
talkie, *s.* *Cin:* Film parlant, film parlé.
tall, *a.* **I.** (*Of pers.*) (*a*) Grand; de haute taille. (*b*) **How tall are you?** quelle est votre taille? **She is growing tall,** elle se fait grande. **2.** (*Of thg*) Haut, élevé. **3.** *F:* Incroyable. **That's a tall story,** celle-là est raide.
tallness, *s.* (*a*) (*Of pers.*) Grande taille. (*b*) Hauteur *f* (d'un édifice).
tallow, *s.* Suif *m.*
tally¹, *s.* (*a*) Compte *m.* (*b*) **To keep tally of goods,** pointer des marchandises.
tally². I. *v.tr.* Pointer, contrôler. **2.** *v.i.* Correspondre (*with,* à); s'accorder (*with,* avec).
tally-ho, *int. & s.* Taïaut (*m*).
talon, *s.* Serre *f*; griffe *f.*
tamarisk, *s.* *Bot:* Tamaris *m.*
tambourine, *s.* *Mus:* Tambour *m* de basque.
tame¹, *a.* **I.** Apprivoisé, domestiqué. **2.** *F:* (*a*) Soumis, dompté. (*b*) Monotone, terne. **-ly,** *adv.* **I.** Sans résistance, lâchement. **2.** Platement.
tame², *v.tr.* (*a*) Apprivoiser. (*b*) Domestiquer (une bête). (*c*) Mater (qn). **taming,** *s.* **I.** (*a*) Apprivoisement *m.* (*b*) Domestication *f.* **2.** Domptement *m.*
tameness, *s.* **I.** (*a*) Nature douce. (*b*) Caractère soumis. **2.** *F:* (*a*) Pusillanimité *f.* (*b*) Monotonie *f,* fadeur *f.*
tamer, *s.* Dompteur, -euse.
tamper, *v.i.* (*a*) **To tamper with sth.,** toucher à (un mécanisme); falsifier (un registre). (*b*) **To tamper with a witness,** suborner un témoin.
tan¹. I. *s.* (*a*) Tan *m.* (*b*) Hâle *m.* **2.** *a.* Tanné; tan *inv.* **Black and tan dog,** chien noir et feu *inv.*
tan², *v.* **I.** *v.tr.* (*a*) Tanner. *F:* **To tan s.o.'s hide,** tanner le cuir à qn. (*b*) Hâler, bronzer

(la peau). **2.** *v.i.* Se hâler, se basaner.
tanning, *s.* **I.** Tannage *m.* **2.** *F:* Tannée *f,* raclée *f.*
tandem. I. *s.* (*a*) *Veh:* Tandem *m.* (*b*) Tandem (bicycle), tandem (de tourisme). **2.** *adv.* **To drive tandem,** conduire en flèche.
tang, *s.* Goût vif; saveur *f.*
tangent, *s.* Tangente *f.* *F:* **To fly off at a tangent,** s'échapper par la tangente.
tangerine, *s.* Mandarine *f.*
tangible, *a.* **I.** Tangible. **2.** *F:* Réel. **-ibly,** *adv.* **I.** Tangiblement. **2.** Sensiblement, manifestement.
Tangier. *Pr.n.* Tanger *m.*
tangle¹, *s.* Embrouillement *m*; emmêlement *m.* **To get into a tangle,** s'embrouiller.
tangle², *v.tr.* **To tangle (up) sth.,** embrouiller, (em)mêler. *F:* **Tangled web,** trame compliquée.
tango¹, *s.* *Danc:* Tango *m.*
tango², *v.i.* Danser le tango.
tank, *s.* **I.** Réservoir *m.* **Water tank,** réservoir à eau; citerne *f.* *I.C.E:* **Petrol tank,** réservoir à essence. **2.** *Mil:* *F:* Char *m* de combat, d'assaut; tank *m.*
tankard, *s.* Pot *m,* chope *f,* en étain.
tanker, *s.* Bateau-citerne *m, pl.* bateaux-citernes.
tanner¹, *s.* Tanneur *m.*
tanner², *s.* *F:* (Pièce *f* de) six pence.
tannery, *s.* Tannerie *f.*
tannin, *s.* Tan(n)in *m.*
tansy, *s.* *Bot:* Tanaisie *f*; sent-bon *m inv.*
tantalize, *v.tr.* Tantaliser, taquiner. **tantalizing,** *a.* Qui tantalise; (sourire) provocant. **-ly,** *adv.* (*a*) Cruellement. (*b*) D'un air provocant.
tantamount, *a.* **To be tantamount to sth.,** équivaloir à qch.
tantrum, *s.* Accès *m* de mauvaise humeur. **To get into a tantrum,** se mettre en colère.
tap¹, *s.* (*a*) Fausset *m* (de fût). (*b*) Robinet *m.* **To turn on the tap,** ouvrir le robinet. **taproom,** *s.* Estaminet *m,* buvette *f.* **tap-root,** *s.* *Bot:* Racine pivotante; pivot *m.*
tap², *v.tr.* (*a*) Percer (un fût). (*b*) **To tap a tree,** inciser, saigner, un arbre. (*c*) *Tp:* **To tap a message,** capter un message. *F:* **To tap a new country,** ouvrir un nouveau pays au commerce. **tapping,** *s.* Mise *f* en perce, perçage *m* (d'un tonneau); incision *f* (d'un arbre).
tap³, *s.* Tape *f*; petit coup. *There was a tap at the door,* on frappa doucement à la porte.
tap⁴, *v.* **I.** *v.tr.* Frapper légèrement; taper, tapoter. **2.** *v.ind.tr.* **To tap at the door,** frapper doucement à la porte.
tape¹, *s.* **I.** (*a*) Ruban *m* de fil, de coton; ganse *f.* (*b*) *Sp:* Bande *f* d'arrivée. **2. Steel tape,** ruban d'acier. **tape-measure,** *s.* Mètre *m* en ruban.
tape², *v.tr.* *F:* **I've got him taped,** j'ai pris mesure.
taper¹, *s.* Bougie filée.

taper², *a. Poet:* Effilé, fuselé.
taper³. **1.** *v.tr.* Effiler; tailler en cône. **2.** *v.i.* To (taper) off, s'effiler; aller en diminuant. **tapering**, *a.* En pointe; effilé, fuselé.
tapestry, *s.* Tapisserie *f.*
tapioca, *s.* Tapioca *m.*
tapir, *s. Z:* Tapir *m.*
tar¹, *s.* **1.** *(a)* Goudron *m. (b) F:* To spoil the ship for a ha'p'orth of tar, faire des économies de bouts de chandelle. **2.** *Nau: F:* (Jack) tar, loup *m* de mer, mathurin *m.*
tar², *v.tr.* Goudronner. *F:* They are all tarred with the same brush, ce sont des gens du même acabit.
tarantula, *s.* Tarentule *f.*
tardiness, *s.* Lenteur *f (in doing sth.,* à faire qch.).
tardy, *a.* **1.** Lent. **2.** Tardif. **-ily**, *adv.* **1.** Lentement. **2.** Tardivement.
tare, *s. Bot:* **1.** Vesce *f.* **2.** *B. & F:* Ivraie *f.*
target, *s.* Cible *f;* but *m,* objectif *m.*
tariff, *s.* **1.** Tarif *m.* **2.** Tableau *m,* liste *f,* des prix.
tarmac, *s.* **1.** *Civ.E:* Tarmac *m.* **2.** *Av:* The tarmac, la piste d'envol.
tarn, *s.* Petit lac (de montagne).
tarnish. **1.** *v.tr.* Ternir. **2.** *v.i.* Se ternir.
tarpaulin, *s. Nau:* (a) Toile goudronnée. *(b)* Bâche *f.*
tarry¹, *a.* Goudronneux, bitumeux.
tarry², *v.i. Lit:* **1.** Rester, demeurer. **2.** Tarder, s'attarder.
tart¹, *s. Cu:* (a) (Open) Tarte *f. Small jam t.,* tartelette *f* aux confitures. *(b)* (Covered) Tourte *f.*
tart², *a.* (a) Au goût âpre, aigrelet. *(b) F:* Aigre; mordant.
tartan, *s. Tex: Cost:* Tartan *m.*
Tartar. **1.** *a. & s. Ethn:* Tatar, -e; Tartare. **2.** *s. F:* Homme *m* intraitable; mégère *f.* To catch a Tartar, trouver à qui parler.
tartaric, *a. Ch:* Tartrique.
Tartary. *Pr.n. A.Geog:* La Tartarie.
tartness, *s.* Acerbité *f; F:* acidité *f,* aigreur *f* (du ton).
task, *s.* **1.** Tâche *f.* (a) *Sch:* Devoir *m.* *(b)* Travail, -aux *m,* ouvrage *m,* besogne *f.* **2.** To take s.o. to task for sth., prendre qn à partie pour avoir fait qch.
taskmaster, *s.* Chef *m* de corvée; surveillant *m. F:* Hard taskmaster, véritable tyran.
Tasmania. *Pr.n.* La Tasmanie.
Tasmanian. *a. & s.* Tasmanien, -ienne.
tassel, *s. Furn:* Gland *m;* houppe *f.*
Tasso. *Pr.n. Lit.Hist:* Le Tasse.
taste¹, *s.* **1.** (a) (Sense of) taste, goût *m.* *(b)* Saveur *f,* goût. *It has a burnt t.,* cela sent le brûlé. *(c) F:* A taste of sth., un petit peu (de fromage). *You'll get a t. of it one of these days,* vous en tâterez un de ces jours. **2.** Goût, prédilection *f* (for, pour). To have a taste

for sth., avoir du goût pour qch. To find sth. to one's taste, trouver qch. à son goût. *Prov:* Tastes differ; everyone to his taste, chacun (à) son goût. **3.** (a) People of taste, les gens de goût. *(b)* It is (in) bad taste to . . ., il est de mauvais goût de. . . .
taste². **I.** *v.tr.* **1.** Percevoir la saveur de; sentir (qch.). **2.** (a) Goûter de, à; manger un petit morceau (d'un mets); tâter de. *(b)* To t. happiness, connaître, goûter, le bonheur. **II.** taste, *v.i.* To taste of sth., avoir un goût de qch. To taste like honey, avoir un goût de miel.
tasteful, *a.* De bon goût. **-fully**, *adv.* Avec goût.
tasteless, *a.* **1.** Sans saveur; fade, insipide. **2.** Qui manque de goût.
tastelessness, *s.* **1.** Insipidité *f,* fadeur *f.* **2.** Manque *m* de goût.
tastiness, *s.* Saveur *f,* goût *m* agréable.
tasty, *a.* Savoureux; succulent.
ta-ta, *int.* Au revoir!
tatter, *s.* Lambeau *m.*
tatterdemalion, *s.* Loqueteux, -euse; déguenillé, -ée; va-nu-pieds *mf inv.*
tattered, *a.* (Vêtement) dépenaillé, en loques; (homme) déguenillé, loqueteux.
tattle¹, *s.* Bavardage *m,* commérage *m.*
tattle², *v.i.* Bavarder; jaser.
tattler, *s.* Bavard, -arde.
tattoo¹, *s. Mil:* **1.** Retraite *f* (du soir). **2.** Torchlight tattoo, retraite aux flambeaux.
tattoo², *v.tr.* Tatouer. **tattooing**, *s.* Tatouage *m.*
taunt¹, *s.* Reproche méprisant; sarcasme *m.*
taunt², *v.tr.* (a) Accabler de sarcasmes. *(b)* To taunt s.o. with sth., reprocher qch. à qn. **taunting**, *a.* (Ton) de sarcasme.
taut, *a.* Tendu, raidi.
tauten, *v.tr.* Raidir.
tautology, *s.* Tautologie *f.*
tavern, *s.* Taverne *f,* cabaret *m.* **tavern-keeper**, *s.* Cabaretier, -ière.
tawdriness, *s.* Clinquant *m;* faux brillant.
tawdry, *a.* D'un mauvais goût criard.
tawny, *a.* (i) Tanné, basané; (ii) fauve.
tax¹, *s.* **1.** Impôt *m,* contribution *f,* taxe *f. Visitors' tax,* taxe de séjour. **2.** Charge *f;* fardeau *m.* To be a tax on s.o., être une charge pour qn. **tax-collector**, *s.* Percepteur *m* des contributions. **tax-payer**, *s* Contribuable *mf.*
tax², *v.tr.* **1.** (a) Taxer; frapper d'un impôt. *(b)* Imposer (qn). *(c) F:* Mettre à l'épreuve. **2.** To tax s.o. with doing sth., taxer, accuser, qn d'avoir fait qch.
taxable, *a.* Imposable.
taxation, *s.* (a) Imposition *f.* *(b)* Charges fiscales. *(c)* Revenu réalisé par les impôts; les impôts *m.*
taxi¹, *s. F:* = TAXI-CAB. **taxi-cab**, *s.* Fiacre *m* automobile; taxi *m.* **taxi-driver**, *s.* Chauffeur *m,* de taxi.
taxi², *v.i.* (Of aircraft) Rouler sur le sol.

taxidermist, *s.* Empailleur *m.*
taxidermy, *s.* Taxidermie *f.*
taximetre, *s.* Taximètre *m.*
tea, *s.* **1.** Thé *m.* (*a*) *Weak tea,* thé léger.
(*b*) **Afternoon tea,** five o'clock *m.* **High tea,**
repas à la fourchette (arrosé de thé). **2.** Tisane
f, infusion *f.* **tea-basket,** *s.* Mallette *f* de
camping. **tea-caddy,** *s.* Boîte *f* à thé.
tea-chest, *s.* Caisse *f* à thé. **tea-cloth,** *s.*
1. Nappe *f* à thé; napperon *m.* **2.** Torchon
m. **tea-cosy,** *s.* Couvre-théière *m.* **tea-
cup,** *s.* Tasse *f* à thé. **tea-kettle,** *s.*
Bouilloire *f.* **tea-leaf,** *s.* Feuille *f* de thé.
(Used) tea-leaves, marc *m* de thé. **tea-
party,** *s.* To give a tea-party, donner un thé.
tea-plant, *s.* Arbre *m* à thé. **tea-planter,**
s. Planteur *m* de thé. **tea-pot,** *s.* Théière *f.*
tea-room, *s.* Salon *m* de thé. **tea-service,**
s. Service *m* à thé. **tea-spoon,** *s.* Cuiller
f à thé. **tea-table,** *s.* Table *f* à thé. **tea-
things,** *s.pl.* Service *m* à thé. **tea-
time,** *s.* L'heure *f* du thé.
teach, *v.tr.* Enseigner; instruire. **To teach
s.o. sth.,** enseigner, apprendre, qch. à qn.
He teaches French, il enseigne, il professe, le
français. **To teach s.o.** (how) **to do sth.,**
apprendre à qn à faire qch. **To teach oneself
sth.,** apprendre qch. tout seul. **That will
teach him!** ça lui apprendra! **To teach s.o.
a thing or two,** dégourdir qn. **teaching,** *s.*
1. Enseignement *m,* instruction *f.* **2. The
teachings of experience,** les leçons *f* de
l'expérience. **3.** Doctrine *f.*
teacher, *s.* (i) Instituteur, -trice; maître, *f.*
maîtresse (d'école); (ii) professeur *m.*
teak, *s.* Teck *m.*
teal, *s.inv. Orn:* Sarcelle *f.*
team, *s.* **1.** Attelage *m.* **2.** Équipe *f.* Football team, équipe de football. **team-work,**
s. Travail *m* d'équipe; collaboration *f.*
tear¹, *s.* Larme *f. To weep tears of joy,*
pleurer de joie. *To laugh till the tears come,*
rire (jusqu')aux larmes. **tear-drop,** *s.*
Larme *f.* **tear-gas,** *s.* Gaz *m* lacrymogène.
tear-stained, *a.* Barbouillé de larmes.
tear², *s.* **1.** Déchirement *m.* **2.** Déchirure *f,*
accroc *m* (dans un vêtement). **3.** *F:* (*a*) **To
go full tear,** aller à toute vitesse. (*b*) Rage *f;*
agitation *f.*
tear³, *v.* **1.** *v.tr.* (*a*) Déchirer. **To tear a hole
in sth.,** faire un trou à qch. *Torn between two
emotions,* tiraillé entre deux émotions.
(*b*) Arracher (*from,* à qn, de qch.). **To tear
(out)** one's hair, s'arracher les cheveux.
2. *v.i. F:* **To tear along,** aller à toute vitesse.
tear away, *v.tr.* Arracher. *He could not t.
himself away,* il ne pouvait se décider à les
quitter. **tear down,** *v.tr.* Arracher. **tear
off,** *v.tr.* Arracher. **tear out,** *v.tr.* Arracher. **tear up,** *v.tr.* **1.** Déchirer; mettre
en pièces. **2. To tear up a tree by the roots,**
déraciner un arbre. **tearing¹,** *s. F:* **1.**
Tearing rage, rage à tout casser. **2.** *F:* **To
be in a tearing hurry,** être terriblement pressé.

tearing², *s.* **1.** Déchirement *m.* **2. Tearing
away, off, out,** arrachement *m.*
tearful, *a.* Éploré; tout en pleurs; larmoyant. *In a t. voice,* (i) avec des larmes dans
la voix; (ii) en pleurnichant. **-fully,** *adv.*
En pleurant; les larmes aux yeux.
tease¹, *s.* Taquin, -ine.
tease² *v.tr.* Taquiner, tourmenter. **teas-
ing¹,** *a.* Taquin; (ton) railleur, *f.* railleuse.
teasing². Taquinerie *f,* taquinage *m.*
teaspoonful, *s.* Cuillerée *f* à thé.
technical, *a.* Technique. **-ally,** *adv.*
Techniquement.
technicality, *s.* Détail *m* technique; considération *f* d'ordre technique.
technician, *s.* Technicien *m.*
technique, *s.* Technique *f.*
Teddy. *Pr.n.* Teddy Bear, ours *m* en peluche.
tedious, *a.* Fatigant, pénible; ennuyeux.
tedium, *s.* Ennui *m;* manque *m* d'intérêt.
tee, *s. Golf:* Dé *m;* tee *m.*
teem, *v.i.* Abonder (*with,* en); foisonner,
fourmiller (*with,* de).
teens, *s.pl. F:* **To be in one's teens,** être
adolescent(e).
teethe, *v.i.* Faire ses (premières) dents.
teething, *s.* Dentition *f.*
teetotal, *a.* Antialcoolique.
teetotalism, *s.* Abstention *f* des liqueurs
alcooliques.
teetotal(l)er, *s.* Abstinent, -ente.
teetotum, *s.* Toton *m.*
telegram, *s.* Télégramme *m;* dépêche *f.*
Wireless telegram, radiotélégramme *m.*
telegraph¹, *s.* Télégraphe *m.* **telegraph
office,** bureau télégraphique. **telegraph
boy,** *s.* Facteur *m* télégraphiste. **telegraph
operator,** *s.* Télégraphiste *mf.* **tele-
graph-pole,** *s.* Poteau *m* télégraphique.
telegraph². **1.** *v.i.* Télégraphier. **2.** *v.tr.*
Télégraphier.
telegraphic, *a.* Télégraphique.
telegraphist, *s.* Télégraphiste *mf.*
telegraphy, *s.* Télégraphie *f.*
telepathic, *a.* Télépathique.
telepathy, *s.* Télépathie *f.*
telephone¹, *s.* Téléphone *m.* **Are you on
the telephone?** avez-vous le téléphone? *You
are wanted on the t.,* on vous demande au
téléphone. **Telephone number,** numéro *m* de
téléphone. **telephone-box,** *s.* Cabine *f*
téléphonique. **telephone girl,** *s.* Demoiselle *f* du téléphone. **telephone operator,** *s.* Téléphoniste *mf.*
telephone². **1.** *v.i.* Téléphoner (*to,* à).
2. *v.tr.* (*a*) Téléphoner. (*b*) Téléphoner à.
telephonic, *a.* Téléphonique.
telephonist, *s.* Téléphoniste *mf.*
telephony, *s.* Téléphonie *f.*
telescope¹, *s.* (*a*) Lunette *f;* longue-vue *f,*
pl. longues-vues. (*b*) Télescope *m.*
telescope². **1.** *v.tr.* Télescoper. **2.** *v.i.* (Se)
télescoper.
telescopic, *a.* Télescopique.

television, *s.* Télévision *f.*
televisor, *s.* Téléviseur *m.*
tell, *v.* I. *v.tr.* **1.** (*a*) Dire. (*b*) To tell s.o.
sth., dire, apprendre, qch. à qn ; faire savoir
qch. à qn. *I have been told,* on m'a dit.
Don't let me have to tell you that again,
tenez-vous cela pour dit. I told you so! je
vous l'avais bien dit ! (*c*) Raconter, conter.
More than words can tell, au delà de tout ce
qui peut se dire. To hear tell of, entendre
parler de. (*d*) Annoncer, proclamer ; révéler
(un secret). (*Of clock*) To tell the time,
marquer l'heure. **2.** (*a*) To tell s.o. about
s.o., parler de qn à qn. (*b*) *He will be furious,
I (can) t. you!* il va être furieux, je vous en
réponds ! **3.** To tell s.o. to do sth., ordonner,
dire, à qn de faire qch. *Do as you are told,*
faites comme on vous l'ordonne. I told him
not to, je le lui ai défendu. **4.** (*a*) Discerner
distinguer, reconnaître. To tell right from
wrong, discerner le bien du mal. One can
tell him by his voice, on le reconnaît à sa voix.
One can tell she is intelligent, on la devine
intelligente. (*b*) Savoir. Who can tell? qui
sait? You never can tell, on ne sait jamais.
I cannot tell, je n'en sais rien. **5.** *Abs.* To
tell of sth., annoncer, révéler, qch. **6.** To
tell (over), compter. All told, tout compris ;
somme toute. II. **tell,** *v.i.* (*a*) Produire son
effet ; porter (coup). Blood will tell, bon
sang ne peut mentir. It tells (up)on his health,
cela affecte sa santé. (*b*) This tells in his
favour, cela milite en sa faveur. *Everything
told against him,* tout témoignait contre lui.
tell off, *v.tr.* **1.** Désigner, affecter (qn pour
une corvée). **2.** *F:* Dire son fait à (qn).
telling[1], *a.* Efficace. Telling blow, coup
qui porte. **telling**[2], *s.* **1.** Récit *m* ; narration
f. **2.** Divulgation *f* (d'un secret). **3.** There
is no telling, on ne sait pas ; qui sait? **4.** Telling (over), dénombrement *m.* **tell-tale,** *s.*
1. (*a*) Rapporteur, -euse ; *Sch:* *F:* cafard,
-arde. (*b*) Tell-tale signs, signes révélateurs.
2. *El.E:* Tell-tale (lamp), lampe témoin.
teller, *s.* **1.** (Ra)conteur, -euse ; narrateur,
-trice. **2.** Caissier *m*, payeur *m* (de banque).
temerity, *s.* Témérité *f*, audace *f.*
temper[1], *s.* **1.** *Metall:* Trempe *f.* **2.** Sang-
froid *m.* To lose one's temper, perdre son
sang-froid ; s'emporter. To be out of temper,
être de mauvaise humeur. To try s.o.'s
temper, énerver qn. **3.** Humeur *f.* (*a*) Caractère *m*, tempérament *m.* To have a bad
temper, avoir le caractère mal fait. (*b*) To
show (ill) temper, montrer de l'humeur. To
be in a good temper, être de bonne humeur.
(*c*) Mauvaise humeur. Outburst of temper,
mouvement *m* d'humeur. To be in a temper,
être en colère.
temper[2], *v.tr.* **1.** *Metall:* Tremper ; donner
la trempe à. **2.** Tempérer ; modérer.
temperament, *s.* Tempérament *m.*
temperamental, *a.* Capricieux, fantasque.
temperance, *s.* Tempérance *f.* **1.** Modéra-

tion *f*, retenue *f.* **2.** Abstention *f* des boissons
alcooliques.
temperate, *a.* **1.** (*a*) Tempérant, sobre.
T. habits, habitudes de sobriété. (*b*) Modéré,
mesuré. **2.** (*Of climate*) Tempéré. -**ly,** *adv.*
Avec modération.
temperature, *s.* Température *f.* *F:* To
have a temperature, avoir de la température.
tempest, *s.* Tempête *f*, tourmente *f.*
tempestuous, *a.* **1.** Tempétueux ; de tempête. **2.** *F:* (*Of meeting*) Orageux.
Templar, *s.* *Hist:* (Knight) Templar,
templier *m* ; chevalier *m* du Temple.
temple[1], *s.* Temple *m.*
temple[2], *s.* *Anat:* Tempe *f.*
tempo, *s.* *Mus:* Tempo *m.*
temporal, *a.* Temporel.
temporary, *a.* (*a*) Temporaire, provisoire.
Temporary appointment, emploi amovible.
(*b*) Momentané. *The improvement is but t.,*
l'amélioration n'est que passagère. -**ily,** *adv.*
(*a*) Temporairement, provisoirement. (*b*)
Pour le moment.
temporize, *v.i.* Temporiser ; chercher à
gagner du temps.
tempt, *v.tr.* Tenter. **1.** To tempt s.o. to do
sth., induire qn à faire qch. *I was greatly
tempted,* l'occasion était bien tentante. **2.** To
tempt providence, tenter la providence.
tempting, *a.* Tentant, alléchant ; (*of offer*)
séduisant, attrayant.
temptation, *s.* Tentation *f.*
tempter, *s.* Tentateur, -trice.
ten, *num. a. & s.* Dix (*m*). *F:* Ten to one he'll
find it out, je vous parie qu'il le découvrira.
tenable, *a.* Tenable ; (théorie) soutenable.
tenacious, *a.* Tenace. -**ly,** *adv.* Obstinément ; avec ténacité.
tenacity, *s.* Ténacité *f.*
tenancy, *s.* Location *f.*
tenant, *s.* Locataire *mf.* Tenant for life,
usufruitier, -ière.
tenantry, *s.* *Coll.* Les tenanciers *m* et fer-
miers *m* (d'un domaine).
tench, *s.* *Ich:* Tanche *f.*
tend[1], *v.tr.* Soigner ; garder (les moutons).
tend[2], *v.i.* **1.** Tendre, se diriger (*towards,*
vers). **2.** To tend to do sth., être sujet(te) à
faire qch.
tendency, *s.* Tendance *f*, inclination *f*, disposition *f* (*to,* à).
tender[1], *s.* (*a*) *Nau:* Bateau *m* annexe ;
tender *m.* (*b*) *Rail:* Tender.
tender[2], *a.* **1.** Tendre. **2.** Tender heart,
cœur tendre, sensible. **3.** (*a*) Délicat, fragile.
(*b*) Jeune, tendre. Child of tender years,
enfant en bas âge. **4.** Tendre, affectueux.
-**ly,** *adv.* **1.** Doucement. **2.** Tendrement ;
avec tendresse. **tender-hearted,** *a.* Compatissant ; au cœur tendre, sensible.
tender[3], *s.* **1.** *Com:* Soumission *f*, offre *f.*
2. Legal tender, cours légal. *To be legal t.,*
avoir cours.
tender[4]. I. *v.tr.* Offrir. *To t. one's resignation,*

offrir de démissionner. **2.** *v.i. Com:* To tender for sth., soumissionner (pour) qch.
tenderness, *s.* **1.** Sensibilité *f.* **2.** Délicatesse *f*, fragilité *f.* **3.** Tendresse *f.*
tendon, *s. Anat:* Tendon *m.*
tendril, *s. Bot:* Vrille *f.*
tenet, *s.* Doctrine *f*, dogme *m.*
tenfold. 1. *a.* Décuple. **2.** *adv.* Dix fois autant. *To increase t.*, décupler.
tennis, *s.* (Lawn-)tennis, (lawn-)tennis *m.* **tennis-ball,** *s.* Balle *f* de tennis. **tennis-court,** *s.* Court *m* (de tennis).
tenor, *s.* **1.** Teneur *f*; contenu *m*, sens général. **2.** *Mus:* Ténor *m.*
tense¹, *s. Gram:* Temps *m.*
tense², *a.* **1.** Tendu. **2.** Tense silence, silence impressionnant. Tense voice, voix étranglée.
tenseness, *s.* **1.** Rigidité *f.* **2.** Tension *f.*
tension, *s.* Tension *f.*
tent, *s.* Tente *f.* **tent-peg,** *s.* Piquet *m* de tente.
tentacle, *s. Nat. Hist:* Tentacule *m.*
tentative. 1. *a.* Expérimental, -aux ; d'essai. **2.** *s.* Tentative *f*, essai *m.* **-ly,** *adv.* En guise d'essai.
tenter-hook, *s. F:* To be on tenter-hooks, être sur des charbons ardents.
tenth, *num. a. & s.* Dixième (*m*). (On) the tenth of March, le dix mars.
tenuous, *a.* Ténu ; délié ; mince.
tenure, *s. Jur:* Jouissance *f*; occupation *f.*
tepid, *a.* Tiède.
term¹, *s.* **1.** Terme *m*, borne *f*, fin *f*, limite *f.* **2.** (*a*) Terme, période *f*, durée *f.* During his term of office, pendant sa période d'activité. (*b*) *Sch:* Trimestre *m.* During term, pendant la période des classes. (*c*) *Jur:* Session *f.* **3.** *pl.* Terms. (*a*) Conditions *f*; clauses *f*, termes. Make your own terms, faites vos conditions vous-même. To dictate terms, imposer des conditions. To come to terms, en venir à un accommodement. (*b*) Terms of payment, conditions de paiement. 'Terms inclusive,' "tout compris." On easy terms, avec facilités de paiement. Not on any terms, à aucun prix. **4.** *pl.* Relations *f*, termes, rapports *m.* To be on friendly terms with s.o., vivre en bonne intelligence avec qn. To be on bad terms with s.o., être mal avec qn. To be on the best of terms with s.o., être au mieux avec qn. **5.** Terme (d'une équation). **6.** (*a*) Terme, mot *m*, expression *f.* (*b*) *pl.* Langage *m*, termes.
term², *v.tr.* Appeler, désigner, nommer.
termagant, *s.* Mégère *f*, virago *f.*
terminable, *a.* Terminable.
terminal. 1. *a.* **1.** Qui borne, qui termine. **2.** *Rail:* (Gare) terminus, de tête de ligne. **II.** **terminal,** *s. El:* Borne *f*; borne d'attache.
terminate. 1. *v.tr.* Terminer. **1.** Délimiter. **2.** (*a*) Mettre fin à. (*b*) Être à la fin de (qch.). **II.** **terminate,** *v.i.* **1.** Se terminer, finir (*in*, en, par). **2.** Aboutir (*in, at*, à).

termination, *s.* **1.** Terminaison *f*, fin *f*; cessation *f.* **2.** *Gram:* Terminaison, désinence *f.*
terminus, *s.* (Gare *f*) terminus *m.*
termite, *s. Ent:* Termite *m*; fourmi blanche.
tern, *s. Orn:* Sterne *m*; hirondelle *f* de mer.
terrace, *s.* **1.** *Const:* Terrasse *f*; terre-plein *m*, *pl.* terre-pleins. **2.** Rangée *f* de maisons formant terrasse.
terra-cotta, *s.* Terre cuite.
terra firma, *s.* Terre *f* ferme.
terrestrial, *a.* Terrestre.
terrible, *a.* (*a*) Terrible. (*b*) Terrible, affreux ; atroce. **-bly,** *adv.* (*a*) Terriblement, affreusement, atrocement. (*b*) *F: T. dangerous*, excessivement dangereux.
terrier, *s.* (Chien *m*) terrier *m.*
terrific, *a.* **1.** Terrifiant, épouvantable. **2.** *F:* Terrible ; énorme. *T. pace*, allure vertigineuse. **-ally,** *adv. F:* Terriblement.
terrify, *v.tr.* Terrifier, effrayer, épouvanter. To terrify s.o. out of their wits, rendre qn fou, *f.* folle, de terreur. **terrifying,** *a.* Terrifiant, terrible, épouvantable.
territorial. 1. *a.* (*a*) Territorial, -aux. (*b*) Terrien. **2.** *s. Mil:* Territorial *m.*
territory, *s.* Territoire *m.*
terror, *s.* **1.** Terreur *f*, effroi *m*, épouvante *f.* To be in terror, être dans la terreur. To be in terror of one's life, craindre pour sa vie. *F:* To go in terror of s.o., avoir une peur bleue de qn. **2.** (*a*) He was the terror of the countryside, c'était la terreur du pays. (*b*) *F:* He's a little terror, c'est un enfant terrible. **terror-struck,** *a.* Saisi de terreur ; épouvanté.
terrorism, *s.* Terrorisme *m.*
terrorize, *v.tr.* Terroriser.
terse, *a.* Concis, net, *f.* nette. **-ly,** *adv.* Avec concision.
terseness, *s.* Concision *f*; netteté *f.*
test¹, *s.* **1.** (*a*) Épreuve *f.* To put s.o. to the test, mettre qn à l'épreuve. (*b*) Essai *m*, épreuve. Endurance test, épreuve d'endurance. The acid test, *F:* l'épreuve concluante. Blood test, examen *m* du sang. **2.** (*a*) Examen. *Aut:* Driving test, examen pour permis de conduire. (*b*) *Psy:* Test *m.* Intelligence test, test de capacité intellectuelle. **test-match,** *s. Cr:* Rencontre internationale. **test-paper,** *s.* **1.** *Ch:* Papier réactif. **2.** *Sch:* Composition *f.* **test-tube,** *s. Ch:* Éprouvette *f.*
test², *v.tr.* (*a*) Éprouver ; mettre à l'épreuve, à l'essai. (*b*) Essayer ; contrôler, vérifier ; examiner.
testacean, *s. Z:* Testacé *m.*
testament, *s.* Testament *m.*
testamentary, *a.* Testamentaire.
testator, *s.* Testateur *m.*
testatrix, *s.* Testatrice *f.*
testifier, *s.* Témoin *m.*
testify. 1. *v.tr.* Témoigner. **2.** *Jur:* (*a*) *v.tr.* Déclarer, affirmer. *Abs.* To testify in

s.o.'s favour, rendre témoignage en faveur de qn. **To testify against s.o.**, déposer contre qn. (b) *v.ind.tr.* **To testify to a fact**, attester un fait.

testimonial, *s.* **1.** Certificat *m*; (lettre *f* de) recommandation *f*. *To show one's testimonials*, exhiber ses certificats. **2.** Témoignage *m* d'estime.

testimony, *s.* Témoignage *m*; *Jur:* attestation *f*; déposition *f*. **To bear testimony to sth.**, rendre témoignage de qch.

testiness, *s.* Irritabilité *f*, irascibilité *f*.

testy, *a.* Irritable, irascible; peu endurant. **-ily,** *adv.* D'un air irrité.

tether¹, *s.* Longe *f*, attache *f*. **To be at the end of one's tether**, être à bout de ressources.

tether², *v.tr.* Attacher, mettre à l'attache.

tetrarch, *s.* Tétrarque *m*.

Teuton. 1. *s.* Teuton, -onne. **2.** *a.* = TEUTONIC.

Teutonic, *a.* Teuton, -onne, teutonique.

text, *s.* **1.** Texte *m.* **2.** *F:* *The t. of his speech*, le sujet de son discours. **To stick to one's text**, ne pas s'écarter de la question.

text-book, *s. Sch:* Manuel *m.*

textile. 1. *a.* Textile. **2.** *s.* (a) Tissu *m*, étoffe *f*. (b) Matière *f* textile; textile *m.*

texture, *s.* Texture *f.*

Thames (the). *Pr.n.* La Tamise. *F:* **He will never set the Thames on fire**, il n'a pas inventé la poudre.

than. I. *conj.* (a) Que; (*with numbers*) de. *I have more, less, t. you*, j'en ai plus, moins, que vous. *More t. twenty*, plus de vingt. *More than once*, plus d'une fois. *I would rather starve than ask him for money*, j'aimerais mieux mourir de faim que de lui demander de l'argent. *No sooner had we entered than the music began*, nous étions à peine entrés que la musique commença. (b) *Any person other than himself*, tout autre que lui. **2.** *quasi-prep.* *A man than whom no one was more respected*, un homme qui était plus respecté que personne.

thank¹, *s.* **Thanks**, remerciement(s) *m.* **Give him my best thanks**, présentez-lui tous mes remerciements. *F:* **Thanks!** merci! **To pass a vote of thanks to s.o.**, voter des remerciements à qn. **Thanks to**, grâce à. *F:* **That's all the thanks I get!** voilà comme on me remercie!

thank², *v.tr.* **1.** (a) Remercier; dire merci à. **To thank s.o. for sth.**, remercier qn de qch. *To t. s.o. effusively*, se confondre en remerciements. **Thank goodness!** Grâce au ciel! (b) **(I) thank you**, je vous remercie; merci. *Will you have some tea?—No, thank you*, prenez-vous du thé?—Merci! **2.** **I'll thank you to mind your own business!** occupez-vous donc de ce qui vous regarde! **3. To have s.o. to thank for sth.**, devoir qch. à qn. *F:* **You have only yourself to thank for it**, c'est à vous seul qu'il faut vous en prendre.

thankful, *a.* Reconnaissant. **-fully,** *adv.* Avec reconnaissance.

thankfulness, *s.* Reconnaissance *f.*

thankless, *a.* Ingrat. **A thankless task**, une tâche ingrate, une vraie corvée.

thanklessness, *s.* Ingratitude *f.*

thanksgiving, *s.* Action *f* de grâce(s).

that¹. I. *Dem. pron.* **1.** Cela, *F:* ça; ce. (a) **Give me that**, donnez-moi cela. **What is that?** qu'est-ce (que c'est) que cela? **Who is that?** qui est-ce là? **That's Mr. Smith**, c'est M. Smith. *T. is my opinion*, voilà mon avis. **After that**, après cela. **With that** *he took himself off*, là-dessus il s'en alla. **What do you mean by that?** qu'entendez-vous par là? **They all think that**, c'est ce qu'ils pensent tous. **Have things come to that?** les choses en sont-elles arrivées là? **That is**, c'est-à-dire. (b) *And so that is settled*, alors quant à cela, c'est décidé. *He is only a fiddler, and a poor one at that*, ce n'est qu'un violoneux, et encore assez piètre. *F:* *Will you help me?—That I will!* voulez-vous m'aider?—Volontiers! *They are fine chaps.—They are that!* ce sont des gaillards.—En effet! **That's right!** that's it! c'est cela! **That's all**, voilà tout. **That's curious!** voilà qui est curieux! **And that's that!** et voilà! **2.** Celui-là, *f.* celle-là; *pl.* ceux-là, *f.* celles-là. *This is new and t. is old*, celui-ci est neuf et celui-là est vieux. **3.** Celui, *f.* celle; *pl.* ceux, *f.* celles. *Those of whom I speak*, ceux dont je parle. **II. that,** *dem.a.* (a) Ce, (before vowel or h 'mute') cet; *f.* cette; *pl.* ces; (for emphasis and in opposition to 'this', 'these') ce . . . -là. **That book, those books**, ce livre(-là), ces livres(-là). **That one**, celui-là, celle-là. *Everybody is agreed on t. point*, tout le monde est d'accord là-dessus. *I only saw him that once*, je ne l'ai vu que cette fois-là. (b) *F:* **Well, how's that leg of yours?** eh bien, et cette jambe? (c) *Those people who take an interest in these things*, les gens, ceux, qui s'intéressent à ces choses-là. **III. that,** *dem. adv. F:* **That high**, aussi haut que ça.

that², *rel. pron. sg. & pl.* **1.** (For subject) Qui; (for object) que. **The house that stands at the corner**, la maison qui se trouve au coin. **The letter (that) I sent you**, la lettre que je vous ai envoyée. **Wretch that I am!** malheureux que je suis! **2.** (Governed by prep.) Lequel, *f.* laquelle; *pl.* lesquels, *f.* lesquelles. *The envelope (that) I put it in*, l'enveloppe dans laquelle je l'ai mis. *The man (that) we are speaking of*, l'homme dont nous parlons. **3.** Où; que. *The night (that) we went to the theatre*, le soir où nous sommes allés au théâtre.

that³, *conj.* **1.** Que. (a) *It was for this t. they fought*, c'est pour cela qu'on s'est battu. (b) *I hope (that) you will have good luck*, j'espère que vous aurez de la chance. (c) (Afin) que, pour que, + *sub.* *Come nearer t. I may see you*, approchez, que je vous voie. *I am* *telling you*, (so) that you may know, je vous préviens pour que vous soyez au courant. **2.** (*a*) *That he should behave like this!* dire qu'il se conduit comme cela! (*b*) *O that it were possible!* oh, si c'était possible!

thatch[1], *s.* Chaume *m.*

thatch[2], *v.tr.* Couvrir (un toit) de, en, chaume. **thatched**, *a.* De chaume. *Thatched cottage*, chaumière *f.*

thatcher, *s.* Couvreur *m* en chaume.

thaw[1], *s.* Dégel *m.*

thaw[2]. **1.** *v.tr.* Dégeler. **2.** *v.i.* (*a*) (*Of snow*) Fondre. (*b*) *Impers.* It is thawing, il dégèle. **thawing**, *s.* **1.** Dégèlement *m.* **2.** Dégel *m*; fonte *f.*

the[1], *def. art.* **1.** Le, *f.* la; (*before vowel or* h '*mute*') l'; *pl.* les. (*a*) *The father and* (*the*) *mother*, le père et la mère. *On the other side*, de l'autre côté. *The Alps*, les Alpes. *I spoke to the coachman*, j'ai parlé au cocher. *Give that to the woman*, donnez cela à la femme. *He has gone to the fields*, il est allé aux champs. *The voice of the people*, la voix du peuple. *The roof of the house*, le toit de la maison. *The arrival of the guests*, l'arrivée des invités. **Edward the Seventh**, Édouard Sept. (*b*) *He is not the person to do that*, ce n'est pas une personne à faire cela. *The impudence of it!* quelle audace! *He hasn't the patience to wait*, il n'a pas assez de patience pour attendre. (*c*) *The beautiful*, le beau. *Coll.* **The poor**, les pauvres. (*d*) *F:* **He has the toothache**, il a mal aux dents. (*e*) *Sixpence the pound*, six pence la livre. *To be employed by the day*, travailler à la journée. **2.** Ce, cet, *f.* cette, *pl.* ces. *I was absent at the time*, j'étais absent à cette époque. *The ladies are in the drawing-room*, ces dames sont au salon. **3.** *Smith's is the shop for furniture*, la maison Smith est la meilleure pour les meubles.

the[2], *adv.* (*a*) *It will be the easier for you*, cela vous sera d'autant plus facile. (*b*) **The sooner the better**, le plus tôt sera le mieux. *The less said about it the better*, moins on en parlera mieux cela vaudra.

theatre, *s.* **1.** (*a*) Théâtre *m*; salle *f* de spectacle. (*b*) **The theatre**, l'art *m* dramatique; le théâtre. **2.** *F:* **The theatre of war**, le théâtre de la guerre. **theatre-goer**, *s.* Amateur, -trice, du théâtre.

theatrical, *a.* **1.** Théâtral, -aux. **2.** (*Of attitude*) Théâtral, histrionique. **-ally**, *adv.* **1.** Théâtralement. **2.** Avec affectation.

theatricals, *s.pl.* *Amateur theatricals*, spectacle *m* d'amateurs.

thee, *pers. pron. Poet:* **1.** Te; (*before a vowel sound*) t'. **2.** (*Stressed*) Toi.

theft, *s.* (*a*) Vol *m.* (*b*) *Petty theft*, larcin *m.*

their, *poss.a.* **1.** (*a*) Leur, *pl.* leurs. (*b*) *Their Majesties*, leurs Majestés. **2.** *F:* *Nobody in their senses*, personne jouissant de son bon sens.

theirs, *poss.pron.* Le leur, la leur, les leurs. *This house is t.*, cette maison est la leur, leur

appartient. *He is a friend of theirs*, c'est un de leurs amis.

them, *pers. pron., pl., objective case.* **1.** (*a*) (*Direct*) Les *mf*; (*indirect*) leur *mf.* *I like them*, je les aime. *I shall tell them so*, je le leur dirai. *Call them*, appelez-les. *Speak to them*, parlez-leur. (*b*) *They took the keys away with them*, ils ont emporté les clefs. **2.** (*Stressed*) Eux, *f.* elles. *Them I do not admire*, je ne les admire pas, eux. **3.** *Many of them*, plusieurs d'entre eux. *Both of them saw me*, ils m'ont vu tous (les) deux. *Give me half of them*, donnez-m'en la moitié. *Every one of them was killed*, ils furent tous tués. *Neither of them*, ni l'un ni l'autre. *Prepare the tables and put some flowers on them*, préparez les tables et mettez-y des fleurs. **4.** *F:* *It's them*, ce sont eux, c'est eux; les voilà!

theme, *s.* **1.** Sujet *m*, thème *m.* **2.** *Sch:* Dissertation *f*; exercice *m* littéraire. **3.** *Mus:* Thème, motif *m.*

themselves, *pers.pron.* *See* SELF 3.

then. **I.** *adv.* **1.** Alors; en ce temps-là. *Then and there*, séance tenante. **2.** Puis, ensuite, alors. *They travelled in France and then in Spain*, ils voyagèrent en France et ensuite en Espagne. *What then?* et puis? et (puis) après? **3.** D'ailleurs; aussi (bien); et puis. *I haven't the time, and then it isn't my business*, je n'ai pas le temps, d'ailleurs, aussi bien, ce n'est pas mon affaire. **II. then**, *conj.* En ce cas, donc, alors. *Go, then*, soit, allez. *But then*, mais c'est que. *You knew all the while then?* vous le saviez donc d'avance? **III. then**, *quasi-s.* Ce temps-là; cette époque-là. *Before then*, avant cela. *By then they had gone*, ils étaient déjà partis. *Till then*, (i) jusqu'alors; (ii) jusque-là. (*Ever*) *since then*, dès lors; depuis ce temps-là. *Between now and then*, d'ici là.

thence, *adv.* **1.** De là. **2.** Pour cette raison; par conséquent.

thenceforth, thenceforward, *adv.* Dès lors; désormais.

theodolite, *s. Surv:* Théodolite *m.*

theologian, *s.* Théologien *m.*

theological, *a.* Théologique.

theology, *s.* Théologie *f.*

theorem, *s.* Théorème *m.*

theoretic(al), *a.* Théorique. *Theoretical chemistry*, chimie pure. **-ally**, *adv.* Théoriquement.

theorist, *s.* Théoriste *mf.*

theorize, *v.tr. & i.* Théoriser.

theorizer, *s.* Théoriste *mf.*

theory, *s.* Théorie *f.* *In theory*, en théorie.

theosophist, *s.* Théosophe *mf.*

theosophy, *s.* Théosophie *f.*

there. **I.** *adv.* **1.** (*a*) Là, y. *Put it there*, mettez-le là. *He is still t.*, il y est toujours. *We are there*, nous voilà rendus. *F:* *He's all t.*, c'est un malin. *He is not all there*, il n'a pas toute sa tête. (*b*) *I am going t.*, j'y

vais. **A hundred miles there and back,** cent
milles aller et retour. (c) F: (*Emphatic*) -là.
That man t. always comes, cet homme-là vient
toujours. **Hurry up there!** dépêchez-vous
là-bas ! (d) **There is, are,** voilà. **There's the
bell ringing,** voilà la cloche qui sonne.
2. (a) There is, are, il est, il y a. **There was
once a king,** il était, il y avait, une fois un roi.
There was singing and dancing, on a chanté
et dansé. *T. is a page missing,* il manque une
page. (b) **There comes a time when,** il arrive
un moment où. **3.** Quant à cela ; en cela.
There we differ, sur ce sujet nous ne sommes
pas d'accord. F: **There you have me!** ça,
ça me dépasse. **II. there,** *int.* Voilà !
There now! (i) voilà ! (ii) allons bon !
There, take this book, tenez ! prenez ce livre.
There! there! don't worry, là là, ne vous
inquiétez pas ! **But there,** *what is the good of
talking!* mais à quoi bon en parler ! **III.
there,** *quasi-s.* He left there *last night,* il
est parti (de là) hier soir. **In there,** là-dedans ;
là.

thereabouts, *adv.* **1.** Près de là ; dans le
voisinage. **Somewhere thereabout,** quelque
part par là. **2.** A peu près ; environ.

thereafter, *adv.* Après (cela) ; par la suite.

thereat, *adv.* Là-dessus.

thereby, *adv.* Par ce moyen ; de cette façon.

therefore, *adv.* Donc ; par conséquent.

therefrom, *adv.* De là.

therein, *adv.* **1.** En cela ; à cet égard.
2. (Là-)dedans.

thereof, *adv.* De cela ; en.

thereon, *adv.* (Là-)dessus.

thereto, *adv.* He put his signature t., il y
apposa sa signature.

thereupon, *adv.* **1.** Sur ce. **2.** *Lit:* Là-
dessus, à ce sujet.

therewith, *adv.* **1.** Avec cela. **2.** = THERE-
UPON 1. **3.** En outre.

thermal, *a.* Thermal, -aux. **Thermal baths,**
thermes *m*.

thermometer, *s.* Thermomètre *m*.

thesis, *s.* (a) Thèse *f*. (b) *Sch:* Dissertation *f*.

thews, *s.pl.* Muscles *m* ; F: nerfs *m*.

they. I. *Pers. pron. nom. pl.* (a) Ils *f*. elles.
T. are dancing, ils, elles, dansent. *Here t.
come,* les voici (qui viennent). *T. are rich
people,* ce sont des gens riches. (b) (*Stressed*)
Eux, *f*. elles. **It is they,** ce sont eux. **If I
were they,** (si j'étais) à leur place. (c) **They
who believe,** ceux, celles, qui croient. **2.**
Indef. pron. On. **They say,** on dit.

thick. I. *a.* **1.** Épais, *f*. épaisse ; (*of book*)
gros, *f*. grosse. *Wall that is two feet thick,*
mur qui a deux pieds d'épaisseur. F: **To
have a thick skin,** être peu sensible. **2.** (*Of
forest*) Épais, serré, touffu. *Bodies lay t. on
the ground,* le sol était encombré de cadavres.
3. (a) (*Of liquid*) Épais, consistant. **Thick
soup,** potage *m* crème. (b) (*Of voice*) Empâté.
To be thick of speech, avoir le parler gras.

(c) F: Obtus. **4.** F: **To be very thick with
s.o.,** être très lié avec qn. **They are as thick
as thieves,** ils s'accordent comme larrons en
foire. **5.** P: **That's a bit thick!** ça c'est un
peu fort ! **-ly,** *adv.* **1.** En couche épaisse.
2. *Snow fell t.,* la neige tombait dru. **3.** D'une
voix empâtée. **II. thick,** *s.* **1.** (a) (La) partie
charnue, le gras. (b) **In the thick of the fight,**
au (plus) fort de la mêlée. **2.** **Through thick
and thin,** à travers toutes les épreuves.
III. thick, *adv.* **1.** En couche épaisse.
2. His blows fell thick and fast, les coups
pleuvaient dru. **thick-headed,** *a.* F:
Bête, stupide. **thick-lipped,** *a.* Lippu ;
à grosses lèvres. **thick-set,** *a.* **1.** (*Of hedge*)
Épais, *f*. épaisse ; dru. **2.** (Short and) thick-
set, trapu. **thick-skinned,** *a.* **1.** A la peau
épaisse ; *Z:* pachyderme. **2.** F: Peu
sensible.

thicken. 1. *v.tr.* Épaissir ; lier (une sauce).
2. *v.i.* (a) (S')épaissir. (b) *The crowd thickens,*
la foule augmente. (c) (*Of plot*) Se corser.

thicket, *s.* Hallier *m*, fourré *m*.

thickness, *s.* **1.** (a) Épaisseur *f* ; grosseur *f*.
(b) Épaisseur (d'une forêt). (c) Consistance
f (d'un liquide) ; épaisseur (du brouillard).
2. Couche *f*.

thief, *s.* Voleur, -euse. *Thieves (as a class),*
F: la pègre. **Stop thief!** au voleur ! *Prov:*
Set a thief to catch a thief, à voleur, voleur et
demi. **Honour among thieves,** foi *f* de
bohème.

thieve, *v.tr.* Voler. *Abs.* Être voleur ; voler.

thieving¹, *a.* Voleur, -euse. **thieving²,** *s.*
Vol *m*, volerie *f*.

thievish, *a.* Voleur, -euse.

thievishness, *s.* Penchant *m* au vol.

thigh, *s.* Cuisse *f*.

thimble, *s.* Dé *m* (à coudre). **thimble-
case,** *s.* Étui *m* à dé.

thimbleful, *s.* F: Doigt *m*, plein un dé à
coudre.

thin¹. a. **1.** (a) Peu épais, *f*. épaisse, mince ;
ténu ; (*of stuff*) léger. (b) Maigre, mince.
To grow thinner, maigrir ; s'amaigrir. **2.** (*Of
hair*) Clairsemé, rare. **3.** Thin voice, voix
fluette, grêle. **4.** F: (a) **Thin excuse,** pauvre
excuse. *That's a bit thin!* c'est peu convaincant ! (b) **To have a thin time of it,** passer
un temps peu agréable. **-ly,** *adv.* **1.** A peine.
Thinly clad, vêtu insuffisamment. **2.** D'une
manière éparse. *Country t. populated,* pays
peu peuplé. **thin-lipped,** *a.* Aux lèvres
minces. **thin-skinned,** *a.* F: Susceptible.

thin². v. 1. *v.tr.* (a) Amincir. (b) Éclaircir
(les arbres). **To thin (out) seedlings,** éclaircir,
repiquer, les jeunes plants. **2.** *v.i.* (a) Maigrir.
(b) S'amincir, s'effiler. (c) (*Of crowd*) S'é-
claircir.

thine. *Poet:* *Poss.pron.* (a) Le tien, la tienne,
les tiens, les tiennes. (b) **For thee and thine,**
pour toi et les tiens. (c) **What is mine is
thine,** ce qui est à moi est à toi.

thing, *s.* **1.** Chose *f*. (a) Objet *m*, article *m*.

(b) *F:* **What's that thing?** qu'est-ce que c'est que ce machin-là? (c) *pl.* Vêtements *m,* effets *m.* **To take off one's things,** se déshabiller. (d) *pl.* Affaires *f,* effets. **To pack up one's things,** faire ses malles. *To put one's things away,* serrer ses affaires. **2.** *F:* Être *m,* créature *f. Poor little things!* pauvres petits êtres! **3.** (a) *You take the t. too seriously,* vous prenez la chose trop sérieusement. **To expect great things,** attendre grand bien. **To talk of one thing and another,** parler de choses et d'autres. **That's the very thing,** c'est juste ce qu'il faut. *That's the t. for me,* voilà mon affaire. **The thing is this,** voici ce dont il s'agit. **Neither one thing nor another,** ni l'un ni l'autre; mi-figue, mi-raisin. **What with one thing and another,** tant et si bien que. **For one thing,** en premier lieu. **He makes a good thing out of it,** ça lui rapporte pas mal. (b) *F:* **To know a thing or two,** en savoir plus d'un(e). *To put s.o. up to a t. or two,* mettre qn à la page. (c) *pl. Things are going badly,* les affaires vont mal. *Since that is how things are,* puisqu'il en est ainsi. *F:* **How are things?** comment ça va? **4.** The latest thing in ties, cravate(s) dernier cri. **5.** *F:* The thing (to do), l'usage *m.* It's not the thing, cela ne se fait pas. It's quite the thing, c'est tout à fait correct. He is not feeling quite the thing, il ne se sent pas dans son assiette.

think¹, *s.* **To have a quiet think,** réfléchir. **think²,** *v.* I. *v.tr. & i.* **1.** Penser, réfléchir. He thinks for himself, il pense par lui-même. *I know what you are thinking,* je connais vos pensées. **To act without thinking,** agir sans réflexion. **Think before you speak,** pesez vos paroles. *Give me time to t.,* laissez-moi me reprendre. *F:* **Think again!** réfléchissez! **2.** Songer, s'imaginer. *One would have thought,* c'était à croire. *Anyone would t. that he was asleep,* on dirait qu'il dort. *Who'd have thought it!* qui l'aurait dit? **Only think!** songez donc! **3.** *I have been thinking that,* l'idée m'est venue que. **Thinking to,** dans l'intention de. **4.** (a) *It is better, don't you think, to get it over?* il vaut mieux, n'est-ce pas, en finir? *What do you t. I ought to do?* que jugez-vous que je doive faire? *I thought all was over,* je me disais que tout était fini. **I think so,** je pense que oui. I should hardly think so, c'est peu probable. **I should (just) think so!** je crois bien! *P:* **I don't think!** jamais de la vie! (b) *Pred.* Juger, trouver, penser. **I think her pretty,** je la trouve jolie. *They were thought to be rich,* ils passaient pour (être) riches. **5.** *I little thought to see him again,* je ne m'attendais guère à le revoir. **I thought so,** je m'y attendais. II. **think of, about,** *v.ind.tr.* **1.** Penser à; songer à. **One can't think of everything,** on ne saurait penser à tout. *I can't t. of the right word,* le mot propre m'échappe. **The best thing I can think of,** ce que je vois de mieux. *That is worth*

thinking about, cela mérite réflexion. *What am I thinking about?* où ai-je la tête? **2.** S'imaginer, se figurer, songer. **3.** Considérer. *To t. of s.o.'s feelings,* avoir égard aux sentiments de qn. **To think of the expense,** regarder à la dépense. **4.** *I couldn't think of it!* il n'y a pas à y songer! **5.** (a) *v.tr.* **What do you think of it?** qu'en pensez-vous? To think too much of oneself, s'en faire accroire. *To t. too much of sth.,* attacher trop d'importance à qch. I told him what I thought of him, je lui ai dit son fait. (b) **To think well of s.o.,** estimer qn. **He is thought well of,** il est bien vu. **think out,** *v.tr.* **1.** Imaginer, méditer. **To think out a plan,** élaborer un plan. *Carefully thought-out answer,* réponse bien pesée. *That wants thinking out,* cela demande mûre réflexion. **2.** *He thinks things out for himself,* il juge des choses par lui-même. **think over,** *v.tr.* Réfléchir sur, aviser à (une question). *T. it over,* réfléchissez-y bien. **thinking¹,** *a.* Pensant; qui pense. **thinking²,** *s.* Pensée(s) *f(pl),* réflexion(s) *f(pl).* **To my thinking,** à mon avis. *That is my way of thinking,* voilà ma façon de penser.

thinkable, *a.* Concevable, imaginable.

thinker, *s.* Penseur, -euse.

thinness, *s.* **1.** (a) Peu *m* d'épaisseur; minceur *f*; légèreté *f.* (b) Maigreur *f.* **2.** Rareté *f* (des cheveux). **3.** Fluidité *f* (d'un liquide). **4.** *F:* Faiblesse *f* (d'une excuse).

third. 1. *Num.a.* Troisième. **Third person,** (i) *Jur:* tierce personne, tiers *m*; (ii) *Gram:* troisième personne. **Edward the Third,** Édouard Trois. **(On) the third of March,** le trois mars. *Rail:* **To travel third,** voyager en troisième (classe). **2.** *s. Mus:* Tierce *f.* **3.** *s.* Tiers *m.* **-ly,** *adv.* Troisièmement; en troisième lieu. **third-class,** *a.* (a) De troisième (classe). (b) De qualité inférieure; d'ordre inférieur. **third-rate,** *a.* De troisième qualité; très inférieur.

thirst¹, *s.* Soif *f. Great t.,* altération *f.*

thirst², *v.i. To t. for blood,* être altéré de sang. **thirsting,** *a.* Altéré, assoiffé (*for,* de).

thirsty, *a.* Altéré. **To be thirsty,** avoir soif. **To make s.o. thirsty,** donner soif à qn; altérer qn. **Thirsty for riches,** assoiffé de richesses. **-ily,** *adv.* Avidement.

thirteen, *num. a. & s.* Treize (*m*).

thirteenth, *num. a. & s.* Treizième *m.* **(On) the thirteenth of May,** le treize mai.

thirtieth, *num. a. & s.* Trentième (*m*). **(On) the thirtieth of June,** le trente juin.

thirty, *num. a. & s.* Trente (*m*). **Thirty-one,** trente et un. **Thirty-first,** trente et unième. *About t. persons,* une trentaine de personnes.

this. I. *Dem. pron.* **1.** Ceci; ce. *This I knew,* ceci, je le savais. **Who is this?** quelle est cette personne? **You will be sorry for this,** vous le regretterez. *It ought to have been done before t.,* cela devrait être déjà fait. **This is curious,** voici qui est curieux. *T. is* *where he lives*, c'est ici qu'il demeure. It was like this, voici comment les choses se sont passées. **The thing is this**, voici ce dont il s'agit. **2. Will you have this or that?** voulez-vous ceci ou cela? **3.** Celui-ci, *f.* celle-ci, *pl.* ceux-ci, *f.* celles-ci. *I prefer these to those*, je préfère ceux-ci à ceux-là. II. **this**, *dem.a.* (*a*) Ce, (*before vowel or h 'mute'*) cet, *f.* cette, *pl.* ces; (*for emphasis*) ce (*etc.*) -ci. T. *book*, *these books*, ce livre(-ci), ces livres(-ci). In **these days**, de nos jours. **This day last year**, l'an dernier à pareil jour. *To run* **this** *way and that*, courir de-ci, de-là. (*b*) **I've been watching you these ten minutes**, voilà dix minutes que je vous observe. III. **this**, *dem.adv.* **This high**, aussi haut que ceci, que ça.

thistle, *s. Bot:* Chardon *m.* **Scotch thistle**, acanthe *f* sauvage. **thistle-down**, *s.* Duvet *m* de chardon.

thither, *adv.* Là; y. **To run hither and thither**, courir çà et là.

thong, *s.* Lanière *f* de cuir; courroie *f.*

thorax, *s. Anat:* Thorax *m.*

thorn, *s.* (*a*) Épine *f. F:* **To be on thorns**, être sur des épines. **A thorn in the flesh**, une épine au pied. (*b*) Arbrisseau épineux; épine.

thorn-bush, *s.* = THORN (*b*).

thorny, *a.* Épineux.

thorough, *a.* (*a*) Minutieux; (*of knowledge*) profond; (*of work*) consciencieux. *To give a room a* t. *cleaning*, nettoyer une chambre à fond. (*b*) **A thorough Frenchman**, un vrai Français. *A* t. *republican*, un républicain convaincu. *A* t. *scoundrel*, un coquin achevé. **-ly**, *adv.* Tout à fait; (*comprendre*) parfaitement; complètement; à fond. **thorough-paced**, *a.* Accompli. *He is a* t.*-p. scoundrel*, c'est un scélérat consommé.

thoroughbred. I. *a.* (Cheval) pur sang *inv*; (chien) de race. **2.** *s.* (*a*) Cheval *m* pur sang. (*b*) Animal, -aux *m*, de race.

thoroughfare, *s.* Voie *f* de communication. **Public thoroughfare**, voie publique. *Busy* t., rue très passante. 'No thoroughfare,' "interdiction de passage."

thoroughness, *s.* Caractère approfondi.

thou, *pers. pron. Poet:* (*a*) Tu. (*b*) (*Stressed*) Toi.

though. I. *conj.* **1.** Quoique, bien que, encore que, + *sub. I am sorry for him, t. he is nothing to me*, je le plains, encore qu'il ne me soit rien. *T. I am a father*, tout père que je suis. *T. small he is none the less brave*, pour être petit il n'en est pas moins brave. **2.** (*a*) **Strange though it may appear**, si étrange que cela paraisse. *I will do it though it cost me my fortune*, je le ferai quand cela me coûterait toute ma fortune. (*b*) **What though the way be long!** qu'importe que le chemin soit long! **3. As though**, comme si. **It looks as though he had gone**, il semble qu'il soit parti. II. **though**, *adv.* (*a*) Cependant,

pourtant. (*b*) **Did he though!** vraiment! il a dit, fait, cela?

thought, *s.* (La) pensée. **I. Capable of thought**, capable de penser. **2.** (*a*) Idée *f.* **Happy thought**, heureuse idée. (*b*) *F:* **A penny for your thoughts**, à quoi pensez-vous? *To read s.o.'s thoughts*, lire dans la pensée de qn. (*c*) **I did not give it another thought**, je n'y ai pas repensé. (*d*) *pl.* Esprit *m*, pensée. *To collect one's thoughts*, rassembler ses idées, ses esprits. **3.** (*a*) Réflexion *f*, considération *f.* **Want of thought**, irréflexion *f.* **After much thought**, après mûre réflexion. **On second thoughts**, (toute) réflexion faite. (*b*) Pensées, rêverie *f*, méditation *f*, recueillement *m.* **4.** (*a*) Intention *f*, dessein *m.* **To have thoughts of doing sth.**, songer à faire qch. **I had no thought of offending you**, je n'avais pas l'intention de vous offenser. (*b*) **I had no thought of meeting you here**, je ne m'attendais pas à vous rencontrer ici. **thought-reader**, *s.* Liseur, -euse, d'âmes. **thought-reading**, *s.* Lecture *f* de la pensée; télépathie *f.*

thoughtful, *a.* **I.** (*a*) Pensif, méditatif; rêveur, -euse. (*b*) Réfléchi, prudent. **2.** Prévenant (*of*, pour). **To be thoughtful of others**, être plein d'égards pour les autres. **-fully**, *adv.* **I.** Pensivement. **2.** D'une manière réfléchie. **3.** Avec prévenance.

thoughtfulness, *s.* **I.** Méditation *f*, recueillement *m.* **2.** Réflexion *f*, prudence *f.* **3.** Prévenance *f*, égards *mpl* (*of*, pour, envers).

thoughtless, *a.* **I.** Irréfléchi; étourdi. **Thoughtless action**, étourderie *f.* **2. Thoughtless of others**, peu soucieux des autres. **-ly**, *adv.* Étourdiment.

thoughtlessness, *s.* **I.** Étourderie *f.* **2.** Manque *m* d'égards (*of*, pour, envers).

thousand, *num. a. & s.* Mille (*m*) *inv*; *s.* millier *m.* **A t. men**, mille hommes. **Thousands of people**, des milliers de gens. **He is one in a thousand**, c'est un homme entre mille. **A thousand apologies!** mille pardons! **A thousand times no!** cent fois non!

thraldom, *s.* Esclavage *m*, servitude *f.*

thrall, *s.* Esclave *m*, serf *m* (*of*, *to*, de).

thrash, *v.tr.* **I.** (*a*) Battre; *F:* rosser. (*b*) Battre à plates coutures. **2.** *Husb:* = THRESH. **thrash out**, *v.tr.* Débattre (une question). **thrashing**, *s.* **I.** Rossée *f*, correction *f.* **To give s.o. a thrashing**, administrer une raclée à qn. **2.** *Husb:* = THRESHING.

thread[1], *s.* **I.** Filament *m*, fil *m. F:* **To hang by a thread**, ne tenir qu'à un fil. **2.** (*a*) *Needlw:* Fil (de coton). **Sewing thread**, fil à coudre. **Lisle thread**, fil d'Écosse. (*b*) *F:* **The thread of life**, la trame de la vie. **To lose the thread of one's discourse**, perdre le fil de son discours. (*c*) (*Length of*) **thread**, brin *m*, bout *m* (de coton). **3.** *Tchn:* Filet *m*, filetage *m*, pas *m* (de vis).

thread[2], *v.tr.* (*a*) Enfiler. (*b*) **To thread one's way**, se faufiler.

threadbare, *a.* Râpé.

threat, *s.* Menace *f.* **There is a threat of rain,** la pluie menace.

threaten, *v.tr.* **I.** Menacer. **To threaten s.o. with sth.,** menacer qn de qch. **To threaten to do sth.,** menacer de faire qch. **2.** *The sky threatens rain,* le ciel annonce la pluie. *Abs.* **A storm is threatening,** la tempête (ou l'orage) menace. **threatening,** *a.* Menaçant. **The weather looks threatening,** le temps menace. **-ly,** *adv.* D'une manière menaçante.

three, *num. a. & s.* Trois (*m*). **three-cornered,** *a.* Triangulaire; (*of hat*) tricorne. **three-legged,** *a.* **Three-legged race,** course à trois pieds. **three-ply,** *attrib.a.* **I. Three-ply wood,** contre-plaqué *m* à trois épaisseurs. **2.** (*Of wool*) A trois fils.

threefold, *a.* Triple.

threepenny, *attrib.a.* **Threepenny bit,** *s.* pièce *f* de trois pence.

thresh, *v.tr.* Battre (le blé). **threshing,** *s.* Battage *m.* **threshing-machine,** *s.* Batteuse *f.*

threshold, *s.* Seuil *m*, pas *m.* **To cross the threshold,** franchir le seuil.

thrice, *adv.* Trois fois.

thrift, *s.* Économie *f*, épargne *f.*

thriftiness, *s.* Économie *f.*

thriftless, *a.* Dépensier, prodigue.

thriftlessness, *s.* Prodigalité *f.*

thrifty, *a.* Économe, ménager. **-ily,** *adv.* Avec économie. *To live t.,* vivre frugalement.

thrill¹, *s.* (*a*) Frisson *m*, tressaillement *m.* (*b*) (Vive) émotion.

thrill². **I.** *v.tr.* (*a*) Faire frissonner, faire frémir. **To be thrilled with joy,** frissonner de joie. (*b*) Émouvoir, empoigner. **2.** *v.i.* Tressaillir, frissonner, frémir. **thrilling,** *a.* Empoignant, émouvant.

thriller, *s.* *P:* Roman sensationnel; pièce *f* mélodramatique, à gros effets.

thrive, *v.i.* (*a*) Se (bien) développer; (*of business*) bien marcher. *He thrives on it,* il s'en trouve bien. (*b*) Prospérer **thriving,** *a.* Vigoureux, prospère.

throat, *s.* (*a*) *Anat:* Gorge *f.* **To grip s.o. by the throat,** empoigner qn à la gorge. *F:* **He is cutting his own throat,** il travaille à sa propre ruine. (*b*) Gorge, gosier *m.* **I have a sore throat,** j'ai mal à la gorge. **To clear one's throat,** s'éclaircir le gosier. **To thrust sth. down s.o.'s throat,** imposer une opinion à qn.

throaty, *a.* D'arrière-gorge; guttural, -aux.

throb¹, *s.* Pulsation *f*, battement *m*; vrombissement *m* (d'une machine).

throb², *v.i.* (*a*) Battre fort; palpiter; (*of engine*) vrombir. (*b*) **My finger is throbbing,** mon doigt lancine. **throbbing,** *s.* (*a*) Battement *m*, pulsation *f*; vrombissement *m.* (*b*) Lancination *f.*

throes, *s.pl.* Douleurs *fpl*, angoisse *f*, agonie *f.* **The throes of death,** les affres *f* de la mort;

l'agonie. **In the throes of,** au beau milieu de.

throne, *s.* Trône *m.*

throng¹, *s.* (*a*) Foule *f*, affluence *f.* (*b*) Cohue *f.*

throng². **I.** *v.i.* S'assembler en foule; affluer. **To throng round s.o.,** se presser autour de qn. **2.** *v.tr.* Encombrer (les rues).

thronged, *a.* Plein de gens; comble, bondé.

throstle, *s.* Grive chanteuse.

throttle¹, *s.* *I.C.E:* Étrangleur *m*; obturateur *m* d'air **To open out the throttle,** mettre les gaz.

throttle², *v.tr.* **I.** Étrangler; serrer à la gorge. **2.** *Mch:* *I.C.E:* Étrangler. **throttling,** *s.* Étranglement *m.*

through. **I.** *prep.* **I.** (*a*) A travers; par. *T. a hedge,* au travers d'une haie. **To look t. a telescope,** regarder dans un télescope. *F:* **To go through s.o.'s pockets,** fouiller qn. *F:* **He's been through it,** il en a vu de dures. **To speak through one's nose,** parler du nez. **I am half through this book,** j'ai lu la moitié de ce livre. (*b*) Pendant, durant. **All through his life,** sa vie durant. **2. Through s.o.,** par qn; par l'entremise de qn. **To send sth. through the post,** envoyer qch. par la poste. **3.** (*a*) En conséquence de, à cause de. **Through ignorance,** par ignorance. **Absent through illness,** absent par suite de maladie. **To act through fear,** agir sous le coup de la peur. (*b*) **It all happened through him,** il est cause de tout. **II. through,** *adv.* **I.** (*a*) A travers. **To let s.o. through,** laisser passer qn. (*b*) **Through (and through),** de part en part. **To run s.o. through,** transpercer qn. (*c*) D'un bout à l'autre; jusqu'au bout. **To see sth. through,** mener qch. à bonne fin. **2.** (*a*) **The train runs through to Paris,** le train va directement à Paris. (*b*) *Tp:* **To get through to s.o.,** obtenir la communication avec qn. **You are through,** vous êtes en communication. **III. through,** *attrib.a. Rail:* **Through carriage,** voiture directe.

throughout. **I.** *prep.* (*a*) **Throughout the country,** dans tout le pays. (*b*) **Throughout the year,** pendant toute l'année. **2.** *adv.* (*a*) Partout. (*b*) Tout le temps.

throw¹, *s.* (*a*) Jet *m*, lancement *m*, lancée *f.* (*b*) *Wr:* Mise *f* à terre.

throw², *v.tr.* **I.** (*a*) Jeter, lancer. *Abs.* **He can throw a hundred yards,** il est capable de lancer à cent mètres. **To throw oneself backwards,** se rejeter en arrière. **To throw temptation in s.o.'s way,** exposer qn à la tentation. **To throw the blame on s.o.,** rejeter la faute sur qn. (*b*) **To be thrown upon one's own resources,** n'avoir plus à compter que sur soi-même. **To throw open the door,** ouvrir la porte toute grande. **2.** Projeter. **To throw a picture on the screen,** projeter une image sur l'écran. **3.** (*a*) *Wr:* **To throw an opponent,** terrasser un adversaire. (*b*) (*Of horse*) **To throw its rider,** démonter son cavalier. **To be thrown,**

être désarçonné. **throw about,** *v.tr.*
I. Jeter çà et là. To throw one's money
about, gaspiller son argent. **2.** To throw
one's arms about, faire de grands gestes.
To throw oneself about, se démener. **throw
away,** *v.tr.* **I.** Jeter; rejeter; mettre au
rebut. **2.** Donner inutilement. To throw
away a chance, laisser passer une occasion.
To throw away one's life, se sacrifier inutilement. **throw down,** *v.tr.* (*a*) Jeter de haut
en bas. (*b*) Jeter à terre. (*c*) To throw down
one's arms, abandonner ses armes. *Ind:* To
throw down one's tools, se mettre en grève.
throw in, *v.tr.* **I.** Jeter dedans. **2.** (*a*)
Ajouter; donner par-dessus le marché.
(*b*) Intercaler (un mot). **3.** To throw in one's
lot with s.o., partager le sort de qn. **4.** To
throw in one's hand, abandonner la partie.
throw off, *v.tr.* **I.** (*a*) Jeter, rendre.
(*b*) Enlever, quitter; se débarrasser de;
abandonner (un déguisement). **2.** To throw
off the scent, dépister. **throw out,** *v.tr.*
I. Jeter dehors; expulser. **2.** Répandre,
émettre. **3.** Rejeter. **4.** To throw out one's
chest, bomber la poitrine. **5.** Lancer, laisser
entendre. **6.** Déconcerter (un orateur).
throw up, *v.tr.* **I.** Jeter en l'air. **2.** Vomir.
3. Lever haut, mettre haut. **4.** Renoncer à,
abandonner. To throw up one's situation,
se démettre de son poste.
thrush, *s. Orn:* Grive *f.*
thrust[1], *s.* (*a*) Poussée *f.* (*b*) Coup *m* de
pointe. *Fenc:* Coup d'estoc. Lance thrust,
coup de lance.
thrust[2], *v.* **I.** *v.tr.* (*a*) Pousser. To thrust
one's hands into one's pockets, fourrer les
mains dans ses poches. To thrust a dagger
into s.o.'s back, enfoncer un poignard dans
le dos de qn. (*b*) To thrust oneself upon s.o.,
s'imposer à qn, chez qn. **2.** *v.i.* To thrust
at s.o., porter un coup de pointe à qn.
thud[1], *s.* Bruit sourd; son mat; floc *m.*
thud[2], *v.i.* Tomber avec un bruit sourd;
émettre un bruit mat.
thug, *s.* **I.** Étrangleur *m.* **2.** Bandit *m.*
thumb, *s.* Pouce *m. F:* His fingers are all
thumbs, il est maladroit de ses mains. To be
under s.o.'s thumb, être sous la domination
de qn. **thumb-nail,** *s.* Ongle *m* du pouce.
Thumb-nail sketch, croquis *m* minuscule.
thumb-screw, *s. Hist:* Poucettes *fpl* (de
torture).
thump[1], *s.* **I.** Coup sourd. **2.** Coup de
poing; bourrade *f.*
thump[2], *v.tr. & i.* Bourrer de coups. *To t.*
(*on*) *the table,* cogner sur la table. My heart
was thumping, mon cœur battait fort.
thumping, *a. F:* Énorme.
thunder[1], *s.* (*a*) Tonnerre *m.* Peal of
thunder, coup *m* de tonnerre. (*b*) *F:* Thunder
of applause, tonnerre d'applaudissements.
thunder-cloud, *s.* Nuage orageux.
thunder-storm, *s.* Orage *m.*
thunder[2], *v.i. & tr.* **I.** Tonner. *It is*

thundering, il tonne. **2.** *F:* To thunder (out)
threats, tonner, fulminer, des menaces.
thundering, *a.* **I.** Tonnant; fulminant.
2. *F:* Formidable.
thunderbolt, *s.* **I.** (Coup *m* de) foudre *f.*
2. *F:* Nouvelle foudroyante.
thunderous, *a.* **I.** Orageux. **2.** (*Of voice*)
Tonnant; (*of applause*) à tout rompre.
thunderstruck, *a.* Confondu, abasourdi.
To be thunderstruck, être atterré.
Thursday, *s.* Jeudi *m.*
thus, *adv.* **I.** Ainsi; de cette façon. **2.** Ainsi,
donc. **3.** Thus far, jusqu'ici; jusque-là.
thwack[1], *s.* **I.** Coup (de bâton). **2.** *int. F:*
V'lan !
thwack[2], *v.tr. F:* Donner des coups à.
thwart[1], *s.* Banc *m* de nage.
thwart[2], *a.* Transversal, -aux; transverse.
thwart[3], *v.tr.* Contrecarrer; déjouer les
menées de. *To t. s.o.'s plans,* circonvenir les
projets de qn. To be thwarted, essuyer un
échec.
thy, *poss.a. Poet:* Ton, *f.* ta, *pl.* tes.
thyme, *s. Bot:* Thym *m.* Wild thyme,
serpolet *m.*
thyroid, *a.* Thyroïde.
thyself, *pron. See* SELF 3.
tiara, *s.* Tiare *f.*
Tiber (the). *Pr.n.* Le Tibre.
Tibet. *Pr.n. Geog:* Le Tibet.
Tibetan, *a. & s.* Tibétain, -aine.
tick[1], *s.* **I.** (*a*) Tic-tac *m. F:* On the tick,
à l'heure sonnante. (*b*) *F:* Moment *m,*
instant *m.* Half a tick! un instant! *He'll do
it in two ticks,* il fera ça en moins de rien.
2. Marque *f,* pointage *m,* trait *m.* To put a
tick against a name, faire une marque à un
nom; pointer un nom. **tick-tack,** *s.* Tic-
tock, *s.* Tic-tac *m.*
tick[2]. **I.** *v.i.* Faire tic-tac. **2.** *v.tr.* = TICK
OFF I. **tick off,** *v.tr.* **I.** Pointer. To *t. off a
name,* faire une marque à un nom. **2.** *F:*
Rembarrer. **ticking,** *s.* Tic-tac *m.*
tick[3], *s. Arach:* Tique *f.*
tick[4], *s. P:* Crédit *m.* On tick, à crédit.
ticker, *s. F:* Montre *f.*
ticket[1], *s.* **I.** Billet *m;* ticket *m* (d'autobus).
Rail: Cloak-room ticket, bulletin *m,* ticket,
de consigne. Platform ticket, billet de quai.
2. *Com:* (Price-)ticket, étiquette *f;* fiche *f.*
3. *P:* That's the ticket! voilà qui fera
l'affaire ! à la bonne heure! **ticket-
collector,** *s. Rail:* Contrôleur *m.* **ticket-
holder,** *s.* Voyageur, -euse, spectateur, -trice,
muni(e) d'un billet. **Season-ticket-holder,**
abonné, -ée. **ticket-inspector,** *s.* Contrôleur *m.*
ticket[2], *v.tr.* Étiqueter, marquer. **ticket-
ing,** *s.* Étiquetage *m.*
tickle[1], *s.* Chatouillement *m.*
tickle[2]. **I.** *v.tr.* (*a*) Chatouiller. *F:* To
tickle the palate, chatouiller le palais. (*b*) *F:*
Amuser. To be tickled to death at sth., se
tordre de rire à l'idée de qch. **2.** *v.i. My*

hand tickles, j'ai des chatouillements à la main.
tickling, *s.* Chatouillement *m.*
ticklish, *a.* **1.** Chatouilleux, -euse. **2.** A ticklish subject, un sujet délicat.
ticklishness, *s.* **1.** Sensibilité *f* au chatouillement. **2.** Délicatesse *f* (d'une tâche).
tidal, *a.* **1.** Tidal wave, vague *f* de fond. **2.** (*Of river*) A marée.
tiddlywinks, *s.* Jeu *m* de la puce.
tide¹, *s.* Marée *f.* **Against the tide**, à contre-marée. **To go with the tide**, suivre le courant. **The tide of battle**, la fortune de la bataille.
tide² over, *v.tr.* Venir à bout. This sum will tide us over, cette somme nous permettra de surmonter nos difficultés.
tidiness, *s.* Bon ordre ; (*of dress*) bonne tenue.
tidings, *s.pl.* Nouvelle(s) *f(pl).*
tidy¹, *a.* **1.** (*a*) Bien rangé, en bon ordre ; (*of dress*) bien tenu. Make yourself t., faites-vous propre. (*b*) Ordonné ; qui a de l'ordre. **2.** *F:* Assez bon ; passable. A tidy sum, une somme rondelette. **-ily**, *adv.* Proprement ; avec ordre. T. dressed, soigneusement mis.
tidy², *v.tr.* Ranger ; arranger (une chambre). To tidy oneself (up), faire un brin de toilette. To tidy away, ranger. *Abs.* To tidy up, tout remettre en place.
tie¹, *s.* **1.** (*a*) Lien *m* ; attache *f.* *F:* Ties of friendship, liens d'amitié. (*b*) Assujettissement *m* ; entrave *f.* **2.** (*a*) Lien (de corde). (*b*) Lacet *m*, cordon *m* (de soulier). (*c*) (Neck-) tie, nœud *m*, cravate *f.* Wearing a white tie, en cravate blanche. **3.** *Mus:* Liaison *f.* **4.** *Sp:* Match *m* ou course *f* à égalité.
tie-clip, *s.* Pince *f* à cravate. **tie-pin**, *s.* Épingle *f* de cravate.
tie², *v.* **I.** *v.tr.* **1.** (*a*) Attacher ; lier. *F:* To tie s.o.'s hands, enlever à qn toute liberté d'action. To be tied to one's work, être toujours à l'attache. (*b*) Lier, nouer. **2.** *Mus:* Lier. **II.** **tie**, *v.i. Sp: etc :* Être, arriver, à égalité (*with*, avec). **tie down**, *v.tr.* **1.** Assujettir. **2.** Tied down to one's duties, assujetti à ses fonctions. **tie up**, *v.tr.* **1.** Attacher, ficeler (un paquet) ; bander, panser. **2.** Attacher (un cheval). **3.** Immobiliser (ses capitaux).
tier, *s.* Rangée *f* ; étage *m.* To rise in tiers, s'étager.
tiff, *s.* Petite querelle ; fâcherie *f.*
tiger, *s.* Tigre *m.* **tiger-cat**, *s.* Chat-tigre *m, pl.* chats-tigres. **tiger-lily**, *s.* Lis tigré.
tight, **I.** *a.* **1.** (*a*) Raide, tendu. To draw a cord tight, serrer un cordon. *F:* To keep a tight hold over s.o., tenir qn serré. (*b*) (*Of clothes*) (Too) tight, trop juste. *F:* To be in a tight corner, être en mauvaise passe. **2.** (*Of money*) Resserré, rare. **3.** *P:* To be tight, être ivre. **-ly**, *adv.* **1.** Eyes t. shut, yeux bien fermés. **2.** (*a*) (Tendre) fortement. (*b*) Étroitement. To hold sth. t., tenir qch. serré. **II.** **tight**, *adv.* **1.** Shut tight, tight shut, (porte) hermétiquement close ; (yeux)

bien fermés. **2.** (*a*) Fortement, fermement. To hold sth. tight, tenir qch. serré. To screw a nut up tight, serrer un écrou à bloc. (*b*) Étroitement. **To fit tight**, être bien ajusté. **tight rope**, *s.* Corde tendue ; corde raide. Tight-rope walker, danseur, -euse, de corde ; funambule *mf.*
tighten, **1.** *v.tr.* (*a*) Serrer, resserrer ; retendre (une courroie). *F:* To tighten one's belt, se serrer la ceinture. (*b*) To tighten (up) restrictions, renforcer des restrictions. **2.** *v.i.* (*a*) Se (res)serrer. (*b*) (*Of cable*) Se tendre ; raidir.
tightness, *s.* (*a*) Tension *f*, raideur *f.* (*b*) Étroitesse *f* (d'un lien).
tights, *s.pl. Th:* Collant *m*, maillot *m.*
tigress, *s.* Tigresse *f.*
Tigris (the). *Pr.n. Geog:* Le Tigre.
tile¹, *s.* **1.** Tuile *f. P:* To have a tile loose, être toqué, timbré. **2.** *P:* Chapeau *m.* **3.** Carreau *m.* Paving tile, brique *f* à paver.
tile², *v.tr.* Carreler. **tiled**, *a.* **1.** (Toit) de, en, tuiles. **2.** (Pavage) carrelé, en carreaux.
tiling, *s.* **1.** (*a*) Pose *f* des tuiles. (*b*) Carrelage *m.* **2.** Coll. (*a*) Couverture *f* en tuiles. (*b*) Carreaux *mpl.*
till¹, *v.tr.* Labourer, cultiver.
till², *s. Com:* Tiroir-caisse *m, pl.* tiroirs-caisses.
till³. **1.** *prep.* (*a*) Jusqu'à. Till now, jusqu'ici. From morning till night, du matin au soir. Good-bye till Thursday! à jeudi ! (*b*) Not till, pas avant. He will not come till after dinner, il ne viendra qu'après le dîner. **2.** *conj.* (*a*) Till the doors are shut, jusqu'à ce que les portes soient fermées. To laugh till one cries, rire aux larmes. (*b*) Not till, pas avant que + *sub.*
tillage, *s.* Labour *m*, culture *f.*
tiller¹, *s. Nau:* Barre franche.
tiller², *s.* Laboureur *m*, cultivateur *m.*
tilt¹, *s.* **1.** Inclinaison *f*, pente *f.* To give a cask a tilt, incliner un tonneau. **2.** (*a*) *F:* To have a tilt at s.o., jouter avec qn. (*b*) (At) full tilt, à toute vitesse. To run full tilt into sth., se jeter tête baissée contre qch.
tilt². **I.** *v.i.* **1.** To tilt (up), s'incliner ; pencher. To tilt over, se renverser. (*Of bench*) To tilt up, basculer. **2.** *A:* (*a*) Jouter. (*b*) To tilt at s.o., *F:* allonger une botte à qn. **II.** **tilt**, *v.tr.* (*a*) Pencher, incliner. To tilt one's chair back, se renverser sur sa chaise. (*b*) Culbuter, faire basculer (une charrette).
tilting, *a.* (i) Incliné ; (ii) inclinable. Tilting seat, strapontin *m* ; siège basculant.
timber¹, *s.* **1.** (*a*) Bois *m* d'œuvre. (*b*) Standing timber, bois sur pied ; arbres *mpl* de haute futaie. **2.** Piece of timber, *F:* timber, poutre *f*, madrier *m.* **timber-raft**, *s.* Train *m* de bois. **timber-tree**, *s.* Arbre *m* de haute futaie. **timber-yard**, *s.* Chantier *m.*
timber², *v.tr.* Boiser. **timbered**, *a.* (*a*) En bois. (*b*) (*Of land*) Boisé.
Timbuctoo. *Pr.n.* Tombouctou *m.*

time[1], *s.* **I. 1.** Temps *m.* Time will show, qui vivra verra. In (the course of) time, avec le temps. **2.** In a short time, en peu de temps; sous peu. In three weeks' time, dans trois semaines. *F:* To do sth. in no time, faire qch. en un rien de temps. Within the required time, dans le délai prescrit. To take a long time over sth., mettre un temps interminable à faire qch. For a long time to come, d'ici à longtemps. *We haven't seen him* for a long time past, voilà longtemps que nous ne l'avons vu. For some time past, depuis quelque temps. For some time to come, pendant quelque temps. All the time, continuellement. **3.** (a) My time is my own, je ne suis pas sujet à l'heure. To have time on one's hands, avoir du temps de reste. *F:* You have heaps of time, vous avez tout le temps voulu. To make up for lost time, rattraper le temps perdu. To lose no time in doing sth., s'empresser de faire qch. To take one's time over sth., mettre le temps à faire qch. *F:* It will take you all your time to, vous aurez fort à faire pour. Time's up! l'heure a sonné! (b) *P:* To do time, faire de la prison. To serve one's time, faire son apprentissage. The house will last our time, la maison durera autant que nous. **4.** *Usu. pl.* Époque *f.* (a) A sign of the times, un signe de l'époque. In times past, autrefois, jadis. In times to come, à l'avenir. In our time, de nos jours. The times we live in, notre époque. (b) To be behind the times, être en retard sur son siècle; être arriéré. **5.** Moment *m.* (a) *I was absent* at the time, j'étais absent alors, à ce moment. At that time, en ce temps-là. At the present time, à l'heure qu'il est; actuellement. At the time fixed, à l'heure dite. At one time . . . at another time. . ., tantôt . . . tantôt. . . . At one time, autrefois, dans le temps. At no time, jamais; à aucun moment. At times, parfois. At various times, à diverses reprises. (At) any time (you like), n'importe quand. He may turn up at any time, il peut arriver d'un moment à l'autre. Some time or other, un jour ou l'autre. By the time (that) I got there, lorsque je suis arrivé. From time to time, de temps en temps. From that time, dès lors; depuis lors. To do sth. when the time comes, faire qch. en son temps. Now is the time to, voilà le moment pour. To choose one's time, choisir son heure. (b) In due time and place, en temps et lieu. **6.** Heure *f.* (a) Summer time, l'heure d'été. (b) What is the time? quelle heure est-il? Watch that keeps (good) time, montre qui est exacte. *F:* To pass the time of day with s.o., échanger quelques mots avec qn. At this time of day, à l'heure actuelle. (c) To be before (one's) time, être en avance. To arrive on time, arriver à l'heure. I was just in time to see it, je suis arrivé juste à temps pour le voir. To start in good time, se mettre en route de bonne heure. *F:* And about time too! c'est pas trop tôt! (d) Time of the year, époque de l'année; saison *f.* At my time of life, à mon âge. (e) To die before one's time, mourir avant l'âge. **7.** *We had a good t.,* on s'est bien amusé. To have a bad time of it, en voir de dures. **8.** Fois *f.* Next time, la prochaine fois. Several times over, à plusieurs reprises. Time after time, à maintes reprises. For weeks at a time, des semaines durant. Four times two is eight, quatre fois deux font huit. Three times as big, trois fois plus grand. **9.** *adv.phr.* At the same time. (a) En même temps. (b) At the same time you must not forget, d'autre part il ne faut pas oublier. **10.** (a) *Mus:* Durée *f.* (b) *Mus:* Mesure *f.* To beat time, battre la mesure. (c) To keep time, suivre la mesure. **time-exposure,** *s. Phot:* Pose *f.* **time-fuse,** *s.* Fusée fusante; fusée à temps. **time-honoured,** *a.* Consacré (par l'usage). **time-keeper,** *s.* Good time-keeper, montre *f* qui est toujours à l'heure. **time-server,** *s.* Opportuniste *mf.* **time-serving,** *s.* Opportunisme *m.* **time-signal,** *s. W.Tel:* Signal *m* horaire, *pl.* signaux horaires. **time-table,** *s.* **I.** Horaire *m;* indicateur *m* (des chemins de fer). **2.** *Sch:* Emploi *m* du temps. **time-worn,** *a.* **I.** Usé par le temps. **2.** Séculaire, vénérable.

time[2], *v.tr.* **I.** (a) Fixer l'heure de. (b) To time a blow, mesurer un coup. (c) *I.C.E:* Régler, ajuster. **2.** Calculer la durée de. **3.** *Sp:* Chronométrer.

timeliness, *s.* Opportunité *f;* à-propos *m.*

timely, *a.* Opportun, à propos.

timepiece, *s.* Pendule *f;* montre *f.*

timid, *a.* Timide, timoré, peureux. **-ly,** *adv.* Timidement.

timidity, *s.* Timidité *f.*

timorous, *a.* Timoré, peureux, craintif. **-ly,** *adv.* Peureusement, craintivement.

tin[1], *s.* **I.** Étain *m.* **2.** Boîte *f* (en fer-blanc). Tin loaf, pain cuit au moule. **3.** *P:* (Money) Galette *f,* braise *f.* **tin-hat,** *s. P:* Casque *m* de tranchée. **tin-opener,** *s.* Ouvre-boîte(s) *m inv.* **tin-plate,** *s.* Fer-blanc *m;* ferblanterie *f.* **tin-tack,** *s.* Broquette *f;* clou *m* de tapisserie. Tin-tacks, semence *f.* **tin-whistle,** *s. F:* Flageolet *m.*

tin[2], *v.tr.* **I.** Étamer. **2.** Mettre en boîtes (de fer-blanc). **tinned,** *a.* **I.** Étamé. **2.** Conservé (en boîtes métalliques). Tinned foods, conserves *f* alimentaires (en boîte).

tincture, *s. Pharm:* Teinture *f.*

tinder, *s.* Amadou *m.* **tinder-box,** *s.* Briquet *m* (à silex).

tine, *s.* **I.** Dent *f,* fourchon *m* (de fourche). **2.** Andouiller *m* (de bois de cerf).

tinfoil, *s.* **I.** Feuille *f* d'étain. **2.** Papier *m* simili-étain.

ting[1], *s.* Tintement *m.*

ting[2], *v.i.* Tinter.

ting-a-ling, *s.* Drelin din din *m.*

tinge[1], *s.* Teinte *f,* nuance *f.*

tinge², *v.tr.* Teinter, nuancer.
tingle, *v.i.* **1.** (*Of ears*) Tinter. **2.** Picoter. Her cheeks tingled, les joues lui picotaient, lui cuisaient. **tingling**, *s.* **1.** Tingling in the ears, tintement *m* d'oreilles. **2.** Picotement *m*, fourmillement *m*.
tinker¹, *s.* Chaudronnier ambulant; rétameur *m*.
tinker². **1.** *v.tr.* To tinker up, retaper, rafistoler. **2.** *v.i.* Bricoler. **tinkering**, *s.* (*a*) Petites besognes d'entretien. (*b*) Rafistolage *m*.
tinkle¹, *s.* Tintin *m*, tintement *m*, drelin *m*.
tinkle². **1.** *v.i.* Tinter. **2.** *v.tr.* Faire tinter. **tinkling**, *s.* = TINKLE¹.
tinniness, *s.* Timbre *m* grêle, métallique.
tinny, *a.* To sound tinny, sonner grêle; rendre un son fêlé.
tinsel, *s.* **1.** (*a*) *Dressm:* Lamé *m*, paillettes *fpl.* (*b*) Clinquant *m.* (*c*) *F:* Faux éclat. **2.** *Attrib.* Faux, *f.* fausse; de clinquant.
tinsmith, *s.* Ferblantier *m.*
tint¹, *s.* Teinte *f*, nuance *f.*
tint², *v.tr.* Teinter, colorer.
tiny, *a.* Minuscule. A tiny bit, un tout petit morceau.
tip¹, *s.* **1.** Bout *m*, extrémité *f*, pointe *f.* Artist to the finger-tips, artiste jusqu'au bout des ongles. On the tip of one's tongue, sur le bout de la langue. **2.** (*a*) Bout ferré, embout *m.* (*b*) *Bill:* Procédé *m* (de la queue). **tiptop**. *F:* **1.** *s.* Sommet *m*, faîte *m.* **2.** *a.* De premier ordre; excellent, extra *inv.* That's tip-top! ça c'est tapé!
tip², *v.tr.* Mettre un bout à; embouter.
tip³, *s.* **1.** Pente *f*, inclinaison *f.* **2.** Coup léger; tape *f.* **3.** (*a*) Pourboire *m*, gratification *f.* (*b*) *F:* Don *m* d'argent de poche. **4.** *Turf:* Tuyau *m.* If you take my tip, si vous m'en croyez. **tip-cat**, *s.* *Games:* Bâtonnet *m.*
tip⁴, *v.* I. *v.tr.* **1.** (*a*) To tip (over), renverser; chavirer, verser. (*b*) To tip (up), soulever; faire basculer (une charrette). (*c*) To tip (out), déverser, décharger. (*d*) Faire pencher, faire incliner. **2.** (*a*) Toucher légèrement, effleurer. (*b*) Donner un pourboire, une gratification à. **3.** *Turf:* Tuyauter. II. **tip**, *v.i.* (*a*) To tip (over), se renverser, basculer; (*of boat*) chavirer, verser. (*b*) To tip (up), (*of plank*) se soulever, basculer. **tipping**, *s.* **1.** (*a*) Inclinaison *f.* (*b*) Tipping (over), renversement *m*; chavirement *m* (d'un canot). (*c*) Basculage *m.* **2.** (Système *m* des) pourboires *m*; distribution *f* de pourboires. **3.** *Turf:* Tuyautage *m.*
tipple¹, *s.* Boisson *f* (alcoolique).
tipple², *v.i.* Se livrer à la boisson.
tippler, *s.* Ivrogne *m*; *F:* poivrot *m.*
tipsiness, *s.* Ivresse *f.*
tipsy, *a.* **1.** Gris, ivre. To get t., se griser. **2.** D'ivrogne.
tiptoe¹, *s.* & *adv.* (On) tiptoe, sur la pointe

des pieds. *F:* To be (up)on the tiptoe of expectation, être dans l'angoisse de l'attente.
tiptoe², *v.i.* Marcher sur la pointe des pieds.
tirade, *s.* Tirade *f.* A violent tirade against s.o., une diatribe contre qn.
tire. **1.** *v.tr.* (*a*) Fatiguer, lasser. (*b*) To tire s.o. out, (i) épuiser, rompre, qn de fatigue; (ii) excéder qn. **2.** *v.i.* To tire of sth., se lasser, se fatiguer, de qch. **tired**, *a.* Fatigué. (*a*) Las, *f.* lasse. Tired out, rompu de fatigue. (*b*) To be tired, être fatigué, avoir sommeil. *F:* You make me tired, tu m'ennuies; tu m'embêtes. (*c*) To be tired of sth., être las de qch.
tiredness, *s.* Lassitude *f*, fatigue *f.*
tireless, *a.* Inlassable, infatigable. **-ly**, *adv.* Infatigablement, inlassablement.
tiresome, *a.* **1.** Fatigant; (*discours*) ennuyeux. **2.** Exaspérant; (*of child*) assommant. How tiresome! quel ennui!
tissue, *s.* **1.** (*a*) Tissu *m*; étoffe *f.* (*b*) *F:* Tissue of lies, tissu de mensonges. **2.** *Biol:* Tissu. **tissue-paper**, *s.* (*a*) Papier *m* de soie. (*b*) Papier pelure.
tit¹, *s.* *Orn:* = TITMOUSE.
tit², *s.* Tit for tat, à bon chat bon rat. To give s.o. tit for tat, rendre à qn la pareille.
Titan, *s.* *Myth:* Titan *m.*
titanic, *a.* Titanique, titanesque.
tit-bit, *s.* Morceau friand; friandise *f.*
tithe, *s.* **1.** Dîme *f.* **2.** Dixième *m.*
Titian. *Pr.n.m.* Le Titien.
titillate, *v.tr.* Titiller, chatouiller.
titillation, *s.* Titillation *f*, chatouillement *m.*
titivate. **1.** *v.tr.* Faire beau; attifer. **2.** *v.i.* & *pr.* Se faire beau.
titlark, *s.* *Orn:* Pipit *m.*
title¹, *s.* **1.** (*a*) Titre *m.* (*b*) Titre de noblesse. Persons of title, les nobles *m*; la noblesse. **2.** Titre (d'un livre). **3.** (*a*) Titre, droit *m.* Title to property, titre de propriété. To have a title to sth., avoir droit, avoir des titres, à qch. (*b*) = TITLE-DEED. **title-deed**, *s.* *Jur:* Titre *m* de propriété. **title-page**, *s.* *Typ:* Page *f* de titre; titre *m.* **title-rôle**, *s.* *Th:* Rôle *m* qui donne le titre à la pièce.
title², *v.tr.* Intituler. **titled**, *a.* Titré.
titmouse, *s.* *Orn:* Mésange *f.*
titter¹, *s.* Rire étouffé.
titter², *v.i.* Avoir un petit rire étouffé. **tittering**, *s.* Petits rires.
tittle, *s.* La moindre partie. Not one tittle, pas un iota. To a tittle, trait pour trait.
tittle-tattle¹, *s.* Potins *mpl*, cancans *mpl.*
tittle-tattle², *v.i.* Potiner, cancaner.
to. I. *prep.* A, à. **1.** (*a*) What school do you go to? à quelle école allez-vous? *He went to France, to Japan, to India*, il est allé en France, au Japon, aux Indes. *She returned home to her family*, elle est rentrée auprès de sa famille. *I am going to the grocer's*, je vais chez l'épicier. *From town to town*, de ville en ville. *Air-lines to and from the Continent*,

lignes aériennes à destination ou en provenance du Continent. (b) *The road to ruin*, le chemin de la ruine. *It is twenty miles to London*, il y a vingt milles d'ici Londres. **2.** Vers, à. *To the east*, vers l'est. *To the right*, à droite. **3.** *To clasp s.o. to one's heart*, serrer qn sur son cœur. **4.** (a) *From morning to night*, du matin au soir. (b) *Ten minutes to six*, six heures moins dix. **5.** (a) *Wet to the skin*, trempé jusqu'aux os. *To this day*, jusqu'à ce jour. (b) *Accurate to a millimetre*, exact à un millimètre près. *A year to the day*, un an jour pour jour. **6.** (a) *To this end*, à cet effet, dans ce but. *To sentence s.o. to death*, condamner qn à mort. (b) *To my despair*, à mon grand désespoir. **7.** (a) En. *To go to ruin*, tomber en ruine. *To put to flight*, mettre en fuite. (b) *To take s.o. to wife*, prendre qn pour femme. **8.** *To the tune of*, sur l'air de. **9.** *Heir to s.o.*, héritier de qn. **10.** (a) *That's nothing to what I have seen*, cela n'est rien auprès de, à côté de, ce que j'ai vu. (b) *Six votes to four*, six voix contre quatre. *One house to the square mile*, une maison par mille carré. **11.** *To all appearances*, selon les apparences. *To write to s.o.'s dictation*, écrire sous la dictée de qn. *To the best of my remembrance*, autant qu'il m'en souvienne. **12.** *To drink to s.o.*, boire à la santé de qn. **13.** *What did he say to my suggestion?* qu'est-ce qu'il a dit de ma proposition? *There's nothing to it*, ça ne vaut pas la peine. **14.** (a) *What is that to you?* qu'est-ce que cela vous fait? (b) Envers, pour. *Good to all*, bon pour tous, envers tous. (c) *Known to the ancients*, connu des anciens. **II. to. 1.** (a) Pour. *He came to help me*, il est venu pour m'aider. *So to speak*, pour ainsi dire. (b) *Happy to do it*, heureux de le faire. *Ready to listen*, prêt à écouter. *Good to eat*, bon à manger. *Too hot to drink*, trop chaud pour qu'on puisse le boire. (c) *To look at her . . .*, à la voir. . . . *He woke to find the lamp still burning*, en s'éveillant il trouva la lampe encore allumée. **2.** (a) *To have much to do*, avoir beaucoup à faire. *Nothing to speak of*, rien qui vaille la peine qu'on en parle. *The first to complain*, le premier à se plaindre. (b) *Tendency to do sth.*, tendance à faire qch. *This is the time to do it*, c'est le moment de le faire. **3.** *To lie is shameful*, il est honteux de mentir. **4.** *I wish him to do it*, je veux qu'il le fasse. **5.** *You ought to*, vous le devriez. *I want to*, je voudrais bien. **III. to**, *adv.* **1.** *To put the horses to*, atteler les chevaux. *To come to*, reprendre connaissance. **2.** *To and fro. To go to and fro*, aller et venir. *The busy hurrying to and fro*, le va-et-vient affairé. **to-do**, *s. F:* Remue-ménage *m*. *To make a to-do*, faire des histoires. *What a to-do!* quelle affaire!

toad, *s.* **1.** (a) Crapaud *m*. (b) *P:* Sale type *m*. **2.** *Cu:* *Toad in the hole*, morceau de viande cuit dans de la pâte.

toadstool, *s.* Champignon vénéneux.

toady[1], *s.* Flagorneur, -euse.

toady[2], *v.tr. & i.* To toady (to) s.o., lécher les bottes à qn; flagorner qn.

toast[1], *s.* **1.** Pain grillé. *Piece, round, of toast*, rôtie *f*. *Anchovies on toast*, anchois sur canapé. *P:* *To have s.o. on toast*, avoir qn à sa merci. **2.** Toast *m*. **toast-rack**, *s.* Porte-rôties *m inv.*

toast[2]. **1.** *v.tr.* (a) Rôtir, griller. (b) *To toast s.o.*, porter un toast à (la santé de) qn. **2.** *v.i.* Rôtir, griller. **toasting-fork**, *s.* Fourchette *f* à rôtir le pain.

toaster, *s.* Grille-pain *m inv.*

tobacco, *s.* Tabac *m* (à fumer). **tobacco-jar**, *s.* Pot *m* à tabac. **tobacco-pouch**, *s.* Blague *f* à tabac.

tobacconist, *s.* Marchand *m* de tabac. *Tobacconist's (shop)*, débit *m* de tabac.

toboggan[1], *s.* Toboggan *m*.

toboggan[2], *v.i.* Faire du toboggan.

to-day, *adv. & s.* Aujourd'hui (*m*). *To-day's paper*, le journal d'aujourd'hui, du jour.

toddle[1], *s.* **1.** Allure chancelante (d'un enfant). **2.** *F:* Petite promenade.

toddle[2], *v.i.* **1.** Marcher à petits pas chancelants. **2.** Marcher à petits pas; trottiner. *To toddle off*, *F:* se trotter.

toddler, *s.* Enfant *mf* qui commence à marcher. *The toddlers*, les tout petits.

toddy, *s.* Grog chaud.

toe[1], *s.* **1.** Orteil *m*; doigt *m* de pied. **2.** Bout *m*, pointe *f* (de soulier). **toe-cap**, *s.* *Bootm:* Bout rapporté. **toe-clip**, *s.* *Cy:* Cale-pied(s) *m inv.* **toe-nail**, *s.* Ongle *m* d'orteil.

toe[2], *v.tr.* *F:* To toe the line, se conformer au mot d'ordre.

toff[1], *s. P:* Dandy *m*, aristo *m*. *The toffs*, la haute gomme.

toff[2], *v.tr.* *F:* To toff up, se faire beau.

toffee, *s.* Caramel *m* au beurre.

tog, *v.tr. & i.* *F:* Attifer, habiller. *To tog (oneself) up*, se faire beau.

toga, *s.* *Rom.Ant:* Toge *f*.

together, *adv.* Ensemble. (a) *Together with*, avec. (b) *To bring together*, rassembler, réunir. (c) *To act together*, agir de concert. *All together*, tous à la fois. (d) *For months together*, pendant des mois entiers.

togs, *s.pl.* *F:* Nippes *f*, frusques *f*.

toil[1], *s.* Travail dur; labeur *m*, peine *f*. **toil-worn**, *a.* Usé par le travail.

toil[2], *v.i.* Travailler, peiner. *To toil up a hill*, gravir péniblement une colline.

toiler, *s.* Travailleur, -euse.

toilet, *s.* **1.** Toilette *f*. **2.** (*In hotels*) Les toilettes, les cabinets *m*. **toilet-paper**, *s.* Papier *m* hygiénique. **toilet-roll**, *s.* Rouleau *m* de papier hygiénique. **toilet-set**, *s.* Garniture *f* de toilette. **toilet-soap**, *s.* Savon *m* de toilette.

toils, *s. pl.* *To be taken in the toils*, se laisser prendre au piège.

toilsome, *a.* Pénible fatigant.

token, *s.* **1.** Signe *m,* marque *f,* témoignage *m.* **In token of,** en signe de ; comme marque de. **2.** (*a*) **Love token,** gage *m* d'amour. (*b*) Jeton *m.* (*c*) **Book tokens,** bons *m* de livres.
Toledo. *Pr.n.* Tolède.
tolerable, *a.* (*a*) Tolérable, supportable. (*b*) Passable ; assez bon. **-ably,** *adv.* **1.** Tolérablement. **2.** Passablement.
tolerance, *s.* Tolérance *f.*
tolerant, *a.* Tolérant (*of,* à l'égard de).
tolerate, *v.tr.* Tolérer, supporter.
toleration, *s.* Tolérance *f.*
toll¹, *s.* **1.** (*a*) Droit *m* de passage ; péage *m.* (*b*) Droit de place (au marché). **2.** Rent takes heavy toll of one's income, le loyer mange une grande partie de nos revenus. **toll-bridge,** *s.* Pont *m* à péage. **toll-call,** *s. Tp:* Conversation interurbaine. **toll-gate,** *s.* Barrière *f* (de péage). **toll-house,** *s.* Bureau *m* de péage ; péage *m.* **toll-keeper,** *s.* Péager, -ère.
toll². 1. *v.tr.* Tinter, sonner (une cloche). *Abs.* **Te toll for the dead,** sonner pour les morts. **2.** *v.i.* (*a*) Tinter, sonner. (*b*) Sonner le glas. **tolling,** *s.* (*a*) Tintement *m* (de cloche). (*b*) Glas *m.*
Tom. 1. *Pr.n.* Thomas *m. F:* **Any Tom, Dick, or Harry,** le premier venu. **2. Tom cat,** *F:* tom, matou *m.* **Tom Thumb.** *Pr.n.* Le petit Poucet. **tom-tit,** *s. Orn:* Mésange azurée.
tomahawk¹, *s.* Hache *f* de guerre, tomahawk *m.*
tomahawk², *v.tr.* Frapper avec un tomahawk.
tomato, *s.* Tomate *f.*
tomb, *s.* Tombe *f* ; tombeau *m.*
tomboy, *s.* Fillette *f* d'allures garçonnières. **She's a regular tomboy,** c'est un garçon manqué.
tombstone, *s.* Pierre tombale.
tome, *s.* Tome *m* ; gros volume.
tomfool¹. 1. *s.* Nigaud *m,* serin *m.* **2.** *Attrib. a.* Stupide, idiot.
tomfool², *v.i.* Faire, dire, des sottises.
tomfoolery, *s.* Nigauderie(s) *f*(*pl*).
Tommy. 1. *Pr.n.* Thomas *m.* **2.** *s. F:* A tommy, un simple soldat. **tommy-gun,** *s.* Mitraillette *f.* **tommy-rot,** *s. F:* Bêtises *f pl.*
to-morrow, *adv. & s.* Demain (*m*). **To-morrow week,** de demain en huit. **The day after to-m.,** après-demain.
tomtom, *s.* Tam-tam *m.*
ton, *s. Meas:* **1.** Tonne *f. F:* **There's tons of it,** il y en a des tas. **2.** *Nau:* Tonneau *m* (de jauge).
tonality, *s.* Tonalité *f.*
tone¹, *s.* **1.** Son *m,* accent *m* ; timbre *m.* **2.** (*a*) Ton *m,* voix *f. F:* **To alter one's tone,** changer de ton, de note. (*b*) *Fin:* **The prevailing tone,** la tendance générale. (*c*) *Med:* Ton. **To lose tone,** se déprimer. **To recover tone,** se retremper. **3.** *Mus:* Ton. **4.** Ton,

nuance *f* (d'une couleur). **5.** *Ling:* Ton ; accent *m* tonique.
tone². 1. *v.tr.* Régler la tonalité. **2.** *v.i.* **To tone (in) with sth.,** s'harmoniser avec qch. **tone down. 1.** *v.tr.* Adoucir, atténuer. **2.** *v.i.* S'adoucir ; le prendre sur un ton plus doux. **toning,** *s. Phot:* Virage *m.*
toneless, *a.* (Voix) veule ; (voix) blanche.
tongs, *s.pl.* **1.** (Fire-)tongs, pincettes *f.* **2.** *Ind:* Pince(s) *f,* tenailles *f pl.*
tongue, *s.* **1.** Langue *f.* (*a*) **To put out one's tongue,** tirer la langue. (*b*) **To have a ready tongue,** avoir la langue bien pendue. **To bridle one's tongue,** tenir sa langue. **To find one's tongue,** retrouver la parole. *F:* **To keep a civil tongue in one's head,** rester courtois. **With one's tongue in one's cheek,** en blaguant. **To give tongue,** donner de la voix. **2.** Langue, idiome *m.* **3.** Langue, languette *f* (de terre) ; patte *f,* languette (de soulier). **tongue-tied,** *a.* Muet, -ette ; interdit.
tonic. 1. *a.* Tonique. **2.** *s.* (*a*) *Med:* Tonique *m,* fortifiant *m.* (*b*) *Mus:* Tonique *f.*
to-night, *adv. & s.* Cette nuit ; ce soir.
tonnage, *s. Nau:* Tonnage *m,* jauge *f.*
tonsil, *s.* Amygdale *f.*
tonsure¹, *s.* Tonsure *f.*
tonsure², *v.tr.* Tonsurer.
too, *adv.* **1.** Trop, par trop. **Too much money,** trop d'argent. **Ten shillings too much,** dix shillings de trop. **The task is too much for me,** la tâche est au-dessus de mes forces. **He was too much for me,** il était trop fort pour moi. *I know him all too well,* je ne le connais que trop. **2.** Aussi ; également. *I too want some,* il m'en faut également ; moi aussi il m'en faut. **3.** (*Moreover*) D'ailleurs ; de plus ; en outre.
tool¹, *s.* **1.** Outil *m* ; instrument *m,* ustensile *m.* **2.** *F:* Instrument, créature *f.* **To make a tool of s.o.,** se servir de qn.
tool², *v.tr.* Ciseler. **tooling,** *s.* Ciselage *m.*
toot¹, *s.* **1.** Son *m,* appel *m* (de clairon). **2.** *Nau:* Coup *m* de sirène. *Aut:* Cornement *m.*
toot². 1. *v.tr. F:* **To toot a horn,** sonner du cor. *Aut:* **To toot the horn,** corner. **2.** *v.i.* Sonner du cor. *Aut:* Corner.
tooth, *s.* **1.** Dent *f.* **A fine set of teeth,** une belle denture. **Set of (false) teeth,** dentier *m.* **To cut one's teeth,** faire, percer, ses dents. **To have a tooth out,** se faire arracher une dent. *F:* **To cast sth. in s.o.'s teeth,** reprocher qch. à qn. **In the teeth of all opposition,** malgré, en dépit de, toute opposition. *F:* **To show one's teeth,** montrer les dents. **To fight tooth and nail,** se battre avec acharnement. **To set one's teeth,** serrer les dents. **2.** Dent (de scie). **The teeth of a wheel,** la denture. **tooth-brush,** *s.* Brosse *f* à dents. **tooth-paste,** *s.* Pâte *f* dentifrice. **tooth-pick,** *s.* Cure-dents *m inv.* **tooth-powder,** *s.* Poudre *f* dentifrice.

toothache, s. Mal m de dents.
toothful, s. F: Goutte f.
toothless, a. Sans dents ; édenté.
toothsome, a. Savoureux. Toothsome morsel, morceau friand.
tootle, v.i. To tootle on the flute, seriner un air de flute.
top[1]. I. s. **1.** Haut m, sommet m, cime f, faîte m. At the top of the tree, en haut de l'arbre. From top to bottom, de haut en bas ; de fond en comble. From top to toe, de la tête aux pieds. To come out on top, avoir le dessus. On top of it all, en sus de tout cela. Mil: To go over the top, monter à l'assaut. **2.** Surface f (de l'eau) ; dessus m (d'une table) ; impériale f (d'un tramway). **3.** Tête f (de page). Bookb: Gilt top, tête dorée. **4.** Haut bout (de la table). **5.** To shout at the top of one's voice, crier à tue-tête, à pleine gorge. **6.** Nau: Hune f. II. top, attrib.a. **1.** Supérieur ; du dessus, du haut, d'en haut. The top floor, le plus haut étage ; le dernier étage. A top garment, un vêtement de dessus. **2.** Premier ; principal, -aux. Sch: The top boy, le premier de la classe. **top-boots,** s.pl. Bottes f à revers. **top-coat,** s. Pardessus m. **top dog,** s. F: Vainqueur m. To be top dog, avoir le dessus. **top-hamper,** s. Superstructure f. Nau: Fardage m. **top-heavy,** a. Trop lourd du haut. **top-note,** s. Plus haute note (d'un registre). The top-notes, les notes hautes. **top-sawyer,** s. Chef m ; personnage.
top[2], v.tr. **1.** Surmonter, couronner, coiffer (with, de). And to top it all, et pour comble. **2.** Dépasser, surpasser. To top s.o. by a head, dépasser qn de la tête. **3.** To top a list, être à la tête d'une liste. **4.** Golf: Calotter. **top up,** v.tr. Remplir (complètement). El: Reniveler (un accumulateur). **topping,** a. P: Excellent, chic m & f. A topping idea, une riche idée. That's topping ! ça c'est fameux ! A topping dinner, un dîner à la hauteur.
top[3], s. Toupie f. To spin a top, faire aller une toupie.
topaz, s. Topaze f.
topee, s. Casque colonial.
toper, s. F: Ivrogne m, buveur m.
topic, s. Matière f ; sujet m, thème m.
topical, a. Topical song, chanson d'actualités. W.Tel: Topical talk, journal parlé. Topical film, film d'actualités.
topmast, s. Mât m de hune.
topmost, a. Le plus haut : le plus élevé.
topography, s. Topographie f.
topper, s. **1.** Type épatant. **2.** Chapeau haut de forme.
topple. 1. v.i. (a) To topple (over), tomber, s'écrouler. (b) Chanceler, branler. **2.** v.tr. To topple sth. over, faire tomber qch.
topsy-turvy, adv. & adj. Sens dessus dessous. To turn everything t.-t., tout bouleverser. Everything is t.-t., tout est en désarroi.
tor, s. Pic m, éminence f conique.

torch, s. **1.** Torche f, flambeau m. **2.** Electric torch, lampe f électrique de poche ; torche électrique. **torch-light,** s. Lumière f de(s) flambeaux.
toreador, s. Toréador m.
torment[1], s. Tourment m, torture f, supplice m. He suffered torments, il souffrait le martyre. To be in torment, être au supplice. F: That child is a torment, cet enfant est assommant.
torment[2], v.tr. Tourmenter, torturer.
tormentor, s. Tourmenteur, -euse.
tornado, s. Tornade f.
torpedo[1], s. Torpille f To make a t. attack, attaquer à la torpille. **torpedo-boat,** s. Torpilleur m. **torpedo-net,** s. Filet m pare-torpilles. **torpedo-tube,** s. Navy: (Tube m) lance-torpille m, pl. lance-torpilles.
torpedo[2], v.tr. Torpiller.
torpid, a. Engourdi, inerte.
torpidity, s. Engourdissement m, inertie f, torpeur f.
torrent, s. Torrent m. To fall in torrents, tomber à torrents, à verse. F: Torrent of abuse, torrent d'injures.
torrential, a. Torrentiel.
torrid, a. Torride.
torso, s. Art: Torse m.
tortoise, s. Z: Tortue f. **tortoise-shell,** s. Écaille f (de tortue). Tortoise-shell cat, chat écaille de tortue.
tortuous, a. Tortueux.
torture[1], s. **1.** Hist: Torture f, question f. **2.** Torture, tourment m, supplice m.
torture[2], v.tr. (a) Hist: Mettre à la question. (b) Torturer ; mettre à la torture, au supplice. Tortured by remorse, tenaillé par le remords.
torturer, s. Hist: Bourreau m.
tosh, s. F: Bêtises fpl, blague(s) f(pl).
toss[1], s. **1.** Action f de jeter en l'air. (a) Lancement m, jet m. (b) Coup m de pile ou face. **2.** Toss of the head, mouvement de tête dédaigneux. **3.** Chute f de cheval.
toss[2], v. **1.** v.tr. (a) Lancer, jeter, en l'air ; (of horse) démonter (un cavalier). To toss sth. to s.o., jeter qch. à qn. Nau: To toss (the) oars, mâter les avirons. (b) To toss (up) a coin, jouer à pile ou face. Abs. To toss for sth., jouer qch. à pile ou face. (c) To toss one's head, relever la tête d'un air dédaigneux. (Of horse) To toss its head, hocher de la tête. (d) Agiter, secouer, ballotter. Tossed on the waves, ballotté par les flots. **2.** v.i. (a) To toss (about) in bed, tourner et se retourner dans son lit. To toss in one's sleep, s'agiter dans son sommeil. (b) (Of ship) To pitch and toss, tanguer. **toss off,** v.tr. Avaler d'un trait ; expédier (une tâche). **toss-up,** s. **1.** (Of coin) Coup m de pile ou face. **2.** Affaire f à issue douteuse. It is a toss-up, les chances sont égales. **tossing,** s. **1.** Lancement m en l'air. **2.** Agitation f, ballottement m.

tot¹, *s.* **1.** Tout(e) petit(e) enfant. Tiny tot, bambin, -ine. **2.** *F:* Goutte *f*, petit verre.
tot², *v.* **1.** *v.tr.* To tot up, additionner. **2.** *v.i.* To tot up, s'élever (*to*, à).
total¹. **1.** *a.* Total, -aux; complet, -ète; global, -aux. (*a*) **Total amount**, somme totale, globale. (*b*) **They were in total ignorance of it**, ils l'ignoraient complètement. **Total failure**, échec complet. **2.** *s.* Total *m*; montant *m*. **Grand total**, total global. **-ally,** *adv.* Totalement, complètement.
total², *v.tr. & i.* **1.** Totaliser, additionner. **2.** To total (up to), s'élever à, se monter à.
totalitarian, *a* Totalitaire.
totalitarianism, *s.* Totalitarisme *m*.
totality, *s.* Totalité *f*.
totalizator, *s. Turf:* Totaliseur *m*, totalisateur *m*.
totem, *s. Anthr:* Totem *m*.
totter, *v.i.* **1.** Chanceler. To totter out, sortir d'un pas mal assuré. **2.** Menacer ruine; chanceler, branler. **tottering,** *a.* Chancelant. *T. steps*, pas mal assurés. **Tottering empire**, empire qui menace ruine, qui croule.
toucan, *s. Orn:* Toucan *m*.
touch¹, *s.* **1.** Attouchement *m*. To give s.o. a touch, toucher qn. *I felt a t. on my arm*, je sentis qu'on me touchait le bras. **2.** (Le sens du) toucher. To know sth. by the touch, reconnaître qch. au toucher. **3.** (*a*) Léger coup. (*b*) Touche *f* (de pinceau). **To add a few touches to a picture**, faire quelques retouches *f* à un tableau. **To give the finishing touch(es) to sth.**, mettre la dernière main à qch. **4.** *Mus:* Toucher *m*. *Typewr:* Frappe *f*. **5.** (*a*) **Touch of satire**, pointe *f* de satire. *T. of rouge*, soupçon *m* de rouge. (*b*) **Touch of fever**, soupçon de fièvre. **6.** Contact *m*. To be in touch with s.o., être en contact avec qn; être en rapport avec qn. **The personal touch**, les rapports personnels. **To be in touch with the situation**, être au courant de la situation. **7.** *F:* It was a near touch, cela n'a tenu qu'à un fil.
touch². **I.** *v.tr.* **1.** (*a*) Toucher. *To t. sth. with one's finger*, toucher qch. du doigt. *To t. s.o. on the shoulder*, toucher qn à l'épaule. *He touched his hat to me*, il m'a salué. *F:* **Touch wood!** touche du bois! *Don't t. those eggs*, ne touchez pas à ces œufs. (*b*) Effleurer. **To touch a spring**, faire jouer un ressort. (*c*) *v.ind.tr.* **To touch on a subject**, toucher, effleurer, un sujet. (*d*) Toucher, atteindre. **The law can't touch him**, la loi ne peut rien contre lui. *F:* **No one can touch him in comedy**, personne ne peut l'approcher dans la comédie. (*e*) **I never touch wine**, jamais je ne bois de vin. **2.** Toucher, émouvoir. **3.** **The question touches you nearly**, la question vous touche de près. **4.** **Flowers touched by the frost**, fleurs atteintes par la gelée. **II.** **touch**, *v.i.* **1.** Se toucher. (*a*) Être en contact. (*b*) Venir en contact. **2.** *Nau:* To touch at a port, faire escale à

un port. **touch up**, *v.tr.* Faire des retouches à (un tableau). **touched,** *a. F:* Toqué, timbré. **touching.** **1.** *a.* Touchant, émouvant. **2.** *prep.* Touchant, concernant. **-ly,** *adv.* D'une manière touchante. **touch and go**, *s.* That was touch and go! *F:* il était moins cinq!
touchiness, *s.* Susceptibilité *f*, irascibilité *f*.
touchy, *a.* Susceptible, ombrageux.
tough, *a.* **1.** Dur, résistant. **Tough meat**, viande coriace. **2.** *F:* He's a tough customer! il est peu commode! **3.** *F:* (*a*) Rude, difficile. (*b*) *That's t.!* c'est dur pour vous!
toughen. **1.** *v.tr.* (*a*) Durcir. (*b*) Endurcir. **2.** *v.i.* (*a*) Durcir. (*b*) S'endurcir.
toughness, *s.* **1.** Dureté *f*; résistance *f*; (*of meat*) coriacité *f*. **2.** (*a*) Force *f*, solidité *f*. (*b*) Résistance *f* à la fatigue.
tour¹, *s.* **1.** Tour *m*; voyage *m* circulaire. **Conducted tours**, excursions accompagnées. **Walking tour**, excursion à pied. **2.** **Tour of inspection**, tournée *f* de visite.
tour², *v.tr. & i.* To tour (through) a country, faire le tour d'un pays. *Touring party*, groupe *m* de touristes. *Th:* **Touring company**, troupe *f* en tournée. **touring-car**, *s.* Automobile *f* de tourisme.
tourist, *s.* Touriste *mf*. **tourist agency**, *s.* Bureau *m* de tourisme. **tourist ticket**, *s.* Billet *m* d'excursion.
tournament, *s.* **1.** *Hist:* (*a*) Tournoi *m*. (*b*) Carrousel *m*. **2.** **Tennis tournament**, tournoi de tennis. **Chess tournament**, concours *m* d'échecs.
tourniquet, *s. Surg:* Tourniquet *m*.
tousle, *v.tr.* Ébouriffer (les cheveux). **tousled,** *a. T. dress*, robe chiffonnée. **Tousled hair**, cheveux ébouriffés.
tout¹, *s.* Racoleur *m*; (*for hotels*) pisteur *m*.
tout², *v.i.* **To tout for customers**, courir après la clientèle.
tow¹, *s.* **1.** (Câble *m* de) remorque *f*. **2.** **To be taken in tow**, se mettre à la remorque. **3.** (*Vessel towed*) Remorque. **tow-boat**, *s.* Remorqueur *m*. **tow-line**, *s.* Remorque *f*; corde *f* de halage. **tow-path**, *s.* Chemin *m* de halage.
tow², *v.tr.* Remorquer (un navire); touer (un chaland); (*from tow-path*) haler. **towing,** *s.* Remorque *f*; touage *m*; (*from tow-path*) halage *m*.
tow³, *s.* Étoupe *f*; filasse *f*. **tow-headed**, *a. F:* Aux cheveux blond filasse.
towards, *prep.* **1.** Vers; du côté de. **2.** Envers, pour, à l'égard de. **3.** Pour. **4.** Vers, sur. *T. noon*, vers midi.
towel¹, *s.* Serviette *f* (de toilette); essuie-main(s) *m inv*. *A clean t.*, une serviette blanche.
towel², *v.tr.* Essuyer, frotter, avec une serviette. **towelling,** *s.* Friction *f* avec une serviette.
tower¹, *s.* (*a*) Tour *f*. (*b*) **Church tower,**

clocher *m.* (*c*) *F:* He is a tower of strength, c'est un puissant appui.

tower², *v.i.* **1.** Dominer. **He towered above the others,** il dominait les autres par la taille. **2.** Monter très haut. **towering,** *a.* **1.** (*a*) Très haut. **A towering height,** une très grande hauteur. (*b*) **Towering ambition,** ambition sans bornes. **2.** *F:* **In a towering passion,** au paroxysme de la colère.

town, *s.* **1.** Ville *f*; cité *f.* **Country town,** ville de province. **2.** (*a*) **A man about town,** un mondain. (*b*) **He is out of town,** il est à la campagne. **3.** **Town life,** vie urbaine. **town-clerk,** *s.* Greffier municipal. **town-council,** *s.* Conseil municipal. **town-councillor,** *s.* Conseiller municipal. **town-hall,** *s.* Hôtel *m* de ville. **town-house,** *s.* Hôtel *m.* **town-planning,** *s.* Urbanisme *m*; aménagement *m* des villes.

township, *s.* Commune *f.*

townsman, *s.* Habitant *m* de la ville; bourgeois *m,* citadin *m.* **Fellow t.,** concitoyen *m.*

townspeople, *s.pl.* **1.** Habitants *m* de la ville; bourgeois *m.* **2.** Concitoyens *m.*

toxic, *a. & s. Med:* Toxique (*m*).

toxicology, *s.* Toxicologie *f.*

toxin, *s.* Toxine *f.*

toy¹, *s.* **1.** Jouet *m*; *F:* joujou *m,* -oux. **2.** *Attrib.* (*a*) **Toy trumpet,** trompette d'enfant. (*b*) **Toy** petit. **Toy dog,** chien de salon. **toy-book,** *s.* Livre *m* d'images. **toy-railway,** *s.* Chemin *m* de fer mécanique (d'enfant). **toy-shop,** *s.* Magasin *m* de jouets.

toy², *v.i.* **1.** **To toy with sth.,** s'amuser, jouer, avec qch. **To toy with one's food,** manger du bout des dents. **To toy with an idea,** caresser une idée. **2.** **To toy with s.o.,** badiner avec qn.

trace¹, *s.* **1.** (*Usu. pl.*) Trace(s) *f(pl).* **2.** Trace, vestige *m.* **There is no trace of it,** il n'en reste pas trace.

trace², *v.tr.* **1.** Tracer. **2.** Calquer (un dessin). **3.** *He has been traced to Paris,* on a suivi sa piste jusqu'à Paris. **4.** Trouver trace de. **5.** Suivre (un chemin). **trace back,** *v.tr.* **To trace sth. back to its source,** remonter jusqu'à l'origine de qch. **tracing,** *s.* **1.** (*a*) Tracé *m.* (*b*) Calquage *m.* **2.** Dessin calqué; calque *m.* **tracing-paper,** *s.* Papier *m* à calquer.

trace³, *s. Harn:* Trait *m.* **In the traces,** attelé. *F:* **To kick over the traces,** s'insurger.

tracer, *s. Mil:* **Tracer bullet,** balle traceuse.

tracery, *s.* **1.** *Arch:* Réseau *m*; découpures *fpl.* **2.** Réseau, nervures *fpl.*

track¹, *s.* **1.** Erre *f*; trace(s) *f(pl),* piste *f.* **To follow in s.o.'s tracks,** suivre la voie tracée par qn. **To be on s.o.'s track,** être sur la trace de qn. **To keep track of s.o.,** ne pas perdre de vue qn. **To throw s.o. off the track,** dépister qn. *P:* **To make tracks,** filer, s'éclipser. **2.** **Mule track,** piste muletière. **3.** Route *f,* chemin *m.* **To put s.o. on the right**

track, mettre qn sur la voie. **4.** *Rac:* Piste. **Motor-racing track,** autodrome *m.* **5.** *Rail:* Voie (ferrée).

track², *v.tr.* Suivre à la piste; traquer. **To track down,** dépister.

tracker, *s.* Traqueur *m.*

trackless, *a.* Sans chemins. **Trackless forest,** forêt vierge.

tract¹, *s.* Étendue *f*; région *f.*

tract², *s.* Petit traité; brochure *f;* tract *m.*

tractability, *s* Humeur *f* traitable; docilité *f.*

tractable, *a.* Docile; traitable.

traction, *s.* Traction *f.* **traction-engine,** *s.* Machine routière; tracteur *m.*

tractor, *s.* Tracteur *m.*

trade¹, *s.* **1.** État *m,* emploi *m*; commerce *m.* **To carry on a trade,** exercer un commerce. **He is a grocer by trade,** il est épicier de son état. **Everyone to his trade,** chacun son métier. **2.** Commerce, négoce *m,* affaires *fpl. Nau:* **Coasting trade,** cabotage *m.* **3.** Commerçants *mpl.* **4.** *Attrib.* **Trade expenses,** frais de bureau. **Trade price,** prix marchand.

trade-mark, *s.* Marque *f* de fabrique. **Registered trade-mark,** marque déposée.

trade-union, *s.* Syndicat ouvrier. **trade-unionism,** *s.* Syndicalisme (ouvrier). **trade-unionist,** *s.* Syndiqué, -ée; syndicaliste *mf.* **trade-wind,** *s.* Vent alizé; alizé *m.*

trade². **1.** *v.i.* (*a*) Faire le commerce, le négoce (*in,* de); trafiquer (*in,* en). (*b*) **To trade on s.o.'s ignorance,** exploiter l'ignorance de qn. **2.** *v.tr.* **To trade sth. for sth.,** troquer qch. contre qch. **trading,** *s.* Commerce *m,* négoce *m.* **Trading concern,** entreprise commerciale.

trader, *s.* Négociant, -ante; commerçant, -ante; marchand, -ande.

tradesfolk, *s.pl.* Commerçants *m.*

tradesman, *s.* Marchand *m,* boutiquier *m,* fournisseur *m.*

tradition, *s.* Tradition *f.*

traditional, *a.* Traditionnel. **-ally,** *adv.* Traditionnellement.

traduce, *v.tr.* Calomnier, diffamer.

traducer, *s.* Calomniateur, -trice.

traffic¹, *s.* **1.** Trafic *m,* négoce *m,* commerce *m* (*in,* de). **2.** Mouvement *m,* circulation *f.* **Block in the traffic,** embouteillage *m Congested t.,* circulation embarrassée. **3.** *Railway* **traffic,** trafic de chemin de fer.

traffic², *v.i.* Trafiquer (*in,* en); faire commerce (*in,* de).

tragedian, *s. Th:* Tragédien, -ienne.

tragedienne, *s. Th:* Tragédienne *f.*

tragedy, *s.* Tragédie *f.*

tragic(al), *a.* Tragique. **-ally,** *adv.* Tragiquement.

trail¹, *s.* **1.** Traînée *f.* **2.** (*a*) Piste *f,* trace *f.* **To pick up the trail,** retrouver la piste. (*b*) Sentier *m*; piste *m.*

trail². **I.** *v.tr.* **1.** **To trail sth. (along),** traîner

qch. après soi. **2.** Traquer. II. **trail**, *v.i.*
I. (*a*) Traîner. (*b*) *With a boat trailing behind,*
avec un bateau à la traîne. **2.** To trail along,
se traîner. **3.** (*Of plant*) Grimper; ramper.
trailing, *a.* Grimpant; rampant.
trailer, *s.* **I.** Traqueur *m.* **2.** *Veh:* Baladeuse *f* (d'auto).
train[1], *s.* **I.** Traîne *f*, queue *f.* **2.** (*a*) Suite *f*,
équipage *m.* (*b*) *Mil:* Baggage train, train *m*
des équipages. (*c*) *War brings famine in its t.*,
la guerre amène la disette. **3.** (*a*) Train,
convoi *m*; succession *f*, série *f.* Train of
thought, chaîne *f* d'idées. (*b*) *Min:* To fire
a train, allumer une traînée de poudre.
(*c*) *F:* To set sth. in train, mettre qch. en
train. **4.** *Rail:* (*a*) Train. Slow train, train
omnibus. To go by train, aller par le train,
par le chemin de fer. *To get into the t.*,
monter en wagon. (*b*) Rame *f* (du Métro).
train-bearer, *s.* Porte-queue *m inv.*
train[2]. I. *v.tr.* **I.** (*a*) Former, instruire;
dresser (un animal); exercer (l'oreille). To
train (up) a child, élever un enfant. (*b*) *Sp:*
Entraîner. (*c*) *Hort:* Diriger, conduire.
2. Pointer (un canon), braquer (une lunette)
(*on*, sur). *Navy:* Orienter (un canon).
II. **train**, *v.i.* (*a*) S'exercer. (*b*) *Sp:* S'entraîner. **trained**, *a.* (*a*) (Soldat) instruit;
(chien) dressé; (domestique) stylé; (œil)
exercé. Trained nurse, infirmière diplômée.
(*b*) *Sp:* Entraîné. **training,** *s.* (*a*) Éducation *f*, instruction *f.* To have had a business
training, être formé aux affaires. (*b*) *Military*
training, dressage *m* militaire. (*c*) *Sp:*
Entraînement *m.* To go into training, s'entraîner. (*d*) Dressage (d'un animal). **train-
ing-college,** *s.* *Sch:* École normale.
training-ship, *s.* Navire *m* école.
trainer, *s.* **I.** Dresseur *m* (d'animaux).
2. *Sp:* Entraîneur *m.*
train-oil, *s.* Huile *f* de baleine.
trait, *s.* Trait *m* (de caractère).
traitor, *s.* Traître *m.* To turn traitor, passer
à l'ennemi; se vendre.
traitorous, *a.* Traître, *f.* traîtresse; perfide.
-ly, *adv.* En traître; traîtreusement.
traitress, *s.* Traîtresse *f.*
trajectory, *s.* Trajectoire *f.*
tram, *s.* = TRAM-CAR. Tram driver, conducteur *m* de tramway; wattman *m.* Tram
conductor, receveur, -euse. **tram-car,** *s.*
(Voiture *f* de) tramway *m.*
trammel, *v.tr.* Entraver.
tramp[1], *s.* **I.** Bruit *m* de pas marqués.
2. (*a*) Marche *f*; promenade *f* à pied.
(*b*) To be on the tramp, *P:* être sur le trimard.
3. Chemineau *m*, vagabond *m.* **4.** *Nau:*
Tramp steamer, *F:* chemineau.
tramp[2], *v.i.* **I.** Marcher à pas marqués;
marcher lourdement. **2.** = TRAMPLE I.
3. (*a*) Marcher; voyager à pied. (*b*) Vagabonder. *v.tr.* To tramp the streets, battre le
pavé
trample. I. *v.i.* To trample on sth., piétiner,

écraser, qch. *F:* To trample on s.o.'s
feelings, fouler aux pieds les susceptibilités
de qn. **2.** *v.tr.* To trample sth. under foot,
fouler qch. aux pieds. **trampling,** *s.*
Piétinement *m*; bruit *m* de pas.
tramway, *s.* Voie *f* de tramway.
trance, *s.* (*a*) *Med:* (i) Extase *f*; (ii) catalepsie *f.* (*b*) (Hypnotic) trance, transe *f*,
hypnose *f.*
tranquil, *a.* Tranquille (et serein); calme,
paisible. **-illy,** *adv.* Tranquillement, paisiblement; avec sérénité.
tranquillity, *s.* Tranquillité *f*, calme *m*,
sérénité *f.*
tranquillize, *v.tr.* Tranquilliser, calmer.
transact, *v.tr.* To transact business with
s.o., faire des affaires avec qn.
transaction, *s.* **I.** Conduite *f.* **2.** The transaction of business, le commerce, les affaires *f.*
2. Cash transaction, opération au comptant.
3. *pl.* Transactions, transactions *f* (d'une
société savante).
transatlantic, *a.* Transatlantique.
transcend, *v.tr.* **I.** Dépasser les bornes de.
2. Surpasser.
transcendent, *a.* Transcendant.
transcribe, *v.tr.* Transcrire.
transcript, *s.* Transcription *f*, copie *f.*
transcription, *s.* Transcription *f.*
transept, *s.* *Ecc.Arch:* Transept *m.*
transfer[1], *s.* **I.** (*a*) Translation *f*, transport
m; déplacement *m* (d'un fonctionnaire).
Rail: Transfer ticket, billet de correspondance. (*b*) *St.Exch:* Transfer of shares,
transfert *m* d'actions. **2.** *Jur:* (Deed of)
transfer, acte *m* de cession. **3.** *Needlew:*
Décalque *m.*
transfer[2], *v.tr.* **I.** Transférer. (*a*) To t. a
civil servant, déplacer un fonctionnaire.
(*b*) *Jur:* Transmettre, céder. **2.** *Needlew:*
Calquer.
transferable, *a.* Transmissible. *Jur:*
(Droit) cessible. 'Not transferable,' strictement personnel.
transferee, *s.* *Jur:* Cessionnaire *mf.*
transferor, *s.* Cédant, -ante.
transfiguration, *s.* Transfiguration *f.*
transfigure, *v.tr.* Transfigurer.
transfix, *v.tr.* **I.** Transpercer. **2.** *F:* He
stood transfixed, il resta cloué au sol.
transform, *v.tr.* **I.** Transformer; *F:*
métamorphoser. **2.** *Ch:* Convertir (*into*, en).
transformation, *s.* **I.** (*a*) Transformation
f; *F:* métamorphose *f.* *Th:* Transformation scene, apothéose *f.* (*b*) Conversion *f.*
2. *Hairdr:* Faux toupet; transformation *f.*
transformer, *s.* *El.E:* Transformateur *m.*
transfuse, *v.tr.* Transfuser.
transfusion, *s.* Transfusion *f.*
transgress, *v.tr.* Transgresser. *Abs.* Pécher.
To t. a rule, violer une règle.
transgression, *s.* (*a*) Transgression *f*,
violation *f.* (*b*) Péché *m*, faute *f.*
transgressor, *s.* Transgresseur *m.*

tranship. **I.** *v.tr.* Transborder. **2.** *v.i.* Changer de vaisseau.

transhipment, *s.* Transbordement *m.*

transient, *a.* Transitoire; passager.

transit, *s.* **I.** Passage *m.* **2.** Transport *m.* Damage in transit, avarie(s) *f(pl)* en cours de route.

transition, *s.* **I.** Transition *f*; passage *m.* **2.** *Mus:* Modulation *f.*

transitive, *a.* (Verbe) transitif.

transitory, *a.* Transitoire; fugitif.

translate, *v.tr.* **I.** Traduire. **2.** Transférer (un évêque) (*to*, à).

translation, *s.* **I.** (*a*) Traduction *f.* (*b*) Traduction; ouvrage traduit. *Sch:* Version *f.* **2.** Translation *f* (d'un évêque).

translator, *s.* Traducteur *m.*

translucence, *s.* Translucidité *f.*

translucent, *a.* Translucide.

transmigration, *s.* **I.** Transmigration *f* (d'un peuple). **2.** Métempsycose *f.*

transmissible, *a.* Transmissible.

transmission, *s.* Transmission *f. El.E:* Transmission of power, transport *m* de force.

transmit, *v.tr.* Transmettre. *El.E:* Transporter (la force). **transmitting,** *a.* (*a*) Transmetteur *m.* (*b*) *W.Tel:* Transmitting station, poste émetteur.

transmitter, *s.* (*a*) *Tg:* Transmetteur *m.* (*b*) *W.Tel:* (Poste) émetteur *m.*

transmutation, *s.* Transmutation *f.*

transmute, *v.tr.* (*a*) Transformer (*into*, en). (*b*) Transmuer (un métal).

transom, *s. Const:* Traverse *f*, linteau *m.* **transom-window,** *s.* Fenêtre *f* à meneau horizontal.

transparency, *s.* (*a*) Transparence *f.* (*b*) Limpidité *f* (de l'eau).

transparent, *a.* **I.** Transparent; (eau) limpide. **2.** *F:* Évident, clair. **-ly,** *adv.* D'une manière transparente; clairement.

transpierce, *v.tr.* Transpercer.

transpiration, *s.* Transpiration *f.*

transpire. (*a*) Transpirer. (*b*) Se passer.

transplant, *v.tr.* Transplanter.

transplantation, *s.* Transplantation *f.*

transport[1], *s.* **I.** Transport *m.* **2.** (*a*) *Nau:* Transport(-vessel), (bâtiment *m* de) transport. (*b*) *Mil:* Les charrois *m.* **3.** Transport (de joie). **She was in transports,** elle était dans le ravissement.

transport[2], *v.tr.* **I.** Transporter. **2.** To be transported with joy, être transporté de joie.

transportation, *s. Jur: A:* Déportation *f.*

transpose, *v.tr.* Transposer.

transposition, *s.* Transposition *f.*

transversal, *a.* Transversal, -aux.

transverse, *a.* Transversal, -aux; en travers. **-ly,** *adv.* Transversalement.

trap[1], *s.* **I.** (*a*) Piège *m*; (*for big game*) trappe *f.* **To set a trap,** armer un piège. **To catch an animal in a trap,** prendre une bête au piège. (*b*) *F:* Piège, ruse *f.* **2.** = TRAP-DOOR.

3. *Veh:* Cabriolet *m.* **trap-door,** *s.* Trappe *f.*

trap[2], *v.tr.* (*a*) Prendre au piège. *F:* **Trapped by the flames,** cerné par les flammes. (*b*) Tendre des pièges dans. (*c*) *Abs.* Trapper.

trapped, *a.* Pris dans un piège; pris au piège.

trape(s), *v.i.* Traîner çà et là; se balader.

trapeze, *s.* Trapèze *m.*

trapper, *s. Ven:* Trappeur *m.*

trappings, *s.pl.* **I.** Harnachement *m*, caparaçon *m.* **2.** *F:* Atours *mpl*; apparat *m.*

trappist, *s. Ecc:* Trappiste *m.*

traps, *s.pl. F:* Effets (personnels). **To pack up one's traps,** faire son paquet.

trash, *s.* (*a*) Chose(s) *f(pl)* sans valeur; camelote *f.* (*b*) Littérature *f* de camelote.

trashy, *a.* Sans valeur; (littérature) de camelote.

travel[1], *s.* (*a*) Voyages *mpl.* **To be fond of t.,** aimer à voyager. (*b*) *pl.* **Is he still on his travels?** est-il toujours en voyage?

travel[2], *v.i.* **I.** (*a*) Voyager; faire des voyages. **He is travelling,** il est en voyage. **To travel over a country,** parcourir un pays. (*b*) Aller, marcher; (*of news*) circuler. **2.** Être voyageur de commerce. **travelling,** *s.* Voyages *mpl.* **Travelling bag,** sac de voyage. **Travelling expenses,** frais de voyage.

traveller, *s.* **I.** Voyageur, -euse. **Traveller's cheque,** chèque de voyage. **2.** (Commercial) traveller, voyageur de commerce; commis voyageur.

traverse, *v.tr.* **I.** Traverser, passer à travers. **2.** *F:* Contrarier, traverser (un dessein).

travesty[1], *s.* Parodie *f*; travestissement *m.*

travesty[2], *v.tr.* Parodier, travestir.

trawl[1], *s.* Trawl(-net), chalut *m*, traille *f.*

trawl[2]. **I.** *v.i. Fish:* Pêcher au chalut; chaluter. **2.** *v.tr.* Traîner (un chalut). **trawling,** *s.* Pêche *f* au chalut.

trawler, *s.* Chalutier *m.*

tray, *s.* Plateau *m.* **tray-cloth,** *s.* Dessus *m*, napperon *m*, de plateau.

treacherous, *a.* Traître; perfide. *T. memory,* mémoire infidèle. **-ly,** *adv.* En traître, perfidement.

treachery, *s.* Trahison *f*, perfidie *f.*

treacle, *s.* Mélasse *f.*

tread[1], *s.* **I.** (*a*) Pas *m. The measured t. of a policeman,* la démarche mesurée d'un agent. (*b*) Bruit *m* de pas. **2.** Tread of a stair, giron *m* d'une marche d'escalier.

tread[2], *v.* **I.** *v.i.* Marcher; poser les pieds. *To t. softly,* marcher à pas feutrés. *To t. on sth.,* mettre le pied sur qch. **2.** *v.tr.* (*a*) To tread sth. under foot, fouler qch. aux pieds. (*b*) To tread (out) grapes, fouler la vendange. *Swim:* **To tread water,** nager debout.

tread down, *v.tr.* Écraser du pied, fouler aux pieds; opprimer.

treadle, *s.* Pédale *f.*

treadmill, *s. A:* Écureuil *m.*

treason, s. *Jur:* Trahison f. **High treason,** haute trahison.

treasonable, a. **1.** De trahison. **2.** Traître, perfide. **-ably,** adv. Traîtreusement.

treasure¹, s. Trésor m. **treasure-house,** s. Trésor m. **treasure-trove,** s. *Jur:* Trésor (découvert par hasard).

treasure², v.tr. **1.** Priser, tenir beaucoup à. **2.** To treasure sth. (up), garder qch. soigneusement.

treasurer, s. Trésorier, -ière.

treasury, s. **1.** Trésor (public); trésorerie f. **2.** Treasury of verse, anthologie f poétique.

treat¹, s. **1.** (a) Régal m, -als; festin m; fête f. (b) *F:* I'll stand treat all round, je paie une tournée générale. **2.** *F:* Plaisir m. A treat in store, un plaisir à venir.

treat². I. v.i. **1.** To treat with s.o., traiter, négocier, avec qn. To treat for peace, traiter la paix. **2.** To treat of a subject, traiter d'un sujet. II. **treat,** v.tr. **1.** Traiter. *To t. s.o. well,* se conduire bien avec qn. To treat sth. as a joke, considérer qch. comme une plaisanterie. **2.** Régaler; payer à boire à. *F:* To treat oneself to an ice, s'offrir, se payer, une glace. **3.** *Med:* Traiter. **4.** Traiter (un thème).

treatise, s. Traité m (on, de).

treatment, s. **1.** (a) Traitement m. *His t. of his friends,* sa manière d'agir envers ses amis. (b) Traitement (d'un sujet). **2.** Traitement médical.

treaty, s. **1.** Traité m; convention f. Treaty obligations, obligations conventionnelles. **2.** Accord m, contrat m. To sell sth. by private treaty, vendre qch. à l'amiable.

treble¹. I. a. **1.** Triple. **2.** *Mus:* Treble voice, (voix f de) soprano m. Treble clef, clef f de sol. II. **treble,** adv. Trois fois autant. III. **treble,** s. **1.** Triple m. **2.** *Mus:* (a) *To sing the t.,* chanter le dessus. (b) Soprano m.

treble². **1.** v.tr. Tripler. **2.** v.i. (Se) tripler.

trebly, adv. Triplement.

tree, s. Arbre m. *To climb a t.,* grimper sur, monter à, un arbre. *F:* To be at the top of the tree, être au haut de l'échelle. *To get to the top of the t.,* arriver. **tree-fern,** s. *Amph:* Rainette f. **tree-frog,** s. *Amph:* **tree-trunk,** s. Tronc m d'arbre.

trefoil, s. *Bot:* Trèfle m.

trek¹, s. Étape f.

trek², v.i. **1.** *F:* Faire route. **2.** *F:* Plier bagage; déguerpir.

trellis, s. Treillis m, treillage m. **trellis-work,** s. Treillis m, treillage m.

tremble¹, s. Frisson m; *(in voice)* tremblotement m. *F:* To be all of a tremble, être tout tremblant.

tremble², v.i. **1.** Trembler, vibrer. **2.** Trembler, frissonner. **trembling¹,** a. Tremblant, tremblotant. **trembling²,** s. Tremblement m; tremblotement m. *F:* In fear and trembling, tout tremblant.

tremendous, a. **1.** Terrible. **2.** *F:* Immense. *There was a t. crowd,* il y avait un monde fou. *T. success,* succès formidable. *T. blow,* coup assommant. **-ly,** adv. **1.** Terriblement. **2.** *F:* Énormément; démesurément.

tremolo, s. *Mus:* Tremolo m.

tremor, s. **1.** Tremblement m, frémissement m. **2.** Earth tremor, secousse f sismique.

tremulous, a. Tremblotant, frémissant. *T. smile,* sourire timide. *T. voice,* voix chevrotante. **-ly,** adv. En tremblant.

trench¹, s. **1.** *Agr:* Tranchée f, fossé m. **2.** *Mil:* Tranchée. **trench-coat,** s. *Mil:* Manteau m imperméable. **trench-mortar,** s. Lance-bombes m inv.

trench². **1.** v.tr. Creuser un fossé, une tranchée, dans. *Abs.* To trench, creuser des fossés. **2.** v.i. To trench (up)on s.o.'s rights, empiéter sur les droits de qn.

trenchant, a. (a) (Ton) tranchant, incisif (b) (Réponse) mordante. **-ly,** adv. D'une manière tranchante.

trend¹, s. Direction f; tendance f. *The t of my thoughts,* le cours de mes pensées.

trend², v.i. Se diriger, tendre.

trepidation, s. Trépidation f.

trespass¹, s. **1.** (a) Contravention f de la loi; délit m. (b) *Theol:* Offense f, péché m. **2.** *Jur:* Violation f des droits de qn.

trespass², v.i. **1.** Pécher (against, contre). **2.** (a) To trespass (up)on s.o.'s property, *abs.* to trespass, s'introduire sans autorisation sur la propriété de qn. *F:* To trespass on s.o.'s preserves, empiéter sur le champ d'activité de qn. (b) *To t.* (up)on s.o.'s kindness, abuser de la bonté de qn.

trespasser, s. **1.** *Theol:* Transgresseur m. **2.** Auteur m d'une violation de propriété. 'Trespassers will be prosecuted,' "défense d'entrer sous peine d'amende."

tress, s. (a) Tresse f, boucle f. (b) pl. **Tresses,** chevelure f.

trestle, s. Tréteau m, chevalet m.

trey, s. *Cards:* (Le) trois.

triad, s. Triade f.

trial, s. *Jur:* (a) Jugement m. They were sent for trial, ils furent renvoyés en jugement. Trial by jury, jugement par jury. (b) Procès m. Famous trials, causes f célèbres. **2.** Essai m. (a) Épreuve f. *Sp:* Trial game, match m de sélection. (b) To give sth. a trial, faire l'essai de qch. On trial, à l'essai. *Book-k:* Trial balance, balance de vérification. **3.** Épreuve douloureuse. To be a trial to, faire le martyre de.

triangle, s. Triangle m.

triangular, a. Triangulaire; en triangle.

tribal, a. **1.** (Of race) Qui vit en tribus. **2.** Qui appartient à la tribu; de tribu.

tribe, s. Tribu f.

tribesman, s. Membre m de la tribu.

tribulation, s. Tribulation f, affliction f.

tribunal, *s.* Tribunal *m*, -aux. **I.** Siège *m* du juge. **2.** Cour *f* de justice ; la cour.

tribune¹, *s.* Tribun *m*.

tribune², *s.* Tribune *f* (d'orateur).

tributary. I. *a.* Tributaire. **2.** *s.* (a) Tributaire *m*. (b) Affluent *m* (d'un fleuve).

tribute, *s.* **I.** Tribut *m*. **2.** Tribut, hommage *m*. *To pay a last t. of respect to s.o.,* rendre à qn les derniers devoirs.

trice, *s.* In a trice, en un clin d'œil.

trick¹, *s.* **I.** (a) Tour *m*, ruse *f* ; supercherie *f*. To play a trick on s.o., jouer un tour à qn. (b) Truc *m*. The tricks of the trade, les trucs du métier. He knows a trick or two, il est roublard. To know the trick of it, avoir le truc. That'll do the trick, ça fera l'affaire. **2.** Farce *f*, tour. Shabby trick, vilain tour. You have been up to your old tricks, vous avez encore fait des vôtres. **3.** Tour d'adresse. Card trick, tour de cartes. *F:* The whole bag of tricks, toute la boutique. *F:* To do the trick, réussir le coup. **4.** Manie *f*, habitude *f* ; tic *m*. He has a trick of (doing sth.), il a la manie de (faire qch). **5.** *Cards:* Levée *f*. The odd trick, le trick, le tri. **6.** *Nau:* Trick at the wheel, tour de barre.

trick², *v.tr.* Attraper, duper. *I've been tricked,* on m'a refait. To trick s.o. out of sth., escroquer qch. à qn.

trickery, *s.* Fourberie *f*, tricherie *f*.

trickiness, *s.* **I.** Fourberie *f*. **2.** *F:* Nature compliquée, difficile.

trickle¹, *s.* Filet *m*.

trickle², *v.i.* Couler (goutte à goutte).

trickling, *s.* Dégouttement *m* ; écoulement *m* goutte à goutte.

trickster, *s.* Fourbe *m*, escroc *m*.

tricky, *a.* **I.** Rusé, astucieux, fin. **2.** *F:* (Mécanisme) d'un maniement délicat.

tricolo(u)r. I. *a.* Tricolore. **2.** *s.* The Tricolour, le drapeau tricolore.

tricycle, *s.* Tricycle *m*.

trident, *s.* Trident *m*.

trier, *s.* *F:* He's a trier, il fait toujours de son mieux.

trifle¹, *s.* **I.** (a) Bagatelle *f*, vétille *f*. (b) He gave the beggar a trifle, il donna quelques sous au mendiant. (c) *Adv.phr.* A trifle, un tout petit peu. *A t. too narrow,* un soupçon trop étroit. **2.** *Cu:* Charlotte *f* russe sur biscuit de Savoie.

trifle². **I.** *v.i.* (a) Jouer, badiner (*with,* avec). To trifle with s.o., se jouer de qn. (b) To trifle with sth., manier nonchalamment (sa canne). *To t. with one's food,* manger du bout des dents. (c) Vétiller ; s'occuper à des riens. **2.** *v.tr.* To trifle one's time away, gâcher son temps. **trifling¹,** *a.* Insignifiant ; peu important. *T. incidents,* menus incidents. Of trifling value, d'une valeur minime. **trifling²,** *s.* **I.** Légèreté *f* d'esprit ; manque *m* de sérieux. **2.** Futilités *fpl*.

trifler, *s.* Personne *f* frivole.

trigger, *s.* (a) Poussoir *m* à ressort. (b) *Sm.a:* Détente *f* ; *F:* gâchette *f*.

trigonometry, *s.* Trigonométrie *f*. Plane trigonometry, trigonométrie rectiligne.

trill¹, *s.* **I.** *Mus:* (a) Trille *m*. (b) Cadence perlée. **2.** Chant perlé.

trill², *v.i.* Faire des trilles.

trilogy, *s.* Trilogie *f*.

trim¹, *s.* **I.** Bon ordre. (a) Everything was in perfect trim, tout était en parfait état. (b) To be in good trim, être gaillard ; être en forme. **2.** *Nau:* Assiette *f*, arrimage *m*. *Av:* Équilibrage *m*. **3.** *Hairdr:* Coupe *f*.

trim², *a.* Soigné ; en bon état. *A t. figure,* une tournure élégante.

trim³, *v.tr.* **I.** (a) Arranger ; mettre en ordre. (b) Tailler ; rafraîchir (la barbe). *To trim one's nails,* se faire les ongles. To trim a lamp, couper la mèche d'une lampe. **2.** *Dressm:* Orner, parer (*with,* de). **3.** *Nau:* (a) Équilibrer. (b) Orienter, appareiller (les voiles).

trimming, *s.* **I.** (a) Arrangement *m*, mise *f* en état (de qch.). (b) Taille *f* (des haies). **2.** (a) Garnissage *m* (de chapeaux). (b) Garniture *f*, ornement *m* (de vêtements, de chapeaux). **3.** *Nau:* Arrimage *m*.

trimness, *s.* Air soigné, air bien tenu. The t. of her figure, sa jolie tournure.

Trinidad. *Pr.n.* (Ile de) la Trinité.

Trinity, *s.* (a) *Theol:* The (blessed) Trinity, la (sainte) Trinité. (b) *F:* Groupe *m* de trois.

trinket, *s.* (a) Petit objet de parure ; breloque *f*. (b) Bibelot *m*.

trio, *s.* Trio *m*.

triolet, *s.* *Pros:* Triolet *m*.

trip¹, *s.* **I.** Excursion *f* ; voyage *m* d'agrément. *Nau:* Round trip, croisière *f*. **2.** (a) Faux pas ; trébuchement *m*. (b) *F:* Faute *f* ; faux pas. (c) Croc-en-jambe *m*.

trip², *v.* **I.** *v.i.* (a) To trip (along), aller d'un pas léger. (b) Trébucher ; faire un faux pas. (c) *F:* Se tromper ; commettre une faute. **2.** *v.tr.* To trip s.o. (up), (i) donner un croc-en-jambe à qn ; (of obstacle) faire trébucher qn ; (ii) *F:* prendre qn en défaut.

tripe, *s.* (a) *Cu:* Tripe(s) *f(pl)* ; gras-double *m*. (b) *P:* Fatras *m*, bêtises *fpl*.

triple¹, *a.* Triple. *Mus:* Triple time, mesure ternaire, à trois temps. **-ply,** *adv.* Triplement.

triple². **I.** *v.tr.* Tripler. **2.** *v.i.* (Se) tripler.

triplet, *s.* **I.** Trio *m*. (a) *Mus:* Triolet *m*. (b) *Pros:* Tercet *m*. **2.** Trijumeau, -elle.

triplicate¹. I. *a.* Triplé ; triple. **2.** *s.* Triple *m* ; triplicata *m*. In triplicate, en triple exemplaire.

triplicate², *v.tr.* **I.** Tripler. **2.** Rédiger en triple expédition.

tripod, *s.* Trépied *m*.

Tripoli. *Pr.n.* Tripoli *m*.

tripper, *s.* Excursionniste *mf*.

triptych, *s.* *Art:* Triptyque *m*.

Tristram. *Pr.n. Lit:* Tristan *m*.

trisyllabic, *a.* Tris(s)yllabique, tris(s)yllabe.

trisyllable, *a.* Tris(s)yllabe *m*.

trite, *a.* Banal, -aux. **Trite subject**, sujet usé, rebattu. **-ly,** *adv.* Banalement.

triteness, *s.* Banalité *f.*

Triton. *Pr.n. Myth:* Triton *m.*

triturate, *v.tr.* Triturer.

trituration, *s.* Trituration *f.*

triumph¹, *s.* (*a*) Triomphe *m*, succès *m.* (*b*) Air *m* de triomphe; jubilation *f.*

triumph², *v.i.* Triompher. **To triumph over one's enemies**, triompher de ses ennemis.

triumphal, *a.* Triomphal, -aux; de triomphe. **Triumphal arch**, arc *m* de triomphe.

triumphant, *a.* Triomphant. **-ly,** *adv.* Triomphalement.

trivet, *s.* Trépied *m*, chevrette *f.*

trivial, *a.* **1.** (*a*) Insignifiant; sans importance. (*b*) (*Of pers.*) Superficiel, léger, futile. **2.** Banal, -aux; trivial, -aux.

triviality, *s.* (*a*) Insignifiance *f.* (*b*) Banalité *f* (d'une observation).

trochaic, *a. & s. Pros:* Trochaïque (*m*).

trochee, *s. Pros:* Trochée *m.*

troglodyte, *s.* Troglodyte *m.*

Trojan, *a. & s.* Troyen, -enne; de Troie. *F:* **To work like a Trojan**, travailler comme un nègre.

troll¹, *s.* Chanson *f* à reprises; canon *m.*

troll². **1.** *v.tr.* Chantonner; *abs.* chantonner. **2.** *v.i. Fish:* **To troll for pike**, pêcher le brochet à la cuiller. **trolling**, *s. Fish:* Pêche *f* à la cuiller.

troll³, *s. Norse Myth:* Troll *m.*

trolley, *s.* **1.** (*a*) *Veh:* Fardier *m*, chariot *m.* (*b*) **Dinner trolley**, serveuse *f.* **2.** *El.E:* (Poulie *f*) de contact (d'un tramway).

trolley-bus, *s.* Autobus *m* à trolley.

trombone, *s.* Trombone *m.*

troop¹, *s.* **1.** Troupe *f*, bande *f.* **In troops**, par bandes. **2.** *Mil:* (*a*) *pl.* **Troops**, troupes. (*b*) Peloton *m* (de cavalerie). **3.** **Troop of boy scouts**, troupe de boy-scouts. **troop-ship**, *s.* Transport *m.* **troop-train**, *s.* Train *m* régimentaire.

troop², *v.i.* (*a*) **To troop together**, s'attrouper, s'assembler. (*b*) **To troop in**, entrer en troupe.

trooper, *s. Mil:* Cavalier *m*; soldat *m* de cavalerie.

trophy, *s.* Trophée *m.*

tropic. **1.** *s.* (*a*) *Geog:* Tropique *m.* (*b*) **The tropics**, les tropiques. **In the tropics**, sous les tropiques. **2.** *a.* Tropical, -aux.

tropical, *a.* Tropical, -aux; des tropiques.

trot¹, *s.* Trot *m.* **To go at a trot**, aller au trot. *F:* **To keep s.o. on the trot**, faire trotter qn.

trot², *v.* **1.** *v.i.* (*a*) Trotter; aller au trot. **To trot away**, partir au trot. (*b*) *F:* **Now I must be trotting**, maintenant il faut que je me trotte. **2.** *v.tr.* Faire trotter (un cheval).

troth, *s. Lit:* **1.** Foi *f.* **By my troth!** sur ma foi! **2.** **In troth**, en vérité.

trouble¹, *s.* **1.** Peine *f*, chagrin *m*; affliction *f*, malheur *m.* **To be in trouble**, être dans la peine; avoir du chagrin. **His troubles are over**, il est au bout de ses peines. **2.** Ennui *m*, difficulté *f.* (*a*) **Money troubles**, soucis *m* d'argent. **The trouble is that**, l'ennui, la difficulté, c'est que. **You will have trouble with him**, il vous donnera du fil à retordre. (*b*) **To get into trouble**, s'attirer une mauvaise affaire. **To get out of trouble**, se tirer d'affaire. **He is looking for trouble**, il se prépare des ennuis. (*c*) **To make trouble**, semer la discorde. **3.** Dérangement *m*, peine. **To take the trouble to do sth.**, prendre la peine de faire qch. **It is not worth the trouble**, ce n'est pas la peine. **To put s.o. to trouble**, déranger qn. **To put oneself to a lot of trouble**, se donner beaucoup de mal. **He thinks nothing too much trouble**, rien ne lui coûte. *F:* **It is no trouble**, cela ne me coûte aucune peine. **To have (had) all one's trouble for nothing**, en être pour sa peine. **4.** (*a*) *Med:* Dérangement. **To have heart trouble**, être malade du cœur. (*b*) *Aut:* **Engine trouble**, panne *f* du moteur. (*c*) *Ind:* **Labour troubles**, conflits *m* entre ouvriers et patrons.

trouble². **1.** *v.tr.* (*a*) Affliger, tourmenter, chagriner; inquiéter, préoccuper, soucier. **To be troubled about s.o.**, se tourmenter au sujet de qn. **That does not t. him much**, cela ne le préoccupe guère. (*b*) Affliger, faire souffrir. (*c*) Déranger, incommoder, gêner. *I shall not t. you with the details*, je ne vous importunerai pas de tous les détails. **May I trouble you to shut the door?** cela vous dérangerait-il de fermer la porte? **To trouble oneself to do sth.**, se donner la peine de faire qch. **2.** *v.i.* (*a*) S'inquiéter. **Don't trouble about it**, ne vous inquiétez pas de cela. (*b*) Se déranger; se mettre en peine. **Don't trouble to write**, ne vous donnez pas la peine d'écrire. **troubled**, *a.* **1.** (*Of liquid*) Trouble. *F:* **To fish in troubled waters**, pêcher en eau trouble. **2.** Inquiet, -ète; agité.

troublesome, *a.* **1.** Ennuyeux, gênant. *T. child*, enfant fatigant. **How troublesome!** quel ennui! **2.** Difficile, pénible.

trough, *s.* **1.** Auge *f. Husb:* **Drinking trough**, abreuvoir *m.* **Feeding trough**, auge. **2.** **Trough of the sea**, creux *m* de la lame.

trounce, *v.tr.* **1.** Rosser, étriller. **2.** Réprimander, semoncer. **trouncing**, *s.* Raclée *f*; étrillage *m.*

troupe, *s.* Troupe *f.*

trouser, *s.* (**Pair of**) **trousers**, pantalon *m.*

trouser-clip, *s.* Pince *f* à pantalon.

trouser-press, *s.* Presse *f* pour pantalons.

trousseau, *s.* Trousseau *m.*

trout, *s.inv. Ich:* Truite *f.* **Trout stream**, ruisseau à truites.

trowel, *s.* **1.** Truelle *f.* **2.** *Hort:* Déplantoir *m*, houlette *f.*

Troy. *Pr.n. A.Geog:* Troie *f.*

truant, *a. & s.* (Élève) absent(e) (de l'école) sans permission. **To play truant**, faire l'école buissonnière.

truce, *s.* Trêve *f.* *F:* A truce to jesting! trêve de plaisanteries!

truck¹, *s.* **1.** Troc *m*, échange *m.* **2.** *F:* I have no truck with him, je n'ai rien à faire avec lui. **3.** (*a*) Articles divers. (*b*) Objets *mpl* de peu de valeur.

truck², *s.* **1.** (*a*) Fardier *m*, camion *m*, chariot *m.* (*b*) **Porter's luggage truck,** (*four-wheeled*) chariot à bagages; (*two-wheeled*) diable *m.* **2.** *Rail:* Wagon *m* (à marchandises).

truckful, *s.* Plein wagon, plein camion.

truckle, *v.i.* **To truckle to s.o.,** ramper, s'abaisser, devant qn.

truckle-bed, *s.* Lit bas à roulettes.

truculence, *s.* Férocité *f*; truculence *f.*

truculent, *a.* Féroce; brutal, -aux; truculent. **-ly,** *adv.* Avec truculence.

trudge¹, *s.* Marche *f* pénible.

trudge², *v.i.* Marcher lourdement, péniblement; clopiner.

true. **I.** *a.* **1.** Vrai; exact. **If it be true that . . .,** s'il est vrai que + *sub.* **True!** c'est (bien) vrai! c'est juste! **To come true,** se réaliser. **2.** Véritable; vrai, réel. **3.** *Mec. E:* Juste, droit. **4.** Fidèle, loyal, -aux (*to*, à). **5.** (*Of voice*) Juste. **6.** *Biol:* **True to type,** conforme au type ancestral. **II. true,** *adv.* **1.** Vraiment; *F:* vrai. **2. To sing true,** chanter juste. **true-born,** *a.* **A true-born Englishman,** un vrai Anglais d'Angleterre. **true-hearted,** *a.* (*a*) Au cœur fidèle; loyal, -aux. (*b*) Sincère, honnête.

truffle, *s.* Truffe *f.*

truism, *s.* Truisme *m*, axiome *m.*

truly, *adv.* **1.** (*a*) Vraiment, véritablement. **I am truly grateful,** je vous suis sincèrement reconnaissant. (*b*) *Corr:* (I am) yours (very) truly, je vous prie de croire à ma parfaite considération. **2.** En vérité. **3.** Fidèlement, loyalement. **4.** Avec vérité; justement.

trump¹, *s.* **1.** *Cards:* Atout *m.* *F:* **He always turns up trumps,** la chance le favorise sans cesse. **2.** *F:* Bon type.

trump², *v.tr.* **1.** *Cards:* Couper. **2. To t. up a charge,** forger une accusation.

trumpery. **1.** *s.* Friperie *f*, camelote *f.* **2.** *a.* (*a*) Sans valeur, de camelote. (*b*) Mesquin, spécieux.

trumpet¹, *s.* Trompette *f.* *F:* **With a flourish of trumpets,** à cor et à cri. **trumpet-call,** *s.* Sonnerie *f* de trompette. **trumpet-major,** *s.* *Mil:* Trompette-major *m.*

trumpet², *v.* **1.** *v.i.* (*a*) Sonner de la trompette. (*b*) (*Of elephant*) Barrir. **2.** *v.tr.* *F:* **To trumpet abroad,** proclamer. **trumpeting,** *s.* **1.** Sonnerie *f* de trompette. **2.** (*Of elephant*) Barrit *m*, barrissement *m.*

trumpeter, *s.* *Mil:* Trompette *m.*

truncate, *v.tr.* Tronquer. **truncated,** *a.* Tronqué.

truncheon, *s.* Bâton *m* (d'agent de police).

trundle, *v.tr.* (*a*) Faire rouler, faire courir. (*b*) Pousser (une brouette).

trunk, *s.* **1.** (*a*) Tronc *m* (d'arbre). (*b*) Tronc (du corps). **2.** Malle *f*, coffre *m.* **To pack one's trunk,** faire sa malle. **3.** Trompe *f* (d'éléphant). **trunk-call,** *s.* *Tp:* Appel *m* à longue distance.

truss¹, *s.* **1.** Botte *f* (de foin). **2.** *Const:* Armature *f* (de poutre).

truss², *v.tr.* **1.** *Const:* Armer, renforcer. **2.** *Cu:* Trousser, brider; *F:* ligoter.

trust¹, *s.* **1.** Confiance *f* (*in*, en) **To take sth. on trust,** ajouter foi à qch. sans examen. **2.** Espérance *f*, espoir *m.* **3.** (*a*) Responsabilité *f*, charge *f.* **Position of trust,** poste de confiance. (*b*) Garde *f*; dépôt *m.* **4.** *Ind:* Trust *m*, syndicat *m.*

trust², **1.** *v.tr.* (*a*) Se fier à; mettre sa confiance en. **He is not to be trusted,** on ne peut pas se fier à lui. **I can scarcely trust my eyes,** c'est à n'en pas croire mes yeux. **To trust s.o. with sth.,** confier qch. à qn. **To trust s.o. to do sth.,** se fier à qn pour que qch. se fasse. **Trust him!** laissez-le faire! *F:* **She won't trust him out of her sight,** elle ne le perd jamais de vue. (*b*) *Com:* *F:* Faire crédit à. (*c*) Espérer (que + *ind.*). *Corr:* **I trust to hear from you soon,** j'espère avoir de vos nouvelles sous peu. **2.** *v.i.* (*a*) Se confier (*in*, en); se fier (*in*, à). (*b*) Mettre ses espérances (*to sth.*, en qch.). **To trust to chance, to luck,** se confier au hasard. **trusted,** *a.* De confiance. **trusting,** *a.* Plein de confiance. **-ly,** *adv.* Avec confiance.

trustee, *s.* **1.** *Jur:* (*a*) Curateur, -trice. (*b*) Dépositaire *mf.* **2.** Administrateur, -trice, curateur.

trustful, *a.* Plein de confiance; confiant. **-fully,** *adv.* Avec confiance.

trustfulness, *s.* Confiance *f.*

trustiness, *s.* Fidélité *f*, loyauté *f.*

trustworthiness, *s.* **1.** Loyauté *f*, fidélité *f.* **2.** Crédibilité *f*, exactitude *f.*

trustworthy, *a.* **1.** Digne de confiance; honnête, fidèle. **2.** Croyable, exact.

truth, *s.* (*a*) Vérité *f.* **The truth (of the matter) is,** pour dire la vérité. **Truth to tell,** en vérité; à vrai dire. **There is some truth in what you say,** il y a du vrai dans ce que vous dites. **Truth will out,** tôt ou tard la vérité se fait jour. (*b*) Vérité; chose vraie. **To tell s.o. some home truths,** dire ses quatre vérités à qn.

truthful, *a.* **1.** Véridique. **2.** Vrai; fidèle. **-fully,** *adv.* **1.** Véridiquement. **2.** Fidèlement.

truthfulness, *s.* Véracité *f.*

try¹, *s.* Essai *m*, tentative *f.* **To have a try at (doing) sth.,** s'essayer à qch. **Let's have a try!** essayons toujours! **At the first try,** du premier coup.

try², *v.* **1.** *v.tr.* **1.** (*a*) Éprouver; mettre à l'épreuve. (*b*) Éprouver; affliger. **A people sorely tried,** une nation durement éprouvée. (*c*) **To try one's eyes** *by reading too much,* se fatiguer les yeux à trop lire. **2.** Essayer, expérimenter; faire l'essai de. **3.** *Jur:* Juger.

4. Essayer, tenter. To try one's strength against s.o., se mesurer avec qn. **5.** To try to do sth., tâcher, essayer, de faire qch. He tried his best *to save them*, il a fait tout son possible pour les sauver. To try again, essayer de nouveau. II. **try,** *v.i.* To try for sth., tâcher d'obtenir qch. **try on,** *v.tr.* **1.** Essayer (un vêtement). **2.** *F:* To try it on with s.o., chercher à mettre qn dedans. **try-on,** *s.* *F:* Tentative *f* de déception. **try out,** *v.tr.* Essayer à fond. **tried,** *a.* Éprouvé. **trying¹,** *a.* **1.** Difficile, pénible. **2.** Vexant; contrariant. **trying²,** *s.* **1.** Essai *m*, épreuve *f*. **2.** *Jur:* Jugement *m*.

tryst, *s.* Rendez-vous *m*.

tsar, *s.*, **tsarevitch,** *s.*, **tsarina,** *s.* = CZAR, CZAREVITCH, CZARINA.

tsetse, *s.* Tsetse(-fly), (mouche *f*) tsé-tsé *f*.

tub, *s.* **1.** (*a*) Baquet *m*, bac *m*. (*b*) (Wash-)tub, baquet, cuvier *m* (à lessive). **2.** (*a*) (Bath-)tub, tub *m*. (*b*) To have a tub, prendre un bain. **3.** *Nau:* *F:* Old tub, vieille coque. **tub-thumper,** *s.* *F:* Orateur *m* de carrefour.

tubby, *a.* *F:* Boulot, -otte.

tube, *s.* **1.** (*a*) Tube *m*, tuyau *m*. (*b*) Tube (de pâte dentifrice). (*c*) *Aut:* *Cy:* Inner tube, chambre *f* à air. **2.** *Anat:* Tube; canal, -aux *m*. **3.** *F:* = TUBE-RAILWAY. **tube-railway,** *s.* *Rail:* Voie souterraine.

tuber, *s.* *Bot:* Racine tubéreuse.

tubercle, *s.* *Bot:* Tubercule *m*.

tubercular, *a.* *Bot:* Tuberculeux.

tuberculosis, *s.* *Med:* Tuberculose *f*.

tuberous, *a.* *Bot:* Tubéreux.

tubing, *s.* *Coll:* Tuyautage *m*, tuyauterie *f*, tubes *mpl*.

tubular, *a.* Tubulaire.

tuck¹, *s.* **1.** *Dressm:* (Petit) pli; rempli *m*, plissé *m*. To take up a tuck in a garment, faire un rempli à un vêtement. **2.** *Sch:* *F:* Mangeaille *f*. Tuck box, boîte à provisions. **tuck-shop,** *s.* *Sch:* *F:* Pâtisserie *f*.

tuck², *v.tr.* **1.** *Dressm:* Faire des plis à. **2.** Replier, rentrer, mettre. To tuck a rug round s.o., envelopper qn d'une couverture. **tuck in.** **1.** *v.tr.* (*a*) Serrer, rentrer; replier (le bord d'un vêtement). To tuck in the bed-clothes, border le lit. (*b*) To tuck s.o. in, border qn (dans son lit). **2.** *v.i.* *F:* Manger à belles dents. **tuck-in,** *s.* *F:* Bombance *f*. **tuck into,** *v.i.* *F:* To tuck into a pie, attaquer un pâté. **tuck up,** *v.tr.* (*a*) Relever, retrousser (sa jupe). (*b*) Border (dans son lit).

Tuesday, *s.* Mardi *m*.

tuft, *s.* **1.** (*a*) Touffe *f* (d'herbe). (*b*) Touffe (de plumes); huppe *f* (d'un oiseau). **2.** (*a*) Barbiche *f*. (*b*) Toupet *m* (de cheveux).

tufted, *a.* **1.** (*a*) Garni de houppes, de glands. (*b*) En touffe; houppé. **2.** *Orn:* Huppé.

tug¹, *s.* **1.** Traction (subite); saccade *f*. To give a good tug, tirer fort. Tug of war, (i) *Sp:* lutte *f* de traction à la corde; (ii) *F:* lutte décisive. **2.** = TUG-BOAT. **tug-boat,** *s.* (Bateau) remorqueur *m*.

tug², *v.tr. & i.* Tirer avec effort. To tug sth. along, traîner qch. To tug at sth., tirer sur qch.

tuition, *s.* Instruction *f*, enseignement *m*.

tulip, *s.* Tulipe *f*.

tulle, *s.* *Tex:* Tulle *m*.

tumble¹, *s.* **1.** Culbute *f*, chute *f*, dégringolade *f*. **2.** Culbute (d'acrobate).

tumble². **1.** *v.i.* (*a*) To tumble (down), tomber (par terre); faire une chute. Building that is tumbling down, édifice qui s'écroule, qui tombe en ruine. (*b*) To tumble (about), s'agiter. (*c*) Se jeter (*into*, dans). To tumble into one's clothes, enfiler ses vêtements à la hâte. (*d*) (*Of acrobat*) Faire des culbutes. (*e*) *F:* To tumble to an idea, saisir une idée. **2.** *v.tr.* (*a*) To tumble sth. over, renverser qch. (*b*) Bouleverser, déranger. **tumble-down,** *attrib.a.* *F:* Croulant, délabré.

tumbler, *s.* Verre *m* sans pied; gobelet *m*.

tumour, *s.* Tumeur *f*.

tumult, *s.* **1.** Tumulte *m*; fracas *m*. **2.** Tumulte, agitation *f*.

tumultuous, *a.* Tumultueux.

tumulus, *s.* Tumulus *m*.

tun, *s.* Tonneau *m*, fût *m*.

tundra, *s.* *Ph.Geog:* Toundra *f*.

tune¹, *s.* **1.** Air *m* (de musique). *F:* Give us a tune! faites-nous un peu de musique! To change one's tune, changer de ton. **2.** Accord *m*. To get out of tune, se désaccorder. (*Of singer*) To be out of tune, détonner. To sing out of t., chanter faux. **3.** Accord, harmonie *f*. To be in tune with one's surroundings, être en bon accord avec son milieu.

tune², *v.tr.* **1.** Accorder, mettre d'accord. **2.** *W.Tel:* To tune in (to) a station, capter un poste. *Abs.* To tune in, accorder le récepteur. **3.** *I.C.E:* To tune (up), caler, régler (un moteur). **tune up,** *v.i.* (*Of orchestra*) S'accorder. **tuning,** *s.* **1.** *Mus:* Accordage *m*, accord *m* (d'un piano). **2.** *I.C.E:* Tuning (up), calage *m*, réglage *m*. **3.** *W.Tel:* Tuning (in), accordage, réglage. **tuning-fork,** *s.* *Mus:* Diapason *m*.

tuneful, *a.* Mélodieux, harmonieux. **-fully,** *adv.* Mélodieusement, harmonieusement.

tuner, *s.* Accordeur *m*.

tunic, *s.* *Cost:* Tunique *f*.

Tunis. *Pr.n.* **1.** La Tunisie. **2.** Tunis.

tunnel¹, *s.* Tunnel *m*; passage souterrain.

tunnel², *v.tr. & i.* To tunnel through a hill, percer un tunnel à travers une colline.

tunnelling, *s.* Percement *m* d'un tunnel.

tunny(-fish), *s.* *Ich:* Thon *m*.

turban, *s.* *Cost:* Turban *m*.

turbid, *a.* Trouble, bourbeux.

turbidity, *s.* Turbidité *f*.

turbine, *s.* Turbine *f*.

turbot, *s.* *Ich:* Turbot *m*.

turbulence, *s.* (*a*) Turbulence *f*, tumulte *m*. (*b*) Indiscipline *f*.

turbulent, *a.* (*a*) Turbulent, tumultueux. (*b*) Insubordonné.

tureen, *s.* Soupière *f.*

turf¹, *s.* (*a*) Gazon *m.* (*b*) Motte *f* de gazon.

turf², *v.tr.* Gazonner.

turgid, *a.* Turgide, enflé, gonflé.

turgidity, *s.* Enflure *f.*

Turk, *s.* Turc, *f.* Turque. *F:* **He's a young Turk**, c'est un enfant terrible.

Turkey¹. *Pr.n.* La Turquie. **Turkey carpet**, *s.* Tapis *m* d'Orient.

turkey², *s.* **1.** Dindon *m.* **Young turkey**, dindonneau *m.* **2.** *Cu:* Dinde *f*, dindonneau. **turkey-cock**, *s.* Dindon *m.* **turkey-hen**, *s.* Dinde *f.*

Turkish. **I.** *a.* Turc, *f.* turque ; de Turquie. **Turkish cigarettes**, cigarettes d'Orient. **2.** *s. Ling:* Le turc. **Turkish delight**, *s.* Rahat loukoum *m.*

turmoil, *s.* (*a*) Trouble *m*, tumulte *m*, agitation *f.* (*b*) Remous *m* (des eaux).

turn¹, *s.* **1.** Tour *m*, révolution *f.* **Meat done to a turn**, viande cuite à point. **2.** (*a*) Changement *m* de direction. *Aut:* Virage *m.* **Turn of the wind**, saute *f* de vent. *F:* **At every turn**, à tout moment, à tout propos. (*b*) Tournure *f.* **Things are taking a turn for the better**, les affaires prennent meilleure tournure. (*c*) **Turn of the tide**, changement de la marée. **The tide is on the turn**, la marée change. **Turn of the scale**, trait *m* de balance. (*d*) **This sight gave me quite a turn**, ce spectacle m'a donné un coup. (*e*) Crise *f*, attaque *f.* **3.** **To take a turn in the garden**, faire un tour dans le jardin. **4.** (*a*) Tour (de rôle). **It is your turn**, c'est votre tour. *It is your t. (to play)*, c'est à vous de jouer. **In turn**, tour à tour ; à tour de rôle. **To speak in one's turn**, parler à son tour. **To play out of one's turn**, jouer avant son tour. **Turn and turn about**, chacun son tour. **To take it in turns to steer**, se relayer à la barre. (*b*) **Music-hall turn**, numéro *m* de music-hall. **5.** (*a*) **To do s.o. a (good) turn**, rendre service à qn. **To do s.o. a bad turn**, jouer un mauvais tour à qn. (*b*) Intention *f*, but *m.* **It will serve my turn**, cela fera mon affaire. **6.** (*a*) Disposition *f* d'esprit. **His turn of mind**, son tour d'esprit. **To have a turn for business**, avoir des dispositions pour le commerce. (*b*) **Turn of a sentence**, tournure *f* d'une phrase. **7.** (*a*) Tournant *m*, coude *m.* **Sharp t.**, crochet *m*, virage *m.* (*b*) Tour (d'une corde). **turn-table**, *s.* **1.** *Rail:* Plaque tournante. **2.** Plateau *m* (tourne-disques).

turn². **I.** *v.tr.* **1.** Tourner, faire tourner. **To turn the key in the lock**, donner un tour de clef à la porte. **To turn the light low**, mettre la lumière en veilleuse. **2.** **To turn (over) a page**, tourner une page. **To turn a garment inside out**, retourner un vêtement. *F:* **Without turning a hair**, sans sourciller. **3.** **He turned his steps homewards**, il dirigea ses pas vers la maison. **To turn a blow**,

détourner un coup. **To turn the conversation**, donner un autre tour à la conversation. **4.** Tourner, retourner (la tête). **5.** **To turn the laughter against s.o.**, retourner les rires contre qn. **6.** (*a*) **To turn the corner**, tourner le coin. (*b*) **He has turned forty**, il a passé la quarantaine. **7.** (*a*) Changer, convertir, transformer (*into*, en). *To t. a sentence into French*, traduire une phrase en français. (*b*) **He has turned his head**, le succès lui a tourné la tête. **8.** Tourner, façonner au tour. **Well-turned sentence**, phrase bien tournée. **II. turn**, *v.i.* **1.** Tourner. (*a*) *The wheel turns*, la roue tourne. (*b*) **The conversation turned on a variety of subjects**, la conversation a roulé sur une variété de sujets. **2.** (*a*) **To toss and turn in bed**, se tourner et se retourner dans son lit. (*b*) **To turn upside down**, (i) (*of boat*) chavirer ; (ii) (*of vehicle*) se retourner. **3.** Se tourner, se retourner. *Mil:* **Right turn!** à droite ! **4.** (*a*) Tourner, se diriger. *He turned to the left*, il tourna, il prit, à gauche. **The wind is turning**, le vent change. (*b*) Se diriger (vers qch.) ; s'adresser (à qn). **I don't know which way to turn**, je ne sais de quel côté (me) tourner. **To turn to s.o.**, avoir recours à qn. **5.** (*a*) **The tide is turning**, la marée change. **His luck has turned**, sa chance a tourné. (*b*) **To turn against s.o.**, se retourner contre qn. **6.** (*a*) Se changer, se convertir (*into*, en). **Everything he touches turns to gold**, tout ce qu'il touche se change en or. (*b*) **The milk has turned (sour)**, le lait a tourné. (*c*) **To turn socialist**, devenir socialiste. **turn aside**. **1.** *v.tr.* Détourner, écarter. **2.** *v.i.* Se détourner, s'écarter. **turn away**. **1.** *v.tr.* (*a*) Détourner. (*b*) Renvoyer, congédier. **2.** *v.i.* Se détourner. **turn back**. **1.** *v.tr.* (*a*) Faire retourner sur ses pas. (*b*) Relever, retrousser (ses manches). **2.** *v.i.* S'en retourner ; rebrousser chemin. **turn down**, *v.tr.* **1.** (*a*) Rabattre. (*b*) Faire un pli, une corne, à (une page). **2.** Baisser (le gaz). **3.** *F:* **To turn down a candidate**, refuser un candidat. **To turn down an offer**, repousser une offre. **turn in**. **1.** *v.tr.* Rentrer (les bouts de qch.). **2.** *v.i.* *F:* **To turn in**, (aller) se coucher. **turn off**. **I.** *v.tr.* **1.** Fermer, couper (l'eau). **2.** Renvoyer, congédier. **II. turn off**, *v.i.* **1.** Changer de route ; tourner. **The car turned off the main road**, l'auto quitta la grande route. **turn on**. **1.** *v.tr.* (*a*) Ouvrir, faire couler (l'eau). (*b*) *F:* **To turn s.o. on to do sth.**, mettre qn à faire qch. **2.** *v.i.* **To turn on s.o.**, attaquer qn. **turn out**. **I.** *v.tr.* **1.** (*a*) **To turn s.o. out**, mettre qn dehors. **To turn out a tenant**, évincer un locataire. **To turn out the government**, renverser le gouvernement. (*b*) Mettre (le bétail) au vert. (*c*) **To turn out the guard**, faire sortir la garde. **2.** Vider (ses poches). **3.** Produire, fabriquer. **4.** **Well turned out**, élégant. **5.** Couper, éteindre (le gaz). **II. turn out**, *v.i.* **1.** *F:* Sortir du lit. **2.** (*a*) **As it turned out**, comme il arriva. **His son turned out badly**, son fils a mal tourné. **The weather has turned out fine**, le temps s'est mis au beau. (*b*) **It turns out that**, il apparaît, il se trouve, que. **turn-out**, *s.* **I.** Concours *m*, assemblée *f*. **2.** (*a*) Tenue *f.* (*b*) Attelage *m*, équipage *m.* **turn over. I.** *v.tr.* (*a*) Retourner; tourner. **To turn over the pages of a book**, feuilleter un livre. **To turn an idea over in one's mind**, ruminer une idée. (*b*) **To turn sth. over to s.o.**, transférer, référer, qch. à qn. **2.** *v.i.* Se tourner, se retourner; (*of vehicle*) verser, capoter. **turn-over**, *s.* **I.** Renversement *m*, culbute *f.* **2.** *Com:* (*a*) Chiffre *m* d'affaires. (*b*) **Rapid turn-over of goods**, écoulement *m* rapide des marchandises. **3.** *Cu:* **Apple turn-over**, chausson *m* aux pommes. **turn round. I.** *v.tr.* Retourner. **2.** *v.i.* (*a*) Tourner. (*b*) Se retourner; faire volte-face. **turn to**, *v.i.* *F:* Se mettre au travail. **turn up. I.** *v.tr.* **I.** (*a*) Relever; retrousser. **Turned-up nose**, nez retroussé. *F:* **To turn up one's nose at sth.**, renifler sur qch. (*b*) **The gardener turned up some human bones**, le jardinier a déterré des ossements humains. (*c*) Trouver, se reporter à (une citation). **2.** Remonter (une lampe). **II. turn up**, *v.i.* **I.** Se relever, se retrousser. **2.** (*a*) **The ten of diamonds turned up**, le dix de carreau est sorti. (*b*) Arriver; faire son apparition. **Something is sure to turn up**, il se présentera sûrement une occasion. **turning**[1], *a.* Tournant; qui tourne. **turning**[2], *s.* **I.** (*a*) Mouvement *m* giratoire; rotation *f.* (*b*) Virage *m*; changement *m* de direction. (*c*) Changement, conversion *f* (*into*, en). **2.** Tournant *m*; coude *m.* *Aut:* Virage. *Take the first t. to the right*, prenez la première à droite. **turning-point**, *s.* Point décisif; moment *m* critique.

turncoat, *s.* Renégat, -ate, apostat, -ate.

turncock, *s.* *Adm:* Fontainier *m.*

turner, *s.* *Ind:* Tourneur *m.*

turnip, *s.* Navet *m.* **turnip-tops**, *s.pl.* Fanes *f* de navets.

turnkey, *s.* Guichetier *m*, porte-clefs *m inv.*

turnpike, *s.* Route *f* à barrière, à péage.

turnspit, *s.* *A:* Tournebroche *m.*

turnstile, *s.* Tourniquet(-compteur) *m.*

turpentine, *s.* Térébenthine *f.*

turquoise, *s.* **I.** Turquoise *f.* **2.** *a.* & *s.* Turquoise(-blue), turquoise (*m*) *inv.*

turret, *s.* Tourelle *f.*

turtle, *s.* Tortue *f* de mer. *F:* **To turn turtle**, chavirer; capoter. **turtle-soup**, *s.* Potage *m* à la tortue.

turtle-dove, *s.* *Orn:* Tourterelle *f.*

Tuscan, *a.* & *s.* Toscan, -ane.

Tuscany. *Pr.n.* La Toscane.

tusk, *s.* Défense *f.*

tusker, *s.* Éléphant *m* (adulte).

tussle[1], *s.* Lutte *f*, mêlée *f*, corps-à-corps *m.* **To have a tussle**, en venir aux mains.

tussle[2], *v.i.* **To tussle with s.o.**, lutter avec qn.

tussock, *s.* Touffe *f* d'herbe.

tut, *int.* (*a*) Quelle bêtise! Tut, tut! ta, ta, ta! (*b*) (*Of impatience*) Zut!

tutelage, *s.* Tutelle *f.*

tutor, *s.* **I.** Directeur *m* des études. **2.** Private tutor, précepteur *m.*

tutorial, *a.* (Cours) d'instruction.

tu-whit, tu-whoo, *int.* Hou hou!

twaddle[1], *s.* Fadaises *fpl*; futilités *fpl.* **To talk twaddle**, débiter des balivernes.

twaddle[2], *v.i.* Dire des sottises.

twain, *a.* & *s.* *Poet:* Deux. **In twain**, en deux.

twang[1], *s.* **I.** Son aigu (d'un banjo). **2.** Nasal twang, ton nasillard. **To speak with a t.**, parler du nez; nasiller.

twang[2], *v.i.* (*Of string*) Résonner.

tweak, *v.tr.* Pincer; serrer entre les doigts.

tweed, *s.* **I.** *Tex:* Cheviote écossaise. **2.** *pl.* Tweeds, complet *m*, costume *m*, de cheviote.

tweet[1], *s.* Pépiement *m*, gazouillement *m.*

tweet[2], *v.i.* Pépier; gazouiller.

tweezers, *s.pl.* Petite pince.

twelfth, *num. a.* & *s.* Douzième. **Louis the Twelfth**, Louis Douze. **Twelfth-night**, *s.* Veille *f* des Rois.

twelve, *num. a.* & *s.* Douze (*m*). **Twelve o'clock**, (i) midi *m*; (ii) minuit *m.* **Half past twelve**, midi, minuit, et demi.

twelvemonth, *s.* Année *f.* **This day twelvemonth**, d'aujourd'hui en un an.

twentieth, *num.a.* & *s.* Vingtième (*m*). **(On) the t. of June**, le vingt juin.

twenty, *num. a.* & *s.* Vingt (*m*). **Twenty-first**, vingt et unième. **The t.-first of May**, le vingt et un mai. **About t. people**, une vingtaine de gens.

twice, *adv.* Deux fois. **Twice as big**, deux fois aussi grand. **Twice over**, à deux reprises. *F:* **To think twice**, y regarder à deux fois. **He did not have to be asked twice**, il ne se fit pas prier.

twiddle, *v.tr.* & *i.* (*a*) Tourner (ses pouces); tortiller (sa moustache). (*b*) Juouer (*with*, avec).

twig[1], *s.* Brindille *f* (de branche); ramille *f.*

twig[2], *v.tr.* *P:* Comprendre, saisir.

twilight, *s.* **I.** Crépuscule *m.* **In the twilight**, au crépuscule; entre chien et loup. **2.** *Attrib.* Crépusculaire.

twill, *s.* *Tex:* Croisé *m*; twill *m.*

twin, *a.* & *s.* **I.** Jumeau, -elle. **Twin(-)brother**, (-)sister, frère jumeau, sœur jumelle. **2.** *a.* Twin beds, lits jumeaux.

twine[1], *s.* Ficelle *f.*

twine[2]. **I.** *v.tr.* Tordre, tortiller. **To twine sth. round sth.**, (en)rouler qch. autour de qch. **2.** *v.i.* (*a*) Se tordre, se tortiller. (*b*) Serpenter.

twinge, *s.* (*a*) Élancement *m.* (*b*) **Twinge of conscience**, remords *m.*

twinkle[1], *s.* **I.** Scintillement *m*, clignotement *m.* **2.** Pétillement *m* (du regard).

twinkle[2], *v.i.* **I.** Scintiller, clignoter. **2.** His eyes twinkled, ses yeux pétillaient. **twink-ling,** s. = TWINKLE[1] I. In the twinkling of an eye, en un clin d'œil.

twirl[1], s. I. Tournoiement m. 2. Volute f (de fumée).

twirl[2]. I. v.tr. (a) Faire tournoyer; faire des moulinets avec (une canne). (b) Tortiller, friser (sa moustache). 2. v.i. Tournoyer.

twist[1], s. I. (a) Fil m retors; cordon m; cordonnet m. (b) Twist of hair, torsade f de cheveux. Twist of paper, cornet m de papier; papillote f. 2. To give sth. a twist, exercer une torsion sur qch. To give one's ankle a twist, se fouler la cheville. 3. Twists and turns, tours et retours. 4. (a) Dévers m, gauchissement m. (b) Perversion f, déformation f, d'esprit.

twist[2]. I. v.tr. (a) Tordre, tortiller. To twist (up) one's handkerchief, tire-bouchonner son mouchoir. F: She can twist him round her little finger, elle lui fait faire ses quatre volontés. (b) To twist one's ankle, se fouler la cheville. To twist s.o.'s arm, tordre le bras à qn. (c) To twist the truth, donner une entorse à la vérité. 2. v.i. (a) Se tordre; se tortiller. (b) (Of road) Tourner; faire des détours. To twist and turn, serpenter.

twisted, a. Tordu, tors.

twister, s. F: He's a twister, il est ficelle.

twit, v.tr. I. Taquiner; railler. 2. To twit s.o. with sth., railler qn de qch.

twitch[1], s. I. Saccade f; petit coup sec. 2. Élancement m (de douleur). 3. Mouvement convulsif.

twitch[2]. I. v.tr. Tirer vivement; donner une saccade à. 2. v.i. (Of face) Se contracter nerveusement; (of hands) se crisper nerveusement.

twitter[1], s. I. Gazouillement m. 2. F: To be all of a twitter, être tout en émoi.

twitter[2], v.i. Gazouiller. **twittering,** s. Gazouillement m.

two, num. a. & s. Deux (m). To walk two by two, marcher deux à deux. F: To put two and two together, tirer ses conclusions (après avoir rapproché les faits). **two-edged,** a. A deux tranchants. **two-faced,** a. = DOUBLE-FACED. **two-handed,** a. (Épée) à deux mains. **two-legged,** a. Bipède. **two-seater,** s. Avion m ou voiture f à deux places; F: un biplace. **two-step,** s. Danc: Pas m de deux.

twofold. I. a. Double. 2. adv. Doublement.

twopence, s. Deux pence m. F: It isn't worth twopence, ça ne vaut pas deux sous.

twopenny, a. A, de, deux pence. **two-penny-halfpenny,** attrib.a. F: Insignifiant; sans importance.

tyke, s. P: I. Chien. 2. Rustre m. 3. (Yorkshire) tyke, homme m du Yorkshire.

type[1], s. I. Type m. People of this t., les individus de ce genre. 2. Typ: (a) Caractère m, type. (b) Coll. Caractères. **type-script,** s. Manuscrit dactylographié.

type[2], v.tr. Écrire à la machine; dactylographier.

typewrite, v.tr. = TYPE[2]. Typewritten document, document transcrit à la machine.

typewriting, s. Dactylographie f.

typewriter, s. Machine f à écrire.

typhoid, a. Med: Typhoïde.

typhoon, s. Meteor: Typhon m.

typhus, s. Med: Typhus m.

typical, a. Typique. The t. Frenchman, le vrai type français. That is t. of him, c'est bien de lui. **-ally,** adv. D'une manière typique.

typify, v.tr. I. Représenter; symboliser. 2. Être caractéristique de.

typist, s. Dactylographe mf, F: dactylo mf. Typist's error, erreur de machine.

typography, s. Typographie f.

tyrannical, a. Tyrannique. **-ally,** adv. Tyranniquement; en tyran.

tyrannize, v.i. Faire le tyran. To tyrannize over s.o., tyranniser qn.

tyrannous, a. Tyrannique.

tyranny, s. Tyrannie f.

tyrant, s. Tyran m.

tyre, s. (a) Bandage m, cercle m. (b) Aut: Rubber tyre, bandage en caoutchouc. Pneumatic tyre, (bandage) pneumatique m; F: pneu m.

tyro, s. Novice mf.

Tyrolese, a. & s. Tyrolien, -ienne.

U

U, u, s. (La lettre) U, u m. F: It's all U.P., tout est perdu. It's all U.P. with him, son affaire est faite. **U-boat,** s. F: Sous-marin allemand.

ubiquitous, a. Qui se trouve partout; que l'on rencontre partout.

ubiquity, s. Ubiquité f.

udder, s. Mamelle f, pis m (de vache).

ugh, int. I. Pouah! 2. Ugh, it's cold! brrr, il fait froid!

ugliness, s. Laideur f.

ugly, a. Laid; disgracieux. Ugly person, laideron, -onne. To grow ugly, enlaidir. P: To cut up ugly, se fâcher.

uhlan, s. Uhlan m.

ukase, s. Ukase m, oukase m.

ulcer, s. Ulcère m.
ulcerate. I. v.tr. Ulcérer. 2. v.i. S'ulcérer.
ulcerated, a. Ulcéré, ulcéreux.
ulterior, a. I. Ultérieur, -eure. 2. Ulterior motive, motif secret, caché. Without u. motive, sans arrière-pensée.
ultimate, a. Final, -als. U. decision, décision définitive. **-ly,** adv. A la fin; en fin de compte.
ultimatum, s. Ultimatum m.
ultimo, adv. Du mois dernier.
ultra. I. a. Extrême. 2. s. Pol: Ultra m.
ultra-fashionable, a. Tout dernier cri.
ultramarine, a. & s. (Bleu m d')outremer m inv.
ultra-violet, a. Opt: Ultra-violet, -ette.
ultra vires. Lt.adj. & adv.phr. Au delà des pouvoirs.
ululation, s. Ululation f, ululement m (du hibou); hurlement m (du chacal).
Ulysses. Pr.n. Ulysse m.
umbel, s. Bot: Ombelle f.
umber, s. Paint: Terre f d'ombre.
umbrage, s. Ombrage m, ressentiment m.
umbrella, s. (a) Parapluie m. (b) Parasol m (de chef de tribu nègre). **umbrella-stand,** s. Porte-parapluies m inv. **umbrella-stick,** s. Manche m, canne f, de parapluie.
umph, int. Hum! hmm!
umpire[1], s. Arbitre m, juge m.
umpire[2], v.tr. Arbitrer.
umpteen, a. & s. P: Je ne sais combien.
unabashed, a. I. Sans perdre contenance. 2. Aucunement ébranlé.
unabated, a. Non diminué. With u. speed, toujours avec la même vitesse.
unable, a. Incapable. Unable to do sth., impuissant à faire qch. We are u. to help you, nous ne pouvons pas vous aider.
unabridged, a. Non abrégé. U. edition, édition intégrale.
unaccented, a. Non accentué.
unacceptable, a. Inacceptable.
unaccommodating, a. Peu accommodant.
unaccompanied, a. I. Inaccompagné, seul 2. Mus: Sans accompagnement.
unaccomplished, a. (a) Inaccompli, non réalisé. (b) (Travail) inachevé.
unaccountable, a. (a) Inexplicable. It is u., explique cela qui pourra. (b) (Conduite) bizarre. **-ably,** adv. Inexplicablement.
unaccustomed, a. Unaccustomed to sth., peu habitué à qch.
unacquainted, a. To be unacquainted with sth., ignorer (un fait).
unadorned, a. Sans ornement; naturel. Beauty unadorned, la beauté sans parure. U. truth, la vérité pure.
unadulterated, a. Pur; sans mélange.
unadvisable, a. Peu sage; imprudent.
unaffected, a. I. Sans affectation. (a) Véritable, sincère. (b) Sans pose. 2. Unaffected by air, inaltérable à l'air. **-ly,** adv. Sans affectation. (a) Sincèrement. (b) Simplement.

unaided, a. Sans aide. He did it u., il l'a fait tout seul. With the unaided eye, à l'œil nu.
unallayed, a. Inapaisé.
unalloyed, a. (Métal) pur, sans alliage. U. happiness, bonheur pur, sans mélange.
unalterable, a. Immuable, invariable. **-ably,** adv. Immuablement, invariablement.
unaltered, a. Toujours le même; sans changement; tel quel.
unambitious, a. I. Sans ambition. 2. (Projet) sans prétention.
unamended, a. Sans modification; tel quel.
unamiable, a. Peu aimable.
unanimity, s. Unanimité f. With unanimity, d'un commun accord.
unanimous, a. Unanime. **-ly,** adv. A l'unanimité; unanimement.
unannounced, a. He marched in u., il entra sans se faire annoncer.
unanswerable, a. Qui n'admet pas de réponse; (argument) sans réplique.
unanswered, a. I. Sans réponse. 2. Irréfuté.
unanticipated, a. Imprévu.
unappeasable, a. (Faim) inapaisable; (appétit) insatiable; (haine) implacable.
unappeased, a. Inapaisé.
unappetizing, a. Peu appétissant.
unappreciated, a. Inapprécié; peu estimé.
unapproachable, a. I. Inabordable, distant. 2. Incomparable; sans pareil.
unappropriated, a. Disponible.
unapt, a. Qui ne convient pas; peu juste.
unarmed, a. Sans armes.
unascertainable, a. Non vérifiab
unascertained, a. Non vérifié.
unashamed, a. Sans honte; cynique.
unasked, a. To do sth. unasked, faire qch. spontanément.
unassailable, a. Inattaquable.
unassertive, a. Modeste, timide.
unassisted, a. = UNAIDED.
unassuaged, a. Inassouvi.
unassuming, a. Sans prétention(s); modeste.
unattached, a. I. Qui n'est pas attaché (to, à); indépendant (to, de). 2. (Officier) disponible.
unattainable, a. Inaccessible (by, à); hors de la portée (by, de).
unattended, a. (a) Seul; sans escorte. (b) Sport not unattended by danger, sport non dépourvu de danger.
unattractive, a. Peu attrayant; (personne) peu sympathique.
unauthorized, a. (a) Inautorisé; sans autorisation. (b) Sans mandat.
unavailing, a. Inutile; (of tears) vain; (of efforts) infructueux. **-ly,** adv. En vain.
unavoidable, a. (a) Inévitable. (b) (Événement) qu'on ne peut prévenir. **-ably,** adv. I. Inévitablement. 2. Unavoidably absent, absent pour raison majeure.
unavowed, a. Inavoué.

unaware, *a.* Ignorant, non informé (*of sth.*, de qch.). To be unaware of sth., ignorer qch.

unawares, *adv.* To take s.o. unawares, prendre qn à l'improviste.

unbalanced, *a.* **1.** (Esprit) déséquilibré, dérangé. **2.** Unbalanced forces, forces non équilibrées.

unbearable, *a.* Insupportable, intolérable. **-ably,** *adv.* Insupportablement.

unbeaten, *a.* Non battu.

unbecoming, *a.* **1.** Peu convenable; déplacé. Unbecoming of s.o., déplacé chez qn. **2.** (*Of garment*) Peu seyant. **-ly,** *adv.* D'une manière peu séante.

unbeknown. **1.** *a.* Inconnu (*to*, de). **2.** *adv.* To do sth. unbeknown to anyone, faire qch. à l'insu de tous.

unbelief, *s.* Incrédulité *f.*

unbelievable, *a.* Incroyable.

unbeliever, *s.* Incrédule *mf.*

unbelieving, *a.* Incrédule.

unbend, *v.i.* S'abandonner un petit peu; se détendre. **unbending,** *a.* Inflexible, ferme, raide.

unbeseeming, *a.* Malséant; peu convenable.

unbias(s)ed, *a.* Impartial, -aux.

unbidden, *a.* **1.** Non invité; (hôte) intrus. **2.** Spontané.

unbind, *v.tr.* Délier.

unbleached, *a.* *Tex:* Écru.

unblemished, *a.* Sans défaut; sans tache.

unblushing, *a.* Sans vergogne; éhonté. **-ly,** *adv.* Sans vergogne; impudemment.

unbolt, *v.tr.* Déverrouiller.

unborn, *a.* Generations yet unborn, générations à venir.

unbosom, *v.tr.* To unbosom oneself to s.o., ouvrir son cœur à qn.

unbounded, *a.* Sans bornes; illimité; (*of conceit*) démesuré.

unbreakable, *a.* Incassable.

unbridled, *a.* Débridé, effréné.

unbroken, *a.* **1.** (*a*) Non brisé, non cassé. (*b*) Intact. Unbroken spirit, courage inentamé. (*c*) Ininterrompu, continu. **2.** (Cheval) non rompu, non dressé. **3.** *Agr:* Unbroken ground, terre vierge.

unbrotherly, *a.* Peu fraternel.

unbuckle, *v.tr.* Déboucler.

unburden, *v.tr.* (*a*) Alléger d'un fardeau. (*b*) To unburden the mind, soulager, alléger, l'esprit. To unburden oneself, se délester le cœur.

unburied, *a.* Sans sépulture; non enterré.

unbusinesslike, *a.* **1.** Peu commerçant. **2.** To conduct one's affairs in an u. way, manquer de méthode.

unbutton, *v.tr.* Déboutonner.

uncalled, *a.* Uncalled for, (*of remark*) déplacé; (*of rebuke*) immérité.

uncanny, *a.* Mystérieux. Uncanny noise, bruit inquiétant.

uncared-for, *a.* Peu soigné. *U.-for child*, enfant délaissé.

unceasing, *a.* (*a*) Incessant, continu. (*b*) (Travail) assidu; (effort) soutenu. **-ly,** *adv.* Sans cesse.

unceremonious, *a.* Sans façon, sans gêne. **-ly,** *adv.* **1.** Sans cérémonie. **2.** Sans façons.

uncertain, *a.* Incertain. **1.** (*a*) Indéterminé. (*b*) (Résultat) douteux. (*c*) Uncertain outline, contour mal défini. **2.** (*a*) Uncertain steps, pas mal assurés. Uncertain temper, humeur inégale. Uncertain health, santé vacillante. (*b*) To be u. of the future, être incertain de l'avenir.

uncertainty, *s.* Incertitude *f.* To remove any uncertainty, pour dissiper toute équivoque.

unchallenged, *a.* **1.** Indisputé. To let (sth.) pass unchallenged, ne pas relever (une affirmation). **2.** *Mil:* Sans interpellation *f.*

unchangeable, *a.* Immuable.

unchanged, *a.* Inchangé; toujours le même.

unchanging, *a.* Invariable, immuable.

uncharitable, *a.* Peu charitable.

uncharted, *a.* **1.** (*Of island*) Non porté sur la carte. **2.** (*Of sea*) Inexploré.

unchecked, *a.* **1.** Sans frein. Unchecked advance, libre marche en avant. **2.** Non vérifié.

unchivalrous, *a.* Peu chevaleresque.

unchristian, *a.* Peu chrétien.

uncivil, *a.* Incivil, impoli. **-illy,** *adv.* Impoliment.

uncivilized, *a.* Incivilisé, barbare.

unclaimed, *a.* Non réclamé. *Post:* Unclaimed letter, lettre de rebut.

uncle, *s.* **1.** Oncle *m.* Yes, uncle! oui, mon oncle! To talk to s.o. like a Dutch uncle, faire la morale à qn. **2.** *P:* My watch is at my uncle's, ma montre est chez ma tante.

unclean, *a.* **1.** Impur, immonde. **2.** Malpropre, sale.

unclench, *v.tr.* Desserrer.

uncloak, *v.tr.* Découvrir (des projets); démasquer, dévoiler.

unclothe, **1.** *v.tr.* Déshabiller, dévêtir. **2.** *v.i.* Se déshabiller.

unclothed, *a.* **1.** Déshabillé. **2.** Nu; sans vêtements.

unclouded, *a.* Sans nuage; (*of liquid*) limpide.

uncoil, **1.** *v.tr.* Dérouler. **2.** *v.i.* Se dérouler.

uncoloured, *a.* Non coloré. *U. account of sth.*, rapport fidèle de qch.

uncomfortable, *a.* **1.** Peu confortable; (chaleur) incommode. **2.** Désagréable. To make things uncomfortable for s.o., faire des histoires à qn. *It makes things u.*, c'est très gênant. **3.** To feel uncomfortable, être mal à l'aise. To be uncomfortable about sth., être inquiet, -ète, au sujet de qch. **-ably,** *adv.* **1.** Peu confortablement; incommodément. **2.** Désagréablement.

uncommon, *a.* Peu commun. (*a*) Uncommon word, mot rare, peu usité. (*b*) Peu ordinaire; singulier. **-ly,** *adv.* **1.** Not uncommonly, assez souvent. **2.** Singulièrement. Uncommonly good, excellent.

uncommunicative, *a.* Peu communicatif.

uncompanionable, *a.* Peu sociable.

uncomplaining, *a.* Qui ne se plaint pas; résigné. **-ly,** *adv.* Sans se plaindre.

uncomplimentary, *a.* Peu flatteur, -euse.

uncompromising, *a.* Intransigeant; intraitable.

unconcealed, *a.* Qui n'est pas caché; fait à découvert.

unconcern, *s.* Insouciance *f*; indifférence *f*.

unconcerned, *a.* Insouciant, indifférent.

unconcernedly, *adv.* D'un air indifférent; avec insouciance.

unconciliatory, *a.* Inconciliant.

unconditional, *a.* (*a*) Absolu. *U. refusal*, refus catégorique. (*b*) *U. acceptance*, acceptation sans conditions. **-ally,** *adv. To accept u.*, accepter sans réserve. *To surrender u.*, se rendre à discrétion.

unconfirmed, *a.* Qui n'est pas confirmé; sujet, -ette, à caution.

uncongenial, *a.* **1.** Peu sympathique. **2.** (*a*) (Climat) peu favorable (*to*, à). (*b*) *U. job*, travail ingrat.

unconnected, *a.* (*a*) Sans rapport, sans lien. (*b*) Décousu, sans suite.

unconquerable, *a.* Invincible.

unconscionable, *a.* **1.** Sans conscience. *U. rogue*, coquin fieffé. **2.** *To take an unconscionable time doing sth.*, mettre un temps déraisonnable à faire qch.

unconscious, *a.* **1.** Inconscient. *To be unconscious of sth.*, (i) ne pas avoir conscience de qch.; (ii) ignorer qch. **2.** Sans connaissance; évanoui. *To become unconscious*, perdre connaissance. **-ly,** *adv.* Inconsciemment.

unconsciousness, *s.* **1.** Inconscience *f* (*of*, de). **2.** Évanouissement *m*.

unconsidered, *a.* **1.** Inconsidéré, irréfléchi. **2.** Auquel on n'attache aucune valeur.

unconstitutional, *a.* Inconstitutionnel.

unconstrained, *a.* Non contraint; libre. *U. manner*, allure désinvolte.

unconstrainedly, *adv.* Sans contrainte, sans aucune gêne; librement.

uncontested, *a.* Incontesté.

uncontrollable, *a.* **1.** (Pouvoir) absolu. **2.** Ingouvernable; irrésistible. *U. laughter*, fou rire. **-ably,** *adv.* Irrésistiblement.

uncontrolled, *a.* **1.** Indépendant. **2.** *U. liberty*, liberté absolue. *U. passions*, passions effrénées.

unconventional, *a.* Qui va à l'encontre des conventions; original, -aux. **-ally,** *adv.* A l'encontre des conventions.

unconvinced, *a.* Sceptique (*of*, à l'égard de).

unconvincing, *a.* Peu convaincant.

uncooked, *a.* Non cuit, cru.

uncork, *v.tr.* Déboucher.

uncouple, *v.tr.* Découpler.

uncouth, *a.* **1.** Grossier, rude. **2.** Malappris, gauche. **-ly,** *adv.* **1.** Grossièrement. **2.** Gauchement.

uncover, *v.tr.* Découvrir (son visage); mettre à découvert. *To u. one's head, abs. to uncover,* se découvrir.

uncovered, *a.* Mis à découvert; découvert.

uncrowned, *a.* **1.** Découronné. **2.** Non couronné.

unction, *s.* Onction *f*.

unctuous, *a.* Onctueux, graisseux. **-ly,** *adv.* Onctueusement.

unctuousness, *s.* Onctuosité *f*.

uncultivated, *a.* Inculte; (personne) sans culture.

uncultured, *a.* (Esprit) incultivé, inculte; (personne) sans culture.

uncurbed, *a.* (*a*) Libre; sans restriction. (*b*) (*Of passion*) Débridé.

undamaged, *a.* Non endommagé; indemne. *U. reputation,* réputation intacte.

undated, *a.* Non daté; sans date.

undaunted, *a.* (*a*) Intrépide. (*b*) Aucunement intimidé. **-ly,** *adv.* Intrépidement.

undeceive, *v.tr.* Désabuser (*of*, de); détromper. *To undeceive oneself,* se désabuser.

undeceived, *a.* **1.** Désabusé; détrompé. **2.** Aucunement trompé (*by*, par).

undecided, *a.* Indécis. (*a*) Mal défini. (*b*) (*Of pers.*) Irrésolu, hésitant.

undecipherable, *a.* Indéchiffrable.

undeciphered, *a.* Indéchiffré.

undefeated, *a.* Invaincu.

undefended, *a.* Sans défense.

undefiled, *a.* Pur; sans souillure.

undefinable, *a.* Indéfinissable.

undefined, *a.* **1.** Non défini. **2.** Indéterminé; vague.

undelivered, *a.* Non délivré. *If u. please return to sender,* en cas de non-délivrance prière de retourner à l'expéditeur.

undemonstrative, *a.* Peu expansif, peu démonstratif; réservé.

undeniable, *a.* Indéniable, incontestable. **-ably,** *adv.* Incontestablement.

under. **I.** *prep.* **1.** Sous; au-dessous de. (*a*) Under water, sous l'eau. *Put it under that,* mettez-le là-dessous. (*b*) To speak under one's breath, parler à demi-voix. He is under thirty, il a moins de trente ans. **2.** (*a*) Under lock and key, sous clef. Visible under the microscope, visible au microscope. *To be under sentence of death,* être condamné à mort. Under his father's will, d'après le testament de son père. *To be under the necessity of,* être dans la nécessité de. (*b*) To be under s.o., être sous le commandement de qn. *F: To be u. the doctor,* être traité par le médecin. **3.** Under repair, en (voie de) réparation. **II.** **under,** *adv.* **1.** (Au-)dessous. As under, comme ci-dessous. **2.** To keep s.o.

under, tenir qn dans la soumission. **under-carriage,** *s. Av:* Châssis *m*, train *m* (d'atterrissage). **under-developed,** *a.* **1.** *Phot:* Insuffisamment développé. **2.** Arrêté dans sa croissance. **under-estimate,** *v.tr.* (*a*) Sous-estimer. (*b*) *To u.-e. the importance of,* faire trop peu de cas de. **under-exposure,** *s. Phot:* Sous-exposition *f.* **under-garment,** *s.* Sous-vêtement *m.* **under-nourished,** *a.* Insuffisamment nourri ; mal nourri. **under-ripe,** *a.* Pas assez mûr. **under-secretary,** *s.* Sous-secrétaire *mf.* **under-sized,** *a.* Rabougri. **under-skirt,** *s.* Jupon *m.*

underbred, *a.* Mal appris ; mal élevé.

undercharge, *v.tr.* Ne pas faire payer assez à.

underclothes, *s.pl.* **underclothing,** *s.* Vêtements *mpl* de dessous ; linge *m* de corps ; (*for women*) lingerie *f.*

undercurrent, *s.* Undercurrent of discontent, courant profond de mécontentement.

undercut[1], *s. Cu:* Filet *m* (de bœuf).

undercut[2], *v.tr.* Vendre moins cher que (qn).

underdone, *a.* **1.** Pas assez cuit. **2.** Pas trop cuit ; (bœuf) saignant.

underfeed, *v.tr.* Nourrir insuffisamment ; mal nourrir. **underfed,** *a.* Mal nourri ; sous-alimenté.

underfoot, *adv.* Sous les pieds.

undergo, *v.tr.* **1.** (*a*) Passer par, subir. Undergoing repairs, en réparation. (*b*) Subir. **2.** Supporter ; essuyer (une perte).

undergraduate, *s.* Étudiant, -ante (qui n'a pas encore pris de grade).

underground. 1. *adv.* (*a*) Sous terre (*b*) Secrètement ; sous main. (*c*) *F:* To go underground, prendre le maquis. **2.** *a.* (*a*) Qui est sous le sol. Underground railway, chemin de fer souterrain. (*b*) Underground forces, maquis *m*. **3.** *s. F:* The Underground = le Métro.

undergrown, *a.* Mal venu ; chétif ; rabougri.

undergrowth, *s. For:* Broussailles *fpl.*

underhand. 1. *adv.* Sous main, sournoisement. **2.** *a.* Secret, -ète ; sournois. Underhand dealings, agissements clandestins.

underlie, *v.tr.* **1.** Être sous. **2.** Être à la base de. **underlying,** *a.* **1.** Au-dessous. **2.** (Principe) fondamental, -aux. **3.** Caché.

underline, *v.tr.* Souligner.

underlinen, *s.* Linge *m* de corps.

underling, *s.* Subordonné, -ée.

undermanned, *a.* A court de personnel. *Nau:* A court d'équipage.

undermentioned, *a.* Sous-mentionné.

undermine, *v.tr.* Miner, saper ; (*of river*) affouiller (les berges). To undermine one's health, s'abîmer lentement la santé.

undermost, *a.* Le plus bas, *f.* la plus basse.

underneath. 1. *prep.* Au-dessous de ; sous. From underneath sth., de dessous qch.

2. *adv.* Au-dessous ; dessous ; par-dessous.
3. *a.* De dessous ; inférieur, -e.

underpaid, *a.* Mal rétribué.

underrate, *v.tr.* Mésestimer, sous-estimer.

undersell, *v.tr.* Vendre à meilleur marché, moins cher, que (qn).

undersigned, *a. & s.* Soussigné, -ée.

understand, *v.tr.* **1.** Comprendre (*a*) I don't understand French, je ne comprends pas le français. To understand horses, connaître en chevaux. To understand sth., se rendre compte de qch. *Abs.* Now I understand! je comprends, j'y suis, maintenant ! I am at a loss to understand it, je n'y comprends rien. *I can't u. why,* je ne m'explique pas pourquoi. (*b*) To give s.o. to understand sth., donner à entendre qch. à qn. Am I to understand? ai-je bien compris (que)? *I u. that he will consent,* je crois savoir qu'il consentira. Now understand me, sachez-le bien. **2.** *Gram:* Sous-entendre. **3.** *v.i.* To understand about an affair, savoir ce qu'il faut faire à propos d'une affaire. **understood,** *a.* **1.** Compris, **2.** Convenu. That is understood, cela va sans dire. **3.** *Gram:* Sous-entendu. **understanding,** *s.* **1.** Entendement *m*, compréhension *f.* **2.** (*a*) Accord *m*, entente *f.* Friendly understanding, entente cordiale. (*b*) Arrangement *m*. To have an understanding with s.o., avoir un arrangement avec qn. To come to an understanding, s'accorder, s'entendre. (*c*) On the understanding that, à condition que.

understandable, *a.* Compréhensible.

understate, *v.tr.* Amoindrir.

understatement, *s.* **1.** Amoindrissement *m*. **2.** Affirmation *f* qui reste au-dessous de la vérité.

understudy[1], *s. Th:* Doublure *f.*

understudy[2], *v.tr.* Doubler.

undertake, *v.tr.* **1.** Entreprendre. **2.** (*a*) Se charger de, s'imposer (une tâche). (*b*) To undertake to do sth., se charger de faire qch.

undertaking, *s.* **1.** (*a*) Entreprise *f.* (*b*) Entreprise de pompes funèbres. **2.** Entreprise (commerciale). *F:* It is quite an undertaking, c'est toute une affaire. **3.** Engagement *m*, promesse *f.*

undertaker, *s.* Entrepreneur *m* de pompes funèbres.

undertone, *s.* To speak in an undertone, parler bas ; parler à demi-voix.

undervalue, *v.tr.* **1.** Sous-estimer **2.** Mésestimer, faire trop peu de cas de.

underwear, *s.* = UNDERCLOTHES.

underwood, *s.* Sous-bois *m*, broussailles *fpl.*

underworld, *s.* **1.** (Les) enfers *m.* **2.** (Les) bas-fonds *m* de la société.

undescribable, *a.* Indescriptible.

undeserved, *a.* Immérité.

undeservedly, *adv.* A tort ; injustement.

undeserving, *a.* (*a*) Peu méritant ; sans mérite. (*b*) Undeserving of attention, indigne d'attention.

undesirable, *a. & s.* Indésirable (*mf*) ; peu désirable.

undetected, *a.* **1.** Qui a échappé à l'attention. **To pass undetected,** passer inaperçu. **2.** (Malfaiteur) insoupçonné.

undeterred, *a.* Non découragé.

undeveloped, *a.* Non développé. Undeveloped land, terrains inexploités.

undeviating, *a.* **1.** Droit, direct. **2.** Constant.

undigested, *a.* Mal digéré. Undigested knowledge, connaissances indigestes.

undignified, *a.* (*a*) Peu digne. (*b*) To be undignified, manquer de dignité, de tenue.

undiluted, *a.* Non dilué ; non étendu (d'eau).

undiplomatic, *a.* Peu diplomatique ; *F:* peu politique, peu adroit.

undiscernible, *a.* Imperceptible.

undiscerning, *a.* Sans discernement.

undisciplined, *a.* Indiscipliné.

undiscovered, *a.* Non découvert ; caché

undiscriminating, *a.* Sans discernement ; (*of taste*) peu averti.

undisguised, *a.* Non déguisé ; (*of feelings*) non dissimulé. To show undisguised satisfaction, témoigner franchement sa satisfaction.

undismayed, *a.* Sans peur, sans terreur.

undisputed, *a.* Incontesté, indisputé.

undistinguishable, *a.* **1.** Indistinguible (*from*, de). **2.** Imperceptible.

undistinguished, *a.* Médiocre ; banal, -aux.

undisturbed, *a.* **1.** Tranquille ; (*of sleep*) paisible. **2.** (*Of peace*) Que rien ne vient troubler. We found everything u., rien n'avait été dérangé.

undivided, *a.* **1.** Indivisé ; entier. **2.** Non partagé. Give me your undivided attention, donnez-moi toute votre attention.

undo, *v.tr.* **1.** Détruire. To undo the mischief, réparer le mal. **2.** Défaire, dénouer. **3.** Perdre, ruiner. **undoing,** *s.* **1.** Action *f* de défaire. **2.** Ruine *f*, perte *f*.

undone, *a.* **1.** (*a*) Défait. To come undone, se défaire. (*b*) Ruiné ; perdu. **2.** Inaccompli ; non accompli. To leave nothing undone, ne rien négliger.

undoubted, *a.* Indiscutable, incontestable. **-ly,** *adv.* Indubitablement, assurément.

undreamt, *a.* Undreamt of, qui passe l'imagination.

undress¹, *s.* **1.** Négligé *m.* **2.** Undress (uniform), petite tenue

undress², *v.* **1.** *v.i. & pr.* Se déshabiller, se dévêtir. **2.** *v.tr.* Déshabiller, dévêtir

undressed, *a.* **1.** Déshabillé, dévêtu **2.** Non préparé ; brut.

undrinkable, *a.* Imbuvable, impotable.

undue, *a.* (*a*) Undue influence, influence *f* illégitime. (*b*) Exagéré, indu.

undulate, *v.i.* Onduler, ondoyer. **undulating,** *a.* Onduleux. U. country, pays ondulé.

undulation, *s.* Ondulation *f*; accident *m* de terrain.

unduly, *adv.* **1.** (*a*) Indûment. (*b*) Sans raison. **2.** A l'excès, outre mesure. Unduly high price, prix exagéré.

undutiful, *a.* Qui ne remplit pas ses devoirs.

undying, *a.* Immortel, impérissable.

unearned, *a.* **1.** Immérité. **2.** Non gagné par le travail.

unearth, *v.tr.* Déterrer.

unearthly, *a.* (*a*) Qui n'est pas de ce monde ; surnaturel. (*b*) Unearthly pallor, pâleur mortelle. *U. light,* lueur sinistre, blafarde. (*c*) *F:* At an unearthly hour, à une heure indue. Unearthly din, vacarme de tous les diables.

uneasiness, *s.* **1.** Gêne *f*, malaise *m*. **2.** Inquiétude *f*.

uneasy, *a.* (*a*) Mal à l'aise ; gêné. Uneasy feeling, sentiment de malaise. (*b*) Inquiet, -ète ; anxieux. Uneasy conscience, conscience agitée. To be uneasy in one's mind, avoir l'esprit inquiet. *To pass an u. night,* passer une nuit tourmentée. **-ily,** *adv.* (*a*) D'un air gêné. (*b*) Avec inquiétude.

uneatable, *a.* Immangeable.

uneducated, *a.* **1.** Sans instruction ; ignorant. **2.** (*Of pronunciation*) Vulgaire.

unemotional, *a.* Peu émotif.

unemployed, *a.* (*a*) Désœuvré. (*b*) *Ind:* Sans emploi. The unemployed, les chômeurs *m*, les sans-travail *m*.

unemployment, *s. Ind:* Chômage *m* (involontaire) ; manque *m* de travail.

unended, *a.* Inachevé.

unending, *a.* **1.** Interminable. Unending complaints, plaintes sans fin. **2.** Éternel.

unendurable, *a.* Insupportable, intolérable.

unenterprising, *a.* Peu entreprenant.

unenviable, *a.* Peu enviable.

unequal, *a.* **1.** (*a*) Inégal, -aux. (*b*) To be unequal to doing sth., ne pas être de force à faire qch. **2.** Inégal, irrégulier. **-ally,** *adv.* Inégalement.

unequalled, *a.* Inégalé ; sans égal.

unequivocal, *a.* Clair, net, *f.* nette ; sans équivoque. **-ally,** *adv.* Sans équivoque.

unerring, *a.* Infaillible, sûr. **-ly,** *adv.* Infailliblement, sûrement.

uneven, *a.* **1.** Inégal, -aux. (*a*) Rugueux. (*b*) (Terrain) accidenté. (*c*) Irrégulier. Uneven temper, humeur inégale. **2.** Impair. **-ly,** *adv.* **1.** Inégalement. **2.** Irrégulièrement.

uneventful, *a.* Sans incidents. Uneventful life, vie calme, unie.

unexampled, *a.* Sans exemple, sans égal, sans pareil ; unique.

unexcelled, *a.* Qui n'a jamais été surpassé.

unexceptionable, *a.* Irréprochable ; (conduite) inattaquable.

unexciting, *a.* Insipide ; peu passionnant.

unexpected, *a.* Inattendu ; (résultat) imprévu ; (secours) inespéré. **Unexpected**

meeting, rencontre inopinée. **-ly,** *adv.* De manière inattendue.

unexpired, *a.* Non expiré ; (billet) encore valable.

unexplained, *a.* Inexpliqué ; inéclairci.

unexplored, *a.* Inexploré.

unexpurgated, *a.* (Livre) non expurgé.

unfailing, *a.* **1.** Qui ne se dément pas ; infaillible, sûr. *U. good humour,* bonne humeur inaltérable. **2.** Intarissable, inépuisable (*of,* de). **-ly,** *adv.* **1.** Infailliblement. **2.** Intarissablement.

unfair, *a.* **1.** Injuste ; peu équitable. **It's unfair!** ce n'est pas juste ! **2.** Inéquitable. **-ly,** *adv.* Injustement ; inéquitablement.

unfairness, *s.* **1.** Injustice *f* ; partialité *f.* **2.** Déloyauté *f* ; mauvaise foi.

unfaithful, *a.* Infidèle.

unfaithfulness, *s.* Infidélité *f.*

unfaltering, *a.* **Unfaltering voice,** voix ferme. **Unfaltering steps,** pas assurés.

unfamiliar, *a.* **1.** Peu familier. *U. face,* visage étranger, inconnu. **2.** *To be u. with the customs,* ne pas être au fait des usages.

unfamiliarity, *s.* **1.** Caractère étranger. **2.** Ignorance *f* (*with,* de).

unfashionable, *a.* Démodé, qui n'est pas de mode.

unfasten, *v.tr.* **1.** *To unfasten sth. from sth.,* détacher qch. de qch. **2.** Défaire ; ouvrir (la porte).

unfathomable, *a.* (Abîme) insondable ; (mystère) impénétrable.

unfathomed, *a.* Insondé.

unfavourable, *a.* Défavorable, peu favorable ; (*of terms*) désavantageux (*to,* à).

unfeeling, *a.* Insensible, impitoyable. *U. heart,* cœur sec, indifférent. *U. language,* langage froid. **-ly,** *adv.* Sans pitié ; froidement.

unfeigned, *a.* Sincère ; non simulé.

unfeignedly, *adv.* Sincèrement ; vraiment.

unfettered, *a.* Libre de tous liens.

unfilial, *a.* Peu filial, -aux.

unfinished, *a.* Inachevé ; (ouvrage) imparfait.

unfit, *a.* **1.** (*a*) Impropre, peu propre (*for,* à). **Road unfit for motor traffic,** chemin impraticable aux automobiles. (*b*) *U. for military service,* inapte au service militaire. **2.** (*a*) *To be unfit,* être en mauvaise santé. (*b*) Faible de constitution.

unfitness, *s.* **1.** *Unfitness for sth.,* inaptitude *f* à qch. **2.** Mauvaise santé.

unfitted, *a.* Impropre (*for sth.,* à qch.); inapte.

unfitting, *a.* Peu convenable ; peu séant.

unflagging, *a.* Inlassable, infatigable ; (intérêt) soutenu.

unflattering, *a.* Peu flatteur, -euse.

unfledged, *a.* **1.** Sans plumes. **2.** *F:* Sans expérience de la vie ; jeune.

unflinching, *a.* **1.** Qui ne bronche pas.

2. Stoïque ; impassible. **-ly,** *adv.* **1.** Sans broncher. **2.** Stoïquement.

unfold, **1.** *v.tr.* (*a*) Déplier. (*b*) Dérouler, déployer. (*c*) Exposer. **To unfold one's plans,** dérouler ses plans. **2.** *v.i.* & *pr.* Se déployer, se dérouler.

unforeseen, *a.* Imprévu, inattendu ; inopiné.

unforgettable, *a.* Inoubliable.

unforgivable, *a.* Impardonnable.

unforgiving, *a.* Implacable.

unforgotten, *a.* Inoublié.

unfortunate, *a.* (*a*) Malheureux, infortuné. *To be u.,* avoir de la malchance. (*b*) (Événement) malencontreux ; (erreur) regrettable. **It is unfortunate that . . .,** il est fâcheux que + *sub.* **How unfortunate!** quel dommage ! **-ly,** *adv.* Malheureusement ; par malheur.

unfounded, *a.* Sans fondement, sans base.

unfrequented, *a.* Peu fréquenté. *U. spot,* endroit solitaire.

unfriendliness, *s.* Manque *m* d'amitié (*towards,* pour) ; hostilité *f* (*towards,* contre).

unfriendly, *a.* Peu amical, -aux. **Unfriendly action,** acte hostile. **To be unfriendly towards s.o.,** être mal disposé pour qn.

unfruitful, *a.* **1.** Stérile, inféconde. **2.** *U. labour,* travail peu fructueux.

unfulfilled, *a.* (*a*) *U. prophecy,* prophétie inaccomplie. (*b*) (Désir) non satisfait, inassouvi. (*c*) *U. promise,* promesse inexécutée.

unfurl, *v.tr.* *Nau:* Déferler (une voile), déployer (un drapeau).

unfurnished, *a.* **1.** Non fourni, dépourvu (*with,* de). **2.** (Appartement) non meublé.

ungainly, *a.* Gauche, lourd ; dégingandé.

ungallant, *a.* Peu galant.

ungenerous, *a.* Peu généreux.

ungentlemanly, *a.* **Ungentlemanly conduct,** conduite indélicate. *It is u. to,* il n'est pas poli de.

ungodliness, *s.* Impiété *f.*

ungodly, *a.* Impie.

ungovernable, *a* *U. passion,* passion effrénée, déréglée.

ungraceful, *a.* Disgracieux ; sans grâce ; gauche. **-fully,** *adv.* Sans grâce ; gauchement.

ungracious, *a.* Malgracieux ; peu aimable. **-ly,** *adv.* Malgracieusement.

ungraciousness, *s.* Mauvaise grâce.

ungrammatical, *a.* Peu grammatical, -aux. **-ally,** *adv.* Incorrectement.

ungrateful, *a.* Ingrat. (*a*) Peu reconnaissant. *U. for favours,* ingrat aux bienfaits. (*b*) *U. soil,* sol ingrat. **-fully,** *adv.* Avec ingratitude.

ungratefulness, *s.* Ingratitude *f.*

ungratified, *a.* Inassouvi, non satisfait.

ungrudging, *a.* **1.** *To give s.o. u. praise,* ne pas ménager ses louanges à qn. **2.** Libéral, -aux ; généreux. **-ly,** *adv.* De bonne grâce ; libéralement.

unguarded, *a.* **1.** Non gardé ; sans garde. **2.** Qui n'est pas sur ses gardes ; (*of speech*) indiscret, -ète. In an unguarded moment, dans un moment d'inattention. **-ly,** *adv.* Inconsidérément.

unguent, *s.* Onguent *m.*

unhallowed, *a.* **1.** Imbéni, profane. **2.** (*Of joy*) Impie.

unhampered, *a.* Libre (de ses mouvements). *U. by rules,* sans être gêné par des règles.

unhappiness, *s.* Chagrin *m* ; soucis *mpl.*

unhappy, *a.* **1.** Malheureux, triste. **2.** Mal inspiré. In an unhappy hour, dans un moment funeste. **-ily,** *adv.* **1.** (*a*) Malheureusement. (*b*) Tristement. **2.** Thought unhappily expressed, pensée mal exprimée.

unharmed, *a.* Sain et sauf ; indemne.

unharness, *v.tr.* Dételer.

unhealthiness, *s.* **1.** Insalubrité *f* (du climat). **2.** (*a*) Mauvaise santé ; état maladif. (*b*) Unhealthiness of mind, esprit malsain.

unhealthy, *a.* **1.** Malsain, insalubre ; (travail) peu hygiénique. **2.** Maladif. *U. complexion,* visage terreux.

unheard, *a.* **1.** To condemn s.o. unheard, condamner qn sans l'entendre. **2.** Unheard of, inouï.

unheeded, *a.* Négligé, dédaigné. To pass unheeded, passer inaperçu.

unheeding, *a.* **1.** Insouciant, distrait. **2.** Inattentif (*of*, à) ; insouciant (*of*, de).

unhesitating, *a.* Qui n'hésite pas ; ferme, résolu. *U. reply,* réponse prompte. **-ly,** *adv.* Sans hésiter.

unhindered, *a.* Sans encombre, sans obstacle, sans empêchement ; librement.

unhinge, *v.tr.* Ébranler, détraquer (l'esprit). His mind is unhinged, il a le cerveau détraqué.

unholy, *a.* **1.** Profane. **2.** *F:* Unholy muddle, désordre affreux.

unhonoured, *a.* Sans être honoré ; qui n'est pas honoré ; dédaigné.

unhook, *v.tr.* (*a*) Décrocher. (*b*) Dégrafer.

unhoped, *a.* Unhoped for, inespéré.

unhorse, *v.tr.* Désarçonner, démonter. To be unhorsed, vider les arçons.

unhurt, *a.* **1.** Sans mal ; indemne. To escape unhurt, s'en tirer sain et sauf. **2.** (*Of thg*) Intact.

unicorn, *s.* *Myth:* Licorne *f.*

unidentified, *a.* Non identifié.

uniform. 1. *a.* Uniforme. Uniform temperature, température constante. **2.** *s.* (*a*) Uniforme *m.* In uniform, en uniforme. (*b*) Costume *m* (d'infirmière). **-ly,** *adv.* Uniformément.

uniformity, *s.* Uniformité *f.*

unify, *v.tr.* Unifier.

unilateral, *a.* Unilatéral, -aux.

unimaginable, *a.* Inimaginable.

unimaginative, *a.* Dénué d'imagination.

unimpaired, *a.* Non affaibli. Unimpaired health, santé non altérée.

unimpeachable, *a.* Incontestable.

unimpeded, *a.* Libre ; sans empêchement.

unimportant, *a.* Sans importance ; peu important.

unimpressed, *a.* I was u. by his speech, son discours m'a laissé froid.

uninhabitable, *a.* Inhabitable.

uninhabited, *a.* Inhabité, désert.

uninitiated, *a.* Non initié (*in,* dans). *s.* The uninitiated, les profanes *m.*

uninjured, *a.* **1.** Sain et sauf ; sans mal ; indemne. **2.** Sans dommage.

uninspired, *a.* Sans inspiration.

unintelligent, *a.* Inintelligent.

unintelligible, *a.* Inintelligible. **-ibly,** *adv.* D'une manière peu intelligible.

unintentional, *a.* Involontaire ; fait sans intention. **-ally,** *adv.* Involontairement.

uninterested, *a.* Non intéressé ; indifférent.

uninteresting, *a.* Peu intéressant ; sans intérêt.

uninterrupted, *a.* **1.** Ininterrompu. **2.** Continu. **-ly,** *adv.* Sans interruption.

uninvited, *a.* Sans être invité. Uninvited guest, hôte inconvié.

uninviting, *a.* Peu attrayant, peu engageant ; (*of food*) peu appétissant.

union, *s.* **1.** Union *f.* **2.** Concorde *f,* harmonie *f.* **Union jack,** *s.* Le pavillon britannique.

unionist, *s.* **1.** *Pol:* Unioniste *mf.* **2.** *Ind:* = TRADE-UNIONIST.

unique, *a.* Unique ; seul en son genre. **-ly,** *adv.* Uniquement.

unison, *s.* **1.** *Mus:* Unisson *m.* In unison, à l'unisson (*with,* de). **2.** To act in unison with s.o., agir de concert avec qn.

unit, *s.* **1.** Unité *f.* **2.** Unité (de longueur).

unite. 1. *v.tr.* (*a*) Unir. (*b*) Mettre d'accord ; unifier. (*c*) Unir en mariage. **2.** *v.i.* S'unir, se joindre (*with,* à). To unite in doing sth., se mettre d'accord pour faire qch. **united,** *a.* Uni, réuni. United efforts, efforts concertés. To present a united front, faire front unique. *Geog:* The United Kingdom, le Royaume-Uni. The United States, les États-Unis (d'Amérique). **-ly,** *adv.* Ensemble ; d'accord.

unity, *s.* Unité *f;* concorde *f,* accord *m.* National u., unité nationale. *Prov:* Unity is strength, l'union fait la force.

universal, *a.* Universel. He is a universal favourite, tout le monde l'aime. **-ally,** *adv.* Universellement.

universe, *s.* Univers *m.*

university, *s.* Université *f.* University professor, professeur de faculté. University town, ville universitaire.

unjust, *a.* Injuste (*to,* envers, avec, pour). My suspicions were u., mes soupçons étaient mal fondés. **-ly,** *adv.* Injustement.

unjustifiable, *a.* Injustifiable, inexcusable.

unjustified, *a.* Non justifié.

unkempt, *a.* **1.** (*Of hair*) Mal peigné. **2.** Peu soigné ; mal tenu.

unkind, *a.* (i) Dur; cruel; (ii) peu aimable. That's very unkind of him, c'est peu aimable de sa part. *Her aunt is u. to her,* sa tante la traite mal. **-ly,** *adv.* (i) Méchamment, durement; (ii) sans bienveillance. Don't take it unkindly, ne le prenez pas en mauvaise part.

unkindness, *s.* **1.** Méchanceté *f.* **2.** Manque *m* de bienveillance.

unknot, *v.tr.* Dénouer.

unknowing, *a.* Ignorant (*of,* de). **-ly,** *adv.* Inconsciemment; sans le savoir.

unknown. 1. *a.* Inconnu (*to,* à, de); ignoré (*to,* de). Unknown writer, écrivain obscur. *adv.* He did it unknown to me, il l'a fait à mon insu. **2.** *s.* (*a*) Inconnu, -ue. (*b*) The unknown, l'inconnu.

unlace, *v.tr.* Délacer, défaire.

unladylike, *a.* Indigne d'une femme bien élevée; peu distingué.

unlatch, *v.tr.* Ouvrir (la porte).

unlawful, *a.* (*a*) Illégal, -aux. (*b*) (Moyen) illicite. **-fully,** *adv.* (*a*) Illégalement. (*b*) Illicitement.

unleash, *v.tr.* Lâcher, découpler.

unleavened, *a.* (Pain) sans levain.

unless. 1. *conj.* A moins que . . . (ne) + *sub.* *You will be late u. you start at once,* vous arriverez trop tard à moins de partir sur-le-champ. Unless I am mistaken, si je ne me trompe (pas). Unless I hear to the contrary, à moins d'avis contraire. **2.** *prep.* Sauf, excepté.

unlettered, *a.* Peu lettré; indocte.

unlicensed, *a.* Non autorisé; illicite.

unlike, *a.* Différent, dissemblable. (*a*) Unlike (to) sth., dissemblable de qch. Not unlike s.o., assez ressemblant à qn. He, unlike his father, lui, à la différence de son père. (*b*) That was very unlike him! je ne le reconnais pas là!

unlikelihood, *s.* Invraisemblance *f,* improbabilité *f.*

unlikely, *a.* **1.** Invraisemblable; peu probable. Most unlikely, très peu probable. It is not at all unlikely that . . ., il se pourrait bien que + *sub.* **2.** The most unlikely man to do such a thing, l'homme le moins fait pour agir de la sorte.

unlimited, *a.* Illimité; sans bornes.

unload, *v.tr.* **1.** (*a*) Décharger. (*b*) To u. one's heart, se soulager le cœur. **2.** Enlever la charge; décharger.

unloaded, *a.* **1.** Déchargé. **2.** (*a*) Non chargé. (*b*) (Fusil) sans charge.

unlock, *v.tr.* Ouvrir (la porte); faire jouer la serrure de (la porte).

unlocked, *a.* Qui n'est pas fermé à clef.

unlooked, *a.* Unlooked for, (événement) inattendu, imprévu.

unlov(e)able, *a.* Peu aimable; peu sympathique.

unlucky, *a.* **1.** (*a*) Malheureux, infortuné. To be unlucky, jouer de malheur. (*b*) Malheureux, malencontreux. Unlucky day, jour néfaste. **2.** Unlucky star, étoile maléfique. It is unlucky, cela porte malheur. Unlucky omen, mauvais augure. **-ily,** *adv.* Malheureusement.

unman, *v.tr.* (*a*) Attendrir. (*b*) Abattre, décourager.

unmanageable, *a.* **1.** Intraitable; (*of child*) indocile; (*of ship*) difficile à manœuvrer. **2.** Difficile à manier.

unmanliness, *s.* (*a*) Manque *m* de virilité; mollesse *f.* (*b*) Lâcheté *f.*

unmanly, *a.* Indigne d'un homme; peu viril.

unmannerliness, *s.* Mauvaises manières.

unmannerly, *a.* Malappris; grossier.

unmarketable, *a.* Invendable.

unmarried, *a.* Célibataire; non marié. Unmarried state, célibat *m.*

unmask. 1. *v.tr.* (*a*) Démasquer. (*b*) F: To unmask a conspiracy, dévoiler un complot. **2.** *v.i.* Se démasquer.

unmatched, *a.* **1.** Sans égal, *pl.* sans égaux; incomparable. **2.** Désassorti, dépareillé.

unmeaning, *a.* Vide de sens.

unmeant, *a.* Involontaire; fait sans intention.

unmeasured, *a.* **1.** (*a*) Non mesuré. (*b*) Infini. **2.** Qui manque de retenue.

unmentionable, *a.* Dont il ne faut pas parler.

unmerciful, *a.* Impitoyable; sans pitié. **-fully,** *adv.* Impitoyablement.

unmerited, *a.* Immérité.

unmethodical, *a.* Peu méthodique.

unmindful, *a.* Unmindful of one's duty, oublieux de son devoir.

unmistakable, *a.* (*a*) Clair; évident. (*b*) Facilement reconnaissable. **-ably,** *adv.* Nettement, évidemment; à ne pas s'y méprendre.

unmitigated, *a.* **1.** (Mal) non mitigé. **2.** *F:* Dans toute la force du terme. Unmitigated ass, parfait imbécile. Unmitigated scoundrel, coquin fieffé.

unmixed, *a.* Sans mélange; pur.

unmolested, *a.* Sans être molesté.

unmounted, *a.* Non monté. **1.** (*a*) (*Of gem*) Non serti. (*b*) (*Of photograph*) Non collé. **2.** (Soldat) à pied.

unmoved, *a.* Impassible. Unmoved by sth., aucunement ému, touché, de, par, qch.

unnamed, *a.* **1.** Au nom inconnu; anonyme. **2.** Innom(m)é; sans nom.

unnatural, *a.* Non naturel. (*a*) Anormal, -aux. (*b*) Contre nature; monstrueux. Unnatural father, père dénaturé. (*c*) U. laugh, rire forcé.

unnavigable, *a.* Innavigable.

unnecessary, *a.* Peu nécessaire; inutile; superflu. **-ily,** *adv.* **1.** Sans nécessité; inutilement. **2.** Plus que de raison.

unneeded, *a.* Inutile; dont on n'a pas besoin.

unneighbourly, *a.* Peu obligeant; de mauvais voisin.
unnerve, *v.tr.* Faire perdre son sang-froid à; effrayer. *Entirely unnerved,* tout à fait démonté.
unnoticed, *a.* **1.** Inaperçu, inobservé. **2.** *To leave a fact u.,* passer un fait sous silence.
unnumbered, *a.* **1.** (*a*) Qui n'est pas compté. (*b*) Sans nombre; innombrable. **2.** Non numéroté.
unobjectionable, *a.* (Personne) à qui on ne peut rien reprocher; (chose) à laquelle on ne peut trouver à redire.
unobservant, *a.* Peu observateur, -trice.
unobserved, *a.* Inobservé, inaperçu.
unobstructed, *a.* **1.** Inobstrué; (*of street*) non encombré; (*of view*) libre. **2.** Sans rencontrer d'obstacles.
unobtainable, *a.* Impossible à obtenir.
unobtrusive, *a.* Discret, -ète; (rôle) effacé, modeste. **-ly,** *adv.* Discrètement.
unoccupied, *a.* Inoccupé. **1.** Sans occupation. *Unoccupied time,* temps libre. **2.** Inhabité. **3.** (*Of seat*) Libre, disponible.
unoffending, *a.* Innocent.
unofficial, *a.* Non officiel. **-ally,** *adv.* A titre officieux.
unopened, *a.* Qui n'a pas été ouvert; (*of letter*) non décacheté.
unopposed, *a.* Sans opposition.
unorthodox, *a.* Peu orthodoxe.
unostentatious, *a.* **1.** Peu fastueux; simple. **2.** Fait sans ostentation. **-ly,** *adv.* Sans ostentation, sans faste.
unpack, *v.tr.* **1.** Déballer, dépaqueter. **2.** Défaire (une malle). *Abs.* Défaire sa malle.
unpaid, *a.* Non payé. **1.** (*Of post*) non rétribué. *U. secretary,* secrétaire sans traitement. *Unpaid services,* services à titre gracieux. **2.** Impayé; non acquitté; (*of letter*) non affranchi.
unpalatable, *a.* (*a*) D'un goût désagréable. (*b*) *F:* Désagréable.
unparalleled, *a.* Incomparable; sans égal, sans pareil.
unpardonable, *a.* Impardonable.
unparliamentary, *a* (Langage) (i) antiparlementaire, (ii) *F:* grossier, injurieux.
unpatriotic, *a.* (*Of pers.*) Peu patriote; (*of action*) peu patriotique.
unperceivable, *a.* Imperceptible.
unperceived, *a.* Inaperçu.
unperturbed, *a.* **1.** Impassible. **2.** Unperturbed by this event, peu ému de cet événement.
unpitying, *a.* Impitoyable.
unpleasant, *a.* Désagréable, déplaisant. **-ly,** *adv.* Désagréablement.
unpleasantness, *s.* **1.** Caractère *m* désagréable. **2.** Désagrément *m,* ennui *m.*
unpleasing, *a.* Peu agréable.; qui manque de grâce.

unpoetic(al), *a.* Peu poétique.
unpolished, *a.* **1.** Non poli; mat; (*of stone*) brut. **2.** Rude, grossier.
unpopular, *a.* Impopulaire. **To make oneself unpopular with everybody,** se faire mal voir de tout le monde.
unpopularity, *s.* Impopularité *f.*
unpopulated, *a.* Non peuplé.
unpractical, *a.* Peu pratique.
unpractised, *a.* Inexercé, inexpert (*in,* à, dans).
unprecedented, *a.* (i) Sans précédent; (ii) inouï.
unprejudiced, *a.* Sans préjugés, impartial, -aux; désintéressé.
unpremeditated, *a.* Inopiné.
unprepared, *a.* **1.** **Unprepared speech,** discours improvisé. **2.** **To catch s.o. unprepared,** prendre qn au dépourvu.
unprepossessing, *a.* Peu engageant.
unpretentious, *a.* Sans prétentions; modeste. **-ly,** *adv.* Modestement.
unprincipled, *a.* Sans principes.
unprocurable, *a.* Impossible à obtenir.
unproductive, *a.* Improductif; stérile.
unprofitable, *a.* Improfitable; peu lucratif; sans profit; (travail) inutile. **-ably,** *adv.* Sans profit; inutilement.
unpromising, *a.* Qui promet peu. (*Of weather*) **To look unpromising,** s'annoncer mal.
unprompted, *a.* Spontané. **To do sth. unprompted,** faire qch. spontanément.
unpronounceable, *a.* Imprononçable.
unpropitious, *a.* Impropice, défavorable.
unprotected, *a.* Inabrité; sans protection, sans défense.
unproved, *a.* **1.** Improuvé; non prouvé. **2.** (*Of fidelity*) Inéprouvé.
unprovided, *a.* **Unprovided with sth.,** dépourvu, dénué, de qch. **To be left unprovided for,** être laissé sans ressources.
unprovoked, *a.* Improvoqué; fait sans provocation.
unpublished, *a.* Inédit; non publié.
unpunctual, *a.* (*a*) Inexact; peu ponctuel. (*b*) En retard; pas à l'heure.
unpunctuality, *s.* Inexactitude *f;* manque *m* de ponctualité.
unpunished, *a.* Impuni.
unqualified, *a.* **1.** (*a*) Incompétent. (*b*) Sans diplômes. **2.** **Unqualified denial,** dénégation catégorique. **Unqualified praise,** éloges sans réserve.
unquenchable, *a.* Inextinguible.
unquestionable, *a.* Indiscutable, indubitable. **Unquestionable fact,** fait hors de doute. **-ably,** *adv.* Indubitablement.
unquestioned, *a.* **1.** Indisputé, incontesté. **2.** *To let a statement pass u.,* laisser passer une affirmation sans la relever
unquestioning, *a.* Aveugle, sans question. **-ly,** *adv.* Aveuglément; sans question.
unquiet, *a.* Inquiet, -ète; agité.

unravel, v. **1.** v.tr. (a) Effiler (un tissu). (b) Débrouiller (des fils). **2.** v.i. (a) S'effiler. (b) Se débrouiller. **unravelling,** s. **1.** Effilage m. **2.** Débrouillement m.

unreadable, a. Illisible.

unreal, a. Irréel ; sans réalité.

unreasonable, a. Déraisonnable. **1.** Don't be unreasonable, soyez raisonnable. **2.** (a) Unreasonable demands, demandes immodérées. (b) At this unreasonable hour, à cette heure indue. **-ably,** adv. Déraisonnablement.

unreasoning, a. Qui ne raisonne pas. Unreasoning hatred, haine aveugle.

unrecognizable, a. Méconnaissable.

unrecognized, a. **1.** (Of genius) Méconnu. **2.** (Of ruler) Non reconnu (by, par).

unrecorded, a. Non enregistré ; dont on ne trouve aucune mention.

unredeemed, a. **1.** Town of u. ugliness, ville uniformément laide. **2.** Unredeemed promise, promesse inaccomplie.

unrefreshed, a. Non rafraîchi.

unregenerate, a. Non régénéré ; inconverti.

unregistered, a. Non enregistré.

unrehearsed, a. Unrehearsed effect, effet non préparé.

unrelated, a. (a) Sans rapport. (b) They are entirely u., il n'y a aucun lien de parenté entre eux.

unrelaxing, a. Sans relâche ; soutenu.

unrelenting, a. (a) Implacable, impitoyable. (b) (Of persecution) Acharné.

unreliability, s. **1.** Inexactitude f. **2.** Instabilité f.

unreliable, a. Sur lequel on ne peut pas compter ; sujet, -ette, à caution. U. map, carte peu fidèle.

unrelieved, a. **1.** Qui reste sans secours. **2.** Monotone. Plain u. by the smallest hillock, plaine ininterrompue par la moindre colline.

unremitting, a. **1.** Ininterrompu ; sans intermission. U. efforts, efforts soutenus. **2.** Infatigable. **-ly,** adv. Sans cesse, sans relâche.

unremunerative, a. Peu rémunérateur, -trice ; peu lucratif ; improfitable.

unrepentant, a. Impénitent.

unrequited, a. **1.** Non récompensé. **2.** Unrequited love, amour non partagé.

unreserved, a. Sans réserve. (a) Franc, f. franche ; expansif. (b) Complet, -ète ; entier.

unreservedly, adv. Sans réserve.

unresisting, a. Soumis, docile.

unresponsive, a. Difficile à émouvoir ; froid.

unrest, a. **1.** Inquiétude f. **2.** Labour unrest, agitation ouvrière.

unrestrained, a. Non restreint ; libre ; intempéré. U. laughter, rires immodérés.

unrestrainedly, adv. Librement ; sans contrainte.

unrestricted, a. Sans restriction ; absolu.

unrevenged, a. Invengé. **1.** Sans être vengé. **2.** Sans s'être vengé.

unrewarded, a. Sans récompense.

unrighteous, a. **1.** Impie. **2.** Inique, injuste. **-ly,** adv. Iniquement, injustement.

unrighteousness, s. Iniquité f, improbité f.

unripe, a. Vert ; qui n'est pas mûr.

unrivalled, a. Sans rival ; sans pareil.

unroll. 1. v.tr. Dérouler. **2.** v.i. & pr. Se dérouler.

unromantic, a. Peu romanesque.

unruffled, a. Calme, placide.

unruly, a. Indiscipliné, insoumis, mutin.

unsafe, a. **1.** Dangereux ; (of ice) peu sûr. **2.** Exposé au danger.

unsaid, a. To leave sth. unsaid, passer qch. sous silence.

unsaleable, a. Invendable.

unsanitary, a. Non hygiénique ; insalubre.

unsatisfactory, a. Peu satisfaisant ; (of explanation) peu convaincant. **-ily,** adv. D'une manière peu satisfaisante.

unsatisfied, a. **1.** Mécontent (with, de). **2.** Inconvaincu. **3.** Inassouvi.

unsatisfying, a. **1.** Peu satisfaisant ; peu convaincant. **2.** Peu rassasiant.

unsavoury, a. **1.** (a) Désagréable. (b) U. smell, mauvaise odeur. **2.** U. business, vilaine affaire.

unsay, v.tr. Se dédire de, rétracter.

unscientific, a. (a) Non scientifique. (b) Peu scientifique.

unscratched, a. Sans égratignure.

unscrew, v.tr. Dévisser.

unscrupulous, a. Peu scrupuleux ; sans scrupules. **-ly,** adv. Peu scrupuleusement ; sans scrupule.

unseal, v.tr. Desceller ; décacheter.

unseasonable, a. **1.** Hors de saison. U. weather, temps qui n'est pas de saison. **2.** Inopportun ; déplacé. **-ably,** adv. **1.** Hors de saison. **2.** Mal à propos.

unseaworthy, a. Hors d'état de prendre la mer ; incapable de tenir la mer.

unseeing, a. Qui ne voit pas ; aveugle.

unseemliness, s. Inconvenance f.

unseemly, a. Inconvenant ; peu convenable.

unseen, a. Inaperçu, invisible.

unselfish, a. Généreux ; sans égoïsme. U. motive, motif désintéressé. **-ly,** adv. Généreusement.

unselfishness, s. Générosité f ; désintéressement m.

unserviceable, a. (a) Inutilisable. (b) Hors d'état de servir.

unsettle, v.tr. Ébranler ; troubler le repos de. **unsettling,** a. Troublant.

unsettled, a. **1.** Troublé ; (temps) variable. **2.** Sans domicile fixe. **3.** (Esprit) indécis. **4.** (a) (Of question) Indécis. (b) Impayé, non réglé.

unshackled, a. Libre ; sans entraves.

unshakeable, a. Inébranlable.

unshaken, *a.* Inébranlé, ferme.
unshapely, *a.* Mal fait ; difforme.
unshaven, *a.* Non rasé.
unsheathe, *v.tr.* Dégainer.
unsheltered, *a.* Sans abri, non abrité (*from,* contre) ; exposé (au vent).
unshrinkable, *a.* Irrétrécissable.
unshrinking, *a.* Hardi ; qui ne bronche pas. **-ly,** *adv.* Hardiment ; sans broncher.
unsightly, *a.* Laid, vilain.
unsigned, *a.* Non signé ; sans signature.
unskilful, *a.* Malhabile, inhabile (*in, at,* à).
unskilled, *a.* Inexpérimenté (*in,* à) ; inexpert (*in,* dans, en). Unskilled labour, main-d'œuvre non spécialisée.
unsleeping, *a* *Lit:* Toujours en éveil ; vigilant.
unsociable, *a.* Insociable ; farouche.
unsoiled, *a.* Propre ; sans tache.
unsold, *a.* Invendu.
unsoldierly, *a.* Peu martial, -aux.
unsolicited, *a.* Non sollicité ; volontaire, spontané. Unsolicited testimonial, lettre d'attestation spontanée.
unsolved, *a.* Non résolu ; (mystère) impénétré.
unsophisticated, *a* Ingénu, naïf ; *F:* innocent.
unsound, *a.* **I.** (*a*) Of unsound mind, non sain d'esprit. (*b*) Gâté ; en mauvais état. **2.** (*a*) (*Of position*) mal affermi ; (*of business*) périclitant. (*b*) Unsound opinions, opinions perverties.
unsoundness, *s.* **I.** (*a*) Unsoundness of mind, faiblesse *f* d'esprit. (*b*) Mauvais état. **2.** (*a*) Manque *m* de solidité. (*b*) Fausseté *f*.
unsparing, *a.* Prodigue (*of,* de). *U. in one's efforts,* infatigable. **-ly,** *adv.* Avec prodigalité ; généreusement.
unspeakable, *a.* **I.** Inexprimable. **2.** *F:* Détestable, inqualifiable. It is unspeakable! ça n'a pas de nom! **-ably,** *adv.* Ineffablement, indiciblement.
unspecified, *a.* Non spécifié.
unspoken, *a.* Non prononcé ; (accord) tacite.
unsportsmanlike, *a.* Indigne d'un sportsman ; peu loyal, -aux.
unstable, *a.* **I.** Instable. **2.** Peu consistant ; (*of character*) inconstant.
unstained, *a.* Propre ; sans tache.
unsteadiness, *s.* **I.** Instabilité *f* ; manque *m* de sûreté (de la main). **2.** (*a*) Irrésolution *f*, indécision *f.* (*b*) Manque de conduite.
unsteady, *a.* **I.** Peu stable, peu solide ; (*of footsteps*) chancelant ; (*of voice*) mal assuré. *F:* To be unsteady on one's legs, avoir une démarche chancelante. **2.** (*a*) Vacillant, irrésolu. (*b*) (*Of pers.*) Dissipé ; déréglé. **-ily,** *adv.* **I.** (Marcher) d'un pas chancelant. **2.** D'une façon irrégulière, inégale.
unstinted, *a.* (*a*) Abondant ; à discrétion. (*b*) To give s.o. unstinted praise, ne pas ménager ses louanges à qn.

unstressed, *a.* Sans accent ; inaccentué ; atone.
unstudied, *a.* (Langage) naturel ; (charme) inétudié.
unsubdued, *a* Non subjugué.
unsuccessful, *a.* **I.** Non réussi ; vain. *U. attempt,* tentative sans succès ; *F:* coup manqué. *The negotiations were u.,* les pourparlers n'ont pas abouti. **2.** Qui n'a pas réussi ; (*of candidate*) refusé, (*at election*) non élu. **-fully,** *adv.* Sans succès ; vainement.
unsuitable, *a.* **I.** Peu fait (*to, for,* pour) ; inapte (à). **2.** (*Of thg*) Impropre, mal adapté. Unsuitable to the occasion, qui ne convient pas à la circonstance. **-ably,** *adv.* D'une manière qui ne convient pas.
unsuited, *a.* Unsuited to sth., peu fait pour qch. ; inapte à qch.
unsullied, *a.* Sans souillure ; sans tache ; immaculé.
unsurpassed, *a.* Qui n'a jamais été surpassé.
unsuspected, *a.* Insoupçonné (*by,* de).
unsuspecting, *a.* Qui ne se doute de rien ; sans soupçons ; sans défiance. **-ly,** *adv.* Sans rien soupçonner ; sans défiance.
unsuspicious, *a.* **I.** = UNSUSPECTING. **2.** To be unsuspicious of sth., ne pas se douter de qch.
unsweetened, *a.* Non sucré.
unswerving, *a.* **I.** Constant, ferme. **2.** To pursue an unswerving course, ne pas s'écarter du but.
unsymmetrical, *a.* Asymétrique.
unsympathetic, *a.* Peu compatissant ; froid ; indifférent. **-ally,** *adv.* D'un air peu compatissant ; froidement.
unsystematic, *a.* Sans système ; sans méthode. **-ally,** *adv.* Sans système ; sans méthode.
untalented, *a.* Sans talents.
untam(e)able, *a.* Inapprivoisable ; indomptable.
untamed, *a.* Inapprivoisé, sauvage ; indompté.
untapped, *a.* Untapped resources, ressources inutilisées.
untarnished, *a.* **I.** Non terni. **2.** (Réputation) sans tache, sans souillure.
untaught, *a.* (*a*) Sans instruction ; illettré, ignorant. (*b*) (*Of skill*) Naturel.
untempting, *a.* Peu tentant.
untenable, *a.* **I.** Intenable. **2.** (*Of theory*) Insoutenable.
untenanted, *a.* Inoccupé ; inhabité.
untested, *a.* Inessayé, inéprouvé.
unthinkable, *a.* Inimaginable ; inconcevable.
unthinking, *a.* Irréfléchi, étourdi. In an unthinking moment, dans un moment d'abstraction. **-ly,** *adv.* Sans réflexion ; étourdiment.
untidiness, *s.* Désordre *m* ; manque *m* d'ordre, de soin.
untidy, *a.* (*a*) En désordre ; mal tenu ; (*of*

hair) ébouriffé. (*b*) Qui manque d'ordre ; sans soin. **-ily,** *adv.* Sans ordre, sans soin.

untie, *v.tr.* Dénouer ; défaire, délier. To come untied, se défaire, se déficeler.

until, *prep. & conj.* = TILL[8].

untilled, *a.* Inculte, incultivé.

untimely[1], *a.* **1.** Prématuré. To come to an untimely end, mourir avant l'âge. **2.** Inopportun, intempestif, mal à propos. **3.** At an untimely hour, à une heure indue.

untimely[2], *adv.* **1.** Prématurément ; avant l'heure. **2.** Inopportunément ; mal à propos.

untiring, *a.* Inlassable, infatigable. **-ly,** *adv.* Inlassablement, infatigablement.

unto, *prep. A : I.* A. And I say unto you, et je vous dis. Let us unto our ships, allons à nos vaisseaux. **2.** Vers. To come nigh unto sth., s'approcher de qch. **3.** Jusqu'à. Unto this day, jusqu'à ce jour même.

untold, *a.* Non computé ; immense. It is worth untold gold, cela vaut une somme fabuleuse. *U. suffering,* souffrances inouïes.

untouched, *a.* **1.** (*a*) Non manié. (*b*) He had left the food u., il n'avait pas touché à la nourriture. **2.** (*a*) To leave sth. untouched, laisser qch. intact. (*b*) Sain et sauf. **3.** Untouched (upon), non mentionné. **4.** Non ému ; indifférent.

untoward, *a.* I hope nothing untoward has happened, il n'est pas arrivé un malheur, j'espère.

untrained, *a.* Inexpert, inexercé ; (domestique) non formé.

untrammelled, *a.* Sans entraves, sans contrainte ; libre (*by,* de).

untransferable, *a.* Intransférable.

untried, *a.* **1.** Inessayé ; non essayé. **2.** Qui n'a pas été mis à l'épreuve.

untrodden, *a.* Impratiqué, non fravé ; (région) inexplorée. *U. snow,* neige immaculée.

untroubled, *a.* Calme, tranquille, paisible.

untrue, *a.* **1.** Faux, *f.* fausse. **2.** Infidèle, déloyal, *-aux* (*to,* à).

untrustworthiness, *s.* **1.** Manque *m* de probité. **2.** Caractère douteux.

untrustworthy, *a.* **1.** Indigne de confiance. *U. memory,* mémoire peu sûre. **2.** (Renseignement) douteux, peu sûr.

untruth, *s.* Mensonge *m.*

untruthful, *a.* **1.** Menteur, *-euse* ; peu véridique. **2.** Mensonger ; faux, *f.* fausse. **-fully,** *adv.* Menteusement, mensongèrement.

untruthfulness, *s.* **1.** Caractère menteur. **2.** Fausseté *f* (d'une histoire).

unusable, *a.* Inutilisable.

unused, *a.* **1.** (*a*) (i) Inutilisé ; non employé ; (ii) hors d'usage. (*b*) Qui n'a pas encore servi ; neuf. **2.** Peu habitué (*to,* à).

unusual, *a.* Peu commun ; exceptionnel ; insolite. Nothing unusual, rien d'anormal. **-ally,** *adv.* Exceptionnellement.

unutterable, *a.* Inexprimable, indicible.

F : U. fool, parfait imbécile. **-ably,** *adv.* Indiciblement.

unvanquished, *a.* Invaincu.

unvaried, *a.* Uniforme, constant.

unvarnished, *a.* **1.** Non verni. **2.** *F :* Simple.

unvarying, *a.* Invariable ; uniforme, constant.

unveil, *v.tr.* Dévoiler. To unveil a statue, inaugurer une statue. **unveiling,** *s.* Inauguration *f.*

unverifiable, *a.* Invérifiable.

unverified, *a.* Invérifié.

unwanted, *a.* **1.** Non désiré, non voulu. **2.** Superflu.

unwarrantable, *a.* Injustifiable, inexcusable.

unwarranted, *a.* Injustifié ; peu justifié ; inautorisé.

unwary, *a.* Imprudent, imprévoyant. **-ily,** *adv.* Imprudemment ; sans précaution.

unwashed, *a.* Non lavé ; malpropre, sale.

unwavering, *a.* Constant, ferme, résolu.

unwearied, *a.* (*a*) Non fatigué. (*b*) Infatigable.

unwearying, *a.* Inlassable, infatigable.

unwelcome, *a.* (*a*) Mal venu, importun. (*b*) Unwelcome news, nouvelle fâcheuse, désagréable.

unwell, *a.* Indisposé ; souffrant.

unwholesome, *a.* Malsain ; (climat) insalubre.

unwieldy, *a.* **1.** Lourd, gauche ; à la démarche lourde. **2.** Peu portatif ; peu maniable.

unwilling, *a.* **1.** Inserviable ; de mauvaise volonté. **2.** To be unwilling to do sth., être peu disposé à faire qch. *U. acquiescence,* assentiment donné à contre-cœur. **-ly,** *adv.* A contre-cœur ; de mauvaise grâce ; à regret.

unwillingness, *s.* **1.** Mauvaise volonté ; manque *m* de bonne volonté. **2.** Répugnance *f* (à faire qch.).

unwind, *v.tr.* Dérouler.

unwise, *a.* **1.** Imprudent ; peu prudent. **2.** Peu sage ; malavisé. **-ly,** *adv.* Imprudemment.

unwitting, *a.* **1.** Inconscient (*of,* de). **2.** Fait sans dessein. **-ly,** *adv.* Sans le savoir ; inconsciemment.

unwomanly, *a.* Peu féminin ; peu digne d'une femme.

unwonted, *a.* Inaccoutumé, inhabituel ; peu commun, insolite.

unworldly, *a.* **1.** (*a*) Peu mondain ; détaché de ce monde. (*b*) Simple, candide. **2.** Céleste ; qui n'est pas de ce monde.

unworthiness, *s.* **1.** Peu *m* de mérite. **2.** Caractère *m* méprisable, peu digne.

unworthy, *a.* Indigne. **1.** Unworthy of sth., indigne de qch. *U. of notice,* qui ne mérite pas qu'on y fasse attention. **2.** Méprisable. **3.** (Travail) peu méritoire.

unwounded, *a.* Non blessé ; sans blessure.

unwrap, *v.tr.* Défaire, désenvelopper.
unwrinkled, *a.* Sans rides ; lisse.
unwritten, *a.* Non écrit ; (*of tradition*) oral, -aux. *F:* The unwritten law, le droit coutumier.
unyielding, *a.* Qui ne cède pas ; raide, ferme ; (*of pers.*) inébranlable ; inflexible.
up. I. *adv.* **1.** (*a*) En montant ; vers le haut. To go up, monter. My room is three flights up, ma chambre est au troisième palier. To throw sth. up (in the air), jeter qch. en l'air. Half-way up, jusqu'à mi-hauteur. (*b*) To walk up and down, se promener de long en large. To go up for an examination, se présenter à un examen. (*c*) From five pounds up, à partir de cinq livres. From my youth up, dès ma jeunesse. **2.** (*a*) Haut ; en haut. What are you doing up there? que faites-vous là-haut? Up above, en haut. Up above sth., au-dessus de qch. The moon is up, la lune est levée. The blinds are up, on a relevé les stores. The shops had their shutters up, les magasins avaient leurs volets mis. The tide is up, la marée est haute. 'Road up,' "route en réparation." (*b*) En dessus. Face up, face en dessus. This side up, haut ; dessus ; ne pas renverser. (*c*) Up in London, à Londres. Relations up from the country, parents de province en visite à la ville. **3.** (*a*) To go up in price, subir une hausse de prix. The thermometer has gone up, le thermomètre a monté. (*b*) To screw up, visser, serrer. *Mch:* Steam is up, nous sommes sous pression. His blood was up, il était monté. (*c*) To be well up in a subject, connaître un sujet à fond. (*d*) To praise s.o. up, vanter qn. To speak up, parler plus haut. **4.** *Put it up beside the other one,* mettez-le tout près de l'autre. To follow s.o. up, suivre qn de près. He came up with me, il me rejoignit. **5.** (*a*) Debout, levé. To get up, se lever. To be up and about, être sur pied. Let us be up and doing, mettons-nous à la besogne. (*b*) To be up all night, ne pas se coucher de la nuit. To stay up, veiller. (*c*) You are up against a strong man, vous avez affaire à forte partie. To be up against difficulties, se heurter à des difficultés. *F:* To be up against it, avoir la déveine. **6.** (*a*) To stir up sediment, remuer, agiter, un dépôt. To be up in arms, être en révolte. (*b*) *F:* What's up? que se passe-t-il? qu'y a-t-il? There is something up, il y a quelque chose. What's up with you? qu'est-ce qui vous prend? **7.** Time is up, il est l'heure. His leave is up, sa permission est expirée. *F:* It's all up, tout est perdu. It's all up with him, son affaire est faite. I thought it was all up with me, j'ai pensé mourir. **8.** Up to. (*a*) Jusqu'à. To go up to s.o., s'approcher de qn. (*b*) Up to now, jusqu'ici. To live up to one's income, dépenser tout son revenu. (*c*) To be up to sth., être capable de qch. To be up to a job, être à la hauteur d'une tâche. To be up to s.o., être de force à lutter avec qn. (*d*) What

are you up to? qu'est-ce que vous faites? He is up to something, il a quelque chose en tête. (*e*) *F:* It is up to him to . . ., c'est à lui de. . . . II. **up,** *prep.* **1.** To go up the stairs, monter l'escalier. The cat is up the tree, le chat est en haut de l'arbre. **2.** Up the river, en amont. Further up the street, plus loin dans la rue. To walk up and down, faire les cent pas. III. **up,** *attrib.a.* Up train, train montant. IV. **up,** *s.* *F:* The ups and downs of life, les vicissitudes *f* de la vie. **up-grade,** *s.* Pente ascendante ; rampe *f.* *F:* To be on the up-grade, (i) (*of prices*) monter ; (ii) (*of business*) reprendre, se relever. **up-stream,** *adv.* (*a*) En amont. (*b*) A contre-fil de l'eau. **up-to-date,** *attrib.a.* *F:* **1.** (*Of pers.*) A la page. **2.** Au goût du jour ; moderne.
upas, *s.* *Bot:* Upas *m.*
upbraid, *v.tr.* Reprocher, faire des reproches à ; gronder.
upbringing, *s.* Éducation *f.*
upheaval, *s.* **1.** *Geol:* (*a*) Soulèvement *m.* (*b*) Commotion *f,* bouleversement *m.* **2.** *F:* Bouleversement, agitation *f.*
up(-)hill. **1.** *a.* (*a*) Montant ; en rampe. (*b*) (*Of task*) Ardu, rude. **2.** *adv.* To go uphill, monter.
uphold, *v.tr.* Supporter, soutenir, maintenir. To uphold the law, faire observer la loi.
upholsterer, *s.* Tapissier *m* (en ameublement).
upholstery, *s.* **1.** Capitonnage *m,* rembourrage *m.* **2.** Tapisserie *f* d'ameublement. **3.** Métier *m* de tapissier ; tapisserie.
upkeep, *s.* (Frais *mpl* d')entretien *m.*
uplift¹, *s.* *F:* Moral uplift, élévation morale.
uplift², *v.tr.* Soulever, élever.
upon, *prep.* = ON I.
upper. I. *a.* **1.** (*a*) Supérieur, -eure ; (plus) haut, (plus) élevé ; de dessus ; d'au-dessus. The upper jaw, la mâchoire supérieure. Upper part of sth., dessus *m* de qch. (*b*) Upper waters of a river, amont *m* d'une rivière. Upper Egypt, la Haute-Égypte. **2.** The upper classes, les hautes classes. To have the upper hand, avoir le dessus. *Sch:* The upper forms, les grandes classes. II. **uppers,** *s.pl.* *Bootm:* Empeignes *f.* *F:* To be (down) on one's uppers, être dans la débine.
uppermost. **1.** *a.* (*a*) Le plus haut, le plus élevé. (*b*) De la plus grande importance ; premier. To be uppermost, prédominer. **2.** *adv.* (*a*) (Le plus) en dessus. Face uppermost, face en dessus. (*b*) His friend's fate was uppermost in his thoughts, le sort de son ami occupait la première place dans ses pensées.
uppish, *a.* *F:* Présomptueux, arrogant.
uppishness, *s.* *F:* Présomption *f,* arrogance *f* ; suffisance *f.*
upright. I. *a.* **1.** Vertical, -aux ; perpendiculaire ; droit. To set sth. upright, mettre qch. debout. *Sitting u. on his chair,* assis raide sur

sa chaise. **2.** Droit, honnête, probe. **-ly,** *adv.*
Avec droiture ; honnêtement. II. **upright,**
s. Const : Montant *m.*
uprightness, *s.* Droiture *f,* honnêteté *f.*
uprising, *s.* **1.** Lever *m.* **2.** Soulèvement *m ;*
insurrection *f.*
uproar, *s.* Vacarme *m,* tapage *m.* **The town
is in an uproar,** la ville est en tumulte.
uproarious, *a.* Tumultueux, tapageur, -euse.
-ly, *adv.* Tumultueusement.
uproot, *v.tr.* Déraciner, extirper.
upset¹, *s.* **1.** Renversement *m ;* chavirement
m (d'un bateau). **2.** (*a*) Désorganisation *f,*
bouleversement *m.* (*b*) Anicroche *f,* ennui *m.*
upset², *v.* **1.** *v.tr.* (*a*) Renverser ; (faire)
chavirer (un bateau). (*b*) Désorganiser,
bouleverser, déranger. (*c*) Troubler, bouleverser. **He is easily upset,** il s'émeut d'un
rien. **Don't upset yourself,** ne vous laissez
pas émouvoir. (*d*) Indisposer (qn) ; dérégler.
déranger (l'estomac). **2.** *v.i.* Se renverser ;
(*of carriage*) verser ; (*of boat*) chavirer.
upset³, *a.* Bouleversé, ému. **To get upset,**
se laisser démonter.
upshot, *s.* Résultat *m,* issue *f,* dénouement *m.*
What will be the upshot of it? à quoi cela
aboutira-t-il ?
upside down, *adv.phr.* (*a*) Sens dessus
dessous ; la tête en bas. (*b*) *F :* En désordre ;
bouleversé. **To turn everything upside down,**
tout bouleverser.
upstairs. 1. *adv.* En haut (de l'escalier).
To go upstairs, monter (l'escalier) ; aller en
haut. **2.** *a.* (*Of room*) D'en haut.
upstanding, *a.* Debout *inv. A fine u. fellow,*
un gaillard bien campé.
upstart, *s.* Parvenu, -ue.
uptake, *s. F :* **To be slow in the uptake,**
avoir la compréhension difficile.
upturned, *a.* (Bord) relevé ; (nez) retroussé ;
(yeux) tournés vers le ciel.
upward. 1. *a.* Upward movement, mouvement ascendant. **Prices show an upward
tendency,** les prix sont à la hausse. **2.** *adv.*
= UPWARDS.
upwards, *adv.* **1.** De bas en haut ; vers le
haut ; en montant. **2.** En dessus. *To lay
sth.* **face upwards,** mettre qch. à l'endroit.
To look upwards, regarder en haut. **3.** Au-
dessus. **Upwards of** *fifty pupils,* plus de
cinquante élèves. **From ten years of age
upwards,** à partir de dix ans.
Ural. *Pr.n.* **The Ural** (river), l'Oural *m.*
The Ural mountains, les monts Ourals.
uranium, *s. Ch :* Uranium *m.*
urban, *a.* Urbain.
urbane, *a.* Courtois, poli, civil. **-ly,** *adv.*
Courtoisement ; avec urbanité.
urbanity, *s.* Urbanité *f ;* courtoisie *f.*
urchin, *s.* (*a*) Galopin *m,* gamin, -ine ; petit(e)
polisson(ne). (*b*) Gosse *mf ;* marmot *m.*
urge¹, *s.* Incitation *f,* impulsion *f ;* poussée *f.*
To feel an urge to do sth., se sentir poussé à
faire qch.

urge², *v.tr.* **1. To urge s.o.** (on), encourager,
exciter, qn. **To urge a horse forward, on,**
pousser un cheval. **To urge s.o. to do sth.,**
pousser, exhorter, qn à faire qch. **2.** Mettre
en avant, alléguer (une raison) ; insister sur
(un point). **3.** Conseiller fortement, recommander. **To urge that sth. should be done,**
insister pour que qch. se fasse.
urgency, *s.* **1.** Urgence *f ;* extrémité *f.*
2. Besoin pressant ; nécessité urgente.
urgent, *a.* Urgent, pressant. *The matter is
u.,* l'affaire presse. *U. entreaty,* prière instante. **-ly,** *adv.* Avec urgence ; avec
instance. *A doctor is u. required,* on demande
instamment un médecin.
urn, *s.* **1.** Urne *f.* **2.** (Tea-)urn, fontaine *f*
(à thé).
us, *pers.pron., objective case.* **1.** (*a*) Nous.
There are three of us, nous sommes trois.
(*b*) (*Refl.*) *We will take the boxes with us,* nous
prendrons les boîtes avec nous. **2.** Nous.
Between you and us, entre vous et nous.
3. (*As a nominative*) *F : He would not believe
that it was us,* il ne voulait pas croire que
c'était nous. **4.** (*With sg. meaning*) *F :* **Let
us have a look,** laissez-moi regarder.
usable, *a.* Utilisable.
usage, *s.* **1.** Traitement *m.* **2.** Usage *m,*
coutume *f.* **3.** Emploi *m,* usage.
use¹, *s.* **1.** (*a*) Emploi *m,* usage *m. A new
use for wireless,* une nouvelle utilisation de la
radio. **To find a use for sth.,** trouver un
moyen de se servir de qch. **To make use of
sth.,** se servir de qch. ; tirer parti de qch.
To make good use of sth., faire bon usage de
qch. **Article of everyday use,** article d'usage
courant. **Word in everyday use,** mot très
usité. **Not in use,** hors d'usage. **Fit for use,**
en état de servir. **Ready for use,** prêt à
servir. '**Directions for use,**' "mode *m*
d'emploi." (*b*) **To improve with use,** s'améliorer à l'usage. **2.** Jouissance *f,* usage.
(*a*) **To have the full use of one's faculties,**
jouir de toutes ses facultés. *He has lost the
use of his left leg,* il est impotent de la jambe
gauche. (*b*) **To have the use of the bathroom,**
avoir le droit de faire usage de la salle de bains.
3. Utilité *f.* **Can I be of any use (to you)?**
puis-je vous être utile en rien ? *It is of no use,*
cela ne sert à rien. **To have no use for sth.,**
n'avoir que faire de qch. *It is no use his
writing to me,* il est inutile qu'il m'écrive.
What's the use of making plans? à quoi bon
faire des projets ? **4.** Usage, coutume *f,*
habitude *f.*
use², *v.tr.* **1.** (*a*) Employer, se servir de.
Are you using this knife? vous servez-vous
de ce couteau ? **To be used for sth.,** servir
à qch. ; être employé à qch. *I used the money
to rebuild my house,* j'ai utilisé l'argent à
rebâtir ma maison. *I use that as a hammer,*
cela me sert de marteau. (*b*) **To use force,**
user de force. **2. To use s.o. well,** en user
bien avec qn ; bien agir envers qn. *To use*

s.o. roughly, maltraiter qn. **3. To use** sth.
(up). (*a*) User, épuiser, qch. *It is all used up*,
il n'en reste plus. (*b*) **To use up the scraps**,
tirer parti des restes. **4.** (*As aux.*) *As children
we used to play together*, quand nous étions
petits nous jouions ensemble. *I used to do it*,
j'avais l'habitude de le faire. *Things aren't
what they used to be*, ce n'est plus comme
autrefois. **She used not to like tobacco**,
autrefois elle n'aimait pas le tabac. **used,** *a*.
1. Usagé ; (timbre-poste) oblitéré. **Used
cars**, voitures d'occasion. **Hardly used**, à
l'état de neuf. **2. To be used to** sth., être
habitué, accoutumé, à qch. **To get used to**
sth., s'habituer, s'accoutumer, à qch. *You
will get u. to it*, vous vous y ferez.
useful, *a*. Utile ; (vêtement) pratique. *This
book was very u. to me*, ce livre m'a été d'une
grande utilité. **To make oneself useful**, se
rendre utile. **-fully,** *adv.* Utilement.
usefulness, *s*. Utilité *f*.
useless, *a*. Inutile ; bon à rien ; (effort) vain.
To be useless, ne servir à rien. *U. regrets*,
regrets superflus. **-ly,** *adv.* Inutilement ;
en vain.
uselessness, *s*. Inutilité *f*.
usher¹, *s*. **1.** (*a*) (Gentleman) usher, huissier
m ; introducteur *m* (à une réception).
(*b*) Theatre usher, ouvreuse *f*. **2.** *Sch: A:*
Surveillant *m* d'études ; *F:* pion *m*.
usher², *v.tr.* **To usher** *s.o.* **into a drawing-
room**, introduire qn dans un salon. **To usher
s.o. out**, reconduire qn.
usherette, *s*. *Cin:* Ouvreuse *f*.
usual, *a*. Usuel, habituel, ordinaire. *At the
u. hour*, à l'heure accoutumée. **It is usual to
pay in advance**, il est d'usage de payer
d'avance. *It is the u. practice*, c'est la pratique
courante. **Earlier than usual**, plus tôt que
de coutume, que d'ordinaire. **As usual**,
comme à l'ordinaire. **-ally,** *adv.* Ordinairement, habituellement ; d'ordinaire. **He was
more than usually polite**, il s'est montré
encore plus poli que d'habitude.
usurer, *s*. Usurier, -ière.
usurious, *a*. **1.** Usuraire. **2.** (Banquier)
usurier.

usurp, *v.tr.* Usurper (*from*, sur). **usurping**,
a. Usurpateur, -trice.
usurpation, *s*. Usurpation *f*.
usurper, *s*. Usurpateur, -trice.
usury, *s*. Usure *f*.
utensil, *s*. (*a*) Ustensile *m*. *Set of kitchen
utensils*, batterie *f* de cuisine. (*b*) Outil *m*,
instrument *m*.
utilitarian, *a*. Utilitaire.
utility, *s*. (*a*) Utilité *f*. (*b*) **Public utility
undertaking**, entreprise *f* de service public.
(*c*) **Utility goods**, articles d'utilité sociale.
utilizable, *a*. Utilisable.
utilization, *s*. Utilisation *f* ; mise *f* en
valeur.
utilize, *v.tr.* Utiliser, se servir de : tirer parti
de, mettre en valeur.
utmost. 1. *a*. Extrême ; dernier. **The
utmost ends of the earth**, les (derniers) confins
de la terre. **It is of the utmost importance
that . . .**, il est de la dernière importance
que + sub. *With the u. ease*, avec la plus
grande facilité. **2.** *s*. Dernière limite ; dernier
degré. **To the utmost**, le plus possible ; au
suprême degré. **To do one's utmost to . . .**, faire
tout son possible pour. . . .
Utopia. *Pr.n.* L'Utopie *f*.
Utopian, *a*. Utopique ; d'utopie.
utter¹, *a*. Complet, -ète ; absolu. *He is an
utter stranger to me*, il m'est complètement
étranger. *U. fool*, sot achevé. **-ly,** *adv.*
Complètement, absolument, tout à fait.
utter², *v.tr.* **1.** (*a*) Pousser, faire entendre ;
prononcer. **Not to utter a word**, ne pas
sonner mot. (*b*) Dire ; exprimer. **2.** Émettre,
mettre en circulation (de la fausse monnaie).
utterance, *s*. **1.** Expression *f* ; émission *f*
(d'un son). **To give utterance to one's
feelings**, exprimer ses sentiments. **2.** Articulation *f*, prononciation *f*. **3.** *pl*. **Utterances**,
propos *m*, paroles *f*.
uttermost, *a. & s.* = UTMOST.
uvula, *s*. Uvule *f* ; luette *f*.
uxorious, *a*. Uxorieux ; (mari) dominé par
sa femme.

V

V, v, *s*. (La lettre) V, v, *m*. *Dressm:* **V neck**,
décolleté *m* en pointe.
vacancy, *s*. **1.** Vide *m*, vacuité *f*. **To stare
into vacancy**, regarder dans le vide, dans le
vague. **2.** Vacance *f* ; poste vacant.
vacant, *a*. **1.** Vacant, vide, libre. *V. space*,
place vide. *V. room*, chambre libre, inoccupée.
2. Vague, sans expression. **Vacant expression**, air hébété. **-ly,** *adv.* D'un regard perdu.
vacate, *v.tr.* (*a*) Quitter. **To vacate office**,

se démettre. (*b*) Quitter ; évacuer (un
appartement).
vacation, *s*. **1.** Vacances *fpl*. **The long
vacation**, les grandes vacances. **2.** Évacuation *f*.
vaccinate, *v.tr.* Vacciner.
vaccination, *s*. Vaccination *f*.
vacillate, *v.i.* Vaciller ; hésiter. **vacillating,** *a*. Vacillant, irrésolu.
vacillation, *s*. Vacillation *f*, hésitation *f*.

vacuity, s. Vacuité f, vide m.
vacuous, a. Vide de pensée, d'expression.
V. laugh, rire niais. *V. look,* air hébété.
vacuum, s. *Ph:* Vide m. **vacuum-cleaning,** s. Nettoyage m par le vide; dépoussiérage m par aspirateur. **vacuum-cleaner,** s. Aspirateur m (de poussière).
vacuum-flask, s. Bouteille isolante.
vagabond. 1. a. Vagabond, errant. **2.** s. (a) Vagabond, -onde; chemineau m. (b) F: Homme sans aveu; vaurien m.
vagabondage, s. Vagabondage m.
vagary, s. Caprice m, fantaisie f, lubie f.
vagrancy, s. (a) *Jur:* Vagabondage m; mendicité f. (b) Vie f de vagabond.
vagrant. 1. a. Vagabond, errant. **2.** s. (a) Vagabond, -onde. (b) Homme sans aveu; chemineau m.
vague, a. Vague; imprécis. **I haven't the vaguest idea,** je n'en ai pas la moindre idée.
-ly, adv. Vaguement.
vagueness, s. Vague m, imprécision f.
vain, a. Vain. **I.** Mensonger, creux. **Vain promises,** vaines promesses. **2.** Inutile, infructueux. **Vain efforts,** efforts vains. **3.** Vaniteux, glorieux. **4. In vain,** en vain. (a) Vainement. *We protested in v. . . .,* nous avons eu beau protester. *. . . To labour in v.,* travailler inutilement. (b) **To take God's name in vain,** prendre le nom de Dieu en vain.
-ly, adv. **I.** Vainement, en vain, inutilement. **2.** Vaniteusement; avec vanité.
vainglorious, a. Vaniteux, glorieux, orgueilleux. **-ly,** adv. Vaniteusement.
vainglory, s. Vaine gloire; gloriole f.
vainness, s. Vanité f.
valance, s. Frange f de lit; lambrequin m.
vale, s. *Poet:* Vallon m; val m, pl. vals.
valediction, s. Adieu(x) m(pl).
valedictory, a. D'adieu.
valerian, s. *Bot:* Valériane f.
valet, s. Valet m de chambre.
valetudinarian, a. & s. Valétudinaire (mf).
valiant, a. Vaillant, valeureux, brave.
-ly, adv. Vaillamment.
valid, a. Valide, valable. **Ticket valid for three months,** billet bon pour trois mois.
validity, s. Validité f.
valise, s. Valise f.
valley, s. Vallée f; (small) vallon m; val m, pl. vals.
valorous, a. Valeureux, vaillant.
valour, s. Valeur f, vaillance f.
valuable. 1. a. Précieux; de valeur, de prix. **2.** s.pl. Valuables, objets m de valeur, de prix.
valuation, s. **I.** (a) Évaluation f, estimation f. **At a valuation,** à dire d'expert. (b) Inventaire m. **2.** Valeur estimée. **To take s.o. at his own valuation,** estimer qn selon l'opinion qu'il a de lui-même.
value¹, s. Valeur f. **I. To be of value,** avoir de la valeur. **Of no value,** sans valeur. **To set a high value on sth.,** faire grand cas de qch. *Com:* **Increase in value,** plus-value f.

2. *Com:* **For value received,** valeur reçue. **To get good value for one's money,** F: en avoir pour son argent. *This article is very good v.,* cet article est très avantageux.
value², v.tr. **I.** Évaluer, estimer. **2.** Estimer, faire grand cas de. **To value one's life,** tenir à la vie. **valued,** a. Estimé, précieux.
valueless, a. Sans valeur.
valuer, s. Estimateur m, expert m.
valve, s. **I.** Soupape f; clapet m; *Cy:* valve f. **2.** Valvule f (du cœur). **3.** *W.Tel:* Lampe f. **Valve set,** appareil m, poste m, à lampes. **4.** *Moll:* Valve. **valve-cap,** s. Capuchon m, chapeau m (d'une valve de pneu).
valvular, a. Valvulaire.
vamp¹, v.tr. *Mus:* F: Tapoter au piano.
vamp², s. F: Aventurière f.
vamp³, v.tr. F: Ensorceler.
vampire, s. **I.** (a) *Myth:* Vampire m; strige f. (b) F: Vampire; extorqueur, -euse. **2.** *Z:* Vampire(-bat), vampire.
van¹, s. (a) Avant-garde f. (b) Front m (de bataille). *F:* **In the van,** en première ligne.
van², s. *Veh:* **I.** (a) Fourgon m. (b) Gipsy van, roulotte f. **2.** *Cin:* Recording van, camion m d'enregistrement. **3.** *Rail:* Wagon m, fourgon. **van-man,** s. Livreur m.
vandal, s. *Hist. & F:* Vandale m.
vandalism, s. Vandalisme m.
vane, s. (Weather-)vane, girouette f.
vanguard, s. *Mil:* Tête f d'avant-garde.
vanilla, s. Vanille f. **Vanilla ice,** glace à la vanille.
vanish, v.i. Disparaître; (of visions) se dissiper, s'évanouir. **vanishing,** s. Disparition f. *Toil:* **Vanishing cream,** crème f de jour.
vanity, s. **I.** Vanité f, vide m. **2.** Vanité; orgueil m. **To do sth. out of vanity,** faire qch. par vanité.
vanquish, v.tr. Vaincre.
vanquisher, s. Vainqueur m.
vantage, s. (Coign of) vantage, position avantageuse; avantage m du terrain.
vapid, a. Plat, insipide. **-ly,** adv. Insipidement.
vapidity, s. Fadeur f, insipidité f.
vaporization, s. **I.** Vaporisation f. **2.** Pulvérisation f (d'un liquide).
vaporize. I. v.tr. (a) Vaporiser. (b) Pulvériser (un liquide); vaporiser. **2.** v.i. Se vaporiser.
vaporizer, s. (a) Vaporis(at)eur m. (b) Pulvérisateur m; atomiseur m.
vaporous, a. Vaporeux
vapour¹, s. Vapeur f.
vapour², v.i. F: Débiter des fadaises.
vapouring, s. F: Platitudes fpl.
variability, s. Variabilité f.
variable, a. Variable; changeant.
variance, s. Désaccord m; discorde f. **To be at variance with s.o.,** être en désaccord avec qn. **To set two people at variance,** mettre la discorde entre deux personnes.

variant. 1. *a. Lit*: Variant reading, variante *f*. **2.** *s*. Variante *f*.

variation, *s*. **1.** Variation *f*, changement *m*. **2.** Différence *f*; écart *m*.

varicose, *a. Med*: Variqueux. **Varicose vein,** varice *f*.

variegate, *v.tr.* **1.** Varier, diversifier. **2.** Bigarrer, barioler. **variegated,** *a*. **1.** Varié; divers. **2.** Bigarré, bariolé.

variegation, *s*. Diversité *f* de couleurs; bigarrure *f*.

variety, *s*. **1.** *(a)* Variété *f*, diversité *f*. To lend variety, donner de la variété. *(b)* A variety of patterns, un assortiment d'échantillons. **2.** *(a) Nat.Hist*: Variété. *(b) Th*: **Variety entertainment,** attractions *f*.

various, *a*. **1.** Varié, divers. Of various kinds, de diverses sortes. **2.** *(a)* Différent, dissemblable; divers. *(b)* Plusieurs; plus d'un. **For various reasons,** pour plusieurs raisons. **At various times,** à différentes reprises. **-ly,** *adv*. Diversement; de diverses manières.

varlet, *s*. **1.** *Hist*: Varlet *m*, page *m*. **2.** *F*: Coquin *m*; vaurien *m*.

varnish¹, *s*. **1.** Vernis *m*. *Toil*: **Nail varnish,** vernis pour les ongles. **2.** (Enduit *m* de) vernis; vernissure *f*.

varnish², *v.tr.* **1.** Vernir; vernisser (la poterie). **2.** *F*: To varnish (over), farder (les faits). **varnishing,** *s*. Vernissage *m*.

vary. 1. *v.tr.* Varier, diversifier; faire varier. To v. one's methods, varier de méthode. **2.** *v.i.* *(a)* Varier, changer; être variable. *(b)* Différer (d'avis). **varied,** *a*. Varié; divers. **varying,** *a*. Variable, changeant; varié, divers.

vase, *s*. Vase *m*.

Vaseline, *s*. (Registered trade mark) Vaseline *f*.

vassal, *a. & s*. Vassal (*m*), -aux; feudataire (*m*) (*to*, de).

vassalage, *s*. *(a)* Vasselage *m*. *(b) F*: Sujétion *f*.

vast, *a*. Vaste, immense. **-ly,** *adv*. Vastement; immensément.

vastness, *s*. Vastitude *f*, immensité *f*.

vat, *s*. Cuve *f*; bac *m*; bain *m*.

Vatican, *s*. The Vatican, le Vatican.

vaudeville, *s*. *Th*: Vaudeville *m*.

vault¹, *s*. **1.** Voûte *f*. *F*: **The vault of heaven,** le dôme des cieux. **2.** *(a)* Souterrain *m*. **Safety vault,** chambre forte. *(b)* **Family vault,** caveau *m* de famille.

vault², *v.tr.* Voûter. **vaulted,** *a*. Voûté; ·en voûte.

vault³. 1. *v.i.* *(a)* To vault over a gate, sauter une barrière. To v. over a stream, sauter un ruisseau à la perche. *(b)* **To vault into the saddle,** sauter en selle. **2.** *v.tr.* Sauter. **vaulting,** *a. Lit*: **Vaulting ambition,** ambition qui vise trop haut.

vaunt¹, *s. Lit*: Vanterie *f*; fanfaronnade *f*.

vaunt², *v.tr. Lit*: *(a)* Vanter. *(b)* Se vanter de; se faire gloire de. **vaunting¹,** *a*. Vantard. **vaunting²,** *s*. Vanterie *f*; jactance *f*.

veal, *s*. *Cu*: Veau *m*.

veer. 1. *v.i.* *(a)* Tourner, sauter. *(b)* Virer; changer de bord. *(c) F*: **To veer round,** changer d'opinion. **2.** *v.tr.* (Faire) virer (un navire) vent arrière.

vegetable. 1. *a*. Végétal, -aux. **2.** *s*. *(a) Bot*: Végétal *m*, -aux. *(b)* Légume *m*. **Early vegetables,** primeurs *f*. **Vegetable garden,** (jardin) potager *m*. **vegetable-dish,** *s*. Légumier *m*.

vegetarian, *a. & s*. Végétarien, -ienne.

vegetarianism, *s*. Végétarisme *m*.

vegetate, *v.i.* Végéter.

vegetation, *s*. Végétation *f*.

vehemence, *s*. Véhémence *f*.

vehement, *a*. Véhément. **-ly,** *adv*. Véhémentement.

vehicle, *s*. **1.** Véhicule *m*, voiture *f*. **2.** Véhicule; moyen *m*.

vehicular, *a*. **Vehicular traffic,** circulation *f* des voitures.

veil¹, *s*. **1.** *(a)* Voile *m*. *Ecc*: **To take the veil,** prendre le voile. *(b)* (Hat-)veil, voilette *f*. **2.** *F*: **To draw a veil over sth.,** jeter un voile sur qch.

veil², *v.tr.* **1.** Voiler. **2.** Voiler, dissimuler.

veiled, *a*. **1.** Voilé; couvert d'un voile. **2.** Voilé, dissimulé. *Hardly v. hostility*, hostilité à peine déguisée.

vein, *s*. **1.** *Anat*: Veine *f*. **2.** Nervure *f* (de feuille). **3.** *Min*: Veine, filon *m*. **4.** *(In marble)* Veine. **5.** Veine, disposition *f*, humeur *f* To be in the vein for doing sth., être en veine de faire qch.

veined, *a*. **1.** Veiné; à veines. **2.** *Bot*: *Ent*: Nervuré.

veld(t), *s*. Veld(t) *m*.

vellum, *s*. Vélin *m*.

velocity, *s*. Vitesse *f*.

velour(s), *s*. **1.** *Tex*: Velouté *m*; velours *m* de laine. **2. Velours hat,** chapeau taupé.

velvet, *s*. **1.** *Tex*: Velours *m*. *F*: **To be on velvet,** être sur le velours. **2.** *Attrib*. *V. coat*, habit de velours.

velveteen, *s*. *Tex*: Velours *m* lisse de coton.

velvety, *a*. Velouté.

venal, *a*. Vénal, -aux; mercenaire. **-ally,** *adv*. Vénalement.

venality, *s*. Vénalité *f*.

vend, *v.tr.* Vendre.

vendetta, *s*. Vendetta *f*.

vendor, *s*. Vendeur, -euse.

veneer¹, *s*. **1.** *(a)* Placage *m*, revêtement *m*. *(b)* Bois *m* de placage. **2.** *F*: Masque *m*; apparence extérieure. *A mere v. of politeness*, une politesse toute en surface.

veneer², *v.tr.* Plaquer.

venerable, *a*. Vénérable.

venerate, *v.tr.* Vénérer.

veneration, *s*. Vénération *f* (*for*, pour). To hold s.o. in veneration, avoir de la vénération pour qn.

Venetian, *a. & s. Geog*: Vénitien, -ienne. **Venetian lace,** point *m* de Venise.

vengeance, *s.* Vengeance *f.* **To take vengeance on s.o.,** se venger sur qn ; se venger de qn. *F:* **With a vengeance,** furieusement ; pour de bon. *It is raining with a v.,* voilà qui s'appelle pleuvoir.

vengeful, *a.* Vindicatif.

venial, *a.* Léger, pardonnable, véniel.

Venice. *Pr.n.* Venise *f.*

venison, *s.* Venaison *f.* **Haunch of venison,** quartier *m* de chevreuil.

venom, *s.* Venin *m.*

venomous, *a.* **1.** Venimeux. **2.** *F:* Venomous tongue, langue de vipère. **-ly,** *adv.* D'une manière venimeuse ; méchamment.

venomousness, *s.* **1.** Nature venimeuse. **2.** Méchanceté *f.*

venous, *a.* Veineux.

vent[1], *s.* **1.** (*a*) Trou *m,* orifice *m* ; évent *m.* (*b*) Lumière *f* (d'une arme à feu). **2.** **To give vent to one's anger,** donner libre cours à sa colère.

vent[2], *v.tr.* **To vent one's anger on s.o.,** décharger sa colère sur qn.

ventilate, *v.tr.* **1.** Aérer (une chambre) ; ventiler (un tunnel). **2.** *F:* Agiter (une question) (au grand jour).

ventilation, *s.* **1.** Aération *f,* aérage *m,* ventilation *f.* **2.** Mise *f* en discussion publique.

ventilator, *s.* **1.** Ventilateur *m* ; soupirail *m,* -aux (d'une cave). **2.** (*Over door*) Vasistas *m.*

ventriloquial, *a.* Ventriloque, de ventriloque.

ventriloquism, *s.* Ventriloquie *f.*

ventriloquist, *s.* Ventriloque *mf.*

venture[1], *s.* **1.** Entreprise risquée. **2.** *Com:* Entreprise, spéculation *f.* **3.** **At a venture,** à l'aventure, au hasard. **To answer at a venture,** répondre au petit bonheur.

venture[2]. **1.** *v.tr.* (*a*) **To venture to do sth.,** oser faire qch. *I v. to write to you,* je me permets de vous écrire. (*b*) **To venture a guess,** hasarder une conjecture. (*c*) Hasarder, aventurer, risquer. **2.** *v.i.* (*a*) **To venture upon sth.,** se risquer à faire qch. *To v. on an opinion,* hasarder une opinion. (*b*) **To venture into an unknown country,** s'aventurer dans un pays inconnu. *To v. out of doors,* se risquer à sortir.

venturesome, *a.* **1.** Aventureux, osé. **2.** Aventuré, risqué.

venturesomeness, *s.* Esprit aventureux.

Venus. *Pr.n.* Vénus *f.*

veracious, *a.* Véridique. **-ly,** *adv.* Véridiquement ; avec véracité.

veraciousness, veracity, *s.* Véracité *f.*

veranda, *s.* Véranda *f.*

verb, *s.* *Gram:* Verbe *m.*

verbal, *a.* (*a*) Verbal, -aux ; oral, -aux. (*b*) *V. dispute,* dispute de mots. **-ally,** *adv.* Verbalement ; de vive voix.

verbatim. **1.** *adv.* Mot pour mot ; textuellement. **2.** *a.* **Verbatim report,** sténogramme *m.*

verbena, *s.* Verveine *f.*

verbiage, *s.* Verbiage *m.*

verbose, *a.* Verbeux, diffus, prolixe. **-ly,** *adv.* Avec verbosité.

verbosity, *s.* Verbosité *f,* prolixité *f.*

verdant, *a.* **1.** Vert, verdoyant. **2.** Inexpérimenté, naïf.

verdict, *s.* **1.** *Jur:* Verdict *m* ; réponse *f* du jury. **To return a verdict,** prononcer un verdict. **2.** Jugement *m,* décision *f*

verdigris, *s.* Vert-de-gris *m.*

verdure, *s.* Verdure *f.*

Verey. *Pr.n.* **Verey light,** étoile éclairante. **Verey pistol,** pistolet *m* à fusée.

verge[1], *s.* (*a*) Bord *m* (d'un fleuve) ; orée *f* (d'une forêt). (*b*) *He is on the v. of ruin,* il est sur le penchant de la ruine. **On the verge of war,** à la veille de la guerre.

verge[2], *v.i.* (*a*) **To verge on sth.,** toucher à, être contigu, -uë, à, qch. (*b*) *That verges on disingenuousness,* cela frise la mauvaise foi.

verger, *s.* *Ecc:* Porte-verge *m inv* ; bedeau *m.*

verification, *s.* Vérification *f,* contrôle *m.*

verify, *v.tr.* **1.** Confirmer. **2.** Vérifier, contrôler (des comptes).

verisimilitude, *s.* Vraisemblance *f.*

veritable, *a.* Véritable. **-ably,** *adv.* Véritablement.

verity, *s.* *Lit:* Vérité *f.*

vermicelli, *s.* Vermicelle *m.*

vermilion. **1.** *s.* Vermillon *m,* cinabre *m.* **2.** *a.* (De) vermillon ; vermeil.

vermin, *s.* **1.** Vermine *f.* **2.** Bêtes puantes.

verm(o)uth, *s.* Vermout(h) *m.*

vernacular. *Ling:* **1.** *a.* Vernaculaire ; indigène. **2.** *s.* (*a*) Vernaculaire *m* ; idiome national. (*b*) La langue vulgaire.

vernal, *a.* Printanier. *Astr:* Vernal, -aux.

veronica, *s.* Véronique *f.*

versatile, *a.* **1.** (*a*) Aux talents variés. (*b*) *V. mind,* esprit souple. **2.** Pivotant ; capable de tourner.

versatility, *s.* Souplesse *f,* universalité *f.*

verse, *s.* **1.** Vers *m.* **2.** (*Of song*) Couplet *m* ; (*of poem*) strophe *f.* **3.** *Coll:* Vers *mpl.* **Light verse,** poésie légère. **4.** *Ecc:* Verset *m.*

versed, *a.* Versé (in, en, dans).

versification, *s.* Versification *f.*

versify, *v.tr. & i.* Versifier ; mettre en vers.

version, *s.* **1.** Version *f,* traduction *f.* **2.** Version ; interprétation *f.* *According to his v.,* d'après lui.

versus, *Lt.prep.* Contre.

vertebra, *s.* Vertèbre *f.*

vertebral, *a.* Vertébral, -aux.

vertebrate, *a. & s.* Vertébré (*m*).

vertex, *s.* Sommet *m.*

vertical. **1.** *a.* Vertical, -aux. *V. cliff,* falaise à pic. **2.** *s.* Verticale *f.* **-ally,** *adv.* Verticalement ; d'aplomb.

vertigo, *s.* *Med:* Vertige *m.*

vervain, *s.* *Bot:* Verveine *f.*

verve, *s.* Verve *f.*

very. **I.** *a.* **1.** Vrai, véritable. **The veriest fool knows that,** le plus parfait nigaud sait cela.

2. (*a*) Même. *You are the v. man I wanted to see*, vous êtes justement l'homme que je voulais voir. *X is the very man*, X est tout indiqué. *At that very moment*, à cet instant même. *To the very day*, jour pour jour. *These are his v. words*, ce sont là ses propres paroles. (*b*) *At the very beginning*, tout au commencement. *He knows our v. thoughts*, il connaît jusqu'à nos pensées. (*c*) *The very thought frightens me*, la seule pensée m'effraie. II. **very,** *adv* **1.** Très; fort, bien. *Very good*, (i) très bon, fort bon; (ii) très bien, fort bien. *You are not very polite*, vous êtes peu poli. *Not v. well pleased*, médiocrement satisfait. *That's very nice of you*, c'est bien gentil de votre part. *It isn't so very difficult*, ce n'est pas tellement difficile. *I was very much surprised*, j'en ai été très surpris. I feel very much better, je me sens beaucoup mieux. **2.** *The very first*, le tout premier. *The very best*, le meilleur de tous. *The v. next day*, dès le lendemain. *At the very most*, tout au plus. *At the very latest*, au plus tard. *The very same*, absolument le même.

vesper. 1. *s. Poet:* Le soir. **2.** *s.pl.* Vespers, vêpres *f*.

vessel, *s.* **1.** Vaisseau *m*, vase *m*, récipient *m*. **2.** Vaisseau, navire *m*, bâtiment *m*. **3.** *Anat:* Vaisseau.

vest[1], *s.* **1.** Gilet *m*. **2.** (Under)vest, gilet de dessous. **vest-pocket,** *s.* Poche *f* du gilet.

vest[2]. 1. *v.tr.* (*a*) *To vest s.o. with authority*, investir qn de l'autorité. (*b*) *Authority vested in the people*, autorité exercée par le peuple. (*c*) Vêtir, revêtir (un dignitaire). **2.** *v.i. To vest in s.o.*, échoir à qn. **vested,** *a.* Dévolu. *Vested interests*, droits acquis.

Vesta. 1. *Pr.n. Rom.Myth:* Vesta *f*. **2.** *s.* (Wax) vesta, allumette-bougie *f*, *pl*. allumettes-bougies.

vestal, *a. & s.* Vestal (virgin), vestale *f*.

vestibule, *s.* Vestibule *m*, antichambre *f*.

vestige, *s.* Vestige *m*, trace *f*. *F: Not a vestige of*, pas la moindre trace de.

vestment, *s.* Vêtement *m* (de cérémonie). *Ecc:* Chasuble *f*. **(Priestly) vestments**, vêtements sacerdotaux.

vestry, *s. Ecc:* Sacristie *f*.

Vesuvius. *Pr.n.* Le Vésuve.

vet, *v.tr. F:* (*a*) Examiner (une bête). (*b*) Examiner médicalement.

veteran. 1. *s.* Vétéran *m*. **2.** *a.* De(s) vétéran(s); aguerri. *A veteran golfer*, un vétéran du golf.

veterinary, *a.* Vétérinaire. *Veterinary surgeon*, *s.* veterinary, vétérinaire *m*.

veto[1], *s.* Veto *m*. *To put a veto on sth.*, mettre le veto à qch. *To have the right of veto*, avoir le veto.

veto[2], *v.tr.* Mettre son veto à; interdire.

vex, *v.tr.* **1.** Vexer, fâcher, chagriner. **2.** *Lit:* Troubler, agiter. **vexed,** *a.* **1.** Vexé, contrarié, chagrin. *To be vexed at sth.*, être vexé de qch. *To be vexed with s.o.*, être fâché contre qn. *To be vexed with oneself*, s'en vouloir. **2.** *Vexed question*, question très débattue, non résolue. **vexing,** *a.* Vexant, chagrinant.

vexation, *s.* **1.** Vexation *f*, tourment *m*. **2.** (*a*) Contrariété *f*, ennui *m*. (*b*) Chagrin *m*, dépit *m*.

vexatious, *a.* Fâcheux, ennuyeux, contrariant. **-ly,** *adv.* **1.** D'une manière contrariante. **2.** A seule fin de contrarier.

via, *prep.* Via; par la voie de; par.

viaduct, *s.* Viaduc *m*.

vial, *s.* Fiole *f*. *F: To pour out the vials of one's wrath*, lâcher la bonde à sa colère.

viand, *s. Lit:* Mets *m*. *Usu. pl.* **Viands,** aliments *m*.

vibrant, *a.* Vibrant.

vibrate. 1. *v.i.* Vibrer; trépider. **2.** *v.tr.* Faire vibrer. **vibrating,** *a.* Vibrant. *Voice vibrating with emotion*, voix vibrante d'émotion.

vibration, *s.* **1.** Vibration *f*; oscillation *f*. **2.** *Mch:* Trépidation *f*.

vibratory, *a.* Vibratoire.

viburnum, *s. Bot:* Viorne *f*.

vicar, *s.* Curé *m*.

vicarage, *s.* Presbytère *m*; cure *f*.

vicarious, *a.* **1.** Délégué. **2.** (*a*) (Châtiment) souffert (i) par un autre, (ii) pour un autre. (*b*) De substitution. **-ly,** *adv.* **1.** Par substitution. **2.** A la place d'un autre.

vice[1], *s.* **1.** Vice *m*. **2.** Défaut *m*.

vice[2], *s. Tls:* Étau *m*.

vice[3], *prep.* A la place de.

In the following compounds of *vice* the noun alone varies in the plural in both English and French:

vice-admiral, *s.* Vice-amiral, -aux *m*.

vice-chairman, *s.* Vice-président *m*.

vice-chairmanship, *s.* Vice-présidence *f*.

vice-chancellor, *s.* **1.** Vice-chancelier *m*. **2.** Recteur *m* (d'une université).

vice-chancellorship, *s.* **1.** Fonction *f*, dignité *f*, de vice-chancelier. **2.** Rectorat *m*.

vice-consul, *s.* Vice-consul *m*.

vice marshal, *s. Mil.Av:* Air vice marshal, général *m*, -aux, de division aérienne.

vice-presidency, *s.* Vice-présidence *f*.

vice-president, *s.* Vice-président *m*.

viceregal, *a.* Du vice-roi.

viceroy, *s.* Vice-roi *m*.

vice versa, *Lt.adv.phr.* Vice versa; réciproquement.

vicinity, *s.* **1.** Voisinage *m*, proximité *f* (*to*, *with*, de). **2.** Abords *mpl*, alentours *mpl*. *In the vicinity of*, à proximité de.

vicious, *a.* **1.** Vicieux. **2.** (i) *V. criticism*, critique méchante. (ii) *To give a vicious tug at the bell*, tirer rageusement la sonnette. **-ly,** *adv.* **1.** Vicieusement. **2.** Méchamment; rageusement.

viciousness, *s.* **1.** Nature vicieuse; vice *m*. **2.** Méchanceté *f*.

vicissitude, *s.* Vicissitude *f. The vicissitudes of fortune,* les retours *m* de la fortune.

victim, *s* Victime *f.* **Victim of an accident,** accidenté, -ée. *To fall a v. to s.o.'s charm,* succomber au charme de qn. *F:* **To make a victim of oneself,** se poser en victime.

victimization, *s.* Oppression *f,* tyrannisation *f.*

victimize, *v.tr.* **1.** Prendre comme victime. **2.** Tromper, escroquer.

victor, *s.* Vainqueur *m.*

Victoria. *Pr.n.* Victoire *f.* **Victoria Cross,** *s.* Croix *f* de Victoria.

Victorian, *a. & s.* Victorien, -ienne.

victorious, *a.* Victorieux; vainqueur *m.* **To be victorious over s.o.,** être victorieux de qn. **-ly,** *adv.* Victorieusement; en vainqueur.

victory, *s.* Victoire *f.* **To gain the victory,** remporter la victoire (*over,* sur).

victual, *v.* **1.** *v.tr.* Approvisionner; ravitailler. **2.** *v.i.* Se ravitailler. **victualling,** *s.* Approvisionnement *m,* ravitaillement *m.*

victualler, *s.* (*a*) Pourvoyeur *m*; fournisseur *m* de vivres. (*b*) **Licensed victualler,** (hôtelier) débitant *m* de boissons.

victuals, *s.pl.* (*a*) Vivres *m,* provisions *f.* (*b*) Victuailles *f.*

videlicet, *adv.* A savoir; c'est-à-dire.

vie, *v.i.* Le disputer (*with s.o.,* à qn); rivaliser (*with s.o.,* avec qn).

view[1], *s.* Vue *f.* **1.** Regard *m*; coup *m* d'œil. **On view,** exposé; ouvert au public **2.** (*a*) **Exposed to view,** exposé aux regards. **In view, en vue.** (*b*) **Field of view** (*of telescope*), champ *m.* **3.** (*a*) Vue, perspective *f.* **Front view of the hotel,** l'hôtel vu de face. *You will get a better v. from here,* vous verrez mieux d'ici. **Point of view,** point *m* de vue. (*b*) *Arch:* **Front view,** élévation *f* du devant. (*c*) **To keep sth. in view,** ne pas perdre qch. de vue. **4.** *To offer a general v. of the subject,* donner un aperçu général de la question. **5.** Manière *f* de voir; opinion *f.* **To take a right view of things,** voir juste. **To hold extreme views,** avoir des idées extrémistes. **In my view,** à mon avis *m.* **To share s.o.'s views,** partager les sentiments *m* de qn. **6.** **In view of,** en considération de; eu égard à. *In v. of the distance,* vu l'éloignement. **7.** Vue, intention *f.* **To fall in with s.o.'s views,** entrer dans les vues de qn. *Will this meet your views?* cela vous conviendra-t-il? **To have sth. in view,** avoir qch. en vue; méditer. **Negotiations with a view to an alliance,** négociations visant une alliance. **view-finder,** *s. Phot:* Viseur *m*; iconoscope *m.* **view-point,** *s.* Point *m* de vue; (*of beauty-spot*) belvédère *m.*

view[2], *v.tr.* **1.** Regarder; examiner; visiter. **2.** Envisager. **3.** Voir, apercevoir.

vigil, *s.* Veille *f.* **To keep vigil,** veiller.

vigilance, *s.* Vigilance *f.*

vigilant, *a.* Vigilant, éveillé, alerte. **-ly,** *adv.* Avec vigilance

vignette, *s.* Vignette *f.*

vigorous, *a.* Vigoureux, robuste. **Vigorous blow,** coup de poing solide. **-ly,** *adv.* Vigoureusement.

vigour, *s.* **1.** Vigueur *f,* énergie *f.* **2.** *Mus:* Brio *m.*

vile, *a.* **1.** Vil; sans valeur. **2.** Vil; bas, *f.* basse, infâme. **3.** *F:* Abominable, exécrable. **Vile weather,** un sale temps. **-ly,** *adv.* **1.** Vilement; bassement. **2.** D'une manière abominable.

vileness, *s.* **1.** Bassesse *f,* caractère *m* ignoble. **2.** *F: The v. of the weather,* le temps abominable.

vilification, *s.* Dénigrement *m.*

vilify, *v.tr.* Vilipender, diffamer.

villa, *s.* Villa *f.*

village, *s.* Village *m.* **Village inn,** auberge *f* de campagne.

villager, *s.* Villageois, -oise.

villain, *s.* (*a*) Scélérat *m*; bandit *m,* gredin *m. F: You little v.!* petit coquin! (*b*) *Th:* **The villain (of the piece),** le traître.

villainous, *a.* **1.** Vil, infâme. *V. deed,* action scélérate. *V. face,* vilain visage. **2.** *F:* = VILE 3. **-ly,** *adv.* **1.** D'une manière infâme. **2.** *F:* D'une manière exécrable.

villainy, *s.* **1.** Scélératesse *f,* infamie *f.* **2.** Action scélérate; infamie.

vim, *s. F:* Vigueur *f,* énergie *f.*

vindicate, *v.tr.* **1.** Défendre, soutenir; justifier. *To v. one's character,* se justifier. **2.** **To vindicate one's rights,** revendiquer ses droits.

vindication, *s.* **1.** Défense *f,* apologie *f.* **In vindication of his conduct,** pour justifier sa conduite. **2.** Revendication *f.*

vindictive, *a.* **1.** Vindicatif; vengeur, -eresse. **2.** Vindicatif, rancunier. **-ly,** *adv.* Vindicativement.

vindictiveness, *s.* Esprit *m* de vengeance; esprit rancunier.

vine, *s.* (Grape-)vine, vigne *f.* **vine-arbour,** *s.* Treille *f.* **vine-grower,** *s.* Viticulteur *m*; vigneron *m.* **vine-growing,** *s.* Viticulture *f.* **vine-plant,** *s.* Cep *m* de vigne.

vinegar, *s.* Vinaigre *m.* **vinegar-cruet,** *s.* Burette *f* à vinaigre. **vinegar-faced,** *a. F:* Au visage revêche.

vinegary, *a. F:* (Visage) revêche; (ton) acerbe.

vineyard, *s.* Clos *m* de vigne; vigne *f,* vignoble *m. The best vineyards,* les meilleurs crus.

vintage, *s.* **1.** (*a*) Récolte *f* du raisin; vendanges *fpl.* (*b*) (*Crop*) Vendange. **2.** Année *f* (de belle récolte). **Vintage wine,** vin de marque; grand vin.

vintager, *s.* Vendangeur, -euse.

vintner, *s.* Négociant *m* en vins.

viola[1], *s. Mus:* Alto *m.* **Viola player,** altiste *mf.*

viola[2], *s. Bot:* Pensée *f* (unicolore).

violate, *v.tr.* Violer; manquer à (une règle).

violation, *s.* Violation *f.* *V. of an order,* infraction *f* à un ordre.

violence, *s.* **I.** (*a*) Violence *f,* intensité *f.* (*b*) *To do v. to one's conscience,* violenter sa conscience. *To do v. to one's feelings,* se faire violence. **2.** *Jur:* **To resort to violence,** se livrer à des voies de fait. **Robbery with violence,** vol *m* à main armée.

violent, *a.* **I.** Violent. **To lay violent hands on s.o.,** attaquer brutalement qn. **2.** Violent, aigu, -uë, fort. *V. dislike,* vive aversion. *In a v. hurry,* extrêmement pressé. **Violent cold,** gros rhume. **-ly,** *adv.* **I.** Violemment; avec violence. **2.** Vivement; extrêmement.

violet. I. *s. Bot:* Violette *f.* **2.** (*a*) *s.* Violet *m.* (*b*) *a.* Violet, -ette. **violet-coloured,** *a.* Violet, -ette ; de couleur violette.

violin, *s.* Violon *m.*

violinist, *s.* Violoniste *mf.*

violoncellist, *s.* Violoncelliste *mf.*

violoncello, *s.* Violoncelle *m.*

viper, *s.* Vipère *f.*

viperish, *a.* *F:* **Viperish tongue,** langue de vipère.

virago, *s.* Mégère *f.*

virgin. I. *s.* Vierge *f.* **2.** *a.* (*a*) De vierge ; virginal, -aux. (*b*) **Virgin forest,** forêt vierge.

virginal, *a.* Virginal, -aux.

Virginia. I. *Pr.n.* Virginie *f.* *Bot:* **Virginia creeper,** vigne *f* vierge. **2.** *s.* Tabac *m* de Virginie ; virginie *m.*

virginity, *s.* Virginité *f.*

virile, *a.* Viril, mâle.

virility, *s.* Virilité *f.*

virtu, *s.* **Articles of virtu,** objets *m* d'art.

virtual, *a.* De fait ; en fait. *This was a v. admission of guilt,* de fait, c'était un aveu. **-ally,** *adv.* Virtuellement ; de fait ; en pratique.

virtue, *s.* **I.** Vertu *f.* **To make a virtue of necessity,** faire de nécessité vertu. **2.** Qualité *f* ; avantage *m.* **3.** **Plants that have healing virtues,** plantes qui ont des propriétés curatives. **4.** *Prep.phr.* **By virtue of,** en vertu de. *By v. of one's office,* à titre d'office.

virtuosity, *s.* Virtuosité *f.*

virtuoso, *s.* **I.** Amateur *m* des arts ; connaisseur *m.* **2.** *Mus:* Virtuose *mf.*

virtuous, *a.* Vertueux. **-ly,** *adv.* Vertueusement.

virulence, *s.* Virulence *f.*

virulent, *a.* Virulent. **-ly,** *adv.* Avec virulence.

virus, *s.* **I.** *Med:* Virus *m.* **2.** *F:* Venin *m.*

visa¹, *a.* *Adm:* Visa *m.*

visa², *v.tr.* Viser ; apposer un visa à.

visage, *s.* Visage *m,* figure *f.*

viscid, *a.* Visqueux.

viscidity, *s.* Viscidité *f,* viscosité *f.*

viscosity, *s.* Viscosité *f.*

viscount, *s.* Vicomte *m.*

viscountess, *s.* Vicomtesse *f.*

viscounty, *s.* Vicomté *f.*

26

viscous, *a.* Visqueux ; gluant.

visibility, *s.* Visibilité *f.*

visible, *a.* Visible. *To become v.,* apparaître. **-ibly,** *adv.* Visiblement, manifestement ; à vue d'œil.

vision, *s.* **I.** (*a*) Vision *f,* vue *f.* **Field of vision,** champ visuel. (*b*) **Man of vision,** homme d'une grande pénétration. **2.** (*a*) Imagination *f,* vision. *Visions of wealth,* visions de richesses. (*b*) Apparition *f,* fantôme *m.*

visionary. I. *a.* (*a*) Visionnaire. (*b*) (Projet) chimérique, fantastique. **2.** *s.* Visionnaire *mf* ; idéologue *m.*

visit¹, *s.* **I.** (Social) visit, visite *f.* **2.** Visite, séjour *m.* **To be on a visit to friends,** être en visite chez des amis. **3.** Tournée *f* d'inspection ; visite d'inspection.

visit², *v.tr.* **I.** (*a*) Rendre visite à ; aller voir. (*b*) Visiter, aller voir. *We visited the museums,* nous avons vu les musées. **2.** Visiter, inspecter. **visiting¹,** *a.* En visite. *Sp:* **Visiting team,** les visiteurs *m.* **visiting²,** *s.* Visites *fpl.* **Visiting hours,** heures de visite. **visiting-card,** *s.* Carte *f* de visite.

visitation, *s.* **I.** (*a*) *F:* Visite fâcheuse. (*b*) Calamité *f.* **2.** Apparition (surnaturelle).

visitor, *s.* (*a*) Visiteur, -euse. *She has visitors,* elle a du monde. (*b*) **Summer visitors,** estivants *m.* **Visitors' book,** livre *m* des voyageurs ; registre *m* des visiteurs.

visor, *s.* *Archeol:* Visière *f.*

vista, *s.* **I.** Échappée *f* de vue ; (*in forest*) percée *f,* éclaircie *f.* **2.** *F:* **To open up new vistas,** ouvrir de nouvelles perspectives.

visual, *a.* Visuel ; perceptible à l'œil.

visualize, *v.tr.* Se représenter ; évoquer l'image de.

vital. I. *a.* **I.** Vital, -aux ; essentiel à la vie. **2.** Essentiel ; capital, -aux. **-ally,** *adv.* D'une manière vitale. **II. vitals,** *s.pl.* Parties vitales.

vitality, *s.* **I.** Vitalité *f.* (d'une race). **2.** Vie *f,* animation *f* (de style).

vitalize, *v.tr.* Vitaliser, vivifier.

vitamin, *s.* *Bio-Ch:* Vitamine *f.*

vitiate, *v.tr.* Vicier, corrompre.

vitiation, *s.* Viciation *f.*

vitreous, *a.* Vitreux.

vitriol, *s.* Vitriol *m.*

vituperate, *v.tr.* Injurier, vilipender.

vituperation, *s.* Injures *fpl,* invectives *fpl.*

vituperative, *a.* Injurieux.

Vitus. *Pr.n.* *Med:* **Saint Vitus's dance,** danse *f* de Saint-Guy.

vivacious, *a.* Vif, animé, enjoué. **-ly,** *adv.* Avec enjouement ; avec verve.

vivacity, *s.* Vivacité *f* ; animation *f.*

viva voce. I. *adv.* De vive voix ; oralement. **2.** *a.* Oral, -aux. **3.** *s.* *Sch :* Examen oral.

vivid, *a.* **I.** Vif, éclatant. **2.** *V. imagination,* imagination vive. **Vivid description,** description vivante. **-ly,** *adv.* Vivement ; avec éclat.

vividness, *s.* Vivacité *f,* éclat *m.*

vivify, *v.tr.* Vivifier, animer.
viviparous, *a.* Vivipare.
vivisect, *v.tr.* Pratiquer des vivisections sur. *Abs.* Faire de la vivisection.
vivisection, *s.* Vivisection *f.*
vixen, *s.* **1.** *Z:* Renarde *f.* **2.** *F:* Mégère *f.*
vixenish, *a.* Acariâtre, méchante.
viz., *adv.* — VIDELICET.
vizier, *s.* Vizir *m.*
vocabulary, *s.* Vocabulaire *m.*
vocal, *a.* **1.** Vocal, -aux. **2.** Doué de voix; capable de produire des sons. **-ally,** *adv.* **1.** Vocalement, oralement. **2.** Par des chants; à l'aide du chant.
vocalist, *s.* Chanteur *m*, cantatrice *f.*
vocation, *s.* **1.** (*a*) Vocation *f.* (*b*) A vocation for literature, la vocation des lettres. **2.** Vocation, profession *f.*
vocative, *a. & s. Gram:* Vocatif (*m*).
vociferate, *v.i. & tr.* Vociférer, crier (*against*, contre).
vociferation, *s.* **1.** Cri *m*, clameur *f.* **2.** Vociférations *fpl*, cris, clameurs.
vociferous, *a.* Vociférant, bruyant. **-ly,** *adv.* En vociférant; bruyamment.
vogue, *s.* Vogue *f*, mode *f.*
voice¹, *s.* **1.** Voix *f.* **1.** To raise one's voice, hausser la voix. In a low voice, à voix basse; à demi-voix. He likes to hear his own voice, il aime à s'entendre parler. **2.** (*a*) Voice, suffrage *m.* (*b*) We have no voice in the matter, nous n'avons pas voix au chapitre. **3.** *Gram:* Voix.
voice², *v.tr.* Exprimer, énoncer.
voiceless, *a.* Sans voix; muet.
void. **I.** *a.* **1.** Vide. **2.** (*Of office*) Vacant, inoccupé. **3.** *Jur:* Nul, *f.* nulle. **4.** Dépourvu, dénué (*of*, de). *Proposal v. of reason,* proposition dénuée de raison. **II. void,** *s.* Vide *m. F:* To have an aching void, avoir l'estomac creux.
voile, *s. Tex:* Voile *m.*
volatile, *a.* **1.** *Ch:* Volatil. **2.** (*a*) Vif, gai. (*b*) Volage, inconstant.
volatilize. **1.** *v.tr.* Volatiliser. **2.** *v.i.* Se volatiliser.
volcanic, *a.* Volcanique.
volcano, *s.* Volcan *m.*
volition, *s.* Volition *f.* To do sth. of one's own volition, faire qch. de son propre gré.
volley¹, *s.* **1.** Volée *f*, salve *f*; grêle *f* (de pierres). **2.** *F:* Volée, bordée *f* (d'injures). **3.** *Ten:* (Balle prise de) volée.
volley², **1.** *v.tr. F:* To volley (forth) abuse, lâcher une bordée d'injures. **2.** *v.i.* (*a*) (*Of guns*) Partir ensemble. (*b*) *F:* Tonner.
volplane¹, *s. Av:* Vol plané.
volplane², *v.i. Av:* **1.** Faire du vol plané; planer. **2.** Descendre en vol plané.
volt, *s. El.Meas:* Volt *m.*
voltage, *s. El.E:* Voltage *m*; tension *f* (en volts).
volubility, *s.* Volubilité *f.*
voluble, *a.* (*Of speech*) Facile, aisé; (langue)

déliée, bien pendue. **-bly,** *adv.* Avec volubilité.
volume, *s.* **1.** Volume *m*, livre *m. F:* It speaks volumes for him, cela en dit long en sa faveur. **2.** *pl.* Volumes of smoke, nuages *m* de fumée. **3.** *Ph:* Volume. *V. of a reservoir,* cubage *m* d'un réservoir. **4.** Volume (d'un son); ampleur *f* (de la voix).
voluminous, *a.* Volumineux.
voluntary. **1.** *a.* (*a*) Volontaire, spontané. (*b*) **Voluntary organization,** organisation bénévole. **2.** *s. Ecc.Mus:* Morceau *m* d'orgue. **-ily,** *adv.* Volontairement, spontanément; de (son) plein gré.
volunteer¹, *s.* (*a*) *Mil:* Volontaire *m.* (*b*) To call for volunteers, demander des hommes de bonne volonté.
volunteer². **1.** *v.tr.* Offrir volontairement, spontanément. *Abs.* S'offrir. To volunteer some information, donner spontanément des renseignements. **2.** *v.i. Mil:* S'engager comme volontaire.
voluptuous, *a.* Voluptueux. **-ly,** *adv.* Voluptueusement.
voluptuousness, *s.* Sensualité *f.*
vomit¹, *s.* Vomissement *m.*
vomit², *v.tr. & i.* Vomir. **vomiting,** *s.* Vomissement *m.*
voracious, *a.* Vorace, dévorant. **Voracious appetite,** appétit de loup. **Voracious reader,** lecteur vorace. **-ly,** *adv.* Avec voracité.
voracity, *s.* Voracité *f.*
vortex, *s.* (*a*) Tourbillonnement *m* (d'air). (*b*) (*Whirlpool*) Tourbillon *m*, gouffre *m.*
votary, *s.* Dévoué, -e (*of*, à); adorateur, -trice (de). *F:* Votary of art, partisan zélé des arts.
vote¹, *s.* **1.** (*a*) Vote *m*, scrutin *m.* **Popular vote,** consultation *f* populaire. **Vote of an assembly,** délibération *f* d'une assemblée. To put a question to the vote, mettre une question aux voix. (*b*) (*Individual*) vote, voix *f*, suffrage *m.* To have a vote, avoir le droit de vote. To record one's vote, voter. **2.** (*a*) Motion *f*, résolution *f.* **Vote of censure,** motion de censure. (*b*) *Parl:* Crédit *m.*
vote². **1.** *v.i.* Voter; donner sa voix, son vote; *abs.* prendre part au vote. **2.** *v.tr.* (*a*) Voter (une somme). (*b*) *F:* I vote that we go, je propose que nous y allions.
voting, *s.* (Participation *f* au) vote; scrutin *m. Result of the v.,* vote. **Voting paper,** bulletin *m* de vote.
voter, *s.* (*a*) Votant, -ante. (*b*) Électeur, -trice.
votive, *a.* Votif. **Votive offering,** offrande votive; ex-voto *m inv.*
vouch. **1.** *v.tr.* (*a*) Affirmer, garantir. (*b*) Prouver, confirmer. **2.** *v.i.* To vouch for s.o., répondre de qn.
voucher, *s.* (*a*) Pièce justificative. *Book-k:* Pièce comptable. (*b*) *Com:* Fiche *f*; reçu *m*, bon *m.* (*c*) *Th:* Contremarque *f.*
vouchsafe, *v.tr.* (*a*) To vouchsafe s.o. sth.,

accorder, octroyer, qch. à qn. (*b*) To vouch-safe to do sth., daigner faire qch.
vow[1], *s.* Vœu *m*, serment *m*. To be under a vow to do sth., avoir fait le vœu de faire qch. To fulfil a vow, accomplir un vœu.
vow[2], *v.tr.* Vouer, jurer. To vow vengeance against s.o., faire vœu de se venger de qn.
vowel, *s.* Voyelle *f.* Vowel sound, son *m* vocalique.
voyage[1], *s.* Voyage *m* sur mer.
voyage[2], *v.i.* Voyager sur mer; naviguer.
voyaging, *s.* Voyage(s) *m*(*pl*) sur mer.
voyager, *s.* Voyageur, -euse, par mer; passager, -ère; navigateur *m.*
vulcanite, *s.* Vulcanite *f*, ébonite *f.*
vulcanize, *v.tr. Ind:* Vulcaniser. **vulcanizing**, *s.* Vulcanisation *f.*

vulgar, *a.* **I.** Vulgaire, commun; de mauvais goût. The vulgar herd, le commun des hommes. **2.** (*a*) Vulgaire; communément reçu. V. errors, erreurs très répandues. (*b*) The vulgar tongue, la langue commune. (*c*) *Ar:* Vulgar fraction, fraction ordinaire. **-ly**, *adv.* **I.** Vulgairement, grossièrement. **2.** Vulgairement, communément.
vulgarian, *s.* Personne vulgaire, commune.
vulgarism, *s.* Expression *f* vulgaire.
vulgarity, *s.* Vulgarité *f*, trivialité *f.*
vulnerability, *s.* Vulnérabilité *f.*
vulnerable, *a.* Vulnérable.
vulpine, *a.* **I.** Qui a rapport au renard. **2.** Qui tient du renard; rusé, astucieux
vulture, *s.* **I.** *Orn:* Vautour *m.* **2.** *F:* Homme *m* rapace.

W

W, w, *s.* (La lettre) W, w *m.*
wad[1], *s.* **I.** (*a*) Tampon *m*, bouchon *m.* (*b*) Liasse *f.* **2.** Bourre *f* (de cartouche).
wad[2], *v.tr. Dressm:* Ouater. **wadding**, *s.* **I.** Ouatage *m*, rembourrage *m.* **2.** (*a*) Ouate *f.* (*b*) Tampon *m* d'ouate.
waddle[1], *s.* Dandinement *m*; tortillement *m* des hanches.
waddle[2], *v.i.* Se dandiner; tortiller les hanches.
wade. I. *v.i.* Marcher dans l'eau. To wade across a stream, passer à gué un cours d'eau. *F:* To wade through a book, venir péniblement à bout d'un livre. **2.** *v.tr.* Passer à gué.
wader, *s.* **I.** Personne *f* qui marche dans l'eau. **2.** *pl.* Waders, bottes cuissardes imperméables.
wadi, *s.* Oued *m*, ravin *m.*
wafer, *s.* **I.** *Cu:* Gaufrette *f.* **2.** *Ecc:* Hostie *f.* **3.** Cachet *m* en papier.
waffle, *s.* *Cu:* Gaufre (américaine).
waft[1], *s.* Bouffée *f*, souffle *m.*
waft[2], *v.tr. Lit:* To waft a scent through the air, porter un parfum dans les airs. *Music wafted on the breeze*, musique qui flotte sur la brise.
wag[1], *s.* **I.** Farceur *m*, blagueur *m.* **2.** *Sch:* To hop (the) wag, faire l'école buissonnière.
wag[2], *s.* Agitation *f*, mouvement *m* (de la queue); hochement *m* (de la tête). (*Of dog*) With a wag of its tail, en remuant la queue.
wag[3], *v.* **I.** *v.tr.* Agiter, remuer. To wag one's tongue, jaser. To wag one's finger at s.o., menacer qn du doigt. To wag one's head, hocher la tête. **2.** *v.i.* (*a*) S'agiter, se remuer. His tongue was beginning to wag, sa langue se déliait. To set (people's) tongues

wagging, faire aller les langues. (*b*) So the world wags, ainsi va le monde.
wage[1], *s.* *Usu. pl.* (*a*) Gages *mpl* (de domestique); salaire *m*, paye *f* (d'ouvrier). A living wage, un salaire qui permet de vivre. (*b*) *Lit:* Prix *m*, salaire. **wage-earner**, *s.* Salarié, -ée.
wage[2], *v.tr.* To wage war, faire la guerre (on, à).
wager[1], *s.* Pari *m*; gageure *f.*
wager[2], *v.tr.* Parier, gager.
waggish, *a.* Plaisant; blagueur, facétieux. **-ly**, *adv.* Plaisamment, facétieusement.
waggishness, *s.* Caractère blagueur; disposition *f* à la plaisanterie.
waggle, *v.tr. & i. F:* = WAG[3].
wag(g)on, *s.* **I.** Charrette *f* (à quatre roues); chariot *m*; camion *m.* **2.** *Mil:* Fourgon *m.* **3.** *Rail:* Wagon découvert (à marchandises). Covered goods waggon, fourgon. **wag(g)onload**, *s.* Charretée *f. Rail:* (Charge *f* de) wagon *m.*
wag(g)oner, *s.* Roulier *m*, voiturier *m*, charretier *m.*
wag(g)onette, *s.* *Veh:* Wagonnette *f*, break *m.*
wagtail, *s.* *Orn:* Hochequeue *m*, bergeronnette *f.*
waif, *s.* *Jur:* Épave *f.* Waifs and strays, (enfants) abandonnés.
wail[1], *s.* (*a*) Cri plaintif; plainte *f*, gémissement *m.* (*b*) Vagissement *m.*
wail[2], *v.i.* (*a*) Gémir. (*b*) To wail over sth., se lamenter sur qch. **wailing**, *a.* (Cri) plaintif; gémissant.
wain, *s.* Charrette *f.*
wainscot[1], *s* Lambris *m.*

wainscot², *v.tr.* Lambrisser. **Wainscot(t)ed room,** chambre lambrissée.

waist, *s.* **I.** Taille *f*, ceinture *f*. Up to the waist, jusqu'à mi-corps. Waist measurement, tour *m* de taille. To put one's arm round **s.o.'s** waist, prendre qn par la taille. **2.** *Dressm:* Dress with a short waist, robe à taille courte. **waist-belt,** *s. Mil:* Ceinturon *m*.

waistband, *s.* Ceinture *f* (de jupe).

waistcoat, *s.* Gilet *m*.

wait¹, *s.* **I.** (*a*) Attente *f*; (*of train*) arrêt *m*. We had a long wait at the station, nous avons dû attendre longtemps à la gare. (*b*) To lie in wait for s.o., se tenir à l'affût de qn. **2.** *pl.* Waits, chanteurs *m* de noëls.

wait², **I.** *v.i.* (*a*) Attendre. To keep s.o. waiting, faire attendre qn. To wait for s.o., attendre qn. He did not wait to be told twice, il ne se le fit pas dire deux fois. *Com:* Repairs while you wait, réparations à la minute. *Prov:* Everything comes to him who waits, tout vient à point à qui sait attendre. Wait and see! il faudra voir! (*b*) To wait at table, servir (à table); faire le service. **2.** *v.tr.* Attendre, guetter. **wait on, upon,** *v.ind.tr.* (*a*) Servir. To wait on s.o. hand and foot, être aux petits soins pour qn. (*b*) To present chez. **wait up,** *v.i.* To wait up for s.o., rester levé à attendre qn. **waiting¹,** *a.* **I.** Qui attend. **2.** De service. **waiting-maid,** femme *f* de chambre. **waiting²,** *s.* **I.** Attente *f*. *We shall lose nothing by w.,* nous ne perdrons rien pour attendre. **2.** Service *m*. In waiting, de service. Lady in waiting, dame d'honneur.

waiting-room, *s.* Salle *f* d'attente; antichambre *f* (chez un médecin).

waiter, *s.* Garçon *m* (de restaurant). Head waiter, maître *m* d'hôtel. Waiter! garçon!

waitress, *s.* Fille *f* de salle (de restaurant); serveuse *f*. Waitress! mademoiselle!

waive, *v.tr.* Renoncer à, abandonner; ne pas insister sur (une condition).

wake¹, *s.* (*a*) *Nau:* Sillage *m*. To be in the wake of a ship, être dans les eaux d'un bâtiment. (*b*) *F:* To follow in s.o.'s wake, marcher à la suite de qn.

wake², *s.* Veillée *f* mortuaire.

wake³, *v.* **I.** *v.i.* (*a*) Être éveillé. Waking or sleeping, éveillé ou endormi. (*b*) To wake (up), se réveiller. He is waking up to the truth, la vérité se fait jour dans son esprit. **2.** *v.tr.* (*a*) To wake s.o. (up), réveiller qn. *He wants something to w. him up,* il lui faut quelque chose qui l'émoustille. (*b*) *F:* To wake the dead, réveiller, ranimer, les morts. **waking¹,** *a.* Éveillé. Waking hours, heures de veille. **waking²,** *s.* **I.** Veille *f*. Between sleeping and waking entre la veille et le sommeil. **2.** Réveil *m*. On waking, au réveil.

wakeful, *a.* **I.** (*a*) Éveillé; peu disposé à dormir. (*b*) Sans sommeil. Wakeful night,

nuit blanche. **2.** Vigilant. **-fully,** *adv.* **I.** Sans dormir. **2.** Avec vigilance.

wakefulness, *s.* **I.** (*a*) Insomnie *f*. (*b*) État *m* de veille. **2.** Vigilance *f*.

waken. **I.** *v.tr.* (*a*) Éveiller, réveiller. (*b*) Éveiller, exciter (une émotion). **2.** *v.i.* Se réveiller, s'éveiller. **wakening,** *s.* Réveil *m*.

wale, *s.* Marque *f*, trace *f* (d'un coup); vergeture *f*.

Wales. *Pr.n.* Le pays de Galles The Prince of Wales, le Prince de Galles.

walk¹, *s.* **I.** Marche *f*. **2.** Promenade *f* (à pied). To go for a walk, aller se promener; faire une promenade. To take s.o. for a walk, emmener qn en promenade. **3.** (*a*) Démarche *f*. I know him by his walk, je le reconnais à sa marche. (*b*) (*Of horse*) To fall into a walk, se mettre au pas. **4.** (*a*) Allée *f* (de jardin); avenue *f*, promenade. (*b*) Allée couverte; promenoir *m*. **5.** Walk of life, position sociale.

walk². **I.** *v.i.* **I.** Marcher, cheminer. To walk in one's sleep, être somnambule. To walk with s.o., accompagner qn. **2.** (*a*) Aller à pied. To walk home, rentrer à pied. You can walk it in ten minutes, vous en avez pour dix minutes à pied. (*b*) Se promener (à pied). To be out walking, être en promenade. **3.** (*Of horse*) Aller au pas. **4.** (*Of ghost*) Revenir. **II.** walk, *v.tr.* **I.** *F:* To walk the boards, être acteur. **2.** To walk s.o. off his legs, exténuer qn à force de le faire marcher. **walk about,** *v.i.* Se promener; circuler. **walk along,** *v.i.* Marcher; s'avancer. **walk away,** *v.i.* S'en aller; partir. **walk in,** *v.i.* Entrer. To ask s.o. to walk in, faire entrer qn. (Please) walk in, entrez sans frapper. **walk into,** *v.tr.* **I.** To walk into the room, entrer dans la salle. **2.** *F:* (*a*) Se heurter à; se trouver nez à nez avec (qn). (*b*) S'attaquer à. **walk off.** **I.** *v.i.* S'en aller; partir. *F:* To walk off with sth., décamper avec (un objet volé). **2.** *v.tr.* To walk s.o. off to prison, emmener qn en prison. **walk out,** *v.i.* (*a*) Sortir. (*b*) To walk out with a young man, être bien avec un jeune homme. **walk-over,** *s. Sp:* Victoire *f* facile. **walk round,** *v.i.* **I.** Faire le tour de. **2.** Faire un détour. **walk up,** *v.i.* To walk up to s.o., s'approcher de qn. To walk up and down, se promener de long en large. **walking,** *s.* Marche *f*; promenades *fpl* à pied. *To like w.,* aimer la marche. It is within walking distance, on peut aisément s'y rendre à pied. **walking-stick,** *s.* Canne *f*.

walker, *s.* **I.** Marcheur, -euse; promeneur, -euse; piéton *m*. He is a fast walker, il marche vite. **2.** *Th:* Walker-on, figurant, -ante.

wall¹, *s.* **I.** (*a*) Mur *m*. Main walls, gros murs. Blank wall, mur plein. Surrounding w., mur d'enceinte. To leave only the bare walls standing, ne laisser que les quatre murs. *F:* To run one's head against a (brick) wall, se buter à l'impossible. *F:* To go to the wall, succomber; perdre la partie. (b) Muraille f. The Great Wall of China, la muraille de Chine. *Pol.Ec:* High tariff walls, hautes murailles douanières. **2.** *Min:* Paroi f. **wall-fruit,** s. Fruit m d'espalier. **wallpaper,** s. Papier peint; (papier) tenture f. **wall²,** v.tr. To wall (in), entourer de murs; murer. **wall up,** v.tr. Murer. **walled,** a. Walled (in), muré; clos de murs.

wallaby, s. Kangourou m de petite taille.

wallet, s. **1.** Besace f (de mendiant). **2.** Sacoche f (de bicyclette). **3.** Portefeuille m.

wallflower, s. **1.** *Bot:* Giroflée f des murailles. **2.** *F:* To be a wallflower, faire tapisserie.

Walloon, a. & s. Wallon, -onne.

wallop¹, s. *F:* **1.** Gros coup. **2.** And down he went with a wallop! et patatras, le voilà qui tombe!

wallop², v.tr. *P:* Rosser. **walloping¹,** a. *P:* Énorme. **walloping²,** s. *P:* Rossée f.

wallow¹, s. Trou bourbeux.

wallow², v.i. Se vautrer; se rouler dans la boue. *F:* To wallow in blood, se baigner dans le sang. To wallow in vice, croupir dans le vice.

walnut, s. **1.** Noix f. **2.** Noyer m. **3.** (Bois m de) noyer. **walnut-juice,** s. Brou m de noix. **walnut-shell,** s. Coquille f de noix. **walnut-tree,** s. Noyer m.

walrus, s. *Z:* Morse m. *F:* Walrus moustache, moustache tombante.

Walter. *Pr.n.* Gauthier m.

waltz¹, s. **1.** Valse f. **2.** *Mus:* Air m de valse.

waltz², v.i. Valser. I waltzed with Miss X, j'ai fait valser Mlle X. **waltzing,** s. Valse f.

wan, a. Pâlot, -otte; blême; blafard. Wan smile, pâle sourire.

wand, s. **1.** Baguette f (de fée). **2.** Bâton m (de commandement); verge f (d'huissier).

wander, v.i. (a) Errer (sans but); se promener au hasard. To wander about, aller à l'aventure. To let one's thoughts wander, laisser vaguer ses pensées. (b) To wander (away) from the subject, s'écarter du sujet. (c) To wander in one's mind, divaguer; avoir le délire. **wandering¹,** a. **1.** (a) Errant, vagabond. W. tribes, nomades m. (b) (Esprit) distrait. **2.** (a) *Med:* Qui a le délire. (b) (Discours) incohérent. **wandering²,** s. **1.** Vagabondage m. To recount one's wanderings, *F:* raconter son odyssée f. **2.** (a) Rêverie f. (b) *Med:* Égarement m. In his wanderings, dans ses divagations. **3.** W. from the subject, déviation f du sujet.

wanderer, s. Vagabond, -e; voyageur, -euse.

wane¹, s. **1.** Déclin m. To be on the wane, (of moon) décroître. *F:* His star is on the wane, son étoile pâlit.

wane², v.i. Décroître, décliner; (of beauty) être sur le retour.

wangle¹, s. *P:* Moyen détourné; truc m.

wangle², v.tr. *P:* **1.** Obtenir par subterfuge.

To wangle a week's leave, carotter huit jours de congé. **2.** Cuisiner (des comptes). **wangling,** s. Carottage m.

wangler, s. *P:* Carotteur, -euse.

wanness, s. Pâleur f.

want¹, s. **1.** (a) Manque m, défaut m. Want of judgment, défaut de jugement. Want of imagination, manque d'imagination. For want of something better, faute de mieux. For w. of something to do, par désœuvrement. (b) To be in want of sth., avoir besoin de qch. **2.** Indigence f, misère f. To be in want, être dans le besoin. **3.** Besoin m. To attend to s.o.'s wants, pourvoir aux besoins de qn. A long-felt want, une lacune à combler.

want². 1. v.i. (a) Manquer (for, de); être dépourvu (de). (b) Être dans le besoin. **2.** v.tr. (a) Manquer de, ne pas avoir. It wants six minutes of ten o'clock, il est dix heures moins six. (b) To want rest, avoir besoin de repos. That work wants a lot of patience, ce travail exige beaucoup de patience. Have you all you want? avez-vous tout ce qu'il vous faut? I've had all I want(ed), j'en ai assez. That's the very thing I want, c'est juste ce qu'il me faut; c'est juste mon affaire. Wanted, a good cook, on demande une bonne cuisinière. (c) Your hair wants cutting, vous avez besoin de vous faire couper les cheveux. It wants some doing, ce n'est pas (si) facile à faire. (d) Désirer, vouloir. He knows what he wants, il sait ce qu'il veut. *Iron:* You don't want much! tu n'es pas dégoûté! You are wanted, on vous demande. We are not wanted here, nous sommes de trop ici. We don't w. you, nous n'avons que faire de vous. What does he want with me? que me veut-il? I want to tell you, je voudrais vous dire (that, que). I want him to come, je désire qu'il vienne. I don't want it known, je ne veux pas que cela se sache. **wanted,** a. **1.** Désiré, voulu, demandé. **2.** (Criminel) que la police recherche. **wanting,** pred.a. (a) Manquant, qui manque. To be wanting, faire défaut. (b) Wanting in intelligence, dépourvu d'intelligence. He was tried and found wanting, il ne supporta pas l'épreuve. (c) *F:* Faible d'esprit.

wanton¹, a. (a) Licencieux, impudique. (b) Wanton winds, vents folâtres. (c) Gratuit; sans motif. Wanton cruelty, cruauté gratuite. **-ly,** adv. **1.** Impudiquement. **2.** De gaieté de cœur. **3.** Gratuitement.

wanton², v.i. Folâtrer; s'ébattre.

wantonness, s. **1.** Libertinage m. **2.** To do sth. in sheer wantonness, faire qch. de gaieté de cœur, par étourderie.

wapiti, s. *Z:* Wapiti m.

war¹, s. Guerre f. To go to war, se mettre en guerre. To make war on s.o., faire la guerre à, contre, qn. War of the elements, conflit m des éléments. War of words, dispute f de mots. *F:* You look as if you had been in the wars, vous avez l'air de vous être battu. **war-cloud,** s. *F:* Menace f de guerre. **war-correspondent,** *s.* Correspondant *m*, journaliste *m*, aux armées **war-cry,** *s.* Cri *m* de guerre. **war-dance,** *s.* Danse guerrière. **war-fever,** *s.* Psychose *f* de la guerre. **war-horse,** *s.* Cheval *m* de bataille. **war-loan,** *s.* *Fin:* Emprunt *m* de guerre. **war-lord,** *s.* Généralissime *m*; chef *m* suprême (de l'armée). **war-monger,** *s.* Agitateur *m* qui pousse à la guerre. **war-mongering,** *s.* Propagande *f* de guerre. **war-paint,** *s.* Peinture *f* de guerre. **war-path,** *s.* *F:* To be on the war-path, chercher noise à tout le monde. *The boss is on the -w.-p.,* le patron est d'une humeur massacrante. **war-plane,** *s.* Avion *m* de guerre. **war-time,** *s.* Temps *m* de guerre. **war-worn,** *a,* Usé par la guerre.

war², *v.i.* To war against s.o., mener une campagne contre qn. *To war against abuses,* faire la guerre aux abus. **warring,** *a.* Warring interests, intérêts contraires.

warble¹, *s.* Gazouillement *m*, ramage *m*.

warble². **1.** *v.i* (a) Gazouiller. (b) *F:* Chanter. **2.** *v.tr.* Chanter en gazouillant.

warbling, *s.* = WARBLE¹.

warbler, *s.* **1.** Oiseau chanteur; *F:* chanteur *m.* **2.** *Orn:* Fauvette *f.*

ward¹, *s.* **1.** (a) Guet *m.* To keep watch and ward, faire bonne garde. (b) Pupille *mf. Jur:* Ward in Chancery, pupille sous tutelle judiciaire. **2.** (a) Hospital ward, salle *f* d'hôpital. (b) Quartier *m* (d'une prison). **3.** Arrondissement *m* (d'une ville). **4.** Wards of a lock, gardes *f* d'une serrure. **ward-room,** *s. Navy:* Carré *m* des officiers.

ward², *v.tr.* To ward off a blow, parer un coup. *To w. off an illness,* prévenir une maladie.

warden, *s.* (a) Directeur *m* (d'une institution). (b) Gardien *m.* (c) Gouverneur *m.* (d) Chef *m* d'îlot. Warden's post, poste de défense passive.

warder, *s.* Gardien *m* (de prison).

wardress, *s.* Gardienne *f* de prison.

wardrobe, *s.* **1.** *Furn:* Armoire *f* (pour garde-robe). **2.** (Ensemble *m* de) vêtements *mpl.* Wardrobe dealer, marchand, -e, de toilette.

ware, *s.* **1.** *Coll.* (a) Articles fabriqués. Toilet ware, ustensiles *mpl* de toilette. (b) Faïence *f.* China ware, porcelaine *f.* **2.** *pl.* Wares, marchandise(s) *f.*

warehouse¹, *s.* **1.** Entrepôt *m*; magasin *m.* **2.** Italian warehouse, magasin de comestibles; épicerie *f.*

warehouse², *v.tr.* **1.** (Em)magasiner; mettre en magasin. **2.** To warehouse one's furniture, mettre son mobilier au garde-meuble.

warehousing, *s.* (Em)magasinage *m*; mise *f* en magasin.

warehouseman, *s.* **1.** Garçon *m* de magasin. **2.** Italian warehouseman, marchand *m* de comestibles.

warfare, *s.* La guerre. Trench warfare, la guerre de tranchées. Naval warfare, guerre maritime. Aerial warfare, guerre aérienne.

wariness, *s.* Circonspection *f*, prudence *f*; défiance *f.*

warlike, *a.* (Maintien) guerrier; (air) martial; (peuple) belliqueux.

warm¹, *a.* **1.** (a) Chaud. *W. water,* eau chaude. *W. night,* nuit tiède. To be warm, (i) (of water) être chaud; (ii) (of pers.) avoir chaud. *I can't get w.,* je ne peux pas me réchauffer. (At games) You are getting warm! vous brûlez! (b) (Vêtement) chaud. (c) It is warm, il fait chaud. **2.** (a) Chaleureux; ardent. *W. thanks,* remerciements chaleureux. (b) Warm heart, cœur généreux, chaud. To meet with a warm reception, (i) être accueilli chaleureusement; (ii) être accueilli par des huées. (c) The argument was getting warm, la discussion s'animait. Warm contest, lutte acharnée, chaude. *F:* It is warm work, c'est une rude besogne. To make it warm for s.o., en faire voir de dures à qn. **-ly,** *adv.* **1.** (Vêtu) chaudement. **2.** (a) (Applaudir) chaudement. To thank s.o. warmly, remercier qn chaleureusement. (b) Vivement, avec chaleur. **warm-blooded,** *a. Z:* A sang chaud. **warm-hearted,** *a.* Au cœur chaud, généreux.

warm², *s. F: Come and have a w.,* venez vous réchauffer. To give sth. a warm, chauffer qch.

warm³. **1.** *v.tr.* (a) Chauffer. To warm oneself at the fire, se chauffer au feu. (b) *F:* To warm s.o.'s jacket, flanquer une tripotée à qn. **2.** *v.i.* (Se) chauffer; se réchauffer. (b) *F:* S'animer. **warm up.** **1.** *v.tr.* (a) Chauffer; réchauffer. (b) (Faire) réchauffer. **2.** *v.i.* S'échauffer; s'animer.

warming, *s.* **1.** Chauffage *m.* **2.** *F:* Rossée *f*, raclée *f.* **warming-pan,** *s.* Bassinoire *f.*

warmth, *s.* **1.** Chaleur *f.* **2.** (a) Ardeur *f*, zèle *m*; chaleur. (b) Cordialité *f*, chaleur (d'un accueil). (c) Emportement *m*, vivacité *f.*

warn, *v.tr.* Avertir. **1.** Prévenir. To warn s.o. of a danger, avertir qn d'un danger. To warn s.o. against sth., mettre qn en garde contre qch. You have been warned! vous voilà prévenu! **2.** To warn the police, avertir la police. **warning¹,** *a.* Avertisseur, d'avertissement. **warning²,** *s.* Avertissement *m.* **1.** Action *f* d'avertir. **2.** (a) Avis *m*, préavis *m.* Without warning, sans préavis. (b) To give s.o. fair warning, donner à qn un avertissement formel. (c) Let this be a warning to you, que cela vous serve de leçon. **3.** Warning to leave, congé *m.* To give an employee warning, donner congé à un employé.

warp¹, *s.* **1.** *Tex:* Chaîne *f.* **2.** *Nau:* Amarre *f*; touée *f.* **3.** Voilure *f*, courbure *f* (d'une planche).

warp². **1.** *v.tr.* **1.** (a) Déjeter, (faire) voiler (le bois). (b) *F:* Fausser, pervertir (l'esprit).

2. *Nau:* Haler, touer. II. **warp,** *v.i.* Se déformer; (*of timber*) se déjeter, gauchir. **warped,** *a.* (*a*) (Bois) déjeté, gauchi. (*b*) (Esprit) perverti, faussé. **warrant**[1], *s.* **I.** Garantie *f.* **2.** Autorisation *f*; justification *f.* **3.** (*a*) Mandat *m*, ordre *m.* A warrant is out against him, il est sous le coup d'un mandat d'amener. (*b*) Autorisation écrite; autorité *f.* (*c*) Certificat *m.* (*d*) Warrant for payment, ordonnance *f* de payement. (*e*) Brevet *m.* Royal warrant, brevet de fournisseur du roi. Warrant-officer, (i) *Mil:* sous-officier *m*; (ii) *Navy:* maître principal. **warrant**[2], *v.tr.* **I.** Garantir, certifier (qch.). *F:* I warrant you, je vous en réponds. **2.** Justifier. **warranted,** *a.* **I.** *Com:* Garanti. **2.** Autorisé.

warranty, *s.* **I.** Autorisation *f*; justification *f* (*for doing sth.*, pour faire qch.). **2.** Garantie *f.*

warren, *s.* (Rabbit-)warren, garenne *f.*

warrior, *s.* Guerrier *m*, soldat *m.*

Warsaw. *Pr.n.* Varsovie *f.*

warship, *s.* Vaisseau *m* de guerre.

wart, *s.* Verrue *f.*

wary, *a.* (*a*) Avisé, prudent. (*b*) To be wary of sth., se méfier de qch. **-ily,** *adv.* Avec circonspection; prudemment.

wash[1], *s.* **I.** (*a*) To give sth. a wash, laver qch. (*b*) Ablutions *fpl.* *F:* To have a wash and brush-up, faire un bout de toilette. (*c*) Lessive *f*, blanchissage *m.* To send clothes to the wash, envoyer du linge au blanchissage. *F:* It will all come out in the w., ça se tassera. **2.** Colour wash, badigeon *m.* **3.** (*a*) The wash of the waves, le bruit des flots. (*b*) *Nau:* Sillage *m*, houache *f*, remous *m.* *Av:* Propeller wash, souffle *m* de l'hélice. **wash-basin,** *s.* Cuvette *f* (de lavabo). **wash-house,** *s.* (*a*) Buanderie *f.* (*b*) Lavoir (public). **wash-leather,** *s.* Peau *f* de chamois. Wash-leather gloves, gants chamois. **wash-tub,** *s.* Cuvier *m*; baquet *m* (à lessive). **wash**[2]. I. *v.tr.* **I.** (*a*) Laver. To wash one's face, se débarbouiller. To wash one's hands, se laver les mains. *F:* To wash one's hands of sth., se laver les mains de qch. (*b*) *v.pr.* & *i.* To wash (oneself), se laver. **2.** (*a*) Blanchir, lessiver, laver (le linge). (*b*) Material that washes well, étoffe très lavable. *F:* That story won't wash! cette histoire-là ne passe pas! **3.** Baigner, arroser (les côtes). **4.** To wash sth. ashore, rejeter qch. sur le rivage. Sailor washed overboard, matelot balayé par une lame. II. **wash,** *v.i.* The waves washed over the deck, les vagues balayaient le pont. **wash away,** *v.tr.* **I.** Enlever par le lavage. **2.** (*a*) River-bank washed away, berge affouillée. (*b*) Emporter, entraîner. **wash off,** *v.tr.* Enlever, effacer, par le lavage It will wash off, cela s'effacera à l'eau **wash out,** *v.tr.* **I.** (*a*) Enlever (une tache). *Lit:* To wash out an insult, laver un affront. *F:* You can wash that right out, il ne faut pas compter

là-dessus. (*b*) Laver, rincer. **2.** (*With passive force*) Partir au lavage. **wash-out,** *s.* *F:* (*a*) Fiasco *m*, four *m.* The play was a wash-out, la pièce a fait four. (*b*) He is a wash-out, c'est un raté. **washed out,** *a.* **I.** (*a*) Délavé. (*b*) *F:* Washed-out complexion, teint de papier mâché. **2.** *F:* Flapi, vanné. To feel washed out, se sentir à plat. **wash up,** *v.tr.* (*a*) To wash up the dishes, *abs.* to wash up, laver la vaisselle. (*b*) Rejeter sur le rivage. **washing,** *s.* **I.** (*a*) Lavage *m.* (*b*) Ablutions *fpl.* **2.** (*a*) Blanchissage *m*, lessive *f* (du linge). (*b*) She takes in washing, elle fait le blanchissage. **washing-day,** *s.* Jour *m* de lessive. **washing-soda,** *s.* Cristaux *mpl.* (de soude). **wash-hand,** *attrib.a.* Wash-hand basin, cuvette *f* (de lavabo). Wash-hand stand, lavabo *m.*

washer, *s.* *Mec.E:* Rondelle *f*; bague *f* d'appui.

washerwoman, *s.* Blanchisseuse *f.*

washstand, *s.* *Furn:* Lavabo *m.*

washy, *a.* *F:* Fade, insipide.

wasp, *s.* Guêpe *f.* Wasps' nest, guêpier *m.*

waspish, *a.* *F:* Méchant; acariâtre. *W. tone,* ton aigre. **-ly,** *adv.* Méchamment.

waspishness, *s.* *F:* Méchanceté *f.*

wastage, *s.* (*a*) Déperdition *f*; perte *f.* (*b*) Gaspillage *m.*

waste[1], *a.* **I.** (*a*) Waste land, terrains *m* vagues. (*b*) To lay waste, dévaster, ravager. **2.** De rebut. Waste paper, vieux papiers. Waste-paper basket, corbeille *f* à papier(s). **waste**[2], *s.* **I.** Région *f* inculte; désert *m.* **2.** Gaspillage *m.* Waste of time, perte *f* de temps. **3.** Déchets *mpl*, rebut *m.* **waste**[3]. I. *v.tr.* **I.** Consumer, user. Patient wasted by disease, malade amaigri par la maladie. **2.** Gaspiller. To waste one's time, perdre son temps. Wasted life, vie manquée. *F:* To waste words, parler en pure perte. Waste not, want not, qui épargne gagne. II. **waste,** *v.i.* **I.** Se perdre; s'user. **2.** To waste (away), dépérir. **wasted,** *a.* **I.** Dévasté, ravagé. **2.** (Malade) amaigri. **3.** Gaspillé. Time wasted, temps perdu. **wasting,** *s.* **I.** Gaspillage *m*, perte *f.* **2.** Wasting (away), dépérissement *m.*

wasteful, *a.* Gaspilleur, -euse; prodigue. *W. habits,* habitudes de gaspillage. **-fully,** *adv.* Avec prodigalité.

wastefulness, *s.* Prodigalité *f*; gaspillage *m.*

waster, *s.* *F:* = WASTREL.

wastrel, *s.* *F:* Vaurien *m*; propre *m* à rien.

watch[1], *s.* **I.** *A:* Veille *f.* **2.** Garde *f*; surveillance *f.* To be on the watch for s.o., guetter qn. To keep watch, monter la garde. To keep a close watch on s.o., surveiller qn de près. **3.** *Hist:* The watch, la ronde de nuit. **4.** *Nau:* Quart *m.* (*b*) The w. on deck, la bordée de quart. **5.** Montre *f.* It is six by my watch, il est six heures à ma montre. **watch-case,** *s.* Boîtier *m* de montre. **watch-chain,** *s.* Chaîne *f* de montre. **watch-dog,** *s.* Chien *m* de garde. **watch-fire,** *s.*

Feu *m* de bivouac. **watch-glass,** *s.* Verre *m* de montre. **watch-maker,** *s.* Horloger *m.* **watch-spring,** *s.* Ressort *m* de montre. **watch-tower,** *s.* Tour *f* d'observation, de guet.

watch². **I.** *v.i.* (*a*) Veiller. (*b*) To watch by a sick person, veiller un malade. To watch over a flock, garder un troupeau. (*c*) To watch, *F:* to watch out, être aux aguets. (*d*) To watch for s.o., attendre qn; guetter qn. **2.** *v.tr.* (*a*) Garder, veiller sur (qn, qch.). (*b*) Observer; regarder attentivement. To watch s.o. narrowly, surveiller qn de près. (*c*) We shall have to watch the expenses, il nous faudra avoir l'œil sur la dépense. (*d*) Regarder; voir. To watch a football match, assister à un match de football. (*e*) To watch one's opportunity, guetter l'occasion.

watcher, *s.* Veilleur, -euse.

watchful, *a.* Vigilant; alerte; attentif. To keep a watchful eye on s.o., surveiller qn de près. **-fully,** *adv.* Avec vigilance. ———

watchfulness, *s.* Vigilance *f.*

watchman, *s.* Gardien *m,* garde *m. Nau:* Homme *m* de garde. *Ind:* Night watchman, veilleur *m* de nuit.

watchword, *s.* Mot *m* d'ordre.

water¹, *s.* Eau *f.* **I.** (*a*) Cold w., eau fraîche. Fresh water, eau douce. *F:* To throw cold water on a scheme, décourager un projet. (*b*) Eaux ménagères. To turn on the water, ouvrir l'eau. To have the water laid on, faire mettre l'eau courante. Water supply, service *m* des eaux. **2.** *Usu. pl.* To take the waters, prendre les eaux. **3.** (*a*) The waters of the Danube, les eaux du Danube. (*b*) To be under water, être inondé, submergé. To swim under water, nager entre deux eaux. Above water, à flot; surnageant. To keep one's head above water, (i) se maintenir à la surface; (ii) *F:* faire face à ses engagements. (*c*) High water, marée haute; haute mer. High-water mark, *F:* apogée *m. F:* He is in low water, il est dans la gêne. **4.** (*a*) Strong waters, eau-de-vie *f.* (*b*) To bring the water to one's eyes, faire venir les larmes aux yeux. **water bottle,** *s.* **I.** Carafe *f* (de toilette). **2.** Gourde *f; Mil:* bidon *m.* **water-can,** *s.* Broc *m.* **water-cart,** *s.* Tonneau *m* d'arrosage. **water-closet,** *s.* Cabinet *m*; les cabinets; water-closet *m,* *pl.* water-closets; (*in hotel*) le numéro cent. **water-colour,** *s. Art:* **I.** *pl.* To paint in water-colours, peindre à l'aquarelle. **2.** A water-colour (painting), une aquarelle. **water-cress,** *s.* Cresson *m* de fontaine. **water-diviner,** *s.* Sourcier *m.* **water-front,** *s.* Partie *f* de la ville faisant face à la mer. **water-glass,** *s. Com:* verre *m* soluble. **water-hen,** *s.* Poule *f* d'eau. **water-ice,** *s. Cu:* Sorbet *m.* **water-jug,** *s.* **I.** Pot *m,* cruche *f,* à eau. **2.** *Toil:* Broc *m.* **water-lily,** *s.* Nénuphar

m; lis *m* d'eau. White water-lily, nymphée *f.* Yellow water-lily, nuphar *m,* lis jaune. **water-line,** *s. Nau:* (Ligne *f* de) flottaison *f.* **water-main,** *s. Hyd.E:* Conduite principale (d'eau). **water-mark,** *s.* Filigrane *m.* **water-melon,** *s.* Melon *m* d'eau; pastèque *f.* **water-mill,** *s.* Moulin *m* à eau. **water-nymph,** *s. Myth:* Naïade *f.* **water-pipe,** *s.* Tuyau *m* d'eau, conduite *f* d'eau. **water-polo,** *s. Sp:* Polo *m* nautique. **water-power,** *s.* Force *f* hydraulique; *F:* houille blanche. **water-rat,** *s. Z:* Rat *m* d'eau; campagnol nageur. **water-spout,** *s.* **I.** Tuyau *m,* descente *f* (d'eau). **2.** Gouttière *f,* gargouille *f.* **3.** *Meteor:* Trombe *f.* **water-sprite,** *s.* Ondin, -ine. **water-way,** *s.* Voie *f* d'eau; voie navigable. **water-wings,** *s.pl.* Flotteur *m* de natation.

water². **I.** *v.tr.* (*a*) Arroser. (*b*) To water one's wine, mouiller, couper, son vin. (*c*) Faire boire, abreuver. **2.** *v.i.* (*a*) My eye is watering, mon œil pleure, larmoie. (*b*) *Nau:* Faire de l'eau. **watered,** *a.* **I.** Arrosé. **2.** Étendu d'eau. **3.** *Tex:* Watered silk, soie moirée. **watering,** *s.* **I.** (*a*) Arrosage *m.* (*b*) Irrigation *f.* **2.** Dilution *f.* **3.** Abreuvage *m* (des bêtes). **watering-can,** *s.* Arrosoir *m.* **watering-cart,** *s.* = WATER-CART. **watering-place,** *s.* **I.** Abreuvoir *m.* **2.** Station *f* balnéaire.

watercourse, *s.* Cours *m* d'eau.

waterfall, *s.* Chute *f* d'eau.

waterfowl, *s.* (*a*) Oiseau *m* aquatique. (*b*) *Coll.* Gibier *m* d'eau; sauvagine *f.*

waterlogged, *a.* (*a*) (Navire) entre deux eaux. (*b*) (Bois) alourdi par absorption d'eau.

Waterloo. *Pr.n. F:* To meet one's Waterloo, arriver au désastre.

waterman, *s.* Batelier *m,* marinier *m.*

waterproof. **I.** *a.* Imperméable. **2.** *s. Cost:* Imperméable *m.*

watershed, *s. Ph.Geog:* Ligne *f* de partage des eaux; ligne de faîte.

watertight, *a.* Étanche (à l'eau). *F:* W. regulations, règlement qui a prévu tous les cas.

waterworks, *s.pl.* Usine *f* de distribution d'eau.

watery, *a.* (*a*) Aqueux; qui contient de l'eau; noyé d'eau. Watery eyes, yeux larmoyants. (*b*) Watery sky, ciel chargé de pluie. (*c*) *Poet:* To find a watery grave, trouver la mort dans les eaux.

watt, *s. El.Meas:* Watt *m*; voltampère *m.*

wattle¹, *s.* (*a*) Wattle(-work), clayonnage *m.* (*b*) Claie *f.*

wattle², *s.* Barbe *f* (d'un coq).

wave¹, *s.* **I.** (*a*) Vague *f; Lit:* lame *f.* (*b*) The waves, *Lit:* les flots *m.* (*c*) *F:* Wave of enthusiasm, vague d'enthousiasme. **2.** *Ph:* Onde *f.* **3.** Ondulation *f* (des cheveux). *Hairdr:* To have a wave, se faire onduler. **4.** (*a*) Balancement *m,* ondoiement *m.* (*b*) With a wave of his hand, d'un geste de la main. **wave-length,** s. *Ph:* Longueur *f* d'onde.

wave². I. *v.i.* **1.** S'agiter; flotter (au vent); *(of plume)* onduler. **2.** To wave to s.o., faire signe à qn (en agitant le bras). **3.** *My hair waves naturally,* mes cheveux ondulent naturellement. II. **wave,** *v.tr.* **1.** Agiter. To wave one's hand, faire signe de la main. To wave one's arms about, battre des bras. **2.** He waved us on, de la main il nous fit signe de continuer. To wave aside an objection, écarter une objection. **3.** *Hairdr:* Onduler. To have one's hair waved, se faire onduler. **waved,** *a.* Ondé, ondulé. **waving,** s. **1.** (a) Agitation *f.* W. *of the hand,* geste *m* de la main. (b) Ondoiement *m* (du blé). **2.** *Hairdr:* Ondulation *f.*

wavelet, s. Petite vague.

waver, *v.i.* Vaciller. **1.** *(Of flame)* Trembloter. **2.** Hésiter; *(of courage)* défaillir.

wavering¹, *a.* **1.** *(Of flame)* Vacillant, tremblotant. **2.** (Homme) irrésolu, hésitant; (voix) défaillante. **-ly,** *adv.* Avec indécision; irrésolument. **wavering²,** s. **1.** Tremblement *m,* vacillement *m* (d'une flamme). **2.** Vacillation *f,* irrésolution *f.*

waverer, s. Indécis, -ise; irrésolu, -ue.

wavy, *a.* Onduleux. Wavy line, ligne tremblée. Wavy hair, chevelure ondoyante.

wax¹, s. Cire *f.* **wax candle,** s. Bougie *f* de cire; *(in church)* cierge *m.* **wax doll,** s. Poupée *f* de cire. **wax taper,** s. Rat *m* de cave.

wax², *v.tr.* Cirer, enduire de cire. **waxed,** *a.* **1.** Ciré; enduit de cire. Waxed moustache, moustache cosmétiquée. **2.** Waxed thread, fil poissé.

wax³, *v.i.* **1.** To wax and wane, croître et décroître. **2.** Devenir, se faire.

wax⁴, s. *F:* Rage *f,* colère *f.* To get into a wax, se mettre en colère.

waxen, *a.* (a) De cire, en cire. (b) Cireux.

waxwork, s. (a) Figure *f* de cire. (b) *pl:* Waxworks, (musée *m* de) figures de cire.

waxy¹, *a.* Cireux.

waxy², *a. F:* En colère.

way, s. **1.** Chemin *m,* route *f,* voie *f.* Over the way, de l'autre côté de la rue. The house across the way, la maison d'en face. *Rail:* Six-foot way, entre-voie *f.* **2.** (a) The way to the station, le chemin de la gare. To show s.o. the way, montrer la route à qn. To ask one's way, demander son chemin. To lose one's way, s'égarer, se perdre. To go the wrong way, faire fausse route. To go the shortest way, prendre par le plus court. *F:* He knows his way about, il sait se débrouiller. To prepare the way, préparer les voies. To start on one's way, se mettre en route. On the way, chemin faisant; en chemin. *On my way home,* en revenant chez moi; en rentrant. To go one's way, passer son chemin. *F:* To go out of one's way, se déranger. Village that is rather out of

the way, village un peu écarté. His talent is nothing out of the way, son talent n'est pas hors ligne. (b) Way in, entrée *f* Way out, sortie *f.* To find a way out, trouver une issue. (c) To find one's way to a place, parvenir à un endroit. To make one's way towards a place, se diriger vers un endroit. How to make one's way in the world, le moyen de parvenir. To work one's way up, s'élever à force de travail. To pay one's way, se suffire. To see one's way to do sth., se croire à même de faire qch. (d) To stand in s.o.'s way, faire obstacle à qn. To put difficulties in s.o.'s way, créer des difficultés à qn. To get in one another's way, se gêner (les uns les autres). To be in s.o.'s way, gêner, embarrasser, qn. To get out of the way, se ranger, s'effacer. To keep out of the way, se tenir à l'écart. To keep out of s.o.'s way, se cacher de qn; éviter qn. To make way for s.o., faire place à qn **3.** *To accompany s.o. a little way,* accompagner qn un bout de chemin. All the way, tout le long du chemin; jusqu'au bout. It's a long way from here, c'est loin d'ici. To have a long way to go, avoir beaucoup de chemin à faire. A little way off, à peu de distance. *F:* He will go a long way, il ira loin; il fera son chemin. To make a penny go a long way, savoir ménager les sous. By a long way, de beaucoup. Not by a long way, il s'en faut de beaucoup. **4.** (a) Côté *m,* direction *f.* *Which way is the wind blowing?* d'où vient le vent? This way out, par ici la sortie. This way and that, de-ci de-là. *F:* Not to know which way to look, être tout décontenancé. To look the other way, détourner les yeux. I have nothing to say one way or the other, je n'ai rien à dire pour ou contre. I am going your way, je vais de votre côté. Such people have not often come my way, je n'ai pas souvent eu affaire à des gens pareils. If the opportunity comes your way, si vous en trouvez l'occasion. (b) Sens *m.* (In) the wrong way, à contre-sens. The wrong way up, sens dessus dessous; à l'envers. Right way up, dans le bon sens. **5.** Moyen *m.* To find a way, trouver (le) moyen (to, de). *Adm:* Ways and means, voies et moyens. **6.** (a) Façon *f,* manière *f.* In this way, de cette façon. In a friendly way, en ami; amicalement. Without in any way wishing to criticize, sans aucunement vouloir critiquer. That's the way! à la bonne heure! To go the right way to work, s'y prendre bien. In one way or another, de façon ou d'autre. There are no two ways about it, il n'y a pas à discuter. The way things are going, l'allure *f* des affaires. Well, it is this way, voici ce que c'est. That's his way, voilà comme il est. That is always the way with him, il est toujours comme ça. To do things in one's own way, faire les choses à sa guise. To be in the way of doing sth., avoir l'habitude de faire qch. *You will get into the way of it,* vous vous y ferez. (b) I know his little ways, je connais ses petites manies. He has a way with him, il est insinuant. (c) To have one's (own) way, agir à sa guise. He wants his own way, il veut (en) faire à sa tête. He had it all his own way, il n'a pas rencontré de résistance. 7. In many ways, à bien des égards. In some ways, à certains points de vue. 8. Cours m, course f. In the ordinary way, de coutume. 9. (a) The flood is making way, l'inondation fait des progrès. (b) Erre f (d'un navire). Ship under way, navire en marche, faisant route. 10. (a) Things seem in a bad way, les choses ont l'air d'aller mal. (b) F: He is in a fine way about it, il a pris la chose très à cœur. (c) In a fair way to succeed, en bonne voie pour réussir. 11. Way of business, genre m d'affaires ; métier m. 12. (a) By the way, incidemment ; en passant. All this is by the way, tout ceci est par parenthèse. By the way! ah, j'y pense ! (b) By way of warning, à titre d'avertissement.

wayfarer, s. Voyageur m ; passant m.

waylay, v.tr. 1. Tendre un guet-apens à. 2. Arrêter au passage.

wayside, s. Bord m de la route.

wayward, a. (a) Volontaire, rebelle. (b) Capricieux, fantasque.

waywardness, s. (a) Entêtement m, obstination f. (b) Caractère m fantasque.

we, pers. pron. nom. pl. (a) Nous. We are playing, nous jouons. Here we are, nous voici. (b) We and they, nous et eux. We lawyers, nous autres avocats. (c) On. As we say, comme on dit.

weak, a. 1. Faible ; (of health) débile ; (of body) infirme, chétif. To grow weak, s'affaiblir. 2. S.o.'s weak side, le côté faible, le faible. de qn. 3. Dilué, étendu. W. tea, thé léger. -ly¹, adv. (a) Faiblement ; sans force. (b) Sans résolution. **weak-kneed,** a. F: Sans caractère.

weaken. 1. v.tr. Affaiblir ; amollir. 2. v.i. S'affaiblir, faiblir. **weakening¹,** a. 1. Affaiblissant. 2. Faiblissant ; qui faiblit. **weakening²,** s. Affaiblissement m.

weakling, s. (a) Être m faible, débile. (b) Homme m faible de caractère.

weakly², a. Débile, faible (de santé).

weakness, s. (a) Faiblesse f. (b) To have a weakness for sth., avoir un faible pour qch.

weal¹, s. Weal and woe, bonheur m et malheur m. For weal or (for) woe, quoi qu'il arrive ; advienne que pourra.

weal², s. = WALE.

wealth, s. 1. Richesse(s) f(pl) ; opulence f. He is rolling in wealth, il roule sur l'or. 2. Abondance f, profusion f.

wealthy, a. Riche, opulent.

wean, v.tr. 1. Sevrer. 2. To wean s.o. from his bad habits, détacher qn de ses mauvaises habitudes.

weapon, s. Arme f.

wear¹, s. 1. (a) Usage m. Frocks for evening

wear, toilettes pour le soir. Ladies' wear, articles m pour dames. (b) Stuff that will stand hard wear, étoffe d'un bon usage. To be the worse for wear, être usé. 2. Usure f. Wear and tear, usure ; avaries fpl.

wear², v. 1. v.tr. Porter. To wear black, porter du noir. What shall I w.? qu'est-ce que je vais mettre? 2. v.tr. User To wear holes in sth., faire des trous à qch. 3. (With passive force) (a) To wear into holes, se trouer. (b) To wear well, (i) être de bon usage ; (ii) bien porter son âge. 4. v.i. (Of time) Traîner. The year was wearing to its close, l'année tirait à sa fin. **wear away.** 1. v.tr. (a) User, ronger. (b) Effacer, détruire. 2. v.i. (a) S'user. (b) S'effacer. **wear off.** 1. v.tr. Faire disparaître (par l'usure). 2. v.i S'effacer, disparaître. The novelty of the sight soon wore off, la nouveauté de ce spectacle passa vite. **wear on,** v.i. As the evening wore on, à mesure que la soirée s'avançait. **wear out.** 1. v.tr (a) User. To wear oneself out, s'user, s'épuiser. (b) Épuiser, lasser (la patience de qn). 2. v.i. S'user. **worn out,** a. 1. Usé. 2. Épuisé ; exténué. The horses are w. out, les chevaux n'en peuvent plus. **wearing¹,** a. Fatigant, lassant, épuisant. **wearing²,** s. Wearing apparel, vêtements mpl, habits mpl.

wearer, s. Personne f qui porte qch.

weariness, s. Lassitude f, fatigue f.

wearisome, a. Ennuyeux, fastidieux. **-ly,** adv. Ennuyeusement.

weary¹, a. 1. Fatigué ; las, f. lasse. 2. Las, dégoûté (of, de). To grow w. of sth., se dégoûter de qch. 3. Fatigant, obsédant. **-ily,** adv. 1. D'un air las, fatigué. 2. Avec fatigue ; péniblement.

weary², v. 1. v.i. (a) Se lasser, se fatiguer. (b) Trouver le temps long. (c) To weary for sth., désirer ardemment qch. ; languir après qch 2. v.tr. Lasser, fatiguer. **wearied,** a. Las, f. lasse ; fatigué. **wearying,** a. Ennuyeux.

weasel, s. Z: Belette f.

weather¹, s. Temps m. In all weathers, par tous les temps In such weather, par le temps qu'il fait. In the hot w., pendant les grandes chaleurs. (Wind and) weather permitting, si le temps le permet. What is the w. like? quel temps fait-il? F: To be under the weather, être indisposé. **weather-beaten,** a. 1. Battu par la tempête. 2. Bronzé, hâlé, basané. **weather-bound,** a. Retenu, arrêté, par le mauvais temps. **weather-forecast,** s. Bulletin m météorologique ; prévisions fpl du temps. **weather-prophet,** s. Personne f qui se pique de prédire le temps.

weather², v.tr. Nau: (a) To weather a headland, doubler un cap (à la voile). (b) To weather (out) a storm, survivre à une tempête.

weathercock, s. Girouette f.

weave, v.tr. (a) Tex: Tisser. (b) F: To

weave a plot, tramer un complot. (c) Tresser ;
entrelacer. **woven**, a Tissé. **weaving**, s.
1. Tissage m. **2.** Entrelacement m.
weaver, s. Tisserand m.
web, s. **1.** Tex: Tissu m. **2.** Spider's web,
toile f d'araignée. **web-footed**, a. Palmi-
pède ; aux pieds palmés.
webbed, a. Palmé, membrané. Webbed feet,
pattes palmées.
wed, v. **1.** v.tr. (a) Épouser ; se marier avec.
(b) (Of priest) To wed a couple, marier un
couple. (c) Unir (to, with, à). To be wedded
to an opinion, être obstinément attaché à une
opinion. **2.** v.i. Se marier. **wedded**, a.
1. Marié. My wedded wife, mon épouse
légitime. **2.** Wedded life, la vie conjugale.
wedding, s. **1.** Noce(s) f(pl) ; mariage m.
2. Attrib. Nuptial -aux ; de noce(s) ; de
mariage. **wedding-breakfast**, s. Repas
m de noces. **wedding-cake**, s. Gâteau m
de noce(s). **wedding-day**, s. **1.** Jour m
des noces. **2.** Anniversaire m du mariage.
wedding-guest, s. Invité, -ée (à un
mariage). **wedding-march**, s. Marche
nuptiale. **wedding-present**, s. Cadeau
m de noces. **wedding-ring**, s. Alliance f.
wedge¹, s. Coin m. **1.** F: It is the thin
end of the wedge, c'est un premier empiétement. **2.** Chose de forme triangulaire.
W. of cake, morceau m (triangulaire) de
gâteau. **wedge-shaped**, a. En (forme de)
coin.
wedge², v.tr. **1.** Coincer, assujettir. **2.** To
wedge (up) a piece of furniture, caler un
meuble. **3.** To wedge sth. in sth., enclaver,
F: enfoncer, serrer, qch. dans qch.
wedlock, s. (a) Mariage m. (b) La vie
conjugale.
Wednesday, s. Mercredi m.
wee, a. F: Petit ; tout petit ; minuscule.
weed¹, s. Bot: Mauvaise herbe ; herbe folle.
weed², v.tr. Sarcler. **weed out**, v.tr.
F: Éliminer ; extirper. **weeding**, s. Sar-
clage m.
weediness, s. F: Maigreur f ; apparence f
malingre.
weeds, s.pl. Vêtements m de deuil.
weedy, a. F: (Homme) malingre.
week, s. Semaine f. (a) What day of the
week is it? quel jour de la semaine sommes-
nous? Twice a week, deux fois par semaine.
(b) F: Huit jours. Every week, tous les
huit jours. Within the week, dans la huitaine.
To-day week, d'aujourd'hui en huit. In a
week or so, dans une huitaine. **week-end**, s.
Fin f de semaine ; week-end m, pl. week-ends.
weekday, s. Jour m ouvrable ; jour de
semaine. On weekdays, en semaine.
weekly. 1. a. (a) (Salaire) de la semaine ;
hebdomadaire. (b) (Pensionnaire) à la
semaine. **2.** s. Journal m hebdomadaire.
3. adv. Par semaine ; tous les huit jours.
weep, v.i. (a) Pleurer. To w. bitterly,
pleurer à chaudes larmes. To weep for joy,

pleurer de joie. (With cogn. acc.) To weep
tears, répandre, verser, des larmes. (b) (Of
tree) Pleurer. Weeping willow, saule pleureur. **weeping**, s. Pleurs mpl, larmes fpl.
weevil, s. Ent: Charançon m.
weft, s. Tex: Trame f.
weigh. 1. v.tr. (a) Peser ; faire la pesée de.
To w. sth. in one's hand, soupeser qch. (b) To
weigh one's words, peser, mesurer, ses
paroles. To weigh sth. (up) in one's mind,
considérer qch. (c) Nau: To weigh anchor,
lever l'ancre ; appareiller. **2.** v.i. (a) Peser ;
avoir du poids. To weigh heavily, peser lourd
inv. (b) The debt is weighing on his mind,
cette dette lui pèse sur l'esprit. Fate weighs
heavily on us, la fatalité s'appesantit sur nous.
(c) The point that weighs with me, ce qui a
du poids pour moi. **weigh down**, v.tr.
Surcharger. F: Weighed down with sorrow,
accablé de chagrin. **weighing**, s. **1.** Pesée f.
2. Levage m (de l'ancre) ; appareillage m.
weighing-machine, s. Appareil m de
pesage ; bascule f (de pesage). **weigh-
bridge**, s. Pont m à bascule.
weight¹, s. **1.** (a) Poids m. To sell by weight,
vendre au poids. Two pounds in weight,
d'un poids de deux livres. F: It is worth
its weight in gold, cela vaut son pesant d'or.
To gain weight, prendre du poids. P: To
throw one's weight about, faire de l'esbrouffe.
To pull one's weight, F: y mettre du sien.
(b) Poids, pesanteur f. To feel the weight of
sth., soupeser qch. Atomic weight, poids
atomique. **2.** Poids. Set of weights, série f
de poids. **3.** Charge f. F: That's a weight
off my mind, voilà qui me soulage l'esprit.
4. Force f (d'un coup). **5.** Importance f.
His word carries weight, sa parole a du poids.
People of weight, gens influents.
weight², v.tr. Attacher un poids à ; charger,
alourdir, d'un poids.
weightiness, s. **1.** Pesanteur f, lourdeur f.
2. F: Importance f, force f.
weighty, a. **1.** Pesant, lourd. **2.** Important,
sérieux. W. arguments, arguments puissants.
For w. reasons, pour des raisons graves.
weir, s. **1.** Barrage m. **2.** Déversoir m.
weird, a. (a) Surnaturel ; mystérieux.
(b) F: Étrange, singulier. **-ly**, adv. Étrangement.
weirdness, s. **1.** Étrangeté inquiétante.
2. F: Caractère singulier.
welcome¹, a. **1.** (a) Bienvenu. To make s.o.
welcome, faire bon accueil à qn. (b) As int.
Welcome! soyez le bienvenu ! To bid s.o.
welcome, souhaiter la bienvenue à qn.
2. Agréable ; acceptable. A welcome change,
un changement agréable **3.** You are welcome
to try, libre à vous d'essayer. You are
welcome to it, (i) c'est à votre service ;
(ii) grand bien vous fasse !
welcome², s. (a) Bienvenue f. (b) Accueil
m. To give s.o. a hearty welcome, faire bon
accueil à qn.

welcome³, *v.tr.* **1.** Souhaiter la bienvenue à ; faire bon accueil à. **2.** (*a*) Recevoir avec plaisir. (*b*) *To w. s.o. with joy,* accueillir qn avec joie.

weld, *v.tr.* (*a*) Souder, unir à chaud. (*b*) *F:* Unir, joindre, étroitement. **welding,** *s.* Soudage *m,* soudure *f.*

welfare, *s.* Bien-être *m* ; prospérité *f.* Public welfare, le salut public. Child welfare, puériculture sociale. Welfare work, assistance sociale.

welkin (the), *s. Poet :* Le firmament.

well¹, *s.* **1.** Puits *m ;* source *f.* **2.** (*a*) Puits, cage *f* (d'un ascenseur). (*b*) Partie encaissée, creux *m.*

well², *v.i.* To well (up), jaillir ; (*of spring*) sourdre.

well³. I. *adv.* Bien. **1.** (*a*) To work well, bien travailler. This lad will do well, ce garçon fera son chemin, ira loin. To do as well as one can, faire de son mieux. Well done ! bravo ! très bien ! *F:* To do oneself well, bien se nourrir. He accepted, as well he might, il accepta, et rien d'étonnant. One might as well say, autant dire. Very well! très bien ! (c'est) entendu ! (*b*) It speaks well for, cela fait honneur à. She deserves well of you, elle mérite bien votre reconnaissance. Well intended, fait à bonne intention. (*c*) You are well out of it, soyez heureux d'en être quitte. Well met! soyez le bienvenu ! **2.** It is well worth trying, cela vaut bien la peine d'essayer. Well on into the small hours, fort avant dans la nuit. Well on in years, avancé en âge. To be well up *in a subject,* bien posséder un sujet. **3.** Pretty well all, presque tout. *F:* It serves him jolly well right, c'est joliment bien fait pour lui. **4.** (*a*) As well, aussi. I want some as well, il m'en faut également. (*b*) As well as, de même que ; comme ; non moins que. **5.** (*a*) Well, as I was telling you, donc, comme je vous disais. *Well, who was it?* eh bien, qui était-ce ? (*b*) Well I never! pas possible ! *Well, it cannot be helped,* ma foi ! on n'y peut rien. Well, well! que voulez-vous ! (*c*) Well then, eh bien, alors. II. **well,** *pred.a.* **1.** To be well, être en bonne santé, être bien portant. Well and strong, robuste. Not to feel well, ne pas se sentir bien. **2.** (*a*) It would be well to, il serait bon de. It would be just as well if you were present, il y aurait avantage à ce que vous soyez présent. (*b*) It was well that you were there, c'est bien heureux que vous vous soyez trouvé là. (*c*) All's well that ends well, tout est bien qui finit bien. (*d*) That's all very well, tout cela est bel et bon. It is all very well for you to say that . . ., libre à vous de dire que. . . . He is all very well in his way, il n'y a rien à dire contre lui. Well and good! soit ! bon ! III. **well,** *s.* To wish s.o. well, vouloir du bien à qn ; être bien disposé (en)vers qn. **well advised,** *pred.a.* (*a*) (*Of pers.*) Bien avisé. (*b*) (*Of action*) Sage, prudent. **well-being,** *s.* Bien-être *m.* **well-born,** *a.* Bien né ; de bonne famille. **well-bred,** *a.* Bien élevé, bien appris. **well-conducted,** *a.* **1.** Qui se conduit bien ; sage. **2.** Bien dirigé. **well directed,** *a.* Bien ajusté. **well disposed,** *a.* Bien disposé, bien porté (*to, towards,* envers). **well-doing,** *s.* **1.** Bien faire *m* ; le bien. **2.** Prospérité *f,* succès *m.* **well earned,** *a.* Bien mérité. **well educated,** *a.* Instruit. **well found,** *a.* Bien équipé ; bien pourvu (*in,* de). **well founded,** *a.* Bien fondé ; légitime. **well informed,** *a.* Bien renseigné, bien informé, instruit. In well-informed quarters, en lieu compétent. **well judged,** *a.* Judicieux ; bien estimé, bien calculé. **well known,** *a.* (Bien) connu ; célèbre ; réputé ; renommé (*for,* pour). As is well known, comme tout le monde le sait. **well made,** *a.* **1.** (Homme) bien découplé. **2.** (Habit) de coupe soignée. **well-mannered,** *a.* Qui a de bonnes manières ; bien élevé. **well marked,** *a.* Bien marqué ; très évident ; accusé. *Well-m. differences,* différences tranchées. **well-matched,** *a.* (Ménage) bien assorti. *The two teams are well-m.,* les deux équipes sont de force (égale). **well-meaning,** *a.* Bien intentionné. **well-meant,** *a.* Fait avec une bonne intention. **well-nigh,** *adv. Lit :* Presque. **well off,** *adj.phr.* **1.** (*a*) To be well off, être dans l'aisance, à l'aise ; être riche. Well-off people, gens aisés. (*b*) Prospère. You don't know when you are well off, vous ne savez pas quand vous êtes bien. **2.** To be well off for sth., être bien pourvu, bien fourni, de qch. **well-ordered,** *a.* Bien ordonné ; méthodique. **well read,** *a.* Instruit ; qui a de la lecture. **well-regulated,** *a.* = WELL-ORDERED. **well spent,** *a.* Bien utilisé ; bien employé. **well-spoken,** *a.* **1.** (*a*) Qui parle bien. (*b*) A la parole affable. **2.** To be well spoken of, avoir une bonne réputation. **well-to-do,** *a.* To be well-to-do, être dans l'aisance ; être à son aise. **well-wisher,** *s.* Ami, -ie, partisan *m.* **well-worn,** *a.* (*a*) (Vêtement) fortement usagé. (*b*) (Argument) rebattu.

Wellingtons, *s.pl. Cost:* Bottes *f* en caoutchouc.

Welsh. I. *a.* Gallois ; du pays de Galles. **2.** *s.* (*a*) *pl.* The Welsh, les Gallois *m.* (*b*) *Ling :* Le gallois.

welsher, *s. Turf :* Bookmaker marron.

Welshman, *s.* Gallois *m.*

Welshwoman, *s.* Galloise *f.*

welter¹, *s. F:* **1.** Confusion *f,* désordre *m.* **2.** Masse confuse, fouillis *m.*

welter², *v.i.* Se vautrer, se rouler. To be weltering in one's blood, baigner dans son sang.

wen, *s.* **1.** *F:* Loupe *f.* **2.** *F:* Goitre *m.*

wench, *s.* (*a*) Jeune fille *f,* jeune femme *f.*

Strapping w., grande gaillarde. *(b) Kitchen w.*, fille de cuisine.

wend, *v.tr.* Lit: To wend one's way, porter, diriger, ses pas (*to,* vers).

werewolf, *s.* Loup-garou *m, pl.* loups-garous.

west. I. *s. (a)* Ouest *m,* occident *m,* couchant *m. (b)* The West, l'Occident. **2.** *adv.* A l'ouest, à l'occident. To travel west, voyager vers l'ouest. *P:* To go west, mourir; *Mil:* passer l'arme à gauche. **3.** *a.* Ouest *inv*; (vent) d'ouest; (pays) de l'ouest, occidental, -aux. **West Indian,** *a.* Des Antilles; antillais.

westerly. I. *a.* Westerly wind, vent d'ouest, qui vient de l'ouest. **2.** *adv.* Vers l'ouest.

western, *a.* Ouest *inv,* de l'ouest; occidental, -aux.

westward. I. *s.* Direction *f* de l'ouest. To westward, vers l'ouest. **2.** *a.* A l'ouest, de l'ouest.

westwards, *adv.* Vers l'ouest, à l'ouest.

wet¹, *a. (a)* Mouillé, humide; imbibé d'eau. To get one's feet wet, se mouiller les pieds. To be wet through, être trempé (jusqu'aux os). Wringing wet, mouillé à tordre. Ink still wet, encre encore fraîche. *(b)* Wet weather, temps humide, pluvieux. *It is going to be wet,* il va pleuvoir. The wet season, la saison des pluies. **wet blanket,** *s. F:* **I.** To throw a wet blanket over the meeting, jeter un froid sur l'assemblée. **2.** Rabat-joie *m inv.* **wet nurse,** *s.* Nourrice *f.*

wet², *s.* **I.** Humidité *f.* **2.** Pluie *f.*

wet³, *v.tr.* Mouiller. *F:* To wet the tea, infuser le thé. **wetting,** *s.* To get a wetting, se faire tremper.

wether, *s.* Mouton *m.*

wetness, *s.* Humidité *f.*

whack¹. I. *s. (a)* Coup *m* (de bâton). *(b) F:* To have a whack at sth., essayer de faire qch. *(c) P:* Part *f,* portion *f.* **2.** *int. F:* V'lan!

whack², *v.tr. F: (a)* Donner des coups à. *(b)* Battre à plates coutures. **whacking¹,** *a. P:* Énorme; colossal, -aux. **whacking²,** *s. F:* Rossée *f,* raclée *f.*

whale¹, *s. Z:* Baleine *f.* **whale-boat,** *s.* Baleinière *f.* **whale-oil,** *s.* Huile *f* de baleine.

whale², *v.i.* Faire la pêche à la baleine. **whaling,** *s.* Pêche *f* à la baleine. Whaling ship, baleinier *m.*

whalebone, *s.* Baleine *f.*

whaler, *s.* **I.** Baleinier *m*; pêcheur *m* de baleines. **2.** *(Ship)* Baleinier.

wharf, *s. Nau:* Appontement *m,* débarcadère *m,* embarcadère *m*; quai *m.*

wharfinger, *s.* Propriétaire *m* d'un quai.

what. I. *a.* **I.** (Ce) que, qui. *He traded with what capital he had,* il faisait le commerce avec ce qu'il possédait de capital. **2.** Quel, *f.* quelle. *Tell me what time it is,* dites-moi l'heure qu'il est. *What right has he to give orders?* de quel droit donne-t-il des ordres? What good is this? à quoi cela est-il bon? What day of the month is it? le combien sommes-nous? **3.** What an idea! quelle idée! *What a fool he is!* qu'il est bête! *What a lot of people!* que de gens! II. **what,** *pron.* **I.** Ce qui, ce que. What is done cannot be undone, ce qui est fait est fait. And what is more, et qui plus est. *This is what it is all about,* voici ce dont il s'agit. Come what may, advienne que pourra. Say what he will, quoi qu'il dise. *What with golf and what with tennis,* entre le golf et le tennis. Not a day but what it rains, il ne se passe pas un jour qu'il ne pleuve. *P:* To give s.o. what for, laver la tête à qn. **2.** *(a)* Qu'est-ce qui? qu'est-ce que? que? quoi? What is it? (i) qu'est-ce? qu'est-ce que c'est? (ii) qu'est-ce qu'il y a? What is the matter? qu'y a-t-il? de quoi s'agit-il? What is that to you? qu'est-ce que cela vous fait? What's the use? à quoi bon? What is to be done? comment faire? que faire? What is he like? comment est-il? What do you take me for? pour qui me prenez-vous? What's it all about? de quoi s'agit-il? What about a game of bridge? si on faisait une partie de bridge? What about you? et vous? Well, what about it? (i) et puis après? (ii) eh bien, qu'en dites-vous? What is that for? à quoi sert cela? What (on earth) for? mais pourquoi donc? What then? et après? et alors? What though we are poor? qu'importe que nous soyons pauvres? What (did you say)? plaît-il? pardon? *F:* comment? What of that? qu'est-ce que cela fait? *(b)* Ce qui, ce que. *I don't know what to do,* je ne sais que faire. *He knows what's what,* il en sait long; il s'y connaît. **3.** *(a) What he has suffered!* ce qu'il a souffert! What next! par exemple! *(b)* What? you can't come! comment! vous ne pouvez pas venir! **what-d'ye-call-her, -him, -it,** *s. P:* Machin, -ine.

whatever. I. *pron. (a)* Whatever you like, tout ce que vous voudrez; n'importe quoi. *(b)* Quoi qui, quoi que + *sub.* Whatever it may be, quoi que ce soit. **2.** *a. (a)* Quelque . . . qui, que + *sub.* Whatever ambition moves him, quelque ambition qui l'agite. *(b)* (i) Aucun. He has no chance whatever, il n'a aucune chance. None whatever, pas un seul. Nothing whatever, absolument rien. (ii) Has he any chance whatever? a-t-il une chance quelconque?

whatsoever, *pron. & a.* = WHATEVER.

wheat, *s.* Blé *m,* froment *m.*

wheaten, *a.* De froment, de blé. Fine wheaten bread, pain de gruau.

wheedle, *v.tr.* Enjôler, cajoler, embobeliner.

wheedling, *a.* Enjôleur, câlin. *W.* voice, voix pateline.

wheedler, *s.* Enjôleur, -euse; patelin, -ine.

wheel¹, *s.* **I.** Roue *f*; roulette *f.* *(a) Veh:* Back wheel, roue arrière. *(b) F:* There are wheels within wheels, il y a toutes sortes de forces en jeu. The wheels of government,

les rouages *m* de l'administration. (*c*) N*au* :
To take the wheel, prendre la barre. **2.** Hist :
To break s.o. on the wheel, rouer qn.

wheel². **I.** **1.** *v.tr.* (*a*) Tourner ; faire pivoter.
(*b*) Rouler. **2.** *v.i.* Tourner en rond ; tournoyer.

wheelbarrow, *s.* Brouette *f.*

wheelwright, *s.* Charron *m.*

wheeze¹, *s.* **1.** Respiration sifflante. **2.** P :
Truc *m.* A good wheeze, une heureuse idée.

wheeze², *v.i.* Respirer péniblement.

wheezy, *a.* Asthmatique ; F : poussif.

whelk, *s.* Moll : Buccin *m.*

whelp, *s.* Petit *m* d'un fauve.

when. I. *adv.* Quand ? **When is the meeting?**
pour quand est la réunion ? **When ever will**
he come? quand donc viendra-t-il ? **II. when,**
conj. **1.** Quand, lorsque. *When he was born,*
lors de sa naissance. *When I was young,* du
temps que j'étais jeune. *He will speak when*
I have done, il parlera après que j'aurai fini.
He looks in when passing, il nous fait une
petite visite en passant. **2.** (*a*) **The day when**
I met you, le jour où je vous ai rencontré.
One day when I was on duty, un jour que
j'étais de service. (*b*) (=*and then*) Et (alors).

whence, *adv.* D'où.

whenever, *adv.* (*a*) Toutes les fois que ;
chaque fois que. (*b*) **Whenever you like,** à
n'importe quel moment.

where, *adv.* **1.** (*a*) Où ? **Where ever have**
you been? mais d'où venez-vous ? (*b*) **Where**
do you come from? d'où venez-vous ?
2. (*a*) (There) where, (là) où. I shall stay
where I am, je resterai (là) où je suis. (*b*) W.
you are mistaken, ce en quoi vous vous
trompez c'est. (*c*) **The house where I was**
born, la maison où, dans laquelle, je suis né.

whereabouts. I. *adv.* Où (donc)? **Where-**
abouts are you? où donc êtes-vous ? **2.** *s.* Lieu
m où se trouve qn, qch. No one knows his
whereabouts, personne ne sait où il est.

whereafter, *rel.adv.* Après quoi.

whereas, *conj.* **1.** Attendu que, vu que,
puisque. **2.** Alors que, tandis que.

whereat, *adv.* A quoi, sur quoi, de quoi, etc.

whereby, *adv.* **1.** Par quoi ? Par quel moyen ?
2. Decision whereby, décision par laquelle.

wherefore. I. *adv.* (*a*) Pourquoi ? pour quelle
raison ? (*b*) = THEREFORE. **2.** *s.* The whys
and wherefores, les pourquoi et les parce que.

wherefrom, *adv.* D'où.

wherein, *adv.* **1.** En quoi ? **2.** Dans lequel ;
où.

whereof, *adv.* **1.** En quoi ? de quoi ?
2. De quoi ; dont.

whereon, *adv.* **1.** Sur quoi ? **2.** Sur quoi,
sur lequel.

wheresoever, *adv.* = WHEREVER.

whereupon, *adv.* **1.** = WHEREON **1. 2.** (*a*)
= WHEREON **2.** (*b*) W. he left us, sur quoi il
nous quitta.

wherever, *adv.* **1.** Partout où ; n'importe
où. *I will go wherever you want me to,*

j'irai où vous voudrez. **2. Wherever they**
come from *they have done well,* d'où qu'ils
viennent ils se sont bien acquittés.

wherewith, *adv.* **1.** Avec quoi ? **2.** (*a*) Avec
lequel ; avec quoi ; au moyen duquel.
(*b*) = WHEREUPON **2** (*b*).

wherewithal, *s.* The wherewithal, le nécessaire ; les moyens *m.*

wherry, *s.* Bachot *m* (de rivière).

whet, *v.tr.* **1.** Aiguiser, repasser. **2.** F :
Stimuler, exciter.

whether, *conj.* **1.** Si. *I don't know w. it is*
true, je ne sais pas si c'est vrai. **2. Whether**
it rains or blows, soit qu'il vente, soit qu'il
pleuve. W. he comes or not, qu'il vienne ou
non. Whether or not, qu'il en soit ainsi ou
non.

whetstone, *s.* Pierre *f* à aiguiser.

whey, *s.* Petit lait.

which. I. *a.* **1.** Quel, *f.* quelle ; *pl.* quels,
f. quelles ? **Which way do we go?** par où
allons-nous ? **Which one?** lequel ? laquelle ?
W. one of us? lequel d'entre nous ? **2.** Lequel,
f. laquelle ; *pl.* lesquels, lesquelles. **Look**
which way you will, de quelque côté que vous
regardiez. **II. which,** *pron.* **1.** Lequel, etc.
Which have you chosen? lequel avez-vous
choisi ? W. of you can answer? lequel d'entre
vous peut répondre ? **I don't mind which,**
cela m'est égal. **2.** (*a*) Qui ; que ; lequel.
The house which is to be sold, la maison qui
est à vendre. *The books w. I possess,* les
livres que je possède. (*b*) Ce qui, ce que.
If this happens, w God forbid, si cela arrive,
ce qu'à Dieu ne plaise. **3.** (*a*) To which,
at which, auquel, *f.* à laquelle, *pl.* auxquels,
auxquelles. Of which, from which, duquel,
f. de laquelle ; *pl.* desquels, desquelles ; dont.
The hotels at which we stayed, les hôtels où
nous sommes descendus. (*b*) In which he
is right, en quoi il a raison.

whichever, *rel. pron.* & *a.* **1.** (*a*) *pron.*
Celui, *f.* celle ; *pl.* ceux, celles qui, celui
que, n'importe lequel, *f.* laquelle, *pl.*
lesquel(le)s. (*b*) *a.* Le . . . que ; n'importe
quel. *Take w. book you like best,*
prenez le livre que vous aimez le
mieux. **2.** *a.* N'importe quel ; quelque
. . . que. *W. way he turned,* de
quelque côté qu'il se tournât, n'importe de
quel côté il se tournait.

whiff, *s.* Bouffée *f.*

while¹, *s.* **1.** (*a*) (Espace *m* de) temps *m.*
After a while, après quelque temps. In a
little while, sous peu ; avant peu. A little
while ago, il y a peu de temps. A long while,
longtemps. For a long while past, depuis
longtemps. **A good while,** pas mal de
temps. Quite a while, pas mal de temps.
(*b*) *Adv.phr.* The while, en attendant ; pendant ce temps. **2. To be worth (one's) while,**
valoir la peine. **I will make it worth your**
while, vous serez bien payé de votre peine.

while², *v.tr.* To while away, faire passer.

while³, *conj.* **1.** (*a*) Pendant que, tandis que. *W. reading I fell asleep,* tout en lisant, je me suis endormi. **While this was going on,** sur ces entrefaites. (*b*) Tant que. **While I live,** tant que je vivrai. **2.** Quoique, bien que, tout en. . . . **While I admit, while admitting, the thing is difficult,** quoique j'admette, tout en reconnaissant, que la chose est difficile. **3.** Tandis que.

whilst, *conj.* = WHILE³.

whim, *s.* Caprice *m*; fantaisie *f*, lubie *f*. **Passing whim,** toquade *f*. **As the whim takes her,** selon son caprice.

whimper¹, *s.* Geignement *m*, plainte *f*.

whimper², *v.i.* (*a*) Pleurnicher, geindre. (*b*) (*Of dog*) Faire entendre une plainte.

whimsical, *a.* Capricieux, fantasque. **-ally,** *adv.* Capricieusement, bizarrement.

whimsicality, *s.* Bizarrerie *f*.

whin, *s.* *Bot:* Ajonc commun.

whine¹, *s.* **1.** Plainte *f*; geignement *m*. **2.** *F:* Jérémiade *f*.

whine², **1.** *v.i.* Se plaindre; (*of infant*) pleurnicher, piauler; (*of dog*) geindre. **2.** *v.tr.* Dire (qch.) d'un ton plaintif.

whining¹, *a.* (*a*) Geignant; (enfant) pleurnicheur, -euse; (ton) plaintif. (*b*) Geignard.

whining², *s.* (*a*) Geignement *m*. (*b*) *F:* Jérémiades *fpl*; plaintes *fpl*. **Stop your whining!** assez de jérémiades !

whinny¹, *s.* Hennissement *m* (de cheval).

whinny², *v.i.* (*Of horse*) Hennir.

whip¹, *s.* Fouet *m.* **whip-hand,** *s.* *F:* **To have the whip-hand,** avoir l'avantage. **whip-lash,** *s.* Mèche *f* de fouet. **whip-top,** *s.* *Toys:* Sabot *m.*

whip², *v.* **I.** *v.tr.* **1.** (*a*) Fouetter; donner le fouet à. (*b*) Whipped cream, crème fouettée. **2.** Mouvoir vivement. **He whipped the revolver out of his pocket,** il sortit vivement le revolver de sa poche. **II. whip,** *v.i.* Fouetter. **The rain whipped against the panes,** la pluie fouettait, cinglait, contre les vitres. **whip off,** *v.tr* Enlever vivement.

whipping, *s.* **1.** (*a*) Fouettage *m.* (*b*) Fouettée *f* **To give a child a whipping,** donner le fouet à un enfant. **2.** Fouettement *m* (de la pluie).

whipper-snapper, *s.* *F:* Freluquet *m*, paltoquet *m.*

whippet, *s.* **1.** (*Dog*) Whippet *m.* **2.** *Mil:* Char *m* d'assaut de modèle léger.

whir¹, ², *s. & v.i.* = WHIRR¹, ³

whirl¹, *s.* (*a*) Mouvement *m* giratoire, giration *f.* (*b*) Tourbillon *m*, tourbillonnement *m*, tournoiement *m* **My head is in a whirl,** la tête me tourne.

whirl², **1.** *v.i.* (*a*) To whirl (around), tourbillonner, tournoyer. (*b*) To whirl along, rouler, filer, à toute vitesse. **2.** *v.tr* (*a*) Faire tournoyer, faire tourbillonner (*b*) The train whirled us along, le train nous emportait à toute vitesse.

whirligig, *s.* **1.** *Toys:* Tourniquet *m.* **2.** Pirouette *f.*

whirlpool, *s.* Tourbillon *m* (d'eau); remous *m*; gouffre *m.*

whirlwind, *s.* Tourbillon *m*; trombe *f.* *F:* To come in like a whirlwind, entrer en trombe, en coup de vent.

whirr¹, *s.* Bruissement *m*; ronronnement *m*; vrombissement *m.*

whirr², *v.i.* Tourner à toute vitesse; ronronner; vrombir.

whisk¹, *s.* Mouvement *m* en coup de fouet. **A whisk of the tail,** un coup de queue.

whisk². **1.** *v.i.* S'élancer. **To whisk away,** filer comme un trait. **To whisk past,** passer comme le vent. **2.** *v.tr.* (*a*) (*Of cow*) **To whisk its tail,** agiter sa queue. (*b*) **To whisk sth. off,** enlever qch. d'un geste rapide.

whisker, *s.* *Usu. pl.* **Whiskers,** favoris *m*; moustache(s) *f* (de chat).

whiskered, *a.* A favoris.

whisky, *s.* Whisky *m.*

whisper¹, *s.* **1.** (*a*) Chuchotement *m.* **To speak in a whisper,** parler bas. (*b*) *F:* Bruissement *m* (des feuilles); murmure *m* (de l'eau). **2.** Rumeur *f*, bruit *m.* **There is a whisper that...,** il court un bruit que....

whisper². **1.** *v.i.* Chuchoter; parler bas; (*of leaves*) susurrer; (*of water*) murmurer. **To whisper to s.o.,** souffler qch. à l'oreille de qn. **2.** *v.tr.* (*a*) Whispered conversation, conversation à voix basse. (*b*) It is whispered that, il court un bruit que. **whispering,** *s.* **1.** Chuchotement *m.* **2.** Bruissement *m*; murmure *m.*

whisperer, *s.* Chuchoteur, -euse.

whist, *s.* Whist *m.* **Whist drive,** tournoi *m* de whist.

whistle¹, *s.* **1.** Sifflement *m*; coup *m* de sifflet. **2.** Sifflet *m.* **To blow a whistle,** donner un coup de sifflet.

whistle². **1.** *v.i.* (*a*) Siffler. **To whistle for one's dog,** siffler son chien *F:* He may whistle for his money, il peut courir après son argent. (*b*) Donner un coup de sifflet. **2.** *v.tr.* Siffler, siffloter.

whistler, *s* Siffleur, -euse.

whit¹, *s* Brin *m*, iota *m*, petit morceau **He is not a whit the better for it,** il ne s'en porte aucunement mieux. *He is every whit as good as you,* il vous vaut bien.

Whit², *a* **Whit Sunday,** (dimanche *m* de) la Pentecôte.

white¹. **I.** *a.* **1.** Blanc, *f.* blanche. **He is going white,** il commence à blanchir **2.** (*a*) White bread, pain blanc White wine, vin blanc. (*b*) The white races, les races blanches. **A white man** (i) un blanc; (ii) un homme loyal. (*c*) White with fear, blanc de peur. **To go white,** pâlir, blêmir **As white as a sheet,** pâle comme la mort. **II. white,** *s.* **1.** Blanc *m*; couleur blanche **2.** Dressed in white, habillé en blanc, de blanc *Com:* **White sale,** vente de blanc. *Sp:* Whites, pantalon *m* de flanelle blanche. **3.** Blanc, *f.* blanche; homme, femme, de la race blanche. **4.** (*a*) White of egg, blanc d'œuf. (*b*) White of the eye, blanc de l'œil. **white-haired,** *a.* Aux cheveux blancs. **white-headed,** *a.* Aux cheveux blancs. **white hot,** *a.* *Metall:* Chauffé à blanc; porté au blanc. **white-lipped,** *a.* Blême, livide. **white-livered,** *a.* *F:* Poltron.

white², *v.tr.* Whited sepulchre, sépulcre blanchi.

whitebait, *s.* *Cu:* Blanchaille *f.*

whiten, *v.tr.* Blanchir.

whiteness, *s.* (*a*) Blancheur *f.* (*b*) Pâleur *f.*

whitethorn, *s.* *Bot:* Aubépine *f.*

whitewash¹, *s.* Blanc *m* de chaux, badigeon blanc.

whitewash², *v.tr.* (*a*) Badigeonner en blanc; blanchir à la chaux. (*b*) *F:* Blanchir, disculper. **whitewashing,** *s.* Peinture *f* à la chaux; badigeonnage *m* en blanc.

whither, *adv.* **1.** Où? vers quel lieu? **2.** (Là) où.

whithersoever, *adv.* N'importe vers quel endroit; n'importe où.

whiting, *s.* *Ich:* Merlan *m.*

whitish, *a.* Blanchâtre.

Whitsun(tide), *s.* (Fête *f* de) la Pentecôte.

whittle, *v.tr.* *F:* To whittle down s.o.'s allowance, rogner la pension de qn.

whizz¹. **1.** *int.* Pan! **2.** *s.* *F:* Sifflement *m.*

whizz², *v.i.* Siffler. **To whizz past,** passer en sifflant; (*of motor cycle*) passer à toute vitesse.

who, *pron. nom.* **1.** (*a*) Qui? qui est-ce qui? *Who is that lady?* qui, quelle, est cette dame? *F:* Who on earth is it? qui cela peut-il bien être? *F:* Who does he think he is? pour qui se prend-il? (*b*) *F:* Who do you want? qui voulez-vous? **2.** (*Relative*) (*a*) Qui. *My friend who came yesterday,* mon ami qui est venu hier. (*b*) Lequel, *f.* laquelle; *pl.* lesquel(le)s. *The father of this girl, who is very rich,* le père de cette jeune fille, lequel est très riche.

whoa, *int.* Ho!

whoever, *pron. nom.* **1.** Celui qui; quiconque. **2.** Qui que + *sub.* *W. you are, speak!* qui que vous soyez, parlez!

whole. **I.** *a.* **1.** (*Of pers.*) Sain et sauf; (*of thg*) intact. **2.** (*a*) Intégral, -aux; entier; complet, -ète. Ox roasted whole, bœuf rôti entier. (*b*) To tell the whole truth, dire toute la vérité. *The w. world,* le monde entier. **wholly,** *adv.* **1.** Tout à fait; complètement, entièrement. **2.** Intégralement; en totalité. *W. or partly,* en tout ou en partie. **II. whole,** *s.* Tout *m,* totalité *f,* ensemble *m.* The whole of the school, l'école entière; toute l'école. The whole amounts to, le total se monte à. Taken as a whole, pris dans sa totalité. (Up)on the whole, à tout prendre; en somme; somme toute. **whole-meal,** *attrib. a.* (Pain) complet. **whole-time,** *attrib. a.* Whole-time work, travail qui occupe la journée entière.

wholesale. **1.** *s.* (Vente *f* en) gros *m.* Wholesale and retail, gros et détail. **2.** *a.* (*a*)Wholesale trade, commerce de gros, en gros. (*b*) *F:* A wholesale slaughter, une tuerie en masse. **3.** *adv.* (Vendre, acheter) en gros.

wholesome, *a.* Sain; (air) salubre.

wholesomeness, *s.* Nature saine; salubrité *f* (du climat).

whom, *pron., objective case.* **1.** Qui? *W. did you see?* qui avez-vous vu? qui est-ce que vous avez vu? **Whom else?** qui d'autre? **2.** (*Relative*) (*a*) (*Direct obj.*) Que; lequel, *f.* laquelle; *pl.* lesquels, *f.* lesquelles. *The man w. you saw,* l'homme que vous avez vu. (*b*) (*Indirect obj. and after prep.*) Qui. *The beggar to w. you gave a penny,* le mendiant à qui vous avez donné deux sous. *The two officers between w. she was sitting,* les deux officiers entre lesquels elle était assise. *The friend of whom I speak,* l'ami dont je parle. *These two men, both of whom were quite young,* ces deux hommes, qui tous deux étaient tout jeunes. **3.** Celui, *f.* celle, que; qui.

whom(so)ever, *pron.* **1.** Celui (quel qu'il soit) que. **2.** N'importe qui que; qui que ce soit que.

whoop¹, *int.* Houp!

whoop², *v.i.* Pousser des houp. **whooping-cough,** *s.* *Med:* Coqueluche *f.*

whop, *v.tr.* *F:* (*a*) Rosser, battre. (*b*) Battre, rouler.

whorl, *s.* **1.** *Bot:* Verticille *m.* **2.** Tour *m;* spire *f,* volute *f.*

whortleberry, *s.* Airelle *f* myrtille *f.*

whose, *poss.pron.* **1.** De qui? à qui? **Whose are these gloves?** à qui sont ces gants? **Whose daughter are you?** de qui êtes-vous la fille? **2.** (*Relative*) (*a*) Dont. (*b*) (*After prep.*) De qui; duquel, *f.* de laquelle; *pl.* desquels, *f.* desquelles.

whosoever, *pron.* = WHOEVER.

why. **1.** *adv.* (*a*) Pourquoi? pour quelle raison? **Why didn't you say so?** que ne le disiez-vous? **Why not?** pourquoi pas? **Why so?** pourquoi cela? (*b*) That is (the reason) why, voilà pourquoi. **2.** *s.* Pourquoi *m.* **3.** *int.* Why, it's Jones! tiens, mais c'est Jones! **Why, you are not afraid, are you?** voyons, vous n'avez pas peur? *Why, what's the matter?* mais qu'avez-vous donc?

wick, *s.* Mèche *f.*

wicked, *a.* **1.** Mauvais, méchant. **2.** *F:* Malicieux. **-ly,** *adv.* **1.** Méchamment. **2.** *F:* (*a*) Terriblement, affreusement. (*b*) Malicieusement.

wickedness, *s.* Méchanceté *f.*

wicker. **1.** *s.* = WICKERWORK. **2.** *Attrib.* D'osier, en osier.

wickerwork, *s.* Vannerie *f;* osier tressé.

wicket, *s.* **1.** Guichet *m* (d'une porte). **2.** (*a*) (*In large door*) Porte à piétons. (*b*) (*Into garden*) Barrière *f.* **3.** *Cr:* Guichet.

wide. **I.** *a.* **1.** Large. The road is twelve feet wide, la route a douze pieds de largeur.

How w. is the room? quelle est la largeur de la pièce? **2.** Étendu, vaste, ample. The wide world, l'univers m. **3.** Ample, large. **4.** Éloigné, loin. **-ly,** adv. Largement. W. known, très connu. W. held opinion, opinion largement répandue. He has travelled widely, il a beaucoup voyagé. W. different versions, versions qui diffèrent du tout au tout. II. **wide,** adv. **1.** Loin. Wide apart, espacé. **2.** Largement. **wide open,** a. (Tout) grand ouvert. To fling the gates wide open, ouvrir les portes toutes grandes. W.-o. eyes, yeux grands ouverts, écarquillés. **widespread,** a. **1.** Étendu. **2.** Répandu; général, -aux.

widen. **1.** v.tr. (a) Élargir. (b) Étendre. **2.** v.i. S'élargir; s'agrandir (en large). **widen out,** v.i. S'élargir; s'épanouir.

widow, s. Veuve f.

widowed, a. Veuve. She was w. early, elle devint veuve de bonne heure. He lives with his w. mother, il habite avec sa mère qui est veuve.

widower, s. Veuf m.

widowhood, s. Veuvage m.

width, s. Largeur f; ampleur f. The footpath is four feet in w., le trottoir a quatre pieds de large.

wield, v.tr. Manier; tenir (le sceptre). To wield power, exercer le pouvoir.

wife, s. Femme f, épouse f. She was his second wife, il l'avait épousée en secondes noces. The farmer's wife, la fermière. To take a wife, se marier; F: prendre femme.

wifely, a. D'épouse, qui conviennent à une femme mariée.

wig, s. **1.** Perruque f. **2.** F: Chevelure f; tignasse f. **wig-maker,** s. Perruquier m.

wigging, s. F: Verte semonce. To give s.o. a good wigging, tancer vertement qn.

wigwam, s. Wigwam m.

wild, a. **1.** Sauvage. **2.** (a) (Vent) furieux. It was a wild night, c'était une nuit de tempête. (b) Farouche, inapprivoisé. (c) Dissipé, dissolu. To lead a wild life, mener une vie déréglée. To run wild, courir en liberté. **3.** (a) Affolé. Wild eyes, yeux égarés. Wild with joy, fou, f. folle, de joie. It makes me wild, cela me fait rager. F: To be w. with s.o., être furieux contre qn. (b) Fantasque; insensé; (conjecture) au hasard. Wild talk, propos en l'air. **4.** s.pl. Wilds, région sauvage. To go out into the wilds, pénétrer dans des régions inexplorées. **-ly,** adv. **1.** D'une manière extravagante. To talk wildly, dire des folies. Her heart was beating w., son cœur battait à se rompre. **2.** (Répondre) au hasard. **wild beast,** s. Bête f sauvage. **wild-cat,** attrib.a. F: Wild-cat scheme, projet dénué de bon sens. **wild-fowl,** s. Coll: Gibier m à plume.

wilderness, s. Désert m; lieu m sauvage; pays m inculte.

wildfire, s. F: To spread like wildfire, se répandre comme une traînée de poudre.

wildness, s. **1.** État m sauvage. **2.** (a) Fureur f (du vent). (b) Dérèglement m (de mœurs). **3.** Extravagance f (de paroles).

wile[1], s. Usu. pl. Ruses f, artifices m.

wile[2], v.tr. Séduire, charmer.

wilful, a. **1.** Entêté, volontaire. **2.** Fait exprès. Jur: Wilful murder, homicide volontaire, prémédité. **-fully,** adv. **1.** Exprès, à dessein, avec intention. **2.** Avec entêtement; volontairement.

wilfulness, s. Obstination f, entêtement m.

wiliness, s. Astuce f.

will[1], s. **1.** (a) Volonté f. He has a will of his own, il est volontaire. Man lacking strength of will, homme qui manque de caractère. The will to win, la volonté de vaincre. To take the will for the deed, accepter l'intention f pour le fait. Where there's a will there's a way, vouloir c'est pouvoir. (b) To work with a will, travailler de bon cœur. **2.** (a) Décision f; volonté. To work one's will upon s.o., faire à sa guise avec qn. (b) Bon plaisir; gré m. At will, à volonté; à discrétion. To do sth. of one's own free will, faire qch. de son plein gré. I did it against my will, je l'ai fait malgré moi, à contre-cœur. **3.** Jur: Testament m. The last will and testament of, les dernières volontés de. To mention s.o. in one's will, mettre qn sur son testament. **will-power,** s. Volonté f.

will[2], v.tr. **1.** (a) Fate willed (it) that he should die, le sort voulut qu'il mourût. (b) To will s.o. to do sth., faire faire qch. à qn par un acte de volonté; (in hypnotism) suggestionner qn. **2.** Léguer.

will[3], modal aux. v. def. I. Vouloir. **1.** (a) Do as you will, faites comme vous voudrez. What would you have me do? que voulez-vous que je fasse? Say what you will, quoi que vous disiez. Look which way you will, de quelque côté que vous regardiez. (b) (I) would (that) I were a bird! je voudrais être un oiseau! Would to heaven, plût au ciel (que). **2.** He could if he would, il le pourrait s'il le voulait. The engine won't start, le moteur ne veut pas démarrer. Just wait a moment, will you? voulez-vous bien attendre un instant? He will have none of it, il refuse d'en entendre parler. I will not have it! je ne le veux pas! Won't you sit down, veuillez (donc) vous asseoir. **3.** Accidents will happen, on ne peut pas éviter les accidents. He will have his little joke, il aime à plaisanter. I quite forgot!—You would! j'ai oublié!—C'est bien de vous! She would often return home exhausted, elle rentrait souvent très fatiguée. **5.** This will be your cousin? c'est là sans doute votre cousin? II. **will** as an auxiliary forming the future tenses. **1.** I will not be caught again, on ne m'y reprendra plus. **2.** (a) Will he be there?—He will, y sera-t-il? —Oui (, il y sera). But I shall starve!—No, you won't, mais je mourrai de faim!—Pas du tout. *You won't forget, will you?* vous n'oublierez pas, hein? *You will write to me, won't you?* vous m'écrirez, n'est-ce pas? (*b*) *I shall dictate and you will write,* je vais dicter et vous allez écrire. (*c*) *You will be here at three o'clock,* soyez ici à trois heures. **3.** *He would come if you invited him,* il viendrait si vous l'invitiez. **willing,** *a.* **1.** (*a*) De bonne volonté; bien disposé; serviable. *W. hands,* mains empressées. (*b*) Consentant. **2.** *Used pred.* To be willing to do sth., vouloir bien faire qch. *W. to oblige,* prêt à rendre service; complaisant. To be able and willing, avoir à la fois le pouvoir et la volonté. Willing or not, bon gré mal gré. **-ly,** *adv.* **1.** De plein gré. **2.** De bon cœur; volontiers.

William. *Pr.n.* Guillaume *m.*

willingness, *s.* **1.** Bonne volonté. *With the utmost w.,* de très bon cœur. **2.** Consentement *m.*

will-o'-the-wisp, *s.* Feu follet.

willow, *s.* *Bot:* Willow(-tree), saule *m.*

willowy, *a.* Souple, svelte, élancé.

willy-nilly, *adv.* Bon gré mal gré.

wilt, *v.i.* (*a*) Se flétrir, se faner. (*b*) (*Of pers.*) Dépérir, languir. (*c*) *P:* Perdre contenance.

wily, *a.* Rusé, astucieux. *He's a wily old bird,* c'est un vieux roublard.

win[1], *s.* Victoire *f.*

win[2], *v.tr. & i.* **1.** Gagner; remporter. To win the prize, remporter le prix. **2.** Acquérir; captiver (l'attention). To win glory, (re)cueillir des lauriers. *This gallant action won him the cross,* cette action d'éclat lui a valu la croix. **3.** To win all hearts, gagner, conquérir, tous les cœurs. **4.** To win one's way to, parvenir à (un endroit). **5.** Extraire (le charbon). **win over,** *v.tr.* Gagner; capter la bienveillance de. *To win over the audience,* se concilier les auditeurs. **win through,** *v.i.* Venir à bout de; parvenir à son but.

winning[1], *a.* **1.** Winning number, numéro gagnant; (*in lottery*) numéro sortant. Winning stroke, coup décisif. **2.** Attrayant, séduisant. **winning**[2], *s.* **1.** Victoire *f*; acquisition *f.* *The w. of the war,* le fait d'avoir gagné la guerre. **2.** *pl.* Winnings, gains *m.*

winning-post, *s.* *Turf:* Poteau *m* d'arrivée.

wince[1], *s.* Crispation *f*; tressaillement *m.* Without a wince, sans sourciller.

wince[2], *v.i.* Faire une grimace de douleur; tressaillir de douleur. Not to wince, ne pas sourciller; ne pas broncher.

winch, *s.* **1.** Manivelle *f.* **2.** Treuil *m.*

wind[1], *s.* **1.** Vent *m.* (*a*) The north wind, le vent du nord; la bise. High wind, vent fort, violent. *The w. is high,* il fait grand vent. *F:* To see which way the wind blows, regarder de quel côté vient le vent. *F:* There's something in the wind, il se manigance quelque chose. *F:* To go like the wind, aller comme le vent. *P:* To raise the wind, se procurer de l'argent. To get the wind up, avoir le trac, la frousse. (*b*) *Nau:*

Head wind, vent debout. To run before the wind, courir vent arrière. In the teeth of the wind, contre le vent. *F:* To sail close to the wind, friser la malhonnêteté. *F:* To take the wind out of s.o.'s sails, déjouer les plans de qn. (*c*) *F:* Chose vaine. *These promises are merely w.,* ce sont des promesses en l'air. **2.** *F:* To get wind of sth., avoir vent de qch. **3.** Souffle *m,* respiration *f,* haleine *f.* To get one's second wind, reprendre haleine. **4.** *Mus:* The wind, les instruments *m* à vent. **wind-instrument,** *s.* *Mus:* Instrument *m* à vent. **wind-jammer,** *s.* *Nau: F:* Voilier *m.* **wind-sleeve,** *s.* *Av:* Sac *m* à vent.

wind[2], *v.tr.* **1.** To wind the horn, sonner du cor. **2.** (*a*) Éventer, flairer. (*b*) Couper la respiration, le souffle, à; essouffler. **winded,** *a.* Hors d'haleine; essoufflé.

wind[3], *v.* I. *v.i.* Tourner; faire des détours; (*of river*) serpenter; (*of staircase*) monter en colimaçon. *The plant winds round the pole,* la plante s'enroule autour de la perche. *The road winds up the hill,* le chemin monte en serpentant. II. **wind,** *v.tr.* **1.** Enrouler. *Tex:* Dévider (le fil). To wind the wool into a ball, enrouler la laine en peloton. **2.** To wind the clock, remonter l'horloge. **wind up.** **1.** *v.tr.* (*a*) Enrouler. (*b*) Remonter (l'horloge). (*c*) Terminer. **2.** *v.i.* (*a*) Finir; terminer. (*b*) *The company wound up,* la société se mit en liquidation. **winding**[1], *a.* Sinueux, plein de détours, qui serpente. *W. streets,* rues tortueuses. **winding**[2], *s.* **1.** Mouvement sinueux; cours sinueux; replis *mpl.* **2.** Remontage *m* (d'une horloge). **3.** *pl.* Windings, sinuosités *f,* replis, méandres *m.* **winding-sheet,** *s.* Linceul *m,* suaire *m.*

windbag, *s.* *F:* Orateur verbeux. *He's a w.,* il parle pour ne rien dire.

windfall, *s.* **1.** Fruit abattu par le vent; fruit tombé. **2.** *F:* Aubaine *f*; bonne fortune.

windlass, *s.* Treuil *m.*

windmill, *s.* Moulin *m* à vent.

window, *s.* **1.** (*a*) Fenêtre *f.* *F:* To look out of the window, regarder par la fenêtre. Attic window, fenêtre en mansarde. *To break the windows,* casser les vitres, les carreaux. (*b*) Stained-glass window, verrière *f*; vitrail, -aux *m.* (*c*) Guichet *m* (d'un bureau de délivrance de billets). (*d*) *Com:* Vitrine *f,* devanture *f,* montre *f.* To put sth. in the window, mettre qch. à l'étalage, en montre. **2.** *Rail: Veh:* Glace *f.* *To close the w.,* remonter la glace. **window-box,** *s.* Caisse *f,* bac *m,* à fleurs **window-dressing,** *s.* **1.** Art *m* de l'étalage **2.** *F:* That's all window-dressing, tout ça, c'est du truquage. **window-frame,** *s.* Dormant *m,* châssis *m,* de fenêtre; chambranle *m.* **window-ledge,** *s.* Rebord *m,* appui *m,* de fenêtre. **window-pane,** *s.* Vitre *f,* carreau *m.* **window-sash,** *s.* Châssis *m* (de fenêtre à guillotine).

window-sill, s. Appui m, rebord m, tablette f, de fenêtre.

windpipe, s F: Gosier m.

windscreen, s. Aut: Pare-brise m inv.

windward. I. a. & adv. Au vent. 2. s. Côté m au vent. To (the) w. of, au vent de

windy, a. I. Venteux. W. day, journée de grand vent. It is very w., il fait beaucoup de vent. 2. (Of speech) Enflé, verbeux.

wine, s. Vin m. To take (a glass of) wine with s.o., trinquer avec qn **wine-cellar,** s. Cave f au vin. **wine-glass,** s. Verre m à vin. **wine-glassful,** s. Plein verre à vin. **wine-list,** s. Carte f des vins. **wine-merchant,** s. Négociant m en vins. **wine-press,** s. Pressoir m. **wine-vault(s),** s.(pl.) Cave f, caveau m (à vin). **wine-waiter,** s. Sommelier m.

wing[1], s. I. Aile f. F: To take s.o. under one's wing, prendre qn sous sa protection. 2. Vol m, essor m To shoot a bird on the wing, tirer un oiseau au vol. (Of bird) To be on the wing, voler. To take wing, s'envoler; prendre son vol. 3. (a) Battant m (d'une porte). (b) Aile (d'un bâtiment); pavillon m (d'un hôpital). 4. Aile (d'un avion) 5. Th: The wings, les coulisses f. **wing-commander,** s. Mil.Av: Lieutenant-colonel m. **wing-rib,** s. Cu: Côte f d'aloyau. **wing-spread,** s. Envergure f.

wing[2], v.tr. (Of bird) To wing its way, voler.

winged, a. Ailé.

wink[1], s. Clignement m d'œil; clin m d'œil. F: To tip s.o. the wink, faire signe de l'œil à qn. With a w., en clignant de l'œil. Without a wink of the eyelid, sans sourciller. F: To have forty winks, faire un petit somme.

wink[2]. I. v.i. (a) Cligner les yeux. (b) To wink at s.o., cligner de l'œil à qn. (c) F: To wink at an abuse, fermer les yeux sur un abus. 2. v.tr. (a) To wink one's eye, cligner de l'œil. (b) To wink assent, signifier son assentiment par un clin d'œil. **winking,** s. Clignement m de l'œil. F: **Like winking,** en un clin d'œil.

winkle, s. Moll: Bigorneau m.

winner, s. Gagnant, -ante. The w. of the race, le vainqueur de l'épreuve.

winnow, v.tr. (a) Vanner. (b) To winnow (out) the true from the false, séparer le vrai d'avec le faux. **winnowing,** s. Vannage m.

winsome, a. Captivant, séduisant.

winter[1], s. Hiver m. In winter, en hiver. Winter resort, station hivernale. Winter visitors, hivernants m. Winter sports, sports d'hiver. **winter-time,** s. Saison f d'hiver.

winter[2], v.i. Hiverner, passer l'hiver (at, à). **wintering,** s. Hivernage m.

wintry, a. D'hiver; hivernal, -aux. F: Wintry smile, sourire décourageant.

wipe[1], s. To give sth. a wipe, essuyer qch.

wipe[2], v.tr. Essuyer. To wipe one's eyes, s'essuyer les yeux. To wipe sth. dry, bien

essuyer qch **wipe away,** v.tr Essuyer. **wipe off,** v.tr. Enlever, essuyer; liquider (une dette) **wipe out,** v.tr. (a) Liquider, amortir (une dette); effacer (une injure). (b) F: Exterminer

wire[1], s. I. Fil m métallique. (a) Copper wire, fil de laiton. Wire mattress, sommier métallique. Mil: Wire entanglement, réseau(x) m(pl) de fil de fer barbelé. (b) Telegraph wires, fils télégraphiques 2. Télégramme m, dépêche f. **wire-netting,** s. Treillis m métallique; treillage m en fil de fer. **wire-puller,** s. F: Intrigant, -ante. **wire-pulling,** s. Art m de tirer les ficelles; intrigues fpl.

wire[2], v.tr. I. El.E: Canaliser (une maison). 2. F: Transmettre par le télégraphe, par fil; télégraphier. To wire to s.o., télégraphier à qn. **wire in,** v.i. F: S'y mettre de tout son cœur. To wire into a meal, abs. to wire in, s'attaquer à un repas. **wiring,** s. El.E: Pose f de fils électriques; canalisation f.

wireless[1], a. Sans fil. Wireless telegraphy, s. wireless, télégraphie f sans fil, abbr. T.S.F. Wireless telegram, radiotélégramme m. W. message, message m par radio; radio m. Nau: Wireless room, poste m de T. S. F. To talk on the wireless, parler au micro. Wireless set, poste m de T. S. F.

wireless[2], v.tr. Envoyer par la radio.

wiriness, s. Vigueur f.

wiry, a. (a) (Of hair) Raide, rude. (b) Sec, f. sèche, et nerveux.

wisdom, s. Sagesse f. Wisdom tooth, dent de sagesse.

wise[1], a. I. Sage; prudent; sagace. The seven wise men, les sept sages. The Wise Men of the East, les (Rois) Mages m. 2. (a) To look wise, prendre un (petit) air entendu. (b) He is none the wiser (for it), il n'en est pas plus avancé. To do sth. without anyone being the wiser, faire qch. à l'insu de tout le monde. No one will be any the wiser, ni vu ni connu. **-ly,** adv. Sagement, prudemment.

wise[2], s. Manière f, façon f; guise f. In no wise, en aucune manière, d'aucune façon.

wiseacre, s. Prétendu sage; pédant m.

wish[1], s. (a) Désir m; vœu m. You shall have your w., votre désir sera exaucé. (b) Souhait m, vœu. To send all good wishes to s.o., adresser tous ses vœux de bonheur à qn. What more can you wish for? que voudriez-vous de plus?

wish-bone, s. Lunette f, fourchette f.

wish[2]. I. v.ind.tr. To wish for sth., désirer, souhaiter, qch. To have everything one can wish for, avoir tout à souhait. What more can you wish for? que voudriez-vous de plus? 2. v.tr. Vouloir. (a) I do not wish it, je ne le veux pas. To wish to do sth., désirer, vouloir, faire qch. (b) I wish I were in your place, je voudrais bien être à votre place. I w. I had seen it! j'aurais bien voulu voir cela! I w. he would come! que ne vient-il? (c) F: Don't you wish you may get it! je vous en souhaite! (d) He wishes me well, il est bien disposé envers moi. **To wish s.o. good night,** souhaiter une bonne nuit à qn ; dire bonsoir à qn. **wishing,** *s.* Désirs *mpl*, souhaits *mpl.*

wishful, *a.* Désireux (*of sth.,* de qch.). **-fully,** *adv.* Avec désir.

wishy-washy, *a. F :* Fade, insipide.

wisp, *s.* (*a*) Bouchon *m*, poignée *f* (de paille). (*b*) **Wisp of hair,** mèche folle.

wistful, *a.* Plein d'un vague désir ou d'un vague regret. *W. smile,* sourire pensif. **-fully,** *adv.* D'un air songeur et triste ; avec un désir silencieux.

wit¹, *s.* **I.** (*Often pl.*) Esprit *m*, entendement *m* ; intelligence *f.* **To sharpen s.o.'s wits,** aiguiser l'intelligence de qn. **To keep one's wits about one,** conserver toute sa présence d'esprit. **To be at one's wit's end,** ne plus savoir de quel côté se tourner. **To have a battle of wits,** jouer au plus fin. **To live by one's wits,** vivre d'expédients. **To set one's wits to work,** s'ingénier. **2.** (Vivacité *f* d')esprit. **Flash of wit,** trait *m* d'esprit.

wit², *s.* Homme *m*, femme *f*, d'esprit.

wit³, *v.tr.* Savoir. *Jur :* To wit, à savoir ; c'est-à-dire. **witting,** *a.* Fait de propos délibéré. **-ly,** *adv.* Sciemment ; à dessein.

witch, *s.* (*a*) Sorcière *f.* (*b*) *F :* Old witch, vieille bonne femme. (*c*) *F :* Charmeuse *f* ; ensorceleuse *f.* **witch-doctor,** *s. Anthr :* Sorcier guérisseur.

witchcraft, *s.* Sorcellerie *f* ; magie noire.

witchery, *s.* (*a*) Ensorcellement *m*, enchantement *m.* (*b*) *F :* Fascination *f* ; charme *m* magique.

with, *prep.* Avec. **I.** (*a*) *He is staying with friends,* il est chez des amis. *Is there someone with you?* êtes-vous accompagné ? **With the colours,** sous les drapeaux. **I shall be with you in a moment,** je serai à vous dans un moment. (*b*) **Girl with blue eyes,** jeune fille aux yeux bleus. **He was speaking with his hat on,** il parlait le chapeau sur la tête. **With your intelligence,** intelligent comme vous l'êtes. (*c*) **To leave a child with s.o.,** laisser un enfant à la garde de qn. **This decision rests with you,** c'est à vous de décider. (*d*) **With all his faults,** malgré tous ses défauts. **2.** (*a*) **To have to do with s.o.,** avoir affaire avec qn. **I can do nothing with him,** je ne peux rien en faire. **To be sincere with oneself,** être sincère envers soi-même. **It is a habit with me,** c'est une habitude chez moi. **To be in favour with the queen,** être en faveur auprès de la reine. (*b*) **I do not agree with you,** je ne suis pas de votre avis. **I am with you there!** j'en conviens ! (*c*) **With these words he dismissed me,** ce disant il me congédia. (*d*) **To wrestle with s.o.,** lutter avec qn. **To fight with s.o.,** se battre contre qn. **3.** *To part with sth.,* se dessaisir, se défaire, de qch. **4.** (*a*) **To walk with (the aid of) a stick,** marcher avec une canne. **To take sth. with both hands,** prendre qch.

à deux mains. *To strike with all one's might,* frapper de toutes ses forces. (*b*) **To tremble with rage,** trembler de rage. **To be stiff with cold,** être engourdi par le froid. **To be ill with typhoid fever,** être malade de la fièvre typhoïde. (*c*) **To fill a vase with water,** remplir un vase d'eau. **It is pouring with rain,** il pleut à verse. **5.** **To work with courage,** travailler avec courage. **To receive s.o. with open arms,** recevoir qn à bras ouverts. **With all due respect,** sauf votre respect. **I say so with regret,** je le dis à regret. **With a few exceptions,** à peu d'exceptions près. **6.** **Away with care!** bannissons les soucis !

withdraw, *v.* **I.** *v.tr.* (*a*) Retirer. (*b*) **To withdraw s.o. from an influence,** soustraire qn à une influence. (*c*) **To withdraw coins from circulation,** retirer des pièces de la circulation. (*d*) Retirer. *Jur :* To withdraw an action, abandonner un procès. **2.** *v.i.* Se retirer (*from,* de) ; s'éloigner. **To withdraw in favour of s.o.,** se désister en faveur de qn. **To withdraw into oneself,** se renfermer en soi-même.

withdrawal, *s.* **I.** (*a*) Retrait *m.* (*b*) Rappel *m* (d'un décret) ; rétractation *f* (d'une promesse). **2.** (*a*) Retraite *f. Mil :* Repli *m.* (*b*) **Withdrawal of a candidate,** désistement *m* d'un candidat.

wither. **I.** *v.i.* Se dessécher, dépérir. **2.** *v.tr.* (*a*) Dessécher, flétrir. (*b*) *F :* To wither s.o. with a look, foudroyer qn du regard. **withering¹,** *a. F :* (Regard) foudroyant, écrasant. **-ly,** *adv. F :* D'un regard foudroyant ; d'un ton de mépris. **withering²,** *s.* Dessèchement *m.*

withhold, *v.tr.* **I.** (*a*) Refuser (*from s.o.,* à qn). (*b*) **To withhold the truth from s.o.,** cacher la vérité à qn. (*c*) **To withhold so much out of s.o.'s pay,** retenir tant sur la paye de qn. **2.** **To withhold s.o. from doing sth.,** retenir, empêcher, qn de faire qch.

within. **I.** *adv.* (*a*) A l'intérieur. **Within and without,** à l'intérieur et à l'extérieur. (*b*) Seen from within, vu de l'intérieur, du dedans. **2.** *prep.* (*a*) A l'intérieur de, en dedans de. **Within four walls,** entre quatre murs. (*b*) **To keep within the law,** rester dans la légalité. **Within the meaning of the Act,** selon les prévisions de l'Acte. **To live within one's income,** ne pas dépasser son revenu. **To be well within the truth,** être au-dessous de la vérité. **Weight within a pound,** poids à une livre près. (*c*) **Within sight,** en vue. **Within call,** à (la) portée de la voix. **Situated within two miles of the town,** situé à moins de deux milles de la ville. **Within a radius of ten miles,** dans un rayon de dix milles. **Within an inch of death,** à deux doigts de la mort. (*d*) **Within an hour,** dans, avant, une heure. **Within the week,** avant la fin de la semaine. *W. the next five years,* d'ici cinq ans. *W. the required time,* dans le délai prescrit. **Within the memory of man,** de mémoire d'homme.

without. **I.** *adv.* A l'extérieur, au dehors. **Seen from without,** vu de l'extérieur, du dehors. **2.** *prep.* (*a*) En dehors de. (*b*) Sans. **To be without friends,** être sans amis. **To be without food,** manquer de nourriture. **Without end,** sans fin. **He passed by without seeing me,** il passa sans me voir. **That goes without saying,** cela va sans dire. **To go without sth.,** se passer de qch.

withstand, *v.tr.* Résister à. *Mil:* **To withstand an attack,** soutenir une attaque.

withy, *s.* **I.** Osier *m.* **2.** Brin *m* d'osier.

witless, *a.* (*a*) Sans intelligence; sot, *f.* sotte. (*b*) Imbécile; faible d'esprit.

witness[1], *s.* **I.** Témoignage *m.* **To bear witness to sth.,** témoigner de qch. **In witness whereof,** en témoignage de quoi. **2.** Témoin *m.* **To call s.o. as a witness,** citer qn comme témoin. **witness-box,** *s.* *Jur:* = Barre *f* des témoins.

witness[2]. **I.** *v.tr.* (*a*) Être témoin de ; assister à. (*b*) Certifier (une signature). **2.** *v.i.* **To witness to sth.,** témoigner de qch.

witticism, *s.* Trait *m* d'esprit ; bon mot.

wittiness, *s.* Esprit *m.*

witty, *a.* Spirituel. **-ily,** *adv.* Spirituellement.

wizard, *s.* Sorcier *m*, magicien *m.*

wizardry, *s.* Sorcellerie *f*, magie *f.*

wizened, *a.* Desséché, ratatiné ; (*of cheeks, etc.*) parcheminé ; (*of face*) vieillot ,-otte.

wobble[1], *s.* **I.** Branlement *m*, oscillation *f.* **2.** *F:* Vacillation *f*, hésitation *f.*

wobble[2], *v.i.* **I.** Ballotter ; trembler ; branler. **2.** *F:* Hésiter, vaciller. **wobbling,** *s.* = WOBBLE[1].

wobbler, *s.* Tergiversateur, -trice.

wobbly, *a.* Branlant, vacillant. **Wobbly chair,** chaise bancale.

woe, *s.* Malheur *m*, chagrin *m*, peine *f.* **Woe is me!** pauvre de moi! **Woe to the vanquished!** malheur aux vaincus! **woebegone,** *a.* Triste, désolé, abattu.

wo(e)ful, *a.* Triste, affligé, malheureux. **-fully,** *adv.* Tristement.

wolf[1], *s.* Loup *m.* **She-wolf,** louve *f.* **Prairie wolf,** coyote *m.* **That will keep the wolf from the door,** cela vous mettra à l'abri du besoin. **A wolf in sheep's clothing,** un loup déguisé en brebis. **wolf-hound,** *s.* Lévrier *m* d'Irlande. **wolf's-bane,** *s.* *Bot:* Aconit *m.*

wolf[2], *v.tr.* To wolf (down) one's food, avaler sa nourriture à grosses bouchées.

wolfish, *a.* De loup ; vorace ; cruel.

woman, *s.* **I.** Femme *f.* **A young woman,** une jeune femme ; (*unmarried*) une jeune personne. **An old woman,** une vieille femme ; *F:* une vieille. **2.** *Attrib.* **Woman doctor,** femme médecin. **woman-hater,** *s.* Misogyne *m.*

womanhood, *s.* **I.** État *m* de femme. *She had now grown to w.,* c'était maintenant une femme (faite). **2.** *Coll:* Les femmes.

womanlike. **I.** *a.* De femme. **2.** *adv.* En femme ; comme une femme.

womanliness, *s.* (*a*) Caractère *m* de femme ; féminité *f.* (*b*) Charme féminin.

womanly, *a.* De femme ; féminin. **She is so womanly,** elle est si femme.

womb, *s.* *Anat:* Matrice *f.* *F:* Sein *m*; entrailles *fpl.*

womenfolk, *s.pl.* One's womenfolk, les femmes *f* de sa famille.

wonder[1], *s.* **I.** Merveille *f*, prodige *m.* **A nine-days' wonder,** la merveille d'un jour. **The wonder is,** ce qu'il y a d'étonnant c'est. **For a wonder,** chose remarquable. **He is ill, and no wonder,** il est malade, et rien d'étonnant. **2.** (i) Étonnement *m*, surprise *f.* (ii) Émerveillement *m.* **To fill s.o. with wonder,** émerveiller qn. **wonder-struck,** *a.* Émerveillé.

wonder[2]. **I.** *v.i.* S'étonner, s'émerveiller (*at*, *de*). **I do not wonder at it,** cela ne m'étonne pas. **That isn't to be wondered at,** ce n'est pas étonnant. **That set me wondering,** cela m'a intrigué. **2.** *v.tr.* (*a*) S'étonner. (*b*) Se demander. *I w. who invented that,* je suis curieux de savoir qui a inventé cela. **wondering,** *a.* Étonné, émerveillé.

wonderful, *a.* Merveilleux, prodigieux. **Wonderful to relate,** chose étonnante, chose remarquable. **It was wonderful!** *F:* c'était épatant! **-fully,** *adv.* Merveilleusement. **Wonderfully well,** à merveille.

wonderment, *s.* Étonnement *m.*

wondrous, *a.* Étonnant ; merveilleux. **-ly,** *adv.* Merveilleusement.

wont[1], *pred.a.* **To be wont to do sth.,** avoir coutume, avoir l'habitude, de faire qch.

wont[2], *s.* Coutume *f*, habitude *f.* *Oftener than was his w.,* plus souvent que d'habitude.

wonted, *a.* Habituel, accoutumé.

woo, *v.tr.* **I.** Faire la cour à, courtiser. **2.** Rechercher, courtiser (la fortune). **wooing,** *s.* Cour *f*; recherche *f* en mariage.

wood, *s.* **I.** Bois *m.* Pine wood, bois de pins. **We are not yet out of the wood,** nous ne sommes pas encore tirés d'affaire. **2.** Bois. **Wood pavement,** pavage en bois. *F:* **Touch wood!** touchez du bois! **3.** Wine in the wood, vin en pièce, en cercles. **wood-carving,** *s.* Sculpture *f* sur bois. **wood-cutter,** *s.* Bûcheron *m.* **wood-engraving,** *s.* Gravure *f* sur bois. **wood-louse,** *s.* Cloporte *m.* **wood-nymph,** *s.* Nymphe *f* des bois. **wood-pigeon,** *s.* *Orn:* (Pigeon *m*) ramier *m*; palombe *f.* **wood-pile,** *s.* Tas *m*, monceau *m*, de bois. **wood-pulp,** *s.* *Paperm:* Pâte *f* de bois. **wood-stack,** *s.* = WOOD-PILE.

woodbine, *s.* *Bot:* Chèvrefeuille *m* des bois.

woodchuck, *s.* Marmotte *f* d'Amérique.

woodcock, *s.* Bécasse *f.*

woodcraft, *s.* Connaissance *f* de la forêt.

woodcut, *s.* Gravure *f* sur bois.

wooded, *a.* Boisé, arbreux.
wooden, *a* **1.** De bois, en bois. **2.** *F:* (*a*) Raide, gauche. (*b*) Sans intelligence ; à l'esprit obtus. **wooden-headed,** *a* Stupide.

woodenness, *s.* (*a*) Raideur *f.* (*b*) Manque *m* d'intelligence.

woodland, *s.* **1.** Pays boisé ; bois *m.* **2.** *Attrib.* Des bois ; sylvestre.

woodlander, *s.* Habitant *m* des bois.

woodman, *s.* Bûcheron *m.*

woodpecker, *s.* *Orn:* Pic *m.* Green woodpecker, pivert *m.*

woodsman, *s.* Homme *m* des bois.

woodwork, *s.* **1.** Travail *m* du bois. **2.** Bois travaillé. (*a*) Boiserie *f.* (*b*) Menuiserie *f.*

wooer, *s.* Amoureux *m* ; prétendant *m.*

woof, *s.* = WEFT.

wool, *s.* **1.** Laine *f.* (*a*) *F:* Keep your wool on! te fâche pas ! (*b*) Knitting wool, laine à tricoter. **2.** (*a*) Pelage *m* (d'animal). (*b*) Cheveux crépus, laine (des nègres). **3.** Steel wool, laine d'acier. **wool-bearing,** *a.* Lanifère.
wool-gathering, *s.* *F:* (*a*) *s.* Rêvasserie *f.* Your wits have gone wool-gathering, *F:* vous êtes dans la lune. (*b*) *a.* Distrait. *You're w.-g.,* vous rêvassez.

woollen, *a.* De laine. Woollen goods, *s.* woollens, lainages *m.*

woolliness, *s* **1.** Nature laineuse (*of*, de). **2.** *F:* Imprécision *f* ; manque *m* de netteté.

woolly. 1. *a.* (*a*) Laineux ; de laine. *F:* Woolly hair, cheveux laineux, crépus. (*b*) Flou, -e ; peu net, *f.* nette. **2.** *s.* (Vêtement *m* en) tricot *m.*

word¹, *s.* **1.** Mot *m.* (*a*) Vocable *m.* Word for word, (répéter qch.) mot pour mot ; (traduire qch.) mot à mot. In a word, en un mot ; bref. In other words, en d'autres termes. In so many words, en termes propres. Bad is not the word for it, mauvais n'est pas assez dire. (*b*) Spoken words, paroles *f.* In the words of, selon l'expression de. Of few words, sobre de paroles. He never said a word, il n'a pas soufflé mot. I can't get a word out of him, je ne peux pas le faire parler. To put one's word in, intervenir ; placer son mot. Without a word, sans mot dire. With these words, ce disant. You have taken the words out of my mouth, c'est justement ce pue j'allais dire. Beyond words, inqualifiable. He is too silly for words, il est d'une bêtise indicible. (*c*) I want (to have) a word with you, j'aurais un mot à vous dire. *I'il have a w. with him about it,* je lui en toucherai deux mots. To say a good word for s.o., dire un mot en faveur de qn. A word in season, un conseil opportun. *Prov:* A word to the wise (is sufficient), à bon entendeur salut. (*d*) To have words with s.o., avoir une altercation avec qn. Words ran high, la querelle s'échauffait. **2.** By word of mouth, de vive voix ; verbalement. **3.** To send s.o. word of sth., faire savoir qch. à qn ; prévenir qn

de qch. Word came, on nous manda. **4.** To keep one's word, tenir (sa) parole. To break one's word, manquer à sa parole. I give you my word for it, croyez-m'en ; je vous en réponds. *I take your w. for it,* je le crois sur votre parole. To take s.o. at his word, prendre qn au mot. Upon my word! ça c'est trop fort ! My word! fichtre ! **5.** Word of command, ordre *m*, commandement *m.* The word has gone round, on s'est donné le mot. *F:* Sharp's the word! (faites) vite !

word², *v.tr.* Formuler par écrit ; énoncer ; rédiger (un télégramme). Thus worded, ainsi conçu. Well worded, bien exprimé. **wording,** *s.* **1.** Rédaction *f*, libellé *m.* **2.** Mots *mpl* ; langage *m* ; termes *mpl.*

wordiness, *s.* Verbosité *f.*

wordy, *a.* **1.** Verbeux, prolixe, diffus. **2.** Wordy warfare, lutte *f* oratoire.

work¹, *s.* **1.** Travail *m*, -aux. The forces at work, les forces en jeu. To go the right way to work, s'y prendre bien. **2.** (*a*) Travail, ouvrage *m*, besogne *f*, tâche *f.* I have so much work to do, j'ai tellement (de travail) à faire. A piece of work, un travail, un ouvrage, une œuvre. The brandy had done its work, l'eau-de-vie avait fait son effet. I have my work cut out, j'ai de quoi faire. Day's work, (travail d'une) journée. *F:* It's all in a day's work, c'est l'ordinaire de mon existence. (*b*) It was thirsty work, c'était un travail qui donnait soif **3.** (*a*) Good works, (les) bonnes œuvres. (*b*) Ouvrage, œuvre. The works of Shakespeare, les œuvres de Shakespeare. A work of art, une œuvre d'art. **4.** To be out of work, être sans travail, sans emploi ; chômer. **5.** *pl.* *Mil:* Defensive works, ouvrages défensifs. **6.** *pl.* *Civ.E:* Constructive works, ouvrages d'art. Public works, travaux publics. **7.** *pl.* Rouages *mpl*, mécanisme *m*, mouvement *m.* **8.** *pl.* Usine *f*, atelier *m.* **9.** *Nau:* Upper works, œuvres mortes. **work-bag,** *s.* Sac *m* à ouvrage.
work-basket, *s.* Corbeille *f*, nécessaire *m*, à ouvrage. **work-bench,** *s.* Établi *m.*
work-box, *s.* Boîte *f* à ouvrage. **work-day,** *s.* Jour *m* ouvrable. **work-room,** *s.* Atelier *m.* **work-table,** *s.* Table *f* à ouvrage.

work², *v.* I. *v.i.* **1.** (*a*) Travailler. To work hard, travailler dur, ferme. To work at music, travailler la musique. (*b*) To work for an end, travailler pour atteindre un but. **2.** (*a*) Fonctionner, aller. System that works well, système qui fonctionne bien *The pump isn't working,* la pompe ne marche pas. (*b*) Drug that works, médicament qui agit. His scheme did not work, son plan a échoué. **3.** (*Of yeast*) Fermenter. **4.** His mouth was working, sa bouche se crispait. II. **work,** *v.tr.* **1.** Faire travailler. *He works his men too hard,* il surmène ses hommes. To work oneself to death, se tuer à force de travailler. **2.** (*a*) Faire fonctionner, faire marcher (une machine); faire jouer (un ressort). (*Of machine*) To be worked by electricity, marcher à l'électricité. (*b*) To work a scheme, mettre un plan à exécution. **3.** (*a*) Faire; opérer; amener (un changement). To work mischief, semer la discorde. *F:* I will work it if I can, je vais tâcher de manigancer ça. (*b*) To work a sum, faire un calcul. **4.** Broder (un dessin). **5.** (*a*) To work one's hands free, parvenir à dégager ses mains. (*b*) He worked his way to the front of the crowd, il se fraya un chemin jusqu'au premier rang de la foule. **6.** (*a*) Travailler, façonner. (*b*) He worked himself into a rage, il se mit peu à peu en colère. **7.** Exploiter (une mine). **8.** *Nau:* To work one's passage, gagner son passage par son travail. **work on,** *v.i.* **1.** Continuer à travailler. **2.** (*a*) *We have no data to w. on,* nous n'avons pas de données sur lesquelles nous baser. (*b*) To work on s.o., agir sur qn. **work out. 1.** *v.tr.* (*a*) Mener à bien. To work out one's salvation, faire son salut. To work out one's time, (*of apprentice*) finir son temps. (*b*) Développer (une idée); élaborer (un projet); (*c*) Supputer (un compte); résoudre (un problème). **2.** *v.i.* (*a*) Sortir peu à peu. (*b*) *It worked out very well for me,* je m'en suis bien trouvé. (*c*) The total works out at six pounds, le total s'élève à six livres. **work up,** *v.tr.* (*a*) Développer (une situation dramatique); élaborer (un article). To work up a connexion, se faire une clientèle. (*b*) Préparer (un sujet). (*c*) Exciter, émouvoir. *To be worked up,* être emballé. **wrought up,** *a. Lit:* Excité, agité. **wrought,** *a.* Ouvré. **working**[1], *a.* **1.** (*a*) Qui travaille; ouvrier. The working classes, la classe ouvrière. Working man, ouvrier *m.* (*b*) *Mil:* Working party, atelier *m,* équipe *f.* **2.** Qui fonctionne. (*a*) Working parts, parties ouvrières. (*b*) Not working, hors d'action. (*c*) Working agreement, modus vivendi *m.* Working majority, majorité suffisante. **working**[2], *s.* **1.** Travail *m.* Working clothes, vêtements de travail. Working day = WORK-DAY. **2.** (*a*) Manœuvre *f* (d'une machine). (*b*) Mise *f* en œuvre (d'un procédé); exploitation *f* (d'une mine). Working expenses, frais généraux. Working capital, capital d'exploitation. **3.** Marche *f,* fonctionnement *m.* In working order, en état de service. **4.** The workings of the mind, le travail de l'esprit.

workable, *a.* **1.** (Bois) ouvrable. **2.** (Mine) exploitable. **3.** (Projet) réalisable.

workaday, *a.* (*a*) De tous les jours. (*b*) This workaday world, ce monde prosaïque.

worker, *s.* **1.** (*a*) Travailleur, -euse. (*b*) Ouvrier, -ère. The workers, les classes laborieuses. **2.** Worker of miracles, faiseur *m* de miracles.

workhouse, *s.* Asile *m* des pauvres; hospice *m.* To end one's days in the workhouse, finir ses jours à l'hôpital.

workman, *s.* Ouvrier *m,* artisan *m.* Workmen's dwellings, habitations ouvrières.

workmanlike, *a.* **1.** Bien fait, bien travaillé. **2.** To do sth. in a workmanlike manner, faire qch. en bon ouvrier.

workmanship, *s. Ind:* Exécution *f;* fini *m* de l'exécution; façon *f.* Of fine workmanship, d'un beau travail.

workpeople, *s.pl.* Ouvriers *m.*

workshop, *s.* Atelier *m.*

workwoman, *s.* Ouvrière *f.*

world, *s.* Monde *m.* **1.** (*a*) In this world, en ce monde; ici-bas. To go to a better world, partir pour l'autre monde. World, without end, jusqu'à la fin des siècles. (*b*) To be alone in the world, être seul au monde. Nothing in the world, rien au monde; rien du tout. *What in the w. is the matter with you?* mais qu'est-ce que vous avez donc? He was for all the world like . . ., il avait exactement l'air de. . . . **2.** To go round the world, faire le tour du monde. He has seen the world, il a vu du pays. Map of the world, carte universelle; (*in two hemispheres*) mappemonde *f.* All the world over, dans le monde entier. **3.** It's the way of the world, ainsi va le monde. Man of the world, homme qui connaît la vie. **4.** (*a*) The theatrical world, le milieu du théâtre. The sporting world, le monde du sport. (*b*) The animal world, le monde animal. **5.** *F:* To give oneself a world of trouble, se donner un mal de chien. To think the world of s.o., avoir une très haute opinion de qn. **world-famous,** *a.* De renommée mondiale. **world-wide,** *a.* Universel; répandu partout; mondial, -aux.

worldliness, *s.* Mondanité *f.*

worldly, *a.* **1.** Du monde, de ce monde, d'ici-bas. **2.** Mondain. **worldly-minded,** *a.* Attaché aux choses matérielles.

worm[1], *s.* Ver *m.* He is a worm, c'est un piètre personnage. **worm-eaten,** *a.* Rongé des vers, piqué des vers; (*of wood*) vermoulu.

worm[2], *v.tr.* (*a*) To worm (one's way), se glisser, se faufiler (*through,* à travers). To worm oneself into s.o.'s favour, s'insinuer dans les bonnes grâces de qn. (*b*) To worm a secret out of s.o., tirer un secret de qn.

wormwood, *s. Bot:* Armoise amère; absinthe *f.*

worry[1], *s.* Ennui *m,* tracasserie *f,* tracas *m.* Money worries, soucis *m* d'argent.

worry[2], *v.* **1.** *v.tr.* (*a*) (*Of dog*) Harceler; prendre avec les dents et secouer (un rat). (*b*) *F:* To worry out a problem, s'évertuer à résoudre un problème. (*c*) Tourmenter, harceler. To worry oneself, se tourmenter. **2.** *v.i.* Se tourmenter, se tracasser, s'inquiéter. Don't (you) worry! soyez tranquille! We'll worry along somehow, on se débrouillera.

worried, *a. To be w.,* être en proie à l'inquiétude.

worse. 1. *a. & s.* Pire; plus mauvais. **This**

ls worse and worse, c'est de mal en pis. To make matters worse, par surcroît de malheur. It might have been worse, ce n'est qu'un demi-mal. He escaped with nothing worse than a fright, il en fut quitte pour la peur. So much the worse, tant pis. *He escaped none the worse*, il s'en est tiré sans aucun mal. **2.** *s.* (*a*) But there was worse to come, mais il y eut plus grave. I have been through worse than that, j'en ai vu bien d'autres. (*b*) **To change for the worse**, s'altérer. **3.** *adv.* Pis ; plus mal. You might do worse, vous pourriez faire pis. To think worse of **s.o.**, avoir plus mauvaise opinion de qn. *He is* worse off *than before*, sa situation a empiré.

worsen. 1. *v.tr.* Empirer ; aggraver. **2.** *v.i.* Empirer.

worship¹, *s.* **1.** Culte *m*, adoration *f*. Place of worship, édifice *m* du culte ; église *f*, temple *m*. *F:* To be an object of worship, être un objet d'adoration. **2.** His 'Worship the Mayor, son Honneur *m* le maire. Yes, your Worship, oui, monsieur le maire, monsieur le juge.

worship², *v.tr.* **1.** Rendre un culte à, adorer. **2.** Adorer ; aimer à l'adoration. *He worships the ground she treads on*, il baise la trace de ses pas.

worshipful, *a.* Honorable.

worshipper, *s.* Adorateur, -trice.

worst¹. 1. *a.* (Le) pire, (le) plus mauvais. *His w. mistake*, sa plus grave erreur. **2.** *s.* The worst of the storm is over, le plus fort de la tempête est passé. That's the worst of cheap shoes, c'est le désavantage des souliers bon marché. When things are at their worst, quand les choses sont au pire. To get the worst of it, avoir le dessous. If the worst comes to the worst, en mettant les choses au pis. Do your worst! faites du pis que vous pourrez ! **3.** *adv.* (Le) pis, (le) plus mal.

worst², *v.tr.* Battre, vaincre. To be worsted, succomber ; avoir le dessous.

worsted, *s.* *Tex:* Laine *f* à tricoter, à tapisserie.

worth. 1. *pred. a.* Valant. (*a*) To be worth so much, valoir tant. *That is* worth something, cela a de la valeur. Whatever it may be worth, vaille que vaille. Worth the money, avantageux. It would be as much as my life is worth, ce serait risquer ma vie. (*b*) It is not worth the trouble, cela ne, n'en, vaut pas la peine. Book worth reading, livre qui mérite d'être lu. *It is w. thinking about*, cela mérite réflexion. *It's w. knowing*, c'est bon à savoir. (*c*) To die worth a million, mourir en laissant un million. *That is all I am w.*, voilà tout mon avoir. *F:* For all one is worth, de toutes ses forces. **2.** *s.* Valeur *f*. Give me two shillings' worth of chocolate, donnez-moi pour deux shillings de chocolat. To want one's money's worth, en vouloir pour son argent.

worthiness, *s.* Mérite *m*.

worthless, *a.* Sans valeur, de nulle valeur ; mauvais. *W. fellow*, vaurien *m*.

worthlessness, *s.* Peu *m* de valeur.

worthy. 1. *a.* Digne. (*a*) *F:* Our worthy friend, notre brave ami. (*b*) To be worthy of sth., être digne de qch. To be worthy of death, mériter la mort. It is worthy of note, il est à noter. **2.** *s.* The village worthies, les gros bonnets du village. **-ily,** *adv.* **1.** Dignement. **2.** A juste titre.

would-be, *a.* Prétendu, soi-disant *inv.*

wound¹, *s.* (*a*) Blessure *f*. *Slight w. in the arm*, atteinte *f* au bras. (*b*) Plaie *f*.

wound², *v.tr.* Blesser ; faire une blessure à. *Wounded in the shoulder*, atteint à l'épaule. The wounded, les blessés.

wrack, *s.* **1.** Varec(h) *m*. **2.** Laisse *f*.

wraith, *s.* (*a*) Apparition spectrale. (*b*) Double spectral d'une personne.

wrangle¹, *s.* Dispute *f*, querelle *f*.

wrangle², *v.i.* Se disputer, se quereller.

wrangling, *s.* Disputes *fpl*, querelles *fpl*.

wrap¹, *s.* (*a*) (*Usu. pl.*) Wraps, couvertures *f* (de voyage) ; châles *m*. (*b*) Pèlerine *f* ; manteau *m*.

wrap², *v.tr.* **1.** (*a*) Envelopper. (*b*) To wrap oneself up, *abs.* to wrap up, s'emmitoufler. **2.** To wrap sth. round sth., enrouler qch. autour de qch. **wrapped,** *a.* **1.** (*a*) *W. in paper*, roulé dans du papier. (*b*) Wrapped up, emmitouflé. (*c*) Affair wrapped in mystery, affaire enveloppée de mystère. **2.** (*a*) Wrapped in meditation, plongé dans ses pensées. (*b*) *He is w. up in his work*, il est entièrement absorbé par son travail. **wrapping,** *s.* (*a*) Enveloppe *f*, couverture *f*. (*b*) Papier *m*, toile *f*, d'emballage. (*c*) *pl.* Bandelettes *f* (de momie). **wrappingpaper,** *s.* Papier *m* d'emballage.

wrapper, *s.* **1.** (*a*) Chemise *f* (d'un dossier). (*b*) Couverture *f* (d'un livre). **2.** Bande *f* (de journal). **3.** Robe *f* de chambre.

wrath, *s.* Colère *f* ; courroux *m*.

wrathful, *a.* Courroucé.

wreak, *v.tr.* To wreak one's wrath upon s.o., décharger sa colère sur qn. To wreak vengeance on s.o., se venger de qn.

wreath, *s.* **1.** Couronne *f*, guirlande *f*. Funeral wreath, couronne mortuaire. **2.** Volute *f*, panache *m* (de fumée).

wreathe, *v.tr.* (*a*) Enguirlander ; couronner (de fleurs). Face wreathed in smiles, visage rayonnant. (*b*) Entrelacer, tresser.

wreck¹, *s.* **1.** Épave *f*. *Ins:* Total wreck, navire entièrement perdu. *F:* The building is a mere wreck, le bâtiment n'est qu'une ruine. To be a nervous wreck, avoir les nerfs détraqués. **2.** Naufrage *m*. *To be saved from the w.*, échapper au naufrage.

wreck², *v.tr.* (*a*) Faire faire naufrage à. To be wrecked, faire naufrage. (*b*) Faire dérailler (un train) ; démolir. (*c*) Faire échouer, *F:* saboter (une entreprise) ; ruiner. **wrecked,**

a. Naufragé. *W. life*, existence brisée. *W. health*, santé ruinée. **wrecking,** *s.* Destruction *f* (d'un navire); déraillement *m* (d'un train); ruine *f.* **wreckage,** *s.* Épaves éparses; débris *mpl.* **Piece of wreckage,** épave. **wrecker,** *s.* **1.** Naufrageur *m*; pilleur *m* d'épaves. **2.** Destructeur *m* (*of*, de). **wren,** *s.* *Orn:* Roitelet *m.* **wrench¹,** *s.* **1.** To give sth. a wrench, tordre qch. violemment. *With a w.*, d'un effort violent. **It will be a wrench**, il m'en coûtera. **2.** Clef *f* (à écrous); tourne-à-gauche *m inv.* **wrench²,** *v.tr.* (*a*) Tordre; tourner violemment. **To wrench the lid open**, forcer le couvercle. **To wrench off**, arracher. (*b*) To wrench sth. from s.o., arracher qch. à qn. **wrest,** *v.tr.* Arracher (*from*, à). **wrestle¹,** *s.* *To have a w. with s.o.*, lutter avec, contre, qn. **wrestle².** **1.** *v.i.* (*a*) To wrestle with s.o., lutter avec, contre, qn. (*b*) To wrestle with sth., lutter contre (les difficultés). **2.** *v.tr.* Lutter avec, contre. **wrestling,** *s.* Sport *m* de la lutte; lutte (corps à corps). Wrestling match, assaut *m* (de lutte). **wrestler,** *s.* Lutteur *m.* **wretch,** *s.* **1.** Malheureux, -euse; infortuné, -ée. **Poor wretch**, pauvre diable *m.* **2.** (*a*) Scélérat, -ate. **You wretch!** misérable! (*b*) **You little wretch!** petit(e) fripon(ne)! **wretched,** *a.* **1.** Misérable, malheureux, infortuné. **2.** Pitoyable; lamentable. **What wretched weather**, quel temps de chien! **-ly,** *adv.* **1.** Misérablement. **2.** De façon pitoyable, lamentable. **3.** *To be w. poor*, être dans la misère. **wretchedness,** *s.* Misère *f*, malheur *m.* **wrick¹,** *s.* To give oneself a wrick, se donner, attraper, un effort. **Wrick in the neck**, torticolis *m.* **wrick²,** *v.tr.* To wrick oneself, se donner un effort. **wriggle¹,** *s.* Tortillement *m.* **wriggle².** **1.** *v.i.* (*a*) Se tortiller; s'agiter. *To w. through a hedge*, se faufiler à travers une haie. (*b*) To wriggle out of a difficulty, se tirer d'une position difficile. (*c*) *F:* Tortiller; tergiverser. **2.** *v.tr.* (*a*) *To w. one's body*, remuer, tortiller, le corps. (*b*) To wriggle one's way, se faufiler, s'insinuer. **wriggling,** *s.* **1.** Tortillement *m.* **2.** *F:* Tergiversation *f.* **wring¹,** *s.* To give the clothes a wring, tordre le linge. **wring²,** *v.tr.* **1.** Tordre. **To wring s.o.'s hand**, étreindre la main de qn. **To wring one's hands**, se tordre les mains, les bras. **It wrings my heart to . . .**, cela me déchire le cœur de. . . . **2.** To wring sth. out of s.o., arracher (un secret à qn). **wringing,** *a.* **Wringing wet**, mouillé à tordre; (*of pers.*) trempé jusqu'aux os. **wrinkle¹,** *s.* **1.** (*a*) (*On face*) Ride *f.* (*b*) Ru-

gosité *f.* (*c*) Faux pli. **2.** *F:* Renseignement *m* utile; *F:* tuyau *m.* **wrinkle².** **1.** *v.tr.* Rider, plisser. **To wrinkle one's forehead**, froncer les sourcils. **2.** *v.i.* To wrinkle (up), se rider; se plisser. **wrist,** *s.* Poignet *m.* **wrist-watch,** *s.* Montre-bracelet *f*, *pl.* montres-bracelets. **wristband,** *s.* *Cost:* Poignet *m*, manchette *f.* **writ,** *s.* **1.** **Holy writ**, les saintes Écritures; l'Écriture sainte. **2.** *Jur:* Acte *m* judiciaire; mandat *m*, ordonnance *f.* **To serve a writ on s.o.**, assigner qn (en justice). **write,** *v.tr.* **1.** Écrire. *That was not written by me*, cela n'est pas écrit de ma main. **He writes a good hand**, il a une belle main. **There's detective written all over him**, il sent son policier d'une lieue. **2.** Écrire; rédiger (un article). **To write for a paper**, faire du journalisme. **He writes**, il est écrivain. *F:* **That's nothing to write home about**, ce n'est pas bien extraordinaire. **I will write (off) for it at once**, je vais le commander tout de suite. **write down,** *v.tr.* Coucher par écrit; inscrire (son nom); marquer, noter. **write out,** *v.tr.* **1.** Transcrire. **2.** To write sth. out in full, écrire qch. en toutes lettres. **3.** (*a*) *Med:* Formuler, rédiger (une ordonnance). (*b*) Libeller, remplir (un chèque). **I'll write you (out) a cheque**, *F:* je vais vous faire un chèque. **written,** *a.* Écrit. **Written consent**, consentement par écrit. **writing,** *s.* **1.** Écriture *f.* (*a*) *Give me writing materials*, donnez-moi de quoi écrire. (*b*) *His w. is bad*, il a une mauvaise écriture. *To answer in writing*, répondre par écrit. **2.** (*a*) The writing profession, le métier d'écrivain. (*b*) Ouvrage *m* littéraire. *pl.* The writings of Bossuet, les écrits *m* de Bossuet. **writing-case,** *s.* Nécessaire *m* (contenant ce qu'il faut pour écrire). **writing-desk,** *s.* Pupitre *m*, bureau *m.* **writing-pad,** *s.* Sous-main *m*, *pl.* sous-mains. **writing-paper,** *s.* Papier *m* à écrire. **writer,** *s.* **1.** To be a good writer, avoir une belle écriture. **2.** The (present) writer, celui qui écrit. **3.** (*a*) Auteur *m.* (*b*) Écrivain *m.* **writhe,** *v.i.* (*a*) Se tordre (de douleur); se tortiller; se crisper. (*b*) To make s.o. writhe, donner des crispations à qn. **writhing,** *s.* Contorsions *fpl.* **wrong¹.** **I.** *a.* **1.** Mauvais; mal *inv.* **It is wrong to steal**, c'est mal de voler. **That was very wrong of you!** c'était très mal de votre part! *P:* A wrong 'un, un mauvais sujet. **2.** (*a*) Incorrect, inexact; faux, *f.* fausse. **My watch is wrong**, ma montre n'est pas à l'heure. *His ideas are all w.*, il a des idées toutes de travers. (*b*) **To be wrong**, avoir tort; se tromper. **3.** (*a*) To be in the wrong place, n'être pas à sa place. **To drive on the wrong side of the road**, circuler à contre-voie. *F:* **To get out of bed on the wrong side**, se lever du pied gauche. **Your shirt is wrong side out**, votre chemise est à l'envers. **To** be wrong side up, être sens dessus dessous. To brush a hat the wrong way, brosser un chapeau à rebours, à contre-poil. F: To be on the wrong side of forty, avoir (dé)passé la quarantaine. (b) I went to the wrong house, je me suis trompé de maison. To be on the wrong track, suivre une mauvaise piste. To say the wrong thing, commettre une gaffe. Tp: Wrong number, erreur f de numéro. Mus: Wrong note, fausse note. 4. What's wrong with you? qu'avez-vous? Something is wrong, il y a quelque chose qui ne va pas. There's something wrong somewhere, il y a quelque chose qui cloche. I hope there is nothing wrong, j'espère qu'il n'est rien arrivé. Things are all wrong, tout va mal, de travers. F: What's wrong with that? qu'avez-vous à redire à cela? -ly, adv. 1. A tort, à faux. Rightly or wrongly, à tort ou à raison. 2. Mal. II. wrong, s. 1. Mal m. Two wrongs do not make a right, deux noirs ne font pas un blanc. 2. Tort m, injustice f. To labour under a sense of wrong, nourrir un sentiment d'injustice. 3. To be in the wrong, être dans son tort; avoir tort. III. wrong, adv. Mal. 1. (a)

Inexactement, incorrectement. To answer wrong, répondre mal, de travers. (b) A tort; à faux. You did wrong, vous avez mal agi. You took me up wrong, vous avez mal pris mes paroles. 2. To go wrong, (a) F: tomber dans le vice. (b) Se déranger, se détraquer. Things are going wrong, les affaires se gâtent. wrong-doer, s. Celui qui commet une infraction à la loi. wrong-doing, s. Infraction f à la loi. wrong-headed, a. Qui a l'esprit pervers, mal fait. wrong-headedness, s. Perversité f de jugement. wrong², v.tr. (a) Faire (du) tort à; faire injure à. (b) Être injuste pour, envers; faire tort à. wrongful, a. 1. Injuste. Wrongful dismissal, renvoi injustifié. 2. Jur: Illégal, -aux. -fully, adv. Injustement; à tort. wroth, pred.a. En colère (at, contre). To wax wroth, entrer en courroux. wrought, See WORK². wry, a. Tordu, tors; de travers. To pull a wry face, faire la grimace. He gave a wry smile, il grimaça un sourire. wryneck, s. Orn: Torcol m. wych-elm, s. Bot: Orme blanc.

X

X, x, s. 1. (La lettre) X, x m. 2. Ph: X rays, rayons m X. X-ray¹, attrib. a. Radiologique. X-ray examination, examen radiographique. X-ray photograph, radiogramme m. X-ray², v.tr. Med: Radiographier.

xylograph, s. Xylographie f; gravure f sur bois; estampe f. xylography, s. Xylographie f. xylonite, s. Xylonite f. xylophone, s. Mus: Xylophone m.

Y

Y, y, s. (La lettre) Y, y m; i grec. yacht¹, s. Yacht m. yacht-club, s. Yacht-club m, pl. yacht-clubs. yacht², v.i. Faire du yachting. yachting, s. Yachting m. Yachting cruise, croisière f en yacht. yachtsman, s. Yachtman m, pl. yachtmen. yah, int 1. (Disgust) Pouah! 2. Oh, là là! yak, s. Z: Ya(c)k m. yam, s. Bot: Igname f. yank¹, s. Secousse f, saccade f. yank², v.tr. Tirer (d'un coup sec). To y. the bed-clothes off s.o., découvrir qn d'une secousse. Yankee, s. P: Américain, -aine (des États-Unis); Yankee m. yap¹, s. Jappement m.

yap², v.i. (a) Japper. (b) F: (Of pers.) Criailler; en dégoiser. yapping, s. = YAP¹. yard¹, s. 1. Meas: Yard m. How many yards do you want? quel métrage désirez-vous? Face a yard long, figure longue d'une aune. 2. Nau: Vergue f. yard-arm, s. Nau: Bout m de vergue. yard², s. 1. Cour f (de maison). 2. (a) Chantier m. (b) Dépôt m. Rail: Goods yard, cour, dépôt, de marchandises. yarn¹, s. 1. Tex: Fil m; filé m (de coton). 2. F: Histoire f, conte m. To spin a yarn, raconter, débiter, une histoire. yarn², v.i. F: Débiter des histoires. yashmak, s. Cost: Yachmak m. yataghan, s. Yatagan m. yaw¹, s. Nau: Embardée f.

yaw², *v.i.* *Nau*: Embarder, faire des embardées.

yawl, *s.* *Nau*: Yole *f.*

yawn¹, *s.* Bâillement *m.* **To give a yawn**, bâiller. **To stifle a y.**, étouffer un bâillement.

yawn². **I.** *v.i.* (*a*) Bâiller. (*b*) Être béant. **The gulf yawned at his feet**, le gouffre s'ouvrait à ses pieds. **2.** *v.tr.* *F*: **To yawn one's head off**, bâiller à se décrocher la mâchoire. **yawning¹**, *a.* Béant, ouvert. **yawning²**, *s.* Bâillement *m.*

ye, *pers.pron.* *A*: Vous. *F*: **How d'ye do?** comment allez-vous?

yea, *adv.* *Lit*: (*a*) Oui. (*b*) En vérité; voire.

year, *s.* An *m*, année *f.* (*a*) **In the year 1850**, en l'an 1850. **Last year**, l'an dernier; l'année dernière. **To be ten years old**, avoir dix ans. **To see the old year out**, réveillonner. (*b*) Année. **Financial year**, année d'exercice. *He is in my y.*, il est de ma promotion. **By the year**, à l'année. **From year's end to year's end**, d'un bout de l'année à l'autre. **Years ago**, il y a bien des années. **In after years**, dans la suite. **From his earliest years**, dès son âge le plus tendre. **Old for his years**, plus vieux que son âge. **To be getting on in years**, prendre de l'âge. **year-book**, *s.* Annuaire *m.*

yearly. **I.** *a.* Annuel. (*a*) Qui se fait, qui revient, chaque année. (*b*) Qui dure un an. **Yearly letting**, location annale. **2.** *adv.* Annuellement.

yearn, *v.i.* **To yearn for sth.**, languir pour qch. **To yearn to do sth.**, avoir bien envie de faire qch. **yearning¹**, *a.* (Désir) vif, ardent; (regard) plein d'envie. **-ly**, *adv.* Avec envie. **yearning²**, *s.* Désir ardent; envie *f* (*for*, de).

yeast, *s.* Levure *f.*

yell¹, *s.* Hurlement *m*; cri aigu.

yell². **I.** *v.i.* Hurler; crier à tue-tête. **2.** *v.tr.* **To y. out abuse**, vociférer, hurler, des injures. **yelling¹**, *s.* Hurlements *mpl.*

yellow¹. **I.** *a.* (*a*) Jaune. **Yellow hair**, cheveux blonds. (*b*) *F*: Poltron, lâche. **2.** *s.* Jaune *m.* **Chrome yellow**, jaune de chrome. **yellow fever**, *s.* Fièvre *f* jaune. **yellow-hammer**, *s.* *Orn*: Bruant *m* jaune.

yellow², *v.tr. & i.* Jaunir.

yellowish, *a.* Jaunâtre.

yellowness, *s.* Ton *m* jaune, teinte *f* jaune (de qch.); teint *m* jaune (de qn).

yelp¹, *s.* Jappement *m*, glapissement *m.*

yelp², *v.i.* Japper, glapir. **yelping**, *s.* Jappement *m*, glapissement *m.*

yeoman, *s.* **I.** Petit propriétaire; gros fermier. *F*: **To do yeoman('s) service**, fournir un effort précieux. **2.** *Navy*: Gardien *m*; magasinier *m.*

yes, *adv.* (*a*) Oui; parfaitement; (*contradicting negation*) si; si fait. **To answer yes or no**, répondre par oui ou non. **Yes, certainly**, mais oui. (*b*) (*Interrogatively*) **Yes?** (i) vraiment? (ii) et puis après?

yesterday, *adv. & s.* Hier (*m*). **The day before yesterday**, avant-hier (*m*).

yet. **I.** *adv.* **I.** (*a*) Encore. *I can see him yet*, je le vois encore. (*b*) **Yet more**, encore plus. **Yet again**, encore une fois. **2.** Déjà; jusqu'ici. **Not yet**, pas encore. *It will not happen just yet*, nous n'en sommes pas encore là. **As yet**, jusqu'à présent, jusqu'ici. **3.** Malgré tout. **I'll do it yet!** j'y arriverai! **II. yet**, *conj.* Néanmoins, cependant; tout de même.

yew, *s.* *Bot*: Yew(-tree), if *m.*

yield¹, *s.* Production *f*; rapport *m* (d'un arbre fruitier); récolte *f* (d'un champ).

yield². **I.** *v.tr.* (*a*) Rendre, donner. (*b*) Rapporter, produire. *Abs.* **Ground that yields well**, terre qui donne un bon rendement. (*c*) Céder. **2.** *v.i.* (*a*) Se rendre; céder (*to*, à). **To yield to temptation**, succomber à la tentation. (*b*) S'affaisser, fléchir, plier. **yielding¹**, *a.* **I.** Facile, complaisant. *In a y. moment*, dans un moment de faiblesse. **2.** (*a*) Mou, *f.* molle. (*b*) Souple, élastique. **yielding²**, *s.* **I.** Rendement *m.* **2.** (*a*) Soumission *f.* (*b*) Cession *f.* **3.** Affaissement *m*, fléchissement *m.*

yodel¹, *s.* *Mus*: Ioulement *m.*

yodel², *v.i.* *Mus*: Iouler.

yoke¹, *s.* **I.** Joug *m.* **Yoke oxen**, bœufs d'attelage. **Yoke of oxen**, couple *f*, attelage *m* (de bœufs). *F*: **To throw off, cast off, the yoke**, secouer le joug. **2.** (*For carrying two pails*) Palanche *f.* **3.** *Dressm*: Empiècement *m*; tour *m* de gorge.

yoke², *v.tr.* Accoupler; mettre au joug: atteler (à la charrue).

yokel, *s.* Rustre *m*; campagnard *m.*

yolk, *s.* Jaune *m* d'œuf.

yonder. **I.** *adv.* **Over yonder**, là-bas. **2.** *a.* Ce . . . -là, *f.* cette . . . -là, *pl.* ces . . . -là.

yore, *s.* *A*: **Of yore**, (d')autrefois. **In days of yore**, au temps jadis; autrefois.

you, *pers.pron.* (i) Vous; (ii) *sg.* (*addressing relatives, children, etc.*) tu, te, toi. **I.** (*a*) (*Nom.*) Vous. *You are, vous voilà*, te voilà. *Tp*: **Are you there?** allô! (*b*) (*As object*) Vous; te. (*c*) **Between you and me**, entre nous soit dit. **There's a fine apple for you!** regardez-moi ça, si ce n'est pas une belle pomme! **Away with you!** allez-vous-en! va-t'en! **2.** (*a*) **You and I will go by train**, vous et moi, nous irons par le train. **If I were you**, (si j'étais) à votre place. **Hi! you there!** eh! dites donc, là-bas! (*b*) **Now you make a speech**, à votre tour de parler. *Never you mind!* ça c'est mon affaire! (*c*) **You Englishmen**, vous autres Anglais. **You idiot (, you)!** idiot que vous êtes! **3. Get you gone**, allez-vous-en. **4.** (*Indefinite*) On. **You never can tell**, on ne sait jamais. *The joy you feel when you meet a friend*, la joie qui vous saisit quand on rencontre un ami.

young. **I.** *a.* (*a*) Jeune; (*of animal*) petit.

Younger son, fils cadet. **We are only young once,** jeunesse n'a qu'un temps. **Young men,** jeunes gens *m.* **Young Mr Smith,** (i) M. Smith fils ; (ii) le jeune M. Smith. (*b*) **To grow young again,** rajeunir. (*c*) **The night is still young,** la nuit n'est que peu avancée. **2.** *s. pl. inv.* (*a*) Les jeunes gens ; la jeunesse. **Old and young,** les grands et les petits. (*b*) **Animal and its young,** animal et ses petits.

youngish, *a.* Assez jeune.

youngster, *s.* (*a*) Jeune personne *f* ; jeune homme *m.* (*b*) Petit, -ite ; *F :* gosse *mf.*

your, *poss.a.* **I.** (i) Votre, *pl.* vos ; (ii) *sg.* (*when addressing relatives, children, etc.*) ton, *f.* ta, *pl.* tes. *Your house,* votre maison, ta maison. *Your friends,* vos ami(e)s, tes ami(e)s. *Have you hurt your hand?* vous vous êtes fait mal à la main? *Games :* **Your turn!** à vous ! **2.** Son, *f.* sa, *pl.* ses. **You cannot alter your nature,** on ne peut pas changer son caractère.

yours, *poss.pron.* (i) Le vôtre, la vôtre, les vôtres ; (ii) *sg.* (*when addressing relatives, children, etc.*) le tien, la tienne, les tiens, les tiennes. (*a*) **This is yours,** ceci est à vous, à toi. *The idea is yours,* l'idée est de vous. **He is a friend of yours,** c'est un de vos amis. *That pride of yours,* votre orgueil. (*b*) **You and yours,** vous et les vôtres.

yourself, *pers. pron. See* SELF 3.

youth, *s.* **I.** Jeunesse *f,* adolescence *f,* jeune âge *m.* **2.** Jeune homme *m,* adolescent *m.* **3.** *Coll.* Jeunes gens *m* ; jeunesse.

youthful, *a.* **I.** Jeune. **2.** De jeunesse.

youthfulness, *s.* Jeunesse *f* ; air *m* de jeunesse.

yowl[1]**,** *s.* Hurlement *m* (de chien) ; miaulement *m* (de chat).

yowl[2]**,** *v.i.* (*Of dog*) Hurler ; (*of cat*) miauler.

Yugoslav, *a. & s.* = JUGOSLAV.

Yugoslavia. *Pr.n.* = JUGOSLAVIA.

Yule, *s.* *A :* Noël *m.* **yule-log,** *s.* Bûche *f* de Noël. **yule-tide,** *s.* L'époque *f* de Noël ; les fêtes *f* de Noël.

Z

Z, z, *s.* (La lettre) Z, z *m.*

zeal, *s.* Zèle *m,* ardeur *f* ; empressement *m.*

zealot, *s.* Fanatique *mf,* zélateur, -trice.

zealous, *a.* Zélé ; empressé. **-ly,** *adv.* Avec zèle.

zebra, *s.* Zèbre *m.*

zenana, *s.* Zénana *m,* harem *m.*

zenith, *s.* *Astr :* Zénith *m. F :* **At the zenith of his fame,** à l'apogée de sa gloire.

zephyr, *s.* Zéphire *m,* zéphyr(e) *m.*

zero, *s.* Zéro *m.* **zero hour,** *s.* *Mil :* L'heure *f* H.

zest, *s.* (*a*) Enthousiasme *m,* entrain *m.* *To eat with z.,* manger avec appétit. (*b*) Saveur *f,* goût *m.* *To add z. to the adventure,* donner du piquant à l'aventure.

Zeus. *Pr.n.* *Myth :* Zeus *m.*

zigzag[1]**,** *s.* Zigzag *m.* *In zigzags,* en zigzag.

zigzag[2]**,** *v.i.* Zigzaguer ; faire des zigzags.

zinc, *s.* Zinc *m*

Zion. *Pr.n.* Sion *m.*

zip[1]**,** *s.* **I.** Sifflement *m* (d'une balle). **2.** *F :* Énergie *f.* **Put a zip into it,** mettez-y du nerf. **3. Zip fastener,** fermeture *f* éclair *inv.*

zip[2]**,** *v.i.* Siffler (comme une balle). **To zip past,** passer comme un éclair.

zither(n), *s.* *Mus :* Cithare *f.*

zodiac, *s.* *Astr :* Zodiaque *m.*

zone, *s.* Zone *f.*

zoo, *s.* *F :* Jardin *m* zoologique.

zoological, *a.* Zoologique.

zoologist, *s.* Zoologiste *m.*

zoology, *s.* Zoologie *f.*

zoom[1]**,** *s.* Bourdonnement *m* ; vrombissement *m.*

zoom[2]**,** *v.i.* **I.** Bourdonner ; vrombir. **2.** *Av :* Monter en chandelle.

zoophyte, *s.* *Biol :* Zoophyte *m.*

zouave, *s.* Zouave *m.*

Zulu, *a. & s.* *Ethn :* Zoulou *m, pl.* -ous.

Zululand. *Pr.n.* Le Zoulouland.

Zuyder Zee (the). *Pr.n.* Le Zuyderzée.